The
American Heritage Dictionary

The American

Heritage Dictionary

BASED ON THE NEW
SECOND COLLEGE EDITION

A Laurel Book
Published by
Dell Publishing
a division of
Bantam Doubleday Dell Publishing Group, Inc.
666 Fifth Avenue
New York, New York 10103

Words that are believed to be registered trademarks have been checked with authoritative sources. No investigation has been made of common-law trademark rights in any word, because such investigation is impracticable. Words that are known to have current registrations are shown with an initial capital and are also identified as trademarks. The inclusion of any word in this Dictionary is not, however, an expression of the Publisher's opinion as to whether or not it is subject to proprietary rights. Indeed, no definition in this Dictionary is to be regarded as affecting the validity of any trademark.

Based on the hardcover SECOND COLLEGE EDITION OF
THE AMERICAN HERITAGE DICTIONARY

All correspondence and inquiries should be directed to
Reference Division, Houghton Mifflin Company, Two Park Street, Boston, MA 02108.

The trademark Laurel® is registered in the U.S. Patent and Trademark Office.

The trademark Dell® is registered in the U.S. Patent and Trademark Office.

ISBN: 0-440-20189-6

Published by arrangement with Houghton Mifflin Company

Printed in the United States of America

Published simultaneously in Canada

Five Previous Dell Editions

New Laurel Edition

July 1989

20   19   18   17   16   15   14   13

OPM

TABLE OF CONTENTS

STAFF

Margery S. Berube
Director of Editorial Operations

Diane J. Neely
Traffic Coordinator

Pamela Burton DeVinne
Project Editor

Editors
Mark Boyer
Kaethe Ellis
Dolores R. Harris
Anne H. Soukhanov

Contributing Editors
Walter Havighurst
Anne D. Steinhardt

Etymologies
Marion Severynse, *Associate Editor*
Rachel Lucas
Lawrence O. Masland

Copy-editing and Proofreading
Trudy Nelson
Caroline L. Becker
Judith L. Drummond
Rhonda L. Holmes

Picture Research and Editing
Carole La Mond, *Picture and Research Editor*
Sarah A. O'Reilly, *Assistant Picture Researcher*
Donna L. Muise

PREFACE

The *American Heritage Dictionary* was revised recently to reflect the language of the '80's. New general and technical words were added to record the language that is used today in the arts, sciences, business, politics, and the media. It is the first major Dictionary in ten years.

This is the paperback edition, prepared by the staff of the *American Heritage Dictionary*. It is an independent reference work embodying in smaller form the additions of the parent book. The definitions have been selected and rewritten or edited to be as lucid and useful as possible. The definitions are enhanced by the use of illustrations, charts, and diagrams. Selected Usage notes derived from the deliberations of the American Heritage Panel on English Usage are included in the text.

GUIDE TO THE DICTIONARY

THE MAIN ENTRY

The main entry is the word or phrase one looks up in the Dictionary. It is printed in boldface type a little to the left of the rest of the type.

Two or more entries that are identical in spelling but have different etymologies are entered separately; each entry bears a superscript number.

bore[1]

bore[2]

bore[3]

The entry word, whether a solid word, syllabicated word, hyphenated compound, or phrase, is alphabetized as if it were written solid. Here is a typical alphabetical sequence: **great, great circle, great-coat, Great Dane, great-grand-child.**

SYLLABICATION

An entry word is divided into syllables by centered dots.

ac·a·de·mi·cian

In a phrasal entry words that appear as separate entries are not syllabicated.

car·bon·ic acid

Acid is a separate entry, **carbonic** is not.

However, when principal parts of regular verbs appear as parts of phrasal entries, they are *not* syllabicated.

VARIANTS

If two or more different spellings of a single word are entered, they are set in boldface type and are treated in two ways:

(1) A variant may follow the main entry, separated from it by "or." This indicates that the two forms are used almost equally frequently.

ax or axe

(2) When one spelling is distinctly preferred, the variant is introduced by "Also."

me·di·e·val . . . Also **me·di·ae·val.**

A large class of variants consists of spellings preferred in British English and sometimes used in American English. Such variants as **colour** and **centre** are labeled *Chiefly Brit*. The variant **-ise,** which occurs in many British spellings where American has **-ize** (for example, **realize, realise**), is not given unless it is also a common American variant.

When a word that has a variant occurs in a compound, the variant is not repeated at the compound; for example, the variant **colour** is given at **color,** but it is not repeated at **colorblind** and other compounds.

A variant spelling that would, if entered, fall within five entries of the preferred spelling is not entered separately.

Apart from variant spellings, which are given at the beginning of an entry, there are often two or more distinct words or phrases that have identical meaning. These alternate names for the same thing are treated as follows:

The alternate name is a main entry, and the preferred form is given as the definition.

ad·ju·tant . . . *n.* 1. . . . 3. The marabou.

darning needle *n.* 1. . . . 2. *Informal.* A dragonfly.

bicarbonate of soda *n.* Sodium bicarbonate.

The preferred form is fully defined as a main entry; if the alternate name is mentioned, it is treated as a regular synonym, i.e., it appears in lightface roman type.

INFLECTED FORMS

Inflected forms regarded as being irregular or offering possible spelling problems are entered in boldface type, usually in shortened form, are syllabicated, and immediately follow the part-of-speech label or the numbered sense of the definition to which they apply.

base . . . bas·er, bas·est.

well . . . bet·ter, best.

fly . . . flew, flown, fly·ing.

Regular inflections are normally not entered with the exception of degrees of adjectives and adverbs. For the purposes of this Dictionary, regular inflections include:

(1) Plurals formed by suffixing *-s* or *-es*. The regular plural is shown, however, when there is an irregular variant plural or when the spelling of the regular plural might present difficulty, as with words ending in *-o*.

cac·tus . . . *pl.* -ti (-tī′) or -tus·es.

to·ma·to . . . *pl.* -toes.

pi·an·o . . . *pl.* -os.

(2) Past tenses and past participles formed by suffixing *-ed* with no other change in the verb form, as **marked, parked,** etc.

(3) Present participles formed by suffixing *-ing* with no other change in the verb form, as **marking, parking,** etc.

(4) Present-tense forms, with the exception of such irregular forms as **is, has,** etc.

The inflected forms of verbs are given in the following order: past tense, past participle (if it differs from the past tense), and present participle.

fly . . . flew, flown, fly·ing.

Irregular inflected forms that would fall within five entries of the main entry are not entered separately. If, however, they fall more than five entries from the main entry (i.e., the infinitive form of a verb, the singular of a noun, etc.), they are separately entered, pronounced, and identified as a part or parts of a verb, comparative of an adjective, plural of a noun, etc.

ORDER OF DEFINITIONS

When an entry has multiple numbered definitions, these are ordered by a method of semantic analysis intended to serve the convenience of the general user of the Dictionary. The numerical order does not indicate the historical sequence in which the senses developed. The first definition, then, is not necessarily the earliest sense of the word, though it may be. Rather, the first definition is the central meaning about which the other senses can most logically be organized. The organization seeks to clarify the fact that despite its various meanings the entry is a single "word" and not a number of separate words that happen to be spelled the same way.

Numbers and Letters

When an entry has more than one definition, these are numbered in sequence. In a *combined entry* (one in which the entry word belongs to more than one part of speech), the definitions are numbered in separate sequences beginning with **1.** after each part of speech.

ef·fect . . . *n.* **1.** Something . . . . **2.** The capacity to . . . . **3.** The condition of . . . . **4.** Basic meaning . . . . **5. effects.** Possessions; belongings. —*v.* **1.** To bring about . . . . **2.** To make. . . .

When a numbered definition has two or more closely related senses, these are marked **a., b.,** etc.

ech·o . . . **1. a.** Repetition of a sound by reflection of sound waves from a surface. **b.** A sound produced in this manner.

When a general definition is further qualified by several specific meanings, the letters **a., b.,** etc., are used.

Numbered Boldface Definitions: Plural Forms

If a noun has, in addition to its ordinary sense, a sense or senses in which it often appears in the plural, this fact is indicated as follows:

glass . . . **1.** . . . **4.** Often **glasses.** A device containing a lens or lenses. . . .

If a noun sense is *always* used in the plural, the plural form appears in boldface before the definition.

gut . . . *n.* **1.** . . . **5. guts.** *Informal.* Courage; fortitude.

Combined Upper-case and Lower-case Forms

When upper-case and lower-case words of the same spelling have the same etymology, both forms are usually included in the same entry.

If the lower-case form is a common word with a specific upper-case sense, the lower-case form is the main entry. Most upper-case and lower-case combinations are of this sort.

com·mon . . . *adj.* **1.** Belonging equally to all; joint . . . —*n.* **1.** A tract of land . . . **2. Commons.** The lower house of Parliament . . .

If, on the other hand, the upper-case form is the original sense and is still current, it is the main entry.

Mes·si·ah . . . . **1.** The expected . . . . **2.** Jesus Christ. **3. messiah.** An expected deliverer or savior.

The word "Often" immediately following a boldface number indicates that a word is often or usually upper-case (or lower-case) in that sense.

cock·ney . . . *n.* **1.** Often **Cockney.** A native of . . . **2.** The dialect . . .

Part-of-Speech Labels

The italicized labels below, which follow the pronunciation of the entry word, are used to indicate parts of speech.

n.	noun	*pron.*	pronoun
adj.	adjective	*conj.*	conjunction
adv.	adverb	*prep.*	preposition

v.	verb	*pref.*	prefix
interj.	interjection	*suff.*	suffix

The following additional italicized labels are used to indicate inflected forms:

pl.	plural	*p.p.*	past participle
sing.	singular	*compar.*	comparative
pres.p.	present participle	*superl.*	superlative
p.t.	past tense		

PART-OF-SPEECH LABELS IN COMBINED ENTRIES

In combined entries the part-of-speech labels that follow the first one are preceded by a dash. Such labels precede all elements that apply to that part of speech and may be followed by any elements (pronunciation, other labels, etc.) that can appear immediately following the main-entry word, its pronunciation, etc.

> **now** . . . *adv.* **1.** At the present. . . . *—conj.* Since; seeing that. *—n.* The present time. . . . *—adj. Informal.* Of the present time; current. . . .

If, however, a language, status, or field label applies to an entire entry, the label precedes all part-of-speech labels.

> **mug²** . . . *Slang.* *—n.* **1.** The face . . . **2.** . . . *—v.* **mugged, mug·ging. 1.** . . .

VERBS

Parentheses are used to indicate a direct object.

> **ad·min·is·ter** . . . *v.* **1.** To manage. **2. a.** To give (a drug) remedially. **b.** To dispense (a sacrament) . . .

Parentheses are also used around a final preposition to indicate that a verb can be used either transitively or intransitively in that sense, i.e., that it can be followed by a direct object or that its object may be omitted entirely.

> **kink** . . . *n.* **1.** A small, tight . . . *—v.* To form kinks (in).

PHRASAL VERBS

Phrasal verbs are alphabetically run in and defined as subentries of their main-entry base words. They are introduced by the italic bold subhead *—phrasal verbs* and follow the last main-entry verb definition.

> **go¹** . . . *v.* . . . *—phrasal verbs.* **go about.** To busy oneself with: *go about one's business.* **go along.** To be in agreement; concur. . . .

IDIOMS

Many entry words are commonly used in phrases the meaning of which is not clear from the meanings of the separate words. Except as noted, such phrases are defined at the entry for the most significant word in the phrase. Idioms are introduced by the boldface italic subhead *—idioms* and are run in alphabetically and defined within main entries; they appear just before the etymologies and after all parts of speech in combined entries. The idioms, like the phrasal verbs, are set in boldface type.

> **go¹** . . . *v.* *—phrasal verbs.* . . . *—n., pl.* **goes.** *Informal.* . . . *—adj. Informal.* . . . *—idioms.* **go far.** To succeed; prosper greatly. **on the go.** *Informal.* Perpetually busy. **to go.** To be taken out, as restaurant food and drink.

Phrases such as **water buffalo**, made up of an attributive (adjective or noun) plus a noun, are separate main entries.

USAGE LABELS

Usage labels are restrictive labels that serve to warn the reader that a term is not properly available for use in all contexts. A usage label applies only to the definition or definitions that follow it. A single entry may have standard (unlabeled) definitions and any combination of labeled definitions.

Informal signifies "cultivated colloquial," that is, the speech of educated persons when they are more interested in what they are saying than in how they are saying it. *Informal* terms are also used in writing that seeks the effect of speech, but they are not used in formal writing.

Slang does not define a level of speech, as does *Informal*, but a style having features that are usually not hard to identify. Slang may occur in all but the most formal language and remain slang. A primary rule to distinguish it from nonstandard speech is that a slang term may not be used merely to indicate the meaning of a word; it always carries some deliberately informal connotation in addition and suggests some intention—however dully conceived—of rhetorical effect, such as incongruity, hyperbole, irreverence, etc.

Nonstandard, unlike *Informal* and *Slang*, indicates usages that are widespread but not acceptable. It includes forms such as "irregardless" and "ain't."

Obsolete (Obs.) is for obsolete words, few of which are entered; in order to be entered an obsolete term must have appeared in standard literature either frequently or prominently. A distinction must be made between a term for an obsolete thing and a term that is itself obsolete. The former is not labeled, but the historical situation is explained in the definition, e.g., "An 18th-cent. hat . . ."

Archaic is used for terms that were once common and continue to have some use, but are now used only to suggest an earlier style. The label does not suggest a date beyond which a word cannot be found, merely that when it is found in a contemporary context, it is readily identifiable as belonging to a style of language no longer in general use.

Poetic is used for such locutions as a shortening (*o'er*) that is or was common in poetry but was never common in prose.

Regional is used for terms that are not common to American speech in general but exist in more than one locality.

Important words belonging to major English dialectal areas of the U.S. or outside the U.S. are so labeled.

FIELD LABELS

An italicized word or abbreviation denoting a specific subject and preceding a definition indicates a specialized sense not identical with any other sense the word may have apart from the labeled field.

ETYMOLOGIES

Etymologies appear in square brackets following the definitions. The symbol < is used to mean "from" and is often an indication that transitional stages have been omitted in order to give a concise history of the word. The etymologies of most basic words are given.

Abbreviations and Symbols

abbr.	abbreviation	freq.	frequentative
adj.	adjective	comp.	comparative
adv.	adverb	dial.	dialectal
cent.	century	dim.	diminutive
fem.	feminine	ety.	etymology

fut.	future	pl.	plural
gerund.	gerundive	poss.	possibly
imit.	imitative	pr.	present
imper.	imperative	pr.p.	present participle
M	Middle	prob.	probably
masc.	masculine	redup.	reduplication
Med.	Medieval	sing.	singular
Mod.	Modern	St.	Saint
n.	noun	superl.	superlative
naut.	nautical	transl.	translation
O	Old	ult.	ultimately
obs.	obsolete	v.	verb
orig.	origin, originally	var.	variant
p.	past		
p.p.	past participle		
p.t.	past tense	<	derived from
perh.	perhaps	+	combined with

Abbreviations of Languages

Afr.	Afrikaans	Louisiana Fr.	Louisiana French
Am. E.	American English	LG	Low German
Am. Sp.	American Spanish	MDu.	Middle Dutch
AN	Anglo-Norman	ME	Middle English
Ar.	Arabic	Med. Lat.	Medieval Latin
Aram.	Aramaic	Mex. Sp.	Mexican Spanish
Balt.	Baltic	MHG	Middle High German
Brit.	British	MLG	Middle Low German
Can. Fr.	Canadian French	NLat.	New Latin
Cant.	Cantonese	Norman Fr.	Norman French
Celt.	Celtic	Norw.	Norwegian
Chin.	Chinese	ODan	Old Danish
Dan.	Danish	OE	Old English
Du.	Dutch	OFr.	Old French
Egypt.	Egyptian	OHG	Old High German
E.	English	OIr.	Old Irish
Finn.	Finnish	OItal.	Old Italian
Flem.	Flemish	ON	Old Norse
Fr.	French	ONFr.	Old North French
G.	German	OProv.	Old Provençal
Gael.	Gaelic	OSp.	Old Spanish
Gk.	Greek	Pers.	Persian
Gmc.	Germanic	Pidgin E.	Pidgin English
Goth.	Gothic	Pol.	Polish
Heb.	Hebrew	Port.	Portuguese
HG	High German	Prov.	Provençal
Hung.	Hungarian	R.	Russian
Icel.	Icelandic	Rum.	Rumanian
Ir.	Irish	Sc.	Scottish
Iran.	Iranian	Scand.	Scandinavian
Ir. Gael.	Irish Gaelic	Sc. Gael.	Scottish Gaelic
Ital.	Italian	Skt.	Sanskrit
J.	Japanese	Slav.	Slavic
Lat.	Latin	Sp.	Spanish
LGk.	Late Greek	Swed.	Swedish
Lith.	Lithuanian	Turk.	Turkish

Biographical Entries, Geographical Entries, and Abbreviations

There are separate A–Z listings in the back of this Dictionary for biographical names, geographical names, and abbreviations.

Pronunciation

Pronunciation is given for all main entries and for other forms as needed. It is indicated in parentheses following the form to which it applies.

The set of symbols used is designed to enable the reader to reproduce a satisfactory pronunciation with no more than quick reference to the key. All pronunciations given are acceptable in all circumstances. When more than one is given, the first is assumed to be the most common, but the difference in frequency may be insignificant.

It is obvious that Americans do not all speak alike. It is equally obvious that Americans can understand one another, at least on the level of speech sounds. In fact, the differences among the major regional varieties of American speech are such that for most words a single set of symbols can represent the pronunciation found in each regional variety, provided the symbols are planned for the purpose stated above: to enable the reader to reproduce a satisfactory pronunciation. When a single pronunciation is offered in this Dictionary, the reader will supply those features of his own regional speech that are called forth by his reading of the key. Apart from regional variations in pronunciation, there are variations among social groups. The pronunciations recorded in this Dictionary are exclusively those of educated speech.

Pronunciation Key

A shorter form of this key appears across the bottom of each lefthand page. The symbols marked with an asterisk are discussed in the explanatory notes following the pronunciation key.

spellings	symbols	spellings	symbols
pat	ă	thing	ng
pay	ā	pot, *horrid	ŏ
care	*âr	toe, *hoarse	ō
father	ä	caught, paw, *for	ô
bib	b	noise	oi
church	ch	took	ŏŏ
deed, milled	d	boot	ōō
pet	ĕ	out	ou
bee	ē	pop	p
fife, phase, rough	f	roar	*r
gag	g	sauce	s
hat	h	ship, dish	sh
which	hw	tight, stopped	t
pit	*ĭ	thin	th
pie, by	ī	this	th
pier	*îr	cut	ŭ
judge	j	urge, term, firm,	*ûr
kick, cat, pique	k	word, heard	
lid, needle	*l (nēd′l)	valve	v
mum	m	with	w
no, sudden	*n (sŭd′n)	yes	y

spellings	symbols	spellings	symbols
		FOREIGN	
abuse, use	yo͞o	*French* feu,	œ
zebra, xylem	z	*German* schön	
vision, pleasure, garage	zh	*French* tu, *German* über	ü
about, item, edible, gallop, circus	*ə	*German* ich, *Scottish* loch	KH
butter	*ər	*French* bon	N

STRESS

Primary stress ′   **bi·ol′o·gy** (bī-ŏl′ə-jē)
Secondary stress ′   **bi′o·log′i·cal** (bī′ə-lŏj′ĭ-kəl)

EXPLANATORY NOTES

ə: This nonalphabetical symbol is called a *schwa*. The symbol is used in the Dictionary to represent only a reduced vowel, i.e., a vowel that receives the weakest level of stress (which can be thought of as no stress) within a word and therefore nearly always exhibits a change in quality from the quality it would have if it were stressed, as in *telegraph* (tĕl′ĭ-grăf′) and *telegraphy* (tə-lĕg′rə-fē). Vowels are never reduced to a single exact vowel; the schwa sound will vary according to its phonetic environment.

ĭ: This symbol is used to represent the second vowel in *artist* (är′tĭst), a vowel that has been only partially reduced and therefore cannot be represented by the schwa. The choice between schwa (ə) and "breve i" (ĭ) to represent reduced vowels is arrived at through a complex set of considerations. In nearly every case in which (ĭ) appears, there is also a variant pronunciation closer to (ə). As long as reduced vowels receive no stress, the surrounding sounds will lead the reader to produce either (ə) or (ĭ), according to his regional speech pattern.

âr   These symbols represent vowels that have been altered by a following *r*.
îr   This situation is traditionally exemplified by the words *Mary, merry,* and
ôr   *marry.* In some regional varieties all three are pronounced alike: (mĕr′ē).
ōr   However, in a broad range of individual American speech patterns cutting
ûr   across regional boundaries the three words are distinguished. It is this pattern that the Dictionary represents, thus: *Mary* (mâr′ē), *merry* (mĕr′ē), *marry* (măr′ē). Some words, however, are heard in all three pronunciations, indistinctly grading one into another. For these words the Dictionary represents only (âr), for example, *care* (kâr), *dairy* (dâr′ē).

In words such as *hear, beer,* and *dear,* the vowel could be represented by (ē) were it not for the effect of the following *r*, which makes it approach (ĭ) in sound. In this Dictionary a special symbol (îr) is used for this combination, as in *beer* (bîr).

There are regional differences in the distinctions among various pronunciations of the syllable *-or.* In pairs such as *for, four; horse, hoarse;* and *morning, mourning,* the vowel varies between (ô) and (ō). In this Dictionary these vowels are represented as follows: *for* (fôr), *four* (fôr, fōr); *horse* (hôrs), *hoarse* (hôrs, hōrs). Other words for which both forms are shown include those such as *more* (môr, mōr) and *glory* (glôr′ē,glōr′-).

Another group of words with variations for the *-or* syllable includes words such as *forest* and *horrid,* in which the pronunciation of *o* before *r* varies between (ô) and (ō). In these words the (ôr) pronunciation is given first: *forest* (fôr′ist, fŏr′-).

The symbol (ûr) is used to represent the sound of the vowel in such words as *her* (hûr) and *fur* (fûr).

xv

Syllabic Consonants

There are two consonants that can represent complete syllables. These are *l* and *n* (called *syllabics*) following stressed syllables ending in *d* or *t* in such words as *bottle* (bŏt′l), *fatal* (fāt′l), *button* (bŭt′n), *ladle* (lād′l), and *hidden* (hĭd′n). Syllabic *n* is not shown after a syllable ending in *-nd* or *-nt: abandon* (ə-băn′dən), *mountain* (moun′tən); but syllabic *l* is shown in that position: *spindle* (spĭn′d′l).

Stress

In this Dictionary stress, the relative degree of loudness with which the syllables of a word (or phrase) are spoken, is indicated in three different ways. An unmarked syllable has the weakest stress in the word. The strongest stress is marked with a bold mark (′). An intermediate level of stress, here called *secondary*, is marked with a similar but lighter mark (′).

Words of one syllable show no stress mark, since there is no other stress level to which the syllable is compared.

The pronunciations are syllabicated for clarity. Syllabication of the pronunciation does not necessarily match the syllabication of the entry word being pronounced. The former follows strict, though not obvious, phonological rules; the latter represents the established practice of printers and editors.

Aa

a or **A** (ā) *n., pl.* **a's** or **A's. 1.** The 1st letter of the English alphabet. **2.** The highest grade in quality. **3.** The 1st in a series.

a (ə; ā *when stressed*) *indef. art.* **1.** One: *I didn't say a word.* **2.** Any: *A dog is a four-legged animal.* —*prep.* Per: *two dollars a gallon.* [< OE ān, one.]

a-¹ *pref.* Without:*amoral.* [Gk.]

a-² *pref.* **1.** On or in the direction of or toward: *aboard.* **2.** In the act of: *a-singing.* [< OE < an, on.]

aard·vark (ärd′värk′) *n.* A burrowing African mammal that has a stocky, hairy body, large ears, and a long, tubular snout. [Obs. Afr.]

ab- *pref.* Away from; from: *abnormal.* [Lat.]

a·back (ə-băk′) *adv.* —**take aback.** To startle.

ab·a·cus (ăb′ə-kəs) *n., pl.* **-cus·es** or **-ci** (-sī′). A manual counting and computing device consisting of a frame holding parallel rods strung with movable beads. [< Gk. *abax,* counting board.]

abacus

a·baft (ə-băft′) *adv.* Toward the stern. —*prep.* Toward the stern from. [A-² + OE *beæftan,* behind.]

ab·a·lo·ne (ăb′ə-lō′nē) *n.* A large, edible salt-water mollusk having an ear-shaped shell. [Am. Sp. *abulón.*]

a·ban·don (ə-băn′dən) *v.* **1.** To desert; forsake. **2.** To give up completely. —*n.* A complete surrender to feeling or impulse. [< OFr. *abandoner < a bandon,* in one's power.] —**a·ban′don·er** *n.* —**a·ban′don·ment** *n.*

Syns: abandon, desert, forsake, leave, quit v.

a·ban·doned (ə-băn′dənd) *adj.* Shamelessly unrestrained.

a·base (ə-bās′) *v.* **a·based, a·bas·ing.** To humble. [OFr. *abaissier.*] —**a·base′ment** *n.*

a·bash (ə-băsh′) *v.* To embarrass; disconcert. [< OFr. *esbahir.*] —**a·bash′ment** *n.*

a·bate (ə-bāt′) *v.* **a·bat·ed, a·bat·ing.** To lessen in amount, degree, or intensity. [< OFr. *abattre,* to beat.] —**a·bat′a·ble** *adj.* —**a·bate′ment** *n.* —**a·bat′er** *n.*

ab·at·toir (ăb′ə-twär′) *n.* A slaughterhouse. [Fr. < *abattre,* to beat.]

ab·ba·cy (ăb′ə-sē) *n., pl.* **-cies.** The office, term, or jurisdiction of an abbot.

ab·bé (ăb′ā′, ă-bā′) *n.* A title used for a French priest.

ab·bess (ăb′ĭs) *n.* A nun who is the head of a convent.

ab·bey (ăb′ē) *n., pl.* **-beys. 1.** A monastery or convent. **2.** An abbey church. [< LLat. *abbatia.*]

ab·bot (ăb′ət) *n.* The superior of a monastery. [< Aram. *abba,* father.]

ab·bre·vi·ate (ə-brē′vē-āt′) *v.* **-at·ed, -at·ing.** To shorten, esp. to an abbreviation. [< LLat. *abbreviare.*] —**ab·bre′vi·a′tor** *n.*

ab·bre·vi·a·tion (ə-brē′vē-ā′shən) *n.* **1.** The act or product of abbreviating. **2.** A shortened form of a word or phrase, as *Mass.* for *Massachusetts.*

ABC (ā′bē′sē′) *n., pl.* **ABC's. 1.** Often **ABC's.** The alphabet. **2.** The rudiments of a subject.

ab·di·cate (ăb′dĭ-kāt′) *v.* **-cat·ed, -cat·ing.** To relinquish (e.g. power) formally. [Lat. *abdicare,* to disclaim.] —**ab′di·ca′tion** *n.* —**ab′di·ca′tor** *n.*

ab·do·men (ăb′də-mən, ăb-dō′mən) *n.* **1.** The part of the body in mammals that lies between the thorax and the pelvis. **2.** In arthropods, the major part of the body behind the thorax. [Lat., belly.] —**ab·dom′i·nal** (-dŏm′ə-nəl) *adj.* —**ab·dom′i·nal·ly** *adv.*

ab·duct (ăb-dŭkt′) *v.* To carry off by force; kidnap. [< Lat. *abducere.*] —**ab·duc′tion** *n.* —**ab·duc′tor** *n.*

a·beam (ə-bēm′) *adv.* At right angles to the keel of a ship.

a·bed (ə-bĕd′) *adv.* In bed.

ab·er·ra·tion (ăb′ə-rā′shən) *n.* **1.** A deviation from the normal, usual, or expected. **2.** *Optics.* A defect of focus, as blurring or distortion, in an image. [Lat. *aberratio,* diversion.] —**ab·er′rant** *adj.*

a·bet (ə-bĕt′) *v.* **a·bet·ted, a·bet·ting.** To encourage; incite. [< OFr. *abeter,* to entice.] —**a·bet′ment** *n.* —**a·bet′tor** or **a·bet′ter** *n.*

a·bey·ance (ə-bā′əns) *n.* The condition of being temporarily suspended. [OFr. *abeance,* desire < *abaer,* to gape at.]

ab·hor (ăb-hôr′) *v.* **-horred, -hor·ring.** To detest; loathe. [< Lat. *abhorrēre,* to shrink from.] —**ab·hor′rer** *n.*

ab·hor·rent (ăb-hôr′ənt, -hôr′-) *adj.* Loathsome; repellent. —**ab·hor′rence** *n.* —**ab·hor′rent·ly** *adv.*

a·bide (ə-bīd′) *v.* **a·bode** (ə-bōd′) or **a·bid·ed, a·bid·ing. 1.** To put up with; endure. **2.** To remain; stay. **3.** To dwell. —**phrasal verb. abide by.** To comply with. [< OE *ābīdan.*] —**a·bid′ance** *n.* —**a·bid′er** *n.*

a·bil·i·ty (ə-bĭl′ĭ-tē) *n., pl.* **-ties.** The power to do something; skill. [< OFr. *habilite < Lat. habilis,* able.]

Syns: ability, capability, competence, faculty, might n.

-ability or **-ibility** *suff.* Capable of or causing: *availability.* [< Lat. *-abilitas, -ibilitas.*]

ab·ject (ăb′jĕkt′, ăb-jĕkt′) *adj.* **1.** Contemptible; base. **2.** Miserable; wretched. [< Lat. *abjicere*, to cast away.] **—ab′ject′ly** *adv.* **—ab·jec′tion** *n.*

ab·jure (ăb-jŏŏr′) *v.* **-jured, -jur·ing. 1.** To recant solemnly; repudiate. **2.** To renounce under oath. [< Lat. *abjurare.*] **—ab′ju·ra′tion** *n.* **—ab·jur′er** *n.*

ab·la·tion (ă-blā′shən) *n.* Removal, esp. by cutting, melting, or vaporization. [Lat. *ablatio*, < *auferre*, to carry away.]

ab·la·tive (ăb′lə-tĭv) *adj.* Designating a grammatical case indicating separation, direction away from, and sometimes manner or agency. [< Lat. *ablativus.*] **—ab′la·tive** *n.*

a·blaze (ə-blāz′) *adj.* On fire; blazing.

a·ble (ā′bəl) *adj.* **a·bler, a·blest. 1.** Having the skill, power, or resources to do something. **2.** Efficiently skillful. [< Lat. *habilis*, manageable < *habēre*, to handle.] **—a′bly** *adv.*

–able *or* **–ible. 1.** Susceptible, capable, or worthy of (an action): *debatable, collapsible.* **2.** Inclined to or liable to: *knowledgeable, fashionable.* [< Lat. *-abilis, -ibilis.*]

a·ble-bod·ied (ā′bəl-bŏd′ēd) *adj.* Strong and healthy.

able-bodied seaman *n.* A merchant seaman certified for all seaman's duties.

a·bloom (ə-blŏōm′) *adj.* In bloom; flowering.

ab·lu·tion (ă-blŏō′shən) *n.* A washing or cleansing of the body or a part of the body. [< Lat. *abluere*, to wash away.]

Ab·na·ki (ăb-nä′kē) *n., pl* **-ki** *or* **-kis. 1.** A tribe of North American Indians of Maine, New Brunswick, and southern Quebec. **2.** A member of the Abnaki. **3.** The Algonquian language of the Abnaki. **—Ab·na′ki** *adj.*

ab·ne·gate (ăb′nĭ-gāt′) *v.* **-gat·ed, -gat·ing.** To deny to oneself; renounce. [Lat. *abnegare*, to refuse.] **—ab′ne·ga′tion** *n.*

ab·nor·mal (ăb-nôr′məl) *adj.* Not normal; deviant. **—ab′nor·mal′i·ty** (-măl′ĭ-tē) *n.* **—ab·nor′mal·ly** *adv.*

a·board (ə-bôrd′, ə-bōrd′) *adv.* On, onto, or inside a ship, train, airplane, etc. *—prep.* On; onto; in.

a·bode (ə-bōd′) *n.* A dwelling place; home. *—v.* A *p.t.* & *p.p.* of **abide.** [< ME *abod.*]

a·bol·ish (ə-bŏl′ĭsh) *v.* To do away with; put an end to. [< Lat. *abolēre*, to destroy.] **—a·bol′ish·a·ble** *adj.* **—a·bol′ish·er** *n.* **—a·bol′ish·ment** *n.* **—ab′o·li′tion** (ăb′ə-lĭsh′ən) *n.*

ab·o·li·tion·ism (ăb′ə-lĭsh′ə-nĭz′əm) *n.* Advocacy of the abolition of slavery. **—ab′o·li′tion·ist** *n.*

A-bomb (ā′bŏm′) *n.* An atomic bomb.

a·bom·i·na·ble (ə-bŏm′ə-nə-bəl) *adj.* Detestable; loathsome. **—a·bom′i·na·bly** *adv.*

abominable snowman *n.* A large, hairy apelike creature that supposedly lives in the Himalayas.

a·bom·i·nate (ə-bŏm′ə-nāt′) *v.* **-nat·ed, -nat·ing.** To detest; abhor. [< Lat. *abominari*, to deprecate as a bad omen.] **—a·bom′i·na′tion** *n.* **—a·bom′i·na′tor** *n.*

ab·o·rig·i·nal (ăb′ə-rĭj′ə-nəl) *adj.* Native; indigenous. **—ab′o·rig′i·nal** *n.* **—ab′o·rig′i·nal·ly** *adv.*

ab·o·rig·i·ne (ăb′ə-rĭj′ə-nē) *n.* A member of a group of the original inhabitants of a given region. [< Lat. *aborigines*, aborigines.]

a·born·ing (ə-bôr′nĭng, -bôr′-) *adv.* While being born or coming into being.

a·bort (ə-bôrt′) *v.* **1.** To terminate pregnancy prematurely. **2.** To terminate completion. [< Lat. *aboriri*, to miscarry.]

a·bor·tion (ə-bôr′shən) *n.* **1.** Induced termination of pregnancy before the embryo or fetus is capable of survival. **2.** A fatally premature expulsion of an embryo or fetus from the uterus. **—a·bor′tive** *adj.* **—a·bor′tive·ly** *adv.* **—a·bor′tive·ness** *n.*

a·bound (ə-bound′) *v.* **1.** To be plentiful in number or amount. **2.** To be fully supplied. [< Lat. *abundare*, to overflow.]

a·bout (ə-bout′) *prep.* **1.** Concerning. **2.** Close or near to. **3.** On the point of: *about to go.* **4.** On all sides of. *—adv.* **1.** Approximately. **2.** To and fro. **3.** In the vicinity. [< OE *onbūtan.*]

a·bout-face (ə-bout′fās′, ə-bout′fās′) *n.* A complete reversal of direction, attitude, or viewpoint. **—a·bout′-face′** *v.*

a·bove (ə-bŭv′) *adv.* **1.** In or to a higher place or position. **2.** In an earlier part of a text. *—prep.* **1.** Over or higher than. **2.** Upstream or uphill from. **3.** Superior to. *—adj.* Appearing or stated earlier. [< OE *abufan.*]

Usage: The use of *above* in referring to earlier material in a text *(the above figures; take note of the above)* is more appropriate to business and legal contexts than to general writing.

a·bove-board (ə-bŭv′bôrd′, -bōrd′) *adv.* & *adj.* Without deceit or trickery.

ab·ra·ca·dab·ra (ăb′rə-kə-dăb′rə) *n.* **1.** A magical charm believed to ward off disease or disaster. **2.** Jargon; gibberish. [LLat.]

a·brade (ə-brād′) *v.* **a·brad·ed, a·brad·ing.** To wear away by friction; erode. [Lat. *abradere*, to scrape off.] **—a·bra′sion** *n.*

a·bra·sive (ə-brā′sĭv, -zĭv) *adj.* **1.** Causing abrasion. **2.** Causing friction or irritation. **—a·bra′sive** *n.* **—a·bra′sive·ly** *adv.* **—a·bra′sive·ness** *n.*

a·breast (ə-brĕst′) *adv.* & *adj.* **1.** Side by side. **2.** Up to date with.

a·bridge (ə-brĭj′) *v.* **a·bridged, a·bridg·ing.** To reduce the length or extent of. [< LLat. *abbreviare*, to abbreviate.] **—a·bridg′er** *n.* **—a·bridg′ment** *or* **a·bridge′ment** *n.*

a·broad (ə-brôd′) *adv.* & *adj.* **1.** In or to foreign places. **2.** Broadly or widely. **3.** Outdoors and about.

ab·ro·gate (ăb′rə-gāt′) *v.* **-gat·ed, -gat·ing.** To abolish by authority. [Lat. *abrogare.*] **—ab′ro·ga′tion** *n.*

a·brupt (ə-brŭpt′) *adj.* **1.** Unexpectedly sudden. **2.** Curt; brusque. **3.** Jerky; disconnected: *abrupt, nervous prose.* **4.** Very steep. [< Lat. *abrumpere*, to break off.] **—a·brupt′ly** *adv.* **—a·brupt′ness** *n.*

ab·scess (ăb′sĕs′) *n.* A collection of pus surrounded by an inflamed area. [< Lat. *abscessus*, departure < *abscedere*, to go away.]

ab·scis·sa (ăb-sĭs′ə) *n., pl.* **-sas** *or* **-scis·sae** (-sĭs′ē). The coordinate representing the distance of a point from the *y*-axis in a plane Cartesian coordinate system, measured along a line parallel to the *x*-axis. [NLat. *(linea) abscissa,* cut-off (line).]

ab·scond (ăb-skŏnd′) *v.* To leave secretly and hide oneself. [Lat. *abscondere,* to hide.]

ab·sence (ăb′səns) *n.* **1.** A state or period of being away. **2.** Lack; dearth.

ab·sent (ăb′sənt) *adj.* **1.** Not present. **2.** Not existent; lacking. **3.** Absorbed in thought. —*v.* (ăb-sĕnt′). To keep (oneself) away. [< Lat. *absens < abesse,* to be away.] —**ab′sent·ly** *adv.*

ab·sen·tee (ăb′sən-tē′) *n.* One that is absent.

ab·sen·tee·ism (ăb′sən-tē′ĭz′əm) *n.* Habitual absence, esp. from work.

ab·sent-mind·ed (ăb′sənt-mīn′dĭd) *adj.* Lost in thought; preoccupied. —**ab′sent-mind′ed·ly** *adv.* —**ab′sent-mind′ed·ness** *n.*

ab·sinthe (ăb′sĭnth) *n.* Also **ab·sinth.** An alcoholic liqueur flavored with wormwood. [< Gk. *apsinthion,* wormwood.]

ab·so·lute (ăb′sə-lōōt′) *adj.* **1.** Perfect in quality or nature; complete. **2.** Not mixed; pure. **3.** Not limited by restrictions, qualifications, or exceptions. **4.** Positive; certain: *absolute proof.* **5.** *Physics.* **a.** Pertaining to measurements or units of measurement derived from fundamental relationships of space, mass, and time. **b.** Pertaining to a temperature scale where zero point is absolute zero. [< Lat. *absolvere,* to free from.] —**ab′so·lute′ly** *adv.* —**ab′so·lute′ness** *n.*

absolute pitch *n.* **1.** The precise pitch of a tone, as established by its rate of vibration measured on a standard scale. **2.** The ability to identify or produce a tone that has been heard or specified.

absolute value *n.* The numerical value or magnitude of a real number without regard to its sign.

absolute zero *n.* The temperature at which a substance contains no thermal energy, equal to −273.15°C or −459.67°F.

ab·so·lu·tion (ăb′sə-lōō′shən) *n.* **1.** The formal release from sin, esp. as given by a priest as part of the sacrament of penance. **2.** Forgiveness.

ab·so·lut·ism (ăb′sə-lōō′tĭz′əm) *n.* A form of government in which a ruler or government has absolute power. —**ab′so·lut′ist** *n.* —**ab′so·lut·is′tic** *adj.*

ab·solve (ăb-zŏlv′, -sŏlv′) *v.* **-solved, -solv·ing.** **1.** To clear of blame or guilt. **2.** To relieve of a requirement or obligation. [< Lat. *absolvere.*] —**ab·solv′a·ble** *adj.* —**ab·solv′er** *n.*

ab·sorb (ăb-sôrb′, -zôrb′) *v.* **1.** To take in; soak up. **2.** To take in and assimilate: *Plants absorb energy from the sun.* **3.** To take in or receive (e.g. sound) with little or none of it being transmitted or reflected. **4.** To occupy completely; take up entirely. [< Lat. *absorbēre.*] —**ab·sorb′a·bil′i·ty** *n.* —**ab·sorb′a·ble** *adj.* —**ab·sorb′ing·ly** *adv.*

ab·sorb·ent (ăb-sôr′bənt, -zôr′-) *adj.* Capable of absorbing. —**ab·sorb′en·cy** *n.* —**ab·sorb′ent** *n.*

ab·sorp·tion (ăb-sôrp′shən, -zôrp′-) *n.* **1.** The act or process of absorbing. **2.** A state of mental concentration. —**ab·sorp′tive** *adj.*

ab·stain (ăb-stān′) *v.* To keep oneself from doing something. [< Lat. *abstinēre.*] —**ab·stain′er** *n.*

ab·ste·mi·ous (ăb-stē′mē-əs) *adj.* Sparing, esp. in the use of alcohol or food. [Lat. *abstemius.*] —**ab·ste′mi·ous·ly** *adv.* —**ab·ste′mi·ous·ness** *n.*

ab·sti·nence (ăb′stə-nəns) *n.* A usu. voluntary refraining, esp. from alcoholic beverages or from specified foods. —**ab′sti·nent** *adj.*

ab·stract (ăb′străkt′, ăb-străkt′) *adj.* **1.** Considered apart from concrete existence or a particular example. **2.** Expressing a quality or property abstracted from the person or thing possessing it. **3.** In art, using forms or designs that have little or no connection with objective or observable reality. —*n.* (ăb′străkt′). **1.** A summary; epitome. **2.** Something abstract, as a term. —*v.* (ăb-străkt′). **1.** To take away; remove. **2.** To steal. **3.** To summarize. [< Lat. *abstrahere,* to remove.] —**ab·stract′er** *n.* —**ab·stract′ly** *adv.* —**ab·stract′ness** *n.*

ab·stract·ed (ăb-străk′tĭd) *adj.* Absentminded. —**ab·stract′ed·ly** *adv.* —**ab·stract′ed·ness** *n.*

ab·strac·tion (ăb-străk′shən) *n.* **1.** The act or process of removing or separating. **2.** An abstract idea. **3.** Preoccupation; absent-mindedness. **4.** An abstract work of art.

ab·struse (ăb-strōōs′) *adj.* Difficult to understand. [< Lat. *abstrudere,* to hide.] —**ab·struse′ly** *adv.* —**ab·struse′ness** *n.*

ab·surd (ăb-sûrd′, -zûrd′) *adj.* Contrary to common sense. [< Lat. *absurdus.*] —**ab·surd′i·ty** *or* **ab·surd′ness** *n.* —**ab·surd′ly** *adv.*

a·bun·dant (ə-bŭn′dənt) *adj.* Richly or plentifully supplied; ample. [Lat. *abundare,* to abound.] —**a·bun′dance** *n.* —**a·bun′dant·ly** *adv.*

a·buse (ə-byōōz′) *v.* **a·bused, a·bus·ing.** **1.** To use wrongly or improperly. **2.** To maltreat. **3.** To attack with insults; revile. —*n.* (ə-byōōs′). **1.** Misuse. **2.** Maltreatment: *His old truck has taken much abuse.* **3.** Insulting or coarse language. [< Lat. *abuti,* to use up.] —**a·bus′er** *n.* —**a·bu′sive** *adj.* —**a·bu′si·ve·ly** *adv.* —**a·bu′sive·ness** *n.*

Syns: **abuse, maltreat, mistreat, misuse** *v.*

a·but (ə-bŭt′) *v.* **a·but·ted, a·but·ting.** To touch at one end or side of something; border upon. [< OFr. *abouter.*] —**a·but′ter** *n.*

a·but·ment (ə-bŭt′mənt) *n.* **1.** The act of abutting. **2.** A structure that supports, as at the end of a bridge.

a·bysm (ə-bĭz′əm) *n.* An abyss. [< OFr. *abisme,* ult. < Gk. *abussos,* bottomless.]

a·bys·mal (ə-bĭz′məl) *adj.* Immeasurably deep; profound. —**a·bys′mal·ly** *adv.*

a·byss (ə-bĭs′) *n.* **1. a.** The primeval chaos. **b.** The bottomless pit; hell. **2.** An unfathomable or immeasurable depth or void. [< Gk. *abussos,* bottomless.]

Ac The symbol for the element actinium.

a·ca·cia (ə-kā′shə) *n.* Any of various chiefly tropical trees with feathery leaves and tight clusters of small yellow or white flowers. [< Gk. *akakia.*]

ac·a·deme (ăk′ə-dēm′) *n.* The scholastic life or environment.

ac·a·dem·ic (ăk′ə-dĕm′ĭk) *adj.* **1.** Of or pertaining to a school or college. **2.** Liberal or classical rather than technical or vocational. **3.** Theoretical; not practical. —**ac′a·dem′i·cal·ly** *adv.*

a·cad·e·mi·cian (ăk′ə-də-mĭsh′ən, ə-kăd′ə-) *n.* A member of an academy or society of learned men or artists.

a·cad·e·mi·cism (ə-kăd′ə-mĭ-sĭz′əm) *n.* Also **a·cad·e·mism** (ə-kăd′ə-mĭz′əm). Traditional formalism, esp. in art.

a·cad·e·my (ə-kăd′ə-mē) *n., pl.* **-mies.** 1. A school for special instruction. 2. A secondary or college-preparatory school, esp. a private one. 3. A society of scholars or artists. [< Gk. *Akadēmia,* the place in Athens where Plato taught.]

a·can·thus (ə-kăn′thəs) *n.* 1. A plant of the Mediterranean region, with large, segmented, thistlelike leaves. 2. Decoration in the form of acanthus leaves. [< Gk. *akanthos.*]

acanthus

Left: Acanthus leaves
Right: Capital of a Corinthian column showing acanthus motif

a cap·pel·la (ä′ kə-pĕl′ə) *adv. Mus.* Without instrumental accompaniment. [Ital.]

ac·cede (ăk-sēd′) *v.* **-ced·ed, -ced·ing.** 1. To give one's assent; agree. 2. To come into an office or dignity. [< Lat. *accedere,* to go near.] **—ac·ced′ence** *n.*

ac·cel·er·an·do (ä-chĕl′ə-rän′dō, ăk-sĕl′ə-) *adv. Mus.* So as to become faster. [Ital.] **—ac·cel′er·an·do** *adj.*

ac·cel·er·ate (ăk-sĕl′ə-rāt′) *v.* **-at·ed, -at·ing.** 1. To make or become faster. 2. To cause to happen sooner. [Lat. *accelerare.*] **—ac·cel·er·a′tion** *n.* **—ac·cel′er·a′tive** *adj.*

ac·cel·er·a·tor (ăk-sĕl′ə-rā′tər) *n.* 1. One that accelerates. 2. A mechanical device, esp. the gas pedal of an automobile, for increasing the speed of a machine. 3. *Physics.* A device, such as a cyclotron, that accelerates charged particles.

ac·cel·er·om·e·ter (ăk-sĕl′ə-rŏm′ĭ-tər) *n.* An instrument that measures acceleration.

ac·cent (ăk′sĕnt′) *n.* 1. Vocal stress or emphasis given to a particular syllable, word, or phrase. 2. A characteristic style of speech or pronunciation: *a southern accent.* 3. A mark placed over a vowel letter to indicate its quality. *—v.* To stress; emphasize. [< Lat. *accentus,* accentuation.]

ac·cen·tu·ate (ăk-sĕn′chōō-āt′) *v.* **-at·ed, -at·ing.** To accent. **—ac·cen′tu·a′tion** *n.*

ac·cept (ăk-sĕpt′) *v.* 1. To receive gladly. 2. To receive into a place or group. 3. To answer affirmatively: *accept an invitation.* 4. To consent to pay, as by a signed agreement. [< Lat. *accipere,* to receive.]

ac·cept·a·ble (ăk-sĕp′tə-bəl) *adj.* Satisfactory; adequate. **—ac·cept′a·bil′i·ty** or **ac·cept′a·ble·ness** *n.* **—ac·cept′a·bly** *adv.*

ac·cep·tance (ăk-sĕp′təns) *n.* 1. The act or process of taking something offered. 2. The condition of being accepted or acceptable. 3. An accepted draft or bill of exchange.

ac·cep·ta·tion (ăk′sĕp-tā′shən) *n.* The usual meaning, as of a word or expression.

ac·cess (ăk′sĕs′) *n.* 1. An act or means of approaching. 2. The right to enter or use. 3. A sudden outburst. [< Lat. *accessus* < *accedere,* to arrive.]

ac·ces·si·ble (ăk-sĕs′ə-bəl) *adj.* Easily approached. **—ac·ces′si·bil′i·ty** *n.* **—ac·ces′si·bly** *adv.*

ac·ces·sion (ăk-sĕsh′ən) *n.* 1. The attainment of rank or dignity. 2. **a.** An increase by means of something added. **b.** An addition. **—ac·ces′sion·al** *adj.*

ac·ces·so·ry (ăk-sĕs′ə-rē) *n., pl.* **-ries.** Also **ac·ces·sa·ry.** 1. Something supplementary. 2. Something nonessential but useful. 3. One who though absent assists or contributes to the commission of a crime. **—ac·ces′so·ry** *adj.*

ac·ci·dence (ăk′sĭ-dəns, -dĕns′) *n.* The section of grammar that deals with the inflections of words.

ac·ci·dent (ăk′sĭ-dənt, -dĕnt′) *n.* 1. An unexpected and undesirable event. 2. Something that occurs unexpectedly. 3. A property or attribute that is nonessential. 4. Fortune; chance. [< Lat. *accidere,* to happen.]

ac·ci·den·tal (ăk′sĭ-dĕn′tl) *adj.* 1. Occurring unexpectedly and unintentionally; by chance. 2. Nonessential; incidental. *—n. Mus.* A sharp, flat, or natural that is not in the key signature. **—ac·ci·den′tal·ly** *adv.*

Syns: *accidental, casual, chance, fluky, fortuitous, inadvertent* **adj.**

ac·claim (ə-klām′) *v.* 1. To praise; applaud. 2. To declare through acclamation. *—n.* Enthusiastic applause, praise, or approval. [Lat. *acclamare,* to shout at.] **—ac·claim′er** *n.*

ac·cla·ma·tion (ăk′lə-mā′shən) *n.* 1. A shout or salute of enthusiastic approval, acceptance, or welcome. 2. An oral vote, esp. a vote of approval taken without formal ballot. **—ac·clam′a·to′ry** (ə-klăm′ə-tôr′ē, -tōr′ē) *adj.*

ac·cli·mate (ə-klī′mĭt, ăk′lə-māt′) *v.* **-mat·ed, -mat·ing.** To make or become accustomed to a new environment or situation. [Fr. *acclimater.*] **—ac′cli·ma′tion** *n.*

ac·cli·ma·tize (ə-klī′mə-tīz′) *v.* **-tized, -tiz·ing.** To acclimate. **—ac·cli′ma·ti·za′tion** *n.*

ac·cliv·i·ty (ə-klĭv′ĭ-tē) *n., pl.* **-ties.** An upward slope. [Lat. *acclivitas* < *acclivis,* uphill.]

ac·co·lade (ăk′ə-lād′, ăk′ə-läd′) *n.* 1. Recognition; acknowledgment. 2. Praise; approval. [< Prov. *acolada,* embrace.]

ac·com·mo·date (ə-kŏm′ə-dāt′) *v.* **-dat·ed, -dat·ing.** 1. To do a favor for; oblige. 2. To provide for; supply with. 3. To contain comfortably. 4. To adapt; adjust. 5. To settle; reconcile. [Lat. *accommodare,* to make fit.]

ac·com·mo·dat·ing (ə-kŏm′ə-dā′tĭng) *adj.* Helpful and obliging. **—ac·com′mo·dat′ing·ly** *adv.*

ac·com·mo·da·tion (ə-kŏm′ə-dā′shən) *n.* 1. The act of accommodating or the condition of being accommodated. 2. Something that meets a need. 3. **accommodations.** Room and board; lodgings.

ac·com·pa·ni·ment (ə-kŭm′pə-nə-mənt, ə-kŭmp′nə-) *n.* 1. Something that accompanies; concomitant. 2. Music played along as support or embellishment.

ac·com·pa·ny (ə-kŭm′pə-nē, ə-kŭmp′nē) *v.*

-nied, -ny-ing. 1. To go along or occur with. 2. To play an accompaniment (for). [< OFr. *accompagner.*]

ac-com-plice (ə-kŏm'plĭs) *n.* One who assists a lawbreaker in a criminal act. [< ME, *a complice,* an associate.]

ac-com-plish (ə-kŏm'plĭsh) *v.* To succeed in completing; achieve. [< OFr. *accomplir.*] —**ac-com'plish-er** *n.*

Syns: accomplish, achieve, attain, reach, realize, score *v.*

ac-com-plished (ə-kŏm'plĭsht) *adj.* 1. Completed; finished. 2. Skilled; expert.

ac-com-plish-ment (ə-kŏm'plĭsh-mənt) *n.* 1. The act of accomplishing or being accomplished. 2. Something completed successfully. 3. A skill that has been acquired.

ac-cord (ə-kôrd') *v.* 1. To make conform or agree. 2. To bestow upon; grant. 3. To be in agreement, unity, or harmony. —*n.* Agreement; harmony. [< OFr. *acorder.*] —**ac-cor'dance** *n.* —**ac-cor'dant** *adj.* —**ac-cor'dant-ly** *adv.*

ac-cord-ing-ly (ə-kôr'dĭng-lē) *adv.* 1. In keeping with what is known, stated, or expected. 2. Consequently; therefore.

according to *prep.* 1. As stated or indicated by: *According to him she lied.* 2. In agreement with: *Proceed according to instructions.*

ac-cor-di-on (ə-kôr'dē-ən) *n.* A portable musical instrument with a small keyboard and free metal reeds that sound when air is forced past them by pleated bellows. [G. *Akkordion,* ult. < OFr. *acorder,* to accord.] —**ac-cor'di-on-ist** *n.*

ac-cost (ə-kôst', ə-kŏst') *v.* To approach and speak to first. [< Med. Lat. *acostare,* to adjoin.]

ac-count (ə-kount') *n.* 1. A description of events; narrative. 2. A set of reasons; explanation. 3. A record or statement, esp. of business dealings or money received or spent. 4. A business arrangement, as with a bank or store, in which money is kept, exchanged, or owed. —*v.* To consider; regard. —*phrasal verb.* **account for.** To give the reason for; explain. —*idiom.* **on account of.** Because of. [< OFr. *acont* < *acompter,* to reckon.]

ac-count-a-ble (ə-koun'tə-bəl) *adj.* Answerable; responsible. —**ac-count'a-bil'i-ty** or **ac-count'a-ble-ness** *n.* —**ac-count'a-bly** *adv.*

ac-count-ant (ə-koun'tənt) *n.* An expert in accounting. —**ac-count'an-cy** *n.*

ac-count-ing (ə-koun'tĭng) *n.* The bookkeeping methods involved in recording business transactions and preparing the financial statements of a business.

ac-cou-ter (ə-kōō'tər) *v.* Also **ac-cou-tre.** To outfit and equip, esp. for a particular purpose. [< OFr. *acoustrer.*] —**ac-cou'ter-ments** or **ac-cou'tre-ments** *n.*

ac-cred-it (ə-krĕd'ĭt) *v.* 1. To credit. 2. To certify as meeting a standard. [Fr. *accréditer.*] —**ac-cred'i-ta'tion** *n.*

ac-cre-tion (ə-krē'shən) *n.* 1. Growth or increase in size by gradual external addition. 2. The result of accretion. [< Lat. *accrescere,* to grow.] —**ac-cre'tion-ar'y** or **ac-cre'tive** *adj.*

ac-crue (ə-krōō') *v.* -**crued,** -**cru-ing.** 1. To come as a gain or increase: *benefits that accrue from scientific research.* 2. To increase by regular growth. [< Lat. *accrescere,* to grow.] —**ac-cru'al** *n.*

ac-cul-tur-a-tion (ə-kŭl'chə-rā'shən) *n.* The process of altering a society, esp. the modification of a primitive culture by contact with an advanced culture.

ac-cu-mu-late (ə-kyōō'myə-lāt') *v.* -**lat-ed,** -**lat-ing.** To amass or collect; mount up. [Lat. *accumulare.*] —**ac-cu'mu-la'tion** *n.* —**ac-cu'mu-la'tor** *n.*

ac-cu-rate (ăk'yər-ĭt) *adj.* Having no errors; correct. [< Lat. *accurare,* to attend to carefully.] —**ac'cu-ra-cy** *n.* —**ac'cu-rate-ly** *adv.* —**ac'cu-rate-ness** *n.*

Syns: accurate, correct, exact, faithful, precise, right, true, veracious *adj.*

ac-curs-ed (ə-kûr'sĭd, ə-kûrst') *adj.* Also **ac-curst** (ə-kûrst'). 1. Under a curse; damned. 2. Hateful; abominable. —**ac-curs'ed-ly** *adv.*

ac-cu-sa-tive (ə-kyōō'zə-tĭv) *adj.* Of or pertaining to the grammatical case of a noun, pronoun, adjective, or participle that is the direct object of a verb or the object of certain prepositions. —*n.* 1. The accusative case. 2. A word in the accusative case. [< Lat. *(casus) accusativus,* (case) of accusation.]

ac-cuse (ə-kyōōz') *v.* -**cused,** -**cus-ing.** To charge with an error or offense. [< Lat. *accusare.*] —**ac'cu-sa'tion** *n.* —**ac-cus'er** *n.* —**ac-cus'ing-ly** *adv.*

ac-cus-tom (ə-kŭs'təm) *v.* To familiarize, as by constant practice. [< OFr. *acoustumer.*]

ac-cus-tomed (ə-kŭs'təmd) *adj.* Usual; habitual.

ace (ās) *n.* 1. A playing card, die, or domino having one spot or pip. 2. In racket games, a point scored by the failure of one's opponent to return a serve. 3. A fighter pilot who has destroyed five or more enemy planes. 4. *Informal.* One who excels in performance. —*v.* **aced, ac-ing.** *Slang.* To get the better of. —*idioms.* **ace in the hole.** A hidden advantage. **within an ace of.** Very near to. [< Lat. *as,* unit.]

ac-er-bate (ăs'ər-bāt') *v.* -**bated,** -**bat-ing.** To vex; annoy. [< Lat. *acerbus,* bitter.]

a-cer-bi-ty (ə-sûr'bĭ-tē) *n., pl.* -**ties.** Bitterness; harshness. [< Lat. *acerbus,* bitter.]

ac-e-tate (ăs'ĭ-tāt') *n.* 1. A salt or ester of acetic acid. 2. Cellulose acetate or any of various products, esp. fibers, derived from it.

a-ce-tic (ə-sē'tĭk, ə-sĕt'ĭk) *adj.* Of, pertaining to, or containing acetic acid or vinegar. [< Lat. *acetum,* vinegar.]

acetic acid *n.* A clear, colorless organic acid, CH_3COOH, with a distinctive pungent odor, that is found in vinegar and used in chemical synthesis and manufacturing.

ac-e-tone (ăs'ĭ-tōn') *n.* A colorless, volatile, extremely flammable liquid, CH_3COCH_3, widely used as an organic solvent.

a-ce-tyl-cho-line (ə-sēt'l-kō'lēn) *n.* A white crystalline compound, $C_7H_{17}NO_3$, that transmits nerve impulses across intercellular gaps.

a-cet-y-lene (ə-sĕt'l-ēn', -ĭn) *n.* A colorless, highly flammable or explosive gas, C_2H_2, used for metal welding and cutting.

a-ce-tyl-sal-i-cyl-ic acid (ə-sēt'l-săl'ĭ-sĭl'ĭk) *n.* Aspirin.

ache (āk) *v.* **ached, ach-ing.** 1. To suffer a dull, sustained pain. 2. *Informal.* To yearn; long. [< OE *ācan.*] —**ache** *n.* —**ach'y** *adj.*

a-chieve (ə-chēv') *v.* **a-chieved, a-chiev-ing.** To attain or get through effort or work. [< OFr. *achever* < *(venir) a chef,* (to come) to a head.] —**a-chiev'a-ble** *adj.* —**a-chieve'ment** *n.* —**a-chiev'er** *n.*

A-chil-les' heel (ə-kĭl'ēz) *n.* A weak point.

[From the myth that Achilles was vulnerable only in the heel.]

Achilles' tendon *n.* The large tendon running from the heel bone to the calf muscle.

ach·ro·mat·ic (ăk′rə-măt′ĭk) *adj.* **1.** Of or designating a color, such as black or white, that has no hue. **2.** *Optics.* Refracting white light without breaking it into the colors of the spectrum. —**ach′ro·mat′i·cal·ly** *adv.*

ac·id (ăs′ĭd) *n.* **1.** *Chem.* Any of a large class of substances, whose aqueous solutions are capable of turning litmus indicators red, of reacting with bases or alkalis to form salts, or that have a sour taste. **2.** A substance having a sour taste. **3.** *Slang.* LSD. —*adj.* **1.** *Chem.* Of or pertaining to an acid. **2.** Having a sour taste. **3.** Biting; caustic: *an acid wit.* [< Lat. *acidus,* sour.] —**a·cid′ic** (ə-sĭd′ĭk) *adj.* —**a·cid′i·ty** (ə-sĭd′ĭ-tē) *n.* —**ac′id·ly** *adv.* —**ac′id·ness** *n.*

ac·id·head (ăs′ĭd-hĕd′) *n. Slang.* One who uses LSD, esp. habitually.

a·cid·i·fy (ə-sĭd′ə-fī′) *v.* **-fied, -fy·ing.** To make or become acid. —**a·cid′i·fi′a·ble** *adj.* —**a·cid′i·fi·ca′tion** *n.* —**a·cid′i·fi′er** *n.*

ac·i·do·sis (ăs′ĭ-dō′sĭs) *n.* A condition of pathologically high acidity of the blood. —**ac′i·dot′ic** (ăs′ĭ-dŏt′ĭk) *adj.*

acid test *n.* A decisive or critical test.

a·cid·u·late (ə-sĭj′ŏŏ-lāt′) *v.* **-lat·ed, -lat·ing.** To make or become slightly acid. [ACIDUL(OUS) + -ATE²] —**a·cid′u·la′tion** *n.*

a·cid·u·lous (ə-sĭj′ə-ləs, ə-sĭd′yə-) *adj.* Somewhat sour. [Lat. *acidulus.*]

ac·knowl·edge (ăk-nŏl′ĭj) *v.* **-edged, -edg·ing.** **1.** To admit the validity, authority, or truth of. **2. a.** To express recognition of. **b.** To express thanks or gratitude for. **3.** To report the receipt of. [Blend of ME *knowlegen,* to acknowledge and ME *aknouen,* to recognize.] —**ac·knowl′edge·a·ble** *adj.* —**ac·knowl′edg·ment** or **ac·knowl′edge·ment** *n.*

Syns: *acknowledge, admit, allow, concede, confess, grant* v.

ac·me (ăk′mē) *n.* The highest point; peak. [Gk. *akmē.*]

ac·ne (ăk′nē) *n.* An inflammatory disease of the oil glands, characterized by pimples, esp. on the face. [Poss. < Gk. *akmē,* point.]

ac·o·lyte (ăk′ə-līt′) *n.* **1.** A person who assists a priest in a religious service. **2.** An attendant; follower. [< Gk. *akolouthos,* attendant.]

ac·o·nite (ăk′ə-nīt′) *n.* **1.** The monkshood. **2.** A medicinal preparation made from the roots of monkshood. [< Gk. *akoniton.*]

a·corn (ā′kôrn′, ā′kərn) *n.* The fruit of the oak tree, consisting of a nut set in a cuplike base. [< OE *æcern.*]

acorn squash *n.* A type of squash shaped somewhat like an acorn with a ridged rind and sweet yellow flesh.

a·cous·tic (ə-kŏŏ′stĭk) or **a·cous·ti·cal** (-stĭ-kəl) *adj.* **1.** Of or pertaining to sound, the sense of hearing, or the science of sound. **2.** Designed to aid in hearing. [Gk. *akoustikos* < *akouein,* to hear.] —**a·cous′ti·cal·ly** *adv.*

a·cous·tics (ə-kŏŏ′stĭks) *n.* **1.** (*used with a sing. verb*). The scientific study of sound. **2.** (*used with a pl. verb*). The qualities of space that make it transmit sound well or poorly.

ac·quaint (ə-kwānt′) *v.* To make familiar or informed. [< Lat. *accognoscere,* to know perfectly.]

ac·quain·tance (ə-kwān′təns) *n.* **1.** Personal knowledge or information. **2.** A person or persons whom one knows. —**ac·quain′tance·ship′** *n.*

ac·qui·esce (ăk′wē-ĕs′) *v.* **-esced, -esc·ing.** To consent or comply without protest. [Lat. *acquiescere.*] —**ac′qui·es′cence** *n.* —**ac′qui·es′cent** *adj.* —**ac′qui·es′cent·ly** *adv.*

Usage: *Acquiesce* takes the prepositions *to* (*acquiesced to their wishes*) or *in* (*acquiesced in the ruling*).

ac·quire (ə-kwīr′) *v.* **-quired, -quir·ing.** **1.** To gain possession of. **2.** To get by one's efforts. [< Lat. *acquirere,* to add to.] —**ac·quir′a·ble** *adj.* —**ac·quire′ment** *n.*

ac·qui·si·tion (ăk′wĭ-zĭsh′ən) *n.* **1.** The act of acquiring. **2.** Something acquired.

ac·quis·i·tive (ə-kwĭz′ĭ-tĭv) *adj.* Eager to acquire possessions; grasping. —**ac·quis′i·tive·ly** *adv.* —**ac·quis′i·tive·ness** *n.*

ac·quit (ə-kwĭt′) *v.* **-quit·ted, -quit·ting.** **1.** To declare free from a charge or accusation. **2.** To conduct (oneself). [< OFr. *aquiter.*] —**ac·quit′tal** *n.*

a·cre (ā′kər) *n.* A unit of area used in land measurement and equal to 4,840 sq. yd. or 43,560 sq. ft. [< OE *æcer.*]

a·cre·age (ā′kər-ĭj) *n.* Land area in acres.

ac·rid (ăk′rĭd) *adj.* **1.** Harsh or bitter in taste or smell. **2.** Biting; caustic. [< Lat. *acer,* bitter.] —**a·crid′i·ty** (ə-krĭd′ĭ-tē) or **ac′rid·ness** *n.* —**ac′rid·ly** *adv.*

ac·ri·mo·ny (ăk′rə-mō′nē) *n.* Bitterness or illnatured animosity, esp. in speech or manner. [Lat. *acrimonia.*] —**ac′ri·mo′ni·ous** *adj.* —**ac′ri·mo′ni·ous·ly** *adv.* —**ac′ri·mo′ni·ous·ness** *n.*

acro- *pref.* **1.** A height or summit: *acrophobia.* **2.** Beginning: *acronym.* [< Gk. *akros,* extreme.]

ac·ro·bat (ăk′rə-băt′) *n.* A person skilled in feats of agility and balance. [< Gk. *akrobatēs* < *akrobatein,* to walk on tiptoe.] —**ac′ro·bat′ic** *adj.* —**ac′ro·bat′i·cal·ly** *adv.*

ac·ro·bat·ics (ăk′rə-băt′ĭks) *pl.n.* The actions of an acrobat.

ac·ro·nym (ăk′rə-nĭm′) *n.* A word formed from the initial letters of a name, as WAC for Women's Army Corps.

ac·ro·pho·bi·a (ăk′rə-fō′bē-ə) *n.* Abnormally intense fear of being in high places.

a·crop·o·lis (ə-krŏp′ə-lĭs) *n.* **1.** The fortified

acropolis
The Acropolis, Athens, Greece

---

height or citadel of an ancient Greek city.
2. Acropolis. The citadel of Athens. [Gk. *akropolis.*]

a·cross (ə-krôs', ə-krŏs') *prep.* **1.** To, from, or on the other side of. **2.** Crosswise. —*adv.* From one side to the other. [< OFr. *a croix,* in the form of a cross.]

a·cross-the-board (ə-krôs'thə-bôrd', -bŏrd', ə-krŏs'-) *adj.* **1.** Combining win, place, or show in one bet. **2.** Including all categories.

a·cros·tic (ə-krŏ'stĭk, ə-krŏs'tĭk) *n.* A poem or series of lines in which certain letters, such as the first in a line of verse, form a name, motto, or message when read in sequence. [< Gk. *akrostikhis.*]

a·cryl·ic (ə-krĭl'ĭk) *n.* **1.** A paint in which the vehicle is acrylic resin. **2.** Acrylic resin. **3.** Acrylic fiber. [*acr(olein)* + -YL + -IC.]

acrylic fiber *n.* Any of numerous synthetic fibers produced from acrylonitrile.

acrylic resin *n.* Any of numerous thermoplastics used to produce synthetic rubbers or clear, lightweight plastics resistant to weather and corrosion.

act (ăkt) *v.* **1.** To perform in a dramatic production. **2.** To behave; conduct oneself. **3.** To perform an action; do something. **4.** To put on a false show; pretend. **5.** To serve; function. **6.** To have an effect on. —*phrasal verb.* **act up.** To behave in an unusual or undesirable way; misbehave. —*n.* **1.** A thing done; deed. **2. a.** A performance that is part of a longer show. **b.** A main division of a dramatic work. **3.** A pretense; false show. **4.** A law; statute. **5. Acts.** See table at **Bible**. [< Lat. *actus,* p.p. of *agere,* to do.] —**act'a·bil'i·ty** *n.* —**act'a·ble** *adj.*

ACTH (ā'sē'tē-āch') *n.* A protein hormone for use in stimulating secretion of cortisone and other adrenal cortex hormones. [< *a(dreno)c(ortico)t(ropic) h(ormone).*]

act·ing (ăk'tĭng) *adj.* Temporarily assuming the duties or authority of another.

ac·ti·nide (ăk'tə-nīd') *n.* Any of a series of chemically similar, mostly synthetic, radioactive elements with atomic numbers ranging from 89 (actinium) through 103 (lawrencium). [< Gk. *aktis,* ray.]

ac·ti·nism (ăk'tə-nĭz'əm) *n.* The property of radiation that produces chemical changes. —**ac·tin'ic** (-tĭn'ĭk) *adj.* —**ac·tin'i·cal·ly** *adv.*

ac·tin·i·um (ăk-tĭn'ē-əm) *n. Symbol* **Ac** A radioactive metallic element found in uranium ores and used as a source of alpha rays. Atomic number 89; longest-lived isotope Ac227. [< Gk. *aktis,* ray.]

ac·tin·o·gen (ăk-tĭn'ō-jən) *n.* A radioactive element. [Gk. *aktis,* ray + -GEN.]

ac·tion (ăk'shən) *n.* **1. a.** A thing done; deed. **b. actions.** Behavior; conduct. **2.** The act, process, or fact of doing something. **3.** Motion; movement: *the constant action of a pendulum.* **4.** The plot of a play, story, etc. **5.** The operating parts of a mechanism: *the action of a piano.* **6.** A lawsuit. **7.** Battle; combat. **8.** *Informal.* Activity.

ac·tion·a·ble (ăk'shə-nə-bəl) *adj.* Giving just cause for legal action. —**ac'tion·a·bly** *adv.*

ac·ti·vate (ăk'tə-vāt') *v.* **-vat·ed, -vat·ing. 1.** To make active: *activate the procedure.* **2.** To create or organize (a military unit). **3.** To purify (sewage). **4.** *Physics.* To make (a substance) radioactive. —**ac'ti·va'tion** *n.* —**ac'ti·va'tor** *n.*

ac·tive (ăk'tĭv) *adj.* **1.** In action; moving.

2. Capable of functioning; working. **3.** Full of energy; lively. **4.** Causing action or change; effective: *active efforts for improvement.* **5.** *Gram.* Showing or expressing action: *an active verb.* —**ac'tive·ly** *adv.* —**ac'tive·ness** *n.*

active immunity *n.* Long-lasting immunity to a disease due to antibody production by the organism.

ac·tiv·ism (ăk'tĭv-ĭz'əm) *n.* A theory or practice based on militant action to achieve a social or political end. —**ac'tiv·ist** *n.*

ac·tiv·i·ty (ăk-tĭv'ĭ-tē) *n., pl.* **-ties. 1.** The condition of being active; action. **2.** A planned or organized thing to do: *extracurricular activities.* **3.** Energetic action; liveliness.

act of God *n. Law.* An unforeseeable or inevitable occurrence, as a tornado, caused by nature.

ac·tor (ăk'tər) *n.* **1.** A theatrical performer. **2.** A participant.

ac·tress (ăk'trĭs) *n.* A female theatrical performer.

ac·tu·al (ăk'chōō-əl) *adj.* **1.** Existing in fact; real. **2.** Existing or acting at the present moment. [< Lat. *actualis.*] —**ac'tu·al'i·ty** *n.* —**ac'tu·al·ly** *adv.*

ac·tu·al·ize (ăk'chōō-ə-līz') *v.* **-ized, -iz·ing.** To realize in action. —**ac'tu·al·i·za'tion** *n.*

ac·tu·ar·y (ăk'chōō-ĕr'ē) *n., pl.* **-ies.** One who computes insurance risks and premiums. [Lat. *actuarius,* secretary of accounts.] —**ac'tu·ar'i·al** (-âr'ē-əl) *adj.*

ac·tu·ate (ăk'chōō-āt') *v.* **-at·ed, -at·ing. 1.** To put into action. **2.** To move to action. [Med. Lat. *actuare.*] —**ac'tu·a'tion** *n.* —**ac'tu·a'tor** *n.*

a·cu·i·ty (ə-kyōō'ĭ-tē) *n.* Keenness of vision or mind. [< Med. Lat. *acuitas.*]

a·cu·men (ə-kyōō'mən, ăk'yə-) *n.* Keenness of insight or judgment. [Lat.]

ac·u·punc·ture (ăk'yōō-pŭngk'chər) *n.* A traditional Chinese therapeutic technique whereby the body is punctured with fine needles. [Lat. *acus,* needle + PUNCTURE.]

a·cute (ə-kyōōt') *adj.* **1.** Having a sharp point. **2.** Keenly perceptive; shrewd. **3.** Sensitive. **4.** Crucial: *an acute need for funds.* **5.** Extremely severe or sharp: *acute pain.* **6.** *Med.* Reaching a crisis rapidly: *acute appendicitis.* **7.** *Geom.* Designating angles that are less than 90°. [< Lat. *acuere,* to sharpen.] —**a·cute'ly** *adv.* —**a·cute'ness** *n.*

acute accent *n.* A mark used over a vowel to indicate sound quality or length.

ad (ăd) *n.* An advertisement.

ad– *pref.* Toward; to: *adsorb.* [Lat.]

ad·age (ăd'ĭj) *n.* A short proverb; saying. [< Lat. *adagium.*]

a·da·gio (ə-dä'jō, -jē-ō') *adv. Mus.* Slowly. —*adj. Mus.* Slow in tempo. —*n., pl.* **-gios.** **1.** *Mus.* An adagio movement. **2.** The slow section of a pas de deux in ballet. [Ital.]

Ad·am (ăd'əm) *n.* In the Old Testament, the first man and progenitor of mankind.

ad·a·mant (ăd'ə-mənt, -mănt') *n.* A legendary stone believed to be impenetrable. —*adj.* Unyielding; inflexible. [< Gk. *adamas.*] —**ad'a·mant·ly** *adv.*

Adam's apple *n.* The projection of cartilage at the front of the throat, most noticeable in men.

a·dapt (ə-dăpt') *v.* To adjust or become adjusted to new or different conditions. [Lat. *adaptare.*] —**a·dapt'a·bil'i·ty** *n.* or **a·dapt'a·ble·ness** *n.* —**a·dapt'a·ble** *adj.*

ad·ap·ta·tion (ăd'ăp-tā'shən) n. 1. a. The condition of being adapted. b. The act or process of adapting. 2. An alteration or adjustment. —**ad'ap·ta'tion·al** adj. —**ad'ap·ta'tion·al·ly** adv.

a·dapt·er (ə-dăp'tər) n. Also **a·dap·tor.** A device used to connect different parts of one or more pieces of apparatus.

a·dap·tive (ə-dăp'tĭv) adj. Tending to adapt: man's adaptive nature. —**a·dap'tive·ly** adv. —**a·dap'tive·ness** n.

A·dar (ä-där') n. The 6th month of the Hebrew year. See table at **calendar.**

add (ăd) v. 1. To join or unite so as to increase in size, quantity, or scope. 2. To combine to form a sum. 3. To say or write further. —**phrasal verbs. add up.** To be reasonable or consistent. **add up to.** To mean; indicate. [< Lat. addere.]

ad·den·dum (ə-dĕn'dəm) n., pl. **-da** (-də). Something added; supplement. [Lat.]

ad·der¹ (ăd'ər) n. 1. Any of various poisonous Old World snakes. 2. Any of several nonpoisonous snakes of North America. [< OE nǣdre.]

adder¹

add·er² (ăd'ər) n. A computer device that performs arithmetic addition.

ad·dict (ə-dĭkt') v. To devote or give (oneself) habitually or compulsively. —n. (ăd'ĭkt). One who is addicted to a harmful substance, esp. to narcotics. [< Lat. addicere, to award to.] —**ad·dic'tion** n. —**ad·dic'tive** adj.

ad·di·tion (ə-dĭsh'ən) n. 1. The act or process of adding. 2. Something that is added. 3. The process of computing with sets of numbers so as to find their sum.

ad·di·tion·al (ə-dĭsh'ə-nəl) adj. Added; extra: additional information. —**ad·di'tion·al·ly** adv.

ad·di·tive (ăd'ĭ-tĭv) adj. Involving addition. —n. A substance added in small amounts to something else to improve or strengthen it.

ad·dle (ăd'l) v. **-dled, -dling.** 1. To make or become confused. 2. To spoil, as an egg. [< OE adela, filth.]

ad·dress (ə-drĕs') v. 1. To speak to. 2. To mark with a destination. 3. To direct one's efforts or attention to. —n. 1. A formal spoken or written communication. 2. (also ăd'rĕs). The indication of destination on mail. 3. (also ăd'rĕs). The location at which an organization or person can be reached. 4. Skillfulness. [< OFr. adresser.]

ad·dress·ee (ăd'rĕs-ē', ə-drĕs'ē') n. One to whom something is addressed.

ad·duce (ə-dōōs', ə-dyōōs', ā-) v. **-duced,** **-duc·ing.** To cite as an example or means of proof. [Lat. adducere, to bring to.]

-ade suff. A sweetened drink of: lemonade. [Fr.]

ad·e·nine (ăd'n-ēn', -ĭn) n. A purine derivative, $C_5H_5N_5$, that is a constituent of nucleic acid in the pancreas, spleen, and other organs. [Gk. adēn, gland + -INE².]

ad·e·noids (ăd'n-oidz') pl.n. Lymphoid tissue growths in the nose above the throat. [Gk. adēn, gland + -OID.] —**ad'e·noid'** or **ad'e·noi'dal** adj.

a·den·o·sine tri·phos·phate (ə-dĕn'ə-sēn' trī-fŏs'fāt') n. ATP.

a·dept (ə-dĕpt') adj. Highly skilled; proficient. —n. (ăd'ĕpt'). An expert. [Lat. adeptus.] —**a·dept'ly** adv. —**a·dept'ness** n.

ad·e·quate (ăd'ĭ-kwĭt) adj. 1. Able to satisfy a requirement. 2. Barely satisfactory; mediocre. [< Lat. adaequare, to make equal to.] —**ad'e·qua·cy** (-kwə-sē) or **ad'e·quate·ness** n. —**ad'e·quate·ly** adv.

ad·here (ăd-hîr') v. **-hered, -her·ing.** 1. To stick or hold fast. 2. To be devoted or loyal to. 3. To follow closely; observe: adhere to a plan. [Lat. adhaerēre.] —**ad·her'ent** adj. & n.

ad·he·sion (ăd-hē'zhən) n. 1. The act or condition of adhering. 2. Bodily tissues that are abnormally joined together.

ad·he·sive (ăd-hē'sĭv) adj. 1. Tending to adhere; sticky. 2. Gummed so as to adhere. —n. An adhesive substance. —**ad·he'sive·ly** adv. —**ad·he'sive·ness** n.

ad hoc (ăd hŏk') adj. & adv. For a specific purpose, case, or situation: an ad hoc committee. [< Lat., to this.]

a·dieu (ə-dōō', ə-dyōō') interj. Good-by; farewell. —n., pl. **a·dieus** or **a·dieux** (ə-dōōz', ə-dyōōz'). A farewell. [< OFr.]

ad in·fi·ni·tum (ăd ĭn'fə-nī'təm) adj. & adv. Without end; limitless. [Lat.]

a·di·os (ä'dē-ōs', ăd'ē-) interj. Good-by; farewell. [Sp.]

ad·i·pose (ăd'ə-pōs') adj. Of or related to animal fat; fatty. [< Lat. adeps, fat.]

ad·ja·cent (ə-jā'sənt) adj. Next to; adjoining. [< Lat. adjacere, to lie near.] —**ad·ja'cen·cy** n. —**ad·ja'cent·ly** adv.

ad·jec·tive (ăj'ĭk-tĭv) n. Any of a class of words used to modify a noun or other substantive by limiting, qualifying, or specifying. [< Lat. adjectivus.] —**ad'jec·ti'val** (-tī'vəl) adj. —**ad'jec·ti'val·ly** adv.

ad·join (ə-join') v. To be next to. [< Lat. adjungere, to join to.]

ad·journ (ə-jûrn') v. 1. To suspend until a later stated time. 2. Informal. To move from one place to another. [OFr. ajourner.] —**ad·journ'ment** n.

ad·judge (ə-jŭj') v. **-judged, -judg·ing.** 1. To determine, rule, or award by law. 2. To regard, consider, or deem. [< Lat. adjudicare.]

ad·ju·di·cate (ə-jōō'dĭ-kāt') v. **-cat·ed, -cat·ing.** To settle by judicial procedure. [Lat. adjudicare.] —**ad·ju'di·ca'tion** n. —**ad·ju'di·ca'tive** adj. —**ad·ju'di·ca'tor** n.

ad·junct (ăj'ŭngkt') n. One attached to another in a subordinate position or relationship. [Lat. adjunctum.]

ad·jure (ə-jŏŏr′) v. **-jured, -jur·ing.** 1. To command or enjoin solemnly, as under oath. 2. To appeal to earnestly. [< Lat. *adjurare.*] —**ad′ju·ra′tion** (ăj′ŏŏ-rā′shən) n.

ad·just (ə-jŭst′) v. 1. To change so as to match or fit. 2. To bring into proper relationship; correct. 3. To adapt or conform, as to new conditions. 4. To regulate: *adjust a watch.* 5. To settle (a claim or debt). [< OFr. *ajoster.*] —**ad·just′a·ble** adj. —**ad·just′er** or **ad·jus′tor** n. —**ad·just′ment** n.

ad·ju·tant (ăj′ə-tənt) n. 1. A military staff officer who helps a commanding officer. 2. An assistant. 3. The marabou. [< Lat. *adjutare,* to assist.] —**ad′ju·tan·cy** n.

ad lib (ăd lĭb′) adv. In an unrestrained manner; spontaneously. [< Lat. *ad libitum,* to pleasure.]

ad-lib (ăd-lĭb′) v. **-libbed, -lib·bing.** To improvise or extemporize. —n. Words, music, or actions ad-libbed.

ad·man (ăd′măn′) n. *Informal.* A person employed in the advertising business.

ad·min·is·ter (ăd-mĭn′ĭ-stər) v. 1. To direct; manage. 2. **a.** To give (a drug) remedially. **b.** To dispense (a sacrament). 3. To mete out. 4. To tender (an oath). 5. To manage or dispose of (an estate). [< Lat. *administrare.*] —**ad·min′is·tra·ble** adj.

ad·min·is·tra·tion (ăd-mĭn′ĭ-strā′shən) n. 1. The act of administering. 2. Management. 3. **a.** Often **Administration.** The executive body of a government. **b.** Its term of office. 4. *Law.* The management and disposal of a trust or estate. —**ad·min′is·tra′tive** adj. —**ad·min′is·tra′tive·ly** adv.

ad·min·is·tra·tor (ăd-mĭn′ĭ-strā′tər) n. 1. One that administers. 2. One appointed to administer an estate.

ad·mi·ra·ble (ăd′mər-ə-bəl) adj. Deserving of admiration; excellent. —**ad′mi·ra·ble·ness** n. —**ad′mi·ra·bly** adv.

ad·mi·ral (ăd′mər-əl) n. 1. The commander in chief of a navy or fleet. 2. A naval officer of the next-to-the-highest rank. [< Ar. *'amīr-al-,* commander of.]

ad·mi·ral·ty (ăd′mər-əl-tē) n., pl. **-ties.** 1. A court that has jurisdiction over all maritime cases. 2. **Admiralty.** The department of the British government that has control over naval affairs.

ad·mire (ăd-mīr′) v. **-mired, -mir·ing.** 1. To regard with wonder and approval. 2. To esteem; respect. [Lat. *admirari.*] —**ad′mi·ra′tion** (ăd′mə-rā′shən) n. —**ad·mir′er** n. —**ad·mir′ing·ly** adv.

ad·mis·si·ble (ăd-mĭs′ə-bəl) adj. Capable or worthy of being accepted or admitted: *admissible evidence.* —**ad·mis′si·bil′i·ty** or **ad·mis′si·ble·ness** n.

ad·mis·sion (ăd-mĭsh′ən) n. 1. The act or process of admitting or the condition of being allowed to enter. 2. Something admitted, as a confession. 3. The right to enter; access: *application for admission.* 4. An entrance fee. [< Lat. *admittere,* to admit.]

ad·mit (ăd-mĭt′) v. **-mit·ted, -mit·ting.** 1. To permit to enter or serve as a means of entrance. 2. To have room for; accommodate. 3. To afford opportunity for; allow: *a problem that admits of no solution.* 4. To acknowledge; confess. 5. To concede. [< Lat. *admittere.*]

ad·mit·tance (ăd-mĭt′ns) n. Permission or right to enter.

ad·mit·ted·ly (ăd-mĭt′ĭd-lē) adv. By general admission.

ad·mix·ture (ăd-mĭks′chər) n. 1. A mixture or blend. 2. Something added in mixing. —**ad·mix′** v.

ad·mon·ish (ăd-mŏn′ĭsh) v. 1. To reprove mildly. 2. To warn, urge, or caution. [< Lat. *admonere.*] —**ad·mo·ni′tion** (-mə-nĭsh′ən) or **ad·mon′ish·ment** n. —**ad·mon′i·to′ry** (-ə-tôr′ē, -tōr′ē) adj.

Syns: *admonish, rebuke, reprimand, reproach, reprove* v.

ad nau·se·am (ăd nô′zē-əm) adv. To a disgusting or ridiculous degree. [Lat., to nausea.]

a·do (ə-dŏŏ′) n. Fuss; trouble. [ME.]

a·do·be (ə-dō′bē) n. 1. **a.** Sun-dried, unburned brick of clay and straw. **b.** Clay or soil from which such bricks are made. 2. A structure built with adobe. [< Ar. *attōba.*]

ad·o·les·cence (ăd′l-ĕs′əns) n. The period of physical and psychological development between childhood and adulthood. [< Lat. *adolescēre,* to grow up.] —**ad′o·les′cent** n. & adj.

A·don·is (ə-dŏn′ĭs, ə-dō′nĭs) n. 1. *Gk. Myth.* A youth loved by Aphrodite for his striking beauty. 2. **adonis.** A young man of great physical beauty.

a·dopt (ə-dŏpt′) v. 1. To take (a child) into one's family legally and raise as one's own. 2. To take and follow by choice or assent. 3. To take up and use as one's own. [Lat. *adoptare.*] —**a·dopt′a·ble** adj. —**a·dopt′er** n. —**a·dop′tion** n.

Usage: One refers to an *adopted* child but to *adoptive* parents.

a·dop·tive (ə-dŏp′tĭv) adj. Acquired by adoption: *adoptive parents.* —**a·dop′tive·ly** adv.

a·dor·a·ble (ə-dôr′ə-bəl, ə-dōr′-) adj. *Informal.* Delightful; lovable; charming. —**a·dor′a·bil′i·ty** or **a·dor′a·ble·ness** n. —**a·dor′a·bly** adv.

a·dore (ə-dôr′, ə-dōr′) v. **a·dored, a·dor·ing.** 1. To worship as divine. 2. To love deeply; idolize. 3. *Informal.* To like very much. [< Lat. *adorare.*] —**ad′o·ra′tion** n. —**a·dor′er** n. —**a·dor′ing·ly** adv.

a·dorn (ə-dôrn′) v. 1. To be a decoration to; enhance. 2. To decorate with or as with ornaments. [< Lat. *adornare.*] —**a·dorn′ment** n.

a·dre·nal (ə-drē′nəl) adj. 1. At, near, or on the kidneys. 2. Pertaining to the adrenal glands or their secretions.

adrenal gland. Either of two small endocrine glands, one located above each kidney.

a·dren·a·line (ə-drĕn′ə-lĭn) n. Epinephrine.

a·drift (ə-drĭft′) adv. & adj. 1. Drifting or floating freely. 2. Without direction or purpose.

a·droit (ə-droit′) adj. 1. Dexterous; deft. 2. Skillful and adept under pressing conditions. [Fr.] —**a·droit′ly** adv. —**a·droit′ness** n.

ad·sorb (ăd-sôrb′, -zôrb′) v. To take up (liquid or gas) on the surface of a solid. [AD- + Lat. *sorbēre,* to suck.] —**ad·sorp′tion** n. —**ad·sorp′tive** adj.

ad·u·late (ăj′ŏŏ-lāt′) v. **-lat·ed, -lat·ing.** To praise excessively or fawningly. [< Lat. *adulari.*] —**ad′u·la′tion** n. —**ad′u·la′tor** n. —**ad′u·la·to′ry** (-lə-tôr′ē, -tōr′ē) adj.

a·dult (ə-dŭlt′, ăd′ŭlt′) n. One that is fully grown or mature, esp. a person who has attained legal age. —adj. 1. Fully developed and mature. **2.** Of or intended for mature persons. [< Lat. *adolescēre*, to grow up.] —**a·dult'hood'**

a·dul·ter·ate (ə-dŭl'tə-rāt') *v.* **-at·ed, -at·ing.** To make impure or inferior by adding unnecessary or improper ingredients. [Lat. *adulterāre.*] —**a·dul'ter·ant** *n.* & *adj.* —**a·dul'ter·a'tion** *n.*

a·dul·ter·y (ə-dŭl'tə-rē, -trē) *n., pl.* **-ries.** Sexual intercourse between a married person and one other than the lawful spouse. [< Lat. *adulterium.*] —**a·dul'ter·er** *n.* —**a·dul'ter·ess** (-trĭs, -tər-ĭs) *n.* —**a·dul'ter·ous** *adj.* —**a·dul'ter·ous·ly** *adv.*

ad·um·brate (ăd'əm-brāt', ə-dŭm'-) *v.* **-brat·ed, -brat·ing. 1.** To give a sketchy outline. **2.** To foreshadow. [Lat. *adumbrāre*, to overshadow.] —**ad·um·bra'tion** *n.* —**ad·um'bra·tive** (-brə-tĭv) *adj.*

ad·vance (ăd-văns') *v.* **-vanced, -vanc·ing. 1.** To move or bring forward or onward. **2.** To propose. **3.** To aid the growth or progress of. **4.** To make progress. **5.** To raise or rise in rank, amount, or value. **6.** To cause to occur sooner; hasten. **7.** To pay (money) before legally due. —*n.* **1.** The act or process of moving or going forward. **2.** Improvement; progress. **3.** An increase of price or value. **4. advances.** Personal approaches made to secure acquaintance, favor, or agreement. **5.** Payment of money before legally due. —*adj.* **1.** Prior: *advance warning.* **2.** Going before. —*idiom.* **in advance. 1.** Ahead of time. **2.** In front. [< Lat. *abante*, from before.] —**ad·vance'ment** *n.* —**ad·vanc'er** *n.*

ad·vanced (ăd-vănst') *adj.* **1.** Highly developed or complex. **2.** At a higher level than others. **3.** Progressive: *advanced ideas.* **4. a.** Far along in course. **b.** Very old.

advance man An agent or assistant who makes arrangements beforehand, as for a political campaign tour.

ad·van·tage (ăd-văn'tĭj) *n.* **1.** A favorable position or factor. **2.** Benefit or profit; gain. **3.** *Tennis.* The first point scored after deuce. —*idiom.* **take advantage of. 1.** To avail oneself of. **2.** To exploit. [< OFr. *avantage* < Lat. *abante*, from before.] —**ad'van·ta'geous** (-văn-tā'jəs, -vən-) *adj.* —**ad'van·ta'geous·ly** *adv.* —**ad'van·ta'geous·ness** *n.*

ad·vent (ăd'vĕnt') *n.* **1.** A coming or arrival: *the advent of the computer.* **2. Advent. a.** The birth of Christ. **b.** The period including four Sundays before Christmas. [< Lat. *advenīre*, to come to.]

ad·ven·ti·tious (ăd'vĕn-tĭsh'əs) *adj.* Not inherent; accidental. [Lat. *adventīcius*, foreign.] —**ad'ven·ti'tious·ly** *adv.*

ad·ven·ture (ăd-vĕn'chər) *n.* **1.** A risky undertaking. **2.** An unusual and exciting experience. **3.** A business venture. —*v.* **-tured, -tur·ing.** To risk; dare. [OFr. *aventure* < Lat. *advenīre*, to arrive.] —**ad·ven'tur·ous·ly** *adv.* —**ad·ven'tur·ous·ness** *n.*

ad·ven·tur·er (ăd-vĕn'chər-ər) *n.* **1.** One who undertakes risky ventures. **2.** A soldier of fortune. **3.** One who seeks wealth and position by unscrupulous means.

ad·ven·tur·ess (ăd-vĕn'chər-ĭs) *n.* A woman who seeks social and financial advancement by dubious means.

ad·verb (ăd'vûrb') *n.* Any of a class of words used to modify a verb, an adjective, or another adverb. [< Lat. *adverbium.*] —**ad·ver'bi·al** *adj.* —**ad·ver'bi·al·ly** *adv.*

ad·ver·sar·y (ăd'vər-sĕr'ē) *n., pl.* **-ies.** An opponent; enemy.

ad·verse (ăd-vûrs', ăd'vûrs') *adj.* **1.** Antagonistic in design or effect; hostile. **2.** Unfavorable; unpropitious. [< OFr. *advers* < Lat. *advertere*, to turn toward.] —**ad·verse'ly** *adv.*

ad·ver·si·ty (ăd-vûr'sĭ-tē) *n., pl.* **-ties. 1.** Great hardship; misfortune. **2.** A calamitous event. [< Lat. *advertere*, to turn toward.]

ad·vert (ăd-vûrt') *v.* To allude; refer. [Lat. *advertere*, to turn toward.]

ad·ver·tise (ăd'vər-tīz') *v.* **-tised, -tis·ing. 1.** To call the attention of the public to a product or business, esp. to promote sales. **2.** To make known. —**ad'ver·tis'er** *n.*

ad·ver·tise·ment (ăd'vər-tīz'mənt, ăd-vûr'tĭs-mənt, -tĭz-) *n.* A notice designed to attract public attention or patronage.

ad·ver·tis·ing (ăd'vər-tī'zĭng) *n.* **1.** The business of preparing and distributing advertisements. **2.** Advertisements collectively.

ad·vice (ăd-vīs') *n.* Opinion about a course of action; counsel. [< Med. Lat. *advisum.*]

ad·vis·a·ble (ăd-vī'zə-bəl) *adj.* Worthy of being recommended; prudent. —**ad·vis'a·bil'i·ty** *n.* —**ad·vis'a·bly** *adv.*

ad·vise (ăd-vīz') *v.* **-vised, -vis·ing. 1.** To offer advice to. **2.** To recommend; suggest. **3.** To inform; notify. [OFr. *adviser.*] —**ad·vis'er** or **ad·vi'sor** *n.*

ad·vis·ed·ly (ăd-vī'zĭd-lē) *adv.* Deliberately.

ad·vise·ment (ăd-vīz'mənt) *n.* Careful consideration.

ad·vi·so·ry (ăd-vī'zə-rē) *adj.* **1.** Empowered to advise. **2.** Of or containing advice. —**ad·vi'so·ry** *n.*

ad·vo·cate (ăd'və-kāt') *v.* **-cat·ed, -cat·ing.** To speak in favor of. —*n.* (ăd'və-kĭt, -kāt'). **1.** One who argues for a cause. **2.** One who pleads in another's behalf. [Lat. *advocāre*, to call to.] —**ad'vo·ca'cy** *n.* —**ad'vo·ca'tor** *n.*

adz or **adze** (ădz) *n.* An axlike tool with a curved blade at right angles to the handle, used for shaping wood. [OE *adesa.*]

ae·gis (ē'jĭs) *n.* **1.** Protection. **2.** Sponsorship; patronage. [Gk. *aigis.*]

Ae·ne·as (ĭ-nē'əs) *n.* Trojan hero, reputed ancestor of the Romans.

ae·on (ē'ŏn', ē'ən) *n.* Var. of **eon.**

aer·ate (âr'āt') *v.* **-at·ed, -at·ing. 1.** To supply or charge (liquid) with a gas. **2.** To expose to the circulation of air. **3.** To supply (blood) with oxygen. —**aer·a'tion** *n.* —**aer'a·tor** *n.*

aer·i·al (âr'ē-əl, ā-îr'ē-əl) *adj.* **1.** Of, in, or caused by the air. **2.** Lofty. **3.** Airy. **4.** Of, for, or by aircraft. —*n.* (âr'ē-əl). An antenna. [< Gk. *aërios.*]

aer·i·al·ist (âr'ē-ə-lĭst) *n.* An acrobat who performs on a tightrope, trapeze, or similar apparatus.

aerialist

aer·ie (âr'ē, ăr'ē, ĭr'ē) *n., pl.* **-ies.** The nest of an eagle or other predatory bird, built on a high place. [OFr. *aire.*]

aero– or **aer–** *pref.* **1.** Air, gas, or the atmosphere: *aerate.* **2.** Aircraft: *aeronautics.* [< Gk. *aēr*, air.]

aer·o·bat·ics (âr'ə-băt'ĭks) *n. (used with a sing. or pl. verb).* The performance of stunts with an airplane. [AERO-+ (ACRO)BATICS.]

aer·o·bic (â-rō'bĭk) *adj.* Requiring or living in the presence of molecular or free oxygen. [AERO- + Gk. *bios*, life.]

aer·o·bics (â-rō'bĭks) *n. (used with a sing. or pl. verb).* An exercise regimen designed to strengthen the cardiovascular system.

aer·o·dy·nam·ics (âr'ō-dī-năm'ĭks) *n. (used with a sing. verb).* The science that deals with the motion of gases and esp. with the atmospheric forces exerted on moving objects. —**aer'o·dy·nam'ic** *adj.*

aer·o·naut (âr'ə-nôt') *n.* A pilot or navigator of a balloon or lighter-than-air craft. [AERO- + Gk. *nautēs*, sailor.]

aer·o·nau·tics (âr'ə-nô'tĭks) *n. (used with a sing. verb).* **1.** The design and construction of aircraft. **2.** Aircraft navigation. —**aer'o·nau'tic** or **aer'o·nau'ti·cal** *adj.* —**aer'o·nau'ti·cal·ly** *adv.*

aer·o·pause (âr'ə-pôz') *n.* The region of the atmosphere above which aircraft cannot fly.

aer·o·plane (âr'ə-plān') *n. Chiefly Brit.* Var. of airplane.

aer·o·sol (âr'ə-sôl', -sŏl', -sōl') *n.* **1.** A gaseous suspension of fine solid or liquid particles. **2.** A substance, such as an insecticide or paint, packaged under pressure for release as an aerosol. [AERO- + SOL(UTION).]

aer·o·space (âr'ə-spās') *n.* The region consisting of the earth's atmosphere and outer space.

aes·thete or **es·thete** (ĕs'thēt') *n.* One who develops a superior appreciation of the beautiful, esp. in art. [< AESTHETIC.]

aes·thet·ic or **es·thet·ic** (ĕs-thĕt'ĭk) *adj.* **1.** Of aesthetics. **2. a.** Of or pertaining to the sense of the beautiful. **b.** Artistic. **3.** Having a love of beauty. [Gk. *aisthētikos*, of sense perception.] —**aes·thet'i·cal·ly** *adv.*

aes·thet·ics or **es·thet·ics** (ĕs-thĕt'ĭks) *n. (used with a sing. verb).* The branch of philosophy that deals with the theories and forms of beauty and of the fine arts.

a·far (ə-fär') *adv.* Far away; far off. [*a-*, of + FAR.]

af·fa·ble (ăf'ə-bəl) *adj.* **1.** Amiable. **2.** Mild; gentle. [Lat. *affabilis.*] —**af'fa·bil'i·ty** *n.* —**af'fa·bly** *adv.*

af·fair (ə-fâr') *n.* **1.** Something done or to be done. **2. affairs.** Business matters. **3.** Private matter. **4.** A love affair. **5.** A social gathering. [OFr. *afaire.*]

af·fect[1] (ə-fĕkt') *v.* **1.** To have an influence on. **2.** To touch the emotions of. [Lat. *afficere.*]

af·fect[2] (ə-fĕkt') *v.* **1.** To simulate; pretend; feign. **2.** To fancy; like: *He affects three-piece suits.* [Lat. *affectare*, to strive < *afficere*, to affect.] —**af·fect'er** *n.*

af·fec·ta·tion (ăf'ĕk-tā'shən) *n.* Artificial behavior adopted to impress others.

af·fect·ed (ə-fĕk'tĭd) *adj.* Assumed or simulated to impress others. —**af·fect'ed·ly** *adv.* —**af·fect'ed·ness** *n.*

af·fect·ing (ə-fĕk'tĭng) *adj.* Full of pathos; touching; moving. —**af·fect'ing·ly** *adv.*

af·fec·tion (ə-fĕk'shən) *n.* A tender feeling toward another; fondness. —**af·fec'tion·ate** *adj.* —**af·fec'tion·ate·ly** *adv.*

af·fer·ent (ăf'ər-ənt) *adj.* Directed toward a central organ or part of an organism. [< Lat. *afferre*, to bring toward.]

af·fi·ance (ə-fī'əns) *v.* **-anced, -anc·ing.** To betroth. [OFr. *affiancer.*]

af·fi·da·vit (ăf'ĭ-dā'vĭt) *n.* A written declaration made under oath. [< Med. Lat. *affidare*, to pledge.]

af·fil·i·ate (ə-fĭl'ē-āt') *v.* **-at·ed, -at·ing.** **1.** To accept as an associate. **2.** To associate (with). —*n.* (ə-fĭl'ē-ĭt, -āt'). An associate or subordinate. [Med. Lat. *affiliare*, to adopt as a son.] —**af·fil'i·a'tion** *n.*

af·fin·i·ty (ə-fĭn'ĭ-tē) *n., pl.* **-ties.** **1.** An attraction or attractive force. **2.** Relationship; kinship. [Lat. *affinitas.*]

af·firm (ə-fûrm') *v.* **1.** To declare or maintain to be true. **2.** To ratify or confirm. [Lat. *affirmare.*] —**af·firm'a·ble** *adj.* —**af·fir'mant** *adj. & n.* —**af'fir·ma'tion** *n.*

af·firm·a·tive (ə-fûr'mə-tĭv) *adj.* **1.** Giving assent. **2.** Confirming. —*n.* **1.** A word or phrase signifying assent. **2.** The side in a debate that upholds a proposition. —**af·firm'a·tive·ly** *adv.*

affirmative action *n.* Specific action taken to provide equal opportunity for members of disadvantaged groups.

af·fix (ə-fĭks') *v.* **1.** To secure; attach. **2.** To append. —*n.* (ăf'ĭks'). **1.** Something affixed. **2.** A word element, such as a prefix or suffix, that is attached to a base, stem, or root. [< Lat. *affigere.*]

af·fla·tus (ə-flā'təs) *n.* A creative impulse; inspiration. [< Lat *afflare*, to breathe on.]

af·flict (ə-flĭkt') *v.* To inflict pain or suffering upon; distress. [Lat. *affligere*, to dash against.] —**af·flic'tion** *n.* —**af·flic'tive** *adj.*

af·flu·ence (ăf'lōō-əns) *n.* **1.** Wealth; riches. **2.** A plentiful supply; abundance. —**af'flu·ent** *adj.* —**af'flu·ent·ly** *adv.*

af·ford (ə-fôrd', ə-fōrd') *v.* **1.** To have the financial means for. **2.** To be able to spare or give up. **3.** To provide. [OE *geforthian*, to carry out.] —**af·ford'a·ble** *adj.*

af·for·es·ta·tion (ə-fôr'ĭ-stā'shən, ə-fŏr'-) *n.* The conversion of open land into forest. —**af·for'est** *v.*

af·fray (ə-frā') *n.* A noisy quarrel or brawl. [OFr. *effray.*]

af·front (ə-frŭnt') *v.* **1.** To insult. **2.** To confront. —*n.* An insult. [OFr. *afronter.*]

af·ghan (ăf'găn', -gən) *n.* A coverlet knitted or crocheted in colorful geometric designs. [< *Afghan*, a native of Afghanistan.]

Afghan hound *n.* A large, slender dog of an ancient breed, with long, thick hair.

af·ghan·i (ăf-găn'ē, -gä'nē) *n.* See table at currency. [Pashto.]

a·fi·ci·o·na·do (ə-fĭsh′ə-nä′dō, ə-fĭs′ē-, ə-fē′sĕ-) *n., pl.* **-dos.** A devotee. [Sp.]

a·field (ə-fēld′) *adv.* **1.** Off the usual or desired track. **2.** Away from one's home. **3.** To or on a field.

a·fire (ə-fīr′) *adj. & adv.* On fire; burning.

a·flame (ə-flām′) *adj. & adv.* On fire; flaming.

a·float (ə-flōt′) *adj. & adv.* **1.** Floating. **2.** At sea. **3.** Flooded.

a·flut·ter (ə-flŭt′ər) *adj.* Nervous and excited.

a·foot (ə-fŏŏt′) *adj. & adv.* **1.** Walking; on foot. **2.** In progress.

a·fore·men·tioned (ə-fôr′mĕn′shənd, ə-fōr′-) *adj.* Mentioned previously or before.

a·fore·said (ə-fôr′sĕd′, ə-fōr′-) *adj.* Spoken of earlier.

a·fore·thought (ə-fôr′thôt′, ə-fōr′-) *adj.* Premeditated: *malice aforethought.*

a for·ti·o·ri (ä fôr′tē-ôr′ē, ā fôr′tē-ô′rī′) *adv.* For a stronger reason. Used of the most logical conclusion. [Lat.]

a·foul (ə-foul′) *prep.* In or into a condition of collision, entanglement, or conflict. —*idiom.* **run** (or **fall**) **afoul of.** To become entangled or in conflict with.

a·fraid (ə-frād′) *adj.* **1.** Filled with fear; frightened. **2.** Reluctant; averse: *not afraid to work.* [< OFr. *affreier*, to startle.]

A-frame (ā′frām′) *n.* A structure with steeply angled sides and a roof that reaches to the ground.

a·fresh (ə-frĕsh′) *adv.* Again; anew. [*a,* of + FRESH.]

Af·ri·can (ăf′rĭ-kən) *n.* **1.** A person born or living in Africa. **2.** A member of one of the indigenous peoples of Africa. —**Af′ri·can** *adj.*

African violet A tropical African plant with violet, white, or pink flowers, widely cultivated as a house plant.

Af·ri·kaans (ăf′rĭ-käns′, -känz′) *n.* A language developed from 17th-cent. Dutch that is now one of the official languages of the Republic of South Africa.

Af·ri·kan·er (ăf′rĭ-kä′nər) *n.* A descendant of the Dutch settlers of South Africa.

Af·ro (ăf′rō′) *n., pl.* **-ros.** A full, bushy hair style in which dense frizzy hair is worn naturally. —*adj.* **1.** Of or pertaining to an Afro. **2.** African in style.

Af·ro-A·mer·i·can (ăf′rō-ə-mĕr′ĭ-kən) *adj.* Of or pertaining to American blacks of African ancestry. —**Af′ro-A·mer′i·can** *n.*

Af·ro-A·si·at·ic (ăf′rō-ā′zhē-ăt′ĭk, -zē-) *n.* A family of languages of southwestern Asia and northern Africa. —**Af′ro-A′si·at′ic** *adj.*

aft (ăft) *adv. & adj.* At, in, toward, or near a ship's stern. [Prob. < ABAFT.]

af·ter (ăf′tər) *prep.* **1.** Behind in a place or order. **2.** In pursuit of. **3.** About; concerning: *I asked after you.* **4.** At a later time than. **5.** With the same name as. —*conj.* Following the time that. —*adv.* **1.** Afterward: *forever after.* **2.** Behind. —*adj.* **1.** Later. **2.** Nearer the rear, esp. of a ship. [OE *æfter.*]

af·ter·birth (ăf′tər-bûrth′) *n.* The placenta and fetal membranes expelled from the uterus after childbirth.

af·ter·burn·er (ăf′tər-bûr′nər) *n.* A device for increasing the thrust of a jet engine by burning additional fuel with the hot exhaust gases.

af·ter·ef·fect (ăf′tər-ĭ-fĕkt′) *n.* A delayed, prolonged, or secondary response to a stimulus.

af·ter·glow (ăf′tər-glō′) *n.* The light remaining after removal of a source of illumination.

af·ter·hours (ăf′tər-ourz′) *adj.* Occurring or operating after the usual or established time.

af·ter·im·age (ăf′tər-ĭm′ĭj) *n.* A visual image that continues after a visual stimulus ceases.

af·ter·life (ăf′tər-līf′) *n.* A life or existence after death.

af·ter·math (ăf′tər-măth′) *n.* **1.** A consequence or result, esp. an unfortunate one. **2.** A second crop of grass in the same season. [AFTER + OE *mǣth,* mowing.]

af·ter·noon (ăf′tər-nōōn′) *n.* The part of the day from noon until sunset.

af·ter·shave (ăf′tər-shāve′) *n.* A usually fragrant lotion used on the face after shaving.

af·ter·taste (ăf′tər-tāst′) *n.* A taste or feeling that persists after the stimulus causing it is no longer there.

af·ter·thought (ăf′tər-thôt′) *n.* An idea or explanation that occurs to one after an event or decision.

af·ter·ward (ăf′tər-wərd) *adv.* Also **af·ter·wards** (-wərdz). In or at a later time; subsequently.

Ag The symbol for the element silver. [Lat. *argentum.*]

a·gain (ə-gĕn′) *adv.* **1.** Once more; anew. **2.** To a previous condition, place, or position: *He never went back again.* **3.** Furthermore. **4.** On the other hand. [OE *ongeagn,* against.]

a·gainst (ə-gĕnst′) *prep.* **1.** In a direction or course opposite to. **2.** So as to come into contact with: *waves dashing against the shore.* **3.** In opposition or resistance to. **4.** Contrary to: *against my better judgment.*

Ag·a·mem·non (ăg′ə-mĕm′nŏn′) *n.* Gk. Myth. The king of Mycenae, leader of the Greeks against Troy.

a·gape (ə-gāp′, ə-găp′) *adj. & adv.* With the mouth wide open, as in wonder.

a·gar (ā′gär′, ä′gär′) *n.* Also **a·gar-a·gar** (ā′-gär-ā′gär′, ä′gär-ä′-). A gelatinous material prepared from certain saltwater algae and used in bacterial cultures and for thickening foods. [Malay.]

ag·ate (ăg′ĭt) *n.* **1.** A variety of chalcedony with bands of color. **2.** A marble made of agate or an imitation of it. [Gk. *akhatēs.*]

a·ga·ve (ə-gä′vē, ə-gā′-) *n.* Any of numerous fleshy-leaved tropical American plants. [< Gk. *agauos,* noble.]

age (āj) *n.* **1.** The period of time during which someone or something exists. **2.** A lifetime. **3.** The time in life when a person assumes certain civil and personal rights and responsibilities. **4.** A period or stage of life. **5.** The latter portion of life. **6.** Often **Age.** A period in history. **7.** *Informal.* A long time. —*v.* **aged, ag·ing.** To grow or cause to grow older or more mature. [Lat. *aetas.*]

-age *suff.* **1.** Collection; mass: *sewerage.* **2.** Relationship; connection with: *parentage.* **3.** Condition; state: *vagabondage.* **4. a.** An action; *blockage.* **b.** Result of an action: *breakage.* **5.** Residence or place of: *vicarage.* **6.** Charge or fee: *cartage.* [< Lat. *-aticum.*]

ag·ed (ā′jĭd) *adj.* **1.** Old; advanced in years.

ă pat ā pay â care ä father ĕ pet ē be ĭ pit ī tie î pier ŏ pot ō toe ô paw, for oi noise ŏŏ took
ōō boot ou out th thin th this ŭ cut û urge yōō abuse zh vision ə about, item, edible, gallop, circus

2. (ājd). Of the age of. —*n.* **the aged.** Very old people. —**age'ed·ness** *n.*

age·ism (ā'jĭz'əm) *n.* Discrimination based on age. —**age'ist** *n.*

age·less (āj'lĭs) *adj.* **1.** Seeming never to grow old. **2.** Existing forever. —**age'less·ly** *adv.*

a·gen·cy (ā'jən-sē) *n., pl.* **-cies. 1.** Action; operation. **2.** A mode of action; means. **3.** A business or service acting for others. **4.** An administrative governmental department. [Med. Lat. *agentia.*]

a·gen·da (ə-jĕn'də) *n. (used with a sing. verb).* A list or program of things to be done. [< Lat. *agere,* to do.]

a·gent (ā'jənt) *n.* **1.** One that acts or has the power to act. **2.** One that acts as the representative of another. **3.** A means of doing something; instrument. [< Lat. *agere,* to do.]

a·gent pro·vo·ca·teur (ä-zhän' prō-vô'kä-tûr') *n., pl.* **a·gents pro·vo·ca·teurs** (ä-zhän' prō-vô'kä-tûr'). One who infiltrates an organization in order to incite its members to commit illegal acts. [Fr.]

ag·er·a·tum (ăj'ə-rā'təm) *n.* Any of various tropical American plants having clusters of violet-blue or white flowers. [< Gk. *agēratos,* ageless.]

ag·gie (ăg'ē) *n.* A playing marble. [AG(ATE) + -IE.]

ag·glom·er·ate (ə-glŏm'ə-rāt') *v.* **-at·ed, -at·ing.** To form into a rounded mass. —*n.* (ə-glŏm'ər-ĭt). A jumbled mass. [Lat. *agglomerare.*] —**ag·glom'er·a'tion** *n.*

ag·glu·ti·nate (ə-glōōt'n-āt') *v.* **-nat·ed, -nat·ing. 1.** To join by causing adhesion. **2.** *Physiol.* To cause (red blood cells or microorganisms) to clump together. [Lat. *agglutinare.*] —**ag·glu'ti·na'tion** *n.* —**ag·glu'ti·na'tive** *adj.*

ag·gran·dize (ə-grăn'dīz', ăg'rən-) *v.* **-dized, -diz·ing.** To make greater; increase. [Fr. *aggrandir.*] —**ag·gran'dize·ment** *n.* —**ag·gran'diz·er** *n.*

ag·gra·vate (ăg'rə-vāt') *v.* **-vat·ed, -vat·ing. 1.** To make worse. **2.** To annoy; irritate. [Lat. *aggravare.*] —**ag'gra·vat'ing·ly** *adv.* —**ag'gra·va'tion** *n.* —**ag'gra·va'tor** *n.*

ag·gre·gate (ăg'rə-gĭt', -gāt') *adj.* Gathered together into a mass so as to constitute a whole; total. —*n.* (ăg'rə-gĭt). An assemblage or group of distinct particulars massed together. —*v.* (ăg'rə-gāt') **-gat·ed, -gat·ing.** To gather into a mass, sum, or whole. [< Lat. *aggregare,* to add to.] —**ag'gre·gate·ly** *adv.* —**ag'gre·ga'tion** *n.* —**ag'gre·ga'tive** *adj.* —**ag'gre·ga'tor** *n.*

ag·gres·sion (ə-grĕsh'ən) *n.* **1.** An unprovoked attack on another. **2.** The habit or practice of launching attacks. **3.** Hostile action or behavior. [Lat. *aggressio.*] —**ag·gres'sor** (-grĕs'ər) *n.*

ag·gres·sive (ə-grĕs'ĭv) *adj.* **1.** Quick to attack or act in a hostile fashion. **2.** Assertive; bold: *an aggressive salesman.* —**ag·gres'sive·ly** *adv.* —**ag·gres'sive·ness** *n.*

ag·grieve (ə-grēv') *v.* **-grieved, -griev·ing. 1.** To distress or afflict. **2.** To injure or treat unjustly; wrong. [Lat. *aggravare,* to aggravate.]

a·ghast (ə-găst') *adj.* Shocked, as by something horrible; appalled. [*a,* intensive + OE *gāst,* ghost.]

ag·ile (ăj'əl, ăj'īl') *adj.* Able to move quickly and easily; nimble. [< Lat. *agilis.*] —**ag'ile·ly** *adv.* —**a·gil'i·ty** (ə-jĭl'ĭ-tē) or **ag'ile·ness** *n.*

ag·i·tate (ăj'ĭ-tāt') *v.* **-tat·ed, -tat·ing. 1.** To move or stir violently. **2.** To upset; disturb. **3.** To arouse or try to arouse public interest. [Lat. *agitare.*] —**ag'i·tat'ed·ly** *adv.* —**ag'i·ta'tion** *n.* —**ag'i·ta'tor** *n.*

a·gleam (ə-glēm') *adj. & adv.* Gleaming.

a·glim·mer (ə-glĭm'ər) *adj. & adv.* Glimmering.

a·glit·ter (ə-glĭt'ər) *adj. & adv.* Glittering.

a·glow (ə-glō') *adj. & adv.* Glowing.

ag·nos·tic (ăg-nŏs'tĭk) *n.* One who believes that there can be no proof of the existence of God but does not deny the possibility that God exists. [< Gk. *agnōstos,* unknown.] —**ag·nos'tic** *adj.* —**ag·nos'ti·cal·ly** *adv.* —**ag·nos'ti·cism** *n.*

Ag·nus De·i (ăg'nəs dē'ī', än'yōōs dā'ē, äg'nōōs) *n.* **1.** The Lamb of God, an emblem of Christ. **2.** A liturgical prayer to Christ. [Lat.]

Agnus Dei

a·go (ə-gō') *adj. & adv.* Gone by; in the past. [< OE *āgān.*]

a·gog (ə-gŏg') *adj.* Eagerly expectant; excited. [OFr. *en gogue,* in merriment.] —**a·gog'** *adv.*

-agogue or **-agog** *suff.* A leader or inciter: *demagogue.* [< Gk. *agōgos,* leading.]

ag·o·nize (ăg'ə-nīz') *v.* **-nized, -niz·ing. 1.** To make a great effort; struggle. **2.** To be in or cause to be in great anguish. [< Gk. *agōnizesthai.*] —**ag'o·niz'ing·ly** *adv.*

ag·o·ny (ăg'ə-nē) *n., pl.* **-nies. 1.** Intense physical or mental pain. **2.** A sudden strong emotion: *an agony of doubt.* [< Gk. *agōn,* contest.]

ag·o·ra (ăg'ə-rä') *n., pl.* **-rot** (-rōt') or **-roth** (-rōt'). See table at **currency.** [Heb. *'agōrāh.*]

ag·o·ra·pho·bi·a (ăg'ə-rə-fō'bē-ə) *n.* Abnormal fear of open spaces. [Gk. *agora,* open space + -PHOBIA.] —**ag'o·ra·pho'bic** (-fō'bĭk, -fōb'ĭk) *adj.*

a·grar·i·an (ə-grâr'ē-ən) *adj.* **1.** Of or pertaining to land and its ownership. **2.** Pertaining to farming; agriculture. —*n.* One who favors equitable distribution of land. [< Lat. *ager,* land.] —**a·grar'i·an·ism** *n.*

a·gree (ə-grē') *v.* **a·greed, a·gree·ing. 1.** To grant consent; accede. **2.** To be in accord. **3.** To come to an understanding or to terms. **4.** To be suitable or beneficial. **5.** *Gram.* To correspond in gender, number, case, or person. [< OFr. *agreer.*]

Syns: **agree, coincide, conform, correspond** *v.*

a·gree·a·ble (ə-grē'ə-bəl) *adj.* **1.** Pleasing; pleasant. **2.** Willing to consent. **3.** In accord; suitable. —**a·gree'a·ble·ness** *n.* —**a·gree'a·bly** *adv.*

a·gree·ment (ə-grē'mənt) *n.* **1.** Harmony of opinion; accord. **2.** An arrangement or understanding between parties; covenant; treaty.

3. *Gram.* Correspondence between words in gender, number, case, or person.

ag·ri·busi·ness (ăg'rə-bĭz'nĭs) *n.* Farming engaged in as big business, including the production, processing, and distribution of farm products and the manufacture of farm equipment. [AGRI(CULTURE) + BUSINESS.]

ag·ri·cul·ture (ăg'rĭ-kŭl'chər) *n.* The science, art, and business of cultivating the soil, producing crops, and raising livestock. [Lat. *agricultura.*] —**ag'ri·cul'tur·al** *adj.* —**ag'ri·cul'tur·al·ly** *adv.* —**ag'ri·cul'tur·ist** *n.*

a·gron·o·my (ə-grŏn'ə-mē) *n.* The application of the various soil and plant sciences to soil management and the raising of crops. [Fr. *agronomie.*] —**ag'ro·nom'ic** (ăg'rə-nŏm'ĭk) or **ag'ro·nom'i·cal** *adj.* —**a·gron'o·mist** *n.*

a·ground (ə-ground') *adv. & adj.* Stranded in shallow water or on a reef or shoal.

a·gue (ā'gyōō) *n.* A fever accompanied by chills or shivering. [< OFr. *(fievre) ague,* sharp (fever).]

ah (ä) *interj.* Used to express surprise, satisfaction, pain, etc.

a·ha (ä-hä') *interj.* Used to express surprise or triumph.

a·head (ə-hĕd') *adv.* **1.** At or to the front. **2.** In advance; before. **3.** Forward or onward. —*idioms.* **be ahead.** *Informal.* To be gaining or winning. **get ahead.** To attain success.

a·hem (ə-hĕm') *interj.* Used to attract attention or to express doubt or warning.

a·hoy (ə-hoi') *interj.* Used as a nautical call or greeting.

aid (ād) *v.* To help; assist. —*n.* **1.** Assistance. **2.** One that provides assistance. [< Lat. *adjutare.*] —**aid'er** *n.*

aide (ād) *n.* An assistant. [Fr.]

aide-de-camp (ād'də-kămp') *n., pl.* **aides-de-camp.** A naval or military officer acting as an assistant to a superior officer. [Fr.]

ai·grette or **ai·gret** (ā-grĕt', ā'grĕt') *n.* An ornamental tuft of plumes. [Fr., egret.]

ail (āl) *v.* **1.** To feel ill. **2.** To make ill or uneasy. [< OE *eglan.*]

ai·lan·thus (ā-lăn'thəs) *n.* A deciduous tree with numerous pointed leaflets and clusters of greenish flowers with an unpleasant odor. [< Amboinese *ai lanto,* tree (of) heaven.]

ai·ler·on (ā'lə-rŏn') *n.* A movable control surface on the trailing edge of an airplane wing. [< Lat. *ala,* wing.]

ail·ment (āl'mənt) *n.* A mild illness.

aim (ām) *v.* **1.** To direct (a weapon, remark, etc.) at someone or something. **2.** To direct a weapon. **3.** To direct one's efforts or purposes. —*n.* **1.** The act of aiming. **2.** The direction of something aimed. **3.** Purpose; intention. [< OFr. *aesmer,* to guess at.]

aim·less (ām'lĭs) *adj.* Without purpose. —**aim'less·ly** *adv.* —**aim'less·ness** *n.*

ain't (ānt). *Nonstandard.* **1.** Am not. **2.** Used also as a contraction of *are not, is not, has not,* and *have not.*

Usage: Even though it would be useful as a contraction for *am not* and also as an alternative form for *isn't, aren't, hasn't,* and *haven't, ain't* is still unacceptable in standard usage.

Ai·nu (ī'nōō) *n., pl.* **Ainu** or **-nus. 1.** A member of an aboriginal Caucasian people inhab-

iting the northernmost islands of Japan. **2.** The language of the Ainus.

air (âr) *n.* **1.** A colorless, odorless, tasteless gaseous mixture chiefly nitrogen (78%) and oxygen (21%). **2.** The earth's atmosphere. **3.** A breeze; wind. **4.** An impression; appearance: *an air of gentility.* **5. airs.** Affectation. **6.** A melody or tune. **7.** The airwaves. **8.** The medium through which aircraft travel. —*v.* **1.** To expose to air; ventilate. **2.** To give public utterance to; circulate. —*idioms.* **in the air.** Abroad; prevalent. **on (or off) the air.** *Radio & TV.* Being (or not being) broadcast. **up in the air.** Not decided; uncertain. [< Gk. *aēr.*]

air bag *n.* An automotive baglike safety device that inflates upon collision and prevents pitching forward.

air·borne (âr'bôrn', -bōrn') *adj.* Carried by or through the air.

air brake *n.* A brake operated by compressed air.

air·brush (âr'brŭsh') *n.* An atomizer that uses compressed air to spray paint. —**air'brush** *v.*

air conditioner *n.* An apparatus for controlling, esp. lowering, the temperature and humidity of an enclosure. —**air'-con·di'tion** *v.* —**air conditioning** *n.*

air·craft (âr'krăft') *n., pl.* **aircraft.** Any machine or device, including airplanes, helicopters, gliders, and dirigibles, capable of atmospheric flight.

aircraft carrier *n.* A warship carrying aircraft.

air·drome (âr'drōm') *n.* An airport.

air·drop (âr'drŏp') *n.* A delivery, as of supplies or troops, by parachute from aircraft in flight. —**air'drop** *v.*

Aire·dale (âr'dāl') *n.* A large terrier with a wiry tan and black coat. [< *Airedale,* a valley in Yorkshire, England.]

air·field (âr'fēld') *n.* **1.** An airport with paved runways. **2.** A landing strip.

air·foil (âr'foil') *n.* An aircraft control part or surface, such as a wing, propeller blade, or rudder.

air force *n.* The aviation branch of a country's armed forces.

air gun *n.* A gun discharged by compressed air.

air lane *n.* A regular route of travel for aircraft.

air·lift (âr'lĭft') *n.* A system of transporting troops or supplies by air when surface routes are blocked. —**air'lift** *v.*

air·line (âr'līn') *n.* **1.** A system for transport of passengers and freight by air. **2.** The shortest, most direct distance between two points.

air·lin·er (âr'lī'nər) *n.* A large passenger airplane.

air lock *n.* An airtight chamber between regions of unequal pressure.

air mail *n.* Also **air·mail** (âr'māl'). **1.** The system of conveying mail by aircraft. **2.** Mail conveyed by aircraft. —**air'mail** *v.*

air·man (âr'mən) *n.* **1.** An enlisted man or woman in the U.S. Air Force. **2.** An aviator.

airman basic *n.* An enlisted person of the lowest rank in the U.S. Air Force.

air mass *n.* A large body of air with only

ă pat ā pay â care ä father ĕ pet ē be ĭ pit ī tie î pier ŏ pot ō toe ô paw, for oi noise ŏŏ took
ōō boot ou out th thin th this ŭ cut û urge yōō abuse zh vision ə about, item, edible, gallop, circus

small horizontal variations of temperature, pressure, and moisture.

air mile *n.* A nautical mile.

air·plane (âr′plān′) *n.* A winged vehicle capable of flight, heavier than air and propelled by jet engines or propellers. [Fr. *aéroplane.*]

air·port (âr′pôrt′, -pōrt′) *n.* A facility that provides space for aircraft to take off and land and accommodations for passengers and cargo.

air raid *n.* A bombing attack by hostile military aircraft. —**air′-raid′** *adj.*

air·ship (âr′shĭp′) *n.* A self-propelled lighter-than-air craft with directional control surfaces; dirigible.

air·sick (âr′sĭk′) *adj.* Suffering from airsickness.

air·sick·ness (âr′sĭk′nĭs) *n.* Nausea resulting from flight in an aircraft.

air·space (âr′spās′) *n.* The portion of the atmosphere above a particular land area, esp. above a nation.

air speed *n.* The speed of an aircraft relative to the air.

air·strip (âr′strĭp′) *n.* A minimally equipped airfield.

air·tight (âr′tīt′) *adj.* 1. Impermeable by air or gas. 2. Unassailable: *an airtight excuse.*

air-to-air missile (âr′tə-âr′) *n.* A missile designed to be fired from aircraft at aircraft.

air-to-surface missile (âr′tə-sûr′fĭs) *n.* A missile designed to be fired from aircraft at ground targets.

air·waves (âr′wāvz′) *pl.n.* The medium used for the transmission of radio and television signals.

air·way (âr′wā′) *n.* An air lane.

air·wor·thy (âr′wûr′thē) *adj.* Fit to fly: *an airworthy old plane.* —**air′wor′thi·ness** *n.*

air·y (âr′ē) *adj.* **-i·er, -i·est.** 1. Of or like the air. 2. Open to the air; breezy. 3. Light as air; graceful or delicate. 4. Insubstantial; unreal. 5. Nonchalant; carefree. —**air′i·ly** *adv.* —**air′i·ness** *n.*

aisle (īl) *n.* A passageway between rows of seats, as in a church or auditorium. [< OFr. *aile,* wing of a building < Lat. *ala,* wing.]

a·jar (ə-jär′) *adv.* & *adj.* Partially opened: *Leave the door ajar.* [ME *on char,* in the act of turning.]

a·kim·bo (ə-kĭm′bō) *adj.* & *adv.* With the hands on the hips and the elbows bowed outward. [ME *in kenebowe,* in a sharp curve.]

a·kin (ə-kĭn′) *adj.* 1. Of the same kin; related. 2. Similar in quality or character. 3. *Ling.* Cognate. [*a-,* of + KIN.]

Ak·ka·di·an (ə-kā′dē-ən) *n.* 1. A native or inhabitant of Akkad, a region of ancient Mesopotamia. 2. The Semitic language of the Akkadians. —**Ak·ka′di·an** *adj.*

Al The symbol for the element aluminum.

-al¹ *suff.* Of, relating to, or characterized by: *adjectival.* [< Lat. *-alis.*]

-al² *suff.* Action; process: *denial; arrival.* [< Lat. *-alis,* adj. suff.]

à la (ä′lä, ä′lə, äl′ə) *prep.* In the style or manner of. [Fr. *à la mode de.*]

al·a·bas·ter (ăl′ə-băs′tər) *n.* A dense, translucent, white or tinted fine-grained gypsum. [< Gk. *alabastros.*]

à la carte (ä′ lä kärt′, ä′lə, äl′ə) *adv.* & *adj.* With a separate price for each item on the menu. [Fr., by the menu.]

a·lac·ri·ty (ə-lăk′rĭ-tē) *n.* Cheerful eagerness; sprightliness. [Lat. *alacritas.*] —**a·lac′ri·tous** *adj.*

à la mode (ä′ lä mōd′, ä′lə, äl′ə) *adj.* 1. Fashionable. 2. Served with ice cream. [Fr.]

a·larm (ə-lärm′) *n.* 1. A sudden feeling of fear. 2. A warning of danger. 3. A device that sounds a warning. 4. The sounding mechanism of a clock. 5. A call to arms. —*v.* To frighten or warn by an alarm. [< OItal. *all′ arme,* to arms.]

a·larm·ing (ə-lär′mĭng) *adj.* Frightening. —**a·larm′ing·ly** *adv.*

a·larm·ist (ə-lär′mĭst) *n.* A person who needlessly alarms others.

a·las (ə-lăs′) *interj.* Used to express regret or anxiety.

alb (ălb) *n.* A long, white linen robe worn by a priest at Mass. [< Lat. *albus,* white.]

al·ba·core (ăl′bə-kôr′, -kōr′) *n.* A large marine fish that is a major source of canned tuna. [< Ar. *al-bakrah.*]

Al·ba·ni·an (ăl-bā′nē-ən, -bān′yən, ôl-) *n.* 1. A native or inhabitant of Albania. 2. The Indo-European language of Albania. —**Al·ba′ni·an** *adj.*

al·ba·tross (ăl′bə-trôs′, -trŏs′) *n.* Any of various large, web-footed, long-winged sea birds. [< Sp. or Port. *alcatraz,* pelican.]

George Miksch Sutton
albatross

al·be·it (ôl-bē′ĭt, ăl-) *conj.* Although. [ME, although it be.]

al·bi·no (ăl-bī′nō) *n., pl.* **-nos.** A person or animal having abnormally pale skin, very light hair, and lacking normal eye coloring. [Port. < Lat. *albus,* white.] —**al′bi·nism** *n.*

al·bum (ăl′bəm) *n.* 1. A book or binder with blank pages for stamps, photographs, etc. 2. One or more phonograph records in one binding. [Lat., blank tablet < *albus,* white.]

al·bu·men (ăl-byōō′mən) *n.* 1. The white of an egg. 2. Albumin. [Lat. < *albus,* white.]

al·bu·min (ăl-byōō′mən) *n.* Any of several proteins found in egg white, blood serum, milk, and various animal and plant tissues. [ALBUM(EN) + -IN.]

al·bu·min·ous (ăl-byōō′mə-nəs) *adj.* Of, like, or pertaining to albumin or albumen.

al·ca·zar (ăl-käz′ər, ăl′kə-zär′) *n.* A Spanish palace or fortress.

al·che·my (ăl′kə-mē) *n.* 1. A medieval chemical philosophy concerned primarily with the conversion of base metals into gold. 2. Any seemingly magical power. [< Ar. *al-kīmiyā′.*] —**al·chem′i·cal** (-kĕm′ĭ-kəl) *or* **al·chem′ic** *adj.* —**al·chem′i·cal·ly** *adv.* —**al′che·mist** *n.*

al·co·hol (ăl′kə-hôl′) *n.* 1. Any of a series of related organic compounds, with the general formula $C_nH_{2n+1}OH$. 2. Ethanol. 3. Intoxicating liquor containing alcohol. [Ar. *al-koḥl,* powder of antimony.]

al·co·hol·ic (ǎl'kə-hô'lǐk, -hǒl'ǐk) *adj.* **1.** Of, containing, or resulting from alcohol. **2.** Suffering from alcoholism. —*n.* One who suffers from alcoholism.

al·co·hol·ism (ǎl'kə-hô-lǐz'əm) *n.* **1.** Habitual excessive drinking of alcoholic beverages. **2.** A chronic pathological condition caused by this.

al·cove (ǎl'kōv') *n.* A small recessed or partly enclosed extension of a room. [< Ar. *al-qubbah*, the vault.]

al·de·hyde (ǎl'də-hīd') *n.* Any of a class of highly reactive organic chemical compounds obtained by oxidation of alcohols. [< NLat. *al(cohol) dehyd(rogenatum)*, dehydrogenized alcohol.]

al·der (ôl'dər) *n.* Any of various shrubs or trees that grow in cool, moist places. [< OE *alor.*]

al·der·man (ôl'dər-mən) *n.* A member of a municipal legislative body. [< OE *ealdormann.*]

ale (āl) *n.* A fermented, bitter alcoholic beverage similar to beer. [< OE *ealu.*]

a·le·a·to·ry (ā'lē-ə-tôr'ē, -tōr'ē) *adj.* Dependent upon chance. [Lat. *aleatorius* < *alea*, dice.]

a·lee (ə-lē') *adv.* Away from the wind.

a·lem·bic (ə-lěm'bǐk) *n.* An apparatus formerly used for distilling. [< Ar. *al-anbīg.*]

a·leph (ä'lěf, -ləf) *n.* Also **a·lef.** The 1st letter of the Hebrew alphabet. See table at **alphabet.** [Heb. *āleph* < *eleph*, ox.]

a·lert (ə-lûrt') *adj.* **1.** Vigilantly attentive. **2.** Mentally responsive; quick. **3.** Lively. —*n.* **1.** A warning signal of attack or danger. **2.** The period of time during which an alert is in effect. —*v.* **1.** To warn. **2.** To make aware of; inform. [< Ital. *all' erta*, on the watch.] —**a·lert′ly** *adv.* —**a·lert′ness** *n.*

Syns: **alert, observant, open-eyed, vigilant, wakeful, wary, watchful, wide-awake** *adj.*

A·leut (ə-lōōt', ǎl'ē-ōōt') *n., pl.* **Aleut** or **A·leuts.** **1.** Also **A·leu·tian** (ə-lōō'shən) An Eskimo native of the Aleutian Islands. **2.** A group of related languages spoken in the Aleutian Islands. —**A·leu′tian** *adj.*

Al·ex·an·dri·an (ǎl'ǐg-zǎn'drē-ən) *adj.* **1.** Of or pertaining to Alexander the Great. **2.** Of or pertaining to Alexandria, Egypt. **3.** Of, characteristic of, or designating a learned school of Hellenistic literature, science, and philosophy located at Alexandria in the last three cent. B.C.

al·ex·an·drine (ǎl'ǐg-zǎn'drǐn) *n.* A line of English verse composed in iambic hexameter. [< OFr. < *Alexandre*, a romance about Alexander the Great.]

al·fal·fa (ǎl-fǎl'fə) *n.* A cloverlike plant with purple flowers, widely cultivated for forage. [< Ar. *al-fasfasah.*]

al·fres·co (ǎl-frěs'kō) *adv. & adj.* In the fresh air; outdoors. [Ital.]

al·ga (ǎl'gə) *n., pl.* **-gae** (-jē). Any of various primitive, chiefly aquatic, one-celled or multicellular plants, as the seaweeds. [Lat., seaweed.] —**al′gal** (ǎl'gəl) *adj.*

al·ge·bra (ǎl'jə-brə) *n.* A branch of mathematics in which symbols represent numbers of a specified set of numbers and are related

by operations that hold for all numbers in the set. [< Ar. *al-jebr.*] —**al′ge·bra′ist** (-brā'ĭst) *n.* —**al·gia** *suff.* Pain or disease of: *neuralgia.* [< Gk. *algos*, pain.]

AL·GOL or **Al·gol** (ǎl'gôl', -gǒl') *n.* A language for programming a computer, used esp. for scientific problems. [*algo(rithmic)* + L(ANGUAGE).]

Al·gon·qui·an (ǎl-gǒng'kwē-ən, -kē-ən) *n., pl.* **-an** or **-ans.** **1.** A principal family of about 50 North American Indian languages spoken in an area from the Atlantic seaboard west to the Rocky Mountains, and from Labrador south to North Carolina and Tennessee. **2.** A member of a tribe using an Algonquian language. —**Al·gon′qui·an** *adj.*

Al·gon·quin (ǎl-gǒng'kwǐn, -kǐn) *n., pl.* **-quin** or **-quins.** Also **Al·gon′kin** (-kǐn). **1.** Any of several North American Indian tribes of southeastern Canada. **2. a.** The Algonquian language of the Algonquin tribes. **b.** An Indian of these tribes.

al·go·rithm (ǎl'gə-rǐth'əm) *n. Math.* A rule or procedure for solving a problem. [< Mohammed ibn-Musa *al-Khwarizmi* (780-850?).]

a·li·as (ā'lē-əs, ǎl'yəs) *n., pl.* **-as·es.** An assumed name. —*adv.* Otherwise named: *Johnson, alias Rogers.* [< Lat., otherwise.]

al·i·bi (ǎl'ə-bī') *n., pl.* **-bis.** **1.** A form of defense whereby a defendant attempts to prove that he was elsewhere when a crime was committed. **2.** *Informal.* An excuse. [< Lat., elsewhere.] —**al′i·bi′** *v.*

a·li·en (ā'lē-ən, āl'yən) *adj.* **1.** Owing allegiance to another country or government. **2.** Not one's own; unfamiliar: *an alien culture.* **3.** Repugnant; adverse: *Lying is alien to his nature.* —*n.* **1.** An unnaturalized resident of a country. **2.** A member of another people, region, etc. **3.** One excluded from some group; an outsider. **4.** *Sci. Fic.* A creature from outer space. [< Lat. *alienus.*]

al·ien·a·ble (āl'yə-nə-bəl, ā'lē-ə-) *adj. Law.* Capable of being transferred to the ownership of another. —**al′ien·a·bil′i·ty** *n.*

al·ien·ate (āl'yə-nāt', ā'lē-ə-) *v.* **-at·ed, -at·ing.** **1.** To cause to become unfriendly or indifferent; estrange: *alienated his friends.* **2.** *Law.* To transfer (property) to the ownership of another. —**al′ien·a′tion** *n.* —**al′ien·a′tor** *n.*

al·ien·ist (āl'yə-nǐst, ā'lē-ə-) *n.* A psychiatrist, esp. one accepted by a court as an expert. [Fr. *aliéniste* < *aliéné*, insane.]

a·light¹ (ə-līt') *v.* **a·light·ed** or **a·lit** (ə-lǐt'), **a·light·ing.** **1.** To come down and settle, as after flight. **2.** To dismount. [< OE *ālīhtan.*]

a·light² (ə-līt') *adj. & adv.* Burning; lighted.

a·lign (ə-līn') *v.* Also **a·line, a·lined, a·lin·ing.** **1.** To arrange in a straight line. **2.** To ally (oneself) with or on the side of an argument, cause, nation, etc. **3.** To adjust (a mechanism or its parts) to produce a proper relationship or condition. [< OFr. *aligner.*] —**a·lign′er** *n.* —**a·lign′ment** *n.*

a·like (ə-līk') *adj.* Having close resemblance; similar. —*adv.* In the same way, manner, or degree. [< OE *gelīc.*] —**a·like′ness** *n.*

al·i·ment (ǎl'ə-mənt) *n.* Food; nourishment. [< Lat. *alimentum.*] —**al′i·men′tal** (-měn'tl) *adj.*

al·i·men·ta·ry (ăl'ə-měn'tə-rē, -trē) *adj.* 1. Of or pertaining to food or nutrition. 2. Providing nourishment.

alimentary canal *n.* The mucous-membrane-lined tube of the digestive system that extends from the mouth to the anus and includes the pharynx, esophagus, stomach, and intestines.

al·i·mo·ny (ăl'ə-mō'nē) *n., pl.* **-nies.** *Law.* An allowance for support paid by one spouse to the other spouse after a divorce or legal separation. [Lat. *alimonia,* nourishment.]

a·line (ə-līn') *v.* Var. of **align.**

al·i·phat·ic (ăl'ə-făt'ĭk) *adj.* Pertaining to organic compounds in which the carbon atoms are linked in open chains rather than rings. [< Gk. *aleiphar,* oil.]

a·lit (ə-lĭt') *v. p.t. & p.p.* of **alight.**

a·live (ə-līv') *adj.* 1. Having life; living. 2. In existence or operation. 3. Full of life; lively. —*idioms.* **alive to.** Sensitive to: *alive to the moods of others.* **alive with.** Swarming with: *a pool alive with fish.* —**a·live'ness** *n.*

a·liz·a·rin (ə-lĭz'ə-rĭn) *n.* An orange-red crystalline compound, $C_{14}H_8O_4$, used in dyes. [< Ar. *al-'aṣārah,* the juice pressed out.]

al·ka·li (ăl'kə-lī') *n., pl.* **-lis** or **-lies.** 1. A hydroxide or carbonate of an alkali metal, the aqueous solution of which is bitter, slippery, caustic, and basic. 2. Any of various basic, soluble mineral salts found in natural water and arid soils. [< Ar. *al qalīy,* the ashes.]

alkali metal *n.* Any of a group of highly reactive metallic elements, including lithium, sodium, potassium, rubidium and cesium.

al·ka·line (ăl'kə-līn, -lĭn) *adj.* 1. Of, pertaining to, or containing an alkali. 2. Basic. —**al'ka·lin'i·ty** (-lĭn'ĭ-tē) *n.*

alkaline-earth metal (ăl'kə-līn-ûrth') *n.* Any of a group of basic metallic elements, esp. calcium, strontium, and barium, but gen. including beryllium, magnesium, and radium.

al·ka·lize (ăl'kə-līz') *v.* **-lized, -liz·ing.** Also **al·ka·lin·ize** (-lĭ-nīz'), **-ized, iz·ing.** To make alkaline or become an alkali. —**al'ka·li·za'tion** or **al'ka·lin·i·za'tion** *n.*

al·ka·loid (ăl'kə-loid') *n.* Any of a class of colorless, bitter, organic compounds that contain nitrogen, are derived from seed plants, and include nicotine, quinine, cocaine, atropine, and morphine. —**al'ka·loi'dal** (-loid'l) *adj.*

al·ka·lo·sis (ăl'kə-lō'sĭs) *n.* Pathologically high alkali content in the blood and tissues.

al·kyd resin (ăl'kĭd) *n.* A widely used durable synthetic resin. [*alkyl*(*l*) + (*aci*)*D* + *resin*.]

all (ôl) *adj.* 1. The total extent or number of: *all Christendom; all men.* 2. Constituting the whole of: *all day.* 3. The utmost possible: *in all truth.* 4. Every: *all kinds.* 5. Any: *proven beyond all doubt.* 6. Nothing but; only: *all skin and bones.* —*pron.* Each and every one: *All aboard the ship were drowned.* —*n.* Everything one has: *He gave his all.* —*adv.* 1. Wholly: *all wrong.* 2. Each; apiece: *a score of five all.* 3. Exclusively: *The cake is all for him.* —*idioms.* **all but.** Very nearly. **all in.** *Informal.* Exhausted. **all out.** With every effort possible. **all over.** 1. Finished. 2. Everywhere. 3. *Informal.* Thoroughly or typically: *That's me all over.* [< OE.]

Al·lah (ăl'ə, ä'lə) *n.* The supreme being in Islam.

all-A·mer·i·can (ôl'ə-měr'ĭ-kən) *adj.* 1. Representing the best of its kind in the United States. 2. *Sports.* Chosen as the best amateur in the United States at a particular position or event. —**all'-A·mer'i·can** *n.*

all-a·round (ôl'ə-round') *adj.* Var. of **all-round.**

al·lay (ə-lā') *v.* 1. To lessen or relieve (e.g. pain). 2. To calm or pacify (e.g. fear). [< OE *ālecgan,* to lay aside.]

all clear *n.* 1. A signal, usu. by siren, that an air raid or air-raid drill is over. 2. A term signifying the absence of immediate obstacles or impending danger.

al·lege (ə-lĕj') *v.* **-leged, -leg·ing.** 1. To declare or assert to be true, usu. without offering proof. 2. To cite as a plea or excuse. [< Lat. *allegare,* to dispatch.] —**al'le·ga'tion** *n.* —**al·leg'ed·ly** (-ĭd-lē) *adv.* —**al·leg'er** *n.*

al·le·giance (ə-lē'jəns) *n.* Obedience or loyalty owed to a nation, sovereign, or cause. [< OFr. *ligeance.*]

al·le·gor·i·cal (ăl'ĭ-gôr'ĭ-kəl, -gōr'-) or **al·le·gor·ic** (-gôr'ĭk, -gōr'ĭk) *adj.* Of, pertaining to, or containing allegory. —**al'le·gor'i·cal·ly** *adv.*

al·le·go·ry (ăl'ĭ-gôr'ē, -gōr'ē) *n., pl.* **-ries.** A literary, dramatic, or pictorial device in which each literal character, object, and event represent symbols illustrating an idea or moral or religious principle. [< Gk. *allēgoria.*] —**al'le·gor'ic** or **al'le·gor'i·cal** *adj.* —**al'le·gor'i·cal·ly** *adv.* —**al'le·go'rist** *n.*

al·le·gret·to (ăl'ĭ-grĕt'ō) *adv.* Slower than allegro but faster than andante. [Ital.] —**al'le·gret'to** *adj.*

al·le·gro (ə-lĕg'rō, ə-lā'grō) *adv.* At a fast tempo. [Ital.] —**al·le'gro** *adj.*

al·lele (ə-lēl') *n.* Any of a group of genes that occur as alternative forms at a given site. [G. *Allel.*] —**al·le'lic** *adj.*

al·le·lu·ia (ăl'ə-lōō'yə) *interj.* Hallelujah.

al·ler·gen (ăl'ər-jən) *n.* A substance that causes an allergy. —**al'ler·gen'ic** (-jĕn'ĭk) *adj.*

al·ler·gist (ăl'ər-jĭst) *n.* A physician who specializes in the treatment of allergies.

al·ler·gy (ăl'ər-jē) *n., pl.* **-gies.** 1. Hypersensitive bodily reaction to environmental factors or substances, such as pollens, foods, dust, or microorganisms, in amounts that do not affect most people. 2. *Informal.* A strong dislike. [G. *Allergie.*] —**al·ler'gic** (ə-lûr'jĭk) *adj.*

al·le·vi·ate (ə-lē'vē-āt') *v.* **-at·ed, -at·ing.** To make more bearable. [LLat. *alleviare,* to lighten.] —**al·le'vi·a'tion** *n.* —**al·le'vi·a'tive** *adj.* —**al·le'vi·a'tor** *n.*

al·ley (ăl'ē) *n., pl.* **-leys.** 1. A narrow street or passageway between or behind buildings. 2. A bowling alley. —*idiom.* **up (one's) alley.** Compatible with one's interests or qualifications. [OFr. *alee* < *aler,* to go.]

alley cat *n.* 1. A homeless cat. 2. A domestic cat with no known ancestry.

al·ley·way (ăl'ē-wā') *n.* A narrow passage between buildings.

al·li·ance (ə-lī'əns) *n.* 1. **a.** A formal pact of union or confederation between nations. **b.** The nations so conjoined. 2. A union, relationship, or connection by kinship, marriage, or common interest.

al·li·ga·tor (ăl'ĭ-gā'tər) *n.* 1. A large amphibious reptile with sharp teeth, powerful jaws, and a broader, shorter snout than the related crocodile. 2. Leather made from the hide of an alligator. [< Sp. *el lagarto,* the lizard.]

alligator pear *n.* The avocado.

all-im·por·tant (ôl'ĭm-pôr'tnt) *adj.* Very important; vital.

al·lit·er·ate (ə-lĭt'ə-rāt') *v.* **-at·ed, -at·ing.** 1. To use alliteration. 2. To form or arrange with alliteration. [< ALLITERATION.]

al·lit·er·a·tion (ə-lĭt'ə-rā'shən) *n.* The repetition of the same initial consonant sound in two or more words in a line of speech or writing for poetic or emphatic effect, as in "When to the sessions of sweet silent thought" (Shakespeare). [< AD- + Lat. *littera,* letter.] **—al·lit'er·a'tive** *adj.* **—al·lit'er·a·tive·ly** *adv.*

allo- *pref.* Divergence, opposition, or difference: *allotrope.* [Gk. < *allos,* other.]

al·lo·cate (ăl'ə-kāt') *v.* **-cat·ed, -cat·ing.** To allot; assign. [< Med. Lat. *allocare,* to place to.] **—al'lo·ca'tion** *n.*

al·lo·morph (ăl'ə-môrf') *n.* *Ling.* Any of the variant forms of a morpheme. For example, the phonetic *s* of *cats,* *z* of *dogs,* and *iz* of *horses* are allomorphs of the plural morpheme *s.* **—al'lo·mor'phic** *adj.*

al·lo·phone (ăl'ə-fōn') *n.* *Ling.* Any of the variant forms of a phoneme. For example, the aspirated *p* of *pit* and the unaspirated *p* of *spit* are allophones of the phoneme *p.* **—al'lo·phon'ic** (-fŏn'ĭk) *adj.*

al·lot (ə-lŏt') *v.* **-lot·ted, -lot·ting.** 1. To distribute by lot. 2. To give or assign. [< OFr. *aloter.*] **—al·lot'ment** *n.* **—al·lot'ter** *n.*

al·lot·ro·py (ə-lŏt'rə-pē) *n.* The existence, esp. in the solid state, of two or more crystalline or molecular structural forms of an element. **—al'lo·trope'** (ăl'ə-trōp') *n.* **—al'lo·trop'ic** (ăl'-ə-trŏp'ĭk) *or* **al'lo·trop'i·cal** (-trŏp'ĭ-kəl) *adj.*

all-out (ôl'out') *adj.* Wholehearted: *an all-out effort.*

al·low (ə-lou') *v.* 1. To let do or happen; permit. 2. To permit to have. 3. To make provision for. 4. To permit the presence of: *No pets allowed.* 5. To provide. 6. To admit: *allow that to be true.* 7. To allow as a discount. **—phrasal verbs. allow for.** To make a provision for: *Allow for bad weather.* **allow of.** To permit: *a treatise allowing of several interpretations.* [< OFr. *allouer.*] **—al·low'a·ble** *adj.* **—al·low'a·bly** *adv.* **—al·low'ed·ly** (-ĭd-lē) *adv.*

al·low·ance (ə-lou'əns) *n.* 1. The act of allowing. 2. A regular provision of money, food, etc. 3. A price discount. **—idiom. make allowance (or allowances) for.** To allow for: *make allowance for his inexperience.*

al·loy (ăl'oi', ə-loi') *n.* 1. A macroscopically homogeneous mixture or solid solution, usu. of two or more metals. 2. Something added that lowers value or purity. [< Lat. *alligare,* to bind to.] **—al·loy'** (ə-loi', ăl'oi') *v.*

all-pur·pose (ôl'pûr'pəs) *adj.* Useful in many ways.

all right *adv.* 1. Satisfactory; average. 2. Correct. 3. Uninjured. 4. Very well; yes. 5. Without a doubt: *That's him all right!*

all-right (ôl'rīt') *adj. Slang.* 1. Dependable; honorable: *an all-right fellow.* 2. Good; excellent: *an all-right movie.*

all-round (ôl'round') *adj.* Also **all-a-round** (ôl'-ə-round'). 1. Comprehensive in extent or depth. 2. Versatile.

All Saints' Day *n.* November 1, a Christian festival in honor of all saints.

All Souls' Day *n.* November 2, observed by the Roman Catholic Church as a day of prayer for souls in purgatory.

all·spice (ôl'spīs') *n.* The aromatic berries of a tropical American tree, used as a spice.

all-star (ôl'stär') *adj.* Made up of star performers.

all-time (ôl'tīm') *adj.* Unsurpassed until now; of all time: *set an all-time attendance record.*

all told *adv.* With everything considered.

al·lude (ə-lōōd') *v.* **-lud·ed, -lud·ing.** To make an indirect reference to. [Lat. *alludere,* to play with.] **—al·lu'sion** *n.* **—al·lu'sive** *adj.* **—al·lu'sive·ly** *adv.*

al·lure (ə-lōōr') *v.* **-lured, -lur·ing.** To entice with something desirable; tempt. **—n.** The power of attracting. [< OFr. *aleurrer.*] **—al·lure'ment** *n.* **—al·lur'er** *n.*

al·lu·vi·um (ə-lōō'vē-əm) *n., pl.* **-vi·ums** *or* **-vi·a** (-vē-ə). Sediment deposited by flowing water, as in a river bed. [Lat. < *alluere,* to wash against.] **—al·lu'vi·al** *adj.*

al·ly (ə-lī', ăl'ī') *v.* **-lied, -ly·ing.** To unite or connect in a formal or close relationship or bond. **—n.** (ăl'ī', ə-lī'), *pl.* **-lies.** One united with another in a formal or close relationship. [< Lat. *alligare,* to bind to.]

al·ma ma·ter (ăl'mə mä'tər, ăl'mə, äl'mə) *n.* 1. The school, college, or university a person attended. 2. The anthem of a school, college, or university. [Lat., fostering mother.]

al·ma·nac (ôl'mə-năk', ăl'-) *n.* An annual publication in calendar form that includes weather forecasts, astronomical information, and often other useful facts. [< Med. Lat. *almanachus.*]

al·might·y (ôl-mī'tē) *adj.* 1. Omnipotent. 2. *Informal.* Great: *an almighty din.* **—n.** the **Almighty.** God. [< OE *ealmihtig.*]

al·mond (ä'mənd, ăm'ənd) *n.* 1. An oval, edible nut with a soft, light-brown shell. 2. A tree bearing almonds. [< LLat. *amandula.*]

al·most (ôl'mōst', ôl-mōst') *adv.* Slightly short of; not quite. [< OE (e)*almǣst.*]

alms (ämz) *pl.n.* Money or goods given to the poor in charity. [< Gk. *eleēmosunē* < *eleos,* pity.]

alms·house (ämz'hous') *n.* A poorhouse.

al·oe (ăl'ō) *n.* Any of various chiefly African plants with fleshy, spiny-toothed leaves. [< Gk. *aloē.*]

a·loft (ə-lôft', ə-lŏft') *adv.* 1. In or into a high place. 2. Toward the upper rigging of a ship. [< ON *ā lopt.*]

a·lo·ha (ä-lō'hä') *interj.* Used to express greeting or farewell. [Hawaiian.]

a·lone (ə-lōn') *adj.* 1. Apart from other people; single; solitary. 2. Excluding anything or anyone else; sole; only. 3. With nothing further added. **—idioms. let alone.** 1. To leave alone. 2. Not to speak of: *I can't even do arithmetic, let alone algebra.* **stand alone.** To be without equal. [ME.] **—a·lone'** *adv.*

a·long (ə-lông', ə-lŏng') *adv.* 1. In a line with; following the length or path of. 2. Forward: *moving along.* 3. In association; together. 4. As company: *Bring your parents along.* 5. Somewhat advanced: *The evening was well* *along.* **6.** Approaching: *along about midnight.* —*prep.* Over, through, or by the length of. —*idioms.* **all along.** All the time: *I was right all along.* **get along. 1.** To go onward. **2.** To survive. **3.** To be compatible. [< OE *andlang.*]

a·long·shore (ə-lông′shôr′, -shôr′, ə-lŏng′-) *adv.* Along, near, or by the shore.

a·long·side (ə-lông′sīd′, ə-lŏng′-) *adv.* Along, near, at, or to the side. —*prep.* By the side of.

a·loof (ə-lōōf′) *adj.* Distant; reserved. —*adv.* At a distance, but within view; apart. [A-² + obs. *loufe,* side of a ship.] —**a·loof′ly** *adv.* —**a·loof′ness** *n.*

a·loud (ə-loud′) *adv.* **1.** In a loud tone. **2.** Orally: *Read this passage aloud.*

alp (ălp) *n.* A high mountain. [< *Alps,* a group of mountains in Europe.]

al·pac·a (ăl-păk′ə) *n.* **1.** A South American mammal related to the llama, having fine, long wool. **2. a.** The silky wool of the alpaca. **b.** Cloth made from this wool. [Sp.]

alpaca

al·pen·horn (ăl′pən-hôrn′) *n.* A curved wooden horn used to call cows to pasture.

al·pen·stock (ăl′pən-stŏk′) *n.* A long staff with an iron point, used by mountain climbers. [G.]

al·pha (ăl′fə) *n.* The 1st letter of the Greek alphabet. See table at **alphabet.** [Gk.]

al·pha·bet (ăl′fə-bĕt′, -bĭt) *n.* **1.** The letters of a language, arranged in the order fixed by custom. **2.** Basic principles; rudiments. [< Gk. *alphabētos.*]

al·pha·bet·i·cal (ăl′fə-bĕt′ĭ-kəl) or **al·pha·bet·ic** (-bĕt′ĭk) *adj.* **1.** Arranged in the customary order of the letters of a language. **2.** Expressed by an alphabet. —**al′pha·bet′i·cal·ly** *adv.*

al·pha·bet·ize (ăl′fə-bĭ-tīz′) *v.* **-ized, -iz·ing.** To arrange in alphabetical order. —**al′pha·bet′i·za′tion** (-bĕt′ĭ-zā′shən) *n.* —**al′pha·bet·iz′er** *n.*

al·pha·nu·mer·ic (ăl′fə-nōō-mĕr′ĭk, -nyōō-) *adj.* Consisting of both alphabetic and numerical symbols. [ALPHA(BET) + NUMERIC(AL).]

alpha particle *n.* A positively charged composite particle, indistinguishable from a helium atom nucleus, consisting of two protons and two neutrons.

alpha ray *n.* A stream of alpha particles.

alpha rhythm *n.* Also **alpha wave.** The most common waveform found in electroencephalograms of the adult cerebral cortex, 8-12 smooth, regular oscillations/second in subjects at rest.

al·pine (ăl′pīn′, -pīn) *adj.* Of or pertaining to high mountains.

al·read·y (ôl-rĕd′ē) *adv.* By this or a specified time; before; previously: *I have already finished the job.* [ME *al redy.*]

al·so (ôl′sō) *adv.* Besides; in addition; too. —*conj.* And in addition. [< OE *alswā.*]

al·so-ran /ôl′sō-răn′) *n. Informal.* One defeated in a competition.

Al·ta·ic (ăl-tā′ĭk) *n.* A language family of Europe and Asia that includes the Turkic, Tungusic, and Mongolic subfamilies. —*adj.* **1.** Of or pertaining to the Altai Mountains. **2.** Of or pertaining to Altaic. [< the *Altai* Mountains.]

al·tar (ôl′tar) *n.* Any elevated structure upon which sacrifices may be offered or before which other religious ceremonies may be enacted. [< Lat. *altare.*]

al·tar·piece (ôl′tər-pēs′) *n.* A painting or carving placed above and behind an altar.

al·ter (ôl′tər) *v.* **1.** To change or become different. **2.** To adjust (a garment) for a better fit. **3.** *Informal.* To castrate or spay (an animal). [< Med. Lat. *alterare* < Lat. *alter,* other.] —**al′ter·a·ble** *adj.* —**al′ter·a·bly** *adv.* —**al′ter·a′tion** *n.*

al·ter·cate (ôl′tər-kāt′) *v.* **-cat·ed, -cat·ing.** To argue or dispute vehemently. [Lat. *altercari* < *alter,* another.] —**al′ter·ca′tion** *n.*

al·ter e·go (ôl′tər ē′gō) *n.* **1.** Another side of oneself. **2.** An intimate friend. [Lat., other I.]

al·ter·nate (ôl′tər-nāt′, ăl′-) *v.* **-nat·ed, -nat·ing. 1.** To occur in successive turns. **2.** To pass from one state, action, or place to a second and back indefinitely. —*adj.* (ôl′tər-nĭt, ăl′-). **1.** Happening or following in turns. **2.** Designating or pertaining to every other one of a series. **3.** Substitute: *an alternate plan.* —*n.* (ôl′tər-nĭt, ăl′-). A person acting in the place of another. [Lat. *alternare* < *alter,* other.] —**al′ter·nate·ly** *adv.* —**al′ter·na′tion** *n.*

alternating current *n.* An electric current that reverses direction at regular intervals.

al·ter·na·tive (ôl-tûr′nə-tĭv, ăl-) *n.* **1.** A choice between two or more possibilities. **2.** One of the things to be chosen. —*adj.* **1.** Allowing or necessitating a choice. **2.** Existing outside conventional institutions or systems. —**al·ter′na·tive·ly** *adv.*

alternative school *n.* A school that is nontraditional in educational values or teaching methods.

al·ter·na·tor (ôl′tər-nā′tər, ăl′-) *n.* An electric generator that produces alternating current.

al·though (ôl-*thō*′) *conj.* Also **al·tho.** Regardless of the fact that; even though. [ME.]

Usage: The words *although* and *though* are interchangeable: *Although* (or *though*) *she was tired, she went to work. Although* usu. occurs first in its clause, but *though* can occur in final position or after a word describing the subject: *We didn't respond, though. We are wiser though poorer.* Do not use the variant *tho* in formal prose.

al·tim·e·ter (ăl-tĭm′ĭ-tər) *n.* An instrument for determining altitude. [Lat. *altus,* high + -METER.] —**al·tim′e·try** *n.*

al·ti·tude (ăl′tĭ-tōōd′, -tyōōd′) *n.* **1.** *Geog.* The height of something measured in relation to a reference level, esp. above the earth's surface. **2.** *Astron.* The angular height of a celestial object above the horizon. **3.** *Geom.* The perpendicular distance from the base of a geo-

TABLE OF ALPHABETS

The transliterations shown are those used in the etymologies of this Dictionary.

Arabic

The different forms in the four numbered columns are used when the letters are (1) in isolation; (2) in juncture with a previous letter; (3) in juncture with the letters on both sides; (4) in juncture with a following letter.

Long vowels are represented by the consonant signs *'alif* (for *ā*), *wāw* (for *ū*), and *yā* (for *ī*). Short vowels are not usually written.

Transliterations with subscript dots represent "emphatic" or pharyngeal consonants, which are pronounced in the usual way except that the pharynx is tightly narrowed during articulation.

Hebrew

Vowels are not represented in normal Hebrew writing, but for educational purposes they are indicated by a system of subscript and superscript dots.

The transliterations shown in parentheses apply when the letter falls at the end of a word. The transliterations with subscript dots are pharyngeal consonants, as in Arabic.

The second forms shown are used when the letter falls at the end of a word.

Greek

The superscript ʻ on an initial vowel or *rhō*, called the "rough breathing," represents an aspirate. Lack of aspiration on an initial vowel is indicated by the superscript ʼ, called the "smooth breathing."

When *gamma* precedes *kappa, xi, khi,* or another *gamma*, it has the value *n* and is so transliterated. The second lower-case form of *sigma* is used only in final position.

Russian

[1] This letter, called *tvordiĭ znak,* "hard sign," is very rare in modern Russian. It indicates that the previous consonant remains hard even though followed by a front vowel.
[2] This letter, called *myakiĭ znak,* "soft sign," indicates that the previous consonant is palatalized even when a front vowel does not follow.

ARABIC

Forms				Name	Sound
1	2	3	4		
ا	ل			'alif	'
ب	ب	ب	ب	bā	b
ت	ت	ت	ت	tā	t
ث	ث	ث	ث	thā	th
ج	ج	ج	ج	jīm	j
ح	ح	ح	ح	ḥā	ḥ
خ	خ	خ	خ	khā	kh
د	د			dāl	d
ذ	ذ			dhāl	dh
ر	ر			rā	r
ز	ز			zāy	z
س	س	س	س	sīn	s
ش	ش	ش	ش	shīn	sh
ص	ص	ص	ص	ṣād	ṣ
ض	ض	ض	ض	ḍād	ḍ
ط	ط	ط	ط	ṭā	ṭ
ظ	ظ	ظ	ظ	ẓā	ẓ
ع	ع	ع	ع	'ayn	'
غ	غ	غ	غ	ghayn	gh
ف	ف	ف	ف	fā	f
ق	ق	ق	ق	qāf	q
ك	ك	ك	ك	kāf	k
ل	ل	ل	ل	lām	l
م	م	م	م	mīm	m
ن	ن	ن	ن	nūn	n
ه	ه	ه	ه	hā	h
و	و			wāw	w
ى	ى	ى	ى	yā	y

HEBREW			GREEK			RUSSIAN	
Forms	Name	Sound	Forms	Name	Sound	Forms	Sound
א	'aleph		A α	alpha	a.	A a	a
ב	bēth	b (bh)	B β	beta	b	Б б	b
						В в	v
ג	gimel	g (gh)	Γ γ	gamma	g (n)	Г г	g
ד	dāleth	d (dh)	Δ δ	delta	d	Д д	d
ה	hē	h	E ε	epsilon	e	E e	e
ו	waw	w	Z ζ	zēta	z	Ж ж	zh
						З з	z
ז	zayin	z	H η	ēta	ē	И и Й й	i, ĭ
ח	ḥeth	ḥ	Θ θ	thēta	th	К к	k
ט	ṭeth	ṭ	I ι	iota	i	Л л	l
י	yodh	y	K κ	kappa	k	М м	m
כ ך	kāph	k (kh)	Λ λ	lambda	l	Н н	n
						O o	o
ל	lāmedh	l	M μ	mu	m	П п	p
מ ם	mēm	m	N ν	nu	n	Р р	r
נ ן	nūn	n	Ξ ξ	xi	x	С с	s
ס	samekh	s	O o	omicron	o	Т т	t
ע	'ayin	'	Π π	pi	p	У у	u
פ ף	pē	p (ph)	P ρ	rhō	r (rh)	Ф ф	f
צ ץ	ṣadhe	ṣ	Σ σ ς	sigma	s	Х х	kh
ק	qōph	q	T τ	tau	t	Ц ц	ts
ר	rēsh	r	Υ υ	upsilon	u	Ч ч	ch
ש	sin	s	Φ φ	phi	ph	Ш ш	sh
ש	shin	sh	X χ	chi khi	kh	Щ щ	shch
ת	tāw	t (th)	Ψ ψ	psi	ps	Ъ ъ	"1
			Ω ω	ōmega	ō	Ы ы	y
						Ь ь	'2
						Э э	e
						Ю ю	yu
						Я я	ya

metric figure to the opposite vertex, parallel side, or parallel surface. [< Lat. *altitudo*.] **—al'ti·tu'di·nal** *adj.*

al·to (ăl'tō) *n., pl.* **-tos.** *Mus.* **1.** A low female singing voice. **2.** A singer having an alto voice. **3.** A part written in the range of the alto voice. **4.** An instrument that sounds within the alto range. [Ital.]

al·to·geth·er (ôl'tə-gĕth'ər, ôl'tə-gĕth'ər) *adv.* **1.** Entirely. **2.** With all included or counted; in all: *Altogether 100 people were there.* **3.** On the whole. [ME *al togeder.*]

al·tru·ism (ăl'trōō-ĭz'əm) *n.* Unselfish concern for the welfare of others; selflessness. [Fr. *altruisme*, ult. < Lat. *alter*, other.] **—al'tru·ist** *n.* **—al'tru·is'tic** *adj.* **—al'tru·is'ti·cal·ly** *adv.*

al·um (ăl'əm) *n.* Any of various double sulfates of a trivalent metal, esp. aluminum potassium sulfate, $AlK(SO_4)_2 \cdot 12H_2O$, used medicinally as topical astringents and styptics. [< Lat. *alumen.*]

a·lu·mi·na (ə-lōō'mə-nə) *n.* Any of several forms of aluminum oxide, Al_2O_3, that occur naturally as corundum, in bauxite, and with various impurities as ruby, sapphire, and emery. [< Lat. *alumen*, alum.]

a·lu·min·i·um (ăl'yə-mĭn'ē-əm) *n.* Chiefly Brit. Var. of **aluminum.**

a·lu·mi·nize (ə-lōō'mə-nīz') *v.* **-nized, -niz·ing.** To coat or treat with aluminum.

a·lu·mi·nous (ə-lōō'mə-nəs) *adj.* Of, pertaining to, or containing aluminum or alum.

a·lu·mi·num (ə-lōō'mə-nəm) *n. Symbol* **Al** A silvery-white, ductile metallic element used to form many hard, light, corrosion-resistant alloys. Atomic number 13; atomic weight 26.98. [< ALUMINA.]

a·lum·na (ə-lŭm'nə) *n., pl.* **-nae** (-nē'). A female graduate of a school, college, or university. [Lat., female pupil.]

a·lum·nus (ə-lŭm'nəs) *n., pl.* **-ni** (-nī'). A male graduate of a school, college, or university. [Lat., male pupil.]

al·ways (ôl'wāz, -wēz, -wĭz) *adv.* **1.** On every occasion. **2.** Continuously; forever. **3.** Without exception. [OE *ealne weg.*]

am (ăm; *unstressed* əm) *v.* 1st person sing. present tense of **be.**

Am The symbol for the element americium.

a·main (ə-mān') *adv.* With full force.

a·mal·gam (ə-măl'gəm) *n.* **1.** An alloy of mercury with another metal or metals. **2.** A mixture of diverse elements. [< Med. Lat. *amalgama.*]

a·mal·ga·mate (ə-măl'gə-māt') *v.* **-mat·ed, -mat·ing.** To form so as to make a whole. **—a·mal'ga·ma'tion** *n.*

a·man·u·en·sis (ə-măn'yōō-ĕn'sĭs) *n., pl.* **-ses** (-sēz'). A secretary. [Lat.]

am·a·ranth (ăm'ə-rănth') *n.* **1.** Any of various, often weedy plants with clusters of small greenish or purplish flowers. **2.** An imaginary flower that never fades. [Gk. *amarantos*, unfading.] **—am'a·ran'thine** *adj.*

am·a·ryl·lis (ăm'ə-rĭl'ĭs) *n.* A bulbous, tropical plant with large, lilylike reddish or white flowers. [< Lat. *Amaryllis*, a name of a shepherdess.]

a·mass (ə-măs') *v.* To accumulate. [OFr. *amasser.*] **—a·mass'er** *n.* **—a·mass'ment** *n.*

am·a·teur (ăm'ə-chŏor', -/ -ə-tər, -ə-tyŏor') *n.* **1.** One who engages in an activity as a pastime rather than as a profession. **2.** One who lacks expertise. [< Lat. *amator*, a lover.] **—am'a·teur'ish** *adj.* **—am'a·teur'ish·ly** *adv.* **—am'a·teur'ism** *n.*

am·a·to·ry (ăm'ə-tôr'ē, -tōr'ē) *adj.* Of or expressive of sexual love. [Lat. *amatorius.*]

a·maze (ə-māz') *v.* **a·mazed, a·maz·ing.** To fill with surprise or wonder; astonish. [< OE *āmasian*, to bewilder.] **—a·maz'ed·ly** (ə-mā'zĭd-lē) *adv.* **—a·maze'ment** *n.* **—a·maz'ing·ly** *adv.*

Am·a·zon (ăm'ə-zŏn', -zən) *n.* **1.** *Gk. Myth.* A member of a nation of female warriors. **2.** **amazon.** A tall, vigorous, aggressive woman. **—Am'a·zo'ni·an** (ăm'ə-zō'nē-ən) *adj.*

Amazon
Amazon fighting Hercules

am·bas·sa·dor (ăm-băs'ə-dər) *n.* A diplomatic official of the highest rank appointed as representative in residence by one government to another. [OFr. *ambassadeur*.] **—am·bas'sa·do'ri·al** (-dôr'ē-əl, -dōr'-) *adj.* **—am·bas'sa·dor·ship'** *n.*

am·ber (ăm'bər) *n.* **1.** A yellow or brownish-yellow fossil resin, used for making ornamental objects. **2.** A brownish yellow. [Ar. *'anbar*.] **—am'ber** *adj.*

am·ber·gris (ăm'bər-grĭs, -grēs') *n.* A waxy substance produced by sperm whales and used in perfumes. [OFr. *ambre gris*.]

ambi- *pref.* Both: *ambidextrous.* [Lat., round.]

am·bi·ance (ăm'bē-əns) *n.* Also **am·bi·ence.** The distinct atmosphere of an environment or setting. [Fr.]

am·bi·dex·trous (ăm'bĭ-dĕk'strəs) *adj.* Capable of using both hands with equal facility. [LLat. *ambidexter.*] **—am'bi·dex·ter'i·ty** (ăm'-bĭ-dĕk-stĕr'ĭ-tē) *n.* **—am'bi·dex'trous·ly** *adv.*

am·bi·ent (ăm'bē-ənt) *adj.* Surrounding. [< Lat. *ambire*, to go around.]

ambiguity error *n.* A gross error, usu. transient, in the readout of an electronic device that is caused by imprecise synchronism, as in analog-to-digital conversion.

am·big·u·ous (ăm-bĭg'yōō-əs) *adj.* **1.** Capable of being interpreted in more than one way. **2.** Doubtful or uncertain. [Lat. *ambiguus*, uncertain.] **—am'bi·gu'i·ty** (-gyōō'ĭ-tē) or **am·big'u·ous·ness** *n.* **—am·big'u·ous·ly** *adv.*

am·bi·tion (ăm-bĭsh'ən) *n.* **1.** A strong desire to achieve something. **2.** An object or goal strongly desired. [< Lat. *ambire*, to solicit.]

am·bi·tious (ăm-bĭsh'əs) *adj.* **1.** Characterized

by ambition. **2.** Challenging: *an ambitious plan.* —**am·bi'tious·ly** *adv.*

am·biv·a·lence (ăm-bĭv'ə-ləns) *n.* The simultaneous existence of two conflicting feelings about a person, object, or idea. —**am·biv'a·lent** *adj.* —**am·biv'a·lent·ly** *adv.*

am·ble (ăm'bəl) *v.* **-bled, -bling.** To move at an easy gait; saunter. [< Lat. *ambulare,* to walk.] —**am'ble** *n.* —**am'bler** *n.*

Am·boi·nese (ăm'boi-nēz', -nēs') *n.* The language of Amboina, an island in the Moluccas, Indonesia.

am·bro·sia (ăm-brō'zhə) *n.* **1.** *Gk. & Rom. Myth.* The food of the gods. **2.** Something of exquisite flavor or fragrance. [Gk.] —**am·bro'sial** *adj.*

am·bu·lance (ăm'byə-ləns) *n.* A vehicle equipped to transport the sick or wounded. [Fr.]

am·bu·lant (ăm'byə-lənt) *adj.* Moving or walking about. [< Lat. *ambulare,* to walk.]

am·bu·la·to·ry (ăm'byə-lə-tôr'ē, -tōr'ē) *adj.* **1.** Of, involving, or for walking. **2.** Capable of walking. **3.** Moving about; not stationary. —*n., pl.* **-ries.** A covered place for walking, as in a cloister. [< Lat. *ambulare,* to walk.]

am·bus·cade (ăm'bə-skād', ăm'bə-skād') *n.* An ambush. [< OItal. *imboscare,* to ambush.] —**am'bus·cade** *v.*

am·bush (ăm'bŏosh') *n.* **1.** The act of lying in wait to attack by surprise. **2.** A surprise attack made from a concealed position. [OFr. *embuschier,* to ambush.] —**am'bush** *v.*

a·me·ba (ə-mē'bə) *n.* Var. of **amoeba.**

a·me·lio·rate (ə-mēl'yə-rāt') *v.* **-rated, -rating.** To make or become better; improve. [Fr. *améliorer.*] —**a·mel'io·ra·ble** (-rə-bəl) *adj.* —**a·mel'io·ra'tion** *n.* —**a·mel'io·ra'tive** *adj.* —**a·mel'io·ra'tor** *n.*

a·men (ā-mĕn', ä-) *interj.* So be it. Used at the end of a prayer or to express approval. [< Heb. *āmēn,* certainly.]

a·me·na·ble (ə-mē'nə-bəl, ə-měn'ə-) *adj.* **1.** Tractable; responsive: *amenable to reason.* **2.** Responsible; accountable. [< Fr. *amener,* to lead.] —**a·me'na·bil'i·ty** *n.* —**a·me'na·bly** *adv.*

a·mend (ə-měnd') *v.* **1.** To correct; rectify. **2.** To alter (a law) formally by adding, deleting, or rephrasing. **3.** To improve. [< Lat. *emendare.*] —**a·mend'a·ble** *adj.*

a·mend·ment (ə-měnd'mənt) *n.* **1.** Improvement. **2.** A correction. **3. a.** A formal alteration of a law. **b.** The parliamentary process whereby such alteration is made.

a·mends (ə-měndz') *pl.n.* Reparation for insult or injury.

a·men·i·ty (ə-měn'ĭ-tē, ə-mē'nĭ-) *n., pl.* **-ties. 1.** Pleasantness; agreeableness. **2.** Something that provides or increases comfort or convenience. **3. amenities.** Social courtesies; manners. [< Lat. *amoenitas.*]

Am·er·a·sian (ăm'ə-rā'zhən, -shən) *n.* A person of mixed American and Asian descent. —**Am'er·a'sian** *adj.*

a·merce (ə-mûrs') *v.* **-merced, -merc·ing. 1.** To punish by a fine imposed arbitrarily by the court. **2.** To punish. [< AN *amercier.*]

A·mer·i·can (ə-měr'ĭ-kən) *n.* A native or inhabitant of the United States or the Americas. —**A·mer'i·can** *adj.*

A·mer·i·ca·na (ə-měr'ĭ-kă'nə, -kăn'ə, -kä'nə) *pl.n.* A collection of things relating to American history, folklore, etc.

American English *n.* The English language as used in the United States.

American Indian *n.* A member of any of the aboriginal peoples of North America (except the Eskimos), South America, and the West Indies.

A·mer·i·can·ism (ə-měr'ĭ-kə-nĭz'əm) *n.* **1.** A custom, trait, or tradition originating in the United States. **2.** A language usage characteristic of American English.

A·mer·i·can·ize (ə-měr'ĭ-kə-nīz') *v.* **-ized, -iz·ing.** To make or become American in culture, customs, or methods. —**A·mer'i·can·i·za'tion** *n.*

American plan *n.* A system of hotel management in which a guest pays a fixed daily rate for room, meals, and service.

American Spanish *n.* The Spanish language as used in the Western Hemisphere.

a·mer·i·ci·um (ăm'ə-rĭsh'ē-əm) *n. Symbol* **Am** A white metallic radioactive element used as a radiation source in research. Atomic number 95; longest-lived isotope Am 243.

Am·er·ind (ăm'ə-rĭnd') *n.* An American Indian or an Eskimo. [AMER(ICAN) + IND(IAN).] —**Am'er·in'di·an** *adj. & n.*

am·e·thyst (ăm'ə-thĭst) *n.* **1.** A purple or violet form of transparent quartz used as a gemstone. **2.** A purple or violet color. [< Gk. *amethustos.*]

Am·har·ic (ăm-hăr'ĭk, äm-hä'rĭk) *n.* A southern Semitic language that is the official language of Ethiopia.

a·mi·a·ble (ā'mē-ə-bəl) *adj.* **1.** Good-natured; friendly: *an amiable couple.* **2.** Pleasant; agreeable. [< Lat. *amicus,* friend.] —**a'mi·a·bil'i·ty** or **a'mi·a·ble·ness** *n.* —**a'mi·a·bly** *adv.*

Syns: *amiable, affable, agreeable, complaisant, cordial, easygoing, genial, good-natured adj.*

am·i·ca·ble (ăm'ĭ-kə-bəl) *adj.* Friendly; peaceable. [< Lat. *amicus,* friend.] —**am'i·ca·bil'i·ty** or **am'i·ca·ble·ness** *n.* —**am'i·ca·bly** *adv.*

am·ice (ăm'ĭs) *n.* A liturgical vestment that consists of an oblong piece of white linen worn around the neck and shoulders and partly under the alb. [< Lat. *amictus,* mantle.]

a·mid (ə-mĭd') *prep.* Also **a·midst** (ə-mĭdst'). In the middle of; among.

a·mid·ships (ə-mĭd'shĭps') *adv.* Also **a·mid·ship** (-shĭp'). Midway between the bow and the stern of a ship.

a·mi·go (ə-mē'gō) *n., pl.* **-gos.** A friend. [Sp.]

a·mi·no acid (ə-mē'nō, ăm'ə-nō') *n.* Any of a class of nitrogenous organic compounds that are essential components of proteins.

A·mish (ä'mĭsh, ăm'ĭsh) *pl.n.* Mennonites of a sect that settled primarily in southeastern Pennsylvania in the late 17th cent. [< Jacob *Amman,* 17th-cent. Mennonite bishop.] —**A'mish** *adj.*

a·miss (ə-mĭs') *adj.* Out of proper order; wrong. —*adv.* In an improper way. [< ON *a mis.*]

am·i·ty (ăm'ĭ-tē) *n., pl.* **-ties.** Friendly relations, as between nations. [< OFr. *amitie* < Lat. *amicus,* friend.]

am·me·ter (ăm'mē'tər) *n.* An instrument that measures electric current in amperes.

am·mo (ăm'ō) *n.* Ammunition.

am·mo·nia (ə-mōn'yə, ə-mō'nē-ə) *n.* **1.** A colorless, pungent gas, NH_3, used to manufacture fertilizers and a wide variety of nitrogen-containing organic and inorganic chemicals. 2. Ammonium hydroxide. [< Lat. (sal) ammoniacus, (salt) of Amen.]

am·mo·ni·um (ə-mō′nē-əm) n. The chemical ion, NH₄⁺. [AMMON(IA) + -IUM.]

ammonium chloride n. A white crystalline compound, NH₄Cl, used in dry cells and as an expectorant.

ammonium hydroxide n. An alkali solution, NH₄OH, formed by dissolving ammonia gas in water, and used as a household cleanser and in a wide variety of products.

am·mu·ni·tion (ăm′yə-nĭsh′ən) n. 1. a. Projectiles that can be fired from guns or otherwise propelled. b. Explosive materials used in war. 2. A means of offense or defense. [< Fr. la munition, the munition.]

am·ne·sia (ăm-nē′zhə) n. Loss of memory. [< Gk. amnēsia.] —**am·ne′si·ac′** (-zē-ăk′, -zhē-ăk′) or **am·ne′sic** (-zĭk, -sĭk) n. & adj. —**am·ne′sic** adj.

am·nes·ty (ăm′nĭ-stē) n., pl. -ties. A general pardon, esp. for political offenses. [< Gk. amnēstos, forgotten.] —**am′nes·ty** v.

am·ni·o·cen·te·sis (ăm′nē-ō-sĕn-tē′sĭs) n., pl. -ses (-sēz′). The surgical withdrawal of a sample of fluid from the uterus of a pregnant female, esp. for use in the determination of sex or genetic disorder in the fetus. [amnio(n) + Gk. kentēsis, a pricking.]

a·moe·ba (ə-mē′bə) n., pl. -bas or -bae (-bē). Also **a·me·ba.** Any of various protozoans of the class Sarcodina, found in water and soil and as internal parasites, characteristically having an indefinite, changeable form. [< Gk. amoibē, change.] —**a·moe′bic** or **a·me′bic** adj.

a·mok (ə-mŭk′, ə-mŏk′) adv. Var. of amuck.

a·mong (ə-mŭng′) prep. Also **a·mongst** (ə-mŭngst′). 1. In or through the midst of. 2. In the number or company of. 3. With portions to each of. 4. Between one another. [< OE on gemang.]

a·mon·til·la·do (ə-mŏn′tə-lä′dō) n., pl. -dos. A pale dry sherry. [Sp. (vino) amontillado, (wine) made in Montilla.]

a·mor·al (ā-môr′əl, ā-mŏr′əl) adj. 1. Neither moral nor immoral. 2. Not caring about right and wrong. —**a′mo·ral′i·ty** (ā′mô-răl′ĭ-tē) n. —**a·mor′al·ly** adv.

am·o·rous (ăm′ər-əs) adj. 1. Inclined to love. 2. Produced by or showing love. 3. Of love. [< Lat. amor, love.] —**am′o·rous·ly** adv. —**am′o·rous·ness** n.

a·mor·phous (ə-môr′fəs) adj. 1. Without definite form. 2. General or vague. 3. Chem. Lacking distinct crystalline structure. [Gk. amorphos.] —**a·mor′phous·ly** adv. —**a·mor′phous·ness** n.

am·or·tize (ăm′ər-tīz′, ə-môr′tīz′) v. -tized, -tiz·ing. To liquidate (a debt) by installment payments. [< OFr. amortir.] —**am′or·ti·za′tion** n.

a·mount (ə-mount′) n. 1. The total quantity or number. 2. A principal plus its interest. —v. 1. To reach as a total. 2. To be equivalent or tantamount. [< OFr. amont, upward.]

a·mour (ə-mŏŏr′) n. A love affair, esp. an illicit one. [< Lat. amor, love.]

a·mour·pro·pre (ə-mŏŏr′prôp′rə) n. Self-respect. [Fr.]

am·per·age (ăm′pər-ĭj, ăm′pîr′ĭj) n. The strength of an electric current expressed in amperes.

am·pere (ăm′pîr′) n. The standard unit for measuring the strength of an electric current, equal to a flow of one Coulomb per second. [< André Marie Ampère (1775–1836).]

am·per·sand (ăm′pər-sănd′) n. The character (&) representing and. [Contraction of and per se and, & (the sign) by itself (equals) and.]

am·phet·a·mine (ăm-fĕt′ə-mēn′, -mĭn) n. A colorless volatile liquid, C₉H₁₃N, used primarily as a central nervous system stimulant. [a(lpha) m(ethyl) ph(enyl) et(hyl) amine.]

am·phib·i·an (ăm-fĭb′ē-ən) n. 1. An organism, such as a frog or toad, having an aquatic early stage and developing air-breathing lungs as an adult. 2. An aircraft that can take off and land either on land or on water. 3. A vehicle that can move over land and on water. —adj. Amphibious. [< Gk. amphibion.]

am·phib·i·ous (ăm-fĭb′ē-əs) adj. 1. Capable of living both on land and in water. 2. Capable of operating on both land and water: amphibious vehicles. [Gk. amphibios.]

am·phi·bole (ăm′fə-bōl′) n. Any of a large group of rock-forming minerals that contain various combinations of sodium, calcium, magnesium, iron, and aluminum. [< Gk. amphibolos, doubtful.] —**am′phi·bor′ic** (-bōl′ĭk) adj.

am·phi·the·a·ter (ăm′fə-thē′ə-tər) n. An oval or round structure having tiers of seats that rise outward from a central open arena. [< Gk. amphitheatron.]

am·pho·ra (ăm′fər-ə) n., pl. -rae (-fə-rē′) or -ras. An ancient Greek jar with two handles and a narrow neck. [< Gk. amphoreus.]

am·ple (ăm′pəl) adj. -pler, -plest. 1. Large; capacious. 2. More than enough; abundant. 3. Sufficient; adequate. [< Lat. amplus.] —**am′ple·ness** n. —**am′ply** (-plē) adv.

am·pli·fy (ăm′plə-fī′) v. -fied, -fy·ing. 1. To make larger or more powerful. 2. To add to; expand. 3. To make louder. 2. Lat. amplificare.] —**am′pli·fi·ca′tion** (-fi-kā′shən) n. —**am′pli·fi′er** n.

am·pli·tude (ăm′plĭ-tōōd′, -tyōōd′) n. 1. Fullness; copiousness. 2. Breadth or range, as of mind. 3. Physics. The maximum value of a periodically varying quantity. [Lat. amplitudo.]

amplitude modulation n. The encoding of a carrier wave by variation of its amplitude in accordance with an input signal.

am·poule or **am·pule** (ăm′pōōl′, -pyōōl′) n. A small sealed vial used as a container for a hypodermic injection. [< Lat. ampulla, a round bottle.]

am·pu·tate (ăm′pyōō-tāt′) v. -tat·ed, -tat·ing. To cut off (a part of the body), esp. by surgery. [Lat. amputare, to cut around.] —**am′pu·ta′tion** n.

am·pu·tee (ăm′pyōō-tē′) n. A person who has had one or more limbs amputated.

a·muck (ə-mŭk′) adv. Also **a·mok** (ə-mŭk′, ə-mŏk′). 1. In a murderous frenzy or in a fit of wildness: run amuck. 2. In a jumbled or faulty manner: Plans went amuck. [Malay amok, furious attack.]

---

am·u·let (ăm′yə-lĭt) n. An object worn as a charm against evil or injury. [Lat. *amuletum*.]

a·muse (ə-myōoz′) v. **a·mused, a·mus·ing. 1.** To entertain; divert. **2.** To cause to laugh. [OFr. *amuser*, to stupefy.] **—a·mus′a·ble** adj. **—a·mus′ed·ly** (-zĭd-lē) adv. **—a·muse′ment** n. **—a·mus′er** n.

am·y·lase (ăm′ə-lās′, -lāz′) n. Any of various enzymes that convert starch to sugar. [*amyl*-, starch + -ASE.]

an (ən; ăn when stressed) indef. art. A form of a used before words beginning with a vowel or with an unpronounced h: an elephant; an hour. [OE ān, one.]

an- pref. Not; without: anaerobe. [Gk.]

-an suff. **1.** Pertaining to, belonging to, or resembling: Mexican. **2.** Believing in or adhering to: Mohammedan. [Lat. -anus, adj. suffix.]

ana- pref. **1.** Upward; up: anabolism. **2.** Again; anew: anaphylaxis. [Gk.]

-ana suff. A collection of items relating to a specified place or person: Americana. [Lat.]

a·nach·ro·nism (ə-năk′rə-nĭz′əm) n. **1.** The representation of something as existing or happening at other than its proper or historical time. **2.** Something out of its proper time. [< Gk. *anakhronismos*.] **—a·nach′ro·nis′tic** or **a·nach′ro·nous** (-nəs) adj. **—a·nach′ro·nis′ti·cal·ly** or **a·nach′ro·nous·ly** adv.

an·a·con·da (ăn′ə-kŏn′də) n. A large, nonvenomous tropical American snake that constricts its prey in its coils. [Prob. < Singhalese *henakandayā*.]

an·aer·o·bic (ăn′ə-rō′bĭk, ăn′â-) adj. Capable of living or growing in an environment lacking free oxygen.

an·aes·the·sia (ăn′ĭs-thē′zhə) n. Var. of **anesthesia.**

an·a·gram (ăn′ə-grăm′) n. A word or phrase formed by reordering the letters of another word or phrase. [Fr. *anagramme*.]

a·nal (ā′nəl) adj. Of or near the anus.

an·al·ge·si·a (ăn′əl-jē′zē-ə, -zhə) n. Inability to feel pain while conscious, a condition usu. produced by a drug. [< Gk. *analgēsia*.] **—an′al·ge′sic** n. & adj.

an·a·log computer (ăn′ə-lôg′, -lŏg′) n. A computer in which numerical data are represented by analogous physical magnitudes or electrical signals.

a·nal·o·gous (ə-năl′ə-gəs) adj. **1.** Alike in certain ways. **2.** Biol. Similar in function but not in origin or structure. [< Gk. *analogos*, proportionate.]

an·a·logue (ăn′ə-lôg′, -lŏg′) n. **1.** Something that is analogous. **2.** Biol. An analogous organ.

a·nal·o·gy (ə-năl′ə-jē) n., pl. -gies. **1.** Correspondence in some respects between things otherwise dissimilar. **2.** An inference that if two things are alike in some respects they must be alike in others. **3.** Biol. Correspondence in function but not in evolutionary origin. [< Gk. *analogia*.] **—an′a·log′i·cal** adj. **—an′a·log′i·cal·ly** adv.

a·nal·y·sis (ə-năl′ĭ-sĭs) n., pl. -ses (-sēz′). **1.** The separation of a whole into constituents with a view to its examination and interpretation. **2.** A statement of the results of such a study. **3.** Psychoanalysis. [Gk. *analusis*, a releasing.] **—an′a·lyst** n. **—an′a·lyt′ic** (-ə-lĭt′-ĭk) or **an′a·lyt′i·cal** adj.

an·a·lyze (ăn′ə-līz′) v. -lyzed, -lyz·ing. **1.** To make an analysis of. **2.** To psychoanalyze. [Prob. < Fr. *analyser*.] **—an′a·lyz′a·ble** adj. **—an′a·lyz′er** n.

an·a·pest (ăn′ə-pĕst′) n. A metrical foot composed of two short syllables followed by one long one. [< Gk. *anapaistos*.] **—an′a·pes′tic** adj.

an·ar·chic (ăn-är′kĭk) or **an·ar·chi·cal** (-kĭ-kəl) adj. Lacking order or control; lawless. **—an·ar′chi·cal·ly** adv.

an·ar·chism (ăn′ər-kĭz′əm) n. **1.** The theory that all forms of government are oppressive and should be abolished. **2.** Terrorism. **—an′ar·chist** n. **—an′ar·chis′tic** adj.

an·ar·chy (ăn′ər-kē) n., pl. -chies. **1.** Absence of any form of governmental authority or law. **2.** Disorder and confusion. [Gk. *anarkhia*.]

a·nath·e·ma (ə-năth′ə-mə) n., pl. -mas. **1.** A formal ecclesiastical ban, curse, or excommunication. **2.** One that is intensely disliked. [< Gk. *anathēma*, a cursed thing.] **—a·nath′e·ma·tize′** v.

An·a·to·li·an (ăn′ə-tō′lē-ən) n. An extinct group of Indo-European languages of ancient Anatolia, including Hittite. **—An′a·to′li·an** adj.

a·nat·o·mize (ə-năt′ə-mīz′) v. -mized, -miz·ing. **1.** To dissect (an animal or plant) in order to study its structure. **2.** To analyze.

a·nat·o·my (ə-năt′ə-mē) n., pl. -mies. **1.** The structure of an organism or organ. **2.** The science of the structure of organisms and their parts. **3.** A detailed analysis. [< Gk. *anatomē*, dissection.] **—an′a·tom′i·cal** (ăn′-ə-tŏm′ĭ-kəl) adj. **—an′a·tom′i·cal·ly** adv. **—a·nat′o·mist** n.

-ance or **-ancy** suff. An action, quality, or condition: riddance, compliancy. [< Lat. -antia, n. suffix.]

an·ces·tor (ăn′sĕs′tər) n. **1.** A person from whom one is descended; forefather. **2.** Biol. The organism or stock from which later kinds have evolved. **3.** A forerunner or predecessor. [< Lat. *antecessor*.] **—an·ces′tral** adj. **—an·ces′tral·ly** adv. **—an′ces·tress** n.

Syns: ancestor, antecedent, forebear, forefather, progenitor n.

an·ces·try (ăn′sĕs′trē) n., pl. -tries. **1.** Descent or lineage. **2.** Ancestors collectively.

an·chor (ăng′kər) n. **1.** A heavy metal device attached to a vessel and cast overboard to keep the vessel in place. **2.** Something that gives stability. **3.** Radio & TV. An anchorman or anchorwoman. —v. **1.** To hold or be held fast by or as if by an anchor. **2.** Radio & TV. To narrate or coordinate (a newscast in which several correspondents give reports). —idiom. **at anchor.** Anchored; held fast. [< Gk. *ankura*.]

an·chor·age (ăng′kər-ĭj) n. A place for anchoring ships.

an·cho·rite (ăng′kə-rīt′) n. A religious hermit. [< LGk. *anakhōrētēs*.] **—an′cho·rit′ic** (-rĭt′ĭk) adj.

an·chor·man (ăng′kər-măn′) n. **1.** Sports. The last runner in a relay race. **2.** Radio & TV. A person who anchors a newscast.

an·chor·wom·an (ăng′kər-wōōm′ən) n. Radio & TV. A woman who anchors a newscast.

an·cho·vy (ăn′chō′vē, ăn-chō′vē) n., pl. -vy or -vies. Any of various small, edible, herringlike saltwater fishes. [Sp. *anchova*.]

an·cien ré·gime (äN-syăN′ rā-zhēm′) n. **1.** The political and social system in France before the Revolution of 1789. **2.** A former sociopolitical system. [Fr.]

an·cient (ān'shənt) *adj.* **1.** Very old; aged. **2.** Of or occurring in times long past, esp. prior to the fall of Rome (A.D. 476). —*n.* **1.** A very old person. **2.** ancients. The ancient Greeks and Romans. [< Lat. *ante,* before.] —**an'cient·ly** *adv.* —**an'cient·ness** *n.*

an·cil·lar·y (ān'sə-lĕr'ē) *adj.* **1.** Subordinate. **2.** Auxiliary; supplementary. [Lat. *ancillaris.*]

-ancy *suff.* Var. of **-ance.**

and (ənd, ən; ănd *when stressed*) *conj.* **1.** Together with or along with; as well as. **2.** Added to; plus. **3.** As a result: *Seek, and ye shall find.* **4.** To. Used between finite verbs: *Try and find it.* [< OE.]

Usage: The use of *and* to begin a sentence has a long and respectable history in English: *"And it came to pass in those days"* (Luke 2:1).

an·dan·te (ān-dän'tā, än-dän'tē) *adv. Mus.* Moderately slow in tempo. [Ital.] —**an·dan'te** *adj.*

an·dan·ti·no (ān'dän-tē'nō, än'dän-tē'nō) *adv. Mus.* Slightly faster than andante in tempo. [Ital.] —**an·dan·ti'no** *adj.*

and·i·ron (ănd'ī'ərn) *n.* One of a pair of metal supports for logs in a fireplace. [< OFr. *andier,* firedog.]

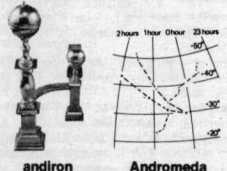

andiron   Andromeda

and/or *conj.* Used to indicate that either *and* or *or* may be used to connect words, phrases, or clauses.

andro- *pref.* Male; masculine: *androgen.* [Gk.]

an·dro·gen (ăn'drə-jən) *n.* A hormone that develops and maintains masculine characteristics. —**an'dro·gen'ic** (-jĕn'ĭk) *adj.*

an·drog·y·nous (ăn-drŏj'ə-nəs) *adj.* Having female and male characteristics in one. —**an·drog'y·ny** *n.*

an·droid (ăn'droid') *n.* An artificially created person.

An·drom·e·da (ăn-drŏm'ĭ-də) *n.* **1.** *Gk. Myth.* The wife of Perseus. **2.** A constellation in the Northern Hemisphere.

-andry *suff.* Number of husbands: *monandry.* [< Gk. *anēr,* man.]

-ane *suff. Chem.* A saturated hydrocarbon: *propane.* [< -ENE.]

an·ec·dote (ăn'ĭk-dōt') *n.* A short account of an interesting or humorous incident. [< Gk. *anekdotos,* unpublished.] —**an'ec·do'tal** *adj.*

an·e·cho·ic (ăn'ĭ-kō'ĭk) *adj.* Neither having nor producing echoes.

a·ne·mi·a (ə-nē'mē-ə) *n.* Pathological deficiency in the oxygen-carrying material of the blood. [< Gk. *anaimia.*] —**a·ne'mic** *adj.*

an·e·mom·e·ter (ăn'ə-mŏm'ĭ-tər) *n.* An instrument for measuring wind force and speed. [Gk. *anemos,* wind + -METER.] —**an·e·mo·met'ric** (-mō-mĕt'rĭk) *adj.*

a·nem·o·ne (ə-nĕm'ə-nē) *n.* **1.** Any of various plants with white, purple, or red cup-shaped flowers. **2.** The sea anemone. [< Gk. *anemōnē.*]

a·nent (ə-nĕnt') *prep.* Regarding; concerning. [< OE *onefn,* near.]

an·er·oid barometer (ăn'ə-roid') *n.* A barometer that measures atmospheric pressure by means of the changes in shape of an elastic metal disk that covers a partially evacuated chamber. [A-¹ + Gk. *nēron,* water.]

an·es·the·sia (ăn'ĭs-thē'zhə) *n.* Also **an·aes·the·sia.** Total or partial loss of physical sensation. [< Gk. *anaisthēsia,* lack of sensation.]

an·es·the·si·ol·o·gy (ăn'ĭs-thē'zē-ŏl'ə-jē) *n.* Also **an·aes·the·si·ol·o·gy.** The medical study and application of anesthetics. —**an'es·the·si·ol'o·gist** *n.*

an·es·thet·ic (ăn'ĭs-thĕt'ĭk) *adj.* Also **an·aes·thet·ic.** Causing anesthesia. —*n.* An agent that causes anesthesia.

an·es·the·tize (ə-nĕs'thĭ-tīz') *v.* **-tized, -tiz·ing.** Also **an·aes·the·tize.** To induce anesthesia in, esp. by means of a drug. —**an·es'the·tist** *n.* —**an·es'the·ti·za'tion** *n.*

an·eu·rysm (ăn'yə-rĭz'əm) *n.* Also **an·eu·rism.** A pathological blood-filled sac formed by the dilation of a blood vessel. [Gk. *aneurusma.*]

a·new (ə-nōō', ə-nyōō') *adv.* **1.** Once more; again. **2.** In a new and different way, form, or manner. [*a-,* of + NEW.]

an·gel (ān'jəl) *n.* **1.** One of the immortal beings attendant upon God. **2.** A kind and lovable person. **3.** A financial backer of an enterprise, esp. a dramatic production. [< Gk. *angelos,* messenger.] —**an·gel'ic** (-jĕl'ĭk) or **an·gel'i·cal** *adj.* —**an·gel'i·cal·ly** *adv.*

an·gel·fish (ān'jəl-fĭsh') *n.* Any of several brightly colored tropical fishes with a flattened body.

an·gel·i·ca (ăn-jĕl'ĭ-kə) *n.* A plant with aromatic seeds that are used as a flavoring.

an·ger (ăng'gər) *n.* A feeling of extreme hostility, indignation, or exasperation; rage; wrath. —*v.* To make or become angry. [< ON *angr,* grief.]

an·gi·na (ăn-jī'nə) *n.* **1.** A disease of the throat or chest in which painful, choking spasms occur. **2.** Angina pectoris. [< Gk. *ankhonē,* a strangling.]

angina pec·to·ris (pĕk'tə-rĭs) *n.* Severe paroxysmal pain in the chest, caused by an insufficient supply of blood to the heart. [ANGINA + Lat. *pectus,* chest.]

an·gi·o·sperm (ăn'jē-ə-spûrm') *n.* A plant characterized by having seeds enclosed in an ovary. [Gk. *angeion,* vessel + SPERM.]

an·gle¹ (ăng'gəl) *v.* **-gled, -gling.** **1.** To fish with a hook and line. **2.** To try to get something by using schemes. —n. A devious method; scheme. [< OE *angul,* fishhook.] —**an'gler** n.

an·gle² (ăng'gəl) n. **1.** *Geom.* **a.** The figure formed by two lines diverging from a common point. **b.** The rotation required to superimpose either of two such lines or angles on the other. **2. a.** The position or direction from which an object is viewed. **b.** A point of view. —*v.* **-gled, -gling. 1.** To move or turn at an angle. **2.** To hit (e.g. a ball or puck) at an angle. [< Lat. *angulus.*]

An·gles (ăng'gəlz) pl.n. A Germanic people who migrated to England in the 5th cent. A.D. and with the Jutes and Saxons formed the Anglo-Saxon peoples.

angle·worm (ăng'gəl-wûrm') n. An earthworm, used as bait in fishing.

An·gli·can (ăng'glĭ-kən) adj. **1.** Of or characteristic of the Anglican Church. **2.** Of or pertaining to England or the English. —**An'gli·can** n. —**An'gli·can·ism** n.

Anglican Church n. The Church of England or any of its related churches, esp. the Protestant Episcopal Church.

An·gli·cism (ăng'glĭ-sĭz'əm) n. A word, phrase, or idiom peculiar to the English language, esp. as spoken in England; Briticism.

An·gli·cize (ăng'glĭ-sīz') v. **-cized, -ciz·ing.** To make or become English in form, idiom, style, or character. —**An'gli·ci·za'tion** n.

Anglo- pref. English; England: *Anglophile.* [< Lat. *Angli,* Angles.]

An·glo-Nor·man (ăng'glō-nôr'mən) n. **1.** A Norman settler in England after 1066. **2.** A dialect of Norman French as used in England. —**An'glo-Nor'man** adj.

An·glo·phile (ăng'glə-fīl') n. An admirer of England and English things. —**An'glo·phil'i·a** (-fĭl'ē-ə) n.

An·glo·phobe (ăng'glə-fōb') n. One who has an aversion to or fear of England or English things. —**An'glo·pho'bi·a** (-fō'bē-ə) n.

An·glo·phone (ăng'glə-fōn') adj. English-speaking. —n. An English-speaking person, esp. in Canada.

An·glo-Sax·on (ăng'glō-săk'sən) n. **1.** A member of one of the Germanic peoples who settled in Britain in the 5th and 6th cent. A.D. **b.** Any of the descendants of these peoples. **2.** Old English. **3.** Any person of English ancestry. —**An'glo-Sax'on** adj.

An·go·ra (ăng-gôr'ə, -gōr'ə) n. **1.** A goat, rabbit, or cat with long, silky hair. **2. angora.** A yarn or fabric made from the hair of an Angora goat or rabbit. [< *Angora,* the former name for Ankara, Turkey.]

an·gry (ăng'grē) adj. **-gri·er, -gri·est. 1.** Feeling, showing, or resulting from anger. **2.** Having a menacing aspect: *angry clouds.* **3.** Inflamed: *an angry sore.* —**an'gri·ly** (-grə-lē) adv. —**an'gri·ness** n.

Syns: *angry, furious, indignant, irate, mad, sore, wrathful adj.*

angst (ängkst) n. A feeling of anxiety. [G.]

ang·strom or **Ång·ström** (ăng'strəm) n. A unit of length equal to one ten-billionth (10^{-10}) of a meter. [< A.J. *Ångström* (1814–74).]

an·guish (ăng'gwĭsh) n. An agonizing physical or mental pain. —v. To feel or cause to feel anguish. [< Lat. *angustia,* narrowness.] —**an'guished** adj.

an·gu·lar (ăng'gyə-lər) adj. **1.** Having an angle or angles. **2.** Measured by an angle. **3.** Bony and lean. **4.** Sharp-cornered. **5.** Awkward: *an angular gait.* —**an·gu·lar'i·ty** (-lăr'ĭ-tē) or **an'gu·lar·ness** n. —**an'gu·lar·ly** adv.

an·hy·dride (ăn-hī'drĭd') n. A chemical compound formed from another by the removal of water. [ANHYDR(OUS) + -IDE.]

an·hy·drous (ăn-hī'drəs) adj. Without water. [Gk. *anudros.*]

an·i·line (ăn'ə-lĭn) n. Also **an·i·lin.** A colorless, oily, poisonous liquid, $C_6H_5NH_2$, used in rubber, dyes, resins, pharmaceuticals, varnishes, and rocket fuels. [G. *Anilin.*]

an·i·mad·vert (ăn'ə-măd-vûrt') v. To comment critically, usu. with disapproval. [Lat. *animadvertere,* to direct the mind to.] —**an'i·mad·ver'sion** n.

an·i·mal (ăn'ə-məl) n. **1.** An organism distinguished from a plant by structural and functional characteristics, such as the ability to move. **2.** A living being other than a human being. **3.** A brutish person. —adj. **1.** Of or relating to animals. **2.** Sensual or physical rather than spiritual. [Lat.]

an·i·mal·cule (ăn'ə-măl'kyōōl') n. A microscopic or minute organism. [NLat. *animalculum.*] —**an'i·mal'cu·lar** (-kyə-lər) adj.

animal husbandry n. The care and breeding of domestic animals.

an·i·mate (ăn'ə-māt') v. **-mat·ed, -mat·ing. 1.** To give life to. **2.** To impart interest to. **3.** To inspire; encourage. **4.** To make or produce (a cartoon) so as to create the illusion of motion. —adj. (-ə-mĭt). **1.** Having life; living. **2.** Of or relating to animal life. [Lat. *animare.*] —**an'i·ma'tion** n.

an·i·mat·ed (ăn'ə-mā'tĭd) adj. **1.** Lively; spirited. **2.** Constructed so as to seem alive and moving: *animated puppets.* —**an'i·mat·ed·ly** adv.

animated cartoon n. A motion picture consisting of a photographed series of drawings.

a·ni·ma·to (ä'nə-mä'tō) adv. *Mus.* In an animated or lively manner. [Ital.] —**a'ni·ma'to** adj.

an·i·ma·tor (ăn'ə-mā'tər) n. Also **an·i·mat·er.** One that animates, esp. an artist or technician who produces animated cartoons.

an·i·mism (ăn'ə-mĭz'əm) n. Belief that natural phenomena and inanimate things have souls. [< Lat. *anima,* soul.] —**an'i·mis'tic** adj.

an·i·mos·i·ty (ăn'ə-mŏs'ĭ-tē) n., pl. **-ties.** Bitter hostility or hatred. [< LLat. *animositas,* courage.]

an·i·mus (ăn'ə-məs) n. Animosity. [Lat., soul.]

an·i·on (ăn'ī'ən) n. A negatively charged ion that migrates to an anode, as in electrolysis. [< Gk. *anienai,* to go up.] —**an'i·on'ic** (-ŏn'ĭk) adj. —**an'i·on'i·cal·ly** adv.

an·ise (ăn'ĭs) n. **1.** A plant having yellowish-white flowers and licorice-flavored seeds. **2.** Aniseed. [< Gk. *anison.*]

an·i·seed (ăn'ĭ-sēd') n. The seed of the anise plant, used for flavoring. [ME *anis seed.*]

an·i·sette (ăn'ə-sĕt', -zĕt') n. An anise-flavored liqueur.

ankh (ăngk) *n.* A cross shaped like a T with a loop at the top. [Of Egypt. orig.]

an·kle (ăng′kəl) *n.* **1.** The joint between the foot and the leg. **2.** The slender section of the leg above the foot. [ME *ancle.*]

an·kle-bone (ăng′kəl-bōn′) *n. Anat.* The talus.

an·klet (ăng′klĭt) *n.* **1.** An ornament worn around the ankle. **2.** A short sock covering the ankle.

an·nals (ăn′əlz) *pl.n.* **1.** A chronological record of the events of successive years. **2.** A descriptive record. **3.** A periodical compiling the records and reports of a learned field. [< Lat. *annalis.*] —**an′nal·ist** *n.* —**an′nal·is′tic** *adj.*

an·neal (ə-nēl′) *v.* **1.** To heat (glass or metal) and slowly cool to toughen it and reduce brittleness. **2.** To temper. [< OE *onǣlan.*]

an·ne·lid (ăn′ə-lĭd) *n.* Any of various worms with cylindrical segmented bodies. [< Lat. *annellus,* small ring.] —**an′ne·lid** *adj.*

an·nex (ə-nĕks′) *v.* **1.** To add or join to, esp. to a larger thing. **2.** To incorporate (territory) into an existing country or state. —*n.* (ăn′ĕks′). A building added on to a larger one or situated near a main one. [< Lat. *annectere.*] —**an′nex·a′tion** *n.*

an·ni·hi·late (ə-nī′ə-lāt′) *v.* -**lat·ed, -lat·ing.** To destroy completely. [LLat. *annihilare.*] —**an·ni′hi·la·bil′i·ty** (-lə-bĭl′ĭ-tē) *n.* —**an·ni′hi·la·ble** (-lə-bəl) *adj.* —**an·ni′hi·la′tion** *n.* —**an·ni′hi·la′tor** *n.*

an·ni·ver·sa·ry (ăn′ə-vûr′sə-rē) *n., pl.* -**ries.** The annual recurrence of the date of an event that took place in a preceding year. [< Med. Lat. *anniversaria.*]

an·no Dom·i·ni (ăn′ō dŏm′ə-nī′, dŏm′ə-nē) *adv.* In a specified year of the Christian era. [Lat., in the year of the Lord.]

an·no·tate (ăn′ō-tāt′) *v.* -**tat·ed, -tat·ing.** To furnish (a literary work) with critical or explanatory notes. [Lat. *annotare,* to note down.] —**an′no·ta′tion** *n.* —**an′no·ta′tive** *adj.* —**an′no·ta′tor** *n.*

an·nounce (ə-nouns′) *v.* -**nounced, -nounc·ing.** **1.** To bring to public notice. **2.** To proclaim the arrival of: *announce a visitor.* **3.** To serve as an announcer. [< Lat. *annuntiare.*] —**an·nounce′ment** *n.*

an·nounc·er (ə-noun′sər) *n.* A radio or television performer who provides program continuity and gives commercial and other announcements.

an·noy (ə-noi′) *v.* To bother or irritate. [< LLat. *inodiare,* to make odious.] —**an·noy′er** *n.* —**an·noy′ing·ly** *adv.*

Syns: *annoy, aggravate, bother, bug, disturb, chafe, exasperate, fret, gall, get, irk, irritate, nettle, peeve, provoke, ruffle, vex* v.

an·noy·ance (ə-noi′əns) *n.* **1.** The act of annoying. **2.** A nuisance. **3.** Vexation; irritation.

an·nu·al (ăn′yōō-əl) *adj.* **1.** Occurring or done every year; yearly. **2.** Of or pertaining to a year: *an annual income.* **3.** *Bot.* Living and growing for only one year or season. —*n.* **1.** A periodical published yearly; yearbook. **2.** *Bot.* An annual plant. [< LLat. *annualis.*] —**an′nu·al·ly** *adv.*

annual ring *n.* A layer of wood, esp. in a tree trunk, that indicates a year's growth.

annual ring
Left: Cross section showing annual rings
Right: Cross section of a tree showing annual rings

an·nu·i·tant (ə-nōō′ĭ-tənt, ə-nyōō′-) *n.* A person who receives an annuity.

an·nu·i·ty (ə-nōō′ĭ-tē, ə-nyōō′-) *n., pl.* -**ties.** **1.** An amount of money paid annually. **2.** An investment on which a person receives fixed payments for a lifetime or a certain number of years. [< Med. Lat. *annuitas.*]

an·nul (ə-nŭl′) *v.* -**nulled, -nul·ling.** To nullify or cancel, as a marriage or a law. [< LLat. *annullare.*] —**an·nul′ment** *n.*

an·nu·lar (ăn′yə-lər) *adj.* Shaped like a ring. [< Lat. *annularis.*] —**an′nu·lar·ly** *adv.*

an·nu·lus (ăn′yə-ləs) *n., pl.* -**lus·es** or -**li** (-lī′). A ringlike part, structure, or marking. [Lat. *anulus,* ring.]

an·nun·ci·ate (ə-nŭn′sē-āt′) *v.* -**at·ed, -at·ing.** To announce. [Lat. *annuntiare.*]

an·nun·ci·a·tion (ə-nŭn′sē-ā′shən) *n.* **1.** The act of announcing. **2.** An announcement. **3. Annunciation. a.** The angel Gabriel's announcement to Mary that she was to bear Jesus. **b.** The festival, on Mar. 25, celebrating this event.

an·ode (ăn′ōd′) *n.* A positively charged electrode. [Gk. *anodos,* a way up.]

an·o·dyne (ăn′ə-dīn′) *n.* **1.** A medicine that relieves pain. **2.** A soothing or comforting agent. [< Gk. *anōdunos,* free from pain.]

a·noint (ə-noint′) *v.* To apply oil, esp. in a religious ceremony. [< Lat. *inunguere.*] —**a·noint′er** *n.* —**a·noint′ment** *n.*

a·nom·a·ly (ə-nŏm′ə-lē) *n., pl.* -**lies.** **1.** Deviation from the normal order, form, or rule; abnormality. **2.** Something unusual, irregular, or abnormal. [< Gk. *anomalos,* uneven.] —**a·nom′a·lis′tic** (-lĭs′tĭk) *adj.* —**a·nom′a·lous** *adj.* —**a·nom′a·lous·ly** *adv.* —**a·nom′a·lous·ness** *n.*

a·non (ə-nŏn′) *adv. Archaic.* Soon. [< OE *onǣn.*]

a·non·y·mous (ə-nŏn′ə-məs) *adj.* Having an unknown or withheld name, authorship, or agency. [< Gk. *anōnumos,* nameless.] —**an′o·nym′i·ty** (ăn′ə-nĭm′ĭ-tē) *n.* —**a·non′y·mous·ly** *adv.* —**a·non′y·mous·ness** *n.*

a·noph·e·les (ə-nŏf′ə-lēz′) *n.* A mosquito that transmits malaria to humans. [< Gk. *anōphelēs,* useless.]

an·o·rex·i·a (ăn′ə-rĕk′sē-ə) *n.* Loss of appetite, esp. as a result of disease. [Gk.]

anorexia nerv·o·sa (nûr-vō'sə) *n.* The pathological loss of appetite occurring chiefly in young women that is thought to be psychological in origin. [NLat., nervous anorexia.]

an·oth·er (ə-nŭth'ər) *adj.* **1.** Different: *another method.* **2.** Changed: *You've been another person since you got that job.* **3. a.** Some other and later: *We'll discuss this at another time.* **b.** Some other and former: *belongs to another era.* **4.** Additional; one more: *another cup of tea.* **5.** New: *He thinks he's another Babe Ruth.* —*pron.* **1.** An additional or different one. **2.** One of a group of things. [ME *an other.*]

an·swer (ăn'sər) *n.* **1.** A spoken or written reply, as to a question. **2.** A solution or result, as to a problem. —*v.* **1.** To reply to. **2.** To respond correctly to. **3.** To serve (a purpose). **4.** To be responsible for. —*phrasal verb.* **answer back.** To reply defiantly. [OE *andswaru.*] —**an'swer·a·bil'i·ty** or **an'swer·a·ble·ness** *n.* —**an'swer·a·ble** *adj.* —**an'swer·a·bly** *adv.*

Syns: *answer, rejoin, reply, respond, retort, return* v.

ant (ănt) *n.* Any of various usu. wingless insects that live in complexly organized colonies. [OE *ǣmete.*]

ant- *pref.* Var. of **anti-**.

-ant *suff.* Performing, promoting, or causing an action: *deodorant.* [< Lat. *-ans,* pr.part. ending.]

ant·ac·id (ănt-ăs'ĭd) *adj.* Counteracting an acid; basic. —*n.* An antacid substance, esp. one that neutralizes excess stomach acid.

an·tag·o·nism (ăn-tăg'ə-nĭz'əm) *n.* Opposition; hostility. —**an·tag'o·nist** *n.* —**an·tag'o·nis'tic** *adj.* —**an·tag'o·nis'ti·cal·ly** *adv.*

an·tag·o·nize (ăn-tăg'ə-nīz') *v.* **-nized, -niz·ing.** To incur the hostility of. [Gk. *antagōnizesthai,* to struggle against.]

Ant·arc·tic (ănt-ärk'tĭk, -är'tĭk) *adj.* Of or pertaining to the regions surrounding the South Pole.

Antarctic Circle *n.* The parallel of latitude 66° 33' south, marking the limit of the South Frigid Zone.

An·tar·es (ăn-târ'ēz') *n.* The brightest star in the southern sky, in the constellation Scorpius.

an·te (ăn'tē) *n.* **1.** *Poker.* A stake put up by each player before receiving a hand or receiving new cards. **2.** *Slang.* An amount to be paid. —*v.* **-ted** or **-teed, -te·ing. 1.** *Poker.* To put up (one's stake). **2.** *Slang.* To pay (one's share). [< Lat. *ante,* before.]

ante- *pref.* **1.** Earlier: *antecedent.* **2.** In front of: *anteroom.* [Lat.]

ant·eat·er (ănt'ē'tər) *n.* Any of various long-snouted animals that feed primarily on ants.

an·te·bel·lum (ăn'tē-bĕl'əm) *adj.* Of the period before the U.S. Civil War. [Lat. *ante bellum,* before the war.]

an·te·ce·dent (ăn'tĭ-sēd'nt) *adj.* Going before; preceding. —*n.* **1.** One that precedes. **2.** An event prior to another. **3. antecedents.** One's ancestors. **4.** The word, phrase, or clause that a relative pronoun refers to. [< Lat. *antecedere,* to go before.] —**an'te·ce'dence** *n.* —**an'te·ce'dent·ly** *adv.*

an·te·cham·ber (ăn'tē-chām'bər) *n.* An anteroom.

an·te·date (ăn'tĭ-dāt') *v.* **-dat·ed, -dat·ing. 1.** To precede in time. **2.** To give a date earlier than the actual date.

an·te·di·lu·vi·an (ăn'tĭ-də-lōō'vē-ən) *adj.* **1.** Of the era before the Biblical Flood. **2.** Antiquated. —*n.* **1.** One that lived or existed before the Biblical Flood. **2.** A very old person. [ANTE- + Lat. *diluvium,* flood.]

an·te·lope (ăn'tə-lōp') *n., pl.* **-lope** or **-lopes.** Any of various slender, swift-running, long-horned, hoofed mammals. [< LGk. *antholops.*]

an·te me·rid·i·em (ăn'tē mə-rĭd'ē-əm) *adv. & adj.* Before noon. [Lat.]

Usage: Although *12 A.M.* denotes noon and *12 P.M.* denotes midnight, it is advisable to use *12 noon* and *12 midnight* to avoid confusion.

an·ten·na (ăn-tĕn'ə) *n.* **1.** *pl.* **-ten·nae** (-tĕn'ē). One of the pair of sensory organs on the head of an insect, crustacean, etc. **2.** *pl.* **-nas.** A metallic apparatus for sending and receiving radio waves; aerial. [Med. Lat.] —**an·ten'nal** *adj.*

an·te·pe·nult (ăn'tē-pē'nŭlt', -pĭ-nŭlt') *n.* The 3rd syllable from the end in a word. [LLat. *antepaenultima.*] —**an'te·pe·nul'ti·mate** *adj. & n.*

an·te·ri·or (ăn-tîr'ē-ər) *adj.* **1.** Located in front. **2.** Prior in time. [Lat.] —**an·te'ri·or·ly** *adv.*

an·te·room (ăn'tē-rōōm', -rŏŏm') *n.* A waiting room.

an·them (ăn'thəm) *n.* **1.** A song of praise or loyalty. **2.** A sacred choral composition. [< LGk. *antiphōnos,* singing in response.]

an·ther (ăn'thər) *n.* The pollen-bearing organ at the end of a stamen. [Ult. < Gk. *anthos,* flower.]

ant·hill (ănt'hĭl') *n.* A mound of earth formed by ants or termites in digging a nest.

an·thol·o·gy (ăn-thŏl'ə-jē) *n., pl.* **-gies.** A collection of literary pieces. [< Gk. *anthologia,* flower gathering.] —**an'tho·log'i·cal** (ăn'thə-lŏj'ĭ-kəl) *adj.* —**an·thol'o·gist** *n.* —**an·thol'o·gize'** *v.*

an·thra·cite (ăn'thrə-sīt') *n.* A hard coal with a high carbon content and little volatile matter. [Gk. *anthrakitēs,* a kind of coal.] —**an'thra·cit'ic** (-sĭt'ĭk) *adj.*

an·thrax (ăn'thrăks') *n.* An infectious, usu. fatal disease of animals, esp. cattle and sheep, characterized by malignant ulcers and transmissible to humans. [Gk., pustule.]

anthropo- *pref.* Human: *anthropology.* [< Gk. *anthrōpos,* man.]

an·thro·po·cen·tric (ăn'thrə-pō-sĕn'trĭk) *adj.* Interpreting reality in terms of human values and experience.

an·thro·poid (ăn'thrə-poid') *adj.* Resembling a human being, as certain apes. —*n.* An anthropoid ape, as a gorilla or chimpanzee. —**an'thro·poid'al** *adj.*

an·thro·pol·o·gy (ăn'thrə-pŏl'ə-jē) *n.* The science of the origin, culture, and development of human beings. —**an'thro·po·log'ic** (-pə-lŏj'ĭk) or **an'thro·po·log'i·cal** *adj.* —**an'thro·po·log'i·cal·ly** *adv.* —**an'thro·pol'o·gist** *n.*

an·thro·po·mor·phism (ăn'thrə-pə-môr'fĭz'əm) *n.* The attribution of human characteristics to nonhuman beings or things. —**an'thro·po·mor'phic** *adj.* —**an'thro·po·mor'phi·cal·ly** *adv.*

an·ti (ăn'tī, -tē) *n., pl.* **-tis.** *Informal.* One who is opposed. [< ANTI-.]

an·ti– or **ant–** *pref.* **1. a.** Opposite: *antiparticle.* **b.** Against; opposing: *anticlerical.* **c.** Counteracting: *antibody.* **2.** Reciprocal: *antilogarithm.* [Gk.]

Usage: Many compounds other than those entered here may be formed with *anti–.* In forming compounds *anti–* is normally joined with the following element without space or hyphen: *antibody.* However, if the second element begins with a capital letter, it is separated with a hyphen: *anti-American.* It is also preferable to use the hyphen if the second element begins with *i: anti-intellectual.* The hyphen may also be used to aid clarity, as in nonce coinage: *anti-antivivisection,* or when the compound brings together three or more vowels: *anti-aesthetic.*

an·ti·a·bor·tion (ăn′tē-ə-bôr′shən) *adj.* Opposing abortions. —**an′ti·a·bor′tion·ist** *n.*

an·ti·air·craft (ăn′tē-âr′krăft′) *adj.* Used against aircraft attack.

an·ti·bal·lis·tic missile (ăn′tĭ-bə-lĭs′tĭk) *n.* A defensive missile designed to intercept and destroy a ballistic missile in flight.

an·ti·bi·ot·ic (ăn′tē-bī-ŏt′ĭk) *n.* Any of various substances, such as penicillin and streptomycin, produced by certain fungi, bacteria, and other organisms, that inhibit the growth of or destroy microorganisms and are widely used to prevent and treat diseases. [ANTI- + Gk. *biōtikos,* of life.] —**an′ti·bi·ot′ic** *adj.*

an·ti·bod·y (ăn′tĭ-bŏd′ē) *n.* Any of various proteins in the blood that are generated in reaction to foreign proteins or carbohydrates, neutralize them, and thus produce immunity against certain microorganisms or their toxins.

an·ti·bus·ing (ăn′tē-bŭs′ĭng) *adj.* Opposed to public-school busing as a way of achieving racial balance.

an·tic (ăn′tĭk) *n.* Often **antics.** A ludicrous act or gesture; caper. —*adj.* Odd; ludicrous. [Ital. *antico,* an ancient.]

an·ti·can·cer (ăn′tĭ-kăn′sər) *adj.* Combating cancer.

An·ti·christ (ăn′tĭ-krīst′) *n.* **1.** Christ's personal antagonist. **2. antichrist.** An enemy of Christ.

an·tic·i·pate (ăn-tĭs′ə-pāt′) *v.* **-pat·ed, -pat·ing. 1.** To foresee. **2.** To look forward to. **3.** To act in advance to prevent; forestall. [Lat. *anticipare,* to take before.] —**an·tic′i·pa′tion** *n.* —**an·tic′i·pa′tor** *n.* —**an·tic′i·pa·to′ry** (-pə-tôr′-ē, -tōr′ē) *adj.*

an·ti·cler·i·cal (ăn′tē-klĕr′ĭ-kəl) *adj.* Opposing the church's influence in politics. —**an′ti·cler′i·cal·ism** *n.*

an·ti·cli·max (ăn′tē-klī′măks′) *n.* **1.** A decline in disappointing contrast to a previous rise. **2.** Something commonplace concluding a series of significant events. —**an′ti·cli·mac′tic** *adj.* —**an′ti·cli·mac′ti·cal·ly** *adv.*

an·ti·co·ag·u·lant (ăn′tē-kō-ăg′yə-lənt) *n.* A substance that counteracts coagulation of the blood.

an·ti·cy·clone (ăn′tē-sī′klōn′) *n.* A system of winds that spirals outward around an area of high barometric pressure. —**an′ti·cy·clon′ic** (-sī-klŏn′ĭk) *adj.*

an·ti·de·pres·sant (ăn′tē-dĭ-prĕs′ənt) *n.* A

drug to prevent or treat depression. —**an′ti·de·pres′sive** *adj.*

an·ti·dote (ăn′tĭ-dōt′) *n.* **1.** An agent that counteracts a poison. **2.** Anything that counteracts something injurious. [< Gk. *antidoton.*] —**an′ti·dot′al** (ăn′tĭ-dōt′l) *adj.*

Usage: Antidote may be followed by *to, for,* or *against: an antidote to snakebite; an antidote for poison; an antidote against infection.*

an·ti·freeze (ăn′tĭ-frēz′) *n.* A substance, such as alcohol, mixed with a liquid to lower the freezing point of the latter.

an·ti·gen (ăn′tĭ-jən) *n.* A substance that when introduced into the body stimulates antibody production. —**an′ti·gen′ic** (-jĕn′ĭk) *adj.* —**an′ti·gen′i·cal·ly** *adv.* —**an′ti·ge·nic′i·ty** (-jə-nĭs′ə-tē) *n.*

an·ti·he·ro (ăn′tĭ-hîr′ō) *n.* A fictional or dramatic character lacking traditional heroic qualities.

an·ti·his·ta·mine (ăn′tē-hĭs′tə-mēn′, -mĭn) *n.* A drug used to reduce physiological effects associated with histamine production in allergies and colds. —**an′ti·his′ta·min′ic** (-mĭn′ĭk) *adj.*

an·ti·knock (ăn′tĭ-nŏk′) *n.* A substance added to gasoline to reduce engine knock.

an·ti·log·a·rithm (ăn′tē-lô′gə-rĭth′əm, -lŏg′ə-) *n.* The number for which a given logarithm stands; e.g. where log *x* equals *y,* the *x* is the antilogarithm of *y.*

an·ti·ma·cas·sar (ăn′tē-mə-kăs′ər) *n.* A small cover to protect the backs or arms of furniture. [ANTI- + *Macassar,* a brand of hair oil.]

an·ti·mat·ter (ăn′tĭ-măt′ər) *n.* Matter consisting of antiparticles and having positron-surrounded nuclei composed of antiprotons and antineutrons.

an·ti·mo·ny (ăn′tə-mō′nē) *n.* *Symbol* **Sb** A metallic element used in a wide variety of alloys, esp. with lead in battery plates, and in paints, semiconductors, and ceramic products. Atomic number 51; atomic weight 121.75. [< Med. Lat. *antimonium.*]

an·ti·neu·tri·no (ăn′tē-nōō-trē′nō, -nyōō-) *n., pl.* **-nos.** *Physics.* The antiparticle of the neutrino.

an·ti·neu·tron (ăn′tē-nōō′trŏn′, -nyōō′-) *n.* *Physics.* The antiparticle of the neutron.

an·ti·nov·el (ăn′tē-nŏv′əl) *n.* A novel lacking the traditional features of a fictional work. —**an′ti·nov′el·ist** *n.*

an·ti·ox·i·dant (ăn′tē-ŏk′sĭ-dənt) *n.* A chemical compound or substance that inhibits oxidation.

an·ti·par·ti·cle (ăn′tē-pär′tĭ-kəl) *n.* A subatomic particle, such as a positron or antineutron, having the same mass, average lifetime, and magnitude of electric charge as the particle to which it corresponds, but having the opposite electric charge, opposite intrinsic parity, and opposite magnetic characteristics.

an·ti·pas·to (ăn′tĭ-pä′stō, -päs′tō) *n., pl.* **-tos** or **-ti** (-tē). An assortment of appetizers often served as a main course. [Ital.]

an·tip·a·thy (ăn-tĭp′ə-thē) *n., pl.* **-thies. 1.** A feeling of aversion. **2.** The object of aversion. [< Gk. *antipatheia.*] —**an·tip′a·thet′ic** (-thĕt′ĭk) or **an·tip′a·thet′i·cal** (-ĭ-kəl) *adj.* —**an·tip′a·thet′i·cal·ly** *adv.*

---

an·ti·per·son·nel (ăn'tē-pûr'sə-nĕl') adj. Designed to kill military or civilian personnel.

an·ti·per·spi·rant (ăn'tē-pûr'spər-ənt) n. A preparation applied to the skin to prevent excessive perspiration.

an·ti·phon (ăn'tə-fŏn') n. A devotional composition sung responsively as part of a liturgy. [< Gk. *antiphōna*, sung responses.] —**an·tiph'o·nal** (-tĭf'ə-nəl) adj.

an·tiph·o·ny (ăn-tĭf'ə-nē) n., pl. -nies. 1. Antiphonal singing. 2. A sound or other effect that echoes or answers another.

an·ti·pode (ăn'tĭ-pōd') n. A direct opposite. [< ANTIPODES.] —**an·tip'o·dal** adj.

an·tip·o·des (ăn-tĭp'ə-dēz') pl.n. 1. Two places or regions on opposite sides of the earth. 2. (*sometimes used with a sing. verb*). One that is the exact opposite of another. [Gk.]

an·ti·pol·lu·tion (ăn'tē-pə-lōō'shən) adj. Intended to counteract or eliminate pollution. —**an'ti·pol·lu'tion·ist** n.

an·ti·pope (ăn'tĭ-pōp') n. One claiming to be pope in opposition to the one chosen by church law.

an·ti·pov·er·ty (ăn'tē-pŏv'ər-tē) adj. Intended to alleviate poverty.

an·ti·pro·ton (ăn'tē-prō'tŏn') n. Physics. The antiparticle of the proton.

an·ti·py·ret·ic (ăn'tĭ-pī-rĕt'ĭk) adj. Reducing or tending to reduce fever. —n. A fever-reducing medication. —**an'ti·py·re'sis** (-rē'sĭs) n.

an·ti·quary (ăn'tĭ-kwĕr'ē) n., pl. -ies. A student of or dealer in antiquities. —**an'ti·quar'i·an** (ăn'tĭ-kwâr'ē-ən) adj. & n.

an·ti·quate (ăn'tĭ-kwāt') v. -quat·ed, -quat·ing. To make obsolete. —**an'ti·qua'tion** n.

an·tique (ăn-tēk') adj. 1. Of ancient times, esp. those of ancient Greece or Rome. 2. Of or typical of an earlier period. —n. An object of special value because of its age, esp. a work of art or handicraft over 100 years old. —v. -tiqued, -tiqu·ing. To give the appearance of an antique to. [< Lat. *antiquus*.] —**an·tique'ly** adv. —**an·tique'ness** n.

an·tiq·ui·ty (ăn-tĭk'wĭ-tē) n., pl. -ties. 1. Ancient times, esp. those preceding the Middle Ages. 2. The quality of being old or ancient: *a carving of great antiquity*.

an·ti-Sem·ite (ăn'tē-sĕm'īt) n. A person hostile toward Jews. —**an'ti-Se·mit'ic** (-sə-mĭt'ĭk) adj. —**an'ti-Sem'i·tism** n.

an·ti·sep·sis (ăn'tĭ-sĕp'sĭs) n. The destruction of microorganisms that cause disease, fermentation, or rot.

an·ti·sep·tic (ăn'tĭ-sĕp'tĭk) adj. 1. Pertaining to or capable of producing antisepsis. 2. Entirely clean. 3. Austere; drab. —n. An antiseptic agent. —**an'ti·sep'ti·cal·ly** adv.

an·ti·se·rum (ăn'tĭ-sîr'əm) n., pl. -rums or -ra (-rə). A serum containing antibodies for at least one antigen.

an·ti·so·cial (ăn'tē-sō'shəl) adj. 1. Not sociable. 2. Interfering with society: *antisocial behavior*. —**an'ti·so'cial·ly** adv.

an·tith·e·sis (ăn-tĭth'ĭ-sĭs) n., pl. -ses (-sēz'). 1. Direct contrast; opposition. 2. The direct opposite. 3. Rhet. Juxtaposition of sharply contrasting ideas. [< Gk.] —**an'ti·thet'i·cal** (ăn'tĭ-thĕt'ĭ-kəl) or **an'ti·thet'ic** (-thĕt'-ĭk) adj. —**an'ti·thet'i·cal·ly** adv.

an·ti·tox·in (ăn'tē-tŏk'sĭn) n. 1. An antibody formed in response to, and capable of neutralizing, a biological poison. 2. An animal serum containing antibodies.

an·ti·trust (ăn'tē-trŭst') adj. Regulating trusts or similar monopolies.

ant·ler (ănt'lər) n. One of the paired, often branched bony growths on the head of a deer. [< OFr. *antoillier*.] —**ant'lered** adj.

ant lion n. 1. An insect, the adults of which resemble dragonflies. 2. The larva of the ant lion, which digs holes to trap ants.

an·to·nym (ăn'tə-nĭm') n. A word having a sense opposite to that of another word. —**an·to·nym'ic** (-nĭm'ĭk) adj. —**an·ton'y·mous** (ăn-tŏn'ə-məs) adj. —**an·ton'y·my** n.

a·nus (ā'nəs) n. The excretory opening of the alimentary canal. [Lat.]

an·vil (ăn'vĭl) n. 1. A heavy iron or steel block with a smooth, flat top on which metals are shaped by hammering. 2. Anat. The incus. [< OE *anfilt*.]

anx·i·e·ty (ăng-zī'ĭ-tē) n., pl. -ties. 1. A state of uneasiness; apprehension; worry. 2. Psychiat. Intense fear or dread that lacks a specific cause. [Lat. *anxietas*.]

Syns: *anxiety, care, concern, disquietude, worry* n.

anx·ious (ăngk'shəs, ăng'shəs) adj. 1. Apprehensive; worried. 2. Eagerly or earnestly desirous. [Lat. *anxius*.] —**anx'ious·ly** adv. —**anx'ious·ness** n.

an·y (ĕn'ē) adj. 1. One, no matter which, from three or more: *Take any book you want*. 2. Every: *Any kid in my gang would do the same*. 3. Some: *Is there any soda?* 4. Much: *You don't need any strength to chop kindling*. —pron. 1. Any one or ones among three or more. 2. Any quantity or part. —adv. At all: *I don't feel any better*. [< OE *ænig*.]

an·y·bod·y (ĕn'ē-bŏd'ē, -bŭd'ē) pron. Any person; anyone. —n. A person of consequence: *everybody who is anybody*.

an·y·how (ĕn'ē-hou') adv. 1. In any case: *It was raining, but I walked home anyhow*. 2. In any way or by any means whatever.

an·y·more (ĕn'ē-môr', -mōr') adv. From now on.

an·y·one (ĕn'ē-wŭn', -wən) pron. Any person; anybody.

an·y·place (ĕn'ē-plās') adv. To, in, or at any place; anywhere.

an·y·thing (ĕn'ē-thĭng') pron. Any object, occurrence, or matter whatever. —idiom. **anything but**. By no means.

an·y·time (ĕn'ē-tīm') adv. At any time whatever.

an·y·way (ĕn'ē-wā') adv. 1. In any case; at any rate; anyhow. 2. Just the same; nevertheless.

an·y·where (ĕn'ē-hwâr', -wâr') adv. 1. To, in, or at any place. 2. To any extent or degree.

an·y·wise (ĕn'ē-wīz') adv. In any manner.

A-one (ā'wŭn') adj. Also **A-1**. Informal. First-class; excellent.

a·or·ta (ā-ôr'tə) n., pl. -tas or -tae (-tē'). The main trunk of the systemic arteries, carrying blood to all bodily organs except the lungs. [< Gk. *aortē*.] —**a·or'tal** or **a·or'tic** adj.

a·ou·dad (ä'ōō-dăd') n. A wild sheep of northern Africa, with long, curved horns and a beardlike growth of hair on the neck and chest. [< Berber *audad*.]

a·pace (ə-pās') adv. At a rapid pace; swiftly. [< OFr. *a pas*.]

A·pach·e (ə-păch'ē) n., pl. **Apache** or -es. 1. a. A formerly nomadic tribe of North

American Indians inhabiting the southwestern United States and northern Mexico. **b.** A member of this tribe. **2.** Any of the Athapascan languages of the Apache.

ap·a·nage (ăp′ə-nĭj) *n.* Var. of **appanage**.

a·part (ə-pärt′) *adv.* **1. a.** In pieces. **b.** To pieces. **2. a.** Separately or at a distance in time, place, or position. **b.** To one side; aside. —*idiom.* **apart from.** With the exception of; aside from. [< OFr. *a part,* to the side.]

a·part·held (ə-pärt′hīt′, -hāt′) *n.* An official policy of racial segregation promulgated in the Republic of South Africa. [Afr.]

a·part·ment (ə-pärt′mənt) *n.* A room or suite designed for dwelling. [< Ital. *appartemento.*]

ap·a·thy (ăp′ə-thē) *n.* **1.** Lack of emotion or feeling. **2.** Indifference. [Gk. *apatheia.*] —**ap′a·thet′ic** *adj.* —**ap′a·thet′i·cal·ly** *adv.*

ape (āp) *n.* **1.** A large primate such as a chimpanzee, gorilla, gibbon, or orangutan. **2.** Any monkey. **3.** A mimic or imitator. **4.** A clumsy, coarse person. —*v.* **aped, ap·ing.** To mimic. [< OE *apa.*] —**ape′like′** *adj.*

ape

Bornean orangutans

a·pé·ri·tif (ä-pĕr′ĭ-tēf′) *n.* A drink of alcoholic liquor taken before a meal. [Fr.]

ap·er·ture (ăp′ər-chər) *n.* An opening; orifice. [Lat. *apertura.*] —**ap′er·tur·al** *adj.*

a·pex (ā′pĕks′) *n., pl.* **-es** or **a·pi·ces** (ā′pĭ-sēz′, ăp′ĭ-). The highest point; peak. [Lat.]

a·pha·sia (ə-fā′zhə) *n.* Loss of the ability to express and understand ideas, resulting from brain damage. [Gk.] —**a·pha′si·ac** (-zē-ăk′) *n.* —**a·pha′sic** (-zĭk, -sĭk) *adj. & n.*

a·phe·li·on (ə-fē′lē-ən, ə-fēl′yən) *n., pl.* **-li·a** (-lē-ə). The point on a planetary orbit farthest from the sun. [Gk. *ap(o)*-, away from + Gk. *hēlios,* sun.]

a·phid (ā′fĭd, ăf′ĭd) *n.* Any of various small insects that suck sap from plants. [Orig. unknown.]

aph·o·rism (ăf′ə-rĭz′əm) *n.* **1.** A brief statement of a principle. **2.** A maxim; adage. [< Gk. *aphorismos.*] —**aph′o·ris′tic** (ăf′ə-rĭs′tĭk) *adj.* —**aph′o·ris′ti·cal·ly** *adv.*

aph·ro·dis·i·ac (ăf′rə-dĭz′ē-ăk′) *adj.* Stimulating or intensifying sexuality. —*n.* An aphrodisiac drug or food. [Gk. *aphrodisiakos.*]

Aph·ro·di·te (ăf′rə-dī′tē) *n. Gk. Myth.* The goddess of love and beauty.

a·pi·ar·y (ā′pē-ĕr′ē) *n., pl.* **-ies.** A place where bees are raised for their honey. [Lat. *apiarium,* beehive.] —**a′pi·ar′i·an** (ā′pē-âr′ē-ən) *adj. & n.* —**a′pi·a·rist** (ā′pē-ə-rĭst) *n.*

a·pi·ces (ā′pĭ-sēz′, ăp′ĭ-) *n.* A pl. of **apex**.

a·pi·cul·ture (ā′pĭ-kŭl′chər) *n.* The raising of bees. [Lat. *apis,* bee + CULTURE.] —**a′pi·cul′tur·al** *adj.* —**a′pi·cul′tur·ist** *n.*

a·piece (ə-pēs′) *adv.* To or for each one.

a·plomb (ə-plŏm′, ə-plŭm′) *n.* Self-confidence; poise. [Fr., balance.]

A·poc·a·lypse (ə-pŏk′ə-lĭps′) *n.* **1.** See table at **Bible.** **2.** apocalypse. A prophetic revelation. [< Gk. *apokalupsis,* revelation.] —**a·poc′a·lyp′tic** or **a·poc′a·lyp′ti·cal** *adj.* —**a·poc′a·lyp′ti·cal·ly** *adv.*

A·poc·ry·pha (ə-pŏk′rə-fə) *pl.n.* (used with a sing. verb). **1.** The 14 Biblical books not included in the Old Testament by Protestants as being of doubtful authorship. Eleven of these books are accepted by the Roman Catholic Church. See table at **Bible.** **2.** apocrypha. Writings of questionable authorship or authenticity. [< Gk. *apokruphos,* hidden.]

a·poc·ry·phal (ə-pŏk′rə-fəl) *adj.* **1.** Of doubtful authorship or authenticity. **2.** False; counterfeit. **3.** Apocryphal. Of or relating to the Apocrypha. —**a·poc′ry·phal·ly** *adv.* —**a·poc′ry·phal·ness** *n.*

ap·o·gee (ăp′ə-jē′) *n.* **1.** The point in the orbit of a natural or artificial satellite most distant from the earth. **2.** The farthest or highest point; apex. [< Gk. *apogaion.*]

a·po·lit·i·cal (ā′pə-lĭt′ĭ-kəl) *adj.* **1.** Having no interest in politics. **2.** Politically unimportant. —**a′po·lit′i·cal·ly** *adv.*

A·pol·lo (ə-pŏl′ō) *n.* **1.** *Gk. Myth.* The god of the sun, prophecy, music, medicine, and poetry. **2.** apollo. A very handsome young man.

a·pol·o·get·ic (ə-pŏl′ə-jĕt′ĭk) *adj.* Making an apology. —*n.* A formal defense or apology. —**a·pol′o·get′i·cal·ly** *adv.*

ap·o·lo·gi·a (ăp′ə-lō′jē-ə, -jə) *n.* A formal defense or justification. [LLat., apology.]

a·pol·o·gize (ə-pŏl′ə-jīz′) *v.* **-gized, -giz·ing.** **1.** To make an apology. **2.** To make a formal defense or justification. —**a·pol′o·giz′er** or **a·pol′o·gist** (-jĭst) *n.*

a·pol·o·gy (ə-pŏl′ə-jē) *n., pl.* **-gies.** **1.** A statement expressing regret for an offense or fault. **2.** A formal justification or defense. **3.** An inferior substitute. [< Gk. *apologiā.*]

ap·o·phthegm (ăp′ə-thěm′) *n.* Var. of **apothegm.**

ap·o·plex·y (ăp′ə-plĕk′sē) *n.* Sudden loss of muscular control, sensation, and consciousness, resulting from rupture or blocking of a blood vessel in the brain. [< Gk. *apoplēxia.*] —**ap′o·plec′tic** *adj.* —**ap′o·plec′ti·cal·ly** *adv.*

a·pos·ta·sy (ə-pŏs′tə-sē) *n., pl.* **-sies.** Abandonment of one's religious faith, political party, or cause. [< Gk. *apostasia,* desertion.] —**a·pos′tate′** (-tāt′, -tĭt) *n. & adj.* —**a·pos′ta·tize′** *v.*

a pos·te·ri·o·ri (ä′ pŏ-stîr′ē-ôr′ē, -ôr′ē, -ôr′ī′, -ôr′ī′, ä′) *adj.* Denoting reasoning from observed facts. [Lat., from the subsequent.]

a·pos·tle (ə-pŏs′əl) *n.* **1.** Often **Apostle.** One of the 12 disciples chosen by Christ to preach the Gospel. **2.** One who leads a cause. [< Gk. *apostolos,* messenger.]

ap·os·tol·ic (ăp′ə-stŏl′ĭk) *adj.* **1.** Of or pertaining to the Apostles or their faith, teachings, etc. **2.** Papal.

a·pos·tro·phe¹ (ə-pŏs′trə-fē) *n.* A mark (') used to indicate omission of a letter or letters from a word, the possessive case, and certain plurals. [< Gk. *apostrophos* < *apostrephein*, to turn away.]

a·pos·tro·phe² (ə-pŏs′trə-fē) *n.* A digression in discourse, esp. a turning away from an audience to address an absent or imaginary person. [Gk. *apostrophē* < *apostrephein*, to turn away.] —**ap′os·troph′ic** (ăp′ə-strŏf′ĭk) *adj.* —**a·pos′tro·phize′** *v.*

a·poth·e·car·ies′ measure (ə-pŏth′ĭ-kĕr′ēz) *n.* A system of liquid volume measure used in pharmacy.

apothecaries′ weight *n.* A system of weights used in pharmacy and based on an ounce equal to 480 grains and a pound equal to 12 ounces.

a·poth·e·car·y (ə-pŏth′ĭ-kĕr′ē) *n.*, *pl.* -**ies.** A druggist; pharmacist. [< Gk. *apothēkē*, storehouse.]

ap·o·thegm (ăp′ə-thĕm′) *n.* Also **ap·o·phthegm.** A maxim; proverb. [Gk. *apophthegma*.] —**ap′o·theg·mat′ic** (-thĕg-măt′ĭk) *or* **ap′o·theg·mat′i·cal** (-ĭ-kəl) *adj.* —**ap′o·theg·mat′i·cal·ly** *adv.*

a·poth·e·o·sis (ə-pŏth′ē-ō′sĭs, ăp′ə-thē′ə-sĭs) *n.*, *pl.* -**ses** (-sēz′). **1.** Exaltation to divine rank or stature; deification. **2.** An exalted or glorified ideal. [< Gk. *apotheōsis.*] —**a·poth′e·o·size′** *v.*

ap·pall (ə-pôl′) *v.* To fill with horror and dismay. [OFr. *apalir.*] —**ap·pall′ing·ly** *adv.*

ap·pa·loo·sa (ăp′ə-lōō′sə) *n.* A horse having a spotted rump. [Prob. < the *Palouse* Indians.]

ap·pa·nage (ăp′ə-nĭj) *n.* Also **ap·a·nage.** **1.** A source of revenue, as land, given by a king for the maintenance of a member of the royal family. **2.** A natural adjunct. [< Med. Lat. *appanare,* to make provisions for.]

ap·pa·ra·tus (ăp′ə-rā′təs, -răt′əs) *n.*, *pl.* -**tus** *or* -**tus·es.** **1.** The means by which a specified function or task is performed. **2.** Equipment, esp. laboratory equipment. **3.** A machine or group of machines. **4.** A system. [< Lat. *apparare,* to prepare.]

ap·par·el (ə-păr′əl) *n.* Clothing, esp. outer garments. —*v.* -**eled** *or* -**elled,** -**el·ing** *or* -**el·ling.** To dress; clothe. [OFr. *apareil,* preparation.]

ap·par·ent (ə-păr′ənt, ə-pâr′-) *adj.* **1.** Readily seen or perceived. **2.** Appearing as such but not necessarily so. [< Lat. *apparēre,* to appear.] —**ap·par′ent·ly** *adv.*

ap·pa·ri·tion (ăp′ə-rĭsh′ən) *n.* **1.** A ghost. **2.** A sudden, unusual sight. [LLat. *apparitio,* appearance.] —**ap′pa·ri′tion·al** *adj.*

ap·peal (ə-pēl′) *n.* **1.** An earnest request. **2.** An application to a higher authority, as for a decision. **3.** The power of arousing interest. **4.** *Law.* **a.** Transfer of a case from a lower to a higher court for a new hearing. **b.** A request for a new hearing. —*v.* **1.** To make an earnest request, as for help. **2.** To be attractive. **3.** To transfer or apply to transfer (a case) to a higher court for rehearing. [< Lat. *appellare,* to entreat.] —**ap·peal′a·ble** *adj.* —**ap·peal′er** *n.* —**ap·peal′ing·ly** *adv.*

ap·pear (ə-pîr′) *v.* **1.** To become visible. **2.** To seem. **3.** To come before the public. **4.** To come formally before an authority. [Lat. *apparēre.*]

ap·pear·ance (ə-pîr′əns) *n.* **1.** The act of appearing. **2.** The outward aspect of something. **3.** A pretense.

ap·pease (ə-pēz′) *v.* -**peased,** -**peas·ing.** To placate, esp. by granting demands. [< OFr. *apaisier.*] —**ap·peas′a·ble** *adj.* —**ap·peas′a·bly** *adv.* —**ap·pease′ment** *n.* —**ap·peas′er** *n.*

ap·pel·lant (ə-pĕl′ənt) *adj.* Appellate. —*n.* One who appeals a court decision.

ap·pel·late (ə-pĕl′ĭt) *adj.* Empowered to hear judicial appeals. [< Lat. *appellare,* to entreat.]

ap·pel·la·tion (ăp′ə-lā′shən) *n.* A name or title. [< Lat. *apellatio.*]

ap·pend (ə-pĕnd′) *v.* To add as a supplement; attach. [Lat. *appendere.*]

ap·pend·age (ə-pĕn′dĭj) *n.* **1.** Something attached to a larger entity. **2.** *Biol.* A subordinate or derivative bodily part, as a finger.

ap·pen·dec·to·my (ăp′ən-dĕk′tə-mē) *n.*, *pl.* -**mies.** Surgical removal of the appendix.

ap·pen·di·ci·tis (ə-pĕn′dĭ-sī′tĭs) *n.* Inflammation of the appendix.

ap·pen·dix (ə-pĕn′dĭks) *n.*, *pl.* -**es** *or* -**di·ces** (-dĭ-sēz′). **1.** Supplementary material at the end of a book. **2.** *Anat.* A slender, closed tube attached to the large intestine near the point at which it joins the small intestine. [Lat., appendage.]

ap·per·tain (ăp′ər-tān′) *v.* To have relation. [< OFr. *apartenir.*]

ap·pe·tite (ăp′ĭ-tīt′) *n.* **1.** A desire for food or drink. **2.** A physical craving or desire. [Lat. *appetitus.*]

ap·pe·tiz·er (ăp′ĭ-tī′zər) *n.* A food or drink served before a meal.

ap·pe·tiz·ing (ăp′ĭ-tī′zĭng) *adj.* Stimulating the appetite. —**ap′pe·tiz′ing·ly** *adv.*

ap·plaud (ə-plôd′) *v.* To express approval (of) by clapping the hands. —**ap·plaud′er** *n.*

ap·plause (ə-plôz′) *n.* Approval expressed esp. by clapping the hands. [< Lat. *applaudere,* to applaud.]

ap·ple (ăp′əl) *n.* **1.** A tree having fragrant pink or white flowers and edible fruit. **2.** The firm, rounded, often red-skinned fruit of the apple tree. —*idiom.* **apple of (one's) eye.** One very much liked or loved. [< OE *æppel.*]

ap·ple·jack (ăp′əl-jăk′) *n.* Brandy distilled from hard cider.

ap·ple·sauce (ăp′əl-sôs′) *n.* **1.** Stewed, sweetened, and blended apples. **2.** *Slang.* Nonsense.

ap·pli·ance (ə-plī′əns) *n.* A device or instrument, esp. one operated by electricity or gas and designed for household use. [< APPLY.]

ap·pli·ca·ble (ăp′lĭ-kə-bəl, ə-plĭk′ə-) *adj.* Capable of being applied. —**ap′pli·ca·bil′i·ty** *n.* —**ap′pli·ca·bly** *adv.*

ap·pli·cant (ăp′lĭ-kənt) *n.* One who applies.

ap·pli·ca·tion (ăp′lĭ-kā′shən) *n.* **1.** The act of applying. **2.** Something applied. **3.** A method of applying or using; specific use. **4.** The capacity of being usable; relevance. **5.** Close attention; diligence. **6. a.** A request, as for a job. **b.** The form on which such a request is made.

ap·pli·ca·tor (ăp′lĭ-kā′tər) *n.* An instrument for applying something, such as medicine.

ap·plied (ə-plīd′) *adj.* Put into practice; used.

ap·pli·qué (ăp′lĭ-kā′) *n.* A cloth decoration cut out and sewn to a larger piece of cloth. [< Fr., decorated with an appliqué.] —**ap′pli·qué′** *v.*

ap·ply (ə-plī′) *v.* -**plied,** -**ply·ing.** **1.** To bring into contact with something. **2.** To adapt for a special use. **3.** To devote (oneself or one's efforts) to something. **4.** To be pertinent. **5.** To make a request, as for a job. [< OFr. *aplier* < Lat. *applicare*.] **—ap·pli′er** *n.*

ap·point (ə-point′) *v.* **1.** To designate for an office or position. **2.** To fix or set by authority. **3.** To furnish; equip. [< OFr. *apointier,* to arrange.]

ap·point·ee (ə-poin′tē′, ăp′oin-) *n.* One who is appointed to an office or position.

ap·point·ive (ə-poin′tĭv) *adj.* Pertaining to or filled by appointment.

ap·point·ment (ə-point′mənt) *n.* **1.** The act of appointing. **2.** The office or position to which one is appointed. **3.** An arrangement for a meeting at a given time and place. **4. appointments.** Furnishings or equipment.

ap·por·tion (ə-pôr′shən, ə-pōr′-) *v.* To divide and assign according to some plan or proportion; allot. [OFr. *apportionner.*] **—ap·por′tion·ment** *n.*

ap·po·site (ăp′ə-zĭt) *adj.* Suitable; appropriate. [< Lat. *apponere,* to place near to.] **—ap′po·site·ly** *adv.* **—ap′po·site·ness** *n.*

ap·po·si·tion (ăp′ə-zĭsh′ən) *n.* **1.** Placement side by side or next to each other. **2.** *Gram.* A construction in which a noun or noun phrase is placed with another as an explanatory equivalent, as in *Copley, the famous painter, was born in Boston.* [< Med. Lat. *appositio* < Lat. *apponere,* to place near to.] **—ap′po·si′tion·al** *adj.* **—ap′po·si′tion·al·ly** *adv.*

ap·pos·i·tive (ə-pŏz′ĭ-tĭv) *adj.* Of, pertaining to, or standing in grammatical apposition. **—ap·pos′i·tive** *n.* **—ap·pos′i·tive·ly** *adv.*

ap·praise (ə-prāz′) *v.* **-praised, -prais·ing.** To put a value on. [< LLat. *appretiare.*] **—ap·prais′a·ble** *adj.* **—ap·prais′al** *n.* **—ap·praise′ment** *n.* **—ap·prais′er** *n.*

ap·pre·cia·ble (ə-prē′shə-bəl) *adj.* Capable of being noticed or measured; noticeable. **—ap·pre′cia·bly** *adv.*

ap·pre·ci·ate (ə-prē′shē-āt′) *v.* **-at·ed, -at·ing. 1.** To estimate the quality or value of. **2.** To value highly. **3.** To be fully aware of; realize. **4.** To be thankful for. **5.** To increase in value or price. [< LLat. *appretiare,* to appraise.] **—ap·pre′ci·a′tion** *n.* **—ap·pre′ci·a′tor** *n.*

Syns: *appreciate, cherish, esteem, prize, respect, treasure, value* **v.**

ap·pre·cia·tive (ə-prē′shə-tĭv, -shē-ā′tĭv) *adj.* Feeling or showing appreciation. **—ap·pre′cia·tive·ly** *adv.*

ap·pre·hend (ăp′rĭ-hĕnd′) *v.* **1.** To arrest. **2.** To understand. **3.** To anticipate with anxiety. [< Lat. *apprehendere,* to seize.] **—ap′pre·hen′sion** *n.*

ap·pre·hen·sive (ăp′rĭ-hĕn′sĭv) *adj.* Fearful; uneasy. **—ap′pre·hen′sive·ly** *adv.* **—ap′pre·hen′sive·ness** *n.*

ap·pren·tice (ə-prĕn′tĭs) *n.* **1.** One who is learning a trade under a skilled craftsman. **2.** A beginner. **—v. -ticed, -tic·ing.** To place or take on as an apprentice. [< Lat. *apprehendere,* to seize.] **—ap·pren′tice·ship′** *n.*

ap·prise (ə-prīz′) *v.* **-prised, -pris·ing.** Also **apprize, -prized, -priz·ing.** To cause to know; inform. [< Lat. *apprehendere,* to seize.]

ap·proach (ə-prōch′) *v.* **1.** To come near or nearer (to). **2.** To come close to in appearance; approximate. **3.** To make a proposal to;

make overtures to. **—n. 1.** The act of coming near. **2.** A fairly close resemblance; approximation. **3.** A way of reaching; access. **4.** Often **approaches.** An advance or overture made by one person to another. [LLat. *appropriare.*] **—ap·proach′a·bil′i·ty** *n.* **—ap·proach′a·ble** *adj.*

ap·pro·ba·tion (ăp′rə-bā′shən) *n.* Approval; sanction. [< Lat. *approbare,* to make good.]

ap·pro·pri·ate (ə-prō′prē-ĭt) *adj.* Suitable; proper; fitting. **—v.** (ə-prō′prē-āt′) **-at·ed, -at·ing. 1.** To set apart for a specific use. **2.** To take possession of, often without permission. [LLat. *appropriare,* to make one's own.] **—ap·pro′pri·ate·ly** *adv.* **—ap·pro′pri·ate·ness** *n.* **—ap·pro′pri·a′tion** *n.* **—ap·pro′pri·a′tor** *n.*

ap·prov·al (ə-prōō′vəl) *n.* **1.** An official approbation; sanction. **2.** Favorable regard. **—idiom. on approval.** Subject to a prospective buyer's rejection or acceptance.

ap·prove (ə-prōōv′) *v.* **-proved, -prov·ing. 1.** To regard favorably. **2.** To consent to officially; sanction. [< Lat. *approbare,* to make good.] **—ap·prov′ing·ly** *adv.*

ap·prox·i·mate (ə-prŏk′sə-mĭt) *adj.* **1.** Almost exact or accurate. **2.** Very similar. **—v.** (ə-prŏk′sə-māt′) **-mat·ed, -mat·ing.** To come close to; be nearly the same as. [< Lat. *approximare,* to approach.] **—ap·prox′i·mate·ly** *adv.* **—ap·prox′i·ma′tion** *n.*

ap·pur·te·nance (ə-pûrt′n-əns) *n.* Something added to another, more important thing; accessory. [< LLat. *appertinēre,* to appertain.] **—ap·pur′te·nant** *adj.*

a·pri·cot (ăp′rĭ-kŏt′, ā′prĭ-) *n.* **1.** A tree widely cultivated for its edible fruit. **2.** The juicy, yellow-orange peachlike fruit of the apricot tree. [Prob. < Ar. *al-birquq,* the apricot.]

A·pril (ā′prəl) *n.* The 4th month of the year, having 30 days. See table at **calendar.** [< Lat. *aprilis.*]

a pri·o·ri (ä′ prē-ôr′ē, -ōr′ē, ā′ prī-ôr′ī′, -ōr′ī′) *adj.* **1.** From a known or assumed cause to a necessarily related effect; deductive. **2.** Based on theory rather than experience. [Lat., from the former.]

a·pron (ā′prən) *n.* **1.** A garment worn over the front of the body to protect clothing. **2.** Something resembling an apron in appearance or function. **3.** The paved strip around airport hangars and terminal buildings. [< ME *a napron,* an apron.]

ap·ro·pos (ăp′rə-pō′) *adj.* Appropriate; pertinent. **—adv. 1.** Appropriately; pertinently. **2.** By the way; incidentally. **—prep.** Concerning; regarding. [Fr. *à propos,* to the purpose.]

apropos of *prep.* With reference to.

apse (ăps) *n.* A semicircular or polygonal, usu. domed projection of a church. [< Gk. *hapsis,* arch.]

apt (ăpt) *adj.* **1.** Exactly suitable; appropriate. **2.** Likely. **3.** Having a tendency; inclined. **4.** Quick to learn or understand: *an apt student.* [< Lat. *aptus* < *apere,* to fasten.] **—apt′ly** *adv.* **—apt′ness** *n.*

Usage: *Apt* is used instead of *likely* to indicate a natural tendency to error or undesirable behavior. *He is apt to lose his temper under severe stress* but *He is likely* (not *apt*) *to remain calm under severe stress.*

ă pat ā pay â care ä father ĕ pet ē be ĭ pit ī tie î pier ŏ pot ō toe ô paw, for oi noise ōō took ōō boot ou out th thin th this ŭ cut û urge yōō abuse zh vision ə about, item, edible, gallop, circus

APT (ā'pē-tē') n. A computer language designed for programming numerically controlled machine tools. [A(UTOMATICALLY) + P(ROGRAMMED) + T(OOL).]

ap·ti·tude (ăp'tĭ-tōōd', -tyōōd') n. 1. A natural talent or ability. 2. Quickness in learning. 3. Suitability; appropriateness. [< LLat. *aptitudo*, fitness.]

aq·ua (ăk'wə, ä'kwə) n., pl. **aq·uae** (ăk'wē, ä'kwī') or **-uas**. 1. Water. 2. An aqueous solution. 3. A light bluish green to light greenish blue. [Lat.] —**aq'ua** adj.

aq·ua·ma·rine (ăk'wə-mə-rēn', ä'kwə-) n. 1. A transparent blue-green beryl, used as a gemstone. 2. A light greenish blue. [Lat. *aqua marina*, sea water.]

aq·ua·naut (ăk'wə-nôt', ä'kwə-) n. One who works in scientific research conducted in underwater installations. [AQUA + (AERO)-NAUT.]

aq·ua·plane (ăk'wə-plān', ä'kwə-) n. A board on which one rides in a standing position while it is towed by a motorboat. —**aq'ua·plane'** v.

aqua re·gi·a (rē'jē-ə) n. A corrosive, fuming mixture of hydrochloric and nitric acids, capable of dissolving platinum and gold. [NLat., royal water.]

a·quar·i·um (ə-kwâr'ē-əm) n., pl. **-ums** or **-i·a** (-ē-ə). 1. A water-filled enclosure in which living aquatic animals and plants are kept. 2. A place where aquatic animals and plants are displayed to the public. [< Lat. *aquarius*, of water.]

A·quar·i·us (ə-kwâr'ē-əs) n. 1. A constellation in the equatorial region of the Southern Hemisphere. 2. The 11th sign of the zodiac.

a·quat·ic (ə-kwŏt'ĭk, ə-kwăt'-) adj. 1. Living or growing in or on the water. 2. Taking place in or on the water. —**a·quat'ic** n.

a·qua·vit (ä'kwə-vēt') n. A strong, clear liquor flavored with caraway seed. [Swed., Dan., and Norw. *akvavit*.]

aqua vi·tae (vī'tē) n. 1. Alcohol. 2. Whiskey, brandy, or other strong liquor. [< Med. Lat., water of life.]

aq·ue·duct (ăk'wĭ-dŭkt') n. 1. A conduit designed to carry water from a distant source. 2. A bridgelike structure supporting a conduit or canal passing over a river or low ground. [Lat. *aquae ductus*.]

aqueduct
1st-cent. B.C. Roman aqueduct

a·que·ous (ā'kwē-əs, ăk'wē-) adj. Of, containing, or dissolved in water; watery. [< Lat. *aqua*, water.]

aqueous humor n. A clear, lymphlike fluid that fills the space between the cornea and the lens of the eye.

aq·ui·line (ăk'wə-līn', -lĭn) adj. 1. Of or similar to an eagle. 2. Curved like an eagle's beak: *an aquiline nose.* [< Lat. *aquila*, eagle.]

-ar suff. Like, pertaining to, or of the nature of: *titular.* [< Lat. *-aris* < *-alis*, -al.]

Ar The symbol for the element argon.

Ar·ab (ăr'əb) n. 1. A native or inhabitant of Arabia. 2. A member of a Semitic people of the Middle East and North Africa. —**Ar'ab** adj. —**A·ra'bi·an** adj. & n.

ar·a·besque (ăr'ə-běsk') n. An ornamental design of interwoven flowers, leaves, and geometric forms. [< Ital. *arabesco*, in the Arabic fashion.]

Ar·a·bic (ăr'ə-bĭk) adj. Of or pertaining to Arabia, the Arabs, their language, or their culture. —n. The Semitic language of the Arabs, consisting of many dialects.

Arabic numeral n. One of the numerical symbols 1, 2, 3, 4, 5, 6, 7, 8, 9, and 0.

ar·a·ble (ăr'ə-bəl) adj. Fit for cultivation. [< Lat. *arare*, to plow.]

a·rach·nid (ə-răk'nĭd) n. One of a group of eight-legged arthropods including the spiders, scorpions, ticks, and mites. [< Gk. *arakhnē*, spider.] —**a·rach'ni·dan** (-nə-dən) adj. & n.

Ar·a·ma·ic (ăr'ə-mā'ĭk) n. A Semitic language used in southwestern Asia from the 7th cent. B.C. to the 7th cent. A.D. —**Ar'a·ma'ic** adj.

A·rap·a·ho (ə-răp'ə-hō') n., pl. **-ho** or **-hos**. Also **A·rap·a·hoe** pl. **-hoe** or **-hoes**. 1. A tribe of North American Indians now settled in Oklahoma and Wyoming. 2. A member of the Arapaho. 3. The Algonquian language of the Arapaho. —**A·rap'a·ho** adj.

Ar·a·wa·kan (ăr'ə-wä'kən) n., pl. **-kan** or **-kans**. 1. A South American Indian language family spoken in a wide area comprising the Amazon basin in Brazil, Venezuela, Colombia, the Guianas, Peru, Bolivia, and Paraguay. 2. An Indian or an Indian people who speak an Arawakan language. —**Ar'a·wa'kan** adj.

ar·ba·lest (är'bə-lĭst) n. Also **ar·be·lest**. A medieval missile launcher designed on the crossbow principle. [< LLat. *arcuballista*.]

ar·bi·ter (är'bĭ-tər) n. One having the power to judge or decide. [< Lat., judge.]

ar·bit·ra·ment (är-bĭt'rə-mənt) n. 1. The act of arbitrating. 2. The judgment of an arbiter. [< OFr. *arbitrement*.]

ar·bi·trary (är'bĭ-trĕr'ē) adj. 1. Determined by whim or caprice. 2. Not limited by law; despotic. [< Lat. *arbitrarius*.] —**ar'bi·trar'i·ly** (-trăr'ə-lē) adv. —**ar'bi·trar'i·ness** n.

ar·bi·trate (är'bĭ-trāt') v. **-trat·ed, -trat·ing**. 1. To judge or decide as an arbitrator. 2. To submit (a dispute) to settlement by arbitration. 3. To serve as an arbitrator. [< Lat. *arbitrari*.] —**ar'bi·tra'tion** n.

ar·bi·tra·tor (är'bĭ-trā'tər) n. A person chosen to settle a dispute or controversy.

ar·bor¹ (är'bər) n. A shady garden shelter or bower. [< OFr. *herbier*, garden.]

ar·bor² (är'bər) n. 1. An axis or shaft supporting a rotating part on a lathe. 2. A bar for supporting cutting tools. 3. A spindle of a wheel, as in watches and clocks. [Lat., tree.]

ar·bo·re·al (är-bôr'ē-əl, -bōr'-) adj. 1. Of or like a tree. 2. Living in trees.

ar·bo·re·tum (är'bə-rē'təm) n., pl. **-tums** or **-ta** (-tə). A place for the study and exhibition of trees. [Lat., a place where trees grow.]

ar·bor·vi·tae (är'bər-vī'tē) n. Also **arbor vi·tae**.

Any of several evergreen trees with small, scalelike leaves. [NLat., tree of life.]

ar·bu·tus (är-byōō'təs) n. The trailing arbutus. [Lat., strawberry tree.]

arc (ärk) n. 1. Something shaped like a bow, curve, or arch. 2. *Geom.* A segment of a curve. 3. A luminous discharge of electric current crossing a gap between two electrodes. —v. arced or arcked, arc·ing or ark·ing. To move in or form an arc. [< Lat. *arcus.*]

ar·cade (är-kād') n. 1. A series of arches supported by columns. 2. A roofed passageway, esp. one with shops on either side. [< Ital. *arcata < arco*, arch.]

ar·cane (är-kān') adj. Secret; esoteric. [Lat. *arcanus < arca*, chest.]

arch¹ (ärch) n. 1. A structural device, esp. of masonry, forming the curved, pointed, or flat upper edge of an opening or a support, as in a bridge or doorway. 2. A structure similar to an arch, as a monument. 3. Something curved like an arch. —v. 1. To supply with an arch. 2. To form or cause to form an arch. [< Lat. *arcus.*] —arched adj.

arch² (ärch) adj. 1. Chief; principal. 2. Mischievous: *an arch glance.* [< ARCH-.] —arch'ly adv. —arch'ness n.

arch- pref. 1. Highest rank or chief status: *archduke.* 2. Ultimate of a kind: *archfiend.* [< Gk. *arkhos*, ruler.]

-arch suff. Ruler; leader: *matriarch.* [< Gk. *arkhos*, ruler.]

ar·chae·ol·o·gy or **ar·che·ol·o·gy** (är'kē-ŏl'ə-jē) n. The systematic recovery and detailed scientific study of material evidence of human life and culture in past ages. [< Gk. *arkhaiologia*, antiquarian lore.] —ar'chae·o·log'i·cal (-ə-lŏj'ĭ-kəl) or ar'chae·o·log'ic adj. —ar'chae·o·log'i·cal·ly adv. —ar'chae·ol'o·gist n.

ar·cha·ic (är-kā'ĭk) adj. 1. Belonging to an earlier time. 2. No longer current; antiquated. 3. Designating words and language that were once common but are now used chiefly to suggest an earlier style. [< Gk. *arkhaikos < arkhē*, beginning.] —ar·cha'i·cal·ly adv.

arch·a·ism (är'kē-ĭz'əm, -kā-) n. An archaic word, phrase, idiom, or expression. —ar'cha·ist n. —ar'cha·is'tic adj.

arch·an·gel (ärk'ān'jəl) n. A celestial being next in rank above an angel. —arch·an'gel'ic n.

arch·bish·op (ärch-bĭsh'əp) n. A bishop of the highest rank. —arch·bish'op·ric n.

arch·dea·con (ärch-dē'kən) n. A church official, chiefly of the Anglican Church, in charge of temporal and other affairs in a diocese. —arch·dea'con·ate (-kə-nĭt) n. —arch·dea'con·ry n. —arch·dea'con·ship' n.

arch·di·o·cese (ärch-dī'ə-sĭs, -sēs', -sēz') n. The area under an archbishop's jurisdiction. —arch'di·oc'e·san (-ŏs'ĭ-sən) adj.

arch·duke (ärch-dōōk', -dyōōk') n. A royal prince, esp. of imperial Austria. —arch·duch'ess n.

arch·en·e·my (ärch-ĕn'ə-mē) n., pl. -mies. 1. A chief enemy. 2. Satan.

ar·che·ol·o·gy (är'kē-ŏl'ə-jē) n. Var. of **archaeology.**

arch·er (är'chər) n. One who shoots with a bow and arrow. [< Lat. *arcus*, bow.] —arch'er·y n.

arche·type (är'kĭ-tīp') n. An original model after which other similar things are patterned. [< Gk. *arkhetupos*, exemplary.] —ar'che·typ'al (-tī'pəl) or ar'che·typ'ic (-tĭp'ĭk) or ar'che·typ'i·cal adj.

arch·fiend (ärch-fēnd') n. 1. A chief fiend. 2. Satan.

arch·e·pis·co·pal (är'kē-ĭ-pĭs'kə-pəl) adj. Pertaining to an archbishop.

archi·man·drite (är'kə-măn'drīt') n. *Gk. Orthodox Ch.* A cleric ranking below a bishop. [< LGk. *arkhimandritēs.*]

archi·pel·a·go (är'kə-pĕl'ə-gō') n., pl. -goes or -gos. 1. A large group of islands. 2. A sea containing a large group of islands. [Ital. *Arcipelago*, the Aegean Sea.]

archi·tect (är'kĭ-tĕkt') n. 1. One who designs and supervises the construction of buildings. 2. A planner or deviser. [< Gk. *arkhitektōn*, master builder.]

archi·tec·ton·ics (är'kĭ-tĕk-tŏn'ĭks) n. (used with a sing. verb). 1. The science of architecture. 2. Structural design, as in a musical work. —ar'chi·tec·ton'ic adj.

archi·tec·ture (är'kĭ-tĕk'chər) n. 1. The art and science of designing and erecting buildings. 2. A style and method of design and construction: *modern architecture.* —ar'chi·tec'tural adj. —ar'chi·tec'tural·ly adv.

archi·trave (är'kĭ-trāv') n. The lowermost part of an entablature, resting directly on top of a column in classical architecture. [< OItal.]

ar·chives (är'kīvz') pl.n. 1. Public records pertaining to an organization or institution. 2. A place where archives are kept. [< Gk. *arkheia.*]

archi·vist (är'kə-vĭst, -kī'-) n. One in charge of archives.

arch·way (ärch'wā') n. 1. A passageway under an arch. 2. An arch covering a passageway.

-archy suff. Rule; government: *oligarchy.* [< Gk. *arkhos*, ruler.]

arcked (ärkt). A p.t. & p.p. of **arc.**

arck·ing (ärk'ĭng). A pr.p. of **arc.**

arc lamp n. An electric lamp in which a current traverses a gas between two incandescent electrodes.

arc·tic (ärk'tĭk, är'tĭk) adj. 1. Extremely cold; frigid. 2. **Arctic.** Of the region lying north of the Arctic Circle. [< Gk. *arktikos < arktos*, bear, Ursa Major.]

Arctic Circle n. The parallel of latitude 66° 33' north, marking the limit of the North Frigid Zone.

-ard or **-art** suff. One who does something to excess: *drunkard.* [< OFr.]

ar·dent (är'dnt) adj. 1. Characterized by warmth of passion, emotion, or desire; passionate. 2. Glowing. 3. Fiery; burning. [< Lat. *ardēre*, to burn.] —ar'den·cy (-dn-sē) n. —ar'dent·ly adv.

ar·dor (är'dər) n. 1. Intensity of emotion, passion, or desire. 2. Intense heat. [< Lat.]

ar·du·ous (är'jōō-əs) adj. 1. Difficult; strenuous. 2. Full of hardships. [Lat. *arduus.*] —ar'du·ous·ly adv. —ar'du·ous·ness n.

are¹ (är) *v.* Present tense indicative pl. and 2nd person sing. present tense of **be.**

are² (âr, är) *n.* A metric unit of area equal to 100 square meters. [< Lat. *area,* open space.]

ar·e·a (âr´ē-ə) *n.* **1.** A flat, open surface or space. **2.** A specific region. **3.** The range or scope of anything. **4.** The measure of a planar region or of the surface of a solid. [Lat.]

area code *n.* A three-digit number assigned to each telephone area in the United States and Canada.

ar·e·a·way (âr´ē-ə-wā´) *n.* A small sunken area allowing access or light and air to a basement.

a·re·na (ə-rē´nə) *n.* **1.** An auditorium for public entertainments, esp. sports events. **2.** A sphere or field of conflict, interest, or activity: *the political arena.* [Lat.]

arena theater *n.* A theater in which the stage is at the center of the auditorium.

aren't (ärnt, är´ənt). Are not.

Ar·es (âr´ēz´) *n. Gk. Myth.* The god of war.

ar·gent (är´jənt) *n. Archaic.* Silver. [Lat. *argentum.*] —**ar´gent** *adj.*

ar·gon (är´gŏn´) *n. Symbol* **Ar** A colorless, odorless, inert gaseous element constituting approximately one per cent of the earth's atmosphere and used in electric lamps, fluorescent tubes, and radio vacuum tubes. Atomic number 18; atomic weight 39.94. [< Gk. *argos,* inert.]

ar·go·sy (är´gə-sē) *n., pl.* **-sies.** **1.** A large merchant ship. **2.** A fleet of large merchant ships. [< Ital. *ragusea,* vessel of *Ragusa,* former name of Dubrovnik, Yugoslavia.]

ar·got (är´gō, -gət) *n.* A specialized vocabulary used by a particular group, esp. the jargon of the underworld. [Fr.]

ar·gue (är´gyōō) *v.* **-gued, -gu·ing.** **1.** To put forth reasons for or against something. **2.** To maintain in argument; contend. **3.** To dispute; quarrel. **4.** To persuade or influence, as by presenting reasons. [< Lat. *arguere,* to prove.] —**ar´gu·a·ble** *adj.* —**ar´gu·a·bly** *adv.* —**ar´gu·er** *n.*

Syns: *argue, bicker, contend, dispute, fight, quarrel, quibble, squabble, wrangle v.*

ar·gu·ment (är´gyə-mənt) *n.* **1.** A discussion of differing points of view; debate. **2.** A quarrel. **3.** A course of reasoning aimed at demonstrating the truth or falsehood of something.

ar·gu·men·ta·tion (är´gyə-mĕn-tā´shən) *n.* The presentation and elaboration of an argument.

ar·gu·men·ta·tive (är´gyə-mĕn´tə-tĭv) *adj.* Given to arguing; disputatious. —**ar´gu·men·ta·tive·ness** *n.*

ar·gyle or **ar·gyll** (är´gīl´) *n.* **1.** A knitting pattern of varicolored, diamond-shaped areas on a solid color background. **2.** An argyle sock. [< the Scottish clan Campbell of *Argyle.*]

a·ri·a (är´ē-ə) *n.* A solo vocal piece with instrumental accompaniment, as in an opera. [Ital. < Lat. *aer,* air.]

-arian *suff.* **1.** Sect: *Unitarian.* **2.** Believer in: *vegetarian.* [< Lat. *-arius.*]

ar·id (är´ĭd) *adj.* **1.** Parched; dry. **2.** Lifeless; dull. [< Lat. *aridus.*] —**a·rid´i·ty** (ə-rĭd´ĭ-tē) *n.*

Ar·ies (âr´ēz´, âr´ē-ēz´) *n.* **1.** A constellation in the Northern Hemisphere. **2.** The 1st sign of the zodiac.

a·right (ə-rīt´) *adv.* Properly; correctly.

a·rise (ə-rīz´) *v.* **a·rose** (ə-rōz´), **a·ris·en** (ə-rĭz´-ən), **a·ris·ing.** **1.** To get up. **2.** To move upward; ascend. **3.** To originate. **4.** To result or proceed. [< OE *ārīsan.*]

ar·is·toc·ra·cy (är´ĭ-stŏk´rə-sē) *n., pl.* **-cies.** **1.** A social class based on inherited wealth, status, and sometimes titles. **2.** Government by the highest social class. **3.** A group or class considered to be superior. [< Gk. *aristokratia,* rule by the best.] —**a·ris´to·crat´** (ə-rĭs´tə-krăt´, är´ĭs-tə-) *n.* —**a·ris´to·crat´ic** *adj.* —**a·ris´to·crat´i·cal·ly** *adv.*

a·rith·me·tic (ə-rĭth´mə-tĭk) *n.* **1.** The mathematics of integers under addition, subtraction, multiplication, division, involution, and evolution. **2.** Computation and problem solving involving real numbers and the arithmetic operations. [< Gk. *arithmētikē (tekhnē),* (the art) of counting.] —**ar´ith·met´ic** (är´ĭth-mĕt´ĭk) or **ar´ith·met´i·cal** (-ĭ-kəl) *adj.* —**ar´ith·met´i·cal·ly** *adv.* —**a·rith´me·ti´cian** (-tĭsh´ən) *n.*

arithmetic mean (är´ĭth-mĕt´ĭk) *n.* The number obtained by dividing the sum of a set of quantities by the number of quantities in the set.

-arium *suff.* A place or device containing or associated with: *planetarium.* [Lat., neuter of *-arius,* -ary.]

ark (ärk) *n.* **1.** In the Old Testament, the ship built by Noah for the Flood. **2. Ark.** The ancient Hebrew chest containing the Ten Commandments on tablets. [< Lat. *arca,* chest.]

arm¹ (ärm) *n.* **1.** An upper limb of the human body. **2.** A part similar to an arm. **3.** Authority; power: *the arm of the law.* —*idiom.* **with open arms.** In a very friendly manner. [< OE *earm.*]

arm² (ärm) *n.* **1.** A weapon. **2.** A branch of a military force. —*v.* **1.** To equip with weapons. **2.** To prepare for or as if for warfare. [< Lat. *arma.*] —**armed** *adj.*

ar·ma·da (är-mä´də, -mā´-) *n.* A fleet of warships. [Sp. < Lat. *armare,* to arm.]

ar·ma·dil·lo (är´mə-dĭl´ō) *n., pl.* **-los.** A burrowing tropical American mammal having a covering of armorlike, bony plates. [Sp., dim. of *armado,* armed.]

Ar·ma·ged·don (är´mə-gĕd´n) *n.* **1.** In the Bible, the scene of a final battle between the forces of good and evil. **2.** A decisive conflict.

ar·ma·ment (är´mə-mənt) *n.* **1.** The weapons and supplies of a military unit. **2.** Often **armaments.** All the military forces and war equipment of a country. **3.** The process of arming for war. [< Lat. *armamenta,* implements.]

ar·ma·ture (är´mə-chŏŏr´, -chər) *n.* **1.** *Elect.* **a.** The rotating part of a dynamo, consisting of copper wire wound around an iron core. **b.** The moving part of an electromagnetic device such as a relay, buzzer, or loudspeaker. **c.** A piece of soft iron connecting the poles of a magnet. **2.** A protective covering; armor. [< Lat. *armare,* to arm.]

arm·chair (ärm´châr´) *n.* A chair with sides for supporting the arms.

armed forces (ärmd) *pl.n.* The military forces of a country.

Ar·me·ni·an (är-mē´nē-ən, -mēn´yən) *n.* **1.** A native or inhabitant of Armenia. **2.** The Indo-European language of the Armenians. —**Ar·me´ni·an** *adj.*

arm·ful (ärm′fŏŏl′) *n., pl.* **-fuls.** As much as an arm can hold.

arm·hole (ärm′hōl′) *n.* An opening for the arm in a garment.

ar·mi·stice (är′mĭ-stĭs) *n.* A temporary suspension of hostilities by mutual consent; truce. [< NLat. *armistitium.*]

arm·let (ärm′lĭt) *n.* A band worn around the upper arm for ornament or identification.

ar·mor (är′mər) *n.* **1.** A protective or defensive covering. **2.** The armored vehicles of an army. [< Lat. *armare,* to arm.] —**ar′mor** *v.* —**ar′-mored** *adj.*

armor

ar·mo·ri·al (är-môr′ē-əl, -mōr′-) *adj.* Of or pertaining to heraldry or coats of arms.

ar·mo·ry (är′mə-rē) *n., pl.* **-ies.** **1.** A storehouse for military weapons. **2.** An arms factory.

arm·pit (ärm′pĭt′) *n.* The hollow under the arm at the shoulder.

arm·rest (ärm′rĕst′) *n.* A support for the arm.

arms (ärmz) *pl.n.* **1.** Weapons. **2.** Warfare. **3.** Heraldic bearings. [< Lat. *arma.*]

ar·my (är′mē) *n., pl.* **-mies.** **1.** A large body of people organized for warfare. **2.** Often **Army.** The entire military land forces of a country. **3.** A large group of people organized for a specific cause. **4.** A multitude, as of people or animals. [< Lat. *armare,* to arm.]

ar·ni·ca (är′nĭ-kə) *n.* **1.** A plant having brightyellow, rayed flowers. **2.** A tincture of dried arnica flower heads, used for sprains and bruises. [Orig. unknown.]

a·ro·ma (ə-rō′mə) *n.* A usu. pleasant characteristic odor. [< Gk. *arōma,* aromatic herb.] —**ar′o·mat′ic** (ăr′ə-măt′ĭk) *adj.*

a·rose (ə-rōz′) *v. p.t.* of **arise.**

a·round (ə-round′) *adv.* **1.** On or to all sides or in all directions. **2.** In a circle or circular motion. **3.** In or toward the opposite direction. **4.** From one place to another: *wander around.* **5.** Close at hand; nearby. —*prep.* **1.** On all sides of. **2.** So as to enclose, surround, or envelop. **3.** About the circumference of; encircling. **4.** About the central point of. **5.** In or to various places within or near. **6.** On or to the farther side of: *the house around the corner.* **7.** *Informal.* Approximately at.

a·rouse (ə-rouz′) *v.* **a·roused, a·rous·ing. 1.** To awaken from or as if from sleep. **2.** To stir up; stimulate; excite. [*a-* (intensive) + ROUSE.] —**a·rous′al** *n.*

ar·peg·gi·o (är-pĕj′ē-ō′, -pĕj′ō) *n., pl.* **-os.** The playing or singing of the notes of a chord in rapid succession rather than all at once. [Ital.]

ar·raign (ə-rān′) *v.* **1.** To summon before a court to answer to an indictment. **2.** To accuse; denounce. [< OFr. *araisnier.*] —**ar′raign′ment** *n.*

ar·range (ə-rānj′) *v.* **-ranged, -rang·ing. 1.** To put into a specific order or relation; dispose. **2.** To agree about; settle. **3.** To reset (music) for other instruments or voices. [< OFr. *arangier.*] —**ar·range′ment** *n.* —**ar·rang′er** *n.*

ar·rant (ăr′ənt) *adj.* Thoroughgoing; out-and-out. [Var. of ERRANT.]

ar·ras (ăr′əs) *n.* **1.** A tapestry. **2.** A wall hanging, esp. of tapestry. [< *Arras,* a city in France.]

ar·ray (ə-rā′) *v.* **1.** To arrange in order. **2.** To deck in finery; adorn. —*n.* **1.** An orderly arrangement, as of troops. **2.** An impressive collection. **3.** Splendid attire; finery. [< OFr. *areer.*]

ar·rears (ə-rîrz′) *pl.n.* **1.** Overdue debts. **2.** The condition of being behind in fulfilling obligations or payments. [< OFr. *arriere,* behind.] —**ar·rear′age** *n.*

ar·rest (ə-rĕst′) *v.* **1.** To stop or check. **2.** To seize and hold by legal authority. **3.** To attract and hold briefly; engage. —*n.* The act of arresting or the condition of being arrested. —*idiom.* **under arrest.** Held in legal custody. [< OFr. *arester.*] —**ar·rest′er** *n.*

ar·rest·ing (ə-rĕs′tĭng) *adj.* Capturing and holding the attention.

ar·riv·al (ə-rī′vəl) *n.* **1.** The act of arriving. **2.** One that arrives or has arrived.

ar·rive (ə-rīv′) *v.* **-rived, -riv·ing. 1.** To reach a destination. **2.** To come finally: *The day of crisis has arrived.* **3.** To achieve success or recognition. [< OFr. *ariver.*]

ar·ro·gant (ăr′ə-gənt) *adj.* Excessively and unpleasantly self-important; haughty. [< Lat. *arrogare,* to claim without right.] —**ar′ro·gance** *n.* —**ar′ro·gant·ly** *adv.*

Syns: *arrogant, disdainful, haughty, insolent, lordly, overbearing, presumptuous, proud, supercilious, superior adj.*

ar·ro·gate (ăr′ə-gāt′) *v.* **-gat·ed, -gat·ing.** To appropriate or claim without right. [Lat. *arrogare.*] —**ar′ro·ga′tion** *n.* —**ar′ro·ga′tive** *adj.* —**ar′ro·ga′tor** *n.*

ar·row (ăr′ō) *n.* **1.** A straight, thin shaft that is shot from a bow and usu. having a pointed head and flight-stabilizing feathers at the end. **2.** A symbol shaped like an arrow, used to indicate direction. [< OE *arwe.*]

ar·row·head (ăr′ō-hĕd′) *n.* The pointed striking tip of an arrow.

ar·row·root (ăr′ō-rōōt′, -rŏŏt′) *n.* **1.** A tropical American plant with roots that yield an edible starch. **2.** The starch from the arrowroot.

ar·roy·o (ə-roi′ō) *n., pl.* **-os.** A deep gully cut by an intermittent stream. [Sp.]

ar·se·nal (är′sə-nəl) *n.* **1.** A place for the storage, manufacture, or repair of arms and ammunition. **2.** A stock or supply, esp. of weapons. [< Ar. *dār-aṣ-ṣinā′ah.*]

ar·se·nic (är′sə-nĭk) *n. Symbol* **As** A highly poisonous metallic element used in insecticides, weed killers, solid-state doping agents, and various alloys. Atomic number 33; atomic weight 74.922. [< Gk. *arsenikon*, a yellow substance.] **—ar'se·nic** *adj.* **—arsen'i·cal** (-sĕn'ĭ-kəl) *adj. & n.* **—arse'ni·ous** (-sē'-nē-əs) *adj.*

ar·son (är'sən) *n.* The crime of intentionally setting fire to buildings or other property. [< Med. Lat. *arsio* < Lat. *ardēre*, to burn.] **—ar'son·ist** *n.*

art¹ (ärt) *n.* **1. a.** The activity of creating beautiful things. **b.** Works, such as paintings or poetry, resulting from such activity. **2.** A branch of artistic activity, as musical composition, using a special medium and technique. **3.** The aesthetic values of an artist as expressed in his works. **4.** Any of various disciplines, as the humanities, that do not rely exclusively on the scientific method. **5.** A craft or trade and its methods. **6.** A practical skill; knack. **7.** Cunning; contrivance. [< Lat. *ars.*]

art² (ärt; ärt *when stressed*) *v. Archaic.* 2nd person sing. present tense of **be.**

-art *suff.* Var. of **-ard.**

art de·co (dĕk'ō) *n.* An early 20th-cent. style of decorative art featuring geometric designs and bold colors. [< Fr. *Exposition Internationale des Arts Décoratifs et Industriels Moderns*, a 1925 exhibition in Paris.]

Arte·mis (är'tə-mĭs) *n. Gk. Myth.* The goddess of the hunt and the moon.

arte·ri·o·scle·ro·sis (är-tîr'ē-ō-sklə-rō'sĭs) *n.* A chronic disease in which thickening and hardening of arterial walls interferes with blood circulation. **—arte'ri·o·scle·rot'ic** (-rŏt'-ĭk) *adj.*

artery (är'tə-rē) *n., pl.* **-ies. 1.** *Anat.* Any of a branching system of muscular tubes that carry blood away from the heart. **2.** A major transportation route into which local routes flow. [< Gk. *artēria.*] **—arte'ri·al** (-tîr'ē-əl) *adj.*

arte·sian well (är-tē'zhən) *n.* A deep drilled well in which water is forced up by internal hydrostatic pressure. [Fr. *(puit) artésien*, (well) of Artois.]

art·ful (ärt'fəl) *adj.* **1.** Skillful; clever; ingenious. **2.** Deceitful; cunning; crafty. **—art'ful·ly** *adv.* **—art'ful·ness** *n.*

ar·thri·tis (är-thrī'tĭs) *n.* Inflammation of a joint or joints. **—ar·thrit'ic** (-thrĭt'ĭk) *adj.*

arthro- or **arthr-** *pref.* Joint: *arthroscopy.* [< Gk. *arthron*, joint.]

arthro·pod (är'thrə-pŏd') *n.* Any of numerous invertebrates, including insects and crustaceans, that have a segmented body and jointed limbs.

arthros·co·py (är-thrŏs'kə-pē) *n., pl.* **-pies.** The endoscopic examination of a joint, as the knee. **—ar'thro·scope'** (är'thrə-skōp') *n.*

Arthur (är'thər) *n.* Legendary king of the Britons in the 6th cent. A.D. **—Arthu'ri·an** (-thŏŏr'ē-ən) *adj.*

arti·choke (är'tĭ-chōk') *n.* **1.** A thistlelike plant having a large flower head with numerous fleshy, scalelike bracts. **2.** The unopened flower head of the artichoke, cooked and eaten as a vegetable. [< Ar. *al-kharshūf.*]

arti·cle (är'tĭ-kəl) *n.* **1.** An individual member of a class; item. **2.** A separate section of a document. **3.** A nonfictional composition that is an independent part of a publication. **4.** *Gram.* Any of a class of words, such as *a* or *the*, that are used with nouns and specify

their application. [< Lat. *articulus*, dim. of *artus*, joint.]

artic·u·lar (är-tĭk'yə-lər) *adj.* Of, pertaining to, or occurring in a joint. [< Lat. *articularis* < *articulus*, small joint.]

artic·u·late (är-tĭk'yə-lĭt) *adj.* **1.** Capable of speech. **2.** Spoken in or divided into clear and distinct words or syllables. **3.** Using or characterized by clear, expressive language. **4.** *Biol.* Jointed. **—v.** (är-tĭk'yə-lāt') **-lat·ed, -lat·ing. 1.** To utter (speech sounds). **2.** To speak distinctly and carefully. **3.** To express in words. **4.** To unite by or form a joint. [< Lat. *articulare*, to divide into joints.] **—artic'u·late·ly** *adv.* **—artic'u·late·ness** *n.* **—artic'u·la'tion** *n.* **—artic'u·la'tor** *n.* **—artic'u·la·to·ry** (-lə-tôr'ē, -tōr'ē) *adj.*

arti·fact (är'tə-făkt') *n.* An object, esp. a tool, produced by human workmanship. [Lat. *ars*, art + Lat. *factum*, something made.]

arti·fice (är'tə-fĭs) *n.* **1.** A crafty device; stratagem. **2.** Deception; trickery. **3.** Ingenuity; cleverness. [< Lat. *artificium.*]

ar·tif·i·cer (är-tĭf'ĭ-sər) *n.* **1.** A skilled worker. **2.** An inventor.

arti·fi·cial (är'tə-fĭsh'əl) *adj.* **1.** Made by man rather than occurring in nature. **2.** Made in imitation of something natural. **3.** Not genuine; pretended. [< Lat. *artificialis* < *artificium*, artifice.] **—ar'ti·fi'ci·al'i·ty** (-ē-ăl'ĭ-tē) *n.* **—ar'ti·fi'cial·ly** *adv.*

Syns: *artificial, ersatz, manmade, synthetic* **adj.**

artificial respiration *n.* A method used to restore normal breathing by rhythmically forcing air into and out of the lungs of a person whose breathing has stopped.

ar·til·lery (är-tĭl'ə-rē) *n.* **1.** Large-caliber, mounted guns, such as cannons. **2.** Troops armed with artillery. [< OFr. *atillier*, to fortify.]

arti·san (är'tĭ-zən, -sən) *n.* A manually skilled worker; craftsman. [< Ital. *artigiano* < Lat. *ars*, art.]

art·ist (är'tĭst) *n.* **1.** One who practices any of the fine arts, esp. painting, sculpture, or music. **2.** One whose work shows skill.

ar·tis·tic (är-tĭs'tĭk) *adj.* **1.** Of art or artists. **2.** Showing skill and good taste. **—ar·tis'ti·cal·ly** *adv.*

art·ist·ry (är'tĭ-strē) *n.* Artistic ability, quality, or workmanship.

art·less (ärt'lĭs) *adj.* **1.** Without cunning or deceit. **2.** Natural; simple. **3.** Lacking art; crude. **—art'less·ly** *adv.* **—art'less·ness** *n.*

arty (är'tē) *adj.* **-i·er, -i·est.** *Informal.* Ostentatiously or affectedly artistic. **—art'i·ness** *n.*

arum (âr'əm, ăr'-) *n.* A plant having small flowers on a clublike spike surrounded by a leaflike part. [< Gk. *aron.*]

-ary *suff.* Of, engaged in, or connected with: *parliamentary.* [< Lat. *-arius*, n. and adj. suffix.]

Ar·yan (âr'ē-ən, ăr'-) *n.* **1.** A member of the prehistoric people that spoke Indo-European. **2.** Indo-European or a language descended from it. **3.** In Nazi ideology, a Caucasian gentile. **—Ar'yan** *adj.*

as (ăz; əz *when unstressed*) *adv.* **1.** To the same extent or degree; equally. **2.** For instance: *large carnivores, as bears.* **—conj. 1.** To the same degree or quantity that: *as sweet as sugar.* **2.** In the same way that: *Think as I think.* **3.** At the same time that;

while. **4.** Since; because. **5.** For the reason that: *Study so as to learn.* **6.** Though: *Pretty as it is, it's worthless.* **7.** That: *I don't know as I can.* —*pron.* **1.** That; which; who: *I received the same grade as you.* **2.** A fact that: *The sun is hot, as everyone knows.* —*prep.* In the role, capacity, or function of: *acting as a mediator.* —**idiom. as is.** Just the way it is or appears. [< OE *eallswā.*]

As The symbol for the element arsenic.

as·a·fet·i·da (ăs′ə-fĕt′ĭ-də) *n.* A yellow-brown, bitter, bad-smelling plant resin formerly used in medicine. [< Med. Lat. *asafoetida.*]

as·bes·tos (ăs-bĕs′təs, ăz-) *n.* An incombustible fibrous mineral used esp. for fireproofing and electrical insulation. [< Gk. *asbestos,* inextinguishable.]

as·cend (ə-sĕnd′) *v.* **1.** To go or move upward; rise. **2.** To come to occupy: *ascended the throne.* [< Lat. *ascendere.*] —**as·cend′a·ble** or **as·cend′i·ble** *adj.*

as·cen·dan·cy (ə-sĕn′dən-sē) *n.* Also **as·cen·den·cy.** The state of being dominant.

as·cen·dant (ə-sĕn′dənt). Also **as·cen·dent.** —*adj.* **1.** Moving upward; rising. **2.** Dominant; superior. —*n.* The state of being dominant or in power.

as·cen·sion (ə-sĕn′shən) *n.* **1.** The act or process of ascending. **2. Ascension.** The bodily ascent of Christ into heaven, celebrated on the 40th day after Easter. —**as·cen′sion·al** *adj.*

as·cent (ə-sĕnt′) *n.* **1.** The act of ascending. **2.** An upward slope or incline.

as·cer·tain (ăs′ər-tān′) *v.* To discover through investigation; find out. [< OFr. *acertainer.*] —**as·cer·tain′a·ble** *adj.* —**as·cer·tain′ment** *n.*

as·cet·ic (ə-sĕt′ĭk) *n.* One who practices rigid self-denial, esp. as an act of religious devotion. [< Gk. *askētēs,* hermit.] —**as·cet′ic** *adj.* —**as·cet′i·cal·ly** *adv.* —**as·cet′i·cism** *n.*

as·cor·bic acid (ə-skôr′bĭk) *n.* A vitamin, $C_6H_8O_6$, found in citrus fruits, tomatoes, potatoes, and leafy green vegetables and used to prevent scurvy. [A-¹ + SCORB(UT)IC.]

as·cot (ăs′kŏt, -kōt′) *n.* A necktie or scarf tied so that the broad ends are laid flat upon each other. [< *Ascot,* England.]

as·cribe (ə-skrīb′) *v.* **-cribed, -crib·ing.** To attribute to a specific cause, source, or origin. [< Lat. *ascribere.*] —**as·crib′a·ble** *adj.* —**as·crip′tion** (ə-skrĭp′shən) *n.*

-ase *suff.* Enzyme: *amylase.* [< *diastase,* amylase found in germinating grains.]

a·sep·tic (ə-sĕp′tĭk, ā-) *adj.* Free from pathogenic organisms. —**a·sep′sis** *n.*

a·sex·u·al (ā-sĕk′shōō-əl) *adj.* **1.** Having no sex or sex organs; sexless. **2.** Not involving sex organs or the union of sex cells. —**a·sex′u·al′i·ty** (-ăl′ĭ-tē) *n.* —**a·sex′u·al·ly** *adv.*

as for *prep.* With regard to.

ash¹ (ăsh) *n.* **1.** The grayish-white to black, soft solid residue of combustion. **2.** Pulverized particles of matter ejected by volcanic eruption. **3. ashes.** Human remains, esp. after cremation. [< OE *asce.*]

ash² (ăsh) *n.* **1.** Any of various trees having compound leaves and strong, durable wood. **2.** The wood of the ash tree. [< OE *æsc.*]

a·shamed (ə-shāmd′) *adj.* **1.** Feeling shame or

guilt. **2.** Reluctant because of shame. [< OE *āscamian,* to feel shame.] —**a·sham′ed·ly** *adv.*

ash·en (ăsh′ən) *adj.* Resembling ashes in color; pale.

ash·lar (ăsh′lər) *n.* **1.** A squared block of building stone. **2.** Masonry made of ashlar stones. [< Lat. *axilla,* dim. of *axis,* board.]

a·shore (ə-shôr′, ə-shōr′) *adv.* Toward or on the shore.

ash·tray (ăsh′trā′) *n.* A container for tobacco ashes.

Ash Wednesday *n.* The first day of Lent.

ash·y (ăsh′ē) *adj.* **-i·er, -i·est. 1.** Of, resembling, or covered with ashes. **2.** Having the color of ashes.

A·sian (ā′zhən, ā′shən) *adj.* Pertaining to Asia or its people. —**A′sian** *n.*

A·si·at·ic (ā′zhē-ăt′ĭk, -shē-, -zē-) *adj.* Asian. —**A′si·at′ic** *n.*

a·side (ə-sīd′) *adv.* **1.** To one side. **2.** Apart. **3.** Out of one's thoughts or mind. —*n.* Words spoken by a character in a play that the other actors on stage are not supposed to hear.

aside from *prep.* Excluding; except for.

as if *conj.* In the same way that it would be if.

as·i·nine (ăs′ə-nīn′) *adj.* Stupid; silly. [Lat. *asininus < asinus,* ass.] —**as′i·nine′ly** *adv.* —**as′i·nin′i·ty** (-nĭn′ĭ-tē) *n.*

ask (ăsk, äsk) *v.* **1.** To put a question to. **2.** To inquire (about). **3.** To request. **4.** To expect or demand. **5.** To invite. [< OE *āscian.*] —**ask′er** *n.*

a·skance (ə-skăns′) *adv.* **1.** With a sidelong glance. **2.** With disapproval or distrust. [Orig. unknown.]

a·skew (ə-skyōō′) *adv. & adj.* Out of line; crooked.

a·slant (ə-slănt′) *adv. & adj.* At a slant.

a·sleep (ə-slēp′) *adj.* **1.** Sleeping. **2.** Inactive. **3.** Numb. —*adv.* Into a condition of sleep.

asp (ăsp) *n.* A venomous African snake. [< Gk. *aspis.*]

as·par·a·gus (ə-spăr′ə-gəs) *n.* A plant having scales or needlelike branchlets rather than true leaves and succulent young stalks that are cooked and eaten as a vegetable. [< Gk. *asparagos.*]

as·pect (ăs′pĕkt) *n.* **1.** An appearance; air. **2.** An element; facet. **3.** A position or side facing a given direction. [< Lat. *aspectus,* view < *aspicere,* to look at.]

as·pen (ăs′pən) *n.* Any of several poplar trees having leaves that flutter readily in the wind. [< OE *æspe.*]

as·per·i·ty (ă-spĕr′ĭ-tē) *n.* **1.** Roughness; harshness. **2.** Ill temper. [< Lat. *asper,* rough.]

as·per·sion (ə-spûr′zhən, -shən) *n.* A slanderous remark. [< Lat. *aspergere,* to scatter.]

as·phalt (ăs′fôlt′) *n.* A brownish-black solid or semisolid mixture of bitumens used in paving, roofing, and waterproofing. [< Gk. *asphaltos,* pitch.] —**as·phal′tic** (ăs-fôl′tĭk) *adj.*

as·pho·del (ăs′fə-dəl′) *n.* Any of several Mediterranean plants having clusters of white or yellow flowers. [Gk. *asphodelos.*]

---

as·phyx·i·a (ăs-fĭk′sē-ə) n. Lack of oxygen or an increase of carbon dioxide in the blood, causing unconsciousness or death. [Gk. *asphuxia*, stopping of the pulse.]

as·phyx·i·ate (ăs-fĭk′sē-āt′) v. **-at·ed, -at·ing.** To suffocate; smother. **—as·phyx′i·a′tion** n. **—as·phyx′i·a′tor** n.

as·pic (ăs′pĭk) n. A jelly made from chilled meat, fish, or vegetable juices. [Fr., asp (from the resemblance of the jelly's coloration to an asp's).]

as·pi·dis·tra (ăs′pĭ-dĭs′trə) n. A plant having long evergreen leaves and widely cultivated as a house plant. [< Gk. *aspis*, shield.]

as·pi·rate (ăs′pər-ĭt) n. **1.** The speech sound represented in English by the *h* in *hand.* **2.** A speech sound that has a puff of breath as its final element. [Lat. *aspirare*, to breathe upon.] **—as′pi·rate′** (-pə-rāt′) v.

as·pi·ra·tion (ăs′pə-rā′shən) n. **1. a.** A strong desire for high achievement. **b.** An object of this desire. **2. a.** The pronunciation of a consonant with an aspirate. **b.** An aspirate. **3.** Removal of liquids or gases by means of suction.

as·pire (ə-spīr′) v. **-pired, -pir·ing.** To have a great ambition. [< Lat. *aspirare*, to desire.] **—as·pir′er** n. **—as·pir′ing·ly** adv.

as·pi·rin (ăs′pə-rĭn, -prĭn) n. **1.** A white crystalline compound of acetylsalicylic acid, $C_9H_8O_4$, used to relieve pain and reduce fever. **2.** A tablet of aspirin. [Orig. a trademark.]

ass (ăs) n., pl. **ass·es** (ăs′ĭz). **1.** A hoofed mammal, resembling and closely related to the horses and zebras; donkey. **2.** A silly or stupid person. [< OE *assa.*]

ass

as·sail (ə-sāl′) v. To attack with violence. [< Lat. *assilire*, to jump on.] **—as·sail′a·ble** adj. **—as·sail′ant** n. **—as·sail′er** n.

as·sas·sin (ə-săs′ĭn) n. A murderer, esp. of a political figure. [< Ar. *hashshāshīn*, user of hashish.]

as·sas·si·nate (ə-săs′ə-nāt′) v. **-nat·ed, -nat·ing.** To murder for political reasons. **—as·sas′si·na′tion** n.

as·sault (ə-sôlt′) n. **1.** A violent physical or verbal attack. **2.** An unlawful attempt or threat to injure another physically. [< Lat. *assultus*, p.p. of *assilire*, to jump on.] **—as·sault′** v. **—as·sault′er** n.

assault and battery n. *Law.* An executed threat to use force upon another.

as·say (ăs′ā′, ă-sā′) n. Qualitative or quantitative analysis of a substance, esp. of an ore or drug. **—v.** (ă-sā′, ăs′ā′). **1.** To subject to or undergo an assay. **2.** To evaluate; assess. **3.** To attempt. [< OFr. *assai*, trial.] **—as·say′er** n.

as·sem·blage (ə-sĕm′blĭj) n. **1.** The act or process of assembling. **2.** A collection of persons or things. **3.** A fitting together of parts, as of a machine. **4.** A work of art consisting of an arrangement of miscellaneous objects, such as scraps of metal, cloth, and string.

as·sem·ble (ə-sĕm′bəl) v. **-bled, -bling. 1.** To bring or gather together into a group. **2.** To fit or join together the parts of. [< OFr. *assembler.*] **—as·sem′bler** n.

as·sem·bly (ə-sĕm′blē) n., pl. **-blies. 1.** The act of assembling or the state of being assembled. **2.** A group of persons gathered together for a common purpose. **3. Assembly.** The lower house of legislature. **4. a.** The putting together of parts to make a completed product. **b.** A set of parts so assembled: *the steering assembly of a truck.* **5.** The signal calling troops to assemble.

assembly line n. A line of factory workers and equipment on which the work passes consecutively from operation to operation until completed.

as·sent (ə-sĕnt′) v. To express agreement; concur. [< Lat. *assentari.*] **—as·sent′** n. **—as·sent′er** or **as·sen′tor** n.

as·sert (ə-sûrt′) v. **1.** To state positively; affirm. **2.** To defend or maintain. [Lat. *asserere.*] **—as·sert′a·ble** or **as·sert′i·ble** adj. **—as·sert′er** or **as·ser′tor** n. **—as·ser′tive** adj. **—as·ser′tive·ly** adv. **—as·ser′tive·ness** n.

Syns: **assert, affirm, declare, hold, maintain** v.

as·ser·tion (ə-sûr′shən) n. A positive declaration.

as·sess (ə-sĕs′) v. **1.** To evaluate, esp. for taxation. **2.** To set the amount of (e.g. a tax). **3.** To charge with a tax, fine, etc. [< Lat. *assidere*, to sit beside (as an assistant judge).] **—as·sess′a·ble** adj. **—as·sess′ment** n. **—as·ses′sor** n.

as·set (ăs′ĕt) n. **1.** A useful or valuable possession. **2. assets.** All the property, such as cash, inventory, or claims against others, that is owned by a person or a business and may be applied to cover liabilities. [< OFr. *asez*, enough.]

as·sev·er·ate (ə-sĕv′ə-rāt′) v. **-at·ed, -at·ing.** To declare positively. [Lat. *asseverare.*] **—as·sev′er·a′tion** n.

as·sid·u·ous (ə-sĭj′ō͞o-əs) adj. Constant in application or attention; diligent. [Lat. *assiduus* < *assidēre*, to attend to.] **—as′si·du′i·ty** (ăs′ĭ-dō͞o′ĭ-tē, -dyō͞o′-) n. **—as·sid′u·ous·ly** adv. **—as·sid′u·ous·ness** n.

as·sign (ə-sīn′) v. **1.** To specify; designate: *assign a day for the examination.* **2.** To select for a duty; appoint. **3.** To give out as a task; allot. **4.** To ascribe; attribute. **5.** *Law.* To transfer (e.g. property) to another. [< Lat. *assignare.*] **—as·sign′a·bil′i·ty** n. **—as·sign′a·ble** adj. **—as·sign′er** n.

as·sig·na·tion (ăs′ĭg-nā′shən) n. An appointment for a meeting between lovers.

as·sign·ment (ə-sīn′mənt) n. **1.** The act of assigning. **2.** Something assigned.

as·sim·i·late (ə-sĭm′ə-lāt′) v. **-lat·ed, -lat·ing.**
1. To take in, digest, and transform (food) into living tissue. 2. To take in; understand. 3. To make or become similar. [< Lat. *assimilare*, to make similar to.] **—as·sim′i·la·ble** *adj.* **—as·sim′i·la′tion** *n.* **—as·sim′i·la′tor** *n.*

As·sin·i·boin (ə-sĭn′ə-boin′) *n., pl.* **-boin** or **-boins.** 1. A tribe of North American Indians of northeastern Montana and adjacent regions of Canada. 2. A member of the Assiniboin. 3. The Siouan language of the Assiniboin. **—As·sin′i·boin′** *adj.*

as·sist (ə-sĭst′) v. To aid; help. **—n.** 1. An act of giving aid. 2. A maneuver, as with a ball or puck, made by a team player that enables a teammate to put out or score against an opponent. [< Lat. *assistere*.] **—as·sis′tance** *n.*

as·sis·tant (ə-sĭs′tənt) *n.* One who assists; helper.

as·size (ə-sīz′) *n.* 1. A judicial inquest. 2. **assizes.** One of the periodic court sessions held in the counties of England and Wales. [< OFr. *asseior*, to seat.]

as·so·ci·ate (ə-sō′shē-āt′, -sē-) v. **-at·ed, -at·ing.** 1. To connect or join in a relationship. 2. To connect in the mind or imagination. **—n.** (ə-sō′shē-ĭt, -āt′, -sē-). 1. A partner; colleague. 2. A companion; comrade. [< Lat. *associare*, to join to.] **—as·so′ci·ate** (ə-sō′-shē-ĭt, -āt′, -sē-) *adj.*

as·so·ci·a·tion (ə-sō′sē-ā′shən, -shē-) *n.* 1. The act of associating. 2. An organized body of people; society.

as·so·ci·a·tive (ə-sō′shē-ā′tĭv, -sē-, -shə-tĭv) *adj.* Of or characterized by association.

as·so·nance (ăs′ə-nəns) *n.* Correspondence or resemblance of repeated vowel sounds, esp. in verse. [< Lat. *assonare*, to respond to.]

as·sort (ə-sôrt′) v. To separate into groups according to kind; classify. [< OFr. *assorter*.] **—as·sort′er** *n.*

as·sort·ed (ə-sôr′tĭd) *adj.* Of different kinds; various.

as·sort·ment (ə-sôrt′mənt) *n.* A collection of various things.

as·suage (ə-swāj′) v. **-suaged, -suag·ing.** 1. To make less severe; ease. 2. To satisfy. [< OFr. *assouagier*.]

as·sume (ə-sōōm′) v. **-sumed, -sum·ing.** 1. To take upon oneself. 2. To take on; adopt. 3. To feign; pretend. 4. To take for granted; suppose. [< Lat. *assumere*, to adopt.] **—as·sum′a·ble** *adj.* **—as·sum′a·bly** *adv.* **—as·sum′ed·ly** (ə-sōō′mĭd-lē) *adv.* **—as·sum′er** *n.*

as·sump·tion (ə-sŭmp′shən) *n.* 1. The act of assuming. 2. A statement accepted as true without proof. 3. **Assumption.** The bodily taking up of the Virgin Mary into heaven after her death, celebrated on Aug. 15.

as·sur·ance (ə-shŏŏr′əns) *n.* 1. The act of assuring. 2. A guarantee; pledge. 3. a. Freedom from doubt; certainty. b. Self-confidence. 4. Boldness; audacity.

as·sure (ə-shŏŏr′) v. **-sured, -sur·ing.** 1. To declare confidently. 2. To cause to feel sure. 3. To make certain; ensure. [< Med. Lat. *assecurare*, to make sure.] **—as·sur′a·ble** *adj.* **—as·sur′er** *n.*

Usage: Assure, ensure, and insure all mean "to make secure or certain." Only *assure,* however, is used with reference to a person in the sense of "to set the mind at rest."

as·ta·tine (ăs′tə-tēn′, -tĭn) *n.* Symbol **At** A highly unstable radioactive element used in medicine as a radioactive tracer. Atomic number 85. [< Gk. *astatos*, unstable.]

as·ter (ăs′tər) *n.* Any of various plants having rayed, daisylike flowers that range in color from white to purplish or pink. [< Gk. *astēr*, star.]

as·ter·isk (ăs′tə-rĭsk′) *n.* A star-shaped character (*) used in printing to indicate an omission or a reference to a footnote. [< Gk. *asteriskos*, dim. of *astēr*, star.]

a·stern (ə-stûrn′) *adv. & adj.* 1. Behind a vessel. 2. At or toward the rear of a vessel.

as·ter·oid (ăs′tə-roid′) *n.* Any of numerous small celestial bodies that orbit the sun, chiefly in the region between Mars and Jupiter. [Gk. *astēr*, star + -OID.] **—as′ter·oid′al** *adj.*

asth·ma (ăz′mə, ăs′-) *n.* A respiratory disease, often arising from allergies, characterized by difficulty in breathing, tightness of the chest, and coughing. [< Gk.] **—asth·mat′ic** *n. & adj.* **—asth·mat′i·cal·ly** *adv.*

as though *conj.* As if.

a·stig·ma·tism (ə-stĭg′mə-tĭz′əm) *n.* A refractive defect of a lens, esp. of the lens of the eye, that prevents focusing of sharp, distinct images. [A-¹ + Gk. *stigma*, mark.] **—as′tig·mat′ic** (ăs′tĭg-măt′ĭk) *adj.*

a·stir (ə-stûr′) *adj.* Moving about. [Sc. *asteer*.]

as to *prep.* With regard to.

as·ton·ish (ə-stŏn′ĭsh) v. To fill with sudden wonder or amazement. [< OFr. *estoner*.] **—as·ton′ish·ing·ly** *adv.* **—as·ton′ish·ment** *n.*

as·tound (ə-stound′) v. To strike with confusion and wonder. [< obs. *astony*, to amaze.]

a·strad·dle (ə-străd′l) *adv. & prep.* Astride.

as·tra·khan (ăs′trə-kăn′, -kən) *n.* A curly fur made from the skins of young lambs from the region of Astrakhan in the USSR.

as·tral (ăs′trəl) *adj.* Of or resembling the stars. [< Lat. *astrum*, star.]

a·stray (ə-strā′) *adv.* 1. Away from the correct direction. 2. Into evil or wrong ways. [< OFr. *estraier*, to stray.]

a·stride (ə-strīd′) *prep.* With a leg on each side of. **—a·stride′** *adv.*

as·trin·gent (ə-strĭn′jənt) *adj.* 1. Tending to draw together or tighten living tissue. 2. Harsh; severe. **—n.** An astringent substance or drug. [< Lat. *astringere*, to bind together.] **—as·trin′gen·cy** (-jən-sē) *n.* **—as·trin′gent·ly** *adv.*

astro– *pref.* 1. Star: *astrophysics*. 2. Outer space: *astronaut*. [< Gk. *astron*, star.]

as·tro·labe (ăs′trə-lāb′) *n.* An instrument used to determine the altitude of a celestial body. [< Gk. (*organon*) *astrolabon*, (instrument) for taking the stars.]

as·trol·o·gy (ə-strŏl′ə-jē) *n.* The study of the positions and aspects of heavenly bodies with a view to predicting their influence on human affairs. **—as·trol′o·ger** *n.* **—as·tro·log′ic** (ăs′trə-lŏj′ĭk) or **as′tro·log′i·cal** *adj.* **—as′tro·log′i·cal·ly** *adv.*

---

as·tro·naut (ăs'trə-nôt') *n.* A person who travels in a spacecraft, esp. as a crew member. [ASTRO- + Gk. *nautēs,* sailor.]

as·tro·nau·tics (ăs'trə-nô'tĭks) *n. (used with sing. verb).* The science and technology of space flight. —**as·tro·nau'tic** or **as·tro·nau'ti·cal** *adj.* —**as·tro·nau'ti·cal·ly** *adv.*

as·tro·nom·i·cal (ăs'trə-nŏm'ĭ-kəl) or **as·tro·nom·ic** (-nŏm'ĭk) *adj.* 1. Of or pertaining to astronomy. 2. Inconceivably large. —**as·tro·nom'i·cal·ly** *adv.*

astronomical unit *n.* A unit of distance equal to the average distance between the earth and the sun, about 150 kilometers or 93 million miles.

as·tron·o·my (ə-strŏn'ə-mē) *n.* The scientific study of the positions, distribution, motion, and composition of celestial bodies. —**as·tron'o·mer** *n.*

as·tro·phys·ics (ăs'trō-fĭz'ĭks) *n. (used with a sing. verb).* The science that studies the physical and chemical nature of celestial bodies. —**as·tro·phys'i·cal** *adj.* —**as·tro·phys'i·cist** (-fĭz'ĭ-sĭst) *n.*

as·tute (ə-stōōt', ə-styōōt') *adj.* Keen in judgment; shrewd. [Lat. *astutus < astus,* craft.] —**as·tute'ly** *adv.* —**as·tute'ness** *n.*

a·sun·der (ə-sŭn'dər) *adv.* 1. Into separate parts or groups. 2. Apart in position or direction. [< OE *onsundran.*]

a·sy·lum (ə-sī'ləm) *n.* 1. An institution for the care of those who are ill or in need. 2. A place of safety; refuge. 3. Protection granted by a government to a political fugitive from another country. [< Gk. *asulon,* sanctuary.]

a·sym·met·ric (ā'sĭ-mĕt'rĭk) or **a·sym·met·ri·cal** (-rĭ-kəl) *adj.* Not symmetrical. —**a·sym·met'ri·cal·ly** *adv.* —**a·sym'me·try** *n.*

as·ymp·tote (ăs'ĭm-tōt', -ĭmp-) *n.* A straight line that is approached but never met by a moving point on a curve as the point moves an infinite distance from the origin. [< Gk. *asumptōtos,* not touching.] —**as'ymp·tot'ic** (-tŏt'ĭk) or **as'ymp·tot'i·cal** *adj.*

at¹ (ăt; *at when unstressed*) *prep.* 1. Used to indicate position, location, or state: *at home; at rest.* 2. Used to indicate a direction or goal: *look at us.* 3. Used to indicate location in time: *at noon.* 4. Used to indicate manner, means, or cause: *getting there at top speed.* [< OE *æt.*]

at² (ăt) *n., pl.* **at.** See table at **currency.** [Thai.]

At The symbol for the element astatine.

at all *adv.* In any situation.

at·a·vism (ăt'ə-vĭz'əm) *n.* The reappearance of a characteristic in an organism after several generations of absence. [< Lat. *atavus,* ancestor.] —**at·a·vis'tic** *adj.* —**at·a·vis'ti·cal·ly** *adv.*

-ate¹ *suff.* 1. a. Having: *nervate.* b. Characterized by: *Latinate.* c. Resembling: *lyrate.* 2. a. One that is characterized by: *laminate.* b. Rank; office: *rabbinate.* 3. To act upon in a specified manner: *acidulate.* [< Lat. *-atus,* p.p. suffix.]

-ate² *suff.* 1. A derivative of a specified chemical compound or element: *aluminate.* 2. A salt or ester of a specified acid: *acetate.* [NLat. *-atum <* Lat. *atus,* p.p. suffix.]

at·el·ier (ăt'l-yā') *n.* 1. A workshop. 2. An artist's studio. [< OFr. *astelier.*]

Ath·a·pas·can (ăth'ə-păs'kən) *n.* Also **Ath·a·bas·can** (-băs'-). 1. A group of related North American Indian languages including Navaho and Apache. 2. A member of an Athapascan-speaking tribe.

a·the·ism (ā'thē-ĭz'əm) *n.* Disbelief in the existence of God. [< Gk. *atheos,* godless.] —**a'the·ist** *n.* —**a'the·is'tic** *adj.*

A·the·na (ə-thē'nə) *n.* Gk. *Myth.* The goddess of wisdom and the arts.

ath·e·nae·um (ăth'ə-nē'əm) *n.* Also **ath·e·ne·um.** 1. An institution for the promotion of learning. 2. A library. [LLat. *Athenaeum,* a Roman school < Gk. *Athēnaion,* the temple of Athena at Athens.]

a·thirst (ə-thûrst') *adj.* Strongly desirous; eager.

ath·lete (ăth'lēt') *n.* 1. One who takes part in competitive sports. 2. One who possesses natural aptitudes for physical exercises and sport. [< Gk. *athlētēs < athlein,* to compete.]

athlete's foot (ăth'lēts') *n.* A contagious skin infection caused by parasitic fungi, usu. affecting the feet and causing itching, blisters, cracking, and scaling.

ath·let·ic (ăth-lĕt'ĭk) *adj.* 1. Of, pertaining to, or for athletics or athletes. 2. Physically strong; muscular. —**ath·let'i·cal·ly** *adv.*

ath·let·ics (ăth-lĕt'ĭks) *n. (used with a pl. verb).* Athletic activities.

athletic supporter *n.* An elastic support for the male genitals, worn during sports or other strenuous activity.

a·thwart (ə-thwôrt') *adv.* From side to side; crosswise. —*prep.* 1. From one side to the other of; across. 2. Contrary to.

a·tilt (ə-tĭlt') *adj. & adv.* In a tilted position.

-ation *suff.* 1. Action or process of: *negotiation.* 2. State, condition, or quality of: *moderation.* 3. Result or product of: *civilization.* [< Lat. *-atio,* n. suffix.]

-ative *suff.* Relation, nature, or tendency: *formative.* [< Lat. *-ativus < -atus,* -ate.]

At·las (ăt'ləs) *n.* 1. Gk. *Myth.* A Titan condemned to support the heavens upon his shoulders. 2. **atlas.** A book or bound collection of maps.

at·mos·phere (ăt'mə-sfîr') *n.* 1. The gaseous mass or envelope surrounding a celestial body in space, esp. the earth. 2. Surroundings; environment. 3. *Physics.* A unit of pressure equal to 1.01325×10^5 newtons per square meter. [Gk. *atmos,* vapor + Lat. *sphaera,* sphere.] —**at'mos·pher'ic** (-sfĕr'ĭk, -sfîr'-) *adj.* —**at'mos·pher'i·cal·ly** *adv.*

at·mos·pher·ics (ăt'mə-sfĕr'ĭks, -sfîr'-) *n. (used with a sing. verb).* Radio interference produced by electromagnetic radiation from natural phenomena.

at·oll (ăt'ôl', -ōl', ă'tôl', ā'tôl') *n.* A ringlike coral island that encloses a lagoon. [Malayalam *atoḷu,* reef.]

at·om (ăt'əm) *n.* 1. The smallest particle. 2. *Physics & Chem.* A unit of matter, the smallest unit of an element, consisting of a dense, positively charged nucleus surrounded by a system of electrons, characteristically remaining undivided in chemical reactions except for limited removal, transfer, or exchange of certain electrons. [< Gk. *atomos,* indivisible.]

a·tom·ic (ə-tŏm'ĭk) *adj.* 1. Of or relating to an atom. 2. Of or employing nuclear energy. 3. Very small; infinitesimal. —**a·tom'i·cal·ly** *adv.*

atomic bomb *n.* An explosive weapon of great destructive power derived from the rapid release of energy in the fission of heavy atomic nuclei.

atomic bomb

atomic energy *n.* The energy released from an atomic nucleus in fission or fusion.

atomic number *n.* The number of protons in an atomic nucleus.

atomic weight *n.* The average weight of an atom of an element, usu. expressed in relation to the isotope of carbon taken to have a standard weight of 12.

at·om·ize (ăt'ə-mīz') *v.* **-ized, -iz·ing.** To reduce or separate into fine or minute particles. —**at'om·i·za'tion** *n.*

at·om·iz·er (ăt'ə-mī'zər) *n.* A device for producing a fine spray of a liquid.

atom smasher *n. Physics.* An accelerator.

a·ton·al (ā-tō'nəl) *adj. Mus.* Lacking a traditional key or tonality. —**a'to·nal'i·ty** (ā'tō-năl'ĭ-tē) *n.* —**a·ton'al·ly** *adv.*

at once *adv.* **1.** At one time; simultaneously. **2.** Immediately.

a·tone (ə-tōn') *v.* **a·toned, a·ton·ing.** To make amends (for). [< AT ONE.] —**a·ton'er** *n.*

a·tone·ment (ə-tōn'mənt) *n.* **1.** Reparation made for an injury or wrong. **2. Atonement.** The reconciliation of God and man brought about by the life and death of Christ.

a·top (ə-tŏp') *prep.* On top of.

-ator *suff.* One that acts in a specified manner: *radiator.* [< Lat.]

-atory *suff.* **1. a.** Of or relating to: *perspiratory.* **b.** Tending to: *amendatory.* **2.** One that is connected with: *reformatory.* [< Lat. *-atorius.*]

ATP (ā'tē-pē') *n.* An adenosine-derived nucleotide, $C_{10}H_{16}N_5O_{13}P_3$, that supplies energy to cells. [A(DENOSINE) T(RI)P(HOSPHATE).]

a·tri·um (ā'trē-əm) *n., pl.* **a·tri·a** (ā'trē-ə) or **-ums. 1.** An open central court, esp. in an ancient Roman house. **2.** A bodily cavity or chamber, as in the heart. [Lat.]

a·tro·cious (ə-trō'shəs) *adj.* **1.** Extremely evil, savage, or cruel. **2.** Exceptionally bad; abominable. [< Lat. *atrox,* horrible.] —**a·tro'cious·ly** *adv.* —**a·tro'cious·ness** *n.*

a·troc·i·ty (ə-trŏs'ĭ-tē) *n., pl.* **-ties. 1.** Atrocious condition or state. **2.** An atrocious action, situation, or object.

at·ro·phy (ăt'rə-fē) *n., pl.* **-phies.** *Pathol.* The emaciation or wasting away of tissues, organs, or the entire body. —*v.* **-phied, -phy·ing.** To waste or cause to waste away; wither. [< Gk. *atrophos,* ill-nourished.] —**a·tro'phic** (ă-trō'fĭk) *adj.*

at·ro·pine (ăt'rə-pēn', -pĭn) *n.* Also **at·ro·pin** (-pĭn). A poisonous, bitter, crystalline alkaloid, $C_{17}H_{23}NO_3$, obtained from belladonna and used to dilate the pupil of the eye. [G. *Atropin,* ult. < Gk. *atropos,* unchangeable.]

at·tach (ə-tăch') *v.* **1.** To fasten; connect; join. **2.** To bind by ties of affection or loyalty. **3.** To seize by legal writ. **4.** To become fastened. [< OFr. *attacher.*] —**at·tach'a·ble** *adj.* —**at·tach'er** *n.*

    Syns: **attach, affix, clip, connect, couple, fasten, fix, secure** *v.*

at·ta·ché (ăt'ə-shā', ă-tă'shā') *n.* A person assigned to a diplomatic mission in a particular capacity. [Fr.]

attaché case *n.* A briefcase resembling a small suitcase, with hinges and flat sides.

at·tach·ment (ə-tăch'mənt) *n.* **1.** The act of attaching or the condition of being attached. **2.** Something that attaches one thing to another. **3.** A bond of affection or loyalty. **4.** A supplementary part, as of a machine or appliance. **5.** The legal seizure of a person or property.

at·tack (ə-tăk') *v.* **1.** To set upon with violent force. **2.** To criticize strongly. **3.** To start work on with vigor. —*n.* **1.** The act of attacking; assault. **2.** Seizure by a disease. [< OItal. *attaccare.*] —**at·tack'er** *n.*

    Syns: **attack, assail, assault, beset, strike** *v.*

at·tain (ə-tān') *v.* **1.** To accomplish; achieve. **2.** To arrive at. [< Lat. *attingere.*] —**at·tain'a·bil'i·ty** or **at·tain'a·ble·ness** *n.* —**at·tain'a·ble** *adj.*

at·tain·der (ə-tān'dər) *n.* The loss of all civil rights by a person sentenced for a serious crime. [< OFr. *ataindre,* to convict.]

at·tain·ment (ə-tān'mənt) *n.* **1.** The act of attaining. **2.** An acquired skill or ability; accomplishment.

at·taint (ə-tānt') *v.* To condemn by a sentence of attainder. [< OFr. *ataindre,* to convict.]

at·tar (ăt'ər) *n.* A fragrant oil obtained from flower petals. [Pers. *'aṭir,* perfumed.]

at·tempt (ə-tĕmpt') *v.* To make an effort to do; try. —*n.* **1.** An effort. **2.** An attack; assault. [< Lat. *attemptare.*]

at·tend (ə-tĕnd') *v.* **1.** To be present (at). **2.** To accompany. **3.** To take care of. **4.** To listen to; heed. **5.** To apply oneself. [< Lat. *attendere,* to heed.]

at·ten·dance (ə-tĕn'dəns) *n.* **1.** The act of attending. **2.** The number of persons present.

at·ten·dant (ə-tĕn'dənt) *n.* **1.** One who attends or waits upon another. **2.** One who is present. **3.** An accompanying circumstance; consequence. —*adj.* Accompanying or consequent: *attendant circumstances.*

at·ten·tion (ə-tĕn'shən) *n.* **1.** Concentration of the mental powers upon an object. **2.** Observant consideration; notice. **3.** Consideration or courtesy. **4. attentions.** Acts of courtesy or consideration. **5.** The erect posture assumed by a soldier on command. —**at·ten'tive** adj. —**at·ten'tive·ly** adv. —**at·ten'tive·ness** n.

at·ten·u·ate (ə-tĕn'yōō-āt') v. -**ated,** -**ating.** 1. To make or become slender, fine, or small. 2. To weaken. 3. To lessen in density; dilute or rarefy (a liquid or gas). [Lat. *attenuare.*] —**at·ten'u·a'tion** n.

at·test (ə-tĕst') v. 1. To affirm to be correct, true, or genuine, esp. by affixing one's signature as witness. 2. To supply evidence of. 3. To bear witness. [< Lat. *attestari.*] —**at'·tes·ta'tion** (ăt'ĕs-tā'shən, ăt'ə-stā'-) n.

at·tic (ăt'ĭk) n. A story, room, or space directly below the roof of a house. [< *Attic story,* a decorative structure ·over an order in a classical style.]

At·tic (ăt'ĭk) adj. 1. Of, pertaining to, or characteristic of ancient Athens or the Athenians. 2. Often **attic.** Characterized by classical purity and simplicity.

at·tire (ə-tīr') v. -**tired,** -**tiring.** To dress; clothe. —n. Clothing; array. [< OFr. *atirier,* to put in order.]

at·ti·tude (ăt'ĭ-tōōd', -tyōōd') n. 1. A position of the body or manner of carrying oneself, indicative of a mood or condition. 2. A state of mind or feeling with regard to a person or thing. 3. The orientation of an aircraft's axes relative to a reference line or plane, as the horizon. [< LLat. *aptitudo,* fitness.]

at·tor·ney (ə-tûr'nē) n., pl. -**neys.** A person legally appointed or empowered to act for another, esp. a lawyer. [< OFr. *atorner,* to appoint.]

attorney general n., pl. **attorneys general.** The chief law officer and legal counsel of the government of a state or the United States.

at·tract (ə-trăkt') v. 1. To cause to draw near or adhere. 2. To draw or direct to oneself by some quality or action. 3. To allure or be alluring. [< Lat. *attrahere.*] —**at·tract'a·ble** adj. —**at·trac'tor** or **at·tract'er** n.

  Syns: *attract, allure, appeal, draw, lure, magnetize, pull* v.

at·trac·tion (ə-trăk'shən) n. 1. The act or power of attracting. 2. A feature, characteristic, or factor that attracts. 3. A public spectacle or entertainment.

at·trac·tive (ə-trăk'tĭv) adj. Capable of attracting. 2. Appealing; charming. —**at·trac'·tive·ly** adv. —**at·trac'tive·ness** n.

at·trib·ute (ə-trĭb'yōōt) v. -**uted,** -**uting.** To regard or assign as belonging to or resulting from someone or something. —n. (ăt'rə-byōōt'). 1. A distinctive feature of or object associated with a person or thing. 2. *Gram.* An adjective or a phrase used as an adjective. [Lat. *attribuere.*] —**at·trib'ut·a·ble** adj. —**at·trib'ut·er** or **at·trib'u·tor** n. —**at'tri·bu'tion** (ăt'rə-byōō'shən) n.

at·trib·u·tive (ə-trĭb'yə-tĭv) n. *Gram.* A word or word group, such as an adjective, that is placed adjacent to the noun it modifies without a linking verb. —adj. 1. *Gram.* Of or functioning as an attribute. 2. Of or having the nature of an attribute. —**at·trib'u·tive·ly** adv.

at·tri·tion (ə-trĭsh'ən) n. 1. A wearing away or rubbing down by friction. 2. A gradual diminution in number or strength due to constant stress: *a war of attrition.* 3. A gradual, natural reduction in membership or personnel, as through retirement, resignation, or death. [< Lat. *atterere,* to rub against.]

at·tune (ə-tōōn', ə-tyōōn') v. -**tuned,** -**tuning.** 1. To tune. 2. To bring into harmony.

a·typ·i·cal (ā-tĭp'ĭ-kəl) adj. Not typical; abnormal. —**a·typ'i·cal·ly** adv.

Au The symbol for the element gold. [Lat. *aurum.*]

au·burn (ô'bərn) n. A reddish brown. [< Med. Lat. *alburnus,* whitish.] —**au'burn** adj.

au cou·rant (ō' kōō-räN') adj. Up-to-date. [Fr.]

auc·tion (ôk'shən) n. A public sale in which items are sold to the highest bidder. —v. To sell at or by an auction. [Lat. *auctio.*] —**auc'·tion·eer'** (-shə-nîr') n.

au·da·cious (ô-dā'shəs) adj. 1. Fearlessly daring; bold. 2. Arrogantly insolent; impudent. [< Lat. *audax,* bold.] —**au·da'cious·ly** adv. —**au·dac'i·ty** (ô-dăs'ĭ-tē) n.

au·di·ble (ô'də-bəl) adj. Capable of being heard. [< Lat. *audire,* to hear.] —**au'di·bil'i·ty** n. —**au'di·bly** adv.

au·di·ence (ô'dē-əns) n. 1. A gathering of spectators or listeners. 2. All those reached by a book, radio broadcast, or television program. 3. A formal hearing or conference. 4. An opportunity to be heard. [< Lat. *audire,* to hear.]

au·di·o (ô'dē-ō') adj. Of or pertaining to sound or to the reproduction of sound. —n. 1. The audio part of television equipment. 2. Audio broadcasting or reception. 3. Audible sound. [< AUDIO-.]

audio- pref. 1. Hearing: *audiology.* 2. Sound: *audiophile.* [< Lat. *audire,* to hear.]

audio frequency n. A range of frequencies, usu. from 15 cycles per second to 20,000 cycles per second, characteristic of signals audible to the normal human ear.

au·di·ol·o·gy (ô'dē-ŏl'ə-jē) n., pl. -**gies.** The science of hearing defects and their treatment. —**au'di·o·log'i·cal** (-ə-lŏj'ĭ-kəl) adj. —**au'di·ol'o·gist** n.

au·di·o·phile (ô'dē-ə-fīl') n. One with an ardent interest in high-fidelity sound reproduction.

au·di·o·vis·u·al (ô'dē-ō-vĭzh'ōō-əl) adj. Of or involving both hearing and sight.

au·di·o·vis·u·als (ô'dē-ō-vĭzh'ōō-əlz) pl.n. Educational materials that present information in audible and visible form.

au·dit (ô'dĭt) n. A formal examination or verification of financial records. —v. 1. To make a formal audit of. 2. To attend (a college course) without receiving academic credit. [< Lat. *auditus,* a hearing.]

au·di·tion (ô-dĭsh'ən) n. A hearing, esp. a trial performance of a performer. —v. To give or be tested in an audition. [< Lat. *audire,* to hear.]

au·di·tor (ô'dĭ-tər) n. 1. A listener. 2. One who audits.

au·di·to·ri·um (ô'dĭ-tôr'ē-əm, -tōr'-) n. 1. A room to accommodate an audience. 2. A building for public gatherings or entertainments.

au·di·to·ry (ô'dĭ-tôr'ē, -tōr'ē) adj. Pertaining to the sense, the organs, or the experience of hearing.

auf Wie·der·seh·en (ouf vē'dər-zā'ən) interj. Farewell. [G.]

au·ger (ô'gər) n. A tool for boring. [< OE *nafogār.*]

aught (ôt) n. A cipher; zero. [< *a naught.*]

aug·ment (ôg-měnt′) v. To make or become greater; enlarge; increase. [< LLat. *augmentare.*] —**aug′men·ta′tion** n.

au gra·tin (ō grät′n, grăt′n) adj. Covered with bread crumbs and often grated cheese and browned. [Fr.]

au·gur (ô′gər) n. A seer; soothsayer. —v. 1. To prognosticate; foretell. 2. To serve as an omen of; betoken. [Lat.]

au·gu·ry (ô′gyə-rē) n., pl. **-ries.** 1. The practice of divination. 2. An omen.

au·gust (ô-gŭst′) adj. Inspiring awe or reverence; majestic. [Lat. *augustus,* venerable.] —**au·gust′ly** adv.

Au·gust (ô′gəst) n. The 8th month of the year, having 31 days. See table at **calendar.** [< Lat. *(mensis) Augustus,* (month) of Augustus.]

auk (ôk) n. A chunky, short-winged sea bird of northern regions. [< ON *álka.*]

auld lang syne (ōld′ lăng zīn′, sīn′) n. The good old days long past. [Sc., old long since.]

aunt (ănt, änt) n. 1. The sister of one's father or mother. 2. The wife of one's uncle. [< Lat. *amita,* paternal aunt.]

au·ra (ôr′ə) n. 1. An invisible breath or emanation. 2. A distinctive quality that characterizes a person or thing. [< Gk., breeze.]

au·ral (ôr′əl) adj. Of, pertaining to, or received through the ear. [< Lat. *auris,* ear.]

au·re·ole (ôr′ē-ōl′) n. Also **au·re·o·la** (ô-rē′ə-lə). A halo. [< Lat. *aureolus,* golden.]

au re·voir (ō′ rə-vwär′) interj. Good-by. [Fr.]

au·ri·cle (ôr′ĭ-kəl) n. 1. a. The e...ernal part of the ear. b. An atrium of the heart. 2. An earlike part or appendage. [Lat. *auricula* < *auris,* ear.]

au·ric·u·lar (ô-rĭk′yə-lər) adj. 1. Aural. 2. Perceived by or spoken into the ear. 3. Having the shape of an ear. 4. Of or pertaining to an atrium of the heart.

au·rif·er·ous (ô-rĭf′ər-əs) adj. Gold-bearing: *auriferous rocks.* [< Lat. *aurifer.*]

Au·ro·ra (ô-rôr′ə, ô-rōr′ə, ə-) n. 1. *Rom. Myth.* The goddess of the dawn. 2. **aurora.** High-altitude, many-colored, flashing luminosity visible in the night skies of polar and sometimes temperate zones, thought to result from electrically charged particles. —**au·ro′ral** adj.

aurora aus·tra·lis (ô-strä′lĭs) n. The aurora of the Southern Hemisphere; southern lights. [NLat., southern dawn.]

aurora bo·re·al·is (bôr′ē-ăl′ĭs, bōr′-) n. The aurora of the Northern Hemisphere; northern lights. [NLat., northern dawn.]

aus·cul·ta·tion (ô′skəl-tā′shən) n. Diagnostic monitoring of the sounds made by internal bodily organs. [< Lat. *auscultare,* to listen to.]

aus·pice (ô′spĭs) n., pl. **aus·pic·es** (ô′spĭ-sēz′, -səz). 1. **auspices.** Protection or support; patronage. 2. A portent or omen. [Lat. *auspicium,* bird divination.]

aus·pi·cious (ô-spĭsh′əs) adj. 1. Favorable; propitious. 2. Successful; prosperous. —**aus·pi′cious·ly** adv. —**aus·pi′cious·ness** n.

aus·tere (ô-stîr′) adj. 1. Severe; stern; somber. 2. Severely simple; ascetic: *an austere lifestyle.* 3. Without adornment; bare: *austere living quarters.* [< Lat. *austērus,* harsh.] —**aus·tere′ly** adv. —**aus·ter′i·ty** (ô-stěr′ĭ-tē) n.

aus·tral (ô′strəl) adj. Southern. [< Lat. *auster,* south.]

Aus·tra·lian (ô-strāl′yən) n. 1. A native or citizen of Australia. 2. An aborigine of Australia. 3. Any of the languages of the Australian aborigines. —**Aus·tra′lian** adj.

Aus·tro-A·si·at·ic (ôs′trō-ā′zhē-ăt′ĭk) n. A family of languages of southeastern Asia once dominant in northeastern India and Indochina. —**Aus′tro-A′si·at′ic** adj.

aut- pref. Var. of **auto-.**

au·then·tic (ô-thĕn′tĭk) adj. 1. Worthy of trust, reliance, or belief 2. Genuine; real. [< Gk. *authentikos* < *authentēs,* author.] —**au·then′ti·cal·ly** adv. —**au·then·tic′i·ty** (-tĭs′ĭ-tē) n.

au·then·ti·cate (ô-thĕn′tĭ-kāt′) v. **-cat·ed, -cat·ing.** 1. To prove. 2. To establish as being genuine. —**au·then′ti·ca′tion** n. —**au·then′ti·ca′tor** n.

au·thor (ô′thər) n. 1. The writer of a literary work. 2. The beginner, originator, or creator of anything. [< Lat. *auctor,* creator.] —**au′thor** v.

au·thor·i·tar·i·an (ə-thôr′ĭ-târ′ē-ən, ə-thôr′-, ô-) adj. Characterized by or favoring absolute obedience to authority. —n. One who believes in authoritarian policies. —**au·thor′i·tar′i·an·ism** n.

au·thor·i·ta·tive (ə-thôr′ĭ-tā′tĭv, ə-thôr′-, ô-) adj. 1. Having or arising from proper authority. 2. Having or showing expert knowledge. —**au·thor′i·ta′tive·ly** adv. —**au·thor′i·ta′tive·ness** n.

au·thor·i·ty (ə-thôr′ĭ-tē, ə-thôr′-, ô-) n., pl. **-ties.** 1. a. The right and power to command, enforce laws, determine, influence, or judge. b. A person or group invested with this right and power. c. **authorities.** Government officials having this right and power. 2. Authorization. 3. a. An accepted source of expert information. b. A citation from such a source. 4. An expert in a given field.

au·thor·ize (ô′thə-rīz′) v. **-ized, -iz·ing.** 1. To grant authority or power to. 2. To sanction. 3. To justify. —**au′thor·i·za′tion** n. —**au′thor·iz′er** n.

au·thor·ship (ô′thər-shĭp′) n. 1. The profession or occupation of writing. 2. A source or origin, as of a book or idea.

au·tism (ô′tĭz′əm) n. 1. Abnormal subjectivity; acceptance of fantasy rather than reality. 2. A form of childhood schizophrenia characterized by acting out and withdrawal; infantile autism. —**au·tis′tic** (ô-tĭs′tĭk) adj.

au·to (ô′tō) n., pl. **-tos.** An automobile.

auto- or **aut-** pref. 1. Acting or directed from within: *autism.* 2. Self; same: *autobiography.* [< Gk. *autos,* self.]

au·to·bi·og·ra·phy (ô′tō-bī-ŏg′rə-fē, -bē-) n., pl. **-phies.** The story of a person's life written by that person; memoirs. —**au′to·bi′o·graph′ic** or **au′to·bi′o·graph′i·cal** adj.

au·toc·ra·cy (ô-tŏk′rə-sē) n., pl. **-cies.** Government by a single person having unlimited power. —**au′to·crat′** n. —**au′to·crat′ic** adj. —**au′to·crat′i·cal·ly** adv.

au·to·graph (ô′tə-grăf′) n. 1. A person's own signature or handwriting. 2. A manuscript in the author's own handwriting. —v. To write one's signature on.

Napoleon

Christopher Columbus

Thomas Jefferson   Gertrude Stein

autograph

au·to·mate (ô'tǝ-māt') v. **-mat·ed, -mat·ing.**
1. To convert to automation. 2. To operate
by automation. [< AUTOMATIC.]

au·to·mat·ic (ô'tǝ-măt'ĭk) adj. 1. Capable of
operating with little or no external control or
influence. 2. Involuntary; reflex. 3. Capable
of firing continuously until out of ammunition. —n. A device, esp. a firearm, that is
automatic. [< Gk. automatos, acting by itself.]
—**au'to·mat'i·cal·ly** adv.

automatic pilot n. A mechanism, as on an
aircraft, that automatically maintains a preset
course.

au·to·ma·tion (ô'tǝ-mā'shǝn) n. 1. The automatic operation or control of a process, machine, equipment, or system. 2. The
mechanical and electronic techniques and
equipment used to achieve automatic operation or control. 3. The condition of being
automatically controlled or operated. —**au'to·
ma'tive** adj.

au·tom·a·tize (ô-tŏm'ǝ-tīz') v. **-tized, -tiz·ing.**
To make automatic. —**au·tom'a·ti·za'tion** n.

au·tom·a·ton (ô-tŏm'ǝ-tǝn, -tŏn') n., pl. **-tons**
or **-ta** (-tǝ). 1. An automatic machine, esp. a
robot. 2. One that behaves in an automatic or
mechanical fashion. [< Gk. automatos, acting
by itself.]

au·to·mo·bile (ô'tǝ-mō-bēl', -mō'bēl') n. A
self-propelled land vehicle, esp. a four-
wheeled passenger vehicle powered by an
internal-combustion engine.

au·to·mo·tive (ô'tǝ-mō'tĭv) adj. 1. Self-
propelling. 2. Of or pertaining to automobiles
or other self-propelled land vehicles.

au·to·net·ics (ô'tō-nĕt'ĭks) n. (used with a
sing. verb). The study of automatic guidance
and control systems. [AUTO- + (CYBER)NET-
ICS.]

au·to·nom·ic nervous system (ô'tǝ-nŏm'ĭk)
n. The division of the vertebrate nervous system that regulates involuntary action, as of
the intestines, heart, and glands, and comprises the sympathetic nervous system and the
parasympathetic nervous system.

au·ton·o·mous (ô-tŏn'ǝ-mǝs) adj. 1. Independent; self-contained. 2. Self-governing.
[Gk. autonomos, self-ruling.] —**au·ton'o·mous·
ly** adv. —**au·ton'o·my** n.

au·top·sy (ô'tŏp'sē, ô'tǝp-) n., pl. **-sies.** The
examination of a dead body to determine the
cause of death. [< Gk. autopsia, a seeing for
oneself.]

au·to·sug·ges·tion (ô'tō-sǝg-jĕs'chǝn) n. Psychol. The process by which a person induces
self-acceptance of an opinion, belief, or plan
of action.

au·tumn (ô'tǝm) n. 1. The season between
summer and winter. 2. A time or period of
maturity verging on decline. [< Lat. autum-
nus.] —**au·tum'nal** (ô-tŭm'nǝl) adj.

aux·il·ia·ry (ôg-zĭl'yǝ-rē, -zĭl'ǝ-) adj. 1. Giving
assistance or support; helping. 2. Subsidiary;
supplementary. —n., pl. **-ries.** 1. One that
acts in an auxiliary capacity. 2. An auxiliary
verb. [< Lat. auxilium, help.]

auxiliary verb n. A verb, such as have, can, or
will, that comes first in a verb phrase and
helps form the tense, mood, or voice of the
main verb.

aux·in (ôk'sĭn) n. A plant hormone that promotes growth. [< Gk. auxein, to grow.]

Av (ŏv, äb) n. The 11th month of the Hebrew
year. See table at **calendar.**

a·vail (ǝ-vāl') v. To be of use or advantage
(to). —n. Use, benefit, or advantage: His
efforts were to no avail. [ME availen.]

a·vail·a·ble (ǝ-vā'lǝ-bǝl) adj. 1. Capable of being used. 2. At hand; accessible. —**a·vail·a·
bil'i·ty** or **a·vail'a·ble·ness** n. —**a·vail'a·bly**
adv.

av·a·lanche (ăv'ǝ-lănch') n. A large mass of
snow, rock, or other material sliding down a
mountainside. [< dial. Fr. avalantse.]

a·vant-garde (ä'vänt-gärd') n. A group, esp.
in the arts, who are the leaders in inventing
and applying unconventional styles and new
techniques in a given field. [Fr., vanguard.]
—**a'vant-garde'** adj.

av·a·rice (ăv'ǝr-ĭs) n. Extreme desire for
wealth; greed. [< Lat. avarus, greedy.] —**av'·
a·ri'cious** (-ǝ-rĭsh'ǝs) adj.

a·vast (ǝ-văst') interj. Naut. Hold on! Stop!
[< Du. houd vast, hold fast.]

a·va·tar (ăv'ǝ-tär') n. 1. One regarded as an
incarnation. 2. An exemplar; archetype. [Skt.
avatāra.]

a·vaunt (ǝ-vônt', ǝ-vänt') interj. Archaic. Be
gone! Go away! [< OFr. avant, forward.]

a·venge (ǝ-vĕnj') v. **a·venged, a·veng·ing.**
1. To take revenge or exact satisfaction for.
2. To take vengeance on behalf of: avenge
one's father. [< OFr. avengier.] —**a·veng'er** n.

av·e·nue (ăv'ǝ-nōō', -nyōō') n. 1. A wide
street or thoroughfare, esp. one lined with
trees. 2. A means of reaching or achieving
something. [< OFr. avenir, to approach.]

a·ver (ǝ-vûr') v. **a·verred, a·ver·ring.** To assert
positively. [< Med. Lat. adverare.] —**a·ver'·
ment** n.

av·er·age (ăv'ǝr-ĭj, ăv'rĭj) n. 1. A number that
typifies a set of numbers of which it is a
function; arithmetic mean. 2. A relative proportion or degree indicating position or
achievement. —adj. 1. Of, pertaining to, or
constituting a mathematical average. 2. Normal or ordinary. 3. Not exceptional; undis-
tinguished. —v. **-aged, -ag·ing.** 1. To
calculate, obtain, or amount to the average of.
2. To distribute proportionately. [Obs. averie,
loss on damaged shipping, ult. < Ar. awārī-
yah, damaged goods.]

a·verse (ǝ-vûrs') adj. Opposed; reluctant. [<
Lat. avertere, avert.] —**a·verse'ly** adv.

a·ver·sion (ǝ-vûr'zhǝn, -shǝn) n. 1. Intense
dislike. 2. A feeling of extreme repugnance.

a·vert (ǝ-vûrt') v. 1. To turn away: avert one's
eyes. 2. To ward off; prevent. [< Lat. avertere.] —**a·vert'i·ble** or **a·vert'a·ble** adj.

A·ves·ta (ǝ-vĕs'tǝ) n. The sacred writings of
the ancient Persians.

a·vi·an (ā'vē-ǝn) adj. Of or pertaining to
birds. [< Lat. avis, bird.]

a·vi·ar·y (ā'vē-ĕr'ē) n., pl. **-ies.** A large enclosure for birds, as in a zoo. [< Lat. *avis*, bird.] —**a'vi·a·rist** (-ə-rĭst, -âr'ĭst) *n.*

a·vi·a·tion (ā'vē-ā'shən, ăv'ē-) *n.* 1. The operation of aircraft. 2. The design and production of aircraft. [< Lat. *avis*, bird.]

a·vi·a·tor (ā'vē-ā'tər, ăv'ē-) *n.* One who flies an aircraft.

a·vi·a·trix (ā'vē-ā'trĭks, ăv'ē-) *n.* A woman who flies an aircraft.

av·id (ăv'ĭd) *adj.* 1. a. Eager. b. Greedy. 2. Enthusiastic; ardent. [< Lat. *avidus*.] —**av'id·ly** *adv.*

a·vi·on·ics (ā'vē-ŏn'ĭks, ăv'ē-) *n.* (used with a *sing. verb*). The science of electronics applied to aeronautics and astronautics. [AVI(ATION) + (ELECTR)ONICS.] —**a'vi·on'ic** *adj.*

a·vo (ä'vōō) *n., pl.* **a·vos.** See table at currency. [Port.]

av·o·ca·do (ăv'ə-kä'dō, ä'və-) *n., pl.* **-dos.** 1. A tropical American tree cultivated for its edible fruit. 2. The fruit of the avocado tree, with leathery skin and bland, greenish-yellow pulp. [< Nahuatl *ahuacatl.*]

av·o·ca·tion (ăv'ō-kā'shən) *n.* An activity engaged in, usu. for enjoyment, in addition to one's regular work; hobby. [< Lat. *avocare*, to call away.]

av·o·cet (ăv'ə-sĕt') *n.* A long-legged shore bird with a long, slender beak. [Ital. *avocetta.*]

a·void (ə-void') *v.* 1. To keep away from; shun. 2. To evade; dodge. 3. To keep from happening; prevent. 4. To refrain from. [< OFr. *esvuidier*, to empty out.] —**a·void'a·ble** *adj.* —**a·void'a·bly** *adv.* —**a·void'ance** *n.* —**a·void'er** *n.*

Syns: *avoid, by-pass, dodge, duck, elude, escape, eschew, evade, shun v.*

av·oir·du·pois weight (ăv'ər-də-poiz') *n.* A system of weights and measures based on one pound containing 16 ounces or 7,000 grains and equal to 453.59 grams. [< OFr. *aver de peis*, goods of weight.]

a·vouch (ə-vouch') *v.* 1. To guarantee. 2. To affirm. [< Lat. *advocare*, to summon.]

a·vow (ə-vou') *v.* To acknowledge openly; confess. [< Lat. *advocare*, to summon.] —**a·vow'al** *n.* —**a·vowed'** *adj.* —**a·vow'ed·ly** (ə-vou'ĭd-lē) *adv.*

a·vun·cu·lar (ə-vŭng'kyə-lər) *adj.* Of, pertaining to, or resembling an uncle. [< Lat. *avunculus*, maternal uncle.]

a·wait (ə-wāt') *v.* 1. To wait (for). 2. To be in store for. [< ONFr. *awaitier.*]

a·wake (ə-wāk') *v.* **a·woke** (ə-wōk'), **a·waked**, **a·wak·ing.** 1. To rouse from sleep. 2. To excite. 3. To stir up. —*adj.* 1. Not asleep. 2. Alert; vigilant. [< OE *āwacian.*]

a·wak·en (ə-wā'kən) *v.* To awake. [< OE *āwæcnian.*] —**a·wak'en·ing** *adj. & n.*

a·ward (ə-wôrd') *v.* 1. To grant or declare as merited or due. 2. To bestow for performance or quality. —*n.* 1. A decision, as one made by a judge or arbitrator. 2. Something awarded. [< AN *awarder*, to decide (a legal question).]

a·ware (ə-wâr') *adj.* Mindful or conscious of; cognizant. [< OE *gewær.*] —**a·ware'ness** *n.*

Syns: *aware, cognizant, conversant, knowing, mindful adj.*

a·wash (ə-wŏsh', ə-wôsh') *adj. & adv.* 1. Level with or washed by waves. 2. Flooded. 3. Afloat.

a·way (ə-wā') *adv.* 1. At or to a distance. 2. In or to a different place or direction. 3. From one's presence or possession: *Take these things away.* 4. Out of existence: *fading away.* 5. Continuously: *working away.* 6. Immediately: *Fire away!* —*adj.* 1. Absent: *He's away from home.* 2. At a distance: *miles away.* 3. Played on the opposing team's home grounds. [< OE *aweg.*]

awe (ô) *n.* 1. An emotion of mingled reverence, dread, and wonder. 2. Respect tinged with fear. —*v.* **awed, aw·ing.** To fill with awe. [< ON *agi.*]

a·weigh (ə-wā') *adj.* Hanging just clear of the bottom, as the anchor of a ship.

awe·some (ô'səm) *adj.* Inspiring or characterized by awe. —**awe'some·ly** *adv.* —**awe'some·ness** *n.*

awe·struck (ô'strŭk') *adj.* Also **awe·strick·en** (ô'strĭk'ən). Filled with awe.

aw·ful (ô'fəl) *adj.* 1. Inspiring awe or fear. 2. Very bad or unpleasant. 3. Dreadful; appalling. 4. Great: *went to an awful lot of trouble.*

aw·ful·ly (ô'fə-lē, ô'flē) *adv.* 1. In an awful manner. 2. Very.

a·while (ə-hwīl', ə-wīl') *adv.* For a short time.

awk·ward (ôk'wərd) *adj.* 1. Lacking grace or dexterity; clumsy. 2. Causing embarrassment. 3. Uncomfortable; inconvenient. 4. Difficult to handle; unwieldy. [ME *awkeward*, in the wrong direction.] —**awk'ward·ly** *adv.* —**awk'ward·ness** *n.*

Syns: *awkward, gawky, graceless, inept, ungainly adj.*

awl (ôl) *n.* A pointed tool for making holes, as in wood or leather. [< OE *æl.*]

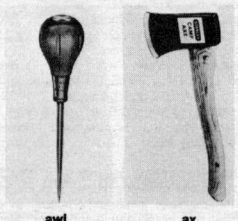

awl   ax

awn (ôn) *n.* One of the bristles on a grass spike. [< ON *ōgn.*]

awn·ing (ô'nĭng) *n.* A structure, as of canvas, stretched over a frame as a shelter from weather.

a·woke (ə-wōk') *v. p.t.* of **awake.**

AWOL (ā'wôl') *adj.* Absent without leave, esp. from military service. —*n.* One that is AWOL.

a·wry (ə-rī') *adv.* 1. Askew. 2. Wrong; amiss.

ax or **axe** (ăks) *n., pl.* **ax·es** (ăk'sĭz). A chopping tool with a bladed head mounted on a

---

ă pat ā pay â care ä father ĕ pet ē be ĭ pit ī tie î pier ŏ pot ō toe ô paw, for oi noise ōō took ōō boot ou out th thin th this ŭ cut û urge yōō abuse zh vision ə about, item, edible, gallop, circus

handle. —v. **axed, ax·ing.** 1. To work on with an ax. 2. To fire; dismiss. [< OE æx.]

ax·i·al (ăk′sē-əl) adj. Of, on, around, or along an axis.

ax·i·om (ăk′sē-əm) n. 1. A self-evident or universally recognized truth; maxim. 2. A statement that is assumed to be true without proof. [Gk. axiōma < axios, worthy.] —**ax′i·o·mat′ic** adj. —**ax′i·o·mat′i·cal·ly** adv.

ax·is (ăk′sĭs) n., pl. **ax·es** (ăk′sēz′). 1. A straight line around which an object rotates or can be conceived to rotate. 2. A line, ray, or line segment with respect to which a figure or object is symmetrical. 3. A reference line from which or along which distances or angles are measured in a system of coordinates. 4. Bot. The main stem or central part about which organs or plant parts such as branches are arranged. [Lat.]

ax·le (ăk′səl) n. A supporting shaft on which a wheel revolves. [< OE eaxl.]

ax·le·tree (ăk′səl-trē′) n. A crossbar that has a spindle at each end on which a wheel turns.

a·ya·tol·lah (ī′ə-tō′lə, -tōl′ə) n. An Islamic religious leader of the Shiite sect. [Pers.]

aye¹ (ī). Also **ay.** —n. An affirmative vote or voter. —adv. Yes. [Prob. < I.]

ax·i·al² (ā) adv. Also **ay.** Poet. Always; ever. [< ON ei.]

a·yin (ī′ĭn) n. The 16th letter of the Hebrew alphabet. See table at **alphabet.** [Heb. 'ayin.]

a·za·le·a (ə-zāl′yə) n. Any of several shrubs cultivated for their showy, variously colored flowers. [< Gk. azaleas, dry.]

az·i·muth (ăz′ə-məth) n. 1. The horizontal angular distance from a fixed reference direction to a position, object, or object referent, as to a great circle intersecting a celestial body, usu. measured clockwise in degrees along the horizon from a point due south. 2. The lateral deviation of a projectile or bomb. [< Ar. as-sumūt.]

Az·tec (ăz′tĕk′) n. 1. A member of an Indian people of central Mexico noted for their advanced civilization before Hernando Cortés invaded Mexico in 1519. 2. Nahuatl. —adj. Also **Az·tec·an** (-ən). Of the Aztecs or their language, culture, or empire.

az·ure (ăzh′ər) n. A light to medium blue. [< Ar. al-lāzaward.] —**az′ure** adj.

Bb

b or **B** (bē) n., pl. **b's** or **B's.** 1. The 2nd letter of the English alphabet. 2. The 2nd in a series. 3. The 2nd-highest grade in quality.

B The symbol for the element boron.

Ba The symbol for the element barium.

baa (bă, bä) n. The bleat of a sheep. —**baa** v.

Ba·al (bā′əl) n., pl. **-al·im** (-ə-lĭm). 1. Any of various fertility and nature gods of the ancient Semitic peoples. 2. A false god or idol.

Bab·bitt (băb′ĭt) n. A smug, provincial member of the American middle class. [< the main character in Babbitt by Sinclair Lewis (1885-1951).]

bab·ble (băb′əl) v. **-bled, -bling.** 1. To utter indistinct, meaningless sounds. 2. To talk foolishly; chatter. 3. To make a continuous low, murmuring sound. [ME babelen.] —**bab′ble** n. —**bab′bler** n.

babe (bāb) n. 1. A baby. 2. An innocent or naive person. [ME.]

Ba·bel (bā′bəl, băb′əl) n. 1. In the Old Testament, the site of a tower where construction was interrupted by God who caused a confusion of tongues. 2. **babel.** A confusion of sounds, voices, or languages.

ba·boon (bă-bōōn′) n. A large African monkey with an elongated, doglike muzzle. [< OFr. babuin.]

ba·bush·ka (bə-bōōsh′kə) n. A head scarf, folded triangularly and tied under the chin. [R., grandmother.]

ba·by (bā′bē) n., pl. **-bies.** 1. A very young child; infant. 2. The youngest member of a family or group. 3. One who acts like a baby. 4. Slang. A young girl or woman. 5. Slang. An object of personal concern: The project was his baby. —v. **-bied, -by·ing.** To treat

oversolicitously. [ME babie.] —**ba′by·hood′** n. —**ba′by·ish** adj. —**ba′by·ish·ly** adv. —**ba′by·ish·ness** n.

Syns: baby, coddle, indulge, mollycoddle, pamper, spoil v.

Bab·y·lo·ni·an (băb′ə-lō′nē-ən) n. 1. A native or inhabitant of Babylonia. 2. The Semitic language of the Babylonians, a form of Akkadian. —**Bab′y·lo′ni·an** adj.

ba·by's-breath (bā′bēz-brĕth′) n. Also **ba·bies'-breath.** A plant with numerous small white flowers.

ba·by-sit (bā′bē-sĭt′) v. To care for children when the parents are not at home. —**baby sitter** n.

bac·ca·lau·re·ate (băk′ə-lôr′ē-ĭt) n. 1. The degree of bachelor conferred upon graduates of colleges and universities. 2. An address delivered to a graduating class at commencement. [Med. Lat. baccalaureatus.]

bac·ca·rat (băk′ə-rä′, băk′ə-) n. A gambling game played with cards. [Fr. baccara.]

bac·cha·nal (băk′ə-năl′, bä′kə-näl′, băk′ə-nəl) n. 1. A drunken or riotous celebration, orig. in honor of Bacchus. 2. A participant in such a celebration. 3. A reveler. —**bac′cha·na′lian** (-nāl′yən, -nā′lē-ən) adj.

Bac·chus (băk′əs) n. Rom. Myth. The god of wine. —**Bac′chic** adj.

bach·e·lor (băch′ə-lər, băch′lər) n. 1. An unmarried man. 2. a. A college or university degree signifying completion of the undergraduate curriculum. b. A person with this degree. [< Med. Lat. baccalarius.] —**bach′e·lor·hood′** n.

bach·e·lor's-but·ton (băch′ə-lərz-bŭt′n, băch′-lərz-) n. The cornflower.

ba·cil·lus (bə-sĭl′əs) *n., pl.* **-cil·li** (-sĭl′ī′). Any of various rod-shaped bacteria. [< Lat. *baculum*, rod.] —**bac′il·lar′y** (băs′ə-lĕr′ē) or **ba·cil′lar** *adj.*

back (băk) *n.* **1. a.** The region of the vertebrate body nearest the spine. **b.** The upper part of the body in invertebrates. **2.** The part farthest from or behind the front; the rear. **3.** The reverse side. **4.** A football player positioned in the backfield. —*v.* **1.** To move backward or in a reverse direction. **2.** To support; strengthen. **3.** To bet on. **4.** To form the back of. —*adj.* **1.** At the rear. **2.** Distant; remote. **3.** Of or for a past date or time. **4.** Backward. —*adv.* **1.** To or toward the rear. **2.** To or toward a former place, state, or time. **3.** In reserve, concealment, or check. **4.** In return. —*phrasal verbs.* **back down.** To withdraw from a former stand. **back off.** To retreat or retire, as from a dangerous position. **back out.** To withdraw from something. **back up. 1.** To assist, esp. as an auxiliary. **2.** To accumulate in a clogged state. —*idioms.* **behind (one's) back.** When one is not present. **go back on. 1.** To fail to keep (a promise or commitment). **2.** To betray or desert (a person). [< OE *bæc.*]

back·ache (băk′āk′) *n.* A pain or discomfort in the region of the spine or back.

back·bench·er (băk′bĕn′chər) *n. Brit.* A junior member of the House of Commons.

back·bite (băk′bīt′) *v.* To speak spitefully or slanderously of a person who is not present. —**back′bit′er** *n.*

back·board (băk′bôrd′, -bōrd′) *n.* **1.** A board placed under or behind something to provide firmness or support. **2.** *Basketball.* The elevated, vertical board from which the basket projects.

back·bone (băk′bōn′) *n.* **1.** The vertebrate spine or spinal column. **2.** A principal support. **3.** Strength of character.

back·break·ing (băk′brā′kĭng) *adj.* Demanding great exertion; arduous.

Syns: *backbreaking, arduous, demanding, difficult, formidable, hard, heavy, laborious, onerous, rigorous, severe, taxing, tough, trying adj.*

back·door (băk′dôr′, -dōr′) *adj.* Secret or surreptitious; clandestine.

back·drop (băk′drŏp′) *n.* A painted curtain hung at the back of a stage.

back·er (băk′ər) *n.* One who supports or gives aid.

back·field (băk′fēld′) *n. Football.* **1.** The players stationed behind the line of scrimmage. **2.** The area occupied by the backfield.

back·fire (băk′fīr′) *n.* An explosion of prematurely ignited fuel or of unburned exhaust. —*v.* **-fired, -fir·ing. 1.** To explode in a backfire. **2.** To produce an unexpected, undesired result.

back·for·ma·tion (băk′fôr-mā′shən) *n.* **1.** A new word created by the deletion of what is construed to be an affix from an existing word, as *laze* from *lazy.* **2.** The process of forming words in this way.

back·gam·mon (băk′găm′ən) *n.* A board game for two, with moves determined by throws of dice.

backgammon

backpack

back·ground (băk′ground′) *n.* **1.** The area, space, or surface against which objects are seen or represented. **2.** Conditions or events forming a setting. **3.** A place or state of relative obscurity. **4.** One's total experience, education, and knowledge. **5.** Subdued music played esp. as an accompaniment to dialogue in a dramatic performance. **6.** Sound or radiation present at a relatively constant low level.

back·ground·er (băk′groun′dər) *n. Slang.* A meeting at which an official provides background information about a governmental issue.

back·hand (băk′hănd′) *n.* **1.** *Sports.* A stroke or motion, as of a racket, made with the back of the hand facing outward and the arm moving forward. **2.** Handwriting characterized by letters that slant to the left. —*adj.* Backhanded. —**back′hand′** *v.*

back·hand·ed (băk′hăn′dĭd) *adj.* **1.** Made with the motion of a backhand. **2.** Containing a disguised insult or rebuke. —**back′hand′ed·ly** *adv.* —**back′hand′ed·ness** *n.*

back·ing (băk′ĭng) *n.* **1.** Material that forms, supports, or strengthens the back of something. **2. a.** Support or aid. **b.** Approval or endorsement. **3.** Supporters or endorsers.

back·lash (băk′lăsh′) *n.* **1.** A sudden or violent backward whipping motion. **2.** Hostile reaction, as in socioeconomic relations.

back·log (băk′lôg′, -lŏg′) *n.* **1.** A reserve supply or source. **2.** An accumulation, esp. of unfinished work or unfilled orders. —**back′-log′** *v.*

back number *n.* **1.** An out-of-date periodical or newspaper. **2.** *Informal.* One that is old-fashioned.

back·pack (băk′păk′) *n.* **1.** A knapsack, often mounted on a lightweight frame. **2.** Any piece of equipment made for use while being carried on the back. —*v.* To hike with or carry in a backpack. —**back′pack′er** *n.*

back·rest (băk′rĕst′) *n.* A support for the back.

back seat *n.* **1.** A seat in the back, esp. of a vehicle. **2.** *Informal.* A subordinate position.

back·side (băk′sīd′) *n.* The buttocks.

back·slide (băk′slīd′) *v.* To revert to wrongdoing; relapse. —**back′slid′er** *n.*

back·spin (băk′spĭn′) *n.* A spin that tends to slow, stop, or reverse the motion of an object, esp. of a ball.

back·stage (băk′stāj′) *adv.* **1.** In or toward the area behind the performing area in a theater. **2.** Secretly; privately.

back·stairs (băk′stârz′) *adj.* Furtively carried on; clandestine: *backstairs gossip.*

back·stop (băk′stŏp′) *n.* **1.** A screen or fence

in back of a playing area used to stop a ball's movement. **2.** *Baseball.* The catcher.

back·stretch (băk′strĕch′) *n.* The part of a racecourse farthest from the spectators and opposite the homestretch.

back·stroke (băk′strŏk′) *n.* **1.** A backhanded stroke. **2.** A swimming stroke executed with the swimmer on his back, using a flutter kick and moving the arms upward and backward.

back·swept (băk′swĕpt′) *adj.* Swept or angled backward.

back talk *n.* An insolent retort.

back·track (băk′trăk′) *v.* **1.** To retrace one's route. **2.** To reverse one's position or policy.

back-up (băk′ŭp′) *n.* **1.** A reserve, as of provisions. **2.** A person standing by and ready to serve as a substitute. **3.** Support or backing. **4.** A background accompaniment, as for a musical performer.

back·ward (băk′wərd) *adv.* Also **back·wards** (-wərdz). **1.** Toward the back. **2.** With the back leading. **3.** In reverse. **4.** Toward a worse condition. —*adj.* **1.** Reversed. **2.** Reluctant; unwilling. **3.** Retarded in development. —*idlom.* **bend over backward.** To do one's utmost. —**back′ward·ly** *adv.* —**back′-ward·ness** *n.*

Usage: The adverb forms *backward* and *backwards* are interchangeable: *leaned backward; moved the chair backwards.* Only *backward* is an adjective: *a backward view.*

back·wash (băk′wŏsh′, -wôsh′) *n.* **1.** A backward flow or motion, as of water or air. **2.** The result of some event; aftermath.

back·wa·ter (băk′wô′tər, -wŏt′ər) *n.* A place or situation of stagnation or arrested progress.

back·woods (băk′wŏŏdz′, -wŏŏdz′) *pl.n.* Heavily wooded, thinly settled areas. —**back′woods′man** *n.*

ba·con (bā′kən) *n.* The salted and smoked meat from the back and sides of a pig. —*idlom.* **bring home the bacon.** *Informal.* **1.** To make a living. **2.** To succeed. [< OFr.]

bac·te·ri·a (băk-tîr′ē-ə) *n.* Pl. of **bacterium.**

bac·te·ri·cide (băk-tîr′ĭ-sīd′) *n.* A substance that destroys bacteria. —**bac·te′ri·ci′dal** *adj.*

bac·te·ri·ol·o·gy (băk-tîr′ē-ŏl′ə-jē) *n.* The scientific study of bacteria. —**bac·te′ri·o·log′ic** (-ə-lŏj′ĭk) or **bac·te′ri·o·log′i·cal** *adj.* —**bac·te′ri·o·log′i·cal·ly** *adv.* —**bac·te′ri·ol′o·gist** *n.*

bac·te·ri·o·phage (băk-tîr′ē-ə-fāj′) *n.* A submicroscopic, usu. viral organism that destroys bacteria.

bac·te·ri·um (băk-tîr′ē-əm) *n., pl.* **-ri·a** (-ē-ə). Any of numerous sometimes parasitic unicellular organisms having various forms and often causing disease. [Gk. *baktērion,* little rod.] —**bac·te′ri·al** *adj.* —**bac·te′ri·al·ly** *adv.*

bad¹ (băd) *adj.* **worse** (wûrs), **worst** (wûrst). **1.** Having undesirable qualities; not good. **2.** Inferior; poor. **3.** Unfavorable. **4.** Rotten; spoiled. **5.** Severe; intense: *a bad cold.* **6.** Sorry; regretful. —*n.* Something bad: *Accept the bad with the good.* —*adv. Informal.* Badly. [ME *badde.*] —**bad′ly** *adv.* —**bad′-ness** *n.*

Usage: The use of *bad* as an adverb, while common in informal speech, should be avoided in writing. Formal usage requires: *My tooth hurts badly* (not *bad*).

bad² (băd) *v. Archaic.* A *p.t.* of **bid.**

bad blood *n.* Bitterness between two or more persons.

bade (băd, bād) *v.* A *p.t.* of **bid.**

badge (băj) *n.* An emblem worn as an insignia of rank, membership, or honor. [ME *bagge.*]

badg·er (băj′ər) *n.* **1.** A burrowing animal with a thick, grizzled coat. **2.** The fur of a badger. —*v.* To trouble or harry; pester. [Orig. unknown.]

bad·i·nage (băd′ə-näzh′) *n.* Light, playful banter. [Fr.]

bad·lands (băd′lăndz′) *pl.n.* An area of barren land characterized by eroded ridges, peaks, and mesas.

bad·min·ton (băd′mĭn′tən) *n.* A net game played with a shuttlecock and long-handled rackets. [< *Badminton,* an estate in Gloucestershire, England.]

bad-mouth (băd′mouth′, -mou*th*′) *v.* Also **bad-mouth.** *Slang.* To criticize or disparage, often spitefully.

baf·fle (băf′əl) *v.* **-fled, -fling. 1.** To puzzle; perplex. **2.** To foil; thwart. —*n.* A structure or enclosure designed to stop, alter, or regulate the movement of a gas, sound, light, or liquid. [Orig. unknown.] —**baf′fle·ment** *n.* —**baf′fler** *n.*

bag (băg) *n.* **1.** A nonrigid container, as of cloth or paper. **2.** A suitcase or purse. **3.** An amount of game taken at a time. **4.** *Baseball.* A base. **5.** *Slang.* An area of interest or skill. **6.** *Slang.* An unattractive woman. —*v.* **bagged, bag·ging. 1.** To put into a bag. **2.** To hang or bulge loosely. **3.** To capture or kill as game. —*idlom.* **in the bag.** *Slang.* Assured of successful outcome. [< ON *baggi.*] —**bag′ful** *n.*

ba·gasse (bə-găs′) *n.* The dry pulp remaining from a plant, as sugar cane, after the juice has been extracted. [< Lat. *baca,* berry.]

bag·a·telle (băg′ə-tĕl′) *n.* A trifle. [< Lat. *baca,* berry.]

ba·gel (bā′gəl) *n.* A tough, chewy ring-shaped roll. [< OHG *boug,* ring.]

bag·gage (băg′ĭj) *n.* **1.** The bags and belongings carried while traveling. **2.** A wanton or impudent woman. [< OFr. *bague,* bundle.]

bag·gy (băg′ē) *adj.* **-gi·er, -gi·est.** Bulging or hanging loosely. —**bag′gi·ly** *adv.* —**bag′gi·ness** *n.*

bag·pipe (băg′pīp′) *n.* Often **bagpipes.** A musical wind instrument with an inflatable bag that produces the different tones. —**bag′pip′-er** *n.*

ba·guette (bă-gĕt′) *n.* A gem cut into a narrow rectangle. [Fr.]

baht (bät) *n., pl.* **bahts** or **baht.** See table at **currency.** [Thai *bāt.*]

bail¹ (bāl) *n.* **1.** Money supplied as a guarantee that an arrested person will appear for trial. **2.** Release obtained by bail. **3.** One providing bail. —*v.* To release by providing or taking bail. —*phrasal verb.* **bail out. 1.** *Informal.* To extricate from a difficult situation. **2.** To parachute from an airplane. [< Lat. *bajulus,* carrier.] —**bail′a·ble** *adj.* —**bail′er** *n.*

bail² (bāl) *v.* To empty a boat of water by scooping or dipping. [< OFr. *baille,* bucket.] —**bail′er** *n.*

bail³ (bāl) *n.* The arched, hooplike handle of a pail, kettle, etc. [ME *bail.*]

bail·ee (bā-lē′) *n.* A person to whom property is bailed.

bail·iff (bā′lĭf) *n.* **1.** A court attendant who has custody of prisoners and maintains order in a courtroom. **2.** An official who assists a British sheriff by executing writs and arrests.

3. *Chiefly Brit.* An overseer of an estate; steward. [< Lat. *bajulus,* carrier.]

bail·i·wick (bā'lə-wīk') *n.* **1.** The office or district of a bailiff. **2.** One's field of interest or authority. [ME *bailliwik.*]

bail·or (bā'lər) *n. Law.* One who bails property for another.

bails·man (bālz'mən) *n. Law.* One who provides bail for another.

bairn (bârn) *n. Scot.* A child. [< OE *bearn.*]

bait (bāt) *n.* **1.** Food or other lure used to catch fish or trap animals. **2.** An enticement; lure. —*v.* **1.** To put bait on. **2.** To lure or entice. **3.** To set dogs upon (a captive animal) for sport. **4.** To harass; persecute. **5.** To tease. [< ON *beita,* to hunt with dogs, and < ON *beita,* food.] —**bait'er** *n.*

Usage: The word *bait* is sometimes used improperly for *bate* in the phrase *bated breath.*

bait and switch *n.* A sales tactic in which a bargain-priced item is used to attract customers who are then encouraged to purchase a more expensive similar item.

bai·za (bī'zä) *n.* See table at **currency.** [Ar.]

baize (bāz) *n.* A thick feltlike cloth. [Fr. *baies.*]

bake (bāk) *v.* **baked, bak·ing. 1.** To cook with continuous dry heat, esp. in an oven. **2.** To harden or dry in or as if in an oven: *bake clay pottery.* —*n.* **1.** The act or process of baking. **2.** A social gathering at which food is baked and served. [< OE *bacan.*] —**bak'er** *n.*

Ba·ke·lite (bā'kə-līt') A trademark for any of a group of thermosetting plastics having high chemical and electrical resistance and used in a variety of manufactured articles.

baker's dozen *n.* A group of 13. [< the former custom among bakers of adding an extra roll as a safeguard against the possibility of 12 weighing light.]

bak·er·y (bā'kə-rē) *n., pl.* **-ies.** A place where products such as bread, cake, and pastries are baked or sold.

baking powder *n.* Any of various powdered mixtures of baking soda, starch, and an acidic compound such as cream of tartar, used as leavening.

baking soda *n.* Sodium bicarbonate.

bak·sheesh (bāk'shēsh', bāk-shēsh') *n.* A gratuity or gift of alms in the Near East. [Pers. *bakhshīsh.*]

bal·a·lai·ka (bāl'ə-lī'kə) *n.* A musical instrument with a triangular body and three strings. [R.]

bal·ance (bāl'əns) *n.* **1.** A weighing device consisting essentially of a lever that is brought into equilibrium by adding known weights to one end while the unknown weight hangs from the other. **2.** Equilibrium. **3.** An influence or force tending to produce equilibrium. **4. a.** Equality of totals in the debit and credit sides of an account. **b.** A difference between such totals. **5.** Anything that remains or is left over. **6.** Equality of symbolic value on each side of an equation. —*v.* **-anced, -anc·ing. 1.** To weight or poise in or as if in a balance. **2.** To bring into or be maintained in equilibrium. **3.** To counterbalance. **4.** To compute the difference between the debits and credits of (an account). —**idiom. In the**

balance. With the result or outcome still uncertain. [< Lat. *bilanx,* having two scales.]

balance sheet *n.* A statement of the assets and liabilities of a business or individual.

balance wheel *n.* A wheel that regulates rate of movement in machine parts, as in a watch.

Bal·bo·a (bāl-bō'ə) *n.* See table at **currency.** [< Vasco Núñez de *Balboa* (1475–1519).]

bal·brig·gan (bāl-brĭg'ən) *n.* A knitted cotton fabric. [< *Balbriggan,* Ireland.]

bal·co·ny (bāl'kə-nē) *n., pl.* **-nies. 1.** A platform that projects from the wall of a building and is surrounded by a railing. **2.** An upper section of seats in a theater or auditorium. [Ital. *balcone,* of Gmc. orig.]

bald (bôld) *adj.* **-er, -est. 1.** Lacking hair on the head. **2.** Lacking natural or usual covering. **3.** Having a white head: *the bald eagle.* **4.** Undisguised; blunt: *a bald statement.* [ME *balled.*] —**bald'ly** *adv.* —**bald'ness** *n.*

bal·da·chin (bôl'də-kĭn, bǎl'-) *n.* Also **bal·da·chi·no** (bôl'də-kē'nō). A canopy esp. of fabric placed over an altar, throne, or dais. [< OItal. *Baldacco,* Baghdad.]

bal·der·dash (bôl'dər-dǎsh') *n.* Words without sense; nonsense. [Orig. unknown.]

bal·dric (bôl'drĭk) *n.* A leather belt worn across the chest to support a sword or bugle. [< OFr. *baudre.*]

bale (bāl) *n.* A large bound package of raw or finished material. —*v.* **baled, bal·ing.** To wrap in bales. [ME.] —**bal'er** *n.*

ba·leen (bə-lēn') *n.* Whalebone. [< Gk. *phalaina.*]

bale·ful (bāl'fəl) *adj.* **1.** Malignant in intent or effect. **2.** Portending evil; ominous. [*bale,* evil + -FUL.] —**bale'ful·ly** *adv.* —**bale'ful·ness** *n.*

balk (bôk) *v.* **1.** To stop short and refuse to go on. **2.** To thwart; check. **3.** *Baseball.* To make an illegal motion before pitching, entitling all runners automatically to advance a base. —*n.* **1.** A hindrance, check, or defeat. **2.** A blunder or failure. **3.** *Baseball.* The act of balking. [< OE *balc,* ridge.] —**balk'er** *n.* —**balk'y** *adj.*

ball¹ (bôl) *n.* **1.** A spherical or almost spherical body or entity. **2. a.** Any of various more or less rounded objects used in games. **b.** A game played with such an object. **3.** *Baseball.* A pitched ball that does not pass through the strike zone and is not swung at by the batter. **4.** A rounded part or protuberance: *the ball of the foot.* —*v.* To form or become formed into a ball. —*phrasal verb.* **ball up.** *Slang.* To confuse or bungle. —*idioms.* **on the ball.** *Slang.* Alert, competent, or efficient. **play ball.** *Informal.* To cooperate. [< ON *böllr.*]

ball² (bôl) *n.* **1.** A formal gathering for social dancing. **2.** *Slang.* An enjoyable time. [< Gk. *ballizein,* to dance.]

bal·lad (bāl'əd) *n.* **1.** A narrative poem, often of folk origin and intended to be sung, consisting of simple stanzas and usu. having a recurrent refrain. **2.** The music for such a poem. **3.** A slow, romantic popular song. [< OProv. *balada,* song sung while dancing.] —**bal'lad·eer** (-ə-dîr') *n.* —**bal'lad·ry** *n.*

bal·last (bāl'əst) *n.* **1.** Heavy material carried in the hold of a ship or the gondola of a balloon to enhance stability. **2.** Coarse gravel or crushed rock laid to form a roadbed. —*v.*

To stabilize or provide with ballast. [Of Scand. orig.]

ball bearing n. 1. A friction-reducing bearing, as for a turning shaft, in which the moving and stationary parts are held apart by freely revolving small, hard balls. 2. A small, hard ball used in a ball bearing.

bal·le·ri·na (băl'ə-rē'nə) n. A female ballet dancer. [Ital.]

bal·let (bă-lā', băl'ā') n. 1. A dance genre characterized chiefly by a highly formalized technique. 2. A choreographic presentation, usually with music, on a narrative or abstract theme. 3. A company that performs ballet. [Fr.]

bal·let·o·mane (bă-lĕt'ə-mān') n. An ardent admirer of the ballet. [< BALLETOMANIA.] —**bal·let'o·ma'ni·a** n.

bal·lis·tic missile n. A projectile that assumes a free-falling trajectory after a controlled, self-powered ascent.

bal·lis·tics (bə-lĭs'tĭks) n. (used with a sing. verb). 1. a. The study of the dynamics of projectiles. b. The study of the flight characteristics of projectiles. 2. a. The study of the functioning of firearms. b. The study of the firing, flight, and effect of ammunition. [< Gk. ballein, to throw.] —**bal·lis'tic** adj. —**bal·lis'ti·cal·ly** adv.

bal·loon (bə-lōōn') n. 1. A flexible bag inflated with a gas, such as helium, that causes it to rise in the atmosphere, esp. such a bag with sufficient capacity to lift a suspended gondola. —v. 1. To expand or cause to expand like a balloon. 2. To ascend or ride in a balloon. [< Ital. pallone.] —**bal·loon'ist** n.

bal·lot (băl'ət) n. 1. A paper or ticket used to cast or register a vote. 2. The act, process, or method of voting. 3. A list of candidates for office. 4. The total of all votes cast in an election. 5. The right to vote; franchise. —v. To cast a ballot; vote. [< Ital. balla, ball.]

ball·park (bôl'pärk') n. A stadium in which ball games are played. —**Idiom. In the ballpark.** Informal. Within the proper range.

ball-point pen (bôl'point') n. A pen with a small ball bearing that serves as its writing point.

ball·room (bôl'rōōm', -rŏŏm') n. A large room for dancing.

bal·ly·hoo (băl'ē-hōō') Informal. —n. 1. Sensational or clamorous advertising. 2. Noisy shouting or uproar. —v. To advertise in a loud or sensational manner. [Orig. unknown.]

balm (bäm) n. 1. An aromatic resin, oil, or ointment used medicinally. 2. Any of several aromatic plants. 3. Something that soothes, heals, or comforts. [< Gk. balsamon, balsam.]

balm·y (bä'mē) adj. **-i·er, -i·est.** 1. Having the quality or fragrance of balm. 2. Mild and pleasant: balmy climates. 3. Slang. Eccentric; crazy. —**balm'i·ly** adv. —**balm'i·ness** n.

ba·lo·ney (bə-lō'nē) n. Slang. Nonsense. [< BOLOGNA.]

bal·sa (bôl'sə) n. 1. A tropical American tree with very light, buoyant wood. 2. The wood of the balsa tree. [Sp.]

bal·sam (bôl'səm) n. 1. An aromatic resin or ointment obtained from various trees or plants. 2. A tree yielding balsam. 3. A plant cultivated for its colorful flowers. [Gk. balsamon.]

balsam fir n. An American evergreen tree widely used as a Christmas tree.

Bal·tic (bôl'tĭk) adj. 1. Of or pertaining to the Baltic Sea or to the Baltic States and their inhabitants or cultures. 2. Of or designating a branch of Indo-European languages consisting of Lithuanian, Latvian, and Old Prussian. —n. The Baltic language branch.

bal·us·ter (băl'ə-stər) n. One of the upright supports of a handrail. [< Ital. balaustro.]

bal·us·trade (băl'ə-strād') n. A handrail and the row of posts that support it. [< Ital. balaustrata.]

balustrade

bam·boo (băm-bōō') n. A tall tropical grass with hollow, jointed stems that have a wide variety of uses. [Orig. unknown.]

bam·boo·zle (băm-bōō'zəl) v. **-zled, -zling.** Informal. To trick; deceive. [Orig. unknown.]

ban¹ (băn) v. **banned, ban·ning.** To prohibit, esp. officially. —n. A prohibition imposed by law or official decree. [< OE bannan, to summon, and < ON banna, to prohibit.]

ban² (băn) n., pl. **ba·ni** (bä'nē). See table at currency. [Rum.]

ba·nal (bə-năl', -näl', bā'nəl) adj. Completely ordinary; trite. [Fr., of Gmc. orig.] —**ba·nal'i·ty** (-năl'ĭ-tē) n. —**ba·nal'ly** adv.

ba·nan·a (bə-năn'ə) n. 1. Any of several treelike tropical or subtropical plants with long, broad leaves and hanging clusters of edible fruit. 2. The crescent-shaped fruit of the banana plant, with white, pulpy flesh and yellow or reddish skin. [Of African orig.]

band¹ (bănd) n. 1. A thin strip of flexible material used to encircle and bind together. 2. A range or interval, esp. of radio wavelengths: the shortwave band. —v. To bind or identify with a band. [OFr. bande.]

band² (bănd) n. 1. A group of people or animals. 2. A group of musicians who play together. —v. To assemble or unite in a group. [OFr. bande.]

band·age (băn'dĭj) n. A strip of material used to protect a wound or other injury. —v. **-daged, -dag·ing.** To apply a bandage to. [Fr.]

Band-Aid (bănd'ād'). A trademark for an adhesive bandage with a gauze pad in the center.

ban·dan·na or **ban·dan·a** (băn-dăn'ə) n. A large handkerchief, usu. patterned and often used as a head scarf. [Prob. < Port.]

band·box (bănd'bŏks') n. A rounded box used to hold small articles of apparel.

ban·de·role or **ban·de·rol** (băn'də-rōl') n. A narrow forked flag or streamer. [< Ital. bandiera, banner.]

ban·di·coot (băn'dĭ-kōōt') n. A ratlike Australian marsupial with a long snout. [Telugu pandi-kokku.]

ban·dit (băn'dĭt) n. A robber; gangster. [Ital. bandito.] —**ban'dit·ry** n.

ban·do·leer or **ban·do·lier** (băn'də-lîr') n. A

military belt for cartridges that is worn across the chest. [Fr. *bandoulière.*]

band saw *n.* A power saw that consists mainly of a continuous toothed metal band.

band-stand (bănd'stănd') *n.* A platform for a band or orchestra, often roofed.

band-wag-on (bănd'wăg'ən) *n.* **1.** A decorated wagon used to transport musicians in a parade. **2.** *Informal.* A cause or party that attracts increasing numbers of adherents.

ban-dy (băn'dē) *v.* **-died, -dy-ing. 1.** To toss back and forth. **2.** To discuss or exchange in a casual or frivolous manner. —*adj.* Bent or curved outward; bowed: *bandy legs.* [Orig. unknown.]

bane (bān) *n.* **1.** A cause of death or ruin. **2.** A deadly poison. [OE *bana.*] —**bane'ful** *adj.*

bang¹ (băng) *n.* **1.** A sudden loud noise or thump. **2.** *Slang.* A sense of excitement; thrill. —*v.* **1.** To hit noisily. **2.** To close or handle noisily or violently. —*adv.* Exactly; precisely. [Prob. of Scand. orig.]

bang² (băng) *n.* Often **bangs.** Hair cut straight across the forehead. [Perh. < ON *banpa,* to cut off.]

ban-gle (băng'gəl) *n.* **1.** A hooplike bracelet or anklet. **2.** A pendent ornament. [Hindi *baṅgrī,* glass bracelet.]

bang-up (băng'ŭp') *adj. Slang.* Excellent.

ban-ian (băn'yən) *n.* Var. of **banyan.**

ban-ish (băn'ĭsh) *v.* **1.** To force to leave a country by official decree; exile. **2.** To drive away; expel. [OFr. *banir,* of Gmc. orig.] —**ban'ish-ment** *n.*

ban-is-ter (băn'ĭ-stər) *n.* Also **ban-nis-ter. 1.** A baluster. **2.** The handrail along a staircase. [Var. of BALUSTER.]

ban-jo (băn'jō) *n., pl.* **-jos** or **-joes.** A fretted stringed instrument having a hollow circular body with a stretched diaphragm of vellum. [Prob. of African orig.] —**ban'jo-ist** *n.*

bank¹ (băngk) *n.* **1.** A piled-up mass, as of snow or clouds. **2.** A steep natural incline. **3.** An artificial embankment. **4.** The slope of land adjoining a lake, river, or sea. **5.** An elevated area of a sea floor. **6.** Lateral tilting of an aircraft in a turn. **7.** The sideways slope of a surface on a curve or of a motor vehicle rounding a curve. —*v.* **1.** To border or protect with a bank. **2.** To pile up; amass. **3.** To cover (a fire) with ashes or fuel for low burning. **4.** To construct with a slope rising to the outside edge. **5.** To tilt (an aircraft) laterally in flight. [Of Scand. orig.]

bank² (băngk) *n.* **1. a.** A business establishment authorized to perform financial transactions, such as receiving and lending money. **b.** The building in which such an establishment is located. **2.** A small container in which money is saved. **3.** The funds owned by a gambling establishment. **4.** A supply for use in emergencies: *a blood bank.* **5.** A place of storage: *a computer's memory bank.* —*v.* **1.** To deposit (money) in a bank. **2.** To transact business with a bank. **3.** To operate a bank. —*phrasal verb.* **bank on.** To rely on; count on. [< Ital. *banca,* moneychanger's table.] —**bank'a-ble** *adj.* —**bank'er** *n.*

bank³ (băngk) *n.* **1.** A set of similar things arranged in a row: *a bank of elevators.* **2.** A

row of oars. —*v.* To arrange in a row. [< OFr. *banc,* bench.]

bank-book (băngk'bŏŏk') *n.* A depositor's booklet in which a bank enters the amounts deposited in or withdrawn from the account.

bank note *n.* A note issued by an authorized bank payable to the bearer on demand and acceptable as money.

bank-roll (băngk'rōl') *n.* **1.** A roll of paper money. **2.** *Informal.* A person's ready cash. —*v.* To underwrite the cost of.

bank-rupt (băngk'rŭpt', -rəpt) *adj.* **1.** Legally declared insolvent and having one's remaining property administered by or divided among one's creditors. **2.** Financially ruined. **3.** Lacking in quality or resources. —*v.* To cause to become bankrupt. —*n.* One who is bankrupt. [< Ital. *bancarotta.*] —**bank'rupt'cy** *n.*

ban-ner (băn'ər) *n.* **1.** A piece of cloth attached to a staff and used as a standard by a monarch, military commander, etc. **2.** A flag. **3.** A headline spanning the width of a newspaper page. —*adj.* Outstanding; superior. [< OFr. *baniere,* of Gmc. orig.]

ban-nis-ter (băn'ĭ-stər) *n.* Var. of **banister.**

ban-nock (băn'ək) *n.* A griddlecake made of oatmeal, barley, or wheat flour. [< Gael. *bannach.*]

banns (bănz) *pl.n.* Also **bans.** Announcement in a church of an intended marriage. [ME.]

ban-quet (băng'kwĭt) *n.* **1.** An elaborate feast. **2.** A ceremonial dinner honoring a guest or occasion. —*v.* To entertain at or partake in a banquet. [OFr.] —**ban'quet-er** *n.*

ban-quette (băng-kĕt') *n.* **1.** A long upholstered bench, either placed against or built into a wall. **2.** A platform lining a trench or parapet for guns or gunners. [Fr.]

ban-shee (băn'shē) *n.* In Gaelic folklore, a female spirit believed to presage a death in the family by wailing. [Ir. Gael. *bean sidhe.*]

ban-tam (băn'təm) *n.* **1.** One of a breed of small domestic fowl. **2.** A small aggressive person. —*adj.* **1.** Diminutive; small. **2.** Spirited or aggressive. [< *Bantam,* Indonesia.]

ban-tam-weight (băn'təm-wāt') *n.* A boxer in the lowest weight class, about 51 to 54 kilograms or 112 to 118 pounds.

ban-ter (băn'tər) *n.* Good-humored teasing. —*v.* To tease or mock gently. [Orig. unknown.] —**ban'ter-er** *n.* —**ban'ter-ing-ly** *adv.*

Ban-tu (băn'tōō) *n., pl.* **-tu** or **-tus. 1.** A member of a group of Negro tribes of central and southern Africa. **2.** A group of languages spoken by the Bantu. —**Ban'tu** *adj.*

ban-yan (băn'yən) *n.* Also **ban-ian.** A tropical tree having many aerial roots that develop into additional trunks. [< Skt. *vāṇiyo,* merchant.]

ban-zai (băn-zī') *n.* A Japanese battle cry or patriotic cheer. [J., ten thousand years.]

ba-o-bab (bā'ō-băb', bä'-) *n.* A tropical tree with a short, swollen trunk and large, hardshelled, hanging fruit. [Prob. a native word in central Africa.]

bap-tism (băp'tĭz'əm) *n.* **1.** A Christian sacrament of spiritual rebirth by which the recipient is cleansed of original sin through the symbolic application of water. **2.** An ordeal of initiation. [< LLat. *baptisma*.] —**bap·tis′mal** *adj*. —**bap·tis′mal·ly** *adv*.

Bap·tist (băp′tĭst) *n*. A member of any of various Protestant denominations practicing baptism by immersion.

bap·tis·ter·y (băp′tĭ-strē) *n., pl*. **-ies**. Also **bap·tis·try** *pl*. **-tries**. 1. A part of a church in which baptism is performed. 2. A baptismal font. 3. A tank for baptizing by total immersion.

bap·tize (băp-tīz′, băp′tīz′) *v*. **-tized, -tiz·ing.** 1. To dip or immerse in water during baptism. 2. a. To cleanse; purify. b. To initiate. 3. To give a first or Christian name to. —*v*. [< Gk. *baptizein*.] —**bap·tiz′er** *n*.

bar (bär) *n*. 1. A relatively long, rigid piece of solid material. 2. A solid oblong block of a substance, as soap. 3. An obstacle. 4. A band, as one formed by light. 5. The nullifying of a claim or action. 6. The railing in a courtroom in front of which the judges, lawyers, and defendants sit. 7. A system of law courts. 8. The legal profession. 9. A vertical line dividing a musical staff into measures. 10. a. A counter at which drinks are served. b. A place having such a counter. —*v*. **barred, bar·ring.** 1. To fasten or obstruct with or as if with bars. 2. To forbid; prohibit. 3. To exclude. 4. To obstruct. —*prep*. Excluding: *my poorest performance, bar none.* [OFr. *barre*.]

barb (bärb) *n*. 1. A sharp backward-pointing projection, as on a weapon, tool, or fishhook. 2. A cutting remark. 3. *Bot*. A hooked bristle or hairlike projection. 4. A parallel filament projecting from the main shaft of a feather. —*v*. To provide with barbs. [< Lat. *barba*, beard.]

bar·bar·i·an (bär-bâr′ē-ən) *n*. 1. A member of a people considered by others to be primitive, uncivilized, or savage. 2. A crude and savage person. [< Lat. *barbaria*, foreign country.] —**bar·bar′i·an** *adj*. —**bar·bar′i·an·ism** *n*.

bar·bar·ic (bär-băr′ĭk) *adj*. 1. Of or typical of a barbarian or barbarians. 2. Savage; cruel.

bar·ba·rism (bär′bə-rĭz′əm) *n*. 1. An act, trait, or custom characterized by brutality or coarseness. 2. The use of words or forms considered nonstandard in a language.

bar·ba·rous (bär′bər-əs) *adj*. 1. Wild; primitive; uncivilized. 2. Brutal; savage; cruel. 3. Uncultured or unrefined, esp. in the use of words. [< Gk. *barbaros*, foreign.] —**bar·bar′i·ty** (bär-băr′ĭ-tē) *n*. —**bar·ba·rize′** *v*. —**bar·ba·rous·ly** *adv*. —**bar·ba·rous·ness** *n*.

bar·be·cue (bär′bĭ-kyōō′) *n*. 1. A grill, pit, or outdoor fireplace for roasting meat. 2. Meat roasted over an open fire. 3. A social gathering at which food is barbecued. —*v*. **-cued, -cu·ing.** To roast (meat) over an open fire. [Prob. < Taino.]

barbed (bärbd) *adj*. 1. Having barbs. 2. Sharp; cutting: *barbed criticism.*

barbed wire *n*. Twisted strands of fence wire with barbs at regular intervals.

bar·bell (bär′bĕl′) *n*. A bar with adjustable weights at each end, lifted for sport or exercise.

bar·ber (bär′bər) *n*. One whose business is cutting hair and shaving or trimming beards. —*v*. To cut the hair or beard of. [< Lat. *barba*, beard.]

bar·ber·ry (bär′bĕr′ē) *n*. Any of various often spiny shrubs with small reddish berries. [< Ar. *barbārīs*.]

bar·bi·can (bär′bĭ-kən) *n*. An outdoor defensive fortification on the approach to a castle or town. [Med. Lat. *barbacana*.]

bar·bi·tal (bär′bĭ-tôl′) *n*. A white crystalline compound, $C_8H_{12}N_2O_3$, used as a sedative. [BARBIT(URIC ACID) + (*veron*)*al*.]

bar·bi·tu·rate (bär-bĭch′ər-ĭt, -ə-rāt′, bär′bĭ-tŏŏr′ĭt, -āt′, -tyŏŏr-) *n*. Any of a group of barbituric acid derivatives used as sedatives or hypnotics. [BARBITUR(IC ACID) + -ATE².]

bar·bi·tu·ric acid (bär-bĭ-tŏŏr′ĭk, -tyŏŏr′-) *n*. An organic acid, $C_4H_4N_2O_3$, used in the manufacture of barbiturates and some plastics. [< G. *Barbitursäure*.]

bar·ca·role (bär′kə-rōl′) *n*. Also **bar·ca·rolle.** A Venetian gondolier's song. [< Ital. *barcaruola*.]

bard (bärd) *n*. 1. One of an ancient Celtic order of singing, narrative poets. 2. A poet, esp. an exalted national poet. [< Ir. Gael. *bárd* and < Welsh *bardd*.] —**bard′ic** *adj*.

bare (bâr) *adj*. **bar·er, bar·est.** 1. Without the usual or appropriate covering or clothing. 2. Exposed to view. 3. Lacking the usual equipment or decoration. 4. Without addition or qualification: *the bare facts*. 5. Just sufficient: *the bare necessities*. —*v*. **bared, bar·ing.** To make bare; reveal. [< OE *bær*.] —**bare′ness** *n*.

Syns: *bare, bald, naked, nude adj.*

bare·back (bâr′băk′) *adj*. Using no saddle: *a bareback rider.* —**bare′back′** *adv*.

bare·faced (bâr′fāst′) *adj*. 1. Without covering or beard on the face. 2. Bold; brazen: *a barefaced lie.* —**bare′fac·ed·ly** (-fā′sĭd-lē, -fāst′lē) *adv*. —**bare′fac·ed·ness** *n*.

bare·foot (bâr′fŏŏt′) *adj*. Also **bare·foot·ed** (-fŏŏt′ĭd). Wearing nothing on the feet. —**bare′foot′** *adv*.

bare·hand·ed (bâr′hăn′dĭd) *adj*. 1. Having no covering on the hands. 2. Unaided by tools or weapons. —**bare′hand′ed** *adv*.

bare·head·ed (bâr′hĕd′ĭd) *adj*. With the head uncovered. —**bare′head′ed** *adv*.

bare·leg·ged (bâr′lĕg′ĭd, -lĕgd′) *adj*. Having the legs uncovered. —**bare′leg′ged** *adv*.

bare·ly (bâr′lē) *adv*. 1. By a very little; hardly. 2. Without disguise; openly.

bar·fly (bär′flī′) *n. Slang*. One who frequents bars.

bar·gain (bär′gĭn) *n*. 1. a. An agreement or contract, esp. one involving the sale and purchase of goods or services. b. The terms or conditions of such an agreement. c. The property acquired or services rendered as a result of such an agreement. 2. Something offered or acquired at a price advantageous to the buyer. —*v*. 1. To negotiate the terms of a sale, exchange, or other agreement. 2. To arrive at an agreement. —*phrasal verb*. **bargain for.** To expect; count on. —*idioms*. **into (or in) the bargain.** More than what is expected. **strike a bargain.** To agree on the terms of a purchase or joint undertaking. [< OFr. *bargaine*, of Gmc. orig.] —**bar′gain·er** *n*.

barge (bärj) *n*. 1. A long usu. flat-bottomed boat for transporting freight. 2. A large pleasure boat for parties. 3. *Naval*. A power boat for the use of a flag officer. —*v*. **barged, barg·ing.** 1. To carry by barge. 2. To move about clumsily. 3. To intrude. [OFr.]

bar graph *n*. A graph consisting of parallel, usu. vertical, bars or rectangles with lengths proportional to specified quantities.

bar·ite (bâr'īt', băr'-) *n.* A colorless crystalline mineral of barium sulfate that is the chief source of barium chemicals. [Gk. *barus,* heavy + -ITE¹.]

bar·i·tone (băr'ĭ-tōn') *n.* **1.** A male singing voice having a range higher than a bass and lower than a tenor. **2.** A singer having a baritone voice. **3.** A part written in the range of a baritone voice. [< Gk. *barutonos,* deep-sounding.]

bar·i·um (bâr'ē-əm, băr'-) *n. Symbol* **Ba** A soft, silvery-white metal, used to deoxidize copper, in various alloys, and in rat poison. Atomic number 56; atomic weight 137.34. [< Gk. *barus,* heavy.]

bark¹ (bärk) *n.* The short, harsh sound characteristically made by a dog. —*v.* **1.** To produce such a sound. **2.** To speak sharply; snap. —**idiom. bark up the wrong tree.** *Informal.* To wastefully misdirect one's energies. [< OE *beorcan,* to bark.]

bark² (bärk) *n.* **1.** The often rough outer covering of the stems and roots of trees and other woody plants. —*v.* **1.** To remove bark from. **2.** To scrape skin from. [< ON *börkr.*]

bark³ (bärk) *n.* Also **barque. 1.** A sailing ship with from three to five masts. **2.** A boat, esp. a small sailing vessel. [< LLat. *barca,* boat.]

bar·keep·er (bär'kē'pər) *n.* Also **bar·keep** (-kēp'). One who owns or runs a bar selling alcoholic beverages.

bark·er (bär'kər) *n.* **1.** One that makes a barking sound. **2.** One who stands at the entrance to a show and solicits customers with a loud sales pitch.

bar·ley (bär'lē) *n.* A cereal grass bearing grain used as food and in making beer and whiskey. [< OE *bære.*]

bar·maid (bär'mād') *n.* A woman who serves drinks in a bar.

bar·man (bär'mən) *n.* A man who serves drinks in a bar.

bar mitz·vah (bär mĭts'və) *n.* Also **bar mizvah. 1.** A thirteen-year-old Jewish boy who ceremonially assumes the religious responsibilities of an adult. **2.** The ceremony confirming a bar mitzvah. [Heb. *bar mitzvāh.*]

barn (bärn) *n.* A large farm building used for storing produce and for sheltering livestock. [< OE *bern.*]

bar·na·cle (bär'nə-kəl) *n.* A small, hard-shelled marine crustacean that attaches itself to submerged surfaces. [< Med. Lat. *bernaca.*] —**bar'na·cled** *adj.*

barnacle

barometer

barn·storm (bärn'stôrm') *v.* **1.** To travel about, presenting plays, lecturing, or making political speeches. **2.** To tour as a stunt flyer. —**barn'storm'er** *n.*

barn·yard (bärn'yärd') *n.* The often enclosed yard surrounding a barn.

ba·rom·e·ter (bə-rŏm'ĭ-tər) *n.* **1.** An instrument for measuring atmospheric pressure, used in weather forecasting and in determining elevation. **2.** An indicator of change. [Gk. *baros,* weight + -METER.] —**bar·o·met·ric** (băr'ə-mĕt'rĭk) or **bar·o·met·ri·cal** *adj.* —**bar·o·met·ri·cal·ly** *adv.* —**ba·rom'e·try** *n.*

bar·on (băr'ən) *n.* **1.** A male member of the lowest rank of nobility in Great Britain, certain European countries, and Japan. **2.** A man with great power in a particular field. [< OFr.] —**ba·ro'ni·al** *adj.* —**bar'o·ny** *n.*

bar·on·age (băr'ə-nĭj) *n.* **1.** The rank, title, or dignity of a baron. **2.** Peerage.

bar·on·ess (băr'ə-nĭs) *n.* **1.** The wife or widow of a baron. **2.** A woman holding a barony in her own right.

bar·on·et (băr'ə-nĭt, băr'ə-nĕt') *n.* An Englishman holding a hereditary title of honor next below a baron. —**bar'on·et·cy** *n.*

ba·roque (bə-rōk') *adj.* **1.** Often **Baroque.** Of an artistic style current in Europe from about 1500 to 1700, marked by extremely elaborate and ornate forms. **2.** Often **Baroque.** Of a musical style current in Europe from about 1600 to 1750, marked by strict forms and elaborate ornamentation. **3.** Irregularly shaped: *a baroque pearl.* **4.** Flamboyant; outlandish. [< Ital. *barocco.*] —**ba·roque'** *n.*

ba·rouche (bə-rōōsh') *n.* A four-wheeled, horse-drawn carriage with a folding top and a driver's seat outside. [G. *Barutsche.*]

barque (bärk) *n.* Var. of **bark³.**

bar·racks (băr'əks) *n.* (*used with a sing. or pl. verb*). A building or group of buildings used to house soldiers. [< Catalan *barraca.*]

bar·ra·cu·da (băr'ə-kōō'də) *n.* A narrow-bodied, chiefly tropical marine fish with very sharp teeth. [Mex. Sp.]

bar·rage (bə-räzh') *n.* **1.** A heavy curtain of missiles or artillery fire. **2.** A rapid outpouring: *a barrage of questions.* —*v.* **-raged, -raging.** To direct a barrage at. [Fr. *(tir de) barrage,* barrier (fire).]

bar·ra·try (băr'ə-trē) *n., pl.* **-tries. 1.** *Law.* The offense of exciting quarrels or groundless lawsuits. **2.** An unlawful breach of duty on the part of a ship's master or crew, resulting in injury to the ship's owner. **3.** The sale or purchase of positions in the church or state. [< OFr. *baraterie,* deception.] —**bar'ra·trous** *adj.*

bar·rel (băr'əl) *n.* **1.** A large cask usu. made of curved wooden staves and having a flat top and bottom. **2.** The quantity that a barrel will hold. **3.** A unit of volume or capacity, varying from about 117 to 159 liters or 31 to 42 gallons, as established by law or usage. **4. a.** The long tube of a gun. **b.** A cylindrical machine part. **5.** *Informal.* A great amount: *a barrel of fun.* —*v.* **-reled** or **-relled, -reling** or **-relling. 1.** To put or pack in a barrel or barrels. **2.** *Slang.* To move at breakneck speed. [< OFr. *bari.*]

barrel organ n. A portable musical instrument similar to a small organ, in which the airflow to the pipes is controlled by valves operated by a hand crank.

barrel roll n. A flight maneuver in which an aircraft makes a complete rotation on its longitudinal axis.

bar·ren (băr′ən) adj. **1. a.** Not producing offspring. **b.** Infertile; sterile. **2.** Lacking vegetation. **3.** Unproductive of results; unprofitable. **4.** Devoid; lacking: *writing barren of insight.* [OFr. *baraigne.*] —**bar′ren·ly** adv. —**bar′ren·ness** n.

Syns: barren, infertile, unproductive adj.

bar·rette (bə-rĕt′, bä-) n. A hair clasp. [Fr.]

bar·ri·cade (băr′ĭ-kād′, băr′ĭ-kād′) n. A makeshift barrier or fortification set up across a route of access. —v. **-cad·ed, -cad·ing. 1.** To block or confine with a barricade. [< OFr. *barrique*, barrel.]

bar·ri·er (băr′ē-ər) n. **1.** A fence, wall, or other structure built to block passage. **2.** A boundary or limit. **3.** Something that hinders or restricts. [OFr. *barriere.*]

barrier reef n. A long narrow ridge of coral parallel to a coastline and separated from it by a lagoon.

bar·ring (băr′ĭng) prep. Apart from the possibility of; excepting.

bar·ri·o (bä′rē-ō′) n., pl. **-os.** A chiefly Spanish-speaking community or neighborhood in a U.S. city. [< Ar. *barr*, open area.]

bar·ris·ter (băr′ĭ-stər) n. Chiefly Brit. A lawyer who argues cases in the superior courts. [Prob. < BAR.]

bar·room (băr′rōōm′, -rŏŏm′) n. A place where alcoholic beverages are sold at a bar.

bar·row¹ (băr′ō) n. **1.** A wheelbarrow. **2.** A flat, rectangular tray or cart with handles at each end. [< OE *bearwe.*]

bar·row² (băr′ō) n. Archaeol. A large mound of earth or stones placed over an ancient burial site. [< OE *beorg.*]

bar·tend·er (băr′tĕn′dər) n. One who mixes and serves alcoholic drinks at a bar.

bar·ter (băr′tər) v. To trade (e.g. goods or services) without using money. —n. **1.** The act of bartering. **2.** Something bartered. [Prob. < OFr. *barater.*] —**bar′ter·er** n.

bar·y·on (băr′ē-ŏn′) n. Any of a family of subatomic particles that are gen. more massive than the proton. [< Gk. *barus*, heavy.]

ba·sal (bā′səl, -zəl) adj. **1.** Pertaining to, located at, or forming a base. **2.** Of primary importance; basic. —**ba′sal·ly** adv.

basal metabolism n. The least amount of energy required to maintain vital functions in an organism at complete rest.

ba·salt (bə-sôlt′, bā′sôlt′) n. A hard, dense, dark volcanic rock. [< Gk. *basanitēs*, touchstone, of Egypt. orig.]

base¹ (bās) n. **1.** The lowest or bottom part. **2.** The fundamental principle or underlying concept of a system or theory. **3.** A chief constituent. **4.** The fact, observation, or premise from which a measurement or reasoning process is begun. **5.** Sports. A goal, starting point, or safety area. **6.** A center of organization, supply, or activity. **7. a.** A fortified center of operations. **b.** A supply center for a large force. **8.** Ling. A morpheme or morphemes regarded as a form to which affixes or other bases may be added. **9.** A line used as a reference for measurement or computations. **10. a.** Any of a large class of compounds, including the hydroxides and oxides of metals, having a bitter taste, a slippery solution, the ability to turn litmus blue, and the ability to react with acids to form salts. **b.** A molecular or ionic substance capable of combining with a proton to form a new substance. **11.** Math. The number that is raised to various powers to generate the principal counting units of a number system. —adj. Forming or serving as a base. —v. **based, bas·ing. 1.** To form or make a base for. **2.** To find a basis for; establish. —idiom. off base. **1.** Baseball. Not touching the base occupied. **2.** Badly mistaken, inaccurate, or unprepared. [< Gk. *basis.*]

base² (bās) adj. **bas·er, bas·est. 1.** Morally bad; contemptible. **2.** Lowly; menial: *base slavery.* **3.** Inferior in quality or value. [LLat. *bassus*, low.] —**base′ly** adv. —**base′ness** n.

base·ball (bās′bôl′) n. **1.** A game played with a usu. wooden bat and hard ball by two opposing teams of nine players, each team playing alternately in the field and at bat, the players at bat having to run a course of four bases laid out in a diamond pattern in order to score. **2.** The ball used in baseball.

base·board (bās′bôrd′, -bōrd′) n. A molding that conceals the joint between an interior wall and the floor.

base·born (bās′bôrn′) adj. **1.** Of humble birth. **2.** Born of unwed parents; illegitimate. **3.** Ignoble; contemptible.

base hit n. Baseball. A hit by which the batter reaches base safely, without an error or force play being made.

base·less (bās′lĭs) adj. Without basis or foundation in fact.

base line n. **1.** A line serving as a base for measurement or comparison. **2.** Baseball. An area within which a base runner must stay when running between successive bases. **3.** A line bounding each back end of a court in games such as tennis.

base·man (bās′mən) n. Baseball. A player assigned to first, second, or third base.

base·ment (bās′mənt) n. **1.** The substructure or foundation of a building. **2.** The lowest story of a building.

ba·sen·ji (bə-sĕn′jē) n., pl. **-jis.** A small dog having a short, smooth coat, and not uttering the barking sound typical of most dogs. [Bantu.]

base on balls n. Baseball. A walk.

base runner n. Baseball. A member of the team at bat who has safely reached or is trying to reach a base.

ba·ses (bā′sēz′) n. Pl. of **basis.**

bash (băsh) v. Informal. To strike with a heavy, crushing blow. —n. **1.** Informal. A heavy, crushing blow. **2.** Slang. A party. [Orig. unknown.]

bash·ful (băsh′fəl) adj. Timid; shy. [< ME *baschen*, to abash.] —**bash′ful·ly** adv. —**bash′ful·ness** n.

ba·sic (bā′sĭk) adj. **1.** Forming a basis. **2.** First and necessary before all else: *basic training.* **3.** Chem. a. Producing an excess of hydroxyl ions in solution. **b.** Of, producing, or resulting from a base. —n. Often **basics.** Something fundamental. —**ba′sic·al·ly** adv.

BA·SIC or **Ba·sic** (bā′sĭk) n. A language for programming a computer. [B(EGINNER'S) A(LL-PURPOSE) S(YMBOLIC) I(NSTRUCTION) C(ODE).]

bas·il (băz′əl, bā′zəl) n. An aromatic herb

with leaves used as seasoning. [< Gk. *basilikon,* royal.]

bas·i·lar (băs'ə-lər) *adj.* Also **bas·i·lar·y** (-lĕr'ē). Of or located at or near the base, esp. of the skull. [< Gk. *basis,* bottom.]

ba·sil·i·ca (bə-sĭl'ĭ-kə) *n.* 1. An oblong building used as a court or place of assembly in ancient Rome. 2. A building of this type used as a Christian church. 3. A church accorded certain ceremonial rights by the pope. [< Gk. *basilikē* (*stoa*), royal portico.]

bas·i·lisk (băs'ə-lĭsk', băz'-) *n.* A legendary serpent with lethal breath and glance. [< Gk. *basiliskos.*]

ba·sin (bā'sən) *n.* 1. A round, open, shallow container used esp. for holding liquids. 2. The amount that a basin holds. 3. An artificially enclosed area of a river or harbor. 4. A small enclosed or partly enclosed body of water. 5. A bowl-shaped depression in a land or ocean-floor surface. [< OFr. *bacin.*]

ba·sis (bā'sĭs) *n., pl.* **-ses** (-sēz'). 1. A foundation; a supporting element. 2. The main part. 3. Principle; criterion. [< Gk.]

bask (băsk) *v.* 1. To expose oneself pleasantly to warmth. 2. To thrive in the presence of a pleasant or advantageous influence. [ME *basken.*]

bas·ket (băs'kĭt) *n.* 1. A container made of interwoven material. 2. The amount a basket holds. 3. *Basketball.* A hoop with an open-ended net suspended from it, serving as a goal. [ME.]

bas·ket·ball (băs'kĭt-bôl') *n.* 1. A game played between two teams of five players each, the object being to throw the ball through an elevated basket on the opponent's side of the rectangular court. 2. The ball used in this game.

basket case *n. Informal.* One who is in a completely hopeless or useless condition.

bas mitz·vah (bäs mĭts'və) *n.* Var. of **bat mitzvah.**

Basque (băsk) *n.* 1. One of a people of unknown origin inhabiting the western Pyrenees in France and Spain. 2. The language of the Basques, of no known linguistic affiliation.

bas·re·lief (bä'rĭ-lēf') *n. Sculpture.* Low relief. [< Ital. *bassorilievo.*]

bass¹ (băs) *n.* Any of several freshwater or marine food fishes. [< OE *bærs.*]

bass² (bās) *n.* 1. A low-pitched tone. 2. The tones in the lowest register of a musical instrument. 3. The lowest part in vocal or instrumental part music. 4. A male singing voice of the lowest range. 5. A singer having a bass voice. 6. A part written in the range of a bass voice. 7. An instrument that sounds within the range of a bass. [ME *bas.*] —**bass** *adj.*

basset hound *n.* A short-haired dog with a long body, short, crooked forelegs, and long, drooping ears. [Fr. *basset,* short + HOUND.]

bas·si·net (băs'ə-nĕt', băs'ə-nĕt') *n.* An oblong basket on legs, used as a crib for an infant. [Fr., a small basin.]

bas·so (băs'ō, bä'sō) *n., pl.* **-sos** or **-si** (-sē). A bass singer. [Ital.]

bas·soon (bə-sōōn', bă-) *n.* A woodwind instrument with a long wooden body connected

to a double reed by a bent metal tube. [< Ital. *bassone.*] —**bas·soon'ist** *n.*

bass viol (bās) *n.* A double bass.

bass·wood (băs'wŏŏd') *n.* A North American linden tree.

bast (băst) *n.* Fibrous plant material used to make cordage and textiles. [< OE *bæst.*]

bas·tard (băs'tərd) *n.* 1. An illegitimate child. 2. *Slang.* A mean person. [< OFr.] —**bas'tard** *adj.* —**bas'tard·ly** *adj.* —**bas'tard·y** *n.*

bas·tard·ize (băs'tər-dīz') *v.* **-ized, -iz·ing.** To debase; corrupt. —**bas'tard·i·za'tion** *n.*

baste¹ (bāst) *v.* **bast·ed, bast·ing.** To sew loosely with large, running, temporary stitches. [< OFr. *bastir.*]

baste² (bāst) *v.* **bast·ed, bast·ing.** To pour liquid over (meat) while cooking. [Orig. unknown.]

baste³ (bāst) *v.* **bast·ed, bast·ing.** 1. To beat vigorously; thrash. 2. To berate. [Orig. unknown.]

bas·ti·na·do (băs'tə-nā'dō, -nä'-) *n., pl.* **-does.** 1. A beating, esp. on the soles of the feet. 2. A stick or cudgel. —*v.* **-doed, -do·ing.** To subject to a beating. [Sp. *bastonada.*]

bas·tion (băs'chən, -tē-ən) *n.* 1. A projecting part of a fortification. 2. A well-defended position. [< OFr. *bastille,* jail.]

bat¹ (băt) *n.* 1. A stout wooden stick or club; cudgel. 2. A sharp blow. 3. a. *Baseball.* A rounded, tapered, usu. wooden club used to strike the ball. b. A flat-surfaced wooden club used in cricket. 4. *Slang.* A binge; spree. —*v.* **bat·ted, bat·ting.** 1. To hit with or as if with a bat. 2. *Baseball.* a. To have (a certain percentage) as a batting average. b. To be the hitting team or hitter. —*idioms.* **at bat.** Having a turn as a hitter in baseball. **go to bat for.** To support or defend. **right off the bat.** Immediately. [< OE *batt.*]

bat² (băt) *n.* A mouselike flying mammal with membranous wings. [Of Scand. orig.]

bat³ (băt) *v.* **bat·ted, bat·ting.** To flutter. [Prob. < *bate,* to flap wings.]

batch (băch) *n.* 1. An amount prepared or produced at one time. 2. A group of persons or things. [< OE *bacan,* to bake.]

bate (bāt) *v.* **bat·ed, bat·ing.** To lessen the force of; restrain; moderate. [< ME *abaten,* to abate.]

ba·teau (bă-tō') *n., pl.* **-teaux** (-tōz'). A light, flat-bottomed boat. [Fr., boat, prob. < OE *bāt.*]

bath (băth, bäth) *n., pl.* **baths** (bă*th*z, bä*th*z, băths, bäths). 1. a. The act of washing or soaking the body in water. b. The water used for bathing. 2. a. A bathtub. b. A bathroom. 3. **baths.** a. A building equipped for bathing: *the ruins of Roman public baths.* b. A spa. 4. A liquid, or a liquid and its container, in which an object is dipped or soaked so as to process it. [OE *bæth.*]

bathe (bā*th*) *v.* **bathed, bath·ing.** 1. To take a bath. 2. To give a bath to. 3. To go swimming. 4. To soak in a liquid for soothing or healing purposes. 5. To make wet; moisten. 6. To suffuse. [< OE *bathian.*] —**bath'er** *n.*

bath·house (băth'hous', bäth'-) *n.* 1. A building equipped for bathing. 2. A building with dressing rooms for swimmers.

bathing suit *n.* A swimsuit.

ă pat ā pay â care ä father ĕ pet ē be ĭ pit ī tie î pier ŏ pot ō toe ô paw, for oi noise ŏŏ took
ŏŏ boot ou out th thin *th* this ŭ cut û urge yŏŏ abuse zh vision ə about, item, edible, gallop, circus

bathos | bayonet

ba·thos (bā'thŏs') *n.* **1.** A ludicrously abrupt transition from an elevated to a commonplace style. **2.** Insincere or grossly sentimental pathos. [Gk., depth.] —**ba·thet'ic** *adj.*

bath·robe (băth'rōb', bäth'-) *n.* A loose-fitting robe worn before and after bathing and for lounging.

bath·room (băth'rŏōm', -rŏōm', bäth'-) *n.* A room equipped with a bathtub or shower and usu. a sink and toilet.

bath salts *pl.n.* Perfumed crystals for softening the water in a bathtub.

bath·tub (băth'tŭb', bäth'-) *n.* A tub to bathe in.

bath·y·scaph (băth'ĭ-skăf') *n.* Also **bath·y·scaphe.** A free-diving, self-contained deep-sea research vessel, consisting of a large flotation hull with a manned observation capsule fixed to its underside. [Fr.]

bath·y·sphere (băth'ĭ-sfîr') *n.* A manned spherical deep-diving chamber lowered by cable. [Gk. *bathus*, deep + SPHERE.]

ba·tik (bə-tēk', băt'ĭk) *n.* **1.** A dyeing method in which designs are made by covering fabric parts with removable wax. **2.** Cloth thus dyed. [Malay.]

ba·tiste (bə-tēst', bă-) *n.* A fine, thin, light fabric usu. of cotton or linen. [Fr.]

bat mitz·vah (băt mĭts'və) *n.* Also **bas mitz·vah** (bäs). **1.** A Jewish girl of 12 to 14 years old who ceremonially assumes her Jewish duties and responsibilities. **2.** The ceremony confirming a bat mitzvah. [Heb. *bat mitzvāh*.]

ba·ton (bə-tŏn', băt'n) *n.* **1.** A thin, tapered stick often used by the conductor in leading an orchestra. **2.** A hollow metal rod with heavy rubber tips twirled by a drum major or majorette. [< LLat. *bastum*, stick.]

bats (băts) *adj. Slang.* Crazy.

bats·man (băts'mən) *n. Baseball & Cricket.* A player at bat.

bat·tal·ion (bə-tăl'yən) *n.* **1.** A tactical military unit, consisting of a headquarters company and four infantry companies or a headquarters battery and four artillery batteries. **2.** A large group of people. [< OItal. *battaglione*.]

bat·ten (băt'n) *n.* A flexible wooden strip for covering, fastening, or flattening parts. —*v.* **1.** To furnish with battens. **2.** To secure with or as if with battens: *batten down the hatches.* [< BATON.]

bat·ter¹ (băt'ər) *v.* To pound or damage with heavy blows. [< Lat. *battuere.*]

bat·ter² (băt'ər) *n. Baseball & Cricket.* A player at bat.

bat·ter³ (băt'ər) *n.* A thick, beaten mixture, as of flour, milk, and eggs, used in cooking. [ME *bater.*]

battered child syndrome *n.* A combination of serious physical injuries inflicted on a child through gross abuse usu. by parents or guardians.

bat·ter·ing-ram (băt'ər-ĭng-răm') *n.* Also **battering ram.** An ancient siege engine used to batter down walls and gates.

bat·ter·y (băt'ə-rē) *n., pl.* **-ies. 1.** The unlawful beating of a person. **2. a.** An artillery emplacement. **b.** A set of artillery pieces, as on a warship. **3.** An array: *a battery of lawyers.* **4.** *Baseball.* The pitcher and catcher. **5.** The percussion section of an orchestra. **6.** A device for generating an electric current. [< OFr. *battre*, to batter.]

bat·ting (băt'ĭng) *n.* Cotton or wool fiber wadded into a flat mass, used to stuff mattresses, line quilts, etc.

batting average *n.* The ratio of the number of a baseball player's hits to the number of times at bat.

bat·tle (băt'l) *n.* **1.** A large-scale combat between two armed forces. **2.** An intense competition or hard struggle. —*v.* **-tled, -tling.** **1.** To engage in or as if in battle. **2.** To fight against. [< LLat. *battualia*, fighting and fencing exercises.] —**bat'tler** *n.*

bat·tle-ax or **bat·tle-axe** (băt'l-ăks') *n.* A heavy ax formerly used as a weapon.

battle cry *n.* **1.** A shout uttered by troops in battle. **2.** A militant slogan.

bat·tle·field (băt'l-fēld') *n.* **1.** A place where a battle is fought. **2.** An area of conflict.

bat·tle·front (băt'l-frŭnt') *n.* The area where opponents meet in battle.

bat·tle·ground (băt'l-ground') *n.* A battlefield.

bat·tle·ment (băt'l-mənt) *n.* Often **battlements.** A parapet on top of a wall, with indentations for defense or decoration. —**bat'tle·ment'ed** (-měn'tĭd) *adj.*

battle royal *n., pl.* **battles royal. 1.** A battle with many combatants. **2.** A bitter quarrel.

bat·tle·ship (băt'l-shĭp') *n.* Any of the largest, most heavily armed and armored class of warships.

bat·tle·wag·on (băt'l-wăg'ən) *n. Slang.* A battleship.

bat·ty (băt'ē) *adj.* **-ti·er, -ti·est.** *Slang.* Insane.

bau·ble (bô'bəl) *n.* A trinket. [< OFr. *baubel*, plaything.]

baux·ite (bôk'sīt') *n.* The principal ore of aluminum, 30 to 75 per cent $Al_2O_3 \cdot nH_2O$, with ferric oxide and silica as impurities. [< Les *Baux*, France.]

bawd (bôd) *n.* **1.** A woman who keeps a brothel. **2.** A prostitute. [ME *bawde.*]

bawd·y (bô'dē) *adj.* **-i·er, -i·est.** Coarsely and humorously indecent. —**bawd'i·ly** *adv.* —**bawd'i·ness** *n.*

bawl (bôl) *v.* To cry out loudly and vehemently; bellow. —*phrasal verb.* **bawl out.** *Informal.* To scold loudly or harshly. —*n.* A bellowing cry. [ME *baulen.*] —**bawl'er** *n.*

bay¹ (bā) *n.* A body of water partly enclosed by land, but having a wide outlet to the sea. [< OFr. *baie.*]

bay² (bā) *n.* **1.** *Archit.* A compartment set off from other compartments making up a given structure. **2.** A projecting compartment containing a window. **3.** An opening or recess in a wall. [< OFr. *baee*, an opening.]

bay³ (bā) *adj.* Reddish brown. —*n.* **1.** A reddish brown. **2.** A reddish-brown animal, esp. a horse. [< Lat. *badius.*]

bay⁴ (bā) *n.* A deep, prolonged barking, esp. of hounds. —*v.* To utter a deep, prolonged bark. —**idiom. at (or to) bay. 1.** Cornered by and facing pursuers. **2.** At a distance so as to ward off danger: *keep trouble at bay.* [< OFr. *baiier.*]

bay⁵ (bā) *n.* A laurel with stiff, glossy, aromatic leaves. **2.** A similar tree or shrub. [< Lat. *baca*, berry.]

bay·ber·ry (bā'běr'ē) *n.* **1.** An aromatic shrub bearing waxy, pleasant-smelling berries. **2.** The fruit of such a shrub.

bay leaf *n.* The dried, aromatic leaf of the laurel, used as seasoning.

bay·o·net (bā'ə-nĭt, -nět', bā'ə-nět') *n.* A knife adapted to fit the muzzle end of a rifle. —*v.*

-net·ed or **-net·ted, -net·ing** or **-net·ting.** To stab with a bayonet. [< *Bayonne,* France.]

bay·ou (bī′ōō, bī′ō) *n., pl.* **-ous.** *Southern U.S.* A marshy, sluggish body of water connected with a lake or river. [< Choctaw *bayuk.*]

bay window *n.* **1.** A large window or group of windows projecting from the outer wall of a building and forming an alcove in the room within. **2.** *Slang.* A protruding belly.

ba·zaar (bə-zär′) *n.* Also **ba·zar. 1.** An Oriental market consisting of a street lined with shops and stalls. **2.** A fair for charity. [< Pers. *bāzār.*]

ba·zoo·ka (bə-zōō′kə) *n.* A portable tube-shaped weapon that fires small, armor-piercing rockets. [< *bazooka,* a crude wind instrument, invented and named by Bob Burns (1896–1956).]

BB *n.* A standard size of lead shot that measures about .46 cm, or 0.18 in., in diameter.

be (bē) *v.*

	1st person	2nd person	3rd person
Present Tense			
singular	am (ăm)	are (är)†	is (ĭz)
plural	are	are	are

†*Archaic 2nd person singular* **art** (ärt)

Past Tense			
singular	was (wŭz, wŏz)	were (wûr)‡	was
plural	were	were	were

‡*Archaic 2nd person singular* **wast** (wŏst) or **wert** (wûrt)

Present Participle: **being** (bē′ĭng) Present Subjunctive: **be**
Past Participle: **been** (bĭn) Past Subjunctive: **were**

1. To exist: *I think, therefore I am.* **2.** To exist in a specified place: *"Oh, to be in England,/ Now that April's there"* (Robert Browning). **3.** To occupy a specified position: *The food is on the table.* **4.** To take place; occur. **5.** To go. Used chiefly in the past and perfect tenses: *Have you ever been to Italy?* **6.** *Archaic.* To belong; befall. Used in the subjunctive: *Peace be unto you.* **7.** Used as a copula linking a subject and a predicate nominative, adjective, or pronoun, as: **a.** To equal in meaning or identity: *"To be a Christian was to be a Roman."* (James Bryce). **b.** To signify; symbolize: *A is excellent, C is passing.* **c.** To belong to a specified class or group: *Man is a primate.* **d.** To have or show a specified quality or characteristic: *She is lovely. All humans are mortal.* **8.** Used as an auxiliary verb, as: **a.** With the past participle of a transitive verb to form the passive voice: *The election is held annually.* **b.** With the present participle of a verb to express a continuing action: *We are working to improve housing conditions.* **c.** With the present participle or the infinitive of a verb to express intention, obligation, or future action: *She is to eat her dinner before she may play. He is leaving next month.* **d.** With the past participle of certain intransitive verbs of motion to form the perfect tense: *"Where be those roses gone which sweetened so our eyes?"* (Philip Sidney). **—idiom. let be.** *Informal.* To let (someone) alone: *Go away and let me be.* [< OE *bēon.*]

Be The symbol for the element beryllium.

be- *pref.* **1.** Completely: *bemoan.* **2.** On; over: *besmear.* **3. a.** Cause to become; make: *besot.* **b.** Affect or provide with: *bedew.* [< OE.]

beach (bēch) *n.* The shore of a body of water. **—v.** To go or haul ashore. [Orig. unknown.]

beach buggy *n.* A dune buggy.

beach·comb·er (bēch′kō′mər) *n.* **1.** A drifter or loafer living on the beach. **2.** A long wave rolling in toward a beach.

beach·head (bēch′hĕd′) *n.* **1.** A position on an enemy shoreline captured by advance troops of an invading force. **2.** A first achievement that opens the way for further development; foothold.

bea·con (bē′kən) *n.* **1.** A signal fire. **2.** A lighthouse. **3.** A radio transmitter that emits a signal to guide aircraft. [< OE *bēacen.*]

bead (bēd) *n.* **1.** A small piece of material pierced for stringing. **2. beads. a.** A necklace made of beads. **b.** A rosary. **3.** Any small, round object. **4.** A narrow projecting strip of molding. **—v. 1.** To decorate with beads. **2.** To collect into beads. **—idioms. count** (or **say** or **tell**) **one's beads.** To pray with a rosary. **draw a bead on.** To take careful aim at. [< OE *gebed,* prayer.] **—bead'y** *adj.*

bea·dle (bēd′l) *n.* A minor parish official in the Church of England. [< OE *bydel.*]

bea·gle (bē′gəl) *n.* A small, smooth-coated hound with pendulous ears, often used as a hunting dog. [ME *begle.*]

beak (bēk) *n.* **1.** The horny, projecting mouth parts of a bird; bill. **2.** A similar part or structure. [< Lat. *beccus,* of Celt. orig.]

beak·er (bē′kər) *n.* **1.** A large drinking cup with a wide mouth. **2.** An open glass cylinder with a pouring lip, used as a laboratory container. [< ON *bikarr.*]

beam (bēm) *n.* **1.** A length of timber forming a supporting member in construction. **2.** *Naut.* A ship's maximum breadth. **3.** A constant directional radio signal for navigational guidance. **4. a.** A ray of light. **b.** A group of particles traveling together in close parallel trajectories. **—v. 1.** To emit or transmit. **2.** To radiate. **3.** To smile radiantly. **—idiom. on the beam. 1.** Following a radio beam, as an aircraft. **2.** *Informal.* On the right track. [< OE *bēam.*]

bean (bēn) *n.* **1.** The often edible seed or seed pod of any of various plants. **2.** A plant bearing such seeds or pods. **3.** *Slang.* The head. **—v.** *Slang.* To hit on the head. **—idiom. spill the beans.** To reveal a secret. [< OE *bēan.*]

bean·bag (bēn′băg′) *n.* A small bag filled with dried beans and used for throwing in games.

bean ball *n.* A baseball pitch aimed at the batter's head.

bean curd *n.* A soft, cheeselike food made from puréed soybeans.

bean·ie (bē′nē) *n.* A small brimless cap.

bean·o (bē′nō) *n., pl.* **-os.** A form of bingo.

bean·pole (bēn′pōl′) *n.* **1.** A pole around which a bean vine twines. **2.** *Slang.* A tall, thin person.

bean sprout *n.* A young, tender shoot of certain beans, such as the soybean.

bear¹ (bâr) *v.* **bore** (bôr, bōr), **borne** (bôrn) or

---

born, bear-ing. 1. a. To carry; support. b. To carry on one's person. 2. To endure. 3. To conduct (oneself). 4. To have; show; exhibit. 5. To transmit: *bear good tidings.* 6. To render; give: *bear witness.* 7. *p.p.* born. To give birth to. 8. To yield; produce. 9. a. To permit of or be liable to: *This will bear investigation.* b. To have relevance; apply. c. To be accountable for: *bear the responsibility.* 10. To exert pressure. 11. To proceed (in a specified direction): *bear right.* —*phrasal verbs.* bear down. 1. To weigh on: *financial pressure bearing down on us.* 2. To exert oneself: *I bore down and got the job done.* bear out. To prove right; confirm. bear up. To endure. bear with. To be patient or tolerant with. —*idioms.* bear in mind. To be careful or vigilant. bring to bear. To exert pressure or influence. [< OE *beran.*] —bear'a-ble *adj.* —bear'a-bly *adv.* —bear'er *n.*

bear² (bâr) *n.* 1. Any of various usu. large mammals having a shaggy coat and a short tail. 2. A clumsy or ill-mannered person. 3. An investor or concern that sells shares in the expectation that prices will fall. [< OE *bera.*]

bear²

beard (bîrd) *n.* 1. The hair on the chin and cheeks of a man. 2. Any similar hairy or hair-like growth, as on an animal or plant. —*v.* To confront boldly. [< OE.]

bear hug *n.* A rough hug.

bear-ing (bâr'ĭng) *n.* 1. Deportment; mien. 2. A device that supports, guides, and reduces friction between fixed and moving machine parts. 3. A supportive element. 4. Relationship or relevance. 5. a. Direction measured relative to geographical or celestial reference lines. b. A navigational determination of position. 6. bearings. Grasp of one's position in relation to one's surroundings. 7. A heraldic emblem.

bear-ish (bâr'ĭsh) *adj.* 1. Clumsy, boorish, or surly. 2. Causing, expecting, or characterized by falling stock-market prices. —bear'ish-ly *adv.* —bear'ish-ness *n.*

béar-naise sauce (bā'ăr-nāz', -ər-) *n.* A sauce flavored with tarragon, chervil, and shallots. [< Fr. *béarnaise,* of Béarn.]

bear-skin (bâr'skĭn') *n.* 1. The skin of a bear. 2. A tall military headdress made of black fur.

beast (bēst) *n.* 1. Any animal, esp. a large, four-footed animal. 2. A brutal person. [< Lat. *bestia.*]

beast-ly (bēst'lē) *adj.* -li-er, -li-est. 1. Of or like a beast; savage. 2. Disagreeable; nasty: *beastly behavior.* —beast'li-ness *n.*

beat (bēt) *v.* beat, beat-en (bēt'n) or beat, beat-ing. 1. To strike repeatedly. 2. To forge. 3. To flatten by trampling; tread. 4. To de-

feat. 5. To excel; surpass. 6. *Slang.* To baffle. 7. To pulsate; throb. 8. To mix rapidly: *beat eggs.* 9. To flap, as wings. 10. To sound (a signal), as on a drum. 11. *Informal.* To counter the effects of; circumvent: *beat the traffic.* —*phrasal verbs.* beat off. To drive away. beat up. *Informal.* To thrash. —*n.* 1. A stroke; blow. 2. A pulsation; throb. 3. A rhythmic stress. 4. A regular round: *the night beat.* —*adj.* Tired; exhausted. —*idioms.* beat about (or around) the bush. To approach a subject in a roundabout manner. beat a retreat. To flee or withdraw. beat it. *Slang.* To get going; go away. beat (one's) brains out. *Informal.* To try energetically. [< OE *bēatan.*] —beat'er *n.*

be-a-tif-ic (bē'ə-tĭf'ĭk) *adj.* Showing or producing extreme joy or bliss: *a beatific smile.* [LLat. *beatificus.*] —be'a-tif'i-cal-ly *adv.*

be-at-i-fy (bē-ăt'ə-fī') *v.* -fied, -fy-ing. 1. To make blissfully happy. 2. *Rom. Cath. Ch.* To proclaim (a deceased person) to be one of the blessed. —be-at'i-fi-ca'tion (-fĭ-kā'shən) *n.*

be-at-i-tude (bē-ăt'ĭ-tōōd', -tyōōd') *n.* Supreme blessedness. [Lat. *beatitudo.*]

beat-nik (bēt'nĭk) *n.* A person who acts and dresses with exaggerated disregard for what is thought proper.

beau (bō) *n.*, *pl.* beaus or beaux (bōz). 1. A suitor. 2. A dandy. [Fr., handsome.]

Beau Brum-mell (brŭm'əl) *n.* A dandy; fop. [< George Bryan ("Beau") Brummell (1778–1840).]

beau geste (bō zhĕst') *n,* *pl.* beaux gestes (bō zhĕst') or beau gestes (bō zhĕst'). 1. A gracious gesture. 2. A gesture that appears noble but is meaningless and empty. [Fr.]

beau i-de-al (bō' ĭ-dē'əl) *n.*, *pl.* beau i-de-als. An ideal type or model. [Fr. *beau idéal.*]

beau monde (bō mŏnd', MÔND') *n.*, *pl.* beaux mondes (bō MÔND') or beau mondes (bō mŏndz'). Fashionable society. [Fr.]

beaut (byōōt) *n.* *Slang.* Something outstanding of its kind. [< BEAUTY.]

beau-te-ous (byōō'tē-əs, -tyəs) *adj.* Beautiful. —beau'te-ous-ly *adv.* —beau'te-ous-ness *n.*

beau-ti-cian (byōō-tĭsh'ən) *n.* One skilled in cosmetic treatments, as in a beauty parlor.

beau-ti-ful (byōō'tə-fəl) *adj.* Having beauty. —beau'ti-ful-ly *adv.* —beau'ti-ful-ness *n.*

Syns: *beautiful, attractive, beauteous, comely, fair[1], good-looking, gorgeous, handsome, lovely, pretty, ravishing adj.*

beautiful people *pl.n.* Also Beautiful People. Prominent members of international society.

beau-ti-fy (byōō'tə-fī') *v.* -fied, -fy-ing. To make or become more beautiful. —beau'ti-fi-ca'tion *n.* —beau'ti-fi'er *n.*

beau-ty (byōō'tē) *n.,* *pl.* -ties. 1. A quality that pleases the senses or mind. 2. One that is beautiful. [< Lat. *bellus,* pretty.]

beauty parlor *n.* An establishment providing women with hair treatment, manicures, facials, etc.

beaux (bō) *n.* A pl. of beau.

beaux-arts (bō-zär') *pl.n.* The fine arts. [Fr.]

bea-ver (bē'vər) *n.* 1. A large aquatic rodent with thick fur, webbed hind feet, a paddlelike tail, and sharp front teeth with which it fells trees to build dams. 2. The fur of a beaver. [< OE *beofor.*]

be-calm (bĭ-käm') *v.* To render motionless for lack of wind.

be-came (bĭ-kām') *v.* *p.t.* of become.

be-cause (bĭ-kôz', -kŭz') *conj.* For the reason

that; since. —*Idiom.* **because of.** By reason of; on account of. [ME *bi cause.*]

Usage: *Because* sometimes occurs in informal speech to mean "just because," as in *Because he works hard he thinks he should be promoted.* This use of *because* should be avoided in formal style.

beck (bĕk) *n.* A summons. —*Idiom.* **at one's beck and call.** Willingly obedient. [ME *bek,* order.]

beck·on (bĕk′ən) *v.* **1.** To summon by nodding or waving. **2.** To attract. [< OE *bēcnan.*]

be·cloud (bĭ-kloud′) *v.* To obscure.

be·come (bĭ-kŭm′) *v.* **-came** (-kām′), **-come, -com·ing. 1.** To grow or come to be. **2.** To be appropriate or suitable to. —*phrasal verb.* **become of.** To be the fate of: *What will become of me?* [< OE *becuman.*]

be·com·ing (bĭ-kŭm′ĭng) *adj.* **1.** Appropriate; suitable. **2.** Attractive. —**be·com′ing·ly** *adv.*

bed (bĕd) *n.* **1.** A piece of furniture for reclining and sleeping. **2.** A small plot of cultivated ground: *flower beds.* **3. a.** The surface at the bottom of a body of water. **b.** A horizontally extending layer of earth or rock. **4.** A foundation. **5.** *Geol.* A deposit, as of ore. —*v.* **bed·ded, bed·ding. 1.** To furnish with a bed. **2.** To put to bed. **3. a.** To prepare (soil) for planting. **b.** To plant in a prepared bed of soil. **4.** To lay flat or arrange in layers. **5.** To embed. [< OE.]

be·daub (bĭ-dôb′) *v.* To smear.

be·daz·zle (bĭ-dăz′əl) *v.* **-zled, -zling.** To dazzle so completely as to confuse or blind.

bed·bug (bĕd′bŭg′) *n.* A wingless, bloodsucking insect that often infests human dwellings.

bed·clothes (bĕd′klōz′, -klōthz′) *pl.n.* Coverings used on a bed.

bed·ding (bĕd′ĭng) *n.* **1.** Bedclothes. **2.** Straw or similar material for animals to sleep on. **3.** A foundation.

be·deck (bĭ-dĕk′) *v.* To adorn.

be·dev·il (bĭ-dĕv′əl) *v.* **-iled** or **-illed, -il·ing** or **-il·ling. 1.** To torment; harass. **2.** To worry or frustrate. —**be·dev′il·ment** *n.*

be·dew (bĭ-dōō′, -dyōō′) *v.* To wet with or as if with dew.

bed·fel·low (bĕd′fĕl′ō) *n.* **1.** One with whom a bed is shared. **2.** A temporary associate.

be·di·zen (bĭ-dī′zən, -dĭz′ən) *v.* To dress or ornament gaudily. [BE- + *dizen,* to dress.]

bed·lam (bĕd′ləm) *n.* **1.** A place of noisy confusion. **2.** A madhouse. [ME *Bedlam,* Hospital of St. Mary of *Bethlehem,* London, an insane asylum.]

Bed·ou·in (bĕd′ōō-ĭn, bĕd′wĭn) *n.* An Arab of any of the nomadic tribes of the deserts of North Africa, Arabia, and Syria. [< Ar. *badāwī.*]

bed·pan (bĕd′păn′) *n.* A receptacle used as a toilet by a bedridden person.

bed·post (bĕd′pōst′) *n.* Any of the four vertical posts at the corners of some beds.

bed·rid·den (bĕd′rĭd′n) *adj.* Confined to bed. [< OE *bedrida,* bedridden person.]

bed·rock (bĕd′rŏk′) *n.* **1.** Solid rock that underlies the earth's surface. **2.** The lowest or bottom level. **3.** Fundamental principles.

bed·roll (bĕd′rōl′) *n.* A portable roll of bedding.

bed·room (bĕd′rōōm′, -rōōm′) *n.* A room for sleeping.

bed·side (bĕd′sīd′) *n.* The space alongside a bed, esp. the bed of a sick person. —**bed′side′** *adj.*

bed·sore (bĕd′sôr′, -sōr′) *n.* A pressure-induced skin ulceration occurring during long confinement to bed.

bed·spread (bĕd′sprĕd′) *n.* A decorative bed covering.

bed·stead (bĕd′stĕd′) *n.* The frame supporting a bed.

bed·time (bĕd′tīm′) *n.* The time when one goes to bed.

bee (bē) *n.* **1.** Any of various winged, usu. stinging insects that gather nectar and pollen from flowers and in some species produce honey. **2.** A gathering where people work together or compete. —*idiom.* **a bee in (one's) bonnet.** An idea that fills most of one's thoughts. [< OE *bēo.*]

beech (bēch) *n.* A tree having light-colored bark, edible nuts, and strong, heavy wood. [< OE *bēce.*]

beech·nut (bēch′nŭt′) *n.* The nut of the beech tree.

beef (bēf) *n., pl.* **beeves** (bēvz). **1.** A full-grown steer, bull, ox, or cow, esp. one intended for use as meat. **2.** The flesh of a slaughtered steer, bull, ox, or cow. **3.** *Informal.* Human muscle; brawn. **4.** *pl.* **beefs.** *Slang.* A complaint. —*v. Slang.* To complain. —*phrasal verb.* **beef up.** *Slang.* To reinforce; build up. [< Lat. *bos.*]

beef·eat·er (bēf′ē′tər) *n.* A yeoman of the royal guard in England or a warder of the Tower of London.

beef·y (bē′fē) *adj.* **-i·er, -i·est.** Muscular in build; heavy; brawny: *a beefy wrestler.* —**beef′i·ness** *n.*

bee·hive (bē′hīv′) *n.* **1.** A hive for bees. **2.** A place teeming with activity.

bee·keep·er (bē′kē′pər) *n.* One who keeps bees.

bee·line (bē′līn′) *n.* A fast, straight course.

Be·el·ze·bub (bē-ĕl′zə-bŭb′) *n.* The Devil. [< Heb. *ba'al zbūb,* lord of the flies.]

been (bĭn) *v. p.p.* of **be.**

beep (bēp) *n.* A signaling or warning sound, as from an electronic device. [Imit.] —**beep** *v.*

beep·er (bē′pər) *n.* A small portable electronic paging device that emits a beeping signal.

beer (bîr) *n.* **1.** An alcoholic beverage brewed from malt and hops. **2.** Any of various carbonated soft drinks. [< OE *bēor.*]

bees·wax (bēz′wăks′) *n.* The wax secreted by bees for making honeycombs and having a variety of commercial uses.

beet (bēt) *n.* A cultivated plant with a fleshy dark-red or whitish root used as a vegetable or as a source of sugar. [< Lat. *beta.*]

bee·tle¹ (bēt′l) *n.* An insect with horny front wings that cover the hind wings when not in flight. [< OE *bitela.*]

bee·tle² (bēt′l) *adj.* Jutting: *beetle brows.* —*v.* **-tled, -tling.** To project. [< ME *bitel-brouwed,* having protruding eyebrows.]

bee·tle³ (bēt′l) *n.* A heavy mallet or similar tool. [< OE *bíetel.*]

ă pat ā pay â care ä father ĕ pet ē be ĭ pit ī tie î pier ŏ pot ō toe ô paw, for oi noise ōō took ōō boot ou out th thin th this ŭ cut û urge yōō abuse zh vision ə about, item, edible, gallop, circus

beeves (bēvz) *n.* A pl. of **beef.**

be-fall (bĭ-fôl') *v.* **-fell** (-fĕl'), **-fall-en** (-fôl'ən), **-fall-ing.** 1. To come to pass; happen. 2. To happen to. [< OE *befeallen,* to fall.]

be-fit (bĭ-fĭt') *v.* **-fit-ted, -fit-ting.** To be suitable or appropriate for.

be-fog (bĭ-fôg', -fŏg') *v.* **-fogged, -fog-ging.** To cover with or as if with fog.

be-fore (bĭ-fôr', -fōr') *adv.* 1. In front; ahead; in advance. 2. In the past; previously. —*prep.* 1. In front of. 2. Prior to. 3. Awaiting. 4. In the presence of. 5. Under the consideration of: *the case before the court.* 6. In preference to; sooner than. 7. In advance of or in precedence of, as in rank, condition, or development. —*conj.* 1. In advance of the time when: *before we went.* 2. Rather than; sooner than: *I would die before I would betray my country.* [< OE *beforan.*]

be-fore-hand (bĭ-fôr'hănd', -fōr'-) *adv.* In advance; early. —**be-fore'hand** *adj.*

be-foul (bĭ-foul') *v.* To sully.

be-friend (bĭ-frĕnd') *v.* To act as a friend to.

be-fud-dle (bĭ-fŭd'l) *v.* **-dled, -dling.** To confuse.

beg (bĕg) *v.* **begged, beg-ging.** 1. To ask for as charity. 2. To entreat. 3. To evade: *beg the question.* —*phrasal verb.* **beg off** (or **out**). To ask to be excused from. [ME *beggen.*]

be-gan (bĭ-găn') *v.* p.t. of **begin.**

be-get (bĭ-gĕt') *v.* **-got** (-gŏt'), **-got-ten** (-gŏt'n) or **-got, -get-ting.** To father; sire. [< OE *begietan,* to obtain.] —**be-get'ter** *n.*

beg-gar (bĕg'ər) *n.* 1. One who solicits alms for a living. 2. A pauper. —*v.* 1. To impoverish. 2. To render impotent. [< OFr. *begart.*] —**beg'gar-li-ness** *n.* —**beg'gar-ly** *adj.* —**beg'gar-y** *n.*

be-gin (bĭ-gĭn') *v.* **-gan** (-găn'), **-gun** (-gŭn'), **-gin-ning.** 1. To commence. 2. To come into being. [< OE *beginnan.*] —**be-gin'ner** *n.*

Syns: *begin, arise, commence, originate, start* **v.**

be-gin-ning (bĭ-gĭn'ĭng) *n.* 1. Commencement. 2. The time when something begins or is begun. 3. The place where something begins or is begun. 4. Source; origin.

be-gone (bĭ-gôn', -gŏn') *interj.* Expressive of dismissal. [BE- + obs. *gone.*]

be-go-nia (bĭ-gōn'yə) *n.* Any of various plants cultivated for their showy leaves and flowers. [< Michel *Bégon* (1638-1710).]

be-got (bĭ-gŏt') *v.* p.t. & a p.p. of **beget.**

be-got-ten (bĭ-gŏt'n) *v.* p.p. of **beget.**

be-grime (bĭ-grīm') *v.* **-grimed, -grim-ing.** To soil with dirt or grime.

be-grudge (bĭ-grŭj') *v.* **-grudged, -grudg-ing.** 1. To envy. 2. To give with reluctance.

be-guile (bĭ-gīl') *v.* **-guiled, -guil-ing.** 1. To deceive; cheat. 2. To divert. —**be-guile'ment** *n.* —**be-guil'er** *n.*

be-gum (bē'gəm, bā'-) *n.* A Moslem lady of rank. [Urdu.]

be-gun (bĭ-gŭn') *v.* p.p. of **begin.**

be-half (bĭ-hăf') *n.* Interest; benefit. —*idioms.* **in behalf of.** In the interest of; for the benefit of. **on behalf of.** On the part of. [ME *bihalfe.*]

be-have (bĭ-hāv') *v.* **-haved, -hav-ing.** 1. To act, react, or function in a particular way. 2. a. To conduct oneself in a specified way. b. To conduct oneself in a proper way. [ME *behaven.*]

be-hav-ior (bĭ-hāv'yər) *n.* 1. Deportment; demeanor. 2. Action, reaction, or function under specified circumstances. [ME *behavour.*] —**be-hav'ior-al** *adj.*

be-hav-ior-ism (bĭ-hāv'yə-rĭz'əm) *n.* The psychological school that believes that objectively observable behavior rather than mental conditions constitutes the essential scientific basis of psychological data and investigation. —**be-hav'ior-ist** *n.* —**be-hav'ior-is'tic** *adj.*

be-head (bĭ-hĕd') *v.* To decapitate.

be-held (bĭ-hĕld') *v.* p.t. & p.p. of **behold.**

be-he-moth (bĭ-hē'məth, bē'ə-) *n.* 1. A huge animal mentioned in the Old Testament. 2. Something enormous. [Heb. *běhēmōth.*]

be-hest (bĭ-hĕst') *n.* An order or authoritative command. [< OE *behaes,* vow.]

be-hind (bĭ-hīnd') *adv.* 1. In, to, or toward the rear: *I walked behind.* 2. In a place or condition that has been passed or left: *I left my gloves behind.* 3. In arrears; late. 4. Slow: *My watch is running behind.* —*prep.* 1. At the back of or in the rear of. 2. On the farther side of. 3. In a former place, time, or situation. 4. After (a set time): *behind schedule.* 5. Below, as in rank. 6. In support of. —*n. Informal.* The buttocks. [< OE *bihindan.*]

be-hind-hand (bĭ-hīnd'hănd') *adv.* 1. In arrears. 2. Behind the times. —**be-hind'hand** *adj.*

be-hold (bĭ-hōld') *v.* **-held** (-hĕld'), **-hold-ing.** To gaze at; look upon. —*interj.* Expressive of amazement. [< OE *behealdan.*]

be-hold-en (bĭ-hōl'dən) *adj.* Obliged; indebted. [ME *biholden.*]

be-hoove (bĭ-hōōv') *v.* **-hooved, -hoov-ing.** To be necessary or proper for: *It behooves us to heed the warning.* [< OE *behōfian.*]

beige (bāzh) *n.* Light grayish brown. [Fr.] —**beige** *adj.*

be-ing (bē'ĭng) *n.* 1. Existence. 2. One that exists. 3. One's essential nature.

be-la-bor (bĭ-lā'bər) *v.* 1. To beat or attack with blows. 2. To harp on.

be-lat-ed (bĭ-lā'tĭd) *adj.* Tardy. [BE- + obs. *lated* < LATE.] —**be-lat'ed-ly** *adv.* —**be-lat'ed-ness** *n.*

be-lay (bĭ-lā') *v.* 1. To make fast; secure. 2. *Naut.* To stop: *Belay there!* —*n.* A hold in mountain climbing. [< OE *belecgan,* to surround.]

belaying pin *n. Naut.* A pin used on shipboard for securing running gear.

belaying pin

belch (bĕlch) *v.* 1. To expel gas from the stomach through the mouth; eruct. 2. To gush forth; erupt. —*n.* A belching; eructation. [< ME *belchen.*] —**belch'er** *n.*

bel·dam (běl'dəm) *n.* Also **bel·dame.** An ugly, loathsome old woman. [ME, grandmother.]

be·lea·guer (bǐ-lē'gər) *v.* 1. To besiege. 2. To harass; beset. [Du. *belegeren.*]

bel·fry (běl'frē) *n., pl.* **-fries.** 1. A church bell tower. 2. The part of a steeple where the bells are hung. [< OFr. *berfrei*, portable siege tower.]

be·lie (bǐ-lī') *v.* **-lied, -ly·ing.** 1. To misrepresent or disguise. 2. To show to be false. 3. To frustrate or disappoint. [< OE *belēogan.*] —**be·li'er** *n.*

be·lief (bǐ-lēf') *n.* 1. Trust or confidence. 2. A conviction or opinion. 3. A tenet or a body of tenets. [< OE *bileafe.*]
    Syns: *belief, conviction, feeling, idea, mind, notion, opinion, sentiment n.*

be·lieve (bǐ-lēv') *v.* **-lieved, -liev·ing.** 1. To accept as true or real. 2. To credit with veracity; have confidence in; trust. 3. To expect or suppose; think. 4. To hold a religious belief. [< OE *belēfan.*] —**be·liev'a·ble** *adj.* —**be·liev'er** *n.*
    Syns: *believe, accept, buy, swallow v.*

be·lit·tle (bǐ-lǐt'l) *v.* **-tled, -tling.** To speak of as small or unimportant; depreciate; disparage. —**be·lit'tle·ment** *n.* —**be·lit'tler** *n.*
    Syns: *belittle, decry, depreciate, derogate, disparage, downgrade, knock v.*

bell (běl) *n.* 1. A hollow metal instrument that rings when struck. 2. Something shaped like a bell. 3. *Naut.* **a.** A stroke on a bell to mark the hour. **b.** The time indicated by the striking of a bell. —*v.* To furnish with a bell. [< OE *belle.*]

bel·la·don·na (běl'ə-dŏn'ə) *n.* 1. A poisonous plant with purplish-red flowers and small black berries. 2. A drug derived from the belladonna plant used to treat asthma. [Ital.]

bell-bot·tom (běl'bŏt'əm) *adj.* Having legs that flare out at the bottom: *bell-bottom trousers.*

bell-bot·toms (běl'bŏt'əmz) *pl.n.* Bell-bottom trousers.

bell·boy (běl'boi') *n.* A hotel porter.

belle (běl) *n.* An attractive and much-admired girl or woman. [< Fr., beautiful.]

belles-let·tres (běl-lět'rə) *pl.n.* (used with a sing. verb). Literature regarded for its artistic value rather than for its didactic or informative content. [Fr.]

bell·hop (běl'hŏp') *n.* A hotel porter.

bel·li·cose (běl'ǐ-kōs') *adj.* Warlike; pugnacious. [< Lat. *bellicosus.*] —**bel·li·cos'i·ty** (-kŏs'ĭ-tē) *n.*

bel·lig·er·ent (bə-lǐj'ər-ənt) *adj.* 1. Aggressively hostile. 2. Waging war. —*n.* One that is engaged in war. [< Lat. *belligerare*, to wage war.] —**bel·lig'er·ence** or **bel·lig'er·en·cy** *n.* —**bel·lig'er·ent·ly** *adv.*

bel·low (běl'ō) *v.* 1. To roar in the manner of a bull. 2. To shout in a deep loud voice. [ME *belwen.*] —**bel'low** *n.*

bel·lows (běl'ōz, -əz) *n.* (used with a sing. or pl. verb). A hand-operated device for directing a strong current of air, as to increase the draft of a fire. [< OE *belg*, bag.]

bell·weth·er (běl'wĕth'ər) *n.* 1. A male sheep that wears a bell and leads a flock. 2. One that leads or initiates.

bel·ly (běl'ē) *n., pl.* **-lies.** 1. The part of the body that contains the intestines; abdomen. 2. The underside of the body of an animal. 3. The stomach. —*v.* **-lied, -ly·ing.** To bulge or cause to bulge. [< OE *belg.*]

bel·ly·ache (běl'ē-āk') *n.* A pain in the abdomen. —*v. Slang.* To grumble; complain.

bel·ly·but·ton (běl'ē-bŭt'n) *n. Informal.* The navel.

belly dance *n.* A dance in which the performer makes sinuous movements of the belly. —**bel'ly-dance'** *v.* —**belly dancer** *n.*

belly laugh *n.* A deep laugh.

be·long (bǐ-lông', -lŏng') *v.* 1. To be the property or concern of. 2. To be part of or in natural association with something. 3. To be a member of an organization. 4. To have a proper or suitable place. [ME *belongen.*]

be·long·ing (bǐ-lông'ĭng, -lŏng'-) *n.* 1. **belongings.** Personal possessions. 2. Close and secure relationship.

be·lov·ed (bǐ-lŭv'ĭd, -lŭvd') *adj.* Dearly loved. —**be·lov'ed** *n.*

be·low (bǐ-lō') *adv.* 1. In or to a lower place or level. 2. On earth: *creatures here below.* —*prep.* 1. Lower than; under. 2. Inferior to. [ME *bilooghe.*]

belt (bĕlt) *n.* 1. A supportive or ornamental band worn around the waist. 2. A continuous moving band used as a machine element. 3. A band of tough material beneath the tread of a tire, used for reinforcement. 4. A geographic region that is distinctive in a specific way. 5. *Slang.* A powerful blow. 6. *Slang.* A drink of hard liquor. —*v.* 1. To encircle; gird. 2. To attach with a belt. 3. To strike with or as if with a belt. 4. To sing loudly. —*idioms.* **below the belt. 1.** *Boxing.* Below the waistline, where a blow is foul. 2. Unfair. **tighten (one's) belt.** To exercise thrift and frugality. [< Lat. *balteus.*]

belt tightening *n.* A decrease in spending.

be·lu·ga (bə-lōō'gə) *n.* 1. The white whale. 2. A sturgeon whose roe is used for caviar. [R. *byelukha.*]

be·moan (bǐ-mōn') *v.* 1. To lament. 2. To express pity or grief for.

be·muse (bǐ-myōōz') *v.* **-mused, -mus·ing.** To confuse; stupefy.

bench (běnch) *n.* 1. A long seat for two or more persons. 2. **a.** The judge's seat in court. **b.** The office or position of a judge. 3. The court or judges. 4. A craftsman's worktable. 5. *Sports.* **a.** The place where the players on a team sit when not participating in a game. **b.** The reserve players on a team. —*v.* 1. To seat on a bench. 2. *Sports.* To remove (a player) from a game. [< OE *benc.*]

bench mark *n.* Also **bench·mark** (běnch'märk'). 1. A surveyor's mark made on a stationary object and used as a reference point. 2. **benchmark.** A standard by which something can be judged.

bench warrant *n. Law.* A warrant issued by a judge or court, ordering the arrest of an offender.

bend (běnd) *v.* **bent** (běnt), **bend·ing.** 1. To tighten (a bow). 2. To curve. 3. To turn or deflect. 4. To coerce or subdue. 5. To concentrate; apply. 6. To fasten. 7. To yield;

submit. —*n.* **1.** The act of bending. **2.** Something bent; curve; crook. **3.** A knot that joins one rope to another or to an object. **4.** bends. Caisson disease. —*Idiom.* **bend over backward.** To make a strong effort. [< OE *bendan.*]

bend·er (bĕn′dər) *n.* **1.** One that bends. **2.** *Slang.* A drinking spree.

be·neath (bĭ-nēth′) *adv.* **1.** In a lower place; below. **2.** Underneath. —*prep.* **1.** Below; under. **2.** Unworthy of. [< OE *binithan.*]

ben·e·dic·tion (bĕn′ĭ-dĭk′shən) *n.* An invocation of divine blessing, esp. at the end of a church service. [< Lat. *benedictio.*] —**ben′e·dic′to·ry** (-tə-rē) *adj.*

ben·e·fac·tion (bĕn′ə-făk′shən, bĕn′ə-făk′-) *n.* **1.** The act of conferring a benefit. **2.** A charitable gift or deed. [LLat. *benefactio.*]

ben·e·fac·tor (bĕn′ə-făk′tər) *n.* One who gives financial or other aid.

ben·e·fac·tress (bĕn′ə-făk′trĭs) *n.* A woman who functions as a benefactor.

ben·e·fi·cence (bə-nĕf′ĭ-səns) *n.* **1.** The quality of charity or kindness. **2.** A charitable act or gift. [< Lat. *beneficentia.*] —**be·nef′i·cent** *adj.* —**be·nef′i·cent·ly** *adv.*

ben·e·fi·cial (bĕn′ə-fĭsh′əl) *adj.* Helpful; advantageous. [< Lat. *beneficus.*] —**ben′e·fi′cial·ly** *adv.*

ben·e·fi·ci·ar·y (bĕn′ə-fĭsh′ē-ĕr′ē, -fĭsh′ə-rē) *n.,* *pl.* **-ies.** One that receives a benefit, as funds or property from an insurance policy, will, or trust fund.

ben·e·fit (bĕn′ə-fĭt) *n.* **1.** An advantage. **2.** An aid; help. **3.** A payment or series of payments to one in need. **4.** A fund-raising public entertainment. —*v.* **1.** To be helpful or advantageous to. **2.** To derive advantage; profit. [< Lat. *benefactum.*]

be·nev·o·lence (bə-nĕv′ə-ləns) *n.* **1.** Charitable good nature. **2.** A charitable act. [< Lat. *benevolens,* well-wishing.] —**be·nev′o·lent** *adj.* —**be·nev′o·lent·ly** *adv.*

Ben·ga·li (bĕn-gô′lē, bĕng-) *n.* **1.** An inhabitant of Bengal or Bangladesh. **2.** The modern Indic language of West Bengal and Bangladesh. —**Ben·ga′li** *adj.*

be·night·ed (bĭ-nī′tĭd) *adj.* Ignorant. —**be·night′ed·ly** *adv.* —**be·night′ed·ness** *n.*

be·nign (bĭ-nīn′) *adj.* **1.** Of a kind disposition. **2.** *Pathol.* Not malignant. [< Lat. *benignus.*] —**be·nign′ly** *adv.*

be·nig·nant (bĭ-nĭg′nənt) *adj.* Kind and gracious. —**be·nig′nan·cy** (-nən-sē) *n.* —**be·nig′nant·ly** *adv.*

bent (bĕnt) *v.* *p.t.* & *p.p.* of **bend.** —*adj.* **1.** Not straight; crooked. **2.** On a fixed course of action; determined. —*n.* An individual tendency, disposition, or inclination.

be·numb (bĭ-nŭm′) *v.* **1.** To make numb, esp. by cold. **2.** To make inactive; stupefy.

benz- or **benzo-** *pref.* Benzene; benzoic acid: *benzoate.* [< BENZOIN.]

Ben·ze·drine (bĕn′zĭ-drēn′). A trademark for a brand of amphetamine.

ben·zene (bĕn′zēn′, bĕn-zēn′) *n.* A clear, colorless, flammable liquid, C_6H_6, derived from petroleum and used to manufacture DDT, detergents, insecticides, and motor fuels.

benzene ring *n.* The hexagonal ring structure in the benzene molecule, each vertex of which is occupied by a carbon atom.

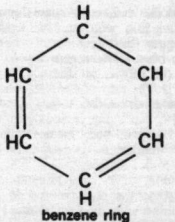

benzene ring

Each C represents a carbon atom, each H a hydrogen atom, and the straight lines are chemical bonds

ben·zine (bĕn′zēn′, bĕn-zēn′) or **ben·zin** (bĕn′-zĭn) *n.* Ligroin.

ben·zo·ate (bĕn′zō-āt′, -ĭt) *n.* A salt or ester of benzoic acid.

ben·zo·ic acid (bĕn-zō′ĭk) *n.* A white crystalline acid, C_6H_5COOH, used in perfumes, germicides, and to season tobacco.

ben·zo·in (bĕn′zō-ĭn, -zoin′) *n.* Any of several balsamlike resins obtained from trees in southern Asia and used in ointments, perfumes, and medicine. [< Ar. *lubān jāwī,* frankincense of Java.]

ben·zol (bĕn′zôl′, -zōl′) *n.* Benzene.

be·queath (bĭ-kwēth′, -kwēth′) *v.* **1.** To leave by will. **2.** To hand down. [< OE *becwethan.*] —**be·queath′al** (bĭ-kwē′thəl, -thŏl) *n.* —**be·queath′er** *n.*

be·quest (bĭ-kwĕst′) *n.* **1.** The act of bequeathing. **2.** Something bequeathed; legacy. [< OE *becwethan,* to bequeath.]

be·rate (bĭ-rāt′) *v.* **-rat·ed, -rat·ing.** To scold harshly. [BE- + RATE².]

Ber·ber (bûr′bər) *n.* **1.** A member of one of several Moslem tribes of North Africa. **2.** Any of the Afro-Asiatic languages of the Berbers.

ber·ceuse (bĕr-sœz′) *n.,* *pl.* **-ceuses** (-sœz′). **1.** A lullaby. **2.** A musical composition with a soothing accompaniment. [Fr.]

be·reave (bĭ-rēv′) *v.* **-reaved** or **-reft** (-rĕft′), **-reav·ing.** To deprive of, as by death. [< OE *berēafian.*] —**be·reave′ment** *n.*

be·ret (bə-rā′, bĕr′ā′) *n.* A round, visorless cloth cap. [< LLat. *birrus,* hooded cloak.]

ber·i·ber·i (bĕr′ē-bĕr′ē) *n.* A thiamine-deficiency disease characterized by partial paralysis, emaciation, and anemia. [Singhalese.]

ber·ke·li·um (bar-kē′lē-əm, bûrk′lē-əm) *n.* Symbol **Bk** A synthetic radioactive element. Atomic number 97. [< *Berkeley,* California.]

Ber·mu·da onion (bər-myōō′də) *n.* A large, mild-flavored, yellow-skinned onion.

Bermuda shorts *pl.n.* Shorts that end slightly above the knees.

Ber·noul·li effect (bər-nōō′lē) *n.* The reduction of internal fluid pressure with increased stream velocity. [< Daniel *Bernoulli* (1700–1782).]

ber·ry (bĕr′ē) *n.,* *pl.* **-ries.** **1.** A usu. small, fleshy, many-seeded fruit. **2.** A seed or dried kernel, as of coffee. —*v.* **-ried, -ry·ing.** To gather or bear berries. [< OE *berie.*]

ber·serk (bər-sûrk′, -zûrk′) *adj.* **1.** Destructively violent. **2.** Crazed; deranged. [< ON *berserkr,* warrior.] —**ber·serk′** *adv.*

berth (bûrth) *n.* **1.** A built-in bed on a ship or train. **2.** *Naut.* **a.** A space at a wharf for a ship to dock. **b.** Enough space for a ship to maneuver. **3.** A job, esp. on a ship. —**v.** **1.** To bring (a ship) to a berth. **2.** To provide with a berth. —**idiom. give a wide berth to.** To stay at a substantial distance from. [Prob. < BEAR[1].]

Ber·til·lon system (bûr'tl-ŏn') *n.* A former system for identifying persons by means of a record of various body measurements, coloring, and markings. [< Alphonse *Bertillon* (1853–1914).]

ber·yl (bĕr'əl) *n.* A hard mineral, essentially $Be_3Al_2Si_6O_{18}$, the chief source of beryllium and used as a gem. [< Gk. *bērullos*.] —**ber'yl·line** (-ə-lĭn, -lĭn') *adj.*

be·ryl·li·um (bə-rĭl'ē-əm) *n.* Symbol **Be** A high-melting, lightweight, corrosion-resistant, rigid, steel-gray metallic element used as an aerospace structural material, as a moderator and reflector in nuclear reactors, and in a copper alloy used for springs, electrical contacts, and nonsparking tools. Atomic number 4; atomic weight 9.0122. [< BERYL.]

be·seech (bĭ-sēch') *v.* **-sought** (-sôt') or **-seeched, -seech·ing.** To request urgently; implore. [< OE *besēcan.*]

be·seem (bĭ-sēm') *v. Archaic.* To be appropriate for.

be·set (bĭ-sĕt') *v.* **-set, -set·ting. 1.** To trouble persistently; harass. **2.** To attack from all sides. [< OE *besettan.*]

be·side (bĭ-sīd') *prep.* **1.** Next to. **2.** In comparison with. **3.** Except for. **4.** Apart from. —*adv.* In addition to. —*idiom.* **beside (oneself).** Extremely agitated. [< OE *be sīdan.*]

be·sides (bĭ-sīdz') *adv.* **1.** In addition; also. **2.** Moreover; furthermore. **3.** Otherwise; else. —*prep.* **1.** In addition to. **2.** Except for.

be·siege (bĭ-sēj') *v.* **-sieged, -sieg·ing. 1.** To lay siege to. **2.** To crowd around. **3.** To harass or importune, as with requests. —**be·sieg'er** *n.*

be·smear (bĭ-smîr') *v.* To smear over.

be·smirch (bĭ-smûrch') *v.* **1.** To soil. **2.** To tarnish; dishonor. —**be·smirch'er** *n.*

be·sot (bĭ-sŏt') *v.* **-sot·ted, -sot·ting.** To muddle or stupefy, esp. with liquor.

be·sought (bĭ-sôt') *v. p.t. & p.p.* of **beseech.**

be·spat·ter (bĭ-spăt'ər) *v.* **1.** To soil, as with mud. **2.** To slander; defame.

be·speak (bĭ-spēk') *v.* **-spoke** (-spōk'), **-spo·ken** (-spō'kən) or **-spoke, -speak·ing. 1.** To be or give a sign of; indicate. **2.** To engage or claim in advance; reserve. **3.** To foretell.

be·spread (bĭ-sprĕd') *v.* To cover or spread over.

be·sprin·kle (bĭ-sprĭng'kəl) *v.* **-kled, -kling.** To sprinkle over.

Bes·se·mer converter (bĕs'ə-mər) *n.* A large container in which molten iron is converted to steel by the Bessemer process.

Bessemer process *n.* A method for making steel by blasting compressed air through molten iron and burning out excess carbon and other impurities. [< Sir Henry *Bessemer* (1813–98).]

best (bĕst) *adj. superl.* of **good. 1.** Surpassing all others in quality. **2.** Most satisfactory or desirable: *the best solution.* **3.** Greatest: *the best part of a week.* —*adv. superl.* of **well[2]. 1.** Most advantageously. **2.** To the greatest

extent; most. —*n.* **1.** The best among several. **2.** The best person or persons. **3.** The best condition: *look your best.* **4.** One's best clothing. **5.** The best effort one can make. **6.** One's regards: *Give them my best.* —*v.* To surpass; defeat. —*idioms.* **as best (one) can.** As well as one can. **at best. 1.** Interpreted most favorably: *Your remark was at best a well-meaning blunder.* **2.** Under the most favorable conditions: *This car does 120 at best.* **for the best.** For the ultimate good. **get the best of.** To outwit. **had best.** Should: *You had best get out of here.* **make the best of it.** To do as well as possible under the circumstances. [< OE *betst.*]

Syns: **best, optimal, optimum, superlative, unsurpassed** *adj.*

bes·tial (bĕs'chəl, bēst'yəl) *adj.* Having the qualities of or behaving in the manner of a brute. [< LLat. *bestialis.*] —**bes·ti·al'i·ty** *n.* —**bes'tial·ly** *adv.*

be·stir (bĭ-stûr') *v.* **-stirred, -stir·ring.** To make active; rouse.

best man *n.* A bridegroom's chief attendant.

be·stow (bĭ-stō') *v.* To present as a gift or honor. [ME *bestowen.*] —**be·stow'al** *n.*

be·strew (bĭ-strōō') *v.* **-strewed, -strewed** or **-strewn** (-strōōn'), **-strew·ing.** To strew or scatter things about.

be·stride (bĭ-strīd') *v.* **-strode** (-strōd'), **-strid·den** (-strĭd'n), **-strid·ing. 1.** To straddle. **2.** To step over.

bet (bĕt) *n.* **1.** A wager. **2.** The event on which a wager is made. **3.** The amount risked in a wager. —*v.* **bet** or **bet·ted, bet·ting. 1.** To make or place a bet (with). **2.** To make a bet on (a contestant or an outcome). —*idiom.* **you bet.** Of course; surely. [Orig. unknown.] —**bet'ter** or **bet'tor** *n.*

be·ta (bā'tə, bē'-) *n.* The 2nd letter of the Greek alphabet. See table at **alphabet.** [Gk. *bēta.*]

be·take (bĭ-tāk') *v.* **-took** (-tōōk'), **-tak·en** (-tā'kən), **-tak·ing.** To cause (oneself) to go.

beta particle *n.* A high-speed electron or positron, esp. one emitted in radioactive decay.

beta ray *n.* A stream of beta particles, esp. of electrons.

beta rhythm *n.* Also **beta wave.** The second most common waveform occurring in electroencephalograms of the adult brain, having a frequency of 18–30 cycles/second and associated with an alert waking state.

be·ta·tron (bā'tə-trŏn', bē'-) *n.* A fixed-radius magnetic induction electron accelerator.

be·tel (bēt'l) *n.* A climbing Asiatic plant whose leaves are chewed with the betel nut to induce both stimulating and narcotic effects. [< Malayalam *vettila.*]

betel nut *n.* Also **be·tel·nut** (bēt'l-nŭt'). The seed of the fruit of the betel palm.

betel palm *n.* A palm tree of tropical Asia, with featherlike leaves and orange fruit.

bête noire (bĕt nwär') *n.* One that is an object of intense dislike or aversion. [Fr.]

beth (bĕth) *n.* The 2nd letter of the Hebrew alphabet. See table at **alphabet.** [Heb. *bēth.*]

be·think (bĭ-thĭngk') *v.* **-thought** (-thôt'), **-think·ing.** To remind (oneself).

be·tide (bĭ-tīd') *v.* **-tid·ed, -tid·ing.** To happen (to); befall. [ME *betiden.*]

be·times (bǐ-tīmz′) *adv.* In good time; early. [ME.]

be·to·ken (bǐ-tō′kən) *v.* To give a sign of; portend.

be·took (bǐ-tŏŏk′) *v. p.t.* of **betake**.

be·tray (bǐ-trā′) *v.* 1. To commit treason against; be a traitor to. 2. To be disloyal or unfaithful to. 3. To make known unintentionally. 4. To show; reveal. 5. To lead astray. [ME *betrayen.*] **—be·tray′al** *n.* **—be·tray′er** *n.*

be·troth (bǐ-trōth′, -trôth′) *v.* To promise to marry. **—be·troth′al** *n.*

be·trothed (bǐ-trōthd′, -trôtht′) *n.* A person who is engaged to be married.

bet·ter (bĕt′ər) *adj.* Compar. of **good**. 1. Greater in excellence or higher in quality. 2. More appropriate or useful. 3. Larger; greater. 4. Healthier than before. **—***adv.* Compar. of **well²**. 1. In a more excellent way. 2. To a greater extent or degree. 3. To greater use or advantage. 4. More: *better than a year.* **—***v.* 1. To make or become better. 2. To surpass or exceed. **—***n.* 1. Something that is better. 2. A superior, as in rank. **—***idiom.* **better off.** In a wealthier or better condition. [< OE *betera.*]

bet·ter·ment (bĕt′ər-mənt) *n.* An improvement.

bet·tor (bĕt′ər) *n.* Also **bet·ter.** One who bets.

be·tween (bǐ-twēn′) *prep.* 1. In the position or interval separating: *between two trees.* 2. **a.** By the combined effort or effect of: *Between them they succeeded.* **b.** In the combined ownership of: *had three dollars between them.* 3. From one or another of: *choose between riding and walking.* **—***idiom.* **between you and me.** In strictest confidence. [< OE *betwēonum.*]

be·twixt (bǐ-twǐkst′) *prep. & adv. Archaic.* Between. [< OE *betwyx.*]

bev·el (bĕv′əl) *n.* 1. The angle or inclination of a line or surface that meets another at any angle but 90 degrees. 2. A rule with an adjustable arm, used to measure or draw angles or to fix a surface at an angle. **—***v.* **-eled** or **-elled, -el·ing** or **-el·ling.** 1. To cut at a bevel. 2. To be inclined; slope. [< OFr. *baif,* openmouthed.]

bev·er·age (bĕv′ər-ĭj, bĕv′rĭj) *n.* Any of various liquids for drinking, usu. excluding water. [< OFr. *bevrage.*]

bev·y (bĕv′ē) *n., pl.* **-ies.** A group or assemblage. [ME.]

be·wail (bǐ-wāl′) *v.* To express sorrow (about); lament.

be·ware (bǐ-wâr′) *v.* **-wared, -war·ing.** To be on guard (against); be wary (of). [ME *be war.*]

be·wil·der (bǐ-wǐl′dər) *v.* To confuse or befuddle, esp. with numerous conflicting situations, objects, or statements. [BE- + obs. *wilder,* to stray.] **—be·wil′der·ment** *n.*

be·witch (bǐ-wǐch′) *v.* 1. To place under one's power by magic. 2. To fascinate; charm. [ME *bewicchen.*] **—be·witch′ing·ly** *adv.* **—be·witch′ment** *n.*

bey (bā) *n.* 1. A provincial governor in the Ottoman Empire. 2. A native ruler of the former kingdom of Tunis. [Turk.]

be·yond (bē-ŏnd′, bǐ-yŏnd′) *prep.* 1. On the far side of; past. 2. Later than. 3. Past the understanding, reach, or scope of. 4. To a degree or amount greater than. 5. In addition to. **—***adv.* 1. Farther along. 2. In addition. [< OE *begeondan.*]

bez·el (bĕz′əl) *n.* 1. A slanting edge on a cutting tool. 2. The faceted portion of a cut gem, esp. above the setting. 3. A groove or flange designed to hold a beveled edge, as of a watch crystal. [Orig. unknown.]

bhang (băng) *n.* A narcotic made from the dried leaves and flowers of the hemp plant. [< Skt. *bhaṅgā.*]

Bi The symbol for the element bismuth.

bi- or **bin-** *pref.* 1. **a.** Two: *bipolar, binaural.* **b.** At intervals of two: *bicentennial.* 2. Twice during: *biweekly.* [< Lat. *bis,* twice.]

bi·an·nu·al (bī-ăn′yōō-əl) *adj.* Happening twice each year; semiannual. **—bi·an′nu·al·ly** *adv.*

bi·as (bī′əs) *n.* 1. A line cutting diagonally across the grain of fabric. 2. Preference or inclination that inhibits impartiality; prejudice. **—***adv.* On a diagonal; aslant. **—***v.* **-ased** or **-assed, -as·ing** or **-as·sing.** To cause to have a bias; prejudice. [< OFr. *biais,* oblique.]

bi·ath·lon (bī-ăth′lən, -lŏn′) *n.* An athletic competition combining events in cross-country skiing and rifle shooting. [BI- + Gk. *athlon,* contest.]

bib (bĭb) *n.* A cloth napkin tied under the chin, worn esp. by children to protect clothing during meals. [Prob. < ME *bibben,* to drink.]

bi·be·lot (bē′bə-lō′, bē-blō′) *n.* A small decorative object or trinket. [< OFr. *beubelet.*]

Bi·ble (bī′bəl) *n.* 1. The sacred book of Christianity, which includes the Old Testament and the New Testament. 2. The Old Testament, the sacred book of Judaism. [< Gk. *biblion,* book.] **—Bib′li·cal** (bĭb′lĭ-kəl) *adj.* **—Bib′li·cal·ly** *adv.*

biblio- *pref.* Books: *bibliophile.* [< Gk. *biblion,* book.]

bib·li·og·ra·phy (bĭb′lē-ŏg′rə-fē) *n., pl.* **-phies.** 1. The description or history of the editions, dates of issue, and authorship of books or other printed material. 2. A list of the works of an author or of sources of information in print on a specific subject. **—bib′li·og′ra·pher** *n.* **—bib′li·o·graph′i·cal** (-ə-grăf′ĭ-kəl) or **bib′li·o·graph′ic** *adj.*

bib·li·o·phile (bĭb′lē-ə-fīl′) *n.* A connoisseur of books.

bib·u·lous (bĭb′yə-ləs) *adj.* Given to convivial, often excessive drinking. [Lat. *bibulus.*] **—bib′u·lous·ly** *adv.*

bi·cam·er·al (bī-kăm′ər-əl) *adj.* Composed of two legislative branches. [BI- + LLat. *camera,* room.]

bi·car·bon·ate (bī-kär′bə-nāt′, -nĭt) *n.* The radical group HCO_3 or a compound containing it.

bicarbonate of soda *n.* Sodium bicarbonate.

bi·cen·te·na·ry (bī′sĕn-tĕn′ə-rē, bī-sĕn′tə-nĕr′ē) *n., pl.* **-ries.** A bicentennial. **—bi′cen·ten′a·ry** *adj.*

bi·cen·ten·ni·al (bī′sĕn-tĕn′ē-əl) *n.* A 200th anniversary or its celebration; bicentenary. **—bi′cen·ten′ni·al** *adj.*

bi·ceps (bī′sĕps′) *n., pl.* **-ceps** or **-ceps·es** (-sĕp′sĭz′). A muscle having two points of origin, esp. the large muscle at the front of the upper arm. [< Lat., two-headed.]

bick·er (bĭk′ər) *v.* To engage in petty quarreling; squabble. **—***n.* A petty quarrel; tiff. [ME *bikeren,* to attack.]

bi·con·cave (bī′kŏn-kāv′, bī-kŏn′kāv′) *adj.*

BOOKS OF THE BIBLE

Bible translation is one of the world's oldest scholarly activities; the tradition runs back to the 3rd century B.C. As of the present date, at least some books of the Bible have been translated into more than 1,400 languages. Since there are more than 3,000 languages in the world, it is reasonable to assume that the field will continue to expand. English has an uncommonly rich heritage in this respect; since the metrical paraphrases and Gospels of Anglo-Saxon times, the entire book has been translated again and again. The Jewish Publication Society *Holy Scriptures According to the Masoretic Text*, issued in 1916 by a committee of Jewish scholars, is accepted as standard in American Judaism, and its contents are listed here. For Roman Catholics the Douay Version (1582–1610) has for many centuries been the text officially approved for teaching and Church use. To serve two pressing needs facing the Church in the second half of the twentieth century—the need to keep abreast of the times and the need to

deepen theological thought—changes have had to be made. The original texts were re-examined and re-evaluated with the assistance of the pioneer work of the School of Biblical Studies in Jerusalem; the result was the publication in France of *La Bible de Jerusalem* in the early 1960's. The English text of the *Jerusalem Bible*, published in 1966, owes a large debt to the work of the many scholars who collaborated to produce *La Bible de Jerusalem*. The *Jerusalem Bible* has gained wide acceptance in the light of the most recent research in the fields of history, archaeology, and literary criticism. Protestants may use either the King James Bible (or Authorized Version, as it is often called, especially in Great Britain) which appeared in 1611 under the patronage of James I; or they may use the Revised Standard Version (1946–52). The following table presents the contents as listed in the Jerusalem Bible and King James versions because they have the sanction of general acceptance.

HEBREW SCRIPTURES

Genesis	II Samuel	Joel	Haggai	Lamentations
Exodus	I Kings	Amos	Zechariah	Ecclesiastes
Leviticus	II Kings	Obadiah	Malachi	Esther
Numbers	Isaiah	Jonah	Psalms	Daniel
Deuteronomy	Jeremiah	Micah	Proverbs	Ezra
Joshua	Ezekiel	Nahum	Job	Nehemiah
Judges	THE TWELVE	Habakkuk	Song of Songs	I Chronicles
I Samuel	Hosea	Zephaniah	Ruth	II Chronicles

OLD TESTAMENT

Jerusalem Version	King James Version	Jerusalem Version	King James Version
Genesis	Genesis	Song of Solomon	Song of Solomon
Exodus	Exodus	Wisdom	
Leviticus	Leviticus	Ecclesiasticus	
Numbers	Numbers	Isaiah	Isaiah
Deuteronomy	Deuteronomy	Jeremiah	Jeremiah
Joshua	Joshua	Lamentations	Lamentations
Judges	Judges	Baruch	
Ruth	Ruth	Ezekiel	Ezekiel
I Samuel	I Samuel	Daniel	Daniel
II Samuel	II Samuel	Hosea	Hosea
I Kings	I Kings	Joel	Joel
II Kings	II Kings	Amos	Amos
I Chronicles	I Chronicles	Obadiah	Obadiah
II Chronicles	II Chronicles	Jonah	Jonah
Ezra	Ezra	Micah	Micah
Nehemiah	Nehemiah	Nahum	Nahum
Tobit		Habakkuk	Habakkuk
Judith		Zephaniah	Zephaniah
Esther	Esther	Haggai	Haggai
Job	Job	Zechariah	Zechariah
Psalms	Psalms	Malachi	Malachi
Proverbs	Proverbs	I Maccabees	
Ecclesiastes	Ecclesiastes	II Maccabees	

NEW TESTAMENT

Matthew	I Corinthians	II Thessalonians	I Peter
Mark	II Corinthians	I Timothy	II Peter
Luke	Galatians	II Timothy	I John
John	Ephesians	Titus	II John
Acts	Philippians	Philemon	III John
	Colossians	Hebrews	Jude
Romans	I Thessalonians	James	Revelation

ă pat ā pay â care ä father ĕ pet ē be ĭ pit ī tie î pier ŏ pot ō toe ô paw, for oi noise ŏŏ took
ōō boot ou out th thin *th* this ŭ cut û urge yōō abuse zh vision ə about, item, edible, gallop, circus

Concave on both sides or surfaces. —**bi'con·cav'i·ty** (-kăv'ĭ-tē) n.

bi·con·vex (bī'kŏn-věks', bī-kŏn'věks') adj. Convex on both sides or surfaces. —**bi'con·vex'i·ty** (-věk'sĭ-tē) n.

bi·cus·pid (bī-kŭs'pĭd) n. One of the two-pointed teeth between the canines and molars in human beings. [BI- + Lat. cuspis, point.]

bi·cy·cle (bī'sĭk'əl, -sĭ-kəl) n. A vehicle consisting of a metal frame mounted on two wheels and having a seat, handlebars for steering, and pedals. —v. **-cled, -cling.** To ride on a bicycle. [Fr.] —**bi'cy·clist** n.

bid (bĭd) v. **bade** (băd, bād) or **bid, bid·den** (bĭd'n) or **bid, bid·ding.** 1. To order; command. 2. To invite to attend; summon. 3. To utter (a greeting or salutation). 4. p.t. & p.p. **bid.** To state one's intention to take (tricks of a certain number or suit) in card games. 5. p.t. & p.p. **bid.** To offer as a price. 6. p.t. & p.p. **bid.** To make an offer to pay or accept a specified price. —n. 1. a. An offer of a price, as for a contract. b. The amount offered. 2. An invitation. 3. a. The act of bidding in card games. b. The number of tricks or points declared. c. A player's turn to bid. 4. An earnest effort to win or attain something. [< OE biddan, to command, and < OE beden, to offer.] —**bid'der** n.

bid·da·ble (bĭd'ə-bəl) adj. 1. Capable of being bid. 2. Docile; obedient.

bid·dy (bĭd'ē) n., pl. **-dies.** A hen; fowl. [Orig. unknown.]

bide (bīd) v. **bid·ed** or **bode** (bōd), **bid·ed, bid·ing.** 1. To remain; stay. 2. To wait; tarry. 3. To await. [< OE bīdan.]

bi·det (bē-dā') n. A basinlike fixture used for bathing the genitals and posterior parts of the body. [Fr.]

bi·en·ni·al (bī-ĕn'ē-əl) adj. 1. Lasting or living for two years. 2. Happening every second year. 3. Producing leaves in the first year and producing fruit and dying in the second year. [< Lat. biennium, a two-year period.] —**bi·en'ni·al** n. —**bi·en'ni·al·ly** adv.

bier (bîr) n. A stand on which a corpse or coffin is placed. [< OE bēr.]

bi·fo·cal (bī-fō'kəl) adj. Having two different focal lengths. —n. **bifocals.** Eyeglasses with lenses that correct for both near and distant vision.

bi·fur·cate (bī'fər-kāt', bī-fûr'-) v. **-cat·ed, -cat·ing.** To divide or separate into two parts or branches. [< Lat. bifurcus, forked.] —**bi'fur·cate'** adj. —**bi'fur·ca'tion** n.

big (bĭg) adj. **big·ger, big·gest.** 1. Of great size, number, quantity, magnitude, or extent; large. 2. Grown-up; adult. 3. Pregnant. 4. Of great significance; important. 5. Informal. Self-important; boastful. —adv. 1. Self-importantly; boastful. 2. With considerable success. [ME, prob. of Scand. orig.] —**big'gish** adj. —**big'ness** n.

Syns: big, extensive, good, great, healthy, large, sizable adj.

big·a·my (bĭg'ə-mē) n., pl. **-mies.** The criminal offense of marrying one person while still legally married to another. [< LLat. bigamus, bigamous.] —**big'a·mist** n. —**big'a·mous** adj.

big bang theory n. A cosmological theory holding that the universe originated billions of years ago from the violent eruption of a point source.

Big Dipper n. An asterism in Ursa Major consisting of seven stars forming a dipper-shaped configuration.

big·horn (bĭg'hôrn') n. A wild mountain sheep of western North America, the male of which has massive, curved horns.

bight (bīt) n. 1. A loop in a rope. 2. a. A curve in a shoreline. b. A bay formed by a bight. [< OE byht, bend.]

big-name (bĭg'nām') adj. Extremely popular: a big-name band.

big·ot (bĭg'ət) n. A person who is intolerant, esp. in matters of religion, race, or politics. [< OFr.] —**big'ot·ed** adj. —**big'ot·ry** n.

big shot n. Slang. An important or influential person.

big time n. Slang. The highest level of attainment in a competitive field or profession. —**big'-time'** adj. —**big'-tim'er** n.

big top n. Informal. 1. The main tent of a circus. 2. The circus.

big·wig (bĭg'wĭg') n. Informal. An important person.

Bi·ha·ri (bĭ-hä'rē) n., pl. **-ris.** 1. A native or inhabitant of Bihar in east-central India. 2. The Indic language of the Biharis.

bike (bīk) n. Informal. A bicycle. —**bike** v.

bi·ki·ni (bĭ-kē'nē) n. A woman's brief two-piece bathing suit. [< Bikini, an atoll in the Marshall Islands.]

bi·lat·er·al (bī-lăt'ər-əl) adj. 1. Of or having two sides. 2. Affecting or undertaken by two sides equally; reciprocal. —**bi·lat'er·al·ly** adv.

bile (bīl) n. 1. A bitter yellow or greenish liquid that is secreted by the liver and aids in the digestion of fats. 2. Ill temper; irascibility. [< Lat. bilis.]

bilge (bĭlj) n. 1. The lowest inner part of a ship's hull. 2. Water that collects in the bilge. 3. Slang. Stupid talk; nonsense. [Prob. < BULGE.]

bi·lin·gual (bī-lĭng'gwəl) adj. Expressed in or able to speak two languages. [Lat. bilinguis.]

bil·ious (bĭl'yəs) adj. 1. Of, pertaining to, or containing bile. 2. Of, pertaining to, or experiencing gastric disorder caused by a malfunction of the liver or gallbladder. 3. Irascible. —**bil'ious·ness** n.

bilk (bĭlk) v. To defraud, cheat, or swindle. [Perh. < BALK.] —**bilk'er** n.

bill¹ (bĭl) n. 1. A statement of charges for goods or services. 2. A list of particulars, as a menu. 3. A public notice such as an advertising poster. 4. A piece of paper money. 5. A commercial note such as a bill of exchange. 6. A draft of a law presented for approval to a legislative body. 7. Law. A document containing a formal statement of a case, complaint, or petition. —v. 1. To present a statement of costs or charges to. 2. To enter on a bill. 3. To advertise by public notice. [< Med. Lat. billa.]

bill² (bĭl) n. 1. The beak of a bird. 2. A beaklike mouth part, as of a turtle. —v. To touch beaks together. [< OE bile.]

bill·board (bĭl'bôrd', -bōrd') n. A structure for the display of advertising posters.

bil·let (bĭl'ĭt) n. 1. A lodging for troops. 2. A written order directing that a billet be provided. 3. A position of employment. —v. To assign quarters to by billet. [< OFr. billette, official register.]

bil·let-doux (bĭl'ā-dōō') n., pl. **bil·lets-doux** (-dōō', -dōōz'). A love letter. [Fr.]

bill·fold (bĭl'fōld') n. A wallet.

bil·liards (bĭl'yərdz) n. (used with a sing. verb). A game in which a cue is used to hit three balls against one another or the side cushions of a rectangular table. [< Fr. *billard*, billiard cue.]

bil·lings·gate (bĭl'ĭngz-gāt', -gĭt) n. Foul-mouthed, abusive language. [After *Billingsgate*, a fishmarket in London.]

bil·lion (bĭl'yən) n. 1. The cardinal number equal to 10⁹. 2. *Chiefly Brit.* The cardinal number equal to 10¹². [Fr., a million million.] —**bil'lion** adj. & pron.

bil·lionth (bĭl'yənth) n. 1. The ordinal number that matches the number one billion in a series. 2. One of a billion equal parts. —**bil'lionth** adj. & adv.

bill of exchange n. A written order directing that a specified sum of money be paid to a particular person.

bill of fare n. A menu.

bill of lading n. A document listing and acknowledging receipt of goods for shipment.

bil·low (bĭl'ō) n. 1. A large wave of water. 2. A great swell or surge, as of smoke. —v. 1. To surge or roll in billows. 2. To swell or cause to swell in billows. [< ON *bylgja*.] —**bil'low·y** adj.

bil·ly (bĭl'ē) n., pl. **-lies.** A short wooden club. [Prob. < *Billy*, nickname for *William*.]

billy goat n. A male goat.

billy goat

bi·me·tal·lic (bī'mĭ-tăl'ĭk) adj. 1. Consisting of two metals. 2. Of, based on, or employing bimetallism.

bi·met·al·lism (bī-mĕt'l-ĭz'əm) n. The use of both gold and silver as the monetary standard of currency.

bi·month·ly (bī-mŭnth'lē) adj. 1. Happening every two months. 2. Happening twice a month. —n., pl. **-lies.** A bimonthly publication. —**bi·month'ly** adv.

bin (bĭn) n. A storage receptacle or container. [< OE *binne*.]

bin- pref. Var. of **bi-**.

bi·na·ry (bī'nə-rē) adj. 1. Of or based on the number 2 or the binary numeration system. 2. Having two distinct parts or components. —**bi'na·ry** n.

binary digit n. Either of the digits 0 or 1 used in representing numbers in the binary numeration system.

binary numeration system n. A system of numeration, based on 2, in which the numerals are represented as sums of powers of 2 and in which all numerals can be written using just the symbols 0 and 1.

binary star n. A system made up of two stars

orbiting about a common center of mass and appearing as a single object.

bin·au·ral (bī-nôr'əl) adj. 1. Of, pertaining to, or hearing with two ears. 2. Of or pertaining to sound transmission from two sources, which may vary acoustically relative to a listener.

bind (bīnd) v. **bound** (bound), **bind·ing.** 1. To tie or encircle with or as if with a rope. 2. To bandage. 3. To hold or restrain. 4. To compel or obligate, as with a sense of duty. 5. To place under legal obligation. 6. To cohere or cause to cohere in a mass. 7. To enclose and fasten (a book) between covers. 8. To reinforce or ornament with an edge or border. 9. To be tight and uncomfortable. 10. To constipate. 11. To be obligatory or compulsory. [< OE *bindan*.] —**bind'er** n.

bind·er·y (bīn'də-rē) n., pl. **-ies.** A place where books are bound.

bind·ing (bīn'dĭng) n. Something that binds, as the cover that holds together the pages of a book or a strip sewn along the edge of something.

binge (bĭnj) n. *Slang.* 1. A spree. 2. A period of uncontrolled self-indulgence. [Dial. *binge*, to soak.]

bin·go (bĭng'gō) n. A game of chance in which players place markers on a pattern of numbered squares according to numbers drawn and announced by a caller. [Orig. unknown.]

bin·na·cle (bĭn'ə-kəl) n. The nonmagnetic stand on which a ship's compass case is supported. [< Lat. *habitaculum*, little house.]

bin·oc·u·lar (bə-nŏk'yə-lər, bī-) adj. Of, used by, or involving both eyes. —n. Often **binoculars.** A binocular optical device, such as a pair of field glasses.

bi·no·mi·al (bī-nō'mē-əl) adj. Consisting of or pertaining to two names or terms. —n. 1. A mathematical expression consisting of two terms connected by a plus or minus sign. 2. A taxonomic plant or animal name consisting of two terms. [< BI- + Gk. *nomos*, part.]

bio- pref. Life or living organisms: *biochemistry*. [< Gk. *bios*, life.]

bi·o·chem·is·try (bī'ō-kĕm'ĭ-strē) n. The chemistry of biological substances and processes. —**bi'o·chem'i·cal** (-ĭ-kəl) adj. —**bi'o·chem'ist** n.

bi·o·de·grad·a·ble (bī'ō-dĭ-grā'də-bəl) adj. Capable of being decomposed by natural biological processes.

bi·o·feed·back (bī'ō-fēd'băk') n. A technique in which an attempt is made to consciously regulate a bodily function thought to be involuntary, as blood pressure, by using an instrument to monitor the function and to signal changes in it.

bi·o·ge·og·ra·phy (bī'ō-jē-ŏg'rə-fē) n. The biological study of the geographic distribution of plants and animals. —**bi'o·ge'o·graph'ic** (-jē'ə-grăf'ĭk) or **bi'o·ge'o·graph'i·cal** adj.

bi·og·ra·phy (bī-ŏg'rə-fē, bē-) n., pl. **-phies.** 1. A written account of a person's life. 2. Biographies in general, esp. when considered as a literary form. —**bi·og'ra·pher** n. —**bi'o·graph'i·cal** (bī'ə-grăf'ĭ-kəl) or **bi'o·graph'ic** adj.

biological warfare n. Warfare in which disease-producing microorganisms and bacteria are used to destroy livestock, crops, or human life.

bi·ol·o·gy (bī-ŏl′ə-jē) *n.* **1.** The scientific study of living things and life processes. **2.** The life processes of a particular group of living organisms. —**bi′o·log′i·cal** (bī′ə-lŏj′ĭ-kəl) or **bi′o·log′ic** *adj.* —**bi′o·log′i·cal·ly** *adv.* —**bi·ol′o·gist** *n.*

bi·o·med·i·cine (bī′ō-mĕd′ĭ-sĭn) *n.* The study of medicine as it relates to all biological systems. —**bi·o′med′i·cal** (-kəl) *adj.*

bi·o·phys·ics (bī′ō-fĭz′ĭks) *n.* (*used with a sing. verb*). The physics of biological processes. —**bi′o·phys′i·cal** *adj.* —**bi′o·phys′i·cist** *n.*

bi·op·sy (bī′ŏp′sē) *n., pl.* **-sies.** The study of tissues removed from the living body as an aid to medical diagnosis.

–biosis *suff.* A way of living: *symbiosis.* [< Gk. *biōsis.*]

bi·o·sphere (bī′ə-sfîr′) *n.* The part of the earth and its atmosphere in which living organisms exist.

bi·ot·ic (bī-ŏt′ĭk) *adj.* Of or pertaining to life or to living organisms. [< Gk. *biōtikos.*]

bi·o·tin (bī′ə-tĭn) *n.* A colorless crystalline vitamin, $C_{10}H_{16}N_2O_3S$, of the vitamin B complex, found esp. in liver, egg yolk, milk, and yeast. [Gk. *biotos,* life + -IN.]

bi·o·tite (bī′ə-tīt′) *n.* A dark-brown to black mica containing iron, potassium, and magnesium. [< Jean Baptiste *Biot* (1774–1862).]

bi·par·ti·san (bī-pär′tĭ-zən, -sən) *adj.* Of, consisting of, or supported by members of two parties. —**bi·par′ti·san·ship′** *n.*

bi·par·tite (bī-pär′tīt′) *adj.* **1.** Having or consisting of two parts. **2.** Having two corresponding parts, one for each party: *a bipartite treaty.*

bi·ped (bī′pĕd′) *n.* A two-footed animal.

bi·plane (bī′plān′) *n.* An airplane with two sets of wings, esp. one above and one below the fuselage.

bi·po·lar (bī-pō′lər) *adj.* **1.** Pertaining to or having two poles. **2.** Relating to or involving both of the earth's poles. —**bi′po·lar′i·ty** (-lăr′ĭ-tē) *n.*

bi·ra·cial (bī-rā′shəl) *adj.* Of, pertaining to, or involving members of two races.

birch (bûrch) *n.* **1.** Any of several deciduous trees with bark that can be separated from the wood in sheets. **2.** The hard wood of a birch tree. **3.** A birch rod used for whipping. —*v.* To whip with a birch rod. [< OE *birce.*]

bird (bûrd) *n.* A warm-blooded, egg-laying, feathered vertebrate with forelimbs modified to form wings. [< OE *brid.*]

bird·bath (bûrd′băth′, -băth′) *n.* A basin filled with water for birds to bathe in.

bird·house (bûrd′hous′) *n.* **1.** An aviary. **2.** A box made as a nesting place for birds.

bird·ie (bûr′dē) *n. Golf.* One stroke under par for any hole.

bird·lime (bûrd′līm′) *n.* A sticky substance smeared on branches or twigs to capture small birds.

bird of paradise *n.* Any of various birds with brilliant plumage native to New Guinea.

bird·seed (bûrd′sēd′) *n.* A mixture of various kinds of seeds used for feeding birds, esp. caged birds.

bird's-eye (bûrdz′ī′) *adj.* **1.** Patterned with spots resembling birds' eyes: *bird's-eye maple.* **2.** Seen from high above: *a bird's-eye view.*

bi·ret·ta (bə-rĕt′ə) *n.* A stiff square cap that is

worn esp. by Roman Catholic clergymen. [< LLat. *birrus,* hooded cloak.]

birr (bîr) *n., pl.* **birr** or **birrs.** See table at **currency.** [Native word in Ethiopia.]

birth (bûrth) *n.* **1.** The fact of being born or act of bearing young. **2.** A beginning; origin. **3.** Ancestry; lineage. [< ON *burdhr.*]

birth control *n.* Voluntary control of the number of children conceived, esp. by use of contraception.

birth·day (bûrth′dā′) *n.* The day or anniversary of a person's birth.

birth·mark (bûrth′märk′) *n.* A mark or blemish present on the body from birth.

birth·place (bûrth′plās′) *n.* The place where someone is born or where something originates.

birth·rate (bûrth′rāt′) *n.* The number of births of a given population in a given interval of time.

birth·right (bûrth′rīt′) *n.* A right or privilege to which a person is entitled by birth.

birth·stone (bûrth′stōn′) *n.* A jewel associated with the specific month of a person's birth.

bis·cuit (bĭs′kĭt) *n.* **1.** A small cake of bread leavened with baking powder or soda. **2.** *Chiefly Brit.* A thin, crisp cracker of unleavened bread. [< Med. Lat. *biscoctus.*]

bi·sect (bī′sĕkt′, bī-sĕkt′) *v.* **1.** To cut or divide into two equal parts. **2.** To split; fork. —**bi·sec′tion** *n.* —**bi·sec′tor** *n.*

bi·sex·u·al (bī-sĕk′shōō-əl) *adj.* **1.** Of or pertaining to both sexes. **2.** Having both male and female organs. **3.** Sexually attracted to members of both sexes. —**bi·sex′u·al** *n.* —**bi·sex′u·al′i·ty** *n.*

bish·op (bĭsh′əp) *n.* **1.** A high-ranking Christian clergyman, usu. in charge of a diocese. **2.** A chessman that can move diagonally across any number of unoccupied spaces of the same color. [< Gk. *episkopos,* overseer.]

bish·op·ric (bĭsh′ə-prĭk) *n.* The office, rank, or diocese of a bishop. [< OE *bisceoprīce,* diocese of a bishop.]

bis·muth (bĭz′məth) *n. Symbol* **Bi** A white, crystalline, brittle metallic element used in medicines and esp. in various low-melting alloys. Atomic number 83; atomic weight 208.980. [< G. *Wismut.*]

bi·son (bī′sən, -zən) *n.* A shaggy-maned, short-horned bovine mammal of western North America. [Lat.]

bisque (bĭsk) *n.* **1.** A cream soup made esp. from meat, fish, or shellfish. **2.** Ice cream mixed with crushed macaroons or nuts. [Fr.]

bis·tro (bē′strō, bĭs′trō) *n., pl.* **-tros.** A small bar, tavern, or nightclub. [Fr.]

bit¹ (bĭt) *n.* **1.** A small piece, portion, or amount. **2.** A moment **3.** An entertainment routine; act. **4.** *Slang.* A particular kind of behavior or activity. **5.** *Informal.* An amount equal to ⅛ of a dollar. [< OE *bita.*]

bit² (bĭt) *n.* **1.** A pointed and threaded tool for drilling and boring that is secured in a brace, bitstock, or drill press. **2.** The metal mouthpiece of a bridle. [< OE *bite,* cut.]

bit³ (bĭt) *n. Computer Sci.* **1.** A single character of a language having just two characters, as either of the binary digits 0 or 1. **2.** A unit of information equivalent to the choice of either of two equally likely alternatives. **3.** A unit of information storage capacity, as of a computer memory. [B(INARY) (DIG)IT.]

bitch (bĭch) *n.* **1.** A female dog. **2.** *Slang.* A spiteful woman. **3.** A complaint. —v. *Slang.* To complain. [< OE *bicce*.]

bite (bīt) v. **bit** (bīt), **bit·ten** (bīt'n) or **bit, bit·ing. 1.** To cut, grip, or tear with or as if with the teeth. **2.** To wound with or as if with fangs. **3.** To cut into with or as if with a sharp instrument. **4.** To corrode. **5.** To sting or cause to sting. **6.** To take or swallow bait. —n. **1.** The act of biting. **2.** A wound or injury resulting from biting. **3. a.** A stinging or smarting sensation. **b.** An incisive, penetrating quality. **4.** A mouthful. **5.** A light meal or snack. **6.** The angle at which the upper and lower teeth meet. [< OE *bītan*.] —**bit'er** n.

bit·ing (bī'tĭng) *adj.* **1.** Incisive; penetrating. **2.** Causing a stinging sensation.

bit·ter (bĭt'ər) *adj.* **1.** Having a taste that is sharp and unpleasant. **2.** Causing sharp pain to the body or discomfort to the mind. **3.** Exhibiting or proceeding from strong animosity. **4.** Having or marked by resentfulness or disappointment. —n. **bitters.** A bitter, usu. alcoholic liquid made with herbs or roots and used in cocktails or as a tonic. [< OE *biter*.] —**bit'ter·ly** *adv.* —**bit'ter·ness** n.

bit·tern (bĭt'ərn) n. Any of several wading birds similar to the heron and noted for its deep, resonant cry. [< OFr. *butor*.]

bit·ter·sweet (bĭt'ər-swēt') n. **1.** A woody vine with orange or yellowish fruits that split open to expose seeds with fleshy scarlet coverings. **2.** A species of nightshade with purple flowers and poisonous scarlet berries. —adj. **1.** Bitter and sweet at the same time. **2.** Producing a mixture of pain and pleasure.

bi·tu·men (bĭ-tōō'mən, -tyōō'-, bī-) n. Any of various mixtures of hydrocarbons and other substances, occurring naturally or obtained from coal or petroleum, found in asphalt and tar. [< Lat.]

bi·tu·mi·nous (bĭ-tōō'mə-nəs, -tyōō'-, bī-) *adj.* Containing or resembling bitumen.

bituminous coal n. A mineral coal that burns with a smoky, yellow flame, yielding volatile bituminous constituents.

bi·va·lent (bī-vā'lənt) *adj.* Having valence 2.

bi·valve (bī'vălv') n. A mollusk, such as a clam, with a shell consisting of two hinged parts. —**bi'valve'** *adj.*

biv·ou·ac (bĭv'ōō-ăk', bĭv'wăk') n. A temporary encampment made by soldiers in the field. —v. **-acked, -ack·ing.** To encamp in a bivouac. [Fr.]

bi·week·ly (bī-wēk'lē) *adj.* **1.** Happening every two weeks. **2.** Happening twice a week. —n., pl. **-lies.** A biweekly publication. —**bi·week'ly** *adv.*

bi·year·ly (bī-yîr'lē) *adj.* **1.** Happening every two years. **2.** Happening twice a year. —**bi·year'ly** *adv.*

bi·zarre (bĭ-zär') *adj.* Strikingly unconventional; odd. [< Sp. *bizarro*, brave.] —**bi·zarre'ly** *adv.*

Bk The symbol for the element berkelium.

blab (blăb) v. **blabbed, blab·bing. 1.** To reveal (a secret), esp. through careless talk. **2.** To chatter indiscreetly. [ME *blabben*.]

black (blăk) n. **1. a.** The darkest of all colors; the opposite of white. **b.** Something, esp. clothing, of this color. **2.** A member of a Ne-

groid people; Negro. —adj. **-er, -est. 1.** Of or nearly of the color black. **2.** Without light: *a black moonless night.* **3.** Belonging to an ethnic group having dark skin, esp. Negroid. **4.** Gloomy; depressing. **5.** Evil; wicked: *black deeds.* **6.** Angry; sullen. —v. To blacken. —**phrasal verb. black out. 1.** To lose consciousness temporarily. **2.** To produce or undergo a blackout. [< OE *blæc*.] —**black'ish** *adj.* —**black'ly** *adv.* —**black'ness** n.

Usage: The term *black* is preferred instead of *Negro*, and it is usually, but not always, written without an initial capital letter: *"Together, blacks and whites can move our country beyond racism"* (Whitney Young, Jr.).

black-and-blue (blăk'ən-blōō') *adj.* Discolored from coagulation of broken blood vessels beneath the skin.

black·ball (blăk'bôl') n. **1.** A small black ball that is used as a negative ballot. **2.** A vote that blocks the admission of an applicant. —**black'ball'** v.

black belt n. The rank of expert in a system of self-defense such as judo or karate.

black·ber·ry (blăk'bĕr'ē) n. **1.** Any of several woody plants with canelike, usu. thorny stems and black, edible berries. **2.** The fruit of a blackberry plant.

blackberry   **black-eyed Susan**

black·bird (blăk'bûrd') n. Any of various birds with black or predominantly black plumage.

black·board (blăk'bôrd', -bōrd') n. A smooth surface for writing on with chalk.

black·bod·y (blăk'bŏd'ē) n. A theoretically perfect absorber of all incident radiation.

black box n. A usu. electronic device with known performance characteristics but unknown constituents.

black·en (blăk'ən) v. **1.** To make or become black. **2.** To defame. —**black'en·er** n.

black eye n. A bruised discoloration of the flesh surrounding the eye.

black-eyed Su·san (sōō'zən) n. A plant having daisylike flowers with orange-yellow rays and dark-brown centers.

Black·foot (blăk'fŏŏt') n., pl. **-foot** or **-feet. 1.** Any of three tribes of Indians formerly inhabiting the regions of Montana, Alberta, and Saskatchewan. **2.** A member of one of the Blackfoot tribes. **3.** The Algonquian language of the Blackfoot. —**Black'foot'** *adj.*

black·guard (blăg'ard, -ärd') n. A low, unprincipled person; scoundrel.

black·head (blăk'hĕd') n. A plug of dried fatty matter that clogs a pore in the skin.

black·jack (blăk'jăk') n. **1.** A small leather-covered club with a short flexible shaft. **2.** A card game in which the object is to accumulate cards with a total count nearer to 21 than that of the dealer.

black light *n.* Invisible ultraviolet or infrared radiation.

black·list (blăk′lĭst′) *n.* A list of disapproved persons or organizations. —**black′list′** *v.*

black magic *n.* Magic in league with the devil; witchcraft.

black·mail (blăk′māl′) *n.* **1.** Extortion by the threat of exposure of something criminal or discreditable. **2.** Something extorted by blackmail. [BLACK + Sc. *mail,* rent.] —**black′mail′** *v.* —**black′mail′er** *n.*

black market *n.* Illegal buying or selling of goods in violation of restrictions.

black·out (blăk′out′) *n.* **1.** The extinguishment or concealment of lights that might be visible to enemy aircraft during an air raid. **2.** A temporary loss of consciousness. **3.** A stoppage, as of electricity.

Black Power *n.* A movement among black Americans to achieve equality through black political and cultural institutions.

black sheep *n.* A person considered undesirable or disgraceful by his family or group.

black·smith (blăk′smĭth′) *n.* One who forges and shapes iron with an anvil and hammer.

black·thorn (blăk′thôrn′) *n.* A thorny Eurasian shrub with clusters of white flowers and bluish-black, plumlike fruit.

black·top (blăk′tŏp′) *n.* A bituminous material, such as asphalt, used to pave roads. —**black′top′** *v.*

black widow *n.* A black and red spider of which the female is extremely venomous.

blad·der (blăd′ər) *n.* Any of various distensible membranous sacs found in most animals, esp. the urinary bladder. [< OE *blǣdre.*]

blade (blād) *n.* **1.** The flat-edged cutting part of a sharpened tool or weapon. **2.** A thin, flat part or structure similar to a blade. **3.** A dashing young man. [< OE *blǣd.*]

blame (blām) *v.* **blamed, blam·ing. 1.** To hold responsible. **2.** To find fault with; censure. —*n.* **1.** Responsibility for a fault or error. **2.** Censure, as for a fault. [< OFr. *blasmer.*] —**blam′a·ble** or **blame′a·ble** *adj.* —**blame′less** *adj.* —**blame′less·ly** *adv.* —**blam′er** *n.* **Syns:** *blame, censure, condemn, criticize, denounce* v.

blame·wor·thy (blām′wûr′thē) *adj.* Deserving blame.

blanch (blănch) *v.* **1.** To bleach. **2.** To make or become pale or white. [< OFr. *blanchir.*]

blanc·mange (blə-mänj′, -mänzH′) *n.* A flavored and sweetened milk pudding thickened with cornstarch. [< OFr. *blanc manger,* white food.]

bland (blănd) *adj.* **1.** Characterized by a moderate or tranquil quality. **2.** Lacking a distinctive character; dull. [Lat. *blandus,* flattering.] —**bland′ly** *adv.* —**bland′ness** *n.*

blan·dish (blăn′dĭsh) *v.* To coax by flattery; cajole. [< Lat. *blandiri.*] —**blan′dish·er** *n.* —**blan′dish·ment** *n.*

blank (blăngk) *adj.* **1.** Bearing no writing or marking. **2.** Not completed or filled in. **3.** Having no finishing grooves or cuts. **4.** Expressing nothing; vacant. **5.** Appearing confused or dazed; bewildered. **6.** Utter; complete: *a blank refusal.* —*n.* **1.** An empty space. **2. a.** A space to be filled in on a document. **b.** A document with such spaces.

3. An unfinished article such as a key form. **4.** A gun cartridge with a charge of powder but no bullet. —*v.* **1.** To remove, as from view; obliterate. **2.** To prevent (an opponent in a game or sport) from scoring. [< OFr. *blanc,* white.] —**blank′ly** *adv.* —**blank′ness** *n.*

blank check *n.* Total freedom of action.

blan·ket (blăng′kĭt) *n.* **1.** A piece of wool or other thick cloth used as a covering. **2.** A thick layer that covers. —*adj.* Applying to or covering a wide range of conditions or requirements: *a blanket insurance policy.* —*v.* To cover with or as if with a blanket. [< OFr. *blanquet* < *blanc,* white.]

blank verse *n.* Verse of unrhymed iambic lines.

blare (blâr) *v.* **blared, blar·ing.** To sound or utter loudly. [< ME *bleren.*] —**blare** *n.*

blar·ney (blär′nē) *n.* Smooth, flattering talk. [< the *Blarney* Stone, Ireland, said to give skill in flattery.]

bla·sé (blä-zā′, blä′zā) *adj.* **1.** Uninterested or bored. **2.** Sophisticated. [Fr.]

blas·pheme (blăs-fēm′, blăs′fēm′) *v.* **-phemed, -phem·ing.** To speak of (God or something sacred) in an irreverent or impious manner. [< Gk. *blasphēmein.*] —**blas·phem·er** *n.* —**blas′phe·mous** *adj.* —**blas′phe·mous·ly** *adv.* —**blas′phe·my** *n.*

blast (blăst) *n.* **1.** A strong gust of wind. **2.** A strong rush or stream of air, gas, steam, etc., from an opening. **3.** The sound produced by blowing a whistle, trumpet, etc. **4.** An explosion: *an atomic blast.* **5.** A violent verbal attack; denunciation. **6.** *Slang.* A gay or wild party. —*v.* **1.** To explode. **2.** To blight or wither. **3.** To criticize vigorously. **4.** *Slang.* To shoot. —*phrasal verb.* **blast off.** To begin flight, as a rocket or space vehicle. —*idiom.* **(at) full blast.** At full speed or capacity. [< OE *blǣst.*] —**blast′er** *n.*

blast furnace *n.* Any furnace in which combustion is intensified by a blast of air.

blast·off (blăst′ôf′, -ŏf′) *n.* Also **blast-off.** The launching of a rocket or space vehicle.

bla·tant (blāt′nt) *adj.* **1.** Unpleasantly loud and noisy. **2.** Offensively conspicuous; obvious: *a blatant lie.* [Prob. < Lat. *blatire,* to blab.] —**bla′tan·cy** *n.* —**bla′tant·ly** *adv.*

blath·er (blăth′ər) *v.* To speak foolishly or nonsensically. [< ON *blathra.*] —**blath′er** *n.* —**blath′er·er** *n.*

blath·er·skite (blăth′ər-skīt′) *n.* A babbling, foolish person. [BLATHER + Sc. dial. *skate,* a contemptible person.]

blaze¹ (blāz) *n.* **1. a.** A brightly burning fire. **b.** A destructive fire. **2.** A bright or direct light: *the blaze of day.* **3.** A brilliant or striking display: *a blaze of color.* **4.** A sudden outburst, as of activity or emotion. **5.** **blazes.** Used as an oath: *What in blazes happened?* —*v.* **blazed, blaz·ing. 1.** To burn brightly. **2.** To shine brightly. **3.** To show strong emotion. **4.** To shoot rapidly and steadily. [< OE *blǣse.*]

blaze² (blāz) *n.* **1.** A white spot on the face of an animal. **2.** A mark cut on a tree to indicate a trail. —*v.* **blazed, blaz·ing.** To indicate (a trail) by marking trees with blazes. [< OHG *plas.*]

blaz·er (blā′zər) *n.* An informal sports jacket.

bla·zon (blā′zən) *n.* **1.** A coat of arms. **2.** An ostentatious display. —*v.* To adorn or embellish with or as if with blazons. [< OFr. *blason*, shield.] —**bla′zon·ry** *n.*

bleach (blēch) *v.* To make or become white or colorless. —*n.* A chemical agent used for bleaching. [< OE *blǣcan.*]

bleach·ers (blē′chərz) *pl.n.* An unroofed outdoor grandstand.

bleak (blēk) *adj.* **-er, -est.** **1.** Exposed to the elements; barren. **2.** Cold and cutting; harsh. **3.** Dreary and somber: *a bleak prognosis.* [< ON *bleikr.*] —**bleak′ly** *adv.* —**bleak′ness** *n.*

blear (blîr) *v.* **1.** To blur (the eyes) with or as if with tears. **2.** To blur; dim; obscure. —*adj.* Indistinct. [< ME *bleren.*] —**blear′i·ly** *adv.* —**blear′i·ness** *n.* —**blear′y** *adj.*

bleat (blēt) *n.* The cry of a goat, sheep, or calf, or a similar sound. [< OE *blǣtan.*] —**bleat** *v.* —**bleat′er** *n.*

bleed (blēd) *v.* **bled** (blĕd), **bleed·ing.** **1.** To lose or extract blood. **2.** To feel sympathetic grief or anguish: *My heart bleeds for you.* **3.** To exude or extract sap. **4.** *Slang.* To obtain or extort money from. **5.** To run or become mixed, as dyes on wet cloth or paper. **6.** To draw or drain liquid or gaseous contents from: *bleed the transmission.* [< OE *blēdan.*]

bleed·er (blē′dər) *n.* A hemophiliac.

bleed·ing-heart (blē′dĭng-härt′) *n.* **1.** A garden plant with nodding pink flowers. **2.** A person who is excessively sympathetic toward others.

blem·ish (blĕm′ĭsh) *v.* To impair or spoil by a flaw. —*n.* A flaw or defect. [< OFr. *blemir,* to make pale.]

blench (blĕnch) *v.* To draw back or flinch, as from fear. [< OE *blencan.*]

blend (blĕnd) *v.* **blend·ed** or **blent** (blĕnt), **blend·ing.** **1.** To make or form a uniform mixture. **2.** To mix (different varieties or grades) to obtain a new mixture: *blend whiskeys.* **3.** To become merged into one; unite. **4.** To pass imperceptibly into one another. —*n.* **1.** Something blended: *a different blend of coffee.* **2.** A word produced by combining parts of other words, as *smog* from *smoke* and *fog.* [< OE *blandan.*] —**blend′er** *n.*

bless (blĕs) *v.* **blessed** or **blest** (blĕst), **bless·ing.** **1.** To make holy by religious rite; sanctify. **2.** To honor as holy; glorify: *Bless the Lord.* **3.** To invoke divine favor upon. **4.** To confer well-being upon. **5.** To favor, as with talent. **6.** To make the sign of the cross over. [< OE *blētsian.*]

bless·ed (blĕs′ĭd) *adj.* **1.** Worthy of worship; holy. **2.** Enjoying happiness; fortunate. **3.** Bringing happiness. **4.** *Rom. Cath. Ch.* Beatified. —**bless′ed·ly** *adv.* —**bless′ed·ness** *n.*

bless·ing (blĕs′ĭng) *n.* **1. a.** The act of one who blesses. **b.** The prescribed words or ceremony for such an act. **2.** An expression or utterance of good wishes. **3.** A special favor granted by God. **4.** Something promoting or contributing to happiness, well-being, or prosperity. **5.** Approbation; approval. **6.** A short prayer before or after a meal.

blew (blōō) *v. p.t.* of **blow.**

blight (blīt) *n.* **1.** A plant disease. **2.** An adverse environmental condition, as air pollution. **3.** Something that withers hopes or

impairs growth. —*v.* **1.** To cause or suffer decay; ruin. **2.** To frustrate. [Orig. unknown.]

blimp (blĭmp) *n.* A nonrigid, buoyant aircraft. [Orig. unknown.]

blimp

blind (blīnd) *adj.* **-er, -est.** **1.** Being without the sense of sight. **2.** Of or for sightless persons. **3.** Performed by instruments and without the use of sight: *blind navigation.* **4.** Unwilling or unable to perceive or understand: *blind to his faults.* **5.** Not based on reason or evidence: *blind faith.* **6.** Hidden or screened from sight: *a blind intersection.* **7. a.** Closed at one end: *a blind alley.* **b.** Having no opening: *a blind wall.* —*n.* **1.** Something that shuts out light. **2.** A shelter for concealing hunters. **3.** A subterfuge. —*v.* **1.** To deprive of sight. **2.** To deprive (a person) of judgment or reason. **3.** To dazzle. [< OE.] —**blind′ly** *adv.* —**blind′ness** *n.*

blind date *n. Informal.* **1.** A social engagement between two persons who have not previously met. **2.** Either of the persons participating in a blind date.

blind·ers (blīn′dərz) *pl.n.* Either of two leather flaps attached to a horse's bridle to curtail side vision.

blind·fold (blīnd′fōld′) *v.* **1.** To cover the eyes with or as if with a bandage. **2.** To mislead; delude. —*n.* A bandage over the eyes to keep someone from seeing. [< OE *geblindfellian,* to strike blind.]

blind side *n.* The side away from which one is directing one's attention.

blind spot *n.* **1.** The small area, insensitive to light, where the optic nerve enters the retina of the eye. **2.** A subject about which a person is ignorant or prejudiced.

blink (blĭngk) *v.* **1.** To close and open (one or both eyes) rapidly. **2.** To flash on and off. —*phrasal verb.* **blink at.** To pretend not to see. —*n.* **1.** A brief closing of the eyes. **2.** A quick look or glimpse. **3.** A flash of light; gleam. —*idiom.* **on the blink.** Out of order. [ME *blinken.*]

blink·er (blĭng′kər) *n.* **1.** A light that blinks in order to convey a signal. **2.** *Slang.* An eye.

blintz (blĭnts) or **blin·tze** (blĭn′tsə) *n.* A thin, rolled pancake usu. filled with cottage cheese and often served with sour cream. [Yiddish *blintse.*]

blip (blĭp) *v.* **blipped, blip·ping.** To interrupt recorded sounds, as on a videotape: *blipped the expletive from the TV show.* —*n.* **1.** A spot of light on a radar screen. **2.** A brief interruption in a broadcast resulting from blipping. [Imit.]

bliss (blĭs) *n.* **1.** Extreme happiness; joy.

2. Religious ecstasy; spiritual joy. [< OE.] —**bliss´ful** adj. —**bliss´ful·ly** adv. —**bliss´ful·ness** n.

blis·ter (blĭs´tər) n. 1. A thin swelling of the skin containing watery matter, caused by burning or irritation. 2. Something resembling a blister. [< OFr. blestre.] —**blis´ter** v. —**blis´ter·y** adj.

blis·ter·ing (blĭs´tər-ĭng) adj. 1. Hot: a blistering sun. 2. Very strong; intense: blistering criticism. 3. Extremely rapid: a blistering pace.

blithe (blīth, blīth) adj. **blīth·er, blīth·est.** Cheerful; carefree. [< OE blīthe.] —**blithe´ly** adv. —**blithe´ness** n.

blithe·some (blīth´səm, blīth´-) adj. Cheerful; merry. —**blithe´some·ly** adv. —**blithe´some·ness** n.

blitz (blĭts) n. 1. A blitzkrieg. 2. An intense air raid. 3. An intense, swift attack: a last-minute campaign blitz. 4. Football. A rushing of the passer by the defensive team. [< BLITZKRIEG.] —**blitz** v.

blitz·krieg (blĭts´krēg´) n. A swift, sudden military attack by air and land forces. [G.]

bliz·zard (blĭz´ərd) n. A very heavy snowstorm with high winds. [Orig. unknown.]

bloat (blōt) v. To make or become swollen or inflated. [< ON blautr, soft.]

blob (blŏb) n. 1. A soft, formless mass: a blob of wax. 2. A splotch of color. [ME blober, bubble.]

bloc (blŏk) n. A group of persons, states, or nations, united by common interests. [< OFr., block.]

block (blŏk) n. 1. A solid piece of wood or other hard substance having one or more flat sides. 2. A stand from which articles are displayed at an auction. 3. A pulley or set of pulleys set in a casing. 4. A set of like items handled as a unit: blocks of tickets. 5. a. An act of obstructing. b. An obstacle or hindrance. 6. a. A section of a town enclosed by four intersecting streets. b. A segment of a street bounded by successive cross streets. 7. Med. An obstruction of a neural, digestive, or other physiological process. 8. Psychol. Sudden cessation of a thought process without an immediate observable cause. 9. Slang. A person's head. —v. 1. To support, strengthen, or retain in place by means of a block. 2. To shape or form with or on a block: block a hat. 3. To stop or impede the passage of: block traffic. 4. Med. To interrupt the proper functioning of (a physiological process). —**phrasal verb. block out.** To plan broadly without details. —**idiom. on the block.** Up for sale. [< MDu. blok.] —**block´age** n. —**block´er** n. —**block´ish** adj.

block·ade (blŏ-kād´) n. 1. The closing off of a city or other area to traffic and communication. 2. The forces used in a blockade. —v. **-ad·ed, -ad·ing.** To set up a blockade against. [BLOCK + (AMBUSC)ADE.] —**block·ad´er** n.

block and tackle n. An apparatus of pulley blocks and ropes or cables used for hauling and hoisting.

block·bust·er (blŏk´bŭs´tər) n. Informal. 1. A bomb capable of destroying a city block. 2. Something extremely impressive or startling.

block·bust·ing (blŏk´bŭs´tĭng) n. Informal. The practice of persuading homeowners to sell quickly and usu. at a loss by appealing to the fear that minority groups will move into the neighborhood with a resulting decline in property values.

block·head (blŏk´hĕd´) n. A stupid person.

block·house (blŏk´hous´) n. 1. A wooden or concrete fortification. 2. A reinforced building from which the launching of rockets or space vehicles is observed.

blond (blŏnd) adj. **-er, -est.** 1. Having fair hair and skin: a blond boy. 2. Light-colored: blond hair; blond furniture. —n. A blond man or boy. [Fr.] —**blond´ish** adj. —**blond´ness** n.

Usage: Blond as an adjective may be used of both sexes. Blonde as a noun is used to refer only to a female.

blonde (blŏnd) adj. **blond·er, blond·est.** Blond. —n. A blonde woman or girl.

blood (blŭd) n. 1. a. The fluid circulated by the heart in a vertebrate, carrying oxygen, nutrients, hormones, etc., throughout the body and waste materials to excretory organs. b. A functionally similar fluid in an invertebrate. c. A fluid resembling blood, such as the juice of certain plants. 2. Life; lifeblood: Energy is the blood of an industrial nation. 3. Bloodshed; murder. 4. Temperament; disposition: hot blood; sporting blood. 5. Kinship: related by blood. 6. Racial or national ancestry. 7. Members as a class: the best young blood of the nation. 8. A dashing young man. —**idiom. in cold blood.** Dispassionately. [< OE blōd.]

blood bank n. A place where whole blood is stored for use in transfusion.

blood bath n. A massacre.

blood count n. A test in which the cells in a blood sample are classified and counted.

blood·cur·dling (blŭd´kûrd´lĭng) adj. Terrifying.

blood·ed (blŭd´ĭd) adj. Thoroughbred: blooded horses.

blood·hound (blŭd´hound´) n. 1. A hound with drooping ears, sagging jowls, and a keen sense of smell. 2. Informal. A relentless pursuer.

blood·line (blŭd´līn´) n. Direct line of descent.

blood poisoning n. 1. Toxemia. 2. Septicemia.

blood pressure n. The pressure of the blood within the arteries.

blood·shed (blŭd´shĕd´) n. 1. The shedding of blood. 2. Carnage.

blood·shot (blŭd´shŏt´) adj. Red and irritated: bloodshot eyes.

blood·stain (blŭd´stān´) n. A discoloration caused by blood. —**blood´stained´** adj.

blood·stream (blŭd´strēm´) n. Also **blood stream.** The blood flowing through a circulatory system.

blood·suck·er (blŭd´sŭk´ər) n. 1. An animal that sucks blood, as a leech. 2. Informal. One who preys upon another. —**blood´suck´ing** adj.

blood·thirst·y (blŭd´thûr´stē) adj. Thirsting for bloodshed. —**blood´thirst´i·ly** adv. —**blood´thirst´i·ness** n.

blood vessel n. An elastic tubular canal, as an artery, vein, or capillary, through which blood circulates.

blood·y (blŭd´ē) adj. **-i·er, -i·est.** 1. Bleeding: a bloody nose. 2. Of, containing, or stained with blood. 3. Causing or marked by bloodshed: a bloody fight. 4. Brit. Slang. Used as an intensive: *a bloody fool.* —*v.* **-ied, -y·ing.** To stain with or as if with blood. —**blood'i·ly** *adv.* —**blood'i·ness** *n.*

bloody mar·y (mâr'ē) *n.* Also **Bloody Mar·y.** A drink made with vodka and tomato juice.

bloom (bloom) *n.* **1.** The flower or blossoms of a plant. **2. a.** The condition or time of being in flower. **b.** A condition or time of great development, vigor, or beauty; prime. **3.** A fresh, rosy complexion. **4.** A delicate, powdery coating on some fruits, leaves, and stems. —*v.* **1.** To bear flowers. **2.** To shine with health and vigor; glow. **3.** To grow or flourish. [< ON *blōmi.*]

bloo·mers (bloo'mərz) *pl.n.* Women's wide, loose pants or underpants, gathered at or above the knee. [< Amelia *Bloomer* (1818–94).]

bloom·ing (bloo'ming) *adj.* **1.** Flowering; blossoming. **2.** Flourishing.

bloop·er (bloo'pər) *n.* **1.** *Baseball.* A short, weakly hit fly ball. **2.** *Informal.* An embarrassing mistake. [< *bloop,* imit. of the sound of such a hit.]

blos·som (blŏs'əm) *n.* **1.** A flower, esp. of a plant that yields edible fruit. **2.** The condition or time of flowering: *peach trees in blossom.* —*v.* **1.** To come into flower; bloom. **2.** To develop; flourish. [< OE *blōstma.*] —**blos'som·y** *adj.*

blot (blŏt) *n.* **1.** A spot; stain: *a blot of ink.* **2.** A moral blemish; disgrace. —*v.* **blot·ted, blot·ting. 1.** To spot or stain. **2.** *Obs.* To bring moral disgrace to. **3.** To obliterate; cancel. **4.** To make obscure; darken. **5.** To dry or soak up with absorbent material. **6.** To make a blot. **7.** To become blotted. —*phrasal verb.* **blot out.** To destroy utterly. [ME.]

blotch (blŏch) *n.* **1.** A spot or blot; splotch. **2.** A discoloration on the skin; blemish. [Prob. a blend of BLOT and BOTCH.] —**blotch** *v.* —**blotch'i·ness** *n.* —**blotch'y** *adj.*

blot·ter (blŏt'ər) *n.* **1.** A piece of blotting paper. **2.** A book containing daily records of occurrences or transactions: *a police blotter.*

blotting paper *n.* Absorbent paper used to dry a surface or absorb excess ink.

blouse (blous, blouz) *n.* **1.** A loosely fitting shirtlike garment. **2.** The jacket of a U.S. Army uniform. —*v.* **bloused, blous·ing.** To hang or drape loosely. [Fr.]

blow¹ (blō) *v.* **blew** (bloo), **blown** (blōn), **blow·ing. 1.** To be in a state of motion, as the wind. **2. a.** To be carried by or as if by the wind. **b.** To cause to move by means of a current of air. **3.** To drive a current of air upon, in, or through. **4.** To expel a current of air, as from a bellows. **5.** To sound or cause to sound by expelling a current of air: *blow a trumpet.* **6.** To pant. **7.** To cause to explode. **8.** To melt (a fuse). **9.** To spout water and air, as a whale. **10.** To shape by forcing air or gas through at the end of a pipe: *blow glass.* **11.** *Slang.* To depart. **12.** *Slang.* To spend (money) freely. **13.** *Slang.* To handle ineptly: *Don't blow this opportunity.* —*phrasal verbs.* **blow in.** To arrive. **blow out. 1.** To extinguish or be extinguished by blowing. **2.** To burst suddenly, as a tire. **3.** To melt, as a fuse. **4.** To fail, as an electrical apparatus. **blow over. 1.** To subside; wane. **2.** To be forgotten. **blow up. 1.** To come into being: *A storm blew up.* **2.** To explode. **3.** To fill with air; inflate. **4.** To enlarge (a photographic image or print). **5.** *Informal.* To lose one's temper. —*n.* **1.** A blast of air or wind. **2.** The act of blowing. —*idiom.* **blow off steam.** To give release to one's anger or other pent-up emotion. [< OE *blāwan.*]

blow² (blō) *n.* **1.** A sudden hard stroke or hit, as with the fist. **2.** A sudden shock or calamity. **3.** A sudden attack. —*idiom.* **come to blows.** To begin to fight. [ME *blaw.*]

blow³ (blō) *v.* **blew** (bloo), **blown** (blōn), **blow·ing.** To bloom. —*n.* A mass of blossoms: *peach blow.* [< OE *blōwan.*]

blow-by-blow (blō'bī-blō') *adj.* Describing in great detail.

blow-dry (blō'drī') *v.* To dry and often style with a hand-held hair dryer. —**blow'-dry'er** *n.*

blow·er (blō'ər) *n.* One that blows, esp. a mechanical device.

blow·gun (blō'gŭn') *n.* A long, narrow pipe through which darts or pellets may be blown.

blow·out (blō'out') *n.* **1.** A sudden bursting, as of an automobile tire. **2.** A sudden escape of confined gas. **3.** *Slang.* A large party or social affair.

blow·torch (blō'tôrch') *n.* A usu. portable gas burner that produces a flame hot enough to melt soft metals.

blow·up (blō'ŭp') *n.* **1.** An explosion. **2.** A violent outburst of temper. **3.** A photographic enlargement.

blow·y (blō'ē) *adj.* **-i·er, -i·est.** Windy; breezy.

blow·zy (blou'zē) *adj.* **-zi·er, -zi·est.** Also **blow·sy.** Disheveled; unkempt. [< obs. *blowse,* beggar girl.]

blub·ber¹ (blŭb'ər) *v.* To weep and sob noisily. —*n.* A loud weeping. [ME *bluberen.*] —**blub'ber·er** *n.*

blub·ber² (blŭb'ər) *n.* **1.** The fat of whales, seals, and other marine mammals. **2.** *Slang.* Excessive body fat. [ME *bluber,* foam.] —**blub'ber·y** *adj.*

blu·cher (bloo'chər, -kər) *n.* A laced shoe having the vamp and tongue made of one piece. [< Gebhard L. von *Blücher* (1742–1819).]

bludg·eon (blŭj'ən) *n.* A short, heavy club that has one end thicker than the other. —*v.* **1.** To hit with or as if with a bludgeon. **2.** To threaten or bully. [Orig. unknown.] —**bludg'eon·er** *n.*

blue (bloo) *n.* **1. a.** Any of a group of colors whose hue is that of the sky on a clear day. **b.** Anything of this color. **2. the blue. a.** The sea. **b.** The sky. —*adj.* **blu·er, blu·est. 1.** Of the color blue. **2.** Having a gray or purplish color, as from cold or bruise. **3.** *Informal.* Gloomy; depressed. **4.** Puritanical; strict. **5.** Indecent; risqué: *a blue joke.* —*v.* **blued, blu·ing. 1.** To make blue. **2.** To use bluing on. —*idioms.* **once in a blue moon.** Rarely. **out of the blue.** At a completely unexpected time. [< OFr. *bleu,* of Gmc. orig.] —**blue'ness** *n.* —**blu'ish** or **blue'ish** *adj.*

blue baby *n.* A newborn baby with bluish skin caused by too little oxygen in its blood.

blue·bell (bloo'bĕl') *n.* Any of various plants with blue, bell-shaped flowers.

ă pat ā pay â care ä father ĕ pet ē be ĭ pit ī tie î pier ŏ pot ō toe ô paw, for oi noise ŏŏ took
ōō boot ou out th thin th this ŭ cut û urge yōō abuse zh vision ə about, item, edible, gallop, circus

blue·ber·ry (blōō'bĕr'ē) *n.* **1.** A juicy, edible blue or purplish berry. **2.** A shrub bearing blueberries.

blue·bird (blōō'bûrd') *n.* A North American bird with blue plumage and usu. a rust-colored breast.

blue blood *n.* **1.** Noble or aristocratic descent. **2.** A member of the aristocracy. —**blue'-blood'ed** (-blŭd'ĭd) *adj.*

blue·bon·net (blōō'bŏn'ĭt) *n.* A plant with compound leaves and clusters of blue flowers.

blue book or **blue-book** (blōō'bŏŏk') *n.* **1.** *Informal.* A book listing the names of socially prominent people. **2.** A blank notebook with blue covers in which to write college examinations.

blue·bot·tle (blōō'bŏt'l) *n.* A fly with a bright metallic-blue body.

blue cheese *n.* A tangy cheese streaked with a bluish mold.

blue chip *n.* A stock that sells at a high price because of its long record of steady earnings. —**blue'-chip'** *adj.*

blue-col·lar (blōō'kŏl'ər) *adj.* Of or pertaining to wage earners doing skilled or semiskilled manual labor.

blue·fish (blōō'fĭsh') *n.* A food and game fish of temperate and tropical waters.

blue·grass (blōō'grăs') *n.* **1.** A lawn and pasture grass with bluish or grayish leaves and stems. **2.** A type of folk music that originated in the southern United States, characterized by rapid tempos and the use of banjos and guitars.

blue·ing (blōō'ĭng) *n.* Var. of **bluing.**

blue·jack·et (blōō'jăk'ĭt) *n.* An enlisted man in the U.S. or British Navy; sailor. [From the blue jacket of the Navy.]

blue jay *n.* A North American bird with a crested head and predominantly blue plumage.

blue jay

blue jeans *pl.n.* Jeans.

blue law *n.* A law designed to regulate Sunday activities.

blue·nose (blōō'nōz') *n.* A puritanical person.

blue-pen·cil (blōō'pĕn'səl) *v.* **-ciled** or **-cilled, -cil·ing** or **-cil·ling.** To edit with or as if with a blue pencil.

blue point *n.* An edible oyster found chiefly off Blue Point, Long Island, New York.

blue·print (blōō'prĭnt') *n.* **1.** A photographic reproduction, as of architectural plans, rendered as white lines on a blue background. **2.** A carefully designed plan.

blue ribbon *n.* The first prize. —**blue'-rib'bon** *adj.*

blues (blōōz) *pl.n.* (*used with a sing. or pl. verb*). **1.** A state of melancholy. **2.** A style of jazz evolved from southern American Negro

secular songs and usu. having a slow tempo. [< *blue devils,* a feeling of depression.]

blue-stock·ing (blōō'stŏk'ĭng) *n.* A pedantic or scholarly woman. [< the *Blue Stocking Society,* a predominantly female literary club of 18th-cent. London.]

blu·et (blōō'ĭt) *n.* A slender, low-growing plant that has small, light-blue flowers. [< Fr., cornflower.]

bluff¹ (blŭf) *v.* To mislead or intimidate, esp. by a false display of confidence. —*n.* **1.** The act or practice of bluffing. **2.** One who bluffs. [Poss. < Du. *bluffen,* to boast.] —**bluff'er** *n.*

bluff² (blŭf) *n.* A steep headland, bank, or cliff. —*adj.* **-er, -est. 1.** Having a rough, blunt but not unkind manner. **2.** Presenting a broad, steep front. [Orig. unknown.] —**bluff'ly** *adv.* —**bluff'ness** *n.*

blu·ing (blōō'ĭng) *n.* Also **blue·ing.** A blue substance added to rinse water to counteract the yellowing of laundered fabrics.

blun·der (blŭn'dər) *n.* A foolish or stupid mistake. —*v.* **1.** To move awkwardly or clumsily. **2.** To make a stupid mistake. [< ME *blunderen.*] —**blun'der·er** *n.* —**blun'der·ing·ly** *adv.*

blun·der·buss (blŭn'dər-bŭs') *n.* **1.** A short musket with a wide muzzle, formerly used to scatter shot at close range. **2.** A stupid, clumsy person. [< Du. *donderbus.*]

blunt (blŭnt) *adj.* **-er, -est. 1.** Having a thick, dull edge or end. **2.** Abrupt and frank in manner; brusque. —*v.* To make or become blunt. [ME.] —**blunt'ly** *adv.* —**blunt'ness** *n.*

blur (blûr) *v.* **blurred, blur·ring. 1.** To make or become indistinct; obscure. **2.** To smear or stain; smudge. **3.** To lessen the perception of; dim. —*n.* **1.** A smear or smudge. **2.** Something that is hazy and indistinct. [Orig. unknown.] —**blur'ry** *adj.*

blurb (blûrb) *n.* A brief, favorable publicity notice, as on a book jacket. [Coined by Frank Gelett Burgess (1866-1951).]

blurt (blûrt) *v.* To say suddenly and impulsively. [Prob. imit.]

blush (blŭsh) *v.* **1.** To become suddenly red in the face from modesty, embarrassment, or shame; flush. **2.** To feel ashamed or regretful about something. **3.** To become red or rosy. [< OE *blyscan.*] —**blush** *n.* —**blush'er** *n.*

blus·ter (blŭs'tər) *v.* **1.** To blow in loud, violent gusts, as wind in a storm. **2.** To speak noisily and boastfully. [ME *blusteren* < MLG.] —**blus'ter** *n.* —**blus'ter·er** *n.* —**blus'ter·y** *adj.*

bo·a (bō'ə) *n.* **1.** A nonvenomous tropical snake, such as the boa constrictor, that coils around and crushes its prey. **2.** A long, fluffy scarf made of fur, feathers, etc. [< Lat. *boa,* a large water snake.]

boar (bôr, bōr) *n.* **1.** An uncastrated male pig. **2.** A wild pig. [< OE *bār.*]

board (bôrd, bōrd) *n.* **1.** A flat length of sawed lumber. **2.** A flat piece of wood or similar material adapted for a special use. **3. a.** A table set for serving a meal. **b.** Food served daily to paying guests: *room and board.* **4.** A table at which official meetings are held. **5.** An organized body of administrators. **6. the boards.** A theater stage. **7.** *Naut.* The side of a ship. —*v.* **1.** To cover or close with boards: *board up the window.* **2.** To provide with or receive food and lodging for a charge. **3.** To go aboard (a ship, train, or plane).

4. To come alongside (a ship). —*Idiom.* **on board.** Aboard. [< OE *bord*.]

board·er (bôr′dər, bōr′-) *n.* One who pays for both meals and lodging at another's home.

boarding house *n.* Also **board·ing·house** (bôr′dĭng-hous′, bōr′-). A house that provides meals and lodging for a charge.

board·walk (bôrd′wôk′, bōrd′-) *n.* A promenade, esp. of planks, along a beach or waterfront.

boast (bōst) *v.* **1.** To talk about or speak with excessive pride. **2.** To take pride in the possession of. —*n.* **1.** An instance of bragging. **2.** A source of pride. [ME *boster*.] —**boast′er** *n.* —**boast′ing·ly** *adv.*

Syns: *boast, brag, crow, vaunt* v.

boast·ful (bōst′fəl) *adj.* Tending to boast or brag. —**boast′ful·ly** *adv.* —**boast′ful·ness** *n.*

boat (bōt) *n.* **1.** A relatively small, usu. open water craft. **2.** A ship. **3.** A dish shaped like a boat: *a gravy boat.* —*Idiom.* **in the same boat.** In the same situation. [< OE *bat*.] —**boat′er** *n.* —**boat′ing** *n.*

boat·man (bōt′mən) *n.* One who works on, deals with, or operates boats.

boat·swain (bō′sən) *n.* Also **bo's'n,** **bos'n,** or **bo·sun.** A warrant officer or petty officer in charge of a ship's deck crew, rigging, anchors, and cables.

bob¹ (bŏb) *v.* **bobbed, bob·bing.** To move or cause to move up and down. —*phrasal verb.* **bob up.** To appear suddenly. —*n.* A quick, jerky movement. [ME *bobben*.]

bob² (bŏb) *n.* **1.** A small knoblike pendent object. **2.** A fishing float. **3.** A short haircut on a woman or child. **4.** The docked tail of a horse. —*v.* **bobbed, bob·bing.** To cut short: *bobbed her hair.* [ME *bobbe.*] —**bob′ber** *n.*

bob³ (bŏb) *n., pl.* **bob.** *Brit. Slang.* A shilling. [Orig. unknown.]

bob·bin (bŏb′ĭn) *n.* A spool or reel for thread, as on a sewing machine. [Fr. *bobine.*]

bob·ble (bŏb′əl) *v.* **-bled, -bling.** **1.** To bob up and down. **2.** To fumble (a ball). [< BOB¹.] —**bob′ble** *n.*

bob·by (bŏb′ē) *n., pl.* **-bies.** *Brit. Slang.* A policeman. [< Sir *Robert* Peel (1788–1850).]

bobby pin *n.* A small metal hair clip with ends pressed tightly together. [< BOB².]

bobby socks *pl.n.* Also **bobby sox.** *Informal.* Ankle socks. [< *Bobby,* nickname for *Robert.*]

bob·by·sox·er (bŏb′ē-sŏk′sər) *n. Informal.* A teen-age girl.

bob·cat (bŏb′kăt′) *n.* A wild cat of North America, with spotted fur, tufted ears, and a short tail.

bob·o·link (bŏb′ə-lĭngk′) *n.* An American migratory songbird. [Imit. of its cry.]

bob·sled (bŏb′slĕd′) *n.* **1.** A long racing sled whose front runners are controlled by a steering wheel. **2. a.** A long sled made of two shorter sleds joined one behind the other. **b.** Either of these sleds. —*v.* **-sled·ded, -sled·ding.** To ride or race in a bobsled.

bob·tail (bŏb′tāl′) *n.* **1.** A short tail or a tail that has been cut short. **2.** An animal, esp. a horse, with a bobtail. —**bob′tailed′** *adj.*

bob·white (bŏb-hwīt′, -wīt′) *n.* A brown and white North American quail. [Imit. of its cry.]

bock beer (bŏk) *n.* A dark springtime beer. [< G. *Einbecker Bier,* beer from Einbeck.]

bod (bŏd) *n. Slang.* Body.

bode¹ (bōd) *v.* **bod·ed, bod·ing.** To be an omen of. [< OE *bodian,* to announce.]

bode² (bōd) *v. A p.t.* of **bide.**

bod·ice (bŏd′ĭs) *n.* The fitted upper part of a dress. [< *bodies,* pl. of BODY.]

bod·i·less (bŏd′ē-lĭs) *adj.* Having no body, form, or substance: *bodiless fears.*

bod·i·ly (bŏd′l-ē) *adj.* **1.** Of or pertaining to the body. **2.** Physical: *bodily welfare.* —*adv.* **1.** In person. **2.** As a complete physical entity: *We carried him bodily from the room.*

bod·kin (bŏd′kĭn) *n.* **1.** A small pointed instrument for making holes in fabric or leather. **2.** A blunt needle for pulling tape or ribbon through loops or a hem. **3.** *Archaic.* A dagger. [ME *boidekyn.*]

bod·y (bŏd′ē) *n., pl.* **-ies.** **1.** The entire physical structure of an organism, esp. a human being or animal. **2.** A corpse or carcass. **3.** The trunk or torso. **4.** Any well-defined object or collection of matter: *a body of water.* **5.** A group of persons considered or acting together: *a governing body.* **6.** A collection of related things: *a body of information.* **7.** The main or central part of something: *the body of a ship.* **8.** Consistency of substance: *a wine with fine body.* **9.** *Informal.* A person. [OE *bodig.*]

body building *n.* The practice of developing the body through physical exercise and diet esp. for competitive exhibition. —**body builder** *n.*

body count *n.* A count of individual bodies, as those killed by enemy soldiers.

body English *n.* The involuntary effort of a person to affect the movement of a propelled object, as a ball, by twisting his body toward the desired goal.

bod·y·guard (bŏd′ē-gärd′) *n.* A person or persons, usu. armed, responsible for the physical safety of one or more specific persons.

body language *n.* The gestures, postures, and facial expressions by which an individual communicates nonverbally with others.

body politic *n.* The whole population of a nation or state, regarded as a political unit.

body shop *n.* A garage where the bodies of automotive vehicles are repaired.

body stocking *n.* A close-fitting, one-piece garment that covers the torso, and sometimes the arms and legs.

bod·y·surf (bŏd′ē-sûrf′) *v.* **-surfed, -surf·ing.** To ride on a wave without a surfboard. —**bod′y·surf′er** *n.*

bobcat

Boer (bôr, bōr, bōōr) *n.* A South African of Dutch descent. —**Boer** *adj.*

bof·fo (bŏf'ō) *adj.* Extremely successful; excellent. [< slang *boffola*, success.]

bog (bŏg, bôg) *n.* Soft, water-soaked ground; marsh. —*v.* **bogged, bog·ging.** To hinder or be hindered. [< Ir. Gael. *bogach*.] —**bog'gy** *adj.*

bo·gey (bō'gē) *n.*, *pl.* **-geys.** 1. *Golf.* One stroke over par on a hole. 2. An unidentified flying aircraft. —*v. Golf.* To shoot (a hole) in one shot over par.

bog·gle (bŏg'al) *v.* **-gled, -gling.** 1. To hesitate or evade as if in fear or doubt. 2. To overwhelm with amazement: *It boggles the mind.* [Poss. < dial. *bogle*, goblin.]

bo·gus (bō'gas) *adj.* Counterfeit; fake. [< *bogus*, a machine for making counterfeit money.]

bo·gy (bō'gē) *n.*, *pl.* **-gies.** Also **bo·gie.** 1. An evil or mischievous spirit; hobgoblin. 2. Something that causes one worry or annoyance. [Orig. unknown.]

Bo·he·mi·an (bō-hē'mē-an) *n.* 1. A native or inhabitant of Bohemia. 2. A Gypsy. 3. The Czech dialects of Bohemia. 4. **bohemian.** A writer or artist who disregards conventional standards of behavior. —**Bo·he'mi·an** *adj.*

boil[1] (boil) *v.* 1. To vaporize a liquid by applying heat. 2. To cook by boiling. 3. To be in a state of agitation, as boiling water. 4. To be greatly excited, as with rage. 5. To heat to the boiling point. 6. To separate by evaporation as a result of boiling. —*phrasal verbs.* **boil down.** 1. To reduce in bulk or size by boiling. 2. To summarize. **boil over.** To explode in rage or passion. —*n.* The condition or act of boiling. [< Lat. *bullire.*]

boil[2] (boil) *n.* A painful, pus-filled swelling of the skin and subcutaneous tissue caused by bacterial infection. [< OE *byl.*]

boil·er (boi'lar) *n.* 1. An enclosed vessel in which water is heated and circulated, either as hot water or as steam, for heating or power. 2. A container for boiling liquids. 3. A storage tank for hot water.

boil·er·room (boi'lar-rōōm', -rŏŏm') *adj. Informal.* Of or involving usu. illegal, high-pressure telephone sales tactics as used in selling commodities or land.

boiling point *n.* 1. The temperature at which a liquid boils, esp. under standard atmospheric conditions. 2. *Informal.* The point at which a person loses his or her temper.

bois·ter·ous (boi'star-as, -stras) *adj.* 1. Rough and stormy. 2. Noisy, high-spirited, and unrestrained. [< ME *boistous*, rude.] —**bois'ter·ous·ly** *adv.* —**bois'ter·ous·ness** *n.*

bo·la (bō'la) *n.* Also **bo·las** (-las). A rope with round weights attached, used to catch cattle or game by entangling the legs. [Am. Sp. *bolas.*]

bold (bōld) *adj.* **-er, -est.** 1. Fearless and daring; courageous. 2. Requiring or exhibiting courage and bravery. 3. Unduly forward and brazen. 4. Clear and distinct to the eye. 5. Steep, as a cliff. [< OE *bald.*] —**bold'ly** *adv.* —**bold'ness** *n.*

bold·face (bōld'fās') *n.* Type with thick, heavy lines.

bole (bōl) *n.* The trunk of a tree. [< ON *bolr.*]

bo·le·ro (bō-lâr'ō, ba-) *n.*, *pl.* **-ros.** 1. A short jacket, usu. with no front fastening. 2. **a.** A Spanish dance in triple meter. **b.** The music for this dance. [Sp.]

bo·li·var (bō-lē'vär', bŏl'a-var) *n.*, *pl.* **bo·li·vars** or **bo·li·va·res** (bō'lē-vä'räs'). See table at **currency.** [< Simón **Bolívar** (1783–1830).]

boll (bōl) *n.* A rounded seedpod, as of the cotton plant. [ME.]

boll weevil *n.* A long-snouted beetle that lays its eggs in cotton bolls and bolls, causing great damage.

bo·lo (bō'lō) *n.*, *pl.* **-los.** A long, heavy, single-edged machete used in the Philippines. [Sp.]

bo·lo·gna (ba-lō'nē, -na, -nya) *n.* A large smoked sausage made of mixed meats. [< *Bologna*, Italy.]

Bol·she·vik (bōl'sha-vĭk', bŏl'-) *n.*, *pl.* **-viks** or **-vi·ki** (-vē'kē). 1. A member of the party that seized power and set up a proletarian dictatorship in Russia (1917–22). 2. A Communist. [R. *Bol'shevik.*] —**Bol'she·vism** *n.* —**Bol'she·vist** *n.* —**Bol'she·vis'tic** *adj.*

bol·ster (bōl'star) *n.* A long, narrow pillow or cushion. —*v.* To support with or as if with a bolster. [< OE.]

bolt[1] (bōlt) *n.* 1. A threaded metal pin used with a nut to hold parts together. 2. A sliding bar for fastening a door or gate. 3. A metal bar in a lock that is pushed out or withdrawn at a turn of the key. 4. A large roll of cloth. 5. A flash of lightning or a thunderbolt. 6. A sudden darting movement; dash. —*v.* 1. To secure or lock with or as if with a bolt. 2. To eat hurriedly; gulp. 3. To desert or withdraw support from (a political party). 4. To utter impulsively. 5. To move or spring suddenly. [< OE, heavy arrow.]

bolt[2] (bōlt) *v.* To sift. [< OFr. *buleter.*]

bo·lus (bō'las) *n.* 1. A small round mass. 2. A large pill or tablet. [< Gk. *bōlos*, lump of earth.]

bomb (bŏm) *n.* 1. **a.** An explosive weapon dropped on or hurled at a target. **b.** An atomic bomb. 2. A container that ejects a spray, foam, or gas under pressure. 3. *Slang.* A dismal failure. —*v.* 1. To attack or destroy with bombs. 2. *Slang.* To fail miserably. [< Ital. *bomba.*]

bom·bard (bŏm-bärd') *v.* 1. To attack with bombs, explosive shells, missiles, etc. 2. To assail persistently. 3. To act on (e.g. an element or atom) with high-energy radiation or particles. [< OFr. *bombarde*, cannon.] —**bom·bard'ment** *n.*

bom·bar·dier (bŏm'bar-dîr') *n.* The member of an aircraft crew who operates the bombing equipment. [< OFr. *bombarde*, cannon.]

bom·bast (bŏm'băst') *n.* Grandiloquent and pompous speech or writing. [< OFr. *bombace*, cotton padding.] —**bom·bas'tic** *adj.* —**bom·bas'ti·cal·ly** *adv.*

bom·ba·zine (bŏm'ba-zēn') *n.* A fine twilled fabric often dyed black. [< Gk. *bombux*, silkworm.]

bomb·er (bŏm'ar) *n.* 1. An aircraft designed to drop bombs. 2. One who bombs.

bomb·shell (bŏm'shĕl') *n.* 1. A bomb. 2. A shocking surprise.

bomb·sight (bŏm'sīt') *n.* A device in an aircraft for aiming bombs.

bo·na fide (bō'na fīd', fī'dē, bŏn'a) *adj.* 1. Done in good faith: *a bona fide offer.* 2. Authentic; genuine: *a bona fide Monet.* [Lat., in good faith.]

bo·nan·za (ba-năn'za) *n.* 1. A rich mine or

vein of ore. **2.** A source of great wealth. [Sp., prosperity.]

bon·bon (bŏn′bŏn′) *n.* A candy with a creamy center, usu. coated with chocolate. [Fr.]

bond (bŏnd) *n.* **1.** Something that binds, ties, or fastens together. **2. bonds.** Shackles. **3.** Often **bonds.** A uniting force or tie; link. **4.** A binding agreement. **5.** The promise or obligation by which one is bound. **6.** A union or cohesion between parts. **7.** A sum of money paid as bail or surety. **8.** One who acts as bail; bondsman. **9.** A certificate of debt issued by a government or corporation, guaranteeing payment of the original investment plus interest by a specified future date. **10.** The state of storing goods in a warehouse until the taxes or duties due on them are paid. **11.** Surety against losses, theft, etc. **12.** A superior grade of white paper. —*v.* **1.** To join securely, as with glue. **2.** To mortgage or place a guaranteed bond on. **3.** To furnish bond or surety for. **4.** To place (an employee or merchandise) under bond or guarantee. [< ON *band.*]

bond·age (bŏn′dĭj) *n.* The condition of a slave or serf; servitude. [< OE *bōnda*, householder.]

Syns: *bondage, servitude, slavery* n.

bond paper *n.* A superior grade of strong white paper made wholly or in part from rag pulp.

bonds·man (bŏndz′mən) *n.* **1.** Also **bond·man** (bŏnd′-). A slave or serf. **2.** One who provides bond or surety for another.

bone (bōn) *n.* **1. a.** The hard, dense, calcified tissue that forms the skeleton of most vertebrates. **b.** A skeletal structure made of this material. **2.** An animal material resembling bone, such as ivory. **3.** Something made of bone or similar material. —*v.* **boned, bon·ing.** To remove the bones from, esp. for cooking. —*phrasal verb.* **bone up on.** *Informal.* To study intensively. —*idioms.* **have a bone to pick with.** To have reason to quarrel with. **make no bones about.** To be completely frank about. [< OE *bān.*] —**bon′y** *adj.*

bone-black (bōn′blăk′) *n.* Also **bone black.** A black material made by roasting animal bones, used esp. as a pigment.

bone-dry (bōn′drī′) *adj.* Very dry.

bone meal *n.* Bones crushed and ground to a coarse powder, used as fertilizer and animal feed.

bon·er (bō′nər) *n. Slang.* A blunder.

bon·fire (bŏn′fīr′) *n.* A large outdoor fire. [ME *bonfir.*]

bon·go (bŏng′gō, bông′-) *n., pl.* **-gos.** One of a pair of connected and tuned drums. [Am. Sp. *bongó.*]

bon·ho·mie (bŏn′ə-mē′) *n.* A pleasant disposition; geniality. [Fr. < *bonhomme*, good-natured man.]

bo·ni·to (bə-nē′tō) *n., pl.* **-to** or **-tos.** Any of several saltwater food and game fishes related to the tuna. [Sp. < *bonito*, pretty.]

bon mot (bōn mō′) *n., pl.* **bons mots** (bōn mō′, mōz′). A clever remark. [Fr.]

bon·net (bŏn′ĭt) *n.* A hat that is held in place by ribbons tied under the chin, esp. one worn by a woman or child. [< OFr. *bonet*, cap.]

bon·ny or **bon·nie** (bŏn′ē) *adj.* **-ni·er, -ni·est.** *Scot.* **1.** Pretty; fair. **2.** Healthy. **3.** Cheerful; pleasant. [Orig. unknown.]

bon·sai (bŏn′sī′, bôn′-) *n., pl.* **-sai.** A dwarfed, ornamentally shaped tree or shrub planted in a shallow pot. [J., potted plant.]

bonsai

bo·nus (bō′nəs) *n.* Something given or paid in addition to what is usual or expected. [< Lat., good.]

bon vi·vant (bŏn′ vē-vänt′, bôN′ vē-väN′) *n., pl.* **bons vi·vants** (bŏn′ vē-vänts′, bôN′ vē-väN′). One who enjoys good living. [Fr.]

bon voy·age (bŏn′ voi-äzh′, bôN′ vwä-yäzh′) *n.* A wish for a pleasant journey extended to a traveler. [Fr.]

boo (bōō) *n., pl.* **boos.** A shout expressing scorn or disapproval. —**boo** *v.*

boo·by (bōō′bē) *n., pl.* **-bies.** A stupid person. [Prob. < Lat. *balbus*, stammering.]

booby prize *n.* An award for the lowest score in a game or contest.

booby trap *n.* A device or situation that catches a person off guard.

boo·dle (bōōd′l) *n. Slang.* **1.** Money accepted as a bribe. **2.** Stolen goods. [< \Du. *boedel*, estate.]

book (bōōk) *n.* **1.** A volume made up of pages fastened along one edge and enclosed between protective covers. **2.** A written or printed literary work. **3.** A main division of a larger written or printed work. **4. the Book.** The Bible. **5.** A volume in which records of financial transactions are kept. **6.** A record of bets placed on a race. —*v.* **1.** To reserve or schedule by or as if by writing in a book. **2.** To record charges against on a police blotter. [< OE *bōc.*]

book·case (bōōk′kās′) *n.* A piece of furniture with shelves for holding books.

book end *n.* A prop for keeping a row of books upright.

book·ie (bōōk′ē) *n. Slang.* A bookmaker.

book·ing (bōōk′ing) *n.* A scheduled engagement, as for a performance.

book·ish (bōōk′ĭsh) *adj.* **1.** Fond of books. **2.** Relying on knowledge gained from books rather than practical experience.

book·keep·ing (bōōk′kē′pĭng) *n.* The recording of the accounts and transactions of a business. —**book′keep′er** *n.*

book·let (bōōk′lĭt) *n.* A small book.

book·mak·er (bōōk′mā′kər) *n.* One who accepts and pays off bets. —**book′mak′ing** *n.*

book·mark (bōōk′märk′) *n.* An object placed

between the pages of a book to mark the place.

book·mo·bile (bŏŏk′mə-bēl′) *n.* A truck equipped for use as a mobile lending library.

book·plate (bŏŏk′plāt′) *n.* A label pasted inside a book and bearing the owner's name.

book value *n.* The worth of a business as shown in the account books as distinguished from the market value.

book·worm (bŏŏk′wûrm′) *n.* **1.** The larva of an insect that infests books and feeds on the paste in the bindings. **2.** One who spends much time reading or studying.

boom¹ (bŏŏm) *v.* **1.** To make a deep, resonant sound. **2.** To flourish or cause to flourish swiftly or vigorously. —*n.* **1.** A booming sound. **2.** A sudden increase, as in growth, wealth, or popularity. [ME *bummen.*]

boom² (bŏŏm) *n.* **1.** A long pole extending from a mast to stretch out the bottom of a sail. **2.** A long pole extending upward and outward from the mast of a derrick and supporting the object being lifted or suspended. **3.** A barrier composed of a chain of floating logs enclosing other free-floating logs. [Du., pole.]

boo·mer·ang (bŏŏ′mə-răng′) *n.* **1.** A flat, curved missile that can be thrown so that it returns to the thrower. **2.** An action that rebounds harmfully against its originator. —*v.* To backfire: *The scheme boomeranged.* [Native word in Australia.]

boon¹ (bŏŏn) *n.* Something beneficial; blessing. [< ON *bōn,* prayer.]

boon² (bŏŏn) *adj.* Jolly; convivial: *a boon companion.* [< Lat. *bonus,* good.]

boon·docks (bŏŏn′dŏks′) *pl.n. Slang.* **1.** A jungle. **2.** Backcountry; hinterland. [Tagalog *bundok,* mountain.]

boon·dog·gle (bŏŏn′dô′gəl, -dŏg′əl) *v.* **-gled,** **-gling.** To waste time on pointless and unnecessary work. —*n.* Time-wasting work. [< *boondoggle,* the plaited leather cord worn by Boy Scouts.]

boor (bŏŏr) *n.* A crude person with rude, clumsy manners. [Du. *boer,* peasant.] —**boor′ish** *adj.* —**boor′ish·ly** *adv.* —**boor′ish·ness** *n.*

boost (bŏŏst) *v.* **1.** To lift by or as if by pushing up from behind or below. **2.** To increase; raise. **3.** To promote; aid. —*n.* **1.** A lift or help. **2.** An increase. [Orig. unknown.]

boost·er (bŏŏ′stər) *n.* **1.** A device for increasing power or effectiveness. **2.** A promoter. **3.** A rocket used to launch a missile or space vehicle. **4.** A supplementary dose of a vaccine.

boot¹ (bŏŏt) *n.* **1.** A kind of shoe that covers the foot and part of the leg. **2.** A protective covering or sheath. **3.** *Chiefly Brit.* An automobile trunk. **4.** *Mil.* A new recruit. **5.** A kick. **6.** A discharge from employment. —*v.* **1.** To put boots on. **2.** To kick. **3.** To discharge; dismiss. [< OFr. *bote.*]

boot² (bŏŏt) *v. Archaic.* To be of help; avail. —*idiom.* **to boot.** In addition; besides. [< OE *bōt,* help.]

boot·black (bŏŏt′blăk′) *n.* One who polishes shoes for a living.

boot·ee or **boot·ie** (bŏŏ′tē) *n.* A soft baby shoe, usu. knitted.

Bo·ö·tes (bō-ō′tēz) *n.* A constellation in the Northern Hemisphere.

booth (bŏŏth) *n., pl.* **booths** (bŏŏthz, bŏŏths).

1. A small enclosed compartment. **2.** A small stall where things are sold. [ME *bothe.*]

boot·leg (bŏŏt′lĕg′) *v.* **-legged,** **-leg·ging.** To make, sell, or transport illegally, as liquor. —**boot′leg′** *n. & adj.* —**boot′leg′ger** *n.*

boot·less (bŏŏt′lĭs) *adj.* Useless; futile. —**boot′less·ly** *adv.* —**boot′less·ness** *n.*

boo·ty (bŏŏ′tē) *n., pl.* **-ties. 1.** Loot taken from an enemy. **2.** Seized or stolen goods. [< MLG *būte,* exchange.]

booze (bŏŏz) *Informal.* —*n.* Intoxicating drink. —*v.* **boozed, booz·ing.** To drink alcoholic beverages excessively. [< MDu. *būse,* drinking vessel.] —**booz′er** *n.*

bop (bŏp) *Informal.* —*v.* **bopped, bop·ping.** To hit or strike. —*n.* A blow; punch. [Imit.]

bo·rate (bôr′āt′, bōr′-) *n.* A salt of boric acid.

bo·rax (bôr′ăks′, -əks, bōr′-) *n.* A crystalline compound, sodium borate, used in manufacturing glass, detergents, and pharmaceuticals. [< Ar. *būraq.*]

bor·del·lo (bôr-dĕl′ō) *n., pl.* **-los.** A house of prostitution. [Ital.]

bor·der (bôr′dər) *n.* **1.** A surrounding margin or rim. **2.** A political or geographic boundary. —*v.* **1.** To put a border on. **2.** To share a boundary with; be next to. —*phrasal verb.* **border on** (or **upon**). **1.** To adjoin. **2.** To be almost like; approach. [< OFr. *border,* to border.]

bor·der·land (bôr′dər-lănd′) *n.* **1.** Land on or near a border or frontier. **2.** An uncertain area or situation.

bor·der·line (bôr′dər-līn′) *n.* A boundary. **2.** A vague or indefinite line between two different conditions. —*adj.* Uncertain; dubious.

bore¹ (bôr, bōr) *v.* **bored, bor·ing.** **1.** To make a hole in or through with or as if with a drill or similar tool. **2.** To make by drilling, digging, or burrowing. —*n.* **1.** A hole made by or as if by drilling. **2.** The interior diameter of a hole, tube, cylinder, etc. **3.** The caliber of a firearm. **4.** A drilling tool. [< OE *borian.*] —**bor′er** *n.*

bore² (bôr, bōr) *v.* **bored, bor·ing.** To tire with repetition or tediousness. —*n.* One that bores. [Orig. unknown.]

Syns: **bore, pall, tire, weary** *v.*

bore³ (bôr, bōr) *v. p.t.* of **bear¹.**

bo·re·al (bôr′ē-əl, bōr′-) *adj.* Pertaining to or located in the north; northern. [< Lat. *Boreas,* the north wind.]

bore·dom (bôr′dəm, bōr′-) *n.* The condition of being bored.

boric acid *n.* A white or colorless crystalline compound, H_3BO_3, used esp. as an antiseptic and preservative.

born (bôrn) *v.* A *p.p.* of **bear¹.** —*adj.* **1.** By birth or natural talent: *a born artist.* **2.** Coming or resulting from: *wisdom born of experience.*

borne (bôrn) *v.* A *p.p.* of **bear¹.**

bo·ron (bôr′ŏn′, bōr′-) *n. Symbol* **B** A soft, brown, amorphous or crystalline, nonmetallic element used in flares, propellant mixtures, nuclear reactor control elements, abrasives, and hard metallic alloys. Atomic number-5; atomic weight 10.811. [BOR(AX) + (CARB)ON.]

bor·ough (bûr′ō, bŭr′ō) *n.* **1.** A self-governing incorporated town, as in certain U.S. states. **2.** One of the five administrative units of New York City. [< OE *burg,* city.]

bor·row (bôr′ō, bŏr′ō) *v.* **1.** To obtain or receive (something) on loan with the intent to return. 2. To adopt or use as one's own: *They borrowed his ideas.* [< OE *borgian.*]

borscht (bôrsht) *n.* Also **borsch** (bôrsh). A beet soup served hot or cold. [R. *borshch.*]

bor-zoi (bôr'zoi') *n.* A rather large, slenderly built dog having a narrow head and a silky coat. [R. *borzaya.*]

bosh (bŏsh) *n. Informal.* Nonsense. [< Turk. *boş*, useless.]

bosk-y (bŏs'kē) *adj.* **-i-er, -i-est.** Covered with bushes, shrubs, or trees; wooded. [< ME *bosk*, bush.]

bo's'n or **bos'n** (bō'sən) *n.* Vars. of **boatswain.**

bos-om (bŏŏz'əm, bŏŏ'zəm) *n.* **1.** The human chest or breast. **2.** The part of a garment that covers the chest. **3.** The heart or center. [< OE *bōsm.*]

boss¹ (bôs, bŏs) *n.* **1.** An employer or supervisor. **2.** A politician who controls a political party or machine. —*v.* **1.** To supervise or control. **2.** To command in a domineering manner. [Du. *baas*, master.] —**boss'y** *adj.*

boss² (bôs, bŏs) *n.* A knoblike ornament or protuberance. —*v.* To decorate with bosses. [< OFr. *boce.*]

bo-sun (bō'sən) *n.* Var. of **boatswain.**

bot-a-ny (bŏt'n-ē) *n.* The scientific study of plants. [< Gk. *botanē*, plant.] —**bo-tan'i-cal** (bə-tăn'ĭ-kəl) or **bo-tan'ic** *adj.* —**bot'a-nist** *n.*

botch (bŏch) *v.* **1.** To ruin through clumsiness; bungle. **2.** To repair clumsily. [ME *bocchen*, to mend.] —**botch** *n.* —**botch'er** *n.* —**botch'i-ly** *adv.* —**botch'y** *adj.*

Syns: *botch, blow, blunder, bungle, foul up, fumble, mess up, mishandle, mismanage, muddle, spoil v.*

both (bōth) *adj.* One and the other; relating to or being two in conjunction: *Both men arrived.* —*pron.* The one and the other: *Both of those men are patriots.* —*conj.* Used with *and* to indicate that each of two things in a coordinated phrase or clause is included: *both men and women.* [< ON *bāthir.*]

both-er (bŏth'ər) *v.* **1.** To irritate or annoy, esp. repeatedly. **2.** To trouble or concern oneself. —*n.* **1.** A nuisance. **2.** Trouble. [Orig. unknown.] —**both'er-some** (-səm) *adj.*

bot-tle (bŏt'l) *n.* **1.** A container, usu. made of glass, with a narrow neck and a mouth that can be capped. **2.** The amount that a bottle holds. **3.** Alcoholic liquor. —*v.* **-tled, -tling.** To put in a bottle. —*phrasal verb.* **bottle up.** To confine in or as if in a bottle. [< LLat. *buttis*, cask.] —**bot'tle-ful** *n.* —**bot'tler** *n.*

bot-tle-neck (bŏt'l-nĕk') *n.* **1.** A narrow passage where movement is slowed down. **2.** A hindrance to production or progress.

bot-tom (bŏt'əm) *n.* **1.** The lowest or deepest part of something. **2.** The underside. **3.** The supporting part of something; base. **4.** The basic underlying quality; essence. **5.** The land below a body of water: *a river bottom.* **6.** *Informal.* The buttocks. —*adj.* Lowest; undermost; fundamental. [< OE *botm.*] —**bot'tom-less** *adj.*

bottom line *n.* **1.** The lowest line in a financial statement, showing net income or loss. **2.** The end result of something. **3.** The main or essential point.

bot-u-lism (bŏch'ə-lĭz'əm) *n.* A serious, often

fatal form of food poisoning caused by bacteria that grow in improperly canned foods. [< Lat. *botulus*, sausage.]

bou-doir (bŏŏ'dwär', -dwôr') *n.* A woman's private room. [< OFr. *bouder*, to pout.]

bouf-fant (bŏŏ-fänt') *adj.* Full and puffed-out: *a bouffant hair style.* [Fr. < *bouffer*, to puff up.]

bough (bou) *n.* A large branch of a tree. [< OE *bōg.*]

bought (bôt) *v. p.t. & p.p.* of **buy.**

bouil-la-baisse (bŏŏ'yə-bäs') *n.* A highly seasoned fish stew made with several kinds of fish. [< Prov. *bouiabaisso.*]

bouil-lon (bŏŏl'yŏn', bŏŏl'-, -yən) *n.* A clear meat broth. [< OFr. *boulir*, to boil.]

boul-der (bōl'dər) *n.* A large, rounded mass of rock. [ME *bulder.*]

boul-e-vard (bŏŏl'ə-värd', bŏŏl'ə-) *n.* A broad city street, often landscaped. [< MDu. *bolwerc*, bulwark.]

bounce (bouns) *v.* **bounced, bounc-ing.** **1.** To rebound elastically from a collision. **2.** To cause to collide and rebound. **3.** To bound in a lively and energetic manner. —*n.* **1.** A bound or rebound. **2.** A spring or leap. **3.** Capacity to bounce. **4.** Liveliness; vivacity. [ME *bounsen*, to beat.] —**bounc'i-ly** *adv.* —**bounc'i-ness** *n.* —**bounc'y** *adj.*

bounc-er (boun'sər) *n.* One employed to throw disorderly persons out of a public place.

bounc-ing (boun'sĭng) *adj.* Healthy; thriving: *a bouncing baby.*

bound¹ (bound) *v.* **1.** To leap or spring. **2.** To move by leaping. **3.** To bounce or rebound. —*n.* **1.** A leap. **2.** A bounce. [< OFr. *bondir*, to rebound.]

bound² (bound) *n.* **1.** Often **bounds.** A boundary; limit. **2. bounds.** The territory on, within, or near limiting lines. —*v.* **1.** To limit. **2.** To constitute the limit of. **3.** To demarcate. —*idiom.* **out of bounds.** Beyond the usual, legal, or safe limits. [< Med. Lat. *bodina*, of Celt. orig.]

bound³ (bound) *v. p.t. & p.p.* of **bind.** —*adj.* **1.** Certain: *We are bound to be late.* **2.** Under obligation; obliged. **3.** Confined by or as if by bonds. **4.** Enclosed in a cover or binding.

bound⁴ (bound) *adj.* On the way: *bound for home.* [< ON *búinn*, p.p. of *búa*, to get ready.]

bound-a-ry (boun'də-rē, -drē) *n., pl.* **-ries.** Something that indicates a border or limit.

bound-en (boun'dən) *adj.* Required; obligatory. [< ME, p.p. of *binden*, to bind.]

bound-er (boun'dər) *n. Brit.* A cad.

bound-less (bound'lĭs) *adj.* Without limit. —**bound'less-ly** *adv.* —**bound'less-ness** *n.*

boun-te-ous (boun'tē-əs) *adj.* **1.** Generous. **2.** Copious; plentiful. —**boun'te-ous-ly** *adv.*

boun-ti-ful (boun'tə-fəl) *adj.* **1.** Bounteous. **2.** Abundant; plentiful: *bountiful rainfall.* —**boun'ti-ful-ly** *adv.*

boun-ty (boun'tē) *n., pl.* **-ties.** **1.** Liberality in giving: *dependent on a patron's bounty.* **2.** Something that is given liberally. **3.** A reward or inducement, esp. one given by a government for performing a service. [< Lat. *bonitas*, goodness.]

bou-quet (bō-kā', bŏŏ-) *n.* **1.** A cluster of

flowers. **2.** (bŏŏ-kā′). A pleasant fragrance, esp. of a wine. [< OFr. *bosquet*, thicket.]

bour·bon (bûr′bən) *n.* A whiskey distilled from a fermented mash. [< *Bourbon* County, Kentucky.]

bour·geois (bŏŏr-zhwä′, bŏŏr′zhwä′) *n., pl.* **-geois.** **1.** One who belongs to the middle class. **2.** A capitalist. —*adj.* **1.** Of or typical of the middle class. **2.** Overly concerned with respectability and possessions. [Fr. < OFr. *bourg,* fortified town.]

bour·geoi·sie (bŏŏr′zhwä-zē′) *n.* The middle class as opposed to the aristocracy or the laboring class. [Fr.]

bourn (bôrn, bōrn, bŏŏrn) *n.* Also **bourne.** *Archaic.* **1.** A boundary. **2.** A goal or destination. [< Med. Lat. *bodina.*]

bout (bout) *n.* **1.** A contest; match. **2.** A period of time spent in a particular way: *a bout of the flu.* [ME, bend.]

bou·tique (bŏŏ-tēk′) *n.* A small retail shop that sells gifts, fashionable clothes, and accessories. [Fr.]

bou·ton·niere or **bou·ton·nière** (bŏŏt′n-îr′, -yâr′) *n.* A flower worn in a buttonhole. [< OFr. < *bouton,* button.]

bo·vine (bō′vīn′, -vēn′) *adj.* **1.** Of, pertaining to, or resembling an ox or cow. **2.** Dull; stolid. [< Lat. *bos,* cow.] —**bo′vine′** *n.*

bow¹ (bō) *n.* **1.** A weapon used to shoot arrows, consisting of a curved stave, strung taut from end to end. **2.** A rod strung with horsehair, used in playing the violin, viola, and related stringed instruments. **3.** A knot tied with a loop or loops at either end. **4.** A curve or arch. **5.** A rainbow. —*v.* **1.** To bend into a bow. **2.** To play (a stringed instrument) with a bow. [< OE *boga.*]

bow² (bou) *v.* **1.** To bend (the head, knee, or body) in order to express greeting, consent, veneration, etc. **2.** To acquiesce; submit. —*phrasal verb.* **bow out.** To withdraw or resign. —*n.* A bending of the body or head, as when showing respect. [< OE *būgan.*]

bow³ (bou) *n.* The front section of a ship or boat. [Poss. of LG orig.]

bowd·ler·ize (bōd′lə-rīz′, boud′-) *v.* **-ized, -iz·ing.** To remove passages considered improper or indecent from. [< Thomas *Bowdler* (1754–1825).] —**bowd′ler·i·za′tion** *n.*

bow·el (bou′əl, boul) *n.* **1.** An intestine, esp. of a human being. **2.** Often **bowels.** The digestive tract below the stomach. **3. bowels.** The inmost depths of something: *in the bowels of the ship.* [< Lat. *botulus,* sausage.]

bow·er (bou′ər) *n.* A shaded, leafy recess; arbor. [< OE *būr,* a dwelling.] —**bow′er·y** *adj.*

bow·ie knife (bō′ē, bŏŏ′ē) *n.* A long single-edged steel hunting knife. [< James *Bowie* (1790?–1836).]

bowl¹ (bōl) *n.* **1.** A rounded, hollow container for liquids or food. **2.** A curved, hollow part, as of a spoon. **3.** A bowl-shaped structure or edifice. [< OE *bolla.*] —**bowl′ful** *n.*

bowl² (bōl) *n.* **1.** A heavy ball rolled in certain games. **2.** A roll of the ball in bowling. —*v.* **1.** To play the game of bowling. **2.** To roll a ball in bowling. —*phrasal verb.* **bowl over. 1.** To knock over. **2.** To take by surprise; astound. [< Lat. *bulla,* bubble.]

bow·leg·ged (bō′lĕg′ĭd, -lĕgd′) *adj.* Having legs that curve outward at or below the knee.

bowl·er¹ (bō′lər) *n.* One that bowls.

bowl·er² (bō′lər) *n.* A man's derby hat. [< John *Bowler,* 19th-cent. London hatmaker.]

bow·line (bō′lĭn, -līn′) *n.* A knot forming a loop that does not slip. [ME *bouline.*]

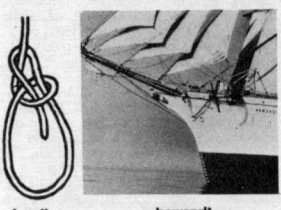

bowline   bowsprit

bowl·ing (bō′lĭng) *n.* **1. a.** A game played by rolling a heavy ball down a wooden alley in an attempt to knock down a triangular formation of ten wooden pins. **b.** A similar game, such as skittles. **2.** A game played on a bowling green, by rolling a wooden ball as close as possible to a target ball.

bowling alley *n.* A level, wooden lane used for bowling.

bowling green *n.* A level grassy area for bowling.

bow·man (bō′mən) *n.* An archer.

bow·sprit (bou′sprĭt, bō′-) *n.* A spar extending forward from the bow of a sailing ship. [ME *bouspret.*]

bow·string (bō′strĭng) *n.* The string of a bow.

box¹ (bŏks) *n.* **1.** A usu. rectangular container, often with a lid. **2.** The amount that a box holds. **3.** A separate seating compartment in a theater. **4.** A booth. **5.** *Baseball.* **a.** An area marked out by chalk lines where the batter stands. **b.** Any of various designated areas for other team members. **6.** An awkward or perplexing situation. —*v.* To place in or as if in a box. [< OE, ult. < Gk. *puxis.*] —**box′ful** *n.*

box² (bŏks) *n.* A blow or slap with the hand. —*v.* **1.** To hit with the hand. **2.** To take part in a boxing match with. [ME.]

box³ (bŏks) *n., pl.* **box** or **box·es.** An evergreen tree or shrub having hard, yellowish wood, used esp. for hedges. [OE, ult. < Gk. *puxos.*]

box·car (bŏks′kär′) *n.* An enclosed railway car used to carry freight.

box·er¹ (bŏk′sər) *n.* One who boxes, esp. professionally.

box·er² (bŏk′sər) *n.* A short-haired dog with a brownish coat and a square-jawed muzzle. [G. < BOXER¹.]

box·ing (bŏk′sĭng) *n.* The sport of fighting with the fists.

box office *n.* A ticket office, as of a theater.

box·wood (bŏks′wŏŏd′) *n.* **1.** The box³. **2.** The hard wood of the box tree.

boy (boi) *n.* **1.** A male child or a youth. —*interj.* A word used as a mild exclamation. [ME *boi.*] —**boy′hood′** *n.* —**boy′ish** *adj.* —**boy′ish·ly** *adv.* —**boy′ish·ness** *n.*

boy·cott (boi′kŏt′) *v.* To abstain from using, buying, or dealing with, as a means of protest. [< Charles C. *Boycott* (1832–97).] —**boy′cott′** *n.*

Boy Scout *n.* A member of a worldwide organization of young men and boys, founded to help develop self-reliance, good citizenship, and outdoor skills.

boy·sen·ber·ry (boi′zən-bĕr′ē) *n.* A prickly bramble hybrid of the loganberry, blackberry, and raspberry, bearing large, wine-red, edible berries. [< Rudolph *Boysen* (d. 1950).]

Br The symbol for the element bromine.

bra (brä) *n.* A brassiere.

brace (brās) *n.* 1. A clamp. 2. A device that steadies or supports a weight. 3. *Med.* A device used to support a part of the body. 4. Often **braces.** An arrangement of wires and bands fixed to crooked teeth in order to straighten them. 5. Either of the symbols, { }, used to connect written or printed lines. 6. A rotating handle for holding and turning a bit. 7. **braces.** *Chiefly Brit.* Suspenders. —*v.* **braced, brac·ing.** 1. To support; strengthen. 2. To prepare for a shock, struggle, or danger. 3. To fill with energy; refresh. [< Gk. *brakhiōn*, arm.] —**brac·ing·ly** *adv.*

brace·let (brās′lĭt) *n.* An ornamental band or chain worn around the wrist. [< Gk. *brakhiōn*, arm.]

brack·en (brăk′ən) *n.* 1. A fern with tough stems and branching, finely divided fronds. 2. An area overgrown with bracken. [ME *braken.*]

brack·et (brăk′ĭt) *n.* 1. A support or fixture fastened to a vertical surface and projecting to support a shelf or other weight. 2. A shelf supported by brackets. 3. Either of a pair of symbols, [ ], used to enclose written or printed material. 4. A classification or grouping, esp. by income, within a series. —*v.* 1. To support with a bracket. 2. To place within brackets. 3. To classify or group together. [< OFr. *braquette*, pouch.]

brack·ish (brăk′ĭsh) *adj.* Containing some salt; briny. [Du. *brak.*] —**brack′ish·ness** *n.*

bract (brăkt) *n.* A leaflike plant part located either below a flower or on the stalk of a flower cluster. [Lat. *bractea*, gold leaf.]

brad (brăd) *n.* A tapered nail with a small head. [< ON *broddr*, spike.]

brae (brā) *n.* *Scot.* A hillside. [< ON *brā*, eyelash.]

brag (brăg) *v.* **bragged, brag·ging.** To talk or declare boastfully. [ME *braggen.*] —**brag** *n.* —**brag′ger** *n.*

brag·ga·do·ci·o (brăg′ə-dō′shē-ō′) *n., pl.* **-os.** 1. A braggart. 2. a. Empty or pretentious bragging. b. Swaggering arrogance; cockiness. [< *Braggadocchio*, the personification of boasting in the *Faerie Queen* by Edmund Spenser.]

brag·gart (brăg′ərt) *n.* One that brags. [Fr. *bragard.*]

Brah·ma (brä′mə) *n. Hinduism.* The personification of divine reality in its creative aspect as a member of the Hindu triad.

Brah·man (brä′mən) *n.* Also **Brah·min.** 1. A member of the highest Hindu caste, orig. composed of priests. 2. One of a breed of domestic cattle developed in the southern United States from stock originating in India.

Brah·man·ism (brä′mə-nĭz′əm) *n.* Also **Brah·min·ism** (brä′mĭ-). 1. The religious practices and beliefs of ancient India. 2. The social caste system of the Brahmans of India. —**Brah′man·ist** *n.*

Brah·min (brä′mən) *n.* 1. A highly cultured and socially exclusive person. 2. Var. of **Brah·man.**

braid (brād) *v.* 1. To interweave strands of; plait. 2. To decorate with an interwoven trim. 3. To make by weaving strands together. —*n.* 1. a. A narrow length of interwoven or braided material. b. A length of hair that has been braided. 2. An ornamental strip of braided material. [< OE *bregdan*, to weave.] —**braid′er** *n.*

Braille or **braille** (brāl) *n.* A system of writing and printing for the blind, in which raised dots represent letters and numerals. [< Louis *Braille* (1809–52).]

brain (brān) *n.* 1. a. The portion of the central nervous system consisting of a large mass of gray nerve tissue enclosed in the skull of a vertebrate, responsible for the interpretation of sensory impulses, the coordination and control of bodily activities, and the exercise of emotion and thought. b. A functionally similar portion of the invertebrate nervous system. 2. Often **brains.** Intellectual capacity; intelligence. —*v.* 1. To smash in the skull of. 2. *Slang.* To hit on the head. [< OE *brægen.*] —**brain′i·ness** *n.* —**brain′ish** *adj.* —**brain′less·ly** *adv.* —**brain′less·ness** *n.* —**brain′y** *adj.*

brain-child (brān′chīld′) *n. Informal.* An original idea, plan, or creation.

brain death *n.* Death as evidenced by the absence of activity of the central nervous system.

brain·storm (brān′stôrm′) *n. Informal.* A sudden inspiration. —*v.* To attempt to solve a problem by a method in which the members of a group spontaneously propose ideas and solutions. —**brain′storm′ing** *n.*

brain·wash (brān′wŏsh′, -wôsh′) *v.* To indoctrinate so as to replace an individual's own beliefs with an opposing set of beliefs.

brain wave *n.* Any of the rhythmically fluctuating voltages that arise from electrical activity in the brain.

braise (brāz) *v.* **braised, brais·ing.** To brown in fat and then simmer in a small amount of liquid in a covered container. [Fr. *braiser.*]

brake¹ (brāk) *n.* A device for slowing or stopping motion. —*v.* **braked, brak·ing.** 1. To reduce the speed of with or as if with a brake. 2. To operate or apply a brake. [Perh. ME *breake*, bridle.]

brake² (brāk) *n.* 1. Any of several ferns, esp. bracken. 2. A densely overgrown area. [ME.]

brake·man (brāk′mən) *n.* A railroad employee who assists the conductor and checks on the operation of the train's brakes.

bram·ble (brăm′bəl) *n.* A prickly plant or shrub, esp. the blackberry or the raspberry. [< OE *bræmbel.*] —**bram′bly** *adj.*

bran (brăn) *n.* The outer husks of cereal grain, sifted out from the flour. [< OFr., of Celt. orig.]

branch (brănch) *n.* 1. a. One of the stem parts dividing out from the stem of a tree or plant. b. A similar structure or part. 2. A part or division of a larger system. 3. A division of a family or tribe. —*v.* To divide or spread out in branches or branchlike parts. [< LLat. *branca*, paw.]

brand (brănd) *n.* **1. a.** A trademark or distinctive name that identifies a product or a manufacturer. **b.** The make of a product so identified. **2.** A distinctive kind or type. **3.** A mark indicating ownership, burned on the hide of an animal. **4.** A mark formerly burned into the flesh of criminals. **5.** A mark of disgrace; stigma. **6.** A piece of burning or charred wood. —*v.* **1.** To mark with or as if with a brand. **2.** To stigmatize. [< OE, torch.]

bran·dish (brăn'dĭsh) *v.* To wave or flourish menacingly, as a weapon. [< OFr. *brand*, sword.] —**bran'dish·er** *n.*

brand-new (brănd'no͞o', -nyo͞o') *adj.* In fresh and unused condition.

bran·dy (brăn'dē) *n., pl. -dies.* An alcoholic liquor distilled from wine or from fermented fruit juice. [< Du. *brandewijn*.] —**bran'dy** *v.*

brash (brăsh) *adj.* **-er, -est.** **1.** Hasty and unthinking; rash. **2.** Impudent; bold. [Orig. unknown.] —**brash'ly** *adv.* —**brash'ness** *n.*

brass (brăs) *n.* **1.** An alloy that contains copper and zinc. **2.** An object made of brass. **3.** *Informal.* Blatant self-assurance; nerve. [< OE *bræs*.] —**brass'y** *adj.*

bras·se·rie (brăs'ə-rē') *n.* A bar serving food as well as alcoholic drinks. [Fr.]

brass hat *n. Slang.* A person of high rank or position, esp. a high-ranking military officer. [< the gold braid on the cap.]

bras·siere (brə-zîr') *n.* A woman's undergarment worn to support the breasts. [Fr. *brassière*.]

brass tacks *pl.n. Informal.* Essential facts; basics.

brat (brăt) *n.* A nasty or spoiled child. [Poss. < OE *bratt*, coarse garment.] —**brat'ty** *adj.*

bra·va·do (brə-vä'dō) *n., pl. -does or -dos.* **1.** A show of courage. **2.** Defiant, swaggering conduct. [Sp. *bravada.*]

brave (brāv) *adj.* **brav·er, brav·est.** **1.** Possessing or showing courage. **2.** Making a fine display; splendid. **3.** *Archaic.* Excellent. —*n.* A North American Indian warrior. —*v.* **braved, brav·ing.** To undergo or face courageously. [< OItal. *bravo.*] —**brave'ly** *adv.* —**brave'ness** *n.*

Syns: brave, audacious, bold, courageous, dauntless, fearless, gallant, heroic, intrepid, plucky, stouthearted, valiant *adj.*

brav·er·y (brā'və-rē, brāv'rē) *n., pl. -ies.* Courage.

bra·vo (brä'vō, brä-vō') *interj.* Excellent; well done. —*n., pl. -vos.* A shout or cry of approval. [Ital.]

bra·vu·ra (brə-vŏŏr'ə, -vyŏŏr'ə) *n.* **1.** Brilliant musical technique or style. **2.** A showy display. [Ital.]

brawl (brôl) *n.* A noisy quarrel or fight. [ME *brall.*] —**brawl** *v.* —**brawl'er** *n.* —**brawl'ing·ly** *adv.*

brawn (brôn) *n.* **1.** Solid and well-developed muscles. **2.** Muscular strength. [< OFr. *braon*, flesh, of Gmc. orig.] —**brawn'y** *adj.*

bray (brā) *n.* The loud, harsh cry of a donkey. [< OFr. *braire*, to cry, of Celt. orig.] —**bray** *v.*

braze (brāz) *v.* **brazed, braz·ing.** To solder together using a solder with a high melting point. [Prob. < OFr. *braser*, to burn.]

bra·zen (brā'zən) *adj.* **1.** Rudely bold; insolent. **2.** Made of or resembling brass. **3.** Having a harsh and loud sound. [OE *bræsen,*

made of brass.] —**bra'zen·ly** *adv.* —**bra'zen·ness** *n.*

bra·zier (brā'zhər) *n.* A metal pan for holding burning coals or charcoal. [Fr.]

Bra·zil nut (brə-zĭl') *n.* The hard-shelled, edible nut of a South American tree.

breach (brēch) *n.* **1.** A violation, as of a law or obligation. **2.** A gap or hole, esp. in a solid structure. **3.** A disruption of a friendly relationship or bond. [< OE *brēc.*] —**breach** *v.*

bread (brĕd) *n.* **1.** A food made chiefly from moistened, usu. leavened, flour or meal kneaded and baked. **2.** Food in general, regarded as necessary to sustain life. **3.** The necessities of life; livelihood: *earn one's bread.* **4.** *Slang.* Money. —*v.* To coat with bread crumbs before cooking. [< OE *brēad.*]

bread·bas·ket (brĕd'băs'kĭt) *n.* A region serving as a major source of grain.

bread·board (brĕd'bôrd', -bōrd') *n.* **1.** A slicing board. **2.** *Slang.* An experimental model, esp. of an electric or electronic circuit; prototype. —**bread'board'** *v.*

bread·fruit (brĕd'fro͞ot') *n.* **1.** A tropical tree that has deeply lobed leaves and round, usu. seedless fruit. **2.** The edible fruit of the breadfruit that has a texture like that of bread, when baked or roasted.

bread·stuff (brĕd'stŭf') *n.* Flour or grain used in making bread.

breadth (brĕdth) *n.* **1.** The measure or dimension from side to side of something, as distinguished from length or thickness; width. **2.** Wide extent or scope. **3.** Freedom from narrowness, esp. in interests or attitudes. [< OE *brēd.*]

bread·win·ner (brĕd'wĭn'ər) *n.* A person whose earnings support a family.

break (brāk) *v.* **broke** (brōk), **bro·ken** (brō'kən), **break·ing.** **1. a.** To separate into or reduce to pieces by sudden force; come apart. **b.** To crack without separating into pieces. **2. a.** To make or become unusable by or as if by breaking. **b.** To give way; collapse. **3.** To force or make a way into, through, or out of. **4.** To pierce the surface of. **5.** To disrupt the continuity or unity of: *break ranks.* **6.** To come into being or notice, esp. suddenly: *The news broke.* **7.** To begin suddenly: *breaks into bloom.* **8.** To change suddenly: *His voice broke.* **9.** To overcome or surpass. **10. a.** To ruin; destroy. **b.** To demote. **11.** To lessen in force: *break a fall.* **12.** *Informal.* To occur. —*phrasal verbs.* **break in. 1.** To train. **2.** To enter forcibly. **3.** To interrupt. **break off. 1.** To stop suddenly. **2.** To discontinue a relationship. **break out. 1.** To erupt. **2.** To escape, as from prison. —*n.* **1.** The act of breaking. **2.** The result of breaking; a fracture or crack. **3.** A disruption of continuity. **4.** An emergence: *the break of day.* **5.** *Informal.* A stroke of luck. [< OE *brecan.*] —**break'a·ble** *adj. & adj.*

break·age (brā'kĭj) *n.* **1.** The act or process of breaking. **2.** A quantity broken. **3. a.** Loss as a result of breaking. **b.** An allowance for such a loss.

break·down (brāk'doun') *n.* **1.** The act or process of failing to function or the condition resulting from this. **2.** A collapse of physical or mental health. **3.** Disintegration or decomposition into parts or elements. **4.** An analysis, outline, or summary consisting of itemized data or essentials.

break·er (brā'kər) *n.* **1.** One that breaks.

2. *Elect.* A circuit breaker. **3.** A wave that breaks into foam, esp. against a shoreline.

break·fast (brĕk′fəst) *n.* The first meal of the day. [ME *brekfast.*] **—break′fast** *v.*

break·front (brāk′frŭnt′) *n.* A cabinet having a central section projecting beyond the end sections.

break·neck (brāk′nĕk′) *adj.* **1.** Reckless; dangerous. **2.** Rapid.

break·through (brāk′thrōō′) *n.* **1.** An act or the place of breaking through an obstacle or restriction. **2.** A sudden achievement or success that promotes further progress.

break·up (brāk′ŭp′) *n.* **1.** A separation; collapse. **2.** Division; dispersal.

break·wa·ter (brāk′wô′tər, -wŏt′ər) *n.* A barrier that protects a harbor or shore from the impact of waves.

bream (brēm) *n., pl.* **bream** or **breams**. Any of several freshwater fishes with a flattened body and silvery scales. [< OFr. *breme,* of Gmc. orig.]

breast (brĕst) *n.* **1.** The mammary gland, esp. of the human female. **2.** The front surface of the body, extending from the neck to the abdomen. *—v.* To boldly meet or confront. [< OE *brēost.*]

breast·bone (brĕst′bōn′) *n.* The sternum.

breast·plate (brĕst′plāt′) *n.* A piece of armor plate that covers the breast.

breast stroke *n.* A swimming stroke in which one lies face down in the water and extends the arms in front of the head, then sweeps them back laterally while kicking the legs.

breast·work (brĕst′wûrk′) *n.* A temporary fortification, usu. breast-high.

breath (brĕth) *n.* **1.** The air inhaled and exhaled in respiration. **2.** The act or process of breathing; respiration. **3.** The ability to breathe. **4.** A slight breeze. **5.** A trace. **6.** A soft-spoken sound. [< OE *brǣth.*] **—breath′less** *adj.* **—breath′less·ly** *adv.*

breathe (brĕth) *v.* **breathed, breath·ing.** **1.** To inhale and exhale air. **2.** To be alive; live. **3.** To pause to rest. **4.** To utter quietly. [ME *brethen.*] **—breath′a·ble** *adj.*

bred (brĕd) *v.* *p.t. & p.p.* of **breed.**

breech (brēch) *n.* **1.** The buttocks. **2.** The part of a firearm to the rear of the barrel or, in a cannon, to the rear of the bore. **3. breech·es** (brĭch′ĭz). **a.** Knee-length trousers. **b.** Trousers. [< OE *brēc,* trousers.]

breed (brēd) *v.* **bred** (brĕd), **breed·ing.** **1.** To produce (offspring); reproduce. **2.** To bring about; engender. **3.** To raise (animals). **4.** To rear; bring up. *—n.* **1.** A genetic strain, esp. of a domestic animal developed and maintained by man. **2.** A kind; sort. [< OE *brēdan.*]

breed·ing (brē′dĭng) *n.* **1.** A line of descent; ancestry. **2.** Training in the proper forms of social and personal conduct.

breeze (brēz) *n.* **1.** A light, gentle wind. **2.** *Informal.* An easily accomplished task. *—v.* **breezed, breez·ing.** *Informal.* To move or do swiftly and effortlessly. [Perh. < OSp. *briza,* northeast wind.] **—breez′i·ly** *adv.* **—breez′i·ness** *n.* **—breez′y** *adj.*

breeze·way (brēz′wā′) *n.* A roofed, open-sided passageway connecting two buildings, such as a house and a garage.

breth·ren (brĕth′rən) *n. Archaic.* Pl. of **brother.**

Bret·on (brĕt′n) *n.* **1.** A native or inhabitant of Brittany. **2.** The Celtic language of Brittany. **—Bret′on** *adj.*

breve (brēv, brĕv) *n.* **1.** A symbol placed over a vowel to show that it has a short sound. **2.** A single musical note equivalent to two whole notes. [< Lat. *brevis,* brief.]

bre·vi·ar·y (brē′vē-ĕr′ē, brĕv′-ē-) *n., pl.* **-ies.** A book containing the hymns, offices, and prayers for the canonical hours. [Lat. *breviarium,* summary.]

brev·i·ty (brĕv′ĭ-tē) *n.* **1.** Briefness of duration. **2.** Concise expression; terseness. [Lat. *brevitas.*]

brew (brōō) *v.* **1.** To make (beer) from malt and hops by infusion, boiling, and fermentation. **2.** To make (a beverage) by boiling or steeping. [< OE *brēowan.*] **—brew** *n.* **—brew′er** *n.*

brew·er·y (brōō′ə-rē, brōōr′ē) *n., pl.* **-ies.** A place where beer or ale is brewed.

bri·ar¹ (brī′ər) *n.* Also **bri·er. 1.** A European heath plant with a woody root used to make tobacco pipes. **2.** A pipe made from this root. [Fr. *bruyère,* heath.]

bri·ar² (brī′ər) *n.* Var. of **brier¹.**

bribe (brīb) *n.* Something, such as money, offered or given to induce or influence a person to act dishonestly. *—v.* **bribed, brib·ing. 1.** To give, offer, or promise a bribe to. **2.** To gain influence over or corrupt by means of a bribe. [< OFr., alms.] **—brib′a·ble** *adj.* **—brib′er·y** *n.*

bric-a-brac (brĭk′ə-brāk′) *n.* Small objects usu. displayed as ornaments. [Fr. *bric-à-brac.*]

brick (brĭk) *n.* A molded rectangular block of clay, baked until hard and used as a construction material. *—v.* To construct or make of brick. [< MDu. *bricke.*]

brick·bat (brĭk′băt′) *n.* **1.** A piece of brick, esp. one used as a missile. **2.** A critical remark.

brick·lay·er (brĭk′lā′ər) *n.* A person skilled in building walls, chimneys, etc., with bricks. **—brick′lay′ing** *n.*

brid·al (brīd′l) *n.* A wedding. [< OE *brȳdealu,* wedding feast.] **—brid′al** *adj.*

bride (brīd) *n.* A woman who has recently been married or is about to be married. [< OE *brȳd.*]

bride·groom (brīd′grōōm′, -grŏŏm′) *n.* A man who has recently been married or is about to be married. [< OE *brȳdguma.*]

brides·maid (brīdz′mād′) *n.* A usu. unmarried woman who attends the bride at a wedding.

bridge¹ (brĭj) *n.* **1.** A structure spanning and providing a way across an obstacle. **2.** The upper bony ridge of the human nose. **3.** *Mus.* A thin, upright piece of wood in a stringed instrument that supports the strings above the sounding board. **4.** A fixed or removable replacement for missing teeth. **5.** *Naut.* A crosswise platform above the deck of a ship. *—v.* **bridged, bridg·ing. 1.** To build a bridge over: *a plan to bridge the bay.* **2.** To cross by or as if by a bridge. [< OE *brycge.*] **—bridge′a·ble** *adj.*

bridge² (brĭj) n. Any of several card games for four people, derived from whist. [Orig. unknown.]

bridge-work (brĭj'wûrk') n. Dental bridges used to replace missing teeth.

bri-dle (brīd'l) n. 1. The harness fitted about a horse's head, used to restrain or guide. 2. A restraint; curb. —v. **-dled, -dling.** 1. To put a bridle on. 2. To check or restrain with or as if with a bridle. 3. To toss the head as an expression of scorn or resentment. [< OE *brīdel.*]

brief (brēf) adj. **-er, -est.** 1. Short in extent or duration. 2. Condensed; concise. —n. 1. A short or condensed statement, esp. of a legal case or argument. 2. **briefs.** Short, tight-fitting underpants. —v. To give instructions or information. [< Lat. *brevis.*] —**brief'ly** adv. —**brief'ness** n.

brief-case (brēf'kās') n. A portable case used esp. for carrying papers.

bri-er¹ (brī'ər) n. Also **bri-ar.** Any of various thorny plants or bushes, esp. a rosebush. [< OE *brēr.*] —**bri'er-y** adj.

bri-er² (brī'ər) n. Var. of **briar¹.**

brig (brĭg) n. 1. A two-masted square-rigged sailing ship. 2. A naval ship's prison. [< BRIGANTINE.]

bri-gade (brĭ-gād') n. 1. A military unit consisting of a variable number of combat battalions, with supporting services. 2. A group of persons organized for a specific purpose: *a fire brigade.* [< Ltal. *briga,* strife.]

brig-a-dier general (brĭg'ə-dîr') n., pl. **briga-dier generals.** An officer ranking above a colonel in the U.S. Army, Air Force, and Marine Corps.

brig-and (brĭg'ənd) n. A bandit. [< Oltal. *brigante,* skirmisher.] —**brig'and-age** (-ən-dĭj), **brig'and-ism** n.

brig-an-tine (brĭg'ən-tēn') n. A two-masted, square-rigged sailing ship having a fore-and-aft mainsail. [< Oltal. *brigantino,* skirmishing ship.]

bright (brīt) adj. **-er, -est.** 1. Emitting or reflecting light; shining. 2. Brilliant in color; vivid. 3. Glorious; splendid. 4. Clever; smart. 5. Happy; cheerful. [< OE *beorht.*] —**bright'ly** adv. —**bright'ness** n.

Syns: *bright, brilliant, incandescent, luminous, lustrous, radiant, shining* adj.

bright-en (brīt'n) v. To make or become bright or brighter.

bril-liant (brĭl'yənt) adj. 1. Shining brightly. 2. Very bright and vivid in color. 3. Extremely intelligent. 4. Splendid; magnificent. —n. A gem cut in any of various forms, with numerous facets. [Fr. *brillant.*] —**bril'liance** or **bril'lian-cy** n. —**bril'liant-ly** adv.

bril-lian-tine (brĭl'yən-tēn') n. An oily, perfumed hairdressing. [Fr. *brillantine.*]

brim (brĭm) n. 1. The rim or uppermost edge of a cup or other vessel. 2. A projecting rim, as on a hat. [ME *brimme.*] —**brim'less** adj.

brim-ful (brĭm'fŏŏl') adj. Completely full.

brim-stone (brĭm'stōn') n. Obs. Sulfur. [< OE *brynstān.*]

brin-dle (brĭn'dl) adj. Also **brin-dled** (-dld). Tawny or grayish with darker streaks or spots. [< ME *brende.*]

brine (brīn) n. 1. Water saturated with salt. 2. The ocean. [< OE *brīne.*] —**brin'i-ness** n. —**brin'y** adj.

bring (brĭng) v. **brought** (brôt), **bring-ing.**

1. To take with oneself to a place. 2. To cause; produce. 3. To sell for. 4. To persuade. 5. To act upon so as to put into a specified situation or condition. —**phrasal verbs. bring about.** To cause to happen. **bring forth.** To produce. **bring off.** To accomplish successfully. **bring on.** To result in; cause. **bring out.** 1. To reveal or expose. 2. To produce or publish. **bring to.** To cause to recover consciousness. **bring up.** 1. To take care of and rear as a parent. 2. To mention. [< OE *bringan.*]

brink (brĭngk) n. 1. The upper edge of a steep place. 2. The verge of something. [ME.]

bri-o (brē'ō) n. Vigor; vivacity. [Ital.]

bri-oche (brē-ōsh', -ôsh') n. A soft roll or bun made from yeast dough containing butter and eggs. [Fr.]

bri-quette or **bri-quet** (brĭ-kĕt') n. A block of compressed coal dust or charcoal, used for fuel and kindling. [Fr.]

brisk (brĭsk) adj. **-er, -est.** 1. Moving or acting quickly; lively. 2. Stimulating and invigorating. [Orig. unknown.] —**brisk'ly** adv. —**brisk'ness** n.

bris-ket (brĭs'kĭt) n. 1. The chest of an animal. 2. The ribs and meat from the brisket. [ME *brusket.*]

bris-ling (brĭz'lĭng, brĭs'-) n. A small sardine. [Norw.]

bris-tle (brĭs'əl) n. A short, coarse, stiff hair. —v. **-tled, -tling.** 1. To raise the bristles stiffly. 2. To react with anger, defiance, or fear. 3. To stand out stiffly. 4. To be covered with or as if with bristles. [< OE *byrst.*] —**bris'tly** adj.

Bri-tan-nia metal (brĭ-tăn'yə, -tăn'ē-ə) n. A white alloy of tin with copper, antimony, and sometimes bismuth and zinc. [< *Britannia,* a poetic term for Great Britain.]

Bri-tan-nic (brĭ-tăn'ĭk) adj. British.

britch-es (brĭch'ĭz) pl.n. Informal. Breeches.

Brit-i-cism (brĭt'ĭ-sĭz-əm) n. A word or phrase peculiar to English as spoken in Great Britain.

Brit-ish (brĭt'ĭsh) n. (used with a pl. verb). 1. The people of Great Britain. 2. British English. —**Brit'ish** adj.

British English n. The English language as used in Great Britain.

British thermal unit n. The quantity of heat required to raise the temperature of one pound of water by one degree Fahrenheit.

Brit-on (brĭt'n) n. 1. A native or inhabitant of Great Britain. 2. A member of the Celtic people of ancient Britain before the Roman invasion.

brit-tle (brĭt'l) adj. Likely to break or snap; fragile. [ME *britel.*] —**brit'tle-ness** n.

broach (brōch) n. 1. A tapered, serrated tool used to shape or enlarge a hole. 2. A gimlet for tapping a cask. —v. 1. To introduce as a subject. 2. To pierce in order to draw off liquid. [< OFr. *broche,* a spit for roasting meat.] —**broach'er** n.

broad (brôd) adj. **-er, -est.** 1. Wide. 2. Large in expanse; spacious. 3. Clear; bright: *broad daylight.* 4. Covering a wide scope; general. 5. Main; essential. 6. Not subtle; obvious. 7. Liberal; tolerant. 8. Coarse; vulgar. [< OE *brād.*] —**broad'ly** adv. —**broad'ness** n.

Syns: *broad, ample, expansive, extensive, spacious* adj.

broad-band (brôd'bănd') adj. Of, having, or

pertaining to a wide band of electromagnetic frequencies.

broad·cast (brôd′kăst′) v. **-cast** or **-cast·ed**, **-cast·ing.** 1. To transmit by radio or television. 2. To make known over a wide area. 3. To sow over a wide area; scatter. —n. 1. Transmission of a radio or television program or signal. 2. A radio or television program. **—broad′cast′er** n.

broad·cloth (brôd′klôth′, -klŏth′) n. 1. A fine woolen cloth with a smooth, glossy texture. 2. A closely woven silk, cotton, or synthetic cloth.

broad·en (brôd′n) v. To make or become broad or broader.

broad·loom (brôd′lōōm′) n. A carpet woven on a wide loom.

broad·mind·ed (brôd′mīn′dĭd) adj. Open-minded and tolerant in attitude. **—broad′mind′ed·ly** adv. **—broad′mind′ed·ness** n.

broad·side (brôd′sīd′) n. 1. The side of a ship above the water line. 2. A firing of all the guns on one side of a warship. 3. An explosive verbal attack or denunciation.

broad·spec·trum (brôd′spĕk′trəm) adj. Widely applicable or effective: a broad-spectrum drug.

broad·sword (brôd′sôrd′, -sōrd′) n. A sword with a wide blade.

broad·tail (brôd′tāl′) n. The flat, glossy, rippled fur from the pelt of a very young or prematurely born karakul lamb.

bro·cade (brō-kād′) n. A heavy fabric with a raised interwoven design. [< Ital. broccato, embossed fabric.]

broc·co·li (brŏk′ə-lē) n. A plant that has densely clustered buds and stalks and is eaten as a vegetable. [Ital.]

bro·chette (brō-shĕt′) n. A skewer. [Fr.]

bro·chure (brō-shōōr′) n. A pamphlet; booklet. [Fr.]

bro·gan (brō′gən) n. A heavy, ankle-high shoe. [Ir. Gael. brógan.]

brogue (brōg) n. 1. A sturdy oxford shoe. 2. A dialectal or regional accent, esp. an Irish accent. [Ir. Gael. and Sc. Gael. bròg, shoe.]

broil (broil) v. To cook by direct radiant heat. [< OFr. bruler.]

broil·er (broi′lər) n. 1. A small electric oven or a specific unit of a stove used for broiling. 2. A tender young chicken suitable for broiling.

broke (brōk) v. p.t. of **break.** —adj. Informal. Without funds.

bro·ken (brō′kən) v. p.p. of **break.** —adj. 1. Shattered; fractured. 2. Not functioning. 3. Not kept; violated. 4. Spoken imperfectly. 5. Overwhelmed. 6. Tamed; subdued. 7. Not continuous.

bro·ken-heart·ed (brō′kən-här′tĭd) adj. Overwhelmed by grief or despair.

bro·ker (brō′kər) n. An agent who negotiates contracts, purchases, or sales in return for a fee or commission. [< AN brocour.]

bro·ker·age (brō′kər-ĭj) n. 1. The business of a broker. 2. A fee or commission paid to a broker.

bro·mide (brō′mīd′) n. 1. A chemical compound of bromine with another element or radical. 2. Potassium bromide. 3. A hackneyed remark or idea.

bro·mid·ic (brō-mĭd′ĭk) adj. Trite; commonplace.

bro·mine (brō′mēn′) n. Symbol **Br** A heavy, volatile, corrosive, reddish-brown, nonmetallic liquid element, used in gasoline antiknock mixtures, fumigants, dyes, and photographic chemicals. Atomic weight 79.909; atomic number 35. [Gk. brōmos, stench + -INE².]

bron·chi (brŏng′kī′, -kē′) n. Pl. of **bronchus.**

bron·chi·al (brŏng′kē-əl) adj. Of or pertaining to the bronchi or their extensions.

bron·chi·tis (brŏng-kī′tĭs) n. Inflammation of the mucous membrane of the bronchial tubes. **—bron·chit′ic** (-kĭt′ĭk) adj.

bron·chus (brŏng′kəs) n., pl. **-chi** (-kī′, -kē′). Either of two main branches of the trachea, leading directly to the lungs. [< Gk. bronkhos, windpipe.]

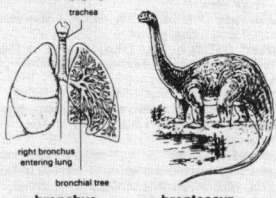

trachea

right bronchus entering lung

bronchial tree

bronchus   **brontosaur**

bron·co (brŏng′kō) n., pl. **-cos.** A small wild or half-wild horse of western North America. [Mex. Sp.]

bron·co-bust·er (brŏng′kō-bŭs′tər) n. A cowboy who breaks wild horses to the saddle.

bron·to·saur (brŏn′tə-sôr′) n. Also **bron·to·sau·rus** (brŏn′tə-sôr′əs). A very large, herbivorous dinosaur. [Gk. brontē, thunder + -SAUR.]

bronze (brŏnz) n. 1. An alloy consisting chiefly of copper and tin. 2. A work of art made of bronze. 3. A yellowish or olive brown. —v. **bronzed, bronz·ing.** To give the appearance or color of bronze to. [< Ital. bronzo.] **—bronze** adj. **—bronz′y** adj.

brooch (brōch, brōōch) n. A decorative pin or clasp. [ME broche, pointed tool.]

brood (brōōd) n. A group of young animals, esp. a group of young birds hatched at one time. —v. 1. To sit on in order to hatch. 2. To think or worry anxiously. [< OE brōd.] **—brood′ing·ly** adv.

brood·er (brōō′dər) n. 1. One that broods. 2. A heated structure in which young chickens or other fowl are raised.

brook¹ (brōōk) n. A small, natural stream. [< OE brōc.]

brook² (brōōk) v. To put up with; tolerate. [< OE brūcan, to enjoy.]

brook·let (brōōk′lĭt) n. A small brook.

brook trout n. A freshwater game fish of eastern North America.

broom (brōōm, brōōm) n. 1. An implement, as of bound twigs or straw attached to a stick, used for sweeping. 2. A shrub native to Eurasia, with compound leaves and yellow or white flowers. [< OE brōm.]

broth (brôth, brŏth) n., pl. **broths** (brôths,

brŏths, brŏthz, brŏthz). The liquid in which meat, fish, or vegetables have been boiled. [< OE.]

broth-el (brŏth'əl, brŏ'thəl) n. A house of prostitution. [ME, prostitute.]

broth-er (brŭth'ər) n. 1. A male having at least one parent in common with another person. 2. A kindred human being. 3. A member of a men's religious order who is not a priest. [< OE brōthor.] —broth'er-li-ness n. —broth'er-ly adj.

broth-er-hood (brŭth'ər-hŏŏd') n. 1. The state of being a brother or brothers. 2. Brotherly feelings or friendship; fellowship. 3. A group of men united for a common purpose. 4. All the members of a profession or trade.

broth-er-in-law (brŭth'ər-ĭn-lô') n., pl. broth-ers-in-law. 1. The brother of one's husband or wife. 2. The husband of one's sister. 3. The husband of the sister of one's brother or wife.

brougham (brŏŏm, brŏŏ'əm, brŏ'əm) n. 1. A closed four-wheeled carriage with an open driver's seat in front. 2. An automobile with an open driver's seat. [< Henry P. Brougham (1778–1868).]

brought (brôt) v. p.t. & p.p. of bring.

brou-ha-ha (brŏŏ'hä-hä') n. An uproar. [Fr.]

brow (brou) n. 1. a. The forehead. b. An eyebrow. c. The ridge over the eyes. 2. The projecting upper edge of a steep place. [< OE brū.]

brow-beat (brou'bēt') v. To intimidate with an overbearing manner; bully.

brown (broun) n. Any of a group of colors between red and yellow in hue. —adj. -er, -est. 1. Of the color brown. 2. Deeply suntanned. —v. To make or become brown. [< OE brūn.] —brown'ish adj. —brown'ness n.

brown-ie (brou'nē) n. 1. A small helpful elf in folklore. 2. A rich, chewy chocolate cookie. 3. Brownie. A junior Girl Scout.

brown-out (broun'out') n. A reduction in electric power, esp. as a result of a shortage. [BROWN + (BLACK)OUT.]

brown rice n. Unpolished rice grains.

brown-stone (broun'stōn') n. 1. A brownish-red sandstone. 2. A house built or faced with brownstone.

brown study n. Deep thought.

brown sugar n. Unrefined or partially refined sugar.

browse (brouz) v. browsed, brows-ing. 1. To inspect in a leisurely and casual way. 2. To feed on leaves, young shoots, and other vegetation; graze (on). [< OFr. brost, twig.] —browse n. —brows'er n.

bru-in (brŏŏ'ĭn) n. A bear. [Du., brown.]

bruise (brŏŏz) v. bruised, bruis-ing. 1. a. To injure the skin without rupture. b. To suffer such injury. 2. To dent or mar. 3. To pound into fragments. 4. To offend. —n. An injury in which the skin is not broken; contusion. [< OE brȳsan, to crush, and < OFr. bruisier, to crush.]

bruis-er (brŏŏ'zər) n. Slang. A large, powerfully built person.

bruit (brŏŏt) v. To spread news of. [< OFr., noise.]

brunch (brŭnch) n. A meal eaten late in the morning as a combination of breakfast and lunch. [BR(EAKFAST) + (L)UNCH.]

bru-net (brŏŏ-nĕt') adj. 1. Of a dark complex-

ion or coloring. 2. Having brown or black eyes or hair. —n. A person with brown hair. [< OFr. brun, brown.]

bru-nette (brŏŏ-nĕt') adj. Having dark or brown hair. —n. A girl or woman with dark or brown hair. [Fr.]

brunt (brŭnt) n. The main impact, force, or burden, as of a blow. [ME.]

brush¹ (brŭsh) n. 1. A device consisting of bristles or other flexible material fastened into a handle, for scrubbing, applying paint, grooming the hair, etc. 2. A light touch in passing. 3. A brief encounter. 4. The bushy tail of a fox or other animal. 5. A sliding connection completing a circuit between a fixed and a moving conductor. —v. 1. To use a brush (on). 2. To apply or remove with or as if with motions of a brush. 3. To touch lightly in passing; graze against. —phrasal verbs. brush off (or aside). To dismiss abruptly. brush up. To refresh one's memory. [< OFr. brosse.]

brush² (brŭsh) n. Also brush-wood (brŭsh'-wŏŏd'). 1. A dense growth of bushes. 2. Cut or broken-off branches. [< OFr. brosse, brushwood.] —brush'y adj.

brush-off (brŭsh'ôf', -ŏf') n. Slang. An abrupt dismissal.

brusque (brŭsk) adj. Abrupt and curt in manner or speech; discourteously blunt. [Fr. < Ital. brusco.] —brusque'ly adv. —brusque'-ness n.

Brus-sels sprouts (brŭs'əlz) pl.n. The edible heads of a variety of cabbage, eaten as a vegetable.

bru-tal (brŏŏt'l) adj. Characteristic of a brute; cruel; harsh; crude. —bru-tal'i-ty (-tăl'ĭ-tē) n. —bru'tal-ly adv.

bru-tal-ize (brŏŏt'l-īz') v. -ized, -iz-ing. 1. To make brutal. 2. To treat in a brutal manner. —bru'tal-i-za'tion n.

brute (brŏŏt) n. 1. An animal; beast. 2. A brutal person. —adj. 1. Of or relating to beasts. 2. Entirely physical or instinctive; not involving intelligence: brute force. [< Lat. brutus, stupid.] —brut'ish adj. —brut'ish-ly adv. —brut'ish-ness n.

bub-ble (bŭb'əl) n. 1. A rounded, generally spherical, hollow, or sometimes solid, object, esp. a small globule of gas trapped in a liquid. 2. A glass or plastic dome. 3. Something that gives early promise of success but comes to nothing. —v. -bled, -bling. To form or give off bubbles. [ME bobelen.] —bub'bly adj.

bu-bo (bŏŏ'bō, byŏŏ'-) n., pl. -boes. An inflamed swelling of a lymphatic gland, esp. near the armpit or groin. [< Gk. boubōn.] —bu-bon'ic (-bŏn'ĭk) adj.

bubonic plague n. A very contagious, usu. fatal epidemic disease caused by bacteria transmitted by fleas from infected rodents and characterized by chills, fever, vomiting, diarrhea, and buboes.

buc-ca-neer (bŭk'ə-nîr') n. A pirate. [< Fr. boucaner, to cure meat.]

buck¹ (bŭk) n. 1. The adult male of some animals, such as the deer or rabbit. 2. A robust or high-spirited young man. —v. 1. To leap forward and upward suddenly; rear up. 2. To butt (against). 3. To jolt. 4. To throw (a rider or burden) by bucking. 5. To oppose directly and stubbornly. —phrasal verbs. buck for. To strive for: bucking for a promotion. buck up. Informal. To raise one's spirits.

—*adj.* Lowest in rank: *a buck private.* [< OE *buc.*] —**buck'er** *n.*

buck² (bŭk) *n. Slang.* A dollar. [< BUCK-SKIN.]

buck·board (bŭk'bôrd', -bōrd') *n.* A four-wheeled open carriage with the seat attached to a flexible board. [Obs. *buck,* body of a wagon + BOARD.]

buck·et (bŭk'ĭt) *n.* 1. A cylindrical vessel used for holding or carrying liquids or solids; pail. 2. Any of various machine compartments that receive and convey material, as the scoop of a steam shovel. [< OFr. *buket.*]

bucket seat *n.* A seat with a molded back, as in sports cars.

buck·eye (bŭk'ī') *n.* A North American tree with erect flower clusters and glossy brown nuts. [< the seed's appearance.]

buck·le¹ (bŭk'əl) *n.* 1. A clasp, esp. a frame with a movable tongue for fastening two strap or belt ends. 2. An ornament that resembles a buckle. —*v.* **-led, -ling.** To fasten or secure with a buckle. —*phrasal verb.* **buckle down.** To begin working hard. [< OFr. *boucle.*]

buck·le² (bŭk'əl) *v.* **-led, -ling.** 1. To bend, warp, or crumple under pressure or heat. 2. To collapse or yield. —*n.* A bend, bulge, or other distortion. [< OFr. *boucler,* to fasten with a buckle.]

buck·ler (bŭk'lər) *n.* A small round shield. [< OFr. *bocler.*]

buck·ram (bŭk'rəm) *n.* A coarse cotton cloth stiffened with glue, used for binding books and lining garments. [< OFr. *boquerant,* fine linen.]

buck·saw (bŭk'sô') *n.* A saw usu. set in an H-shaped frame. [< back, sawhorse.]

buck·shot (bŭk'shŏt') *n.* A large lead shot for shotgun shells.

buck·skin (bŭk'skĭn') *n.* Strong, grayish-yellow leather orig. made from deerskin.

buck·tooth (bŭk'tōōth') *n.* A prominent, projecting upper front tooth. —**buck'toothed'** (-tōōtht') *adj.*

buck·wheat (bŭk'hwēt', -wēt') *n.* 1. A plant with small triangular seeds. 2. The seeds of the buckwheat, often ground into flour. [< MDu. *boecweite.*]

bu·col·ic (byōō-kŏl'ĭk) *adj.* Pastoral; rustic. [< Gk. *boukolikos.*]

bud (bŭd) *n.* 1. A small, protuberant plant structure containing undeveloped flowers, leaves, etc. 2. A budlike part, as an asexually produced reproductive structure. 3. An undeveloped or incipient stage. —*v.* **bud·ded, bud·ding.** 1. To form or produce a bud. 2. To develop from or as if from a bud. [ME *budde.*] —**bud'der** *n.* —**bud'like'** *adj.*

Bud·dhism (bōō'dĭz'əm, bŏŏd'ĭz'-) *n.* The doctrine, attributed to Buddha, that suffering is inseparable from existence but that inward extinction of the self and the senses culminates in a state of illumination called nirvana. —**Bud'dhist** *n.* —**Bud·dhis'tic** *adj.*

bud·dy (bŭd'ē) *n., pl.* **-dies.** *Informal.* A close friend; comrade. [Prob. < BROTHER.]

budge (bŭj) *v.* **budged, budg·ing.** 1. To move or cause to move slightly. 2. To alter or cause to alter a position or attitude. [OFr. *bouger.*]

budg·er·i·gar (bŭj'ə-rē-gär') *n.* A small, color-ful parakeet popular as a cage bird. [Native word in Australia.]

budg·et (bŭj'ĭt) *n.* 1. An itemized list of probable expenditures and income for a given period. 2. The sum of money allocated for a particular purpose or time period. —*v.* 1. To make a budget. 2. To enter or plan for in a budget. [< Lat. *bulga,* leather bag, of Celt. orig.] —**budg'et·ar'y** (-ĭ-tĕr'ē) *adj.*

buff¹ (bŭf) *n.* 1. A soft, thick, undyed leather made from the skins of buffalo, elk, or oxen. 2. A yellowish tan. —*adj.* Yellowish tan. —*v.* To polish or shine with a buff. [OFr. *buffle,* buffalo.]

buff² (bŭf) *n. Informal.* One who is enthusiastic and knowledgeable about a particular subject. [< the buff uniforms worn at one time by New York volunteer firemen.]

buf·fa·lo (bŭf'ə-lō') *n., pl.* **-loes** or **-los** or **-lo.** 1. Any of several oxlike African or Asian mammals. 2. The American bison. —*v. Slang.* To intimidate, confuse, or bewilder. [< Gk. *boubalos.*]

buffalo

buff·er¹ (bŭf'ər) *n.* Something used to shine or polish, as a soft cloth or a machine with a moving head. [< BUFF¹.]

buff·er² (bŭf'ər) *n.* 1. One that lessens, absorbs, or protects against the shock of an impact. 2. A substance capable of stabilizing the acidity or alkalinity of a solution by neutralizing, within limits, any acid or base that is added. [Prob. < *buff,* to deaden the shock of.]

buf·fet¹ (bə-fā', bŏŏ-) *n.* 1. A sideboard. 2. A counter for meals and refreshments. 3. A meal at which guests serve themselves from dishes arranged on a table or sideboard. [Fr.]

buf·fet² (bŭf'ĭt) *n.* A blow or cuff with or as if with the hand. —*v.* 1. To hit or strike against repeatedly. 2. To force (one's way). [< OFr. *bufet.*] —**buf'fet·er** *n.*

buf·foon (bə-fōōn') *n.* A clown; jester. [< Ital. *buffone.*] —**buf·foon'er·y** *n.*

bug (bŭg) *n.* 1. Any of various often harmful insects. 2. Any insect, spider, etc. 3. *Informal.* A disease-producing microorganism; germ. 4. A mechanical, electrical, or other systemic defect. 5. *Slang.* An enthusiast; buff. 6. A small hidden microphone or other device used for eavesdropping. —*v.* **bugged, bug·ging.** 1. *Slang.* To annoy; pester. 2. To equip (e.g. a telephone circuit) with a concealed electronic listening device. [Orig. unknown.]

bug·a·boo (bŭg'ə-bōō') *n., pl.* **-boos.** A steady source of annoyance or concern. [Perh. of Celt. orig.]

bug·bear (bŭg′bâr′) n. An object of excessive concern or fear. [ME *bugge,* hobgoblin + BEAR.]

bug·eyed (bŭg′īd′) adj. Slang. Agog.

bug·gy (bŭg′ē) n., pl. **-gies.** A small, light, four-wheeled carriage. [Orig. unknown.]

bu·gle (byōō′gəl) n. A trumpetlike instrument without keys or valves. [< OFr.] **—bu′gle** v. **—bu′gler** n.

build (bĭld) v. **built** (bĭlt), **build·ing.** 1. To erect; construct. 2. To fashion; create. 3. To add to; develop. 4. To establish a basis for. **—phrasal verb. build up.** To construct in stages or by degrees. —n. The physical make-up of a person or thing. [< OE *bold,* a dwelling.] **—build′er** n.

build·ing (bĭl′dĭng) n. 1. A structure; edifice. 2. The act, process, art, or occupation of constructing.

build·up (bĭld′ŭp′) n. Also **build-up.** 1. The act of amassing or increasing. 2. Widely favorable publicity, esp. by a systematic campaign.

built-in (bĭlt′ĭn′) adj. 1. Constructed as a nondetachable part of a larger unit. 2. Natural; inherent.

bulb (bŭlb) n. 1. A rounded, modified underground stem, such as that of the onion or tulip, from which a new plant develops. 2. A rounded object, projection, or part. 3. An incandescent lamp or its glass housing. [< Gk. *bolbos,* bulbous plant.] **—bulb′ar** adj.

bul·bous (bŭl′bəs) adj. 1. Shaped like a bulb. 2. Growing from bulbs.

Bul·gar·i·an (bŭl-gâr′ē-ən, bōōl-) n. 1. Also **Bul·gar** (bŭl′gər, bōōl′gär′). A native of Bulgaria. 2. The Slavic language of the Bulgarians. **—Bul·gar′i·an** adj.

bulge (bŭlj) n. A protruding part; a swelling. —v. **bulged, bulg·ing.** To swell or cause to swell out. [< Lat. *bulga,* bag, of Celt. orig.] **—bulg′y** adj.

bulk (bŭlk) n. 1. Great size, mass, or volume. 2. The major portion of something. —v. To be or appear to be great in size or importance; loom. **—idiom. in bulk.** Unpackaged; loose. [< ON *bulki,* cargo.] **—bulk′i·ly** adv. **—bulk′i·ness** n. **—bulk′y** adj.

> **Syns:** bulk, amplitude, magnitude, mass, size, volume n.

bulk·head (bŭlk′hĕd′) n. 1. An upright partition that divides the inside of a ship into compartments. 2. A wall or embankment constructed in a mine or tunnel. [Orig. unknown.]

bull¹ (bōōl) n. 1. a. The adult male of cattle or certain other large mammals. b. The uncastrated adult male of domestic cattle. 2. One who buys commodities or securities in anticipation of a rise in prices. 3. Slang. A police officer. 4. Slang. Empty talk; nonsense. —adj. 1. Male. 2. Large and strong. 3. Characterized by rising prices: *a bull market.* **—idiom. shoot the bull.** Slang. To spend time talking. [< ON *boli.*]

bull² (bōōl) n. A papal document. [< Med. Lat. *bulla.*]

bull·dog (bōōl′dôg′, -dŏg′) n. A stocky, short-haired dog with a large head and strong, square jaws. —adj. Resembling a bulldog; stubborn. —v. **-dogged, -dog·ging.** To throw (a steer) by seizing its horns and twisting its neck.

bull·doze (bōōl′dōz′) v. **-dozed, -doz·ing.**

1. To dig up or move with a bulldozer. 2. Slang. To bully. [Poss. < obs. *bulldose,* severe beating.]

bull·doz·er (bōōl′dō′zər) n. A large, powerful tractor having a vertical metal scoop in front for moving earth and rocks.

bul·let (bōōl′ĭt) n. A cylindrical usu. metal projectile that is fired from a firearm. [< Lat. *bulla,* ball.] **—bul′let·proof** adj.

bul·le·tin (bōōl′ĭ-tn, -tĭn) n. 1. A printed or broadcast statement on a matter of public interest. 2. A periodical issued by an organization. [Fr.]

bulletin board n. A board mounted on a wall, on which notices are posted.

bull·fight (bōōl′fīt′) n. A public spectacle, esp. in Spain and Mexico, in which a matador engages and usu. kills a fighting bull. **—bull′fight′er** n. **—bull′fight′ing** n.

bullfight

bull·finch (bōōl′finch′) n. A European songbird with a short, thick bill and a red breast.

bull·frog (bōōl′frôg′, -frŏg′) n. A large frog with a deep, resonant croak.

bull·head (bōōl′hĕd′) n. A North American freshwater catfish.

bull·head·ed (bōōl′hĕd′ĭd) adj. Very stubborn; headstrong. **—bull′head′ed·ly** adv. **—bull′head′ed·ness** n.

bul·lion (bōōl′yən) n. Gold or silver bars or ingots. [OFr. *bille,* stick, and < OFr. *boillon,* molten metal.]

bull·ish (bōōl′ĭsh) adj. 1. Like a bull. 2. Stubborn. 3. a. Expecting a rise in stock-market prices. b. Optimistic. **—bull′ish·ly** adv. **—bull′ish·ness** n.

bul·lock (bōōl′ək) n. A steer or young bull. [< OE *bulluc.*]

bull·pen (bōōl′pĕn′) n. Baseball. An area where relief pitchers warm up during a game.

bull session n. Informal. An informal group discussion.

bull's eye n. Also **bull's-eye** (bōōlz′ī′) n. The small central circle on a target or a shot that hits this circle.

bul·ly (bōōl′ē) n., pl. **-lies.** One who is habitually cruel to smaller or weaker people. —v. **-lied, -ly·ing.** To behave like a bully. —adj. Informal. Excellent; splendid. —interj. Used to express approval. [Poss. < MDu. *boele,* sweetheart.]

bul·rush (bōōl′rŭsh′) n. Any of various tall grasslike sedges or similar marsh plants. [ME *bulrish.*]

bul·wark (bōōl′wərk, bŭl′-, -wôrk′) n. 1. A wall or similar structure for defense; rampart. 2. Something serving as a defense against attack or encroachment. [< MHG *bolwerc.*]

bum (bŭm) n. 1. A tramp; hobo. 2. One who seeks to live off others. —v. **bummed, bum·ming.** Informal. 1. To live or acquire by begging and scavenging. **2.** To loaf. —*adj. Slang.* **1.** Of poor quality. **2.** Disabled; malfunctioning. [Prob. < G. *Bummler,* lazy person.]

bum·ble (bŭm'bəl) *v.* **-bled, -bling.** To speak or behave in a clumsy manner. [Prob. < BUNGLE.] —**bum'bler** *n.*

bum·ble·bee (bŭm'bəl-bē') *n.* Any of various large, hairy bees. [ME *bomblen,* to buzz + BEE.]

bump (bŭmp) *v.* **1.** To strike or collide (with). **2.** To knock. **3.** To displace; oust. —*phrasal verbs.* **bump into.** To meet by chance. **bump off.** *Slang.* To murder. —*n.* **1.** A light blow, collision, or jolt. **2.** A slight swelling or lump. [Imit.] —**bump'i·ness** *n.* —**bump'y** *adj.*

bump·er¹ (bŭm'pər) *n.* A device, esp. a horizontal bar, attached to the front and rear of an automobile to absorb the impact of a collision.

bump·er² (bŭm'pər) *n.* A drinking vessel filled to the top. —*adj.* Unusually abundant: *a bumper crop.* [Perh. < BUMP.]

bump·kin (bŭmp'kĭn, bŭm'-) *n.* An awkward or unsophisticated person. [Orig. unknown.]

bump·tious (bŭmp'shəs) *adj.* Crudely forward and self-assertive in behavior; pushy. [Perh. a blend of BUMP and FRACTIOUS.] —**bump'·tious·ly** *adv.* —**bump'tious·ness** *n.*

bun (bŭn) *n.* **1.** A small bread roll, often sweetened. **2.** A roll of hair worn at the back of the head. [ME *bunne.*]

bunch (bŭnch) *n.* A group, cluster, or tuft. [ME *bunche.*] —**bunch** *v.* —**bunch'y** *adj.*

bun·co (bŭng'kō) *n., pl.* **-cos.** A swindle; confidence game. [Sp. *banca,* card game.] —**bun'co** *v.*

bun·dle (bŭn'dl) *n.* **1.** A number of objects bound, wrapped, or otherwise held together; package. **2.** *Slang.* A large sum of money. —*v.* **-dled, -dling. 1.** To tie, wrap, fold, or otherwise secure together. **2.** To dress warmly. [ME *bundel.*] —**bun'dler** *n.*

bung (bŭng) *n.* A stopper for a bunghole. [< MDu. *bonge.*]

bun·ga·low (bŭng'gə-lō') *n.* A small cottage, usu. of one story. [Hindi *banglā.*]

bung·hole (bŭng'hōl') *n.* The hole in a cask, keg, or barrel through which the liquid is poured or drained.

bun·gle (bŭng'gəl) *v.* **-gled, -gling.** To work, manage, or act ineptly or inefficiently. [Perh. of Scand. orig.] —**bun'gler** *n.*

bun·ion (bŭn'yən) *n.* A painful, inflamed swelling at the bursa of the big toe. [Prob. < obs. *bunny,* swelling.]

bunk¹ (bŭngk) *n.* **1.** A narrow built-in bed. **2.** A double-decker bed. **3.** *Informal.* A place for sleeping. [Orig. unknown.] —**bunk** *v.*

bunk² (bŭngk) *n. Slang.* Empty talk; nonsense. [< *Buncombe* County, North Carolina.]

bun·ker (bŭng'kər) *n.* **1.** A bin or tank for fuel storage, as on a ship. **2.** *Golf.* An obstacle, usu. a sandtrap. **3.** A fortified earthwork. [Sc. *bonker,* chest.]

bunk·house (bŭngk'hous') *n.* Sleeping quarters on a ranch or in a camp.

bun·ny (bŭn'ē) *n., pl.* **-nies.** *Informal.* A rabbit. [Dial. *bun,* rabbit.]

Bun·sen burner (bŭn'sən) *n.* A small, adjustable gas-burning laboratory burner. [< Robert W. Bunsen (1811–99).]

bunt (bŭnt) *v.* **1.** To butt (something) with the head. **2.** *Baseball.* To bat (a pitched ball) with a half swing so that the ball rolls slowly in front of the infielders. —*n.* **1.** A bunt with the head. **2.** *Baseball.* **a.** The act of bunting. **b.** A bunted ball. [Orig. unknown.]

bunt·ing¹ (bŭn'tĭng) *n.* **1.** A light cloth used for making flags. **2.** Flags collectively. **3.** Long, colored strips of cloth for holiday decoration. [Orig. unknown.]

bunt·ing² (bŭn'tĭng) *n.* Any of various birds with short, cone-shaped bills. [ME.]

buoy (boo'ē, boi) *n. Naut.* A float anchored in water as a warning of danger or as a marker for a channel. **2.** A device made of buoyant material for keeping a person afloat; life preserver. —*v.* **1.** *Naut.* To mark (a water hazard or a channel) with a buoy. **2.** To keep afloat. **3.** To cheer; hearten. [< OFr. *boie.*]

buoy·an·cy (boi'ən-sē, boo'yən-) *n.* **1.** The tendency to remain afloat in a liquid or to rise in air or gas. **2.** The upward force of a fluid. **3.** The ability to recover quickly from setbacks. **4.** Cheerfulness. —**buoy'ant** *adj.* —**buoy'ant·ly** *adv.*

bur¹ (bûr) *n.* Also **burr. 1.** The rough, prickly, or spiny covering enclosing a seed, fruit, etc. **2.** A rotary cutting tool designed to be attached to a drill. [ME *burre,* of Scand. orig.]

bur² (bûr) *n.* Var. of **burr¹** and **burr².**

bur·den¹ (bûr'dn) *n.* **1.** Something that is carried. **2.** Something that is difficult to bear. **3.** A responsibility or duty. **4.** The amount of cargo a vessel can carry. —*v.* **1.** To load or overload. **2.** To weigh down; oppress. [< OE *byrthen.*] —**bur'den·some** *adj.* —**bur'den·some·ness** *n.*

bur·den² (bûr'dn) *n.* **1.** *Mus.* A chorus or refrain. **2.** A main idea or theme. [< OFr. *bourdon,* drone.]

bur·dock (bûr'dŏk') *n.* A weedy plant having large leaves and purplish flowers surrounded by bristles. [BUR¹ + DOCK⁴.]

bu·reau (byoor'ō) *n., pl.* **-reaus** or **bu·reaux** (byoor'ōz). **1.** A chest of drawers. **2.** A government department or subdivision of a department: *the tax bureau.* **3.** An office or business that performs a specific duty: *a travel bureau.* [Fr.]

bu·reauc·ra·cy (byoo-rŏk'rə-sē) *n., pl.* **-cies. 1. a.** Government administered through bureaus and departments. **b.** The departments and their officials as a group. **2.** An unwieldy administrative system. —**bu'reau·crat'** *n.* —**bu'reau·crat'ic** *adj.* —**bu'reau·crat'i·cal·ly** *adv.*

bu·rette (byoo-rĕt') *n.* Also **bu·ret.** A graduated glass tube with a small aperture used for measuring and dispensing fluids. [Fr.]

burg (bûrg) *n. Informal.* A city or town. [< OE.]

bur·geon (bûr'jən) *v.* **1.** To put forth new buds, leaves, or greenery; begin to sprout or grow. **2.** To develop rapidly; flourish. [< OFr. *borjoner.*]

burg·er (bûr'gər) *n. Informal.* A hamburger.

bur·gess (bûr'jĭs) *n.* A freeman, citizen, or representative of an English borough. [< OFr. *burgeis.*]

---

burgh (bûrg) *n.* A chartered town in Scotland. [Sc.]

burgh·er (bûr′gər) *n.* A solid citizen; bourgeois. [G. *Bürger* or Du. *burger.*]

bur·glar (bûr′glər) *n.* One who commits burglary; housebreaker. [AN *burgler.*] —**bur′glar·i·ous** —**bur′glar·ize′** *v.* —**bur′glar·proof** *adj.* —**bur′gla·ry** *n.*

bur·gle (bûr′gəl) *v.* **-gled, -gling.** *Informal.* To commit burglary (on). [< BURGLAR.]

bur·go·mas·ter (bûr′gə-măs′tər) *n.* The principal magistrate of some European cities, comparable to a mayor. [Du. *burgemeester.*]

bur·i·al (bĕr′ē-əl) *n.* The interment of a dead body. [< OE *byrgels.*]

burl (bûrl) *n.* **1.** A large, rounded outgrowth on a tree. **2.** The wood from a burl, used as veneer. [< OFr. *bourle.*]

bur·lap (bûr′lăp′) *n.* A coarse cloth made of jute, flax, or hemp. [Orig. unknown.]

bur·lesque (bər-lĕsk′) *n.* **1.** A ludicrous or mocking imitation. **2.** Vaudeville entertainment characterized by ribald comedy and display of nudity. —*v.* **-lesqued, -lesqu·ing.** To imitate mockingly. —*adj.* **1.** Mockingly and ludicrously imitative. **2.** Of or characteristic of theatrical burlesque. [< Ital. *burlesco.*] —**bur·lesqu′er** *n.*

bur·ly (bûr′lē) *adj.* **-li·er, -li·est.** Heavy and strong. [ME *burlich.*] —**bur′li·ness** *n.*

Bur·mese (bər-mēz′, -mēs′) *n., pl.* **-mese. 1.** A native of Burma. **2.** The Sino-Tibetan language of Burma. —**Bur·mese′** *adj.*

burn (bûrn) *v.* **burned** or **burnt** (bûrnt), **burn·ing. 1.** To undergo or cause to undergo combustion. **a.** To destroy or be destroyed by fire. **b.** To damage or be damaged by fire or heat. **c.** *Slang.* To execute, esp. by electrocution. **2.** To produce by fire or heat: *burn a clearing in the brush.* **4.** To use as a fuel. **5.** To impart a sensation of intense heat to: *The chili burned my mouth.* **6.** To emit heat or light by or as if by means of fire. **7.** To feel or look hot. **8.** To be consumed with strong emotion. **9.** To waste: *money to burn.* —*phrasal verbs.* **burn out. 1.** To stop burning from lack of fuel. **2.** To wear out or fail, esp. because of heat. **3.** To become exhausted from long-term stress. **burn up. 1.** To consume or be consumed by fire or heat. **2.** *Slang.* To make or become very angry. —*n.* **1.** An injury produced by fire or heat. **2.** A sunburn. **3.** *Aerospace.* One firing of a rocket. [< OE *beornan* and *bærnan.*]

burn·er (bûr′nər) *n.* **1.** One that burns something. **2.** The part of a stove, furnace, or lamp that is lighted to produce a flame. **3.** A device in which something is burned: *an oil burner.*

bur·nish (bûr′nĭsh) *v.* To polish or become polished by or as if by rubbing. —*n.* A smooth, glossy finish; luster. [< OFr. *burnir.*] —**bur′nish·er** *n.*

bur·noose (bər-nōōs′) *n.* A long, hooded cloak worn by Arabs. [< Ar. *bournous.*]

burn·out (bûrn′out′) *n.* **1.** A failure in a device caused by excessive heat or friction. **2.** *Aerospace.* **a.** Termination of rocket or jet-engine operation due to fuel exhaustion or shutoff. **b.** The point at which this occurs. **3. a.** Physical or emotional exhaustion from long-term stress. **b.** One who is burned out.

burnt (bûrnt) *v.* A *p.t. & p.p.* of **burn.**

burp (bûrp) *Informal.* —*n.* A belch. —*v.* To belch or cause (a baby) to belch. [Imit.]

burr[1] (bûr) Also **bur.** —*n.* **1.** A rough edge on metal or other material after it has been cast, cut, or drilled. **2.** A rough outgrowth, esp. on a tree. —*v.* **1.** To form a rough edge on. **2.** To remove a rough edge or edges from. [ME *burre.*]

burr[2] (bûr) Also **bur.** —*n.* **1.** A rough trilling of the letter *r,* as in Scottish pronunciation. **2.** A buzzing or whirring sound. —*v.* To pronounce or speak with a burr. [Imit.]

burr[3] (bûr) *n.* Var. of **burr**[1].

bur·ro (bûr′ō, bōōr′ō, bŭr′ō) *n., pl.* **-ros.** A small donkey. [Sp.]

bur·row (bûr′ō, bŭr′ō) *n.* A hole or tunnel dug in the ground by an animal. —*v.* **1.** To dig a burrow. **2.** To move or form by or as if by tunneling. [ME *borow.*] —**bur′row·er** *n.*

bur·sa (bûr′sə) *n., pl.* **-sae** (-sē′) or **-sas.** A saclike body cavity, esp. one located between joints. [< Gk., purse.]

bur·sar (bûr′sər, -sär′) *n.* A treasurer, as at a college. [< Gk. *bursa,* purse.] —**bur′sa·ry** *n.*

bur·si·tis (bər-sī′tĭs) *n.* Inflammation of a bursa, esp. in the shoulder, elbow, or knee joints.

burst (bûrst) *v.* **burst, burst·ing. 1.** To force open or fly apart suddenly, esp. from internal pressure. **2.** To be full to the breaking point. **3.** To emerge suddenly and in full force. **4.** To become audible or visible suddenly. **5.** To give sudden utterance or expression: *burst into song.* **6.** *Computer Sci.* To separate (a continuous print-out) into sheets. —*n.* **1.** The act or result of bursting; a rupture or explosion. **2.** A sudden outbreak. [< OE *berstan.*]

bur·y (bĕr′ē) *v.* **-ied, -y·ing. 1.** To place in the ground and cover with earth. **2.** To place (a dead body) in a grave or tomb. **3.** To hide; conceal. **4.** To embed; sink: *found dead with a knife buried in his heart.* **5.** To occupy (oneself) with deep concentration; absorb: *buried myself in my books.* **6.** To put an end to; abandon: *bury an old quarrel.* [< OE *byrgan.*]

bus (bŭs) *n., pl.* **bus·es** or **bus·ses.** A long motor vehicle for carrying passengers. —*v.* **bused** or **bussed, bus·ing** or **bus·sing.** To transport or travel in a bus. [< OMNIBUS.]

bus boy *n.* A waiter's assistant.

bus·by (bŭz′bē) *n., pl.* **-bies.** A tall fur hat worn in certain regiments of the British Army. [Orig. unknown.]

bush (bŏŏsh) *n.* **1.** A low, branching, woody plant; shrub. **2.** Land covered with dense shrubby growth. **3.** A dense growth or tuft. —*v.* To form a dense, tufted growth. —*idiom.* **beat around (or about) the bush.** To delay in getting to the point. [ME.] —**bush′i·ness** *n.* —**bush′y** *adj.*

bushed (bŏŏsht) *adj. Informal.* Extremely tired.

bush·el (bŏŏsh′əl) *n.* **1.** A unit of volume or capacity used in dry measure in the United States and equal to 4 pecks, 35.24 liters, or 2,150.42 cubic inches. **2.** A container with approximately this capacity. [< OFr. *boissel,* of Celt. orig.]

bush·ing (bŏŏsh′ĭng) *n.* A fixed or removable metal lining used to constrain, guide, or reduce friction. [MDu. *busse.*]

bush-league (bŏŏsh′lēg′) *adj. Slang.* Second-rate. —**bush′-leagu′er** *n.*

bush·mas·ter (bŏŏsh′măs′tər) *n.* A large, venomous tropical American snake.

bush pilot *n.* A pilot who flies a small airplane to and from otherwise inaccessible areas.

bush·whack (bŏŏsh′hwăk′, -wăk′) *v.* 1. To travel through thick woods by cutting away bushes and branches. 2. To ambush. —**bush′whack′er** *n.*

busi·ness (bĭz′nĭs) *n.* 1. The occupation in which a person is engaged. 2. Commercial, industrial, or professional dealings. 3. A commercial establishment. 4. Volume of commercial trade. 5. Commercial policy or practice. 6. One's concern or interest. 7. An affair or matter: *a peculiar business.* 8. An incidental action performed by an actor on the stage to fill a pause between lines or to provide interesting detail. —**idiom. give (someone) the business.** To upbraid or treat roughly. **mean business.** To be in earnest.
Syns: business, commerce, industry, trade, traffic *n.*

business administration *n.* A college-level course offering instruction in general business principles and practices.

business card *n.* A small card conveying information about a business or its representative.

busi·ness·like (bĭz′nĭs-līk′) *adj.* Methodical; efficient.

busi·ness·man (bĭz′nĭs-măn′) *n.* A man engaged in business.

busi·ness·wom·an (bĭz′nĭs-wŏŏm′ən) *n.* A woman engaged in business.

bus·ing (bŭs′ĭng) *n.* Also **bus·sing.** The transportation of children by bus to schools outside their neighborhoods, esp. as a means of achieving racial integration.

bus·kin (bŭs′kĭn) *n.* 1. A laced halfboot worn by actors of Greek and Roman tragedies. 2. Tragedy. [OFr. *bouzequin.*]

bus·man's holiday (bŭs′mənz) *n. Informal.* A vacation on which a person engages in recreation similar to his or her usual work.

buss (bŭs) *v.* To kiss loudly. —*n.* A smacking kiss. [Perh. imit.]

bus·ses (bŭs′ĭz) *n.* A pl. of **bus.**

bust[1] (bŭst) *n.* 1. A woman's bosom. 2. A sculpture of a person's head and torso. [< Ital. *busto.*]

bust[2] (bŭst) *Informal.* —*v.* 1. To burst or break. 2. To make or become short of money. 3. To demote. 4. To punch. 5. To place under arrest. 6. To break or tame (a horse). —*n.* 1. A failure. 2. A time of widespread financial depression. 3. An arrest. [< BURST.]

bus·tle[1] (bŭs′əl) *v.* **-tled, -tling.** To hurry energetically and busily. —*n.* Commotion; stir. [Prob. < *busk,* to prepare.]

bus·tle[2] (bŭs′əl) *n.* A frame or pad worn to puff out the back of a woman's skirt. [Orig. unknown.]

bus·y (bĭz′ē) *adj.* **-er, -est.** 1. Actively engaged in some form of work. 2. Crowded with activity. 3. Meddlesome; prying. 4. Temporarily in use, as a telephone line. 5. Cluttered with minute detail: *a busy design.* —*v.* **-ied, -y·ing.** To make busy. [< OE *bisig.*] —**bus′i·ly** *adv.* —**bus′y·ness** *n.*

bus·y·bod·y (bĭz′ē-bŏd′ē) *n., pl.* **-ies.** A meddlesome person.

but (bŭt; *unstressed* bət) *conj.* 1. On the contrary. 2. Contrary to expectation; however. 3. Except; save. 4. Except that: *They should have resisted but they lacked courage.* 5. Without the result that: *It never rains but it pours.* 6. Other than: *I have no goal but to end war.* 7. That. Often used after a negative. 8. That . . . not. Used after a negative or question: *There never is a tax law presented but someone will oppose it.* 9. Who . . . not; which . . . not: *None came to them but were treated well.* —*prep.* With the exception of; barring; save. —*n.* An objection, restriction, or exception: *no ifs, ands, or buts.* [< OE *būtan.*]
Usage: In informal speech *but* is often used together with a negative in sentences like *It won't take but an hour.* This construction should be avoided in formal style; instead, use *It will take only an hour.*

bu·ta·di·ene (byŏŏ′tə-dī′ēn′, -dī-ēn′) *n.* A colorless, highly flammable hydrocarbon, C_4H_6, obtained from petroleum and used in the manufacture of synthetic rubber. [BUTA(NE) + DI- + -ENE.]

bu·tane (byŏŏ′tān′) *n.* Either of two isomers of a gaseous hydrocarbo.., C_4H_{10}, produced synthetically from petroleum and used as a household fuel, refrigerant, and aerosol propellant. [*but(yric acid)* + -ANE.]

butch·er (bŏŏch′ər) *n.* 1. One who slaughters and dresses animals for food. 2. One who sells meat. 3. A cruel or wanton killer. 4. *Informal.* A person who bungles; botcher. —*v.* 1. To slaughter or dress (animals). 2. To kill cruelly or wantonly. 3. To spoil by botching; bungle. [< OFr. *bouchier.*] —**butch′er·er** *n.* —**butch′ery** *n.*

but·ler (bŭt′lər) *n.* The chief male servant of a household. [< OFr. *bouteillier,* a bottle bearer.]

butt[1] (bŭt) *v.* To hit with the head or horns; ram. —**phrasal verb. butt in (or into).** *Informal.* To meddle. —*n.* A push or blow with the head or horns. [< OFr. *bouter,* to strike, of Gmc. orig.]

butt[2] (bŭt) *v.* To attach the ends of; abut. [< OFr. *bouter,* to adjoin.]

butt[3] (bŭt) *n.* One serving as an object of ridicule. [< OFr. *butte.*]

butt[4] (bŭt) *n.* 1. The larger end: *the butt of a rifle.* 2. An unburned end, as of a cigarette. 3. A short or broken remnant; stub. 4. *Slang.* A cigarette. 5. *Informal.* The buttocks. [ME *butte.*]

butte (byŏŏt) *n.* A hill that rises sharply from the surrounding area and has a flat top. [< OFr. *butt,* mound behind targets.]

but·ter (bŭt′ər) *n.* 1. A soft, yellowish, fatty substance churned from milk or cream and used as a food. 2. A similar substance. —*v.* 1. To put butter on. 2. *Informal.* To flatter. [< Gk. *bouturon.*] —**but′tery** *adj.*

but·ter·cup (bŭt′ər-kŭp′) *n.* A plant with glossy yellow flowers.

but·ter·fat (bŭt′ər-făt′) *n.* The oily content of milk from which butter is made.

but·ter·fin·gers (bŭt′ər-fĭng′gərz) *n. (used with a sing. verb).* A clumsy, awkward person who drops things.

but·ter·fish (bŭt′ər-fĭsh′) *n.* A North American marine food fish with a flattened body. [< its slippery mucous coating:]

but·ter·fly (bŭt′ər-flī′) n. Any of various narrow-bodied insects with four broad, usu. colorful wings. [< OE buttorflēoge.]

but·ter·milk (bŭt′ər-mĭlk′) n. The thick, sour liquid that remains after the butterfat has been removed from whole milk or cream by churning.

but·ter·nut (bŭt′ər-nŭt′) n. 1. An eastern North American tree with compound leaves and egg-shaped nuts. 2. The edible, oily nut of the butternut tree. 3. The hard, grayish-brown wood of the butternut tree. [< the nut's oiliness.]

butternut squash n. A small, pear-shaped winter squash.

but·ter·scotch (bŭt′ər-skŏch′) n. 1. A syrup, sauce, or flavoring made by melting butter and brown sugar. 2. A candy made from these ingredients.

but·tock (bŭt′ək) n. 1. Either of the two rounded fleshy parts of the rump. 2. **buttocks.** The rump. [ME.]

but·ton (bŭt′n) n. 1. A small knob or disk, esp. one sewn on a garment as a fastener or trimming. 2. Any of various objects of similar appearance. —v. To fasten with a button or buttons. —*Idiom.* **on the button.** *Informal.* Exactly; precisely. [< OFr. bouton.] —**but′ton·er** n.

but·ton-down (bŭt′n-doun′) adj. 1. Having the ends of the collar fastened down by buttons. 2. Conservative, conventional, and unimaginative.

but·ton·hole (bŭt′n-hōl′) n. A slit or hole in a garment or in cloth used to hold and fasten a button. —v. **-holed, -hol·ing.** 1. To make a buttonhole (in). 2. To stop and detain in conversation.

but·tress (bŭt′rĭs) n. 1. A structure, usu. brick or stone, built against a wall for support. 2. Something that serves to support. —v. To brace or reinforce with or as if with a buttress. [< OFr. bouter, to strike against.]

bu·tut (boō′toōt′) n., pl. **-tut** or **-tuts.** See table at **currency.** [Native word in Gambia.]

bux·om (bŭk′səm) adj. Ample of figure, esp. in the bosom. [ME, obedient.]

buy (bī) v. **bought** (bôt), **buy·ing.** 1. To acquire in exchange for money; purchase. 2. To be capable of purchasing. 3. To acquire by sacrifice or exchange. 4. To bribe. 5. *Slang.* To accept the truth or feasibility of; believe: *I'll never buy that story.* —*phrasal verbs.* **buy in.** To purchase stock or interest, as in a company. **buy off.** To bribe. **buy out.** To purchase the controlling stock, business rights, or interests of (a person). **buy up.** To purchase all that is available (of). —n. 1. Something bought. 2. *Informal.* A bargain. [< OE bycgan.] —**buy′a·ble** adj. —**buy′er** n.

buzz (bŭz) v. 1. To make a low droning or vibrating sound like that of a bee. 2. To talk excitedly in low tones. 3. To move quickly and busily; bustle. 4. To signal (a person) with a buzzer. 5. *Informal.* To telephone (a person): *Buzz me later.* —n. 1. A rapidly vibrating, humming, or droning sound. 2. A low murmur. 3. *Informal.* A telephone call. 4. *Slang.* Pleasant intoxication. [ME bussen.]

buz·zard (bŭz′ərd) n. 1. Any of various North American vultures. 2. *Chiefly Brit.* Any of various broad-winged hawks. [< OFr. busard.]

buzz·er (bŭz′ər) n. An electric signaling device that makes a buzzing sound.

buzz saw n. A circular saw.

buzz word n. A usu. important-sounding word connected with a specialized field that is used esp. to impress laypersons.

by (bī) prep. 1. Next to. 2. With the use of; through. 3. Up to and beyond; past. 4. In the period of; during: *sleeping by day.* 5. Not later than: *by 5:00 P.M.* 6. In the amount of: *letters by the thousands.* 7. To the extent of: *shorter by two inches.* 8. According to: *by my own account.* 9. In the presence or name of. 10. Through the agency or action of: *killed by a bullet.* 11. In succession to; after: *day by day.* 12. In behalf of; for: *You do well by your employees.* 13. Used to link certain expressions to be taken together and indicating: **a.** multiplication of quantities. **b.** coordination of measurements: *a room 12 by 18 feet.* —adv. 1. On hand; nearby: *stand by.* 2. Aside; away: *putting it by for later.* 3. Up to, alongside, and past: *The car raced by.* 4. Into the past: *as years go by.* —*idioms.* **by and by.** Before long. **by and large.** On the whole. **by the way.** Incidentally. [< OE bi.]

by- pref. 1. By: bygone. 2. Secondary: byway. [ME.]

by-and-by (bī′ən-bī′) n. 1. Some future time. 2. The hereafter.

bye (bī) n. 1. A secondary matter; side issue. 2. *Sports.* The position of one who draws no opponent for a round in a tournament and so advances to the next round. —*Idiom.* **by the bye.** Incidentally. [< BY.]

bye-bye (bī′bī′) interj. *Informal.* Used to express farewell. [< GOOD-BYE.]

by·gone (bī′gôn′, -gŏn′) adj. Past; former: *bygone days.* —n. A past occurrence. —*Idiom.* **let bygones be bygones.** To forget past differences.

by·law (bī′lô′) n. A law or rule governing the internal affairs of an organization. [ME bilawe, local regulation.]

by-line (bī′līn′) n. Also **by·line.** A line at the head of a newspaper or magazine article with the author's name. —**by′-lin′er** n.

by-pass (bī′păs′). Also **by·pass.** —n. 1. A road or highway that passes around or to one side of an obstructed or congested area. 2. *Elect.* A shunt. 3. **a.** A surgically created alternative passage between two blood vessels. **b.** An operation to create a by-pass. —v. To go around instead of through.

by-path (bī′păth′, -päth′) n. A side path.

by-play (bī′plā′) n. Theatrical action or speech taking place while the main action proceeds.

by-prod·uct (bī′prŏd′əkt) n. 1. Something produced in the making of something else. 2. A side effect.

by·stand·er (bī′stăn′dər) n. One who is present at some event without participating in it.

byte (bīt) n. A sequence of adjacent binary digits operated on as a unit by a computer and usu. shorter than a word. [< BIT[3] and BITE.]

by·way (bī′wā′) n. 1. A side road. 2. A secondary or overlooked field of study.

by·word (bī′wûrd′) n. 1. A proverb. 2. One that proverbially represents a type, class, or quality: *Quisling has become a byword for traitor.*

Byz·an·tine (bĭz'ən-tēn', -tīn', bĭ-zăn'tĭn) *adj.*
1. Of, pertaining to, or characteristic of Byzantium, its inhabitants, or their culture.
2. Of or designating the ornate, intricate style of architecture developed from the 5th cent. A.D. in Byzantium. 3. Of the Eastern Orthodox Church or the rites performed in it.
4. **a.** Characterized by intrigue. **b.** Highly complex: *a Byzantine plot.* —*n.* A native or inhabitant of Byzantium.

Byzantine

Cc

c or **C** (sē) *n.*, *pl.* **c's** or **C's.** 1. The 3rd letter of the English alphabet. 2. The 3rd in a series. 3. The 3rd-highest in quality or rank. 4. **C** The Roman numeral for 100.
C The symbol for the element carbon.
Ca The symbol for the element calcium.
cab (kăb) *n.* 1. A taxicab. 2. A compartment for the operator of a heavy vehicle or machine. [< TAXICAB.]
ca·bal (kə-băl') *n.* 1. A conspiratorial group. 2. A secret plot. —*v.* **-balled, -bal·ling.** To form a cabal. [< Heb. *qabbālāh*, tradition.]
cab·a·la (kăb'ə-lə, kə-bä'-) *n.* 1. An occult theosophy of rabbinical origin based on an esoteric interpretation of the Hebrew Scriptures. 2. An esoteric or occult doctrine. [< Heb. *qabbālāh*, tradition.] —**cab'a·lism** *n.* —**cab'a·list** *n.* —**cab·a·lis'tic** (kăb'ə-lĭs'tĭk) *adj.* —**cab·a·lis'ti·cal·ly** *adv.*
ca·ban·a (kə-băn'ə, -băn'yə) *n.* A shelter on a beach, used as a bathhouse. [Sp. *cabaña.*]
cab·a·ret (kăb'ə-rā') *n.* 1. A restaurant providing short programs of live entertainment. 2. The floor show in a cabaret. [< ONFr., a shop selling liquor.]
cab·bage (kăb'ĭj) *n.* A plant with a short, thick stalk and a large head formed by tightly overlapping leaves, eaten as a vegetable. [< OFr. *caboce*, head.]

cabbage   cabin

cab·by or **cab·bie** (kăb'ē) *n.*, *pl.* **-bies.** *Informal.* A cab driver.
cab·in (kăb'ĭn) *n.* 1. A small, simply built house. 2. **a.** A room used as living quarters on a ship. **b.** An enclosed compartment on a boat or airplane. [LLat. *capanna*, hut.]

cabin boy *n.* A boy functioning as a servant on a ship.
cabin class *n.* A class of accommodations on some passenger ships, lower than first class and higher than tourist class.
cabin cruiser *n.* A powerboat with a cabin.
cab·i·net (kăb'ə-nĭt) *n.* 1. An upright case or cupboard with shelves, drawers, or compartments for the safekeeping or display of objects. 2. Often **Cabinet.** The body of persons appointed by a chief of state or a prime minister to head the executive departments of the government and to act as official advisers. [< ONFr. *cabine*, gambling house.]
cab·i·net·mak·er (kăb'ə-nĭt-mā'kər) *n.* A craftsman who makes fine articles of wooden furniture. —**cab'i·net·mak'ing** *n.*
cab·i·net·work (kăb'ə-nĭt-wûrk') *n.* Finished furniture made by a cabinetmaker.
cabin fever *n.* Uneasiness due to a lack of environmental stimulation.
ca·ble (kā'bəl) *n.* 1. A large-diameter steel or fiber rope. 2. A bound or sheathed group of mutually insulated conductors. 3. A cablegram. 4. Cable television. —*v.* **-bled, -bling.** To send a cablegram to. [Med. Lat. *capulum*, lasso.]
cable car *n.* A vehicle pulled by a cable that moves in an endless loop.
ca·ble·cast (kā'bəl-kăst') *n.* A telecast by cable television. —**ca'ble·cast'** *v.* —**ca'ble·cast'er** *n.*
ca·ble·gram (kā'bəl-grăm') *n.* A telegram sent by underwater cable.
cable television *n.* A commercial television system in which signals are received by a single antenna and delivered to subscribers' receivers by means of a cable.
ca·ble·vi·sion (kā'bəl-vĭzh'ən) *n.* Cable television.
cab·o·chon (kăb'ə-shŏn') *n.* A highly polished, convex-cut, unfaceted gem. [OFr.]
ca·boo·dle (kə-bōōd'l) *n.* *Informal.* The whole lot, group, or bunch. [Perh. a blend of KIT + BOODLE.]
ca·boose (kə-bōōs') *n.* The last car on a freight train, with kitchen and sleeping facilities for the train crew. [Perh. < Du. *kabuis*, a ship's galley.]

cab·ri·o·let (kăb′rē-ə-lā′) *n.* **1.** A light, two-wheeled one-horse carriage with two seats and a folding top. **2.** A convertible coupé. [Fr.]

ca·ca·o (kə-kā′ō, -kä′ō) *n., pl.* **-os.** **1.** An evergreen tropical American tree having yellowish flowers and reddish-brown seed pods. **2.** The seed of this tree, used in making chocolate, cocoa, and cocoa butter. [< Nahuatl *cacahuati,* cacao bean.]

cach·a·lot (kăsh′ə-lŏt′, -lō′) *n.* The sperm whale. [Fr.]

cache (kăsh) *n.* **1.** A hiding place used for storage. **2.** A place for concealing and safekeeping valuables. **3.** A store of goods hidden in a cache. —*v.* **cached, cach·ing.** To store in a hiding place for future use. [Fr.]

ca·chet (kă-shā′) *n.* **1.** A seal on a letter or document. **2.** A mark of distinction, individuality, or authenticity. [< OFr.]

cack·le (kăk′əl) *v.* **-led, -ling.** **1.** To make the shrill cry characteristic of a hen after laying an egg. **2.** To laugh or talk in a shrill, broken manner. —*n.* **1.** The act or sound of cackling. **2.** Shrill, brittle laughter. [ME *cakelen.*] —**cack′ler** *n.*

ca·coph·o·ny (kə-kŏf′ə-nē) *n., pl.* **-nies.** Harsh, jarring, discordant sound; dissonance. [< Gk. *kakophōnos,* dissonant.] —**ca·coph′o·nous** *adj.* —**ca·coph′o·nous·ly** *adv.*

cac·tus (kăk′təs) *n., pl.* **-ti** (-tī′) or **-tus·es.** Any of various leafless, fleshy-stemmed, often spiny plants of arid regions. [< Gk. *kaktos,* a kind of plant.]

cad (kăd) *n.* An ungentlemanly man. [< CADDIE.] —**cad′dish** *adj.* —**cad′dish·ly** *adv.* —**cad′dish·ness** *n.*

ca·dav·er (kə-dăv′ər) *n.* A dead body. [Lat.] —**ca·dav′er·ic** *adj.*

ca·dav·er·ous (kə-dăv′ər-əs) *adj.* Resembling a corpse; pale and gaunt. —**ca·dav′er·ous·ly** *adv.* —**ca·dav′er·ous·ness** *n.*

cad·die (kăd′ē). Also **cad·dy.** —*n., pl.* **-dies.** A person hired by a golfer to carry the clubs. —*v.* **-died, -dy·ing.** To serve as a caddie. [Fr. *cadet.*]

Cad·do·an (kăd′ō-ən) *n.* A family of North American Indian languages formerly spoken in the Dakotas, Nebraska, Kansas, Oklahoma, Arkansas, Texas, and Louisiana.

cad·dy (kăd′ē) *n., pl.* **-dies.** A small container, esp. for tea. [< Malay *kati,* a unit of weight.]

ca·dence (kād′ns) *n.* Also **ca·den·cy** (kād′n-sē) *pl.* **-cies.** **1.** Balanced, rhythmic flow or movement. **2.** Vocal inflection or modulation. **3.** *Mus.* A progression of chords moving to a harmonic close. [< Lat. *cadere,* to fall.]

ca·den·za (kə-děn′zə) *n.* An ornamental flourish or section, as near the end of a movement of a concerto. [Ital.]

ca·det (kə-dět′) *n.* **1.** A student training to be an officer at a military or naval academy. **2.** A younger son or brother. [Fr.]

cadge (kăj) *v.* **cadged, cadg·ing.** *Informal.* To get by begging; mooch. [< ME *cadgear,* peddler.]

cad·mi·um (kăd′mē-əm) *n. Symbol* **Cd** A soft, bluish-white metallic element used in low-friction alloys, solders, dental amalgams, and nickel-cadmium storage batteries. Atomic number 48; atomic weight 112.40. [< Lat. *cadmia,* zinc ore.] —**cad′mic** (-mĭk) *adj.*

ca·dre (kăd′rē) *n.* A nucleus of trained personnel. [< Lat. *quadrum,* square.]

ca·du·ce·us (kə-dōō′sē-əs, -dyōō′-) *n., pl.* **-ce·i** (-sē-ī′). A winged staff with two serpents twined around it, used as the symbol of the medical profession. [Lat.]

cae·cum (sē′kəm) *n.* Var. of cecum.

Cae·sar (sē′zər) *n.* **1.** A title of the Roman emperors after Augustus. **2.** A dictator or autocrat.

Cae·sar·e·an (sĭ-zâr′ē-ən) *adj.* Also **Cae·sar·i·an** or **Ce·sar·e·an** or **Ce·sar·i·an.** Pertaining to Julius Caesar or the Caesars. —*n.* A Caesarean section.

Caesarean section or **caesarean section** *n.* A surgical incision through the abdominal wall and uterus, performed to extract a fetus.

cae·si·um (sē′zē-əm) *n.* Var. of cesium.

cae·su·ra (sĭ-zhōōr′ə, -zōōr′ə) *n., pl.* **-ras** or **-su·rae** (-zhōōr′ē, -zōōr′ē). A pause in phrasing a metrical line. [Lat.] —**cae·su′ral** or **cae·su′ric** *adj.*

ca·fé (kă-fā′, kə-) *n.* **1.** A restaurant. **2.** A bar. **3.** A cabaret. [Fr.]

café au lait (ō lā′) *n.* **1.** Coffee with hot milk. **2.** A light yellowish brown. [Fr.]

caf·e·te·ri·a (kăf′ĭ-tîr′ē-ə) *n.* A restaurant in which the customers are served at a counter and carry their meals on trays to tables. [Sp. *cafetería,* coffee shop.]

caf·feine (kă-fēn′, kăf′ēn′, -ē-ĭn) *n.* Also **caf·fein.** A bitter white alkaloid, $C_8H_{10}N_4O_2 \cdot H_2O$, derived from coffee, tea, and cola nuts, and used as a stimulant and diuretic. [G. *Kaffein.*]

caf·tan (kăf′tən, kăf-tän′) *n.* A full-length tunic with long sleeves, worn esp. in the Near East. [< Turk. *caftan.*]

cage (kāj) *n.* **1. a.** A barred or grated enclosure for confining birds or animals. **b.** A similar enclosure or structure. **2.** *Baseball.* **a.** A backstop used for batting practices. **b.** A catcher's mask. **3.** *Basketball.* The basket. **4.** *Hockey.* The goal. —*v.* **caged, cag·ing.** To put in a cage. [< Lat. *cavea.*]

ca·gey (kā′jē) *adj.* **-gi·er, -gi·est.** Also **ca·gy.** Wary; careful; shrewd. [Orig. unknown.] —**ca′gi·ly** *adv.* —**ca′gi·ness** *n.*

ca·hoots (kə-hōōts′) *pl.n. Informal.* Partnership. —*idiom.* **in cahoots.** Working together secretly. [Orig. unknown.]

Ca·huil·la (kə-wē′ə) *n.* A Shoshonean language of southeastern California.

cai·man (kā′mən, kā-măn′, kī-) *n., pl.* **-mans.** Any of various tropical American reptiles closely related to the alligators. [< Carib *acayuman.*]

Cain (kān) *n.* **1.** In the Bible, the eldest son of Adam and Eve, who killed his brother Abel. **2.** A murderer. —*idiom.* **raise Cain.** *Slang.* To create a disturbance; make trouble.

cairn (kârn) *n.* A mound of stones erected as a landmark or memorial. [ME *carne,* of Celt. orig.]

cais·son (kā′sŏn′, -sən) *n.* **1.** A watertight structure within which underwater construction work is done. **2.** A watertight compartment used to raise a sunken ship. **3.** *Mil.* **a.** A large box used to hold ammunition. **b.** A horse-drawn two-wheeled vehicle formerly used for carrying ammunition. [Fr.]

caisson disease *n.* A disorder caused by too rapid a return from high pressure to atmospheric pressure, characterized by cramps, paralysis, and eventual death unless treated by gradual decompression.

cal·tiff (kă′tĭf) *adj.* Base and cowardly. [< Lat. *captivus,* captive.] —**cal′tiff** *n.*

ca·jole (kə-jōl′) *v.* **-joled, -jol·ing.** To coax;

wheedle. [Fr. *cajoler*.] —**ca·jol′er** *n.* —**ca·jol′-er·y** *n.*

Ca·jun (kā′jən) *n.* A native of Louisiana believed to be descended from the French exiles from Acadia.

cake (kāk) *n.* **1.** A sweet food made from baked batter or dough. **2.** A thin baked or fried portion of batter or other food. **3.** A shaped mass, as of soap. —*v.* **caked, cak·ing.** To make or become a hard or compact mass. [ON *kaka*.]

cal·a·bash (kăl′ə-băsh′) *n.* A large, hard-shelled gourd often used as a utensil. [< Sp. *calabaza*.]

cal·a·boose (kăl′ə-bōōs′) *n.* Slang. A jail. [< Sp. *calabozo*, dungeon.]

cal·a·mine (kăl′ə-mīn′, -mĭn) *n.* Pharm. A pink powder of zinc oxide with a small amount of ferric oxide, dissolved in mineral oils and used in skin lotions. [Med. Lat. *calamina*.]

ca·lam·i·ty (kə-lăm′ĭ-tē) *n., pl.* **-ties.** **1.** A disaster. **2.** Great distress. [< Lat. *calamitas*.] —**ca·lam′i·tous** *adj.* —**ca·lam′i·tous·ly** *adv.* —**ca·lam′i·tous·ness** *n.*

cal·car·e·ous (kăl-kâr′ē-əs) *adj.* Of or containing calcium carbonate, calcium, or limestone; chalky. [Lat. *calcarius*.]

cal·ces (kăl′sēz′) *n.* A pl. of **calx.**

calci– or **calc–** *pref.* Calcium: *calciferous.* [< Lat. *calx*, limestone.]

cal·cif·er·ous (kăl-sĭf′ər-əs) *adj.* Of, forming, or containing calcium or calcium carbonate.

cal·ci·fy (kăl′sə-fī′) *v.* **-fied, -fy·ing.** To make or become calcareous. —**cal′ci·fi·ca′tion** *n.*

cal·ci·mine (kăl′sə-mīn′) *n.* A white or tinted mixture of zinc oxide, water, and glue, used to coat walls and ceilings. [Orig. unknown.]

cal·cine (kăl′sīn′) *v.* **-cined, -cin·ing.** To heat to a high temperature but below the melting or fusing point, causing loss of moisture, reduction, or oxidation. —**cal′ci·na′tion** (kăl′sə-nā′shən) *n.*

cal·cite (kăl′sīt′) *n.* A common crystalline form of calcium carbonate. —**cal·cit′ic** (-sĭt′-ĭk) *adj.*

cal·ci·um (kăl′sē-əm) *n.* Symbol **Ca** A silvery metallic element that occurs in bone, shells, limestone, and gypsum and forms compounds used to make plaster, quicklime, cement, and metallurgic and electronic materials. Atomic number 20; atomic weight 40.08.

calcium carbonate *n.* A colorless or white crystalline compound, $CaCO_3$, occurring naturally as chalk, limestone, and marble, and used in commercial chalk, medicines, and dentifrices.

calcium chloride *n.* A white deliquescent compound, $CaCl_2$, used chiefly as a drying agent, refrigerant, and preservative and for controlling dust and ice on roads.

calcium hydroxide *n.* A soft white powder, $Ca(OH)_2$, used in making mortar, cements, calcium salts, paints, and petrochemicals.

calcium oxide *n.* A white caustic lumpy powder, CaO, used as a refractory, as a flux, in manufacturing steel, glassmaking, waste treatment, and insecticides.

cal·cu·late (kăl′kyə-lāt′) *v.* **-lat·ed, -lat·ing.** **1.** To compute mathematically. **2.** To estimate; reckon. **3.** To intend; plan. [Lat. *calcu-*

lare.] —**cal′cu·la·ble** *adj.* —**cal′cu·la·bly** *adv.* —**cal′cu·la′tive** *adj.*

cal·cu·lat·ed (kăl′kyə-lā′tĭd) *adj.* Estimated with careful forethought: *a calculated risk.* —**cal′cu·lat′ed·ly** *adv.*

cal·cu·lat·ing (kăl′kyə-lā′tĭng) *adj.* **1.** Used in or for performing calculations. **2.** Coldly scheming or conniving.

cal·cu·la·tion (kăl′kyə-lā′shən) *n.* **1.** The act, process, or result of calculating. **2.** Deliberation; foresight.

cal·cu·la·tor (kăl′kyə-lā′tər) *n.* **1.** One who performs calculations. **2.** A mechanical or electronic machine that automatically performs mathematical operations.

cal·cu·lus (kăl′kyə-ləs) *n., pl.* **-li** (-lī′) or **-lus·es.** **1.** Med. An abnormal mineral concretion in the body, such as a stone in the gallbladder. **2.** The combined mathematics of differential and integral calculus. [Lat., pebble.]

cal·dron (kôl′drən) *n.* Also **caul·dron.** A large kettle or vat. [< LLat. *caldaria*.]

cal·en·dar (kăl′ən-dər) *n.* **1.** A system of reckoning time divisions and days. **2.** A table showing such divisions, usu. for a year. **3.** A chronological list or schedule. —*v.* To enter on a calendar. [< Lat. *calendarium*, moneylender's account book.]

cal·en·der (kăl′ən-dər) *n.* A machine in which paper or cloth is given a smooth, glossy finish by being pressed between rollers. —*v.* To treat with a calender. [< Gk. *kulindros*, roller.]

cal·ends (kăl′əndz, kā′ləndz) *n., pl.* **-ends.** The 1st day of the month in the ancient Roman calendar. [< Lat. *kalendae*.]

calf¹ (kăf, käf) *n., pl.* **calves** (kăvz, kävz). **1.** The young of cattle or certain other large mammals, as the elephants. **2.** Calfskin. [< OE *cealf.*]

calf² (kăf, käf) *n., pl.* **calves** (kăvz, kävz). The fleshy, muscular back part of the human leg between the knee and ankle. [< ON *kalfi.*]

calf·skin (kăf′skĭn′, käf′-) *n.* **1.** The hide of a calf. **2.** Fine leather made from the hide of a calf.

cal·i·ber (kăl′ə-bər) *n.* Also *chiefly Brit.* **cal·i·bre.** **1.** The diameter of the inside of a tube, esp. the bore of a firearm. **2.** The diameter of a bullet or shell. **3.** Degree of worth or distinction. [< Ar. *qālib*, mold.]

cal·i·brate (kăl′ə-brāt′) *v.* **-brat·ed, -brat·ing.** **1.** To check or adjust the graduations of a quantitative measuring instrument. **2.** To measure the caliber of. —**cal′i·bra′tion** *n.* —**cal′i·bra′tor** *n.*

cal·i·co (kăl′ĭ-kō′) *n., pl.* **-coes** or **-cos.** A coarse cloth, usu. printed with bright designs. —*adj.* Covered with spots of different colors; mottled: *a calico cat.* [< *Calicut* (Kozhikode), India.]

Cal·i·for·nia poppy (kăl′ə-fôr′nyə) *n.* A plant of the Pacific Coast of North America, with bluish-green leaves and orange-yellow flowers.

cal·i·for·ni·um (kăl′ə-fôr′nē-əm) *n.* Symbol **Cf** A synthetic radioactive element produced in trace quantities by helium isotope bombardment of curium. Atomic number 98; longest-lived isotope Cf 251. [< *California.*]

cal·i·per (kăl′ə-pər) *n.* Also **cal·li·per.** **1.** Often **calipers** (*used with a pl. verb*). An instrument consisting of two curved hinged legs or jaws,

MONTHS OF THREE PRINCIPAL CALENDARS

GREGORIAN		HEBREW		MOSLEM	
		Months correspond approximately to those in parentheses		Beginning of year retrogresses through the solar year of the Gregorian calendar	
name	number of days	name	number of days	name	number of days
January	31	Tishri (September–October)	30	Muharram	30
February in leap year	28 29	Heshvan in some years (October–November)	29 30	Safar	29
March	31	Kislev in some years (November–December)	29 30	Rabi I	30
April	30	Tevet (December–January)	29	Rabi II	29
May	31	Shevat (January–February)	30	Jumada I	30
June	30	Adar* in leap year (February–March)	29 30	Jumada II	29
July	31	Nisan (March–April)	30	Rajab	30
August	31	Iyar (April–May)	29	Sha`ban	29
September	30	Sivan (May–June)	30	Ramadan	30
October	31	Tammuz (June–July)	29	Shawwal	29
November	30	Av (July–August)	30	Dhu'l-Qa dah	30
December	31	Elul (August–September)	29	Dhu'l-Hijja in leap year	29 30

*Adar is followed in leap year by the intercalary month Veadar, or Adar Sheni, having 29 days.

used to measure internal and external dimensions. **2.** A vernier caliper. [< CALIBER.]

ca·liph (kā′lĭf, kăl′ĭf) *n.* Also **ca·lif.** The political and religious head of a Moslem state. [< Ar. *khalīfa.*] —**ca·liph·ate** (-fāt′, -fĭt) *n.*

cal·is·then·ics (kăl′ĭs-thĕn′ĭks) *n. (used with a sing. or pl. verb).* Exercises designed to develop muscular tone and to promote physical well-being. [Gk. *kallos,* beauty + Gk. *sthenos,* strength.] —**cal·is·then·ic** *adj.*

calk (kôk) *v.* Var. of caulk.

call (kôl) *v.* **1.** To cry or utter loudly or clearly. **2.** To summon. **3.** To telephone. **4.** To name; designate. **5.** To consider; estimate. **6.** To pay a brief visit. **7.** To demand payment of (a loan or bond issue). **8.** *Baseball.* To stop (a game) officially. **9.** *Poker.* To demand that an opponent show his cards. —*phrasal verbs.* **call back.** To telephone in return. **call down. 1.** To invoke, as from heaven. **2.** To find fault with. **call for. 1.** To go and get or stop for. **2.** To be appropriate for; warrant. **call forth.** To evoke. **call in. 1.** To take out of circulation: *call in silver dollars.* **2.** To summon for assistance or consultation. **call off. 1.** To cancel or postpone.

2. To recall; restrain: *Call off your hounds!* **call on** (or **upon**). **1.** To pay a short visit to. **2.** To appeal to (someone) to do something. **call out. 1.** To cause to assemble; summon. **call up. 1.** To summon into military service. **2.** To remember or cause to remember: *call up old times.* **3.** To telephone. —*n.* **1. a.** A shout or loud cry. **b.** A characteristic cry, esp. of a bird. **2.** A summons or invitation. **3.** Demand; need. **4.** A short visit. **5.** A communication by telephone. —*idioms.* **call into question.** To raise doubts about. **call to mind.** To remind of. **close call.** A narrow escape. **on call. 1.** Available when summoned. **2.** Payable on demand. **within call.** Accessible. [< ON *kalla.*] —**call′er** *n.*

cal·la (kăl′ə) *n.* Also **calla lily.** A plant with a showy, usu. white petallike leaf enclosing a clublike flower stalk. [< Gk. *kallaia,* rooster's wattle.]

call·back (kôl′băk′) *n.* A recall of a recently sold product by the manufacturer to correct a defect.

cal·lig·ra·phy (kə-lĭg′rə-fē) *n.* **1.** The art of fine handwriting. **2.** Penmanship; handwriting. [Gk. *kalligraphia.*] —**cal·lig′ra·pher** or

call·lig'ra·phist n. —**cal'li·graph'ic** (kăl'ĭ-grăf'-ĭk) adj.

call·in (kôl'ĭn') adj. Inviting listeners to make broadcasted telephone calls: a call-in radio show.

call·ing (kô'lĭng) n. 1. An inner urge; strong impulse. 2. An occupation; vocation.

cal·li·o·pe (kə-lī'ə-pē', kăl'ē-ōp') n. A musical instrument fitted with steam whistles, played from a keyboard. [< Calliope, Muse of epic poetry.]

call·li·per (kăl'ə-pər) n. Var. of caliper.

call letters·pl.n. The series of letters or letters and numbers that identifies a radio or television station.

call loan n. A loan repayable on demand at any time.

call number n. A set of letters and numbers used to indicate the placement of a library book on the shelves.

cal·los·i·ty (kă-lŏs'ĭ-tē, kə-) n., pl. -ties. 1. a. A callus. b. The condition of having calluses. 2. Lack of feeling; hardheartedness.

cal·lous (kăl'əs) adj. 1. Having calluses; toughened. 2. Insensitive; unfeeling. —v. To make or become callous. [< Lat. callosus.] —**cal'lous·ly** adv. —**cal'lous·ness** n.

cal·low (kăl'ō) adj. Immature; inexperienced: a callow youth. [< OE calu, bald.] —**cal'low·ly** adv. —**cal'low·ness** n.

call·up (kôl'ŭp') n. An order to report for military service.

cal·lus (kăl'əs) n., pl. -lus·es. A localized thickening and enlargement of the horny layer of the skin. —v. To form or develop a callus. [Lat.]

calm (käm) adj. -er, -est. 1. Nearly or completely motionless and undisturbed: calm seas. 2. Not excited; quiet; serene. —n. 1. An absence of motion; stillness. 2. Serenity; tranquility; peace. —v. To make or become calm. [< OItal. calma.] —**calm'ly** adv. —**calm'ness** n.
Syns: calm, peaceful, placid, quiet, serene, still, tranquil adj.

cal·o·mel (kăl'ə-měl', -məl) n. A white, tasteless compound, Hg_2Cl_2, formerly used as a purgative. [Fr.]

cal·o·rie (kăl'ə-rē) n. 1. The amount of heat required to raise the temperature of 1 gram of water by 1°C at 1 atmosphere pressure; small calorie. 2. The amount of heat required to raise the temperature of 1 kilogram of water by 1°C at 1 atmosphere pressure; large calorie. [< Lat. calor, heat.] —**ca·lor'ic** (kə-lôr'ĭk, -lŏr'-) adj.

cal·o·rif·ic (kăl'ə-rĭf'ĭk) adj. Pertaining to heat.

cal·o·rim·e·ter (kăl'ə-rĭm'ĭ-tər) n. An instrument that measures and indicates heat.

cal·u·met (kăl'yə-mět', kăl'yə-mět') n. A long-stemmed pipe smoked by North American Indians for ceremonial purposes. [< dial. Fr., straw.]

ca·lum·ni·ate (kə-lŭm'nē-āt') v. -at·ed, -at·ing. To make malicious false statements about; slander. —**ca·lum'ni·a'tion** n. —**ca·lum'ni·a'tor** n.

cal·um·ny (kăl'əm-nē) n., pl. -nies. A maliciously false and injurious statement; slander.

[< Lat. calumnia.] —**ca·lum'ni·ous** adj. —**ca·lum'ni·ous·ly** adv.

calve (kăv, käv) v. calved, calv·ing. To give birth to a calf.

calves (kăvz, kävz) n. Pl. of calf.

Cal·vin·ism (kăl'və-nĭz'əm) n. The doctrine of John Calvin (1509–64), esp. his affirmation of predestination and redemption by grace alone. —**Cal'vin·ist** n. —**Cal'vin·is'tic** adj.

calx (kălks) n., pl. calx·es or cal·ces (kăl'sēz'). 1. The crumbly residue left after a mineral or metal has been calcined. 2. Calcium oxide. [< Gk. khalix, pebble.]

ca·lyp·so (kə-lĭp'sō) n. A type of West Indian music with improvised lyrics on topical or humorous subjects. [< Calypso, a sea nymph in Homer's Odyssey.]

ca·lyx (kā'lĭks, kăl'ĭks) n., pl. -lyx·es or ca·ly·ces (kā'lĭ-sēz', kăl'ĭ-). The usu. green segmented outer envelope of a flower. [< Gk. kalux.]

cam (kăm) n. A multiply curved wheel mounted on a rotating shaft and used to produce reciprocating motion. [Du., comb.]

ca·ma·ra·de·rie (kä'mə-rä'də-rē, kăm'ə-räd'ə-) n. Comradely good will among friends. [Fr.]

cam·ber (kăm'bər) n. 1. A slightly arched surface, as of a road. 2. The adjustment of automobile wheels so that they are closer together at the bottom than at the top. [< OFr. cambre.] —**cam'ber** n.

cam·bi·um (kăm'bē-əm) n. A layer of cells in the stems and roots of vascular plants that gives rise to phloem and xylem. [< Med. Lat., change.] —**cam'bi·al** adj.

Cam·bri·an (kăm'brē-ən) adj. Of or belonging to the geologic time, rock system, or sedimentary deposits of the first period of the Paleozoic era. —n. The Cambrian period.

cam·bric (kăm'brĭk) n. A fine white linen or cotton fabric. [< Cambrai, France.]

cam·e (kăm) v. p.t. of come.

cam·el (kăm'əl) n. A long-necked, humped ruminant mammal of northern Africa and western Asia, used in desert regions as a beast of burden. [< Gk. kamēlos, of Semitic orig.]

ca·mel·lia (kə-mēl'yə, -mēl'ē-ə) n. 1. The showy, many-petaled flower of an evergreen shrub. 2. The shrub itself. [< George J. Kamel (1661–1706).]

Cam·e·lot (kăm'ə-lŏt') n. 1. A legendary town where King Arthur had his court. 2. A place or time marked by idealized beauty, peacefulness, and enlightenment.

camel's hair n. Also camel hair. 1. The soft, fine hair of a camel or a substitute for it. 2. A soft, heavy cloth, usu. light tan, made chiefly of camel's hair.

cam·e·o (kăm'ē-ō') n., pl. -os. A gem or medallion with a design cut in raised relief, usu. of a contrasting color. [< OSp. camafeo.]

cam·er·a (kăm'ər-ə, kăm'rə) n. 1. An apparatus consisting of a lightproof enclosure having an aperture with a shuttered lens through which the image of an object is focused and recorded on a photosensitive film or plate. 2. The part of a television transmitting apparatus that receives the primary image and transforms it into electrical impulses. [< Gk. kamara, vault.]

cam·er·a·man (kăm'ər-ə-măn', kăm'rə-) n.

The operator of a motion-picture or television camera.

cam·i·sole (kăm'ĭ-sōl') n. A woman's short, sleeveless undergarment. [< LLat. *camisia*, shirt.]

cam·o·mile (kăm'ə-mīl') n. Var. of **chamomile**.

cam·ou·flage (kăm'ə-fläzh', -fläj') n. A means of concealment that creates the effect of being part of the natural surroundings. —v. **-flaged, -flag·ing.** To conceal by such means. [< Ital. *camuffare*, to disguise.] —**cam'ou·flag'er** n.

camp¹ (kămp) n. 1. a. A place where a group of people is temporarily lodged in makeshift shelters. b. The shelters in such a place or the persons using them. 2. A place consisting of more or less permanent vacation cabins. 3. A group favorable to a common cause, doctrine, or political system. —v. To shelter or lodge in a camp; encamp. [< Lat. *campus*, field.]

camp² (kămp) n. Artificiality of manner or style, appreciated for its humor, triteness, or vulgarity. —*adj.* Having the qualities of such a manner or style: *a camp movie.* [Orig. unknown.] —**camp'i·ly** *adv.* —**camp'i·ness** n. —**camp'y** *adj.*

cam·paign (kăm-pān') n. 1. A series of military operations undertaken to achieve a specific objective within a given area. 2. An organized activity or operation to attain a political, social, or commercial goal. —v. To engage in a campaign. [< OItal. *campagna*, battlefield.] —**cam·paign'er** n.

cam·pa·ni·le (kăm'pə-nē'lē) n. A bell tower, esp. one near but not attached to a church. [Ital.]

camp·er (kăm'pər) n. 1. A person who camps outdoors or who attends a camp. 2. a. A vehicle resembling an automobile-and-trailer combination, designed to serve as a dwelling and used for camping or long motor trips. b. A portable shelter resembling the top part of a trailer, made to be mounted on a pickup truck to form such a vehicle.

camp·fire (kămp'fīr') n. 1. An outdoor fire in a camp, used for warmth or cooking. 2. A meeting held around such a fire.

Camp Fire Girl n. A member of an organization for girls that provides recreation and develops practical skills.

camp·ground (kămp'ground') n. An area used for setting up a camp.

cam·phor (kăm'fər) n. A volatile crystalline compound, $C_{10}H_{16}O$, used as an insect repellent. [< Ar. *kāfūr.*] —**cam'phor·at'ed** (-fə-rā'tĭd) *adj.* —**cam·phor'ic** (-fôr'ĭk, -fŏr'-) *adj.*

camp meeting n. An evangelistic meeting held in a tent or outdoors.

camp·site (kămp'sīt') n. An area used or suitable for camping.

cam·pus (kăm'pəs) n., pl. **-pus·es.** The grounds of a school, college, or university. [Lat., field.]

cam·shaft (kăm'shăft') n. An engine shaft fitted with one or more cams.

can¹ (kăn; kən *when unstressed*) v. Past tense **could** (kood; kəd *when unstressed*). 1. Used as an auxiliary to indicate: a. Physical or mental ability: *I can meet you today.* b. Possession of a power, right, or privilege: *The President can veto bills.* c. Possession of a capacity or skill: *He can tune pianos.* 2. Used to indicate possibility or probability: *I wonder if she can be ill.* 3. Used to request or grant permission: *Can I*

be excused? Yes, you can. [< OE *cunnan*, to know how.]

Usage: In speech *can* is used more frequently than *may* to express permission, even though traditionalists insist that *can* should be used only to express the capacity to do something. Technically, correct usage therefore requires: *May I have the car tonight?* Because the contraction *mayn't* is felt to be stilted, however, the negative form of this question is usually expressed as *Can't I have the car tonight?*

can² (kăn) n. 1. A metal container. 2. a. An airtight storage container usu. made of tincoated iron. b. The amount that a can holds. —v. **canned, can·ning.** 1. To seal in a can or jar. 2. *Slang.* a. To dismiss; fire. b. To dispense with: *can the chatter.* [< OE *canne,* water container.] —**can'ner** n.

Canada goose n. A common wild goose of North America, with grayish plumage, a black neck and head, and a white face patch.

Ca·na·di·an French (kə-nā'dē-ən) n. French as used in Canada.

ca·naille (kə-nī', -nāl') n. The common people. [< Ital. *canaglia.*]

ca·nal (kə-năl') n. 1. A man-made waterway. 2. *Anat.* A tube or duct. [< Lat. *canalis*, channel.] —**ca·nal'i·za'tion** n. —**ca·nal'ize'** v.

can·a·pé (kăn'ə-pā', -pē) n. A cracker or small, thin piece of bread or toast topped with a spread or a tidbit, and served as an appetizer. [Fr.]

ca·nard (kə-närd') n. A false or unfounded story. [Fr.]

ca·nary (kə-nâr'ē) n., pl. **-ies.** A usu. yellow songbird popular as a cage bird. [< the *Canary* Islands.] —**ca·nary** *adj.*

ca·nas·ta (kə-năs'tə) n. A card game related to rummy and requiring two decks of cards. [Sp.]

can·can (kăn'kăn') n. An exuberant exhibition dance marked by high kicking. [Fr.]

can·cel (kăn'səl) v. **-celed** or **-celled, -cel·ing** or **-cel·ling.** 1. To cross out with lines or other markings. 2. To annul or invalidate. 3. To mark or perforate (e.g. a postage stamp) to insure against its further use. 4. To neutralize; offset. 5. *Math.* a. To remove a common factor from the numerator and denominator of a fraction. b. To remove a common factor or term from both members of an equation or inequality. [< Lat. *cancellare.*] —**can'cel·a·ble** *adj.* —**can'cel·er** n. —**can'cel·la'tion** n.

can·cer (kăn'sər) n. 1. a. A malignant tumor that tends to invade healthy tissue and spread to new sites. b. The pathological condition characterized by such growths. 2. A pernicious, spreading evil. 3. **Cancer.** A constellation in the Northern Hemisphere. 4. **Cancer.** The 4th sign of the zodiac. [Lat.] —**can'cer·ous** (-sər-əs) *adj.*

can·de·la (kăn-dēl'ə) n. *Physics.* A unit of luminous intensity equal to 1/60 of the intensity of the light emitted per square centimeter by a blackbody heated to a temperature of 1,773°C. [Lat., candle.]

can·de·la·brum (kăn'dl-ä'brəm, -āb'rəm, -ä'brəm) n., pl. **-bra** (-brə) or **-brums.** Also **can·de·la·bra** pl. **-bras.** A large candlestick with arms for holding several candles. [Lat.]

can·des·cent (kăn-děs'ənt) *adj.* Glowing or dazzling with great heat; incandescent. [<

Lat. *candescere,* to shine.] —**can·des'cence** *n.* —**can·des'cent·ly** *adv.*

can·did (kăn'dĭd) *adj.* **1.** Direct and frank; straightforward. **2.** Not posed or rehearsed: *a candid photograph.* **3.** Without prejudice; impartial. [< Lat. *candidus.*] —**can'did·ly** *adv.* —**can'did·ness** *n.*

can·di·date (kăn'dĭ-dāt', -dĭt) *n.* One who seeks or is nominated for an office, prize, honor, etc. [< Lat. *candidatus,* clothed in white.] —**can'di·da·cy** (-də-sē) or **can'di·da·ture'** (-də-chŏŏr', -chər) *n.*

can·dle (kăn'dl) *n.* A solid, usu. cylindrical mass of tallow, wax, or other fatty substance with an embedded wick that is burned to provide light. —*v.* **-dled, -dling.** To examine (an egg) in front of a light. [< Lat. *candela.*] —**can'dler** *n.*

can·dle·light (kăn'dl-līt') *n.* **1.** Illumination from a candle or candles. **2.** Dusk; twilight.

can·dle·pin (kăn'dl-pĭn') *n.* A slender bowling pin used in a variation of the game of ten-pins.

can·dle·pow·er (kăn'dl-pou'ər) *n.* The intensity of a light source expressed in candelas.

can·dle·stick (kăn'dl-stĭk') *n.* A holder for a candle.

can·dle·wick (kăn'dl-wĭk') *n.* The wick of a candle.

can·dor (kăn'dər) *n.* Also *chiefly Brit.* **can·dour.** Frankness of expression; sincerity; straightforwardness. [Lat.]

can·dy (kăn'dē) *n., pl.* **-dies.** A sweet confection food made of sugar and a variety of other ingredients. —*v.* **-died, -dying.** To cook, preserve, or coat with sugar or syrup. [Ult. < Ar. *gand,* cane sugar.]

candy striper *n.* A usu. teen-age volunteer nurse's aide in a hospital.

can·dy·tuft (kăn'dē-tŭft') *n.* Any of various plants with clusters of white, red, or purplish flowers. [Obs. *Candy,* Crete + TUFT.]

cane (kān) *n.* **1. a.** A slender, often hollow or flexible woody or pithy stem. **b.** A plant with such stems. **c.** Interwoven strips of such stems, esp. rattan. **2.** A walking stick or similar rod. **3.** Sugar cane. —*v.* **caned, caning. 1.** To make or repair (furniture) with cane. **2.** To hit or beat with a walking stick. [Gk. *kanna,* reed.]

cane·brake (kān'brāk') *n.* A dense thicket of cane.

cane sugar *n.* Sugar obtained from sugar cane.

ca·nine (kā'nīn') *adj.* Of or pertaining to dogs or related animals; doglike. —*n.* **1.** One of the conical teeth between the incisors and the bicuspids. **2.** A canine animal. [Lat. *caninus.*]

Ca·nis Ma·jor (kā'nĭs mā'jər, kăn'ĭs) A constellation in the Southern Hemisphere.

Canis Mi·nor (mī'nər) *n.* A constellation in the equatorial region of the Southern Hemisphere.

can·is·ter (kăn'ĭ-stər) *n.* **1.** A container, usu. of thin metal, for holding dry foods. **2.** A metallic cylinder that, when fired from a gun, bursts and scatters the shot packed inside it. **3.** The part of a gas mask containing a filter for poison gas. [< Gk. *kanastron,* reed basket.]

can·ker (kăng'kər) *n.* Also **canker sore.** An ulcerous sore in the mouth or on the lips. [< Lat. *cancer.*] —**can'ker·ous** *adj.*

can·na (kăn'ə) *n.* Any of various tropical plants with large leaves and showy red or yellow flowers. [< Lat., reed.]

can·na·bis (kăn'ə-bĭs) *n.* The hemp plant; marijuana. [Lat.]

canned (kănd) *adj.* **1.** Preserved and sealed in an airtight can or jar. **2.** *Informal.* Recorded or taped: *canned laughter.*

can·ner·y (kăn'ə-rē) *n., pl.* **-ies.** A factory where meat, vegetables, or other foods are canned.

can·ni·bal (kăn'ə-bəl) *n.* **1.** A person who eats the flesh of human beings. **2.** An animal that feeds on others of its own kind. [< Arawakan *Caniba,* Carib.] —**can'ni·bal·ism** *n.* —**can'ni·bal·is'tic** *adj.*

can·ni·bal·ize (kăn'ə-bə-līz') *v.* **-ized, -iz·ing.** To remove serviceable parts from (damaged or worn-out equipment) for use in the repair of other equipment. —**can'ni·bal·i·za'tion** *n.*

can·non (kăn'ən) *n., pl.* **-non** or **-nons. 1.** A weapon for firing projectiles, consisting of a heavy metal tube mounted on a carriage. **2.** Any heavy firearm whose caliber is .60 or larger. [< OItal. *cannone.*] —**can'non·eer'** *n.*

can·non·ade (kăn'ə-nād') *v.* **-ad·ed, -ad·ing.** To bombard with cannon fire. —*n.* An extended discharge of artillery.

can·non·ball (kăn'ən-bôl') *n.* **1.** A round projectile for firing from a cannon. **2.** Something, such as a fast train, moving with great speed. —**can'non·ball** *v.*

can·not (kăn'ŏt', kă-nŏt', kə-) *v.* The negative form of **can.**

Usage: In the phrase *cannot but,* which is sometimes criticized as a double negative, *but* is used in the sense of "except." *One cannot but admire his courage* is therefore acceptable.

can·ny (kăn'ē) *adj.* **-ni·er, -ni·est. 1.** Careful and shrewd. **2.** Skillful; competent. [< Lat. *canna.*] —**can'ni·ly** *adv.* —**can'ni·ness** *n.*

ca·noe (kə-nōō') *n.* A light, slender boat with pointed ends, propelled by paddles. —*v.* **-noed, -noe·ing.** To carry or travel by canoe. [< Sp. *canoa,* of Cariban orig.] —**ca·noe'ist** *n.*

can·on¹ (kăn'ən) *n.* **1.** A law or code of laws established by a church council. **2.** A basic principle or standard; criterion. **3.** The books of the Bible officially recognized by a Christian church. **4.** *Rom. Cath. Ch.* **a.** Often **Canon.** The most important part of the Mass. **b.** The accepted calendar of saints. **5.** *Mus.* A round. [< LLat., ult. < Gk. *kanōn,* rule.]

can·on² (kăn'ən) *n.* A member of the clergy serving in a cathedral or collegiate church. [< LLat. *canonicus,* ult. < Gk. *kanōn,* rule.]

ca·ñon (kăn'yən) *n.* Var. of **canyon.**

ca·non·i·cal (kə-nŏn'ĭ-kəl) or **ca·non·ic** (-nŏn'ĭk) *adj.* **1.** Pertaining to, required by, or abiding by canon law. **2.** Authoritative; orthodox. —**ca·non'i·cal·ly** *adv.* —**can'on·ic'i·ty** (kăn'ə-nĭs'ĭ-tē) *n.*

canonical hours *pl.n.* A form of prayer, prescribed by canon law, normally to be recited at specified times of the day.

can·on·ize (kăn'ə-nīz') *v.* **-ized, -iz·ing. 1.** To declare (a deceased person) a saint. **2.** To glorify; exalt. —**can'on·i·za'tion** *n.*

ă pat ā pay â care ä father ĕ pet ē be ĭ pit ī tie î pier ŏ pot ō toe ô paw, for oi noise ŏŏ took ŏŏ boot ou out th thin *th* this ŭ cut û urge yŏŏ abuse zh vision ə about, item, edible, gallop, circus

canon law *n.* The body of officially established rules governing a Christian church.

can·o·py (kăn′ə-pē) *n., pl.* **-pies.** 1. A cloth covering fastened or held horizontally over a bed, entrance, sacred object or carried over an important person. 2. *Archit.* An ornamental rooflike structure. 3. *Aviation.* **a.** The transparent, movable enclosure over an aircraft's cockpit. **b.** The hemispherical surface of a parachute. —*v.* **-pied, -py·ing.** To spread over with or as if with a canopy. [< Gk. *kōnōpion*, mosquito net.]

canopy
19th-cent. American canopy bed

canst (kănst) *v. Archaic.* 2nd person sing. present tense of **can.**

cant¹ (kănt) *n.* 1. Angular deviation from a vertical or horizontal plane or surface. 2. The tilt caused by such a motion. 3. A slanted edge or surface. —*v.* To cause to slant or tilt. [< Norman Fr.]

cant² (kănt) *n.* 1. Wheedling speech. 2. Discourse recited mechanically. 3. Hypocritically pious language. 4. The special vocabulary peculiar to the members of a group. —*v.* 1. To speak in a whining, pleading tone. 2. To speak sententiously; moralize. [Prob. < Norman Fr., singing.] —**cant′ing·ly** *adv.*

can't (kănt, känt). Cannot.

can·ta·bi·le (kän-tä′bĕ-lā′, -bi-, kən-) *adv. Mus.* In a smooth, lyrical, flowing style. [Ital.] —**can·ta′bi·le′** *adj.* & *n.*

can·ta·loupe or **can·ta·loup** (kăn′tl-ōp′) *n.* A melon with a ribbed, rough rind and orange flesh. [< *Cantalupo,* a papal villa near Rome.]

can·tan·ker·ous (kăn-tăng′kər-əs) *adj.* Ill-tempered and quarrelsome. [Perh. ult. < ME *contek,* contentious.] —**can·tan′ker·ous·ly** *adv.* —**can·tan′ker·ous·ness** *n.*

can·ta·ta (kən-tä′tə) *n. Mus.* A vocal and instrumental composition consisting of choruses, solos, and recitatives. [Ital.]

can·teen (kăn-tēn′) *n.* 1. A small container for carrying drinking water, used esp. by soldiers and campers. 2. **a.** A store for on-base military personnel. **b.** *Chiefly Brit.* A club for soldiers. 3. An institutional recreation hall or cafeteria. 4. A temporary, often mobile eating place set up esp. in an emergency. [< Ital. *cantina,* wine cellar.]

can·ter (kăn′tər) *n.* A gait slower than the gallop but faster than the trot. —*v.* To move or cause to move at a canter. [< *Canterbury gallop.*]

can·thus (kăn′thəs) *n., pl.* **-thi** (-thī′). The corner at either side of the eye, formed by the meeting of the upper and lower eyelids. [< Gk. *kanthos.*]

can·ti·cle (kăn′tĭ-kəl) *n.* A liturgical chant. [< LLat. *canticulum.*]

can·ti·le·ver (kăn′tl-ē′vər, -ĕv′ər) *n.* A projecting beam or other structure supported only at one end. —*v.* To extend outward or build as a cantilever. [Poss. CANT¹ + LEVER.]

can·tle (kăn′təl) *n.* The rear part of a saddle. [< Norman Fr. *cantel,* corner.]

can·to (kăn′tō) *n., pl.* **-tos.** A principal division of a long poem. [< Lat. *cantus,* song.]

can·ton (kăn′tən, -tŏn′) *n.* A small division of a country, esp. one of the states of Switzerland. —*v.* 1. To divide into parts, esp. into cantons. 2. To assign quarters to. [Fr.] —**can′ton·al** *adj.*

Can·ton·ese (kăn′tə-nēz′, -nēs′) *n.* The dialect of Chinese spoken in and around Guangzhou, China. [< *Canton* (Guangzhou), China.] —**Can′ton·ese′** *adj.*

can·ton·ment (kăn-tōn′mənt, -tŏn′-) *n.* 1. A group of temporary buildings for housing troops. 2. Assignment of troops to temporary quarters.

can·tor (kăn′tər) *n.* The official who leads the congregation in prayer and sings the music used in a Jewish religious service. [Lat., singer.]

can·vas (kăn′vəs) *n.* 1. A heavy, closely woven fabric of cotton, hemp, or flax, used for making tents and sails. 2. A piece of such material used as the surface for a painting. 3. Sailcloth. 4. Sails. 5. The floor of a boxing or wrestling ring. [< Norman Fr. *canevas.*]

can·vas·back (kăn′vəs-băk′) *n.* A North American duck with a reddish head and neck and a whitish back.

can·vass (kăn′vəs) *v.* 1. To scrutinize. 2. **a.** To go through in order to solicit votes, orders, subscriptions, etc. **b.** To conduct a survey. —*n.* 1. An examination or discussion. 2. A solicitation of votes, sales orders, or opinions. [< obs. *canvas,* to toss a person in a canvas sheet.] —**can′vass·er** *n.*

can·yon (kăn′yən) *n.* Also **ca·ñon.** A narrow chasm with steep cliff walls. [Sp. *cañon.*]

cap (kăp) *n.* 1. A usu. close-fitting covering for the head, with or without a visor. 2. Any of numerous objects similar to a head covering in form, use, or position: *a bottle cap.* 3. **a.** A percussion cap. **b.** A small explosive charge enclosed in paper for use in a toy gun. —*v.* **capped, cap·ping.** 1. To put a cap on. 2. To lie over or on top of: *Snow capped the hills.* [< LLat. *cappa.*]

ca·pa·ble (kā′pə-bəl) *adj.* Having capacity or ability; competent. —*idiom.* **capable of.** 1. Qualified for. 2. Open to: *an error capable of remedy.* [< Lat. *capabilis,* spacious.] —**ca′pa·bil′i·ty** or **ca′pa·ble·ness** *n.* —**ca′pa·bly** *adv.*

ca·pa·cious (kə-pā′shəs) *adj.* Spacious; roomy. [< Lat. *capax.*] —**ca·pa′cious·ly** *adv.* —**ca·pa′cious·ness** *n.*

ca·pac·i·tance (kə-păs′ĭ-təns) *n.* 1. The ability of a conductor or dielectric to store electric charge. 2. A measure of this ability equal to the ratio of stored charge to electric potential. —**ca·pac′i·tive** *adj.* —**ca·pac′i·tive·ly** *adv.*

ca·pac·i·tor (kə-păs′ĭ-tər) *n.* An electric circuit element used to store charge temporarily, consisting in general of two metallic plates separated by a dielectric.

ca·pac·i·ty (kə-păs′ĭ-tē) *n., pl.* **-ties.** 1. The ability to receive, hold, or absorb. 2. The maximum amount that can be contained. 3. The maximum or optimum amount of production. 4. The ability to learn or retain knowledge. **5.** The quality of being suitable for or receptive to specified treatment: *the capacity of elastic to be stretched.* **6.** The position in which one functions; role. **7.** *Elect.* Capacitance. —*adj.* As large or numerous as possible: *a capacity crowd.* [< Lat. *capacitas.*]

ca·par·i·son (kə-pǎr'ĭ-sən) *n.* **1.** A decorative cover placed over a saddle or harness. **2.** Richly ornamented clothing; finery. —*v.* To outfit with a caparison. [< Sp. *caparazón.*]

cape¹ (kāp) *n.* A sleeveless garment worn hanging over the shoulders. [< LLat. *cappa.*]

cape² (kāp) *n.* A point or head of land projecting into a sea or other body of water. [< OProv. *cap.*]

ca·per¹ (kā'pər) *n.* **1.** A playful leap or hop. **2.** A wild escapade. —*v.* To leap or frisk about. [< CAPRIOLE.]

ca·per² (kā'pər) *n.* A pickled flower bud of a Mediterranean shrub, used as a condiment. [< Gk. *kapparis.*]

cap·il·lar·i·ty (kǎp'ə-lǎr'ĭ-tē) *n., pl.* **-ties.** The interaction between contacting surfaces of a liquid and a solid that distorts the liquid surface from a planar shape.

cap·il·lary (kǎp'ə-lěr'ē) *adj.* **1.** Pertaining to or resembling a hair; fine and slender. **2.** Having a very small internal diameter, as a tube. **3.** *Anat.* In, of, or pertaining to the capillaries. **4.** *Physics.* Of or pertaining to capillarity. —*n., pl.* **-ies.** **1.** Any of the tiny blood vessels that connect the arteries and veins. **2.** A tube with a small internal diameter. [< Lat. *capillaris,* hairlike.]

capillary attraction *n.* The force that causes a liquid to be raised against a vertical surface, as is water in a close glass tube.

cap·i·tal¹ (kǎp'ĭ-tl) *n.* **1.** A town or city that is the official seat of government in a political entity. **2.** Wealth in the form of money or property. **3. a.** The net worth of a business. **b.** The funds invested in a business by the owners or stockholders. **4.** Capitalists considered as a class. **5.** An asset or advantage. **6.** A capital letter. —*adj.* **1.** First and foremost; chief; principal. **2.** Pertaining to a political capital. **3.** First-rate; excellent: *a capital fellow.* **4.** Extremely serious: *a capital blunder.* **5.** Punishable by or involving death: *capital punishment.* **6.** Pertaining to capital. [< Lat. *capitalis,* principal.]

Usage: A city or town serving as the seat of a government is a *capital;* the building in which a legislative assembly meets is a *capitol.*

cap·i·tal² (kǎp'ĭ-tl) *n. Archit.* The top part of a pillar or column. [< LLat. *capitellum.*]

capital goods *pl.n.* Goods used in the production of commodities.

cap·i·tal·ism (kǎp'ĭ-tl-ĭz'əm) *n.* An economic system, characterized by a free market and open competition, in which goods are produced for profit, labor is performed for wages, and the means of production and distribution are privately owned.

cap·i·tal·ist (kǎp'ĭ-tl-ĭst) *n.* **1.** An investor of capital in business. **2.** One who supports capitalism. **3.** A person of great wealth. —**cap'i·tal·is'tic** *adj.* —**cap'i·tal·is'ti·cal·ly** *adv.*

cap·i·tal·i·za·tion (kǎp'ĭ-tl-ĭ-zā'shən) *n.* **1.** The act, practice, or result of capitalizing. **2.** The total investment of owners in a business.

cap·i·tal·ize (kǎp'ĭ-tl-īz') *v.* **-ized, -iz·ing.** **1.** To convert into capital. **2.** To supply with capital. **3.** To turn to advantage; exploit: *capitalize on an opponent's error.* **4.** To write or print in upper-case letters.

capital letter *n.* A letter written or printed in a size larger than and often in a form differing from its corresponding smaller letter; upper-case letter.

capital punishment *n.* The death penalty.

capital stock *n.* **1.** The total amount of stock authorized for issue by a corporation. **2.** The total value of the permanently invested capital of a corporation.

cap·i·ta·tion (kǎp'ĭ-tā'shən) *n.* A tax fixed at an equal sum per person; a per capita tax. [Lat. *capitatio.*]

cap·i·tol (kǎp'ĭ-tl) *n.* The building in which a legislature assembles. [< Lat. *Capitolium,* Jupiter's temple in Rome.]

ca·pit·u·late (kə-pĭch'ə-lāt') *v.* **-lat·ed, -lat·ing.** **1.** To surrender under stated conditions. **2.** To give up all resistance; acquiesce. [Med. Lat. *capitulare,* to draw up in chapters.] —**ca·pit'u·la'tion** *n.*

ca·pon (kā'pŏn', -pən) *n.* A castrated rooster raised for food. [< Lat. *capo.*]

ca·pric·cio (kə-prē'chō, -chē-ō') *n., pl.* **-cios.** *Mus.* An instrumental work written in a whimsical style and a free form. [Ital.]

ca·price (kə-prēs') *n.* **1. a.** An impulsive change of mind. **b.** An inclination to change one's mind impulsively. **2.** *Mus.* A capriccio. [< Ital. *capriccio.*] —**ca·pri'cious** *adj.* —**ca·pri'cious·ly** *adv.* —**ca·pri'cious·ness** *n.*

Cap·ri·corn (kǎp'rĭ-kôrn') *n.* **1.** A constellation in the equatorial region of the Southern Hemisphere. **2.** The 10th sign of the zodiac.

cap·ri·ole (kǎp'rē-ōl') *n.* **1.** An upward leap made by a trained horse without moving forward. **2.** A leap or jump. [< Ital. *capriola,* somersault.]

cap·size (kǎp'sīz', kǎp-sīz') *v.* **-sized, -siz·ing.** To overturn or cause to overturn. [Orig. unknown.]

cap·stan (kǎp'stən, -stǎn') *n.* **1.** *Naut.* A vertical revolving cylinder for hoisting weights by winding in a cable. **2.** A small cylindrical pulley used to regulate the speed of magnetic tape in a tape recorder. [< Lat. *capistrum,* halter.]

cap·su·lar (kǎp'sə-lər, -syōo-) *adj.* Of or like a capsule.

cap·su·late (kǎp'sə-lāt', -syōo-, -lĭt) *adj.* Also **cap·su·lat·ed** (-lā'tĭd). In or formed into a capsule.

capital²   capitol

cap·sule (kăp′səl, -syŏŏl) n. 1. A soluble container, usu. of gelatin, enclosing a dose of an oral medicine. 2. A fibrous, membranous, or fatty sac enclosing a bodily organ or part. 3. A seed case that dries and splits open. 4. A pressurized compartment of an aircraft or spacecraft. —adj. Condensed; brief. [< Lat. capsula.]

cap·tain (kăp′tən) n. 1. One who commands, leads, or guides. 2. The officer in command of a ship. 3. a. A commissioned officer in the Army, Air Force, or Marine Corps who ranks above a first lieutenant. b. A commissioned officer in the Navy who ranks above a commander. 4. A leading figure in a given field: a captain of industry. —v. To command or direct. [< LLat. capitaneus.] —cap′tain·cy n. —cap′tain·ship′ n.

cap·tion (kăp′shən) n. 1. A short legend or description, as of an illustration or photograph. 2. A subtitle in a motion picture. 3. A title, as of a document or chapter. —v. To furnish a caption for. [< Lat. captio, arrest.]

cap·tious (kăp′shəs) adj. 1. Inclined to find fault. 2. Intended to entrap or confuse. [< Lat. captiosus.] —cap′tious·ly adv. —cap′tious·ness n.

cap·ti·vate (kăp′tĭ-vāt′) v. -vat·ed, -vat·ing. To fascinate or charm with wit, beauty, or intelligence. —cap′ti·va′tion n. —cap′ti·va′tor n.

cap·tive (kăp′tĭv) n. 1. A prisoner. 2. One who is enslaved by a strong emotion. —adj. 1. Held as prisoner. 2. Under restraint or control: a captive nation. 3. Enraptured. 4. Obliged to be present or attentive: a captive audience. —cap′tiv′i·ty n.

cap·tor (kăp′tər, -tôr′) n. One who captures.

cap·ture (kăp′chər) v. -tured, -tur·ing. 1. To take captive. 2. To win possession or control of. —n. 1. The act of capturing; seizure. 2. One that is seized, caught, or won. [< Lat. capere, to seize.]

car (kär) n. 1. An automobile. 2. A conveyance with wheels that runs along tracks, as a railroad car. 3. A boxlike enclosure for passengers on a conveyance, as an elevator car. [< Lat. carrus, cart.]

car·a·cul (kăr′ə-kəl) n. Var. of karakul.

ca·rafe (kə-răf′, -räf′) n. A glass bottle for serving water or wine at the table. [< Ar. gharrāf.]

car·a·mel (kăr′ə-məl, -mĕl′, kär′məl) n. 1. A smooth, chewy candy made of sugar, butter, cream or milk, and flavoring. 2. Burnt sugar, used for coloring and sweetening. [< Sp. caramel.]

car·a·pace (kăr′ə-pās′) n. Zool. A hard outer covering, as the upper shell of a turtle. [< Sp. carapacho.]

car·at (kăr′ət) n. 1. A unit of weight for precious stones, equal to 200 milligrams. 2. Var. of karat. [< Ar. qīrāt, a small weight.]

car·a·van (kăr′ə-văn′) n. 1. A company of travelers journeying together, esp. across a desert. 2. A single file of vehicles or pack animals. 3. A large covered vehicle; van. [< Pers. kārwān.]

car·a·van·sa·ry (kăr′ə-văn′sə-rē) n., pl. -ries. Also car·a·van·se·rai (-rī′). 1. An inn for accommodating caravans in the Near or Far East. 2. A large inn. [Pers. kārwān, caravan + Pers. serāī, inn.]

car·a·vel (kăr′ə-vĕl′) n. A small, light sailing ship used by the Spanish and Portuguese in the 15th and 16th cent. [< OPort. caravela.]

car·a·way (kăr′ə-wā′) n. 1. A plant with pungent, aromatic seeds. 2. The seeds of the caraway plant, used in cooking. [ME carowei.]

car·bide (kär′bīd′) n. A binary compound of carbon and a more electropositive element.

car·bine (kär′bīn′, -bēn′) n. A light shoulder rifle with a short barrel. [Fr. carabine]

carbo- or **carb-** pref. Carbon: carbohydrate. [Fr.]

car·bo·hy·drate (kär′bō-hī′drāt′, -bə-) n. Any of a group of chemical compounds, including sugars, starches, and cellulose, containing carbon, hydrogen, and oxygen only, with the ratio of hydrogen to oxygen atoms usu. 2:1.

car·bol·ic acid (kär-bŏl′ĭk) n. Phenol. [CARB(O)- + Lat. oleum, oil + -IC.]

car·bon (kär′bən) n. Symbol **C** 1. A naturally abundant nonmetallic element that occurs in many inorganic and in all organic compounds, exists in amorphous, graphitic, and diamond allotropes, and is capable of chemical self-bonding to form an enormous number of chemically, biologically, and commercially important long-chain molecules. Atomic number 6; atomic weight 12.01115. 2. a. A sheet of carbon paper. b. A carbon copy. [< Lat. carbo, charcoal.] —car′bon·i·za′tion n. —car′bon·ize′ v.

carbon 14 n. A naturally radioactive carbon isotope with atomic mass 14 and half-life 5,700 years, used in dating ancient carbon-containing objects.

car·bo·na·ceous (kär′bə-nā′shəs) adj. Consisting of, containing, pertaining to, or yielding carbon.

car·bon·ate (kär′bə-nāt′) v. -at·ed, -at·ing. To charge with carbon dioxide gas. —car·bon·a′tion n.

carbon black n. A finely divided form of carbon derived from the incomplete combustion of hydrocarbons and used principally in rubber and ink.

carbon copy n. 1. A replica, as of a letter, made by using carbon paper. 2. Informal. A close copy.

carbon dating n. The estimation of age, as of a fossil, by determination of carbon 14 content.

carbon dioxide n. A colorless, odorless, incombustible gas, CO_2, formed during respiration, combustion, and organic decomposition.

car·bon·ic acid (kär-bŏn′ĭk) n. A weak, unstable acid, H_2CO_3, present in solutions of carbon dioxide in water.

car·bon·if·er·ous (kär′bə-nĭf′ər-əs) adj. 1. Producing, containing, or pertaining to carbon or coal. 2. Carboniferous. Of, designating, or belonging to a division of the Paleozoic era, including the Mississippian and Pennsylvanian periods, characterized by dense plant growth that eventually sank into swamps and later hardened into coal. —n. Carboniferous. The Carboniferous period.

carbon monoxide n. A colorless, odorless, highly poisonous gas, CO, formed by the incomplete combustion of carbon.

carbon paper n. A lightweight paper faced on one side with a dark waxy pigment that is transferred to a copying surface by the impact of typewriter keys or by writing pressure.

carbon tet·ra·chlo·ride (tĕt′rə-klôr′īd′, -klōr′-) n. A poisonous, nonflammable, colorless liquid, CCl_4, used as a solvent.

Car·bo·run·dum (kär′bə-rŭn′dəm). A trademark for a silicon carbide abrasive.

car·boy (kär′boi′) n. A large bottle, usu. encased in a protective covering and often used to hold corrosive liquids. [Pers. *qarāba*.]

car·bun·cle (kär′bŭng′kəl) n. A painful, localized, pus-producing infection of the skin. [< Lat. *carbunculus*.] —**car·bun′cu·lar** (-kyə-lər) adj.

car·bu·re·tor (kär′bə-rā′tər, -byə-) n. A device used in gasoline engines to produce an efficient explosive vapor of fuel and air. [< obs. *carburet*, carbide.]

car·cass (kär′kəs) n. A dead body, esp. of an animal. [Fr. *carcasse*.]

car·cin·o·gen (kär-sĭn′ə-jən, kär′sə-nə-jěn′) n. A cancer-causing substance. [Gk. *karkinos*, cancer + -GEN.] —**car′cin·o·gen′e·sis** n. —**car′cin·o·gen′ic** adj. —**car′ci·no·gen′ic′i·ty** (-jə-nĭs′ĭ-tē) n.

car·ci·no·ma (kär′sə-nō′mə) n., pl. -**mas** or -**ma·ta** (-mə-tə). A malignant tumor derived from epithelial tissue. [< Gk. *karkinōma*.] —**car′ci·nom′a·tous** (-nŏm′ə-təs, -nō′mə-) adj.

car coat n. A three-quarter-length coat.

card[1] (kärd) n. 1. A small, flat piece of stiff paper or thin pasteboard with numerous uses: **a.** One of a set of playing cards. **b.** A post card. **c.** One bearing a greeting and an illustration, as for Christmas. **d.** A business card. 2. **cards.** A game using playing cards. 3. A program of events, as at horse races. 4. *Informal.* An amusing or eccentric person. —v. 1. To furnish with or attach to a card. 2. To list on a card or cards; catalogue. —*idioms.* **have a card up (one's) sleeve.** To have a secret resource or plan in reserve. **in the cards.** Likely to occur. **put (or lay) (one's) cards on the table.** To reveal frankly and clearly, as one's motives. [< Gk. *khartēs*, leaf of papyrus.]

card[2] (kärd) n. A wire-toothed brush used to disentangle textile fibers or raise the nap on a fabric. —v. To comb out or brush with a card. [< Lat. *carere*, to card.] —**card′er** n.

car·da·mom or **car·da·mum** (kär′də-məm) n. Also **car·da·mon** (-mən). A tropical Asiatic perennial plant with large, hairy leaves and capsular fruit whose seeds are used as a condiment and in medicine. [< Gk. *kardamōmon.*]

card·board (kärd′bôrd′, -bōrd′) n. A stiff pasteboard made of paper pulp.

card-car·ry·ing (kärd′kăr′ē-ĭng) adj. 1. Being an enrolled member of an organization, esp. the Communist party. 2. Strongly identified with a particular cause or issue.

card catalog n. A listing, esp. of books in a library, made with a separate card for each item and arranged in alphabetical order.

car·di·ac (kär′dē-ăk′) adj. Of or near the heart. [< Gk. *kardiakos.*]

cardiac massage n. Resuscitation marked by rhythmic compression of the chest in order to restore proper circulation and respiration.

car·di·gan (kär′dĭ-gən) n. A sweater or knitted jacket without a collar, opening down the front. [< the 7th Earl of *Cardigan* (1797–1868).]

car·di·nal (kär′dn-əl, kärd′nəl) adj. 1. Of foremost importance. 2. Of a dark to deep or

vivid red color. —n. 1. *Rom. Cath. Ch.* An official ranking just below the pope. 2. Dark to deep or vivid red. 3. A North American bird with a crested head and bright-red plumage in the male. [< Lat. *cardinalis.*]

car·di·nal·ate (kär′dn-əl-ĭt, kärd′nəl-, -āt′) n. *Rom. Cath. Ch.* The position, rank, dignity, or term of a cardinal.

cardinal number n. A number, such as 3 or 11 or 412, used to indicate quantity but not order.

cardio- pref. Heart: cardiogram. [< Gk. *kardia*, heart.]

car·di·o·gram (kär′dē-ə-grăm′) n. The curve traced by a cardiograph, used to diagnose heart defects.

car·di·o·graph (kär′dē-ə-grăf′) n. An instrument used to record graphically the movements of the heart.

car·di·ol·o·gy (kär′dē-ŏl′ə-jē) n. The study of the diseases and functioning of the heart. —**car′di·ol′o·gist** n.

car·di·o·pul·mo·nary (kär′dē-ō-pŏol′mə-něr′ē) adj. Of or pertaining to the heart and lungs.

cardiopulmonary resuscitation n. A procedure employed after cardiac arrest in which cardiac massage, drugs, and mouth-to-mouth resuscitation are used to restore breathing.

car·di·o·vas·cu·lar (kär′dē-ō-văs′kyə-lər) adj. Involving the heart and the blood vessels.

card·sharp (kärd′shärp′) n. A person expert in cheating at cards. —**card′sharp′ing** n.

care (kâr) n. 1. Mental distress and grief. 2. An object or source of attention or solicitude. 3. Caution: *handle with care.* 4. Supervision; charge: *in the care of a nurse.* —v. **cared, car·ing.** 1. To be concerned or interested. 2. To object; mind. [< OE *cearu.*]

ca·reen (kə-rēn′) v. 1. To move rapidly and in an uncontrolled manner. 2. To cause (a ship) to lean to one side; tilt. [< Fr. *(en) carène*, (on) the keel.]

ca·reer (kə-rîr′) n. 1. A chosen pursuit; lifework. 2. A person's progress in his or her occupation. —v. To move or run at full speed; rush. [Fr. *carrière.*]

care·free (kâr′frē′) adj. Free of worries and responsibilities.

care·ful (kâr′fəl) adj. 1. Cautious in thought, speech, or action. 2. Thorough; painstaking; conscientious. —**care′ful·ly** adv. —**care′ful·ness** n.

Syns: careful, cautious, chary, circumspect, prudent adj.

care·less (kâr′lĭs) adj. 1. Inattentive; negligent. 2. Marked by or resulting from lack of thought. 3. Inconsiderate: *a careless remark.* 4. Free from cares; cheerful. —**care′less·ly** adv. —**care′less·ness** n.

Syns: careless, messy, slapdash, sloppy, slovenly, untidy adj.

ca·ress (kə-rĕs′) n. A gentle touch or gesture of fondness. —v. To touch or stroke fondly. [< Ital. *carezza.*] —**ca·ress′er** n.

car·et (kăr′ĭt) n. A proofreading symbol used to indicate where something is to be inserted in a line of printed or written matter. [< Lat., there is lacking.]

care·tak·er (kâr′tā′kər) n. One employed to look after or take charge of goods, property, or a person; custodian.

care·worn (kâr'wôrn', -wōrn') *adj.* Showing signs of worry or care.

car·fare (kär'fâr') *n.* The fare charged a passenger for transportation, as on a bus or subway.

cargo (kär'gō) *n., pl.* **-goes** or **-gos.** The freight carried by a ship, airplane, or other vehicle. [Sp.]

car·hop (kär'hŏp') *n.* A waitress or waiter at a drive-in restaurant.

Carib (kăr'ĭb) *n., pl.* **-ib** or **-ibs. 1. a.** A group of peoples of American Indians of northern South America and the Lesser Antilles. **b.** A member of one of these peoples. **2.** Any of the languages of the Carib. **—Car'ib** *adj.*

Car·i·ban (kăr'ə-bən, kə-rē'bən) *n., pl.* **-ban** or **-bans.** A language family comprising the Carib languages. **—Car'i·ban** *adj.*

car·i·bou (kăr'ə-bōō') *n.* A New World arctic deer considered identical to the reindeer. [Can. Fr., of Algonquian orig.]

car·i·ca·ture (kăr'ĭ-kə-chōōr', -chər) *n.* **1.** A representation, esp. pictorial, in which a subject's distinctive features or peculiarities are exaggerated for comic or grotesque effect. **2.** An imitation so inferior as to be absurd. **—v.** **-tured, -tur·ing.** To represent or imitate in or as if in a caricature. [< Ital. *caricatura.*] **—car'i·ca·tur·ist** *n.*

caries (kâr'ēz') *n., pl.* **-ies.** Decay of a bone or tooth. [Lat.]

car·il·lon (kăr'ə-lŏn', -lən) *n.* A set of bells hung in a tower and played from a keyboard. [Fr.]

Ca·ri·na (kə-rī'nə) *n.* A constellation in the Southern Hemisphere.

car·load (kär'lōd') *n.* The amount a car carries or is able to carry.

carmine (kär'mĭn, -mīn') *n.* A strong to vivid red color. [Med. Lat. *carminium.*] **—car'mine** *adj.*

car·nage (kär'nĭj) *n.* Massive slaughter, as in war. [< Oltal. *carnaggio.*]

car·nal (kär'nəl) *adj.* **1.** Relating to the desires of the flesh; sensual. **2.** Not spiritual. [Med. Lat. *carnalis.*] **—car·nal'i·ty** (kär-năl'ĭ-tē) *n.* **—car'nal·ly** *adv.*

car·na·tion (kär-nā'shən) *n.* A plant cultivated for its fragrant flowers with fringed petals. [Prob. < OFr., flesh-colored.]

car·nel·ian (kär-nēl'yən) *n.* A reddish variety of clear chalcedony, used in jewelry. [< OFr. *corneline.*]

car·ni·val (kär'nə-vəl) *n.* **1.** The season just before Lent, marked by merrymaking and feasting. **2.** A traveling amusement show. [Ital. *carnevale.*]

car·ni·vore (kär'nə-vôr', -vōr') *n.* A flesh-eating mammal, esp. one of a group including dogs, cats, and bears.

car·niv·o·rous (kär-nĭv'ər-əs) *adj.* **1.** Belonging or pertaining to the carnivores. **2.** Flesh-eating or predatory. [Lat. *carnivorus.*] **—car·niv'o·rous·ly** *adv.* **—car·niv'o·rous·ness** *n.*

carny (kär'nē) *n., pl.* **-nies.** Also **carney** *pl.* **-neys.** *Slang.* **1.** A carnival. **2.** One who works with a carnival.

carol (kăr'əl) *n.* A song of praise or joy, esp. for Christmas. **—v.** **-oled** or **-olled, -ol·ing** or **-ol·ling. 1.** To celebrate in song. **2.** To sing joyously. [< OFr. *carole.*] **—car'ol·er** *n.*

carom (kăr'əm) *n.* **1.** A billiards shot in which the cue ball successively strikes two other balls. **2.** A collision followed by a rebound. **—v.** **1.** To collide with another.

2. To make a carom in billiards. [< Fr. *carambole.*]

car·o·tene (kăr'ə-tēn') *n.* An orange-yellow to red hydrocarbon, $C_{40}H_{56}$, occurring in many plants and converted to vitamin A by the liver. [< Lat. *carota,* carrot.]

ca·rot·id (kə-rŏt'ĭd) *n.* Either of the two major arteries in the neck that carry blood to the head. [< Gk. *karōtides.*] **—ca·rot'id** or **ca·rot'id·al** *adj.*

ca·rouse (kə-rouz') *n.* Boisterous, drunken merrymaking. **—v.** **-roused, -rous·ing. 1.** To drink excessively. **2.** To go on a drinking spree. [G. *garaus (trinken),* (to drink) all out.] **—ca·rous'al** *n.* **—ca·rous'er** *n.*

carou·sel or **carou·sel** (kăr'ə-sĕl', -zĕl') *n.* A merry-go-round. [Fr. *carrousel.*]

carp¹ (kärp) *v.* To find fault and complain constantly. [< ON *karpa,* boast.] **—carp'er** *n.*

carp² (kärp) *n.* An edible freshwater fish. [< Med. Lat. *carpa,* of Gmc. orig.]

—carp *suff. Bot.* Fruit; fruitlike structure: *endocarp.* [< Gk. *karpos,* fruit.]

car·pal (kär'pəl) *adj. Anat.* Of or near the carpus. **—n.** A bone of the carpus.

car·pel (kär'pəl) *n. Bot.* The central, seed-bearing female organ of a flower, consisting of a modified leaf forming one or more sections of the pistil. [< Gk. *karpos,* fruit.]

car·pen·ter (kär'pən-tər) *n.* One whose occupation is constructing, finishing, and repairing wooden objects and structures. [Lat. *carpentarius (artifax),* (maker) of a carriage.] **—car'pen·ter** *v.* **—car'pen·try** *n.*

carpet (kär'pĭt) *n.* **1.** A heavy usu. woven covering for a floor. **2.** The fabric used for a carpet. **—v.** To cover with or as if with a carpet. **—idiom. on the carpet.** In the position of being reprimanded by one in authority. [< Oltal. *carpita.*]

carpet·bag (kär'pĭt-băg') *n.* A traveling bag made of carpet fabric.

carpet·bag·ger (kär'pĭt-băg'ər) *n.* A Northerner who went to the South after the Civil War for political or financial advantage. **—car'pet·bag'ger·y** *n.*

car·pool (kär'pōōl') *n.* **1.** An arrangement whereby several commuters share a car and expenses. **2.** A group participating in a car-pool. **—car'-pool'** *v.* **—car'-pool'er** *n.*

car·port (kär'pôrt', -pōrt') *n.* A roof projecting from the side of a building, used as a shelter for an automobile.

car·pus (kär'pəs) *n., pl.* **-pi** (-pī'). *Anat.* **1.** The wrist. **2.** The bones of the wrist. [Gk. *karpos.*]

car·rel (kăr'əl) *n.* Also **car·rell.** A nook near the stacks in a library, used for private study. [OFr. *carole.*]

car·riage (kăr'ĭj) *n.* **1.** A four-wheeled horse-drawn passenger vehicle. **2.** A wheeled vehicle for a baby that is pushed by someone on foot. **3.** A wheeled support or frame for moving a heavy object, such as a cannon. **4.** A moving part of a machine for holding or shifting another part. **5. a.** The act or process of transporting or carrying. **b.** (kăr'ē-ĭj). The cost or charge for transporting. **6.** Posture; bearing. [< Norman Fr. *cariage.*]

carriage trade *n.* Wealthy patrons, as of a restaurant.

car·ri·er (kăr'ē-ər) *n.* **1.** One that carries or conveys. **2.** One that transports passengers or goods. **3.** *Med.* An immune organism that transmits a pathogen to others. **4.** An aircraft carrier.

carrier pigeon *n.* A homing pigeon, esp. one trained to carry messages.

carrier wave *n.* An electromagnetic wave that can be modulated to transmit sound or images.

car·ri·on (kăr′ē-ən) *n.* Dead and decaying flesh. [< AN *careine.*]

car·rot (kăr′ət) *n.* **1.** The edible, yellow-orange root of a widely cultivated plant. **2.** Something held out as an attractive but often illusory inducement. [< Gk. *karōton.*]

carrot-and-stick (kăr′ət-ən-stĭk′) *adj.* Combining a promised reward with a threat or punishment.

car·rou·sel (kăr′ə-sĕl′, -zĕl′) *n.* Var. of **carousel.**

car·ry (kăr′ē) *v.* **-ried, -ry·ing.** **1.** To bear; convey; transport. **2.** To win over. **3.** To take; seize; capture. **4.** To keep or have on one's person. **5.** To involve; imply. **6.** To conduct (oneself) in a specified manner. **7.** To sustain; support. **8.** To offer for sale or keep in stock. **9.** To cover a range; reach. **10.** To secure the adoption of. **11.** To win most of the votes of. **12.** To keep in one's accounts. **13.** To print or broadcast: *All the papers carried the story.* —*phrasal verbs.* **carry away.** To move or excite greatly. **carry forward.** To progress with. **2.** *Accounting.* To transfer (an entry) to the next column, page, book, or to another account. **carry off.** **1.** To cause the death of: *carried off by a fever.* **2.** To handle (e.g. a situation) successfully. **3.** To win: *carried off first prize.* **4.** To seize and detain (a person) unlawfully. **carry on.** **1.** To conduct; administer. **2.** To engage in: *carry on a conversation.* **3.** To continue without halting: *carry on in the face of disaster.* **4.** To behave in an excited, improper, or silly way. **carry out.** **1.** To put into practice. **2.** To follow or obey. **3.** To bring to a conclusion; accomplish. **carry over.** **1.** *Accounting.* To transfer (an entry) to another column, page, book, or account. **2.** To continue at another time. **carry through.** **1.** To accomplish; complete. **2.** To enable to endure; sustain. —*n., pl.* **-ries.** **1.** A portage, as between two navigable rivers. **2.** The range of a gun or projectile. [< Norman Fr. *carier.*]

car·ry·all (kăr′ē-ôl′) *n.* A large bag, basket, or pocketbook.

carrying charge *n.* The interest charged on the balance owed when paying in installments.

car·ry·on (kăr′ē-ŏn′) *n.* An item small enough to be carried aboard an airplane.

car·ry·out (kăr′ē-out′) *adj.* Take-out. —**car·ry·out′** *n.*

car·sick (kär′sĭk′) *adj.* Nauseated by vehicular motion. —**car′sick′ness** *n.*

cart (kärt) *n.* **1.** A two-wheeled vehicle. **2.** A small, light vehicle moved by hand. —*v.* **1. a.** To convey in a cart. **b.** To convey laboriously; lug. **2.** To remove or transport unceremoniously. [ON *kartr.*] —**cart′a·ble** *adj.* —**cart′er** *n.*

cart·age (kär′tĭj) *n.* **1.** The act or process of transporting by cart. **2.** The cost of transporting by cart.

carte blanche (kärt′ blänsh′, blänch′) *n., pl.* **cartes blanches** (blänsh′, blän′shĭz, blänch′, blän′chĭz). Unrestricted authority. [Fr.]

car·tel (kär-tĕl′) *n.* A monopolistic combination of independent business organizations. [< Fr.]

Car·te·sian coordinates (kär-tē′zhən) *pl.n.* The numbers locating a point in a Cartesian coordinate system, as the abscissa and the ordinate in a plane system.

Cartesian coordinate system *n.* **1.** A two-dimensional coordinate system in which the coordinates of a point are its distances from two intersecting, usu. perpendicular straight lines, the distance from each being measured along a straight line parallel to the other. **2.** A three-dimensional coordinate system in which the coordinates of a point are its distances from each of three intersecting, usu. mutually perpendicular planes along lines parallel to the intersection of the other two. [< René *Descartes* (1595-1650).]

car·ti·lage (kär′tl-ĭj) *n.* A tough white fibrous connective tissue attached to the articular surfaces of bones. [Lat. *cartilago.*] —**car′ti·lag′i·nous** (-ăj′ə-nəs) *adj.*

car·tog·ra·phy (kär-tŏg′rə-fē) *n.* The making of maps. [Fr. *cartographie.*] —**car·tog′ra·pher** *n.* —**car′to·graph′ic** (kär′tə-grăf′ĭk) or **car′to·graph′i·cal** *adj.*

car·ton (kär′tn) *n.* A cardboard box or other container. [< Ital. *cartone,* pasteboard.]

car·toon (kär-tōōn′) *n.* **1.** A satirical drawing or caricature. **2.** A preliminary sketch, as for a fresco. **3.** A comic strip. [Ital. *cartone.*] —**car·toon′ist** *n.*

car·tridge (kär′trĭj) *n.* **1.** A tubular case containing the propellant powder and bullet or shot of a small firearm. **2.** A small modular unit of equipment to be inserted into a larger piece of equipment, esp. a cassette for a tape recorder or a case with photographic film that can be loaded directly into a camera. [< Ital. *cartoccio.*]

cart·wheel (kärt′hwēl′, -wēl′) *n.* **1.** A handspring in which the body turns over sideways with the arms and legs extended. **2.** A silver dollar.

carve (kärv) *v.* **carved, carv·ing.** **1.** To divide into pieces by cutting; slice. **2.** To slice and serve meat or poultry. **3.** To produce or form by or as if by cutting. [< OE *ceorfan.*] —**carv′er** *n.*

car·y·at·id (kär′ē-ăt′ĭd) *n., pl.* **-ids** or **-at·i·des** (-ăt′ĭ-dēz′). A supporting column sculptured in the form of a woman. [< Gk. *karuatidēs,* caryatids.]

ca·sa·ba (kə-sä′bə) *n.* A melon with a yellow rind and sweet, whitish flesh. [< *Kassaba,* former name for *Turgutlu,* Turkey.]

cas·cade (kă-skād′) *n.* **1.** A waterfall or series of small waterfalls. **2.** A structure or phenomenon resembling a cascade. —*v.* **-cad·ed, -cad·ing.** To fall in or as if in a cascade. [< Ital. *cascata.*]

cas·car·a (kă-skăr′ə) *n.* **1.** A buckthorn shrub or tree of northwestern North America. **2.** The dried bark of the cascara, used as a laxative. [Sp. *cáscara,* bark.]

case¹ (kās) *n.* **1.** A specific instance; example. **2. a.** An occurrence of disease or injury. **b.** A client, as of a physician or attorney. **3.** A set of circumstances or state of affairs; situation. **4.** A persuasive argument, demonstration, or justification. **5.** A question or problem; matter. **6.** *Law.* An action or suit or just grounds for an action. **7.** *Ling.* An inflectional pattern or form of nouns, pronouns, and adjectives to express syntactic functions in a sentence. —*v.* **cased, cas·ing.** *Slang.* To examine carefully, as in planning a crime. —**idioms. in any case.** Regardless of what occurred or will occur. **in case.** If it happens that. [< Lat. *casus.*]

case² (kās) *n.* **1.** A container or receptacle. **2.** A covering. **3.** A set or pair. **4.** The frame or framework of a window or door. **5.** A shallow, compartmented tray for storing printing type. —*v.* **cased, cas·ing.** To put into, cover, or protect with a case. [< Lat. *capsa.*]

case history *n.* The facts relevant to the development of an individual or group condition under study or treatment.

ca·sein (kā′sēn′, -sē-ĭn) *n.* A white, tasteless, odorless milk protein used to make plastics, adhesives, paints, and foods. [< Lat. *caseus,* cheese.]

case·ment (kās′mənt) *n.* **1.** A window sash that opens outward by means of hinges. **2.** A window with casements. [< Med. Lat. *casamentum.*]

case·work (kās′wûrk′) *n.* Social work dealing with the problems of a particular case. —**case′work′er** *n.*

cash (kăsh) *n.* **1.** Money in the form of currency. **2.** Immediate payment for goods or services. —*v.* To exchange for or convert into ready money. [< Lat. *capsa,* case.]

cash·ew (kăsh′ōō, kə-shōō′) *n.* **1.** A tropical American tree bearing kidney-shaped nuts. **2.** The nut of the cashew. [< Tupi *acajú.*]

cash·ier¹ (kă-shîr′) *n.* **1.** The officer of a bank or business concern in charge of paying and receiving money. **2.** An employee, as in a shop, responsible for cash transactions. [< Fr. *caissier.*]

ca·shier² (kă-shîr′) *v.* To dismiss in disgrace from a position of responsibility. [< LLat. *cassare,* to quash.]

cashier's check *n.* A check drawn by a bank on its own funds and signed by the bank's cashier.

cash·mere (kăzh′mîr′, kăsh′-) *n.* **1.** Fine wool from an Asian goat. **2.** A soft fabric made from cashmere. [< *Kashmir,* India.]

cash register *n.* A machine that tabulates the amount of sales transactions and makes a record of them.

cas·ing (kā′sĭng) *n.* An outer cover; case.

ca·si·no (kə-sē′nō) *n., pl.* **-nos.** A public room or house for entertainment, esp. for gambling. [Ital.]

cask (kăsk) *n.* **1.** A barrel of any size. **2.** The amount a cask holds. [Sp. *casco,* helmet.]

cas·ket (kăs′kĭt) *n.* **1.** A small case or chest, as for jewels. **2.** A coffin. [ME.]

casque (kăsk) *n.* A helmet. [< Sp. *casco.*]

Cas·san·dra (kə-săn′drə) *n.* One who utters unheeded prophecies. [< *Cassandra,* a Trojan prophetess.]

cas·sa·va (kə-sä′və) *n.* A tropical American plant with a starchy root from which tapioca is derived. [< Taino *caçábi.*]

cas·se·role (kăs′ə-rōl′) *n.* **1.** A dish in which food is baked and served. **2.** Food baked and served in a casserole. [Fr., saucepan.]

cas·sette (kə-sĕt′, kă-) *n.* A cartridge for film or magnetic tape. [Fr., small box.]

cas·sia (kăsh′ə) *n.* **1.** Any of various chiefly tropical trees, shrubs, and plants with compound leaves, usu. yellow flowers, and long pods. **2.** A tropical Asian tree with cinnamonlike bark. [Gk. *kassia.*]

Cas·si·o·pe·ia (kăs′ē-ə-pē′ə) *n.* A W-shaped constellation in the Northern Hemisphere.

cas·sit·er·ite (kə-sĭt′ə-rīt′) *n.* A dark mineral, SnO₂, that is an important tin ore. [< Gk. *kassiteros,* tin.]

cas·sock (kăs′ək) *n.* A long garment worn by clergymen. [< Pers. *kazagand,* padded jacket.]

cast (kăst) *v.* **cast, cast·ing.** **1.** To throw; fling. **2.** To shed; discard. **3.** To turn; direct: *cast a glance at her.* **4.** To give or deposit (a ballot). **5. a.** To assign a role to. **b.** To choose actors for. **6.** To form by molding. **7.** To add up (a column of figures); compute. —*n.* **1.** A throw. **2.** A throw of the dice. **3.** The group of actors assigned roles, as in a play. **4.** A rigid plaster dressing, as for immobilizing and protecting a broken bone. **5.** A mold. **6.** A hue; shade. **7.** Outward appearance; look. **8.** Something shed or thrown off. [< ON *kasta.*]

cas·ta·nets (kăs′tə-nĕts′) *pl.n.* A pair of shells of ivory or hardwood held in the hand and clicked in accompaniment to music and dancing. [Sp. *castañeta.*]

cast·a·way (kăst′ə-wā′) *adj.* **1.** Cast adrift or ashore; shipwrecked. **2.** Thrown away; discarded. —**cast′a·way′** *n.*

caste (kăst) *n.* **1.** One of the major hereditary classes into which Hindu society is divided. **2. a.** A social class separated from the others by distinctions of hereditary rank, profession, or wealth. **b.** Social status; position. [Port. *casta.*]

cast·er (kăs′tər) *n.* Also **cas·tor.** **1.** A small wheel on a swivel attached to the underside of a heavy object to make it easier to move. **2.** A small bottle or cruet for condiments.

cas·ti·gate (kăs′tĭ-gāt′) *v.* **-gat·ed, -gat·ing.** To chastise or criticize severely. [Lat. *castigare.*] —**cas′ti·ga′tion** *n.* —**cas′ti·ga′tor** *n.*

cast·ing (kăs′tĭng) *n.* **1.** Something cast off or out. **2.** Something cast in a mold.

cast iron *n.* A hard, brittle nonmalleable iron-carbon alloy containing 2.0–4.5% carbon and 0.5–3% silicon.

cas·tle (kăs′əl) *n.* **1.** A fort or fortified group of buildings. **2.** A building resembling a castle. **3.** The rook in chess. [< Lat. *castellum.*]

cast·off (kăst′ôf′, -ŏf′) *n.* One that has been discarded.

cast-off (kăst′ôf′, -ŏf′) *adj.* Discarded.

cas·tor (kăs′tər) *n.* Var. of **caster.**

castor oil *n.* An oil extracted from the seeds of a tropical plant and used as a cathartic and a fine lubricant. [Prob. < *castor,* an oily brown substance.]

cas·trate (kăs′trāt′) *v.* **-trat·ed, -trat·ing.** To remove the testicles or ovaries of. [Lat. *castrare.*] —**cas·tra′tion** *n.*

ca·su·al (kăzh′ōō-əl) *adj.* **1.** Happening by chance. **2.** Nonchalant; offhand. **3. a.** Informal. **b.** Designed for informal wear or use. **4.** Not thorough; superficial. [< Lat. *casualis.*] —**ca′su·al·ly** *adv.* —**ca′su·al·ness** *n.*

ca·su·al·ty (kăzh′ōō-əl-tē) *n., pl.* **-ties. 1.** One injured or killed in an accident. **2.** One injured, killed, captured, or missing in action against an enemy. **3.** A disastrous accident.

ca·su·ist·ry (kăzh′ōō-ĭ-strē) *n.* A subtle but misleading or false application of ethical principles. [< Lat. *casus,* case.] —**ca′su·ist** *n.* —**ca′su·is′tic** *adj.* —**ca′su·is′ti·cal·ly** *adv.*

cat (kăt) *n.* **1. a.** A carnivorous mammal domesticated as a catcher of rats and mice and as a pet. **b.** An animal related to the cat, as the lion, tiger, or leopard. **2.** A spiteful woman. **3.** *Slang.* A person. [< OE *catt.*]

ca·tab·o·lism (kə-tăb′ə-lĭz′əm) *n.* The metabolic change of complex into simple molecules. [< Gk. *katabolē,* a throwing down.] —**cat′a·bol′ic** (kăt′ə-bŏl′ĭk) *adj.*

cat·a·clysm (kăt′ə-klĭz′əm) *n.* A violent and sudden upheaval. [< Gk. *kataklusmos,* flood.] —**cat′a·clys′mic** (-klĭz′mĭk) or **cat′a·clys′mal** (-məl) *adj.*

cat·a·comb (kăt′ə-kōm′) *n.* Often **catacombs.** An underground chamber with recesses for graves. [< LLat. *catacumba.*]

cat·a·falque (kăt′ə-fălk′, -fôlk′) *n.* The structure on which a coffin rests during a state funeral. [< Ital. *catafalco.*]

catafalque

Cat·a·lan (kăt′l-ăn′, -ən) *n.* **1.** A native or inhabitant of Catalonia. **2.** The Romance language of Catalonia. —**Cat′a·lan′** *adj.*

cat·a·lep·sy (kăt′l-ĕp′sē) *n.* Muscular rigidity, lack of awareness of environment, and lack of response to external stimuli. [< Gk. *katalēpsis.*] —**cat′a·lep′tic** *adj.*

cat·a·logue or **cat·a·log** (kăt′l-ôg′, -ŏg′) *n.* **1.** An itemized, often descriptive list. **2.** A publication containing a catalogue. **3.** A card catalog. —*v.* **-logued** or **-loged, -logu·ing** or **-log·ing.** To list·in or make a catalogue. [< Gk. *katalegein,* to list.] —**cat′a·logu′er** or **cat′a·log′er** *n.*

ca·tal·pa (kə-tăl′pə, -tôl′-) *n.* A tree with large leaves, showy flower clusters, and long, slender pods. [Creek *kutuhlpa.*]

ca·tal·y·sis (kə-tăl′ĭ-sĭs) *n.* The action of a catalyst, esp. in modifying the rate of a chemical reaction. [Gk. *katalusis,* dissolution.] —**cat′a·lyt′ic** (kăt′l-ĭt′ĭk) *adj.* —**cat′a·lyt′i·cal·ly** *adv.*

cat·a·lyst (kăt′l-ĭst) *n.* A substance that modifies and esp. increases the rate of a chemical reaction without being consumed in the process. [< CATALYSIS.]

cat·a·lyze (kăt′l-īz′) *v.* **-lyzed, -lyz·ing.** To modify the rate of (a chemical reaction) as a catalyst. —**cat′a·lyz′er** *n.*

cat·a·ma·ran (kăt′ə-mə-răn′) *n.* A boat with two parallel hulls. [Tamil *kaṭṭumaran.*]

cat·a·mount (kăt′ə-mount′) *n.* A mountain lion or lynx. [< *cat of the mountain.*]

cat·a·pult (kăt′ə-pŭlt′, -pŏŏlt′) *n.* **1.** An ancient military machine for hurling large missiles. **2.** A mechanism for launching aircraft from the deck of a ship. [< Gk. *katapaltēs.*] —**cat′a·pult′** *v.*

cat·a·ract (kăt′ə-răkt′) *n.* **1.** A great waterfall or downpour. **2.** Opacity of the lens or capsule of the eye, causing partial or total blindness. [< Gk. *katauraktēs.*]

ca·tarrh (kə-tär′) *n.* Inflammation of mucous membranes, esp. of the nose and throat. [< Gk. *katarrhous.*] —**ca·tarrh′al** (-əl) *adj.*

ca·tas·tro·phe (kə-tăs′trə-fē) *n.* A great and sudden calamity; disaster. [Gk. *katastrophē.*] —**cat′a·stroph′ic** (kăt′ə-strŏf′ĭk) *adj.* —**cat′a·stroph′i·cal·ly** *adv.*

cat·a·ton·ic (kăt′ə-tŏn′ĭk) *adj.* Of or pertaining to a schizophrenic disorder characterized by immobility, stupor, negativism, and silence. —*n.* One who is catatonic. [< G. *Katatonie,* a catatonic condition.]

Ca·taw·ba (kə-tô′bə) *n.* **1. a.** A tribe of Indians formerly living along the Catawba River in the Carolinas. **b.** A member of this tribe. **2.** The Siouan language of the Catawba.

cat·bird (kăt′bûrd′) *n.* A dark-gray North American songbird with a call like the mewing of a cat.

cat·call (kăt′kôl′) *n.* A shrill call or cry of derision. —**cat′call′** *v.*

catch (kăch, kĕch) *v.* **caught** (kôt), **catch·ing.** **1.** To capture, esp. after a chase. **2.** To snare or trap. **3.** To come upon suddenly, unexpectedly, or accidentally. **4.** To take or apprehend suddenly. **5.** To grasp. **6.** To snatch; grab. **7.** To intercept. **8.** To become ensnared. **9.** To fasten. **10.** To take in and retain. **11.** To get to in time: *catch a plane.* **12.** To become subject to; contract, as by contagion. **13.** *Informal.* To watch: *caught the late movie.* —*phrasal verbs.* **catch on.** *Informal.* **1.** To understand or perceive. **2.** To become popular. **catch up. 1.** To come up from behind; overtake. **2.** To bring up to date: *catch up on his correspondence.* —*n.* **1.** The act of catching. **2.** A fastening or checking device. **3.** Something caught. **4.** *Informal.* One worth catching. **5.** *Informal.* An unsuspected drawback. **6.** A game of throwing and catching a ball. [< Lat. *captare,* to chase.]

catch·all (kăch′ôl′, kĕch′-) *n.* A receptacle for odds and ends.

catch·er (kăch′ər, kĕch′-) *n.* **1.** One that catches. **2.** The baseball player whose position is behind home plate.

catch·ing (kăch′ĭng, kĕch′-) *adj.* **1.** Infectious; contagious. **2.** Attractive; alluring.

catch·up (kăch′əp, kĕch′-) *n.* Var. of ketchup.

catch·y (kăch′ē, kĕch′-) *adj.* **-i·er, -i·est. 1.** Easily remembered: *a catchy tune.* **2.** Tricky; deceptive.

cat·e·chism (kăt′ĭ-kĭz′əm) *n.* An instructional summary of the basic principles of a religion in question-and-answer form. [< LGk. *katēkhismos.*] —**cat′e·chist** *n.* —**cat′e·chize′** *v.*

cat·e·chu·men (kăt′ĭ-kyōō′mən) *n.* A convert receiving religious instruction before a baptism. [< Gk. *katēkhein,* to instruct.]

cat·e·gor·i·cal (kăt′ĭ-gôr′ĭ-kəl, -gôr′-) or **cat·e·gor·ic** (-ĭk) *adj.* **1.** Without qualification; absolute. **2.** Of, concerning, or included in a category. **—cat′e·gor′i·cal·ly** *adv.*

cat·e·go·rize (kăt′ĭ-gə-rīz′) *v.* **-rized, -riz·ing.** To put into categories; classify. **—cat′e·go·ri·za′tion** *n.*

cat·e·go·ry (kăt′ĭ-gôr′ē, -gôr′ē) *n., pl.* **-ries.** A specific division in a system of classification; class. [< Gk. *katēgoria.*]

ca·ter (kā′tər) *v.* **1.** To provide food. **2.** To provide something wished for or needed. [< Norman Fr. *acatour,* caterer.] **—ca′ter·er** *n.*

cat·er-cor·nered (kăt′ər-kôr′nərd, kăt′ē-) *& adv.* Var. of **catty-cornered.**

cat·er·pil·lar (kăt′ər-pĭl′ər, kăt′ə-) *n.* The wormlike, often hairy larva of a butterfly or moth. [< OFr. *chatepelose.*]

cat·er·waul (kăt′ər-wôl′) *v.* To make a discordant sound or shriek. [ME *caterwawen.*] **—cat′er·waul′** *n.*

cat·fish (kăt′fĭsh′) *n.* Any of various scaleless fishes with whiskerlike feelers near the mouth.

cat·gut (kăt′gŭt′) *n.* A tough cord made from the dried intestines of certain animals.

ca·thar·sis (kə-thär′sĭs) *n., pl.* **-ses** (-sēz′). **1.** Purgation, esp. for the digestive system. **2.** A purifying or figurative cleansing of the emotions. [Gk. *katharsis.*]

ca·thar·tic (kə-thär′tĭk) *adj.* Inducing catharsis; purgative. **—n.** A cathartic agent, as a laxative.

ca·the·dral (kə-thē′drəl) *n.* The principal church of a bishop's see. [< Gk. *kathedra,* seat.]

cath·e·ter (kăth′ĭ-tər) *n.* A slender, flexible tube inserted into a bodily channel to distend or maintain an opening to an internal cavity. [< Gk. *kathetēr.*]

cath·ode (kăth′ōd′) *n.* **1.** A negatively charged electrode, as of an electrolytic cell. **2.** The positively charged terminal of a primary cell or of a storage battery. [Gk. *kathodos,* descent.] **—ca·thod′ic** (kă-thŏd′ĭk) *adj.*

cath·o·lic (kăth′ə-lĭk, kăth′lĭk) *adj.* **1.** Universal; general. **2. Catholic.** Of or pertaining to Catholics or the Roman Catholic Church. **—n. Catholic.** A member of the Roman Catholic Church. [< Gk. *katholikos.*] **—ca·thol′i·cal·ly** (kə-thŏl′ĭ-klē) *adv.*

Ca·thol·i·cism (kə-thŏl′ə-sĭz′əm) *n.* The faith, doctrine, system, and practice of the Roman Catholic Church.

cat·i·on (kăt′ī′ən) *n.* An ion having a positive charge and, in electrolytes, characteristically moving toward a negative electrode. [Gk. *kation,* (thing) going down.] **—cat′i·on′ic** (-ŏn′ĭk) *adj.*

cat·kin (kăt′kĭn) *n.* A dense cluster of scalelike flowers, as of a birch.

cat·nap (kăt′năp′) *n.* A short nap; light sleep. **—cat′nap′** *v.*

cat·nip (kăt′nĭp′) *n.* An aromatic plant to which cats are strongly attracted.

cat-o'-nine-tails (kăt′ə-nīn′tālz′) *n.* A whip consisting of nine knotted cords fastened to a handle.

cat's cradle *n.* A game in which an intricately looped string is transferred from the hands of one player to another.

cat's-eye (kăts′ī′) *n.* Any of various semiprecious gems displaying a band of reflected light that shifts position as the gem is turned.

cat's-paw (kăts′pô′) *n.* Also **cats·paw.** A person used by another as a dupe or tool.

cat·sup (kăt′səp, kăch′əp, kĕch′-) *n.* Var. of **ketchup.**

cat·tail (kăt′tāl′) *n.* A tall-stemmed, long-leaved marsh plant with a dense brown cylindrical head.

cat·tle (kăt′l) *pl.n.* Horned, hoofed mammals, as cows, bulls, and oxen, esp. those domesticated for meat and dairy products. [< Med. Lat. *capitale,* property.]

cat·ty (kăt′ē) *adj.* **-ti·er, -ti·est.** Subtly malicious; spiteful. **—cat′ti·ly** *adv.* **—cat′ti·ness** *n.*

cat·ty-cor·nered (kăt′ē-kôr′nərd) *adj. & adv.* Also **cat·er-cor·nered** (kăt′ər-kôr′nərd, kăt′ē-) or **cat·ty-cor·ner** (kăt′ē-kôr′nər). In a diagonal position. [< obs. *cater,* four at dice.]

cat·walk (kăt′wôk′) *n.* A narrow walk, as on the sides of a bridge.

Cau·ca·sian (kô-kā′zhən, -kăzh′ən) *n.* **1.** A native of the Caucasus. **2.** A member of the Caucasoid ethnic division. **—Cau·ca′sian** *adj.*

Cau·ca·soid (kô′kə-soid′) *adj.* Of or pertaining to a major ethnic division of the human species having skin color varying from very light to brown. **—Cau′ca·soid′** *n.*

cau·cus (kô′kəs) *n., pl.* **-cus·es** or **-cus·ses.** A meeting of the members of a political party to decide questions of policy and the selection of candidates. [Poss. of Algonquian orig.] **—cau′cus** *v.*

cau·dal (kôd′l) *adj.* Of, at, or near the tail or hind parts; posterior. [< Lat. *cauda,* tail.] **—cau′dal·ly** *adv.*

caught (kôt) *v. p.t. & p.p.* of **catch.**

caul·dron (kôl′drən) *n.* Var. of **caldron.**

cau·li·flow·er (kô′lĭ-flou′ər, kŏl′ĭ-) *n.* **1.** A cabbagelike plant with a large, compact whitish flower head eaten as a vegetable. **2.** The flower head of the cauliflower. [Prob. < Ital. *cavolofiore.*]

cauliflower ear *n.* An ear deformed by repeated blows.

caulk (kôk) *v.* Also **calk. 1.** To make (a boat) watertight by packing seams with oakum or tar. **2.** To make (pipes) tight against leakage by sealing. [< OFr. *cauquer,* to press.] **—caulk′er** *n.*

caus·al (kô′zəl) *adj.* **1.** Being or constituting a cause. **2.** Indicating or expressing a cause. **—cau·sal′i·ty** (-zăl′ĭ-tē) *n.* **—caus′al·ly** *adv.*

cau·sa·tion (kô-zā′shən) *n.* **1.** The act or process of causing. **2.** A causal agency.

cause (kôz) *n.* **1.** A person or thing responsible for an action or result. **2.** A reason; motive. **3.** Good or sufficient reason. **4.** A goal or principle. **5. a.** The ground for legal action. **b.** A lawsuit. **—v. caused, caus·ing.** To be the cause of; bring about. [< Lat. *causa,* reason.] **—cause′less** *adj.* **—caus′er** *n.*

cause cé·lè·bre (kôz′ sā-lĕb′rə) *n., pl.* **causes cé·lè·bres** (kôz′ sā-lĕb′rə). **1.** A celebrated legal case. **2.** An issue arousing heated debate. [Fr.]

cau·se·rie (kōz-rē′) *n.* **1.** A chat. **2.** A short, conversational piece of writing. [Fr.]

cause·way (kôz′wā′) *n.* A raised roadway across water or marshland. [ME *caucewei.*]

caus·tic (kô′stĭk) *adj.* **1.** Able to burn, corrode, or dissolve. **2.** Marked by sharp and bitter wit; cutting. **—n.** A caustic material or substance. [< Gk. *kaustikos.*]

cau·ter·ize (kô′tə-rīz′) *v.* **-ized, -iz·ing.** To burn or sear so as to stop bleeding or prevent infection. [< Gk. *kautēriazein,* to brand.] **—cau′ter·i·za′tion** *n.*

cau·tion (kô′shən) *n.* **1.** Forethought to avoid

danger or harm. **2.** A warning; admonishment. **3.** *Informal.* One that is striking or alarming. —*v.* To warn against danger; put on guard. [< Lat. *cavēre,* to take care.] —**cau'tion·ar·y** (-shə-nĕr'ē) *adj.*

cau·tious (kô'shəs) *adj.* Showing or practicing caution; careful. —**cau'tious·ly** *adv.* —**cau'tious·ness** *n.*

cav·al·cade (kăv'əl-kād', kăv'əl-kād') *n.* **1.** A ceremonial procession, esp. of horsemen. **2.** A colorful procession or display. [< OItal. *cavalcare,* to ride on horseback.]

cav·a·lier (kăv'ə-lîr') *n.* **1.** An armed horseman; knight. **2.** A gallant gentleman. **3. Cavalier.** A supporter of Charles I of England. —*adj.* **1.** Haughty; disdainful. **2.** Carefree and gay; offhand. [< Lat. *caballarius,* horseman.] —**cav'a·lier'ly** *adv.*

cav·al·ry (kăv'əl-rē) *n., pl.* **-ries.** Troops trained to fight on horseback or in armored vehicles. [< OItal. *cavalleria* < Lat. *caballarius,* horseman.] —**cav'al·ry·man** *n.*

cave (kāv) *n.* A hollow beneath the earth's surface, often having an opening in the side of a hill or cliff. —*v.* **caved, cav·ing. 1.** To fall in; collapse. **2.** To give up all opposition; yield. [< Lat. *cava.*]

ca·ve·at (kă'vē-ăt', kăv'ē-, kä'vē-ät') *n.* A warning. [Lat., let him beware.]

cave-in (kāv'ĭn') *n.* **1.** An action of caving in. **2.** A place where the ground has caved in.

cave man *n.* **1.** A prehistoric man who lived in caves. **2.** *Informal.* One who is crude or brutal, esp. toward women.

cav·ern (kăv'ərn) *n.* A large cave. [< Lat. *caverna.*] —**cav'ern·ous** *adj.*

cav·i·ar (kăv'ē-är') *n.* Also **cav·i·are.** The roe of a sturgeon or other large fish, salted and eaten as a delicacy. [Prob. < Turk. *havyār.*]

cav·il (kăv'əl) *v.* **-iled** or **-illed, -il·ing** or **-il·ling.** To find fault unnecessarily; raise trivial objections. [< Lat. *cavillari,* to criticize.] —**cav'il** *n.* —**cav'il·er** *n.*

cav·i·ty (kăv'ĭ-tē) *n., pl.* **-ties. 1.** A hollow or hole. **2.** A pitted area in a tooth caused by decay. [< LLat. *cavitas.*]

ca·vort (kə-vôrt') *v.* To prance about; caper. [Perh. < CURVET.]

caw (kô) *n.* The hoarse, raucous sound uttered by a crow or similar bird. [Imit.] —**caw** *v.*

cay (kē, kā) *n.* An islet of coral or sand; key. [Sp. *cayo.*]

cay·enne pepper (kī-ĕn', kā-) *n.* A pungent condiment made from the fruit of a variety of the pepper plant. [< Tupi *kyinha.*]

Ca·yu·ga (kā-yōō'gə, kī-) *n., pl.* **-ga** or **-gas. 1. a.** A tribe of Indians formerly living around Cayuga and Seneca lakes in central New York. **b.** A member of this tribe. **2.** The Iroquoian language of the Cayuga.

Cay·use (kī-yōōs', kī'yōōs') *n., pl.* **-use** or **-us·es. 1. a.** A tribe of Indians of Oregon. **b.** A member of this tribe. **2.** The Sahaptin language of the Cayuse.

Cb The symbol for the element columbium.

Cd The symbol for the element cadmium.

Ce The symbol for the element cerium.

cease (sēs) *v.* **ceased, ceas·ing.** To bring or come to an end; stop. [< Lat. *cessare.*]

cease-fire (sēs'fîr') *n.* A suspension of active hostilities; truce.

cease·less (sēs'lĭs) *adj.* Without stop; endless. —**cease'less·ly** *adv.*

ce·cum (sē'kəm) *n., pl.* **-ca** (-kə). Also **cae·cum.** The large blind pouch forming the beginning of the large intestine. [< Lat. (*intestinum*) *caecum,* blind (intestine).] —**ce'cal** (-kəl) *adj.*

ce·dar (sē'dər) *n.* **1.** Any of various evergreen trees with aromatic, often reddish wood. **2.** The wood of a cedar. [Gk. *kedros.*]

cede (sēd) *v.* **ced·ed, ced·ing. 1.** To relinquish, as by treaty. **2.** To transfer; assign. [< Lat. *cedere.*]

ce·di (sā'dē) *n., pl.* **-di** or **-dis.** See table at **currency.** [Native word in Ghana.]

ce·dil·la (sĭ-dĭl'ə) *n.* A mark (¸) placed beneath the letter *c* to indicate that the letter is to be pronounced (s). [Obs. Sp., dim. of *ceda,* the letter *z.*]

ceil·ing (sē'lĭng) *n.* **1.** The interior upper surface of a room. **2.** A vertical boundary, as of operable aircraft altitude. **3.** A maximum limit: *wage and price ceilings.* [ME *celing.*]

-cele or **-coel** or **-coele** *suff.* A hollow chamber: *blastocoel.* [< Gk. *koilos,* hollow.]

cel·e·brate (sĕl'ə-brāt') *v.* **-brat·ed, -brat·ing. 1.** To observe (a day or event) with ceremonies of respect or festivity. **2.** To perform (a religious ceremony). **3.** To extol; praise. [Lat. *celebrare.*] —**cel'e·brant** *n.* —**cel'e·bra'tion** *n.* —**cel'e·bra'tor** *n.*

cel·e·brat·ed (sĕl'ə-brā'tĭd) *adj.* Famous.

ce·leb·ri·ty (sə-lĕb'rĭ-tē) *n., pl.* **-ties. 1.** A famous person. **2.** Renown; fame. [Lat. *celebritas,* fame.]

ce·ler·i·ty (sə-lĕr'ĭ-tē) *n.* Swiftness; speed. [< Lat. *celeritas.*]

cel·er·y (sĕl'ə-rē) *n.* A plant cultivated for its succulent, edible stalks. [< Gk. *selinon.*]

ce·les·ta (sə-lĕs'tə) *n.* Also **ce·leste** (sə-lĕst'). A keyboard instrument with metal plates struck by hammers. [Fr. *célesta.*]

ce·les·tial (sə-lĕs'chəl) *adj.* **1.** Of or pertaining to the sky or the heavens. **2.** Of or suggestive of heaven; heavenly. [< Lat. *caelestis.*]

celestial navigation *n.* Navigation based on the positions of celestial bodies.

celestial sphere *n.* An imaginary sphere of infinite extent with the earth at its center.

cel·i·ba·cy (sĕl'ə-bə-sē) *n.* The condition of being celibate. [Lat. *caelibatus.*]

cel·i·bate (sĕl'ə-bĭt) *adj.* **1.** Unmarried, esp. by reason of religious vows. **2.** Sexually abstinent. [Lat. *caelebs.*] —**cel'i·bate** *n.*

cell (sĕl) *n.* **1.** A narrow, confining room, as in a prison or convent. **2.** The basic organizational unit of a movement, esp. of a revolutionary political party. **3.** *Biol.* The smallest structural unit of an organism that is capable of independent functioning, consisting of nuclei, cytoplasm, various organelles, and inanimate matter, all surrounded by a membrane. **4.** A small, enclosed cavity or space, as in a honeycomb. **5. a.** A single unit for electrolysis or for conversion of chemical into electric energy, usu. consisting of a container with electrodes and an electrolyte. **b.** A single unit that converts radiant energy into electric energy. [< Lat. *cella,* chamber.]

cell

cel·lar (sĕl′ər) *n.* 1. An underground room, usu. beneath a building. 2. A stock of wines. [LLat. *cellarium*, pantry.]

cel·lo (chĕl′ō) *n., pl.* **-los.** An instrument of the violin family, pitched lower than the viola but higher than the double bass. [< VIOLON-CELLO.] **—cel′list** *n.*

cel·lo·phane (sĕl′ə-fān′) *n.* A thin, flexible, transparent cellulose material used as a moistureproof wrapping. [Orig. a trademark.]

cel·lu·lar (sĕl′yə-lər) *adj.* Of, pertaining to, or resembling a cell. 2. Consisting of cells.

cel·lu·loid (sĕl′yə-loid′) *n.* A colorless, flammable material made from nitrocellulose and camphor. [Orig. a trademark.]

cel·lu·lose (sĕl′yə-lōs′, -lōz′) *n.* An amorphous polymer, $(C_6H_{10}O_5)_x$, the main constituent of all plant tissues and fibers, used in the manufacture of paper, textiles, and explosives. [Fr.] **—cel′lu·lo′sic** (-lō′sĭk, -zĭk) *adj.*

Cel·si·us (sĕl′sē-əs, -shəs) *adj.* Of or pertaining to a temperature scale that registers the freezing point of water at 0°C and the boiling point at 100°C under normal atmospheric pressure. [< Anders *Celsius* (1701–44).]

Celt (kĕlt, sĕlt) *n.* 1. One of an ancient people of western and central Europe, including the Britons and the Gauls. 2. A speaker of a Celtic language.

Celt·ic (kĕl′tĭk, sĕl′-) *n.* A subfamily of the Indo-European language family, including Welsh, Irish Gaelic, and Scottish Gaelic. **—Cel′tic** *adj.*

cem·ba·lo (chĕm′bə-lō′) *n., pl.* **-los.** A harpsichord. [Ital.] **—cem′ba·list** *n.*

ce·ment (sĭ-mĕnt′) *n.* 1. A construction adhesive consisting essentially of powdered rock and clay substances that forms a paste with water and sets as a solid mass. 2. A substance that hardens to act as an adhesive; glue. **—v.** 1. To bind with or as if with cement. 2. To cover or coat with cement. [< Lat. *caementum*, rough stone.] **—ce·ment′er** *n.*

ce·men·tum (sĭ-mĕn′təm) *n.* A bony substance covering the root of a tooth. [< Lat. *caementum*, rough stone.]

cem·e·tery (sĕm′ĭ-tĕr′ē) *n., pl.* **-ies.** A graveyard. [< Gk. *koimētērion.*]

-cene *suff.* A recent geologic period: *Eocene.* [< Gk. *kainos*, new.]

cen·o·taph (sĕn′ə-tăf′) *n.* A monument erected in honor of a dead person whose remains lie elsewhere. [< Gk. *kenotaphion.*]

Ce·no·zo·ic (sē′nə-zō′ĭk, sĕn′ə-) *adj.* Pertaining to the most recent era of geologic time, which includes the Tertiary and Quaternary periods and is characterized by the evolution of mammals, birds, plants, modern conti-

nents, and glaciation. **—n.** The Cenozoic era. [Gk. *kainos*, new + -ZOIC.]

cen·ser (sĕn′sər) *n.* A vessel in which incense is burned, esp. in a religious ceremony. [< Norman Fr. *encensier.*]

cen·sor (sĕn′sər) *n.* 1. A person authorized to examine printed or other materials and remove or suppress what he considers objectionable. 2. One of two Roman officials responsible for supervising the census. **—v.** To examine and expurgate. [Lat., Roman censor.] **—cen·so′ri·al** (-sôr′ē-əl, -sōr′-) *adj.*

cen·so·ri·ous (sĕn-sôr′ē-əs, -sōr′-) *adj.* Tending to censure; critical. **—cen·so′ri·ous·ly** *adv.* **—cen·so′ri·ous·ness** *n.*

cen·sor·ship (sĕn′sər-shĭp′) *n.* 1. The act or process of censoring. 2. The office of a Roman censor.

cen·sure (sĕn′shər) *n.* 1. An expression of blame or disapproval. 2. An official rebuke. **—v. -sured, -sur·ing.** To criticize severely; blame. **—cen′sur·a·ble** *adj.* **—cen′sur·er** *n.*

cen·sus (sĕn′səs) *n.* A periodic official count of population. [Lat., registration of citizens.]

cent (sĕnt) *n.* See table at **currency.** [< Lat. *centum*, hundred.]

cent- *pref.* Var. of **centi-**.

cen·taur (sĕn′tôr′) *n. Gk. Myth.* One of a race of monsters having the head, arms, and trunk of a man and the body and legs of a horse. [< Gk. *Kentauros.*]

Cen·tau·rus (sĕn-tôr′əs) *n.* A constellation in the Southern Hemisphere.

cen·ta·vo (sĕn-tä′vō) *n., pl.* **-vos.** See table at **currency.** [Sp.]

cen·te·nar·i·an (sĕn′tə-nâr′ē-ən) *n.* A person 100 years old or older. **—cen·te·nar′i·an** *adj.*

cen·ten·a·ry (sĕn-tĕn′ə-rē, sĕn′tə-nĕr′ē) *n., pl.* **-ries.** A centennial. [< Lat. *centenarius*, of a hundred.] **—cen·ten′a·ry** *adj.*

cen·ten·ni·al (sĕn-tĕn′ē-əl) *n.* A 100th anniversary or celebration. [CENT- + (BI)ENNIAL.] **—cen·ten′ni·al** *adj.*

cen·ter (sĕn′tər). Also *chiefly Brit.* **cen·tre.** **—n.** 1. A point equidistant from all points on the sides or outer boundaries of something; middle. 2. **a.** A point equidistant from the vertexes of a regular polygon. **b.** A point equidistant from all points on the circumference of a circle or on the surface of a sphere. 3. A point around which something revolves; axis. 4. A place of concentrated activity or influence. 5. One that occupies a middle position. 6. A group whose political views are midway between liberal and conservative. 7. A player who holds a middle position. **—v.** 1. To place in or on a center. 2. To gather or concentrate at a center. 3. To have a center; focus. [< Gk. *kentron.*]

center field *n. Baseball.* The middle part of the outfield, behind second base. **—center fielder** *n.*

cen·ter·piece (sĕn′tər-pēs′) *n.* A decorative object or arrangement placed at the center of a table.

cen·tes·i·mal (sĕn-tĕs′ə-məl) *adj.* Pertaining to or divided into hundredths. [< Lat. *centesimus.*]

cen·tes·i·mo¹ (sĕn-tĕs′ə-mō′) *n., pl.* **-mos** or **-mi** (-mē). See table at **currency.** [Ital.]

cen·tes·i·mo² (sĕn-tĕs′ə-mō′) *n., pl.* **-mos.** See table at **currency.** [Sp.]

centi- or **cent-** *pref.* A hundredth: *centimeter.* [< Lat. *centum*, hundred.]

cen·ti·grade (sĕn'tĭ-grād', sän'-) *adj.* Celsius. [Fr.]

cen·ti·gram (sĕn'tĭ-grăm') *n.* A unit of mass or weight equal to one hundredth (10^{-2}) of a gram.

cen·time (sän'tēm', sĕn'-) *n.* See table at currency. [Fr.]

cen·ti·me·ter (sĕn'tə-mē'tər, sän'-) *n.* A unit of length equal to $1/100$ of a meter or 0.3937 inch.

cen·ti·mo (sĕn'tə-mō') *n., pl.* **-mos.** See table at currency. [Sp. *céntimo.*]

cen·ti·pede (sĕn'tə-pēd') *n.* A wormlike arthropod with many legs and body segments. [Lat. *centipeda.*]

centr– *pref.* Var. of centro-.

cen·tral (sĕn'trəl) *adj.* **1.** At, in, near, or being the center. **2.** Principal; essential. —*n.* **1.** A telephone exchange. **2.** A telephone operator. —**cen'tral·ly** *adv.*

cen·tral·ize (sĕn'trə-līz') *v.* **-ized, -iz·ing.** To bring or come to a center or under a central authority. —**cen'tral·i·za'tion** *n.*

central nervous system *n.* The portion of the vertebrate nervous system consisting of the brain and spinal cord.

cen·tre (sĕn'tər) *n. & v. Chiefly Brit.* Var. of center.

cen·trif·u·gal (sĕn-trĭf'yə-gəl, -trĭf'ə-) *adj.* **1.** Moving or directed away from a center or axis. **2.** Operated by means of centrifugal force. [< Lat. *centrum,* center + *fugere,* to flee.] —**cen·trif'u·gal·ly** *adv.*

centrifugal force *n.* The apparent force, as observed from a body that is moving in a curve or rotating, that acts outward from the center of the curve or the axis of rotation.

cen·tri·fuge (sĕn'trə-fyōōj') *n.* A compartment spun about a central axis to separate contained materials of different density or to simulate gravity with centrifugal force. [Fr.]

cen·trip·e·tal (sĕn-trĭp'ĭ-tl) *adj.* Directed or moving toward a center or axis. [< Lat. *centrum,* center + Lat. *petere,* to seek.] —**cen·trip'e·tal·ly** *adv.*

centripetal force *n.* The force acting on a body that moves in a curve or rotates about an axis that acts toward the center of the curve or the axis of rotation.

cen·trist (sĕn'trĭst) *n.* One who takes a position in the political center; moderate.

centro– or **centr–** *pref.* Center: centrist. [< Gk. *kentron.*]

cen·tu·ri·on (sĕn-tŏŏr'ē-ən, -tyŏŏr'-) *n.* An officer commanding a century in the ancient Roman army. [< Lat. *centurio.*]

cen·tu·ry (sĕn'chə-rē) *n., pl.* **-ries.** **1.** A period of 100 years. **2.** A unit of the ancient Roman army. [Lat. *centuria,* a group of a hundred.]

ce·phal·ic (sə-făl'ĭk) *adj.* Of or relating to the head or skull. [< Gk. *kephalē,* head.]

ce·ram·ic (sə-răm'ĭk) *n.* **1.** Any of various hard, brittle, heat-resistant and corrosion-resistant materials made by firing clay or other minerals. **2. a.** An object made of ceramic. **b. ceramics** (*used with a sing. verb*). The art or technique of making objects of ceramic, esp. from fired clay or porcelain. [< Gk. *keramos,* clay.] —**ce·ram'ist** *n.*

ce·re·al (sîr'ē-əl) *n.* **1.** An edible grain, as wheat or corn. **2.** A food prepared from such grain. [< Lat. *cerealis,* of grain.]

cer·e·bel·lum (sĕr'ə-bĕl'əm) *n., pl.* **-lums** or **-bel·la** (-bĕl'ə). The structure of the brain responsible for coordination of muscular movement. [< Lat. *cerebrum,* brain.] —**cer·e·bel'lar** (-bĕl'ər) *adj.*

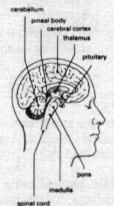

cerebellum

cer·e·bral (sĕr'ə-brəl, sə-rē'-) *adj.* Of or pertaining to the brain or cerebrum. —**cer·e·bral·ly** *adv.*

cerebral cortex *n.* The outer layer of gray tissue that covers the two parts of the cerebrum, largely responsible for higher nervous functions.

cerebral palsy *n.* Impaired muscular power and coordination from brain damage usu. at or before birth.

cer·e·brum (sĕr'ə-brəm, sə-rē'-) *n., pl.* **-brums** or **-bra** (-brə). The large, rounded structure of the brain occupying most of the cranial cavity and divided into two cerebral hemispheres. [Lat., brain.]

cere·cloth (sîr'klôth', -klŏth') *n.* Cloth coated with wax, formerly used for wrapping the dead. [< *cered cloth,* waxed cloth.]

cere·ment (sîr'mənt) *n.* A shroud. [< Fr. *cirement.*]

cer·e·mo·ni·al (sĕr'ə-mō'nē-əl) *adj.* Of or characterized by ceremony. —*n.* **1.** A ceremony; rite. **2.** A set of ceremonies for an occasion; rite. —**cer·e·mo'ni·al·ly** *adv.*

cer·e·mo·ni·ous (sĕr'ə-mō'nē-əs) *adj.* **1.** Fond of ceremony. **2.** Characterized by ceremony; formal. —**cer·e·mo'ni·ous·ly** *adv.* —**cer·e·mo'ni·ous·ness** *n.*

cer·e·mo·ny (sĕr'ə-mō'nē) *n., pl.* **-nies.** **1.** A formal act or set of acts prescribed by ritual, custom, or etiquette. **2.** A conventionally polite social gesture or act. **3.** Strict observance of formalities or etiquette. [< Lat. *caerimonia,* religious rite.]

Ce·res (sîr'ēz) *n. Rom. Myth.* The goddess of agriculture.

ce·re·us (sîr'ē-əs) *n.* Any of several tall tropical American cacti. [Lat., taper.]

ce·rise (sə-rēs', -rēz') *n.* A purplish red. [Fr.]

ce·ri·um (sîr'ē-əm) *n. Symbol* **Ce** A lustrous, iron-gray, malleable metallic element, used in various metallurgical and nuclear applications. Atomic number 58; atomic weight 140.12. [< the asteroid *Ceres.*]

cer·tain (sûr'tn) *adj.* **1.** Having no doubt; positive. **2.** Definite. **3.** Inevitable. **4.** Not identified but assumed to be known: *a certain* woman. **5.** Limited: *to a certain degree.* **—pron.** An indefinite number; some. [< OFr.] **—cer′tain·ly** *adv.*

cer·tain·ty (sûr′tn-tē) *n., pl.* **-ties. 1.** The condition or quality of being certain. **2.** An established fact.

Syns: *certainty, certitude, confidence, conviction n.*

cer·tif·i·cate (sər-tĭf′ĭ-kĭt) *n.* **1.** A document testifying to a fact, qualification, or promise. **2.** A document certifying completion of requirements, as of a course of study. **3.** A document certifying ownership.

cer·ti·fi·ca·tion (sûr′tə-fĭ-kā′shən) *n.* **1.** The act of certifying. **2.** The state of being certified. **3.** A certified statement.

certified check *n.* A check guaranteed by a bank to be covered by sufficient funds on deposit.

certified public accountant *n.* An accountant with a certificate stating he has met the state's legal requirements.

cer·ti·fy (sûr′tə-fī′) *v.* **-fied, -fy·ing. 1.** To confirm formally as true, accurate, or genuine. **2.** To acknowledge on (a check) that the maker has funds for its payment. **3.** To declare legally insane. [< LLat. *certificare.*] **—cer′ti·fi′a·ble** *adj.* **—cer′ti·fi′a·bly** *adv.* **—cer′ti·fi′er** *n.*

cer·ti·tude (sûr′tĭ-tōōd′, -tyōōd′) *n.* The condition of being certain. [< LLat. *certitudo.*]

ce·ru·le·an (sə-rōō′lē-ən) *adj.* Sky-blue. [Lat. *caeruleus,* dark blue.]

ce·ru·men (sə-rōō′mən) *n.* Earwax. [< Lat. *cera,* wax.]

cer·vi·cal (sûr′vĭ-kəl) *adj.* Of or pertaining to a neck or a cervix.

cer·vix (sûr′vĭks) *n., pl.* **-vix·es** or **-vi·ces** (-vĭ-sēz′, sûr-vī′sēz′). **1.** The neck. **2.** A neck-shaped anatomical structure, as the narrow outer end of the uterus. [Lat.]

Ce·sar·e·an or **Ce·sar·i·an** (sĭ-zâr′ē-ən) *adj.* Vars. of **Caesarean.**

ce·si·um (sē′zē-əm) *n.* Also **cae·si·um.** Symbol **Cs** A soft, silvery-white ductile metal, liquid at room temperature, used in photoelectric cells. Atomic number 55; atomic weight 132.905. [< Lat. *caesius,* bluish-gray.]

ces·sa·tion (sĕ-sā′shən) *n.* The act of ceasing; a temporary or complete halt. [< Lat. *cessare,* to stop.]

ces·sion (sĕsh′ən) *n.* An act of ceding, as of territory to another country by treaty. [< Lat. *cedere,* to yield.]

cess·pool (sĕs′pōōl′) *n.* A covered hole or pit for receiving waste or sewage. [< ME *suspiral,* drainpipe.]

Cf The symbol for the element californium.

Cha·blis (shă-blē′, shă-, shăb′lē) *n.* A very dry white Burgundy wine. [< *Chablis,* France.]

chafe (chāf) *v.* **chafed, chaf·ing. 1.** To make or become worn or sore from rubbing. **2.** To annoy; vex. **3.** To heat or warm by rubbing. [< Lat. *calefacere,* to warm.]

chaff¹ (chăf) *n.* **1.** Grain husks after separation from the seed. **2.** Trivial or worthless matter. [< OE *ceaf.*]

chaff² (chăf) *v.* To tease good-naturedly. **—n.** Good-natured teasing. [Perh. < CHAFE.]

chaf·fer (chăf′ər) *v.* To haggle; bargain. [ME *chaffaren.*] **—chaf′fer·er** *n.*

chaf·finch (chăf′ĭnch) *n.* A small European songbird with reddish-brown plumage. [ME *chaffinche.*]

chafing dish *n.* A utensil used to cook food at the table.

cha·grin (shə-grĭn′) *n.* A feeling of embarrassment or humiliation. **—v.** To cause to feel chagrin. [Fr.]

chain (chān) *n.* **1.** A connected, flexible series of links. **2. chains. a.** Bonds, fetters, or shackles. **b.** Bondage. **3.** A series of related things. **4.** A number of commercial establishments under common ownership. **5. a.** A measuring instrument consisting of 100 linked pieces of iron or steel. **b.** A unit of length equal to 100 links, or about 20 meters, or 66 feet. **—v. 1.** To bind or make fast with a chain. **2.** To bind or fetter. [< Lat. *catena.*]

chain gang *n.* A group of convicts chained together.

chain mail *n.* Flexible armor of joined metal links or scales.

chain reaction *n.* **1.** A series of events each of which induces or otherwise influences its successor. **2.** *Physics.* A multistage nuclear reaction, esp. a self-sustaining series of fissions in which the average number of neutrons produced per unit of time exceeds the number absorbed or lost. **3.** *Chem.* A series of reactions in which one product of a reacting set is a reactant in the following set. **—chain′-re·act′** *v.*

chain saw *n.* A power saw with teeth linked in an endless chain.

chair (châr) *n.* **1.** A seat with a back, designed for one person. **2. a.** A seat of office, authority, or dignity, as that of a bishop or chairman. **b.** One who holds such an office. **3.** *Slang.* The electric chair. **4.** A sedan chair. **—v.** To preside over as chairman. [< Gk. *kathedra.*]

chair lift *n.* A cable-suspended, power-driven chair assembly used to transport people up or down mountains.

chair·man (châr′mən) *n.* One who presides over an assembly, meeting, committee, or board. **—chair′man·ship′** *n.* **—chair′per·son** *n.* **—chair′wom·an** *n.*

chaise (shāz) *n.* **1.** A two-wheeled carriage with a collapsible hood. **2.** A post chaise. [Fr., chair.]

chaise longue (shāz lông′) *n., pl.* **chaise longues** or **chaises longues** (shāz lông′). A chair with a seat long enough to support the sitter's outstretched legs. [Fr.]

chal·ced·o·ny (kăl-sĕd′n-ē) *n., pl.* **-nies.** A translucent to transparent milky or grayish quartz. [< Gk. *khalkēdōn,* a mystical stone.]

cha·let (shă-lā′) *n.* **1.** A dwelling with a sloping overhanging roof, common in Alpine regions. **2.** The hut of a herdsman in the Alps. [Fr.]

chal·ice (chăl′ĭs) *n.* **1.** A goblet. **2.** A cup for the consecrated wine of the Eucharist. [< Lat. *calix.*]

chalk (chôk) *n.* **1.** A soft, compact calcium carbonate derived mainly from fossil seashells. **2.** A piece of chalk used for marking on a surface such as a blackboard. **—v. 1.** To mark, draw, or write with chalk. **—phrasal verb. chalk up. 1.** To earn or score. **2.** To credit. [< Gk. *khalix,* stone.] **—chalk′y** *adj.*

chalk·board (chôk′bôrd′, -bōrd′) *n.* A blackboard.

chal·lenge (chăl′ənj) *n.* **1.** A call to engage in a contest. **2.** A demand for an explanation. **3.** A sentry's demand for identification. **4.** A formal objection, esp. to the qualifications of

a juror or voter. —v **-lenged, -leng·ing.**
1. To call to engage in a contest. **2.** To take
exception to; dispute. **3.** To order to halt and
be identified. **4.** To object formally to (a
juror or voter). **5.** To summon to action or
effort; stimulate. [< Lat. *calumnia,* calumny.]
—**chal'leng·er** n.

chal·lis (shăl'ē) n. A light, usu. printed fabric
of wool, cotton, or rayon. [Poss. < the surname *Challis.*]

cham·ber (chām'bər) n. **1.** A room, esp. a
bedroom. **2.** Often **chambers.** A judge's office. **3.** A hall, esp. for the meeting of a legislative assembly. **4.** A legislative, judicial, or
deliberative assembly. **5.** An enclosed space;
cavity. **6.** An enclosed space at the bore of a
gun that holds the charge. [LLat. *camera.*]

cham·ber·lain (chām'bər-lĭn) n. **1.** A chief
steward. **2.** A treasurer. **3.** A high-ranking officer in a royal court. [< OFr. *chamberlenc.*]

cham·ber·maid (chām'bər-mād') n. A maid
who cleans bedrooms, as in hotels.

chamber music n. Music appropriate for
performance in a small concert hall and composed for a group of instruments such as a
quartet.

chamber of commerce n. An association of
businesses for the promotion of their interests
in a community.

cham·bray (shăm'brā') n. A lightweight fabric
woven with white threads across a colored
warp. [< *Cambrai,* France.]

cha·me·leon (kə-mēl'yən, -mē'lē-ən) n.
1. Any of various lizards capable of changing
color. **2.** A changeable person. [< Gk. *kha-
maileōn.*]

cham·fer (chăm'fər) v. **1.** To cut off the edge
or corner of; bevel. **2.** To cut a groove in;
flute. —n. A surface made by chamfering.
[Prob. ult. < OFr. *chanfreindre.*]

cham·ois (shăm'ē) n., pl. **cham·ois** (shăm'ēz).
1. A goatlike mammal of mountainous regions
of Europe. **2.** Also **cham·my** or **sham·my** pl.
-mies. Soft leather made from the hide of a
chamois. [OFr.]

cham·o·mile or **cam·o·mile** (kăm'ə-mīl') n.
An aromatic plant with daisylike white flowers. [< Gk. *khamaimēlon.*]

champ¹ (chămp) v. Also **chomp** (chŏmp). To
chew noisily. [Perh. imit.]

champ² (chămp) n. *Informal.* A champion.

cham·pagne (shăm-pān') n. A sparkling
white wine orig. produced in Champagne,
France.

cham·paign (shăm-pān') n. Leve and open
country. [< LLat. *campania.*]

cham·pi·on (chăm'pē-ən) n. **1.** One that holds
first place or wins first prize in a contest.
2. One who fights for or defends a cause or
another person. —v. To fight a champion
of; defend. [< OFr.]

cham·pi·on·ship (chăm'pē-ən-shĭp') n.
1. a. The position or title of a champion. **b.** A
contest held to determine a champion. **2.** Defense or support.

chance (chăns) n. **1. a.** The abstract nature
shared by unexpected, random, or unpredictable events. **b.** This quality regarded as a
cause of such events; luck. **2.** The likelihood
of occurrence of an event; probability. **3.** An
opportunity. **4.** A risk. **5.** A raffle ticket.

6. An unexpected or fortuitous event. —v.
chanced, chanc·ing. 1. To happen by accident. **2.** To risk. —**phrasal verb. chance on**
(or **upon**). To happen upon. [< OFr. < Lat.
cadere, to fall.]

chan·cel (chăn'səl) n. The space around the
altar of a church for the clergy and choir. [<
OFr. < LLat. *cancellus,* lattice.]

chan·cel·ler·y (chăn'sə-lə-rē, -slə-rē) n., pl.
-ies. 1. The rank or position of a chancellor.
2. The office of an embassy or consulate.

chan·cel·lor (chăn'sə-lər, -slər) n. **1.** The chief
minister of state in some countries. **2.** The
head of a university. **3.** The presiding judge
of a court of equity. [< LLat. *cancellarius,*
doorkeeper.] —**chan'cel·lor·ship'** n.

chan·cer·y (chăn'sə-rē) n., pl. **-ies. 1.** A court
with jurisdiction in equity. **2.** An office of
archives. **3.** Chancellery (sense 2). [< OFr.
chancelerie, chancellery.]

chan·cre (shăng'kər) n. A dull-red, hard, insensitive sore that is an early sign of syphilis.
[< Lat. *cancer,* ulcer.]

chanc·y (chăn'sē) adj. **-i·er, -i·est.** Uncertain;
hazardous.

chan·de·lier (shăn'də-lîr') n. A branched fixture for lights, usu. suspended from a ceiling.
[< Lat. *candelabrum,* candelabrum.]

chan·dler (chănd'lər) n. **1.** One that makes or
sells candles. **2.** A dealer in goods or equipment of a specified kind, esp. for ships. [<
Lat. *candela,* candle.] —**chan'dler·y** n.

change (chānj) v. **changed, chang·ing. 1.** To
be or cause to be different; alter. **2.** To give
and receive reciprocally; interchange. **3.** To
exchange for or replace by another. **4.** To
give or receive an equivalent sum of money in
lower denominations or in foreign currency.
5. To put fresh clothes or coverings on. —n.
1. The act, process, or result of changing.
2. Money of smaller denomination exchanged
for a unit of higher denomination. **3.** Coins.
4. A different or fresh set of clothing. [<
LLat. *cambiare.*] —**change'a·bil'i·ty** or
change'a·ble·ness n. —**change'a·ble** adj.
—**change'a·bly** adv. —**change'less** adj.
—**chang'er** n.

Syns: *change, alter, modify, mutate, transform, turn, vary* v.

change·ful (chānj'fəl) adj. Given to frequent
changes. —**change'ful·ness** n.

change·ling (chānj'lĭng) n. A child secretly
exchanged for another.

change of life n. The menopause.

change·o·ver (chānj'ō'vər) n. A change from
one activity or system to another.

chan·nel (chăn'əl) n. **1.** The bed of a stream.
2. The deeper part of a river or harbor. **3.** A
strait. **4.** A tubular passage. **5.** A means of
passage. **6. channels.** Official routes of communication. **7.** A specified frequency band
for the transmission and reception of electromagnetic signals. **8.** A trench, furrow, or
groove. —v. **-neled** or **-nelled, -nel·ing** or
-nel·ling. 1. To make or form channels in.
2. To direct or guide along a channel. [< Lat.
canalis, canal.] —**chan'nel·i·za'tion** n.
—**chan'nel·ize'** v.

chan·son (shän-sôn') n. A song. [Fr. < Lat.
cantare, to sing.]

chant (chănt) n. **1. a.** A melody in which a

number of words are sung on each note. **b.** A canticle sung thus. **2.** A monotonous rhythmic voice. —*v.* **1.** To sing (a chant). **2.** To say or sing in the manner of a chant. **3.** To celebrate in song. [< Lat. *cantus,* song.] —**chant'er** *n.*

chan·teuse (shăn-tœz') *n.* A woman singer, esp. a nightclub singer. [Fr.]

chan·tey (shăn'tē, chăn'-) *n., pl.* -**teys.** A song sailors sing to the rhythm of their work. [Prob. < Fr. *chanter,* to sing.]

chan·ti·cleer (chăn'tĭ-klĭr', shăn'-) *n.* A rooster. [< OFr. *chantecler.*]

Cha·nu·kah (KHä'nŏŏ-kə) *n.* An eight-day Jewish festival commemorating the rededication of the Temple at Jerusalem. [Heb. *ḥanukkāh,* consecration.]

cha·os (kā'ŏs') *n.* **1.** Total disorder and confusion. **2.** Often **Chaos.** The amorphous void supposed to have existed before the creation of the universe. [< Gk. *khaos,* unformed matter.] —**cha·ot'ic** *adj.* —**cha·ot'i·cal·ly** *adv.*

chap¹ (chăp) *v.* **chapped, chap·ping.** To split or roughen, esp. from cold or exposure. [ME *chappen.*]

chap² (chăp) *n. Informal.* A man or boy; fellow. [< CHAPMAN.]

chap·ar·ral (shăp'ə-răl', chăp'-) *n.* A dense thicket of shrubs. [Sp. < *chaparro,* evergreen oak.]

cha·peau (shă-pō') *n., pl.* -**peaux** (-pōz') or -**peaus** (-pōz'). A hat. [Fr.]

chap·el (chăp'əl) *n.* **1. a.** A small church. **b.** A place of worship subordinate to a church, esp. in a college, hospital, etc. **2.** The services held at a chapel. **3.** In England, a place of worship for those not members of the Established Church. [< OFr. *chapele.*]

chap·er·on (shăp'ə-rōn') *n.* Also **chap·er·one.** One, esp. an older woman, who accompanies and supervises young unmarried people. —*v.* To act as a chaperon to or for. [< OFr., hood.] —**chap'er·on'age** *n.*

chap·lain (chăp'lən) *n.* A member of the clergy attached to a chapel, legislative assembly, or military unit. [< Med. Lat. *cappellanus < cappella,* chapel.] —**chap'lain·cy** or **chap'lain·ship** *n.*

chap·let (chăp'lĭt) *n.* **1.** A wreath for the head. **2. a.** A string of prayer beads having one third the number of a rosary's beads. **b.** The prayers counted on such beads. **3.** A string of beads. [< OFr. *chapelet.*]

chap·man (chăp'mən) *n. Chiefly Brit.* A peddler. [< OE *cēapmann.*]

chaps (chăps, shăps) *pl.n.* Heavy leather trousers without a seat, worn by cowboys. [< Mex. Sp. *chaparreras.*]

chap·ter (chăp'tər) *n.* **1.** A main division of a book. **2.** A local branch of a club, fraternity, etc. **3.** An assembly of members, as of a religious order. [< OFr. *chapitre.*]

char¹ (chär) *v.* **charred, char·ring.** **1.** To scorch or become scorched. **2.** To reduce or be reduced to charcoal by incomplete combustion. [< CHARCOAL.]

char² (chär) *n., pl.* **char** or **chars.** Any of several fishes related to the trout. [Orig. unknown.]

char³ (chär) *n.* **1.** A chore or odd job, esp. a household task. **2.** A charwoman. —*v.* **charred** or **chared, char·ring** or **char·ing.** **1.** To do small chores. **2.** To work as a charwoman. [< OE *cierr,* piece of work.]

char·ac·ter (kăr'ĭk-tər) *n.* **1.** A distinguishing

feature or attribute; characteristic. **2.** The moral or ethical structure of a person or group. **3.** Moral strength; integrity. **4.** Reputation. **5.** *Informal.* An eccentric person. **6.** A person portrayed in a drama, novel, etc. **7.** A symbol in a writing system. **8.** A structure, function, or attribute determined by a gene or group of genes. [< Gk. *kharaktēr.*]

char·ac·ter·is·tic (kăr'ĭk-tə-rĭs'tĭk) *adj.* Distinctive; typical. —*n.* A distinguishing feature or attribute. —**char·ac·ter·is'ti·cal·ly** *adv.* **Syns:** *characteristic, distinctive, individual, peculiar, typical* **adj.**

char·ac·ter·ize (kăr'ĭk-tə-rīz') *v.* -**ized, -iz·ing.** **1.** To describe the qualities of. **2.** To be a characteristic or quality of. **3.** To give character to, as on the stage. —**char'ac·ter·i·za'tion** *n.* —**char'ac·ter·iz'er** *n.*

cha·rade (shə-rād') *n.* **1. charades** (*used with a sing. or pl. verb*). A game in which words or phrases are acted out in pantomime until guessed by the other players. **2.** A pretense. [Fr.]

char·broil (chär'broil') *v.* To broil over charcoal: *charbroil a steak.*

char·coal (chär'kōl') *n.* **1.** A black, porous carbon-containing material produced by the destructive distillation of wood and used as a fuel, a filter, and an absorbent. **2.** A drawing pencil made from charcoal. **3.** A dark gray. [< ME *charcole.*]

chard (chärd) *n.* A variety of beet with large, succulent leaves eaten as a vegetable. [Fr. *carde.*]

charge (chärj) *v.* **charged, charg·ing.** **1.** To entrust with a duty, responsibility, etc. **2.** To command. **3.** To blame or accuse. **4.** To set as a price. **5.** To demand payment from. **6.** To record as a debt. **7.** To attack violently. **8.** To load or fill with; impregnate. **9. a.** To cause formation of a net electric charge on or in (a conductor). **b.** To energize (a storage battery). —*n.* **1.** Care, custody, or responsibility. **2.** One that is entrusted to another's care. **3.** A command or injunction. **4.** An accusation or indictment. **5.** Cost; price. **6. a.** A debit in an account. **b.** An attack. **7.** A load; burden. **8.** The quantity needed to fill an apparatus or container. **10. a.** The intrinsic property of matter responsible for all electric phenomena, occurring in two forms arbitrarily designated *negative* and *positive.* **b.** A measure of this property. **11.** *Informal.* A feeling of pleasant excitement; thrill. [< LLat. *carricare,* to load.] —**charge'a·ble** *adj.*

charge account *n.* A business arrangement, as with a store, in which a customer receives goods or services and pays for them at a later time.

char·gé d'af·faires (shär-zhā' də-fâr') *n., pl.* **char·gés d'af·faires** (shär-zhā', shär-zhāz') An official temporarily in charge of an embassy or legation. [Fr.]

charg·er (chär'jər) *n.* **1.** One that charges. **2.** A war-horse (sense 1). **3.** A device for charging electric storage batteries.

char·i·ot (chăr'ē-ət) *n.* An ancient two-wheeled horse-drawn vehicle used in battle, races, and processions. [< Lat. *carrus,* vehicle.] —**char'i·o·teer'** *n.*

cha·ris·ma (kə-rĭz'mə) *n.* A quality attributed to those with exceptional ability to secure the devotion of large numbers of people. [< Gk. *kharisma,* divine gift.] —**char'is·mat'ic** (kăr'-ĭz-măt'ĭk) *adj.*

char·i·ta·ble (chăr'ĭ-tə-bəl) *adj.* 1. Generous to the needy. 2. Tolerant in judging others. 3. Of or for charity. —**char'i·ta·ble·ness** *n.* —**char'i·ta·bly** *adv.*

char·i·ty (chăr'ĭ-tē) *n., pl.* -**ties.** 1. Help or alms given to the poor. 2. An organization or fund that helps the poor. 3. An act or feeling of benevolence. 4. Forbearance in judging others. 5. *Theol.* **a.** The benevolence of God toward man. **b.** Good will or brotherly love. [< Lat. *caritas,* affection.]

char·la·tan (shär'lə-tən) *n.* A person who deceives others by falsely claiming to have expert knowledge or skill. [< Ital. *ciarlatano.*] —**char'la·tan·ism** or **char'la·tan·ry** *n.*

Charles·ton (chärl'stən) *n.* A fast ballroom dance popular in the 1920's. [< *Charleston,* South Carolina.]

char·ley horse (chär'lē) *n. Informal.* A muscle cramp. [Orig. unknown.]

char·lotte russe (shär'lət rōōs') *n.* A cold dessert of Bavarian cream set in a mold lined with ladyfingers. [Fr.]

charm (chärm) *n.* 1. The power or quality of pleasing or attracting. 2. A small ornament worn on a bracelet. 3. Anything worn for its supposed magical effect; an amulet. 4. An action or formula thought to have magical power. —*v.* 1. To be alluring or pleasing; attract. 2. To act on as if with magic; bewitch. —*idiom.* **like a charm.** Exceedingly well. [< Lat. *carmen,* incantation.] —**charm'er** *n.* —**charm'ing** *adj.*

Syns: *charm, bewitch, enchant, enthrall, entrance, spellbind v.*

charm
Left: From the New Hebrides
Right: 18th-century silver charm
from New Hampshire

char·nel (chär'nəl) *n.* Also **charnel house.** A building, room, or vault in which bones or corpses are placed. [< Lat. *caro,* flesh.]

Char·on (kâr'ən, kăr'-) *n. Gk. Myth.* The ferryman of Hades.

chart (chärt) *n.* 1. A map. 2. A sheet with information in the form of graphs or tables. —*v.* 1. To make a chart of. 2. To plan. [< Gk. *khartēs,* papyrus leaf.]

char·ter (chär'tər) *n.* 1. A document issued by a governmental authority, creating a corporation and defining its rights and privileges. 2. A document outlining the organization of a corporate body. 3. An authorization from an organization to establish a local chapter. 4. **a.** The hiring or leasing of an aircraft, vessel, etc. **b.** The aircraft or vessel so hired. —*v.* 1. To grant a charter to. 2. To hire or lease by charter. [< OFr. *chartre.*] —**char'ter·er** *n.*

charter member *n.* An original member of an organization.

char·treuse (shär-trōōz', -trōōs', -trœz') *n.* A light yellowish green. [< Chartreuse.] —**char·treuse'** *adj.*

Chartreuse. A trademark for a green or yellow liqueur.

char·wom·an (chär'wŏŏm'ən) *n. Chiefly Brit.* A cleaning woman.

char·y (châr'ē) *adj.* -**i·er,** -**i·est.** 1. Cautious; wary. 2. Not wasteful; sparing. [< OE *cearig,* sorrowful.] —**char'i·ly** *adv.* —**char'i·ness** *n.*

chase¹ (chās) *v.* **chased, chas·ing.** 1. To pursue; follow. 2. To hunt. 3. To put to flight; drive away. 4. *Informal.* To rush. —*n.* 1. The act of chasing. 2. **the chase.** The sport of hunting. 3. One that is hunted. [< Lat. *captare,* to seize.]

chase² (chās) *n.* 1. A groove cut in an object; slot. 2. A trench or channel for drainpipes or wiring. —*v.* **chased, chas·ing.** To decorate (metal) with engraved or embossed designs. [Prob. < OFr. *chas,* enclosure.]

chas·er (chā'sər) *n.* 1. One that chases. 2. *Informal.* A drink of water, beer, etc., taken after hard liquor.

chasm (kăz'əm) *n.* 1. A deep crack in the earth's surface; gorge. 2. A marked difference of opinion, interests, or loyalty. [< Gk. *khasma.*] —**chas'mal** *adj.*

Chas·sid (KHä'sĭd) *n., pl.* **Chas·si·dim** (KHä-sē'dĭm). A member of a sect of orthodox Jewish mystics, founded in Poland about 1750. [Heb. *hasidh,* pious.] —**Chas·si'dic** (-dĭk) *adj.*

chas·sis (shăs'ē, chăs'ē) *n., pl.* **chas·sis** (shăs'-ēz, chăs'ēz). 1. The rectangular steel frame that holds the body and motor of an automotive vehicle. 2. The landing gear of an aircraft, including the wheels, floats, and other structures. 3. The framework that holds the functioning parts of a radio, television set, etc. [Fr. *châssis.*]

chaste (chāst) *adj.* 1. Morally pure; modest. 2. Abstaining from sexual intercourse. 3. Celibate. 4. Simple in style; not ornate. [< Lat. *castus.*] —**chaste'ly** *adv.* —**chaste'ness** or **chas'ti·ty** *n.*

chas·ten (chā'sən) *v.* 1. To punish; discipline. 2. To restrain; moderate. 3. To refine; purify. [< Lat. *castigare.*] —**chas'ten·er** *n.*

chas·tise (chăs-tīz') *v.* -**tised, -tis·ing.** 1. To punish, usu. by beating. 2. To criticize severely. [< OFr. *chastiier.*] —**chas·tis'a·ble** *adj.* —**chas·tise'ment** (chăs-tīz'mənt, chăs'-tīz-) *n.* —**chas·tis'er** *n.*

chas·u·ble (chăz'ə-bəl, chăzh'-, chăs'-) *n.* A long, sleeveless vestment worn over the alb by the priest at Mass. [< LLat. *casubla,* hooded garment.]

chat (chăt) *v.* **chat·ted, chat·ting.** To converse in an easy manner. —*n.* 1. A relaxed, informal conversation. 2. Any of several birds known for their chattering call. [ME *chatten,* to jabber.]

cha·teau or **châ·teau** (shă-tō') *n., pl.* -**teaux**

(-tōz'). **1.** A French castle. **2.** A large country house.

chat·e·laine (shăt'l-ān') n. **1.** The lady of a chateau. **2.** The mistress of a large, fashionable house. **3.** A clasp or chain worn at a woman's waist for holding keys or a watch. [Fr. *châtelaine.*]

chat·tel (chăt'l) n. **1.** An article of movable personal property. **2.** A slave. [< Med. Lat. *capitale*, capital.]

chat·ter (chăt'ər) v. **1.** To utter inarticulate speechlike sounds. **2.** To talk rapidly, incessantly, and inanely. **3.** To click together repeatedly, as the teeth from cold. [ME *chatteren.*] —**chat'ter** n. —**chat'ter·er** n.

chat·ter·box (chăt'ər-bŏks') n. A very talkative person.

chat·ty (chăt'ē) adj. **-ti·er, -ti·est.** Given to informal conversation. —**chat'ti·ly** adv. —**chat'ti·ness** n.

chauf·feur (shō'fər, shō-fûr') n. One who is hired to drive an automobile. [Fr., stoker.] —**chauf'feur** v.

chau·vin·ism (shō'və-nĭz'əm) n. **1.** Fanatical patriotism. **2.** Prejudiced belief in the superiority of one's own group: *male chauvinism.* [< Nicolas *Chauvin*, a legendary French soldier.] —**chau'vin·ist** n. —**chau'vin·is'tic** adj. —**chau'vin·is'ti·cal·ly** adv.

cheap (chēp) adj. **-er, -est. 1.** Inexpensive. **2.** Charging low prices. **3.** Requiring little effort: *a cheap victory.* **4.** Of little value. **5.** Of poor quality; inferior. **6.** Vulgar: *cheap humor.* **7.** Stingy. —adv. At a low price. [< OE *cēap*, trade < Lat. *caupo*, tradesman.] —**cheap'en** v. —**cheap'en·er** n. —**cheap'ly** adv. —**cheap'ness** n.

cheap shot n. An unjust action or statement directed at a vulnerable target.

cheap·skate (chēp'skāt') n. *Slang.* A miser. [CHEAP + *skate*, fellow.]

cheat (chēt) v. **1.** To deceive by trickery; swindle. **2.** To act dishonestly. **3.** To elude as if by trickery or deception: *The mountain climbers cheated death.* —n. **1.** A fraud or swindle. **2.** One guilty of swindle or dishonesty. [ME *cheten*, to revert.] —**cheat'er** n. —**cheat'ing·ly** adv.

check (chĕk) n. **1.** An abrupt halt or stop. **2.** A restraint. **3.** A standard of comparison to verify accuracy. **4.** A mark to show verification. **5.** A slip for identification: *a baggage check.* **6.** A bill at a restaurant. **7.** Also *chiefly Brit.* **cheque.** A written order to a bank to pay an amount from funds on deposit. **8. a.** A pattern of small squares. **b.** A fabric with such a pattern. **9.** *Chess.* A move in which an opponent's king is attacked. **10.** *Ice Hockey.* The act of impeding an opponent in control of the puck, either by blocking his progress with the body or by jabbing at the puck with the stick. —v. **1.** To arrest the motion of abruptly. **2.** To hold in restraint. **3.** To examine, as for accuracy. **4.** To make a check mark on. **5.** To deposit for temporary safekeeping: *check one's hat.* **6.** To have item-for-item correspondence. **7.** *Ice Hockey.* To impede an opponent in control of the puck, either by using the body to block the opponent or by jabbing at the puck with the stick. —*phrasal verbs.* **check in.** To register, as at a hotel. **check out. 1.** To pay one's bill and leave, as from a hotel. **2.** To take, after a recording procedure: *check out a book from a library.* —*idiom.* **in check.** Under

control. [< Ar. *shāh*, check (in chess) < Pers., king.]

check·book (chĕk'bŏŏk') n. A booklet containing blank checks, given by a bank to a depositor who has a checking account.

check·er (chĕk'ər) n. Also *chiefly Brit.* **chequer. 1. a. checkers** (*used with a sing. verb*). A game played on a checkerboard by two players, each using 12 pieces. **b.** One of the round, flat pieces used in this game. **2.** One of the squares in a pattern of many squares. **3.** A person who receives items for temporary storage or safekeeping: *a baggage checker.* **4.** A cashier. —v. To mark with a pattern of squares. [< OFr. *eschequier*, chessboard.]

check·er·board (chĕk'ər-bôrd', -bōrd') n. A game board divided into 64 squares of alternating colors, on which checkers or chess may be played.

check·ered (chĕk'ərd) adj. **1.** Divided into squares. **2.** Having light and dark patches. **3.** Full of many changes in fortune: *a checkered career.*

checking account n. A bank account from which money may be withdrawn or payments made from the amount on deposit by writing checks.

check·mate (chĕk'māt') v. **-mat·ed, -mat·ing. 1.** *Chess.* To attack (an opponent's king) so that no escape or defense is possible, thus ending the game. **2.** To defeat completely. —n. **1.** A chess move that places an opponent's king under direct and inescapable attack. **2.** A situation in which one is completely foiled or defeated. [< Ar. *shāh māt* < Pers., the king is dead.]

check·off (chĕk'ôf', -ŏf') n. The collecting of dues from members of a union by authorized deduction from their wages.

check·out (chĕk'out') n. **1.** The act or process of checking out, as at a supermarket, library, or hotel. **2.** A place where merchandise may be checked out. **3.** A test or inspection, as of a machine, for proper working condition.

check·point (chĕk'point') n. A place where surface traffic is stopped for inspection.

check·rein (chĕk'rān') n. A short rein connected from a horse's bit to the saddle to keep a horse from lowering its head.

check·room (chĕk'rŏŏm', -rŏŏm') n. A room where items may be left temporarily.

check·up (chĕk'ŭp') n. **1.** An examination or inspection, as for general working condition or accuracy. **2.** A physical examination.

Ched·dar (chĕd'ər) n. Also **ched·dar.** Any of several types of firm, usu. yellowish cheese. [< *Cheddar*, England.]

cheek (chēk) n. **1.** The part of the face below the eye and between the nose and ear on either side. **2.** Impudence. —*idiom.* **cheek by jowl.** In close contact. [< OE *cēce.*]

cheek·bone (chēk'bōn') n. The zygomatic bone.

cheek·y (chē'kē) adj. **-i·er, -i·est.** Impertinent. —**cheek'i·ly** adv. —**cheek'i·ness** n.

cheep (chēp) n. A faint, shrill chirp as of a young bird; chirp. [Imit.] —**cheep'** v. —**cheep'er** n.

cheer (chĭr) n. **1.** Gaiety; happiness. **2.** Anything that gives happiness or comfort. **3.** A shout of encouragement or congratulation. —v. **1.** To fill with happiness. **2. a.** To encourage or acclaim with cheers. **b.** To shout cheers. [< OFr. *chiere*, face.] —**cheer'er** n.

—**cheer·ing·ly** adv. —**cheer·less** adj.
—**cheer·less·ly** adv. —**cheer·less·ness** n.
cheer·ful (chîr'fəl) adj. **1.** In good spirits.
2. Producing cheer. —**cheer·ful·ly** adv.
—**cheer·ful·ness** n.
   Syns: cheerful, bright, cheery, chipper, happy,
sunny adj.
cheer·lead·er (chîr'lē'dər) n. One who starts
and leads the cheering of spectators at a
game.
cheer·y (chîr'ē) adj. **-i·er, -i·est.** Cheerful.
—**cheer'i·ly** adv. —**cheer'i·ness** n.
cheese (chēz) n. A solid food made from the
pressed curd of milk. [< Lat. caseus.]
cheese·burg·er (chēz'bûr'gər) n. A hamburger topped with melted cheese.
cheese·cake (chēz'kāk') n. **1.** Also **cheese
cake.** A cake made of cream or cottage
cheese, eggs, milk, and sugar. **2.** Slang. **a.** A
photograph of a pretty girl or woman scantily
clothed. **b.** Such photographs collectively.
cheese·cloth (chēz'klôth', -klŏth') n. A thin,
loosely woven cotton gauze.
cheese·par·ing (chēz'pâr'ĭng) n. **1.** Something
of negligible value. **2.** Parsimony. —adj.
Stingy.
chees·y (chē'zē) adj. **-i·er, -i·est.** **1.** Like
cheese. **2.** Slang. Of poor quality; shoddy.
—**chees'i·ness** n.
chee·tah (chē'tə) n. A long-legged, swift-
running spotted wild cat of Africa and southwestern Asia. [< Skt. citrakāya, tiger.]
chef (shĕf) n. A cook, esp. a chief cook. [<
OFr., chief.]
chef-d'oeu·vre (shĕ-dœ'vr'ə) n., pl.
chefs-d'oeu·vre (shĕ-). A masterpiece. [Fr.]
chef's salad n. A tossed salad usu. containing raw vegetables, hard-boiled eggs, and
small strips of cheese and meat.
chem- or **chemi-** pref. Vars. of **chemo-**.
chem·i·cal (kĕm'ĭ-kəl) adj. **1.** Pertaining to
chemistry. **2.** Involving or produced by
chemicals. —n. A substance produced by or
used in a chemical process. [< Med. Lat.
alchimia, alchemy.] —**chem'i·cal·ly** adv.
chemical bond n. Any of several forces or
mechanisms, esp. the ionic bond, covalent
bond, and metallic bond, by which atoms or
ions are bound in a molecule or crystal.
chemical engineering n. The technology of
large-scale chemical production. —**chemical
engineer** n.
Chemical Mace. A trademark for a mixture
of organic chemicals used in aerosol form as
a weapon to disable by causing intense burning eye pain, acute bronchitis, and respiratory
irritation.
chemical warfare n. Warfare using chemicals
other than explosives as weapons.
chem·i·lu·mi·nes·cence (kĕm'ĭ-lōō'mə-nĕs'-
əns) n. The emission of light as a result of a
chemical reaction at environmental temperatures. —**chem'i·lu·mi·nes'cent** adj.
che·mise (shə-mēz') n. **1.** A woman's loose,
shirtlike undergarment. **2.** A dress that hangs
straight from the shoulders. [< OFr., shirt.]
chem·ist (kĕm'ĭst) n. **1.** A scientist who specializes in chemistry. **2.** Chiefly Brit. A pharmacist.
chem·is·try (kĕm'ĭ-strē) n., pl. **-tries.** **1.** The
scientific study of the composition, structure,

properties, and reactions of matter, esp. at the
level of atomic and molecular systems. **2.** The
composition, structure, properties, and reactions of a substance: blood chemistry. **3.** Behavior or functioning, as of a complex of
emotions: the chemistry of love.
chemo- or **chemi-** or **chem-** pref. Chemicals; chemical: chemotherapy. [< Gk. khē-
meia, alchemy.]
che·mo·re·cep·tion (kē'mō-rĭ-sĕp'shən, kĕm'-
ō-rĭ-) n. The reaction of a sense organ to a
chemical stimulus. —**che'mo·re·cep'tive** adj.
—**che'mo·re·cep'tor** n.
che·mo·sur·ger·y (kē'mō-sûr'jə-rē, kĕm'ō'-) n.
Selective destruction of tissue by use of
chemicals.
che·mo·syn·the·sis (kē'mō-sĭn'thə-sĭs, kĕm'ō-)
n. A process, carried on by some living
things, in which nutrients or other organic
substances are manufactured using the energy
of chemical reactions.
che·mo·ther·a·py (kē'mō-thĕr'ə-pē, kĕm'ō-) n.
The use of chemicals in treating diseases.
—**che'mo·ther'a·peu'tic** (-pyōō'tĭk) adj.
chem·ur·gy (kĕm'ər-jē, kĕ-mûr'-) n. The development of new industrial chemical products from organic raw materials, esp. from
those of agricultural origin. —**chem·ur'gic**
(kĕ-mûr'jĭk) or **chem·ur'gi·cal** adj.
che·nille (shə-nēl') n. **1.** A soft, tufted cord of
silk, cotton, or worsted. **2.** Fabric made of
chenille. [Fr., caterpillar.]
cheque (chĕk) n. Chiefly Brit. Var. of **check**
(sense 7).
chequ·er (chĕk'ər) n. & v. Chiefly Brit. Var.
of **checker**.
cher·ish (chĕr'ĭsh) v. To hold dear. [< OFr.
cherir.] —**cher'ish·er** n.
Cher·o·kee (chĕr'ə-kē', chĕr'ə-kē') n., pl. **-kee**
or **-kees.** **1. a.** A tribe of Indians formerly
inhabiting North Carolina and northern
Georgia, now settled in Oklahoma. **b.** A
member of this tribe. **2.** The Iroquoian language of the Cherokee. —**Cher'o·kee'** adj.
che·root (shə-rōōt', chə-) n. A cigar with
square-cut ends. [Tamil śuruṭṭu.]
cher·ry (chĕr'ē) n., pl. **-ries.** **1.** A small, fleshy,
rounded fruit with a hard stone. **2.** A tree
bearing such fruit. **3.** The wood of such a
tree. **4.** Deep or purplish red. [< Gk. kerasos,
cherry tree.]
cher·ub (chĕr'əb) n. **1.** pl. **cher·u·bim** (chĕr'-
ə-bĭm, -yə-bĭm). Theol. One of the 2nd order
of angels. **2.** An angelic cherub portrayed as
a winged child with a chubby, rosy face.
[Heb. kärübh.] —**che·ru'bic** adj.
cher·vil (chûr'vəl) n. An aromatic Eurasian
plant with leaves used in soups and salads.
[< Gk. khairephullon.]
chess (chĕs) n. A game played on a chessboard between two players, each starting with
16 pieces, the object of which is to put the
opponent's king out of action. [< Ar. shāh,
check (in chess) < Pers., king.]
chess·board (chĕs'bôrd', -bōrd') n. A board
with 64 squares in alternating colors, used in
chess.
chess·man (chĕs'măn', -mən) n. One of the
pieces used in chess.
chest (chĕst) n. **1.** The part of the body between the neck and abdomen. **2.** A sturdy

box with a lid, used for storage. **3.** A bureau or dresser. [< OE *cest.*]

ches·ter·field (chĕs′tər-fēld′) *n.* An overcoat with a velvet collar. [< a 19th-cent. Earl of *Chesterfield.*]

chest·nut (chĕs′nŭt′, -nət) *n.* **1.** An edible nut enclosed in a prickly bur. **2.** A tree bearing such nuts. **3.** The wood of such a tree. **4.** Reddish brown. **5.** An old, stale joke or story. [< Gk. *kastenea*, chestnut tree.]

chev·a·lier (shĕv′ə-lîr′) *n.* A member of certain orders of knighthood or merit. [< OFr., horseman.]

chev·i·ot (shĕv′ē-ət, chĕv′-) *n.* A heavy, twilled woolen fabric used chiefly for suits and overcoats. [< the *Cheviot* Hills, England.]

chev·ron (shĕv′rən) *n.* A badge made up of stripes meeting at an angle, worn on the sleeve of a military, naval, or police uniform to show rank, merit, or length of service. [< OFr., rafter.]

chew (chōō) *v.* To grind (something) with the teeth. —*phrasal verb.* **chew out.** *Slang.* To scold. —*n.* **1.** The act of chewing. **2.** Something chewed. —*idiom.* **chew the fat (or rag).** *Slang.* To talk casually or idly. [< OE *cēowan.*] —**chew′er** *n.* —**chew′y** *adj.*

chewing gum *n.* A sweetened, flavored preparation for chewing, usu. made of chicle.

Chey·enne (shī-ăn′, -ĕn′) *n., pl.* **-enne** or **-ennes. 1. a.** A tribe of Indians formerly inhabiting central Minnesota and the Dakotas, now settled in Montana and Oklahoma. **b.** A member of this tribe. **2.** The Algonquian language of the Cheyenne. —**Chey·enne′** *adj.*

Cheyne-Stokes respiration (chān′stōks′, chā′nē-stōks′) *n.* Abnormal breathing marked by slow rhythmic waxing and waning of respiratory depth. [< John *Cheyne* (1777–1836) and William *Stokes* (1804–78).]

chi (kī) *n.* The 22nd letter of the Greek alphabet. See table at **alphabet.** [< Gk. *khi.*]

chi·a·ro·scu·ro (kē-är′ə-skŏŏr′ō, -skyŏŏr′ō) *n., pl.* **-ros.** The technique of using light and shade in pictorial representation. [Ital.] —**chi′a·ro·scu′rist** *n.*

chic (shēk) *adj.* Stylish; fashionable. [Fr.] —**chic** *n.*

chi·cane (shĭ-kān′) *v.* **-caned, -can·ing.** To trick or deceive in order to outwit or gain an advantage. [< OFr. *chicaner*, to quibble.] —**chi·cane′** or **chi·can′er·y** *n.*

Chi·ca·no (shĭ-kä′nō, chĭ-) *n., pl.* **-nos.** A Mexican-American. —*adj.* Of or pertaining to Mexican-Americans.

chi·chi (shē′shē) *adj.* Ostentatiously stylish. [Fr.]

chick (chĭk) *n.* **1.** A young chicken. **2.** The young of any bird. **3.** A child. **4.** *Slang.* A young woman; girl.

chick·a·dee (chĭk′ə-dē′) *n.* A small, gray, dark-crowned North American bird. [Imit. of its cry.]

Chick·a·saw (chĭk′ə-sô′) *n., pl.* **-saw** or **-saws. 1. a.** A tribe of Indians, orig. from Mississippi, later removed to Oklahoma. **b.** A member of this tribe. **2.** The Muskhogean language of the Chickasaw.

chick·en (chĭk′ən) *n.* **1.** The common domestic fowl or its young. **2.** The edible flesh of a chicken. —*adj. Slang.* Afraid. —*phrasal verb.* **chicken out.** To lose one's nerve. [< OE *cīcen.*]

chicken feed *n. Slang.* A trifling amount of money.

chicken hawk *n.* Any of various hawks that prey on chickens.

chick·en-heart·ed (chĭk′ən-här′tĭd) *adj.* Cowardly.

chick·en-liv·ered (chĭk′ən-lĭv′ərd) *adj.* Cowardly; timid.

chicken pox *n.* A contagious virus disease, mainly of children, characterized by skin eruption and mild fever.

chick·pea (chĭk′pē′) *n.* The edible, pealike seed of a bushy Old World plant. [< Lat. *cicer*, chickpea + PEA.]

chick·weed (chĭk′wĕd′) *n.* A low, weedy plant with small white flowers.

chi·cle (chĭk′əl) *n.* The coagulated milky juice of a tropical American tree, used as the principal ingredient of chewing gum. [< Nahuatl *chictli.*]

chic·o·ry (chĭk′ə-rē) *n., pl.* **-ries. 1.** A plant with blue, daisylike flowers and leaves used as salad. **2.** The ground, roasted root of this plant, used as a coffee admixture or substitute. [< Gk. *kikhora.*]

chide (chīd) *v.* **chid·ed** or **chid** (chĭd), **chid·ed** or **chid** or **chid·den** (chĭd′n), **chid·ing.** To scold; reprimand. [< OE *cīdan.*] —**chid′er** *n.* —**chid′ing·ly** *adv.*

chief (chēf) *n.* **1.** One who is highest in rank or authority. **2.** Often **Chief.** The chief engineer of a ship. —*adj.* **1.** Highest in rank or authority. **2.** Most important. [< Lat. *caput*, head.] —**chief′ly** *adv. & adj.*

chief justice *n.* Also **Chief Justice.** The presiding judge of a court of several judges, esp. of the U.S. Supreme Court.

chief of staff *n.* **1.** *Mil.* **a.** The senior staff officer at the division level or higher. **b.** A senior administrator on an executive staff. **2. Chief of Staff.** The ranking officer of the U.S. Army, Navy, or Air Force, responsible to the secretary of his branch and to the President.

chief of state *n.* One who serves as the formal head of a nation.

chief·tain (chēf′tən) *n.* The leader of a clan, tribe, or similar group. [< LLat. *capitaneus.*]

chif·fon (shĭ-fŏn′, shĭf′ŏn′) *n.* A soft, filmy fabric of silk or rayon. [Fr.]

chif·fo·nier (shĭf′ə-nîr′) *n.* Also **chif·fon·nier.** A narrow, high chest of drawers. [Fr. < *chiffon*, rag.]

chig·ger (chĭg′ər) *n.* **1.** A mite that lodges on the skin and causes intense itching. **2.** The chigoe. [< CHIGOE.]

chi·gnon (shēn′yŏn′, shēn-yŏn′) *n.* A knot of hair worn at the back of the head. [< OFr. *chaignon*, chain.]

chig·oe (chĭg′ō, chē′gō) *n.* A small tropical flea, the fertile female of which burrows under the skin, causing intense irritation and sores. [Of Cariban orig.]

Chi·hua·hua (chĭ-wä′wä, -wə) *n.* A very small dog with pointed ears and a smooth coat. [< *Chihuahua*, Mexico.]

chil·blain (chĭl′blān′) *n.* An inflammation of the hands, feet, or ears, resulting from exposure to damp cold. [CHIL(L) + *blain*, a sore.]

child (chīld) *n., pl.* **chil·dren** (chĭl′drən). **1.** A person between birth and puberty. **2.** A son or daughter. **3.** An immature person. [< OE *cild.*] —**child′hood′** *n.* —**child′less** *adj.*

child-bear·ing (chīld′bâr′ĭng) *n.* Pregnancy and childbirth.

child·birth (chīld′bûrth′) *n.* Parturition.

child·ish (chīl′dĭsh) *adj.* **1.** Of, similar to, or suitable for a child. **2.** Immature in behavior. —**child′ish·ly** *adv.* —**child′ish·ness** *n.*

child·like (chīld′līk′) *adj.* Like or befitting a child.

child-proof (chīld′prŏŏf′) *adj.* Designed to resist tampering by children.

chil·dren (chĭl′drən) *n.* Pl. of **child.**

child's play *n.* **1.** Something very easy to do. **2.** A trivial matter.

chil·e con car·ne (chĭl′ē kŏn kär′nē) *n.* Also **chil·i con car·ne.** A highly spiced dish made of red peppers, meat, and sometimes beans. [Sp.]

chil·i (chĭl′ē) *n., pl.* **-ies.** Also **chil·e** or **chil·li. 1. a.** The very pungent pod of a variety of red pepper. **b.** A condiment made from the dried fruits of this plant. **2.** Chile con carne. [< Nahuatl *chilli.*]

chil·i·bur·ger (chĭl′ē-bûr′gər) *n.* A hamburger covered with chili.

chil·i·dog (chĭl′ē-dôg′, -dŏg′) *n.* A hot dog covered with chili.

chili sauce *n.* A spiced sauce made of chilies and tomatoes.

chill (chĭl) *n.* **1.** A moderate but penetrating coldness. **2.** A sensation of coldness or a similar feeling, as from fever or fear. **3.** A dampening of enthusiasm or spirit. —*adj.* Chilly. —*v.* **1.** To make or become cold. **2.** To dispirit. [< OE *cēle.*] —**chill′ness** *n.*

chil·ly (chĭl′ē) *adj.* **-i·er, -i·est. 1.** Cold enough to cause shivering. **2.** Seized with cold. **3.** Distant and cool; unfriendly. —**chill′i·ly** *adv.* —**chill′i·ness** *n.*

chime (chīm) *n.* **1.** Often **chimes.** A set of bells tuned to the musical scale. **2.** The musical sound produced by a bell or bells. —*v.* **chimed, chim·ing. 1.** To sound with a harmonious ring when struck. **2.** To agree; harmonize. **3.** To make (the hour) known by ringing bells. —*phrasal verb.* **chime in.** To interrupt, as a conversation. [< Lat. *cymbalum,* cymbal.]

chi·me·ra (kĭ-mîr′ə, kə-) *n.* **1. Chimera.** *Gk. Myth.* A fire-breathing monster with the head of a lion, the body of a goat, and the tail of a serpent. **2.** An impossible or foolish fantasy.

chimera

5th-century B.C. bronze Chimera
from Arezzo, Italy

chi·mer·i·cal (kĭ-mĕr′ĭ-kəl, -mîr′-, kə-) *adj.* **1.** Imaginary; unreal. **2.** Given to unrealistic fantasies. —**chi·mer′i·cal·ly** *adv.*

chim·ney (chĭm′nē) *n., pl.* **-neys.** **1.** A usu. vertical passage through which smoke and gases escape from a fire or furnace. **2.** A glass tube for enclosing the flame of a lamp. [< Lat. *caminus,* furnace.]

chim·ney·piece (chĭm′nē-pēs′) *n.* **1.** A fireplace mantel. **2.** A decoration over a fireplace.

chimney pot *n.* A pipe placed on the top of a chimney to improve the draft.

chimney sweep *n.* A worker employed to clean soot from chimneys.

chimney swift *n.* A small, dark, swallowlike New World bird that often nests in chimneys.

chimp (chĭmp) *n.* *Informal.* A chimpanzee.

chim·pan·zee (chĭm′păn-zē′, chĭm-păn′zē) *n.* A dark-haired, gregarious African ape. [Of Bantu orig.]

chin (chĭn) *n.* The central forward portion of the lower jaw. —*v.* **chinned, chin·ning.** To grasp an overhead horizontal bar and pull oneself up until one's chin is level with it. [< OE *cin.*]

chi·na (chī′nə) *n.* **1.** High-quality porcelain or ceramic ware. **2.** Any porcelain ware. [< *China.*]

chinch (chĭnch) *n.* A bedbug. [< Lat. *cimex,* bug.]

chinch bug *n.* A small black and white insect that is very destructive to grains and grasses.

chin·chil·la (chĭn-chĭl′ə) *n.* **1. a.** A squirrellike South American rodent with soft pale-gray fur. **b.** The fur of this animal. **2.** A thick wool cloth used for overcoats. [Sp.]

chine (chīn) *n.* **1.** The backbone; spine. **2.** A cut of meat containing part of the backbone. **3.** A ridge or crest. [< OFr. *eschine,* of Gmc. orig.]

Chi·nese (chī-nēz′, -nēs′) *adj.* Of or pertaining to China, its culture, people, or languages. —*n., pl.* **Chinese.** **1. a.** A native or inhabitant of China. **b.** A person of Chinese ancestry. **2. a.** A branch of the Sino-Tibetan language family that consists of the various dialects spoken by the Chinese people. **b.** The standard vernacular language of China, based on the principal dialect spoken in and around Beijing (formerly Peking). **c.** Any of the dialects spoken by the Chinese people.

Chinese cabbage *n.* A plant related to the common cabbage, with a cylindrical head of crisp, edible leaves.

Chinese lantern *n.* A decorative, collapsible lantern of thin, brightly colored paper.

Chinese puzzle *n.* **1.** A very intricate puzzle. **2.** A very difficult problem.

chink¹ (chĭngk) *n.* A crack or narrow fissure. —*v.* To fill cracks or chinks in. [Poss. < obs. *chine.*]

chink² (chĭngk) *n.* A short, clinking sound. —*v.* To make a chink. [Imit.]

chi·no (chē′nō, shē′-) *n., pl.* **-nos. 1.** A coarse, twilled cotton fabric. **2. chinos.** Trousers of this material. [Am. Sp., toasted.]

Chi·nook (shə-nŏŏk′, chə-) *n., pl.* **-nook** or **-nooks. 1. a.** A tribe of Indians formerly inhabiting Oregon. **b.** A member of this tribe. **2.** The Chinookan language of the Chinook.

Chi·nook·an (shĭ-nŏŏk′ən, chĭ-) *n.* A North American Indian language family of Washington and Oregon. —*adj.* Of or pertaining to the Chinook.

chintz (chĭnts) *n.* A printed and glazed cotton

fabric, usu. of bright colors. [< Skt. *citra-*, variegated.]

chintz·y (chĭnt'sē) *adj.* **-i·er, -i·est.** Gaudy; cheap.

chip (chĭp) *n.* **1.** A small piece broken or cut off. **2.** A mark made by the breaking of such a piece. **3.** A coinlike disk used as a counter, as in poker. **4.** A thin, crisp piece of food. **5.** *Electronics.* A minute square of a thin semiconducting material processed to have specified electrical characteristics, esp. such a square before attachment of electrical leads and packaging as an electronic component or integrated circuit. —*v.* **chipped, chip·ping.** To break or cut so as to form a chip or chips. —*phrasal verb.* **chip in.** *Informal.* To contribute. —*idioms.* **a chip off the old block.** A child that resembles either of its parents. **a chip on (one's) shoulder.** A persistent feeling of resentment or bitterness. [< OE *cipp*, beam.]

Chip·e·wy·an (chĭp'ə-wī'ən) *n., pl.* **-an** or **-ans. 1. a.** A tribe of Indians living in Canada in the area between Great Slave Lake and Lake Athabasca on the west and Hudson Bay on the east. **b.** A member of this tribe. **2.** The Athapascan language of the Chipewyan.

chip·munk (chĭp'mŭngk') *n.* A small squirrellike rodent having a striped back. [Of Algonquian orig.]

chipped beef *n.* Dried beef smoked and sliced very thin.

chip·per (chĭp'ər) *adj. Informal.* Cheerful; brisk. [Orig. unknown.]

Chip·pe·wa (chĭp'ə-wô', -wä', -wä') *n., pl.* **-wa** or **-was.** Also **Chip·pe·way** (-wä'). Ojibwa.

chiro- *pref.* Hand: *chiropractic.* [< Gk. *kheir.*]

chi·rop·o·dy (kə-rŏp'ə-dē, shə-) *n.* Podiatry. —**chi·rop'o·dist** *n.*

chi·ro·prac·tic (kī'rə-prăk'tĭk) *n.* A system of therapy in which manipulation of the spinal column and other bodily structures is the preferred method of treatment. [CHIRO- + Gk. *praktikos,* effective.] —**chi'ro·prac'tor** *n.*

chirp (chûrp) *n.* A short, high-pitched sound, as that made by a small bird. —*v.* **1.** To utter a chirp. **2.** To speak in a quick, sprightly manner. [Imit.] —**chirp'er** *n.*

chis·el (chĭz'əl) *n.* A metallic cutting and shaping tool with a sharp, beveled edge. —*v.* **-eled** or **-elled, -el·ing** or **-el·ling. 1.** To shape or cut with a chisel. **2.** *Slang.* To swindle or obtain by swindling. [< OFr.] —**chis'el·er** *n.*

chit¹ (chĭt) *n.* **1.** A voucher for an amount owed for food and drink. **2.** *Chiefly Brit.* A note; memo. [< Hindi *ciṭṭhi,* note.]

chit² (chĭt) *n.* A pert girl. [ME, young animal.]

chit·chat (chĭt'chăt') *n.* Casual conversation; small talk. [Redup. of CHAT.]

chi·tin (kī'tĭn) *n.* A horny substance that is the principal component of crustacean shells and insect exoskeletons. [< Gk. *khitōn,* ton.]

chi·ton (kīt'n, kī'tŏn') *n.* **1.** A tunic worn by men and women in ancient Greece. **2.** Any of various marine mollusks living on rocks and having shells consisting of eight overlapping transverse plates. [< Gk. *khitōn.*]

chit·ter·lings (chĭt'lĭnz) *pl.n.* Also **chit·lins** or **chit·lings.** The intestines of pigs prepared as food. [ME *chiterling.*]

chiv·al·rous (shĭv'əl-rəs) *adj.* Also **chiv·al·ric** (shĭ-văl'rĭk, shĭv'əl-). **1.** Having the qualities of gallantry and honor attributed to an ideal knight. **2.** Of or pertaining to chivalry. —**chiv'al·rous·ly** *adv.*

chiv·al·ry (shĭv'əl-rē) *n., pl.* **-ries. 1.** The qualities, as bravery and courtesy, idealized by knighthood. **2.** The medieval institution of knighthood. **3.** A chivalrous act. [< LLat. *caballarius,* horseman.]

chive (chīv) *n.* A plant with grasslike onion-flavored leaves used as seasoning. [< Lat. *cepa,* onion.]

chlor- *pref.* Var. of **chloro-.**

chlo·ral (klôr'əl, klōr'-) *n.* A colorless, oily liquid, CCl_3CHO, used to manufacture DDT and chloral hydrate. [CHLOR- + AL(COHOL).]

chloral hydrate *n.* A colorless crystalline compound, $CCl_3CH(OH)_2$, used as a sedative and hypnotic.

chlo·rate (klôr'āt, klōr'-) *n.* The inorganic group ClO_3 or a compound containing it.

chlor·dane (klôr'dān, klōr'-) *n.* Also **chlor·dan** (-dän'). A colorless, odorless viscous liquid, $C_{10}H_6Cl_8$, used as an insecticide. [CHLOR- + *(in)d(ene)* + -ANE.]

chlo·rel·la (klə-rĕl'ə) *n.* Any of various green algae widely used in studies of photosynthesis. [CHLOR- + *-ella,* dim. suffix.]

chlo·ric acid (klôr'ĭk, klōr'-) *n.* A strongly oxidizing unstable acid, $HClO_3·7H_2O.$

chlo·ride (klôr'īd', klōr'-) *n.* A binary compound of chlorine.

chlo·rin·ate (klôr'ə-nāt', klōr'-) *v.* **-at·ed, -at·ing.** To treat or combine with chlorine or a chlorine compound. —**chlo'ri·na'tion** *n.* —**chlo'rin·a'tor** *n.*

chlo·rine (klôr'ēn', klōr'-, -ĭn) *n. Symbol* **Cl** A highly irritating, greenish-yellow gaseous element, used to purify water, as a disinfectant, a bleaching agent, and in the manufacture of chloroform and carbon tetrachloride. Atomic number 17; atomic weight 35.45.

chloro- or **chlor-** *pref.* **1.** Green: *chlorosis.* **2.** Chlorine: *chloroform.* [< Gk. *khlōros,* green.]

chlo·ro·form (klôr'ə-fôrm', klōr'-) *n.* A clear, colorless liquid, $CHCl_3,$ used in refrigerants, propellants, and resins and as an anesthetic. —*v.* To anesthetize or kill with chloroform. [CHLORO- + FORM(YL).]

chlo·ro·phyll (klôr'ə-fĭl, klōr'-) *n.* A green plant pigment essential in photosynthesis.

chlor·tet·ra·cy·cline (klôr'tĕt-rə-sī'klēn', klōr'tĕt-) *n.* An antibiotic, $C_{22}H_{23}ClN_2O_8,$ obtained from a soil bacterium.

chock (chŏk) *n.* A block or wedge placed under something, as a boat or wheel, to keep it from moving. —*v.* To secure by a chock or chocks. [Orig. unknown.]

chock-a-block (chŏk'ə-blŏk') *adj.* Jammed together.

chock-full (chŏk'fŏŏl', chŭk'-) *adj.* Also **chuck-full.** Completely filled. [ME *chokeful.*]

choc·o·late (chô'kə-lĭt, chŏk'ə-, chôk'lĭt, chŏk'-) *n.* **1.** Husked, roasted, and ground cacao seeds. **2.** A candy or beverage made from chocolate. **3.** A deep reddish or grayish brown. [< Aztec *xocolatl.*] —**choc'o·late** *adj.*

Choc·taw (chŏk'tô') *n., pl.* **-taw** or **-taws. 1. a.** A tribe of Indians, formerly living in southern Mississippi and Alabama, now settled in Oklahoma. **b.** A member of this tribe. **2.** The Muskhogean language of the Choctaw.

choice (chois) *n.* **1.** The act of choosing; selection. **2.** The power or right to choose. **3.** One chosen. **4.** A number or variety from which to choose. **5.** The best part. —*adj.* **1.** Of fine quality. **2.** Selected with care. [< OFr. *choisir*, to choose.]

Syns: *choice, election, option, preference, selection* **n.**

choir (kwīr) *n.* **1.** An organized group of singers, esp. in a church. **2.** The part of a church used by singers. **3.** A group or section of orchestral instruments. [< Lat. *chorus*, choral dance.]

choke (chōk) *v.* **choked, chok·ing.** **1.** To terminate, interfere with, or have difficulty in breathing, as by constricting or breaking the windpipe; suffocate. **2.** To repress or check forcefully. **3.** To block up; obstruct; clog. **4.** To reduce the air intake of a carburetor), thereby enriching the fuel mixture. —*phrasal verb.* **choke up.** *Informal.* To be unable to speak because of strong emotion. —*n.* **1.** The act or sound of choking. **2.** A device used in an internal-combustion engine to enrich the fuel mixture by reducing the air flow to the carburetor. [< OE *ācēocian*.]

chok·er (chō′kər) *n.* A short, close-fitting necklace.

chol·er (kŏl′ər, kō′lər) *n.* Anger; irritability. [< Lat. *cholera*, jaundice.]

chol·er·a (kŏl′ər-ə) *n.* An acute, infectious, often fatal epidemic disease characterized by watery diarrhea, vomiting, cramps, and suppression of urine. [< Gk. *kholera*, jaundice.]

chol·er·ic (kŏl′ə-rĭk, kə-lĕr′ĭk) *adj.* Bad-tempered; irritable.

cho·les·ter·ol (kə-lĕs′tə-rôl′, -rōl′) *n.* A glistening white soapy crystalline substance, $C_{27}H_{45}OH$, occurring notably in bile, gallstones, the brain, blood cells, plasma, egg yolk, and seeds. [Gk. *kholē*, bile + Gk. *stereos*, solid + -OL.]

chomp (chŏmp) *v.* Var. of **champ**[1].

chon (chŏn) *n., pl.* **chon.** See table at currency. [Korean.]

choose (chōōz) *v.* **chose** (chōz), **cho·sen** (chō′zən), **choos·ing.** **1.** To decide on and pick out. **2.** To prefer; desire. [< OE *cēosan*.] —**choos·er** *n.*

Syns: *choose, desire, like, please, want, will, wish* **v.**

choos·y (chōō′zē) *adj.* **-i·er, -i·est.** Also **choos·ey.** Hard to please. —**choos′i·ness** *n.*

chop[1] (chŏp) *v.* **chopped, chop·ping.** **1.** To cut by striking with a heavy, sharp tool. **2.** To cut into bits; mince. **3.** To hit with a short, swift downward stroke. —*n.* **1.** A swift, short blow or stroke. **2.** A cut of meat, usu. taken from the rib, shoulder, or loin and containing a bone. **3.** A short, irregular motion of waves. [ME *choppen*.]

chop·house (chŏp′hous′) *n.* A restaurant specializing in chops and steaks.

chop·per (chŏp′ər) *n.* **1.** *Slang.* A helicopter. **2.** A customized motorcycle.

chop·py (chŏp′ē) *adj.* **-pi·er, -pi·est.** Abruptly shifting or breaking, as waves. —**chop′pi·ly** *adv.* —**chop′pi·ness** *n.*

chops (chŏps) *pl.n.* The jaws, cheeks, or jowls. [Orig. unknown.]

chop·sticks (chŏp′stĭks′) *pl.n.* A pair of slender sticks used as eating utensils chiefly in the Orient. [Pidgin E. *chop*, fast + STICKS.]

chop su·ey (chŏp sōō′ē) *n.* A Chinese-American dish consisting of small pieces of meat or chicken cooked with bean sprouts and other vegetables and served with rice. [Cant. *tsap² sui⁴*, mixed pieces.]

cho·ral (kôr′əl, kōr′-) *adj.* Of, pertaining to, or for a chorus or choir. —*n.* Var. of **cho·rale.**

cho·rale (kə-răl′, -räl′) *n.* Also **cho·ral.** A hymn harmonized for four voices. [G. *Choral(gesang)*, choral (song).]

chord[1] (kôrd, kōrd) *n.* A combination of three or more musical tones sounded simultaneously. [< OFr. *accord*, agreement.]

chord[2] (kôrd, kōrd) *n.* **1.** A line segment that joins two points on a curve. **2.** A string or cord, esp. a cordlike anatomical structure. [< CORD.]

chore (chôr, chōr) *n.* **1.** A daily or routine task. **2.** An unpleasant task. [< CHAR[3].]

cho·re·a (kə-rē′ə, kô-) *n.* A nervous disorder, esp. of children, marked by uncontrollable movements of the arms, legs, and face; St. Vitus' dance. [< Gk. *khoreia*, choral dance.]

cho·re·og·ra·phy (kôr′ē-ŏg′rə-fē, kōr′-) *n.* The art of creating and arranging ballets or dances. [Fr. *chorégraphie.*] —**cho′re·o·graph′** (kôr′ē-ə-grăf′, -gräf′, kōr′-) *v.* —**cho′re·og′ra·pher** *n.* —**cho′re·o·graph′ic** (-ə-grăf′ĭk) *adj.*

cho·ris·ter (kôr′ĭ-stər, kŏr′-, kōr′-) *n.* A choir singer. [< Med. Lat. *chorista.*]

cho·roid (kôr′oid′, kōr′-) *n.* Also **cho·roi·de·a** (kô-roi′dē-ə, kō-). The dark-brown vascular membrane of the eye between the sclera and the retina. [< Gk. *khoroeidēs*, like an afterbirth.]

chor·tle (chôr′tl) *v.* **-tled, -tling.** To chuckle throatily. [Blend of CHUCKLE and SNORT.] —**chor′tle** *n.* —**chor′tler** *n.*

cho·rus (kôr′əs, kōr′-) *n., pl.* **-rus·es.** **1. a.** A group of singers who perform together. **b.** Music for such a group. **2.** A group of dancers in a musical comedy or revue. **3.** A group speaking or reciting together. **4.** The simultaneous utterance of several voices. **5.** A repeated refrain or melodic section of a song. —*v.* **-rused** or **-russed, -rus·ing** or **-rus·sing.** To sing or utter in chorus. [Lat., choral dance < Gk. *khoros.*] —**chor′ic** *adj.*

chose (chōz) *v. p.t.* of **choose.**

cho·sen (chō′zən) *v. p.p.* of **choose.** —*adj.* Selected from or preferred above others.

chow[1] (chou) *n.* A heavy-set dog with a long, dense, reddish-brown or black coat. [Prob. < Chin. *kou³*, dog.]

chow[2] (chou) *n. Slang.* Food. [Pidgin E., prob. < Chin. *chao³*, to stir-fry.]

chow·der (chou′dər) *n.* A thick seafood soup often in a milk base. [< Lat. *caldaria*, stew pot.]

chow mein (chou′ mān′) *n.* A Chinese-American dish consisting of various stewed vegetables and meat, served over fried noodles. [Chin. *chao³ mian⁴.*]

ă pat ā pay â care ä father ĕ pet ē be ĭ pit ī tie î pier ŏ pot ō toe ô paw, for oi noise ōŏ took
ōō boot ou out th thin *th* this ŭ cut û urge yōō abuse zh vision ə about, item, edible, gallop, circus

chrism (krĭz′əm) *n*. Consecrated oil and balsam used for anointing, esp. in baptism and confirmation. [< Gk. *khrisma*, ointment.] —**chris′mal** *adj*.

Christ (krīst) *n*. Jesus, the son of Mary, regarded by Christians as being the Son of God and the Messiah foretold by the prophets of the Old Testament. [< Gk. *khristos*, anointed.] —**Christ′like′** *adj*. —**Christ′like′ness** *n*. —**Christ′ly** *adj*.

chris·ten (krĭs′ən) *v*. **1.** To baptize. **2.** To give a name to at baptism. **3.** To name and dedicate ceremonially: *christen a ship*. [< OE *cristnian*.] —**chris′ten·er** *n*.

Chris·ten·dom (krĭs′ən-dəm) *n*. **1.** Christians collectively. **2.** The Christian world.

chris·ten·ing (krĭs′ə-nĭng) *n*. The Christian sacrament of baptism.

Chris·tian (krĭs′chən) *n*. One who believes in Christianity. —*adj*. **1.** Professing belief in Christianity. **2.** Pertaining to Jesus or His teachings. **3.** Pertaining to Christianity or its adherents. —**Chris′tian·i·za′tion** *n*. —**Chris′tian·ize′** *v*. —**Chris′tian·iz′er** *n*.

Christian era *n*. The period beginning with the birth of Jesus (conventionally A.D. 1).

chris·ti·a·ni·a (krĭs′tē-ă′nē-ə, -chē-ăn′ē-ə) *n*. A ski turn in which the body is swung from a crouching position to change direction or to stop. [< *Christiania*, former name for Oslo.]

Chris·ti·an·i·ty (krĭs′chē-ăn′ĭ-tē) *n*. **1.** The Christian religion, founded on the teachings of Jesus. **2.** Christendom. **3.** The state or fact of being a Christian.

Christian name *n*. A name given at birth or baptism.

Christian Science *n*. The church and the religious system founded by Mary Baker Eddy that emphasizes healing through spiritual means as an important element of Christianity and teaches pure divine goodness as underlying the scientific reality of existence. —**Christian Scientist** *n*.

Christ·mas (krĭs′məs) *n*. December 25, a holiday celebrated by Christians as the anniversary of the birth of Jesus. [< OE *Crīstesmæsse*.]

Christ·mas·tide (krĭs′məs-tīd′) *n*. The season of Christmas.

Christmas tree *n*. An evergreen or artificial tree decorated during the Christmas season.

chrom- *pref*. Var. of **chromo-**.

chro·mat·ic (krō-măt′ĭk) *adj*. **1.** Pertaining to colors or color. **2.** *Mus*. Proceeding by half tones: *a chromatic scale*. [< Gk. *khrōma*, color.] —**chro·mat′i·cal·ly** *adv*. —**chro·mat′i·cism** *n*.

chrome (krōm) *n*. **1.** Chromium. **2.** Something plated with a chromium alloy. [< Gk. *khrōma*, color.]

chro·mi·um (krō′mē-əm) *n*. *Symbol* **Cr** A lustrous, hard, steel-gray metallic element used to harden steel alloys, to produce stainless steels, and in corrosion-resistant decorative platings. Atomic number 24; atomic weight 51.996.

chromo- or **chrom-** *pref*. Color: *chromosome*. [Gk. *khrōma*, color.]

chro·mo·some (krō′mə-sōm′) *n*. A DNA-containing linear body of the cell nuclei of plants and animals, responsible for determination and transmission of hereditary characteristics. —**chro′mo·som′al** (-sō′məl) *adj*.

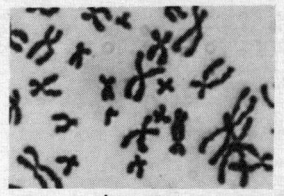

chromosome
Chromosomes from a female human

chron·ic (krŏn′ĭk) *adj*. Of long duration; continuing; lingering. [< Gk. *khronos*, time.] —**chron′i·cal·ly** *adv*.

chron·i·cle (krŏn′ĭ-kəl) *n*. **1.** A chronological record of historical events. **2. Chronicles.** See table at **Bible**. —*v*. **-cled, -cling.** To record in or in the form of a chronicle. [< Gk. *khronika*, annals.] —**chron′i·cler** (-klər) *n*.

chrono- *pref*. Time: *chronometer*. [< Gk. *khronos*.]

chron·o·log·i·cal (krŏn′ə-lŏj′ĭ-kəl, krō′nə-) or **chron·o·log·ic** (-lŏj′ĭk) *adj*. **1.** Arranged in order of time of occurrence. **2.** In accordance with or relating to chronology. —**chron′o·log′i·cal·ly** *adv*.

chro·nol·o·gy (krə-nŏl′ə-jē) *n*., *pl*. **-gies.** **1.** The determination of dates and sequences of events. **2.** The arrangement of events in time. **3.** A chronological list or table. —**chro·nol′o·gist** *n*.

chro·nom·e·ter (krə-nŏm′ĭ-tər) *n*. An exceptionally precise timepiece.

chrys·a·lis (krĭs′ə-lĭs) *n*. **1.** The pupa of a moth or butterfly, enclosed in a firm case or cocoon. **2.** Something still in the process of development. [< Gk. *khrusallis*.]

chry·san·the·mum (krĭ-săn′thə-məm) *n*. A plant cultivated in various forms for its showy flowers. [< Gk. *khrusanthemon*, a kind of flower.]

chub (chŭb) *n*., *pl*. **chub** or **chubs.** Any of various freshwater fishes related to the carps and minnows. [ME *chubbe*.]

chub·by (chŭb′ē) *adj*. **-bi·er, -bi·est.** Rounded and plump. [Prob. < CHUB.] —**chub′bi·ly** *adv*. —**chub′bi·ness** *n*.

chuck[1] (chŭk) *v*. **1.** To pat or squeeze playfully, esp. under the chin. **2.** To toss. **3.** *Informal*. To throw out; discard. [Orig. unknown.] —**chuck** *n*.

chuck[2] (chŭk) *n*. **1.** A cut of beef extending from the neck to the ribs. **2.** A clamp that holds a tool, or the material being worked, in a machine such as a drill or a lathe. [Dial. *chuck*, lump.]

chuck-full (chŏk′fŏŏl′, chŭk′-) *adj*. Var. of **chock-full.**

chuck·le (chŭk′əl) *v*. **-led, -ling.** To laugh quietly. —*n*. A quiet laugh. [Prob. imit.] —**chuck′ler** *n*.

chug (chŭg) *n*. A brief, dull, explosive sound made by or as if by a laboring engine. —*v*. **chugged, chug·ging.** **1.** To make chugs. **2.** To move while making chugs. [Imit.]

chuk·ka (chŭk′ə) *n*. A short, ankle-length boot with two pairs of eyelets. [< CHUKKER.]

chuk·ker (chŭk′ər) *n*. Also **chuk·kar.** A period

of play in a polo match. [< Skt. *cakram*, circle.]

chum (chŭm) *n.* A close friend. —*v.* **chummed, chum·ming.** To be a close friend. [Prob. < *chamber fellow.*]

chum·my (chŭm'ē) *adj.* **-mi·er, -mi·est.** Intimate; friendly. —**chum'mi·ly** *adv.* —**chum'mi·ness** *n.*

chump (chŭmp) *n.* A dupe. [Prob. a blend of CHUNK and LUMP or STUMP.]

chunk (chŭngk) *n.* 1. A thick mass or piece. 2. A substantial amount. [Poss. < CHUCK2.]

chunk·y (chŭng'kē) *adj.* **-i·er, -i·est.** Thickset; stocky. —**chunk'i·ness** *n.*

church (chûrch) *n.* 1. Often **Church.** All Christians regarded as a spiritual body. 2. A building for public worship. 3. A congregation. 4. A religious service. 5. Ecclesiastical power as distinguished from the secular: *the separation of church and state.* 6. The clergy. [< Gk. *kuriakos,* of the lord.]

church·go·er (chûrch'gō'ər) *n.* One who at-tends church regularly. —**church'go'ing** *adj.*

church key *n. Informal.* A can or bottle opener with a triangular head.

church·man (chûrch'mən) *n.* 1. A clergyman; priest. 2. A member of a church.

Church of Christ, Scientist *n.* The official name of the Christian Science Church.

Church of England *n.* The episcopal and liturgical national church of England.

Church of Jesus Christ of Latter-day Saints *n.* The official name of the Mormon Church.

church·war·den (chûrch'wôrd'n) *n.* A lay of-ficer who handles the secular affairs of an Anglican or Episcopal church.

church·wom·an (chûrch'wŏŏm'ən) *n.* A woman who is a member of a church.

church·yard (chûrch'yärd') *n.* A yard adja-cent to a church.

churl (chûrl) *n.* 1. A rude, surly person. 2. A medieval peasant. [< OE *ceorl,* peasant.] —**churl'ish** *adj.* —**churl'ish·ly** *adv.* —**churl'ish·ness** *n.*

churn (chûrn) *n.* A device in which cream or milk is agitated to make butter. —*v.* 1. To stir or agitate (milk or cream) in a churn. 2. To make (butter) by churning. 3. To move or be moved with great agitation. —*phrasal verb.* **churn out.** To produce automatically and in great volume: *churn out a novel.* [< OE *cyrn.*]

chute (shōōt) *n.* 1. An inclined trough or pas-sage down which things can pass. 2. *Informal.* A parachute. [< Fr. *cheoir,* to fall.]

chut·ney (chŭt'nē) *n.* A pungent relish made of fruits, spices, and herbs. [Hindi *catṇi.*]

chutz·pah (KHŎŏt'spə) *n. Slang.* Gall; nerve. [Yiddish.]

ciao (chou) *interj.* Used to express greeting or farewell. [Ital.]

ci·bo·ri·um (sĭ-bôr'ē-əm, -bōr'-) *n., pl.* **-bo·ri·a** (-bôr'ē-ə, -bōr'-).** 1. A vaulted canopy over an altar. 2. A covered receptacle for holding the consecrated wafers of the Eucharist. [< Lat., drinking cup.]

ci·ca·da (sĭ-kā'də, -kä'-) *n., pl.* **-das** or **-dae** (-dē').** A large insect with membranous wings and specialized organs producing a shrill, droning sound. [Lat.]

cic·a·trix (sĭk'ə-trĭks', sĭ-kā'trĭks) *n., pl.* **-tri·ces** (-trī'sēz', -trĭ-sēz').** Recently formed connec-tive tissue on a healing wound. [Lat.] —**cic'-a·tri'cial** (sĭk'ə-trĭsh'əl) *adj.*

-cide *suff.* 1. Killer: *insecticide.* 2. Killing of: *genocide.* [< Lat. *caedere,* to kill.]

ci·der (sī'dər) *n.* The juice pressed from ap-ples, used to produce vinegar or a beverage. [< Heb. *shēkār,* intoxicating drink.]

ci·gar (sĭ-gär') *n.* A small, compact roll of tobacco leaves prepared for smoking. [Sp. *cigarro.*]

cig·a·rette (sĭg'ə-rĕt', sĭg'ə-rĕt') *n.* Also **cig·a·ret.** A small roll of finely cut tobacco for smoking, usu. enclosed in a wrapper of thin paper. [Fr., dim. of *cigare,* cigar.]

cil·i·a (sĭl'ē-ə) *n.* Pl. of **cilium.**

cil·i·ar·y (sĭl'ē-ĕr'ē) *adj.* 1. Of, pertaining to, or resembling cilia. 2. Of or pertaining to the ciliary body.

ciliary body *n.* The thickened part of the vascular layer of the eye that connects the choroid with the iris.

cil·i·ate (sĭl'ē-ĭt, -āt') *adj.* Also **cil·i·at·ed** (-ā'-tĭd).** Having cilia. —**cil'i·ate·ly** *adv.*

cil·i·um (sĭl'ē-əm) *n., pl.* **-i·a** (-ē-ə).** 1. A mi-croscopic hairlike process extending from a cell and often capable of motion. 2. An eye-lash. [< Lat., eyelid.]

cinch (sĭnch) *n.* 1. A girth for holding a pack or saddle in place. 2. *Informal.* A firm grip. 3. *Slang.* Something easy to accomplish. —*v.* 1. To put a saddle girth on. 2. *Slang.* To make certain of. [< Lat. *cingula.*]

cin·cho·na (sĭn-kō'nə, -chō'-, sĭng-) *n.* 1. A South American tree whose bark yields qui-nine and other medicinal alkaloids. 2. The dried bark of such a tree. [< Francisca Hen-riquez de Ribera (1576–1639), Countess of *Chinchón.*]

cinc·ture (sĭngk'chər) *n.* A belt; girdle. [Lat. *cinctura.*] —**cinc'ture** *v.*

cin·der (sĭn'dər) *n.* 1. A burned substance that is not reduced to ashes but cannot be burned further. 2. A partly charred substance that can burn further but without flame. 3. **cinders.** Ashes. [< OE *sinder,* dross.] —**cin'der·y** *adj.*

cinder block *n.* A hollow, concrete building block made with coal cinders.

cin·e·ma (sĭn'ə-mə) *n.* 1. A motion picture. 2. A motion-picture theater. 3. **the cinema. a.** Motion pictures collectively. **b.** The motion-picture industry. 4. The art of making motion pictures. [< CINEMATOGRAPH.] —**cin'e·mat'ic** (sĭn'ə-mǎt'ĭk) *adj.* —**cin'e·mat'i·cal·ly** *adv.*

cin·e·mat·o·graph (sĭn'ə-mǎt'ə-grǎf') *n.* A motion-picture camera or projector. [Fr. *ciné-matographe.*] —**cin'e·mat'o·graph'ic** *adj.* —**cin'e·mat'o·graph'i·cal·ly** *adv.*

cin·e·ma·tog·ra·phy (sĭn'ə-mə-tŏg'rə-fē) *n.* The making of motion pictures. —**cin'e·ma·tog'ra·pher** *n.*

ci·né·ma vé·ri·té (sĕ'nä-mä' vä'rĕ-tā') *n.* Film-making that stresses unbiased realism. [Fr.]

cin·e·rar·i·a (sĭn'ə-râr'ē-ə) *n.* A tropical plant cultivated as a house plant, with flat clusters of blue or purplish daisylike flowers. [< Lat. *cinerarius,* of ashes.]

cin·e·rar·i·um (sĭn'ə-râr'ē-əm) *n., pl.* **-i·a** (-ē-ə).**

A place for keeping the ashes of a cremated body. [Lat.]

cin·na·bar (sĭn'ə-bär') n. A heavy reddish compound, HgS, that is the principal ore of mercury. [< Gk. kinnabari.]

cin·na·mon (sĭn'ə-mən) n. 1. The aromatic reddish or yellowish-brown bark of a tropical Asian tree, dried and often ground for use as a spice. 2. A reddish or light yellowish brown. [< Gk. kinnamōmon.]

ci·pher (sī'fər) n. 1. The mathematical symbol (0) denoting absence of quantity; zero. 2. An Arabic numeral or figure. 3. a. A system of secret writing in which units of plain text are substituted according to a predetermined key. b. The key to such a system. c. A message in cipher. 4. One that is without influence or value; nonentity. 5. A monogram. —v. To compute arithmetically. [< Ar. ṣifr.]

cir·ca (sûr'kə) prep. About: a house built circa 1750. [Lat.]

cir·cle (sûr'kəl) n. 1. A plane curve everywhere equidistant from a given fixed point, the center. 2. A planar region bounded by such a curve. 3. Something shaped like a circle. 4. A group of people sharing an interest, activity, or achievement. 5. A sphere of influence or interest. —v. -cled, -cling. 1. To make a circle around. 2. To move in a circle. [< Lat. circus, ring.] —cir'cler (-klər) n.

cir·clet (sûr'klĭt) n. A small circle.

cir·cuit (sûr'kĭt) n. 1. a. A closed, usu. circular, curve. b. The region enclosed by such a curve. 2. A closed path or route. 3. a. A closed path followed by an electric current. b. A configuration of electrically or electromagnetically connected components or devices. 4. a. A regular or accustomed course from place to place, as that of a salesman. b. The area or district thus covered, esp. a territory under the jurisdiction of a judge, in which he holds periodic court sessions. —v. 1. To make a circuit of. 2. To move in a circuit. [< Lat. circumire, to go around.]

circuit breaker n. An automatic switch that interrupts an overloaded electric circuit.

cir·cu·i·tous (sər-kyŏŏ'ĭ-təs) adj. Being or taking a roundabout course. —cir·cu'i·tous·ly adv. —cir·cu'i·ty or cir·cu'i·tous·ness n.

cir·cuit·ry (sûr'kĭ-trē) n. 1. The detailed design of an electric or electronic circuit. 2. Electric or electronic circuits in general.

cir·cu·lar (sûr'kyə-lər) adj. 1. Pertaining to a circle. 2. Shaped like a circle. 3. Forming or moving in a circle. 4. Circuitous. —n. A printed advertisement for public distribution. —cir'cu·lar'i·ty or cir'cu·lar·ness n. —cir'cu·lar·ly adv.

circular saw n. A power saw consisting of a toothed disk rotated at a high speed.

cir·cu·late (sûr'kyə-lāt') v. -lat·ed, -lat·ing. 1. To move in or flow through a circle or circuit. 2. To move around, as from person to person or place to place. 3. To move or cause to move, as air. 4. To spread or distribute widely; disseminate. —cir'cu·la'tive adj. —cir'cu·la'tor n. —cir'cu·la·to'ry (-lə-tôr'ē, -tŏr'ē) adj.

cir·cu·la·tion (sûr'kyə-lā'shən) n. 1. Movement in a circle or circuit. 2. The movement of blood through bodily vessels as a result of the heart's pumping action. 3. a. The distribution of a periodical publication. b. The number of copies sold or distributed.

circulatory system n. The heart, blood vessels, and lymphatic system of the body.

circum- pref. Around; about: circumnavigate. [< Lat. circum, around.]

cir·cum·cise (sûr'kəm-sīz') v. -cised, -cis·ing. 1. To remove the prepuce of (a male). 2. To remove the clitoris of (a female). [< Lat. circumcidere, to cut around.] —cir'cum·ci'sion (-sĭzh'ən) n.

cir·cum·fer·ence (sər-kŭm'fər-əns) n. 1. a. The boundary line of a circle. b. A perimeter. 2. The length of such a boundary or perimeter. [< Lat. circumferre, to carry around.] —cir·cum'fer·en'tial (-fə-rĕn'shəl) adj.

cir·cum·flex (sûr'kəm-flĕks') n. A mark (ˆ) used over a vowel to indicate quality of pronunciation. [< Lat. circumflectere, to bend around.]

cir·cum·lo·cu·tion (sûr'kəm-lō-kyŏŏ'shən) n. A roundabout expression.

cir·cum·lu·nar (sûr'kəm-lōō'nər) adj. Around the moon.

cir·cum·nav·i·gate (sûr'kəm-năv'ĭ-gāt') v. -gat·ed, -gat·ing. To sail completely around. —cir'cum·nav'i·ga'tion n. —cir'cum·nav'i·ga'tor n.

cir·cum·scribe (sûr'kəm-skrīb') v. -scribed, -scrib·ing. 1. To draw a line around. 2. To confine within bounds; restrict. [< Lat. circumscribere.] —cir'cum·scrip'tion (-skrĭp'-shən) n.

cir·cum·so·lar (sûr'kəm-sō'lər) adj. Around the sun.

cir·cum·spect (sûr'kəm-spĕkt') adj. Heedful of consequences. [< Lat. circumspicere, to take heed.] —cir'cum·spec'tion n. —cir'cum·spect'ly adv.

cir·cum·stance (sûr'kəm-stăns') n. 1. One of the conditions or facts attending an event and having bearing on it. 2. The sum of determining factors beyond willful control. 3. Often **circumstances.** Financial status or means. 4. Formal display; ceremony: pomp and circumstance. —**idioms. under no circumstances.** Never. **under (or in) the circumstances.** Given these conditions. [< Lat. circumstare, to stand around.]

cir·cum·stan·tial (sûr'kəm-stăn'shəl) adj. 1. Of or dependent upon circumstances. 2. Not of primary importance; incidental. 3. Complete and detailed: a circumstantial account. —cir'cum·stan'tial·ly adv.

circumstantial evidence n. Evidence not bearing directly on the facts in a legal dispute but on various attendant circumstances from which a judge or jury might infer the occurrence of the facts in dispute.

cir·cum·stan·ti·ate (sûr'kəm-stăn'shē-āt') v. -at·ed, -at·ing. To give detailed proof or description of. —cir'cum·stan'ti·a'tion n.

cir·cum·ter·res·tri·al (sûr'kəm-tə-rĕs'trē-əl) adj. Around the earth.

cir·cum·vent (sûr'kəm-vĕnt', sûr'kəm-vĕnt') v. 1. To entrap or overcome by ingenuity. 2. To avoid: circumvent a problem. [Lat. circumvenire.] —cir'cum·ven'tion n. —cir'cum·ven'tive adj.

cir·cus (sûr'kəs) n., pl. -cus·es. 1. A traveling show of acrobats, clowns, trained animals, etc., often performing under a tent. 2. Informal. A humorous or rowdy occurrence. [Lat., circle.]

cirque (sûrk) n. A steep hollow, often containing a small lake, at the upper end of a mountain valley. [< Lat. *circus*, circle.]

cir·rho·sis (sĭ-rō′sĭs) *n.* A chronic disease of the liver that ultimately results in liver failure and death. [Gk. *kirrhos*, tawny + -OSIS.] —**cir·rhot′ic** (sĭ-rŏt′ĭk) *adj.*

cir·ri (sĭr′ī′) *n.* Pl. of **cirrus.**

cir·ro·cu·mu·lus (sĭr′ō-kyōō′myə-ləs) *n.* A high-altitude cloud composed of a series of small, regularly arranged parts in the form of ripples or grains. [CIRR(US) + CUMULUS.]

cirrocumulus   cirrus

cir·ro·stra·tus (sĭr′ō-strā′təs, -străt′əs) *n.* A high-altitude, thin, hazy cloud, often covering the sky and producing a halo effect. [CIRR(US) + STRATUS.]

cir·rus (sĭr′əs) *n., pl.* **cir·ri** (sĭr′ī′). A high-altitude cloud composed of narrow bands or patches of thin, gen. white, fleecy parts. [Lat., curl.]

cis·tern (sĭs′tərn) *n.* A receptacle for holding water, esp. rainwater. [< Lat. *cisterna*.] —**cis·ter′nal** *adj.*

cit·a·del (sĭt′ə-dl, -děl′) *n.* 1. A fortress in a commanding position in or near a city. 2. A stronghold. [< Oltal. *citadella*.]

cite (sīt) *v.* **cit·ed, cit·ing.** 1. To quote as an authority or example. 2. To mention as support, illustration, or proof. 3. To commend for meritorious action, esp. in military service. 4. To summon before a court of law. [< Lat. *citare*.] —**ci·ta′tion** *n.*

cit·i·fy (sĭt′ə-fī′) *v.* **-fied, -fy·ing.** 1. To make urban. 2. To mark with the styles and manners of the city. —**cit′i·fi·ca′tion** *n.* —**cit′i·fied′** *adj.*

cit·i·zen (sĭt′ĭ-zən) *n.* 1. A person owing loyalty to and entitled by birth or naturalization to the protection of a given country. 2. A resident of a city or town. [< OFr. *citeain*.]

cit·i·zen·ry (sĭt′ĭ-zən-rē) *n., pl.* **-ries.** Citizens collectively.

citizen's band *n.* A radio-frequency band allocated for private use by individuals.

cit·i·zen·ship (sĭt′ĭ-zən-shĭp′) *n.* The status of a citizen with its duties, rights, and privileges.

cit·rate (sĭt′rāt′) *n.* A salt or ester of citric acid.

cit·ric (sĭt′rĭk) *adj.* Of or obtained from citrus fruits.

citric acid *n.* A colorless acid, $C_6H_8O_7 \cdot H_2O$, occurring in lemon, lime, and pineapple juices.

cit·rine (sĭt′rĭn, -rēn′) *n.* 1. A pale-yellow quartz. 2. A light yellow. —*adj.* Light yellow. [< Lat. *citrus*, a citrus.]

cit·ro·nel·la (sĭt′rə-něl′ə) *n.* A light-yellow, aromatic oil obtained from a tropical grass and used in insect repellents and perfumery. [< Fr. *citronelle*, lemon oil.]

cit·rus (sĭt′rəs) *adj.* Also **cit·rous.** Of or pertaining to related trees or fruit such as the orange, lemon, lime, and grapefruit. —*n., pl.* **-rus·es** or **-rus.** A citrus tree. [< Lat., citrus tree.]

cit·y (sĭt′ē) *n., pl.* **-ies.** 1. A town of significant size. 2. An incorporated municipality with definite boundaries and legal powers set forth in a state charter. 3. The inhabitants of a city as a group. —*adj.* Of or in a city. [< Lat. *civitas*.]

city council *n.* The governing body of a city.

city father *n.* A city official.

city hall *n.* 1. The building housing the administrative offices of a municipal government. 2. A municipal government.

cit·y-state (sĭt′ē-stāt′) *n.* A sovereign state consisting of an independent city and its surrounding territory.

civ·et (sĭv′ĭt) *n.* 1. A catlike African mammal that secretes a musky fluid. 2. This fluid, used in making perfumes. [< Ar. *zabād*.]

civ·ic (sĭv′ĭk) *adj.* Of a city, citizens, or citizenship. —*n.* **civics** (*used with a sing. verb*). The study of civic affairs, esp. the rights and duties of citizenship. [Lat. *civicus*.]

civ·ies (sĭv′ēz) *pl.n.* Var. of **civvies.**

civ·il (sĭv′əl) *adj.* 1. Of a citizen or citizens. 2. Of ordinary community life, as distinct from the military or ecclesiastical. 3. Civilized. 4. Polite. [< Lat. *civilis*.] —**civ′il·ly** *adv.* —**civ′il·ness** *n.*

civil engineer *n.* An engineer trained in the design and construction of public works. —**civil engineering** *n.*

ci·vil·ian (sĭ-vĭl′yən) *n.* One not serving in the armed forces.

ci·vil·i·ty (sĭ-vĭl′ĭ-tē) *n., pl.* **-ties.** 1. Politeness; courtesy. 2. An act or expression of courtesy.

civ·i·li·za·tion (sĭv′ə-lə-zā′shən) *n.* 1. A human society having an advanced stage of development in the arts and sciences and social, political, and cultural complexity. 2. The type of culture developed by a particular people or in a particular epoch. —**civ′i·liz′a·ble** *adj.* —**civ′i·lize′** *v.* —**civ′i·liz′er** *n.*

civil law *n.* The body of law dealing with the rights of private citizens.

civil liberty *n.* The legal guarantee of individual rights such as freedom of speech, thought, and action.

civil rights *pl.n.* Rights belonging to an individual by virtue of his or her status as a citizen.

civil service *n.* All branches of public service that are not legislative, judicial, or military. —**civil servant** *n.*

civil war *n.* 1. A war between factions or regions of one country. 2. **Civil War.** The war between the Union and the Confederacy lasting from 1861 to 1865.

civ·vies (sĭv′ēz) *pl.n.* Also **civ·ies.** *Slang.* Civilian clothes.

Cl The symbol for the element chlorine.

clab·ber (klăb′ər) *n.* Sour, curdled milk. —*v.* To curdle. [< Ir. Gael. *bainne clabair*.]

clack (klăk) *v.* 1. To make or cause to make

an abrupt, dry sound, as by the collision of hard surfaces. **2.** To chatter. —*n.* A clacking sound. [< ON *klaka.*] —**clack′er** *n.*

clad (klăd) *v.* A *p.t. & p.p.* of **clothe.**

claim (klām) *v.* **1.** To demand as one's due. **2.** To state to be true. **3.** To call for; require. —*n.* **1.** A demand for something as one's due. **2.** Title or right. **3.** Something claimed. **4.** A statement of something as a fact. —*idiom.* **lay claim to.** To assert one's right to or ownership of. [< Lat. *clamare,* to call.] —**claim′-a·ble** *adj.*

claim·ant (klā′mənt) *n.* One making a claim.

clair·voy·ance (klâr-voi′əns) *n.* The supposed power to perceive things that are out of the range of human senses. [Fr.] —**clair·voy′ant** *n. & adj.*

clam (klăm) *n.* Any of various bivalve mollusks, many of which are edible. —*v.* **clammed, clam·ming.** To hunt for clams. —*phrasal verb.* **clam up.** To refuse to talk. [< ME *clam,* clamp.]

clam·bake (klăm′bāk′) *n.* A picnic where clams, corn, and other foods are baked in layers on buried hot stones.

clam·ber (klăm′bər, klăm′ər) *v.* To climb with difficulty, esp. on all fours. [ME *clambren.*] —**clam′ber·er** *n.*

clam·my (klăm′ē) *adj.* **-mi·er, -mi·est.** Unpleasantly damp and usu. cold. [ME *clammy.*] —**clam′mi·ness** *n.*

clam·or (klăm′ər) *n.* **1.** A loud outcry; hubbub. **2.** A vehement protest or outcry. —*v.* To make a clamor. [< Lat., shout.] —**clam′orous** *adj.*

clamp (klămp) *n.* A device used to join, grip, support, or compress mechanical parts. —*v.* To grip, fasten, or support with or as if with a clamp. —*phrasal verb.* **clamp down.** To become more strict or repressive. [< MDu. *klampe.*]

clan (klăn) *n.* **1.** A group of families, as in the Scottish Highlands, claiming a common ancestor. **2.** A large group of relatives or associates. [< Sc. Gael. *clann.*] —**clan′nish** *adj.* —**clan′nish·ly** *adv.* —**clans′man** *n.*

clan·des·tine (klăn-dĕs′tĭn) *adj.* Done secretly or kept secret. [< Lat. *clandestinus.*]

clang (klăng) *v.* To make or cause to make a loud, ringing, metallic sound. —*n.* A clanging sound. [Lat. *clangere.*]

clan·gor (klăng′ər, -gər) *n.* A clang or repeated clanging. [Lat.] —**clan′gor** *v.*

clank (klăngk) *n.* A quick, sharp, metallic sound. [Imit.] —**clank** *v.*

clap (klăp) *v.* **clapped, clap·ping. 1.** To strike (the palms of the hands) together with an abrupt loud sound. **2.** To come together suddenly with a sharp noise. **3.** To tap with the open hand, as in greeting. **4.** To put or send promptly or suddenly: *clapped him in jail.* —*n.* **1.** The act or sound of clapping the hands. **2.** A loud or explosive noise. **3.** A slap. [< OE *clappan.*]

clap·board (klăb′ərd, klăp′bôrd′, -bōrd′) *n.* A long, narrow board with one edge thicker than the other, overlapped to cover the outer walls of a house. [< MDu. *clapholt.*] —**clap′board** *v.*

clap·per (klăp′ər) *n.* One that claps, esp. the hammerlike object inside a bell.

clap·trap (klăp′trăp′) *n.* Pretentious or empty speech.

claque (klăk) *n.* A group hired to applaud at a performance. [Fr.]

clar·et (klăr′ĭt) *n.* A dry red table wine. [< OFr. *vin claret,* light-colored wine.]

clar·i·fy (klăr′ə-fī′) *v.* **-fied, -fy·ing.** To make or become clear or pure. [< LLat. *clarificare.*] —**clar·i·fi·ca′tion** *n.* —**clar′i·fi′er** *n.*

clar·i·net (klăr′ə-nĕt′) *n.* A woodwind instrument with a single-reed mouthpiece, a cylindrical body, and a flaring bell. [< Lat. *clarus,* clear.] —**clar′i·net′ist** or **clar′i·net′tist** *n.*

clar·i·on (klăr′ē-ən) *adj.* Shrill and clear. [< Lat. *clarus,* clear.]

clar·i·ty (klăr′ĭ-tē) *n.* Clearness; lucidity. [< Lat. *claritas.*]

clash (klăsh) *v.* **1.** To collide or strike together with a loud, harsh noise. **2.** To conflict; disagree. —*n.* **1.** A loud metallic sound. **2.** A usu. hostile conflict. [Imit.]

clasp (klăsp) *n.* **1.** A fastener, such as a hook, used to hold two objects or parts together. **2. a.** An embrace. **b.** A grip of the hand. —*v.* **1.** To fasten with or as if with a clasp. **2.** To hold in a tight grasp; embrace. **3.** To grip firmly in or with the hand. [ME *claspe.*] —**clasp′er** *n.*

class (klăs) *n.* **1.** A group whose members have at least one attribute in common; kind; sort. **2.** A division by quality or grade. **3.** A social stratum whose members share similar characteristics. **4. a.** A group of students graduated in the same year. **b.** A group of students meeting to study the same subject. **5.** *Slang.* High style in manner or dress. —*v.* To classify. [< Lat. *classis,* class of citizens.]

class action *n.* A lawsuit in which the plaintiff or plaintiffs bring suit both on their own behalf and on behalf of many others who have the same claim against the defendant.

clas·sic (klăs′ĭk) *adj.* **1.** Of the highest rank or class. **2.** Serving as a model of its kind. **3.** Pertaining to ancient Greek or Roman literature or art. **4.** Of or in accordance with established principles and methods. **5.** Of lasting historical or literary significance. —*n.* **1.** An artist, author, or work of the highest rank. **2. classics.** The literature of ancient Greece and Rome. **3.** A traditional event, as in sports.

clas·si·cal (klăs′ĭ-kəl) *adj.* **1.** Of, pertaining to, or in the style of ancient Greek and Roman art, literature, or culture. **2.** Pertaining to or versed in studies of antiquity. **3. a.** Of the musical style that prevailed in Europe in the late part of the 18th cent. **b.** Of concert music or all music other than popular music and folk music. **4.** Standard or traditional rather than new or experimental. —**clas′si·cal·ly** *adv.*

clas·si·cism (klăs′ĭ-sĭz′əm) *n.* **1.** Aesthetic attitudes and principles based on the culture, art, and literature of ancient Greece and Rome and characterized by emphasis on form, simplicity, proportion, and restrained emotion. **2.** The use of such rules or principles in artistic creation. **3.** Classical scholarship. —**clas′si·cist** (klăs′ĭ-sĭst) *n.*

clas·si·fied (klăs′ə-fīd′) *adj.* Available only to authorized persons; secret.

clas·si·fy (klăs′ə-fī′) *v.* **-fied, -fy·ing. 1.** To arrange in classes or assign to a class. **2.** To designate (information) as secret and available only to authorized persons. —**clas′si·fi′a·ble** *adj.* —**clas′si·fi·ca′tion** (-fĭ-kā′shən) *n.* —**clas′si·fi′er** *n.*

class·mate (klăs′māt′, klăs′-) *n.* A member of the same academic class.

class·room (klăs'rōōm', -rōōm', klăs'-) *n.* A room in which academic classes meet.

class·y (klăs'ē) *adj.* **-i·er, -i·est** *Slang.* Stylish; elegant.

clat·ter (klăt'ər) *v.* To make or cause to make a rattling sound. —*n.* **1.** A rattling sound. **2.** A loud disturbance. [ME *clateren.*]

clause (klôz) *n.* **1.** *Gram.* A group of words that contains a subject and a predicate and forms part of a compound or complex sentence. **2.** A distinct article, stipulation, or provision of a document. [< Med. Lat. *clausa*, close of a rhetorical period.]

claus·tro·pho·bi·a (klô'strə-fō'bē-ə) *n.* An abnormal fear of being enclosed in a small space. [Lat. *claustrum*, enclosed place + -PHOBIA.] —**claus'tro·pho'bic** (-fō'bĭk) *adj.*

clav·i·chord (klăv'ĭ-kôrd') *n.* An early musical keyboard instrument. [Med. Lat. *clavichordium.*]

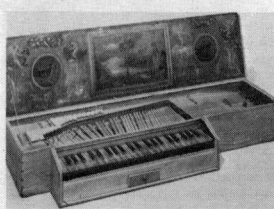

clavichord

clav·i·cle (klăv'ĭ-kəl) *n.* A bone that connects the sternum and the scapula. [< Lat. *clavicula*, dim. of *clavis*, key.] —**cla·vic'u·lar** (klə-vĭk'yə-lər) *adj.*

cla·vier (klə-vîr', klă'vē-ər, klăv'ē-) *n.* **1.** A keyboard. **2.** A stringed keyboard musical instrument. [Fr., ult. < Lat. *clavis*, key.]

claw (klô) *n.* **1.** A sharp, often curved nail on the toe of an animal. **2.** A pincerlike part, as of a lobster. **3.** Something resembling a claw. —*v.* To scratch or dig with or as if with claws. [< OE *clawu.*]

clay (klā) *n.* **1.** A firm, fine-grained earth that is soft and pliable when wet, used in making bricks, pottery, and tiles. **2.** Moist earth; mud. **3.** The mortal human body. [< OE *clæg.*] —**clay'ey** (klā'ē) *adj.* —**clay'ish** *adj.*

clay pigeon *n.* A disk-shaped target for skeet and trapshooting.

clean (klēn) *adj.* **-er, -est. 1.** Free from dirt or impurities. **2.** Morally decent; honorable. **3.** Even; regular. **4.** Thorough; complete. **5.** Obeying the rules; fair. —*adv.* **1.** In a clean manner. **2.** *Informal.* Entirely; completely. —*v.* To make or become clean. —*phrasal verbs.* **clean out. 1.** To drive or force out. **2.** *Informal.* To deprive completely, as of money. **clean up.** *Informal.* To make a large sum of money in a short period of time. —*idiom.* **come clean.** *Slang.* To admit the truth. [< OE *clæne.*] —**clean'a·ble** *adj.* —**clean'er** *n.* —**clean'ness** *n.*

Syns: *clean, antiseptic, immaculate, spotless, stainless* **adj.**

clean-cut (klēn'kŭt') *adj.* **1.** Clearly defined. **2.** Wholesome.

clean·ly (klĕn'lē) *adj.* **-li·er, -li·est.** Habitually neat and clean. —*adv.* (klēn'lē). In a clean manner. —**clean'li·ness** (klĕn'lē-nĭs) *n.*

cleanse (klĕnz) *v.* **cleansed, cleans·ing.** To free from dirt, defilement, or guilt. [< OE *clænsian.*] —**cleans'er** *n.*

clean·up (klēn'ŭp') *n.* **1.** The act or process of cleaning up. **2.** *Informal.* A large profit. —*adj. Baseball.* Being 4th in the batting order.

clear (klîr) *adj.* **-er, -est. 1.** Free from anything that dims or obscures. **2.** Free from impediment; open. **3.** Easily perceptible; distinct. **4.** Discerning or perceiving easily: *a clear mind.* **5.** Free from doubt or confusion. **6.** Free from qualification or limitation. **7.** Freed from contact or connection; disengaged: *clear of danger.* **8.** Freed from burden or obligation. —*adv.* **1.** Distinctly. **2.** *Informal.* Entirely. —*v.* **1.** To make or become clear, light, or bright. **2.** To rid of impurities or blemishes. **3.** To rid of obstructions. **4.** To free from a charge of guilt. **5.** To pass by, under, or over without contact. **6.** To gain as net profit or earnings. **7.** To pass through a clearinghouse, as a check. **8.** To free (the throat) of phlegm. —*phrasal verb.* **clear out.** *Informal.* To leave a place, often quickly. [< Lat. *clarus.*] —**clear'a·ble** *adj.* —**clear'ly** *adv.* —**clear'ness** *n.*

clear·ance (klîr'əns) *n.* **1.** The act of clearing. **2.** The amount by which a moving object clears something. **3.** Permission to proceed.

clear-cut (klîr'kŭt') *adj.* **1.** Distinctly defined. **2.** Plain; evident.

clear·ing (klîr'ĭng) *n.* An area of land from which trees have been removed.

clear·ing·house (klîr'ĭng-hous') *n.* An office where banks exchange checks, drafts, and other notes and settle accounts.

cleat (klēt) *n.* A wooden or metallic projection used to grip, provide support, or prevent slipping. [ME *clete.*]

cleav·age (klē'vĭj) *n.* **1.** The act, process, or result of splitting. **2.** A fissure or division.

cleave¹ (klēv) *v.* **cleft** (klĕft) or **cleaved** or **clove** (klōv), **cleft** or **cleaved** or **clo·ven** (klō'vən), **cleav·ing. 1.** To split or separate. **2.** To pierce or penetrate. [< OE *clēofan.*]

cleave² (klēv) *v.* **cleaved, cleav·ing.** To adhere; cling. [< OE *clifian.*]

cleav·er (klē'vər) *n.* A heavy knife or hatchet used by butchers.

clef (klĕf) *n.* A symbol on a musical staff that indicates which pitch each of the various lines and spaces represents. [Fr. < Lat. *clavis*, key.]

cleft (klĕft) *v. p.t.* & *p.p.* of **cleave¹.** —*adj.* Divided; split. —*n.* A crack; crevice.

clem·a·tis (klĕm'ə-tĭs) *n.* Any of various vines with white or variously colored flowers and plumelike seeds. [< Gk. *klēma*, twig.]

clem·en·cy (klĕm'ən-sē) *n., pl.* **-cies. 1.** Leniency; mercy. **2.** Mildness, esp. of weather.

clem·ent (klĕm'ənt) *adj.* **1.** Lenient; merciful. **2.** Pleasant; mild. [< Lat. *clemens.*] —**clem'ent·ly** *adv.*

clench (klĕnch) *v.* **1.** To bring together (a hand or the teeth) tightly. **2.** To grasp or grip tightly. **3.** To clinch. —*n.* **1.** A tight grip or grasp. 2. Something that clenches, as a mechanical device. [< OE *beclencan*.]

clere·sto·ry (klîr'stôr'ē, -stōr'ē) n. A windowed wall that rises above the roofed section of a building. [ME *clerestorie*.]

cler·gy (klûr'jē) n., pl. **-gies.** The body of people ordained for religious service. [< OFr. *clergie*, learning.]

cler·gy·man (klûr'jē-mən) n. A member of the clergy.

cler·ic (klĕr'ĭk) n. A clergyman. [< LLat. *clericus* < Gk. *klērikos*, of inheritance.]

cler·i·cal (klĕr'ĭ-kəl) adj. 1. Of or relating to clerks or office workers. 2. Of, relating to, or characteristic of the clergy or a clergyman.

cler·i·cal·ism (klĕr'ĭ-kə-lĭz'əm) n. A policy of supporting the influence of the clergy in political or secular matters.

clerk (klûrk; Brit. klärk) n. 1. One who performs such business tasks as keeping records and filing. 2. A salesperson in a store. —v. To work as a clerk. [< LLat. *clericus*, clergyman.] —**clerk'ship'** n.

clev·er (klĕv'ər) adj. **-er, -est.** 1. Mentally quick and resourceful. 2. Quick-witted. 3. Dexterous. [Poss. < ME *cliver*, expert in seizing.] —**clev'er·ly** adv. —**clev'er·ness** n.

Syns: clever, alert, bright, intelligent, sharp, smart adj.

clev·is (klĕv'ĭs) n. A U-shaped metal piece used for attaching parts. [Prob. of Scand. orig.]

clew (klōō) n. 1. A ball of yarn or thread. 2. Naut. A metal loop in the corner of a sail. [< OE *clewe*.]

cli·ché (klē-shā', klĭ-) n. A trite expression or idea. [Fr.]

click (klĭk) n. A brief, sharp sound. —v. 1. To make or cause to make a click or a series of clicks. 2. Informal. **a.** To be completely successful. **b.** To function well together. [Imit.]

cli·ent (klī'ənt) n. 1. One for whom professional services are rendered. 2. A customer or patron. [< Lat. *cliens*, a dependent.]

cli·en·tele (klī'ən-tĕl', klē'ən-) n. Clients or customers in general. [Fr. *clientèle*.]

cliff (klĭf) n. A high, steep, or overhanging face of rock. [< OE *clif*.]

cliff·hang·er (klĭf'hăng'ər) n. 1. A melodrama serial in which each episode ends in suspense. 2. A contest whose outcome is uncertain until the end.

cli·mac·ter·ic (klī-măk'tər-ĭk, klī'măk-tĕr'ĭk) n. 1. A period of life when physiological changes, esp. menopause, take place. 2. A critical period. [< Gk. *klimaktēr*, rung of a ladder, crisis.]

cli·mac·tic (klī-măk'tĭk) adj. Pertaining to or forming a climax. —**cli·mac'ti·cal·ly** adv.

cli·mate (klī'mĭt) n. 1. The prevailing weather conditions of a particular region. 2. A region having certain weather conditions: *a polar climate.* 3. A general atmosphere or attitude: *a climate of fear.* [< Gk. *klima*, region of the earth.] —**cli·mat'ic** (klī-măt'ĭk) or **cli·mat'i·cal** adj. —**cli·mat'i·cal·ly** adv.

cli·ma·tol·o·gy (klī'mə-tŏl'ə-jē) n. The scientific study of climate. —**cli'ma·to·log'ic** (-tə-lŏj'ĭk) or **cli'ma·to·log'i·cal** adj. —**cli'ma·tol'o·gist** n.

cli·max (klī'măks') n. 1. The point in a series of events or statements marked by greatest intensity or effect. 2. The stage at which a

community of plants and animals reaches its fullest development. —v. To reach or bring to a climax. [< Gk. *klimax*, ladder.]

climb (klīm) v. 1. To move up or ascend, esp. by using the hands and feet. 2. To rise in rank or fortune. 3. To slope upward. 4. To grow upward. —n. 1. The act of climbing. 2. A place to be climbed. [< OE *climban*.] —**climb'a·ble** (klī'mə-bəl) adj. —**climb'er** n.

clime (klīm) n. Poetic. Climate.

clinch (klĭnch) v. 1. To fasten securely, as with a nail or bolt. 2. To settle decisively. 3. To embrace so as to immobilize an opponent's arms. —n. 1. The act, process, or result of clinching. 2. Slang. An amorous embrace. [< CLENCH.]

clinch·er (klĭn'chər) n. One that clinches, esp. a decisive point, fact, or remark.

cling (klĭng) v. clung (klŭng), cling·ing. 1. To hold tight or adhere to something. 2. To remain emotionally attached. [< OE *clingan*.] —**cling'er** n.

cling·stone (klĭng'stōn') n. A fruit, esp. a peach, with pulp that does not separate easily from the stone.

clin·ic (klĭn'ĭk) n. 1. A training session in which medical students observe while patients are examined and treated. 2. An institution associated with a hospital that deals mainly with outpatients. 3. A medical institution run by several specialists working in cooperation. 4. A center that provides special counseling or training. [< Gk. *klinikos*, physician.]

clin·i·cal (klĭn'ĭ-kəl) adj. 1. Of or connected with a clinic. 2. Of or related to direct examination and treatment of patients. 3. Objective; analytical. —**clin'i·cal·ly** adv.

clinical pathology n. The scientific study of the diagnosis and treatment of disease through laboratory analysis of clinical specimens, as tissue.

cli·ni·cian (klĭ-nĭsh'ən) n. A physician, psychologist, or psychiatrist specializing in clinical studies or practice.

clink¹ (klĭngk) v. To make or cause to make a light, sharp, ringing sound. [< MDu. *clinken*.] —**clink** n.

clink² (klĭngk) n. Slang. A prison. [< *Clink*, a London prison.]

clink·er (klĭng'kər) n. 1. A lump of incombustible matter that remains after coal has burned. 2. Slang. A mistake or error. [Obs. Du. *klinckœrd*.]

cli·o·met·rics (klī'ə-mĕt'rĭks) n. (used with a sing. verb). The study of history using advanced mathematical methods of data processing and analysis. [*Clio*, the Muse of history + -METRICS.] —**cli'o·met'ric** adj.

clip¹ (klĭp) v. clipped, clip·ping. 1. To cut off or out with shears. 2. To make shorter by cutting. 3. Informal. To strike with a sharp blow. 4. Slang. To cheat or overcharge. —n. 1. Something clipped off, as a sequence clipped from a movie film. 2. Informal. A sharp blow. 3. Informal. A brisk pace. [< ON *klippa*.]

clip² (klĭp) n. 1. A device for gripping or clasping; fastener. 2. A container for holding cartridges. —v. clipped, clip·ping. 1. To grip securely; fasten. 2. Football. To block (an opponent) illegally. [< OE *clyppan*.]

clip·board (klĭp'bôrd', -bōrd') n. A portable writing board with a spring clip at the top for holding papers.

clip·per (klĭp′ər) *n.* **1. clippers.** An instrument for cutting, clipping, or shearing. **2.** A sailing vessel built for great speed.

clipper

clip·ping (klĭp′ĭng) *n.* Something cut off or out, esp. an item from a newspaper.

clip-sheet (klĭp′shĕt′) *n.* A sheet containing news items, usu. printed on only one side for convenience in clipping and reprinting.

clique (klĕk, klĭk) *n.* An exclusive group of people. [Fr.] **—cliqu′ey** or **cliqu′y** *adj.*

cli·to·ris (klĭt′ər-ĭs, klī′tər-) *n.* A small erectile organ at the upper end of the vulva, homologous with the penis. [Gk. *kleitoris.*] **—clit′o·ral** (-əl) *adj.*

cloak (klōk) *n.* **1.** A loose outer garment. **2.** Something that covers or conceals. **—***v.* **1.** To cover with a cloak. **2.** To conceal. [< Med. Lat. *clocca,* bell.]

cloak-and-dag·ger (klōk′ən-dăg′ər) *adj.* Marked by melodramatic intrigue and spying.

clob·ber (klŏb′ər) *v. Slang.* **1.** To hit or pound with great force. **2.** To defeat completely. [Orig. unknown.]

cloche (klōsh) *n.* A close-fitting woman's hat. [< OFr., bell.]

clock¹ (klŏk) *n.* An instrument for measuring or indicating time. **—***v.* To record the time or speed of. [< Med. Lat. *clocca,* bell.] **—clock′er** *n.*

clock² (klŏk) *n.* An embroidered or woven design on a stocking or sock. [Poss. < CLOCK¹, bell (obs.).]

clock·wise (klŏk′wīz′) *adv.* In the same direction as the rotating hands of a clock. **—clock′wise** *adj.*

clock·work (klŏk′wûrk′) *n.* The mechanism of a clock or a similar mechanism or process.

clod (klŏd) *n.* **1.** A lump of earth or clay. **2.** A dull, ignorant, or stupid person. [< OE.] **—clod′dish** *adj.* **—clod′dish·ly** *adv.* **—clod′dish·ness** *n.*

clod·hop·per (klŏd′hŏp′ər) *n.* **1.** A clumsy, coarse person. **2. clodhoppers.** Big, heavy shoes.

clog (klŏg) *n.* **1.** A heavy thick-soled shoe. **2.** An obstacle. **3.** A weight attached to the leg of an animal to hinder movement. **—***v.* **clogged, clog·ging.** To impede or encumber. **2.** To make or become obstructed. [ME *clogge,* block attached to an animal's leg.]

cloi·son·né (kloi′zə-nā′, klə-wä′-) *n.* Enamelware in which the surface decoration is formed by different colors of enamel separated by thin strips of metal. [< Fr. *cloisonner,* to partition.]

clois·ter (kloi′stər) *n.* **1.** A covered walk with an open colonnade on one side, running along the inside wall of a building. **2.** A monastery or convent. **—***v.* To confine in or as if in a cloister; seclude. [< Lat. *claustrum,* enclosed place.] **—clois′tral** (-strəl) *adj.*

clone (klōn) *n.* One or more identical organisms descended asexually from a single ancestor. **—***v.* **cloned, clon·ing.** To create a genetic duplicate of (an individual organism) asexually. [< Gk. *klōn,* twig.] **—clon′al** (klō′nəl) *adj.* **—clon′al·ly** *adv.* **—clon′er** *n.*

clop (klŏp) *n.* The drumming sound of a horse's hoofs as they strike the pavement. **—***v.* **clopped, clop·ping.** To make or move with a clop. [Imit.]

close (klōs) *adj.* **clos·er, clos·est.** **1.** Proximate in time, space, or relation; near. **2.** Compact: *a close weave.* **3.** Near a surface, as of the skin: *a close haircut.* **4.** Nearly equivalent or even, as a contest. **5.** Fitting tightly. **6.** Not deviating from an original: *a close copy.* **7.** Precise. **8.** Complete; thorough: *close attention.* **9.** Bound by mutual interests or affections; intimate. **10.** Shut or shut in. **11.** Confined in space. **12.** Confined to specific persons; restricted. **13.** Hidden; secluded. **14.** Taciturn in manner; reticent. **15.** Miserly. **16.** Lacking fresh or circulating air. **—***v.* (klōz) **closed, clos·ing.** **1.** To shut or become shut. **2.** To fill up. **3.** To end; finish. **4.** To join or unite; bring into contact. **5.** To enclose; shut in. **6.** To reach an agreement. **—***phrasal verbs.* **close down.** To stop operating. **close out.** To sell at a reduced price in order to dispose of quickly. **—***n.* (klōz). A conclusion; finish. **—***adv.* (klōs). In a close manner. [< Lat. *claudere,* to close.] **—close′ly** (klōs′lē) *adv.* **—close′ness** (klōs′nĭs) *n.* **—clos′er** (klō′zər) *n.*

closed-cap·tioned (klōzd-kăp′shənd) *adj.* Designating a telecast with captions that can be seen only on a specially equipped receiver.

closed circuit *n.* Television that is transmitted to a limited number of receivers.

closed shop *n.* A company in which only union members may be hired.

close-fist·ed (klōs′fĭs′tĭd) *adj.* Stingy; miserly.

close-mouthed (klōs′mouthd′, -moutht′) *adj.* Giving away very little information.

close-out (klōz′out′) *n.* A sale in which all goods are disposed of, usu. at greatly reduced prices.

clos·et (klŏz′ĭt) *n.* **1.** A small room for storing supplies or clothing. **2.** A small private room. **—***v.* To enclose in a private room, as for discussion. [< OFr., dim. of *clos,* enclosure.]

close-up (klōs′ŭp′) *n.* **1.** A picture taken at close range. **2.** A close or intimate look or view.

clo·sure (klō′zhər) *n.* **1.** The act of closing or the condition of being closed. **2.** Something that closes. **3.** Cloture.

clot (klŏt) *n.* A thick or solid mass or lump formed from liquid. [< OE.] **—clot** *v.*

cloth (klôth, klŏth) *n., pl.* **cloths** (klôths, klôthz, klŏths, klŏthz). **1.** Fabric produced by weaving, knitting, or matting natural or manmade fibers. **2.** A piece of cloth used for a special purpose, as a washcloth. **3.** Professional mode of dress. **4. the cloth.** The clergy. [< OE *clāth.*]

clothe (klōth) *v.* **clothed** or **clad** (klăd), **cloth·ing.** **1.** To put clothes on; dress. **2.** To cover as if with clothes; invest. [< OE *clathian.*]

clothes (klōz, klōthz) *pl.n.* Articles of dress; garments.

clothes·horse (klōz′hôrs′, klōthz′-) *n.* **1.** A frame on which clothes are hung. **2.** One considered excessively concerned with dress.

clothes·pin (klōz′pĭn, klōthz′-) *n.* A clip for fastening clothes to a line.

cloth·ier (klōth′yər, klō′thē-ər) *n.* One who makes or sells clothing or cloth.

cloth·ing (klō′thĭng) *n.* Clothes collectively.

clo·ture (klō′chər) *n.* A procedure in a legislative body by which debate is ended and an immediate vote is taken. [< OFr. *closure,* closure.] —**clo′ture** *v.*

cloud (kloud) *n.* **1. a.** A visible body of fine water droplets or ice particles in the earth's atmosphere. **b.** A similar mass in the air, as of dust. **2.** A swarm. **3.** Something that darkens or fills with gloom. —*v.* **1.** To cover with or as if with clouds. **2.** To become overcast. **3.** To make or become gloomy or troubled. **4.** To cast aspersions on. [< OE *clūd,* hill.] —**cloud′less** *adj.*

cloud·burst (kloud′bûrst′) *n.* A sudden rainstorm.

cloud chamber *n.* A device in which the paths of charged subatomic particles are made visible as trails of droplets in a supersaturated vapor.

cloud·y (klou′dē) *adj.* **-i·er, -i·est.** **1.** Full of or covered with clouds. **2.** Of or like clouds. **3.** Not transparent. **4.** Obscure; vague. —**cloud′i·ly** *adv.* —**cloud′i·ness** *n.*

clout (klout) *n.* **1.** A blow, esp. with the fist. **2.** *Informal.* Influence; pull. —*v.* To hit, esp. with the fist. [ME.]

clove¹ (klōv) *n.* An evergreen tree whose aromatic unopened flower buds are used as a spice. [< OFr. *clou (de girofle),* nail (of the clove tree).]

clove² (klōv) *n.* A separable section of a bulb, as of garlic. [< OE *clufu.*]

clove³ (klōv) *v.* A *p.t.* of **cleave¹.**

clo·ven (klō′vən) *v.* A *p.p.* of **cleave¹.** —*adj.* Split; divided.

clo·ver (klō′vər) *n.* Any of various plants having compound leaves with three leaflets and tight heads of small flowers. [< OE *clæfre.*]

clo·ver·leaf (klō′vər-lēf′) *n.* A highway interchange at which two highways crossing each other on different levels are provided with curving access and exit ramps, enabling vehicles to go in any of four directions.

clown (kloun) *n.* **1.** A buffoon or jester who entertains in a circus or other presentation. **2.** A coarse, rude person. —*v.* To behave like a clown. [Perh. of LG orig.] —**clown′ish** *adj.* —**clown′ish·ly** *adv.* —**clown′ish·ness** *n.*

cloy (kloi) *v.* To surfeit, esp. with something too rich or sweet. [< ME *acloien.*]

cloy·ing (kloi′ĭng) *adj.* Excessive to the point of being distasteful: *cloying praise.* —**cloy′ing·ly** *adv.* —**cloy′ing·ness** *n.*

club (klŭb) *n.* **1.** A heavy stick suitable for use as a weapon. **2.** A stick used to drive a ball in certain games. **3.** Any of a suit of playing cards marked with a black figure shaped like a cloverleaf. **4.** A group of people organized for a common purpose. **5.** The facilities used for the meetings of a club. —*v.*

clubbed, club·bing. 1. To strike or beat with or as if with a club. **2.** To contribute or combine for a common purpose. [< ON *klubba.*]

club car *n.* A railroad passenger car equipped with a buffet or bar and other extra comforts.

club·foot (klŭb′fŏŏt′) *n.* **1.** A congenital deformity of the foot, marked by a misshapen appearance often resembling a club. **2.** A foot so deformed. —**club′foot′ed** *adj.*

club·house (klŭb′hous′) *n.* **1.** A building occupied by a club. **2.** The locker room for a sports team.

club sandwich *n.* A sandwich, usu. of three slices of bread, with a filling of various meats, tomato, lettuce, and dressing.

club soda *n.* A carbonated unflavored water used in various alcoholic and nonalcoholic drinks.

club steak *n.* A small beefsteak.

cluck (klŭk) *n.* The low, short, throaty sound made by a brooding hen. [Imit.] —**cluck** *v.*

clue (klōō) *n.* Something that guides or directs in the solution of a problem or mystery. —*v.* **clued, clue·ing** or **clu·ing.** To give (someone) guiding information. [< CLEW.]

clump (klŭmp) *n.* **1.** A clustered mass or thick grouping; lump. **2.** A heavy dull sound. —*v.* **1.** To walk with a heavy dull sound. **2.** To form clumps (of). [Prob. < MLG *klumpe.*]

clum·sy (klŭm′zē) *adj.* **-si·er, -si·est.** **1.** Lacking physical coordination, skill, or grace; awkward. **2.** Gauche; inept: *a clumsy excuse.* [< ME *clumsen,* to be numb with cold.] —**clum′si·ly** *adv.* —**clum′si·ness** *n.*

clung (klŭng) *v. p.t. & p.p.* of **cling.**

clus·ter (klŭs′tər) *n.* A group of things growing or gathered closely together; bunch. —*v.* To gather, grow, or form into clusters. [< OE *clyster.*]

clutch (klŭch) *v.* To grasp or attempt to grasp and hold tightly. —*n.* **1.** The hand, claw, talon, paw, etc., in the act of grasping. **2.** A tight grasp. **3.** Often **clutches.** Control or power. **4.** A device for engaging and disengaging two working parts of a shaft or of a shaft and a driving mechanism. **5.** A tense or critical situation. [< OE *clyccan.*]

clut·ter (klŭt′ər) *n.* A confused or disordered state or collection; jumble. —*v.* To litter or pile in a disordered state. [< ME *cloteren,* to clot.]

Cm The symbol for the element curium.

Co The symbol for the element cobalt.

co- *pref.* **1.** With; together; joint; jointly: *co-education.* **2. a.** Partner or associate in an activity: *co-author.* **b.** Subordinate or assistant: *copilot.* **3.** To the same extent or degree: *coextensive.* **4.** Complement of an angle: *cotangent.* [< Lat.]

coach (kōch) *n.* **1.** A large closed carriage with four wheels. **2.** A motorbus. **3.** A railroad passenger car. **4.** One who trains athletes or athletic teams. **5.** One who gives private instruction. —*v.* To teach or train; tutor. [< Hung. *kocsi.*]

coach·man (kōch′mən) *n.* One who drives a coach.

co·ad·ju·tor (kō′ə-jōō′tər, kō-ăj′ə-tər) *n.* A coworker; assistant, esp. to a bishop. [< Lat.]

co·ag·u·lant (kō-ăg′yə-lənt) *n.* An agent that causes coagulation.

co·ag·u·late (kō-ăg′yə-lāt′) *v.* **-lat·ed, -lat·ing.** To form a soft, semisolid, or solid mass. [< Lat. *coagulare.*] —**co·ag′u·la′tion** *n.*

coal (kōl) *n.* **1.** A natural dark-brown to

black, carbon-containing solid used as a fuel.
2. An ember. —*v.* To provide with or take
on coal. [< OE *col.*]

co·a·lesce (kō′ə-lĕs′) *v.* **-lesced, -lesc·ing.** To
grow or come together so as to form one
whole; fuse; unite. [< Lat. *coalescere.*] —**co′-
a·les′cence** *n.*

coal gas *n.* A gaseous mixture distilled from
bituminous coal and used as a fuel.

co·a·li·tion (kō′ə-lĭsh′ən) *n.* An alliance or
union, esp. a temporary one. [< Lat. *coalescere*, to coalesce.]

coal tar *n.* A thick, viscous black liquid distilled from bituminous coal and used in dyes,
drugs, organic chemicals, paints, and industrial materials.

coarse (kôrs, kōrs) *adj.* **coars·er, coars·est.**
1. Of common or inferior quality. 2. Lacking
in delicacy or refinement. 3. Consisting of
large particles: *coarse sand.* 4. Rough; harsh:
coarse cloth. [ME *cors.*]
   Syns: *coarse, boorish, churlish, crass, crude,
earthy, gross, rough, rude, uncouth, vulgar adj.*

coars·en (kôr′sən, kōr′-) *v.* To make or become coarse.

coast (kōst) *n.* 1. The seashore. 2. A slope
down which one may coast, as on a sled.
3. The act of sliding or coasting. —*v.* 1. To
slide down an inclined slope, as on a sled.
2. To move without further acceleration.
3. To move aimlessly. [< Lat. *costa*, side.]
—**coast′al** (-əl) *adj.*

coast·er (kō′stər) *n.* 1. One that coasts. 2. A
small tray or disk used to protect a table top
or other surface.

coast guard *n.* Also **Coast Guard.** The military or naval coastal patrol of a nation.

coast·line (kōst′līn′) *n.* The shape or outline
of a coast.

coat (kōt) *n.* 1. An outer garment covering
the body from the shoulders to the waist or
below. 2. A natural or outer covering, as the
fur of an animal. 3. A layer of some material
covering something else. —*v.* To provide or
cover with a coat or layer. [< OFr. *cote.*]

coat·ing (kō′tĭng) *n.* A coat (sense 3).

coat of arms *n.* 1. A shield blazoned with
heraldic bearings. 2. A representation of a
coat of arms.

coat of mail *n., pl.* **coats of mail.** An armored
coat made of chain mail.

co·au·thor (kō-ô′thər, kō′ô′-) *n.* A collaborat-
ing or joint author. —**co·au′thor** *v.*

coax (kōks) *v.* 1. To persuade or try to persuade by pleading or flattery. 2. To obtain by
persistent persuasion. [Obs. *cokes*, to fool.]

co·ax·i·al (kō-ăk′sē-əl) *adj.* Having a common
axis.

coaxial cable *n.* A transmission cable consisting of a conducting outer metal tube enclosing and insulated from a central
conducting core.

cob (kŏb) *n.* 1. The central core of an ear of
corn. 2. A male swan. 3. A thick-set, short-
legged horse. [Prob. < obs. *cob*, round object.]

co·balt (kō′bôlt′) *n.* Symbol **Co** A hard, brittle metallic element, used chiefly for magnetic
alloys, high-temperature alloys, and for blue
glass and ceramic pigments. Atomic number

27; atomic weight 58.9332. [< MHG *kobolt*,
goblin.]

cob·ble (kŏb′əl) *v.* **-bled, -bling.** 1. To mend
(boots or shoes). 2. To put together clumsily.
[Prob. < COBBLER[1].]

cob·bler[1] (kŏb′lər) *n.* One who mends boots
and shoes. [ME *cobelere.*]

cob·bler[2] (kŏb′lər) *n.* A deep-dish fruit pie
with a thick top crust. [Orig. unknown.]

cob·ble·stone (kŏb′əl-stōn′) *n.* A naturally
rounded stone, formerly used for paving
streets. [ME *cobelston.*]

CO·BOL or **Co·bol** (kō′bôl′) *n.* A language
based on English words and phrases, used in
programming digital computers. [CO(MMON)
B(USINESS) O(RIENTED) L(ANGUAGE).]

co·bra (kō′brə) *n.* A venomous snake of Asia
and Africa capable of expanding the skin of
the neck to form a flattened hood. [< Port.
cobra (de capello), snake (with a hood).]

cob·web (kŏb′wĕb′) *n.* **1. a.** The web spun by
a spider. **b.** A single thread of such a web.
2. Something resembling a cobweb in gauzi-
ness or flimsiness. 3. A plot; snare. [ME
coppeweb.] —**cob′web′** *v.*

co·caine (kō-kān′, kō′kān′) *n.* A narcotic alkaloid, $C_{17}H_{21}NO_4$, extracted from a South
American tree and used as a surface anesthetic. [Sp. *coca*, the tree whose leaves contain cocaine + -INE[2].]

coc·cus (kŏk′əs) *n., pl.* **coc·ci** (kŏk′sī′, kŏk′ī′).
A bacterium with a spherical shape. [< Gk.
kokkos, grain.]

-coccus *suff.* A microorganism that is
spherical in shape: *streptococcus.* [< COCCUS.]

coc·cyx (kŏk′sĭks) *n., pl.* **coc·cy·ges** (kŏk-sī′-
jēz, kŏk′sĭ-jēz′). A small bone at the base of
the spinal column. [< Gk. *kokkux.*]

coch·i·neal (kŏch′ə-nēl′, kŏch′ə-nēl′) *n.* A
brilliant-red dye made from the dried bodies
of a tropical American insect. [< Lat. *cocci-
nus*, scarlet < Gk. *kokkos*, a kind of berry.]

coch·le·a (kŏk′lē-ə) *n., pl.* **-le·ae** (-lē-ē′) or **-le·as.** A
spiral tube of the inner ear containing nerve
endings essential for hearing. [< Gk. *ko-
khlias*, snail.] —**coch′le·ar** (-lē-ər) *adj.*

cock[1] (kŏk) *n.* 1. A male bird, esp. the adult
male of the domestic fowl. 2. A faucet or
valve. 3. **a.** The hammer in a firearm. **b.** Its
position when ready for firing. —*v.* 1. To set
the hammer of (a firearm) in position for
firing. 2. To tilt or turn up or to one side.
3. To raise or draw back in preparation to
throw or hit. [< OE *coc.*]

cock[2] (kŏk) *n.* A cone-shaped pile of straw or
hay. [ME *cok.*]

cock·ade (kō-kād′) *n.* A rosette or knot of
ribbon usu. worn on the hat as a badge. [<
OFr. *coquarde*, vain.]

cock·a·too (kŏk′ə-tōō′) *n.* A crested Australian parrot. [< Malay *kakatua.*]

cock·a·trice (kŏk′ə-trĭs, -trīs′) *n.* A mythical
serpent having the power to kill with its
glance. [< Lat. *calcare*, to track.]

cocked hat *n.* A three-cornered hat.

cock·er·el (kŏk′ər-əl) *n.* A young rooster.
[ME *cokerel*, dim. of *cok*, male bird.]

cock·er spaniel (kŏk′ər) *n.* A dog with long,
drooping ears and a silky coat. [< its use in
hunting woodcocks.]

cocker spaniel

cock·eyed (kŏk′īd′) *adj.* **1.** Cross-eyed. **2.** *Slang.* **a.** Crooked; askew. **b.** Foolish; ridiculous: *a cockeyed idea.*

cock·fight (kŏk′fīt′) *n.* A fight between gamecocks that are usu. fitted with metal spurs. —**cock′fight′ing** *n.*

cock·le (kŏk′əl) *n.* Any of various bivalve mollusks with ribbed, heart-shaped shells. [< Gk. *konkhulion.*]

cock·le·shell (kŏk′əl-shĕl′) *n.* **1.** The shell of a cockle. **2.** A small, light boat.

cock·ney (kŏk′nē) *n., pl.* -**neys**. **1.** Often **Cockney**. A native of the East End of London. **2.** The dialect or accent of cockneys. [ME *cokenei*, pampered child.]

cock·pit (kŏk′pĭt′) *n.* **1.** A pit or enclosed space for cockfights. **2.** The space in an airplane for the pilot and crew.

cock·roach (kŏk′rōch′) *n.* An oval, flat-bodied insect common as a household pest. [< Sp. *cucaracha.*]

cocks·comb (kŏks′kōm′) *n.* **1.** The fleshy comb on the head of a rooster. **2.** The cap of a jester, decorated to resemble the comb of a rooster. **3.** Also **cox·comb**. A pretentious fop.

cock·sure (kŏk′shŏŏr′) *adj.* **1.** Completely sure. **2.** Overconfident.

cock·tail (kŏk′tāl′) *n.* **1.** A mixed alcoholic drink. **2.** An appetizer, such as seafood.

cock·y (kŏk′ē) *adj.* -**i·er,** -**i·est**. Cheerfully self-confident or conceited. —**cock′i·ly** *adv.* —**cock′i·ness** *n.*

co·co (kō′kō) *n., pl.* -**cos**. The coconut or the coconut palm. [< Port.]

co·coa (kō′kō) *n.* **1.** A powder made from cacao seeds. **2.** A beverage made by combining cocoa powder with water or milk and sugar. [< CACAO.]

co·co·nut (kō′kə-nŭt′, -nət) *n.* Also **co·coa·nut**. The large, hard-shelled, edible nut of a tropical palm tree, the coconut palm, having a hollow center filled with milky fluid.

co·coon (kə-kōōn′) *n.* The silky or fibrous pupal case spun by the larvae of moths and other insects. [< Prov. *coco,* shell.]

cod (kŏd) *n., pl.* **cod** or **cods**. A commercially important food fish of Northern Atlantic waters. [ME.]

co·da (kō′də) *n. Mus.* The final passage of a movement or composition. [Ital.]

cod·dle (kŏd′l) *v.* -**dled,** -**dling.** **1.** To cook in water just below the boiling point. **2.** To treat indulgently; baby. [< *caudle,* a kind of beverage.] —**cod′dler** *n.*

code (kōd) *n.* **1.** A systematically arranged and comprehensive collection of laws or rules and regulations. **2.** A system of signals used in transmitting messages. **3.** An arbitrary system of symbols, letters, or words used for transmitting brief or secret messages. —*v.* **cod·ed, cod·ing.** To systematize, arrange, or convert into a code. [< Lat. *codex.*]

co·deine (kō′dēn′, -dē-ĭn) *n.* An alkaloid narcotic derived from opium or morphine, used esp. for relieving pain. [< Gk. *kōdeia,* poppy head.]

co·dex (kō′dĕks′) *n., pl.* **co·di·ces** (kō′dĭ-sēz′, kŏd′ĭ-). A manuscript volume, esp. of a classic work or of the Scriptures. [Lat.]

cod·fish (kŏd′fĭsh′) *n.* The cod.

codg·er (kŏj′ər) *n. Informal.* An odd or eccentric man. [Poss. < obs. *cadger,* peddler.]

cod·i·cil (kŏd′ĭ-səl) *n.* A supplement or appendix to a will. [< Lat. *codex.*]

cod·i·fy (kŏd′ə-fī′, kō′də-) *v.* -**fied,** -**fy·ing.** To arrange or systematize. —**cod′i·fi·ca′tion** *n.*

co·ed (kō′ĕd′) *Informal.* —*n.* A woman student attending a coeducational college or university. —*adj.* Coeducational. [< *coeducational student.*]

co·ed·u·ca·tion (kō′ĕj-ōō-kā′shən) *n.* The education of both men and women at the same institution. —**co′ed·u·ca′tion·al** *adj.*

co·ef·fi·cient (kō′ə-fĭsh′ənt) *n.* **1. a.** A numerical factor of an elementary algebraic term, as 4 in the term $4x$. **b.** The product of all but one of the factors of a mathematical expression. **2.** A numerical measure of a physical or chemical property that is constant for a specified system.

—**coel** or —**coele** *suff.* Vars. of -**cele**.

co·e·qual (kō-ē′kwəl) *adj.* Equal with one another. —*n.* An equal. —**co′e·qual′i·ty** *n.* —**co·e′qual·ly** *adv.*

co·erce (kō-ûrs′) *v.* -**erced,** -**erc·ing.** **1.** To force to act or think in a given manner. **2.** To dominate, restrain, or control by force. **3.** To bring about by force. [< Lat. *coercēre,* to confine.] —**co·erc′er** *n.* —**co·erc′i·ble** *adj.* —**co·er′cion** *n.* —**co·er′cive** *adj.* —**co·er′cive·ly** *adv.*

co·e·val (kō-ē′vəl) *adj.* Of the same period or time. [< Lat. *coaevus.*] —**co·e′val** *n.* —**co·e′val·ly** *adv.*

co·ex·ist (kō′ĭg-zĭst′) *v.* **1.** To exist together, at the same time, or in the same place. **2.** To live in peace with another or others despite differences. —**co′ex·is′tence** *n.*

co·ex·ten·sive (kō′ĭk-stĕn′sĭv) *adj.* Having the same limits, boundaries, or scope. —**co′ex·ten′sive·ly** *adv.*

cof·fee (kô′fē, kŏf′ē) *n.* **1. a.** An aromatic, mildly stimulating beverage prepared from the beanlike seeds of a tropical tree. **b.** The seeds themselves. **2.** A dark yellowish brown. —*adj.* Dark yellowish brown. [< Ar. *qahwah.*]

coffee cake *n.* A cake made of sweetened yeast dough, often containing nuts or raisins.

cof·fee·house (kô′fē-hous′, kŏf′ē-) *n.* A restaurant where coffee and other refreshments are served.

coffee klatch (klăch, kläch) *n.* A casual gathering for coffee and conversation. [< G. *Kaffeeklatsch.*]

cof·fee·pot (kô′fē-pŏt′, kŏf′ē-) *n.* A pot for brewing or serving coffee.

coffee shop *n.* A small restaurant in which light meals are served.

coffee table *n.* A long, low table, often placed before a sofa.

cof·fer (kô′fər, kŏf′ər) *n.* **1.** A strongbox. **2. coffers.** Financial resources; funds. [< Gk. *kophinos,* basket.]

cof·fer·dam (kŏ′fər-dăm′, kŏf′ər-) n. A temporary watertight enclosure built in the water and pumped dry to expose the bottom so that construction, as of piers, may be undertaken.

cof·fin (kŏ′fĭn, kŏf′ĭn) n. A box in which a corpse is buried. [< Gk. *kophinos*, basket.]

cog (kŏg) n. 1. A tooth or notch on the rim of a wheel or gear. 2. *Informal.* A subordinate member of an organization. [ME *cogge*.]

co·gen·er·a·tion (kō-jĕn′ə-rā′shən) n. A process in which an industrial facility utilizes its waste energy to produce electricity.

co·gent (kō′jənt) adj. Forcefully convincing. [< Lat. *cogere*, to force.] —**co′gen·cy** (-jən-sē) n. —**co′gent·ly** adv.

cog·i·tate (kŏj′ĭ-tāt′) v. -tat·ed, -tat·ing. 1. To meditate; ponder. 2. To think carefully about. [< Lat. *cogitare*.] —**cog′i·ta′tion** n. —**cog′i·ta′tor** n.

co·gnac (kōn′yăk, kŏn′-) n. A fine French brandy. [< *Cognac*, France.]

cog·nate (kŏg′nāt′) adj. 1. Having a common ancestor or origin, esp. culturally or linguistically akin. 2. Analogous in nature. [< Lat. *cognatus*.] —**cog′nate′** n. —**cog·na′tion** n.

cog·ni·tion (kŏg-nĭsh′ən) n. 1. The mental process or faculty by which knowledge is acquired. 2. Knowledge. [< Lat. *cognoscere*, to learn.] —**cog′ni·tive** (kŏg′nĭ-tĭv) adj.

cog·ni·zance (kŏg′nĭ-zəns) n. 1. Conscious knowledge or recognition; awareness. 2. Observance; notice. [< Lat. *cognoscere*, to know.] —**cog′ni·zant** adj.

cog·no·men (kŏg-nō′mən) n., pl. -mens or -nom·i·na (-nŏm′ə-nə). 1. A surname. 2. A nickname. [Lat.]

co·gno·scen·te (kŏn′yə-shĕn′tē) n., pl. -ti (-tē). A connoisseur. [Obs. Ital. < Lat. *cognoscere*, to learn.]

cog·wheel (kŏg′hwēl′, -wēl′) n. A cogged wheel within a given mechanism.

co·hab·it (kō-hăb′ĭt) v. To live together as lovers when not legally married. [LLat. *cohabitare*.] —**co·hab′i·ta′tion** n.

co·here (kō-hîr′) v. -hered, -her·ing. 1. To stick or hold together. 2. To be logically connected. [Lat. *cohaerēre*.]

co·her·ent (kō-hîr′ənt, -hĕr′-) adj. 1. Sticking together; cohering. 2. Logically connected. —**co·her′ence** or **co·her′en·cy** n. —**co·her′ent·ly** adv.

co·he·sion (kō-hē′zhən) n. 1. The process or condition of cohering. 2. *Physics.* The mutual attraction by which the elements of a body are held together. —**co·he′sive** (-sĭv) adj. —**co·he′sive·ly** adv. —**co·he′sive·ness** n.

co·hort (kō′hôrt′) n. 1. A group or band united in some struggle. 2. A companion or associate. [< Lat. *cohors*, an army division.]

coif (koif) n. 1. A tight-fitting cap. 2. A coiffure. [< Lat. *cofea*, helmet.]

coif·feur (kwä-fûr′) n. A hairdresser. [Fr.]

coif·fure (kwä-fyŏŏr′) n. A way of arranging the hair.

coil (koil) n. 1. A series of connected spirals or concentric rings formed by gathering or winding. 2. A spiral or ring. 3. *Elect.* A wound spiral of insulated wire. —v. To wind in coils. [< Lat. *colligere*, to gather.]

coin (koin) n. 1. A piece of metal issued by a government as money. 2. Metal money collectively. —v. 1. To make (coins) from metal. 2. To invent (a word or phrase). [< Lat. *cuneus*, wedge.] —**coin′er** n.

coin·age (koi′nĭj) n. 1. The process of making coins. 2. Metal currency. 3. A coined word or phrase.

co·in·cide (kō′ĭn-sīd′) v. -cid·ed, -cid·ing. 1. To occupy the same position simultaneously. 2. To happen at the same time. 3. To correspond exactly. [< Med. Lat. *coincidere*.]

co·in·ci·dence (kō-ĭn′sĭ-dəns, -dĕns′) n. 1. A combination of accidental circumstances that seems to have been planned or arranged. 2. The condition of coinciding. —**co·in′ci·den′tal** or **co·in′ci·dent** adj. —**co·in′ci·den′tal·ly** adv.

co·i·tus (kō′ĭ-təs) n. Also **co·i·tion** (kō-ĭsh′ən). Sexual intercourse. [Lat.] —**co′i·tal** adj.

coke (kōk) n. The solid residue of coal after all volatile material has been removed, used as fuel. [Poss. < ME *colk*, core.]

co·la¹ (kō′lə) n. A carbonated soft drink containing an extract prepared from kola nuts.

co·la² (kō′lə) n. A pl. of **colon²**.

col·an·der (kŭl′ən-dər, kŏl′-) n. A perforated, bowl-shaped kitchen utensil for draining food. [< Lat. *colare*, to strain.]

cold (kōld) adj. -er, -est. 1. Having a low temperature. 2. Having a subnormal body temperature. 3. Feeling no warmth; uncomfortably chilled. 4. Not affected by emotion; objective. 5. Not interested; indifferent. b. *Informal.* Unconscious; insensible: *knocked cold.* —adv. Completely; thoroughly. —n. 1. Relative lack of warmth. 2. The sensation resulting from lack of warmth. 3. A viral infection of the mucous membranes of the respiratory passages. —**idioms. in cold blood.** Without feeling or regret. **out in the cold.** Neglected; ignored. [OE *ceald*.] —**cold′ly** adv. —**cold′ness** n.

Syns: *cold, chill, chilly, cool, nippy* adj.

cold-blood·ed (kōld′blŭd′ĭd) adj. 1. Having a body temperature that changes according to the temperature of the surroundings, as fish and reptiles. 2. Ruthless; heartless. —**cold′-blood′ed·ly** adv. —**cold-blood′ed·ness** n.

cold cream n. An emulsion for cleansing and softening the skin.

cold cuts pl.n. Slices of assorted cold meats.

cold duck n. A beverage made of sparkling burgundy and champagne. [Transl. of G. *Kalte Ente*.]

cold feet n. *Slang.* Failure of nerve.

cold frame n. A structure consisting of a wooden frame and a glass top, used for protecting young plants.

cold front n. The forward edge of a cold air mass.

cold-heart·ed (kōld′här′tĭd) adj. Lacking sympathy or feeling; callous. —**cold′-heart′ed·ly** adv. —**cold′-heart′ed·ness** n.

cold shoulder n. Deliberate coldness or disregard. —**cold′shoul′der** v.

cold sore n. A small sore on the lips that often accompanies a fever or cold.

cold turkey n. *Informal.* Immediate, complete withdrawal from use of something, as an addictive drug.

cold war *n.* A state of political tension and military rivalry between nations, stopping short of actual full-scale war.

cole·slaw (kōl′slô′) *n.* Also **cole slaw.** A salad of shredded raw cabbage. [Du. *koolsla.*]

co·le·us (kō′lē-əs) *n.* A plant cultivated for its showy leaves. [< Gk. *koleos*, sheath.]

col·ic (kōl′ĭk) *n.* A sharp, acute pain in the abdomen. [< Gk. *kōlon*, colon.] —**col′ick·y** (kōl′ĭ-kē) *adj.*

col·i·se·um (kōl′ĭ-sē′əm) *n.* A large public amphitheater. [< the *Colosseum*, an amphitheater in Rome.]

co·li·tis (kō-lī′tĭs, kə-) *n.* An inflammation of the mucous membrane of the colon.

col·lab·o·rate (kə-lăb′ə-rāt′) *v.* **-rat·ed, -rat·ing.** 1. To work together, esp. in a joint intellectual effort. 2. To cooperate treasonably. [LLat. *collaborare*.] —**col·lab′o·ra′tion** *n.* —**col·lab′o·ra′tor** *n.*

col·lage (kō-läzh′, kə-) *n.* An artistic composition of materials and objects pasted over a surface. [Fr. < *coller*, to glue.]

col·la·gen (kōl′ə-jən) *n.* The fibrous albuminlike constituent of bone, cartilage, and connective tissue.

col·lap·sar (kə-lăp′sär′) *n.* A black hole. [COLLAPS(E) + (QUAS)AR.]

col·lapse (kə-lăps′) *v.* **-lapsed, -laps·ing.** 1. To fall down or inward suddenly; cave in. 2. To cease to function; break down suddenly. 3. To break down mentally or physically. 4. To fold compactly. [< Lat. *collabi*, to fall together.] —**col·lapse′** *n.* —**col·laps′i·ble** *adj.*

col·lar (kōl′ər) *n.* 1. The part of a garment that encircles the neck. 2. *Biol.* An encircling bandlike part or structure suggestive of a collar. 3. A ringlike device used to limit, guide, or secure a part. 4. An arrest. —*v.* To seize or detain. [< Lat. *collum*, neck.]

col·lar·bone (kōl′ər-bōn′) *n.* The clavicle.

col·lard (kōl′ərd) *n.* Often **collards.** A smooth-leaved variety of kale. [< *colewort*, a kind of cabbage.]

col·late (kə-lāt′, kō-, kōl′āt′) *v.* **-lat·ed, -lat·ing.** 1. To examine and compare (texts) carefully. 2. To assemble in proper sequence. [< Lat. *collatus*, p.p. of *conferre*, to bring together.]

col·lat·er·al (kə-lăt′ər-əl) *adj.* 1. Situated or running side by side. 2. Serving to corroborate. 3. Of a secondary nature; subordinate. 4. Of, designating, or guaranteed by a security pledged against the performance of an obligation. 5. Having an ancestor in common but descended from a different line. —*n.* Property acceptable as security for a loan or other obligation. [< Med. Lat. *collateralis.*]

col·la·tion (kə-lā′shən, kō-, kŏ-) *n.* 1. The act or process of collating. 2. A light meal.

col·league (kōl′ēg′) *n.* A fellow member, esp. in a profession; associate. [< Lat. *collega.*]

col·lect¹ (kə-lĕkt′) *v.* 1. To bring or come together in a group; assemble. 2. To accumulate: *collect stamps.* 3. To call for and obtain payment of: *collect taxes.* 4. To recover control of: *collect one's thoughts.* —*adj.* With payment to be made by the receiver: *a collect call.* —*adv.* So that the receiver is charged: *send a telegram collect.* [< Lat. *colligere.*] —**col·lect′i·ble** or **col·lect′a·ble** *adj.* —**col·lec′tion** *n.* —**col·lec′tor** *n.*

col·lect² (kōl′ĭkt, -ĕkt′) *n.* A brief prayer used before the epistle at Mass, varying with the day. [< Med. Lat. *(oratio ad) collectam*, (prayer at the) gathering.]

col·lect·ed (kə-lĕk′tĭd) *adj.* Self-possessed; composed.

col·lec·tive (kə-lĕk′tĭv) *adj.* 1. Formed by collecting. 2. Of, pertaining to, or made by a number of individuals acting as one: *a collective opinion.* —*n.* A collective business or undertaking or those working in it. —**col·lec′tive·ly** *adv.*

collective bargaining *n.* Negotiation between the representatives of organized workers and an employer.

collective noun *n.* A noun that denotes a collection of persons or things regarded as a unit.

Usage: A collective noun takes a singular verb when reference is made to the group as a whole and a plural verb when reference is made to the members of a group as single individuals: *The orchestra was playing. The orchestra have all gone home.*

col·lec·tiv·ism (kə-lĕk′tə-vĭz′əm) *n.* The principle or system of ownership and control of the means of production and distribution by the people collectively.

col·leen (kŏ-lēn′, kŏl′ēn′) *n.* An Irish girl. [Ir. Gael. *cailín.*]

col·lege (kōl′ĭj) *n.* 1. A school of higher learning that grants a bachelor's degree. 2. Any of the undergraduate divisions or schools of a university. 3. A technical or professional school, often affiliated with a university. 4. The building or buildings occupied by any such school. 5. A body of persons having a common purpose or common duties. [< Lat. *collegium*, association.] —**col·le′giate** (kə-lē′jĭt, -jē-ĭt) *adj.*

col·le·gian (kə-lē′jən, -jē-ən) *n.* A college student or recent college graduate.

col·le·gi·um (kə-lē′jē-əm, -lĕg′ē-) *n., pl.* **-gi·a** (-lē′jē-ə, -lĕg′ē-ə) or **-ums.** A governing council in which all members have equal authority, esp. one in the USSR. [R. *kollegya* < Lat. *collegium*, association.]

col·lide (kə-līd′) *v.* **-lid·ed, -lid·ing.** 1. To come together with violent, direct impact. 2. To clash; conflict. [< Lat. *collidere.*] —**col·li′sion** (-lĭzh′ən) *n.*

col·lie (kōl′ē) *n.* A large, long-haired dog orig. used to herd sheep. [Sc.]

col·lier (kōl′yər) *n. Chiefly Brit.* 1. A coal miner. 2. A coal ship. [< OE *col*, coal.]

col·lier·y (kōl′yə-rē) *n., pl.* **-ies.** *Chiefly Brit.* A coal mine.

col·lin·e·ar (kə-lĭn′ē-ər, kō-) *adj.* 1. Lying on the same line. 2. Containing a common line; coaxial.

col·lo·cate (kōl′ə-kāt′) *v.* **-cat·ed, -cat·ing.** To place together, esp. side by side. [< Lat. *collocare.*] —**col′lo·ca′tion** *n.*

col·lo·di·on (kə-lō′dē-ən) *n.* A highly flammable colorless or yellowish syrupy solution, used to hold surgical dressings, as a medicinal coating, and in making photographic plates. [< Gk. *kollōdēs*, gluelike.]

col·loid (kōl′oid′) *n.* A substance in the form of finely divided particles that do not settle out of and cannot be readily filtered from the uniform medium in which they are suspended. [< Gk. *kolla*, glue.] —**col·loid′al** (kə-loi′dl) *adj.*

col·lo·qui·al (kə-lō′kwē-əl) *adj.* Of, pertaining to, or suitable to informal speech and writing. —**col·lo′qui·al·ism** *n.* —**col·lo′qui·al·ly** *adv.* —**col·lo′qui·al·ness** *n.*

col·lo·qui·um (kə-lō′kwē-əm) *n., pl.* **-ums** or

-qui·a (-kwē-ə). **1.** An informal conference. **2.** An academic seminar. [Lat.]

col·lo·quy (kŏl'ə-kwē) *n., pl.* **-quies.** A conversation, esp. a formal one. [Lat. *colloquium.*]

col·lude (kə-lōōd') *v.* **-lud·ed, -lud·ing.** To be in collusion; connive. [Lat. *colludere.*]

col·lu·sion (kə-lōō'zhən) *n.* A secret agreement for a deceitful or fraudulent purpose. —col·lu'sive *adj.* —col·lu'sive·ly *adv.*

co·logne (kə-lōn') *n.* A scented liquid made of alcohol and fragrant oils. [< Fr. *eau de Cologne,* water of Cologne.]

co·lon¹ (kō'lən) *n.* A punctuation mark (:) used to introduce a quotation, explanation, example, or series. [< Gk. *kōlon,* metrical unit.]

co·lon² (kō'lən) *n., pl.* **-lons** or **-la** (-lə). The section of the large intestine from the cecum to the rectum. [< Gk. *kolon.*] —co·lon'ic (kə-lŏn'ĭk) *adj.*

co·lón³ (kō-lōn') *n., pl.* **-lons** or **-lo·nes** (-lō'-nās'). See table at **currency.** [Sp. *colón* < *Christóbal Colón,* Christopher Columbus.]

colo·nel (kûr'nəl) *n.* An officer, as in the army, ranking immediately above a lieutenant colonel. [< OItal. *colonello,* dim. of *colonna,* column of soldiers.]

co·lo·ni·al (kə-lō'nē-əl) *adj.* **1.** Of, pertaining to, or possessing colonies. **2.** Often **Colonial.** Of or pertaining to the 13 original American colonies. —*n.* An inhabitant of a colony.

co·lo·ni·al·ism (kə-lō'nē-ə-lĭz'əm) *n.* A governmental policy of acquiring or controlling foreign territory. —co·lo'ni·al·ist *n.*

col·o·nist (kŏl'ə-nĭst) *n.* **1.** An original settler or founder of a colony. **2.** A colonial.

col·o·nize (kŏl'ə-nīz') *v.* **-nized, -niz·ing. 1.** To establish a colony in. **2.** To settle in a colony. —col'o·ni·za'tion *n.* —col'o·niz'er *n.*

col·on·nade (kŏl'ə-nād') *n.* Archit. A series of regularly spaced columns. [< Ital. *colonna,* column.] —col'on·nad'ed *adj.*

col·o·ny (kŏl'ə-nē) *n., pl.* **-nies. 1.** A group of people who settle in a distant land but remain subject to a parent country. **2.** A territory ruled by a distant power. **3.** A group of people with similar interests concentrated in one area: *the American colony in Paris.* **4.** A group of the same kind of organisms living or growing together. [< Lat. *colonia.*]

col·o·phon (kŏl'ə-fŏn', -fən) *n.* An inscription placed usu. at the end of a book, giving facts pertaining to its publication. [< Gk. *kolophōn,* finishing touch.]

col·or (kŭl'ər) *n.* **1.** The aspect of things that is caused by differing qualities of the light reflected or emitted by them. **2.** A dye, paint, etc., that imparts color. **3.** Skin tone. **4.** colors. A flag or banner, as of a country or military unit. **5.** Outward, often deceptive, appearance. **6.** Vividness or picturesqueness. —*v.* **1.** To impart color to; change the color of. **2.** To give a distinctive character to; influence. **3.** To misrepresent. **4.** To blush. [< Lat.] —col'or·er *n.* —col'or·less *adj.* —col'or·less·ly *adv.* —col'or·less·ness *n.*

col·or·a·tu·ra (kŭl'ər-ə-tōōr'ə, -tyōōr'ə) *n.* **1.** Florid ornamentation in vocal music. **2.** A

singer, esp. a soprano, who specializes in coloratura. [Obs. Ital.]

col·or·blind (kŭl'ər-blīnd') *adj.* Partially or totally unable to see differences in colors. —col'or·blind'ness *n.*

col·or·cast (kŭl'ər-kăst') *n.* A television broadcast in color. [COLOR + (BROAD)CAST.] —col'or·cast' *v.*

col·or·code (kŭl'ər-kōd') *v.* **-cod·ed, -cod·ing.** To color, as wires or papers, according to a code for easy identification.

col·ored (kŭl'ərd) *adj.* **1.** Having color. **2. a.** Of an ethnic group not regarded as Caucasian, esp. Negro. **b.** Of mixed racial strains. **3.** Distorted or biased, as by irrelevant or incorrect information. —*n.* A colored person.

col·or·fast (kŭl'ər-făst') *adj.* Having color that will not run or fade. —col'or·fast'ness *n.*

col·or·ful (kŭl'ər-fəl) *adj.* **1.** Full of color. **2.** Rich in variety or vivid detail. —col'or·ful·ly *adv.* —col'or·ful·ness *n.*

color line *n.* A barrier, created by custom, law, or economic differences, that separates nonwhite persons from whites.

co·los·sal (kə-lŏs'əl) *adj.* Enormous in size or degree. [< Lat. *colossus,* colossus.]

Co·los·sians (kə-lŏsh'ənz, -lŏs'ē-ənz) *pl.n.* (*used with a sing. verb*). See table at **Bible.**

co·los·sus (kə-lŏs'əs) *n., pl.* **-los·si** (-lŏs'ī') or **-sus·es. 1.** A huge statue. **2.** Something of enormous size or importance. [Lat. < Gk. *kolossos.*]

col·our (kŭl'ər) *n. & v. Chiefly Brit.* Var. of **color.**

colt (kōlt) *n.* A young male horse or related animal. [< OE.] —colt'ish *adj.* —colt'ish·ly *adv.* —colt'ish·ness *n.*

col·um·bine (kŏl'əm-bīn') *n.* Any of several plants with variously colored flowers that have five spurred petals. [< Lat. *columba,* dove.]

co·lum·bi·um (kə-lŭm'bē-əm) *n. Symbol* **Cb** Niobium. [< NLat. *Columbia,* the United States.]

Co·lum·bus Day (kə-lŭm'bəs) *n.* Oct. 12, a holiday celebrated officially on the 2nd Monday in Oct. in the United States in honor of Christopher Columbus.

col·umn (kŏl'əm) *n.* **1.** A pillar used in a building as a support or as a decoration. **2.** Something that resembles a pillar in shape or use. **3.** One of two or more vertical sections of a page. **4.** A feature article that appears regularly in a periodical. **5.** A long row, as of soldiers. [< Lat. *columna.*] —co·lum'nar (kə-lŭm'nər) *adj.*

col·um·nist (kŏl'əm-nĭst, -ə-mĭst) *n.* A writer of a newspaper or magazine column.

com— or col— or con— *pref.* Together; jointly: *commingle.* [< Lat.]

co·ma (kō'mə) *n., pl.* **-mas.** A deep, prolonged unconsciousness, usu. the result of injury, disease, or poison. [Gk. *kōma,* deep sleep.]

Co·man·che (kə-măn'chē) *n., pl.* **-che** or **-ches. 1. a.** A tribe of Indians formerly ranging over the western plains from Wyoming to Texas, now living in Oklahoma. **b.** A member of this tribe. **2.** The Uto-Aztecan language of the Comanche. —Co·man'che *adj.*

co·ma·tose (kō'mə-tōs', kŏm'ə-) *adj.* **1.** Of,

ă pat ā pay â care ä father ĕ pet ē be ĭ pit ī tie î pier ŏ pot ō toe ô paw, for oi noise ŏŏ took
ōŏ boot ou out th thin th this ŭ cut û urge yōō abuse zh vision ə about, item, edible, gallop, circus

pertaining to, or affected with coma. **2.** Lethargic; torpid.

comb (kōm) *n.* **1.** A thin, toothed strip of plastic or other material, used to arrange the hair. **2.** Something resembling a comb in shape or use. **3.** A fleshy crest on the top of the head of a rooster, hen, or certain other birds. **4.** A honeycomb. —*v.* **1.** To arrange with or as if with a comb. **2.** To card (wool or other fiber). **3.** To search thoroughly; look through. [< OE.]

com·bat (kəm-băt′, kŏm′băt′) *v.* **-bat·ed** or **-bat·ted, -bat·ing** or **-bat·ting. 1.** To fight against; contend with. **2.** To oppose vigorously. —*n.* (kŏm′băt′). Fighting, esp. armed battle. [<OFr. *combattre.*] —**com·bat′ant** *n.* —**com·bat′ive** *adj.* —**com·bat′ive·ly** *adv.* —**com·bat′ive·ness** *n.*

combat fatigue *n.* A nervous disorder involving anxiety, depression, and irritability, induced by combat.

comb·er (kō′mər) *n.* **1.** One that combs. **2.** A long, cresting wave of the sea.

com·bi·na·tion (kŏm′bə-nā′shən) *n.* **1.** The act of combining or state of being combined. **2.** Something resulting from combining; aggregate. **3.** A sequence of numbers or letters used to open certain locks.

com·bine (kəm-bīn′) *v.* **-bined, -bin·ing. 1.** To make or become united. **2.** To form a chemical compound. —*n.* (kŏm′bīn′). **1.** A machine that harvests and threshes grain. **2.** An association of persons united for commercial or political interests. [< Lat. *combinare.*]

comb·ings (kō′mĭngz) *pl.n.* Hairs, wool, or other material removed with a comb.

combining form *n.* A word element that combines with other word forms to create compounds.

com·bo (kŏm′bō) *n., pl.* **-bos.** A small group of musicians. [< COMBINATION.]

com·bus·ti·ble (kəm-bŭs′tə-bəl) *adj.* Capable of catching fire and burning. —*n.* A combustible substance. —**com·bus′ti·bil′i·ty** *n.* —**com·bus′ti·bly** *adv.*

com·bus·tion (kəm-bŭs′chən) *n.* **1.** The process of burning. **2.** A chemical reaction, esp. oxidation, accompanied by the production of light and heat. [< Lat. *comburere.*] —**com·bus′tive** (-tĭv-) *adj.*

come (kŭm) *v.* **came** (kām), **come, com·ing. 1.** To advance; approach. **2.** To arrive. **3.** To reach a particular result, state, or position. **4.** To move into view. **5.** To exist at a particular point or place. **6.** To happen: *How did you come to know that?* **7.** To issue from; originate. **8.** To be obtainable: *It comes in two sizes.* —*phrasal verbs.* **come about.** To occur; take place; happen. **come across. 1.** To meet by chance. **2.** *Slang.* To do or give what is wanted. **come around** (or **round**). **1.** To recover. **2.** To change one's opinion or position. **come by.** To acquire. **come into.** To inherit. **come off. 1.** To happen; occur. **2.** To turn out. **come out. 1.** To be disclosed. **2.** To make a formal social debut. **come through. 1.** To succeed. **2.** *Informal.* To do as expected. **come to.** To regain consciousness. **come up with.** *Informal.* To propose; produce. [< OE *cuman.*]

come·back (kŭm′băk′) *n.* **1.** A return to former prosperity or status. **2.** A retort.

co·me·di·an (kə-mē′dē-ən) *n.* **1.** A professional entertainer who tells jokes or performs various other comic acts. **2.** A person who

amuses or tries to be amusing; clown. **3.** An actor in comedy. **4.** A comedy writer.

co·me·di·enne (kə-mē′dē-ĕn′) *n.* A female entertainer who tells jokes or performs various other comic acts. [Fr. *comédienne.*]

come·down (kŭm′doun′) *n.* **1.** A decline in status or level. **2.** A cause or feeling of depression or disappointment.

com·e·dy (kŏm′ĭ-dē) *n., pl.* **-dies. 1.** A play, motion picture, or similar entertainment in which the story and characters are humorous and that ends happily. **2.** A literary composition having a comedic theme or using the methods of comedy. **3.** A comic occurrence or situation in real life. [< Gk. *kōmōidia.*] —**co·me·dic** (kə-mē′dĭk) *adj.*

come·ly (kŭm′lē) *adj.* **-li·er, -li·est.** Attractive; handsome. [< OE *cȳmlic.*] —**come′li·ness** *n.*

come-on (kŭm′ŏn′, -ôn′) *n.* Something offered to attract or allure; inducement.

com·er (kŭm′ər) *n.* One showing promise of attaining success.

co·mes·ti·ble (kə-mĕs′tə-bəl) *adj.* Edible. —*n.* Something edible. [< Lat. *comedere,* to eat up.]

com·et (kŏm′ĭt) *n.* A celestial body having a solid head surrounded by a nebulous luminescent cloud and an elongated curved vapor tail arising when the head approaches the sun. [< Gk. *(astēr) komētēs,* long-haired (star).]

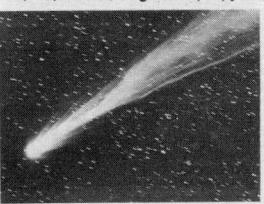

comet

come·up·pance (kŭm-ŭp′əns) *n.* Punishment that one deserves.

com·fit (kŭm′fĭt, kŏm′-) *n.* A candy; confection. [< Lat. *conficere,* to prepare.]

com·fort (kŭm′fərt) *v.* To soothe in time of grief or fear. —*n.* **1.** A condition of ease or well-being. **2.** Consolation; solace. **3.** One that brings ease or relief. **4.** Capacity to give physical ease. [< LLat. *confortare,* to strengthen.] —**com′fort·ing·ly** *adv.*

com·fort·a·ble (kŭm′fər-tə-bəl, kŭmf′tə-bəl) *adj.* **1.** Providing comfort. **2.** In a state of comfort. **3.** Sufficient; adequate: *comfortable earnings.* —**com′fort·a·ble·ness** *n.* —**com′fort·a·bly** *adv.*

com·fort·er (kŭm′fər-tər) *n.* **1.** One that comforts. **2.** A thick quilt.

com·fy (kŭm′fē) *adj.* **-fi·er, -fi·est.** *Informal.* Comfortable.

com·ic (kŏm′ĭk) *adj.* **1.** Of or characteristic of comedy. **2.** Funny; amusing; humorous. —*n.* **1.** One who is comical. **2. comics.** *Informal.* Comic strips. [< Gk. *kōmos,* revel.]

com·i·cal (kŏm′ĭ-kəl) *adj.* Causing amusement; funny. —**com′i·cal′i·ty** or **com′i·cal·ness** *n.* —**com′i·cal·ly** *adv.*

comic book *n.* A book of comic strips.

comic strip *n.* A narrative series of cartoons.

com·ing (kŭm′ĭng) *adj.* **1.** Approaching; next.

2. *Informal.* Showing promise of success. —*n.* Arrival; advent.

com·i·ty (kŏm′ĭ-tē) *n., pl.* **-ties.** Civility; courtesy. [Lat. *comitas.*]

com·ma (kŏm′ə) *n.* A punctuation mark (,) used to indicate a separation of ideas or elements within the structure of a sentence. [< Gk. *komma,* short clause.]

com·mand (kə-mănd′) *v.* **1.** To give orders (to). **2.** To exercise authority (over). **3.** To dominate by position; overlook. —*n.* **1.** The act of commanding. **2.** An order given with authority. **3.** A signal that activates a device such as a computer. **4.** Ability to control; mastery. **5.** *Mil.* **a.** The forces and areas under the control of one officer. **b.** A group of officers with authority to command. [< OFr. *comander.*]

Syns: *command, bid, charge, direct, enjoin, instruct, order, require, tell v.*

com·man·dant (kŏm′ən-dănt′) *n.* A commanding officer of a military organization.

com·man·deer (kŏm′ən-dîr′) *v.* To seize arbitrarily, esp. for public use; confiscate. [Afr. *kommanderen.*]

com·mand·er (kə-măn′dər) *n.* **1.** One who commands. **2.** An officer in the navy ranking above a lieutenant commander.

commander in chief *n., pl.* **commanders in chief.** The supreme commander of all the armed forces of a nation.

com·mand·ing (kə-măn′dĭng) *adj.* **1.** Having command; in charge. **2.** Impressive. **3.** Dominating. —**com·mand′ing·ly** *adv.*

com·mand·ment (kə-mănd′mənt) *n.* **1.** A command. **2.** Often **Commandment.** Any of the Ten Commandments.

command module *n.* The portion of a spacecraft in which the astronauts live and operate controls during a flight.

com·man·do (kə-măn′dō) *n., pl.* **-dos** or **-does.** A member of a small military unit specially trained to make quick raids. [Afr. *kommando.*]

com·mem·o·rate (kə-mĕm′ə-rāt′) *v.* **-rat·ed, -rat·ing.** **1.** To honor the memory of. **2.** To be a memorial to. [< Lat. *commemorare.*] —**com·mem′o·ra′tion** *n.* —**com·mem′o·ra·tive** (-ər-ə-tĭv, -ə-rā′-) *adj. & n.* —**com·mem′o·ra′tor** *n.*

com·mence (kə-mĕns′) *v.* **-menced, -menc·ing.** To begin; start. [< OFr. *comencier.*] —**com·menc′er** *n.*

com·mence·ment (kə-mĕns′mənt) *n.* **1.** A beginning; start. **2.** A graduation ceremony, as of a college.

com·mend (kə-mĕnd′) *v.* **1.** To praise. **2.** To represent as worthy or qualified; recommend. **3.** To put in the care of another. [< Lat. *commendare.*] —**com·mend′a·ble** *adj.* —**com·mend′a·ble·ness** *n.* —**com·mend′a·bly** *adv.* —**com′men·da′tion** (kŏm′ən-dā′shən) *n.*

com·men·da·to·ry (kə-mĕn′də-tôr′ē, -tōr′ē) *adj.* Approving.

com·men·su·ra·ble (kə-mĕn′sər-ə-bəl, -shər-) *adj.* Able to be measured by a common standard or unit. [Lat. *commensurabilis.*] —**com·men′su·ra·bil′i·ty** *n.* —**com·men′su·ra·bly** *adv.*

com·men·su·rate (kə-mĕn′sər-ĭt, -shər-) *adj.* **1.** Of the same size, extent, or duration. **2.** Corresponding in scale; proportionate.

—**com·men′su·rate·ly** *adv.* —**com·men′su·ra′tion** *n.*

com·ment (kŏm′ĕnt) *n.* **1.** An expression of criticism, analysis, or observation. **2.** A statement of opinion. [< Lat. *commentum,* interpretation.] —**com′ment′** *v.*

com·men·tar·y (kŏm′ən-tĕr′ē) *n., pl.* **-ies.** A series of explanations or interpretations.

com·men·tate (kŏm′ən-tāt′) *v.* **-tat·ed, -tat·ing.** To make a commentary on or serve as a commentator.

com·men·ta·tor (kŏm′ən-tā′tər) *n.* A radio or television reporter and news analyst.

com·merce (kŏm′ərs) *n.* The buying and selling of goods; trade; business. [< Lat. *commercium.*]

com·mer·cial (kə-mûr′shəl) *adj.* **1.** Of, pertaining to, or engaged in commerce. **2.** Having profit as a chief aim. **3.** Supported by advertising. —*n.* An advertisement on radio or television. —**com·mer′cial·ism** *n.* —**com·mer′cial·ist** *n.* —**com·mer′cial·is′tic** *adj.* —**com·mer′cial·ly** *adv.*

commercial bank *n.* A bank whose principal functions are to receive demand deposits and make short-term loans.

com·mer·cial·ize (kə-mûr′shə-līz′) *v.* **-ized, -iz·ing.** To make commercial, esp. for profit. —**com·mer′cial·i·za′tion** *n.*

com·min·gle (kə-mĭng′gəl) *v.* **-gled, -gling.** To blend together; mix.

com·mis·er·ate (kə-mĭz′ə-rāt′) *v.* **-at·ed, -at·ing.** To feel or express sympathy (for). [Lat. *commiserari.*] —**com·mis′er·a′tion** *n.* —**com·mis′er·a′tive·ly** *adv.* —**com·mis′er·a′tor** *n.*

com·mis·sar (kŏm′ĭ-sär′) *n.* A Communist Party official in charge of indoctrination and enforcement of Party loyalty. [R. *komissar.*]

com·mis·sar·i·at (kŏm′ĭ-sâr′ē-ət) *n.* An army department in charge of food and supplies. [< Med. Lat. *commissarius,* agent.]

com·mis·sar·y (kŏm′ĭ-sĕr′ē) *n., pl.* **-ies.** A store where food and supplies are sold, esp. on a military post. [< Med. Lat. *commissarius,* agent.]

com·mis·sion (kə-mĭsh′ən) *n.* **1. a.** Authorization to carry out a task. **b.** The authority so granted. **c.** The task so entrusted. **d.** A document conferring such authorization. **2.** A group authorized to perform certain duties or functions. **3.** A committing; perpetration: *commission of a crime.* **4.** An allowance to a salesman or agent for services rendered. **5.** A document conferring the rank of a military officer. —*v.* **1.** To grant a commission to. **2.** To place an order for. —*idioms.* **in commission.** In use or in usable condition. **out of commission.** Not in use or in working condition. [< Lat. *committere,* to entrust.]

commissioned officer *n.* An officer who holds a commission and ranks above an enlisted man or a warrant officer.

com·mis·sion·er (kə-mĭsh′ə-nər) *n.* **1.** A member of a commission. **2.** An official in charge of a governmental department. **3.** An administrative head of a professional sport.

com·mit (kə-mĭt′) *v.* **-mit·ted, -mit·ting.** **1.** To do, perform, or perpetrate: *commit perjury; commit suicide.* **2.** To consign; entrust. **3.** To place in confinement or custody. **4.** To pledge (oneself) to a position on some issue. [< Lat. *committere*, to entrust.] —**com·mit'ment** *n.* —**com·mit'ta·ble** *adj.* —**com·mit'tal** *n.*

com·mit·tee (kə-mĭt'ē) *n.* A group of people chosen to do a particular job or fulfill specified duties: *the membership committee of our club.* —**com·mit'tee·man** *n.* —**com·mit'tee·wom'an** *n.*

com·mode (kə-mōd') *n.* **1.** A low cabinet or chest of drawers. **2.** A movable stand containing a washbowl. **3.** A toilet. [< Fr., convenient.]

com·mo·di·ous (kə-mō'dē-əs) *adj.* Roomy; spacious. [< Lat. *commodus*, convenient.] —**com·mo'di·ous·ly** *adv.* —**com·mo'di·ous·ness** *n.*

com·mod·i·ty (kə-mŏd'ĭ-tē) *n., pl.* **-ties.** **1.** Something that is useful. **2.** A transportable article of trade or commerce, esp. an agricultural or mining product. [< Lat. *commoditas*.]

com·mo·dore (kŏm'ə-dôr', -dōr') *n.* **1.** Formerly, a naval officer ranking below a rear admiral. **2. a.** The senior captain of a naval squadron or merchant fleet. **b.** The presiding officer of a yacht club. [Prob. < Du. *komandeur*, commander.]

com·mon (kŏm'ən) *adj.* **-er, -est. 1.** Belonging equally to all; joint. **2.** Pertaining to the whole community; public: *the common good.* **3.** Widespread; prevalent; general. **4.** Usual; ordinary. **5.** Most widely known; occurring most frequently. **6.** Without special characteristics; average; standard. **7.** Unrefined; coarse. —*n.* **1.** A tract of land belonging to a whole community. **2. Commons.** The House of Commons. —*idiom.* **in common.** Equally with or by all. [< Lat. *communis*.] —**com'mon·ly** *adv.* —**com'mon·ness** *n.*

Syns: common, everyday, familiar, frequent, regular, routine, widespread *adj.*

common denominator *n.* **1.** A number that contains the denominator of each of a set of fractions as a factor. **2.** A commonly shared theme or trait.

com·mon·er (kŏm'ə-nər) *n.* A person without noble rank.

common fraction *n.* A fraction whose numerator and denominator are both integers.

common law *n.* An unwritten system of law based on court decisions, customs, and usages. —**com'mon-law'** *adj.*

common logarithm *n.* A logarithm to the base 10.

common market *n.* A customs union.

common multiple *n.* A number that contains each of a set of given numbers as a factor.

com·mon·place (kŏm'ən-plās') *adj.* Ordinary; common. —*n.* Something ordinary or common, esp. a trite or obvious remark. —**com'mon·place'ness** *n.*

common sense *n.* Native good judgment.

com·mon·weal (kŏm'ən-wēl') *n.* **1.** The public good. **2.** *Archaic.* A commonwealth.

com·mon·wealth (kŏm'ən-wĕlth') *n.* **1.** The people of a nation or state. **2.** A nation or state governed by the people; republic. **3.** A union or federation of self-governing states. [ME *commune welthe*, common well-being.]

com·mo·tion (kə-mō'shən) *n.* Violent or turbulent motion; agitation; tumult. [< Lat. *commovēre*, to disturb.]

com·mu·nal (kə-myōō'nəl, kŏm'yə-nəl) *adj.* **1.** Of or pertaining to a commune or community. **2.** Public. —**com·mu'nal·ly** *adv.*

com·mune[1] (kə-myōōn') *v.* **-muned, -mun·ing.** To converse intimately. [< OFr. *communier*.]

com·mune[2] (kŏm'yōōn') *n.* **1.** The smallest local political division of various European countries. **2. a.** A place used for group living. **b.** The people of a commune. [< Lat. *communis*, common.]

com·mu·ni·ca·ble (kə-myōō'nĭ-kə-bəl) *adj.* **1.** Capable of being communicated or transmitted. **2.** Talkative. —**com·mu'ni·ca·bil'i·ty** *n.* —**com·mu'ni·ca·bly** *adv.*

com·mu·ni·cant (kə-myōō'nĭ-kənt) *n.* **1.** One who receives Communion. **2.** One who communicates.

com·mu·ni·cate (kə-myōō'nĭ-kāt') *v.* **-cat·ed, -cat·ing. 1.** To make known; impart. **2.** To transmit, as a disease. **3.** To receive Communion. [< Lat. *communicare*.] —**com·mu'ni·ca'tor** *n.*

com·mu·ni·ca·tion (kə-myōō'nĭ-kā'shən) *n.* **1.** The act of communicating; transmission. **2.** The exchange of thoughts, messages, or information. **3.** Something communicated; message. **4. communications. a.** A system for communicating. **b.** The art and technology of communicating. —**com·mu'ni·ca'tive** (-kā'tĭv, -kə-tĭv) *adj.* —**com·mu'ni·ca'tive·ly** *adv.* —**com·mu'ni·ca'tive·ness** *n.*

communications satellite *n.* An artificial satellite used to aid communications, as by relaying a radio signal.

com·mun·ion (kə-myōōn'yən) *n.* **1.** A sharing of thoughts or feelings. **2. a.** A religious or spiritual fellowship. **b.** A Christian denomination. **3. Communion. a.** The Eucharist. **b.** The consecrated elements of the Eucharist. [< Lat. *communio*, mutual participation.]

com·mu·ni·qué (kə-myōō'nĭ-kā', kə-myōō'nĭ-kā') *n.* An official communication. [Fr., p.p. of *communiquer*, to inform.]

com·mu·nism (kŏm'yə-nĭz'əm) *n.* **1.** A system characterized by the absence of social classes and by common ownership of production means. **2. Communism. a.** The theory of revolutionary struggle toward communism. **b.** Socialism as exemplified in countries ruled by Communist parties. [< Lat. *communis*, common.] —**com'mu·nist** *n.* —**com·mu·nis'tic** *adj.* —**com'mu·nis'ti·cal·ly** *adv.*

Communist Party *n.* A Marxist-Leninist party, esp. the official state party of the USSR.

com·mu·ni·ty (kə-myōō'nĭ-tē) *n., pl.* **-ties. 1. a.** A group of people living in the same locality and under the same government. **b.** The locality in which they live. **2.** A social group or class. **3.** Similarity: *a community of interests.* **4.** Society as a whole; the public. [< Lat. *communitas*.]

community college *n.* A junior college without residential facilities that is often government-funded.

community property *n.* Property owned jointly by a husband and wife.

com·mu·nize (kŏm'yə-nīz') *v.* **-nized, -niz·ing. 1.** To subject to public ownership or management. **2.** To convert to Communist principles or control. —**com'mu·ni·za'tion** *n.*

com·mu·ta·tion (kŏm'yə-tā'shən) *n.* **1.** A substitution or exchange. **2.** *Law.* A reduction of a penalty to a less severe one. **3.** The travel of a commuter.

com·mu·ta·tive (kə-myōō'tə-tĭv, kŏm'yə-tā'tĭv) *adj.* 1. Pertaining to, involving, or characterized by substitution, interchange, or exchange. 2. Logically or mathematically independent of order.

com·mu·ta·tor (kŏm'yə-tā'tər) *n.* A device connected to the coils of an electric motor or generator to provide a unidirectional current from the generator or a reversal of current into the coils of the motor.

com·mute (kə-myōōt') *v.* **-mut·ed, -mut·ing.** 1. To substitute; interchange. 2. To change (a penalty or payment) to a less severe one. 3. To travel as a commuter. —*n. Informal.* The distance traveled by a commuter. [< Lat. *commutare.*]

com·mut·er (kə-myōō'tər) *n.* One who travels regularly between a home in one community and work in another.

com·pact¹ (kəm-păkt', kŏm-, kŏm'păkt') *adj.* 1. Closely and firmly united or packed. 2. Arranged within a small space. 3. Expressed briefly. —*v.* (kəm-păkt'). To press or join firmly together. —*n.* (kŏm'păkt'). 1. A small cosmetic case. 2. A small automobile. [< Lat. *compactus,* p.p. of *compingere,* to join together.] —**com·pact'er** *n.* —**com·pact'ly** *adv.* —**com·pact'ness** *n.*

com·pact² (kŏm'păkt') *n.* An agreement or covenant. [< Lat. *compactus,* p.p. of *compacisci,* to make an agreement.]

com·pac·tor (kəm-păk'tər, kŏm'păk'-) *n.* A device that compresses refuse into relatively small packages.

com·pan·ion (kəm-păn'yən) *n.* 1. A comrade; associate. 2. A person employed to live or travel with another. 3. One of a pair or set of things. [< OFr. *compaignon.*] —**com·pan'ion·ship'** *n.*

com·pan·ion·a·ble (kəm-păn'yə-nə-bəl) *adj.* Sociable; friendly. —**com·pan'ion·a·bly** *adv.*

com·pan·ion·way (kəm-păn'yən-wā') *n.* A staircase leading from a ship's deck to the cabins or area below. [Obs. Du. *kompanje,* poop deck.]

com·pa·ny (kŭm'pə-nē) *n., pl.* **-nies.** 1. A group of people. 2. People assembled for a social purpose. 3. A guest or guests. 4. Companionship; fellowship. 5. A business enterprise; firm. 6. A troupe of dramatic or musical performers: *a repertory company.* 7. *Mil.* A subdivision of a regiment or battalion. 8. A ship's crew and officers. [< OFr. *compagnie.*]

com·pa·ra·ble (kŏm'pər-ə-bəl) *adj.* 1. Capable of being compared. 2. Worthy of comparison. —**com·pa·ra·bil'i·ty** *n.* —**com·pa·ra·bly** *adv.*

com·par·a·tive (kəm-păr'ə-tĭv) *adj.* 1. Of, based on, or involving comparison. 2. Relative. 3. Designating a degree of comparison of adjectives and adverbs higher than positive and lower than superlative. —*n. Gram.* 1. The comparative degree. 2. An adjective or adverb expressing the comparative degree. —**com·par'a·tive·ly** *adv.*

com·pare (kəm-pâr') *v.* **-pared, -par·ing.** 1. To represent as similar, equal, or analogous; liken. 2. To examine in order to note the similarities or differences of. 3. To form the positive, comparative, or superlative degrees of (an adjective or adverb). —*n.* Comparison: *a pianist who is beyond compare.* [< Lat. *comparare.*]

com·par·i·son (kəm-păr'ĭ-sən) *n.* 1. The act of comparing. 2. Similarity. 3. The modification or inflection of an adjective or adverb to denote the positive, comparative, or superlative degree. [< Lat. *comparatio.*]

com·part·ment (kəm-pärt'mənt) *n.* One of the parts or spaces into which an area is subdivided. [< LLat. *compartiri,* to share.]

com·part·men·tal·ize (kŏm-pärt-mĕn'tl-īz', kəm-pärt'-) *v.* **-ized, -iz·ing.** To divide into compartments.

com·pass (kŭm'pəs, kŏm'-) *n.* 1. A device used to determine geographic direction, esp. a magnetic needle horizontally mounted or suspended and free to pivot until aligned with the magnetic field of the earth. 2. Often **com·passes.** A V-shaped device used for drawing circles or arcs of circles. 3. An enclosing line or boundary; girth. 4. An enclosed space or area. 5. A range or scope; extent. —*v.* 1. To make a circuit of; circle. 2. To surround; encircle. 3. To accomplish. 4. To scheme; plot. [< OFr. *compasser,* to measure.] —**com·pass·a·ble** *adj.*

compass

com·pas·sion (kəm-păsh'ən) *n.* The deep feeling of sharing the suffering of another; mercy. [< LLat. *compati,* to sympathize with.] —**com·pas'sion·ate** *adj.* —**com·pas'sion·ate·ly** *adv.*

com·pat·i·ble (kəm-păt'ə-bəl) *adj.* Capable of living or performing harmoniously with another or others. [< LLat. *compati,* to sympathize with.] —**com·pat'i·bil'i·ty** or **com·pat'i·ble·ness** *n.* —**com·pat'i·bly** *adv.*

com·pa·tri·ot (kəm-pā'trē-ət, -ŏt') *n.* A fellow countryman.

com·peer (kəm-pîr', kŏm'pîr') *n.* A peer; equal.

com·pel (kəm-pĕl') *v.* **-pelled, -pel·ling.** To force; constrain. [< Lat. *compellere.*]

com·pen·di·um (kəm-pĕn'dē-əm) *n., pl.* **-ums** or **-di·a** (-dē-ə). A short, complete summary. [Lat., shortening.]

com·pen·sate (kŏm'pən-sāt') *v.* **-sat·ed, -sat·ing.** 1. To make up for; counterbalance. 2. To make payment to; recompense. [Lat. *compensare.*] —**com·pen'sa·to·ry** (kəm-pĕn'sə-tôr'ē, -tōr'ē) *adj.*

com·pete (kəm-pēt') *v.* **-pet·ed, -pet·ing.** To strive or contend with another. [Lat. *competere,* to strive together.]

com·pe·tence (kŏm'pĭ-təns) *n.* Also **com·pe·ten·cy** (-tən-sē). 1. The state or condition of being competent. **2.** Sufficient means for a comfortable existence.

com·pe·tent (kŏm'pĭ-tənt) *adj.* **1.** Properly or well qualified; capable. **2.** Adequate for a purpose. **3.** Legally qualified. [< Lat. *compe-tere*, to be suitable.] —**com'pe·tent·ly** *adv.*

com·pe·ti·tion (kŏm'pĭ-tĭsh'ən) *n.* **1.** The act of competing. **2.** A contest. —**com·pet'i·tive** *adj.* —**com·pet'i·tive·ly** *adv.* —**com·pet'i·tive·ness** *n.*

com·pet·i·tor (kəm-pĕt'ĭ-tər) *n.* One who competes, as in sports or business; rival.

com·pile (kəm-pīl') *v.* **-piled, -pil·ing. 1.** To gather into a single book or record. **2.** To compose from materials gathered from several sources. [< OFr. *compiler.*] —**com'pi·la'tion** (kŏm'pə-lā'shən) *n.* —**com·pil'er** *n.*

com·pla·cence (kəm-plā'səns) *n.* Also **com·pla·cen·cy** (-sən-sē). **1.** Contentment; satisfaction. **2.** Self-satisfaction; smugness. [< Lat. *complacēre*, to please.] —**com·pla'cent** *adj.* —**com·pla'cent·ly** *adv.*

com·plain (kəm-plān') *v.* **1.** To express feelings of pain, dissatisfaction, or resentment. **2.** To make a formal accusation. [< OFr. *complaindre.*] —**com·plain'er** *n.*

com·plain·ant (kəm-plā'nənt) *n.* A person who makes a formal charge, as in a court of law; plaintiff.

com·plaint (kəm-plānt') *n.* **1.** An expression of pain, dissatisfaction, or grief. **2.** A cause or reason for complaining; grievance. **3.** A disease; illness. **4.** *Law.* A formal accusation or charge. [< OFr. *complainte.*]

com·plai·sance (kəm-plā'səns) *n.* Willing compliance. [< Lat. *complacēre*, to please.] —**com·plai'sant** *adj.* —**com·plai'sant·ly** *adv.*

com·ple·ment (kŏm'plə-mənt) *n.* **1.** Something that completes or makes up a whole. **2.** The quantity or number needed to make up a whole. **3.** *Geom.* An angle related to another with the sum of their measures being 90°. **4.** A word or group of words that completes a predicate or sentence. —*v.* (kŏm'plə-mĕnt'.) To add or serve as a complement to. [< Lat. *complementum.*] —**com'ple·men'ta·ry** (-tə-rē, -trē) *adj.*

Usage: Complement means "something that completes or brings to perfection": *The wine was a complement to the delicious dinner.* Compliment means "an expression of courtesy or praise": *He paid her a great compliment.*

com·plete (kəm-plēt') *adj.* **1.** Having all necessary or normal parts. **2.** Concluded; ended. **3.** Thorough; perfect. —*v.* **-plet·ed, -plet·ing. 1.** To make whole or complete. **2.** To end; conclude. [< Lat. *complēre*, to fill up.] —**com·plete'ly** *adv.* —**com·plete'ness** *n.* —**com·ple'tion** *n.*

com·plex (kəm-plĕks', kŏm'plĕks') *adj.* **1.** Consisting of two or more parts. **2.** Intricate; complicated. —*n.* (kŏm'plĕks'). **1.** A whole composed of intricate parts. **2.** A group of repressed emotions, desires, and memories that influences a person's personality and behavior. [Lat. *complecti*, to entwine.] —**com·plex'i·ty** (kəm-plĕk'sĭ-tē) *n.* —**com·plex'ly** *adv.* —**com·plex'ness** *n.*

Syns: *complex, complicated, elaborate, intricate, knotty* **adj.**

complex fraction *n.* A fraction in which the numerator or denominator or both contain fractions.

com·plex·ion (kəm-plĕk'shən) *n.* **1.** The natural color, texture, and appearance of the skin. **2.** General character or appearance. [< Lat. *complexio*, combination.]

complex number *n.* A number that can be expressed as $a + bi$, where a and b are real numbers and $i^2 = -1$.

complex sentence *n.* A sentence containing an independent clause and one or more dependent clauses.

com·pli·ance (kəm-plī'əns) *n.* Also **com·pli·an·cy** (-ən-sē). **1.** A complying with a wish, request, or demand. **2.** A disposition or tendency to yield to others. —**com·pli'ant** *adj.* —**com·pli'ant·ly** *adv.*

com·pli·cate (kŏm'plĭ-kāt') *v.* **-cat·ed, -cat·ing.** To make or become complex or intricate. [Lat. *complicare*, to fold up.] —**com'pli·ca'tion** *n.*

com·plic·i·ty (kəm-plĭs'ĭ-tē) *n.* Involvement as an accomplice in a crime or wrongdoing.

com·pli·ment (kŏm'plə-mənt) *n.* **1.** An expression of praise or admiration. **2.** **compliments.** A formal expression of courtesy or greeting. [< Lat. *complēre*, to fill up.]

com·pli·men·ta·ry (kŏm'plə-mĕn'tə-rē, -trē) *adj.* **1.** Expressing a compliment. **2.** Given free as a favor or courtesy. —**com'pli·men'ta·ri·ly** *adv.*

com·ply (kəm-plī') *v.* **-plied, -ply·ing.** To agree or acquiesce, as to a command or wish. [< Lat. *complēre*, to fill up.]

com·po·nent (kəm-pō'nənt) *n.* A constituent part. —*adj.* Being or functioning as a part or constituent of. [< Lat. *componere*, to put together.]

com·port (kəm-pôrt', -pōrt') *v.* **1.** To conduct or behave (oneself) in a particular manner. **2.** To agree; harmonize. [< Lat. *comportare*, to bring together.]

com·port·ment (kəm-pôrt'mənt, -pōrt'-) *n.* Bearing; deportment.

com·pose (kəm-pōz') *v.* **-posed, -pos·ing. 1.** To make up; constitute: *an exhibit composed of French Impressionist paintings.* **2.** To make by putting together parts or elements. **3.** To create (e.g. music). **4.** To make calm or tranquil. **5.** To settle; adjust. **6.** To arrange or set (e.g. type). [< Lat. *componere*, to put together.] —**com·posed'** *adj.* —**com·pos'ed·ly** (-pō'zĭd-lē) *adv.* —**com·pos'er** *n.*

com·pos·ite (kəm-pŏz'ĭt) *adj.* **1.** Made up of distinctly different parts or elements; compound. **2.** Of, belonging to, or characteristic of a family of flowering plants, such as the daisy, characterized by flower heads consisting of many small, densely clustered flowers that give the impression of a single bloom. —*n.* **1.** A composite structure or entity. **2.** A composite plant. [< Lat. *componere*, to put together.] —**com·pos'ite·ly** *adv.*

com·po·si·tion (kŏm'pə-zĭsh'ən) *n.* **1.** The act or product of composing, esp. a literary or artistic work. **2.** Constitution; make-up. **3.** The arrangement of artistic parts so as to form a unified whole. **4.** A short essay. **5.** The setting of type. —**com'po·si'tion·al** *adj.*

com·pos·i·tor (kəm-pŏz'ĭ-tər) *n.* A typesetter.

com·post (kŏm'pōst') *n.* A mixture of decaying organic matter used as fertilizer. [< OFr. *composte*, compote.]

com·po·sure (kəm-pō'zhər) *n.* Calmness and self-possession.

com·pote (kŏm'pōt') *n.* **1.** Fruit stewed or cooked in syrup. **2.** A long-stemmed dish used for holding fruit, nuts, or candy. [< OFr. *composte*.]

com·pound¹ (kŏm'pound') *n.* **1.** A combination of two or more parts, ingredients, etc. **2.** A combination of two or more words or word elements, written solid or with a hyphen. **3.** A substance that consists of atoms of at least two different elements combined in definite proportions, usu. having properties different from any of its constituent elements. —*v.* (kŏm-pound', kəm-). **1.** To combine; mix. **2.** To produce by combining. **3.** To compute (interest) on the principal and accrued interest. **4.** To make greater; increase. —*adj.* (kŏm'pound', kŏm-pound') Consisting of two or more parts. [< Lat. *componere*, to put together.] —**com·pound'a·ble** *adj.* —**com·pound'er** *n.*

com·pound² (kŏm'pound) *n.* A group of buildings set off and enclosed by a barrier. [Malay *kampong*, village.]

compound interest *n.* Interest computed on accumulated unpaid interest as well as on the original principal.

compound sentence *n.* A sentence of two or more independent clauses.

com·pre·hend (kŏm'prĭ-hĕnd') *v.* **1.** To understand. **2.** To take in; include. [< Lat. *comprehendere*.] —**com'pre·hen'sion** *n.*

com·pre·hen·si·ble (kŏm'prĭ-hĕn'sə-bəl) *adj.* Capable of being understood; intelligible. —**com'pre·hen'si·bil'i·ty** *n.* —**com'pre·hen'si·bly** *adv.*

com·pre·hen·sive (kŏm'prĭ-hĕn'sĭv) *adj.* Including or comprehending much; large in scope or content. —**com'pre·hen'sive·ly** *adv.* —**com'pre·hen'sive·ness** *n.*

com·press (kəm-prĕs') *v.* **1.** To press together or force into smaller space; condense. —*n.* (kŏm'prĕs'). A soft pad applied to some part of the body to control bleeding or reduce pain or infection. [< LLat. *compressare*.] —**com·press'i·bil'i·ty** *n.* —**com·press'i·ble** *adj.* —**com·pres'sion** *n.*

com·pres·sor (kəm-prĕs'ər) *n.* Something that compresses, esp. a device used to compress gases.

com·prise (kəm-prīz') *v.* -**prised, -pris·ing.** **1.** To consist of. **2.** To include; contain. [< Lat. *comprehendere*.]
Usage: The traditional rule states that the whole *comprises* the parts; the parts *compose* the whole. *Comprise,* however, is increasingly used in place of *compose: The Union is comprised of 50 states.* This example is considered unacceptable by a majority of the Usage Panel.

com·pro·mise (kŏm'prə-mīz') *n.* **1.** A settlement of differences in which each side makes concessions. **2.** Something that combines the qualities of different things. —*v.* -**mised, -mis·ing.** **1.** To settle by or agree to concessions. **2.** To expose to danger, suspicion, or dishonor. [< Lat. *compromissum*.] —**com'pro·mis'er** *n.*

comp·trol·ler (kən-trō'lər) *n.* A business executive or government official who supervises financial affairs. [ME, controller.]

com·pul·sion (kəm-pŭl'shən) *n.* **1.** The act of compelling or forcing. **2.** The state of being compelled. **3.** A strong, irresistible impulse to

act. [< Lat. *compellere*, to compel.] —**com·pul'sive** *adj.* —**com·pul'sive·ly** *adv.* —**com·pul'sive·ness** *n.*

com·pul·so·ry (kəm-pŭl'sə-rē) *adj.* **1.** Employing or exerting compulsion; coercive. **2.** Obligatory. —**com·pul'so·ri·ly** *adv.*
Syns: compulsory, imperative, mandatory, necessary, obligatory, required **adj.**

com·punc·tion (kəm-pŭngk'shən) *n.* Uneasiness caused by guilt; remorse. [< Lat. *compungere*, to sting.]

com·pute (kəm-pyōōt') *v.* -**put·ed, -put·ing.** To determine by mathematics, esp. by numerical methods. [Lat. *computare*.] —**com·put'a·bil'i·ty** *n.* —**com·put'a·ble** *adj.* —**com'pu·ta'tion** *n.*

com·put·er (kəm-pyōō'tər) *n.* **1.** A person who computes. **2.** A device that computes, esp. an electronic machine that performs high-speed mathematical or logical calculations and assembles, stores, correlates, or otherwise processes and prints data.

com·put·er·ize (kəm-pyōō'tə-rīz') *v.* -**ized, -iz·ing.** **1.** To process or store (information) with or in an electronic computer or system of computers. **2.** To furnish with a computer or computer system. —**com·put'er·i·za'tion** *n.*

computer language *n.* A code used to provide data and instructions to computers.

com·rade (kŏm'rād', -rəd) *n.* A friend, associate, or companion. [< OFr. *camarade*, roommate.] —**com'rade·ship'** *n.*

con¹ (kŏn) *adv.* Against. —*n.* An argument, opinion, etc., against something. [< CONTRA-.]

con² (kŏn) *v.* **conned, con·ning.** To study or examine carefully, esp. to memorize. [< OE *cunnan*, to know.]

con³ (kŏn) *Slang.* —*v.* **conned, con·ning.** To swindle or defraud; dupe. —*n.* A swindle. [< CONFIDENCE.]

con⁴ (kŏn) *n. Slang.* A convict.

con- *pref.* Var. of com-.

con·cat·e·nate (kŏn-kăt'n-āt', kən-) *v.* -**nat·ed, -nat·ing.** To connect or link in a series. [< LLat. *concatenare*.] —**con·cat'e·nate** (-ĭt, -āt') *adj.* —**con·cat'e·na'tion** *n.*

con·cave (kŏn-kāv', kŏn'kāv') *adj.* Curved like the inner surface of a sphere. [< Lat. *concavus*, vaulted.] —**con·cave'ly** *adv.* —**con·cav'i·ty** (-kăv'ĭ-tē) *or* **con·cave'ness** *n.*

con·ceal (kən-sēl') *v.* To keep from observation, discovery, or understanding. [< Lat. *concelare*.] —**con·ceal'a·ble** *adj.* —**con·ceal'er** *n.* —**con·ceal'ment** *n.*

con·cede (kən-sēd') *v.* -**ced·ed, -ced·ing.** **1.** To admit as true or real; acknowledge. **2.** To yield, as a right. [< Lat. *concedere*.] —**con·ced'er** *n.*

con·ceit (kən-sēt') *n.* **1.** Too high an opinion of oneself; vanity. **2.** An elaborate or extended metaphor. [ME *conceite*, mind.]

con·ceit·ed (kən-sē'tĭd) *adj.* Vain. —**con·ceit'ed·ly** *adv.* —**con·ceit'ed·ness** *n.*

con·ceiv·a·ble (kən-sē'və-bəl) *adj.* Imaginable; possible. —**con·ceiv'a·bil'i·ty** *n.* —**con·ceiv'a·bly** *adv.*

con·ceive (kən-sēv') *v.* -**ceived, -ceiv·ing.** **1.** To become pregnant (with). **2.** To form in the mind; devise. **3.** To think; imagine. [< Lat. *concipere*.] —**con·ceiv'er** *n.*

con·cen·trate (kŏn'sən-trāt') *v.* -**trat·ed, -trat-**

ing. 1. To direct or draw toward a common center; focus. **2.** *Chem.* To increase the concentration. —*n. Chem.* A product of concentration. [Lat. *com-*, together + Lat. *centrum*, center.] —**con'cen·tra'tive** *adj.* —**con'cen·tra'tor** *n.*

con·cen·tra·tion (kŏn'sən-trā'shən) *n.* **1.** The act of concentrating or state of being concentrated. **2.** Something concentrated. **3.** The amount of a specified substance in a unit amount of another substance.

concentration camp *n.* A camp where prisoners of war, enemy aliens, and political prisoners are confined.

con·cen·tric (kən-sĕn'trĭk) *or* **con·cen·tri·cal** (-tĭ-kəl) *adj.* Having a center in common. [Med. Lat. *concentricus.*] —**con·cen'tri·cal·ly** *adv.* —**con'cen·tric'i·ty** (-trĭs'ĭ-tē) *n.*

con·cept (kŏn'sĕpt') *n.* A general idea or understanding, esp. one derived from specific instances. [LLat. *conceptus.*] —**con·cep'tu·al** *adj.* —**con·cep'tu·al·ly** *adv.*

con·cep·tion (kən-sĕp'shən) *n.* **1.** The fusing of a sperm and egg to form a zygote capable of developing into a new organism. **2.** A beginning; start. **3.** The ability to form or understand mental concepts. **4.** A concept, plan, design, or thought. [< Lat. *concipere*, to conceive.] —**con·cep'tion·al** *adj.*

con·cep·tu·al·ize (kən-sĕp'chōō-ə-līz') *v.* **-ized, -iz·ing.** To form concepts (of). —**con·cep'tu·al·i·za'tion** *n.*

con·cern (kən-sûrn') *v.* **1.** To pertain or relate to; affect. **2.** To engage the interests of. **3.** To cause anxiety or uneasiness in. —*n.* **1.** Something of interest or importance. **2.** Earnest regard: *concern for one's well-being.* **3.** Relation; reference. **4.** Anxiety; worry. **5.** A business establishment. [< Med. Lat. *concernere.*]

con·cerned (kən-sûrnd') *adj.* Anxious; disturbed; troubled.

con·cern·ing (kən-sûr'nĭng) *prep.* In reference to; regarding.

con·cert (kŏn'sûrt', -sərt) *n.* **1.** A public musical performance. **2.** Agreement in purpose, feeling, or action. —*v.* (kən-sûrt'). **1.** To plan or arrange by mutual agreement. **2.** To act or contrive together. —*idiom.* **in concert.** All together; in agreement. [< Ital. *concerto.*]

con·cert·ed (kən-sûr'tĭd) *adj.* **1.** Planned or accomplished together. **2.** Using all available energies and resources: *a concerted effort.*

con·cer·ti·na (kŏn'sər-tē'nə) *n.* A small, hexagonal accordion with buttons for keys.

con·cert·mas·ter (kŏn'sərt-măs'tər) *n.* The first violinist and assistant conductor in a symphony orchestra.

con·cer·to (kən-chěr'tō) *n., pl.* **-tos** *or* **-ti** (-tē). A composition for an orchestra and one or more solo instruments. [Ital.]

con·ces·sion (kən-sĕsh'ən) *n.* **1.** The act of conceding. **2.** Something conceded. **3.** Something granted by a government to be used for a specific purpose. **4.** The privilege of operating a subsidiary business in a certain place. [< Lat. *concedere*, to concede.]

con·ces·sion·aire (kən-sĕsh'ə-nâr') *n.* The operator or holder of a concession. [Fr.]

con·ces·sive (kən-sĕs'ĭv) *adj.* Of the nature of or containing a concession.

conch (kŏngk, kŏnch) *n., pl.* **conchs** (kŏngks) *or* **conch·es** (kŏn'chĭz). A tropical marine mollusk with a large, brightly colored spiral shell. [< Gk. *konkhē*, mussel.]

conch

con·cierge (kŏn-syârzh') *n.* A person, esp. in France, who lives in a building, attends the entrance, and serves as a janitor. [< Lat. *conservus*, fellow slave.]

con·cil·i·ate (kən-sĭl'ē-āt') *v.* **-at·ed, -at·ing. 1.** To win over; placate. **2.** To gain or win, as favor. [Lat. *conciliare.*] —**con·cil'i·a'tion** *n.* —**con·cil'i·a'tor** *n.* —**con·cil'i·a·to'ry** (-ə-tôr'ē, -tôr'ē) *adj.*

con·cise (kən-sīs') *adj.* Expressing much in few words; brief and clear. [Lat. *concisus*, p.p. of *concidere*, to cut up.] —**con·cise'ly** *adv.* —**con·cise'ness** *n.*

Syns: *concise, condensed, laconic, pithy, succinct, terse* **adj.**

con·clave (kŏn'klāv', kŏng'-) *n.* A secret meeting, esp. one in which the cardinals of the Roman Catholic Church meet to elect a pope. [< Lat., *private chamber.*]

con·clude (kən-klōōd') *v.* **-clud·ed, -clud·ing. 1.** To bring or come to an end; close. **2.** To come to an agreement or settlement of. **3.** To reach a decision about. **4.** To determine; resolve. [< Lat. *concludere.*] —**con·clu'sion** *n.*

con·clu·sive (kən-klōō'sĭv) *adj.* Decisive; final. —**con·clu'sive·ly** *adv.*

con·coct (kən-kŏkt') *v.* **1.** To prepare by mixing ingredients. [< Lat. *concoquere*, to cook together.] —**con·coct'er** *or* **con·coc'tor** *n.* —**con·coc'tion** *n.*

con·com·i·tant (kən-kŏm'ĭ-tənt) *adj.* Existing or occurring concurrently. —*n.* An accompanying state or thing. [< Lat. *concomitari*, to accompany.] —**con·com'i·tance** *n.*

con·cord (kŏn'kôrd', kŏng'-) *n.* Agreement of interests or feelings; concurrence; accord. [< Lat. *concordia.*]

con·cor·dance (kən-kôr'dns) *n.* **1.** A state of agreement. **2.** An index of words in a written work or works, showing the context in which they occur.

con·cor·dant (kən-kôr'dnt) *adj.* Harmonious; agreeing. —**con·cor'dant·ly** *adv.*

con·cor·dat (kən-kôr'dăt') *n.* A formal agreement; compact. [< Med. Lat. *concordatum.*]

con·course (kŏn'kôrs', -kôrs, kŏng'-) *n.* **1.** A crowd; throng. **2. a.** A large open space for the gathering or passage of crowds. **b.** A broad thoroughfare. [< Lat. *concursus.*]

con·cres·cence (kən-krĕs'əns) *n.* The uniting, esp. the growing together, of related parts. [Lat. *concrescentia.*]

con·crete (kŏn-krēt', kŏn'krēt) *adj.* **1.** Relating to an actual, specific thing or instance; not general; particular. **2.** Existing in reality or in real experience. **3.** Formed by the coalescence of separate particles or parts into one mass; solid. **4.** Made of concrete. —*n.* (kŏn'krēt, kŏn-krēt'). **1.** A construction material consisting of conglomerate gravel, pebbles, broken stone, or slag in a mortar or cement matrix. **2.** A mass formed by the coalescence of particles. —*v.* (kŏn′krēt, kŏn-krēt′) **-cret·ed, -cret·ing. 1.** To form into a mass by coalescence or cohesion of particles. **2.** To build, treat, or cover with concrete. [< Lat. *concretus*, p.p. of *concrescere*, to grow together.] —**con·crete′ly** *adv.* —**con·crete′ness** *n.*

con·cre·tion (kŏn-krē′shən) *n.* **1.** A hard, solid mass. **2.** The act or process of concreting; coalescence.

con·cu·bine (kŏng′kyə-bīn′, kŏn′-) *n.* A woman who cohabits with a man without being married to him. [< Lat. *concubina.*]

con·cu·pis·cence (kŏn-kyōō′pĭ-səns) *n.* Sexual desire; lust. [LLat. *concupiscentia.*] —**con·cu′pis·cent** *adj.*

con·cur (kən-kûr′) *v.* **-curred, -cur·ring. 1.** To have the same opinion; agree. **2.** To act together. **3.** To occur at the same time. [< Lat. *concurrere*, to meet.] —**con·cur′rence** *n.*

con·cur·rent (kən-kûr′ənt) *adj.* **1.** Happening at the same time or place. **2.** Acting in conjunction. **3.** Meeting or tending to meet at the same point. —**con·cur′rent·ly** *adv.*

con·cus·sion (kən-kŭsh′ən) *n.* **1.** A violent jarring; shock. **2.** An injury to a soft bodily tissue, esp. the brain, resulting from a violent blow. [< Lat. *concutere*, to shake violently.] —**con·cus′sive** (-kŭs′ĭv) *adj.*

con·demn (kən-dĕm′) *v.* **1.** To express disapproval of; denounce. **2. a.** To convict. **b.** To sentence to a punishment. **3.** To declare unfit for use. **4.** To declare legally appropriated for public use. [< Lat. *condemnare.*] —**con·demn′a·ble** (-dĕm′nə-bəl) *adj.* —**con·dem·na·tion** *n.* —**con·dem′na·to·ry** (-tôr′ē, -tōr′ē) *adj.*

con·dense (kən-dĕns′) *v.* **-densed, -dens·ing. 1.** To make or become more compact. **2.** To abridge. **3.** To form a liquid from a vapor. [< Lat. *condensare.*] —**con·dens·a·bil′i·ty** *n.* —**con·dens′a·ble** or **con·dens′i·ble** *adj.* —**con·den·sa′tion** (kŏn′dĕn-sā′shən) *n.* —**con·dens′er** *n.*

con·de·scend (kŏn′dĭ-sĕnd′) *v.* **1.** To agree to do something one regards as beneath one's rank or dignity; deign. **2.** To treat in a patronizing manner. [< LLat. *condescendere.*] —**con·de·scend′ing·ly** *adv.* —**con′de·scen′sion** *n.*

con·dign (kən-dīn′) *adj.* Deserved; merited: *condign censure.* [< Lat. *condignus.*] —**con·dign′ly** *adv.*

con·di·ment (kŏn′də-mənt) *n.* A seasoning for food, as mustard. [< Lat. *condimentum.*]

con·di·tion (kən-dĭsh′ən) *n.* **1.** The particular state of being of a person or thing. **2.** A state of health. **3.** *Informal.* A disease or ailment: *a heart condition.* **4.** A prerequisite. **5.** A qualification. **6.** Often **conditions.** The existing circumstances: *poor driving conditions.* **7.** *Gram.* The dependent clause of a conditional sentence. —*v.* **1.** To make conditional. **2.** To put into good or proper condition. **3.** To adapt. **4.** *Psychol.* To cause to respond in a specific manner to a specific stimulus. [< Lat. *conditio*, stipulation.]

con·di·tion·al (kən-dĭsh′ə-nəl) *adj.* **1.** Imposing, depending on, or containing a condition or conditions. **2.** Tentative. **3.** *Gram.* Stating

or implying a condition. —*n.* *Gram.* A mood, tense, clause, or word expressing a condition. —**con·di′tion·al·ly** *adv.*

con·di·tioned (kən-dĭsh′ənd) *adj.* **1.** Subject to conditions. **2.** Prepared for a specific action. **3.** *Psychol.* Exhibiting or trained to exhibit a new or modified response.

con·dole (kən-dōl′) *v.* **-doled, -dol·ing.** To express sympathy or sorrow. [LLat. *condolēre.*] —**con·do′lence** *n.* —**con·dol′er** *n.*

con·dom (kŏm′dəm) *n.* A rubber sheath for covering the penis during sexual intercourse to prevent disease or conception. [Orig. unknown.]

con·do·min·i·um (kŏn′də-mĭn′ē-əm) *n.* **1.** Joint sovereignty. **2. a.** An apartment building in which the apartments are owned individually. **b.** An apartment in such a building. [COM- + Lat. *dominium*, property.]

con·done (kən-dōn′) *v.* **-doned, -don·ing.** To forgive, overlook, or disregard (an offense) without protest or censure. [Lat. *condonare.*] —**con·don′er** *n.*

con·dor (kŏn′dôr′, -dər) *n.* A very large vulture of the Andes or the mountains of California. [< Quechua *kúntur.*]

con·duce (kən-dōōs′, -dyōōs′) *v.* **-duced, -duc·ing.** To contribute or lead to. [< Lat. *conducere.*] —**con·du′cive** *adj.*

con·duct (kən-dŭkt′) *v.* **1.** To direct the course of; control. **2.** To lead or guide. **3.** To serve as a medium for conveying; transmit. **4.** To behave. —*n.* (kŏn′dŭkt′). **1.** The way one acts; behavior. **2.** Management. **3.** The act of leading or guiding. [< Lat. *conducere.*] —**con·duct′i·bil′i·ty** *n.* —**con·duct′i·ble** *adj.*

con·duc·tance (kən-dŭk′təns) *n.* The measure of a material's ability to conduct an electric charge.

con·duc·tive (kən-dŭk′tĭv) *adj.* Having the ability or power to conduct or transmit. —**con·duc′tiv′i·ty** *n.*

con·duc·tor (kən-dŭk′tər) *n.* **1.** One who conducts or leads. **2.** The person in charge of a train, bus, or streetcar. **3.** The director of a musical ensemble. **4.** A substance or medium that conducts heat, light, sound, or esp. an electric charge.

con·duit (kŏn′dĭt, -dōō-ĭt) *n.* **1.** A channel or pipe for conveying fluids. **2.** A tube or duct for enclosing electric wires or cable. [< OFr., conveyance.]

cone (kōn) *n.* **1.** A surface generated by a straight line passing through a fixed point and moving along the intersection with a fixed curve. **2.** The figure formed by such a surface bound by its vertex and an intersecting plane. **3.** A scaly, rounded or cylindrical seed-bearing structure, as of a pine. **4.** A photoreceptor in the retina. [< Gk. *kōnos.*]

Con·es·to·ga wagon (kŏn′ĭ-stō′gə) *n.* A heavy covered wagon with broad wheels, used by American pioneers. [< *Conestoga,* Pennsylvania.]

co·ney (kō′nē, kŭn′ē) *n.* Var. of **cony.**

con·fab·u·late (kən-făb′yə-lāt′) *v.* **-lat·ed, -lat·ing.** To talk informally; chat. [Lat. *confabulari.*] —**con·fab′u·la′tion** *n.* —**con·fab′u·la′tor** *n.* —**con·fab′u·la·to′ry** (-lə-tôr′ē, -tōr′ē) *adj.*

con·fec·tion (kən-fĕk′shən) *n.* A sweet preparation, such as candy or preserves. [< Lat. *conficere*, to prepare.]

con·fec·tion·er (kən-fĕk'shə-nər) *n.* One who makes or sells confections.

con·fec·tion·er·y (kən-fĕk'shə-nĕr'ē) *n., pl.* **-ies.** **1.** Candies and other confections collectively. **2.** A confectioner's shop.

con·fed·er·a·cy (kən-fĕd'ər-ə-sē) *n., pl.* **-cies.** A political union of several peoples, parties, or states.

con·fed·er·ate (kən-fĕd'ər-ĭt) *n.* **1.** An associate; ally. **2.** An accomplice. **3.** A member of a confederacy. —*v.* (kən-fĕd'ə-rāt') **-at·ed, -at·ing.** To form into or become part of a confederacy. [< LLat. *confoederare*, to unite.] —**con·fed'er·ate** *adj.*

con·fed·er·a·tion (kən-fĕd'ə-rā'shən) *n.* A confederacy.

con·fer (kən-fûr') *v.* **-ferred, -fer·ring. 1.** To bestow (e.g. an honor). **2.** To hold a conference. [< Lat. *conferre*, to bring together.] —**con·fer'ment** or **con·fer'ral** *n.* —**con·fer'ra·ble** *adj.* —**con·fer'rer** *n.*

con·fer·ence (kŏn'fər-əns, -frəns) *n.* **1.** A meeting to discuss something. **2.** A regional association of athletic teams.

con·fess (kən-fĕs') *v.* **1.** To disclose or acknowledge one's misdeed or fault. **2.** To concede the truth or validity of. **3.** To make known (one's sins), esp. to a priest for absolution. [< Lat. *confitēri*, to acknowledge.] —**con·fess'ed·ly** (-ĭd-lē) *adv.*

con·fes·sion (kən-fĕsh'ən) *n.* **1.** An act of confessing. **2.** Something confessed. **3.** A formal declaration of guilt. **4.** The disclosure of sins to a priest for absolution. **5.** A religious group that adheres to a particular creed.

con·fes·sion·al (kən-fĕsh'ə-nəl) *n.* A small booth in which a priest hears confessions.

con·fes·sor (kən-fĕs'ər) *n.* **1.** A priest who hears confessions. **2.** One who confesses.

con·fet·ti (kən-fĕt'ē) *pl.n.* (*used with a sing. verb*). Small pieces of colored paper scattered on festive occasions. [Ital., candies.]

con·fi·dant (kŏn'fĭ-dănt', -dänt', kŏn'fĭ-dănt', -dänt') *n.* A person to whom one confides personal matters or secrets.

con·fide (kən-fīd') *v.* **-fid·ed, -fid·ing. 1.** To tell in confidence. **2.** To put into another's keeping. [< Lat. *confidere*.] —**con·fid'er** *n.*

con·fi·dence (kŏn'fĭ-dəns) *n.* **1.** Self-assurance. **2.** Trust or reliance. **3.** A trusting relationship. **4.** The assurance that someone will keep a secret. **5.** Something confided. —**con·fi·dent** *adj.* —**con·fi·dent·ly** *adv.*

Syns: *confidence, aplomb, assurance, security, self-confidence, self-possession* n.

con·fi·den·tial (kŏn'fĭ-dĕn'shəl) *adj.* **1.** Told in confidence; secret. **2.** Entrusted with private information or matters. —**con·fi·den'ti·al'i·ty** *n.* —**con·fi·den'tial·ly** *adv.*

con·fig·u·ra·tion (kən-fĭg'yə-rā'shən) *n.* The arrangement of the parts or elements of something. [< LLat. *configuratio*, to form.] —**con·fig'u·ra'tion·al·ly** *adv.* —**con·fig'u·ra'tive** (-rā'tĭv) or **con·fig'u·ra'tion·al** *adj.*

con·fine (kən-fīn') *v.* **-fined, -fin·ing. 1.** To limit in area, extent, or manner; restrict. **2.** To imprison. [< Lat. *confinis*, adjoining.] —**con·fin'a·ble** or **con·fine'a·ble** *adj.* —**con·fine'ment** *n.* —**con·fin'er** *n.*

con·fines (kŏn'fīnz') *pl.n.* The limits of a space or area; borders.

con·firm (kən-fûrm') *v.* **1.** To corroborate;

verify. **2.** To strengthen; establish. **3.** To ratify. **4.** To administer the rite of confirmation. [< Lat. *confirmare*.] —**con·firm'a·ble** *adj.* —**con·fir'ma·to'ry** (-fûr'mə-tôr'ē, -tōr'ē) or **con·fir'ma·tive** *adj.* —**con·firm'er** *n.*

con·fir·ma·tion (kŏn'fər-mā'shən) *n.* **1.** The act of confirming. **2.** A verification. **3.** A rite admitting a baptized person to full membership in a church.

con·fis·cate (kŏn'fĭ-skāt') *v.* **-cat·ed, -cat·ing. 1.** To seize (private property) for the public treasury. **2.** To seize by or as if by authority. [< Lat. *confiscare*.] —**con·fis·ca'tion** *n.* —**con·fis·ca'tor** *n.*

con·fla·gra·tion (kŏn'flə-grā'shən) *n.* A large and destructive fire. [< Lat. *conflagrare*, to burn up.]

con·flict (kŏn'flĭkt') *n.* **1.** Prolonged warfare. **2.** A clash of opposing ideas, interests, etc.; disagreement. —*v.* (kən-flĭkt'). To be in opposition; differ. [< Lat. *confligere*, to strike together.] —**con·flic'tive** *adj.*

Syns: *conflict, clash, contention, difficulty, disaccord, discord, dissension, dissent, dissidence, friction, strife* n.

con·flu·ence (kŏn'flōō-əns) *n.* **1. a.** A flowing together of two or more streams. **b.** The point where such streams come together. **2.** A crowd. —**con·flu'ent** *adj. & n.*

con·flux (kŏn'flŭks') *n.* A confluence.

con·form (kən-fôrm') *v.* **1.** To make or become similar. **2.** To act or be in agreement; comply. **3.** To act in accordance with current attitudes or practices. [< Lat. *conformare*, to fashion.] —**con·form'a·bil'i·ty** *n.* —**con·form'a·ble** *adj.* —**con·form'a·bly** *adv.* —**con·form'er** *n.* —**con·form'ist** *n.*

con·for·mance (kən-fôr'məns) *n.* Conformity.

con·for·ma·tion (kŏn'fər-mā'shən) *n.* The way something is formed; shape or structure.

con·for·mi·ty (kən-fôr'mĭ-tē) *n., pl.* **-ties. 1.** Similarity in form or character; correspondence. **2.** Action or behavior in agreement with current customs, rules, principles, etc.

con·found (kən-found', kŏn-) *v.* **1.** To bewilder, puzzle, or perplex. **2.** To mix up; mistake (one thing) for another. [Lat. *confundere*, to mix together.] —**con·found'er** *n.*

con·fra·ter·ni·ty (kŏn'frə-tûr'nĭ-tē) *n., pl.* **-ties.** An association of people united in a common purpose or profession.

con·frere (kŏn'frâr') *n.* A colleague. [< OFr.]

con·front (kən-frŭnt') *v.* **1.** To come or bring face to face with. **2.** To meet or face boldly or defiantly. [< Med. Lat. *confrontare*.] —**con·fron·ta'tion** (kŏn'frən-tā'shən) *n.* —**con·fron·ta'tion·al** *adj.* —**con·front'er** *n.*

Con·fu·cian·ism (kən-fyōō'shə-nĭz'əm) *n.* The principles of conduct based on the teachings of Confucius. —**Con·fu'cian** *n. & adj.*

con·fuse (kən-fyōōz') *v.* **-fused, -fus·ing. 1.** To mislead; mix up. **2.** To fail to distinguish between. **3.** To make unclear; blur. [< Lat. *confundere*, to mix together.] —**con·fus'ed·ly** (-fyōō'zĭd-lē) *adv.* —**con·fus'ing·ly** *adv.*

Syns: *confuse, addle, befuddle, bewilder, confound, fuddle, mix up, perplex* v.

con·fu·sion (kən-fyōō'zhən) *n.* The act of confusing or the condition of being confused.

con·fute (kən-fyōōt') *v.* **-fut·ed, -fut·ing.** To prove to be wrong or false; refute. [Lat. *confutare*.] —**con·fut'a·ble** *adj.* —**con·fu·ta'tion** (kŏn'-) *n.* —**con·fu'ta·tive** *adj.* —**con·fut'er** *n.*

con·geal (kən-jēl') *v.* **1.** To solidify or cause

to solidify, as by freezing. **2.** To coagulate; jell. [< Lat. *congelare.*] **—con·geal′a·ble** *adj.* **—con·geal′ment** *n.*

con·gen·ial (kən-jēn′yəl) *adj.* **1.** Having the same tastes or temperament. **2.** Friendly. **3.** Suited to one's nature or needs; agreeable. **—con·ge·ni·al′i·ty** (-jē′nē-ăl′ĭ-tē) *or* **con·gen′ial·ness** *n.* **—con·gen′ial·ly** *adv.*

con·gen·i·tal (kən-jĕn′ĭ-tl) *adj.* **1.** Existing at birth but not hereditary. **2.** Being such as if by nature: *a congenital thief.* [< Lat. *congenitus.*] **—con·gen′i·tal·ly** *adv.*

con·ger (kŏng′gər) *n.* A large, scaleless eel. [< Gk. *gongros.*]

con·ge·ries (kŏn′jə-rēz′, kən-jîr′ēz′) *n. (used with a sing. verb).* A collection of things heaped together; aggregation. [Lat.]

con·gest (kən-jĕst′) *v.* **1.** To overfill. **2.** To cause excessive blood to accumulate in (a bodily vessel or organ). [Lat. *congerere.*] **—con·ges′tion** *n.* **—con·ges′tive** *adj.*

con·glom·er·ate (kən-glŏm′ə-rāt′) *v.* **-at·ed, -at·ing.** To form or collect into an adhering or rounded mass. **—***n.* (kən-glŏm′ər-ĭt). **1.** A collected heterogeneous mass; cluster. **2.** *Geol.* A rock consisting of pebbles and gravel embedded in a loosely cementing material. **3.** A business corporation made up of a number of different companies that operate in diversified fields. [Lat. *conglomerare.*] **—con·glom′er·ate** (-ər-ĭt) *adj.* **—con·glom·er·a′tion** *n.*

con·grat·u·late (kən-grăch′ə-lāt′) *v.* **-lat·ed, -lat·ing.** To express praise or acknowledgment for the achievement or good fortune of. [Lat. *congratulari.*] **—con·grat·u·la′tion** *n.* **—con·grat′u·la·to′ry** (-lə-tôr′ē, -tōr′ē) *adj.*

con·gre·gate (kŏng′grĭ-gāt′) *v.* **-gat·ed, -gat·ing.** To come or bring together in a crowd. [< Lat. *congregare.*] **—con′gre·ga′tor** *n.*

con·gre·ga·tion (kŏng′grĭ-gā′shən) *n.* **1.** An act of congregating. **2.** An assemblage; gathering. **3.** A group of people gathered for religious worship.

con·gre·ga·tion·al (kŏng′grĭ-gā′shə-nəl) *adj.* **1.** Of or pertaining to a congregation. **2.** **Congregational.** Of or pertaining to a Protestant denomination in which each member church is self-governing. **—con′gre·ga′tion·al·ism** *n.* **—con′gre·ga′tion·al·ist** *n.*

con·gress (kŏng′grĭs) *n.* **1.** A formal assembly or meeting to discuss problems. **2.** A national legislature, esp. of a republic. **3. Congress.** The U.S. legislature, consisting of the Senate and House of Representatives. [< Lat. *congressus.*]

con·gres·sion·al (kən-grĕsh′ə-nəl) *adj.* **1.** Of or pertaining to a congress. **2. Congressional.** Of or pertaining to the U.S. Congress.

con·gress·man *or* **Con·gress·man** (kŏng′-grĭs-mən) *n.* A member of the U.S. Congress. **con·gress·wom·an** *or* **Con·gress·wom·an** (kŏng′grĭs-wŏom′ən) *n.* A female member of the U.S. Congress.

con·gru·ent (kŏng′grōō-ənt, kən-grōō′ənt) *adj.* **1.** Corresponding; congruous. **2.** Coinciding exactly when superimposed: *congruent triangles.* [< Lat. *congruere,* to agree.] **—con·gru′ence** *n.* **—con′gru·ent·ly** *adv.*

con·gru·ous (kŏng′grōō-əs) *adj.* **1.** Corre-

sponding in character or kind; harmonious. **2.** Congruent.

con·ic (kŏn′ĭk) *or* **con·i·cal** (-ĭ-kəl) *adj.* Of or shaped like a cone.

co·ni·fer (kŏn′ə-fər, kō′nə-) *n.* A cone-bearing tree, as a pine or fir. [< Lat., cone-bearing.] **—co·nif′er·ous** (kō-nĭf′ər-əs, kə-) *adj.*

con·jec·ture (kən-jĕk′chər) *n.* Inference based on inconclusive evidence; guesswork. [< Lat. *conicere,* to infer.] **—con·jec′tur·a·ble** *adj.* **—con·jec′tur·al** *adj.* **—con·jec′ture** *v.* **—con·jec′tur·er** *n.*

con·join (kən-join′) *v.* To join together; connect; unite. **—con·join′er** *n.* **—con·joint′** *adj.* **—con·joint′ly** *adv.*

con·ju·gal (kŏn′jŏō-gəl, -jə-) *adj.* Of marriage or the marital relationship. [< Lat. *conjunx,* spouse.] **—con′ju·gal·ly** *adv.*

con·ju·gate (kŏn′jə-gāt′) *v.* **-gat·ed, -gat·ing.** To inflect a verb. **—***adj.* (kŏn′jə-gĭt, -gāt′). **1.** Joined together, esp. in pairs. **2.** Pertaining to words having the same derivation and usu. a related meaning. **—***n.* (kŏn′jə-gĭt, -gāt′). One of two or more conjugate words. [< Lat. *conjugare,* to yoke together.] **—con′ju·ga′tive** *adj.* **—con′ju·ga′tor** *n.*

con·ju·ga·tion (kŏn′jə-gā′shən) *n.* **1. a.** The inflection of a verb. **b.** A presentation of the complete set of inflected forms of a verb. **2.** An act or process of sexual joining in reproduction. **—con′ju·ga′tion·al** *adj.* **—con′ju·ga′tion·al·ly** *adv.*

con·junct (kən-jŭngkt′, kŏn′jŭngkt′) *adj.* Joined together; united. [< Lat. *conjunctus.*] **—con·junct′ly** *adv.*

con·junc·tion (kən-jŭngk′shən) *n.* **1.** A joining together; combination or association. **2.** The occurrence together of two events, conditions, etc. **3.** A word that connects other words, phrases, clauses, or sentences. **—con·junc′tion·al** *adj.* **—con·junc′tion·al·ly** *adv.*

con·junc·ti·va (kŏn′jŭngk-tī′və) *n., pl.* **-vas** *or* **-vae** (-vē′). The mucous membrane that lines the inner surface of the eyelid and the exposed surface of the eyeball. [< Med. Lat. *(membrana) conjunctiva,* connective (membrane).] **—con′junc·ti′val** *adj.*

con·junc·tive (kən-jŭngk′tĭv) *adj.* **1.** Connective. **2.** Joined together; combined. **3.** Used as a conjunction. **—***n.* A connective word, esp. a conjunction. **—con·junc′tive·ly** *adv.*

con·junc·ti·vi·tis (kən-jŭngk′tə-vī′tĭs) *n.* Inflammation of the conjunctiva.

con·junc·ture (kən-jŭngk′chər) *n.* **1.** A combination of circumstances or events. **2.** A critical set of circumstances.

con·jure (kŏn′jər, kən-jōōr′) *v.* **-jured, -jur·ing.** **1.** To entreat solemnly, esp. by an oath. **2.** To summon (a spirit) by sorcery. **3.** To effect by magic or legerdemain. **—***phrasal verb.* **conjure up.** To contrive, imagine, or evoke. [< Lat. *conjurare,* to swear together.] **—con′ju·ra′tion** *n.* **—con′jur·er** *or* **con′jur·or** *n.*

conk (kŏngk, kôngk) *v. Slang.* To hit, esp. on the head. **—***phrasal verb.* **conk out.** To fail suddenly. [Orig. unknown.]

con·nect (kə-nĕkt′) *v.* **1.** To join or become joined; link; unite. **2.** To associate or think of as related. [< Lat. *connectere.*] **—con·nec′tor** *or* **con·nect′er** *n.*

con·nec·tion (kə-nĕk′shən) *n.* **1.** Union; junction. **2.** A bond; link. **3.** An association or relation. **4.** Logical ordering of words or ideas; coherence. **5.** The relation of a word to its context. **6.** connections. People with whom one is associated. **7.** A distant relative. **8.** A transfer from one plane, train, or bus to another.

con·nec·tive (kə-nĕk′tĭv) *adj.* Serving or tending to connect. —*n.* A connecting word, such as a conjunction. —**con·nec′tive·ly** *adv.* —**con·nec·tiv′i·ty** *n.*

con·nip·tion (kə-nĭp′shən) *n. Informal.* A fit of violent emotion. [Orig. unknown.]

con·nive (kə-nīv′) *v.* **-nived, -niv·ing. 1.** To feign ignorance of a wrong, thus implying consent. **2.** To cooperate secretly; conspire. [Lat. *connivēre.*] —**con·niv′ance** *n.*

con·nois·seur (kŏn′ə-sûr′) *n.* An informed and astute judge in matters of taste; expert. [Obs. Fr., ult. < Lat. *cognoscere,* to learn.]

con·no·ta·tion (kŏn′ə-tā′shən) *n.* A secondary meaning suggested by a word in addition to its literal meaning. —**con′no·ta′tive** *adj.* —**con′no·ta′tive·ly** *adv.*

con·note (kə-nōt′) *v.* **-not·ed, -not·ing. 1.** To suggest or imply in addition to literal meaning. **2.** To involve as a condition or consequence. [< Med. Lat. *connotare,* to mark in addition.]

con·nu·bi·al (kə-nōō′bē-əl, -nyōō′-) *adj.* Of marriage or the married state; conjugal. [Lat. *connubialis.*] —**con·nu′bi·al·ly** *adv.*

con·quer (kŏng′kər) *v.* **1.** To defeat or subdue, as by force of arms. **2.** To overcome. [< Lat. *conquirere,* to procure.] —**con′quer·a·ble** *adj.* —**con′quer·or** *n.*

con·quest (kŏn′kwĕst′, kŏng′-) *n.* **1.** The act or process of conquering. **2.** Something acquired by conquering.

con·quis·ta·dor (kŏn-kwĭs′tə-dôr′, kŏng-kēs′-) *n., pl.* **-dors** or **-do·res** (-dôr′ās, -ēz). One of the Spanish conquerors of Mexico and Peru in the 16th cent. [Sp.]

con·san·guin·e·ous (kŏn′săng-gwĭn′ē-əs) *adj.* Related by blood. [Lat. *consanguineus.*] —**con′san·guin′i·ty** *n.*

con·science (kŏn′shəns) *n.* **1.** The faculty of recognizing the distinction between right and wrong in regard to one's own conduct. **2.** Conformity to one's own sense of right conduct. [< Lat. *conscire,* to know wrong.]

con·sci·en·tious (kŏn′shē-ĕn′shəs) *adj.* **1.** Scrupulous; honest. **2.** Thorough and painstaking; careful. —**con′sci·en′tious·ly** *adv.* —**con′sci·en′tious·ness** *n.*

conscientious objector *n.* One who refuses to serve in the armed forces on the basis of moral or religious beliefs.

con·scious (kŏn′shəs) *adj.* **1. a.** Having an awareness of one's own existence and environment. **b.** Capable of complex response to environment. **c.** Not asleep; awake. **2.** Subjectively known: *conscious remorse.* **3.** Intentional; deliberate: *a conscious insult.* [Lat. *conscius,* knowing with others.] —**con′scious·ly** *adv.* —**con′scious·ness** *n.*

consciousness-raising *n.* A process of achieving greater awareness of one's needs in order to fulfill one's potential as an individual. **2.** A technique whereby one is made aware of discrimination against a particular class of people who have been oppressed.

con·script (kən-skrĭpt′) *v.* To enroll compulsorily for service in the armed forces; draft. —*n.* (kŏn′skrĭpt′). One who is drafted into

the armed forces. [< Lat. *conscribere,* to enroll.] —**con·scrip′tion** *n.*

con·se·crate (kŏn′sĭ-krāt′) *v.* **-crat·ed, -crat·ing. 1.** To make or declare sacred. **2.** *Theol.* To change (the elements of the Eucharist) into the body and blood of Christ. **3.** To initiate (a priest) into the order of bishops. **4.** To dedicate to some service or goal. [< Lat. *consecrare.*] —**con′se·cra′tion** *n.* —**con′se·cra′tor** *n.*

con·sec·u·tive (kən-sĕk′yə-tĭv) *adj.* Following successively without interruption. [< Lat. *consequi,* to follow up.] —**con·sec′u·tive·ly** *adv.* —**con·sec′u·tive·ness** *n.*

con·sen·sus (kən-sĕn′səs) *n.* Collective opinion; general agreement. [Lat. < *consentire,* to agree.]
Usage: The phrase *consensus of opinion* is considered to be redundant because *consensus* by itself denotes a general opinion.

con·sent (kən-sĕnt′) *v.* To give assent or permission; agree. —*n.* Agreement and acceptance. [< Lat. *consentire.*]

con·se·quence (kŏn′sĭ-kwĕns′, -kwəns) *n.* **1.** An effect; result. **2.** Significance; importance: *an issue of consequence.*

con·se·quent (kŏn′sĭ-kwĕnt′, -kwənt) *adj.* Following as an effect, result, or conclusion. [< Lat. *consequi,* to follow up.] —**con′se·quent′ly** *adv.*

con·se·quen·tial (kŏn′sĭ-kwĕn′shəl) *adj.* **1.** Having important consequences. **2.** Conceited; pompous. —**con′se·quen′ti·al′i·ty** *n.* —**con′se·quen′tial·ly** *adv.*

con·ser·va·tion (kŏn′sər-vā′shən) *n.* **1.** The act or process of conserving. **2.** The controlled use and systematic protection of natural resources. —**con′ser·va′tion·al** *adj.* —**con′ser·va′tion·ist** *n.*

con·ser·va·tism (kən-sûr′və-tĭz′əm) *n.* The tendency to maintain the existing order and resist change.

con·ser·va·tive (kən-sûr′və-tĭv) *adj.* **1.** Favoring preservation of the existing order. **2.** Moderate; prudent; cautious. **3.** Traditional in manner or style. **4.** Tending to conserve; preservative. —*n.* A conservative person. —**con·ser′va·tive·ly** *adv.* —**con·ser′va·tive·ness** *n.*

con·ser·va·tor (kən-sûr′və-tər, kŏn′sər-vā′tər) *n.* **1.** A protector. **2.** *Law.* A guardian.

con·ser·va·to·ry (kən-sûr′və-tôr′ē, -tōr′ē) *n., pl.* **-ries. 1.** A glass-enclosed room or greenhouse in which plants are grown. **2.** A school of music or drama.

con·serve (kən-sûrv′) *v.* **-served, -serv·ing. 1.** To protect from loss or depletion; preserve. **2.** To preserve (fruits). —*n.* (kŏn′sûrv). A jam made of two or more fruits stewed in sugar. [< Lat. *conservare.*] —**con·serv′a·ble** *adj.* —**con·serv′er** *n.*

con·sid·er (kən-sĭd′ər) *v.* **1.** To deliberate upon; examine. **2.** To think or deem. **3.** To believe; judge. [< Lat. *considerare.*]

con·sid·er·a·ble (kən-sĭd′ər-ə-bəl) *adj.* **1.** Fairly large in amount, extent, or degree. **2.** Worthy of consideration; important; significant. —**con·sid′er·a·bly** *adv.*

con·sid·er·ate (kən-sĭd′ər-ĭt) *adj.* Having regard for the needs or feelings of others; thoughtful. —**con·sid′er·ate·ly** *adv.* —**con·sid′er·ate·ness** *n.*

con·sid·er·a·tion (kən-sĭd′ə-rā′shən) *n.* **1.** Deliberation. **2.** A factor to be considered in making a decision. **3.** Thoughtful concern for others. **4.** Recompense.

con·sid·ered (kən-sĭd′ərd) *adj.* Reached after careful thought.

con·sid·er·ing (kən-sĭd′ər-ĭng) *prep.* In view of. —*adv. Informal.* All things considered.

con·sign (kən-sīn′) *v.* **1.** To give over to the care of another; entrust. **2.** To deliver (merchandise) for sale. **3.** To assign to a less important position; relegate. [< Lat. *consignare,* to attest.] —**con·sign′a·ble** *adj.* —**con·sign′ee** *n.* —**con·sig′nor** or **con·sign′er** *n.*

con·sign·ment (kən-sīn′mənt) *n.* A shipment of goods or a cargo to an agent for sale or custody. —*idiom.* **on consignment.** Sent to a retailer with payment due following sale.

con·sist (kən-sĭst′) *v.* **1.** To be made up of composed: *New York City consists of five boroughs.* **2.** To be inherent. [Lat. *consistere,* to stand still.]

con·sis·ten·cy (kən-sĭs′tən-sē) *n., pl.* -**cies.** Also **con·sis·tence** (-təns). **1.** Agreement or compatibility among things or parts. **2.** Uniformity. **3.** Degree of texture or firmness. —**con·sis′tent** *adj.* —**con·sis′tent·ly** *adv.*

con·sis·to·ry (kən-sĭs′tə-rē) *n., pl.* -**ries.** A session of cardinals presided over by the pope.

con·sole[1] (kən-sōl′) *v.* -**soled, -sol·ing.** To comfort; solace. [< Lat. *consolari.*] —**con·sol′a·ble** *adj.* —**con·so·la′tion** *n.* —**con·sol′er** *n.* —**con·sol′ing·ly** *adv.*

con·sole[2] (kŏn′sōl′) *n.* **1.** A cabinet for a radio or television set, designed to stand on the floor. **2.** The part of an organ containing the keyboard, stops, and pedals. **3.** A control panel. [Fr.]

con·sol·i·date (kən-sŏl′ĭ-dāt′) *v.* -**dat·ed, -dat·ing. 1.** To form into a compact mass; solidify. **2.** To unite into one system or body; combine. [Lat. *consolidare.*] —**con·sol′i·da′tion** *n.* —**con·sol′i·da′tor** *n.*

con·som·mé (kŏn′sə-mā′) *n.* A clear soup made of meat or vegetable stock. [Fr., p.p. of *consommer,* to use up.]

con·so·nance (kŏn′sə-nəns) *n.* **1.** Agreement; harmony. **2.** A repetition of terminal consonant sounds of words, as *rain* and *tone.*

con·so·nant (kŏn′sə-nənt) *adj.* **1.** In agreement or accord. **2.** Harmonious in sound. —*n.* **1.** A speech sound produced by a partial or complete obstruction of the stream of air. **2.** A letter or character representing a consonant. [< Lat. *consonare,* to agree.] —**con′so·nan′tal** (-năn′tl) *adj.* —**con′so·nan′tal·ly** *adv.* —**con′so·nant·ly** *adv.*

con·sort (kŏn′sôrt′) *n.* A husband or wife, esp. of a monarch. —*v.* (kən-sôrt′). **1.** To keep company; associate. **2.** To be in agreement. [< Lat. *consors,* partner.]

con·sor·ti·um (kən-sôr′tē-əm, -shē-) *n., pl.* -**ti·a** (-tē-ə, -shē-ə). **1.** A usu. international association of banks, corporations, or other financial institutions to effect a venture, such as an industry, requiring extensive capital investments. **2.** A conglomerate or partnership. [Lat., fellowship.]

con·spic·u·ous (kən-spĭk′yōō-əs) *adj.* **1.** Obvious. **2.** Prominent; remarkable. [< Lat. *conspicere,* to observe.] —**con·spic′u·ous·ly** *adv.* —**con·spic′u·ous·ness** *n.*

con·spir·a·cy (kən-spĭr′ə-sē) *n., pl.* -**cies.** A plot, esp. an illegal one. [< Lat. *conspiratio.*] —**con·spir′a·tor** *n.* —**con·spir′a·to′ri·al** *adj.* —**con·spir′a·to′ri·al·ly** *adv.*

con·spire (kən-spīr′) *v.* -**spired, -spir·ing. 1.** To plan together secretly to commit an illegal act. **2.** To work or act together; combine. [< Lat. *conspirare.*]

con·sta·ble (kŏn′stə-bəl, kŭn′-) *n.* A peace officer or policeman. [< LLat. *comes stabuli,* officer of the stable.]

con·stab·u·lar·y (kən-stăb′yə-lĕr′ē) *n., pl.* -**ies. 1.** The body of constables of a district or city. **2.** An armed police force organized like a military unit.

con·stant (kŏn′stənt) *adj.* **1.** Continually recurring; persistent. **2.** Unchanging; invariable. **3.** Steadfast. —*n.* **1.** A thing that is unchanging or invariable. **2.** A condition, factor, or quantity that is invariant in specified circumstances. [< Lat. *constare,* to stand together.] —**con′stan·cy** *n.* —**con′stant·ly** *adv.*

constant dollars *pl.n.* A measure of the cost of goods or services with the effects of inflation removed.

con·stel·la·tion (kŏn′stə-lā′shən) *n.* **1.** Any of 88 groups of stars considered to resemble and named after various mythological characters, inanimate objects, and animals. **2.** The position of the stars at the time of one's birth, regarded as determining one's character or fate. **3.** A grouping or configuration. [< LLat. *constellatio.*]

con·ster·na·tion (kŏn′stər-nā′shən) *n.* Great confusion or dismay. [< Lat. *consternare,* to perplex.]

con·sti·pa·tion (kŏn′stə-pā′shən) *n.* Difficult, incomplete, or infrequent movement of the bowels. [< Lat. *constipare,* to press together.] —**con′sti·pate′** *v.*

con·stit·u·en·cy (kən-stĭch′ōō-ən-sē) *n., pl.* -**cies. 1.** A body of voters. **2.** A district represented by an elected legislator. **3.** A group of supporters.

con·stit·u·ent (kən-stĭch′ōō-ənt) *adj.* **1.** Serving as part of a whole; component. **2.** Empowered to elect. **3.** Authorized to make or amend a constitution. —*n.* **1.** One represented by an elected official. **2.** A component. [< Lat. *constituere,* to set up.] —**con·stit′u·ent·ly** *adv.*

con·sti·tute (kŏn′stĭ-tōōt′, -tyōōt′) *v.* -**tut·ed, -tut·ing. 1.** To make up; compose. **2.** To set up; establish. **3.** To appoint, as to an office; designate. [< Lat. *constituere,* to set up.]

con·sti·tu·tion (kŏn′stĭ-tōō′shən, -tyōō′-) *n.* **1.** The act or process of constituting. **2. a.** The composition of something; make-up. **b.** The physical make-up of a person. **3.** The basic law of a politically organized body. **4. the Constitution.** The written constitution of the United States, adopted in 1787 and put into effect in 1789.

con·sti·tu·tion·al (kŏn′stĭ-tōō′shə-nəl, -tyōō′-) *adj.* **1.** Basic; essential. **2.** Contained in, consistent with, or operating under a constitution. —*n.* A walk taken regularly for one's health. —**con′sti·tu′tion·al′i·ty** *n.* —**con′sti·tu′tion·al·ly** *adv.*

con·sti·tu·tive (kŏn′stĭ-tōō′tĭv, -tyōō′-) *adj.* Essential. —**con′sti·tu′tive·ly** *adv.*

con·strain (kən-strān′) *v.* **1.** To compel;

oblige. **2.** To confine. **3.** To restrain. [< Lat. *constringere,* to compress.] —**con·strain'er** *n.*

con·strained (kən-strānd') *adj.* Forced; unnatural. —**con·strain·ed·ly** (-strā'nĭd-lē) *adv.*

con·straint (kən-strānt') *n.* **1.** Compulsion. **2.** Something that restricts. **3.** Restraint. **4.** Lack of ease; embarrassment.

con·strict (kən-strĭkt') *v.* To compress, contract, or squeeze. [< Lat. *constringere.*] —**con·stric'tion** *n.* —**con·stric'tive** *adj.* —**con·stric'tive·ly** *adv.*

con·struct (kən-strŭkt') *v.* To build; erect; make. [< Lat. *construere.*] —**con·struc'ti·ble** *adj.* —**con·struc'tor** or **con·struct'er** *n.*

con·struc·tion (kən-strŭk'shən) *n.* **1.** The act, process, or business of building. **2.** A structure. **3.** *Gram.* The arrangement of words to form a meaningful phrase, clause, or sentence. —**con·struc'tion·al** *adj.* —**con·struc'tion·al·ly** *adv.*

con·struc·tive (kən-strŭk'tĭv) *adj.* **1.** Useful; helpful. **2.** Structural. —**con·struc'tive·ly** *adv.* —**con·struc'tive·ness** *n.*

con·strue (kən-strōō') *v.* **-strued, -stru·ing. 1.** *Gram.* **a.** To analyze the structure of (a clause or sentence). **b.** To use syntactically. **2.** To interpret. **3.** To translate. [< Lat. *construere,* to build.]

con·sul (kŏn'səl) *n.* **1.** Either of the two chief magistrates of the Roman Republic, elected for a term of one year. **2.** An official appointed by a government to reside in a foreign city and represent its citizens there. [< Lat.] —**con'su·lar** *adj.* —**con'sul·ship'** *n.*

con·su·late (kŏn'sə-lĭt) *n.* The building or offices occupied by a consul.

con·sult (kən-sŭlt') *v.* **1.** To seek advice or information of. **2.** To exchange views; confer. [< Lat. *consulere,* to take counsel.] —**con·sult'ant** *n.* —**con·sul·ta'tion** *n.* —**con·sult'a·tive** *adj.*

con·sume (kən-sōōm') *v.* **-sumed, -sum·ing. 1.** To eat or drink up; ingest. **2.** To use up; expend. **3.** To waste; squander. **4.** To destroy, as by fire. **5.** To absorb; engross. [< Lat. *consumere.*] —**con·sum'a·ble** *adj.* & *n.*

con·sum·er (kən-sōō'mər) *n.* **1.** One that consumes. **2.** A buyer.

con·sum·er·ism (kən-sōō'mə-rĭz'əm) *n.* A movement seeking to protect the rights of consumers by requiring honest advertising, fair pricing, and improved safety standards. —**con·sum'er·ist** *n.*

consumer price index *n.* An index of prices used to measure the change in the cost of basic goods and services in comparison with a fixed base period.

con·sum·mate (kŏn'sə-māt') *v.* **-mat·ed, -mat·ing. 1.** To bring to completion; conclude. **2.** To fulfill (a marriage) with the first act of sexual intercourse. —*adj.* (kən-sŭm'ĭt). **1.** Perfect. **2.** Complete; utter. [< Lat. *consummare.*] —**con·sum'mate·ly** *adv.* —**con'sum·ma'tion** *n.* —**con'sum·ma'tor** *n.*

con·sump·tion (kən-sŭmp'shən) *n.* **1. a.** The act or process of consuming. **b.** The amount consumed. **2.** The using up of consumer goods and services. **3.** *Pathol.* **a.** A wasting away of tissues. **b.** Tuberculosis. [< Lat. *consumptio.*]

con·sump·tive (kən-sŭmp'tĭv) *adj.* **1.** Wasteful; destructive. **2.** *Pathol.* Of or afflicted with consumption. —*n.* One who has consumption. —**con·sump'tive·ly** *adv.*

con·tact (kŏn'tăkt') *n.* **1.** A coming together or touching of objects or surfaces. **2.** A relationship; association. **3.** Connection. **4.** A conducting connection between two electric conductors. —*v.* (kŏn'tăkt, kən-tăkt'). **1.** To come or put into contact. **2.** To get in touch with. —*adj.* (kŏn'tăkt'). **1.** Of or making contact. **2.** Caused or transmitted by touching. [< Lat. *contactus,* p.p. of *contingere,* to touch.]

contact lens *n.* A thin corrective lens worn directly on the cornea.

con·ta·gion (kən-tā'jən) *n.* **1. a.** The transmission of disease by contact. **b.** A disease so transmitted. **2.** The tendency to spread, as of an emotional state. [Lat. *contagio.*]

con·ta·gious (kən-tā'jəs) *adj.* **1.** Transmissible by contact. **2.** Carrying or capable of carrying disease. **3.** Tending to spread; catching. —**con·ta'gious·ly** *adv.* —**con·ta'gious·ness** *n.*

con·tain (kən-tān') *v.* **1.** To enclose. **2.** To comprise; include. **3.** To be able to hold. **4.** To hold back; restrain. [< Lat. *continēre.*] —**con·tain'a·ble** *adj.*

con·tain·er (kən-tā'nər) *n.* A receptacle.

con·tain·er·ize (kən-tā'nə-rīz') *v.* **-ized, -iz·ing.** To package (cargo) in standardized containers to facilitate shipping and handling. —**con·tain'er·i·za'tion** *n.*

container ship *n.* A ship for carrying containerized cargo.

con·tam·i·nate (kən-tăm'ə-nāt') *v.* **-nat·ed, -nat·ing.** To make impure by contact or mixture; pollute. [< Lat. *contaminare.*] —**con·tam'i·nant** *n.* —**con·tam'i·na'tion** *n.* —**con·tam'i·na·tive** *adj.* —**con·tam'i·na'tor** *n.*

con·temn (kən-tĕm') *v.* To view with contempt; despise. [< Lat. *contemnere.*]

con·tem·plate (kŏn'təm-plāt') *v.* **-plat·ed, -plat·ing. 1.** To ponder or consider thoughtfully. **2.** To intend or anticipate. [< Lat. *contemplari.*] —**con'tem·pla'tion** *n.* —**con·tem'pla·tive** (kən-tĕm'plə-tĭv) *adj.* & *n.* —**con·tem'pla·tive·ly** *adv.* —**con·tem·pla'tor** *n.*

con·tem·po·ra·ne·ous (kən-tĕm'pə-rā'nē-əs) *adj.* Contemporary. [Lat. *contemporaneus.*] —**con·tem'po·ra'ne·ous·ly** *adv.* —**con·tem'po·ra'ne·ous·ness** *n.*

con·tem·po·rar·y (kən-tĕm'pə-rĕr'ē) *adj.* **1.** Living or happening during the same period of time. **2.** Current; modern. —*n., pl.* **-ies. 1.** One of the same time or age as another. **2.** A person of the present time.

con·tempt (kən-tĕmpt') *n.* **1. a.** A feeling that someone or something is inferior and undesirable. **b.** The condition of being regarded in this way. **2.** Open disrespect or willful disobedience. [< Lat. *contemptus,* p.p. of *contemnere,* to scorn.]

con·tempt·i·ble (kən-tĕmp'tə-bəl) *adj.* Deserving contempt; despicable. —**con·tempt'i·bil'i·ty** or **con·tempt'i·ble·ness** *n.* —**con·tempt'i·bly** *adv.*

con·temp·tu·ous (kən-tĕmp'chōō-əs) *adj.* Manifesting or feeling contempt; scornful. —**con·temp'tu·ous·ly** *adv.* —**con·temp'tu·ous·ness** *n.*

con·tend (kən-tĕnd') *v.* **1.** To strive, vie, or dispute. **2.** To maintain or assert. [< Lat. *contendere.*] —**con·tend'er** *n.*

con·tent¹ (kŏn'tĕnt') *n.* **1.** Often **contents.** Something contained in a receptacle. **2.** Often **contents.** Subject matter, as of a written work. **3.** Meaning or significance. **4.** The proportion of a specified substance. [< Lat. *contentus,* p.p. of *continēre,* to contain.]

con·tent² (kən-tĕnt´) *adj.* Satisfied. —*v.* To make satisfied. —*n.* Satisfaction. [< Lat. *contentus*, p.p. of *continēre*, to contain.]

con·tent·ed (kən-tĕn´tĭd) *adj.* Satisfied. —**con·tent´ed·ly** *adv.* —**con·tent´ed·ness** *n.*

con·ten·tion (kən-tĕn´shən) *n.* Dispute; controversy. [< Lat. *contendere*, to contend.] —**con·ten´tious** *adj.* —**con·ten´tious·ly** *adv.* —**con·ten´tious·ness** *n.*

con·tent·ment (kən-tĕnt´mənt) *n.* The condition of being contented.

con·ter·mi·nous (kən-tûr´mə-nəs) *adj.* Having a boundary in common; contiguous. [Lat. *conterminus*.] —**con·ter´mi·nous·ly** *adv.*

con·test (kŏn´tĕst´) *n.* 1. A struggle; fight. 2. A competition. —*v.* (kən-tĕst´, kŏn´tĕst´). 1. To compete or strive for. 2. To dispute; challenge. [< Lat. *contestari*, to call to witness.] —**con·test´a·ble** *adj.* —**con·test´er** *n.*

con·test·ant (kən-tĕs´tənt, kŏn´tĕs´tənt) *n.* A competitor or challenger.

con·text (kŏn´tĕkst´) *n.* 1. The setting of words and ideas in which a particular word or statement appears. 2. The overall situation in which an event occurs. [< Lat. *contexere*, to weave.] —**con·tex´tu·al** (kən-tĕks´chōō-əl) *adj.* —**con·tex´tu·al·ly** *adv.*

con·tig·u·ous (kən-tĭg´yōō-əs) *adj.* 1. Touching. 2. Next or adjacent to; nearby. [< Lat. *contingere*, to touch.] —**con·ti·gu´i·ty** (kŏn´-tĭ-gyōō´ĭ-tē) *n.* —**con·tig´u·ous·ly** *adv.* —**con·tig´u·ous·ness** *n.*

con·ti·nence (kŏn´tə-nəns) *n.* 1. Self-restraint, esp. abstention from sexual activity. 2. Ability to control bladder or bowel functions. [< Lat. *continēre*, to contain.] —**con´ti·nent** *adj.*

con·ti·nent (kŏn´tə-nənt) *n.* 1. One of the principal land masses of the earth. 2. **the Continent**. The mainland of Europe. [< Lat. *(terra) continens*, continuous (land).]

con·ti·nen·tal (kŏn´tə-nĕn´tl) *adj.* 1. Of or like a continent. 2. Often **Continental**. European. 3. **Continental**. Of or pertaining to the American colonies during the Revolution. —*n.* **Continental**. A soldier in the Continental Army. —**con·ti·nen´tal·ly** *adv.*

continental divide *n.* An extensive stretch of high ground from each side of which the river systems of a continent flow in opposite directions.

continental shelf *n.* A gen. flat, shallow submerged portion of a continent.

con·tin·gen·cy (kən-tĭn´jən-sē) *n., pl.* **-cies**. A fortuitous or possible event.

con·tin·gent (kən-tĭn´jənt) *adj.* 1. Liable to occur but not certain; possible. 2. Conditional. 3. Accidental. —*n.* 1. A quota, as of troops. 2. A representative group. [< Lat. *contingere*, to touch.]

con·tin·u·al (kən-tĭn´yōō-əl) *adj.* 1. Recurring frequently. 2. Continuous; incessant. —**con·tin´u·al·ly** *adv.*

con·tin·u·ance (kən-tĭn´yōō-əns) *n.* 1. The act or fact of continuing. 2. Duration. 3. Unbroken sequence. 4. Postponement or adjournment of legal proceedings.

con·tin·u·a·tion (kən-tĭn´yōō-ā´shən) *n.* 1. The act, state, or fact of continuing. 2. A sequel or supplement.

con·tin·ue (kən-tĭn´yōō) *v.* **-ued, -u·ing**. 1. To persist. 2. To endure; last. 3. To remain in a state, capacity, or place. 4. To go on after an interruption; resume. 5. To extend. 6. To retain. 7. *Law*. To postpone or adjourn. [< Lat. *continuare*.] —**con·tin´u·er** *n.*

con·ti·nu·i·ty (kŏn´tə-nōō´ĭ-tē, -nyōō´-) *n., pl.* **-ties**. 1. The condition or quality of being continuous. 2. An uninterrupted succession.

con·tin·u·ous (kən-tĭn´yōō-əs) *adj.* Continuing without interruption or cessation. —**con·tin´u·ous·ly** *adv.* —**con·tin´u·ous·ness** *n.*

Syns: *continuous, ceaseless, constant, continual, endless, eternal, everlasting, incessant, interminable, nonstop, perpetual, relentless, timeless adj.*

con·tin·u·um (kən-tĭn´yōō-əm) *n., pl.* **-u·a** (-yōō-ə) *or* **-ums**. Something in which no part can be distinguished from neighboring parts except by arbitrary division. [< Lat. *continuus*, continuous.]

con·tort (kən-tôrt´) *v.* To twist or wrench out of shape. [< Lat. *contorquēre*, to twist together.] —**con·tor´tion** *n.*

con·tor·tion·ist (kən-tôr´shə-nĭst) *n.* One who performs acrobatic feats involving extraordinary postures. —**con·tor´tion·is´tic** *adj.*

contortionist

con·tour (kŏn´tōōr´) *n.* 1. The outline of a figure, body, or mass. 2. Often **contours**. The surface of a curving form. —*adj.* Following the contour or form of something. [< Ital. *contornare*, to draw in outline.] —**con´tour** *v.*

contra- *pref.* Against, opposing, or contrary: *contradistinction*. [< Lat. *contra*, against.]

con·tra·band (kŏn´trə-bănd´) *n.* 1. Goods prohibited in trade. 2. Smuggled goods. [< Ital. *contrabbando*.]

con·tra·cep·tion (kŏn´trə-sĕp´shən) *n.* The prevention of conception. —**con´tra·cep´tive** (-tĭv) *adj. & n.*

con·tract (kŏn´trăkt´) *n.* An enforceable agreement; covenant. —*v.* (kən-trăkt´, kŏn´-trăkt´). 1. To enter into or establish by contract. 2. To catch (a disease). 3. To shrink by drawing together. 4. To shorten (a word or words) by omitting or combining some of the letters. [< Lat. *contrahere*, to draw together.] —**con·tract´i·bil´i·ty** *n.* —**con·tract´i·ble** *adj.* —**con·trac´tion** *n.* —**con·trac´tor** *n.*

Syns: *contract, compress, condense, constrict, shrink v.*

con·trac·tile (kən-trăk´təl, -tīl´) *adj.* Capable of contracting.

con·trac·tu·al (kən-trăk´chōō-əl) *adj.* Of or having the nature of a contract. —**con·trac´tu·al·ly** *adv.*

con·tra·dict (kŏn'trə-dĭkt') v. **1.** To assert the opposite of. **2.** To deny the statement of. **3.** To be contrary to or inconsistent with. [< Lat. *contradicere*, to speak against.] —**con'tra·dict'a·ble** adj. —**con'tra·dict'er** or **con'tra·dic'tor** n. —**con'tra·dic'tion** n. —**con'tra·dic'to·ri·ness** n. —**con'tra·dic'to·ry** adj.

con·tra·dis·tinc·tion (kŏn'trə-dĭ-stĭngk'shən) n. Distinction by contrast. —**con'tra·dis·tinc'tive** adj.

con·trail (kŏn'trāl') n. A visible trail of water droplets or ice crystals formed in the wake of an aircraft. [CON(DENSATION) + TRAIL.]

con·tra·in·di·cate (kŏn'trə-ĭn'dĭ-kāt') v. **-cat·ed, -cat·ing.** To indicate the inadvisability of. —**con'tra·in'di·ca'tion** n.

con·tral·to (kən-trăl'tō) n., pl. **-tos.** Mus. **1.** The lowest female voice or voice part. **2.** A singer having a contralto voice. [Ital.]

con·trap·tion (kən-trăp'shən) n. Informal. A mechanical device; gadget. [Perh. blend of CONTRIVE and TRAP + -TION.]

con·tra·pun·tal (kŏn'trə-pŭn'tl) adj. Mus. Of or using counterpoint. [< Ital. *contrapunto*, counterpoint.] —**con'tra·pun'tal·ly** adv.

con·tra·ri·e·ty (kŏn'trə-rī'ĭ-tē) n., pl. **-ties.** The condition of being contrary.

con·trar·i·wise (kŏn'trĕr'ē-wīz') adv. **1.** Oppositely. **2.** On the contrary.

con·trar·y (kŏn'trĕr'ē) adj. **1.** Opposite, as in character or direction. **2.** Adverse; unfavorable. **3.** Perverse; willful. **4.** Opposed; counter. —n., pl. **-ies.** Something that is contrary; the opposite. —adv. In opposition; contrariwise. [< Lat. *contra*, against.] —**con'trar·i·ly** adv. —**con'trar·i·ness** n.

con·trast (kən-trăst') v. **1.** To set in opposition in order to show differences. **2.** To show differences when compared. —n. (kŏn'trăst'). **1.** Dissimilarity between things compared. **2.** Something strikingly different from something else. [< Med. Lat. *contrastare*.] —**con·trast'a·ble** adj. —**con·trast'ing·ly** adv.

con·tra·vene (kŏn'trə-vēn') v. **-vened, -ven·ing. 1.** To act or be counter to. **2.** To contradict. [< LLat. *contravenire*, to oppose.] —**con'tra·ven'er** n.

con·tre·temps (kŏn'trə-tŏN', kŏN'trə-täN') n., pl. **-temps** (-tŏNz', -täNz'). An inopportune or embarrassing occurrence. [Fr.]

con·trib·ute (kən-trĭb'yōot) v. **-ut·ed, -ut·ing.** To give up a share to or participate in. [< Lat. *contribuere*, to unite.] —**con'tri·bu'tion** n. —**con·trib'u·tive** adj. —**con·trib'u·tive·ly** adv. —**con·trib'u·tor** n. —**con·trib'u·to·ry** (-tôr'ē, -tōr'ē) adj.

con·trite (kən-trīt', kŏn'trīt') adj. Repentant; penitent. [< Lat. *contritus*, p.p. of *conterere*, to crush.] —**con·trite'ly** adv. —**con·tri'tion** (-trĭsh'ən) n.

con·triv·ance (kən-trī'vəns) n. **1.** A scheme; plan. **2.** A mechanical device.

con·trive (kən-trīv') v. **-trived, -triv·ing. 1.** To devise; plan. **2.** To manage or effect. **3.** To fabricate or make. [< LLat. *contropare*, to compare.] —**con·triv'ed·ly** (-trī'vĭd-lē) adv. —**con·triv'er** n.

con·trol (kən-trōl') v. **-trolled, -trol·ling. 1.** To exercise authority or influence over; direct. **2.** To verify or regulate by systematic comparison. —n. **1.** Power to regulate, direct, or dominate. **2.** Restraint; reserve. **3.** A standard of comparison for verifying the results of an experiment. **4.** Often **controls.** A set of instruments for regulating a machine. [<

Med. Lat. *contrarotulare*, to check by a duplicate register.] —**con·trol'la·bil'i·ty** n. —**con·trol'la·ble** adj.

con·trol·ler (kən-trō'lər) n. **1.** One that controls, esp. an automatic device that regulates the operation of a machine. **2.** A comptroller.

con·tro·ver·sy (kŏn'trə-vûr'sē) n., pl. **-sies.** A dispute, esp. a public one between sides holding opposing views. [< Lat. *controversus*, turned against.] —**con'tro·ver'sial** (-vûr'shəl, -sē-əl) adj. —**con'tro·ver'sial·ly** adv.

con·tro·vert (kŏn'trə-vûrt') v. To contradict; deny. —**con'tro·vert'i·ble** adj.

con·tu·ma·cious (kŏn'tə-mā'shəs) adj. Stubbornly disobedient or rebellious; insubordinate. [< Lat. *contumax*.] —**con'tu·ma'cious·ly** adv. —**con'tu·ma·cy** (-mə-sē) n.

con·tu·me·ly (kŏn'tōō-mə-lē, -tyōō-, -təm-lē) n., pl. **-lies.** Insulting treatment; insolence. [< Lat. *contumelia*.] —**con'tu·me'li·ous** (kŏn'tə-mē'lē-əs) adj. —**con'tu·me'li·ous·ly** adv.

con·tuse (kən-tōōz', -tyōōz') v. **-tused, -tus·ing.** To injure without breaking the skin; bruise. [< Lat. *contundere*, to drink.] —**con·tu'sion** n.

co·nun·drum (kə-nŭn'drəm) n. A riddle. [Orig. unknown.]

con·ur·ba·tion (kŏn'ər-bā'shən) n. A predominantly urban region including adjacent towns. [CON- + Lat. *urbs*, city + -ATION.]

con·va·lesce (kŏn'və-lĕs') v. **-lesced, -lesc·ing.** To recuperate from an illness or injury. [Lat. *convalescere*.] —**con'va·les'cence** n. —**con'va·les'cent** adj. & n.

con·vec·tion (kən-vĕk'shən) n. The transfer of heat by fluid motion between regions of unequal density that result from nonuniform heating. [< LLat. *convectus*, p.p. of *convehere*, to carry together.] —**con·vec'tion·al** adj. —**con·vec'tive** adj.

con·vene (kən-vēn') v. **-vened, -ven·ing.** To assemble, meet, or convoke. [< Lat. *convenire*.] —**con·ven'a·ble** adj. —**con·ven'er** n.

con·ven·ience (kən-vēn'yəns) n. **1.** Suitability or handiness. **2.** Personal comfort; material advantage. **3.** Something that increases comfort or makes work less difficult.

con·ven·ient (kən-vēn'yənt) adj. **1.** Suited to one's comfort or needs. **2.** Easy to reach; accessible. [< Lat. *convenire*, to be suitable.] —**con·ven'ient·ly** adv.

Syns: convenient, appropriate, fit[1], good, suitable, useful adj.

con·vent (kŏn'vənt, -vĕnt') n. A monastic community or house, esp. of nuns. [< Lat. *conventus*, assembly.] —**con·ven'tu·al** (kən-vĕn'chōō-əl) adj.

con·ven·ti·cle (kən-vĕn'tĭ-kəl) n. A religious meeting, esp. a secret one. [< Lat. *conventiculum*, dim. of *conventus*, assembly.]

con·ven·tion (kən-vĕn'shən) n. **1. a.** A formal assembly, as of a political party. **b.** The delegates attending such an assembly. **2.** An international agreement or compact. **3.** General usage or custom. **4.** An accepted or prescribed practice. [< Lat. *convenire*, to meet.]

con·ven·tion·al (kən-vĕn'shə-nəl) adj. **1.** Following accepted practice; customary. **2.** Commonplace; ordinary. —**con·ven'tion·al'i·ty** n. —**con·ven'tion·al·ly** adv.

con·ven·tion·al·ize (kən-vĕn'shə-nə-līz') v. **-ized, -iz·ing.** To make conventional. —**con·ven'tion·al·i·za'tion** n.

con·verge (kən-vûrj') v. **-verged, -verg·ing.**

To tend or move toward a common point or result. [LLat. *convergere,* to incline together.] —**con·ver'gence** or **con·ver'gen·cy** *n.* —**con·ver'gent** *adj.*

con·ver·sant (kən-vûr'sənt, kŏn'vər-) *adj.* Familiar, as by study or experience. —**con·ver'sant·ly** *adv.*

con·ver·sa·tion (kŏn'vər-sā'shən) *n.* An informal spoken exchange. —**con'ver·sa'tion·al** *adj.* —**con'ver·sa'tion·al·ly** *adv.*

con·ver·sa·tion·al·ist (kŏn'vər-sā'shə-nə-list) *n.* One given to or skilled at conversation.

conversation piece *n.* An unusual object that arouses comment.

con·verse¹ (kən-vûrs') *v.* **-versed, -vers·ing.** 1. To engage in conversation. 2. To interact with a computer on-line. —*n.* (kŏn'vûrs'). Conversation. [< Lat. *conversari,* to associate with.]

con·verse² (kŏn'vûrs') *n.* The opposite or reverse of something. —*adj.* (kən-vûrs', kŏn'-vûrs'). Opposite; contrary. [< Lat. *conversus,* p.p. of *convertere,* to turn around.] —**con·verse'ly** (kən-vûrs'lē) *adv.*

con·ver·sion (kən-vûr'zhən, -shən) *n.* 1. The act of converting or the condition of being converted. 2. A change in which a person adopts a new religion. 3. The unlawful appropriation of another's property. 4. *Football.* A score made on a try for a point or points after a touchdown.

con·vert (kən-vûrt') *v.* 1. To change into another form, substance, or condition; transform. 2. To persuade or be persuaded to adopt a given religion or belief. 3. To adapt to a new or different purpose. 4. To exchange for something of equal value. 5. To misappropriate. 6. *Football.* To score a point or points after a touchdown. —*n.* (kŏn'vûrt'). One who has adopted a new religion or belief. [< Lat. *convertere,* to turn around.] —**con·vert'er** or **con·ver'tor** *n.*

con·vert·i·ble (kən-vûr'tə-bəl) *adj.* Capable of being converted. —*n.* 1. An automobile with a top that can be folded back or taken off. 2. Something that can be converted.

convertible
1953 Eldorado

con·vex (kŏn-vĕks', kŏn'vĕks') *adj.* Curved outward, as the exterior of a sphere. [Lat. *convexus.*] —**con·vex'i·ty** *n.* —**con·vex'ly** *adv.*

con·vey (kən-vā') *v.* 1. To carry; transport. 2. To transmit. 3. To communicate; impart. [< Med. Lat. *conviare,* to escort.] —**con·vey'a·ble** *adj.* —**con·vey'er** or **con·vey'or** *n.*

con·vey·ance (kən-vā'əns) *n.* 1. The act of conveying. 2. A vehicle. 3. A legal document effecting the transfer of title to property.

con·vict (kən-vĭkt') *v.* To find or prove guilty of an offense or crime. —*n.* (kŏn'vĭkt'). A person found guilty of a crime, esp. one serving a prison sentence. [< Lat. *convicere.*]

con·vic·tion (kən-vĭk'shən) *n.* 1. The act of

convicting or condition of being convicted. 2. A strong opinion or belief.

con·vince (kən-vĭns') *v.* **-vinced, -vinc·ing.** To bring to belief by argument and evidence; persuade. [Lat. *convincere.*] —**con·vinc'er** *n.* —**con·vinc'ing** *adj.* —**con·vinc'ing·ly** *adv.*

con·viv·i·al (kən-vĭv'ē-əl) *adj.* Sociable; jovial. [< Lat. *convivium,* banquet.] —**con·viv·i·al'i·ty** (-ăl'ĭ-tē) *n.* —**con·viv'i·al·ly** *adv.*

con·vo·ca·tion (kŏn'və-kā'shən) *n.* 1. The act of convoking. 2. A formal assembly.

con·voke (kən-vōk') *v.* **-voked, -vok·ing.** To cause to assemble; convene. [< Lat. *convocare.*] —**con·vok'er** *n.*

con·vo·lut·ed (kŏn'və-lōō'tĭd) *adj.* 1. Coiled; twisted. 2. Intricate; complicated. [< Lat. *convolvere,* to interweave.]

con·vo·lu·tion (kŏn'və-lōō'shən) *n.* 1. A tortuous winding, folding, or twisting together. 2. An intricacy. 3. One of the convex folds of the surface of the brain.

con·voy (kŏn'voi', kən-voi') *v.* To escort for protection. —*n.* (kŏn'voi'). 1. A group of ships or vehicles, protected on their way by an armed escort. 2. A group, as of vehicles or people, traveling together for convenience. [< Med. Lat. *conviare,* to escort.]

con·vulse (kən-vŭls') *v.* **-vulsed, -vuls·ing.** 1. To disturb or agitate violently. 2. To cause to have convulsions. [< Lat. *convulsus,* p.p. of *convellere,* to pull violently.] —**con·vul'sive** *adj.* —**con·vul'sive·ly** *adv.*

con·vul·sion (kən-vŭl'shən) *n.* 1. A violent involuntary muscular contraction or a series of such contractions. 2. A violent disturbance. 3. An uncontrolled fit of laughter.

co·ny (kō'nē, kŭn'ē) *n., pl.* **-nies.** Also **co·ney** *pl.* **-neys.** 1. A rabbit or similar animal. 2. The fur of a rabbit. [< Lat. *cuniculus.*]

coo (kōō) *n.* 1. The low, murmuring sound made by a pigeon or dove. 2. A sound similar to a coo. [Imit.] —**coo** *v.*

cook (kŏŏk) *v.* 1. To prepare food for eating by applying heat. 2. To prepare or treat by heating. —*phrasal verb.* **cook up.** *Informal.* To invent; concoct: *cook up an excuse.* —*n.* One who prepares food for eating. [< Lat. *coquere.*]

cook·book (kŏŏk'bŏŏk') *n.* A book of cooking recipes.

cook·er·y (kŏŏk'ə-rē) *n., pl.* **-ies.** The art or practice of preparing food.

cook·out (kŏŏk'out') *n.* A meal cooked and eaten outdoors.

cook·y or **cook·ie** (kŏŏk'ē) *n., pl.* **-ies.** A small, sweet, usu. flat cake. [Du. *koekje,* dim. of *koek,* cake.]

cool (kōōl) *adj.* **-er, -est.** 1. Moderately cold. 2. Giving or allowing relief from heat. 3. Calm; controlled. 4. Indifferent or disdainful; unenthusiastic. 5. Impudent. 6. *Slang.* Excellent. —*v.* 1. To make or become less warm. 2. To make or become less intense. —*n.* 1. Moderate cold. 2. *Slang.* Composure: *lost his cool.* —*idiom.* **cool it.** *Slang.* To calm down; relax. [< OE *cōl.*] —**cool'ly** *adv.* —**cool'ness** *n.*

cool·ant (kōō'lənt) *n.* Something that cools, esp. a fluid that draws off heat by circulating through a machine or over some of its parts.

cool·er (kōō′lər) *n.* 1. A device that cools or keeps something cool. 2. *Slang.* Jail.

coo·lie (kōō′lē) *n.* An unskilled Oriental laborer. [Hindi *kulī.*]

coon (kōōn) *n. Informal.* A raccoon. [< RACCOON.]

coon·skin (kōōn′skĭn′) *n.* 1. The pelt of a raccoon. 2. An article made of coonskin.

coop (kōōp) *n.* A cage, esp. one for poultry. —*v.* To confine in or as if in a coop. [ME *coupe.*]

co·op (kō′ŏp′, kō-ŏp′) *n.* A cooperative.

coo·per (kōō′pər) *n.* One who makes wooden tubs and casks. [< MDu. *cūper* < *cūpe,* cask.] —**coo′per** *v.* —**coo′per·age** (-ĭj) *n.*

co·op·er·ate (kō-ŏp′ə-rāt′) *v.* -at·ed, -at·ing. To work with another toward a common end. [Lat. *cooperari.*] —**co·op′er·a′tion** *n.* —**co·op′er·a′tor** *n.*

co·op·er·a·tive (kō-ŏp′ər-ə-tĭv, -ŏp′rə-, -ə-rā′tĭv) *adj.* 1. Willing to help or cooperate. 2. Engaged in joint economic activity. —*n.* An enterprise owned and operated jointly by those who use its facilities or services. —**co·op′er·a·tive·ly** *adv.* —**co·op′er·a·tive·ness** *n.*

co-opt (kō-ŏpt′) *v.* 1. To elect or appoint as a fellow member or colleague. 2. To appropriate. 3. To take over through assimilation into an established group or culture. [Lat. *cooptare.*] —**co-op·ta′tion** (kō′ŏp-tā′shən) *n.* —**co-op·ta′tive** (-tə-tĭv) *adj.*

co·or·di·nate (kō-ŏr′dn-āt, -ĭt′) *n.* 1. One that is equal in rank or order. 2. *Math.* One of a set of numbers that determines the location of a point in a space of a given dimension. —*adj.* (-ĭt, -āt′). 1. Of equal rank or order. 2. Of or involving coordination. 3. Of or based on coordinates. —*v.* (-āt′) -nat·ed, -nat·ing. 1. To place in the same rank or order. 2. To arrange in proper relative position. 3. To harmonize in a common action. [< CO-ORDINATION.] —**co·or′di·nate·ly** *adv.* —**co·or′di·na·tive** *adj.* —**co·or′di·na·tor** *n.*

co·or·di·na·tion (kō-ŏr′dn-ā′shən) *n.* 1. The act of coordinating or state of being coordinated. 2. The organized action of muscles in the performance of complicated movements. [< Lat. *coordinatio.*]

coot (kōōt) *n.* 1. A short-billed, dark-gray water bird. 2. *Informal.* A foolish old man. [ME *coote.*]

coot

coo·tie (kōō′tē) *n. Slang.* A body louse. [Poss. < Malay *kutu.*]

cop (kŏp) *n. Informal.* A policeman. —*v.* **copped, cop·ping.** *Slang.* 1. To steal. 2. To seize; catch. —*phrasal verb.* **cop out.** *Slang.* To fail or refuse to commit oneself. —**idiom.**

cop a plea. *Slang.* To plead guilty. [Prob. < Du. *kapen,* to catch.]

cope¹ (kōp) *v.* **coped, cop·ing.** To contend or strive, esp. successfully. [< OFr. *couper* < *coup,* blow.]

cope² (kōp) *n.* A long capelike garment worn by priests or bishops. [< LLat. *capa,* cloak.]

cop·i·er (kŏp′ē-ər) *n.* One that copies, esp. an office machine that makes copies.

co·pi·lot (kō′pī′lət) *n.* The second or relief pilot of an aircraft.

cop·ing (kō′pĭng) *n.* The top part of a wall. [< COPE².]

co·pi·ous (kō′pē-əs) *adj.* Ample; abundant. [< Lat. *copia,* abundance.] —**co′pi·ous·ly** *adv.* —**co′pi·ous·ness** *n.*

cop-out (kŏp′out′) *n. Slang.* A failure or refusal to commit oneself.

cop·per (kŏp′ər) *n.* 1. *Symbol* **Cu** A ductile, malleable, reddish-brown metallic element that is an excellent conductor of heat and electricity and is used for electrical wiring, water piping, and corrosion-resistant parts. Atomic number 29; atomic weight 63.54. 2. A copper object or coin. [< Lat. *Cyprium (aes),* (metal) of Cyprus.] —**cop′per·y** *adj.*

cop·per·as (kŏp′ər-əs) *n.* A greenish, crystalline compound, FeSO₄·7H₂0, used in fertilizers and inks and in water purification. [< Med. Lat. *cuperosa.*]

cop·per·head (kŏp′ər-hĕd′) *n.* A venomous reddish-brown snake of eastern United States.

cop·ra (kŏp′rə) *n.* Dried coconut meat from which coconut oil is extracted. [< Malayalam *koppara.*]

copse (kŏps) *n.* A thicket. [< OFr. *couper,* to cut.]

cop·ter (kŏp′tər) *n. Informal.* A helicopter.

cop·u·la (kŏp′yə-lə) *n., pl.* **-las** *or* **-lae** (-lē). A verb, as a form of *be* or *feel,* that identifies the predicate of a sentence with the subject. [Lat., link.] —**cop′u·lar** *adj.* —**cop′u·la·tive** *adj.* —**cop′u·la·tive·ly** *adv.*

cop·u·late (kŏp′yə-lāt′) *v.* **-lat·ed, -lat·ing.** To engage in sexual intercourse. [Lat. *copulare.*] —**cop′u·la′tion** *n.*

cop·y (kŏp′ē) *n., pl.* **-ies.** 1. An imitation or reproduction of something original; duplicate. 2. One specimen of a printed text or picture. 3. A manuscript or other material to be set in type. 4. Suitable source material, as for journalism. —*v.* **-ied, -y·ing.** 1. To make a copy of. 2. To follow as a model; imitate. [< Lat. *copia,* abundance.]

cop·y·book (kŏp′ē-bŏŏk′) *n.* A book of models of penmanship for imitation.

cop·y·cat (kŏp′ē-kăt′) *n.* An imitator.

copy desk *n.* The desk in a newspaper office where copy is edited and prepared for typesetting.

cop·y·right (kŏp′ē-rīt′) *n.* The legal right to exclusive publication, sale, or distribution of a literary or artistic work. —*adj.* Also **copy·right·ed** (-rī′tĭd). Protected by copyright. —*v.* To secure a copyright for.

cop·y·writ·er (kŏp′ē-rī′tər) *n.* One who writes advertising copy.

co·quette (kō-kĕt′) *n.* A flirt. [Fr. < *coq,* cock.] —**co·quet′tish** *adj.* —**co·quet′tish·ly** *adv.* —**co·quet′tish·ness** *n.*

cor·a·cle (kôr′ə-kəl, kŏr′-) *n.* A boat made of waterproof material stretched over a wicker or wooden frame. [Welsh *corwgl.*]

cor·al (kôr′əl, kŏr′-) *n.* 1. A hard, stony substance, often used for jewelry, formed by the skeletons of tiny sea animals massed together in great numbers. **2.** A yellowish pink or red. [< Gk. *korallion*.] —**cor'al** *adj.*

coral snake *n.* A venomous snake having red, black, and yellow banded markings.

cor·bel (kôr′bəl, -bĕl′) *n.* A usu. stone bracket projecting from the face of a wall and used to support a cornice or an arch. [< OFr., dim. of *corp*, raven.]

cord (kôrd) *n.* **1.** A string or small rope of twisted strands or fibers. **2.** An insulated, flexible electric wire fitted with a plug. **3. a.** A raised rib on the surface of cloth. **b.** A fabric or cloth, as corduroy, with such ribs. **4.** A unit of quantity for cut fuel wood, equal to 128 cubic feet in a stack measuring 4 by 4 by 8 feet. —*v.* **1.** To fasten with a cord. **2.** To pile (wood) in cords. [< Gk. *khordē*.] —**cord'er** *n.*

cord·age (kôr′dĭj) *n.* Cords or ropes, esp. the ropes in the rigging of a ship.

cor·dial (kôr′jəl) *adj.* Hearty; warm; sincere. —*n.* **1.** A stimulant, such as a medicine or drink. **2.** A liqueur. [< Lat. *cor*, heart.] —**cor·dial'i·ty** (kôr′jăl′ĭ-tē, kôr-ăl′-, -dē-ăl′-) *n.* —**cor'dial·ly** *adv.*

cor·dil·le·ra (kôr-dĭl-yâr′ə, kôr-dĭl′ər-ə) *n.* A chain of mountains. [Sp. < *cuerda*, cord.] —**cor'dil·ler'an** (-yâr′ən) *adj.*

cord·ite (kôr′dīt′) *n.* A smokeless explosive powder consisting of nitrocellulose, nitroglycerin, and petrolatum.

cord·less (kôrd′lĭs) *adj.* **1.** Having no cord. **2.** Using batteries as a source of power: *a cordless drill.*

cor·do·ba (kôr′də-bə, -və) *n.* See table at **currency.** [< Francisco de Córdoba (1475–1526).]

cor·don (kôr′dn) *n.* **1.** A line, as of people or ships, stationed around an area to enclose it. **2.** A ribbon worn as an ornament or decoration. —*v.* To form a cordon around. [< OFr. < *corde*, cord.]

cor·do·van (kôr′də-vən) *n.* A soft, fine-grained leather. [< *Córdoba*, Spain.]

cor·du·roy (kôr′də-roi′, kôr′də-roi′) *n.* **1.** A durable, ribbed cotton fabric. **2. corduroys.** Corduroy trousers. [Prob. CORD + obs. *duroy*, coarse woolen fabric.]

core (kôr, kōr) *n.* **1.** The hard or fibrous central part of certain fruits, such as the apple. **2.** The innermost or most important part of anything; heart. **3.** An internal computer memory. —*v.* **cored, cor·ing.** To remove the core of. [ME.]

co·re·spon·dent (kō′rĭ-spŏn′dənt) *n.* A person charged with having committed adultery with the defendant in a suit for divorce.

co·ri·an·der (kôr′ē-ăn′dər, kōr′-) *n.* An herb with aromatic seeds used as a condiment. [Gk. *koriandron*.]

Co·rin·thi·ans (kə-rĭn′thē-ənz) *n.* See table at **Bible.**

co·ri·um (kôr′ē-əm, kōr′-) *n., pl.* **-ri·a** (-ē-ə). The skin layer beneath the epidermis, containing nerve endings, sweat glands, and blood and lymph vessels. [Lat., skin.]

cork (kôrk) *n.* **1.** The light, porous, elastic outer bark of a Mediterranean tree, the cork oak. **2.** Something made of cork, esp. a bottle

stopper. —*v.* To stop or seal with or as if with a cork. [< Sp. *alcorque*, cork-soled shoe.] —**cork'y** *adj.*

cork·screw (kôrk′skrōō′) *n.* A device for drawing corks from bottles. —*adj.* Spiral in shape.

corm (kôrm) *n.* A rounded underground plant stem similar to a bulb. [< Gk. *kormos*, a trimmed tree trunk.]

cor·mo·rant (kôr′mar-ənt) *n.* A water bird with dark plumage, webbed feet, and a hooked bill. [< OFr. *cormorant.*]

corn¹ (kôrn) *n.* **1. a.** A tall, widely cultivated cereal plant bearing seeds or kernels on large ears. **b.** The seeds or ears of this plant. **2.** A seed or fruit of various cereal plants. **3.** *Slang.* Something trite, melodramatic, or too sentimental. —*v.* To preserve in brine. [< OE, grain.]

corn² (kôrn) *n.* A horny thickening of the skin, usu. on or near a toe, resulting from pressure or friction. [< Lat. *cornu*, horn.]

corn bread *n.* Also **corn·bread** (kôrn′brĕd′.) A bread made from cornmeal.

corn·cob (kôrn′kŏb′) *n.* The woody core of an ear of corn.

corn·crib (kôrn′krĭb′) *n.* A ventilated structure for storing and drying corn.

cor·ne·a (kôr′nē-ə) *n.* The tough, transparent membrane covering the lens of the eye. [< Med. Lat. *cornea (tela)*, horny (tissue).] —**cor'ne·al** *adj.*

cor·ner (kôr′nər) *n.* **1. a.** The position at which two lines or surfaces meet. **b.** The immediate interior or exterior region of the angle formed at this position, bounded by the two lines or surfaces. **2.** The place where two streets meet. **3.** A position from which escape is difficult. **4.** Any part or region. **5.** A remote or secret place or area. **6.** Speculation in a stock or commodity by controlling the available supply so as to raise its price. —*v.* **1.** To place or drive into a corner. **2.** To form a corner in (a stock or commodity). —**idiom. cut corners.** *Informal.* To reduce expenses; economize. [< OFr. < Lat. *cornu*, horn.]

cor·ner·stone (kôr′nər-stōn′) *n.* **1.** A stone at one of the corners of a building's foundation, esp. one set in place with a special ceremony. **2.** The fundamental basis of something.

cor·net (kôr-nĕt′) *n.* A three-valved instrument resembling a trumpet. [< Lat. *cornu*, horn.] —**cor·net'ist** or **cor·net'tist** *n.*

corn·flow·er (kôrn′flou′ər) *n.* A garden plant with blue, purple, pink, or white flowers.

cor·nice (kôr′nĭs) *n.* A horizontal molded projection that crowns or completes a building or wall. [< OItal.]

cornice

Cor·nish (kôr′nĭsh) *n.* The extinct Celtic language of Cornwall. —**Cornish** *adj.*

corn·meal (kôrn′mēl′) *n.* Coarse meal made from corn.

corn·stalk (kôrn′stôk′) *n.* A stalk of corn, esp. maize.

corn·starch (kôrn′stärch′) *n.* A purified starchy flour made from corn, used as a thickener in cooking.

corn syrup *n.* A syrup prepared from corn and containing glucose, dextrin, and maltose.

cor·nu·co·pi·a (kôr′nə-kō′pē-ə) *n.* 1. A cone-shaped container overflowing with fruit, flowers, and corn. 2. An abundance. [LLat., horn of plenty.]

corn·y (kôr′nē) *adj.* **-i·er, -i·est.** *Slang.* Trite, outdated, or mawkish.

co·rol·la (kə-rŏl′ə, -rōl′ə) *n.* The outer part of a flower, consisting of fused or separate petals. [Lat., small garland.]

cor·ol·lar·y (kôr′ə-lĕr′ē, kŏr′-) *n.,* pl. **-ies.** 1. A proposition that follows with little or no proof from one already proven. 2. A natural consequence or effect; result. [< Lat. *corollarium,* gratuity.]

co·ro·na (kə-rō′nə) *n.,* pl. **-nas** or **-nae** (-nē). A faintly colored luminous ring around a celestial body visible through a haze or thin cloud. [< Gk. *koronē,* crown.]

cor·o·nar·y (kôr′ə-nĕr′ē, kŏr′-) *adj.* 1. Pertaining to either of two arteries that originate in the aorta and supply blood directly to the heart tissues. 2. Pertaining to the heart. [Lat. *coronarius,* of a garland.]

coronary thrombosis *n.* The blockage of a coronary artery by a blood clot, often leading to destruction of heart muscle.

cor·o·na·tion (kôr′ə-nā′shən, kŏr′-) *n.* The act or ceremony of crowning a sovereign. [< Lat. *coronare,* to crown.]

cor·o·ner (kôr′ə-nər, kŏr′-) *n.* A public officer whose function is to investigate any death thought to be of other than natural causes. [< AN *corouner,* officer of the Crown.]

cor·o·net (kôr′ə-nĕt′, kŏr′-) *n.* 1. A small crown worn by nobles below the rank of sovereign. 2. A gold or jeweled headband. [< OFr. *coronette.*]

cor·po·ra (kôr′pər-ə) *n.* Pl. of **corpus.**

cor·po·ral¹ (kôr′pər-əl) *adj.* Of the body; bodily. [< Lat. *corporalis.*] —**cor′po·ral′i·ty** (-pə-răl′ĭ-tē) *n.* —**cor′po·ral·ly** *adv.*

cor·po·ral² (kôr′pər-əl, -prəl) *n.* A noncommissioned officer of the lowest rank, as in the army. [< OItal. *caporal.*]

cor·po·rate (kôr′pər-ĭt, -prĭt) *adj.* 1. Formed into a corporation; incorporated. 2. Of a corporation. 3. United or combined into one body; collective. [< Lat. *corporare,* to make into a body.] —**cor′po·rate·ly** *adv.*

cor·po·ra·tion (kôr′pə-rā′shən) *n.* 1. A body of persons acting under a legal charter as a separate entity with privileges and liabilities. 2. Such a body created for purposes of government.

cor·po·re·al (kôr-pôr′ē-əl, -pōr′-) *adj.* 1. Pertaining to or characteristic of the body. 2. Of a material nature; tangible. [< Lat. *corporeus.*] —**cor·po′re·al·ly** *adv.*

corps (kôr, kōr) *n.,* pl. **corps** (kôrz, kōrz). 1. A specialized section or branch of the armed forces. 2. A group of persons under common direction. [Fr.]

corpse (kôrps) *n.* A dead body, esp. of a human being. [< Lat. *corpus.*]

cor·pu·lence (kôr′pyə-ləns) *n.* Fatness; obesity. [< Lat. *corpulentia.*] —**cor′pu·lent** *adj.* —**cor′pu·lent·ly** *adv.*

cor·pus (kôr′pəs) *n.,* pl. **-po·ra** (-pər-ə). 1. *Anat.* A structure constituting the main part of an organ. 2. A large collection of specialized writings. [Lat.]

cor·pus·cle (kôr′pə-səl, -pŭs′əl) *n.* 1. A cell capable of free movement in a fluid or matrix as distinguished from a cell fixed in tissue. 2. A minute particle. [Lat. *corpusculum,* little particle.] —**cor·pus′cu·lar** (-pŭs′kyə-lər) *adj.*

corpus de·lic·ti (də-lĭk′tī′) *n.* 1. *Law.* Evidence of the fact that a crime has been committed. 2. The victim's corpse in a murder case. [NLat., body of the crime.]

cor·ral (kə-răl′) *n.* An enclosure for confining livestock. —*v.* **-ralled, -ral·ling.** 1. To drive into and hold in a corral. 2. *Informal.* To seize; capture. [Sp.]

cor·rect (kə-rĕkt′) *v.* 1. To remove the errors or mistakes from. 2. To mark the errors in. 3. To admonish or punish in order to improve. 4. To remedy or counteract. —*adj.* 1. True or accurate. 2. Conforming to standards; proper. [< Lat. *corrigere.*] —**cor·rect′a·ble** or **cor·rect′i·ble** *adj.* —**cor·rec′tive** *adj. & n.* —**cor·rect′ly** *adv.* —**cor·rect′ness** *n.*

Syns: correct, amend, mend, rectify, remedy, right *v.*

cor·rec·tion (kə-rĕk′shən) *n.* 1. The act or process of correcting. 2. Something offered or substituted for a mistake or fault. 3. Punishment intended to improve. 4. A quantity added or subtracted to improve accuracy. —**cor·rec′tion·al** *adj.*

cor·re·la·tion (kôr′ə-lā′shən, kŏr′-) *n.* A complementary, parallel, or reciprocal relationship: *a direct correlation between recession and unemployment.* [Med. Lat. *correlatio.*] —**cor·re·late′** *v. & adj.* —**cor′re·la′tion·al** *adj.*

cor·rel·a·tive (kə-rĕl′ə-tĭv) *adj.* 1. Related; corresponding. 2. Reciprocally related. —*n.* 1. Either of two correlative entities. 2. A correlative word or expression, as *neither* and *nor.* —**cor·rel′a·tive·ly** *adv.*

cor·re·spond (kôr′ĭ-spŏnd′, kŏr′-) *v.* 1. To be in agreement, harmony, or conformity. 2. To be similar or equal (to). 3. To communicate by letter. [< Med. Lat. *correspondēre.*] —**cor′re·spond′ing·ly** *adv.*

cor·re·spon·dence (kôr′ĭ-spŏn′dəns, kŏr′-) *n.* 1. The act, fact, or state of agreeing or conforming. 2. Similarity; analogy. 3. a. Communication by exchange of letters. b. The letters written or received.

cor·re·spon·dent (kôr′ĭ-spŏn′dənt, kŏr′-) *n.* 1. One who communicates by letter. 2. One employed by the media to supply news, esp. from a distant place. 3. One that corresponds; correlative. —*adj.* Corresponding.

cor·ri·dor (kôr′ĭ-dər, -dôr′, kŏr′-) *n.* 1. A narrow passageway, usu. with rooms opening onto it. 2. A narrow strip of land, esp. through a foreign country. 3. A long, narrow, densely populated area having two or more major cities. [< OItal. *corridore.*]

cor·ri·gen·dum (kôr′ə-jĕn′dəm, kŏr′-) *n.,* pl. **-da** (-də). 1. An error in a book. 2. **corrigenda.** A list of errors in a book with their corrections. [< Lat. *corrigendum,* thing to be corrected.]

cor·rob·o·rate (kə-rŏb'ə-rāt') v. **-rat·ed, -rat·ing.** To support or confirm (other evidence). [< Lat. *corroborare.*] **—cor·rob'o·ra'tion** n. **—cor·rob'o·ra'tive** adj. **—cor·rob'o·ra'tor** n.

cor·rode (kə-rōd') v. **-rod·ed, -rod·ing.** To wear away or cause to wear away gradually, esp. by chemical action. [< Lat. *corrodere,* to gnaw away.] **—cor·rod'i·ble** or **cor·ro'si·ble** (-rō'sə-bəl) adj. **—cor·ro'sion** n. **—cor·ro'sive** adj. & n. **—cor·ro'sive·ly** adv. **—cor·ro'sive·ness** n.

cor·ru·gate (kôr'ə-gāt', kŏr'-) v. **-gat·ed, -gat·ing.** To make folds or parallel and alternating ridges and grooves (in). [Lat. *corrugare,* to wrinkle up.] **—cor'ru·ga'tion** n.

cor·rupt (kə-rŭpt') adj. **1.** Immoral; depraved. **2.** Open to bribery; dishonest: *a corrupt judge.* **3.** Decaying; putrid. **—v.** To make or become corrupt. [< Lat. *corrumpere,* to destroy.] **—cor·rupt'er** or **cor·rup'tor** n. **—cor·rupt'i·bil'i·ty** or **cor·rupt'i·ble·ness** n. **—cor·rupt'i·ble** adj. **—cor·rupt'i·bly** adv. **—cor·rup'tion** n. **—cor·rupt'ly** adv. **—cor·rupt'ness** n.

cor·sage (kôr-säzh') n. A small bouquet worn usu. at the shoulder. [< OFr., torso.]

cor·sair (kôr'sâr') n. **1.** A pirate. **2.** A swift pirate ship. [< Med. Lat. *cursarius.*]

cor·set (kôr'sĭt) n. A close-fitting undergarment, often reinforced by stays, worn to support and shape the waist and hips. [< OFr.]

cor·tege (kôr-tĕzh', -tāzh') n. **1.** A train of attendants; retinue. **2.** A ceremonial procession. [< Lat. *cohors,* throng.]

cor·tex (kôr'tĕks') n., pl. **-ti·ces** (-tĭ-sēz') or **-tex·es.** The outer layer of a bodily organ or part. [Lat., bark.] **—cor'ti·cal** adj. **—cor'ti·cal·ly** adv.

cor·ti·sone (kôr'tĭ-sōn', -zōn') n. An adrenal hormone, $C_{21}H_{28}O_5$, active in carbohydrate metabolism and used to treat rheumatoid arthritis, diseases of connective tissue, and gout. [< *corticosterone,* a kind of hormone.]

co·run·dum (kə-rŭn'dəm) n. An extremely hard mineral, aluminum oxide, occurring in gem varieties and in a common form used chiefly in abrasives. [Tamil *kuruntam.*]

cor·us·cate (kôr'ə-skāt', kŏr'-) v. **-cat·ed, -cat·ing.** To sparkle; glitter. [Lat. *coruscare.*] **—cor'us·ca'tion** n.

cor·vette (kôr-vĕt') n. **1.** A fast, lightly armed warship smaller than a destroyer. **2.** An obsolete warship smaller than a frigate. [Fr., a kind of warship.]

corvette

co·ry (kô'rē, kŏr'ē) n. See table at **currency.**

co·ry·za (kə-rī'zə) n. An acute inflammation of the nasal mucous membrane, marked by discharge of mucus, sneezing, and watering of the eyes. [< Gk. *koruza,* catarrh.]

co·sig·na·to·ry (kō-sĭg'nə-tôr'ē, -tōr'ē) adj. Signed jointly with another or others. **—n., pl. -ries.** One who cosigns.

cos·met·ic (kŏz-mĕt'ĭk) n. A preparation, such as skin cream, designed to beautify the body. [< Gk. *kosmētikos,* skilled in arranging.] **—cos·met'ic** adj. **—cos·met'i·cal·ly** adv.

cos·me·tol·o·gy (kŏz'mĭ-tŏl'ə-jē) n. The study or art of cosmetics and their use. [Fr. *cosmétologie.*] **—cos'me·tol'o·gist** n.

cos·mic (kŏz'mĭk) adj. **1.** Pertaining to the universe, esp. as distinct from the earth. **2.** Vast; grand. **—cos'mi·cal·ly** adv.

cosmic ray n. A stream of ionizing radiation, consisting of high-energy atomic nuclei, alpha particles, fragments, particles, and some electromagnetic waves, that enters the atmosphere from outer space.

cosmo- or **cosm-** pref. World; universe: *cosmology.* [< Gk. *kosmos,* universe.]

cos·mo·chem·is·try (kŏz'mō-kĕm'ĭ-strē) n. The science of the chemical composition of the universe. **—cos'mo·chem'i·cal** adj.

cos·mog·o·ny (kŏz-mŏg'ə-nē) n. The astrophysical study of the evolution of the universe. [Gk. *kosmogonia,* creation of the world.]

cos·mog·ra·phy (kŏz-mŏg'rə-fē) n., pl. **-phies. 1.** The study of the constitution of nature. **2.** A description of the world or universe. **—cos·mog'ra·pher** n.

cos·mol·o·gy (kŏz-mŏl'ə-jē) n. **1.** A branch of philosophy dealing with the origin, processes, and structure of the universe. **2.** The study of the structure and constituent dynamics of the universe. **—cos'mo·log'ic** (-mə-lŏj'ĭk) or **cos'-mo·log'i·cal** adj.

cos·mo·naut (kŏz'mə-nôt') n. A Russian astronaut. [R. *kosmonaut.*]

cos·mo·pol·i·tan (kŏz'mə-pŏl'ĭ-tn) adj. **1.** Common to the whole world. **2.** Of the entire world or from many different parts of the world. **3.** At home in all parts of the world or in many spheres of interest. **—n.** A cosmopolitan person.

cos·mop·o·lite (kŏz-mŏp'ə-līt') n. A cosmopolitan person. [Gk. *kosmopolitēs.*]

cos·mos (kŏz'məs, -mōs) n. **1.** The universe regarded as an orderly, harmonious whole. **2.** Any system regarded as ordered, harmonious, and whole. **3.** A garden plant with variously colored daisylike flowers. [Gk. *kosmos.*]

co·spon·sor (kō-spŏn'sər) n. A joint sponsor. [Gk. *kosmopolitēs.*] **—co·spon'sor** v. **—co·spon'sor·ship** n.

Cos·sack (kŏs'ăk') n. A member of a people of the southern USSR, noted as cavalrymen. **—Cos'sack'** adj.

cost (kôst) n. **1.** An amount paid or required in payment for a purchase. **2.** A loss, sacrifice, or penalty. **—v.** To require a specified payment, expenditure, effort, or loss. [< Lat. *constare,* to cost.]

co·star (kō'stär'). Also **co-star. —n.** A starring actor or actress given equal status with another or others in a play or motion picture. **—v.** **-starred, -star·ring.** To act or present as a costar.

cost·ly (kôst'lē) adj. **-li·er, -li·est. 1.** Of high price or value. **2.** Entailing great loss or sacrifice. **—cost'li·ness** n.

cost of living *n.* **1.** The average cost of the basic necessities of life, such as food, shelter, and clothing. **2.** The cost of basic necessities as defined by an accepted standard.

cost-of-liv·ing adjustment (kôst′əv-lĭv′ĭng) *n.* An adjustment made in wages that corresponds with a change in the cost of living.

cost-of-living index *n.* The consumer price index.

cost-plus (kôst′plŭs′, kôst′-) *n.* The cost of production plus a fixed rate of profit. —**cost′-plus′** *adj.*

cost-push (kôst′pŏosh′, kôst′-) *adj.* Designating inflation in which increased production costs tend to drive prices up.

cos·tume (kôs′tōōm′, -tyōōm′) *n.* **1.** A style of dress characteristic of a particular country or period. **2.** A set of clothes for a particular occasion or season. **3.** An outfit worn by one playing a part. [< Ital.] —**cos′tum·er** *n.*

co·sy (kō′zē) *adj. & n.* Var. of **cozy.**

cot (kŏt) *n.* A narrow bed, esp. a collapsible one. [< Skt. *khatva,* couch.]

cote (kōt) *n.* A small shed or shelter for sheep or birds. [< OE.]

co·te·rie (kō′tə-rē) *n.* A small group of persons who associate frequently. [Fr.]

co·til·lion (kō-tĭl′yən, kə-) *n.* **1.** A lively dance having varied patterns and steps. **2.** A formal debutante ball. [Fr. *cotillon.*]

cot·tage (kŏt′ĭj) *n.* A small house. [ME *cotage.*] —**cot′tag·er** *n.*

cottage cheese *n.* An extremely soft, mild white cheese made of strained and seasoned curds of skim milk.

cot·ter (kŏt′ər) *n.* A bolt, wedge, key, or pin inserted through a slot to hold parts together. [Orig. unknown.]

cotter pin *n.* A split cotter inserted through holes in two or more pieces and bent at the ends to fasten them together.

cot·ton (kŏt′n) *n.* **1.** Any of various plants or shrubs cultivated in warm climates for the fiber surrounding their seeds. **2.** The soft, white, downy fiber attached to the seeds of the cotton plant, used esp. in making textiles. **3.** Thread or cloth made from cotton fiber. —*v. Informal.* To take a liking to; become friendly. [< Ar. *quṭn.*] —**cot′ton·y** *adj.*

cot·ton·mouth (kŏt′n-mouth′) *n.* The water moccasin.

cot·ton·seed (kŏt′n-sēd′) *n.* The seed of cotton, used as a source of oil and meal.

cot·ton·tail (kŏt′n-tāl′) *n.* A New World rabbit having a tail with a white underside.

cot·y·le·don (kŏt′l-ēd′n) *n.* An embryonic plant leaf, the first to appear from a sprouting seed. [Lat., a kind of plant.] —**cot′y·le′don·al** or **cot′y·le′do·nous** *adj.*

couch (kouch) *n.* A piece of furniture, usu. upholstered, on which one may sit or recline; sofa. —*v.* To word in a certain manner; phrase. [< OFr. *couche.*]

couch·ant (kou′chənt) *adj. Heraldry.* Lying down with the head raised. [< OFr.]

cou·gar (kōō′gər) *n.* The mountain lion. [Ult. < Tupi *suasuarana.*]

cough (kôf, kŏf) *v.* **1.** To expel air from the lungs suddenly and noisily. **2.** To expel by coughing. [ME *coughen.*] —**cough** *n.*

could (kŏod) *v. p.t.* of **can.**

could·n't (kŏod′nt). Could not.

cou·lee (kōō′lē) *n.* A deep gulch or ravine. [Can. Fr. *coulée.*]

cou·lomb (kōō′lŏm′, -lōm′) *n.* A unit of electrical charge equal to the quantity of charge transferred in one second by a steady current of one ampere. [< Charles A. de *Coulomb* (1736–1806).]

coun·cil (koun′səl) *n.* **1.** An assembly called together for consultation, deliberation, etc. **2.** An administrative, legislative, or advisory body. [< Lat. *concilium.*] —**coun′cil·man** *n.* —**coun′cil·wom′an** *n.*

Usage: Council and *counsel* are not interchangeable although they are related terms. A *council* is a deliberative assembly, such as a city council. *Counsel* pertains chiefly to advice and guidance in general.

coun·cil·or (koun′sə-lər) *n.* Also **coun·cil·lor.** A member of a council.

coun·sel (koun′səl) *n.* **1.** An exchange of opinions and ideas; discussion. **2.** Advice or guidance. **3.** A deliberate resolution; plan. **4.** A private opinion or purpose: *keep one's own counsel.* **5.** *pl.* **counsel.** A lawyer or group of lawyers. —*v.* **-seled** or **-selled, -sel·ing** or **-sel·ling.** **1.** To give counsel (to); advise. **2.** To urge the adoption of; recommend. [< Lat. *consilium.*]

coun·sel·or (koun′sə-lər, -slər) *n.* Also **coun·sel·lor. 1.** An adviser. **2.** An attorney, esp. a trial lawyer. —**coun′se·lor·ship′** *n.*

count¹ (kount) *v.* **1.** To name or list one by one in order to determine a total. **2.** To recite numerals in ascending order. **3.** To include in a reckoning: *ten dogs, counting the puppies.* **4.** To believe or consider to be. **5.** To merit consideration. **6.** To be of value or importance: *His opinions count for little.* —*phrasal verb.* **count on.** To rely; depend on. —*n.* **1.** The act of counting. **2.** A number reached by counting. **3.** *Law.* Any of the charges in an indictment. [< Lat. *computare,* to compute.] —**count′a·ble** *adj.*

count² (kount) *n.* In some European countries, a nobleman whose rank corresponds to that of an English earl. [< LLat. *comes,* occupant of a state office.]

count·down (kount′doun′) *n.* The act of counting backward to indicate the time remaining before a scheduled event, as the firing of a rocket.

coun·te·nance (koun′tə-nəns) *n.* **1.** Appearance, esp. the expression of the face. **2.** The face. **3.** Support or approval; encouragement. —*v.* **-nanced, -nanc·ing.** To approve; sanction. [< OFr. *contenance.*]

coun·ter¹ (koun′tər) *adj.* Contrary; opposing. —*v.* To move or act in opposition (to). —*n.* One that is counter; opposite. —*adv.* In a contrary manner or direction. [< COUNTER–.]

count·er² (koun′tər) *n.* **1.** A table or similar flat surface on which money is counted, business transacted, or food served. **2.** A piece, as of wood or ivory, used for keeping a count or a place in games. [< Med. Lat. *computatorium,* place of accounts.]

count·er³ (koun′tər) *n.* One that counts, esp. an electrical or electronic device that automatically counts occurrences or repetitions of phenomena or events.

counter– *pref.* **1.** Opposition, as in direction or purpose: *counteract.* **2.** Reciprocation: *countersign.* [< Lat. *contra,* against.]

coun·ter·act (koun′tər-ăkt′) *v.* To oppose and lessen the effects of by contrary action. —**coun′ter·ac′tion** *n.*

coun·ter·at·tack (koun'tər-ə-tăk') *n.* A return attack. —**coun'ter·at·tack'** *v.*

coun·ter·bal·ance (koun'tər-băl'əns) *n.* **1.** A force or influence equally counteracting another. **2.** A weight that balances another. —**coun'ter·bal'ance** *v.*

coun·ter·claim (koun'tər-klām') *n.* A claim filed in opposition to another claim, esp. in a lawsuit. —**coun'ter·claim'** *v.* —**coun'ter·claim'ant** *n.*

coun·ter·clock·wise (koun'tər-klŏk'wīz') *adv. & adj.* In a direction opposite to that of the movement of the hands of a clock.

coun·ter·cul·ture (koun'tər-kŭl'chər) *n.* A culture created by or for the alienated young in opposition to traditional values.

coun·ter·es·pi·o·nage (koun'tər-ĕs'pē-ə-näzh', -nĭj) *n.* Espionage undertaken to counteract enemy espionage.

coun·ter·feit (koun'tər-fĭt) *v.* **1.** To make a copy of, usu. with intent to defraud; forge. **2.** To feign; pretend. —*adj.* **1.** Made in imitation of what is genuine, usu. with intent to defraud. **2.** Simulated; feigned. —*n.* A fraudulent imitation or facsimile. [< OFr. *contrefaire.*] —**coun'ter·feit·er** *n.*

coun·ter·in·sur·gen·cy (koun'tər-ĭn-sûr'jən-sē) *n.* Political and military action undertaken to counter insurgency. —**coun'ter·in·sur'gent** *n.*

coun·ter·in·tel·li·gence (koun'tər-ĭn-tĕl'ə-jəns) *n.* The branch of an intelligence service charged with keeping valuable information from an enemy and preventing subversion and sabotage.

coun·ter·man (koun'tər-măn', -mən) *n.* One who tends a counter, as in a luncheonette.

coun·ter·mand (koun'tər-mănd') *v.* **1.** To reverse (a command). **2.** To recall by a contrary order. [< OFr. *contremander.*]

coun·ter·mea·sure (koun'tər-mĕzh'ər) *n.* A measure or action taken to oppose or offset another.

coun·ter·of·fen·sive (koun'tər-ə-fĕn'sĭv) *n.* A large-scale attack by an army, designed to stop the offensive of an enemy force.

coun·ter·pane (koun'tər-pān') *n.* A bedspread. [< Med. Lat. *culcita puncta,* stitched quilt.]

coun·ter·part (koun'tər-pärt') *n.* One that is exactly or very much like another, as in function or relation.

coun·ter·point (koun'tər-point') *n.* **1.** A musical technique in which two or more melodic lines are combined so that they establish a harmonic relationship while retaining their individuality. **2.** A contrasting but parallel element, item, or theme.

coun·ter·poise (koun'tər-poiz') *n.* **1.** A counterbalancing weight. **2.** A force or influence that balances or counteracts another. **3.** The state of being balanced or in equilibrium. —*v.* **-poised, -pois·ing.** To oppose with an equal weight, force, or power.

coun·ter·rev·o·lu·tion (koun'tər-rĕv'ə-lōō'-shən) *n.* A movement arising in opposition to a revolution. —**coun'ter·rev·o·lu'tion·ar·y** *adj. & n.*

coun·ter·sign (koun'tər-sīn') *v.* To sign (a previously signed document), as for authentication. —*n.* **1.** A second or confirming signature, as on a previously signed document.

2. A secret sign or signal given in order to obtain passage; password.

coun·ter·sink (koun'tər-sĭngk') *v.* **1.** To enlarge the top part of (a hole) so that a screw or bolthead will lie flush with or below the surface. **2.** To drive a screw or bolt into (such a hole). —*n.* **1.** A tool for making such a hole. **2.** A hole so made.

coun·ter·spy (koun'tər-spī') *n.* A spy working in opposition to enemy espionage.

coun·ter·ten·or (koun'tər-tĕn'ər) *n.* A male singer with a range above that of tenor.

coun·ter·weight (koun'tər-wāt') *n.* A weight used as a counterbalance.

count·ess (koun'tĭs) *n.* **1.** The wife or widow of a count or earl. **2.** A woman holding the title of count or earl in her own right.

counting house *n.* Also **count·ing-house** (koun'tĭng-hous'). An office in which a business firm carries on operations such as accounting and correspondence.

count·less (kount'lĭs) *adj.* Innumerable.

coun·tri·fied (kŭn'trĭ-fīd') *adj.* Also **coun·try·fied. 1.** Having the characteristics of country life; rural. **2.** Lacking in sophistication.

coun·try (kŭn'trē) *n., pl.* **-tries. 1.** A large tract of land distinguishable by features of topography, biology, or culture. **2.** A rural area. **3. a.** A nation or state. **b.** The territory of a nation or state. **4.** The land of a person's birth or citizenship. [< LLat. *contrata.*]

country and western *n.* Country music.

country club *n.* A suburban club with facilities for outdoor sports and social activities.

coun·try·man (kŭn'trē-mən) *n.* **1.** A man from one's own country. **2.** A rustic. —**coun'try·wom'an** *n.*

country music *n.* Folk music of the rural United States, esp. the southern or southwestern United States.

coun·try·side (kŭn'trē-sīd') *n.* **1.** A rural region. **2.** The inhabitants of such an area.

coun·ty (koun'tē) *n., pl.* **-ties.** An administrative subdivision of a state or territory. [< Med. Lat. *comitatus,* territory of a count.]

coup (kōō) *n., pl.* **coups** (kōōz). A brilliantly executed stratagem. [< OFr., blow.]

coup de grâce (kōō' də gräs') *n., pl.* **coups de grâce** (kōō' də gräs'). **1.** A death blow or finishing stroke, as delivered to one who is mortally wounded. **2.** A finishing or decisive stroke. [Fr.]

coup d'é·tat (kōō' dā-tä') *n., pl.* **coups d'état** (kōō' dā-tä'). A sudden, unconstitutional overthrow of a government by a group of persons in or previously in authority. [Fr.]

cou·pé (kōō-pā') *n.* Also **coupe** (kōōp). A closed two-door automobile. [Fr.]

cou·ple (kŭp'əl) *n.* **1.** Two items of the same kind. **2.** Something that joins two things. **3.** *(used with a sing. or pl. verb).* A man and woman united, as by marriage. **4.** *Informal.* A few; several: *a couple of days.* —*v.* **-pled, -pling. 1.** To link together. **2.** To form pairs. [< Lat. *copula,* bond.] —**cou'pler** *n.*

Usage: When referring to a man and woman together, *couple* may be used with either a singular or plural verb. Whatever the choice, usage should be consistent: *The newlywed couple is* (or *are*) *spending its* (or *their*) *honeymoon in Europe.*

cou·plet (kŭp′lĭt) *n.* Two successive lines of verse, usu. rhyming and having the same meter. [OFr.]

cou·pon (kōō′pŏn′, kyōō′-) *n.* **1.** A negotiable certificate attached to a bond that represents a sum of interest due at a stated maturity. **2.** A certificate entitling the bearer to certain benefits, such as a cash refund or a gift. **3.** A printed form, as in an advertisement, on which to write one's name and address when sending away for something. [Fr.]

cour·age (kûr′ĭj, kŭr′-) *n.* The quality of mind that enables one to face danger with confidence, resolution, and firm control of oneself; bravery. [< Lat. *cor*, heart.] —**cou·ra′geous** *adj.* —**cou·ra′geous·ly** *adv.*

cou·ri·er (kōōr′ē-ər, kûr′-) *n.* A messenger, esp. one on urgent or official business. [OItal. *corriere*.]

course (kôrs, kōrs) *n.* **1.** Onward movement in a particular direction. **2.** The route or path taken by something that moves, as a stream. **3.** Duration: *in the course of a year.* **4.** A mode of action or behavior. **5.** Regular development. **6. a.** A body of prescribed studies: *a premed course.* **b.** A unit of such studies. **7.** A part of a meal served as a unit at one time. —*v.* **coursed, cours·ing. 1.** To move swiftly (through or over); traverse. **2.** To hunt (game) with hounds. **3.** To follow a direction. **4.** To flow. —**idioms. in due course.** At the right time. **of course.** Without any doubt; certainly. [< Lat. *cursus.*]

cours·er (kôr′sər, kōr′-) *n.* A swift horse.

court (kôrt, kōrt) *n.* **1.** A courtyard. **2.** A short street. **3.** A royal mansion or palace. **4.** The retinue of a sovereign. **5.** A sovereign's governing body, including ministers and state advisers. **6. a.** A person or body of persons appointed to hear and submit a decision on legal cases. **b.** The room in which such cases are heard. **c.** The regular session of a judicial assembly. **7.** An open, level area marked with lines, upon which tennis, handball, basketball, etc. are played. —*v.* **1.** To attempt to gain the favor of by flattery or attention. **2.** To attempt to gain the love of; woo. **3.** To invite, often unwittingly or foolishly: *court disaster.* —**idiom. pay court to. 1.** To flatter with solicitous overtures in an attempt to obtain something. **2.** To woo. [< Lat. *cohors.*]

cour·te·ous (kûr′tē-əs) *adj.* Gracious and considerate toward others. —**cour′te·ous·ly** *adv.* —**cour′te·ous·ness** *n.*

cour·te·san (kôr′tĭ-zən, kōr′-) *n.* A prostitute, esp. one associating with men of rank or wealth. [< OItal. *cortigiana.*]

cour·te·sy (kûr′tĭ-sē) *n.*, *pl.* **-sies. 1.** Polite behavior; gracious manner or manners. **2.** A polite gesture or remark. [< OFr. *courtesie.*]

court·house (kôrt′hous′, kōrt′-) *n.* A building housing judicial courts.

court·i·er (kôr′tē-ər, kōr′-) *n.* An attendant at a sovereign's court.

court·ly (kôrt′lē, kōrt′-) *adj.* **-li·er, -li·est.** Elegant in manners; polite; refined. —**court′li·ness** *n.*

court-mar·tial (kôrt′mär′shəl, kōrt′-) *n.*, *pl.* **courts-martial.** A military court of officers appointed to try persons for offenses under military law. **2.** A trial by court-martial. —*v.* **-tialed** or **-tialled, -tial·ing** or **-tial·ling.** To try by court-martial.

court·room (kôrt′rōōm′, -rōōm′, kōrt′-) *n.* A room for court proceedings.

court·ship (kôrt′shĭp′, kōrt′-) *n.* The act or period of wooing.

court·yard (kôrt′yärd′, kōrt′-) *n.* An open space surrounded by walls or buildings.

cous·in (kŭz′ĭn) *n.* **1.** A child of one's aunt or uncle. **2.** A relative descended from a common ancestor. **3.** A member of a kindred group or country. [< Lat. *consobrinus.*]

cou·ture (kōō-tōōr′) *n.* The business of a couturier or the work of dressmaking and fashion design. [Fr., sewing.]

cou·tu·ri·er (kōō-tōōr′ē-ər, -ē-ā′) *n.* A fashion designer, esp. of women's clothing. [Fr.]

co·va·lent bond (kō-vā′lənt) *n.* A chemical bond formed by the sharing of one or more electrons, esp. pairs, between atoms.

cove (kōv) *n.* A small, sheltered bay. [< OE *cofa*, cave.]

cov·en (kŭv′ən, kō′vən) *n.* An assembly of 13 witches. [Perh. < ME *covent*, assembly.]

cov·e·nant (kŭv′ə-nənt) *n.* A formal binding agreement; compact; contract. [< OFr.] —**cov′e·nant** *v.* —**cov′e·nant·er** *n.*

cov·er (kŭv′ər) *v.* **1.** To place upon, over, or in front of (something) so as to protect, shut in, or conceal. **2.** To clothe. **3.** To occupy the surface of: *Dust covered the table.* **4.** To extend over: *a farm covering 100 acres.* **5.** To hide or conceal, as a fact or crime. **6.** To protect by insurance. **7.** To defray (an expense). **8.** To deal with; treat of. **9.** To travel or pass over. **10.** To hold within the range and aim of a firearm. **11.** To report the details of (an event or situation). **12.** *Informal.* To act as a substitute during someone's absence. —*n.* **1.** Something that covers. **2.** Shelter of any kind. **3.** Something that conceals or disguises. **4.** A table setting for one person. **5.** An envelope or wrapper for mail. —**idioms. under cover. 1.** Operating secretly or under a guise; covert. **2.** Hidden; protected. **under separate cover.** Within a separate envelope. [< Lat. *cooperire*, to cover completely.] —**cov′er·er** *n.*

cov·er·age (kŭv′ər-ĭj) *n.* **1.** The extent or degree to which something is observed, analyzed, and reported. **2.** The protection given by an insurance policy.

cov·er·alls (kŭv′ər-ôlz′) *pl.n.* A loose-fitting one-piece garment worn to protect clothing.

coveralls　　　　**cowboy**

cover charge *n.* A fixed amount added to the bill at a nightclub for entertainment or services.

cover crop *n.* A crop, such as winter rye, planted to prevent winter erosion and provide humus or nitrogen when plowed under.

cov·er·let (kŭv′ər-lĭt) *n.* A bedspread.

cov·ert (kŭv′ərt, kō′vərt) *adj.* 1. Sheltered. 2. Concealed; hidden; secret. —*n.* 1. A covered shelter or hiding place. 2. Thick underbrush affording cover for game. [< OFr.] —**cov′ert·ly** *adv.* —**cov′ert·ness** *n.*

cov·er-up (kŭv′ər-ŭp′) *n.* Also **cov·er·up.** An effort or strategy designed to conceal something, such as a crime or scandal.

cov·et (kŭv′ĭt) *v.* 1. To desire (that which is another's). 2. To wish for excessively; crave. [< OFr. *coveitier*.] —**cov′et·er** *n.* —**cov′et·ous** *adj.* —**cov′et·ous·ly** *adv.* —**cov′et·ous·ness** *n.*

cov·ey (kŭv′ē) *n., pl.* **-eys.** A small flock or group, as of birds or persons: [< OFr. *covee*, brood.]

cow[1] (kou) *n.* 1. The mature female of cattle or of other animals such as whales or elephants. 2. *Informal.* Any domesticated bovine. [< OE *cū.*]

cow[2] (kou) *v.* To frighten with threats or a show of force; intimidate. [Prob. of Scand. orig.]

cow·ard (kou′ərd) *n.* One who lacks courage in the face of danger, pain, or hardship. [< OFr. *couard.*] —**cow′ard·ly** *adj. & adv.*

cow·ard·ice (kou′ər-dĭs) *n.* Lack of courage or resoluteness.

cow·bird (kou′bûrd′) *n.* A blackbird that lays its eggs in other birds' nests.

cow·boy (kou′boi′) *n.* One who tends cattle and performs many of his duties on horseback. —**cow′girl**′ *n.*

cow·er (kou′ər) *v.* To crouch or shrink, as from fear; cringe. [ME *couren,* of Scand. orig.]

cow·hand (kou′hănd′) *n.* A cowboy or cowgirl.

cow·hide (kou′hīd′) *n.* 1. a. The hide of a cow. b. The leather made from this hide. 2. A strong, heavy, flexible whip, usu. made of braided leather.

cowl (koul) *n.* 1. The hood worn by monks. 2. The top portion of the front part of an automobile, supporting the windshield and dashboard. [< Lat. *cucullus,* hood.]

cow·lick (kou′lĭk′) *n.* A projecting tuft of hair that will not lie flat.

cowl·ing (kou′lĭng) *n.* A removable metal covering for an aircraft engine.

co·work·er (kō′wûrk′ər) *n.* A fellow worker.

cow·poke (kou′pōk′) *n. Informal.* A cowboy or cowgirl.

cow·pox (kou′pŏks′) *n.* A skin disease of cattle caused by a virus that is isolated and used to vaccinate humans against smallpox.

cow·punch·er (kou′pŭn′chər) *n. Informal.* A cowboy or cowgirl.

cow·ry (kou′rē) *n., pl.* **-ries.** Any of various tropical marine mollusks with glossy, often brightly marked shells. [< Skt. *kapardah,* shell, or Dravidian orig.]

cow·slip (kou′slĭp′) *n.* 1. An Old World primrose with yellow flowers. 2. The marsh marigold. [< OE *cūslyppe.*]

cox·comb (kŏks′kōm′) *n.* 1. A conceited dandy; fop. 2. Var. of **cockscomb** (sense 3). [ME *cokkes comb,* cock's comb.]

cox·swain (kŏk′sən, -swān′) *n.* One who steers a boat or racing shell. [ME *cokswaynne.*]

coy (koi) *adj.* **-er, -est.** Shy, esp. affectedly so. [< Lat. *quietus.*] —**coy′ly** *adv.* —**coy′ness** *n.*

coy·o·te (kī-ō′tē, kī′ōt′) *n.* A wolflike animal common in western North America. [< Nahuatl *coyotl.*]

coz·en (kŭz′ən) *v.* To deceive; cheat. [Poss. < Ital. *cozzone,* horse-trader.] —**coz′en·age** *n.*

co·zy (kō′zē) *adj.* **-zi·er, -zi·est.** Also **co·sy, -si·er, -si·est.** Snug and comfortable. —*n., pl.* **-zies.** Also **co·sy** *pl.* **-sies.** A padded covering for a teapot to keep the tea hot. [Prob. of Scand. orig.] —**co′zi·ly** *adv.* —**co′zi·ness** *n.*

Cr The symbol for the element chromium.

crab[1] (krăb) *n.* Any of various chiefly marine crustaceans having a broad body with a shell-like covering. [< OE *crabba.*]

crab[2] (krăb) *n. Informal.* A quarrelsome, ill-tempered person. [ME.] —**crab** *v.*

crab apple *n.* 1. A small, tart applelike fruit. 2. A tree bearing crab apples.

crab·bed (krăb′ĭd) *adj.* 1. Irritable; ill-tempered. 2. Difficult to read, as handwriting. [ME.] —**crab′bed·ly** *adv.* —**crab′bed·ness** *n.*

crab·by (krăb′ē) *adj.* **-bi·er, -bi·est.** Grouchy; ill-tempered.

crab·grass (krăb′grăs′) *n.* A coarse grass that spreads and displaces other grasses in lawns.

crab louse *n.* A body louse that infests the pubic region of humans.

crack (krăk) *v.* 1. To break or cause to break with a sharp sound; snap. 2. To break or cause to break without dividing into parts. 3. To change sharply in pitch or timbre, as the voice from emotion. 4. To strike. 5. To break open or into. 6. To discover the solution to, esp. after considerable effort. 7. *Informal.* To tell (a joke). 8. To decompose (petroleum) into simpler compounds. —*phrasal verbs.* **crack down.** *Informal.* To become more demanding, severe, or strict. **crack up.** *Informal.* 1. To crash; collide. 2. To have a mental or physical breakdown. 3. To laugh or cause to laugh boisterously. —*n.* 1. A sharp, snapping sound. 2. A partial split or break; fissure. 3. A narrow space: *The window was open a crack.* 4. A sharp, resounding blow. 5. A cracking vocal tone or sound. 6. An attempt or chance: *gave him a crack at the job.* 7. A sarcastic remark. —*adj.* Superior; first-rate. [< OE *cracian.*]

crack·down (krăk′doun′) *n.* An act or instance of cracking down.

crack·er (krăk′ər) *n.* 1. A thin, crisp wafer or biscuit. 2. A firecracker.

crack·er·jack (krăk′ər-jăk′) *n. Slang.* One that is excellent. —**crack′er·jack′** *adj.*

crack·le (krăk′əl) *v.* **-led, -ling.** 1. To make or cause to make a succession of slight sharp, snapping noises. 2. To develop a network of fine cracks in a surface. [< CRACK.] —**crack′le** *n.* —**crack′ly** *adj.*

crack·pot (krăk′pŏt′) *n.* An eccentric person.

crack·up (krăk′ŭp′) *n. Informal.* 1. A collision, as of an automobile. 2. A mental or physical breakdown.

-cracy *suff.* Government or rule: *technocracy.* [< Gk. *kratos,* power.]

cra·dle (krād′l) *n.* 1. An infant's low bed with rockers. 2. A place of origin. 3. The part of a telephone on which the receiver and mouthpiece unit is supported. 4. A frame projecting above a scythe, used to catch grain as it is cut. —v. **-died, -dling.** 1. To place in or as if into a cradle. 2. To care for or nurture in infancy. [< OE *cradel.*]

craft (krăft) n. 1. Skill or ability, esp. in handwork or the arts. 2. Skill in evasion or deception; cunning. 3. a. A trade, esp. one requiring manual dexterity. b. The membership of such a trade; guild. 4. *pl.* **craft.** A boat, ship, or aircraft. [< OE *cræft.*]

crafts·man (krăfts'mən) n. A skilled worker who practices a craft; artisan. —**crafts'man·ship'** n. —**crafts'wom'an** n.

craft·y (krăf'tē) adj. **-i·er, -i·est.** Underhanded and deceptive; cunning. —**craft'i·ly** adv. —**craft'i·ness** n.

crag (krăg) n. A steeply projecting rock mass. [ME.] —**crag'gy** adj.

cram (krăm) v. **crammed, cram·ming.** 1. To squeeze into an insufficient space; stuff. 2. To fill too tightly. 3. To gorge with food. 4. *Informal.* To study intensively just before an examination. [< OE *crammian.*]

cramp¹ (krămp) n. 1. A sudden, painful involuntary muscular contraction. 2. A temporary partial paralysis of habitually or excessively used muscles. 3. **cramps.** Sharp, persistent abdominal pains. —v. 1. To cause or be affected with or as if with a cramp. [< OFr. *crampe,* of Gmc. orig.]

cramp² (krămp) n. Something that compresses or restrains. —v. 1. To restrict; hamper. 2. To jam (the wheels of a car) hard to the right or left. [MDu. *crampe,* hook.]

cran·ber·ry (krăn'bĕr'ē) n. 1. The tart red, edible berry of a trailing North American plant. 2. The plant that bears cranberries. [< LG *kraanbere.*]

crane (krān) n. 1. A large wading bird with a long neck, long legs, and a long bill. 2. A machine for hoisting heavy objects. —v. **craned, cran·ing.** To stretch one's neck for a better view. [< OE *cran.*]

cra·ni·um (krā'nē-əm) n., *pl.* **-ums** or **-ni·a** (-nē-ə). 1. The skull of a vertebrate. 2. The part of the skull enclosing the brain. [< Gk. *kranion.*] —**cra'ni·al** adj.

crank (krăngk) n. 1. A device for transmitting rotary motion, consisting of a handle attached at right angles to a shaft. 2. *Informal.* An eccentric idea or person. —v. To start or operate by turning a crank. [< OE *cranc.*]

crank·case (krăngk'kās') n. The metal case enclosing a crankshaft.

crank·shaft (krăngk'shăft') n. A shaft that turns or is turned by a crank.

crank·y (krăng'kē) adj. **-i·er, -i·est.** 1. Ill-tempered; peevish. 2. Eccentric; odd.

cran·ny (krăn'ē) n., *pl.* **-nies.** A small crevice; fissure. [< OFr. *cran,* notch.]

crape (krāp) n. Var. of **crepe.**

craps (krăps) n. (*used with a sing. or pl. verb*). A gambling game played with a pair of dice. [Louisiana Fr.]

crap·shoot·er (krăp'shōō'tər) n. One who plays craps.

crash¹ (krăsh) v. 1. To fall, break, or collide noisily. 2. To make a sudden loud noise. 3. To fail suddenly, as a business. 4. *Informal.* To join or enter without paying or without invitation: *crash a party.* —n. 1. A sudden loud noise. 2. A collision. 3. A sudden, severe business failure. —adj. *Informal.* Marked by an intensive effort to produce or

accomplish something quickly: *a crash program.* [ME *crasschen.*]

crash² (krăsh) n. A coarse cotton or linen fabric used for towels and curtains. [R. *krashenina,* colored linen.]

crash-land (krăsh'lănd') v. To land and usu. damage an aircraft under emergency conditions. —**crash'-land'ing** n.

crass (krăs) adj. **-er, -est.** Crude and undiscriminating; coarse. [Lat. *crassus,* dense.] —**crass'ly** adv. —**crass'ness** n.

-crat *suff.* A participant in or supporter of a class or form of government: *technocrat.* [< Gk. *-kratēs.*]

crate (krāt) n. An often slatted wooden container. —v. **crat·ed, crat·ing.** To pack into a crate. [Lat. *cratis,* wickerwork.]

cra·ter (krā'tər) n. 1. A bowl-shaped depression at the mouth of a volcano. 2. A depression or pit resembling a crater. [< Gk. *kratēr,* mixing vessel.]

cra·vat (krə-văt') n. A necktie. [Fr. *cravate.*]

crave (krāv) v. **craved, crav·ing.** 1. To have an intense desire for. 2. To beg earnestly for. [< OE *crafian,* to beg.]

cra·ven (krā'vən) adj. Cowardly. —n. A coward. [ME *cravant.*] —**cra'ven·ly** adv.

crav·ing (krā'vĭng) n. A consuming desire; longing.

craw (krô) n. The crop of a bird or stomach of an animal. [ME *crawe.*]

craw·fish (krô'fĭsh') n. A crayfish.

crawl (krôl) v. 1. To move slowly by dragging the body along the ground; creep. 2. To advance slowly, feebly, or laboriously. 3. To be or feel as if covered with crawling things. —n. 1. A very slow pace. 2. A rapid swimming stroke performed face down. [ON *krafla.*]

cray·fish (krā'fĭsh') n. A small, lobsterlike freshwater crustacean. [< OFr. *crevise,* of Gmc. orig.]

cray·on (krā'ŏn', -ən) n. A stick of colored wax, charcoal, or chalk used for drawing. [< Lat. *creta,* chalk.] —**cray'on** v.

craze (krāz) v. **crazed, craz·ing.** 1. To be or cause to become insane. —n. A short-lived fashion; fad. [ME *crasen,* of Scand. orig.]

cra·zy (krā'zē) adj. **-zi·er, -zi·est.** 1. Mentally unbalanced; insane. 2. *Informal.* Immoderately fond. 3. *Informal.* Extremely impractical. —**cra'zi·ly** adv. —**cra'zi·ness** n.

creak (krēk) v. To make or move with a grating or squeaking sound. [ME *creken.*] —**creak** n. —**creak'i·ly** adv. —**creak'i·ness** n. —**creak'y** adj.

cream (krēm) n. 1. The yellowish fatty part of milk. 2. A yellowish white color. 3. A substance resembling cream, as certain foods or cosmetics. 4. The choicest part. —v. 1. To beat (butter) to a creamy consistency. 2. To prepare in a cream sauce. [< LLat. *cramum.*]

cream cheese A soft white cheese made of cream and milk.

cream·er·y (krē'mə-rē) n., *pl.* **-ies.** An establishment where dairy products are prepared or sold.

crease (krēs) n. A line or mark made by pressing, folding, or wrinkling. [< ME *crest,* ridge.] —**crease** v.

cre·ate (krē-āt') v. **-at·ed, -at·ing.** 1. To cause to exist; originate. 2. To bring about; produce. [< Lat. *creare.*]

cre·a·tion (krē-ā'shən) n. 1. The act or

process of creating. **2.** Something created. **3.** The world and all things in it.

cre·a·tive (krē-ā'tǐv) *adj.* Characterized by originality; imaginative. **—cre'a·tiv'i·ty** *n.*

cre·a·tor (krē-ā'tər) *n.* **1.** One that creates. **2.** Creator. God.

crea·ture (krē'chər) *n.* **1.** A living being, esp. an animal. **2.** A human being. **3.** One that is dependent upon or subservient to another.

crèche (krěsh) *n.* A representation of the Nativity scene. [Fr., of Gmc. orig.]

cre·dence (krēd'ns) *n.* Acceptance as true; belief. [< Lat. *credere*, to believe.]

cre·den·tial (krǐ-děn'shəl) *n.* Something that entitles one to credit or authority.

cre·den·za (krǐ-děn'zə) *n.* A buffet or sideboard, esp. one without legs. [Ital.]

cred·i·ble (krěd'ə-bəl) *adj.* **1.** Believable; plausible. **2.** Trustworthy; reliable. [< Lat. *credibilis.*] **—cred'i·bil'i·ty** *n.* **—cred'i·bly** *adv.*

cred·it (krěd'ĭt) *n.* **1.** Belief; trust. **2.** The quality of being trustworthy. **3.** A source of honor: *a credit to his family.* **4.** Approval; respect. **5.** Certification of completion of a course of study. **6.** Reputation for financial solvency and integrity. **7.** Time allowed for payment of something sold on trust. **8.** Entry in an account of payment received. **9.** The balance in a person's bank account. *—v.* **1.** To believe; trust. **2.** To give credit to. [< Lat. *creditum,* loan.]

cred·it·a·ble (krěd'ĭ-tə-bəl) *adj.* Deserving commendation. **—cred'it·a·bly** *adv.*

credit card *n.* A card authorizing the holder to buy goods or services on credit.

cred·i·tor (krěd'ĭ-tər) *n.* One to whom money is owed.

cre·do (krē'dō, krā'-) *n., pl.* **-dos.** A statement of belief; creed. [Lat., I believe.]

cred·u·lous (krěj'ə-ləs) *adj.* Tending to believe too readily; gullible. [Lat. *credulus.*] **—cre·du'li·ty** (krǐ-dōō'lǐ-tē, -dyōō'-) *or* **cred·u'lous·ness** *n.* **—cred'u·lous·ly** *adv.*

Cree (krē) *n., pl.* **Cree** *or* **Crees. 1. a.** A tribe of Indians formerly living in central Canada. **b.** A member of the Cree. **2.** The Algonquian language of the Cree.

creed (krēd) *n.* A statement of the essential articles of a religious belief. [< OE *crēda* < Lat. *credo,* I believe.]

creek (krēk, krĭk) *n.* A small stream, often a tributary to a river. [ME *creke.*]

Creek (krēk) *n., pl.* **Creek** *or* **Creeks. 1. a.** A confederacy of Indian tribes formerly inhabiting parts of the southeastern United States. **b.** A member of the Creek. **2.** The Muskhogean language of the Creek.

creel (krēl) *n.* A wicker basket used esp. for carrying fish. [ME *crelle.*]

creep (krēp) *v.* **crept** (krěpt), **creep·ing. 1.** To move on hands and knees with the body close to the ground. **2.** To move furtively or slowly. **3.** To grow along a surface, as a vine. **4.** To have a tingling sensation. [< OE *crēopan.*] **—creep** *n.* **—creep'er** *n.*

creep·y (krē'pē) *adj.* **-i·er, -i·est.** *Informal.* Inducing or having a sensation of fear, as of things crawling on the skin.

cre·mate (krē'māt', krǐ-māt') *v.* **-mat·ed, -mat·ing.** To burn (a corpse) to ashes. [Lat. *cremare.*] **—cre·ma'tion** *n.*

cre·ma·to·ry (krē'mə-tôr'ē, -tōr'ē, krěm'ə-) *n., pl.* **-ries.** A furnace or establishment for the cremation of corpses.

cren·e·lat·ed (krěn'ə-lā'tĭd) *adj.* Having battlements. [< Fr. *crenel,* crenelation.] **—cren'e·la'tion** *n.*

Cre·ole (krē'ōl') *n.* **1.** A person of European descent born in the West Indies or Spanish America. **2. a.** A person descended from the original French settlers of Louisiana. **b.** The French dialect spoken by the Creoles. **3.** A person of European and Negro ancestry.

cre·o·sote (krē'ə-sōt') *n.* An oily liquid obtained from coal tar and used as a wood preservative and disinfectant. [G. *Kreosot.*]

crepe (krāp) *n.* *Also* **crepe, crêpe.** A thin, crinkled fabric of silk, cotton, wool, or other fiber. [Fr. *crêpe.*]

crept (krěpt) *v.* *p.t. & p.p.* of **creep.**

cre·pus·cu·lar (krǐ-pǔs'kyə-lər) *adj.* **1.** Of or like twilight. **2.** Active at twilight, as certain insects. [< Lat. *crepusculum,* twilight.]

cres·cen·do (krə-shěn'dō, -sěn'-) *n., pl.* **-dos.** A gradual increase in the volume of sound. *—adj.* Gradually increasing in volume. [Ital.] **—cres·cen'do** *adv.*

cres·cent (krěs'ənt) *n.* **1.** The figure of the moon in its first quarter, with concave and convex edges terminating in points. **2.** Something shaped like a crescent. [< OFr. *creissant.*] **—cres'cent** *adj.*

cress (krěs) *n.* Any of various related plants with pungent leaves often used in salads. [< OE *cærse.*]

crest (krěst) *n.* **1.** A tuft or similar projection on the head of a bird or other animal. **2.** The top of something, as a wave; peak. **3.** A heraldic device above the shield on a coat of arms. *—v.* **1.** To reach the crest of. **2.** To form into a crest. [< Lat. *crista.*]

crest·fall·en (krěst'fô'lən) *adj.* Dejected; dispirited.

Cre·ta·ceous (krǐ-tā'shəs) *adj.* Of or belonging to the geologic time, system of rocks, or sedimentary deposits of the most recent period of the Mesozoic era, characterized by the development of flowering plants and the disappearance of dinosaurs. *—n.* The Cretaceous period.

cre·tin (krēt'n) *n.* A person afflicted with cretinism. [< dial. Fr. *crestin,* Christian, deformed idiot.]

cre·tin·ism (krēt'n-ĭz'əm) *n.* A thyroid deficiency causing arrested mental and physical development.

cre·tonne (krǐ-tŏn', krē'tŏn') *n.* A heavy unglazed cotton or linen fabric used for draperies and slipcovers. [< *Creton,* France.]

creel   crescent

ă pat   ā pay   â care   ä father   ě pet   ē be   ĭ pit   ī tie   î pier   ŏ pot   ō toe   ô paw, for   oi noise   ōō took
ōō boot   ou out   th thin   th this   ŭ cut   û urge   yōō abuse   zh vision   ə about, item, edible, gallop, circus

cre·vasse (krə-văs′) n. 1. A deep fissure, as in a glacier. 2. A crack in a levee. [Fr.]

crev·ice (krĕv′ĭs) n. A narrow crack; fissure. [< Lat. *crepare*, to crack.]

crew[1] (krōō) n. 1. A group of people working together. 2. The personnel manning a ship or aircraft. 3. A team of oarsmen. [ME *creue*, military reinforcement.]

crew[2] (krōō) v. A p.t. of *crow*[2].

crew·el (krōō′əl) n. Loosely twisted worsted yarn used for embroidery. [ME *crule*.]

crib (krĭb) n. 1. A child's bed with high sides. 2. A small building for storing corn. 3. A rack or trough for fodder. 4. *Informal.* A petty theft, as of another's work; plagiarism. 5. *Informal.* A translation or synopsis consulted dishonestly by students during an examination. —v. **cribbed, crib·bing.** 1. To confine in or as if in a crib. 2. *Informal.* To plagiarize. 3. *Informal.* To steal. 4. *Informal.* To use a crib in examinations. [< OE *cribb*, manger.] —**crib′ber** n.

crib·bage (krĭb′ĭj) n. A card game scored by inserting pegs into holes on a board. [< CRIB.]

crick (krĭk) n. A painful cramp, as in the back. [ME *crike*.]

crick·et[1] (krĭk′ĭt) n. A leaping insect the male of which produces a shrill, chirping sound. [< OFr. *criquet*.]

crick·et[2] (krĭk′ĭt) n. A game played with bats, a ball, and wickets by two teams of 11 players each. [Poss. < OFr. *criquet*, target stick in a bowling game.]

cri·er (krī′ər) n. One who shouts out public announcements.

cries (krīz) n. Pl. of *cry*.

crime (krīm) n. An act committed or omitted in violation of the law. [< Lat. *crimen*.]

crim·i·nal (krĭm′ə-nəl) n. One who has committed a crime. —adj. 1. Of, involving, or being a crime. 2. Guilty of crime. —**crim′i·nal·i·ty** (-năl′ĭ-tē) n. —**crim′i·nal·ly** adv.
Syns: criminal, illegal, illegitimate, illicit, lawless, unlawful, wrongful adj.

crim·i·nol·o·gy (krĭm′ə-nŏl′ə-jē) n. The scientific study of crime and criminals. —**crim′i·no·log′i·cal** (-nə-lŏj′ĭ-kəl) adj. —**crim′i·nol′o·gist** n.

crimp (krĭmp) v. 1. To press into small folds or ridges; corrugate. 2. To curl (hair). —n. Something, as hair, that has been crimped. [ME *crimpen*, to wrinkle.] —**crimp′er** n.

crim·son (krĭm′zən, -sən) n. A vivid purplish red. —v. To make or become crimson. [< Ar. *qirmizī*.] —**crim′son** adj.

cringe (krĭnj) v. **cringed, cring·ing.** To shrink back, as in fear; cower. [ME *crengen*.]

crin·kle (krĭng′kəl) v. **-kled, -kling.** To form into many wrinkles or ripples. [ME *crinkelen*.] —**crin′kle** n. —**crin′kly** adj.

crin·o·line (krĭn′ə-lĭn) n. 1. A fabric used to line and stiffen garments. 2. A hoop skirt. [< Ital. *crinolino*.]

crip·ple (krĭp′əl) n. One who is disabled or lame. —v. **-pled, -pling.** To disable or damage. [< OE *crypel*.]

cri·sis (krī′sĭs) n., pl. **-ses** (-sēz′). 1. A crucial or decisive point or situation; turning point. 2. A sudden change in the course of an acute disease toward improvement or deterioration. [< Gk. *krisis*.]

crisp (krĭsp) adj. **-er, -est.** 1. Firm but easily broken; brittle. 2. Firm and fresh: *crisp cel·ery.* 3. Brisk; invigorating. 4. Having small curls or waves. —v. To make or become crisp. [< Lat. *crispus*, curly.] —**crisp′ly** adv. —**crisp′ness** n. —**crisp′y** adj.

criss·cross (krĭs′krôs′, -krŏs′) v. 1. To mark with crossing lines. 2. To move crosswise through or over. —n. A pattern made of crossing lines. [< obs. *christcross*, mark of a cross.] —**criss′cross′** adj. & adv.

cri·te·ri·on (krī-tîr′ē-ən) n., pl. **-te·ri·a** (-tîr′ē-ə) or **-ons.** A standard on which a judgment can be based. [< Gk. *kritērion*.]
Usage: Criteria is a plural form and should not be substituted for the singular *criterion*.

crit·ic (krĭt′ĭk) n. 1. One who forms and expresses judgments, esp. of literary or artistic works. 2. One who finds fault. [< Gk. *kritikos*, able to discern.]

crit·i·cal (krĭt′ĭ-kəl) adj. 1. Of or pertaining to critics or criticism. 2. Tending to criticize. 3. Characterized by or requiring careful evaluation and judgment. 4. Forming or of the nature of a crisis. —**crit′i·cal·ly** adv.
Syns: critical, acute, crucial, desperate, dire, exigent adj.

crit·i·cism (krĭt′ĭ-sĭz′əm) n. 1. The act of making judgments and evaluations. 2. Censure; disapproval. 3. A review or article expressing the judgments of a critic.

crit·i·cize (krĭt′ĭ-sīz′) v. **-cized, -ciz·ing.** 1. To judge the merits and faults of; evaluate. 2. To find fault with.

cri·tique (krĭ-tēk′) n. A critical review or commentary. [Fr.] —**cri·tique′** v.

crit·ter (krĭt′ər) n. *Informal.* A creature, esp. a domestic animal. [< CREATURE.]

croak (krōk) n. A low, hoarse sound, as that made by a frog. —v. 1. To utter or utter with a croak. 2. *Slang.* To die. [< ME *croken*, to croak.]

Croat (krōt, krō′ăt) n. Croatian or a Croatian.

Cro·a·tian (krō-ā′shən) n. 1. A native or inhabitant of Croatia. 2. Serbo-Croatian as used in Croatia. —**Cro·a′tian** adj.

cro·chet (krō-shā′) v. **-cheted** (-shād′), **-chet·ing** (-shā′ĭng). To make (a piece of needlework) by looping thread with a hooked needle. —n. Needlework made by crocheting. [< Fr., hook.]

crock (krŏk) n. An earthenware vessel. [< OE *crocc.*]

crock·er·y (krŏk′ə-rē) n. Earthenware.

croc·o·dile (krŏk′ə-dīl′) n. A large tropical aquatic reptile with armorlike skin and long, tapering jaws. [< Gk. *krokodilos*.]

crocodile

cro·cus (krō′kəs) n., pl. **-cus·es.** A garden plant with showy, variously colored early-blooming flowers. [< Gk. *krokos*, of Semitic orig.]

crois·sant (krwä-säN′) *n.* A rich crescent-shaped roll. [Fr.]

crone (krōn) *n.* A withered, witchlike old woman. [ME.]

cro·ny (krō′nē) *n., pl.* **-nies.** A close friend or companion, esp. of long standing. [Poss. < Gk. *khronios,* long-lasting.]

crook (krŏŏk) *n.* **1.** Something bent or curved. **2.** A bent or curved implement. **3.** A curve or bend. **4.** *Informal.* A thief; swindler. —*v.* To curve; bend. [< ON *krōkr,* hook.]

crook·ed (krŏŏk′ĭd) *adj.* **1.** Having bends or curves. **2.** *Informal.* Dishonest; fraudulent. —**crook′ed·ly** *adv.* —**crook′ed·ness** *n.*

croon (krōōn) *v.* To sing or hum softly. —*n.* A crooning sound. [< MDu. *kronen,* to lament.] —**croon′er** *n.*

crop (krŏp) *n.* **1. a.** Agricultural produce. **b.** A specific yield of such produce. **2.** A short haircut. **3.** A short riding whip. **4.** A pouchlike enlargement of a bird's esophagus in which food is partially digested. —*v.* **cropped, crop·ping. 1.** To cut off the ends of. **2.** To cut very short. **3.** To reap; harvest. —*phrasal verb.* **crop up.** To appear unexpectedly. [< OE *cropp,* ear of corn.]

crop·per (krŏp′ər) *n.* A sharecropper.

cro·quet (krō-kā′) *n.* An outdoor game in which wooden balls are driven through a series of wickets with mallets. [< ONFr., hook.]

cro·quette (krō-kĕt′) *n.* A small cake of minced food fried in deep fat. [Fr.]

cro·sier (krō′zhər) *n.* Also **cro·zier.** A bishop's staff. [< OFr. *crosse.*]

cross (krôs, krŏs) *n.* **1.** An upright post with a transverse piece near the top. **2.** A trial or affliction. **3.** A symbolic representation of the cross upon which Christ was crucified. **4.** A pattern formed by two intersecting lines. **5. a.** A hybrid plant or animal. **b.** The process of hybridization. —*v.* **1.** To go or extend across. **2.** To intersect. **3.** To draw a line across. **4.** To place crosswise. **5.** To thwart or obstruct. **6.** To breed by hybridizing. —*adj.* **1.** Lying crosswise. **2.** Contrary or opposing. **3.** Showing ill humor; annoyed. **4.** Hybrid. [< Lat. *crux.*] —**cross′ly** *adv.* —**cross′ness** *n.*

cross·bar (krôs′bär′, krŏs′-) *n.* A horizontal bar or line.

cross·bones (krôs′bōnz′, krŏs′-) *n.* Two bones placed crosswise, usu. under a skull.

cross·bow (krôs′bō′, krŏs′-) *n.* A medieval weapon consisting of a bow fixed crosswise on a stock.

cross·breed (krôs′brēd′, krŏs′-) *v.* **-bred** (-brĕd′), **-breed·ing.** To hybridize. —*n.* A hybrid.

cross·coun·try (krôs′kŭn′trē, krŏs′-) *adj.* **1.** Moving across open country rather than roads. **2.** From one side of a country to the opposite side. —**cross′-coun′try** *adv.*

cross·cur·rent (krôs′kûr′ənt, -kûr′-, krŏs′-) *n.* **1.** A current flowing across another. **2.** A conflicting tendency.

cross·cut (krôs′kŭt′, krŏs′-) *v.* To cut or run crosswise. —*adj.* **1.** Used for cutting crosswise: *a crosscut saw.* **2.** Cut across the grain.

cross-ex·am·ine (krôs′ĭg-zăm′ĭn, krŏs′-) *v.* **-ined, -in·ing. 1.** To question (someone) closely, esp. in order to compare the resulting answers with previous responses. —**cross′-ex·am′i·na′tion** *n.*

cross-eye (krôs′ī′, krŏs′ī′) *n.* A form of strabismus in which one or both eyes turn inward toward the nose. —**cross′-eyed** *adj.*

cross·fire (krôs′fīr′, krŏs′-) *n.* **1.** Lines of fire crossing each other. **2.** A rapid, often agitated discussion.

cross·hatch (krôs′hăch′, krŏs′-) *v.* To shade with sets of intersecting parallel lines.

cross·ing (krô′sĭng, krŏs′ĭng) *n.* **1.** An intersection, as of roads. **2.** The place at which something, as a river, can be crossed.

cross·piece (krôs′pēs′, krŏs′-) *n.* A transverse piece, as of a structure.

cross-pol·li·nate (krôs′pŏl′ə-nāt′, krŏs′-) *v.* **-nat·ed, -nat·ing.** To fertilize (a plant or flower) with pollen from another. —**cross′pol·li·na′tion** *n.*

cross-pur·pose (krôs′pûr′pəs, krŏs′-) *n.* A conflicting or contrary purpose.

cross-re·fer (krôs′rĭ-fûr′, krŏs′-) *v.* **-ferred, -fer·ring.** To refer from one part or passage, as of a book, to another. —**cross′-ref′er·ence** (-rĕf′ər-əns, -rĕf′rəns) *n.*

cross·road (krôs′rōd′, krŏs′-) *n.* **1.** A road that intersects another. **2.** Often **crossroads.** A place where two or more roads meet.

cross section *n.* **1. a.** A section formed by a plane cutting through an object, usu. at right angles to an axis. **b.** A piece so cut or a graphic representation of it. **2.** A representative sample meant to be typical of the whole.

cross·walk (krôs′wôk′, krŏs′-) *n.* A street crossing marked for pedestrians.

cross·wise (krôs′wīz′, krŏs′-) *adv.* Also **cross·ways** (-wāz′). Across; running transversely. —**cross′wise′** *adj.*

cross·word puzzle (krôs′wûrd′, krŏs′-) *n.* A puzzle with an arrangement of numbered squares to be filled with words in answer to clues.

crotch (krŏch) *n.* The angle or fork formed by the junction of parts, as two branches or legs. [Poss. < CRUTCH.]

crotch·et (krŏch′ĭt) *n.* An odd or whimsical notion. [< OFr. *crochet.*] —**crotch′et·y** *adj.*

crouch (krouch) *v.* **1.** To stoop with the limbs close to the body. **2.** To cringe. [< OFr. *crochir,* to be bent.] —**crouch** *n.*

croup (krōōp) *n.* Laryngitis in children, characterized by respiratory difficulty and a harsh cough. [Orig. unknown.] —**croup′y** *adj.*

crou·pi·er (krōō′pē-ər, -pē-ā′) *n.* An attendant at a gaming table who collects and pays bets. [Fr.]

crou·ton (krōō′tŏn′, krōō-tŏn′) *n.* A small crisp piece of toast used as a garnish. [< Lat. *crusta,* crust.]

crow¹ (krō) *n.* A large, glossy black bird with a raucous call. [< OE *crāwe.*]

crow² (krō) *n.* **1.** The cry of a rooster. **2.** An inarticulate sound of pleasure or delight. —*v.* **1.** *p.t.* **crowed** or **crew** (krōō). To utter the cry of a rooster. **2.** To make an inarticulate sound of pleasure or delight. **3.** To boast; exult. [< OE *crāwan.*]

Crow (krō) *n., pl.* **Crow** or **Crows. 1. a.** A tribe of Indians now settled in southeastern Montana. **b.** A member of this tribe. **2.** The Siouan language of the Crow.

ă pat ā pay â care ä father ĕ pet ē be ĭ pit ī tie î pier ŏ pot ō toe ô paw, for oi noise ŏŏ took ōō boot ou out th thin *th* this ŭ cut û urge yōō abuse zh vision ə about, item, edible, gallop, circus

crow·bar (krō′bär′) n. A metal bar with the working end shaped like a forked chisel, used as a lever.

crowd (kroud) n. 1. A large number of persons or things gathered together; throng. 2. A particular group; clique. —v. -1. To gather in numbers; throng. 2. To press or shove; push. 3. To cram tightly together. [< OE *crūdan*, to hasten.]

crown (kroun) n. 1. A head covering worn as a symbol of sovereignty. 2. The power of a monarch. 3. A wreath worn on the head as a symbol of victory, honor, or distinction. 4. Something resembling a crown in shape or position. 5. a. A former British coin. b. See table at **currency**. 6. The highest point of something, as the head. 7. The part of a tooth that is covered by enamel and projects beyond the gum line. —v. 1. To invest with royal power. 2. To put a crown upon. 3. To confer honor upon. 4. To be the highest part of; surmount. [< Gk. *korōnē*, wreath.]

crow's-foot (krōz′fŏŏt′) n., pl. **-feet** (-fēt′). A wrinkle at the outer corner of the eye.

crow's-nest (krōz′nĕst′) n. A lookout platform near the top of a ship's mast.

cro·zier (krō′zhər) n. Var. of **crosier**.

cru·ces (krōō′sēz) n. A pl. of **crux**.

cru·cial (krōō′shəl) adj. 1. Of decisive importance; critical. 2. Difficult; trying. [OFr., cross-shaped.] —**cru′cial·ly** adv.

cru·ci·ble (krōō′sə-bəl) n. A vessel made of a refractory substance used for melting materials at high temperatures. [< Med. Lat. *crucibulum*.]

cru·ci·fix (krōō′sə-fīks′) n. An image of Christ on the cross. [< OFr.]

cru·ci·fix·ion (krōō′sə-fīk′shən) n. 1. The act of crucifying. 2. A representation of Christ on the cross. 3. **Crucifixion**. The crucifying of Christ.

cru·ci·form (krōō′sə-fôrm′) adj. Cross-shaped. [Lat. *crux*, cross + -FORM.]

cru·ci·fy (krōō′sə-fī′) v. **-fied, -fy·ing.** 1. To put to death by nailing or binding to a cross. 2. To torment; torture. [< LLat. *crucifigere*.]

crude (krōōd) adj. **crud·er, crud·est.** 1. In an unrefined or natural state; raw. 2. Lacking finish, tact, or taste. 3. Roughly made. —n. Unrefined petroleum. [< Lat. *crudus*.] —**crude′ly** adv. —**cru′di·ty** n.

cru·el (krōō′əl) adj. **-el·er** or **-el·ler, -el·est** or **-el·lest.** Causing pain or suffering. [< Lat. *crudelis*.] —**cru′el·ly** adv. —**cru′el·ty** n.

cru·et (krōō′ĭt) n. A small glass bottle for holding vinegar or oil. [< OFr. *crue*, flask, of Gmc. orig.]

cruise (krōōz) v. **cruised, cruis·ing.** 1. To sail or travel over or about, as for pleasure. 2. To travel at a maximally efficient speed. [< MDu. *crucen*, to cross.] —**cruise** n.

cruis·er (krōō′zər) n. 1. One of a class of fast warships of medium tonnage. 2. A large motorboat whose cabin has living facilities. 3. A police squad car.

crul·ler (krŭl′ər) n. A small cake of sweet dough, usu. twisted, fried in deep fat. [< MDu. *crul*, curly.]

crumb (krŭm) n. 1. A small piece broken or fallen, as from bread. 2. A fragment or scrap. —v. 1. To break into crumbs. 2. To cover with crumbs. [< OE *cruma*.]

crum·ble (krŭm′bəl) v. **-bled, -bling.** 1. To break or cause to break into small parts. 2. To disintegrate. [< OE *(ge)crymian*.] —**crum′bly** adj.

crum·my (krŭm′ē) adj. **-mi·er, -mi·est.** Also **crumb·y, -i·er, -i·est.** Slang. 1. Miserable; wretched. 2. Shabby; cheap. [< CRUMB.]

crum·pet (krŭm′pĭt) n. A soft, muffinlike bread cooked on a griddle. [Poss. < ME *crompid (cake)*, curled (cake).]

crum·ple (krŭm′pəl) v. **-pled, -pling.** 1. To crush together into wrinkles; rumple. 2. To fall down; collapse. [Prob. < ME *crampen*, to curl up.]

crunch (krŭnch) v. 1. To chew with a noisy, grinding sound. 2. To crush or grind noisily. [Imit.] —**crunch** n. —**crunch′y** adj.

cru·sade (krōō-sād′) n. 1. **Crusade.** Any of the military expeditions undertaken by Christians in the 11th, 12th, and 13th cent. to recover the Holy Land. 2. A vigorous concerted movement for a cause or against an abuse. —v. **-sad·ed, -sad·ing.** To engage in a crusade. [< Lat. *crux*, cross.] —**cru·sad′er** n.

crush (krŭsh) v. 1. To press or squeeze so as to break or injure. 2. To extract or obtain by pressure. 3. To reduce to fine particles. 4. To break, pound, or grind into small fragments or powder. 5. To put down; subdue. —n. 1. The act of crushing. 2. A great crowd. 3. Informal. An infatuation. [< OFr. *croissir*.]

crust (krŭst) n. 1. The hard outer part of bread. 2. A piece of bread consisting mostly of crust. 3. A hard covering or surface. 4. A pastry shell, as of a pie. —v. To cover or become covered with a crust. [< Lat. *crusta*, shell.] —**crust′y** adj.

crus·ta·cean (krŭ-stā′shən) n. Any of various chiefly aquatic arthropods having a segmented body with a hard outer covering, as a lobster, crab, or shrimp. [< Lat. *crusta*, shell.]

crutch (krŭch) n. 1. A support used as an aid in walking, usu. having a crosspiece to fit under the armpit. 2. Something depended upon for support. [< OE *crycc*.]

crux (krŭks, krŏŏks) n., pl. **-es** or **cru·ces** (krōō′sēz). 1. A critical or crucial point. 2. A puzzling problem. [Lat., cross.]

cru·zei·ro (krōō-zâr′ō, -roŏ) n., pl. **-ros.** See table at **currency**. [Port.]

cry (krī) v. **cried, cry·ing.** 1. To shed tears and make inarticulate sobbing sounds; weep. 2. To utter loudly; shout. 3. To utter a characteristic sound or call, as an animal does. 4. To proclaim or announce in public. —n., pl. **cries.** 1. A loud utterance; shout. 2. A fit of weeping. 3. An urgent appeal. 4. The characteristic call of an animal. —idiom. **a far cry.** A long way. [< OFr. *crier*.]

cry·ba·by (krī′bā′bē) n. One who cries or complains frequently with little cause.

cryo- pref. Cold, freezing, or frost: *cryogenics*. [< Gk. *kruos*, frost.]

cry·o·gen·ics (krī′ə-jĕn′ĭks) n. (used with a sing. verb). The science of low-temperature phenomena. —**cry·o·gen′ic** adj.

crypt (krĭpt) n. An underground vault, esp. one used as a burial place. [< Gk. *kruptē*.]

cryp·tic (krĭp′tĭk) adj. Having an ambiguous or hidden meaning. [< Gk. *kruptikos*.]

crypto- pref. Hidden or secret: *cryptography*. [< Gk. *kruptos*, hidden.]

cryp·to·gram (krĭp′tə-grăm′) n. Something written in code or cipher.

cryp·tog·ra·phy (krĭp-tŏg′rə-fē) n. The study

or process of writing in or deciphering secret code. —**cryp·tog'ra·pher** *n.*

crys·tal (krĭs'tal) *n.* **1. a.** A three-dimensional atomic, ionic, or molecular structure of periodically repeated, identically constituted, congruent unit cells. **b.** The unit cell of such a structure. **c.** A body, such as a piece of quartz, having such a structure. **2.** Something similar to crystal, as in transparency. [< Gk. *krustallos*.] —**crys'tal·line** *adj.*

crys·tal·lize (krĭs'tə-līz') *v.* **-lized, -liz·ing. 1.** To form or cause to form a crystalline structure. **2.** To assume or cause to assume a definite and permanent form. —**crys'tal·li·za'tion** *n.*

crys·tal·log·ra·phy (krĭs'tə-lŏg'rə-fē) *n.* The science of crystal structure and phenomena. —**crys'tal·log'ra·pher** *n.* —**crys'tal·lo·graph'ic** (-lə-grăf'ĭk) or **crys'tal·lo·graph'i·cal** *adj.*

Cs The symbol for the element cesium.

Cu The symbol for the element copper. [Lat. *cuprum.*]

cub (kŭb) *n.* **1.** The young of certain animals, such as the bear. **2.** A novice, esp. in newspaper reporting. [Orig. unknown.]

cub·by·hole (kŭb'ē-hōl') *n.* A small compartment, cupboard, or closet. [< obs. *cub*, stall.]

cube (kyōōb) *n.* **1. a.** *Geom.* A solid having six congruent square faces. **b.** Something shaped like a cube. **2.** The product that results when the same number is used three times as a factor. —*v.* **cubed, cub·ing. 1.** To raise (a quantity or number) to the third power. **2.** To form or cut into a cube. [< Gk. *kubos*, six-sided die.]

cu·bic (kyōō'bĭk) *adj.* **1.** Having the shape of a cube. **2. a.** Having three dimensions. **b.** Having volume equal to a cube whose edge is of a stated length. **3.** *Math.* Of the third power, order, or degree. —**cu'bi·cal** *adj.*

cu·bi·cle (kyōō'bĭ-kəl) *n.* A small compartment, esp. a sleeping compartment. [Lat. *cubiculum.*]

cub·ism (kyōō'bĭz'əm) *n.* An early 20th-cent. school of painting and sculpture in which the subject matter is portrayed by geometric forms without realistic detail. —**cub'ist** *n.* —**cu·bis'tic** *adj.*

cubism
Detail from "Nature Morte" by
Georges Braque

cu·bit (kyōō'bĭt) *n.* An ancient unit of linear measure approx. 17 to 22 inches. [< Lat. *cubitum.*]

cuck·old (kŭk'əld, kōōk'-) *n.* A man whose wife has committed adultery. [< OFr. *cucu*, cuckoo.] —**cuck'old** *v.*

cuck·oo (kōō'kōō, kōōk'ōō) *n., pl.* **-oos.** An Old World bird with grayish plumage and a characteristic two-note call. —*adj.* Crazy or foolish. [ME *cuccu.*]

cu·cum·ber (kyōō'kŭm'bər) *n.* **1.** A vine cultivated for its edible fruit. **2.** The cylindrical green-skinned, white-fleshed edible fruit of the cucumber. [< Lat. *cucumis.*]

cud (kŭd) *n.* Food regurgitated from the first stomach to the mouth of a ruminant and chewed again. [< OE *cudu.*]

cud·dle (kŭd'l) *v.* **-dled, -dling. 1.** To hug tenderly. **2.** To nestle; snuggle. [Orig. unknown.] —**cud'dly** *adj.*

cudg·el (kŭj'əl) *n.* A short, heavy club. [< OE *cycgel.*] —**cudg'el** *v.*

cue[1] (kyōō) *n.* A long, tapered rod used to propel the ball in billiards and pool. [< Lat. *cauda*, tail.]

cue[2] (kyōō) *n.* **1.** A word or signal to begin or enter, as in a play. **2.** A hint or reminder. [Orig. unknown.] —**cue** *v.*

cue ball *n.* A white ball propelled with the cue in billiards and pool.

cuff[1] (kŭf) *n.* **1.** A fold or band at the bottom of a sleeve. **2.** The turned-up fold at the bottom of a trouser leg. [ME *cuffe*, mitten.]

cuff[2] (kŭf) *v.* To strike with the open hand; slap. [Orig. unknown.] —**cuff** *n.*

cui·sine (kwĭ-zēn') *n.* **1.** A manner or style of preparing food. **2.** The food prepared. [< LLat. *coquina*, kitchen.]

cul-de-sac (kŭl'dĭ-săk', kōōl'-) *n.* **1.** A dead-end street. **2.** An impasse. [Fr.]

cu·li·nary (kyōō'lə-nĕr'ē, kŭl'ə-) *adj.* Of or pertaining to cookery. [< Lat. *culina*, kitchen.]

cull (kŭl) *v.* **1.** To pick out from others; select. **2.** To gather; collect. [< Lat. *colligere*, to collect.] —**cull'er** *n.*

cul·mi·nate (kŭl'mə-nāt') *v.* **-nat·ed, -nat·ing.** To reach the highest point or degree; climax. [< LLat. *culminare*.] —**cul'mi·na'tion** *n.*

cu·lottes (kōō-lŏts', kyōō-) *pl.n.* A woman's full trousers cut to resemble a skirt. [Fr., dim. of *cul*, rump.]

cul·pa·ble (kŭl'pə-bəl) *adj.* Responsible for wrong or error. [< Lat. *culpare*, to blame.] —**cul'pa·bil'i·ty** *n.* —**cul'pa·bly** *adv.*

cul·prit (kŭl'prĭt) *n.* A person charged with or guilty of a crime. [Orig. unknown.]

cult (kŭlt) *n.* **1.** A system or community of religious worship and ritual. **2. a.** Obsessive devotion to a person or ideal. **b.** A group of persons sharing such devotion. [< Lat. *cultus*, worship.] —**cult'ish** *adj.* —**cult'ist** *n.*

cul·ti·vate (kŭl'tə-vāt') *v.* **-vat·ed, -vat·ing. 1.** To improve and prepare (land) for raising crops. **2.** To grow or tend (a plant or crop). **3.** To form and refine, as by education. **4.** To seek the acquaintance or good will of. [Med. Lat. *cultivare* < Lat. *colere*.] —**cul'ti·va·ble** or **cul'ti·vat'a·ble** *adj.* —**cul'ti·va'tion** *n.* —**cul'ti·va'tor** *n.*

cul·ture (kŭl'chər) *n.* **1.** Development of the intellect through education and training.

2. Intellectual and artistic taste and refinement. **3.** The arts, beliefs, customs, institutions, and all other products of human work and thought created by a people or group at a particular time. **4. a.** The raising of animals or growing of plants, esp. to improve stock. **b.** Cultivation of the soil. **5.** A growth or colony of microorganisms in a nutrient medium. —*v.* **-tured, -tur-ing.** **1.** To grow (microorganisms, tissues, etc.) in a nutrient medium. **2.** To cultivate. [< Lat. *cultura.*] —**cul'tur-al** *adj.* —**cul'tured** *adj.*

cul-vert (kŭl'vərt) *n.* A drain crossing under a road or embankment. [Orig. unknown.]

cum-ber (kŭm'bər) *v.* To weigh down. [ME *combren,* to annoy.] —**cum'brous** *adj.* —**cum'brous-ly** *adv.*

cum-ber-some (kŭm'bər-səm) *adj.* Unwieldy and burdensome. —**cum'ber-some-ly** *adv.*

cum-mer-bund (kŭm'ər-bŭnd') *n.* A broad, pleated sash worn as a waistband, esp. by men. [Hindi *kamarband.*]

cu-mu-la-tive (kyōōm'yə-lā'tĭv, -lə-tĭv) *adj.* Increasing or enlarging by successive addition. [< Lat. *cumulare,* to heap up.] —**cu'mu-la'tive-ly** *adv.* —**cu'mu-la'tive-ness** *n.*

cu-mu-lo-nim-bus (kyōōm'yə-lō-nĭm'bəs) *n., pl.* **-bus-es** or **-bi** (-bī'). A very dense cloud with massive projections that billow upward. [CUMUL(US) + NIMBUS.]

cu-mu-lus (kyōōm'yə-ləs) *n., pl.* **-li** (-lī'). A dense white, fluffy, flat-based cloud with a multiple rounded top and a well-defined outline. [Lat., heap.]

cu-ne-i-form (kyōō-nē'ə-fôrm', kyōō-nē'-) *adj.* Wedge-shaped, as the characters used in ancient Mesopotamian writings. —*n.* Cuneiform writing. [< Lat. *cuneus,* wedge.]

cuneiform

cun-ning (kŭn'ĭng) *adj.* **1.** Shrewd; crafty. **2.** Exhibiting ingenuity. **3.** *Informal.* Delicately pleasing; charming. —*n.* **1.** Skill in deception; guile. **2.** Dexterity. [< OE *cunnan,* to know.] —**cun'ning-ly** *adv.*

cup (kŭp) *n.* **1.** A small, open container used for drinking. **2.** The amount a cup holds. **3.** The wine used in the Eucharist. **4.** A measure of capacity equal to about 237 milliliters, 8 ounces, or 16 tablespoons. **5.** Something resembling a cup. —*v.* **cupped, cup-ping.** To form or shape like a cup: *cupped his hands.* [< LLat. *cuppa,* drinking vessel.] —**cup'ful'** (-fōōl') *n.*

cup-board (kŭb'ərd) *n.* A storage closet or cabinet.

cup-cake (kŭp'kāk') *n.* A small cup-shaped cake.

cu-pid (kyōō'pĭd) *n.* A representation of the Roman god of love, portrayed as a winged boy with a bow and arrow.

cu-pid-i-ty (kyōō-pĭd'ĭ-tē) *n.* Excessive desire, esp. for wealth; greed. [< Lat. *cupiditas.*]

cu-po-la (kyōō'pə-lə) *n.* A small, usu. domed structure surmounting a roof. [Ital.]

cur (kûr) *n.* **1.** A mongrel dog. **2.** A base person. [ME *curre.*]

cu-ra-re (kyōō-rä'rē, kōō-) *n.* A resinous extract obtained from various South American trees, used medicinally as a muscle relaxant. [< Carib *kurari.*]

cu-rate (kyōōr'ĭt) *n.* **1.** A clergyman who assists a rector or vicar. **2.** A clergyman who has charge of a parish. [< Med. Lat. *curatus* < Lat. *cura,* care.] —**cu'ra-cy** *n.*

cu-ra-tive (kyōōr'ə-tĭv) *adj.* Serving or tending to cure. —**cu'ra-tive-ly** *adv.*

cu-ra-tor (kyōō-rā'tər, kyōōr'ā-tər) *n.* The director of an institution such as a museum. [< Lat., overseer.] —**cu'ra-to'ri-al** (kyōōr'ə-tôr'-ē-əl, -tōr'-) *adj.* —**cu-ra'tor-ship'** *n.*

curb (kûrb) *n.* **1.** A concrete or stone edging along a sidewalk. **2.** Something that checks or restrains. **3.** A chain or strap used together with a bit to restrain a horse. —*v.* To check, restrain, or control. [< Lat. *curvus,* curved.]

curb-ing (kûr'bĭng) *n.* **1.** The material used to construct a curb. **2.** A curb.

curb-stone (kûrb'stōn') *n.* A stone or row of stones that constitutes a curb.

curd (kûrd) *n.* The thick part of milk that separates from the whey, used to make cheese. [ME *crud.*]

cur-dle (kûr'dl) *v.* **-dled, -dling.** To change or cause to change into curd.

cure (kyōōr) *n.* **1.** A method or course of medical treatment. **2.** Restoration of health. **3.** An agent, such as a drug, used to restore health. —*v.* **cured, cur-ing.** **1.** To restore to health. **2.** To rid of (disease). **3.** To preserve (e.g. meat or fish), as by salting, smoking, or aging. [< Lat. *cura,* care.] —**cur'a-ble** *adj.* —**cure'less** *adj.*

cure-all (kyōōr'ôl') *n.* Something that cures all diseases or evils; panacea.

cu-ret-tage (kyōōr'ĭ-täzh') *n.* Surgical scraping of a bodily cavity. [Fr. < *curette,* a surgical scoop.]

curfew (kûr'fyōō) *n.* **1.** A regulation requiring specified groups of people to retire from the streets at a prescribed hour. **2.** A signal, as a bell, announcing the hour of a curfew. [< OFr. *cuevrefeu.*]

cu-ri-a (kyōōr'ē-ə) *n., pl.* **-ri-ae** (-ē-ē'). Often **Curia.** The central administration governing the Roman Catholic Church. [Lat., council.]

cu-rie (kyōōr'ē, kyōō-rē') *n.* A unit of radioactivity, the amount of any nuclide that undergoes exactly 3.7×10^{10} radioactive disintegrations per second. [< Marie *Curie* (1867–1934).]

cu-ri-o (kyōōr'ē-ō') *n., pl.* **-os.** A rare or unusual object of art. [< CURIOSITY.]

cu-ri-ous (kyōōr'ē-əs) *adj.* **1.** Eager to know or learn. **2.** Excessively inquisitive; nosy. **3.** Unusual or extraordinary; singular. [< Lat. *curiosus.*] —**cu'ri-os'i-ty** (-ŏs'ĭ-tē) *n.* —**cu'ri-ous-ly** *adv.*

cu-ri-um (kyōōr'ē-əm) *n. Symbol* **Cm** A silvery, metallic synthetic radioactive element. Atomic number 96; longest-lived isotope Cm 247. [< Marie (1867–1934) and Pierre *Curie* (1859–1906).]

curl (kûrl) v. **1.** To form or twist into ringlets. **2.** To assume or form into a curved or spiral shape. —n. **1.** A ringlet of hair. **2.** Something with a spiral or coiled shape. [ME *curlen*.] —**curl'i·ness** n. —**curl'y** adj.

cur·lew (kûr'lyōō, kûr'lōō) n. A brownish, long-legged, long-billed shore bird. [< OFr. *courlieu.*]

curl·i·cue (kûr'lĭ-kyōō') n. A fancy twist or flourish. [CURLY + CUE¹.]

cur·mudg·eon (kər-mŭj'ən) n. A cantankerous person. [Orig. unknown.]

cur·rant (kûr'ənt, kŭr'-) n. **1. a.** Any of various usu. prickly shrubs bearing clusters of red, black, or greenish fruit. **b.** The small, sour fruit of any of these plants. **2.** A small seedless raisin. [ME *(raysons of) Coraunte,* (raisins of) Corinth.]

cur·ren·cy (kûr'ən-sē, kŭr'-) n., pl. **-cies. 1.** A form of money in actual use as a medium of exchange. **2.** General acceptance; prevalence.

cur·rent (kûr'ənt, kŭr'-) adj. **1.** Belonging to the present time; present-day. **2.** Commonly accepted; prevalent. —n. **1.** A steady and smooth onward movement, as of water. **2.** The part of a body of liquid or gas that has a continuous onward motion. **3. a.** A flow of electric charge. **b.** The amount of electric charge that passes a point in a unit of time. [< Lat. *currere,* to run.] —**cur'rent·ly** adv.

cur·ric·u·lum (kə-rĭk'yə-ləm) n., pl. **-la** (-lə) or **-lums. 1.** The courses of study offered by an educational institution. **2.** A particular course of study. [Lat., course.] —**cur·ric'u·lar** adj.

cur·ry¹ (kûr'ē, kŭr'ē) v. **-ried, -ry·ing. 1.** To groom (a horse) with a currycomb. **2.** To prepare (tanned hides) for use, as by soaking. [< AN *curreier,* to arrange.]

cur·ry² (kûr'ē, kŭr'ē) n., pl. **-ries. 1.** A pungent condiment made from a powdered blend of spices. **2.** A sauce or dish seasoned with curry. —v. **-ried, -ry·ing.** To season with curry. [Tamil *kari,* relish.]

cur·ry·comb (kûr'ē-kōm', kŭr'-) n. A comb with metal teeth used for grooming horses. —**cur'ry·comb'** v.

curse (kûrs) n. **1. a.** An appeal to a supernatural power for evil to befall someone or something. **b.** The evil thus invoked. **2.** A swear word; oath. **3.** Something that causes great harm; scourge. —v. **cursed** or **curst** (kûrst), **curs·ing. 1.** To invoke evil on; damn. **2.** To bring evil upon; afflict. **3.** To swear (at); blaspheme. [< OE *curs.*]

cur·sive (kûr'sĭv) adj. Designating handwriting or printing in which the letters are joined together. [< Med. Lat. *(scripta) cursiva,* flowing (script).]

cur·so·ry (kûr'sə-rē) adj. Hasty and superficial; not thorough. [LLat. *cursorius,* of running.] —**cur'so·ri·ly** adv.

curt (kûrt) adj. **-er, -est.** Rudely brief and abrupt; brusque. [Lat. *curtus,* cut short.] —**curt'ly** adv. —**curt'ness** n.

cur·tail (kər-tāl') v. To cut short; abbreviate. [< OFr. *courtault,* horse with a cropped tail.] —**cur·tail'ment** n.

cur·tain (kûr'tn) n. A piece of material hanging in a window or other opening as a deco-

ration, shade, or screen. [< LLat. *cortina.*] —**cur'tain** v.

curt·sy (kûrt'sē) n., pl. **-sies.** A gesture of respect or reverence made by women by bending the knees with one foot forward. [< COURTESY.] —**curt'sy** v.

cur·va·ceous (kûr-vā'shəs) adj. Having a full or voluptuous figure; shapely.

cur·va·ture (kûr'və-chōōr', -chər) n. An act, instance, or amount of curving.

curve (kûrv) n. **1. a.** A line that deviates from straightness in a smooth, continuous fashion. **b.** A surface that deviates from planarity in a smooth, continuous fashion. **2.** Something that has the shape of a curve. —v. **curved, curv·ing.** To move in, form, or cause to form a curve. [< Lat. *curvus.*]

cush·ion (kōōsh'ən) n. **1.** A soft pad or pillow to sit, lie, or rest on. **2.** Something that absorbs or softens an impact. **3.** The rim bordering a billiard table. —v. **1.** To provide with a cushion. **2.** To protect against or absorb the impact of. [< Lat. *coxa,* hip.]

cusp (kŭsp) n. A point or pointed end. [< Lat. *cuspis.*]

cus·pid (kŭs'pĭd) n. A canine tooth. [< BICUSPID.]

cus·pi·dor (kŭs'pĭ-dôr') n. A spittoon. [Port. < *cuspir,* to spit.]

cuss (kŭs) v. Informal. To curse. [< CURSE.] —**cuss** n.

cus·tard (kŭs'tərd) n. A dessert of milk, sugar, eggs, and flavoring cooked until set. [< Lat. *crusta,* crust.]

cus·to·di·an (kŭ-stō'dē-ən) n. **1.** One who has charge of something; caretaker. **2.** A janitor. —**cus·to'di·an·ship'** n.

cus·to·dy (kŭs'tə-dē) n., pl. **-dies. 1.** The act or right of caring for or guarding. **2.** The condition of being detained or held under guard, esp. by the police. [< Lat. *custos,* guard.] —**cus·to'di·al** (kŭ-stō'dē-əl) adj.

cus·tom (kŭs'təm) n. **1. a.** A practice followed as a matter of course; convention. **2.** A habit of an individual. **3. customs.** A duty or tax on imported goods. **4.** Habitual patronage, as of a store. —adj. **1.** Made to order. **2.** Specializing in made-to-order goods. [< Lat. *consuetudo.*]

cus·tom·ar·y (kŭs'tə-mĕr'ē) adj. **1.** Established by custom. **2.** Commonly practiced or used; usual. —**cus'tom·ar'i·ly** (-mâr'ə-lē) adv.

cus·tom-built (kŭs'təm-bĭlt') adj. Built according to the specifications of the buyer.

cus·tom·er (kŭs'tə-mər) n. One who buys goods or services, esp. on a regular basis.

cus·tom·house (kŭs'təm-hous') n. A building where customs are collected.

cus·tom-made (kŭs'təm-mād') adj. Made according to the specifications of the buyer.

customs union n. An international association organized to eliminate customs restrictions between member nations and to establish a tariff policy toward nonmember nations.

cut (kŭt) v. **cut, cut·ting. 1.** To penetrate with or as if with a sharp edge. **2.** To separate into parts with a sharp-edged instrument; sever. **3.** To separate by or as if by cutting; remove. **4.** To shorten; trim. **5.** To harvest. **6.** To un-

---

ă pat ā pay â care ä father ĕ pet ē be ĭ pit ī tie î pier ŏ pot ō toe ô paw, for oi noise ōō took
ōō boot ou out th thin th this ŭ cut û urge yōō abuse zh vision ə about, item, edible, gallop, circus

CURRENCY

Basic Unit or Subdivision	Country	Basic Unit	Subdivision
afghani	Afghanistan		100 puls
agora	Israel	shekel	100 agorot
at	Laos	kip	100 at
avo	Macao	pataca	100 avos
baht	Thailand		100 satang
baiza	Oman	riyal-omani	1000 baiza
balboa	Panama		100 centesimos
ban	Rumania	leu	100 bani
birr	Ethiopia		100 cents
bolivar	Venezuela		100 centimos
butut	Gambia	dalasi	100 bututs
cedi	Ghana		100 pesewas
cent	Australia	dollar	100 cents
	Bahamas	dollar	100 cents
	Barbados	dollar	100 cents
	Belize	dollar	100 cents
	Brunei	dollar	100 cents
	Canada	dollar	100 cents
	Cayman Islands	dollar	100 cents
	China, Republic of (Taiwan)	yuan	100 cents
	Dominica	dollar	100 cents
	Ethiopia	birr	100 cents
	Fiji	dollar	100 cents
	Grenada	dollar	100 cents
	Guyana	dollar	100 cents
	Hong Kong	dollar	100 cents
	Kenya	shilling	100 cents
	Liberia	dollar	100 cents
	Malta	pound	100 cents
	Mauritius	rupee	100 cents
	Nauru	dollar	100 cents
	Netherlands	guilder	100 cents
	Netherlands Antilles	guilder	100 cents
	New Zealand	dollar	100 cents
	Saint Lucia	dollar	100 cents
	Saint Vincent	dollar	100 cents
	Seychelles	rupee	100 cents
	Sierra Leone	leone	100 cents
	Singapore	dollar	100 cents
	Solomon Islands	dollar	100 cents
	Somalia	schilling	100 cents
	South Africa	rand	100 cents
	Sri Lanka	rupee	100 cents
	Surinam	guilder	100 cents
	Swaziland	lilangeni	100 cents
		rand	100 cents
	Tanzania	shilling	100 cents
	Trinidad and Tobago	dollar	100 cents
	Uganda	shilling	100 cents
	United States	dollar	100 cents
	Western Samoa	tala	100 cents
	Zimbabwe	dollar	100 cents
centavo	Argentina	peso	100 centavos
	Bolivia	peso	100 centavos
	Brazil	cruzeiro	100 centavos
	Cape Verde	escudo	100 centavos
	Chile	peso	100 centavos
	Colombia	peso	100 centavos
	Cuba	peso	100 centavos
	Dominican Republic	peso	100 centavos
	Ecuador	sucre	100 centavos
	El Salvador	colon	100 centavos

CURRENCY *(continued)*

Basic Unit or Subdivision	Country	Basic Unit	Subdivision
	Guatemala	quetzal	100 centavos
	Guinea-Bissau	peso	100 centavos
	Honduras	lempira	100 centavos
	Mexico	peso	100 centavos
	Nicaragua	cordoba	100 centavos
	Peru	sol	100 centavos
	Philippines	peso	100 centavos
	Portugal	escudo	100 centavos
centesimo	Italy	lira	100 centesimi
	Panama	balboa	100 centesimos
	San Marino	lira	100 centesimi
	Uruguay	peso	100 centesimos
	Vatican City	lira	100 centesimi
centime	Algeria	dinar	100 centimes
	Andorra	franc	100 centimes
	Belgium	franc	100 centimes
	Benin	franc	100 centimes
	Burundi	franc	100 centimes
	Cameroon	franc	100 centimes
	Central African Republic	franc	100 centimes
	Chad	franc	100 centimes
	Comoros	franc	100 centimes
	Congo	franc	100 centimes
	Djibouti	franc	100 centimes
	France	franc	100 centimes
	Gabon	franc	100 centimes
	Haiti	gourde	100 centimes
	Ivory Coast	franc	100 centimes
	Liechtenstein	franc	100 centimes
	Luxembourg	franc	100 centimes
	Madagascar	franc	100 centimes
	Mali	franc	100 centimes
	Monaco	franc	100 centimes
	Morocco	dirham	100 centimes
	Niger	franc	100 centimes
	Rwanda	franc	100 centimes
	Senegal	franc	100 centimes
	Switzerland	franc	100 centimes
	Togo	franc	100 centimes
	Upper Volta	franc	100 centimes
	Vanuatu	franc	100 centimes
centimo	Andorra	peseta	100 centimos
	Costa Rica	colon	100 centimos
	Equatorial Guinea	ekpwele	100 centimos
	Paraguay	guarani	100 centimos
	São Tomé and Principe	dobra	100 centimos
	Spain	peseta	100 centimos
	Venezuela	bolivar	100 centimos
chao	Vietnam	dong	10 chao
chetrum	Bhutan	ngultrum	100 chetrums
chiao	China, People's Republic of	renminbi	10 chiao
chon	South Korea	won	100 chon
colon	Costa Rica		100 centimos
	El Salvador		100 centavos
cordoba	Nicaragua		100 centavos
cory	Guinea	syli	100 cory
crown	Czechoslovakia		100 halers
cruzeiro	Brazil		100 centavos
dalasi	Gambia		100 bututs
deutsche mark	West Germany		100 pfennigs
dinar	Algeria		100 centimes
	Bahrain		100 fils
	Iran	rial	100 dinars
	Iraq		1000 fils
	Jordan		1000 fils

CURRENCY *(continued)*

Basic Unit or Subdivision	Country	Basic Unit	Subdivision
	Kuwait		1000 fils
	Libya		1000 dirhams
	Southern Yemen		1000 fils
	Tunisia		1000 milliemes
	Yugoslavia		100 para
dirham	Morocco		100 centimes
	Qatar	riyal	100 dirhams
	United Arab Emirates		100 fils
dobra	São Tomé and Principe		100 centimos
dollar	Australia		100 cents
	Bahamas		100 cents
	Barbados		100 cents
	Brunei		100 cents
	Canada		100 cents
	Cayman Islands		100 cents
	Dominica		100 cents
	Fiji		100 cents
	Grenada		100 cents
	Guyana		100 cents
	Hong Kong		100 cents
	Jamaica		100 cents
	Liberia		100 cents
	Nauru		100 cents
	New Zealand		100 cents
	Saint Lucia		100 cents
	Saint Vincent		100 cents
	Singapore		100 cents
	Solomon Islands		100 cents
	Trinidad and Tobago		100 cents
	United States		100 cents
	Zimbabwe		100 cents
dong	Vietnam		10 chao
drachma	Greece		100 lepta
ekpwele	Equatorial Guinea		100 cents
escudo	Cape Verde		100 centavos
	Portugal		100 centavos
eyrir	Iceland	krona	100 aurar
fil	Bahrain	dinar	1000 fils
	Iraq	dinar	1000 fils
	Jordan	dinar	1000 fils
	Kuwait	dinar	1000 fils
	Southern Yemen	dinar	1000 fils
	United Arab Emirates	dinar	100 fils
	Yemen	riyal	100 fils
fillér	Hungary	forint	100 fillér
forint	Hungary		100 fillér
franc	Andorra		100 centimes
	Belgium		100 centimes
	Benin		100 centimes
	Burundi		100 centimes
	Cameroon		100 centimes
	Central African Republic		100 centimes
	Chad		100 centimes
	Comoros		100 centimes
	Congo		100 centimes
	Djibouti		100 centimes
	France		100 centimes
	Gabon		100 centimes
	Ivory Coast		100 centimes
	Liechtenstein		100 centimes
	Luxembourg		100 centimes
	Madagascar		100 centimes
	Mali		100 centimes
	Monaco		100 centimes
	Niger		100 centimes
	Rwanda		100 centimes

CURRENCY (continued)

Basic Unit or Subdivision	Country	Basic Unit	Subdivision
	Senegal		100 centimes
	Switzerland		100 centimes
	Togo		100 centimes
	Upper Volta		100 centimes
	Vanuatu		100 centimes
gourde	Haiti		100 centimes
groschen	Austria	schilling	100 groschen
grosz	Poland	zloty	100 groszy
guarani	Paraguay		100 centimos
guilder	Netherlands		100 cents
	Netherlands Antilles		100 cents
	Surinam		100 cents
haler	Czechoslovakia	crown	100 halers
jun	North Korea	won	100 jun
khoum	Mauritania	ouguiya	5 khoums
kina	Papua New Guinea		100 toea
kip	Laos		100 at
kobo	Nigeria	naira	100 kobo
kopeck	U.S.S.R.	rouble	100 kopecks
krona	Iceland		100 aurar
	Sweden		100 öre
krone	Norway		100 öre
kroner	Denmark		100 öre
kuru	Turkey	pound	100 kurus
kwacha	Malawi		100 tambala
	Zambia		100 ngwee
kwanza	Angola		100 lwei
kyat	Burma		100 pyas
laree	Maldives	rupee	100 larees
lek	Albania		100 quintar
lempira	Honduras		100 centavos
leone	Sierra Leone		100 cents
lepton	Greece	drachma	100 lepta
leu	Rumania		100 bani
lev	Bulgaria		100 stotinki
likuta	Zaire	zaire	100 makuta
lilangeni	Swaziland		100 cents
lira	Italy		100 centesimi
	San Marino		100 centesimi
	Vatican City		100 centesimi
lisente	Lesotho	loti	100 lisente
loti	Lesotho		100 lisente
lwei	Angola	kwanza	100 lwei
mark	East Germany		100 pfennigs
markka	Finland		100 penni
mil	Cyprus	pound	1000 mils
millieme	Tunisia	dinar	1000 milliemes
mongo	Mongolia	tugrik	100 mongo
naira	Nigeria		100 kobo
ngultrum	Bhutan		100 chetrums
ngwee	Zambia	kwacha	100 ngwee
öre	Denmark	kroner	100 öre
	Norway	krone	100 öre
	Sweden	krona	100 öre
ouguiya	Mauritania		5 khoums
pa'anga	Tonga		100 seniti
paisa	Bangladesh	taka	100 paisas
	India	rupee	100 paise
	Nepal	rupee	100 paisas
	Pakistan	rupee	100 paisas
para	Yugoslavia	dinar	100 para
pataca	Macao		100 avos
penni	Finland	markka	100 penni
penny	Ireland, Republic of	pound	100 pence
	United Kingdom	pound	100 pence
peseta	Andorra		100 centimos

CURRENCY *(continued)*

Basic Unit or Subdivision	Country	Basic Unit	Subdivision
	Spain		100 centimos
pesewa	Ghana	cedi	100 pesewas
peso	Argentina		100 centavos
	Bolivia		100 centavos
	Chile		100 centavos
	Colombia		100 centavos
	Cuba		100 centavos
	Dominican Republic		100 centavos
	Guinea-Bissau		100 centavos
	Mexico		100 centavos
	Philippines		100 centavos
	Uruguay		100 centesimos
pfennig	East Germany	mark	100 pfennigs
	West Germany	deutsche mark	100 pfennigs
piaster	Egypt	pound	100 piasters
	Lebanon	pound	100 piasters
	Sudan	pound	100 piasters
	Syria	pound	100 piasters
pound	Cyprus		1000 mils
	Egypt		100 piasters
	Ireland, Republic of		100 pence
	Israel		100 agorot
	Lebanon		100 piasters
	Malta		100 cents
	Sudan		100 piasters
	Syria		100 piasters
	Turkey		100 kurus
	United Kingdom		100 pence
pul	Afghanistan	afghani	100 puls
pya	Burma	kyat	100 pyas
quetzal	Guatemala		100 centavos
quintar	Albania	lek	100 quintar
qurush	Saudi Arabia	riyal	20 qurush
rand	South Africa		100 cents
	Swaziland		100 cents
renminbi	China, People's Republic of		10 chiao
rial	Iran		100 dinars
riel	Cambodia		100 sen
riyal	Qatar		100 dirhams
	Saudi Arabia		20 qurush
	Yemen		100 fils
riyal-omani	Oman		1000 baiza
rouble	U.S.S.R.		100 kopecks
rupee	India		100 paise
	Maldives		100 larees
	Mauritius		100 cents
	Nepal		100 paisas
	Pakistan		100 paisas
	Seychelles		100 cents
	Sri Lanka		100 cents
rupiah	Indonesia		100 sen
satang	Thailand	baht	100 satang
schilling	Austria		100 groschen
	Somalia		100 cents
sen	Cambodia	riel	100 sen
	Indonesia	rupiah	100 sen
	Japan	yen	100 sen
	Malaysia	ringgit	100 sen
sene	Western Samoa	tala	100 sene
seniti	Tonga	pa'anga	100 seniti
shekel	Israel		100 agorot
shilling	Kenya		100 cents
	Tanzania		100 cents
	Uganda		100 cents
sol	Peru		100 centavos

CURRENCY (continued)

Basic Unit or Subdivision	Country	Basic Unit	Subdivision
stotinki	Bulgaria	lev	100 stotinki
sucre	Ecuador		100 centavos
syli	Guinea		100 cory
taka	Bangladesh		100 paise
tala	Western Samoa		100 sene
tambala	Malawi	kwacha	100 tambala
toea	Papua New Guinea	kina	100 toea
tugrik	Mongolia		100 mongo
won	North Korea		100 jun
	South Korea		100 chon
yen	Japan		100 sen
yuan	China, Republic of (Taiwan)		100 cents
zaire	Zaire		100 makuta
zloty	Poland		100 groszy

dergo the growth of a tooth through the gums. **7.** To cause to cease; stop. **8.** To reduce the size, amount, or strength of. **9.** *Informal.* To fail deliberately to attend: *cut a class.* —*phrasal verbs.* **cut in. 1.** To interrupt. **2.** To interrupt a dancing couple in order to dance with one of them. **cut out. 1.** To be suited: *not cut out for city life.* **2.** *Informal.* To depart. **cut up.** *Informal.* To misbehave. —*n.* **1.** The act or result of cutting. **2.** A part that has been cut from an animal: *cuts of pork.* **3.** A reduction: *a pay cut.* **4.** The style in which something, as a garment, is cut. **5.** An insult. **6.** A passage, as a channel, resulting from excavating. **7.** *Informal.* A share, as of earnings. **8.** *Informal.* An unexcused absence, as from class. **9. a.** An engraved block or plate. **b.** A print made from such a block. [ME *cutten.*]

cut-and-dried (kŭt′n-drīd′) *adj.* In accordance with a formula; routine.

cu·ta·ne·ous (kyōō-tā′nē-əs) *adj.* Of or affecting the skin. [< Lat. *cutis,* skin.] —**cu·ta′ne·ous·ly** *adv.*

cut·back (kŭt′băk′) *n.* A decrease, as of personnel; curtailment.

cute (kyōōt) *adj.* **cut·er, cut·est. 1.** Delightfully pretty or dainty. **2.** Shrewd; clever. [< ACUTE.]

cu·ti·cle (kyōō′tǐ-kəl) *n.* **1.** The epidermis. **2.** The strip of hardened skin at the base of a fingernail or toenail. [< Lat. *cutis,* skin.]

cut·lass (kŭt′ləs) *n.* A short, heavy sword with a curved blade. [< Lat. *cultellus,* dim. of *culter,* knife.]

cut·ler·y (kŭt′lə-rē) *n.* Cutting instruments and tools, esp. implements used as tableware. [< OFr. *coutel,* knife.]

cut·let (kŭt′lĭt) *n.* A thin slice of meat, as veal or lamb, cut from the leg or ribs. [< OFr. *costelette.*]

cut·off (kŭt′ôf′, -ŏf′) *n.* **1.** A designated limit or point of termination. **2.** A short cut or by-pass. **3.** A device for cutting off a flow, as of water.

cut·out (kŭt′out′) *n.* Something cut out or intended to be cut out.

cut-rate (kŭt′rāt′) *adj.* Sold or on sale at a reduced price.

cut·ter (kŭt′ər) *n.* **1.** A device that cuts. **2.** A ship's boat for transporting stores or passengers. **3.** A small, lightly armed motorboat. **4.** A small sleigh.

cut·throat (kŭt′thrōt′) *n.* A murderer. —*adj.* **1.** Cruel; murderous. **2.** Ruthless; merciless: *cutthroat competition.*

cut·ting (kŭt′ĭng) *n.* A part cut off from a main body, esp. a shoot removed from a plant for rooting or grafting. —*adj.* **1.** Piercing and cold: *a cutting wind.* **2.** Sarcastic: *a cutting remark.*

cut·tle·bone (kŭt′l-bōn′) *n.* The chalky internal shell of the cuttlefish, used to supply calcium to caged birds.

cut·tle·fish (kŭt′l-fĭsh′) *n.* A ten-armed, squid-like marine mollusk that has a chalky internal shell and secretes a dark, inky fluid. [< OE *cudele,* cuttlefish + FISH.]

cut·up (kŭt′ŭp′) *n.* *Informal.* One that cuts up; prankster.

-cy *suff.* **1.** A quality or condition: *bankruptcy.* **2.** Office or rank: *baronetcy.* **3.** An action or practice: *mendicancy.* [< Lat. *-cia* < Gk. *-kia.*]

cy·a·nide (sī′ə-nīd′) *n.* Also **cy·an·id** (-nĭd). Any of various compounds containing a CN group, esp. the poisonous compounds potassium cyanide and sodium cyanide.

cyano- or **cyan-** *pref.* **1.** A blue or dark-blue coloring: *cyanosis.* **2.** *Chem.* Cyanide: *cyanogen.* [< Gk. *kuanos,* blue.]

cy·an·o·gen (sī-ăn′ə-jən) *n.* The univalent radical CN found in simple and complex cyanide compounds.

cy·a·no·sis (sī′ə-nō′sĭs) *n.* A condition in which the skin appears blue as a result of too little oxygen in the blood. —**cy·a·not′ic** (-nŏt′ĭk) *adj.*

cy·ber·net·ics (sī′bər-nĕt′ĭks) *n.* *(used with a sing. verb).* The theoretical study of control processes in electronic, mechanical, and biological systems. [< Gk. *kubernētēs,* governor.] —**cy·ber·net′ic** *adj.* —**cy·ber·net′i·cist** *n.*

cyc·la·mate (sĭk′lə-māt′, sī′klə-) *n.* A salt of

cyclamic acid, used formerly as noncaloric sweetening agents.

cyc·la·men (sĭk′lə-mən, sī′klə-) *n.* A plant with showy white, pink, or red flowers. [< Gk. *kuklaminos.*]

cyc·la·mic acid (sĭk′lə-mĭk, sī′klə-). A sour-sweet crystalline acid, $C_6H_{13}NO_3S$.

cy·cle (sī′kəl) *n.* **1. a.** A single occurrence of a periodically repeated phenomenon. **b.** The time during which this phenomenon occurs. **2.** A periodically repeated sequence of events. **3.** A group of literary or musical works on a single theme or hero. **4.** A bicycle or motorcycle. —*v.* **-cled, -cling. 1.** To occur in or pass through a cycle. **2.** To ride a bicycle or motorcycle. [< Gk. *kuklos,* circle.]

cy·clic (sī′klĭk, sĭk′lĭk) or **cy·cli·cal** (sī′klĭ-kəl, sĭk′lĭ-) *adj.* **1.** Of or occurring in cycles. **2.** *Chem.* Of compounds that have atoms arranged in a ring. —**cy′cli·cal·ly** *adv.*

cy·clist (sī′klĭst) *n.* One who rides a vehicle such as a bicycle or motorcycle.

cyclo- *pref.* A circle: *cyclometer.* [< Gk. *kuklos.*]

cy·clom·e·ter (sī-klŏm′ĭ-tər) *n.* **1.** An instrument that records the revolutions of a wheel in order to indicate distance traveled. **2.** An instrument that measures circular arcs. —**cy′clo·met′ric** (-klə-mĕt′rĭk) *adj.*

cy·clone (sī′klōn′) *n.* **1.** An atmospheric disturbance characterized by masses of air rapidly rotating about a low-pressure center. **2.** A violent rotating windstorm, such as a tornado. [< Gk. *kuklōma,* coil.] —**cy·clon·ic** (-klŏn′ĭk) *adj.*

cy·clo·pe·di·a (sī′klə-pē′dē-ə) *n.* Also **cy·clo·pae·di·a.** An encyclopedia. [< ENCYCLOPEDIA.] —**cy·clo·pe′dic** *adj.* —**cy′clo·pe′dist** *n.*

cy·clo·tron (sī′klə-trŏn′) *n.* A device that accelerates atomic particles in a spiral path by means of a fixed magnetic field and a variable electric field.

cyg·net (sĭg′nĭt) *n.* A young swan. [< Gk. *kuknos,* swan.]

Cyg·nus (sĭg′nəs) *n.* A constellation in the Northern Hemisphere.

cyl·in·der (sĭl′ən-dər) *n.* **1. a.** A surface generated by a straight line moving parallel to a fixed straight line and intersecting a plane curve. **b.** A solid bounded by two parallel planes and such a surface having a closed curve, esp. a circle. **2.** Something shaped like a cylinder. **3.** A chamber in which a piston moves. **4.** The rotating chamber of a revolver that holds the cartridges. [< Gk. *kulindros.*] —**cy·lin′dri·cal** (sə-lĭn′drĭ-kəl) or **cy·lin′dric** *adj.* —**cy·lin′dri·cal·ly** *adv.*

cym·bal (sĭm′bəl) *n.* One of a pair of concave brass plates that are struck together as percussion instruments. [< Gk. *kumbalon.*]

cymbal

cyn·ic (sĭn′ĭk) *n.* One who believes all people are motivated by selfishness. [< Gk. *kunikos,* like a dog.] —**cyn′i·cal** *adj.* —**cyn′i·cal·ly** *adv.* —**cyn′i·cism** *n.*

cy·no·sure (sī′nə-shoŏr′, sĭn′ə-) *n.* A center of interest or attraction. [< Gk. *kunosura,* Ursa Minor.]

cy·press (sī′prəs) *n.* Any of various chiefly evergreen trees with small, scalelike needles. [< Gk. *kuparissos.*]

cyst (sĭst) *n.* An abnormal, usu. fluid-containing membranous bodily sac. [< Gk. *kustis,* bladder.] —**cys′tic** *adj.*

cystic fibrosis *n.* A congenital disease of mucous glands of the body, causing pancreatic insufficiency and pulmonary disorders.

cys·to·scope (sĭs′tə-skōp′) *n.* A tubular instrument used to examine the urinary bladder. [Gk. *kustis,* bladder + -SCOPE.] —**cys′to·scop′ic** (-skŏp′ĭk) *adj.*

-cyte *suff.* A cell: *leukocyte.* [< Gk. *kutos,* hollow vessel.]

cyto- *pref.* A cell: *cytoplasm.* [< Gk. *kutos,* hollow vessel.]

cy·tol·o·gy (sī-tŏl′ə-jē) *n.* The biology of the formation, structure, and function of cells. —**cy′to·log′i·cal** (-tə-lŏj′ĭ-kəl) or **cy′to·log′ic** *adj.* —**cy·tol′o·gist** *n.*

cy·to·plasm (sī′tə-plăz′əm) *n.* The protoplasm outside a cell nucleus. —**cy′to·plas′mic** (-plăz′mĭk) *adj.*

cy·to·sine (sī′tə-sēn′) *n.* A pyrimidine base, $C_4H_5N_3O$, that is an essential constituent of both ribonucleic and deoxyribonucleic acids.

czar (zär) *n.* Also **tsar** or **tzar. 1.** A king or emperor, esp. one of the former emperors of Russia. **2.** A tyrant. **3.** *Informal.* One in authority; leader. [< R. *tsar′.*]

cza·ri·na (zä-rē′nə) *n.* The wife of a czar. [< R. *tsarina.*]

czar·ism (zär′ĭz′əm) *n.* The system of government in Russia under the czars; autocracy. —**czar′ist** *n.*

Czech (chĕk) *n.* **1.** A native or inhabitant of Czechoslovakia. **2.** The Slavic language of the Czechs. —**Czech** *adj.*

Dd

d or **D** (dē) *n., pl.* **d's** or **D's**. **1.** The 4th letter of the English alphabet. **2.** The 4th in a series. **3.** D The lowest passing grade given to a student. **4.** D The Roman numeral for 500.

dab (dăb) *v.* **dabbed, dab·bing**. **1.** To apply with short, light strokes. **2.** To pat quickly and lightly. —*n.* **1.** A small amount. **2.** A quick, light pat. [ME *dabben*.] —**dab'ber** *n.*

dab·ble (dăb'əl) *v.* **-bled, -bling**. **1.** To splash or spatter with or as with a liquid. **2.** To splash in and out of water playfully. **3.** To undertake something superficially or without serious intent. [Poss. < Du. *dabbelen.*] —**dab'bler** *n.*

da ca·po (dä kä'pō, də) *adv. Mus.* From the beginning. [Ital.]

dace (dās) *n., pl.* **dace** or **dac·es**. A small freshwater fish related to the minnows. [< OFr. *dars.*]

da·cha (dä'chə) *n.* A Russian country house.

dachs·hund (däks'hŏŏnt', däks'hŏŏnd') *n.* A small dog with a long body, drooping ears, and very short legs. [G.]

dachshund

Da·cron (dā'krŏn', dăk'rŏn'). A trademark for a synthetic polyester textile fiber.

dac·tyl (dăk'təl) *n.* A metrical foot of one accented syllable followed by two unaccented ones. [< Gk. *daktulos*, finger, dactyl.] —**dac·tyl'ic** (-tĭl'ĭk) *adj.* —**dac·tyl'i·cal·ly** *adv.*

dad (dăd) *n. Informal.* Father. [Of baby-talk orig.]

Da·da (dä'dä) *n.* Also **Da·da·ism** (-ĭz'əm). A western European artistic and literary movement (1916–23) that sought the discovery of authentic reality through the abolition of traditional cultural and aesthetic forms. [Fr.] —**Da'da·ist** *n.* —**Da'da·is'tic** *adj.*

dad·dy (dăd'ē) *n., pl.* **-dies**. *Informal.* Father.

daddy long·legs (lông'lĕgz', lŏng'-) *n., pl.* **daddy longlegs**. A spiderlike arachnid with a small, rounded body and long, slender legs.

da·do (dā'dō) *n., pl.* **-does**. **1.** The section of a pedestal between the base and crown. **2.** The lower portion of a wall, decorated differently from the upper section. [Ital.]

daf·fo·dil (dăf'ə-dĭl) *n.* A plant cultivated for its showy, usu. yellow flowers with a trumpet-shaped central crown. [< ME *affodyle*, asphodel.]

daf·fy (dăf'ē) *adj.* **-fi·er, -fi·est**. *Informal.* **1.** Silly; zany. **2.** Crazy. [< ME *daff*, fool.]

daft (dăft) *adj.* **-er, -est**. **1.** Crazy; mad. **2.** Foolish. [< OE *gedæfte*, meek.] —**daft'ly** *adv.* —**daft'ness** *n.*

dag·ger (dăg'ər) *n.* **1.** A short pointed weapon with sharp edges. **2.** A symbol (†) used as a reference mark. [ME *daggere.*]

da·guerre·o·type (də-gâr'ə-tīp') *n.* A photograph made by an early process on a light-sensitive silver-coated metallic plate and developed by mercury vapor. [< Louis J.M. *Daguerre* (1787–1851).]

dag·wood (dăg'wŏŏd') *n.* Also **Dag·wood**. A multilayered sandwich. [< *Dagwood* Bumstead, a comic-strip character.]

dahl·ia (dăl'yə, däl'-, däl'-) *n.* A plant cultivated for its showy, variously colored flowers. [< Anders *Dahl* (d. 1789).]

dai·ly (dā'lē) *adj.* Of, pertaining to, occurring, or published every day. —*adv.* **1.** Every day. **2.** Once a day. —*n., pl.* **-lies**. A daily publication, esp. a newspaper. [< OE *dælic.*]

daily double *n.* A bet won by choosing both winners of two specified races on one day, as in horse racing.

daily dozen *n.* A set of daily exercises.

dain·ty (dān'tē) *adj.* **-ti·er, -ti·est**. **1.** Delicately beautiful. **2.** Delicious; choice. **3.** Of refined taste. **4.** Too fastidious; squeamish. —*n., pl.* **-ties**. Something delicious; delicacy. [< Lat. *dignitas*, dignity.] —**dain'ti·ly** *adv.* —**dain'ti·ness** *n.*

dai·qui·ri (dī'kə-rē, dăk'ə-) *n., pl.* **-ris**. An iced cocktail of rum, lime or lemon juice, and sugar. [< *Daiquiri*, Cuba.]

dair·y (dâr'ē) *n., pl.* **-ies**. **1.** An establishment that processes or sells milk and milk products. **2.** A farm where milk and milk products are produced. [< OE *dæge*, dairymaid.]

dairy cattle *n.* Cows raised for milk rather than meat.

dairy farm *n.* A farm for producing milk and milk products.

dair·y·ing (dâr'ē-ĭng) *n.* The business of running a dairy.

dair·y·man (dâr'ē-mən) *n.* One who owns, manages, or works in a dairy.

da·is (dā'ĭs, dăs) *n.* A raised platform, as in a lecture hall, for honored guests. [< LLat. *discus*, table, ult. < Gk. *diskos*, quoit.]

dai·sy (dā'zē) *n., pl.* **-sies**. Any of several related plants having flowers with petallike rays surrounding a central disk, esp. a common species with white rays and a yellow center. [< OE *dægeseage.*]

Da·ko·ta (də-kō'tə) *n., pl.* **-tas**. **1. a.** A large group of tribes of Plains Indians, commonly called Sioux. **b.** A member of any of these tribes. **2.** The Siouan language of the Dakota. —**Da·ko'tan** *adj. & n.*

---

da·la·si (dä-lä′sē) n., pl. **-si.** See table at currency. [Native word in Gambia.]

dale (dāl) n. A valley. [< OE dæl.]

da·leth (dä′leth) n. The 4th letter of the Hebrew alphabet. See table at **alphabet.** [Heb. dāleth.]

dal·ly (dăl′ē) v. **-lied, -ly·ing.** 1. To flirt playfully. 2. To waste time; dawdle. [< OFr. dalier.] **—dal′li·ance** n. **—dal′li·er** n.

Dal·ma·tian (dăl-mā′shən) n. A dog with a short white coat covered with black spots. [< Dalmatia, region of Yugoslavia.]

dam¹ (dăm) n. 1. A barrier built across a waterway to control the flow of water. **—v.** **dammed, dam·ming.** 1. To build a dam across. 2. To hold back; check. [ME.]

dam² (dăm) n. A female parent of a four-footed animal. [< Lat. domina, mistress.]

dam·age (dăm′ĭj) n. 1. Impairment of the usefulness or value of person or property; loss; harm. 2. **damages.** Law. Money to be paid as compensation for injury or loss. **—v.** **-aged, -ag·ing.** To cause injury to. [< Lat. damnum, loss.] **—dam′age·a·ble** adj. **—dam′ag·ing·ly** adv.

Da·mas·cus steel (də-măs′kəs) n. An early form of steel with wavy markings, used chiefly for making sword blades.

dam·ask (dăm′əsk) n. 1. A rich patterned fabric of cotton, silk, etc. 2. A fine twilled table linen. [< Med. Lat. (pannus de) damasco, (cloth of) Damascus.] **—dam′ask** adj.

damask rose n. A rose with fragrant red or pink flowers used as a source of attar. [< obs. Damask, of Damascus.]

dame (dām) n. 1. Brit. A woman's title, equivalent to that of a knight. 2. Slang. A woman. [< Lat. domina, mistress.]

damn (dăm) v. 1. To criticize adversely; condemn. 2. To condemn to everlasting punishment or a similar fate. 3. To swear at by saying "damn." **—interj.** Used to express anger or disappointment. **—adj. & adv.** Informal. Used as an intensive: You're damn right. **—n.** Informal. The least bit; jot: not worth a damn. [< Lat. damnum, damage.] **—dam′na′tion** n. **—damn′ing** adj. **—damn′ing·ly** adv.

dam·na·ble (dăm′nə-bəl) adj. Deserving condemnation; odious. **—dam′na·bly** adv.

damned (dămd) adj. **-er, -est.** 1. Condemned or doomed: damned souls. 2. Informal. **a.** Dreadful; awful. **b.** Used as an intensive: a damned fool. **—adv.** Informal. Used as an intensive: a damned good idea.

damp (dămp) adj. **-er, -est.** Slightly wet; moist. **—n.** 1. Moisture; humidity. 2. Foul or poisonous gas. **—v.** 1. To dampen. 2. To restrain or check. 3. To decrease the amplitude of. [< ME, poison gas.] **—damp′ish** adj. **—damp′ly** adv. **—damp′ness** n.

damp·en (dăm′pən) v. 1. To make or become damp. 2. To depress: dampen one's spirits. **—damp′en·er** n.

damp·er (dăm′pər) n. 1. One that restrains or depresses. 2. An adjustable plate in a flue for controlling the draft.

dam·sel (dăm′zəl) n. A young woman or girl. [< Lat. domina, lady.]

dam·sel·fly (dăm′zəl-flī′) n. A slender-bodied insect related to the dragonfly.

dam·son (dăm′zən) n. A small, oval, bluish-black plum. [< Lat. (prunum) Damascenum, (plum) of Damascus.]

dance (dăns) v. **danced, danc·ing.** 1. To move rhythmically to music. 2. To leap or skip about. 3. To bob up and down. **—n.** 1. A set of rhythmic steps and motions, usu. to music. 2. A party at which people dance. 3. One round or turn of dancing. 4. The art of dancing. [< OFr. danser.] **—danc′er** n. **—danc′ing·ly** adv.

dan·de·li·on (dăn′dl-ī′ən) n. A common weedy plant with many-rayed yellow flowers. [< OFr. dent-de-lion, lion's tooth.]

dan·der (dăn′dər) n. Informal. Temper. [Orig. unknown.]

dan·dle (dăn′dl) v. **-dled, -dling.** To move (a small child) up and down on one's knees. [Orig. unknown.] **—dan′dler** n.

dan·druff (dăn′drəf) n. Small white scales of dead skin shed from the scalp. [Orig. unknown.]

dan·dy (dăn′dē) n., pl. **-dies.** 1. A man who affects extreme elegance. 2. Informal. Something very good of its kind. **—adj. -di·er, -di·est.** 1. Like or dressed like a dandy. 2. Informal. Fine; good. [Perh. < jack-a-dandy, fop.] **—dan′di·fi·ca′tion** n. **—dan′di·fy′** v. **—dan′dy·ism** n.

Dane (dān) n. A native or inhabitant of Denmark.

dan·ger (dān′jər) n. 1. Exposure or liability to evil, injury, or harm. 2. A possible cause or chance of harm. [< OFr. dangier < Lat. dominium, sovereignty.]

Syns: danger, hazard, jeopardy, peril, risk n.

dan·ger·ous (dān′jər-əs) adj. 1. Full of danger. 2. Able or likely to cause harm. **—dan′ger·ous·ly** adv. **—dan′ger·ous·ness** n.

dan·gle (dăng′gəl) v. **-gled, -gling.** To hang or cause to hang loosely and swing to and fro. [Poss. of Scand. orig.] **—dan′gler** n.

dangling participle n. Gram. A participle that is not clearly connected with the word it modifies. In the sentence "Sitting at my desk, a loud noise startled me," sitting is a dangling participle.

Dan·iel (dăn′yəl) n. See table at **Bible.**

Dan·ish (dā′nĭsh) adj. Of or pertaining to Denmark, the Danes, or their language. **—n.** 1. The Germanic language of the Danes. 2. Danish pastry.

Danish pastry n. A sweet pastry made with raised dough.

dank (dăngk) adj. **-er, -est.** Uncomfortably damp; chilly and wet. [ME.] **—dank′ly** adv. **—dank′ness** n.

dap·per (dăp′ər) adj. 1. Neatly dressed; trim. 2. Small and active. [ME dapyr, elegant.] **—dap′per·ly** adv. **—dap′per·ness** n.

dap·ple (dăp′əl) v. **-pled, -pling.** To mark or mottle with spots. [< dapple-gray, gray with darker gray markings.] **—dap′ple** or **dap′pled** adj.

dare (dâr) v. **dared, dar·ing.** 1. To have the courage required for. 2. To challenge (someone) to do something requiring boldness. **—n.** A challenge. **—idiom. dare say** or **dare·say** (dâr′sā′). To consider very likely. [< OE durran.] **—dar′er** n.

Usage: The idiomatic form dare say (or daresay) is more common in British than in American English. The expression occurs only with I as the subject and only in the present tense. It is never followed by that: I daresay he'll be sorry tomorrow.

dare·dev·il (dâr′dĕv′əl) *n.* One who is recklessly bold. —**dare′dev′il** *adj.*

daredevil

A rope walker sits on the roof of a 1,350-foot building after walking along the rope from another building

dar·ing (dâr′ĭng) *adj.* Fearless; bold. —*n.* Bravery. —**dar′ing·ly** *adv.*

dark (därk) *adj.* **-er, -est. 1.** Lacking light or brightness. **2.** Somber in color. **3.** Gloomy; threatening. **4.** Obscure; cryptic. **5.** Ignorant; uncivilized: *a dark era.* **6.** Evil; sinister. —*n.* **1.** Absence of light. **2.** Night; nightfall. —**idiom. in the dark. 1.** In secret. **2.** In ignorance; uninformed. [< OE *deorc.*] —**dark′ish** *adj.* —**dark′ly** *adv.* —**dark′ness** *n.*

Syns: *dark, dim, dusky, murky, obscure* **adj.**

Dark Ages *pl.n.* The early part of the Middle Ages from about A.D. 500 to about A.D. 1000.

dark·en (där′kən) *v.* **1.** To make or become dark or darker. **2.** To make or become sad. —**dark′en·er** *n.*

dark horse *n.* A little-known entrant or unexpected winner in a race or contest.

dark·room (därk′rōōm′, -rŏŏm′) *n.* A darkened or specially illuminated room in which photographic materials are processed.

dar·ling (där′lĭng) *n.* **1.** One who is dearly loved. **2.** A favorite. —*adj.* **1.** Dearest; beloved. **2.** *Informal.* Charming; adorable. [< OE *dēorling.*]

darn¹ (därn) *v.* To mend by weaving thread across a hole. —*n.* A place repaired by darning. [Dial. Fr. *darner.*] —**darn′er** *n.*

darn² (därn) *v. & interj. & adj. & adv.* Damn. [< DAMN.] —**darned** *adj. & adv.*

dar·nel (där′nəl) *n.* Any of several weedy grasses. [ME.]

darning needle *n.* **1.** A long, large-eyed needle used in darning. **2.** *Informal.* A dragonfly.

dart (därt) *n.* **1.** A small, arrowlike missile with a sharp point to be thrown or shot. **2. darts** *(used with a sing. verb).* A game in which darts are thrown at a target. **3.** Anything resembling a dart. **4.** A quick, rapid movement. **5.** A tapered tuck taken in a garment. —*v.* To move or shoot out suddenly. [< OFr., of Gmc. orig.]

dart·er (där′tər) *n.* Any of various small, often brightly colored freshwater fishes.

Dar·win·ism (där′wə-nĭz′əm) *n.* A theory of biological evolution developed by Charles Darwin and others, stating that species of plants and animals develop through natural selection of variations that increase the organism's ability to survive and reproduce.

—**Dar·win′i·an** (-wĭn′ē-ən) *adj.* —**Dar′win·ist** *n.* —**Dar·win·is′tic** *adj.*

dash (dăsh) *v.* **1.** To break; smash; destroy. **2.** To hurl, knock, or thrust violently. **3.** To splash. **4.** To perform or complete hastily: *dash off a letter.* **5.** To move with haste; rush. —*n.* **1.** A swift blow or stroke. **2.** A splash. **3.** A small amount of an ingredient. **4.** A sudden movement; rush. **5.** A short foot race. **6.** Vigor; verve. **7.** A punctuation mark (—) used to indicate a break or omission. **8.** A long sound or signal used in combination with the dot and silent intervals to represent letters or numbers in Morse Code. [ME *dashen.*] —**dash′er** *n.*

dash·board (dăsh′bôrd′, -bōrd′) *n.* A panel beneath the windshield of an automobile, containing instruments, dials, and controls.

da·shi·ki (də-shē′kē) *n.* A loose, often brightly colored African tunic, usu. worn by men. [Yoruba *danshiki.*]

dash·ing (dăsh′ĭng) *adj.* **1.** Brave, bold, and daring. **2.** Showy or stylish. —**dash′ing·ly** *adv.*

das·tard (dăs′tərd) *n.* A mean, sneaking coward. [ME.] —**das′tard·li·ness** *n.* —**das′tard·ly** *adj.*

da·ta (dā′tə, dăt′ə, dä′tə) *pl.n.* **1.** Information, esp. information organized for analysis or decision-making. **2.** Numerical information suitable for computer processing. **3.** Pl. of **datum** (sense 1). [Lat., pl. of *datum,* something given < p.p. of *dare,* to give.]

Usage: Data is the plural form of *datum* and traditionally takes a plural verb: *These data are inconclusive.* It is now widely used also with a singular verb: *This data is inconclusive.*

data bank *n.* **1.** A data base. **2.** An organization concerned with building, maintaining, and using a data base.

data base *n.* A collection of data arranged for computer retrieval.

data carrier *n.* The medium, as magnetic tape, selected to transport or communicate data.

data processing *n.* Sorting, classification, storage, and analysis of information, esp. when done by or for computers. —**data processor** *n.*

date¹ (dāt) *n.* **1.** The particular time at which something happens. **2.** The period to which something belongs. **3.** The day of the month. **4.** An inscription or statement indicating when a thing was made or written. **5.** *Informal.* **a.** An appointment to meet socially. **b.** A person so met, esp. one of the opposite sex. —*v.* **dat·ed, dat·ing. 1.** To mark with a date, as a letter. **2.** To determine the date of. **3.** To betray the age of. **4.** To originate in a particular time in the past: *a statue dating from 500 B.C.* **5.** *Informal.* To make or have social engagements with (persons of the opposite sex). —**idioms. out of date.** No longer current, valid, or useful. **to date.** Up to the present time. **up to date.** Modern; current. [< Med. Lat. *data Romae,* issued at Rome (on a certain day).]

date² (dāt) *n.* The sweet, oblong, edible fruit of a tropical palm tree. [< Gk. *daktulos,* finger.]

ă pat ā pay â care ä father ĕ pet ē be ĭ pit ī tie î pier ŏ pot ō toe ô paw, for oi noise ōō took ōō boot ou out th thin *th* this ŭ cut û urge yōō abuse zh vision ə about, item, edible, gallop, circus

dat·ed (dā′tĭd) *adj.* **1.** Marked with a date. **2.** Old-fashioned. —**dat′ed·ness** *n.*

date·line (dāt′līn′) *n.* A phrase in a news story that gives its date and place of origin.

dating bar *n.* A singles bar.

da·tive (dā′tĭv) *adj.* Designating or belonging to a grammatical case that principally marks the indirect object of a verb. —*n.* The dative case. [< Lat. *(casus) dativus*, (case) of giving.]

da·tum (dā′təm, dăt′əm, dä′təm) *n.* **1.** *pl.* **-ta** (-tə). A fact or proposition used to draw a conclusion or to make a decision. **2.** *pl.* **-tums.** A point, line, or surface used as a reference, as in surveying. [Lat., something given.]

daub (dôb) *v.* **1.** To cover or smear with an adhesive substance. **2.** To paint crudely. —*n.* **1.** The act or a stroke of daubing. **2.** A soft adhesive coating. **3.** A crude painting. [< Lat. *dealbare*, to whitewash.] —**daub′er** *n.* —**daub′ing·ly** *adv.*

daugh·ter (dô′tər) *n.* **1.** A female offspring. **2.** A female descendant. **3.** A girl or woman considered as if in a relationship of child to parent: *a daughter of the nation.* [< OE *dohtor.*] —**daugh′ter·ly** *adj.*

daugh·ter-in-law (dô′tər-ĭn-lô′) *n.*, *pl.* **daughters-in-law.** The wife of one's son.

daunt (dônt, dänt) *v.* **1.** To intimidate. **2.** To discourage. [< Lat. *domitare*, to tame.]

daunt·less (dônt′lĭs, dänt′-) *adj.* Fearless. —**daunt′less·ly** *adv.* —**daunt′less·ness** *n.*

dau·phin (dô′fĭn) *n.* The eldest son of a king of France. [< OFr. *dalphin*, title of the lords of Dauphiné.]

dav·en·port (dăv′ən-pôrt′, -pōrt′) *n.* A large sofa. [Orig. unknown.]

dav·it (dăv′ĭt, dā′vĭt) *n.* One of a pair of curved arms attached to the side of a ship, used esp. for hoisting boats. [< OFr. *daviot*, dim. of *David*, David.]

daw·dle (dôd′l) *v.* **-dled, -dling.** To waste time by trifling or idling. [Orig. unknown.] —**daw′dler** *n.*

dawn (dôn) *n.* **1.** The first appearance of daylight in the morning. **2.** A first appearance; beginning. —*v.* **1.** To begin to grow light in the morning. **2.** To come into existence. —*phrasal verb.* **dawn on.** To begin to be perceived or understood. [< OE *dagian*, to dawn.]

day (dā) *n.* **1.** The period of light between dawn and nightfall. **2.** The 24-hour period during which the earth completes one rotation on its axis. **3.** The portion of a day devoted to work. **4.** A period of activity or prominence: *a writer who has had his day.* **5.** Often **days.** A period of time; age; era. **6.** The contest or issue at hand: *carry the day.* —*idioms.* **call it a day.** *Informal.* To stop one's work for the day. **day in, day out.** Continuously. [< OE *dæg.*]

day bed *n.* A couch convertible into a bed.

day·book (dā′bŏŏk′) *n.* A journal or diary.

day·break (dā′brāk′) *n.* Dawn.

day care *n.* The providing of daytime supervision, training, medical care, etc., esp. for preschool children. —**day′-care′** *adj.*

day·dream (dā′drēm′) *n.* A dreamlike musing or fantasy. —*v.* To have daydreams. —**day′dream′er** *n.*

day labor *n.* Labor hired and paid by the day. —**day laborer** *n.*

day letter *n.* A telegram sent during the day,

usu. less expensive but slower than a regular telegram.

day·light (dā′līt′) *n.* **1.** The light of day. **2.** Dawn. **3.** Daytime. **4.** An understanding of what was formerly obscure. **5. daylights.** *Slang.* Wits; sense: *scared the daylights out of me.*

day·light-sav·ing time (dā′līt-sā′vĭng) *n.* Time during which clocks are set one hour ahead of standard time.

day nursery *n.* A nursery providing day care for preschool children.

Day of Atonement *n.* Yom Kippur.

day school *n.* A private school for pupils living at home.

day student *n.* A nonresident student at a college or preparatory school.

day·time (dā′tīm′) *n.* The time between dawn and dark. —**day′time′** *adj.*

day-to-day (dā′tə-dā′) *adj.* Occurring on a routine or daily basis.

day-trip·per (dā′trĭp′ər) *n.* One who makes a trip during the day without staying overnight.

daze (dāz) *v.* **dazed, daz·ing.** **1.** To stun or confuse, as with a blow or shock. **2.** To dazzle, as with strong light. —*n.* A stunned or confused condition. [ME *dasen*, of Scand. orig.] —**daz′ed·ly** (dā′zĭd-lē) *adv.*

daz·zle (dăz′əl) *v.* **-zled, -zling.** **1.** To overpower or be overpowered with intense light. **2.** To bewilder or amaze with a spectacular display. [Freq. of DAZE.] —**daz′zler** *n.* —**daz′zling·ly** *adv.*

D-day (dē′dā′) *n.* The unnamed day on which an operation, as a military offensive, is launched. [*D* (abbr. for *day*) + DAY.]

DDT (dē′dē-tē′) *n.* A colorless insecticide, C₁₄H₉Cl₅, toxic to man and animals when swallowed or absorbed through the skin. [*D(I-CHLORO)D(IPHENYL)T(RICHLOROETHANE).*]

de- *pref.* **1.** Reverse: *decode.* **2.** Remove: *delouse.* **3.** Reduce: *degrade.* [< Lat. *de,* from.]

Usage: Many compounds are formed with *de-.* Normally, *de-* combines with a second element without an intervening hyphen. Exceptions include: **a.** a second element beginning with *e,* as *de-escalate;* **b.** a second element beginning with two vowels, as *deaerate;* **c.** a second element beginning with a capital letter, as *de-Americanize.*

dea·con (dē′kən) *n.* **1.** A clergyman ranking just below a priest. **2.** A lay assistant to a minister. [< Gk. *diakonos,* attendant.] —**dea′con·ry** *n.*

dea·con·ess (dē′kə-nĭs) *n.* A woman appointed or elected to serve as an assistant in a church.

de·ac·ti·vate (dē-ăk′tə-vāt′) *v.* **1.** To render inactive. **2.** *Mil.* To remove from active status. —**de·ac′ti·va′tion** *n.*

dead (dĕd) *adj.* **-er, -est.** **1.** No longer alive; lifeless. **2.** Inanimate. **3.** Lacking feeling; unresponsive. **4.** No longer in existence or use. **5.** Devoid of interest. **6.** Not productive. **7.** Weary and worn-out. **8.** Lacking some important or previously evident quality. **9.** Suggestive of death. **10.** Exact: *dead center.* **11. a.** Lacking connection to a source of electric current. **b.** Discharged, as a battery. **12.** Having little or no bounce: *a dead ball.* —*n.* A period of greatest intensity: *the dead of winter.* —*adv.* **1.** Absolutely; altogether. **2.** Directly; exactly. [< OE *dēad.*] —**dead′ness** *n.*

dead·beat (dĕd′bĕt′) *n.* *Slang.* **1.** One who

does not pay his debts. **2.** A lazy person; loafer.

dead-en (dĕd'n) *v.* **1.** To make less intense, keen, or strong. **2.** To make soundproof. —**dead'en-er** *n.*

dead end *n.* **1.** A passage that is closed at one end. **2.** An impasse.

dead-head (dĕd'hĕd') *n. Informal.* **1.** One who uses a free ticket for admittance or accommodation. **2.** A vehicle, such as an aircraft, carrying no passengers or freight. —**dead'head'** *v. & adj.*

dead heat *n.* A race in which two or more contestants finish at the same time; tie.

dead letter *n.* An unclaimed or undelivered letter.

dead-line (dĕd'līn') *n.* A set time by which something must be done.

dead-lock (dĕd'lŏk') *n.* A standstill resulting from the opposition of two unrelenting forces. —*v.* To bring or come to a deadlock.

dead-ly (dĕd'lē) *adj.* **-li-er, -li-est. 1.** Causing or capable of causing death. **2.** Suggesting death. **3.** Implacable; mortal. **4.** Destructive in effect. **5.** Absolute; unqualified. —*adv.* **1.** So as to suggest death. **2.** To an extreme: *deadly earnest.* —**dead'li-ness** *n.*

deadly sins *pl.n.* The seven deadly sins.

dead-pan (dĕd'păn') *adj. & adv. Informal.* With a blank face or manner. —**dead'pan'** *v.*

dead reckoning *n.* Essentially nonobservational navigation by computations of position based on course and distance traveled from a known position.

dead spot *n.* A region where the reception of radio waves over a given frequency range is very weak.

dead weight *n.* **1.** The unrelieved weight of a heavy, motionless mass. **2.** An oppressive burden or difficulty.

dead-wood (dĕd'wŏŏd') *n.* Anything burdensome or superfluous.

deaf (dĕf) *adj.* **-er, -est. 1.** Partially or completely unable to hear. **2.** Unwilling to listen.

[< OE *dēaf.*] —**deaf'en** *v.* —**deaf'ly** *adv.* —**deaf'ness** *n.*

deaf-mute (dĕf'myōōt') *n.* Also **deaf mute.** One who can neither speak nor hear. —**deaf-mute'** *adj.*

deal¹ (dēl) *v.* **dealt** (dĕlt), **deal-ing. 1.** To apportion or distribute. **2.** To administer; deliver. **3.** To distribute (playing cards) among players. **4.** To be occupied or concerned; treat. **5.** To behave in a specified way toward another or others. **6.** To take action. **7.** To do business; trade. —*n.* **1.** The act of dealing. **2. a.** Cards dealt in a card game; hand. **b.** The right or turn of a player to distribute cards. **3.** An indefinite quantity, extent, or degree. **4.** *Informal.* A secret agreement. **5.** An agreement or business transaction. **6.** A bargain or favorable sale. **7.** *Informal.* Treatment received, esp. as the result of an agreement. **8.** *Slang.* An important issue: *big deal.* —**idiom. a great (or good) deal. 1.** A lot. **2.** Much: *a good deal thinner.* [< OE *dǣlan.*]

deal² (dēl) *n.* Fir or pine wood. [< MLG *dele,* plank.]

deal-er (dē'lər) *n.* **1.** One who buys and sells. **2.** One who deals the cards in a card game.

deal-er-ship (dē'lər-shĭp') *n.* **1.** An agency or distributor that is authorized to sell a particular item in a certain area. **2.** Authorization to sell in this way.

deal-ings (dē'lĭngz) *pl.n.* Agreements or relations with others, esp. when involving money or trade.

dean (dēn) *n.* **1.** An administrative officer in a university, college, or high school. **2.** The head of the chapter of canons governing a cathedral. **3.** The senior member of a group or profession. [< LLat. *decanus,* chief of ten < Lat. *decem,* ten.] —**dean'ship** *n.*

dean-er-y (dē'nə-rē) *n., pl.* **-ies.** The office, official residence, jurisdiction, or authority of a dean.

dear (dîr) *adj.* **-er, -est. 1.** Beloved; precious. **2.** Highly esteemed or regarded. **3.** High-priced. —*n.* A greatly loved person;

de-a-cid'i-fy' *v.*
de-aer'ate' *v.*
de'-aer-a'tion *n.*
de'-A-mer'i-can-i-za'tion *n.*
de'-A-mer'i-can-ize' *v.*
de-ash' *v.*
de'as-sim'i-la'tion *n.*
de-car'bon-ate' *v.*
de-cer'ti-fi-ca'tion *n.*
de-cer'ti-fy' *v.*
de-chlor'i-nate' *v.*
de-col'or *v.*
de-col'or-a'tion *n.*
de-com-mis'sion *n.*
de-com'pen-sate' *v.*
de-com'pound' *v.*
de-con-di'tion *v.*
de-con-ges'tion *n.*
de-con-ges'tive *adj.*
de-con'se-crate' *v.*
de-em'pha-size' *v.*
de-en'er-gize' *v.*
de-horn' *v.*

de-hull' *v.*
de-lam'i-nate' *v.*
de-lam'i-na'tion *n.*
de-lead' *v.*
de-lime' *v.*
de-lint' *v.*
de-lo'cal-ize' *v.*
de-louse' *v.*
de-lus'ter *v.*
de-mast' *v.*
de-ma-te'ri-al-i-za'tion *n.*
de-ma-te'ri-al-ize' *v.*
de-mes'mer-ize' *v.*
de-mount' *v.*
de-na'tion-al-i-za'tion *n.*
de-na'tion-al-ize' *v.*
de-nat'u-ral-i-za'tion *n.*
de-nat'u-ral-ize' *v.*
de-ni'trate' *v.*
de-pas'ture *v.*
de-pig'ment *v.*
de-plume' *v.*
de-po'lar-i-za'tion *n.*

de-po'lar-ize' *v.*
de-pol'ish *v.*
de-pres'sur-ize' *v.*
de-ra'tion *v.*
de-req'ui-si'tion *v.*
de're-strict' *v.*
de-salt' *v.*
de-sanc'ti-fy' *v.*
de-sat'u-rate' *v.*
de-scale' *v.*
de-scram'ble *v.*
de-sil'ver *v.*
de-size' *v.*
de-so'cial-ize' *v.*
de-soil' *v.*
de-sta'bi-lize' *v.*
de-sug'ar *v.*
de-sul'fur-i-za'tion *n.*
de-sul'fur-ize' *v.*
de-vol'a-til-ize' *v.*
de-vow' *v.*
de-wool' *v.*
de-worm' *v.*

darling. —*interj.* Used to express surprise or distress. [< OE *dēore*.] —**dear'ness** *n.*

Dear John (jŏn) *n.* A letter, as to a soldier, in which a wife requests a divorce or a girlfriend ends a close relationship.

dearth (dûrth) *n.* Scarcity; paucity. [< ME *dere*, expensive.]

death (dĕth) *n.* **1.** The act of dying or condition of being dead. **2.** Termination; extinction. **3.** A cause or manner of dying. —*idiom.* **to death.** To an extreme degree: *bored to death.* [< OE *dēath.*]

death·bed (dĕth'bĕd') *n.* **1.** The bed on which a person dies. **2.** One's last hours of life.

death·blow (dĕth'blō') *n.* A fatal blow or event.

death·less (dĕth'lĭs) *adj.* Undying; immortal. —**death'less·ness** *n.*

death·ly (dĕth'lē) *adj.* Resembling or characteristic of death; fatal. —*adv.* **1.** In the manner of death. **2.** Extremely; very.

death rattle. A rattling in the throat of a dying person, caused by loss of the cough reflex and passage of air through accumulating mucus in the throat.

death row. A cell block in which condemned prisoners await execution.

death's-head (dĕths'hĕd') *n.* The human skull as a symbol of death.

death·watch (dĕth'wŏch') *n.* A vigil kept beside a dying or dead person.

de·ba·cle (dĭ-bä'kəl, -băk'əl) *n.* A sudden, disastrous collapse, downfall, or defeat. [< OFr. *desbacler*, to unbar.]

de·bar (dĭ-bär') *v.* **-barred, -barring.** To forbid, exclude, or bar. [< OFr. *desbarrer.*] —**de·bar'ment** *n.*

de·bark (dĭ-bärk') *v.* To unload; disembark. [< OFr. *debarquer.*] —**de·bar·ka'tion** (dē'bär-kā'shən) *n.*

de·base (dĭ-bās') *v.* **-based, -basing.** To lower in character, quality, or value; degrade. —**de·base'ment** *n.* —**de·bas'er** *n.*

de·bate (dĭ-bāt') *v.* **-bated, -bating. 1.** To deliberate; consider. **2.** To discuss opposing points. **3.** To discuss or argue formally. —*n.* **1.** The act of debating. **2.** A formal contest of argumentation in which two opposing teams defend and attack a given proposition. [< OFr. *debattre.*] —**de·bat'a·ble** *adj.* —**de·bat'a·bly** *adv.* —**de·bat'er** *n.*

de·bauch (dĭ-bôch') *v.* To corrupt morally. [< OFr. *desbaucher*, to roughhew timber.] —**de·bauch'er** *n.* —**de·bauch'er·y** *n.*

de·ben·ture (dĭ-bĕn'chər) *n.* A certificate acknowledging a debt, esp. a bond issued by a civil or governmental agency. [< Lat. *debentur*, they are due.]

de·bil·i·tate (dĭ-bĭl'ĭ-tāt') *v.* **-tated, -tating.** To make feeble; weaken. [Lat. *debilitare.*] —**de·bil'i·ta'tion** *n.* —**de·bil'i·ta'tive** *adj.*

de·bil·i·ty (dĭ-bĭl'ĭ-tē) *n., pl.* **-ties.** Feebleness.

deb·it (dĕb'ĭt) *n.* An item of debt, esp. one recorded in an account. —*v.* **1.** To enter a debit in an account. **2.** To charge with a debit. [< Lat. *debitum.*]

deb·o·nair or **deb·o·naire** (dĕb'ə-nâr') *adj.* **1.** Gracious and charming. **2.** Carefree and gay; jaunty. [< OFr. *de bonne aire*, of good disposition.] —**deb'o·nair'ly** *adv.* —**deb'o·nair'ness** *n.*

de·brief (dē-brēf') *v.* To question to obtain knowledge gathered, esp. on a military mission. —**de·brief'ing** *n.*

de·bris or **dé·bris** (də-brē', dā'brē') *n.* The scattered remains of something broken, destroyed, or discarded. [< OFr. *desbrisier*, to break into pieces.]

debt (dĕt) *n.* **1.** Something owed, as money, goods, or services. **2.** The condition of owing; indebtedness. [< Lat. *debitum* < *debēre*, to owe.] —**debt'or** *n.*

de·bug (dē-bŭg') *v.* **1.** To remove insects from. **2.** To remove a hidden electronic eavesdropping device from. **3.** To search for and eliminate malfunctioning elements or errors in.

de·bunk (dē-bŭngk') *v. Informal.* To expose or ridicule the falseness or pretensions of. —**de·bunk'er** *n.*

de·but or **dé·but** (dā-byōō', dĭ-, dā'byōō') *n.* **1.** A first public appearance. **2.** The formal presentation of a girl to society. **3.** The beginning of a career. [Fr. < *débuter*, to begin.] —**de·but'** *v.*

deb·u·tante or **dé·bu·tante** (dĕb'yōō-tänt', dā'byōō-, dĕb'yōō-tänt') *n.* A young woman making a debut into society. [Fr. < *débuter*, to begin.]

deca- or **dec-** or **deka-** *pref.* Ten: *decahedron.* [< Gk. *deka*, ten.]

dec·ade (dĕk'ād', dĕ-kād') *n.* A period of ten years. [< Gk. *dekas* < *deka*, ten.]

dec·a·dence (dĕk'ə-dəns, dĭ-kād'ns) *n.* A process, condition, or period of deterioration; decay. [< Med. Lat. *decadentia.*] —**dec'a·dent** *adj.* —**dec'a·dent·ly** *adv.*

dec·a·gon (dĕk'ə-gŏn') *n.* A polygon with ten sides.

dec·a·gram or **dek·a·gram** (dĕk'ə-grăm') *n.* Ten grams.

dec·a·he·dron (dĕk'ə-hē'drən) *n., pl.* **-drons** or **-dra** (-drə). A polyhedron with ten faces.

de·cal (dē'kăl', dĭ-kăl') *n.* A design transferred by decalcomania.

de·cal·ci·fy (dē-kăl'sə-fī') *v.* To remove calcium or calcareous matter from. —**de·cal'ci·fi·ca'tion** *n.*

de·cal·co·ma·ni·a (dĭ-kăl'kə-mā'nē-ə) *n.* **1.** The process of transferring designs printed on specially prepared paper to glass, metal, or other material. **2.** A decal. [< Fr. *décalquer*, to transfer by tracing.]

Dec·a·logue or **Dec·a·log** (dĕk'ə-lôg', -lŏg') *n.* The Ten Commandments. [< Gk. *dekalogos.*]

dec·a·me·ter or **dek·a·me·ter** (dĕk'ə-mē'tər) *n.* Ten meters.

de·camp (dĭ-kămp') *v.* **1.** To break camp. **2.** To depart suddenly. [< OFr. *descamper.*] —**de·camp'ment** *n.*

de·cant (dĭ-kănt') *v.* To pour off, as wine, without disturbing the sediment. [< Med. Lat. *decanthare.*] —**de·can·ta'tion** (dē'kăn-tā'shən) *n.*

de·cant·er (dĭ-kăn'tər) *n.* A decorative bottle for serving liquids, esp. wine.

de·cap·i·tate (dĭ-kăp'ĭ-tāt') *v.* **-tated, -tating.** To behead. [LLat. *decapitare.*] —**de·cap'i·ta'tion** *n.* —**de·cap'i·ta'tor** *n.*

dec·a·syl·la·ble (dĕk'ə-sĭl'ə-bəl) *n.* A line of verse having ten syllables. —**dec'a·syl·lab'ic** (-sə-lăb'ĭk) *adj.*

de·cath·lon (dĭ-kăth'lŏn, -lŏn') *n.* An athletic contest in which contestants compete in ten events. [DEC- + Gk. *athlon*, contest.]

de·cay (dĭ-kā') *v.* **1.** To decompose; rot. **2.** To decrease or decline in quality or quantity. **3.** *Physics.* To lose radioactive atoms as a result of nuclear disintegrations. —*n.* **1.** Decomposition. **2.** Deterioration. **3.** *Physics.* Radioactive decay. [< AN *decair.*]

de·cease (dĭ-sēs') *v.* **-ceased, -ceas·ing.** To die. —*n.* Death. [< Lat. *decedere,* to depart.]

de·ceased (dĭ-sēst') *adj.* No longer living; dead. —*n.* A dead person.

de·ceit (dĭ-sēt') *n.* **1.** Misrepresentation; deception. **2.** A stratagem; trick. [< Lat. *decepta,* fem. p.p of *decipere,* to deceive.] —**de·ceit'ful** *adj.* —**de·ceit'ful·ly** *adv.* —**de·ceit'ful·ness** *n.*

de·ceive (dĭ-sēv') *v.* **-ceived, -ceiv·ing.** To delude; mislead. [< Lat. *decipere.*] —**de·ceiv'er** *n.* —**de·ceiv'ing·ly** *adv.*

Syns: *deceive, betray, delude, double-cross, mislead v.*

de·cel·er·ate (dē-sĕl'ə-rāt') *v.* **-at·ed, -at·ing.** To decrease in speed. [DE- + (AC)CELERATE.] —**de·cel'er·a'tion** *n.*

De·cem·ber (dĭ-sĕm'bər) *n.* The 12th month of the year, having 31 days. See table at **cal·endar.** [< Lat., the 10th month.]

de·cen·ni·al (dĭ-sĕn'ē-əl) *adj.* **1.** Of or lasting for ten years. **2.** Occurring once every ten years. —*n.* A tenth anniversary or its celebration. [< Lat. *decennium,* decade.] —**de·cen'ni·al·ly** *adv.*

de·cent (dē'sənt) *adj.* **1.** Conforming to the standards of propriety; proper. **2.** Free from indelicacy; modest. **3.** Adequate; passable. **4.** Kind; generous. **5.** Properly dressed. [< Lat. *decere,* to be fitting.] —**de'cen·cy** *n.* —**de'cent·ly** *adv.* —**de'cent·ness** *n.*

de·cen·tral·ize (dē-sĕn'trə-līz') *v.* **-ized, -iz·ing.** **1.** To distribute the functions of (a central authority) among local authorities. **2.** To cause to withdraw from an area of concentration. —**de·cen'tral·i·za'tion** *n.*

de·cep·tion (dĭ-sĕp'shən) *n.* **1.** The use of deceit. **2.** The fact or state of being deceived. [< Lat. *decipere,* to deceive.]

de·cep·tive (dĭ-sĕp'tĭv) *adj.* Intended or tending to deceive. —**de·cep'tive·ly** *adv.* —**de·cep'tive·ness** *n.*

deci- *pref.* One-tenth: *decimeter.* [< Lat. *decimus,* tenth.]

dec·i·bel (dĕs'ə-bəl, -bĕl') *n.* A unit used to express relative difference in power, usu. between acoustic or electric signals, equal to ten times the common logarithm of the ratio of the two levels.

de·cide (dĭ-sīd') *v.* **-cid·ed, -cid·ing.** **1.** To conclude, settle, or announce a verdict. **2.** To influence or determine the conclusion of. **3.** To make up one's mind. [< Lat. *decidere.*] —**de·cid'a·ble** *adj.* —**de·cid'er** *n.*

Syns: *decide, conclude, determine, resolve, settle v.*

de·cid·ed (dĭ-sī'dĭd) *adj.* **1.** Clear-cut; definite. **2.** Resolute. —**de·cid'ed·ly** *adv.* —**de·cid'ed·ness** *n.*

de·cid·u·ous (dĭ-sĭj'ōō-əs) *adj.* **1.** Falling off at a specific season or stage of growth: *deciduous leaves.* **2.** Shedding foliage at the end of the growing season: *deciduous trees.* [Lat. *deciduus.*] —**de·cid'u·ous·ly** *adv.* —**de·cid'u·ous·ness** *n.*

dec·i·gram (dĕs'ĭ-grăm') *n.* One-tenth of a gram.

dec·i·li·ter (dĕs'ə-lē'tər) *n.* One-tenth of a liter.

de·cil·lion (dĭ-sĭl'yən) *n.* **1.** The cardinal number equal to 10^{33}. **2.** *Chiefly Brit.* The cardinal number equal to 10^{60}. [DEC- + (M)ILLION.] —**de·cil'lionth** *adj. & n.*

dec·i·mal (dĕs'ə-məl) *n.* **1.** A linear array of integers that represents a fraction, every decimal place indicating a multiple of a positive or negative power of 10. For example, the decimal .1 = $^1/_{10}$, .12 = $^{12}/_{100}$, .003 = $^3/_{1000}$. **2.** A number written using base 10; a number containing a decimal point. —*adj.* **1.** Expressed or expressible as a decimal. **2. a.** Based on 10. **b.** Numbered or ordered by 10's. **3.** Not integral; fractional. [< Lat. *decimus,* tenth.] —**dec'i·mal·ly** *adv.*

decimal place *n.* The position of a digit to the right of a decimal point, usu. identified by successive ascending ordinal numbers with the digit immediately to the right of the decimal point being first.

decimal point *n.* A period placed at the left of a decimal.

dec·i·mate (dĕs'ə-māt') *v.* **-mat·ed, -mat·ing.** To destroy or kill a large part of. [Lat. *decimare* < *decimus,* tenth.] —**dec'i·ma'tion** *n.* —**dec'i·ma'tor** *n.*

Usage: Decimate originally meant to kill every 10th person, but its meaning has been extended to include the destruction of any large proportion of a group. The Usage Panel accepts a sentence such as *Famine decimated the population,* but considers that *decimate* should not be used to describe the destruction of a single person, an entire group, or any specified percentage other than 10%.

dec·i·me·ter (dĕs'ə-mē'tər) *n.* One-tenth of a meter.

de·ci·pher (dĭ-sī'fər) *v.* **1.** To decode. **2.** To read or interpret (something obscure or illegible). —**de·ci'pher·a·ble** *adj.* —**de·ci'pher·ment** *n.*

de·ci·sion (dĭ-sĭzh'ən) *n.* **1.** A final conclusion or choice; judgment. **2.** Firmness of character or action; determination. [< Lat. *decidere,* to decide.]

de·ci·sive (dĭ-sī'sĭv) *adj.* **1.** Conclusive. **2.** Resolute; determined. **3.** Beyond doubt; unquestionable. —**de·ci'sive·ly** *adv.* —**de·ci'sive·ness** *n.*

deck¹ (dĕk) *n.* **1. a.** A platform extending horizontally from one side of a ship to the other. **b.** A similar platform or surface. **2.** A pack of playing cards. [< MDu. *dec,* covering.]

deck² (dĕk) *v.* To clothe with finery; adorn. [< MDu. *dekken,* to cover.]

deck chair *n.* A folding chair, usu. with arms and a leg rest.

deck hand *n.* A member of a ship's crew who works on deck.

deck tennis *n.* A game in which a small ring or quoit is tossed back and forth over a net.

de·claim (dĭ-klām') *v.* To speak loudly and with rhetorical effect. [< Lat. *declamare.*] —**de·claim'er** *n.* —**dec·la·ma'tion** (dĕk'lə-mā'shən) *n.*

de·clam·a·to·ry (dĭ-klăm'ə-tôr'ē, -tōr'ē) *adj.* **1.** Of or pertaining to declamation. **2.** Loud and rhetorical, esp. when bombastic. —**de·clam'a·to'ri·ly** *adv.*

Declaration of Independence *n.* A proclamation issued in 1776, declaring the independence of the 13 American colonies from Great Britain.

de·clare (dĭ-klâr′) *v.* **-clared, -clar·ing.** **1.** To state officially, formally, or authoritatively. **2.** *Bridge.* To make the final bid that establishes trump or no-trump. [< Lat. *declarare.*] —**dec′la·ra′tion** *n.* —**de·clar′a·tive** *adj.* —**de·clar′er** *n.*

de·clas·si·fy (dē-klăs′ə-fī′) *v.* To remove official security classification from (a document). —**de·clas′si·fi·ca′tion** *n.*

de·clen·sion (dĭ-klĕn′shən) *n.* **1. a.** The systematic inflection of nouns, pronouns, and adjectives. **b.** A class of such words with similar inflections. **2.** A descent. **3.** A decline or deterioration. [< Lat. *declinatio,* a sloping downward.] —**de·clen′sion·al** *adj.*

de·cline (dĭ-klīn′) *v.* **-clined, -clin·ing.** **1.** To refuse to do or accept (something). **2.** To slope downward. **3.** To deteriorate gradually; wane. **4.** To give the declension of. —*n.* **1.** The process or result of declining. **2.** A downward slope. **3.** A disease that gradually weakens the body. [< Lat. *declinare,* to turn aside.] —**de·clin′a·ble** *adj.* —**dec′li·na′tion** *n.* —**dec′li·na′tion·al** *adj.* —**de·clin′er** *n.*

de·cliv·i·ty (dĭ-klĭv′ĭ-tē) *n., pl.* **-ties.** A steep downward slope. [< Lat. *declivitas.*]

de·code (dē-kōd′) *v.* To convert from a code into plain text. —**de·cod′er** *n.*

dé·col·le·tage (dā′kŏl-täzh′) *n.* A low neckline. [Fr.]

dé·col·le·té (dā′kŏl-tā′) *adj.* Having a low neckline. [Fr., p.p. of *décolleter,* to cut a low neckline.]

de·col·o·nize (dē-kŏl′ə-nīz′) *v.* To free (e.g. a colony) from colonial status. —**de·col′o·ni·za′tion** *n.*

de·com·pose (dē′kəm-pōz′) *v.* **1.** To separate into component parts or basic elements. **2.** To rot or cause to rot. —**de′com·pos′a·ble** *adj.* —**de·com′po·si′tion** (dē-kŏm′pə-zĭsh′ən) *n.*

de·com·press (dē′kəm-prĕs′) *v.* To relieve of pressure. —**de′com·pres′sion** *n.*

de·con·ges·tant (dē′kən-jĕs′tənt) *n.* A medication that breaks up congestion, esp. in the sinuses.

de·con·tam·i·nate (dē′kən-tăm′ə-nāt′) *v.* To free of contamination or of dangerous or harmful elements. —**de′con·tam′i·nant** *n.* —**de′con·tam′i·na′tion** *n.*

de·con·trol (dē′kən-trōl′) *v.* To free esp. from government control.

dé·cor or **de·cor** (dā′kôr′, dā-kôr′) *n.* A decorative style or scheme, as of a room, home, stage setting, etc. [Fr.]

dec·o·rate (dĕk′ə-rāt′) *v.* **-rat·ed, -rat·ing.** **1.** To furnish with something attractive. **2.** To confer a medal or honor on. [< Lat. *decorare.*] —**dec′o·ra′tion** *n.*

dec·o·ra·tive (dĕk′ər-ə-tĭv, -ə-rā′-) *adj.* Ornamental. —**dec′o·ra·tive·ly** *adv.* —**dec′o·ra·tive·ness** *n.*

dec·o·ra·tor (dĕk′ə-rā′tər) *n.* One who decorates architectural interiors.

dec·o·rous (dĕk′ər-əs, dĭ-kôr′-, -kōr′-) *adj.* Marked by decorum; proper. [< Lat. *decor,* seemliness.] —**dec′o·rous·ly** *adv.* —**dec′o·rous·ness** *n.*

de·co·rum (dĭ-kôr′əm, -kōr′-) *n.* Conformity to social conventions; propriety. [Lat.]

de·coy (dē′koi′, dĭ-koi′) *n.* **1.** A living or artificial animal used to entice game. **2.** One who leads another into danger, deception, or a trap. —*v.* (dĭ-koi′). To lure or entrap by or as if by a decoy. [Poss. < Du. *de kooi,* the cage.] —**de·coy′er** *n.*

decoy

de·crease (dĭ-krēs′) *v.* **-creased, -creas·ing.** To diminish gradually; reduce. —*n.* (dē′krēs′). The act or process of decreasing or the resulting condition. [< Lat. *decrescere.*] —**de·creas′ing·ly** *adv.*

Syns: *decrease, abate, diminish, dwindle, ebb, lessen, reduce* v.

de·cree (dĭ-krē′) *n.* **1.** An authoritative order; edict. **2.** The judgment of a court. —*v.* **-creed, -cree·ing.** To ordain, establish, or decide by decree. [< Lat. *decretum* < *decernere,* to decide.]

dec·re·ment (dĕk′rə-mənt) *n.* **1.** A gradual decrease. **2.** The amount lost by gradual diminution or waste. [Lat. *decrementum* < *decrescere,* to decrease.]

de·crep·it (dĭ-krĕp′ĭt) *adj.* Weakened by old age, illness, or hard use. [< Lat. *decrepitus,* very old.] —**de·crep′it·ly** *adv.* —**de·crep′i·tude**′ *n.*

de·cre·scen·do (dē′krə-shĕn′dō, dā′-) *Mus.* —*n., pl.* **-dos.** **1.** A gradual decrease in loudness. **2.** A decrescendo passage. —*adj.* Gradually decreasing in loudness. —*adv.* With a decrescendo. [Ital.]

de·crim·i·nal·ize (dē-krĭm′ə-nə-līz′) *v.* To make no longer illegal or criminal. —**de·crim′i·nal·i·za′tion** *n.*

de·cry (dĭ-krī′) *v.* To belittle publicly; censure. [OFr. *descrier.*] —**de·cri′er** *n.*

ded·i·cate (dĕd′ĭ-kāt′) *v.* **-cat·ed, -cat·ing.** **1.** To set apart for a special purpose. **2.** To commit (oneself) fully; devote. **3.** To inscribe (e.g. a book) to someone. [< Lat. *dedicare.*] —**ded′i·ca′tion** *n.* —**ded′i·ca·tive** or **ded′i·ca·to′ry** (-kə-tôr′ē, -tōr′ē) *adj.* —**ded′i·ca′tor** *n.*

de·duce (dĭ-dōōs′, -dyōōs′) *v.* **-duced, -duc·ing.** **1.** To reach (a conclusion) by reasoning. **2.** To trace the origin of. [< Lat. *deducere,* to lead away.] —**de·duc′i·ble** *adj.*

de·duct (dĭ-dŭkt′) *v.* To subtract. [< Lat. *deducere.*] —**de·duct′i·ble** *adj.*

de·duc·tion (dĭ-dŭk′shən) *n.* **1.** The act of deducting; subtraction. **2.** Something that is or may be deducted. **3. a.** The act or process of reasoning, esp. a logical method in which a conclusion necessarily follows from the propositions stated. **b.** A conclusion reached by deduction. —**de·duc′tive** *adj.* —**de·duc′tive·ly** *adv.*

deed (dēd) *n.* **1.** An act; feat; exploit. **2.** Action or performance in general: *in word and deed.* **3.** A document sealed as an instrument of bond, contract, or conveyance, esp. pertaining to property. —*v.* To transfer by means of a deed. [< OE *dæd.*]

deem (dēm) v. To judge; consider; think. [< OE *dēman.*]

deep (dēp) adj. -er, -est. 1. Extending to or located at a distance below a surface. 2. Extending from front to rear or inward from the outside. 3. Arising from or penetrating to a depth. 4. Far distant; obscure. 5. Learned; profound. 6. Intense; extreme. 7. Dark rather than pale in shade. 8. Low in pitch; resonant. —n. 1. A deep place on land or in a body of water, esp. in the ocean and over 3,000 fathoms in depth. 2. The most intense or extreme part. 3. the deep. The ocean. —adv. 1. Profoundly. 2. Well on in time; late. —idiom. in deep. Informal. Completely committed. [< OE *dēop.*] —deep'ly adv. —deep'ness n.

deep-en (dē'pən) v. To make or become deep or deeper. —deep'en-er n.

Deep-freeze (dēp'frēz'). A trademark for a refrigerator designed to freeze food for long periods.

deep-fry (dēp'frī') v. To fry by immersing in a deep pan of fat or oil.

deep-rooted (dēp'rōō'tĭd, -rōōt'ĭd) adj. Deep-seated.

deep-sea (dēp'sē') adj. Of, pertaining to, or occurring in deep parts of the sea.

deep-seated (dēp'sē'tĭd) adj. Deeply entrenched; ingrained.

deep-six (dēp'sĭks') v. -sixed, -six-ing. Slang. 1. To toss overboard. 2. To get rid of.

deep space n. The regions beyond the moon, including interplanetary, interstellar, and intergalactic space.

deer (dîr) n., pl. deer. Any of various hoofed mammals of which the males characteristically have seasonally shed antlers. [< OE *dēor.*]

deer-skin (dîr'skĭn') n. 1. The skin of a deer. 2. Leather made from this skin.

de-es-ca-late (dē-ĕs'kə-lāt') v. To lessen the scope or intensity of. —de'es-ca-la'tion n.

de-face (dĭ-fās') v. -faced, -fac-ing. To spoil or mar the surface or appearance of. —de-face'ment n. —de-fac'er n.

de fac-to (dĭ fäk'tō, dā) adv. In reality or fact; actually. —adj. 1. Actual. 2. Actually exercising power. [Lat., according to the fact.]

de-fal-cate (dĭ-fäl'kāt', -fôl'-, dĕf'əl-kāt') v. -cat-ed, -cat-ing. To embezzle. [< Med. Lat. *defalcare,* to cut off.] —de-fal-ca'tion n. —de-fal'ca-tor n.

de-fame (dĭ-fām') v. -famed, -fam-ing. To attack the good name of by slander or libel. [< Lat. *diffamare.*] —def'a-ma'tion (dĕf'ə-mā'shən) n. —de-fam'a-to'ry (dĭ-făm'ə-tôr'ē, -tōr'ē) adj. —de-fam'er n.

de-fault (dĭ-fôlt') n. 1. A failure to perform a task or fulfill an obligation. 2. Loss by failure to appear. 3. Failure to participate in or complete a contest. —v. 1. To fail to do what is required. 2. To lose by not appearing, completing, or participating. [< OFr. *defaute.*] —de-fault'er n.

de-feat (dĭ-fēt') v. 1. To win victory over; beat. 2. To prevent the success of; thwart: *defeat one's purposes.* —n. The act of defeating or the condition of being defeated. [< OFr. *desfait,* p.p. of *desfaire,* to destroy.] —de-feat'er n.

Syns: *defeat, beat, best, conquer, lick, overcome, rout, shellac, subdue, thrash, trounce, vanquish, whip* v.

de-feat-ism (dĭ-fē'tĭz'əm) n. Acceptance of the prospect of defeat. —de-feat'ist n.

def-e-cate (dĕf'ĭ-kāt') v. -cat-ed, -cat-ing. To empty the bowels of waste matter. [< Lat. *defaecare.*] —def-e-ca'tion n. —def'e-ca'tor n.

de-fect (dē'fĕkt', dĭ-fĕkt') n. 1. Lack of something necessary or desirable. 2. An imperfection; fault. —v. (dĭ-fĕkt'). To desert one's country, party, etc., in order to adopt or join another. [< Lat. *defectus* < p.p. of *deficere,* to fail.] —de-fec'tion n. —de-fec'tor n.

de-fec-tive (dĭ-fĕk'tĭv) adj. Having a defect. —de-fec'tive-ly adv. —de-fec'tive-ness n.

de-fend (dĭ-fĕnd') v. 1. To protect from danger; guard. 2. To support or maintain; justify. 3. a. To represent (the defendant) in a civil or criminal case. b. To contest (a legal action or claim). [< Lat. *defendere,* to ward off.] —de-fend'a-ble adj. —de-fend'er n.

Syns: *defend, guard, protect, safeguard, secure, shield* v.

de-fen-dant (dĭ-fĕn'dənt) n. Law. One against whom a suit or criminal charge is brought.

de-fense (dĭ-fĕns') n. Also chiefly Brit. de-fence. 1. The act of defending. 2. One that defends or protects. 3. An argument in support or justification. 4. Sports. The team attempting to stop the opposition from scoring. 5. A defendant and his or her legal counsel. [< Lat. *defensa.*] —de-fense'less adj. —de-fense'less-ly adv. —de-fense'less-ness n.

defense mechanism n. A physical or psychological reaction of an organism used in self-defense, as against germs.

de-fen-si-ble (dĭ-fĕn'sə-bəl) adj. Capable of being defended or justified. —de-fen'si-bil'i-ty n. —de-fen'si-bly adv.

de-fen-sive (dĭ-fĕn'sĭv) adj. Of, intended, or done for defense. —idiom. on the defensive. Expecting attack. —de-fen'sive-ly adv. —de-fen'sive-ness n.

de-fer¹ (dĭ-fûr') v. -ferred, -fer-ring. To put off; postpone. [< Lat. *diferre.*] —de-fer'ra-ble adj. —de-fer'rer n.

de-fer² (dĭ-fûr') v. -ferred, -fer-ring. To comply with or submit to the opinion or decision of another. [< Lat. *deferre,* to carry away.] —de-fer'rer n.

def-er-ence (dĕf'ər-əns) n. 1. Courteous submission to the opinion, wishes, or judgment of another. 2. Courteous respect. —def'er-en'tial adj. —def'er-en'tial-ly adv.

de-fer-ment (dĭ-fûr'mənt) n. Also de-fer-ral (-fûr'əl). 1. An act or instance of deferring. 2. Postponement of compulsory military service.

de-fi-ant (dĭ-fī'ənt) adj. 1. Marked by resistance to authority. 2. Intentionally provocative. —de-fi'ance n. —de-fi'ant-ly adv.

deficiency disease n. A disease, such as pellagra, that results from a diet lacking in essential nutrients.

de-fi-cient (dĭ-fĭsh'ənt) adj. 1. Lacking an important element; inadequate. 2. Defective; imperfect. [< Lat. *deficere,* to fail.] —de-fi'cien-cy n. —de-fi'cient-ly adv.

def-i-cit (dĕf'ĭ-sĭt) n. The amount by which a

sum of money falls short of the required or expected amount; shortage. [< Lat., it is lacking.]

deficit spending *n.* The spending of money obtained by borrowing.

de-file¹ (dǐ-fīl') *v.* **-filed, -fil·ing.** 1. To make filthy or dirty. 2. To corrupt. 3. To profane (e.g. a good name). 4. To desecrate. 5. To violate the chastity of. [ME *defilen* < *filen*, to defile, and *defoulen*, to injure.] —**de·file'ment** *n.* —**de·fil'er** *n.* —**de·fil'ing·ly** *adv.*

de-file² (dǐ-fīl') *v.* **-filed, -fil·ing.** To march in single file or in columns. —*n.* A narrow passage. [Fr. *défiler.*]

de-fine (dǐ-fīn') *v.* **-fined, -fin·ing.** 1. To state the precise meaning of (a word). 2. To describe the basic qualities of a word. 3. To delineate. 4. To specify distinctly; fix definitely. [< Lat. *definire.*] —**de·fin'a·ble** *adj.* —**de·fin'a·bly** *adv.* —**de·fin'er** *n.*

def·i·nite (děf'ə-nǐt) *adj.* 1. Having distinct limits. 2. Known positively. 3. Clearly defined; precise. [< Lat. *definire*, to define.] —**def'i·nite·ly** *adv.* —**def'i·nite·ness** *n.*

definite article *n.* Gram. The word *the*, used to introduce an identified or immediately identifiable noun or noun phrase.

def·i·ni·tion (děf'ə-nǐsh'ən) *n.* 1. a. The act of defining a word, phrase, or term. b. The statement of the meaning of a word, phrase, or term. 2. The act of making clear and distinct. 3. A determining of outline, extent, or limits. —**def'i·ni'tion·al** *adj.*

de·fin·i·tive (dǐ-fǐn'ǐ-tǐv) *adj.* 1. Precisely defining or outlining. 2. Final; conclusive. 3. Authoritative and complete: *a definitive biography.* —**de·fin'i·tive·ly** *adv.* —**de·fin'i·tive·ness** *n.*

de·flate (dǐ-flāt') *v.* **-flat·ed, -flat·ing.** 1. a. To release contained air or gas from. b. To collapse by such a release. 2. To lessen the confidence, pride, or certainty of. 3. Econ. To reduce the value or amount of (currency), effecting a decline in prices. [DE- + (IN)FLATE.] —**de·fla'tion** *n.* —**de·fla'tion·ar·y** (-shə-něr'ē) *adj.* —**de·fla'tor** *n.*

de·flect (dǐ-flěkt') *v.* To cause to swerve; turn aside. [Lat. *deflectere.*] —**de·flect'a·ble** *adj.* —**de·flec'tion** *n.* —**de·flec'tive** *adj.* —**de·flec'tor** *n.*

de·fog (dē-fôg', -fŏg') *v.* To remove fog from. —**de·fog'ger** *n.*

de·fo·li·ant (dē-fō'lē-ənt) *n.* A chemical sprayed or dusted on plants to make their leaves fall off.

de·fo·li·ate (dē-fō'lē-āt') *v.* **-at·ed, -at·ing.** To deprive of leaves, esp. by the use of a chemical. —**de·fo'li·a'tion** *n.* —**de·fo'li·a'tor** *n.*

de·for·est (dē-fôr'ĭst, -fŏr'-) *v.* To clear away the forests from. —**de·for'es·ta'tion** *n.* —**de·for'est·er** *n.*

de·form (dǐ-fôrm') *v.* 1. To spoil the natural form or appearance of; disfigure. 2. To become changed in shape. —**de·form'a·bil'i·ty** *n.* —**de·for·ma'tion** (dē'fôr-mā'shən, děf'ər-) *n.*

de·for·mi·ty (dǐ-fôr'mǐ-tē) *n., pl.* **-ties.** 1. The condition of being deformed. 2. A part of the body that is deformed. 3. One that is deformed.

de·fraud (dǐ-frôd') *v.* To swindle. —**de·fraud·a'tion** (dē'frô-dā'shən) *n.* —**de·fraud'er** *n.*

de·fray (dǐ-frā') *v.* To meet or satisfy by payment; pay. [< OFr. *desfrayer.*] —**de·fray'a·ble** *adj.* —**de·fray'al** *n.*

de·frock (dē-frŏk') *v.* To unfrock.

de·frost (dē-frôst', -frŏst') *v.* 1. To remove ice or frost from. 2. To cause to thaw. 3. To become free of ice or frost. —**de·frost'er** (-frô'stər, -frŏst'ər) *n.*

deft (děft) *adj.* **-er, -est.** Skillful; adroit. [ME *defte.*] —**deft'ly** *adv.* —**deft'ness** *n.*

de·funct (dǐ-fŭngkt') *adj.* No longer in existence, operation, or use. [Lat. *defunctus*, p.p. of *defungi*, to finish.] —**de·funct'ness** *n.*

de·fuse (dē-fyōōz') *v.* 1. To remove the fuse from (an explosive). 2. To make less dangerous or tense.

de·fy (dǐ-fī') *v.* **-fied, -fy·ing.** 1. To confront or stand up to; challenge. 2. To resist successfully; withstand. 3. To dare (someone) to perform something deemed impossible. [< OFr. *desfier.*] —**de·fi'er** *n.*

de·gauss (dē-gous') *v.* To neutralize the magnetic field of. [DE- + *gauss*, an electromagnetic unit.]

de·gen·er·ate (dǐ-jěn'ə-rāt') *v.* **-at·ed, -at·ing.** To deteriorate or decay. —*adj.* (dǐ-jěn'ər-ǐt). Morally degraded or sexually deviant. —*n.* (dǐ-jěn'ər-ǐt). A morally degraded or sexually deviant person. [Lat. *degenerare.*] —**de·gen'er·a·cy** or **de·gen'er·ate·ness** *n.* —**de·gen'er·ate·ly** *adv.* —**de·gen'er·a'tion** *n.* —**de·gen'er·a·tive** (-ər-ə-tǐv') *adj.*

de·glu·ti·nate (dǐ-glōōt'n-āt') *v.* **-nat·ed, -nat·ing.** To extract the gluten from: *deglutinate wheat flour.* [Lat. *deglutinare.*] —**de·glu'ti·na'tion** *n.*

de·glu·ti·tion (dē'glōō-tǐsh'ən) *n.* The act or process of swallowing. [< Lat. *deglutire*, to swallow.] —**de·glu·ti'tious** *adj.*

de·grade (dǐ-grād') *v.* **-grad·ed, -grad·ing.** 1. To reduce in rank, status, or position. 2. To debase; corrupt. 3. Chem. To decompose (a compound) by stages. —**de·grad'a·ble** *adj.* —**deg·ra·da'tion** (děg'rə-dā'shən) *n.* —**de·grad'ed·ly** *adv.* —**de·grad'ed·ness** *n.* —**de·grad'er** *n.*

de·gree (dǐ-grē') *n.* 1. One of a series of steps or stages. 2. Relative social or official rank or position. 3. Relative intensity. 4. Relative condition or extent. 5. The extent or measure of a state of being, action, etc. 6. A unit division of a temperature scale. 7. A unit of angular measure equal in magnitude to the central angle subtended by 1/360 of the circumference of a circle. 8. A unit of latitude or longitude, 1/360 of a great circle. 9. The greatest sum of the exponents of the variables in a term of a polynomial or polynomial equation. 10. An academic title given to one who has completed a course of study or as an honorary distinction. 11. Law. A classification of a crime according to its seriousness. 12. Gram. One of the forms used in the comparison of adjectives and adverbs. 13. Mus. One of the seven notes of a diatonic scale. [< OFr. *degre.*]

de·gree-day (dǐ-grē'dā') *n.* 1. An indication of the extent of departure from a standard of mean daily temperature. 2. A unit used in estimating quantities of fuel and power consumption, based on a daily ratio of consumption and the mean temperature below 65°F.

de·hu·man·ize (dē-hyōō'mə-nīz') *v.* To deprive of human qualities or attributes, esp. to render mechanical and routine. —**de·hu'man·i·za'tion** *n.*

de·hu·mid·i·fy (dē'hyōō-mǐd'ə-fī') *v.* To decrease the humidity of. —**de·hu·mid'i·fi·ca'tion** *n.* —**de·hu·mid'i·fi·er** *n.*

de·hy·drate (dē-hī'drāt') v. -drat·ed, -drat·ing. To remove or lose water. —**de·hy·dra'tion** n.

de·hy·dro·ge·nate (dē'hī-drŏj'ə-nāt', dē-hī'drə-jə-) v. *Chem.* To remove hydrogen from. —**de·hy·dro·ge·na'tion** n.

de·ice (dē-īs') v. 1. To remove ice from, esp. by melting. 2. To prevent formation of ice on. —**de·ic'er** n.

de·i·fy (dē'ə-fī') v. -fied, -fy·ing. 1. To make a god of. 2. To worship; glorify. [< Lat. *deificare.*] —**de·i·fi·ca'tion** n. —**de'i·fi'er** n.

deign (dān) v. To condescend to give or grant. [< Lat. *dignari,* to regard as worthy.]

de·in·sti·tu·tion·al·ize (dē-ĭn'stĭ-tōō'shə-nə-līz', -tyōō'-) v. 1. To remove the status of an institution from. 2. To enable (one who is mentally ill or developmentally disabled) to live away from an institution. —**de·in'sti·tu'tion·al·i·za'tion** n.

de·ism (dē'ĭz'əm) n. An 18th-cent. system of natural religion affirming the existence of God while denying the validity of revelation. [< Lat. *deus,* god.] —**de'ist** n. —**de·is'tic** (dē-ĭs'tĭk) adj. —**de·is'ti·cal·ly** adv.

de·i·ty (dē'ĭ-tē) n., pl. -ties. 1. A god or goddess. 2. Divinity. 3. **the Deity.** God. [< Lat. *deus.*]

dé·jà vu (dā'zhä vū') n. The illusion of having already experienced something actually being experienced for the first time. [Fr., already seen.]

de·ject (dĭ-jĕkt') v. To dishearten; dispirit. [< Lat. *deicere,* to cast down.] —**de·jec'tion** n.

de·ject·ed (dĭ-jĕk'tĭd) adj. Depressed; disheartened. —**de·ject'ed·ly** adv. —**de·ject'ed·ness** n.

de ju·re (dē jōōr'ē, dä yōōr'ā) adv. & adj. According to law; by right. [Lat.]

deka- pref. Var. of **deca-.**

dek·a·gram (dĕk'ə-grăm') n. Var. of **decagram.**

dek·a·me·ter (dĕk'ə-mē'tər) n. Var. of **decameter.**

Del·a·ware (dĕl'ə-wâr') n., pl. -ware or -wares. 1. a. A group of Indian tribes formerly inhabiting the Delaware River valley. b. A member of any of these tribes. 2. The Algonquian language of the Delaware.

de·lay (dĭ-lā') v. 1. To postpone; defer. 2. To cause to be late. 3. To procrastinate; linger. —n. 1. The act of delaying or condition of being delayed. 2. The period of time one is delayed. [< OFr. *deslaier.*] —**de·lay'er** n.

Syns: *delay, dally, dawdle, dilly-dally, drag, lag, linger, loiter, poke, procrastinate, tarry* v.

de·le (dē'lē) n. A sign indicating that something is to be deleted from typeset matter. [Lat., imper. of *delēre,* to delete.] —**de'le** v.

de·lec·ta·ble (dĭ-lĕk'tə-bəl) adj. 1. Delightful. 2. Delicious. [< Lat. *delectare,* to please.] —**de·lec'ta·bil'i·ty** n. —**de·lec'ta·bly** adv.

de·lec·ta·tion (dē'lĕk-tā'shən) n. Pleasure; delight.

del·e·gate (dĕl'ĭ-gāt', -gĭt) n. 1. One authorized to act as a representative for another or others. 2. A member of the lower house of the Maryland, Virginia, and West Virginia legislatures. —v. (dĕl'ĭ-gāt') -gat·ed, -gat·ing. 1. To authorize and send (a person) as one's representative. 2. To commit to one's representative. [< Lat. *delegare,* to send away.]

del·e·ga·tion (dĕl'ĭ-gā'shən) n. 1. The act of delegating or condition of being delegated. 2. A group of persons authorized to represent another or others.

de·lete (dĭ-lēt') v. -let·ed, -let·ing. To strike out; omit. [< Lat. *delēre.*] —**de·le'tion** n.

del·e·te·ri·ous (dĕl'ĭ-tîr'ē-əs) adj. Harmful; injurious. [< Gk. *dēlētērios.*] —**del'e·te'ri·ous·ly** adv. —**del'e·te'ri·ous·ness** n.

delft (dĕlft) n. Also **delf** (dĕlf). A style of glazed earthenware, usu. blue and white. [< *Delft,* the Netherlands.]

delft
Bristol delft plate

del·i (dĕl'ē) n., pl. -is. *Informal.* A delicatessen.

de·lib·er·ate (dĭ-lĭb'ə-rāt') v. -at·ed, -at·ing. 1. To consider or discuss (a matter) carefully. 2. To take careful thought; reflect. —adj. (dĭ-lĭb'ər-ĭt). 1. Intentional. 2. a. Careful in deciding. b. Not hastily determined: *a deliberate choice.* 3. Slow. [Lat. *deliberare.*] —**de·lib'er·ate·ly** adv. —**de·lib'er·ate·ness** n.

de·lib·er·a·tion (dĭ-lĭb'ə-rā'shən) n. 1. Careful consideration. 2. Often **deliberations.** Careful discussion of an issue. —**de·lib'er·a'tive** (-lĭb'-ə-rā'tĭv, -ər-ə-tĭv) adj. —**de·lib'er·a'tive·ly** adv. —**de·lib'er·a'tive·ness** n.

del·i·ca·cy (dĕl'ĭ-kə-sē) n., pl. -cies. 1. The quality of being delicate. 2. A choice food.

del·i·cate (dĕl'ĭ-kĭt) adj. 1. Exquisitely or pleasingly fine. 2. Frail in constitution. 3. Easily damaged. 4. Requiring or marked by tact. 5. Keenly sensitive or accurate. 6. Requiring great skill and expertise. [< Lat. *delicatus.*] —**del'i·cate·ly** adv. —**del'i·cate·ness** n.

del·i·ca·tes·sen (dĕl'ĭ-kə-tĕs'ən) n. A shop that sells freshly prepared foods ready for serving. [< G. *Delikatessen,* delicacies.]

de·li·cious (dĭ-lĭsh'əs) adj. Very pleasing to taste. [< LLat. *deliciosus.*] —**de·li'cious·ly** adv. —**de·li'cious·ness** n.

Syns: *delicious, delectable, luscious, savory, scrumptious, tasty, yummy* adj.

de·light (dĭ-līt') n. 1. Great pleasure; joy. 2. Something that gives great pleasure or enjoyment. —v. 1. To take great pleasure or joy. 2. To give (someone) great pleasure or joy. [< Lat. *delectare,* to please < *delicere,* to allure.] —**de·light'ed·ly** adv. —**de·light'ed·ness** n.

de·light·ful (dĭ-līt′fəl) *adj.* Giving delight. —**de·light′ful·ly** *adv.* —**de·light′ful·ness** *n.*

de·lim·it (dĭ-lĭm′ĭt) *v.* To establish the limits of. [< Lat. *delimitare*.] —**de·lim′i·ta′tion** *n.* —**de·lim′i·ta′tive** *adj.*

de·lin·e·ate (dĭ-lĭn′ē-āt′) *v.* -at·ed, -at·ing. 1. To draw or outline accurately. 2. To describe broadly but accurately. [Lat. *delineare*.] —**de·lin′e·a′tion** *n.* —**de·lin′e·a′tive** *adj.*

de·lin·quent (dĭ-lĭng′kwənt) *adj.* 1. Failing to do what is required. 2. Overdue in payment: *a delinquent account.* —*n.* 1. One who fails to do what is required. 2. A juvenile delinquent. [< Lat. *delinquere*, to offend.] —**de·lin′quen·cy** *n.* —**de·lin′quent·ly** *adv.*

del·i·quesce (dĕl′ĭ-kwĕs′) *v.* -quesced, -quesc·ing. *Chem.* To dissolve and become liquid by absorbing moisture from the air. [Lat. *deliquescere*.] —**del′i·ques′cence** *n.* —**del′i·ques′cent** *adj.*

de·lir·i·um (dĭ-lîr′ē-əm) *n.,* pl. -ums or -a (-ē-ə). 1. A condition of temporary mental confusion resulting from high fever, intoxication, or shock, and characterized by anxiety, tremors, hallucinations, delusions, and incoherence. 2. Uncontrolled excitement or emotion. [Lat. < *delirare*, to be deranged.] —**de·lir′i·ous** *adj.* —**de·lir′i·ous·ly** *adv.* —**de·lir′i·ous·ness** *n.*

delirium tre·mens (trē′mənz) *n.* An acute delirium caused by alcohol poisoning. [NLat., trembling delirium.]

de·liv·er (dĭ-lĭv′ər) *v.* 1. To take to an intended recipient or place. 2. To throw or hurl. 3. To utter. 4. To set free. 5. a. To assist in the birth of. b. To assist (a female) in giving birth. 6. To do what is expected; make good. [< LLat. *deliberare*.] —**de·liv′er·a·bil′i·ty** *n.* —**de·liv′er·a·ble** *adj.* —**de·liv′er·ance** *n.* —**de·liv′er·er** *n.*

de·liv·er·y (dĭ-lĭv′ə-rē) *n.,* pl. -ies 1. The act of delivering. 2. Something delivered. 3. Childbirth. 4. Manner of speaking or singing. 5. The act or manner of throwing or discharging, esp. a ball.

dell (dĕl) *n.* A small, secluded valley. [< OE.]

del·phin·i·um (dĕl-fĭn′ē-əm) *n.* A tall cultivated plant with spikes of showy, variously colored spurred flowers. [< Gk. *delphinion*, dim. of *delphis*, dolphin.]

del·ta (dĕl′tə) *n.* 1. The 4th letter of the Greek alphabet. See table at **alphabet.** 2. A usu. triangular deposit at the mouth of a river. [Gk.]

del·toid (dĕl′toid′) *n.* A thick, triangular muscle covering the shoulder joint, used to raise the arm from the side. [< Gk. *deltoeidēs,* triangular.] —**del′toid** *adj.*

de·lude (dĭ-lōōd′) *v.* -lud·ed, -lud·ing. To mislead; deceive. [< Lat. *deludere*.] —**de·lud′er** *n.* —**de·lud′ing·ly** *adv.*

del·uge (dĕl′yōōj) *n.* 1. A flood; downpour. 2. An overwhelming influx. —*v.* -uged, -ug·ing. To overrun with or as if with water. [< Lat. *diluvium.*]

de·lu·sion (dĭ-lōō′zhən) *n.* 1. The act of deluding or the state of being deluded. 2. A false belief held in spite of invalidating evidence. —**de·lu′sive** or **de·lu′sion·al** *adj.* —**de·lu′sive·ly** *adv.* —**de·lu′sive·ness** *n.*

de luxe (dĭ lōōks′, lŭks′). Also **de·luxe.** —*adj.* Exceptionally elegant or luxurious. —*adv.* In a sumptuous manner. [Fr., of luxury.]

delve (dĕlv) *v.* delved, delv·ing. To search deeply and laboriously. [< OE *delfan.*]

de·mag·net·ize (dē-măg′nĭ-tīz′) *v.* To remove magnetic properties from. —**de·mag′net·i·za′tion** *n.*

dem·a·gogue (dĕm′ə-gôg′, -gŏg′) *n.* Also **dem·a·gog.** A leader who obtains power by means of appeals to the emotions and prejudices of the populace. [Gk. *dēmagōgos,* popular leader.] —**dem′a·gog′ic** (-gŏj′ĭk) or **dem·a·gog′i·cal** (-gŏj′ĭ-kəl) *adj.* —**dem′a·gog′i·cal·ly** *adv.* —**dem′a·gogu′er·y** *n.* —**dem′a·gog′y** *n.*

de·mand (dĭ-mănd′) *v.* 1. To ask for urgently or insistently. 2. To claim as just or due. 3. To need or require. —*n.* 1. The act of demanding. 2. Something that is demanded. 3. a. The condition of being sought after. b. An urgent need. 4. *Econ.* a. The desire to possess something combined with the ability to purchase it. b. The amount of any commodity that people are ready to buy at a given time for a given price. [< Lat. *demandare,* to entrust.] —**de·mand′a·ble** *adj.* —**de·mand′er** *n.*

de·mand·ing (dĭ-măn′dĭng, dĭ-män′-) *adj.* 1. Making rigorous demands. 2. Requiring careful attention or constant effort. —**de·mand′ing·ly** *adv.*

de·mar·cate (dĭ-mär′kāt′, dē′mär-kāt′) *v.* -cat·ed, -cat·ing. To mark with or as with boundaries. [< DEMARCATION.] —**de·mar′ca·tor** *n.*

de·mar·ca·tion (dē′mär-kā′shən) *n.* 1. The setting or marking of boundaries or limits. 2. A separation. [Sp. *demarcación* < *demarcar,* to mark boundaries.]

de·mean (dĭ-mēn′) *v.* To debase in dignity or stature.

de·mean·or (dĭ-mē′nər) *n.* A person's manner toward others. [< OFr. *demener,* to govern.]

de·ment·ed (dĭ-mĕn′tĭd) *adj.* 1. Insane. 2. *Informal.* Foolish. [< *dement,* to make insane < LLat. *dementare.*]

de·men·tia (dĭ-mĕn′shə) *n.* Deterioration of mental faculties along with emotional disturbance resulting from organic brain disorder. [Lat., madness.]

dementia prae·cox (prē′kŏks′) *n.* Schizophrenia. [NLat., premature dementia.]

de·mer·it (dĭ-mĕr′ĭt) *n.* A mark made against a person's record for bad conduct or failure. [< Lat. *demeritum,* neuter p.p. of *demerēre,* to deserve.]

Dem·er·ol (dĕm′ə-rôl′, -rŏl′). A trademark for a synthetic morphine.

de·mesne (dĭ-mān′, -mēn′) *n.* 1. The lands of an estate. 2. An extensive piece of landed property. 3. Any district; territory. [< OFr. *demaine,* domain.]

De·me·ter (dĭ-mē′tər) *n.* Gk. Myth. The goddess of agriculture.

dem·i·god (dĕm′ē-gŏd′) *n.* 1. *Myth.* a. The offspring of a god and a mortal. b. An inferior or minor deity. 2. A person with godlike attributes. [*demi-,* partly + GOD.]

dem·i·john (dĕm′ē-jŏn′) *n.* A large bottle usu. encased in wickerwork. [Prob. < Fr. *dame-Jeanne,* Lady Jane.]

de·mil·i·ta·rize (dē-mĭl′ĭ-tə-rīz′) *v.* To prohibit or eliminate military forces or installations. —**de·mil′i·ta·ri·za′tion** *n.*

dem·i·mon·daine (dĕm′ē-mŏn-dān′, -mŏn′dān′) *n.* A woman belonging to the demimonde. [Fr.]

dem·i·monde (dĕm′ē-mŏnd′) *n.* 1. The social class of those who are kept by wealthy lovers or protectors. 2. Any group that exists on the fringes of respectability. [Fr.]

de·mise (dĭ-mīz′) *n.* Death. [< Lat. *demittere,* to release.]

dem·i·tasse (dĕm′ē-tăs′, -täs′) *n.* A small cup of strong black coffee. [Fr.]

de·mo·bi·lize (dē-mō′bə-līz′) *v.* **1.** To discharge from military service or use. **2.** To change (e.g. an economy) from a wartime to peacetime condition. —**de·mo′bi·li·za′tion** *n.*

de·moc·ra·cy (dĭ-mŏk′rə-sē) *n., pl.* **-cies.** **1. a.** Government by the people, exercised either directly or through elected representatives. **b.** A political unit with this form of government. **2.** Social and political equality and respect for the individual within the community. [< Gk. *dēmokratia.*]

dem·o·crat (dĕm′ə-krăt′) *n.* **1.** An advocate of democracy. **2. Democrat.** A member of the Democratic Party.

dem·o·crat·ic (dĕm′ə-krăt′ĭk) *adj.* **1.** Of, characterized by, or advocating political, economic, or social democracy. **2.** Pertaining to or promoting the interests of the people. **3.** Practicing social equality; not snobbish. **4. Democratic.** Of or pertaining to the Democratic Party. —**dem′o·crat′i·cal·ly** *adv.*

Democratic Party *n.* One of the two major U.S. political parties.

de·moc·ra·tize (dĭ-mŏk′rə-tīz′) *v.* **-tized, -tizing.** To make democratic. —**de·moc′ra·ti·za′tion** *n.*

de·mod·u·late (dē-mŏj′ōō-lāt′, -mŏd′yə-) *v.* **-lated, -lating.** To extract (information from a modulated carrier wave. —**de·mod′u·la′tion** *n.* —**de·mod′u·la′tor** *n.*

de·mog·ra·phy (dĭ-mŏg′rə-fē) *n.* The statistical study of human populations. [Gk. *dēmos,* people + -GRAPHY.] —**de·mog′ra·pher** *n.* —**dem′o·graph′ic** (dĕm′ə-grăf′ĭk) *adj.* —**dem′o·graph′i·cal·ly** *adv.*

de·mol·ish (dĭ-mŏl′ĭsh) *v.* To tear down completely; destroy. [< Lat. *demoliri.*]

dem·o·li·tion (dĕm′ə-lĭsh′ən) *n.* The act or process of demolishing; esp. destruction by explosives. [< Lat. *demoliri,* to demolish.] —**dem′o·li′tion·ist** *n.*

de·mon (dē′mən) *n.* **1.** A devil or evil being. **2.** A persistently tormenting person, force, or passion. **3.** One who is extremely zealous or skillful in a given activity. [< Gk. *daimōn,* divine power.]

de·mon·e·tize (dĭ-mŏn′ĭ-tīz′, -mŭn′-) *v.* **1.** To divest (currency) of its standard monetary value. **2.** To stop using as money. —**de·mon′e·ti·za′tion** *n.*

de·mo·ni·ac (dĭ-mō′nē-ăk′) *or* **de·mo·ni·a·cal** (dē′mə-nī′ə-kəl) *adj.* **1.** Possessed by or as if by a demon; wild. **2.** Devilish; fiendish. [< Gk. *daimoniakos.*] —**de′mo·ni′a·cal·ly** (dē′mə-nī′ə-kə-lē) *adv.*

de·mon·ic (dĭ-mŏn′ĭk) *adj.* **1.** Befitting a demon; fiendish. **2.** Inspired by a spiritual force or genius.

de·mon·ol·o·gy (dē′mə-nŏl′ə-jē) *n.* The study of demons.

de·mon·stra·ble (dĭ-mŏn′strə-bəl) *adj.* Capable of being shown or proved. —**de·mon′stra·bil′i·ty** *n.* —**de·mon′stra·bly** *adv.*

dem·on·strate (dĕm′ən-strāt′) *v.* **-strated, -strating.** **1.** To prove or make manifest by reasoning or evidence. **2.** To manifest or reveal. **3.** To display, operate, and explain (a product). **4.** To make a public display of opinion. [Lat. *demonstrare.*] —**dem′on·stra′-**

tion *n.* —**de·mon′stra·tive** *adj.* —**de·mon′stra·tive·ly** *adv.* —**de·mon′stra·tive·ness** *n.* —**dem′on·stra′tor** *n.*

de·mor·al·ize (dĭ-môr′ə-līz′, -mŏr′-) *v.* **-ized, -izing.** **1.** To weaken the confidence or morale of; dishearten. **2.** To corrupt. —**de·mor′al·i·za′tion** *n.* —**de·mor′al·iz′er** *n.*

de·mote (dĭ-mōt′) *v.* **-moted, -moting.** To lower in rank or grade. [DE- + (PRO)MOTE.] —**de·mo′tion** *n.*

de·mot·ic (dĭ-mŏt′ĭk) *adj.* **1.** Of or pertaining to the common people; popular. **2.** Of or pertaining to a form of modern Greek based on colloquial use. —*n.* Demotic Greek. [< Gk. *dēmos,* people.]

de·mul·cent (dĭ-mŭl′sənt) *adj.* Soothing. —*n.* A soothing, usu. jellylike or oily substance. [< Lat. *demulcēre,* to soothe.]

de·mur (dĭ-mûr′) *v.* **-murred, -murring.** To take exception; object. [< Lat. *demorari,* to delay.]

de·mure (dĭ-myōōr′) *adj.* **-murer, -murest.** **1.** Modest in manner; reserved. **2.** Affectedly modest; coy. [ME.] —**de·mure′ly** *adv.* —**de·mure′ness** *n.*

de·my·thol·o·gize (dē′mĭ-thŏl′ə-jīz′) *v.* **-gized, -gizing.** To remove mythical aspects from. —**de′my·thol′o·gi·za′tion** *n.* —**de′my·thol·o·giz′er** *n.*

den (dĕn) *n.* **1.** The shelter of a wild animal; lair. **2.** A small, usu. secluded place, esp. when used as a hideout or for an illegal activity. **3.** A small secluded room for study or relaxation. **4.** A unit of about eight to ten Cub Scouts. [< OE *denn.*]

de·na·ture (dē-nā′chər) *v.* **-tured, -turing.** To render unfit to eat or drink, esp. to add methanol to for this purpose. —**de·na′tura′tion** *n.*

den·drite (dĕn′drīt′) *n.* A branched part of a nerve cell that transmits impulses toward the cell body. —**den·drit′ic** (-drĭt′ĭk) *or* **den·drit′i·cal** *adj.*

dendro- *or* **dendr-** *pref.* Tree; treelike: *dendrology.* [< Gk. *dendron,* tree.]

den·drol·o·gy (dĕn-drŏl′ə-jē) *n.* The botanical study of trees. —**den′dro·log′ic** (-drə-lŏj′ĭk) *or* **den′dro·log′i·cal** *adj.* —**den·drol′o·gist** *n.*

den·gue (dĕng′gē, -gā) *n.* A severe infectious disease of tropical and subtropical regions, transmitted by mosquitoes and marked by fever and severe pains in the joints. [Sp.]

de·ni·al (dĭ-nī′əl) *n.* **1.** A negative reply, as to a request. **2.** Refusal to grant the truth of a statement. **3.** A disavowal; repudiation. **4.** Self-denial.

de·nic·o·tin·ize (dē-nĭk′ə-tĭ-nīz′) *v.* **-ized, -izing.** To remove nicotine from.

den·ier (dĕn′yər) *n.* A unit of fineness for rayon, nylon, and silk yarns. [< OFr., a coin < Lat. *denarius.*]

den·i·grate (dĕn′ĭ-grāt′) *v.* **-grated, -grating.** To belittle maliciously; defame. [Lat. *denigrare,* to blacken.] —**den′i·gra′tion** *n.* —**den′i·gra′tor** *n.*

den·im (dĕn′əm) *n.* **1.** A coarse, heavy cotton cloth used for work clothes and sportswear. **2. denims.** Garments made of denim. [Fr. *(serge) de Nîmes,* serge of Nîmes.]

de·ni·tri·fy (dē-nī′trə-fī′) *v.* **-fied, -fying.** **1.** To remove nitrogen or its compounds from.

2. To convert (a nitrate) into a compound having a lower level of oxidation. —**de·ni'tri·fi·ca'tion** n.

den·i·zen (dĕn'ĭ-zən) n. An inhabitant; resident. [< LLat. *deintus,* from within.]

den mother n. A woman who supervises a Cub Scout den.

de·nom·i·na·tion (dĭ-nŏm'ə-nā'shən) n. **1.** A name, esp. the name of a class or group. **2.** A unit having a specified value in a system of currency or weights. **3.** An organized group of religious congregations. [< Lat. *denominare,* to designate.] —**de·nom'i·na'tion·al** adj. —**de·nom'i·na'tion·al·ly** adv.

de·nom·i·na·tor (dĭ-nŏm'ə-nā'tər) n. **1.** The quantity below the line indicating division in a fraction; the quantity that divides the numerator. **2.** A characteristic or quality held in common.

de·note (dĭ-nōt') v. **-not·ed, -not·ing. 1.** To reveal or indicate plainly. **2.** To refer to specifically; mean explicitly. [< Lat. *denotare.*] —**de·no'ta·tion** n. —**de·no'ta·tive** adj. —**de·no'ta·tive·ly** adv.
Usage: In speaking of words, *denote* is used to indicate the object a word names and *connote* to indicate our associations with that object: *The word bachelor denotes an unmarried man and connotes a life of parties and carefree amusements.*

dé·noue·ment (dā'nōō-mäN') n. The solution or outcome of a literary work. [Fr. < OFr. *desnouement,* an untying.]

de·nounce (dĭ-nouns') v. **-nounced, -nounc·ing. 1.** To express vehement disapproval of openly. **2.** To accuse formally; inform against. [< Lat. *denuntiare.*] —**de·nounce'ment** n. —**de·nounc'er** n.

dense (dĕns) adj. **dens·er, dens·est. 1.** Having relatively high density. **2.** Crowded together. **3.** Thick; impenetrable. **4.** Stupid. [Lat. *densus,* thick.] —**dense'ly** adv. —**dense'ness** n.

den·si·ty (dĕn'sĭ-tē) n., pl. **-ties. 1. a.** The amount of something per unit measure, esp. per unit length, area, or volume. **b.** The mass per unit volume of a substance under specified conditions of pressure and temperature. **2.** Thickness of consistency; impenetrability. **3.** Stupidity.

dent (dĕnt) n. A depression in a surface made by pressure or a blow. [< OE *dynt,* blow.]

den·tal (dĕn'tl) adj. **1.** Of or pertaining to the teeth. **2.** *Phonet.* Produced with the tip of the tongue near or against the upper front teeth. —n. A dental consonant.

dental floss n. A thread used to clean between the teeth.

dental hygienist n. One who assists a dentist.

denti- or **dent-** pref. Tooth: *dentine.* [< Lat. *dens,* tooth.]

den·ti·frice (dĕn'tə-frĭs) n. A substance, as paste, for cleaning the teeth. [< Lat. *dentifricium.*]

den·tine (dĕn'tēn') n. Also **den·tin** (-tĭn). The calcified part of a tooth, beneath the enamel. —**den'ti·nal** adj.

den·tist·ry (dĕn'tĭ-strē) n. The diagnosis, prevention, and treatment of diseases of the teeth and gums. —**den'tist** n.

den·ti·tion (dĕn-tĭsh'ən) n. The type, number, and arrangement of teeth.

den·ture (dĕn'chər) n. A set of artificial teeth.

de·nude (dĭ-nōōd', -nyōōd') v. **-nud·ed, -nud·ing.** To strip the covering of; make bare.
[Lat. *denudare.*] —**den'u·da'tion** (dĕn'yōō-dā'shən) n.

de·nun·ci·a·tion (dĭ-nŭn'sē-ā'shən, -shē-) n. The act of denouncing.

de·ny (dĭ-nī') v. **-nied, -ny·ing. 1.** To declare untrue; contradict. **2.** To refuse to believe; reject. **3.** To refuse to recognize or acknowledge; disavow. **4.** To refuse to grant. [< Lat. *denegare.*]

de·o·dor·ant (dē-ō'dər-ənt) n. A substance used to counteract undesirable odors.

de·o·dor·ize (dē-ō'də-rīz') v. **-ized, -iz·ing.** To cover or absorb the odor of. —**de·o'dor·i·za'tion** n. —**de·o'dor·iz'er** n.

de·ox·y·ri·bo·nu·cle·ic acid (dē-ŏk'sē-rī'bō-nōō-klē'ĭk, -nyōō-) n. DNA.

de·part (dĭ-pärt') v. **1.** To go away; leave. **2.** To vary or deviate: *depart from custom.* **3.** To die. [< OFr. *departir,* to divide.]

de·part·ment (dĭ-pärt'mənt) n. **1.** A distinct usu. specialized division of an organization, government, or business. **2.** An area of expertise or activity; sphere. [Fr. *département.*] —**de·part·men'tal** (dē'pärt-mĕn'tl) adj.

de·part·men·tal·ize (dē'pärt-mĕn'tl-īz') v. **-ized, -iz·ing.** To divide into departments. —**de·part·men'tal·i·za'tion** n.

department store n. A large retail store offering a variety of merchandise.

de·par·ture (dĭ-pär'chər) n. **1.** The act of leaving. **2.** A starting out, as on a trip. **3.** A divergence.

de·pend (dĭ-pĕnd') v. **1.** To rely, as for support: *depends on his scholarship.* **2.** To place trust: *You can depend on her reliability.* **3.** To be determined or dependent. **4.** To hang down. [< Lat. *dependere.*]
Usage: Depend, indicating a condition or contingency, is always followed by *on* or *upon,* as in *The outcome of the election depends on the labor-union vote.*

de·pend·a·ble (dĭ-pĕn'də-bəl) adj. Reliable; trustworthy. —**de·pend'a·bil'i·ty** n.

de·pend·ence (dĭ-pĕn'dəns) n. Also **de·pend·ance. 1.** The condition of being dependent, esp. for support. **2.** The condition of being determined, influenced, or controlled by something else. **3.** Trust; reliance.

de·pend·en·cy (dĭ-pĕn'dən-sē) n., pl. **-cies.** Also **de·pend·an·cy. 1.** Dependence. **2.** A territory or state under the jurisdiction of another country from which it is separated geographically.

de·pend·ent (dĭ-pĕn'dənt) adj. Also **de·pend·ant. 1.** Determined or influenced by another. **2.** Subordinate. **3.** Relying on or requiring the aid of another for support: *dependent children.* **4.** Hanging down. —n. One who relies on another for support. —**de·pend'ent·ly** adv.

de·pict (dĭ-pĭkt') v. **1.** To represent in a picture. **2.** To represent in words. [Lat. *depingere.*] —**de·pic'tion** n.

de·pil·a·to·ry (dĭ-pĭl'ə-tôr'ē, -tōr'ē) n., pl. **-ries.** An agent used to remove hair. [< Lat. *depilare,* to remove hair.]

de·plane (dē-plān') v. **-planed, -plan·ing.** To disembark from an airplane.

de·plete (dĭ-plēt') v. **-plet·ed, -plet·ing.** To use up or exhaust. [Lat. *deplēre,* to empty.] —**de·ple'tion** n.

de·plore (dĭ-plôr', -plōr') v. **-plored, -plor·ing. 1.** To feel or express strong disapproval of. **2.** To feel or express deep sorrow over; lament. [< Lat. *deplorare.*] —**de·plor'a·ble** adj. —**de·plor'a·bly** adv.

de·ploy (dǐ-ploi') v. To spread out (persons or forces) systematically over an area. [< Lat. *displicare*, to scatter.] —**de·ploy'ment** n.

de·po·nent (dǐ-pō'nənt) n. One who testifies under oath, esp. in writing. [< Lat. *deponere*, to put down.]

de·pop·u·late (dē-pŏp'yə-lāt') v. To reduce sharply the population of. —**de·pop'u·la'tion** n. —**de·pop'u·la'tor** n.

de·port (dǐ-pôrt', -pōrt') v. To expel from a country. [< Lat. *deportare*, to carry away.] —**de·por·ta'tion** (dē'pôr-tā'shən, -pōr-) n. —**de·port·ee'** n.

de·port·ment (dǐ-pôrt'mənt, -pōrt'-) n. Behavior; demeanor: *aristocratic deportment.*

de·pose (dǐ-pōz') v. **-posed, -pos·ing.** 1. To remove from office or a position of power. 2. To testify, esp. in writing. [< OFr. *deposer*.] —**de·pos'a·ble** adj. —**de·pos'al** n.

de·pos·it (dǐ-pŏz'ǐt) v. 1. To place for safekeeping, as money in a bank. 2. To lay or set down. 3. To put down in layers by a natural process. 4. To give (money) as partial payment or security. —n. 1. Something entrusted for safekeeping, esp. money in a bank. 2. The condition of being deposited: *a thousand dollars on deposit.* 3. Money given as partial payment or as security. 4. Something deposited, esp. mineral or sandy matter settled by moving water. [< Lat. *deponere*, to put aside.] —**de·pos'i·tor** n.

dep·o·si·tion (dĕp'ə-zĭsh'ən) n. 1. The act of deposing, as from high office. 2. The act of depositing. 3. *Law.* Testimony under oath, esp. a written statement admissible in court. 4. A deposit.

de·pos·i·to·ry (dǐ-pŏz'ǐ-tôr'ē, -tōr'ē) n., pl. **-ries.** A place where something is held for safekeeping.

de·pot (dē'pō) n. 1. A railroad or bus station. 2. A warehouse or storehouse. 3. A military installation where supplies are stored or troops are assembled and assigned. [< Lat. *depositum*, deposit.]

depot
In Boise, Idaho

de·prave (dǐ-prāv') v. **-praved, -prav·ing.** To corrupt morally; debase. [< Lat. *depravare*.] —**de·praved'** adj. —**de·prav'i·ty** (-prăv'ǐ-tē) n.

dep·re·cate (dĕp'rǐ-kāt') v. **-cat·ed, -cat·ing.** 1. To express disapproval of. 2. To depreciate; belittle. [Lat. *deprecari*, to ward off by prayer.] —**dep're·ca'tion** n. —**dep're·ca'tor** n.

dep·re·ca·to·ry (dĕp'rǐ-kə-tôr'ē, -tōr'ē) adj. Expressing disapproval; disparaging.

de·pre·ci·ate (dǐ-prē'shē-āt') v. **-at·ed, -at·ing.** 1. To make or become less in price or value. 2. To belittle. [< LLat. *depretiare*.] —**de·pre'ci·a'tion** n. —**de·pre'cia·to'ry** (-shə-tôr'ē, -tōr'-) adj.

dep·re·da·tion (dĕp'rǐ-dā'shən) n. The act or an instance of destruction, plunder, or ravaging. [< LLat. *depraedari*, to plunder.]

de·press (dǐ-prĕs') v. 1. To make sad or dejected; sadden. 2. To press down; lower. 3. To lower or lessen in value or price. [< Lat. *deprimere*.] —**de·pres'sor** n.

de·pres·sant (dǐ-prĕs'ənt) adj. Tending to slow vital body processes. —n. A depressant drug.

de·pressed (dǐ-prĕst') adj. 1. Gloomy; dejected. 2. Suffering economic hardship.

Syns: *depressed, backward, disadvantaged, underprivileged* adj.

de·pres·sion (dǐ-prĕsh'ən) n. 1. The act of depressing or condition of being depressed. 2. A mental condition of gloom or sadness; dejection. 3. An area that is sunk below its surroundings; hollow. 4. A region of low barometric pressure. 5. A period of drastic decline in the national economy. —**de·pres'sive** adj.

de·prive (dǐ-prīv') v. **-prived, -priv·ing.** 1. To take something away from; divest. 2. To keep from the possession of something. [< Med. Lat. *deprivare*.] —**dep'ri·va'tion** (dĕp'rə-vā'shən) n.

de·pro·gram (dē-prō'grăm', -grəm) v. To counteract the effect of a previous indoctrination, esp. a religious indoctrination. —**de·pro'gram·mer** or **de·pro'gram·er** n.

depth (dĕpth) n. 1. The quality of being deep. 2. The distance or dimension downward, backward, or inward. 3. Often **depths.** The inner or most remote part. 4. The most profound or intense part or stage. 5. Intellectual complexity or penetration. 6. The range of one's understanding or competence: *beyond one's depth.* 7. Richness; intensity: *depth of color.* [ME *depthe*.]

depth charge n. A charge designed for explosion under water, used esp. against submarines.

dep·u·ta·tion (dĕp'yə-tā'shən) n. 1. A group appointed to represent others. 2. The act of deputing.

de·pute (dǐ-pyōōt') v. **-put·ed, -put·ing.** To delegate. [< LLat. *deputare*, to allot.]

dep·u·tize (dĕp'yə-tīz') v. **-tized, -tiz·ing.** To appoint as a deputy.

dep·u·ty (dĕp'yə-tē) n., pl. **-ties.** 1. One empowered to act for another. 2. An assistant exercising full authority in the absence of his superior. 3. A legislative representative in certain countries.

de·rail (dē-rāl') v. To run off or cause to run off the rails. —**de·rail'ment** n.

de·rail·leur (dǐ-rā'lər) n. A gear mechanism on a bicycle that changes bicycle gear ratio by moving the chain from one sprocket to another. [Fr. *dérailler*, to become derailed.]

de·range (dǐ-rānj') v. **-ranged, -rang·ing.** 1. To disarrange. 2. To make insane. [< OFr. *desrengier*.] —**de·range'ment** n.

der·by (dûr'bē; *Brit.* där'bē) n., pl. **-bies.** 1. A

horse race, usu. for three-year-olds, held annually. **2.** A race open to all contestants. **3.** A stiff felt hat with a round crown and narrow brim. [< 12th Earl of *Derby* (1752–1834).]

der·e·lict (děr'ə-lĭkt) *n.* **1.** A homeless or jobless person. **2.** Abandoned property, esp. a ship abandoned at sea. —*adj.* **1.** Neglectful of duty; remiss. **2.** Abandoned by an owner. [< Lat. *derelinquere*, to abandon.]

der·e·lic·tion (děr'ə-lĭk'shən) *n.* **1.** Willful failure or neglect, as of duty. **2.** Abandonment.

de·ride (dĭ-rīd') *v.* **-rid·ed, -rid·ing.** To speak of or treat with scorn; scoff at. [Lat. *deridēre*.] —**de·ri'sion** (dĭ-rĭzh'ən) *n.* —**de·ri'sive** (dĭ-rī'sĭv) *adj.* —**de·ri'sive·ly** *adv.*

de ri·gueur (də rē-gûr') *adj.* Required by the current fashion or custom. [Fr.]

der·i·va·tion (děr'ə-vā'shən) *n.* **1.** The act or process of deriving or the condition or fact of being derived. **2.** The origin or source of something. **3.** The historical origin and development of a word; etymology.

de·riv·a·tive (dĭ-rĭv'ə-tĭv) *adj.* Resulting from derivation. —*n.* **1.** Something derived. **2.** A word formed from another by derivation.

de·rive (dĭ-rīv') *v.* **-rived, -riv·ing. 1.** To obtain or issue from a source. **2.** To deduce; infer. **3.** To trace the origin or development of. **4.** To produce or obtain (a compound) from another substance by chemical reaction. [< Lat. *derivare*.] —**de·riv'a·ble** *adj.*

der·ma (dûr'mə) *n.* The corium. [< Gk. *derma*, skin.] —**der'mal** *adj.*

der·ma·ti·tis (dûr'mə-tī'tĭs) *n.* Inflammation of the skin.

der·ma·tol·o·gy (dûr'mə-tŏl'ə-jē) *n.* The medical study of the skin and its diseases. —**der'ma·tol'o·gist** *n.*

der·mis (dûr'mĭs) *n.* The corium. [< Gk. *derma*, skin.]

der·o·gate (děr'ə-gāt') *v.* **-gat·ed, -gat·ing. 1.** To detract; take away. **2.** To disparage; belittle. [Lat. *derogare*.] —**der'o·ga'tion** *n.*

de·rog·a·to·ry (dĭ-rŏg'ə-tôr'ē, -tōr'ē) *adj.* Tending to derogate; disparaging. —**de·rog'a·to'ri·ly** *adv.*

der·rick (děr'ĭk) *n.* **1.** A large crane for hoisting and moving heavy objects. **2.** A tall framework over the opening of an oil well, used to support equipment. [Obs. *derick*, gallows.]

der·ri·ère (děr'ē-âr') *n.* The buttocks. [Fr., behind.]

der·ring-do (děr'ĭng-dōō') *n.* Daring spirit and action. [ME.]

der·rin·ger (děr'ĭn-jər) *n.* A small pistol. [< Henry *Deringer*, 19th-cent. U.S. gunsmith.]

derringer

der·vish (dûr'vĭsh) *n.* A member of any of various Moslem orders of ascetics, some of which use whirling dances to achieve ecstasy. [< Pers. *dārvīsh*, mendicant.]

de·sal·i·nate (dē-săl'ə-nāt') *v.* **-nat·ed, -nat·ing.** To remove salts and other chemicals from (e.g. sea water). —**de·sal'i·na'tion** *n.*

des·cant (děs'kănt') *v.* **1.** To comment at

length; discourse. **2.** To sing or play part music. [< Med. Lat. *discantus*, refrain.]

de·scend (dĭ-sěnd') *v.* **1.** To move from a higher to a lower level; come or go down. **2.** To slope, extend, or incline downward. **3.** To be derived from ancestors. **4.** To pass by inheritance or transmission. **5.** To arrive in an overwhelming manner: *Tourists descended on the town.* [< Lat. *descendere*.]

de·scen·dant (dĭ-sěn'dənt) *n.* One descended from specified ancestors. —*adj.* Descendent.

de·scen·dent (dĭ-sěn'dənt) *adj.* **1.** Moving downward. **2.** Proceeding from an ancestor.

de·scent (dĭ-sěnt') *n.* **1.** The act or an instance of descending. **2.** A downward incline. **3.** Family origin; ancestry. **4.** A decline, as in status. **5.** A sudden attack. [< OFr.]

de·scribe (dĭ-skrīb') *v.* **-scribed, -scrib·ing. 1.** To give a verbal account of. **2.** To trace the outline of. [Lat. *describere*, to write down.] —**de·scrib'a·ble** *adj.* —**de·scrib'er** *n.*

de·scrip·tion (dĭ-skrĭp'shən) *n.* **1.** The act of describing; verbal representation. **2.** An account describing something. **3.** A kind; sort: *costumes of every description.* —**de·scrip'tive** *adj.*

de·scry (dĭ-skrī') *v.* **-scried, -scry·ing. 1.** To espy or catch sight of. **2.** To discover by careful observation. [< ME *discrien*, to proclaim.] —**de·scri'er** *n.*

des·e·crate (děs'ĭ-krāt') *v.* **-crat·ed, -crat·ing.** To abuse the sacredness of; profane. [DE- + (CON)SECRATE.] —**des'e·cra'tion** *n.*

de·seg·re·gate (dē-sěg'rĭ-gāt') *v.* To abolish racial segregation in. —**de·seg're·ga'tion** *n.*

de·sen·si·tize (dē-sěn'sĭ-tīz') *v.* **-tized, -tiz·ing.** To make less sensitive. —**de·sen'si·ti·za'tion** *n.* —**de·sen'si·tiz·er** *n.*

des·ert¹ (děz'ərt) *n.* A dry, barren region, often covered with sand, and with little or no vegetation. [< LLat. *desertum*.]

de·sert² (dĭ-zûrt') *n.* Often **deserts.** Something that is deserved or merited, esp. a punishment. [< OFr. *deserte* < p.p. of *deservir*, to deserve.]

de·sert³ (dĭ-zûrt') *v.* **1.** To forsake or leave; abandon. **2.** To forsake one's duty or post. [< LLat. *desertare*.] —**de·sert'er** *n.* —**de·ser'tion** *n.*

de·serve (dĭ-zûrv') *v.* **-served, -serv·ing.** To be worthy of; merit. [< Lat. *deservire*, to serve zealously.]

de·served (dĭ-zûrvd') *adj.* Merited or earned. **de·serv·ed·ly** (dĭ-zûr'vĭd-lē) *adv.* As is right and fair.

de·serv·ing (dĭ-zûr'vĭng) *adj.* Worthy; meritorious. —**de·serv'ing·ly** *adv.*

des·ic·cant (děs'ĭ-kənt) *n.* A substance used to absorb moisture.

des·ic·cate (děs'ĭ-kāt') *v.* **-cat·ed, -cat·ing.** To make or become thoroughly dry. [Lat. *desicare*.] —**des'ic·ca'tion** *n.*

de·sid·er·a·tum (dĭ-sĭd'ə-rā'təm, -rä'-) *n., pl.* **-ta** (-tə). Something needed and desired. [Lat.]

de·sign (dĭ-zīn') *v.* **1.** To conceive; invent. **2.** To draw up plans for, esp. by means of sketches or drawings. **3.** To have as a goal or purpose; intend. —*n.* **1.** A drawing or sketch giving the details of how something is to be made. **2.** The arrangement of the parts or details of something according to a plan. **3.** A decorative pattern. **4.** The art of creating designs. **5.** A plan or project. **6.** A reasoned

des·ig·nate (dĕz′ĭg-nāt′) v. **-nat·ed**, **-nat·ing.**
1. To indicate or specify. 2. To give a name
to. 3. To appoint. —*adj.* (dĕz′ĭg-nĭt). Appointed but not yet installed in office. [< Lat.
designare.] —**des′ig·na′tion** n.

designated hitter n. *Baseball.* A player designated to bat regularly for the pitcher.

de·sign·ing (dĭ-zī′nĭng) *adj.* Conniving.

de·sir·a·ble (dĭ-zīr′ə-bəl) *adj.* 1. Attractive;
fine. 2. Advantageous; advisable: *a desirable
reform.* —**de·sir′a·bil′i·ty** or **de·sir′a·ble·ness**
n. —**de·sir′a·bly** *adv.*

de·sire (dĭ-zīr′) v. **-sired, -sir·ing.** 1. To wish
or long for; want; crave. 2. To express a wish
for. —n. 1. A wish, longing, or craving. 2. A
request. 3. Something longed for. 4. Sexual
appetite. [< Lat. *desiderare.*] —**de·sir′er** n.

de·sir·ous (dĭ-zīr′əs) *adj.* Desiring; wishing.

de·sist (dĭ-zĭst′, -sĭst′) v. To cease doing
something; stop. [< Lat. *desistere.*]

desk (dĕsk) n. 1. A piece of furniture usu.
with a flat top for writing. 2. A counter or
booth at which specified services are performed. 3. A specialized department of an
organization: *city desk.* [< OItal. *desco,* table.]

des·o·late (dĕs′ə-lĭt) *adj.* 1. Devoid of inhabitants; deserted. 2. Rendered unfit for habitation or use. 3. Dreary; dismal; gloomy.
4. Forlorn; lonely. —v. (dĕs′ə-lāt′) **-lat·ed,
-lat·ing.** To make desolate. [< Lat. *desolatus.*]
—**des′o·late·ly** *adv.*

des·o·la·tion (dĕs′ə-lā′shən) n. 1. The act of
making desolate. 2. The condition of being
desolate; ruin. 3. A wasteland. 4. Loneliness
or misery; wretchedness.

de·spair (dĭ-spâr′) n. 1. Utter lack of hope.
2. Something that causes great grief or torment. —v. To lose all hope. [< Lat. *desperare,* to despair.]

des·per·a·do (dĕs′pə-rä′dō, -rä′-) n., pl. **-does**
or **-dos.** A desperate, dangerous criminal. [<
DESPERATE.]

des·per·ate (dĕs′pər-ĭt, -prĭt) *adj.* 1. Reckless
or violent because of despair. 2. Nearly hopeless; grave. 3. Extreme; great: *desperate need.*
[Lat. *desperatus,* p.p. of *desperare,* to despair.]
—**des′per·ate·ly** *adv.* —**des′per·ate·ness** n.

des·per·a·tion (dĕs′pə-rā′shən) n. 1. The condition of being desperate. 2. Recklessness
arising from despair.

des·pi·ca·ble (dĕs′pĭ-kə-bəl, dĭ-spĭk′ə-) *adj.*
Deserving contempt or disdain. [LLat. *despicabilis.*] —**des′pi·ca·bly** *adv.*

de·spise (dĭ-spīz′) v. **-spised, -spis·ing.** To
regard with contempt or disdain. [< Lat. *despicere.*] —**de·spis′er** n.

Syns: *despise, abhor, disdain, scorn* v.

de·spite (dĭ-spīt′) *prep.* In spite of. [< OFr.
despit, spite.]

de·spoil (dĭ-spoil′) v. To deprive of possessions by force; plunder. [< Lat. *despoliare.*]
—**de·spoil′er** n. —**de·spoil′ment** n.

de·spo·li·a·tion (dĭ-spō′lē-ā′shən) n. The act
of despoiling or the condition of being despoiled; plunder.

de·spond (dĭ-spŏnd′) v. To become disheartened. [Lat. *despondēre.*] —**de·spond′ing·ly**
adv.

de·spon·den·cy (dĭ-spŏn′dən-sē) n., pl. **-cies.**
Depression; dejection. —**de·spon′dent** *adj.*
—**de·spon′dent·ly** *adv.*

des·pot (dĕs′pət) n. An autocratic or oppressive ruler; tyrant. [< Gk. *despotēs.*] —**des·pot′ic** (dĭ-spŏt′ĭk) *adj.* —**des·pot′i·cal·ly** *adv.*
—**des′pot·ism** n.

des·sert (dĭ-zûrt′) n. A usu. sweet food served
as the last course of a meal. [< OFr. *desservir,* to clear the table.]

des·ti·na·tion (dĕs′tə-nā′shən) n. 1. The place
or point to which one is going. 2. An ultimate goal or purpose. 3. An act of appointing or setting aside for a purpose.

des·tine (dĕs′tĭn) v. **-tined, -tin·ing.** 1. To determine beforehand. 2. To assign or set apart
for a specific end or purpose. 3. To direct
toward a given destination. [< Lat. *destinare.*]

des·ti·ny (dĕs′tə-nē) n., pl. **-nies.** 1. The inevitable fate to which one is destined; fortune.
2. The seemingly preordained or inevitable
course of events.

des·ti·tute (dĕs′tĭ-tōōt′, -tyōōt′) *adj.* 1. Altogether lacking; devoid: *destitute of experience.*
2. Completely impoverished; penniless. [<
Lat. *destitutus,* p.p. of *destituere,* to desert.]
—**des′ti·tu′tion** n.

de·stroy (dĭ-stroi′) v. 1. To ruin completely.
2. To tear down; demolish. 3. To kill. [< Lat.
destruere.]

Syns: *destroy, demolish, level, raze* v.

de·stroy·er (dĭ-stroi′ər) n. 1. One that destroys. 2. A small, fast warship.

destroyer

de·struct (dĭ-strŭkt′) n. The intentional destruction of a space vehicle, rocket, or missile
after launching.

de·struc·ti·ble (dĭ-strŭk′tə-bəl) *adj.* Capable
of being destroyed. —**de·struc′ti·bil′i·ty** n.

de·struc·tion (dĭ-strŭk′shən) n. 1. The act of
destroying or the condition of being destroyed; ruin. 2. A means or cause of destroying. [< Lat. *destructio.*] —**de·struc′tive**
adj. —**de·struc′tive·ly** *adv.* —**de·struc′tiveness** n.

destructive distillation n. The chemical decomposition by heat and distillation of organic substances such as wood and coal to
produce useful by-products.

des·ue·tude (dĕs′wĭ-tōōd′, -tyōōd′) n. The
condition of disuse. [< Lat. *desuetudo.*]

des·ul·to·ry (dĕs′əl-tôr′ē, -tōr′ē) *adj.* Progressing aimlessly from one thing to another. [Lat.
desultorius, of a leaper.]

de·tach (dĭ-tăch′) v. To separate; disconnect.
[< OFr. *destachier.*] —**de·tach′a·ble** *adj.*
—**de·tach′a·bly** *adv.*

de·tached (dĭ-tăcht′) *adj.* 1. Separate from

others; disconnected. **2.** Free from emotional involvement.

de·tach·ment (dǐ-tǎch′mənt) n. **1.** The act or process of detaching; separation. **2.** Disinterest; impartiality. **3.** Indifference to worldly affairs; aloofness. **4.** *Mil.* **a.** The dispatch of troops or ships from a larger unit for a special duty. **b.** A small permanent unit organized for special duties.

de·tail (dǐ-tāl′, dē′tāl′) n. **1.** An individual part or item. **2.** Itemized or minute treatment of particulars. **3. a.** A group of military personnel selected to do a specified task. **b.** The task assigned. —v. **1.** To relate item by item. **2.** To assign (military personnel) to a specified task. [< OFr., piece cut off.]

de·tain (dǐ-tān′) v. **1.** To keep from proceeding; delay. **2.** To keep in custody; confine. [< Lat. *detinēre.*] —**de·tain′ment** n.

de·tect (dǐ-těkt′) v. To discover or discern the existence, presence, or fact of. [< Lat. *detegere,* to uncover.] —**de·tect′a·ble** or **de·tect′i·ble** adj. —**de·tec′tion** n. —**de·tec′tor** n.

de·tec·tive (dǐ-těk′tǐv) n. One whose work is investigating crimes, obtaining evidence, etc.

dé·tente (dā-tänt′, -tänt′) n. A relaxing of tension between nations. [Fr.]

de·ten·tion (dǐ-těn′shən) n. **1.** The act of detaining or condition of being detained. **2.** A period of being kept in confinement or temporary custody. [< LLat. *detentio.*]

de·ter (dǐ-tûr′) v. -**terred,** -**ter·ring.** To prevent or discourage (someone) from acting by means of fear or doubt. [Lat. *deterrēre.*] —**de·ter′ment** n.

de·ter·gent (dǐ-tûr′jənt) n. A cleansing agent, esp. a synthetic one that is chemically different from soap. [< Lat. *detergēre,* to wipe off.]

de·te·ri·o·rate (dǐ-tîr′ē-ə-rāt′) v. -**rat·ed,** -**rat·ing.** To make or become worse. [< LLat. *deteriorare.*] —**de·te·ri·o·ra′tion** n.

de·ter·mi·nant (dǐ-tûr′mə-nənt) n. An influencing or determining factor. —adj. Serving to determine.

de·ter·mi·nate (dǐ-tûr′mə-nǐt) adj. **1.** Precisely limited or defined; definite. **2.** Settled; final.

de·ter·mi·na·tion (dǐ-tûr′mə-nā′shən) n. **1. a.** The act of arriving at a decision. **b.** The decision arrived at. **2.** Firmness of purpose; resoluteness. **3.** The calculation of the extent, quality, position, or character of something.

de·ter·mine (dǐ-tûr′mǐn) v. -**mined,** -**min·ing.** **1.** To decide, establish, or ascertain authoritatively or conclusively. **2.** To limit or regulate. **3.** To affect as a causative factor; influence. **4.** To resolve firmly. [< Lat. *determinare,* to limit.] —**de·ter′mi·na·ble** adj. —**de·ter′mi·na·bly** adv.

de·ter·mined (dǐ-tûr′mǐnd) adj. Fixed in purpose; resolute; firm. —**de·ter′mined·ly** adv.

de·ter·min·er (dǐ-tûr′mə-nər) n. A word, such as *the* or *her,* belonging to a group of noun modifiers that usu. precede the descriptive adjectives in a noun phrase.

de·ter·min·ism (dǐ-tûr′mə-nĭz′əm) n. The philosophical doctrine asserting a mechanical correspondence between determining causes and effects.

de·ter·rent (dǐ-tûr′ənt, -tûr′-) n. One that deters. —adj. Tending to deter or restrain.

de·test (dǐ-těst′) v. To dislike intensely; loathe; hate. [Lat. *detestari,* to curse.] —**de·test′a·ble** adj. —**de·test′a·bly** adv. —**de·tes·ta′tion** n.

de·throne (dē-thrōn′) v. -**throned,** -**thron·ing.** To remove from a throne; depose. —**de·throne′ment** n.

det·o·nate (dět′n-āt′) v. -**nat·ed,** -**nat·ing.** To explode or cause to explode. [Lat. *detonare,* to thunder down.] —**det′o·na′tion** n. —**det′o·na′tor** n.

de·tour (dē′tŏŏr′, dĭ-tŏŏr′) n. A roundabout way, esp. one used temporarily instead of a main route. —v. To go or cause to go by a detour. [< OFr. *destorner,* to turn away.]

de·tox·i·fy (dē-tŏk′sə-fī′) v. -**fied,** -**fy·ing.** To remove poison or the effects of poison from. —**de·tox′i·fi·ca′tion** n.

de·tract (dǐ-trăkt′) v. To take away from; diminish. [< Lat. *detrahere,* to remove.] —**de·trac′tion** n. —**de·trac′tive** adj. —**de·trac′tor** n.

de·train (dē-trān′) v. To leave or cause to leave a railroad train.

det·ri·ment (dět′rə-mənt) n. **1.** Damage, harm, or loss. **2.** Something that causes damage, harm, or loss. [< Lat. *detrimentum.*] —**det′ri·men′tal** adj. —**det′ri·men′tal·ly** adv.

de·tri·tus (dǐ-trī′təs) n. **1.** Fragments formed by the disintegration of rocks. **2.** Debris: *the detritus of a past civilization.* [< Lat. *deterere,* to wear away.]

deuce¹ (dōōs, dyōōs) n. **1.** A playing card or side of a die bearing two spots. **2.** *Tennis.* A score in which each player or side has 40 points. [< Lat. *duo,* two.]

deuce² (dōōs, dyōōs) n. The devil. Used as a mild oath. [Prob. < LG *duus,* a throw of two in dice games.]

deu·te·ri·um (dōō-tîr′ē-əm, dyōō-) n. An isotope of hydrogen having an atomic weight of 2.0141. [< Gk. *deuteros,* second.]

deut·sche mark (doi′chə märk′) n. Also **deut·sche·mark.** See *table* at **currency.** [G., German mark.]

de·val·u·ate (dē-văl′yōō-āt′) v. -**at·ed,** -**at·ing.** Also **de·val·ue** (-yōō), -**ued,** -**u·ing.** **1.** To lessen the value of. **2.** To lower the exchange value of (currency). —**de·val′u·a′tion** n.

dev·as·tate (dĕv′ə-stāt′) v. -**tat·ed,** -**tat·ing.** **1.** To lay waste; ruin. **2.** *Informal.* To overwhelm; confound. [Lat. *devastare.*] —**dev′as·ta′tion** n.

de·vel·op (dǐ-věl′əp) v. **1.** To bring, grow, or evolve to a more complete, complex, or desirable state. **2.** To appear, disclose, or acquire gradually. **3.** To elaborate; expand. **4.** To make available or usable. **5.** To process (a photosensitive material) chemically in order to render a recorded image visible. [< OFr. *desvoloper.*] —**de·vel′op·er** n. —**de·vel′op·ment** n. —**de·vel′op·men′tal** adj. —**de·vel′op·men′tal·ly** adv.

de·vi·ant (dē′vē-ənt) n. One whose behavior differs from accepted social or moral standards. —**de′vi·ance** n. —**de′vi·ant** adj.

de·vi·ate (dē′vē-āt′) v. -**at·ed,** -**at·ing.** To differ or move away from an established course or prescribed mode of behavior. —n. (dē′vē-ĭt). A deviant. [LLat. *deviare.*] —**de′vi·a′tion** n.

de·vice (dǐ-vīs′) n. **1.** Something devised for a particular purpose, esp. a machine. **2.** A plan or scheme; trick. **3.** A graphic symbol or motto, esp. in heraldry. [< OFr. *deviser,* to devise.]

dev·il (dĕv′əl) n. **1. a.** Often **Devil.** The major spirit of evil, esp. in Christian theology. **b.** A demon or similar evil spirit. **2.** A wicked or destructively mischievous person. **3.** A dashing or daring person. **4.** An unfortunate per-

son; wretch. **5.** A printer's apprentice. —v.
-iled or **-illed, -il·ing** or **-il·ling. 1.** To annoy;
torment. **2.** To prepare (food) with pungent
seasoning. [< Gk. *diabolos,* slanderer.]

dev·il·ish (dĕv′ə-lĭsh) *adj.* **1.** Of or like a
devil; fiendish. **2.** Mischievous or playful.
3. Excessive; extreme: *devilish heat.* —*adv.
Informal.* Extremely; very. —**dev′il·ish·ly** *adv.*
—**dev′il·ish·ness** *n.*

dev·il·try (dĕv′əl-trē) *n., pl.* **-tries. 1.** Wanton
mischief. **2.** Wickedness. **3.** Evil magic.

de·vi·ous (dē′vē-əs) *adj.* **1.** Deviating from the
straight or direct course. **2.** Not straightforward; deceitful. [Lat. *devius,* out-of-the-way.]
—**de′vi·ous·ly** *adv.* —**de′vi·ous·ness** *n.*

de·vise (dĭ-vīz′) *v.* **-vised, -vis·ing. 1.** To plan;
invent; contrive. **2.** *Law.* To transmit (real
property) by will. —*n.* **1.** The act of transmitting real property by will. **2.** A will or
clause in a will devising real property. [< Lat.
dividere, to divide.] —**de·vis′a·ble** *adj.* —**de·
vis′er** *n.*

de·vi·tal·ize (dē-vīt′l-īz′) *v.* To lower or destroy the life or vitality of.

de·void (dĭ-void′) *adj.* Completely lacking;
destitute: *a novel devoid of wit.* [< OFr. *des-
voidier,* to remove.]

de·volve (dĭ-vŏlv′) *v.* **-volved, -volv·ing.** To
pass on or be passed on to a substitute or
successor. [< Lat. *devolvere,* to roll down.]

De·vo·ni·an (dĭ-vō′nē-ən) *adj.* Of or belonging to the geologic time, system of rocks, or
sedimentary deposits of the 4th period of the
Paleozoic era, characterized by the appearance of forests and amphibians. —*n.* The
Devonian period. [< *Devon,* England.]

de·vote (dĭ-vōt′) *v.* **-vot·ed, -vot·ing. 1.** To give
or apply (e.g. oneself or one's time) entirely.
2. To dedicate; consecrate. **3.** To set apart for
a specific purpose. [Lat. *devovēre,* to vow.]

de·vot·ed (dĭ-vō′tĭd) *adj.* **1.** Loving; affectionate. **2.** Zealous; ardent. —**de·vot′ed·ly** *adv.*

dev·o·tee (dĕv′ə-tē′, -tā′) *n.* An enthusiast.

de·vo·tion (dĭ-vō′shən) *n.* **1.** Ardent attachment or affection. **2.** Religious ardor. **3.** Often **devotions.** Prayers, esp. when private.

de·vour (dĭ-vour′) *v.* **1.** To eat up greedily.
2. To destroy, consume, or waste. **3.** To take
in eagerly. **4.** To swallow up; engulf. [< Lat.
devorare.] —**de·vour′er** *n.*

de·vout (dĭ-vout′) *adj.* **1.** Deeply religious; pious. **2.** Sincere; earnest. [< LLat. *devotus.*]
—**de·vout′ly** *adv.* —**de·vout′ness** *n.*

dew (dōō, dyōō) *n.* **1.** Water droplets condensed from the air, usu. at night, onto cool
surfaces. **2.** Something resembling or suggestive of dew. [< OE *dēaw.*] —**dew′i·ly** *adv.*
—**dew′i·ness** *n.* —**dew′y** *adj.*

dew·ber·ry (dōō′bĕr′ē, dyōō′-) *n.* **1.** Any of
several trailing blackberry plants. **2.** The edible fruit of the dewberry.

dew·claw (dōō′klô′, dyōō′-) *n.* A vestigial
digit on the foot of certain mammals.

dew·drop (dōō′drŏp′, dyōō′-) *n.* A drop of
dew.

dew·lap (dōō′lăp′, dyōō′-) *n.* A fold of loose
skin hanging from the neck of certain animals. [ME *dewlappe.*]

dew point *n.* The temperature at which air
becomes saturated and produces dew.

dex·ter·i·ty (dĕk-stĕr′ĭ-tē) *n.* **1.** Skill in the use

of the hands or body; adroitness. **2.** Mental
skill or cleverness.

dex·te·rous (dĕk′stər-əs, -strəs) *adj.* Also **dex·
trous** ( ). **1.** Adroit or skillful in the use
of the hands or mind. **2.** Done with dexterity.
[< Lat. *dexter.*] —**dex′ter·ous·ly** *adv.* —**dex′-
ter·ous·ness** *n.*

dex·trin (dĕk′strĭn) *n.* A powder formed by
the hydrolysis of starch, used mainly as an
adhesive. [Fr. *dextrine.*]

dex·trose (dĕk′strōs′) *n.* A colorless sugar,
$C_6H_{12}O_6·H_2O$, found in animal and plant tissue and also made synthetically from starch.
[Lat. *dexter,* right + -OSE.]

dhar·ma (dûr′mə, där′-) *n. Hinduism & Buddhism.* The ultimate law of all things. [Skt.
darmah.]

Dhe·gi·ha (dā′jē-hä′) *n., pl.* **-ha** or **-has. 1.** A
Siouan language of the Osage, Omaha and
other neighboring tribes. **2. a.** The tribes
speaking Dhegiha. **b.** A member of any of
these tribes.

Dhul-Hij·ja (dūl-hĭj′ä) *n.* The 12th month of
the Moslem year. See table at **calendar.** [Ar.
dhū′l-hijja.]

Dhul-Qa·dah (dūl-kä′dä) *n.* The 11th month
of the Moslem year. See table at **calendar.**
[Ar. *dhu′l-ga′dah.*]

Di The symbol for the element didymium.

di- *pref.* **1.** Twice, double, or two: *dicotyledon.*
2. Having two atoms, molecules, or radicals:
dioxide. [Gk.]

di·a·be·tes (dī′ə-bē′tĭs, -tēz) *n.* Any of several
metabolic disorders marked by excessive discharge of urine, esp. diabetes mellitus. [< Gk.
diabētēs, passing through.] —**di′a·bet′ic** (-bĕt′-
ĭk) *adj. & n.*

diabetes mel·li·tus (mə-lī′təs) *n.* A chronic
disease of pancreatic origin, characterized by
insulin deficiency, excess sugar in the blood
and urine, weakness, and emaciation. [DIABE-
TES + Lat. *mellitus,* sweet.]

di·a·bol·ic (dī′ə-bŏl′ĭk) or **di·a·bol·i·cal**
(-ĭ-kəl) *adj.* Devilish; wicked; fiendish. [<
LLat. *diabolicus.*] —**di′a·bol′i·cal·ly** *adv.*

di·a·crit·i·cal (dī′ə-krĭt′ĭ-kəl). Also **di·a·crit·ic**
(-ĭk). —*adj.* Marking a distinction; distinguishing. —*n.* Also **diacritical mark.** A mark
added to a letter to indicate a special phonetic value. [Gk. *diakritikos.*]

di·a·dem (dī′ə-dĕm′) *n.* A crown or headband
worn as a sign of royalty. [< Gk. *diadēma.*]

di·aer·e·sis (dī-ĕr′ĭ-sĭs) *n.* Var. of **dieresis.**

di·ag·no·sis (dī′əg-nō′sĭs) *n., pl.* **-ses** (-sēz′).
Identification, esp. of a disease, by examination or analysis. [< Gk. *diagnōsis,* discernment.] —**di′ag·nose′** *v.* —**di′ag·nos′tic**
(-nŏs′tĭk) *adj.* —**di′ag·nos′ti·cal·ly** *adv.* —**di′-
ag·nos·ti′cian** (-stĭsh′ən) *n.*

di·ag·o·nal (dī-ăg′ə-nəl) *adj.* **1.** Joining two
vertices that are not adjacent. **2.** Having a
slanted or oblique direction. —*n.* A diagonal
line or plane. [< Gk. *diagōnios,* from angle to
angle.] —**di·ag′o·nal·ly** *adv.*

di·a·gram (dī′ə-grăm′) *n.* A schematic plan or
drawing designed to explain how something
works or to clarify the relationship between
the parts of a whole. —*v.* **-grammed** or
-gramed, -gram·ming or **-gram·ing.** To represent by a diagram. [< Gk. *diagramma.*] —**di′-**

ă pat ā pay â care ä father ĕ pet ē be ĭ pit ī tie î pier ŏ pot ō toe ô paw, for oi noise ōō took
ōō boot ou out th thin th this ŭ cut û urge yōō abuse zh vision ə about, item, edible, gallop, circus

a·gram·mat·ic or **di·a·gram·mat·i·cal** *adj.* —**di·a·gram·mat·i·cal·ly** *adv.*

di·al (dī′əl) *n.* **1.** A marked disk or plate on which a measurement, as of time, speed, or temperature, is indicated by a moving pointer. **2.** A rotatable disk, as of a telephone or radio, for making connections, changing frequency, etc. **3.** A sundial. —*v.* **-aled** or **-alled, -al·ing** or **-al·ling. 1.** To indicate or select by means of a dial. **2.** To call on a telephone. [< Med. Lat. *dialis,* daily.]

di·a·lect (dī′ə-lĕkt′) *n.* **1.** A regional variety of a language. **2.** A language considered as part of a larger family. [< Gk. *dialektos,* speech.] —**di·a·lect′al** *adj.*

di·a·lec·tic (dī′ə-lĕk′tĭk) *n.* Also **di·a·lec·tics** (-tĭks). A method of logical argument in which contradictions are disclosed and synthetically resolved. [< Gk. *dialektikē (tekhnē),* (the art) of debate.] —**di·a·lec′ti·cal** or **di·a·lec′tic** *adj.* —**di·a·lec′ti·cian** (-tĭsh′ən) *n.*

di·a·logue or **di·a·log** (dī′ə-lôg′, -lŏg′) *n.* **1.** A conversation between two or more people. **2.** A conversational passage in a play or narrative. **3.** An exchange of ideas or opinions. [< Gk. *dialogos.*]

di·al·y·sis (dī-ăl′ĭ-sĭs) *n., pl.* **-ses** (-sēz′). The separation of molecular or particulate constituents in a solution by selective diffusion through a semipermeable membrane. —**di·a·lyt′ic** (dī′ə-lĭt′ĭk) *adj.*

di·a·mag·net·ic (dī′ə-măg-nĕt′ĭk) *adj.* Of or pertaining to a substance in which the magnetic field is in the opposite direction to and weaker than the magnetizing field. [Gk. *dia,* through + MAGNETIC.] —**di·a·mag′net·ism** (-nə-tĭz′əm) *n.*

di·am·e·ter (dī-ăm′ĭ-tər) *n.* **1. a.** A straight line segment passing through the center of a figure, esp. of a circle or sphere. **b.** The length of such a segment. **2.** The thickness or width of something. [< Gk. *diametros.*] —**di·a·met′ri·cal** (-ə-mĕt′rĭ-kəl) or **di·a·met′ric** *adj.* —**di·a·met′ri·cal·ly** *adv.*

di·a·mond (dī′mənd, dī′ə-) *n.* **1.** An extremely hard, colorless or white crystalline form of carbon, the hardest of all known substances, used as a gemstone when pure and chiefly in abrasives otherwise. **2.** A rhombus or lozenge. **3.** Any of a suit of playing cards marked with a red, diamond-shaped symbol. **4.** *Baseball.* **a.** The infield. **b.** The whole playing field. [< Gk. *adamas.*]

di·a·mond·back (dī′mənd-băk′, dī′ə-) *n.* A large, venomous rattlesnake of the southern and western United States and Mexico.

Di·an·a (dī-ăn′ə) *n. Rom. Myth.* The goddess of chastity, hunting, and the moon.

Diana

di·a·pa·son (dī′ə-pā′zən, -sən) *n.* **1.** Either of the two principal stops on a pipe organ. **2.** The entire range of an instrument or voice. [< Gk. *(hē) dia pasōn (khordōn sumphonia),* (concord) through all (the notes).]

di·a·per (dī′ə-pər, dī′pər) *n.* A piece of cloth or other absorbent material, folded and pinned around a baby to serve as underpants. —*v.* To put a diaper on (a baby). [Med. Gk. *diapros,* pure white.]

di·aph·a·nous (dī-ăf′ə-nəs) *adj.* Of such fine texture as to be translucent. [< Gk. *diaphanēs.*] —**di·aph′a·nous·ly** *adv.*

di·a·pho·re·sis (dī′ə-fə-rē′sĭs) *n.* Copious perspiration, esp. when medically induced. [< Gk. *diaphorēsis.*] —**di·a·pho·ret′ic** (-rĕt′ĭk) *adj.*

di·a·phragm (dī′ə-frăm′) *n.* **1.** A muscular membrane that separates the organs of the chest from those of the abdomen and acts in forcing air into and out of the lungs. **2.** Any similar membrane that divides or separates. **3.** A thin disk, as in a microphone, whose vibrations convert electric signals to sound waves or sound waves to electric signals. **4.** A contraceptive device consisting of a flexible disk that covers the uterine cervix. **5.** A disk used to restrict the amount of light that passes through a lens or optical system. [< Gk. *diaphragma.*] —**di·a·phrag·mat·ic** (dī′-ə-frăg-măt′ĭk) *adj.*

di·ar·rhe·a or **di·ar·rhoe·a** (dī′ə-rē′ə) *n.* Abnormally frequent bowel movements. [< Gk. *diarrhoia.*]

di·a·ry (dī′ə-rē) *n., pl.* **-ries. 1.** A daily record, esp. of personal experiences and observations. **2.** A book for keeping such a record. [Lat. *diarium.*] —**di·a·rist** *n.*

di·as·to·le (dī-ăs′tə-lē′) *n.* The normal rhythmically occurring relaxation and dilatation of the heart cavities during which the cavities fill with blood. [Gk. *diastolē,* dilation.] —**di·a·stol′ic** (dī′ə-stŏl′ĭk) *adj.*

di·a·ther·my (dī′ə-thûr′mē) *n.* The therapeutic generation of local heat in bodily tissues by high-frequency electromagnetic waves. [Gk. *dia,* through + Gk. *thermē,* heat.] —**di·a·ther′mic** *adj.*

di·a·tom (dī′ə-tŏm′, -təm) *n.* Any of various minute, single-celled algae with cell walls consisting mainly of silica. [< Gk. *diatomos,* cut in half.]

di·a·tom·ic (dī′ə-tŏm′ĭk) *adj.* Made up of two atoms in a molecule.

di·a·ton·ic (dī′ə-tŏn′ĭk) *adj.* Of or using the eight tones of a standard major or minor scale. [< Gk. *diatonikos.*] —**di·a·ton′i·cal·ly** *adv.*

di·a·tribe (dī′ə-trīb′) *n.* A bitter and abusive attack. [< Gk. *diatribē,* lecture.]

di·az·e·pam (dī-ăz′ə-păm′) *n.* An antianxiety drug. [*diaz(o)* + *ep(oxide)* + AM(MONIA).]

dib·ble (dĭb′əl) *n.* A pointed implement used to make holes in soil, esp. for planting bulbs. [ME *debylle.*] —**dib′ble** *v.*

dice (dīs) *n., pl.* **dice. 1.** Pl. of **die**² (sense 2). **2.** Small cubes marked on each side with from one to six dots, used in games of chance. **3.** *pl.* also **dic·es.** A small cube, as of food. —*v.* **diced, dic·ing. 1.** To gamble with dice. **2.** To cut into cubes. [Pl. of DIE².]

di·chot·o·my (dī-kŏt′ə-mē) *n., pl.* **-mies.** Division into two usu. contradictory parts or categories. [< Gk. *dikhotomia.*] —**di·chot′o·mous** *adj.* —**di·chot′o·mous·ly** *adv.*

dick (dĭk) n. Slang. A detective.

dick·ens (dĭk'ǝnz) interj. Devil. Used as an oath. [Perh. < Old Nick, Satan.]

dick·er (dĭk'ǝr) v. To bargain; barter. [Orig. unknown.]

dick·ey (dĭk'ē) n., pl. **-eys.** Also **dick·y** pl. **-ies.** 1. A separate shirt, often worn under a jacket, sweater, etc. 2. A small bird. [< Dick, nickname for Richard.]

di·cot·y·le·don (dī-kŏt'l-ēd'n) n. A plant with a pair of embryonic seed leaves that appear at germination. —**di·cot'y·le'don·ous** adj.

dic·tate (dĭk'tāt', dĭk-tāt') v. **-tat·ed, -tat·ing.** 1. To say or read aloud for transcription. 2. To prescribe or command with authority. —n. (dĭk'tāt'). An order; directive. [< Lat. dictare.] —**dic·ta'tion** n.

dic·ta·tor (dĭk'tā'tǝr, dĭk-tā'-) n. 1. A ruler having complete authority and unlimited power, esp. a tyrant. 2. One who dictates. —**dic·ta'tor·ship'** n.

dic·ta·to·ri·al (dĭk'tǝ-tôr'ē-ǝl, -tōr-) adj. Pertaining to or characteristic of a dictator; autocratic. —**dic·ta·to'ri·al·ly** adv. —**dic·ta·to'ri·al·ness** n.

dic·tion (dĭk'shǝn) n. 1. The choice and use of words in speaking or writing. 2. Clarity and distinctness of pronunciation. [Lat. dictio.]

dic·tion·ar·y (dĭk'shǝ-něr'ē) n., pl. **-ies.** A reference book containing an alphabetical list of words with definitions or equivalent translations into another language.

dic·tum (dĭk'tǝm) n., pl. **-ta** (tǝ) or **-tums.** 1. An authoritative pronouncement. 2. A maxim. [Lat.]

did (dĭd) v. p.t. of **do.**

di·dac·tic (dī-dăk'tĭk) or **di·dac·ti·cal** (-tĭ-kǝl) adj. 1. Intended to teach. 2. Morally instructive. [Gk. didaktikos, skillful in teaching.] —**di·dac'ti·cal·ly** adv.

didn't (dĭd'nt). Did not.

di·do (dī'dō) n., pl. **-dos** or **-does.** Informal. A mischievous prank. [Orig. unknown.]

didst (dĭdst) v. Archaic. 2nd person sing. past tense of **do**[1].

die[1] (dī) v. **died, dy·ing.** 1. To cease living. 2. To lose force or vitality. 3. To cease existing. 4. Informal. To desire greatly. [< ON deyja.]

Syns: die, decease, depart, expire, go, pass away, perish, succumb v.

die[2] (dī) n. 1. pl. **dies.** A device that shapes materials by stamping, cutting, or punching. 2. pl. **dice** (dīs). One of a pair of dice. [< OFr. de, gaming dice.]

die-hard (dī'härd') n. One who stubbornly resists change.

di·e·lec·tric (dī'ĭ-lĕk'trĭk) n. A nonconductor of direct current. [Gk. dia, through + ELECTRIC.] —**di·e·lec'tric** adj. —**di·e·lec'tri·cal·ly** adv.

di·er·e·sis (dī-ĕr'ĭ-sĭs) n., pl. **-ses** (-sēz'). Also **di·aer·e·sis.** A mark (¨) placed over the second of two adjacent vowels to indicate that it is pronounced in a separate syllable. [< Gk. diairesis, separation.]

die·sel (dē'zǝl, -sǝl) n. A vehicle powered by a diesel engine.

diesel engine n. An internal-combustion engine in which the fuel is sprayed directly into the cylinder and ignited by the heat of air

that has been highly compressed by the piston. [< Rudolf Diesel (1858–1913).]

di·et[1] (dī'ĭt) n. 1. One's usual food and drink. 2. A regulated selection of foods, often prescribed for medical reasons. —v. To eat and drink a prescribed selection of foods. [< Gk. diaita.] —**di·e·tar'y** adj. —**di·et·er** n.

di·et[2] (dī'ĭt) n. A legislature; assembly. [< Med. Lat. dieta.]

di·e·tet·ic (dī'ĭ-tĕt'ĭk) adj. Of or for a restricted nutritional diet.

di·e·tet·ics (dī'ĭ-tĕt'ĭks) n. (used with a sing. verb). The study of diet and nutrition.

di·e·ti·tian (dī'ĭ-tĭsh'ǝn) n. Also **di·e·ti·cian.** A specialist in dietetics.

dif·fer (dĭf'ǝr) v. 1. To be unlike. 2. To disagree. [< Lat. differre.]

dif·fer·ence (dĭf'ǝr-ǝns, dĭf'rǝns) n. 1. The fact, condition, or degree of being different. 2. A disagreement; quarrel. 3. a. The amount by which one quantity is greater or less than another. b. The number that results when one number is subtracted from another.

dif·fer·ent (dĭf'ǝr-ǝnt, dĭf'rǝnt) adj. Unlike; dissimilar. 2. Distinct; separate. 3. Unusual; distinctive. —**dif'fer·ent·ly** adv. —**dif'fer·ent·ness** n.

dif·fer·en·tial (dĭf'ǝ-rĕn'shǝl) adj. Of, showing, or constituting a difference. —n. 1. An amount or degree of difference between similar kinds or individuals: a wage differential. 2. A differential gear.

differential gear n. An arrangement of gears that allows one turning shaft to drive two others at two different speeds.

dif·fer·en·ti·ate (dĭf'ǝ-rĕn'shē-āt') v. **-at·ed, -at·ing.** 1. To constitute or perceive a distinction. 2. To make or become different, distinct, or specialized —**dif'fer·en'ti·a'tion** n.

dif·fi·cult (dĭf'ĭ-kŭlt', -kǝlt) adj. 1. Hard to do, achieve, or comprehend. 2. Hard to manage or satisfy. —**dif'fi·cult·ly** adv.

Syns: difficult, hard, knotty, tough adj.

dif·fi·cul·ty (dĭf'ĭ-kŭl'tē, -kǝl-tē) n., pl. **-ties.** 1. The condition or quality of being difficult. 2. Great effort and trouble. 3. a. A troublesome or embarrassing state of affairs: financial difficulties. b. Problems or conflicts: emotional difficulties. [< Lat. difficultas.]

dif·fi·dent (dĭf'ĭ-dǝnt, -dĕnt') adj. Lacking self-confidence; timid. [< Lat. diffidere, to mistrust.] —**dif'fi·dence** n. —**dif'fi·dent·ly** adv.

dif·frac·tion (dĭ-frăk'shǝn) n. The bending or deflection of light or other radiation as it passes an obstacle such as the edge of a slit or aperture. [< Lat. diffractus, p.p. of diffringere, to shatter.]

dif·fuse (dĭ-fyōoz') v. **-fused, -fus·ing.** To pour out, spread, and disperse. —adj. (dĭ-fyōos'). 1. Widely spread or scattered. 2. Wordy. [< Lat. diffundere.] —**dif·fuse'ly** (dĭ-fyōos'lē) adv. —**dif·fus'i·ble** adj. —**dif·fu'sion** n.

dig (dĭg) v. **dug** (dŭg), **dig·ging.** 1. To break up, turn over, or remove (earth, sand, etc.) with a tool or the hands. 2. To make (an excavation) by or as by digging. 3. To learn or discover: dig up information. 4. To thrust against: digging me in the ribs. 5. Slang. To understand or enjoy. —phrasal verb. **dig in.** Informal. To begin to work in earnest. —n.

1. A poke. **2.** A sarcastic remark; gibe. **3.** An archaeological excavation. [ME *diggen*.] —**dig′ger** n.

di-gest (dī-jĕst′, dĭ-) v. **1.** To change food into a form that is easily absorbed into the body. **2.** To absorb mentally; comprehend. **3.** To organize into a systematic arrangement. —n. (dī′jĕst′) A synopsis of written materials or data. [< Lat. *digere*, to separate.] —**di-gest′er** n. —**di-gest′i-bil′i-ty** n. —**di-gest′i-ble** adj. —**di-ges′tion** n. —**di-ges′tive** adj.

digestive system n. The alimentary canal along with the glands, such as the liver, salivary glands, and pancreas, that produce substances needed in digestion.

dig-it (dĭj′ĭt) n. **1.** A finger or toe. **2.** Any of the Arabic numerals 0 through 9. [< Lat. *digitus*, finger.]

dig-i-tal (dĭj′ĭ-tal) adj. **1.** Of or involving a digit. **2.** Expressed as, using, or giving a readout in digits: *a digital clock.* —**dig′i-tal-ly** adv.

digital computer A computer that performs operations on data represented as series of digits.

dig-i-tal-is (dĭj′ĭ-tăl′ĭs) n. A drug prepared from the seeds and leaves of the foxglove, used as a powerful heart stimulant. [< Lat. *digitalis*, digital.]

dig-ni-fied (dĭg′nə-fīd′) adj. Having or expressing dignity. —**dig′ni-fied′ly** adv.

dig-ni-fy (dĭg′nə-fī′) v. -**fied**, -**fy-ing.** To give dignity or honor to. [< LLat. *dignificare*.]

dig-ni-tary (dĭg′nĭ-tĕr′ē) n., pl. -**ies.** A person of high rank or position.

dig-ni-ty (dĭg′nĭ-tē) n., pl. -**ties. 1.** The condition of being worthy or honorable. **2.** A high office or rank. **3.** Nobility of character or language. [< Lat. *dignitas*.]

di-graph (dī′grăf′) n. A pair of letters that represents one sound. —**di-graph′ic** adj.

di-gress (dī-grĕs′, dĭ-) v. To stray from the main subject in writing or speaking. [Lat. *digredi*.] —**di-gres′sion** n. —**di-gres′sive** adj. —**di-gres′sive-ly** adv.

dike (dīk) n. Also **dyke. 1.** A wall or embankment built to hold back water and prevent floods. **2.** A ditch or channel. [< OE *dīc*, trench.] —**dik′er** n.

di-lap-i-dat-ed (dĭ-lăp′ĭ-dā′tĭd) adj. In partial ruin or disrepair. [Lat. *dilapidatus*, p.p. of *dilapidare*, to destroy.] —**di-lap′i-da′tion** n.

di-late (dī-lāt′, dī′lāt′) v. -**lat-ed**, -**lat-ing.** To make or become wider or larger; expand. [< Lat. *dilatare*.] —**di-lat′a-ble** adj. —**di-la′tion** or **di-la′ta′tion** n. —**di-la′tor** n.

dil-a-to-ry (dĭl′ə-tôr′ē, -tōr′ē) adj. Tending to delay. [< Lat. *dilatus*, p.p. of *differe*, to delay.] —**dil′a-to′ri-ly** adv. —**dil′a-to′ri-ness** n.

di-lem-ma (dĭ-lĕm′ə) n. A situation that requires a choice between two equal, usu. unpleasant alternatives. [< Gk. *dilēmma*, ambiguous proposition.]

dil-et-tante (dĭl′ĭ-tänt′, -tän′tē, -tänt′, -tän′tē, dĭl′ĭ-tänt′) n., pl. -**tantes** or -**tan-ti** (-tän′tē, -tän′-). One with an amateurish or superficial interest in the arts or a branch of knowledge. [Ital.] —**dil′et-tan′tism** n.

dil-i-gent (dĭl′ə-jənt) adj. Done with or characterized by great effort and care; assiduous. [< Lat. *diligere*, to love.] —**dil′i-gence** n. —**dil′i-gent-ly** adv.

dill (dĭl) n. An herb with aromatic leaves and seeds used as seasoning. [< OE *dile*.]

dil-ly (dĭl′ē) n., pl. -**lies.** Slang. Something remarkable. [< DELIGHTFUL.]

dil-ly-dal-ly (dĭl′ē-dăl′ē) v. -**lied**, -**ly-ing. 1.** To waste time. **2.** To vacillate. [< DALLY.]

di-lute (dī-lōōt′, dĭ-) v. -**lut-ed**, -**lut-ing.** To make thinner or weaker as by mixing or dispersing. —adj. Weakened; diluted. [Lat. *diluere*.] —**di-lut′er** n. —**di-lu′tion** n.

dim (dĭm) adj. **dim-mer, dim-mest. 1.** Faintly lighted. **2.** Obscure or indistinct; faint. **3.** Lacking luster; dull. **4.** Lacking sharpness or clarity in sight or understanding. **5.** Negative or unpromising. —v. **dimmed, dim-ming. 1.** To make or become dim. **2.** To put on low beam: *dim the headlights.* [< OE *dimm*.] —**dim′ly** adv. —**dim′ness** n.

dime (dīm) n. A U.S. coin worth ten cents. [< Lat. *decima (pars)*, tenth (part).]

di-men-sion (dĭ-mĕn′shən) n. **1.** A measure of spatial extent, esp. width, height, or length. **2.** Often **dimensions.** Extent; magnitude; size; scope. **3. a.** Any of the least number of independent coordinates required to specify a point in space uniquely. **b.** A physical property, often mass, length, time, or some combination thereof, regarded as a fundamental measure. [< Lat. *dimensio*.] —**di-men′sion-al** adj. —**di-men′sion-al′i-ty** (-shə-năl′ĭ-tē) n. —**di-men′sion-al-ly** adv.

di-min-ish (dĭ-mĭn′ĭsh) v. **1.** To make or become smaller or less important. **2.** To taper. [ME *diminishen*.] —**di-min′ish-a-ble** adj. —**di-min′ish-ment** n.

di-min-u-en-do (dĭ-mĭn′yōō-ĕn′dō) n., pl. -**dos.** Decrescendo. [Ital.] —**di-min′u-en′do** adj. & adv.

dim-i-nu-tion (dĭm′ə-nōō′shən, -nyōō′-) n. The act, process, or result of diminishing. [< Lat. *deminuere*, to diminish.]

di-min-u-tive (dĭ-mĭn′yə-tĭv) adj. **1.** Of very small size; tiny. **2.** Expressing smallness or affection, as the suffix -*let* in *booklet.* —n. A diminutive suffix, word, or name.

dim-i-ty (dĭm′ĭ-tē) n., pl. -**ties.** A thin, crisp, corded cotton cloth. [< Med. Gk. *dimitos*, double-threaded.]

dim-mer (dĭm′ər) n. A rheostat or other device used to reduce the brightness of electric lights.

dim-ple (dĭm′pəl) n. **1.** A small natural indentation in the flesh, esp. on the cheek. **2.** A slight depression in a surface. —v. -**pled**, -**pling.** To form dimples, as by smiling. [ME *dimpel*.]

din (dĭn) n. Loud, confused, prolonged noise. —v. **dinned, din-ning.** To impart by wearying repetition. [< OE *dyne*.]

di-nar (dĭ-när′, dē′när′) n. See table at **currency.** [Ar. *dīnār*.]

dine (dīn) v. **dined, din-ing. 1.** To eat dinner. **2.** To give dinner to. [< OFr. *diner*.]

din-er (dī′nər) n. **1.** A person eating dinner. **2.** A railroad dining car. **3.** A restaurant shaped like a railroad car.

di-nette (dī-nĕt′) n. A nook or alcove for meals.

din-ghy (dĭng′ē) n., pl. -**ghies.** A small boat, esp. a rowboat. [Hindi *ḍiṅgī*.]

din-go (dĭng′gō) n., pl. -**goes.** A yellowish-brown wild dog of Australia. [A native word in Australia.]

din-gus (dĭng′əs) n. Slang. A gadget or other article whose name is unknown or forgotten. [Du. *dinges*.]

din-gy (dĭn′jē) adj. -**gi-er**, -**gi-est. 1.** Dirty; soiled; grimy. **2.** Drab; squalid. [Orig. unknown.] —**din′gi-ly** adv. —**din′gi-ness** n.

din·ky (dĭng'kē) adj. **-ki·er, -ki·est.** Informal. Of small size or consequence; insignificant. [Prob. < Sc. dink, neat.]

din·ner (dĭn'ər) n. **1.** The main meal of the day. **2.** A formal banquet. [< OFr. diner.]

dinner jacket n. A tuxedo.

di·no·saur (dī'nə-sôr') n. Any of various prehistoric, extinct, often gigantic reptiles. [Gk. deinos, monstrous + -SAUR.]

dint (dĭnt) n. **1.** Force or effort: succeeded by dint of hard work. **2.** A dent. [< OE dynt.]

di·o·cese (dī'ə-sĭs, -sēs', -sēz') n. The district or churches under the leadership of a bishop. [< Gk. dioikesis, administration.] —di·oc'e·san (dī-ŏs'ə-sən) adj.

di·ode (dī'ōd') n. **1.** An electron tube with two electrodes, esp. a tube that allows current to flow in one direction only. **2.** A semiconductor with two terminals, used as a rectifier.

Di·o·nys·i·an (dī'ə-nĭsh'ən, -nĭzh'-, -nĭs'ē-ən) adj. **1.** Of or relating to Dionysus. **2.** Of an ecstatic, orgiastic, or irrational character.

Di·o·ny·sus (dī'ə-nī'səs) n. Gk. Myth. The god of wine.

Dionysus

di·o·ram·a (dī'ə-răm'ə, -rä'mə) n. A three-dimensional miniature scene with painted modeled figures and background. [Gk. dia, through + (PAN)ORAMA.]

di·ox·ide (dī-ŏk'sīd') n. An oxide with two atoms of oxygen per molecule.

dip (dĭp) v. **dipped, dip·ping. 1.** To plunge briefly into a liquid. **2.** To immerse (an animal) in a disinfectant solution. **3.** To scoop up (liquid). **4.** To lower and raise (a flag) in salute. **5.** To drop or sink suddenly. **6.** To slope downward; decline. **7.** To look casually into a subject or source of information. —n. **1.** A brief plunge or immersion. **2.** A liquid into which something is dipped. **3.** A creamy food mixture into which crackers, chips, etc. may be dipped. **4.** An amount taken up by dipping. **5.** A decline or drop: a dip in the price of sugar. **6.** A downward slope or sloping. **7.** A hollow; depression. [< OE dyppan.]

diph·the·ri·a (dĭf-thîr'ē-ə, dĭp-) n. A serious contagious bacterial disease marked by high fever, weakness, and the formation in the throat and other air passages of false membranes that cause difficulty in breathing. [< Gk. diphthera, piece of leather.] —diph'the·rit'ic (dĭf'thə-rĭt'ĭk) or diph·ther'ic (-thĕr'ĭk) or diph·the'ri·al (-thîr'ē-əl) adj.

diph·thong (dĭf'thông', -thŏng', dĭp'-) n. **1.** A complex speech sound beginning with one vowel sound and moving to another vowel or semivowel position within the same syllable, as oy in the word boy. **2.** A ligature. [< Gk. diphthongos.]

dip·loid (dĭp'loid') adj. Having double the basic number of chromosomes. [< Gk. diploos, double.]

di·plo·ma (dĭ-plō'mə) n. **1.** A document showing that a person has earned a degree from or completed a course of study at a school, college, or university. **2.** A certificate conferring a privilege or honor. [< Gk. diplōma, document.]

di·plo·ma·cy (dĭ-plō'mə-sē) n., pl. -cies. **1.** The art or practice of conducting international relations. **2.** Skill in dealing with others; tact. [Ult. < Gk. diplōma, document.]

dip·lo·mat (dĭp'lə-măt') n. One skilled or working in diplomacy.

dip·lo·mat·ic (dĭp'lə-măt'ĭk) adj. **1.** Of or pertaining to diplomacy. **2.** Tactful. —dip'lo·mat'i·cal·ly adv.

dip·per (dĭp'ər) n. One that dips, esp. a long-handled cup for taking up water.

dip·so·ma·ni·a (dĭp'sə-mā'nē-ə, -mān'yə) n. An uncontrollable craving for alcoholic liquors. [Gk. dipsa, thirst + -MANIA.] —dip'so·ma'ni·ac' n. & adj.

dip·stick (dĭp'stĭk') n. A graduated rod for measuring the depth of liquid in a container.

dire (dīr) adj. **dir·er, dir·est. 1.** Warning of disaster. **2.** Dreadful; disastrous. **3.** Urgent; grave: in dire need. [Lat. dirus.] —dire'ful adj. —dire'ful·ly adv. —dire'ly adv.

di·rect (dĭ-rĕkt', dī-) v. **1.** To conduct the affairs of; manage. **2.** To take charge of with authority; control. **3.** To conduct (musicians) in a rehearsal or performance. **4.** To aim, guide, or address (something or someone) toward a goal. **5.** To give interpretative dramatic supervision to the actors in a play or film. —adj. **1.** Proceeding or lying in a straight course or line. **2.** Straightforward. **3.** Without intervening persons, conditions, or agencies; immediate. **4.** By action of voters, rather than through elected delegates. **5.** Absolute; total: direct opposites. **6.** Receiving the action of a transitive verb: direct object. **7.** Varying in the same manner as another quantity, esp. increasing if another quantity increases or decreasing if it decreases. —adv. In a direct manner; straight; directly. [< Lat. dirigere.] —di·rect'ness n.

direct current n. An electric current flowing in one direction.

di·rec·tion (dĭ-rĕk'shən, dī-) n. **1.** The act or function of directing. **2.** Often directions. An instruction or series of instructions for doing something. **3.** A command. **4. a.** The distance-independent relationship between two points that specifies the angular position of either with respect to the other. **b.** A position to which motion or another position is referred. **c.** The line or course along which a person or thing moves. **5.** Tendency toward a particular end or goal. —di·rec'tion·al adj. —di·rec'tion·al'i·ty n.

di·rec·tive (dĭ-rĕk'tĭv, dī-) n. An order or instruction.

di·rect·ly (dĭ-rĕkt'lē, dī-) adv. **1.** In a direct line or manner. **2.** Without anything or anyone intervening. **3.** Exactly. **4.** Instantly.

di·rec·tor (dĭ-rĕk′tər, dī-) n. 1. A manager. 2. One who supervises or guides the performers in a play, film, or similar performance. —**di·rec′to′ri·al** adj. —**di·rec′tor·ship′** n.

di·rec·to·rate (dĭ-rĕk′tər-ĭt, dī-) n. 1. The office or position of a director. 2. A board of directors.

di·rec·to·ry (dĭ-rĕk′tə-rē, dī-) n., pl. **-ries.** An alphabetical or classified list of names and addresses.

dirge (dûrj) n. A sad, solemn piece of music. [< Lat. *dirige*, direct (the first word in a Med. Lat. antiphon).]

dir·ham (də-răm′) n. See table at **currency.** [Ar.]

dir·i·gi·ble (dĭr′ə-jə-bəl, dĭ-rĭj′ə-) n. An early type of rigid lighter-than-air craft that could be steered. [< Lat. *dirigere*, to direct.]

dirk (dûrk) n. A dagger. [Sc. *durk*.]

dirn·dl (dûrn′dəl) n. A full-skirted dress with a tight bodice. [G.]

dirt (dûrt) n. 1. Earth or soil. 2. A filthy or soiling substance, such as mud. 3. Obscene language. 4. Malicious or scandalous gossip. [< ON *drit*.]

dirt·y (dûr′tē) adj. **-i·er, -i·est.** 1. Soiled; grimy. 2. Dull in color. 3. Threatening: *a dirty look.* 4. Stormy: *dirty weather.* 5. Dishonorable; unfair: *a dirty fighter.* 6. Obscene or indecent. —v. **-ied, -y·ing.** To make or become soiled. —**dirt′i·ly** adv. —**dirt′i·ness** n.

Syns: *dirty, filthy, grimy, grubby, soiled, unclean* **adj.**

dirty work n. 1. Foul play; deceit. 2. A difficult or distasteful task.

dis- *pref.* 1. Negation, lack, invalidation, or deprivation: *distrust.* 2. Reversal: *disunite.* 3. Removal or rejection: *disbar.* [< Lat. *dis*, apart.]

dis·a·bil·i·ty (dĭs′ī-bĭl′ĭ-tē) n., pl. **-ties.** 1. A disabled condition; incapacity. 2. Something that disables or disqualifies.

dis·a·ble (dĭs-ā′bəl) v. **-bled, -bling.** 1. To weaken or incapacitate. 2. To render legally disqualified.

dis·a·buse (dĭs′ə-byōōz′) v. **-bused, -bus·ing.** To free from a falsehood or misconception. [Fr. *désabuser*.]

dis·ad·van·tage (dĭs′əd-văn′tĭj) n. 1. An unfavorable condition or circumstance; handicap. 2. Damage; harm; loss. —**dis·ad·van·ta′geous** adj. —**dis·ad·van·ta′geous·ly** adv.

dis·ad·van·taged (dĭs′əd-văn′tĭjd) adj. Underprivileged; poor.

dis·af·fect (dĭs′ə-fĕkt′) v. To alienate the affection or loyalty of. —**dis·af·fect′ed** adj. —**dis·af·fect′ed·ly** adv. —**dis·af·fec′tion** n.

dis·a·gree (dĭs′ə-grē′) v. 1. To fail to correspond 2. To have a different opinion. 3. To dispute; quarrel. 4. To have bad effects. —**dis·a·gree′ment** n.

dis·a·gree·a·ble (dĭs′ə-grē′ə-bəl) adj. 1. Unpleasant; distasteful. 2. Bad-tempered. —**dis·a·gree′a·ble·ness** n. —**dis·a·gree′a·bly** adv.

dis·al·low (dĭs′ə-lou′) v. To refuse to allow; reject: *disallow a motion.* —**dis·al·low′ance** n.

dis·ap·pear (dĭs′ə-pîr′) v. 1. To pass out of sight; vanish. 2. To cease to exist. —**dis·ap·pear′ance** n.

dis·ap·point (dĭs′ə-point′) v. To fail to satisfy the hope or expectation of. [< OFr. *desapointier*.] —**dis·ap·point′ing·ly** adv. —**dis·ap·point′ment** n.

dis·ap·pro·ba·tion (dĭs-ăp′rə-bā′shən) n. Disapproval; condemnation.

dis·ap·prov·al (dĭs′ə-prōō′vəl) n. Unfavorable judgment; condemnation.

dis·ap·prove (dĭs′ə-prōōv′) v. 1. To have an unfavorable opinion (of). 2. To refuse to approve. —**dis·ap·prov′ing·ly** adv.

dis·arm (dĭs-ärm′) v. 1. To deprive of weapons. 2. To render helpless or harmless. 3. To overcome the hostility of. 4. To reduce one's armaments or armed forces.

dis·ar·ma·ment (dĭs-är′mə-mənt) n. A reduction of armed forces or armaments.

dis·ar·range (dĭs′ə-rānj′) v. To upset the arrangement of. —**dis·ar·range′ment** n.

dis·ar·ray (dĭs′ə-rā′) v. 1. Disorder or confusion. 2. Disordered or insufficient dress. —v. To throw into confusion.

dis·as·sem·ble (dĭs′ə-sĕm′bəl) v. To take apart.

dis·as·so·ci·ate (dĭs′ə-sō′shē-āt′, -sē-) v. To dissociate. —**dis·as·so′ci·a′tion** n.

dis·as·ter (dĭ-zăs′tər) n. Great destruction, distress, or misfortune. [< Ital. *disastro*.] —**dis·as′trous** adj. —**dis·as′trous·ly** adv.

---

dis′ac·com′mo·date′ v.	**dis·bal′ance** n.	**dis′em·broil′** v.
dis′ac·cord′ n. & v.	**dis·branch′** v.	**dis′em·broil′ment** n.
dis′ac·cred′it v.	**dis·bud′** v.	**dis′em·ploy′** v.
dis′ac·cus′tom v.	**dis·bur′den** v.	**dis′em·ploy′ment** n.
dis′a·cid′i·fy′ v.	**dis′com·mend′** v.	**dis′en·a′ble** v.
dis′ac·knowl′edge v.	**dis′com·mend′a·ble** adj.	**dis′en·cour′age** v.
dis′ac·knowl′edg·ment n.	**dis′com·mod′i·ty** n.	**dis′en·cour′age·ment** n.
dis′ac·quaint′ance n.	**dis′con·firm′** v.	**dis′en·dow′** v.
dis′ac·quaint′ed adj.	**dis′con·fir·ma′tion** n.	**dis′en·dow′ment** n.
dis′ad·vise′ v.	**dis′con·firm′** v.	**dis′en·joy′** v.
dis′af·fil′i·ate′ v.	**dis′con·gru′i·ty** n.	**dis′en·joy′ment** n.
dis′af·fil′i·a′tion n.	**dis′con·gru′ous** adj.	**dis′en·roll′** v.
dis′af·firm′ v.	**dis′con·sid′er** v.	**dis′en·roll′ment** n.
dis′af·fir·ma′tion n.	**dis′con·so′nant** adj.	**dis′en·tail′** v.
dis′ag·gre·gate′ v.	**dis·crown′** v.	**dis′en·thrall′** v.
dis′ag·gre·ga′tion n.	**dis′e·con′o·my** n.	**dis′en·thrall′ment** n.
dis′al·ly′ v.	**dis·edge′** v.	**dis′en·ti′tle** v.
dis′a·men′i·ty n.	**dis·ed′i·fy′** v.	**dis′en·tomb′** v.
dis·an′chor v.	**dis′em·balm′** v.	**dis′en·tomb′ment** n.
dis·an′nex′ v.	**dis′em·bar′rass** v.	**dis′en·trance′** v.
dis′a·noint′ v.	**dis′em·bar·rass·ment** n.	**dis′en·twine′** v.
dis′as·sem′bly n.	**dis′em·bel′lish** v.	**dis′e·qui·lib′ri·um** n.
	dis′em·bel′lish·ment n.	

Syns: disaster, calamity, cataclysm, catastrophe, tragedy.

dis·a·vow (dĭs′ə-vou′) *v.* To disclaim knowledge of, responsibility for, or association with. —**dis′a·vow′al** *n.*

dis·band (dĭs-bănd′) *v.* To dissolve or become dissolved. —**dis·band′ment** *n.*

dis·bar (dĭs-bär′) *v.* To expel (a lawyer) from the legal profession. —**dis·bar′ment** *n.*

dis·be·lieve (dĭs′bĭ-lēv′) *v.* To refuse to believe (in). —**dis′be·lief′** *n.* —**dis′be·liev′er** *n.*

dis·burse (dĭs-bûrs′) *v.* **-bursed, -burs·ing.** To pay out, as from a fund. [< OFr. *desbourser.*] —**dis·burse′ment** or **dis·bur′sal** *n.* —**dis·burs′er** *n.*

disc (dĭsk) *n.* **1.** Also **disk.** *Informal.* A phonograph record. **2.** Var. of **disk.** [< Gk. *diskos,* quoit.]

dis·card (dĭs-kärd′) *v.* **1.** To throw away; reject; dismiss. **2. a.** To throw out (an undesired card or cards). **b.** To play (a card other than a trump and different in suit from the card led). —*n.* (dĭs′kärd′). **1.** The act of discarding. **2.** A person or thing discarded.

dis·cern (dĭ-sûrn′, -zûrn′) *v.* **1.** To detect or perceive with the eye or mind. **2.** To perceive the distinctions of; discriminate. [< Lat. *discernere.*] —**dis·cern′er** *n.* —**dis·cern′i·ble** *adj.* —**dis·cern′ment** *n.*

dis·cern·ing (dĭ-sûr′nĭng, -zûr′-) *adj.* Insightful; perceptive. —**dis·cern′ing·ly** *adv.*

dis·charge (dĭs-chärj′) *v.* **-charged, -charg·ing. 1.** To relieve or be relieved of a burden or contents. **2.** To unload or empty (contents). **3.** To release or dismiss, as from employment. **4.** To send or pour forth; emit. **5.** To shoot (a projectile or weapon). **6.** To perform the obligations or demands of (a duty). **7.** To acquit oneself of (an obligation). **8.** To cause or undergo electrical discharge. —*n.* (dĭs′chärj′, dĭs-chärj′). **1.** The act of removing a load or burden. **2.** The act of shooting a projectile or weapon. **3.** A pouring forth; emission. **4.** The amount or rate of emission or ejection. **5.** Something that is discharged. **6.** A relieving from an obligation. **7. a.** Dismissal or release from employment, service, etc. **b.** A

document certifying such release, esp. from military service. **8. a.** The release of stored energy in a capacitor by the flow of electric current between its terminals. **b.** The conversion of chemical energy to electric energy in a storage battery. **c.** A flow of electricity in a dielectric, esp. in a rarefied gas. [< OFr. *descharger.*]

dis·ci·ple (dĭ-sī′pəl) *n.* **1. a.** One who accepts the teachings of a master and often assists in spreading them. **b.** An active adherent. **2. Disciple.** One of the companions of Christ. [< Lat. *discipulus,* pupil < *discere,* to learn.]

dis·ci·pli·nar·i·an (dĭs′ə-plə-nâr′ē-ən) *n.* One who enforces or believes in strict discipline.

dis·ci·pli·nary (dĭs′ə-plə-nĕr′ē) *adj.* Pertaining to or used for discipline.

dis·ci·pline (dĭs′ə-plĭn) *n.* **1. a.** Training intended to produce a specified character or pattern of behavior. **b.** Controlled behavior resulting from such training. **2.** A state of order based on submission to rules and authority. **3.** Punishment intended to correct or train. **4.** A set of rules or methods. **5.** A branch of knowledge or teaching. —*v.* **-plined, -plin·ing. 1.** To train by instruction and control. **2.** To punish. [Lat. *disciplina* < *discere,* to learn.] —**dis′ci·plin′er** *n.*

disc jockey *n.* A radio announcer who presents phonograph records.

dis·claim (dĭs-klām′) *v.* **1.** To deny or renounce a claim to or connection with. **2.** To renounce a legal right or claim (to).

dis·claim·er (dĭs-klā′mər) *n.* A denial or repudiation of a claim.

dis·close (dĭs-klōz′) *v.* **-closed, -clos·ing. 1.** To expose to view. **2.** To make known; divulge.

dis·co (dĭs′kō) *n., pl.* **-cos.** A discotheque.

dis·col·or (dĭs-kŭl′ər) *v.* To change or spoil in color. —**dis·col′or·a′tion** *n.*

dis·com·bob·u·late (dĭs′kəm-bŏb′yə-lāt′) *v.* **-lat·ed, -lat·ing.** To confuse; upset. [Poss. < DISCOMPOSE.]

dis·com·fit (dĭs-kŭm′fĭt) *v.* **1.** To defeat or frustrate. **2.** To make uneasy or confused;

ă pat ā pay â care ä father ĕ pet ē be ĭ pit ī tie î pier ŏ pot ō toe ô paw, for oi noise ŏŏ took
ōō boot ou out th thin *th* this ŭ cut û urge yōō abuse zh vision ə about, item, edible, gallop, circus

disconcert. [< OFr. *disconfit*, p.p. of *desconfire*, to defeat.] —**dis·com'fi·ture'** *n.*

Usage: Discomfit was once used strictly in the sense of "to defeat or frustrate," but through confusion with the unrelated word *discomfort*, it has also come to mean "to disconcert or make uncomfortable." A large majority of the Usage Panel accepts this newer meaning.

dis·com·fort (dĭs-kŭm'fərt) *n.* **1.** The condition of being uncomfortable in body or mind. **2.** Something that disturbs comfort. —*v.* To make uncomfortable.

dis·com·mode (dĭs'kə-mōd') *v.* **-mod·ed, -mod·ing.** To inconvenience; disturb. [Fr. *discommoder.*]

dis·com·pose (dĭs'kəm-pōz') *v.* **1.** To disturb the composure of. **2.** To disorder; disarrange. —**dis'com·po'sure** (-pō'zhər) *n.*

dis·con·cert (dĭs'kən-sûrt') *v.* To perturb; upset. —**dis'con·cert'ing·ly** *adv.*

dis·con·nect (dĭs'kə-nĕkt') *v.* To break or interrupt the connection of or between. —**dis'con·nec'tion** *n.*

dis·con·nect·ed (dĭs'kə-nĕk'tĭd) *adj.* **1.** Not connected. **2.** Lacking order; incoherent. —**dis'con·nect'ed·ly** *adv.*

dis·con·so·late (dĭs-kŏn'sə-lĭt) *adj.* **1.** Hopelessly sad. **2.** Gloomy; dismal. [< Med. Lat. *disconsolatus.*] —**dis·con'so·late·ly** *adv.* —**dis·con'so·late·ness** *n.*

dis·con·tent (dĭs'kən-tĕnt') *n.* The absence of contentment; dissatisfaction. —*adj.* Discontented. —*v.* To make discontented.

dis·con·tent·ed (dĭs'kən-tĕn'tĭd) *adj.* Not satisfied; unhappy. —**dis'con·tent'ed·ly** *adv.* —**dis'con·tent'ed·ness** *n.*

dis·con·tin·ue (dĭs'kən-tĭn'yōō) *v.* **1.** To put a stop to. **2.** To give up; abandon. **3.** To come to an end. —**dis'con·tin'u·ance** or **dis'con·tin'u·a'tion** *n.*

dis·con·tin·u·ous (dĭs'kən-tĭn'yōō-əs) *adj.* Marked by breaks or interruptions. —**dis'con·ti·nu'i·ty** (dĭs-kŏn'tə-nōō'ĭ-tē, -nyōō'-) *n.* —**dis'con·tin'u·ous·ly** *adv.*

dis·cord (dĭs'kôrd') *n.* **1.** Lack of agreement or accord; dissension. **2.** A harsh mingling of sounds. **3.** *Mus.* A harsh combination of simultaneously sounded tones; dissonance. [< Lat. *discordia.*] —**dis·cor'dant** *adj.* —**dis·cor'dant·ly** *adv.*

dis·co·theque (dĭs'kə-tĕk', dĭs'kə-tĕk') *n.* A club that features dancing to recorded music. [Fr. *discothèque.*]

dis·count (dĭs'kount', dĭs-kount') *v.* **1.** To deduct, as from a cost or price. **2. a.** To purchase or sell (a commercial paper) after deducting the interest. **b.** To lend money after deducting the interest. **3.** To disregard as being untrustworthy or exaggerated. **4.** To anticipate and make allowance for. —*n.* (dĭs'kount'). **1.** A reduction from the full amount of a price or debt. **2.** The interest deducted in advance in purchasing or selling a commercial paper. **3.** The rate of interest so deducted. **4.** The act or an instance of discounting. [< Med. Lat. *discomputare.*] —**dis'count'a·ble** *adj.* —**dis'count'er** *n.*

dis·coun·te·nance (dĭs-koun'tə-nəns) *v.* **1.** To view with disfavor. **2.** To disconcert.

discount store *n.* A store that sells merchandise below the suggested retail price.

dis·cour·age (dĭ-skûr'ĭj, -skûr'-) *v.* **-aged, -ag·ing.** **1.** To make less hopeful or enthusiastic.

---

2. To try to dissuade. **3.** To hamper. —**dis·cour'age·ment** *n.* —**dis·cour'ag·ing·ly** *adv.*

dis·course (dĭs'kôrs', -kōrs') *n.* **1.** Verbal exchange; conversation. **2.** A formal discussion of a subject, either spoken or written. —*v.* (dĭs-kôrs', -kōrs') **-coursed, -cours·ing.** To speak or write formally and at length. [< LLat. *discursus.*] —**dis·cours'er** *n.*

dis·cour·te·ous (dĭs-kûr'tē-əs) *adj.* Lacking courtesy; not polite. —**dis·cour'te·ous·ly** *adv.* —**dis·cour'te·ous·ness** *n.* —**dis·cour'te·sy** *n.*

dis·cov·er (dĭ-skŭv'ər) *v.* **1.** To arrive at through search or study. **2.** To be the first to find, learn of, or observe. [< LLat. *discooperire*, to reveal.] —**dis·cov'er·a·ble** *adj.* —**dis·cov'er·er** *n.*

dis·cov·er·y (dĭ-skŭv'ə-rē) *n., pl.* **-ies.** **1.** The act of discovering. **2.** Something that has been discovered.

dis·cred·it (dĭs-krĕd'ĭt) *v.* **1.** To disgrace; dishonor. **2.** To cast doubt on. **3.** To disbelieve. —*n.* **1.** Damage to one's reputation. **2.** Lack or loss of trust or belief. —**dis·cred'it·a·ble** *adj.* —**dis·cred'it·a·bly** *adv.*

dis·creet (dĭ-skrēt') *adj.* Having or showing good judgment and self-restraint in speech or behavior; prudent. [< Med. Lat. *discretus* < Lat. *discernere*, to discern.] —**dis·creet'ly** *adv.* —**dis·creet'ness** *n.*

dis·crep·an·cy (dĭ-skrĕp'ən-sē) *n., pl.* **-cies.** Also **dis·crep·ance** (-əns). Lack of agreement; difference; inconsistency. [< Lat. *discrepare*, to disagree.]

dis·crete (dĭ-skrēt') *adj.* **1.** Individually distinct; separate. **2.** Consisting of unconnected distinct parts. [< Lat. *discretus*, p.p. of *discernere*, to separate.]

dis·cre·tion (dĭ-skrĕsh'ən) *n.* **1.** The quality of being discreet. **2.** Freedom of action or judgment: *leave the choice to your discretion.* —**dis·cre'tion·ar'y** (-ə-nĕr'ē) *adj.*

dis·crim·i·nate (dĭ-skrĭm'ə-nāt') *v.* **-nat·ed, -nat·ing.** **1.** To make a clear distinction; differentiate. **2.** To act on the basis of prejudice. [Lat. *discriminare.*] —**dis·crim'i·nate·ly** *adv.* —**dis·crim'i·na'tion** *n.* —**dis·crim'i·na'tive** or **dis·crim'i·na·to'ry** (-nə-tôr'ē, -tōr'ē) *adj.*

dis·crim·i·nat·ing (dĭ-skrĭm'ə-nā'tĭng) *adj.* **1.** Able to recognize fine distinctions; discerning. **2.** Fastidiously selective.

dis·cur·sive (dĭ-skûr'sĭv) *adj.* Rambling; digressive. [< LLat. *discursus*, discussion.] —**dis·cur'sive·ly** *adv.* —**dis·cur'sive·ness** *n.*

dis·cus (dĭs'kəs) *n.* A disk, usu. wooden with a metal rim, that is thrown for distance in athletic contests. [Lat. < Gk. *diskos.*]

discus

dis·cuss (dĭ-skŭs') *v.* **1.** To speak together about. **2.** To examine (a subject) in speech or writing; treat of. [< Lat. *discutere.*] —**dis·cuss'i·ble** *adj.* —**dis·cus'sion** *n.*

dis·cuss·ant (dĭ-skŭs′ənt) *n.* One who participates in a discussion.

dis·dain (dĭs-dān′) *v.* **1.** To show contempt for. **2.** To refuse aloofly. —*n.* Mild contempt and aloofness. [< Lat. *dedignari.*] —**dis·dain′ful** *adj.* —**dis·dain′ful·ly** *adv.*

dis·ease (dĭ-zēz′) *n.* A condition of an organism that impairs normal physiological functioning. [< OFr. *disese,* misery.] —**dis·eased** (-zēzd′) *adj.*

dis·em·bark (dĭs′ĕm-bärk′) *v.* To put, go, or cause to go ashore from a ship. —**dis·em·bar·ka′tion** *n.*

dis·em·bod·y (dĭs′ĕm-bŏd′ē) *v.* **-ied, -y·ing.** To free (the spirit) from the body. —**dis·em·bod′i·ment** *n.*

dis·em·bow·el (dĭs′ĕm-bou′əl) *v.* To remove the entrails from. —**dis·em·bow′el·ment** *n.*

dis·en·chant (dĭs′ĕn-chănt′) *v.* To free from false belief or enchantment; disillusion. —**dis·en·chant′ment** *n.*

dis·en·cum·ber (dĭs′ĕn-kŭm′bər) *v.* To free from something that hinders or burdens.

dis·en·fran·chise (dĭs′ĕn-frăn′chīz′) *v.* To disfranchise.

dis·en·gage (dĭs′ĕn-gāj′) *v.* To release from something that holds, connects, or obliges. —**dis·en·gage′ment** *n.*

dis·en·tan·gle (dĭs′ĕn-tăng′gəl) *v.* To free or become free from entanglement; extricate. —**dis·en·tan′gle·ment** *n.*

dis·es·tab·lish (dĭs′ĭ-stăb′lĭsh) *v.* To remove the established status of, esp. of a nationally established church. —**dis·es·tab′lish·ment** *n.*

dis·fa·vor (dĭs-fā′vər) *n.* **1.** Disapproval. **2.** The condition of being disliked or disapproved of. —**dis·fa′vor** *v.*

dis·fig·ure (dĭs-fĭg′yər) *v.* **-ured, -ur·ing.** To spoil the appearance or shape of; mar. —**dis·fig′ure·ment** *n.*

dis·fran·chise (dĭs-frăn′chīz′) *v.* To deprive of a right or privilege, esp. the right to vote. —**dis·fran′chise′ment** *n.*

dis·gorge (dĭs-gôrj′) *v.* **-gorged, -gorg·ing.** **1.** To vomit. **2.** To discharge violently; spew.

dis·grace (dĭs-grās′) *n.* **1.** Loss of honor, respect, or reputation. **2.** Something that brings disgrace. —*v.* **-graced, -grac·ing.** To bring shame or dishonor upon. [< Ital. *disgrazia.*] —**dis·grace′ful** *adj.* —**dis·grace′ful·ly** *adv.* **Syns: disgrace, discredit, dishonor, disrepute, ignominy, shame** *n.*

dis·grun·tle (dĭs-grŭn′tl) *v.* **-tled, -tling.** To make discontented; upset. [DIS- + dial. *gruntle,* to grumble.]

dis·guise (dĭs-gīz′) *n.* **1.** Clothes or accessories worn to conceal one's true identity. **2.** Concealment or camouflage. —*v.* **-guised, -guis·ing.** **1.** To change the manner or appearance of in order to prevent recognition. **2.** To conceal or obscure by false show. [< OFr. *disguiser,* to disguise.] —**dis·guis′er** *n.*

dis·gust (dĭs-gŭst′) *v.* To make (someone) feel sick, annoyed, averse, or offended. —*n.* A feeling of annoyance, aversion, or repugnance. [< OFr. *desgouster.*] —**dis·gust′ed** *adj.* —**dis·gust′ed·ly** *adv.*

dish (dĭsh) *n.* **1. a.** A flat or shallow container for holding or serving food. **b.** The amount that a dish holds. **2.** A particular preparation of food. **3.** Something shaped like a dish.

—*v.* **1.** To serve in or as if in a dish. **2.** *Informal.* To give out; dispense. [< OE *disc* < Lat. *discus,* quoit.]

dis·ha·bille (dĭs′ə-bēl′) *n.* The condition of being dressed in a sloppy or casual way. [Fr. *déshabillé* < p.p. of *déshabiller,* to undress.]

dis·har·mo·ny (dĭs-här′mə-nē) *n.* Lack of harmony. —**dis·har·mo′ni·ous** (-mô′nē-əs) *adj.*

dish·cloth (dĭsh′klôth′, -klŏth′) *n.* A cloth for washing dishes.

dis·heart·en (dĭs-här′tn) *v.* To shake or destroy the courage or spirit of. —**dis·heart′en·ing·ly** *adv.*

di·shev·el (dĭ-shĕv′əl) *v.* **-eled** or **-elled, -el·ing** or **-el·ling.** To put into disarray or disorder, esp. hair or clothing. [< OFr. *descheveler,* to disarrange the hair.] —**di·shev′el·ment** *n.*

dis·hon·est (dĭs-ŏn′ĭst) *adj.* **1.** Lacking honesty; untrustworthy. **2.** Showing or resulting from fraud. —**dis·hon′est·ly** *adv.* —**dis·hon′es·ty** *n.*

dis·hon·or (dĭs-ŏn′ər) *n.* **1.** Loss of honor, respect, or reputation; disgrace. **2.** Something that causes loss of honor. **3.** Failure to pay a note, bill, or other commercial obligation. —*v.* **1.** To deprive of honor; disgrace. **2.** To fail to pay. —**dis·hon′or·a·ble** *adj.* —**dis·hon′or·a·bly** *adv.*

dish·rag (dĭsh′răg′) *n.* A dishcloth.

dish·wash·er (dĭsh′wŏsh′ər, -wô′shər) *n.* A person or machine that washes dishes.

dis·il·lu·sion (dĭs′ĭ-lōō′zhən) *v.* To free or deprive of illusion. —**dis·il·lu′sion·ment** *n.*

dis·in·cline (dĭs′ĭn-klīn′) *v.* To make or be reluctant. —**dis·in′cli·na′tion** (-klə-nā′shən) *n.*

dis·in·fect (dĭs′ĭn-fĕkt′) *v.* To rid of disease-causing microorganisms. —**dis·in·fec′tant** *n. & adj.* —**dis·in·fec′tion** *n.*

dis·in·gen·u·ous (dĭs′ĭn-jĕn′yōō-əs) *adj.* Not straightforward; crafty. —**dis·in·gen′u·ous·ly** *adv.* —**dis·in·gen′u·ous·ness** *n.*

dis·in·her·it (dĭs′ĭn-hĕr′ĭt) *v.* To prevent from inheriting.

dis·in·te·grate (dĭs-ĭn′tĭ-grāt′) *v.* **-grat·ed, -grat·ing.** **1.** To separate into pieces; fragment. **2.** To decay or undergo a transformation, as an atomic nucleus. —**dis·in′te·gra′tion** *n.* —**dis·in′te·gra′tor** *n.*

dis·in·ter (dĭs′ĭn-tûr′) *v.* To remove from or as if from a grave or tomb. —**dis·in·ter′ment** *n.*

dis·in·ter·est·ed (dĭs-ĭn′trĭ-stĭd, -tə-rĕs′tĭd) *adj.* **1.** Free of bias and self-interest; impartial. **2.** Indifferent. —**dis·in′ter·est** *n.* —**dis·in′ter·est·ed·ly** *adv.* —**dis·in′ter·est·ed·ness** *n.*

Usage: According to traditional rule, a *disinterested* party is one who has no stake in a dispute and is therefore presumed to be impartial. One is *uninterested* in something, by contrast, when one is indifferent to it. There is an increasing tendency to use the two words interchangeably, although a majority of the Usage Panel insists that *disinterested* should not be used for *uninterested.*

dis·join (dĭs-join′) *v.* To separate.

dis·joint (dĭs-joint′) *v.* **1.** To take apart at the join/s. **2.** To separate; disconnect.

dis·joint·ed (dĭs-join′tĭd) *adj.* **1.** Separated. **2.** Lacking order or coherence. —**dis·joint′ed·ly** *adv.* —**dis·joint′ed·ness** *n.*

disk (dĭsk) *n.* Also **disc.** **1.** A thin, flat, circular plate. **2.** The central part of a composite flower, as the daisy. **3.** Var. of **disc** (sense 1). [< Gk. *diskos*, quoit.]

dis·like (dĭs-līk') *v.* To regard with distaste or aversion. —*n.* A feeling of distaste or aversion; antipathy.

dis·lo·cate (dĭs'lō-kāt', dĭs-lō'kāt') *v.* **-cated, -cating. 1.** To move out of the normal position, esp. to displace (a bone) from a socket or joint. **2.** To disturb. —**dis·lo·ca'tion** *n.*

dis·lodge (dĭs-lŏj') *v.* To remove or force out from a position previously occupied.

dis·loy·al (dĭs-loi'əl) *adj.* Lacking in loyalty. —**dis·loy'al·ly** *adv.* —**dis·loy'al·ty** *n.*

dis·mal (dĭz'məl) *adj.* Causing or showing gloom or depression. [< Med. Lat. *dies mali*, evil days.] —**dis·mal·ly** *adv.*

dis·man·tle (dĭs-măn'tl) *v.* **-tled, -tling. 1.** To strip of furnishings or equipment. **2.** To take apart; tear down. [OFr. *desmanteler*.] —**dis·man'tle·ment** *n.*

dis·may (dĭs-mā') *v.* To fill with dread or apprehension; daunt. —*n.* Consternation; apprehension. [ME *dismaien*.]

dis·mem·ber (dĭs-mĕm'bər) *v.* **1.** To cut, tear, or pull off the limbs of. **2.** To divide into pieces. —**dis·mem'ber·ment** *n.*

dis·miss (dĭs-mĭs') *v.* **1.** To discharge, as from employment. **2.** To direct or allow to leave: *dismiss troops.* **3.** To reject; repudiate. **4.** To put (a claim or action) out of court without further hearing. [< Lat. *dimittere,* to dismiss.] —**dis·miss'al** *n.* —**dis·miss'i·ble** *adj.*

dis·mount (dĭs-mount') *v.* **1.** To get off or down, as from a horse. **2.** To remove (a rider) from a horse. **3.** To remove (something) from its support or mounting. **4.** To disassemble. —**dis·mount'a·ble** *adj.*

dis·o·be·di·ence (dĭs'ə-bē'dē-əns) *n.* Refusal or failure to obey. —**dis·o·be'di·ent** *adj.* —**dis·o·be'di·ent·ly** *adv.*

dis·o·bey (dĭs'ə-bā') *v.* To refuse or fail to obey.

dis·or·der (dĭs-ôr'dər) *n.* **1.** A lack of order. **2.** A public disturbance. **3.** An illness. —*v.* To throw into disorder.

dis·or·der·ly (dĭs-ôr'dər-lē) *adj.* **1.** Not neat or tidy. **2.** Unruly; riotous. **3.** Disturbing the public peace. —**dis·or·der·li·ness** *n.*

   Syns: *disorderly, riotous, rowdy, unruly* **adj.**

dis·or·gan·ize (dĭs-ôr'gə-nīz') *v.* To destroy the organization of. —**dis·or'gan·i·za'tion** *n.*

dis·o·ri·ent (dĭs-ôr'ē-ĕnt', -ŏr'-) *v.* To cause to lose orientation. —**dis·o'ri·en·ta'tion** *n.*

dis·own (dĭs-ōn') *v.* To refuse to claim or accept as one's own; repudiate.

dis·par·age (dĭ-spăr'ĭj) *v.* **-aged, -aging.** To speak of as unimportant or inferior; belittle. [< OFr. *desparager,* to degrade.] —**dis·par'age·ment** *n.* —**dis·par'ag·ing·ly** *adv.*

dis·pa·rate (dĭs'pər-ĭt, dĭ-spăr'-) *adj.* Completely distinct or different; dissimilar. [Lat. *disparatus,* p.p. of *disparare,* to separate.] —**dis'pa·rate·ly** *adv.* —**dis·par'i·ty** (-ĭ-tē) *n.*

dis·pas·sion·ate (dĭs-păsh'ə-nĭt) *adj.* Not influenced by emotion; impartial. —**dis·pas'sion·ate·ly** *adv.* —**dis·pas'sion·ate·ness** *n.*

dis·patch (dĭ-spăch') *v.* **1.** To send. **2.** To perform promptly. **3.** To kill. —*n.* **1.** The act of dispatching. **2.** Efficient, expeditious performance. **3.** A message. **4.** A shipment. **5.** A news item sent to a newspaper by a correspondent. [< OFr. *despeechier,* to set free.] —**dis·patch'er** *n.*

dis·pel (dĭ-spĕl') *v.* **-pelled, -pelling.** To rid of by or as if by scattering; drive away. [Lat. *dispellere.*]

dis·pen·sa·ble (dĭ-spĕn'sə-bəl) *adj.* Capable of being dispensed with.

dis·pen·sa·ry (dĭ-spĕn'sə-rē) *n., pl.* **-ries.** A place where medicine and medical aid are dispensed.

dis·pen·sa·tion (dĭs'pən-sā'shən, -pĕn-) *n.* **1.** The act of dispensing. **2.** Something distributed. **3.** An official exemption or release from an obligation or rule. **4.** A system for ordering or administering affairs. **5.** A religious system considered to have been divinely appointed.

dis·pense (dĭ-spĕns') *v.* **-pensed, -pensing. 1.** To deal out in portions. **2.** To prepare and give out (medicines). **3.** To carry out; administer. —*phrasal verb.* **dispense with. 1.** To manage without. **2.** To dispose of. [< Lat. *dispensare < dispendere,* to weigh out.] —**dis·pen'ser** *n.*

dis·perse (dĭ-spûrs') *v.* **-persed, -persing. 1.** To break up and scatter. **2.** To disseminate or distribute. [< Lat. *dispergere.*] —**dis·pers'i·ble** *adj.* —**dis·per'sion** or **dis·per'sal** *n.*

dis·pir·it (dĭ-spĭr'ĭt) *v.* To dishearten. [DI(S)- + SPIRIT.] —**dis·pir'it·ed·ly** *adv.*

dis·place (dĭs-plās') *v.* **1.** To remove from the usual place or position of. **2.** To take the place of; supplant. **3.** To cause a displacement of (e.g. a body).

dis·place·ment (dĭs-plās'mənt) *n.* **1.** The act of displacing. **2.** The weight or volume of a fluid displaced by a floating body. **3.** The distance from an initial position to a subsequent position assumed by a body.

dis·play (dĭ-splā') *v.* To put on view; exhibit. —*n.* **1.** The act of displaying. **2.** Something displayed. [< Lat. *displicare,* to scatter.]

dis·please (dĭs-plēz') *v.* To annoy or irritate. —**dis·pleas'ing·ly** *adv.* —**dis·pleas'ure** (-plĕzh'ər) *n.*

dis·port (dĭ-spôrt', -pôrt') *v.* To play; frolic. [< OFr. *desporter,* to divert.]

dis·pos·al (dĭs-pō'zəl) *n.* **1.** A particular order, distribution, or placement. **2.** The act of throwing out or away. **3.** An apparatus for getting rid of something. **4.** Administration; management. **5.** The act of transferring ownership by sale or gift. **6.** The power to use something.

dis·pose (dĭs-spōz') *v.* **-posed, -posing. 1.** To place in a particular order; arrange. **2.** To incline: *disposed to laughter.* —*phrasal verb.* **dispose of.** To get rid of, as by attending to or selling. [< Lat. *disponere.*] —**dis·pos'a·ble** (-spō'zə-bəl) *adj.* —**dis·pos'er** *n.*

dis·po·si·tion (dĭs'pə-zĭsh'ən) *n.* **1.** Temperament. **2.** A tendency or inclination. **3.** Arrangement or distribution. **4.** A final settlement. **5.** An act of disposing of.

   Syns: *disposition, humor, nature, temper, temperament* **n.**

dis·pos·sess (dĭs'pə-zĕs') *v.* To deprive of possession of, as land. —**dis'pos·ses'sion** *n.*

dis·praise (dĭs-prāz') *v.* To disparage. —*n.* Reproach.

dis·pro·por·tion (dĭs'prə-pôr'shən, -pōr'-) *n.* A lack of proper proportion or harmonious relationship. —**dis'pro·por'tion·al** or **dis'pro·por'tion·ate** *adj.* —**dis'pro·por'tion·al·ly** or **dis'pro·por'tion·ate·ly** *adv.*

dis·prove (dǐs-prōōv′) *v.* To prove to be false. —**dis·prov′al** *n.*

Syns: disprove, belie, discredit, rebut, refute *v.*

dis·pu·ta·tion (dǐs′pyōō-tā′shən) *n.* 1. An argument or debate. 2. An academic exercise consisting of an oral defense of a thesis.

dis·pu·ta·tious (dǐs′pyōō-tā′shəs) *adj.* Inclined to dispute; contentious. —**dis′pu·ta′tious·ly** *adv.* —**dis′pu·ta′tious·ness** *n.*

dis·pute (dǐs-spyōōt′) *v.* -put·ed, -put·ing. 1. To argue; debate. 2. To question the truth or validity of; doubt. 3. To strive against; oppose. —*n.* 1. An argument; debate. 2. A quarrel. [< Lat. *disputare*, to examine.] —**dis·put′a·ble** *adj.* —**dis·put′a·bly** *adv.* —**dis·pu′tant** *or* **dis·put′er** *n.*

dis·qual·i·fy (dǐs-kwŏl′ə-fī′) *v.* To declare or render unqualified. —**dis·qual′i·fi·ca′tion** *n.*

dis·qui·et (dǐs-kwī′ĭt) *v.* To make uneasy; trouble. —*n.* Disquietude. —**dis·qui′et·ing·ly** *adv.*

dis·qui·e·tude (dǐs-kwī′ĭ-tōōd′, -tyōōd′) *n.* A condition of worry or uneasiness.

dis·qui·si·tion (dǐs′kwĭ-zĭsh′ən) *n.* A formal discourse or treatise. [< Lat. *disquirere*, to investigate.]

dis·re·gard (dǐs′rĭ-gärd′) *v.* To pay no attention to; ignore. —*n.* A lack of regard, esp. when willful. —**dis′re·gard′ful** *adj.*

dis·re·pair (dǐs′rĭ-pâr′) *n.* The condition of being in need of repairs.

dis·rep·u·ta·ble (dǐs-rĕp′yə-tə-bəl) *adj.* Not respectable in character, action, or appearance. —**dis·rep′u·ta·bly** *adv.*

dis·re·pute (dǐs′rĭ-pyōōt′) *n.* Absence or loss of reputation; disgrace.

dis·re·spect (dǐs′rĭ-spĕkt′) *n.* Lack of respect; rudeness. —**dis′re·spect′ful** *adj.* —**dis′re·spect′ful·ly** *adv.*

dis·robe (dǐs-rōb′) *v.* -robed, -rob·ing. To undress.

dis·rupt (dǐs-rŭpt′) *v.* 1. To throw into confusion. 2. To break apart. [Lat. *disrumpere*, to break apart.] —**dis·rupt′er** *or* **dis·rup′tor** *n.* —**dis·rup′tion** *n.* —**dis·rup′tive** *adj.*

dis·sat·is·fac·tion (dǐs-săt′ĭs-făk′shən) *n.* Discontent.

dis·sat·is·fy (dǐs-săt′ĭs-fī′) *v.* To fail to meet the expectations or desires of; disappoint.

dis·sect (dǐ-sĕkt′, dī-, dī′sĕkt′) *v.* 1. To cut apart or separate (tissue), esp. for anatomical study. 2. To analyze in minute detail. [Lat. *dissecare*, to cut apart.] —**dis·sec′tion** *n.*

dis·sem·ble (dǐ-sĕm′bəl) *v.* -bled, -bling. 1. To disguise the real nature of. 2. To simulate; feign. [< OFr. *dessembler*, to be different.] —**dis·sem′bler** *n.*

dis·sem·i·nate (dǐ-sĕm′ə-nāt′) *v.* -nat·ed, -nat·ing. To spread widely; distribute. [Lat. *disseminare*.] —**dis·sem′i·na′tion** *n.* —**dis·sem′i·na′tor** *n.*

dis·sen·sion (dǐ-sĕn′shən) *n.* A difference of opinion, esp. one that causes strife within a group. [< Lat. *dissentire*, to dissent.]

dis·sent (dǐ-sĕnt′) *v.* 1. To disagree; differ. 2. To withhold assent. —*n.* 1. Difference of opinion. 2. The refusal to conform to the authority or doctrine of an established church. [< Lat. *dissentire*.] —**dis·sent′er** *n.*

dis·ser·ta·tion (dǐs′ər-tā′shən) *n.* A treatise,

esp. one written as a doctoral thesis. [< Lat. *dissertare*, to converse < *disserere*.]

dis·serv·ice (dǐs-sûr′vĭs) *n.* A harmful action.

dis·si·dent (dǐs′ĭ-dənt) *adj.* Disagreeing, as in opinion or belief. —*n.* One who disagrees; dissenter. [< Lat. *dissidēre*, to disagree.] —**dis′si·dence** *n.*

dis·sim·i·lar (dǐ-sǐm′ə-lər) *adj.* Unlike; distinct. —**dis·sim′i·lar′i·ty** (-lâr′ə-tē) *n.* —**dis·sim′i·lar·ly** *adv.*

dis·si·mil·i·tude (dǐs′ə-mǐl′ĭ-tōōd′, -tyōōd′) *n.* Difference; dissimilarity.

dis·sim·u·late (dǐ-sǐm′yə-lāt′) *v.* -lat·ed, -lat·ing. To disguise under a feigned appearance; dissemble. [< Lat. *dissimulare*.] —**dis·sim′u·la′tion** *n.* —**dis·sim′u·la′tor** *n.*

dis·si·pate (dǐs′ə-pāt′) *v.* -pat·ed, -pat·ing. 1. To break up and drive away. 2. To waste; squander. 3. To vanish; disappear. 4. To indulge in extravagant pursuit of pleasure. [< Lat. *dissipare*.] —**dis′si·pat′ed** *adj.* —**dis·si·pa′tion** *n.*

dis·so·ci·ate (dǐ-sō′shē-āt′, -sē-) *v.* -at·ed, -at·ing. To separate. [Lat. *dissociare*.] —**dis·so′ci·a′tion** *n.* —**dis·so′ci·a′tive** *adj.*

dis·so·lute (dǐs′ə-lōōt′) *adj.* Lacking in moral restraint; wanton. [< Lat. *dissolutus*, p.p. of *dissolvere*, to dissolve.] —**dis′so·lute′ly** *adv.* —**dis′so·lute′ness** *n.*

dis·so·lu·tion (dǐs′ə-lōō′shən) *n.* 1. Decomposition; disintegration. 2. Termination or extinction by dispersion. 3. Death. 4. Termination of a legal bond. 5. Formal dismissal of an assembly. 6. Reduction to a liquid form; liquefaction.

dis·solve (dǐ-zŏlv′) *v.* -solved, -solv·ing. 1. To enter or cause to enter into solution. 2. To melt. 3. To dispel. 4. To break into component parts. 5. To terminate or dismiss. 6. To collapse emotionally. [< Lat. *dissolvere*.] —**dis·solv′a·ble** *adj.* —**dis·solv′er** *n.*

dis·so·nance (dǐs′ə-nəns) *n.* 1. Discord. 2. *Mus.* A combination of tones that sounds harsh and is often suggestive of an unrelieved tension. [< Lat. *dissonare*, to be dissonant.] —**dis′so·nant** *adj.* —**dis′so·nant·ly** *adv.*

dis·suade (dǐ-swād′) *v.* -suad·ed, -suad·ing. To discourage or deter from a purpose or course of action. [Lat. *dissuadēre*.] —**dis·sua′sion** (-swā′zhən) *n.* —**dis·sua′sive** *adj.*

dis·taff (dǐs′tăf′) *n.* 1. A staff having a cleft end that holds flax, wool, etc. in spinning. 2. Women in general. —*adj.* Female. [< OE *distæf.*]

distaff side *n.* The maternal branch of a family.

dis·tal (dǐs′təl) *adj.* Anatomically located far from the origin or line of attachment, as a bone. [DIST(ANT) + -AL.]

dis·tance (dǐs′təns) *n.* 1. Separation in space or time. 2. The length of a line segment joining two points. 3. The interval separating any two specified instants in time. 4. a. The degree of deviation or difference that separates two things in relationship. b. The degree of progress between two points in a trend or course. 5. Coldness; aloofness. 6. The whole way: *go the distance.* —*v.* -tanced, -tanc·ing. To outrun; outstrip.

dis·tant (dǐs′tənt) *adj.* 1. Separate in space or time. 2. Far removed. 3. Located at, coming from, or going to a distance. **4.** Remote in relationship: *a distant cousin.* **5.** Aloof; cold. [< Lat. *distare*, to be remote.] **—dis'tant·ly** *adv.*

dis·taste (dĭs-tāst') *n.* Dislike.

dis·taste·ful (dĭs-tāst'fəl) *adj.* Unpleasant; disagreeable. **—dis·taste'ful·ly** *adv.* **—dis·taste'ful·ness** *n.*

dis·tem·per (dĭs-tĕm'pər) *n.* A contagious, often fatal virus disease occurring in dogs and certain other mammals.

dis·tend (dĭ-stĕnd') *v.* To expand or swell. [< Lat. *distendere.*] **—dis·ten'si·ble** *adj.* **—dis·ten'tion** or **dis·ten'sion** *n.*

dis·till (dĭ-stĭl') *v.* **1.** To subject to or derive by means of distillation. **2.** To separate from. **3.** To exude in drops. [< Lat. *distillare*, to trickle.] **—dis·till'er** *n.* **—dis·till'er·y** *n.*

dis·til·late (dĭs'tə-lāt', -lĭt, dĭ-stĭl'ĭt) *n.* The liquid condensed from vapor in distillation.

dis·til·la·tion (dĭs'tə-lā'shən) *n.* Any of several processes in which a complex mixture or substance is broken up into relatively pure or individual components by being heated until the components vaporize one by one and are made to condense individually.

dis·tinct (dĭ-stĭngkt') *adj.* **1.** Individual; separate. **2.** Easily perceived; clear. **3.** Explicit; unquestionable: *a distinct disadvantage.* [< Lat. *distinctus*, p.p. of *distinguere*, to distinguish.] **—dis·tinct'ly** *adv.* **—dis·tinct'ness** *n.*

dis·tinc·tion (dĭ-stĭngk'shən) *n.* **1.** The act of distinguishing; differentiation. **2.** A difference. **3.** A distinguishing factor or characteristic. **4.** Excellence or eminence. **5.** Honor: *graduate with distinction.*

dis·tinc·tive (dĭ-stĭngk'tĭv) *adj.* Serving to distinguish or set apart from others. **—dis·tinc'tive·ly** *adv.* **—dis·tinc'tive·ness** *n.*

dis·tin·guish (dĭ-stĭng'gwĭsh) *v.* **1.** To recognize as being distinct. **2.** To perceive distinctly; discern. **3.** To discriminate. **4.** To set apart. **5.** To make eminent. [< Lat. *distinguere.*] **—dis·tin'guish·a·ble** *adj.* **—dis·tin'guish·a·bly** *adv.*

dis·tin·guished (dĭ-stĭng'gwĭsht) *adj.* **1.** Characterized by excellence or distinction; eminent. **2.** Dignified in conduct or appearance.

dis·tort (dĭ-stôrt') *v.* **1.** To twist out of a proper or natural shape. **2.** To give a false account of; misrepresent. [< Lat. *distorquere.*] **—dis·tor'tion** *n.*

dis·tract (dĭ-străkt') *v.* **1.** To sidetrack; divert. **2.** To upset emotionally; unsettle. [< Lat. *distrahere*, to pull away.] **—dis·tract'ing·ly** *adv.* **—dis·trac'tion** *n.*

dis·traught (dĭ-strôt') *adj.* **1.** Anxious or agitated; harried. **2.** Crazed; mad. [< ME *distract*, p.p. of *distracten*, to distract.]

dis·tress (dĭ-strĕs') *n.* **1.** Pain or suffering of mind or body. **2.** Severe psychological strain. **3.** The condition of being in need of immediate assistance. **—v.** To cause anxiety or suffering to. [< Lat. *districtus*, p.p. of *distringere*, to draw tight.] **—dis·tress'ing·ly** *adv.*

Syns: *distress, agony, anguish, hurt, misery, pain, woe* n.

dis·trib·ute (dĭ-strĭb'yŏŏt) *v.* **-ut·ed, -ut·ing.** **1.** To divide and give out in portions. **2.** To hand out; deliver. **3.** To spread or scatter over an area. **4.** To market, esp. as a wholesaler. **5.** To classify. [< Lat. *distribuere.*] **—dis·tri·bu'tion** *n.* **—dis·trib'u·tive** *adj.*

dis·trib·u·tor (dĭ-strĭb'yə-tər) *n.* **1.** One that

distributes. **2.** A device that applies electric current to the spark plugs of an engine.

dis·trict (dĭs'trĭkt) *n.* **1.** A part of a geographic unit marked out by law for a particular purpose. **2.** A distinctive area: *the lake district.* **—v.** To divide into districts. [< Med. Lat. *districtus*, area of jurisdiction < Lat. *distringere*, to hinder.]

district attorney *n.* The prosecuting attorney of a given judicial district.

dis·trust (dĭs-trŭst') *n.* Lack of trust; suspicion. **—v.** To lack confidence in. **—dis·trust'ful** *adj.* **—dis·trust'ful·ly** *adv.* **—dis·trust'ful·ness** *n.*

Syns: *distrust, doubt, mistrust, suspicion* n.

dis·turb (dĭ-stûrb') *v.* **1.** To destroy the tranquillity or settled condition of. **2.** To trouble emotionally or mentally. **3.** To intrude upon; interrupt. **4.** To disarrange. [< Lat. *disturbare.*] **—dis·turb'ance** *n.* **—dis·turb'er** *n.* **—dis·turb'ing·ly** *adv.*

dis·u·nite (dĭs'yŏŏ-nīt') *v.* To separate; divide.

dis·u·ni·ty (dĭs-yŏŏ'nĭ-tē) *n.* Lack of unity; dissension.

dis·use (dĭs-yŏŏs') *n.* The condition of being no longer in use.

ditch (dĭch) *n.* A trench dug in the ground. **—v.** **1.** To dig or make a ditch in or around. **2.** To drive (a vehicle) into a ditch. **3.** *Slang.* To discard. [< OE *dīc.*]

dith·er (dĭth'ər) *n.* A condition of agitation or indecision. [< ME *didderen*, to tremble.]

dit·to (dĭt'ō) *n., pl.* **-tos.** **1.** The same as stated above or before. **2.** The pair of small marks (") used as a symbol for the word *ditto.* **3.** A duplicate or copy. [Dial. Ital., said.]

dit·ty (dĭt'ē) *n., pl.* **-ties.** A short, simple song. [< Lat. *dictatum*, p.p. of *dictare*, to dictate.]

di·u·ret·ic (dī'ə-rĕt'ĭk) *adj.* Tending to increase the discharge of urine. [< Gk. *diourētikos < diourein*, to urinate.] **—di'u·ret'ic** *n.*

di·ur·nal (dī-ûr'nəl) *adj.* **1.** Pertaining to or occurring in a day or each day; daily. **2.** Occurring or active during the daytime rather than at night. [< Lat. *diurnus.*] **—di·ur'nal·ly** *adv.*

di·va (dē'və) *n., pl.* **-vas** or **-ve** (-vā'). An operatic prima donna. [Ital. < Lat., goddess.]

di·va·gate (dī'və-gāt', dĭv'ə-) *v.* **-gat·ed, -gat·ing.** To wander or drift about. [LLat. *divagari.*] **—di'va·ga'tion** *n.*

di·van (dī'văn, dĭ-văn') *n.* A long couch; sofa. [< Turk.]

dive (dīv) *v.* **dived** or **dove** (dōv), **dived, div·ing.** **1.** To plunge headfirst into water. **2.** To submerge: *dive for pearls.* **3.** To fall or drop sharply and rapidly; plummet. **4.** To lunge,

dive
Diver

leap, or dash. **5.** To plunge into a question or activity. —*n.* **1.** An act or instance of diving. **2.** A quick, pronounced drop. **3.** *Slang.* A disreputable or run-down bar or nightclub. [< OE *dȳfan,* to dip.] —**div'er** *n.*

di·verge (dǐ-vûrj', dī-) *v.* **-verged, -verg·ing. 1.** To extend in different directions from a common point. **2.** To differ, as in opinion. **3.** To deviate, as from a norm. [LLat. *divergere,* to turn aside.] —**di·ver'gence** *n.* —**di·ver'gent** *adj.*

di·vers (dī'vərz) *adj.* Various; sundry.

di·verse (dǐ-vûrs', dī-, dī'vûrs') *adj.* **1.** Distinct in kind; unlike. **2.** Having variety in form; diversified. [< Lat. *diversus.*] —**di·verse'ness** *adv.* —**di·verse'ness** *n.*

di·ver·si·fy (dǐ-vûr'sə-fī', dī-) *v.* **-fied, -fy·ing. 1.** To make diverse; vary. **2.** To spread out activities or investments, esp. in business. —**di·ver'si·fi·ca'tion** (-fǐ-kā'shən) *n.*

di·ver·sion (dǐ-vûr'zhən, -shən, dī-) *n.* **1.** An act or instance of diverting. **2.** Something that diverts; distraction or pastime. —**di·ver'sion·ar'y** (-zhə-nĕr'ē) *adj.*

di·ver·si·ty (dǐ-vûr'sǐ-tē, dī-) *n., pl.* **-ties. 1.** The fact or quality of being diverse; difference. **2.** Variety; multiformity.

di·vert (dǐ-vûrt', dī-) *v.* **1.** To turn aside from a course or direction. **2.** To distract. **3.** To amuse or entertain. [< Lat. *divertere.*]

di·ver·ti·men·to (dǐ-vûr'tə-mĕn'tō) *n., pl.* **-tos** or **-ti** (-tē). An instrumental chamber work, usu. with several short movements. [Ital.]

di·vest (dǐ-vĕst', dī-) *v.* **1.** To strip, as of clothes. **2.** To deprive, as of rights; dispossess. [< OFr. *desvestir,* to undress.]

di·vide (dǐ-vīd') *v.* **-vid·ed, -vid·ing. 1.** To separate or become separated into parts, sections, or groups. **2.** To classify. **3.** To set at odds; disunite. **4.** To cause to be separate from; cut off. **5.** To distribute among a number; apportion. **6.** *Math.* **a.** To subject to the process of division. **b.** To be an exact divisor of. **7.** To branch out. —*n.* A watershed. [< Lat. *dividere.*] —**di·vid'a·ble** *adj.*

div·i·dend (dǐv'ǐ-dĕnd') *n.* **1.** A quantity to be divided. **2.** A share of profits received by a stockholder. **3.** *Informal.* A bonus. [< Lat. *dividendum,* thing to be divided.]

di·vid·er (dǐ-vī'dər) *n.* **1.** One that divides, esp. a partition. **2. dividers.** A device resembling a compass, used for dividing lines and transferring measurements.

div·i·na·tion (dǐv'ə-nā'shən) *n.* **1.** The art or act of foretelling future events or revealing occult knowledge by means of augury or alleged supernatural agency. **2.** Inspired insight or intuition.

di·vine[1] (dǐ-vīn') *adj.* **-vin·er, -vin·est. 1.** Being or having the nature of a deity. **2.** Of or relating to a deity. **3.** Superhuman; godlike. **4.** Supremely good; magnificent. —*n.* **1.** A clergyman. **2.** A theologian. [< Lat. *divinus.*] —**di·vine'ly** *adv.*

di·vine[2] (dǐ-vīn') *v.* **-vined, -vin·ing. 1.** To foretell or prophesy. **2.** To guess, infer, or conjecture. [< Lat. *divinare.*] —**di·vin'er** *n.*

divining rod *n.* A forked rod that allegedly indicates underground water or minerals by bending downward when held over a source.

di·vin·i·ty (dǐ-vǐn'ǐ-tē) *n., pl.* **-ties. 1.** The state or quality of being divine. **2. Divinity.** God. **3.** Theology.

di·vis·i·ble (dǐ-vǐz'ə-bəl) *adj.* Capable of being divided. —**di·vis'i·bil'i·ty** *n.*

di·vi·sion (dǐ-vǐzh'ən) *n.* **1.** The act or process of dividing or the state of being divided. **2.** Something that serves to divide or separate. **3.** One of the parts, sections, or groups into which something is divided. **4.** A self-contained military unit smaller than a corps. **5.** Disagreement; disunion. **6.** *Math.* The operation of determining how many times one quantity is contained in another. [< Lat. *dividere,* to divide.] —**di·vi'sion·al** *adj.*

di·vi·sive (dǐ-vī'sǐv) *adj.* Creating or tending to create discord or dissension. —**di·vi'sive·ly** *adv.* —**di·vi'sive·ness** *n.*

di·vi·sor (dǐ-vī'zər) *n.* The quantity by which another, the dividend, is to be divided.

di·vorce (dǐ-vôrs', -vōrs') *n.* **1.** The legal dissolution of a marriage. **2.** A complete separation. [< Lat. *divortium,* separation.] —**di·vorce'** *v.*

di·vor·cée (dǐ-vôr-sā', -sē', -vōr-, -vôr'sā', -sē', -vôr'-) *n.* A divorced woman. [Fr.]

div·ot (dǐv'ət) *n.* A piece of turf torn up by a golf club in striking the ball. [Sc.]

di·vulge (dǐ-vǔlj') *v.* **-vulged, -vulg·ing.** To disclose; reveal. [< Lat. *divulgare,* to publish.]

Dix·ie (dǐk'sē) *n.* The Southern states, esp. those that joined the Confederacy. [< *Dixie,* a song by Daniel D. Emmett (1815–1904).]

Dix·ie·land (dǐk'sē-lǎnd') *n.* A style of instrumental jazz characterized by a two-beat rhythm and improvisation.

diz·zy (dǐz'ē) *adj.* **-zi·er, -zi·est. 1.** Having a whirling sensation. **2.** Producing or produced by giddiness. **3.** *Informal.* Scatterbrained; silly. [< OE *dysig,* foolish.] —**diz'zi·ly** *adv.* —**diz'zi·ness** *n.* —**diz'zy** *v.*

DNA (dē'ĕn-ā') *n.* A nucleic acid that is the main constituent of the chromosomes of living cells, consisting of two long chains of phosphate and sugar units twisted into a double helix and joined by hydrogen bonds in a sequence that determines individual heredity characteristics. [D(EOXYRIBO)N(UCLEIC) A(CID).]

DNA
Model of DNA molecule showing
the double helix configuration of
two long chains joined by
hydrogen bonds.

do¹ (dōō) *v.* **did** (dĭd), **done** (dŭn), **do·ing, does** (dŭz). **1.** To perform or execute. **2.** To fulfill; complete. **3.** To produce: *did some sketches.* **4.** To bring about; effect. **5.** To put into action; exert. **6.** To deal with so as to prepare: *did the dishes.* **7.** To render: *did me a big favor.* **8.** To work at: *What do you do?* **9.** To work out; solve: *did a math problem.* **10.** To have the role of; play. **11.** To travel (through), esp. as a tourist. **12.** To meet the needs of sufficiently; suit. **13.** *Informal.* To serve out in prison. **14.** *Slang.* To cheat or swindle: *did him out of his inheritance.* **15.** To behave; act: *Do as you are told.* **16.** To decorate. **17.** To get along; fare: *doing well.* **18.** To be adequate. —*aux.* Used: **1.** In questions, negative statements, and inverted phrases: *Do you understand? I did not sleep well. Little did he suspect.* **2.** As a substitute for an antecedent verb: *She tries as hard as they do.* **3.** For emphasis: *I do want to be sure.* —**phrasal verbs. do away with. 1.** To dispose of; eliminate. **2.** To destroy; kill. **do in.** *Slang.* **1.** To tire completely; exhaust. **2.** To kill. —*n., pl.* **do's** or **dos.** A statement of what should be done: *do's and don'ts.* [< OE *dōn.*]

do² (dō) *n., pl.* **dos.** *Mus.* The first tone of the diatonic scale. [Ital.]

dob·bin (dŏb'ĭn) *n.* A horse, esp. a work-horse. [< *Dobbin,* nickname for *Robert.*]

Do·ber·man pin·scher (dō'bər-mən pĭn'shər) *n.* A fairly large dog of a breed originating in Germany, with a smooth, short-haired coat. [G. *Dobermann* < Ludwig *Dobermann,* 19th-cent. German dog breeder) + G. *Pinscher,* terrier.]

do·bra (dō'brə) *n.* See table at **currency.** [Port.]

do·cent (dō'sənt, dō-sĕnt') *n.* A teacher or lecturer who is not a regular faculty member. [Obs. G. < Lat. *docēre,* to teach.]

doc·ile (dŏs'əl, -īl') *adj.* Easily managed or taught; tractable. [Lat. *docilis* < *docēre,* to teach.] —**doc·il'i·ty** (dŏ-sĭl'ĭ-tē, dō-) *n.*

dock¹ (dŏk) *n.* **1.** The area of water between two piers or alongside a pier that receives a ship. **2.** A pier or wharf. **3.** A wharflike loading platform. —*v.* **1.** To maneuver into or next to a dock. **2.** To couple (two or more spacecraft) in space. [MDu. *docke.*]

dock² (dŏk) *v.* **1.** To clip short or cut off. **2.** To withhold a part of; deduct. [ME *dok.*]

dock³ (dŏk) *n.* An enclosed place where the defendant stands or sits in a criminal court. [Flem. *docke,* cage.]

dock⁴ (dŏk) *n.* A weedy plant with clusters of small, usu. greenish flowers. [< OE *docce.*]

dock·age (dŏk'ĭj) *n.* **1.** A charge for docking privileges. **2.** Facilities for docking vessels.

dock·et (dŏk'ĭt) *n.* **1. a.** A brief entry of the proceedings in a court of justice. **b.** The book containing such entries. **c.** A calendar of the cases awaiting court action. **2.** A list of things to be done; agenda. **3.** A label on a package listing contents or directions. [ME *doggett.*] —**dock'et** *v.*

dock·hand (dŏk'hănd') *n.* A longshoreman.

dock·yard (dŏk'yärd') *n.* A shipyard.

doc·tor (dŏk'tər) *n.* **1.** One trained in the healing arts, esp. a physician, surgeon, dentist, or veterinarian. **2.** One holding the highest academic degree awarded by a college or university. —*v.* **1.** To give medical treatment to. **2.** To practice medicine. **3.** To repair, esp. in a makeshift manner. **4.** To alter or falsify.

5. To add ingredients to. [< Lat., teacher.] —**doc'tor·al** *adj.*

doc·tor·ate (dŏk'tər-ĭt) *n.* The degree or status of a doctor.

doc·tri·naire (dŏk'trə-nâr') *n.* One inflexibly attached to a practice or theory without regard to its practicality. [Fr.]

doc·trine (dŏk'trĭn) *n.* **1.** Something that is taught. **2.** A tenet; dogma. [< Lat. *doctrina,* teaching.] —**doc·tri'nal** *adj.*

doc·u·ment (dŏk'yə-mənt) *n.* A paper that provides evidence, information, or proof about something. [< Lat. *documentum,* lesson < *docēre,* to teach.] —**doc·u·ment'** (-mĕnt') *v.* —**doc'u·men·ta'tion** *n.*

doc·u·men·ta·ry (dŏk'yə-mĕn'tə-rē) *adj.* **1.** Of or pertaining to documents. **2.** Presenting facts objectively in artistic form: *a documentary film.* —**doc'u·men'ta·ry** *n.*

dod·der¹ (dŏd'ər) *v.* To shake or move shakily, as from age. [ME *daderen.*]

dod·der² (dŏd'ər) *n.* A parasitic vine with few leaves and small whitish flowers. [< MLG, yolk of an egg.]

dodge (dŏj) *v.* **dodged, dodg·ing.** **1.** To avoid by moving quickly aside. **2.** To evade by cunning, trickery, or deceit. **3.** To move aside quickly. —*n.* **1.** A quick move or shift. **2.** A clever or evasive trick; stratagem. **3.** A method; technique. [Orig. unknown.] —**dodg'er** *n.*

do·do (dō'dō) *n., pl.* **-does** or **-dos.** **1.** A large flightless bird extinct since the 17th cent. **2.** *Informal.* **a.** One who is hopelessly passé. **b.** A stupid person; simpleton. [Port. *doudo.*]

doe (dō) *n., pl.* **does** or **doe.** The female of a deer or of certain other animals, such as the hare. [< OE *dā.*]

do·er (dōō'ər) *n.* One that does, esp. an active and energetic person.

does (dŭz) *v.* 3rd person sing. present tense of **do¹.**

doe·skin (dō'skĭn') *n.* **1.** Soft leather made from the skin of a doe. **2.** A soft, napped woolen fabric.

does·n't (dŭz'ənt). Does not.

do·est (dōō'ĭst) *v. Archaic.* 2nd person sing. present tense of **do¹.**

do·eth (dōō'əth) *v. Archaic.* 3rd person sing. present tense of **do¹.**

doff (dŏf, dôf) *v.* **1.** To take off: *doffed his clothes.* **2.** To lift or tip (one's hat). **3.** To discard. [< ME *don off,* to do off.]

dog (dôg, dŏg) *n.* **1. a.** A domesticated carnivorous mammal related to wolves and foxes. **b.** The male of such an animal. **2.** *Informal.* A fellow: *a lucky dog.* **3.** *Informal.* An inferior product or creation. **4.** A contemptible person. **5.** A metallic device used to grip or hold heavy objects. —*v.* **dogged, dog·ging.** **1.** To track or trail persistently. **2.** To hound; harry. [< OE *docga.*] —**dog'gy** *adj.*

dog·bane (dôg'bān', dŏg'-) *n.* Any of a genus of usu. poisonous plants with milky juice.

dog·cart (dôg'kärt', dŏg'-) *n.* A one-horse vehicle for two persons seated back to back.

dog·catch·er (dôg'kăch'ər, -kĕch'-, dŏg'-) *n.* One appointed or elected to impound stray dogs.

doge (dōj) *n.* The elected chief magistrate of the former republics of Venice and Genoa. [< dial. Ital. < Lat. *dux,* leader.]

dog-ear (dôg'ĭr', dŏg'-) *n.* A turned-down

corner of the page of a book. —**dog'-eared'** *adj.*

dog-fight (dôg'fīt', dŏg'-) *n.* A battle involving two or more fighter planes at close quarters.

dog-fish (dôg'fĭsh', dŏg'-) *n.* Any of various small sharks.

dog-ged (dô'gĭd, dŏg'ĭd) *adj.* Not yielding readily; stubbornly tenacious. —**dog'ged-ly** *adv.* —**dog'ged-ness** *n.*

dog-ger-el (dô'gər-əl, dŏg'ər-) *n.* Light verse in a loose, irregular rhythm. [ME. worthless.]

dog-gy or **dog-gie** (dô'gē, dŏg'ē) *n., pl.* **-gies.** A dog, esp. a small one.

dog-house (dôg'hous', dŏg'-) *n.* A shelter for a dog. —**idiom. in the doghouse.** *Slang.* In disfavor.

do-gie (dō'gē) *n.* *Western U.S.* A motherless or stray calf. [Orig. unknown.]

dog-leg (dôg'lĕg', dŏg'-) *n.* An abrupt or sharp angle or bend. —**dog'leg** *v.*

dog-ma (dôg'mə, dŏg'-) *n.* **1.** A system of doctrines proclaimed by a church. **2.** A principle or system of principles. [< Gk., opinion < *dokein*, to seem.]

dog-mat-ic (dôg-măt'ĭk, dŏg-) *adj.* Marked by an authoritarian, often arrogant assertion of principles. —**dog-mat'i-cal-ly** *adv.*

dog-ma-tism (dôg'mə-tĭz'əm, dŏg'-) *n.* Dogmatic assertion of opinion or belief.

dog-tooth violet (dôg'tōōth', dŏg'-) *n.* Any of several plants with nodding, lilylike yellow flowers.

dog-trot (dôg'trŏt', dŏg'-) *n.* A steady trot.

dog-wood (dôg'wŏŏd', dŏg'-) *n.* A tree with small greenish flowers surrounded by showy white or pink petallike bracts.

doi-ly (doi'lē) *n., pl.* **-lies.** A small ornamental mat. [< *Doyly* or *Doily*, an 18th-cent. London draper.]

do-ings (dōō'ĭngz) *pl.n.* Activities, esp. social activities.

do-it-your-self (dōō'ĭt-yər-sĕlf') *adj.* *Informal.* Of, pertaining to, or designed to be done by an amateur or as a hobby.

dol-drums (dōl'drəmz', dŏl'-, dōl'-) *n.* (*used with a sing. verb*). **1.** Ocean regions near the equator, marked by calms. **2. a.** A period of listlessness or depression. **b.** A period of inactivity or recession. [< obs. *doldrum*, dullard.]

dole (dōl) *n.* **1. a.** The distribution esp. of money, food, or clothing to the poor. **b.** Something so distributed. **2.** *Chiefly Brit.* Government distribution of relief payments to the unemployed. —*v.* **doled, dol-ing. 1.** To distribute to the poor. **2.** To distribute in small portions: *doled out rice.* [< OE *dāl*, portion.]

dole-ful (dōl'fəl) *adj.* Mournful; sad. —**dole'-ful-ly** *adv.* —**dole'ful-ness** *n.*

doll (dŏl) *n.* **1.** A figure representing a human being, used esp. as a child's toy. **2.** *Slang.* **a.** A pretty woman. **b.** An attractive person. —*v.* *Slang.* To dress up smartly. [< *Doll,* nickname for *Dorothy.*]

dol-lar (dŏl'ər) *n.* See table at **currency.** [< LG *daler,* a silver coin.]

dol-lop (dŏl'əp) *n.* A lump, helping, or portion, as of ice cream. [Orig. unknown.]

dol-ly (dŏl'ē) *n., pl.* **-lies.** **1.** A doll. **2.** A low mobile platform that rolls on casters. **3.** A

wheeled apparatus used to move a motion-picture or television camera.

dol-men (dōl'mən, dŏl'-) *n.* A prehistoric structure consisting of two or more upright stones supporting a horizontal slab. [Fr.]

dol-o-mite (dō'lə-mīt', dŏl'ə-) *n.* A magnesia-rich sedimentary rock resembling limestone. [< Déodat de *Dolomieu* (1705–1801).]

do-lor (dō'lər, dŏl'ər) *n.* Anguish; sorrow. [< Lat., pain.] —**do'lor-ous** *adj.* —**do'lor-ous-ly** *adv.* —**do'lor-ous-ness** *n.*

dol-phin (dŏl'fĭn, dôl'-) *n.* **1.** A marine mammal related to the whales but gen. smaller and with a beaklike snout. **2.** A marine fish with iridescent coloring. [< Gk. *delphis.*]

dolphin   **dome**

dolt (dōlt) *n.* A stupid person; blockhead. [Perh. < ME *dol,* dull.] —**dolt'ish** *adj.*

-dom *suff.* **1.** The condition of being: *bore-dom.* **2.** The domain, position, or rank of: *dukedom.* [< OE *-dōm.*]

do-main (dō-mān') *n.* **1.** A territory or range of control or rule. **2.** A sphere of interest or action; field. [< Lat. *dominium,* property.]

dome (dōm) *n.* **1.** A hemispheric roof or vault. **2.** Something resembling a dome. [< Lat. *domus,* house.]

do-mes-tic (də-mĕs'tĭk) *adj.* **1.** Of or pertaining to the family or household. **2.** Fond of home life and household affairs. **3.** Domesticated; tame. **4.** Of or pertaining to a country's internal affairs. **5.** Produced in or native to a particular country; indigenous. —*n.* A household servant. [< Lat. *domesticus* < *domus,* house.] —**do-mes'ti-cal-ly** *adv.*

do-mes-ti-cate (də-mĕs'tĭ-kāt') *v.* **-cat-ed, -cat-ing.** To adapt to life with and usefulness to human beings; tame. —**do-mes'ti-ca'tion** *n.*

do-mes-tic-i-ty (dō'mĕ-stĭs'ĭ-tē) *n., pl.* **-ties.** **1.** The quality or condition of being domestic. **2.** Home life or activities.

dom-i-cile (dŏm'ĭ-sīl', -səl, dō'mĭ-) *n.* A home, dwelling place, or legal residence. [< Lat. *domicilium.*] —**dom'i-cile'** *v.* —**dom'i-cil'i-ar-y** (-sĭl'ē-ĕr'ē) *adj.*

dom-i-nant (dŏm'ə-nənt) *adj.* **1.** Exercising the most influence or control. **2.** Pre-eminent in position. **3.** Producing the same phenotypic effect when paired with an identical or a dissimilar gene. —**dom'i-nance** *n.* —**dom'i-nant-ly** *adv.*

dom-i-nate (dŏm'ə-nāt') *v.* **-nat-ed, -nat-ing.** **1.** To control, govern, or rule. **2.** To occupy the pre-eminent position in or over. **3.** To overlook from a height. **4.** To be dominant in position or authority. [< Lat. *dominari.*] —**dom'i-na'tion** *n.* —**dom'i-na'tor** *n.*

dom-i-neer (dŏm'ə-nîr') *v.* **1.** To rule arrogantly; tyrannize. **2.** To be arrogant or tyrannical. [Du. *domineren*, ult. < Lat. *dominari*, to rule.]

do·min·ion (də-mĭn′yən) *n.* **1.** Control or the exercise of control; sovereignty. **2.** A sphere of influence or control; domain. **3.** Often **Dominion.** A self-governing nation within the British Commonwealth. [< Lat. *dominium*, property.]

dom·i·no¹ (dŏm′ə-nō′) *n., pl.* **-noes** or **-nos. 1. a.** A hooded robe worn with an eye mask at a masquerade. **b.** The mask itself. **2.** One wearing a domino. [< Lat. *benedicamus domino*, let us bless the Lord.]

dom·i·no² (dŏm′ə-nō′) *n., pl.* **-noes** or **-nos. 1.** A small, rectangular block marked with dots. **2. dominoes** (*used with a sing. verb*). A game played with dominoes. [< Lat.]

don¹ (dŏn) *n.* **1. Don.** Sir. A Spanish title formerly affixed to a Christian name. **2.** A Spanish gentleman. **3.** A tutor or fellow at a college of Oxford or Cambridge.

don² (dŏn) *v.* **donned, don·ning.** To put on (an article of clothing). [< *do on*.]

do·ña (dōn′yə) *n.* **1. Doña.** Lady. A Spanish title of courtesy used with a woman's given name. **2.** A Spanish gentlewoman.

do·nate (dō′nāt′, dō-nāt′) *v.* **-nated, -nating.** To give to a fund or cause; contribute. [< Lat. *donare*, to give.] —**do·na′tion** *n.* —**do′na·tor** *n.*

done (dŭn) *v.* *p.p.* of **do¹.** —*adj.* **1.** Completely accomplished or finished. **2.** Sufficiently cooked. **3.** Socially acceptable.

dong (dŏng, dông) *n.* See table at **currency.** [Vietnamese.]

don·key (dŏng′kē, dŭng′-, dông′-) *n., pl.* **-keys. 1.** The domesticated ass. **2.** An obstinate or stupid person. [Perh. DUN² + *-key* as in *monkey*.]

don·ny·brook (dŏn′ē-brŏŏk′) *n.* A brawl; free-for-all. [< *Donnybrook* fair, Ireland.]

do·nor (dō′nər) *n.* One who contributes, gives, or donates. [< Lat. *donator* < *donare*, to give.]

don't (dōnt). Do not.

do·nut (dō′nŭt′, -nət) *n.* Var. of **doughnut.**

doo·dad (dōō′dăd′) *n. Informal.* An unnamed or nameless gadget or trinket. [Orig. unknown.]

doo·dle (dōōd′l) *v.* **-dled, -dling.** To draw or scribble while preoccupied. [Dial. E., to waste time.] —**doo′dle** *n.*

doom (dōōm) *n.* **1.** A terrible and inescapable fate. **2.** Disaster; ruin. **3.** Condemnation to a severe penalty. —*v.* To condemn to ruination or death. [< OE *dōm.*]

dooms·day (dōōmz′dā′) *n.* The day of the Last Judgment. [< OE *dōmes dæg.*]

door (dôr, dōr) *n.* **1.** A movable panel used to open or close an entranceway. **2.** An entranceway to a room, building, or passage. **3.** A means of approach or access. [< OE *duru.*]

door·jamb (dôr′jăm′, dōr′-) *n.* Either of the two vertical pieces framing a doorway.

door·keep·er (dôr′kē′pər, dōr′-) *n.* One employed to guard an entrance or gateway.

door·knob (dôr′nŏb′, dōr′-) *n.* A handle for opening and closing a door.

door·man (dôr′măn′, -mən, dōr′-) *n.* One employed to attend the entrance of a building, as a hotel.

door·mat (dôr′măt′, dōr′-) *n.* A mat placed before a doorway for wiping the shoes.

door·step (dôr′stĕp′, dōr′-) *n.* A step leading to a door.

door·way (dôr′wā′, dōr′-) *n.* An entranceway.

door·yard (dôr′yärd′, dōr′-) *n.* A yard in front of or behind the door of a house.

dope (dōp) *n.* **1.** A usu. liquid preparation added to produce desired properties; additive. **2.** *Informal.* A narcotic or stimulant. **3.** *Slang.* A very stupid person. **4.** *Slang.* Factual information. —*v.* **doped, dop·ing. 1.** To add or apply dope to. **2.** *Informal.* To administer a narcotic to. **3.** *Informal.* To figure out (an outcome or puzzle). [Du. *doop*, sauce.]

dop·ey (dō′pē) *adj.* **-i·er, -i·est.** Also **dop·y.** *Slang.* **1.** Dazed or lethargic as if drugged. **2.** Stupid.

Dor·ic (dôr′ĭk, dōr′-) *n.* A dialect of ancient Greek spoken in the Peloponnese, southern Italy, Sicily, and some of the Aegean islands.

dorm (dôrm) *n. Informal.* A dormitory.

dor·mant (dôr′mənt) *adj.* **1.** In a state resembling sleep. **2.** In a state of suspended activity or development; inactive. [< Lat. *dormire*, to sleep.] —**dor′man·cy** *n.*

dor·mer (dôr′mər) *n.* A window set vertically in a gable projecting from a sloping roof. [OFr. *dormeor*, bedroom < *dormir*, to sleep.]

dor·mi·to·ry (dôr′mĭ-tôr′ē, -tōr′ē) *n., pl.* **-ries. 1.** A bedroom for a number of persons. **2.** A residence hall, as at a school. [< Lat. *dormire*, to sleep.]

dor·mouse (dôr′mous′) *n.* A small, squirrel-like Old World rodent. [ME *dormowse.*]

dor·sal (dôr′səl) *adj.* Of, toward, on, or in the back. [< Lat. *dorsum*, back.]

do·ry (dôr′ē, dōr′ē) *n., pl.* **-ries.** A flat-bottomed boat with high sides. [Mosquito *dóri.*]

dose (dōs) *n.* A specified quantity of a therapeutic agent to be administered or taken at one time or at stated intervals. —*v.* **dosed, dos·ing. 1.** To give a dose of medicine to. **2.** To give or prescribe in doses. [< Gk. *dosis* < *didonai*, to give.] —**dos′age** *n.*

do·sim·e·ter (dō-sĭm′ĭ-tər) *n.* A device that measures doses of x-rays or radioactivity.

dos·si·er (dŏs′ē-ā′, dô′sē-ā′) *n.* A file of documents pertaining to a particular person or subject. [< OFr., bundle of papers labeled on the back < *dos*, back.]

dost (dŭst) *v. Archaic.* 2nd person sing. present tense of **do¹.**

dot (dŏt) *n.* **1.** A round mark made by or as if by a pointed instrument; spot. **2.** A short sound or signal used in combination with the dash to represent letters or numbers in a code. **3.** *Mus.* A mark after a note indicating an increase in time value by half. —*v.* **dot·ted, dot·ting. 1.** To mark with a dot. **2.** To cover with or as if with dots: *Campfires dotted the night.* [< OE *dott*, head of a boil.]

dot·age (dō′tĭj) *n.* A condition of feeblemindedness, often caused by old age; senility. [< *dote.*]

dot·ard (dō′tərd) *n.* A senile person. [< ME *doten*, to dote.]

dote (dōt) *v.* **dot·ed, dot·ing. 1.** To be feebleminded, esp. from old age. **2.** To lavish excessive love. [ME *doten.*] —**dot′er** *n.*

doth (dŭth) *v. Archaic.* 2nd person sing. present tense of **do¹.**

dot·ty (dŏt′ē) *adj.* **-ti·er, -ti·est.** Eccentric; daft; crazy. [< ME *doten*, to dote.]

dou·ble (dŭb′əl) *adj.* **1.** Twice as much in size, strength, number, or amount. **2.** Composed of two parts or members. **3.** Twofold; dual. **4.** Designed for two: *a double bed.* **5. a.** Acting two parts: *a double agent.* **b.** Deceitful: *double talk.* **6.** Having numerous overlapping petals. —*adv.* **1. a.** To twice the extent; doubly. **b.** To twice the amount. **2.** Two together: *sleep double.* **3.** In two: *bent double in pain.* —*n.* **1.** Something increased twofold. **2.** A duplicate or counterpart. **3.** An actor's understudy. **4.** A sharp turn; reversal. **5.** **doubles.** A game, such as tennis, having two players on each side. **6.** *Baseball.* A two-base hit. **7.** *Bridge.* A bid doubling one's opponent's bid. —*v.* **1.** To make or become twice as great. **2.** To be twice as much as. **3.** To fold in two. **4.** *Baseball.* To make a two-base hit. **5.** *Bridge.* To challenge with a double. **6.** To turn sharply backward; reverse: *double back.* **7.** To serve in an additional capacity. [< Lat. *duplus.*] —**dou'bly** *adv.*

double bass *n.* The largest member of the violin family, shaped like a cello and having a low range.

double bass

dou·ble-cross (dŭb'əl-krôs', -krŏs') *v. Slang.* To betray by acting in contradiction to an agreed course of action. —**dou'ble-cross'** *n.* —**dou'ble-cross'er** *n.*

dou·ble-deal·ing (dŭb'əl-dē'lĭng) *n.* Treachery; duplicity. —**dou'ble-deal'er** *n.*

dou·ble-deck·er (dŭb'əl-dĕk'ər) *n.* **1.** Something, as a bus or bed, with two tiers or decks. **2.** A sandwich with two layers.

double-decker

dou·ble-en·ten·dre (dŭb'əl-än-tän'drə, dŏŏ-blän-tän'dr') *n.* A word or phrase with more than one interpretation, esp. when one is risqué. [Fr.]

dou·ble-head·er (dŭb'əl-hĕd'ər) *n.* Two

games or events held in succession on the same program, esp. in baseball.

dou·ble-joint·ed (dŭb'l-join'tĭd) *adj.* Having a flexible joint that facilitates unusual mobility of connected parts.

double negative *n.* A syntactic construction in which two negatives are used when only one should be, as in the sentence *He didn't say nothing.*

Usage: A *double negative* is considered unacceptable in standard usage. Formerly, however, such constructions occurred frequently in good writing for purposes of intensification or emphasis; an example is Hamlet's advice to the players: *"Be not too tame neither, but let your discretion be your tutor."*

double play *n. Baseball.* A play in which two players are put out.

double star *n.* A binary star.

dou·blet (dŭb'lĭt) *n.* **1.** A close-fitting jacket formerly worn by men. **2.** One of a pair of identical or similar things. [< OFr.]

double take *n.* A delayed reaction to an unusual remark or circumstance.

double talk *n.* Meaningless speech that consists of nonsense syllables mixed with intelligible words; gibberish.

dou·bloon (dŭ-blŏŏn') *n.* An obsolete Spanish gold coin. [Sp. *doblón.*]

doubt (dout) *v.* **1.** To be uncertain or skeptical (about). **2.** To distrust. —*n.* **1.** A lack of conviction or certainty. **2.** An uncertain condition; uncertainty. [< Lat. *dubitare.*] —**doubt'er** *n.*

Usage: *Doubt* often occurs in informal speech, both as a verb and noun, with *but: I don't doubt but* (or *but what) he'll come. There is no doubt but it will be difficult.* These usages should be avoided in formal style; substitute *that* or *whether* as the case requires.

doubt·ful (dout'fəl) *adj.* **1.** Causing doubt; uncertain. **2.** Experiencing or showing doubt; undecided. **3.** Of uncertain outcome. **4.** Questionable in character; suspicious. —**doubt'ful·ly** *adv.* —**doubt'ful·ness** *n.*

doubt·less (dout'lĭs) *adj.* Certain; assured. —*adv.* **1.** Certainly; assuredly. **2.** Presumably; probably. —**doubt'less·ly** *adv.*

douche (dōōsh) *n.* **1.** A stream of water or air applied to a bodily part or cavity for cleansing or medicinal purposes. **2.** The application of a douche. **3.** An instrument for applying a douche. [Fr., shower.]

dough (dō) *n.* **1.** A thick, pliable mixture of flour and other ingredients that can be rolled or kneaded, as to make pastry. **2.** A pasty mass similar to dough. **3.** *Slang.* Money. [< OE *dāg.*] —**dough'y** *adj.*

dough·boy (dō'boi') *n.* An American infantryman in World War I.

dough·nut (dō'nŭt', -nət) *n.* Also **do·nut.** A small, ring-shaped cake made of dough that is fried in deep fat.

dough·ty (dou'tē) *adj.* **-ti·er, -ti·est.** Stouthearted; courageous. [< OE *dohtig.*]

Doug·las fir (dŭg'ləs) *n.* A tall evergreen timber tree of northwestern North America.

dour (dŏŏr, dour) *adj.* **1.** Harsh; stern. **2.** Glum; sullen. [< Lat. *durus,* hard.]

douse (dous) *v.* **doused, dous·ing.** **1.** To

plunge into liquid; immerse. **2.** To wet thoroughly; drench. **3.** To put out; extinguish. [Perh. < obs. *douse,* to strike.]

dove¹ (dŭv) *n.* **1.** A pigeon or related bird, esp. an undomesticated species. **2.** One who advocates peace and conciliation. [< OE *dūfe.*]

dove² (dōv) *v.* A *p.t.* of **dive.**

dove·tail (dŭv′tāl′) *n.* A fan-shaped tenon that forms a tight interlocking joint when fitted into a corresponding mortise. —*v.* **1.** To join by means of dovetails. **2.** To combine or interlock into a unified whole.

dow·a·ger (dou′ə-jər) *n.* **1.** A widow with a title or property derived from her husband. **2.** An elderly woman of high social station. [< OFr. *douage,* dowry, ult. < Lat. *dos.*]

dow·dy (dou′dē) *adj.* -**di·er,** -**di·est.** Lacking in stylishness or neatness; shabby or untidy. [< ME *doude,* unattractive woman.]

dow·el (dou′əl) *n.* A usu. round pin that fits into a corresponding hole to fasten or align two adjacent pieces. [ME *doule,* part of a wheel.] —**dow′el** *v.*

dow·er (dou′ər) *n.* **1.** The part of a man's real estate allotted by law to his widow for her lifetime. **2.** A dowry. —*v.* To assign a dower to; endow. [< Lat. *dos.*]

down¹ (doun) *adv.* **1.** From a higher to a lower place. **2.** In or to a lower position, point, or condition. **3.** From an earlier to a later time. **4.** In partial payment at the time of purchase: *five dollars down.* **5.** Seriously or vigorously: *got down to work.* **6.** In writing; on paper: *took her statement down.* —*adj.* **1. a.** Moving or directed downward: *a down elevator.* **b.** In a low position; not up. **2. a.** Sick: *down with a cold.* **b.** Low in spirits; depressed. **3.** Being the first installment in a series of payments. —*prep.* In a descending direction upon, along, through, or into. —*n.* **1. a.** A downward movement; descent. **b.** A low or bad phase: *ups and downs.* **2.** Football. One of four plays during which a team must advance at least ten yards to retain the ball. —*v.* **1.** To come, bring, put, strike, or throw down. **2.** To swallow hastily. **3.** To defeat. [< OE *adūne.*]

down² (doun) *n.* **1.** Fine, soft, fluffy feathers. **2.** A soft covering or substance similar to down. [< ON *dūnn.*] —**down′y** *adj.*

down³ (doun) *n.* Often **downs.** A rolling, grassy upland area. [< OE *dūn.*]

down·beat (doun′bēt′) *n.* The downward stroke of a conductor indicating the first beat of a measure of music.

down·cast (doun′kăst′) *adj.* **1.** Directed downward: *downcast eyes.* **2.** Dejected; sad.

down·er (dou′nər) *n.* Slang. **1.** A depressant drug, esp. a barbiturate. **2.** A depressing experience.

down·fall (doun′fôl′) *n.* **1.** A sudden fall, as from high position; ruin. **2.** Something causing a downfall. **3.** A heavy, usu. sudden fall, as of rain. —**down′fall′en** *adj.*

down·grade (doun′grād′) *n.* A descending slope, as in a road. —*v.* To lower the status, importance, or reputation of.

down·heart·ed (doun′här′tĭd) *adj.* Low in spirit; discouraged.

down·hill (doun′hĭl′) *adv.* Down the slope of a hill. —**down′hill′** *adj.*

down·pour (doun′pôr′, -pōr′) *n.* A heavy fall of rain.

down·range (doun′rānj′) *adv. & adj.* In a di-

rection away from the launch site and along the flight line of a missile test range.

down·right (doun′rīt′) *adj.* **1.** Thorough; unequivocal: *a downright lie.* **2.** Frank; candid: *a downright answer.* —*adv.* Thoroughly; absolutely.

Down's syndrome (dounz) *n.* A congenital disorder characterized by moderate to severe mental retardation, a short, flattened skull, and slanting eyes. [< John L.H. *Down* (1828–96).]

down·stage (doun′stāj′) *adv. & adj.* Toward or at the front part of a stage.

down·stairs (doun′stârz′) *adv.* **1.** Down the stairs. **2.** To or on a lower floor. —**down′stairs′** *n.*

down·stream (doun′strēm′) *adv. & adj.* In the direction of a stream's current.

down·swing (doun′swĭng′) *n.* **1.** A swing downward; as of a golf club. **2.** A business decline.

down-to-earth (doun′tə-ûrth′) *adj.* Realistic; sensible.

down·town (doun′toun′) *adv.* To, toward, or in the lower part or the business center of a city or town. —*n.* (-toun′). The lower part or business center of a city or town. —**down′town′** *adj.*

down·trod·den (doun′trŏd′n) *adj.* Oppressed; tyrannized.

down·turn (doun′tûrn′) *n.* A tendency downward, esp. in business or economic activity.

down·ward (doun′wərd) *adv.* Also **downwards** (-wərdz). **1.** From a higher to a lower place, level, or condition. **2.** From an earlier to a more recent time. —**down′ward** *adj.*

down·wind (doun′wĭnd′) *adv. & adj.* In the direction in which the wind blows.

dow·ry (dou′rē) *n., pl.* -**ries.** Money or property brought by a bride to her husband. [< DOWER.]

dowse (douz) *v.* **dowsed, dows·ing.** To use a divining rod, esp. to search for water. [Orig. unknown.] —**dows′er** *n.*

dox·ol·o·gy (dŏk-sŏl′ə-jē) *n., pl.* -**gies.** A liturgical formula of praise to God. [< Gk. *doxologia,* praise.]

doze (dōz) *v.* **dozed, doz·ing.** To sleep lightly and intermittently. [Prob. of Scand. orig.] —**doze** *n.*

doz·en (dŭz′ən) *n., pl.* -**en** or -**ens.** A set of 12. —*adj.* Twelve. [< Lat. *duodecim,* twelve.] —**doz′enth** *adj.*

drab (drăb) *adj.* **drab·ber, drab·best. 1.** Of a light grayish or olive brown color. **2.** Dull; dreary. —*n.* A light grayish or olive brown. [< OFr. *drap,* cloth < LLat. *drappus.*] —**drab′ness** *n.*

drach·ma (drăk′mə) *n., pl.* -**mas** or -**mae** (-mē). **1.** See table at **currency. 2.** A silver coin of ancient Greece. [< Gk. *drakhmē,* a silver coin.]

Dra·co (drā′kō) *n.* A constellation in the polar region of the Northern Hemisphere.

draft (drăft, dräft). Also *chiefly Brit.* **draught** (drăft). —*n.* **1.** A current of air. **2.** A device in a flue controlling air circulation. **3. a.** A pull or traction of a load. **b.** The load pulled or drawn. **4.** A preliminary outline, plan, or picture; version. **5. a.** The selection of personnel from a group, esp. conscription for military service. **b.** The body of people so selected. **6. a.** A gulp, swallow, or inhalation. **b.** The amount taken in by such an act. **7.** A document for transferring money: *a bank* *draft.* 8. The depth of a vessel's keel below the water line. 9. A heavy demand on resources. —*v.* 1. To select from a group for a specific duty, as military service. 2. To draw up a preliminary plan for or version of. —*adj.* 1. Suited or used for drawing heavy loads. 2. Drawn from a cask or tap. [ME.] —**draft′er** *n.*

draft·ee (drăf-tē′, dräf-) *n.* One drafted for military service.

drafts·man (drăfts′mən, dräfts′-) *n.* One who draws plans or designs, as of buildings or machinery. —**drafts′man·ship′** *n.*

draft·y (drăf′tē, dräf′-) *adj.* -**i·er,** -**i·est.** Having or exposed to drafts of air. —**draft′i·ness** *n.*

drag (drăg) *v.* **dragged, drag·ging.** 1. To pull or draw along, esp. by force; haul. 2. To trail along the ground. 3. To search the bottom of (a body of water), as with a grappling hook. 4. To bring forcibly to or into. 5. To move slowly or with difficulty. 6. To lag behind. 7. To prolong tediously: *dragged the report out.* 8. *Slang.* To draw on a cigarette or pipe; puff. —*n.* 1. The act of dragging. 2. Something, as a harrow, dragged along a surface. 3. Something that retards motion or progress. 4. The force that tends to slow a body in motion through a fluid, as air or water. 5. *Slang.* One that is obnoxiously tiresome. 6. *Slang.* A puff, as on a cigarette. 7. *Slang.* A street or road: *the main drag.* 8. *Slang.* The clothing of one sex when worn by a homosexual member of the opposite sex. [< ON *draga.*] —**drag′ger** *n.*

drag·net (drăg′nĕt′) *n.* 1. A net, esp. one for trawling. 2. A system of procedures used to apprehend criminal suspects.

drag·o·man (drăg′ə-mən) *n., pl.* -**mans** or -**men.** An interpreter, as of Arabic, esp. in the Middle East. [< Ar. *targumān.*]

drag·on (drăg′ən) *n.* A fabulous monster usu. represented as a gigantic winged reptile with a lion's claws. [< Gk. *drakōn,* serpent.]

drag·on·fly (drăg′ən-flī′) *n.* A large, narrow-bodied, four-winged insect.

dra·goon (drə-gōōn′, drǎ-) *n.* A heavily armed mounted trooper. —*v.* To coerce by violent measures; harass. [< OFr. *dragon,* dragon.]

drag race *n.* An acceleration race between cars.

drain (drān) *v.* 1. To draw or flow off by a gradual process. 2. To make or become empty or dry. 3. To remove water through natural channels of (a tract of land). 4. To consume totally; exhaust. —*n.* 1. A pipe or channel by which liquid is drained off. 2. An act or instance of draining. 3. A strain or something that causes a strain; burden: *a drain on the national treasury.* [< OE *drēahnian.*] —**drain′er** *n.*

drain·age (drā′nĭj) *n.* 1. The action or a method of draining. 2. A system of drains. 3. Something that is drained off.

drain·pipe (drān′pīp′) *n.* A pipe for drainage.

drake (drāk) *n.* A male duck. [ME.]

dram (drăm) *n.* 1. **a.** A unit of avoirdupois weight equal to 27.344 grains, 0.0625 ounce, or 1.772 grams. **b.** A unit of apothecary weight equal to 60 grains. 2. A small drink, as of alcohol. [< Gk. *drakhmē,* a silver coin.]

dra·ma (drä′mə, drăm′ə) *n.* 1. A prose or verse composition, esp. one for performance by actors; play. 2. Plays of a given type or period. 3. A situation that involves conflicts and builds to a climax. [< Gk.] —**dra·mat′ic** (drə-măt′ĭk) *adj.* —**dra·mat′i·cal·ly** *adv.*

dram·a·tist (drăm′ə-tĭst, drä′mə-) *n.* A playwright.

dram·a·tize (drăm′ə-tīz′, drä′mə-) *v.* -**tized, -tiz·ing.** 1. To adapt for theatrical presentation. 2. To present or view in a dramatic or highly emotional way. —**dram′a·ti·za′tion** *n.*

drank (drăngk) *v.* *p.t.* of **drink.**

drape (drāp) *v.* **draped, drap·ing.** 1. To cover or hang with or as if with cloth in loose folds. 2. To arrange in loose, graceful folds. 3. To hang or rest limply: *draped his legs over the chair.* —*n.* 1. A drapery. 2. The way in which cloth falls or hangs. [< LLat. *drappus,* cloth, of Celt. orig.]

drap·er (drā′pər) *n.* *Chiefly Brit.* A dealer in cloth and dry goods.

drap·er·y (drā′pə-rē) *n., pl.* -**ies.** 1. Cloth arranged in loose folds. 2. Often **draperies.** A curtain that hangs straight in loose folds. 3. *Chiefly Brit.* The business of a draper.

dras·tic (drăs′tĭk) *adj.* Extreme or severe; radical. [Gk. *drastikos,* active < *dran,* to do.] —**dras′ti·cal·ly** *adv.*

draught (drăft) *n., v.,* & *adj. Chiefly Brit.* Var. of **draft.**

draughts (drăfts, dräfts) *n. (used with a sing. verb). Chiefly Brit.* The game of checkers. [< ME *draught,* a move at chess.]

Dra·vid·i·an (drə-vĭd′ē-ən) *n.* 1. A large non-Indo-European family of languages including Tamil and Malayalam. 2. One who speaks a Dravidian language. —**Dra·vid′i·an** *adj.*

draw (drô) *v.* **drew** (drōō), **drawn** (drôn), **draw·ing.** 1. **a.** To pull or move in a given direction or to a given position. **b.** To cause to move in a given direction: *drew us into the room.* 2. To take or pull out; extract. 3. **a.** To bring in; earn: *draw interest.* **b.** To withdraw (money). 4. To take in; inhale: *drew a deep sigh.* 5. To produce by marking a surface, as with a pen; sketch. 6. To elicit: *drew laughter.* 7. To receive on a regular basis: *draw a salary.* 8. To take or accept by chance or in a chance drawing: *draw lots.* 9. To attract; entice. 10. To deduce from evidence; formulate: *draw a conclusion.* 11. To eviscerate; disembowel. 12. To displace (a specified depth of water) in floating. 13. To induce to act. 14. To bring on; provoke: *drew enemy fire.* 15. To end (a game) in a draw; tie. 16. To write in set or proper form: *drew up the contract.* 17. To distort the shape of. 18. To proceed or move steadily: *The boat drew near the shore.* —*phrasal verbs.* **draw on** (or **upon**). To use as a source; call upon. **draw out.** To cause to converse freely. —*n.* 1. The act or result of drawing. 2. A special advantage; edge. 3. A contest ending in a tie. 4. Something that attracts. [< OE *dragan.*]

draw·back (drô′băk′) *n.* A disadvantage or inconvenience.

draw·bridge (drô′brĭj′) *n.* A bridge that can be raised, lowered, or drawn aside.

draw·er *n.* 1. (drô′ər). 1. One that draws. 2. **drawer** (drôr). A sliding boxlike compartment in a bureau or table. **3. drawers** (drôrz). Underpants.

draw·ing (drô′ĭng) n. **1.** The act of one that draws. **2.** The art of depicting forms or figures by means of lines on a surface. **3.** A portrayal in lines on a surface of a form or figure. **4.** A lottery.

drawing card n. Something that attracts attention or business.

drawing room n. **1.** A formal reception room or living room. **2.** A private room on a railroad sleeping car. [< *withdrawing room.*]

drawl (drôl) v. To speak or utter with lengthened or drawn-out vowels. [Poss. < DRAW.] —**drawl** n.

drawn (drôn) v. *p.p.* of **draw.**

draw·string (drô′strĭng′) n. A cord or ribbon run through a hem or casing and pulled to tighten or close an opening.

dray (drā) n. A low cart used for heavy loads. [< OE *dræge,* dragnet.]

dread (drĕd) n. **1.** Profound fear; terror. **2.** Anxious or fearful anticipation. **3.** Awe; reverence. —v. **1.** To be in terror of; fear greatly. **2.** To anticipate with anxiety or reluctance. —*adj.* **1.** Terrifying; fearsome. **2.** Awesome; revered. [< OE *drædan,* to fear.]

dread·ful (drĕd′fəl) adj. **1.** Inspiring dread; terrible. **2.** Extremely unpleasant; distasteful or shocking. —**dread′ful·ly** adv. —**dread′ful·ness** n.

dread·nought (drĕd′nôt′) n. A heavily armed battleship.

dreadnought

dream (drēm) n. **1.** A series of mental images, ideas, and emotions that occur during sleep. **2.** A daydream; reverie. **3.** A wild fancy or hope. **4.** An aspiration; ambition. **5.** One that is extremely beautiful, fine, or pleasant. —v. **dreamed** or **dreamt** (drĕmt), **dream·ing. 1.** To experience a dream (of). **2.** To daydream. **3.** To conceive of; imagine. **4.** To pass (time) idly or in reverie. —*phrasal verb.* **dream up.** To invent; concoct. [< OE *drēam,* joy.] —**dream′er** n. —**dream′y** adj.

dream·land (drēm′lănd′) n. An ideal or imaginary land.

drear (drĭr) adj. Dreary.

drea·ry (drĭr′ē) adj. **-ri·er, -ri·est. 1.** Bleak; dismal. **2.** Boring; dull. [< OE *drēorig,* bloody.] —**drear′i·ly** adv. —**drear′i·ness** n.

dredge¹ (drĕj) n. **1.** A machine or implement that removes mud or silt from the bottom of a body of water. **2.** A ship or barge equipped with a dredge. —v. **dredged, dredg·ing.** To clean or dig up with or as if with a dredge. [Sc. *dreg.*]

dredge² (drĕj) v. **dredged, dredg·ing.** To coat

(food) by sprinkling, as with flour. [< Gk. *tragēmata,* sweetmeats < *trōgein,* to gnaw.]

dregs (drĕgz) pl.n. **1.** The sediment of a liquid; lees. **2.** The basest or least desirable part of something. [< ON *dregg.*]

drench (drĕnch) v. To wet thoroughly; saturate. [< OE *drencan,* to cause to drink.]

dress (drĕs) n. **1.** A one-piece, skirted outer garment for women. **2.** Clothing; apparel. —v. **1.** To put clothes on; clothe. **2.** To decorate or trim; adorn. **3.** To arrange or style (the hair). **4.** To apply therapeutic materials to. **5.** To make ready for use; finish: *dress a hide.* **6.** To prepare for cooking or sale: *dress a turkey.* **7.** To put on or wear formal clothes. —*phrasal verb.* **dress down.** To scold; reprimand. —*adj.* **1.** Suitable for a formal occasion: *a dress shirt.* **2.** Requiring formal clothing: *a dress reception.* [< OFr. *dresser,* to dress < Lat. *dirigere,* to direct.]

dres·sage (drə-säzh′, drĕ-) n. The guiding of a horse through a series of complex maneuvers by slight movements of the hands, legs, and weight.

dress·er¹ (drĕs′ər) n. One that dresses or assists in dressing.

dress·er² (drĕs′ər) n. A chest of drawers, usu. with a mirror. [< OFr. *dreceur,* table for preparing food < *dresser,* to arrange.]

dress·ing (drĕs′ĭng) n. **1.** Therapeutic material applied to a wound. **2.** A sauce, as for a salad. **3.** A stuffing, as for poultry.

dressing gown n. A robe worn informally at home.

dress·mak·er (drĕs′mā′kər) n. One who makes women's clothes. —**dress′mak′ing** n.

dress·y (drĕs′ē) adj. **-i·er, -i·est. 1.** Elaborate in dress. **2.** Smart; stylish. —**dress′i·ly** adv. —**dress′i·ness** n.

drew (drōō) v. *p.t.* of **draw.**

drib·ble (drĭb′əl) v. **-bled, -bling. 1.** To fall or let fall in drops. **2.** To drool; trickle. **3.** To move (a ball) by repeated light bounces or kicks, as in basketball. —n. **1.** A trickle. **2.** A small quantity. **3.** The act of dribbling a ball. [Freq. of *drib,* var. of DRIP.]

drib·let (drĭb′lĭt) n. **1.** A falling drop of liquid. **2.** A small amount or portion.

dri·er¹ (drī′ər) n. **1.** A substance added to paint, varnish, or ink to speed drying. **2.** Var. of **dryer.**

dri·er² (drī′ər) adj. A compar. of **dry.**

dri·est (drī′ĭst) adj. A superl. of **dry.**

drift (drĭft) v. **1.** To carry or be carried along by or as if by a current. **2.** To move about without a goal; wander. **3.** To pile up in banks or heaps, as by the force of the wind. —n. **1.** The act or process of drifting. **2.** Something that drifts. **3.** A bank or pile, as of snow or sand, heaped up by the wind. **4.** A general meaning or purport; tenor. **5.** Lateral displacement or deviation of an object or vehicle from a planned course. **6.** The rate of flow of a current of water. [< ME *drift,* the act of driving.]

drift·er (drĭf′tər) n. A person who lacks aspirations, goals, or enterprise.

drift·wood (drĭft′wŏŏd′) n. Wood floating in or washed up by water.

drill¹ (drĭl) n. **1.** An implement that bores holes in solid materials. **2.** Disciplined, repetitious exercise as a means of training. **3.** A specific task or exercise designed to develop a skill. —v. **1.** To bore with a drill. **2.** To train by repetition. [Du. *dril.*]

drill (drĭl) *n.* **1.** A trench or furrow in which seeds are planted. **2.** An implement for planting seeds in drills. [Orig. unknown.]

drill³ (drĭl) *n.* Strong cotton or linen twill. [< Lat. *trilix*, triple-twilled.]

drill-mas-ter (drĭl'măs'tər) *n.* A military drill instructor.

drill press *n.* A powered vertical drilling machine in which the drill is forced into metal by power or a hand lever.

drink (drĭngk) *v.* **drank** (drăngk), **drunk** (drŭngk), **drink-ing.** **1.** To swallow (liquid). **2.** To soak up (liquid or moisture); absorb. **3. a.** To propose (a toast). **b.** To salute with a toast. **4.** To take in eagerly through the senses or intellect: *drank in every word.* **5.** To imbibe alcoholic beverages, esp. to excess. —*n.* **1.** A liquid for drinking; beverage. **2.** Alcoholic liquor. **3.** An amount of liquid swallowed. **4.** Excessive use of alcoholic beverages. [< OE *drincan.*] —**drink'a-ble** *adj.* —**drink'er** *n.*

drip (drĭp) *v.* **dripped, drip-ping.** **1.** To fall or let fall in drops. **2.** To shed drops. —*n.* **1.** The process of falling in drops. **2.** Liquid that falls in drops. **3.** The sound made by dripping liquid. **4.** *Slang.* An unpleasant or tiresomely boring person. [< OE *dryppan.*]

drip-pings (drĭp'ĭngz) *pl.n.* The fat and juice from roasting meat.

drive (drīv) *v.* **drove** (drōv), **driv-en** (drĭv'ən), **driv-ing.** **1.** To push, propel, or press forcibly. **2.** To force into a particular condition: *drives me crazy.* **3.** To force to go through or penetrate: *drive a nail.* **4. a.** To guide, control, and direct (a vehicle). **b.** To operate or be transported in a vehicle. **c.** To cause to function; motivate. **6.** To carry through vigorously to a conclusion. **7.** To propel (a ball) with speed and force. **8.** To rush or advance violently: *a driving wind.* —*n.* **1.** A ride, trip, or journey in a vehicle. **2.** A road, esp. a driveway. **3.** The means or apparatus for transmitting motion to a machine or machine part. **4.** An organized effort to accomplish a purpose; campaign. **5.** Energy; initiative. **6.** A strong motivating tendency or instinct. **7.** A massive, sustained military offensive. **8.** The act of propelling a ball forcefully. **9. a.** The act of driving cattle. **b.** The act of driving logs down a river. [< OE *drīfan.*]

drive-in (drīv'ĭn') *n.* A business establishment that accommodates customers who remain in their automobiles.

driv-el (drĭv'əl) *v.* **-eled** or **-elled, -el-ing** or **-el-ling.** **1.** To slobber; drool. **2.** To talk or utter stupidly, childishly, or senselessly. [< OE *dreflian.*] —**driv'el** *n.* —**driv'el-er** *n.*

driv-er (drī'vər) *n.* **1.** One that drives, as a chauffeur. **2.** A wooden-headed golf club used for making long shots from the tee.

drive-way (drīv'wā') *n.* An often short private road.

driz-zle (drĭz'əl) *v.* **-zled, -zling.** To rain gently in fine, mistlike drops. [Perh. < ME *dresen,* to fall.] —**driz'zle** *n.* —**driz'zly** *adj.*

drogue (drōg) *n.* A parachute used to slow down a fast-moving object, as a space vehicle during re-entry. [Poss. < DRAG.]

droll (drōl) *adj.* **-er, -est.** Amusingly odd, whimsical, or comical. [Fr. *drôle* < MDu. *drol,* little man.] —**droll'er-y** *n.* —**drol'ly** *adv.*

-drome *suff.* A large field or arena: *airdrome.* [< Gk. *dromos,* race.]

drom-e-dar-y (drŏm'ĭ-dĕr'ē, drŭm'-) *n., pl.* **-ies.** The one-humped domesticated camel of northern Africa and western Asia. [< LLat. *dromedarius* < Gk. *dromas,* running.]

dromedary

drone¹ (drōn) *n.* **1.** A male bee, esp. a honeybee. **2.** One who is lazy; loafer. **3.** A pilotless remote-control aircraft. [< OE *drān.*]

drone² (drōn) *v.* **droned, dron-ing.** **1.** To make a continuous low, dull humming sound. **2.** To speak in a monotonous tone. · [< DRONE¹.] —**drone** *n.*

drool (drōol) *v.* **1.** To let saliva run from the mouth; drivel. **2.** *Informal.* To talk nonsense. [< DRIVEL.] —**drool** *n.*

droop (drōop) *v.* **1.** To bend or hang downward. **2.** To appear dejected or listless; languish. [< ON *drūpa.*] —**droop** *n.* —**droop'i-ness** *n.* —**droop'y** *adj.*

drop (drŏp) *v.* **dropped, drop-ping.** **1.** To fall or let fall in drops. **2.** To fall or let fall from a higher to a lower place. **3.** To become less, as in number or amount; decrease. **4.** To descend. **5.** To sink into a state of exhaustion. **6.** To pass into a specified condition: *dropped into a doze.* **7.** To say or offer casually: *drop a hint.* **8.** To send: *drop me a line.* **9.** To bring or come to an end; cease: *dropped the subject.* **10.** To stop participating in; quit: *drop a course.* **11.** To dismiss or reject. **12.** To omit (a letter) in speaking or writing. —**phrasal verbs. drop by** (or **in** or **over**). To visit informally and unexpectedly. **drop off.** To fall asleep. **drop out.** **1.** To leave school without graduating. **2.** To withdraw from organized society. —*n.* **1.** A quantity of liquid heavy enough to fall in a spherical mass. **2.** Something resembling a drop. **3.** A small amount of liquid. **4.** A sudden decline or decrease, as in quantity. **5.** The act of falling. **6.** A steep or sheer descent. **7.** The vertical distance from a higher to a lower level. **8.** Something arranged to be lowered, as a stage curtain. **9.** Men and equipment landed by parachute. [< OE *dropa.*]

drop-let (drŏp'lĭt) *n.* A tiny drop.

drop-out (drŏp'out') *n.* One who drops out.

drop-per (drŏp'ər) *n.* A small tube with a suction bulb at one end for drawing in a liquid and releasing it in drops.

drop-sy (drŏp'sē) *n.* Pathological accumulation of diluted lymph in body tissues and cavities. [< Gk. *hudrōpsis* < *hudōr,* water.] —**drop'si-cal** (-sĭ-kəl) *adj.*

dro·soph·i·la (drō-sŏf'ə-lə, drə-) *n.* A fruit fly used extensively in genetic studies. [< Gk. *drosos*, dew + Gk. *philos*, loving.]

dross (drôs, drŏs) *n.* **1.** The waste material that forms on the surface of a molten metal. **2.** Worthless material; rubbish. [< OE *drōs*, dregs.]

drought (drout) *n.* Also **drouth** (drouth). A long period of little or no rain. [< OE *drūgoth*.]

drove¹ (drōv) *v.* *p.t.* of **drive.**

drove² (drōv) *n.* A flock, herd, or large group driven or moving in a body. [< OE *draf* < *drifan*, to drive.]

drov·er (drō'vər) *n.* A driver of cattle, sheep, or horses.

drown (droun) *v.* **1.** To die or kill by suffocating in water or other liquid. **2.** To cover with or as if with water. **3.** To overpower; overcome. [ME *drounen*.]

drowse (drouz) *v.* **drowsed, drows·ing.** To be half asleep; doze. [< OE *drusian*, to be sluggish.] **—drowse** *n.*

drows·y (drou'zē) *adj.* **-i·er, -i·est. 1.** Sleepy. **2.** Causing sleepiness. **—drows'i·ly** *adv.* **—drows'i·ness** *n.*

drub (drŭb) *v.* **drubbed, drub·bing. 1.** To beat with or as if with a stick. **2.** To defeat thoroughly. [Ar. *dáraba*, to beat.] **—drub'ber** *n.*

drudge (drŭj) *n.* One who does tedious, menial, or unpleasant work. **—v.** **drudged, drudg·ing.** To do the work of a drudge. [< ME *druggen*, to labor.] **—drudg'er·y** *n.*

drug (drŭg) *n.* **1.** A substance used as medicine in the treatment of disease. **2.** A narcotic. **—v.** **drugged, drug·ging. 1.** To administer a drug to. **2.** To mix a drug into. **3.** To stupefy or dull with or as if with a drug. [< OFr. *drogue*, a chemical substance.]

drug·gist (drŭg'ĭst) *n.* A pharmacist.

drug·store (drŭg'stôr', -stōr') *n.* A store where prescriptions are filled and drugs are sold.

dru·id (drōō'ĭd) *n.* Also **Dru·id.** A member of an order of priests in ancient Gaul and Britain who appear in legend as prophets and sorcerers. [Lat. *druides*, druids, prob. of Celt. orig.]

drum (drŭm) *n.* **1.** A musical percussion instrument consisting of a hollow cylinder with a membrane stretched tightly over its ends, played by beating with the hands or sticks. **2.** The sound produced by beating a drum. **3.** Something shaped like a drum. **—v.** **drummed, drum·ming. 1.** To play or perform on a drum. **2.** To thump or tap rhythmically; beat. **3.** To summon by or as if by beating a drum. **4.** To instill by constant repetition or effort: *drummed the answers into his head.* **5.** To expel, esp. in disgrace: *drummed out of the army.* **—phrasal verb. drum up.** To obtain by persevering effort: *drumming up new business.* [Perh. < Du.]

drum·beat (drŭm'bēt') *n.* The sound made by beating a drum.

drum·lin (drŭm'lĭn) *n.* An oval hill formed from material left by a glacier. [< Ir. Gael. *drum*, ridge.]

drum major *n.* A man who leads a marching band.

drum majorette *n.* A girl who prances and twirls a baton at the head of a marching band.

drum·mer (drŭm'ər) *n.* **1.** One who plays a drum. **2.** A traveling salesman.

drum·stick (drŭm'stĭk') *n.* **1.** A stick for beating a drum. **2.** The lower part of the leg of a cooked fowl.

drunk (drŭngk) *v.* *p.p.* of **drink.** **—adj. 1.** Intoxicated with alcoholic liquor; inebriated. **2.** Overcome by emotion: *drunk with happiness.* **—n. 1.** A drunkard. **2.** A bout of drinking.

drunk·ard (drŭng'kərd) *n.* One who is habitually drunk.

drunk·en (drŭng'kən) *adj.* **1.** Drunk; intoxicated. **2.** Of, caused by, or happening during intoxication: *a drunken rage.* **—drunk'en·ly** *adv.* **—drunk'en·ness** *n.*

drupe (drōōp) *n.* A fleshy fruit, as a peach, with a single hard stone that encloses a seed. [< Gk. *drupepēs*, overripe.]

dry (drī) *adj.* **dri·er** or **dry·er, dri·est** or **dry·est. 1.** Free or freed from liquid or moisture. **2.** Not under water: *dry land.* **3.** Of or pertaining to solid rather than liquid commodities. **4.** Marked by little or no rainfall; arid. **5.** Needing drink; thirsty. **6.** Lacking natural secretion: *a dry cough.* **7.** Not yielding milk: *a dry cow.* **8.** Quietly ironic: *a dry wit.* **9.** Matter-of-fact; impersonal. **10.** Not sweet: *a dry wine.* **11.** Prohibiting the sale of alcoholic beverages. **—v.** **dried, dry·ing.** To make or become dry. [< OE *dryge*.] **—dry'ly** or **dri'ly** *adv.* **—dry'ness** *n.*

dry·ad (drī'əd, -ăd') *n.* A wood nymph. [< Gk. *druas* < *drus*, tree.]

dry cell *n.* A primary battery that has an electrolyte in the form of moist paste.

dry-clean (drī'klēn') *v.* To clean (fabrics) with chemical solvents having little or no water. **—dry cleaning** *n.*

dry dock *n.* A large floating or stationary dock used for ship maintenance, repair, or construction.

dry dock

dry·er (drī'ər) *n.* Also **dri·er.** An appliance that removes moisture.

dry farming *n.* Farming without irrigation practiced in arid areas. **—dry farmer** *n.*

dry goods *pl.n.* Textiles, clothing, and related articles of trade.

dry ice *n.* Solid carbon dioxide used primarily as a refrigerant.

dry measure *n.* A system of units for measuring dry quantities, such as grains, by volume.

dry run *n.* A trial run or rehearsal, as a military exercise without live ammunition.

D.T.'s (dē-tēz') *pl.n.* Delirium tremens.

du·al (dōō'əl, dyōō'-) *adj.* **1.** Composed of two parts; double. **2.** Having a double nature, character, or purpose. [Lat. *dualis* < *duo*, two.] **—du'al·ism** or **du·al'i·ty** (-ăl'ĭ-tē) *n.*

dub¹ (dŭb) v. **dubbed, dub·bing. 1.** To confer knighthood on. **2.** To give a nickname to. [< OE *dubbian.*]

dub² (dŭb) v. **dubbed, dub·bing. 1.** To add (sound) to an existing recording. **2.** To provide (a film) with a new sound track, often in a different language. [< DOUBLE.]

dub·bin (dŭb'ĭn) n. An application of tallow and oil for dressing leather. [< DUB¹.]

du·bi·e·ty (dōō-bī'ĭ-tē, dyōō-) n., pl. -ties. **1.** The quality of being dubious. **2.** A matter of doubt; uncertainty. [LLat. *dubietas* < Lat. *dubius,* dubious.]

du·bi·ous (dōō'bē-əs, dyōō'-) adj. **1.** Fraught with uncertainty; undecided. **2.** Arousing doubt; questionable. **3.** Skeptical; doubtful. [Lat. *dubius.*] —**du'bi·ous·ly** adv. —**du'bi·ous·ness** n.

du·cal (dōō'kəl, dyōō'-) adj. Of or pertaining to a duke or dukedom.

duc·at (dŭk'ət) n. Any of various gold coins formerly used in Europe. [< Med. Lat. *ducatus,* duchy.]

duch·ess (dŭch'ĭs) n. **1.** The wife or widow of a duke. **2.** A woman holding title to a duchy. [< Med. Lat. *ducissa* < Lat. *dux,* leader.]

duch·y (dŭch'ē) n., pl. -ies. The territory ruled by a duke or duchess; dukedom. [< Med. Lat. *ducatus* < Lat. *dux,* leader.]

duck¹ (dŭk) n. Any of various water birds with a broad, flat bill, short legs, and webbed feet. [< OE *duce.*]

duck² (dŭk) v. **1.** To lower quickly, esp. so as to avoid something. **2.** To evade; dodge. **3.** To submerge briefly in water. [ME *douken.*]

duck³ (dŭk) n. **1.** A durable, closely woven cotton fabric. **2.** ducks. Clothing made of duck. [Du. *doek,* cloth.]

duck·bill (dŭk'bĭl') n. The platypus.

duck·board (dŭk'bôrd', -bōrd') n. A board or boardwalk laid across a wet or muddy surface.

duck·ling (dŭk'lĭng) n. A young duck.

duck·pin (dŭk'pĭn') n. **1.** A bowling pin shorter and squatter than a tenpin. **2.** duck·pins (*used with a sing. verb*). A bowling game played with duckpins.

duct (dŭkt) n. **1.** A tubular passage through which a substance, esp. a fluid, is conveyed. **2.** A tube or pipe for electrical cables or wires. [Lat. *ductus,* act of leading < *ducere,* to lead.]

duc·tile (dŭk'tĭl) adj. **1.** Capable of being drawn out, as into wire, or being hammered thin. **2.** Readily controlled; tractable. [< Lat. *ductilis* < *ducere,* to lead.] —**duc·til'i·ty** (-tĭl'-ĭ-tē) n.

duct·less gland (dŭkt'lĭs) n. An endocrine gland.

dud (dŭd) n. Informal. **1.** A bomb, shell, etc., that fails to explode. **2.** One that is a total failure. **3.** duds. Clothing or personal belongings. [ME *dudde,* article of clothing.]

dude (dōōd, dyōōd) n. Informal. **1.** An Easterner or city person staying in the West. **2.** Informal. A dandy. [Orig. unknown.]

dude ranch n. A resort patterned after a Western ranch, with outdoor activities such as horseback riding.

dudg·eon (dŭj'ən) n. A sullen or indignant anger; resentment. [Orig. unknown.]

due (dōō, dyōō) adj. **1.** Payable immediately or on demand. **2.** Owed as a debt or right; owing. **3.** Fitting or appropriate. **4.** Sufficient or adequate. **5.** Expected or scheduled. —n. **1.** Something owed or deserved. **2.** dues. A charge or fee, as for membership. —adv. Straight; directly: *due west.* [< Lat. *debitus,* p.p. of *debere,* to owe.]

du·el (dōō'əl, dyōō'-) n. **1.** A prearranged combat between two persons, fought esp. to settle a point of honor. **2.** A struggle between two persons or groups. —v. -eled or -elled, -el·ing or -el·ling. To fight in a duel. [< Lat. *duellum,* war.] —**du'el·ist** n.

du·en·na (dōō-ĕn'ə, dyōō-) n. **1.** An elderly woman who acts as governess and companion to the daughters in a Spanish or Portuguese family. **2.** A chaperon. [Sp. *dueña* < Lat. *domina,* lady.]

due process of law n. Proceedings in judicial activity that do not violate the legal rights of the individual.

du·et (dōō-ĕt', dyōō-) n. A musical composition for two voices or instruments. [Ital. *duetto,* dim. of *duo,* two.]

due to prep. Because of.

Usage: Objection is often made when *due to* is used as a prepositional phrase: *He hesitated due to fear.* Although widely used, this construction is unacceptable to a large majority of the Usage Panel.

duffel bag n. A large cloth bag for personal belongings. [< *Duffel,* Belgium.]

duf·fer (dŭf'ər) n. An inept or incompetent person. [Orig. unknown.]

dug (dŭg) v. p.t. & p.p. of **dig.**

dug·out (dŭg'out') n. **1.** A boat or canoe made by hollowing out a log. **2.** A shelter dug into the ground or in a hillside. **3.** A long, low shelter for the players at the side of a baseball field.

duke (dōōk, dyōōk) n. **1.** A nobleman with the highest hereditary rank, esp. in Great Britain. **2.** A prince who rules an independent duchy. [< Lat. *dux,* leader.] —**duke'dom** n.

dul·cet (dŭl'sĭt) adj. **1.** Pleasing to the ear. **2.** Soothing and agreeable. [< Lat. *dulcis,* sweet.]

dul·ci·mer (dŭl'sə-mər) n. A musical instrument with wire strings of graduated lengths, played with two padded hammers. [< OFr. *doulcemer.*]

dull (dŭl) adj. -er, -est. **1.** Not sharp; blunt. **2.** Not keenly or intensely felt. **3.** Not exciting; boring. **4.** Not brisk; sluggish. **5.** Slow to learn or understand; stupid. **6.** Slow to respond; insensitive. **7.** Not bright or vivid. **8.** Cloudy or overcast; gloomy. **9.** Muffled; indistinct. —v. To make or become dull. [< OE *dol.*] —**dull'ness** n. —**dul'ly** adv.

dull·ard (dŭl'ərd) n. A dull or stupid person; dolt.

du·ly (dōō'lē, dyōō'-) adv. **1.** In a proper manner; fittingly. **2.** At the expected time.

dumb (dŭm) adj. -er, -est. **1.** Lacking the power or faculty of speech; mute. **2.** Temporarily speechless, as from fear; silent. **3.** *In-*

formal. Stupid. [< OE.] —**dumb′ly** *adv.*
—**dumb′ness** *n.*

dumb·bell (dŭm′bĕl′) *n.* **1.** A weight lifted for
muscular exercise, consisting of a short bar
with a metal ball at each end. **2.** *Slang.* A
stupid person; dolt.

dumb·wait·er (dŭm′wā′tər) *n.* A small elevator for conveying food or other goods from
one floor of a building to another.

dum·dum (dŭm′dŭm′) *n.* A bullet with a soft
nose designed to expand upon contact. [<
Dum-Dum, India.]

dum·found (dŭm′found′) *v.* Also **dumb·found.**
To strike dumb with astonishment; nonplus.
[DUM(B) + (CON)FOUND.]

dum·my (dŭm′ē) *n., pl.* **-mies. 1.** An imitation
of a real object used as a substitute. **2.** A
model of the human figure, esp. one used to
display clothes. **3.** *Informal.* A blockhead;
dolt. **4.** One who is secretly in the service of
another. **5.** A sample page to be reproduced
by printing. **6. a.** The partner in a bridge
game who exposes his hand to be played by
the declarer. **b.** The hand thus exposed. [<
DUMB.]

dump (dŭmp) *v.* **1.** To drop in a large mass.
2. To empty (material), as from a container.
3. To get rid of by or as if by dumping;
dispose of. **4.** To place (large quantities of
goods) on the market at a low price. —*n.*
1. A place where refuse is dumped. **2.** A storage place; depot. **3.** *Slang.* A dilapidated or
disreputable place. [ME *dumpen.*]

dump·ling (dŭmp′lĭng) *n.* **1.** A small ball of
dough cooked with stew or soup. **2.** A baked
dessert of fruit wrapped in dough. [Orig. unknown.]

dumps (dŭmps) *pl.n. Informal.* A gloomy,
melancholy state of mind. [< Du. *domp,*
haze.]

dump truck *n.* A heavy-duty truck with a bed
that tilts to dump loose material.

dump·y (dŭm′pē) *adj.* **-i·er, -i·est.** Short and
stout; squat. [< dial. *dump,* lump.] —**dump′-
i·ness** *n.*

dun¹ (dŭn) *v.* **dunned, dun·ning.** To ask (a
debtor) persistently for payment. [Orig. unknown.] —**dun** *n.*

dun² (dŭn) *n.* A dull grayish-brown color. [<
OE *dunn.*] —**dun** *adj.*

dunce (dŭns) *n.* A stupid person. [< John
Duns Scotus (1265?–1308).]

dun·der·head (dŭn′dər-hĕd′) *n.* A numbskull;
dunce. [Perh. Du. *donder,* thunder + HEAD.]

dune (dōōn, dyōōn) *n.* A hill or ridge of
wind-blown sand. [< MDu. *dūne.*]

dune buggy *n.* A small light automobile with
oversized tires for driving on sand.

dung (dŭng) *n.* Animal excrement; manure.
[< OE.]

dun·ga·ree (dŭng′gə-rē′) *n.* **1.** A sturdy, usu.
blue denim fabric. **2. dungarees.** Overalls or
trousers made from dungaree. [Hindi *dungri.*]

dun·geon (dŭn′jən) *n.* A dark, often underground prison or cell. [< Med. Lat. *dominio,*
lordship < Lat. *dominus,* lord.]

dung·hill (dŭng′hĭl′) *n.* A heap of dung.

dunk (dŭngk) *v.* **1.** To plunge into liquid; immerse. **2.** To dip (food) into liquid before
eating it. **3.** To submerge oneself briefly in
water. [Pennsylvania Dutch *dunke.*]

du·o (dōō′ō, dyōō′ō) *n., pl.* **-os. 1.** A duet.
2. A pair. [Ital. < Lat., two.]

du·o·dec·i·mal (dōō′ō-dĕs′ə-məl, dyōō′-) *adj.*

Of, pertaining to, or based on the number 12.
[< Lat. *duodecim,* twelve.]

du·o·de·num (dōō′ə-dē′nəm, dyōō′-, dōō-ŏd′-
n-əm, dyōō-) *n., pl.* **-o·de·na** (-ə-dē′nə, -ŏd′-
n-ə). The portion of the small intestine just
below the stomach. [< Med. Lat. *duodenum
digitorum,* intestine of 12 fingers length.]
—**du′o·de′nal** *adj.*

dupe (dōōp, dyōōp) *n.* One who is easily
deceived or used. —*v.* **duped, dup·ing.** To
make a dupe of. [< OFr.]

du·ple (dōō′pəl, dyōō′-) *adj. Mus.* Having two
beats or a multiple of two beats to the
measure. [Lat. *duplus.*]

du·plex (dōō′plĕks, dyōō′-) *adj.* Twofold or
double. —*n.* A house divided into two living
units. [Lat.]

du·pli·cate (dōō′plĭ-kĭt, dyōō′-) *adj.* **1.** Identical to another. **2.** Existing in two corresponding parts; double. —*n.* Something that
corresponds exactly to something else; copy.
—*v.* (-kāt′) **-cat·ed, -cat·ing. 1.** To make an
identical copy of. **2.** To make or perform
again. [< Lat. *duplicare.*] —**du′pli·ca′tion** *n.*

du·pli·ca·tor (dōō′plĭ-kā′tər) *n.* A machine that reproduces printed or written material.

du·plic·i·ty (dōō-plĭs′ĭ-tē, dyōō-) *n., pl.* **-ties.**
Deliberate deceptiveness in behavior or
speech. [< LLat. *duplicitas.*]

du·ra·ble (dŏŏr′ə-bəl, dyŏŏr′-) *adj.* Able to
withstand wear and tear. [< Lat. *durare,* to
last.] —**du′ra·bil′i·ty** *n.*

du·ra ma·ter (dŏŏr′ə mā′tər, dyŏŏr′ə-) *n.* A
tough fibrous membrane that covers the brain
and spinal cord. [< Med. Lat. *dura mater
(cerebri),* hard mother (of the brain).]

du·rance (dŏŏr′əns, dyŏŏr′-) *n.* Imprisonment. [< Lat. *durare,* to last.]

du·ra·tion (dōō-rā′shən, dyōō-) *n.* **1.** Continu-
ance in time. **2.** The time during which something exists or persists. [< Lat. *durare,* to
last.]

du·ress (dŏŏ-rĕs′, dyŏŏ-) *n.* **1.** Constraint by
threat; coercion. **2.** Illegal coercion or confinement. [< Lat. *duritia,* hardness < *durus,*
hard.]

dur·ing (dŏŏr′ĭng, dyŏŏr′-) *prep.* **1.** Throughout the course of. **2.** At some time in. [< ME
duren, to last.]

du·rum (dŏŏr′əm, dyŏŏr′-) *n.* A hardy wheat
used chiefly in making pasta. [< Lat. *durus,*
hard.]

dusk (dŭsk) *n.* The darker stage of twilight.
[< OE *dox.*]

dusk·y (dŭs′kē) *adj.* **-i·er, -i·est. 1.** Rather
dark in color. **2.** Lacking adequate light; dim.
—**dusk′i·ness** *n.*

dust (dŭst) *n.* **1.** Fine particulate matter.
2. The earthy remains of a human body.
3. The surface of the ground. **4.** Something of
no worth. —*v.* **1.** To remove dust (from).
2. To sprinkle with a powdery substance. [<
OE *dūst.*] —**dust′y** *adj.*

dust bowl *n.* A region reduced to aridity by
drought and dust storms.

dust devil *n.* A small whirlwind that swirls
dust and debris.

dust·er (dŭs′tər) *n.* **1.** One that dusts. **2.** A
cloth or brush used to remove dust. **3.** A
smock worn to protect clothing from dust.
4. A woman's dress-length housecoat.

dust·pan (dŭst′păn′) *n.* A shovellike pan into
which dust is swept.

dust storm *n.* A severe windstorm that sweeps clouds of dust across an arid region.

dust storm
In Elkhart, Kansas, 1937

Dutch (dŭch) *n.* **1.** (*used with a pl. verb*). The people of the Netherlands. **2.** The Germanic language of the Netherlands. —**Dutch** *adj.* —**Dutch'man** *n.*

Dutch door *n.* A door divided horizontally so that either part may be left open or closed.

Dutch elm disease *n.* A disease of elms caused by a fungus and resulting in brown streaks in the wood and eventual death.

Dutch oven *n.* A heavy kettle with a tight lid, used for slow cooking.

Dutch treat *n. Informal.* An outing, as for dinner or a movie, for which each person pays his own expenses.

du·te·ous (dōō'tē-əs, dyōō'-) *adj.* Obedient; dutiful. —**du'te·ous·ly** *adv.*

du·ti·a·ble (dōō'tē-ə-bəl, dyōō'-) *adj.* Subject to import tax.

du·ti·ful (dōō'tĭ-fəl, dyōō'-) *adj.* **1.** Careful to perform one's duties. **2.** Expressing or filled with a sense of duty. —**du'ti·ful·ly** *adv.* —**du'ti·ful·ness** *n.*

du·ty (dōō'tē, dyōō'-) *n., pl.* **-ties.** **1.** An act or a course of action that one should or must do. **2.** A moral obligation. **3.** A task assigned to or demanded of one, esp. in the armed forces. **4.** A tax charged by a government, esp. on imports. **5.** Function or work; service: *a heavy-duty washer.* [< OFr. *deu,* due, ult. < Lat. *debēre,* to owe.]

dwarf (dwôrf) *n., pl.* **dwarfs** or **dwarves** (dwôrvz). An atypically small person, animal, or plant. —*v.* **1.** To check the natural growth or development of; stunt. **2.** To cause to appear small by comparison. [< OE *dweorh.*] —**dwarf'ish** *adj.*

dwell (dwĕl) *v.* **dwelt** (dwĕlt) or **dwelled, dwell·ing.** **1.** To live; reside. **2.** To be present; exist. **3.** To linger over or emphasize in thought, speech, or writing. [< OE *dwellan,* to delay.] —**dwell'er** *n.*

dwell·ing (dwĕl'ĭng) *n.* A place to live in; residence.

dwin·dle (dwĭn'dəl) *v.* **-dled, -dling.** To make or become gradually less; diminish. [< OE *dwīnan,* to shrink.]

Dy The symbol for the element dysprosium.

dyb·buk (dĭb'ək) *n.* In Jewish folklore, the soul of a dead person that enters and takes control of the body of a living person. [< Heb. *dibbúq.*]

dye (dī) *n.* **1.** A substance used for coloring materials. **2.** A color imparted with a dye. —*v.* **dyed, dye·ing.** **1.** To color (a material) with a dye. **2.** To take on or impart color. [< OE *dēah,* color.] —**dy'er** *n.*

dye-stuff (dī'stŭf') *n.* Material used as or yielding a dye.

dy·ing (dī'ĭng) *adj.* **1.** About to die. **2.** Done or uttered just before death. **3.** Drawing to an end; declining.

dyke (dīk) *n.* Var. of **dike.**

dy·nam·ic (dī-năm'ĭk) *adj.* **1.** Marked by energy and vigor; forceful. **2.** Of or pertaining to energy, force, or motion in relation to force. —*n.* **dynamics.** (*used with a sing. verb*). **1.** The study of the relationship between motion and the forces affecting motion. **2.** The physical or moral forces that produce motion, activity, and change in a field or system. **3.** Variation in force or intensity, esp. in musical sound. [< Gk. *dunamikos,* powerful < *dunamis,* power.] —**dy·nam'i·cal·ly** *adv.*

dy·na·mite (dī'nə-mīt') *n.* A powerful explosive made of nitroglycerin combined with an absorbent material. —*v.* **-mit·ed, -mit·ing.** **1.** To blow up with dynamite. **2.** To destroy completely; blast. [Swed. *dynamit.*]

dy·na·mo (dī'nə-mō') *n., pl.* **-mos.** **1.** A generator, esp. one for producing direct current. **2.** *Informal.* An extremely energetic and forceful person. [< *dynamoelectric machine.*]

dy·na·mom·e·ter (dī'nə-mŏm'ĭ-tər) *n.* An instrument used to measure force or power. [Fr. *dynamomètre.*]

dy·nas·ty (dī'nə-stē) *n., pl.* **-ties.** **1.** A succession of rulers from the same family or line. **2.** A family or group that maintains power or position for several generations. [< Gk. *dunasteia,* lordship.] —**dy·nas'tic** (dī-năs'tĭk) *adj.*

dys- *pref.* Diseased, difficult, faulty, or bad: *dyslexia.* [< Gk. *dus-.*]

dys·en·ter·y (dĭs'ən-tĕr'ē) *n.* An infection of the lower intestinal tract producing severe diarrhea, often with blood and mucus. [< Gk. *dusenteria.*]

dys·lex·i·a (dĭs-lĕk'sē-ə) *n.* Impairment of the ability to read. [DYS- + Gk. *lexis,* speech.] —**dys·lex'ic** *adj.*

dys·pep·sia (dĭs-pĕp'shə, -sē-ə) *n.* Indigestion. [< Gk. *duspepsia.*] —**dys·pep'tic** *adj.*

dys·pro·si·um (dĭs-prō'zē-əm) *n. Symbol* **Dy** A soft, silvery rare-earth metal used in nuclear research. Atomic number 66; atomic weight 162.50. [< Gk. *dusprositos,* difficult to approach.]

dys·tro·phy (dĭs'trə-fē) *n.* **1.** Defective nutrition. **2.** A disorder caused by defective nutrition. —**dys·troph'ic** (-trŏf'ĭk, -trō'fĭk) *adj.*

Ee

e or **E** (ē) *n.*, *pl.* **e's** or **E's**. 1. The 5th letter of the English alphabet. 2. The 5th in a series.

each (ēch) *adj.* Being one of two or more considered individually; every. —*pron.* Every one of a group considered individually; each one. —*adv.* For or to each one; apiece. [< OE *ælc.*]

Usage: When the subject of a sentence begins with *each*, it is traditionally held to be grammatically singular, and the verb and following pronouns must be singular as well: *Each of the boys has his job to do.* When *each* follows a plural subject, however, the verb and following pronouns are in the plural: *The boys each have their jobs to do.*

each other *pron.* Each the other. Used to indicate a reciprocal relationship or action: *met each other on the beach.*

Usage: The possessive form of *each other* is written *each other's: The boys wore each other's* (not *each others'*) *coats.*

ea·ger (ē'gər) *adj.* **-er, -est.** Marked by or full of intense or enthusiastic interest or desire: *eager to study.* [< Lat. *acer*, sharp.] —**ea'ger·ly** *adv.* —**ea'ger·ness** *n.*

ea·gle (ē'gəl) *n.* 1. A large bird of prey with a hooked bill and strong, soaring flight. 2. A former U.S. gold coin worth ten dollars. 3. *Golf.* A score of two below par on a hole. [< Lat. *aquila.*]

eagle

ea·glet (ē'glĭt) *n.* A young eagle.

-ean *suff.* Var. of **-ian.**

ear[1] (îr) *n.* 1. a. The organ of hearing in vertebrates, responsible for maintaining equilibrium and sensing sound. b. The visible outer part of this organ. 2. The sense of hearing. 3. Aural sensitivity, as to differences in musical pitch. 4. Attention; heed. 5. Something resembling the vertebrate ear. [< OE *ēare.*] —**eared** *adj.* —**ear'less** *adj.*

ear[2] (îr) *n.* The seed-bearing spike of a cereal plant, as corn. [< OE *ear.*]

ear·ache (îr'āk') *n.* An ache in the ear.

ear·drum (îr'drŭm') *n.* The thin membrane that separates the outer and middle ear and vibrates when struck by sound waves.

ear·flap (îr'flăp') *n.* Either of two cloth or fur tabs on a cap that may be turned down over the ears.

earl (ûrl) *n.* A British peer ranking above a viscount and below a marquis. [< OE *eorl,* nobleman.] —**earl'dom** *n.*

ear·lobe (îr'lōb') *n.* The soft, fleshy tissue at the lowest part of the outer ear.

ear·ly (ûr'lē) *adj.* **-li·er, -li·est.** 1. Near the beginning of a series, period of time, or course of events. 2. In or belonging to a distant or remote period or stage of development; primitive. 3. Occurring, developing, or appearing before the usual time. 4. Occurring in the near future. —*adv.* **-li·er, -li·est.** 1. Near the beginning of a series, period of time, or course of events. 2. Far back in time. 3. Before the usual time. [< OE *ælīce.*] —**ear'li·ness** *n.*

ear·mark (îr'märk') *n.* An identifying mark or characteristic. —*v.* 1. To mark for identification. 2. To set aside for a particular purpose.

ear·muff (îr'mŭf') *n.* Either of a pair of ear coverings worn to protect against the cold.

earn (ûrn) *v.* 1. To receive in return for services or labor. 2. To gain or acquire as a result of one's efforts or behavior. [< OE *earnian.*] —**earn'er** *n.*

ear·nest[1] (ûr'nĭst) *adj.* 1. Serious and determined. 2. Showing or expressing deep sincerity or feeling. 3. Of an important nature; grave. —*idiom.* **in earnest.** With serious purpose or intent. [< OE *eornost,* zeal.] —**ear'nest·ly** *adv.* —**ear'nest·ness** *n.*

ear·nest[2] (ûr'nĭst) *n.* Something, as money paid in advance, given by a purchaser to a seller to bind a contract. [< Heb. *'ērābhôn.*]

earn·ings (ûr'nĭngz) *pl.n.* Something earned, as salary, wages, or profit.

ear·phone (îr'fōn') *n.* A device that converts electric signals to audible sound and is worn near or in contact with the ear.

ear·ring (îr'rĭng, îr'ĭng) *n.* An ornament worn on the earlobe.

ear·shot (îr'shŏt') *n.* The range within which sound can be heard.

ear·split·ting (îr'splĭt'ĭng) *adj.* Unbearably loud and shrill.

earth (ûrth) *n.* 1. **Earth.** The planet on which human beings live, the 3rd planet from the sun. 2. The land surface of the world; ground. 3. Soil; dirt. —*idiom.* **down to earth.** Sensible; realistic. [< OE *eorthe.*]

earth·en (ûr'thən, -thən) *adj.* Made of earth or baked clay.

earth·en·ware (ûr'thən-wâr', -thən-) *n.* Pottery made of coarse, porous baked clay.

earth·ling (ûrth'lĭng) *n.* One who inhabits the earth.

earth·ly (ûrth'lē) *adj.* 1. Of or pertaining to the earth; terrestrial. 2. Conceivable; possible: *no earthly meaning.* —**earth'li·ness** *n.*

earth·quake (ûrth'kwāk') *n.* A series of vibrations in the crust of the earth.

earthquake
The aftermath of the 1906
earthquake in San Francisco

earth science *n.* Any of several sciences, such as geology, concerned with the origin, structure, and physical nature of the earth.

earth·shak·ing (ûrth'shā'kĭng) *adj.* Of enormous or fundamental importance.

earth·ward (ûrth'wərd) *adv.* Also **earth·wards** (-wərdz). To or toward the earth.

earth·work (ûrth'wûrk') *n.* An earthen embankment or fortification.

earth·worm (ûrth'wûrm') *n.* A round-bodied segmented worm that burrows into soil.

earth·y (ûr'thē) *adj.* **-i·er, -i·est.** 1. Consisting of or resembling earth or soil. 2. Crude or coarse; unrefined. —**earth'i·ness** *n.*

ear·wax (îr'wăks') *n.* The waxlike secretion of certain glands lining the canal of the outer ear.

ear·wig (îr'wĭg') *n.* An insect with pincerlike appendages protruding from the rear of the body. [< OE *ēarwicga.*]

ease (ēz) *n.* 1. Freedom from pain, worry, or discomfort. 2. Freedom from constraint or awkwardness; naturalness. 3. Freedom from difficulty; comfort. —*v.* **eased, eas·ing.** 1. To free or become free from pain, worry, or trouble; comfort. 2. To make or become less troublesome or difficult. 3. To slacken the strain, pressure, or tension; loosen. 4. To move into place slowly and carefully. [< Lat. *adjacens,* nearby.]

ea·sel (ē'zəl) *n.* A frame to support an artist's canvas or a picture. [< MDu. *ezel,* ass.]

east (ēst) *n.* 1. a. The direction in which the earth rotates on its axis. b. The point on the mariner's compass 90° clockwise from north. 2. Often **East.** A region or area lying to the east of a particular point. 3. **East.** Asia; the Orient. —*adj.* To, toward, of, from, facing, or in the east. —*adv.* In, from, or toward the east. [< OE *ēast.*]

Eas·ter (ē'stər) *n.* A Christian festival commemorating the Resurrection of Christ. [< OE *ēastre.*]

east·er·ly (ē'stər-lē) *adj.* 1. In or toward the east. 2. From the east. —**east'er·ly** *adv.*

east·ern (ē'stərn) *adj.* 1. Of, in, or toward the east. 2. From the east. Often **Eastern.** a. Characteristic of or found in eastern regions. b. Of Asia and the Eastern Hemisphere; Oriental. [< OE *ēasterne.*]

east·ern·er (ē'stər-nər) *n.* Often **Easterner.** A native or inhabitant of an eastern region.

east·ward (ēst'wərd) *adv.* Also **east·wards** (-wərdz). To or toward the east. —**east'ward** *adj.* —**east'ward·ly** *adj. & adv.*

eas·y (ē'zē) *adj.* **-i·er, -i·est.** 1. Capable of being accomplished without difficulty: *an easy job.* 2. Free from worry, anxiety, trouble, or pain. 3. Pleasant and relaxing. 4. Relaxed; easygoing. 5. Not strict; lenient. 6. Not strenuous or hurried; moderate. —*adv. Informal.* Without strain or difficulty; in a relaxed manner. [< OFr. *aisie,* p.p. of *aisier,* to put at ease.] —**eas'i·ly** *adv.* —**eas'i·ness** *n.*

Syns: *easy, effortless, facile, ready, simple, smooth adj.*

eas·y·go·ing (ē'zē-gō'ĭng) *adj.* Living without worry or concern; carefree.

eat (ēt) *v.* **ate** (āt), **eat·en** (ēt'n), **eat·ing.** 1. To consume (food). 2. To consume or ravage as if by eating. 3. To erode or corrode. [< OE *etan.*] —**eat'a·ble** *adj.* —**eat'er** *n.*

eaves (ēvz) *pl.n.* The projecting overhang at the edge of a roof. [< OE *efes.*]

eaves·drop (ēvz'drŏp') *v.* **-dropped, -drop·ping.** To listen secretly to a private conversation. [< ME *evesdrop,* place where water falls from eaves.] —**eaves'drop'per** *n.*

ebb (ĕb) *v.* 1. To recede, as the tide does after reaching its highest point. 2. To decline or diminish. —*n.* 1. The period of a tide between high tide and a succeeding low tide. 2. A period of decline. [< OE *ebba,* low tide.]

eb·o·nite (ĕb'ə-nīt') *n.* Hard rubber, esp. when black.

eb·o·ny (ĕb'ə-nē) *n., pl.* **-nies.** The hard, dark wood of a tropical Asian tree. —*adj.* Suggesting ebony; black. [< Gk. *ebeninos,* of ebony, of Egypt. orig.]

e·bul·lient (ĭ-bool'yənt, ĭ-bŭl'-) *adj.* 1. Filled with excitement; exuberant. 2. Boiling, as a liquid; bubbling. [< Lat. *ebullire,* to boil over.] —**e·bul'lience** *n.* —**e·bul'lient·ly** *adv.*

e·bul·li·tion (ĕb'ə-lĭsh'ən) *n.* 1. The bubbling or effervescence of a liquid. 2. A sudden outpouring, as of emotion or violence.

ec·cen·tric (ĭk-sĕn'trĭk) *adj.* 1. Deviating from a conventional or established pattern. 2. Deviating from a circular form, as in an elliptical orbit. 3. Not situated at or in the center. 4. Not having the same center. —*n.* 1. One who deviates from a conventional or established pattern. 2. A disk or wheel whose axis of revolution is displaced from its center so that it is capable of imparting reciprocating motion. [< Gk. *ekkentros,* not having the same center.] —**ec·cen'tri·cal·ly** *adv.* —**ec'cen·tric'i·ty** (ĕk'sĕn-trĭs'ĭ-tē) *n.*

Ec·cle·si·as·tes (ĭ-klē'zē-ăs'tēz') *n.* See table at **Bible.**

ec·cle·si·as·tic (ĭ-klē'zē-ăs'tĭk) *adj.* Ecclesiastical. —*n.* A clergyman; priest. [< Gk. *ekklēsiastikos.*]

ec·cle·si·as·ti·cal (ĭ-klē'zē-ăs'tĭ-kəl) *adj.* Of or pertaining to a church, esp. as an organized institution.

ech·e·lon (ĕsh'ə-lŏn') *n.* 1. A steplike formation, as of troops or aircraft. 2. A subdivision of a military force. 3. A level, as of authority, in a hierarchy. [< OFr. *eschelon,* rung of a ladder.]

ech·o (ĕk'ō) *n., pl.* **-oes.** 1. a. Repetition of a sound by reflection of sound waves from a surface. b. A sound produced in this manner.

2. A reflected wave received by a radio or radar. —v. **1.** To repeat or be repeated by or as if by an echo. **2.** To imitate: *echoing the leader's ideas.* [< Gk. *ēkhō.*]

ech·o·lo·ca·tion (ĕk'ō-lō-kā'shən) n. **1.** The ability of an animal such as a bat to orient itself by the reflections of the sounds it has produced. **2.** *Electronics.* Ranging by acoustical echo analysis.

é·clair (ā-klâr', ā'klâr') n. A light, tubular pastry filled with cream or custard. [< OFr. *esclair*, lightning.]

é·clat (ā-klä') n. **1.** A brilliant success, as in performance. **2.** Great acclaim. [< OFr. *esclater*, to burst.]

ec·lec·tic (ĭ-klĕk'tĭk) adj. Choosing or consisting of what appears to be the best from diverse sources. [< Gk. *eklektikos*, selective.] —**ec·lec'tic** n.

e·clipse (ĭ-klĭps') n. **1. a.** The partial or complete obscuring of one celestial body by another. **b.** The period of time during which such an obscuring occurs. **2.** A decline into obscurity, disuse, or disgrace. —v. **e·clipsed,**

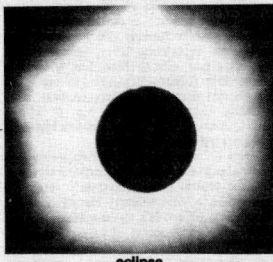

eclipse
Solar eclipse

e·clips·ing. To cause an eclipse of. [< Gk. *ekleipsis.*]

e·clip·tic (ĭ-klĭp'tĭk) n. The apparent path of the sun among the stars; the intersection plane of the earth's solar orbit with the celestial sphere. [< LLat. *ecliptica (linea)*, (line) of eclipses.]

ec·logue (ĕk'lôg', -lŏg') n. A pastoral poem. [< Gk. *eklogē*, selection.]

e·col·o·gy (ĭ-kŏl'ə-jē) n. **1.** The science of the relationships between organisms and their environments. **2.** The relationship between organisms and their environment. [G. *Ökologie.*] —**ec·o·log'i·cal** (ĕk'ə-lŏj'ĭ-kəl, ē'kə-) or **ec·o·log'ic** adj. —**ec·o·log'i·cal·ly** adv. —**e·col'o·gist** n.

ec·o·nom·ic (ĕk'ə-nŏm'ĭk, ē'kə-) adj. **1.** Of or pertaining to the production, development, and management of material wealth, as of a country. **2.** Of or pertaining to the necessities of life.

ec·o·nom·i·cal (ĕk'ə-nŏm'ĭ-kəl, ē'kə-) adj. **1.** Not wasteful; frugal. **2.** Operating inexpensively or at a saving. —**ec·o·nom'i·cal·ly** adv.

ec·o·nom·ics (ĕk'ə-nŏm'ĭks, ē'kə-) n. (used with a sing. verb). The science of the production, distribution, and consumption of goods and services. —**e·con'o·mist** (ĭ-kŏn'ə-mĭst) n.

e·con·o·mize (ĭ-kŏn'ə-mīz') v. **-mized, -miz·ing.** To be thrifty or frugal; practice economy. —**e·con'o·miz'er** n.

e·con·o·my (ĭ-kŏn'ə-mē) n., pl. **-mies. 1. a.** The careful or thrifty management of resources. **b.** An instance of this. **2.** A system for the management and development of resources: *an agricultural economy.* [< Gk. *oikonomia*, management of a household.]

ec·o·sys·tem (ĕk'ō-sĭs'təm) n. An ecological community together with its environment, considered as a unit. [ECO(LOGY) + SYSTEM.]

ec·ru (ĕk'rōō, ā'krōō) n. A light tan color. [Fr. *écru.*]

ec·sta·sy (ĕk'stə-sē) n., pl. **-sies.** A state of intense or extreme emotion, esp. rapture. [< Gk. *ekstasis.*] —**ec·stat'ic** (ĭk-stăt'ĭk) adj. —**ec·stat'i·cal·ly** adv.

-ectomy suff. Removal by surgery: *tonsillectomy.* [< Gk. *ek-*, out + NLat. *-tomia*, a cutting.]

ec·u·men·i·cal (ĕk'yə-mĕn'ĭ-kəl) adj. **1.** Worldwide in range or applicability; universal. **2.** Of or pertaining to ecumenism. [< Gk. *oikoumenē*, the inhabited world < *oikein*, to inhabit.]

ec·u·men·ism (ĕk'yə-mə-nĭz'əm, ĭ-kyōō'-) n. A movement seeking to achieve worldwide Christian unity. —**ec'u·men'ist** n.

ec·ze·ma (ĕk'sə-mə, ĭg-zē'-) n. A noncontagious skin inflammation marked by itching and sores that become crusted and scaly. [< Gk. *ekzema.*]

-ed¹ suff. **1.** Used to form the past participle of regular verbs: *absorbed.* **2.** Having; characterized by; resembling: *blackhearted.* [OE *-ad, -ed, -od.*]

-ed² suff. Used to form the past tense of regular verbs: *inhabited.* [< OE *-ade, -ede, -ode.*]

E·dam (ē'dəm, ē'dăm') n. A yellow Dutch cheese pressed into balls. [< *Edam*, Netherlands.]

ed·dy (ĕd'ē) n., pl. **-dies.** A current, as of water, moving contrary to the direction of a main current, esp. in a circular motion. —v. **-died, -dy·ing.** To move in an eddy. [ME *ydy.*]

e·del·weiss (ā'dəl-vīs', -wīs') n. An Alpine plant with downy leaves and small whitish flowers. [G.]

e·de·ma (ĭ-dē'mə) n. An excessive accumulation of serous fluid in the tissues. [< Gk. *oidēma*, a swelling.]

E·den (ēd'n) n. **1.** The first home of Adam and Eve; Paradise. **2.** A state of bliss or ultimate happiness.

edge (ĕj) n. **1.** The line or point where something begins or ends. **2.** A dividing line or point of transition; border. **3.** The sharp side of a cutting blade. **4.** An advantage. **5.** Keenness; zest. —v. **edged, edg·ing. 1.** To give an edge to. **2.** To advance or move gradually. —**idiom. on edge.** Highly tense or nervous; irritable. [< OE *ecg.*]

edge·wise (ĕj'wīz') adv. Also **edge·ways** (-wāz'). With the edge foremost.

edg·ing (ĕj'ĭng) n. Something that forms an edge or border.

edg·y (ĕj'ē) adj. **-i·er, -i·est. 1.** Tense and nervous. **2.** Having a sharp edge. —**edg'i·ness** n.

  Syns: *edgy, jittery, jumpy, nervous, restless, skittish, tense, uneasy, uptight* **adj.**

ed·i·ble (ĕd'ə-bəl) adj. Fit to be eaten. [< Lat. *edere*, to eat.] —**ed'i·bil'i·ty** n.

e·dict (ē'dĭkt') n. A decree; proclamation. [Lat. *edictum* < *edicere*, to proclaim.]

ed·i·fice (ĕd'ə-fĭs) *n.* A building, esp. one of imposing size. [< Lat. *aedificium.*]

ed·i·fy (ĕd'ə-fī') *v.* **-fied, -fy·ing.** To instruct, esp. so as to encourage moral improvement. [< Lat. *aedificare,* to build.] —**ed'i·fi·ca'tion** *n.* —**ed'i·fi'er** *n.*

ed·it (ĕd'ĭt) *v.* **1.** To prepare for publication, as by revising. **2.** To supervise the publication of. **3.** To put together the parts of (a film, an electronic tape, or a sound track) by cutting, combining, and splicing. [< Lat. *edere,* to publish.] —**ed'i·tor** *n.* —**ed'i·tor·ship'** *n.*

e·di·tion (ĭ-dĭsh'ən) *n.* **1.** The form in which a book is published. **2.** The entire number of copies of a publication printed at one time. **3.** One similar to an original; version.

ed·i·to·ri·al (ĕd'ĭ-tôr'ē-əl, -tōr'-) *n.* An article, as in a newspaper, expressing the opinion of its editors or publishers. —*adj.* **1.** Of or pertaining to an editor. **2.** Characteristic of or being an editorial. —**ed'i·to'ri·al·ly** *adv.*

ed·i·to·ri·al·ize (ĕd'ĭ-tôr'ē-ə-līz', -tōr'-) *v.* **-ized, -iz·ing. 1.** To express an opinion in or as if in an editorial. **2.** To express an opinion in a factual report. —**ed'i·to'ri·al·iz'er** *n.*

ed·u·ca·ble (ĕj'ə-kə-bəl) *adj.* Capable of being educated. [EDUC(ATE) + -ABLE.]

ed·u·cate (ĕj'ə-kāt') *v.* **-cat·ed, -cat·ing. 1.** To provide with esp. formal schooling; teach. **2.** To stimulate or develop the mental or moral growth of. [< Lat. *educare.*] —**ed'u·ca'tor** *n.*

ed·u·ca·tion (ĕj'ə-kā'shən) *n.* **1. a.** The act or process of educating. **b.** The process of being educated. **c.** The knowledge or skills obtained. **2.** The study of the teaching and learning processes; pedagogy. —**ed'u·ca'tion·al** *adj.* —**ed'u·ca'tion·al·ly** *adv.*

e·duce (ĭ-dōōs', ĭ-dyōōs') *v.* **e·duced, e·duc·ing. 1.** To evoke; elicit. **2.** To work out from given facts; deduce. [Lat. *educere.*]

-ee[1] *suff.* **1.** The recipient of an action: *addressee.* **2.** One who is in a specified condition: *standee.* [< Lat. *-atus, -ate.*]

-ee[2] *suff.* **1. a.** One resembling: *goatee.* **b.** A particular kind of: *bootee.* Used often as a diminutive. **2.** One connected with: *bargee.* [< -Y!.]

eel (ēl) *n., pl.* **eel** or **eels.** Any of various long, snakelike marine or freshwater fishes. [< OE *æl.*]

eel

-eer *suff.* One who works with or is concerned with: *auctioneer.* [< Lat. *-arius, -ary.*]

ee·rie or **ee·ry** (îr'ē) *adj.* **-ri·er, -ri·est. 1.** Inspiring fear or dread. **2.** Uncanny; mysteri-

ous. [< OE *earg,* timid.] —**ee'ri·ly** *adv.* —**ee'ri·ness** *n.*

ef·face (ĭ-fās') *v.* **-faced, -fac·ing.** To obliterate or make indistinct by or as if by rubbing out. [OFr. *effacer.*] —**ef·face'ment** *n.*

ef·fect (ĭ-fĕkt') *n.* **1.** Something brought about by a cause or agent; result. **2.** The capacity to achieve a desired result; influence. **3.** The condition of being operative or in full force. **4.** Basic meaning; purport: *said something to that effect.* **5. effects.** Possessions; belongings. —*v.* **1.** To bring about; accomplish. **2.** To make; execute. —*idiom.* **in effect. 1.** In fact; actually. **2.** In essence; virtually. **3.** In active force; in operation. [< Lat. *effectus,* p.p. of *efficere,* to accomplish.]

ef·fec·tive (ĭ-fĕk'tĭv) *adj.* **1.** Having an intended or desired effect. **2.** Producing a desired impression; striking. **3.** In effect; operative. —**ef·fec'tive·ly** *adv.* —**ef·fec'tive·ness** *n.*

ef·fec·tor (ĭ-fĕk'tər) *n.* An organ at the end of a nerve that activates gland secretion or muscular contraction.

ef·fec·tu·al (ĭ-fĕk'chōō-əl) *adj.* Producing or sufficient to produce a desired effect; fully adequate. —**ef·fec'tu·al·ly** *adv.*

ef·fec·tu·ate (ĭ-fĕk'chōō-āt') *v.* **-at·ed, -at·ing.** To bring about; effect. [Med. Lat. *effectuare.*]

ef·fem·i·nate (ĭ-fĕm'ə-nĭt) *adj.* Having qualities associated more with women than men; unmanly. [Lat. *effeminatus,* p.p. of *effeminare,* to make effeminate.] —**ef·fem'i·na·cy** *n.* —**ef·fem'i·nate·ly** *adv.*

ef·fer·ent (ĕf'ər-ənt) *adj.* Directed away from a central organ or area, esp. carrying impulses from the central nervous system to an effector. [< Lat. *efferre,* to carry away.]

ef·fer·vesce (ĕf'ər-vĕs') *v.* **-vesced, -vesc·ing. 1.** To emit small bubbles of gas, as a carbonated liquid does. **2.** To be lively or vivacious. [Lat. *effervescere,* to boil over.] —**ef'fer·ves'cence** *n.* —**ef'fer·ves'cent** *adj.*

ef·fete (ĭ-fēt') *adj.* **1.** Exhausted of vitality or effectiveness; worn-out. **2.** Decadent. [Lat. *effetus,* worn out by childbearing.]

ef·fi·ca·cious (ĕf'ĭ-kā'shəs) *adj.* Producing or capable of producing a desired effect. [< Lat. *efficax.*] —**ef'fi·ca·cy** (-kə-sē) *n.*

ef·fi·cien·cy (ĭ-fĭsh'ən-sē) *n., pl.* **-cies. 1.** The condition or quality of being efficient. **2.** The ratio of the effective or useful output to the total input in a system.

ef·fi·cient (ĭ-fĭsh'ənt) *adj.* **1.** Acting or producing effectively with a minimum of waste or effort. **2.** Exhibiting a high ratio of output to input. [< Lat. *efficere,* to bring about.] —**ef·fi'cient·ly** *adv.*

ef·fi·gy (ĕf'ə-jē) *n., pl.* **-gies.** An image of a person, esp. a crude image of a hated or despised person. [< Lat. *effigies,* likeness.]

ef·flo·resce (ĕf'lə-rĕs') *v.* **-resced, -resc·ing.** To blossom; bloom. [Lat. *efflorescere.*]

ef·flo·res·cence (ĕf'lə-rĕs'əns) *n.* **1.** A state or time of flowering. **2. a.** A gradual process of developing. **b.** The highest point; culmination. —**ef'flo·res'cent** *adj.*

ef·flu·ence (ĕf'lōō-əns) *n.* **1.** The act or process of flowing out. **2.** Something that flows out. [< Lat. *effluere,* to flow out.] —**ef'flu·ent** *adj. & n.*

ă pat ā pay â care ä father ĕ pet ē be ĭ pit ī tie î pier ŏ pot ō toe ô paw, for oi noise ōō took ōō boot ou out th thin th this ŭ cut û urge yōō abuse zh vision ə about, item, edible, gallop, circus

ef·flu·vi·um (ĭ-flōō'vē-əm) *n.*, *pl.* **-vi·a** (-vē-ə) or **-ums.** An often foul or harmful emanation. [Lat., a flowing out.]

ef·fort (ĕf'ərt) *n.* **1.** The applied use of physical or mental energy. **2.** Exertion. **3.** An attempt. **4.** Something done or produced through effort; achievement. [< Med. Lat. *exfortiare,* to force.] **—ef'fort·ful** *adj.* **—ef'fort·less** *adj.*

Syns: *effort, endeavor, exertion, pains, strain, struggle, trouble* **n.**

ef·fron·ter·y (ĭ-frŭn'tə-rē) *n.*, *pl.* **-ies.** Impudent boldness; insolence. [< LLat. *effrons,* shameless.]

ef·ful·gent (ĭ-fŏŏl'jənt, ĭ-fŭl'-) *adj.* Shining brilliantly; radiant. [< Lat. *effulgēre,* to shine out.] **—ef·ful'gence** *n.*

ef·fu·sion (ĭ-fyōō'zhən) *n.* **1.** A pouring forth. **2.** An unrestrained outpouring.

ef·fu·sive (ĭ-fyōō'sĭv) *adj.* Unrestrained in emotional expression. **—ef·fu'sive·ly** *adv.* **—ef·fu'sive·ness** *n.*

eft (ĕft) *n.* A newt. [< OE *efeta,* lizard.]

e·gal·i·tar·i·an (ĭ-găl'ĭ-târ'ē-ən) *adj.* Advocating political, economic, and legal equality for all. [< Lat. *aequalis,* equal.] **—e·gal'i·tar'i·an** *n.* **—e·gal'i·tar'i·an·ism** *n.*

egg¹ (ĕg) *n.* **1.** A female reproductive cell; ovum. **2.** The oval, thin-shelled ovum of a bird, esp. that of a domestic fowl, used as food. [< ON, a bird's egg.]

egg² (ĕg) *v.* To encourage or incite to action: *Egged on by him, I played a shameful trick on the old man.* [< ON *eggja.*]

egg·beat·er (ĕg'bē'tər) *n.* A kitchen utensil with rotating blades for beating or whipping.

egg·head (ĕg'hĕd') *n. Slang.* An intellectual; highbrow.

egg·nog (ĕg'nŏg') *n.* A drink consisting of milk, beaten eggs, and often liquor. [EGG + obs. *nog,* ale.]

egg·plant (ĕg'plănt') *n.* **1.** A plant cultivated for its large, ovoid purple-skinned fruit. **2.** The fruit of the eggplant.

egg·shell (ĕg'shĕl') *n.* The brittle outer covering of an egg.

e·gis (ē'jĭs) *n.* Var. of **aegis.**

eg·lan·tine (ĕg'lən-tīn', -tēn') *n.* The sweetbrier. [< OFr. *aiglent.*]

e·go (ē'gō, ĕg'ō) *n.* **1.** The self as distinguished from all others. **2.** The personality component that is conscious, most immediately controls behavior, and is most in touch with external reality. **3.** Conceit; egotism. [Lat., I.] **—e·go·cen'tric** *adj.*

e·go·cen·tric (ē'gō-sĕn'trĭk, ĕg'ō-) *adj.* Thinking or acting with one's self as the major concern; self-centered. **—e'go·cen'tric** *n.* **—e'go·cen·tric'i·ty** (-trĭs'ĭ-tē) *n.*

e·go·ism (ē'gō-ĭz'əm, ĕg'ō-) *n.* **1.** The belief that self-interest is the just and proper motive force. **2.** Egotism. **—e'go·ist** *n.* **—e'go·is'tic** or **e·go·is'ti·cal** *adj.* **—e'go·is'ti·cal·ly** *adv.*

e·go·tism (ē'gə-tĭz'əm, ĕg'ə-) *n.* **1.** The tendency to speak or write excessively about oneself. **2.** An exaggerated sense of self-importance; conceit. **—e'go·tist** *n.* **—e'go·tis'tic** or **e·go·tis'ti·cal** *adj.* **—e'go·tis'ti·cal·ly** *adv.*

ego trip *n. Slang.* An experience or act that boosts or gratifies the ego.

e·gre·gious (ĭ-grē'jəs, -jē-əs) *adj.* Conspicuously bad; flagrant; outrageous. [Lat. *egregius,* distinguished.] **—e·gre'gious·ly** *adv.* **—e·gre'gious·ness** *n.*

e·gress (ē'grĕs') *n.* A path or means of going out; exit. [Lat. *egressus.*]

e·gret (ē'grĭt, ĕg'rĭt) *n.* A heronlike, usu. white wading bird with long, showy, drooping plumes. [< Prov. *aigron,* heron.]

E·gyp·tian (ĭ-jĭp'shən) *n.* **1.** A native or inhabitant of Egypt. **2.** The Afro-Asiatic language spoken by the ancient Egyptians. **—E·gyp'tian** *adj.*

ei·der (ī'dər) *n.* A sea duck of northern regions, with soft, fine down. [< ON *æðhr.*]

eider

ei·der·down (ī'dər-doun') *n.* The down of the eider.

eight (āt) *n.* **1.** The cardinal number equal to the sum of 7 + 1. **2.** The 8th in a set or sequence. **3.** Something having eight parts, units, or members. [< OE *eahta.*] **—eight** *adj. & pron.*

eight ball *n.* A black pool ball bearing the number 8. **—idiom. behind the eight ball.** *Slang.* In an unfavorable position.

eigh·teen (ā-tēn') *n.* **1.** The cardinal number equal to the sum of 17 + 1. **2.** The 18th in a set or sequence. **—eight·een'** *adj. & pron.*

eigh·teenth (ā-tēnth') *n.* **1.** The ordinal number that matches the number 18 in a series. **2.** One of 18 equal parts. **—eight·eenth'** *adj. & adv.*

eighth (ātth, āth) *n.* **1.** The ordinal number that matches the number 8 in a series. **2.** One of eight equal parts. **—eighth** *adj. & adv.*

eight·i·eth (ā'tē-ĭth) *n.* **1.** The ordinal number that matches the number 80 in a series. **2.** One of 80 equal parts. **—eight'i·eth** *adj. & adv.*

eight·y (ā'tē) *n.* The cardinal number equal to 8 × 10. **—eight'y** *adj. & pron.*

ein·stein·i·um (īn-stī'nē-əm) *n. Symbol* **Es** A synthetic element first produced by neutron irradiation of uranium in a thermonuclear explosion. Atomic number 99; longest-lived isotope Es 254. [< Albert *Einstein* (1879–1955).]

ei·ther (ē'thər, ī'thər) *pron.* One or the other of two. **—adj.** **1.** One or the other of two: *Wear either coat.* **2.** The one and the other: *candles on either side of the centerpiece.* **—conj.** Used correlatively with *or* to introduce alternatives: *Either we go now or spend the night here.* **—adv.** Likewise; also: *If you don't go, I won't either.* [< OE *ægther.*]

Usage: *Either* is normally used to mean "one of two," although it is sometimes used of three or more: *either corner of the triangle.* When referring to one of more than two, *any* or *any one* is preferred.

e·jac·u·late (ĭ-jăk'yə-lāt') *v.* **-lat·ed, -lat·ing.** **1.** To eject abruptly, esp. to discharge semen.

2. To utter suddenly and passionately; exclaim. [Lat. *ejaculari*.] —e·jac'u·la'tion *n.* —e·jac'u·la·to'ry (-lə-tôr'ē, -tôr'ē) *adj.*

e·ject (ĭ-jĕkt') *v.* To discharge or throw out forcefully; expel. [< Lat. *ejicere*.] —e·jec'tion *n.* —e·jec'tor *n.*

ejection seat *n.* A seat that ejects clear of an aircraft and parachutes to the ground in an emergency.

eke (ēk) *v.* **eked, ek·ing.** To make or supplement with difficulty or effort: *eke out a living.* [< OE *ēacan*, to increase.]

e·kis·tics (ĭ-kĭs'tĭks) *n. (used with a sing. verb).* The science of human settlements, including city or community planning and design. [< Gk. *oikistikos*, of settlements.] —e·kis'tic *adj.*

ek·pwe·le (ĕk-pwĕ'lē) *n.* See table at **currency.** [Native word in Equatorial Guinea.]

e·lab·o·rate (ĭ-lăb'ər-ĭt) *adj.* **1.** Planned or executed with painstaking attention to detail. **2.** Very complex and usu. ornate. —*v.* (-ə-rāt') **-rat·ed, -rat·ing. 1.** To work out with care and detail; develop thoroughly. **2.** To express oneself at greater length or in greater detail. [Lat. *elaboratus*, p.p. of *elaborare*, to work out.] —e·lab'o·rate·ly *adv.* —e·lab'o·rate·ness *n.* —e·lab'o·ra'tion *n.*

é·lan (ā-län', ā-län') *n.* Enthusiasm; ardor. [< OFr. *eslancer*, to throw out.]

e·land (ē'lənd, ē'länd') *n.* A large African antelope with spirally twisted horns. [Afr.]

e·lapse (ĭ-lăps') *v.* **e·lapsed, e·laps·ing.** To slip by; pass, as time. [Lat. *elabi.*]

e·las·tic (ĭ-lăs'tĭk) *adj.* **1.** Returning or capable of returning to an initial form or shape after deformation. **2.** Adaptable to change; flexible. **3.** Quick to recover or revive. —*n.* **1.** An elastic fabric or tape. **2.** A rubber band. [< Gk. *elastos*, impulsive.] —e·las·tic'i·ty (ĭ-lă-stĭs'ĭ-tē, ē'lă-) *n.*

e·late (ĭ-lāt') *v.* **e·lat·ed, e·lat·ing.** To fill with happiness or joy. [< Lat. *elatus*, p.p. of *efferre*, to carry away.] —e·la'tion *n.*

el·bow (ĕl'bō') *n.* **1. a.** The joint or bend of the arm between the forearm and upper arm. **b.** The bony outer projection of this joint. **2.** Something, esp. a length of pipe, having a bend similar to an elbow. —*v.* **1.** To push or jostle with the elbow. **2.** To make one's way by elbowing. [< OE *elnboga.*]

elbow grease *n. Informal.* Strenuous effort.

el·bow·room (ĕl'bō-rōōm', -rŏŏm') *n.* Room enough to move around or function in.

eld·er¹ (ĕl'dər) *adj.* A compar. of **old.** —*n.* **1.** An older person. **2.** An older, influential member of a family, tribe, or community. **3.** One of the governing officers of a church. [< OE *eldra.*]

Usage: *Elder* and *eldest* apply only to persons, unlike *older* and *oldest*, which also apply to things. *Elder* and *eldest* are used principally with reference to seniority: *elder brother; elder statesman.*

el·der² (ĕl'dər) *n.* A shrub with clusters of small white flowers and red or blackish berries. [< OE *ellen.*]

el·der·ber·ry (ĕl'dər-bĕr'ē) *n.* **1.** The small, edible fruit of an elder. **2.** The elder.

eld·er·ly (ĕl'dər-lē) *adj.* **1.** Approaching old

age. **2.** Of, pertaining to, or characteristic of old age.

eld·est (ĕl'dĭst) *adj.* A superl. of **old.**

El Do·ra·do (ĕl' də-rä'dō) *n.* A place of fabulous wealth. [Sp., the gilded (land).]

e·lect (ĭ-lĕkt') *v.* **1.** To select by vote, as for office or membership. **2.** To choose; pick. —*adj.* **1.** Chosen deliberately; singled out. **2.** Elected but not yet installed in office: *the governor-elect.* —*n.* **1.** A selected person. **2.** *(used with a pl. verb).* The members of a wealthy or privileged group. [< Lat. *eligere.*]

e·lec·tion (ĭ-lĕk'shən) *n.* **1.** The act or process of electing. **2.** The fact of being elected.

e·lec·tion·eer (ĭ-lĕk'shə-nîr') *v.* To work actively for a candidate or political party.

e·lec·tive (ĭ-lĕk'tĭv) *adj.* **1.** Filled or chosen by election. **2.** Having the power to elect. **3.** Optional. —*n.* An elective course in an academic curriculum.

e·lec·tor (ĭ-lĕk'tər) *n.* **1.** A qualified voter. **2.** A member of the Electoral College. —e·lec'tor·al *adj.*

Electoral College *n.* A group of electors chosen to elect the President and Vice President of the United States.

e·lec·tor·ate (ĭ-lĕk'tər-ĭt) *n.* All those persons qualified to vote.

electr- *pref.* Var. of **electro-.**

e·lec·tric (ĭ-lĕk'trĭk) or **e·lec·tri·cal** (-trĭ-kəl) *adj.* **1.** Of, pertaining to, derived from, producing, produced, powered, or operated by electricity. **2.** Charged with emotion; thrilling. —e·lec'tri·cal·ly *adv.*

electric chair *n.* A chair used to electrocute a person sentenced to death.

electric eye *n.* A photoelectric cell.

e·lec·tri·cian (ĭ-lĕk-trĭsh'ən, ē'lĕk-) *n.* One whose occupation is the installation, repair, or operation of electric equipment and circuitry.

e·lec·tric·i·ty (ĭ-lĕk-trĭs'ĭ-tē, ē'lĕk-) *n.* **1.** The class of physical phenomena arising from the existence and interactions of electric charge. **2.** Electric current used or regarded as a source of power.

e·lec·tri·fy (ĭ-lĕk'trə-fī') *v.* **-fied, -fy·ing. 1.** To produce electric charge on or in. **2.** To wire or equip for the use of electric power. **3.** To thrill, startle, or shock. —e·lec'tri·fi·ca'tion *n.*

electro- or **electr-** *pref.* **1.** Electricity: *electromagnet.* **2.** Electric; electrically: *electrocute.* **3.** Electrolysis: *electrolyte.* [< Gk. *ēlektron*, amber.]

e·lec·tro·car·di·o·gram (ĭ-lĕk'trō-kär'dē-ə-grăm') *n.* The curve traced by an electrocardiograph, used to diagnose heart disease.

e·lec·tro·car·di·o·graph (ĭ-lĕk'trō-kär'dē-ə-grăf') *n.* An instrument that records electric potentials associated with the electric currents that traverse the heart. —e·lec'tro·car'di·og'ra·phy (-ŏg'rə-fē) *n.*

e·lec·tro·chem·is·try (ĭ-lĕk'trō-kĕm'ĭ-strē) *n.* The science of the interaction of electricity and chemical reactions or changes. —e·lec'tro·chem'i·cal (-ĭ-kəl) *adj.*

e·lec·tro·cute (ĭ-lĕk'trə-kyōōt') *v.* **-cut·ed, -cut·ing. 1.** To kill with electricity. **2.** To execute (a condemned criminal) by electricity. [ELECTRO- + (EXE)CUTE.] —e·lec'tro·cu'tion *n.*

e·lec·trode (ĭ-lĕk'trōd') *n.* A solid electric conductor through which an electric current enters or leaves a medium such as an electrolyte, a nonmetallic solid, a molten metal, a gas, or a vacuum.

e·lec·tro·dy·nam·ics (ĭ-lĕk'trō-dī-năm'ĭks) *n.* *(used with a sing. verb).* The scientific study of the relationships between electric, magnetic, and mechanical phenomena. —**e·lec'tro·dy·nam'ic** *adj.*

e·lec·tro·en·ceph·a·lo·gram (ĭ-lĕk'trō-ĕn-sĕf'ə-lə-grăm') *n.* A graphic record of the electrical activity of the brain as recorded by an electroencephalograph.

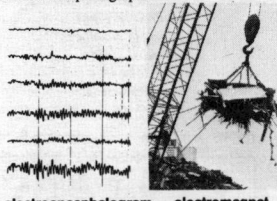

electroencephalogram   **electromagnet**

e·lec·tro·en·ceph·a·lo·graph (ĭ-lĕk'trō-ĕn-sĕf'ə-lə-grăf') *n.* An instrument that records the electrical activity of the brain. —**e·lec'tro·en·ceph'a·log'ra·phy** (-lŏg'rə-fē) *n.*

e·lec·trol·o·gist (ĭ-lĕk-trŏl'ə-jĭst, ē'lĕk-) *n.* One that removes esp. body hair by means of an electric current.

e·lec·trol·y·sis (ĭ-lĕk-trŏl'ĭ-sĭs, ē'lĕk-) *n.* **1.** Chemical change, esp. decomposition, produced in an electrolyte by an electric current. **2.** Destruction of living tissue, as hair roots, by an electric current.

e·lec·tro·lyte (ĭ-lĕk'trə-līt') *n.* A substance that dissociates into ions in solution or when fused, thereby becoming electrically conductive.

e·lec·tro·lyt·ic (ĭ-lĕk'trə-lĭt'ĭk) *adj.* **1.** Of or pertaining to electrolysis. **2.** Of or pertaining to an electrolyte. —**e·lec'tro·lyt'i·cal·ly** *adv.*

e·lec·tro·mag·net (ĭ-lĕk'trō-măg'nĭt) *n.* A device consisting essentially of a soft-iron core wound with a current-carrying coil of insulated wire.

e·lec·tro·mag·net·ic (ĭ-lĕk'trō-măg-nĕt'ĭk) *adj.* Of or exhibiting electromagnetism. —**e·lec'tro·mag·net'i·cal·ly** *adv.*

electromagnetic radiation *n.* A series of electromagnetic waves.

e·lec·tro·mag·net·ism (ĭ-lĕk'trō-măg'nĭ-tĭz'əm) *n.* **1.** Magnetism arising from electric charges in motion. **2.** The physics of electricity and magnetism.

e·lec·tro·mo·tive (ĭ-lĕk'trō-mō'tĭv) *adj.* Of, pertaining to, or producing electric current.

electromotive force *n.* **1.** A force that tends to produce an electric current. **2.** The energy per unit of charge that is converted into electrical form by a device such as a battery or generator.

e·lec·tron (ĭ-lĕk'trŏn') *n.* A subatomic particle having a unit negative electric charge of about 1.602×10^{-19} coulomb and a mass, when at rest, of 9.1066×10^{-28} gram.

e·lec·tron·ic (ĭ-lĕk-trŏn'ĭk, ē'lĕk-) *adj.* Of, pertaining to, or involving electrons or electronics. —**e·lec·tron'i·cal·ly** *adv.*

e·lec·tron·ics (ĭ-lĕk-trŏn'ĭks, ē'lĕk-) *n.* *(used with a sing. verb).* **1.** The science and technology of electronic devices and systems. **2.** The commercial industry of electronic devices and systems.

electron microscope *n.* A microscope that uses a beam of electrons rather than a beam of visible light to produce magnified images.

electron tube *n.* A sealed, enclosed space, containing either a vacuum or a small amount of gas, in which electrons act as the main carriers of current between at least two electrodes.

e·lec·tro·pho·re·sis (ĭ-lĕk'trō-fə-rē'sĭs) *n.* The motion of charged particles through a relatively stationary liquid under the influence of an applied electric field. —**e·lec'tro·pho·ret'ic** (-rĕt'ĭk) *adj.*

e·lec·tro·plate (ĭ-lĕk'trə-plāt') *v.* **-plat·ed, -plat·ing.** To coat or cover electrolytically with a thin layer of metal.

e·lec·tro·pos·i·tive (ĭ-lĕk'trō-pŏz'ĭ-tĭv) *adj.* **1.** Having a positive electric charge. **2.** Tending to release electrons to form a chemical bond.

e·lec·tro·shock (ĭ-lĕk'trō-shŏk') *n.* A form of shock therapy in which an electric current is passed through the brain.

e·lec·tro·stat·ic (ĭ-lĕk'trō-stăt'ĭk) *adj.* **1.** Of, pertaining to, or produced by static electric charges. **2.** Of or pertaining to electrostatics.

e·lec·tro·stat·ics (ĭ-lĕk'trō-stăt'ĭks) *n.* *(used with a sing. verb).* The scientific study of static electricity.

e·lec·tro·type (ĭ-lĕk'trə-tīp') *n.* A duplicate metal plate used in letterpress printing, made by electroplating a mold of the original plate.

el·ee·mos·y·nary (ĕl'ə-mŏs'ə-nĕr'ē, ĕl'ē-ə-) *adj.* Of, pertaining to, supported by, or contributed as charity. [< Gk. *eleēmosunē*, alms.]

el·e·gance (ĕl'ĭ-gəns) *n.* **1.** Refinement and grace, as in appearance or manners. **2.** Tasteful opulence in form, decoration, or presentation. **3.** Something characterized by elegance. [< Lat. *eligere*, to choose.] —**el'e·gant** *adj.* —**el'e·gant·ly** *adv.*

el·e·gi·ac (ĕl'ə-jī'ăk, ĭ-lē'jē-ăk') *adj.* **1.** Of or pertaining to an elegy. **2.** Expressing sorrow; mournful.

el·e·gy (ĕl'ə-jē) *n.*, *pl.* **-gies.** A mournful poem, esp. one lamenting the dead. [< Gk. *elegeia.*]

el·e·ment (ĕl'ə-mənt) *n.* **1.** *Chem. & Physics.* A substance composed of atoms having an identical number of protons in each nucleus and not separable into a less complex substance. **2.** A fundamental or essential part of a whole. **3. a.** *Math.* A member of a set. **b.** A point, line, or plane. **c.** A part of a geometric configuration, as an angle in a triangle. **4. elements.** The forces that collectively constitute the weather, esp. inclement weather. **5.** An environment natural to or associated with an individual. [< Lat. *elementum*, first principle.]

el·e·men·tal (ĕl'ə-mĕn'tl) *adj.* **1.** Of, pertaining to, or being an element. **2.** Fundamental or essential. **3.** Rudimentary or simple. **4.** Of or resembling a force of nature in power or effect.

el·e·men·ta·ry (ĕl'ə-mĕn'tə-rē, -trē) *adj.* **1.** Fundamental, essential, or irreducible. **2.** Of, involving, or introducing the funda-

PERIODIC TABLE OF THE ELEMENTS

KEY

Atomic Number	→	1
		H	← Symbol
		Hydrogen
		1.00797

Atomic Weight (or Mass Number of most stable isotope if in parentheses)

1a								
1 **H** Hydrogen 1.00797	2a							
3 **Li** Lithium 6.939	4 **Be** Beryllium 9.0122	3b	4b	5b	6b	7b		8
11 **Na** Sodium 22.9898	12 **Mg** Magnesium 24.312							
19 **K** Potassium 39.102	20 **Ca** Calcium 40.08	21 **Sc** Scandium 44.956	22 **Ti** Titanium 47.90	23 **V** Vanadium 50.942	24 **Cr** Chromium 51.996	25 **Mn** Manganese 54.9380	26 **Fe** Iron 55.847	27 **Co** Cobalt 58.9332
37 **Rb** Rubidium 85.47	38 **Sr** Strontium 87.62	39 **Y** Yttrium 88.905	40 **Zr** Zirconium 91.22	41 **Nb** Niobium 92.906	42 **Mo** Molybdenum 95.94	43 **Tc** Technetium (97)	44 **Ru** Ruthenium 101.07	45 **Rh** Rhodium 102.905
55 **Cs** Cesium 132.905	56 **Ba** Barium 137.34	57–71* Lanthanides	72 **Hf** Hafnium 178.49	73 **Ta** Tantalum 180.948	74 **W** Tungsten 183.85	75 **Re** Rhenium 186.2	76 **Os** Osmium 190.2	77 **Ir** Iridium 192.2
87 **Fr** Francium (223)	88 **Ra** Radium (226)	89–103** **Actinides						

*Lanthanides	57 **La** Lanthanum 138.91	58 **Ce** Cerium 140.12	59 **Pr** Praseodymium 140.907	60 **Nd** Neodymium 144.24	61 **Pm** Promethium (145)	62 **Sm** Samarium 150.35	63 **Eu** Europium 151.96
**Actinides	89 **Ac** Actinium (227)	90 **Th** Thorium 232.038	91 **Pa** Protactinium (231)	92 **U** Uranium 238.03	93 **Np** Neptunium (237)	94 **Pu** Plutonium (244)	95 **Am** Americium (243)

				3a	4a	5a	6a	7a	0
									2 **He** Helium 4.0026
				5 **B** Boron 10.811	6 **C** Carbon 12.01115	7 **N** Nitrogen 14.0067	8 **O** Oxygen 15.9994	9 **F** Fluorine 18.9984	10 **Ne** Neon 20.183
	1b	**2b**		13 **Al** Aluminum 26.9815	14 **Si** Silicon 28.086	15 **P** Phosphorus 30.9738	16 **S** Sulfur 32.064	17 **Cl** Chlorine 35.453	18 **Ar** Argon 39.948
28 **Ni** Nickel 58.71	29 **Cu** Copper 63.546	30 **Zn** Zinc 65.37	31 **Ga** Gallium 69.72	32 **Ge** Germanium 72.59	33 **As** Arsenic 74.9216	34 **Se** Selenium 78.96	35 **Br** Bromine 79.904	36 **Kr** Krypton 83.80
46 **Pd** Palladium 106.4	47 **Ag** Silver 107.868	48 **Cd** Cadmium 112.40	49 **In** Indium 114.82	50 **Sn** Tin 118.69	51 **Sb** Antimony 121.75	52 **Te** Tellurium 127.60	53 **I** Iodine 126.9044	54 **Xe** Xenon 131.30
78 **Pt** Platinum 195.09	79 **Au** Gold 196.967	80 **Hg** Mercury 200.59	81 **Tl** Thallium 204.37	82 **Pb** Lead 207.19	83 **Bi** Bismuth 208.980	84 **Po** Polonium (210)	85 **At** Astatine (210)	86 **Rn** Radon (222)

64 **Gd** Gadolinium 157.25	65 **Tb** Terbium 158.924	66 **Dy** Dysprosium 162.50	67 **Ho** Holmium 164.930	68 **Er** Erbium 167.26	69 **Tm** Thulium 168.934	70 **Yb** Ytterbium 173.04	71 **Lu** Lutetium 174.97
96 **Cm** Curium (247)	97 **Bk** Berkelium (247)	98 **Cf** Californium (251)	99 **Es** Einsteinium (254)	100 **Fm** Fermium (257)	101 **Md** Mendelevium (258)	102 **No** Nobelium (254)	103 **Lw** Lawrencium (257)

mental or simplest aspects of a subject; rudimentary.

elementary particle *n.* A subatomic particle.

elementary school *n.* A school attended for the first six to eight years of a child's formal education.

el·e·phant (ĕl'ə-fənt) *n.* A very large Asian or African mammal with a long, flexible trunk and long tusks. [< Gk. *elephas.*]

elephant

el·e·phan·ti·a·sis (ĕl'ə-fən-tī'ə-sĭs) *n.* Enlargement and hardening of tissues, esp. of the lower body, as a result of the blockage of lymph ducts by parasitic worms. [< Gk.]

el·e·phan·tine (ĕl'ə-făn'tēn, -tīn', ĕl'ə-fən-) *adj.* 1. Of or pertaining to an elephant. 2. a. Enormous in size. b. Ponderous; clumsy.

el·e·vate (ĕl'ə-vāt') *v.* **-vat·ed, -vat·ing.** 1. To raise to a higher position; lift up. 2. To promote to a higher rank. 3. To raise to a higher level; exalt. 4. To lift the spirits of; elate. [< Lat. *elevare.*]

el·e·va·tion (ĕl'ə-vā'shən) *n.* 1. The act of elevating or the condition of being elevated. 2. An elevated place or position. 3. A height, as above sea level, to which something is elevated.

el·e·va·tor (ĕl'ə-vā'tər) *n.* 1. A platform or enclosure raised and lowered to transport freight or people. 2. A granary with devices for hoisting and discharging grain. 3. A movable control surface on an aircraft that moves the craft upward or downward.

el·e·ven (ĭ-lĕv'ən) *n.* 1. The cardinal number equal to the sum of 10 + 1. 2. The 11th in a set or sequence. 3. Something having 11 parts, units, or members, esp. a football team. [< OE *endleofan.*] **—e·lev'en** *adj. & pron.*

el·e·venth (ĭ-lĕv'ənth) *n.* 1. The ordinal number that matches the number 11 in a series. 2. One of 11 equal parts. **—e·lev'enth** *adj. & adv.*

elf (ĕlf) *n., pl.* **elves** (ĕlvz). A small, mischievous fairy. [< OE *ælf.*] **—elf'in** *adj.* **—elf'ish** *adj.*

e·lic·it (ĭ-lĭs'ĭt) *v.* 1. To bring out; evoke. 2. To call forth. [< Lat. *elicere.*]

e·lide (ĭ-līd') *v.* **e·lid·ed, e·lid·ing.** 1. To omit or slur over (a vowel or syllable) in pronunciation. 2. To eliminate or leave out. [Lat. *elidere*, to strike out.] **—e·li'sion** (ĭ-lĭzh'ən) *n.*

el·i·gi·ble (ĕl'ĭ-jə-bəl) *adj.* 1. Qualified, as for an office or position. 2. Worthy of being chosen, esp. for marriage. [< Lat. *eligere*, to choose.] **—el'i·gi·bil'i·ty** *n.* **—el'i·gi·ble** *n.*

e·lim·i·nate (ĭ-lĭm'ə-nāt') *v.* **-nat·ed, -nat·ing.** 1. To get rid of; remove. 2. To leave out; omit. 3. To excrete (wastes) from the body. [< Lat. *eliminare.*] **—e·lim'i·na'tion** *n.*

e·lite or **é·lite** (ĭ-lēt', ā-lēt') *n.* 1. *(used with a pl. verb).* a. The superior members of a social group. b. A small but powerful group. 2. A type face for typewriters, providing 12 characters to the inch. [< OFr. *eslire*, to choose.]

e·lit·ism or **é·lit·ism** (ĭ-lē'tĭz'əm, ā-lē'-) *n.* 1. Rule or domination by an elite. 2. Belief in elitism. **—e·lit'ist** *n.*

e·lix·ir (ĭ-lĭk'sər) *n.* 1. A sweetened solution of alcohol and water containing medicine. 2. A medicine believed to cure all ills; panacea. [< Ar. *al-iksīr*, the elixir.]

E·liz·a·be·than (ĭ-lĭz'ə-bē'thən) *adj.* Of, pertaining to, or characteristic of the reign of Elizabeth I of England. **—E·liz'a·be'than** *n.*

elk (ĕlk) *n., pl.* **elks** or **elk.** 1. The wapiti. 2. A large European deer related to the North American moose. [< ON *elgr.*]

ell¹ (ĕl) *n.* An extension of a building at right angles to the main structure. [From its resemblance to the letter L.]

ell² (ĕl) *n.* A former English linear measure equal to 45 inches. [< OE *eln*, the length from elbow to finger tips.]

el·lipse (ĭ-lĭps') *n.* A plane curve formed by the locus of points the sum of the distances of each of which from two fixed points is the same constant. [< ELLIPSIS.]

el·lip·sis (ĭ-lĭp'sĭs) *n., pl.* **-ses** (-sēz'). 1. The omission of a word not necessary for the comprehension of a sentence. 2. A mark or series of marks (. . . or ***) used to indicate an omission. [< Gk. *elleipsis.*]

el·lip·soid (ĭ-lĭp'soid') *n.* A geometric surface whose plane sections are all ellipses or circles. **—el'lip·sol'dal** (ĕl'ĭp-soid'l) *adj.*

el·lip·tic (ĭ-lĭp'tĭk) or **el·lip·ti·cal** (-tĭ-kəl) *adj.* 1. Of, pertaining to, or having the shape of an ellipse. 2. Containing an ellipsis. [Gk. *elleiptikos*, defective.]

elm (ĕlm) *n.* A shade tree with arching or curving branches. [< OE.]

el·o·cu·tion (ĕl'ə-kyōō'shən) *n.* The art of public speaking. [< Lat. *eloqui*, to speak out.] **—el'o·cu'tion·ist** *n.*

e·lon·gate (ĭ-lông'gāt', ĭ-lŏng'-) *v.* **-gat·ed, -gat·ing.** To make or grow longer. [< LLat. *elongare.*] **—e·lon'ga'tion** *n.*

e·lope (ĭ-lōp') *v.* **e·loped, e·lop·ing.** To run away, esp. in order to be married. [AN *aloper*, to run away from one's husband with a lover.] **—e·lope'ment** *n.*

el·o·quent (ĕl'ə-kwənt) *adj.* 1. Fluent and persuasive in discourse. 2. Movingly expressive. [< Lat. *eloqui*, to speak out.] **—el'o·quence** *n.* **—el'o·quent·ly** *adv.*

else (ĕls) *adj.* 1. Other; different: *somebody else.* 2. In addition; more: *Would you like anything else?* **—adv.** 1. In a different time, place, or manner; differently: *How else could it be done?* 2. If not; otherwise: *Be careful or else you will make a mistake.* [< OE *elles.*]

Usage: When a pronoun is followed by *else*, the possessive form is generally written thus: *someone else's* (not *someone's else*). Both *who else's* and *whose else* are in use but not *whose else's: Who else's book could it have been? Whose else could it have been?*

else·where (ĕls'hwâr', -wâr') *adv.* To or in a different or other place.

e·lu·ci·date (ĭ-lōō'sĭ-dāt') *v.* -dat·ed, -dat·ing. To make clear or plain; clarify. [LLat. *elucidare.*] —**e·lu'ci·da'tion** *n.*

e·lude (ĭ-lōōd') *v.* e·lud·ed, e·lud·ing. 1. To manage to get away from; evade. 2. To escape the understanding or detection of. [Lat. *eludere*, to cheat.]

E·lul (ĕ-lōōl', ĕl'ōōl) *n.* The 12th month of the Hebrew calendar. See table at **calendar.** [Heb. *'Elul.*]

e·lu·sive (ĭ-lōō'sĭv, -zĭv) *adj.* Tending to elude. —**e·lu'sive·ly** *adv.* —**e·lu'sive·ness** *n.*

el·ver (ĕl'vər) *n.* A young or immature eel. [< *eelfare*, the migration of eels.]

elves (ĕlvz) *n.* Pl. of **elf.**

E·ly·si·um (ĭ-lĭz'ē-əm, ĭ-lĭzh'-) *n.* A place or condition of ideal happiness; paradise. [< Gk. *Elysium*, the abode of the blessed after death.] —**E·ly'sian** (ĭ-lĭzh'ən) *adj.*

em (ĕm) *n. Printing.* A unit of measure describing the line space occupied by the body size of a piece of type that is as long as it is wide, esp. of a pica M.

'em (əm) *pron. Informal.* Them. [< OE *heom.*]

em-1 *pref.* Var. of **en-**1.

em-2 *pref.* Var. of **en-**2.

e·ma·ci·ate (ĭ-mā'shē-āt') *v.* -at·ed, -at·ing. To cause to become thin and wasted. [Lat. *emaciare.*] —**e·ma'ci·a'tion** *n.*

em·a·nate (ĕm'ə-nāt') *v.* -nat·ed, -nat·ing. To come forth from a source; issue or originate. [< Lat. *emanare.*] —**em'a·na'tion** *n.*

e·man·ci·pate (ĭ-măn'sə-pāt') *v.* -pat·ed, -pat·ing. To free from oppression, bondage, or restraint. [Lat. *emancipare.*] —**e·man'ci·pa'tion** *n.* —**e·man'ci·pa'tor** *n.*

e·mas·cu·late (ĭ-măs'kyə-lāt') *v.* -lat·ed, -lat·ing. 1. To castrate. 2. To make weak. [Lat. *emasculare.*] —**e·mas'cu·la'tion** *n.*

em·balm (ĕm-bäm') *v.* To prevent or retard the decay of (a corpse) by treatment with preservatives. [< OFr. *embasmer.*] —**em·balm'er** *n.* —**em·balm'ment** *n.*

em·bank (ĕm-băngk') *v.* To confine, support, or protect with a bank, as of earth or stone. —**em·bank'ment** *n.*

em·bar·go (ĕm-bär'gō) *n., pl.* -goes. 1. A government order prohibiting merchant ships from entering or leaving its ports. 2. A prohibition or restriction. —*v.* To impose an embargo upon. [Sp. < *embargar*, to impede.]

em·bark (ĕm-bärk') *v.* 1. To board or cause to board a vessel, esp. at the start of a journey. 2. To set out on a venture; commence. [< LLat. *imbarcare.*] —**em'bar·ka'tion** *n.*

em·bar·rass (ĕm-băr'əs) *v.* 1. To cause to feel ill at ease; disconcert. 2. To hamper with financial difficulties. 3. To impede. [< Fr. *embarrazzare*, to impede.] —**em·bar'rass·ing·ly** *adv.* —**em·bar'rass·ment** *n.*

em·bas·sy (ĕm'bə-sē) *n., pl.* -sies. 1. The position or function of an ambassador. 2. A mission headed by an ambassador. 3. An ambassador and his staff. 4. The official headquarters of an ambassador. [< OFr. *ambassee.*]

em·bat·tle (ĕm-băt'l) *v.* -tled, -tling. To prepare or array for battle. [< OFr. *embataillier.*]

em·bed (ĕm-bĕd') *v.* -bed·ded, -bed·ding. To

fix or become fixed firmly in a surrounding mass.

em·bel·lish (ĕm-bĕl'ĭsh) *v.* 1. To make more beautiful; adorn. 2. To add fictitious details to: *embellished the truth.* [< OFr. *embellir.*] —**em·bel'lish·ment** *n.*

em·ber (ĕm'bər) *n.* 1. A piece of live coal or wood from a fire. 2. **embers.** The smoldering remains of a fire. [< OE *æmerge.*]

em·bez·zle (ĕm-bĕz'əl) *v.* -zled, -zling. To take (money or property) in violation of a trust. [< AN *enbesiler.*] —**em·bez'zle·ment** *n.* —**em·bez'zler** *n.*

em·bit·ter (ĕm-bĭt'ər) *v.* 1. To make bitter. 2. To cause bitter feelings in.

em·bla·zon (ĕm-blā'zən) *v.* 1. To ornament richly, esp. with heraldic devices. 2. To make resplendent with brilliant colors. 3. To exalt.

em·blem (ĕm'bləm) *n.* 1. Something, as an object, that represents something else; symbol. 2. An identifying badge, design, or device. [< Gk. *emblēma*, raised ornament.] —**em'blem·at'ic** (-blə-măt'ĭk) or **em'blem·at'i·cal** *adj.*

em·bod·y (ĕm-bŏd'ē) *v.* -ied, -y·ing. 1. To invest with or as with bodily form. 2. To personify. 3. To make or include as part of a united whole. —**em·bod'i·ment** *n.*

em·bold·en (ĕm-bōl'dən) *v.* To instill courage in; encourage.

em·bo·lism (ĕm'bə-lĭz'əm) *n.* The obstruction of a blood vessel by a mass of material such as an air bubble or a detached blood clot. [< Gk. *embolismos*, insertion.]

em·boss (ĕm-bôs', -bŏs') *v.* 1. To mold or carve in relief. 2. To decorate with a raised design. [< OFr. *embocer.*]

em·bou·chure (äm'bōō-shŏŏr') *n.* 1. The mouthpiece of a wind instrument. 2. The manner in which the lips and tongue are applied to an embouchure. [< OFr. *emboucher*, to stop up.]

em·bow·er (ĕm-bou'ər) *v.* To enclose or shelter in a bower.

em·brace (ĕm-brās') *v.* -braced, -brac·ing. 1. To clasp or hold in the arms; hug. 2. To encircle; surround. 3. To take in; include. 4. To take up willingly; adopt. 5. To accept eagerly; welcome. 6. To join in an act of embracing. —*n.* The act of embracing. [< OFr. *embracer.*]

em·bra·sure (ĕm-brā'zhər) *n.* 1. A recess for a door or window. 2. An opening for a gun in a wall or parapet. [Fr.]

em·bro·cate (ĕm'brə-kāt') *v.* -cat·ed, -cat·ing. To moisten and rub (a part of the body) with a lotion or liniment. [< Gk. *embrekhein.*] —**em'bro·ca'tion** *n.*

em·broi·der (ĕm-broi'dər) *v.* 1. To ornament (fabric) with needlework; do embroidery. 2. To add fictitious details to; embellish. [< OFr. *embroder.*]

em·broi·der·y (ĕm-broi'də-rē) *n., pl.* -ies. 1. The art or act of embroidering. 2. Something that has been embroidered.

em·broil (ĕm-broil') *v.* 1. To involve in argument, contention, or conflict. 2. To throw into confusion or disorder. [Fr. *embrouiller.*] —**em·broil'ment** *n.*

em·bry·o (ĕm'brē-ō') *n., pl.* -os. 1. An organism in its earliest stages of development, esp. before birth or hatching. 2. A rudimentary or beginning stage. [< Gk. *embruon.*] —**em'bry·on'ic** (-ŏn'ĭk) *adj.*

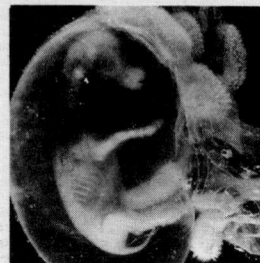

embryo
Cow embryo

em·bry·ol·o·gy (ĕm'brē-ŏl'ə-jē) n. The science dealing with the formation and development of embryos. —**em'bry·o·log'ic** (-ə-lŏj'ĭk) or **em'bry·o·log'i·cal** adj. —**em'bry·ol'o·gist** n.

em·cee (ĕm'sē') n. Informal. A master of ceremonies. [Pronunciation of M.C., abbr. of master of ceremonies.] —**em'cee'** v.

e·meer (ĕ-mîr') n. Var. of emir.

e·mend (ĭ-mĕnd') v. To improve (a text) by critical editing. [< Lat. emendare.] —**e'men·da'tion** (ē'mĕn-dā'shən) n.

em·er·ald (ĕm'ər-əld, ĕm'rəld) n. 1. A brilliant, transparent green beryl used as a gem. 2. A strong yellowish green. [< Gk. smaragdos.] —**em'er·ald** adj.

e·merge (ĭ-mûrj') v. **e·merged, e·merg·ing.** 1. To rise up or come forth into view; appear. 2. To come into existence. 3. To become known or evident. [Lat. emergere.] —**e·mer'gence** n. —**e·mer'gent** adj.

e·mer·gen·cy (ĭ-mûr'jən-sē) n., pl. **-cies.** An unexpected situation or occurrence that demands immediate attention.

e·mer·i·tus (ĭ-mĕr'ĭ-təs) adj. Retired but retaining an honorary title: a professor emeritus. [Lat., p.p. of emereri, to earn by service.]

em·er·y (ĕm'ə-rē, ĕm'rē) n. A fine-grained impure corundum used for grinding and polishing. [< Gk. smuris.]

e·met·ic (ĭ-mĕt'ĭk) adj. Causing vomiting. [< Gk. emein, to vomit.] —**e·met'ic** n.

-emia suff. Blood: leukemia. [< Gk. haima, blood.]

em·i·grate (ĕm'ĭ-grāt') v. **-grat·ed, -grat·ing.** To leave one country or region to settle in another. [Lat. emigrare.] —**em'i·grant** n. —**em'i·gra'tion** n.

é·mi·gré (ĕm'ĭ-grā') n. An emigrant, esp. a refugee from a revolution. [Fr.]

em·i·nence (ĕm'ə-nəns) n. 1. A position of great distinction or superiority. 2. A rise or elevation of ground; hill.

em·i·nent (ĕm'ə-nənt) adj. 1. Outstanding, as in reputation; distinguished. 2. Towering above others; projecting. [< Lat. eminēre, to stand out.] —**em'i·nent·ly** adv.

eminent domain n. Law. The right of a government to appropriate private property for public use.

e·mir (ĕ-mîr') n. Also **e·meer.** An Arabian prince, chieftain, or governor. [< Ar. 'amīr, commander.]

em·is·sary (ĕm'ĭ-sĕr'ē) n., pl. **-ies.** A messenger or agent, esp. one representing a government. [Lat. emissarius.]

e·mit (ĭ-mĭt') v. **e·mit·ted, e·mit·ting.** 1. To release, give off, or send out: emit light. 2. To utter; express. 3. To put (e.g. paper money) into circulation. [Lat. emittere.] —**e·mis'sion** (ĭ-mĭsh'ən) n.

e·mol·lient (ĭ-mŏl'yənt) adj. Producing softness and smoothness, esp. of the skin. [< Lat. emollire, to soften.] —**e·mol'lient** n.

e·mol·u·ment (ĭ-mŏl'yə-mənt) n. Compensation or profit derived from one's employment or office. [< Lat. emolumentum.]

e·mote (ĭ-mōt') v. **e·mot·ed, e·mot·ing.** To express emotion in an exaggerated and theatrical manner. [< EMOTION.]

e·mo·tion (ĭ-mō'shən) n. 1. Agitation of the passions or sensibilities. 2. A strong, complex feeling, as of joy, sorrow, or hate. [< Lat. emovēre, to excite.]

em·pa·thy (ĕm'pə-thē) n. Identification with and understanding of another's situation, feelings, and motives. [EM-² + -PATHY.] —**em·path'ic** (-păth'ĭk) adj. —**em'pa·thize'** (-thīz') v.

em·per·or (ĕm'pər-ər) n. The ruler of an empire. [< Lat. imperator.]

em·pha·sis (ĕm'fə-sĭs) n., pl. **-ses** (-sēz'). 1. Special importance or significance placed on or imparted to something. 2. Stress given to a syllable, word, or phrase. [< Gk. emphainein, to indicate.]

em·pha·size (ĕm'fə-sīz') v. **-sized, -siz·ing.** To give emphasis to; stress. [< EMPHASIS.]

em·phat·ic (ĕm-făt'ĭk) adj. Expressed or performed with emphasis. [< Gk. emphatikos.] —**em·phat'i·cal·ly** adv.

em·phy·se·ma (ĕm'fĭ-sē'mə) n. A disease in which the air sacs of the lungs lose their elasticity, resulting in an often severe loss of breathing ability. [< Gk. emphusēma.]

em·pire (ĕm'pīr') n. 1. A political unit, usu. larger than a kingdom and often comprising a number of territories or nations, ruled by a single central authority. 2. Imperial dominion, power, or authority. [< Lat. imperium.]

em·pir·i·cal (ĕm-pîr'ĭ-kəl) adj. Also **em·pir·ic** (-pîr'ĭk). 1. Based on observation or experiment. 2. Relying on practical experience rather than theory. [< Gk. empeirikos, experienced.] —**em·pir'i·cal·ly** adv.

em·pir·i·cism (ĕm-pîr'ĭ-sĭz'əm) n. 1. The view that experience, esp. of the senses, is the only source of knowledge. 2. The employment of empirical methods, as in science. —**em·pir'i·cist** n.

em·place·ment (ĕm-plās'mənt) n. 1. A prepared position for guns within a fortification. 2. Placement. [Fr.]

em·ploy (ĕm-ploi') v. 1. To engage or use the services of. 2. To put to service; use. 3. To devote or apply (one's time or energies) to an activity. —n. Employment. [< Lat. implicare, to involve.] —**em·ploy'a·ble** adj.

em·ploy·ee (ĕm-ploi'ē, ĕm'ploi-ē') n. Also **em·ploye.** One who works for another.

em·ploy·er (ĕm-ploi'ər) n. One that employs others.

em·ploy·ment (ĕm-ploi'mənt) n. 1. The act of

employing. **2.** The state of being employed. **3.** An activity or occupation.

em·po·ri·um (ĕm-pôr′ē-əm, -pōr′-) *n., pl.* **-ums** or **-po·ri·a** (-pôr′ē-ə, -pōr′-). A store carrying a wide variety of merchandise. [< Gk. *emporion*, market.]

em·pow·er (ĕm-pou′ər) *v.* To invest with legal power; authorize.

em·press (ĕm′prĭs) *n.* **1.** The female sovereign of an empire. **2.** The wife or widow of an emperor. [< OFr. *emperesse*.]

emp·ty (ĕmp′tē) *adj.* **-ti·er, -ti·est. 1.** Containing nothing. **2.** Having no occupants or inhabitants; unoccupied. **3.** Lacking purpose, substance, value, or effect. —*v.* **-tied, -ty·ing. 1.** To make or become empty. **2.** To discharge or flow: *a river that empties into a bay.* —*n., pl.* **-ties.** An empty container, esp. a bottle. [< OE *æmtig*.] —**emp′ti·ness** *n.*

emp·ty-hand·ed (ĕmp′tē-hăn′dĭd) *adj.* **1.** Bearing nothing in the hands. **2.** Having gained or accomplished nothing.

em·py·re·an (ĕm′pī-rē′ən) *n.* **1.** The highest reaches of heaven. **2.** The sky or firmament. [< Gk. *empurios*, fiery.]

e·mu (ē′myōō) *n.* A large, flightless Australian bird related to and resembling the ostrich. [Port. *ema*, flightless bird of South America.]

em·u·late (ĕm′yə-lāt′) *v.* **-lat·ed, -lat·ing.** To strive to equal or excel, esp. through imitation. [Lat. *aemulari.*] —**em′u·la′tion** *n.*

e·mul·si·fy (ĭ-mŭl′sə-fī′) *v.* **-fied, -fy·ing.** To make into or become an emulsion. —**e·mul′si·fi·ca′tion** *n.* —**e·mul′si·fi′er** *n.*

e·mul·sion (ĭ-mŭl′shən) *n.* **1.** A suspension of small globules of one liquid in a second liquid with which the first does not mix. **2.** A light-sensitive coating, usu. of silver halide grains in a thin gelatin layer, on photographic film, paper, or glass. [< Lat. *emulgēre*, to drain out.] —**e·mul′sive** *adj.*

en (ĕn) *n.* Printing. A unit of measure equal to half the width of an em.

en-¹ or **em-** *pref.* **1. a.** To put into or on: *enthrone.* **b.** To go into or on: *entrain.* **2.** To cover or provide with: *enrobe.* **3.** To cause to be: *endear.* **4.** Thoroughly. Used often as an intensive: *entangle.* [< Lat. *in*, in.]

en-² or **em-** *pref.* In; into; within: *empathy.* [< Gk.]

-en¹ *suff.* **1. a.** To cause to be: *cheapen.* **b.** To become: *redden.* **2. a.** To cause to have: *hearten.* **b.** To come to have: *lengthen.* [< OE *-nian.*]

-en² *suff.* Made of or resembling: *wooden.* [< OE.]

en·a·ble (ĕn-ā′bəl) *v.* **-bled, -bling. 1.** To provide with the means, knowledge, or opportunity; make possible. **2.** To give legal power, capacity, or sanction to.

en·act (ĕn-ăkt′) *v.* **1.** To make (a bill) into a law. **2.** To act out, as on a stage. —**en·act′ment** *n.*

en·am·el (ĭ-năm′əl) *n.* **1.** A vitreous, usu. opaque coating baked on metal, glass, or ceramic ware. **2.** A paint that dries to a hard, glossy surface. **3.** The hard substance that covers the exposed portion of a tooth. —*v.* **-eled** or **-elled, -el·ing** or **-el·ling.** To coat or decorate with enamel. [< AN *enamailler*, to put on enamel.] —**en·am′el·ware**′ *n.*

en·am·or (ĭ-năm′ər) *v.* Also *chiefly Brit.* **en·am·our.** To inspire with love; captivate. [< OFr. *enamourer.*]

en bloc (ăn blŏk′) *adv.* All together; as a whole. [Fr.]

en·camp (ĕn-kămp′) *v.* To set up or live in a camp. —**en·camp′ment** *n.*

en·cap·su·late (ĕn-kăp′sə-lāt′) *v.* **-lat·ed, -lat·ing.** To encase or become encased in a capsule. —**en·cap′su·la′tion** *n.*

en·case (ĕn-kās′) *v.* **-cased, -cas·ing.** To enclose in or as if in a case. —**en·case′ment** *n.*

-ence or **-ency** *suff.* Action, state, quality, or condition: *reference.* [< Lat. *-entia.*]

en·ceph·a·li·tis (ĕn-sĕf′ə-lī′tĭs) *n.* Inflammation of the brain. —**en·ceph′a·lit′ic** (-lĭt′ĭk) *adj.*

encephalo- or **encephal-** *pref.* The brain: *encephalitis.* [< Gk. *enkephalos*, in the head.]

en·ceph·a·lon (ĕn-sĕf′ə-lŏn′) *n., pl.* **-la** (-lə). The brain of a vertebrate. [Gk. *enkephalon.*]

en·chain (ĕn-chān′) *v.* To bind with or as if with chains; fetter.

en·chant (ĕn-chănt′) *v.* **1.** To cast under a spell; bewitch. **2.** To delight completely; enrapture. [< Lat. *incantare.*] —**en·chant′er** *n.* —**en·chant′ment** *n.*

en·chi·la·da (ĕn′chə-lä′də) *n.* A rolled tortilla with a meat or cheese filling, served with a sauce spiced with chili. [Mex. Sp.]

en·ci·pher (ĕn-sī′fər) *v.* To put (a message) into cipher. —**en·ci′pher·ment** *n.*

en·cir·cle (ĕn-sûr′kəl) *v.* **-cled, -cling. 1.** To form a circle around; surround. **2.** To move or go around; make a circuit of. —**en·cir′cle·ment** *n.*

en·clave (ĕn′klāv′, ŏn′-) *n.* A country or part of a country lying entirely within the boundaries of another. [< OFr. *enclaver*, to enclose.]

en·close (ĕn-klōz′) *v.* **-closed, -clos·ing.** Also **in·close** (ĭn-). **1.** To surround on all sides; fence in. **2.** To include in the same container with a package or letter. [< Lat. *includere*, to include.] —**en·clo′sure** (-klō′zhər) *n.*

en·code (ĕn-kōd′) *v.* **-cod·ed, -cod·ing.** To put (a message) into code. —**en·cod′er** *n.*

en·co·mi·um (ĕn-kō′mē-əm) *n., pl.* **-ums** or **-mi·a** (-mē-ə). Lofty praise; eulogy. [< Gk. *enkōmios*, of the victory procession.]

en·com·pass (ĕn-kŭm′pəs, -kŏm′-) *v.* **1.** To surround. **2.** To comprise or contain; include.

en·core (ŏn′kôr′, -kōr′) *n.* **1.** A demand by an audience for an additional performance. **2.** An additional performance in response to an audience's demand. —*v.* **-cored, -cor·ing.** To demand an encore of or from. [< Fr., again.]

en·coun·ter (ĕn-koun′tər) *n.* **1.** A casual or unexpected meeting. **2.** A hostile confrontation, as between enemies; clash. —*v.* **1.** To meet, esp. unexpectedly. **2.** To confront in battle. [< OFr. *encontre.*]

en·cour·age (ĕn-kûr′ĭj, -kŭr′-) *v.* **-aged, -ag·ing. 1.** To inspire with courage or confidence. **2.** To help bring about; foster. [< OFr. *encoragier.*] —**en·cour′age·ment** *n.* —**en·cour′ag·ing·ly** *adv.*

en·croach (ĕn-krōch′) *v.* To intrude or infringe gradually upon the property or rights of another; trespass. [< OFr. *encrochier*, to seize.] —**en·croach′ment** *n.*

en·crust (ĕn-krŭst′) *v.* Also **in·crust** (ĭn-). To cover or become covered with or as if with a crust. —**en′crus·ta′tion** (ĕn′krŭ-stā′shən) *n.*

en·cum·ber (ĕn-kŭm′bər) *v.* **1.** To weigh down excessively; burden. **2.** To hinder; impede. [< OFr. *encombrer*, to block up.] —**en·cum′brance** (-brəns) *n.*

-ency *suff.* Var. of **-ence.**

en·cyc·li·cal (ĕn-sĭk′lĭ-kəl) *n. Rom. Cath. Ch.* A papal letter addressed to the bishops. [Gk. *enkuklios,* circular.]

en·cy·clo·pe·di·a or **en·cy·clo·pae·di·a** (ĕn-sī′klə-pē′dē-ə) *n.* A comprehensive reference work with articles on many subjects or numerous aspects of a particular field. [< Gk. *enkuklios paideia,* general education.] —**en·cy′clo·pe′dic** *adj.*

en·cyst (ĕn-sĭst′) *v.* To enclose or become enclosed in a cyst. —**en·cyst′ment** *n.*

end (ĕnd) *n.* **1.** An extremity; tip. **2.** The point at which something ceases or is completed; conclusion. **3. a.** A result; outcome. **b.** A purpose; goal. **4.** Death. **5.** A point that marks the extent or limit of something. **6.** A remainder or remnant. **7.** *Informal.* A share in a responsibility. **8.** *Football.* Either of the players in the outermost position at the line of scrimmage. —*v.* **1.** To bring or come to an end; conclude. **2.** To be at or form the end of. **3.** To cause the death or ruin of; destroy. [< OE *ende.*]
  Syns: end, close, complete, conclude, finish, terminate, wind up, wrap up *v.*

en·dan·ger (ĕn-dān′jər) *v.* To expose to danger; imperil. —**en·dan′ger·ment** *n.*

endangered species *n.* A species in danger of extinction.

en·dear (ĕn-dîr′) *v.* To cause to be held dear.

en·dear·ment (ĕn-dîr′mənt) *n.* A word or expression of affection.

en·deav·or (ĕn-dĕv′ər) *v.* Also *chiefly Brit.* **en·deav·our.** To make an earnest attempt; strive. [< ME *putten in dever,* to put in duty.] —**en·deav′or** *n.*

en·dem·ic (ĕn-dĕm′ĭk) *adj.* Prevalent in or peculiar to a particular locality or people. [< Gk. *endēmos.*]

en·dive (ĕn′dīv′, ŏn′dēv′) *n.* **1.** A plant with crisp succulent leaves used in salads. **2.** A plant related to the endive, with a narrow, pointed cluster of whitish leaves. [< Lat. *bum.*]

end·less (ĕnd′lĭs) *adj.* **1.** Having or seeming to have no end; infinite. **2.** Formed with the ends joined; continuous. —**end′less·ly** *adv.*

end man *n.* One of two men in a minstrel show at the end of the line of performers who engage in banter with the interlocutor.

end·most (ĕnd′mōst′) *adj.* Being at or closest to the end.

endo- *pref.* Inside or within: *endogenous.* [< Gk. *endon,* within.]

en·do·crine (ĕn′də-krĭn, -krēn′, -krīn′) *adj.* **1.** Secreting internally rather than through a duct. **2.** Of or pertaining to any of the ductless or endocrine glands. [ENDO- + Gk. *krinein,* to separate.]

endocrine gland *n.* Any of the ductless glands, such as the thyroid or adrenal, whose secretions pass directly into the bloodstream.

en·do·cri·nol·o·gy (ĕn′də-krə-nŏl′ə-jē) *n.* The medical study of the endocrine glands, their functions, and their diseases. —**en′do·cri·nol′o·gist** *n.*

en·dog·e·nous (ĕn-dŏj′ə-nəs) *adj.* Originating within an organ or part.

en·do·plasm (ĕn′də-plăz′əm) *n.* The inner,

relatively viscous portion of the continuous phase of cytoplasm.

en·dorse (ĕn-dôrs′) *v.* **-dorsed, -dors·ing.** Also **in·dorse** (ĭn-). **1.** To write one's signature on the back of (e.g. a check) in return for the cash or credit indicated on its face. **2.** To give approval of; support. [< Med. Lat. *indorsare.*] —**en·dorse′ment** *n.*

en·do·ther·mic (ĕn′də-thûr′mĭk) *adj.* Also **en·do·ther·mal** (-məl). Characterized by or causing the absorption of heat.

en·dow (ĕn-dou′) *v.* **1.** To provide with income or a source of income. **2.** To provide or equip with a talent or quality. [< AN *endouer.*] —**en·dow′ment** *n.*

en·due (ĕn-dōō′, -dyōō′) *v.* **-dued, -du·ing.** To provide with some quality or trait. [< Lat. *inducere,* to lead in, and < Lat. *induere,* to clothe.]

en·dur·ance (ĕn-dōōr′əns, -dyōōr′-) *n.* **1.** The power to withstand hardship or stress. **2.** The state or fact of persevering.

en·dure (ĕn-dōōr′, -dyōōr′) *v.* **-dured, -dur·ing.** **1.** To bear up under. **2.** To bear with tolerance; put up with; undergo. **3.** To continue to exist; last. [< Lat. *indurare,* to make hard.] —**en·dur′a·ble** *adj.*

en·du·ro (ĕn-dōōr′ō, -dyōōr′ō) *n., pl. -os.* A race, as of runners, that tests endurance. [< ENDURANCE.]

end·wise (ĕnd′wīz′) *adv.* Also **end·ways** (-wāz′). **1.** On end. **2.** With the end foremost. **3.** Lengthwise.

-ene *suff.* Unsaturation of an organic compound, esp. one having a double bond: *ethylene.* [< Gk. *-ēnē,* fem. adj. suffix.]

en·e·ma (ĕn′ə-mə) *n.* **1.** The injection of a liquid into the rectum for cleansing or other therapeutic purposes. **2.** The liquid used for an enema. [< Gk.]

en·e·my (ĕn′ə-mē) *n., pl. -mies.* **1.** One that shows hostility toward another. **2.** A hostile power or military force. [< Lat. *inimicus.*]

en·er·get·ic (ĕn′ər-jĕt′ĭk) *adj.* Having, exerting, or displaying energy; vigorous. [Gk. *energētikos.*] —**en′er·get′i·cal·ly** *adv.*

en·er·gize (ĕn′ər-jīz′) *v.* **-gized, -giz·ing.** To give or supply energy to. —**en′er·giz′er** *n.*

en·er·gy (ĕn′ər-jē) *n., pl. -gies.* **1.** The work that a physical system is capable of doing in changing from its actual state to a specified reference state. **2.** Capacity for action or accomplishment. **3.** Strength and vigor; force. [< Gk. *energeia,* vigor.]

en·er·vate (ĕn′ər-vāt′) *v.* **-vat·ed, -vat·ing.** To deprive of strength or vitality; weaken. [Lat. *enervare.*] —**en′er·va′tion** *n.*

en·fee·ble (ĕn-fē′bəl) *v.* **-bled, -bling.** To make feeble. [< OFr. *enfeblir.*] —**en·fee′ble·ment** *n.*

en·fi·lade (ĕn′fə-lād′, -läd′) *n.* Gunfire that sweeps the length of a target, as a column of troops. [< OFr. *enfiler,* to thread.]

en·fold (ĕn-fōld′) *v.* Also **in·fold** (ĭn-). **1.** To cover with or as if with folds; envelop. **2.** To embrace.

en·force (ĕn-fôrs′, -fōrs′) *v.* **-forced, -forc·ing.** **1.** To compel observance of or obedience to. **2.** To compel. —**en·force′a·ble** *adj.* —**en·force′ment** *n.* —**en·forc′er** *n.*

en·fran·chise (ĕn-frăn′chīz′) *v.* **-chised, -chis-**

ing. 1. To endow with the rights of citizenship, esp. the right to vote. **2.** To free, as from slavery. —**en·fran'chise·ment** n.

en·gage (ĕn-gāj') v. **-gaged, -gag·ing. 1.** To hire; employ. **2.** To attract and hold; engross: *a project that engaged her interest.* **3.** To pledge, esp. to promise to marry. **4.** To enter or bring into conflict. **5.** To interlock or cause to interlock; mesh. **6.** To participate or cause to participate; involve. [< OFr. *engager,* to pledge something as security for repayment of a debt.]

en·gage·ment (ĕn-gāj'mənt) n. **1.** An act of engaging or the state of being engaged. **2.** Betrothal. **3.** A commitment to appear at a certain time; appointment. **4.** Employment. **5.** A battle or encounter.

en·gag·ing (ĕn-gā'jĭng) adj. Tending to attract; charming. —**en·gag'ing·ly** adv.

en·gen·der (ĕn-jĕn'dər) v. **1.** To give rise to; produce. **2.** To procreate; beget. [< Lat. *ingenerare.*]

en·gine (ĕn'jən) n. **1.** A machine that converts energy into mechanical motion. **2.** A mechanical device, instrument, or tool: *engines of destruction.* **3.** A locomotive. [< Lat. *ingenium,* skill.]

engine block n. The cast metal block containing the cylinders of an internal-combustion engine.

en·gi·neer (ĕn'jə-nîr') n. **1.** One skilled at or professionally engaged in a branch of engineering. **2.** One who operates an engine, esp. a locomotive. —v. **1.** To plan, construct, and manage as an engineer. **2.** To plan or accomplish by skill or contrivance. [< Med. Lat. *ingeniator,* contriver.]

en·gi·neer·ing (ĕn'jə-nîr'ĭng) n. The application of scientific principles to practical purposes, as the design, construction, and operation of efficient and economical structures, equipment, and systems.

Eng·lish (ĭng'glĭsh) adj. Of, pertaining to, derived from, or characteristic of England and its inhabitants. —n. **1.** The people of England. **2.** The Germanic language of the peoples of Britain, the United States, and many other countries. —**Eng'lish·man** n. —**Eng'lish·wom'an** n.

English horn n. A double-reed woodwind instrument similar to but larger than the oboe and lower in pitch and timbre.

English setter n. A dog of a breed developed in England that has a silky white coat usu. with black or brownish markings.

en·graft (ĕn-grăft') v. To graft (a shoot) onto a plant.

en·grave (ĕn-grāv') v. **-graved, -grav·ing. 1.** To carve, cut, or etch (a design or letters) into a surface. **2.** a. To carve, cut, or etch (a design or letters) into a block or surface used for printing. **b.** To print from a block or plate thus made. —**en·grav'er** n.

en·grav·ing (ĕn-grā'vĭng) n. **1.** The art or technique of one that engraves. **2.** An engraved surface for printing. **3.** A print made from an engraved plate.

en·gross (ĕn-grōs') v. **1.** To occupy the complete attention of; absorb wholly. **2.** a. To write or transcribe in a large, clear hand. **b.** To prepare the text of (an official document). [< OFr. *en gros,* in large quantity.]

en·gulf (ĕn-gŭlf') v. **1.** To surround and enclose completely. **2.** To overwhelm by or as if by overflowing and enclosing.

en·hance (ĕn-hăns') v. **-hanced, -hanc·ing.** To make greater, as in value or beauty. [< OFr. *enhaucier.*] —**en·hance'ment** n.

e·nig·ma (ĭ-nĭg'mə) n. One that is puzzling, ambiguous, or inexplicable. [< Gk. *ainigma.*]

e·nig·mat·ic (ĕn'ĭg-măt'ĭk) adj. Like an enigma; puzzling. —**en'ig·mat'i·cal·ly** adv.

en·join (ĕn-join') v. **1.** To direct with authority and emphasis; command. **2.** To prohibit, esp. by legal action. [< Lat. *injungere.*] —**en·join'der** n.

en·joy (ĕn-joi') v. **1.** To experience satisfaction or pleasure from; relish: *enjoy good food.* **2.** To have the use or benefit of: *enjoys good health.* [< OFr. *enjoir.*] —**en·joy'a·ble** adj. —**en·joy'a·bly** adv. —**en·joy'ment** n.

en·large (ĕn-lärj') v. **-larged, -larg·ing. 1.** To make or become larger. **2.** To speak or write at greater length or in greater detail. —**en·large'ment** n. —**en·larg'er** n.

en·light·en (ĕn-līt'n) v. **1.** To furnish with spiritual understanding. **2.** To inform. —**en·light'en·ment** n.

en·list (ĕn-lĭst') v. **1.** To engage for service in the armed forces. **2.** To engage the assistance or cooperation of. **3.** To enter the armed forces voluntarily. —**en·list'ment** n.

enlisted man n. One in the armed forces who ranks below a warrant officer or a commissioned officer.

en·liv·en (ĕn-lī'vən) v. To make lively or spirited; animate. —**en·liv'en·ment** n.

en masse (ŏn măs') adv. In one group or body; all together. [Fr.]

en·mesh (ĕn-mĕsh') v. To entangle or catch in or as if in a mesh.

en·mi·ty (ĕn'mĭ-tē) n., pl. **-ties.** Deep-seated hatred or hostility, as between enemies or opponents. [< Lat. *inimicus,* enemy.]

en·no·ble (ĕn-nō'bəl) v. **-bled, -bling. 1.** To invest with nobility; exalt. **2.** To confer a rank of nobility upon. —**en·no'ble·ment** n.

en·nui (ŏn-wē', ŏn'wē) n. Boredom. [< Lat. *in odio,* odious.]

e·nor·mi·ty (ĭ-nôr'mĭ-tē) n., pl. **-ties. 1.** Extreme wickedness. **2.** A monstrous offense or evil; outrage.

e·nor·mous (ĭ-nôr'məs) adj. Of very great size, extent, number, or degree; immense. [< Lat. *enormis.*] —**e·nor'mous·ly** adv.

e·nough (ĭ-nŭf') adj. Sufficient to meet a need or satisfy a desire. —pron. An adequate quantity. —adv. **1.** To a satisfactory amount or degree. **2.** Very; quite: *glad enough to leave.* **3.** Tolerably; rather: *sang well enough.* [< OE *genōg.*]

en·quire (ĕn-kwīr') v. Var. of **inquire.**

en·rage (ĕn-rāj') v. **-raged, -rag·ing.** To put in a rage; infuriate.

en·rap·ture (ĕn-răp'chər) v. **-tured, -tur·ing.** To fill with rapture or delight.

en·rich (ĕn-rĭch') v. **1.** To make rich or richer. **2.** To add to the beauty of; adorn. —**en·rich'ment** n.

en·roll or **en·rol** (ĕn-rōl') v. **-rolled, -rol·ling. 1.** To enter the name of in a register, record, or roll. **2.** To place one's name on a roll or register. —**en·roll'ment** or **en·rol'ment** n.

en route (ŏn rōōt', ĕn) adv. & adj. On or along the way. [Fr.]

en·sconce (ĕn-skŏns') v. **-sconced, -sconc·ing. 1.** To settle securely or comfortably. **2.** To place or conceal in a secure place. [EN-¹ + *sconce,* small fort.]

en·sem·ble (ŏn-sŏm′bəl) *n.* **1.** A unit or group of complementary parts that contribute to a single effect. **2.** A complete outfit of coordinated clothing. **3.** A group of musicians, singers, dancers, or actors who perform together. **4.** Music for two or more performers. [< LLat. *insimul*, at the same time.]

en·shrine (ĕn-shrīn′) *v.* **-shrined, -shrin·ing.** **1.** To enclose in or as if in a shrine. **2.** To cherish as sacred.

en·shroud (ĕn-shroud′) *v.* To cover with or as if with a shroud.

en·sign (ĕn′sən) *n.* **1.** (*also* ĕn′sīn′). A flag or banner. **2.** A commissioned officer of the lowest rank in the U.S. Navy, ranking below a lieutenant. **3.** (*also* ĕn′sīn′). A badge or emblem of rank. [< Lat. *insignia*, insignia.]

en·si·lage (ĕn′sə-lĭj) *n.* Green fodder preserved in a silo.

en·sile (ĕn-sīl′) *v.* **-siled, -sil·ing.** To preserve and store (fodder) in a silo. [< Sp. *ensilar*.]

en·slave (ĕn-slāv′) *v.* **-slaved, -slav·ing.** To make a slave of. **—en·slave′ment** *n.*

en·snare (ĕn-snâr′) *v.* **-snared, -snar·ing.** To catch in or as if in a snare.

en·sue (ĕn-sōō′) *v.* **-sued, -su·ing.** **1.** To take place subsequently. **2.** To follow as a consequence; result. [< Lat. *insequi*, to pursue.]

en·sure (ĕn-shŏŏr′) *v.* **-sured, -sur·ing.** To make sure or certain; insure.

-ent *suff.* **1.** Having a specified quality: *effervescent.* **2.** One that performs, promotes, or causes a specified action: *referent.* [< Lat. *-ens,* pr.p. suffix.]

en·tail (ĕn-tāl′) *v.* **1.** To have as a necessary accompaniment or consequence. **2.** To limit the inheritance of (property) to a specified unalterable succession of heirs. [ME *entaillen,* to limit inheritance to specific heirs.] **—en·tail′ment** *n.*

en·tan·gle (ĕn-tăng′gəl) *v.* **-gled, -gling.** **1.** To make tangled; snarl. **2.** To complicate; confuse. **—en·tan′gle·ment** *n.*

en·tente (ŏn-tŏnt′) *n.* **1.** An agreement between two or more governments for cooperative action. **2.** The parties to an entente. [Fr.]

en·ter (ĕn′tər) *v.* **1.** To come or go into. **2.** To penetrate; pierce. **3.** To embark upon; begin. **4.** To become a member of or participant in. **5.** To register or enroll in. **6.** To inscribe; record. **7.** *Law.* **a.** To place formally before a court or on record. **b.** To go upon or into (real property) as a trespasser or with felonious intent. **c.** To go upon (land) to take possession. [< Lat. *intrare.*]

en·ter·i·tis (ĕn′tə-rī′tĭs) *n.* Inflammation of the intestinal tract. [Gk. *enteron,* intestine + -ITIS.]

en·ter·prise (ĕn′tər-prīz′) *n.* **1. a.** An undertaking; venture. **b.** Readiness for adventure or risk; initiative. **2.** A business organization. [< OFr. *enterprendre,* to undertake.]

en·ter·pris·ing (ĕn′tər-prī′zĭng) *adj.* Showing imagination, initiative, and boldness in action.

en·ter·tain (ĕn′tər-tān′) *v.* **1.** To hold the attention of; amuse. **2.** To extend hospitality to. **3.** To hold in the mind. [< OFr. *entretenir.*] **—en′ter·tain′er** *n.* **—en′ter·tain′ment** *n.*

en·ter·tain·ing (ĕn′tər-tā′nĭng) *adj.* Amusing; diverting. **—en′ter·tain′ing·ly** *adv.*

en·thrall (ĕn-thrôl′) *v.* **-thralled, -thrall·ing.** **1.** To hold spellbound. **2.** To enslave. **—en·thrall′ment** *n.*

en·throne (ĕn-thrōn′) *v.* **-throned, -thron·ing.** **1.** To place upon or as if upon a throne. **2.** Exalt; revere. **—en·throne′ment** *n.*

en·thuse (ĕn-thōōz′) *v.* **-thused, -thus·ing.** *Informal.* To make or act enthusiastic. [< ENTHUSIASM.]

en·thu·si·asm (ĕn-thōō′zē-ăz′əm) *n.* **1.** Great or fervent interest or excitement. **2.** A cause of keen or lively interest. [< Gk. *enthousiasmos.*] **—en·thu′si·ast′** *n.* **—en·thu′si·as′ti·cal·ly** *adv.*

en·tice (ĕn-tīs′) *v.* **-ticed, -tic·ing.** To attract by arousing hope or desire; lure. [< OFr. *enticier.*] **—en·tice′ment** *n.* **—en·tic′er** *n.* **—en·tic′ing·ly** *adv.*

en·tire (ĕn-tīr′) *adj.* Having no part missing; complete: *my entire approval; his entire attention.* [< Lat. *integer.*] **—en·tire′ly** *adv.*

en·tire·ty (ĕn-tīr′ə-tē) *n., pl.* **-ties.** **1.** Completeness. **2.** Something entire; totality.

en·ti·tle (ĕn-tīt′l) *v.* **-tled, -tling.** **1.** To give a name to. **2.** To give a right. [< LLat. *intitulare.*] **—en·ti′tle·ment** *n.*

en·ti·ty (ĕn′tĭ-tē) *n., pl.* **-ties.** **1.** The fact of existence. **2.** Something that exists independently. [< Lat. *ens,* pr.p. of *esse,* to be.]

en·tomb (ĕn-tōōm′) *v.* To place in or as if in a tomb; bury. [< OFr. *entomber.*] **—en·tomb′ment** *n.*

en·to·mol·o·gy (ĕn′tə-mŏl′ə-jē) *n.* The scientific study of insects. [Gk. *entomon,* insect + -LOGY.] **—en′to·mo·log′ic** (-mə-lŏj′ĭk) *or* **en′to·mo·log′i·cal** *adj.* **—en′to·mo·log′i·cal·ly** *adv.* **—en′to·mol′o·gist** *n.*

en·tou·rage (ŏn′tŏŏ-räzh′) *n.* A group of attendants accompanying an important person. [< OFr. *entour,* surroundings.]

en·tr'acte (ŏn′trăkt′, äN-trăkt′) *n.* **1.** The interval between two acts of a theatrical performance. **2.** An entertainment provided between two acts. [Fr.]

en·trails (ĕn′trālz′, -trəlz) *pl.n.* The internal organs, esp. the intestines. [< Lat. *interaneus,* interior.]

en·train (ĕn-trān′) *v.* To board a train.

en·trance¹ (ĕn′trəns) *n.* **1.** The act or an instance of entering. **2.** A place or means of entry. **3.** The permission or right to enter. [< OFr. *entrer,* to enter.]

en·trance² (ĕn-trăns′) *v.* **-tranced, -tranc·ing.** To fill with delight or wonder. **—en·trance′ment** *n.* **—en·tranc′ing·ly** *adv.*

en·trant (ĕn′trənt) *n.* A person who enters a competition.

en·trap (ĕn-trăp′) *v.* **-trapped, -trap·ping.** To catch in or as if in a trap. **—en·trap′ment** *n.*

en·treat (ĕn-trēt′) *v.* To ask earnestly; implore. [< OFr. *entraitier.*] **—en·treat′ing·ly** *adv.* **—en·treat′ment** *n.*

en·treat·y (ĕn-trē′tē) *n., pl.* **-ies.** An earnest request; plea.

en·trée (ŏn′trā′, ŏn-trā′) *n.* **1.** The power or right to enter. **2.** The main course of a meal. [Fr.]

en·trench (ĕn-trĕnch′) *v.* **1.** To place in a trench. **2.** To establish firmly. **3.** To encroach. **—en·trench′ment** *n.*

en·tre·pre·neur (ŏn′trə-prə-nûr′) *n.* One who

organizes, operates, and esp. assumes the risk of a business venture. [< OFr. *entreprendre*, to undertake.]

en·tro·py (ĕn'trə-pē) *n.* **1.** A measure of the capacity of a system to undergo spontaneous change. **2.** A measure of the randomness, disorder, or chaos in a system. [G. *Entropie*.]

en·trust (ĕn-trŭst') *v.* **1.** To turn over to another for care or action. **2.** To turn something over to as a trust.

en·try (ĕn'trē) *n., pl.* -**tries**. **1.** The act or right of entering. **2.** A means of entrance. **3. a.** The inclusion of an item in a record. **b.** An item thus entered. **4.** A word, term, or phrase entered or defined, as in a dictionary. **5.** One entered in a race or contest.

en·twine (ĕn-twīn') *v.* -**twined**, -**twin·ing**. To twine or twist around or together.

entwine

e·nu·mer·ate (ĭ-nōō'mə-rāt', ĭ-nyōō'-) *v.* -**at·ed**, -**at·ing**. **1.** To list. **2.** To determine the number of; count. [Lat. *enumerare*.] —**e·nu'mer·a'tion** *n.* —**e·nu'mer·a'tor** *n.*

e·nun·ci·ate (ĭ-nŭn'sē-āt', -shē-) *v.* -**at·ed**, -**at·ing**. **1.** To pronounce, esp. with clarity; articulate. **2.** To declare definitely; proclaim. [Lat. *enuntiare*.] —**e·nun'ci·a'tion** *n.*

en·vel·op (ĕn-vĕl'əp) *v.* To cover with or as if with a covering. [< OFr. *enveloper*.] —**en·vel'op·ment** *n.*

en·ve·lope (ĕn'və-lōp', ŏn'-) *n.* **1.** Something that envelops; cover. **2.** A flat paper container, used esp. for mailing letters. **3.** The bag containing the gas in a balloon. [< OFr. *enveloper*, to envelop.]

en·ven·om (ĕn-vĕn'əm) *v.* **1.** To fill with venom. **2.** To embitter.

en·vi·a·ble (ĕn'vē-ə-bəl) *adj.* Extremely desirable. —**en'vi·a·bly** *adv.*

en·vi·ous (ĕn'vē-əs) *adj.* Feeling or displaying envy. —**en'vi·ous·ly** *adv.* —**en'vi·ous·ness** *n.*

en·vi·ron·ment (ĕn-vī'rən-mənt) *n.* Surroundings. —**en·vi'ron·men'tal** (-mĕn'tl) *adj.* —**en·vi'ron·men'tal·ly** *adv.*

en·vi·ron·men·tal·ist (ĕn-vī'rən-mĕn'tl-ĭst) *n.* A person who seeks to protect the natural environment. —**en·vi'ron·men'tal·ism** *n.*

en·vi·rons (ĕn-vī'rənz) *pl.n.* The surrounding areas, esp. of a city; outskirts. [< OFr. *environ*, around.]

en·vis·age (ĕn-vĭz'ĭj) *v.* -**aged**, -**ag·ing**. To picture in the mind. [OFr. *envisager*.]

en·voi (ĕn'voi', ŏn'-) *n.* Also **en·voy**. A short concluding passage, as of a poem or book. [< OFr. *envoier*, to send.]

en·voy¹ (ĕn'voi', ŏn'-) *n.* **1.** A diplomatic representative of a government. **2.** A messenger; agent. [< OFr. *envoier*, to send < LLat. *inviare*, to put on the way.]

en·voy² (ĕn'voi', ŏn'-) *n.* Var. of **envoi**.

en·vy (ĕn'vē) *n., pl.* -**vies**. **1.** Discontented desire or resentment aroused by another's possessions, achievements, or advantages. **2.** An object of envy. —*v.* -**vied**, -**vy·ing**. To feel envy toward or because of. [< Lat. *invidia*.] —**en'vi·er** *n.* —**en'vy·ing·ly** *adv.*

en·zyme (ĕn'zīm') *n.* Any of numerous proteins that are produced in the cells of living organisms and function as catalysts in the chemical processes of those organisms. [< Med. Gk. *enzumos*, leavened.] —**en'zy·mat'ic** (ĕn'zə-măt'ĭk) *adj.*

eo- *pref.* Earliest: *Eolithic*. [< Gk. *ēōs*, dawn.]

E·o·cene (ē'ə-sēn') *adj.* Of or belonging to the geologic time, rock series, or sedimentary deposits of the second epoch of the Cenozoic era, characterized by the rise of mammals. —*n.* The Eocene epoch.

e·o·li·an (ē-ō'lē-ən) *adj.* Pertaining to, caused by, or carried by the wind. [< *Aeolus*, god of the winds in classical myth.]

E·o·lith·ic (ē'ə-lĭth'ĭk) *adj.* Relating to the era considered to be the earliest period of human culture preceding the Paleolithic. —*n.* The Eolithic era.

e·on (ē'ŏn', ē'ən) *n.* **1.** An indefinitely long period of time; age. **2.** The longest division of geologic time, containing two or more eras. [< Gk. *aiōn*.]

E·os (ē'ŏs') *n. Gk. Myth.* The goddess of the dawn.

Eos   epaulet

-eous *suff.* Resembling; having the nature of: *beauteous*. [Lat. *-eus*.]

ep·au·let or **ep·au·lette** (ĕp'ə-lĕt', ĕp'ə-lĕt') *n.* A shoulder ornament, esp. on a uniform. [< Fr. *épaule*, shoulder.]

é·pée or **e·pee** (ā-pā') *n.* A fencing sword with a bowl-shaped guard and a long, narrow blade that has no cutting edge. [Fr. < Lat. *spatha*, sword.]

e·phed·rine (ĭ-fĕd'rĭn, ĕf'ĭ-drēn') *n.* A white, odorless, alkaloid, $C_{10}H_{15}NO$, used as a drug to treat allergies and asthma. [< Lat. *ephedra*, horsetail.]

e·phem·er·al (ĭ-fĕm'ər-əl) *adj.* Lasting for a brief time; short-lived. [< Gk. *ephēmeros*.]

epi- or **ep-** *pref.* **1.** Over; above: *epicenter*. **2.** Around; covering: *epithelium*. **3.** Besides; in addition: *epoxy*. [< Gk.]

ep·ic (ĕp'ĭk) *n.* **1.** A long narrative poem that celebrates episodes of a people's heroic tradition. **2.** A literary or dramatic work that suggests the characteristics of epic poetry. —*adj.* Of or resembling an epic; grand; heroic. [< Gk. *epos*, word, poem.]

ep·i·cene (ĕp'ĭ-sēn') *adj.* **1.** Having the characteristics of both the male and the female. **2.** Effeminate. **3.** Sexless. —*n.* An epicene person or object. [< Gk. *epikoinos*.]

ep·i·cen·ter (ĕp'ĭ-sĕn'tər) *n.* The part of the

earth's surface directly above the point or origin of an earthquake.

ep·i·cure (ĕp'ĭ-kyŏŏr') *n.* A person with refined taste esp. in food and wine. [< *Epicurus* (341-270 B.C.), a Greek philosopher.]

ep·i·cu·re·an (ĕp'ĭ-kyŏŏ-rē'ən) *adj.* **1.** Devoted to the pursuit of pleasure. **2.** Suited to the tastes of an epicure. —**ep'i·cu·re'an** *n.*

ep·i·dem·ic (ĕp'ĭ-dĕm'ĭk) *adj.* Spreading rapidly among many individuals in an area. —*n.* **1.** A contagious disease that spreads rapidly. **2.** A rapid spread or development. [< Gk. *epidēmos,* prevalent.]

ep·i·der·mis (ĕp'ĭ-dûr'mĭs) *n.* The outer, protective layer of the skin. —**ep'i·der'mal** *adj.*

ep·i·glot·tis (ĕp'ĭ-glŏt'ĭs) *n.* An elastic flap of cartilage located at the base of the tongue that prevents food from entering the windpipe during swallowing.

ep·i·gram (ĕp'ĭ-grăm') *n.* A short, witty poem or remark. [< Gk. *epigramma,* inscription.] —**ep'i·gram·mat'ic** *adj.* —**ep'i·gram·mat'i·cal·ly** *adv.*

e·pig·ra·phy (ĭ-pĭg'rə-fē) *n.* The study of inscriptions, esp. ancient inscriptions. [< Gk. *epigraphē,* inscription.] —**e·pig'ra·pher** *n.*

ep·i·lep·sy (ĕp'ə-lĕp'sē) *n.* A disorder of the nervous system marked by loss of consciousness or convulsions. [< Gk. *epilēpsia.*] —**ep'i·lep'tic** *n. & adj.*

ep·i·logue (ĕp'ə-lôg', -lŏg') *n.* A short poem or speech to the audience at the end of a play. [< Gk. *epilogos.*]

ep·i·neph·rine (ĕp'ə-nĕf'rĕn', -rĭn) or **ep·i·neph·rin** (-rĭn) *n.* An adrenal hormone that constricts blood vessels and raises blood pressure. [EPI- + NEPHR(O)- + -INE.]

E·piph·a·ny (ĭ-pĭf'ə-nē) *n., pl.* **-nies.** A Christian festival occurring on Jan. 6 and celebrating the visit of the Magi to Christ. [< Gk. *epiphaneia,* appearance.]

e·pis·co·pa·cy (ĭ-pĭs'kə-pə-sē) *n., pl.* **-cies. 1.** The government of a church by bishops. **2.** An episcopate.

e·pis·co·pal (ĭ-pĭs'kə-pəl) *adj.* **1.** Of or pertaining to a bishop or bishops. **2.** Governed by bishops. **3. Episcopal.** Of or pertaining to the Anglican Church or the Protestant Episcopal Church. [< Gk. *episkopos,* overseer.]

E·pis·co·pa·li·an (ĭ-pĭs'kə-pā'lē-ən, -pāl'yən) *n.* A member of the Protestant Episcopal Church. —**E·pis·co·pa'li·an** *adj.* —**E·pis'co·pa'li·an·ism** *n.*

e·pis·co·pate (ĭ-pĭs'kə-pĭt, -pāt') *n.* **1.** The rank, position, or term of office of a bishop. **2.** The jurisdiction of a bishop. **3.** Bishops collectively.

ep·i·sode (ĕp'ĭ-sōd') *n.* **1.** An incident in the course of an experience. **2.** An incident that forms a unit in a narrative or dramatic work. [Gk. *epeisodion,* part of a Greek tragedy.] —**ep'i·sod'ic** (-sŏd'ĭk) *adj.*

e·pis·tle (ĭ-pĭs'əl) *n.* **1.** A letter. **2.** Often **Epistle.** In the New Testament, a letter written by an Apostle. [< Gk. *epistolē.*] —**e·pis'to·lar'y** (-tə-lĕr'ē) *adj.*

ep·i·taph (ĕp'ĭ-tăf') *n.* An inscription, as on a tombstone, in memory of a dead person. [< Gk. *epitaphion,* funeral oration.]

ep·i·the·li·um (ĕp'ə-thē'lē-əm) *n., pl.* **-ums** or **-li·a** (-lē-ə). A thin, membranous tissue, usu.

in a single layer, that covers most internal surfaces and organs and the outer surface of an animal body. [< EPI- + Gk. *thēlē,* nipple.] —**ep'i·the'li·al** *adj.*

ep·i·thet (ĕp'ə-thĕt') *n.* A term, often of an abusive nature, used to characterize a person or thing. [< Gk. *epitheton.*]

e·pit·o·me (ĭ-pĭt'ə-mē) *n.* **1.** A summary; abridgement. **2.** A typical or perfect example of a type. [< Gk. *epitomē.*]

e·pit·o·mize (ĭ-pĭt'ə-mīz') *v.* **-mized, -miz·ing. 1.** To make an epitome of; sum up. **2.** To typify; embody.

ep·och (ĕp'ək) *n.* A particular period of history, esp. one that is characteristic or memorable; era. [Gk. *epokhē,* pause.] —**ep'och·al** *adj.* —**ep'och·al·ly** *adv.*

ep·ox·y (ĕp'ŏk'sē, ĭ-pŏk'-) *n., pl.* **-ies.** Any of various usu. thermosetting resins used esp. in surface coatings and adhesives. [EP(I)- + OXY(GEN).] —**ep'ox'y** *v.*

ep·si·lon (ĕp'sə-lŏn') *n.* The 5th letter in the Greek alphabet. See table at **alphabet.** [Gk. *e psilon,* simple e.]

Ep·som salts (ĕp'səm) *pl.n.* Hydrated magnesium sulfate, used esp. as a cathartic. [< *Epsom,* England.]

eq·ua·ble (ĕk'wə-bəl, ē'kwə-) *adj.* **1.** Unvarying; even. **2.** Even-tempered. [< Lat. *aequus,* even.] —**eq'ua·bil'i·ty** *n.* —**eq'ua·bly** *adv.*

e·qual (ē'kwəl) *adj.* **1.** Having the same capability, quantity, effect, or value as another. **2.** Having the same privileges, status, or rights. **3.** Having the necessary qualities for a task or situation. —*n.* One that is equal to another. —*v.* **equaled** or **equalled, equal·ing** or **e·qual·ling. 1.** To be equal to, esp. in value. **2.** To do, make, or produce something equal to. [< Lat. *aequalis.*] —**e'qual·ly** *adv.*

e·qual·i·ty (ĭ-kwŏl'ĭ-tē) *n., pl.* **-ties. 1.** The condition of being equal. **2.** A mathematical statement, usu. an equation, that one thing equals another.

e·qual·ize (ē'kwə-līz') *v.* **-ized, -iz·ing.** To make equal. —**e'qual·i·za'tion** *n.* —**e'qual·iz'er** *n.*

e·quate (ĭ-kwāt') *v.* **e·quat·ed, e·quat·ing.** To make, treat, or regard as equal or equivalent. [< Lat. *aequare.*]

e·qua·tion (ĭ-kwā'zhən, -shən) *n.* **1.** The process or act of equating. **2.** The condition of being equated; equilibrium. **3.** A statement, as in mathematics, that two expressions are equal. —**e·qua'tion·al** *adj.*

e·qua·tor (ĭ-kwā'tər) *n.* An imaginary great circle whose plane is perpendicular to the earth's axis of rotation, whose circumference coincides with the earth's surface, and which divides the earth into the Northern Hemisphere and the Southern Hemisphere. [< Med. Lat. *(circulus) aequator (diei et nocis),* (circle) equalizing (day and night).] —**e'qua·to'ri·al** (ē'kwə-tôr'ē-əl, -tōr'-, ĕk'wə-) *adj.*

e·quer·ry (ĕk'wə-rē) *n., pl.* **-ries. 1.** An officer in charge of the horses in a royal or noble household. **2.** An attendant to the royal English household. [< OFr. *escuier,* squire.]

e·ques·tri·an (ĭ-kwĕs'trē-ən) *adj.* **1.** Of or pertaining to horsemanship. **2.** Depicted or represented on horseback. —*n.* One who rides a horse or performs on horseback. [< Lat. *equester*.]

equi- *pref.* Equal; equally: *equiangular*. [< Lat. *aequus*.]

e·qui·an·gu·lar (ē'kwē-ăng'gyə-lər, ĕk'wē-) *adj.* Having all angles equal.

e·qui·dis·tant (ē'kwə-dĭs'tənt, ĕk'wə-) *adj.* Equally distant.

e·qui·lat·er·al (ē'kwə-lăt'ər-əl, ĕk'wə-) *adj.* Having all sides equal. —**e'qui·lat'er·al** *n.*

e·qui·lib·ri·um (ē'kwə-lĭb'rē-əm, ĕk'wə-) *n.* A condition of balance between opposed forces, influences, or actions. [Lat. *aequilibrium*.]

e·quine (ē'kwīn') *adj.* Of, pertaining to, or characteristic of a horse. [Lat. *equinus*.] —**e'·quine** *n.*

e·qui·noc·tial (ē'kwə-nŏk'shəl, ĕk'wə-) *adj.* Of or pertaining to an equinox.

e·qui·nox (ē'kwə-nŏks', ĕk'wə-) *n.* Either of the two times during a year when the sun crosses the celestial equator and the length of day and night are approx. equal. [< Lat. *aequinoctium*.]

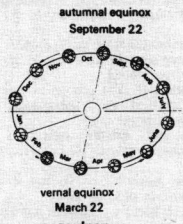

autumnal equinox
September 22

vernal equinox
March 22

equinox

e·quip (ĭ-kwĭp') *v.* **e·quipped, e·quip·ping.** To supply with the necessary materials for an undertaking. [Fr. *équiper*.]

eq·ui·page (ĕk'wə-pĭj) *n.* A horse-drawn carriage, usu. attended by footmen.

e·quip·ment (ĭ-kwĭp'mənt) *n.* **1.** The things with which one is equipped. **2.** The act of equipping or the condition of being equipped.

e·qui·poise (ē'kwə-poiz', ĕk'wə-) *n.* **1.** Balance; equilibrium. **2.** A counterbalance.

eq·ui·ta·ble (ĕk'wĭ-tə-bəl) *adj.* Just and fair; impartial. [< OFr. *equite*, equity.] —**eq'ui·ta·ble·ness** *n.* —**eq'ui·ta·bly** *adv.*

eq·ui·ta·tion (ĕk'wĭ-tā'shən) *n.* The practice or art of riding a horse; horsemanship. [< Lat. *equitare*, to ride.]

eq·ui·ty (ĕk'wĭ-tē) *n., pl.* **-ties. 1.** The condition or quality of being just, impartial, and fair. **2.** Something that is just, impartial, and fair. **3.** The value of a business or property beyond any mortgage or liability. **4.** A system of rules and principles supplementing civil and common law. [< Lat. *aequitas*.]

e·quiv·a·lent (ĭ-kwĭv'ə-lənt) *adj.* **1.** Equal. **2.** Almost identical in function or effect. [< Lat. *aequivalēre*, to be equal in value.] —**e·quiv'a·lence** or **e·quiv'a·len·cy** *n.* —**e·quiv'a·lent** *n.* —**e·quiv'a·lent·ly** *adv.*

e·quiv·o·cal (ĭ-kwĭv'ə-kəl) *adj.* **1.** Ambiguous. **2.** Questionable; inconclusive. [< LLat. *aequivocus*.] —**e·quiv'o·cal·ly** *adv.*

e·quiv·o·cate (ĭ-kwĭv'ə-kāt') *v.* **-cat·ed, -cat·ing.** To use ambiguous language; hedge. [< Med. Lat. *aequivocare*.]

Er The symbol for the element erbium.

-er¹ *suff.* **1. a.** One that performs a specified

action: *swimmer*. **b.** One that undergoes or is capable of undergoing a specified action: *broiler*. **c.** One that has: *ten-pounder*. **2. a.** One associated or involved with: *banker*. **b.** Native or resident of: *New Yorker*. **c.** One that is: *foreigner*. [< Lat. *-arius*, -ary.]

-er² *suff.* Used to form the comparative degree of adjectives and adverbs: *darker; faster*. [< OE *-ra*.]

e·ra (îr'ə, ĕr'ə) *n.* **1.** A period of time using a specific point in history as a basis. **2.** A period of time distinguished by a particular aspect or feature. [< Lat. *aera*, counters.]

e·rad·i·cate (ĭ-răd'ĭ-kāt') *v.* **-cat·ed, -cat·ing.** To remove completely; uproot. [< Lat. *eradicare*.] —**e·rad'i·ca·ble** *adj.* —**e·rad'i·ca'tion** *n.* —**e·rad'i·ca'tor** *n.*

e·rase (ĭ-rās') *v.* **e·rased, e·ras·ing. 1.** To remove (something written or drawn) by or as if by rubbing. **2.** To remove all traces of. [< Lat. *eradere*.] —**e·ras'a·ble** *adj.* —**e·ras'er** *n.* —**e·ra'sure** *n.*

er·bi·um (ûr'bē-əm) *n.* Symbol **Er** A soft, silvery rare-earth element. Atomic number 68; atomic weight 167.26. [< *Ytterby*, Sweden.]

ere (âr) *Archaic.* —*prep.* Previous to; before. —*conj.* **1.** Before. **2.** Sooner than; rather than. [< OE *ær*.]

e·rect (ĭ-rĕkt') *adj.* Directed or pointing upward; upright. —*v.* **1.** To build; construct. **2.** To raise upright. **3.** To set up; establish. [< Lat. *erectus*, p.p. of *erigere*, to raise up.] —**e·rect'ly** *adv.* —**e·rect'ness** *n.* —**e·rec'tor** *n.*

e·rec·tile (ĭ-rĕk'təl, -tīl') *adj.* Of or relating to vascular tissue that is capable of filling with blood and becoming rigid.

e·rec·tion (ĭ-rĕk'shən) *n.* **1.** The act of erecting or the condition of being erected. **2.** *Physiol.* The condition of erectile tissue when filled with blood.

ere·long (âr-lông', -lŏng') *adv. Archaic.* Before long; soon.

er·e·mite (ĕr'ə-mīt') *n.* A hermit. [< Gk. *erēmitēs* < Gk. *erēmia*, desert.]

erg (ûrg) *n.* A unit of energy or work equal to the work done by a force of 1 dyne acting over a distance of 1 centimeter. [Gk. *ergon*, work.]

er·go (ûr'gō, âr'-) *conj. & adv.* Consequently; therefore. [Lat.]

er·got (ûr'gət, -gŏt') *n.* **1. a.** A fungus that infects rye and other cereal plants. **b.** The disease caused by such a fungus. **2.** A drug or medicine made from dried ergot. [< OFr. *argot*, cock's spur.]

er·mine (ûr'mĭn) *n.* **1.** A weasel with brownish fur that turns white in winter. **2.** The white fur of the ermine. [< OFr. *ermin*.]

ermine

e·rode (ĭ-rōd') *v.* **e·rod·ed, e·rod·ing. 1.** To wear away or destroy gradually by or as if by abrasion. 2. To eat into or away. [Lat. *erodere*, to eat away.]

e·rog·e·nous (ĭ-rŏj′ə-nəs) *adj.* Of, pertaining to, or arousing sexual desire. [Gk. *erōs*, love + -GENOUS.]

Er·os (ĭr′ŏs′, ĕr′-) *n.* *Gk. Myth.* The god of love.

e·ro·sion (ĭ-rō′zhən) *n.* The process of eroding or the condition of being eroded.

e·ro·sive (ĭ-rō′sĭv, -zĭv) *adj.* Causing erosion; eroding.

e·rot·ic (ĭ-rŏt′ĭk) *adj.* 1. Of, concerning, or tending to arouse sexual desire. 2. Dominated by sexual desire. [Gk. *erōtikos*.] —**e·rot′i·cal·ly** *adv.* —**e·rot′i·cism** *n.*

err (ûr, ĕr) *v.* 1. To make an error. 2. To be wrong. 3. To sin. [< Lat. *errare*.]

er·rand (ĕr′ənd) *n.* 1. A short trip taken to perform a specific task. 2. The purpose or object of an errand. [< OE *ǣrend.*]

er·rant (ĕr′ənt) *adj.* 1. Roving, esp. in search of adventure. 2. Straying from proper moral standards. 3. Roving aimlessly. [< OFr.] —**er′rant·ry** *n.*

er·rat·ic (ĭ-răt′ĭk) *adj.* 1. Not consistent or uniform; irregular. 2. Unconventional; eccentric. [< Lat. *erraticus*, wandering.] —**er·rat′i·cal·ly** *adv.*

er·ra·tum (ĭ-rä′təm, ĭ-rä′-) *n.*, *pl.* -ta (-tə). An error in a printed text. [Lat.]

er·ro·ne·ous (ĭ-rō′nē-əs) *adj.* Incorrect; mistaken. [< Lat. *erroneus*.] —**er·ro′ne·ous·ly** *adv.* —**er·ro′ne·ous·ness** *n.*

er·ror (ĕr′ər) *n.* 1. An unintentional deviation from what is correct, right, or true. 2. The condition of being incorrect or wrong. 3. *Baseball.* A defensive misplay. [< Lat.]
Syns: *error, lapse, misstep, mistake, slip* *n.*

er·satz (ĕr′zäts, -zäts′) *adj.* Substitute; artificial. [< G., replacement.]

erst (ûrst) *adv.* *Archaic.* Formerly. [< OE *ǣrest*, earliest.]

erst·while (ûrst′hwīl′, -wīl′) *adj.* Former. —**erst′while′** *adv.*

e·ruct (ĭ-rŭkt′) *v.* To belch. [Lat. *eructare.*] —**e·ruc′ta′tion** *n.*

er·u·dite (ĕr′yə-dīt′, ĕr′ə-) *adj.* Very learned; scholarly. [< Lat. *eruditus*, p.p. of *erudire*, to polish.] —**er′u·dite′ly** *adv.*

er·u·di·tion (ĕr′yə-dĭsh′ən, ĕr′ə-) *n.* Extensive learning; scholarship.

e·rupt (ĭ-rŭpt′) *v.* 1. To give or force out violently from limits or restraint; explode. 2. To become violently active. 3. To break out in or as if in a skin blemish or rash. [Lat. *erumpere*.] —**e·rup′tion** *n.* —**e·rup′tive** *adj.*

-ery or **-ry** *suff.* 1. A place for a specified activity or function: *bakery.* 2. A collection or class of objects: *finery.* 3. A craft, study, or practice: *husbandry.* 4. Certain characteristics: *snobbery.* 5. Condition or status: *slavery.* [< OFr. *-erie.*]

er·y·sip·e·las (ĕr′ĭ-sĭp′ə-ləs, ĭr′ĭ-) *n.* An acute disease of the skin caused by a streptococcus and marked by spreading inflammation. [< Gk. *erusipelas.*]

e·ryth·ro·cyte (ĭ-rĭth′rə-sīt′) *n.* A red blood cell. [Gk. *eruthros*, red + -CYTE.]

Es The symbol for the element einsteinium.

-es[1] *suff.* Var. of **-s**[1].

-es[2] *suff.* Var. of **-s**[2].

es·ca·late (ĕs′kə-lāt′) *v.* -lat·ed, -lat·ing. To increase or intensify. [< ESCALATOR.] —**es′ca·la′tion** *n.*

es·ca·la·tor (ĕs′kə-lā′tər) *n.* A moving stairway consisting of steps attached to a continuously circulating belt. [Orig. a trademark.]

es·cal·lop (ĭ-skŏl′əp, ĭ-skăl′-) *n.* & *v.* Var. of scallop.

es·ca·pade (ĕs′kə-pād′) *n.* A reckless adventure. [< OItal. *scappare*, to escape.]

es·cape (ĭ-skāp′) *v.* -caped, -cap·ing. 1. To break out (of). 2. To avoid capture, danger, or harm. 3. To succeed in avoiding. 4. To elude. 5. To issue involuntarily from. —*n.* 1. The act, an instance, or a means of escaping. 2. A leakage. [< ONFr. *escaper.*] —**es·cap′er** *n.*

es·cap·ee (ĕs′kă-pē′, ĭ-skā′pē′) *n.* One that has escaped, esp. an escaped prisoner.

es·cap·ism (ĭ-skā′pĭz′əm) *n.* The avoidance of reality through fantasy or other forms of diversion. —**es·cap′ist** *n.*

es·ca·role (ĕs′kə-rōl′) *n.* A salad plant with densely clustered, ruffled leaves. [< Lat. *esca*, food.]

es·carp·ment (ĭ-skärp′mənt) *n.* 1. A long cliff. 2. A steep slope in front of a fortification. [< Ital. *scarpa*, slope.]

-escence *suff.* The process of emitting light in a specified way: *fluorescence.* [< Lat. *-escentia*, beginning.]

-escent *suff.* Emitting light in a specified way: *phosphorescent.* [< Lat. *-escens*, beginning.]

es·chew (ĕs-chōō′) *v.* To avoid; shun. [< OFr. *eschivir*, of Gmc. orig.]

es·cort (ĕs′kôrt′) *n.* 1. One or more persons or vehicles that accompany another to give guidance or protection or to pay honor. 2. A man who is the companion of a woman, esp. socially. —*v.* (ĭ-skôrt′). To accompany as an escort. [< OItal. *scorta.*]

es·cri·toire (ĕs′krĭ-twär′) *n.* A writing table or desk. [< OFr. *escriptoire*, study.]

es·crow (ĕs′krō′, ĭ-skrō′) *n.* A written agreement, such as a deed, put into the custody of a third party until certain conditions are fulfilled. [< OFr. *escroe*, scroll.]

es·cu·do (ĭ-skōō′dō) *n.*, *pl.* -dos. See table at currency. [Port. and Sp.]

es·cutch·eon (ĭ-skŭch′ən) *n.* A shield or shield-shaped emblem bearing a coat of arms. [Lat. *scutum*, shield.]

-ese *suff.* 1. A native or inhabitant: *Sudanese.* 2. A language or dialect: *Japanese.* 3. A literary style or diction: *journalese.* [< Lat. *-ensis*, of.]

Es·ki·mo (ĕs′kə-mō′) *n.*, *pl.* -mo or -mos. 1. One of a people native to the Arctic coastal regions of North America and to parts of Greenland and Siberia. 2. The language of the Eskimos. —**Es′ki·mo′** *adj.*

e·soph·a·gus (ĭ-sŏf′ə-gəs) *n.*, *pl.* -gi (-jī′). A muscular tube through which food passes from the pharynx to the stomach. [< Gk. *oisophagos*.] —**e·soph′a·ge′al** (ĭ-sŏf′ə-jē′əl) *adj.*

es·o·ter·ic (ĕs′ə-tĕr′ĭk) *adj.* 1. Intended for or understood by only a small group. 2. Not publicly disclosed; private; confidential. [Gk. *esōterikos*.] —**es·o·ter′i·cal·ly** *adv.*

es·pa·drille (ĕs′pə-drĭl′) *n.* A sandal with a

rope sole and a canvas upper. [< Prov. *espardilho.*]

es·pal·ier (ĭ-spăl′yər, -yā′) *n.* A tree or shrub trained to grow horizontally against a wall or framework, often in a pattern. [< Ital. *spalla*, shoulder.] —**es·pal′ier** *v.*

es·pe·cial (ĭ-spĕsh′əl) *adj.* Standing apart from others; particular; exceptional. [< Lat. *specialis.*] —**es·pe′cial·ly** *adv.*

Es·pe·ran·to (ĕs′pə-răn′tō, -răn′-) *n.* An artificial international language based on word roots common to many European languages. [< Dr. *Esperanto*, pseudonym of L.L. Zamenhof (1859–1917).]

es·pi·o·nage (ĕs′pē-ə-näzh′, -nĭj) *n.* The act or practice of spying. [< OItal. *spione*, spy, of Gmc. orig.]

es·pla·nade (ĕs′plə-näd′, -nād′) *n.* A flat, open stretch of pavement or grass used as a promenade. [< Ital. *spianare*, to level.]

esplanade

es·pou·sal (ĭ-spou′zəl) *n.* 1. Adoption of or support for an idea or cause: *espousal of women's rights.* 2. Often **espousals. a.** An engagement; betrothal. **b.** A wedding ceremony.

es·pouse (ĭ-spouz′) *v.* -**poused,** -**pous·ing.** 1. To give one's loyalty or support to; adopt. 2. To marry. [< Lat. *spondēre*, to betroth.]

es·pres·so (ĕ-sprĕs′ō) *n., pl.* -**sos.** A strong coffee brewed by forcing steam through long-roasted, powdered beans. [< Ital., p.p. of *esprimere*, to press out.]

es·prit (ĕ-sprē′) *n.* Liveliness of mind and expression; spirit. [< Lat. *spiritus*, spirit.]

es·prit de corps (ĕ-sprē′ də kôr′) *n.* A common spirit of devotion and enthusiasm among members of a group. [Fr.]

es·py (ĭ-spī′) *v.* -**pied,** -**py·ing.** To catch sight of; glimpse. [< OFr. *espier*, to watch, of Gmc. orig.]

-esque *suff.* Manner or quality: *statuesque.* [< Ital. *-esco*, of Gmc. orig.]

es·quire (ĭ-skwīr′, ĕs′kwīr′) *n.* 1. A candidate for knighthood serving a knight as attendant. 2. A member of the English gentry ranking just below a knight. 3. **Esquire.** A title of courtesy used after the full name of a person, esp. an attorney. (*also* ĕ-sā′). [< LLat. *scutarius*, squire.]
   Usage: The term *Esquire*, and its abbreviation *Esq.*, traditionally reserved for men, is now sometimes used in correspondence addressed to women, especially attorneys: *Jane Roe, Esq.*

-ess *suff.* Female: *lioness.* [< Gk. *-issa.*]

es·say (ĕs′ā) *n.* 1. A short literary composition on a single subject, usu. presenting the personal views of the author. 2. An attempt; endeavor. —*v.* (ĕ-sā′). To make an attempt at; try. [< OFr. *essai*, trial.] —**es′say·er** *n.*

es·say·ist (ĕs′ā-ĭst) *n.* A writer of essays.

es·sence (ĕs′əns) *n.* 1. The intrinsic or indispensable properties of a thing. 2. A concentrated extract of a substance that retains its fundamental properties. 3. A perfume. [< Lat. *essentia.*]

es·sen·tial (ĭ-sĕn′shəl) *adj.* 1. Constituting or part of the essence of something; inherent. 2. Basic or indispensable; necessary. —*n.* Something essential. —**es·sen′ti·al′i·ty** or **es·sen′tial·ness** *n.* —**es·sen′tial·ly** *adv.*

-est¹ *suff.* The superlative degree of adjectives and adverbs: *greatest, earliest.* [< OE.]

-est² or **-st** *suff.* Used to form the archaic 2nd person sing. of English verbs: *comest.* [< OE.]

es·tab·lish (ĭ-stăb′lĭsh) *v.* 1. To settle securely in a position. 2. To found or create. 3. To cause to be recognized or accepted. 4. To prove the truth of. [< Lat. *stabilire*, to make firm.] —**es·tab′lish·er** *n.*

es·tab·lish·ment (ĭ-stăb′lĭsh-mənt) *n.* 1. The act of establishing or the condition of being established. 2. A business firm or residence, including its members, staff, and possessions. 3. **the Establishment.** An exclusive or powerful group who control or strongly influence a government, society, or field of activity.

es·tate (ĭ-stāt′) *n.* 1. A sizable piece of land with a large house. 2. All of one's possessions, esp. those left by a deceased person. 3. A stage, condition, or status of life. [< Lat. *status*, condition.]

es·teem (ĭ-stēm′) *v.* 1. To place a high value on; respect; prize. 2. To judge to be; consider. —*n.* Favorable regard; respect. [< Lat. *aestimare*, to appraise.]

es·ter (ĕs′tər) *n.* Any of a class of organic compounds chemically corresponding to inorganic salts. [G.]

es·the·sia (ĕs-thē′zhə, -zhē-ə) *n.* The ability to receive sense impressions. [< ANESTHESIA.]

es·thet·ic (ĕs-thĕt′ĭk) *adj.* Var. of **aesthetic.**

es·thet·ics (ĕs-thĕt′ĭks) *n.* Var. of **aesthetics.**

es·ti·mate (ĕs′tə-māt′) *v.* -**mat·ed,** -**mat·ing.** 1. To make a judgment as to the likely or approximate cost, quantity, or extent of. 2. To evaluate. —*n.* (ĕs′tə-mĭt). 1. A rough calculation. 2. A preliminary calculation of the cost of work to be undertaken. 3. An opinion. [Lat. *aestimare.*] —**es′ti·ma·ble** (-mə-bəl) *adj.* —**es′ti·ma·bly** *adv.* —**es′ti·ma′tion** *n.* —**es′ti·ma′tor** *n.*

Es·to·ni·an (ĕ-stō′nē-ən) *n.* 1. A native or inhabitant of Estonia. 2. The Finno-Ugric language of Estonia. —**Es·to′ni·an** *adj.*

es·trange (ĭ-strānj′) *v.* -**tranged,** -**trang·ing.** To alienate the affections of. [< Lat. *extraneare.*] —**es·trange′ment** *n.*

es·tro·gen (ĕs′trə-jən) *n.* Any of several hormones, produced chiefly in the ovaries, that act to regulate certain reproductive functions and maintain female secondary sex characteristics. [*estrus*, regularly recurring mammalian estrus + -GEN.] —**es′tro·gen′ic** (-jĕn′ĭk) *adj.*

es·tu·ar·y (ĕs′chŏō-ĕr′ē) *n., pl.* -**ies.** 1. The wide lower course of a river where its current is met by the tides. 2. An inland arm of the sea that meets the mouth of a river. [Lat. *aestuarium.*]

-et *suff.* Small: *baronet.* [< OFr.]

e·ta (ā′tə, ē′tə) *n.* The 7th letter of the Greek alphabet. See table at **alphabet.** [< Gk. *ēta.*]

et cet·er·a (ĕt sĕt′ər-ə, -sĕt′rə). Also **et-cet-**

er·a. And other unspecified things; and so forth. [Lat., and the rest.]

etch (ĕch) *v.* **1.** To make (a pattern) on a surface with acid. **2.** To impress or imprint clearly. [G. *ätzen*.] —**etch′er** *n.*

etch·ing (ĕch′ĭng) *n.* **1.** The art or technique of preparing etched metal plates. **2.** A design etched on a plate. **3.** An impression made from an etched plate.

e·ter·nal (ĭ-tûr′nəl) *adj.* **1.** Without beginning or end. **2.** Lasting; timeless. **3.** Seemingly endless; interminable. **4.** Of or relating to existence after death. —*n.* **the Eternal.** God. [Lat. *aeternus*.] —**e·ter′nal·ly** *adv.* —**e·ter′nal·ness** *n.*

e·ter·ni·ty (ĭ-tûr′nĭ-tē) *n., pl.* **-ties. 1.** The totality of time without beginning or end. **2.** The condition or quality of being eternal. **3.** Immortality. **4.** A very long or seemingly very long time. [< Lat. *aeternitas*.]

-eth¹ *suff.* Used to form the archaic 3rd person sing. of English verbs: *cometh.* [< OE.]

-eth² *suff.* Var. of **-th².**

eth·ane (ĕth′ān′) *n.* A colorless, odorless gas, C_2H_6, occurring in natural gas and used as a fuel and refrigerant. [ETH(YL) + -ANE.]

eth·a·nol (ĕth′ə-nôl′, -nōl′) *n.* A colorless flammable liquid, C_2H_5OH, obtained from fermentation of sugars and starches, and used as a solvent, in drugs, and in intoxicating beverages. [ETHAN(E) + -OL.]

e·ther (ē′thər) *n.* **1.** Any of a class of organic compounds in which two hydrocarbon groups are linked by an oxygen atom. A highly flammable liquid, $C_4H_{10}O$, widely used in industry and as an anesthetic. **3.** The regions of space beyond the earth's atmosphere; the clear sky. **4.** An all-pervading, infinitely elastic, massless medium formerly postulated as the medium of propagation of electromagnetic waves. [< Gk. *aithēr*, upper air.]

e·the·re·al (ĭ-thîr′ē-əl) *adj.* **1.** Highly refined; delicate. **2.** Heavenly. [< Gk. *aitherios*.] —**e·the′re·al·ly** *adv.*

eth·ic (ĕth′ĭk) *n.* **1.** A principle of right or good conduct or a body of such principles. **2.** A system of moral principles or values. **3. ethics.** *(used with a sing. verb).* The study of the general nature of morals and of specific moral choices. **4. ethics.** The rules or standards governing the conduct of the members of a profession. [< Gk. *ēthikē*.]

eth·i·cal (ĕth′ĭ-kəl) *adj.* **1.** Of or dealing with ethics. **2.** In accordance with accepted principles governing the conduct of a group. —**eth′i·cal·ly** *adv.*

eth·nic (ĕth′nĭk) *adj.* Of or pertaining to a group of people recognized as a class on the basis of certain distinctive characteristics, such as religion, language, ancestry, culture, or national origin. —**eth′ni·cal·ly** *adv.*

eth·nic·i·ty (ĕth-nĭs′ĭ-tē) *n.* **1.** The condition of belonging to a particular ethnic group. **2.** Ethnic pride.

ethno- or **ethn-** *pref.* Race or people: *ethnology.* [< Gk. *ethnos.*]

eth·nol·o·gy (ĕth-nŏl′ə-jē) *n.* **1.** The anthropological study of socioeconomic systems and cultural heritage in technologically primitive societies, esp. the study of origins and factors influencing cultural growth and change.

2. The branch of anthropology that deals with the characteristics and origins of ethnic groups and the relations among them. —**eth′no·log′ic** (-nə-lŏj′ĭk) or **eth′no·log′i·cal** *adj.* —**eth′no·log′i·cal·ly** *adv.*

e·thol·o·gy (ē-thŏl′ə-jē) *n.* The scientific study of animal behavior. [< ETHO(S) + -LOGY.] —**e′tho·log′i·cal** (ē′thə-lŏj′ĭ-kəl) *adj.* —**e·thol′o·gist** *n.*

e·thos (ē′thŏs′) *n.* The character or attitude peculiar to a specific culture or group. [Gk. *ēthos*, custom.]

eth·yl (ĕth′əl) *n.* An organic radical, C_2H_5. [ETH(ER) + -YL.]

ethyl alcohol *n.* Ethanol.

eth·yl·ene (ĕth′ə-lēn′) *n.* **1.** A colorless, flammable gas, C_2H_4, derived from natural gas and petroleum. **2.** An organic radical, C_2H_4.

ethylene glycol *n.* A colorless, syrupy, poisonous alcohol, $C_2H_6O_2$, used as an antifreeze.

e·ti·ol·o·gy (ē′tē-ŏl′ə-jē) *n.* **1.** The study of causes, origins, or reasons. **2.** The cause of a disease or disorder as determined by medical diagnosis. [< Gk. *aitiologia*.] —**e′ti·o·log′ic** (-ə-lŏj′ĭk) or **e′ti·o·log′i·cal** *adj.* —**e′ti·o·log′i·cal·ly** *adv.* —**e′ti·ol′o·gist** *n.*

et·i·quette (ĕt′ĭ-kĕt′, -kĭt) *n.* The practices and forms prescribed by social convention or by authority. [Fr. *étiquette*.]

E·trus·can (ĭ-trŭs′kən) *n.* **1.** One of a people of ancient Etruria. **2.** The extinct language of the Etruscans, of unknown linguistic affiliation. —**E·trus′can** *adj.*

-ette *suff.* **1.** Small: *novelette.* **2.** Female: *usherette.* [< OFr.]

é·tude or **e·tude** (ā′tōōd′, -tyōōd′) *n.* A piece of music for the development of a given point of technique. [Fr.]

et·y·mol·o·gy (ĕt′ə-mŏl′ə-jē) *n., pl.* **-gies. 1.** The origin and historical development of a word. **2.** An account of the history of a specific word. **3.** The branch of linguistics that studies the derivation of words. [< Gk. *etumologia*.] —**et′y·mo·log′i·cal** (-mə-lŏj′ĭ-kəl) *adj.* —**et′y·mol′o·gist** *n.*

Eu The symbol for the element europium.

eu- *pref.* Well, pleasant, or beneficial: *eucalyptus.* [< Gk. *eus*, good.]

eu·ca·lyp·tus (yōō′kə-lĭp′təs) *n., pl.* **-es** or **-ti** (-tī′). Any of numerous Australian trees yielding valuable timber and an aromatic medicinal oil. [EU- + Gk. *kaluptos*, covered.]

Eu·cha·rist (yōō′kər-ĭst) *n.* **1.** The Christian sacrament commemorating Christ's Last Supper; Communion. **2.** The consecrated elements of bread and wine used in the Eucharist. [< Gk. *eukharistia*, gratitude.] —**Eu′cha·ris′tic** *adj.*

eu·chre (yōō′kər) *n.* A card game played with the 32 highest cards of the deck. [Orig. unknown.]

Eu·clid·e·an (yōō-klĭd′ē-ən) *adj.* Of or pertaining to Euclid's geometric principles.

eu·gen·ics (yōō-jĕn′ĭks) *n.* *(used with a sing. verb).* The study of hereditary improvement of a breed or race, esp. of human beings, by genetic control. —**eu·gen′ic** *adj.*

eu·lo·gize (yōō′lə-jīz′) *v.* **-gized, -giz·ing.** To write or deliver a eulogy about or for; praise highly; extol.

---

eu·lo·gy (yōō′lə-jē) n., pl. **-gies.** A public speech or written tribute honoring a person or thing, esp. a person who has recently died. [< Gk. *eulogia*, praise.] **—eu′lo·gist** or **eu′lo·giz′er** n. **—eu′lo·gis′tic** adj. **—eu′lo·gize′** v.

eu·nuch (yōō′nək) n. A castrated man. [< Gk. *eunoukhos*.]

eu·phe·mism (yōō′fə-mĭz′əm) n. An inoffensive term substituted for one considered offensively explicit. [Gk. *euphēmismos*.] **—eu′phe·mist** n. **—eu′phe·mis′tic** adj. **—eu′phe·mis′ti·cal·ly** adv.

eu·pho·ny (yōō′fə-nē) n., pl. **-nies.** Pleasing or agreeable sound, esp. of words pleasing the ear. **—eu·pho′ni·ous** adj. **—eu·pho′ni·ous·ly** adv.

eu·pho·ri·a (yōō-fôr′ē-ə, -fōr′-) n. A feeling of great happiness or well-being. [Gk.] **—eu·phor′ic** (-fôr′ĭk, -fōr′-) adj.

Eur·a·sian (yōō-rā′zhən, -shən) adj. 1. Of, pertaining to, or originating in Eurasia. 2. Of mixed European and Asian ancestry. **—Eur·a′sian** n.

eu·re·ka (yōō-rē′kə) interj. Used to express triumph upon discovering something. [Gk. *heurēka*, I have found (it).]

Eu·ro·bond (yōō′rō-bŏnd′) n. A bond of a U.S. corporation issued in Europe. [EURO(PE) + BOND.]

eu·ro·cur·ren·cy (yōō′rō-kûr′ən-sē, -kŭr′-) n., pl. **-cies.** Currency used in the European money market. [EURO(PE) + CURRENCY.]

Eu·ro·dol·lar (yōō′rō-dŏl′ər) n. A U.S. dollar on deposit with a bank abroad, esp. in Europe. [EURO(PE) + DOLLAR.]

Eu·ro·pe·an (yōō′rə-pē′ən) n. 1. A native or inhabitant of Europe. 2. A person of European descent. **—adj.** Of Europe or its peoples, cultures, or languages.

European plan n. A hotel plan in which payment for room and services is separate from payment for meals.

eu·ro·pi·um (yōō-rō′pē-əm) n. Symbol Eu A silvery-white, soft element, used to absorb neutrons in research. Atomic number 63; atomic weight 151.96. [< *Europe*.]

Eu·sta·chian tube (yōō-stā′shən, -shē-ən, -stā′kē-ən) n. The narrow tube that connects the middle ear and the pharynx and allows the pressures on both sides of the eardrum to equalize. [< B. *Eustachio* (1524?–74).]

eu·tha·na·sia (yōō′thə-nā′zhə, -shə) n. 1. The act of killing a person painlessly for reasons of mercy. 2. A painless death. [Gk.]

eu·then·ics (yōō-thĕn′ĭks) n. (used with a sing. or pl. verb). The study of the improvement of human functioning and well-being by the control or adjustment of the environment. [< Gk. *euthenein*, to flourish.] **—eu·then′ist** n.

e·vac·u·ate (ĭ-văk′yōō-āt′) v. **-at·ed, -at·ing.** 1. a. To remove the contents of. b. To create a vacuum in. 2. To excrete or discharge waste matter from (the bowels). 3. To withdraw, esp. from a threatened area. [< Lat. *evacuare*.] **—e·vac′u·a′tion** n. **—e·vac′u·a′tor** n.

e·vac·u·ee (ĭ-văk′yōō-ē′) n. One evacuated from a threatened area.

e·vade (ĭ-vād′) v. **e·vad·ed, e·vad·ing.** To escape or avoid by cleverness or deceit. [< Lat. *evadere*.] **—e·vad′er** n.

e·val·u·ate (ĭ-văl′yōō-āt′) v. **-at·ed, -at·ing.** To ascertain or fix the value or worth of. [< OFr. *evaluer*.] **—e·val′u·a′tion** n. **—e·val′u·a′tor** n.

ev·a·nesce (ĕv′ə-nĕs′) v. **-nesced, -nesc·ing.**

To disappear gradually; fade away; vanish. [Lat. *evanescere*.]

ev·a·nes·cence (ĕv′ə-nĕs′əns) n. 1. Gradual disappearing; dissipation. 2. The condition or quality of being insubstantial or transitory.

ev·a·nes·cent (ĕv′ə-nĕs′ənt) adj. Vanishing or likely to vanish; transitory; fleeting. **—ev′a·nes′cence** n. **—ev′a·nes′cent·ly** adv.

e·van·gel·i·cal (ē′văn-jĕl′ĭ-kəl) or **e·van·gel·ic** (-jĕl′ĭk) adj. 1. Of or in accordance with the Christian gospel, esp. the Gospels of the New Testament. 2. Of or being a Protestant group emphasizing the authority of the Gospel. [< Gk. *euangelos*, bring good news.] **—e′van·gel′i·cal·ism** n. **—e′van·gel′i·cal·ly** adv.

e·van·gel·ism (ĭ-văn′jə-lĭz′əm) n. The zealous preaching and dissemination of the Gospel, as through missionary work.

e·van·gel·ist (ĭ-văn′jə-lĭst) n. 1. Often **Evangelist.** Any of the authors of the New Testament Gospels; Matthew, Mark, Luke, or John. 2. A Protestant who practices evangelism. **—e·van′gel·is′tic** adj. **—e·van′gel·is′ti·cal·ly** adv.

e·vap·o·rate (ĭ-văp′ə-rāt′) v. **-rat·ed, -rat·ing.** 1. To convert or change into a vapor. 2. To remove or be removed in or as a vapor. 3. To vanish. [< Lat. *evaporare*.] **—e·vap′o·ra′tion** n. **—e·vap′o·ra′tor** n.

e·va·sion (ĭ-vā′zhən) n. 1. The act of evading. 2. A means of evading. [< LLat. *evasio*.]

e·va·sive (ĭ-vā′sĭv) adj. 1. Characterized by evasion. 2. Intentionally vague. **—e·va′sive·ly** adv. **—e·va′sive·ness** n.

eve (ēv) n. 1. Often **Eve.** The evening or day preceding a holiday. 2. The period immediately preceding a certain event: *the eve of war.* 3. *Poet.* Evening. [< OE *æfen.*]

e·ven[1] (ē′vən) adj. **-er, -est.** 1. a. Flat: *an even floor.* b. Smooth. c. Level: *The picture is even with the window.* 2. Uniform; steady; regular: *an even rate of speed.* 3. Tranquil; calm: *an even temper.* 4. Equal in degree, extent, or amount; balanced. 5. a. *Math.* Exactly divisible by 2. b. Characterized by a number exactly divisible by 2. 6. a. Having an even number in a series. b. Having an even number of members. 7. Exact: *an even pound.* **—adv.** 1. To a higher degree: *an even worse condition.* 2. At the same time as: *Even as we watched, the building collapsed.* 3. In spite of: *Even with his head start, I overtook him.* 4. In fact: *unhappy, even weeping.* **—v.** To make or become even. **—idioms. break even.** *Informal.* To have neither losses nor gains. **get even.** To take revenge. [< OE *efen.*] **—e′ven·ly** adv. **—e′ven·ness** n.

e·ven[2] (ē′vən) n. *Archaic & Poetic.* Evening. [< OE *æfen.*]

e·ven·hand·ed (ē′vən-hăn′dĭd) adj. Impartial; just. **—e′ven·hand′ed·ly** adv. **—e′ven·hand′ed·ness** n.

eve·ning (ēv′nĭng) n. Late afternoon and early night. [< OE *æfnung.*]

evening star n. A planet, esp. Mercury or Venus, that shines brightly in the western sky after sunset.

e·vent (ĭ-vĕnt′) n. 1. An occurrence or incident, esp. one of significance. 2. One of the items in a sports program. [Lat. *eventus.*]

e·vent·ful (ĭ-vĕnt′fəl) adj. 1. Full of events. 2. Important; momentous. **—e·vent′ful·ly** adv. **—e·vent′ful·ness** n.

e·ven·tide (ē′vən-tīd′) n. Poet. Evening. [< OE ǣfentīd.]

e·ven·tu·al (ĭ-vĕn′chōō-əl) adj. Occurring at an unspecified time in the future: his eventual death. [< EVENT.] —**e·ven′tu·al·ly** adv.

e·ven·tu·al·i·ty (ĭ-vĕn′chōō-ăl′ĭ-tē) n., pl. **-ties.** Something that may occur.

e·ven·tu·ate (ĭ-vĕn′chōō-āt′) v. **-at·ed, -at·ing.** To result ultimately; culminate.

ev·er (ĕv′ər) adv. 1. At all times: He is ever courteous. 2. At any time: Have you ever seen a circus? 3. In any way or case; at all. —Idiom. **ever so.** To an extreme degree: ever so glad. [< OE ǣfre.]

ev·er·glade (ĕv′ər-glād′) n. A tract of usu. submerged swampland.

ev·er·green (ĕv′ər-grēn′) adj. Bot. Having foliage that remains green throughout the year. —n. An evergreen tree, shrub, or plant.

ev·er·last·ing (ĕv′ər-lăs′tĭng) adj. Lasting forever; eternal. —n. 1. **the Everlasting.** God. 2. Eternity. 3. A plant, such as the strawflower, that retains form and color after it is dry. —**ev′er·last′ing·ly** adv.

ev·er·more (ĕv′ər-môr′, -mōr′) adv. Forever; always.

ev·er·y (ĕv′rē) adj. 1. Each without exception: every student in the class. 2. Each in a specified series: every third seat; every two hours. 3. Entire; utmost: was given every care. —Idioms. **every bit.** Informal. In all ways; equally. **every so often.** Occasionally. [< OE ǣfre ǣlc, ever each.]

ev·er·y·bod·y (ĕv′rē-bŏd′ē) pron. Every person; everyone.

ev·er·y·day (ĕv′rē-dā′) adj. 1. Suitable for ordinary occasions. 2. Commonplace; usual.

ev·er·y·one (ĕv′rē-wŭn′) pron. Every person; everybody.

Usage: Everyone is one of a large class of English words and expressions such as anyone, somebody, none, or whoever that are singular in form but felt to be plural in sense, so that speakers are uncertain as to whether to use a singular or plural pronoun in referring to them. For example, strict grammarians have long insisted that it is correct to say everyone took his coat, not their coat or their coats, and that we should say no one is happy when he is abandoned and not when they are abandoned. The application of this traditional rule may be politically offensive to many, especially in cases that involve reference to a group consisting of both men and women. Those who find the singular he and his distasteful in such cases have the choice of flying in the face of traditional grammar and using they or their or of using the somewhat clumsy alternatives his and her or her and his. The entire matter is properly outside the scope of grammar. In the end, as Fowler says, "everyone must decide for himself (or for himself and herself, or for themselves)."

ev·er·y·place (ĕv′rē-plās′) adv. Everywhere.

ev·er·y·thing (ĕv′rē-thĭng′) pron. All things that exist or are relevant.

ev·er·y·where (ĕv′rē-hwâr′, -wâr′) adv. In every place.

Usage: The use of that with everywhere (everywhere that I go) is superfluous.

e·vict (ĭ-vĭkt′) v. To expel (a tenant) by legal process. [< Lat. evincere, to conquer.] —**e·vic′tion** n. —**e·vic′tor** n.

ev·i·dence (ĕv′ĭ-dəns) n. 1. The data on which a judgment can be based or proof established. 2. Something that serves to indicate: His reaction was evidence of guilt. —v. **-denced, -denc·ing.** To indicate clearly. —Idiom. **in evidence.** Plainly visible; conspicuous.

ev·i·dent (ĕv′ĭ-dənt) adj. Easily recognized or perceived; obvious. [< Lat. evidens.] —**ev′i·dent·ly** adv. —**ev′i·dent·ness** n.

e·vil (ē′vəl) adj. **-er, -est.** 1. Morally bad or wrong; wicked. 2. Harmful; injurious. —n. 1. Something that is morally bad or wrong; wickedness. 2. Something that causes misfortune, suffering, or difficulty. [< OE yfel.] —**e′vil·ly** adv. —**e′vil·ness** n.

e·vil·do·er (ē′vəl-dōō′ər) n. A person who does evil. —**e′vil·do′ing** n.

e·vince (ĭ-vĭns′) v. **e·vinced, e·vinc·ing.** To show or demonstrate; manifest. [Lat. evincere.] —**e·vinc′i·ble** adj.

e·vis·cer·ate (ĭ-vĭs′ə-rāt′) v. **-at·ed, -at·ing.** 1. To remove the entrails of. 2. To take away a vital or essential part of. [Lat. eviscerare.] —**e·vis′cer·a′tion** n.

ev·o·ca·tion (ĕv′ə-kā′shən) n. The act of calling forth or conjuring up: an evocation of childhood memories.

e·voc·a·tive (ĭ-vŏk′ə-tĭv) adj. Tending or having the power to evoke. —**e·voc′a·tive·ly** adv.

e·voke (ĭ-vōk′) v. **e·voked, e·vok·ing.** To summon or call forth; elicit: evoke memories. [Lat. evocare.] —**ev′o·ca′tion** n. —**e·voc′a·tive** adj. —**e·voc′a·tive·ly** adv.

ev·o·lu·tion (ĕv′ə-lōō′shən) n. 1. A gradual process in which something changes esp. into a more complex form. 2. Biol. The theory that groups of organisms, such as species, may change or develop over a long period of time so that descendants differ morphologically and physiologically from their ancestors. 3. The extraction of a root of a mathematical quantity. [Lat. evolutio, an unrolling.] —**ev′o·lu′tion·ar·y** adj. —**ev′o·lu′tion·ism** n. —**ev′o·lu′tion·ist** n.

e·volve (ĭ-vŏlv′) v. **e·volved, e·volv·ing.** 1. To develop or work out; arrive at gradually: evolve a plan. 2. To develop biologically by evolutionary processes. [Lat. evolvere, to unroll.] —**e·volve′ment** n.

ewe (yōō) n. A female sheep. [< OE ēowu.]

E·we (ā′wā′, ā′vā′) n. 1. a. A Negro people of Togo, Ghana, and parts of Dahomey. b. A member of the Ewe people. 2. The language of the Ewe people.

ew·er (yōō′ər) n. A large, wide-mouthed pitcher. [< Lat. aqua, water.]

ex¹ (ĕks) prep. Finance. Without; not including; not participating in: ex dividend. [Lat., out of.]

ex² (ĕks) n. The letter x.

ex³ (ĕks) n. Slang. A former wife or husband. [< EX-.]

ex- pref. 1. Out of or from: exurbia. 2. Former: ex-president. [< Lat. ex, out of.]

ex·ac·er·bate (ĭg-zăs′ər-bāt′, ĭk-săs′-) v. **-bat·ed, -bat·ing.** To increase the severity of; aggravate: exacerbate tensions; exacerbate pain. [Lat. exacerbare.] —**ex·ac′er·bat′ing·ly** adv. —**ex·ac′er·ba′tion** n.

ex·act (ĭg-zăkt′) *adj.* Strictly accurate; precise. —*v.* **1.** To obtain by or as if by force or authority. **2.** To call for or require. [Lat. *exāctus*, p.p. of *exigere*, to demand.] —**ex·act′ly** *adv.* —**ex·act′ness** *n.*

ex·act·ing (ĭg-zăk′tĭng) *adj.* **1.** Making rigorous demands. **2.** Requiring great care or effort. —**ex·act′ing·ly** *adv.*

ex·act·i·tude (ĭg-zăk′tĭ-tōōd′, -tyōōd′) *n.* The condition or quality of being exact.

ex·ag·ger·ate (ĭg-zăj′ə-rāt′) *v.* **-at·ed, -at·ing.** To enlarge (something) disproportionately; overstate. [Lat. *exaggerare*.] —**ex·ag′ger·a′tion** *n.* —**ex·ag′ger·a·tive** or **ex·ag·ger·a·to·ry** (-ə-tôr′ē, -tōr′ē) *adj.* —**ex·ag′ger·a′tor** *n.*

ex·alt (ĭg-zôlt′) *v.* **1.** To raise in position, status, etc.; elevate. **2.** To glorify; praise. **3.** To fill with pride, delight, etc.; elate. [< Lat. *exaltare*.] —**ex′al·ta′tion** *n.*

ex·am (ĭg-zăm′) *n. Informal.* An examination.

ex·am·i·na·tion (ĭg-zăm′ə-nā′shən) *n.* **1.** The act or process of examining. **2.** A set of questions designed to test knowledge. —**ex·am′i·na′tion·al** *adj.*

ex·am·ine (ĭg-zăm′ĭn) *v.* **-ined, -in·ing. 1.** To inspect or analyze (a person, thing, or situation) in detail. **2.** To test knowledge or skills by questioning. **3.** To interrogate formally to elicit facts. [< Lat. *examinare*.] —**ex·am′in·ee′** *n.* —**ex·am′in·er** *n.*

ex·am·ple (ĭg-zăm′pəl) *n.* **1.** One representative of a group as a whole; sample. **2.** One that is worthy of imitation; model. **3.** One that serves as a warning. **4.** A problem that illustrates a principle. [< Lat. *exemplum*.]

ex·as·per·ate (ĭg-zăs′pə-rāt′) *v.* **-at·ed, -at·ing.** To make angry or irritated; provoke. [Lat. *exasperare*.] —**ex·as′per·a′tion** *n.*

ex·ca·vate (ĕk′skə-vāt′) *v.* **-vat·ed, -vat·ing. 1.** To dig out; hollow out. **2.** To remove (soil) by digging or scooping out. **3.** To uncover by digging. [< Lat. *excavare*.] —**ex′ca·va′tion** *n.* —**ex′ca·va′tor** *n.*

excavate

ex·ceed (ĭk-sēd′) *v.* **1.** To be greater than; surpass. **2.** To go or be beyond the limits of: *exceed one's authority.* [< Lat. *excedere*.]

ex·ceed·ing (ĭk-sē′dĭng) *adj.* Extreme; extraordinary. —**ex·ceed′ing·ly** *adv.*

ex·cel (ĭk-sĕl′) *v.* **-celled, -cel·ling.** To be superior to (others); surpass; outdo. [< Lat. *excellere*.]

ex·cel·lence (ĕk′sə-ləns) *n.* **1.** The quality or condition of being excellent; superiority. **2.** Something in which one excels. **3.** **Excellence.** Excellency.

Ex·cel·len·cy (ĕk′sə-lən-sē) *n., pl.* **-cies.** A title for certain high officials.

ex·cel·lent (ĕk′sə-lənt) *adj.* Of the highest or finest quality; exceptionally good; superb. —**ex′cel·lent·ly** *adv.*

   Syns: *excellent, capital, dandy, fine, first-class, great, prime, splendid, super, superb, swell, terrific, top, topflight, topnotch* adj.

ex·cel·si·or (ĭk-sĕl′sē-ər) *n.* Wood shavings used esp. for packing. [Lat., higher.]

ex·cept (ĭk-sĕpt′) *prep.* With the exclusion of; but. —*conj.* Were it not for the fact that; only. —*v.* To leave out; exclude. [< Lat. *exceptus*, p.p. of *excipere*, to take out.]

   Usage: *Except* in the sense of "with the exclusion of" is generally construed as a preposition, not a conjunction. A personal pronoun that follows *except* is therefore in the objective case: *Every member of the original cast was signed except her.*

ex·cept·ing (ĭk-sĕp′tĭng) *prep.* Excluding; except.

ex·cep·tion (ĭk-sĕp′shən) *n.* **1.** The act of excepting. **2.** One that is excepted. **3.** An objection.

ex·cep·tion·a·ble (ĭk-sĕp′shə-nə-bəl) *adj.* Open to objection. —**ex·cep′tion·a·bly** *adv.*

ex·cep·tion·al (ĭk-sĕp′shə-nəl) *adj.* Uncommon; extraordinary. —**ex·cep′tion·al·ly** *adv.*

ex·cerpt (ĕk′sûrpt′) *n.* A passage selected from a speech, book, film, etc. [Lat. *excerptum*.] —**ex′cerpt′** *v.*

ex·cess (ĭk-sĕs′, ĕk′sĕs′) *n.* **1.** An amount or quantity beyond what is required; superfluity. **2.** Intemperance; overindulgence. —*adj.* Exceeding what is required. [< Lat. *excessus*, p.p. of *excedere*, to exceed.]

   Syns: *excess, glut, overage, overflow, overstock, superfluity, surplus* n.

ex·ces·sive (ĭk-sĕs′ĭv) *adj.* Exceeding what is usual, necessary, or proper.

ex·change (ĭks-chānj′) *v.* **-changed, -chang·ing. 1.** To give and receive reciprocally; trade. **2.** To replace (one thing by another). —*n.* **1.** An act or instance of exchanging. **2.** A place where things are exchanged, esp. a center where securities are traded. **3.** A central system that establishes connections between individual telephones. [< OFr. *eschangier*.] —**ex·change′a·ble** *adj.*

ex·cheq·uer (ĭks-chĕk′ər, ĕks′chĕk′ər) *n.* A treasury, as of a nation or an organization. [< OFr. *eschequier*, counting table.]

ex·cise[1] (ĕk′sīz′, ĭk-sīz′) *n.* A tax on the production, sale, or consumption of certain commodities within a country. [Obs. Du. *excijs*.]

ex·cise[2] (ĭk-sīz′) *v.* **-cised, -cis·ing.** To remove by or as if by cutting. [Lat. *excidere*.] —**ex·ci′sion** (-sĭzh′ən) *n.*

ex·cit·a·ble (ĭk-sī′tə-bəl) *adj.* Capable of being easily excited. —**ex·cit′a·bil′i·ty** or **ex·cit′a·ble·ness** *n.* —**ex·cit′a·bly** *adv.*

ex·cite (ĭk-sīt′) *v.* **-cit·ed, -cit·ing. 1.** To stir to activity; stimulate. **2.** To arouse strong feeling in (a person); provoke. **3.** *Physics.* To raise (e.g. an atom or molecule) to a higher energy level. [< Lat. *excitare*.] —**ex·ci′ta·tion** *n.* —**ex·cit′ed·ly** *adv.* —**ex·cite′ment** *n.* —**ex·cit′ing·ly** *adv.*

ex·claim (ĭk-sklām′) *v.* To cry out or speak suddenly or vehemently. [< Lat. *exclamare*.]

ex·cla·ma·tion (ĕks′klə-mā′shən) *n.* **1.** A sudden utterance. **2.** An interjection. —**ex·clam′a·to·ry** (-ə-tôr′ē, -tōr′ē) *adj.*

exclamation point *n.* A punctuation mark (!) used after an exclamation.

ex·clude (ĭk-sklōōd′) *v.* **-clud·ed, -clud·ing. 1.** To prevent from entering a place, group, activity, etc.; bar. **2.** To put out; expel. [< Lat. *excludere.*] —**ex·clu'sion** *n.*

ex·clu·sive (ĭk-sklōō'sĭv) *adj.* **1.** Not divided or shared with others. **2.** Admitting only certain people; select. **3.** Expensive; chic: *exclusive shops.* —*n.* A news item released to only one person or publication. —*idiom.* **exclusive of.** Not including; besides: *exclusive of other factors.* —**ex·clu'sive·ly** *adv.* —**ex·clu'sive·ness** *or* **ex'clu·siv'i·ty** (-sĭv'ĭ-tē) *n.*

ex·com·mu·ni·cate (ĕks'kə-myōō'nĭ-kāt') *v.* **-cat·ed, -cat·ing.** To exclude from membership in a church by ecclesiastical authority. [< LLat. *excommunicare.*] —**ex'com·mu'ni·ca'tion** *n.* —**ex'com·mu'ni·ca'tor** *n.*

ex·co·ri·ate (ĭk-skôr'ē-āt', -skōr'-) *v.* **-at·ed, -at·ing.** **1.** To tear or wear off the skin of. **2.** To censure strongly; denounce. [< Lat. *excoriare,* to strip of skin.] —**ex·co'ri·a'tion** *n.*

ex·cre·ment (ĕk'skrə-mənt) *n.* Bodily waste, esp. fecal matter. [Lat. *excrementum.*] —**ex'cre·men'tal** (-mĕn'tĭl) *adj.*

ex·cres·cence (ĭk-skrĕs'əns) *n.* An abnormal outgrowth or enlargement. [< Lat. *excrescentia.*] —**ex·cres'cent** *adj.*

ex·cre·ta (ĭk-skrē'tə) *pl.n.* Waste matter, such as sweat, urine, or feces, expelled from the body. [Lat.] —**ex·cre'tal** *adj.*

ex·crete (ĭk-skrēt') *v.* **-cret·ed, -cret·ing.** To separate and eliminate (waste matter) from the blood, tissues, or organs. [Lat. *excernere.*] —**ex·cre'tion** *n.* —**ex'cre·to'ry** (-skrĭ-tôr'ē, -tōr'ē) *or* **ex·cre'tive** *adj.*

ex·cru·ci·at·ing (ĭk-skrōō'shē-ā'tĭng) *adj.* Intensely painful or distressing. [< Lat. *excruciare,* to torture.] —**ex·cru'ci·at'ing·ly** *adv.*

ex·cul·pate (ĕk'skəl-pāt', ĭk-skŭl'-) *v.* **-pat·ed, -pat·ing.** To clear of guilt or blame. [< Med. Lat. *exculpatus.*] —**ex·cul·pa'tion** *n.* —**ex·cul'pa·to'ry** (ĭk-skŭl'pə-tôr'ē, -tōr'ē) *adj.*

ex·cur·sion (ĭk-skûr'zhən) *n.* **1.** A usu. brief journey; outing. **2.** A short, inexpensive pleasure tour. **3.** A digression from the main topic. [Lat. *excursio.*] —**ex·cur'sion·ist** *n.*

ex·cur·sive (ĭk-skûr'sĭv) *adj.* Characterized by digression; rambling. —**ex·cur'sive·ly** *adv.* —**ex·cur'sive·ness** *n.*

ex·cuse (ĭk-skyōōz') *v.* **-cused, -cus·ing.** **1.** To pardon; forgive. **2.** To overlook; condone. **3.** To justify. **4.** To release, as from an obligation. **5.** To apologize. —*n.* (ĭk-skyōōs') **1.** An explanation to elicit pardon. **2.** A ground for being excused. **3.** *Informal.* One that falls short of expectations. [< Lat. *excusare.*] —**ex·cus'a·ble** *adj.* —**ex·cus'a·bly** *adv.* —**ex·cus'er** *n.*

Usage: The expression **excuse away** has no meaning beyond that of **excuse** and is unacceptable to a large majority of the Usage Panel: *His behavior cannot be excused* (not *excused away*).

ex·e·cra·ble (ĕk'sĭ-krə-bəl) *adj.* **1.** Detestable; abhorrent. **2.** Extremely inferior. [< Lat. *execrabilis.*] —**ex'e·cra·bly** *adv.*

ex·e·crate (ĕk'sĭ-krāt') *v.* **-crat·ed, -crat·ing.** **1.** To protest vehemently against; denounce. **2.** To loathe; hate. [Lat. *execrari.*] —**ex'e·cra'tion** *n.* —**ex'e·cra'tor** *n.*

ex·e·cute (ĕk'sĭ-kyōōt') *v.* **-cut·ed, -cut·ing.** **1.** To carry out; perform. **2.** To make valid or legal, as by signing: *execute a deed.* **3.** To

carry out what is required by: *execute a will.* **4.** To subject to capital punishment. [< Med. Lat. *executare.*] —**ex'e·cut'er** *n.* —**ex·e·cu'tion** *n.*

ex·e·cu·tion·er (ĕk'sĭ-kyōō'shə-nər) *n.* One who administers capital punishment.

ex·ec·u·tive (ĭg-zĕk'yə-tĭv) *n.* **1.** A person or group having administrative or managerial authority in an organization. **2.** The branch of government concerned with putting a country's laws into effect. —*adj.* **1.** Pertaining to or capable of carrying out plans, duties, etc. **2.** Of or pertaining to the executive branch of government.

ex·ec·u·tor (ĭg-zĕk'yə-tər) *n.* A person designated to execute the terms of a will. —**ex·ec'u·trix** *n.*

ex·e·ge·sis (ĕk'sə-jē'sĭs) *n., pl.* **-ses** (-sēz'). Critical explanation or analysis of a text, esp. the Bible. [Gk. *exēgēsis.*] —**ex'e·get'ic** (-jĕt'ik) *or* **ex'e·get'i·cal** *adj.*

ex·em·plar (ĭg-zĕm'plär', -plər) *n.* **1.** One worthy of being imitated; model. **2.** One that is typical; example. [< LLat. *exemplarium.*] —**ex·em'pla·ry** *adj.*

ex·em·pli·fy (ĭg-zĕm'plə-fī') *v.* **-fied, -fy·ing.** **1.** To illustrate by example. **2.** To serve as an example of. [< Med. Lat. *exemplificare.*] —**ex·em'pli·fi·ca'tion** *n.*

ex·empt (ĭg-zĕmpt') *v.* To free from an obligation or duty required of others. [< Lat. *eximere.*] —*adj.* —**ex·empt'i·ble** *adj.* —**ex·emp'tion** *n.*

ex·er·cise (ĕk'sər-sīz') *n.* **1.** An act of using or putting into effect. **2.** Physical activity to develop fitness. **3.** A lesson, problem, etc., designed to develop understanding or a skill. **4.** **exercises.** A public ceremony that includes speeches, awards, etc. —*v.* **-cised, -cis·ing.** **1.** To put into operation; employ. **2.** To subject to or engage in. **3.** To worry, upset, or make anxious. [< Lat. *exercitium.*] —**ex'er·cis'er** *n.*

ex·ert (ĭg-zûrt') *v.* **1.** To bring to bear. **2.** To make a strenuous effort. [Lat. *exserere,* to put forth.] —**ex·er'tion** *n.*

ex·hale (ĕks-hāl', ĕk-sāl') *v.* **-haled, -hal·ing.** **1.** To breathe out. **2.** To emit (e.g. smoke). [< Lat. *exhalare.*] —**ex'ha·la'tion** (-lā'shən) *n.*

ex·haust (ĭg-zôst') *v.* **1.** To draw off or release (a liquid or gas). **2.** To use up; consume. **3.** To wear out completely; tire. **4.** To deal with comprehensively: *exhaust all possibilities.* —*n.* **1. a.** The escape or release of waste gases or vapors, as from an engine. **b.** Vapor or gases so released. **2.** A device or system that pumps gases out or allows them to escape. [Lat. *exhaurire.*] —**ex·haust'i·bil'i·ty** *n.* —**ex·haust'i·ble** *adj.* —**ex·haus'tion** *n.*

ex·haus·tive (ĭg-zô'stĭv) *adj.* Comprehensive; thorough: *exhaustive tests.* —**ex·haus'tive·ly** *adv.* —**ex·haus'tive·ness** *n.*

ex·hib·it (ĭg-zĭb'ĭt) *v.* **1.** To show or display, esp. to public view. —*n.* **1.** An act of exhibiting. **2.** Something exhibited. **3.** Something introduced as evidence in court. [< Lat. *exhibēre.*] —**ex'hi·bi'tion** *n.* —**ex·hib'i·tor** *n.*

ex·hi·bi·tion·ism (ĕk'sə-bĭsh'ə-nĭz'əm) *n.* The practice of behaving so as to attract attention. —**ex'hi·bi'tion·ist** *n.* —**ex'hi·bi'tion·is'tic** *adj.*

ex·hil·a·rate (ĭg-zĭl'ə-rāt') *v.* **-rat·ed, -rat·ing.**

1. To make cheerful; elate. 2. To invigorate. [Lat. *exhilarare*.] —**ex·hil'a·ra'tion** *n.* —**ex·hil'a·ra'tive** *adj.*

ex·hort (ĭg-zôrt') *v.* To urge by strong argument or appeal; admonish earnestly. [< Lat. *exhortari*.] —**ex'hor·ta'tion** *n.* —**ex·hor'ta·tive** *adj.* —**ex·hort'er** *n.*

ex·hume (ĭg-zyōōm', ĕks-hyōōm') *v.* -**humed,** -**hum·ing.** To remove from a grave. [Med. Lat. *exhumare*.] —**ex'hu·ma'tion** *n.*

ex·i·gen·cy (ĕk'sə-jən-sē, ĕg'zə-) *n., pl.* -**cies.** Also **ex·i·gence** (-jəns). 1. A situation demanding swift attention or action. 2. Often **exigencies.** Urgent requirements. [< Lat. *exigere*, to demand.] —**ex'i·gent** *adj.* —**ex'i·gent·ly** *adv.*

ex·ig·u·ous (ĭg-zĭg'yōō-əs, ĭk-sĭg'-) *adj.* Scanty; meager. [Lat. *exiguus*, measured.] —**ex·i·gu'i·ty** *n.* —**ex·ig'u·ous·ly** *adv.*

ex·ile (ĕg'zīl', ĕk'sīl') *n.* 1. Enforced removal or voluntary separation from one's native country. 2. One who has been separated from his country. —*v.* -**iled, -il·ing.** To send (someone) into exile; banish. [< Lat. *exilium*.]

ex·ist (ĭg-zĭst') *v.* 1. To have material or spiritual being; be or live. 2. To occur. [< Lat. *existere*.] —**ex·is'tence** *n.* —**ex·is'tent** *adj.*

ex·is·ten·tial·ism (ĕg'zĭ-stĕn'shə-lĭz'əm, ĕk'sĭ-) *n.* A 20th-cent. philosophy that views the individual as being unique and alone in an indifferent and even hostile universe. —**ex'is·ten'tial·ist** *n.*

ex·it (ĕg'zĭt, ĕk'sĭt) *n.* 1. A passage or way out. 2. The act of going out. 3. The departure of a performer from the stage. [Lat. *exitus*.] —**ex'it** *v.*

exo- *pref.* Outside; external: *exosphere.* [< Gk. *exō*, outside of.]

ex·o·bi·ol·o·gy (ĕk'sō-bī-ŏl'ə-jē) *n.* Extraterrestrial biology. —**ex'o·bi·ol'o·gist** *n.*

ex·o·crine (ĕk'sə-krĭn, -krēn, -krīn') *adj.* Having or secreting through a duct: *exocrine gland.* [EXO- + Gk. *krinein,* to separate.]

ex·o·dus (ĕk'sə-dəs) *n.* 1. A mass departure or emigration. 2. **Exodus.** See table at **Bible.** [< Gk. *exodos.*]

ex of·fi·ci·o (ĕks' ə-fĭsh'ē-ō') *adj. & adv.* By virtue of one's office or position. [Lat.]

ex·og·e·nous (ĕk-sŏj'ə-nəs) *adj.* Having a cause outside the body. [Fr. *exogène.*]

ex·on·er·ate (ĭg-zŏn'ə-rāt') *v.* -**at·ed, -at·ing.** To free from blame. [< Lat. *exonerare,* to free from a burden.] —**ex·on'er·a'tion** *n.* —**ex·on'er·a'tor** *n.*

ex·or·bi·tant (ĭg-zôr'bĭ-tənt) *adj.* Exceeding reasonable limits; excessive. [< Med. Lat. *exorbitare,* to deviate.] —**ex·or'bi·tance** *n.* —**ex·or'bi·tant·ly** *adv.*

ex·or·cise (ĕk'sôr-sīz', -sər-) *v.* -**cised, -cis·ing.** 1. To expel (an evil spirit) by or as if by incantation. 2. To free from evil spirits. [< Gk. *exorkizein.*] —**ex'or·cis'er** *n.* —**ex'or·cism** *n.* —**ex'or·cist** *n.*

ex·o·sphere (ĕk'sō-sfîr') *n.* The outermost layer of the atmosphere.

ex·o·ther·mic (ĕk'sō-thûr'mĭk) *adj.* Also **ex·o·ther·mal** (-məl). Releasing or giving off heat.

ex·ot·ic (ĭg-zŏt'ĭk) *adj.* 1. From another part of the world; foreign. 2. Intriguingly unusual or beautiful. [< Gk. *exōtikos.*] —**ex·ot'ic** *n.* —**ex·ot'i·cal·ly** *adv.*

ex·pand (ĭk-spănd') *v.* 1. To unfold; spread out. 2. To increase in size, extent, etc. 3. To express in detail; enlarge upon. [< Lat. *expandere.*]

ex·panse (ĭk-spăns') *n.* A wide and open extent, as of land, sky, or water. [Lat. *expansum.*]

ex·pan·sion (ĭk-spăn'shən) *n.* 1. The act or process of expanding. 2. The state of being expanded. 3. A product of expanding.

ex·pan·sive (ĭk-spăn'sĭv) *adj.* 1. Capable of expanding or tending to expand. 2. Wide; sweeping. 3. Kind and generous; outgoing. —**ex·pan'sive·ly** *adv.* —**ex·pan'sive·ness** *n.*

ex parte (ĕks pär'tē) *adj. & adv. Law.* From or on one side only; partisan. [Med. Lat.]

ex·pa·ti·ate (ĭk-spā'shē-āt') *v.* -**at·ed, -at·ing.** To speak or write at length; elaborate. [Lat. *exspatiari.*] —**ex·pa'ti·a'tion** *n.*

ex·pa·tri·ate (ĕks-pā'trē-āt') *v.* -**at·ed, -at·ing.** 1. To banish; exile. 2. To leave one's country to reside in another country. —*n.* (-ĭt, -āt'). An expatriated person. [Med. Lat. *expatriare.*] —**ex·pa'tri·a'tion** *n.*

ex·pect (ĭk-spĕkt') *v.* 1. To look forward to the occurrence or appearance of. 2. To consider reasonable or due. 3. *Informal.* To think or suppose. [Lat. *expectare.*] —**ex·pect'er** *n.*

ex·pec·tan·cy (ĭk-spĕk'tən-sē) *n., pl.* -**cies.** 1. Expectation. 2. Something expected.

ex·pec·tant (ĭk-spĕk'tənt) *adj.* Expecting. —**ex·pec'tant·ly** *adv.*

ex·pec·ta·tion (ĕk'spĕk-tā'shən) *n.* 1. The act or condition of expecting. 2. Anticipation. 3. **expectations.** Prospects; hopes, as of success, profits, etc.

ex·pec·to·rant (ĭk-spĕk'tər-ənt) *adj.* Easing or increasing secretion or discharge from the mucous membranes of the respiratory system. —**ex·pec'to·rant** *n.*

ex·pec·to·rate (ĭk-spĕk'tə-rāt') *v.* -**rat·ed, -rat·ing.** To eject from the mouth; spit. [< Lat. *expectorare,* to drive from the breast.] —**ex·pec'to·ra'tion** *n.*

ex·pe·di·en·cy (ĭk-spē'dē-ən-sē) *n., pl.* -**cies.** Also **ex·pe·di·ence** (-dē-əns). 1. Appropriateness to a purpose. 2. Adherence to self-serving means.

ex·pe·di·ent (ĭk-spē'dē-ənt) *adj.* 1. Appropriate to a particular purpose. 2. Serving narrow or selfish interests. —*n.* Something expedient. [< Lat. *expedire,* to make ready.] —**ex·pe'di·ent·ly** *adv.*

ex·pe·dite (ĕk'spĭ-dīt') *v.* -**dit·ed, -dit·ing.** 1. To speed the progress of; facilitate. 2. To perform quickly. [Lat. *expedire,* to make ready.] —**ex'pe·dit'er** or **ex'pe·dit'tor** *n.*

Syns: *expedite, accelerate, hasten, hurry, quicken, speed* v.

ex·pe·di·tion (ĕk'spĭ-dĭsh'ən) *n.* 1. a. A journey undertaken with a definite objective. b. A group making such a journey. 2. Speed in performance; promptness. [< Lat. *expeditio.*]

ex·pe·di·tion·ar·y (ĕk'spĭ-dĭsh'ə-nĕr'ē) *adj.* Of or being an expedition, esp. a military one.

ex·pe·di·tious (ĕk'spĭ-dĭsh'əs) *adj.* Acting or done with speed and efficiency. —**ex'pe·di'tious·ly** *adv.* —**ex'pe·di'tious·ness** *n.*

ex·pel (ĭk-spĕl') *v.* -**pelled, -pel·ling.** 1. To force or drive out; eject forcefully. 2. To dismiss officially. [< Lat. *expellere.*] —**ex·pel'la·ble** *adj.* —**ex·pel'ler** *n.*

ex·pend (ĭk-spĕnd') *v.* 1. To spend. 2. To use up; waste. [< Lat. *expendere.*]

ex·pend·a·ble (ĭk-spĕn'də-bəl) *adj.* Subject to discard or sacrifice; nonessential.

ex·pen·di·ture (ĭk-spĕn'də-chər) *n.* 1. The act or process of expending. 2. Something expended, esp. money.

ex·pense (ĭk-spĕns´) n. 1. a. Something paid out to accomplish a purpose. b. Something given up for something else; sacrifice. 2. **expenses.** a. Charges incurred by an employee in the performance of work. b. *Informal.* Money allotted for payment of such charges. 3. Something requiring the expenditure of money. [< Lat. *expensa.*]

ex·pen·sive (ĭk-spĕn´sĭv) adj. High-priced; costly.

ex·pe·ri·ence (ĭk-spîr´ē-əns) n. 1. Apprehension through the mind, senses, or emotions. 2. a. Activity or practice through which knowledge or skill is gained. b. Knowledge or skill thus gained. 3. a. An event, circumstance, etc., undergone or lived through. b. The sum or cumulative effect of such events. —v. -enced, -encing. To have as an experience; undergo. [< Lat. *experiri,* to try, test.]

ex·pe·ri·enced (ĭk-spîr´ē-ənst) adj. Skilled through long experience.

ex·per·i·ment (ĭk-spĕr´ə-mənt, -mĕnt´) n. A test made to demonstrate a known truth, examine the validity of a hypothesis, or determine the nature of something not yet known. —v. To conduct an experiment. [< Lat. *experimentum.*] —**ex·per·i·men´tal** adj. —**ex·per·i·men´tal·ly** adv. —**ex·per·i·men·ta´tion** n.

ex·pert (ĕk´spûrt´) n. A person with a high degree of knowledge or skill in a particular field. —adj. (ĭk-spûrt´, ĕk´spûrt´). Highly skilled or knowledgeable. [< Lat. *experiri,* to try.] —**ex·pert´ly** adv. —**ex·pert´ness** n.

ex·per·tise (ĕk´spər-tēz´) n. Expert skill or knowledge. [< OFr.]

ex·pi·ate (ĕk´spē-āt´) v. -at·ed, -at·ing. To atone or make amends for. [< Lat. *expiare.*] —**ex´pi·a´tor** n. —**ex´pi·a·to·ry** (-ə-tôr´ē, -tōr´ē) adj.

ex·pire (ĭk-spîr´) v. -pired, -pir·ing. 1. To come to an end; terminate. 2. To die. 3. To breathe out; exhale. [< Lat. *exspirare.*] —**ex´pi·ra´tion** n.

ex·plain (ĭk-splān´) v. 1. To make plain or comprehensible. 2. To offer reasons for; account for. [< Lat. *explanare.*] —**ex·plain´a·ble** adj. —**ex·plain´er** n. —**ex´pla·na´tion** n. —**ex·plan·a·to·ry** (-splăn´-ə-tôr´ē, -tōr´ē) adj.

ex·ple·tive (ĕks´plĭ-tĭv) n. An exclamation or oath. [LLat. *expletivus.*]

ex·pli·ca·ble (ĕk´splĭ-kə-bəl) adj. Capable of being explained.

ex·pli·cate (ĕk´splĭ-kāt´) v. -cat·ed, -cat·ing. To explain, esp. in detail. [Lat. *explicare,* to unfold.] —**ex´pli·ca´tion** n. —**ex´pli·ca´tive** adj. —**ex´pli·ca´tor** n.

ex·plic·it (ĭk-splĭs´ĭt) adj. Clearly defined; specific; precise. [< Lat. *explicitus,* p.p. of *explicare,* to unfold.] —**ex·plic´it·ly** adv. —**ex·plic´it·ness** n.

Syns: *explicit, categorical, clear-cut, decided, definite, express, positive, precise, specific, unequivocal* **adj.**

Usage: *Explicit* and *express* both apply to something clearly stated rather than implied. *Explicit* applies more particularly to that which is carefully spelled out: *explicit instructions. Express* applies particularly to a clear expression of intention: *an express promise.*

ex·plode (ĭk-splōd´) v. -plod·ed, -plod·ing. 1. To cause or undergo an explosion. 2. To burst or cause to burst by explosion. 3. To burst forth or break out suddenly. 4. To increase suddenly, sharply, and without control. 5. To expose as false; refute: *explode a theory.* [Lat. *explodere,* to drive out by clapping.] —**ex·plod´er** n.

ex·ploit (ĕk´sploit´) n. A notable act or deed, esp. a heroic feat. —v. (ĭk-sploit´). 1. To utilize fully or advantageously. 2. To make selfish or unethical use of. [< Lat. *explicitum.*] —**ex·ploit´a·ble** adj. —**ex´ploi·ta´tion** n. —**ex·ploit´a·tive** adj. —**ex·ploit´er** n.

ex·plore (ĭk-splôr´, -splōr´) v. -plored, -plor·ing. 1. To travel into or wander through (an area) for the purpose of discovery. 2. To investigate systematically. [Lat. *explorare.*] —**ex´plo·ra´tion** n. —**ex·plor´a·to·ry** (-ə-tôr´ē, -tōr´ē) adj. —**ex·plor´er** n.

ex·plo·sion (ĭk-splō´zhən) n. 1. a. A sudden, violent release of mechanical, chemical, or nuclear energy. b. The loud sound accompanying such a release. 2. A sudden outbreak. 3. A sudden and sharp outburst or increase: *the population explosion.* [Lat. *explosio.*]

ex·plo·sive (ĭk-splō´sĭv) adj. 1. Of, pertaining to, or causing an explosion. 2. Tending to explode. —n. A substance, esp. a prepared chemical, that explodes or causes explosion. —**ex·plo´sive·ly** adv. —**ex·plo´sive·ness** n.

ex·po·nent (ĭk-spō´nənt) n. 1. One who explains, interprets, or advocates. 2. A number or symbol, as *3* in (*x + y*)³, placed to the right of and above another number, symbol, or expression, denoting the power to which the latter is to be raised. [< Lat. *exponere,* to expound.] —**ex´po·nen´tial** (-nĕn´shəl) adj. —**ex´po·nen´tial·ly** adv.

ex·port (ĭk-spôrt´, -spōrt´, ĕk´spôrt´, -spōrt´) v. To send or carry abroad, esp. for sale or trade. —n. (ĕk´spôrt, -spōrt). 1. The act of exporting. 2. Something exported. [Lat. *exportare.*] —**ex·port´a·ble** adj. —**ex´por·ta´tion** n. —**ex·port´er** n.

ex·pose (ĭk-spōz´) v. -posed, -pos·ing. 1. To uncover; lay bare. 2. To lay open or subject, as to a force, influence, etc. 3. To make visible or known; reveal. 4. To subject (a photographic film or plate) to the action of light. [< Lat. *exponere.*] —**ex·pos´er** n.

ex·po·sé (ĕk´spō-zā´) n. A public revelation of something discreditable. [Fr.]

ex·po·si·tion (ĕk´spə-zĭsh´ən) n. 1. A setting forth of meaning or intent. 2. The presentation of information in clear, precise form. 3. A public exhibition of broad scope. —**ex·pos´i·tor** n. —**ex·pos´i·to·ry** (-tôr´ē, -tōr´ē) adj.

ex post fac·to (ĕks´ pōst făk´tō) adj. Formulated, enacted, or operating retroactively. [Med. Lat., from what is done afterwards.]

ex·pos·tu·late (ĭk-spŏs´chə-lāt´) v. -lat·ed, -lat·ing. To reason earnestly with someone, esp. to dissuade. [Lat. *expostulare,* to demand strongly.] —**ex·pos´tu·la´tion** n. —**ex·pos´tu·la´tor** n. —**ex·pos´tu·la·to·ry** adj.

ex·po·sure (ĭk-spō´zhər) n. 1. An act or example of exposing. 2. The condition of being exposed. 3. A position in relation to direction of weather conditions. 4. a. The act or time

of exposing a photographic film or plate.
b. A film or plate so exposed.

ex·pound (ĭk-spound′) v. To give a detailed statement (of); explain. [< Lat. *exponere*.] **—ex·pound′er** n.

ex·press (ĭk-sprĕs′) v. **1.** To make known or indicate, as by words, facial aspect, or symbols. **2.** To press out, as juice. **3.** To send by rapid transport. *—adj.* **1.** Clearly stated; explicit. **2.** Sent by rapid direct transportation: *an express package.* **3.** Direct, rapid, and usu. not making local stops: *an express train.* *—adv.* By express transportation. *—n.* **1.** An express train, bus, etc. **2.** A rapid, efficient system for the delivery of goods and mail. [< Med. Lat. *expressare.*] **—ex·press′i·ble** *adj.* **—ex·press′ly** *adv.*

ex·pres·sion (ĭk-sprĕsh′ən) n. **1.** Communication of an idea, emotion, etc., esp. by words. **2.** A symbol; sign; indication. **3.** A manner of expressing, esp. in speaking or performing. **4.** A facial aspect or tone of voice conveying feeling. **5.** A word or phrase. **6.** A symbolic mathematical form, such as an equation. **—ex·pres′sion·less** *adj.*

ex·pres·sion·ism (ĭk-sprĕsh′ə-nĭz′əm) n. A movement in the fine arts that emphasized the expression of inner experience rather than solely realistic portrayal. **—ex·pres′sion·ist** n. **—ex·pres′sion·is′tic** *adj.* **—ex·pres′sion·is′ti·cal·ly** *adv.*

ex·pres·sive (ĭk-sprĕs′ĭv) *adj.* **1.** Expressing or tending to express. **2.** Full of meaning; significant. **—ex·pres′sive·ly** *adv.* **—ex·pres′sive·ness** n.

ex·press·way (ĭk-sprĕs′wā′) n. A multilane usu. divided highway designed for fast travel.

ex·pro·pri·ate (ĕks-prō′prē-āt′) v. **-at·ed, -at·ing.** To acquire or take (land or other property) from another, esp. for public use. [Med. Lat. *expropriare.*] **—ex·pro′pri·a′tion** n. **—ex·pro′pri·a′tor** n.

ex·pul·sion (ĭk-spŭl′shən) n. The act of expelling or condition of being expelled.

ex·punge (ĭk-spŭnj′) v. **-punged, -pung·ing.** To strike out; erase. [Lat. *expungere.*] **—ex·pung′er** n.

ex·pur·gate (ĕk′spər-gāt′) v. **-gat·ed, -gat·ing.** To remove obscene or objectionable passages from. [Lat. *expurgare,* to purify.] **—ex′pur·ga′tion** n. **—ex′pur·ga′tor** n.

ex·qui·site (ĕk′skwĭ-zĭt, ĭk-skwĭz′ĭt) *adj.* **1.** Beautifully made or designed. **2.** Delicately or poignantly beautiful. **3.** Acutely discriminating; refined. **4.** Intense; keen. [< Lat. *exquisitus,* p.p. of *exquirere,* to search out.] **—ex′qui·site·ly** *adv.* **—ex′qui·site·ness** n.

ex·tant (ĕk′stənt, ĭk-stănt′) *adj.* Still in existence; not destroyed, lost, or extinct. [< Lat. *extare,* to stand out.]

ex·tem·po·ra·ne·ous (ĭk-stĕm′pə-rā′nē-əs) *adj.* Not rehearsed or prepared in advance; impromptu. [< Lat. *ex tempore,* extemporary.] **—ex·tem′po·ra′ne·ous·ly** *adv.* **—ex·tem′po·ra′ne·ous·ness** n.

ex·tem·po·re (ĭk-stĕm′pə-rē) *adj.* Extemporaneous. *—adv.* Extemporaneously. [Lat. *ex tempore,* out of the time.]

ex·tem·po·rize (ĭk-stĕm′pə-rīz′) v. **-rized, -riz·ing.** To do or perform (something) extemporaneously; improvise. **—ex·tem′po·ri·za′tion** n. **—ex·tem′po·riz′er** n.

ex·tend (ĭk-stĕnd′) v. **1.** To spread, stretch, or enlarge to greater length, area, or scope. **2.** To exert vigorously or to full capacity.

3. To offer; tender. [< Lat. *extendere.*] **—ex·tend′i·bil′i·ty** or **ex·ten′si·bil′i·ty** n. **—ex·tend′i·ble** or **ex·ten′si·ble** *adj.*

ex·ten·sion (ĭk-stĕn′shən) n. **1.** The act of extending or condition of being extended. **2.** An extended or added part. [< Lat. *extensio.*]

ex·ten·sive (ĭk-stĕn′sĭv) *adj.* Large in area, range, or amount. **—ex·ten′sive·ly** *adv.* **—ex·ten′sive·ness** n.

ex·tent (ĭk-stĕnt′) n. **1.** The area or distance over which something extends; size. **2.** The range or degree to which something extends; scope. [< Lat. *extendere,* to extend.]

ex·ten·u·ate (ĭk-stĕn′yōō-āt′) v. **-at·ed, -at·ing.** To excuse by minimizing the seriousness of: *extenuate his guilt.* [Lat. *extenuare.*] **—ex·ten′u·a′tion** n. **—ex·ten′u·a′tor** n.

ex·te·ri·or (ĭk-stîr′ē-ər) *adj.* Outer; external. *—n.* An outer part, surface, or aspect. [< Lat. *exterus,* outward.]

ex·ter·mi·nate (ĭk-stûr′mə-nāt′) v. **-nat·ed, -nat·ing.** To destroy completely; wipe out. [Lat. *exterminare,* to drive out.] **—ex·ter′mi·na′tion** n. **—ex·ter′mi·na′tor** n.

ex·ter·nal (ĭk-stûr′nəl) *adj.* **1.** Of, on, or for the outside or an outer part. **2.** Acting or coming from the outside. **3.** For outward show; superficial. **4.** Not internal or domestic; foreign. *—n.* **externals.** Outward appearances. [< Lat. *externus.*] **—ex·ter′nal·ly** *adv.*

ex·tinct (ĭk-stĭngkt′) *adj.* **1.** No longer existing in living or active form. **2.** Not burning; extinguished. [< Lat. *extinctus,* p.p. of *extinguere,* to extinguish.] **—ex·tinc′tion** n.

ex·tin·guish (ĭk-stĭng′gwĭsh) v. **1.** To put out (a fire or flame). **2.** To put an end to; destroy. [Lat. *extinguere.*] **—ex·tin′guish·a·ble** *adj.* **—ex·tin′guish·er** n.

ex·tir·pate (ĕk′stər-pāt′, ĭk-stûr′-) v. **-pat·ed, -pat·ing.** **1.** To uproot or cut out. **2.** To destroy the whole of. [Lat. *extirpare,* to root out.] **—ex′tir·pa′tion** n. **—ex′tir·pa′tive** *adj.* **—ex′tir·pa′tor** n.

ex·tol or **ex·toll** (ĭk-stōl′) v. **-tolled, -tol·ling.** To praise lavishly; eulogize. [< Lat. *extollere,* to lift up.] **—ex·tol′ler** n. **—ex·tol′ment** n.

ex·tort (ĭk-stôrt′) v. To obtain (e.g. money) by coercion or intimidation. [Lat. *extorquēre,* to wrench out.] **—ex·tor′tion** n. **—ex·tor′tion·ate (-ĭt)** *adj.* **—ex·tor′tion·ist** n. **—ex·tor′tive** *adj.*

ex·tra (ĕk′strə) *adj.* More than what is usual, expected, etc.; additional. *—adv.* Especially; unusually. *—n.* **1.** Something additional, esp. for which an added charge is made. **2.** A special edition of a newspaper. **3.** An actor hired to play a minor part, as in a crowd scene. [Prob. < EXTRAORDINARY.]

extra- or **extro-** *pref.* Outside a boundary or scope: *extrasensory.* [< Lat. *extra,* outside.]

ex·tract (ĭk-străkt′) v. **1.** To draw out or forth forcibly. **2.** To obtain despite resistance, as by a threat. **3.** To obtain by a chemical or physical process. **4.** To remove, select, or quote (a passage from a literary work). **5.** *Math.* To determine or calculate (a root). *—n.* (ĕk′străkt). **1.** A literary excerpt. **2.** A concentrated substance prepared by extracting; essence: *vanilla extract.* [< Lat. *extrahere.*] **—ex·tract′a·ble** or **ex·tract′i·ble** *adj.* **—ex·trac′tor** n.

ex·trac·tion (ĭk-străk′shən) n. **1.** The act or process of extracting. **2.** Something obtained by extracting; extract. **3.** Descent; lineage.

ex·tra·cur·ric·u·lar (ĕk′strə-kə-rĭk′yə-lər) *adj.* Not part of a regular course of study.

ex·tra·dite (ĕk'strə-dīt') v. -dit·ed, -dit·ing. To surrender or obtain the surrender of (an alleged criminal) for trial by another judicial authority. [Ult. < Fr. *extradition*, extradition.] —**ex'tra·dit'a·ble** adj. —**ex'tra·di'tion** n.

ex·tra·ga·lac·tic (ĕk'strə-gə-lăk'tĭk) adj. Located or originating beyond the galaxy.

ex·tra·mar·i·tal (ĕk'strə-măr'ə-təl) adj. Adulterous.

ex·tra·mu·ral (ĕk'strə-myŏŏr'əl) adj. Of or between participants, teams, etc., from more than one school: *extramural sports.*

ex·tra·ne·ous (ĭk-strā'nē-əs) adj. **1.** Coming from without; foreign. **2.** Not essential. [Lat. *extraneus*.] —**ex·tra'ne·ous·ly** adv. —**ex·tra'ne·ous·ness** n.

ex·traor·di·nar·y (ĭk-strôr'dn-ĕr'ē, ĕk'strə-ôr'-) adj. Beyond what is ordinary or usual; exceptional; remarkable. —**ex·traor'di·nar'i·ly** (-nâr'ə-lē) adv.

ex·trap·o·late (ĭk-străp'ə-lāt') v. -lat·ed, -lat·ing. To infer (unknown information) from known information. [EXTRA- + (INTER)PO-LATE.] —**ex·trap'o·la'tion** n.

ex·tra·sen·so·ry (ĕk'strə-sĕn'sə-rē) adj. Outside the range of normal sense perception.

ex·tra·ter·res·tri·al (ĕk'strə-tə-rĕs'trē-əl) adj. Outside the earth or its atmosphere.

ex·tra·ter·ri·to·ri·al (ĕk'strə-tĕr'ĭ-tôr'ē-əl, -tōr'-) adj. Located outside the territorial boundaries of a nation or state.

ex·tra·ter·ri·to·ri·al·i·ty (ĕk'strə-tĕr'ĭ-tôr'ē-ăl'-ĭ-tē, -tōr'-) n. Immunity from local legal jurisdiction, esp. as granted to foreign diplomats.

ex·trav·a·gant (ĭk-străv'ə-gənt) adj. **1.** Lavish, wasteful, or imprudent in the spending of money. **2.** Excessive; unrestrained. [< Med. Lat. *extravagari*, to wander.] —**ex·trav'a·gance** n. —**ex·trav'a·gant·ly** adv.

ex·trav·a·gan·za (ĭk-străv'ə-găn'zə) n. A lavish, spectacular entertainment. [Ital. *estravaganza.*]

ex·tra·ve·hic·u·lar activity (ĕk'strə-vē-hĭk'yə-lər) n. Maneuvers performed by an astronaut outside a spacecraft in space.

ex·treme (ĭk-strēm') adj. **1.** Outermost or farthest; most remote. **2.** Final; last. **3.** Very great; intense. **4.** To the utmost degree; radical. **5.** Drastic; severe. —n. **1.** The greatest or utmost degree. **2.** Either of the two ends of a scale, series, or range. **3.** An extreme condition. **4.** A drastic expedient. [< Lat. *extremus.*] —**ex·treme'ly** adv. —**ex·treme'ness** n.

ex·trem·ist (ĭk-strē'mĭst) n. A person with extreme views, esp. in politics. —**ex·trem'ism** n.

ex·trem·i·ty (ĭk-strĕm'ĭ-tē) n., pl. -ties. **1.** The outermost or farthest point or part. **2.** The utmost degree. **3.** Extreme danger, need, or distress. **4.** An extreme or severe measure. **5. a.** A bodily limb or appendage. **b. extremities.** The hands or feet.

ex·tri·cate (ĕk'strĭ-kāt') v. -cat·ed, -cat·ing. To release from entanglement or difficulty; disengage. [Lat. *extricare.*] —**ex'tri·ca'tion** n.

ex·trin·sic (ĭk-strĭn'sĭk, -zĭk) adj. **1.** Not inherent or essential. **2.** Originating from the outside; external. [LLat. *extrinsecus*, from outside.] —**ex·trin'si·cal·ly** adv.

extro- pref. Var. of **extra-.**

ex·tro·vert (ĕk'strə-vûrt') n. One interested in others or in the environment rather than self.

[EXTRO- + Lat. *vertere*, to turn.] —**ex'tro·ver'sion** n.

ex·trude (ĭk-strōōd') v. -trud·ed, -trud·ing. **1.** To push or thrust out. **2.** To shape (metal, plastic, etc.) by forcing through a die. [Lat. *extrudere.*] —**ex·tru'sion** n. —**ex·tru'sive** adj.

ex·u·ber·ant (ĭg-zōō'bər-ənt) adj. **1.** High-spirited; lively. **2.** Lavish; effusive. **3.** Growing abundantly; prolific. [< Lat. *exuberare*, to be exuberant.] —**ex·u'ber·ance** n. —**ex·u'ber·ant·ly** adv.

ex·ude (ĭg-zōōd', ĭk-sōōd') v. -ud·ed, -ud·ing. **1.** To ooze or pour forth gradually. **2.** To give off; radiate. [Lat. *exudare.*] —**ex'u·da'tion** n. —**ex'u·date'** n.

ex·ult (ĭg-zŭlt') v. To rejoice greatly, as in triumph. [Lat. *exultare.*] —**ex·ul'tant** adj. —**ex·ul'tant·ly** adv. —**ex'ul·ta'tion** n. —**ex·ult'ing·ly** adv.

ex·ur·bi·a (ĕk-sûr'bē-ə, ĕg-zûr'-) n. A mostly rural residential area beyond the suburbs of a city. [EX- + (SUB)URBIA.] —**ex·ur'ban·ite'** n. -ey suff. Var. of -y1.

eye (ī) n. **1.** An organ of vision or of light sensitivity. **2.** Sight; vision. **3.** A look; gaze. **4.** Ability to perceive or discern. **5.** Viewpoint; opinion. **6.** Something suggestive of an eye. —v. **eyed, eye·ing** or **ey·ing.** To look at; regard. —*idioms.* **catch (someone's) eye.** *Informal.* To attract someone's attention. **eye to eye.** In agreement. [< OE *ēage.*]

eye·ball (ī'bôl') n. The ball-shaped portion of the eye enclosed by the socket and eyelids.

eye·brow (ī'brou') n. The hairs covering the bony ridge over the eye.

eye·ful (ī'fŏŏl') n. **1.** A good look. **2.** *Informal.* A pleasing sight.

eye·glass (ī'glăs') n. **1.** A lens used to improve vision. **2. eyeglasses.** A pair of lenses worn to improve faulty vision.

eye·lash (ī'lăsh') n. One of the short hairs fringing the edge of an eyelid.

eye·let (ī'lĭt) n. **1.** A small hole for a lace, cord, or hook to fit through. **2.** A metal ring used to strengthen such a hole. [< OFr. *oillet*, dim. of *oil*, eye.]

eye·lid (ī'lĭd') n. Either of two folds of skin and muscle that can be closed over an eye.

eye opener n. Something startling or shocking; revelation.

eye·piece (ī'pēs') n. The lens or group of lenses closest to the eye in an optical instrument.

eye shadow n. A cosmetic used to color the eyelids.

eye·sight (ī'sīt') n. The faculty or range of sight; vision.

eye·sore (ī'sôr', ī'sōr') n. An ugly sight.

eye·strain (ī'strān') n. Fatigue of one or more of the eye muscles.

eye·tooth (ī'tōōth') n. A canine tooth of the upper jaw.

eye·wash (ī'wŏsh', -wôsh') n. **1.** A medicated solution for washing the eyes. **2.** Nonsense; meaningless talk.

eye·wit·ness (ī'wĭt'nəs) n. One who has personally seen something and can bear witness to the fact.

ey·rir (ā'rĭr') n., pl. **au·rar** (ou'rär', œ'-). See table at **currency.** [Icel.]

E·ze·ki·el (ĭ-zē'kē-əl). See table at **Bible.**

Ff

f or **F** (ĕf) *n.*, *pl.* **f's** or **F's**. **1.** The 6th letter of the English alphabet. **2. F** A failing grade. **F** The symbol for the element fluorine.

fa (fä) *n. Mus.* The 4th tone of the diatonic scale.

fa·ble (fā'bəl) *n.* **1.** A fictitious story, often with animal characters, that teaches a lesson. **2.** A story about legendary persons and feats. **3.** A falsehood. —*v.* **-bled, -bling.** To tell or write about as if true. [< Lat. *fabula.*] —**fab'u·list** (fāb'yə-lĭst) *n.*

fa·bled (fā'bəld) *adj.* **1.** Made known by fable; legendary. **2.** Existing only in fable; fictitious.

fab·ric (fāb'rĭk) *n.* **1.** Cloth produced by joining fibers, as by weaving or knitting. **2.** A structure; framework: *the fabric of society.* [< Lat. *fabrica,* workshop.]

fab·ri·cate (fāb'rĭ-kāt') *v.* **-cat·ed, -cat·ing.** **1. a.** To fashion or make. **b.** To construct; build. **2.** To make up (a deception). —**fab'ri·ca'tion** *n.*

fab·u·lous (fāb'yə-ləs) *adj.* **1.** Of the nature of a fable; legendary. **2.** Told of or celebrated in fables. **3.** Barely credible; astonishing. **4.** *Informal.* Extremely exciting or excellent. [< Lat. *fabulosus.*] —**fab'u·lous·ly** *adv.* —**fab'u·lous·ness** *n.*
Syns: *fabulous, amazing, astonishing, fantastic, incredible, marvelous, miraculous, phenomenal, stupendous, unbelievable, wonderful* **adj.**

fa·çade or **fa·cade** (fə-säd') *n.* **1.** The main face or front of a building. **2.** An artificial or false appearance. [< Ital. *facciata.*]

façade

face (fās) *n.* **1.** The surface of the front of the head. **2.** A facial expression; countenance. **3.** A grimace. **4.** An outward appearance; aspect. **5.** Dignity; prestige. **6.** Effrontery; impudence. **7.** A planar surface bounding a solid. **8.** The appearance and geologic surface features of an area of land; topography. —*v.* **faced, fac·ing.** **1.** To turn or be turned in the direction of. **2.** To front on: *a window facing the south.* **3. a.** To meet; encounter. **b.** To confront; meet boldly. **4.** To furnish with a surface or cover of a different material. **5.** To provide the edges of (a cloth or garment) with finishing or trimming. —*phrasal verbs.* **face down.** To overcome by a stare or a resolute manner. **face off.** To start play, as in ice hockey, by releasing the puck between two opposing players. **face up.** **1.** To recognize the existence or importance of. **2.** To confront bravely. —*idioms.* **face the music.** *Slang.* To face unpleasant circumstances. **face to face.** **1.** In each other's presence. **2.** Directly confronting. **in the face of.** Despite the opposition of. **in view of. on the face of it.** From all appearances. **to (one's) face.** In one's presence. [< Lat. *facies.*] —**face'a·ble** *adj.* —**face'less** *adj.*

face card *n.* A king, queen, or jack of a deck of playing cards.

face lifting *n.* Also **face-lift** (fās'lĭft'). **1.** Plastic surgery to tighten facial tissue. **2.** A renovation of a building's exterior.

face-off (fās'ôf', -ŏf', -ŏf') *n.* **1.** A method of starting play in ice hockey by releasing the puck between two opposing players. **2.** A confrontation.

fac·et (fās'ĭt) *n.* **1.** One of the flat surfaces cut on a gemstone. **2.** A small planar or rounded smooth surface on a bone or tooth. **3.** An aspect; phase. [< OFr.] —**fac'et·ed** or **fac'et·ted** *adj.*

fa·ce·tious (fə-sē'shəs) *adj.* Playfully jocular; flippant. [< Lat. *facetus.*] —**fa·ce'tious·ly** *adv.* —**fa·ce'tious·ness** *n.*

face value *n.* The value printed on a bill, bond, etc.

fa·cial (fā'shəl) *adj.* Of the face. —*n.* A cosmetic treatment for the face. —**fa'cial·ly** *adv.*

fac·ile (fās'əl) *adj.* **1. a.** Done with little effort. **b.** Arrived at without due care or effort; superficial. **2.** Effortlessly fluent. [< Lat. *facilis.*] —**fac'ile·ly** *adv.* —**fac'ile·ness** *n.*

fa·cil·i·tate (fə-sĭl'ĭ-tāt') *v.* **-tat·ed, -tat·ing.** To make easier; assist. [< Ital. *facilitare.*] —**fa·cil'i·ta'tion** *n.*

fa·cil·i·ty (fə-sĭl'ĭ-tē) *n.*, *pl.* **-ties.** **1.** Ease in doing, resulting from skill or aptitude. **2.** Often **facilities.** The means to facilitate an action or process.

fac·ing (fā'sĭng) *n.* **1. a.** A piece of material sewn to the edge of a garment as lining or decoration. **b.** Fabric used for this. **2.** A coating of different material applied to a surface.

fac·sim·i·le (fāk-sĭm'ə-lē) *n.* **1.** An exact copy or reproduction **2.** Electronic transmission of images or printed matter. [< Lat. *fac simile,* make (it) similar.]

fact (fākt) *n.* **1.** Something true and accurate. **2.** Something having real, demonstrable existence; reality. **3.** An act considered with regard to its legality: *after the fact.* [Lat. *factum,* a deed.]

fact-find·ing (fākt'fīn'dĭng) *n.* The discovery or determination of facts. —**fact-find'ing** *adj.*

fac·tion (fāk'shən) *n.* **1.** A united and usu. troublesome minority within a larger group. **2.** Internal discord. [< Lat. *facere,* to do.] —**fac'tion·al** *adj.*

-faction *suff.* Production; making: *petrifaction.* [< Lat. *-factio.*]

fac-tious (făk′shəs) *adj.* 1. Produced or characterized by faction. 2. Tending to cause conflict or discord; divisive. —**fac′tious·ly** *adv.* —**fac′tious·ness** *n.*

fac-ti-tious (făk-tĭsh′əs) *adj.* Artificial; false. [Lat. *facticius*, made by art.] —**fac·ti′tious·ly** *adv.* —**fac·ti′tious·ness** *n.*

fac-tor (făk′tər) *n.* 1. One who acts for another; agent. 2. One that actively contributes to a result or process. 3. *Math.* One of two or more quantities having a designated product: *2 and 3 are factors of 6.* —*v. Math.* To determine the factors of. [< Lat., maker.]

fac-to-ry (făk′tə-rē) *n., pl.* -**ries.** A building or group of buildings in which goods are manufactured; plant.

fac-to-tum (făk-tō′təm) *n.* An employee with a wide range of duties. [< Lat. *fac totum*, do everything.]

facts of life *pl.n.* The basic physiological functions involved in sex and reproduction.

fac-tu-al (făk′chōō-əl) *adj.* Based on or containing facts. —**fac′tu·al·ly** *adv.*

fac-ul-ty (făk′əl-tē) *n., pl.* -**ties.** 1. An inherent power or ability. 2. A special aptitude. 3. A division of learning at a college or university. 4. The teachers in a college or school. [< Lat. *facultas.*]

fad (făd) *n.* A briefly popular fashion. [Orig. unknown.] —**fad′dish** *adj.* —**fad′dist** *n.*

fade (fād) *v.* **fad·ed, fad·ing.** 1. To lose or cause to lose brightness or brilliance; dim. 2. To lose strength or freshness; wither. 3. To disappear gradually; vanish. —*phrasal verbs.* **fade in.** To make (an image or sound) appear gradually, as in television, films, or radio broadcasting. **fade out.** To make (an image or sound) change or disappear gradually, as in television, films, or radio broadcasting. —*n.* A gradual change from one image or sound to another, as in television, films, or radio broadcasting. [< OFr. *fader.*] —**fade′less** *adj.* —**fade′less·ly** *adv.*

fa·e·rie (fā′ə-rē, fâr′ē) *n.* Also **fa·er·y** *pl.* -**ies.** 1. A fairy. 2. Fairyland. [ME *fairie.*]

fag¹ (făg) *n. Chiefly Brit.* A student at an English public school who is required to perform menial tasks for an upperclassman. —*v.* **fagged, fag·ging.** 1. To work to exhaustion; toil. 2. *Chiefly Brit.* To serve as the fag of another student. 3. To exhaust from long work; fatigue. [Orig. unknown.]

fag² (făg) *n. Slang.* A cigarette. [< FAG END.]

fag end *n.* 1. The untwisted end of a rope. 2. The last and least useful part. [ME *fag.*]

fag·ot *or* **fag·got** (făg′ət) *n.* A bundle of twigs or sticks. [< OFr.] —**fag′ot** *v.*

Fahr·en·heit (făr′ən-hīt′) *adj.* Of or concerning a temperature scale that indicates the freezing point of water as 32° and the boiling point of water as 212° under standard atmospheric pressure. [< Gabriel *Fahrenheit* (1686–1736).]

fa·ience *or* **fa·ence** (fī-äns′, -äns′, fä-) *n.* An often colorfully decorated earthenware with a tin glaze. [Fr.]

fail (fāl) *v.* 1. To be deficient or unsuccessful. 2. To decline, weaken, or cease to function. 3. To disappoint or forsake. 4. To omit or neglect: *failed to appear.* 5. To give or receive an unacceptable academic grade. —*idiom.*

without fail. Definitely; positively. [< Lat. *fallere*, to deceive.]

fail-ing (fā′lĭng) *n.* A shortcoming. —*prep.* In the absence of.

faille (fīl) *n.* A ribbed fabric of silk, rayon, etc. [< OFr.]

fail-safe (fāl′sāf′) *adj.* 1. Capable of compensating automatically for a failure. 2. Acting to stop a military attack on the occurrence of a predetermined condition. —**fail′-safe′** *v.*

fail-ure (fāl′yər) *n.* 1. The act, condition, or fact of failing. 2. One that has failed. 3. The act or fact of becoming bankrupt.

fain (fān) *Archaic.* —*adv.* Willingly; gladly. —*adj.* 1. Willing; glad. 2. Obliged or required. [< OE *fægen*, glad.]

faint (fānt) *adj.* -**er, -est.** 1. Lacking strength or vigor; feeble. 2. Indistinct; dim. 3. Suddenly dizzy and weak. —*n.* An abrupt, usu. brief loss of consciousness. —*v.* To fall into a faint. [< OFr. *faindre*, to feign.] —**faint′ly** *adv.* —**faint′ness** *n.*

faint-heart·ed (fānt′här′tĭd) *adj.* Lacking conviction or courage; timid. —**faint-heart′ed·ly** *adv.* —**faint-heart′ed·ness** *n.*

fair¹ (fâr) *adj.* -**er, -est.** 1. Beautiful; lovely. 2. Clear and sunny. 3. Light in color, as hair. 4. Just; equitable. 5. Consistent with rules; permissible. 6. Moderately good; average. 7. Unblemished; clean. 8. Favorable; propitious. —*adv.* 1. In a fair manner; properly. 2. Directly; squarely. —*idioms.* **fair and square.** Just and honest. **fair to middling.** So-so. [< OE *fæger.*] —**fair′ness** *n.*

Syns: *fair, dispassionate, equitable, fair-minded, impartial, just, objective* **adj.**

fair² (fâr) *n.* 1. A gathering for buying and selling goods. 2. A public exhibition at which various products, handicrafts, etc., are displayed or judged competitively. 3. A fund-raising sale, as for charity. [< Lat. *feriae*, holidays.]

fair catch *n. Football.* A catch of a punt by a defensive player who has signaled that he will not run with the ball and who therefore may not be tackled.

fair-ground (fâr′ground′) *n.* Often **fair-grounds.** An open area where fairs are held.

fair-haired (fâr′hârd′) *adj.* 1. Having blond hair. 2. Favorite: *mother's fair-haired boy.*

fair-ly (fâr′lē) *adv.* 1. In a fair or just manner; equitably. 2. Moderately; rather. 3. Quite; completely.

fair-mind·ed (fâr′mīn′dĭd) *adj.* Just and impartial. —**fair′-mind′ed·ness** *n.*

fair-trade (fâr′trād′) *adj.* Of, relating to, or being an agreement under which retailers sell a given item at no less than a minimum price set by the manufacturer.

fair-way (fâr′wā′) *n.* The mowed area of a golf course from the tee to the putting green.

fair-weath·er (fâr′wĕth′ər) *adj.* Loyal and dependable only in good times: *fair-weather friends.*

fair-y (fâr′ē) *n., pl.* -**ies.** An imaginary being supposed to have magical powers. [< Lat. *fata*, Fates.]

fair-y-land (fâr′ē-lănd′) *n.* 1. The imaginary land of the fairies. 2. A charming place.

fairy tale *n.* 1. A story about fairies. 2. A fictitious fanciful story.

---

fait ac·com·pli (fĕt′ä-kôN-plē′, făt′-) *pl.* **faits ac·com·plis** (fĕt′ä-kôN-plē′, făt′-). An accomplished fact. [Fr.]

faith (fāth) *n.* **1. a.** Confident belief; trust. **b.** Belief in God; religious conviction. **2.** Loyalty; allegiance. **3.** A religion. [< Lat. *fides.*]

faith·ful (fāth′fəl) *adj.* **1.** Loyal. **2.** Worthy of trust. **3.** Accurate; truthful. —**faith′ful·ly** *adv.* —**faith′ful·ness** *n.*

Syns: *faithful, constant, fast¹, firm¹, loyal, resolute, staunch, steadfast, steady, true adj.*

faith·less (fāth′lĭs) *adj.* **1.** Breaking faith; disloyal. **2.** Lacking faith. —**faith′less·ly** *adv.* —**faith′less·ness** *n.*

Syns: *faithless, disloyal, false, false-hearted, traitorous, treacherous, unfaithful, untrue adj.*

fake (fāk) *adj.* Not genuine; false; fraudulent. —*n.* **1.** Something not genuine or authentic; a counterfeit. **2.** An impostor; fraud. —*v.* **faked, fak·ing. 1.** To contrive and present as genuine; counterfeit. **2.** To pretend; feign. [Orig. unknown.] —**fak′er** *n.* —**fak′er·y** *n.*

fa·kir (fə-kîr′) *n.* A Moslem or Hindu religious mendicant, esp. one who performs feats of magic or endurance. [Ar. *faqīr.*]

fal·con (fāl′kən, fôl′-, fô′kən) *n.* A long-winged, swift-flying hawk, esp. one trained to hunt small game. [< LLat. *falco.*] —**fal′con·er** *n.* —**fal′con·ry** *n.*

falcon

fall (fôl) *v.* **fell** (fĕl), **fall·en** (fô′lən), **fall·ing. 1.** To move under the influence of gravity, esp. to drop without restraint. **2.** To come down from an erect position; collapse. **3.** To be killed or severely wounded in battle. **4.** To hang down: *Her hair fell in ringlets.* **5.** To assume an expression of disappointment: *His face fell.* **6.** To be conquered or overthrown. **7.** To slope. **8.** To diminish. **9.** To decline in rank, status, or importance. **10.** To err or sin. **11.** To pass into a less active condition: *The crowd fell silent.* **12.** To arrive and pervade: *A hush fell on the crowd.* **13.** To occur at a specified time or place. **14.** To be allotted: *The task fell to me.* **15.** To divide naturally: *They fall into three categories.* **16.** To be directed by chance: *My gaze fell on a book.* **17.** To be uttered as if involuntarily. —*phrasal verbs.* **fall back.** To retreat. **fall back on.** To turn to for help. **fall behind.** To fail to keep up with. **fall for.** *Informal.* **1.** To become infatuated or fall in love with. **2.** To be taken in by. **fall in.** To take one's place in a military formation. **fall in with. 1.** To meet by chance. **2.** To agree to. **fall on** (or **upon**). To attack suddenly. **fall out.** To quarrel. **fall through.** To fail; collapse. **fall to.** To begin vigorously. —*n.* **1.** The act or an instance of falling. **2.** Something that has fallen: *a fall of hail.* **3. a.** The amount of what has fallen: *a light fall of rain.* **b.** The distance that something falls. **4.** Often **Fall.** Autumn. **5.** Often **falls.** A waterfall. **6.** A woman's hair piece with long, free-hanging hair. **7.** An overthrow or collapse: *the fall of a government.* **8.** A decline or reduction. **9.** A loss of moral innocence. —*idioms.* **fall flat.** *Informal.* To fail. **fall short.** To fail to reach or attain. [< OE *feallan.*]

fal·la·cious (fə-lā′shəs) *adj.* **1.** Containing or based on a fallacy. **2.** Deceptive in appearance or meaning. —**fal·la′cious·ly** *adv.*

fal·la·cy (făl′ə-sē) *n., pl.* **-cies. 1.** A false idea or notion. **2.** A fallacious belief or argument. [Lat. *fallacia, deceit.*]

fall·back (fôl′băk′) *n.* **1.** A mechanism for carrying on programmed instructions despite failure or malfunction of the primary device. **2.** A retreat or last resort.

fall guy *n. Slang.* **1.** A dupe. **2.** A scapegoat.

fal·li·ble (făl′ə-bəl) *adj.* Capable of erring. [< Lat. *fallere,* to deceive.] —**fal′li·bil′i·ty** *n.* —**fal′li·bly** *adv.*

falling-out (fô′lĭng-out′) *n., pl.* **fallings-out** or **falling-outs.** A quarrel.

falling star *n.* A meteor.

fall line *n.* The transition area between lowlands and uplands.

Fal·lo·pi·an tube (fə-lō′pē-ən) *n.* Either of a pair of slender ducts that connect the uterus to the region of each of the ovaries in the female reproductive system of humans and higher vertebrates. [< Gabriello *Fallopio* (1523–62).]

fall·out (fôl′out′) *n.* **1. a.** The slow descent of minute particles of radioactive debris in the atmosphere following a nuclear explosion. **b.** The particles so descending. **2.** Incidental results or side effects: *political fallout.*

fal·low (făl′ō) *adj.* Plowed and tilled but left unseeded during a growing season. [< OE *fealg,* plowed land.] —**fal′low·ness** *n.*

fallow deer (făl′ō) *n.* An Old World deer with a white-spotted summer coat and broad, flat antlers. [OE *fealo,* reddish-yellow + DEER.]

false (fôls) *adj.* **fals·er, fals·est. 1.** Contrary to fact or truth. **2.** Unfaithful; disloyal. **3.** Not natural; artificial. **4.** *Mus.* Wrong in pitch. [< Lat. *falsus,* p.p. of *fallere,* to deceive.] —**false′ly** *adv.* —**false′ness** *n.*

Syns: *false, erroneous, inaccurate, incorrect, specious, untruthful, wrong adj.*

false arrest *n. Law.* An unlawful arrest.

false-heart·ed (fôls′här′tĭd) *adj.* Deceitful.

false·hood (fôls′hŏŏd′) *n.* **1.** Lack of conformity with truth or fact. **2.** The act of lying. **3.** A lie.

fal·set·to (fôl-sĕt′ō) *n., pl.* **-tos. 1.** An artificially high voice, esp. that of a tenor. **2.** One who sings in falsetto. —*adv.* In falsetto. [Ital.]

fal·si·fy (fôl′sə-fī′) *v.* **-fied, -fy·ing. 1.** To state untruthfully. **2.** To alter (a document) so as to deceive. [< Med. Lat. *falsificare.*] —**fal′si·fi·ca′tion** *n.* —**fal′si·fi′er** *n.*

fal·si·ty (fôl′sĭ-tē) *n., pl.* **-ties. 1.** The condition of being false. **2.** A lie.

fal·ter (fôl′tər) *v.* **1.** To waver or weaken in purpose, force, etc. **2.** To stammer. **3.** To stumble. —*n.* **1.** Unsteadiness in speech or action. **2.** A faltering sound. [ME *falteren,* to stagger.] —**fal′ter·ing·ly** *adv.*

fame (fām) *n.* Great reputation and recognition; renown. [< Lat. *fama.*] —**famed** *adj.*

fa·mil·iar (fə-mĭl′yər) *adj.* **1.** Often encountered; common. **2.** Having knowledge of something. **3.** Intimate. **4.** Unduly forward; bold. [< Lat. *familiaris.*] **—fa·mil'iar·ly** *adv.*

fa·mil·i·ar·i·ty (fə-mĭl'ē-ăr'ĭ-tē) *n., pl.* **-ties.** **1.** Substantial acquaintance with or knowledge of something. **2.** Close friendship. **3.** Undue liberty; forwardness.

fa·mil·iar·ize (fə-mĭl'yə-rīz') *v.* **-ized, -iz·ing.** To make (oneself or another) acquainted with. **—fa·mil'iar·i·za'tion** *n.*

fam·i·ly (făm'ə-lē, făm'lē) *n., pl.* **-lies.** **1.** Parents and their children. **2.** A group of persons related by blood or marriage. **3.** The members of one household. **4.** A group of things with common characteristics. **5.** *Biol.* A group of related plants or animals ranking between a genus and an order. [< Lat. *familia.*] **—fa·mil'ial** (fə-mĭl'yəl) *adj.*

family name *n.* A surname.

family planning *n.* The planning of the number of one's children through birth-control techniques.

family room *n.* A recreation room for family members.

family tree *n.* A genealogical diagram of a family.

fam·ine (făm'ĭn) *n.* **1.** A drastic, wide-reaching shortage of food. **2.** A drastic scarcity. [< Lat. *fames,* hunger.]

fam·ished (făm'ĭsht) *adj.* Extremely hungry.

fa·mous (fā'məs) *adj.* Well-known; renowned. [< Lat. *famosus.*] **—fa'mous·ly** *adv.* **—fa'mous·ness** *n.*

Syns: *famous, celebrated, distinguished, eminent, famed, illustrious, noted, pre-eminent, prestigious, prominent, redoubtable, renowned adj.*

fan¹ (făn) *n.* **1. a.** A hand-held, flat, light implement for creating a cool breeze. **b.** An electrical device that circulates air by rapidly rotating thin, rigid blades attached to a central hub. **2.** Something resembling a fan. **—v.** **fanned, fan·ning.** **1.** To direct a current of air upon. **2.** To stir up: *fan resentment.* **3.** *Baseball.* To strike out. **4.** To spread like a fan: *soldiers fanning out in all directions.* [< Lat. *vannus.*]

fan² (făn) *n. Informal.* An ardent admirer. [< FANATIC.]

fa·nat·ic (fə-năt'ĭk) *n.* One possessed by excessive or irrational zeal. [< Lat. *fanaticus,* inspired by a god.] **—fa·nat'i·cal** or **fa·nat'ic** *adj.* **—fa·nat'i·cal·ly** *adv.* **—fa·nat'i·cism** *n.*

fan·ci·er (făn'sē-ər) *n.* One who has a special enthusiasm, as raising a specific kind of plant or animal.

fan·ci·ful (făn'sĭ-fəl) *adj.* **1.** Full of fancy; imaginary. **2.** Tending to indulge in fancy. **3.** Quaint and whimsical in design. **—fan'ci·ful·ly** *adv.* **—fan'ci·ful·ness** *n.*

fan·cy (făn'sē) *n., pl.* **-cies.** **1.** Imagination, esp. of a playful or whimsical sort. **2.** An unfounded opinion. **3.** A notion; whim. **4.** Capricious or sudden liking. **—adj.** **-ci·er, -ci·est.** **1.** Elaborate in design. **2.** Marked by great technical skill. **3.** Illusory: *fancy notions.* **4.** Of superior grade: *fancy preserves.* **—v.** **-cied, -cy·ing.** **1.** To imagine. **2.** To be fond of. **3.** To have an unfounded belief. [ME *fansy.*] **—fan'ci·ly** *adv.* **—fan'ci·ness** *n.*

fancy dress *n.* A masquerade costume. **—fan'cy-dress'** *adj.*

fan·cy-free (făn'sē-frē') *adj.* Without emotional commitment; unattached.

fan·cy·work (făn'sē-wûrk') *n.* Decorative needlework, as embroidery.

fan·dan·go (făn-dăng'gō) *n., pl.* **-gos.** A lively Spanish dance. [Sp.]

fan·fare (făn'fâr') *n.* **1.** A flourish of trumpets. **2.** Spectacular display. [Fr.]

fang (făng) *n.* A long, pointed tooth, as that with which a poisonous snake injects its venom. [< OE, capture.] **—fanged** *adj.*

fang

fan·jet (făn'jĕt') *n.* An aircraft powered by turbofan engines.

fan·light (făn'līt') *n.* A half-circle window with radiating sash bars like the ribs of an open fan.

fan mail *n.* Letters to a public figure from admirers.

fan·tail (făn'tāl') *n.* Something that resembles a fan. **—fan'tailed'** *adj.*

fan·ta·sia (făn-tā'zhə, -zhē-ə, făn'tə-zē'ə) *n. Mus.* A freeform composition. [Ital.]

fan·ta·size (făn'tə-sīz') *v.* **-sized, -siz·ing.** To indulge in fantasies; daydream.

fan·tas·tic (făn-tăs'tĭk) or **fan·tas·ti·cal** (-tĭ-kəl) *adj.* **1.** Bizarre; grotesque. **2.** Unreal; illusory. **3.** Capricious or eccentric: *a fantasic old person.* **4.** *Informal.* Wonderful or superb. [< Gk. *phantastikos,* imaginary.] **—fan·tas'ti·cal·ly** *adv.*

fan·ta·sy (făn'tə-sē, -zē) *n., pl.* **-sies.** **1.** The creative imagination. **2.** A product of the imagination; illusion. **3.** A delusion. **4.** A capricious or whimsical notion or idea; conceit. **5.** A daydream. **6.** A fantasia. [< Gk. *phantasia,* appearance.]

far (fär) *adv.* **far·ther** (fär'thər) or **fur·ther** (fûr'thər), **far·thest** (fär'thĭst) or **fur·thest** (fûr'thĭst). **1.** To, from, or at a considerable distance. **2.** To or at a considerable distance or degree. **3.** Not at all: *far from happy.* **—adj.** **far·ther** or **fur·ther, far·thest** or **fur·thest.** **1.** Being a considerable distance: *a far country.* **2.** More distant or remote: *the far corner.* **3.** Extensive; long: *a far trek.* **—idioms. as far as.** To the extent that. **by far.** To a considerable degree. **far and away.** By a great margin. **far and wide.** Everywhere. **go far.** To be successful. **in so far** (or **insofar**) **as.** To the degree or extent that. **so far.** **1.** Up to now. **2.** To a certain limit. **so far as.** To the extent that. [< OE *feor,* distant.]

Syns: *far, distant, faraway, far-off, remote, removed adj.*

far·ad (făr′əd, -ăd′) *n.* A unit of capacitance equal to that of a capacitor that will accumulate a charge of 1 coulomb when a potential difference of 1 volt is applied to it. [< Michael *Faraday* (1791–1867).]

far·a·way (făr′ə-wā′) *adj.* 1. Distant; remote. 2. Dreamy; abstracted.

farce (färs) *n.* 1. A play marked by slapstick humor and wild improbabilities of plot. 2. An empty show; mockery. [< Lat. *farcire,* to stuff.] —**far′ci·cal** *adj.* —**far′ci·cal′i·ty** (-kăl′ĭ-tē) *n.* —**far′ci·cal·ly** *adv.*

fare (fâr) *v.* **fared, far·ing.** 1. To get along. 2. To turn out; go: *How does it fare with you?* —*n.* 1. **a.** Transportation charge. **b.** A passenger who pays a fare. 2. Food and drink. [< OE *faran.*] —**far′er** *n.*

fare-well (fâr-wĕl′) *interj.* Used to say goodby. —*n.* 1. A good-by. 2. A leave-taking. —**fare′well′** *adj.*

far-fetched (fär′fĕcht′) *adj.* Implausible.

far-flung (fär′flŭng′) *adj.* Wide-ranging.

fa·ri·na (fə-rē′nə) *n.* Fine meal, as of cereal grain, often used as a cooked cereal or in puddings. [Lat.]

far·i·na·ceous (făr′ə-nā′shəs) *adj.* 1. Made from or containing starch. 2. Mealy or powdery in texture. [LLat. *farinaceus,* mealy.]

farm (färm) *n.* 1. **a.** An area of land on which crops or animals are raised. **b.** The fields, buildings, animals, and personnel appurtenant to a farm. 2. An area or tract of water used for raising aquatic animals: *a fish farm.* 3. Also **farm team.** *Baseball.* A minor-league team affiliated with a major-league team for training recruits. —*v.* 1. To raise crops or livestock as a business. 2. To use (land) for this purpose. —*phrasal verb.* **farm out.** To send out (work) to be done elsewhere. 2. *Baseball.* To assign (a player) to a farm team. [ME, lease.] —**farm′er** *n.*

farm hand *n.* A hired farm laborer.

farm·house (färm′hous′) *n.* The house on a farm.

farm·land (färm′lănd′, -lənd) *n.* Land suitable for farming.

farm·stead (färm′stĕd′) *n.* A farm and its buildings.

farm·yard (färm′yärd′) *n.* An area adjacent to farm buildings.

faro (fâr′ō) *n.* A card game in which the players bet on cards drawn from a dealing box. [< PHARAOH.]

far-off (fär′ôf′, -ŏf′) *adj.* Remote in space or time; distant.

far-out (fär′out′) *adj.* *Slang.* Extremely unconventional; avant-garde.

far·ra·go (fə-rä′gō, -rā′gō) *n., pl.* **-goes.** A medley; conglomeration. [Lat.]

far-reach·ing (fär′rē′chĭng) *adj.* Having a wide range or effect.

far·row (făr′ō) *n.* A litter of pigs. —*v.* To give birth to a farrow. [< OE *fearh,* pig.]

far·see·ing (fär′sē′ĭng) *adj.* Foresighted.

far·sight·ed (fär′sī′tĭd) *adj.* 1. Able to see objects better from a distance than from short range. 2. Planning wisely for the future; foresighted. —**far·sight′ed·ly** *adv.* —**far·sight′ed·ness** *n.*

far·ther (fär′thər) *adv.* 1. To a greater distance. 2. In addition. 3. To a greater extent. —*adj.* 1. More distant. 2. Additional. [< OE *furthor.*]

far·ther·most (fär′thər-mōst′) *adj.* Farthest.

far·thest (fär′thĭst) *adj.* Most remote or distant. —*adv.* To or at the most distant or remote point in space or time. [ME *ferthest.*]

far·thing (fär′thĭng) *n.* 1. A former British coin worth one-fourth of a penny. 2. Something of little value. [< OE *fēorthing.*]

far·thin·gale (fär′thĭng-gāl′) *n.* A support, such as a hoop, worn by women in the 16th and 17th cent. to make skirts stand out. [< OSp. *verdugado.*]

fas·ci·cle (făs′ĭ-kəl) *n.* 1. One of the separately published installments of a book. 2. *Bot.* A bundlelike cluster, as of stems, flowers, or leaves. [Lat. *fasciculus,* small bundle.] —**fas′ci·cled** *adj.* —**fas·cic′u·lar** (fə-sĭk′yə-lər) *adj.* —**fas·cic′u·late** *adj.*

fas·ci·nate (făs′ə-nāt′) *v.* **-nat·ed, -nat·ing.** 1. To attract irresistibly. 2. To spellbind or mesmerize. [Lat. *fascinare,* to enchant.] —**fas′ci·nat′ing·ly** *adv.* —**fas′ci·na′tion** *n.* —**fas′ci·na′tor** *n.*

fas·cism (făsh′ĭz′əm) *n.* A system of government that exercises a dictatorship of the extreme right, typically through the merging of state and business leadership, together with belligerent nationalism. [< Ital. *fascio,* group.] —**fas′cist** *n.* —**fas·cis′tic** (fə-shĭs′tĭk) *adj.*

fash·ion (făsh′ən) *n.* 1. The configuration or aspect of something. 2. Kind; sort. 3. Manner; way. 4. The current style. —*v.* 1. To make into a particular shape or form. 2. To make suitable; adapt. —*idiom.* **after a fashion.** To a limited extent. [< Lat. *facere,* to make.] —**fash′ion·a·ble** *adj.* —**fash′ion·a·ble·ness** *n.* —**fash′ion·a·bly** *adv.*

Syns: **fashion, craze, mode, rage, style, thing, vogue** *n.*

fast¹ (făst) *adj.* **-er, -est.** 1. Swift; rapid. 2. Done quickly. 3. Indicating a time ahead of the correct time: *a fast clock.* 4. Adapted to rapid travel: *a fast turnpike.* 5. Flouting conventional mores, esp. in sexual matters. 6. Resistant: *acid-fast.* 7. Firmly fixed or fastened. 8. Secure. 9. Loyal; constant: *fast friends.* 10. Proof against fading. 11. Deep; sound: *a fast sleep.* 12. *Photog.* **a.** Compatible with a high shutter speed: *a fast lens.* **b.** Designed for short exposure; highly sensitive: *fast film.* —*adv.* 1. Firmly; securely; tightly. 2. Deeply; soundly: *fast asleep.* 3. Quickly; rapidly. 4. In a dissipated way: *living fast.* [< OE *fæst.*] —**fast′ness** *n.*

Syns: **fast, breakneck, fleet², quick, rapid, speedy, swift** *adj.*

fast² (făst) *v.* To abstain from eating all or certain foods. —*n.* The act or a period of fasting. [< OE *fæstan.*]

fast·back (făst′băk′) *n.* An automobile with a curving downward slope from roof to rear.

fast-breed·er reactor (făst′brē′dər) *n.* A breeder reactor requiring high-energy neutrons to produce fissionable material.

fas·ten (făs′ən) *v.* 1. To attach or become attached to something else; join; connect. 2. **a.** To make fast or secure. **b.** To close, as by shutting. 3. To fix or focus steadily. [< OE *fæstnian.*] —**fas′ten·er** *n.*

fast food *n.* Restaurant food prepared and served quickly. —**fast′-food′** *adj.*

fas·tid·i·ous (fă-stĭd′ē-əs, fə-) *adj.* 1. Careful in all details; meticulous. 2. Very difficult to please. [< Lat. *fastidiosus.*] —**fas·tid′i·ous·ly** *adv.* —**fas·tid′i·ous·ness** *n.*

fast-talk (făst′tôk′) *v.* **-talked, -talk·ing.** To influence or persuade, esp. by smooth, deceptive talk. —**fast'-talk'er** n.

fat (făt) n. **f. a.** Any of various energy-rich semisolid organic compounds occurring widely in animal and plant tissue. **b.** Organic tissue containing such substances. **c.** A solidified animal or vegetable oil. **2.** Plumpness; obesity. **3.** The best part: *the fat of the land.* —adj. **fat'ter, fat'test. 1.** Having too much flesh. **2.** Oily; greasy.~ **3.** Abounding in desirable elements. **4.** Fertile or productive; rich. **5.** Ample; well-stocked: *a fat larder.* **6.** Thick; broad; large: *a fat plank.* —v. **fat'ted, fat'ting.** To make or become fat. —*idiom.* **chew the fat.** *Slang.* To have a leisurely conversation. [< OE *fǣtt,* fattened.] —**fat'ly** adv. —**fat'ness** n. —**fat'ti-ly** adv. —**fat'ti-ness** n. —**fat'ty** adj.

Syns: *fat, corpulent, fleshy, gross, obese, overweight, portly, stout, weighty* adj.

fa-tal (fāt'l) adj. **1.** Deadly; mortal. **2.** Ruinous; disastrous. **3.** Most decisive; fateful. **4.** Controlling destiny. [< Lat. *fatalis.*] —**fa-tal'ly** adv.

Usage: The contrast between *fatal* in the sense of "leading to death or destruction" and *fateful* in the sense of "affecting one's destiny or future" is illustrated by the following sentence: *The fateful decision to relax safety standards led directly to the fatal crash.*

fa-tal-ism (fāt'l-ĭz'əm) n. The belief that all events are predetermined by fate. —**fa'tal-ist** n. —**fa'tal-is'tic** adj. —**fa'tal-is'ti-cal-ly** adv.

fa-tal-i-ty (fā-tăl'ĭ-tē, fə-) n., pl. **-ties. 1.** An accidental death. **2.** Liability to disaster.

fat-back (făt'băk') n. Salt-cured fat from the upper part of a side of pork.

fat cat n. *Slang.* **1.** A rich, powerful person. **2.** A rich, heavy contributor to a political party.

fate (fāt) n. **1.** The supposed power or force that predetermines events. **2.** Lot; fortune. **3.** A final outcome. **4.** Doom or ruin. **5.** Fates. *Gk. & Rom. Myth.* The three goddesses who govern human destiny. [< Lat. *fatum.*]

fate-ful (fāt'fəl) adj. **1.** Decisively important. **2.** Controlled by fate. **3.** Portentous; ominous. **4.** Bringing death or disaster; fatal. —**fate'ful-ly** adv. —**fate'ful-ness** n.

fat-head (făt'hĕd') n. *Slang.* A stupid person. —**fat'head'ed** adj.

fa-ther (fä'thər) n. **1. a.** A male parent. **b.** A male ancestor. **2.** An originator. **3. Father.** God, esp. the first member of the Trinity. **4. Father.** A title used for a priest. **5.** Often **Father.** One of the authoritative early codifiers of Christian doctrines and observances. **6.** An elderly or venerable man. **7.** A leading citizen: *the town fathers.* —v. **1.** To beget. **2.** To act or serve as a father to. [< OE *fæder.*] —**fa'ther-less** adj. —**fa'ther-li-ness** n. —**fa'ther-ly** adj.

fa-ther-hood (fä'thər-hood') n. The condition of being a father; paternity.

fa-ther-in-law (fä'thər-ĭn-lô') n., pl. **fa-thers-in-law.** The father of one's spouse.

fa-ther-land (fä'thər-lănd') n. One's native land.

fath-om (făth'əm) n., pl. **-oms** or **-om.** A unit of length equal to about 1.83 meters or 6 feet, used mainly in measuring the depth of water.

—v. **1.** To measure the depth of; sound. **2.** To understand. [< OE *fæthm,* outstretched arms.] —**fath'om-a-ble** adj.

fath-om-less (făth'əm-lĭs) adj. Too deep to be fathomed.

fa-tigue (fə-tēg') n. **1.** Weakness or weariness resulting from exertion or prolonged stress. **2.** Manual or menial labor assigned to soldiers. **3. fatigues.** Military dress for work and field duty. —v. **-tigued, -tigu-ing.** To tire out; exhaust. [< Lat. *fatigare,* to fatigue.] —**fat'i-ga-ble** (făt'ĭ-gə-bəl, fə-tē'-) adj.

threaded spindle

disk washer

brass screw

flow opening

fatigue **faucet**

Fatigues

fat-ten (făt'n) v. To make or become fat. —**fat'ten-er** n.

fatty acid n. Any of a large group of monobasic acids having the general formula $C_nH_{2n+1}COOH$, esp. any of a commercially important subgroup obtained from animals and plants.

fa-tu-i-ty (fə-tōō'ĭ-tē, -tyōō'-) n. Stupidity; foolishness.

fat-u-ous (făch'ōō-əs) adj. Foolish; inane. [Lat. *fatuus.*] —**fat'u-ous-ly** adv. —**fat'u-ous-ness** n.

fau-cet (fô'sĭt) n. A device for drawing liquid, as from a pipe. [< OFr. *fausser,* to break in.]

fault (fôlt) n. **1.** A failing, defect, or impairment. **2.** A mistake or minor transgression. **3.** Responsibility for something wrong. **4. Geol.** A break in the continuity of a rock formation, caused by a shifting or dislodging of the earth's crust, in which adjacent surfaces are differentially displaced parallel to the plane of fracture. **5. Sports.** A bad service, as in tennis. —v. **1.** To find a fault in. **2.** To produce a geologic fault in. **3.** To commit a fault; err. —*idioms.* **at fault.** Guilty. **find fault.** To carp. **to a fault.** Excessively. [< Lat. *fallere,* to fail.] —**fault'i-ly** adv. —**fault'less** adj. —**fault'less-ly** adv. —**fault'y** adj.

fault-find-er (fôlt'fīn'dər) n. One who continually carps. —**fault'find'ing** n.

faun (fôn) n. *Rom. Myth.* One of a group of rural deities represented as part man and part goat. [< Lat. *Faunus,* Roman god of nature.]

fau-na (fô'nə) n., pl. **-nas** or **-nae** (-nē'). Animals, esp. of a region or time. [< Lat. *Fauna,* Roman goddess of nature.] —**fau'nal** adj.

Faust (foust) n. A legendary magician who sold his soul to the devil in exchange for power and knowledge. —**Faust'i-an** adj.

fau-vism (fō'vĭz'əm) n. An art movement of

the early 20th cent., characterized by the use of exuberant colors and distorted forms. [< Fr. *fauve*, wild.]

faux pas (fō′ pä′) *pl.* **faux pas** (fō′ päz′, pä′). A social blunder. [Fr.]

fa·vor (fā′vər). Also *chiefly Brit.* **fa·vour.** —*n.* **1.** A friendly attitude. **2.** An act of kindness. **3.** An indulgence. **4. a.** Friendly regard shown by a superior. **b.** A state of being held in such regard. **5.** Approval or support. **6. favors.** Sexual privileges. ′ **7.** A token of love. **8.** A small, decorative gift handed out at a party. **9.** Advantage; benefit. —*v.* **1.** To oblige. **2.** To like. **3.** To support. **4.** To aid or facilitate. **5.** To resemble: *She favors her father.* **6.** To be gentle with; spare: *favor a sore foot.* —**idiom. in favor of. 1.** In support of. **2.** To the advantage of. [< Lat.] —**fa′vor·er** *n.* —**fa′vor·ing·ly** *adv.*

Syns: *favor, admiration, esteem, estimation, honor, regard, respect n.*

fa·vor·a·ble (fā′vər-ə-bəl, fāv′rə-) *adj.* **1.** Helpful; advantageous: *favorable winds; a favorable climate.* **2.** Encouraging; promising. **3.** Expressing approval. —**fa′vor·a·ble·ness** *n.* —**fa′vor·a·bly** *adv.*

Syns: *favorable, auspicious, beneficial, bright, propitious adj.*

fa·vor·ite (fā′vər-ĭt, fāv′rĭt) *n.* **1.** One liked or favored above all others. **2.** A person esp. indulged by a superior: *a favorite of the queen.* **3.** A contestant regarded most likely to win. [< OItal. *favorito*, p.p. of *favorire*, to favor.] —**fa′vor·ite** *adj.*

favorite son *n.* A candidate supported by the delegates from his state at a national political convention.

fa·vor·it·ism (fā′vər-ĭ-tĭz′əm, fāv′rə-) *n.* A display of partiality.

fawn¹ (fôn) *n.* **1.** A young deer. **2.** A light yellowish brown. [< Lat. *fetus*, offspring.] —**fawn** *adj.*

fawn² (fôn) *v.* **1.** To exhibit affection, as a dog. **2.** To seek favor by obsequious behavior. [< OE *fagnian*, to rejoice.] —**fawn′er** *n.* —**fawn′ing·ly** *adv.*

fay (fā) *n.* **1.** A fairy. **2.** An elf. [< Lat. *fata*, Fates.]

faze (fāz) *v.* **fazed, faz·ing.** To disconcert. [< ME *fesen*, to drive away.]

Fe The symbol for the element iron. [< Lat. *ferrum*, iron.]

fe·al·ty (fē′əl-tē) *n., pl.* **-ties. 1.** Loyalty. **2.** The obligation of feudal allegiance. [< Lat. *fidelitas*, faithfulness.]

fear (fîr) *n.* **1. a.** A feeling of alarm or disquiet caused by awareness or expectation of danger. **b.** An instance or manifestation of such a feeling. **2.** A state of dread. **3.** Concern; solicitude. **4.** Awe; reverence: *fear of God.* —*v.* **1.** To be afraid of. **2.** To be apprehensive. **3.** To be in awe of. **4.** To suspect: *I fear you are wrong.* [< OE *fǣr*.] —**fear′er** *n.* —**fear′ful** *adj.* —**fear′ful·ly** *adv.* —**fear′ful·ness** *n.* —**fear·less** *adj.* —**fear′less·ly** *adv.* —**fear′less·ness** *n.*

fear·some (fîr′səm) *adj.* **1.** Causing fear. **2.** Fearful; timid. —**fear′some·ly** *adv.* —**fear′some·ness** *n.*

fea·si·ble (fē′zə-bəl) *adj.* **1.** Capable of being accomplished or carried out. **2.** Suitable. **3.** Plausible. [< OFr. *faisible*.] —**fea·si·bil′i·ty** or **fea′si·ble·ness** *n.* —**fea′si·bly** *adv.*

feast (fēst) *n.* **1.** A large, elaborate meal; banquet. **2.** A religious festival. —*v.* **1.** To enter-

tain or feed sumptuously. **2.** To delight; gratify. **3.** To partake of a feast. [< Lat. *festum*.] —**feast′er** *n.*

feat (fēt) *n.* A particularly remarkable exploit or achievement. [< Lat. *factum*.]

feath·er (fĕth′ər) *n.* **1.** One of the light hollow-shafted structures forming the outer covering of birds. **2. feathers.** Plumage. **3. feathers.** Clothing; attire. **4.** Character; kind. —*v.* **1.** To cover, dress, or line with feathers. **2.** To fit (an arrow) with a feather. **3.** To turn (an oar) so that its blade is parallel to the surface of the water between strokes. **4.** To turn the blades of (an aircraft propeller) so that they are parallel to the direction of flight. —**idioms. a feather in (one's) cap.** An achievement of which one can be proud. **feather (one's) nest.** To accumulate wealth esp. by abusing a position of trust. **in fine feather.** In excellent condition or humor. [< OE *fether*.] —**feath′er·i·ness** *n.* —**feath′er·less** *adj.* —**feath′er·y** *n.*

feath·er·bed (fĕth′ər-bĕd′) *v.* **-bed·ded, -bed·ding. 1.** To employ more workers than are actually needed for a given purpose or to limit their production. **2.** To be so employed.

feather bed *n.* A mattress stuffed with feathers or down.

feath·er·brain (fĕth′ər-brān′) *n.* A flighty, empty-headed person. —**feath′er·brained′** *adj.*

feath·er·edge (fĕth′ər-ĕj′) *n.* A thin, fragile edge.

feath·er·stitch (fĕth′ər-stĭch′) *n.* An embroidery stitch that produces a decorative zigzag line. —**feath′er·stitch′** *v.*

feath·er·weight (fĕth′ər-wāt′) *n.* **1.** A boxer weighing between approx. 54 and 57 kilograms or 118 and 127 pounds. **2.** One of little intelligence or importance.

fea·ture (fē′chər) *n.* **1. a.** The shape or aspect of the face. **b. features.** The face or its lineaments: *regular features.* **2.** A prominent or distinctive characteristic. **3.** The main film at a motion-picture theater. **4.** A prominent article in a newspaper or periodical. **5.** A special sales inducement. —*v.* **-tured, -tur·ing. 1.** To make prominent; publicize. **2.** To be a prominent part of. **3.** To draw the features of. [< Lat. *factura*.]

feb·ri·fuge (fĕb′rə-fyōōj′) *n.* A medicine that reduces a fever. [Lat. *febris*, fever + Lat. *fugare*, to drive away.]

fe·brile (fĕb′rəl, fē′brəl) *adj.* Of or having a fever. [< Lat. *febris*, fever.]

Feb·ru·ar·y (fĕb′rōō-ĕr′ē, fĕb′yōō-) *n., pl.* **-ies** or **-ys.** The 2nd month of the year, having 28 days, 29 in leap years. See table at **calendar.** [< Lat. *Februarius*.]

fe·ces (fē′sēz) *pl.n.* Waste excreted from the bowels; excrement. [< Lat. *faex*, dregs.] —**fe′cal** (-kəl) *adj.*

feck·less (fĕk′lĭs) *adj.* **1.** Lacking purpose or vitality; ineffective. **2.** Careless; irresponsible. [Sc. *feck*, efficacy + -LESS.] —**feck′less·ly** *adv.* —**feck′less·ness** *n.*

fe·cund (fē′kənd, fĕk′ənd) *adj.* Productive; fertile; fruitful. [< Lat. *fecundus*.] —**fe·cun′di·ty** (fĭ-kŭn′dĭ-tē) *n.*

fe·cun·date (fē′kən-dāt′, fĕk′ən-) *v.* **-dat·ed, -dat·ing. 1.** To impregnate; fertilize.

fed (fĕd) *v.* p.t. & p.p. of **feed.**

fed·er·al (fĕd′ər-əl) *adj.* **1.** Of or constituting a form of government in which separate states are united under one central authority while retaining certain regulatory powers. **2.** Often **Federal.** Of or relating to the central government of the United States. **3. Federal.** Of, relating to, or supporting the Union during the Civil War. —*n.* A supporter of federation or federal government. [< Lat. *foedus*, league.] —**fed'er·al·ly** *adv.*

fed·er·al·ism (fĕd'ər-ə-lĭz'əm) *n.* **1.** The doctrine or system of federal government. **2.** The advocacy of such a government.

fed·er·al·ist (fĕd'ər-ə-lĭst) *n.* **1.** An advocate of federalism. **2. Federalist.** A member of a U.S. political party of the 1790's, advocating a strong federal government. —**fed'er·al·ist** *adj.*

fed·er·al·ize (fĕd'ər-ə-līz') *v.* **-ized, -iz·ing.** **1.** To unite in a federal union. **2.** To put under federal control. —**fed'er·al·i·za'tion** *n.*

fed·er·ate (fĕd'ə-rāt') *v.* **-at·ed, -at·ing.** To join or unite in a league, federal union, or similar association. [< Lat. *foederare.*] —**fed'er·a'tion** *n.* —**fed'er·a·tive** (fĕd'ə-rā'tĭv, fĕd'ər-ə-tĭv) *adj.*

fe·do·ra (fĭ-dôr'ə, -dōr'ə) *n.* A soft felt hat with a flexible brim and a low crown creased lengthwise. [< *Fédora*, play by Victorien Sardou (1831-1908).]

fed up *adj.* Extremely tired or disgusted.

fee (fē) *n.* **1.** A fixed charge. **2.** A payment for professional service. **3.** *Law.* An inherited or heritable estate in land. [< OFr. *fie, fief*, of Gmc. orig.]

fee·ble (fē'bəl) *adj.* **-bler, -blest.** **1.** Lacking strength; frail. **2.** Lacking vigor or force; ineffective: *a feeble answer.* **3.** Faint: *a feeble cry.* [< Lat. *flebilis*, lamentable.] —**fee'ble·ness** *n.* —**fee'bly** *adv.*

fee·ble-mind·ed (fē'bəl-mīn'dĭd) *adj.* Mentally deficient. —**fee'ble-mind'ed·ly** *adv.* —**fee'ble-mind'ed·ness** *n.*

feed (fēd) *v.* **fed** (fēd), **feed·ing.** **1.** To give food to or provide as food or nourishment. **2.** To eat. **3.** To supply a flow of (a material to be consumed or utilized). —*n.* **1.** Food for animals. **2.** *Informal.* A meal. **3. a.** Material supplied, as to a machine. **b.** An apparatus that supplies such material. [< OE *fēdan.*] —**feed'er** *n.*

feed·back (fēd'băk') *n.* **1.** The return of a part of the output of a system or process to the input. **2. a.** The return of information to the source of a process or action for the purpose of control or correction. **b.** The information so transmitted. —**feed'back'** *adj.*

feed·lot (fēd'lŏt') *n.* A lot on which livestock are fattened for market.

feed·stock (fēd'stŏk') *n.* Raw materials for an industrial process.

feed·stuff (fēd'stŭf') *n.* Feed (sense 1).

feel (fēl) *v.* **felt** (fĕlt), **feel·ing.** **1.** To perceive, give, or produce through the sense of touch. **2. a.** To touch. **b.** To examine by touching. **3. a.** To experience (an emotion). **b.** To be aware of; sense. **c.** To suffer from. **4.** To believe or consider. **5.** To have compassion or sympathy. —*phrasal verb.* **feel out.** To sound out in order to ascertain another's position or opinion. —*n.* **1.** Perception by touching or feeling. **2.** The sense of touch. **3.** The nature or quality of something perceived. —*idiom.* **feel like.** *Informal.* To be in the mood for. [< OE *fēlan.*]

feel·er (fē'lər) *n.* **1.** An exploratory suggestion

or remark. **2.** A sensory organ such as an antenna or tentacle.

feel·ing (fē'lĭng) *n.* **1. a.** The sensation involving perception by touch. **b.** A sensation perceived by touch. **c.** A physical sensation. **2. a.** An affective state or disposition. **b.** Emotion. **3.** An awareness; impression. **4. feelings.** Sensibilities. **5.** Opinion. **6.** Sympathy. **7.** A bent; aptitude. —*adj.* **1. a.** Sensitive. **b.** Easily moved emotionally. **2.** Sympathetic. —**feel'ing·ly** *adv.*

feet (fēt) *n.* Pl. of **foot.**

feign (fān) *v.* **1.** To give a false appearance (of). **2.** To make a false show; pretend. [< Lat. *fingere*, to form.] —**feign'er** *n.*

feint (fānt) *n.* A feigned attack designed to draw defensive action away from an intended target. [< OFr. *feinte.*] —**feint** *v.*

feis·ty (fī'stē) *adj.* **-i·er, -i·est.** *Informal.* **1.** Touchy; quarrelsome. **2.** Spirited; frisky. [< dial. *feist*, small dog.]

feld·spar (fĕld'spär', fĕl'spär') *n.* Any of a group of abundant rock-forming minerals consisting of silicates of aluminum with potassium, sodium, calcium, and rarely barium. [Obs. G. *Feldspath*, fieldspar.]

fe·lic·i·tate (fĭ-lĭs'ĭ-tāt') *v.* **-tat·ed, -tat·ing.** To congratulate. —**fe·lic'i·ta'tion** *n.* —**fe·lic'i·ta'tor** *n.*

fe·lic·i·tous (fĭ-lĭs'ĭ-təs) *adj.* **1.** Well-chosen; apt. **2.** Having an agreeable manner or style. —**fe·lic'i·tous·ly** *adv.* —**fe·lic'i·tous·ness** *n.*

fe·lic·i·ty (fĭ-lĭs'ĭ-tē) *n.*, *pl.* **-ties.** **1.** Great happiness. **2.** A cause of happiness. **3.** Appropriateness and aptness of expression or an instance of it. [< Lat. *felicitas.*]

fe·line (fē'līn') *adj.* **1.** Of or pertaining to cats or related animals, as lions and tigers. **2.** Catlike, as in slyness or suppleness. —*n.* A feline animal. [Lat. *felinus.*] —**fe'line·ly** *adv.* —**fe'line'ness** or **fe·lin'i·ty** (fĭ-lĭn'ĭ-tē) *n.*

fell¹ (fĕl) *v.* **1.** To cut or knock down. **2.** To kill. **3.** To sew (a seam) by turning under and then stitching down the raw edges. [< OE *fyllan.*] —**fell'a·ble** *adj.* —**fell'er** *n.*

fell² (fĕl) *adj.* **1.** Cruel; fierce. **2.** Deadly; lethal. [< OFr. *fel.*] —**fell'ness** *n.*

fell³ (fĕl) *n.* The hide of an animal; pelt. [< OE.]

fell⁴ (fĕl) *v.* *p.t.* of **fall.**

fel·lah (fĕl'ə) *n.*, *pl.* **-lahs** or **fel·la·hin** (fĕl'ə-hēn') or **-la·heen.** A peasant or agricultural laborer in Arab countries. [< Ar. *fellāh.*]

fel·low (fĕl'ō) *n.* **1.** A man or boy. **2.** *Informal.* A boyfriend. **3.** An individual. **4.** A comrade; associate. **5.** One of a pair; mate. **6.** A member of a learned society. **7.** A recipient of a grant for advanced study. [< ON *félagi*, business partner.]

fel·low·ship (fĕl'ō-shĭp') *n.* **1.** Companionship. **2.** A union of friends or equals; fraternity. **3. a.** A graduate stipend. **b.** A foundation awarding such grants.

fellow traveler *n.* One who sympathizes with the beliefs and programs of an organized group, such as the Communist Party, without actually joining it.

fel·on¹ (fĕl'ən) *n.* One who has committed a felony. [< Med. Lat. *fello*, villain.]

fel·on² (fĕl'ən) *n.* A pus-filled infection near

the nail or the end of a finger or toe. [ME *feloun.*]

fel·o·ny (fĕl'ə-nē) *n., pl.* **-nies.** A serious crime, such as murder, rape, or burglary. **—fe·lo'ni·ous** *adj.* **—fe·lo'ni·ous·ly** *adv.* **—fe·lo'ni·ous·ness** *n.*

felt¹ (fĕlt) *n.* **1.** A fabric of matted, compressed fibers, as wool or fur. **2.** A material resembling felt. [< OE.]

felt² (fĕlt) *v. p.t. & p.p.* of **feel.**

fe·male (fē'māl') *adj.* **1. a.** Of or characteristic of the sex that produces ova or bears young. **b.** Consisting of members of this sex. **2.** *Bot.* **a.** Pertaining to or designating an organ, such as a pistil or ovary, that functions in producing seeds or spores after fertilization. **b.** Bearing pistils but not stamens. **3.** Having a hollow part into which a projecting part, such as a plug or prong, fits. **—n.** A female person, animal, or plant. [< Lat. *femella,* girl.] **—fe'male·ness** *n.*

fem·i·nine (fĕm'ə-nĭn) *adj.* **1.** Of or belonging to the female sex. **2.** Marked by qualities attributed to women. **3.** *Gram.* Of or belonging to the gender of words or grammatical forms that are classified as female. **—n.** *Gram.* **1.** The feminine gender. **2.** A word or form of this gender. [< Lat. *femininus.*] **—fem'i·nine·ly** *adv.* **—fem'i·nine·ness** *n.* **—fem'i·nin'i·ty** *n.*

fem·i·nism (fĕm'ə-nĭz'əm) *n.* Advocacy of the political, social, and economic equality of men and women. **—fem'i·nist** *n.* **—fem'i·nis'tic** *adj.*

femme fa·tale (fĕm' fə-tăl', făm' fə-tăl') *n., pl.* **femmes fa·tales** (fĕm' fə-tăl', făm' fə-tăl'). A seductive woman. [Fr.]

fe·mur (fē'mər) *n., pl.* **-murs** or **fem·o·ra** (fĕm'ər-ə). **1.** The proximal bone of the lower or hind limb in vertebrates, situated between the pelvis and knee in humans. **2.** The thigh. [Lat.] **—fem'o·ral** (fĕm'ər-əl) *adj.*

fen (fĕn) *n.* Low, swampy land; bog. [< OE *fenn.*] **—fen'ny** *adj.*

fence (fĕns) *n.* **1.** An enclosure, barrier, or boundary made of posts, boards, wire, stakes, or rails. **2. a.** A receiver of stolen goods. **b.** A place where such goods are received and sold. **—v. fenced, fenc·ing. 1.** To surround, close in, or close off by a fence. **2.** To practice the art of fencing. **3.** To be evasive. **4.** To act as a fence for stolen goods. **—idiom. on the fence.** *Informal.* Undecided; neutral. [< DE-FENSE.] **—fenc'er** *n.*

fenc·ing (fĕn'sĭng) *n.* **1.** The art of using a

fencing

foil, épée, or saber. **2.** Material used in constructing fences.

fend (fĕnd) *v.* To ward off; repel. **—idiom.**

fend for (oneself). To get along without help. [< DEFEND.]

fend·er (fĕn'dər) *n.* **1.** A guard device over the wheel of a vehicle. **2.** A screen in front of a fireplace.

fen·es·tra·tion (fĕn'ə-strā'shən) *n.* The design and placement of windows. [< Lat. *fenestra,* window.]

Fe·ni·an (fē'nē-ən) *n.* **1. Fenians.** A legendary group of heroic Irish warriors of the 2nd and 3rd cent. A.D. **2.** A member of a secret Irish and Irish-American organization of the mid-19th cent. whose goal was the overthrow of British rule in Ireland.

fen·nel (fĕn'əl) *n.* **1.** A plant with aromatic seeds used as flavoring. **2.** The seeds or edible stalks of this plant. [< Lat. *faeniculum.*]

-fer *suff.* One that bears: *aquifer.* [< Lat. *ferre,* to bear.]

fe·ral (fîr'əl, fĕr'-) *adj.* **1.** Reverted to an untamed state from domestication. **2.** Of or characteristic of a wild animal; savage. [< Lat. *ferus,* wild.]

fer·de·lance (fĕr'də-lăns', -läns') *n.* A poisonous tropical snake with brown and grayish markings. [Fr.]

fer·ment (fûr'mĕnt') *n.* **1.** Something that causes fermentation, as a yeast or enzyme. **2.** A state of agitation or unrest. **—v.** (fər-mĕnt'). **1.** To produce by or as if by fermentation. **2.** To undergo or cause to undergo fermentation. **3.** To be turbulent; seethe. [< Lat. *fermentum.*] **—fer·ment'a·bil'i·ty** *n.* **—fer·ment'a·ble** *adj.* **—fer·ment'er** *n.*

fer·men·ta·tion (fûr'mĕn-tā'shən) *n.* **1.** Chemical splitting of complex organic compounds into relatively simple substances, esp. the conversion of sugar to carbon dioxide and alcohol by yeast. **2.** Unrest; commotion. **—fer·men'ta·tive** (fər-mĕn'tə-tĭv) *adj.*

fer·mi·um (fûr'mē-əm) *n. Symbol* **Fm** A synthetic metallic element. Atomic number 100; longest-lived isotope Fm 257. [< Enrico Fermi (1901-54).]

fern (fûrn) *n.* Any of numerous flowerless plants characteristically having fronds with divided leaflets and reproducing by means of spores. [< OE *fearn.*] **—fern'y** *adj.*

fe·ro·cious (fə-rō'shəs) *adj.* **1.** Extremely fierce and cruel; savage. **2.** Extreme; intense: *ferocious energy.* [< Lat. *ferox,* fierce.] **—fe·ro'cious·ly** *adv.* **—fe·ro'cious·ness** or **fe·roc'i·ty** (fə-rŏs'ĭ-tē) *n.*

-ferous *suff.* Bearing; producing; containing: *carboniferous.* [-FER + -OUS.]

fer·ret (fĕr'ĭt) *n.* **1.** A domesticated, usu. white form of the Old World polecat, often trained to hunt rats or rabbits. **2.** A related weasellike North American mammal. **—v. 1.** To hunt with a ferret. **2.** To drive out; expel. **3.** To uncover and bring to light by searching: *ferret out a secret.* [< Lat. *fur,* thief.] **—fer'ret·er** *n.* **—fer'ret·y** *adj.*

fer·ric (fĕr'ĭk) *adj.* Of or containing iron, esp. with valence 3.

ferric oxide *n.* A dark compound, Fe_2O_3, that occurs naturally as hematite ore and rust.

Fer·ris wheel (fĕr'ĭs) *n.* Also **ferris wheel.** A large upright, rotating wheel with suspended cars in which passengers ride for amusement. [< George W.G. *Ferris* (1859-96).]

ferro– or **ferr–** *pref.* **1.** Iron: *ferromagnetic.* **2.** Ferrous iron: *ferromanganese.* [< Lat. *ferrum,* iron.]

ferro·mag·net·ic (fĕr′ō-măg-nĕt′ĭk) *adj.* Of or characteristic of substances, as iron, nickel, cobalt, and various alloys, that have magnetic properties. **—fer′ro·mag′net n. —fer′ro·mag′ne·tism** *n.*

fer·ro·man·ga·nese (fĕr′ō-măng′gə-nēz′, -nēs′) *n.* An alloy of iron and manganese, used in making steel.

fer·rous (fĕr′əs) *adj.* Of or containing iron, esp. with valence 2.

ferrous oxide *n.* A black powdery compound, FeO, used in the manufacture of steel.

fer·rule (fĕr′əl, -ōōl′) *n.* A metal ring or cap attached to or near the end of a cane or wooden handle to prevent splitting. [< Lat. *viriola,* little bracelet.]

ferret   ferrule

fer·ry (fĕr′ē) *v.* **-ried, -ry·ing. 1.** To transport by boat across a body of water. **2.** To cross on a ferry. **3.** To transport from one point to another. **—n.,** *pl.* **-ries. 1.** A ferryboat. **2.** The place where a ferryboat embarks. **3.** A service for transporting esp. an aircraft under its own power to its eventual user. [< OE *ferian.*]

fer·ry·boat (fĕr′ē-bōt′) *n.* A boat used to ferry passengers or goods.

fer·tile (fûr′tl) *adj.* **1.** Capable of initiating, sustaining, or supporting reproduction. **2.** Rich in material needed to sustain plant growth: *fertile soil.* **3.** Highly or continuously productive; prolific: *a fertile imagination.* [< Lat. *fertilis.*] **—fer′tile·ly** *adv.* **—fer·til′i·ty** or **fer′tile·ness** *n.*

  Syns: *fertile, fecund, fruitful, productive, prolific, rich adj.*

fer·til·ize (fûr′tl-īz′) *v.* **-ized, -iz·ing. 1.** To initiate biological reproduction, esp. to provide with sperm or pollen. **2.** To make fertile, as by spreading fertilizer. **—fer′til·iz·a·ble** *adj.* **—fer′til·i·za′tion** *n.*

fer·til·iz·er (fûr′tl-ī′zər) *n.* **1.** A material, as manure, compost, or a chemical compound, added to soil to increase its fertility. **2.** One that fertilizes.

fer·ule (fĕr′əl, -ōōl′) *n.* A flat stick or ruler used in punishing children. [Lat. *ferula.*]

fer·vent (fûr′vənt) *adj.* **1.** Passionate; ardent. **2.** Extremely hot; glowing. [< Lat. *fervēre,* to boil.] **—fer′ven·cy** or **fer′vent·ness** *n.* **—fer′vent·ly** *adv.*

fer·vid (fûr′vĭd) *adj.* **1.** Fervent; impassioned. **2.** Extremely hot. [Lat. *fervidus.*] **—fer′vid·ly** *adv.* **—fer′vid·ness** *n.*

fer·vor (fûr′vər) *n.* **1.** Intensity of emotion; ardor. **2.** Intense heat. [< Lat.]

fes·tal (fĕs′tal) *adj.* Festive. [< Lat. *festa,* feast.] **—fes′tal·ly** *adv.*

fes·ter (fĕs′tər) *v.* **1.** To generate pus. **2.** To be or become a source of irritation; rankle. [< Lat. *fistula,* fistula.]

fes·ti·val (fĕs′tə-vəl) *n.* **1.** A day of religious feasting or special observances. **2.** A programmed series of related cultural events: *a film festival.* **3.** Conviviality; revelry.

fes·tive (fĕs′tĭv) *adj.* **1.** Of or suited to a feast or festival. **2.** Merry; joyous. [Lat. *festivus.*] **—fes′tive·ly** *adv.* **—fes′tive·ness** *n.*

fes·tiv·i·ty (fĕ-stĭv′ĭ-tē) *n., pl.* **-ties. 1.** A joyous feast, holiday, or celebration; festival. **2.** Often **festivities.** The activities during a festival or feast. **3.** The merriment of a festival.

fes·toon (fĕ-stōōn′) *n.* **1.** A decorative garland hung between two points. **2.** An ornament in the shape of a festoon. **—v. 1.** To decorate with festoons. **2.** To form festoons. [< Ital. *festone,* festal ornament.] **—fes·toon′er·y** *n.*

fe·tal (fēt′l) *adj.* Also **foe·tal.** Of or relating to a fetus.

fetal alcohol syndrome *n.* A complex of birth defects that occur in infants born to alcoholic mothers.

fetch (fĕch) *v.* **1.** To go after and return with. **2.** To cause to come forth. **3.** To bring as a price. **4. a.** To draw in (breath); inhale. **b.** To heave (a sigh). **5.** To deal (a blow). [< OE *feccean.*] **—fetch′er** *n.*

fetch·ing (fĕch′ĭng) *adj.* *Informal.* Attractive; charming. **—fetch′ing·ly** *adv.*

fete or **fête** (fāt, fĕt) *n.* **1.** A festival. **2.** An elaborate outdoor party. **—v. fet·ed, fet·ing.** To honor or celebrate with a fete. [< OFr. *feste,* feast.]

fet·id (fĕt′ĭd, fē′tĭd) *adj.* Foul-smelling; stinking. [< Lat. *fetidus.*] **—fet′id·ly** *adv.* **—fet′id·ness** *n.*

fet·ish (fĕt′ĭsh) *n.* **1.** An object believed to have magical power. **2.** An object of obsessive attention or reverence. [< Lat. *factitius,* made by art.] **—fet′ish·ism** *n.* **—fet′ish·ist** *n.*

fet·lock (fĕt′lŏk′) *n.* A projection above and behind the hoof of a horse or related animal. [ME *fitlok.*]

fet·ter (fĕt′ər) *n.* **1.** A chain or shackle attached to the ankles. **2. fetters.** Something that restricts or restrains. **—v. 1.** To shackle. **2.** To restrict or restrain. [< OE *feter.*]

fet·tle (fĕt′l) *n.* Condition: *in fine fettle.* [< ME *fetlen,* to shape.]

fe·tus (fē′təs) *n., pl.* **-es.** Also **foe·tus.** The unborn young of a viviparous vertebrate; in humans, the unborn young from the end of the 8th week to the moment of birth as distinguished from the earlier embryo. [Lat., offspring.]

feud (fyōōd) *n.* A prolonged quarrel; vendetta. [< OFr. *faide,* of Gmc. orig.] **—feud** *v.*

feu·dal (fyōōd′l) *adj.* Of or relating to feudalism. [Med. Lat. *feudalis.*] **—feu′dal·i·za′tion** *n.* **—feu′dal·ize′** *v.* **—feu′dal·ly** *adv.*

feu·dal·ism (fyōōd′l-ĭz′əm) *n.* A political and economic system in medieval Europe by which a landowner granted land to a vassal in exchange for homage and military service. **—feu′dal·ist** *n.* **—feu′dal·is′tic** *adj.*

feu·da·to·ry (fyōō′də-tôr′ē, -tōr′ē) *n., pl.* **-ries. 1.** A vassal. **2.** A feudal fee. **—adj.** Owing feudal allegiance.

fe·ver (fē′vər) *n.* **1.** Abnormally high body temperature. **2.** A disease marked by an abnormally high body temperature. **3.** Heightened activity or excitement. **4.** An intense usu. short-lived enthusiasm; craze. [< Lat. *febris*.] —**fe′ver·ish** *adj.* —**fe′ver·ish·ly** *adv.* —**fe′ver·ish·ness** *n.*

fever blister *n.* A cold sore.

few (fyōō) *adj.* **-er, -est.** Amounting to or consisting of a small number. —*n.* (*used with a pl. verb*). **1.** An indefinitely small number: *Only a few came to my party.* **2.** A select or elite group: *the happy few.* —*pron.* (*used with a pl. verb*). A small number: *Few of them were able to read.* [< OE *fēawe.*]

Usage: Few and fewer are correctly used in writing only before a plural noun: *few cars; fewer books.*

fey (fā) *adj.* **1.** Clairvoyant. **2.** Enchanted. [< OE *fǣge.*]

fez (fĕz) *n., pl.* **fez·zes.** A brimless, usu. red felt hat with a flat top and a black tassel, worn chiefly by men in eastern Mediterranean countries. [< *Fez*, Morocco.]

fi·an·cé (fē′än-sā′, fē-än′sā′) *n.* A man engaged to be married. [Fr., p.p. of *fiancer*, to betroth.]

fi·an·cée (fē′än-sā′, fē-än′sā′) *n.* A woman engaged to be married.

fi·as·co (fē-ăs′kō, -ăs′-) *n., pl.* **-coes** or **-cos.** A complete failure. [< Ital.]

fi·at (fē′ăt′, fī′ăt′, -ət) *n.* An arbitrary order or decree. [< Lat., let it be done.]

fib (fĭb) *n.* A small or trivial lie. —*v.* **fibbed, fib·bing.** To tell a fib. [Orig. unknown.] —**fib′ber** *n.*

fi·ber (fī′bər) *n.* **1.** A slender, threadlike strand. **2.** A number of fibers forming a single substance: *muscle fiber; flax fiber.* **3.** Inner strength; toughness. [< Lat. *fibra.*]

fi·ber·board (fī′bər-bôrd′, -bōrd′) *n.* A building material composed of fibers compressed into rigid sheets.

fiber glass *n.* A composite material of glass fibers in resin.

fi·bril (fī′brəl, fĭb′rəl) *n.* A tiny, slender, often microscopic fiber, as a root hair. [< Lat. *fibra*, fiber.] —**fi′bril·lar** *adj.*

fi·bril·la·tion (fĭb′rə-lā′shən, fī′brə-) *n.* An uncoordinated twitching of the muscle fibers of the ventricles of the heart.

fi·brin (fī′brĭn) *n.* An elastic, insoluble, fibrous protein that forms a blood clot.

fi·brin·o·gen (fī-brĭn′ə-jən) *n.* A soluble protein normally present in the blood plasma, which is converted to fibrin when blood clots.

fibro- or **fibr-** *pref.* **1.** Fiber: *fibrous.* **2.** Fibrous tissue: *fibroma.* [< Lat. *fibra*, fiber.]

fi·broid (fī′broid′) *adj.* Resembling or composed of fibrous tissue. —*n.* A benign tumor of smooth muscle.

fi·bro·ma (fī-brō′mə) *n., pl.* **-mas** or **-ma·ta** (-mə-tə). A benign neoplasm derived from fibrous tissue. —**fi·brom′a·tous** *adj.*

fi·bro·sis (fī-brō′sĭs) *n.* The formation of excess fibrous tissue.

fi·brous (fī′brəs) *adj.* Of, resembling, or having fibers.

fi·bro·vas·cu·lar (fī′brō-văs′kyə-lər) *adj.* Having fibrous tissue and vascular tissue.

fib·u·la (fĭb′yə-lə) *n., pl.* **-lae** (-lē′) or **-las.** The outer and smaller of two bones of the human leg or the hind leg of an animal. [Lat.]

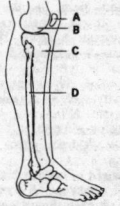

fibula

A. Patella   C. Tibia
B. Femur   D. Fibula

-fic *suff.* Causing; making: *honorific.* [< Lat. *facere*, to make.]

-fication *suff.* Production; making: *amplification.* [< Lat. *facere*, to make.]

fiche (fēsh) *n.* A microfiche.

fi·chu (fĭsh′ōō, fē′shōō) *n.* A woman's triangular scarf, worn over the shoulders and fastened at the breast. [Fr.]

fick·le (fĭk′əl) *adj.* Changeable; inconstant. [< OE *ficol*, deceitful.] —**fick′le·ness** *n.*

fic·tion (fĭk′shən) *n.* **1.** A product of the imagination. **2. a.** The category of literature with imaginary characters and events, including novels, short stories, etc. **b.** A work of this category. [< Lat. *fictus*, p.p. of *fingere*, to form.] —**fic′tion·al** *adj.* —**fic′tion·al·ly** *adv.*

fic·ti·tious (fĭk-tĭsh′əs) *adj.* **1.** Nonexistent; imaginary; unreal. **2.** Purposefully deceptive; false: *a fictitious name.* —**fic·ti′tious·ly** *adv.* —**fic·ti′tious·ness** *n.*

fid·dle (fĭd′l) *n. Informal.* A violin. —*v.* **-dled, -dling. 1.** *Informal.* To play a violin. **2.** To fidget. **3.** To tinker with. [< Lat. *vitulari*, to celebrate a victory.] —**fid′dler** *n.*

fiddler crab *n.* A burrowing crab with one of the front claws much enlarged in the male.

fid·dle·sticks (fĭd′l-stĭks′) *interj.* Used to express mild annoyance or impatience.

fi·del·i·ty (fĭ-dĕl′ĭ-tē, fī-) *n., pl.* **-ties. 1.** Faithfulness; loyalty. **2.** Conformity to truth; accuracy. **3.** The degree to which an electronic system reproduces sound without distortion. [< Lat. *fidelitas.*]

fidg·et (fĭj′ĭt) *v.* To move uneasily, nervously, or restlessly. —*n.* **fidgets.** A condition of nervousness or restlessness. [Obs. *fidge*, to move about restlessly.] —**fidg′et·er** *n.* —**fidg′et·i·ness** *n.* —**fidg′et·y** *adj.*

fi·du·ci·ar·y (fĭ-dōō′shē-ĕr′ē, -dyōō′-, fī-) *adj.* **1.** Pertaining to the holding of something in trust. **2.** Held in trust. —*n., pl.* **-ies.** A trustee. [Lat. *fiduciarius.*]

fie (fī) *interj.* Used to express distaste or shock.

fief (fēf) *n.* A feudal estate. [< OFr.]

field (fēld) *n.* **1.** A broad, level expanse of open land. **2.** Land devoted to a particular crop. **3.** Land containing a specified natural resource: *an oil field.* **4.** An airfield or airport. **5.** *Sports.* A background area, as on a flag. **6.** *Sports.* **a.** An area in which a sports event takes place; ground; stadium. **b.** All the contestants in an event. **7.** An area of activity or knowledge. **8.** A battlefield. **9.** A region of space characterized by a physical property, such as gravitational force, having a determinable

value at every point in the region. —v.
1. *Sports.* To retrieve (a ball) and perform the required maneuver. 2. *Sports.* To put (a team) into a contest. 3. To respond to adequately: *field questions.* [< OE *feld.*] —**field'er** n.

field day n. 1. A day spent outdoors in a planned activity such as athletic competition, nature study, etc. 2. *Informal.* An occasion of great pleasure or triumph.

field event n. A track event other than a race.

field glasses pl.n. Portable binoculars.

field goal n. 1. *Football.* A score worth three points made on an ordinary down by kicking the ball over the crossbar and between the goal posts. 2. *Basketball.* A score worth two points made by throwing the ball through the basket in regulation play.

field magnet n. A magnet used to provide a magnetic field needed for the operation of a machine such as a generator or motor.

field marshal n. An officer of the highest rank in some European armies.

field mouse n. Any of various small mice inhabiting meadows and fields.

field of force n. A region of space throughout which the force produced by a single agent, such as an electric current, is operative.

field-test (fēld'tĕst') v. To test in natural operating conditions.

field trial n. A test for young, untried hunting dogs to determine their competence in pointing and retrieving.

field trip n. A group excursion to observe and learn, as to a museum.

field work n. Work done or observations made in the field.

fiend (fēnd) n. 1. An evil spirit; demon. 2. An extremely evil or cruel person. 3. *Informal.* An addict: *a dope fiend; a fresh-air fiend.* [< OE *fēond.*] —**fiend'ish** adj. —**fiend'ish·ly** adv. —**fiend'ish·ness** n.

fierce (fîrs) adj. **fierc·er, fierc·est.** 1. Wild and savage: *a fierce beast.* 2. Extremely severe or violent: *a fierce storm.* 3. Intense or ardent: *fierce loyalty.* [< Lat. *ferus.*] —**fierce'ly** adv. —**fierce'ness** n.

Syns: *fierce, bestial, cruel, feral, ferocious, inhuman, savage, vicious* **adj.**

fier·y (fīr'ē, fī'ə-rē) adj. **-i·er, -i·est.** 1. Of, consisting of, or like fire. 2. a. Filled with or exhibiting intense emotion. b. Easily provoked: *a fiery temper.* [< ME *fiere,* fire.] —**fier'i·ly** adv. —**fier'i·ness** n.

fi·es·ta (fē-ĕs'tə) n. 1. A religious feast or holiday. 2. A celebration or festival. [< Lat. *festus,* joyous.]

fife (fīf) n. A musical instrument similar to a flute but higher in range. [< OHG *pfifa.*]

fif·teen (fĭf-tēn') n. The cardinal number equal to the sum of 14 + 1. —**fif·teen'** adj. & pron.

fif·teenth (fĭf-tēnth') n. 1. The ordinal number that matches 15 in a series. 2. One of 15 equal parts. —**fif·teenth'** adj. & adv.

fifth (fĭfth) n. 1. The ordinal number that matches 5 in a series. 2. One of 5 equal parts. 3. A measure of liquid capacity equal to ⅕ of a gallon or ¾ of a liter, used mainly for alcoholic beverages. [< OE *fifta.*] —**fifth** adj. & adv.

fifth column n. A secret organization that works within a country to further the military and political aims of an enemy. [First applied in 1936 to rebel sympathizers in Madrid when four columns of rebel troops were attacking that city.] —**fifth columnist** n.

fifth wheel n. One that is unnecessary.

fif·ti·eth (fĭf'tē-ĭth) n. 1. The ordinal number that matches the number 50. 2. One of 50 equal parts. —**fif'ti·eth** adj. & adv.

fif·ty (fĭf'tē) n. The cardinal number equal to 5 × 10. [< OE *fiftig.*] —**fif'ty** adj. & pron.

fif·ty-fif·ty (fĭf'tē-fĭf'tē) adj. *Informal.* Divided or shared in two equal portions. —**fif'ty-fif'ty** adv.

fig (fĭg) n. 1. a. The pear-shaped, many-seeded, edible fruit of a widely cultivated tree. b. A tree bearing such fruit. 2. A trivial amount; whit: *not care a fig.* [< Lat. *ficus.*]

fight (fīt) v. **fought** (fôt), **fight·ing.** 1. To participate in combat or battle. 2. To struggle; contend (with). 3. To quarrel; argue. 4. To box or wrestle (against) in a ring. 5. To prevent; oppose. 6. To wage (a battle). 7. To make (one's way), as by combat. —**phrasal verb. fight off.** To defend against or drive off. —n. 1. A battle; combat. 2. A struggle or conflict. 3. A boxing match; bout. 4. Inclination to fight; pugnacity. [< OE *feohtan.*]

fight·er (fī'tər) n. 1. One that fights. 2. A boxer or wrestler. 3. A fast, maneuverable combat aircraft.

fig·ment (fĭg'mənt) n. 1. Something imagined. 2. An arbitrary notion. [< Lat. *figmentum.*]

fig·u·ra·tive (fĭg'yər-ə-tĭv) adj. 1. Based on figures of speech; metaphorical. 2. Represented by a figure; emblematic. —**fig'u·ra·tive·ly** adv.

fig·ure (fĭg'yər) n. 1. a. A written or printed symbol. b. A numeral. 2. **figures.** Arithmetic calculations. 3. An amount represented in numbers. 4. The outline, form, or silhouette of a thing, esp. of a human body. 5. An individual, esp. a well-known personage. 6. The impression an individual makes: *cuts a dashing figure.* 7. A diagram, design, or pattern. 8. A group of steps in a dance. 9. A figure of speech. —v. **-ured, -ur·ing.** 1. To calculate with numbers; compute. 2. To make a likeness of; represent. 3. To adorn with a design. 4. *Informal.* To conclude, believe, or predict. 5. To be pertinent or involved. —**phrasal verbs. figure on** (or **upon**). *Informal.* 1. To depend on. 2. To plan on; expect. **figure out.** *Informal.* To solve, decipher, or comprehend. [< Lat. *figura.*]

figure eight n. A figure in the shape of the number 8.

fig·ure·head (fĭg'yər-hĕd') n. 1. A person with nominal leadership but no actual authority. 2. A figure on the prow of a ship.

figure of speech n. An expression, such as a metaphor or hyperbole, in which the literal meanings of words are distorted to create vivid or dramatic effects.

fig·u·rine (fĭg'yə-rēn') n. A small sculptured figure; statuette. [< Ital. *figurina.*]

fil·a·ment (fĭl'ə-mənt) n. 1. A fine, thin thread or threadlike structure. 2. A fine wire heated electrically to incandescence in an electric lamp. [< Lat. *filum,* thread.] —**fil'a·men'ta·ry** adj. —**fil'a·men'tous** adj.

ă pat ā pay â care ä father ĕ pet ē be ĭ pit ī tie î pier ŏ pot ō toe ô paw, for oi noise ŏŏ took
ŏŏ boot ou out th thin th this ŭ cut û urge yŏŏ abuse zh vision ə about, item, edible, gallop, circus

fi·lar·i·a (fĭ-lâr′ē-ə) *n., pl.* **-i·ae** (-ē-ē′). Any of various parasitic nematode worms that infest humans and other vertebrates and are often transmitted by biting insects. [< Lat. *filum,* thread.] —**fi·lar′i·al** *adj.*

fil·bert (fĭl′bərt) *n.* The rounded, smooth-shelled edible nut of an Old World hazel. [< AN < St. *Philbert* (d. A.D. 684).]

filch (fĭlch) *v.* To steal; pilfer. [ME *filchen.*] —**filch′er** *n.*

file¹ (fīl) *n.* **1.** A receptacle for keeping papers, cards, etc., in useful order. **2.** A collection of objects kept thus: *the accounts-due file.* **3.** A line of persons, animals, or things positioned one behind another. —*v.* **filed, fil·ing. 1.** To put in useful order; catalogue. **2.** To enter (e.g. a legal document) on public record. **3.** To transmit (copy) to a newspaper. **4.** To march or walk in a line. —**idiom. on file.** Catalogued in a file; on hand. [< Lat. *filum,* thread.] —**fil′er** *n.*

file² (fīl) *n.* A tool with a series of sharp ridged edges, used in smoothing, shaping, or grinding. —*v.* **filed, fil·ing.** To smooth, grind, or remove with a file. [< OE *fīl.*] —**fil′er** *n.*

file clerk *n.* One who is employed to maintain the files of an office.

fi·let¹ (fĭ-lā′, fĭl′ā′) *n.* A lace with a simple pattern of squares. [< Lat. *filum,* thread.]

fi·let² (fĭ-lā′, fĭl′ā′) *n.* Var. of **fillet** (sense 2). —*v.* Var. of **fillet** (sense 2).

fil·i·al (fĭl′ē-əl) *adj.* Of or befitting a son or daughter: *filial obedience.* [< Lat. *filius,* son.]

fil·i·bus·ter (fĭl′ə-bŭs′tər) *n.* **1.** Obstructionist tactics, such as a long speech, for the purpose of delaying or preventing legislative action. **2.** An adventurer who engages in private warfare in a foreign country. [Sp. *filibustero,* freebooter.] —**fil′i·bus′ter·er** *n.*

fil·i·gree (fĭl′ə-grē′) *n.* Lacelike ornamental work of twisted gold or silver wire. [< Ital. *filigrana.*] —**fil′i·gree′** *v. & adj.*

fil·ing (fī′lĭng) *n.* Often **filings.** A particle scraped off with a file.

Fil·i·pi·no (fĭl′ə-pē′nō) *n., pl.* **-nos.** A native or inhabitant of the Philippines. —**Fil′i·pi′no** *adj.*

fill (fĭl) *v.* **1.** To make or become full. **2.** To stop or plug up. **3.** To satisfy; fulfill: *fill the requirements.* **4.** To supply the necessary materials for: *fill a prescription.* **5.** To supply (an empty space) with material. **6.** To put someone into a (specific office or position). **7.** To occupy a (specific office or position). —*phrasal verb.* **fill in.** To substitute for. —*n.* **1.** A full supply: *eat one's fill.* **2.** Material used to fill holes or depressions in the ground. [< OE *fyllan.*]

fill·er (fĭl′ər) *n.* **1.** Something added in order to increase weight or size or to fill space. **2.** A material used to fill pores, cracks, or holes in a surface.

fil·lér (fĭl′ār′) *n.* See table at **currency.** [Hung.]

fil·let *n.* **1.** (fĭl′ĭt). A narrow strip of material, as a band or ribbon. **2.** (fĭ-lā′, fĭl′ā′). Also **fi·let.** A boneless piece of meat or fish. —*v.* **1.** fil·let·ed (fĭl′ĭt-tĭd), fil·let·ing (fĭl′ĭt-tĭng). To bind or decorate with or as with a fillet. **2.** fil·leted (fĭ-lād′, fĭl′ād′), fil·let·ing (fĭ-lā′ĭng, fĭl′ā′-ĭng). Also **fi·let.** To cut into fillets. [< Lat. *filum,* thread.]

fill·ing (fĭl′ĭng) *n.* **1.** Something used to fill a space or cavity: *a gold filling in a tooth.* **2.** An

edible mixture used to fill something: *pie filling.* **3.** The threads that cross the warp in weaving; weft.

filling station *n.* A gas station.

fil·lip (fĭl′əp) *n.* **1.** A snap of the fingers. **2.** An incentive; stimulus. [Imit.] —**fil′lip** *v.*

fil·ly (fĭl′ē) *n., pl.* **-lies.** A young female horse. [< ON *fylja.*]

film (fĭlm) *n.* **1.** A thin skin or membrane. **2.** A thin covering or coating. **3.** A thin sheet or strip of flexible cellulose material coated with a photosensitive emulsion, used to make photographic negatives or transparencies. **4. a.** A motion picture. **b.** Motion pictures as an art. —*v.* **1.** To cover with or as if with a film. **2.** To make a motion picture of. [< OE *filmen,* thin coating.] —**film′y** *adj.*

film·strip (fĭlm′strĭp′) *n.* A strip of film with photographs prepared for still projection one picture at a time.

fil·ter (fĭl′tər) *n.* **1.** A porous substance through which a liquid or gas is passed in order to remove unwanted components, esp. suspended material. **2.** A device that operates on electric currents, electromagnetic waves, sound waves, etc., in a way that allows waves of certain frequencies to pass while those of other frequencies are blocked. —*v.* **1.** To pass through a filter. **2.** To remove by passing through a filter. [< Med. Lat. *filtrum,* of Gmc. orig.] —**fil′ter·a·bil′i·ty** *n.* —**fil′ter·a·ble** or **fil′tra·ble** *adj.*

filter bed *n.* A layer of sand or gravel on the bottom of a reservoir or tank used to filter water or sewage.

filth (fĭlth) *n.* **1.** Foul or dirty matter. **2.** Corruption; foulness. **3.** Something that disgusts or offends, esp. obscenity. [< OE *fȳlth.*] —**filth′i·ness** *n.* —**filth′y** *adj.*

fil·trate (fĭl′trāt′) *v.* **-trat·ed, -trat·ing.** To pass through a filter. —*n.* The portion of material that has passed through a filter. [< Med. Lat. *filtrum,* filter.] —**fil·tra′tion** *n.*

fin (fĭn) *n.* **1.** One of the thin, external membranous swimming and balancing appendages extending from the body of a fish or other aquatic animal. **2.** Something resembling a fin. **3.** A flexible piece of rubber attached to each foot to give added propulsion while swimming. [< OE *finn.*]

fi·na·gle (fĭ-nā′gəl) *v.* **-gled, -gling.** *Informal.* To get or achieve by dubious or crafty methods; wangle. [Prob. < dial. *fainaigue,* to cheat.] —**fi·na′gler** *n.*

fi·nal (fī′nəl) *adj.* **1.** Coming at the end; concluding. **2.** Ultimate and definitive; decisive. **3.** Of or constituting an ultimate goal or purpose. —*n.* **1.** The last game in a series of games or a tournament. **2.** The last examination of an academic course. [< Lat. *finalis.*] —**fi·nal′i·ty** (fī-năl′ə-tē, fĭ-) *n.* —**fi′nal·ly** *adv.*

fi·na·le (fĭ-năl′ē, -nä′lē) *n.* The final section, esp. of a musical composition. [Ital.]

fi·nal·ist (fī′nə-lĭst) *n.* A contestant in the finals of a competition.

fi·nal·ize (fī′nə-līz′) *v.* **-ized, -iz·ing.** To put into final form. —**fi′nal·iz′er** *n.*

Usage: Many object to the use of *finalize* because it is associated with the language of bureaucracy. While there is no one word that is an exact synonym for *finalize,* those who wish to avoid this term can substitute an expression such as *complete, conclude, make final,* or *put into final form.*

fi·nance (fĭ-năns′, fī-, fī′năns′) *n.* **1.** The management of money and other assets. **2. fi-nances.** Money and other resources; funds. —*v.* **-nanced, -nanc-ing. 1.** To provide the funds or capital for. **2.** To furnish with on credit. [< OFr. *finer*, to pay ransom.] —**fi-nan'cial** *adj.* —**fi-nan'cial-ly** *adv.*

fin-an-cier (fĭn'ən-sîr', fī-năn'-, fī'nən-) *n.* One who deals in large-scale financial affairs. [Fr.]

finch (fĭnch) *n.* Any of various small birds with a short, stout bill. [< OE *finc.*]

find (fīnd) *v.* **found** (found), **find-ing. 1.** To come upon by accident or after a search. **2.** To attain: *found contentment at last.* **3.** To determine; ascertain. **4.** To consider; regard. **5.** To recover; regain. **6.** To declare as a verdict or conclusion. —*phrasal verb.* **find out.** To get information about something; ascertain. —*n.* **1.** An act of finding. **2.** An unexpectedly valuable discovery. [< OE *findan.*]

find-er (fīn'dər) *n.* **1.** One that finds. **2.** A lens on a camera that shows what will appear in a photograph.

finder's fee *n.* A fee paid to one who finds financial backing for or brings the principals together in a venture.

fin de siè-cle (făɴ' də sē-ĕk'lə) *adj.* Of or characteristic of the sophistication and decadence that marked the last part of the 19th cent. [Fr.]

find-ing (fīn'dĭng) *n.* **1.** The act or an example of discovering. **2. findings.** The results of an investigation.

fine¹ (fīn) *adj.* **fin-er, fin-est. 1.** Of superior quality, skill, or appearance. **2.** Most enjoyable; pleasant. **3.** Sharp: *a blade with a fine edge.* **4.** Consisting of extremely small particles: *fine dust.* **5.** Subtle or precise: *a fine shade of meaning.* **6.** Of refined manners; elegant. **7.** Having no clouds; clear: *a fine day.* **8.** *Informal.* Quite well; in satisfactory health. —*adv. Informal.* Very well: *doing fine.* [< Lat. *finis*, end.] —**fine'ly** *adv.* —**fine'ness** *n.*

fine² (fīn) *n.* A sum of money imposed as a penalty for an offense. —*v.* **fined, fin-ing.** To impose a fine on. [< Lat. *finis*, limit.]

fine arts *n.* The arts of painting, sculpture, and architecture.

fin-er-y (fī'nə-rē) *n., pl.* **-ies.** Fine clothes and ornaments.

fi-nesse (fĭ-nĕs') *n.* **1.** Delicacy and refinement of performance or execution: *played the nocturne with finesse.* **2.** Subtlety; tact. [< OFr. *fin*, fine.]

fin-ger (fĭng'gər) *n.* **1.** Any of the five digits of the hand. **2.** The part of a glove that fits over a finger. **3.** Something resembling a finger. —*v.* **1.** *Mus.* To play (an instrument) by using the fingers in a particular order. **2.** To handle or touch with the fingers. [< OE.]

fin-ger-board (fĭng'gər-bôrd', -bōrd') *n.* The part of a stringed instrument against which the strings are pressed in playing.

finger bowl *n.* A small bowl to hold water for rinsing the fingers at table.

fin-ger-ing (fĭng'gər-ĭng) *n.* Symbols on a musical score that indicate which fingers are to be used in playing.

fin-ger-ling (fĭng'gər-lĭng) *n.* A young or small fish.

fin-ger-nail (fĭng'gər-nāl') *n.* The thin sheet of

horny, transparent material that covers the dorsal tip of each finger.

fin-ger-print (fĭng'gər-prĭnt') *n.* An impression formed by the curves in the ridges of the skin on the tips of the fingers. —**fin'ger-print** *v.*

finger tip *n.* Also **fin-ger-tip** (fĭng'gər-tĭp'). The tip of a finger.

fin-i-al (fĭn'ē-əl) *n.* An ornamental projection or terminating part, as on an arch. [ME.]

fin-icky (fĭn'ĭ-kē) *adj.* Difficult to please; fussy. [Prob. ult. < FINE¹.] —**fin'ick-i-ness** *n.*

fi-nis (fĭn'ĭs, fī'nĭs) *n.* The end. [Lat.]

fin-ish (fĭn'ĭsh) *v.* **1.** To reach the end of. **2.** To bring to an end; complete. **3.** To consume all of; use up. **4.** To kill, destroy, or wear out completely. **5.** To give (a surface) a desired texture. —*n.* **1.** The final part or conclusion; end: *a close finish in the race.* **2.** Surface texture. **3.** Smoothness of execution. **4.** Polish or refinement in speech, manners, or comportment. [< Lat. *finire*, to complete.] —**fin'ish-er** *n.*

fi-nite (fī'nīt') *adj.* **1.** Having bounds; limited. **2.** Neither infinite nor infinitesimal. [< Lat. *finire*, limit.] —**fi'nite-ly** *adv.* —**fi'nite-ness** *n.*

fink (fĭngk). *Slang.* —*n.* **1.** An informer. **2.** An undesirable person. —*v.* To inform against another. [Orig. unknown.]

Finn (fĭn) *n.* A native or inhabitant of Finland.

fin-nan had-die (fĭn'ən hăd'ē) *n.* Smoked haddock. [Obs. *findhorn haddock.*]

Finn-ish (fĭn'ĭsh) *adj.* Of or pertaining to Finland, its language, or its people. —*n.* The Finno-Ugric language of the Finns.

Fin-no-U-gric (fĭn'ō-ōō'grĭk, -yōō'-) *n.* A subfamily of the Uralic language family that includes Finnish, Hungarian, and other languages of eastern Europe and northwestern USSR. —**Fin'no-U'gric** *adj.*

fin-ny (fĭn'ē) *adj.* **-ni-er, -ni-est. 1.** Having or resembling fins. **2.** Of or pertaining to fish.

fiord (fyôrd, fyōrd) *n.* Var. of **fjord.**

fir (fûr) *n.* **1.** An evergreen tree with flat needles and erect cones. **2.** The wood of a fir tree. [< OE *fyrh.*]

fire (fīr) *n.* **1.** A rapid, self-sustaining chemical reaction that releases light and heat, esp. the burning of something with oxygen. **2.** A destructive burning: *insured the house against fire.* **3.** Great enthusiasm; ardor. **4.** The discharge of firearms. —*v.* **fired, fir-ing. 1.** To ignite. **2.** To maintain a fire in. **3.** To bake in a kiln. **4.** To arouse the emotions of. **5.** To detonate or discharge (a weapon). **6.** *Informal.* To hurl suddenly and forcefully. **7.** To discharge from a job; dismiss. —*idiom.* **play with fire.** To take part in a dangerous or risky situation. **under fire.** Subjected to critical attack or censure. [< OE *fȳr.*]

fire-arm (fīr'ärm') *n.* A weapon capable of firing a missile, esp. a pistol or rifle.

fire-ball (fīr'bôl') *n.* **1.** A brilliantly burning sphere. **2.** An exceptionally bright meteor. **3.** A highly luminous, intensely hot spherical cloud generated by a nuclear explosion. **4.** *Informal.* An energetic person.

fire-box (fīr'bŏks') *n.* **1.** A chamber, as a furnace, in which fuel is burned. **2.** A box containing a device for sounding a fire alarm.

ă pat ā pay â care ä father ĕ pet ē be ĭ pit ī tie î pier ŏ pot ō toe ô paw, for oi noise ōō took
ōō boot ou out th thin th this ŭ cut û urge yōō abuse zh vision ə about, item, edible, gallop, circus

fire-brand (fīr′brănd′) n. 1. A piece of burning wood. 2. One who stirs up trouble.

fire-break (fīr′brāk′) n. A strip of cleared or plowed land used to stop the spread of a fire.

fire-brick (fīr′brĭk′) n. A refractory brick made of fire clay, used for lining furnaces, chimneys, or fireplaces.

fire-bug (fīr′bŭg′) n. Informal. One who deliberately sets fires; arsonist.

fire clay n. A type of heat-resistant clay used esp. in the making of firebricks.

fire-crack-er (fīr′krăk′ər) n. A small explosive charge in a cylinder of heavy paper, used to make noise, as at celebrations.

fire-damp (fīr′dămp′) n. A combustible gas, chiefly methane, that occurs in coal mines and forms an explosive mixture with air.

fire engine n. A large truck that carries firefighters and equipment to a fire.

fire escape n. An outside stairway for emergency exit in the event of fire.

fire extinguisher n. A portable apparatus containing chemicals that can be discharged in a jet to extinguish a small fire.

fire-fight-er (fīr′fī′tər) n. One who fights fires, esp. for a living.

fire-flood (fīr′flŭd′) n. A procedure for extracting additional oil from producing wells by injecting compressed air and burning some of the oil from the petroleum reservoir and burning some of the fuel.

fire-fly (fīr′flī′) n. A nocturnal beetle with luminous abdominal organs that produce a flashing light.

fire-house (fīr′hous′) n. A fire station.

fire irons pl.n. Equipment used to tend a fireplace, including a shovel, a poker, and tongs.

fire-man (fīr′mən) n. 1. A firefighter. 2. One who tends fires; stoker.

fire-place (fīr′plās′) n. An open recess for holding a fire at the base of a chimney; hearth.

fire-plug (fīr′plŭg′) n. A pipe from which water may be drawn for use in extinguishing a fire; hydrant.

fire-pow-er (fīr′pou′ər) n. The capacity, as of a military unit, for discharging fire.

fire-proof (fīr′prŏŏf′) adj. Capable of withstanding fire. —v. To make fireproof.

fire-side (fīr′sīd′) n. 1. The area around a fireplace. 2. Home.

fire station n. A building for fire equipment and firefighters.

fire tower n. A tower in which a lookout for fires is posted.

fire-trap (fīr′trăp′) n. A building likely to catch fire easily or difficult to escape from in the event of fire.

fire wall n. A fireproof wall used in buildings and machinery to prevent the spread of a fire.

fire-wood (fīr′wŏŏd′) n. Wood used as fuel.

fire-works (fīr′wûrks′) pl.n. 1. Explosives and combustibles used to produce lights, smoke, and noise for entertainment. 2. An exciting or dramatic display: *musical fireworks*.

firing line n. 1. The line of positions from which gunfire is directed against a target. 2. The foremost position of an activity.

firing pin n. The part of the bolt of a firearm that strikes the primer and explodes the charge of the projectile.

firm¹ (fûrm) adj. **-er, -est.** 1. Unyielding to pressure; solid. 2. Exhibiting the tone and resiliency characteristic of healthy tissue: *firm muscles.* 3. Securely fixed in place. 4. Constant; steadfast. 5. Not changing; fixed: *a firm belief.* 6. Strong and sure: *a firm grasp.* 7. Showing resolution or determination. —adv. Without wavering; resolutely. —v. To make or become firm. [< Lat. *firmus.*] —**firm′ly** adv. —**firm′ness** n.

firm² (fûrm) n. A commercial partnership of two or more persons. [< Ital. *firmare,* to ratify by signature, ult. < Lat. *firmus,* solid.]

fir-ma-ment (fûr′mə-mənt) n. The vault or expanse of the heavens; sky. [< Lat. *firmamentum,* support.]

first (fûrst) adj. 1. Coming or located before all others. 2. Prior to all others; earliest. 3. Foremost in importance or quality. —adv. 1. Before or above all others in time or rank. 2. For the first time. 3. Preferably; rather. —n. 1. The ordinal number that matches the number 1 in a series. 2. The one coming, occurring, or ranking first. 3. The beginning; outset: *from the first.* 4. The lowest forward gear in an automotive vehicle. 5. The winning position in a contest. [< OE *fyrst.*]
Syns: first, initial, maiden, original, primary, prime adj.

first aid n. Emergency treatment administered to injured or sick persons.

first base n. 1. *Baseball.* The first of the bases in the infield, counterclockwise from home plate. 2. *Informal.* The first stage in a procedure. —**first baseman** n.

first-born (fûrst′bôrn′) adj. First in order of birth. —n. The first-born child.

first class n. 1. The first, highest, or best group of a specified category. 2. A class of mail sealed against inspection. —**first′-class** adj. & adv.

first-de-gree burn (fûrst′dĭ-grē′) n. A mild burn that produces redness of the skin.

first-hand (fûrst′hănd′) adj. Received from the original source. —**first′hand′** adv.

first lieutenant n. A military officer ranking above a second lieutenant.

first-ly (fûrst′lē) adv. In the first place.

first mate n. A ship's officer ranking immediately below the captain.

first person n. A set of grammatical forms designating the speaker of the sentence in which they appear.

first-rate (fûrst′rāt′) adj. Foremost in importance, rank, or quality. —**first′-rate′** adv.

first sergeant n. In the U.S. Army, the highest-ranking noncommissioned officer of a company or other military unit.

first-string (fûrst′strĭng′) adj. Being a regular performer as distinguished from a substitute.

firth (fûrth) n. A narrow inlet of the sea. [< ON *fjordhr.*]

fis-cal (fĭs′kəl) adj. 1. Of or pertaining to the public treasury or finances. 2. Of or pertaining to finances in general. [< Lat. *fiscus,* treasury.] —**fis′cal-ly** adv.

fish (fĭsh) n., pl. **fish** or **fish-es.** 1. Any of numerous cold-blooded aquatic vertebrates characteristically having fins, gills, and a streamlined body. 2. The edible flesh of a fish. —v. 1. To catch or try to catch fish. 2. To look for something by feeling one's way; grope. 3. To seek something indirectly: *fish for compliments.* [< OE *fisc.*] —**fish′er** n. —**fish′ing** n.

fish-bowl (fĭsh′bōl′) n. 1. A bowl in which live fish are kept. 2. An activity or position that is open to public view.

fish-er-man (fĭsh′ər-mən) n. 1. One who

fishes as an occupation or sport. **2.** A commercial fishing vessel.

fish·er·y (fĭsh'ə-rē) n., pl. **-ies. 1.** The industry of catching fish. **2.** A fishing ground.

fish-hook (fĭsh'hŏŏk') n. A barbed hook for catching fish.

fishing rod n. A rod used with a line for catching fish.

fish ladder n. A steplike series of pools by which fish can pass around a dam.

fish-meal (fĭsh'mēl') n. Ground, dried fish used as animal feed and fertilizer.

fish story n. *Informal.* An implausible and boastful story. [< stories of fishermen who exaggerate the size of their catch.]

fish-wife (fĭsh'wīf') n. **1.** A woman who sells fish. **2.** A coarse, abusive woman.

fish·y (fĭsh'ē) adj. **-i-er, -i-est. 1.** Resembling or suggestive of fish. **2.** Suspicious or questionable. —**fish'i-ness** n.

fis·sile (fĭs'əl, -īl') adj. **1.** Capable of being split. **2.** *Physics.* Fissionable, esp. by neutrons of all energies. [< Lat. *fissus,* p.p. of *findere,* to split.] —**fis·sil'i·ty** (fĭ-sĭl'ĭ-tē) n.

fis·sion (fĭsh'ən) n. **1.** The act or process of splitting into parts. **2.** *Physics.* A nuclear reaction in which an atomic nucleus splits into fragments, generating approx. 100 million to several hundred million electron volts of energy. —**fis·sion·a·ble** adj.

fis·sure (fĭsh'ər) n. A narrow crack, usu. of considerable size. —**fis'sure** v.

fist (fĭst) n. The hand closed tightly, with the fingers bent against the palm. [< OE *fȳst.*]

fist·ful (fĭst'fŏŏl') n. A handful.

fist·i·cuffs (fĭs'tĭ-kŭfs') pl.n. A fist fight.

fis·tu·la (fĭs'chŏŏ-lə, -chə-) n., pl. **-las** or **-lae** (-lē'). An abnormal bodily duct or passage from an abscess, cavity, or hollow organ. [< Lat.] —**fis'tu·lous** adj.

fit¹ (fĭt) v. **fit·ted** or **fit, fit·ting. 1.** To be the proper size and shape (for). **2.** To be suitable (to). **3.** To make suitable; adjust. **4.** To equip; outfit: *fit out a ship.* **5.** To provide a place or time for: *The doctor can fit you in this afternoon.* —adj. **fit·ter, fit·test. 1.** Suited or acceptable for a given circumstance or purpose. **2.** Appropriate; proper. **3.** Physically sound; healthy. —n. The manner in which something fits: *a good fit.* [ME *fitten,* to be suitable.] —**fit'ly** adv. —**fit'ness** n. —**fit'ter** n.

Usage: Either *fitted* or *fit* is correct as the past tense of *fit: The suit fitted* (or *fit*) *her beautifully.* In the sense of "to cause to fit," only *fitted* is used as the past tense: *The tailor fitted* (not *fit*) *the suit in a few minutes.*

fit² (fĭt) n. **1.** *Med.* **a.** A sudden, acute attack of a disease or disorder. **b.** A convulsion. **2.** A sudden outburst: *a fit of jealousy.* **3.** A sudden period of vigorous activity. [ME, hardship.]

fitch (fĭch) n. The fur of the Old World polecat. [ME *fiche.*]

fit·ful (fĭt'fəl) adj. Intermittent; irregular. —**fit'ful·ly** adv. —**fit'ful·ness** n.

fit·ting (fĭt'ĭng) n. **1.** The act of trying on clothes for fit. **2.** A small accessory part. —adj. Suitable; appropriate. —**fit'ting·ly** adv. —**fit'ting·ness** n.

five (fīv) n. The cardinal number equal to the sum of 4 + 1. [< OE *fīf.*] —**five** adj. & pron.

fix (fĭks) v. **1.** To place or fasten securely. **2.** To put into a stable or unalterable form, as: **a.** To make a substance nonvolatile or solid. **b.** To convert (nitrogen) into stable, biologically assimilable compounds. **c.** To prevent discoloration of (a photographic image) by washing or coating with a chemical preservative. **3.** To direct (e.g. the gaze) steadily. **4.** To establish definitely; settle: *fix a time.* **5.** To ascribe; place: *fix blame.* **6.** To rectify; adjust. **7.** To set right; repair. **8.** To make ready; put together; prepare. **9.** *Informal.* To take revenge upon; get even with. **10.** To prearrange the outcome of (a contest) by unlawful means. —n. **1.** A difficult or embarrassing position. **2.** The position, as of a ship or aircraft, as determined by observations or radio. **3.** An instance of collusion to predetermine a result. **4.** *Slang.* A dose of a narcotic. [< Lat. *fixus,* p.p. of *figere,* to fasten.] —**fix'a·ble** adj. —**fix'er** n.

fix·a·tion (fĭk-sā'shən) n. A strong, usu. unhealthy attachment or interest. —**fix'ate'** v.

fix·a·tive (fĭk'sə-tĭv) n. A substance used to fix or stabilize. —**fix'a·tive** adj.

fixed (fĭkst) adj. **1.** Firmly in position; stationary. **2.** Not subject to change or variation; constant. **3.** Firmly held in the mind: *a fixed notion.* **4.** *Chem.* **a.** Nonvolatile: *fixed oils.* **b.** In a stable combined form. —**fix'ed·ly** (fĭk'sĭd-lē) adv. —**fix'ed·ness** (-sĭd-nĭs) n.

fix·ings (fĭk'sĭngz) pl.n. *Informal.* Accessories; trimmings: *a big meal with all the fixings.*

fix·i·ty (fĭk'sĭ-tē) n., pl. **-ties.** The quality or condition of being fixed; stability.

fix·ture (fĭks'chər) n. **1.** Something installed or fixed as a part of a larger system. **2.** One considered to be permanently established or fixed. [< LLat. *fixura.*]

fizz (fĭz) n. A hissing or bubbling sound. [Imit.] —**fizz** v.

fiz·zle (fĭz'əl) v. **-zled, -zling. 1.** To make a hissing or sputtering sound. **2.** To fail or die out, esp. after a hopeful beginning. —n. A failure. [Prob. < obs. *fist,* to break wind.]

fjord or **fiord** (fyôrd, fyōrd) n. A long, narrow inlet of the sea between steep cliffs and slopes. [< ON *fjördhr.*]

fjord

flab·ber·gast (flăb'ər-găst') v. To overwhelm with astonishment; astound. [Orig. unknown.]

flab·by (flăb'ē) adj. **-bi·er, -bi·est. 1.** Lacking firmness; loose and soft. **2.** Lacking force;

feeble. [< *flappy*, tending to flap < FLAP.] **—flab'bi-ly** adv. **—flab'bi-ness** n.

flac-cid (flăk'sĭd, flăs'ĭd) adj. Soft and limp. [< Lat. *flaccus*.] **—flac-cid'i-ty** n. **—flac'cid-ly** adv.

flac-on (flăk'ən, -ŏn') n. A small stoppered bottle. [< LLat. *flasco*, flask.]

flag¹ (flăg) n. 1. A piece of cloth of individual size, color, and design, used as a symbol, signal, or emblem. 2. Something resembling a flag in function or appearance. —v. **flagged, flag-ging.** 1. To mark with a flag. 2. To signal with or as if with a flag. [Orig. unknown.]

flag² (flăg) n. A plant, such as an iris, having long bladelike leaves. [ME *flagge*, reed.]

flag³ (flăg) v. **flagged, flag-ging.** 1. To hang limply; droop. 2. To decline in vigor or strength; weaken. [Orig. unknown.]

flag⁴ (flăg) n. Flagstone, slab of stone. [< ON *flaga*, slab of stone.]

flag-el-late (flăj'ə-lāt') v. **-lat-ed, -lat-ing.** To whip or flog; scourge. [Lat. *flagellare*.] **—flag-el-la'tion** n.

flag-on (flăg'ən) n. A large vessel for liquids that has a handle and spout. [< LLat. *flasco*, bottle.]

flag-pole (flăg'pōl') n. A pole for displaying a flag.

fla-grant (flā'grənt) adj. Conspicuously bad; shocking. [< Lat. *flagrare*, to burn.] **—fla'gran-cy** or **fla'grance** n. **—fla'grant-ly** adv.

flag-ship (flăg'shĭp') n. A ship bearing the flag of a fleet or squadron commander.

flag-staff (flăg'stăf') n. A flagpole.

flag-stone (flăg'stōn') n. A flat, evenly layered paving stone.

flail (flāl) n. A hand tool for threshing grain. —v. To beat or thrash with or as if with a flail. [< Lat. *flagrum*, whip.]

flair (flâr) n. 1. A natural talent or aptitude. 2. Instinctive discernment; keenness. [< Lat. *fragrare*, to emit a smell.]

flak (flăk) n. a. Antiaircraft artillery. b. The bursting shells fired from such artillery. 2. *Slang.* Excessive criticism. [G.]

flake (flāk) n. A flat, thin piece. —v. **flaked, flak-ing.** To form into or come off in flakes. [ME, of Scand. orig.]

flak-y (flā'kē) adj. **-i-er, -i-est.** 1. Made of or resembling flakes. 2. Forming or tending to form flakes. 3. *Informal.* Eccentric; odd. **—flak'i-ly** adv. **—flak'i-ness** n.

flam-bé (fläm-bā', flän-) adj. Served flaming in ignited liquor: *steak flambé.* [Fr., p.p. of *flamber*, to flame.] **—flam-bé** v.

flam-boy-ant (flăm-boi'ənt) adj. 1. Highly elaborate; showy. 2. Richly colored; vivid. [< OFr. *flamboyer*, to blaze.] **—flam-boy'ance** or **flam-boy'an-cy** n. **—flam-boy'ant-ly** adv.

flame (flām) n. 1. The zone of burning gases and fine suspended particles that forms as a result of fire. 2. A condition of active combustion. 3. Something flamelike in appearance or intensity. 4. A violent or intense passion. 5. *Informal.* A sweetheart. —v. **flamed, flam-ing.** 1. To burn with a flame; blaze. 2. To break into or as if into flames. [< Lat. *flamma*.]

fla-men-co (flə-mĕng'kō) n. A dance style of the Andalusian Gypsies characterized by forceful often improvised rhythms. [Sp., Flemish.]

flame-out (flām'out') n. The failure of a jet aircraft engine in flight.

flame thrower n. A weapon that projects burning fuel in a steady stream.

fla-min-go (flə-mĭng'gō) n., pl. **-gos** or **-goes.** A large wading bird of tropical regions, with reddish or pinkish plumage, long legs, and a long, flexible neck. [Prob. < OProv. *flamenc*.]

flam-ma-ble (flăm'ə-bəl) adj. Capable of igniting easily and burning rapidly. [< Lat. *flamma*, flame.] **—flam'ma-bil'i-ty** n.

flange (flănj) n. A protruding rim or edge, as on a wheel, used to strengthen an object or hold it in place. [Prob. < *flanch*, to widen out.]

flank (flăngk) n. 1. The fleshy section of the side between the last rib and the hip. 2. A cut of meat from the flank section of an animal. 3. A side or lateral part. 4. *Mil.* The right or left side of a formation. —v. 1. To protect or guard the flank of. 2. To attack or maneuver around the flank of. 3. To be placed or situated at the flank of. [< OFr. *flanc*, of Gmc. orig.]

flan-nel (flăn'əl) n. 1. A soft woven cloth of wool or a wool blend. 2. **flannels** Trousers or underclothing made of flannel. [ME.]

flan-nel-ette (flăn'ə-lĕt') n. A soft, napped cotton cloth.

flap (flăp) v. **flapped, flap-ping.** 1. To move up and down, as wings; beat. 2. To swing or sway loosely. 3. To hit with something broad and flat. —n. 1. A flat, loose piece attached along one side, as on an envelope. 2. A hinged section on the rear edge of an aircraft wing, used primarily to increase lift or drag. 3. The sound or action of flapping. 4. A blow given with something flat. 5. *Slang.* A condition of nervous excitement or distress. [ME *flappen*.]

flap-jack (flăp'jăk') n. A pancake.

flap-per (flăp'ər) n. 1. One that flaps. 2. *Informal.* A young woman of the 1920's who flaunted her disdain for conventional dress and behavior.

flare (flâr) v. **flared, flar-ing.** 1. To burn with a bright, wavering light. 2. To erupt into sudden or intense emotion or activity: *Tempers flared.* 3. To expand outward, as a skirt. —n. 1. A brief, wavering blaze. 2. A device that produces a bright flame for signaling or illumination. 3. An outbreak, as of emotion or activity. 4. An expanding contour. [Orig. unknown.]

flare-up (flâr'ŭp') n. A sudden outbreak, as of flame or resentment.

flash (flăsh) v. 1. To occur or emerge suddenly in or as if in flame. 2. To appear or cause to appear briefly. 3. To be lighted intermittently; sparkle. 4. To cause (light) to appear in intermittent bursts. 5. To move rapidly. 6. To signal with light. 7. To communicate (information) at great speed. 8. To display ostentatiously; flaunt. —n. 1. A sudden brief, intense display of light. 2. A sudden, brief display, as of a mental faculty. 3. An instant: *in a flash.* 4. A brief news dispatch or transmission. 5. a. Instantaneous illumination for photography. b. A device used to produce such illumination. [ME *flashen*, to splash.]

flash-back (flăsh'băk') n. The interruption of a narrative to show or tell about an incident from the past.

flash bulb n. A glass bulb filled with finely shredded metal foil that is ignited by electricity to produce a bright flash of light for taking photographs.

flash-cube (flăsh'kyōōb') n. A small rotating cube that contains four flash bulbs.

flash flood n. A sudden, violent flood.

flash gun n. A portable device used in photography to hold a flash bulb and fire it electrically.

flash lamp n. An electric lamp that produces a bright light for use in photography.

flash-light (flăsh'līt') n. **1.** A small, portable lamp consisting of a bulb and dry batteries. **2.** A brief, brilliant flood of light from a photographic lamp.

flash point n. The lowest temperature at which the vapor of a combustible liquid can be made to ignite.

flash-y (flăsh'ē) adj. **-i-er, -i-est. 1.** Momentarily or superficially brilliant. **2.** Showy; gaudy. **—flash'i-ly** adv. **—flash'i-ness** n.

flask (flăsk) n. A small, flat, bottle-shaped container. [< LLat. flasca.]

flat¹ (flăt) adj. **flat-ter, flat-test. 1. a.** Having no curves. **b.** Having a smooth, even, level surface. **2.** Shallow; low: a flat box. **3.** Lying prone; prostrate. **4.** Unequivocal; absolute: a flat refusal. **5.** Fixed: a flat rate. **6.** Uninteresting; dull; vapid. **7.** Lacking zest; flavorless. **8.** Deflated, as a tire. **9.** Mus. **a.** Being one half step lower than the corresponding natural key. **b.** Being below the intended pitch. **—adv. 1.** Horizontally; level with the ground. **2.** So as to be flat. **3.** Directly; completely. **4.** Mus. Below the intended pitch. **—n. 1.** A flat object, surface, or part. **2.** Often **flats.** A stretch of level ground. **3.** A shallow frame or box for seeds or seedlings. **4.** A deflated tire. **5. flats.** Women's shoes with flat heels. **6.** Mus. **a.** A sign (♭) affixed to a note to indicate that it is to be lowered by a half step. **b.** A note that is lowered a half step. **—v. flat-ted, flat-ting. 1.** To make flat; flatten. **2.** Mus. **a.** To lower (a note) a half step. **b.** To sing or play below the proper pitch. [< ON flatr.] **—flat'ly** adv. **—flat'ness** n.

flat² (flăt) n. An apartment on one floor. [< OE flet, inner part of a house.]

flat-bed (flăt'bĕd') n. A truck or trailer having a rear platform without sides.

flat-boat (flăt'bōt') n. A flat-bottomed barge for transporting freight.

flatboat

flat-car (flăt'kär') n. A railroad freight car without sides or roof.

flat-fish (flăt'fĭsh') n. A fish, as a flounder or sole, having a flattened body with the eyes on the upper side.

flat-foot (flăt'fŏŏt') n. **1.** pl. **-feet** (-fēt'). A condition in which the arch of the foot is flattened so that the entire sole makes contact with the ground. **2.** pl. **-foots.** Slang. A policeman. **—flat'-foot'ed** adj.

flat-i-ron (flăt'ī'ərn) n. A heated iron for pressing clothes.

flat-ten (flăt'n) v. To make or become flat or flatter. **—flat'ten-er** n.

flat-ter (flăt'ər) v. **1.** To compliment excessively and often insincerely. **2.** To please or gratify. **3.** To portray too favorably. **4.** To persuade (oneself) that something one wants to believe is the case. [< OFr. flater, of Gmc. orig.] **—flat'ter-er** n. **—flat'ter-ing** adj.

flat-ter-y (flăt'ə-rē) n. **1.** The act or practice of flattering. **2.** Insincere praise.

flat-top (flăt'tŏp') n. An aircraft carrier.

flat-u-lent (flăch'ə-lənt) adj. **1.** Having or causing excessive gas in the digestive tract. **2.** Inflated with self-importance; pompous. [< Lat. flatus, a breaking wind.] **—flat'u-lence** n. **—flat'u-lent-ly** adv.

flat-ware (flăt'wâr') n. **1.** Tableware that is fairly flat and formed usu. of a single piece, as plates. **2.** Table utensils such as knives, forks, and spoons.

flaunt (flônt) v. To exhibit ostentatiously; show off. [Orig. unknown.] **—flaunt'ing-ly** adv.

Usage: Flaunt and flout are often confused. Flaunt means "to exhibit ostentatiously": She flaunted her diamonds. Flout means "to defy openly": She flouted the proprieties.

flau-tist (flô'tĭst, flou'-) n. A flutist. [< OProv. flaut, flute.]

fla-vor (flā'vər). Also chiefly Brit. **fla-vour.** **—n. 1.** Distinctive taste; savor. **2.** A seasoning; flavoring. **3.** A characteristic quality. **—v.** To give flavor to. [< Lat. flare, to blow.] **—fla'vor-ful** adj. **—fla'vor-less** adj.

fla-vor-ing (flā'vər-ĭng) n. A substance that imparts flavor, as an extract or spice.

flaw (flô) n. **1.** An imperfection; defect. **2.** A crack or blemish. **—v.** To make or become defective. [< ON flaga, slab of stone.] **—flaw'less** adj. **—flaw'less-ly** adv. **—flaw'less-ness** n.

flax (flăks) n. **1.** Any of several plants with blue flowers and slender stems from which a fine fiber is obtained. **2.** The textile fiber obtained from flax. [< OE fleax.]

flax-en (flăk'sən) adj. **1.** Made of or resembling flax. **2.** Having the pale-yellow color of flax fiber.

flay (flā) v. **1.** To strip off the skin of. **2.** To criticize or scold harshly. [< OE flēan.] **—flay'er** n.

flea (flē) n. Any of various small, wingless, bloodsucking insects that are parasitic on warm-blooded animals. [< OE flēah.]

flea market n. A usu. open market selling antiques, secondhand goods, and curios.

fleck (flĕk) n. **1.** A tiny mark or spot. **2.** A small bit or flake. **—v.** To spot or streak. [Prob. < ON flekkr, spotted.]

fledg-ling or **fledge-ling** (flĕj'lĭng) n. **1.** A young bird that has recently acquired its flight feathers. **2.** A young and inexperienced person. [Prob. < OE flycge, feathered.]

flee (flē) v. **fled** (flĕd), **flee-ing. 1.** To run away, as from trouble or danger. **2.** To pass swiftly; vanish. [< OE *flēon.*] **—flē'er** n.

fleece (flēs) n. **1.** The coat of wool of a sheep or similar animal. **2.** A soft, woolly covering or fabric. —v. **fleeced, fleec-ing. 1.** To shear the fleece from. **2.** To swindle. [< OE *flēos.*] **—fleec'er** n. **—fleec'y** adj.

fleet¹ (flēt) n. **1.** A group of warships operating together under one command. **2.** A group of vehicles owned or operated as a unit. [< OE *flēot.*]

fleet² (flēt) adj. **-er, -est.** Moving swiftly; rapid or nimble. [Prob. < OE *flēotan,* to float.] **—fleet'ly** adv. **—fleet'ness** n.

Flem-ish (flĕm'ĭsh) adj. Of or pertaining to Flanders, its inhabitants, or their language. —n. The Germanic language of Flanders.

flesh (flĕsh) n. **1.** The soft tissue of the body, esp. the skeletal muscles. **2.** The meat of animals as distinguished from the edible tissue of fish or fowl. **3.** The pulpy part of a fruit or vegetable. **4.** The body as distinguished from the mind or soul. **5.** Mankind in general; humanity. —v. To fill out (a structure or framework). **—idioms. flesh and blood.** A blood relative or relatives. **in the flesh.** In person. [< OE *flæsc.*]

flesh-ly (flĕsh'lē) adj. **-i-er, -i-est. 1.** Physical; corporeal. **2.** Carnal; sensual. **3.** Not spiritual; worldly. **—flesh'li-ness** n.

flesh-y (flĕsh'ē) adj. **-i-er, -i-est. 1.** Of or resembling flesh. **2.** Fat; plump. **3.** Firm and pulpy, as fruit. **—flesh'i-ness** n.

fleur-de-lis (flûr'də-lē', flōōr'-) n., pl. **fleurs-de-lis** (flûr'də-lēz', flōōr'-). A heraldic device consisting of a stylized three-petaled iris. [< OFr. *flor de lis,* flower of the lily.]

flew (flōō) v. p.t. of **fly¹.**

flex (flĕks) v. **1.** To bend. **2.** To contract (a muscle). [< Lat. *flexus,* p.p. of *flectere,* to bend.]

flex-i-ble (flĕk'sə-bəl) adj. **1.** Capable of being flexed; pliable. **2.** Capable of or responsive to change; adaptable. **—flex'i-bil'i-ty** n. **—flex'i-bly** adv.

Syns: flexible, elastic, plastic, pliable, pliant, resilient, supple adj.

flex-time (flĕks'tīm') n. Also **flex-i-time** (flĕk'sə-tīm'). An arrangement by which employees set their own work schedules. [FLEX(IBLE) + TIME.]

flex-ure (flĕk'shər) n. A bend, curve, or turn.

flick¹ (flĭk) n. **1.** A light, quick blow or stroke. —v. **1.** To strike with a flick. **2.** To cause to move with a light flick; snap. [Imit.]

flick² (flĭk) n. Slang. A motion picture. [< FLICKER.]

flick-er (flĭk'ər) v. **1.** To give off irregular, intermittent light. **2.** To move waveringly; flutter. —n. **1.** A wavering or unsteady light. **2.** A brief or slight sensation. [< OE *flicerian,* to flutter.]

flied (flīd) v. p.t. & p.p. of **fly¹** (sense 7).

fli-er (flī'ər) n. Also **fly-er. 1.** One that flies, esp. a pilot. **2.** A daring financial venture. **3.** A circular for mass distribution.

flight¹ (flīt) n. **1.** The act or process of flying. **2.** A scheduled airline trip. **3.** A group, esp. of birds or aircraft, flying together. **4.** A swift passage or movement: *the flight of time.* **5.** An effort or display that surpasses the usual bounds: *a flight of imagination.* **6.** A series of stairs rising from one landing to another. [< OE *flyht.*]

flight² (flīt) n. An act of running away. [ME.]

flight-less (flīt'lĭs) adj. Incapable of flying, as certain birds.

flight-y (flī'tē) adj. **-i-er, -i-est. 1.** Capricious or impulsive. **2.** Irresponsible; silly. **3.** Easily excited. **—flight'i-ness** n.

flim-flam (flĭm'flăm') n. Informal. **1.** Nonsense. **2.** A deception; swindle. [Prob. of Scand. orig.] **—flim'flam'** v.

flim-sy (flĭm'zē) adj. **-si-er, -si-est. 1.** Lacking solidity or strength. **2.** Implausible; unconvincing. [Orig. unknown.] **—flim'si-ness** n.

flinch (flĭnch) v. To draw back or away, as from pain or fear. [OFr. *flenchir.*] **—flinch** n. **—flinch'er** n.

fling (flĭng) v. **flung** (flŭng), **fling-ing. 1.** To throw or move suddenly or forcefully. **2.** To throw (oneself) into some activity with abandon and energy. **3.** To toss aside; discard. —n. **1.** A toss; throw. **2.** A brief period of indulging one's impulses; spree. **3.** Informal. A brief attempt. [ME *flingen,* of Scand. orig.]

flint (flĭnt) n. **1.** A very hard, fine-grained quartz that sparks when struck with steel. **2.** A small solid cylinder of a spark-producing alloy. [< OE.] **—flint'y** adj.

flint-lock (flĭnt'lŏk') n. **1.** An obsolete gunlock in which a flint sparks the charge. **2.** A firearm with a flintlock.

flintlock

flip (flĭp) v. **flipped, flip-ping. 1.** To toss or turn with a light, quick motion. **2.** To strike with a light, quick blow; flick. **3.** Slang. **a.** To go crazy. **b.** To react strongly and esp. enthusiastically. —n. A quick, turning movement. —adj. **flip-per, flip-pest.** Informal. Disrespectful; impertinent. [Orig. unknown.]

flip-pant (flĭp'ənt) adj. Casually disrespectful; pert. [Prob. < FLIP.] **—flip'pan-cy** n. **—flip'pant-ly** adv.

flip-per (flĭp'ər) n. **1.** A wide, flat limb, as of a seal, adapted for swimming. **2.** A wide, flat, finlike rubber shoe used in swimming.

flirt (flûrt) v. **1.** To play lightly or mockingly at courtship. **2.** To deal casually or coyly; toy: *flirt with danger.* **3.** To move jerkily. —n. **1.** One given to flirting. **2.** An abrupt jerking movement. [Orig. unknown.] **—flir-ta'tion** n. **—flir-ta'tious** adj. **—flir-ta'tious-ly** adv. **—flir-ta'tious-ness** n.

flit (flĭt) v. **flit-ted, flit-ting.** To move quickly and nimbly; dart. [< ON *flytja.*] **—flit'ter** n.

float (flōt) v. **1. a.** To remain or cause to remain suspended in or on the surface of a liquid without sinking. **b.** To be or cause to be suspended unsupported in space. **2.** To move from position to position at random; drift. **3.** To move easily and lightly as if suspended. **4.** To release (a security) for sale. —n. **1.** Something that floats. **2.** A small floating object on a fishing line. **3.** A large, flat vehicle bearing an exhibit in a parade. **4.** A soft drink with ice cream floating in it. [< OE *flotian*.] —**float′er** *n.*

flock (flŏk) *n.* **1.** A group of animals, as birds or sheep, that live, travel, or feed together. **2.** A group of people under the leadership of one person. **3.** A large crowd or number. —*v.* To congregate or travel in a flock or crowd. [< OE *floc*.]

floe (flō) *n.* A large, flat mass of floating ice. [Prob. < ON *flō*, layer.]

flog (flŏg, flôg) *v.* **flogged, flog·ging.** To beat severely with a whip or rod. [Perh. < Lat. *flagrum*, whip.] —**flog′ger** *n.*

flood (flŭd) *n.* **1.** An overflowing of water onto normally dry land. **2.** An abundant flow or outpouring: *a flood of applications.* **3.** Flood. The universal deluge recorded in the Old Testament. —*v.* **1.** To cover or submerge with a flood; inundate. **2.** To fill with an abundance or excess. [< OE *flōd*.]

flood-gate (flŭd′gāt′) *n.* A gate used to control the flow of a body of water.

flood-light (flŭd′līt′) *n.* **1.** Artificial light in an intensely bright and broad beam. **2.** A unit that produces such a beam. —*v.* To illuminate with a floodlight.

flood plain *n.* A plain bordering a river, subject to flooding.

floor (flôr, flōr) *n.* **1.** The surface of a room on which one stands. **2.** The ground or lowermost surface, as of a forest or ocean. **3.** The lower part of a room, as a legislative chamber, where business is conducted. **4. a.** The right to address an assembly. **b.** The body of assembly members. **5.** A story of a building. —*v.* **1.** To provide with a floor. **2.** To knock down. **3.** To stun; overwhelm. [< OE *flōr*.]

floor leader *n.* A member of a legislative body chosen by fellow party members to be in charge of the party's activities on the floor.

floor show *n.* The entertainment presented in a nightclub.

floor-walk-er (flôr′wô′kər, flōr′-) *n.* One who supervises sales personnel and assists customers in a department store.

floo-zy (flōō′zē) *n., pl.* **-zies.** *Slang.* A slovenly or vulgar woman. [Orig. unknown.]

flop (flŏp) *v.* **flopped, flop·ping.** **1.** To fall heavily and noisily; plop. **2.** To move about in a clumsy, noisy way. **3.** *Informal.* To fail utterly. —*n.* **1.** The act or sound of flopping. **2.** *Informal.* An utter failure. [< FLAP.]

flop-house (flŏp′hous′) *n.* A cheap hotel.

flop-py (flŏp′ē) *adj.* **-pi-er, -pi-est.** Tending to flop; loose and flexible. —**flop′pi-ly** *adv.* —**flop′pi-ness** *n.*

flo-ra (flôr′ə, flōr′ə) *n., pl.* **-ras** or **flo-rae** (flôr′ē′, flōr′ē′). Plants, esp. of a particular region or period. [< Lat. *flos*, flower.]

flo-ral (flôr′əl, flōr′-) *adj.* Of or pertaining to flowers.

flo-res-cence (flô-rĕs′əns, flə-) *n.* The condition or period of blossoming. [< Lat. *florescere*, to begin to bloom.]

flor-id (flôr′ĭd, flŏr′-) *adj.* **1.** Flushed; ruddy. **2.** Heavily embellished; flowery. [< Lat. *floridus*.] —**flo-rid′i-ty** (flô-rĭd′ĭ-tē) or **flor′id-ness** *n.* —**flor′id-ly** *adv.*

flo-rin (flôr′ĭn, flŏr′-) *n.* **1.** A guilder. **2.** A former British coin. [< Ital. *fiore*, flower.]

flo-rist (flôr′ĭst, flŏr′-, flōr′-) *n.* One who raises or sells flowers.

floss (flôs, flŏs) *n.* **1.** Short fibers or waste silk. **2.** A soft, loosely twisted thread. **3.** A soft, silky, fibrous substance. [Perh. < OFr. *flosche*, down.]

floss-y (flô′sē, flŏs′ē) *adj.* **-i-er, -i-est.** **1.** Made of or resembling floss. **2.** *Slang.* Ostentatiously stylish; flashy. —**floss′i-ness** *n.*

flo-ta-tion (flō-tā′shən) *n.* **1.** The act or condition of floating. **2.** A process in which different materials, esp. pulverized minerals, are separated from a fluid-mixture by agitation.

flo-til-la (flō-tĭl′ə) *n.* **1.** A fleet of small ships. **2.** A small fleet. [< OSp. *floti*, fleet.]

flot-sam (flŏt′səm) *n.* Floating wreckage or cargo from a ship. [< OFr. *floter*, to float, of Gmc. orig.]

flounce[1] (flouns) *n.* A strip of material, such as a ruffle, attached along its upper edge to a skirt, curtain, etc. [< OFr. *fronce*, pleat.]

flounce[2] (flouns) *v.* **flounced, flounc·ing.** To move with exaggerated motions expressive of displeasure or impatience. —*n.* The act or motion of flouncing. [Poss. of Scand. orig.]

floun-der[1] (floun′dər) *v.* **1.** To move clumsily or with difficulty. **2.** To proceed clumsily and in confusion. [Prob. < FOUNDER.]

floun-der[2] (floun′dər) *n.* Any of various saltwater flatfishes used as food. [ME, of Scand. orig.]

flour (flour) *n.* **1.** A fine, powdery substance obtained -by grinding grain, esp. wheat. **2.** Any similar soft, fine powder. —*v.* To cover or coat with flour. [ME.] —**flour′y** *adj.*

flour-ish (flûr′ĭsh, flŭr′-) *v.* **1.** To grow well or luxuriantly; thrive. **2.** To fare well; succeed. **3.** To wield dramatically: *flourish a baton.* —*n.* **1.** An embellishment or ornamentation, esp. in handwriting. **2.** A dramatic action or gesture. [< Lat. *florēre*, to bloom.]

flout (flout) *v.* To show contempt for; scoff at. [Prob. < ME *flouten*, to play the flute.] —**flout′er** *n.*

flow (flō) *v.* **1.** To move or run freely in or as if in a stream. **2.** To circulate, as the blood in the body. **3.** To proceed steadily and continuously. **4.** To appear smooth, harmonious, or graceful. **5.** To rise, as the tide. **6.** To arise; derive. **7.** To abound or be plentiful. **8.** To hang loosely and gracefully. —*n.* **1. a.** The smooth motion characteristic of fluids. **b.** The act of flowing. **2.** A stream. **3. a.** A continuous outpouring: *a flow of ideas.* **b.** A continuous movement or circulation: *the flow of traffic.* **4.** The amount that flows in a given period of time. **5.** The rising of the tide. [< OE *flōwan*.]

flow chart *n.* A schematic representation of a sequence of operations.

flow-er (flou′ər) *n.* **1.** The reproductive structure of a seed-bearing plant, having specialized male and female organs and usu. colorful petals. **2.** A plant conspicuous for its blossoms. **3.** The period of highest development; peak. **4.** The highest example or best representative of something. —*v.* **1.** To produce flowers; bloom. **2.** To develop fully; reach a peak. [< Lat. *flos.*]

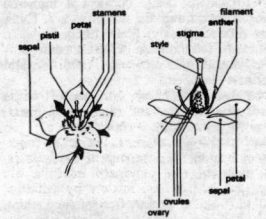

flower
Left: Flower
Right: Cross section showing
details

fluke²
Left: Fluke of a harpoon
Center: Fluke of an anchor
Right: Fluke of a sperm whale

flower girl *n.* A young girl who carries flowers at a wedding.

flow·er·pot (flou′ər-pŏt′) *n.* A pot in which plants are grown.

flow·er·y (flou′ə-rē) *adj.* **-i·er, -i·est. 1.** Full of or suggestive of flowers. **2.** Full of figurative or ornate expressions. **—flow′er·i·ness** *n.*

flown (flōn) *v. p.p.* of **fly¹.**

flu (flōō) *n. Informal.* Influenza.

flub (flŭb) *v.* **flubbed, flub·bing.** To botch or bungle. [Orig. unknown.] **—flub** *n.*

fluc·tu·ate (flŭk′chōō-āt′) *v.* **-at·ed, -at·ing. 1.** To change or vary irregularly. **2.** To rise and fall like waves. [Lat. *fluctuare.*] **—fluc′tu·a′tion** *n.*

flue (flōō) *n.* A pipe, tube, etc., through which air, gas, steam, or smoke can pass, as in a chimney. [Orig. unknown.]

flu·ent (flōō′ənt) *adj.* **1.** Having facility in the use of a language. **2.** Smoothly and naturally flowing; polished. **3.** Flowing or capable of flowing; fluid. [< Lat. *fluere,* to flow.] **—flu′en·cy** *n.* **—flu′ent·ly** *adv.*

fluff (flŭf) *n.* **1.** Light down or nap. **2.** Something having a light, soft, or frothy consistency or appearance. **3.** Something of little consequence. **4.** *Informal.* An error or lapse of memory, esp. by an actor or announcer. *—v.* **1.** To make light and puffy by shaking or patting into a soft, loose mass: *fluffed up the pillow.* **2.** *Informal.* To misread or forget, as dialogue. [Orig. unknown.] **—fluff′i·ness** *n.* **—fluff′y** *adj.*

flu·id (flōō′ĭd) *n.* A substance, such as air or water, that flows relatively easily and tends to take on the shape of its container. *—adj.* **1.** Capable of flowing, as a liquid. **2.** Smooth and effortless. **3.** Easily changed or readily changing; adaptable. **4.** Convertible into cash: *fluid assets.* [< Lat. *fluere,* to flow.] **—flu·id′i·ty** (flōō-ĭd′ĭ-tē) or **flu′id·ness** *n.* **—flu′id·ly** *adv.*

fluid ounce *n.* **1.** A unit of volume or capacity in the U.S. Customary System, used in liquid measure, equal to 29.574 milliliters, 1.804 cubic inches, or ¹⁄₁₆ of a pint. **2.** A unit of volume or capacity in the British Imperial System, used in liquid and dry measure, equal to 3.552 cubic centimeters or 1.734 cubic inches.

fluke¹ (flōōk) *n.* Any of various flatfishes, esp. a flounder. [< OE *flōc.*]

fluke² (flōōk) *n.* **1.** The triangular blade at the end of either arm of an anchor. **2.** A barb or barbed head, as on a harpoon. **3.** One of the two flattened divisions of a whale's tail. [Poss. < **FLUKE¹.**]

fluke³ (flōōk) *n.* An accidental stroke of good luck. [Orig. unknown.] **—fluk′y** *adj.*

flume (flōōm) *n.* **1.** A narrow gorge, usu. with a stream flowing through it. **2.** An artificial channel or chute for a stream of water. [< Lat. *fluere,* to flow.]

flum·mox (flŭm′əks) *v. Slang.* To confuse; perplex. [Orig. unknown.]

flung (flŭng) *v. p.t. & p.p.* of **fling.**

flunk (flŭngk) *v. Informal.* To fail an examination, course, etc. [Orig. unknown.]

flun·ky (flŭng′kē) *n., pl.* **-kies.** Also **flun·key** *pl.* **-keys. 1.** A servile or fawning person; a toady. **2.** A person who does menial or trivial work. [Sc.]

fluor— *pref.* Var. of **fluoro—.**

flu·o·resce (flōō′ə-rĕs′, flōō-rĕs′) *v.* **-resced, -resc·ing.** To undergo, produce, or show fluorescence. [< **FLUORESCENCE.**]

flu·o·res·cence (flōō′ə-rĕs′əns, flōō-rĕs′-) *n.* **1.** The emission of electromagnetic radiation, esp. of visible light, resulting from the absorption of incident radiation and persisting only as long as the stimulating radiation is continued. **2.** The radiation emitted during fluorescence. [*fluor,* mineral containing fluorine + **-ESCENCE.**] **—flu·o·res′cent** *adj.*

fluorescent lamp *n.* A lamp consisting of a glass tube, the inner wall of which is coated with a material that fluoresces when bombarded with secondary radiation generated within the tube.

fluor·i·date (flōōr′ĭ-dāt′, flôr′-, flōr′-) *v.* **-dat·ed, -dat·ing.** To add a fluorine compound to (a water supply) for the purpose of preventing tooth decay. **—fluor·i·da′tion** *n.*

flu·o·ride (flōō′ə-rīd′, flōōr′ĭd′, flôr′-, flōr′-) *n.* A binary compound of fluorine with another element.

flu·o·rine (flōō′ə-rēn′, -rĭn, flōōr′ēn′, -ĭn, flôr′-, flōr′-) *n. Symbol* F A pale-yellow, highly corrosive, highly poisonous, gaseous element, used in a wide variety of industrially important compounds. Atomic number 9; atomic weight 18.9984. [*fluor,* mineral containing fluorine + **-INE².**]

fluoro— or **fluor—** *pref.* **1.** Fluorine: *fluoride.* **2.** Fluorescence: *fluoroscope.* [< **FLUORINE.**]

fluor·o·car·bon (flōōr′ō-kär′bən) *n.* Any of various compounds in which fluorine replaces hydrogen, used as aerosol propellants, refrigerants, solvents, and lubricants, and in making plastics and resins.

fluor·o·scope (flōōr′ə-skōp′, flôr′-, flōr′-, flōō′ər-ə-) *n.* A mounted fluorescent screen on which the internal structure or parts of an optically opaque object may be viewed as shadows formed by the transmission of x-rays through the object. **—fluor'o·scope'** v. **—fluor'o·scop'ic** (-skŏp'ĭk) adj. **—fluo·ros'co·py** (flŏŏ-rŏs'kə-pē) n.

flur·ry (flûr'ē, flŭr'ē) n., pl. **-ries.** 1. A sudden gust of wind. 2. A light snowfall. 3. A sudden burst of activity: a flurry of preparations. [< obs. flurr, to scatter.] **—flur'ry** v.

flush¹ (flŭsh) v. 1. To flow suddenly and abundantly. 2. To redden; blush. 3. To glow, esp. with a reddish color. 4. To wash out or clean by a rapid, brief gush of water. 5. To excite or elate. **—n.** 1. A brief but copious flow or gushing, as of water. 2. A reddish tinge; a blush. 3. A feeling of animation or exhilaration. 4. A sudden freshness, development, or growth. **—adj.** 1. Having a reddish color; blushing. 2. Abundant; plentiful. 3. Prosperous; affluent. 4. a. Having surfaces in the same plane; even. b. Arranged with adjacent sides, surfaces, or edges close together. 5. Direct; straightforward. **—adv.** 1. So as to be even, in one plane, or aligned with a margin. 2. Squarely; solidly: a hit flush on the face. [Prob. < flush, to dart out.]

flush² (flŭsh) n. A hand in certain card games in which all the cards are of the same suit. [< Lat. fluxus, flux.]

flush³ (flŭsh) v. To fly from or cause to fly from cover, as a game bird. [ME flusshen.]

flus·ter (flŭs'tər) v. To become or make confused, nervous, or upset. **—n.** A state of agitation or confusion. [Prob. of Scand. orig.]

flute (flŏŏt) n. 1. A high-pitched tubular woodwind instrument. 2. One of the long parallel grooves on the shaft of a column. 3. A groove in cloth, as a pleat. [< OFr. floute.] **—flut'ed** adj. **—flut'ing** n.

flut·ist (flŏŏ'tĭst) n. One who plays the flute.

flut·ter (flŭt'ər) v. 1. To wave or flap lightly, rapidly, and irregularly. 2. To fly with a quick, light flapping of the wings. 3. To vibrate or beat rapidly or erratically. 4. To move or behave in a restless or excited fashion. **—n.** 1. An act of fluttering. 2. A condition of nervous excitement or agitation. [< OE flotorian.] **—flut'ter·y** adj.

flux (flŭks) n. 1. a. A flow or flowing. b. A continued flow or flood. 2. Change regarded as an abstract influence or condition persisting in time. 3. A substance applied to prevent oxide formation and facilitate flowing, as of solder. **—v.** 1. To melt; fuse. 2. To apply a flux to. [< Lat. fluxus.]

fly¹ (flī) v. **flew** (flŏŏ), **flown** (flōn), **fly·ing.** 1. To engage in flight, esp.: a. To move through the air with the aid of wings or winglike parts. b. To travel by air. c. To pilot an aircraft. 2. To rise, float, or cause to float in the air. 3. To flee; try to escape. 4. To hasten; rush. 5. To pass by swiftly. 6. To disappear rapidly; vanish. 7. p.t. & p.p. **flied.** To bat a baseball in a high arc. **—n.,** pl. **flies.** 1. An overlapping fold of cloth that hides the fastening on a garment. 2. A cloth flap that covers an entrance, as of a tent. 3. A baseball batted in a high arc. 4. **flies.** The area directly over the stage and behind the proscenium of a theater. **—idioms. fly in the face** (or **teeth**) **of.** To resist or defy openly. **fly off the handle.** To lose control of one's temper. [< OE flēogan.] **—fly'a·ble** adj.

fly² (flī) n., pl. **flies.** 1. Any of numerous winged insects, esp. the housefly. 2. A fishing lure simulating a fly. [< OE flēoge.]

fly-blown (flī'blōn') adj. Spoiled; tainted.

fly-by-night (flī'bī-nīt') adj. 1. Of unreliable business character. 2. Temporary.

fly-catch·er (flī'kăch'ər) n. Any of various birds that fly after and catch flying insects.

fly·er (flī'ər) n. Var. of flier.

flying buttress n. An arch extending from a separate supporting structure to brace part of the main structure.

flying buttress   flying squirrel

flying fish n. A marine fish with enlarged, winglike fins that aid in brief, gliding flights over the water.

flying saucer n. Any of various unidentified flying objects typically reported and described as luminous disks.

flying squirrel n. Any of various squirrels having membranes between the forelegs and hind legs that enable them to glide through the air.

fly·leaf (flī'lēf') n. A blank page at the beginning or end of a book.

fly·pa·per (flī'pā'pər) n. Paper coated with a sticky substance for catching flies.

fly·speck (flī'spĕk') n. 1. A speck or mark made by the excrement of a fly. 2. A minute spot.

fly·weight (flī'wāt') n. A boxer of the lightest weight class, weighing 112 pounds or less.

fly·wheel (flī'hwēl', -wēl') n. A heavy-rimmed rotating wheel used to keep a shaft of a machine turning at a steady speed.

Fm The symbol for the element fermium.

foal (fōl) n. The young offspring of an equine animal, esp. one less than a year old. **—v.** To give birth to a foal. [< OE fola.]

foam (fōm) n. 1. A mass of gas bubbles in a liquid-film matrix. 2. Any of various light, bulky, more or less rigid materials used as thermal or mechanical insulators, esp. in packaging and containers. **—v.** To form or come forth in foam. [< OE fām.] **—foam'i·ness** n. **—foam'y** adj.

foam rubber n. A light, firm, spongy rubber, used in upholstery and for insulation.

fob¹ (fŏb) n. 1. A short chain or ribbon attached to a pocket watch. 2. An ornament attached to a watch chain. [Prob. of Gmc. orig.]

fob² (fŏb) v. **fobbed, fob·bing.** To dispose of (something) by fraud or deception: fobbed off the zircon as a diamond. [ME fobben.]

---

fo·cal length *n.* The distance of the focus from the surface of a lens or mirror.

focal point *n.* A point on the axis of symmetry of an optical system to which parallel incident rays converge or from which they appear to diverge after passing through the system.

fo·cus (fō′kəs) *n., pl.* **-cus·es** or **-ci** (-sī′). 1. A point to which something converges or from which it diverges. 2. a. Focal point. b. Focal length. c. The distinctness or clarity with which an optical system renders an image. d. Adjustment for distinctness or clarity. 3. A center of interest or activity. —*v.* **-cused** or **-cussed, -cus·ing** or **cus·sing.** 1. a. To produce a clear image of. b. To adjust the setting of (a lens) to produce a clear image. 2. To concentrate on. 3. To converge at a focus. [Lat., hearth.] —**fo′cal** *adj.* —**fo′cal·ly** *adv.*

fod·der (fŏd′ər) *n.* Feed for livestock, often consisting of coarsely chopped stalks of corn and hay. [< OE *fōdor.*]

foe (fō) *n.* 1. a. A personal enemy. b. An enemy in war. 2. An adversary; opponent. [< OE *gefā,* foe, and < OE *fāh,* hostile.]

foe·tal (fēt′l) *adj.* Var. of **fetal.**

foe·tus (fē′təs) *n.* Var. of **fetus.**

fog (fŏg, fôg) *n.* 1. A cloudlike mass of condensed water vapor close to the ground. 2. Confusion or bewilderment. 3. A dark blur on a developed photographic negative. —*v.* **fogged, fog·ging.** To cover or be obscured with or as if with fog. [Perh. of Scand. orig.] —**fog′gi·ly** *adv.* —**fog′gy** *adj.*

fog·horn (fŏg′hôrn′, fôg′-) *n.* A horn used to warn ships of danger in fog or darkness.

fo·gy (fō′gē) *n., pl.* **-gies.** Also **fo·gey** *pl.* **-geys.** A person of old-fashioned habits or attitudes. [Orig. unknown.] —**fo′gy·ish** *adj.*

foi·ble (foi′bəl) *n.* A minor weakness of character. [< OFr. *feble,* feeble.]

foil[1] (foil) *v.* To prevent from being successful; thwart. [ME *foilen,* to trample.]

foil[2] (foil) *n.* 1. A thin, flexible leaf or sheet of metal. 2. One that by contrast enhances the distinctive characteristics of another. [< Lat. *folium,* leaf.]

foil[3] (foil) *n.* A light fencing sword with a thin, flexible blade and a blunt point. [Orig. unknown.]

foist (foist) *v.* 1. To pass off as genuine, valuable, or worthy. 2. To force upon another, as by trickery. [< Du. *vuist,* fist.]

fold[1] (fōld) *v.* 1. To bend over or double up so that one part lies on another. 2. To bring from an extended to a closed position. 3. To place together and intertwine: *fold one's arms.* 4. To wrap; envelop. 5. To mix in (an ingredient) by slowly and gently turning one part over another. 6. *Informal.* To fail or collapse. —*n.* 1. A line, layer, pleat, or crease formed by folding. 2. A folded edge or piece. [< OE *fealdan.*]

fold[2] (fōld) *n.* 1. A fenced enclosure for domestic animals, esp. sheep. 2. A flock of sheep. 3. A group of people bound together by common beliefs and aims. [< OE *fald.*]

-fold *suff.* 1. Division into a specified number of parts: *fivefold.* 2. Multiplication by a specified number: *tenfold.* [< OE *-feald.*]

fold·er (fōl′dər) *n.* 1. One that folds. 2. A booklet made of one or more folded sheets of paper. 3. A folded sheet of cardboard or heavy paper used as a container.

fol·de·rol (fŏl′də-rŏl′) *n.* 1. Nonsense. 2. A trinket; bauble. [< a refrain in some old songs.]

fo·li·age (fō′lē-ĭj) *n.* The leaves of growing plants. [< Lat. *folium,* leaf.]

fo·li·o (fō′lē-ō′) *n., pl.* **-os.** 1. A large sheet of paper folded once in the middle. 2. A book of the largest common size, having such folded sheets. 3. A page number in a book. [Lat. *folium,* leaf.]

folk (fōk) *n., pl.* **folk** or **folks.** 1. A people or nation. 2. People of a specified group or kind: *country folk.* 3. **folks.** *Informal.* One's family or relatives. 4. **folks.** *Informal.* People in general. —*adj.* Of, occurring in, or originating among the common people: *folk art.* [< OE *folc.*]

folk·lore (fōk′lôr′, -lōr′) *n.* The traditional beliefs, practices, legends, and tales of a people, passed down orally. —**folk′lor·ist** *n.*

folk music *n.* Music originating among the common people of a nation or region.

folk rock *n.* Popular music that combines elements of rock 'n' roll and folk music.

folk singer *n.* A singer of folk songs.

folk song *n.* A song belonging to the folk music of a people or area, characterized chiefly by directness and simplicity.

folk·sy (fōk′sē) *adj.* **-si·er, -si·est.** *Informal.* Simple and unpretentious. —**folk′si·ness** *n.*

folk·way (fōk′wā′) *n.* A way of thinking or acting shared by the members of a group as part of their common culture.

fol·li·cle (fŏl′ĭ-kəl) *n.* 1. A tiny bodily cavity or sac, such as the depression in the skin from which a hair grows. 2. An ova-containing structure in an ovary. [Lat. *folliculus,* little bag.]

fol·low (fŏl′ō) *v.* 1. To come or go after. 2. To pursue. 3. To accompany; attend. 4. To move along the course of. 5. To obey; comply with. 6. To succeed to the place or position of. 7. To engage in. 8. To result; ensue. 9. To be attentive to. 10. To grasp the meaning or logic of; understand. [< OE *folgian.*]

fol·low·er (fŏl′ō-ər) *n.* 1. One that follows. 2. An attendant or subordinate. 3. One who subscribes to the teachings or methods of another; adherent.

fol·low·ing (fŏl′ō-ĭng) *adj.* 1. Coming next in time or order. 2. Now to be mentioned or listed. —*n.* A group of followers.

fol·low-through (fŏl′ō-thrōō′) *n.* 1. The act or process of carrying to completion. 2. The concluding part of a stroke, after a ball has been hit.

fol·low-up (fŏl′ō-ŭp′) *n.* 1. The act of repeating or adding to previous action so as to increase effectiveness. 2. The means used to do this.

fol·ly (fŏl′ē) *n., pl.* **-lies.** 1. Lack of good sense, understanding, or foresight. 2. An act or example of foolishness. 3. A costly undertaking having an absurd or ruinous outcome. [< OFr. *fol,* foolish.]

fo·ment (fō-mĕnt′) *v.* 1. To stir up; arouse. 2. To treat with heat and moisture. [< Lat. *fomentum,* poultice.] —**fo′men·ta′tion** *n.* —**fo·ment′er** *n.*

fond (fŏnd) *adj.* **-er, -est.** 1. Affectionate; tender. 2. Having a strong affection or liking: *fond of ballet.* 3. Foolishly affectionate; doting. 4. Deeply felt; dear. [Prob. < ME *fon,* fool.] —**fond′ly** *adv.* —**fond′ness** *n.*

fon·dle (fŏn′dl) *v.* **-dled, -dling.** To handle or

stroke affectionately; caress. [< obs. *fond*, to show affection for.]

fon·due (fŏn-dōō′) *n.* A hot dish made of melted cheese and wine. [Fr.]

font¹ (fŏnt) *n.* **1.** A basin for baptismal or holy water. **2.** A source of abundance. [< Lat. *fons*, fountain.]

font² (fŏnt) *n.* A complete set of printing type of one size and face. [< OFr. *fondre*, to melt.]

food (fōōd) *n.* **1.** A substance taken in and assimilated by an organism to maintain life and growth; nourishment. **2.** A particular kind of nourishment: *plant food.* **3.** Solid nourishment as distinguished from liquid nourishment. **4.** Something that stimulates or encourages: *food for thought.* [< OE *fōda.*]

food chain *n.* A series of plants and animals within an environment, each kind serving as a source of nourishment for the next in the series.

food poisoning *n.* Poisoning caused by eating food contaminated by natural toxins or bacteria, characterized by vomiting, diarrhea, and prostration.

food·stuff (fōōd′stŭf′) *n.* A substance that can be used or prepared for use as food.

fool (fōōl) *n.* **1.** One who is deficient in judgment, sense, or understanding. **2.** A jester. **3.** One who can easily be deceived; dupe. —*v.* To deceive or trick; dupe. **1.** To take unawares; surprise. **2.** To act or speak in jest; joke. —*phrasal verbs.* **fool around.** *Informal.* **1.** To waste time; idle. **2.** To mess around; play. **fool with** (or **around with**). To toy or meddle with. [< Lat. *follis*, bellows.]

fool·er·y ((fōō′lə-rē) *n., pl.* **-ies.** Foolish behavior; nonsense.

fool·har·dy (fōōl′här′dē) *adj.* **-di·er, -di·est.** Foolishly bold or daring; rash. [< OFr. *fol hardi*, bold fool.] —**fool′har′di·ly** *adv.* —**fool′har′di·ness** *n.*

fool·ish (fōō′lĭsh) *adj.* **1.** Having or resulting from poor judgement; unwise. **2.** Silly; ridiculous. —**fool′ish·ly** *adv.* —**fool′ish·ness** *n.*

Syns: *foolish, absurd, crazy, harebrained, idiotic, nonsensical, preposterous, sappy, silly, wacky, zany adj.*

fool·proof (fōōl′prōōf′) *adj.* Designed to be proof against error, misuse, or failure.

fools·cap (fōōlz′kăp′) *n.* A sheet of writing paper approx. 13 x 16 inches. [< the watermark orig. marking this type of paper.]

foot (fōōt) *n., pl.* **feet** (fēt). **1.** The lower extremity of the leg that is in direct contact with the ground in standing or walking. **2.** Something resembling or suggestive of a foot in position or function: *the foot of a mountain.* **3.** *Pros.* A metrical unit consisting of a stressed or unstressed syllable or syllables. **4.** A unit of length equal to ¹/₃ yard or 12 inches. —*v.* **1.** To go on foot; walk. **2.** To dance. **3.** To add up; total: *Foot up the bill.* **4.** *Informal.* To pay. —**idioms. on foot.** Walking or running rather than riding. **put (one's) best foot forward.** *Informal.* To make a good first impression. **put (one's) foot down.** *Informal.* To take a firm stand. **put (one's) foot in (one's) mouth.** *Informal.* To say something by mistake that causes embar-

rassment or hurt feelings. [< OE *fōt.*] —**foot′less** *adj.* —**foot′less·ly** *adv.*

foot·age (fōōt′ĭj) *n.* **1.** The length or extent of something as expressed in feet. **2.** A portion of motion-picture film or videotape.

foot·ball (fōōt′bôl′) *n.* **1. a.** A game played by two teams of 11 players on a long field with goals at either end. **b.** The inflated oval ball used in football. **2.** *Brit.* **a.** Soccer or rugby. **b.** The ball used in soccer or rugby.

foot·board (fōōt′bôrd′, -bōrd′) *n.* **1.** A board or small raised platform on which to support or rest the feet. **2.** An upright board across the foot of a bedstead.

foot·bridge (fōōt′brĭj′) *n.* A narrow bridge for pedestrians.

foot·ed (fōōt′ĭd) *adj.* **1.** Having a foot or feet. **2.** Having a specified kind or number of feet: *web-footed.*

foot·fall (fōōt′fôl′) *n.* **1.** A footstep. **2.** The sound made by a footstep.

foot·hill (fōōt′hĭl′) *n.* A low hill near the base of a mountain.

foot·hold (fōōt′hōld′) *n.* **1.** A place providing support for the foot in climbing or standing. **2.** A secure position that provides a base for further advancement.

foot·ing (fōō′tĭng) *n.* **1.** A secure placement of the feet. **2.** A basis; foundation. **3.** A basis for social or business transactions with others; standing.

foot·lights (fōōt′līts′) *pl.n.* **1.** Lights placed in a row along the front of a stage floor. **2.** The theater as a profession.

foot·lock·er (fōōt′lŏk′ər) *n.* A small trunk for personal belongings.

foot·loose (fōōt′lōōs′) *adj.* Having no attachments or ties.

foot·man (fōōt′mən) *n.* A male servant who waits at table, attends the door, and runs various errands.

foot·note (fōōt′nōt′) *n.* **1.** A note of comment or reference at the bottom of a page of a book. **2.** An afterthought. —**foot′note′** *v.*

foot·path (fōōt′păth′, -päth′) *n.* A narrow path for pedestrians.

foot·print (fōōt′prĭnt′) *n.* An outline or indentation of a foot.

foot·rest (fōōt′rĕst′) *n.* A support on which to rest the feet.

foot·sore (fōōt′sôr′, -sōr′) *adj.* Having sore or tired feet.

foot·step (fōōt′stĕp′) *n.* **1.** A step with the foot. **2.** The distance covered by one step: *a footstep away.* **3.** The sound of a foot stepping. **4.** A footprint.

foot·stool (fōōt′stōōl′) *n.* A low stool for supporting the feet.

foot·wear (fōōt′wâr′) *n.* Coverings for the feet.

foot·work (fōōt′wûrk′) *n.* The manner in which the feet are used or maneuvered, as in boxing.

fop (fŏp) *n.* A man who is preoccupied with his clothes and manners; dandy. [ME. fool.] —**fop′pish** *adj.* —**fop′pish·ness** *n.*

for (fôr; far *when unstressed*) *prep.* **1.** Used to indicate the recipient, object, or goal of an action or activity: *studied for the ministry; swimming for fun; fight for one's life.* **2.** Used to indicate a destination: *set off for town.*

ă pat ā pay â care ä father ĕ pet ē be ĭ pit ī tie î pier ŏ pot ō toe ô paw, for oi noise ōō took
ōō boot ou out th thin th this ŭ cut û urge yōō abuse zh vision ə about, item, edible, gallop, circus

3. As a result of: *weep for joy.* **4.** Used to indicate amount, extent, or duration: *a bill for three dollars; talked for ten minutes.* **5.** Considering the normal character of: *His book is short for a novel.* **6.** In spite of: *For all her experience she does a poor job.* **7. a.** On behalf of: *a collection for the poor.* **b.** In favor, defense, or support of. **8.** As equivalent or equal to: *word for word.* **9.** As against: *pound for pound.* **10.** As being: *took him for a fool.* **11.** As the duty or task of: *That's for you to decide.* —*conj.* Because; since. [< OE.]

for·age (fôr′ĭj, fŏr′-) *n.* **1.** Food for domestic animals, esp. plants or grass eaten while grazing. **2.** A search for food or provisions. —*v.* **-aged, -ag·ing.** **1.** To search for food or provisions. **2.** To raid; plunder. **3.** To rummage through, esp. in search of provisions. [< OFr. *feurre*, fodder.] —**for′ag·er** *n.*

for·ay (fôr′ā′, fŏr′ā′) *n.* **1.** A sudden raid. **2.** A first venture or attempt. [< ME *forraien*, to plunder.] —**for′ay′** *v.*

for·bear¹ (fôr-bâr′) *v.* **-bore** (-bôr′, -bōr′), **-borne** (-bôrn′, -bōrn′), **-bear·ing.** **1.** To refrain or desist from. **2.** To be tolerant or patient. [< OE *forberan.*] —**for·bear′ance** *n.*

for·bear² (fôr′bâr′, fŏr′-) *n.* Var. of **forebear.**

for·bid (fər-bĭd′, fôr-) *v.* **-bade** (-băd′, -bād′) or **-bad** (-băd′), **-bid·den** (-bĭd′n) or **-bid, -bid·ding.** **1.** To command (someone) not to do something. **2.** To prohibit. **3.** To preclude. [< OE *forbēodan.*]

Syns: forbid, ban, disallow, enjoin, outlaw, prohibit, proscribe *v.*

for·bid·ding (fər-bĭd′ĭng, fôr-) *adj.* Tending to frighten with; threatening or ominous.

force (fôrs, fōrs) *n.* **1. a.** Strength; power. **b.** The exertion of such power. **2.** Intellectual vigor or persuasiveness, as of a statement. **3.** A body of persons organized for a certain purpose, esp. for the use of military power. **4.** A vector quantity that tends to produce an acceleration of a body in the direction of its application. —*v.* **forced, forc·ing.** **1.** To compel to perform an action. **2.** To obtain by force; extort. **3.** To produce by effort: *force a tear from one's eye.* **4.** To move (something) against resistance. **5.** To break down or open by force: *force a lock.* **6.** To inflict or impose. **7.** To cause to grow rapidly by artificial means. —**idiom. in force. 1.** In full strength. **2.** In effect; operative: *a rule no longer in force.* [< Lat. *fortis,* strong.] —**forc′er** *n.*

force·ful (fôrs′fəl, fōrs′-) *adj.* Effective: *a forceful speaker.* —**force′ful·ly** *adv.* —**force′ful·ness** *n.*

for·ceps (fôr′səps) *n.* (used with a pl. verb).

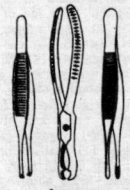

forceps
Left: Mouse-tooth forceps
Center: Lion-jaw bone-holding forceps
Right: Thumb forceps

An instrument used for grasping, manipulating, or extracting, esp. in surgery. [Lat.]

forc·i·ble (fôr′sə-bəl, fōr′-) *adj.* **1.** Accomplished through force. **2.** Characterized by force. —**forc′i·bly** *adv.*

ford (fôrd, fōrd) *n.* A shallow place in a body of water where a crossing can be made on foot or horseback. —*v.* To cross (a body of water) at a ford. [< OE.] —**ford′a·ble** *adj.*

fore (fôr, fōr) *adj. & adv.* At, in, or toward the front. —*n.* The front part. —*interj.* Golf. Used to warn those ahead that a ball is about to be driven in their direction. [< OE, beforehand.]

fore- *pref.* **1.** Before in time: *foresight.* **2.** The front or first part: *foredeck.* [< OE.]

fore-and-aft (fôr′ən-ăft′, fōr′-) *adj.* Parallel with the keel of a ship.

fore·arm¹ (fôr-ärm′, fōr′-) *v.* To prepare in advance for a conflict.

fore·arm² (fôr′ärm′, fōr′-) *n.* The part of the arm between the wrist and elbow.

fore·bear (fôr′bâr′, fōr′-) *n.* Also **forebear.** A forefather; ancestor. [ME.]

fore·bode (fôr-bōd′, fōr-) *v.* **-bod·ed, -bod·ing. 1.** To give a warning or hint of; portend. **2.** To have a premonition of (a future misfortune). —**fore·bod′ing** *n.*

fore·cast (fôr′kăst′, fōr′-) *v.* **-cast** or **-cast·ed, -cast·ing. 1.** To calculate or predict in advance, esp. the weather. **2.** To serve as an advance indication of; foreshadow. —*n.* A prediction. [ME *forecasten,* to plan beforehand.] —**fore′cast′er** *n.*

fore·cas·tle (fōk′səl, fôr′kăs′əl, fōr′-) *n.* **1.** The section of the upper deck of a ship located forward of the foremast. **2.** The crew's quarters at the bow of a merchant ship. [< AN.]

fore·close (fôr-klōz′, fōr-) *v.* **-closed, -clos·ing. 1.** To end (a mortgage), taking possession of the mortgaged property when regular payments are not made. **2.** To exclude or rule out; bar. [< OFr. *forclore,* to exclude from an inheritance.]

fore·clo·sure (fôr-klō′zhər, fōr-) *n.* The act of foreclosing, esp. a legal proceeding by which a mortgage is foreclosed.

fore·fa·ther (fôr′fä′thər, fōr′-) *n.* An ancestor.

fore·fin·ger (fôr′fĭng′gər, fōr′-) *n.* The index finger.

fore·foot (fôr′fŏŏt′, fōr′-) *n.* One of the front feet of an animal.

fore·front (fôr′frŭnt′, fōr′-) *n.* **1.** The foremost part or area of something. **2.** The most important position.

fore·go (fôr-gō′, fōr-) *v.* **-went** (-wĕnt′), **-gone** (-gôn′, -gŏn′), **-go·ing.** To precede. —**fore·go′er** *n.*

fore·go² (fôr-gō′, fōr-) *v.* Var. of **forgo.**

fore·go·ing (fôr-gō′ĭng, fōr-, fôr′gō′ĭng, fōr′-) *adj.* Just past; previous.

fore·gone (fôr′gôn′, -gŏn′, fōr′-) *adj.* So certain as to be known in advance: *a foregone conclusion.* [< FOREGO¹.]

fore·ground (fôr′ground′, fōr′-) *n.* **1.** The part of a view or picture nearest to the viewer. **2.** The most important or prominent position.

fore·hand (fôr′hănd′, fōr′-) *n. Sports.* A stroke, as of a racket, made with the palm of the hand moving forward. —**fore′hand′** *adj.*

fore·head (fôr′ĭd, fôr′-, fôr′hĕd′, fōr′-) *n.* The part of the face between the eyebrows and the normal hairline. [< OE *forehēafod.*]

for·eign (fôr′ĭn, fŏr′-) *adj.* **1.** Located away from one's native country: *foreign parts.* **2.** Of a country other than one's own: *a foreign* *custom.* **3.** Conducted or involved with other nations: *foreign trade.* **4.** Situated in an abnormal or improper place. **5.** Not germane; extraneous. [< Lat. *foras,* outside.] —**for′eign·ness** *n.*

for·eign·er (fôr′ə-nər, fŏr′-) *n.* A person from a foreign country.

fore·knowl·edge (fôr-nŏl′ĭj, fŏr-) *n.* Knowledge of something prior to its occurrence.

fore·leg (fôr′lĕg′, fŏr′-) *n.* A front leg of an animal.

fore·limb (fôr′lĭm′, fŏr′-) *n.* A front part such as an arm, wing, foreleg, or flipper.

fore·lock (fôr′lŏk′, fŏr′-) *n.* A lock of hair that grows or falls on the forehead.

fore·man (fôr′mən, fŏr′-) *n.* **1.** A person in charge of a group of workers, as at a factory or ranch. **2.** The spokesman for a jury. —**fore′wom′an** *n.*

fore·mast (fôr′məst, -măst′, fŏr′-) *n.* The forward mast of a sailing ship.

fore·most (fôr′mōst′, fŏr′-) *adj. & adv.* First in rank or position. [< OE *forma,* first.]

fore·noon (fôr′nōōn′, fŏr′-) *n.* The period between sunrise and noon.

fo·ren·sic (fə-rĕn′sĭk, -zĭk) *adj.* Of or used in legal proceedings or in public debate. [Lat. *forensis.*] —**fo·ren′si·cal·ly** *adv.*

fore·or·dain (fôr′ôr-dān′, fŏr′-) *v.* To appoint or ordain beforehand; predestine.

fore·part (fôr′pärt′, fŏr′-) *n.* The first or foremost part.

fore·quar·ter (fôr′kwôr′tər, fŏr′-) *n.* The region including the front leg and shoulder of an animal or side of meat.

fore·run·ner (fôr′rŭn′ər, fŏr′-) *n.* **1.** A predecessor. **2.** One that provides advance notice of the coming of others; harbinger.

fore·sail (fôr′səl, -sāl′, fŏr′-) *n.* The principal square sail hung to the foremast of a square-rigged vessel.

fore·see (fôr-sē′, fŏr-) *v.* To see or know beforehand. —**fore·see′a·ble** *adj.* —**fore·se′er** *n.*

fore·shad·ow (fôr-shăd′ō, fŏr-) *v.* To present a warning, sign, or hint of beforehand.

fore·shore (fôr′shôr′, fŏr′shōr′) *n.* The part of a shore that is covered at high tide.

fore·short·en (fôr-shôr′tn, fŏr-) *v.* In drawing or painting, to shorten certain lines in (e.g. a figure or design) so as to give the illusion of depth or distance.

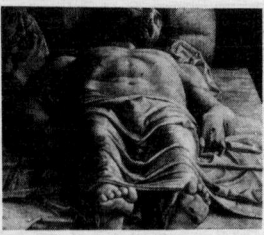

foreshorten
Foreshortened figure of the dead
Christ; detail of a painting by
Mantegna

fore·sight (fôr′sīt′, fŏr′-) *n.* **1.** The act or ability to foresee. **2.** The act of looking forward. **3.** Concern or prudence with respect to the future. —**fore′sight′ed** *adj.* —**fore′sight′ed·ly** *adv.* —**fore′sight′ed·ness** *n.*

fore·skin (fôr′skĭn′, fŏr′-) *n.* The prepuce.

for·est (fôr′ĭst, fŏr′-) *n.* A dense growth of trees covering a large area. [< Lat. *foris,* outside.]

fore·stall (fôr-stôl′, fŏr-) *v.* To prevent or delay by taking precautionary measures against beforehand. [< OE *foresteall,* highway robbery.] —**fore·stall′er** *n.*

for·est·ry (fôr′ĭ-strē, fŏr′-) *n.* The science that deals with the development, maintenance, and management of forests. —**for′est·er** *n.*

fore·taste (fôr′tāst′, fŏr′-) *n.* An advance realization. —**fore·taste′** *v.*

fore·tell (fôr-tĕl′, fŏr-) *v.* To tell of or indicate beforehand; predict. —**fore·tell′er** *n.*

fore·thought (fôr′thôt′, fŏr′-) *n.* Thought, planning, or preparation beforehand.

fore·to·ken (fôr-tō′kən, fŏr-) *v.* To foreshadow; presage. —**fore′to′ken** *n.*

for·ev·er (fôr-ĕv′ər, fər-) *adv.* **1.** Eternally. **2.** Incessantly.

for·ev·er·more (fôr-ĕv′ər-môr′, -mōr′, fər-) *adv.* Forever.

fore·warn (fôr-wôrn′, fŏr-) *v.* To warn in advance.

fore·word (fôr′wûrd′, -wərd, fŏr′-) *n.* A preface or introductory text, esp. in a book.

for·feit (fôr′fĭt) *n.* **1.** Something surrendered as punishment; penalty .r fine. **2.** Something placed in escrow and then redeemed after payment of a fine. **3.** A forfeiture. —*v.* To surrender or be forced to surrender as a forfeit. [< OFr. *forsfaire,* to commit a crime.]

for·fei·ture (fôr′fĭ-chōōr′, -char) *n.* **1.** The act of forfeiting. **2.** Something forfeited.

for·gath·er (fôr-găth′ər, fŏr-) *v.* To gather together; assemble. [Sc.]

for·gave (fər-gāv′, fŏr-) *v. p.t.* of **forgive.**

forge¹ (fôrj, fōrj) *n.* A furnace or hearth where metals are heated and wrought; smithy. —*v.* **forged, forg·ing.** **1.** To form (metal) by heating and hammering. **2.** To give form or shape to; devise: *forge a treaty.* **3.** To fashion or reproduce for fraudulent purposes; counterfeit: *forge a signature.* [< Lat. *fabrica.*] —**forg′er** *n.* —**for′ger·y** *n.*

forge² (fôrj, fōrj) *v.* **forged, forg·ing.** **1.** To advance gradually but steadily. **2.** To advance quickly and suddenly. [Orig. unknown.]

for·get (fər-gĕt′, fŏr-) *v.* **-got** (-gŏt′), **-got·ten** (-gŏt′n) **or -got, -get·ting.** **1.** To be unable to remember or call to mind. **2.** To treat with inattention; neglect. **3.** To fail or neglect to become aware at the proper moment. —*idiom.* **forget (oneself).** To lose one's inhibitions or self-restraint. [< OE *forgetan.*] —**for·get′ful** *adj.* —**for·get′ful·ly** *adv.* —**for·get′ful·ness** *n.* —**for·get′ta·ble** *adj.*

for·get-me-not (fər-gĕt′mē-nŏt′, fŏr-) *n.* A low-growing plant with small blue flowers.

for·give (fər-gĭv′, fŏr-) *v.* **-gave** (-gāv′), **-giv·en** (-gĭv′ən), **-giv·ing.** **1.** To excuse for a fault or offense. **2.** To stop feeling anger for or resentment against. **3.** To absolve from payment of. [< OE *forgifan.*] —**for·giv′a·ble** *adj.* —**for·give′ness** *n.* —**for·giv′er** *n.*

for·go (fôr-gō′, fôr-) v. **-went** (-wĕnt′), **-gone** (-gôn′, -gŏn′), **-go·ing.** Also **fore·go.** To give up; relinquish. [< OE *forgān.*] **—for·go′er** n.

for·got (fər-gŏt′, fôr-) v. *p.t.* & *a p.p.* of **forget.**

for·got·ten (fər-gŏt′n, fôr-) v. A *p.p.* of **forget.**

fo·rint (fôr′ĭnt′) n. See table at **currency.** [Hung.]

fork (fôrk) n. **1.** A utensil with several tines for use in eating food. **2.** A large farm tool of similar shape used esp. for digging. **3. a.** A separation into two or more branches. **b.** The place at which such a separation occurs. **c.** One of the branches: *the right fork.* —v. **1.** To raise, carry, etc. with a fork. **2.** To give the shape of a fork to. **3.** To divide into branches. [< Lat. *furca.*] **—fork′ful′** n.

forked (fôrkt, fôr′kĭd) *adj.* Having or shaped like a fork.

fork lift n. A vehicle with a power-operated pronged platform for lifting and carrying loads.

for·lorn (fôr-lôrn′, fər-) *adj.* **1.** Deserted; abandoned. **2.** Pitiful in appearance. **3.** Nearly hopeless. [< OE *forlēosan,* to abandon.] **—for·lorn′ly** *adv.* **—for·lorn′ness** n.

form (fôrm) n. **1.** The contour and structure of something. **2.** The body, esp. of a person. **3.** The essence of something. **4.** The mode in which a thing exists; kind; variety: *a form of animal life.* **5.** Procedure as determined by regulation or custom. **6.** Manners as governed by etiquette. **7.** Performance according to recognized criteria. **8.** Fitness with regard to health or training. **9.** A fixed order of words or procedures, as in a ceremony. **10.** A document with blanks for the insertion of requested information. **11.** Style or manner in literary or musical composition. **12.** The structure of a work of art. **13.** A model for making a mold. **14.** A grade in a British school or in some American private schools. —v. **1.** To shape or become shaped. **2.** To shape into or assume a particular form. **3.** To develop by instruction or precept: *form the mind.* **4.** To develop; acquire: *form a habit.* **5.** To constitute a part of. **6.** To develop in the mind: *form an opinion.* **7.** To draw up; arrange. [< Lat. *forma.*]

-form *suff.* Having the form of: *cuneiform.*

for·mal (fôr′məl) *adj.* **1.** Pertaining to the outward aspect of something. **2.** Pertaining to the essential form of something: *a formal principle.* **3.** Following accepted conventions or proper forms. **4.** Characterized by strict observation of forms. **5.** Stiff or cold: *a formal manner.* **6.** Done for the sake of form only: *a purely formal greeting.* —n. An occasion requiring formal attire. **—for′mal·ly** *adv.*

for·mal·de·hyde (fôr-măl′də-hīd′) n. A colorless gaseous compound, HCHO, used in aqueous solution as a preservative and disinfectant. [*form*(*ic acid*) + ALDEHYDE.]

for·mal·ism (fôr′mə-lĭz′əm) n. Strict or excessive observance of recognized forms, esp. in religion or art. **—for′mal·ist** n. **—for′mal·is′tic** *adj.*

for·mal·i·ty (fôr-măl′ĭ-tē) n., pl. **-ties. 1.** The condition or quality of being formal. **2.** Strict or ceremonious compliance with established rules. **3.** An established rule.

for·mal·ize (fôr′mə-līz′) v. **-ized, -iz·ing. 1.** To make formal. **2.** To give formal endorsement to. **—for′mal·i·za′tion** n.

for·mat (fôr′măt′) n. **1.** A plan for the organization and arrangement of something. **2.** The layout of a publication. [< Lat. *forma,* form.]

for·ma·tion (fôr-mā′shən) n. **1.** The process of forming. **2.** Something that is formed. **3.** The manner in which something is formed. **4.** A specified arrangement, as of troops. **—for·ma′tion·al** *adj.*

for·ma·tive (fôr′mə-tĭv) *adj.* **1.** Forming or capable of forming. **2.** Of or relating to formation or growth: *a formative stage.*

for·mer (fôr′mər) *adj.* **1.** Occurring earlier in time. **2.** Coming before in place or order. **3.** Being first or first mentioned of two. [< OE *forma,* first.]

Usage: The former is used when reference is to the first of two persons or things mentioned, but not when referring to the first of three or more. In the latter case, use *the first* or *the first named.*

for·mer·ly (fôr′mər-lē) *adv.* At a former time; once.

form-fit·ting (fôrm′fĭt′ĭng) *adj.* Closely fitted to the body.

For·mi·ca (fôr-mī′kə) n. A trademark for any of various laminated plastic coverings, used esp. for chemical- and heat-resistant surfaces.

for·mi·da·ble (fôr′mĭ-də-bəl, fôr-mĭd′ə-bəl) *adj.* **1.** Arousing fear, dread, or awe. **2.** Difficult to surmount. [< Lat. *formido,* fear.] **—for′mi·da·bil′i·ty** n. **—for′mi·da·bly** *adv.*

form·less (fôrm′lĭs) *adj.* Having no definite form. **—form′less·ness** n.

for·mu·la (fôr′myo-lə) n., pl. **-las** or **-lae** (-lē′). **1.** A set form of words, symbols, or rules for use in a ceremony. **2.** *Chem.* A set of symbols that show the composition or the composition and structure of a chemical compound. **3.** A mathematical statement, as an equation, of some logical relation. **4.** A recipe. **5.** A liquid food prescribed for an infant. [< Lat. *forma,* form.] **—for′mu·la′ic** (-lā′ĭk) *adj.*

for·mu·late (fôr′myə-lāt′) v. **-lat·ed, -lat·ing. 1.** To state as a formula. **2.** To express in systematic terms or concepts. **3.** To prepare according to a formula. **—for′mu·la′tion** n. **—for′mu·la′tor** n.

for·ni·ca·tion (fôr′nĭ-kā′shən) n. Sexual intercourse between persons not married to each other. [< Lat. *fornix,* brothel.] **—for′ni·cate′** v. **—for′ni·ca′tor** n.

for·sake (fôr-sāk′, fər-) v. **-sook** (-sŏŏk′), **-sak·en** (-sā′kən), **-sak·ing. 1.** To give up; renounce. **2.** To leave altogether; desert. [< OE *forsacan.*]

for·sooth (fôr-sŏŏth′, fər-) *adv.* Archaic. In truth; indeed. [< OE *forsōth.*]

for·swear (fôr-swâr′, fər-) v. **-swore** (-swôr′, -swōr′), **-sworn** (-swôrn′, -swōrn′), **-swear·ing. 1.** To give up; renounce. **2.** To commit perjury. [< OE *forswerian.*]

for·syth·i·a (fôr-sĭth′ē-ə, fər-) n. A widely cultivated shrub with early-blooming yellow flowers. [< William *Forsyth* (1737–1804).]

fort (fôrt, fōrt) n. A fortified place, esp. a permanent post. [< Lat. *fortis,* strong.]

forte¹ (fôrt, fōrt, fôr′tā′) n. Something in which a person excels. [< OFr. *fort,* strong.]

for·te² (fôr′tā′) *adv. Mus.* Loudly; forcefully. [Ital.] **—for′te′** *adj.*

forth (fôrth, fōrth) *adv.* **1.** Out into view. **2.** Forward or onward. **—idiom. and so forth.** And the like; et cetera. [< OE.]

forth·com·ing (fôrth-kŭm′ĭng, fôrth-) *adj.* **1.** About to appear or take place. **2.** Available when required.

forth·right (fôrth′rīt′, fôrth′-) *adj.* Straightforward; frank; candid. —**forth′right′ly** *adv.* —**forth′right′ness** *n.*

forth·with (fôrth-wĭth′, -wĭth′, fôrth′-) *adv.* At once; immediately.

for·ti·eth (fôr′tē-ĭth) *n.* **1.** The ordinal number that matches the number 40 in a series. **2.** One of 40 equal parts. —**for′ti·eth** *adj.* & *adv.*

for·ti·fy (fôr′tə-fī′) *v.* **-fied, -fy·ing. 1.** To strengthen and secure (a position) militarily. **2.** To strengthen physically; invigorate. **3.** To give moral or mental strength to; encourage. **4.** To increase the amount of an important ingredient in (a substance): *fortify bread with vitamins.* [< LLat. *fortificare.*] —**for′ti·fi·ca′tion** *n.* —**for′ti·fi′er** *n.*

for·tis·si·mo (fôr-tĭs′ə-mō′) *adv. Mus.* Very loudly. [Ital.] —**for·tis′si·mo′** *adj.*

for·ti·tude (fôr′tĭ-tōōd′, -tyōōd′) *n.* Strength of mind that allows one to endure pain or adversity with courage. [< Lat. *fortitudo.*]

fort·night (fôrt′nīt′) *n.* A period of 14 days; two weeks. [< OE *fēowertīene niht,* 14 nights.]

fort·night·ly (fôrt′nīt′lē) *adj.* Happening or appearing once every two weeks. —**fort′night·ly** *adv.*

FOR·TRAN or **For·tran** (fôr′trăn′) *n.* A computer programming language. [FOR(MULA) + TRAN(SLATION).]

for·tress (fôr′trĭs) *n.* A fort. [< Lat. *fortis,* strong.]

for·tu·i·tous (fôr-tōō′ĭ-təs, -tyōō′-) *adj.* Happening by accident or chance; unplanned. [< Lat. *forte,* by chance.] —**for·tu′i·tous·ly** *adv.* —**for·tu′i·tous·ness** *n.*

for·tu·i·ty (fôr-tōō′ĭ-tē, -tyōō′-) *n., pl.* **-ties. 1.** An accidental occurrence; chance. **2.** The condition or quality of being fortuitous.

for·tu·nate (fôr′chə-nĭt) *adj.* **1.** Occurring by good fortune. **2.** Lucky. —**for′tu·nate·ly** *adv.* —**for′tu·nate·ness** *n.*

for·tune (fôr′chən) *n.* **1.** A hypothetical force that governs the events of one's life. **2.** Good or bad luck. **3.** Luck, esp. when good; success. **4.** Wealth; riches. [< Lat. *fortuna.*]

fortune hunter *n.* A person who seeks to become wealthy, esp. through marriage. —**for′tune-hunt′ing** *n.*

for·tune-tell·er (fôr′chən-tĕl′ər) *n.* A person who, usu. for a fee, will undertake to predict one's future. —**for′tune-tell′ing** *n.* & *adj.*

for·ty (fôr′tē) *n., pl.* **-ties.** The cardinal number equal to 4 x 10. [< OE *fēowertig.*] —**for′ty** *adj.* & *pron.*

for·ty-five (fôr′tē-fīv′) *n.* **1.** A .45-caliber pistol. **2.** A phonograph record designed to be played at 45 revolutions per minute.

for·ty-nin·er (fôr′tē-nī′nər) *n.* One who took part in the 1849 California gold rush.

forty winks *pl.n. Informal.* A short nap.

fo·rum (fôr′əm, fōr′-) *n., pl.* **-rums** or **fo·ra** (fôr′ə, fōr′ə). **1.** The public square or marketplace of an ancient Roman city. **2.** A public place or medium for open discussion. **3.** A court of law. [Lat.]

for·ward (fôr′wərd) *adj.* **1.** At, near, belonging to, or located in the front. **2.** Going, tending, or moving toward the front. **3.** Presumptuous; bold. **4.** Progressive, esp. technologically, politically, or economically. **5.** Mentally, physically, or socially advanced; precocious.

—*adv.* **1.** Also **forwards** (-wərdz). Toward the front; frontward: *Please step forward.* **2.** In or toward the future: *I look forward to seeing you.* **3.** Into view; forth: *Come forward out of the shadows so I can see you.* —*n. Sports.* A player in the front line, as in basketball. —*v.* **1.** To send on to a subsequent destination: *forward mail.* **2.** To advance; promote. [< OE *foreweard.*] —**for′ward·er** *n.* —**for′ward·ness** *n.*

Usage: **Forward** and **forwards** as adverbs are interchangeable only in the sense of "toward the front": *moved forward* (or *forwards*).

forward pass *n. Football.* A pass thrown in the direction of the opponent's goal.

for·went (fôr-wĕnt′, fōr-) *v. p.t.* of **forgo.**

fos·sil (fŏs′əl) *n.* **1.** A remnant or trace of an organism of a past geologic age, as a footprint or leaf imprint, embedded in the earth's crust. **2.** One that is outdated. [< Lat. *fossus,* p.p. of *fodere,* to dig.] —**fos·sil·if′er·ous** *adj.*

fossil

fos·sil·ize (fŏs′ə-līz′) *v.* **-ized, -iz·ing. 1.** To convert into or become a fossil. **2.** To make or become outmoded, rigid, or fixed. —**fos′sil·i·za′tion** *n.*

fos·ter (fô′stər, fŏs′tər) *v.* **1.** To bring up; rear. **2.** To encourage; cultivate. —*adj.* Receiving or giving parental care although not related through legal or blood ties: *a foster child; a foster mother.* [< OE *fōster,* food.] —**fos′ter·age** *n.* —**fos′ter·er** *n.*

fos·ter·ling (fô′stər-lĭng, fŏs′tər-) *n.* A foster child.

foul (foul) *adj.* **-er, -est. 1.** Offensive to the senses; disgusting: *a foul flavor.* **2.** Having an offensive odor. **3.** Spoiled; rotten. **4.** Dirty; filthy. **5.** Immoral; wicked. **6.** Vulgar; obscene. **7.** Unpleasant: *a foul day.* **8.** Unfair; dishonorable: *win by foul means.* **9.** *Sports.* **a.** Designating lines that limit the playing area: *foul lines.* **b.** Contrary to the rules or outside the limits set. **10.** Entangled, as a rope. —*n.* **1.** *Sports.* **a.** A foul ball, hit, move, etc. **b.** An infraction of the rules. **2.** An entanglement or collision. —*adv.* In a foul manner. —*v.* **1.** To make or become foul; soil. **2.** To bring into dishonor. **3.** To clog or obstruct. **4.** To entangle or become entangled, as a rope. **5.** *Sports.* To commit a foul. —*phrasal verb.* **foul up.** *Slang.* To blunder or cause to blunder because of mistakes or poor judgment. [< OE *fūl.*] —**foul′ly** *adv.* —**foul′ness** *n.*

fou·lard (fōō-lärd′) *n.* A lightweight twill or

plain-woven fabric of silk usu. having a printed design. [Fr.]

foul-mouthed (foul′mou*t*hd′, -moutht′) *adj.* Using obscene language.

foul play *n.* Unfair or treacherous action, esp. involving violence.

foul-up (foul′ŭp′) *n. Informal.* 1. A condition of confusion caused by poor judgment or mistakes. 2. Mechanical trouble.

found¹ (found) *v.* 1. To originate or establish (e.g. a college). 2. To establish the foundation or basis of. [< Lat. *fundare*.] —**found′er** *n.*

found² (found) *v.* 1. To melt (metal or glass) and pour into a mold. 2. To make (objects) by founding. [< Lat. *fundere*.] —**found′er** *n.*

found³ (found) *v. p.t. & p.p.* of **find**.

foun-da-tion (foun-dā′shən) *n.* 1. The act of founding or the condition of being founded. 2. The basis on which a thing stands; underlying support. 3. a. An endowment. b. An endowed institution. 4. A cosmetic base for facial make-up. —**foun-da′tion-al** *adj.*

foun-der (foun′dər) *v.* 1. To go lame, as a horse. 2. To fail utterly; collapse. 3. To sink below the water. [< OFr. *fondrer*, to sink to the ground.]

found-ling (found′lĭng) *n.* A child abandoned by unknown parents. [ME.]

foun-dry (found′drē) *n., pl.* **-dries.** An establishment in which metals are cast and molded.

fount (found) *n.* 1. A fountain. 2. A source; wellspring. [< Lat. *fons.*]

foun-tain (foun′tən) *n.* 1. A spring of water from the earth. 2. a. An artificially created stream of water. b. The structure or device from which such a stream rises and flows. 3. A source; point of origin. 4. A soda fountain. [< Lat. *fons.*]

foun-tain-head (foun′tan-hĕd′) *n.* 1. A spring that is the source of a stream. 2. A primary source or origin.

fountain pen *n.* A pen containing a reservoir of ink that automatically feeds the writing point.

four (fôr, fōr) *n.* The cardinal number equal to the sum of 3 + 1. [< OE *fēower.*] —**four** *adj. & pron.*

four-flush-er (fôr′flŭsh′ər, fōr′-) *n. Slang.* A bluffer; faker. [< *four-flush*, to bluff in poker with a five-card hand having only four cards of the same suit.]

four-fold (fôr′fōld′, fōr′-) *adj.* 1. Having four units or aspects; quadruple. 2. Being four times as much or as many. —**four′fold′** *adv.*

Four-H Club (fôr′āch′, fōr′-) *n.* A youth organization sponsored by the Department of Agriculture and offering instruction in agriculture and home economics. [< its four goals of improving head, heart, hands, and health.]

four hundred *n.* The wealthiest and most exclusive social set.

four-in-hand (fôr′ĭn-hănd′, fōr′-) *n.* 1. A team of four horses driven by one person. 2. A necktie tied in a slipknot with the ends left hanging and overlapping.

four-leaf clover (fôr′lēf′, fōr′-) *n.* A clover leaf with four leaflets instead of three, considered an omen of good luck.

four-o'clock (fôr′ə-klŏk′, fōr′-) *n.* A plant with variously colored tubular flowers that open in the late afternoon.

four-post-er (fôr′pō′stər, fōr′-) *n.* A bed with

---

tall corner posts orig. intended to support curtains or a canopy.

four-score (fôr′skôr′, fōr′skōr′) *adj.* Four times 20; 80.

four-some (fôr′səm, fōr′-) *n.* 1. A group of four persons. 2. The players in a golf match played by four persons.

four-square (fôr′skwâr′, fōr′-) *adj.* 1. Square. 2. Unyielding; firm. 3. Forthright; frank. —**four′square′** *adv.*

four-teen (fôr-tēn′, fōr-) *n.* The cardinal number equal to the sum of 13 + 1. —**fourteen′** *adj. & pron.*

four-teenth (fôr-tēnth′, fōr-) *n.* 1. The ordinal number that matches the number 14 in a series. 2. One of 14 equal parts. —**four′teenth′** *adj. & adv.*

fourth (fôrth, fōrth) *n.* 1. The ordinal number that matches the number 4 in a series. 2. One of four equal parts; one quarter. —**fourth** *adj. & adv.*

fourth dimension *n.* Time regarded as a co-ordinate dimension and required by geometry, along with three spatial dimensions, to specify completely the location of any event.

fourth estate *n.* The public press; journalism or journalists.

Fourth of July *n.* Independence Day.

Fourth World *n.* The least-developed countries of the Third World, esp. in Africa and Asia.

fowl (foul) *n., pl.* **fowl** or **fowls.** 1. A bird used as food or hunted as game, esp. the common domesticated chicken. 2. The edible flesh of such a bird. —*v.* To hunt wild fowl. [< OE *fugol.*] —**fowl′er** *n.*

fox (fŏks) *n.* 1. A mammal related to the dogs and wolves, having a pointed snout and a long, bushy tail. 2. The fur of a fox. 3. A crafty or sly person. —*v.* To trick or fool by ingenuity or cunning; outwit. [< OE.]

Fox (fŏks) *n., pl.* **Fox-es** or **Fox.** 1. A tribe of Algonquian-speaking Indians mainly of southwestern Wisconsin who merged with the Sauk in 1760. 2. A member of the Fox.

foxed (fŏkst) *adj.* Discolored with yellowish-brown stains, as an old book.

fox-fire (fŏks′fīr′) *n.* A phosphorescent glow on rotting wood.

fox-glove (fŏks′glŭv′) *n.* A plant with a long cluster of large, tubular, pinkish-purple flowers and leaves that are the source of the medicinal drug digitalis.

fox-hole (fŏks′hōl′) *n.* A pit dug for protection against enemy fire.

fox terrier *n.* A small dog with a smooth or wiry white coat with dark markings.

fox terrier

fox trot *n.* A ballroom dance in 2/4 or 4/4 time. —**fox′-trot′** *v.*

fox-y (fŏk′sē) *adj.* **-i-er, -i-est.** 1. Suggestive of a fox; sly; clever. **2.** *Informal.* Sensually attractive; sexy. **—fox'i·ly** *adv.* **—fox'i·ness** *n.*

foy·er (foi'ər, foi'ā') *n.* **1.** The lobby of a public building. **2.** The entrance hall of a private dwelling. [< Lat. *focus,* hearth.]

Fr The symbol for the element francium.

fra·cas (frā'kəs) *n.* A brawl. [< Ital. *fracasso.*]

frac·tion (frăk'shən) *n.* **1.** A small part of something. **2.** A disconnected piece of something. **3.** *Math.* An indicated quotient of two quantities shown as a numerator over a denominator. **4.** *Chem.* A component separated by distillation, crystallization, etc. [< Lat. *fractus,* p.p. of *frangere,* to break.] **—frac'tion·al** *adj.* **—frac'tion·al·ly** *adv.*

frac·tious (frăk'shəs) *adj.* **1.** Inclined to make trouble; unruly. **2.** Cranky; irritable. [< FRACTION.] **—frac'tious·ly** *adv.* **—frac'tious·ness** *n.*

frac·ture (frăk'chər) *n.* **1. a.** The act or process of breaking. **b.** The condition of being broken. **2.** A break, rupture, or crack, as in bone or cartilage. **—v. -tured, -tur·ing.** To break or crack. [< Lat. *fractus,* p.p. of *frangere,* to break.]

frag·ile (frăj'əl, -īl') *adj.* **1.** Easily broken or damaged; delicate. **2.** Tenuous; flimsy: *a fragile claim.* [< Lat. *fragilis* < *frangere,* to break.] **—frag'ile·ly** *adv.* **—fra·gil'i·ty** (frə-jĭl'ĭ-tē) or **frag'ile·ness** *n.*

frag·ment (frăg'mənt) *n.* **1.** A part broken off. **2.** Something incomplete. **—v.** (frăg'mĕnt'). To break into pieces. [< Lat. *fragmentum* < *frangere,* to break.] **—frag'men·ta'tion** *n.*

frag·men·tar·y (frăg'mən-tĕr'ē) *adj.* Consisting of fragments. **—frag'men·tar'i·ly** (-târ'ə-lē) *adv.* **—frag'men·tar'i·ness** *n.*

fra·grant (frā'grənt) *adj.* Having a pleasant odor; sweet-smelling. [< Lat. *fragrare,* to emit an odor.] **—fra'grance** *n.* **—fra'grant·ly** *adv.*

frail (frāl) *adj.* **-er, -est. 1.** Having a delicate constitution. **2.** Slight; weak. **3.** Easily broken. [< Lat. *fragilis,* fragile.] **—frail'ly** *adv.* **frail·ty** (frāl'tē) *n., pl.* **-ties. 1.** The condition or quality of being frail. **2.** Often **frailties.** A fault arising from human weakness.

frame (frām) *v.* **framed, fram·ing. 1.** To construct; build. **2.** To design; draw up. **3.** To arrange or adjust for a purpose: *The question was framed to draw only one answer.* **4.** To put into words; compose. **5.** To provide with a frame; enclose. **6.** *Slang.* To rig evidence or events so as to incriminate (a person) falsely. **—n.** Something composed of parts fitted and joined together; a structure, such as: **a.** A skeletal structure: *the frame of a house.* **b.** An open structure or rim: *a window frame.* **c.** The human body. **2.** A machine built upon or utilizing a frame. **3.** The general structure of something: *the frame of government.* **4.** A single exposure on a roll of motion-picture film. [< ME, structure.] **—fram'er** *n.*

frame-up (frām'ŭp') *n.* *Slang.* A fraudulent scheme, esp. one involving falsified charges or evidence.

frame·work (frām'wûrk') *n.* **1.** A structure for supporting or enclosing something. **2.** A basic system or design.

franc (frăngk) *n.* See table at **currency.** [< OFr.]

fran·chise (frăn'chīz') *n.* **1.** A privilege granted a person or group; charter. **2.** A constitutional or statutory right, as the right to vote. **3.** Authorization granted by a manufacturer to sell his products. **4.** The territory or limits within which a privilege may be exercised. **—v. -chised, -chis·ing.** To endow with a franchise; enfranchise. [< OFr., freedom.] **—fran'chis·ee'** *n.* **—fran'chis·er** *n.*

fran·ci·um (frăn'sē-əm) *n.* *Symbol* **Fr** An extremely unstable radioactive metallic element. Atomic number 87; longest-lived isotope Fr 223. [< *France.*]

fran·gi·ble (frăn'jə-bəl) *adj.* Easily broken; breakable. [< Lat. *frangere,* to break.] **—fran'gi·bil'i·ty** or **fran'gi·ble·ness** *n.*

frank (frăngk) *adj.* **-er, -est.** Open and sincere in expression; straightforward. **—v. 1.** To put an official mark on (a piece of mail) so that it can be sent and delivered free. **2.** To send (mail) free of charge. **—n. 1.** A mark or signature on a piece of mail to indicate the right to send it free. **2.** The right to send mail free. [< OFr. *franc,* of Gmc. orig.] **—frank'ly** *adv.* **—frank'ness** *n.*

frank·furt·er (frăngk'fər-tər) *n.* A smoked sausage of beef or beef and pork made in long, reddish links. [< *Frankfurt am Main,* West Germany.]

frank·in·cense (frăng'kĭn-sĕns') *n.* An aromatic gum resin used chiefly as incense. [< OFr. *franc encens,* superior incense.]

fran·tic (frăn'tĭk) *adj.* Distraught, as from fear or worry. [ME *frantik.*] **—fran'ti·cal·ly** or **fran'tic·ly** *adv.* **—fran'tic·ness** *n.*

frap·pé (fră-pā', frăp) *n.* **1.** A frozen mixture similar to sherbet. **2.** A beverage poured over shaved ice. **3.** A milk shake with ice cream. [< Fr., chilled.]

fra·ter·nal (frə-tûr'nəl) *adj.* **1. a.** Of brothers. **b.** Showing comradeship. **2.** Pertaining to or constituting a fraternity. **3.** Of or concerning a twin or twins developed from separately fertilized ova. [< Lat. *frater,* brother.] **—fra·ter'nal·ism** *n.* **—fra·ter'nal·ly** *adv.*

fra·ter·ni·ty (frə-tûr'nĭ-tē) *n., pl.* **-ties. 1.** A group of people associated or linked by similar backgrounds, interests, or professions. **2.** A chiefly social organization of male college students. **3.** Brotherhood; brotherliness.

frat·er·nize (frăt'ər-nīz') *v.* **-nized, -niz·ing. 1.** To associate with (others) in a brotherly or congenial way. **2.** To associate with the people of an enemy or conquered country. **—frat'er·ni·za'tion** *n.* **—frat'er·niz'er** *n.*

frat·ri·cide (frăt'rĭ-sīd') *n.* **1.** The act of killing one's brother or sister. **2.** One who has killed a brother or sister. [Lat. *frater,* brother + -CIDE.] **—frat'ri·cid'al** *adj.*

Frau (frou) *n., pl.* **Frau·en** (frou'ən). A married woman in a German-speaking area.

fraud (frôd) *n.* **1.** A deliberate deception for unfair or unlawful gain. **2.** A swindle; trick. **3.** One who practices deception; imposter. [< Lat. *fraus.*]

fraud·u·lent (frô'jə-lənt) *adj.* Characterized by, constituting, or gained by fraud. [< Lat. *fraudulentus.*] **—fraud'u·lence** *n.* **—fraud'u·lent·ly** *adv.*

fraught (frôt) *adj.* Attended; accompanied: *an*

occasion fraught with peril. [< MDu. *vracht,* freight.]

Fräu·lein (froi′lĭn′) *n., pl.* **-lein.** An unmarried girl or woman in a German-speaking area.

fray¹ (frā) *n.* **1.** A fight or scuffle. **2.** A heated dispute. [< OFr. *effrei.*]

fray² (frā) *v.* **1.** To unravel, wear away, or tatter by rubbing. **2.** To strain or irritate; chafe: *frayed nerves.* [< Lat. *fricare,* to rub.]

fraz·zle (frăz′əl) *v.* **-zled, -zling.** *Informal.* **1.** To wear out; fray. **2.** To tire out completely. [Perh. blend of FRAY² and dial. *fazzle,* to tangle.] **—fraz′zle** *n.*

freak (frēk) *n.* **1.** A person, thing, or occurrence that is abnormal or very unusual. **2.** A whim; vagary. **3.** *Slang.* **a.** A drug addict. **b.** A fan or enthusiast. **—phrasal verb. freak out.** *Slang.* **1.** To experience or cause to experience a negative reaction, as hallucinations, induced by a drug. **2.** To make or become wild or agitated. [Orig. unknown.] **—freak′i·ly** *adv.* **—freak′ish** *adj.* **—freak′ish·ly** *adv.* **—freak′ish·ness** *n.* **—freak′y** *adj.*

freak-out (frēk′out′) *n. Slang.* An act or instance of freaking out.

freck·le (frĕk′əl) *n.* A precipitation of pigment in the skin. **—v. -led, -ling.** To dot or become dotted with freckles or spots. [< ON *freknur,* freckles.] **—freck′ly** *adj.*

free (frē) *adj.* **fre·er, fre·est.** **1.** At liberty; not bound or constrained. **2.** Not under obligation or necessity. **3. a.** Politically independent. **b.** Governed by consent and possessing civil liberties. **4. a.** Not affected by a given condition or circumstance. **b.** Exempt: *duty-free.* **5.** Not literal: *a free translation.* **6.** Costing nothing; gratuitous. **7. a.** Unoccupied. **b.** Unobstructed. **8.** Guileless; frank. **9.** Taking undue liberties. **10.** Liberal or lavish. **—adv. 1.** In a free manner. **2.** Without charge. **—v. freed, free·ing. 1.** To set at liberty. **2.** To rid or release. **3.** To disengage; untangle. **—idioms. make free with.** To take liberties with. **set free.** To liberate. [< OE *frēo.*] **—free′ly** *adv.* **—free′ness** *n.*

free·bie (frē′bē) *n.* Also **free·bee.** *Slang.* Something given or received gratis. [< FREE.]

free·board (frē′bôrd′, -bōrd′) *n. Naut.* The distance between the water line and the uppermost deck.

free·boot·er (frē′bōō′tər) *n.* One who plunders; pirate. [< Du. *vribuit,* plunder.]

free·born (frē′bôrn″) *adj.* **1.** Born as a free person. **2.** Of or befitting a person born free.

freed·man (frēd′mən) *n.* One freed from bondage. **—freed′wom′an** *n.*

free·dom (frē′dəm) *n.* **1.** The condition of being free. **2. a.** Political independence. **b.** Possession of civil rights. **3.** Facility, as of motion. **4.** Frankness. **5.** Unrestricted use or access. [< OE *frēodom.*]

Syns: *freedom, autonomy, independence, liberty, sovereignty* **n.**

free enterprise *n.* The freedom of private business to operate competitively with minimal government regulation.

free fall *n.* The fall of a body toward the earth without a drag-producing device such as a parachute.

free-for-all (frē′fər-ôl′) *n.* A brawl or competition in which many take part.

free·hand (frē′hănd′) *adj.* Drawn by hand without mechanical aids. **—free′hand′** *adv.*

free hand *n.* Full liberty to do as one sees fit.

free·hand·ed (frē′hăn′dĭd) *adj.* Generous. **—free′hand′ed·ly** *adv.* **—free′hand′ed·ness** *n.*

free·hold (frē′hōld′) *n.* **1.** An estate held in fee or for life. **2.** The tenure by which such an estate is held. **—free′hold′er** *n.*

free lance *n.* A person, esp. a writer, artist, or musician, who does not work for one employer only but sells his services to several employers as those services are needed. **—free′-lance′** *v.* **&** *adj.*

free·load (frē′lōd′) *v. Slang.* To live off the generosity or hospitality of others; sponge. **—free′load′er** *n.*

free love *n.* The practice of living together without marriage.

free·man (frē′mən) *n.* **1.** A person not in bondage or slavery. **2.** A person who possesses the rights or privileges of a citizen.

Free·ma·son (frē′mā′sən) *n.* A member of the Free and Accepted Masons, an international secret fraternity. **—Free′ma′son·ry** *n.*

fre·er (frē′ər) *adj.* Compar. of **free.**

fre·est (frē′ĭst) *adj.* Superl. of **free.**

free·stand·ing (frē′stăn′dĭng) *adj.* Standing without support or attachment.

free·stone (frē′stōn′) *n.* **1.** A fruit with a stone that does not adhere to the pulp. **2.** A stone, such as limestone, soft enough to be cut easily without shattering.

free·think·er (frē′thĭng′kər) *n.* One who has rejected authority and dogma, esp. in religious matters. **—free′think′ing** *adj.* **&** *n.*

free trade *n.* Trade between nations or states without protective customs tariffs.

free verse *n.* Verse without a conventional metrical pattern and with either an irregular rhyme or no rhyme.

free·way (frē′wā′) *n.* A highway with several lanes; expressway.

free·wheel·ing (frē′hwē′lĭng, -wē′-) *adj.* **1.** Free of restraints or rules in organization, methods, or procedure. **2.** Heedless; carefree.

free·will (frē′wĭl′) *adj.* Voluntary.

free will *n.* **1.** The power or discretion to choose. **2.** The belief that man's choices are or can be voluntary.

freeze (frēz) *v.* **froze** (frōz), **fro·zen** (frō′zən), **freez·ing. 1. a.** To pass or cause to pass from liquid to solid by loss of heat. **b.** To acquire a surface of ice. **2.** To preserve by subjecting to cold. **3.** To make or become inoperative through the formation of frost or ice. **4.** To damage or be damaged by cold. **5. a.** To be at that degree of temperature at which ice forms. **b.** To be uncomfortably cold. **6.** To make or become rigid or inflexible. **7.** To become paralyzed through fear or shyness. **8.** To become icily silent. **9.** To fix (prices or wages) at a current level. **10.** To prohibit further manufacture or use of. **11.** To prevent or restrict the exchange, liquidation, or granting of by law. **12.** To anesthetize by freezing. **—n. 1.** An act of freezing or a condition of being frozen. **2.** A period of cold weather; frost. [< OE *frēosan.*]

freeze-dry (frēz′drī′) *v.* To preserve by rapid freezing and drying in a vacuum.

freez·er (frē′zər) *n.* One that freezes, esp. an insulated cabinet or room for the rapid freezing and storing of perishable food.

freezing point *n.* The temperature at which a given liquid changes to a solid under a specified pressure, esp. a pressure equal to that of the atmosphere.

freight (frāt) *n.* **1.** Goods carried by a vessel

or vehicle; cargo. **2.** The commercial transportation of goods. **3.** The charge for transporting goods by cargo carrier. **4.** A railway train carrying goods only. —v. **1.** To convey commercially as cargo. **2.** To load with cargo. [< MDu. *vrecht*.]

freight·er (frā'tər) n. A vehicle, esp. a ship, for carrying freight.

French (frĕnch) adj. Of or characteristic of France, its people, language, or culture. —n. **1.** The Romance language of France, Switzerland, parts of Belgium, and various former French possessions. **2.** (used with a pl. verb). The people of France. —**French'man** n. —**French'wom'an** n.

French-Ca·na·di·an (frĕnch'kə-nā'dē-ən) n. Also **French Canadian.** A Canadian of French descent. —**French'-Ca·na'di·an** adj.

French door n. A door with glass panes extending the full length.

French fries pl.n. Strips of potatoes fried in deep fat.

French-fry (frĕnch'frī') v. To fry in deep fat.

French horn n. A valved brass wind instrument that tapers from a narrow mouthpiece to a flaring bell.

French horn

French leave n. An unauthorized departure.

French toast n. Sliced bread soaked in a milk and egg batter and lightly fried.

fre·net·ic (frə-nĕt'ĭk) adj. Frantic; frenzied. [< Gk. *phrenitis*, insanity.] —**fre·net'i·cal·ly** adv.

fren·zy (frĕn'zē) n., pl. -**zies. 1.** A seizure of violent agitation or wild excitement. **2.** Temporary madness. [< Gk. *phrenēsis*.] —**fren'zied** adj. —**fren'zied·ly** adv.

fre·quen·cy (frē'kwən-sē) n., pl. -**cies. 1.** The number of occurrences of a specified event within a given interval, as: **a.** The number of complete cycles of a wave that occur within a period of time. **b.** The number of complete oscillations or vibrations that a body undergoes in a given period of time. **2.** The condition of occurring repeatedly at short intervals. [< Lat. *frequentia*, multitude.]

frequency modulation n. The encoding of a carrier wave by variation of its frequency in accordance with an input signal.

fre·quent (frē'kwənt) adj. Occurring or appearing quite often or at close intervals. —v. (frē-kwĕnt', frē'kwənt). To pay frequent visits to. [< Lat. *frequens*, numerous.] —**fre·quent'er** n. —**fre'quent·ly** adv. —**fre'quent·ness** n.

fres·co (frĕs'kō) n., pl. -**coes** or -**cos. 1.** The art of painting on fresh plaster with colors

mixed in water. **2.** A painting executed in this manner. [< Ital., fresh, of Gmc. orig.]

fresh (frĕsh) adj. -**er, -est. 1.** Recently made, produced, or harvested; not stale or spoiled. **2.** Not preserved, as by canning. **3.** Not saline: *fresh water.* **4.** Additional; new: *fresh evidence.* **5.** New and unusual; novel: *a fresh approach to old problems.* **6.** Not yet used or soiled; clean: *a fresh towel.* **7.** Bright and clear; not dull or faded: *a fresh memory.* **8.** Having just arrived: *fresh from Paris.* **9.** Revived; refreshed. **10.** Giving energy or strength; invigorating: *a fresh spring morning.* **11.** *Informal.* Bold and saucy; impudent. [< OFr. *fres,* of Gmc. orig.] —**fresh'ly** adv. —**fresh'ness** n.

Syns: fresh, inventive, new, newfangled, novel, original adj.

fresh·en (frĕsh'ən) v. To make or become fresh. —**fresh'en·er** n.

fresh·et (frĕsh'ĭt) n. A sudden overflow of a stream resulting from heavy rain or a thaw.

fresh·man (frĕsh'mən) n. **1.** A first-year student at a high school, college, or university. **2.** A novice; beginner.

fresh·wa·ter (frĕsh'wô'tər, -wŏt'ər) adj. **1.** Of, living in, or consisting of water that is not salty. **2.** Accustomed to sailing on inland waters only: *a freshwater sailor.*

fret¹ (frĕt) v. **fret·ted, fret·ting. 1.** To be or cause to be uneasy or distressed; vex. **2. a.** To gnaw or wear away. **b.** To be worn or eaten away. —n. A condition of being troubled; worry. [< OE *fretan,* to devour.]

fret² (frĕt) n. One of several ridges set across the fingerboard of a stringed instrument. [Orig. unknown.] —**fret'ted** adj.

fret³ (frĕt) n. A design within a band or border, consisting of repeated symmetrical figures. [< OFr. *frete.*] —**fret** v.

fret·ful (frĕt'fəl) adj. Inclined to fret; peevish. —**fret'ful·ly** adv. —**fret'ful·ness** n.

fret·work (frĕt'wûrk') n. **1.** Ornamental work consisting of three-dimensional frets. **2.** Fretwork represented two-dimensionally.

Freud·i·an (froi'dē-ən) adj. Pertaining to or in accordance with the psychoanalytic theories of Sigmund Freud. —n. One who applies or believes in the psychoanalytic methods or theories of Freud.

fri·a·ble (frī'ə-bəl) adj. Readily crumbled; brittle. [< Lat. *friare,* to crumble.] —**fri'a·bil'i·ty** or **fri'a·ble·ness** n.

fri·ar (frī'ər) n. A member of certain, usu. mendicant Roman Catholic orders. [< Lat. *frater,* brother.]

fric·as·see (frĭk'ə-sē', frĭk'ə-sē') n. Poultry or meat cut into pieces, stewed, and served with a thick gravy. —v. -**seed, -see·ing.** To prepare as a fricassee. [< Fr. *fricasser,* to fry.]

fric·tion (frĭk'shən) n. **1.** The rubbing of one object or surface against another. **2.** A clash; conflict. **3.** *Physics.* A force that acts to resist or retard the relative motion of two objects that are in contact. [< Lat. *frictus,* p.p. of *fricare,* to rub.] —**fric'tion·al** adj.

friction tape n. A sturdy moisture-resistant adhesive tape used chiefly to insulate electrical conductors.

Fri·day (frī'dē, -dā') n. The 6th day of the week. [< OE *Frīgedæg.*]

friend (frĕnd) *n.* **1.** A person whom one knows, likes, and trusts. **2.** One that supports or patronizes a group or cause. **3. Friend.** A member of the Society of Friends; Quaker. [< OE *frēond.*] —**friend′less** *adj.* —**friend′-less-ness** *n.* —**friend′r′hip′** *n.*

friend·ly (frĕnd′lē) *adj.* **-li·er, -li·est. 1.** Of or befitting a friend. **2.** Favorably disposed; not antagonistic. **3.** Warm; comforting. —**friend′li-ness** *n.*

Syns: friendly, amiable, amicable, chummy, congenial, warmhearted adj.

fri·er (frī′ər) *n.* Var. of **fryer.**

frieze (frēz) *n.* A decorative horizontal band, as along the upper part of a wall in a room. [OFr. *frise.*]

frig·ate (frĭg′ĭt) *n.* **1.** A fast-sailing, square-rigged warship built between the 17th and mid-19th cent. **2.** A U.S. warship intermediate in size between a cruiser and destroyer. [< Ital. *fregata.*]

frigate

fright (frīt) *n.* **1.** Sudden, intense fear. **2.** *Informal.* Something extremely unsightly or alarming. [< OE *fyrhto.*]

fright·en (frīt′n) *v.* **1.** To make suddenly afraid. **2.** To drive or force by arousing fear. —**fright′en·ing·ly** *adv.*

Syns: frighten, alarm, panic, scare, startle, terrify, terrorize v.

fright·ful (frīt′fəl) *adj.* **1.** Causing disgust or shock. **2.** Causing fright. **3.** *Informal.* **a.** Excessive; extreme. **b.** Disagreeable; distressing. —**fright′ful·ly** *adv.* —**fright′ful·ness** *n.*

frig·id (frĭj′ĭd) *adj.* **1.** Extremely cold. **2.** Lacking warmth of feeling; cold in manner. [< Lat. *frigus,* the cold.] —**fri·gid′i·ty** (frĭ-jĭd′ĭ-tē) or **frig′id·ness** *n.* —**frig′id·ly** *adv.*

frill (frĭl) *n.* **1.** A ruffled, gathered, or pleated border or edging. **2.** Something fancy but not essential. [Orig. unknown.] —**frill′y** *adj.*

fringe (frĭnj) *n.* **1.** A decorative border or edging of hanging threads, cords, or loops. **2.** Something like a fringe along an edge. **3.** A marginal or peripheral part. [< LLat. *fimbria.*] —**fringe** *v.*

fringe benefit *n.* An employment benefit given in addition to wages or salary.

frip·per·y (frĭp′ə-rē) *n., pl.* **-ies. 1.** Cheap, showy ornaments or dress. **2.** An ostentatious display. [< OFr. *frepe,* rag.]

frisk (frĭsk) *v.* **1.** To move about briskly and playfully. **2.** To search (a person) for something concealed, esp. weapons, by passing the hands quickly over clothes. [< OFr. *frisque,* lively.] —**frisk′er** *n.*

frisk·y (frĭs′kē) *adj.* **-i·er, -i·est.** Energetic and playful. —**frisk′i·ly** *adv.* —**frisk′i·ness** *n.*

frit·ter¹ (frĭt′ər) *v.* To reduce or squander little by little. [< obs. *fritter,* fragment.]

frit·ter² (frĭt′ər) *n.* A small fried cake made of batter that often contains fruit, vegetables, or fish. [< Lat. *frigere,* to fry.]

friv·o·lous (frĭv′ə-ləs) *adj.* **1.** Insignificant; trivial. **2.** Not serious or sensible: *frivolous conversation.* [< Lat. *frivolus.*] —**fri·vol′i·ty** (-vŏl′ĭ-tē) *n.* —**friv′o·lous·ly** *adv.*

frizz (frĭz) *v.* To form or be formed into small, tight curls. —*n.* A tight curl of hair or fabric. [Fr. *friser.*] —**friz′zi·ly** *adv.* —**friz′zi-ness** *n.* —**friz′zy** *adj.*

friz·zle¹ (frĭz′əl) *v.* **-zled, -zling. 1.** To fry until crisp and curled. **2.** To cook with a sizzling noise. [Perh. blend of FRY¹ and SIZZLE.]

friz·zle² (frĭz′əl) *v.* **-zled, -zling.** To frizz. —*n.* A small, tight curl. [Orig. unknown.]

fro (frō) *adv.* Away; back: *moving to and fro.* [< OE *fram* and < ON *frām.*]

frock (frŏk) *n.* **1.** A woman's or girl's dress. **2.** A long, loose outer garment; smock. **3.** A robe worn by monks and other clerics. [< OFr. *froc,* of Gmc. orig.]

frog (frôg, frŏg) *n.* **1.** Any of numerous tailless, chiefly aquatic amphibians that characteristically have a smooth, moist skin, webbed feet, and long hind legs adapted for leaping. **2.** An ornamental looped braid or cord with a button or knot for fastening the front of a garment. **3.** A device on intersecting railroad tracks that permits wheels to cross the junction. **4.** A spiked or perforated object placed in a container and used to support stems in a flower arrangement. **5.** Hoarseness in the throat. [< OE *frogga.*]

frog·man (frôg′măn′, -mən, frŏg′-) *n.* A swimmer equipped to execute underwater maneuvers, esp. military maneuvers.

frol·ic (frŏl′ĭk) *n.* **1.** Gaiety; merriment. **2.** A gay, carefree time. —*v.* **-icked, -ick·ing. 1.** To behave playfully; romp. **2.** To engage in merrymaking. [< MDu. *vrolijc.*] —**frol′ick·er** *n.* —**frol′ic·some** *adj.*

from (frŭm, frŏm; frəm *when unstressed*) *prep.* **1.** Beginning at a specified place or time. **2.** With a specified time or point as the first of two limits. **3.** With a person, place, or thing as the source or instrument. **4.** Out of. **5.** Out of the jurisdiction, control, or possession of. **6.** So as not to be engaged in: *keep someone from making a mistake.* **7.** Measured by reference to: *far away from home.* **8.** As opposed to: *know right from wrong.* [< OE.]

frond (frŏnd) *n.* The usu. divided leaf of a fern, palm tree, etc. [Lat. *frons, frond-,* foliage.]

front (frŭnt) *n.* **1.** The forward part or surface. **2.** The area, location, or position directly ahead. **3.** A position of superiority or leadership. **4.** The first part. **5.** Demeanor; bearing: *kept up a brave front.* **6.** A false appearance or manner. **7.** Land bordering a lake, river, street, etc. **8.** An area where major fighting is taking place. **9.** An area or scene of a particular activity: *life on the home front.* **10.** The boundary between two masses of air that are at different temperatures: *a cold front.* **11.** An outwardly respectable person or business that serves as a cover for secret or illegal activity. —*adj.* In or facing the front. —*v.* **1.** To have a front (on); face. **2.** To serve as a front for. **3.** To confront. [< Lat. *frons, front-.*] —**fron′tal** *adj.* —**fron′tal·ly** *adv.*

front·age (frŭn′tĭj) *n.* **1. a.** The front part of a piece of property. **b.** The dimensions of such a part. **2.** Land adjacent to a building, street, or body of water.

fron·tier (frŭn-tîr′, frŏn-) *n.* **1.** An international border or the area along it. **2.** A region in a country that marks the point of farthest settlement. **3.** An undeveloped area or field for discovery or research. [< Lat. *frons, front.*] **—fron·tiers′man** *n.*

fron·tis·piece (frŭn′tĭ-spēs′) *n.* An illustration that faces or immediately precedes the title page of a book. [< Med. Lat. *frontispicium,* façade.]

front-run·ner (frŭnt′rŭn′ər) *n.* One that is leading in a race or competition.

frost (frôst, frŏst) *n.* **1.** A covering of small ice crystals formed from frozen water vapor. **2.** The atmospheric conditions below the freezing point of water. *—v.* **1.** To cover or become covered with frost. **2.** To damage or kill by frost. **3.** To cover or decorate with icing. [< OE.] **—frost′i·ly** *adv.* **—frost′i·ness** *n.* **—frost′y** *adj.*

frost·bite (frôst′bīt′, frŏst′-) *n.* Local destruction of body tissue as a result of freezing. **—frost′bite′** *v.*

frost heave *n.* An uplifting of a surface, such as pavement, caused by freezing beneath the surface.

frost·ing (frô′stĭng, frŏs′tĭng) *n.* **1.** A glaze of sugar and other ingredients used to decorate cakes. **2.** A roughened or speckled surface imparted to glass or metal.

frost line *n.* The limit to which frost penetrates the earth.

froth (frôth, frŏth) *n.* **1.** A mass of bubbles in or on a liquid; foam. **2.** A salivary foam resulting from disease or exhaustion. **3.** Something that is lacking in substance or depth. *—v.* To exude or expel froth. [< ON *frodha.*] **—froth′i·ly** *adv.* **—froth′i·ness** *n.* **—froth′y** *adj.*

frou-frou (frōō′frōō) *n.* **1.** A rustling sound, as of silk. **2.** Showy or fussy dress or ornamentation. [Fr.]

fro·ward (frō′wərd, frō′ərd) *adj.* Stubbornly contrary and disobedient. [ME.]

frown (froun) *v.* **1.** To wrinkle the brow, as in thought or displeasure. **2.** To regard with disapproval or distaste. *—n.* The act of wrinkling the brow. [< OFr. *froigner,* of Celt. orig.] **—frown′ing·ly** *adv.*

frow·zy (frou′zē) *adj.* **-zi·er, -zi·est.** Also **frow·sy.** Unkempt in appearance; slovenly. [Orig. unknown.] **—frow′zi·ly** *adv.* **—frow′zi·ness** *n.*

froze (frōz) *v. p.t.* of **freeze.**

fro·zen (frō′zən) *v. p.p.* of **freeze.** *—adj.* **1.** Made into, covered with, or surrounded by ice. **2.** Very cold. **3.** Preserved by freezing. **4.** Rendered immobile. **5.** Expressive of cold unfriendliness. **6. a.** Kept at an arbitrary level, as wages. **b.** Incapable of being withdrawn, sold, or liquidated, as assets.

fruc·ti·fy (frŭk′tə-fī′, frōōk′-) *v.* **-fied, -fy·ing.** To bear or cause to bear fruit. [< Lat. *fructificare.*] **—fruc′ti·fi·ca′tion** *n.*

fruc·tose (frŭk′tōs′, frōōk′-, frōōk′-) *n.* A very sweet sugar, $C_6H_{12}O_6$, found in many fruits and honey. [Lat. *fructus,* fruit + -OSE².]

fru·gal (frōō′gəl) *adj.* **1.** Thrifty. **2.** Not very abundant; meager; economical. [< Lat. *frux,*

success.] **—fru·gal′i·ty** (-găl′ĭ-tē) *or* **fru′gal·ness** *n.* **—fru′gal·ly** *adv.*

fruit (frōōt) *n., pl.* **fruit** *or* **fruits.** **1.** The ripened, seed-bearing part of a plant, esp. when fleshy and edible. **2.** The fertile, often spore-bearing structure of a plant that does not bear seeds. **3.** A result; outcome. *—v.* To produce fruit. [< Lat. *frui,* to enjoy.]

fruit·cake (frōōt′kāk′) *n.* A heavy cake that contains citron, nuts, and preserved fruits.

fruit fly *n.* Any of various small flies that have larvae that feed on ripening or fermenting fruit.

fruit·ful (frōōt′fəl) *adj.* **1.** Producing fruit. **2.** Producing results; profitable. **—fruit′ful·ly** *adv.* **—fruit′ful·ness** *n.*

fru·i·tion (frōō-ĭsh′ən) *n.* **1.** The achievement of something desired or worked for. **2.** The condition of bearing fruit.

fruit·less (frōōt′lĭs) *adj.* **1.** Unproductive. **2.** Producing no fruit. **—fruit′less·ly** *adv.* **—fruit′less·ness** *n.*

fruit·y (frōō′tē) *adj.* **-i·er, -i·est.** Tasting or smelling of fruit. **—fruit′i·ness** *n.*

frump·y (frŭmpē) *adj.* **-i·er, -i·est.** Dull and staid; dowdy. [Orig. unknown.] **—frump** *n.* **—frump′i·ly** *adv.* **—frump′i·ness** *n.*

frus·trate (frŭs′trāt′) *v.* **-trat·ed, -trat·ing.** **1.** To prevent from accomplishing a purpose or fulfilling a desire. **2.** To prevent the accomplishment of; nullify. [< Lat. *frustrare,* to disappoint.] **—frus·tra′tion** *n.*

fry[1] (frī) *v.* **fried, fry·ing.** To cook over direct heat in hot oil or fat. *—n., pl.* **fries.** **1.** A dish of fried food. **2.** A social gathering featuring fried food. [< Lat. *frigere.*]

fry[2] (frī) *n., pl.* **fry.** **1.** A small fish, esp. a recently hatched fish. **2.** Individuals; persons: *young fry.* [Prob. < AN *fri.*]

fry·er (frī′ər) *n.* Also **fri·er.** **1.** A young chicken suitable for frying. **2.** A deep pot for frying foods.

fuch·sia (fyōō′shə) *n.* **1.** A widely cultivated plant with showy, drooping purplish, reddish, or white flowers. **2.** A vivid purplish red. [< Leonhard *Fuchs* (1501-66).] **—fuch′sia** *adj.*

fud·dle (fŭd′l) *v.* **-dled, -dling.** To confuse with or as if with liquor; intoxicate. [Orig. unknown.]

fud·dy-dud·dy (fŭd′ē-dŭd′ē) *n., pl.* **-dies.** An old-fashioned, conservative, or very fussy person. [Orig. unknown.]

fudge (fŭj) *n.* **1.** A soft rich candy made of sugar, butter, and flavoring. **2.** Nonsense; humbug. *—v.* **fudged, fudg·ing.** **1.** To fake or falsify. **2.** To evade; dodge. [Orig. unknown.]

fu·el (fyōō′əl) *n.* Something consumed to produce energy, esp.: **1.** A material such as wood or oil burned to produce heat. **2.** Fissionable material·used in a nuclear reactor. **3.** Nutritive material metabolized by a living organism. *—v.* **-eled** *or* **-elled, -el·ing** *or* **-el·ling.** To provide with or take in fuel. [< Lat. *focus,* hearth.] **—fu′el·er** *n.*

fuel cell *n.* A device in which a fuel and an oxidizing agent react and release energy in the form of electricity.

fu·gi·tive (fyōō′jĭ-tĭv) *adj.* **1.** Running or having run away, as from justice. **2.** Passing quickly; fleeting: *fugitive dreams.* *—n.* One who flees. [< Lat. *fugere,* to flee.]

fugue (fyōōg) *n.* A musical composition in which one or more themes are stated and then developed by means of imitation and elaborate counterpoint. [< Lat. *fuga*, flight.]

füh·rer (fyŏŏr'ər) *n.* Also **fueh·rer.** 1. A leader, esp. one exercising the powers of a tyrant. 2. Führer. The title of Adolf Hitler as leader of Nazi Germany. [G.]

-ful *suff.* 1. Fullness or abundance: *playful.* 2. Having the characteristics of: *masterful.* 3. Tendency or ability: *useful.* 4. The amount or number that will fill: *armful.* [< OE.]

ful·crum (fŏŏl'krəm, fŭl'-) *n., pl.* **-crums** or **-cra** (-krə). The support on which a lever turns. [Lat., support.]

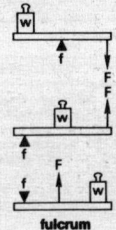

fulcrum

Black triangles represent the fulcrums of three basic levers

ful·fill or **ful·fil** (fŏŏl-fĭl') *v.* **-filled, -fill·ing.** 1. To bring into actuality; effect. 2. To carry out. 3. To satisfy. [< OE *fullfyllan.*] —**ful·fill'er** *n.* —**ful·fill'ment** or **ful·fil'ment** *n.*

full¹ (fŏŏl) *adj.* **-er, -est.** 1. Containing all that is normal or possible; complete. 2. Of maximum or highest degree. 3. Having a great deal or many: *full of errors.* 4. Totally qualified or unanimously accepted: *a full member.* 5. a. Rounded in shape. b. Of generous proportions; wide. 6. Satiated, esp. with food or drink. 7. Having depth and body. —*adv.* 1. To a complete extent; entirely: *knew full well that he was wrong.* 2. Exactly; directly: *a blow that caught him full on the chin.* —*n.* The maximum or complete size, amount, or development. —**idiom. in full.** Completely; with nothing lacking: *paid in full.* [< OE.] —**full'ness** or **ful'ness** *n.*

full² (fŏŏl) *v.* To increase the weight and bulk of (cloth) by shrinking and beating or pressing. [< Lat. *fullo*, fuller.] —**full'er** *n.*

full·back (fŏŏl'băk') *n.* Football. An offensive backfield player whose position is behind the quarterback and halfbacks.

full-blood·ed (fŏŏl'blŭd'ĭd) *adj.* 1. Of unmixed ancestry; purebred. 2. Vigorous and energetic.

full-blown (fŏŏl'blŏn') *adj.* 1. In full blossom. 2. Fully developed or matured.

full-bod·ied (fŏŏl'bŏd'ēd) *adj.* Having richness of flavor.

full dress *n.* The attire required for formal occasions.

full-fledged (fŏŏl'flĕjd') *adj.* 1. Having fully developed adult plumage. 2. Having full status or rank.

full moon *n.* The phase of the moon when it is seen as a fully lighted disk.

full-scale (fŏŏl'skāl') *adj.* 1. Of the actual or full size. 2. Employing all resources.

ful·ly (fŏŏl'ē) *adv.* 1. Totally or completely. 2. At least.

ful·mi·nate (fŏŏl'mə-nāt', fŭl'-) *v.* **-nat·ed, -nat·ing.** 1. To denounce severely. 2. To explode. [< Lat. *fulminare*, to strike with lightning.] —**ful'mi·na'tor** *n.* —**ful'mi·na'tion** *n.*

ful·some (fŏŏl'səm) *adj.* Offensively excessive or insincere: *fulsome praise.* [ME *fulsom*, loathsome.] —**ful'some·ly** *adv.* —**ful'some·ness** *n.*

fum·ble (fŭm'bəl) *v.* **-bled, -bling.** 1. To touch or handle nervously or idly. 2. To grope awkwardly or uncertainly; blunder. 3. Sports. To mishandle or drop a ball. —*n.* 1. The act or an example of fumbling. 2. Sports. A ball that has been fumbled. [Perh. of Scand. orig.] —**fum'ble** *n.* —**fum'bler** *n.*

fume (fyōōm) *n.* Often **fumes.** A usu. irritating smoke, vapor, or gas. —*v.* **fumed, fuming.** 1. To subject to or treat with fumes. 2. To give off in or as if in fumes. 3. To feel or show agitation or anger. [< Lat. *fumus.*]

fu·mi·gate (fyōō'mĭ-gāt') *v.* **-gat·ed, -gat·ing.** To treat with fumes in order to kill germs, insects, rats, or other pests. [Lat. *fumigare*, to smoke.] —**fu'mi·ga'tion** *n.* —**fu'mi·ga'tor** *n.*

fun (fŭn) *n.* 1. Enjoyment, pleasure, or amusement. 2. Excited, noisy activity. —**idiom. make fun of.** To tease or ridicule. [Perh. < ME *fon*, fool.]

func·tion (fŭngk'shən) *n.* 1. The proper, normal, or characteristic activity of a person or thing. 2. The duty, occupation, or role of a person. 3. An official ceremony or elaborate social occasion. 4. Math. A rule of correspondence between two sets such that there is a unique element in one set assigned to each element in the other set. —*v.* To have or perform a function; serve. [< Lat. *functio*, performance.] —**func'tion·less** *adj.*

func·tion·al (fŭngk'shə-nəl) *adj.* 1. Of or concerning a function. 2. Designed for or adapted to a particular purpose. 3. Capable of performing; operative. 4. Path. Existing with no apparent change in the structure of an organism. —**func'tion·al·ly** *adv.*

func·tion·ar·y (fŭngk'shə-nĕr'ē) *n., pl.* **-ies.** One who holds a position of trust; official.

function word *n.* A word that expresses grammatical function rather than content or meaning.

fund (fŭnd) *n.* 1. A source of supply; stock. 2. A sum of money or other resources set aside for a specific purpose. 3. **funds.** Available money; ready cash. —*v.* 1. To furnish money for. 2. To make provision for paying off (a debt). [Lat. *fundus*, piece of land.]

fun·da·men·tal (fŭn'də-mĕn'tl) *adj.* 1. a. Elemental; basic. b. Central; key. 2. Generative; primary. 3. Physics. a. Of or pertaining to the component of lowest frequency of a periodic wave or quantity. b. Of or pertaining to the lowest possible frequency of a vibrating element or system. [< Lat. *fundamentum*, foundation.] —*n.* —**fun'da·men'tal·ly** *adv.*

fun·da·men·tal·ism (fŭn'də-mĕn'tl-ĭz'əm) *n.* A Protestant movement holding the Bible to be the sole historical and prophetic authority. —**fun'da·men'tal·ist** *n.*

fu·ner·al (fyōō'nər-əl) *n.* 1. The ceremonies held in connection with the burial or cremation of the dead. 2. A procession accompanying a body to the grave. [< Lat. *funus.*]

fu·ne·re·al (fyōō-nîr'ē-əl) *adj.* 1. Of or suitable

for a funeral. **2.** Mournful; sorrowful. [< Lat. *funus,* funeral.] **—fu·ne're·al·ly** *adv.*

fun·gi·cide (fŭn'jĭ-sīd', fŭng'gĭ-) *n.* A substance that destroys fungi.

fun·go (fŭng'gō) *n., pl.* **-goes.** *Baseball.* A practice fly ball hit to a fielder with a specially designed bat. [Orig. unknown.]

fun·gus (fŭng'gəs) *n., pl.* **fun·gi** (fŭn'jī') or **-gus·es.** Any of numerous plants, including the yeasts, molds, and mushrooms, that lack chlorophyll. [Lat.] **—fun'gous** or **fun'gal** *adj.*

fu·nic·u·lar (fyŏo-nĭk'yə-lər, fə-) *n.* A cable railway on a steep incline, esp. one with simultaneously ascending and descending cars counterbalancing one another. [< Lat. *funiculus,* thin rope.]

funk (fŭngk) *n.* **1.** A state of cowardly fright. **2.** A state of depression. [Perh. < obs. Flem. *fonck.*]

funk·y (fŭng'kē) *adj.* **-i·er, -i·est.** *Slang.* **1.** Having an earthy, unpolished quality characteristic of the blues: *funky music.* **2.** Unconventional or outlandishly vulgar, often in a humorous manner. [< *funk,* strong smell.] **—funk'i·ness** *n.*

fun·nel (fŭn'əl) *n.* **1.** A conical utensil with a narrow tube at the bottom, used to channel a substance into a small-mouthed container. **2.** A shaft or flue; smokestack. —*v.* **-neled** or **-nelled, -nel·ing** or **-nel·ling.** To move or cause to move through or as if through a funnel. [< Lat. *infundibulum.*]

fun·ny (fŭn'ē) *adj.* **-ni·er, -ni·est. 1.** Causing laughter or amusement. **2.** Strange; odd; curious. —*pl.n.* **funnies.** Comic strips. **—fun'ni·ly** *adv.* **—fun'ni·ness** *n.*

funny bone *n.* A point near the elbow where pressure on a nerve can produce a numb or a tingling feeling.

fur (fûr) *n.* **1. a.** The thick coat of soft hair covering the body of various animals. **b.** The pelts of fur-bearing animals used for clothing, trimming, etc. **2.** A furlike covering. [Prob. < OFr. *forreure,* of Gmc. orig.] **—furred** *adj.*

fur·be·low (fûr'bə-lō') *n.* **1.** A ruffle on a garment. **2.** A small piece of showy ornamentation. [< Fr. *falbala.*]

fur·bish (fûr'bĭsh) *v.* **1.** To brighten by cleaning or rubbing; burnish. **2.** To renovate. [< OFr. *fourbir,* of Gmc. orig.] **—fur'bish·er** *n.*

Fu·ries (fyŏor'ēz) *pl.n. Gk. & Rom. Myth.* The three terrible, winged goddesses who punish doers of unavenged crimes.

fu·ri·ous (fyŏor'ē-əs) *adj.* **1.** Extremely angry; raging. **2.** Fierce; intense: *a furious speed.* [< Lat. *furia,* fury.] **—fu'ri·ous·ly** *adv.*

furl (fûrl) *v.* **1.** To roll up and secure (a flag or sail) to a pole, yard, or mast. **2.** To fold. [< OFr. *ferlier.*] **—furl** *n.*

fur·long (fûr'lông', -lŏng') *n.* A unit of distance, equal to about 201 meters or 220 yards. [< OE *furlang.*]

fur·lough (fûr'lō) *n.* A leave of absence from duty, esp. one granted to military personnel. [Du. *verlof.*] **—fur'lough** *v.*

fur·nace (fûr'nĭs) *n.* An enclosed chamber in which a fuel is consumed, usu. by burning, to produce heat. [< Lat. *fornax.*]

fur·nish (fûr'nĭsh) *v.* **1.** To equip, esp. with furniture. **2.** To supply; give. [< OFr. *furnir,* of Gmc. orig.] **—fur'nish·er** *n.*

fur·nish·ings (fûr'nĭ-shĭngz) *pl.n.* **1.** Furniture and other equipment for a home or office. **2.** Clothes and accessories.

fur·ni·ture (fûr'nə-chər) *n.* **1.** Movable articles for a room or establishment. **2.** Necessary equipment, as for a ship. [< OFr. *furnir,* to furnish.]

fu·ror (fyŏor'ôr', -ər) *n.* **1.** Violent anger; frenzy. **2.** A state of intense excitement. **3.** A public uproar. [Lat. < *furere,* to rage.]

fur·ri·er (fûr'ē-ər) *n.* One who designs, sells, or repairs furs. [< AN *furrer.*]

fur·ring (fûr'ĭng) *n.* Strips of wood or metal applied to a wall to provide a level surface.

fur·row (fûr'ō, fŭr'ō) *n.* **1.** A trench made in the ground by or as if by a plow or other tool. **2.** A deep wrinkle in the skin. [< OE *furh.*] **—fur'row** *v.*

furrow

fur·ry (fûr'ē) *adj.* **-ri·er, -ri·est.** Consisting of, covered with, or resembling fur or a furlike coating. **—fur'ri·ness** *n.*

fur·ther (fûr'thər) *adj.* **1.** More distant in space, time, or degree. **2.** Additional. —*adv.* **1.** To a greater extent; more. **2.** In addition; furthermore. **3.** At or to a more distant point in space or time. —*v.* To help the progress of. [< OE *furthor.*] **—fur'ther·ance** *n.*

fur·ther·more (fûr'thər-môr', -mōr') *adv.* In addition; moreover.

fur·ther·most (fûr'thər-mōst') *adj.* Most distant or remote.

fur·thest (fûr'thĭst) *adj.* Most distant in space, time, or degree. —*adv.* **1.** To the greatest extent or degree. **2.** At or to the most distant point in space or time. [ME.]

fur·tive (fûr'tĭv) *adj.* Marked by stealth; surreptitious. [< Lat. *fur,* thief.] **—fur'tive·ly** *adv.* **—fur'tive·ness** *n.*

fu·ry (fyŏor'ē) *n., pl.* **-ries. 1.** Violent rage. **2.** Uncontrolled action; turbulence. [< Lat. *furere,* to rage.]

furze (fûrz) *n.* Gorse. [< OE *fyrs.*]

fuse¹ (fyŏoz) *n.* **1.** A length of easily burned material that is lighted at one end to carry a flame to and detonate an explosive charge at the other. **2.** Var. of **fuze.** [< Lat. *fusus,* spindle.] **—fuse** *v.*

fuse² (fyŏoz) *v.* **fused, fus·ing. 1.** To liquefy or reduce to a plastic state by heating; melt. **2.** To mix together or unite by or as if by melting; blend. —*n.* A protective device for an electric circuit that melts when the current becomes too strong and thus opens the circuit. [< Lat. *fusus,* p.p. of *fundere,* to melt.] **—fus'i·bil'i·ty** *n.* **—fus'i·ble** *adj.*

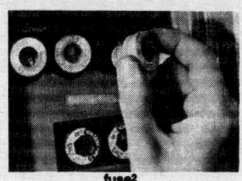

fuse²

fu·see (fyōō-zē′) n. Also **fu·zee.** 1. A friction match with a large head capable of burning in a wind. 2. A colored flare used as a railway warning signal. [< Lat. *fusus,* spindle.]

fu·se·lage (fyōō′sə-läzh′, -zə-) n. The body of an airplane, to which the wings and tail assembly are attached. [< Fr. *fuselé,* spindle-shaped.]

fu·sil·lade (fyōō′sə-läd′, -läd′, -zə-) n. 1. A simultaneous or rapid discharge of many firearms. 2. A rapid outburst or barrage. [< Fr. *fusiller,* to shoot.]

fu·sion (fyōō′zhən) n. 1. The act or process of melting by heat. 2. A mixture or blend formed by fusing. 3. A reaction in which atomic nuclei combine to form more massive nuclei, gen. leaving some excess mass that is converted into energy.

fuss (fŭs) n. 1. Needlessly nervous or useless activity. 2. Needless concern or worry. 3. A protest; complaint. —v. 1. To be in a state of nervous or useless activity. 2. To show excessive care. 3. To complain. [Orig. unknown.] —**fuss′er** n.

fuss-budg·et (fŭs′bŭj′ĭt) n. One who fusses over unimportant matters.

fuss·y (fŭs′ē) adj. **-i·er, -i·est.** 1. Given to fussing; easily upset. 2. Frequently complaining or making demands. 3. Fastidious; meticulous. 4. Requiring attention to small details. —**fuss′i·ly** adv. —**fuss′i·ness** n.

fus·tian (fŭs′chən) n. 1. *Obs.* A coarse, sturdy cloth. 2. Pompous language. [< Med. Lat. *fustaneum.*] —**fus′tian** adj.

fus·ty (fŭs′tē) adj. **-ti·er, -ti·est.** 1. Smelling of mildew or decay. 2. Old-fashioned; antique. [< OFr. *fuste,* wine cask.] —**fus′ti·ly** adv. —**fus′ti·ness** n.

fu·tile (fyōōt′l, fyōō′tīl′) adj. Having no useful result; useless. [Lat. *futilis.*] —**fu′tile·ly** adv. —**fu·til′i·ty** (-tĭl′ĭ-tē) n.

fu·ture (fyōō′chər) n. 1. The period of time yet to be. 2. Something that will happen in time to come. 3. Chance of success or advancement. 4. *Gram.* The future tense. —adj. That is to be or come in the future. [< Lat. *futurus.*]

future shock n. A condition of distress and disorientation brought on by an inability to cope with rapid societal and technological change. [< the book *Future Shock* by Alvin Toffler (b. 1928).]

future tense n. A verb tense used to express action in the future.

fu·tur·is·tic (fyōō′chə-rĭs′tĭk) adj. Of or pertaining to the future, esp. to the forecasting or depiction of life and society in the future.

fu·tu·ri·ty (fyōō-tŏŏr′ĭ-tē, -tyŏŏr′-, -chŏŏr′-) n., pl. **-ties.** 1. The future. 2. The condition or quality of being in or of the future. 3. A future event or possibility.

fu·tur·ol·o·gy (fyōō′chə-rŏl′ə-jē) n. The study or forecast of potential developments, as in science and technology, using current conditions or trends as a point of departure. —**fu′tu·rol′o·gist** n.

fuze (fyōōz) n. Also **fuse.** A mechanical or electrical device used to detonate an explosive. [< FUSE¹.]

fu·zee (fyōō-zē′) n. Var. of **fusee.**

fuzz¹ (fŭz) n. A mass of soft, light particles, fibers, or hairs; fine down. [Perh. < FUZZY.]

fuzz² (fŭz) n. *Slang.* The police. [Orig. unknown.]

fuzz·y (fŭz′ē) adj. **-i·er, -i·est.** 1. Covered with fuzz. 2. Of or resembling fuzz. 3. Indistinct; blurred. [Perh. < LG *fussig,* spongy.] —**fuzz′i·ly** adv. —**fuzz′i·ness** n.

-fy suff. Make; cause to become: *calcify.* [< Lat. *facere,* to make.]

Gg

g or **G** (jē) n., pl. **g's** or **G's.** 1. The 7th letter of the English alphabet. 2. **G.** A unit of force equal to the gravity exerted on a body at rest.

G (jē) adj. Indicating a rating given motion pictures considered appropriate for all ages. [< GENERAL.]

Ga The symbol for the element gallium.

gab (găb) v. **gabbed, gab·bing.** *Informal.* To talk idly or thoughtlessly; chatter. [Perh. < Sc. *gab,* mouthful.] —**gab** n. —**gab′ber** n.

gab·ar·dine (găb′ər-dēn′, găb′ər-dēn′) n. A worsted cotton, wool, or rayon twill, used in making dresses, suits, and coats. [< OFr. *gauvardine,* a long cloak.]

gab·ble (găb′əl) v. **-bled, -bling.** 1. To speak or say rapidly and unclearly. 2. To make repeated cackling noises, as a goose or duck. [MDu. *gabbelen.*] —**gab′ble** n.

gab·by (găb′ē) adj. **-bi·er, -bi·est.** *Informal.* Tending to talk too much. —**gab′bi·ness** n.

ga·ble (gā′bəl) n. A triangular wall section at the end of a pitched roof, bounded by the two roof slopes. [< OFr.] —**ga′bled** adj.

gad (găd) v. **gad·ded, gad·ding.** To move about restlessly and with little purpose; rove. [ME *gadden.*] —**gad′der** n.

gad·a·bout (găd′ə-bout′) n. One who wanders about looking for fun, excitement, or gossip.

gad·fly (găd′flī′) n. 1. A fly that bites or annoys animals, esp. livestock. 2. One that acts as a provocative stimulus. [*gad,* spike + FLY.]

gadg·et (găj′ĭt) n. *Informal.* A small specialized mechanical device. [Orig. unknown.] —**gadg′et·ry** n.

gad·o·lin·i·um (găd′l-ĭn′ē-əm) n. *Symbol* **Gd** A silvery-white, malleable, ductile, metallic element, used to improve the high-temperature characteristics of iron, chromium, and related metallic alloys. Atomic number 64; atomic weight 157.25. [< Johann *Gadolin* (1760–1852).]

Gael (gāl) *n.* A Celt of Scotland, Ireland, or the Isle of Man.

Gael·ic (gā'lĭk) *n.* 1. A branch of the Celtic languages. 2. One of the languages of the Gaels. —**Gael'ic** *adj.*

gaff (găf) *n.* 1. An iron hook attached to a pole and used for landing large fish. 2. A spar used to extend the top edge of a fore-and-aft sail. 3. *Slang.* Harshness of treatment; abuse. [< OFr. *gaffe.*] —**gaff** *v.*

gaff

gaffe (găf) *n.* A clumsy social error. [Fr.]

gaf·fer (găf'ər) *n.* 1. An old man. 2. An electrician in charge of lighting on a film or television set. [Perh. < GODFATHER.]

gag (găg) *n.* 1. Something forced into or put over the mouth to prevent speech. 2. Any obstacle to free speech. 3. A device placed in the mouth to keep it open, as in dentistry. 4. a. A practical joke. b. A comic remark. —*v.* **gagged, gag·ging.** 1. To prevent from uttering sounds by using a gag. 2. To repress (free speech). 3. To block off or obstruct. 4. To choke or retch. 5. To make jokes. [ME *gaggen,* to suffocate.]

gage¹ (gāj) *n.* 1. Something deposited or given as security; pledge. 2. Something, such as a glove, thrown down as a challenge to fight. [< OFr.]

gage² (gāj) *n.* Var. of **gauge.**

gag·gle (găg'əl) *n.* A flock of geese. [ME *gagel.*]

gag order *n.* An order forbidding reporting or public commentary on a case currently before a court.

gag rule *n.* A rule, as in a legislature, limiting discussion or debate.

gai·e·ty (gā'ĭ-tē) *n., pl.* **-ties.** 1. The condition of being gay or merry. 2. Festive or joyful activity. [< OFr. *gaie,* cheerful.]

Syns: *gaiety, glee, hilarity, jollity, merriment, mirth* n.

gai·ly (gā'lē) *adv.* 1. In a joyful, cheerful, or happy manner. 2. Colorfully; showily.

gain (gān) *v.* 1. To become the owner of; acquire; get. 2. To win. 3. To earn. 4. To build up an increase of, as weight. 5. To arrive at. 6. To advance or progress. 7. To come nearer or closer. —*n.* Something gained; profit; advantage; increase. [OFr. *gaaignier.*]

gain·er (gā'nər) *n.* 1. One that gains. 2. A dive in which the diver leaves the board facing forward, does a back somersault, and enters the water feet first.

gain·ful (gān'fəl) *adj.* Providing an income. —**gain'ful·ly** *adv.* —**gain'ful·ness** *n.*

gain·say (gān-sā') *v.* **-said** (-sĕd'), **-say·ing.** To

contradict; deny. [ME *gainsayen.*] —**gain·say'er** *n.*

gait (gāt) *n.* 1. A way of moving on foot. 2. Any of the ways a horse can move by lifting the feet in a certain order or rhythm. [< ON *gata,* path.]

gai·ter (gā'tər) *n.* 1. A leather or cloth covering for the legs from the knee to the instep. 2. A smaller covering worn over a shoe and extending from the ankle to the instep; spat. 3. An ankle-high shoe with elastic sides. 4. An overshoe with a cloth top. [Fr. *guêtre.*]

gal (găl) *n. Informal.* A girl.

ga·la (gā'lə, găl'ə, gä'lə) *n.* A festive occasion or celebration. [< OSp.] —**ga'la** *adj.*

ga·lac·tose (gə-lăk'tōs') *n., pl.* A simple sugar, $C_6H_{12}O_6$, commonly occurring in lactose. [Gk. *gala,* milk + -OSE².]

Gal·a·had (găl'ə-hăd') *n.* A model of chivalrous virtue. [< Sir *Galahad,* knight of Arthurian legend.]

Ga·la·tian (gə-lā'shən) *n.* 1. A native or inhabitant of ancient Galatia. 2. **Galatians.** See table at **Bible.** —**Ga·la'tian** *adj.*

gal·ax·y (găl'ək-sē) *n., pl.* **-ies.** 1. a. Any of numerous large-scale aggregates of stars, gas, and dust, containing an average of 100 billion solar masses and ranging in diameter from 1,500 to 300,000 light-years. b. **Galaxy.** The galaxy of which the earth's sun is a part; the Milky Way. 2. An assembly of brilliant, beautiful, or distinguished persons or things. [< Gk. *galaxias,* milky.] —**ga·lac'tic** *adj.*

galaxy

gale (gāl) *n.* 1. A very strong wind, esp. one having a speed between 51.5 and 101.5 kilometers or 32 and 63 miles per hour. 2. A forceful outburst, as of hilarity. [Orig. unknown.]

ga·le·na (gə-lē'nə) *n.* A gray mineral, essentially PbS, the principal ore of lead. [Lat., lead ore.]

Ga·li·bi (gə-lē'bē, găl'ə-bē) *n., pl.* **-bi** or **-bis.** 1. A member of the Carib people of French Guiana. 2. The language of the Galibi.

gall¹ (gôl) *n.* 1. a. Liver bile. b. The gallbladder. 2. Bad feeling; bitterness. 3. Something bitter to endure. 4. Impudence; effrontery. [< OE *gealla.*]

gall² (gôl) *n.* 1. A skin sore caused by rubbing. 2. Exasperation; irritation; vexation. —*v.* 1. To make or become sore by rubbing; chafe. 2. To irritate; vex. [< OE *gealla.*] —**gall'ing** *adj.* —**gall'ing·ly** *adv.*

gall³ (gôl) *n.* An abnormal swelling on a

plant, caused by insects, disease organisms, or external injury. [< Lat. *galla*.]

gal·lant (găl'ənt) *adj.* **1.** Showy and gay in appearance; dashing. **2.** Stately; majestic; noble. **3.** High-spirited and courageous; daring. **4.** (*also* gə-lănt', -länt') **a.** Chivalrous; courteous. **b.** Flirtatious. —*n.* (gə-lănt', -länt', găl'ənt) **1.** A fashionable young man. **2. a.** A man courteously attentive to women. **b.** A paramour. [< OFr. *galer*, to rejoice.] —**gal'lant·ly** *adv.*

gal·lant·ry (găl'ən-trē) *n., pl.* -ries. **1.** Bravery; courage. **2.** Polite or complimentary attention to women. **3.** A gallant act or speech.

gall-blad·der (gôl'blăd'ər) *n.* Also **gall bladder.** A small muscular sac under the right lobe of the liver, in which bile secreted by the liver is stored.

gal·le·on (găl'ē-on, găl'yən) *n.* A large three-masted sailing ship used during the 15th and 16th cent. for trading and warfare. [< OFr. *galie*, galley.]

gal·ler·y (găl'ə-rē, găl'rē) *n., pl.* -ies. **1.** A long balcony, often with a roof. **2.** Any enclosed narrow passageway; esp. one used for a specified purpose: *a shooting gallery.* **3.** A porch; verandah. **4. a.** The balcony of a theater. **b.** The seats in such a section. **c.** The audience occupying these seats. **d.** A similar balcony, as in a church. **5.** A large audience, as in a stadium. **6. a.** A building or hall in which artistic work is displayed. **b.** An institution that sells works of art. **7.** An underground tunnel or other passageway. [< Med. Lat. *galeria*, portico.]

gal·ley (găl'ē) *n., pl.* -leys. **1.** A long, ancient or medieval ship propelled by sails and oars or by oars alone. **2.** The kitchen of a ship or airliner. **3. a.** A long tray used in printing for holding set type. **b.** A printer's proof taken from such a tray. [Med. Gk. *galea*.]

Gal·lic (găl'ĭk) *adj.* Of ancient Gaul or modern France; French.

gal·li·um (găl'ē-əm) *n.* Symbol **Ga** A rare metallic element used in semiconductor technology and as a component of various low-melting alloys. Atomic number 31; atomic weight 69.72. [< Lat. *gallus*, cock.]

gal·li·vant (găl'ə-vănt') *v.* **1.** To roam about in search of amusement; traipse. **2.** To flirt. [Perh. < GALLANT.]

gal·lon (găl'ən) *n.* **1.** A U.S. Customary System unit of volume or capacity, used in liquid measure, equal to 4 quarts or 231 cubic inches. **2.** A British Imperial System unit of volume, used in liquid and dry measure, equal to 277.420 cubic inches. [< ONFr. *galon*, a liquid measure.]

gal·lop (găl'əp) *n.* **1.** A three-beat gait of a horse, faster than a canter and slower than a run. **2.** A fast running pace. [< OFr. *galoper*, to gallop, of Gmc. orig.] —**gal'lop** *v.*

gal·lows (găl'ōz) *n., pl.* -lows or -lows·es. **1.** A framework from which a noose is suspended, used for hanging condemned persons. **2.** Execution by hanging. [< OE *galga*.]

gallows humor *n.* Humorous treatment of a desperate or grave situation.

gall·stone (gôl'stōn') *n.* A small, hard mass that forms in the gallbladder or in a bile duct.

ga·lore (gə-lôr', -lōr') *adj. Informal.* In great numbers; in abundance: *opportunities galore.* [Ir. Gael. *go leór*, to sufficiency.]

ga·losh (gə-lŏsh') *n.* A waterproof overshoe. [< Lat. *gallica (solea)*, Gaulish (sandals).]

gal·van·ic (găl-văn'ĭk) *adj.* **1.** Of direct-current electricity, esp. when produced chemically. **2.** Having or suggesting the effect of an electric shock; jolting. [Fr. *galvanique*.] —**gal·van'i·cal·ly** *adv.* —**gal'va·nism** *n.*

gal·va·nize (găl'və-nīz') *v.* -nized, -niz·ing. **1.** To stimulate or shock with an electric current. **2.** To arouse to awareness or action; spur; startle. **3.** To coat (iron or steel) with rust-resistant zinc. —**gal'va·ni·za'tion** *n.* —**gal'va·niz'er** *n.*

gal·va·nom·e·ter (găl'və-nŏm'ĭ-tər) *n.* A device for detecting or measuring small electric currents by means of mechanical effects produced by the current to be measured. [GALVAN(ISM) + -METER.] —**gal'va·no·met'ric** (-nŏ-mĕt'rĭk) or **gal'va·no·met'ri·cal** *adj.*

gam·bit (găm'bĭt) *n.* **1.** A chess opening in which a pawn or piece is offered in exchange for a favorable position. **2.** An opening remark or stratagem. [< OItal. *gamba*, leg.]

gam·ble (găm'bəl) *v.* -bled, -bling. **1. a.** To bet (money) on the outcome of a game, contest, or other event. **b.** To play a game of chance. **2.** To take a risk; speculate. **3.** To expose to hazard; risk. —*n.* **1.** A bet or wager. **2.** A risk. [Prob. < OE *gamian*, to play.] —**gam'bler** *n.*

gam·bol (găm'bəl) *v.* -boled or -bolled, -bol·ing or -bol·ling. To leap about playfully; frolic. [< OItal. *gamba*, leg.] —**gam'bol** *n.*

gam·brel roof (găm'brəl) *n.* A roof having two slopes on each side, the lower slope steeper than the upper. [< *gambrel*, hock of an animal.]

game[1] (gām) *n.* **1.** A way of amusing oneself; pastime; diversion. **2.** A sport or other competitive activity. **3.** A single contest between opposing players or teams. **4.** The total number of points required to win a game. **5.** The equipment needed for playing certain games. **6.** A particular style or manner of playing a game. **7.** A scheme; plan. **8.** Wild animals, birds, or fish hunted for food or sport. **9. a.** Something hunted; prey. **b.** An object of ridicule, teasing, or scorn. **10.** *Informal.* An occupation or business. —*v.* gamed, gam·ing. To gamble. —*adj.* gam·er, gam·est. **1.** Plucky; courageous. **2.** *Informal.* Ready and willing. [< OE *gamen*.] —**game'ly** *adv.* —**game'ness** *n.*

game[2] (gām) *adj.* gam·er, gam·est. Lame. [Orig. unknown.]

game·cock (gām'kŏk') *n.* A rooster trained for cockfighting.

game·keep·er (gām'kē'pər) *n.* One employed to protect and maintain wildlife, esp. on an estate or preserve.

games·man·ship (gāmz'mən-shĭp') *n.* Skill at winning advantages, esp. by dubious means.

game·some (gām'səm) *adj.* Frolicsome; playful; merry. —**game'some·ly** *adv.* —**game'some·ness** *n.*

game·ster (gām'stər) *n.* A habitual gambler.

gam·ete (găm'ēt', gə-mēt') *n.* A germ cell, esp. a mature sperm or egg, capable of participating in fertilization. [< Gk. *gametēs*, husband.]

game theory *n.* The mathematical analysis of abstract models of strategic competition.

gam·in (găm'ĭn) *n.* A boy who roams the streets; street urchin. [Fr.]

gam·ma (găm'ə) *n.* **1.** The 3rd letter of the Greek alphabet. See table at **alphabet.** **2.** A gamma ray. [Gk.]

gamma globulin *n.* Any of several globulin fractions of blood serum associated with immune bodies and used to treat measles, poliomyelitis, and other infectious diseases.

gamma ray *n.* An electromagnetic radiation with energy greater than several hundred thousand electron volts.

gam-mon¹ (găm'ən) *n.* A victory in backgammon occurring before the loser has removed a single man. [Prob. < ME *gamen*, game.]

gam-mon² (găm'ən) *n.* Chiefly *Brit. Informal.* Misleading or nonsensical talk; blather. [Orig. unknown.] **—gam'mon** *v.*

gam-mon³ (găm'ən) *n.* 1. A cured or smoked ham. 2. The lower part of a side of bacon. [< LLat. *gamba*, hoof.]

-gamous *suff.* Having a specified number of marriages: *monogamous.* [< Gk. *gamos*, marriage.]

gam-ut (găm'ət) *n.* A complete range; entire extent. [< Med. Lat. *gamma* + *ut*, notes of the medieval and diatonic scales.]

gam-y (gā'mē) *adj.* **-i-er, -i-est.** 1. Having the strong flavor or odor of game, esp. slightly spoiled game. 2. Spirited; plucky. 3. a. Disreputable. b. Racy; risqué. **—gam'i-ness** *n.*

-gamy *suff.* Marriage or sexual union: *misogamy.* [< Gk. *gamos*, marriage.]

gan-der (găn'dər) *n.* 1. A male goose. 2. *Slang.* A quick look. [< OE *gandra.*]

gang (găng) *n.* 1. A group of people who associate or work together. 2. A group of criminals or hoodlums. 3. A set, esp. of matched tools. **—v.** To band together as a group or gang. **—phrasal verb. gang up on.** *Informal.* To harass or attack as a group. [< OE, journey.]

gan-gling (găng'glĭng) *adj.* Also **gan-gly** (-glē), **-gli-er, -gli-est.** Tall, thin, and ungraceful. [Perh. < dial. *gang*, to go.]

gan-gli-on (găng'glē-ən) *n., pl.* **-gli-a** (-glē-ə) or **-ons.** A group of nerve cells, as one located outside the brain or spinal cord, in vertebrates. [Gk., cystlike tumor.] **—gan'gli-on'ic** (-ŏn'ĭk) *adj.*

gang-plank (găng'plăngk') *n.* A board or ramp used as a removable footway between a ship and a pier.

gan-grene (găng'grēn', găng-grēn') *n.* Death and decay of bodily tissue caused by failure of blood supply, injury, or disease. [< Gk. *gangraina.*] **—gan'grene** *v.* **—gan'gre-nous** (-grə-nəs) *adj.*

gang-ster (găng'stər) *n.* A member of an organized group of criminals; racketeer.

gang-way (găng'wā') *n.* 1. A passageway, as through a crowd or an obstructed area. 2. A gangplank.

gan-net (găn'ĭt) *n.* A large sea bird of northern coastal regions with white plumage and black wing tips. [< OE *ganot.*]

gant-let (gônt'lĭt, gănt'-) *n.* 1. Var. of **gauntlet¹.** 2. Var. of **gauntlet².**

gan-try (găn'trē) *n., pl.* **-tries.** A frame or support, esp. a large vertical structure used in assembling or servicing rockets. [Prob. dial. *gawn*, gallon + TREE.]

gap (găp) *n.* 1. An opening, as in a wall. 2. A break or pass through mountains. 3. An empty space; blank. 4. A wide difference; disparity. [< ON, chasm.]

gape (gāp, găp) *v.* **gaped, gap-ing.** 1. To open the mouth wide; yawn. 2. To stare wonderingly, as with the mouth open. 3. To gape widely. **—n.** 1. An act of gaping. 2. A large opening. [< ON *gapa.*] **—gap'er** *n.*

gar (gär) *n.* A fish having an elongated body covered with bony plates and a long snout. [< *garfish.*]

ga-rage (gə-räzh', -räj') *n.* 1. A structure for housing cars. 2. A commercial establishment where cars are repaired and serviced. [< OFr. *garer,* to protect.] **—ga-rage'** *v.*

garage sale *n.* A sale of used household items held at one's home.

garb (gärb) *n.* Clothing, esp. a distinctive way of dressing. **—v.** To dress; clothe. [Prob. < OItal. *garbo,* grace.]

gar-bage (gär'bĭj) *n.* 1. Waste material, esp. scraps of food. 2. Worthless matter; trash. [ME, refuse of fowls.]

gar-ble (gär'bəl) *v.* **-bled, -bling.** 1. To distort or scramble (an account or message) so that it cannot be understood. 2. To pronounce indistinctly. [< Ar. *gharbala,* he selected.] **—gar'ble** *n.* **—gar'bler** *n.*

gar-çon (gär-sŏn') *n., pl.* **-çons** (-sŏn'). A waiter. [Fr.]

gar-den (gär'dn) *n.* 1. A plot of land used for growing flowers, vegetables, or fruit. 2. A planted tract used for public enjoyment. 3. A yard; lawn. 4. A fertile, well-cultivated region. **—adj.** Of, pertaining to, or found in a garden. **—v.** To work in a garden. [< ONFr. *gardin.*] **—gar'den-er** *n.*

gar-de-ni-a (gär-dēn'yə, -dē'nē-ə) *n.* 1. A shrub with glossy, evergreen leaves and large, fragrant white flowers. 2. The flower of this shrub. [< Alexander *Garden* (1731-90).]

gardenia   gargoyle

gar-den-va-ri-e-ty (gär'dn-və-rī'ĭ-tē) *adj.* Common; unremarkable.

gar-gan-tu-an or **Gar-gan-tu-an** (gär-găn'chŏŏ-ən) *adj.* Enormous; huge. [< the hero of *Gargantua and Pantagruel,* by Rabelais.]

gar-gle (gär'gəl) *v.* **-gled, -gling.** 1. To exhale air through a liquid held in the back of the mouth in order to cleanse or medicate the mouth or throat. 2. To produce the sound of gargling when speaking or singing. **—n.** A medicated solution for gargling. 2. A gargling sound. [OFr. *gargouiller.*]

gar-goyle (gär'goil') *n.* A roof spout carved to represent a grotesque figure. [< OFr. *gargole.*]

gar-ish (găr'ĭsh) *adj.* Too bright and flashy; gaudy. [Orig. unknown.] **—gar'ish-ly** *adv.* **—gar'ish-ness** *n.*

gar-land (gär'lənd) *n.* 1. A wreath or crown of flowers, leaves, etc. 2. Something resembling a garland. **—v.** To decorate with a garland. [< OFr. *garlande.*]

gar-lic (gär'lĭk) *n.* 1. A plant related to the

onion, having a bulb with a strong, distinctive odor and flavor. **2.** The bulb of this plant, used as a seasoning. [< OE *gārlēac*.] —**gar'licky** *adj.*

gar·ment (gär'mənt) *n.* An article of clothing, esp. of outer clothing. [< OFr. *garnir*, to equip.] —**gar'ment** *v.*

gar·ner (gär'nər) *v.* To amass; acquire. [< Lat. *granum*, grain.]

gar·net (gär'nĭt) *n.* **1.** Any of several common, widespread silicate minerals, colored red, brown, black, green, yellow, or white, and used as gemstones and abrasives. **2.** A dark to very dark red. [< OFr. *grenat*, pomegranate-colored.] —**gar'net** *adj.*

gar·nish (gär'nĭsh) *v.* **1.** To add a decorative or flavorsome touch to (food or drink). **2.** To embellish; adorn. [< OFr. *garnir*, to equip.] —**gar'nish** *n.*

gar·nish·ee (gär'nĭ-shē') *v.* **-eed, -ee·ing.** *Law.* To attach (a debtor's pay or property) by garnishment.

gar·nish·ment (gär'nĭsh-mənt) *n.* *Law.* A proceeding in which money or property due or belonging to a debtor is turned over to the creditor.

gar·ret (gär'ĭt) *n.* An attic room; loft. [< OFr. *garir*, to protect.]

gar·ri·son (gär'ĭ-sən) *n.* A permanent military post or the troops stationed there. —*v.* To assign (troops) to a military post. [< OFr. *garir*, to protect.]

gar·rote or **gar·rotte** (gə-rŏt', -rōt') *n.* **1. a.** A method of execution by strangulation with an iron collar. **b.** A collar used for this. **2.** Strangulation, esp. in order to rob. [< OFr. *garrot*, instrument of torture.] —**gar·rote'** or **gar·rotte'** *v.* —**gar·rot'er** *n.*

gar·ru·lous (găr'ə-ləs, -yə-) *adj.* Habitually talkative; chatty. [Lat. *garrulus*.] —**gar·ru'li·ty** (gə-rōō'lə-tē) or **gar'ru·lous·ness** *n.*

gar·ter (gär'tər) *n.* An elastic band or suspender worn to hold up hose. [< OFr. *garet*, bend of the knee.]

garter snake *n.* A nonvenomous North American snake with longitudinal stripes.

gas (găs) *n., pl.* **gas·es** or **gas·ses.** **1. a.** The state of matter distinguished from the solid and liquid states by very low density and viscosity, the ability to diffuse readily, and the spontaneous tendency to become distributed uniformly throughout any container. **b.** A substance in this state. **2.** Gasoline. **3.** A poisonous, irritating, or choking gas used as a weapon: *tear gas.* **4.** A gaseous anesthetic. **5.** *Slang.* Thoughtless or boastful talk. **6.** *Slang.* One that provides great fun or amusement. —*v.* **gassed, gas·sing.** **1.** To supply with gas or gasoline. **2.** To treat chemically with gas. **3.** To poison with gas. [< Gk. *khaos*, unformed matter.] —**gas'e·ous** (găs'ē-əs, -yəs, găsh'əs) *adj.*

gas chamber *n.* A sealed enclosure in which prisoners are executed by a poisonous gas.

gash (găsh) *n.* A long, deep cut. [< ONFr. *garser*, to cut.] —**gash** *v.*

gas·ket (găs'kĭt) *n.* Any of a variety of seals or packings used between matched machine parts or around pipe joints to prevent the escape of a fluid. [< Fr. *garce*, girl.]

gas·light (găs'līt') *n.* **1.** Light made by burning gas in a lamp. **2.** A gas burner or lamp.

gas·o·hol (găs'ə-hôl) *n.* A blend of gasoline and ethanol used as a motor fuel. [GAS(O-LINE) + (ALC)OHOL.]

gas·o·line (găs'ə-lēn', găs'ə-lēn') *n.* A volatile mixture of flammable liquid hydrocarbons derived chiefly from crude petroleum and used principally as a fuel for internal-combustion engines and as a solvent and thinner.

gasp (găsp) *v.* **1.** To draw in or catch the breath sharply. **2.** To make violent or labored attempts at breathing. [< ON *geispa*, to yawn.] —**gasp** *n.*

gas·sy (găs'ē) *adj.* **-si·er, -si·est.** Containing, full of, or resembling gas.

gas·tric (găs'trĭk) *adj.* Of or concerning the stomach.

gastric juice *n.* The colorless, watery, acidic digestive fluid secreted by the stomach glands.

gas·tri·tis (gă-strī'tĭs) *n.* Chronic or acute inflammation of the stomach.

gastro- or **gastr-** *pref.* Stomach: *gastritis.* [< Gk. *gastēr*.]

gas·tro·in·tes·ti·nal (găs'trō-ĭn-tĕs'tə-nəl) *adj.* Of the stomach and intestines.

gas·tron·o·my (gă-strŏn'ə-mē) *n.* **1.** The art of good eating. **2.** Cooking, as of a particular region. [Fr. *gastronomie*.] —**gas·tro·nome'** (găs'trə-nōm') *n.* —**gas·tro·nom'ic** (-nŏm'ĭk) *adj.* —**gas·tro·nom'i·cal·ly** *adv.*

gas·tro·pod (găs'trə-pŏd') *n.* A snail or related mollusk having a single, usually coiled shell and a broad, muscular organ of locomotion. —**gas·trop'o·dous** (gă-strŏp'ə-dəs) *adj.*

gas·works (găs'wûrks') *n.* (*used with a sing. or pl. verb*) A factory where gas for heating and lighting is produced.

gate (gāt) *n.* **1.** A structure that may be swung, drawn, or lowered to block an entrance or passageway. **2.** The total admission receipts or attendance at a public spectacle. **3.** A circuit extensively used in computers that has an output dependent on some function of its input. [< OE *geat*.]

gate-crash·er (gāt'krăsh'ər) *n. Slang.* One who gains admittance without being invited or without paying.

gate·way (gāt'wā') *n.* **1.** An opening, as in a wall or fence, that may be closed by a gate. **2.** A means of access.

gath·er (găth'ər) *v.* **1.** To bring or come together. **2.** To accumulate gradually; collect. **3.** To harvest or pick. **4.** To increase by degrees: *gather velocity.* **5.** To pull (cloth) along a thread to create small folds. **6.** To draw (a garment) about or closer to something. **7.** To infer: *I gather he's ready.* —*n.* **1.** An act of gathering. **2.** A small tuck or pucker in cloth. [< OE *gadrian*.] —**gath'er·er** *n.* —**gath'er·ing** *n. & adj.*

Syns: *gather, call, convene, convoke, muster, summon v.*

gauche (gōsh) *adj.* Lacking social grace; tactless. [Fr.] —**gauche'ly** *adv.* —**gauche'ness** or **gau·che·rie'** (gō'shə-rē') *n.*

gau·cho (gou'chō) *n., pl.* **-chos.** A cowboy of the South American pampas. [Am. Sp.]

gaud·y (gô'dē) *adj.* **-i·er, -i·est.** Too brightly colored and showy; garish. [< ME *gaud*, trinket.]

gauge (gāj) *n.* Also **gage. 1. a.** A standard or scale of measurement. **b.** A standard dimension, quantity, or capacity. **2.** An instrument for measuring or testing. **3.** A means of estimating or evaluating. **4. a.** The distance between the two rails of a railroad. **b.** The distance between two wheels on an axle. **5.** The diameter of a shotgun barrel. **6.** Thickness or diameter, as of sheet metal or wire. —*v.* **gauged, gaug·ing. 1.** To measure precisely. **2.** To determine the capacity, volume, or contents of. **3.** To evaluate. [< ONFr.] —**gaug′er** *n.*

gaunt (gônt) *adj.* **-er, -est. 1.** Thin and bony; emaciated. **2.** Bleak and desolate. [ME.] —**gaunt′ly** *adv.* —**gaunt′ness** *n.*

gaunt·let¹ (gônt′lĭt, gänt′-) *n.* Also **gant·let. 1.** A protective glove. **2.** A challenge to fight or compete. [< OFr. *gant,* glove.]

gaunt·let² (gônt′lĭt, gänt′-) *n.* Also **gant·let. 1.** An old form of punishment in which two lines of men facing each other and armed with clubs beat a person forced to run between them. **2.** A severe trial; ordeal: *The candidate had to run the gauntlet of questions from the press.* [< Swed. *gatlopp.*]

gauze (gôz) *n.* A thin, transparent fabric with a loose open weave. [OFr. *gaze.*] —**gauz′i·ly** *adv.* —**gauz′i·ness** *n.* —**gauz′y** *adj.*

gave (gāv) *v.* *p.t.* of **give.**

gav·el (găv′əl) *n.* The mallet or hammer used by a presiding officer or auctioneer to signal for attention or order. [Orig. unknown.] —**gav′el** *v.*

ga·votte (gə-vŏt′) *n.* A French peasant dance resembling the minuet. [< Prov. *gavoto.*]

gawk (gôk) *v.* To stare stupidly; gape. —*n.* An awkward, stupid person; oaf. [Perh. < obs. *gaw,* to stare.] —**gawk′y** *adj.*

gay (gā) *adj.* **-er, -est. 1.** Merry; lighthearted. **2.** Bright or lively, esp. in color. **3.** Homosexual. —*n.* A homosexual. [< OFr. *gai.*] —**gay′ness** *n.*

gaze (gāz) *v.* **gazed, gaz·ing.** To look intently or steadily; stare. [ME *gasen.*] —**gaze** *n.* —**gaz′er** *n.*

Syns: *gaze, gape, gawk, goggle, ogle, peer, stare* **v.**

ga·ze·bo (gə-zē′bō, -zä′-) *n., pl.* **-bos** or **-boes.** A small, open-sided, roofed structure in a garden or park. [Orig. unknown.]

ga·zelle (gə-zĕl′) *n.* Any of various slender, swift-running horned mammals of Africa and Asia. [Prob. ult. < Ar. *ghazāl.*]

ga·zette (gə-zĕt′) *n.* **1.** A newspaper. **2.** An official journal. [< Ital. *gazetta.*]

gaz·et·teer (găz′ĭ-tîr′) *n.* A geographic dictionary or index.

gaz·pa·cho (gə-spä′chō, gäz-pä′-) *n.* A chilled soup made with tomatoes, onions, green peppers, and herbs. [Sp.]

G clef *n.* The treble clef.

Gd The symbol for the element gadolinium.

Ge The symbol for the element germanium.

gear (gîr) *n.* **1. a.** A toothed wheel or other machine element that meshes with another toothed element to transmit motion or change speed or direction. **b.** A transmission configuration for a specific ratio of engine to axle torque in a motor vehicle. **2.** Equipment, as tools or clothing, required for a particular activity. —*v.* **1. a.** To provide with or connect by gears. **b.** To put into gear. **2.** To adjust or adapt. —*idiom.* **in (or out of) gear. 1.** Having the gears that transmit power engaged (or not engaged). **2.** Ready (or not ready) for effective operation. [< ON *gervi,* equipment.]

gear·box (gîr′bŏks′) *n.* An automotive transmission.

gear·shift (gîr′shĭft′) *n.* A device for changing from one gear to another, as in a car.

gee (jē) *interj.* An exclamation of surprise. [< JESUS.]

geese (gēs) *n.* Pl. of **goose.**

gee·zer (gē′zər) *n. Slang.* An eccentric old man. [Poss. < dial. *guiser,* masquerader.]

Gei·ger counter (gī′gər) *n.* An instrument used to detect, measure, and record nuclear emanations, cosmic rays, and artificially produced subatomic particles. [< Hans *Geiger* (1882–1945).]

gei·sha (gā′shə, gē′-) *n., pl.* **-sha** or **-shas.** A Japanese girl trained to provide entertainment esp. for men. [J.]

gel (jĕl) *n.* A colloid in which the disperse phase has combined with the continuous phase to produce a semisolid material such as a jelly. [< GELATIN.]

gel·a·tin (jĕl′ə-tən) *n.* Also **gel·a·tine.** A transparent, brittle protein formed by boiling the specially prepared skin, bones, and connective tissue of animals and used in foods, drugs, and photographic film. [< Lat. *gelare,* to freeze.] —**ge·lat′i·nous** (jĕ-lăt′n-əs) *adj.* —**ge·lat′i·nous·ly** *adv.* —**ge·lat′i·nous·ness** *n.*

geld (gĕld) *v.* To castrate (a horse or other animal). [< ON *gelda.*]

geld·ing (gĕl′dĭng) *n.* A castrated animal, esp. a horse. [< ON *geldingr.*]

gel·id (jĕl′ĭd) *adj.* Very cold; icy. [< Lat. *gelidus.*] —**ge·lid′i·ty** (jə-lĭd′ĭ-tē) or **gel′id·ness** *n.* —**gel′id·ly** *adv.*

gem (jĕm) *n.* **1.** A precious or semiprecious stone, esp. one that has been cut and polished. **2.** One that is valued highly. [< Lat. *gemma.*]

gem·i·nate (jĕm′ə-nāt′) *v.* **-nat·ed, -nat·ing.** To arrange or occur in pairs. [Lat. *geminare.*] —**gem′i·nate** (-nĭt, -nāt′) *adj.*

Gem·i·ni (jĕm′ə-nī′, -nē′) *n.* **1.** A constellation in the Northern Hemisphere. **2.** The 3rd sign of the zodiac.

gem·ol·o·gy or **gem·mol·o·gy** (jĕ-mŏl′ə-jē) *n.* The study of gems. —**gem·o·log′i·cal** (jĕm′ə-lŏj′ĭ-kəl) *adj.* —**gem·ol′o·gist** *n.*

gem·stone (jĕm′stōn′) *n.* A precious or semiprecious stone that can be used as a jewel when cut and polished.

-gen or **-gene** *suff.* **1.** That which produces: *carcinogen.* **2.** Something produced: *antigen.* [< Gk. *-genēs,* born.]

gen·darme (zhän′därm′) *n.* A French policeman. [< Fr. *gens d'armes,* men of arms.]

gen·der (jĕn′dər) *n.* **1.** *Gram.* Any of two or more categories, such as masculine, feminine, and neuter, into which words are divided and that determine agreement with or the selection of modifiers or grammatical forms. **2.** Classification of sex. [< Lat. *genus,* kind.]

gene (jēn) *n.* A functional hereditary unit that occupies a fixed location on a chromosome, has a specific influence on phenotype, and is capable of mutation to various allelic forms. [G. *Gen.*]

ge·ne·al·o·gy (jē′nē-ăl′ə-jē, -ŏl′-, jĕn′ē-) *n., pl.* **-gies. 1.** A record or table of ancestry. **2.** Direct descent from an ancestor. **3.** The study of ancestry. [LLat. *genealogia.*] —**ge′ne·a-**

log'i·cal (-ə-lŏj'ĭ-kəl) *adj.* —**ge·ne·a·log'i·cal·ly** *adv.* —**ge'ne·al'o·gist** *n.*

gen·er·a (jĕn'ər-ə) *n.* Pl. of **genus.**

gen·er·al (jĕn'ər-əl) *adj.* 1. Applicable to or involving the whole or every member of a group. 2. Widespread; prevalent. 3. Not restricted or specialized. 4. True or applicable in most but not all cases. 5. Not precise or detailed. 6. Diversified. 7. Highest or superior in rank: *the general manager.* —*n.* Any of several high-ranking officers in the U.S. Army, Air Force, or Marine Corps ranking above a colonel. —**idiom. in general.** For the most part; on the whole. [< Lat. *generalis.*] —**gen'er·al·ly** *adv.*

Syns: *general, broad, comprehensive, expansive, extensive, inclusive, overall, sweeping, widespread* **adj**

general assembly *n.* 1. A legislative body. 2. **General Assembly.** The main body of the United Nations, in which each member nation is represented and has one vote.

gen·er·al·is·si·mo (jĕn'ər-ə-lĭs'ə-mō') *n., pl.* **-mos.** The commander in chief of all the armed forces in certain countries. [Ital.]

gen·er·al·i·ty (jĕn'ə-răl'ĭ-tē) *n., pl.* **-ties.** 1. The condition or quality of being general. 2. An observation or principle having general application. 3. An imprecise or vague statement or idea. 4. The majority.

gen·er·al·ize (jĕn'ər-ə-līz') *v.* **-ized, -iz·ing.** 1. To render general rather than specific. 2. To draw inferences or a general conclusion (from). 3. To speak or think in generalities. —**gen'er·al·i·za'tion** *n.*

General of the Air Force *n.* A general having the highest rank in the U.S. Air Force.

General of the Army *n.* A general having the highest rank in the U.S. Army.

general practitioner *n.* A physician who does not specialize in a particular area but treats a variety of medical problems.

general relativity *n.* The geometric theory of gravitation developed by Albert Einstein, incorporating and extending the special theory of relativity to accelerated frames of reference and introducing the principle that gravitational and inertial forces are equivalent.

gen·er·al·ship (jĕn'ər-əl-shĭp') *n.* 1. The rank or office of a general. 2. Skill in the conduct of a war. 3. Leadership.

gen·er·ate (jĕn'ə-rāt') *v.* **-at·ed, -at·ing.** To bring into existence; produce. [Lat. *generare.*] —**gen'er·a'tive** (-ə-rə-tĭv) *adj.*

gen·er·a·tion (jĕn'ə-rā'shən) *n.* 1. The act or process of generating. 2. Offspring having common parentage and constituting a stage of descent. 3. A group of contemporaneous individuals. 4. The average time interval between the birth of parents and the birth of their offspring. —**gen'er·a'tion·al** *adj.*

gen·er·a·tor (jĕn'ə-rā'tər) *n.* One that generates, esp. a machine that converts mechanical energy into electrical energy.

ge·ner·ic (jĭ-nĕr'ĭk) *adj.* 1. Of, including, or indicating an entire group. 2. Not protected by a trademark or trade name: *a generic drug.* 3. Of or relating to a biological genus. [< Lat. *genus*, a kind.] —**ge·ner'i·cal·ly** *adv.*

gen·er·ous (jĕn'ər-əs) *adj.* 1. Willing to give or share; unselfish. 2. Lacking pettiness or meanness. 3. Abundant; ample. [< Lat. *generosus*, of noble birth.] —**gen'er·os'i·ty** (-ə-rŏs'-ĭ-tē) *n.* —**gen'er·ous·ly** *adv.*

Syns: *generous, big, big-hearted, magnanimous, unselfish* **adj.**

gen·e·sis (jĕn'ĭ-sĭs) *n., pl.* **-ses** (-sēz'). 1. The beginning; origin. 2. **Genesis.** See table at **Bible.** [< Gk.]

—**genesis** *suff.* Generation: *parthenogenesis.* [< Gk.]

ge·net·ic (jə-nĕt'ĭk) or **ge·net·i·cal** (-ĭ-kəl) *adj.* 1. Of or relating to the origin or development of something. 2. **a.** Of genetics. **b.** Affecting or affected by genes. [< GENESIS.] —**ge·net'i·cal·ly** *adv.*

ge·net·ics (jə-nĕt'ĭks) *n.* (*used with a sing. verb*). The biology of heredity, esp. the study of hereditary transmission and variation. —**ge·net'i·cist** (-ĭ-sĭst) *n.*

ge·ni·al (jēn'yəl, jē'nē-əl) *adj.* 1. Cordial; kindly. 2. Warm and pleasant. [Lat. *genialis*, festive.] —**ge'ni·al'i·ty** (jē'nē-ăl'ĭ-tē) *n.* —**gen'ial·ly** *adv.* —**gen'ial·ness** *n.*

—**genic** *suff.* Generation or production: *antigenic.* 2. Suitable for reproduction by a specified medium: *photogenic.* [-GEN + -IC.]

ge·nie (jē'nē) *n.* A supernatural creature who grants the wishes of the one who summons him. [< Lat. *genius*, guardian spirit.]

gen·i·tal (jĕn'ĭ-təl) *adj.* 1. Of or relating to biological reproduction. 2. Of the genitalia. —*n.* **genitals.** The genitalia. [< Lat. *genitalis.*]

gen·i·ta·li·a (jĕn'ĭ-tā'lē-ə, -tāl'yə) *pl.n.* The reproductive organs, esp. the external sex organs. [Lat. *genitalia (membra)*, genital (members).]

gen·i·tive (jĕn'ĭ-tĭv) *adj.* Of or designating a grammatical case that indicates possession or source. —*n.* The genitive case. [< Lat. *(casus) genitivus*, (case) of origin.] —**gen'i·ti'val** *adj.*

gen·i·to·u·ri·nary (jĕn'ĭ-tō-yŏŏr'ə-nĕr'ē) *adj.* Of or pertaining to the genital and urinary organs or their functions.

gen·ius (jēn'yəs) *n.* 1. Brilliant mental ability or outstanding creative power. 2. A person of the highest mental ability or the greatest creative power. 3. A strong natural talent. 4. The prevailing spirit of a place, person, time, or group. 5. A person who has great influence over another. 6. *pl.* **ge·ni·i** (jē'nē-ī'). *Rom. Myth.* The guardian spirit of a person or place. [Lat., guardian spirit.]

gen·o·cide (jĕn'ə-sīd') *n.* The systematic, planned annihilation of a racial, political, or cultural group. [Gk. *genos*, race + -CIDE.] —**gen'o·cid'al** (-sīd'l) *adj.*

gen·o·type (jĕn'ə-tīp') *n.* 1. The genetic constitution of an organism, esp. as distinguished from its physical appearance. 2. A group or class of organisms having the same genetic constitution. [Gk. *genos*, race + TYPE.] —**gen'o·typ'ic** (-tĭp'ĭk) or **gen'o·typ'i·cal** *adj.* —**gen'o·typ'i·cal·ly** *adv.*

—**genous** *suff.* 1. Producing: *erogenous.* 2. Produced by or in a specified manner: *hypogenous.* [-GEN + -OUS.]

gen·re (zhän'rə) *n.* 1. Type; class. 2. A style of painting depicting scenes of common everyday life. 3. A particular type or category of literary work. [< OFr., a kind < Lat. *genus.*]

gent (jĕnt) *n. Informal.* A man; fellow. [< GENTLEMAN.]

gen·teel (jĕn-tēl') *adj.* 1. Refined and polite in manner; well-bred. 2. Fashionable; elegant. 3. Trying to seem refined but in an artificial or prudish way. [OFr. *gentil*, noble.] **—gen·teel'ly** *adv.* **—gen·teel'ness** *n.*

gen·tian (jĕn'shən) *n.* Any of numerous plants characteristically having showy blue flowers. [< Lat. *gentiana*.]

Gen·tile (jĕn'tīl') *n.* **1.** A Christian as distinguished from a Jew. **2. gentile.** A pagan or heathen. [< LLat. *gentilis*, pagan.]

gen·til·i·ty (jĕn-tĭl'ĭ-tē) *n.* **1.** The condition of being genteel. **2.** Gentle birth. [< Lat. *gentilis*, of the same clan.]

gen·tle (jĕn'tl) *adj.* **-tler, -tlest. 1.** Considerate or kindly. **2.** Not harsh, severe, or violent; mild; soft. **3.** Easily managed or handled. **4.** Gradual; not steep or sudden. **5.** Of good family; well-born. [< Lat. *gentilis*, of the same clan.] **—gen'tle** *v.* **—gen'tle·ness** *n.* **—gen'tly** *adv.*

Syns: *gentle, mild, soft, softhearted, tender, tenderhearted adj.*

gen·tle·man (jĕn'tl-mən) *n.* **1.** A man of high or noble birth. **2.** A polite or well-bred man. **3.** Any man spoken of in a polite way. **—gen'tle·man·ly** *adj.*

gen·tle·wom·an (jĕn'tl-wŏom'ən) *n.* **1.** A woman of high or noble birth. **2.** A polite or well-bred woman.

gen·try (jĕn'trē) *n.* **1.** People of good family and high social standing. **2.** A social class ranking next below the nobility. [< OFr. *gentil*, noble.]

gen·u·flect (jĕn'yə-flĕkt') *v.* To bend one knee, as in worship. [LLat. *genuflectere*.] **—gen'u·flec'tion** *n.*

gen·u·ine (jĕn'yŏo-ĭn) *adj.* **1.** Actually being what it seems or claims to be; real. **2.** Sincere; frank. [Lat. *genuinus*, natural.] **—gen'u·ine·ly** *adv.* **—gen'u·ine·ness** *n.*

ge·nus (jē'nəs) *n., pl.* **gen·er·a** (jĕn'ər-ə). **1.** A category of related organisms usually including several species. **2.** A class or kind with common attributes. [Lat., a kind.]

-geny *suff.* Production; origin: *ontogeny.* [< Gk. *-genēs,* born.]

geo- *pref.* Earth: *geology.* [< Gk. *gē*.]

ge·o·cen·tric (jē'ō-sĕn'trĭk) *adj.* **1.** Of or from the center of the earth. **2.** Having the earth as a center. **—ge'o·cen'tri·cal·ly** *adv.*

ge·o·chro·nol·o·gy (jē'ō-krə-nŏl'ə-jē) *n.* The chronology of the earth's history as determined by geologic data.

ge·ode (jē'ōd') *n.* A small, hollow, usu. spheroidal rock with crystals lining the inside wall. [< Gk. *geōdēs,* earthlike.]

ge·o·des·ic (jē'ə-dĕs'ĭk, -dē'sĭk) *adj.* Made of light-weight straight elements that form interlocking polygons: *a geodesic dome.*

ge·od·e·sy (jē-ŏd'ĭ-sē) *n.* The geologic science of the size and shape of the earth. [< Gk. *geōdaisia.*] **—ge·od'e·sist** (-sĭst) *n.*

ge·og·ra·phy (jē-ŏg'rə-fē) *n., pl.* **-phies. 1.** The study of the earth and its features and of the distribution on the earth of life, including human life and the effects of human activity. **2.** The location and natural features of any area. **3.** A book on geography. **—ge·og'ra·pher** *n.* **—ge'o·graph'ic** (-ə-grăf'ĭk) *or* **ge'o·graph'i·cal** *adj.* **—ge'o·graph'i·cal·ly** *adv.*

ge·ol·o·gy (jē-ŏl'ə-jē) *n., pl.* **-gies. 1.** The scientific study of the origin, history, and structure of the earth. **2.** The structure of a specific region. **—ge'o·log'ic** (jē'ə-lŏj'ĭk) *or* **ge'o·log'i·cal** *adj.* **—ge'o·log'i·cal·ly** *adv.* **—ge·ol'o·gist** *n.*

ge·o·mag·ne·tism (jē'ō-măg'nĭ-tĭz'əm) *n.* The magnetism of the earth. **—ge'o·mag·net'ic** (-măg-nĕt'ĭk) *adj.* **—ge'o·mag·net'i·cal·ly** *adv.*

geometric progression *n.* A sequence of terms, such as 1, 3, 9, 27, 81, each of which is a constant multiple of the immediately preceding term.

ge·om·e·try (jē-ŏm'ĭ-trē) *n., pl.* **-tries. 1.** The mathematics of the properties, measurement, and relationships of points, lines, angles, surfaces, and solids. **2.** Configuration; arrangement. **3.** A surface shape. [< Gk. *geōmetrein,* to measure land.] **—ge'o·met'ric** (jē'ə-mĕt'rĭk) *or* **ge'o·met'ri·cal** *adj.* **—ge'o·met'ri·cal·ly** *adv.* **—ge·om'e·tri'cian** (jē-ŏm'ə-trĭsh'ən, jē'ə-mə-) *or* **ge·om'e·ter** *n.*

ge·o·phys·ics (jē'ō-fĭz'ĭks) *n.* (*used with a sing. verb*). The physics of geologic phenomena. **—ge'o·phys'i·cal** (-ĭ-kəl) *adj.* **—ge'o·phys'i·cist** (-ĭ-sĭst) *n.*

ge·o·pol·i·tics (jē'ō-pŏl'ĭ-tĭks) *n.* (*used with a sing. verb*). The study of how geography influences international relations. **—ge'o·po·lit'i·cal** (-pə-lĭt'ĭ-kəl) *adj.*

ge·o·ther·mal (jē'ō-thûr'məl) *adj.* Also **ge·o·ther·mic** (-mĭk). Of or relating to the internal heat of the earth.

ge·ra·ni·um (jĭ-rā'nē-əm) *n.* **1.** A widely cultivated plant with rounded leaves and showy clusters of red, pink, or white flowers. **2.** A related plant with divided leaves and pink or purplish flowers. [< Gk. *geranos,* crane.]

ger·bil (jûr'bĭl) *n.* A mouselike rodent of desert regions of Africa and Asia Minor. [< Ar. *yerbō',* jerboa.]

ger·i·at·rics (jĕr'ē-ăt'rĭks) *n.* (*used with a sing. verb*). The medical study of the biological processes and diseases of old age. **—ger'i·at'ric** *adj. & n.* **—ger'i·a·tri'cian** (-ə-trĭsh'ən) *n.*

germ (jûrm) *n.* **1.** A small organic structure or cell from which a new organism may develop. **2.** The beginning or first form from which something larger develops. **3.** A microorganism, esp. a pathogen. [< Lat. *germen,* bud.]

German (jûr'mən) *n.* **1. a.** A native or citizen of Germany. **b.** A person of German descent. **2.** The Germanic language of Germany, Austria, and part of Switzerland. **—German** *adj.*

ger·mane (jər-mān') *adj.* Closely or naturally related; pertinent. [< Lat. *germanus,* having the same parents.]

Ger·man·ic (jûr-măn'ĭk) *n.* A branch of the Indo-European language family that includes English, German, Dutch, Afrikaans, Flemish, the Scandinavian languages, and Gothic. **—adj. 1.** Of or characteristic of Germany, any of the German people, or their culture. **2.** Of or relating to Germanic.

ger·ma·ni·um (jər-mā'nē-əm) *n. Symbol* **Ge** A brittle, crystalline, gray-white metalloid element, widely used as a semiconductor and as an alloying agent and catalyst. Atomic number 32; atomic weight 72.59. [< Lat. *Germania,* Germany.]

German measles *n.* A mild, contagious, eruptive disease caused by a virus spread in droplet sprays from the nose and throat.

German shepherd *n.* A large dog with a

ă pat ā pay â care ä father ĕ pet ē be ĭ pit ī tie î pier ŏ pot ō toe ô paw, for oi noise ŏŏ took ŏŏ boot ou out th thin *th* this ŭ cut û urge yŏŏ abuse zh vision ə about, item, edible, gallop, circus

dense brownish or black coat, often trained to assist the police and the blind.

germ cell *n.* A cell, esp. an egg or sperm cell, having reproduction as its principal function.

ger·mi·cide (jûr′mĭ-sīd′) *n.* An agent that kills germs. —**ger′mi·cid′al** *adj.*

ger·mi·nal (jûr′mə-nəl) *adj.* 1. Of or having the nature of a germ cell. 2. Of or in the earliest stage of development. [< Lat. *germen*, offshoot.]

ger·mi·nate (jûr′mə-nāt′) *v.* -nat·ed, -nat·ing. To begin to grow; sprout. [Lat. *germinare.*] —**ger′mi·na′tion** *n.* —**ger′mi·na′tive** *adj.* —**ger′mi·na′tor** *n.*

ger·on·tol·o·gy (jĕr′ən-tŏl′ə-jē) *n.* The scientific study of aging and the problems of the old. [Gk. *gerōn*, old man + -LOGY.] —**ge·ron′to·log′i·cal** (jə-rŏn′tə-lŏj′ĭ-kəl) *adj.* —**ger′on·tol′o·gist** *n.*

ger·ry·man·der (jĕr′ē-măn′dər, gĕr′-) *v.* To divide into voting districts that give unfair advantage to one political party. [Elbridge *Gerry* (1744-1814) + (SALA)MANDER.] —**ger′ry·man′der** *n.*

gerrymander
Contemporary political cartoon
showing a gerrymandered
Massachusetts election district in
the shape of a monster

ger·und (jĕr′ənd) *n.* The form of a verb ending in *-ing* when used as a noun. [< Lat. *gerundum*, acting < *gerere*, to act.] —**ge·run′di·al** (jə-rŭn′dē-əl) *adj.*

ge·run·dive (jə-rŭn′dĭv) *n.* A Latin verbal adjective with the construction of a future passive participle, suggesting fitness or necessity. [< LLat. *gerundivus.*]

Ge·sta·po (gə-stä′pō, -shtä′-) *n.* The secret police force of Nazi Germany. [G. *Ge(heime) Sta(ats)po(lizei)*, secret state police.]

ges·ta·tion (jĕ-stā′shən) *n.* The period of carrying developing offspring in the uterus after conception; pregnancy. [< Lat. *gestare*, to bear.] —**ges′tate** *v.* —**ges·ta′tion·al** *adj.*

ges·tic·u·late (jĕ-stĭk′yə-lāt′) *v.* -lat·ed, -lat·ing. To make gestures, esp. while speaking. [< Lat. *gesticulari.*] —**ges·tic′u·la′tion** *n.* —**ges·tic′u·la′tor** *n.*

ges·ture (jĕs′chər) *n.* 1. A motion of the limbs or body made to express thought or to emphasize speech. 2. An act or expression made as a sign of one's intentions or attitude. [< Lat. *gerere*, to behave.] —**ges′ture** *v.* —**ges′tur·er** *n.*

Ge·sund·heit (gə-zŏŏnt′hīt′) *interj.* Used to wish good health to a person who has just sneezed. [G.]

get (gĕt) *v.* **got** (gŏt), **got** or **got·ten** (gŏt′n), **get·ting.** 1. To obtain or acquire. 2. To pro-

cure; secure. 3. To go after; fetch. 4. To make contact with by or as if by radio or telephone. 5. To receive. 6. To receive. 7. To buy. 8. To catch; contract: *get chicken pox.* 9. To reach by calculation. 10. To have: *I've got a large collection of books.* 11. To understand: *Do you get his point?* 12. *Informal.* To register, as by eye or ear: *I didn't get your name.* 13. To cause to be in a specific condition: *He can't get the hook loose.* 14. To cause to move, come, or go: *Get that dog out of here!* 15. To bring or take: *I'll get him in here.* 16. To prevail upon: *I'll get my friend to agree.* 17. To capture. 18. *Slang.* To repay or requite harmfully: *I'll get you for that remark.* 19. *Informal.* To strike or hit. 20. *Slang.* To puzzle: *Her attitude gets me.* 21. To have the obligation: *I have got to go.* 22. To become or grow: *I got well again.* 23. To arrive: *When will we get to New York?* 24. To betake oneself: *Get out!* 25. *Informal.* To start: *Get going!* —*phrasal verbs.* **get across.** To make or be understandable or clear. **get along.** 1. To be on friendly terms. 2. To manage with reasonable success. 3. To advance in years. **get around.** 1. To evade; circumvent. 2. *Informal.* To convince or win over by flattering or cajoling. **get around to.** To consider or deal with after a postponement. **get away.** To escape. **get away with.** *Informal.* To succeed in doing without being found out or punished. **get by.** To manage; survive. **get down to.** To concentrate on. **get off.** 1. To get down from or out of. 2. To write and send. 3. To escape, as from punishment or labor. **get on.** 1. To climb onto or into; enter. 2. To get along. **get out.** 1. To leave. 2. To become public: *The secret got out.* **get out of.** 1. To avoid. 2. To escape. **get over.** To recover from. **get through.** To undergo and survive: *I wonder if that tree will get through the winter.* **get through to.** 1. To make contact with. 2. To make understandable or apparent to. **get to.** 1. To be able to. 2. To reach. 3. *Informal.* To happen to start; begin: *Then we got to remembering good times.* 4. To have an effect on: *His conceit really gets to me.* **get up.** 1. To arise, as from bed. 2. To create; make. 3. *Informal.* To dress or make up: *was got up as an Arabian princess.* —*n.* Progeny; offspring. —**idioms. get it.** 1. *Informal.* To understand: *I just don't get it.* 2. *Informal.* To be punished or scolded. **get nowhere.** To make no progress or have no success. [< ON *geta.*] —**get′ter** *n.*

get·a·way (gĕt′ə-wā′) *n.* 1. An act of escaping. 2. The start, as of a race; takeoff. —**get′a·way′** *adj.*

get-to·geth·er (gĕt′tə-gĕth′ər) *n.* An informal social gathering.

get-up (gĕt′ŭp′) *n.* An outfit or costume.

gew·gaw (gyōō′gô′) *n.* A trinket; bauble. [Orig. unknown.]

gey·ser (gī′zər) *n.* A natural hot spring that throws out a spray of steam and water from time to time. [< ON *geysa*, to gush.]

ghast·ly (găst′lē) *adj.* -li·er, -li·est. 1. Terrifying; dreadful. 2. Deathly pale. 3. Extremely unpleasant. [< OE *gæstan*, to terrify.] —**ghast′li·ness** *n.*

Syns: *ghastly, grim, grisly, gruesome, hideous, horrible, horrid, macabre adj.*

gher·kin (gûr′kĭn) *n.* A small cucumber, esp. one used for pickling. [Du. *agurkje.*]

ghet·to (gĕt'ō) n., pl. **-tos** or **-toes.** A section of a city to which an ethnic or economically depressed minority group is restricted, as by poverty or social pressure. [Ital.]

ghost (gōst) n. **1.** The spirit of a dead person, supposed to haunt or appear to living persons. **2.** A slight trace or vestige. **3.** A false image, often faint, produced along with the correct television or photographic image. **4.** Informal. A ghostwriter. [< OE gāst.] —**ghost'ly** adj.

ghost·writ·er (gōst'rī'tər) n. A person who writes for and gives credit of authorship to another person. —**ghost'write'** v.

ghoul (gōōl) n. **1.** An evil spirit in Moslem folklore that plunders graves and feeds on corpses. **2.** A grave robber. [Ar. ghūl.] —**ghoul'ish** adj. —**ghoul'ish·ly** adv. —**ghoul'·ness** n.

GI (jē'ī') n., pl. **GIs** or **GI's.** An enlisted person in any of the U.S. armed forces. [Abbr. for government issue.] —**GI** adj.

gi·ant (jī'ənt) n. **1.** A legendary manlike being of enormous size and strength. **2.** One of unusually great size or importance. —adj. Gigantic; huge. [< Gk. gigas.] —**gi'ant·ess** n.
Syns: giant, colossal, elephantine, enormous, gargantuan, gigantic, herculean, huge, immense, jumbo, mammoth, massive, mighty, monstrous, monumental, mountainous, stupendous, titanic, tremendous, vast adj.

gib·ber (jĭb'ər, gĭb'-) v. To speak rapidly and unintelligibly. [Imit.] —**gib'ber** n.

gib·ber·ish (jĭb'ər-ish, gĭb'-) n. Rapid, meaningless speech.

gib·bet (jĭb'ĭt) n. A gallows. —v. **-bet·ed** or **-bet·ted, -bet·ing** or **-bet·ting. 1.** To execute by hanging. **2.** To expose to public ridicule. [< OFr. gibe, staff.]

gib·bon (gĭb'ən) n. An ape of tropical Asia with a slender body and long arms. [Fr.]

gib·bous (gĭb'əs) adj. More than half but less than fully illuminated: the gibbous moon. [< Lat. gibbus, hump.] —**gib'bous·ly** adv. —**gib'bous·ness** n.

gibe (jīb) v. **gibed, gib·ing.** To taunt with heckling or mocking remarks. [Poss. < OFr. giber, to handle roughly.] —**gibe** n. —**gib'er** n. —**gib'ing·ly** adv.

gib·let (jĭb'lĭt) n. The heart, liver, or gizzard of a fowl. [< OFr. gibelet.]

gid·dy (gĭd'ē) adj. **-di·er, -di·est. 1. a.** Dizzy. **b.** Causing dizziness: a giddy climb. **2.** Frivolous; flighty. [< OE gidig.] —**gid'di·ly** adv. —**gid'di·ness** n.

gift (gĭft) n. **1.** Something given; present. **2.** The act, right, or power of giving. **3.** A special ability; talent. [< ON.]

gift·ed (gĭf'tĭd) adj. Endowed with great natural ability; talented. —**gift'ed·ness** n.

gig¹ (gĭg) n. **1.** A light, two-wheeled horse-drawn carriage. **2.** A long, light ship's boat. [< obs. gig, spinning top.]

gig² (gĭg) n. A pronged spear for fishing. [< fishgig, spear for fishing.] —**gig** v.

gig³ (gĭg) n. Slang. A job, esp. an engagement for a musician. [Orig. unknown.]

gi·gan·tic (jī-găn'tĭk) adj. Extremely large or extensive; huge. [< Gk. gigas, giant.] —**gi·gan'ti·cal·ly** adv.

gig·gle (gĭg'əl) v. **-gled, -gling.** To laugh in a half-suppressed or nervous way. [Imit.] —**gig'gle** n. —**gig'gler** n. —**gig'gling·ly** adv. —**gig'gly** adj.

gig·o·lo (jĭg'ə-lō', zhĭg'-) n., pl. **-los.** A man paid to be a woman's escort or lover. [Fr.]

Gi·la monster (hē'lə) n. A venomous lizard of the southwestern United States. [< the Gila River, Arizona.]

Gila monster

gild (gĭld) v. **gild·ed** or **gilt** (gĭlt), **gild·ing. 1.** To cover with or as with a thin layer of gold. **2.** To give a deceptively attractive appearance to. [< OE gyldan.] —**gild'er** n.

gill¹ (gĭl) n. The respiratory organ of fishes and various aquatic invertebrates. [ME gille.]

gill² (jĭl) n. **1.** A U.S. Customary System unit of volume or capacity used in liquid measure, equal to 4 fluid ounces (¼ pint) or 7.216 cubic inches. **2.** A corresponding British Imperial System unit used in dry and liquid measure, equal to 5 fluid ounces (¼ pint) or 8.670 cubic inches. [< Med. Lat. gillo, pot.]

gil·ly·flow·er (gĭl'ē-flou'ər) n. Also **gil·li·flow·er.** A carnation or other plant with fragrant flowers. [< Gk. karuophullon, clove.]

gilt (gĭlt) v. A p.t. & p.p. of **gild.** —adj. Gilded. —n. A thin layer of gold or gold-colored material applied to a surface.

gilt-edged (gĭlt'ĕjd') adj. Of the highest quality or value: gilt-edged securities.

gim·bals (jĭm'bəlz, gĭm'-) pl.n. Two rings mounted on axes at right angles to each other so that an object such as a ship's compass will remain suspended in a horizontal plane between the two rings regardless of the motion of the ship. [< Lat. gemellus, twin.]

gim·crack (jĭm'krăk') n. A cheap, showy, useless object. [Orig. unknown.]

gim·el (gĭm'əl) n. The 3rd letter of the Hebrew alphabet. See table at **alphabet.** [Heb. gîmel.]

gim·let (gĭm'lĭt) n. A small boring tool with a pointed spiral tip. [< Anglo-Norm. guimbelet.]

gim·mick (gĭm'ĭk) n. Informal. **1.** A tricky, deceptive, often dishonest device. **2.** A concealed disadvantage; catch. **3.** An attention-getting stratagem or inducement. **4.** A gadget. [Orig. unknown.] —**gim'mick·ry** n. —**gim'mick·y** adj.

gimp (gĭmp) n. Slang. A limp or limping gait. [Orig. unknown.] —**gimp** v. —**gimp'y** adj.

gin¹ (jĭn) n. An alcoholic liquor distilled from grain and flavored with juniper berries. [< Lat. juniperus, juniper.]

gin² (jĭn) n. **1.** A machine for removing seeds from cotton fibers. **2.** A snare or trap for game —v. ginned, gin·ning. To remove the seeds from (cotton) with a gin. [< ME engin, engine.]

gin³ (jĭn) n. Gin rummy.

gin·ger (jĭn'jər) n. 1. a. The pungent, aromatic root of a tropical Asian plant, used as flavoring. b. The plant itself. 2. Informal. Liveliness; pep. [< Gk. zingiberis.] —gin'ger·y adj.

ginger ale n. A carbonated soft drink flavored with ginger.

gin·ger·bread (jĭn'jər-brĕd') n. 1. A dark molasses cake flavored with ginger. 2. Elaborate ornamentation, esp. in architecture.

gin·ger·ly (jĭn'jər-lē) adj. Cautious; careful. [Poss. < OFr. gensor, gentler.] —gin'ger·li·ness n. —gin'ger·ly adv.

gin·ger·snap (jĭn'jər-snăp') n. A flat, brittle cookie spiced with ginger and sweetened with molasses.

ging·ham (gĭng'əm) n. A light cotton cloth with a woven, often checked pattern. [Malay ginggang.]

gin·gi·vi·tis (jĭn'jə-vī'tĭs) n. Inflammation of the gums. [Lat. gingiva, gum + -ITIS.]

gink·go (gĭng'kō) n., pl. -goes. Also ging·ko pl. -koes. A widely planted Chinese tree with fan-shaped leaves. [J. ginkyō.]

gin rummy n. A variety of rummy in which a player may win by matching all his cards or may end the game by melding.

gin·seng (jĭn'sĕng') n. A Chinese herb with a forked root believed to have medicinal properties. [Chin. ren² shen!.]

Gip·sy (jĭp'sē) n. & adj. Var. of Gypsy.

gi·raffe (jĭ-răf') n. An African mammal with a very long neck and legs and a tan coat with brown blotches. [< Ar. zirāfah.]

gird (gûrd) v. gird·ed or girt (gûrt), gird·ing. 1. To encircle with or as if with a belt or band. 2. To fasten with a belt. 3. To equip or prepare for action. [< OE gyrdan.]

gird·er (gûr'dər) n. A strong horizontal beam used as a main support in building.

gir·dle (gûr'dl) n. 1. A belt, sash, or band worn around the waist. 2. A supporting undergarment worn over the waist and hips. —v. -dled, -dling. To encircle with or as if with a belt. [< OE gyrdel.] —gir'dler n.

girl (gûrl) n. 1. A female child or young unmarried woman. 2. Informal. A woman. 3. A sweetheart. 4. A female servant. [ME girle.] —girl'hood n. —girl'ish adj. —girl'ish·ly adv. —girl'ish·ness n.

girl Friday n. A female assistant who performs a wide variety of duties.

girl·friend (gûrl'frĕnd') n. Also girl friend. 1. A female friend. 2. Informal. A sweetheart or favored female companion of a man.

Girl Scout n. A member of the Girl Scouts, an organization for girls between 7 and 17 that stresses physical fitness, good character, and homemaking ability.

girt (gûrt) v. A p.t. & p.p. of gird.

girth (gûrth) n. 1. Size measured by encircling something; circumference. 2. A strap encircling an animal's body to secure a load or saddle. [< ON györth.]

gist (jĭst) n. The central idea; essence. [< OFr., it lies.]

give (gĭv) v. gave (gāv), giv·en (gĭv'ən), giv·ing. 1. a. To make a present of: give flowers. b. To make gifts. c. To deliver in exchange or in recompense: give five dollars for the book. 2. To entrust to your care or keeping: Give me the scissors. 3. To convey: Give him my best wishes. 4. To grant: give permission. 5. To expose or subject one to: She gave him the measles. 6. To produce: This cow gives three gallons of milk per day. 7. To provide (something required or expected): give one's name and address. 8. To administer. 9. To accord; concede. 10. To relinquish; yield: give ground. 11. To emit or issue: give a sigh. 12. To allot; assign: give her five minutes to finish. 13. To award. 14. To submit for consideration or acceptance; tender: give an opinion. 15. To stage: give a dinner party. 16. To afford a view of or access to; open: The French doors give onto a terrace. —phrasal verbs. give away. 1. To make a gift of. 2. To present (a bride) to the bridegroom at a wedding ceremony. 3. To betray. give back. To return. give in. To surrender; yield. give out. 1. To distribute. 2. To break down. 3. To become used up. give up. 1. To surrender. 2. To stop: give up smoking. 3. To part with; relinquish. —n. Informal. Elasticity; springiness. [< OE giefan.] —giv'er n.

give-and-take (gĭv'ən-tāk') n. Lively exchange of opinions or conversation.

give·a·way (gĭv'ə-wā') n. Informal. 1. Something given away at no charge. 2. Something that betrays or exposes.

giv·en (gĭv'ən) adj. 1. Specified; fixed: a given date. 2. Granted as an assumption; acknowledged. 3. Having a tendency; inclined: given to brooding. —giv'en n.

given name n. A name given at birth or at baptism as distinguished from a surname.

giz·zard (gĭz'ərd) n. A muscular enlargement of the digestive tract in birds. [< Lat. gigeria, cooked entrails of poultry.]

gla·cial (glā'shəl) adj. 1. Of, relating to, or derived from glaciers. 2. Often Glacial. Characterized or dominated by the existence of glaciers. 3. Extremely cold. [Lat. glacialis, icy.] —gla'cial·ly adv.

gla·ci·ate (glā'shē-āt', -sē-) v. -at·ed, -at·ing. 1. To subject to glacial action. 2. To freeze. [Lat. glaciare, to freeze.] —gla'ci·a'tion n.

gla·cier (glā'shər) n. A large mass of slowly moving ice, formed from compacted snow. [< Lat. glacies, ice.]

glad (glăd) adj. glad·der, glad·dest. 1. Feeling, showing, or giving joy and pleasure; happy. 2. Pleased; willing: glad to help. [< OE glæd.] —glad'ly adv. —glad'ness n.
Syns: glad, cheerful, cheery, festive, gay, joyful, joyous adj.

glad·den (glăd'n) v. To make or become glad.

glade (glād) n. An open space in a forest. [Perh. < GLAD, shining (obs.).]

glad hand n. A hearty, effusive greeting. —glad'-hand' v.

glad·i·a·tor (glăd'ē-ā'tər) n. 1. A man trained to entertain the public by engaging in fights to the death in ancient Roman arenas. 2. A person who engages in a sensational struggle. [Lat.] —glad'i·a·to'ri·al (-ə-tôr'ē-əl, -tōr'-) adj.

glad·i·o·lus (glăd'ē-ō'ləs) n., pl. -li (-lī', -lē') or -lus·es. A widely cultivated plant with sword-shaped leaves and a spike of showy, variously colored flowers. [< Lat. gladius, sword.]

glad·some (glăd'səm) adj. Glad; joyful. —glad'some·ly adv. —glad'some·ness n.

glam·or·ize (glăm'ə-rīz') v. -ized, -iz·ing. Also glam·our·ize. To make glamorous. —glam'or·i·za'tion n. —glam'or·iz'er n.

glam·our (glăm'ər) n. Also glam·or. An air of

compelling charm, romance, and excitement. [Sc., var. of GRAMMAR.] —**glam'or·ous** adj. —**glam'or·ous·ly** adv. —**glam'or·ous·ness** n.

glance (glăns) v. **glanced, glanc·ing.** **1.** To look briefly or hastily. **2.** To strike a surface and be deflected. **3.** To glitter. —n. **1.** A brief look. **2.** A gleam. [ME *glansen,* to strike obliquely.]

gland (glănd) n. An organ or structure that secretes a substance, esp. one that extracts specific substances from the blood for subsequent secretion. [< Lat. *glans,* acorn.] —**glan'du·lar** (glăn'jə-lər) adj.

glans (glănz) n. **1.** The head of the penis. **2.** The tip of the clitoris. [Lat., acorn.]

glare (glâr) v. **glared, glar·ing.** **1.** To stare fixedly and angrily. **2.** To shine intensely and blindingly. —n. **1.** A fixed, angry stare. **2.** An intense and blinding light. [ME *glaren,* to shine brightly.]

glar·ing (glâr'ĭng) adj. **1.** Staring fixedly and angrily. **2.** Blindingly bright; dazzling. **3.** Obtrusively conspicuous. —**glar'ing·ly** adv.

glass (glăs) n. **1.** Any of a large class of materials that solidify from the molten state without crystallization, are generally transparent or translucent, and are regarded physically as supercooled liquids rather than true solids. **2.** Also **glass·ware** (glăs'wâr', -wăr'-). Objects made of glass. **3.** Something made of glass, as a drinking vessel or mirror. **4.** Often **glasses.** A device containing a lens or lenses and used as an aid to vision. **5.** Also **glass·ful** (glăs'fŏŏl', glăs'-). The quantity contained by a drinking glass. [< OE *glæs.*] —**glass** adj. —**glass'y** adj.

glau·co·ma (glou-kō'mə, glô-) n. A disease of the eye characterized by high intraocular pressure, hardening of the eyeball, and partial or complete loss of vision. [< Gk. *glaukōma,* cataract.] —**glau·co'ma·tous** adj.

glaze (glāz) n. A thin, smooth, shiny coating, as on ceramics or ice. —v. **glazed, glaz·ing.** **1.** To furnish with glass: *glaze a window.* **2.** To apply a glaze to. **3.** To become glassy. [< OE *glæs,* glass.] —**glaz'er** n.

gla·zier (glā'zhər) n. A person who cuts and fits window glass.

gleam (glēm) n. **1.** A brief flash of light. **2.** A steady but subdued glow of light. **3.** A brief or dim indication: *a gleam of intelligence.* —v. **1.** To flash or glow. **2.** To show briefly or faintly. [< OE *glæm.*]

glean (glēn) v. **1.** To gather (grain) left behind by reapers. **2.** To collect bit by bit. [< LLat. *glennare.*] —**glean'er** n. —**glean'ings** pl.n.

glee (glē) n. **1.** Merriment; joy. **2.** An unaccompanied song for three or more voices. [< OE *glēo.*] —**glee'ful** adj. —**glee'ful·ly** adv. —**glee'ful·ness** n.

glee club n. A group of singers who perform usu. short pieces of choral music.

glen (glĕn) n. A valley. [< OIr. *glend.*]

glib (glĭb) adj. **glib·ber, glib·best.** Easy, fluent, and often superficial, as in speech. [Poss. of LG orig.] —**glib'ly** adv. —**glib'ness** n.

glide (glīd) v. **glid·ed, glid·ing.** **1.** To move or pass smoothly and easily. **2.** To fly without propulsion. —n. **1.** A smooth, effortless movement. **2.** An act of flying without propulsion. [< OE *glīdan.*]

glid·er (glī'dər) n. **1.** One that glides. **2.** A light, engineless aircraft designed to glide after being towed aloft. **3.** A swinging couch that hangs in a vertical frame.

glim·mer (glĭm'ər) n. **1.** A dim or unsteady light. **2.** A faint suggestion or indication. —v. **1.** To give off a dim or unsteady light. **2.** To appear faintly. [< ME *glimeren,* to shine.]

glimpse (glĭmps) n. A brief look. —v. **glimpsed, glimps·ing.** To obtain a glimpse of. [ME *glimsen,* to glance.]

glint (glĭnt) n. A small, brief flash of light; sparkle. [ME *glent.*] —**glint** v.

glis·san·do (glĭ-sän'dō) n., pl. **-di** (-dē) or **-dos.** A rapid glide through a series of consecutive musical tones. [Prob. < Fr. *glissade,* sliding motion.]

glis·ten (glĭs'ən) v. To shine with reflected light. [< OE *glisnian.*] —**glis'ten** n.

glitch (glĭch) n. **1.** A minor malfunction or irregularity. **2.** A false electronic signal caused by an unwanted surge of power. [Prob. < Yiddish *glitsh,* slippery area.]

glit·ter (glĭt'ər) n. **1.** A sparkling light or brightness. **2.** Brilliant or showy attractiveness. **3.** Small pieces of light-reflecting decorative material. —v. To sparkle brilliantly; glisten. [ME *gliteren* < ON *glitra.*] —**glit'ter·ing·ly** adv. —**glit'ter·y** adj.

gloam·ing (glō'mĭng) n. Twilight. [< OE *glōm,* dusk.]

gloat (glōt) v. To feel or express great, often malicious pleasure or self-satisfaction. [Perh. of Scand. orig.] —**gloat'er** n.

glob (glŏb) n. A drop or rounded mass. [< Lat. *globus,* globular mass.]

glob·al (glō'bəl) adj. Worldwide. —**glob'al·ize** v. —**glob'al·ly** adv.

globe (glōb) n. **1.** A spherical object, as a representation of the earth in the form of a hollow ball. **2.** The earth. **3.** A globelike article, as a fishbowl. [< Lat. *globus.*]

globe-trot·ter (glōb'trŏt'ər) n. One who travels widely. —**globe'trot'ting** n. & adj.

glob·u·lar (glŏb'yə-lər) adj. **1.** Spherical. **2.** Consisting of globules. —**glob'u·lar·ly** adv. —**glob'u·lar·ness** n.

glob·ule (glŏb'yŏŏl) n. A small, spherical mass. [Lat. *globulus.*]

glob·u·lin (glŏb'yə-lĭn) n. Any of a class of simple proteins found extensively in blood, milk, muscle, and plant leaves.

glock·en·spiel (glŏk'ən-spēl', -shpēl') n. A musical instrument having a series of metal bars played with two light hammers. [G.]

glockenspiel

gloom (glōōm) *n.* **1.** Partial or total darkness. **2.** An appearance or atmosphere of melancholy or depression. **3.** Low spirits; dejection. [Prob. < ME *gloumen,* to become dark.]

gloom·y (glōō′mē) *adj.* **-i·er, -i·est.** **1.** Dismal, dark, or dreary. **2.** Causing or marked by gloom. —**gloom′i·ly** *adv.* —**gloom′i·ness** *n.* —**Syns:** *gloomy, blue, depressed, downhearted, low, melancholy, sad, unhappy* **adj.**

glo·ri·fy (glôr′ə-fī′, glōr′-) *v.* **-fied, -fy·ing.** **1.** To give honor or high praise to; exalt. **2.** To exaggerate the glory or excellence of. **3.** To worship; extol. [LLat. *glorificare.*] —**glo′ri·fi·ca′tion** *n.* —**glo′ri·fi′er** *n.*

glo·ri·ous (glôr′ē-əs, glōr′-) *adj.* **1.** Having, deserving, or giving glory; illustrious. **2.** Magnificent; resplendent. **3.** *Informal.* Delightful. —**glo′ri·ous·ly** *adv.* —**glo′ri·ous·ness** *n.*

glo·ry (glôr′ē, glōr′ē) *n., pl.* **-ries.** **1.** Great honor or distinction; renown. **2.** Adoration and praise offered in worship. **3.** Magnificent splendor. **4.** A praiseworthy attribute. **5.** The height of achievement, triumph, etc. —*v.* **-ried, -ry·ing.** To rejoice triumphantly; exult. [< Lat. *gloria.*]

gloss¹ (glôs, glŏs) *n.* **1.** Surface shine; luster. **2.** A superficially attractive appearance. —*v.* To attempt to excuse or ignore: *gloss over a friend's weakness.* [Prob. of Scand. orig.]

gloss² (glôs, glŏs) *n.* **1.** A brief explanatory note or translation of a difficult or technical expression. **2.** A translation or commentary accompanying a text. —*v.* To annotate or translate briefly. [< Gk. *glōssa,* word requiring explanation.] —**gloss′er** *n.*

glos·sa·ry (glôs′ə-rē, glŏs′ə-) *n., pl.* **-ries.** A list of difficult or specialized words with their definitions. [Lat. *glossarium.*]

glot·tal stop (glŏt′l) *n.* A speech sound produced by momentarily closing the glottis and then releasing the breath explosively.

glot·tis (glŏt′ĭs) *n., pl.* **-tis·es** or **glot·ti·des** (glŏt′ĭ-dēz′). The space between the vocal cords at the upper part of the larynx. [Gk. *glōttis.*] —**glot′tal** *adj.*

glove (glŭv) *n.* **1.** A fitted covering for the hand having a separate section for each finger. **2.** An oversized padded leather covering for the hand, as one used in baseball or boxing. [< OE *glōf.*] —**gloved** *adj.*

glow (glō) *v.* **1.** To shine brightly and steadily, esp. without a flame. **2.** To have a bright or ruddy color. **3.** To be bright or radiant: *glowing with pride.* —*n.* **1.** A light produced by a heated body. **2.** Brilliance or warmth of color, esp. redness. **3.** A warm feeling. [< OE *glowan.*] —**glow′ing** *adj.* —**glow′ing·ly** *adv.*

glow·er (glou′ər) *v.* To look or stare angrily or sullenly; scowl. [ME *gloren.*] —**glow′er** *n.* —**glow′er·ing·ly** *adv.*

glow·worm (glō′wûrm′) *n.* The luminous larva or grublike female of a firefly.

glu·cose (glōō′kōs′) *n.* **1.** A sugar, dextrose. **2.** A colorless to yellowish syrupy mixture of dextrose and maltose with about 20% water, used in confectionery, alcoholic fermentation, tanning, and treating tobacco. [< Gk. *gleukos,* sweet wine.]

glue (glōō) *n.* Any of various thick, sticky liquids used to hold things together. —*v.* **glued, glu·ing.** To stick or fasten together with or as with glue. [< Lat. *gluten.*] —**glu′ey** (glōō′ē) *adj.* —**glu′i·ness** *n.*

glum (glŭm) *adj.* **glum·mer, glum·mest.** In low spirits; dejected. [Orig. unknown.] —**glum′ly** *adv.* —**glum′ness** *n.*

glut (glŭt) *v.* **glut·ted, glut·ting.** **1.** To eat or fill to excess; satiate. **2.** To flood (a market) with a supply that exceeds demand. —*n.* An oversupply. [< Lat. *gluttire,* to eat greedily.]

glu·ten (glōōt′n) *n.* A nutritious mixture of plant proteins occurring in cereal grains. [Lat. *glue.*] —**glu′ten·ous** *adj.*

glu·te·us (glōō′tē-əs, glōō-tē′-) *n., pl.* **-te·i** (-tē-ī′, -tēī′). Any of three large muscles of the buttocks. [< Gk. *gloutos,* buttock.] —**glu′te·al** *adj.*

glu·ti·nous (glōōt′n-əs) *adj.* Sticky; adhesive. [Lat. *glutinosus.*] —**glu′ti·nous·ly** *adv.* —**glu′ti·nous·ness** or **glu′ti·nos′i·ty** (-ŏs′ĭ-tē) *n.*

glut·ton (glŭt′n) *n.* One who eats too much or is too greedy. [< Lat. *glutto.*] —**glut′ton·ous** *adj.* —**glut′ton·ous·ly** *adv.* —**glut′ton·y** *n.*

glyc·er·in (glĭs′ər-ĭn) *n.* Also **glyc·er·ine** (-ə-rēn′). Glycerol. [< Gk. *glukeros,* sweet.]

glyc·er·ol (glĭs′ə-rôl′, -rŏl′, -rōl′) *n.* A syrupy liquid, $C_3H_8O_3$, obtained from fats and oils and used as a solvent, antifreeze, and sweetener, and in making dynamite, liquid soaps, and lubricants. [GLYCER(IN) + -OL.]

gly·co·gen (glī′kə-jən) *n.* A white powder, $(C_6H_{10}O_5)_n$, occurring as the chief animal storage carbohydrate, primarily in the liver. [Gk. *glukus,* sweet + -GEN.] —**gly′co·gen′ic** (-jĕn′ĭk) *adj.*

gnarl (närl) *n.* A protruding knot on a tree. [< ME *knor,* a swelling.] —**gnarled** *adj.*

gnash (năsh) *v.* To grind (the teeth) together. [ME *gnasten.*]

gnat (năt) *n.* Any of numerous small, winged insects. [< OE *gnæt.*]

gnaw (nô) *v.* **1.** To bite or chew persistently (on). **2.** To consume, wear away, or produce by or as if by nibbling. **3.** To cause persistent pain or distress. [< OE *gnagan.*] —**gnaw′er** *n.* —**gnaw′ing·ly** *adv.*

gneiss (nīs) *n.* A banded metamorphic rock, usu. of the same composition as granite. [G. *Gneis.*]

gnome (nōm) *n.* One of a fabled race of dwarflike creatures who live underground and guard treasure hoards. [< NLat. *gnomus.*] —**gnom′ish** *adj.*

gnu (nōō, nyōō) *n.* A large bearded African antelope with curved horns. [Xhosa *i-gnu.*]

gnu

go (gō) *v.* **went** (wĕnt), **gone** (gôn, gŏn), **go·ing.** **1.** To proceed. **2.** To move or start to move. **3.** To move to or from a given place, or out of someone's presence. **4.** Used in the form *be going* followed by an infinitive to indicate the indefinite future: *He's going to go home.* **5.** To engage in a specified activity: *go riding.* **6.** To function. **7.** To make a specified sound: *The glass went crack.* **8.** To belong (somewhere). **9.** To extend or spread. **10.** To be allotted. **11.** To serve: *It all goes to show.* **12.** To harmonize: *The rug goes well with this room.* **13.** To die. **14.** To come apart or cave in. **15.** To fail: *Her eyes are going.* **16.** To be used up. **17.** To disappear. **18.** To be abolished: *War must go.* **19.** To pass, as time. **20.** To become: *go crazy.* **21.** To be or continue to be: *go unchallenged.* **22.** To fare. **23.** To hold out or endure: *go without water.* **24.** To wager; bid. **25.** To furnish: *go bail for a client.* **26.** To participate to the extent of: *go halves on a deal.* **27.** *Informal.* To say. —*phrasal verbs.* **go about.** To busy oneself with: *go about one's business.* **go along.** To be in agreement; concur. **go back on.** To abandon or betray. **go for. 1.** To try to obtain. **2.** *Informal.* To enjoy or appreciate. **go in for.** *Informal.* To enjoy participating in or partaking of. *go into.* To investigate; inquire about. **go off. 1.** To happen; take place. **2.** To be fired or shot; explode. *The alarm went off at 6 o'clock.* **go on. 1.** To proceed. **2.** To continue to exist. **3.** To happen. **go over. 1.** To check or examine. **2.** To gain acceptance or approval. **go through. 1.** To search or examine thoroughly. **2.** To suffer; undergo; experience. **go under.** To fail or be ruined. —*n., pl.* **goes.** *Informal.* **1.** A try; venture. **2.** A turn, as in a game. **3.** Energy; vitality. —*idioms.* **go far.** To succeed; prosper greatly. **on the go.** *Informal.* Perpetually busy. **to go.** To be taken out, as restaurant food and drink. [< OE *gān.*]

goad (gōd) *n.* **1.** A long, pointed stick for prodding animals. **2.** One that prods or urges; stimulus. [< OE *gād.*] —**goad** *v.*

go-a-head (gō'ə-hĕd') *n.* *Informal.* Permission to proceed.

goal (gōl) *n.* **1.** A desired result or purpose; objective. **2.** The finish line of a race. **3. a.** In certain sports, a structure or area into which players must propel the ball or puck in order to score. **b.** The score awarded for this. [ME *gol,* boundary.]

goal-ie (gō'lē) *n.* A goalkeeper.

goal-keep-er (gōl'kē'pər) *n.* A player assigned to protect the goal in soccer, hockey, and other sports.

goat (gōt) *n.* **1.** A horned, bearded mammal orig. of mountainous regions and now widely domesticated. **2.** A lecherous man. [< OE *gāt.*] —**goat'ish** *adj.*

goat-ee (gō-tē') *n.* A small pointed chin beard.

goat-skin (gōt'skĭn') *n.* **1.** The skin of a goat, used for leather. **2.** A container, as for wine, made from goatskin.

gob¹ (gŏb) *n.* A small piece or lump. [< OFr. *gobet.*]

gob² (gŏb) *n.* *Slang.* A sailor. [Orig. unknown.]

gob-ble¹ (gŏb'əl) *v.* **-bled, -bling. 1.** To devour greedily. **2.** To snatch greedily; grab. [Perh. < GOB¹.]

gob-ble² (gŏb'əl) *v.* **-bled, -bling.** To make the throaty, chortling sound of a male turkey. [Imit.] —**gob'ble** *n.* —**gob'bler** *n.*

gob-ble-dy-gook (gŏb'əl-dē-gŏŏk') *n.* Also **gob-ble-de-gook.** Unclear, wordy jargon. [Coined by Maury Maverick (1895-1954).]

go-be-tween (gō'bĭ-twēn') *n.* An intermediary between two sides.

gob-let (gŏb'lĭt) *n.* A drinking glass with a stem and base. [< OFr. *gobelet.*]

gob-lin (gŏb'lĭn) *n.* **1.** A grotesque elf said to work mischief or evil. **2.** A haunting ghost. [< Med. Lat. *gobelinus.*]

god (gŏd) *n.* **1.** A being of supernatural powers or attributes, believed in and worshiped by a people. **2.** One that is worshiped or idealized as a god. **3. God.** A being conceived as the perfect, omnipotent, omniscient originator and ruler of the universe, the principal object of faith and worship in monotheistic religions. [< OE.] —**god'hood'** *n.* —**god'like'** *adj.*

god-child (gŏd'chīld') *n.* A child for whom a person serves as sponsor at baptism.

god-daugh-ter (gŏd'dô'tər) *n.* A female godchild.

god-dess (gŏd'ĭs) *n.* **1.** A female deity. **2.** A woman of great beauty or grace.

god-fa-ther (gŏd'fä'thər) *n.* A man who sponsors a child at baptism.

god-head (gŏd'hĕd') *n.* **1.** Divinity; godhood. **2. Godhead.** God or the essential and divine nature of God. [ME *godhede.*]

god-less (gŏd'lĭs) *adj.* **1.** Recognizing or worshiping no god. **2.** Irreverent; wicked. —**god'less-ly** *adv.* —**god'less-ness** *n.*

god-ly (gŏd'lē) *adj.* **-li-er, -li-est. 1.** Pious. **2.** Divine. —**god'li-ness** *n.*

god-moth-er (gŏd'mŭth'ər) *n.* A woman who sponsors a child at baptism.

god-par-ent (gŏd'pâr'ənt, -păr'-) *n.* A godfather or godmother.

god-send (gŏd'sĕnd') *n.* An unexpected stroke of luck; windfall.

god-son (gŏd'sŭn') *n.* A male godchild.

go-get-ter (gō'gĕt'ər) *n.* *Informal.* An enterprising, hustling person.

gog-gle (gŏg'əl) *v.* **-gled, -gling.** To stare with wide and bulging eyes. —*n.* **goggles.** Large, usu. tinted eyeglasses worn as a protection against wind, dust, or glare. [ME *gogelen,* to squint.] —**gog'gly** *adj.*

go-go (gō'gō') *adj.* **1.** Of, for, or employed in rock 'n' roll dancing at discotheques. **2.** Enterprising or speculative.

go-ing (gō'ĭng) *n.* **1.** Departure. **2.** The condition underfoot as it affects walking or riding. **3.** *Informal.* Progress toward a goal; headway. —*adj.* **1.** Working; running. **2.** Current; prevailing: *the going rates are high.*

goi-ter (goi'tər) *n.* A chronic, noncancerous enlargement of the thyroid gland, visible as a swelling at the front of the neck. [< Lat. *guttur,* throat.] —**goi'trous** (-trəs) *adj.*

gold (gōld) *n.* **1.** *Symbol* **Au** A soft, yellow, corrosion-resistant, highly malleable and ductile metallic element that is used as an international monetary standard, in jewelry, for decoration, and as a plated coating on a wide variety of electrical and mechanical components. Atomic number 79; atomic weight 196.967. **2. a.** Coinage made of gold. **b.** A gold standard. **3.** Money; riches. **4.** A moderate to vivid yellow. [< OE.] —**gold** *adj.*

gold-brick (gōld'brĭk') *n.* Also **gold-brick-er** (-brĭk'ər). *Slang.* One who avoids performing duties or work; shirker. —**gold'brick'** *v.*

gold-en (gōl'dən) *adj.* **1.** Made of or containing gold. **2.** Having the color of gold. **3.** Suggestive of gold, as in richness or splendor: *a golden voice.* **4.** Precious: *golden memories.* **5.** Marked by prosperity. **6.** Favorable or advantageous; excellent: *a golden opportunity.* **7.** Promising. —**gold'en·ly** *adv.*

golden mean *n.* The medium course between extremes; moderation.

gold·en·rod (gōl'dən-rŏd') *n.* A North American plant with branching clusters of small yellow flowers.

gold·finch (gōld'fĭnch') *n.* A small New World bird having yellow plumage with a black forehead, wings, and tail.

gold·fish (gōld'fĭsh') *n.* A reddish or brass-colored freshwater fish often kept in home aquariums.

gold leaf *n.* Gold beaten into extremely thin sheets, used for gilding.

gold mine *n.* **1.** A mine yielding gold ore. **2.** *Informal.* A source of great profit.

gold rush *n.* A rush of migrants to an area where gold has been discovered.

gold·smith (gōld'smĭth') *n.* One who makes or deals in gold articles.

gold standard *n.* A monetary standard under which the basic unit of currency is equal in value to a specified amount of gold.

golf (gŏlf, gôlf) *n.* A game played on an outdoor course that has 9 or 18 holes spaced far apart, the object being to propel a small ball with the use of a club into each hole with as few strokes as possible. [ME.] —**golf** *v.* —**golf'er** *n.*

-gon *suff.* A figure having a designated number of angles: *pentagon.* [< Gk. *gōnia,* angle.]

go·nad (gō'năd', gŏn'ăd') *n.* The organ that produces gametes; testis or ovary. [< Gk. *gonos,* procreation.] —**go·nad'al** (gō-năd'l) *or* **go·nad'ic** (-năd'ĭk) *adj.*

gon·do·la (gŏn'dl-ə, gŏn-dō'lə) *n.* **1.** A long, narrow boat used on the canals of Venice. **2.** An open, shallow freight car with low sides. **3.** A compartment suspended under a balloon or dirigible. [Ital.]

gondola

gon·do·lier (gŏn'dl-îr') *n.* The boatman of a gondola.

gone (gôn, gŏn) *v. p.p.* of **go.** —*adj.* **1.** Past; bygone. **2.** Dying or dead. **3.** Ruined; lost. **4.** Carried away; absorbed. **5.** Used up; exhausted. **6.** *Slang.* Infatuated.

gon·er (gô'nər, gŏn'ər) *n. Slang.* One that is ruined or doomed.

gong (gông, gŏng) *n.* A metal disk struck to produce a loud, sonorous tone. [Malay *gong.*]

gon·or·rhe·a (gŏn'ə-rē'ə) *n.* An infectious disease of the genitourinary tract, rectum, and cervix, caused by a bacterium and transmitted chiefly by sexual intercourse. [< Gk. *gonorrhoia.*]

goo (gōō) *n. Informal.* A sticky, wet substance. [Orig. unknown.] —**goo'ey** *adj.*

good (gŏŏd) *adj.* **bet·ter** (bĕt'ər), **best** (bĕst). **1.** Having positive or desirable qualities. **2.** Suitable; serviceable. **3. a.** Not spoiled. **b.** Whole; sound. **4.** Superior to the average: *a good student.* **5. a.** Of high quality. **b.** Discriminating: *good taste.* **6.** Suitable for formal occasions: *good clothes.* **7.** Beneficial; salutary: *a good night's rest.* **8.** Competent; skilled. **9.** Complete; thorough. **10. a.** Safe; sure. **b.** Valid or sound. **c.** Genuine; real. **11. a.** Ample; substantial; considerable. **b.** Bountiful. **12.** Full: *a good mile from here.* **13. a.** Pleasant; enjoyable. **b.** Propitious; favorable. **14. a.** Virtuous; upright. **b.** Benevolent; cheerful. **c.** Loyal; staunch. **15. a.** Well-behaved; obedient. **b.** Socially correct; proper. —*n.* **1.** That which is good. **2.** Welfare; benefit. **3.** Goodness; virtue. —*idioms.* **a good deal.** A lot; a considerable amount. **as good as. 1.** Equal or equivalent to. **2.** Nearly; almost. **for good.** Permanently; forever. **make good. 1.** To fulfill: *made good his promise.* **2.** To compensate for. **3.** To be successful. [< OE *gōd.*]

Usage: *Good* is properly used as an adjective with linking verbs such as *be, seem, appear: The future looks good.* It should not be used as an adverb with other verbs: *The dress fits well* (not *good*) *and looks good.*

good-by *or* **good-bye** (gŏŏd-bī') *interj.* Used to express farewell. [< *God be with you.*] —**good'-by'** *or* **good'-bye'** *n.*

Good Friday *n.* The Friday before Easter, observed in commemoration of the Crucifixion of Jesus.

good·heart·ed (gŏŏd'här'tĭd) *adj.* Kind and generous. —**good'heart'ed·ly** *adv.* —**good'-heart'ed·ness** *n.*

good-hu·mored (gŏŏd'hyōō'mərd) *adj.* Cheerful; amiable. —**good'-hu'mored·ly** *adv.* —**good'-hu'mored·ness** *n.*

good-look·ing (gŏŏd'lŏŏk'ĭng) *adj.* Of a pleasing appearance; attractive.

good·ly (gŏŏd'lē) *adj.* **-li·er, -li·est. 1.** Of pleasing appearance; comely. **2.** Somewhat large; considerable. —**good'li·ness** *n.*

good-na·tured (gŏŏd'nā'chərd) *adj.* Having an easygoing, cheerful disposition. —**good'-na'tured·ly** *adv.* —**good'-na'tured·ness** *n.*

good·ness (gŏŏd'nĭs) *n.* **1.** The condition or quality of being good. **2.** Virtuousness. **3.** Kindness; benevolence. **4.** The good part of something. —*interj.* A euphemism for God.

goods (gŏŏdz) *pl.n.* **1.** Merchandise; wares. **2.** Personal belongings. **3.** Fabric; cloth.

Good Sa·mar·i·tan (sə-măr'ĭ-tən) *n.* A person who unselfishly helps others. [< the parable of the *good Samaritan* in the New Testament.]

good will *n.* Also **good·will** (gŏŏd'wĭl'). **1.** Benevolence. **2.** Cheerful willingness. **3.** A good relationship, as of a business enterprise with its customers or a nation with other nations.

goody (gŏŏd'ē) *n., pl.* **-ies.** *Informal.* Something attractive or delectable, esp. something sweet to eat. —**goody** *interj.*

good·y-good·y (gŏŏd'ē-gŏŏd'ē) *adj.* Affectedly sweet or good. —**good'y-good'y** *n.*

goof (gŏŏf) *Slang.* —*n.* **1.** An incompetent, foolish, or stupid person. **2.** A careless mistake. —*v.* **1.** To blunder. **2.** To waste or kill time: *goofed off all afternoon.* [< obs. *goff,* fool.] —**goof'i·ness** *n.* —**goof'y** *adj.*

gook (gŏŏk) *n. Slang.* A dirty, sludgy, or slimy substance. [Poss. < GOO.]

goon (gōōn) *n. Slang.* 1. A thug hired to intimidate or harm people. 2. A stupid or oafish person. [Perh. < dial. *gooney,* fool.]

goose (gōōs) *n., pl.* **geese** (gēs). 1. A water bird related to the ducks and swans. 2. The female of such a bird. 3. The edible flesh of such a bird. 4. *Informal.* A silly person. [< OE *gōs.*]

goose-ber-ry (gōōs'bĕr'ē, gōōz'-) *n.* 1. The edible greenish berry of a spiny shrub. 2. A shrub bearing such berries.

goose flesh *n.* Also **goose bumps** or **goose pimples.** Momentary roughness of skin in response to cold or fear.

goose-neck (gōōs'nĕk') *n.* A slender, curved object or part, such as the flexible shaft of a type of desk lamp.

go-pher (gō'fər) *n.* Any of various burrowing North American rodents with pocketlike cheek pouches. [Orig. unknown.]

gopher

gore¹ (gôr, gōr) *v.* **gored, gor-ing.** To stab with a horn or tusk. [< OE *gār,* spear.]

gore² (gôr, gōr) *n.* A triangular or tapering piece of cloth, as in a skirt, umbrella, or sail. [< OE *gāra,* triangular piece of land.] —**gore** *v.* —**gored** *adj.*

gore³ (gôr, gōr) *n.* Blood, esp. from a wound. [< OE *gor,* filth.]

gorge (gôrj) *n.* 1. A deep, narrow passage with steep sides. 2. The throat; gullet. 3. A mass obstructing a narrow passage: *an ice gorge.* —*v.* **gorged, gorg-ing.** 1. To stuff; satiate. 2. To eat greedily. [< Lat. *gurges,* gulf.] —**gorg'er** *n.*

gor-geous (gôr'jəs) *adj.* 1. Dazzlingly brilliant; magnificent: *gorgeous jewels.* 2. Strikingly attractive. [< OFr. *gorrias,* elegant.] —**gor'geous-ly** *adv.* —**gor'geous-ness** *n.*

go-ril-la (gə-rĭl'ə) *n.* A large African ape with a stocky body and dark hair. [< Gk. *Gorillai,* a tribe of hairy women.]

gor-man-dize (gôr'mən-dīz') *v.* **-dized, -diz-ing.** To eat gluttonously. [< Fr. *gourmandise,* gluttony.] —**gor'man-diz'er** *n.*

gorse (gôrs) *n.* A spiny European shrub with fragrant yellow flowers. [< OE *gors.*]

gor-y (gôr'ē, gōr'ē) *adj.* **-i-er, -i-est.** 1. Bloody; bloodstained. 2. Characterized by much bloodshed or physical violence. —**gor'i-ly** *adv.* —**gor'i-ness** *n.*

gosh (gŏsh) *interj.* Used to express mild surprise. [< GOD.]

gos-hawk (gŏs'hôk') *n.* A large hawk with broad, rounded wings and gray or brownish plumage. [< OE *goshafoc.*]

gos-ling (gŏz'lĭng) *n.* A young goose. [< ON *gæslingr.*]

gos-pel (gŏs'pəl) *n.* 1. Often **Gospel.** The teachings of Christ and the Apostles. 2. **Gospel.** Any of the first four books of the New Testament. 3. Something accepted as unquestionably true. 4. A style of singing characterized by strong Christian evangelical feeling and popular or jazz rhythms and phrasing. [< OE *ōdspel.*]

gos-sa-mer (gŏs'ə-mər) *n.* 1. A fine film of cobwebs often seen floating or caught on bushes or grass. 2. A sheer, gauzy cloth. 3. Anything delicate, light, or insubstantial. [ME *gossomer.*] —**gos'sa-mer** or **gos'sa-mer-y** (-mə-rē) *adj.*

gos-sip (gŏs'əp) *n.* 1. Trivial talk, often involving personal or sensational rumors. 2. One who habitually engages in gossip. —*v.* To engage in or spread gossip. [< OE *godsibb.*] —**gos'sip-er** *n.* —**gos'sip-y** *adj.*

got (gŏt) *v. p.t. & p.p.* of **get.**

Goth (gŏth) *n.* 1. A member of the Germanic people that invaded the Roman Empire in the early centuries of the Christian era. 2. Often **goth.** An uncivilized person; barbarian.

Goth-ic (gŏth'ĭk) *adj.* 1. a. Of the Goths or their language. b. Germanic. 2. Of the Middle Ages; medieval. 3. Of an architectural style prevalent in western Europe from the 12th through the 15th cent. 4. Often **gothic.** Of a style of fiction that emphasizes the grotesque and mysterious: *a gothic novel.* 5. Often **gothic.** Barbarous; uncivilized. —*n.* 1. The extinct Germanic language of the Goths. 2. Gothic architecture. —**Goth'i-cal-ly** *adv.*

got-ten (gŏt'n) *v. p.p.* of **get.**

gouge (gouj) *n.* 1. A chisel with a rounded, troughlike blade. 2. A groove or hole scooped with or as if with a gouge. —*v.* **gouged, goug-ing.** 1. To cut or scoop out with or as if with a gouge. 2. To overcharge deliberately. [< LLat. *gubia.*] —**goug'er** *n.*

gou-lash (gōō'läsh, -läsh) *n.* A meat and vegetable stew seasoned mainly with paprika. [Hung. *gulyás (hus),* herdsman's (meat).]

gourd (gôrd, gōrd, gōōrd) *n.* 1. A vine related to the pumpkin, squash, and cucumber, bearing fruits with a hard rind. 2. The fruit of such a vine. 3. The dried, hollowed-out shell of such a fruit, used as a drinking utensil. [< Lat. *cucurbita.*]

gourde (gōōrd) *n.* See table at **currency.** [Haitian.]

gour-mand (gōōr'mənd, -mänd') *n.* A person who delights in eating well and heartily. [< OFr. *gourmant,* glutton.]

gour-met (gōōr-mā', gōōr'mā') *n.* A person who knows and appreciates fine food and drink; epicure. [< OFr., wine merchant's servant.]

gout (gout) *n.* 1. A disturbance of the uric-acid metabolism occurring predominantly in males and marked by arthritic attacks. 2. A blob, clot, or splash. [< Lat. *gutta,* drop.] —**gout'y** *adj.*

gov-ern (gŭv'ərn) *v.* 1. To control; guide; direct. 2. To rule by exercise of sovereign authority. 3. To regulate or determine. 4. To restrain. 5. To decide; determine. [< Lat. *gubernare.*] —**gov'ern-a-bil'i-ty** or **gov'ern-a-ble-ness** *n.* —**gov'ern-a-ble** *adj.*

gov-ern-ess (gŭv'ər-nĭs) *n.* A woman employed to educate and train the children of a private household.

gov·ern·ment (gŭv′ərn-mənt) n. 1. The act or process of governing, esp. the political administration of an area. 2. A system by which a political unit is governed. 3. A governing body or organization. 4. Political science. —**gov·ern·men·tal** (gŭv′ərn-mĕn′tl) adj. —**gov·ern·men·tal·ly** adv.

Usage: In American usage *government* takes a singular verb: *The government is determined to stop inflation.* In British usage, however, government takes a plural verb: *The government are determined to follow this course.*

gov·er·nor (gŭv′ər-nər) n. 1. One who governs, esp. the chief executive of a U.S. state. 2. The manager or administrative head of an organization or institution. 3. A military commandant. 4. A device that automatically regulates the operation of a machine. [< Lat. *gubernator.*] —**gov′er·nor·ship** n.

gown (goun) n. 1. A long, loose, flowing garment, as a robe or nightgown. 2. A woman's formal dress. 3. A special outer robe worn on ceremonial occasions, as by scholars or clergymen. 4. Professors and students distinguished from townspeople: *town and gown.* [< Med. Lat. *gunna,* fur robe.]

grab (grăb) v. **grabbed, grab·bing.** 1. To take or grasp suddenly; snatch. 2. To capture or restrain; arrest. 3. To seize unlawfully or forcibly. [MLG *grabben.*] —**grab** n. —**grab′ber** n. —**grab′by** adj.

grace (grās) n. 1. Seemingly effortless beauty or charm of movement, form, or proportion. 2. A pleasing characteristic or quality. 3. Skill at avoiding the inept or clumsy course. 4. a. Good will. b. Mercy; clemency. 5. Temporary immunity or respite: *a period of grace.* 6. a. Divine love and protection bestowed freely upon mankind. b. A virtue or gift granted by God. 7. A short prayer at mealtime. 8. Often **Grace.** A title of courtesy for a duke, duchess, or archbishop: *His Grace the Duke of Leeds.* —v. **graced, grac·ing.** 1. To honor; favor. 2. To embellish. —**idiom. in the good (or bad) graces of.** In (or out) of favor with. [< Lat. *gratia.*] —**grace′ful** adj. —**grace′ful·ly** adv. —**grace′ful·ness** n. —**grace′less** adj. —**grace′less·ly** adv. —**grace′less·ness** n.

gra·cious (grā′shəs) adj. 1. Characterized by kindness and warm courtesy. 2. Merciful; compassionate. 3. Suggesting good taste and breeding. —interj. Used to express surprise or mild emotion. [< Lat. *gratiosus,* pleasing.] —**gra′cious·ly** adv. —**gra′cious·ness** n.

grack·le (grăk′əl) n. Any of several New World blackbirds with iridescent blackish plumage. [Lat. *graculus,* jackdaw.]

grad (grăd) n. Informal. A graduate of a school or college.

gra·da·tion (grā-dā′shən) n. 1. A series of gradual, successive stages. 2. A degree or stage in such a progression. 3. The act of arranging in grades. [Lat. *gradatio.*] —**gra·da′tion·al** adj. —**gra·da′tion·al·ly** adv.

grade (grād) n. 1. A stage or degree in a process. 2. A position in a scale. 3. A standard of quality: *not up to grade.* 4. A group all falling in the same specified limits; a class. 5. A class at an elementary school. 6. A mark showing the quality of a student's work. 7. A military, naval, or civil-service rank. 8. The degree of inclination of a slope. 9. A slope or

gradual inclination, esp. of a road or railroad track. —v. **grad·ed, grad·ing.** 1. To arrange in degrees; rank; sort. 2. To evaluate. 3. To assign an academic grade to. 4. To level or smooth to a desired gradient: *grade a road.* [< Lat. *gradus,* step.]

gra·di·ent (grā′dē-ənt) n. A slope or degree of slope. [< Lat. *gradi,* to walk.]

grad·u·al (grăj′ōō-əl) adj. Occurring in small stages or degrees or by even, continuous change. [< Lat. *gradus,* step.] —**grad′u·al·ism** n. —**grad′u·al·ly** adv. —**grad′u·al·ness** n.

grad·u·ate (grăj′ōō-āt′) v. **-at·ed, -at·ing.** 1. To grant or be granted an academic degree or diploma. 2. To divide into categories, steps, or grades. 3. To divide into marked intervals, esp. for use in measurement. —n. (grăj′ōō-ĭt). 1. A recipient of an academic degree or diploma. 2. A graduated container. —adj. (grăj′ōō-ĭt). 1. Possessing an academic degree or diploma. 2. Of or relating to studies beyond a bachelor's degree. [< Med. Lat. *graduare.*] —**grad′u·a′tor** n.

Usage: A strict traditionalist would insist that *she was graduated from college* is the only correct usage, but the usage *she graduated from college* is now entirely acceptable, and the variant *she graduated college* is rapidly gaining ground.

grad·u·a·tion (grăj′ōō-ā′shən) n. 1. The giving or receiving of an academic degree or diploma marking completion of studies. 2. A commencement ceremony. 3. A mark or series of marks on a graduated scale.

graf·fi·to (grə-fē′tō) n., pl. **-ti** (-tē). A crude drawing or inscription, as on a wall. [Ital.]

graft¹ (grăft) v. 1. To unite (a shoot, bud, or plant) with a growing plant by insertion or placing in close contact. 2. To transplant or implant (tissue) into a bodily part. —n. 1. a. A detached shoot or bud grafted onto a growing plant. b. The point of union of such plant parts. 2. Material, esp. tissue or an organ, grafted onto a bodily part. [< OFr. *grafe,* stylus.] —**graft′er** n.

graft¹
Left to right: Cleft graft, whip graft, bud graft

graft² (grăft) n. 1. The unscrupulous use of one's public position to derive profit or advantage. 2. Money or advantage thus gained. [Perh. < GRAFT¹.] —**graft** v. —**graft′er** n.

gra·ham (grā′əm) adj. Made from or consisting of whole-wheat flour. [< Sylvester *Graham* (1794–1851).]

Grail (grāl) n. The legendary cup or chalice used by Christ at the Last Supper and later searched for by medieval knights. [< Med. Lat. *gradalis,* dish.]

grain (grān) n. 1. a. A small, hard seed or fruit, esp. of a cereal grass such as wheat, rice, etc. **b.** The seeds of such plants collectively. **2.** Cereal grasses collectively. **3.** A small hard particle similar to a seed: *a grain of sand.* **4.** A tiny quantity. **5.** A U.S. Customary System avoirdupois unit of weight equal to 0.002285 ounce or 0.036 dram. **6.** The arrangement, direction, or pattern formed by the constituents in wood, leather, stone, cloth, or other material. **7.** Texture. **8.** Natural disposition; temperament. [< Lat. *granum.*] —**grain′i·ness** *n.* —**grain′y** *adj.*

grain alcohol *n.* Ethanol.

gram (grăm) *n.* A metric unit of mass and weight equal to one-thousandth of a kilogram. [< Gk. *gramma,* a small weight.]

-**gram** *suff.* Something written or drawn: *telegram.* [< Gk. *gramma,* letter.]

gram atom *n.* The mass in grams of an element numerically equal to the atomic weight.

gram·mar (grăm′ər) *n.* **1.** The study of language as a body of words that exhibit regularity of structure and arrangement into sentences. **2.** The system of rules used by the speakers of a language for making sentences. **3.** A book containing the syntactic and inflectional rules for a given language. **4.** Writing or speech judged with regard to such rules: *bad grammar.* [< Gk. *gramma,* letter.] —**gram·mar′i·an** (grə-mâr′ē-ən) *n.* —**gram·mat′i·cal** (-măt′ĭ-kəl) *adj.* —**gram·mat′i·cal′i·ty** (-kăl′ĭ-tē) *n.* —**gram·mat′i·cal·ly** *adv.*

grammar school *n.* **1.** An elementary school. **2.** A British secondary or preparatory school.

gram molecule *n. Chem.* A mole.

gram·o·phone (grăm′ə-fōn′) *n.* A phonograph. (Once a trademark.)

gram·pus (grăm′pəs) *n.* A whalelike marine mammal. [< OFr. *craspois.*]

gran·a·ry (grăn′ə-rē, grā′nə-) *n., pl.* -**ries.** A building for storing grain. [< Lat. *granarium.*]

grand (grănd) *adj.* -**er,** -**est.** **1.** Large and impressive in size, scope, or extent. **2.** Magnificent; splendid. **3.** Having higher rank than others of the same category: *a grand duke.* **4.** Most important; main: *the grand ballroom.* **5.** Illustrious. **6.** Dignified and admirable. **7.** Stately; regal. **8.** Lofty; noble. **9.** Inclusive; complete: *the grand total.* —*n.* **1.** A grand piano. **2.** *Slang.* A thousand dollars. [< Lat. *grandis.*] —**grand′ly** *adv.* —**grand′ness** *n.*

Syns: *grand, baronial, grandiose, imposing, lordly, magnificent, majestic, princely, regal, royal, stately adj.*

gran·dam (grăn′dăm′) *n.* Also **gran·dame** (-dām′). **1.** A grandmother. **2.** An old woman. [< OFr. *grand dame,* great lady.]

grand·child (grănd′chīld′, grăn′-) *n.* A child of one's son or daughter.

grand·daugh·ter (grănd′dô′tər) *n.* The daughter of one's son or daughter.

gran·deur (grăn′jər, -joŏr′) *n.* Greatness; splendor. [< OFr.]

grand·fa·ther (grănd′fä′thər, grăn′-) *n.* **1.** The father of one's mother or father. **2.** A forefather; ancestor.

gran·dil·o·quence (grăn-dĭl′ə-kwəns) *n.* Pompous or bombastic eloquence. [< Lat. *grandiloquus,* speaking loftily.] —**gran·dil′o·quent** *adj.* —**gran·dil′o·quent·ly** *adv.*

gran·di·ose (grăn′dē-ōs′, grăn′dē-ōs′) *adj.* **1.** Grand and imposing. **2.** Affectedly grand; pompous. [< Lat. *grandis,* large.] —**gran′di·ose′ly** *adv.* —**gran·di·os′i·ty** (-ŏs′ĭ-tē) or **gran′di·ose′ness** *n.*

grand·ma (grănd′mä′, grăn′-, grăm′mä′, grăm′-) *n. Informal.* Grandmother.

grand mal (grănd′ măl′, grăn′, grän măl′) *n.* A form of epilepsy characterized by severe seizures and loss of consciousness. [Fr.]

grand·moth·er (grănd′mŭth′ər, grăn′-) *n.* **1.** The mother of one's father or mother. **2.** A female ancestor.

grand·pa (grănd′pä′, grăn′-, grăm′pä′, grăm′-pə) *n. Informal.* Grandfather.

grand·par·ent (grănd′pâr′ənt, grăn′-, grăn′-) *n.* A parent of one's mother or father.

grand piano *n.* A piano whose strings are stretched out in a horizontal frame.

grand slam *n.* **1.** *Bridge.* The taking of all the tricks. **2.** *Baseball.* A home run hit when three runners are on base.

grand·son (grănd′sŭn′, grăn′-) *n.* The son of one's son or daughter.

grand·stand (grănd′stănd′, grăn′-) *n.* A roofed stand for spectators at a stadium or racetrack.

grange (grānj) *n.* **1. Grange.** A U.S. farmers' association or one of its branch lodges. **2.** *Chiefly Brit.* A farm with its buildings. [< Lat. *granum,* grain.]

gran·ite (grăn′ĭt) *n.* A common, coarse-grained, light-colored, hard igneous rock consisting chiefly of quartz, orthoclase, and mica, used in monuments and for building. [< Ital. *granito,* grained.] —**gra·nit′ic** (grə-nĭt′ĭk) *adj.*

gran·ny or **gran·nie** (grăn′ē) *n., pl.* -**nies.** **1.** *Informal.* A grandmother. **2.** An old woman. [< GRANDMOTHER.]

gra·no·la (grə-nō′lə) *n.* A mixture of rolled oats, dried fruit, seeds, and other ingredients, eaten esp. as a breakfast and snack food. [Orig. a trademark.]

grant (grănt) *v.* **1.** To allow; consent to. **2.** To accord, as a favor. **3. a.** To bestow; confer. **b.** To transfer (property) by a deed. **4.** To concede; acknowledge. —*n.* **1.** The act of granting. **2.** Something granted. **3. a.** A transfer of property by deed. **b.** The instrument of such transfer. **c.** Land thus bestowed. —**idiom. take for granted.** To assume without question or full appreciation. [< OFr. *creanter,* to assure.] —**grant′er** or **grant′or** *n.*

gran·u·lar (grăn′yə-lər) *adj.* **1.** Composed of granules or grains. **2.** Grainy. —**gran·u·lar′i·ty** (-lăr′ĭ-tē) *n.* —**gran′u·lar·ly** *adv.*

gran·u·late (grăn′yə-lāt′) *v.* -**lat·ed,** -**lat·ing.** **1.** To form into grains or granules. **2.** To make or become rough and grainy. —**gran′u·la′tion** *n.*

gran·ule (grăn′yŏŏl) *n.* A small grain or particle. [< Lat. *granum,* grain.]

grape (grāp) *n.* **1.** A juicy, smooth-skinned, edible fruit borne in clusters on a woody vine. **2.** A vine bearing such fruit. **3.** Grapeshot. [< OFr., bunch of grapes.]

grape·fruit (grāp′frŏŏt′) *n.* **1.** A large, round, yellow-skinned, acid-flavored citrus fruit. **2.** A tree bearing such fruit.

ă pat ā pay â care ä father ĕ pet ē be ĭ pit ī tie î pier ŏ pot ō toe ô paw, for oi noise ŏŏ took ŏŏ boot ou out th thin *th* this ŭ cut û urge yŏŏ abuse zh vision ə about, item, edible, gallop, circus

grape-shot (grāp′shŏt′) n. A cluster of small iron balls formerly used as a cannon charge.

grape sugar n. Dextrose.

grape-vine (grāp′vīn′) n. 1. A vine on which grapes grow. 2. An informal means of transmitting information or rumor.

graph (grăf) n. 1. A drawing that exhibits a relationship between two sets of numbers. 2. Any drawing or diagram used to display numerical data. —v. 1. To represent by a graph. 2. To plot (a function) on a graph. [< *graphic formula.*]

-graph suff. 1. An apparatus that writes or records: *telegraph.* 2. Something drawn or written: *monograph.* [< Gk. *graphein,* to write.]

-grapher suff. 1. One who writes about a specific subject: *biographer.* 2. One who employs a specific means to write, draw, or record: *stenographer.* [< Gk. *graphein,* to write.]

graph-ic (grăf′ĭk) or **graph-i-cal** (-ĭ-kəl) adj. 1. Written, printed, drawn, or engraved. 2. Vividly outlined or set forth: *a graphic account.* 3. Of or pertaining to the graphic arts. [< Gk. *graphikos.*] —**graph′i-cal-ly** adv. —**graph′ic-ness** n.

graphic arts pl.n. The arts that involve representing, writing, or printing on two-dimensional surfaces, as painting, drawing, and engraving.

graph-ics (grăf′ĭks) n. (used with a sing. or pl. verb). 1. The making of drawings or blueprints, as in engineering or architecture. 2. The graphic arts.

graph-ite (grăf′īt′) n. The soft, steel-gray to black form of carbon used in lead pencils, lubricants, paints, and coatings. [< Gk. *graphein,* to write.] —**gra-phit′ic** (grə-fĭt′ĭk) adj.

graph-ol-o-gy (gră-fŏl′ə-jē) n. The study of handwriting. —**graph′o-log′i-cal** (grăf′ə-lŏj′-ĭ-kəl) adj. —**graph-ol′o-gist** n.

-graphy suff. 1. A specific process or method of writing or representation: *stenography.* 2. A writing about a specific subject: *oceanography.* [< Gk. *graphein,* to write.]

grap-nel (grăp′nəl) n. A small anchor with three or more flukes, esp. for anchoring a vessel. [Prob. < OFr. *grapin,* hook.

grap-ple (grăp′əl) n. 1. a. A clawed implement formerly used to hold an enemy ship alongside for boarding. b. A grapnel. 2. Hand-to-hand combat. —v. -**pled,** -**pling.** 1. To lay hold on, make fast, or drag with or as if with a grapple. 2. To seize firmly with the hands. 3. To come to grips; wrestle. [< OFr. *grape,* hook.] —**grap′pler** n.

grappling iron n. Also **grappling hook.** A grapple (sense 1).

grasp (grăsp) v. 1. a. To seize and hold firmly. b. To make a motion of seizing; clutch. 2. To comprehend. —n. 1. Hold; grip. 2. The ability to seize and hold. 3. Comprehension. [ME *graspen.*]

grasp-ing (grăs′pĭng) adj. Greedy. —**grasp′ing-ly** adv. —**grasp′ing-ness** n.

grass (grăs) n. 1. Any of numerous plants with narrow leaves, jointed stems, and spikes or clusters of inconspicuous flowers. 2. Such plants collectively. 3. Ground, as a lawn or pasture, covered with such plants. 4. *Slang.* Marijuana. [< OE *græs.*] —**grass′y** adj.

grass-hop-per (grăs′hŏp′ər) n. Any of various related insects with long hind legs adapted for jumping.

grasshopper

grass-land (grăs′lănd′) n. An area, such as a prairie, of grass or grasslike vegetation.

grass-roots (grăs′rōōts′, -rŏŏts′) pl.n. (used with a sing. or pl. verb). People in local, outlying, or rural areas. —**grass′roots′** adj.

grate¹ (grāt) v. **grat-ed, grat-ing.** 1. To shred or pulverize by rubbing. 2. To make or cause to make a rasping sound. 3. To irritate. —n. A rasping noise. [< OFr. *grater,* to scrape.] —**grat′er** n.

grate² (grāt) n. 1. A framework of parallel or crossed bars over an opening. 2. Such a framework of metal, used to hold burning fuel. [< Lat. *cratis,* wickerwork.]

grate-ful (grāt′fəl) adj. 1. Appreciative; thankful. 2. Expressing gratitude. 3. Pleasing. [< obs. *grate,* pleasing.] —**grate′ful-ly** adv. —**grate′ful-ness** n.

grat-i-fy (grăt′ə-fī′) v. -**fied, -fy-ing.** 1. To please or satisfy. 2. To give what is desired to; indulge. [< Lat. *gratificare,* to oblige.] —**grat′i-fi-ca′tion** n. —**grat′i-fi′er** n.

grat-ing¹ (grā′tĭng) adj. 1. Rasping. 2. Irritating. —**grat′ing-ly** adv.

grat-ing² (grā′tĭng) n. A framework of bars; grate.

gra-tis (grăt′ĭs, grā′tĭs) adv. Freely; without charge. —adj. Free. [< Lat.]

grat-i-tude (grăt′ĭ-tōōd′, -tyōōd′) n. Thankfulness. [< Lat. *gratus,* pleasing.]

gra-tu-i-tous (grə-tōō′ĭ-təs, -tyōō′-) adj. 1. Free; gratis. 2. Unnecessary or unwarranted: *gratuitous criticism.* [Lat. *gratuitus,* voluntary.] —**gra-tu′i-tous-ly** adv. —**gra-tu′i-tous-ness** n.

gra-tu-i-ty (grə-tōō′ĭ-tē, -tyōō′-) n., pl. -**ties.** A tip for service. [< Med. Lat. *gratuitas,* gift.]

grave¹ (grāv) n. 1. An excavation for the burial of a corpse. 2. Any place of burial. [< OE *græf.*]

grave² (grāv) adj. **grav-er, grav-est.** 1. Extremely serious. 2. Bringing death or great danger; critical. 3. Dignified; solemn. 4. (also grāv). Of, being, or written with the mark, as the è in *Sèvres.* —n. (grāv, grăv). The grave accent. [< Lat. *gravis,* heavy.] —**grave′ly** adv. —**grave′ness** n.

grave³ (grāv) n. **graved, grav-en** (grā′vən), **grav-ing.** To engrave. [< OE *grafan.*] —**grav′er** n.

grav-el (grăv′əl) n. A loose mixture of rock fragments or pebbles. [< OFr. *grave,* coarse sand.]

grave-stone (grāv′stōn′) n. A tombstone.

grave-yard (grāv′yärd′) n. A cemetery.

grav-id (grăv′ĭd) adj. Pregnant. [Lat. *gravidus.*] —**gra-vid′i-ty** (grə-vĭd′ĭ-tē) or **grav′id-ness** n.

grav-i-met-ric (grăv′ĭ-mĕt′rĭk) or **grav-i-met-ri-cal** (-rĭ-kəl) adj. Of measurement by weight. [Lat. *gravis,* heavy + METRIC.] —**grav′i-met′-ri-cal-ly** adv. —**gra-vim′e-try** (grə-vĭm′ĭ-trē) n.

grav·i·tate (grăv'ĭ-tāt') v. **-tat·ed, -tat·ing. 1.** To move in response to the force of gravity. **2.** To be attracted. **—grav'i·tat'er** n.

grav·i·ta·tion (grăv'ĭ-tā'shən) n. **1. a.** The attraction that tends to draw together any pair of material objects. **b.** The force involved in this attraction; gravity. **2.** The act or process of gravitating. **—grav'i·ta'tion·al** or **grav'i·ta'tive** (-tā'tĭv) adj. **—grav'i·ta'tion·al·ly** adv.

grav·i·ton (grăv'ĭ-tŏn') n. A particle postulated to be the quantum of gravitational interaction and presumed to have zero electric charge and zero rest mass. [GRAVIT(ATION) + -ON.]

grav·i·ty (grăv'ĭ-tē) n. **1. a.** The force of gravitation, being, for any two sufficiently massive bodies, directly proportional to the product of their masses and inversely proportional to the square of the distance between them; esp. the attractive central gravitational force exerted by a celestial body such as the earth. **b.** Gravitation. **c.** Weight. **2.** Graveness; seriousness. [< Lat. *gravitas.*]

gra·vure (grə-vyŏŏr') n. **1.** A method of printing using photomechanically prepared plates or cylinders. **2.** Photogravure. [< OFr. *graver,* to engrave.]

gra·vy (grā'vē) n., pl. **-vies. 1.** The juices that drip from cooking meat. **2.** A sauce made from these juices. [< OFr. *grave.*]

gray (grā). Also **grey.** —adj. **-er, -est. 1.** Of a neutral color ranging between black and white. **2.** Dull or dark; gloomy. **3.** Having gray hair. —n. **1.** A neutral color ranging between black and white. **2.** An object or animal of this color. [< OE *græg.*] **—gray'ish** adj. **—gray'ness** n.

gray·beard (grā'bîrd') n. An old man.

gray matter n. The brownish-gray nerve tissue of the brain and spinal cord.

graze¹ (grāz) v. **grazed, graz·ing.** To feed on growing grasses and herbage. [< OE *grasian.*] **—graz'er** n.

graze² (grāz) v. **grazed, graz·ing.** To touch or scrape lightly in passing. [Perh. < GRAZE¹.] **—graze** n.

grease (grēs) n. **1.** Melted animal fat. **2.** Any thick oil or viscous lubricant. —v. **greased, greas·ing.** To coat, smear, lubricate, or soil with grease. [< Lat. *crassus,* fat.] **—grease'i·ness** n.

grease paint n. Theatrical make-up.

grease paint

greas·y (grē'sē, -zē) adj. **-i·er, -i·est. 1.** Coated or soiled with grease. **2.** Containing grease, esp. too much grease. **—greas'i·ly** adv. **—greas'i·ness** n.

great (grāt) adj. **-er, -est. 1.** Extremely large; notably big. **2.** Remarkable; outstanding: a great work of art. **3.** Eminent; distinguished: a great leader. **4.** Informal. First-rate; very good: feeling great. **5.** Being one generation removed from the relative specified: a great uncle. —n. One that is great. [< OE *grēat,* thick.] **—great'ly** adv. **—great'ness** n.

great circle n. A circle that is the intersection of the surface of a sphere with a plane passing through the center of the sphere.

great·coat (grāt'kōt') n. A heavy overcoat.

Great Dane n. A large and powerful dog with a smooth, short coat.

great-grand·child (grāt'grănd'chīld', -grăn'-) n. A child of a grandchild.

great-grand·par·ent (grāt'grănd'pâr'ənt,-pâr'-, -grăn'-) n. Either of the parents of a grandparent.

grebe (grēb) n. A diving bird with lobed, fleshy membranes along each toe and a pointed bill. [Fr. *grèbe.*]

Gre·cian (grē'shən) n. A native of Greece. —adj. Greek.

Grec·o-Ro·man (grĕk'ō-rō'mən, grē'kō-) adj. Of or relating to both Greece and Rome.

greed (grēd) n. A selfish desire for more than one needs or deserves; avarice. [< GREEDY.]

greed·y (grē'dē) adj. **-i·er, -i·est.** Wanting more than is needed or reasonable; avaricious. [< OE *grǣdig.*] **—greed'i·ly** adv. **—greed'i·ness** n.

Greek (grēk) n. **1.** A native or inhabitant of Greece. **2.** The Indo-European language of the Greeks. **—Greek** adj.

Greek Orthodox Church n. A division of the Eastern Orthodox Church that is the national church of Greece.

green (grēn) n. **1.** The color of most plant leaves and growing grass. **2. greens.** Leafy plants or plant parts used as food or for decoration. **3.** A grassy lawn or plot: a putting green. —adj. **-er, -est. 1.** Of the color green. **2.** Covered with green growth or foliage. **3.** Not ripe; immature. **4.** Lacking experience. —v. To make or become green. [< OE *grēne.*] **—green'ish** adj. **—green'ness** n.

green·back (grēn'băk') n. A legal-tender note of U.S. currency.

green·er·y (grē'nə-rē) n., pl. **-ies.** Green plants or leaves.

green-eyed (grēn'īd') adj. **1.** Having green eyes. **2.** Jealous.

green·horn (grēn'hôrn') n. An inexperienced or immature person. [Obs. *greynhorne,* animal with immature horns.]

green·house (grēn'hous') n. A glass-enclosed room or building for growing plants that need an even, usu. warm temperature.

green·sward (grēn'swôrd') n. Turf covered with green grass.

green thumb n. A knack for making plants grow well.

Green·wich time (grĭn'ĭj, -ĭch, grĕn'-) n. The time at the meridian at Greenwich, England (0° longitude), used as a basis for calculating time throughout most of the world.

green·wood (grēn'wŏŏd') n. A leafy forest.

greet (grēt) v. **1.** To address in a friendly and respectful way; welcome. **2.** To receive with a specified reaction. **3.** To be perceived by: A din greeted our ears. [< OE *grētan.*] **—greet'er** n.

greet·ing (grē'tĭng) n. A gesture or word of welcome or salutation.

gre·gar·i·ous (grĭ-gâr'ē-əs) adj. 1. Tending to live or move in groups. 2. Seeking and enjoying the company of others; sociable. [Lat. *gregarius.*] —**gre·gar'i·ous·ly** adv. —**gre·gar'i·ous·ness** n.

Gre·go·ri·an calendar (grĭ-gôr'ē-ən, -gôr'-) n. The calendar in use throughout most of the world, sponsored by Gregory XIII in 1582.

grem·lin (grĕm'lĭn) n. An imaginary mischievous elf. [Orig. unknown.]

gre·nade (grə-nād') n. A small bomb detonated by a fuse, designed to be thrown by hand or fired from a rifle. [< OFr. *grenate,* pomegranate.]

gren·a·dier (grĕn'ə-dîr') n. A member of a regiment formerly armed with grenades. [< Fr. *grenade,* grenade.]

gren·a·dine (grĕn'ə-dēn', grĕn'ə-dēn') n. A syrupy flavoring made from pomegranates or red currants. [< OFr. *grenate,* pomegranate.]

grew (grōō) v. p.t. of grow.

grey (grā) n. & adj. Var. of gray.

grey·hound (grā'hound') n. A slender, swift-running dog with long legs, a smooth coat, and a narrow head. [< OE *grīghund.*]

grid (grĭd) n. 1. A framework of parallel or crisscrossed bars. 2. A pattern of horizontal and vertical lines forming squares on a map, used as a reference for locating points. 3. a. An interconnected system of electric cables and power stations over a large area. b. A corrugated or perforated conducting plate in a storage battery. 4. A fine wire screen or coil placed between the plate and filament in an electron tube. [< GRIDIRON.]

grid·dle (grĭd'l) n. A flat pan used for cooking pancakes, bacon, etc. [< OFr. *gridil,* gridiron.]

grid·dle·cake (grĭd'l-kāk') n. A pancake.

grid·i·ron (grĭd'ī'ərn) n. 1. A flat framework of parallel metal bars used for broiling. 2. Any framework or network of crossing straight lines. 3. A football field. [< Lat. *cratis,* wickerwork.]

grief (grēf) n. 1. Deep sadness, as over a loss; sorrow. 2. A cause of sorrow. [< OFr. *grever,* to grieve.]

griev·ance (grē'vəns) n. 1. A circumstance regarded as just cause for protest. 2. A complaint based on such a circumstance.

grieve (grēv) v. **grieved, griev·ing.** 1. To cause to be sorrowful; distress. 2. To feel grief; mourn. [< Lat. *gravare,* to oppress.]

griev·ous (grē'vəs) adj. 1. Causing grief, pain, or anguish. 2. Serious; grave. —**griev'ous·ly** adv. —**griev'ous·ness** n.

grif·fin (grĭf'ĭn) n. Also **grif·fon** or **gryph·on**

griffin
1st-century B.C. Roman frieze

(grĭf'ən). A fabled beast with the head and wings of an eagle and the body of a lion. [< Gk. *grups.*]

grill (grĭl) n. 1. A cooking utensil containing metal bars; gridiron. 2. Food cooked on a grill. 3. A restaurant where grilled foods are served. 4. Var. of **grille.** —v. 1. To broil on a grill. 2. *Informal.* To question relentlessly; cross-examine. [< Lat. *cratis,* wickerwork.]

grille (grĭl) n. Also **grill.** A framework of metal bars used as a barrier, as in a window or gateway. [Fr., ult. < Lat. *cratis,* wickerwork.]

grim (grĭm) adj. **grim·mer, grim·mest.** 1. Unrelenting; rigid; stern. 2. Forbidding; terrible. 3. Ghastly; sinister. 4. Dismal; gloomy. [< OE. *fierce.*] —**grim'ly** adv. —**grim'ness** n.

grim·ace (grĭm'əs, grĭ-mās') n. A contortion of the face expressive of pain, contempt, or disgust. [< OFr.] —**grim'ace** v.

grime (grīm) n. Black dirt or soot on a surface. [< MLG.] —**grim'i·ly** adv. —**grim'i·ness** n. —**grim'y** adj.

grin (grĭn) v. **grinned, grin·ning.** To smile broadly, showing the teeth. —n. The expression of the face produced by grinning. [< OE *grennian,* to grimace.] —**grin'ner** n.

grind (grīnd) v. **ground (ground), grind·ing.** 1. To crush into fine particles. 2. To shape, sharpen, or refine with friction: *grind a lens.* 3. To rub together; gnash: *grind the teeth.* 4. To move with noisy friction: *grind to a halt.* 5. To bear down on harshly; crush. 6. To operate or produce by turning a crank. 7. To produce mechanically or without inspiration: *grinding out cheap novels.* 8. *Informal.* To devote oneself to study or work. —n. 1. The act of grinding. 2. A specific degree of pulverization, as of coffee beans. 3. *Informal.* a. A laborious task, routine, or study. b. One who works or studies excessively. [< OE *grindan.*] —**grind'er** n. —**grind'ing·ly** adv.

grind·stone (grīnd'stōn') n. 1. A stone disk turned on an axle for grinding, polishing, or sharpening tools. 2. A millstone.

grip (grĭp) n. 1. A tight hold; firm grasp. 2. The manner or power of grasping and holding. 3. Mastery; command. 4. A part to be grasped and held; handle. 5. A suitcase. —v. **gripped, grip·ping.** 1. To get and maintain a tight hold on. 2. To hold the interest or attention of. —*idiom.* **come to grips.** 1. To engage in combat. 2. To deal directly or boldly; confront. [< OE *gripe.*] —**grip'ping·ly** adv.

gripe (grīp) v. **griped, grip·ing.** 1. To cause or suffer sharp pain in the bowels. 2. *Informal.* To irritate; annoy. 3. *Informal.* To complain naggingly; grumble. —n. 1. *Informal.* A complaint. 2. **gripes.** Sharp, repeated pains in the bowels. [< OE *grīpan.*]

grippe (grĭp) n. Influenza. [< OFr. *gripper,* to seize.] —**grip'py** adj.

gris·ly (grĭz'lē) adj. **-li·er, -li·est.** Horrifying; gruesome: *a grisly murder.* [< OE *grislic.*]

grist (grĭst) n. Grain to be ground or already ground. [< OE *grīst.*]

gris·tle (grĭs'əl) n. Cartilage, esp. in meat. [< OE.] —**gris'tly** adj.

grit (grĭt) n. 1. Tiny rough particles, as of sand or stone. 2. *Informal.* Indomitable spirit; pluck. —v. **grit·ted, grit·ting.** To clamp (the teeth) together. [< OE *grēot.*] —**grit'ty** adj.

grits (grĭts) pl.n. Coarsely ground grain, esp. corn. [< OE *grytta,* coarse meal.]

griz·zly (grĭz'lē) *adj.* **-zli·er, -zli·est.** Grayish or flecked with gray. —*n., pl.* **-zlies.** A grizzly bear. [< OFr. *gris,* gray.]

grizzly bear *n.* A large grayish bear of North America.

groan (grōn) *v.* To utter a deep, prolonged sound expressive of pain, grief, annoyance, or disapproval. [< OE *grānian.*] —**groan** *n.*

groats (grōts) *pl.n.* Hulled, usu. crushed grain, esp. oats. [< OE *grotan.*]

gro·cer (grō'sər) *n.* A storekeeper who sells foodstuffs and household supplies. [< Med. Lat. *grossarius,* wholesale dealer.]

gro·cer·y (grō'sə-rē) *n., pl.* **-ies.** 1. A store selling foodstuffs and household supplies. 2. **groceries.** The goods sold by a grocer.

grog (grŏg) *n.* Rum or other alcoholic liquor diluted with water. [< Old *Grog,* nickname of Admiral Edward Vernon (1684–1757).]

grog·gy (grŏg'ē) *adj.* **-gi·er, -gi·est.** Unsteady and dazed; shaky. —**grog'gi·ly** *adv.* —**grog'gi·ness** *n.*

groin (groin) *n.* 1. The crease where the thigh meets the trunk, together with the area nearby. 2. *Archit.* The curved edge at the junction of two intersecting vaults. [< OE *grynde,* abyss.]

grom·met (grŏm'ĭt) *n.* A reinforced eyelet, as in a garment, through which a fastener is passed. [Prob. < obs. Fr. *gormette,* chain joining the ends of a bit.]

groom (grōōm, grŏŏm) *n.* 1. A man or boy employed to take care of horses. 2. A bridegroom. —*v.* 1. To make neat and trim. 2. To clean and brush (an animal). 3. To train, as for a specific position. [ME *grom.*]

groove (grōōv) *n.* 1. A long, narrow furrow or channel. 2. A settled, humdrum routine. 3. *Slang.* A pleasurable experience. —*v.* **grooved, groov·ing.** To cut a groove in. [ME *groof,* mining shaft.]

groov·y (grōō'vē) *adj.* **-i·er, -i·est.** *Slang.* Delightful; satisfying.

grope (grōp) *v.* **groped, grop·ing.** 1. To reach about uncertainly; feel one's way. 2. To search blindly or uncertainly: *grope for an answer.* —*n.* The act of groping. [< OE *grāpian.*] —**grop'ing·ly** *adv.*

gros·beak (grōs'bēk') *n.* Any of several often colorful birds with a thick, rounded bill. [< Fr. *grosbec.*]

gro·schen (grō'shən) *n., pl.* **-schen.** See table at **currency.** [G.]

gross (grōs) *adj.* **-er, -est.** 1. Exclusive of deductions; total; entire: *gross profits.* 2. Glaringly obvious; flagrant. 3. Coarse; vulgar. 4. Overweight; corpulent. 5. Broad; general. —*n.* 1. *pl.* **gross·es.** The entire body or amount; a total. 2. *pl.* **gross.** A group of 144 or 12 dozen items. —*v.* To earn as a total before deductions. —*phrasal verb.* **gross out.** *Slang.* To fill with disgust. [< LLat. *grossus,* thick.] —**gross'ly** *adv.* —**gross'ness** *n.*

grosz (grôsh) *n., pl.* **gro·szy** (grô'shē). See table at **currency.** [Pol.]

gro·tesque (grō-tĕsk') *adj.* 1. Characterized by ludicrous or incongruous distortion. 2. Extravagant; outlandish; bizarre. [< Ital. *grottesco,* of a grotto.] —**gro·tesque'** *n.* —**gro·tesque'ly** *adv.* —**gro·tesque'ness** *n.* —**gro·tes'que·ry** *n.*

grot·to (grŏt'ō) *n., pl.* **-toes** or **-tos.** A cave or cavelike excavation. [Ital., ult. < Gk. *kruptē,* crypt.]

grouch (grouch) *v.* To complain; grumble. —*n.* 1. A grumbling or sulky mood. 2. A habitually complaining person. [Prob. < obs. *grutch,* to complain.] —**grouch'i·ly** *adv.* —**grouch'i·ness** *n.* —**grouch'y** *adj.*

ground¹ (ground) *n.* 1. The solid surface of the earth. 2. Soil; earth. 3. Often **grounds.** An area of land designated for a particular purpose. 4. **grounds.** The land surrounding a building. 5. Often **grounds.** The foundation or basis for an argument, belief, or action. 6. A background. 7. **grounds.** The sediment at the bottom of a liquid, esp. coffee. 8. **a.** The position or portion of an electric circuit that is at zero potential with respect to the earth. **b.** A conducting connection to such a position or to the earth. **c.** A large conducting body, such as the earth, used as a return for electric currents and as an arbitrary zero of potential. —*v.* 1. To place or set on the ground. 2. To provide a basis for; base. 3. To instruct in fundamentals. 4. To prevent (an aircraft, pilot, or crew) from flying. 5. To connect (an electric current) to a ground. 6. To run (a vessel) aground. 7. *Baseball.* To hit (a ball) on the ground. [< OE *grund.*]

ground² (ground) *v. p.t. & p.p.* of **grind.**

ground hog *n.* A woodchuck.

ground·less (ground'lĭs) *adj.* Having no ground or foundation; unsubstantiated. —**ground'less·ly** *adv.* —**ground'less·ness** *n.*

ground rule *n.* 1. A rule governing the playing of a game on a particular field, course, or court. 2. A basic rule.

ground swell *n.* 1. A deep swell in the ocean. 2. A strong, rapid growth or surge.

ground water *n.* Water beneath the earth's surface that supplies wells and springs.

ground·work (ground'wûrk') *n.* Preliminary work; basis.

group (grōōp) *n.* A number of persons or things gathered, located, or classified together. —*v.* To place in or form a group or groups. [< Ital. *gruppo,* of Gmc. orig.]

grou·per (grōō'pər) *n.* Any of various large, chiefly tropical marine fishes. [Port. *garoupa.*]

group·ie (grōō'pē) *n. Slang.* A female fan of a rock group, esp. one who follows the group around on tours.

grouse¹ (grous) *n., pl.* **grouse.** A plump, chickenlike bird with mottled brown or grayish plumage. [Orig. unknown.]

grouse¹   **grove**

grouse² (grous) v. **groused, grous·ing.** To complain; grumble. [Orig. unknown.] —**grous'er** n.

grout (grout) n. A thin mortar used to fill cracks, as between tiles. —v. To fill or finish with grout. [< OE *grūt*, coarse meal.] —**grout'er** n.

grove (grōv) n. A small group of trees lacking dense undergrowth. [< OE *gráf.*]

grov·el (grŭv'əl, grŏv'-) v. **-eled** or **-elled, -el·ing** or **-el·ling.** To humble oneself abjectly; cringe. [< ON *grufa*, to lie face down.] —**grov'el·er** n.

grow (grō) v. **grew** (grōō), **grown** (grōn), **grow·ing.** 1. To increase or cause to increase in size by natural processes. 2. To cultivate; raise: *grow tulips.* 3. To develop and reach maturity. 4. To be capable of growth; thrive; flourish. 5. To become: *grow angry; grow cold.* —**phrasal verbs. grow on** (or **upon**). To become more pleasurable, acceptable, or essential to: *a style that grows on one.* **grow up.** To reach maturity; become an adult. [< OE *grōwan.*] —**grow'er** n.

growl (groul) n. A low, guttural, menacing sound, as of a dog. [Perh. imit.] —**growl** v. —**growl'er** n.

grown (grōn) v. p.p. of **grow.** —adj. Mature; adult.

grown-up (grōn'ŭp') adj. Adult; mature. —**grown'-up'** or **grown'up'** n.

growth (grōth) n. 1. a. The process of growing or developing. b. A stage in the process of growing. 2. An increase, as in size or number. 3. Something that has grown: *a growth of grass.* 4. An abnormal tissue formation.

grub (grŭb) v. **grubbed, grub·bing.** 1. To clear of roots. 2. To dig up by the roots. 3. a. To search laboriously; rummage. b. To toil arduously; drudge. 4. Slang. To obtain by begging: *grub a cigarette.* —n. 1. The thick, wormlike larva of certain insects. 2. Slang. Food. [ME *grubben.*] —**grub'ber** n.

grub·by (grŭb'ē) adj. **-bi·er, -bi·est.** Dirty; unkempt. —**grub'bi·ly** adv. —**grub'bi·ness** n.

grub·stake (grŭb'stāk') n. Supplies or funds advanced to a mining prospector or a person starting a business in return for a share of the profits. —**grub'stake'** v. —**grub'stak'er** n.

grudge (grŭj) v. **grudged, grudg·ing.** To be reluctant to give or admit. —n. A feeling of resentment or rancor. [< 'OFr. *grouchier,* to complain.] —**grudg'er** n. —**grudg'ing·ly** adv.

gru·el (grōō'əl) n. A thin, watery porridge. [<OFr. *gru,* groats.]

gru·el·ing (grōō'ə-lĭng) adj. Also **gru·el·ling.** Exhausting. —**gru'el·ing·ly** adv.

grue·some (grōō'səm) adj. Causing horror and repugnance; frightful and shocking. [Obs. *grue,* to shudder + -SOME¹.] —**grue'some·ly** adv. —**grue'some·ness** n.

gruff (grŭf) adj. **-er, -est.** 1. Brief and unfriendly; stern. 2. Hoarse; harsh. [< MDu.] —**gruff'ly** adv. —**gruff'ness** n.

Syns: *gruff, bluff, blunt, brusque, curt* adj.

grum·ble (grŭm'bəl) v. **-bled, -bling.** To mumble in discontent. [< ME *grummen.*] —**grum'ble** n. —**grum'bler** n. —**grum'bly** adj.

grump·y (grŭm'pē) adj. **-i·er, -i·est.** Irritable; cranky. —**grump'i·ly** adv. —**grump'i·ness** n.

grun·ion (grŭn'yən) n. A small fish of California coastal waters that spawns along beaches during high tides at the time of the full moon. [Perh. < Sp. *gruñón,* grumbler.]

grunt (grŭnt) v. To utter (with) a low, gut-

tural sound, as does a hog. [< OE *grunnettan.*] —**grunt** n.

gryph·on (grĭf'ən) n. Var. of **griffin.**

gua·nine (gwä'nēn') n. A purine, $C_5H_5N_5O$, that is a constituent of both ribonucleic and deoxyribonucleic acids. [< GUANO.]

gua·no (gwä'nō) n. The excrement of sea birds or bats, used as fertilizer. [< Quechua *huanu,* dung.]

gua·ra·ni (gwä'rə-nē') n., pl. **-ni** or **-nis.** See table at **currency.** [Sp. *guaraní,* Guarani.]

Gua·ra·ni (gwä'rə-nē') n., pl. **-nis** or **Guarani.** 1. a. A group of South American Indians of Paraguay, Bolivia, and southern Brazil. b. A member of any of these tribes. 2. The language of the Guarani.

guar·an·tee (găr'ən-tē') n. 1. A formal assurance that something is as represented or that a specified act will be performed. 2. A guaranty. 3. A guarantor. —v. **-teed, -tee·ing.** 1. To assume responsibility for the debt or default of: 2. To undertake to accomplish. 3. To furnish security for. [< GUARANTY.]

guar·an·tor (găr'ən-tər, -tôr') n. One that gives a guarantee or guaranty.

guar·an·ty (găr'ən-tē) n., pl. **-ties.** 1. An undertaking to answer for another's debts or obligations in the event of default. 2. a. Anything held as security for something. b. The act of providing such security. 3. A guarantor. [< OFr. *garant,* warrant.]

guard (gärd) v. 1. To protect from harm; watch over. 2. To watch over to prevent escape. 3. To keep watch at (a door or gate). 4. To take precautions: *guard against infection.* —n. 1. One that guards. 2. Watchful care: *under close guard.* 3. A defensive posture or stance. 4. Football. One of the two players on either side of the center. 5. Basketball. Either of the two players stationed near the middle of the court. 6. A device that prevents injury, damage, or loss. [< OFr. *guarder.*] —**guard'er** n.

guard·ed (gär'dĭd) adj. 1. Protected; defended. 2. Cautious; restrained.

guard·house (gärd'hous') n. 1. A building that accommodates a military guard. 2. A military jail.

guard·i·an (gär'dē-ən) n. 1. One that guards. 2. A person who is legally responsible for the person or property of another person, such as a child, who cannot manage his own affairs. —**guard'i·an·ship'** n.

gua·va (gwä'və) n. The yellow-skinned fruit of a tropical American tree, used for jellies and preserves. [Sp. *guayaba.*]

gu·ber·na·to·ri·al (gōō'bər-nə-tôr'ē-əl, -tôr'-, gyōō'-) adj. Of or relating to a governor. [< Lat. *gubernator,* governor.]

Guern·sey (gûrn'zē) n., pl. **-seys.** One of a

Guernsey

breed of brown and white dairy cattle orig. developed on the Isle of Guernsey.

guer·ril·la or **gue·ril·la** (gə-rĭl'ə) *n.* A member of an irregular military force that uses harassing tactics against an enemy army. [< Sp. *guerra,* war.]

guess (gĕs) *v.* **1.** To predict or assume (an event or fact) without enough information to be sure. **2.** To estimate correctly. **3.** To suppose; judge: *I guess you're right.* —*n.* **1.** An act of guessing: *taking a guess.* **2.** A judgment or estimate arrived at by guessing. [ME *gessen.*] —**guess'er** *n.*

guess·work (gĕs'wûrk') *n.* The process or result of making guesses.

guest (gĕst) *n.* **1.** A visitor who receives hospitality, as at the home or table of another. **2.** A patron of a hotel, restaurant, etc. **3.** A visiting participant, as in a television program. [< ON *gestr.*]

guf·faw (gə-fô') *n.* A hearty or coarse burst of laughter. [Imit.] —**guf·faw'** *v.*

guid·ance (gĭd'ns) *n.* **1.** The act or an example of guiding. **2.** Counseling; advice.

guide (gĭd) *n.* **1.** One that shows the way by leading, directing, or advising, esp. a person employed to lead a tour, expedition, or similar group. **2. a.** A sign or mark that serves to direct. **b.** An example or model to be followed. **3.** A device that acts as an indicator or regulates motion. —*v.* **guid·ed, guid·ing.** **1.** To show the way to; conduct. **2.** To direct the course of; steer. **3.** To manage the affairs of; govern. [< OProv. *guida.*] —**guid'er** *n.*

guide·book (gĭd'bŏŏk') *n.* A handbook of information, as for travelers or students.

guided missile Any missile capable of being guided while in flight.

guide·line (gĭd'līn') *n.* A policy or rule intended to give practical guidance.

guide·post (gĭd'pōst') *n.* A post with a directional sign.

gui·don (gī'dŏn', gīd'n) *n.* A small flag carried as a standard by a military unit. [< OProv. *guida,* guide.]

guild (gĭld) *n.* An association of persons of the same trade formed for their mutual aid and protection, esp. a medieval society of merchants or artisans. [< ON *gildi.*]

guil·der (gĭl'dər) *n.* See table at **currency.** [< MDu. *gulden (florijn),* golden (florin).]

guile (gīl) *n.* Deceitful cunning; craftiness. [< OFr.] —**guile'ful** *adj.* —**guile'ful·ly** *adv.* —**guile'ful·ness** *n.* —**guile'less** *adj.* —**guile'·less·ly** *adv.* —**guile'less·ness** *n.*

guil·lo·tine (gĭl'ə-tēn', gē'ə-) *n.* A machine for beheading condemned prisoners by means of a heavy blade that falls freely between upright posts. —*v.* **-tined, -tin·ing.** To behead with a guillotine. [< Joseph I. *Guillotin* (1738–1814).]

guilt (gĭlt) *n.* **1.** The fact of being responsible for a crime or wrongdoing. **2.** Regretful awareness of having done something wrong; remorse. [< OE *gylt.*] —**guilt'less** *adj.* —**guilt'less·ly** *adv.* —**guilt'less·ness** *n.*

guilt·y (gĭl'tē) *adj.* **-i·er, -i·est.** **1.** Responsible for a crime or wrongdoing. **2.** Burdened with or showing a sense of guilt. —**guilt'i·ly** *adv.* —**guilt'i·ness** *n.*

guin·ea (gĭn'ē) *n. Chiefly Brit.* **1.** A former gold coin worth one pound and five pence. **2.** The sum of one pound and five pence. [< the *Guinea* coast of Africa.]

guinea fowl *n.* Also **guinea hen.** A domesticated pheasantlike bird having blackish plumage marked with many small white spots. [< the *Guinea* coast of Africa.]

George Miksch Sutton
guinea fowl

guinea pig *n.* **1.** A variously colored, seemingly tailless rodent often kept as a pet or used for biological experiments. **2.** A subject for experimentation. [Prob. < *Guiana.*]

guise (gīz) *n.* **1.** Outward appearance; aspect. **2.** False appearance; pretense. **3.** Mode of dress; garb. [< OFr., manner.]

gui·tar (gĭ-tär') *n.* A musical instrument with a large flat-backed sound box and usu. six strings, played by strumming or plucking. [< Gk. *kithara,* lyre.] —**gui·tar'ist** *n.*

gulch (gŭlch) *n.* A small, shallow canyon; ravine. [Orig. unknown.]

gulf (gŭlf) *n.* **1.** A large area of a sea or ocean partially enclosed by land. **2.** A deep, wide hole in the earth; abyss. **3.** A separating distance; wide gap. [< Gk. *kolphos,* fold.]

gulf·weed (gŭlf'wēd') *n.* A brownish seaweed often forming dense, floating masses in tropical Atlantic waters.

gull¹ (gŭl) *n.* Any of various chiefly coastal water birds with long wings, webbed feet, and usu. gray and white plumage. [ME, of Celt. orig.]

gull² (gŭl) *n.* A person who is easily fooled; dupe. —*v.* To deceive; dupe. [Orig. unknown.]

gul·let (gŭl'ĭt) *n.* **1.** The esophagus. **2.** The throat. [< Lat. *gula,* throat.]

gul·li·ble (gŭl'ə-bəl) *adj.* Easily deceived or duped. —**gul'li·bil'i·ty** *n.* —**gul'li·bly** *adv.*

gul·ly (gŭl'ē) *n., pl.* **-lies.** A deep channel cut in the earth by running water. [< GULLET.]

gulp (gŭlp) *v.* **1.** To swallow greedily or rapidly in large amounts. **2.** To choke or gasp, as in nervousness. —*n.* **1.** An act of gulping. **2.** A large mouthful. [ME *gulpen.*]

gum¹ (gŭm) *n.* **1.** Any of various viscous plant substances that dry into water-soluble, non-crystalline, brittle solids. **2.** Any of various trees yielding gum. **3.** Chewing gum. —*v.* **gummed, gum·ming.** **1.** To cover, seal, or fill with gum. **2.** To become sticky or clogged with gum. [< Gk. *kommi.*] —**gum'my** *adj.*

gum² (gŭm) *n. Often* **gums.** The firm connective tissue that surrounds the bases of the teeth. [< OE *gōma*, palate.]

gum ara·bic (ăr'ə-bĭk) *n.* A gum exuded by various African trees and used esp. in the manufacture of mucilage and candies.

gum·bo (gŭm'bō) *n., pl.* **-bos.** A soup or stew thickened with okra. [Louisiana Fr. *gombo.*]

gum·drop (gŭm'drŏp') *n.* A small candy made of sweetened gum arabic or gelatin.

gump·tion (gŭmp'shən) *n. Informal.* Boldness of enterprise; initiative. [Orig. unknown.]

gum·shoe (gŭm'shōō') *n.* **1.** A rubber overshoe. **2.** *Slang.* A detective.

gun (gŭn) *n.* **1.** A weapon consisting essentially of a metal tube from which a projectile is fired. **2.** A portable firearm. **3.** A device that shoots or discharges: *a spray gun.* —*v.* **gunned, gun·ning. 1.** To shoot: *gun down a fugitive.* **2.** To open the throttle of: *gun an engine.* —*phrasal verb.* **gun** for. To seek to catch, overcome, or gain. [ME *gunne.*]

gun·boat (gŭn'bōt') *n.* A small armed vessel.

gun·cotton (gŭn'kŏt'n) *n.* Nitrocellulose.

gun·fight (gŭn'fīt') *n.* A fight with firearms. —**gun'fight'er** *n.*

gun·fire (gŭn'fīr') *n.* The firing of guns.

gung ho (gŭng' hō') *adj. Slang.* Extremely dedicated or enthusiastic. [Pidgin E., prob. < Chin. *gōng¹ he²,* to work together.]

gun·lock (gŭn'lŏk') *n.* A device for igniting the gunpowder in some firearms.

gun·man (gŭn'mən) *n.* **1.** A professional killer. **2.** A criminal armed with a gun.

gun·metal (gŭn'mĕt'l) *adj.* Dark gray.

gun·nel (gŭn'əl) *n.* Var. of **gunwale.**

gun·ner (gŭn'ər) *n.* **1.** A soldier, sailor, or airman who aims or fires a gun. **2.** One who hunts with a gun.

gun·nery (gŭn'ə-rē) *n.* The science of constructing and operating guns.

gun·ny (gŭn'ē) *n.* **1.** A coarse fabric made of jute or hemp. **2.** Burlap. [< Skt. *goṇī,* sack.]

gunny sack *n.* A sack made of burlap or gunny.

gun·powder (gŭn'pou'dər) *n.* An explosive powder used to propel projectiles from guns.

gun·shot (gŭn'shŏt') *n.* Shot or a shot fired from a gun.

gun-shy (gŭn'shī') *adj.* Afraid of gunfire or other loud noises.

gun·smith (gŭn'smĭth') *n.* A person who makes or repairs firearms.

gun·wale (gŭn'əl) *n.* Also **gun·nel.** The upper edge of the side of a ship or boat.

gup·py (gŭp'ē) *n., pl.* **-pies.** A small, brightly colored tropical freshwater fish. [After R.J.L. *Guppy* (1836–1916).]

gur·gle (gûr'gəl) *v.* **-gled, -gling.** To flow in a broken, uneven current, making low sounds. [Prob. imit.] —**gur'gle** *n.* —**gur'gling·ly** *adv.*

gu·ru (gŏō'rōō', gŏō-rōō') *n.* **1.** Often **Guru.** A Hindu spiritual teacher. **2.** Any revered guru or mentor. [< Skt. *guru-,* venerable.]

gush (gŭsh) *v.* **1.** To emit or flow forth suddenly and violently. **2.** To make an effusive display of sentiment or enthusiasm. —*n.* A sudden, violent outflow. [ME *gushen.*]

gush·er (gŭsh'ər) *n.* **1.** One that gushes. **2.** A gas or oil well with an abundant flow.

gush·y (gŭsh'ē) *adj.* **-i·er, -i·est.** Characterized by excessive displays of sentiment or enthusiasm. —**gush'i·ly** *adv.* —**gush'i·ness** *n.*

gus·set (gŭs'ĭt) *n.* A triangular insert for

strengthening or enlarging a garment. [< OFr. *gosset.*]

gus·sy (gŭs'ē) *v.* **-sied, -sy·ing.** To dress up showily. [Orig. unknown.]

gust (gŭst) *n.* **1.** A sudden, strong rush of wind. **2.** An outburst of emotion. —*v.* To blow in gusts. [< ON *gustr.*] —**gust'i·ly** *adv.* —**gust'y** *adj.*

gus·ta·to·ry (gŭs'tə-tôr'ē, -tōr'ē) *adj.* Of or relating to the sense of taste. [< Lat. *gustare,* to taste.]

gus·to (gŭs'tō) *n.* Vigorous enjoyment. [Ital.]

gut (gŭt) *n.* **1.** The alimentary canal or any of its parts, esp. the stomach or intestines. **2. guts.** The bowels; entrails. **3. guts.** The essential contents of something. **4.** Strong cord made from animal intestines. **5. guts.** *Informal.* Courage; fortitude. —*v.* **gut·ted, gut·ting. 1.** To disembowel. **2.** To destroy the contents or interior of. —*adj. Slang.* Deeply felt: *a gut response.* [< OE *guttas,* entrails.]

gut·less (gŭt'lĭs) *adj. Informal.* Lacking courage. —**gut'less·ly** *adv.* —**gut'less·ness** *n.*

guts·y (gŭt'sē) *adj.* **-i·er, -i·est.** *Informal.* Full of courage; plucky. —**guts'i·ness** *n.*

gut·ta-per·cha (gŭt'ə-pûr'chə) *n.* A rubbery substance derived from the latex of certain tropical trees, used as electrical insulation for waterproofing. [Malay *gĕtah percha.*]

gut·ter (gŭt'ər) *n.* A channel for draining off water, as at the edge of a street or a roof. —*v.* **1.** To flow in small streams or channels. **2.** To melt away rapidly: *The candle guttered and died.* [< Lat. *gutta,* drop.]

gut·ter·snipe (gŭt'ər-snīp') *n.* A street urchin.

gut·tur·al (gŭt'ər-əl) *adj.* **1.** Of or relating to the throat. **2.** Produced in the throat. [< Lat. *guttur,* throat.] —**gut'tur·al·ly** *adv.*

guy¹ (gī) *n.* A rope, cord, or cable used for steadying or guiding. —*v.* To steady or guide with a guy. [Prob. of LG orig.]

guy² (gī) *n. Informal.* A man; fellow. [< *Guy* Fawkes (1570–1606).]

guz·zle (gŭz'əl) *v.* **-zled, -zling.** To drink greedily or excessively. [Orig. unknown.] —**guz'zler** *n.*

gym (jĭm) *n. Informal.* A gymnasium.

gym·na·si·um (jĭm-nā'zē-əm) *n., pl.* **-ums** or **-si·a** (-zē-ə). **1.** A room or building equipped for gymnastics and sports. **2.** (gĭm-nä'zē-ōōm'). An academic high school in various central European countries. [< Gk. *gumnasion,* school.]

gym·nas·tics (jĭm-năs'tĭks) *n.* (*used with a sing. or pl. verb*). Body-building exercises, esp. those performed with special apparatus in a gymnasium. [< Gk. *gumnastēs,* gymnast.] —**gym'nast'** *n.* —**gym·nas'tic** *adj.* —**gym·nas'ti·cal·ly** *adv.*

gy·ne·col·o·gy (gī'nĭ-kŏl'ə-jē, jī'-, jĭn'ĭ-) *n.* The medical science of disease, reproductive physiology, and endocrinology in females. [Gk. *gunē* + -LOGY.] —**gy'ne·co·log'i·cal** (-kə-lŏj'ĭ-kəl) or **gy'ne·co·log'ic** *adj.* —**gy'ne·col'o·gist** *n.*

gyp (jĭp) *Informal.* —*v.* **gypped, gyp·ping.** To swindle, cheat, or defraud. —*n.* **1.** A swindle. **2.** A swindler. [Prob. < GYPSY.] —**gyp'per** *n.*

gyp·sum (jĭp'səm) *n.* A white mineral, $CaSO_4 \cdot 2H_2O$, used in the manufacture of plasters, wallboards, and fertilizers. [< Gk. *gupsos.*]

Gyp·sy (jĭp'sē) *n., pl.* **-sies.** Also **Gip·sy. 1.** One of a nomadic people orig. migrating from the border region between Iran and

India to Europe in the 14th or 15th cent.
2. Often **gypsy.** A wanderer; vagabond.
—**Gyp'sy** or **Gip'sy** adj.

gypsy moth n. A moth having hairy caterpillars very destructive to trees.

gy·rate (jī'rāt') v. **-rat·ed, -rat·ing.** 1. To revolve on or around a center or axis. 2. To circle or spiral. [< Lat. *gyrare.*] —**gy·ra'tion** n. —**gy'ra·tor** n.

gyr·fal·con (jûr'făl'kən, -fôl'-, -fô'kən) n. A large falcon of northern regions, with white or grayish plumage. [< OFr. *girfaut.*]

gy·ro (jī'rō) n., pl. **-ros.** A gyroscope.

gy·ro·com·pass (jī'rō-kŭm'pəs, -kŏm'-) n. A navigational device in which a gyroscope acts to maintain a pointer's north-south orientation.

gy·ro·scope (jī'rə-skōp') n. A device consisting essentially of a spinning mass, typically a disk or wheel, suspended so that its spin axis maintains a fixed angular orientation when not subjected to external torques. [Gk. *guros,* circle + -SCOPE.] —**gy·ro·scop'ic** (-skŏp'ĭk) adj. —**gy·ro·scop'i·cal·ly** adv.

Hh

h or **H** (āch) n., pl. **h's** or **H's.** 1. The 8th letter of the English alphabet. 2. The 8th in a series. 3. Something shaped like the letter H. **H** The symbol for the element hydrogen.

ha (hä) interj. Also **hah.** Used to express surprise, laughter, or triumph.

Ha·bak·kuk (hăb'ə-kŭk', hə-băk'ək) n. See table at **Bible.**

ha·be·as cor·pus (hā'bē-əs kôr'pəs) n. *Law.* A writ issued to bring a party before a court to prevent unlawful restraint. [< Med. Lat., you should have the body.]

hab·er·dash·er (hăb'ər-dăsh'ər) n. A dealer in men's furnishings. [< AN *haberdassher.*]

hab·er·dash·er·y (hăb'ər-dăsh'ə-rē) n., pl. **-ies.** A haberdasher's shop.

ha·bil·i·ment (hə-bĭl'ə-mənt) n. 1. The dress typical of an office, rank, or occasion. 2. **habiliments.** Clothes. [< OFr. *habiller,* to clothe.]

hab·it (hăb'ĭt) n. 1. A pattern of behavior acquired by frequent repetition. 2. Customary manner or practice. 3. An addiction. 4. A distinctive dress or costume. [< Lat. *habitus,* p.p. of *habēre,* to have.]

hab·it·a·ble (hăb'ĭ-tə-bəl) adj. Suitable to live in. [< Lat. *habitare,* to inhabit.] —**hab'it·a·bil'i·ty** or **hab'it·a·ble·ness** n. —**hab'it·a·bly** adv.

hab·i·tat (hăb'ĭ-tăt') n. 1. The area or natural environment in which an organism normally lives or grows. 2. The place where a person or thing is most likely to be found. [< Lat. *habitare,* to inhabit.]

hab·i·ta·tion (hăb'ĭ-tā'shən) n. 1. The act of inhabiting or the condition of being inhabited. 2. **a.** Natural environment or locality. **b.** Dwelling place.

hab·it-form·ing (hăb'ĭt-fôr'mĭng) adj. Leading to physiological addiction.

ha·bit·u·al (hə-bĭch'ōō-əl) adj. 1. Established by or acting according to habit. 2. Inveterate. 3. Customary; usual. —**ha·bit'u·al·ly** adv. —**ha·bit'u·al·ness** n.

ha·bit·u·ate (hə-bĭch'ōō-āt') v. **-at·ed, -at·ing.** To accustom by repetition or exposure. [< LLat. *habituare.*] —**ha·bit'u·a'tion** n.

hab·i·tude (hăb'ĭ-tōōd', -tyōōd') n. A customary behavior or manner. [< Lat. *habitudo.*]

ha·bit·u·é (hə-bĭch'ōō-ā', hə-bĭch'ōō-ā') n. One who frequents a particular place. [Fr.]

ha·ci·en·da (hä'sē-ĕn'də, ä'sē-) n. 1. In Spanish-speaking countries, a large estate. 2. The main house of such an estate.

hack[1] (hăk) v. 1. To cut with irregular and heavy blows; chop roughly. 2. To cough in short, dry-throated spasms. —n. 1. A notch made by hacking. 2. A tool used for hacking. 3. A rough, dry cough. [< OE *haccian.*] —**hack'er** n.

hack[2] (hăk) n. 1. A horse for hire. 2. A worn-out horse. 3. A vehicle for hire. 4. One hired to do routine writing. 5. A taxicab. —v. 1. To employ or work as a hack. 2. *Informal.* To manage or cope with. —adj. 1. For or by a hack. 2. Banal; trite. [< HACKNEY.] —**hack'man** n.

hack·ie (hăk'ē) n. *Slang.* A taxicab driver.

hack·le (hăk'əl) n. 1. One of the long, slender feathers on the neck of a bird. 2. **hackles.** **a.** The erectile hairs at the back of the neck, esp. of a dog. **b.** Temper; rage. [ME *hakell.*]

hack·ney (hăk'nē) n., pl. **-neys.** 1. A horse for riding or driving. 2. A coach or carriage for hire. —v. To cause to become banal and trite. [ME *hackenei.*]

hack·neyed (hăk'nēd) adj. Trite; banal.

hack·saw (hăk'sô') n. A tough, fine-toothed saw stretched taut in a frame, used for cutting metal.

hacksaw

had (hăd) v. *p.t. & p.p.* of **have.**

had·dock (hăd'ək) n., pl. **-dock** or **-docks.** A food fish of northern Atlantic waters, related to and resembling the cod. [ME *haddok.*]

Ha·des (hā'dēz) n. 1. *Gk. Myth.* The nether world. 2. Often **hades.** Hell.

had·n't (hăd'nt). Had not.

hadst (hădst) v. *Archaic.* p.t. & p.p. of **have**.

haf·ni·um (hăf'nē-əm) n. *Symbol* **Hf** A brilliant, silvery metallic element used in nuclear reactor control rods and in the manufacture of tungsten filaments. Atomic number 72; atomic weight 178.49. [< Lat. *Hafnia*, Copenhagen, Denmark.]

haft (hăft) n. A handle or hilt, as of a sword or knife. [< OE *hæft.*]

hag (hăg) n. 1. An ugly old woman. 2. A witch; sorceress. [Perh. < OE *hægtesse*, witch.]

Hag·ga·i (hăg'ē-ī', hăg'ī') n. See table at **Bible**.

hag·gard (hăg'ərd) adj. Appearing worn and exhausted; gaunt. [OFr. *hagard*, wild.] —**hag'gard·ly** adv. —**hag'gard·ness** n.
    Syns: *haggard, gaunt, wan, worn* adj.

hag·gle (hăg'əl) v. -**gled**, -**gling**. To argue or dispute in an attempt to bargain. [< ON *hŏggva*, to cut.] —**hag'gle** n. —**hag'gler** n.

hag·i·og·ra·phy (hăg'ē-ŏg'rə-fē, hā'jē-) n., pl. -**phies.** Biography of saints. [Gk. *hagios*, holy + -GRAPHY.] —**hag'i·og'ra·pher** n. —**hag'i·o·graph'ic** (-ə-grăf'ĭk) or **hag'i·o·graph'i·cal** adj.

hah (hä) interj. Var. of **ha**.

Hai·da (hī'də) n., pl. -**da** or -**das**. 1. a. Any of the Indian tribes inhabiting the Queen Charlotte Islands, British Columbia, and Prince of Wales Island, Alaska. b. A member of the Haida. 2. a. A language family of the Nadene phylum. b. The language of the Haida and the only surviving language of the Haida language family. —**Hai'dan** adj.

hai·ku (hī'kōō) n., pl. -**ku**. An unrhymed Japanese poem of a fixed, 17-syllable form, usu. on a subject drawn from nature. [J.]

hail¹ (hāl) n. 1. a. Precipitation in the form of pellets of ice and hard snow. b. A hailstone. 2. Something with the effect of a shower of hail. —v. 1. To precipitate hail. 2. To pour down or out. [< OE *hægel.*]

hail² (hāl) v. 1. a. To salute or greet. b. To acclaim enthusiastically. 2. To signal or call to. —n. 1. A greeting or expression of acclaim. 2. Hailing distance. —interj. Used to express a greeting or tribute. [< ON *heill*, healthy.] —**hail'er** n.

hail·stone (hāl'stōn') n. A hard pellet of snow and ice.

hail·storm (hāl'stôrm') n. A storm in which hail falls.

hair (hâr) n. 1. A fine, threadlike outgrowth, esp. from the skin of a mammal. 2. A covering of such outgrowth, as on the human head. 3. A minute distance or narrow margin. —adj. 1. Made of or with hair. 2. For the hair: *a hair dryer*. —**idioms. get in (someone's) hair.** To upset or annoy. **let one's hair down.** To drop one's guard or reserve. **split hairs.** To make trifling distinctions. **turn a hair.** To show distress or embarrassment: *accepted the challenge without turning a hair*. [< OE *hær.*] —**hair'less** adj.

hair·breadth (hâr'brĕdth') adj. Extremely close: *a hairbreadth escape.*

hair·brush (hâr'brŭsh') n. A brush for grooming hair.

hair·cloth (hâr'klôth', -klŏth') n. A stiff, wiry fabric usu. having a cotton or linen warp with a horsehair filler.

hair·cut (hâr'kŭt') n. 1. A shortening of the hair by cutting. 2. The style in which one's hair is cut.

hair·do (hâr'dōō) n., pl. -**dos**. A hair style; coiffure.

hair·dress·er (hâr'drĕs'ər) n. One who cuts or arranges hair.

hair·dress·ing (hâr'drĕs'ĭng) n. 1. The occupation of a hairdresser. 2. The act of dressing or arranging the hair. 3. A preparation used for dressing or arranging the hair.

hair·line (hâr'līn') n. 1. The front edge of hair growing on the head. 2. A very thin line. —**hair'line'** adj.

hair·piece n. 1. A toupee. 2. A small wig or thick bunch of real or artificial hair used to supplement a woman's hairdo.

hair·pin (hâr'pĭn') n. A thin, U-shaped pin used to hold the hair in place. —adj. Doubled back in a deep U: *a hairpin curve.*

hair·rais·ing (hâr'rā'zĭng) adj. Horrifying.

hair·split·ting (hâr'splĭt'ĭng) n. The making of unreasonably fine distinctions; quibbling. —adj. Concerned with petty distinctions. —**hair'split'ter** n.

hair spray n. A preparation sprayed on the hair to keep it neat.

hair·spring (hâr'sprĭng') n. A fine coiled spring that regulates the movement of the balance wheel in a watch or clock.

hair trigger n. A gun trigger adjusted to respond to a very slight pressure.

hair-trig·ger (hâr'trĭg'ər) adj. Responding to the slightest provocation or stimulus: *a hairtrigger temper.*

hair·weav·ing (hâr'wē'vĭng) n. The process of interweaving a hair piece with a balding person's own hair. —**hair'weave'** v.

hair·y (hâr'ē) adj. -**i·er**, -**i·est**. 1. Covered with hair. 2. Of or like hair. 3. *Slang.* Causing anxiety or fear. —**hair'i·ness** n.

hake (hāk) n., pl. **hake** or **hakes**. A marine food fish related to and resembling the cod. [ME.]

hal- pref. Var. of **halo-**.

hal·berd (hăl'bərd) n. A weapon of the 15th and 16th cent. having an axlike blade and a steel spike mounted on the end of a long shaft. [< MHG *helmbarde.*]

hal·cy·on (hăl'sē-ən) adj. Calm and peaceful. [< Gk. *alkuŏn*, mythical bird.]

hale¹ (hāl) adj. **hal·er**, **hal·est**. Sound in health. [< ON *heill.*] —**hale'ness** n.

hale² (hāl) v. **haled**, **hal·ing**. To compel to go. [< OFr. *haler*, of Gmc. orig.]

ha·ler (hä'lər, -lĕr') n., pl. -**lers** or -**le·ru** (-lə-rōō'). See table at **currency**. [Czech.]

half (hăf, häf) n., pl. **halves** (hăvz, hävz). 1. One of two equal parts. 2. A part of something approx. equal to the remainder. 3. *Sports.* Either of the two time periods that make up a game, as in football. —adj. 1. Being a half. 2. Being approx. a half. 3. Partial; incomplete. —adv. 1. To the extent of exactly or nearly a half. 2. Not completely; partly. —**idiom. go halves.** To share equally. [< OE *healf.*]

half·back (hăf'băk', häf'-) n. 1. *Football.* One of the two players positioned near the flanks behind the line of scrimmage. 2. One of several players in various sports stationed behind the forward line. 3. The position played by a halfback.

half-baked (hăf'bākt', häf'-) adj. 1. Only partly baked. 2. *Informal.* Ill-conceived; foolish. 3. *Informal.* Lacking good judgment or common sense.

half boot *n.* A low boot extending just above the ankle.

half-breed (hăf'brēd', häf'-) *n.* A person having parents of different ethnic types.

half brother *n.* A brother related through one parent only.

half-caste (hăf'kăst', häf'-) *n.* A half-breed.

half-cocked (hăf'kŏkt', häf'-) *Informal.* —*adj.* Inadequately conceived; not fully thought out. —*adv.* Hastily; carelessly.

half dollar *n.* A U.S. silver coin worth 50 cents.

half-heart-ed (hăf'här'tĭd, häf'-) *adj.* Exhibiting or having little interest or enthusiasm. —**half'heart'ed·ly** *adv.* —**half'heart'ed·ness** *n.*

half-life (hăf'līf', häf'-) *n. Physics.* The time required for half the nuclei in a sample of a specific isotopic species to undergo radioactive decay.

half-mast (hăf'măst', häf'-) *n.* The position about halfway up a mast or pole at which a flag is flown as a sign of mourning or a signal of distress.

half-moon (hăf'mōōn', häf'-) *n.* 1. The moon when only half its disk is illuminated. 2. Something shaped like a crescent. —**half'moon'** *adj.*

half nel·son (nĕl'sən) *n.* A wrestling hold in which one arm is passed under the opponent's arm from behind to the back of his neck.

half sister *n.* A sister related through one parent only.

half-slip (hăf'slĭp', häf'-) *n.* A woman's underskirt that extends from the waist to the hem of the outer garment.

half sole *n.* A shoe sole extending from the shank to the toe.

half-staff (hăf'stăf', häf'-) *n.* Half-mast.

half step *n.* An interval equal to half a tone in the diatonic scale.

half time *n. Sports.* The intermission between halves in a game.

half-track (hăf'trăk', häf'-) *n.* A lightly armored military vehicle having front wheels and propelled by caterpillarlike treads.

half-truth (hăf'trōōth', häf'-) *n.* A statement that is only partially true, usu. intended to deceive.

half-way (hăf'wā', häf'-) *adj.* 1. Midway between two points or conditions. 2. Partial: *halfway measures.* —**half'way'** *adv.*

half-wit (hăf'wĭt', häf'-) *n.* 1. A mentally retarded person. 2. A stupid, foolish, or frivolous person. —**half'-wit'ted** (-wĭt'ĭd) *adj.* —**half'-wit'ted·ly** *adv.* —**half'-wit'ted·ness** *n.*

hal·i·but (hăl'ə-bət, hŏl'-) *n., pl.* **-but** or **-buts.** A large, edible flatfish of northern marine waters. [ME.]

hal·ide (hăl'īd', hā'līd') *n.* A binary compound of a halogen with an electropositive element or radical.

hal·ite (hăl'īt', hā'līt') *n.* Rock salt.

hal·i·to·sis (hăl'ĭ-tō'sĭs) *n.* Bad breath. [Lat. *halitus,* breath + -OSIS.]

hall (hôl) *n.* 1. a. A corridor; hallway. b. A large entrance room; lobby. 2. A large public building. 3. A large room for meetings, meals, etc. 4. A college or university building. 5. a. The main house on a landed estate.

b. The main residence of a medieval nobleman. [< OE *heall.*]

hal·le·lu·jah (hăl'ə-lōō'yə) *interj.* Used to express praise or joy. —*n.* An expression or exclamation of "hallelujah." [Heb. *hallelūyāh,* praise God.]

hall·mark (hôl'märk') *n.* 1. A mark placed on an article to indicate purity, quality, etc. 2. Any indication of quality or excellence. [< Goldsmith's *Hall,* London, where gold and silver articles were appraised and stamped.]

hall of fame *n.* 1. A room or building housing memorials to famous persons. 2. A group of persons judged outstanding in a particular category.

hal·loo (hə-lōō') *interj.* Used to attract attention. [< obs. *holla,* stop!] —**hal·loo'** *n.*

hal·low (hăl'ō) *v.* 1. To make or set apart as holy; consecrate. 2. To honor or regard as holy; revere. [< OE *hālgian.*]

Hal·low·een (hăl'ō-ēn', hŏl'-) *n.* Also **Hal·low·e'en.** October 31, the eve of All Saints' Day. [< *All Hallow Even.*]

hal·lu·ci·na·tion (hə-lōō'sə-nā'shən) *n.* 1. An illusion of seeing, hearing, or otherwise sensing something that does not really exist. 2. Something, as a vision or image, that occurs as a hallucination. 3. A false notion; delusion. [< Lat. *hallucinari,* to dream.] —**hal·lu'ci·nate'** *v.* —**hal·lu'ci·na'tion·al** *adj.* —**hal·lu'ci·na·tive** *adj.* —**hal·lu'ci·na·to·ry** (-nə-tôr'ē, -tōr'ē) *adj.*

hal·lu·ci·no·gen (hə-lōō'sə-nə-jən) *n.* A drug that induces hallucination. [HALLUCIN(ATION) + -GEN.] —**hal·lu'ci·no·gen'ic** (-jĕn'ĭk) *adj.*

hall·way (hôl'wā') *n.* 1. A corridor or passageway. 2. An entranceway.

ha·lo (hā'lō) *n., pl.* **-los** or **-loes.** 1. A disk or ring of light surrounding the head, as in a representation of a holy person. 2. A circular band of light around a light source, as around the sun or moon. [< Gk. *halōs,* band of light surrounding sun or moon.] —**ha'lo** *v.*

halo   halter

halo– or **hal–** *pref.* 1. Salt: *halite.* 2. Halogen: *halocarbon.* [< Gk. *hals,* salt.]

ha·lo·car·bon (hăl'ō-kär'bən) *n.* A compound consisting of carbon and a halogen.

hal·o·gen (hăl'ə-jən) *n.* Any of a group of five chemically related nonmetallic elements that includes fluorine, chlorine, bromine, iodine, and astatine. —**ha·log'e·nous** (hə-lŏj'ə-nəs) *adj.*

halt¹ (hôlt) *n.* A suspension of movement or progress; stop. —*v.* To bring or come to a stop. [G.]

halt² (hôlt) *v.* To limp or hobble. [< OE *healtian.*] —**halt** *adj.*

hal·ter (hôl′tər) n. 1. A rope or leather strap that fits around the head or neck of an animal, such as a horse, used to lead or secure it. 2. A noose used for execution by hanging. 3. A bodice for women held in place by ties behind the neck and across the back. —v. To put a halter on; control with a halter. [< OE *hælftre*.]

halt·ing (hôl′tĭng) adj. 1. Limping; lame. 2. Hesitant or wavering.

halve (hăv, häv) v. **halved, halv·ing.** 1. To divide or separate into two equal parts. 2. To reduce or lessen by half. 3. *Informal.* To share equally.

halves (hăvz, hävz) n. Pl. of **half.**

hal·yard (hăl′yərd) n. A rope used to raise or lower a sail, flag, or yard. [< ME *halen,* to pull.]

ham (hăm) n. 1. A cut of meat consisting of the thigh of the hind leg of a hog. 2. The back of the knee. 3. The back of the thigh. 4. **hams.** The buttocks. 5. *Slang.* A performer who overacts. 6. *Informal.* A licensed amateur radio operator. —v. **hammed, ham·ming.** To exaggerate or overact. [< OE *hamm.*]

ham·a·dry·ad (hăm′ə-drī′əd) n., pl. **-ads** or **-a·des** (-ə-dēz′) n. *Gk. & Rom. Myth.* A wood nymph. [< Gk. *Hamadruas.*]

ham·burg·er (hăm′bûr′gər) n. Also **ham·burg** (-bûrg′). 1. Ground beef. 2. A cooked patty of ground meat. 3. A sandwich consisting of a hamburger patty usu. in a roll or bun. [< *Hamburg,* Germany.]

Ham·ite (hăm′īt′) n. A member of a group of related peoples of northern and northeastern Africa, including the Berbers and the descendants of the ancient Egyptians.

Ha·mit·ic (hă-mĭt′ĭk, hə-) adj. Of or relating to the Hamites or the language of the Hamites. —n. A subfamily of the Afro-Asiatic language family that includes Berber and Egyptian.

ham·let (hăm′lĭt) n. A small village. [< OFr. *hamelet,* of Gmc. orig.]

ham·mer (hăm′ər) n. 1. A hand tool used to exert an impulsive force by striking. 2. A tool or device of analogous function or action, as: **a.** The part of a gunlock that hits the primer or firing pin or explodes the percussion cap. **b.** One of the padded wooden pieces of a piano that strike the strings. **c.** A part of an apparatus that strikes a gong or bell, as in a clock. —v. 1. To strike; pound. 2. To shape or flatten with a hammer. —*idiom.* **hammer and tongs.** With tremendous energy; vigorously. [< OE *hamor.*] —**ham′mer·er** n.

ham·mer·head (hăm′ər-hĕd′) n. 1. The head of a hammer. 2. A shark whose eyes are set into elongated, fleshy extensions at the sides of the head.

hammer lock n. A wrestling hold in which an opponent's arm is pulled behind his back and twisted upward.

ham·mer·toe (hăm′ər-tō′) n. A toe, usu. the second, that is congenitally bent downward.

ham·mock (hăm′ək) n. A hanging bed of canvas or netting suspended between two supports. [< Taino.]

ham·per¹ (hăm′pər) v. To impede. [ME *hamperen.*]

ham·per² (hăm′pər) n. A large basket, usu. with a cover. [< OFr. *hanapier,* a case for holding goblets.]

ham·ster (hăm′stər) n. A rodent with large cheek pouches and a short tail, often kept as

a pet or used in laboratory research. [< OHG *hamustro,* of Slav. orig.]

ham·string (hăm′strĭng′) n. 1. Either of two tendons at the rear hollow of the human knee. 2. The large sinew in the back of the hock of a quadruped. —v. 1. To cripple by cutting the hamstring. 2. To impede the efficiency of.

hand (hănd) n. 1. The terminal part of the arm below the wrist. 2. A unit of length equal to 4 in. or 10.16 cm., used esp. to specify the height of a horse. 3. Something suggesting the shape or function of the human hand. 4. A pointer on a clock or instrument. 5. A lateral direction: *at my right hand.* 6. Handwriting; penmanship. 7. A round of applause. 8. Assistance; help. 9. *Card Games.* **a.** The cards held by or dealt to a player. **b.** A round of play. 10. A laborer. 11. A member of a group or crew. 12. A participant; contributor. 13. Skill; ability. 14. Often **hands. a.** Possession or keeping. **b.** Control. 15. A source of information: *at first hand.* 16. A pledge to marry. —v. 1. To give or pass with or as with the hands. 2. To aid, direct, or conduct with the hands. 3. *Naut.* To roll up and secure (a sail); furl. —*phrasal verbs.* **hand down.** 1. To pass on, as from parent to child. 2. To deliver (a verdict). **hand in.** To submit; turn in. **hand out.** To give out; distribute. **hand over.** To yield control of. —*idioms.* **at hand.** 1. Close by; accessible. 2. Soon in time. **by hand.** By using one's hands. **hand in glove.** In close association. **hand in hand.** 1. Holding each other's hand. 2. Closely linked or associated. **hand over fist.** *Informal.* At a tremendous rate. **hands down.** By a comfortable margin; easily: *won the beauty contest hands down.* **have a hand in.** To have a share or part in. **have (one's) hands full.** To be fully occupied. **in hand.** Under control: *kept the situation in hand.* **lay hands (or a hand) on.** 1. To grasp or seize. 2. To touch or handle, esp. so as to harm. **off (one's) hands.** Out of one's care or responsibility. **on hand.** Available for use. **on (one's) hands.** In one's care or possession, usu. as a responsibility or burden. **out of hand.** Out of control. **out of (one's) hands.** Not under one's control or jurisdiction. **show (or tip) (one's) hand.** To reveal one's intentions. **take in hand.** To take control of. **throw up (one's) hands.** To give up in despair. [< OE.]

hand·bag (hănd′băg′) n. 1. A woman's bag for carrying small personal articles. 2. A small suitcase.

hand·ball (hănd′bôl′) n. 1. A game in which two or more players bat a ball against the wall with their hands. 2. The small rubber ball used in handball.

hand·bill (hănd′bĭl′) n. A printed sheet or pamphlet distributed by hand.

hand·book (hănd′bŏŏk′) n. A manual or reference book that provides information or instruction on a particular subject.

hand·car (hănd′kär′) n. A small open railroad car propelled by a hand pump or a small motor.

hand·cart (hănd′kärt′) n. A small cart pulled or pushed by hand.

hand·clasp (hănd′klăsp′) n. A handshake.

hand·cuff (hănd′kŭf′) n. Often **handcuffs.** A pair of metal bracelets chained together that can be locked around the wrists. —*v.* To put handcuffs on.

hand·ed (hăn'dĭd) *adj.* **1.** Of or pertaining to dexterity or preference as regards a hand or hands: *one-handed; left-handed.* **2.** Pertaining to a specified number of people: *a four-handed card game.*

hand·ful (hănd'fŏŏl') *n., pl.* **-fuls. 1.** The quantity or number that can be held in the hand. **2.** A small but unspecified quantity or number: *a handful of requests.* **3.** *Informal.* One that is too difficult to control easily.

hand·gun (hănd'gŭn') *n.* A firearm that can be used with one hand.

hand·i·cap (hăn'dē-kăp') *n.* **1.** A race or contest in which advantages or compensations are given different contestants to equalize the chances of winning. **2.** Such an advantage or penalty. **3.** An anatomical, physiological, or mental deficiency that prevents or restricts normal achievement. —*v.* **-capped, -cap·ping. 1.** To assign a handicap or handicaps to (a contestant). **2.** To hinder. [< obs. *hand in cap,* a lottery game in which forfeits were held in a cap.] —**hand'i·cap'per** *n.*

hand·i·capped (hăn'dē-kăpt') *adj.* Suffering from a handicap. —*n.* Handicapped persons collectively.

hand·i·craft (hăn'dē-krăft') *n.* **1.** Skill with the hands. **2.** A trade, craft, or occupation requiring such skill. **3.** The work so produced.

hand·i·work (hăn'dē-wûrk') *n.* **1.** Work performed by hand. **2.** Work accomplished by a single person. **3.** The result of one's efforts.

hand·ker·chief (hăng'kər-chĭf, -chēf') *n.* **1.** A small square of cloth used esp. for wiping the nose or mouth. **2.** A square piece of cloth worn as a decorative article; kerchief.

han·dle (hăn'dl) *v.* **-dled, -dling. 1.** To touch, lift, or turn with the hands. **2.** To operate with the hands; manipulate. **3.** To manage; deal with or in: *handle corporation law.* —*n.* **1.** A part that is held or manipulated with the hand. **2.** *Slang.* A person's name. —*idiom.* **fly off the handle.** *Informal.* To become violently and suddenly angry. [< OE *handlian.*] —**han'dler** *n.*

Syns: handle, manipulate, ply, wield *v.*

han·dle·bar (hăn'dl-bär') *n.* Often **handlebars.** A curved steering bar, as on a bicycle.

hand·made (hănd'mād') *adj.* Made or prepared by hand rather than by machine.

hand·maid (hănd'mād') *n.* Also **hand·maid·en** (hănd'mād'n). A female attendant.

hand-me-down (hănd'mē-doun') *adj.* Handed down from one person to another after being used and discarded. —*n.* Something used and then handed down from one person to another.

hand·off (hănd'ôf', -ŏf') *n.* A football play in which one player hands the ball to another.

hand·out (hănd'out') *n.* **1.** Food, clothing, or money given to a destitute person. **2.** A folder or leaflet circulated free of charge. **3.** A press release.

hand·pick (hănd'pĭk') *v.* To select carefully and personally. —**hand'-picked'** *adj.*

hand·rail (hănd'rāl') *n.* A narrow rail to be grasped with the hand for support.

hand·shake (hănd'shāk') *n.* The grasping of hands by two people, as in greeting, leave-taking, or congratulation.

hands-off (hăndz'ôf', -ŏf') *adj.* Marked by nonintervention.

hand·some (hăn'səm) *adj.* **-som·er, -som·est. 1.** Pleasing and dignified in appearance. **2.** Generous; liberal: *a handsome reward.* [ME *handsom,* handy.] —**hand'some·ly** *adv.* —**hand'some·ness** *n.*

hands-on (hăndz'ŏn', -ôn') *adj.* Involving active participation; applied as opposed to theoretical: *hands-on engineering.*

hand·spring (hănd'sprĭng') *n.* The act of flipping the body completely forward or backward from an upright position, landing first on the hands, then on the feet.

hand·stand (hănd'stănd') *n.* The act of balancing on the hands with the feet in the air.

hand-to-hand (hănd'tə-hănd') *adj.* At close quarters.

hand-to-mouth (hănd'tə-mouth') *adj.* Having barely enough to live on.

hand·work (hănd'wûrk') *n.* Work done by hand.

hand·writ·ing (hănd'rī'tĭng) *n.* **1.** Writing done with the hand. **2.** The writing characteristic of a particular person.

hand·y (hăn'dē) *adj.* **-i·er, -i·est. 1.** Manually adroit. **2.** Readily accessible. **3.** Easy to use. —**hand'i·ly** *adv.* —**hand'i·ness** *n.*

hand·y·man (hăn'dē-măn') *n.* One who performs odd jobs.

hang (hăng) *v.* **hung** (hŭng), **hang·ing. 1.** To fasten or be fastened from above with no support from below. **2.** To suspend or be suspended so as to allow free movement at or about the point of suspension. **3.** *p.t. & p.p.* **hanged** or **hung.** To execute or be executed by suspending by the neck. **4.** To attach at an appropriate angle. **5. a.** To furnish by suspending objects about: *hang the room with curtains.* **b.** To attach to a wall: *hang wallpaper.* **6.** To hold downward. **7.** To deadlock (a jury). —*phrasal verbs.* **hang around.** *Informal.* **1.** To loiter. **2.** To keep company. **hang back.** To hesitate; hold back. **hang on. 1.** To cling to something. **2.** To persevere. **hang out.** *Slang.* To spend one's time in a certain place. **hang up. 1.** To impede; hinder. **2.** To end a telephone conversation. —*n.* **1.** The way in which something hangs. **2.** The particular meaning or significance. **3.** *Informal.* The proper method of doing or using something. —*idioms.* **give (or care) a hang.** To be concerned. **hang by a thread.** To be in an extremely precarious position. **let it all hang out.** *Slang.* **1.** To be completely relaxed. **2.** To be completely frank or candid. [< OE *hon,* to hang, and < OE *hangian,* to hang.]

Usage: In the sense of "to put to death by hanging," *hanged* is used as the past tense and past participle of *hang.* In all other senses of the word, *hung* is the preferred form for the past tense and past participle.

han·gar (hăng'ər) *n.* A structure for housing, servicing, or repairing aircraft. [Prob. < Med. Lat. *angarium,* shed for shoeing horses.]

hang·dog (hăng'dôg', -dŏg') *adj.* **1.** Shame-faced or guilty. **2.** Downcast; abject.

hang·er (hăng'ər) *n.* **1.** One that hangs. **2.** A

device to which something hangs or by which something is hung.

hang·er-on (hăng′ər-ŏn′, -ôn′) *n., pl.* **hang·ers-on.** A sycophant.

hang glider *n.* A kitelike device from which a harnessed rider hangs while gliding in flight.

hang glider

hang·ing (hăng′ĭng) *n.* **1.** An execution on a gallows. **2.** Often **hangings.** Something hung, as draperies or a tapestry.

hang·man (hăng′mən) *n.* An executioner who hangs condemned prisoners.

hang·nail (hăng′nāl′) *n.* A small, partly detached piece of dead skin at the side or base of a fingernail. [< OE *angnægl,* a sore under the nail.]

hang·out (hăng′out′) *n.* A favorite meeting or gathering place.

hang·o·ver (hăng′ō′vər) *n.* **1.** Unpleasant aftereffects as a result of drinking too much alcohol. **2.** Something left from an earlier time; holdover.

hang-up (hăng′ŭp′) *n. Informal.* **1.** An inhibition. **2.** An obstacle.

hank (hăngk) *n.* A coil or loop. [< ON *hönk.*]

han·ker (hăng′kər) *v.* To have a longing; crave. [Perh. < dial. Du. *hankeren.*] —**hank′er·er** *n.* —**hank′er·ing** *n.*

han·ky-pan·ky (hăng′kē-păng′kē) *n. Slang.* Devious or mischievous activity. [Perh. < HOCUS-POCUS.]

han·som (hăn′səm) *n.* A two-wheeled covered carriage with the driver's seat above and behind. [< Joseph A. Hansom (1803–82).]

Ha·nuk·kah or **Ha·nu·kah** (KHÄ′nŏŏ-kä′, -nə-kə, hä′-) *n.* Vars. of **Chanukah.**

hap (hăp) *n.* **1.** Fortune; chance. **2.** An occurrence. [< ON *happ.*]

hap·haz·ard (hăp-hăz′ərd) *adj.* Characterized by lack of order or plan. —**hap·haz′ard·ly** *adv.* —**hap·haz′ard·ness** *n.*

hap·less (hăp′lĭs) *adj.* Luckless; unfortunate. —**hap′less·ly** *adv.* —**hap′less·ness** *n.*

hap·loid (hăp′loid′) *adj. Genetics.* Having the number of chromosomes present in the normal germ cell, equal to half the number in the normal somatic cell. [Gk. *haplous,* single + -OID.]

hap·ly (hăp′lē) *adv.* By chance or accident.

hap·pen (hăp′ən) *v.* **1.** To take place. **2.** To take place by chance. **3.** To come upon something by chance. **4.** To appear by chance; turn up. [< HAP.]

hap·pen·ing (hăp′ə-nĭng) *n.* **1.** An event. **2.** An event of particular importance. **3.** An improvised, often spontaneous spectacle.

hap·pen·stance (hăp′ən-stăns′) *n.* A chance occurrence. [HAPPEN + (CIRCUM)STANCE.]

hap·py (hăp′ē) *adj.* **-pi·er, -pi·est.** **1.** Characterized by good fortune. **2.** Having, showing, or marked by pleasure. **3.** Apt; appropriate.

4. Cheerfully willing. [< HAP.] —**hap′pi·ly** *adv.* —**hap′pi·ness** *n.*

hap·py-go-luck·y (hăp′ē-gō-lŭk′ē) *adj.* Carefree; easygoing.

happy hour *n.* A period of time during which a bar features drinks at reduced prices.

ha·ra-ki·ri (hä′rə-kĭr′ē, hăr′ə-) *n.* Ritual suicide by disembowelment. [J.]

ha·rangue (hə-răng′) *n.* A long, pompous speech; tirade. [< Med. Lat. *harenga.*] —**ha·rangue′** *v.* —**ha·rangu′er** *n.*

ha·rass (hə-răs′, hăr′əs) *v.* **1.** To disturb or irritate persistently. **2.** To wear out; exhaust. **3.** To enervate (an enemy) by repeated raids. [Prob. < OFr. *harer,* to set a dog on.] —**har′ass·er** *n.* —**har′ass·ment** *n.*

har·bin·ger (här′bən-jər) *n.* A forerunner. [< OFr. *herberge,* lodging, of Gmc. orig.]

har·bor (här′bər) *n.* **1.** A sheltered part of a body of water deep enough to serve as a port for ships. **2.** A place of shelter; refuge. —*v.* **1.** To give shelter to; protect; keep. **2.** To hold a thought or feeling about. [ME *herberwe.*] —**har′bor·er** *n.*

hard (härd) *adj.* **-er, -est.** **1.** Resistant to pressure; firm; rigid: *a hard surface.* **2.** Physically or mentally toughened. **3.** Difficult to do, understand, or endure. **4.** Powerful; intense: *a hard blow.* **5.** Energetic. **6.** Bitter; severe; harsh. **7.** Callous; unfeeling. **8.** Cruel; unjust. **9.** Real: *hard facts.* **10.** Having a high alcoholic content. **11.** Containing salts that interfere with the lathering of soap. **12.** Backed by bullion rather than by credit: *hard currency.* **13.** Physically addictive and harmful: *hard drugs.* —**idioms. hard and fast.** Fixed; rigid: *hard and fast rules.* **hard up.** *Informal.* Short of money. [< OE *heard.*] —**hard** *adv.* —**hard′ness** *n.*

hard·back (härd′băk′) *adj.* Bound in cloth, cardboard, or leather rather than paper: *a hardback novel.* —**hard′back′** *n.*

hard-bit·ten (härd′bĭt′n) *adj.* Toughened by experience.

hard-boiled (härd′boild′) *adj.* **1.** Cooked to a solid consistency by boiling. **2.** *Informal.* Callous; tough.

hard cash *n.* Ready money; cash.

hard cider *n.* Fermented cider.

hard coal *n.* Anthracite.

hard copy *n.* Readable printed copy of the output of a computer.

hard-core (härd′kôr′) *adj.* Also **hard-core. 1.** Stubbornly resistant or inveterate: *a hard-core criminal.* **2.** Held to constitute an intractable social problem: *hard-core poverty.*

hard·en (här′dn) *v.* **1.** To make or become firm or firmer. **2.** To toughen mentally or physically. **3.** To make or become unfeeling, unsympathetic, or callous. —**hard′en·er** *n.*

hard hat *n.* **1.** A protective helmet worn esp. by construction workers. **2.** *Informal.* A construction worker. **3.** *Informal.* A very conservative person. **4.** *Slang.* A very patriotic person. —**hard′hat′** *adj.*

hard-head·ed (härd′hĕd′ĭd) *adj.* **1.** Stubborn; willful. **2.** Realistic; practical. —**hard′head′ed·ly** *adv.* —**hard′head′ed·ness** *n.*

hard-heart·ed (härd′här′tĭd) *adj.* Unfeeling; cold. —**hard′heart′ed·ly** *adv.* —**hard′heart′ed·ness** *n.*

har·di·hood (här′dē-hŏŏd′) *n.* Boldness and daring; audacity. [HARDY + -HOOD.]

hard line *n.* An uncompromising position or

stance. **—hard'-line'** or **hard'line'** adj. **—hard'-lin'er** n.

hard-ly (härd'lē) adv. **1.** Barely; just. **2.** To almost no degree. **3.** Probably or almost certainly not. [< OE *heardlice*, boldly.]

Usage: Hardly has the force of a negative; therefore it is not used with another negative: *I could hardly see* (not *couldn't hardly see*).

hard-nosed (härd'nōzd') adj. Hardheaded.

hard palate n. The relatively hard, bony anterior portion of the palate.

hard-pan (härd'păn') n. A layer of hard subsoil or clay.

hard rock n. Rock music marked by harsh, amplified sound, feedback, and other electronic modulations.

hard sauce n. A creamy dessert sauce of butter and sugar flavored with rum, brandy, or vanilla.

hard sell n. *Informal.* Aggressive, high-pressure selling or advertising.

hard-shell (härd'shĕl') adj. Unyieldingly orthodox; uncompromising.

hard-ship (härd'shĭp') n. **1.** Extreme privation; suffering. **2.** A cause of privation or suffering.

hard-tack (härd'tăk') n. A hard biscuit made only with flour and water. [HARD + *tack*, food.]

hard-top (härd'tŏp') n. A car with a rigidly fixed hard top designed to look like that of a convertible.

hard-ware (härd'wâr') n. **1.** Metal goods and utensils. **2. a.** A computer and the associated physical equipment directly involved in communications or data processing. **b.** Machines and other physical equipment directly involved in performing an industrial, technological, or military function.

hard-wood (härd'wŏŏd') n. The wood of a broad-leaved flowering tree as distinguished from that of a conifer.

har-dy (här'dē) adj. **-di-er, -di-est. 1.** Stalwart and rugged; strong. **2.** Capable of surviving severely unfavorable conditions, as cold weather. **3.** Courageous; intrepid; stouthearted. **4.** Audacious; hotheaded. [< OFr. *hardir*, to harden, of Gmc. orig.] **—har'di-ly** adv. **—har'di-ness** n.

hare (hâr) n. A mammal related to and resembling the rabbits but usu. larger and with longer ears. [< OE *hara*.]

hare-brained (hâr'brānd') adj. Giddy; flighty.

Ha-re Krish-na (hä'rē krĭsh'nə) n., pl. **Ha-re Krish-nas.** A member of a religious group devoted to the Hindu god Krishna. [Hindi *hare*, invocation to God + KRISHNA.]

hare-lip (hâr'lĭp') n. A congenital fissure or pair of fissures in the upper lip. **—hare'-lipped'** adj.

har-em (hâr'əm, hăr'-) n. **1.** A house or rooms reserved for women members of a Moslem household. **2.** The women who live in a harem. [Ar. *ḥarīm*.]

hark (härk) v. To listen carefully. **—phrasal verb. hark back.** To return to a previous point or event. [ME *herken*.]

har-le-quin (här'lə-kwən, -kən) n. A clown; buffoon. **—adj.** Having a pattern of brightly colored diamond shapes; parti-colored. [< OFr. *Helquin*, a demon.]

har-lot (här'lət) n. A prostitute. [< OFr. *arlot*, vagabond.] **—har'lot-ry** (-lə-trē) n.

harm (härm) n. Physical or psychological injury or damage. **—v.** To cause harm to; hurt. [< OE *hearm*.] **—harm'ful** adj. **—harm'ful-ly** adv. **—harm'ful-ness** n. **—harm'less** adj. **—harm'less-ly** adv. **—harm'less-ness** n.

Syns: harm, damage, detriment, hurt, injury, outrage n.

har-mon-ic (här-mŏn'ĭk) adj. Of or pertaining to musical harmony or harmonics. **—n. 1.** A musical overtone. **2. harmonics.** *(used with a sing. verb).* The theory or study of the physical properties of musical sound. **—harmon'i-cal-ly** adv.

har-mon-i-ca (här-mŏn'ĭ-kə) n. A small musical instrument played by exhaling and inhaling through a row of reeds. [< Ital. *armonica*, harmonious.]

har-mo-ni-ous (här-mō'nē-əs) adj. **1.** Marked by agreement and accord. **2.** Having elements pleasingly combined. **3.** Marked by harmony of sound. **—har-mo'ni-ous-ly** adv. **—har-mo'ni-ous-ness** n.

har-mo-ni-um (här-mō'nē-əm) n. An organlike keyboard instrument with metal reeds. [< Lat. *harmonia*, harmony.]

har-mo-ny (här'mə-nē) n., pl. **-nies. 1.** Agreement or accord, as of feeling or opinion. **2.** A pleasing combination of parts or elements. **3.** Combination and progression of chords in musical structure. [< Gk. *harmonia.*] **—har'mo-nize'** v.

har-ness (här'nĭs) n. Gear by which a draft animal pulls a vehicle or implement. **—v. 1.** To put a harness on. **2.** To control and direct the force. **—idiom. in harness.** Engaged in one's usual work. [< OFr. *harneis.*] **—har'ness-er** n.

harp (härp) n. A musical instrument having an upright frame with strings played by plucking. **—v.** To play a harp. **—phrasal verb. harp on.** To discourse tediously on. [< OE *hearpe.*] **—harp'er** n. **—harp'ist** n.

har-poon (här-pōōn') n. A spear with an attached rope and a barbed head used esp. in whaling. **—v.** To strike, kill, or capture with or as if with a harpoon. [Prob. < OFr. *harper*, to seize.] **—har-poon'er** or **har'poon-eer'** (här'pōō-nîr') n.

harp-si-chord (härp'sĭ-kôrd') n. A keyboard instrument in which the strings are sounded by means of a plucking mechanism. [Ital. *arpicordo.*]

har-py (här'pē) n., pl. **-pies. 1.** A shrewish woman. **2.** A predatory person. [< Gk. *Harpuiai*, voracious monsters of Greek myth.]

har-que-bus (här'kə-bəs, -kwĭ-bŭs') n. A heavy gun used during the 15th and 16th cent. [< MLG *hakebusse.*]

har-ri-dan (hăr'ĭ-dən) n. A disagreeable old woman. [Poss. < Fr. *haridelle*, thin woman.]

har-ri-er¹ (hăr'ē-ər) n. **1.** One that harries. **2.** A slender, narrow-winged hawk.

har-ri-er² (hăr'ē-ər) n. **1.** A small hound orig. used in hunting hares. **2.** A cross-country runner. [Prob. < HARE.]

har-row (hăr'ō) n. A farm implement having a heavy frame with teeth or upright disks, used to break up plowed ground. **—v. 1.** To break up (soil) with a harrow. **2.** To distress greatly; torment. [ME *harwe*.]

harrow

har·row·ing (hăr′ō-ĭng) *adj.* Extremely frightening and upsetting.

har·ry (hăr′ē) *v.* **-ried, -ry·ing. 1.** To raid; sack. **2.** To disturb or annoy or as by constant attacks. [< OE *hergian*.]

harsh (härsh) *adj.* **-er, -est. 1.** Unpleasant, esp. to the sense of hearing. **2.** Extremely severe or exacting; stern. [ME *harsk*, of Scand. orig.] **—harsh′ly** *adv.* **—harsh′ness** *n.*

Syns: *harsh, discordant, hoarse, rough, strident adj.*

hart (härt) *n., pl.* **harts** or **hart.** An adult male deer. [< OE *heorot*.]

har·um-scar·um (hâr′əm-skâr′əm, hăr′əm-skăr′əm) *adj.* Reckless. **—adv.** Recklessly. [Perh. < HARE + SCARE.]

har·vest (här′vĭst) *n.* **1.** The gathering in of a crop. **2.** A gathered crop. **—v. 1.** To gather (a crop). **2.** To gain, win, or acquire as by gathering. [< OE *herfest*.] **—har′vest·er** *n.*

harvest moon *n.* The full moon that occurs nearest the autumnal equinox.

has (hăz) *v.* 3rd person sing. present tense of **have.**

has-been (hăz′bĭn′) *n. Informal.* One that is no longer famous, successful, or useful.

ha·sen·pfef·fer (hä′zən-fĕf′ər) *n.* A highly seasoned rabbit stew. [G.]

hash[1] (hăsh) *n.* **1.** Chopped meat and potatoes mixed together and browned. **2.** A jumble; hodgepodge. **—v. 1.** To chop up; mince. **2.** To discuss; go over: *hash over future plans.* [< OFr. *hache*, ax, of Gmc. orig.]

hash[2] (hăsh) *n. Informal.* Hashish.

hash·ish (hăsh′ēsh′, -ĭsh) *n.* A narcotic extract prepared from the dried flowers of the hemp plant. [Ar. *ḥashīsh.*]

hash mark *n. Mil. Slang.* A service stripe on the sleeve of an enlisted person's uniform.

has·n't (hăz′ənt). Has not.

hasp (hăsp) *n.* A metal fastener that is passed over a staple and secured by a pin, bolt, or padlock. [< OE *hæpse.*]

Has·sid (KHä′sĭd) *n.* Var. of **Chassid.**

has·sle (hăs′əl) *Slang.* **—n. 1.** An argument or squabble. **2.** Trouble; bother. **—v. -sled, -sling. 1.** To argue or fight. **2.** To bother or harass. [Perh. blend of HAGGLE + TUSSLE.]

has·sock (hăs′ək) *n.* A cushion used as a footstool or for kneeling. [< OE *hassuc*, clump of grass.]

hast (hăst) *v. Archaic.* 2nd person sing. present tense of **have.**

haste (hāst) *n.* **1.** Swiftness; rapidity. **2.** Eagerness to act; urgency. **3.** Rash or headlong action. **—idiom. make haste.** To hurry. [< OFr., of Gmc. orig.]

Syns: *haste, celerity, dispatch, expedition, hurry, hustle, rapidity, speed n.*

has·ten (hā′sən) *v.* To move or cause to move swiftly.

hast·y (hā′stē) *adj.* **-i·er, -i·est. 1.** Characterized by speed; swift. **2.** Done too quickly to be accurate or wise; rash. **—hast′i·ly** *adv.* **—hast′i·ness** *n.*

hat (hăt) *n.* A covering for the head, usu. with a shaped crown and brim. **—idioms. at the drop of a hat.** At the slightest pretext or provocation. **pass the hat.** To take up a collection of money. **take (one's) hat off to.** To respect, admire, or congratulate. **throw (or toss) (one's) hat into the ring.** To enter a political race. [< OE *hæt.*]

hat·box (hăt′bŏks′) *n.* A round box for a hat.

hatch[1] (hăch) *n.* **1.** An opening, as in the deck of a ship or in an airplane. **2.** A hatchway. [< OE *hæc*, small door.]

hatch[2] (hăch) *v.* **1.** To emerge from or cause to emerge from an egg. **2.** To cause (an egg) to produce young. **3.** To devise or originate, esp. in secret. [ME *hacchen.*] **—hatch′er** *n.*

hatch[3] (hăch) *v.* To shade by drawing or etching fine parallel or crossed lines on. [< OFr. *hachier.*]

hatch·back (hăch′băk′) *n.* A car having a hatch opening upward in a sloping back.

hatch·er·y (hăch′ə-rē) *n., pl.* **-ies.** A place where eggs, esp. those of fish or poultry, are hatched.

hatch·et (hăch′ĭt) *n.* **1.** A short-handled ax. **2.** A tomahawk. **—idioms. bury the hatchet.** To make peace. [< OFr. *hache*, ax, of Gmc. orig.]

hatchet man *n. Slang.* **1.** A hired killer. **2.** One hired to carry out unpleasant jobs.

hatch·way (hăch′wā′) *n.* **1.** A hatch leading to a hold, compartment, or cellar. **2.** A ladder or stairway within such an opening.

hate (hāt) *v.* **hat·ed, hat·ing. 1.** To loathe; detest. **2.** To dislike: *hates washing dishes.* **—n. 1.** Intense dislike or animosity; hatred. **2.** An object of hatred. [< OE *hatian.*] **—hate′ful** *adj.* **—hate′ful·ly** *adv.* **—hate′ful·ness** *n.* **—hat′er** *n.*

Syns: *hate, abominate, despise, detest, execrate, loathe v.*

hath (hăth) *v. Archaic.* 3rd person sing. present tense of **have.**

ha·tred (hā′trĭd) *n.* Violent hostility or animosity. [ME.]

hau·berk (hô′bûrk) *n.* A tunic of chain mail. [< OFr. *hauberc.*]

haugh·ty (hô′tē) *adj.* **-ti·er, -ti·est.** Proud and vain to the point of arrogance. [< Lat. *altus*, high.] **—haugh′ti·ly** *adv.* **—haugh′ti·ness** *n.*

haul (hôl) *v.* **1.** To pull or drag; tug. **2.** To provide transportation; cart. **—phrasal verb. haul off.** To draw back slightly, as in preparation for initiating an action: *hauled off and socked him.* **—n. 1.** The act of hauling. **2.** The distance over which something is hauled. **3.** Something that is hauled. **4.** An amount collected or acquired: *a haul of fish.* [< OFr. *haler*, of Gmc. orig.]

haul·age (hô′lĭj) *n.* **1.** The act or process of hauling. **2.** The charge made for hauling.

haunch (hônch, hŏnch) *n.* The hip, buttock, and upper thigh. [< Med. Lat. *hancha*, of Gmc. orig.]

haunt (hônt, hŏnt) *v.* **1.** To visit or appear to as a ghost or spirit. **2.** To frequent. **3.** To recur to continually. **—n.** (hônt, hŏnt). A place visited frequently. [< OFr. *hanter*, to frequent.] **—haunt'ing·ly** *adv.*

haute cou·ture (ōt' kōō-tōōr') *n.* 1. The leading designers of high-fashion garments. 2. a. Creation of high-fashion garments. b. High-fashion garments. [Fr.]

haute cui·sine (ōt' kwĭ-zēn') *n.* Elaborately or skillfully prepared cuisine. [Fr.]

hau·teur (hō-tûr', hō-) *n.* Haughtiness; arrogance. [Fr.]

have (hăv) *v.* **had, hav·ing, has.** 1. To possess; own. 2. To stand in relationship to. 3. To be obliged to. 4. To hold in one's mind; entertain. 5. a. To win a victory over. b. *Informal.* To cheat or trick. 6. To possess sexually. 7. To keep in a specified place. 8. To accept or take. 9. To partake of; consume. 10. To be made of, consist of, or contain. 11. To exercise or exhibit: *have mercy.* 12. To allow; permit. 13. To cause to. 14. To experience: *have a good summer.* 15. To beget or give birth to. 16. To be in command of: *have the necessary technique.* 17. To receive as a guest. 18. Used as an auxiliary with a past participle to form the following tenses: **a.** Present perfect: *have gone.* **b.** Past perfect: *had gone.* **c.** Future perfect: *will have gone.* **—phrasal verbs. have at.** To attack. **have on.** 1. To be wearing. 2. To be scheduled for: *I have a dinner party on tomorrow.* **—n.** One that possesses material wealth. **—idioms. had better.** Ought to. **have done with.** To stop; cease. **have it in for.** To have a grudge against. **have it out.** To settle decisively, esp. by argument. **have to do with.** To be concerned or associated with. [< OE *habban.*]

Usage: When *have* occurs in speech as one element of a verb phrase such as *might have done* or *could have seen,* it is usually unstressed, leading some to write these phrases incorrectly as *might of done* or *could of seen.*

ha·ven (hā'vən) *n.* 1. A harbor or port. 2. A place of sanctuary. [< OE *hæfen.*]

have-not (hăv'nŏt') *n.* One that possesses little or no material wealth.

have·n't (hăv'ənt). Have not.

hav·er·sack (hăv'ər-săk') *n.* A bag worn over one shoulder, used for carrying supplies. [< G. *Habersack.*]

hav·oc (hăv'ək) *n.* Widespread destruction or confusion. **—idiom. play havoc with.** To destroy or ruin. [< AN *havok.*]

haw (hô) *n.* 1. The fruit of a hawthorn. 2. A hawthorn. [< OE *haga.*]

Ha·wai·ian (hə-wä'yən) *n.* 1. A native or inhabitant of Hawaii. 2. The Polynesian language of Hawaii. **—Ha·wai'ian** *adj.*

hawk¹ (hôk) *n.* 1. Any of various day-flying birds of prey characteristically having a short, hooked bill and strong claws adapted for seizing. 2. A member of a group advocating a militaristic foreign policy. [< OE *hafoc.*] **—hawk'ish** *adj.*

hawk² (hôk) *v.* To peddle (goods), esp. in the streets. [Prob. < MLG *hōken,* to peddle.] **—hawk'er** *n.*

hawk-eyed (hôk'īd') *adj.* Having very sharp eyesight.

haw·ser (hô'zər) *n.* A cable or rope used in mooring or towing a ship. [< OFr. *haucier,* to hoist.]

haw·thorn (hô'thôrn') *n.* A thorny tree or shrub with white or pinkish flowers and reddish fruit. [< OE *hagathorn.*]

hay (hā) *n.* Grass or other forage plants cut and dried for fodder. **—v.** To mow and cure grass and herbage for hay. **—idiom. hit the hay.** *Slang.* To go to bed. [< OE *hīeg.*]

hay fever *n.* An acute allergic condition of the mucous membranes of the upper respiratory tract and the eyes, caused by abnormal sensitivity to certain airborne pollens, esp. of the ragweed and related plants.

hay·fork (hā'fôrk') *n.* 1. A pitchfork. 2. A machine-operated fork for moving hay.

hay·loft (hā'lôft',-lŏft') *n.* A loft for storing hay.

hay·seed (hā'sēd') *n.* *Slang.* A country bumpkin; yokel.

hay·stack (hā'stăk') *n.* A large stack of hay stored in the open.

hay·wire (hā'wīr') *adj. Informal.* 1. Not functioning properly; broken. 2. Crazy.

haz·ard (hăz'ərd) *n.* 1. A chance; accident. 2. A danger; risk. 3. An obstacle on a golf course. **—v.** To run the risk of; venture. [< Ar. *azzahr,* gaming die.] **—haz'ard·ous** *adj.* **—haz'ard·ous·ly** *adv.*

haze¹ (hāz) *n.* 1. Atmospheric moisture, dust, smoke, and vapor suspended to form a partially opaque condition. 2. A vague state of mind. [Prob. < HAZY.]

haze² (hāz) *v.* **hazed, haz·ing.** To persecute or harass with meaningless, difficult, or humiliating tasks. [Orig. unknown.] **—haz'er** *n.*

ha·zel (hā'zəl) *n.* 1. A shrub or small tree bearing smooth-shelled edible nuts enclosed in a leafy husk. 2. A light or yellowish brown. [< OE *hæsel.*] **—ha'zel** *adj.*

ha·zel·nut (hā'zəl-nŭt') *n.* The nut of a hazel.

ha·zy (hā'zē) *adj.* **-i·er, -i·est.** 1. Marked by the presence of haze. 2. Not clearly defined; vague. [Orig. unknown.] **—haz'i·ly** *adv.* **—haz'i·ness** *n.*

H-bomb (āch'bŏm') *n.* A hydrogen bomb.

he¹ (hē) *pron.* 1. The male that is neither the speaker nor the hearer. 2. Used to refer to any person whose sex is not specified: *He who hesitates is lost.* **—n.** A male animal or person: *Is the cat a he?* [< OE *hē.*]

he² (hā) *n.* The 5th letter of the Hebrew alphabet. See table at **alphabet.** [Heb. *hē.*]

He The symbol for the element helium.

head (hĕd) *n.* 1. The upper or anterior bodily extremity, containing the brain or the principal ganglia and in vertebrates the eyes, ears, nose, mouth, and jaws. 2. a. Intellect; mind. b. Aptitude. 3. Self-control. 4. Freedom of choice or action. 5. The obverse side of a coin. 6. a. Each individual within a group. b. *pl.* **head.** A single animal within a herd. 7. A leader; chief. 8. The foremost position: *the head of the line.* 9. A turning point; crisis. 10. A projecting or striking part of something. 11. The upper or higher end of something. 12. Either end, as of a drum. 13. Pressure: *a head of steam.* 14. A rounded, compact mass of leaves, as of cabbage, or flowers, as of clover. 15. *Slang.* A drug user. **—adj.** 1. Foremost in importance. 2. Placed at the top or front. 3. Coming from the front: *head winds.* **—v.** 1. To be chief of; command.

2. To assume or be placed in the first or foremost position of. **3.** To aim: *head the horse for home.* **4.** To proceed or set out: *head for town.* —*phrasal verb.* **head off.** To intercept. —*idioms.* **go to (one's) head. 1.** To make one lightheaded or drunk. **2.** To make conceited. **head over heels. 1.** Rolling, as in a somersault. **2.** Completely; hopelessly: *head over heels in love.* **off (or out of) (one's) head.** Insane; crazy. **over (one's) head. 1.** Beyond one's ability to understand or deal with. **2.** To a higher-ranking person: *went over the boss's head and spoke to the manager.* [< OE *hēafod.*] —**head'less** *adj.*

Usage: The use of the expression *head up* in place of the verb *head* is unacceptable to a large majority of the Usage Panel: *She heads* (not *heads up*) *the committee.*

head·ache (hĕd'āk') *n.* **1.** A pain in the head. **2.** *Informal.* An annoying problem. —**head'ach'y** (-ā'kē) *adj.*

head·band (hĕd'bănd') *n.* A band worn around the head.

head·board (hĕd'bôrd', -bōrd') *n.* A board that forms the head of a bed.

head·dress (hĕd'drĕs') *n.* A covering or ornament for the head.

head·first (hĕd'fûrst') *adv.* **1.** With the head leading; headlong. **2.** Impetuously. —**head'first'** *adj.*

head·gear (hĕd'gîr') *n.* A covering, such as a hat or helmet, for the head.

head·hunt·ing (hĕd'hŭn'tĭng) *n.* **1.** The custom of cutting off and preserving the heads of enemies as trophies. **2.** *Slang.* An attempt to recruit executive personnel for a company. —**head'hunt'er** *n.*

head·ing (hĕd'ĭng) *n.* **1.** The title, subtitle, or topic that stands at the top or beginning, as of a text. **2.** The direction in which a ship or aircraft is moving.

head·land (hĕd'lənd, -lănd') *n.* A point of land extending into a body of water; promontory.

head·light (hĕd'līt') *n.* A light on the front of a vehicle.

head·line (hĕd'līn') *n.* The title or caption of a newspaper article set in large type. —*v.* **-lined, -lin·ing. 1.** To supply (an article or page) with a headline. **2.** To present or serve as the chief performer. —**head'lin'er** *n.*

head·lock (hĕd'lŏk') *n.* A wrestling hold in which the head of one wrestler is encircled by the arm of the other.

head·long (hĕd'lŏng', -lŏng') *adv.* **1.** Headfirst. **2.** At breakneck speed. [ME *hedling.*] —**head'long'** *adj.*

head·man (hĕd'măn') *n.* A chief, as in a tribe or clan.

head·mas·ter (hĕd'măs'tər) *n.* A man who is a principal, usu. of a private school.

head·mis·tress (hĕd'mĭs'trĭs) *n.* A woman who is a principal, usu. of a private school.

head·on (hĕd'ŏn', -ôn') *adj.* **1.** Facing forward; frontal. **2.** With the front end foremost. —**head'-on'** *adv.*

head·phone (hĕd'fōn') *n.* A receiver held to the ear by a headband.

head·piece (hĕd'pēs') *n.* **1.** A protective covering for the head. **2.** A headset.

head pin *n. Bowling.* The front pin in a triangle of bowling pins.

head·quar·ters (hĕd'kwôr'tərz) *pl.n.* (*used with a sing. or pl. verb*). **1.** The command

center, as of a military unit. **2.** A center of operations or administration.

Usage: *Headquarters* usually takes the plural form of the verb when reference is to a location or place: *Our headquarters are in Boston.* The singular form of the verb often occurs when reference is to authority or function: *Headquarters has issued a new set of orders.*

head·rest (hĕd'rĕst') *n.* A support for the head.

head·set (hĕd'sĕt') *n.* A pair of headphones.

head shop *n. Slang.* A store selling drug paraphernalia.

head·stall (hĕd'stôl') *n.* The part of a bridle that fits over a horse's head.

head·stand (hĕd'stănd') *n.* The act of balancing the body with all the weight resting on the top of the head and the arms.

head start *n.* **1.** A start before other contestants in a race. **2.** An early, advantageous start.

head·stone (hĕd'stōn') *n.* A stone set at the head of a grave.

head·strong (hĕd'strŏng', -strông') *adj.* Willful; obstinate.

head·wait·er (hĕd'wā'tər) *n.* A waiter in charge of the other waiters in a restaurant.

head·wa·ters (hĕd'wô'tərz, -wŏt'ərz) *pl.n.* The waters from which a river rises.

head·way (hĕd'wā') *n.* **1.** Movement forward. **2.** Progress. **3.** Overhead clearance.

head wind *n.* A wind blowing directly opposite to the course of a plane or ship.

head·work (hĕd'wûrk') *n.* Mental activity. —**head'work'er** *n.*

head·y (hĕd'ē) *adj.* **-i·er, -i·est. 1.** Intoxicating. **2.** Headstrong; obstinate. —**head'i·ly** *adv.* —**head'i·ness** *n.*

heal (hēl) *v.* **1.** To restore or return to health; cure. **2.** To set right; amend. [< OE *hǣlan.*] —**heal'a·ble** *adj.* —**heal'er** *n.*

health (hĕlth) *n.* **1.** The overall condition of an organism at a given time. **2.** Optimal functioning with freedom from disease or abnormality. **3.** A wish for someone's good health, often expressed as a toast. [< OE *hǣlth.*] —**health'ful** *adj.* —**health'ful·ly** *adv.* —**health'ful·ness** *n.*

health food *n.* A food believed to be beneficial to one's health.

health·y (hĕl'thē) *adj.* **-i·er, -i·est. 1.** Possessing good health. **2.** Conducive to good health. **3.** Indicative of good health. **4.** Sizable; considerable: *a healthy portion.* —**health'i·ly** *adv.* —**health'i·ness** *n.*

Syns: *healthy, fit, hale, sound, well* **adj.**

heap (hēp) *n.* **1.** A haphazard or disorderly collection of things; pile. **2.** Often **heaps.** *Informal.* A great deal; lots. —*v.* **1.** To put or throw in a heap. **2.** To fill to overflowing. [< OE *hēap.*]

hear (hîr) *v.* **heard** (hûrd), **hear·ing. 1.** To perceive by the ear. **2.** To listen to attentively. **3.** To learn by hearing. **4.** To listen to in an official capacity, as in a court. [< OE *hīeran.*] —**hear'er** *n.*

hear·ing (hîr'ĭng) *n.* **1.** The capacity to hear. **2.** Range of audibility. **3.** An opportunity to be heard. **4.** A session for listening to arguments or testimony. **5.** A preliminary examination of an accused person.

hearing aid *n.* A small electronic amplifying device that is worn to aid poor hearing.

heark·en (här'kən) *v.* To listen carefully or attentively. [< OE *hercnian.*]

hear·say (hîr'sā') n. Information heard from another.

hearse (hûrs) n. A vehicle for carrying a corpse to a church or cemetery. [ME *herse*, a frame for holding candles.]

heart (härt) n. 1. The hollow muscular organ that pumps blood received from the veins into the arteries, thereby supplying the entire circulatory system. 2. The heart regarded as the seat of emotions, as: **a.** Mood. **b.** Compassion. **c.** Affection. **d.** Character or fortitude. 3. The most central and material part: *the heart of the problem.* 4. Any of a suit of playing cards marked with a red, heart-shaped symbol. —**Idioms. by heart.** By memory. **heart and soul.** Completely; entirely. **with all (one's) heart.** 1. With great sincerity. 2. Very gladly. [< OE *heorte.*]

Syns: *heart, core, essence, gist, kernel, marrow, meat, nub, pith, root, stuff, substance* n.

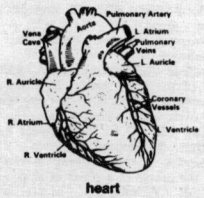

heart

heart·ache (härt'āk') n. Emotional anguish; sorrow.

heart attack n. 1. Partial failure of the pumping action of the heart. 2. A seizure of abnormal heart functioning, as a coronary thrombosis.

heart·beat (härt'bēt') n. A single complete pulsation of the heart.

heart·break (härt'brāk') n. Intense grief; crushing disappointment. —**heart'break'ing** *adj.* —**heart'break'ing·ly** *adv.*

heart·bro·ken (härt'brō'kən) *adj.* Suffering from heartbreak. —**heart'bro'ken·ly** *adv.* —**heart'bro'ken·ness** n.

heart·burn (härt'bûrn') n. A burning sensation in the stomach and esophagus, usu. caused by excess stomach acid.

heart·en (härt'n) v. To encourage; cheer.

heart·felt (härt'fĕlt') *adj.* Deeply or sincerely felt.

hearth (härth) n. 1. The floor of a fireplace, usu. extending into a room. 2. The fireside as a symbol of home or family life. 3. The lowest part of a blast furnace, from which the molten metal flows. [< OE *heorth.*]

hearth·stone (härth'stōn') n. 1. Stone used in the construction of a hearth. 2. The fireside; home.

heart·land (härt'lănd') n. An important central region, esp. one considered vital to a nation.

heart·less (härt'lĭs) *adj.* Without compassion; pitiless; cruel. —**heart'less·ly** *adv.* —**heart'less·ness** n.

heart·rend·ing (härt'rĕn'dĭng) *adj.* Causing anguish or deep sympathy.

heart·sick (härt'sĭk') *adj.* Profoundly depressed. —**heart'sick'ness** n.

heart·strings (härt'strĭngz') *pl.n.* The deepest feelings or affections.

heart·throb (härt'thrŏb') n. 1. A heartbeat. 2. A sweetheart.

heart-to-heart (härt'tə-härt') *adj.* Candid; frank.

heart·wood (härt'wŏod') n. The inactive central wood of a tree or woody plant.

heart·y (här'tē) *adj.* **-i·er, -i·est.** 1. Expressed with warmth of feeling; exuberant. 2. Complete or thorough. 3. Vigorous; robust. 4. Nourishing: *a hearty meal.* —**heart'i·ly** *adv.* —**heart'i·ness** n.

heat (hēt) n. 1. The energy associated with the motion of atoms or molecules in solids, which can be transmitted through solid and fluid media by conduction, through fluid media by convection, and through empty space by radiation. 2. The perceptible, sensible, or measurable effect of such energy so transmitted, esp. a physiological sensation of being hot. 3. A recurrent condition of sexual activity in female mammals. 4. *Slang.* **a.** Pressure, as from police pursuing criminals. **b.** The police. 5. *Sports.* **a.** A single division in a competition. **b.** A preliminary race to determine finalists. [< OE *hǣtu.*]

heat·er (hē'tər) n. An apparatus providing heat.

heat exhaustion n. A reaction to excessive heat, marked by prostration, weakness, and collapse due to dehydration.

heath (hēth) n. 1. An open, uncultivated tract of land covered with heather or similar plants. 2. A plant, as heather, that grows on such land. [< OE *hǣth.*]

hea·then (hē'thən) n., *pl.* **-thens** or **-then.** 1. One who adheres to a religion that does not acknowledge the God of Judaism, Christianity, or Islam. 2. An irreligious, uncivilized, or unenlightened person. [< OE *hǣthen.*] —**hea'then** or **hea'then·ish** *adj.* —**hea'then·dom** (-dəm) or **hea'then·ism** or **hea'then·ry** n.

heath·er (hĕth'ər) n. A low evergreen shrub that grows in a dense mass and has small purplish flowers. [ME *hathir.*] —**heath'er·y** *adj.*

heat lightning n. Intermittent flashes of light without thunder.

heat shield n. A barrier, as on a spacecraft or missile, that is designed to protect against excessive heat.

heat stroke n. A condition caused by exposure to excessively high temperatures and characterized by severe headache, high fever, rapid pulse, and, in serious cases, collapse and coma.

heave (hēv) v. **heaved** or *Naut.* **hove** (hōv), **heav·ing.** 1. To raise or lift. 2. To throw, esp. with great effort. 3. *Naut.* **a.** To pull on or haul. **b.** To push. 4. *Naut.* To come to be in a specified position: *The ship hove alongside.* 5. To breathe or emit: *heaved a sigh.* 6. To rise up or swell. 7. *Informal.* To vomit. —n. 1. The act or strain of heaving. 2. *Informal.* A throw. 3. **heaves** (*used with a sing.* or *pl. verb*) A respiratory disease of horses characterized by coughing and irregular breathing. [< OE *hebban.*]

heav·en (hĕv′ən) *n.* **1.** Often **heavens.** The sky; firmament. **2.** The abode of God, the angels, and the souls granted salvation. **3. Heaven.** The divine Providence. **4.** A place or state of great happiness or bliss. [< OE *heofan.*]   **—heav′en·li·ness** *n.*   **—heav′en·ly** *adj.* **—heav′en·ward** *adv. & adj.*

heav·y (hĕv′ē) *adj.* **-i·er, -i·est. 1.** Having relatively great weight. **2.** Having relatively high density. **3. a.** Large in number or volume: *heavy rainfall; a heavy turnout.* **b.** Intense or sustained: *heavy activity.* **4.** Dense or thick: *heavy fog; a heavy coat.* **5. a.** Concerted or powerful; severe: *a heavy punch.* **b.** Rough; violent: *heavy seas.* **6.** To a great or excessive degree: *a heavy drinker.* **7. a.** Of great import or seriousness; grave. **b.** Causing sorrow; painful: *heavy news.* **8. a.** Hard to do. **b.** Oppressive; burdensome: *heavy taxes.* **9. a.** Substantial: *a heavy breakfast.* **b.** Not easily or quickly digested. **10.** Having large or marked physical features. **11.** Weighed with concern or sadness. **12.** Ponderous. **13. a.** Weighed down; laden. **b.** Exhibiting weariness. **14.** Involving large-scale manufacturing. **15.** Bearing heavy arms or armor: *heavy cavalry.* **16.** *Slang.* Of great significance and profundity. **—adv.** Heavily. **—n., pl. -vies. 1.** A villain in a story or play. **2.** A villain. **3.** *Slang.* One that is very important or influential. [< OE *hefig.*] **—heav′i·ly** *adv.* **—heav′i·ness** *n.*

  Syns: *heavy, hefty, massive, ponderous, weighty adj.*

heav·y-du·ty (hĕv′ē-dōō′tē, -dyōō′-) *adj.* Made for hard use.

heav·y-hand·ed (hĕv′ē-hăn′dĭd) *adj.* **1.** Awkward; clumsy. **2.** Oppressive. **3.** Tactless. **—heav′y-hand′ed·ly** *adv.* **—heav′y-hand′ed·ness** *n.*

heav·y-heart·ed (hĕv′ē-här′tĭd) *adj.* Melancholy. **—heav′y-heart′ed·ly** *adv.* **—heav′y-heart′ed·ness** *n.*

heav·y-set (hĕv′ē-sĕt′) *adj.* Having a heavy, compact build.

heavy water *n.* Any of several isotopic varieties of water, esp. deuterium oxide.

heav·y-weight (hĕv′ē-wāt′) *n.* **1.** One of above average weight. **2.** One who competes in the heaviest class, esp. a boxer who weighs more than 175 pounds or 81 kilograms. **3.** *Informal.* One of great importance or influence.

He·bra·ic (hĭ-brā′ĭk) or **He·bra·i·cal** (-ĭ-kəl) *adj.* Of or characteristic of the Hebrews or their language or culture. **—He·bra′i·cal·ly** *adv.* **—He′bra·ism** (hē′brā-ĭz′əm, hē′brə-) *n.*

He·bra·ist (hē′brā′ĭst) *n.* A Hebrew scholar. **—He·bra·is′tic** or **He·bra·is′ti·cal** *adj.* **—He′bra·is′ti·cal·ly** *adv.*

He·brew (hē′brōō) *n.* **1.** One of the Semitic people claiming descent from Abraham, Isaac, and Jacob; Israelite. **2. a.** The Semitic language of the ancient Hebrews, used in most of the Old Testament. **b.** Any of various later forms of this language, esp. the language of the Israelis. **3. Hebrews.** See table at **Bible.** **—adj.** Of or having to do with the Hebrews.

heck (hĕk) *interj. & n.* Hell.

heck·le (hĕk′əl) *v.* **-led, -ling.** To harass persistently, as with questions, taunts, or comments. [ME *hekelen,* to comb flax.] **—heck′ler** *n.*

hec·tare (hĕk′târ′) *n.* A metric measure of area equal to 100 ares or 2.471 acres.

hec·tic (hĕk′tĭk) *adj.* **1.** Marked by intense ac-

tivity, confusion, or excitement. **2.** Marked by a fluctuating and persistent fever. [< Gk. *hektikos,* habitual.] **—hec′ti·cal·ly** *adv.*

hecto- or **hect-** *pref.* One hundred: *hectoliter.* [< Gk. *hekaton,* hundred.]

hec·to·gram (hĕk′tə-grăm′) *n.* A metric unit of mass equal to 100 grams or 3.527 avoirdupois ounces.

hec·to·li·ter (hĕk′tə-lē′tər) *n.* A metric unit of capacity or volume equal to 100 liters or 26.42 gallons.

hec·to·me·ter (hĕk′tə-mē′tər, hĕk-tŏm′ĭ-tər) *n.* A metric unit of length equal to 100 meters or approx. 328 feet.

hec·tor (hĕk′tər) *v.* To intimidate by blustering. [< HECTOR.]

Hec·tor (hĕk′tər) *n. Gk. Myth.* The Trojan prince and champion killed by Achilles in Homer's *Iliad.*

Hector

he'd (hēd). **1.** He had. **2.** He would.

hedge (hĕj) *n.* **1.** A row of closely planted shrubs forming a boundary. **2.** Protection, esp. against financial loss. **3.** A purposely indirect statement. **—v.** hedged, hedg·ing. **1.** To enclose or protect with or as if with a hedge. **2.** To counterbalance (a bet) with other transactions so as to limit risk. **3.** To avoid making a clear, direct response or statement. [< OE *hecg.*] **—hedg′er** *n.*

hedge·hog (hĕj′hŏg′, -hôg′) *n.* A small Old World mammal having the back covered with dense spines.

hedge-hop (hĕj′hŏp′) *v.* To fly an airplane close to the ground.

he·don·ism (hēd′n-ĭz′əm) *n.* **1.** Pursuit of or devotion to pleasure. **2.** The ethical doctrine that only that which is pleasurable is good. [Gk. *hēdonē,* pleasure + -ISM.]

-hedral *suff.* Having a specified kind or number of surfaces: *dihedral.* [< -HEDRON.]

-hedron *suff.* A crystal or geometric figure having a specified kind or number of surfaces: *pentahedron.* [< Gk. *hedra,* base.]

hee·bie-jee·bies (hē′bē-jē′bēz) *pl.n. Slang.* A feeling of uneasiness or nervousness. [Coined by Billy De Beck (1890–1942).]

heed (hēd) *v.* To pay attention (to). **—n.** Careful attention. [< OE *hēdan.*] **—heed′ful** *adj.* **—heed′ful·ly** *adv.* **—heed′ful·ness** *n.* **—heed′less** *adj.* **—heed′less·ly** *adv.* **—heed′less·ness** *n.*

heel¹ (hēl) *n.* **1. a.** The rounded posterior portion of the human foot under and behind the ankle. **b.** The corresponding part of the hind foot of other vertebrates. **2.** That part of footwear which covers the heel. **3.** A lower, rearward surface of a thing. **4.** A dishonorable man. **—v. 1.** To furnish with a heel or heels. **2.** *Slang.* To furnish (a person), esp. with money. **3.** To follow at the heels of. —*idioms.* **on** (or **upon**) **the heels of.** Immediately following in space or time. **take to** (one's) **heels.** To flee. [< OE *hēla.*] —**heel'less** *adj.*

heel² (hēl) *v.* To tilt or cause to tilt to one side, esp. a ship. —*n.* A tilt to one side. [< OE *hieldan.*]

heft (hĕft) *n. Informal.* Weight; heaviness. —*v.* **1.** To determine the weight of by lifting. **2.** To hoist; heave. [< HEAVE.]

heft-y (hĕf'tē) *adj.* **-i-er, -i-est. 1.** Weighty; heavy. **2.** Large and powerful.

he-gem-o-ny (hĭ-jĕm'ə-nē, hĕj'ə-mō'nē) *n., pl. -nies.* Predominance of one state over others. [< Gk. *hēgemonia.*] —**heg'e-mon'ic** (hĕj'ə-mŏn'ĭk) *adj.*

he-gi-ra (hĭ-jī'rə, hĕj'ər-ə) *n.* Flight, as from danger or hardship. [< Ar. *alhijrat.*]

heif-er (hĕf'ər) *n.* A young cow, esp. one that has not yet borne a calf. [< OE *hēahfore.*]

height (hīt) *n.* **1.** The highest or uppermost point. **2. a.** The most advanced degree; zenith. **b.** The point of highest intensity; climax. **3. a.** The distance from the base to the top of something. **b.** The elevation of something above a given level; altitude. **4. a.** The condition of being relatively tall. **b.** Stature, esp. of the human body. **5.** An eminence. [< OE *hēahthu.*]

height-en (hīt'n) *v.* **1.** To make or become greater in quantity or degree. **2.** To make high or higher. —**height'en-er** *n.*

Heim-lich maneuver (hīm'lĭkH') *n.* A maneuver designed to dislodge an object, as food, from a choking person's windpipe, in which the victim is clasped from behind, a closed fist is placed below the rib cage, and air is forced out of the lungs with a hard upward thrust. [< Henry J. *Heimlich,* 20th-cent. U.S. surgeon.]

hei-nous (hā'nəs) *adj.* Grossly wicked or abominable. [< OFr. *hair,* to hate.] —**hei'-nous-ly** *adv.* —**hei'nous-ness** *n.*

heir (âr) *n.* One who inherits or is legally entitled to inherit the property, rank, title, or office of another. [< Lat. *heres.*]

heir apparent *n., pl.* **heirs apparent.** An heir whose right to inheritance is certain, provided he survives his ancestor.

heir-ess (âr'ĭs) *n.* A female heir, esp. to great wealth.

heir-loom (âr'lōōm') *n.* **1.** A valued possession passed down in a family through succeeding generations. **2.** *Law.* An article of personal property included in an inherited estate. [ME *heirlome.*]

heir presumptive *n., pl.* **heirs presumptive.** An heir whose right to inherit may be canceled by the birth of a relative with a stronger claim to the inheritance.

heist (hīst) *Slang.* —*v.* To rob; steal. —*n.* A robbery. [< HOIST.]

held (hĕld) *v. p.t. & p.p.* of **hold.**

Hel-en of Troy (hĕl'ən) *n. Gk. Myth.* The wife of King Menelaus whose abduction by Paris caused the Trojan War.

hel-i-cal (hĕl'ĭ-kəl) *adj.* Shaped like a helix. [< Gk. *helix,* spiral.] —**hel'i-cal-ly** *adv.*

hel-i-ces (hĕl'ĭ-sēz', hē'lĭ-) *n.* A pl. of **helix.**

hel-i-cop-ter (hĕl'ĭ-kŏp'tər) *n.* An aircraft that derives its lift from horizontal blades that ro-

tate about an approx. vertical central axis. [Fr. *hélicoptère.*]

helio- *pref.* The sun: *heliograph.* [< Gk. *hēlios,* sun.]

he-li-o-cen-tric (hē'lē-ō-sĕn'trĭk) or **he-li-o-cen-tri-cal** (-trĭ-kəl) *adj.* Having the sun as a center. —**he'li-o-cen'tric'i-ty** (-trĭs'ĭ-tē) *n.*

he-li-o-graph (hē'lē-ə-grăf') *n.* A signaling apparatus that reflects sunlight with a movable mirror. —**he'li-o-graph'** *v.* —**he'li-og'ra-pher** (-ŏg'rə-fər) *n.* —**he'li-o-graph'ic** *adj.* —**he'li-og'ra-phy** *n.*

he-li-o-trope (hē'lē-ə-trōp', hēl'yə-) *n.* A cultivated plant with small, fragrant purplish flowers. [< Gk. *hēliotropion.*]

hel-i-port (hĕl'ə-pôrt', -pōrt') *n.* An airport for helicopters. [HELI(COPTER) + PORT.]

he-li-um (hē'lē-əm) *n. Symbol* **He** A colorless, odorless, tasteless, inert gaseous element used to provide lift for balloons and as an inert component of various artificial atmospheres. Atomic number 2; atomic weight 4.0026. [< Gk. *hēlios,* sun.]

he-lix (hē'lĭks) *n., pl.* **-es** or **hel-i-ces** (hĕl'ĭ-sēz', hē'lĭ-). **1.** A three-dimensional curve that lies on a cylinder or cone and cuts the elements at a constant angle. **2.** A spiral form or object. [< Gk.]

hell (hĕl) *n.* **1.** The abode of the dead; underworld. **2.** Often **Hell.** The place of punishment of the wicked after death. **3.** A place or situation of evil, misery, discord, or destruction. **4. a.** Torment; anguish. **b.** Something that causes trouble or agony. —*interj.* Used to express anger, impatience, or dismay. [< OE *helle.*]

he'll (hĕl). **1.** He will. **2.** He shall.

hell-bent (hĕl'bĕnt') *adj.* Impetuously determined to do something. —**hell'-bent'** *adv.*

hell-cat (hĕl'kăt') *n.* A bad-tempered and evil woman.

hel-le-bore (hĕl'ə-bôr', -bōr') *n.* Any of various chiefly poisonous plants with white or greenish flowers. [< Gk. *helleboros.*]

Hel-lene (hĕl'ēn') *n.* Also **Hel-le-ni-an** (hə-lē'nē-ən). A Greek.

Hel-len-ic (hə-lĕn'ĭk) *adj.* Of or relating to the ancient Greeks or their language. —*n.* The branch of the Indo-European language family that consists only of Greek.

Hel-len-ism (hĕl'ə-nĭz'əm) *n.* **1.** An idiom peculiar to the Greeks. **2.** The civilization and culture of ancient Greece. **3.** The adoption of Greek ideas, style, or culture. —**Hel'le-nist** *n.* —**Hel'le-nis'tic** *adj.*

hell-gram-mite (hĕl'grə-mīt') *n.* A large, brownish aquatic insect larva, often used as fishing bait. [Orig. unknown.]

hel-lion (hĕl'yən) *n. Informal.* A mischievous, troublesome person. [Prob. < dial. *hallion,* worthless person.]

hell-ish (hĕl'ĭsh) *adj.* **1.** Of, like, or worthy of hell. **2.** *Informal.* Devilish. —**hell'ish-ly** *adv.* —**hell'ish-ness** *n.*

hel-lo (hĕ-lō', hə-) *interj.* Used to greet someone, attract attention, or express surprise. —*n., pl.* **-loes.** A call or greeting of "hello." [< obs. *holla,* stop!]

helm (hĕlm) *n.* **1.** The steering gear of a ship, esp. the tiller or wheel. **2.** A position of leadership or control. [< OE *helma.*]

hel·met (hěl′mĭt) *n.* A protective head covering of metal, leather, or plastic. [ME.]

hel·minth (hěl′mĭnth′) *n.* A parasitic worm, esp. an intestinal worm. [Gk. *helmis.*]

helms·man (hělmz′mən) *n.* One who steers a ship.

helmsman

hel·ot (hěl′ət, hē′lət) *n.* A serf; bondsman. [< Gk. *Heilōtes*, helots.] —**hel′ot·ry** *n.*

help (hělp) *v.* **1.** To give assistance (to); aid. **2.** To contribute to; further. **3.** To give relief to. **4.** To improve; benefit. **5.** To be able to prevent, change, or rectify. **6.** To refrain from; avoid. **7.** To wait on; serve. —*n.* **1.** Aid; assistance. **2.** Relief; remedy. **3.** One that helps. **4.** a. A person employed to help. **b.** Such employees in general. —*idiom.* **cannot help but.** To be unable to avoid or resist. [< OE *helpan*, and < ON *hjalpa.*] —**help′er** *n.*

help·ful (hělp′fəl) *adj.* Providing help; useful. —**help′ful·ly** *adv.* —**help′ful·ness** *n.*

help·ing (hěl′pĭng) *n.* A portion of food for one person.

help·less (hělp′lĭs) *adj.* **1.** Unable to manage by oneself; dependent. **2.** Lacking power or strength; impotent; weak. —**help′less·ly** *adv.* —**help′less·ness** *n.*

help·mate (hělp′māt′) *n.* A helper and companion, esp. a spouse. [< HELPMEET.]

help·meet (hělp′mēt′) *n.* A helpmate. [HELP + MEET².]

hel·ter-skel·ter (hěl′tər-skěl′tər) *adv.* **1.** In disorderly haste. **2.** Haphazardly. **3.** In confusion. —*adj.* **1.** Hurried and confused. **2.** Haphazard. —*n.* Turmoil; confusion. [Orig. unknown.]

hem¹ (hěm) *n.* A smooth, even edge of a garment or piece of cloth, made by folding the raw edge under and sewing it down. —*v.* **hemmed, hem·ming.** To fold back and sew down the edge of. —*phrasal verb.* **hem in.** To surround and shut in; enclose. [< OE.] —**hem′mer** *n.*

hem² (hěm) *n.* A short cough or clearing of the throat made to gain attention, fill a pause, etc. —*v.* **hemmed, hem·ming.** To make this sound. —*idiom.* **hem and haw.** To be hesitant and indecisive. [Imit.]

he-man (hē′măn′) *n. Informal.* A strong, muscular, virile man.

hemat– *pref.* Blood: *hematology.* [Gk. *haima.*]

hem·a·tite (hěm′ə-tīt′, hē′mə-) *n.* A blackish-red to brick-red mineral, Fe₂O₃, the chief ore of iron. [< Gk. *(lithos) haimatitēs*, bloodlike (stone).]

he·ma·tol·o·gy (hē′mə-tŏl′ə-jē) *n.* The science concerning the generation, anatomy, physiology, pathology, and therapeutics of blood. —**he′ma·tol′o·gist** *n.*

he·ma·to·ma (hē′mə-tō′mə) *n.* A localized swelling containing blood.

heme (hēm) *n.* The nonprotein, iron-containing pigment of hemoglobin. [< Gk. *haima,* blood.]

hem·i·sphere (hěm′ĭ-sfîr′) *n.* **1. a.** A half of a sphere bounded by a great circle. **b.** A symmetrical half of an approx. symmetrical object. **2.** Either of the halves into which the earth is divided by the equator or by a great circle that passes through the poles. [< Gk. *hēmisphairion.*] —**hem′i·spher′ic** (-sfîr′ĭk, -sfěr′ĭk) or **hem′i·spher′i·cal** *adj.*

hem·lock (hěm′lŏk′) *n.* **1. a.** An evergreen tree with short, flat needles and small cones. **b.** The wood of a hemlock. **2. a.** A poisonous plant with compound leaves and small whitish flowers. **b.** A poison extracted from the hemlock. [< OE *hymlīc*, poisonous hemlock.]

he·mo·glo·bin (hē′mə-glō′bĭn, hěm′ə-) *n.* The oxygen-bearing, iron-containing protein in the red blood cells of vertebrates. [< obs. *hematoglobulin.*]

he·mo·phil·i·a (hē′mə-fĭl′ē-ə, hěm′ə-) *n.* A hereditary blood disease, principally of males but transmitted by females, characterized by excessive, sometimes spontaneous bleeding. [Gk. *haima,* blood + Gk. *philia,* friendship.] —**he′mo·phil′i·ac′** *n.*

hem·or·rhage (hěm′ər-ĭj) *n.* Bleeding, esp. severe or heavy bleeding. —*v.* **-rhaged, -rhag·ing.** To bleed copiously. [< Gk. *haimorrhagia.*] —**hem′or·rhag′ic** (-răj′ĭk) *adj.*

hem·or·rhoids (hěm′ə-roidz′) *pl.n.* An itching or painful mass of dilated veins on or within the anus. [< Gk. *haimorrhoides.*]

hemp (hěmp) *n.* **1.** A tall Asian plant that yields a coarse fiber used to make cordage. **2.** The fiber of the hemp plant. [< OE *hænep.*]

hem·stitch (hěm′stĭch′) *n.* A decorative stitch usu. bordering a hem, made by drawing out several parallel threads and catching together the cross threads in uniform groups to create a design. —**hem′stitch′** *v.* —**hem′stitch′er** *n.*

hen (hěn) *n.* A female bird, esp. the adult female of the domestic fowl. [< OE.]

hence (hěns) *adv.* **1.** For this reason; therefore. **2.** From this time; from now. **3.** From this place; away. [< OE *heonon*, from here.]

hence·forth (hěns′fôrth′) *adv.* Also **hence·forward** (hěns-fôr′wərd). From this time on.

hence·for·ward (hěns-fôr′wərd) *adv.* Henceforth.

hench·man (hěnch′mən) *n.* A loyal follower or supporter. [ME *hencheman,* squire.]

hen·na (hěn′ə) *n.* **1.** A tree or shrub with fragrant white or reddish flowers. **2.** A reddish dyestuff obtained from the leaves of the henna plant, used as a cosmetic dye. **3.** A reddish brown. —*v.* To dye or treat with henna. [Ar. *ḥinnā'.*] —**hen′na** *adj.*

hen·peck (hěn′pěk′) *v. Informal.* To dominate (one's husband) by scolding or nagging.

hen·ry (hěn′rē) *n., pl.* **-ries** or **-rys.** The unit of inductance in which an induced electromotive force of one volt is produced when the current changes at the rate of one ampere per second. [< Joseph *Henry* (1797-1878).]

hep (hěp) *adj.* Var. of **hip².**

hep·a·rin (hěp′ər-ĭn) *n.* An organic acid, found esp. in lung and liver tissue, that slows blood clotting. [Gk. *hēpar,* liver + -IN.]

he·pat·ic (hĭ-păt′ĭk) *adj.* **1.** Of or resembling

the liver. **2.** Acting on or affecting the liver. [< Gk. *hēpatikos.*]

he·pat·i·ca (hǐ-pǎt′ǐ-kə) *n.* A woodland plant with three-lobed leaves and white or lavender flowers. [Med. Lat., liverwort.]

hep·a·ti·tis (hěp′ə-tī′tǐs) *n.* Inflammation of the liver, often caused by a virus, characterized by jaundice and usu. fever. [Gk. *hēpar,* liver + -ITIS.]

He·phaes·tus (hǐ-fěs′təs) *n.* Gk. Myth. The god of fire and metalworking.

her (hûr; hər, ər *when unstressed*) *pron.* **1.** The objective case of **she.** Used: **a.** As the direct object of a verb: *They saw her in the library.* **b.** As the indirect object of a verb: *They gave her a book.* **c.** As the object of a preposition: *This letter is addressed to her.* **2.** The possessive form of **she.** Used as a modifier before a noun: *her purse; her tasks; her first rebuff.* [< OE *hire.*]

He·ra (hîr′ə) *n.* Gk. Myth. The sister and wife of Zeus.

her·ald (hěr′əld) *n.* **1.** One who announces important news. **2.** One that gives a sign or indication of what is to follow; harbinger. **3.** An official formerly responsible for announcing royal proclamations. —*v.* To proclaim; announce. [< AN, of Gmc. orig.]

he·ral·dic (hə-rǎl′dǐk) *adj.* Of or pertaining to heralds or heraldry.

her·ald·ry (hěr′əl-drē) *n., pl.* **-ries. 1.** The study or art of tracing genealogies, of determining, designing, and granting coats of arms, and of ruling on questions of rank or protocol. **2.** Armorial ensigns or devices. **3.** Heraldic ceremony; pageantry.

herb (ûrb, hûrb) *n.* **1.** A plant with a fleshy rather than woody stem that usu. dies back at the end of each growing season. **2.** An often aromatic plant used in medicine or as seasoning. [< Lat. *herba.*] —**herb′al** *adj. & n.*

her·ba·ceous (hûr-bā′shəs) *adj.* **1.** Of, like, or consisting of herbs as distinguished from woody plants. **2.** Green and leaflike in appearance or texture.

herb·age (ûr′bǐj, hûr′-) *n.* **1.** Grass or leafy plants, used esp. for pasturage. **2.** The fleshy parts of herbaceous plants.

herb·al·ist (hûr′bə-lǐst, ûr′-) *n.* One who grows or deals in herbs, esp. medicinal herbs.

her·bar·i·um (hûr-bâr′ē-əm) *n., pl.* **-ums** or **-i·a** (-ē-ə). **1.** A collection of dried plants, as for use in scientific study. **2.** A place where such a collection is kept. [LLat.]

her·bi·cide (hûr′bǐ-sīd′) *n.* A substance used to destroy plants, esp. weeds. —**her′bi·cid′al** (-sīd′l) *adj.*

her·bi·vore (hûr′bə-vôr′, -vōr′) *n.* A plant-eating animal. [< Lat. *herbivorus,* herbivorous.]

her·biv·o·rous (hûr-bǐv′ər-əs) *adj.* Feeding on plants.

Her·cu·les (hûr′kyə-lēz′) *n.* Often **hercules.** A man of prodigious strength. [< *Hercules,* Greco-Roman mythological hero noted for his strength.] —**her·cu·le′an** *adj.*

herd (hûrd) *n.* **1.** A group of animals, as domestic cattle, kept or living together. **2.** A large number of people; crowd. —*v.* **1.** To come together in a herd. **2.** To gather, keep, or drive in or as if in a herd. [< OE *heord.*] —**herd′er** *n.* —**herds′man** *n.*

here (hîr) *adv.* **1.** At or in this place: *Let's stay here.* **2.** At this time; now: *We'll adjourn the meeting here.* **3.** At or on this point or item: *Here I must disagree.* **4.** To this place: *Come here.* —*interj.* Used to respond to a roll call, attract attention, command an animal, or rebuke or admonish. —*idiom.* **neither here nor there.** Not important or relevant. [< OE *hēr.*]

Usage: In constructions introduced by *here* the number of the verb is governed by the subject that occurs after the verb: *Here is the zebra; here are the zebras.*

here·a·bout (hîr′ə-bout′) *adv.* Also **here·a·bouts** (-bouts′). In this vicinity; near or around here.

here·af·ter (hîr-ǎf′tər) *adv.* **1.** After this; from now on. **2.** In the afterlife. —*n.* Life after death.

here·by (hîr-bī′, hîr′bī′) *adv.* By this means.

he·red·i·tar·y (hə-rěd′ǐ-těr′ē) *adj.* **1.** Law. **a.** Passing down by inheritance. **b.** Having title or possession through inheritance. **2.** Genetically transmitted or transmissible. **3.** Derived from or fostered by one's ancestors. —**he·red′i·tar′i·ly** (-tǎr′ə-lē) *adv.*

he·red·i·ty (hə-rěd′ǐ-tē) *n., pl.* **-ties. 1.** The genetic transmission of characteristics from parent to offspring. **2.** The set of characteristics transmitted to an individual organism by heredity. [< Lat. *hereditas,* inheritance.]

here·in (hîr-ǐn′) *adv.* In or into this.

here·of (hîr-ǔv′, -ŏv′) *adv.* Of or concerning this.

here·on (hîr-ŏn′, -ôn′) *adv.* On this.

her·e·sy (hěr′ǐ-sē) *n., pl.* **-sies. 1.** An opinion or doctrine at variance with established religious beliefs. **2. a.** A controversial or unorthodox opinion or doctrine, as in politics, philosophy, or science. **b.** Adherence to such opinion. [< Gk. *hairesis,* faction.]

her·e·tic (hěr′ǐ-tǐk) *n.* One who holds opinions that differ from established beliefs, esp. religious beliefs. [< Gk. *hairetikos,* factious.] —**he·ret′i·cal** *adj.* —**he·ret′i·cal·ly** *adv.*

here·to (hîr-tōō′) *adv.* To this.

here·to·fore (hîr′tə-fôr′, -fōr′) *adv.* Before this; previously. [ME.]

here·un·to (hîr-ǔn′tōō, hîr′ǔn-tōō′) *adv.* Hereto.

here·up·on (hîr′ə-pŏn′, -pôn′, hîr′ə-pŏn′, -pôn′) *adv.* Immediately after this; at this.

here·with (hîr-wǐth′, -wǐth′) *adv.* **1.** Along with this. **2.** By this means; hereby.

her·i·ta·ble (hěr′ǐ-tə-bəl) *adj.* Capable of being inherited; hereditary. [< Lat. *heres,* heir.]

her·i·tage (hěr′ǐ-tǐj) *n.* **1.** Property that is or can be inherited. **2.** Something passed down from preceding generations; tradition. [< Lat. *heres,* heir.]

her·maph·ro·dite (hər-mǎf′rə-dīt′) *n.* One that has the sex organs and many of the secondary characteristics of both male and female. [< *Hermaphroditos,* son of Hermes and Aphrodite.] —**her·maph′ro·dit′ic** (-dǐt′ǐk) *adj.* —**her·maph′ro·dit′i·cal·ly** *adv.*

Her·mes (hûr′mēz′) *n.* Gk. Myth. The god of commerce, invention, and theft.

her·met·ic (hər-mět′ǐk) or **her·met·i·cal** (-ǐ-kəl) *adj.* **1.** Completely sealed, esp. against the escape or entry of air. **2.** Insulated against or resistant to outside influences. [< *Hermes* Trismegistus, legendary alchemist.] —her·met′i·cal·ly *adv.*

her·mit (hûr′mĭt) *n.* One who lives a solitary existence, esp. for religious reasons; recluse. [< Gk. *erēmos*, solitary.] —her·mit′ic (hər-mĭt′ĭk) or her·mit′i·cal *adj.* —her·mit′i·cal·ly *adv.*

her·mit·age (hûr′mĭ-tĭj) *n.* 1. The habitation of a hermit. 2. A retreat or hideaway.

her·ni·a (hûr′nē-ə) *n., pl.* -as or -ni·ae (-nē-ē′). Protrusion of an organ or organic part through the wall that normally encloses it; rupture. [< Lat.] —her′ni·al (-əl) *adj.*

he·ro (hîr′ō) *n., pl.* -roes. 1. In mythology and legend, a man celebrated for his strength and bold exploits. 2. A man noted for his special achievements. 3. The principal male character in a literary work. 4. *Slang.* A large sandwich made with a long crusty roll split lengthwise and filled with a variety of meats and cheeses, lettuce, tomato, and onion. [< Gk. *hērōs.*]

he·ro·ic (hĭ-rō′ĭk) or he·ro·i·cal (-ĭ-kəl) *adj.* 1. Of or appropriate to a hero; courageous; noble. 2. Larger than life; grand or grandiose: *heroic sculpture.* —*n.* heroics. Melodramatic behavior or language. —he·ro′i·cal·ly *adv.* —he·ro′i·cal·ness *n.*

heroic couplet *n.* A verse unit of two rhymed lines in iambic pentameter.

her·o·in (hĕr′ō-ĭn) *n.* A white, odorless, highly addictive narcotic, $C_{17}H_{17}NO(C_2H_3O_2)_2$, that is derived from morphine.

her·o·ine (hĕr′ō-ĭn) *n.* 1. A woman noted for courageous and daring acts. 2. A woman noted for her special achievements. 3. The principal female character in a literary work. [< Gk. *hērōinē.*]

her·o·ism (hĕr′ō-ĭz′əm) *n.* 1. Heroic conduct or behavior. 2. Heroic traits or qualities; courage.

her·on (hĕr′ən) *n.* A wading bird with a long neck, long legs, and a long, pointed bill. [< OFr., of Gmc. orig.]

her·pes (hûr′pēz′) *n.* Any of several viral diseases characterized by the eruption of blisters of the skin or mucous membrane. [< Gk. *herpēs.*] —her·pet·ic (-pĕt′ĭk) *adj.*

her·pe·tol·o·gy (hûr′pĭ-tŏl′ə-jē) *n.* The zoological study of reptiles and amphibians. [Gk. *herpeton,* reptile + -LOGY.] —her′pe·to·log′ic (-tə-lŏj′ĭk) or her′pe·to·log′i·cal (-ĭ-kəl) *adj.* —her′pe·to·log′i·cal·ly *adv.* —her′pe·tol′o·gist *n.*

her·ring (hĕr′ĭng) *n., pl.* -ring or -rings. A commercially important food fish of Atlantic and Pacific waters. [< OE *hǣring.*]

her·ring·bone (hĕr′ĭng-bōn′) *n.* 1. A zigzag pattern made up of short parallel lines arranged in rows that slant first one way, then another. 2. A fabric woven in this pattern.

hers (hûrz) *pron.* Used to indicate the one or ones belonging to her: *If you can't find your hat, take hers.* [ME.]

her·self (hər-sĕlf′) *pron.* 1. That one identical with her. Used: **a.** Reflexively as the direct or indirect object of a verb or as the object of a preposition: *She hurt herself.* **b.** For emphasis: *She herself wasn't certain.* 2. Her normal or healthy condition: *She isn't herself today.*

hertz (hûrts) *n.* A unit of frequency equal to one cycle per second. [< Heinrich *Hertz* (1857–94).]

he's (hēz). 1. He is. 2. He has.

Hesh·van (κHĕsh′vən) *n.* The 2nd month of the Hebrew calendar. See table at **calendar.** [Heb. *heshwān.*]

hes·i·tant (hĕz′ĭ-tənt) *adj.* Inclined or tending to hesitate. —hes′i·tan·cy *n.* —hes′i·tant·ly *adv.*

hes·i·tate (hĕz′ĭ-tāt′) *v.* -tat·ed, -tat·ing. 1. To be slow to act, speak, or decide; waver. 2. To be reluctant: *Don't hesitate to ask for help.* 3. To speak haltingly; falter. [Lat. *haesitare.*] —hes′i·tat′er *n.* —hes′i·tat′ing·ly *adv.* —hes′i·ta′tion *n.*

Syns: *hesitate, falter, halt, pause, vacillate, waver v.*

Hes·ti·a (hĕs′tē-ə) *n.* Gk. *Myth.* The goddess of the hearth.

hetero– or heter– *pref.* Other; different: *heterosexual.* [< Gk. *heteros,* other.]

het·er·o·dox (hĕt′ər-ə-dŏks′) *adj.* 1. Not in agreement with accepted beliefs, esp. departing from religious doctrine. 2. Holding unorthodox opinions. [< Gk. *heterodoxos.*] —het′er·o·dox′y *n.*

het·er·o·ge·ne·ous (hĕt′ər-ə-jē′nē-əs, -jēn′yəs) *adj.* Also het·er·og·e·nous (-ə-rŏj′ə-nəs). Consisting of dissimilar elements or parts; not homogeneous: *a heterogeneous collection.* —het′er·o·ge·ne′i·ty (-ə-rō-jə-nē′ĭ-tē) *n.* —het′er·o·ge′ne·ous·ly *adv.* —het′er·o·ge′ne·ous·ness *n.*

het·er·o·sex·u·al (hĕt′ə-rō-sĕk′shōō-əl) *adj.* 1. Characterized by attraction to the opposite sex. 2. Pertaining to different sexes. —*n.* A heterosexual person. —het′er·o·sex·u·al′i·ty (-ăl′ĭ-tē) *n.*

heth (κHät, κHäth, κHĕt, κHĕth) *n.* The 8th letter of the Hebrew alphabet. See table at **alphabet.** [Heb. *hēth.*]

hew (hyōō) *v.* hewed, hewn (hyōōn) or hewed, hew·ing. 1. To make or shape with or as if with an ax. 2. To cut down with an ax. 3. To adhere or conform strictly: *hew to the line.* [< OE *hēawan.*]

hex (hĕks) *n.* 1. An evil spell; curse. 2. One that brings bad luck. —*v.* 1. To put a hex on. 2. To wish or bring bad luck to. [< G. *Hexe,* witch.]

hexa– *pref.* Six: *hexagon.* [< Gk. *hex,* six.]

hex·a·gon (hĕk′sə-gŏn′) *n.* A polygon with six sides and six angles. —hex·ag′o·nal (-săg′ə-nəl) *adj.*

hex·am·e·ter (hĕk-săm′ĭ-tər) *n.* A verse line having six metrical feet.

hey (hā) *interj.* Used to attract attention or to express surprise, appreciation, or pleasure: *Hey you! Hey, that's nice!*

hey·day (hā′dā′) *n.* The period of greatest popularity, success, or power; prime. [Orig. unknown.]

Hf The symbol for the element hafnium.

Hg The symbol for the element mercury. [Lat. *hydrargyrus,* artificial mercury.]

hi (hī) *interj.* *Informal.* Used as a greeting.

hi·a·tus (hī-ā′təs) *n.* A gap or interruption in space, time, or continuity. [Lat. < *hiare,* to gape.]

hi·ba·chi (hĭ-bä′chē) *n., pl.* -chis. A portable charcoal-burning brazier. [J.]

hi·ber·nate (hī′bər-nāt′) *v.* -nat·ed, -nat·ing. To spend the winter in a dormant or torpid state. [< Lat. *hibernare.*] —hi′ber·na′tion *n.* —hi′ber·na′tor *n.*

hi·bis·cus (hī-bĭs′kəs, hĭ-) *n.* Any of various chiefly tropical plants, shrubs, or trees with large, showy, variously colored flowers. [< Gk. *hibiskos*, marsh mallow.]

hic·cup (hĭk'ŭp). Also **hic·cough** (hĭk'ŭp). —*n.*
1. A spasm of the diaphragm causing a sudden inhalation that is quickly cut off by another spasm in the glottis. **2. hiccups.** An attack of such spasms. —*v.* **-cupped, -cupping.** To have the hiccups. [Imit.]

hick (hĭk) *n. Informal.* A gullible, provincial person; yokel. —*adj.* Provincial; unsophisticated. [< *Hick,* a nickname for *Richard.*]

hick·o·ry (hĭk'ə-rē) *n., pl.* **-ries. 1.** Any of several North American trees with smooth or shaggy bark, compound leaves, and hard nuts with an edible kernel. **2.** The wood of a hickory tree. [Of Algonquian orig.]

hide¹ (hīd) *v.* **hid** (hĭd), **hid·den** (hĭd'n) or **hid, hid·ing. 1.** To put or keep out of sight; secrete. **2.** To keep secret; conceal. **3.** To cut off from sight; cover up. **4** To seek refuge. [< OE *hȳdan.*] —**hid'er** *n.*

hide² (hīd) *n.* The skin of an animal, esp. of a large animal. [< OE *hȳd.*]

hide-and-seek (hīd'n-sēk') *n.* A children's game in which one player tries to find and catch others who are hiding.

hide·a·way (hīd'ə-wā') *n.* **1.** A hide-out. **2.** A secluded or isolated place.

hide·bound (hīd'bound') *adj.* Prejudiced or narrow-minded.

hid·e·ous (hĭd'ē-əs) *adj.* Extremely unpleasant, esp. to the sight; repulsive. [< OFr. *hide, fear.*] —**hid'e·ous·ly** *adv.*

hide·out (hīd'out') *n.* A place of shelter or concealment.

hie (hī) *v.* **hied, hie·ing** or **hy·ing.** To hasten; hurry. [< OE *hīgian.*]

hi·er·ar·chy (hī'ə-rär'kē, hī'rär'-) *n., pl.* **-chies. 1.** A body of persons, as clergy, organized or classified according to rank or authority. **2.** An arrangement of persons or things in a graded series. [< Gk. *hierarkhia,* rule of a high priest.] —**hi'er·ar'chi·cal** or **hi'er·ar'chic** *adj.* —**hi'er·ar'chi·cal·ly** *adv.*

hi·er·o·glyph·ic (hī'ər-ə-glĭf'ĭk, hī'rə-) *n.* **1.** A picture or symbol used in writing, esp. in the writing system of ancient Egypt. **2. hieroglyphics.** Illegible or undecipherable symbols. [< Gk. *hierogluphikos.*]

hieroglyphic
16th- to 14th-century B.C.
Egyptian hieroglyphics

hi-fi (hī'fī') *n., pl.* **-fis. 1.** High fidelity. **2.** An electronic system for reproducing sound with high fidelity. [HI(GH) FI(DELITY).]

hig·gle·dy-pig·gle·dy (hĭg'əl-dē-pĭg'əl-dē) *adv.*

In utter disorder or confusion. [Orig. unknown.]

high (hī) *adj.* **-er, -est. 1.** Tall; elevated. **2.** Being at or near a peak or culmination. **3.** Far removed in time; remote. **4.** Piercing in tone or sound. **5.** Situated far from the equator. **6.** Of great moment or importance; serious; weighty: *high treason.* **7.** Lofty or exalted in quality. **8.** Of great quantity, magnitude, or degree. **9.** Costly; expensive. **10.** In a state of excitement or euphoria. **11.** *Informal.* Intoxicated. —*n.* **1.** A high degree, level, or point. **2.** The transmission gear of an automotive vehicle producing maximum speed. **3.** A center of high atmospheric pressure. **4.** *Informal.* Intoxication or euphoria. —*adv.* **-er, -est.** At, in, or to a high position, price, or level. —*idioms.* **high and dry.** Helpless; alone. **high and mighty.** Arrogant; domineering. [< OE *hēah.*] —**high'ly** *adv.*

high-ball (hī'bôl') *n.* A mixed alcoholic beverage served in a tall glass.

high-born (hī'bôrn') *adj.* Of noble birth.

high-boy (hī'boi') *n.* A tall chest of drawers supported on long legs.

high-bred (hī'brĕd') *adj.* Of superior breed or stock.

high-brow (hī'brou') *n. Informal.* One who has or affects superior learning or culture. —**high'brow'** or **high'browed'** *adj.*

high·er-up (hī'ər-ŭp', hī'ər-ŭp') *n. Informal.* One who has a superior rank, position, or status.

high-fa·lu·tin (hī'fə-lōōt'n) *adj. Informal.* Pompous or pretentious. [Orig. unknown.]

high fashion *n.* The latest in trend-setting fashion or design.

high fidelity *n.* The electronic reproduction of sound with minimal distortion. —**high'-fi·del'i·ty** *adj.*

high-flown (hī'flōn') *adj.* Pretentious.

high frequency *n.* A radio frequency in the range between 3 and 30 megacycles per second.

High German *n.* **1.** German as indigenously spoken and written in central and southern Germany. **2.** German (sense 2).

high-hand·ed (hī'hăn'dĭd) *adj.* Arrogant or overbearing in manner. —**high'hand'ed·ly** *adv.* —**high'hand'ed·ness** *n.*

high-hat (hī'hăt') *n. Slang.* A snob. —*v.* To treat in a condescending or supercilious way. —**high'-hat'** *adj.*

high·land (hī'lənd) *n.* **1.** Elevated land. **2. highlands.** A mountainous region or part of a country. —**high'land·er** *n.*

high·light (hī'līt') *n.* An outstanding event or occurrence. —*v.* **1.** To emphasize; make prominent. **2.** To be the highlight of.

high-mind·ed (hī'mīn'dĭd) *adj.* Characterized by elevated ideals or conduct; noble. —**high'mind'ed·ly** *adv.* —**high'-mind'ed·ness** *n.*

high·ness (hī'nĭs) *n.* **1.** Tallness; height. **2. Highness.** A title of honor for royalty.

high-pres·sure (hī'prĕsh'ər) *Informal.* —*adj.* Using aggressive and persistent methods of persuasion. —*v.* To convince or influence by using high-pressure methods.

high-rise (hī'rīz') *n.* A multistoried building equipped with elevators.

high-road (hī'rōd') *n.* **1.** *Chiefly Brit.* A main road; highway. **2.** A direct or sure path.

high school *n.* A secondary school that includes grades 9 or 10 through 12 or grades 7 through 12.

high seas *pl.n.* The open waters beyond the territorial limits of a country.

high-sound-ing (hī'soun'dĭng) *adj.* Pretentious; pompous.

high-spir-it-ed (hī'spĭr'ĭ-tĭd) *adj.* **1.** Brave. **2.** Vivacious; lively.

high-strung (hī'strŭng') *adj.* Tending to be extremely nervous and sensitive.

high-tail (hī'tāl') *v. Slang.* To go or clear out in a great hurry.

high-ten-sion (hī'tĕn'shən) *adj.* Having a high voltage.

high-test (hī'tĕst') *adj.* Of or pertaining to highly volatile high-octane gasoline.

high tide *n.* **1. a.** The highest level of the tide. **b.** The time at which this occurs. **2.** A point of culmination; climax.

high-toned (hī'tōnd') *adj.* **1.** Intellectually, morally, or socially superior. **2.** *Informal.* Pretentiously elegant or fashionable.

high-way (hī'wā') *n.* A main public road.

high-way-man (hī'wā'mən) *n.* A robber who holds up travelers on a highway.

hi-jack (hī'jăk') *v. Informal.* **1.** To steal (goods) from a vehicle in transit. **2.** To seize forcibly or commandeer (a vehicle, esp. an airplane). [Orig. unknown.] —**hi'jack'er** *n.*

hike (hīk) *v.* **hiked, hik-ing.** **1.** To go on an extended walk for pleasure or exercise. **2.** To increase or raise in amount. **3.** To pull up or raise with a sudden motion: *hiked up his pants.* —*n.* **1.** A long walk or march. **2.** An upward movement or rise, as in prices. [Orig. unknown.] —**hik'er** *n.*

hi-lar-i-ous (hĭ-lâr'ē-əs, -lâr'-, hī-) *adj.* Boisterously funny. [< Gk. *hilaros,* cheerful.] —**hi-lar'i-ous-ly** *adv.* —**hi-lar'i-ty** *n.*

hill (hĭl) *n.* **1.** A well-defined natural elevation smaller than a mountain. **2.** A small heap, pile, or mound. [< OE *hyll.*] —**hill'i-ness** *n.* —**hill'y** *adj.*

hill-bil-ly (hĭl'bĭl'ē) *n., pl.* **-lies.** *Informal.* A person from the backwoods or a remote mountain area. [HILL + *Billy,* a nickname for *William.*]

hill-ock (hĭl'ək) *n.* A small hill. [ME *hillok.*]

hill-side (hĭl'sīd') *n.* The side or slope of a hill.

hill-top (hĭl'tŏp') *n.* The crest or top of a hill.

hilt (hĭlt) *n.* The handle of a weapon or tool, esp. of a sword or dagger. —**idiom.** to the hilt. To the limit; completely. [< OE.]

him (hĭm) *pron.* The objective case of **he.** Used: **1.** As the direct object of a verb: *They assisted him.* **2.** As the indirect object of a verb: *They offered him a ride.* **3.** As the object of a preposition: *This letter is addressed to him.* [< OE.]

him-self (hĭm-sĕlf') *pron.* **1.** That one identical with him. Used: **a.** Reflexively as the direct or indirect object of a verb or as the object of a preposition: *He hurt himself.* **b.** For emphasis: *He himself wasn't certain.* **2.** His normal or healthy condition or state: *He hasn't been himself lately.*

hind¹ (hīnd) *adj.* At the back or rear; posterior: *hind legs.* [< OE *bihindan.*]

hind² (hīnd) *n.* A female red deer. [< OE.]

hin-der (hĭn'dər) *v.* **1.** To get in the way of;

hamper. **2.** To check or delay the progress of. [< OE *hindrian.*] —**hin'der-er** *n.*

Syns: *hinder, encumber, hamper, impede, obstruct, retard* **v.**

Hin-di (hĭn'dē) *n.* **1. a.** A group of vernacular Indic dialects spoken in northern India. **b.** A literary and official language based on these dialects. **2.** A member of a cultural group of northern India speaking a Hindi dialect. —**Hin'di** *adj.*

hind-most (hīnd'mōst') *adj.* Also **hind-er-most** (hīn'dər-). Farthest to the rear.

hind-quar-ter (hīnd'kwôr'tər) *n.* **1.** The back portion of a side of meat. **2.** Often **hindquarters.** The rump of a four-footed animal.

hin-drance (hĭn'drəns) *n.* **1.** An act of hindering or a condition of being hindered. **2.** One that hinders. [ME *hindraunce,* harm.]

hind-sight (hīnd'sīt') *n.* An understanding of events after they have occurred.

Hin-du (hĭn'dōo) *n.* **1.** A native of India, esp. northern India. **2.** A believer in Hinduism. —**Hin'du** *adj.*

Hin-du-ism (hĭn'dōo-ĭz'əm) *n.* A syncretistic body of religious, philosophical, and social doctrines native to India.

Hin-du-sta-ni (hĭn'dōo-stä'nē, -stän'ē) *n.* **1.** A native of Hindustan. **2.** A group of Indic dialects that includes Urdu and Hindi. —**Hin-du-sta'ni** *adj.*

hinge (hĭnj) *n.* **1.** A jointed device permitting a part, such as a door, to turn or pivot on a stationary frame. **2.** A similar structure or part. —*v.* **hinged, hing-ing.** **1.** To attach by or equip with a hinge. **2.** To depend; be contingent. [ME.]

hint (hĭnt) *n.* **1.** A slight suggestion or indication; clue. **2.** A barely perceptible amount: *just a hint of color.* —*v.* **1.** To make known by a hint. **2.** To give a hint. [Orig. unknown.] —**hint'er** *n.*

hin-ter-land (hĭn'tər-lănd') *n.* **1.** The area inland from a coast. **2.** A region remote from urban areas. [G.]

hip¹ (hĭp) *n.* **1.** The part of the human body that projects outward over the hipbone between the waist and the thigh. **2.** The hip joint. [< OE *hype.*]

hip² (hĭp) *adj.* **hip-per, hip-pest.** Also **hep** (hĕp). *Slang.* Aware of the most recent developments or trends. **2.** Cognizant; wise. [Orig. unknown.]

hip³ (hĭp) *n.* The berrylike seed case of a rose. [< OE *hēopa.*]

hip-bone (hĭp'bōn') *n.* Either of the large, flat, irregularly shaped bones that form the two halves of the pelvis.

hip joint *n.* The joint between the hipbone and the femur.

hip-pie (hĭp'ē) *n.* Also **hip-py** *pl.* **-pies.** *Informal.* A usu. young person who opposes or rejects the conventional standards and customs. [< HIP².]

Hip-po-crat-ic oath (hĭp'ə-krăt'ĭk) *n.* An oath made by new physicians that sets forth a code of ethical conduct. [< *Hippocrates,* Greek physician of the 5th-4th cent. B.C.]

hip-po-drome (hĭp'ə-drōm') *n.* An arena for spectacles, such as circuses and horse shows. [< Gk. *hippodromos.*]

hip-po-pot-a-mus (hĭp'ə-pŏt'ə-məs) *n., pl.* **-es** or **-mi** (-mī'). A large African river mammal with dark, thick, almost hairless skin, short legs, a broad snout, and a wide mouth. [< LGk. *hippopotamos.*]

hip·ster (hĭp′stər) n. Slang. One who is hip.

hire (hīr) v. **hired, hir·ing.** To engage the services or use of for a fee: hired a new salesman; hire a car for the day. —n. 1. The payment for services or use of something. 2. The act of hiring or the condition of being hired. [< OE hȳrian.] —hir′er n.

hire·ling (hīr′lĭng) n. A mercenary.

hir·sute (hûr′sōōt′, hûr-sōōt′) adj. Hairy. [Lat. hirsutus.] —hir′sute′ness n.

his (hĭz) pron. Used to indicate the one or ones belonging to him: a friend of his. The brown boots are his. He wants to make my car instead of his. If you can't find your hat, take his. [< OE.]

His·pan·ic (hĭ-spăn′ĭk) adj. Of or pertaining to the language, people, and culture of Spain, Portugal, or Latin America.

hiss (hĭs) n. 1. A sharp, sibilant sound similar to a sustained s. 2. An expression of disapproval or contempt conveyed by a hiss. —v. 1. To make a hiss. 2. To show disapproval by hissing. [ME hissen.] —hiss′er n.

his·ta·mine (hĭs′tə-mēn′, -mĭn) n. A white crystalline compound, $C_5H_9N_3$, found in plant and animal tissue, that is used as a vasodilator. [Gk. histos, web + AMINE.] —his′ta·min′ic (-mĭn′ĭk) adj.

his·tol·o·gy (hĭ-stŏl′ə-jē) n. 1. The anatomical study of the microscopic structure of animal and plant tissues. 2. The microscopic structure of tissue. [Gk. histos, web + -LOGY.] —his′to·log′i·cal (hĭs′tə-lŏj′ĭ-kəl) adj. —his′to·log′i·cal·ly adv. —his·tol′o·gist n.

his·to·ri·an (hĭ-stôr′ē-ən, -stōr′-) n. A writer or student of history.

his·tor·ic (hĭ-stôr′ĭk, -stŏr′-) adj. Having importance, esp. in history; famous; renowned.

Usage: Historic and historical are differentiated in usage, although their senses overlap. Historic is used to refer to what is important in history: the historic occasion of the first trip to the moon. Historical is used to refer to whatever existed or took place in the past, whether regarded as important or not: a historical character.

his·tor·i·cal (hĭ-stôr′ĭ-kəl, -stŏr′-) adj. 1. Of or relating to history. 2. Based on or concerned with events in history. 3. Historic. —his·tor′i·cal·ly adv. —his·tor′i·cal·ness n.

his·to·ri·og·ra·phy (hĭ-stôr′ē-ŏg′rə-fē, -stōr′-) n. 1. The principles or methodology of historical study. 2. The writing of history. 3. Historical literature. —his·to′ri·og′ra·pher n. —his·to′ri·o·graph′ic (-ē-ə-grăf′ĭk) or his·to′ri·o·graph′i·cal adj.

his·to·ry (hĭs′tə-rē) n., pl. **-ries.** 1. A narrative of events; chronicle. 2. A chronological record of events. 3. The branch of knowledge that records and analyzes past events. 4. The events of the past. 5. An interesting past: a house with a history. [< Gk. historia.]

his·tri·on·ic (hĭs′trē-ŏn′ĭk) adj. 1. Of or pertaining to actors or acting. 2. Overdramatic or theatrical; affected. [< Lat. histrio, actor.] —his·tri·on′i·cal·ly adv.

his·tri·on·ics (hĭs′trē-ŏn′ĭks) n. (used with a pl. verb.) Exaggerated dramatic or emotional behavior.

hit (hĭt) v. **hit, hit·ting.** 1. To come or cause to come in contact with forcefully; strike. 2. To

affect adversely. 3. To arrive at. 4. To appeal. 5. To propel with a blow. 6. Baseball. To succeed in getting (a base hit). —n. 1. A collision or impact. 2. A successfully executed shot, blow, or throw. 3. A successful or popular venture. 4. Baseball. A base hit. —idi·oms. hit it off. To get along well together. hit the road. To depart or set out. [< ON hitta.] —hit′ter n.

Syns: hit, bash, belt, bop, clip, clobber, clout, knock, paste, slam, slug, smack, smash, smite, sock, strike, swat, wallop, whack, wham v.

hit-and-run (hĭt′n-rŭn′) adj. Of or designating the operator of a vehicle who drives on after striking a pedestrian or another vehicle.

hitch (hĭch) v. 1. To fasten or tie temporarily, as with a loop, hook, or noose. 2. To connect or attach. 3. Informal. To join in marriage. 4. To raise by pulling or jerking. 5. Informal. To secure (a free ride). —n. 1. A knot used as a temporary fastening. 2. A short pull or jerk; tug. 3. A hobble or limp. 4. An impediment or delay. 5. A term of military service. [Orig. unknown.]

hitch·hike (hĭch′hīk′) v. To solicit or get free rides along a road. —hitch′hik′er n.

hith·er (hĭth′ər) adv. To or toward this place: Come hither. —adj. Located on the near side. [< OE hider.]

hith·er·to (hĭth′ər-tōō′) adv. Until this time.

hit-or-miss (hĭt′ər-mĭs′) adj. Haphazard.

Hit·tite (hĭt′īt′) n. 1. A member of an ancient people living in Asia Minor and northern Syria about 2000-1200 B.C. 2. The Indo-European language of the Hittites.

hive (hīv) n. 1. A natural or artificial structure for housing bees, esp. honeybees. 2. A colony of bees living in a hive. 3. A place crowded with busy people. [< OE hȳf.] —hive v.

hives (hīvz) pl.n. (used with a sing. or pl. verb). A skin rash marked by itching welts, usu. caused by an allergic reaction. [Orig. unknown.]

Ho The symbol for the element holmium.

hoa·gie (hō′gē) n. Slang. A hero sandwich. [Orig. unknown.]

hoard (hôrd, hōrd) n. A hidden or secret supply stored up for future use; cache. —v. To accumulate a hoard. [< OE hord.] —hoard′er n.

hoar·frost (hôr′frôst′, -frŏst′, hōr′-) n. Frozen dew that forms a white coating on a surface. [< OE hār.]

hoarse (hôrs, hōrs) adj. **hoars·er, hoars·est.** Low and grating in sound; husky. [< OE hās.] —hoarse′ly adv. —hoarse′ness n.

hoar·y (hôr′ē, hōr′ē) adj. **-i·er, -i·est.** 1. Gray or white with or as if with age. 2. Very old; ancient. [< OE hār.] —hoar′i·ness n.

hoax (hōks) n. Something, as a joke or fraud, that is intended to deceive or trick others. —v. To deceive or cheat by using a hoax. [Perh. < HOCUS-POCUS.] —hoax′er n.

hob (hŏb) n. A hobgoblin, sprite, or elf. —idiom. play (or raise) hob (with). To make mischief or trouble. [< ME Hobbe, nickname for Robin.]

hob·ble (hŏb′əl) v. **-bled, -bling.** 1. To walk or move awkwardly or with difficulty; limp. 2. To fetter; restrain; impede. —n. 1. An awkward, clumsy, or irregular walk or gait.

ă pat ā pay â care ä father ĕ pet ē be ĭ pit ī tie î pier ŏ pot ō toe ô paw, for oi noise ŏŏ took ŏŏ boot ou out th thin th this ŭ cut û urge yŏŏ abuse zh vision ə about, item, edible, gallop, circus

2. A device used to hobble an animal. [< MDu. *hobbelen*.] **—hob′bler** *n.*

hob·by (hŏb′ē) *n., pl.* **-bies.** An activity, as stamp-collecting or gardening, carried on primarily for pleasure; pastime. [< ME *hobi*, small horse.] **—hob′by·ist** *n.*

hob·by·horse (hŏb′ē-hôrs′) *n.* 1. A toy consisting of a long stick with an imitation horse's head on one end. 2. A rocking horse. 3. A favorite topic.

hob·gob·lin (hŏb′gŏb′lĭn) *n.* 1. An ugly, mischievous elf or goblin. 2. A usu. imaginary source of anxiety, fear, or dread.

hob·nail (hŏb′nāl′) *n.* A short nail with a thick head used to protect the soles of shoes or boots. [*hob*, a projection + NAIL.]

hob·nob (hŏb′nŏb′) *v.* **-nobbed, -nob·bing.** To associate familiarly: *hobnobbing with some influential politicians.* [< (drink) *hob* or *nob*, (toast) one another alternately.]

ho·bo (hō′bō) *n., pl.* **-boes** or **-bos.** A tramp. [Orig. unknown.]

hock¹ (hŏk) *n.* The joint of the hind leg of a four-footed animal, as a horse, that corresponds to the human ankle. [< OE *hōh*, heel.]

hock² (hŏk) *Informal.* **—***v.* To pawn. **—***n.* The condition of being pawned. **—idiom. in hock.** In debt. [< Du. *hok*, prison.]

hock·ey (hŏk′ē) *n.* 1. A game played on ice in which two opposing teams of skaters each use curved sticks to try to drive a puck into the opponents' goal. 2. A form of hockey played on foot on a turf field and using a ball rather than a puck. [Orig. unknown.]

hockey
Field hockey

ho·cus-po·cus (hō′kəs-pō′kəs) *n.* 1. Nonsense words or phrases used when performing magic tricks. 2. Deception or trickery. [Poss. < Lat. *hoc est corpus*, this is the body (a phrase used in the Eucharist).]

hod (hŏd) *n.* 1. A V-shaped trough carried over the shoulder for transporting loads, such as bricks or mortar. 2. A coal scuttle. [Perh. < OFr. *hotte*, pannier.]

hodge·podge (hŏj′pŏj′) *n.* A haphazard mixture; jumble. [< HOTCHPOTCH.]

Hodg·kin's disease (hŏj′kĭnz) *n.* A usu. chronic, progressive, ultimately fatal disease of unknown etiology, marked by inflammatory enlargement of the lymph nodes, spleen, liver, and kidneys. [< Thomas *Hodgkin* (1798–1866).]

hoe (hō) *n.* A tool with a flat blade and a long handle, used for weeding, cultivating, and breaking up the soil. [< OFr. *houe*, of Gmc. orig.] **—hoe** *v.* **—ho′er** *n.*

hog (hôg, hŏg) *n.* 1. A pig, esp. a full-grown

domesticated one. 2. A gluttonous, greedy, or filthy person. **—***v.* **hogged, hog·ging.** To take more than one's share of. **—idiom. high off (or on) the hog.** In a lavish or extravagant manner. [< OE *hogg*.] **—hog′gish** *adj.* **—hog′gish·ly** *adv.* **—hog′gish·ness** *n.*

hogs·head (hôgz′hĕd′, hŏgz′-) *n.* 1. A large barrel or cask, esp. one with a capacity ranging from 63 to 140 gallons, or from approx. 238 to 530 liters. 2. A unit of liquid measure in the United States, equal to 63 gallons, or approx. 238 liters.

hog-tie or **hog·tie** (hôg′tī′, hŏg′-) *v.* 1. To tie together the legs of. 2. To impede in movement or action.

hog·wash (hôg′wŏsh′, -wôsh′, hŏg′-) *n.* 1. Garbage or slop fed to hogs. 2. False or nonsensical language.

hoi pol·loi (hoi′ pə-loi′) *n.* The common people. [Gk., the many.]

hoist (hoist) *v.* To raise or haul up. **—***n.* 1. An apparatus for lifting heavy or cumbersome objects. 2. The act of hoisting; lift. [< dial. *hoise.*] **—hoist′er** *n.*

hold¹ (hōld) *v.* **held** (hĕld), **hold·ing.** 1. To have and keep in or as if in one's possession. 2. To support; keep up. 3. To put or maintain in a certain position or relationship; keep. 4. To contain; have or receive as contents. 5. **a.** To own. **b.** To maintain for use; wield. 6. To control; restrain. 7. To retain the attention or interest of. 8. To defend against attack. 9. To stop or delay. 10. To have the position of; occupy. 11. To keep or bind to: *held him to his promise.* 12. To keep in the mind. 13. **a.** To consider; judge. **b.** To assert; affirm. 14. To cause to take place; conduct: *hold a conference.* 15. To adhere closely; keep: *They held to a southwesterly course.* 16. To remain firm or secure. 17. To be valid, correct, or true. **—phrasal verbs. hold out.** 1. To last or endure. 2. To continue to resist. **hold over.** To postpone or delay action. **hold up.** 1. To endure. 2. To rob. **hold with.** To agree with; support. **—***n.* 1. The act or a means of grasping; grip. 2. A controlling influence; power. 3. Something held for support. 4. A prison cell. 5. *Archaic.* A fortified place; stronghold. 6. An instruction to delay, set aside, or halt. **—idioms. hold forth.** To talk at great length. **hold water.** To stand up to critical examination. [< OE *healdan*.] **—hold′er** *n.*

hold² (hōld) *n.* The interior of a ship or airplane in which cargo is stored. [< OE *hulu*, hull.]

hold·ing (hōl′dĭng) *n.* 1. Land rented or leased from another. 2. Often **holdings.** Legally owned property.

holding company *n.* A company that controls a partial or complete interest in other companies.

hold-out (hōld′out′) *n.* One who withholds or delays cooperation or agreement.

hold·o·ver (hōld′ō′vər) *n.* One that remains from an earlier time.

hold·up (hōld′ŭp′) *n.* 1. A delay; interruption. 2. A robbery, esp. an armed robbery.

hole (hōl) *n.* 1. A cavity in a solid. 2. An opening or perforation; gap. 3. A hollow place. 4. An animal's burrow. 5. An ugly, squalid, or depressing place. 6. A fault; defect: *the holes in his argument.* 7. A bad situation; predicament. 8. *Golf.* **a.** The small hollow lined with a cup into which the ball must be hit. **b.** One of the divisions of a golf course, from tee to cup. [< OE *hol.*]

hol·i·day (hŏl′ĭ-dā′) *n.* **1.** A day free from work, esp. a day set aside to celebrate a particular event. **2.** A holy day. **3.** A vacation. [< OE *hālig dæg,* holy day.]

ho·li·ness (hō′lē-nĭs) *n.* **1.** The quality of being holy; sanctity. **2. Holiness.** A title of address used for the pope.

hol·lan·daise sauce (hŏl′ən-dāz′, hŏl′ən-dāz′) *n.* A sauce of butter, egg yolks, and lemon juice or vinegar. [< Fr. *Hollandais,* Dutch.]

hol·ler (hŏl′ər) *v.* To yell or shout. [< OFr. *holà,* stop!] —**hol′ler** *n.*

hol·low (hŏl′ō) *adj.* **-er, -est. 1.** Having a cavity or space within. **2.** Concave: *a hollow basin.* **3.** Sunken; indented: *hollow cheeks.* **4.** Without substance or character; shallow. **5.** Deep, low, and booming; echoing. —*n.* **1.** An indentation or space within something. **2.** A valley. —*v.* To make hollow. [< OE *holh,* hole.] —**hol′low·ness** *n.*

hol·ly (hŏl′ē) *n., pl.* **-lies.** A tree or shrub characteristically having prickly-edged evergreen leaves and bright-red berries. [< OE *holen.*]

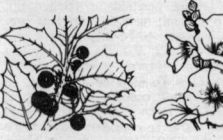

holly   hollyhock

hol·ly·hock (hŏl′ē-hŏk′) *n.* A tall plant with a spike of showy, variously colored flowers. [ME *holihocke,* marsh mallow.]

Hol·ly·wood (hŏl′ē-wŏŏd′) *n.* The U.S. motion-picture industry.

hol·mi·um (hōl′mē-əm) *n. Symbol* **Ho** A relatively soft, malleable, rare-earth element. Atomic number 67; atomic weight 164.930. [< NLat. *Holmia* (Stockholm), Sweden.]

holo- *pref.* Whole: *hologram.* [< Gk. *holos.*]

hol·o·caust (hŏl′ə-kôst′, hō′lə-) *n.* **1.** Great or total destruction, esp. by fire. **2. Holocaust.** The mass murder of the Jews carried out by the Nazi government of Germany. [< Gk. *holokaustos,* burnt whole.]

hol·o·gram (hŏl′ə-grăm′, hō′lə-) *n.* A photographic film or plate that is a record of the light wave interference pattern of an object illuminated by a split coherent beam of light, such as a laser beam.

hol·o·graph (hŏl′ə-grăf′, hō′lə-) *n.* A document written wholly in the handwriting of the person whose signature it bears. —**hol′o·graph′ic** or **hol′o·graph′i·cal** *adj.*

ho·log·ra·phy (hō-lŏg′rə-fē) *n.* The method of producing a three-dimensional image without a lens, using a coherent light beam to illuminate a hologram in order to reconstruct the image.

Hol·stein (hōl′stīn′) *n.* Any of a breed of large black and white dairy cattle. [< *Holstein,* a region in West Germany.]

hol·ster (hōl′stər) *n.* A leather case for carry-

ing tools or a pistol. [Du.] —**hol′stered** *adj.*

ho·ly (hō′lē) *adj.* **-li·er, -li·est. 1.** Of or associated with a divine power or religious beliefs and traditions. **2.** Spiritually pure; saintly. **3.** Worthy of special respect or awe. [< OE *hālig.*]

Holy Communion *n.* The Eucharist.

holy day *n.* A day specified for religious observance.

Holy Ghost *n.* The 3rd person of the Christian Trinity.

Holy Spirit *n.* The Holy Ghost.

holy water *n.* Water blessed by a priest.

hom·age (hŏm′ĭj, ŏm′-) *n.* Special honor or respect shown or expressed publicly. [< Lat. *homo,* man.]

hom·bre (ŏm′brā′, -brē) *n. Western U.S. Slang.* A man; fellow. [Sp.]

hom·burg (hŏm′bûrg′) *n.* A man's felt hat with dented crown and a slightly rolled brim. [< *Homburg,* West Germany.]

home (hōm) *n.* **1.** A place where one lives; residence. **2.** A house. **3.** A dwelling place together with the family that lives there. **4.** A place of origin. **5.** The native habitat, as of a plant or animal. **6.** A goal or place of safety in certain games. **7.** An institution where people are cared for. —*adv.* **1.** At or to one's home. **2.** On target: *The arrow struck home.* **3.** To the very center. —*v.* **homed, hom·ing. 1.** To go or return home. **2.** To be guided to a target automatically, as by means of radio waves. —**idiom. at home.** Comfortable and relaxed. [< OE *hām.*] —**home′less** *adj.*

home base *n.* **1.** *Baseball.* Home plate. **2.** A base of operations; headquarters.

home·bod·y (hōm′bŏd′ē) *n.* One whose interests are in domestic matters.

home·com·ing (hōm′kŭm′ĭng) *n.* **1.** A return home. **2.** In some colleges, an annual celebration for visiting alumni.

home economics *n.* The science and art of home management.

home·land (hōm′lănd′) *n.* One's native land.

home·ly (hōm′lē) *adj.* **-li·er, -li·est. 1.** Characteristic of the home. **2.** Simple or unpretentious; plain: *homely truths.* **3.** Not handsome or good-looking. —**home′li·ness** *n.*

home·made (hōm′mād′) *adj.* **1.** Made or prepared in the home. **2.** Crudely or simply made.

home·mak·er (hōm′mā′kər) *n.* One who manages a household.

homeo- *pref.* Like: *homeostasis.* [< Gk. *homoios.*]

ho·me·op·a·thy (hō′mē-ŏp′ə-thē, hŏm′ē-) *n.* A system of medical treatment based on the use of small quantities of drugs that in massive doses produce symptoms similar to those of the disease under treatment. —**ho′me·o·path** *n.* —**ho′me·o·path′ic** *adj.*

ho·me·o·sta·sis (hō′mē-ō-stā′sĭs, hŏm′ē-) *n.* A state of physiological equilibrium produced by a balance of functions and of chemical composition within an organism. —**ho′me·o·stat′ic** (-stăt′ĭk) *adj.*

home plate *n. Baseball.* The base at which a batter stands to hit the ball and which a runner must cross safely to score a run.

home rule *n.* Self-government with respect to

ă pat ā pay â care ä father ĕ pet ē be ĭ pit ī tie î pier ŏ pot ō toe ô paw, for oi noise ŏŏ took
ŏŏ boot ou out th thin th this ŭ cut û urge yŏŏ abuse zh vision ə about, item, edible, gallop, circus

the internal affairs of a political unit within a larger unit.

home run *n.* Also **hom·er** (hō'mər). *Baseball.* A hit that allows the batter to touch all the bases and score a run.

home·sick (hōm'sĭk') *adj.* Longing for home. —**home'sick·ness** *n.*

home·spun (hōm'spŭn') *adj.* 1. Spun or woven in the home. 2. Made of a homespun fabric. 3. Simple and homely. —*n.* A plain coarse woolen cloth made of homespun yarn.

home·stead (hōm'stĕd') *n.* A house, esp. a farmhouse, with adjoining buildings and land. —*v.* To claim and settle farmland. —**home'stead·er** *n.*

home·stretch (hōm'strĕch') *n.* 1. The part of a racetrack from the last turn to the finish line. 2. The final stage of an undertaking.

home·ward (hōm'wərd) *adv.* Also **home·wards** (-wərdz). Toward home. —**home'ward** *adj.*

home·work (hōm'wûrk') *n.* 1. Work, such as schoolwork, done at home. 2. Work of a preparatory nature.

home·y (hō'mē) *adj.* **-i·er, -i·est.** Also **hom·y.** Having a feeling of home; homelike. —**hom'ey·ness** *n.*

hom·i·cide (hŏm'ĭ-sīd', hō'mĭ-) *n.* 1. The killing of one person by another. 2. A person who kills another. [< Lat. *homicidium.*] —**hom'i·cid'al** *adj.*

hom·i·let·ics (hŏm'ə-lĕt'ĭks) *n.* (*used with a sing. verb*). The art of preaching. [< Gk. *homilētos,* conversation.] —**hom'i·let'ic** *adj.*

hom·i·ly (hŏm'ə-lē) *n., pl.* **-lies.** 1. A sermon. 2. A tedious moralizing lecture. [< Gk. *homilia,* discourse.]

homing pigeon *n.* A pigeon trained to return to its home roost.

hom·i·ny (hŏm'ə-nē) *n.* Hulled and dried kernels of corn. [Perh. of Algonquian orig.]

homo- *pref.* Same: *homophone.* [< Gk. *homos.*]

ho·mo·ge·ne·ous (hō'mə-jē'nē-əs, -jēn'yəs, hōm'ə-) *adj.* 1. Of the same or similar nature or kind. 2. Uniform throughout in composition. —**ho'mo·ge·ne'i·ty** (-jə-nē'ĭ-tē) —**ho'mo·ge'ne·ous·ly** *adv.* —**ho'mo·ge'ne·ous·ness** *n.*

ho·mog·e·nize (hō-mŏj'ə-nīz', hə-) *v.* **-nized, -niz·ing.** 1. To make homogeneous. 2. a. To reduce to particles and distribute evenly throughout. b. To make (milk) uniform in consistency by breaking up the fat globules into particles of extremely small size. [< HOMOGENEOUS.] —**ho·mog'e·ni·za'tion** *n.* —**ho·mog'e·niz'er** *n.*

hom·o·graph (hŏm'ə-grăf', hō'mə-) *n.* One of two or more words that are spelled alike but differ in origin and meaning.

ho·mol·o·gous (hō-mŏl'ə-gəs, hə-) *adj.* Corresponding or similar in position, value, structure, or function. [Gk. *homologos,* agreeing.] —**hom'o·logue'** or **hom'o·log** (hŏm'ə-lôg', hō'mə-) *n.* —**ho·mol'o·gy** *n.*

hom·o·nym (hŏm'ə-nĭm, hō'mə-) *n.* One of two or more words that have the same sound and often the same spelling but differ in meaning. [< Gk. *homōnumon.*]

hom·o·phone (hŏm'ə-fōn', hō'mə-) *n.* One of two or more words that have the same sound but differ in spelling, origin, and meaning, as English *sum* and *some.*

Ho·mo sa·pi·ens (hō'mō sā'pē-ĕnz', -ənz) *n.* Modern man. [Lat. *homo,* man + Lat. *sapiens,* wise.]

ho·mo·sex·u·al (hō'mə-sĕk'shōō-əl, -mō-,

hōm'ə-) *adj.* Of or relating to sexual desire for a member of the same sex. —*n.* A homosexual person. —**ho'mo·sex'u·al'i·ty** *n.*

hom·y (hō'mē) *adj.* Var. of **homey.**

hone (hōn) *n.* A fine-grained whetstone for sharpening a tool. —*v.* **honed, hon·ing.** To sharpen on or as if on a hone. [< OE *hān.*]

hon·est (ŏn'ĭst) *adj.* 1. Marked by truthfulness and integrity; upright. 2. Not deceptive or fraudulent; genuine. 3. True; not false: *honest reporting.* 4. Frank and straightforward; sincere. 5. Without disguise or pretense: *honest pleasure.* [< Lat. *honos,* honor.] —**hon'est·ly** *adv.* —**hon'es·ty** *n.*

hon·ey (hŭn'ē) *n., pl.* **-eys.** 1. A sweet, thick, syrupy substance made by bees from the nectar of flowers. 2. Sweetness; pleasantness. 3. *Informal.* Darling. [< OE *hunig.*]

hon·ey·bee (hŭn'ē-bē') *n.* Any of several social bees that produce honey.

hon·ey·comb (hŭn'ē-kōm') *n.* A structure of hexagonal, thin-walled cells constructed from beeswax by honeybees to hold honey and eggs. —*v.* To fill with or as if with holes.

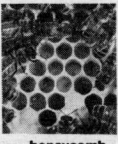
honeycomb

honeysuckle

hon·ey·dew (hŭn'ē-dōō', -dyōō') *n.* A sweet, sticky substance excreted by various insects, esp. aphids.

honeydew melon *n.* A melon with a smooth, whitish rind and green flesh.

hon·eyed (hŭn'ēd) *adj.* Sweet; sugary: *honeyed words.*

hon·ey·moon (hŭn'ē-mōōn') *n.* 1. A vacation taken by a newly married couple. 2. The early harmonious period of a relationship. —**hon'ey·moon'** *v.*

hon·ey·suck·le (hŭn'ē-sŭk'əl) *n.* A shrub or vine with tubular, often fragrant yellowish, white, or pink flowers.

honk (hŏngk, hôngk) *n.* The harsh cry of a goose or a similar harsh resonant sound. [Imit.] —**honk** *v.* —**honk'er** *n.*

hon·ky-tonk (hŏng'kē-tôngk', hông'kē-tŏngk') *n.* A cheap, noisy saloon or dance hall. [Orig. unknown.]

hon·or (ŏn'ər) *n.* 1. Esteem; respect. 2. a. Glory; distinction. b. A token or gesture of respect or distinction: *the place of honor.* 3. Great privilege. 4. Honor. A title of address often accorded to mayors and judges. 5. Personal integrity maintained without legal or other obligation. 6. **honors.** a. Special recognition for unusual academic achievement. b. A program of individual advanced study for exceptional students. —*v.* 1. a. To esteem. b. To show respect for. 2. To confer distinction upon. 3. To accept or pay as valid: *honor a check.* [< Lat.] —**hon'or·er** *n.*
Syns: *honor, dignity, prestige, reputation, repute, status n.*

hon·or·a·ble (ŏn'ər-ə-bəl) *adj.* 1. Worthy of honor and respect. 2. Bringing distinction or honor. 3. Possessing integrity. 4. Illustrious. 5. **Honorable.** Used as a title for a person of high rank. —**hon'ora·ble·ness** n. —**hon'ora· bly** adv.

hon·o·rar·i·um (ŏn'ə-râr'ē-əm) n., pl. **-ums** or **-i·a** (-ē-ə). A payment made to a professional person for services for which fees are not legally or traditionally required. [< Lat. *honorarius*, honorary.]

hon·or·ary (ŏn'ə-rĕr'ē) adj. Held or given as an honor, without fulfillment of the usual requirements. [Lat. *honorarius.*]

hon·or·if·ic (ŏn'ə-rĭf'ĭk) adj. Conferring or showing respect or honor.

hon·our (ŏn'ər) n. & v. Chiefly Brit. Var. of honor.

hood¹ (hŏŏd) n. **1.** A loose, pliable covering for the head and neck. **2.** Something resembling a hood in shape or function. **3.** The hinged metal covering of an automobile engine. [< OE *hōd.*] —**hood'ed** adj.

hood² (hŏŏd) n. Slang. A hoodlum; thug. —**hood** suff. **1.** State, condition, or quality: *manhood.* **2.** A group of a specified nature: *neighborhood.* [< OE *-hād.*]

hood·lum (hŏŏd'ləm, hŏŏd'-) n. **1.** A gangster or thug. **2.** A wild, destructive youth. [Orig. unknown.]

hoo·doo (hŏŏ'dŏŏ) n. **1.** Voodoo. **2.** a. Bad luck. b. One that brings bad luck. [Of African orig.] —**hoo'doo** v.

hood·wink (hŏŏd'wĭngk') v. To deceive; cheat.

hoo·ey (hŏŏ'ē) n. Slang. Nonsense. [Orig. unknown.]

hoof (hŏŏf, hŏŏf) n., pl. **hooves** (hŏŏvz, hŏŏvz) or **hoofs.** **1.** The horny sheath covering the foot of some mammals. **2.** A hoofed foot, esp. of a horse. —v. Slang. To dance. [< OE *hōf.*] —**hoofed** adj.

hook (hŏŏk) n. **1.** A curved or sharply bent device, often of metal, used to catch, pull, or hold something. **2.** Something that resembles a hook. **3.** Sports. A thrown or struck ball that moves in a curve. **4.** Boxing. A short, swinging blow delivered with a bent arm. —v. **1.** To get hold of or catch with or as with a hook. **2.** Slang. To become addicted. **3.** Slang. To steal; snatch. **4.** To fasten by means of a hook and eye. —**phrasal verb. hook up. 1.** To assemble and install. **2.** To connect to a source of power. —**idioms. by hook or (by) crook.** By any means possible. **off the hook.** Out of difficulty. [< OE *hōc.*]

hoo·kah (hŏŏk'ə) n. A smoking pipe in which the smoke is cooled by passing through a long tube submerged in a container of water. [< Ar. *ḥuqqah*, the hookah's water urn.]

hook and eye n. A fastener consisting of a small hook with a corresponding loop.

hook·er (hŏŏk'ər) n. Slang. A prostitute.

hook·up (hŏŏk'ŭp') n. An arrangement or connection of parts that functions as a unit.

hook·worm (hŏŏk'wûrm') n. A parasitic worm with hooked mouth parts that fasten to the intestinal walls of a host.

hoo·li·gan (hŏŏ'lĭ-gən) n. Informal. A ruffian; hoodlum. [Orig. unknown.]

hoop (hŏŏp, hŏŏp) n. **1.** A circular band used esp. to bind together the staves of a cask or barrel. **2.** Something that resembles a hoop. **3.** A circular support for a hoop skirt. **4.** Informal. The basket in basketball. [ME *hop.*]

hoop·la (hŏŏp'lä', hŏŏp'-) n. Slang. **1.** Great commotion or fuss. **2.** Deceptive or ostentatious publicity. [Fr. *houp-là*, an interjection.]

hoop skirt n. A long, full skirt worn over a framework of hoops.

hoop skirt

hoo·ray (hŏŏ-rā') interj. Var. of hurrah.

hoose·gow (hŏŏs'gou') n. Slang. A jail. [< Sp. *juzgado.*]

hoot (hŏŏt) v. **1.** To utter the characteristic cry of an owl. **2.** To make a loud, derisive, or contemptuous cry. **3.** To drive off with jeering cries. [ME *houten.*] —**hoot** n.

hoo·te·nan·ny (hŏŏt'n-ăn'ē) n., pl. **-nies.** Also **hoot·nan·ny** (hŏŏt'năn'ē). An informal performance by folk singers. [Orig. unknown.]

hooves (hŏŏvz, hŏŏvz) n. A pl. of hoof.

hop¹ (hŏp) v. **hopped, hop·ping. 1.** To move with a short skip or leap. **2.** To jump on one foot. **3.** To jump aboard. —n. **1.** A motion made by or as if by hopping. **2.** Informal. A dance. **3.** A trip, esp. by air. [< OE *hoppian.*]

hop² (hŏp) n. **1.** A twining vine with lobed leaves and green, conelike flowers. **2.** hops. The dried flowers of this plant used as a flavoring in brewing beer. —v. **hopped, hop·ping.** To flavor with hops. —**phrasal verb. hop up.** Slang. **1.** To increase the power or energy of. **2.** To stimulate with or as if with a narcotic. [< MDu. *hoppe.*]

hope (hōp) v. **hoped, hop·ing.** To wish for (something) with expectation. —n. **1.** A desire accompanied by some confident expectation. **2.** Something that is desired. **3.** One that is a source of or reason for hope. [< OE *hopian.*] —**hope'ful** adj. & n. —**hope'ful·ly** adv. —**hope'ful·ness** n. —**hope'less** adj. —**hope'less·ly** adv. —**hope'less·ness** n.

Ho·pi (hō'pē) n., pl. **-pi** or **-pis. 1.** A tribe of Indians now inhabiting a reservation in northeastern Arizona. **b.** A member of the Hopi. **2.** The Uto-Aztecan language of the Hopi.

hop·per (hŏp'ər) n. **1.** One that hops. **2.** A container in which materials are held ready for dispensing.

hop·scotch (hŏp'skŏch') n. A children's game in which players toss a small object into the numbered spaces of a pattern of rectangles outlined on the ground and then hop or jump through the spaces to retrieve the object.

horde (hôrd, hōrd) n. A throng; swarm. [< Turk. *ordū*, camp.]

hore·hound (hôr'hound', hōr'-) n. A downy, aromatic plant that yields bitter extract used as flavoring and as a cough remedy. [< OE *hārhūne.*]

ho·ri·zon (hə-rī′zən) n. **1.** The apparent line along which the earth and sky seem to meet. **2.** The range of a person's knowledge, experience, or interest. [< Gk. *horizein*, to limit.]

hor·i·zon·tal (hôr′ĭ-zŏn′tl, hŏr′-) adj. **1.** Of, relating to, or near the horizon. **2.** Parallel to or in the plane of the horizon. —n. Something horizontal. [< HORIZON.] —**hor′i·zon′tal·ly** adv.

hor·mone (hôr′mōn′) n. A substance produced by living cells that is transported, as by blood or sap, and stimulates other cells by means of chemical action. [< Gk. *horman*, to urge on.] —**hor·mon′al** or **hor·mon′ic** (-mŏn′-ĭk) adj.

horn (hôrn) n. **1.** One of the hard, usu. permanent structures projecting from the head of certain mammals, such as cattle or antelopes. **2.** A structure, object, or growth similar to or suggestive of a horn. **3.** The hard, smooth material that forms the outer covering of an animal horn. **4.** A container made from a horn: *a powder horn*. **5.** *Mus.* **a.** A wind instrument made of brass, esp. a French horn. **b.** *Informal.* A trumpet. **6.** A usu. electrical device that produces a sound similar to that of a horn: *a fog horn*. [< OE.] —**horned** adj. —**horn′less** adj. —**horn′y** adj.

horned toad n. A lizard with hornlike projections on the head and a spiny body.

hor·net (hôr′nĭt) n. Any of various large social wasps. [< OE *hyrnet*.]

horn of plenty n. A cornucopia.

horn·pipe (hôrn′pīp′) n. A lively British folk dance.

ho·rol·o·gy (hə-rŏl′ə-jē) n. **1.** The science of measuring time. **2.** The art of making timepieces. [Gk. *hōra*, hour + -LOGY.] —**hor′o·log′i·cal** adj. —**ho·rol′o·gist** n.

hor·o·scope (hôr′ə-skōp′, hŏr′-) n. A diagram that shows the position of the planets in relation to the twelve signs of the zodiac at a particular time, used by astrologers to forecast a person's future. [< Gk. *hōro·skopos*.]

hor·ren·dous (hô-rĕn′dəs, hŏ-) adj. Hideous; dreadful. [< Lat. *horrēre*, to tremble.] —**hor·ren′dous·ly** adv.

hor·ri·ble (hôr′ə-bəl, hŏr′-) adj. **1.** Arousing horror; dreadful. **2.** Very unpleasant; disagreeable. [< Lat. *horribilis*.] —**hor′ri·ble·ness** n. —**hor′ri·bly** adv.

hor·rid (hôr′ĭd, hŏr′-) adj. **1.** Causing horror; dreadful. **2.** Extremely disagreeable; offensive. [Lat. *horridus*.] —**hor′rid·ly** adv. —**hor′rid·ness** n.

hor·ri·fy (hôr′ə-fī′, hŏr′-) v. **-fied, -fy·ing. 1.** To cause to feel horror. **2.** To cause unpleasant surprise; shock. [Lat. *horrificare*.]

hor·ror (hôr′ər, hŏr′-) n. **1.** An intense feeling of repugnance and fear. **2.** Intense dislike; abhorrence. **3.** One that causes horror. [< Lat.]

hors de com·bat (ôr′ də kôN-bä′) adj. & adv. Disabled. [Fr.]

hors d'oeuvre (ôr dûrv′) n., pl. **hors d'oeuvres** (ôr dûrvz′) or **hors d'oeuvre.** An appetizer served before a meal. [Fr.]

horse (hôrs) n. **1.** A large four-legged hoofed mammal, domesticated for riding and for drawing or carrying loads. **2.** A supporting frame, usu. with four legs. **3.** Often **horses.** Horsepower. —**idioms. hold (one's) horses.** To restrain oneself. **the horse's mouth.** The original source. [< OE *hors*.]

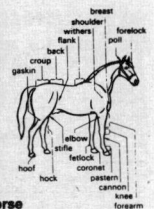

horse
Left: Arabian horse
Right: Anatomical diagram

horse·back (hôrs′băk′) adv. On the back of a horse.

horse·car (hôrs′kär′) n. **1.** A streetcar drawn by horses. **2.** A car for transporting horses.

horse chestnut n. **1.** A tree with erect clusters of white flowers and brown, shiny inedible nuts. **2.** The nut of the horse chestnut.

horse·flesh (hôrs′flĕsh′) n. Horses for riding or racing.

horse·fly (hôrs′flī′) n. A large fly, the female of which sucks the blood of various mammals.

horse·hair (hôrs′hâr′) n. **1.** The hair of a horse, esp. from the mane or tail. **2.** Cloth made of horsehair.

horse·hide (hôrs′hīd′) n. **1.** The hide of a horse. **2.** Leather made from the hide of a horse.

horse·man (hôrs′mən) n. One who rides a horse or is skilled at horsemanship.

horse·man·ship (hôrs′mən-shĭp′) n. The art of horseback riding.

horse·play (hôrs′plā′) n. Rowdy, rough play.

horse·pow·er (hôrs′pou′ər) n. A unit of power equal to 745.7 watts, or 33,000 foot-pounds per minute.

horse·rad·ish (hôrs′răd′ĭsh) n. **1.** A coarse plant with a thick, whitish, pungent root. **2.** The grated root of the horseradish, often used as a condiment.

horse sense n. *Informal.* Common sense.

horse·shoe (hôrs′shōō′, hôrsh′-) n. **1.** A narrow U-shaped iron plate fitted and nailed to a horse's hoof. **2. horseshoes** *(used with a sing. verb).* A game in which players try to toss horseshoes so that they encircle a stake.

horseshoe crab n. A marine arthropod with a large, rounded body and a stiff, pointed tail.

horse·tail (hôrs′tāl′) n. A nonflowering plant with a jointed, hollow stem and narrow leaves.

horse·whip (hôrs′hwĭp′, -wĭp′) n. A whip used to control a horse. —**horse′whip′** v.

hors·y (hôr′sē) adj. **-i·er, -i·est.** Also **hors·ey. 1.** Of, pertaining to, or characteristic of a horse. **2.** Devoted to horses or horsemanship.

hor·ta·to·ry (hôr′tə-tôr′ē, -tōr′ē) adj. Marked by exhortation. [Lat. *hortari*, to urge.]

hor·ti·cul·ture (hôr′tĭ-kŭl′chər) n. The science or art of cultivating fruits, vegetables, flowers, and plants. [Lat. *hortus*, garden + (AGRI)CULTURE.] —**hor′ti·cul′tural** adj. —**hor′ti·cul′tur·ist** n.

ho·san·na (hō-zăn′ə) *interj.* Used to express

praise or adoration to God. [< Heb. *hosh'ă-hanna,* save us.]

hose (hōz) *n.* **1.** *pl.* **hose.** Stockings or socks. **2.** *pl.* **hos·es.** A flexible tube for conveying fluids. —*v.* **hosed, hos·ing.** To water, drench, or wash with a hose. [< OE.]

Ho·se·a (hō-zē'ə, -zā'ə) *n.* See table at **Bible.**

ho·sier·y (hō'zhə-rē) *n.* Stockings and socks. [< OE *hose,* a stocking.]

hos·pice (hŏs'pĭs) *n.* A shelter or lodging for travelers. [< Lat. *hospitium,* hospitality.]

hos·pi·ta·ble (hŏs'pĭ-tə-bəl, hŏ-spĭt'ə-bəl) *adj.* **1.** Cordial and generous to guests. **2.** Open-minded; receptive. [< Lat. *hospes,* host.] —**hos'pi·ta·bly** *adv.*

hos·pi·tal (hŏs'pĭ-təl, -pĭt'l) *n.* An institution that provides medical or surgical care for the sick and injured. [< Lat. *hospitalis,* of a guest.]

hos·pi·tal·i·ty (hŏs'pĭ-tăl'ĭ-tē) *n., pl.* **-ties.** Cordial and generous reception of guests.

hos·pi·tal·ize (hŏs'pĭ-tə-līz') *v.* **-ized, -iz·ing.** To put into a hospital for treatment. —**hos'pi·tal·i·za'tion** *n.*

host¹ (hōst) *n.* **1.** One who entertains guests. **2.** *Biol.* An organism on or in which a parasite lives. —*v.* To serve as host for. [< Lat. *hospes.*]

host² (hōst) *n.* **1.** An army. **2.** A great number. [< Lat. *hostis,* enemy.]

host³ (hōst) *n.* Also **Host.** The consecrated bread or wafer of the Eucharist. [< Lat. *hostia,* sacrifice.]

hos·tage (hŏs'tĭj) *n.* A person held as a pledge that certain terms will be fulfilled. [< Lat. *hospes,* guest, host.]

hos·tel (hŏs'təl) *n.* **1.** A supervised lodging for youthful travelers. **2.** An inn. [< Med. Lat. *hospitale,* inn.] —**hos'tel·er** *n.*

hos·tel·ry (hŏs'təl-rē) *n., pl.* **-ries.** An inn; hotel.

host·ess (hōs'tĭs) *n.* A woman who entertains guests.

hos·tile (hŏs'təl, -tīl') *adj.* **1.** Of or pertaining to an enemy. **2.** Feeling or showing enmity; antagonistic. [< Lat. *hostis,* enemy.] —**hos'tile·ly** *adv.*

hos·til·i·ty (hŏ-stĭl'ĭ-tē) *n., pl.* **-ties. 1.** Antagonism; enmity. **2. a.** A hostile act. **b. hostilities.** Open warfare.

hos·tler (hŏs'lər) *n.* One who takes charge of horses, as at an inn. [< Med. Lat. *hospitale,* inn.]

hot (hŏt) *adj.* **hot·ter, hot·test. 1. a.** Possessing great heat. **b.** Yielding much heat. **c.** At a high temperature. **2.** Warmer than is normal or desirable. **3.** Pungent; spicy. **4. a.** Charged or as if charged with electricity. **b.** Radioactive. **5.** Angry: *a hot dispute.* **6.** *Slang.* Recently stolen: *hot goods.* **7.** *Informal.* **a.** New; fresh: *hot off the press.* **b.** Currently popular: *a hot sales item.* **8.** *Slang.* **a.** Performing with unusual skill. **b.** Lucky. —**idioms. hot under the collar.** *Informal.* Angry. **in hot water.** *Informal.* In trouble. [< OE *hāt.*]

Syns: *hot, blistering, fiery, red-hot, sultry, torrid* *adj.*

hot air *n. Slang.* Empty, often boastful talk.

hot·bed (hŏt'bĕd') *n.* **1.** A glass-covered, heated bed of soil used for the germination of seeds or for protecting tender plants. **2.** An

environment conducive to rapid growth and development.

hot-blood·ed (hŏt'blŭd'ĭd) *adj.* Easily excited or aroused. —**hot'blood'ed·ly** *adv.* —**hot'blood'ed·ness** *n.*

hot·box (hŏt'bŏks') *n.* An overheated axle or journal box, as on a railway car, caused by excessive friction.

hot cake *n.* A pancake. —**idiom. sell** (or **go**) **like hot cakes.** To be in great demand.

hot dog *n.* A frankfurter, usu. served in a long soft roll.

ho·tel (hō-tĕl') *n.* A public house that provides lodging and usu. meals and other services. [< Med. Lat. *hospitale.*]

hot·foot (hŏt'fŏŏt') *v.* To go in haste.

hot·head·ed (hŏt'hĕd'ĭd) *adj.* **1.** Easily angered or excited. **2.** Impetuous; rash. —**hot'head'** *n.* —**hot'head'ed·ly** *adv.* —**hot'head'ed·ness** *n.*

hot·house (hŏt'hous') *n.* A greenhouse.

hot line *n.* A communications line for use in a crisis or emergency.

hot plate *n.* A portable device for cooking food.

hot rod *n.* An automobile rebuilt or modified for increased speed and acceleration. —**hot rod·der** *n.*

hot seat *n. Slang.* **1.** The electric chair. **2.** A position of stress or embarrassment.

hot·shot (hŏt'shŏt') *n. Slang.* An ostentatiously skillful person.

hound (hound) *n.* **1.** A dog of any of various breeds used for hunting, usu. having drooping ears. **2.** A scoundrel. **3.** An enthusiast or addict. —*v.* **1.** To pursue relentlessly. **2.** To nag. [< OE *hund.*]

hour (our) *n.* **1.** One of the 24 parts of a day. **2.** The time of day. **3. a.** A customary time: *the dinner hour.* **b. hours.** A specified time: *bank hours.* [< Gk. *hōra.*]

hour·glass (our'glăs') *n.* An instrument that measures time by the trickling of sand from an upper to a lower glass compartment.

hou·ri (hŏŏr'ē, hŏŏr'ē) *n., pl.* **-ris.** One of the beautiful virgins of the Koranic paradise. [< Ar. *haurā'.*]

hour·ly (our'lē) *adj.* **1. a.** Every hour. **b.** Frequent; continual. **2.** By the hour as a unit: *hourly pay.* —*adv.* **1.** At or during every hour. **2.** Frequently; continually.

house (hous) *n., pl.* **hous·es** (hou'zĭz). **1. a.** A building used as a dwelling by one or more families. **b.** A household. **2. a.** A building used for a particular purpose: *a movie house.* **b.** Audience or patrons: *a full house.* **3. House.** A noble family. **4.** A commercial firm: *a brokerage house.* **5.** A legislative assembly. —*v.* (houz) **housed, hous·ing. 1.** To provide living or working quarters for. **2.** To shelter, keep, or store. **3.** To contain; harbor. —**idioms. clean house.** To eliminate or discard undesirable people, items, or situations. **on the house.** Free. [< OE *hūs.*]

house·boat (hous'bōt') *n.* A barge equipped for use as a home or cruiser.

house·break·ing (hous'brā'kĭng) *n.* The unlawful breaking into of another's house for the purpose of committing a felony. —**house'break'er** *n.*

house·bro·ken (hous'brō'kən) *adj.* **1.** Trained

in habits of excretion appropriate for a house pet. **2.** Compliant.

house-fly (hous'flī') *n.* A common fly that frequents human dwellings and is a transmitter of a wide variety of diseases.

house-hold (hous'hōld') *n.* The members of a family and others who live under the same roof. [ME.] —**house'hold'er** *n.*

house-keep-er (hous'kē'pər) *n.* One hired to perform domestic tasks in a household. —**house'keep'ing** *n.*

house-moth-er (hous'mŭth'ər) *n.* A woman employed as supervisor of a residence for young people.

house organ *n.* A periodical published by an organization for its employees or clients.

house-wares (hous'wârz') *pl.n.* (*used with a sing. or pl. verb*). Articles for use in the home.

house-warm-ing (hous'wôr'mĭng) *n.* A party to celebrate the occupancy of a new home.

house-wife (hous'wīf') *n.* **1.** A married woman who runs a household. **2.** (hŭz'ĭf). A small container for sewing equipment. —**house'wife'li-ness** *n.* —**house'wife'ly** *adj.* —**house'wif'ery** *n.*

house-work (hous'wûrk') *n.* The tasks of housekeeping, esp. cleaning.

hous-ing (hou'zĭng) *n.* **1.** Residences or dwelling places for people. **2.** A dwelling. **3.** Something that covers, protects, or supports, esp. something that protects a mechanical part.

hove (hōv) *v. Naut. p.t. & p.p.* of **heave.**

hov-el (hŭv'əl, hŏv'-) *n.* A small, miserable dwelling. [ME. hut.]

hov-er (hŭv'ər, hŏv'-) *v.* **1.** To remain floating or suspended in the air. **2.** To linger in a place. **3.** To be in a state of uncertainty; waver. [ME hoveren.] —**hov'er-er** *n.* —**hov'er-ing-ly** *adv.*

how (hou) *adv.* **1.** In what manner or way; by what means. **2.** In what state or condition. **3.** To what extent, amount, or degree. **4.** For what reason or purpose; why. **5.** With what meaning: *How should I interpret this?* —*conj.* **1.** In what way or manner: *forgot how it was accomplished.* **2.** In whatever way or manner: *did it how he liked.* —**idioms. how about.** What do you feel or think about: *How about a cup of tea?* **how come.** *Informal.* For what reason; why. [< OE hū.]

how-be-it (hou-bē'ĭt) *Archaic.* —*adv.* Nevertheless. —*conj.* Although.

how-dah (hou'də) *n.* A covered seat on the back of an elephant or camel. [< Ar. *haudaj.*]

how-ev-er (hou-ev'ər) *adv.* **1.** By whatever manner or means. **2.** To whatever degree or extent. —*conj.* Nevertheless; yet.

Usage: Although some grammarians have ruled to the contrary, the use of *however* as the first word of a sentence is now generally considered to be acceptable.

how-it-zer (hou'ĭt-sər) *n.* A cannon that delivers shells at a high trajectory. [< Czech *houfnice.*]

howl (houl) *v.* **1.** To utter a long, mournful sound. **2.** To cry or wail loudly. **3.** *Slang.* To laugh heartily. [< ME *houlen.*] —**howl** *n.*

howl-er (hou'lər) *n.* **1.** One that howls. **2.** An amusing or stupid blunder.

how-so-ev-er (hou'sō-ev'ər) *adv.* **1.** To whatever degree or extent. **2.** By whatever means.

hoy-den (hoid'n) *n.* A high-spirited, often boisterous woman. [Prob. MDu. *heiden*, heathen.]

hub (hŭb) *n.* **1.** The center portion of a wheel, fan, or propeller. **2.** A center of activity or interest. [Prob. < *hob*, projection.]

hub-bub (hŭb'ŭb') *n.* **1.** A confused din; uproar. **2.** Confusion; tumult. [Perh. of Ir. orig.]

hub-cap (hŭb'kăp') *n.* A round metal covering clamped over the hub of an automobile wheel.

hu-bris (hyōō'brĭs) *n.* Excessive pride; arrogance. [Gk., violence.]

huck-le-ber-ry (hŭk'əl-bĕr'ē) *n.* **1.** A glossy, blackish, edible berry related to the blueberry. **2.** A shrub bearing huckleberries. [Prob. < obs. *hurtleberry*, a kind of berry.]

huck-ster (hŭk'stər) *n.* **1.** A peddler; hawker. **2.** *Slang.* A writer of advertising copy. [ME *hukster.*]

hud-dle (hŭd'l) *n.* **1.** A densely packed group. **2.** *Football.* A brief gathering of a team's players behind the line of scrimmage to prepare for the next play. **3.** A small private conference. —*v.* **-dled, -dling. 1.** To crowd together. **2.** To curl up; crouch. **3.** To gather together for consultation. [Orig. unknown.]

hue (hyōō) *n.* **1.** The property of color that is perceived and measured on a scale ranging from red through yellow, green, and blue to violet. **2.** A particular gradation of color; tint; shade. **3.** Color. [< OE *hīw.*]

hue and cry *n.* A public clamor, as of protest or demand. [ME *heu*, a loud cry + CRY.]

huff (hŭf) *n.* A fit of anger or annoyance; pique. —*v.* To puff; blow. [Imit.] —**huff'i-ly** *adv.* —**huff'i-ness** *n.* —**huff'y** *adj.*

hug (hŭg) *v.* **hugged, hug-ging. 1.** To clasp or hold closely; embrace. **2.** To hold or keep close to. **3.** To cherish. —*n.* An affectionate embrace. [Prob. of Scand. orig.] —**hug'ger** *n.*

huge (hyōōj) *adj.* **hug-er, hug-est.** Exceedingly large; tremendous. [< OFr. *ahuge.*] —**huge'ly** *adv.* —**huge'ness** *n.*

Hu-gue-not (hyōō'gə-nŏt') *n.* A French Protestant of the 16th and 17th cent.

huh (hŭ) *interj.* Used to express interrogation, surprise, or contempt.

hu-la (hōō'lə) *n.* A Polynesian dance characterized by rhythmic movements of the hips, arms, and hands. [Hawaiian.]

hulk (hŭlk) *n.* **1.** A heavy, unwieldy ship. **2.** An old, unseaworthy ship. **3.** One that is bulky, clumsy, or awkward. —*v.* To appear exaggeratedly large; loom. [< OE *hulc.*]

hulk-ing (hŭl'kĭng) *adj.* Unwieldy or bulky; massive.

hull (hŭl) *n.* **1.** The dry or leafy outer covering of certain fruits, seeds, or nuts. **2.** The frame or body of a ship. **3.** The outer casing of a rocket, guided missile, or spaceship. —*v.* To remove the hull from. [< OE *hulu.*]

hul-la-ba-loo (hŭl'ə-bə-lōō') *n.* Great noise or excitement; uproar. [Orig. unknown.]

hum (hŭm) *v.* **hummed, hum-ming. 1.** To make a continuous low droning sound. **2.** To be in a state of busy activity. **3.** To sing without opening the lips. —*n.* **1.** The act or sound of humming. [ME *hummen.*] —**hum'mer** *n.*

hu-man (hyōō'mən) *adj.* **1.** Of, relating to, or characteristic of human beings. **2.** Made up of people: *formed a human bridge.* —*n.* A person. [< Lat. *humanus.*] —**hu'man-ness** *n.*

hu-mane (hyōō-mān') *adj.* **1.** Characterized by kindness or compassion. **2.** Marked by an emphasis on humanistic values and concerns.

[< Lat. *humanus*, human.] —hu·mane'ly *adv.* —hu·mane'ness *n.*

hu·man·ism (hyoō'mə-nĭz'əm) *n.* 1. A doctrine or attitude concerned primarily with human beings and their values, capacities, and achievements. 2. Often **Humanism.** A Renaissance movement that emphasized secular concerns as a result of the study of classical art and civilization. —hu'man·ist *n.* —hu'man·is'tic *adj.* —hu'man·is'ti·cal·ly *adv.*

hu·man·i·tar·i·an (hyoō-mǎn'ĭ-târ'ē-ən) *n.* One devoted to the promotion of human welfare. —hu·man'i·tar'i·an *adj.* —hu·man'i·tar'i·an·ism *n.*

hu·man·i·ty (hyoō-mǎn'ĭ-tē) *n., pl.* **-ties.** 1. Human beings collectively; mankind. 2. The condition or quality of being human. 3. The quality of being humane. 4. **humanities.** Philosophy, literature, and the fine arts as distinguished from the sciences.

hu·man·ize (hyoō'mə-nĭz') *v.* **-ized, -iz·ing.** To make human or humane. —hu'man·i·za'tion *n.* —hu'man·iz'er *n.*

hu·man·kind (hyoō'mən-kīnd') *n.* The human race.

hu·man·ly (hyoō'mən-lē) *adv.* 1. In a human way. 2. Within the scope of human means or powers.

hu·man·oid (hyoō'mə-noid') *adj.* Resembling a human being in appearance. —*n.* An android.

hum·ble (hŭm'bəl) *adj.* **-bler, -blest.** 1. Marked by meekness or modesty. 2. Showing submissive respect. 3. Of low rank or station. —*v.* **-bled, -bling.** 1. To humiliate. 2. To make lower in condition or station. [< Lat. *humilis.*] —hum'ble·ness *n.* —hum'bler *n.* —hum'bly *adv.*

Syns: humble, lowly, meek, modest *adj.*

hum·bug (hŭm'bŭg') *n.* 1. A hoax; imposture. 2. One who tries to trick or deceive. 3. Nonsense; rubbish. —*v.* **-bugged, -bug·ging.** To deceive or trick. [Orig. unknown.] —hum'bug'ger *n.* —hum'bug'ger·y *n.*

hum·ding·er (hŭm'dĭng'ər) *n. Slang.* One that is outstanding. [Orig. unknown.]

hum·drum (hŭm'drŭm') *adj.* Monotonous; uneventful. [Orig. unknown.]

hu·mer·us (hyoō'mər-əs) *n., pl.* **-meri** (-mə-rī'). The long bone of the upper part of the arm, extending from the shoulder to the elbow. [< Lat., upper arm.] —hu'mer·al *adj.*

hu·mid (hyoō'mĭd) *adj.* Containing a large amount of water or water vapor. [< Lat. *humēre*, to be moist.] —hu·mid'i·ty *n.*

hu·mid·i·fy (hyoō-mĭd'ə-fī') *v.* **-fied, -fy·ing.** To make humid. —hu·mid'i·fi'er *n.*

hu·mi·dor (hyoō'mĭ-dôr') *n.* A storage container for cigars that has a humidifying device. [< HUMID.]

hu·mil·i·ate (hyoō-mĭl'ē-āt') *v.* **-at·ed, -at·ing.** To lower the pride or dignity of; mortify. [< LLat. *humiliare.*] —hu·mil'i·at'ing·ly *adv.* —hu·mil'i·a'tion *n.*

hu·mil·i·ty (hyoō-mĭl'ĭ-tē) *n., pl.* **-ties.** The quality or condition of being humble. [< Lat. *humilitas.*]

hum·ming·bird (hŭm'ĭng-bûrd') *n.* An extremely small bird with brilliant plumage and a long bill.

hummingbird

hum·mock (hŭm'ək) *n.* A low mound or ridge, esp. of earth; knoll. [Orig. unknown.] —hum'mock·y *adj.*

hu·mor (hyoō'mər) *n.* 1. The quality of being amusing or comical. 2. The ability to perceive, enjoy, or express what is comical or funny. 3. A state of mind; mood: *in a bad humor.* 4. A sudden inclination; whim. 5. *Physiol.* A body fluid, such as blood or bile. —*v.* To comply with the wishes of; indulge. [< Lat., fluid.] —hu'mor·ist *n.* —hu'mor·less *adj.* —hu'mor·less·ly *adv.* —hu'mor·less·ness *n.*

hu·mor·ous (hyoō'mər-əs) *adj.* Comical; amusing; funny. —hu'mor·ous·ly *adv.* —hu'mor·ous·ness *n.*

hump (hŭmp) *n.* 1. A rounded mass, as on the back of a camel. 2. A difficult stage: *over the hump.* [Orig. unknown.]

hump·back (hŭmp'bǎk') *n.* 1. An abnormally curved or humped back. 2. A hunchback. —hump'backed' *adj.*

hu·mus (hyoō'məs) *n.* A brown or black organic substance consisting of decomposed animal or vegetable matter. [Lat., soil.]

Hun (hŭn) *n.* A member of a nomadic Asiatic people who invaded Europe in the 4th and 5th cent. A.D.

hunch (hŭnch) *n.* An intuitive feeling. —*v.* 1. To bend or draw up into a hump. 2. To push or thrust forward. [Orig. unknown.]

hunch·back (hŭnch'bǎk') *n.* 1. An individual with a humpback. 2. An abnormally curved or humped back. —hunch'backed' *adj.*

hun·dred (hŭn'drĭd) *n., pl.* **-dreds** or **-dred.** 1. The cardinal number equal to 10 × 10, or 10². 2. **hundreds.** The numbers between 100 and 999: *The dress was valued in the hundreds.* [< OE.] —hun'dred *adj. & pron.*

hun·dredth (hŭn'drĭdth) *n.* 1. The ordinal number that matches the number 100 in a series. 2. One of 100 equal parts. —hun'dredth *adj. & adv.*

hun·dred·weight (hŭn'drĭd-wāt') *n., pl.* **-weight** or **-weights.** 1. A unit of weight equal to approx. 45.6 kilograms or 100 pounds. 2. *Chiefly Brit.* A unit of weight equal to approx. 50.8 kilograms or 112 pounds.

hung (hŭng) *v. p.t.* & *p.p.* of **hang.**

Hun·gar·i·an (hŭng-gâr'ē-ən) *n.* 1. A native or inhabitant of Hungary. 2. Magyar (sense 2). —Hun·gar'i·an *adj.*

hun·ger (hŭng'gər) *n.* 1. a. A strong desire for food. b. The discomfort, weakness, or pain caused by a lack of food. 2. A strong desire or craving. —*v.* 1. To have a need or desire for food. **2.** To have a strong desire or craving. [< OE *hungor*.] —**hun'gri·ly** *adv.* —**hun'gry** *adj.*

hunk (hŭngk) *n. Informal.* **1.** A large piece. **2.** An attractive man. [Perh. < Flem. *hunke*, a piece of food.]

hun·ker (hŭng'kər) *v.* To squat; crouch. [Prob. of Scand. orig.]

hun·ky-do·ry (hŭng'kē-dôr'ē, -dōr'ē) *adj.* Quite satisfactory; fine. [Obs. *hunk*, goal + *-dory*, of unknown orig.]

hunt (hŭnt) *v.* **1. a.** To pursue (game) for food or sport. **b.** To search (for); seek. **2.** To search through, as for game or prey. —*n.* **1.** The act or sport of hunting. **2.** A hunting expedition or outing. **3.** A diligent search or pursuit. [< OE *huntian*.] —**hunt'er** *n.* —**hunt'ress** *n.*

hunts·man (hŭnts'mən) *n.* One who hunts, esp. one who manages a pack of hunting hounds.

hur·dle (hûr'dl) *n.* **1.** A framelike barrier to be jumped over in obstacle races. **2.** An obstacle or difficulty. —*v.* **-dled, -dling. 1.** To jump over (a barrier). **2.** To overcome (an obstacle). [< OE *hyrdel*.] —**hur'dler** *n.*

hur·dy-gur·dy (hûr'dē-gûr'dē, hûr'dē-gûr'-) *n.,* *pl.* **-dies.** A musical instrument, such as a barrel organ, played by turning a crank. [Prob. imit.]

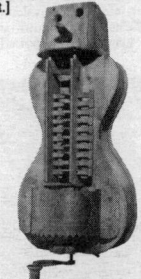

hurdy-gurdy

hurl (hûrl) *v.* **1.** To throw forcefully; fling. **2.** To utter vehemently: *hurl insults.* **3.** To pitch a baseball. [ME *hurlen*.] —**hurl** *n.* —**hurl'er** *n.*

hur·ly-bur·ly (hûr'lē-bûr'lē) *n.,* *pl.* **-lies.** An uproar; commotion. [< HURL.]

Hu·ron (hyŏŏr'ən, -ŏn') *n.,* *pl.* **-ron** or **-rons. 1. a.** A confederation of four tribes of Indians formerly inhabiting the region east of Lake Huron and the St. Lawrence Valley. **b.** A member of any of the Huron. **2.** The Iroquoian language of the Huron. —**Hu'ron** *adj.*

hur·rah (hŏŏ-rä', -rô') *interj.* Also **hoo·ray** (-rā'). Used to express pleasure, approval, or triumph. —**hurrah'** *n. & v.*

hur·ri·cane (hûr'ĭ-kān', hûr'-) *n.* A cyclone with heavy rains and winds exceeding 75 miles per hour. [< Carib *huracan*.]

hur·ry (hûr'ē, hŭr'ē) *v.* **-ried, -ry·ing. 1.** To move or cause to move with speed or haste. **2.** To proceed or press to proceed with great or undue rapidity; rush. —*n., pl.* **-ries. 1.** The act of hurrying. **2.** Haste. [Perh.< ME *horien*.] —**hur'ried** *adj.* —**hur'ried·ly** *adv.* —**hur'ried·ness** *n.*

hurt (hûrt) *v.* **hurt, hurt·ing. 1.** To feel or cause to feel pain. **2.** To offend; distress. **3.** To damage or impair. —*n.* **1.** Something that hurts. **2.** Mental suffering; anguish. **3.** Damage; harm. [Perh. < OFr. *hurter*, to bang into.] —**hurt'ful** *adj.*

hur·tle (hûr'tl) *v.* **-tled, -tling. 1.** To move with or as with great speed. **2.** To throw forcefully; hurl. [ME *hurtlen*, to collide.]

hus·band (hŭz'bənd) *n.* A married man. —*v.* To manage or use economically: *husband one's energy.* [< ON *hūsbōndi*.]

hus·band·man (hŭz'bənd-mən) *n.* A farmer.

hus·band·ry (hŭz'bən-drē) *n.* **1.** Farming; agriculture. **2.** Careful management of resources; economy.

hush (hŭsh) *v.* **1.** To make or become silent. **2.** To calm; soothe. **3.** To suppress; conceal. —*n.* A silence; stillness. [Prob. < ME *husht*, silent.]

hush-hush (hŭsh'hŭsh') *adj. Informal.* Secret; confidential.

hush-pup·py (hŭsh'pŭp'ē) *n.* A fried cornmeal fritter.

husk (hŭsk) *n.* **1.** The dry thin outer covering of certain fruits and seeds, as of an ear of corn or a nut. **2.** A shell or outer layer that is often worthless. —*v.* To remove the husk from. [ME.] —**husk'er** *n.*

husk·y¹ (hŭs'kē) *adj.* **-i·er, -i·est.** Hoarse or throaty. [< HUSK.] —**husk'i·ly** *adv.* —**husk'i·ness** *n.*

husk·y² (hŭs'kē) *adj.* **-i·er, -i·est.** Rugged and strong. [Perh. < HUSK.] —**husk'i·ness** *n.*

hus·ky³ (hŭs'kē) *n., pl.* **-kies.** An Arctic sled dog with a dense, furry, variously colored coat. [Prob. < ESKIMO.]

hus·sar (hŏŏ-zär', -sär') *n.* A member of any of various European units of light cavalry. [< OItal. *corsaro*, corsair.]

hus·sy (hŭz'ē, hŭs'ē) *n., pl.* **-sies. 1.** A saucy or mischievous girl. **2.** An immoral woman. [< HOUSEWIFE.]

hus·tings (hŭs'tĭngz) *n.* (*used with a sing. verb*). A political campaign. [< ON *hūsthing*, assembly.]

hus·tle (hŭs'əl) *v.* **-tled, -tling. 1.** To jostle; shove. **2.** To hurry along. **3.** To work busily. **4.** *Slang.* To make money by questionable means. —*n.* Busy activity. [< MDu. *hustelen*.] —**hus'tler** *n.*

hut (hŭt) *n.* A makeshift or crude dwelling; shack. [Fr. *hutte*, of Gmc. orig.]

hutch (hŭch) *n.* **1.** A coop for small animals. **2.** A low cupboard usu. with open shelves above. **3.** A hut. [< OFr. *huche*, fishpond.]

huz·za (hə-zä') *n.* Also **huz·zah.** *Archaic.* A shout of encouragement or triumph; cheer. —**huz·za'** *interj.*

hy·a·cinth (hī'ə-sĭnth) *n.* A bulbous plant with a cluster of variously colored, fragrant flowers. [< Gk. *huakinthos*, a kind of flower.]

hy·brid (hī'brĭd) *n.* **1.** The offspring of genetically dissimilar parents, esp. of plants or animals that are of different varieties, species, or races. **2.** Something of mixed origin or composition. [Lat. *hybrida*.] —**hy'brid·ism** *n.* —**hy'brid'i·ty** *n.*

hy·brid·ize (hī'brĭ-dīz') *v.* **-ized, -iz·ing.** To produce or cause to produce hybrids; crossbreed. —**hy'brid·i·za'tion** *n.*

hydr- *pref.* Var. of hydro-.

hy·dra (hī'drə) *n., pl.* **-dras** or **-drae** (-drē). A small freshwater polyp with a cylindrical body and a mouth surrounded by tentacles. [< Gk. *Hudra,* a many-headed monster.]

hy·dran·gea (hī-drān'jə, -jē-ə, -drăn'-) *n.* A shrub or tree with large, rounded clusters of white, pink, or blue flowers. [Gk. *hudōr,* water + Gk. *angos,* vessel.]

hy·drant (hī'drənt) *n.* An upright pipe with a nozzle for drawing water from a water main.

hy·drate (hī'drāt') *n.* A chemical compound that contains water combined in a definite ratio, regarded as being retained in its molecular state. —*v.* **-drat·ed, -drat·ing.** To combine with water to form a hydrate. —**hy·dra'tion** *n.*

hy·drau·lic (hī-drô'lĭk) *adj.* **1.** Of, involving, or operated by a liquid, esp. water or oil, under pressure. **2.** Of or pertaining to hydraulics. **3.** Capable of setting and hardening under water, as Portland cement. [< Gk. *hudraulis,* water organ.] —**hy·drau'li·cal·ly** *adv.*

hy·drau·lics (hī-drô'lĭks) *n. (used with a sing. verb).* The science and technology of the static and dynamic behavior of liquids.

hydro– or **hydr–** *pref.* **1.** Water: *hydroelectric.* **2.** Liquid: *hydrostatics.* **3.** Hydrogen: *hydrocarbon.* [< Gk. *hudōr,* water.]

hy·dro·car·bon (hī'drə-kär'bən) *n.* An organic compound, such as benzene and methane, that contains only carbon and hydrogen.

hy·dro·ceph·a·lus (hī'drō-sĕf'ə-ləs) *n.* Also **hy·dro·ceph·a·ly** (-lē). An abnormal condition in which an accumulation of fluid in the cerebral ventricles causes enlargement of the skull and compression of the brain. [< Gk. *hudrokephalon.*] —**hy'dro·ce·phal'ic** (-sə-făl'ĭk) or **hy'dro·ceph'a·loid'** (-sĕf'ə-loid') or **hy'dro·ceph'a·lous** (-ləs) *adj.*

hy·dro·chlo·ric acid (hī'drə-klôr'ĭk, -klōr'-) *n.* A clear, colorless, fuming aqueous solution of hydrogen chloride, HCl, used in petroleum production, food processing, pickling, and metal cleaning.

hy·dro·dy·nam·ics (hī'drō-dī-năm'ĭks) *n. (used with a sing. verb).* The scientific study of the dynamics of fluids, esp. incompressible fluids, in motion.

hy·dro·e·lec·tric (hī'drō-ĭ-lĕk'trĭk) *adj.* Of or relating to electricity generated by conversion of the energy of running water. —**hy'dro·e·lec'tric'i·ty** (-trĭs'ĭ-tē) *n.*

hy·dro·foil (hī'drə-foil') *n.* **1.** One of a set of blades attached to the hull of a boat to lift it out of the water for efficient high-speed operation. **2.** A boat equipped with hydrofoils.

hy·dro·gen (hī'drə-jən) *n. Symbol* **H** A colorless, highly flammable gaseous element, used in the production of synthetic ammonia and methanol, in petroleum refining, as a reducing atmosphere, in oxyhydrogen torches, and in rocket fuels. Atomic number 1; atomic weight 1.00797. —**hy·drog'e·nous** (-drŏj'ə-nəs) *adj.*

hy·dro·gen·ate (hī'drə-jə-nāt', hī-drŏj'ə-) *v.* **-at·ed, -at·ing.** To combine with or subject to the action of hydrogen. —**hy·dro·gen·a'tion** *n.*

hydrogen bomb *n.* A bomb whose explosive power is derived from the sudden release of atomic energy in the fusion of hydrogen nuclei to form helium nuclei.

hydrogen peroxide *n.* An unstable compound, H_2O_2, used chiefly in aqueous solution as an antiseptic, bleaching agent, oxidizing agent, and laboratory reagent.

hy·drol·y·sis (hī-drŏl'ĭ-sĭs) *n.* Decomposition of a chemical compound by reaction with water. —**hy'dro·lize'** *v.* —**hy'dro·lyt'ic** (hī'drə-lĭt'ĭk) *adj.*

hy·drom·e·ter (hī-drŏm'ĭ-tər) *n.* An instrument used to determine the specific gravity of a liquid. —**hy'dro·met'ric** (hī'drə-mĕt'rĭk) or **hy'dro·met'ri·cal** *adj.* —**hy·drom'e·try** *n.*

hy·dro·pho·bi·a (hī'drə-fō'bē-ə) *n.* **1.** Fear of water. **2.** Rabies. —**hy'dro·pho'bic** *adj.*

hy·dro·plane (hī'drə-plān') *n.* **1.** A seaplane. **2.** A motorboat designed to skim the water surface at high speeds.

hy·dro·pon·ics (hī'drə-pŏn'ĭks) *n. (used with a sing. verb).* The cultivation of plants in a nutrient solution rather than in soil. [HYDRO- + Gk. *ponein,* to work.] —**hy'dro·pon'ic** *adj.* —**hy'dro·pon'i·cal·ly** *adv.*

hy·dro·stat·ics (hī'drə-stăt'ĭks) *n. (used with a sing. verb).* The science dealing with the characteristics of fluids at rest. —**hy'dro·stat'ic** or **hy'dro·stat'i·cal** *adj.*

hy·dro·ther·a·py (hī'drə-thĕr'ə-pē) *n., pl.* **-pies.** The use of water in the treatment of diseases.

hy·drous (hī'drəs) *adj.* Containing water, esp. water of crystallization or hydration.

hy·drox·ide (hī-drŏk'sīd') *n.* A chemical compound containing the univalent group OH.

hy·e·na (hī-ē'nə) *n.* A carnivorous African and Asian mammal with powerful jaws. [< Gk. *huaina.*]

hyena

hy·giene (hī'jēn') *n.* **1.** Practices and conditions for the promotion of health and the prevention of disease. **2.** The science of good health and the prevention of disease. [< Gk. *hugiēs,* healthy.] —**hy'gi·en'ic** (-jē-ĕn'ĭk) *adj.* —**hy'gi·en'i·cal·ly** *adv.* —**hy·gien'ist** (hī-jē'nĭst, hī'jē'-) *n.*

hy·grom·e·ter (hī-grŏm'ĭ-tər) *n.* Any of several instruments that measure atmospheric humidity. [Gk. *hugros,* wet + -METER.] —**hy·grom'e·try** *n.*

hy·men (hī'mən) *n.* A membranous fold of tissue partly closing the external opening of the vagina. [< Gk. *humēn,* membrane.]

hy·me·ne·al (hī'mə-nē'əl) *adj.* Of or pertaining to a wedding or marriage. [< Gk. *Humēn,* god of marriage.]

hymn (hĭm) *n.* A song of praise or thanksgiving, esp. to God. [< Gk. *humnos.*]

hym·nal (hĭm'nəl) *n.* A book or collection of hymns. [< Med. Lat. *hymnale.*]

hyp– *pref.* Var. of **hypo-**.

hype (hīp) *n. Slang.* **1.** Deception. **2.** Extravagant claims made esp. in advertising. [Orig. unknown.] —**hype** *v.*

hyper– *pref.* **1.** Over, above, or beyond: *hypersonic.* **2.** Excessive or excessively: *hyperactive.* [< Gk. *huper*, over.]

hy·per·ac·tive (hī'pər-ăk'tĭv) *adj.* Excessively or abnormally active. —**hy'per·ac·tiv'i·ty** (-ăk-tĭv'ĭ-tē) *n.*

hy·per·bo·la (hī-pûr'bə-lə) *n. Geom.* A plane curve having two branches, formed by the locus of points related to two given points such that the difference in the distances of each point from the two given points is a constant. [< Gk. *huperbolē.*]

hy·per·bo·le (hī-pûr'bə-lē) *n.* An exaggerated statement often used as a figure of speech. [< Gk. *huperbolē.*]

hy·per·bol·ic (hī'pər-bŏl'ĭk) or **hy·per·bol·i·cal** (-ĭ-kəl) *adj.* **1.** Of, pertaining to, or employing hyperbole. **2.** *Geom.* Of or pertaining to a hyperbola.

hy·per·crit·i·cal (hī'pər-krĭt'ĭ-kəl) *adj.* Overcritical; captious. —**hy'per·crit'i·cal·ly** *adv.*

hy·per·gly·ce·mi·a (hī'pər-glī-sē'mē-ə) *n.* An excess of glucose in the blood. [HYPER- + Gk. *glukus*, sweet + -EMIA.] —**hy'per·gly·ce'mic** *adj.*

hy·per·sen·si·tive (hī'pər-sĕn'sĭ-tĭv) *adj.* Abnormally sensitive. —**hy'per·sen'si·tive·ness** or **hy'per·sen'si·tiv'i·ty** *n.*

hy·per·son·ic (hī'pər-sŏn'ĭk) *adj.* Of or relating to speed equal to or exceeding five times the speed of sound. —**hy'per·son'ics** *n.*

hy·per·ten·sion (hī'pər-tĕn'shən) *n.* **1.** Abnormally high arterial blood pressure. **2.** A state of high emotional tension.

hy·per·thy·roid·ism (hī'pər-thī'roi-dĭz'əm) *n.* Pathologically excessive activity of the thyroid.

hy·per·tro·phy (hī-pûr'trə-fē) *n.* Abnormal increase in the size of an organ or bodily part. [HYPER- + Gk. *trophē*, food.] —**hy'per·troph'ic** (-trŏf'ĭk) *adj.* —**hy·per'tro·phy** *v.*

hy·phen (hī'fən) *n.* A punctuation mark (-) used between the parts of a compound word or between syllables of a word, esp. of a word divided at the end of a line. [< Gk. *huphen*, together.]

hy·phen·ate (hī'fə-nāt') *v.* **-at·ed, -at·ing.** To divide or connect with a hyphen. —**hy'phen·a'tion** *n.*

hyp·no·sis (hĭp-nō'sĭs) *n., pl.* **-ses** (-sēz'). An induced sleeplike condition in which an individual is extremely responsive to suggestions made by the hypnotist. [Gk. *hupnos*, sleep + -OSIS.]

hyp·not·ic (hĭp-nŏt'ĭk) *adj.* **1.** Of or relating to hypnosis. **2.** Causing or producing sleep. —*n.* An agent that causes sleep. [< Gk. *hupnōtikos*, sleepy.] —**hyp·not'i·cal·ly** *adv.*

hyp·no·tism (hĭp'nə-tĭz'əm) *n.* **1.** The study, practice, or act of inducing hypnosis. **2.** Hypnosis. —**hyp'no·tist** *n.*

hyp·no·tize (hĭp'nə-tīz') *v.* **-tized, -tiz·ing.** **1.** To induce hypnosis in. **2.** To fascinate. —**hyp'no·tiz'a·ble** *adj.* —**hyp'no·ti·za'tion** *n.* —**hyp'no·tiz'er** *n.*

hy·po (hī'pō) *n., pl.* **-pos.** *Informal.* A hypodermic syringe or injection.

hypo– or **hyp–** *pref.* **1.** Below or beneath: *hypodermic.* **2.** Abnormally low: *hypoglycemia.* [< Gk. *hupo*, beneath.]

hy·po·chon·dri·a (hī'pə-kŏn'drē-ə) *n.* A condition marked by depression and a preoccupation with imaginary illnesses. [< Gk. *hupokhondrion*, abdomen.] —**hy'po·chon'dri·ac'** (-ăk') *n. & adj.* —**hy'po·chon·dri'a·cal** (-kən-drī'ə-kəl) *adj.*

hy·poc·ri·sy (hĭ-pŏk'rĭ-sē) *n., pl.* **-sies.** The professing of virtues and beliefs that one does not possess. [< Gk. *hupokrisis*, pretense.]

hyp·o·crite (hĭp'ə-krĭt') *n.* A person given to hypocrisy. [< Gk. *hupokritēs*, actor.] —**hyp'o·crit'i·cal** *adj.* —**hyp'o·crit'i·cal·ly** *adv.*

hy·po·der·mic (hī'pə-dûr'mĭk) *adj.* Injected beneath the skin. —*n.* **1.** A hypodermic injection. **2.** A hypodermic needle or syringe. —**hy'po·der'mi·cal·ly** *adv.*

hypodermic needle *n.* **1.** A hollow needle used with a hypodermic syringe. **2.** A hypodermic syringe complete with needle.

hypodermic syringe *n.* A syringe fitted with a hypodermic needle for injections.

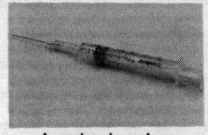

hypodermic syringe

hy·po·gly·ce·mi·a (hī'pō-glī-sē'mē-ə) *n.* An abnormally low level of sugar in the blood. [HYPO- + Gk. *glukus*, sweet + -EMIA.] —**hy'po·gly·ce'mic** *adj.*

hy·pot·e·nuse (hī-pŏt'n-ōōs', -yōōs') *n. Geom.* The side of a right triangle opposite the right angle. [< Gk. *hupoteinousa.*]

hy·po·thal·a·mus (hī'pō-thăl'ə-məs) *n.* The part of the brain that lies below the thalamus and regulates bodily temperature, certain metabolic processes, and other autonomic activities. —**hy'po·tha·lam'ic** (-thə-lăm'ĭk) *adj.*

hy·poth·e·sis (hī-pŏth'ĭ-sĭs) *n., pl.* **-ses** (-sēz'). An explanation or assumption that accounts for a set of facts and that can be tested by further investigation. [< Gk. *hupothesis.*]

hy·poth·e·size (hī-pŏth'ĭ-sīz') *v.* **-sized, -siz·ing.** To assert as or form a hypothesis.

hy·po·thet·i·cal (hī'pə-thĕt'ĭ-kəl) or **hy·po·thet·ic** (-thĕt'ĭk) *adj.* Of, relating to, or founded on a hypothesis; conjectural. [< Gk. *hupothetikos.*] —**hy'po·thet'i·cal·ly** *adv.*

hy·po·thy·roid·ism (hī'pō-thī'roi-dĭz'əm) *n.* **1.** Deficient activity of the thyroid gland. **2.** A pathological condition resulting from hypothyroidism, marked by loss of energy and a lowered rate of metabolism.

hys·sop (hĭs'əp) *n.* A woody, aromatic plant with spikes of small blue flowers. [< Gk. *hussōpos*, of Semitic orig.]

hys·ter·ec·to·my (hĭs'tə-rĕk'tə-mē) *n., pl.* **-mies.** Surgical removal of the uterus. [Gk. *hustera*, uterus + -ECTOMY.]

hys·te·ri·a (hĭ-stĕr'ē-ə, -stîr'-) *n.* **1.** A neurosis characterized by physical symptoms, such as blindness or paralysis, without apparent organic cause. **2.** Excessive or uncontrollable emotion, such as fear or panic. [< Gk. *hustera*, womb.] —**hys·ter'ic** *n. & adj.* —**hys·ter'i·cal** *adj.* —**hys·ter'i·cal·ly** *adv.*

hys·ter·ics (hĭ-stĕr'ĭks) *n.* *(used with a sing. verb).* **1.** A fit of uncontrollable laughing and crying. **2.** An attack of hysteria.

Ii

I or **i** (ī) *n., pl.* **I's** or **i's.** 1. The 9th letter of the English alphabet. 2. Something shaped like the letter I. 3. The Roman numeral for 1.

I¹ (ī) *pron.* The one that is the speaker or writer. [< OE *ic.*]

Usage: When the subject of a sentence is a compound phrase in which *I* is joined to other elements by *and* or *or*, the pronoun is part of the subject proper and the subjective form should be used: *He and I* (not *me*) *will meet you.* In an effort to get the pronouns right, some err by using a construction such as *between you and I* (properly *between you and me*).

I² The symbol for the element iodine.

-ia¹ *suff.* 1. Diseases and disorders: *diphtheria.* 2. Areas and countries: *Manchuria.* [< Lat. and Gk.]

-ia² *suff.* Something relating or belonging to: *orthodontia.* [< Lat. and Gk.]

-ial *suff.* Of, pertaining to, or characterized by: *residential.* [< Lat. *-ialis.*]

i-amb (ī′ămb′) *n.* A metrical foot in which a stressed syllable follows an unstressed syllable. [< Gk. *iambos.*] **—i-am′bic** *adj. & n.*

-ian *suff.* 1. Of, relating to, or resembling: *Bostonian.* 2. One relating to, belonging to, or resembling: *academician.* [< Lat. *-ianus.*]

-iana *suff.* Var. of **-ana.**

-iatric *suff.* Pertaining to a specific kind of medical treatment: *geriatric.* [< Gk. *iatrikos*, medical.]

-iatrics *suff.* A specific kind of medical treatment: *pediatrics.* [< -IATRIC.]

-iatry *suff.* A specific kind of medical treatment: *psychiatry.* [< Gk. *iatros*, physician.]

i-bex (ī′bĕks′) *n.* An Old World mountain goat with long, curving horns. [Lat.]

ib-i-dem (ĭb′ĭ-dĕm′, ĭb-ī′dəm) *adv.* In the same place, as in a book cited before. [Lat.]

-ibility *suff.* Var. of **-ability.**

i-bis (ī′bĭs) *n.* A large wading bird with a long, downward-curving bill. [< Gk., of Egypt. orig.]

George Miksch Sutton
ibis

-ible *suff.* Var. of **-able.**

-ic *suff.* 1. Of, pertaining to, or characteristic of: *seismic.* 2. Having or taking a valence higher than in corresponding *-ous* compounds: *ferric.* [< Lat. *-icus.*]

ice (īs) *n.* 1. Water frozen solid. 2. A dessert consisting of sweetened and flavored crushed ice. 3. *Slang.* Diamonds. 4. *Informal.* Unfriendliness or reserve. *—v.* **iced, ic-ing.** 1. To form ice. 2. To coat with ice. 3. To chill or freeze. 4. To cover or decorate with icing. [< OE *īs.*] **—ic′i-ly** *adv.* **—ic′i-ness** *n.* **—ic′y** *adj.*

ice age *n.* Any of a series of cold periods marked by extensive glaciation.

ice bag *n.* A small waterproof bag filled with ice and applied to sore or swollen parts of the body.

ice-berg (īs′bûrg′) *n.* A massive floating body of ice that has broken away from a glacier. [< Dan. and Norw. *isberg.*]

ice-boat (īs′bōt′) *n.* 1. A boatlike vehicle with runners that sails on ice. 2. An icebreaker.

ice-bound (īs′bound′) *adj.* Locked in or obstructed by ice.

ice-box (īs′bŏks′) *n.* A refrigerator.

ice-break-er (īs′brā′kər) *n.* 1. A ship built for breaking a passage through icebound waters. 2. A protective pier or dock apron used as a buffer against floating ice.

ice cap *n.* An extensive perennial cover of ice and snow.

ice cream *n.* A sweet frozen food made of milk products, sugar, eggs, and flavoring.

ice hockey *n.* Hockey (sense 1).

ice-house (īs′hous′) *n.* A building where ice is stored.

Ice-land-ic (ī-slăn′dĭk) *adj.* Of or pertaining to Iceland, its inhabitants, their language, or their culture. *—n.* The Germanic language of Iceland.

ice pick *n.* An awl for chipping ice.

ice skate *n.* A boot with a runner permanently fixed to it for skating on ice.

ice-skate (īs′skāt′) *v.* **-skat-ed, -skat-ing.** To skate on ice. **—ice skater** *n.*

ice storm *n.* A storm in which snow or rain freezes on contact.

ice water *n.* Very cold or iced drinking water.

ichthyo- *pref.* Fish: *ichthyology.* [< Gk. *ikhthus.*]

ich-thy-ol-o-gy (ĭk′thē-ŏl′ə-jē) *n.* Zoology specializing in the study of fishes. **—ich′thy-ol′o-gist** *n.*

-ician *suff.* A person who practices or is a specialist in a given field: *beautician.* [< OFr. *-icien.*]

i-ci-cle (ī′sĭ-kəl) *n.* A tapering spike of ice formed by the freezing of dripping water. [ME *isikel.*]

ic-ing (ī′sĭng) *n.* A sweet, usu. creamy glaze used on cakes and cookies.

i-con (ī′kŏn′) *n.* Also **i-kon.** An image, esp. a religious image painted on a wooden panel. [< Gk. *eikōn*, likeness.]

i-con-o-clast (ī-kŏn′ə-klăst′) *n.* 1. One who destroys sacred images. 2. One who attacks

---

ă pat ā pay â care ä father ĕ pet ē be ĭ pit ī tie î pier ŏ pot ō toe ô paw, for oi noise ŏŏ took
ŏŏ boot ou out th thin th this ŭ cut û urge yŏŏ abuse zh vision ə about, item, edible, gallop, circus

and seeks to overthrow traditional or popular ideas or institutions. [< Med. Gk. *eikonoklastēs*.] **—i·con'o·clasm** *n.* **—i·con'o·clas'tic** (-klăs'tĭk) *adj.*

-ics *suff.* **1.** The science or art of: *graphics.* **2.** The act, practices, or activities of: *athletics.* [< -IC.]

ic·tus (ĭk'təs) *n., pl.* **-tus·es** or **-tus.** *Pathol.* A sudden attack. [Lat., stroke.]

id (ĭd) *n.* The division of the psyche associated with instinctual impulses and the satisfaction of primitive needs. [Lat., it.]

I'd (īd). **1.** I had. **2.** I would. **3.** I should.

-id *suff.* Body; particle: *chromatid.* [< Gk. *-is,* fem. patronymic suffix.]

-ide *suff.* Chemical compound: *chloride.* [< Fr. *acide,* acid.]

i·de·a (ī-dē'ə) *n.* **1.** A product of mental activity; thought. **2.** An opinion, conviction, or principle. **3.** A plan or method. **4.** A basic meaning or purpose. [< Gk.]

i·de·al (ī-dē'əl, ī-dēl') *n.* **1.** A standard or model of perfection, excellence, or beauty. **2.** An ultimate objective; goal. **3.** An honorable or worthy principle. —*adj.* **1.** Perfect or near-perfect. **2.** Existing only in the mind; imaginary. [< LLat. *idealis.*] **—i·de'al·ly** *adv.*

i·de·al·ism (ī-dē'ə-lĭz'əm) *n.* **1.** The practice of seeing things as they ought to be rather than as they actually are. **2.** Pursuit of one's ideals. **3.** A theory identifying reality with perception or ideation. **—i·de'al·ist** *n.* **—i·de'al·is'tic** *adj.*

i·de·al·ize (ī-dē'ə-līz') *v.* **-ized, -iz·ing.** To regard, envision, or represent as ideal. **—i·de'al·i·za'tion** *n.*

i·de·ate (ī'dē-āt') *v.* **-at·ed, -at·ing.** To form an idea (of). **—i·de·a'tion** *n.* **—i·de·a'tion·al** *adj.*

i·dem (ī'dĕm') *pron.* Something previously mentioned. [Lat., the same.]

i·den·ti·cal (ī-dĕn'tĭ-kəl) *adj.* **1.** Being the same. **2.** Being exactly equal and alike. **3.** Of or pertaining to a twin or twins developed from the same ovum. [< Med. Lat. *identicus.*] **—i·den'ti·cal·ly** *adv.*

i·den·ti·fi·ca·tion (ī-dĕn'tə-fĭ-kā'shən) *n.* **1.** The act of identifying. **2.** The state of being identified. **3.** Proof of identity.

i·den·ti·fy (ī-dĕn'tə-fī') *v.* **-fied, -fy·ing. 1.** To ascertain or establish the identity of. **2.** To be or cause to be identical; regard as the same. **3.** To associate; connect. [Med. Lat. *identificare.*] **—i·den'ti·fi'a·ble** *adj.*

i·den·ti·ty (ī-dĕn'tĭ-tē) *n., pl.* **-ties. 1.** The collective aspect of the set of characteristics by which a thing is recognizable or known. **2.** The distinct personality of an individual; individuality. **3.** The quality or condition of being exactly the same as something else. **4.** A mathematical equation that remains true for all values of the variables it contains. [LLat. *identitas.*]

ideo- *pref.* Idea: *ideograph.* [< Gk. *idea.*]

id·e·o·gram (ĭd'ē-ə-grăm', ī'dē-) *n.* **1.** A character or symbol representing an idea or thing without expressing a particular word or phrase for it. **2.** A graphic symbol, as &, $, and @.

i·de·ol·o·gy (ī'dē-ŏl'ə-jē, ĭd'ē-) *n., pl.* **-gies.** The body of ideas reflecting the social needs and aspirations of an individual, group, class, or culture. **—i·de·o·log'i·cal** (-ə-lŏj'ĭ-kəl) *adj.* **—i·de·o·log'i·cal·ly** *adv.*

Ides (īdz) *n. (used with a sing. verb).* The 15th day of Mar., May, July, or Oct. or the 13th day of the other months in the ancient Roman calendar. [< Lat. *idus.*]

id·i·o·cy (ĭd'ē-ə-sē) *n., pl.* **-cies. 1.** A condition of extreme mental retardation. **2.** Something extremely foolish or stupid.

id·i·om (ĭd'ē-əm) *n.* **1.** An expression having a special meaning not obtainable or not clear from the usual meaning of the words in the expression, as *fly off the handle* (lose one's temper). **2.** The specific grammatical, syntactic, and structural character of a given language. **3.** A regional speech or dialect. **4.** A specialized vocabulary: *legal idiom.* [< Gk. *idiōma.*] **—id'i·o·mat'ic** (-ə-măt'ĭk) *adj.* **—id'i·o·mat'i·cal·ly** *adv.*

id·i·op·a·thy (ĭd'ē-ŏp'ə-thē) *n.* A disease of unknown cause. [Gk. *idios,* own + -PATHY.] **—id'i·o·path'ic** (-ə-păth'ĭk) *adj.*

id·i·o·syn·cra·sy (ĭd'ē-ō-sĭng'krə-sē, -sĭn'-) *n., pl.* **-sies.** A structural or behavioral peculiarity; eccentricity. [Gk. *idiosunkrasia.*] **—id'i·o·syn·crat'ic** (-sĭn-krăt'ĭk) *adj.* **—id'i·o·syn·crat'i·cal·ly** *adv.*

id·i·ot (ĭd'ē-ət) *n.* **1.** A mentally deficient person with intelligence in the lowest measurable range, being unable to guard against common dangers and incapable of learning connected speech. **2.** A foolish or stupid person. [< Gk. *idiōtēs,* a man not holding public office.] **—id'i·ot'ic** (-ŏt'ĭk) *adj.* **—id'i·ot'i·cal·ly** *adv.*

i·dle (īd'l) *adj.* **i·dler, i·dlest. 1.** Not working; inactive. **2.** Avoiding work; lazy. **3.** Useless or groundless: *idle talk; idle threat.* —*v.* **i·dled, i·dling. 1.** To pass time without working. **2.** To move lazily. **3.** To run or cause to run at a slow speed or out of gear. **4.** To cause to be unemployed or inactive. [< OE *īdel.*] **—i'dle·ness** *n.* **—i'dler** *n.* **—i'dly** *adv.*

Usage: In the sense of "to make inactive or unemployed," *idle* is acceptable on all levels of spoken or written English.

i·dol (īd'l) *n.* **1.** An image used as an object of worship. **2.** One that is adored. [< Gk. *eidōlon,* image.]

i·dol·a·try (ī-dŏl'ə-trē) *n.* **1.** The worship of idols. **2.** Blind admiration or devotion. [< Gk. *eidōlolatria.*] **—i·dol'a·ter** *n.* **—i·dol'a·trous** *adj.* **—i·dol'a·trous·ly** *adv.*

i·dol·ize (īd'l-īz') *v.* **-ized, -iz·ing. 1.** To regard with blind admiration or devotion. **2.** To worship as an idol.

i·dyll (īd'l) *n.* Also **i·dyl. 1.** A short poem about rustic life. **2.** A scene or event of rustic simplicity. **3.** A romantic interlude. [< Gk. *eidullion.*] **—i·dyl'lic** (ī-dĭl'ĭk) *adj.* **—i·dyl'li·cal·ly** *adv.*

-ie *suff.* Var. of -y³.

if (ĭf) *conj.* **1.** In the event that: *If I were to go, I would be late.* **2.** Granting that: *If that's true, what will we do?* **3.** On condition that: *She will sing only if she is paid.* **4.** Although possibly; even though: *a handsome if useless trinket.* **5.** Whether: *Ask if he will come.* **6.** Used to introduce an exclamatory clause indicating a wish: *If she had only come earlier!* —*n.* A possibility, condition, or stipulation: *no ifs, ands, or buts.* [< OE *gif.*]

Usage: There is a growing tendency to use *would have* in place of *had* in contrary-to-fact *if* clauses, but this usage is still considered to be nonstandard. Instead of *if I would have been born in the 12th century,* use *if I had been born in the 12th century.*

if·fy (ĭf'ē) *adj. Informal.* Characterized by doubt, uncertainty, or chance.

ig·loo (ĭg'lōō) *n.* An Eskimo house, sometimes built of blocks of ice or hard snow. [Eskimo *iglu,* house.]

ig·ne·ous (ĭg'nē-əs) *adj.* 1. Of or relating to fire. 2. Solidified from a molten state. [< Lat. *igneus.*]

ig·nite (ĭg-nīt') *v.* **-nit·ed, -nit·ing.** To set fire to or catch fire. [LLat. *ignire.*]

ig·ni·tion (ĭg-nĭsh'ən) *n.* 1. An act or instance of igniting. 2. An electrical system that ignites the fuel mixture in an internal-combustion engine.

ig·no·ble (ĭg-nō'bəl) *adj.* 1. Not having a noble character or purpose; dishonorable. 2. Not of the nobility; common. [Lat. *ignobilis.*] **—ig·no'ble·ness** *n.* **—ig·no'bly** *adv.*

ig·no·min·i·ous (ĭg'nə-mĭn'ē-əs) *adj.* 1. Characterized by dishonor. 2. Despicable. 3. Degrading; humiliating. [< Lat. *ignominia,* dishonor.] **—ig'no·min'i·ous·ly** *adv.* **—ig'no·min'y** *n.*

ig·no·ra·mus (ĭg'nə-rā'məs) *n.* An ignorant person. [< Lat., we do not know.]

ig·no·rant (ĭg'nər-ənt) *adj.* 1. Without education or knowledge. 2. Exhibiting lack of education or knowledge. 3. Unaware or uninformed. [< Lat. *ignorare,* to be ignorant.] **—ig'no·rance** *n.* **—ig'no·rant·ly** *adv.*

ig·nore (ĭg-nôr', -nōr') *v.* **-nored, -nor·ing.** To refuse to pay attention to; disregard. [< Lat. *ignorare.*] **—ig·nor'a·ble** *adj.*

i·gua·na (ĭ-gwä'nə) *n.* A large tropical American lizard. [Sp.]

Iguana

i·kon (ī'kŏn') *n.* Var. of **icon.**

il-¹ *pref.* Var. of **in-¹.**

il-² *pref.* Var. of **in-².**

-ile *suff.* Relationship with, similarity to, or capability of: *contractile.* [< Lat. *-ilis.*]

il·e·i·tis (ĭl'ē-ī'tĭs) *n.* Inflammation of the ileum. [ILE(UM) + -ITIS.]

il·e·um (ĭl'ē-əm) *n., pl.* **-e·a** (-ē-ə). The portion of the small intestine extending from the jejunum to the beginning of the large intestine. [< Lat., groin.] **—il'e·al** or **il'e·ai** *adj.*

ilk (ĭlk) *n.* Type or kind: *a remark of that ilk.* [OE *ilca,* same.]

ill (ĭl) *adj.* **worse** (wûrs), **worst** (wûrst). 1. Not healthy; sick. 2. Not normal; unsound: *ill health.* 3. Resulting in suffering; distressing. 4. Hostile; unfriendly. 5. Not favorable; unpropitious. 6. Not up to recognized standards of excellence or conduct. 7. Cruel; harmful. **—adv. worse, worst.** 1. In an ill manner; not well. 2. Scarcely or with diffi-

culty. **—n.** 1. Evil. 2. Disaster or harm. 3. An ailment. [< ON *illr,* bad.]

I'll (ĭl). 1. I will. 2. I shall.

ill-ad·vised (ĭl'əd-vīzd') *adj.* Done without wise counsel or careful deliberation. **—ill-ad·vis'ed·ly** (-vī'zĭd-lē') *adv.*

ill-bred (ĭl'brĕd') *adj.* Badly brought up; ill-mannered; impolite.

il·le·gal (ĭ-lē'gəl) *adj.* 1. Prohibited by law. 2. Prohibited by official rules. **—il'le·gal'i·t** (ĭl'ē-găl'ĭ-tē) *n.* **—il·le'gal·ly** *adv.*

il·leg·i·ble (ĭ-lĕj'ə-bəl) *adj.* Not legible. **—il·leg'i·bil'i·ty** *n.* **—il·leg'i·bly** *adv.*

il·le·git·i·mate (ĭl'ə-jĭt'ə-mĭt) *adj.* 1. Against the law; illegal. 2. Born of parents not married to each other. 3. Incorrectly deduced; illogical. **—il'le·git'i·ma·cy** (-mə-sē) *n.* **—il'le·git'i·mate·ly** *adv.*

ill-fat·ed (ĭl'fā'tĭd) *adj.* Marked by or destined for misfortune; unfortunate.

ill-fa·vored (ĭl'fā'vərd) *adj.* 1. Ugly or unattractive. 2. Objectionable; offensive.

ill-got·ten (ĭl'gŏt'n) *adj.* Obtained by evil or dishonest means.

ill-hu·mored (ĭl'hyōō'mərd) *adj.* Irritable and surly. **—ill'hu'mored·ly** *adv.*

il·lib·er·al (ĭ-lĭb'ər-əl) *adj.* Narrow-minded; bigoted.

il·lic·it (ĭ-lĭs'ĭt) *adj.* Not permitted by custom or law; unlawful. **—il·lic'it·ly** *adv.*

Il·li·nois (ĭl'ə-noi', -noiz') *n., pl.* **-nois.** 1. a. A confederacy of Indian tribes that inhabited Illinois and parts of Iowa, Wisconsin, and Missouri. b. A member of this confederacy. 2. An Algonquian language of the Illinois and Miami peoples.

il·lit·er·ate (ĭ-lĭt'ər-ĭt) *adj.* 1. Having little or no formal education, esp. unable to read and write. 2. Showing a lack of familiarity with language or literature. 3. Ignorant of the fundamentals of a given art or branch of knowledge. **—il·lit'er·a·cy** (-ə-sē) *n.* **—il·lit'er·ate** *n.*

ill-man·nered (ĭl'măn'ərd) *adj.* Lacking or indicating a lack of good manners; rude.

ill-na·tured (ĭl'nā'chərd) *adj.* Disagreeable; surly. **—ill'na'tured·ly** *adv.*

ill·ness (ĭl'nĭs) *n.* Sickness.

il·log·i·cal (ĭ-lŏj'ĭ-kəl) *adj.* Contradicting or disregarding the principles of logic. **—il·log'i·cal'i·ty** (-kăl'ĭ-tē) *n.* **—il·log'i·cal·ly** *adv.*

ill-starred (ĭl'stärd') *adj.* Ill-fated; unlucky.

ill-tem·pered (ĭl'tĕm'pərd) *adj.* Having a bad temper; irritable.

ill-treat (ĭl'trēt') *v.* To treat harmfully or wrongly; maltreat. **—ill'-treat'ment** *n.*

il·lu·mi·nate (ĭ-lōō'mə-nāt') *v.* **-nat·ed, -nat·ing.** 1. To provide or brighten with light. 2. To make understandable; clarify. 3. To enable to understand; enlighten. 4. To decorate (a manuscript or initial letter) with pictures or designs in brilliant colors. [Lat. *illuminare.*] **—il·lu'mi·na'tion** *n.* **—il·lu'mi·na'tor** *n.*

il·lu·mine (ĭ-lōō'mĭn) *v.* **-mined, -min·ing.** To illuminate. [< Lat. *illuminare.*]

ill-us·age *n.* (ĭl'yōō'sĭj', -zĭj) *n.* Bad treatment; abuse.

ill-use (ĭl'yōōz') *v.* **-used, -us·ing.** To treat badly; abuse. **—ill'-use'** (-yōōs') *n.*

il·lu·sion (ĭ-lōō'zhən) *n.* 1. a. An erroneous perception of reality. b. An erroneous concept or belief. **2.** A misleading visual image. [< Lat. *illudere*, to mock.]

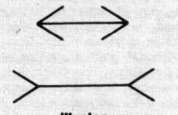

Illusion

Müller-Lyer illusion: an optical illusion in which two lines of the same length appear unequal

il·lu·sion·ism (ĭ-lōō′zhə-nĭz′əm) *n.* The use of techniques such as foreshortening to produce the illusion of reality, esp. in a painting. **—il·lu′sion·ist** *n.*

il·lu·sive (ĭ-lōō′sĭv) *adj.* Illusory.

il·lu·so·ry (ĭ-lōō′sə-rē, -zə-) *adj.* Produced by, based on, or of the nature of an illusion.

il·lus·trate (ĭl′ə-strāt′, ĭ-lŭs′trāt′) *v.* **-trat·ed, -trat·ing. 1. a.** To clarify or explain, as by using examples. **b.** To serve as an example or comparison; exemplify. **2.** To provide (a text) with explanatory or decorative pictures, photographs, or diagrams. [Lat. *illustrare*.] **—il′lus·tra′tor** *n.*

il·lus·tra·tion (ĭl′ə-strā′shən) *n.* **1. a.** The act of illustrating. **b.** The state of being illustrated. **2.** A picture, diagram, or chart serving to explain or decorate a text. **3.** Something serving to clarify or explain; example.

il·lus·tra·tive (ĭ-lŭs′trə-tĭv, ĭl′ə-strā′tĭv) *adj.* Designed or serving to illustrate. **—il·lus′tra·tive·ly** *adv.*

il·lus·tri·ous (ĭ-lŭs′trē-əs) *adj.* Famous; celebrated. [< Lat. *illustris*, bright.] **—il·lus′tri·ous·ly** *adv.* **—il·lus′tri·ous·ness** *n.*

ill will *n.* Unfriendly feeling; hostility.

im-[1] *pref.* Var. of **in-**[1].

im-[2] *pref.* Var. of **in-**[2].

I'm (īm). I am.

im·age (ĭm′ĭj) *n.* **1.** A reproduction of the form of a person or thing, esp. a sculptured likeness. **2.** An optically formed counterpart of an object, esp. one formed by a lens or mirror. **3.** A mental picture of something not present or real. **4.** One that closely resembles another: *the very image of his grandfather.* **5.** A personification: *He is the image of health.* **6.** A vivid description or representation. **—v.** **-aged, -ag·ing. 1.** To make a likeness of. **2.** To mirror; reflect. **3.** To picture mentally; imagine. **4.** To describe in words, esp. vividly. [< Lat. *imago.*]

im·age·ry (ĭm′ĭj-rē) *n., pl.* **-ries. 1.** Mental images. **2.** Figures of speech or vivid descriptions conveying poetic images.

i·mag·in·a·ble (ĭ-măj′ə-nə-bəl) *adj.* Capable of being imagined. **—i·mag′in·a·bly** *adv.*

i·mag·i·nar·y (ĭ-măj′ə-nĕr′ē) *adj.* **1.** Having existence only in the imagination. **2.** Of, pertaining to, or being an imaginary number.

imaginary number *n.* A complex number in which the real part is zero and the coefficient of the imaginary unit is not zero.

imaginary unit *n.* The positive square root of minus 1.

i·mag·i·na·tion (ĭ-măj′ə-nā′shən) *n.* **1.** The process or power of forming a mental image of something not real or present. **2.** Creativity; inventiveness. **3.** Resourcefulness. **—i·**

mag′i·na·tive *adj.* **—i·mag′i·na·tive·ly** *adv.* **—i·mag′i·na·tive·ness** *n.*

i·mag·ine (ĭ-măj′ĭn) *v.* **-ined, -in·ing. 1.** To form a mental picture or image of; fancy. **2.** To think; suppose. [< Lat. *imaginari*.]

i·ma·go (ĭ-mā′gō) *n., pl.* **-goes** or **i·mag·i·nes** (ĭ-măj′ə-nēz′). An insect in its sexually mature adult stage. [< Lat., image.]

im·bal·ance (ĭm-băl′əns) *n.* A lack of balance, as in distribution.

im·be·cile (ĭm′bə-sĭl, -səl) *n.* **1.** A feebleminded person. **2.** A stupid person; dolt. [< Lat. *imbecillus*, feeble.] **—im·be·cil′ic** (-sĭl′ĭk) *adj.* **—im′be·cil′i·ty** (-sĭl′ĭ-tē) *n.*

im·bed (ĭm-bĕd′) *v.* Var. of **embed**.

im·bibe (ĭm-bīb′) *v.* **-bibed, -bib·ing. 1.** To drink. **2.** To take in as if by drinking; absorb. [< Lat. *imbibere*.] **—im·bib′er** *n.*

im·bro·glio (ĭm-brōl′yō) *n., pl.* **-glios. 1. a.** A difficult or intricate situation. **b.** An embarrassing misunderstanding. **2.** A confused heap; tangle. [Ital.]

im·bue (ĭm-byōō′) *v.* **-bued, -bu·ing. 1.** To stain or dye deeply. **2.** To permeate or pervade. [Lat. *imbuere*.]

im·i·ta·ble (ĭm′ĭ-tə-bəl) *adj.* Capable or worthy of being imitated.

im·i·tate (ĭm′ĭ-tāt′) *v.* **-tat·ed, -tat·ing. 1. a.** To copy the actions, appearance, function, or sounds of. **b.** To model oneself after. **2.** To reproduce; copy. **3.** To look like; resemble. [Lat. *imitari*.] **—im′i·ta′tor** *n.*

im·i·ta·tion (ĭm′ĭ-tā′shən) *n.* **1.** An act of imitating. **2.** Something derived or copied from an original. **3.** A counterfeit.

im·i·ta·tive (ĭm′ĭ-tā′tĭv) *adj.* **1.** Of or involving imitation. **2.** Not original; derivative. **3.** Tending to imitate. **4.** Onomatopoeic. **—im′i·ta·tive·ly** *adv.* **—im′i·ta·tive·ness** *n.*

im·mac·u·late (ĭ-măk′yə-lĭt) *adj.* **1.** Free from sin or error; pure. **2.** Impeccably clean. [< Lat. *immaculatus*.] **—im·mac′u·late·ly** *adv.*

im·ma·nent (ĭm′ə-nənt) *adj.* **1.** Existing or remaining within; inherent. **2.** Residing or functioning in and in the human soul. [< Lat. *immanēre*, to remain in.] **—im′ma·nence** or **im′ma·nen·cy** *n.*

im·ma·te·ri·al (ĭm′ə-tîr′ē-əl) *adj.* **1.** Having no material body or form. **2.** Of no importance; inconsequential. **—im′ma·te′ri·al·ly** *adv.* **—im′ma·te′ri·al·ness** *n.*

im·ma·ture (ĭm′ə-tŏŏr′, -tyŏŏr′, -chŏŏr′) *adj.* **1.** Not fully grown or developed. **2.** Marked by or suggesting a lack of normal maturity. **—im′ma·ture′ly** *adv.* **—im′ma·tur′i·ty** *n.*

im·meas·ur·a·ble (ĭ-mĕzh′ər-ə-bəl) *adj.* **1.** Incapable of being measured. **2.** Vast; limitless. **—im·meas′ur·a·bil′i·ty** or **im·meas′ur·a·ble·ness** *n.* **—im·meas′ur·a·bly** *adv.*

im·me·di·a·cy (ĭ-mē′dē-ə-sē) *n., pl.* **-cies. 1.** Directness. **2.** Urgency.

im·me·di·ate (ĭ-mē′dē-ĭt) *adj.* **1.** Occurring or accomplished without delay; instant. **2.** Close at hand; nearby: *our immediate surroundings.* **3.** Coming next or very soon: *the immediate future.* **4.** Next in line or relation: *an immediate successor.* **5.** Being without interposition; direct: *the immediate cause of death.* [LLat. *immediatus*.] **—im·me′di·ate·ly** *adv.*

im·me·mo·ri·al (ĭm′ə-môr′ē-əl, -mōr′-) *adj.* Reaching beyond the limits of memory, tradition, or recorded history.

im·mense (ĭ-mĕns′) *adj.* **1.** Extremely large; huge. **2.** *Informal.* Excellent. [< Lat. *immensus*.] **—im·mense′ly** *adv.* **—im·men′si·ty** *n.*

im·merse (ĭ-mûrs′) v. **-mersed, -mers·ing.**
1. To plunge into a fluid. 2. To baptize by
submerging in water. 3. To absorb; engross.
[Lat. *immergere*.] —**im·mer′sion** n.

im·mi·grant (ĭm′ĭ-grənt) n. 1. One who immi-
grates. 2. An organism that appears where it
was formerly unknown.

im·mi·grate (ĭm′ĭ-grāt′) v. **-grat·ed, -grat·ing.**
To enter and settle permanently in a foreign
country. [Lat. *immigrare*.] —**im′mi·gra′tion** n.

im·mi·nent (ĭm′ə-nənt) adj. About to occur;
impending. [< Lat. *imminēre*, to threaten.]
—**im′mi·nence** n. —**im′mi·nent·ly** adv.

im·mo·bile (ĭ-mō′bəl, -bēl′, -bīl′) adj. 1. Not
movable; fixed. 2. Not moving; motionless.
—**im′mo·bil′i·ty** (ĭm′ō-bĭl′ĭ-tē) n.

im·mo·bi·lize (ĭ-mō′bə-līz′) v. **-lized, -liz·ing.**
To make immobile. —**im·mo′bi·li·za′tion** n.

im·mod·er·ate (ĭ-mŏd′ər-ĭt) adj. Extreme or
excessive. —**im·mod′er·ate·ly** adv. —**im·mod′-
er·ate·ness** or **im·mod′er·a′tion** n.

im·mod·est (ĭ-mŏd′ĭst) adj. Lacking modesty;
indecent or offensive. —**im·mod′est·ly** adv.
—**im·mod′es·ty** n.

im·mo·late (ĭm′ə-lāt′) v. **-lat·ed, -lat·ing.** To
kill as a sacrifice. [Lat. *immolare*.] —**im′mo·
la′tion** n. —**im′mo·la′tor** n.

im·mor·al (ĭ-môr′əl, ĭ-mŏr′-) adj. Contrary to
accepted moral principles. —**im·mor′al·ly** adv.

im·mo·ral·i·ty (ĭm′ə-răl′ĭ-tē, ĭm′ô-) n., pl. **-ties.**
1. The quality or state of being immoral.
2. Behavior or an act that is immoral.

im·mor·tal (ĭ-môr′tl) adj. 1. Not subject to
death. 2. Having enduring fame; imperish-
able. —n. 1. One exempt from death. 2. One
whose fame is enduring. 3. **Immortals.** The
gods of ancient Greece and Rome. [< Lat.
immortalis.] —**im·mor′tal·ly** adv.

im·mor·tal·i·ty (ĭm′ôr-tăl′ĭ-tē) n. The quality
or state of being immortal.

im·mor·tal·ize (ĭ-môr′tl-īz′) v. **-ized, -iz·ing.**
To make immortal.

im·mov·a·ble (ĭ-mōō′və-bəl) adj. 1. Incapable
of moving or of being moved. 2. Unyielding;
steadfast. 3. Unimpressionable or impassive.
—**im·mov′a·bil′i·ty** n. —**im·mov′a·bly** adv.

im·mune (ĭ-myōōn′) adj. 1. Exempt.
2. Resistant, esp. to a specific disease. [Lat.
immunis.] —**im·mu′ni·ty** (ĭ-myōō′nĭ-tē) n.

im·mu·nize (ĭm′yə-nīz′) v. **-nized, -niz·ing.** To
render immune. —**im′mu·ni·za′tion** n.

im·mu·nol·o·gy (ĭm′yə-nŏl′ə-jē) n. The medical study of immunity. —**im′mu·no·log′ic**
(-nə-lŏj′ĭk) or **im′mu·no·log′i·cal** adj. —**im′-
mu·no·log′i·cal·ly** adv. —**im′mu·nol′o·gist** n.

im·mu·no·sup·pres·sive (ĭm′yə-nō-sə-prĕs′ĭv)
adj. Tending to suppress a natural immune
response of an organism to an antigen.

im·mure (ĭ-myōōr′) v. **-mured, -mur·ing.** 1. To
confine within or as if within walls; imprison.
2. To build into a wall; entomb in a wall.
[Med. Lat. *immurare*.]

im·mu·ta·ble (ĭ-myōō′tə-bəl) adj. Not susceptible to change; unchanging or unchangeable.
[< Lat. *immutabilis*.] —**im·mu′ta·bil′i·ty** n.
—**im·mu′ta·bly** adv.

imp (ĭmp) n. 1. A mischievous child. 2. A
small demon. [< OE *impa*, young shoot.]

im·pact (ĭm′păkt′) n. 1. a. A collision. b. The
force transmitted by or as if by a collision.
2. The effect or impression of one thing on

another. —v. (ĭm-păkt′). 1. To pack firmly
together. 2. To strike forcefully. 3. *Informal.*
To have an effect or impact (on). [< Lat.
impactus, p.p. of *impingere*, to push against.]

im·pact·ed (ĭm-păk′tĭd) adj. Wedged inside
the gum in a manner prohibiting eruption
into a normal position: *an impacted tooth.*

im·pair (ĭm-pâr′) v. To diminish in strength,
value, quantity, or quality; damage. [< OFr.
empeirer.] —**im·pair′ment** n.

im·pa·la (ĭm-pä′lə, -păl′ə) n. An African antelope, with ridged, curved horns in the male.
[Zulu *im-pala.*]

im·pale (ĭm-pāl′) v. **-paled, -pal·ing.** 1. To
pierce with or as if with a sharp point. 2. To
torture or kill by impaling. [Med. Lat. *impa-
lare*.] —**im·pale′ment** n.

im·pal·pa·ble (ĭm-păl′pə-bəl) adj. 1. Not perceptible to the touch; intangible. 2. Not easily perceived or grasped by the mind.
—**im·pal′pa·bil′i·ty** n. —**im·pal′pa·bly** adv.

im·pan·el (ĭm-păn′əl) v. **-eled** or **-elled, -el·ing**
or **-el·ling.** To enroll (a jury) on a panel or
list. —**im·pan′el·ment** n.

im·part (ĭm-pärt′) v. 1. To grant a share of;
bestow. 2. To make known; disclose. [Lat.
impartire.]

im·par·tial (ĭm-pär′shəl) adj. Not partial or
biased; unprejudiced. —**im·par′ti·al′i·ty**
(-shē-ăl′ĭ-tē) n. —**im·par′tial·ly** adv.

im·pass·a·ble (ĭm-păs′ə-bəl) adj. Impossible
to pass or cross.

im·passe (ĭm′păs′) n. 1. A road or passage
having no exit. 2. A difficult situation offering no workable escape. [Fr.]

im·pas·si·ble (ĭm-păs′ə-bəl) adj. 1. Not subject to suffering or pain. 2. Impassive.

im·pas·sioned (ĭm-păsh′ənd) adj. Filled with
passion; ardent.

im·pas·sive (ĭm-păs′ĭv) adj. Revealing no
emotion; expressionless. —**im·pas′sive·ly** adv.
—**im·pas′siv′i·ty** (-pă-sĭv′ĭ-tē) n.

im·pa·tience (ĭm-pā′shəns) n. 1. The inability
to wait patiently. 2. The inability to endure
irritation or opposition. 3. Restless eagerness,
desire, or anticipation. —**im·pa′tient** adj.
—**im·pa′tient·ly** adv.

im·peach (ĭm-pēch′) v. 1. To charge with mal-
feasance in office before a proper tribunal.
2. To challenge or discredit; attack. [< Lat.
impedicare, to put in fetters.] —**im·peach′a·
ble** adj. —**im·peach′er** n. —**im·peach′ment** n.

im·pec·ca·ble (ĭm-pĕk′ə-bəl) adj. 1. Without
flaw; faultless. 2. Not capable of sin or
wrongdoing. [Lat. *impeccabilis*.] —**im·pec′ca·
bil′i·ty** or **im·pec′ca·ble·ness** n. —**im·pec′ca·
bly** adv.

im·pe·cu·ni·ous (ĭm′pĭ-kyōō′nē-əs) adj. Lacking money; penniless. [ɪᴍ-¹ + obs. *pecunious*,
rich.] —**im′pe·cu′ni·ous·ly** adv. —**im′pe·cu′ni·
ous·ness** n.

im·ped·ance (ĭm-pēd′ns) n. A measure of the
total opposition to current flow in an
alternating-current circuit.

im·pede (ĭm-pēd′) v. **-ped·ed, -ped·ing.** To retard or obstruct the progress of; block. [<
Lat. *impedire*, to entangle.]

im·ped·i·ment (ĭm-pĕd′ə-mənt) n. 1. A hindrance; obstruction. 2. Something that impedes, esp. a speech defect. [< Lat.
impedimentum.]

ă pat ā pay â care ä father ĕ pet ē be ĭ pit ī tie î pier ŏ pot ō toe ô paw, for oi noise ōō took
ōō boot ou out th thin th this ŭ cut û urge yōō abuse zh vision ə about, item, edible, gallop, circus

im·ped·i·men·ta (ĭm-pĕd'ə-mĕn'tə) *pl.n.* Objects, as provisions or baggage, that impede or encumber. [Lat.]

im·pel (ĭm-pĕl') *v.* **-pelled, -pel·ling.** 1. To urge to action; spur. 2. To drive forward; propel. [Lat. *impellere.*]

im·pel·ler (ĭm-pĕl'ər) *n.* A rotor or rotor blade.

im·pend (ĭm-pĕnd') *v.* 1. To hang or hover menacingly. 2. To be about to take place. [Lat. *impendēre.*]

im·pen·e·tra·ble (ĭm-pĕn'ĭ-trə-bəl) *adj.* 1. Not capable of being penetrated or entered. 2. Incomprehensible; unfathomable. —**im·pen'e·tra·bil'i·ty** *n.* —**im·pen'e·tra·bly** *adv.*

im·pen·i·tent (ĭm-pĕn'ĭ-tənt) *adj.* Not penitent; unrepentant. —**im·pen'i·tence** *n.* —**im·pen'i·tent·ly** *adv.*

im·per·a·tive (ĭm-pĕr'ə-tĭv) *adj.* 1. Expressing a command, request, or plea: *an imperative sentence.* 2. Having the power or authority to command or control. 3. Obligatory; mandatory. [LLat. *imperativus.*] —**im·per'a·tive** *n.* —**im·per'a·tive·ly** *adv.*

im·per·cep·ti·ble (ĭm'pər-sĕp'tə-bəl) *adj.* 1. Not perceptible. 2. Barely perceptible. —**im'per·cep'ti·bly** *adv.*

im·per·fect (ĭm-pûr'fĭkt) *adj.* 1. Not perfect. 2. *Gram.* Of or being a verb tense expressing incomplete or continuous action. —*n. Gram.* 1. The imperfect tense. 2. A verb in the imperfect tense. —**im·per'fect·ly** *adv.*

im·per·fec·tion (ĭm'pər-fĕk'shən) *n.* 1. The quality or state of being imperfect. 2. A defect; flaw.

im·pe·ri·al (ĭm-pîr'ē-əl) *adj.* 1. Of or pertaining to an empire or emperor. 2. Designating a nation or government having sovereign rights over colonies or dependencies. 3. Regal; majestic. [< LLat. *imperialis.*] —**im·pe'ri·al·ly** *adv.*

im·pe·ri·al·ism (ĭm-pîr'ē-ə-lĭz'əm) *n.* The policy of extending a nation's territory or power by establishing dominance over other nations. —**im·pe'ri·al·ist** *n.* —**im·pe'ri·al·is'tic** *adj.* —**im·pe'ri·al·is'ti·cal·ly** *adv.*

im·per·il (ĭm-pĕr'əl) *v.* **-iled** or **-illed, -il·ing** or **-il·ling.** To endanger.

im·pe·ri·ous (ĭm-pîr'ē-əs) *adj.* 1. Domineering; overbearing. 2. Urgent; pressing. [Lat. *imperiosus.*] —**im·pe'ri·ous·ly** *adv.* —**im·pe'ri·ous·ness** *n.*

im·per·ish·a·ble (ĭm-pĕr'ĭ-shə-bəl) *adj.* Not perishable. —**im·per'ish·a·bly** *adv.*

im·per·ma·nent (ĭm-pûr'mə-nənt) *adj.* Not permanent; transient. —**im·per'ma·nence** *n.* —**im·per'ma·nent·ly** *adv.*

im·per·me·a·ble (ĭm-pûr'mē-ə-bəl) *adj.* Not permeable. —**im·per'me·a·bil'i·ty** *n.* —**im·per'me·a·bly** *adv.*

im·per·mis·si·ble (ĭm'pər-mĭs'ə-bəl) *adj.* Not permissible.

im·per·son·al (ĭm-pûr'sə-nəl) *adj.* 1. Not referring to or intended for any particular person. 2. Exhibiting no emotion: *an impersonal manner.* —**im·per'son·al'i·ty** (-năl'ĭ-tē) *n.* —**im·per'son·al·ly** *adv.*

im·per·son·ate (ĭm-pûr'sə-nāt') *v.* **-at·ed, -at·ing.** To act the character or part of. —**im·per'son·a'tion** *n.* —**im·per'son·a'tor** *n.*

im·per·ti·nent (ĭm-pûr'tn-ənt) *adj.* 1. Impudent; insolent. 2. Not pertinent; irrelevant. [LLat. *impertinens,* irrelevant.] —**im·per'ti·nence** *n.* —**im·per'ti·nent·ly** *adv.*

im·per·turb·a·ble (ĭm'pər-tûr'bə-bəl) *adj.* Unshakably calm and collected. —**im'per·turb·a·bil'i·ty** or **im'per·turb'a·ble·ness** *n.* —**im'per·turb'a·bly** *adv.*

im·per·vi·ous (ĭm-pûr'vē-əs) *adj.* 1. Incapable of being penetrated, as by water. 2. Incapable of being affected: *impervious to fear.* [Lat. *impervius.*] —**im·per'vi·ous·ly** *adv.* —**im·per'vi·ous·ness** *n.*

im·pe·ti·go (ĭm'pĭ-tē'gō, -tī'-) *n.* A contagious skin disease characterized by pustules. [Lat.]

im·pet·u·ous (ĭm-pĕch'ŏŏ-əs) *adj.* 1. Characterized by sudden intensity; impulsive. 2. Having or marked by violent force. [< Lat. *impetuosus.*] —**im·pet'u·os'i·ty** (-ŏs'ĭ-tē) *n.* —**im·pet'u·ous·ly** *adv.*

im·pe·tus (ĭm'pĭ-təs) *n., pl.* **-tus·es.** 1. a. An impelling force; impulse. b. Something that incites; stimulus. 2. Force or energy associated with a moving body. [Lat., attack.]

im·pi·e·ty (ĭm-pī'ĭ-tē) *n., pl.* **-ties.** 1. The quality or state of being impious. 2. An impious act.

im·pinge (ĭm-pĭnj') *v.* **-pinged, -ping·ing.** 1. To collide or strike. 2. To encroach or trespass. [Lat. *impingere,* to push against.] —**im·pinge'ment** *n.*

im·pi·ous (ĭm'pē-əs, ĭm-pī'-) *adj.* Not pious; irreverent. —**im'pi·ous·ly** *adv.*

imp·ish (ĭm'pĭsh) *adj.* Of or befitting an imp; mischievous. —**imp'ish·ly** *adv.* —**imp'ish·ness** *n.*

im·pla·ca·ble (ĭm-plă'kə-bəl, -plăk'ə-) *adj.* Not capable of being pacified, appeased, or altered: *implacable opposition.* —**im·pla'ca·bil'i·ty** *n.* —**im·pla'ca·bly** *adv.*

im·plant (ĭm-plănt') *v.* 1. To fix or set firmly. 2. To inculcate; instill. 3. To insert or embed surgically, as in grafting. —**im'plant'** *n.* —**im'plan·ta'tion** *n.*

im·plau·si·ble (ĭm-plô'zə-bəl) *adj.* Not plausible; difficult to believe. —**im·plau'si·bil'i·ty** *n.* —**im·plau'si·bly** *adv.*

im·ple·ment (ĭm'plə-mənt) *n.* A tool or utensil. —*v.* (-mĕnt'). 1. To put into practice. 2. To supply with implements. [< Lat. *implēre,* to fill up.] —**im'ple·men·ta'tion** *n.*

im·pli·cate (ĭm'plĭ-kāt') *v.* **-cat·ed, -cat·ing.** 1. To involve, esp. incriminatingly. 2. To imply. [Lat. *implicare.*] —**im'pli·ca'tion** *n.*

im·plic·it (ĭm-plĭs'ĭt) *adj.* 1. Contained in the nature of something though not readily apparent. 2. Implied or understood though not directly expressed. 3. Complete; absolute: *implicit obedience.* [Lat. *implicitus.*] —**im·plic'it·ly** *adv.*

Syns: implicit, implied, tacit, understood, unsaid, unspoken adj.

im·plode (ĭm-plōd') *v.* **-plod·ed, -plod·ing.** To burst inward. [IM-² + (EX)PLODE.] —**im·plo'sion** *n.*

im·plore (ĭm-plôr', -plōr') *v.* **-plored, -plor·ing.** To entreat; beseech. [Lat. *implorare.*] —**im·plor'er** *n.* —**im·plor'ing·ly** *adv.*

im·ply (ĭm-plī') *v.* **-plied, -ply·ing.** 1. To involve or suggest by logical necessity; entail. 2. To express indirectly; suggest without stating. [< Lat. *implicare,* to involve.]

im·po·lite (ĭm'pə-līt') *adj.* Not polite; discourteous. —**im'po·lite'ly** *adv.* —**im'po·lite'ness** *n.*

im·pol·i·tic (ĭm-pŏl'ĭ-tĭk) *adj.* Not wise or expedient; injudicious.

im·pon·der·a·ble (ĭm-pŏn'dər-ə-bəl) *adj.* Incapable of being weighed or measured with preciseness. —**im·pon'der·a·bil'i·ty** *n.* —**im·pon'der·a·ble** *n.* —**im·pon'der·a·bly** *adv.*

im·port (ĭm-pôrt′, -pōrt′, ĭm′pôrt′, -pōrt′) v.
1. To bring in from an outside source or a
foreign country, esp. for sale. 2. To mean;
signify. 3. To be significant; matter. —n.
(ĭm′pôrt′, -pōrt′). 1. Something imported.
2. Meaning; signification. 3. Importance; significance. [< Lat. *importare*.] —im·port′er n.

im·por·tance (ĭm-pôr′tns) n. The state or
quality of being important; significance.

im·por·tant (ĭm-pôr′tnt) adj. 1. Significant;
noteworthy. 2. Having an air of importance.
[< Lat. *importare*, to be significant.] —im-
por′tant·ly adv.

Syns: important, consequential, historic, momentous, significant, weighty adj.

im·por·ta·tion (ĭm′pôr-tā′shən, -pôr-) n.
1. The act or business of importing. 2. Something imported.

im·por·tu·nate (ĭm-pôr′chə-nĭt) adj. Stubbornly or unreasonably persistent. —im·por′-
tu·nate·ly adv.

im·por·tune (ĭm′pôr-tōōn′, -tyōōn′, ĭm-pôr′-
chən) v. -tuned, -tun·ing. To beset with repeated and insistent requests. [< Lat.
importunus, unsuitable.] —im′por·tu′ni·ty
(-tōō′nĭ-tē, -tyōō′-) n.

im·pose (ĭm-pōz′) v. -posed, -pos·ing. 1. To
inflict: *work that imposed a strain on us.* 2. To
apply or make prevail by or as if by authority. 3. To establish or apply as compulsory;
levy: *impose a tax.* 4. To pass off on others.
5. To take unfair advantage of: *imposing on a
friend's hospitality.* [< Lat. *imponere*.] —im′-
po·si′tion (-pə-zĭsh′ən) n.

im·pos·ing (ĭm-pō′zĭng) adj. Impressive.

im·pos·si·ble (ĭm-pŏs′ə-bəl) adj. 1. Not capable of existing or happening. 2. Having little
likelihood of happening or being accomplished. 3. Unacceptable. 4. Not capable of
being dealt with or tolerated; objectionable.
—im·pos′si·bil′i·ty n. —im·pos′si·bly adv.

im·post (ĭm′pōst′) n. A tax or duty. [< Lat.
imponere, to impose.]

im·pos·tor (ĭm-pŏs′tər) n. A person who deceives under an assumed identity. [< LLat.]

im·pos·ture (ĭm-pŏs′chər) n. Deception or
fraud, esp. assumption of a false identity.
[LLat. *impostura*.]

im·po·tent (ĭm′pə-tənt) adj. 1. Lacking physical strength or vigor. 2. Powerless; ineffectual. 3. Incapable of sexual intercourse.
—im′po·tence n. —im′po·tent·ly adv.

im·pound (ĭm-pound′) v. 1. To confine in or
as if in a pound: *The city impounds stray dogs.*
2. To seize and retain in legal custody. 3. To
accumulate (water) in a reservoir. —im-
pound′ment n.

im·pov·er·ish (ĭm-pŏv′ər-ĭsh, -pŏv′rĭsh) v.
1. To reduce to poverty. 2. To deprive of
natural richness or strength. [< OFr. *empo-
vrir*.] —im·pov′er·ish·ment n.

im·prac·ti·ca·ble (ĭm-prăk′tĭ-kə-bəl) adj. Not
capable of being done, carried out, or used.

im·prac·ti·cal (ĭm-prăk′tĭ-kəl) adj. 1. Unwise
to implement or maintain in practice. 2. Incapable of dealing efficiently with practical
matters. 3. Impracticable. —im·prac′ti·cal′i·ty
(-kăl′ĭ-tē) n.

im·pre·cise (ĭm′prĭ-sīs′) adj. Not precise.
—im′pre·cise′ly adv. —im′pre·ci′sion n.

im·preg·na·ble (ĭm-prĕg′nə-bəl) adj. Capable

of resisting attack; unconquerable. [< OFr.
imprenable.] —im·preg′na·bil′i·ty n.

im·preg·nate (ĭm-prĕg′nāt′) v. -nat·ed, -nat-
ing. 1. To make pregnant; inseminate. 2. To
fertilize (an ovum). 3. To fill, permeate, or
saturate. [< LLat. *impraegnare*.] —im′preg-
na′tion n.

im·pre·sa·ri·o (ĭm′prĭ-sär′ē-ō′, -sär′-) n., pl.
-os. One who sponsors or produces entertainment, esp. the director of an opera company.
[Ital. < *impresa*, undertaking.]

im·press[1] (ĭm-prĕs′) v. 1. To produce or apply with pressure. 2. To mark or stamp with
or as if with pressure. 3. To produce a vivid,
often favorable effect on. 4. To establish
firmly in the mind. —n. (ĭm′prĕs′). 1. The
act of impressing. 2. A mark or pattern produced by impressing. 3. A stamp or seal
meant to be impressed. [< Lat. *impressus*,
p.p. of *imprimere*.] —im·press′i·ble adj.

im·press[2] (ĭm-prĕs′) v. 1. To compel (a person) to serve in a military force. 2. To confiscate (property). [IM-[2] + *press*, to force into
service.] —im·press′ment n.

im·pres·sion (ĭm-prĕsh′ən) n. 1. A mark or
imprint made on a surface by pressure. 2. An
effect, image, or feeling retained as a consequence of experience. 3. A vague notion, remembrance, opinion, or belief. 4. A
humorous imitation of a famous person done
esp. by a professional entertainer. 5. a. All
the copies of a publication printed at one
time from the same set of type. b. A single
copy of this printing.

im·pres·sion·a·ble (ĭm-prĕsh′ə-nə-bəl) adj.
Readily or easily influenced; suggestible.

im·pres·sion·ism (ĭm-prĕsh′ə-nĭz′əm) n. A
style of painting characterized chiefly by concentration on the general impression produced by a scene or object and the use of
unmixed primary colors and small strokes to
simulate actual reflected light. —im·pres′-
sion·ist n. —im·pres′sion·is′tic adj.

Impressionism
"The Laundresses" by Edgar
Degas

im·pres·sive (ĭm-prĕs′ĭv) adj. Making or
tending to make a strong impression: *an impressive ceremony.* —im·pres′sive·ly adv.
—im·pres′sive·ness n.

im·pri·ma·tur (ĭm′prə-mä′tŏŏr′) n. 1. Official
approval or license to print or publish. 2. Official sanction; authorization. [< NLat., let it
be printed.]

im·print (ĭm-prĭnt′, ĭm′prĭnt′) v. 1. To produce
or impress (a mark or pattern) on a surface.

2. To establish firmly, as on the mind. —*n.* (ĭm′prĭnt′). **1.** A mark or pattern produced by imprinting. **2.** A distinguishing influence or effect: *the imprint of defeat.* **3.** A publisher's name, often with the date, address, and edition of a publication, printed at the bottom of a title page. [< Lat. *imprimere.*]

im·pris·on (ĭm-prĭz′ən) *v.* To put in or as if in prison. [< OFr. *emprisoner.*] —**im·pris′on·ment** *n.*

im·prob·a·ble (ĭm-prŏb′ə-bəl) *adj.* Not probable; unlikely. —**im·prob′a·bil′i·ty** *n.* —**im·prob′a·bly** *adv.*

im·promp·tu (ĭm-prŏmp′tōō, -tyōō) *adj.* Performed or conceived without rehearsal or preparation. [< Lat. *in promptu,* at hand.] —**im·promp′tu** *adv. & n.*

im·prop·er (ĭm-prŏp′ər) *adj.* **1.** Not suited to needs or circumstances; unsuitable. **2.** Not conforming to social or moral conventions; indecorous. **3.** Not consistent with fact; incorrect. —**im·prop′er·ly** *adv.*

improper fraction *n.* A fraction in which the numerator is larger than or equal to the denominator.

im·pro·pri·e·ty (ĭm′prə-prī′ĭ-tē) *n., pl.* **-ties. 1.** The quality or condition of being improper. **2.** An improper act or expression.

im·prove (ĭm-prōōv′) *v.* **-proved, -prov·ing. 1.** To make or become better. **2.** To increase the productivity or value of (land). [< AN *emprouer,* to enclose land for cultivation.] —**im·prov′a·ble** *adj.*

im·prove·ment (ĭm-prōōv′mənt) *n.* **1.** The act or procedure of improving. **2.** The condition of being improved. **3.** A change or addition that improves.

im·prov·i·dent (ĭm-prŏv′ĭ-dənt) *adj.* Not providing for the future; thriftless. —**im·prov′i·dence** *n.* —**im·prov′i·dent·ly** *adv.*

im·pro·vise (ĭm′prə-vīz′) *v.* **-vised, -vis·ing. 1.** To invent, compose, or recite without preparation. **2.** To make or provide from available materials: *improvised a hasty meal.* [< Ital. *improvisare.*] —**im·prov′i·sa′tion** (ĭm-prŏv′-ĭ-zā′shən, ĭm′prə-vĭ-) *n.* —**im′pro·vis′er** *n.*

im·pru·dent (ĭm-prōōd′nt) *adj.* Not prudent; unwise or injudicious. —**im·pru′dence** *n.* —**im·pru′dent·ly** *adv.*

im·pu·dent (ĭm′pyə-dənt) *adj.* Marked by brash behavior or impertinent disrespect. [< Lat. *impudens.*] —**im′pu·dence** *n.* —**im′pu·dent·ly** *adv.*

Syns: *impudent, audacious, bold, brazen, cheeky, forward, fresh, impertinent, insolent, presumptuous, sassy, saucy, smart, wise* **adj.**

im·pugn (ĭm-pyōōn′) *v.* To oppose or attack as false; cast doubt on. [< Lat. *impugnare,* to fight against.]

im·pulse (ĭm′pŭls′) *n.* **1. a.** An impelling force. **b.** The motion it produces. **2.** A sudden spontaneous inclination or urge. **3.** A motivating force; incentive. **4.** A general tendency or spirit; current. **5.** A transmission of energy from one neuron to another. [Lat. *impulsus < impellere,* to impel.]

im·pul·sive (ĭm-pŭl′sĭv) *adj.* **1.** Tending to act on impulse rather than thought. **2.** Produced by impulse; uncalculated. **3.** Having the power to impel. —**im·pul′sive·ly** *adv.* —**im·pul′sive·ness** *n.*

im·pu·ni·ty (ĭm-pyōō′nĭ-tē) *n.* Exemption from punishment or penalty. [Lat. *impunitas.*]

im·pure (ĭm-pyōōr′) *adj.* **1.** Not pure or clean; contaminated. **2.** Immoral or obscene.

3. Mixed with another substance; adulterated. —**im·pure′ly** *adv.* —**im·pu′ri·ty** *n.*

im·pute (ĭm-pyōōt′) *v.* **-put·ed, -put·ing. 1.** To ascribe (a crime or fault) to another; charge. **2.** To attribute to a cause or source; credit. [< Lat. *imputare,* to bring into the reckoning.] —**im·put′a·ble** *adj.* —**im′pu·ta′tion** *n.*

in (ĭn) *prep.* **1.** Within the limits or boundaries: *was hit in the head; was ready in a few minutes.* **2.** Toward the inside of; into: *ran in the house.* **3.** Used to indicate a condition, state, or attribute: *in a rage; in command; dressed in black.* **4.** To the state or condition of: *torn in shreds.* **5.** By means of: *paid in cash.* **6.** With reference to: *equal in speed.* —*adv.* **1.** To or toward the inside or center. **2.** Into or toward a given space or position. **3.** Indoors. —*adj.* **1.** Extremely fashionable. **2.** Available or at home: *He wasn't in.* **3.** Incoming. **4.** Having power; incumbent. —*n.* **1.** One in power or having the advantage. **2.** *Informal.* Influence. [< OE.]

In The symbol for the element indium.

in-[1] or **il-** or **im-** or **ir-** *pref.* Not: *inarticulate.* [< Lat.]

in-[2] or **il-** or **im-** or **ir-** *pref.* **1.** In, into; within: *intubation.* **2.** Var. of **en-**[1]. [< Lat.]

-in *suff.* **1.** Also **-ine.** A neutral chemical compound: *globulin.* **2.** Enzyme: *pancreatin.* **3. a.** A pharmaceutical: *niacin.* **b.** An antibiotic: *penicillin.* **4.** Var. of **-ine**[2] (sense 3). [< Lat. *-inus.*]

in·a·bil·i·ty (ĭn′ə-bĭl′ĭ-tē) *n.* Lack of ability or means.

in ab·sen·tia (ĭn′ ăb-sĕn′shə, -shē-ə) *adv.* While or although not present. [Lat., in absence.]

in·ac·ces·si·ble (ĭn′ăk-sĕs′ə-bəl) *adj.* Not accessible; unapproachable. —**in′ac·ces′si·bil′i·ty** *n.* —**in′ac·ces′si·bly** *adv.*

in·ac·cu·rate (ĭn-ăk′yər-ĭt) *adj.* **1.** Not accurate. **2.** Mistaken or incorrect. —**in·ac′cu·ra·cy** *n.* —**in·ac′cu·rate·ly** *adv.*

in·ac·tion (ĭn-ăk′shən) *n.* Lack or absence of action.

in·ac·ti·vate (ĭn-ăk′tə-vāt′) *v.* **-vat·ed, -vat·ing.** To render inactive. —**in·ac′ti·va′tion** *n.*

in·ac·tive (ĭn-ăk′tĭv) *adj.* **1.** Not active or tending not to be active. **2.** Retired from duty or service. —**in·ac′tive·ly** *adv.* —**in·ac′tiv′i·ty** or **in·ac′tive·ness** *n.*

Syns: *inactive, dormant, idle, inert, inoperative, unused* **adj.**

in·ad·e·quate (ĭn-ăd′ĭ-kwĭt) *adj.* Not adequate; insufficient. —**in·ad′e·qua·cy** *n.* —**in·ad′e·quate·ly** *adv.*

in·ad·mis·si·ble (ĭn′əd-mĭs′ə-bəl) *adj.* Not admissible. —**in′ad·mis′si·bil′i·ty** *n.* —**in′ad·mis′si·bly** *adv.*

in·ad·ver·tent (ĭn′əd-vûr′tnt) *adj.* **1.** Not duly attentive. **2.** Accidental; unintentional. [< Med. Lat. *inadvertentia,* inadvertence.] —**in′ad·ver′tence** *n.* —**in′ad·ver′tent·ly** *adv.*

in·ad·vis·a·ble (ĭn′əd-vī′zə-bəl) *adj.* Not recommended; unwise. —**in′ad·vis′a·bil′i·ty** *n.*

in·al·ien·a·ble (ĭn-āl′yə-nə-bəl) *adj.* Incapable of being given up, taken away, or transferred to another. —**in·al′ien·a·bil′i·ty** *n.* —**in·al′ien·a·bly** *adv.*

in·ane (ĭ-nān′) *adj.* Lacking sense or substance; silly or empty. [Lat. *inanis,* empty.] —**in·ane′ly** *adv.* —**in·an′i·tē** *n.*

in·an·i·mate (ĭn-ăn′ə-mĭt) *adj.* Not animate; lacking the qualities associated with active, living organisms. —**in·an'i·mate·ly** *adv.* —**in·an'i·mate·ness** *n.*

in·a·ni·tion (ĭn'ə-nĭsh'ən) *n.* Exhaustion and weakness, as from lack of nourishment. [< Lat. *inanire*, to make empty.]

in·ap·pli·ca·ble (ĭn-ăp'lĭ-kə-bəl) *adj.* Not applicable. —**in·ap'pli·ca·bil'i·ty** *n.*

in·ap·pre·ci·a·ble (ĭn'ə-prē'shə-bəl) *adj.* Too small to be noticed; negligible. —**in'ap·pre'ci·a·bly** *adv.*

in·ap·pro·pri·ate (ĭn'ə-prō'prē-ĭt) *adj.* Not appropriate; unsuitable or improper. —**in'ap·pro'pri·ate·ly** *adv.* —**in'ap·pro'pri·ate·ness** *n.*

in·ar·tic·u·late (ĭn'är-tĭk'yə-lĭt) *adj.* 1. Uttered without the use of normal words or syllables. 2. Unable to speak; mute. 3. Unable to speak with clarity or eloquence. 4. Unexpressed: *inarticulate sorrow.* —**in'ar·tic'u·late·ly** *adv.* —**in'ar·tic'u·late·ness** *n.*

in·as·much as (ĭn'əz-mŭch') *conj.* Because of the fact that; since.

in·at·ten·tion (ĭn'ə-tĕn'shən) *n.* Lack of attention or notice; disregard. —**in'at·ten'tive** *adj.* —**in'at·ten'tive·ly** *adv.*

in·au·di·ble (ĭn-ô'də-bəl) *adj.* Not audible; incapable of being heard. —**in·au'di·bly** *adv.*

in·au·gu·ral (ĭ-nô'gyər-əl) *adj.* 1. Of or pertaining to an inauguration. 2. Initial; first. —*n.* An inaugural speech.

in·au·gu·rate (ĭ-nô'gyə-rāt') *v.* -rat·ed, -rat·ing. 1. To install in office with a formal ceremony. 2. To begin; launch. 3. To open formally with a ceremony; dedicate. [< Lat. *inaugurare*.] —**in·au'gu·ra'tion** *n.*

inaugurate
Inauguration of Ronald Reagan as President of the United States,

in·aus·pi·cious (ĭn'ô-spĭsh'əs) *adj.* Not auspicious; unfavorable. —**in'aus·pi'cious·ly** *adv.*

in·board (ĭn'bôrd', -bōrd') *adj.* 1. Within the hull of a ship. 2. Near the fuselage of an aircraft. —**in'board'** *adv.*

in·born (ĭn'bôrn') *adj.* Hereditary.

in·bound (ĭn'bound') *adj.* Incoming: *inbound traffic.*

in·bred (ĭn'brĕd') *adj.* 1. Produced by inbreeding. 2. Innate; inborn.

in·breed (ĭn'brēd', ĭn-brēd') *v.* To produce by the continued breeding of closely related individuals.

In·ca (ĭng'kə) *n., pl.* -ca or -cas. A member of a powerful Indian people who ruled Peru before the Spanish conquest.

in·cal·cu·la·ble (ĭn-kăl'kyə-lə-bəl) *adj.* 1. Incapable of being calculated, esp. too great to be calculated or conceived. 2. Unpredictable; uncertain. —**in·cal'cu·la·bly** *adv.*

in·can·des·cent (ĭn'kən-dĕs'ənt) *adj.* 1. Emitting visible light as a result of being heated. 2. Shining brilliantly; very bright. [< Lat. *incandescere*, to glow.] —**in'can·des'cence** *n.*

incandescent lamp *n.* An electric lamp in which a filament is heated to incandescence by an electric current.

in·can·ta·tion (ĭn'kăn-tā'shən) *n.* 1. A recitation of verbal charms or spells to produce a magical effect. 2. A formula of words or sounds recited in an incantation. [< Lat. *incantare*, to enchant.]

in·ca·pa·ble (ĭn-kā'pə-bəl) *adj.* Not capable; lacking the necessary ability, power, or capacity for a particular aim or purpose. —**in·ca'pa·bil'i·ty** *n.*

in·ca·pac·i·tate (ĭn'kə-păs'ĭ-tāt') *v.* -tat·ed, -tat·ing. To deprive of strength or ability; disable. —**in'ca·pac'i·ta'tion** *n.*

in·ca·pac·i·ty (ĭn'kə-păs'ĭ-tē) *n., pl.* -ties. Lack of capacity; inadequate strength or ability.

in·car·cer·ate (ĭn-kär'sə-rāt') *v.* -at·ed, -at·ing. 1. To imprison. 2. To confine. [< Lat. *incarcerare*.] —**in·car'cer·a'tion** *n.*

in·car·nate (ĭn-kär'nĭt, -nāt') *adj.* 1. Invested with bodily nature and form. 2. Personified: *wisdom incarnate.* —*v.* (-nāt') -nat·ed, -nat·ing. 1. To give bodily nature and form to. 2. To personify. [< LLat. *incarnatus*, p.p. of *incarnare*, to make flesh.] —**in·car·na'tion** *n.*

in·case (ĭn-kās') *v.* Var. of **encase.**

in·cen·di·ar·y (ĭn-sĕn'dē-ĕr'ē) *adj.* 1. Producing intensely hot fire, as a military weapon. 2. Of or involving arson. 3. Tending to inflame; inflammatory. [Lat. *incendiarius.*] —**in·cen'di·ar·y** *n.*

in·cense¹ (ĭn-sĕns') *v.* -censed, -cens·ing. To cause to be angry; enrage. [< Lat. *incendere*, to set on fire.]

in·cense² (ĭn'sĕns') *n.* 1. An aromatic substance burned to produce a pleasant odor. 2. The smoke or odor produced by the burning of incense. [< LLat. *incensum.*]

in·cen·tive (ĭn-sĕn'tĭv) *n.* Something inciting or tending to incite to action or effort. [< Lat. *incentivus*, inciting.]

in·cep·tion (ĭn-sĕp'shən) *n.* The beginning; commencement. [< Lat. *incipere*, to begin.] —**in·cep'tive** *adj.*

in·cer·ti·tude (ĭn-sûr'tĭ-tōōd', -tyōōd') *n.* 1. Uncertainty. 2. Insecurity or instability.

in·ces·sant (ĭn-sĕs'ənt) *adj.* Continuing without interruption; unceasing. [< LLat. *incessans.*] —**in·ces'sant·ly** *adv.*

in·cest (ĭn'sĕst') *n.* Sexual intercourse between persons so closely related that their marriage is illegal or forbidden by custom. [< Lat. *incestus*, impure.] —**in·ces'tu·ous** (ĭn-sĕs'chōō-əs) *adj.* —**in·ces'tu·ous·ly** *adv.*

inch (ĭnch) *n.* A unit of length equal to $1/12$ of a foot. —*v.* To move or cause to move slowly or by small degrees. [< Lat. *uncia*, 12th part.]

in·cho·ate (ĭn-kō'ĭt) *adj.* In an initial or early stage; incipient. [< Lat. *inchoare*, to begin.]

inch·worm (ĭnch'wûrm') *n.* A caterpillar that moves by alternately looping and stretching out its body.

in·ci·dence (ĭn'sĭ-dəns) *n.* The extent or frequency with which something occurs.

in·ci·dent (ĭn'sĭ-dənt) n. 1. An occurrence; event. 2. An occurrence or event causing or likely to cause a crisis. —adj. 1. Tending to arise or occur as a concomitant. 2. Physics. Falling upon; striking: incident radiation. [< Lat. incidere, to happen.]

in·ci·den·tal (ĭn'sĭ-dĕn'tl) adj. 1. Occurring or likely to occur at the same time or as a consequence. 2. Of a minor or casual nature: incidental expenses. —n. Often incidentals. A minor concomitant circumstance, event, item, or expense. —in·ci·den'tal·ly adv.

in·cin·er·ate (ĭn-sĭn'ə-rāt') v. -at·ed, -at·ing. To consume by burning. [Med. Lat. incinerare.] —in·cin'er·a'tion n.

in·cin·er·a·tor (ĭn-sĭn'ə-rā'tər) n. A furnace or other apparatus for burning waste.

in·cip·i·ent (ĭn-sĭp'ē-ənt) adj. Beginning to exist or appear. [< Lat. incipere, to begin.] —in·cip'i·ence n. —in·cip'i·ent·ly adv.

in·cise (ĭn-sīz') v. -cised, -cis·ing. 1. To cut into or mark with a sharp instrument. 2. To carve (designs or writing) into a surface; engrave. [< Lat. incidere.]

in·ci·sion (ĭn-sĭzh'ən) n. 1. The act of incising. 2. A cut, esp. a surgical cut into soft tissue.

in·ci·sive (ĭn-sī'sĭv) adj. 1. Cutting; penetrating. 2. Direct and effective; telling: incisive comments. —in·ci'sive·ly adv. —in·ci'sive·ness n.

in·ci·sor (ĭn-sī'zər) n. A tooth adapted for cutting, located at the apex of the dental arch in mammals.

in·cite (ĭn-sīt') v. -cit·ed, -cit·ing. To provoke to action; stir up. [< Lat. incitare.] —in·cite'ment n.

in·clem·ent (ĭn-klĕm'ənt) adj. 1. Stormy; severe: inclement weather. 2. Unmerciful. —in·clem'en·cy n. —in·clem'ent·ly adv.

in·cli·na·tion (ĭn'klə-nā'shən) n. 1. An attitude or disposition toward something. 2. A tendency; propensity. 3. A preference or leaning. 4. The act of inclining, as a bow. 5. A slope; slant.

in·cline (ĭn-klīn') v. -clined, -clin·ing. 1. To depart or cause to depart from the horizontal or vertical; slant. 2. To dispose or be disposed; tend. 3. To lower or bend (the head or body), as in a nod; bow. —n. (ĭn'klīn'). An inclined surface; slope. [< Lat. inclinare.]

in·close (ĭn-klōz') v. Var. of enclose.

in·clude (ĭn-klōōd') v. -clud·ed, -clud·ing. 1. To have as a part or member of a whole; contain. 2. To put into a group, class, or total. [< Lat. includere.] —in·clu'sion n. —in·clu'sive adj. —in·clu'sive·ly adv.

in·cog·ni·to (ĭn'kŏg-nē'tō, ĭn-kŏg'nĭ-tō) adv. & adj. With one's identity disguised or concealed. [< Lat. incognitus, unknown.]

in·co·her·ent (ĭn'kō-hîr'ənt, -hĕr'-) adj. 1. Not coherent; lacking order or connection. 2. Unable to express one's thoughts in an orderly manner. —in'co·her'ence n. —in'co·her'ent·ly adv.

in·com·bus·ti·ble (ĭn'kəm-bŭs'tə-bəl) adj. Incapable of burning. —in'com·bus'ti·ble n.

in·come (ĭn'kŭm') n. Money or its equivalent received in exchange for labor or services, from the sale of goods or property, or as profit from financial investment.

income tax n. A tax levied on annual income.

in·com·ing (ĭn'kŭm'ĭng) adj. Coming in or about to come in.

in·com·men·su·rate (ĭn'kə-mĕn'shər-ĭt, -sər-) adj. 1. Not commensurate; disproportionate. 2. Inadequate. —in'com·men'su·rate·ly adv.

in·com·mode (ĭn'kə-mōd') v. -mod·ed, -mod·ing. To disturb; inconvenience.

in·com·mu·ni·ca·do (ĭn'kə-myōō'nĭ-kä'dō) adv. & adj. Without the means or right of communicating with others, as one held in solitary confinement. [Sp., p.p. of incomunicar, to deny communication.]

in·com·pa·ra·ble (ĭn-kŏm'pər-ə-bəl) adj. 1. Incapable of being compared. 2. Beyond compare; matchless. —in·com'pa·ra·bly adv.

in·com·pat·i·ble (ĭn'kəm-păt'ə-bəl) adj. Not compatible; not in harmony or agreement: incompatible colors; conduct incompatible with self-respect. —in'com·pat'i·bil'i·ty n. —in'com·pat'i·bly adv.

in·com·pe·tent (ĭn-kŏm'pĭ-tənt) adj. Not competent. —in·com'pe·tence n. or in·com'pe·ten·cy n. —in·com'pe·tent·ly adv.

in·com·plete (ĭn'kəm-plēt') adj. Not complete. —in'com·plete'ly adv. —in'com·plete'·ness n.

in·com·pre·hen·si·ble (ĭn-kŏm'prĭ-hĕn'sə-bəl, ĭn'kŏm-) adj. Incapable of being comprehended; unintelligible. —in·com'pre·hen·si·bil'i·ty n. —in·com'pre·hen·si·bly adv. —in·com'pre·hen'sion n.

in·com·press·i·ble (ĭn'kəm-prĕs'ə-bəl) adj. Incapable of being compressed. —in'com·press'i·bil'i·ty n.

in·con·ceiv·a·ble (ĭn'kən-sē'və-bəl) adj. Incapable of being conceived of; unimaginable. —in'con·ceiv'a·bly adv.

in·con·clu·sive (ĭn'kən-klōō'sĭv) adj. Not conclusive. —in'con·clu'sive·ly adv. —in'con·clu'sive·ness n.

in·con·gru·ent (ĭn-kŏng'grōō-ənt, ĭn'kŏn-grōō'ənt) adj. Not congruent. —in·con'gru·ence n. —in'con·gru'ent·ly adv.

in·con·gru·ous (ĭn-kŏng'grōō-əs) adj. 1. Not consistent with what is logical, customary, or expected; inappropriate. 2. Made up of disparate members, qualities, or parts. —in·con·gru'i·ty (-kən-grōō'ĭ-tē, -kŏn-) n. —in·con'gru·ous·ly adv.

in·con·se·quen·tial (ĭn-kŏn'sĭ-kwĕn'shəl) adj. Without consequence; unimportant. —in·con'se·quence (-kwəns) n. —in·con'se·quen'ti·al'i·ty (-shē-ăl'ĭ-tē) n.

in·con·sid·er·a·ble (ĭn'kən-sĭd'ər-ə-bəl) adj. Unimportant. —in'con·sid'er·a·bly adv.

in·con·sid·er·ate (ĭn'kən-sĭd'ər-ĭt) adj. Not considerate; thoughtless. —in'con·sid'er·ate·ly adv. —in'con·sid'er·ate·ness n.

in·con·sis·tent (ĭn'kən-sĭs'tənt) adj. Not consistent, esp. incompatible, contradictory, or erratic. —in'con·sis'ten·cy n. —in'con·sis'tent·ly adv.

in·con·sol·a·ble (ĭn'kən-sō'lə-bəl) adj. Incapable of being consoled; despondent. —in'con·sol'a·bly adv.

in·con·spic·u·ous (ĭn'kən-spĭk'yōō-əs) adj. Not readily noticeable. —in'con·spic'u·ous·ly adv. —in'con·spic'u·ous·ness n.

in·con·stant (ĭn-kŏn'stənt) adj. Not constant; likely to change. —in·con'stan·cy n. —in·con'stant·ly adv.

in·con·test·a·ble (ĭn'kən-tĕs'tə-bəl) adj. Indisputable; unquestionable. —in'con·test'a·bil'i·ty n. —in'con·test'a·bly adv.

in·con·ti·nent (ĭn-kŏn'tə-nənt) adj. Not continent, esp.: 1. Lacking in restraint. 2. Incapa-

ble of controlling the excretory functions.
—in·con'ti·nence n. **—in·con'ti·nent·ly** adv.
in·con·tro·vert·i·ble (ĭn-kŏn'trə-vûr'tə-bəl) adj.
Indisputable; unquestionable. **—in·con'tro·vert'i·bly** adv.
in·con·ven·ience (ĭn'kən-vēn'yəns) n. **1.** Lack of ease or comfort. **2.** Something that is inconvenient. **—**v. **-ienced, -ienc·ing.** To cause inconvenience to.
in·con·ven·ient (ĭn'kən-vēn'yənt) adj. Not convenient; causing annoyance or difficulty. **—in'con·ven'ient·ly** adv.
in·cor·po·rate (ĭn-kôr'pə-rāt') v. **-rat·ed, -rat·ing. 1.** To form or form into a legal corporation. **2.** To combine or blend into a unified whole; unite. **3.** To give material form to; embody. [< LLat. incorporare, to form into a body.] **—in·cor'po·ra'tion** n. **—in·cor'po·ra'tor** n.
in·cor·po·re·al (ĭn'kôr-pôr'ē-əl, -pōr'-) adj. Lacking material form or substance. **—in'cor·po're·al·ly** adv.
in·cor·rect (ĭn'kə-rĕkt') adj. **1.** Not correct; erroneous. **2.** Improper; unbecoming. **—in'cor·rect'ly** adv. **—in'cor·rect'ness** n.
in·cor·ri·gi·ble (ĭn-kôr'ĭ-jə-bəl, -kŏr'-) adj. Incapable of being corrected or reformed. [< LLat. incorrigibilis.] **—in·cor'ri·gi·bil'i·ty** n. **—in·cor'ri·gi·ble** n. **—in·cor'ri·gi·bly** adv.
in·cor·rupt·i·ble (ĭn'kə-rŭp'tə-bəl) adj. **1.** Incapable of being corrupted morally. **2.** Not subject to decay. **—in'cor·rupt'i·bil'i·ty** n. **—in'cor·rupt'i·bly** adv.
in·crease (ĭn-krēs') v. **-creased, -creas·ing. 1.** To make or become greater or larger. **2.** To multiply; reproduce. **—**n. (ĭn'krēs'). **1.** The act of increasing. **2.** The amount or rate by which something is increased. [< Lat. increscere.] **—in·creas'ing·ly** adv.

Syns: *increase, augment, enlarge, expand, extend, magnify, mount, snowball, swell* **v.**

in·cred·i·ble (ĭn-krĕd'ə-bəl) adj. **1.** Too implausible to be believed; unbelievable. **2.** Hard to believe; astonishing. **—in·cred'i·bil'i·ty** n. **—in·cred'i·bly** adv.
in·cred·u·lous (ĭn-krĕj'ə-ləs) adj. **1.** Disbelieving; skeptical. **2.** Expressing disbelief. **—in'cre·du'li·ty** (ĭn'krĭ-dōo'lĭ-tē, -dyōo'-) n. **—in·cred'u·lous·ly** adv.
in·cre·ment (ĭn'krə-mənt) n. **1.** An increase in number, size, or extent; enlargement. **2.** Something added or gained, esp. one of a series of regular, usu. small additions. [< Lat. incrementum.] **—in'cre·men'tal** (-mĕn'tl) adj.
in·crim·i·nate (ĭn-krĭm'ə-nāt') v. **-nat·ed, -nat·ing.** To charge with or involve in a crime or wrongful act. [LLat. incriminare.] **—in·crim'i·nat'ing·ly** adv. **—in·crim'i·na'tion** n. **—in·crim'i·na·to'ry** (-nə-tôr'ē, -tōr'ē) adj.
in·crust (ĭn-krŭst') v. Var. of encrust.
in·cu·bate (ĭn'kyə-bāt', ĭng'-) v. **-bat·ed, -bat·ing. 1.** To warm and hatch eggs, as by bodily heat. **2.** To maintain in favorable environmental conditions for development. [Lat. incubare, to lie down on.] **—in·cu·ba'tion** n.
in·cu·ba·tor (ĭn'kyə-bā'tər, ĭng'-) n. **1.** A device in which a uniform temperature can be maintained, used in growing bacterial cultures. **2.** A device used for maintaining a premature infant in an environment of controlled temperature, humidity, and oxygen.

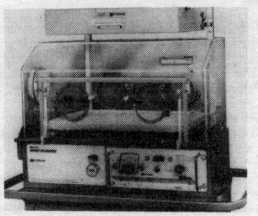

Incubator

in·cu·bus (ĭn'kyə-bəs, ĭng'-) n., pl. **-bus·es** or **-bi** (-bī'). **1.** An evil spirit believed to descend upon sleeping persons. **2.** A nightmare. **3.** Something nightmarishly burdensome. [< LLat.]
in·cu·des (ĭng-kyōo'dēz) n. Pl. of incus.
in·cul·cate (ĭn-kŭl'kāt') v. **-cat·ed, -cat·ing.** To teach or impress by frequent urging or repetition; instill. [Lat. inculcare, to force upon.] **—in'cul·ca'tion** n.
in·cul·pa·ble (ĭn-kŭl'pə-bəl) adj. Free from guilt; blameless.
in·cul·pate (ĭn-kŭl'pāt') v. **-pat·ed, -pat·ing.** To incriminate. [LLat. inculpare.]
in·cum·bent (ĭn-kŭm'bənt) adj. **1.** Lying, leaning, or resting on something else. **2.** Imposed as an obligation or duty; required. **3.** Currently holding a specified office. **—**n. A person who holds an office. [< Lat. incumbere, to lean upon.] **—in·cum'ben·cy** n.
in·cu·nab·u·lum (ĭn'kyə-năb'yə-ləm, ĭng'-) n., pl. **-la** (-lə). A book printed from movable type before 1501. [< Lat. incunabula, cradle.]
in·cur (ĭn-kûr') v. **-curred, -cur·ring. 1.** To meet with; run into: incurring difficulties. **2.** To become liable or subject to, esp. as a result of one's actions; bring upon oneself. [Lat. incurrere.]
in·cur·a·ble (ĭn-kyōor'ə-bəl) adj. Not capable of being cured: an incurable disease. **—in·cur'a·bil'i·ty** n. **—in·cur'a·bly** adv.
in·cu·ri·ous (ĭn-kyōor'ē-əs) adj. Not curious; uninterested.
in·cur·sion (ĭn-kûr'zhən) n. A sudden attack or invasion; raid. [< Lat. incurrere, to attack.]
in·cus (ĭng'kəs) n., pl. **in·cu·des** (ĭng-kyōo'dēz). An anvil-shaped bone in the middle ear. [Lat., anvil.]
in·debt·ed (ĭn-dĕt'ĭd) adj. Obligated to another; beholden. **—in·debt'ed·ness** n.
in·de·cent (ĭn-dē'sənt) adj. **1.** Offensive to good taste; unseemly. **2.** Morally offensive. **—in·de'cen·cy** n. **—in·de'cent·ly** adv.
in·de·ci·pher·a·ble (ĭn'dĭ-sī'fər-ə-bəl) adj. Incapable of being deciphered.
in·de·ci·sion (ĭn'dĭ-sĭzh'ən) n. Inability to make a decision; irresolution.
in·de·ci·sive (ĭn'dĭ-sī'sĭv) adj. **1.** Not decisive; inconclusive. **2.** Characterized by indecision; irresolute. **—in'de·ci'sive·ly** adv. **—in'de·ci'sive·ness** n.
in·dec·o·rous (ĭn-dĕk'ər-əs) adj. Lacking propriety or good taste; unseemly. **—in·dec'o·rous·ly** adv. **—in·dec'o·rous·ness** n.
in·deed (ĭn-dēd') adv. **1.** Without a doubt;

certainly. **2.** In fact; in reality. **3.** Admittedly; unquestionably. —*interj.* Used to express surprise, skepticism, or irony. [ME *indede.*]

in·de·fat·i·ga·ble (ĭn′dĭ-făt′ĭ-gə-bəl) *adj.* Untiring; tireless. [Lat. *indefatigabilis.*] —**in′de·fat′i·ga·bly** *adv.*

in·de·fen·si·ble (ĭn′dĭ-fĕn′sə-bəl) *adj.* **1.** Not capable of being defended. **2.** Inexcusable. —**in′de·fen′si·bly** *adv.*

in·de·fin·a·ble (ĭn′dĭ-fī′nə-bəl) *adj.* Not capable of being defined, described, or analyzed. —**in′de·fin′a·ble·ness** *n.* —**in′de·fin′a·bly** *adv.*

in·def·i·nite (ĭn-dĕf′ə-nĭt) *adj.* **1.** Unclear; vague. **2.** Lacking precise limits. **3.** Uncertain; undecided. —**in·def′i·nite·ly** *adv.* —**in·def′i·nite·ness** *n.*

indefinite article *n. Gram.* An article, as *a* or *an,* that does not fix the identity of the noun modified.

in·del·i·ble (ĭn-dĕl′ə-bəl) *adj.* **1.** Incapable of being removed, erased, or washed away. **2.** Making a mark not easily erased or washed away: *an indelible laundry pencil.* [Lat. *indelebilis.*] —**in·del′i·bly** *adv.*

in·del·i·cate (ĭn-dĕl′ĭ-kĭt) *adj.* **1.** Offensive to propriety; coarse. **2.** Tactless. —**in·del′i·ca·cy** *n.* —**in·del′i·cate·ly** *adv.*

in·dem·ni·fy (ĭn-dĕm′nə-fī′) *v.* **-fied, -fy·ing. 1.** To protect against possible damage; insure. **2.** To make compensation to for damage suffered. [< Lat. *indemnis,* uninjured.] —**in·dem′ni·fi·ca′tion** *n.*

in·dem·ni·ty (ĭn-dĕm′nĭ-tē) *n., pl.* **-ties. 1.** Insurance against possible damage or loss. **2.** A legal exemption from liability for damages. **3.** Compensation for damage, loss, or injury suffered. [< LLat. *indemnitas.*]

in·dent¹ (ĭn-dĕnt′) *v.* **1.** To set in (the first line of a paragraph) from the margin. **2.** To notch the edge of; serrate. —*n.* An indentation. [< OFr. *endenter,* to notch.]

in·dent² (ĭn-dĕnt′) *v.* **1.** To press down on so as to form an impression. **2.** To make a dent in. —**in·den′tion** *n.*

in·den·ta·tion (ĭn′dĕn-tā′shən) *n.* **1.** The act of indenting or condition of being indented. **2.** A notch or jagged cut in an edge. **3.** A deep recess in a boundary such as a coastline. **4.** The blank space between a margin and the beginning of an indented line.

in·den·ture (ĭn-dĕn′chər) *n.* **1.** A written deed or contract. **2.** Often **indentures.** A contract binding one party into the service of another for a specified term. —*v.* **-tured, -tur·ing.** To bind by indenture. [< OFr. *endenture.*]

in·de·pend·ence (ĭn′dĭ-pĕn′dəns) *n.* The condition or quality of being independent.

Independence Day *n.* July 4, a U.S. legal holiday celebrating the anniversary of the adoption of the Declaration of Independence in 1776.

in·de·pend·ent (ĭn′dĭ-pĕn′dənt) *adj.* **1.** Politically autonomous; self-governing. **2.** Free from the influence, guidance, or control of others; self-reliant. **3.** Not committed to any one political party. **4. a.** Financially self-sufficient. **b.** Providing or being sufficient income to enable one to live without working. —*n.* One that is independent, esp. a voter not committed to any one political party. —**in′de·pend′ent·ly** *adv.*

in-depth (ĭn′dĕpth′) *adj.* Detailed; thorough: *an in-depth study.*

in·de·scrib·a·ble (ĭn′dĭ-skrī′bə-bəl) *adj.* **1.** In-

capable of being described. **2.** Beyond description. —**in′de·scrib′a·bly** *adv.*

in·de·struc·ti·ble (ĭn′dĭ-strŭk′tə-bəl) *adj.* Incapable of being destroyed. —**in′de·struc′ti·bil′i·ty** or **in′de·struc′ti·ble·ness** *n.* —**in′de·struc′ti·bly** *adv.*

in·de·ter·mi·nate (ĭn′dĭ-tûr′mə-nĭt) *adj.* **1. a.** Incapable of being determined. **b.** Not precisely determined. **2.** Lacking clarity or precision; vague. —**in′de·ter′mi·na·cy** *n.* —**in′de·ter′mi·nate·ly** *adv.*

in·dex (ĭn′dĕks′) *n., pl.* **-dex·es** or **-di·ces** (-dĭ-sēz′). **1.** An alphabetized listing of the names, places, and subjects in a printed work, giving the page on which each can be found. **2.** Something that reveals or indicates; sign. **3.** *Printing.* A character used to direct attention, as to a particular paragraph. **4.** A number or symbol used to indicate an operation or relationship involving a particular mathematical expression. **5.** A number derived from a formula used to characterize a set of data: *the cost-of-living index.* —*v.* **1.** To furnish with or enter in an index. **2.** To indicate or signal. [Lat., forefinger.]

index finger *n.* The finger next to the thumb.

index number *n.* A number indicating change in magnitude, as of prices, relative to the magnitude at a specified point usu. taken as 100.

index of refraction *n.* The ratio of the speed of light in a vacuum to the speed of light in a medium under consideration.

In·di·an (ĭn′dē-ən) *n.* **1.** A native or inhabitant of India or of the East Indies. **2.** A member of any of the aboriginal peoples of the Americas. —**In′di·an** *adj.*

Indian corn *n.* A tall, widely cultivated cereal plant that bears seeds on large ears.

Indian meal *n.* Cornmeal.

Indian pipe *n.* A waxy white woodland plant with scalelike leaves and a nodding flower.

Indian summer *n.* A period of mild weather occurring in late autumn or early winter.

In·dic (ĭn′dĭk) *n.* A branch of the Indo-European language family that comprises the languages of the Indian subcontinent and Sri Lanka. —**In′dic** *adj.*

in·di·cate (ĭn′dĭ-kāt′) *v.* **-cat·ed, -cat·ing. 1.** To demonstrate or point out. **2.** To serve as a sign, symptom, or token of; signify. **3.** To suggest the necessity or advisability of. **4.** To state or express briefly. [Lat. *indicare.*] —**in′-di·ca′tion** *n.* —**in′di·ca′tor** *n.*

in·dic·a·tive (ĭn-dĭk′ə-tĭv) *adj.* **1.** Serving to indicate. **2.** *Gram.* Of, pertaining to, or being a verb mood used to indicate that a denoted act or condition is an objective fact. —*n. Gram.* **1.** The indicative mood. **2.** A verb in the indicative mood.

in·di·ces (ĭn′dĭ-sēz′) *n.* A pl. of **index.**

in·dict (ĭn-dīt′) *v.* **1.** To accuse of an offense. **2.** To charge formally with a crime by the findings of a grand jury. [< Lat. *enditer.*] —**in·dict′a·ble** *adj.* —**in·dict′er** or **in·dic′tor** *n.* —**in·dict′ment** *n.*

in·dif·fer·ent (ĭn-dĭf′ər-ənt) *adj.* **1.** Having no interest or concern; apathetic. **2.** Showing no bias or preference; impartial. **3.** Neither good nor bad; mediocre. **4.** Not mattering one way or the other; of no great importance. **5.** Having no marked feeling one way or the other; without a preference. —**in·dif′fer·ence** *n.* —**in·dif′fer·ent·ly** *adv.*

in·dig·e·nous (ĭn-dĭj′ə-nəs) *adj.* Occurring or

living naturally in an area; native. [< Lat. *indigena*, a native.]

in·di·gent (ĭn'də-jənt) *adj.* Lacking the means of subsistence; impoverished; needy. [< Lat. *indigēre*, to lack.] —**in'di·gence** *n.* —**in'di·gent·ly** *adv.*

in·di·gest·i·ble (ĭn'dī-jĕs'tə-bəl, -dĭ-) *adj.* Difficult or impossible to digest.

in·di·ges·tion (ĭn'dī-jĕs'chən, -dĭ-) *n.* 1. The inability to digest food. 2. Discomfort or illness resulting from indigestion.

in·dig·nant (ĭn-dĭg'nənt) *adj.* Feeling or expressing indignation. [< Lat. *indignari*, to deem unworthy.] —**in·dig'nant·ly** *adv.*

in·dig·na·tion (ĭn'dĭg-nā'shən) *n.* Anger aroused by something unjust, mean, or unworthy. [< Lat. *indignari*, to deem unworthy.]

in·dig·ni·ty (ĭn-dĭg'nĭ-tē) *n., pl.* **-ties.** 1. Humiliating or degrading treatment. 2. Something that offends one's pride or sense of dignity; affront.

in·di·go (ĭn'dĭ-gō') *n., pl.* **-gos** or **-goes.** 1. A plant that yields a blue dyestuff. 2. A blue dye obtained from an indigo plant or produced synthetically. 3. A dark blue. [< Gk. *indikon (pharmakon)*, Indian (dye).]

Indigo

Indigo bunting *n.* A small bird of North and Central America, the male of which has deep-blue plumage.

Indigo snake *n.* A nonvenomous bluish-black snake of the southern United States.

in·di·rect (ĭn'də-rĕkt', -dī-) *adj.* 1. Not being or taking a direct course; roundabout. 2. **a.** Not straight to the point; circumlocutory. **b.** Not forthright and candid; devious. 3. Not clearly planned for; secondary: *indirect benefits.* —**in'di·rec'tion** *n.* —**in'di·rect'ly** *adv.*

Indirect object *n.* A grammatical object indirectly affected by the action of a verb, as *me* in *Sing me a song.*

in·dis·creet (ĭn'dĭ-skrēt') *adj.* Lacking discretion; imprudent. —**in'dis·creet'ly** *adv.* —**in'dis·cre'tion** (-skrĕsh'ən) *n.*

in·dis·crim·i·nate (ĭn'dĭ-skrĭm'ə-nĭt) *adj.* 1. Lacking in discrimination. 2. Chaotic; confused. 3. Random; haphazard. —**in'dis·crim'i·nate·ly** *adv.*

in·dis·pen·sa·ble (ĭn'dĭ-spĕn'sə-bəl) *adj.* Incapable of being dispensed with; essential. —**in'dis·pen'sa·bil'i·ty** *n.* —**in'dis·pen'sa·ble** *n.* —**in'dis·pen'sa·bly** *adv.*

in·dis·posed (ĭn'dĭ-spōzd') *adj.* 1. Mildly ill. 2. Disinclined; unwilling. —**in·dis'po·si'tion** (-dĭs'pə-zĭsh'ən) *n.*

in·dis·put·a·ble (ĭn'dĭ-spyōō'tə-bəl) *adj.* Be-

yond doubt; undeniable. —**in'dis·put'a·ble·ness** *n.* —**in'dis·put'a·bly** *adv.*

in·dis·sol·u·ble (ĭn'dĭ-sŏl'yə-bəl) *adj.* Incapable of being dissolved, broken, or undone.

in·dis·tinct (ĭn'dĭ-stĭngkt') *adj.* 1. Not sharply delineated; blurred. 2. Not clearly heard, seen, or understood. —**in'dis·tinct'ly** *adv.* —**in'dis·tinct'ness** *n.*

in·dis·tin·guish·a·ble (ĭn'dĭ-stĭng'gwĭ-shə-bəl) *adj.* 1. Not readily perceptible. 2. Without distinctive qualities.

in·dite (ĭn-dīt') *v.* **-dit·ed, -dit·ing.** 1. To write; compose. 2. To set down in writing. [< Lat. *indicere*, to proclaim.] —**in·dit'er** *n.*

in·di·um (ĭn'dē-əm) *n.* Symbol **In** A soft, malleable, silvery-white metallic element used as a plating over silver in making mirrors and in transistor compounds. Atomic number 49; atomic weight 114.82. [INDI(GO) + -IUM.]

in·di·vid·u·al (ĭn'də-vĭj'ōō-əl) *adj.* 1. **a.** Of or relating to a single human being. **b.** By or for one person: *an individual portion.* 2. Existing as a distinct entity; separate: *individual words.* 3. Distinguished by particular attributes; distinctive: *an individual way of dressing.* —*n.* 1. A single person or organism considered separately. 2. A particular person: *a disagreeable individual.* [< Lat. *individuus.*] —**in'di·vid'u·al·ly** *adv.*

in·di·vid·u·al·ism (ĭn'də-vĭj'ōō-ə-lĭz'əm) *n.* 1. The assertion of one's own will and personality. 2. Individuality. 3. The theory that the interests of the individual take precedence over those of the state.

in·di·vid·u·al·ist (ĭn'də-vĭj'ōō-ə-lĭst) *n.* 1. A person of independent thought and action. 2. One who advocates individualism. —**in'di·vid'u·al·is'tic** *adj.*

in·di·vid·u·al·i·ty (ĭn'də-vĭj'ōō-ăl'ĭ-tē) *n.* 1. The quality of being individual. 2. The aggregate of qualities that distinguish one individual from others.

in·di·vid·u·al·ize (ĭn'də-vĭj'ōō-ə-līz') *v.* **-ized, -iz·ing.** 1. To give individuality to. 2. To consider or treat individually. 3. To modify or adapt to suit a particular individual.

in·di·vis·i·ble (ĭn'də-vĭz'ə-bəl) *adj.* Incapable of being divided.

in·doc·tri·nate (ĭn-dŏk'trə-nāt') *v.* **-nat·ed, -nat·ing.** 1. To instruct in a body of doctrine. 2. To teach to accept a system of thought uncritically. —**in·doc'tri·na'tion** *n.*

In·do-Eu·ro·pe·an (ĭn'dō-yŏŏr'ə-pē'ən) *n.* 1. **a.** A family of languages consisting of most of the languages of Europe as well as those of Iran, the Indian subcontinent, and other parts of Asia. **b.** Proto-Indo-European. 2. A member of a people speaking an Indo-European language. —**In'do-Eu'ro·pe'an** *adj.*

in·do·lent (ĭn'də-lənt) *adj.* Disinclined to work; habitually lazy. [LLat. *indolens.*] —**in'do·lence** *n.*

in·dom·i·ta·ble (ĭn-dŏm'ĭ-tə-bəl) *adj.* Incapable of being overcome; unconquerable. [LLat. *indomitabilis.*] —**in·dom'i·ta·bly** *adv.*

In·do·ne·sian (ĭn'də-nē'zhən, -shən) *n.* 1. **a.** A native or inhabitant of the Republic of Indonesia. 2. A group of languages that includes Malay, Tagalog, and the languages of Indonesia. —*adj.* Of or pertaining to Indonesia, its people, or their languages.

in·door (ĭn'dôr', -dōr') *adj.* Of, pertaining to, situated in, or carried on within the interior of a building.

in·doors (ĭn-dôrz', -dōrz') *adv.* In or into a building.

in·dorse (ĭn-dôrs') *v.* Var. of **endorse**.

in·du·bi·ta·ble (ĭn-dōō'bĭ-tə-bəl, -dyōō'-) *adj.* Too apparent to be doubted; unquestionable. —**in·du'bi·ta·bly** *adv.*

in·duce (ĭn-dōōs', -dyōōs') *v.* **-duced, -duc·ing.** 1. To prevail upon; persuade or influence. 2. To stimulate the occurrence of; cause: *induce childbirth.* 3. To infer by inductive reasoning. [< Lat. *inducere.*] —**in·duc'er** *n.*

in·duce·ment (ĭn-dōōs'mənt, -dyōōs'-) *n.* 1. The act or process of inducing. 2. Something that induces; incentive.

in·duct (ĭn-dŭkt') *v.* 1. To place formally in office; install. 2. To admit as a member; initiate. 3. To call into military service; draft. [Lat. *inducere,* to lead in.] —**in·duc·tee'** *n.*

in·duc·tance (ĭn-dŭk'təns) *n.* A circuit element, as a conducting coil, in which electromotive force is generated by electromagnetic induction.

in·duc·tion (ĭn-dŭk'shən) *n.* 1. The act of inducting or the process of being inducted. 2. Reasoning in which general principles are derived from particular facts or instances. 3. a. The generation of electromotive force in a closed circuit by a varying magnetic flux through the circuit. b. The charging of an isolated conducting object by momentarily grounding it while a charged body is nearby. **in·duc·tive** (ĭn-dŭk'tĭv) *adj.* 1. Of, pertaining to, or utilizing reasoning by induction. 2. Of or arising from inductance. —**in·duc'tive·ly** *adv.* —**in·duc'tive·ness** *n.*

in·dulge (ĭn-dŭlj') *v.* **-dulged, -dulg·ing.** 1. To yield to the desires or whims of; pamper. 2. To gratify; satisfy: *indulge a craving for chocolate.* 3. To allow oneself a special pleasure. [Lat. *indulgēre.*] —**in·dulg'er** *n.*

in·dul·gence (ĭn-dŭl'jəns) *n.* 1. The act of indulging or state of being indulgent. 2. Something indulged in. 3. Something granted as a favor or privilege. 4. Liberal or lenient treatment; tolerance. 5. *Rom. Cath. Ch.* The remission of temporal punishment due for a sin after the guilt has been forgiven.

in·dul·gent (ĭn-dŭl'jənt) *adj.* Showing, characterized by, or given to indulgence; lenient. —**in·dul'gent·ly** *adv.*

in·du·rate (ĭn'dōō-rāt', -dyōō-) *v.* **-rat·ed, -rat·ing.** 1. To make or become hard; harden. 2. To make or become stubborn, unfeeling, or obstinate. —*adj.* (-rĭt). Emotionally or physically hardened. [Lat. *indurare,* to harden.] —**in'du·ra'tion** *n.*

in·dus·tri·al (ĭn-dŭs'trē-əl) *adj.* 1. Of or pertaining to industry. 2. Having highly developed industries. 3. Used in industry: *industrial diamonds.* —**in·dus'tri·al·ly** *adv.*

in·dus·tri·al·ist (ĭn-dŭs'trē-ə-lĭst) *n.* One who owns or manages an industrial enterprise.

in·dus·tri·al·ize (ĭn-dŭs'trē-ə-līz') *v.* **-ized, -iz·ing.** To make or become industrial. —**in·dus'tri·al·i·za'tion** *n.*

in·dus·tri·ous (ĭn-dŭs'trē-əs) *adj.* Hard-working; diligent. —**in·dus'tri·ous·ly** *adv.* —**in·dus'tri·ous·ness** *n.*

in·dus·try (ĭn'də-strē) *n., pl.* **-tries.** 1. The production and sale of goods and services. 2. A specific branch of manufacture and trade. 3. Industrial management as distinguished

from labor. 4. Hard work; diligence. [< Lat. *industria,* diligence.]

-ine¹ *suff.* 1. Of, pertaining to, or belonging to: *Byzantine.* 2. Made of or resembling: *opaline.* [< Gk. *-inos.*]

-ine² *suff.* 1. A chemical substance: *adrenaline.* 2. A halogen: *chlorine.* 3. Also **-in.** Alkaloid: *quinine.* 4. A mixture of compounds: *gasoline.* 5. Commercial material: *glassine.* 6. Var. of **-in** (sense 1). [< Lat. *-inus.*]

in·e·bri·ate (ĭ-nē'brē-āt') *v.* **-at·ed, -at·ing.** To make drunk; intoxicate. —*n.* (-ĭt). An intoxicated person, esp. a drunkard. [Lat. *inebriare.*] —**in·e'bri·a'tion** *n.*

in·ed·i·ble (ĭn-ĕd'ə-bəl) *adj.* Not edible.

in·ef·fa·ble (ĭn-ĕf'ə-bəl) *adj.* 1. Beyond expression; indescribable or unspeakable: *ineffable delight; ineffable loathing.* 2. Not to be uttered; taboo: *the ineffable name of God.* [< Lat. *ineffabilis.*] —**in·ef'fa·bly** *adv.*

in·ef·face·a·ble (ĭn'ĭ-fā'sə-bəl) *adj.* Not effaceable; indelible.

in·ef·fec·tive (ĭn'ĭ-fĕk'tĭv) *adj.* 1. Not effective; ineffectual. 2. Incompetent. —**in·ef·fec'tive·ly** *adv.* —**in·ef·fec'tive·ness** *n.*

in·ef·fec·tu·al (ĭn'ĭ-fĕk'chōō-əl) *adj.* 1. Not having an intended effect; vain. 2. Powerless; impotent. —**in·ef·fec'tu·al·ly** *adv.*

in·ef·fi·cient (ĭn'ĭ-fĭsh'ənt) *adj.* Not efficient; wasteful of time, energy, or materials. —**in·ef·fi'cien·cy** *n.* —**in·ef·fi'cient·ly** *adv.*

in·el·e·gant (ĭn-ĕl'ĭ-gənt) *adj.* 1. Lacking elegance. 2. Coarse; vulgar. —**in·el'e·gance** *n.*

in·el·i·gi·ble (ĭn-ĕl'ə-jə-bəl) *adj.* Not qualified for an office or privilege. —**in·el'i·gi·bil'i·ty** *n.* —**in·el'i·gi·ble** *n.*

in·e·luc·ta·ble (ĭn'ĭ-lŭk'tə-bəl) *adj.* Not to be avoided or overcome; inevitable. [Lat. *ineluctabilis.*] —**in·e·luc'ta·bly** *adv.*

in·ept (ĭn-ĕpt') *adj.* 1. Not apt or fitting; inappropriate or unsuitable. 2. Lacking skill or competence; awkward or bungling. 3. Foolish; absurd. [Lat. *ineptus.*] —**in·ept'i·tude** (-ĕp'tĭ-tōōd', -tyōōd') *n.* —**in·ept'ly** *adv.* —**in·ept'ness** *n.*

in·e·qual·i·ty (ĭn'ĭ-kwŏl'ĭ-tē) *n., pl.* **-ties.** 1. The condition of being unequal. 2. Lack of regularity; unevenness. 3. Social or economic disparity. 4. A mathematical statement that two numbers are not equal.

in·eq·ui·ta·ble (ĭn-ĕk'wĭ-tə-bəl) *adj.* Not equitable; unfair. —**in·eq'ui·ta·bly** *adv.*

in·eq·ui·ty (ĭn-ĕk'wĭ-tē) *n., pl.* **-ties.** 1. Lack of equity; injustice; unfairness. 2. An instance of unfairness.

in·ert (ĭn-ûrt') *adj.* 1. Unable to move or act. 2. Moving or acting slowly; sluggish. 3. Exhibiting no chemical activity; completely unreactive. [Lat. *iners,* inactive.] —**in·ert'ly** *adv.* —**in·ert'ness** *n.*

in·er·tia (ĭ-nûr'shə, -shē-ə) *n.* 1. The tendency of a body to remain at rest or continue in motion unless disturbed by an external force. 2. Resistance to motion, action, or change. [Lat., idleness.] —**in·er'tial** *adj.*

in·es·cap·a·ble (ĭn'ĭ-skā'pə-bəl) *adj.* Incapable of being escaped; inevitable. —**in·es·cap'a·bly** *adv.*

in·es·ti·ma·ble (ĭn-ĕs'tə-mə-bəl) *adj.* 1. Incapable of being estimated. 2. Of incalculable value. —**in·es'ti·ma·bly** *adv.*

in·ev·i·ta·ble (ĭn-ĕv'ĭ-tə-bəl) *adj.* Incapable of being avoided or prevented. —**in·ev'i·ta·bil'i·ty** *n.* —**in·ev'i·ta·bly** *adv.*

in·ex·act (ĭn'ĭg-zăkt') *adj.* Not exact; not

quite accurate or precise. —**in'ex·act'iv** adv.
—**in'ex·act'ness** n.

in·ex·cus·a·ble (ĭn'ĭk-skyōō'zə-bəl) adj. Not
excusable; unpardonable. —**in'ex·cus'a·ble·
ness** n. —**in'ex·cus'a·bly** adv.

in·ex·haust·i·ble (ĭn'ĭg-zôs'stə-bəl) adj. 1. Incapable of being used up; limitless. 2. Tireless; indefatigable. —**in'ex·haust'i·bly** adv.

in·ex·o·ra·ble (ĭn-ĕk'sər-ə-bəl) adj. Not capable of being persuaded by entreaty; unyielding. [Lat. *inexorabilis.*] —**in·ex'o·ra·bly** adv.

in·ex·pen·sive (ĭn'ĭk-spĕn'sĭv) adj. Not expensive; low-priced. —**in'ex·pen'sive·ly** adv.

in·ex·pe·ri·ence (ĭn'ĭk-spîr'ē-əns) n. Lack of
experience. —**in'ex·pe'ri·enced** adj.

in·ex·pert (ĭn-ĕk'spûrt') adj. Not expert; unskilled. —**in'ex·pert'ly** adv.

in·ex·pli·ca·ble (ĭn-ĕk'splĭ-kə-bəl, ĭn'ĭk-splĭk'-
ə-) adj. Incapable of being explained or interpreted. —**in·ex'pli·ca·bly** adv.

in·ex·press·i·ble (ĭn'ĭk-sprĕs'ə-bəl) adj. Not
capable of being expressed; indescribable.
—**in'ex·press'i·bly** adv.

in·ex·tin·guish·a·ble (ĭn'ĭk-stĭng'gwĭ-shə-bəl)
adj. Not capable of being extinguished.

in ex·tre·mis (ĭn' ĕk-strē'mĭs) adv. At the
point of death. [Lat.]

in·ex·tri·ca·ble (ĭn-ĕk'strĭ-kə-bəl) adj. 1. Incapable of being disentangled or untied.
2. Too intricate or complex to solve. —**in·ex'-
tri·ca·bly** adv.

in·fal·li·ble (ĭn-făl'ə-bəl) adj. 1. Incapable of
erring. 2. Incapable of failing; certain: an *infallible antidote.* —**in·fal'li·bil'i·ty** n. —**in·fal'li·
bly** adv.

in·fa·mous (ĭn'fə-məs) adj. 1. Having an exceedingly bad reputation; notorious.
2. Grossly shocking; loathsome. —**in'fa·mous·
ly** adv.

in·fa·my (ĭn'fə-mē) n., pl. **-mies.** 1. Evil fame
or reputation. 2. The condition of being infamous. 3. An infamous act. [< Lat. *infamia.*]

in·fan·cy (ĭn'fən-sē) n., pl. **-cies.** 1. The condition or period of being an infant. 2. An early
stage of existence.

in·fant (ĭn'fənt) n. 1. A child in the earliest
period of its life; baby. 2. *Law.* A minor. [<
Lat. *infans.*]

in·fan·ti·cide (ĭn-făn'tĭ-sīd') n. 1. The killing
of an infant. 2. One who kills an infant.

in·fan·tile (ĭn'fən-tīl', -tĭl) adj. 1. Of or pertaining to infants or infancy. 2. Lacking maturity; childish.

infantile paralysis n. Poliomyelitis.

in·fan·try (ĭn'fən-trē) n., pl. **-tries.** The branch
of an army made up of units trained to fight
on foot. [< Ital. *infante,* youth.] —**in'fan·try·
man** n.

in·farct (ĭn'färkt', ĭn-färkt') n. A necrotic area
of tissue resulting from failure of local blood
supply. [< Lat. *infarcire,* to cram.] —**in·
farct'ed** adj. —**in·farc'tion** n.

in·fat·u·ate (ĭn-făch'ōō-āt') v. **-at·ed, -at·ing.**
To inspire with foolish and unreasoning love
or attraction. [Lat. *infatuare.*] —**in·fat'u·at'ed**
adj. —**in·fat'u·a'tion** n.

in·fect (ĭn-fĕkt') v. 1. To contaminate with
pathogenic microorganisms. 2. To communicate a disease to. 3. To affect as if by contagion: *That fear infected us all.* [< Lat.
inficere, to stain.] —**in·fec'tive** adj.

in·fec·tion (ĭn-fĕk'shən) n. 1. Invasion of a
bodily part by pathogenic microorganisms.
2. The pathological condition resulting from
infection. 3. An infectious disease.

in·fec·tious (ĭn-fĕk'shəs) adj. 1. Capable of
causing infection. 2. Caused or spread by infection, as a disease. 3. Easily or readily communicated, as laughter. —**in·fec'tious·ly** adv.

in·fe·lic·i·tous (ĭn'fĭ-lĭs'ĭ-təs) adj. Not suitable,
as in expression; inappropriate. —**in'fe·lic'i·ty**
n. —**in'fe·lic'i·tous·ly** adv.

in·fer (ĭn-fûr') v. **-ferred, -fer·ring.** 1. To conclude from evidence; deduce. 2. To have as a
logical consequence. [< Lat. *inferre.*] —**in·
fer'a·ble** adj.

in·fer·ence (ĭn'fər-əns) n. 1. The act or
process of inferring. 2. Something inferred;
conclusion. —**in·fer·en'tial** (-fə-rĕn'shəl) adj.

in·fe·ri·or (ĭn-fîr'ē-ər) adj. 1. Situated under or
beneath; lower. 2. Low or lower in order,
degree, rank, quality, or estimation. [< Lat.
lower.] —**in·fe'ri·or** n. —**in·fe'ri·or'i·ty** (-ôr'-
ĭ-tē, -ŏr'-) n.

in·fer·nal (ĭn-fûr'nəl) adj. 1. Of, pertaining to,
or resembling hell. 2. Abominable; damnable.
[< Lat. *infernus,* lower.] —**in·fer'nal·ly** adv.

in·fer·no (ĭn-fûr'nō) n., pl. **-nos.** 1. Hell. 2. A
place likened to or resembling hell. [Ital.]

in·fer·tile (ĭn-fûr'tl) adj. Not fertile; unproductive or barren. —**in'fer·til'i·ty** n.

in·fest (ĭn-fĕst') v. To spread in or overrun so
as to be harmful or unpleasant. [< Lat. *infes-
tus,* hostile.] —**in'fes·ta'tion** (ĭn'fĕ-stā'shən) n.

in·fi·del (ĭn'fĭ-dəl, -dĕl') n. 1. One who has no
religious beliefs. 2. One who does not accept
a particular religion, esp. Christianity. [< Lat.
infidelis, unfaithful.]

in·fi·del·i·ty (ĭn'fĭ-dĕl'ĭ-tē) n., pl. **-ties.** 1. Lack
of religious faith. 2. Lack of fidelity or loyalty; unfaithfulness.

in·field (ĭn'fēld') n. 1. The area of a baseball
field within the base lines. 2. The defensive
positions of first base, second base, third
base, and shortstop. —**in'field'er** n.

in·fight·ing (ĭn'fī'tĭng) n. 1. Fighting at close
range. 2. Contention among associates in a
group or organization. —**in'fight'er** n.

in·fil·trate (ĭn-fĭl'trāt', ĭn'fĭl-) v. **-trat·ed, -trat·
ing.** 1. To pass or cause (a liquid or gas) to
pass into. 2. To pass, enter, or join gradually
or surreptitiously. —**in'fil·tra'tion** n.

in·fi·nite (ĭn'fə-nĭt) adj. 1. Having no bounds
or limits; endless. 2. Immeasurably great or
large; immense. 3. *Math.* a. Existing beyond
or being greater than any arbitrarily large
value. b. Unlimited in spatial extent. —**in'fi·
nite** n. —**in'fi·nite·ly** adv.

in·fin·i·tes·i·mal (ĭn-fĭn'ĭ-tĕs'ə-məl) adj. 1. Immeasurably or incalculably small; minute.
2. *Math.* Capable of having values arbitrarily
close to zero. [< Lat. *infinitus,* infinite.] —**in·
fin'i·tes'i·mal·ly** adv.

in·fin·i·tive (ĭn-fĭn'ĭ-tĭv) n. A verb form that
functions as a substantive while retaining certain verbal characteristics and in English is
usu. used with *to.* [LLat. *infinitivus,* unlimited, indefinite.]

in·fin·i·ty (ĭn-fĭn'ĭ-tē) n., pl. **-ties.** 1. Un-
bounded space, time, or quantity. 2. The
quality of being infinite. 3. An indefinitely
large number or amount.

in·firm (ĭn-fûrm′) *adj.* **1.** Weak in body, esp. from old age; feeble. **2.** Not stable; insecure.

in·fir·ma·ry (ĭn-fûr′mə-rē) *n., pl.* **-ries.** A place for the care of the sick or injured.

in·fir·mi·ty (ĭn-fûr′mĭ-tē) *n., pl.* **-ties. 1.** The condition of being infirm; feebleness. **2.** An ailment; disease. **3.** A character failing or defect; weak point.

in·flame (ĭn-flām′) *v.* **-flamed, -flam·ing. 1.** To set on fire; kindle. **2.** To arouse to strong emotion. **3.** To intensify. **4.** To produce or be affected by inflammation. [< Lat. *inflammare.*]

in·flam·ma·ble (ĭn-flăm′ə-bəl) *adj.* **1.** Tending to ignite easily; flammable. **2.** Easily aroused to strong emotion. [< Lat. *inflammare*, to inflame.]

in·flam·ma·tion (ĭn′flə-mā′shən) *n.* Localized heat, redness, swelling, and pain resulting from injury, infection, or irritation.

in·flam·ma·to·ry (ĭn-flăm′ə-tôr′ē, -tōr′ē) *adj.* **1.** Tending to arouse strong emotion, as passion or anger. **2.** Characterized or caused by inflammation.

in·flate (ĭn-flāt′) *v.* **-flat·ed, -flat·ing. 1.** To fill and swell with a gas. **2.** To cause to puff up: *Early success inflated his ego.* **3.** To raise (prices, wages, or currency) abnormally. **4.** To become inflated. [Lat. *inflare.*]

in·fla·tion (ĭn-flā′shən) *n.* **1.** The act of inflating or condition of being inflated. **2.** An abnormal increase in available currency and credit, resulting in a rise in price levels. —**in·fla′tion·ar·y** (-shə-něr′ē) *adj.*

in·flect (ĭn-flĕkt′) *v.* **1.** To turn from a course; bend. **2.** To alter (the voice) in tone or pitch; modulate. **3.** *Gram.* To subject to or be modified by inflection. [< Lat. *inflectere*, to bend.] —**in·flec′tive** *adj.*

in·flec·tion (ĭn-flĕk′shən) *n.* **1.** An alteration in pitch or tone of voice. **2.** *Gram.* **a.** An alteration of the form of a word to indicate number, tense, person, voice, or mood. **b.** A word element involved in such an alteration. **c.** An inflected form of a word. —**in·flec′tion·al** *adj.*

in·flex·i·ble (ĭn-flĕk′sə-bəl) *adj.* **1.** Not flexible; rigid. **2.** Incapable of being changed; unalterable. **3.** Unyielding. —**in·flex′i·bil′i·ty** *n.* —**in·flex′i·bly** *adv.*

in·flict (ĭn-flĭkt′) *v.* **1.** To cause or carry out by aggressive action. **2.** To impose; afflict. [Lat. *infligere.*] —**in·flict′er** or **in·flic′tor** *n.* —**in·flic′tion** *n.*

in·flo·res·cence (ĭn′flə-rĕs′əns) *n.* A characteristic arrangement of flowers on a stalk or in a cluster. [< LLat. *inflorescere*, to begin to flower.] —**in′flo·res′cent** *adj.*

in·flow (ĭn′flō′) *n.* An influx.

in·flu·ence (ĭn′flōō-əns) *n.* **1.** A power indirectly or intangibly affecting a person or course of events. **2. a.** Power to sway or affect based on prestige, wealth, ability, or position. **b.** One exercising such power. —*v.* **-enced, -enc·ing. 1.** To have influence over; affect. **2.** To modify. [< Lat. *influere*, to flow in.] —**in′flu·en′tial** (-ĕn′shəl) *adj.*

in·flu·en·za (ĭn′flōō-ĕn′zə) *n.* An acute infectious viral disease characterized by inflammation of the respiratory tract, fever, muscular pain, and intestinal irritation. [< Med. Lat. *influentia*, influence.]

in·flux (ĭn′flŭks′) *n.* A flowing in. [Lat. *influere*, to flow in.]

in·fold (ĭn-fōld′) *v.* **1.** To fold inward. **2.** Var. of **enfold.**

in·form (ĭn-fôrm′) *v.* **1.** To impart information to; tell. **2.** To disclose or give information, esp. incriminating information. [< Lat. *informare*, to give form to.]

in·for·mal (ĭn-fôr′məl) *adj.* **1.** Not according to prescribed regulations or forms. **2.** Marked by lack of formality. **3.** Of or for ordinary use; casual: *informal clothes.* —**in·for′mal·i·ty** (ĭn′fôr-măl′ĭ-tē) *n.* —**in·for′mal·ly** *adv.*

Syns: *informal, casual, easy, easygoing, laidback, relaxed* **adj.**

in·for·mant (ĭn-fôr′mənt) *n.* One who communicates information.

in·for·ma·tion (ĭn′fər-mā′shən) *n.* **1.** The act of informing or condition of being informed; communication or reception of knowledge. **2.** Knowledge derived from study, experience, or instruction; facts. **3.** A nonaccidental signal used as an input to a computer or communications system. —**in′for·ma′tion·al** *adj.*

in·for·ma·tive (ĭn-fôr′mə-tĭv) *adj.* Providing or disclosing information; instructive.

in·formed (ĭn-fôrmd′) *adj.* Based on, possessing, displaying, or making use of factual information: *an informed consumer.*

in·form·er (ĭn-fôr′mər) *n.* **1.** An informant. **2.** One who secretly informs against others.

in·fra- *pref.* Below; beneath; inferior to: *infrared.* [< Lat. *infra*, below.]

in·frac·tion (ĭn-frăk′shən) *n.* An infringement, as of a rule; violation.

in·fra·red (ĭn′frə-rĕd′) *adj.* Of, pertaining to, or being electromagnetic radiation with wavelengths greater than those of visible light and shorter than those of microwaves.

in·fra·son·ic (ĭn′frə-sŏn′ĭk) *adj.* Generating or using waves or vibrations with frequencies below that of audible sound.

in·fre·quent (ĭn-frē′kwənt) *adj.* **1.** Not frequent; rare. **2.** Not steady; occasional. —**in·fre′quen·cy** *n.* —**in·fre′quent·ly** *adv.*

in·fringe (ĭn-frĭnj′) *v.* **-fringed, -fring·ing. 1.** To break or ignore the terms of; violate. **2.** To trespass; encroach. [Lat. *infringere.*] —**in·fringe′ment** *n.*

in·fu·ri·ate (ĭn-fyŏŏr′ē-āt′) *v.* **-at·ed, -at·ing.** To make furious; enrage. [Med. Lat. *infuriare.*] —**in·fu′ri·at′ing·ly** *adv.*

in·fuse (ĭn-fyŏŏz′) *v.* **-fused, -fus·ing. 1.** To fill; imbue. **2.** To instill; inculcate. **3.** To steep or soak without boiling. [< Lat. *infundere*, to pour in.] —**in·fu′sion** *n.*

in·fus·i·ble (ĭn-fyŏŏ′zə-bəl) *adj.* Incapable of being fused.

-ing¹ *suff.* **1.** Used to form the present participle of verbs: *going.* **2.** Used to form adjectives resembling participial adjectives but not derived from verbs: *swashbuckling.* [< OE *-ende.*]

-ing² *suff.* **1.** An action or process: *dancing.* **2.** Something necessary to perform an action or process: *mooring.* **3.** The result of an action or process: *a drawing.* **4.** Something connected with a specified thing or concept: *siding.* [< OE *-ung.*]

in·gen·ious (ĭn-jēn′yəs) *adj.* **1.** Showing special skill in creating or devising; creative. **2.** Showing originality and resourcefulness. [< Lat. *ingenium*, skill.] —**in·gen′ious·ly** *adv.* —**in·gen′ious·ness** *n.*

in·gé·nue (ăn′zhə-nōō′) *n.* **1.** An artless, innocent girl or young woman. **2.** An actress playing an ingénue. [< Fr., guileless.]

in·ge·nu·i·ty (ĭn′jə-nōō′ĭ-tē, -nyōō′-) n., pl. -ties. Inventive skill or imagination; cleverness. [Lat. *ingenuitas*, frankness.]

in·gen·u·ous (ĭn-jĕn′yōō-əs) adj. 1. Without sophistication; artless. 2. Straightforward; candid. [Lat. *ingenuus*, honest.] —in·gen′u·ous·ly adv. —in·gen′u·ous·ness n.

in·gest (ĭn-jĕst′) v. To take in by or as if by swallowing. [< Lat. *ingestus*, p.p. of *ingerere*, to carry in.] —in·ges′tion n.

in·gle·nook (ĭng′gəl-nōōk′) n. 1. A nook or corner beside a fireplace. 2. A bench placed in an inglenook. [Sc. Gael. *aingeal*, flame + NOOK.]

in·glo·ri·ous (ĭn-glôr′ē-əs, -glōr′-) adj. 1. Not glorious. 2. Dishonorable; shameful. —in·glo′ri·ous·ly adv.

in·got (ĭng′gət) n. A mass of metal shaped for convenient storage or transportation. [< OFr. *lingot*.]

ingot

in·grain (ĭn-grān′) v. To impress indelibly on the mind or nature; imbue. —n. Yarn or fiber dyed before use in spinning, weaving, etc. [IN-2 + GRAIN, dye (obs.)]

in·grained (ĭn-grānd′) adj. 1. Imbued; deep-seated: *ingrained faults.* 2. Complete; utter.

in·grate (ĭn′grāt′) n. An ungrateful person. [< Lat. *ingratus*, ungrateful.]

in·gra·ti·ate (ĭn-grā′shē-āt′) v. -at·ed, -at·ing. To bring (oneself) purposely into the favor of another. [IN-2 + Lat. *gratia*, favor.] —in·gra′ti·at·ing·ly adv. —in·gra′ti·a′tion n.

in·grat·i·tude (ĭn-grăt′ĭ-tōōd′, -tyōōd′) n. Lack of gratitude; ungratefulness.

in·gre·di·ent (ĭn-grē′dē-ənt) n. Something that is an element in a mixture or compound; constituent. [< Lat. *ingredi*, to enter.]

in·gress (ĭn′grĕs′) n. 1. An entrance. 2. Access. [< Lat. *ingredi*, to enter.]

in·grown (ĭn′grōn′) adj. Grown abnormally into the flesh.

in·gui·nal (ĭng′gwə-nəl) adj. Of, relating to, or located in the groin. [< Lat. *inguen*, groin.]

in·hab·it (ĭn-hăb′ĭt) v. To live or reside in. [< Lat. *inhabitare*.] —in·hab′it·a·ble adj.

in·hab·i·tant (ĭn-hăb′ĭ-tənt) n. A permanent resident.

in·ha·la·tor (ĭn′hə-lā′tər) n. A device that produces a vapor to be inhaled.

in·hale (ĭn-hāl′) v. -haled, -hal·ing. 1. To draw in by breathing. 2. To breathe in. [Lat. *inhalare*.] —in·ha·la′tion (-hə-lā′shən) n.

in·hal·er (ĭn-hā′lər) n. 1. One that inhales. 2. An inhalator.

in·here (ĭn-hîr′) v. -hered, -her·ing. To be inherent or innate. [Lat. *inhaerēre*.]

in·her·ent (ĭn-hîr′ənt, -hĕr′-) adj. Existing as an essential constituent or characteristic; intrinsic. —in·her′ent·ly adv.

in·her·it (ĭn-hĕr′ĭt) v. 1. To come into possession of, esp. by legal succession or will. 2. To receive by genetic transmission from an ancestor. [< LLat. *inhereditare*.] —in·her′it·a·ble adj. —in·her′i·tance n. —in·her′i·tor n.

in·hib·it (ĭn-hĭb′ĭt) v. 1. To restrain or hold back; prevent. 2. To prohibit; forbid. [< Lat. *inhibēre*.] —in·hib′it·er n. —in·hib′i·tive or in·hib′i·to·ry (-tôr′ē, -tōr′ē) adj.

in·hi·bi·tion (ĭn′hĭ-bĭsh′ən, ĭn′ĭ-) n. 1. The act of inhibiting or condition of being inhibited. 2. The frequent or habitual suppression of a feeling, urge, or drive.

in·hos·pi·ta·ble (ĭn-hŏs′pĭ-tə-bəl, ĭn′hŏ-spĭt′ə-) adj. 1. Displaying no hospitality; unfriendly. 2. Not affording shelter or sustenance; barren.

in·house (ĭn′hous′) adj. Being or coming from within an organization.

in·hu·man (ĭn-hyōō′mən) adj. 1. a. Lacking kindness or pity; brutal. b. Deficient in emotional warmth; cold. 2. Not in accord with human needs. 3. Not of ordinary human form; monstrous. —in·hu′man·ly adv.

in·hu·mane (ĭn′hyōō-mān′) adj. Not humane; lacking in pity or compassion.

in·hu·man·i·ty (ĭn′hyōō-măn′ĭ-tē) n., pl. -ties. 1. The quality or condition of being inhumane; cruelty. 2. An inhumane or cruel act.

in·im·i·cal (ĭ-nĭm′ĭ-kəl) adj. 1. Harmful; adverse. 2. Unfriendly; hostile. [< Lat. *inimicus*, enemy.] —in·im′i·cal·ly adv.

in·im·i·ta·ble (ĭ-nĭm′ĭ-tə-bəl) adj. Defying imitation; matchless. —in·im′i·ta·bly adv.

in·iq·ui·ty (ĭ-nĭk′wĭ-tē) n., pl. -ties. 1. Wickedness; sinfulness. 2. A wicked act; sin. [< Lat. *iniquus*, unjust.] —in·iq′ui·tous adj.

in·i·tial (ĭ-nĭsh′əl) adj. Of, pertaining to, being, or occurring at the beginning; first. —n. The first letter of a name or a word. —v. -tialed or -tialled, -tial·ing or -tial·ling. To mark or sign with initials. [< Lat. *initium*, beginning.] —in·i′tial·ly adv.

in·i·ti·ate (ĭ-nĭsh′ē-āt′) v. -at·ed, -at·ing. 1. To begin or originate. 2. To introduce (a person) to a new field, interest, skill, or activity. 3. To admit into membership, as with ceremonies or ritual. —n. (-ĭt). 1. One who has been initiated. 2. A novice; beginner. [Lat. *initiare*.] —in·i′ti·a′tion n. —in·i′ti·a′tor n. —in·i′ti·a·to·ry (-ə-tôr′ē, -tōr′ē) adj.

in·i·ti·a·tive (ĭ-nĭsh′ē-ə-tĭv, ĭ-nĭsh′ə-) n. 1. The power or ability to begin or follow through with a 'an or task; enterprise. 2. A first step or action. 3. The procedure by which citizens can propose a law by petition and ensure its submission to the electorate.

in·ject (ĭn-jĕkt′) v. 1. To force or drive (a fluid) into. 2. To introduce into conversation or consideration: *inject a note of humor.* 3. To place into an orbit, trajectory, or stream. [< Lat. *injectus*, p.p. of *inicere*, to put in.] —in·jec′tion n.

in·junc·tion (ĭn-jŭngk′shən) n. 1. A command, directive, or order. 2. A court order prohibiting or requiring a certain action. [< Lat. *injungere*, to enjoin.] —in·junc′tive adj.

in·jure (ĭn'jər) v. **-jured, -jur·ing. 1.** To cause harm or damage to. **2.** To commit an injustice or offense against. [< INJURY.]

in·ju·ri·ous (ĭn-jŏor'ē-əs) adj. Causing injury; harmful. **—in·ju'ri·ous·ly** adv.

in·ju·ry (ĭn'jə-rē) n., pl. **-ries. 1.** An act that harms or damages. **2.** A wound or other specific damage. **3.** Injustice. [< Lat. injurius, unjust.]

in·jus·tice (ĭn-jŭs'tĭs) n. **1.** Violation of another's rights or of what is right. **2.** An unjust act; wrong.

ink (ĭngk) n. A pigmented liquid or paste used esp. for writing or printing. **—v.** To cover or stain with ink. [< Gk. enkauston, purple ink.] **—ink'y** adj.

ink·horn (ĭngk'hôrn') n. A small container, usu. of horn, for holding ink.

ink·ling (ĭngk'lĭng) n. **1.** A hint or intimation. **2.** A vague idea or notion. [Perh. < ME inklen, to mention.]

ink·stand (ĭngk'stănd') n. **1.** A stand for bottles of ink, pens, etc. **2.** An inkwell.

ink·well (ĭngk'wĕl') n. A small reservoir for ink.

in·laid (ĭn'lād') adj. Decorated with a pattern set into a surface.

in·land (ĭn'lənd) adj. **1.** Of or located in the interior part of a country. **2.** Operating or applying within a country; domestic. **—adv.** In, toward, or into the interior of a country. **—n.** The interior of a country.

in·law (ĭn'lô') n. A relative by marriage.

in·lay (ĭn'lā', ĭn-lā') v. To set into a surface to form a design. **—n.** (ĭn'lā'). **1.** An inlaid object or design. **2.** A filling, as of gold, molded and cemented to a tooth.

inlay
1st-century B.C. Roman mosaic

in·let (ĭn'lĕt', -lĭt) n. **1.** A stream or bay leading inland. **2.** A narrow passage of water, as between two islands.

in·mate (ĭn'māt') n. **1.** A resident in a building. **2.** A person confined to an institution such as a prison or asylum.

in me·di·as res (ĭn mĕd'ē-əs rās', mĕ'dē-əs rēz') adv. In or into the middle of a sequence of events. [Lat., in the middle of things.]

in me·mo·ri·am (ĭn' mə-môr'ē-əm, -môr'-) prep. In memory of. [Lat.]

inn (ĭn) n. **1.** A hotel. **2.** A tavern. [< OE.]

in·nards (ĭn'ərdz) pl.n. Informal. **1.** Internal bodily organs; viscera. **2.** The inner parts, as of a machine. [< inwards, entrails.]

in·nate (ĭ-nāt', ĭn'āt') adj. **1.** Possessed at birth; inborn. **2.** Possessed as an essential characteristic; inherent. [< Lat. innatus, p.p. of innasci, to be born in.] **—in·nate'ly** adv.

in·ner (ĭn'ər) adj. **1.** Located farther inside: an inner room. **2.** Of or pertaining to the spirit or mind. **3.** More exclusive, influential, or important: the inner circles of government. [< OE innera.]

in·ner-di·rect·ed (ĭn'ər-dĭ-rĕk'tĭd, -dī-) adj. Guided, as in behavior, by one's own set of values rather than by external standards.

inner ear n. The part of the vertebrate ear consisting of the cochlea, vestibule, and semicircular canals.

in·ner·most (ĭn'ər-mōst') adj. **1.** Farthest within. **2.** Most intimate.

in·ning (ĭn'ĭng) n. A division or period of a baseball game in which each team has a turn at bat. [< IN.]

inn·keep·er (ĭn'kē'pər) n. One who manages an inn.

in·no·cent (ĭn'ə-sənt) adj. **1.** Uncorrupted by evil, malice, or wrongdoing; sinless. **2.** Not guilty of a specific crime; legally blameless. **3.** Causing no harm; innocuous. **4.** Not experienced or worldly; naive. **5.** Without deception or guile; artless. [< Lat. innocens.] **—in'no·cence** n. **—in'no·cent** n. **—in'no·cent·ly** adv.

in·noc·u·ous (ĭ-nŏk'yŏo-əs) adj. **1.** Having no adverse effect; harmless. **2.** Lacking impact; insipid. [Lat. innocuus.] **—in·noc'u·ous·ly** adv. **—in·noc'u·ous·ness** n.

in·nom·i·nate (ĭ-nŏm'ə-nĭt) adj. **1.** Having no name. **2.** Anonymous. [LLat. innominatus.]

in·no·vate (ĭn'ə-vāt') v. **-vat·ed, -vat·ing. 1.** To begin or introduce (something new). **2.** To be creative. [Lat. innovare, to renew.] **—in'no·va'tive** adj. **—in'no·va'tor** n.

in·no·va·tion (ĭn'ə-vā'shən) n. **1.** The act of innovating. **2.** Something, as a method or product, newly introduced.

in·nu·en·do (ĭn'yŏo-ĕn'dō) n., pl. **-does.** An indirect, subtle, usu. derogatory insinuation. [< Lat. innuere, to nod to.]

In·nu·it (ĭn'yŏo-ĭt) n., pl. **-it** or **-its. 1.** An Eskimo of North America and Greenland as distinguished from one of Asia and the Aleutian Islands. **2.** The language of the Innuits.

in·nu·mer·a·ble (ĭ-nŏo'mər-ə-bəl, ĭ-nyŏo'-) adj. Too many to be counted or numbered.

in·oc·u·late (ĭ-nŏk'yə-lāt') v. **-lat·ed, -lat·ing.** To introduce the virus of a disease into in order to immunize, cure, or experiment. [< Lat. inoculare, to engraft.] **—in·oc'u·la'tion** n.

in·of·fen·sive (ĭn'ə-fĕn'sĭv) adj. Giving no offense; unobjectionable.

in·op·er·a·ble (ĭn-ŏp'ər-ə-bəl, -ŏp'rə-) adj. **1.** Not operable. **2.** Not capable of being treated surgically.

in·op·er·a·tive (ĭn-ŏp'ər-ə-tĭv, -ŏp'rə-) adj. Not working or functioning.

in·op·por·tune (ĭn-ŏp'ər-tŏon', -tyŏon') adj. Not opportune; ill-timed. **—in·op'por·tune'ly** adv. **—in·op'por·tune'ness** n.

in·or·di·nate (ĭn-ôr'dn-ĭt) adj. **1.** Exceeding reasonable limits; immoderate. **2.** Not regulated; disorderly. [< Lat. inordinatus.] **—in·or'di·nate·ly** adv.

in·or·gan·ic (ĭn'ôr-găn'ĭk) adj. **1.** Involving neither organic life nor the products of organic life. **2.** Not composed of organic matter; mineral. **3.** Of or pertaining to the chemistry of compounds not usu. classified as organic.

in·pa·tient (ĭn'pā'shənt) n. A patient staying in a hospital for treatment.

in·put (ĭn'pŏot') n. **1.** Something that is put in. **2.** Energy, work, or power put into a system or machine. **3.** Information put into a data-processing system. 4. Contribution to or participation in a common effort. —**in'put'** v.

in·quest (ĭn'kwĕst) n. 1. A judicial inquiry, usu. conducted before a jury. 2. An investigation; inquiry.

in·quire (ĭn-kwīr') v. -quired, -quir·ing. 1. To ask or ask about. 2. To make a search or study; investigate. [< Lat. *inquirere*.] —**in·quir'er** n. —**in·quir'ing·ly** adv.

in·quir·y (ĭn-kwīr'ē, ĭn'kwə-rē) n., pl. -ies. 1. The act or process of inquiring. 2. A question; query. 3. A close examination of a matter; investigation.

in·qui·si·tion (ĭn'kwĭ-zĭsh'ən) n. 1. An official investigation, as an inquest. 2. **Inquisition.** A former Roman Catholic tribunal established to suppress heresy. 3. A severe scrutiny. [< Lat. *inquirere*, to inquire.] —**in'qui·si'tion·al** adj. —**in·quis'i·tor** n. —**in·quis'i·to'ri·al** (-kwĭz'ĭ-tôr'ē-əl, -tōr'-) adj.

in·quis·i·tive (ĭn-kwĭz'ĭ-tĭv) adj. 1. Unduly curious. 2. Eager to learn. —**in·quis'i·tive·ly** adv. —**in·quis'i·tive·ness** n.

in re (ĭn rā', rē') prep. In the matter or case of. [Lat.]

in·road (ĭn'rōd') n. 1. A hostile invasion; raid. 2. An advance, esp. at another's expense; encroachment. [IN + ROAD, raid (obs).]

in·rush (ĭn'rŭsh') n. A sudden influx.

in·sa·lu·bri·ous (ĭn'sə-lōō'brē-əs) adj. Unhealthful; unwholesome.

in·sane (ĭn-sān') adj. 1. Of, exhibiting, or afflicted with mental disorder. 2. Characteristic of, used by, or for the insane. 3. Very foolish; absurd. —**in·sane'ly** adv. —**in·san'i·ty** (-săn'ĭ-tē) n.

Syns: **insane, batty, crazy, cuckoo, deranged, loco, loony, lunatic, mad, maniacal, nuts, screwy, unbalanced** adj.

in·sa·tia·ble (ĭn-sā'shə-bəl, -shē-ə-) adj. Incapable of being satiated; never satisfied.

in·scribe (ĭn-skrīb') v. -scribed, -scrib·ing. 1. To write, print, or engrave (words or letters) on or in a surface. 2. To mark or engrave with words or letters. 3. To enter (a name) on a list. 4. To dedicate to another. 5. To enclose (e.g. a polygon) within a closed configuration of lines, curves, or surfaces so that every vertex of the enclosed figure touches the enclosing configuration. [< Lat. *inscribere.*] —**in·scrib'er** n. —**in·scrip'tion** (-skrĭp'shən) n.

in·scru·ta·ble (ĭn-skrōō'tə-bəl) adj. Difficult to understand or fathom; enigmatic. [Lat. *inscrutabilis.*] —**in·scru'ta·bil'i·ty** or **in·scru'ta·ble·ness** n. —**in·scru'ta·bly** adv.

in·sect (ĭn'sĕkt') n. Any of numerous small, usu. winged invertebrate animals with three pairs of legs and a three-segmented body. [Lat. *insectum.*]

in·sec·ti·cide (ĭn-sĕk'tĭ-sīd') n. A substance used to kill insects. —**in·sec'ti·cid'al** adj.

in·sec·tiv·o·rous (ĭn'sĕk-tĭv'ər-əs) adj. Feeding on insects.

in·se·cure (ĭn'sĭ-kyŏŏr') adj. 1. Inadequately guarded or protected; unsafe. 2. Unstable; shaky. 3. Lacking self-confidence; uncertain. —**in'se·cure'ly** adv. —**in'se·cu'ri·ty** n.

in·sem·i·nate (ĭn-sĕm'ə-nāt') v. -nat·ed, -nat·ing. To introduce semen into the uterus of (a

female). [Lat. *inseminare.*] —**in·sem'i·na'tion** n. —**in·sem'i·na'tor** n.

in·sen·sate (ĭn-sĕn'sāt', -sĭt) adj. 1. Inanimate. 2. Unconscious. 3. Lacking sensibility; unfeeling. 4. Lacking sense; foolish.

in·sen·si·ble (ĭn-sĕn'sə-bəl) adj. 1. Imperceptible. 2. Unconscious. 3. a. Unsusceptible; unaffected. b. Unheeding; unmindful. c. Unfeeling; callous. —**in·sen'si·bil'i·ty** n. —**in·sen'si·bly** adv.

in·sen·si·tive (ĭn-sĕn'sĭ-tĭv) adj. 1. Not physically sensitive; numb. 2. a. Lacking in sensitivity. b. Lacking in responsiveness. —**in·sen'si·tiv'i·ty** n.

in·sen·tient (ĭn-sĕn'shənt) adj. Without sensation or consciousness. —**in·sen'tience** n.

in·sep·a·ra·ble (ĭn-sĕp'ər-ə-bəl) adj. Incapable of being separated. —**in·sep'a·ra·bil'i·ty** n. —**in·sep'a·ra·bly** adv.

in·sert (ĭn-sûrt') v. 1. To put, place, or thrust in: *insert a key in a lock.* 2. To interpolate. —n. (ĭn'sûrt'). Something inserted or intended for insertion, as a chart into written material. [Lat. *inserere.*] —**in·ser'tion** n.

in·set (ĭn-sĕt', ĭn'sĕt') v. To set in; insert. —**in'set'** n.

in·shore (ĭn'shôr', -shōr') adj. Close to or coming toward a shore. —**in'shore'** adv.

in·side (ĭn-sīd', ĭn'sīd') n. 1. An inner or interior part. 2. An inner side or surface. 3. **insides.** *Informal.* a. The inner organs; entrails. b. The inner parts or workings. 4. *Slang.* A position of confidence or influence: *on the inside.* —adv. (ĭn-sīd'). Into or in the interior; within. —prep. (ĭn-sīd'). 1. Within: *inside an hour.* 2. Into: *went inside the house.* —**in'side'** adj.

inside of prep. Inside.

in·sid·er (ĭn-sī'dər) n. One who is in a position of influence or has access to confidential information.

in·sid·i·ous (ĭn-sĭd'ē-əs) adj. 1. Working or spreading harmfully in a subtle or stealthy manner. 2. Intended to entrap; treacherous. 3. Beguiling but harmful; seductive. [Lat. *insidiosus.*] —**in·sid'i·ous·ly** adv. —**in·sid'i·ous·ness** n.

in·sight (ĭn'sīt') n. The capacity to discern the true nature of a situation; penetration.

in·sig·ni·a (ĭn-sĭg'nē-ə) n., pl. -nia or -ni·as. Also **in·sig·ne** (-nē). A distinguishing sign, esp. of office, rank, or honor; badge or emblem. [< Lat. *insignis,* remarkable.]

in·sig·nif·i·cant (ĭn'sĭg-nĭf'ĭ-kənt) adj. 1. Lacking in importance; trivial. 2. Small in size, power, or value. 3. Lacking in meaning; meaningless. —**in'sig·nif'i·cance** n. —**in'sig·nif'i·cant·ly** adv.

in·sin·cere (ĭn'sĭn-sîr') adj. Not sincere; hypocritical. —**in'sin·cere'ly** adv. —**in'sin·cer'i·ty** (-sĕr'ĭ-tē) n.

in·sin·u·ate (ĭn-sĭn'yōō-āt') v. -at·ed, -at·ing. 1. a. To introduce gradually and insidiously. b. To introduce (oneself) by subtle and artful means. 2. To hint. [Lat. *insinuare.*] —**in·sin'u·a'tion** n.

in·sip·id (ĭn-sĭp'ĭd) adj. 1. Lacking flavor or zest; tasteless. 2. Lacking excitement or interest; dull. [LLat. *insipidus.*] —**in·sip'id·ly** adv.

in·sist (ĭn-sĭst') v. 1. To be firm in one's demand. 2. To assert or demand vehemently and persistently. [Lat. *insistere*, to persist.] —**in·sis'tence** or **in·sis'ten·cy** *n.* —**in·sis'tent** *adj.* —**in·sis'tent·ly** *adv.*

in·si·tu (ĭn sī'tŏŏ, sĭt'ŏŏ) *adj. & adv.* In its original place. [Lat.]

in·so·far as (ĭn'sō-fär') *adv.* To the extent that.

in·sole (ĭn'sōl') *n.* 1. The inner sole of a shoe or boot. 2. An extra strip put inside a shoe for comfort.

in·so·lent (ĭn'sə-lənt) *adj.* Disrespectfully arrogant; impudent; rude. [< Lat. *insolens*.] —**in'so·lence** *n.* —**in'so·lent·ly** *adv.*

in·sol·u·ble (ĭn-sŏl'yə-bəl) *adj.* 1. Incapable of being dissolved. 2. Incapable of being solved or explained. [< Lat. *insolubilis*, irrefutable.] —**in·sol'u·bil'i·ty** or **in·sol'u·ble·ness** *n.* —**in·sol'u·bly** *adv.*

in·sol·vent (ĭn-sŏl'vənt) *adj.* Unable to pay one's debts; bankrupt. —**in·sol'ven·cy** *n.* —**in·sol'vent** *n.*

in·som·ni·a (ĭn-sŏm'nē-ə) *n.* Chronic inability to sleep. [< Lat. *insomnis*, sleepless.] —**in·som'ni·ac'** (-ǎk') *n.*

in·so·much as (ĭn'sō-mŭch') *conj.* Inasmuch as; since.

in·sou·ci·ant (ĭn-sŏŏ'sē-ənt) *adj.* Blithely indifferent; carefree. [Fr.] —**in·sou'ci·ance** *n.* —**in·sou'ci·ant·ly** *adv.*

in·spect (ĭn-spĕkt') *v.* 1. To examine carefully and critically. 2. To review or examine officially. [Lat. *inspectare*.] —**in·spec'tion** *n.* —**in·spec'tor** *n.*

in·spi·ra·tion (ĭn'spə-rā'shən) *n.* 1. a. Stimulation of the mind or emotions to a high level. b. The condition of being so stimulated. 2. One that inspires. 3. Something that is inspired. 4. Inhalation. [< Lat. *inspirare*.] —**in'spi·ra'tion·al** *adj.* —**in'spi·ra'tion·al·ly** *adv.*

in·spire (ĭn-spīr') *v.* **-spired, -spir·ing.** 1. To fill with noble or reverent emotion; exalt. 2. To stimulate to creativity or action. 3. To elicit or create in another. 4. To inhale. [Lat. *inspirare*.] —**in·spir'er** *n.* —**in·spir'ing·ly** *adv.*

in·spir·it (ĭn-spĭr'ĭt) *v.* To animate; enliven.

in·sta·bil·i·ty (ĭn'stə-bĭl'ĭ-tē) *n., pl.* **-ties.** Lack of stability.

in·stall (ĭn-stôl') *v.* 1. To set in position and adjust for use. 2. To put in an office, rank, or position. 3. To settle; place. —**in'stal·la'tion** (-stə-lā'shən) *n.* —**in·stall'er** *n.*

in·stall·ment (ĭn-stôl'mənt) *n.* Also **in·stal·ment.** 1. One of several successive payments of a debt. 2. A portion of anything issued at intervals.

in·stance (ĭn'stəns) *n.* 1. A case or example. 2. An occasion. 3. A prompting; request: *He called at the instance of his wife.* —*v.* **-stanced, -stanc·ing.** To offer as an example; cite.

in·stant (ĭn'stənt) *n.* 1. A very brief time; moment. 2. A particular point in time. —*adj.* 1. Immediate. 2. Imperative; urgent. 3. Designed for quick preparation: *instant coffee.* [< Lat. *instans*, present.]

in·stan·ta·ne·ous (ĭn'stən-tā'nē-əs) *adj.* 1. Occurring or completed without perceptible delay. 2. Present or occurring at a specific instant. —**in'stan·ta'ne·ous·ly** *adv.* —**in'stan·ta'ne·ous·ness** *n.*

in·stant·ly (ĭn'stənt-lē) *adv.* At once.

in·stead (ĭn-stĕd') *adv.* In the place of that previously mentioned. —**idiom. instead of.** In place of; rather than.

in·step (ĭn'stĕp') *n.* The arched middle part of the human foot.

in·sti·gate (ĭn'stĭ-gāt') *v.* **-gat·ed, -gat·ing.** 1. To urge on; goad. 2. To incite. [Lat. *instigare*.] —**in'sti·ga'tion** *n.* —**in'sti·ga'tor** *n.*

in·still (ĭn-stĭl') *v.* 1. To introduce gradually; implant. 2. To pour in drop by drop. [Lat. *instillare*, to drip in.] —**in·stil·la'tion** (ĭn'stə-lā'shən) *n.* —**in·still'er** *n.*

in·stinct (ĭn'stĭngkt') *n.* 1. An inner influence, feeling, or drive that is not learned and that results in complex animal behavior such as building of nests or nursing of young. 2. A powerful motivation or impulse. 3. A natural talent or ability. [Lat. *instinguere*, to urge on.] —**in·stinc'tive** *adj.* —**in·stinc'tive·ly** *adv.* —**in·stinc'tu·al** (-chŏŏ-əl) *adj.*

in·sti·tute (ĭn'stĭ-tŏŏt', -tyŏŏt') *v.* **-tut·ed, -tut·ing.** 1. To establish and set in operation. 2. To initiate; begin. —*n.* 1. Something instituted, esp. an authoritative rule. 2. An organization founded to promote some cause. 3. An educational institution. 4. A seminar or workshop. [< Lat. *instituere*.]

in·sti·tu·tion (ĭn'stĭ-tŏŏ'shən, -tyŏŏ'-) *n.* 1. The act of instituting. 2. An established custom or practice in a society. 3. a. An organization, esp. one dedicated to public service. b. The buildings housing such an organization. —**in'sti·tu'tion·al** *adj.* —**in'sti·tu'tion·al·ism** *n.*

in·sti·tu·tion·al·ize (ĭn'stĭ-tŏŏ'shə-nə-līz', -tyŏŏ'-) *v.* **-ized, -iz·ing.** 1. To make into an institution. 2. To confine in an institution.

in·struct (ĭn-strŭkt') *v.* 1. To teach; educate. 2. To give orders to; direct. [< Lat. *instruere*, to prepare.] —**in·struc'tive** *adj.* —**in·struc'tive·ly** *adv.*

in·struc·tion (ĭn-strŭk'shən) *n.* 1. The act, practice, or profession of instructing; education. 2. a. A lesson. b. Something learned. 3. **instructions.** Directions; orders. —**in·struc'tion·al** *adj.*

in·struc·tor (ĭn-strŭk'tər) *n.* One who instructs, esp. a college teacher below the rank of assistant professor. —**in·struc'tor·ship'** *n.*

in·stru·ment (ĭn'strə-mənt) *n.* 1. A means by which something is done; agency. 2. A mechanical implement. 3. A device for recording or measuring, esp. one functioning as part of a control system. 4. A device for producing music. 5. A legal document. —*v.* To equip with instruments. [< Lat. *instrumentum*, tool.]

in·stru·men·tal (ĭn'strə-mĕn'tl) *adj.* 1. Serving as a means or agency. 2. Performed on or written for a musical instrument. —**in'stru·men'tal·ly** *adv.*

in·stru·men·tal·ist (ĭn'strə-mĕn'tl-ĭst) *n.* One who plays a musical instrument.

in·stru·men·tal·i·ty (ĭn'strə-mĕn-tǎl'ĭ-tē) *n., pl.* **-ties.** Agency; means.

in·stru·men·ta·tion (ĭn'strə-mĕn-tā'shən) *n.* 1. The application or use of instruments. 2. The arrangement of music for instruments.

in·sub·or·di·nate (ĭn'sə-bôr'dn-ĭt) *adj.* Not submissive to authority. —**in'sub·or'di·nate·ly** *adv.* —**in'sub·or'di·na'tion** *n.*

in·sub·stan·tial (ĭn'səb-stǎn'shəl) *adj.* 1. Lacking substance or reality. 2. Not firm; flimsy. —**in'sub·stan'ti·al'i·ty** (-shē-ǎl'ĭ-tē) *n.*

in·suf·fer·a·ble (ĭn-sŭf'ər-ə-bəl) *adj.* Incapable of being endured; intolerable. —**in·suf'fer·a·bly** *adv.*

in·suf·fi·cient (ĭn'sə-fĭsh'ənt) *adj.* Not sufficient; inadequate. —**in·suf'fi·cien·cy** *n.* —**in'suf·fi'cient·ly** *adv.*

in·su·lar (ĭn'sə-lər, ĭns'yə-) *adj.* 1. Of or constituting an island or islands: *an insular na-*

tion. 2. a. Isolated. b. Narrow-minded. [< Lat. *insula,* island.]

in·su·late (ĭn'sə-lāt', ĭns'yə-) v. -lat·ed, -lat·ing. 1. To detach; isolate. 2. To prevent the passage of heat, electricity, or sound into or out of, esp. by interposition of an insulating material. [< Lat. *insula,* island.] —in'su·la'tion n. —in'su·la'tor n.

in·su·lin (ĭn'sə-lĭn, ĭns'yə-) n. A pancreatic hormone that regulates carbohydrate metabolism by controlling blood glucose levels. [Lat. *insula,* island + -IN.]

insulin shock n. Hypoglycemia resulting from excessive insulin in the blood.

in·sult (ĭn-sŭlt') v. To speak to or treat with disrespect or contempt. —n. (ĭn'sŭlt'). A disrespectful or contemptuous action or remark. [< Lat. *insultare,* to revile.]

Syns: *insult, affront, offend, outrage* v.

in·su·per·a·ble (ĭn-sōō'pər-ə-bəl) adj. Incapable of being overcome; insurmountable. —in·su'per·a·bil'i·ty n. —in·su'per·a·bly adv.

in·sup·port·a·ble (ĭn'sə-pôr'tə-bəl, -pôr'-) adj. 1. Unbearable; intolerable. 2. Unjustifiable; indefensible.

in·sur·ance (ĭn-shŏŏr'əns) n. 1. The act of insuring or condition of being insured. 2. The business of insuring persons or property. 3. A contract binding a company to indemnify an insured party against specified loss. 4. The sum for which something is insured. 5. A protective measure or device.

in·sure (ĭn-shŏŏr') v. -sured, -sur·ing. 1. To protect against risk or loss with insurance. 2. To make certain; guarantee. [< OFr. *enseurer,* to guarantee.] —in·sur'a·ble adj. —in·sur'er n.

Usage: Although *ensure* and *insure* are generally interchangeable, only *insure* is now widely used in the commercial sense of "to guarantee persons or property against risk."

in·sured (ĭn-shŏŏrd') n. One that is covered by insurance.

in·sur·gent (ĭn-sûr'jənt) adj. Rising in revolt; rebellious. —n. One who revolts against authority, esp. a member of a political party who rebels against its leadership. [< Lat. *surgere,* to rise up.] —in·sur'gence or in·sur'gen·cy n.

in·sur·mount·a·ble (ĭn'sər-moun'tə-bəl) adj. Incapable of being surmounted; insuperable. —in'sur·mount'a·bly adv.

in·sur·rec·tion (ĭn'sə-rĕk'shən) n. The act of open revolt against civil authority or a constituted government. [< Lat. *insurgere,* to rise up.] —in'sur·rec'tion·ist n.

in·tact (ĭn-tăkt') adj. Not impaired in any way. [< Lat. *intactus.*] —in·tact'ness n.

in·ta·glio (ĭn-tăl'yō, -tăl'-) n., pl. -glios. A figure or design carved deep into the surface of hard metal or stone. [< Ital. *intagliare,* to engrave.]

in·take (ĭn'tāk') n. 1. An opening through which a fluid enters a container or pipe. 2. a. The act of taking in. b. The amount taken in.

in·tan·gi·ble (ĭn-tăn'jə-bəl) adj. 1. Not capable of being touched; lacking physical substance. 2. Not capable of being perceived; vague. —n. Something intangible. —in·tan'-

gi·bil'i·ty or in·tan'gi·ble·ness n. —in·tan'gi·bly adv.

in·te·ger (ĭn'tĭ-jər) n. A member of the set of positive whole numbers (1, 2, 3, . . .), negative whole numbers (-1, -2, -3, . . .), and zero (0). [< Lat., whole.]

in·te·gral (ĭn'tĭ-grəl, ĭn-tĕg'rəl) adj. 1. Forming a necessary part of a whole; constituent. 2. Whole; entire. 3. Expressed or expressible as or in terms of integers. —n. A complete unit; whole. [< Lat. *integer,* whole.]

in·te·grate (ĭn'tĭ-grāt') v. -grat·ed, -grat·ing. 1. To make into a whole; unify. 2. To join with something else; unite. 3. To open to all ethnic groups. [Lat. *integrare.*] —in'te·gra'tion n. —in'te·gra'tive adj.

in·teg·ri·ty (ĭn-tĕg'rĭ-tē) n. 1. Strict personal honesty and independence. 2. Completeness; unity. 3. Soundness. [< Lat. *integritas,* soundness.]

in·teg·u·ment (ĭn-tĕg'yə-mənt) n. An outer covering, as skin or a seed coat. [< Lat. *integere,* to cover.]

in·tel·lect (ĭn'tl-ĕkt') n. 1. a. The ability of the mind to think, reason, and learn. b. The ability to think abstractly or deeply. 2. A person of great intellectual ability. [< Lat. *intellegere,* to perceive.]

in·tel·lec·tu·al (ĭn'tl-ĕk'chōō-əl) adj. 1. a. Of, relating to, or requiring use of the intellect. b. Rational. 2. a. Having superior intelligence. b. Given to learning, thinking, and judging ideas. —n. A person of trained intelligence. —in'tel·lec'tu·al·ly adv.

in·tel·lec·tu·al·ize (ĭn'tl-ĕk'chōō-ə-līz') v. -ized, -iz·ing. 1. To make rational. 2. To avoid emotional insight into (an emotional problem) by performing an intellectual analysis. —in'tel·lec'tu·al·i·za'tion n.

in·tel·li·gence (ĭn-tĕl'ə-jəns) n. 1. a. The capacity to acquire and apply knowledge. b. The faculty of thought and reason. c. Superior powers of mind. 2. Received information; news. 3. a. Secret information, esp. about an enemy. b. The work of gathering such information.

in·tel·li·gent (ĭn-tĕl'ə-jənt) adj. 1. Having intelligence. 2. Having a high degree of intelligence. 3. Showing intelligence: *an intelligent choice.* [< Lat. *intellegere,* to perceive.] —in·tel'li·gent·ly adv.

in·tel·li·gent·si·a (ĭn-tĕl'ə-jĕnt'sē-ə, -gĕnt'-) n. The intellectual class within a society. [R. *intelligentsiya.*]

in·tel·li·gi·ble (ĭn-tĕl'ə-jə-bəl) adj. Comprehensible. —in·tel'li·gi·bil'i·ty n. —in·tel'li·gi·bly adv.

in·tem·per·ance (ĭn-tĕm'pər-əns) n. Lack of moderation, esp. in the drinking of alcoholic beverages. —in·tem'per·ate adj. —in·tem'per·ate·ly adv.

in·tend (ĭn-tĕnd') v. 1. To have in mind; plan. 2. To design for a specific purpose. 3. To signify; mean. [< Lat. *intendere.*]

Usage: *Intend* may be followed by an infinitive (*intended to go*), a gerund (*intended going*), or by a *that* clause with a subjunctive (*intended that he be informed*).

in·tend·ed (ĭn-tĕn'dĭd) adj. 1. Deliberate; intentional. 2. Prospective; future. —n. *Informal.* A person's prospective spouse.

in·tense (ĭn-tĕns′) *adj.* **1.** Of great intensity. **2.** Extreme in degree, strength, or size. **3.** Involving or showing great concentration or strain. **4.** Deeply felt; profound. [< Lat. *intendere,* to intend.] —**in·tense′ly** *adv.* —**in·tense′ness** *n.*

 Syns: *intense, desperate, fierce, furious, terrible, vehement, violent* *adj.*

in·ten·si·fy (ĭn-tĕn′sə-fī′) *v.* **-fied, -fy·ing.** To make or become intense or more intense. —**in·ten′si·fi·ca′tion** *n.* —**in·ten′si·fi′er** *n.*

in·ten·si·ty (ĭn-tĕn′sĭ-tē) *n., pl.* **-ties. 1.** Exceptionally great concentration, power, or force. **2.** Degree; strength. **3.** *Physics.* The measure of effectiveness of a force field given by the force per unit test element.

in·ten·sive (ĭn-tĕn′sĭv) *adj.* **1.** Marked by a full and thorough application of resources: *intensive care.* **2.** Adding emphasis. —*n.* A word or word element that adds emphasis but no new meaning. —**in·ten′sive·ly** *adv.*

in·tent (ĭn-tĕnt′) *n.* **1.** Aim; purpose. **2.** The state of mind operative at the time of an action. **3. a.** Meaning; significance. **b.** Connotation. —*adj.* **1.** Firmly fixed; concentrated. **2.** Engrossed. **3.** Determined. [< Lat. *intendere,* to intend.] —**in·tent′ly** *adv.* —**in·tent′ness** *n.*

in·ten·tion (ĭn-tĕn′shən) *n.* **1.** A plan of action; design. **2.** An aim that guides action; object. **3.** The import; meaning.

in·ten·tion·al (ĭn-tĕn′shə-nəl) *adj.* Done deliberately; intended. —**in·ten′tion·al′i·ty** (-năl′ĭ-tē) *n.* —**in·ten′tion·al·ly** *adv.*

in·ter (ĭn-tûr′) *v.* **-terred, -ter·ring.** To place in a grave; bury. [< Med. Lat. *interrare.*]

inter- *pref.* **1.** Between or among: *international.* **2.** Mutually or together: *interact.* [< Lat. *inter,* among.]

in·ter·act (ĭn′tər-ăkt′) *v.* To act on each other. —**in′ter·ac′tion** *n.* —**in′ter·ac′tive** *adj.*

in·ter al·i·a (ĭn′tər ā′lē-ə, ä′lē-ə) *adv.* Among other things. [Lat.]

in·ter·breed (ĭn′tər-brēd′) *v.* **1.** To crossbreed. **2.** To breed within a narrow range; inbreed.

in·ter·cede (ĭn′tər-sēd′) *v.* **-ced·ed, -ced·ing. 1.** To plead on another's behalf. **2.** To mediate. [Lat. *intercedere,* to intervene.]

in·ter·cel·lu·lar (ĭn′tər-sĕl′yə-lər) *adj.* Among or between cells.

in·ter·cept (ĭn′tər-sĕpt′) *v.* **1.** To stop or interrupt the progress of. **2.** To intersect. **3.** *Math.* To cut off or bound a part of (a line, plane, surface, or solid). [Lat. *intercipere.*] —**in′ter·cept′** *n.* —**in′ter·cep′tion** *n.*

in·ter·cep·tor (ĭn′tər-sĕp′tər) *n.* A fast-climbing, highly maneuverable fighter plane designed to intercept enemy aircraft.

in·ter·ces·sion (ĭn′tər-sĕsh′ən) *n.* **1.** Entreaty on another's behalf. **2.** Mediation. [< Lat. *intercedere,* to intervene.] —**in′ter·ces′sion·al** *adj.* —**in′ter·ces′sor·y** *adj.*

in·ter·change (ĭn′tər-chānj′) *v.* **1.** To switch each into the place of the other. **2.** To exchange. **3.** To alternate. —*n.* (ĭn′tər-chānj′). **1.** An exchange. **2.** A highway intersection designed to permit traffic to move freely by means of separate levels from one road to another. —**in′ter·change′a·ble** *adj.* —**in′ter·change′a·bly** *adv.*

in·ter·col·le·giate (ĭn′tər-kə-lē′jĭt, -jē-ĭt) *adj.* Involving two or more colleges.

in·ter·com (ĭn′tər-kŏm′) *n.* A system for two-way communication, as between two rooms. [< INTERCOMMUNICATION.]

in·ter·com·mu·ni·cate (ĭn′tər-kə-myōō′nĭ-kāt′) *v.* **-cat·ed, -cat·ing. 1.** To communicate with each other. **2.** To be adjoined. —**in′ter·com·mu′ni·ca′tion** *n.* —**in′ter·com·mu′ni·ca′tive** *adj.*

in·ter·con·ti·nen·tal (ĭn′tər-kŏn′tə-nĕn′tl) *adj.* **1.** Extending or traveling from one continent to another. **2.** Carried on between continents.

in·ter·cos·tal (ĭn′tər-kŏs′tal) *adj.* Located or occurring between the ribs. [INTER- + Lat. *costa,* rib + -AL¹.]

in·ter·course (ĭn′tər-kôrs′, -kōrs′) *n.* **1.** Social interchange; communication. **2.** Coitus. [< Lat. *intercurrere,* to mingle with.]

in·ter·de·pend·ent (ĭn′tər-dĭ-pĕn′dənt) *n.* Mutually dependent. —**in′ter·de·pend′ence** *n.*

in·ter·dict (ĭn′tər-dĭkt′) *v.* To prohibit or forbid, esp. by official sanction. —*n.* (ĭn′tər-dĭkt′). A prohibition. [< Lat. *interdicere.*] —**in′ter·dic′tion** *n.* —**in′ter·dic′tor** *n.* —**in′ter·dic′to·ry** *adj.*

in·ter·est (ĭn′trĭst, -tər-ĭst) *n.* **1. a.** Willingness to give special attention to something. **b.** Something that arouses such willingness. **2.** Often **interests.** Advantage; benefit. **3.** A right, claim, or legal share in something: *an interest in a business.* **4.** A charge paid for borrowing money, usu. a percentage of the amount borrowed. —*v.* **1.** To arouse interest in. **2.** To cause to become involved or concerned. [< Lat., it is of importance.]

in·ter·est·ed (ĭn′trĭ-stĭd, -tər-ĭ-stĭd, -tə-rĕs′tĭd) *adj.* **1.** Having or showing interest. **2.** Possessing a right, claim, or share.

in·ter·est·ing (ĭn′trĭ-stĭng, -tər-ĭ-stĭng, -tə-rĕs′tĭng) *adj.* Arousing or holding attention. —**in′ter·est·ing·ly** *adv.*

in·ter·face (ĭn′tər-fās′) *n.* **1.** A surface forming a common boundary between adjacent regions. **2. a.** A point at which independent systems or diverse groups interact. **b.** The device or system by which interaction at an interface is effected. —**in′ter·face′** *v.* —**in′ter·fa′cial** (-fā′shəl) *adj.*

in·ter·fere (ĭn′tər-fîr′) *v.* **-fered, -fer·ing. 1.** To hinder; impede. **2.** *Sports.* To impede illegally the catching of a pass or the playing of a ball or puck. **3.** To intervene or intrude in the affairs of others; meddle. **4.** To inhibit or prevent clear reception of broadcast signals. [< OFr. *entreferer,* to meddle.] —**in′ter·fer′ence** *n.* —**in′ter·fer′er** *n.*

in·ter·fer·on (ĭn′tər-fîr′ŏn′) *n.* A cellular protein produced in response to and acting to prevent replication of an infectious viral form within an infected cell. [< INTERFERE.]

in·ter·ga·lac·tic (ĭn′tər-gə-lăk′tĭk) *adj.* Between galaxies.

in·ter·im (ĭn′tər-ĭm) *n.* An intervening period of time. —*adj.* Temporary. [< Lat., in the meantime.]

in·te·ri·or (ĭn-tîr′ē-ər) *adj.* **1.** Of or located in the inside; inner. **2.** Inland. —*n.* **1.** The inner part of something; inside. **2.** One's mental or spiritual being. **3.** A representation of the inside of a building or room. **4.** The inland part of a geographic area. [< Lat. *inter,* within.]

interior decorator *n.* One who plans and executes the layout and decoration of an architectural interior. —**interior decoration** *n.*

in·ter·ject (ĭn′tər-jĕkt′) *v.* To put in between or among other things; insert. [Lat. *interjicere.*] —**in′ter·jec′tor** *n.* —**in′ter·jec′to·ry** *adj.*

in·ter·jec·tion (ĭn′tər-jĕk′shən) *n.* **1.** A word that expresses some abrupt emotion and that

stands alone grammatically, as *Ouch!* or *Oh!*
2. Any exclamation. —**in'ter·jec'tion·al** *adj.*

in·ter·lin·ing (ĭn'tər-lī'nĭng) *n.* An extra lining between the outer fabric and the regular lining of a garment.

in·ter·lock (ĭn'tər-lŏk') *v.* To join or unite closely.

Interlock
Interlocking logs

in·ter·loc·u·tor (ĭn'tər-lŏk'yə-tər) *n.* One who takes part in a conversation or dialogue. [< Lat. *interloqui,* to interrupt.]

in·ter·loc·u·to·ry (ĭn'tər-lŏk'yə-tôr'ē, -tōr'ē) *adj.* Of or relating to a temporary decree made during the course of a suit or trial.

in·ter·lope (ĭn'tər-lōp', ĭn'tər-lōp') *v.* **-loped, -lop·ing. 1.** To violate the legally established trading rights of others. **2.** To interfere; meddle. [INTER- + Du. *loopen,* to run.] —**in'ter·lop'er** *n.*

in·ter·lude (ĭn'tər-lōōd') *n.* **1.** An intervening episode, feature, or period of time. **2.** An entertainment between the acts of a play. **3.** A short musical piece inserted between the parts of a longer composition. [< Med. Lat. *interludium,* dramatic entertainment.]

in·ter·mar·ry (ĭn'tər-măr'ē) *v.* **1.** To marry one of another religion, nationality, race, or group. **2.** To be bound together by the marriages of members: *The two clans intermarried.* **3.** To marry within one's own group. —**in'ter·mar'riage** *n.*

in·ter·me·di·ar·y (ĭn'tər-mē'dē-ĕr'ē) *n., pl.* **-ies. 1.** A mediator; go-between. **2.** An intermediate state or stage. —*adj.* **1.** Acting as a mediator. **2.** In between; intermediate.

in·ter·me·di·ate (ĭn'tər-mē'dē-ĭt) *adj.* Lying, occurring, or being between two extremes; in between. —*n.* **1.** One that is intermediate. **2.** An intermediary. [< Lat. *intermedius.*] —**in'ter·me'di·ate·ly** *adv.*

in·ter·ment (ĭn-tûr'mənt) *n.* The act of interring; burial.

in·ter·mez·zo (ĭn'tər-mĕt'sō, -mĕd'zō) *n., pl.* **-zos** or **-zi** (-sē, -zē). *Mus.* **1.** A short movement separating sections of a larger work. **2.** A short independent instrumental composition. [Ital.]

in·ter·mi·na·ble (ĭn-tûr'mə-nə-bəl) *adj.* Tiresomely long; endless. —**in'ter'mi·na·bly** *adv.*

in·ter·min·gle (ĭn'tər-mĭng'gəl) *v.* To mix or mingle.

in·ter·mis·sion (ĭn'tər-mĭsh'ən) *n.* A temporary suspension of activity, esp. the period between the acts of a theatrical performance. [< Lat. *intermittere,* to suspend.]

in·ter·mit·tent (ĭn'tər-mĭt'nt) *adj.* Stopping and starting at intervals. [< Lat. *intermittere,* to suspend.] —**in'ter·mit'tent·ly** *adv.*

in·ter·mo·lec·u·lar (ĭn'tər-mə-lĕk'yə-lər) *adj.* Between molecules.

in·tern (ĭn'tûrn') *n.* Also **in·terne.** An advanced student or recent graduate, as of a medical school, undergoing supervised practical training. —*v.* **1.** (ĭn'tûrn'). To train or serve as an intern. **2.** (ĭn-tûrn'). To detain or confine, esp. in wartime. [< Lat. *internus,* internal.] —**in·tern'ment** *n.* —**in·tern'ship'** *n.*

in·ter·nal (ĭn-tûr'nəl) *adj.* **1.** Inner; interior. **2.** Intrinsic; inherent. **3.** Located, acting, or effective within the body: *internal bleeding.* **4.** Of or relating to the domestic affairs of a country. [< Lat. *internus.*] —**in·ter'nal·ly** *adv.*

in·ter·nal-com·bus·tion engine (ĭn-tûr'nəl-kəm-bŭs'chən) *n.* An engine in which fuel is burned within the engine itself.

internal revenue *n.* Governmental income from taxes levied within the country.

in·ter·na·tion·al (ĭn'tər-năsh'ə-nəl) *adj.* Of, relating to, or involving two or more nations or nationalities. —**in'ter·na'tion·al·ly** *adv.*

in·ter·na·tion·al·ism (ĭn'tər-năsh'ə-nə-lĭz'əm) *n.* A theory that promotes cooperation among nations, esp. in politics and economy. —**in'ter·na'tion·al·ist** *n.*

in·ter·na·tion·al·ize (ĭn'tər-năsh'ən-ə-līz') *v.* **-ized, -iz·ing.** To put under international control. —**in'ter·na'tion·al·i·za'tion** *n.*

international law *n.* A set of rules gen. regarded and accepted as binding in relations between states and nations.

in·terne (ĭn'tûrn') *n.* Var. of **intern.**

in·ter·ne·cine (ĭn'tər-nĕs'ēn', -īn', -īn, -nē'sīn') *adj.* **1.** Mutually destructive. **2.** Involving conflict within a group: *internecine squabbles within the department.* [< Lat. *internecare,* to slaughter.]

in·tern·ee (ĭn-tûr-nē') *n.* One who is interned, esp. during a war.

in·tern·ist (ĭn-tûr'nĭst, ĭn-tûr'-) *n.* A physician who specializes in internal medicine. [INTERN(AL MEDICINE) + -IST.]

in·ter·of·fice (ĭn'tər-ô'fĭs, -ŏf'ĭs) *adj.* Taking place between offices, esp. of an organization.

in·ter·per·son·al (ĭn'tər-pûr'sə-nəl) *adj.* Of, relating to, involving, or being relations between persons. —**in'ter·per'son·al·ly** *adv.*

in·ter·plan·e·tary (ĭn'tər-plăn'ĭ-tĕr'ē) *adj.* Between planets.

in·ter·play (ĭn'tər-plā') *n.* Reciprocal action and reaction; interaction. —**in'ter·play'** *v.*

in·ter·po·late (ĭn-tûr'pə-lāt') *v.* **-lat·ed, -lat·ing. 1.** To insert or introduce between other things or parts. **2.** To change (a text) by introducing new or false material. [Lat. *interpolare.*] —**in·ter'po·la'tion** *n.* —**in·ter'po·la'tor** *n.*

in·ter·pose (ĭn'tər-pōz') *v.* **-posed, -pos·ing. 1.** To insert or introduce between parts. **2.** To introduce or interject into a conversation or speech. **3.** To intrude. **4.** To intervene. [< Lat. *interponere.*] —**in'ter·pos'er** *n.* —**in'ter·po·si'tion** (-pə-zĭsh'ən) *n.*

in·ter·pret (ĭn-tûr'prĭt) *v.* **1.** To explain or clarify the meaning of. **2.** To perform or present according to one's artistic understanding: *an actor interpreting a role.* **3.** To translate. **4.** To offer an explanation. [< Lat. *interpres,*

ă pat ā pay â care ä father ĕ pet ē be ĭ pit ī tie î pier ŏ pot ō toe ô paw, for oi noise ŏŏ took
ŏŏ boot ou out th thin *th* this ŭ cut û urge yŏŏ abuse zh vision ə about, item, edible, gallop, circus

negotiator.] —**in·ter·pret·a·ble** adj. —**inter·preter** n.

in·ter·pre·ta·tion (ĭn-tûr′prĭ-tā′shən) n. 1. An explanation. 2. A concept of a work of art as expressed by its representation or performance. —**in·ter·pre·ta′tion·al** adj.

in·ter·pre·ta·tive (ĭn-tûr′prĭ-tā′tĭv) adj. Also **in·ter·pre·tive** (-prĭ-tĭv). Expository; explanatory. —**in·ter′pre·ta′tive·ly** adv.

in·ter·ra·cial (ĭn′tər-rā′shəl) adj. Of or between different races.

in·ter·reg·num (ĭn′tər-rĕg′nəm) n., pl. -**nums** or -**na** (-nə). 1. The interval of time between two successive reigns or governments. 2. A gap in continuity. [Lat.] —**in′ter·reg′nal** adj.

in·ter·re·late (ĭn′tər-rĭ-lāt′) v. To place in or come into mutual relationship. —**in′ter·re·la′tion** n. —**in′ter·re·la′tion·ship′** n.

in·ter·ro·gate (ĭn-tĕr′ə-gāt′) v. -**gat·ed**, -**gat·ing**. 1. To question formally. 2. Computer Sci. To send out or give a signal to for setting off an appropriate response. [Lat. interrogare.] —**in·ter′ro·ga′tion** n. —**in·ter′ro·ga′tor** n.

in·ter·rog·a·tive (ĭn′tə-rŏg′ə-tĭv) adj. 1. Of the nature of a question. 2. Used in asking a question: an interrogative pronoun. —**in′ter·rog′a·tive** n. —**in′ter·rog′a·tive·ly** adv.

in·ter·rog·a·to·ry (ĭn′tə-rŏg′ə-tôr′ē, -tōr′ē) adj. Interrogative. —n., pl. -**ries**. Law. A formal question, as to an accused person. —**in′ter·rog′a·to′ri·ly** adv.

in·ter·rupt (ĭn′tə-rŭpt′) v. 1. To break the continuity or uniformity of. 2. To stop by breaking in. 3. To break in on another's speech or action. [< Lat. interrumpere, to break off.] —**in′ter·rupt′er** or **in′ter·rup′tor** n. —**in′ter·rup′tion** n. —**in′ter·rup′tive** adj.

in·ter·sect (ĭn′tər-sĕkt′) v. 1. To cut across or through. 2. To form an intersection with. [Lat. intersecare.]

in·ter·sec·tion (ĭn′tər-sĕk′shən) n. 1. a. The act or process of intersecting. b. A place where things intersect. 2. The point or locus of points common to two or more geometric figures.

in·ter·sperse (ĭn′tər-spûrs′) v. -**spersed**, -**spers·ing**. 1. To scatter here and there among other things. 2. To give variety to by distributing things here and there. [< Lat. interspersus, interspersed.] —**in′ter·sper′sion** (-spûr′zhən, -shən) n.

in·ter·state (ĭn′tər-stāt′) adj. Of, between, or connecting two or more states.

in·ter·stel·lar (ĭn′tər-stĕl′ər) adj. Between the stars.

in·ter·stice (ĭn-tûr′stĭs) n., pl. -**sti·ces** (-stĭ-sēz′, -sĭz). A narrow or small space between things or parts. [< Lat. intersistere, to stand in the middle.] —**in′ter·sti′tial** (ĭn′tər-stĭsh′əl) adj.

in·ter·twine (ĭn′tər-twīn′) v. To join by twining together.

in·ter·ur·ban (ĭn′tər-ûr′bən) adj. Between urban areas.

in·ter·val (ĭn′tər-vəl) n. 1. A period of time between two events or occurrences. 2. A space between two points or objects. 3. a. The set of all numbers that lie between two given numbers, sometimes including either or both of the given numbers. b. A line segment that represents the numbers in this set. 4. The difference in pitch between two musical tones. [< Lat. intervallum.]

in·ter·vene (ĭn′tər-vēn′) v. -**vened**, -**ven·ing**. 1. To occur or come between two things, points, or events. 2. a. To enter a course of

events so as to hinder or change it: The governor intervened to delay the execution. b. To interfere, usu. with force, in the affairs of another nation. [Lat. intervenire.] —**in·ter·ven′tion** (-vĕn′shən) n.

in·ter·view (ĭn′tər-vyōō′) n. 1. a. A face-to-face meeting. b. Such a meeting arranged for formal discussion. 2. A conversation between a reporter and one from whom information is sought. [< Fr. entrevoir, to see.] —**in′ter·view′** v. —**in′ter·view′er** n.

in·ter·weave (ĭn′tər-wēv′) v. 1. To weave together. 2. To intertwine.

in·tes·tate (ĭn-tĕs′tāt′, -tĭt) adj. 1. Having made no legal will. 2. Not disposed of by a legal will. [< Lat. intestatus.] —**in·tes′ta·cy** (-tə-sē) n.

in·tes·tine (ĭn-tĕs′tĭn) n. The portion of the alimentary canal extending from the outlet of the stomach to the anus. [Lat. intestinum.] —**in·tes′ti·nal** n. —**in·tes′ti·nal·ly** adv.

in·ti·mate¹ (ĭn′tə-mĭt) adj. 1. Marked by close acquaintance or familiarity. 2. Essential; innermost. 3. Characterized by informality and privacy. 4. Very personal; private. —n. A close friend or confidant. [< Lat. intimus.] —**in′ti·ma·cy** or **in′ti·mate·ness** n. —**in′ti·mate·ly** adv.

in·ti·mate² (ĭn′tə-māt′) v. -**mat·ed**, -**mat·ing**. To imply subtly. [LLat. intimare.] —**in′ti·mat′er** n. —**in′ti·ma′tion** n.

in·tim·i·date (ĭn-tĭm′ĭ-dāt′) v. -**dat·ed**, -**dat·ing**. 1. To make timid; frighten. 2. To discourage or inhibit by or as if by threats. [Med. Lat. intimidare.] —**in·tim′i·da′tion** n. —**in·tim′i·da′tor** n.

in·to (ĭn′tōō) prep. 1. To the inside of. 2. To the action or occupation of: go into banking. 3. To the condition or form of. 4. So as to be in or within. 5. To a time or place in the course of: well into the week. 6. Against: ram into a tree. 7. Toward. 8. Informal. Interested in or involved with: They are into vegetarianism. [< OE intō.]

in·tol·er·a·ble (ĭn-tŏl′ər-ə-bəl) adj. 1. Unbearable. 2. Inordinate; extravagant. —**in·tol′er·a·bly** adv.

in·tol·er·ant (ĭn-tŏl′ər-ənt) adj. 1. Not tolerant of others; bigoted. 2. Unable to endure: intolerant of certain drugs. —**in·tol′er·ance** n. —**in·tol′er·ant·ly** adv.

in·to·na·tion (ĭn′tō-nā′shən) n. 1. The way in which the speaking voice emphasizes words, makes pauses, or rises and falls in pitch in order to convey meaning. 2. a. A particular quality or tone of voice. b. Expression or expressiveness. 3. The manner in which musical tones are produced, sung, chanted, etc., esp. with respect to accuracy of pitch.

in·tone (ĭn-tōn′) v. -**toned**, -**ton·ing**. To recite in a singing or chanting voice. [< Med. Lat. intonare.] —**in·ton′er** n.

in to·to (ĭn tō′tō) adv. Totally. [Lat.]

in·tox·i·cate (ĭn-tŏk′sĭ-kāt′) v. -**cat·ed**, -**cat·ing**. 1. To make drunk. 2. To stimulate or excite. [Med. Lat. intoxicare.] —**in·tox′i·cant** (-kənt) n. —**in·tox′i·ca′tion** n.

intra- pref. 1. In, within, or inside of: intracellular. [< Lat. intra.]

in·tra·cel·lu·lar (ĭn′trə-sĕl′yə-lər) adj. Within a cell or cells.

in·trac·ta·ble (ĭn-trăk′tə-bəl) adj. Difficult to manage or govern; stubborn.

in·tra·mu·ral (ĭn′trə-myōōr′əl) adj. Existing or carried on within an institution, esp. a school.

in·tran·si·gent (in-trăn'sə-jənt) *adj.* Refusing to moderate an extreme position; uncompromising. [< Sp. *intransigente*.] —**in·tran'si·gence** or **in·tran'si·gen·cy** *n.* —**in·tran'si·gent** *n.* —**in·tran'si·gent·ly** *adv.*

in·tran·si·tive (in-trăn'sĭ-tĭv) *Gram.* —*adj.* Not requiring a direct object to complete its meaning. —*n.* An intransitive verb. —**in·tran'si·tive·ly** *adv.* —**in·tran'si·tive·ness** or **in·tran'si·tiv·i·ty** *n.*

in·tra·state (in'trə-stāt') *adj.* Within the boundaries of a state.

in·tra·u·ter·ine (in'trə-yōō'tər-ĭn, -tə-rīn') *adj.* Within the uterus.

in·tra·ve·nous (in'trə-vē'nəs) *adj.* Within a vein or veins. —**in'tra·ve'nous·ly** *adv.*

in·trep·id (in-trĕp'ĭd) *adj.* Resolutely courageous; fearless; bold. [< Lat. *intrepidus*.] —**in·trep'id·ly** *adv.* —**in·trep'id·ness** *n.*

in·tri·cate (in'trĭ-kĭt) *adj.* 1. Having many complexly arranged elements. 2. Comprehensible only with painstaking effort: *intricate instructions*. [< Lat. *intricare*, to entangle.] —**in'tri·ca·cy** (-kə-sē) *n.* —**in'tri·cate·ly** *adv.*

in·trigue (in'trēg', in-trēg') *n.* 1. A concealed or underhand maneuver or scheme. 2. A secret love affair. 3. Mystery; suspense. —*v.* (in-trēg') **-trigued, -trigu·ing.** 1. To engage in secret or underhand schemes; plot. 2. To accomplish by scheming. 3. To arouse the interest or curiosity of. [< Ital. *intrigo*.] —**in·trigu'er** *n.*

in·trin·sic (in-trĭn'sĭk) *adj.* Belonging to the essential nature of a thing; inherent. [< Lat. *intrinsecus*, inward.] —**in·trin'si·cal·ly** *adv.*

intro- *pref.* 1. In or into: *introjection*. 2. Inward: *introvert*. [Lat.]

in·tro·duce (in'trə-dōōs', -dyōōs') *v.* **-duced, -duc·ing.** 1. To identify and present, esp. to make (strangers) acquainted. 2. To present and recommend, as a plan. 3. To originate. 4. To insert or inject. 5. To inform of something for the first time. 6. To preface. [Lat. *introducere*, to bring in.] —**in'tro·duc'er** *n.* —**in'tro·duc'tion** (-dŭk'shən) *n.* —**in'tro·duc'to·ry** *adj.*

Syns: *introduce, inaugurate, initiate, institute, launch, originate* *v.*

in·tro·mit (in'trə-mĭt') *v.* **-mit·ted, -mit·ting.** To cause or permit to enter. [Lat. *intromittere*, to send in.] —**in'tro·mis'sion** (-mĭsh'ən) *n.* —**in'tro·mit'tent** *adj.*

in·tro·spec·tion (in'trə-spĕk'shən) *n.* Contemplation of one's own thoughts and feelings; self-examination. [< Lat. *introspicere*, to look into.] —**in'tro·spect'** *v.* —**in'tro·spec'tive** *adj.* —**in'tro·spec'tive·ly** *adv.*

in·tro·vert (in'trə-vûrt') *n.* One whose thoughts and interests are directed inward. [INTRO- + Lat. *vertere*, to turn.] —**in'tro·ver'sion** *n.* —**in'tro·vert'ed** *adj.*

in·trude (in-trōōd') *v.* **-trud·ed, -trud·ing.** To put or force in without being wanted or asked. [Lat. *intrudere*, to thrust in.] —**in·trud'er** *n.* —**in·tru'sion** *n.* —**in·tru'sive·ly** *adv.*

in·trust (in-trŭst') *v.* Var. of **entrust**.

in·tu·it (in-tōō'ĭt, in-tyōō'-) *v.* To know or sense by intuition. [< INTUITION.]

in·tu·i·tion (in'tōō-ĭsh'ən, -tyōō-) *n.* 1. a. The

faculty of knowing as if by instinct, without conscious reasoning. b. A perception based on this faculty. 2. Sharp insight. [< Lat. *intueri*, to look at.] —**in·tu'i·tive** *adj.* —**in·tu'i·tive·ly** *adv.* —**in·tu'i·tive·ness** *n.*

in·un·date (in'ən-dāt') *v.* **-dat·ed, -dat·ing.** To cover or overwhelm with or as if with a flood. [Lat. *inundare*.] —**in'un·da'tion** *n.* —**in'un·da'tor** *n.*

in·ure (in-yōōr') *v.* **-ured, -ur·ing.** To make used to something undesirable; harden. [< ME *in ure*, customary.] —**in·ure'ment** *n.*

in·vade (in-vād') *v.* **-vad·ed, -vad·ing.** 1. To enter by force in order to conquer. 2. To get into and spread harm through. 3. To overrun or infest. 4. To trespass or intrude upon; violate. [< Lat. *invadere*.] —**in·vad'er** *n.*

in·va·lid¹ (in'və-lĭd) *n.* A chronically ill or disabled person. —*adj.* Disabled by illness or injury. [< Lat. *invalidus*, weak.]

in·val·id² (in-văl'ĭd) *adj.* 1. Not legally valid; null. 2. Falsely based or reasoned; unjustified. —**in·val'id·ly** *adv.*

in·val·i·date (in-văl'ĭ-dāt') *v.* **-dat·ed, -dat·ing.** To make void; render invalid. —**in·val'i·da'tion** *n.* —**in·val'i·da'tor** *n.* —**in'va·lid'i·ty** (-və-lĭd'ĭ-tē) *n.*

in·val·u·a·ble (in-văl'yōō-ə-bəl) *adj.* 1. Having great value; priceless. 2. Indispensable; much appreciated: *an invaluable service.* —**in·val'u·a·bly** *adv.*

in·var·i·a·ble (in-vâr'ē-ə-bəl) *adj.* Not changing or subject to change; constant. —**in·var'i·a·bil'i·ty** or **in·var'i·a·ble·ness** *n.* —**in·var'i·a·bly** *adv.*

in·va·sion (in-vā'zhən) *n.* 1. The act of invading, esp. entrance by force. 2. The onset of something harmful, as of a disease. [< Lat. *invadere*, to invade.]

in·vec·tive (in-vĕk'tĭv) *n.* Sharp, harsh, insulting words used to attack; violent denunciation. [< Lat. *invectivus*, reproachful.]

in·veigh (in-vā') *v.* To protest vehemently; rail. [Lat. *invehi*, to attack.]

in·vei·gle (in-vē'gəl, -vā'-) *v.* **-gled, -gling.** 1. To lead astray or win over by flattering or deceiving. 2. To obtain by deceiving or flattery. [< OFr. *aveugler*, to blind.] —**in·vei'gle·ment** *n.* —**in·vei'gler** *n.*

in·vent (in-vĕnt') *v.* 1. To conceive of or devise first; originate. 2. To fabricate; make up: *invent an excuse.* [< Lat. *invenire*, to find.] —**in·ven'tor** *n.*

in·ven·tion (in-vĕn'shən) *n.* 1. The act or process of inventing. 2. A new device, method, or process developed from study and experimentation. 3. Something made up or untrue; falsehood. 4. Skill in inventing.

in·ven·tive (in-vĕn'tĭv) *adj.* 1. Of or characterized by invention. 2. Skillful at inventing. —**in·ven'tive·ly** *adv.* —**in·ven'tive·ness** *n.*

in·ven·to·ry (in'vən-tôr'ē, -tōr'ē) *n., pl.* **-ries.** 1. a. A detailed list of things, esp. a periodic survey of all goods and materials in stock. b. The process of making such a survey. c. The items so listed. 2. The supply of goods on hand; stock. —**in·ven'to·ry** *v.*

in·verse (in-vûrs', in'vûrs') *adj.* Reversed in order, nature, or effect. —*n.* Something opposite in effect or character; reverse. [Lat. *inversus*, p.p. of *invertere*, to invert.] —**In·verse·ly** *adv.*

in·ver·sion (ĭn-vûr′zhən, -shən) *n.* **1.** The act of inverting or the condition of being inverted. **2.** An interchange of position, order, etc. **3.** A weather condition in which the air temperature increases with increasing altitude, holding surface air down along with its pollutants.

in·vert (ĭn-vûrt′) *v.* **1.** To turn inside out or upside down. **2.** To reverse the position, order, or condition of. [Lat. *invertere*.] —**in·vert·er** *n.* —**In·vert′i·ble** *adj.*

In·ver·te·brate (ĭn-vûr′tə-brĭt, -brāt′) *adj.* Having no backbone or spinal column; not vertebrate. —**In·ver′te·brate** *n.*

In·vest (ĭn-vĕst′) *v.* **1.** To commit (money or capital) in order to gain profit or interest. **2.** To spend or utilize (time or effort) for future benefit. **3.** To endow with rank, authority, or power. **4.** To install in office; inaugurate. **5.** To cover completely; envelop; shroud. [< Lat. *investire*, to surround.] —**In·ves′tor** *n.*

In·ves·ti·gate (ĭn-vĕs′tĭ-gāt′) *v.* **-gat·ed, -gat·ing.** To observe or inquire into carefully; examine systematically. [< Lat. *investigare.*] —**In·ves′ti·ga′tion** *n.* —**In·ves′ti·ga′tive** *adj.* —**In·ves′ti·ga′tor** *n.*

In·ves·ti·ture (ĭn-vĕs′tə-chōōr′, -chər) *n.* The act or ceremony of conferring the authority and symbols of a high office. [< Med. Lat. *investitura.*]

In·vest·ment (ĭn-vĕst′mənt) *n.* **1.** The act of investing or the condition of being invested. **2.** An amount invested. **3.** Property acquired for future income. **4.** Investiture.

In·vet·er·ate (ĭn-vĕt′ər-ĭt) *adj.* **1.** Firmly established by long standing. **2.** Persisting in an ingrained habit: *an inveterate liar.* [< Lat. *inveterare*, to make old.] —**In·vet′er·a·cy** (-ər-ə-sē) or **In·vet′er·ate·ness** *n.* —**In·vet′er·ate·ly** *adv.*

In·vid·i·ous (ĭn-vĭd′ē-əs) *adj.* **1.** Tending to stir up ill will, envy, or resentment. **2.** Containing or implying a slight. [Lat. *invidiosus*, envious.] —**In·vid′i·ous·ly** *adv.* —**In·vid′i·ous·ness** *n.*

In·vig·o·rate (ĭn-vĭg′ə-rāt′) *v.* **-rat·ed, -rat·ing.** To give vigor or vitality to; animate. —**In·vig′o·rat′ing·ly** *adv.* —**In·vig′o·ra′tion** *n.* —**In·vig′o·ra′tive** *adj.*

In·vin·ci·ble (ĭn-vĭn′sə-bəl) *adj.* Unconquerable. [< Lat. *invincibilis.*] —**In·vin′ci·bil′i·ty** *n.* —**In·vin′ci·bly** *adv.*

In·vi·o·la·ble (ĭn-vī′ə-lə-bəl) *adj.* **1.** Safe from violation or profanation. **2.** Impregnable. —**In·vi′o·la·bil′i·ty** *n.* —**In·vi′o·la·bly** *adv.*

In·vi·o·late (ĭn-vī′ə-lĭt) *adj.* Not violated or profaned; intact. —**In·vi′o·late·ly** *adv.* —**In·vi′o·late·ness** *n.*

In·vis·i·ble (ĭn-vĭz′ə-bəl) *adj.* **1.** Incapable of being seen; not visible. **2.** Not accessible to view; hidden. **3.** Inconspicuous. —**In·vis′i·bil′i·ty** *n.* —**In·vis′i·bly** *adv.*

In·vite (ĭn-vīt′) *v.* **-vit·ed, -vit·ing.** **1.** To request the presence or participation of. **2.** To request formally. **3.** To welcome. **4.** To tend to bring on; provoke. **5.** To lure; entice. —*n.* (ĭn′vīt′). *Informal.* An invitation. [< Lat. *invitare.*]

In·vit·ing (ĭn-vī′tĭng) *adj.* Attractive; tempting. —**In·vit′ing·ly** *adv.* —**In·vit′ing·ness** *n.*

In·vo·ca·tion (ĭn′və-kā′shən) *n.* **1.** The act of invoking, esp. an appeal to a higher power. **2.** A prayer or other formula used in invoking. [< Lat. *invocare*, to invoke.]

In·voice (ĭn′vois′) *n.* **1.** A detailed list of goods shipped or services rendered, with an account of all costs. **2.** The goods or services so itemized. [< OFr. *envoyer*, to send.] —**In′voice′** *v.*

In·voke (ĭn-vōk′) *v.* **-voked, -vok·ing.** **1.** To call upon (a higher power) for help or inspiration. **2.** To appeal to; petition. **3.** To call for earnestly; solicit. **4.** To conjure. **5.** To resort to; use or apply: *invoked the veto power.* [< Lat. *invocare.*] —**In·vok′er** *n.*

In·vol·un·tary (ĭn-vŏl′ən-tĕr′ē) *adj.* **1.** Not performed willingly. **2.** Not subject to control: *an involuntary twitch.* —**In·vol′un·tar′i·ly** (-târ′ə-lē) *adv.* —**In·vol′un·tar′i·ness** *n.*

In·vo·lu·tion (ĭn′və-lōō′shən) *n.* **1.** The act of involving or condition of being involved. **2.** Something complex or involved, esp. a complicated grammatical construction. **3.** *Math.* The multiplying of a quantity by itself a specified number of times; raising to a power. [< Lat. *involvere*, to enwrap.]

In·volve (ĭn-vŏlv′) *v.* **-volved, -volv·ing.** **1.** To contain or include as a part. **2.** To have as a necessary feature or consequence. **3.** To draw in; embroil. **4.** To engross. **5.** To make complex; complicate. [< Lat. *involvere*, to enwrap.] —**In·volved′** *adj.* —**In·volve′ment** *n.*

In·vul·ner·a·ble (ĭn-vŭl′nər-ə-bəl) *adj.* **1.** Immune to attack; impregnable. **2.** Incapable of being damaged, injured, or wounded. —**In·vul′ner·a·bil′i·ty** *n.* —**In·vul′ner·a·bly** *adv.*

In·ward (ĭn′wərd) *adj.* **1.** Located inside; inner. **2.** Directed or moving toward the interior. **3.** Existing in the mind. —*adv.* Also **In·wards** (-wərdz). **1.** Toward the inside or center. **2.** Toward the mind or the self.

In·ward·ly (ĭn′wərd-lē) *adv.* **1.** On or in the inside; within. **2.** Privately; to oneself.

Iod- *pref.* Iodine: *iodide.* [Fr. *iode.*]

I·o·dide (ī′ə-dīd′) *n.* A binary compound of iodine with a more electropositive atom or group.

I·o·dine (ī′ə-dīn′, -dĭn, -dēn′) *n.* **1.** *Symbol* **I** A lustrous, grayish-black, corrosive, poisonous element having radioactive isotopes used as tracers and in thyroid disease diagnosis and therapy, and compounds used as germicides, antiseptics, and dyes. Atomic number 53; atomic weight 126.9044. **2.** A tincture of iodine and sodium iodide, NaI, or potassium iodide, KI, used as an antiseptic. [< Gk. *iōdēs*, violet-colored.]

I·o·dize (ī′ə-dīz′) *v.* **-dized, -diz·ing.** To treat or combine with iodine or an iodide.

I·on (ī′ən, ī′ŏn′) *n.* An atom, group of atoms, or molecule having a net electric charge acquired by gaining or losing electrons from an initially neutral configuration. [< Gk., something that goes.] —**I·on′ic** *adj.*

-ion *suff.* **1.** An act or process or the outcome of an act or process: *invention.* **2.** A state or condition: *cohesion.* [< Lat. *-io.*]

I·on·ic bond *n.* A chemical bond formed by the complete transfer of one or more electrons from one kind of atom to another.

I·on·ize (ī′ə-nīz′) *v.* **-ized, -iz·ing.** To convert or become converted totally or partially into ions. —**I′o·ni·za′tion** *n.*

i·on·o·sphere (ī-ŏn′ə-sfîr′) n. An electrically conducting set of layers of the earth's atmosphere, extending from altitudes of approx. 30 miles to more than 250 miles.

i·o·ta (ī-ō′tə) n. 1. The 9th letter of the Greek alphabet. See table at **alphabet**. 2. A very small amount. [Gk. *iōta*.]

IOU (ī′ō-yōō′) n., pl. **IOU's** or **IOUs**. A promise to pay a debt. [< *I owe you*.]

-lous suff. Characterized by or full of: *bilious*. [< Lat. *-ius* and *-iosus*.]

I·o·wa (ī′ə-wə) n., pl. **-wa** or **-was**. 1. a. A tribe of Indians formerly inhabiting the region of Minnesota, Iowa, and Missouri. b. A member of this tribe. 2. The Siouan language of the Iowas. —**I′o·wa** adj.

ip·so fac·to (ĭp′sō făk′tō) adv. By the fact itself; by that very fact. [Lat.]

Ir The symbol for the element iridium.

ir-1 pref. Var. of **in-1**.

ir-2 pref. Var. of **in-2**.

I·ra·ni·an (ĭ-rā′nē-ən, -rä′-) n. 1. A native or inhabitant of Iran. 2. A branch of the Indo-European language family that includes Persian, Kurdish, and Pashto. —**I·ra′ni·an** adj.

i·ras·ci·ble (ĭ-răs′ə-bəl, ī-răs′-) adj. Prone to outbursts of temper; easily angered. [< LLat. *irascibilis*.] —**i·ras′ci·bil′i·ty** or **i·ras′ci·ble·ness** n. —**i·ras′ci·bly** adv.

i·rate (ī-rāt′, ī′rāt′) adj. Angry; enraged. [Lat. *iratus*.] —**i·rate′ly** adv.

ire (īr) n. Wrath; anger. [< Lat. *ira*.] —**ire′ful** adj. —**ire′ful·ly** adv. —**ire′ful·ness** n.

ir·i·des·cent (ĭr′ĭ-dĕs′ənt) adj. Producing a display of lustrous, rainbowlike colors: *iridescent butterfly wings*. [Gk. *iris*, rainbow + -ESCENT.] —**ir′i·des′cence** n.

i·rid·i·um (ĭ-rĭd′ē-əm, ī-rĭd′-) n. Symbol **Ir** A hard, brittle, exceptionally corrosion-resistant whitish-yellow metallic element used to harden platinum and in high-temperature materials, electrical contacts, and wear-resistant bearings. Atomic number 77; atomic weight 192.2. [< Gk. *iris*, rainbow.]

i·ris (ī′rĭs) n., pl. **-es** or **i·ri·des** (ī′rĭ-dēz′, ĭr′ĭ-). 1. The pigmented, round, contractile membrane of the eye, situated between the cornea and lens and perforated by the pupil. 2. A plant with narrow sword-shaped leaves and showy, variously colored flowers. [< Gk.]

iris   Irish setter

I·rish (ī′rĭsh) adj. Of or relating to Ireland, its people, or their language. —n. 1. The inhabitants of Ireland or their descendants. 2. Irish Gaelic. 3. English as spoken in Ireland. 4. *Informal.* Fieriness of temper or passion. —**I′rish·man** n. —**I′rish·wom′an** n.

Irish bull n. An apparently consistent but actually illogical or inconsistent statement.

Irish Gaelic n. The Celtic language of Ireland.

Irish setter n. A setter with a silky reddish-brown coat.

irk (ûrk) v. To annoy; irritate. [ME *irken*.] **irk·some** (ûrk′səm) adj. Causing annoyance or bother; tedious. —**irk′some·ly** adv. —**irk′some·ness** n.

i·ron (ī′ərn) n. 1. Symbol **Fe** A silvery-white, lustrous, malleable, ductile, magnetic or magnetizable metallic element used alloyed in many important structural materials. Atomic number 26; atomic weight 55.847. 2. Great hardness or strength: *a will of iron*. 3. An implement made of iron alloy or similar metal. 4. A golf club with a metal head. 5. An appliance with a weighted flat bottom, used when heated to press fabric. 6. **irons.** Fetters; shackles. —adj. Of or like iron. —v. To press and smooth with a heated iron. —*phrasal verb.* **iron out.** To discuss and settle. [< OE *īsern*.] —**i′ron·er** n. —**i′ron·ing** n.

i·ron·bound (ī′ərn-bound′) adj. Rigid and unyielding.

i·ron·clad (ī′ərn-klăd′) adj. 1. Covered with iron plates for protection. 2. Rigid: *an ironclad rule*.

Iron Curtain n. Also **iron curtain.** A social, political, or military barrier that prevents free exchange or comunication, esp. the political and ideological barrier between the Soviet bloc and western Europe after World War II.

i·ron·ic (ī-rŏn′ĭk) or **i·ron·i·cal** (-ĭ-kəl) adj. 1. Characterized by or showing irony. 2. Given to irony. —**i·ron′i·cal·ly** adv. —**i·ron′i·cal·ness** n.

iron lung n. A tank in which the body except the head is enclosed and by means of which pressure is regularly increased and decreased to provide artificial respiration.

i·ron·stone (ī′ərn-stōn′) n. 1. An iron ore with admixtures of silica and clay. 2. A hard white pottery.

i·ron·ware (ī′ərn-wâr′) n. Iron utensils and other products made of iron.

i·ron·work (ī′ərn-wûrk′) n. 1. Work in iron, as gratings and rails. 2. **ironworks** (*used with a sing. verb*). A building or establishment where iron is smelted or iron products are made.

i·ro·ny (ī′rə-nē) n., pl. **-nies** 1. The use of words to convey the opposite of their literal meaning. 2. Incongruity between what might be expected and what actually occurs. [< Gk. *eirōneia*, feigned ignorance.]

Iro·quoi·an (ĭr′ə-kwoi′ən) n. 1. A family of Indian languages spoken in Canada and eastern United States. 2. A member of a tribe using a language of the Iroquoian family. —**Ir′o·quoi′an** adj.

Iro·quois (ĭr′ə-kwoi′) n., pl. **-quois** (-kwoi′, -kwoiz′). 1. a. Any of several Indian tribes formerly inhabiting New York State. b. A member of any of these tribes. 2. Any of the languages of the Iroquois. —**Ir′o·quois′** adj.

ir·ra·di·ate (ĭ-rā′dē-āt′) v. **-at·ed, -at·ing.** 1. To expose to or treat with radiation. 2. To emit in or as if in rays; radiate. [Lat. *irradiare*, to shine forth.] —ir·ra'di·a'tion n. —ir·ra'di·a'-tive adj. —ir·ra'di·a'tor n.

ir·ra·tion·al (ĭ-răsh'ə-nəl) adj. 1. a. Not endowed with reason. b. Incoherent, as from shock. c. Illogical: *an irrational dislike.* 2. *Math.* Incapable of being expressed as an integer or a quotient of integers. —ir·ra'tion·al'i·ty n. —ir·ra'tion·al·ly adv.

irrational number n. A member of the set of real numbers that is not a member of the set of rational numbers.

ir·rec·on·cil·a·ble (ĭ-rĕk'ən-sī'lə-bəl, ĭ-rĕk'-ən-sī'-) adj. 1. Incapable of being reconciled. 2. Incompatible; incongruous. —ir·rec·on·cil'-a·bil'i·ty n. —ir·rec'on·cil'a·bly adv.

ir·re·cov·er·a·ble (ĭr'ĭ-kŭv'ər-ə-bəl) adj. Incapable of being recovered; irreparable. —ir·re·cov'er·a·ble·ness n. —ir·re·cov'er·a·bly adv.

ir·re·deem·a·ble (ĭr'ĭ-dē'mə-bəl) adj. 1. Incapable of being bought back or paid off. 2. Not convertible into coin. 3. Incapable of being saved or reformed.

ir·re·den·tist (ĭr'ĭ-dĕn'tĭst) n. One who advocates the recovery of territory culturally or historically related to his nation but now subject to a foreign government. [Ital. *irredentista.*] —ir·re·den'tism n.

ir·re·duc·i·ble (ĭr'ĭ-dōō'sə-bəl, -dyōō'-) adj. Incapable of being reduced to a simpler or smaller form or amount. —ir·re·duc'i·bil'i·ty n. —ir·re·duc'i·bly adv.

ir·ref·u·ta·ble (ĭ-rĕf'yə-tə-bəl, ĭr'ĭ-fyōō'tə-bəl) adj. Incapable of being refuted or disproved: *irrefutable arguments.* —ir·ref'u·ta·bil'i·ty n. —ir·ref'u·ta·bly adv.

ir·re·gard·less (ĭr'ĭ-gärd'lĭs) adv. *Nonstandard.* Regardless.
Usage: Irregardless, a double negative, is only acceptable when the intent is clearly humorous.

ir·reg·u·lar (ĭ-rĕg'yə-lər) adj. 1. Not according to accepted rules, practice, or order. 2. Not straight, uniform, or symmetrical. 3. Of uneven rate, occurrence, or duration. 4. Asymmetrically arranged or atypical. 5. Not up to standard because of imperfection. —n. 1. One that is irregular. 2. A guerrilla. —ir·reg'u·lar·ly (-lär'ĭ-tē) n. —ir·reg'u·lar·ly adv.

ir·rel·e·vant (ĭ-rĕl'ə-vənt) adj. Having no relation to the subject or situation; not applicable: *an irrelevant question.* —ir·rel'e·vance or ir·rel'e·van·cy n. —ir·rel'e·vant·ly adv.

Syns: *irrelevant, extraneous, immaterial, inapplicable* adj.

ir·re·li·gious (ĭr'ĭ-lĭj'əs) adj. Hostile or indifferent to religion. —ir·re·li'gious·ly adv. —ir·re·li'gious·ness n.

ir·re·me·di·a·ble (ĭr'ĭ-mē'dē-ə-bəl) adj. Impossible to remedy, correct, or repair; incurable. —ir·re·me'di·a·bly adv.

ir·re·mis·si·ble (ĭr'ĭ-mĭs'ə-bəl) adj. Not remissible; unpardonable. —ir·re·mis'si·bil'i·ty n. —ir·re·mis'si·bly adv.

ir·re·mov·a·ble (ĭr'ĭ-mōō'və-bəl) adj. Not removable. —ir·re·mov'a·bly adv.

ir·rep·a·ra·ble (ĭ-rĕp'ər-ə-bəl) adj. Incapable of being repaired, rectified, or amended. —ir·rep'a·ra·bil'i·ty or ir·rep'a·ra·ble·ness n. —ir·rep'a·ra·bly adv.

ir·re·place·a·ble (ĭr'ĭ-plā'sə-bəl) adj. Incapable of being replaced.

ir·re·press·i·ble (ĭr'ĭ-prĕs'ə-bəl) adj. Impossible to control or restrain. —ir·re·press'i·bil'i·ty n. —ir·re·press'i·bly adv.

ir·re·proach·a·ble (ĭr'ĭ-prō'chə-bəl) adj. Beyond reproach. —ir·re·proach'a·ble·ness n. —ir·re·proach'a·bly adv.

ir·re·sist·i·ble (ĭr'ĭ-zĭs'tə-bəl) adj. 1. Too strong or compelling to be resisted. 2. Having an overpowering appeal. —ir·re·sist'i·bil'i·ty or ir·re·sist'i·ble·ness n. —ir·re·sist'i·bly adv.

ir·res·o·lute (ĭ-rĕz'ə-lōōt') adj. Undecided or showing uncertainty about what to do. —ir·res'o·lute'ly adv. —ir·res'o·lute'ness or ir·res'o·lu'tion n.

ir·re·spec·tive of (ĭr'ĭ-spĕk'tĭv) prep. Regardless of; without consideration of.

ir·re·spon·si·ble (ĭr'ĭ-spŏn'sə-bəl) adj. Unreliable. —ir·re·spon'si·bil'i·ty or ir·re·spon'si·ble·ness n. —ir·re·spon'si·bly adv.

ir·re·triev·a·ble (ĭr'ĭ-trē'və-bəl) adj. Not capable of being retrieved or recovered. —ir·re·triev'a·ble·ness or ir·re·triev'a·bil'i·ty n. —ir·re·triev'a·bly adv.

ir·rev·er·ence (ĭ-rĕv'ər-əns) n. 1. Lack of reverence or due respect. 2. A disrespectful act or remark. —ir·rev'er·ent adj. —ir·rev'er·ent·ly adv.

ir·re·vers·i·ble (ĭr'ĭ-vûr'sə-bəl) adj. Incapable of being reversed. —ir·re·vers'i·bil'i·ty n. —ir·re·vers'i·bly adv.

ir·rev·o·ca·ble (ĭ-rĕv'ə-kə-bəl) adj. Incapable of being retracted or revoked. —ir·rev'o·ca·bil'i·ty or ir·rev'o·ca·ble·ness n. —ir·rev'o·ca·bly adv.

ir·ri·ga·ble (ĭr'ĭ-gə-bəl) adj. Capable of being irrigated.

ir·ri·gate (ĭr'ĭ-gāt') v. -gat·ed, -gat·ing. 1. To supply (land or crops) with water by means of ditches, pipes, or streams. 2. To wash out with water or a medicated fluid. [Lat. *irrigare.*] —ir'ri·ga'tion n. —ir'ri·ga'tion·al adj. —ir'ri·ga'tor n.

ir·ri·ta·ble (ĭr'ĭ-tə-bəl) adj. 1. Easily annoyed; ill-tempered. 2. *Pathol.* Abnormally sensitive. 3. *Biol.* Responsive to stimuli. [Lat. *irritabilis.*] —ir'ri·ta·bil'i·ty or ir'ri·ta·ble·ness n. —ir'ri·ta·bly adv.

Syns: *irritable, cantankerous, cross, disagreeable, grouchy, grumpy, ill-tempered, irascible, peevish, petulant, querulous, surly, testy* adj.

ir·ri·tant (ĭr'ĭ-tənt) adj. Causing irritation. —n. Something that causes irritation. [< Lat. *irritare,* to irritate.]

ir·ri·tate (ĭr'ĭ-tāt') v. -tat·ed, -tat·ing. 1. To make angry or impatient; annoy or bother. 2. To chafe or inflame. [Lat. *irritare.*] —ir'ri·tant adj. & n. —ir'ri·tat'ing·ly adv. —ir'ri·ta'tion n. —ir'ri·ta'tor n.

ir·rupt (ĭ-rŭpt') v. To break or burst in; invade. [Lat. *irrumpere.*] —ir·rup'tion n. —ir·rup'tive adj. —ir·rup'tive·ly adv.

is (ĭz) v. 3rd person sing. present tense of **be**. —**idiom. as is.** In its present condition; without change, repair, etc.

I·sa·iah (ī-zā'ə, ī-zī'ə) n. See table at **Bible.**

-i·sa·tion suff. Chiefly *Brit.* Var. of **-ization.**

-ise suff. Chiefly *Brit.* Var. of **-ize.**

-ish suff. 1. Of, pertaining to, or being: *Swedish.* 2. a. Characteristic of: *girlish.* b. Having the qualities of: *peevish.* 3. Approximately; somewhat: *greenish.* 4. Tending toward; preoccupied with: *selfish.* [< OE *-isc.*]

i·sin·glass (ī'zĭng-glăs', ī'zən-) n. A transparent, almost pure gelatin prepared from the air bladder of certain fishes, as the sturgeon. [< obs. Du. *huizenblas.*]

I·sis (ī'sĭs) *n.* *Egypt.* *Myth.* The goddess of fertility and queen of the underworld.

Isis

Is·lam (ĭs'ləm, ĭz'-, ĭ-släm') *n.* **1.** A Moslem religion based on the teachings of Mohammed, embodying a belief in one God (Allah). **2.** Moslems or Moslem nations viewed collectively. **—Is·lam'ic** (-lăm'ĭk,-lä'mĭk) *adj.*

is·land (ī'lənd) *n.* **1.** A land mass, esp. one smaller than a continent, surrounded by water. **2.** Something completely isolated or surrounded. [< OE *īegland*.] **—is'land·er** *n.*

isle (īl) *n.* An island, esp. a small one. [< Lat. *insula*.]

is·let (ī'lĭt) *n.* A little island.

ism (ĭz'əm) *n.* *Informal.* A distinctive doctrine, system, or theory. [< -ISM.]

-ism *suff.* **1.** An action, practice, or process: *terrorism.* **2.** A state or condition of being: *parallelism.* **3.** A characteristic behavior or quality: *heroism.* **4.** A distinctive usage or feature: *malapropism.* **5.** A doctrine, theory, system, or principle: *capitalism.* [< Gk. *-ismos,* n. suffix.]

is·n't (ĭz'ənt). Is not.

iso- *pref.* **1.** Equal, identical, or similar: *isotope.* **2.** Isomeric: *isopropyl alcohol.* [< Gk.]

i·so·bar (ī'sə-bär') *n.* A line on a weather map connecting points of equal barometric pressure. [ISO- + Gk. *baros,* weight.] **—i'so·bar'ic** (-bär'ĭk, -băr'-) *adj.*

i·so·late (ī'sə-lāt', ĭs'ə-) *v.* **-lat·ed, -lat·ing.** **1.** To separate from a group or whole and set apart. **2.** To place in quarantine. [< Lat. *insula,* island.] **—i'so·la'tion** *n.* **—i'so·la'tor** *n.*

i·so·la·tion·ism (ī'sə-lā'shə-nĭz'əm, ĭs'ə-) *n.* A national policy of remaining aloof from political entanglements with other countries. **—i'so·la'tion·ist** *n.*

i·so·mer (ī'sə-mər) *n.* **1.** A compound having the same percentage composition and molecular weight as another compound but differing in chemical or physical properties. **2.** An atom whose nucleus can exist in any of several bound excited states for a measurable period of time. **—i'so·mer'ic** *adj.*

i·so·met·ric (ī'sə-mĕt'rĭk) or **i·so·met·ri·cal** (-rĭ-kəl) *adj.* **1.** Exhibiting equality in dimensions or measurements. **2.** Involving muscle contractions in which the ends of the muscle are held in place so that there is an increase in tension rather than a shortening of the muscle: *isometric exercises.* **—n.** **1.** A line connecting isometric points. **2.** **Isometrics.** (*used with a sing. verb*). Isometric exercise. [< Gk. *isometros.*]

Isometric exercise *n.* Exercise involving isometric contraction.

i·so·morph (ī'sə-môrf') *n.* An object, organism, or group exhibiting isomorphism.

i·so·oc·tane (ī'sō-ŏk'tān') *n.* A highly flammable liquid, C_8H_{18}, used to determine the octane numbers of fuels.

i·so·pro·pyl alcohol (ī'sə-prō'pəl) *n.* A clear, colorless, mobile flammable liquid, C_3H_8O, used in antifreeze compounds, lotions, and cosmetics and as a solvent.

i·sos·ce·les (ī-sŏs'ə-lēz') *adj.* Having two equal sides: *an isosceles triangle.* [< Gk. *isoskelēs.*]

i·so·ther·mal (ī'sə-thûr'məl) *adj.* With or at equal temperatures. **—i'so·therm'** *n.*

i·so·tope (ī'sə-tōp') *n.* One of two or more atoms whose nuclei have the same number of protons but different numbers of neutrons. [ISO- + Gk. *topos,* place.] **—i'so·top'ic** (-tŏp'-ĭk) *adj.* **—i'so·top'i·cal·ly** *adv.*

i·so·trop·ic (ī'sə-trŏp'ĭk) *adj.* Invariant with respect to direction. **—i·sot'ro·py** (ī-sŏt'rə-pē) or **i·sot'ro·pism** (-pĭz'əm) *n.*

Is·ra·el (ĭz'rē-əl) *n.* **1.** The descendants of Jacob. **2.** The whole Hebrew people, past, present, and future, regarded as the chosen people of Jehovah by virtue of the covenant of Jacob.

Is·rae·li (ĭz-rā'lē) *adj.* Of or relating to Israel or its people. **—n.,** *pl.* **-li** or **-lis.** A native or inhabitant of Israel.

Is·ra·el·ite (ĭz'rē-ə-līt') *n.* A Hebrew. **—Is'ra·el·ite'** *adj.*

is·sue (ĭsh'ōō) *n.* **1.** An act or instance of flowing, passing, or giving out. **2.** Something produced, published, or offered, as stamps or coins. **3.** The result of an action. **4.** Proceeds from estates or fines. **5.** Something proceeding from a specified source. **6.** Offspring. **7.** A point of discussion. **8.** An outlet. **9.** A discharge, as of blood. **—v.** **-sued, -su·ing.** **1.** To go or come out. **2.** To come forth or cause to come forth. **3.** To give or distribute, as supplies. **4.** To be descended. **5.** To result from. **6.** To result in. **7.** To publish or be published. **8.** To circulate or be circulated, as coins. **—idioms. at issue.** In dispute. **take issue.** To disagree. [< Lat. *exire,* to go out.] **—is'su·ance** *n.* **—is'su·er** *n.*

-ist *suff.* **1.** One who produces or is connected with a specified thing: *dramatist.* **2.** A specialist in a specified field: *biologist.* **3.** An adherent or proponent of a doctrine, system, or school of thought: *anarchist.* **4.** One who is characterized by a certain trait or quality: *romanticist.* [< Gk. *-istēs,* n. suffix.]

isth·mus (ĭs'məs) *n.* **1.** A narrow strip of land connecting two larger masses of land. **2.** *Anat.* **a.** A narrow strip of tissue joining two larger organs or parts of an organ. **b.** A narrow passage connecting two larger cavities. [< Gk. *isthmos.*] **—isth'mi·an** *adj.*

it (ĭt) *pron.* **1.** Used to refer to a nonhuman being, to an animal or a human being whose sex is unknown, to a group of persons, or to an abstraction. **2.** Used as the subject of an impersonal verb: *It is raining.* **3.** Used to refer to a general situation or state of affairs: *He just couldn't take it.* **—n.** The player in children's games who must perform a certain act, such as chasing the other players. [< OE *hit.*]

I·tal·ian (ĭ-tăl′yən) *n.* **1.** A native or inhabitant of Italy or a person of Italian descent. **2.** The Romance language of Italy and one of the three official languages of Switzerland. —**I·tal′ian** *adj.*

i·tal·ic (ĭ-tăl′ĭk, ī-tăl′-) *adj.* Of or being a style of printing type with the letters slanting to the right, used to emphasize a word or passage. —*n.* **1.** Often **italics.** Italic print or typeface. **2. Italic.** A branch of Indo-European that includes Latin. [< *Italy.*]

i·tal·i·cize (ĭ-tăl′ĭ-sīz′, ī-tăl′-) *v.* **-cized, -ciz·ing.** To print in italic type. —**i·tal′i·ci·za′tion** *n.*

itch (ĭch) *n.* **1.** A skin sensation causing a desire to scratch. **2.** A contagious skin disease marked by itching. **3.** A restless desire or craving. [< OE *giccan.*] —**itch** *v.* —**itch′i·ness** *n.* —**itch′y** *adj.*

-ite[1] *suff.* **1.** A native or resident of a specified place: *New Jerseyite.* **2.** An adherent of someone specified: *Benthamite.* **3.** A part of an organ or body: *somite.* **4.** A mineral or rock: *graphite.* **5.** A commercial product: *ebonite.* [< Gk. *-itēs.*]

-ite[2] *suff.* A salt or ester of an acid whose adjectival denomination ends in *-ous: sulfite.* [Fr.]

i·tem (ī′təm) *n.* **1.** A single article or unit in a group, series, or list. **2. a.** A bit of information. **b.** A short piece in a newspaper or magazine. [< Lat., also.]

i·tem·ize (ī′tə-mīz′) *v.* **-ized, -iz·ing.** To set down item by item; list. —**i′tem·i·za′tion** *n.* —**i′tem·iz′er** *n.*

it·er·ate (ĭt′ə-rāt′) *v.* **-at·ed, -at·ing.** To say or perform again; repeat. [< Lat. *iterum,* again.] —**it′er·a′tion** *n.*

i·tin·er·ant (ī-tĭn′ər-ənt, ĭ-tĭn′-) *adj.* Traveling from place to place, esp. to perform some duty or work. —*n.* An itinerant person. [< Lat. *itinerari,* to travel.] —**i·tin′er·an·cy** or **i·tin′er·a·cy** *n.*

i·tin·er·ar·y (ī-tĭn′ə-rĕr′ē, ĭ-tĭn′-) *n., pl.* **-ies.** **1.** A route or proposed route of a journey. **2.** An account or record of a journey. **3.** A guidebook. [< LLat. *itinerarium.*]

-itis *suff.* Inflammation of cr inflammatory disease: *laryngitis.* [< Gk., n. suffix.]

it′ll (ĭt′l). **1.** It will. **2.** It shall.

its (ĭts). The possessive form of **it,** used as a modifier before a noun: *We opposed the bill and worked for its defeat.*

Usage: As the possessive form of *it, its* is never written with an apostrophe. The written form *it's* is a contraction of *it is* or *it has.*

it's (ĭts). **1.** It is. **2.** It has.

It·self (ĭt-sĕlf′) *pron.* **1.** The one identical with it. Used: **a.** Reflexively as the direct or indirect object of a verb or the object of a preposition: *This record player turns itself off.* **b.** For emphasis: *The trouble is in the machine itself.* **2.** Its normal or healthy condition: *The computer is acting itself again since the program was corrected.* —**idiom. by itself. 1.** Alone. **2.** Without help.

-ity *suff.* State or quality: *authenticity.* [< Lat. *-itas.*]

-ium *suff.* An element or chemical group: *barium.* [< Gk. *-ion,* dim. suffix.]

I've (īv). I have.

-ive *suff.* Having a tendency toward or inclination to perform a specified action: *disruptive.* [< Lat. *-ivus.*]

i·vo·ry (ī′və-rē, īv′rē) *n., pl.* **-ries. 1.** The hard, smooth, yellowish-white substance forming the tusks of certain animals, esp. the elephant. **2.** A substance resembling ivory. **3.** An article made of ivory. **4.** A yellowish white. [< Lat. *ebur.*] —**i′vo·ry** *adj.*

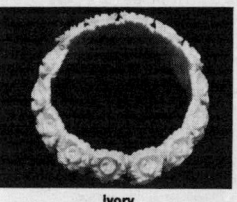

ivory

i·vy (ī′vē) *n., pl.* **i·vies. 1.** A climbing or trailing plant with lobed evergreen leaves. **2.** Any of various similar plants. [< OE *īfig.*]

I·yar (ē-yär′, ē′yär′) *n.* Also **Iy·yar.** The 8th month of the Hebrew year. See table at **calendar.** [Heb. *iyyār.*]

-ization *suff.* Also *chiefly Brit.* **-isation.** Action, process, or result of doing or making: *colonization.* [-IZ(E) + -ATION.]

-ize *suff.* Also *chiefly Brit.* **-ise. 1. a.** To cause to be or to become; make into: *dramatize.* **b.** To cause to conform to or resemble: *Hellenize.* **c.** To treat as: *idolize.* **2. a.** To treat or affect with: *anesthetize; magnetize.* **b.** To subject to: *tyrannize.* **3.** To treat according to or practice the method of: *pasteurize.* **4.** To become or become like: *materialize.* **5.** To perform, engage in, or produce: *theorize.* [< Gk. *-izein,* v. suffix.]

Jj

J or **J** (jā) *n., pl.* **j's** or **J's. 1.** The 10th letter of the English alphabet. **2.** The 10th in a series. **3.** Something shaped like the letter J.

jab (jăb) *v.* **jabbed, jab·bing. 1.** To poke abruptly, esp. with something sharp. **2.** To punch with short blows. —*n.* A quick stab or blow. [ME *jobben.*]

jab·ber (jăb'ər) *v.* To talk rapidly, unintelligibly, or idly. [Imit.] —**jab'ber·er** *n.*

jab·ot (zhă-bō', jă-) *n.* A series of ruffles down the front of a shirt. [Fr.]

jack (jăk) *n.* **1.** Often **Jack.** A fellow; chap. **2.** A playing card showing the figure of a knave and ranking below a queen. **3.** A usu. portable device for raising heavy objects. **4.** A male donkey; jackass. **5. a. jacks** *(used with a sing. verb).* A game played with a small ball and a set of small six-pointed metal pieces that one must pick up in various combinations. **b.** One of the metal pieces used. **6.** A socket that accepts a plug at one end and attaches to another circuit at the other. **7.** A small flag flown by a ship, usu. to indicate nationality. —*v.* **1.** To hoist with or as if with a jack. **2.** To raise. [< the name *Jack.*]

jack·al (jăk'əl, -ôl') *n.* A doglike carnivorous mammal of Africa and Asia. [Turk. *chakāl.*]

jack·ass (jăk'ăs') *n.* **1.** A male ass or donkey. **2.** A foolish or stupid person.

jack·daw (jăk'dô') *n.* A crowlike Eurasian bird. [JACK + *daw,* jackdaw.]

jack·et (jăk'ĭt) *n.* **1.** A short coat, usu. extending to the hip. **2.** An outer covering or casing. [< OFr. *jaque,* short jacket.] —**jack'et·ed** *adj.*

jack·ham·mer (jăk'hăm'ər) *n.* A hand-held pneumatic machine for drilling rock.

jack-in-the-pul·pit (jăk'ĭn-thə-pŏŏl'pĭt, -pŭl'-) *n.* A plant with a leaflike spathe enclosing a clublike flower stalk.

jack-in-the-pulpit

jack·knife (jăk'nīf') *n.* **1.** A large pocketknife. **2.** A dive in which one bends over, touches the toes, and then straightens out. —*v.* To bend or fold like a jackknife.

jack-of-all-trades (jăk'əv-ôl'trădz') *n., pl.* **jacks-of-all-trades.** One who can do many kinds of work.

jack-o'-lan·tern (jăk'ə-lăn'tərn) *n.* A lantern made from a hollowed pumpkin with a carved face.

jack·pot (jăk'pŏt') *n.* The top prize or cumulative stakes in various games.

jack rabbit *n.* A large hare of western North America. [JACK(ASS) + RABBIT.]

jack·screw (jăk'skrŏŏ') *n.* A screw-operated jack.

Ja·cob's ladder (jā'kəbz) *Naut.* A rope or chain ladder with rigid rungs. [From the ladder seen by the patriarch *Jacob* in the Old Testament.]

jade¹ (jād) *n.* Either of two distinct minerals, nephrite and jadeite, both green. [< Sp. *(piedra de) ijada,* (stone of) the flank.]

jade² (jād) *n.* **1.** A broken-down horse; nag. **2.** A disreputable woman. —*v.* **jad·ed, jad·ing. 1.** To exhaust or wear out. **2.** To become weary or spiritless. [ME.]

jad·ed (jā'dĭd) *adj.* **1.** Wearied; worn out. **2.** Dulled, as by overindulgence; sated. **3.** Insensitive; callous. —**jad'ed·ly** *adv.* —**jad'ed·ness** *n.*

jade·ite (jā'dīt') *n.* A rare, emerald to light-green, white, red-brown, yellow-brown, or violet jade, NaAlSi₂O₆.

jag¹ (jăg) *n.* A sharp projecting point. [ME *jagge.*]

jag² (jăg) *n. Slang.* A binge; spree. [Orig. unknown.]

jag·ged (jăg'ĭd) *adj.* Notched or rough. —**jag'ged·ly** *adv.* —**jag'ged·ness** *n.*

jag·uar (jăg'wär', -yŏŏ-är') *n.* A large leopard-like tropical American wildcat. [< Guarani *jaguá,* dog.]

jai a·lai (hī' lī', hī' ə-lī', hī' ə-lī') *n.* A court game in which players use a hand-shaped basket to propel the ball against a wall. [< Basque.]

jail (jāl) *n.* A place for the confinement of persons in lawful detention. —*v.* To put in jail; imprison. [< OFr. *jaiole.*]

jail·bird (jāl'bûrd') *n.* A prisoner or ex-convict.

jail·break (jāl'brāk') *n.* An escape from jail.

jail·er (jā'lər) *n.* Also **jail·or.** The keeper of a jail.

ja·lop·y (jə-lŏp'ē) *n., pl.* **-ies.** An old, dilapidated automobile. [Orig. unknown.]

ja·lou·sie (jăl'ə-sē) *n.* A blind or shutter with adjustable horizontal slats. [< Fr., jealousy.]

jam¹ (jăm) *v.* **jammed, jam·ming. 1.** To drive or squeeze into a tight space. **2.** To activate or apply suddenly. **3.** To lock or cause to lock in an unworkable position. **4.** To fill to excess; cram. **5.** To block or clog. **6.** To crush or bruise. **7.** To interfere with the reception of (broadcast signals) by electronic means. **8.** *Mus.* To play jazz improvisations. —*n.* **1.** The act of jamming or the condition of being jammed. **2.** A crush or congestion. **3.** *Informal.* A predicament. [Orig. unknown.]

jam² (jăm) *n.* A preserve made by boiling fruit with sugar. [Perh. < JAM¹.]

ā pat ā pay â care ä father ĕ pet ē be ĭ pit ī tie î pier ŏ pot ō toe ô paw, for oi noise ŏŏ took
ŏŏ boot ou out th thin th this ŭ cut û urge yŏŏ abuse zh vision ə about, item, edible, gallop, circus

jamb (jăm) n. One of the vertical posts of a door or window frame. [< LLat. *gamba*, hoof.]

jam·bo·ree (jăm'bə-rē') n. 1. A noisy gathering. 2. A large assembly, as of Boy Scouts. [Orig. unknown.]

James (jāmz) n. See table at **Bible.**

jam session n. A gathering at which musicians improvise together.

jan·gle (jăng'gəl) v. **-gled, -gling.** 1. To make or cause to make a harsh, metallic sound. 2. To grate on: *jangle one's nerves.* [< OFr. *jangler.*] **—jan'gle** n. **—jan'gler** n.

jan·i·tor (jăn'ĭ-tər) n. One employed to maintain and clean a building. [Lat., doorkeeper.] **—jan'i·to'ri·al** (-tôr'ē-əl, -tōr'-) adj.

Jan·u·ar·y (jăn'yōō-ĕr'ē) n., pl. **-ies.** The 1st month of the year, having 31 days. See table at **calendar.** [< Lat. *Januarius (mensis),* (month) of Janus.]

Ja·nus (jā'nəs) n. Rom. Myth. The god of gates and doorways, depicted with two opposite faces.

ja·pan (jə-păn') n. A black lacquer or enamel producing a durable glossy finish. [< Japan.] **—ja·pan'** v.

Jap·a·nese (jăp'ə-nēz', -nēs') n., pl. **-nese.** 1. A native or inhabitant of Japan. 2. The language of Japan. **—Jap'a·nese'** adj.

Japanese beetle n. A metallic-green beetle that is a serious plant pest in North America.

jape (jāp) v. **japed, jap·ing.** To joke or quip. **—n.** A joke or quip. [< OFr. *japer,* to chatter.] **—jap'er** n. **—jap'er·y** n.

jar¹ (jär) n. A cylindrical glass or earthenware vessel with a wide mouth. [< Ar. *jarrah,* earthen vessel.]

jar² (jär) v. **jarred, jar·ring.** 1. To make or utter a harsh sound. 2. To disturb or irritate. 3. To shake from impact. 4. To clash or conflict. 5. To bump or cause to move or shake from impact. **—n.** 1. A jolt. 2. A harsh or grating sound. [Perh. imit.]

jar·di·nie·re (jär'dn-îr', zhär'dən-yâr') n. A large, decorative stand or pot for plants. [< Fr. *jardin,* garden.]

jar·gon (jär'gən) n. 1. Nonsensical or incoherent talk. 2. The specialized or technical language of a profession or group. [< OFr.]

jas·mine (jăz'mĭn) n. Also **jes·sa·mine** (jĕs'ə-mĭn). Any of several vines or shrubs with fragrant white or yellow flowers. [< Pers. *yasmīn.*]

jas·per (jăs'pər) n. An opaque reddish, brown, or yellow quartz. [< Gk. *iaspis,* of Semitic orig.]

ja·to (jā'tō) n. An auxiliary rocket engine used as an aid to an aircraft in taking off. [J(ET)-A(SSISTED) T(AKE)O(FF).]

jaun·dice (jôn'dĭs, jän'-) n. Path. Yellowish discoloration of tissues and bodily fluids with bile pigment. [< Lat. *galbus,* yellow.]

jaun·diced (jôn'dĭst, jän'-) adj. 1. Affected with jaundice. 2. Affected by envy, jealousy, or malice.

jaunt (jônt, jänt) n. A short trip or excursion. [Orig. unknown.] **—jaunt** v.

jaun·ty (jôn'tē, jän'-) adj. **-ti·er, -ti·est.** 1. Having a carefree or self-confident air. 2. Stylish; dapper. [< OFr. *gentil,* noble.] **—jaun'ti·ly** adv. **—jaun'ti·ness** n.

ja·va (jăv'ə, jä'və) n. Informal. Coffee. [< Java.]

Jav·a·nese (jăv'ə-nēz', -nēs') n., pl. **-nese.** 1. A native of Java. 2. The Indonesian language of Java. **—Jav'a·nese'** adj.

jave·lin (jăv'lən, jăv'ə-) n. 1. A light spear, used as a weapon. 2. A lightweight spear used in contests of distance throwing. [< OFr. *javeline.*]

jaw (jô) n. 1. Either of two bony or cartilaginous structures in most vertebrates forming the framework of the mouth and holding the teeth. 2. Either of two hinged parts in a mechanical device: *the jaws of a wrench.* 3. **jaws.** A dangerous situation. 4. a. Back talk. b. Chatter. **—v.** To talk; converse. [ME *jowe.*]

jaw·bone (jô'bōn') n. A bone of the jaw, esp. of the lower jaw. **—v. -boned, -bon·ing.** To try to influence or pressure through strong persuasion.

jaw·break·er (jô'brā'kər) n. 1. A hard, round candy. 2. Slang. A word that is difficult to pronounce.

jay (jā) n. Any of various birds related to the crows, often having a loud, harsh call. [< LLat. *gaius.*]

jay·walk (jā'wôk') v. To cross a street in violation of traffic regulations. [*jay,* newcomer + WALK.] **—jay'walk'er** n.

jazz (jăz) n. 1. A kind of native American music marked by a strong but flexible rhythmic understructure with solo and ensemble improvisations and a highly sophisticated harmonic idiom. 2. Slang. a. Extreme exaggeration. b. Nonsense. [Orig. unknown.] **—jazz'y** adj.

jeal·ous (jĕl'əs) adj. 1. Fearful of losing what one has to another, esp. someone's love or affection. 2. Resentful of another's success, advantages, etc. 3. Arising from feelings of envy, apprehension, or bitterness. 4. Intolerant of disloyalty. [< Gk. *zēlos,* zeal.] **—jeal'ous·ly** adv. **—jeal'ous·ness** or **jeal'ous·y** (-ə-sē) n.

jean (jēn) n. 1. A strong cotton. 2. **jeans.** Clothes, esp. pants, made of jean. [< ME *Jene,* Genoa.]

jeep (jēp) n. A small, durable motor vehicle with four-wheel drive, used esp. by the armed forces. [From G.P., "general purpose."]

jeer (jîr) v. To speak or shout derisively. [Orig. unknown.] **—jeer** n. **—jeer'er** n.

Je·ho·vah (jĭ-hō'və) n. In the Old Testament, God. [< Heb. *Yahweh.*]

je·june (jĭ-jōōn') adj. 1. Lacking in nutrition; insubstantial. 2. Not interesting. 3. Childish; immature. [< Lat. *jejunus,* hungry.]

je·ju·num (jĭ-jōō'nəm) n., pl. **-na** (-nə). The section of the small intestine between the duodenum and the ileum. [< Lat. *jejunus,* hungry, fasting.]

jell (jĕl) v. 1. To become or cause to become firm or gelatinous; congeal. 2. To take shape; crystallize. [< JELLY.]

jel·ly (jĕl'ē) n., pl. **-lies.** 1. A soft, semisolid food substance with a springy consistency, made by causing a liquid containing pectin or gelatin to set, esp. such a substance made by boiling fruit juice with sugar. 2. A substance with the consistency of jelly. **—v. -lied, -ly·ing.** To make into or become jelly. [< Lat. *gelare,* to freeze.]

jel·ly·bean (jĕl'ē-bēn') n. A small, chewy candy.

jel·ly·fish (jĕl′ē-fĭsh′) *n.* A gelatinous, free-swimming saltwater animal with a bell-shaped body.

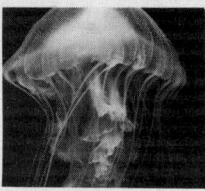

jellyfish

jeop·ard·ize (jĕp′ər-dīz′) *v.* **-ized, -iz·ing.** To expose to loss or injury; imperil.

jeop·ard·y (jĕp′ər-dē) *n.* Danger or risk of loss or injury. [< OFr. *jeu parti*, even game.]

jer·bo·a (jər-bō′ə) *n.* A small, mouselike, leaping rodent of Asia and Africa. [< Ar. *yerbō*.]

jer·e·mi·ad (jĕr′ə-mī′ad) *n.* A prolonged lamentation or a tale of woe. [< Fr. *jérémie,* Jeremiah.]

Jer·e·mi·ah (jĕr′ə-mī′ə) *n.* See table at **Bible.**

jerk (jûrk) *v.* **1.** To give an abrupt thrust, pull, or twist to. **2.** To move in sudden abrupt motions. —*n.* **1.** A sudden yank, tug, or twist. **2.** A sudden spasmodic, muscular movement. **3.** *Slang.* A stupid or foolish person. [Orig. unknown.] —**jerk′i·ly** *adv.* —**jerk′i·ness** *n.* —**jerk′y** *adj.*
Syns: jerk, snap, tug, wrench, yank *v.*

jer·kin (jûr′kĭn) *n.* A short, close-fitting coat, usu. sleeveless. [Orig. unknown.]

jerk·wa·ter (jûrk′wô′tər, -wŏt′ər) *adj. Informal.* Remote and insignificant: *a jerkwater town.*

jer·ry-built (jĕr′ē-bĭlt′) *adj.* Built hastily, cheaply, and poorly. [Orig. unknown.]

jer·sey (jûr′zē) *n., pl.* **-seys. 1. a.** A soft, elastic, knitted fabric. **b.** A garment made of jersey. **2. Jersey.** A breed of light-brown dairy cattle. [< *Jersey,* a Channel Island.]

jes·sa·mine (jĕs′ə-mĭn) *n.* Var. of **jasmine.**

jest (jĕst) *n.* **1.** Something said or done to provoke amusement and laughter. **2.** A playful manner: *spoken in jest.* **3.** A taunt. —*v.* **1.** To joke. **2.** To jeer or ridicule. [< Lat. *gesta,* deeds.]

jest·er (jĕs′tər) *n.* One who jests, esp. a paid fool at medieval courts.

Jes·u·it (jĕzh′ōō-ĭt, jĕz′yōō-) *n. Rom. Cath. Ch.* A member of the Society of Jesus, an order founded by St. Ignatius Loyola in 1534.

Je·sus (jē′zəs) *n.* The founder of Christianity, regarded by Christians as the son of God and the Messiah.

jet¹ (jĕt) *n.* **1.** A dense black coal that takes a high polish and is used for jewelry. **2.** A deep black. [< Gk. *gagatēs* < *Gagai,* a town in Asia Minor.] —**jet** *adj.*

jet² (jĕt) *n.* **1. a.** A high-velocity stream of liquid or gas forced through a narrow opening under pressure. **b.** Something emitted in or as if in such a stream. **c.** An outlet for emitting such a stream. **2.** A jet-propelled aircraft or

other vehicle. —*v.* **jet·ted, jet·ting. 1.** To propel outward. **2.** To travel by jet plane. [< Lat. *jactare,* to throw.]

jet engine *n.* **1.** An engine that develops thrust by ejecting a jet of fluid, esp. a jet of gaseous combustion products. **2.** A jet engine equipped to consume a mixture of fuel and atmospheric oxygen, used esp. in aircraft.

jet lag *n.* The disruption of bodily rhythms caused by high-speed travel in a jet airplane.

jet-pro·pelled (jĕt′prə-pĕld′) *adj.* Propelled by one or more jet engines. —**jet propulsion** *n.*

jet·sam (jĕt′səm) *n.* **1.** Cargo or equipment thrown overboard to lighten a ship in distress. **2.** Discarded odds and ends. [< JETTISON.]

jet set *n.* A social set of wealthy people who travel from one fashionable place to another. —**jet setter** *n.*

jet·ti·son (jĕt′ĭ-sən, -zən) *v.* **1.** To cast off or overboard. **2.** To discard. [< Lat. *jactatio,* a throwing.]

jet·ty (jĕt′ē) *n., pl.* **-ties. 1.** A structure projecting into a body of water to influence the current or protect a harbor or shoreline. **2.** A wharf; pier. [< OFr. *jeter,* to project.]

Jew (jōō) *n.* **1.** An adherent of Judaism. **2.** A descendant of the Hebrew people.

jew·el (jōō′əl) *n.* **1.** A precious stone; gem. **2.** An ornament of precious metal set with gems. **3.** A small gem or gem substitute used as a bearing, as in a watch. **4.** A person or thing that is greatly admired or valued. —*v.* **-eled** or **-elled, -el·ing** or **-el·ling.** To adorn or set with jewels. [< OFr. *jöel.*] —**jew′el·ry** *n.*

jew·el·er (jōō′ə-lər) *n.* Also **jew·el·ler.** One who makes, repairs, or deals in jewelry.

Jew·ish (jōō′ĭsh) *adj.* Of, concerning, or characteristic of the Jews, their customs, or their religion. —**Jew′ish·ness** *n.*

Jew·ry (jōō′rē) *n.* The Jewish people.

jew's-harp (jōōz′härp′) *n.* A small musical instrument with a flexible steel tongue, held between the teeth when played.

jez·e·bel (jĕz′ə-bĕl′, -bəl) *n.* A scheming, wicked woman. [< *Jezebel,* a queen of Israel in the Old Testament.]

jib (jĭb) *n.* A triangular sail set forward of the mast of a sailing vessel. [Perh. < obs. Du. *gijben.*]

jibe¹ (jīb) *v.* **jibed, jib·ing.** To shift a fore-and-aft sail from one side of a vessel to the other while sailing before the wind. [Perh. < obs. Du. *gijben.*]

jibe² (jīb) *v. & n.* Var. of **gibe.**

jibe³ (jīb) *v.* **jibed, jib·ing.** *Informal.* To be in accord; agree. [Orig. unknown.]

jif·fy (jĭf′ē) *n., pl.* **-fies.** Also **jiff** (jĭf). *Informal.* A moment; instant. [Orig. unknown.]

jig (jĭg) *n.* **1.** Any of various lively dances in triple time. **2.** A device for guiding a tool or for holding work as it is fed to a tool. —*v.* **jigged, jig·ging. 1.** To dance a jig. **2.** To operate a jig. [Orig. unknown.]

jig·ger (jĭg′ər) *n.* A small measure for liquor, usu. holding 1¹/₂ ounces.

jig·gle (jĭg′əl) *v.* **-gled, -gling.** To move or cause to move jerkily up and down or to and fro. —*n.* A jiggling motion. [Freq. of JIG.]

jig·saw (jĭg′sô′) *n.* A saw with a narrow, vertically fixed blade, used to cut curves.

jigsaw puzzle *n.* A game consisting of a

mass of irregularly shaped pieces that are fitted together to form a picture.

jilt (jilt) *v.* To cast aside (a lover). —*n.* One who discards a lover. [Orig. unknown.]

Jim Crow *n.* The practice of discriminating against and segregating black people. [< the title of a 19th-cent. song.] —**Jim'-Crow'** *adj.*

jim·my (jĭm'ē) *n., pl.* **-mies.** A short crowbar with curved ends. —*v.* **-mied, -my·ing.** To pry open with or as if with a jimmy. [< *Jimmy*, nickname for *James*.]

jim·son·weed (jĭm'sən-wēd') *n.* A coarse, poisonous plant with large, trumpet-shaped white or purplish flowers. [< *Jamestown weed*.]

jin·gle (jĭng'gəl) *v.* **-gled, -gling.** To make or cause to make a tinkling or ringing metallic sound. —*n.* **1.** A jingling sound. **2.** A simple, repetitious, catchy rhyme or tune: *an advertising jingle.* [ME *ginglen*.]

jin·go·ism (jĭng'gō-ĭz'əm) *n.* Extreme chauvinism or patriotism, esp. the advocacy of an aggressive foreign policy. [< the phrase *by jingo*, used in a bellicose British song.] —**jin'go** or **jin'go·ist** *n.* —**jin'go·is'tic** *adj.*

jin·ni (jĭn'ē, jĭ-nē') *n., pl.* **jinn** (jĭn). A supernatural being in Moslem legend. [Ar. *jinnīy*.]

jin·rik·sha (jĭn-rĭk'shô') *n.* A small, two-wheeled, Oriental carriage drawn usu. by one person. [J. *jinrikisha.*]

jinriksha

jinx (jĭngks) *n. Informal.* **1.** One believed to bring bad luck. **2.** A spell of bad luck. —*v.* To bring bad luck to. [Poss. < Gk. *iunx*, a bird used in magic.]

jit·ney (jĭt'nē) *n., pl.* **-neys.** *Informal.* A small vehicle that transports passengers for a low fare. [Orig. unknown.]

jit·ter·bug (jĭt'ər-bŭg') *n.* **1.** A lively dance consisting of various two-step patterns often with twirls and acrobatic maneuvers. **2.** One who dances the jitterbug. —**jit'ter·bug'** *v.*

jit·ters (jĭt'ərz) *pl.n. Informal.* A fit of nervousness. [Orig. unknown.] —**jit'ter·y** *adj.*

jive (jīv) *n. Slang.* **1.** Jazz or swing music. **2.** The jargon of jazz musicians and enthusiasts. **3.** Deceptive, nonsensical, or glib talk. [Orig. unknown.]

job (jŏb) *n.* **1.** An action or piece of work that needs to be done; task. **2.** A regular activity performed for payment. **3.** A specific piece of work to be done for a set fee. **4.** A position of employment. **5.** A duty or responsibility. —*v.* **jobbed, job·bing. 1.** To work by the piece or at odd jobs. **2.** To act as a middleman or jobber. **3.** To subcontract (work). [Perh. < obs. *job*, piece.] —**job'less** *adj.* —**job'less·ness** *n.*

Job (jōb) *n.* See table at **Bible.**

job action *n.* A temporary action, as a strike

or slowdown, by workers as a protest or to exact demands.

job·ber (jŏb'ər) *n.* **1.** One who buys merchandise from manufacturers and sells it to retailers. **2.** One who works by the piece.

job·hold·er (jŏb'hōl'dər) *n.* One who has a regular job.

job lot *n.* Miscellaneous merchandise sold in one lot.

jock¹ (jŏk) *n.* **1.** A jockey. **2.** A disc jockey. [< JOCKEY.]

jock² (jŏk) *n.* **1.** A male athlete. **2.** One characterized by excessive concern for machismo. [< JOCKSTRAP.]

jock·ey (jŏk'ē) *n., pl.* **-eys.** One who rides horses in races, esp. as a profession. —*v.* **-eyed, -ey·ing. 1.** To ride (a horse) as jockey. **2.** To direct or maneuver by cleverness or skill. **3.** To maneuver in order to gain an advantage. [Dim. of Sc. *Jock*, nickname for *John.*]

jock·strap (jŏk'străp') *n.* An athletic supporter. [Slang *jock*, penis + STRAP.]

jo·cose (jō-kōs') *adj.* Merry; humorous. [Lat. *jocosus.*] —**jo·cose'ness** or **jo·cos'i·ty** (-kŏs'ĭ-tē) *n.*

joc·u·lar (jŏk'yə-lər) *adj.* Humorous; facetious; merry. [Lat. *jocularis.*] —**joc'u·lar'i·ty** (-lăr'ĭ-tē) *n.* —**joc'u·lar·ly** *adv.*

joc·und (jŏk'ənd, jō'kənd) *adj.* Cheerful; merry; gay. [< Lat. *jucundus.*] —**jo·cun'di·ty** (jō-kŭn'dĭ-tē) *n.* —**joc'und·ly** *adv.*

jodh·purs (jŏd'pərz) *pl.n.* Riding breeches that fit loosely above the knees and tightly from the knees to the ankles. [< *Jodhpur*, a region in India.]

Jo·el (jō'əl) *n.* See table at **Bible.**

jog¹ (jŏg) *v.* **jogged, jog·ging. 1.** To jar or move by shoving, bumping, or jerking. **2.** To nudge. **3.** To run or ride at a steady slow trot, esp. for exercise or sport. **4.** To proceed leisurely. —*n.* **1.** A slight nudge. **2.** A slow steady pace. [Orig. unknown.] —**jog'ger** *n.*

jog² (jŏg) *n.* **1.** A protruding or receding part in a surface or line. **2.** An abrupt change in direction. [Perh. var. of JAG¹.]

jog·gle (jŏg'əl) *v.* **-gled, -gling.** To shake slightly. [Freq. of JOG¹.] —**jog'gle** *n.*

John (jŏn) *n.* See table at **Bible.**

John Doe (dō') *n.* A name used in legal proceedings to designate a fictitious or unidentified person.

john·ny·cake (jŏn'ē-kāk') *n.* A thin, flat cornmeal bread, often baked on a griddle.

joie de vi·vre (zhwä də vē'vrə) *n.* Carefree enjoyment of life. [Fr.]

join (join) *v.* **1.** To put or bring together. **2.** To put or bring into close association or relationship. **3.** To meet and unite with. **4.** To become a part or member of. **5.** To connect, as with a straight line. **6.** To come or act together. **7.** To take part; participate. [< Lat. *jungere.*]

join·er (joi'nər) *n.* **1.** A skilled carpenter who makes indoor woodwork and furniture. **2.** *Informal.* A person given to joining groups.

joint (joint) *n.* **1.** A point or position at which two or more things are joined. **2.** A point of connection or articulation between more or less movable bodily parts. **3.** A cut of meat for roasting. **4.** *Slang.* A cheap or disreputable public establishment. **5.** *Slang.* A marijuana cigarette. —*adj.* **1.** Shared by or common to two or more. **2.** Formed or char-

acterized by cooperation or united action.
—v. 1. To provide with a joint. 2. To cut
(meat) into joints. —**idiom. out of joint.**
1. Dislocated, as a bone. 2. Not harmonious;
inconsistent. 3. Out of order; unsatisfactory.
[< OFr. < *joindre*, to join.] —**joint'ly** *adv.*

joist (joist) *n.* Any of the parallel horizontal
beams set from wall to wall to support the
boards of a floor or ceiling. [< OFr. *giste.*]

joke (jōk) *n.* 1. A short story, esp. one with a
humorous punch line. 2. A mischievous trick.
3. A ludicrous incident or situation. 4. A
laughingstock. —v. **joked, jok·ing.** 1. To tell
or play jokes. 2. To speak in fun; be facetious. [Lat. *jocus.*] —**jok'ing·ly** *adv.*

jok·er (jō'kər) *n.* 1. One who tells or plays
jokes. 2. A playing card, used in certain
games as the highest ranking card or as a
wild card. 3. A minor clause in a document
such as a legislative bill that voids or changes
its original or intended purpose.

jol·li·fi·ca·tion (jŏl'ə-fĭ-kā'shən) *n.* Festivity;
merrymaking.

jol·li·ty (jŏl'ĭ-tē) *n.* Gaiety; merriment.

jol·ly (jŏl'ē) *adj.* **-li·er, -li·est.** 1. Merry; fun-
loving. 2. Festive. —*adv. Chiefly Brit. Informal.* Very: *a jolly good cook.* [< OFr. *joli.*]
—**jol'ly** v.

jolt (jōlt) v. 1. To shake violently with a sudden, sharp blow. 2. To move in a bumpy or
jerky fashion. —n. 1. A sudden jerk or
bump. 2. An abrupt shock or reversal. [Orig.
unknown.]

Jo·nah (jō'nə) *n.* See table at **Bible.**

jon·quil (jŏng'kwĭl, jŏn'-) *n.* A cultivated
plant related to the daffodil, with short-tubed,
fragrant yellow flowers. [< Lat. *juncus,* reed.]

josh (jŏsh) v. To tease good-humoredly.
[Orig. unknown.]

Josh·u·a (jŏsh'ōō-ə) *n.* See table at **Bible.**

jos·tle (jŏs'əl) v. **-tled, -tling.** 1. To come in
contact or collide. 2. To make one's way by
pushing or elbowing. 3. To vie for an advantage or favorable position. [< OFr. *juster,* to
joust.] —**jos'tle** *n.*

jot (jŏt) *n.* The smallest bit or particle; iota.
—v. **jot·ted, jot·ting.** To write down briefly
and hastily. [< Gk. *iōta,* iota.]

joule (jōōl, joul) *n.* A unit of energy, equal to
the work done when the point of application
of a force of 1 newton is displaced 1 meter in
the direction of the force. [< James P. *Joule*
(1818–89).]

jounce (jouns) v. **jounced, jounc·ing.** To
move with bumps and jolts. [ME *jouncen.*]
—**jounce** *n.* —**jounc'y** *adj.*

jour·nal (jûr'nəl) *n.* 1. A daily record of occurrences or observations. 2. An official record of daily proceedings or transactions, as of
a legislative body. 3. A newspaper. 4. A specialized periodical. 5. The part of a shaft or
axle supported by a bearing. [< LLat. *diurna-
lis,* daily.]

jour·nal·ese (jûr'nə-lēz', -lēs') *n.* The slick,
superficial style of writing often held to be
characteristic of newspapers and magazines.

jour·nal·ism (jûr'nə-lĭz'əm) *n.* 1. The collecting, writing, editing, and publishing of news
for periodicals or broadcasting. 2. Written
material of current interest or wide popular

appeal. —**jour'nal·ist** *n.* —**jour'nal·is'tic** *adj.*
—**jour'nal·is'ti·cal·ly** *adv.*

jour·ney (jûr'nē) *n., pl.* **-neys.** Travel from
one place to another. —v. To travel. [< Lat.
diurnus, of a day.]

jour·ney·man (jûr'nē-mən) *n.* 1. One who has
mastered a trade and works in another's employ. 2. A competent worker.

joust (joust, jŭst, jōōst) *n.* A combat with
lances between two mounted knights. —v.
To engage in a joust. [< OFr. *juste,* ult. <
Lat. *juxta,* close together.]

Jove (jōv) *n. Rom. Myth.* The god Jupiter.

jo·vi·al (jō'vē-əl) *adj.* Marked by good humor;
jolly. [< Ital. *giovale,* born under the planet
Jupiter.] —**jo'vi·al'i·ty** (-ăl'ĭ-tē) *n.*

jowl[1] (joul) *n.* 1. The jaw, esp. the lower jaw.
2. The cheek. [< OE *ceafl.*]

jowl[2] (joul) *n.* The flesh under the lower jaw,
esp. when plump or flabby. [ME *cholle.*]

joy (joi) *n.* 1. A feeling of great pleasure or
happiness. 2. A source of pleasure. —v. To
rejoice. [< Lat. *gaudia.*] —**joy'less** *adj.*
—**joy'less·ly** *adv.* —**joy'less·ness** *n.*

joy·ful (joi'fəl) *adj.* Feeling, causing, or showing joy. —**joy'ful·ly** *adv.* —**joy'ful·ness** *n.*

joy·ous (joi'əs) *adj.* Joyful. —**joy'ous·ly** *adv.*
—**joy'ous·ness** *n.*

joy ride *n.* An often reckless automobile ride
taken for fun and thrills.

ju·bi·lant (jōō'bə-lənt) *adj.* Feeling or expressing great joy. [< Lat. *jubilare,* to shout for
joy.] —**ju'bi·lance** *n.* —**ju'bi·lant·ly** *adv.*

ju·bi·la·tion (jōō'bə-lā'shən) *n.* 1. Exultation.
2. A joyful celebration.

ju·bi·lee (jōō'bə-lē') *n.* 1. A special anniversary, esp. a 50th anniversary. 2. A season or
occasion of joyful celebration. 3. Jubilation;
rejoicing. [< Heb. *yōbhēl,* the Jewish year of
jubilee.]

Ju·da·ic (jōō-dā'ĭk) or **Ju·da·i·cal** (-ĭ-kəl) *adj.*
Of or pertaining to Jews or Judaism.

Ju·da·ism (jōō'dē-ĭz'əm) *n.* The monotheistic
religion of the Jewish people, that has its
spiritual and ethical principles embodied
chiefly in the Bible and the Talmud.

Ju·das (jōō'dəs) *n.* One who betrays under
the appearance of friendship. [< *Judas* Iscariot, a disciple who betrayed Jesus.]

Jude (jōōd) *n.* See table at **Bible.**

judge (jŭj) v. **judged, judg·ing.** 1. To pass
judgment upon in a court of law. 2. To determine or settle authoritatively after deliberation. 3. To form an opinion about. 4. To
criticize; censure. 5. To think; consider; suppose. —n. 1. A public official who hears and
decides cases brought before a court of law.
2. An appointed arbiter in a contest or competition. 3. One whose critical judgment or
opinion is sought; connoisseur. 4. **Judges.**
See table at **Bible.** [< Lat. *judex,* judge.]
—**judge'ship** *n.*

Syns: *judge, arbitrate, decide, decree, determine, referee, rule, umpire* v.

judg·ment (jŭj'mənt) *n.* Also **judge·ment.**
1. The capacity to perceive, discern, or make
reasonable decisions. 2. The act of or an instance of judging. 3. A decision, opinion, or
conclusion reached after due consideration,
esp. a formal decision of an arbiter 4. A

ă pat ā pay â care ä father ĕ pet ē be ĭ pit ī tie î pier ŏ pot ō toe ô paw, for oi noise ōō took
ōō boot ou out th thin th this ŭ cut û urge yōō abuse zh vision ə about, item, edible, gallop, circus

rough estimation or guess. **5.** *Law.* A judicial decision.

ju·di·ca·ture (jōō′dĭ-kə-chŏŏr′, -chər) *n.* **1.** The administering of justice. **2.** A system of law courts and their judges. [< Lat. *judicare,* to judge.]

ju·di·cial (jōō-dĭsh′əl) *adj.* **1.** Of, pertaining to, or proper to courts of law or to the administration of justice. **2.** Decreed by or proceeding from a court of justice. **3.** Characterized by or expressing judgment. [< Lat. *judicium,* judgment.]

ju·di·ci·ar·y (jōō-dĭsh′ē-ĕr′ē) *adj.* Of or pertaining to courts, judges, or the administration of justice. —*n., pl.* **-ies. 1.** The judicial branch of government. **2.** A system of courts of justice. **3.** Judges in general.

ju·di·cious (jōō-dĭsh′əs) *adj.* Having or exhibiting sound judgment. —**ju·di′cious·ly** *adv.* —**ju·di′cious·ness** *n.*

ju·do (jōō′dō) *n.* A modern form of jujitsu applying principles of balance and leverage. [J. *jūdō.*]

judo

jug (jŭg) *n.* **1.** A tall, often rounded vessel of earthenware, glass, or metal with a small mouth and handle, made for holding liquids. **2.** *Slang.* A jail. [Orig. unknown.]

jug·ger·naut (jŭg′ər-nôt′) *n.* A massive advancing force or object that crushes anything in its path. [< Skt. *jagannāthaḥ,* lord of the world.]

jug·gle (jŭg′əl) *v.* **-gled, -gling. 1.** To keep (two or more objects) in the air at one time by alternately tossing and catching them. **2.** To manipulate in order to deceive. [< Lat. *joculari,* to jest.] —**jug′gler** *n.*

jug·u·lar (jŭg′yə-lər) *adj.* Of or located in the neck or throat. —*n.* A jugular vein. [< Lat. *jugulum,* collarbone.]

juice (jōōs) *n.* **1.** A fluid naturally contained in plant or animal tissue. **2.** A bodily secretion. **3. a.** Electric current. **b.** Fuel for an engine. —*v.* **juiced, juic·ing.** To extract the juice from. [< Lat. *jus.*] —**juice′less** *adj.*

juic·er (jōō′sər) *n.* An appliance for extracting juice from fruits and vegetables.

juic·y (jōō′sē) *adj.* **-i·er, -i·est. 1.** Full of juice; succulent. **2.** Interesting, colorful, or racy. —**juic′i·ness** *n.*

ju·jit·su (jōō-jĭt′sōō) *n.* Also **ju·jut·su.** A Japanese art of self-defense or hand-to-hand combat based on set maneuvers that force an opponent to use his weight and strength against himself. [J. *jūjitsu.*]

ju·jube (jōō′jōōb, -jōō-bē) *n.* A fruit-flavored, usu. chewy candy. [< Gk. *zizuphon,* a fruit tree.]

juke box (jōōk) *n.* A coin-operated phonograph. [< *juke-house,* a roadhouse with music and dancing.]

ju·lep (jōō′ləp) *n.* A mint julep. [< Pers. *gulāb,* a sugar syrup.]

ju·li·enne (jōō′lē-ĕn′) *adj.* Cut into long thin strips: *julienne potatoes.* [Fr.]

Ju·ly (jōō-lī′, jōō-) *n.* The 7th month of the year, having 31 days. See table at **calendar.** [< Lat. *Julius (mensis),* (month) of Julius Caesar.]

Ju·ma·da (jōō-mä′dä) *n.* Either the 5th or 6th month of the Moslem calendar. See table at **calendar.** [Ar. *Jumādā.*]

jum·ble (jŭm′bəl) *v.* **-bled, -bling. 1.** To mix in a disordered mass. **2.** To confuse. [Orig. unknown.] —**jum′ble** *n.*

jum·bo (jŭm′bō) *n., pl.* **-bos.** An unusually large person, animal, or thing. [< *Jumbo,* a large elephant exhibited by P.T. Barnum (1810–91).] —**jum′bo** *adj.*

jump (jŭmp) *v.* **1.** To spring off the ground or other base by a muscular effort of the legs and feet. **2.** To throw oneself down, off, out, or into something. **3.** To spring at or upon with the intent to assail or censure. **4.** To arrive at hastily or haphazardly: *jump to conclusions.* **5.** To grab at eagerly: *jump at a bargain.* **6.** To start involuntarily. **7.** To rise suddenly and pronouncedly. **8.** To skip over, leaving a break in continuity. **9.** *Checkers.* To take (an opponent's piece) by moving over it with one's own checker. **10.** To leave (a course or track) through mishap. **11.** *Slang.* To have a lively, pulsating quality. —*n.* **1.** The act of jumping; leap. **2.** A sudden, involuntary movement. **3.** A sudden, pronounced rise, as in price. **4.** A step or level. —*idioms.* **get (or have) a jump on one.** *Informal.* To have a head start over another. **jump down one's throat.** To answer sharply or angrily. **jump the gun.** To start something too soon. [Perh. imit.]

jump·er¹ (jŭm′pər) *n.* **1.** One that jumps. **2.** A short length of wire used temporarily to complete or by-pass a circuit.

jump·er² (jŭm′pər) *n.* **1.** A sleeveless dress worn over a blouse or sweater. **2.** A loose smock, blouse, or jacket. **3. jumpers.** A child's overalls. [Prob. < *jump,* loose jacket.]

jump shot *n. Basketball.* A shot made by a player at the highest point of his jump.

jump suit *n.* **1.** A parachutist's uniform. **2.** A one-piece garment consisting of a blouse or shirt with attached slacks or shorts.

jump·y (jŭm′pē) *adj.* **-i·er, -i·est.** On edge; nervous. —**jump′i·ness** *n.*

jun (jōōn) *n., pl.* **jun.** See table at **currency.** [Korean.]

jun·co (jŭng′kō) *n., pl.* **-cos.** A North American bird with predominantly gray plumage. [< Lat. *juncus,* reed.]

junc·tion (jŭngk′shən) *n.* **1.** The act of joining or the condition of being joined. **2.** The place where two things join or meet. [< Lat. *jungere,* to join.]

junc·ture (jŭngk′chər) *n.* **1.** The act of joining or the condition of being joined. **2.** The line or point at which two things join; joint. **3.** A point in time, esp. a turning point.

June (jōōn) *n.* The 6th month of the year, having 30 days. See table at **calendar.** [< Lat. *Junius (mensis),* (month) of Juno.]

jun·gle (jŭng′gəl) *n.* **1.** Land densely overgrown with tropical vegetation and trees. **2.** A dense or uncontrolled overgrowth. **3.** A place of ruthless competition or struggle for survival. **4.** *Slang.* A rendezvous for hoboes. [< Skt. *jāṅgala-*, wild.]

jun·ior (jōōn'yər) *adj.* **1.** Younger, esp. when used to distinguish the son from the father of the same name: *William Jones, Jr.* **2.** Of or for younger persons: *junior dresses.* **3.** Of lower rank or shorter length of service. **4.** Of or pertaining to the 3rd year of a U.S. high school or college. **5.** Lesser in scale than the usual. —*n.* **1.** A person who is younger than another. **2.** A person lower in rank or length of service; subordinate. **3.** A 3rd-year student in a U.S. high school or college. [Lat.]

junior college *n.* A school offering a two-year course that is the equivalent of the first two years of a four-year college.

junior high school *n.* A school including the 7th, 8th, and sometimes 9th grades.

ju·ni·per (jōō'nə-pər) *n.* An evergreen tree or shrub with scalelike foliage and aromatic, bluish-gray, berrylike fruit. [< Lat. *juniperus.*]

junk¹ (jŭngk) *n.* **1.** Scrap materials that can be converted into something usable. **2.** Rubbish; trash. **3.** *Slang.* Heroin. —*v.* To throw away or discard as useless. [ME *jonk,* an old rope.]

junk² (jŭngk) *n.* A Chinese flat-bottomed sailing ship. [< Javanese *djong.*]

junk¹

jun·ket (jŭng'kĭt) *n.* **1.** A sweet custardlike food made from flavored milk and rennet. **2.** An outing; picnic. **3.** A trip taken by a public official or businessperson and paid for with public or corporate funds. **4.** An excursion. [< Lat. *juncus,* reed.] —**jun'ket** *v.*

junk·ie or **junk·y** (jŭng'kē) *n., pl.* **-ies.** *Slang.* A narcotics addict, esp. one using heroin.

Ju·no (jōō'nō) *n. Rom. Myth.* The principal goddess of the pantheon, wife and sister of Jupiter.

jun·ta (hōōn'tə, hŏŏn'-, jŭn'-) *n.* A group of persons who govern a country, esp. after a coup d'état. [< Lat. *jungere,* to join.]

Ju·pi·ter (jōō'pĭ-tər) *n.* **1.** *Rom. Myth.* The supreme god. **2.** The 5th planet from the sun, the largest and most massive in the solar system, that has a diameter of approx. 86,000 miles and a mass approx. 318 times that of Earth, and that orbits the sun once every 11.86 years at a mean distance of 483 million miles.

ju·rid·i·cal (jōō-rĭd'ĭ-kəl) or **ju·rid·ic** (-ĭk) *adj.* Of or pertaining to the law and its administration. [< Lat. *juridicus.*]

ju·ris·dic·tion (jōōr-ĭs-dĭk'shən) *n.* **1.** The authority to interpret and apply the law. **2.** The power of authority or control. **3.** The limit within which an authority or control may operate. **4.** The territory under a given authority or control. [< Med. Lat. *jurisdictio.*] —**ju'ris·dic'tion·al** *adj.*

ju·ris·pru·dence (jōōr'ĭs-prōōd'ns) *n.* **1.** The science or philosophy of law. **2.** A system of laws. [LLat. *jurisprudentia.*]

ju·rist (jōōr'ĭst) *n.* One skilled in the law. [< Lat. *jus,* law.]

ju·ris·tic (jōō-rĭs'tĭk) or **ju·ris·ti·cal** (-tĭ-kəl) *adj.* **1.** Of or pertaining to a jurist or to jurisprudence. **2.** Of or pertaining to law or legality.

ju·ror (jōōr'ər, -ôr') *n.* A member of a jury.

ju·ry (jōōr'ē) *n., pl.* **-ries.** **1.** A body of persons summoned by law and sworn to hear and hand down a verdict upon a case presented in court. **2.** A committee to select winners and award prizes. [< Lat. *jus,* law.] —**ju'ry·man** *n.*

just (jŭst) *adj.* **1.** Honest and impartial in one's dealings and actions. **2.** Consistent with standards of what is moral and proper. **3.** Properly due or merited: *just deserts.* **4.** Legitimate. **5.** Suitable; fitting. **6.** Sound; well-founded. **7.** Exact; accurate: *a just account.* —*adv.* (jŭst; *unstressed* jəst, jĭst). **1.** Precisely; exactly. **2.** At that instant. **3.** Quite recently. **4.** Barely; shortly. **5.** Only a little distance; immediately. **6.** Merely; simply. **7.** Really; certainly: *It's just beautiful.* [< Lat. *justus.*] —**just'ly** *adv.* —**just'ness** *n.*

jus·tice (jŭs'tĭs) *n.* **1.** Moral or absolute rightness. **2.** The upholding of what is just; fair treatment and due reward in accordance with honor, standards, or law. **3.** Something just or due: *Justice was served by his downfall.* **4.** Good reason or sound basis; validity. **5.** The administration and procedure of law. **6.** A judge. —*idiom.* **do justice to. 1.** To enjoy fully. **2.** To show to full advantage. [< Lat. *justitia.*]

justice of the peace *n.* A local magistrate with the authority to act upon minor offenses, perform marriages, and administer oaths.

jus·ti·fy (jŭs'tə-fī') *v.* **-fied, -fy·ing. 1.** To demonstrate to be just, right, or valid. **2.** To provide sound reasons for; warrant. **3.** To declare free of blame; absolve. [< LLat. *justificare,* to act justly toward.] —**jus'ti·fi'a·ble** *adj.* —**jus'ti·fi'a·bly** *adv.* —**jus'ti·fi·ca'tion** *n.*

jut (jŭt) *v.* **jut·ted, jut·ting.** To project; protrude. [< JET².] —**jut** *n.*

jute (jōōt) *n.* **1.** Either of two Asian plants that yield a fiber used to make rope, twine, and burlap. **2.** The fiber obtained from the jute. [< Skt. *jūṭaḥ,* twisted hair.]

ju·ve·nile (jōō'və-nəl, -nīl') *adj.* **1.** Young; youthful. **2.** Immature; childish. **3.** Intended for or appropriate to children or young people. —*n.* **1. a.** A young person; child. **b.** A young animal that has not reached sexual maturity. **2.** An actor or actress who plays children or young persons. **3.** A children's book. [Lat. *juvenilis.*] —**ju've·nile·ness** *n.*

jux·ta·pose (jŭk'stə-pōz') *v.* **-posed, -pos·ing.** To place side by side. [Fr. *juxtaposer.*] —**jux'ta·po·si'tion** (-pə-zĭsh'ən) *n.*

Kk

k or **K** (kā) *n.*, *pl.* **k's** or **K's.** The 11th letter of the English alphabet.

K The symbol for the element potassium. [NLat. *kalium.*]

ka·bob (kə-bŏb′) *n.* Shish kebab.

ka·bu·ki (kä-bōō′kē, kə-) *n.* A Japanese popular drama in which gestures, dances, and songs are performed in a formal and stylized manner. [J.]

kabuki

Kad·dish (kä′dĭsh) *n. Judaism.* A prayer recited in the daily synagogue services and by mourners after the death of a close relative. [Aram. *qaddīsh.*]

kaf·fee klatsch (kŏ′fē klăch′, kä′fē kläch′) *n.* Var. of **coffee klatch.**

kaf·tan (kăf′tən, kăf-tăn′) *n.* Var. of **caftan.**

Kai·ser (kī′zər) *n.* The title of the ruler of Germany (1871–1918). [< Lat. *Caesar,* title of Roman emperors.]

kale (kāl) *n.* A variety of cabbage with ruffled or crinkled leaves that do not form a tight head. [< Lat. *caulis,* cabbage.]

ka·lei·do·scope (kə-lī′də-skōp′) *n.* **1.** A small tube in which mirrors reflect light transmitted through bits of loose colored glass contained at one end, causing them to appear as symmetrical designs when viewed at the other. **2.** A constantly changing set of colors. **3.** A series of changing phases or events. [Gk. *kalos,* beautiful + Gk. *eidos,* form + -SCOPE.] **—ka·lei′do·scop′ic** (-skŏp′ĭk) or **ka·lei′do·scop′i·cal** *adj.* **—ka·lei′do·scop′i·cal·ly** *adv.*

kal·ends (kăl′əndz, kā′ləndz) *n.* Var. of **calends.**

ka·mi·ka·ze (kä′mĭ-kä′zē) *n.* **1.** A Japanese pilot trained to make a suicidal crash attack. **2.** An airplane loaded with explosives used by a kamikaze. [J.]

kan·ga·roo (kăng′gə-rōō′) *n., pl.* **-roos.** A marsupial with short forelimbs, large hind limbs that are adapted for leaping, and a long, tapered tail. [Prob. < a native word in Australia.]

kangaroo court *n.* A court set up in violation of established legal procedure, characterized by dishonesty or incompetence.

ka·o·lin (kā′ə-lĭn) *n.* Also **ka·o·line.** A fine clay used in ceramics and refractories. [< Chin. *gao¹ ling³,* a hill in China.]

kaph (käf) *n.* The 11th letter of the Hebrew alphabet. See table at **alphabet.** [Heb. *kāph.*]

ka·pok (kā′pŏk′) *n.* A silky fiber obtained from the fruit of a tropical tree and used as padding in pillows, mattresses, and life preservers. [Malay.]

kap·pa (kăp′ə) *n.* The 10th letter of the Greek alphabet. See table at **alphabet.** [Gk.]

ka·put (kä-pŏŏt′) *adj. Informal.* **1.** Destroyed; ruined. **2.** Incapacitated. [< Fr. *capot,* not having won a trick at cards.]

kar·a·kul (kăr′ə-kəl) *n.* **1.** A central Asian sheep with wool that is curled and glossy in the young but wiry and coarse in the adult. **2.** Fur made from the pelt of a karakul lamb. [< *Kara Kul,* a lake in the USSR.]

kar·at (kăr′ət) *n.* A measure of the proportion of gold in an alloy equal to 1/24 part of pure gold; for example, 12 karat gold is 50% pure gold. [< CARAT.]

ka·ra·te (kə-rä′tē, kä-rä′tä) *n.* A Japanese art of unarmed self-defense that stresses efficiently struck blows. [J.]

kar·ma (kär′mə, kûr′mə) *n.* **1.** *Hinduism & Buddhism.* The total effect of a person's actions and conduct during the successive phases of his existence. **2.** Fate; destiny. [Skt. *karman,* deed.] **—kar′mic** (-mĭk) *adj.*

karst (kärst) *n.* A limestone region characterized by sinkholes, underground streams, caverns, and the absence of surface streams and lakes. [G.]

kart (kärt) *n.* A miniature car used in racing. [Prob. < *Go-Kart,* a trademark.]

Ka·tha·rev·u·sa (kä′thə-rĕv′ə-sä′) *n.* The official form of Modern Greek, which contains morphological and lexical features borrowed from classical Greek. [< Gk. *katharos,* pure.]

ka·ty·did (kä′tē-dĭd′) *n.* A green insect related to the grasshoppers, with specialized organs that produce a shrill sound when rubbed together. [Imit. of its sound.]

kay·ak (kī′ăk′) *n.* **1.** An Eskimo canoe with a deck covering that closes around the waist of the paddler. **2.** A covered canoe similar to a kayak. [Eskimo *qajaq.*]

kay·o (kā′ō, kā′ō′) *n., pl.* **-os.** *Slang.* A knockout. [< K(NOCKO(UT).] **—kay′o** *v.*

ka·zoo (kə-zōō′) *n., pl.* **-zoos.** A toy musical instrument in which a paper membrane is vibrated by the performer's voice. [Imit.]

ke·bab or **ke·bob** (kə-bŏb′) *n.* Shish kebab.

kedge (kĕj) *n.* A light anchor used for warping a vessel. [Poss. < ME *caggen,* to tie.] **—kedge** *v.*

keel (kēl) *n.* **1. a.** The principal structure of a ship, running lengthwise along the center line from bow to stern, to which the frames are attached. **b.** A corresponding structure in an aircraft. **2.** *Poet.* A ship. **3.** A structure similar to a ship's keel in form or function, such as the breastbone of a flying bird. **4.** A pair of united petals in certain flowers, such as those of the pea. **—v.** To capsize. **—phrasal verb. keel over.** **1.** To collapse or fall. **2.** To faint. [< ON *kjǫlr.*]

keel·haul (kēl'hôl') v. To punish by dragging under the keel of a ship. [Du. *kielhalen.*]

keen¹ (kēn) adj. **-er, -est. 1.** Having a fine, sharp edge or point. **2.** Intellectually acute. **3.** Acutely sensitive: *a keen sense of smell.* **4.** Sharp; vivid. **5.** Intense; piercing: *a keen wind.* **6.** Pungent; acrid. **7. a.** Ardent; enthusiastic. **b.** Eagerly desirous: *keen on going.* **8.** *Slang.* Great; splendid. [< OE *cēne,* brave.] **—keen'ly** adv. **—keen'ness** n.

keen² (kēn) n. A loud wailing lament for the dead. [Ir. Gael. *caoine.*] **—keen** v.

keep (kēp) v. **kept** (kĕpt), **keep·ing. 1.** To retain possession of. **2.** To store; put customarily. **3.** To take in one's charge temporarily. **4.** To provide with the necessities of life; support; raise and feed. **5.** To manage; tend; maintain. **6.** To remain, continue, or cause to continue in some condition or position. **7.** To preserve and protect; save. **8.** To detain; confine. **9.** To adhere to; fulfill. **10.** To refrain from divulging. **11.** To celebrate. **12.** To remain fresh or unspoiled. **—phrasal verbs. keep down.** To prevent from accomplishing or succeeding. **keep from.** To deter or prevent. **keep up. 1.** To maintain. **2.** To persevere in. **3.** To continue at the same level or pace. **—n. 1.** Care; charge. **2.** A means of support. **3.** The stronghold of a castle. **4.** A jail. **—idioms. for keeps. 1.** For an indefinitely long period. **2.** Seriously and permanently: *We're separating for keeps.* **keep at it.** To persevere in a course of action. [< OE *cēpan,* to observe.] **—keep'er** n.

keep·sake (kēp'sāk') n. Something given or kept as a reminder; memento.

keg (kĕg) n. A small barrel. [< ON *kaggi.*]

kelp (kĕlp) n. Any of various large brown seaweeds. [ME *culp.*]

Kelt (kĕlt) n. Var. of **Celt.**

Kelt·ic (kĕl'tĭk) n. & adj. Var. of **Celtic.**

Kel·vin (kĕl'vĭn) adj. Pertaining to a temperature scale, the zero point of which is equivalent to −273.16°C. [< 1st Baron *Kelvin* (1824–1907).]

ken (kĕn) v. **kenned, ken·ning.** *Scot.* To know. **—n. 1.** Understanding. **2.** Range of vision. [< OE *cennan,* to declare.]

ken·nel (kĕn'əl) n. **1.** A shelter for a dog. **2.** An establishment where dogs are bred, trained, or boarded. [< Lat. *canis,* dog.] **—ken'nel** v.

ke·pi (kā'pē, kĕp'ē) n., pl. **-is.** A French military cap with a flat, circular top and a visor. [< LLat. *cappa,* cloak.]

kepi   kerf

kept (kĕpt) v. *p.t. & p.p.* of **keep.**

ker·a·tin (kĕr'ə-tən) n. A tough, fibrous protein that forms the outer layer of epidermal structures such as hair, nails, horns, and hoofs. [Gk. *keras,* horn + -IN.] **—ke·rat'i·nous** (kə-rǎt'n-əs) adj.

kerb (kûrb) n. *Chiefly Brit.* Var. of **curb.**

ker·chief (kûr'chĭf) n. **1.** A square scarf, often worn by a woman as a head covering. **2.** A handkerchief. [< OFr. *couvrechef.*]

kerf (kûrf) n. A groove or notch made by a saw or ax. [< OE *cyrf,* act of cutting.]

ker·nel (kûr'nəl) n. **1.** A grain or seed of a cereal plant. **2.** The inner, usu. edible part of a nut or fruit stone. **3.** The central part; core. [< OE *corn.*]

ker·o·sene (kĕr'ə-sēn', kĕr'ə-sēn') n. Also **ker·o·sine.** A thin oil distilled from petroleum or shale oil, used as a fuel and alcohol denaturant. [Gk. *kēros,* wax + -ENE.]

ketch (kĕch) n. A two-masted fore-and-aft-rigged sailing vessel with a smaller mast aft of the mainmast and forward of the tiller. [ME *cache.*]

ketch·up (kĕch'əp, kăch'-) n. A condiment consisting of a thick, smooth, spicy sauce usu. made from tomatoes. [Dial. Chin. *ketsiap,* a kind of sauce.]

ket·tle (kĕt'l) n. A metal pot for boiling. [< ON *ketill.*]

ket·tle·drum (kĕt'l-drŭm') n. A large copper or brass drum with a parchment head.

key¹ (kē) n., pl. **keys. 1.** A notched metallic implement designed to open or close a lock. **2.** Any means of control, esp. of entry or possession. **3. a.** A small instrument for winding a spring. **b.** A slotted metal strip used to open cans. **4. a.** A crucial fact. **b.** A set of answers to a test. **c.** A table, gloss, or cipher for decoding or interpreting. **5.** A pin inserted to lock together mechanical or structural parts. **6. a.** A control button or lever on a hand-operated machine. **b.** A button or lever on a musical instrument, used to produce or modulate a sound. **7.** *Mus.* A tonal system consisting of seven tones in fixed relationship to a tonic; tonality. **8.** The pitch of a voice or other sound. **9.** A general tone or level of intensity. **—v. 1.** To bring into harmony; adjust; adapt. **2.** To supply an explanatory key for. **—phrasal verb. key up.** To make tense or nervous. **—adj.** Of crucial importance; essential; major. [< OE *cæg.*]

key² (kē) n., pl. **keys.** A low offshore island or reef. [Sp. *cayo.*]

key·board (kē'bôrd', -bōrd') n. A set of keys, as on a piano or typewriter. **—v.** To set (copy) by means of a typesetting machine with a keyboard.

key club n. A private club featuring liquor and entertainment. [< KEY¹.]

key·hole (kē'hōl') n. The hole in a lock into which a key fits.

key·note (kē'nōt') n. **1.** The tonic of a musical key. **2.** A prime or central element.

keynote address n. An opening address, as at a political convention.

key punch n. A keyboard machine that is used to punch holes in cards or tapes for data-processing systems.

key signature n. The sharps or flats at the right of the clef on a musical staff that identify the key.

key·stone (kē'stōn') n. The central wedge-shaped stone of an arch that locks its parts together.

khak·i (kăk´ē, kä´kē) *n., pl.* **-is.** **1.** A yellowish brown. **2. a.** A sturdy wool or cotton cloth of khaki color. **b. khakis.** A uniform of this cloth. [< Pers. *khāk,* dust.] **—khak´i** *adj.*

khan (kän, kăn) *n.* **1.** A ruler, official, or man of rank in India and some central Asian countries. **2.** A medieval ruler of a Mongol, Tartar, or Turkish tribe. [< Turk. *khān.*]

khi (kī) *n.* Var. of **chi.**

khoum (kōōm, kōŏm) *n.* See table at **currency.** [Native word in Mauritania.]

kib·butz (kĭ-bŏŏts´) *n., pl.* **-but·zim** (-bŏŏt´sĕm´). A collective farm or settlement in Israel. [< Heb. *qibbūtz,* gathering.]

kib·itz (kĭb´ĭts) *v. Informal.* To look on and offer unwanted advice to others, esp. at a card game. [< G. *kiebitzen,* to look on.] **—kib´itz·er** *n.*

ki·bosh (kī´bŏsh´) *n.* Something that checks or stops. [Orig. unknown.]

kick (kĭk) *v.* **1.** To strike or strike out with the foot. **2.** *Sports.* To strike a ball with the foot. **3.** To recoil, as a gun when fired. **4.** *Informal.* To object vigorously; protest. **—phrasal verbs. kick back.** To pay a kickback. **kick in.** *Slang.* To contribute (a share). **kick off. 1.** To begin or resume play with a kickoff. **2.** To begin. **kick over.** To start to fire, as an internal-combustion engine. **kick up.** *Informal.* To stir up trouble. **—n. 1.** A blow with the foot. **2.** The recoil of a gun. **3.** *Slang.* A complaint or objection. **4.** *Slang.* A feeling of pleasurable stimulation. **5.** *Slang.* A temporary enthusiasm. **—idiom. kick the bucket.** *Slang.* To die. [ME *kiken.*]

Kick·a·poo (kĭk´ə-pōō´) *n., pl.* **-poo** or **-poos. 1. a.** A tribe of Indians formerly living in northern Illinois and southern Wisconsin. **b.** A member of this tribe. **2.** The Algonquian language of the Kickapoo.

kick·back (kĭk´băk´) *n.* **1.** A sharp response or reaction; repercussion. **2.** *Slang.* A percentage payment to a person able to influence or control a source of income.

kick·off (kĭk´ôf´, -ŏf´) *n.* **1.** A place kick in football or soccer with which play is begun. **2.** A beginning.

kid (kĭd) *n.* **1.** A young goat. Also **kid·skin** (kĭd´skĭn´). Leather made from the skin of a young goat. **2.** *Slang.* A child. **—v. kid·ded, kid·ding.** *Informal.* **1.** To make fun of; tease. **2.** To deceive in fun; fool. [< ON *kidh.*] **—kid´der** *n.*

kid·nap (kĭd´năp´) *v.* **-naped** or **-napped, -naping** or **-nap·ping.** To seize and detain unlawfully. [KID + obs. *napper,* thief.] **—kid´nap´er** or **kid´nap´per** *n.*

kid·ney (kĭd´nē) *n., pl.* **-neys. 1.** *Anat.* Either of a pair of organs in the dorsal region of the vertebrate abdominal cavity that function to maintain proper water balance, regulate acid-base concentration, and excrete metabolic wastes as urine. **2.** The kidney of certain animals, eaten as food. **3.** Disposition; temperament. [ME *kidenei.*]

kidney bean *n.* A bean cultivated in many forms for its edible seeds.

kill (kĭl) *v.* **1. a.** To put to death; slay. **b.** To deprive of life. **2. a.** To put an end to. **b.** To thwart; veto: *kill a congressional bill.* **3.** To use up: *kill two hours.* **4.** To cause extreme discomfort to. **5.** To mark for deletion; rule out. **—n. 1.** The act of killing. **2.** Something

that is killed or destroyed, as an animal in hunting. [ME *killen.*] **—kill´er** *n.*

Syns: kill, destroy, dispatch, finish, slay *v.*

kill·deer (kĭl´dîr´) *n., pl.* **-deers** or **-deer.** A wading bird with a distinctive wailing cry. [Imit. of its cry.]

kill·ing (kĭl´ĭng) *n.* **1.** A murder; homicide. **2.** A sudden large profit. **—adj. 1.** Fatal. **2.** Exhausting. **3.** *Informal.* Hilarious.

kill·joy (kĭl´joi´) *n.* One who spoils the enjoyment of others.

kiln (kĭl, kĭln) *n.* An oven for hardening, firing, or drying. [< Lat. *culina,* kitchen.]

ki·lo (kē´lō, kĭl´ō) *n., pl.* **-los.** A kilogram.

kilo- *pref.* 1,000 (10³): *kilowatt.* [< Gk. *khilioi,* thousand.]

ki·lo·cy·cle (kĭl´ə-sī´kəl) *n.* **1.** A unit equal to 1,000 cycles. **2.** 1,000 cycles per second.

ki·lo·gram (kĭl´ə-grăm´) *n.* The basic unit of mass in the metric system, equal to 1,000 grams or about 2.2046 pounds.

ki·lo·hertz (kĭl´ə-hûrts´) *n.* 1,000 hertz.

ki·lo·li·ter (kĭl´ə-lē´tər) *n.* 1,000 liters.

ki·lo·me·ter (kĭl´ə-mē´tər, kĭ-lŏm´ĭ-tər) *n.* 1,000 meters, approx. 0.62137 mile. **—kil´o·met´ric** (-mĕt´rĭk) *adj.*

ki·lo·ton (kĭl´ə-tŭn´) *n.* **1.** 1,000 tons. **2.** An explosive force equivalent to that of 1,000 tons of TNT.

ki·lo·watt (kĭl´ə-wŏt´) *n.* 1,000 watts.

ki·lo·watt-hour (kĭl´ə-wŏt´our´) *n.* A unit of energy equal to the power of one kilowatt acting for one hour.

kilt (kĭlt) *n.* A knee-length, pleated skirt, usu. of tartan, worn esp. as part of the dress for men in Scotland. [< ME *kilten,* to tuck up, of Scand. orig.]

kilt

kil·ter (kĭl´tər) *n.* Proper condition: *out of kilter.* [Orig. unknown.]

ki·mo·no (kə-mō´nə, -nō) *n., pl.* **-nos. 1.** A wide-sleeved Japanese robe, worn with a broad sash. **2.** A dressing gown similar to a kimono. [J.]

kin (kĭn) *n.* A person's relatives. **—adj.** Related; akin. [< OE *cynn.*]

-kin *suff.* Small or diminutive: *lambkin.* [< MDu.]

ki·na (kē´nə) *n., pl.* **-na** or **-nas.** See table at **currency.** [Native word in Papua New Guinea.]

kind¹ (kīnd) *adj.* **-er, -est.** Showing sympathy, concern, or understanding. [< OE *gecynde,* natural.] **—kind´ness** *n.*

kind² (kīnd) *n.* A class or category of similar or related individuals; sort; type. **—idioms. in kind. 1.** With produce or commodities rather than with money. **2.** With something equivalent. **kind of.** *Informal.* Somewhat: *I'm kind of hungry.* [< OE *gecynd,* nature.]

Syns: kind², breed, feather, ilk, sort, species, stripe, type, variety n.

Usage: The use of the plurals these and those with kind, as in these kind of books, although an acceptable and sensible idiom with respectable literary antecedents, often offends traditionalists. Therefore it is probably best avoided by substituting this (or that) kind of and these (or those) kinds of and ensuring that a following noun or verb agrees in number with kind: This kind of book is always in demand. Those are the kinds of books I like.

kin-der-gar-ten (kĭn'dər-gärt'n) n. A class for four- to six-year-old children. [G.]

kin-der-gar-ten-er (kĭn'dər-gärt'nər) n. Also **kin-der-gar-ten-er** (-gärt'n-ər). A child who attends kindergarten.

kind-heart-ed (kīnd'här'tĭd) adj. Kind and sympathetic in nature. —**kind'heart'ed-ly** adv. —**kind'heart'ed-ness** n.

kin-dle (kĭnd'l) v. -dled, -dling. 1. To start (a fire); begin to burn. 2. To glow or cause to glow. 3. To arouse; excite. [< ON kynda.]

kin-dling (kĭnd'lĭng) n. Material that burns easily, used to start a fire.

kind-ly (kīnd'lē) adj. -li-er, -li-est. Showing sympathy, considerateness, or helpfulness. —adv. 1. In a kind way or manner. 2. As a kindness; please: Would you kindly close the door? —**kind'li-ness** n.

kin-dred (kĭn'drĭd) n. 1. A group of related persons. 2. A person's relatives. —adj. Being similar or related. [ME.] —**kin'dred-ness** n.

kine (kīn) n. Archaic. Pl. of cow¹.

kin-e-mat-ics (kĭn'ə-măt'ĭks) n. (used with a sing. verb). The study of motion exclusive of the influences of mass and force. [< Gk. kinēma, motion.] —**kin'e-mat'ic** or **kin'e-mat'i-cal** adj. —**kin'e-mat'i-cal-ly** adv.

kin-e-scope (kĭn'ə-skōp') n. 1. The cathode-ray tube of a television receiver on which the picture appears. 2. A film of a transmitted television program. [Orig. a trademark.]

ki-net-ic (kĭ-nĕt'ĭk) adj. Of, relating to, or produced by motion. [Gk. kinētikos.]

kinetic energy n. Energy associated with the motion of material bodies.

ki-net-ics (kĭ-nĕt'ĭks) n. (used with a sing. verb). 1. The study of all aspects of motion, comprising both kinematics and dynamics. 2. The study of the relationship between motion and the forces affecting motion.

kin-folk (kĭn'fōk') or **kin-folks** (-fōks') pl.n. Vars. of kinsfolk.

king (kĭng) n. 1. A male sovereign. 2. The most eminent of a group, category, etc. 3. A playing card bearing a picture of a king. 4. Chess. The principal piece. 5. Checkers. A piece that has been crowned. 6. Kings. See table at Bible. [< OE cyning.] —**king'li-ness** n. —**king'ly** adj. & adv. —**king'ship'** n.

king-bolt (kĭng'bōlt') n. A vertical bolt used for such purposes as joining the body of a vehicle to the front axle, and usu. serving as a pivot.

king-dom (kĭng'dəm) n. 1. A country ruled by a king or queen. 2. An area in which one thing is dominant. 3. A broad, general category of living or natural forms: the mineral kingdom.

king-fish-er (kĭng'fĭsh'ər) n. A crested, large-billed bird that feeds on fish.

King James Bible n. An Anglican translation of the Bible published in 1611. See table at Bible.

king-pin (kĭng'pĭn') n. 1. Bowling. The foremost or central pin. 2. The most important or essential person or thing. 3. A kingbolt.

kink (kĭngk) n. 1. A tight curl or twist. 2. A painful muscle spasm; crick. 3. A slight flaw, as in a plan or system. 4. A quirk of personality. —v. To form a kink (in). [LG kinke, a twist in a rope.] —**kink'i-ly** adv. —**kink'i-ness** n. —**kink'y** adj.

kink-a-jou (kĭng'kə-jōō') n. A furry, long-tailed tropical American mammal. [Fr. quincajou, of Algonquian orig.]

kins-folk (kĭnz'fōk') pl.n. Also informal **kin-folk** (kĭn'-) or **kin-folks** (kĭn'fōks'). Members of one's family.

kin-ship (kĭn'shĭp') n. The quality or condition of being kin.

kins-man (kĭnz'mən) n. A male blood relation. —**kins'wom'an** n.

ki-osk (kē-ŏsk', kē'ŏsk') n. A small structure used as a newsstand, refreshment booth, etc. [< Pers. kūshk, portico.]

Ki-o-wa (kī'ə-wô', -wä', -wā') n., pl. -wa or -was. 1. a. A tribe of Plains Indians formerly of Colorado, Oklahoma, Kansas, New Mexico, and Texas. b. A member of this tribe. 2. The Uto-Aztecan language of the Kiowa.

kip¹ (kĭp) n., pl. kip. See table at currency. [Thai.]

kip² (kĭp) n. The untanned hide of a small or young animal. [Obs. Du.]

kip-per (kĭp'ər) n. A herring that has been split, salted, and smoked. [< OE cypera.] —**kip'per** v.

kirk (kûrk) n. Scot. A church. [< OE cirice.]

Kis-lev (kĭs'ləf) n. The 3rd month of the Hebrew year. See table at calendar.

kis-met (kĭz'mĭt, kĭs'-) n. Fate; fortune. [< Ar. qismah, lot.]

kiss (kĭs) v. To touch with the lips as a sign of affection, greeting, etc. —n. 1. A touch with the lips. 2. A gentle touch. 3. A small piece of candy. [< OE cyssan.]

kiss-er (kĭs'ər) n. 1. One that kisses. 2. Slang. a. The mouth. b. The face.

kit (kĭt) n. 1. A set of instruments or tools. 2. A set of parts or materials to be assembled. 3. A container, such as a box or case, for a kit. —idiom. the whole kit and caboodle. Informal. The entire collection. [< MDu. kitte, jug.]

kitch-en (kĭch'ən) n. 1. An area in which food is cooked or prepared. 2. A department, as of an institution, that prepares, cooks, and serves food. [< LLat. coquina.]

kitch-en-ette (kĭch'ə-nĕt') n. A small kitchen.

kitchen police n. Mil. 1. Kitchen tasks connected with preparing meals. 2. Personnel assigned to perform kitchen tasks.

kitch-en-ware (kĭch'ən-wâr') n. Utensils for use in the kitchen.

kite (kīt) n. 1. A light frame covered with paper or cloth and often with a tail for balance, designed to hover in the air at the end of a long string. 2. A predatory bird with a long, often forked tail. [< OE *cȳta*, predatory bird.]

kith (kĭth) *n.* Friends and neighbors: *kith and kin.* [< OE *cȳth.*]

kit·ten (kĭt′n) *n.* A young cat. [ME *kitoun.*]

kit·ten·ish (kĭt′n-ĭsh) *adj.* Playful; coy. —**kit′-ten·ish·ly** *adv.* —**kit′ten·ish·ness** *n.*

kit·ty¹ (kĭt′ē) *n., pl.* **-ties.** A pool or fund of money. [< KIT.]

kit·ty² (kĭt′ē) *n., pl.* **-ties.** A kitten or cat. [< KITTEN.]

ki·wi (kē′wē) *n.* A flightless New Zealand bird with a long, slender bill and brownish hairlike feathers. [Maori.]

George Miksch Sutton
kiwi

Kleen·ex (klē′nĕks′). A trademark for a soft cleansing tissue.

klep·to·ma·ni·a (klĕp′tə-mā′nē-ə) *n.* An obsessive impulse to steal, esp. in the absence of economic need. [Gk. *kleptein*, to steal + MANIA.] —**klep′to·ma′ni·ac′** *n.*

klieg light (klēg) *n.* A carbon-arc lamp used esp. in making movies. [< John H. *Kliegl* (1869–1959) and Anton T. *Kliegl* (1872–1927).]

klutz (klŭts) *n. Slang.* **1.** A clumsy or dim-witted person. **2.** A bungler. [< MHG *kloz*, block.] —**klutz′i·ness** *n.* —**klutz′y** *adj.*

knack (năk) *n.* **1.** A clever, expedient method of doing something. **2.** A specific talent or skill. [ME *knak.*]

knap·sack (năp′săk′) *n.* A case or bag, usu. strapped to the back, for carrying supplies and equipment. [LG *knappsack.*]

knave (nāv) *n.* **1.** An unprincipled crafty man. **2.** *Cards.* The jack. [< OE *cnafa*, boy.] —**knav′er·y** *n.* —**knav′ish** *adj.* —**knav′ish·ly** *adv.* —**knav′ish·ness** *n.*

knead (nēd) *v.* **1.** To mix and work (a substance) into a uniform mass. **2.** To massage. [< OE *cnedan.*] —**knead′er** *n.*

knee (nē) *n.* The joint or region between the upper and lower parts of the leg. [< OE *cnēo.*] —**knee** *v.* —**kneed** *adj.*

knee·cap (nē′kăp′) *n.* The patella.

kneel (nēl) *v.* **knelt** (nĕlt) or **kneeled, kneel·ing.** To fall or rest on bent knees. [< OE *cnēowlian.*]

knell (nĕl) *v.* **1.** To ring or sound a bell, esp. for a funeral; toll. **2.** To signal, summon, or proclaim by or as if by tolling. —*n.* **1.** A stroke or toll of a bell esp. for a death. **2.** An omen of disaster, failure. [< OE *cnyllan.*]

knew (nōō) *v. p.t.* of **know.**

knick·ers (nĭk′ərz) *pl.n.* Loose pants gathered just below the knee. [< *knickerbockers.*]

knick·knack (nĭk′năk′) *n.* A small, ornamental article. [< KNACK.]

knife (nīf) *n., pl.* **knives** (nīvz). **1.** A cutting instrument consisting of a sharp blade with a handle. **2.** A cutting edge or blade. —*v.* **knifed, knif·ing. 1.** To cut or stab with a

knife. **2.** *Informal.* To betray by underhand means. [< OE *cnif.*]

knight (nīt) *n.* **1.** A medieval gentleman-soldier. **2.** The holder of a nonhereditary dignity conferred by a sovereign. **3.** A member of any of several orders or brotherhoods. **4.** A chess piece usu. representing a horse's head. —*v.* To raise (a person) to knighthood. [< OE *cniht.*] —**knight′ly** *adj.*

knight·hood (nīt′hōōd) *n.* **1.** The rank or dignity of a knight. **2.** Knights collectively.

knish (kə-nĭsh′) *n.* A piece of dough stuffed with filling, as of meat or cheese, and baked or fried. [< R.]

knit (nĭt) *v.* **knit** or **knit·ted, knit·ting. 1.** To make (a fabric or garment) by intertwining yarn or thread in a series of connected loops. **2.** To join closely. **3.** To draw (the brow) together in wrinkles. —*n.* A fabric or garment made by knitting. [< OE *cnyttan*, to tie in a knot.] —**knit′ter** *n.*

knob (nŏb) *n.* **1. a.** A rounded protuberance. **b.** A rounded handle. **2.** A rounded hill or mountain. [MLG *knobbe.*] —**knobbed** *adj.* —**knob′bi·ness** *n.* —**knob′by** *adj.*

knock (nŏk) *v.* **1.** To strike with a blow or series of blows. **2.** To produce by hitting: *knock a hole in the wall.* **3.** *Slang.* To criticize adversely. **4.** To collide; bump. **5.** To make the pounding noise of a laboring or defective engine. —*phrasal verbs.* **knock about** (or **around**). **1.** To be physically brutal with. **2.** *Informal.* To wander aimlessly from place to place. **knock down. 1.** To sell to the highest bidder at an auction. **2.** To take apart. **knock off. 1.** *Informal.* To stop or cease. **2.** *Informal.* To make or do hastily. **3.** *Informal.* To deduct: *knocked a few dollars off the bill.* **4.** *Slang.* To kill. **knock out. 1.** *Boxing.* To knock (an opponent) unconscious. **2.** To put out of commission; make inoperative or useless. [< OE *cnocian.*] —**knock** *n.*

knock·down (nŏk′doun′) *adj.* **1.** Strong enough to knock down or overwhelm: *a knockdown blow.* **2.** Quickly and easily assembled or disassembled: *knockdown furniture.*

knock·er (nŏk′ər) *n.* A hinged device attached to a door, used for knocking.

knock-knee (nŏk′nē′) *n.* An abnormal condition in which one or both legs turn inward at the knee. —**knock′-kneed′** *adj.*

knock·out (nŏk′out′) *n.* **1.** A blow that causes unconsciousness. **2.** *Boxing.* The act of knocking out an opponent. **3.** *Slang.* One that is very impressive or attractive.

knoll (nōl) *n.* A small rounded hill; hillock. [< OE *cnoll.*]

knot (nŏt) *n.* **1.** A compact intersection of interlaced string, rope, etc. **2.** A tie or bond, esp. a marriage bond. **3.** A cluster of persons or things. **4.** A difficulty; problem. **5.** A hard, dark marking at a point from which a tree branch grows. **6.** A growth on or enlargement of a gland, muscle, etc. **7.** A unit of speed, one nautical mile per hour, about 1.15 statute miles per hour. —*v.* **knot·ted, knot·ting. 1.** To make or become snarled or entangled. **2.** To form a knot (in). —*idiom.* **tie the knot.** *Slang.* To get married. [< OE *cnotta.*] —**knot′ti·ness** *n.* —**knot′ty** *adj.*

Usage: In nautical usage *knot* is a unit of speed, not distance, and has a built-in meaning of "per hour." Therefore, a ship would be said to travel *at ten knots* (not *at ten knots per hour*).

knot·hole (nŏt′hōl′) *n.* A hole in a piece of lumber where a knot once was.

knout (nout) *n.* A leather scourge formerly used for flogging criminals. [< R. *knut.*] —**knout** *v.*

know (nō) *v.* **knew** (nōō, nyōō), **known, know·ing.** **1.** To perceive directly with the senses or mind; be aware of as true or factual. **2.** To be capable of: *know how to swim.* **3.** To have a practical understanding of. **4.** To be subjected to. **5.** To have firmly secured in the mind or memory. **6.** To be able to distinguish. **7.** To be acquainted or familiar with. —**idiom. in the know.** Possessing special or confidential information. [< OE *cnāwan.*] —**know′a·ble** *adj.* —**know′er** *n.*

know-how (nō′hou′) *n. Informal.* Skill or ingenuity.

know·ing (nō′ĭng) *adj.* **1.** Possessing or showing knowledge or understanding. **2.** Suggestive of private information. **3.** Clever; shrewd. —**know′ing·ly** *adv.* —**know′ing·ness** *n.*

knowl·edge (nŏl′ĭj) *n.* **1.** The state or fact of knowing. **2.** Familiarity, awareness, or understanding gained through experience or study. **3.** The sum or range of what has been perceived, discovered, or inferred. **4.** Learning; erudition. [< ME *knowelechen,* to recognize.] —**knowl′edge·a·ble** *adj.*

Syns: *knowledge, education, erudition, instruction, learning, scholarship n.*

known (nōn) *v. p.p.* of **know.**

knuck·le (nŭk′əl) *n.* A joint or region around a joint of a finger, esp. one of the joints connecting the fingers to the hand. —*v.* **-led, -ling.** To press, rub, or hit with the knuckles. —*phrasal verbs.* **knuckle down.** To apply oneself earnestly. **knuckle under.** To yield to pressure. [ME *knokel.*]

knuck·le·bone (nŭk′əl-bōn′) *n.* A knobbed bone, as of a knuckle or joint.

knurl (nûrl) *n.* **1.** A knob or knot. **2.** One of a series of small ridges along the edge of a metal object. [Prob. < ME *knor,* a swelling.] —**knurl′y** *adj.*

ko·a·la (kō-ä′lə) *n.* A furry tree-dwelling Australian marsupial. [Native word in Australia.]

ko·bo (kō′bō′) *n., pl.* **-bo.** See table at currency. [< COPPER.]

kohl·ra·bi (kōl-rä′bē, kōl′rä′-) *n., pl.* **-bies.** A plant with a thickened basal part that is eaten as a vegetable. [< Ital. *cavolo rapa.*]

ko·peck (kō′pĕk′) *n.* See table at currency. [R. *kopeĭka.*]

Ko·ran (kō-rän′, -răn′, kō-) *n.* The sacred text of Islam, believed to contain the revelations made by Allah to Mohammed.

Ko·re·an (kə-rē′ən, kō-, kō-) *n.* The language of the Koreans, which is of no known linguistic affiliation. —**Ko·re′an** *adj.*

ko·sher (kō′shər) *adj.* **1.** Conforming to or prepared in accordance with Jewish dietary laws. **2.** *Slang.* Proper; legitimate. [Heb. *kāshēr,* proper.]

kow·tow (kou′tou′, kō′-) *n.* **1.** A salutation in which one touches the forehead to the ground. **2.** An obsequious act. [Chin. *ke¹ tou².*] —**kow′tow′** *v.*

Kr The symbol for the element krypton.

kraal (kräl) *n.* **1.** A village of southern African natives. **2.** An enclosure for livestock in southern Africa. [Afr. < Port. *curral,* pen.]

Krem·lin (krĕm′lən) *n.* **1.** The citadel of Moscow, housing the offices of the Soviet government. **2.** The Soviet government. [< R. *kreml′,* citadel.]

Krem·lin·ol·o·gy (krĕm′lə-nŏl′ə-jē) *n.* The study of the policies of the Soviet government. —**Krem′lin·o·log′i·cal** (-nə-lŏj′ĭ-kəl) *adj.* —**Krem′lin·ol′o·gist** *n.*

Krish·na (krĭsh′nə) *n. Hinduism.* The 8th and principal avatar of the god Vishnu.

Krishna

kro·na¹ (krō′nə) *n., pl.* **-nur** (-nər). See table at currency. [Icel. *króna.*]

kro·na² (krō′nə) *n., pl.* **-nor** (-nôr′, -nər). See table at currency. [Swed.]

kro·ne (krō′nə) *n., pl.* **-ner** (-nər). See table at currency. [Norw.]

kro·ner (krō′nər) *n.* **1.** See table at currency. **2.** Pl. of **krone.** [Dan.]

kryp·ton (krĭp′tŏn′) *n. Symbol* **Kr** A whitish, inert gaseous element used chiefly in gas-discharge lamps, fluorescent lamps, and electronic flash tubes. Atomic number 36; atomic weight 83.80. [< Gk. *kruptos,* hidden.]

ku·dos (kyōō′dŏs′, -dōs′) *n.* Acclaim or prestige in recognition of achievement. [Gk.]

ku·lak (kōō-läk′, -lăk′) *n.* A prosperous or landed peasant in czarist Russia and during the October Revolution. [R.]

kum·quat (kŭm′kwŏt′) *n.* **1.** A small, thin-skinned edible orangelike fruit. **2.** A tree that bears kumquats. [Cant. *kam kwat.*]

kung fu (kōōng′ fōō′, gōōng′-) *n.* A Chinese system of self-defense similar to karate. [Chin. *gong¹ fu².*]

Kurd (kûrd, kōōrd) *n.* One of a nomadic Moslem people living chiefly in Kurdistan.

Kurd·ish (kûr′dĭsh, kōōr′-) *n.* The Iranian language of the Kurds. —**Kurd′ish** *adj.*

ku·ru (kōō′rōō) *n.* See table at currency. [Turk. *kuruş.*]

kwa·cha (kwä′chə) *n.* See table at currency. [Native word in Zambia.]

kwan·za (kwän′zə) *n., pl.* **-za** or **-zas.** See table at currency. [Swahili.]

kwash·i·or·kor (kwäsh′ē-ôr′kôr, kwä′shē-) *n.* A disease of infants and young children caused by a protein deficiency. [Native word in Ghana.]

kyat (chät) *n.* See table at currency. [Burmese.]

LI

I or **L** (ĕl) *n., pl.* **I's** or **L's. 1.** The 12th letter of the English alphabet. **2.** Something shaped like the letter L. **3.** The Roman numeral for 50.

la (lä) *n. Mus.* The 6th tone of the diatonic scale.

La The symbol for the element lanthanum.

lab (lăb) *n. Informal.* A laboratory.

la·bel (lā′bəl) *n.* **1.** Something, such as a small piece of paper or cloth, attached to an article to identify it or its owner. **2.** A descriptive term; epithet. —*v.* **-beled** or **-belled, -bel·ing** or **-bel·ling. 1.** To attach a label to. **2.** To identify or classify. [< OFr., ribbon.] —**la′bel·er** or **la′bel·ler** *n.*

la·bi·al (lā′bē-əl) *adj.* **1.** Of the lips or labia. **2.** *Phonet.* Formed mainly with the lips, as *b, m, v,* and *w.* —*n.* A labial sound. [< Lat. *labium,* lip.]

la·bi·um (lā′bē-əm) *n., pl.* **-bi·a** (-bē-ə) Any of four folds of tissue of the female external genitalia. [< Lat., lip.]

la·bor (lā′bər) *n.* **1.** Physical or mental exertion. **2.** A specific task. **3.** Work for wages. **4.** The physical efforts of childbirth. —*v.* **1.** To work; toil. **2.** To strive painstakingly. **3.** To proceed slowly; plod. **4.** To suffer from a burden or disadvantage: *labor under a misconception.* **5.** To overstress. [< Lat.] —**la′bor·er** *n.*

Syns: *labor, drudgery, toil, travail, work* n.

lab·o·ra·to·ry (lăb′rə-tôr′ē, -tōr′ē) *n., pl.* **-ries. 1.** A place equipped for scientific experimentation, research, or testing. **2.** A place where drugs and chemicals are manufactured.

Labor Day *n.* The first Monday in Sept., a legal holiday in honor of working people.

la·bored (lā′bərd) *adj.* Lacking natural ease; strained.

la·bo·ri·ous (lə-bôr′ē-əs, -bōr′-) *adj.* Requiring much hard or tedious work. —**la·bo′ri·ous·ly** *adv.* —**la·bo′ri·ous·ness** *n.*

la·bor·sav·ing (lā′bər-sā′vĭng) *adj.* Designed to conserve or decrease the amount of human labor needed.

la·bur·num (lə-bûr′nəm) *n.* A tree or shrub cultivated for its drooping clusters of yellow flowers. [Lat.]

lab·y·rinth (lăb′ə-rĭnth′) *n.* A network of winding, interconnected passages through which it is difficult to find one's way; maze. [< Gk. *laburinthos.*] —**lab′y·rin′thine** (-rĭn′thĭn′, -thēn′) *adj.*

lac (lăk) *n.* A resinous secretion of an Asian insect, used in making shellac. [< Skt. *lākṣā,* resin.]

lace (lās) *n.* **1.** A cord threaded through eyelets or around hooks to pull and tie opposite edges together. **2.** A delicate fabric woven in an open weblike pattern. —*v.* **laced, lac·ing. 1.** To fasten or be fastened with a lace. **2.** To intertwine: *lacing strands into a braid.* **3.** To add liquor to (a beverage). [< Lat. *laqueus,* noose.] —**lac′er** *n.* —**lac′y** *adj.*

lac·er·ate (lăs′ə-rāt′) *v.* **-at·ed, -at·ing** To rip or tear; mangle. [< Lat. *lacerare.*] —**lac′er·a′tion** *n.* —**lac′er·a′tive** *adj.*

lach·ry·mal (lăk′rə-məl) *adj.* Of tears or the tear-producing glands. [< Lat. *lacrima,* tear.]

lach·ry·mose (lăk′rə-mōs′) *adj.* Tearful. [Lat. *lacrimosus.*] —**lach′ry·mose′ly** *adv.*

lack (lăk) *n.* A deficiency or absence. —*v.* **1.** To be entirely without or have very little of. **2.** To be wanting or deficient. [ME.]

lack·a·dai·si·cal (lăk′ə-dā′zĭ-kəl) *adj.* Lacking spirit, liveliness, or interest. [< *lackaday,* an exclamation of regret.] —**lack′a·dai′si·cal·ly** *adv.* —**lack′a·dai′si·cal·ness** *n.*

lack·ey (lăk′ē) *n., pl.* **-eys. 1.** A footman. **2.** A servile follower; toady. [< Catalan *alacay.*]

lack·lus·ter (lăk′lŭs′tər) *adj.* Lacking luster, brightness, or vitality; dull.

la·con·ic (lə-kŏn′ĭk) *adj.* Sparing of words; terse. [< Gk. *Lakōnikos,* Spartan.] —**la·con′i·cal·ly** *adv.*

lac·quer (lăk′ər) *n.* Any of various clear or colored synthetic or resinous coatings used to give wood and metal surfaces a high gloss. [< Skt. *lākṣā,* resin.] —**lac′quer** *v.*

la·crosse (lə-krôs′, -krŏs′) *n.* A game played on a field by two teams using long-handled sticks with webbed pouches and a hard rubber ball. [< Fr. *(le jeu de) la crosse,* (the game of) the hooked stick.]

lacrosse

lact– *pref.* Milk: *lactate.* [< Lat. *lac.*]

lac·tate (lăk′tāt′) *v.* **-tat·ed, -tat·ing.** To secrete or produce milk. —**lac·ta′tion** *n.*

lac·te·al (lăk′tē-əl) *adj.* Of or like milk; milky. [< Lat. *lacteus.*]

lac·tic (lăk′tĭk) *adj.* Of or derived from milk.

lactic acid *n.* A syrupy liquid, $C_3H_6O_3$, present in sour milk, molasses, various fruits, and wines.

lac·tose (lăk′tōs′) *n.* A white crystalline sugar, $C_{12}H_{22}O_{11}$, made from whey and used in pharmaceuticals, infant foods, bakery foods, and confections.

la·cu·na (lə-kyōō′nə) *n., pl.* **-nae** (-nē) or **-nas. 1.** An empty space; gap. **2.** *Anat.* A cavity or depression. [< Lat., pool.]

lad (lăd) *n.* A boy or young man. [ME *ladde.*]

lad·der (lăd′ər) *n.* **1.** A device for climbing, consisting of two long structural members crossed by equally spaced rungs. **2.** A series of ascending stages or levels. [< OE *hlæder.*]

lade (lād) *v.* **lad·ed, lad·en** (lād′n) or **lad·ed,**

lad·ing. 1. To load or be loaded with or as if with cargo: *lade a ship.* 2. To burden; oppress. [< OE *hladan.*] —**lad'en** *adj.*

lad·ing (lā'dǐng) *n.* Cargo; freight.

La·di·no (lə-dē'nō) *n.* A Romance language with elements borrowed from Hebrew that is spoken by Sephardic Jews esp. in the Balkans.

la·dle (lād'l) *n.* A long-handled spoon with a deep bowl for serving liquids. [< OE *hladan,* to lade.] —**la'dle** *v.* —**la'dler** *n.*

la·dy (lā'dē) *n., pl.* -**dies.** 1. A woman of refinement and good manners. 2. The female head of a household: *the lady of the house.* 3. A polite term for an adult member of the feminine sex. 4. **Lady.** *Chiefly Brit.* The general feminine title of nobility and other rank. [< OE *hlǣfdige.*] —**la'dy·like** *adj.*

la·dy·bug (lā'dē-bŭg') *n.* Also **la·dy·bird** (-bûrd'). A small, usu. reddish, black-spotted beetle.

la·dy·fin·ger (lā'dē-fǐng'gər) *n.* A small, finger-shaped sponge cake.

lady in waiting *n., pl.* **ladies in waiting.** A lady appointed to attend a queen or princess.

la·dy's-slip·per (lā'dēz-slǐp'ər) *n.* An orchid with an inflated, pouchlike lip.

La·e·trile (lā'ə-trǐl). A trademark for an alleged anticancer drug.

lag (lăg) *v.* **lagged, lag·ging.** 1. To fail to keep up a pace; fall behind. 2. To weaken; slacken. —*n.* 1. The act or condition of lagging. 2. An extent or duration of lagging. [Orig. unknown.]

la·ger (lä'gər) *n.* Beer aged from six weeks to six months to allow sedimentation. [< G. *lagerbier.*]

lag·gard (lăg'ərd) *n.* One that lags behind.

la·gniappe (lăn-yăp', lăn'yăp') *n.* An extra or unexpected gift. [< Quechua *yapay,* to give more.]

la·goon (lə-gōōn') *n.* A shallow body of water, esp. one separated from the sea by sandbars or coral reefs. [< Lat. *lacuna,* pool.] —**la·goon'al** *adj.*

laid (lād) *v. p.t. & p.p.* of **lay**[1].

laid-back (lād'băk') *adj. Informal.* Having a relaxed or casual atmosphere or character; easygoing.

lain (lān) *v. p.p.* of **lie**[1].

lair (lâr) *n.* A den or hidden dwelling, as of a wild animal. [< OE *leger.*]

lais·sez faire (lĕs'ā fâr') *n.* Noninterference, esp. the economic doctrine that government should not interfere with commerce. [< Fr., let (people) do (as they choose).] —**lais'sez-faire'ism** *n.*

la·i·ty (lā'ĭ-tē) *n., pl.* -**ties.** 1. The lay people of a religious group as distinguished from the clergy. 2. Nonprofessionals.

lake (lāk) *n.* 1. A large inland body of water. 2. A large pool of any liquid. [< Lat. *lacus.*]

lam (lăm) *Slang.* —*v.* **lammed, lam·ming.** To escape, as from prison. —*n.* In flight, esp. from the law: *on the lam.* [Orig. unknown.]

la·ma (lä'mə) *n.* A Buddhist monk of Tibet or Mongolia. [Tibetan *blama.*]

La·ma·ism (lä'mə-ĭz'əm) *n.* Buddhism as practiced in Tibet and Mongolia. —**La'ma·ist** *n.* —**La'ma·is'tic** *adj.*

lamb (lăm) *n.* 1. **a.** A young sheep. **b.** The

flesh of a young sheep used as meat. 2. A sweet, mild-mannered person. [< OE.]

lam·baste (lăm-bāst') *v.* -**bast·ed, -bast·ing.** *Slang.* 1. To thrash; beat. 2. To find fault with sharply. [Perh. *lam,* to beat + BASTE[3].]

lamb·da (lăm'də) *n.* The 11th letter of the Greek alphabet. See table at **alphabet.** [Gk.]

lam·bent (lăm'bənt) *adj.* 1. Flickering or glowing gently. 2. Light and effortless: *lambent wit.* [< Lat. *lambere,* to lick.] —**lam'ben·cy** *n.* —**lam'bent·ly** *adv.*

lamb·skin (lăm'skĭn') *n.* The hide of a lamb or a fine leather made from it.

lame (lām) *adj.* **lam·er, lam·est.** 1. Disabled in one or more limbs, esp. so as to impair walking. 2. Weak and ineffectual: *a lame excuse.* —*v.* **lamed, lam·ing.** To make lame. [< OE *lama.*] —**lame'ly** *adv.* —**lame'ness** *n.*

la·mé (lă-mā', lä-) *n.* A fabric woven with metallic threads. [Fr., ult. < Lat. *lamina,* thin plate.]

la·med (lä'mĕd) *n.* Also **la·medh.** The 12th letter of the Hebrew alphabet. See table at **alphabet.** [Heb. *lāmedh.*]

lame duck *n.* An elected officeholder continuing in office during the period between the election and inauguration of a successor.

la·mel·la (lə-mĕl'ə) *n., pl.* -**mel·lae** (-mĕl'ē) or -**las.** A thin scale, plate, or layer. [Lat.] —**la·mel'lar** or **lam'el·late** (lăm'ə-lāt', lə-mĕl'āt') *adj.* —**la·mel'lar·ly** *adv.*

la·ment (lə-mĕnt') *v.* 1. To express sorrow or deep regret (over); mourn. 2. To wail; complain. —*n.* 1. An expression of sorrow or mourning. 2. A dirge or elegy. [< Lat. *lamentari.*] —**la·men'ta·ble** (lə-mĕn'-, lăm'ən-) *adj.* —**la·men'ta·bly** *adv.* —**la·ment'er** *n.*

lam·en·ta·tion (lăm'ən-tā'shən) *n.* 1. The act of lamenting; an expression of sorrow. 2. **Lamentations.** See table at **Bible.**

lam·i·na (lăm'ə-nə) *n., pl.* -**nae** (-nē') or -**nas.** A thin plate, sheet, or layer. [Lat.] —**lam'i·nar** or **lam'i·nal** *adj.*

lam·i·nate (lăm'ə-nāt') *v.* -**nat·ed, -nat·ing.** 1. To form into or bond together in thin layers. 2. To divide into thin layers. —*adj.* (-nĭt, -nāt'). Also **lam·i·nat·ed** (-nā'tĭd). Consisting of thin layers. —**lam'i·na'tion** *n.* —**lam'i·na'tor** *n.*

lamp (lămp) *n.* 1. A device, as one equipped with an electric bulb or wick, for providing light. 2. A similar device, as for therapeutic radiation. [< Gk. *lampas,* torch.]

lamp·black (lămp'blăk') *n.* A gray or black pigment made from soot.

lam·poon (lăm-pōōn') *n.* Broad satire, esp. when intended to ridicule an individual. [< Fr. *lampons,* let us drink.] —**lam·poon'** *v.* —**lam·poon'er** or **lam·poon'ist** *n.* —**lam·poon'er·y** *n.*

lam·prey (lăm'prē) *n., pl.* -**preys.** An eellike primitive fish with a jawless sucking mouth. [< Med. Lat. *lampreda.*]

la·nai (lə-nī', lä-) *n.* A verandah or patio. [Hawaiian.]

lance (lăns) *n.* 1. A thrusting weapon with a long shaft and a sharp metal head. 2. A similar implement, as one for spearing fish. 3. A lancet. —*v.* **lanced, lanc·ing.** 1. To pierce with a lance. 2. To cut into with a lancet. [< Lat. *lancea.*]

lance corporal n. An enlisted man in the U.S. Marine Corps ranking above a private first class.

lanc·er (lăn'sər) n. A cavalryman armed with a lance.

lan·cet (lăn'sĭt) n. A surgical knife with a short, wide, pointed double-edged blade.

land (lănd) n. 1. The solid ground of the earth, esp. as distinguished from the sea. 2. A distinct region or area: *desert land.* 3. A nation, country, or realm. 4. A tract owned or sold as property. —v. 1. To put or arrive on land after traveling by water or air. 2. To arrive or cause to arrive at a certain place. 3. To come to rest; alight. 4. To catch by or as by fishing. [< OE.]

land·ed (lăn'dĭd) adj. 1. Owning land. 2. Consisting of land.

land·fall (lănd'fôl') n. 1. The sighting or reaching of land on a voyage or flight. 2. The land sighted or reached.

land grant n. A government grant of public land for a railroad, highway, state college, etc. —**land'grant'** adj.

land·hold·er (lănd'hōl'dər) n. One who owns land. —**land'hold'ing** n.

land·ing (lăn'dĭng) n. 1. The act or site of coming to land or rest. 2. A platform at the top, bottom, or between flights of a staircase.

landing gear n. The structure that supports an aircraft and its load on the ground.

landing strip n. An aircraft runway without airport facilities.

land·locked (lănd'lŏkt') adj. 1. Entirely or almost entirely surrounded by land. 2. Confined to inland waters, as certain salmon.

land·lord (lănd'lôrd') n. 1. One who owns and rents real estate, buildings, or dwelling units. 2. An innkeeper. —**land'la·dy** (-lā'dē) n.

land·lub·ber (lănd'lŭb'ər) n. A person unfamiliar with the sea or seamanship. [LAND + lubber, clumsy fellow.]

land·mark (lănd'märk') n. 1. A fixed marker indicating a boundary line. 2. A prominent and identifying feature of a landscape. 3. A historically significant event, building, or site.

land·mass (lănd'măs') n. A large land area.

land-of·fice business (lănd'ô'fĭs, -ŏf'ĭs) n. Thriving or rapidly moving volume of trade.

land-poor (lănd'pōōr') adj. Owning much land but lacking capital.

land·scape (lănd'skāp') n. 1. A view or vista of scenery on land. 2. A painting, photograph, etc., depicting such a scene. —v. **-scaped, -scap·ing.** To improve the appearance of (a piece of ground) by contouring and decorative planting. [Du. *landschap.*] —**land'scap'er** n.

land·slide (lănd'slīd') n. 1. The fall or slide of a mass of earth and rock down a slope. 2. An overwhelming victory, esp. in an election.

land·ward (lănd'wərd) adj. & adv. To or toward land. —**land'wards** adv.

lane (lān) n. 1. A narrow way or road. 2. A set course or passageway designated for vehicles, ships, etc. [< OE.]

lan·guage (lăng'gwĭj) n. 1. a. The use by human beings of voice sounds, and often of written symbols that represent these sounds, to express and communicate thoughts and feelings. b. A system of such voice sounds, used by a people with a shared history or set of traditions. 2. A system of signs, symbols, etc., used for communication. 3. The special vocabulary, usage, or style of a particular

group or individual. 4. A particular manner of utterance: *gentle language.* 5. The manner or means of communication between living creatures other than man. [< OFr. *langage.*]

lan·guid (lăng'gwĭd) adj. 1. Lacking energy or vitality; weak. 2. Listless; spiritless; apathetic. 3. Slow; sluggish. [< Lat. *languidus.*] —**lan'guid·ly** adv. —**lan'guid·ness** n.

lan·guish (lăng'gwĭsh) v. 1. To lose strength or vigor; decline. 2. To become listless and depressed; pine. 3. To assume a wistful or languid air. [< Lat. *languēre.*] —**lan'guish·er** n. —**lan'guish·ment** n.

lan·guor (lăng'gər, lăng'ər) n. Languidness; indolence. [Lat. < *languēre*, to be languid.] —**lan'guor·ous** adj. —**lan'guor·ous·ly** adv.

lank (lăngk) adj. **-er, -est.** 1. Long and lean; gaunt. 2. Long, straight, and limp: *lank hair.* [< OE *hlanc.*] —**lank'ly** adv. —**lank'ness** n.

lank·y (lăng'kē) adj. **-i·er, -i·est.** Tall, thin, and ungainly. —**lank'i·ly** adv. —**lank'i·ness** n.

lan·o·lin (lăn'ə-lĭn) n. A yellowish-white fatty substance obtained from wool and used in soaps, ointments, etc. [< Lat. *lana*, wool.]

lan·tern (lăn'tərn) n. A case with transparent or translucent sides for holding and protecting a light. [< Gk. *lamptēr.*]

lan·tha·nide (lăn'thə-nīd') n. A rare-earth element. [LANTHAN(UM) + -IDE.]

lan·tha·num (lăn'thə-nəm) n. *Symbol* La A soft, silvery-white metallic element used in glass manufacture and lighting. Atomic number 57; atomic weight 138.91. [< Gk. *lanthanein*, to hide.]

lan·yard (lăn'yərd) n. 1. A short rope used on ships to secure the rigging. 2. A braided cord worn around the neck for carrying a knife, whistle, keys, etc. [< OFr. *lanière*, strap.]

lap¹ (lăp) n. 1. The level plane formed by the front part of the legs above the knees of a seated person. 2. The part of a person's clothing that covers the lap. [< OE *læppa*, flap of a garment.]

lap² (lăp) v. **lapped, lap·ping.** 1. To fold or wrap over or around something. 2. To place or extend so as to overlap. —n. 1. An overlapping part. 2. A complete turn or circuit, as of a racetrack. 3. A segment or stage, as of a journey. [Prob. < LAP¹.]

lap³ (lăp) v. **lapped, lap·ping.** 1. To take in (a liquid or food) with the tongue. 2. To wash against with a gentle slapping sound: *waves lapping the shore.* —**phrasal verb. lap up.** To take in eagerly. —n. The act or sound of lapping. [< OE *lapian.*] —**lap'per** n.

lap·board (lăp'bôrd', -bōrd') n. A board held on the lap and used as a table or desk.

lap dog n. A small, easily held pet dog.

la·pel (lə-pĕl') n. Either of two flaps that extend down from the collar of a garment and fold back against the chest. [< LAP¹.]

lap·i·dar·y (lăp'ĭ-dĕr'ē) n., pl. **-ies.** One who cuts and polishes precious stones. —adj. 1. Of precious stones or the art of working with them. 2. Suitable for engraving on stone: *lapidary prose.* [Lat. *lapidarius*, stoneworker.]

lap·in (lăp'ĭn) n. Rabbit fur. [Fr., rabbit.]

lap·is laz·u·li (lăp'ĭs lăz'yə-lē, lăzh'ə-) n. An opaque, deep-blue gemstone. [< Med. Lat.]

Lapp (lăp) n. 1. A member of a nomadic people that inhabits Lapland. 2. The Finno-Ugric language of the Lapps. —**Lapp** or **Lap'pish** (lăp'ĭsh) adj.

lapse (lăps) n. 1. A minor slip, error, or failure. 2. A slipping into a lower state; decline.

3. An interval of passing time. 4. The termination of a right, privilege, custom, etc., through neglect, disuse, or the passage of time. —v. lapsed, laps·ing. 1. To fall away by degrees. 2. To elapse. 3. To become invalid, as through the passage of time. [< Lat. *lapsus*, p.p. of *labi*, to slip.] —laps′er n.

lap·wing (lăp′wĭng′) n. Any of several crested Old World birds related to the plovers. [< OE *hlēapewince*.]

lar·board (lär′bərd) n. Naut. The port side. [ME *laddebord*.] —lar′board adj.

lar·ce·ny (lär′sə-nē) n., pl. -nies. The crime of stealing; theft. [< Lat. *latrocinium*.] —lar′ce·nous (-nəs) adj.

larch (lärch) n. A cone-bearing tree with deciduous needles and heavy, durable wood. [< Lat. *larix*.]

lard (lärd) n. The white rendered fat of a hog. —v. 1. To insert strips of fat in (lean meat or poultry) before cooking. 2. To enrich (e.g. speech or writing) with additions; embellish. [< Lat. *lardum*.] —lard′y adj.

lar·der (lär′dər) n. A room, cupboard, etc., where meat and other foods are kept.

la·ree (lär′ē) n. See table at **currency**. [Pers. *Lārī*.]

large (lärj) adj. larg·er, larg·est. 1. Of a size or amount greater than average; big. 2. Broad; comprehensive. 3. Tolerant; liberal. —idioms. at large. 1. At liberty; free. 2. As a whole; in general. 3. Not assigned to or representing any particular country, district, etc. by and large. For the most part; on the whole. [< Lat. *largus*.] —large′ness n.

large intestine n. The portion of the intestine that extends from the end of the small intestine to the anus.

large·ly (lärj′lē) adv. 1. For the most part; mainly. 2. On a large scale; amply.

large-scale (lärj′skāl′) adj. 1. Of large scope; extensive. 2. Drawn or made large to show detail: *a large-scale map.*

lar·gess (lär-zhĕs′, -jĕs′, lär′jĕs′) n. Also lar·gesse. 1. Liberality in giving. 2. Money or gifts bestowed. [< OFr. *largece*.]

lar·go (lär′gō) adv. Mus. In a slow, solemn manner. [Ital.] —lar′go adj. & n.

lar·i·at (lăr′ē-ət) n. A rope with a running noose; lasso. [Sp. *la reata*, the lariat.]

lark[1] (lärk) n. 1. An Old World bird with a sustained, melodious song. 2. Any of several similar birds. [< OE *lāwerce*.]

lark[2] (lärk) n. A carefree adventure or prank. —v. To engage in fun or pranks. [Prob. < ON *leika*, to play.]

lark·spur (lärk′spûr′) n. A plant with spurred, usu. blue or purplish flowers.

lar·va (lär′və) n., pl. -vae (-vē). 1. The wingless, often wormlike form of a newly hatched insect. 2. The newly hatched stage of any of various animals that differ markedly in the adult form, as a tadpole. [< Lat. *ghost*.] —lar′val adj.

lar·yn·gi·tis (lăr′ən-jī′tĭs) n. Inflammation of the larynx. —lar′yn·git′ic (-jĭt′ĭk) adj.

lar·ynx (lăr′ĭngks) n., pl. la·ryn·ges (lə-rĭn′jēz) or -es. The upper part of the respiratory tract between the pharynx and the trachea,

containing the vocal cords. [Gk. *larunx*.] —la·ryn′ge·al (lə-rĭn′jē-əl) adj.

la·sa·gna (lə-zän′yə) n. Also la·sa·gne. Flat wide noodles, usu. baked with tomato sauce and cheese. [Ital.]

las·civ·i·ous (lə-sĭv′ē-əs) adj. Of or characterized by lust; lewd. [< Lat. *lascivus*.] —las·civ′i·ous·ly adv. —las·civ′i·ous·ness n.

la·ser (lā′zər) n. Any of several devices that convert incident electromagnetic radiation of mixed frequencies to one or more discrete frequencies of highly amplified and coherent radiation. [L(IGHT) A(MPLIFICATION BY) S(TIMULATED) E(MISSION OF) R(ADIATION).]

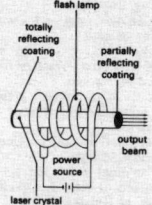

laser
Simplified diagram of a crystal laser

lash[1] (lăsh) n. 1. A stroke or blow with or as if with a whip. 2. A whip or its thongs. 3. An eyelash. —v. 1. To strike with or as if with a whip. 2. To strike against with force or violence: *sleet lashing the roof.* 3. To move or wave rapidly to and fro. 4. To attack verbally. [ME *lashe*.] —lash′er n.

lash[2] (lăsh) v. To secure or bind, as with a rope. [< Lat. *laqueare*, to ensnare.]

lass (lăs) n. 1. A girl or young woman. 2. A sweetheart. [ME *las*.]

las·sie (lăs′ē) n. A lass.

las·si·tude (lăs′ĭ-tōōd′, -tyōōd′) n. A state of listless weakness, exhaustion, or torpor. [Lat. *lassitudo*.]

las·so (lăs′ō, lă-sōō′) n., pl. -sos or -soes. A long rope or thong with an adjustable noose at one end, used esp. to catch horses and cattle. [< Lat. *laqueus*, snare.] —las′so v.

last[1] (lăst) adj. 1. Being, coming, or remaining after all others. 2. Most recent; latest. 3. Conclusive and authoritative. 4. Least likely or expected: *the last person we would have suspected.* —adv. 1. After all others. 2. Most recently. 3. In conclusion. —n. 1. One that is last. 2. The end. —idiom. at last. Finally. [< OE *latost*.] —last′ly adv. Syns: *last, closing, concluding, final, terminal, ultimate* adj.

last[2] (lăst) v. 1. To continue in existence; go on. 2. To remain adequate or sufficient. [< OE *lēstan*.]

last[3] (lăst) n. A foot-shaped block or form used in making or repairing shoes. [< OE *lēst*, sole of the foot.]

last·ing (lăs′tĭng) adj. Continuing or remaining for a long time. —last′ing·ly adv. —last′ing·ness n.

Last Judgment n. The final judgment by God of all mankind.

Last Supper n. Christ's supper with his disciples on the night before the Crucifixion.

latch (lăch) n. A fastening or lock, usu. consisting of a movable bar that fits into a notch. —v. To close with a latch. **—phrasal verb. latch on to** (or **onto**). Informal. 1. To cling to. 2. To get possession of; obtain. [< OE læc-can, to seize.]

late (lāt) adj. **lat·er, lat·est.** 1. Coming, occurring, or remaining after the usual or expected time. 2. Being or occurring toward the end. 3. Recent. 4. Recently deceased: the late Mr. Foster. —adv. **lat·er, lat·est.** 1. After the usual or expected time. 2. At or into an advanced period or part. 3. Recently. —idiom. **of late.** Recently. [< OE læt.] —**late'ness** n. **Syns: late, belated, overdue, tardy adj.**

Late Greek n. Greek from the 4th to the 9th cent. A.D.

Late Latin n. Latin from the 3rd to the 7th cent. A.D.

late·ly (lāt'lē) adv. Not long ago; recently.

la·tent (lāt'nt) adj. Present or potential but not evident or active. [< Lat. latēre, to lie hidden.] —**la'ten·cy** n. —**la'tent·ly** adv.

lat·er·al (lăt'ər-əl) adj. On, of, toward, or from the side. —n. Also **lateral pass.** A football pass thrown sideways or backward. [Lat. lateralis.] —**lat'er·al·ly** adv.

la·tex (lā'tĕks') n. 1. The milky, viscous sap of certain trees and plants, as the rubber tree. 2. An emulsion of rubber or plastic globules in water, used in paints, adhesives, etc. [< Lat., fluid.]

lath (lăth) n., pl. **laths** (lăthz, lăths). 1. A narrow, thin strip of wood or metal, used esp. in making a supporting structure for plaster, shingles, or tiles. 2. A similarly used building material. [< OE lætt.]

lathe (lāth) n. A machine on which a piece of wood, metal, etc., is spun and shaped by a tool. [Orig. unknown.] —**lathe** v.

lath·er (lăth'ər) n. 1. Foam or froth, esp. that formed by soap and water. 2. Frothy sweat. 3. A dither. —v. 1. To produce lather. 2. To apply lather to. [< OE lēathor.] —**lath'er·er** n. —**lath'er·y** adj.

Lat·in (lăt'n) adj. 1. Of or relating to ancient Rome, its culture, or its language. 2. Of or relating to peoples using Romance languages. 3. Of the Roman Catholic Church. —n. 1. The Italic language of ancient Rome. 2. A member of a Latin people.

Latin American n. A native or inhabitant of any of the Spanish- or Portuguese-speaking countries of the Western Hemisphere. —**Lat'in-A·mer'i·can** adj.

lat·i·tude (lăt'ĭ-tōōd', -tyōōd') n. 1. Extent; range. 2. Freedom from limitations. 3. a. The angular distance north or south of the equator, measured in degrees along a meridian. b. A region considered in relation to this distance. [< Lat. latitudo.] —**lat'i·tu'di·nal** adj. —**lat'i·tu'di·nal·ly** adv.

lat·i·tu·di·nar·i·an (lăt'ĭ-tōōd'n-âr'ē-ən, -tyōōd'-) adj. Favoring freedom of thought and behavior, esp. in religion. —n. A latitudinarian person. —**lat'i·tu'di·nar'i·an·ism** n.

la·trine (lə-trēn') n. A communal toilet. [< Lat. latrina.]

lat·ter (lăt'ər) adj. 1. Being the second of two

persons or things mentioned. 2. Closer to the end. [< OE lætra.] —**lat'ter·ly** adv.

Usage: Latter refers to the second of two: Jones and Smith were nominated, but only the latter has the support of labor. When more than two are specified, latter is not appropriate: The president, secretary, and treasurer all serve on the board. To refer to the treasurer, use the last, the last of these, the last named, or repeat the term.

lat·ter-day (lăt'ər-dā') adj. Of present or recent time; modern.

Latter-day Saint n. A Mormon.

lat·tice (lăt'ĭs) n. 1. a. An open framework made of interwoven strips, as of wood or metal. b. Something resembling this, as a window. 2. Physics. A regular periodic configuration throughout an area or space. [< OFr. latiz.] —**lat'ticed** adj. —**lat'tice·work'** n.

Lat·vi·an (lăt'vē-ən) n. 1. A native of Latvia. 2. The Baltic language of the Latvians. —**Lat'vi·an** adj.

laud (lôd) v. To praise highly. —n. 1. Praise. 2. **lauds.** A morning church service at which psalms of praise are sung. [Lat. laudare.] —**lau·da'tion** (lô-dā'shən) n. —**laud'er** n.

laud·a·ble (lô'də-bəl) adj. Commendable; praiseworthy. —**laud'a·bil'i·ty** or **laud'a·ble·ness** n. —**laud'a·bly** adv.

lau·da·num (lôd'n-əm) n. A tincture of opium. [NLat.]

lau·da·to·ry (lô'də-tôr'ē, -tōr'ē) adj. Expressing praise; eulogistic.

laugh (lăf, läf) v. 1. To produce inarticulate sounds expressive of mirth, joy, or derision. 2. To drive or influence by or as if by laughing: laughed him off the stage. —n. 1. The sound or act of laughing. 2. Something amusing or ridiculous. [< OE hlæhhan.] —**laugh'er** n. —**laugh'ing·ly** adv.

laugh·a·ble (lăf'ə-bəl, läf'-) adj. Causing or deserving laughter or derision. —**laugh'a·ble·ness** n. —**laugh'a·bly** adv.

Syns: laughable, comic, comical, funny, laughing, ludicrous, ridiculous, risible adj.

laugh·ing·stock (lăf'ĭng-stŏk', läf'ĭng-) n. An object of jokes, laughter, or ridicule.

laugh·ter (lăf'tər, läf'-) n. The act or sound of laughing. [< OE hleahtor.]

launch¹ (lônch, länch) v. 1. To set in motion; propel. 2. To move (a boat) into the water. 3. To put into action; inaugurate; initiate. [< LLat. lanceare, to wield a lance.] —**launch** n. —**launch'er** n.

launch² (lônch, länch) n. An open motorboat. [Port. lancha.]

launching pad n. The platform from which a rocket or space vehicle is launched.

laun·der (lôn'dər, län'-) v. 1. To wash or wash and iron (clothes or linens). 2. To conceal the source of (money), as by channeling it through an intermediary. [< Lat. lavanda, things to be washed.] —**laun'der·er** n. —**laun'dress** (-drĭs) n.

Laun·dro·mat (lôn'drə-măt', län'-). A trademark for a commercial establishment equipped with washing machines and dryers.

laun·dry (lôn'drē, län'-) n., pl. **-dries.** 1. Soiled or laundered clothes. 2. A place where laundering is done.

lau·re·ate (lôr'ē-ĭt, lŏr'-) n. One receiving highest honors, as a poet or scientist. [< Lat. laureatus, crowned with laurel.] —**lau're·ate** adj. —**lau're·ate·ship'** n.

lau·rel (lôr′əl, lŏr′-) n. 1. a. A shrub or tree of the Mediterranean region, having aromatic evergreen leaves. b. Any of several similar shrubs or trees. 2. Often **laurels.** A wreath of laurel leaves. 3. **laurels.** Honor; glory. [< Lat. *laurus.*]

laurel

lavender

la·va (lä′və, lăv′ə) n. 1. Molten rock from a volcano or a crack in the earth's surface. 2. The rock formed by the cooling and hardening of lava. [< Lat. *labes,* fall.]

la·vage (lə-väzh′) n. A washing out. [< Lat. *lavare,* to wash.]

lav·a·liere (lăv′ə-lîr′) n. A pendant worn on a chain around the neck. [< Louise de *la Vallière* (1644–1710).]

lav·a·to·ry (lăv′ə-tôr′ē, -tōr′ē) n., pl. **-ries.** A room equipped with washing and toilet facilities. [< LLat. *lavatorium.*]

lave (lāv) v. **laved, lav·ing.** To wash or bathe. [< Lat. *lavare.*]

lav·en·der (lăv′ən-dər) n. 1. Any of various aromatic plants having small fragrant purplish flowers. 2. A pale to light purple. [< Med. Lat. *lavendula.*] —**lav′en·der** adj.

lav·ish (lăv′ĭsh) adj. 1. Extravagant; profuse. 2. Luxurious. —v. To give forth unstintingly. [< OFr. *lavasse,* downpour.] —**lav′ish·er** n. —**lav′ish·ly** adv. —**lav′ish·ness** n.

law (lô) n. 1. a. A rule established by authority, society, or custom. b. A body of such rules. 2. The science or study of such rules; jurisprudence. 3. A judicial system or its workings. 4. A formulation or generalization based on observed phenomena. 5. A code of ethics or behavior. 6. Avowed or undisputed authority. [< OE *lagu.*]

law-a·bid·ing (lô′ə-bī′dĭng) adj. Obeying the law.

law·break·er (lô′brā′kər) n. A person who breaks the law. —**law′break′ing** n.

law·ful (lô′fəl) adj. Allowed or recognized by law. —**law′ful·ly** adv. —**law′ful·ness** n.

law·giv·er (lô′gĭv′ər) n. 1. One who establishes a code of laws for a people. 2. A lawmaker.

law·less (lô′lĭs) adj. 1. Disregarding or violating the law. 2. Disobedient. —**law′less·ly** adv. —**law′less·ness** n.

law·mak·er (lô′mā′kər) n. One who drafts laws; legislator. —**law′mak′ing** n.

lawn¹ (lôn) n. A piece of ground planted with grass and mowed regularly. [< OFr. *lande,* glade.]

lawn² (lôn) n. A fine, thin fabric of cotton or linen. [< *Laon,* France.]

law·ren·ci·um (lô-rĕn′sē-əm, lō-) n. *Symbol* **Lw** A synthetic radioactive element. Atomic number 103; mass number 257. [< Ernest O. *Lawrence* (1901–58).]

law·suit (lô′sōōt′) n. A case brought before a court of law for settlement.

law·yer (lô′yər, loi′ər) n. One who gives legal advice to clients and represents them in court. [ME *lawyere.*]

lax (lăks) adj. **-er, -est.** 1. a. Remiss; negligent. b. Not strict; lenient. 2. Not taut; slack. [< Lat. *laxus,* loose.] —**lax′i·ty** or **lax′ness** n. —**lax′ly** adv.

lax·a·tive (lăk′sə-tĭv) n. A medicine that stimulates bowel movements. [< Lat. *laxare,* to relax.] —**lax′a·tive** adj.

lay¹ (lā) v. **laid** (lād), **lay·ing.** 1. a. To place or rest on a surface. b. *Nonstandard.* To recline; lie. 2. To knock down: *laid him out flat.* 3. To calm; allay. 4. To produce and deposit (eggs). 5. To bet. 6. To spread: *lay paint on a canvas.* 7. To apply, assign, or locate. 8. To bring into a specified condition. 9. To set or place in a desired position. 10. To prepare; contrive: *lay plans.* 11. To sink in the ground: *lay a cable.* 12. To impose: *laid a heavy fine on him.* 13. To put forth or submit: *laid the case before us.* —**phrasal verbs. lay aside.** 1. To give up; abandon. 2. To put aside for the future; save. **lay away.** To reserve for the future; save. **lay by.** To save. **lay down.** 1. To set forth; establish. 2. To give up. **lay in.** To obtain and store. **lay off.** 1. To dismiss or suspend from a job. 2. *Slang.* To cease. **lay out.** 1. To arrange according to a plan. 2. To spend or supply (money). 3. To prepare for burial. **lay over.** To make an intermediate stop. **lay up.** 1. To store for future needs. 2. *Informal.* To keep in bed or out of action. —n. General manner, position, or appearance. [< OE *lecgan.*]

lay² (lā) adj. 1. Of or belonging to the laity. 2. Nonprofessional. [< Gk. *laos,* the people.]

lay³ (lā) n. A ballad. [< OFr. *lai.*]

lay⁴ (lā) v. p.t. of **lie¹.**

lay·er (lā′ər) n. 1. A single thickness, coating, or sheet of material. 2. One that lays, esp. a hen. [< ME *leier,* one who lays stones.]

lay·ette (lā-ĕt′) n. Clothing and other supplies for a newborn child. [< OFr. *laie,* box.]

lay·man (lā′mən) n. 1. One who is not a member of the religious clergy. 2. A nonprofessional.

lay·off (lā′ôf′, -ŏf′) n. 1. A temporary dismissal of employees. 2. A period of temporary inactivity or rest.

lay·out (lā′out′) n. 1. An arrangement or plan. 2. A set of tools.

lay·o·ver (lā′ō′vər) n. An intermediate stop in a journey.

laze (lāz) v. **lazed, laz·ing.** To loaf; idle. [< LAZY.]

la·zy (lā′zē) adj. **-zi·er, -zi·est.** 1. Not willing to work or to be energetic; slothful. 2. Slow-moving; sluggish. [Prob. of LG orig.] —**la′zi·ly** adv. —**la′zi·ness** n.

Syns: *lazy, idle, indolent, shiftless, slothful, sluggish* adj.

lazy Su·san (sōō′zən) n. A revolving tray for condiments or food.

lea (lē, lā) n. A meadow. [< OE *lēa.*]

leach (lēch) v. To remove or be removed from by the action of a percolating liquid. [Orig. unknown.] —**leach′er** n.

lead¹ (lēd) v. **led** (lĕd), **lead·ing. 1.** To guide, conduct, escort, or direct. **2.** To influence; induce. **3.** To be ahead or at the head of: *His name led the list.* **4.** To pursue; live: *lead a hectic life.* **5.** To tend toward a certain goal or result: *led to complications.* **6.** To make the initial play, as in a card game. **—phrasal verbs. lead off. 1.** To begin; start. **2.** *Baseball.* To bat first. **lead on. 1.** To lure; entice. **lead up to.** To proceed toward (one's true purpose or subject) with lengthy preliminaries. **—n. 1.** The first place; foremost position. **2.** The margin by which one is ahead. **3.** A clue. **4.** Command; leadership. **5.** An example; precedent. **6.** The principal role in a play. **7. a.** The prerogative or turn to make the first play in a card game. **b.** The card played. **8.** A leash for leading an animal. [< OE *lǣdan.*] **—lead'er** n. **—lead'er·ship'** n.

lead² (lĕd) n. **1. Symbol Pb** A soft, bluish-white, dense metallic element, used in solder and type metal, bullets, radiation shielding, and paints. Atomic number 82; atomic weight 207.19. **2.** A weight used to make soundings. **3.** A thin metal strip used to separate lines of type. **4.** A thin stick of graphitic marking substance in a pencil. **—v. 1.** To cover, line, or weight with lead. **2.** To add lead to. **3.** To secure (window glass) with lead. [< OE *lēad.*]

lead·en (lĕd'n) adj. **1.** Made of lead. **2.** Dark gray: *a leaden sky.* **3.** Heavy like lead. **4.** Burdened; weighted down. **—lead'en·ly** adv. **—lead'en·ness** n.

lead-in (lēd'ĭn') n. **1.** An introduction. **2.** A program, as on television, that precedes another.

lead·ing¹ (lē'dĭng) adj. **1.** In the first or front position. **2.** Most important; main. **3.** Playing a lead in a theatrical production. **4.** Encouraging a desired response: *a leading question.*

lead·ing² (lĕd'ĭng) n. **1.** A border of lead, as around a windowpane. **2.** The strips of lead used to separate lines of type.

lead-time (lĕd'tīm') n. The time needed between the decision to start a project and the completion of the work.

leaf (lēf) n., pl. **leaves** (lēvz). **1.** A usu. green, flattened plant structure attached to a stem and functioning as a principal organ of photosynthesis. **2.** A leaflike part. **3.** Leaves collectively; foliage. **4.** One of the sheets constituting the pages of a book. **5.** A very thin sheet of gold. **6.** A movable section of a table top. **7.** A movable section of a folding door, shutter, or gate. **—v. 1.** To produce leaves. **2.** To turn pages rapidly: *leaf through a book.* [< OE *lēaf.*] **—leaf'i·ness** n. **—leaf·less** adj. **—leaf·y** adj.

leaf·age (lē'fĭj) n. Leaves; foliage.

leaf·let (lēf'lĭt) n. **1.** A small leaf or leaflike part. **2.** A printed handbill or circular.

leaf spring n. A spring that consists of several layers of flexible metallic strips.

league¹ (lēg) n. **1.** An association or alliance for common action. **2.** An association of sports teams. **3.** *Informal.* A level of competition. [< Ital. *liga.*] **—league** v.

league² (lēg) n. A unit of distance equal to 3 miles or approx. 4.8 kilometers. [< Med. Lat. *leuga,* a unit of distance.]

leak (lēk) n. **1. a.** A hole, crack, or similar opening through which something can escape or pass. **b.** Such an escape or passage. **2.** A disclosure of confidential information. **—v. 1.** To escape or pass through a leak. **2.** To allow something passage through a leak. **3.** To disclose or become known through a breach of secrecy. [ME *leke.*] **—leak'i·ness** n. **—leak·y** adj.

leak·age (lē'kĭj) n. **1.** The process of leaking. **2.** A thing or amount that escapes by leaking.

lean¹ (lēn) v. **leaned** or **leant** (lĕnt), **lean·ing. 1.** To bend away from the vertical; incline. **2.** To incline one's weight so as to be supported. **3.** To rely on for assistance or support. **4.** To have a tendency or preference. [< OE *hleonian.*]

lean² (lēn) adj. **-er, -est. 1.** Not fleshy or fat; thin. **2.** Containing little or no fat: *a lean steak.* **3.** Not productive or abundant. **—n.** Meat with little or no fat. [< OE *hlǣne.*] **—lean'ly** adv. **—lean'ness** n.

lean·ing (lē'nĭng) n. A tendency; preference.

lean-to (lēn'tōō') n., pl. **-tos. 1.** A shed with a sloping roof, built against a wall or the side of a building. **2.** A shelter resembling this.

leap (lēp) v. **leaped** or **leapt** (lĕpt, lēpt), **leap·ing. 1.** To jump off the ground with a spring of the legs. **2.** To jump over. **3.** To move quickly, abruptly, or impulsively. **—n.** A jump or bound. [< OE *hlēapan.*] **—leap'er** n.

leap·frog (lēp'frŏg', -frôg') n. A game in which one player bends over while the next jumps over him. **—leap'frog'** v.

leapt (lĕpt, lēpt) v. A p.t. & p.t. of **leap.**

leap year n. A year having 366 days, with Feb. 29 as the extra day.

learn (lûrn) v. **learned** or **learnt** (lûrnt), **learn·ing. 1.** To gain knowledge, comprehension, or mastery (of) through experience or study. **2.** To memorize. **3.** To become informed (of). [< OE *leornian.*]

learn·ed (lûr'nĭd) adj. Erudite; scholarly. **—learn'ed·ly** adv. **—learn'ed·ness** n.

learn·ing (lûr'nĭng) n. Acquired knowledge; erudition.

lease (lēs) n. A contract granting use or occupation of land or holdings during a specified period in exchange for rent. **—v. leased, leas·ing. 1.** To grant by lease. **2.** To hold under lease. [< Lat. *laxare,* to loosen.]

lease·hold (lēs'hōld') n. **1.** Possession by lease. **2.** Property held by lease. **—lease'·hold'er** n.

leash (lēsh) n. A restraining chain, rope, or strap attached to the collar or harness of an animal. [<. Lat. *laxare,* to loosen.] **—leash** v.

least (lēst) adj. A superl. of **little. —adj. 1.** Lowest in importance or rank. **2.** Smallest. **—adv.** To or in the smallest degree. **—n.** The smallest or slightest. **—idioms. at least. 1.** At the lowest. **2.** In any event. **in the least.** At all. [< OE *lǣst.*]

least common multiple n. The smallest number that is exactly divisible by each of two or more designated quantities.

leath·er (lĕth'ər) n. The dressed or tanned hide of an animal, usu. with the hair removed. [< OE *lether.*] **—leather** adj. **—leath'er·y** adj.

leath·er·neck (lĕth'ər-nĕk') n. *Slang.* A U.S. Marine. [< the leather neckband that was once part of the uniform.]

leave¹ (lēv) v. **left** (lĕft), **leav·ing. 1.** To go out or away (from). **2. a.** To let or cause to re-

main. **b.** To deliver. **3.** To have as a remainder. **4.** To forgo moving or interfering with. **5.** To bequeath. **6.** To abandon; forsake. **—phrasal verbs. leave off.** To stop; cease. **leave out.** To omit. [< OE *lǣfan.*]
Usage: In formal style *leave* is not an acceptable substitute for *let* in the sense of "to allow or permit." Only *let* is acceptable in the following examples: *Let us go. Let it lie.*

leave² (lēv) *n.* **1.** Permission. **2.** Official permission to be absent from work or duty. **3.** Farewell or departure. [< OE *lēaf.*]

leaved (lēvd) *adj.* Having a specified number or kind of leaves: *three-leaved; wide-leaved.*

leav-en (lĕv'ən) *n.* Also **leav-en-ing** (lĕv'-ə-nĭng). **1.** A substance, such as yeast, used as an ingredient in batters and doughs to cause them to rise. **2.** A lightening or enlivening element. **—v.** **1.** To add yeast or another fermenting agent to. **2.** To lighten or enliven. [< Lat. *levare,* to raise.] **—leav'ened** *adj.*

leaves (lēvz) *n.* Pl. of **leaf.**

leave-tak-ing (lēv'tā'kĭng) *n.* A departure or farewell.

leav-ings (lē'vĭngz) *pl.n.* Scraps or remains; leftovers.

lech-er (lĕch'ər) *n.* A man given to excessive sexual activity. [< OFr.] **—lech'er-ous** *adj.* **—lech'er-ous-ly** *adv.* **—lech'er-y** *n.*

lec-i-thin (lĕs'ə-thĭn) *n.* Any of a group of fatty compounds found in plant and animal tissues and used esp. in the processing of foods, pharmaceuticals, and cosmetics. [Gk. *lekithos,* egg yolk + -IN.]

lec-tern (lĕk'tərn) *n.* A reading stand for a public speaker. [< Lat. *legere,* to read.]

lec-ture (lĕk'chər) *n.* **1.** A speech providing information about a given subject, delivered before an audience or class. **2.** A solemn scolding. [< Lat. *legere,* to read.] **—lec'ture** *v.* **—lec'tur-er** *n.*

led (lĕd) *v.* *p.t.* & *p.p.* of **lead¹.**

ledge (lĕj) *n.* **1.** A shelflike projection on a wall or cliff. **2.** A reef. [ME, piece of wood.]

ledg-er (lĕj'ər) *n.* An account book in which sums received and paid out are recorded. [ME *legger,* breviary.]

lee (lē) *n.* **1.** The side or quarter away from the wind; the sheltered side. **2.** Cover; shelter. [< OE *hlēo,* shelter.]

leech (lēch) *n.* **1.** Any of various aquatic bloodsucking worms, of which one species was formerly used by physicians to bleed patients. **2.** One who preys on or lives off others. [< OE *lǣce.*]

leek (lēk) *n.* A vegetable related to the onion, having a white, slender bulb and dark-green leaves. [< OE *lēac.*]

leer (lîr) *n.* A suggestive, cunning, or malicious look. [< OE *hlēor,* cheek.] **—leer** *v.*

leer-y (lîr'ē) *adj.* **-i-er, -i-est.** *Informal.* Suspicious; wary. **—leer'i-ly** *adv.* **—leer'i-ness** *n.*

lees (lēz) *pl.n.* Dregs. [< Med. Lat. *lia.*]

lee-ward (lē'wərd, loo'ərd) *adj.* Facing away from the wind. **—lee'ward** *n.* & *adv.*

lee-way (lē'wā') *n.* **1.** The drift of a ship or plane to leeward of true course. **2.** A margin of freedom or variation; latitude.

left¹ (lĕft) *adj.* **1. a.** Of, at, or on the side of

the body that faces north when the subject is facing east. **b.** Of, at, or on the corresponding side of anything that can be said to have a front. **2.** Often *Left.* Of or belonging to the political Left. **—n.** **1. a.** The direction or position on the left side of something. **b.** The left side or hand. **c.** A turn in this direction: *take a left.* **2. the Left.** The persons and groups pursuing egalitarian political goals by reformist or revolutionary means. **—adv.** Toward or on the left. [ME.]

left² (lĕft) *v.* *p.t.* & *p.p.* of **leave¹.**

left field *n.* **1.** *Baseball.* The third of the outfield that is to the left, looking from home plate. **2.** A position far from the mainstream, as of opinion. **—left fielder** *n.*

left-hand (lĕft'hănd') *adj.* **1.** Of or on the left. **2.** Turning from right to left.

left-hand-ed (lĕft'hăn'dĭd) *adj.* **1.** Using the left hand more naturally and easily than the right. **2.** Executed with the left hand. **3.** Awkward; clumsy. **4.** Turning or spiraling from right to left. **—adv.** With the left hand. **—left'-hand'ed-ly** *adv.* **—left'-hand'ed-ness** *n.*

left-hand-er (lĕft'hăn'dər) *n.* A left-handed person.

left-ist (lĕf'tĭst) *n.* A person with political views associated with the Left. **—left'ism** *n.* **—left'ist** *adj.*

left-o-ver (lĕft'ō'vər) *adj.* Remaining unused or uneaten. **—n.** Often **leftovers.** Something that is leftover.

left wing *n.* The leftist faction of a group. **—left'-wing'** *adj.* **—left'-wing'er** *n.*

left-y (lĕf'tē) *n., pl.* **-ies.** *Slang.* A left-handed person.

leg (lĕg) *n.* **1.** A limb of an animal, used for locomotion and support. **2.** Something resembling a leg in shape or function. **3.** The part of a pair of trousers that covers the leg. **4.** A stage of a journey or course. **—v.** **legged, leg-ging.** To use one's legs, esp. to run: *legged it out of there.* [< ON *leggr.*]

leg-a-cy (lĕg'ə-sē) *n., pl.* **-cies.** **1.** Money or property bequeathed to someone by will. **2.** Something handed on from those who have come before. [< Lat. *legare,* to bequeath as a legacy.]

le-gal (lē'gəl) *adj.* **1.** Of or relating to law or lawyers. **2. a.** Authorized by or based on law. **b.** Established by law; statutory. **3.** In conformity with or permitted by law. [< Lat. *lex,* law.] **—le-gal'i-ty** (lē-găl'ə-tē) *n.* **—le-gal-i-za'-tion** *n.* **—le'gal-ize'** *v.* **—le'gal-ly** *adv.*

le-gal-ism (lē'gə-lĭz'əm) *n.* Strict, literal adherence to law. **—le'gal-ist** *n.* **—le'gal-is'tic** *adj.* **—le'gal-is'ti-cal-ly** *adv.*

leg-ate (lĕg'ĭt) *n.* An official emissary, esp. of the pope. [< Lat. *legare,* to send as ambassador.] **—leg'ate-ship'** *n.*

leg-a-tee (lĕg'ə-tē') *n.* One who is the inheritor of a legacy.

le-ga-tion (lĭ-gā'shən) *n.* A diplomatic mission headed by a minister.

le-ga-to (lĭ-gä'tō) *adv. Mus.* In a smooth, even style. [Ital.] **—le-ga'to** *adj.* & *n.*

leg-end (lĕj'ənd) *n.* **1.** An unverifiable popular story handed down from the past. **2.** A person or circumstance often spoken of.

3. An inscription on an object. 4. An explanatory caption. [< Lat. *legenda*, things to be read.] —**leg'en·dar·y** *adj.*

leg·er·de·main (lĕj'ər-də-mān') *n.* Tricks performed with the hands, as by a magician. [< OFr. *leger de main*, light of hand.]

leg·ged (lĕg'ĭd, lĕgd) *adj.* Having a specified number or kind of legs: *six-legged.*

leg·gings (lĕg'ĭngz) *n.* Leg coverings.

leg·gy (lĕg'ē) *adj.* -gi·er, -gi·est. Having long, slender legs. —**leg'gi·ness** *n.*

leg·horn (lĕg'hôrn', -ərn) *n.* 1. Often **Leghorn.** One of a breed of domestic fowl raised esp. for production of eggs. 2. A hat of finely plaited straw. [< *Leghorn*, Italy.]

leg·i·ble (lĕj'ə-bəl) *adj.* Capable of being read. [< Lat. *legere*, to read.] —**leg'i·bil'i·ty** or **leg'i·ble·ness** *n.* —**leg'i·bly** *adv.*

le·gion (lē'jən) *n.* 1. A Roman army unit consisting of 3,000 to 6,000 infantrymen and more than 100 cavalrymen. 2. A large number; multitude. [< Lat. *legere*, to gather.] —**le'gion·ar'y** *n. & adj.* —**le'gion·naire'** *n.*

leg·is·late (lĕj'ĭ-slāt') *v.* -lat·ed, -lat·ing. 1. To pass a law. 2. To enact into law. [< Lat. *legislator*, legislator.] —**leg'is·la'tor** *n.*

leg·is·la·tion (lĕj'ĭ-slā'shən) *n.* 1. The act or process of legislating; lawmaking. 2. A proposed or enacted law or group of laws.

leg·is·la·tive (lĕj'ĭ-slā'tĭv) *adj.* 1. Of or relating to legislation or a legislature. 2. Having the power to create laws.

leg·is·la·ture (lĕj'ĭ-slā'chər) *n.* A body of persons empowered to make laws.

le·git·i·mate (lə-jĭt'ə-mĭt) *adj.* 1. Lawful. 2. In accordance with accepted standards. 3. Reasonable: *a legitimate solution.* 4. Authentic; genuine. 5. Born in wedlock. —*v.* (lə-jĭt'ə-māt') -mat·ed, -mat·ing. To justify as legitimate. [< Lat. *legitimus.*] —**le·git'i·ma·cy** (-mə-sē) *n.* —**le·git'i·mate·ly** *adv.*

leg·ume (lĕg'yōōm', lə-gyōōm') *n.* 1. A bean, pea, or related plant bearing pods that split in two when mature. 2. The edible pod or seeds of a legume. [< Lat. *legumen.*] —**le·gu'mi·nous** (lə-gyōō'mə-nəs) *adj.*

leg·work (lĕg'wûrk') *n. Informal.* Work, such as collecting information, that involves walking or traveling about.

lei¹ (lā, lā'ē) *n.* A garland of flowers, esp. one worn around the neck. [Hawaiian.]

lei² (lā) *n.* Pl. of **leu.**

lei·sure (lē'zhər, lĕzh'ər) *n.* 1. Freedom from work or time-consuming duties. 2. Free time. —*idiom.* **at (one's) leisure.** At one's convenience. [< Lat. *licēre*, to be allowed.] —**lei'sured** *adj.* —**lei'sure·ly** *adj. & adv.*

leit·mo·tif (līt'mō-tēf') *n.* Also **leit·mo·tiv.** A dominant and recurring theme, as in a novel. [G. *Leitmotiv.*]

lek (lĕk) *n.* See table at **currency.** [Albanian.]

lem·ming (lĕm'ĭng) *n.* A rodent of northern regions, noted for its periodic mass migrations. [Norw.]

lem·on (lĕm'ən) *n.* 1. a. An egg-shaped yellow citrus fruit with acid, juicy pulp. b. A tree bearing such fruit. 2. *Slang.* Something chronically defective or unsatisfactory. [< Pers. *līmūn.*]

lem·on·ade (lĕm'ə-nād') *n.* A drink made of lemon juice, water, and sugar.

lem·pi·ra (lĕm-pîr'ə) *n.* See table at **currency.** [Am. Sp.]

le·mur (lē'mər) *n.* A small African primate with large eyes, soft fur, and a long tail. [< Lat. *lemures*, ghosts.]

lemur

lend (lĕnd) *v.* **lent** (lĕnt), **lend·ing.** 1. To give or allow the use of temporarily. 2. To provide (money) temporarily, usu. at interest. 3. To contribute; impart. 4. To accommodate. [< OE *lǣnan.*] —**lend'er** *n.*

length (lĕngkth, lĕngth) *n.* 1. a. The measure of something along its greatest dimension. b. The measure of something from back to front as distinguished from its width or height. 2. Measured distance or dimension. 3. Duration or extent: *the length of a meeting.* —*idiom.* **at length.** 1. Eventually. 2. Fully. [< OE *lengthu.*] —**length'y** *adj.*

length·en (lĕngk'thən, lĕng'-) *v.* To make or become longer.

length·wise (lĕngkth'wīz', lĕngth'-) *adv.* Also **length·ways** (-wāz'). Along the direction of the length. —**length'wise'** *adj.*

le·ni·ent (lē'nē-ənt, lēn'yənt) *adj.* 1. Merciful. 2. Not strict; generous. [< Lat. *lenire*, to soothe.] —**le'ni·en·cy** or **le'ni·ence** *n.* —**le'ni·ent·ly** *adv.*

lens (lĕnz) *n.* 1. A piece of glass or other transparent material made so that either or both of its opposite surfaces are curved, used to make light rays converge or diverge to form an image. 2. A combination of two or more such lenses used to form an image for viewing or photographing. 3. A transparent part of the eye that focuses light rays to form an image on the retina. [Lat., *lentil.*]

lent (lĕnt) *v. p.t. & p.p.* of **lend.**

Lent (lĕnt) *n.* The 40 weekdays from Ash Wednesday until Easter, observed by Christians as a season of penitence. [< OE *lencten*, spring.] —**Lent'en** *adj.*

len·til (lĕn'təl) *n.* 1. The round, flattened, edible seed of a pealike Old World plant. 2. The plant itself. [< Lat. *lens.*]

len·to (lĕn'tō) *adv. Mus.* Slowly. [Ital.] —**len'to** *adj.*

Le·o (lē'ō) *n.* 1. A constellation in the Northern Hemisphere near Cancer and Virgo. 2. The 5th sign of the zodiac.

le·one (lē-ōn') *n.* See table at **currency.** [< *Sierra Leone.*]

le·o·nine (lē'ə-nīn') *adj.* Of or characteristic of a lion. [< Lat. *leoninus.*]

leop·ard (lĕp'ərd) *n.* 1. A large wild cat of Africa and Asia, usu. having a tawny black-spotted coat. 2. The pelt of a leopard. [< LGk. *leopardos.*]

le·o·tard (lē'ə-tärd') *n.* Often **leotards.** A

snugly fitting one-piece garment that covers the torso, worn esp. by dancers. [< Jules *Léotard* (1830–70).]

lep·er (lĕp′ər) *n.* A person afflicted with leprosy. [< Gk. *lepros*, scaly.]

lep·re·chaun (lĕp′rĭ-kŏn′, -kŏn′) *n.* An elf of Irish folklore. [Ir. Gael. *lupracán*.]

lep·ro·sy (lĕp′rə-sē) *n.* An infectious bacterial disease that causes ulcers and sores on the body and in its severe forms causes progressive destruction of tissue. **—lep′rous** *adj.*

lep·ton (lĕp′tŏn′) *n., pl.* **-ta** (-tə). See table at currency. [Mod. Gk.]

les·bi·an (lĕz′bē-ən) *n.* A female homosexual. [< *Lesbos*, an island in the Aegean.] **—les′bi·an** *adj.* **—les′bi·an·ism** *n.*

le·sion (lē′zhən) *n.* 1. A wound or injury. 2. An area of diseased tissue. [< Lat. *laesio*.]

less (lĕs). A compar. of **little.** *—adj.* 1. Smaller. 2. Lower in importance, esteem, or rank. *—adv.* To a smaller extent, degree, or frequency. *—n.* A smaller amount. *—prep.* Minus. [< OE *lǣssa*.]

-less *suff.* Lacking: *sleepless.* [< OE *lēas*, without.]

les·see (lĕ-sē′) *n.* A tenant holding a lease. [< OFr. *lesser*, to lease.]

less·en (lĕs′ən) *v.* To make or become less.

less·er (lĕs′ər) *adj.* Smaller in size or importance.

les·son (lĕs′ən) *n.* 1. Something to be learned. 2. a. A period of instruction. b. An instructional exercise. 3. An edifying example or experience. 4. A reprimand or punishment. 5. A reading from sacred writings as part of a religious service. [< Lat. *lectio*.]

les·sor (lĕs′ôr′, lĕ-sôr′) *n.* A person who rents property to another by a lease. [< OFr. *lesser*, to lease.]

lest (lĕst) *conj.* For fear that. [< OE *thy lǣs the.*]

let¹ (lĕt) *v.* **let, let·ting.** 1. To grant permission to; allow: *She let him continue.* 2. To cause; make: *Let me know what happened.* 3. To assume; suppose. 4. To rent or lease. 5. Used as an auxiliary verb in the imperative to indicate: A request or command: *Let's get going.* b. A warning or threat. c. Resignation. **—phrasal verbs. let down.** 1. To slow down; ease up. 2. To disappoint. **let off.** 1. To emit or release. 2. To release with little or no punishment. **let on.** To allow it to be known. **let out.** 1. To give forth; emit. 2. To loosen or widen by releasing material from a seam: *let out a tight dress.* **let up.** To diminish; subside: *The rain has begun to let up a bit.* [< OE *lǣtan.*]

Usage: In speech *let's* has come increasingly to be used as a mere indication that a suggestion is being made, so that one hears such examples as *let's us go* and *let's get yourself ready for the doctor.* These usages are best avoided in formal writing.

let² (lĕt) *n.* 1. Obstacle; obstruction. 2. A stroke in tennis or a similar net game that is invalid and must be replayed. [< OE *lettan*, to hinder.]

-let *suff.* 1. Small: *booklet.* 2. An article worn on: *anklet.* [< OFr.]

let·down (lĕt′doun′) *n.* 1. A decrease, decline,

or relaxation, as of effort or energy. 2. A disappointment.

le·thal (lē′thəl) *adj.* Causing or capable of causing death. [< Lat. *lethum*, death.] **—le·thal′i·ty** (lē-thăl′ĭ-tē) or **le·thal·ness** *n.* **—le′thal·ly** *adv.*

leth·ar·gy (lĕth′ər-jē) *n., pl.* **-gies.** Drowsy or sluggish indifference; apathy. [< Gk. *lēthargia*.] **—le·thar·gic** (lə-thär′jĭk) *adj.* **—le·thar′gi·cal·ly** *adv.*

Le·the (lē′thē) *n.* Gk. Myth. The river of forgetfulness in Hades.

let's (lĕts). Let us.

let·ter (lĕt′ər) *n.* 1. A written symbol representing a speech sound and constituting a unit of an alphabet. 2. A written or printed communication. 3. The literal meaning of something. 4. **letters.** Literature or learning. *—v.* To write letters (on); inscribe. [< Lat. *littera*.] **—let′ter·er** *n.* **—let′ter·ing** *n.*

let·tered (lĕt′ərd) *adj.* 1. Literate. 2. Erudite. 3. Inscribed with letters.

let·ter·head (lĕt′ər-hĕd′) *n.* 1. Stationery with a printed or engraved heading. 2. The heading itself.

let·ter-per·fect (lĕt′ər-pûr′fĭkt) *adj.* Correct to the last detail.

let·ter·press (lĕt′ər-prĕs′) *n.* The process of printing from a raised inked surface.

let·tuce (lĕt′əs) *n.* A plant cultivated for its edible leaves, eaten as salad. [< Lat. *lactuca*.]

let·up (lĕt′ŭp′) *n.* 1. A slackening or slowdown. 2. A pause.

leu (lĕ′ŏŏ) *n., pl.* **lei** (lā). See table at currency. [Rum.]

leu·ke·mi·a (lōō-kē′mē-ə) *n.* Any of a group of diseases in which the leukocytes increase in uncontrolled numbers.

leuko- or **leuk-** or **leuco-** *pref.* 1. White or colorless: *leukocyte.* 2. Leukocyte: *leukemia.* [< Gk. *leukos.*]

leu·ko·cyte (lōō′kə-sīt′) *n.* Also **leu·co·cyte.** Any of the white or colorless nucleated cells occurring in blood. **—leu′ko·cyt′ic** (-sĭt′ĭk) or **leu′ko·cyt′oid** *adj.*

lev (lĕf) *n., pl.* **lev·a** (lĕv′ə). See table at currency. [Bulgarian.]

lev·ee (lĕv′ē) *n.* 1. An embankment raised to prevent a river from overflowing. 2. A landing place on a river. [< OFr. *lever*, to raise.]

lev·el (lĕv′əl) *n.* 1. Relative position or rank on a scale. 2. A natural or proper position, place, or stage. 3. Position along a vertical axis; elevation; height. 4. a. A horizontal line or plane at right angles to the plumb. b. The position or height of such a line or plane: *eye level.* 5. A flat, horizontal surface. 6. A tract of land of uniform elevation. 7. An instrument for ascertaining whether a surface is horizontal. 8. Computer Sci. A bit, element, channel, or row of information. *—adj.* 1. Having a flat, smooth surface. 2. Horizontal. 3. At the same height as another; even. 4. Uniform; consistent. 5. Steady; cool. *—v.* **-eled** or **-elled, -el·ing** or **-el·ling.** 1. To make or become horizontal, flat, or even. 2. To knock down or raze. 3. To equalize. 4. To aim or direct. **—phrasal verb. level off.** To move toward stability or consistency. **—idiom. on the level.** *Informal.* Without deception or dishonesty. [< Lat. *libra*, balance.]

—**lev'el·er** n. —**lev'el·ly** adv. —**lev'el·ness** n.
Syns: level, even, flat, flush, plane, smooth, straight adj.

level

lev·el·head·ed (lĕv'əl-hĕd'ĭd) adj. Characteristically self-composed and sensible. —**lev'el·head'ed·ness** n.

lev·er (lĕv'ər, lē'vər) n. 1. A simple machine consisting of a rigid bar or rod that turns on a fixed fulcrum. 2. A projecting handle used to operate a device or machine. —v. To move or lift with a lever. [< OFr. lever, to raise.]

lev·er·age (lĕv'ər-ĭj, lē'vər-) n. 1. The action or mechanical advantage of a lever. 2. Positional advantage.

le·vi·a·than (lə-vī'ə-thən) n. 1. A huge sea monster. 2. Something very large or monstrous. [< Heb. liwhyāthān.]

Le·vi's (lē'vīz'). A trademark for close-fitting trousers of heavy denim.

lev·i·tate (lĕv'ĭ-tāt') v. -tat·ed, -tat·ing. To rise or raise in the air in apparent defiance of gravity. [< LEVITY.] —**lev'i·ta'tion** n. —**lev'i·ta'tor** n.

Le·vit·i·cus (lə-vĭt'ĭ-kəs) n. See table at **Bible**.

lev·i·ty (lĕv'ĭ-tē) n., pl. -ties. Lightness of speech or attitude; frivolity. [< Lat. levitas.]

lev·y (lĕv'ē) v. -ied, -y·ing. 1. To impose or collect (a tax). 2. To draft into military service. 3. To wage (a war). 4. To confiscate property. —n. 1. The act or process of levying. 2. Money, troops, or property levied. [< OFr. lever, to raise.] —**lev'i·er** n.

lewd (lood) adj. -er, -est. 1. Obscene; indecent. 2. Lustful. [< OE lǣwede, ignorant.] —**lewd'ly** adv. —**lewd'ness** n.

lex·i·cog·ra·phy (lĕk'sĭ-kŏg'rə-fē) n. The process or work of writing dictionaries. [LEXICO(N) + -GRAPHY.] —**lex'i·cog'ra·pher** n. —**lex'i·co·graph'ic** (-kə-grăf'ĭk) or **lex'i·co·graph'i·cal** adj. —**lex'i·co·graph'i·cal·ly** adv.

lex·i·con (lĕk'sĭ-kŏn') n. 1. A dictionary. 2. A specialized vocabulary. [< Gk. lexikos, of words.] —**lex'i·cal** adj.

Li The symbol for the element lithium.

li·a·bil·i·ty (lī'ə-bĭl'ĭ-tē) n., pl. -ties. 1. A debt. 2. Legal responsibility to fulfill some contract or obligation. 3. A hindrance; handicap. 4. A tendency; susceptibility.

li·a·ble (lī'ə-bəl) adj. 1. Legally obligated; responsible. 2. Susceptible; subject. 3. Likely; apt. [Perh. < OFr. lier, to bind.]

li·ai·son (lē'ā-zŏn', lē-ā'zŏn', lē'ə-) n. 1. Communication between groups or units. 2. A channel or means of communication. 3. A love affair. [< OFr. lier, to bind.]

li·ar (lī'ər) n. A person who tells lies.

li·ba·tion (lī-bā'shən) n. 1. A sacrificial pouring of a liquid or the liquid thus poured. 2. Informal. An alcoholic drink. [< Lat. libare, to pour out as an offering.]

li·bel (lī'bəl) n. 1. A written, printed, or pictorial statement that unjustly damages a person's reputation. 2. The action or crime of presenting such a statement to the public. —v. -beled or -belled, -bel·ing or -bel·ling. To make or publish a libel (about). [< Lat. libellus, petition.] —**li'bel·er** or **li'bel·ist** n. —**li'bel·ous** adj.

lib·er·al (lĭb'ər-əl, lĭb'rəl) adj. 1. Generous in amount or in giving. 2. Approximate; loose. 3. Of or relating to the cultivation of general knowledge and the humanities: the liberal arts. 4. Broad-minded; tolerant. 5. Favoring civil liberties, democratic reforms, and the use of public resources to promote social progress. —n. One holding liberal political or cultural views. [< Lat. liber, free.] —**lib'er·al·ism** n. —**lib'er·al'i·ty** (lĭb'ə-răl'ĭ-tē) n. —**lib'er·al·ize'** v. —**lib'er·al·ly** adv.

lib·er·ate (lĭb'ə-rāt') v. -at·ed, -at·ing. To set free, as from oppression or confinement. [Lat. liberare.] —**lib'er·a'tion** n. —**lib'er·a'tion·ist** n. —**lib'er·a'tor** n.

lib·er·tar·i·an (lĭb'ər-târ'ē-ən) n. A person who believes in freedom of action and thought. —**lib'er·tar'i·an·ism** n.

lib·er·tine (lĭb'ər-tēn') n. A sexually promiscuous person. [< Lat. libertinus, freed slave.] —**lib'er·tine'** adj. —**lib'er·tin·ism** n.

lib·er·ty (lĭb'ər-tē) n., pl. -ties. 1. a. The condition of being free from restriction or control; freedom. b. The right to act as one chooses. 2. Freedom from confinement or servitude. 3. Permission to do something; authorization or privilege. 4. Often liberties. Unwarranted familiarity. 5. Authorized leave from naval duty. [< Lat. libertas.]

li·bi·do (lĭ-bē'dō, -bī'-) n., pl. -dos. 1. The psychic and emotional energy associated with basic biological drives. 2. Sexual desire. [Lat., desire.] —**li·bid'i·nal** adj. —**li·bid'i·nous** adj.

Li·bra (lī'brə, lē'-) n. 1. A constellation in the Southern Hemisphere near Scorpio and Virgo. 2. The 7th sign of the zodiac.

li·brar·i·an (lī-brâr'ē-ən) n. A custodian of a library. —**li·brar'i·an·ship'** n.

li·brar·y (lī'brĕr'ē) n., pl. -ies. 1. A place to keep literary and artistic materials, such as books, periodicals, and prints, for reading, reference, or borrowing. 2. A collection of such materials. [< Lat. libraria, bookshop.]

li·bret·to (lĭ-brĕt'ō) n., pl. -tos or -bret·ti (-brĕt'ē). The text of an opera or other dramatic musical work. [Ital., dim. of libro, book.] —**li·bret'tist** n.

lice (līs) n. A pl. of **louse**.

li·cense (lī'səns) n. Also chiefly Brit. **li·cence**. 1. a. Official or legal permission to do or own a specified thing. b. Proof of permission granted, usu. in the form of a document, card, plate, or tag. 2. Deviation from normal rules, practices, or methods. 3. Latitude of action, esp. in behavior or speech. 4. Excessive freedom. —v. -censed, -cens·ing. 1. To give permission to or for. 2. To grant a license to or for; authorize. [< Lat. licēre, to be allowed.] —**li'cens·a·ble** adj. —**li'cens·ee'** n. —**li'cens·er** n.

li·cen·tious (lī-sĕn'shəs) adj. Morally unrestrained; immoral. [Lat. licentiosus.] —**li·cen'tious·ly** adv. —**li·cen'tious·ness** n.

li·chee (lē'chē) n. Var. of **litchi**.

li·chen (lī'kən) n. A plant consisting of a fungus in close combination with certain algae and forming a scaly or branching growth on rocks or tree trunks. [< Gk. leikhēn.] —**li'chen·ous** adj.

lic·it (lĭs′ĭt) *adj.* Lawful. [< Lat. *licēre*, to be allowed.] —**lic′it·ly** *adv.* —**lic′it·ness** *n.*

lick (lĭk) *v.* **1.** To pass the tongue over. **2.** To flicker over like a tongue. **3.** *Slang.* To thrash or defeat. —*n.* **1.** The act of licking. **2.** A small quantity. **3.** A place frequented by animals that lick an exposed salt deposit. **4.** A blow. [< OE *liccian.*] —**lick′er** *n.*

lick·e·ty·split (lĭk′ĭ-tē-splĭt′) *adv. Informal.* With great speed. [< LICK and SPLIT.]

lick·ing (lĭk′ĭng) *n. Slang.* **1.** A beating; thrashing. **2.** A severe loss or defeat.

lic·o·rice (lĭk′ər-ĭs, -ĭsh) *n.* **1.** A plant with a sweet, distinctively flavored root. **2.** A candy made from or flavored with this root. [< Gk. *glukurrhiza.*]

lid (lĭd) *n.* **1.** A removable cover for a hollow receptacle. **2.** An eyelid. [< OE *hlid.*] —**lid′ded** *adj.* —**lid′less** *adj.*

lie¹ (lī) *v.* **lay** (lā), **lain** (lān), **ly·ing.** **1.** To be in or place oneself in a flat, horizontal, or recumbent position; recline. **2.** To be or remain in a specific condition. **3.** To occupy a place. **4.** To extend. —*n.* The position in which something is situated. [< OE *licgan.*]

lie² (lī) *n.* A deliberate falsehood. —*v.* **lied, ly·ing.** To tell a lie or convey a false image or impression. [< OE *lēogan.*]

Syns: *lie, falsehood, falsity, fib, fiction, story, tale, untruth* n.

lied (lēd, lēt) *n., pl.* **lie·der** (lē′dər). A German lyric song.

lie detector *n.* A machine used to detect lying by recording the physiological functions of a subject being interrogated.

lief (lēf) *adv.* Readily; willingly. [< OE *lēof,* dear.]

liege (lēj) *n.* **1.** A feudal lord. **2.** A vassal. —*adj.* Loyal; faithful. [< LLat. *laetus,* serf, of Gmc. orig.]

lien (lēn, lē′ən) *n.* The legal right to take or hold the property of a debtor as a payment or security for the debt. [< Lat. *ligamen,* bond.]

lieu (lōō) *n. Archaic.* Place; stead. —**idiom. in lieu of.** In place of; instead of. [OFr.]

lieu·ten·ant (lōō-tĕn′ənt) *n.* **1.** A military officer ranking next below a captain. **2.** A naval officer ranking next below a lieutenant commander. **3.** An officer in a police or fire department ranking below a captain. **4.** One who can act in place of a superior; deputy. [< OFr., deputy.] —**lieu·ten′an·cy** *n.*

lieutenant colonel *n.* A military officer ranking next below a colonel.

lieutenant commander *n.* A naval officer ranking next below a commander.

lieutenant general *n.* A military officer ranking next below a general.

life (līf) *n., pl.* **lives** (līvz). **1.** The quality manifested in functions such as metabolism, growth, response to stimulation, and reproduction by which living organisms are distinguished from dead organisms or inanimate matter. **2.** Living organisms collectively: *plant life.* **3.** A living being. **4.** The interval between the birth or inception of an organism and its death. **5.** A biography. **6.** Human activities and relationships: *everyday life.* **7.** A manner of living: *country life.* **8.** Animation; liveliness. [< OE *līf.*] —**life′less** *adj.* —**life′less·ly** *adv.* —**life′less·ness** *n.* —**life′like′** *adj.*

life-blood (līf′blŭd′) *n.* The indispensable vital part of a thing.

life·boat (līf′bōt′) *n.* A boat used for abandoning ship or for rescue service.

lifeboat   **life preserver**

life·guard (līf′gärd′) *n.* An expert swimmer employed to safeguard bathers.

life line *n.* **1.** A line thrown to a person in danger of drowning or falling. **2.** A means or route by which necessary supplies are transported.

life·long (līf′lông′, -lŏng′) *adj.* Continuing for a lifetime.

life preserver *n.* A buoyant device designed to keep a person afloat in water.

life-size (līf′sīz′) *adj.* Also **life-sized** (-sīzd′). Being of the same size as the original: *a life-size statue.*

life·style (līf′stīl′) *n.* Also **life-style** or **life style.** A way of life that reflects the attitudes and values of an individual or a group.

life·time (līf′tīm′) *n.* The time during which an individual is alive.

life·work (līf′wûrk′) *n.* The chief or entire work of a person's lifetime.

lift (lĭft) *v.* **1. a.** To raise; elevate. **b.** To ascend; rise. **2. a.** To revoke; rescind. **b.** To put an end to. **3.** *Informal.* To steal. **4.** To pay off (a debt). —*phrasal verb.* **lift off.** To begin flight. —*n.* **1.** The act or process of raising or rising. **2.** Power or force available for raising. **3.** A load. **4.** The extent or height something is raised. **5.** A rise in the level of the ground. **6.** A rising of spirits. **7.** A machine designed to raise or carry something. **8.** *Chiefly Brit.* An elevator. **9.** Help or a ride along one's way. **10.** The component of the aerodynamic force acting on an aircraft, perpendicular to the relative wind and normally exerted in an upward direction. [< ON *lypta.*] —**lift′er** *n.*

lift-off (lĭft′ôf′, -ŏf′) *n.* The initial movement in the flight of a rocket or other craft.

lig·a·ment (lĭg′ə-mənt) *n.* A sheet or band of tough, fibrous tissue that connects bones or cartilages or supports an organ. [< Lat. *ligamentum,* bond.] —**lig′a·men′tous** *adj.*

lig·a·ture (lĭg′ə-chŏŏr′, -chər) *n.* **1.** The act of tying together or binding. **2.** A cord, wire, or bandage used for tying. **3.** A character combining two or more letters, as æ.

light¹ (līt) *n.* **1.** Electromagnetic radiation that can be perceived by the human eye. **2.** The sensation of the perception of such radiation; brightness. **3.** A source of illumination, such as the sun or an electric lamp. **4.** The illumination derived from such a source. **5.** Daylight. **6.** Dawn; daybreak. **7.** A means or agent, as a match or cigarette lighter, for igniting a fire. **8.** A way of looking at or considering something; aspect. **9.** Understanding; enlightenment. **10.** A prominent or distinguished person. —*adj.* **-er, -est. 1.** Not dark; bright. **2.** Mixed with white: *a light pink.* —*v.* **lighted** or **lit** (lĭt), **light·ing. 1.** To set or be set on fire; ignite. **2.** To cause to give out light: *light a lamp.* **3.** To illuminate. —*idioms.* **come to light.** To be revealed. **in (the) light of.** In consideration of. **see the light.** To perceive a hitherto hidden meaning. [< OE *lēoht.*] —**light'ness** *n.*

Usage: Lighted and *lit* are equally acceptable as past tense and past participle of *light.* When used as an adjective, *lighted* is more common: *a lighted window.* But *lit* is the usual form in combinations: *moonlit; starlit.*

light² (lĭt) *adj.* **-er, -est. 1.** Not heavy. **2.** Of relatively low density. **3.** Having less force, quantity, intensity, or volume than normal. **4.** Moderate; mild. **5.** Not serious or profound. **6.** Free from worries or troubles; blithe. **7.** Frivolous; silly; trivial. **8.** Quick to change or be swayed; fickle. **9.** Dizzy. **10.** Moving quickly and easily; graceful. —*adv.* **1.** Lightly. **2.** With little weight or few burdens: *traveling light.* —*v.* **lighted** or **lit** (lĭt), **light·ing. 1.** To dismount; alight. **2.** To perch; land. —*phrasal verb.* **light into.** To assail. —*idiom.* **make light of.** To minimize. [< OE *lēoht.*] —**light'ly** *adv.* —**light'ness** *n.*

light·en¹ (lĭt'n) *v.* To make or become light or lighter; brighten. —**light'en·er** *n.*

light·en² (lĭt'n) *v.* **1.** To make or become less heavy. **2.** To make or become less oppressive, burdensome, or severe.

light·er¹ (lī'tər) *n.* **1.** One that ignites. **2.** A device for lighting a cigarette, cigar, or pipe.

light·er² (lī'tər) *n.* A barge used to unload cargo from a larger ship unable to enter a harbor. [ME.]

light·face (lĭt'fās') *n.* A typeface with relatively thin, light lines. —**light'faced'** *adj.*

light·head·ed (lĭt'hĕd'ĭd) *adj.* **1.** Dizzy, giddy, or faint. **2.** Frivolous; silly. —**light'head'ed·ly** *adv.* —**light'head'ed·ness** *n.*

light·heart·ed (lĭt'här'tĭd) *adj.* Blithe; carefree; gay. —**light'heart'ed·ly** *adv.* —**light'heart'ed·ness** *n.*

light·house (lĭt'hous') *n.* A tall structure topped by a powerful light that guides ships.

light·ing (lī'tĭng) *n.* **1.** The state of being lighted; illumination. **2.** The method or equipment used to provide artificial illumination. **3.** The act or process of igniting.

light·ning (lĭt'nĭng) *n.* A large-scale high-tension natural electric discharge in the atmosphere, accompanied by a visible flash. —*adj.* Very fast or sudden. [< LIGHT¹.]

lightning bug *n.* A firefly.

lightning rod *n.* A metal rod placed high on a structure to prevent damage by conducting lightning to ground.

light·weight (lĭt'wāt') *n.* **1.** One that weighs relatively little, esp. a boxer or wrestler weighing between 127 and 135 pounds. **2.** A person of little ability, intelligence, influence, or importance. —**light'weight'** *adj.*

light-year (lĭt'yîr') *n.* Also **light year.** The distance that light travels through empty space in one year, approx. 5.878 trillion miles or 9.458 trillion kilometers.

lig·nite (lĭg'nīt') *n.* A low-grade, brownish-black coal. [< Lat. *lignum,* wood.]

lig·num vi·tae (lĭg'nəm vī'tē) *n.* **1.** A tropical American tree with very hard, heavy wood. **2.** The wood of such a tree. [NLat., wood of life.]

lig·ro·in (lĭg'rō-ĭn) *n.* A volatile, flammable fraction of petroleum, obtained by distillation, and used as a solvent. [Orig. unknown.]

lik·a·ble (lī'kə-bəl) *adj.* Also **like·a·ble.** Easy to like; pleasing. —**lik'a·ble·ness** *n.*

like¹ (līk) *v.* **liked, lik·ing. 1.** To find pleasant; enjoy. **2.** To want, wish, or prefer. **3.** To be fond of. —*n.* **likes.** The things one enjoys; preferences. [< OE *līcian.*] —**lik'er** *n.*

Syns: like, enjoy, relish, savor v.

like² (līk) *prep.* **1.** Similar or similarly to. **2.** In the typical manner of: *That's not like you.* **3.** Disposed to: *feel like eating.* **4.** Indicative of: *It looks like rain.* —*adj.* **1.** Similar. **2.** Equivalent; equal. —*adv.* As if: *He ran like crazy.* —*n.* Similar or related persons or things: *bills, coins, and the like.* —*conj. Nonstandard.* **1.** In the same way; as: *Tell it like it is.* **2.** As if: *It rained like the skies were falling.* [< OE *gelīc,* similar.]

Syns: like, alike, analogous, comparable, corresponding, equivalent, parallel, uniform adj.

Usage: Like has been used as a conjunction since Shakespeare's time by the best writers. But the usage has come under such heavy fire from purists in recent times that it is best avoided on grounds of prudence. Therefore, use *The engine responds as* (not *like*) *it should.* There can be no objection to the use of *like* when no verb follows: *He took to politics like a duck to water.*

-like *suff.* Resembling or characteristic of: *ladylike.* [< LIKE².]

like·li·hood (līk'lē-hŏŏd') *n.* **1.** The chance of a certain thing happening; probability. **2.** Something that is probable.

like·ly (līk'lē) *adj.* **-li·er, -li·est. 1.** Apparently destined; apt: *likely to be successful.* **2.** Expected to occur. **3.** Credible; plausible: *a likely excuse.* **4.** Apparently suitable: *a likely place.* **5.** Apparently capable of doing well; promising: *a likely lad.* —*adv.* Probably.

like·mind·ed (līk'mīn'dĭd) *adj.* Of the same way of thinking or turn of mind.

lik·en (lī'kən) *v.* To see, mention, or show as like or similar; compare.

like·ness (līk'nĭs) *n.* **1.** Similarity or resemblance. **2.** An imitative appearance; guise. **3.** A copy or picture of something; image.

like·wise (līk'wīz') *adv.* **1.** In the same way; similarly. **2.** As well; also.

Usage: Likewise, since it is not a conjunction, cannot take the place of *and,* as in *He risked his fortune, likewise his honor;* properly, *He risked his fortune and likewise his honor.*

lik·ing (lī'kĭng) *n.* **1.** A feeling of fondness or affection. **2.** Preference; inclination.

li·ku·ta (lē-kŏŏ'tä) *n., pl.* **ma·ku·ta** (mä-). See table at **currency.** [Native word in Zaire.]

li·lac (lī'lək, -lŏk', -lăk') *n.* **1.** A shrub widely cultivated for its clusters of fragrant purplish or white flowers. **2.** A pale purple. [< Ar. *līlak.*] —**li'lac** *adj.*

li·lan·ge·ni (lĭ-läng'gĕ-nē) *n.* See table at **currency.** [Native word in Swaziland.]

lilt (lĭlt) *n.* **1.** A light, happy tune or song. **2.** A cheerful, rhythmic, or lively manner of speaking. [< ME *lilten,* to sound an alarm.]

lil·y (lĭl'ē) *n., pl.* **-ies. 1.** Any of various related plants with showy, often trumpet-shaped flowers. **2.** Any of various similar plants. [< Lat. *lilium*.]

lil·y-liv·ered (lĭl'ē-lĭv'ərd) *adj.* Cowardly.

lily of the valley *n., pl.* **lilies of the valley.** A plant with a slender cluster of fragrant, bell-shaped white flowers

lily of the valley   lily pad

lily pad *n.* One of the floating leaves of a water lily.

li·ma bean (lī'mə) *n.* **1.** A plant having flat pods containing large, light-green, edible seeds. **2.** The seed of such a plant. [< *Lima*, Peru.]

limb (lĭm) *n.* **1.** A large tree branch. **2.** One of the jointed appendages of an animal, as an arm, leg, wing, or flipper. [< OE *lim*.]

lim·ber (lĭm'bər) *adj.* **1.** Bending or flexing readily; pliable. **2.** Capable of moving, bending, or contorting easily; agile. **—***v.* To make or become limber: *limbering up before running.* [Orig. unknown.] **—lim'ber·ness** *n.*

lim·bo (lĭm'bō) *n., pl.* **-bos.** **1.** Often **Limbo.** In some Christian theologies, the abode of souls kept from heaven by circumstance, such as lack of baptism. **2.** A place or condition of neglect, stagnation, or prolonged uncertainty. [< Lat. *limbus*, border.]

Lim·burg·er (lĭm'bûr'gər) *n.* A soft white cheese with a strong odor and flavor. [< *Limburg*, Belgium.]

lime¹ (lĭm) *n.* **1.** A green, egg-shaped citrus fruit with acid juice used as flavoring. **2.** A tree bearing limes. [< Ar. *līmah*.]

lime² (lĭm) *n.* An Old World linden tree. [< OE *lind*.]

lime³ (lĭm) *n.* **1.** Calcium oxide. **2.** Birdlime. [< OE *līm*.] **—lim'y** *adj.*

lime·light (lĭm'līt') *n.* **1.** A bright light produced by directing a flame at a cylinder of heated lime, formerly used in the theater. **2.** A focus of public attention or notoriety: *in the limelight.*

lim·er·ick (lĭm'ər-ĭk) *n.* A light humorous or nonsensical verse of five lines with the rhyme scheme *aabba.* [< *Limerick*, Ireland.]

lime·stone (lĭm'stōn') *n.* A shaly or sandy sedimentary rock composed chiefly of calcium carbonate.

lim·it (lĭm'ĭt) *n.* **1.** The point, edge, or line beyond which something cannot or may not proceed. **2.** Often **limits.** A boundary; bounds: *within city limits.* **3.** The greatest amount or number allowed. **—***v.* To confine or restrict within limits. [< Lat. *limes*.] **—lim'it·a·ble** *adj.* **—lim'i·ta'tion** *n.* **—lim'it·er** *n.* **—lim'it·less** *adj.* **—lim'it·less·ly** *adv.*

lim·it·ed (lĭm'ĭ-tĭd) *adj.* **1.** Having a limit or limits. **2.** Chiefly *Brit.* Limiting the liability of each stockholder to his actual investment: *a limited company.* **3.** Designating trains or

buses that make few stops. **—lim'i·ted·ly** *adv.* **—lim'i·ted·ness** *n.*

lim·ou·sine (lĭm'ə-zēn', lĭm'ə-zēn') *n.* **1.** A large, luxurious automobile. **2.** A small bus used to carry passengers to airports, hotels, etc. [< *Limousin*, a region of France.]

limp (lĭmp) *v.* To walk lamely, favoring one leg. **—***n.* An irregular, jerky, or awkward gait. **—***adj.* **-er, -est.** Lacking rigidity; flabby. [Prob. < obs. *limphalt*, lame.] **—limp'ly** *adv.* **—limp'ness** *n.*

lim·pet (lĭm'pĭt) *n.* A marine mollusk that has a tent-shaped shell and adheres to rocks of tidal areas. [Poss. < ME *lempet*.]

lim·pid (lĭm'pĭd) *adj.* Crystal clear; transparent. [< Lat. *limpidus*.] **—lim·pid'i·ty** or **lim'pid·ness** *n.* **—lim'pid·ly** *adv.*

lin·age (lī'nĭj) *n.* Also **line·age.** The number of lines of printed or written material.

linch·pin (lĭnch'pĭn') *n.* A metal pin inserted in the end of a shaft, as in an axle, to prevent a wheel from slipping off. [OE *lynis*, linchpin + PIN.]

lin·den (lĭn'dən) *n.* A shade tree with heart-shaped leaves and yellowish, often fragrant flowers. [< OE *lind*.]

line¹ (lĭn) *n.* **1. a.** The locus of a point having one degree of freedom; curve. **b.** A set of points (x, y) that satisfy the equation $ax + by + c = 0$, where a and b are not both zero. **2.** A thin, continuous mark, as that made by a pen, pencil, or brush. **3.** A crease in the skin; wrinkle. **4.** A border or limit. **5.** A contour or outline. **6.** A cable, rope, string, cord, wire, etc. **7.** An electric-power transmission cable. **8.** A telephone connection. **9.** A system of transportation, 'esp. a company owning such a system. **10.** A course of progress or movement: *line of flight.* **11.** A general manner or course of procedure: *different lines of thought.* **12.** An official or prescribed policy: *the party line.* **13.** Alignment: *bring the wheels into line.* **14. a.** One's trade or occupation. **b.** The range of one's competence: *out of my line.* **15.** Merchandise of a similar nature: *a line of small tools.* **16.** A group of persons or things arranged in a row: *stand in line.* **17.** A row of words printed or written across a page. **18.** A brief letter or note. **19.** Often **lines.** The dialogue of a play or other theatrical presentation. **20.** A calculated or glib way of speaking. **21.** *Football.* **a.** A line of scrimmage. **b.** The linemen. **—***v.* **lined, lin·ing.** **1.** To mark with lines. **2.** To place in a series or row. **3.** To form a row or rows (along). **—phrasal verb.** **line up.** **1.** To align. **2.** To secure; gain: *lined up considerable support.* **—idioms. hold the line.** To stand firm. **in line. 1.** Behaving properly. **2.** Consistent; in accordance. **in line for.** Due for: *in line for a promotion.* **on the line.** *Informal.* **1.** Immediately available. **2.** At stake; out of line. **1.** Improper; uncalled-for. **2.** Not in agreement; inconsistent. [< Lat. *linea*, cord < *linum*, thread.]

line² (lĭn) *v.* **lined, lin·ing.** **1.** To sew or fit a covering to the inside surface of. **2.** To cover the inner surface of. [< OE *līn*, flax < Lat. *linum*.]

lin·e·age¹ (lĭn'ē-ĭj) *n.* Direct descent from a

particular ancestor; ancestry. [< OFr. *linage*, ult. < Lat. *linum*, thread.]

line·age² (lĭ'nĭj) *n.* Var. of **linage**.

lin·e·al (lĭn'ē-əl) *adj.* **1.** In the direct line of descent from an ancestor. **2.** Linear. **—lin'e·al·ly** *adv.*

lin·e·a·ment (lĭn'ē-ə-mənt) *n.* A distinctive shape, contour, or feature, esp. of the face. [< Lat. *lineare*, to make straight.]

lin·e·ar (lĭn'ē-ər) *adj.* **1.** Of, relating to, or resembling a line or lines. **2.** Narrow and elongated; *a linear leaf.* [< Lat. *linea*, line.] **—lin'e·ar·ly** *adv.*

line·back·er (lĭn'băk'ər) *n.* A defensive football player positioned just behind the line.

line drive *n.* A batted baseball hit in a roughly straight horizontal line.

line·man (lĭn'mən) *n.* **1.** One who installs or repairs telephone, telegraph, or other electric power lines. **2.** A football player positioned on the forward line.

lin·en (lĭn'ən) *n.* **1.** Thread or cloth made of flax. **2.** Often **linens.** Cloth household articles, such as sheets and towels, made of linen or of other fabrics. [< Lat. *linum*, thread.] **—lin'en** *adj.*

line of scrimmage *n.* An imaginary line across a football field on which the ball rests and where the teams line up for each play.

lin·er¹ (lĭ'nər) *n.* **1.** A commercial ship or airplane, esp. one carrying passengers on a regular route. **2.** One that makes lines. **3.** *Baseball.* A line drive.

lin·er² (lĭ'nər) *n.* **1.** One who puts in linings. **2.** Something used as a lining.

lines·man (lĭnz'mən) *n.* **1.** A football official who marks the downs. **2.** An official in various court games whose chief duty is to call shots that fall out of bounds.

line·up (lĭn'ŭp') *n.* Also **line-up. 1.** A line of persons formed for inspection or identification. **2.** The members of a team chosen to start a game. **3.** A list of personnel.

-ling *suff.* **1.** One who belongs to or is connected with: *hireling.* **2.** One that is small: *duckling.* **3.** One having a specified quality: *underling.* [< OE.]

lin·ger (lĭng'gər) *v.* **1.** To remain as though reluctant to leave; tarry. **2.** To persist: *The memory still lingers.* **3.** To be tardy in acting; procrastinate. [< OE *lengra*, longer.] **—lin'ger·er** *n.* **—lin'ger·ing·ly** *adv.*

lin·ge·rie (län'zhə-rē', län'zhə-rā') *n.* Women's underwear and sleeping garments. [< Lat. *linum*, thread.]

lin·go (lĭng'gō) *n., pl.* **-goes. 1.** Specialized language; jargon. **2.** Unintelligible language. [< Lat. *lingua*, language.]

lin·gua fran·ca (lĭng'gwə frăng'kə) *n.* A language used between people who normally speak different languages. [Ital.]

lin·gual (lĭng'gwəl) *adj.* Of or pronounced with the tongue. [< Lat. *lingua*, tongue.] **—lin'gual·ly** *adv.*

lin·guist (lĭng'gwĭst) *n.* **1.** One who speaks several languages fluently. **2.** A specialist in linguistics. [Lat. *lingua*, language + -IST.]

lin·guis·tics (lĭng-gwĭs'tĭks) *n.* (*used with a sing. verb*). The study of the nature and structure of human speech. **—lin·guis'tic** *adj.* **—lin·guis'ti·cal·ly** *adv.*

lin·i·ment (lĭn'ə-mənt) *n.* A soothing liquid medicine rubbed on the skin. [< Lat. *linere*, to anoint.]

lin·ing (lĭ'nĭng) *n.* A covering or coating for an inside surface.

link (lĭngk) *n.* **1.** One of the rings or loops that form a chain. **2.** One of a connected series of things: *a sausage link.* **3.** A bond or tie. **—v.** To connect or become connected with or as if with links. [ME *linke*, of Scand. orig.]

link·age (lĭng'kĭj) *n.* **1.** The act or process of linking or the condition of being linked. **2.** A system of interconnected elements.

linking verb *n.* A verb that connects the subject of a sentence with a predicate adjective or predicate nominative.

links (lĭngks) *pl.n.* A golf course. [< OE *hlinc*, ridge.]

lin·net (lĭn'ĭt) *n.* A small, brownish Old World songbird. [< Lat. *linum*, flax.]

li·no·le·um (lĭ-nō'lē-əm) *n.* A durable, washable material made in sheets, used as a floor and counter-top covering. [Orig. a trademark.]

Li·no·type (lĭ'nə-tīp'). A trademark for a keyboard-operated machine that sets a line of type on a single metal slug.

lin·seed (lĭn'sēd') *n.* The seed of flax, esp. as the source of a yellowish oil used as a drying agent in paints, varnishes, etc. [< OE *līnsǣd.*]

lint (lĭnt) *n.* Clinging bits of fiber and fluff; fuzz. [< Lat. *linteum*, linen cloth.]

lin·tel (lĭn'tl) *n.* The horizontal beam over the top of a door or window. [< Lat. *limitaris*, a boundary.]

li·on (lī'ən) *n.* **1.** A large carnivorous cat of Africa and India, having a short tawny coat and a thick mane in the male. **2. Lion.** Leo. **3.** A celebrity. [< Gk. *leōn*.] **—li'on·ess** *n.*

lion

li·on·heart·ed (lī'ən-här'tĭd) *adj.* Extraordinarily courageous.

li·on·ize (lī'ə-nīz') *v.* **-ized, -iz·ing.** To treat as a celebrity.

lip (lĭp) *n.* **1. a.** Either of the fleshy, muscular folds of tissue that together surround the mouth. **b.** A part or structure that similarly encircles an opening. **2.** A protruding part of certain flowers. **3.** The tip of a pouring spout. **4.** *Slang.* Insolent talk. [< OE *lippa*.]

lip reading *n.* The interpretation of inaudible speech by watching lip and facial movements. **—lip'-read'** (lĭp'rēd') *v.* **—lip reader** *n.*

lip service *n.* Insincere agreement or payment of respect.

lip·stick (lĭp'stĭk') *n.* A stick of waxy lip coloring enclosed in a small case.

liq·ue·fy (lĭk'wə-fī') *v.* **-fied, -fy·ing.** Also **liq·ui·fy.** To make or become liquid. [< Lat. *liquefacere*.] **—liq'ue·fac'tion** (-făk'shən) *n.*

li·queur (lĭ-kûr', -kyōōr') *n.* A sweet, syrupy alcoholic beverage. [< Lat. *liquor*, a liquid.]

liq·uid (lĭk'wĭd) *n.* A substance capable of flowing or of being poured. —*adj.* 1. Of or being a liquid. 2. Liquefied, esp.: **a.** Melted by heating: *liquid wax.* **b.** Condensed by cooling: *liquid oxygen.* 3. Readily converted into cash: *liquid assets.* [< Lat. *liquēre*, to be liquid.] —**li·quid'i·ty** (lĭ-kwĭd'ĭ-tē) *n.*

liq·ui·date (lĭk'wĭ-dāt') *v.* -**dat·ed**, -**dat·ing.** 1. To pay off or settle (e.g. a debt). 2. To wind up the affairs of: *liquidate a business.* 3. To convert (assets) into cash. 4. To put an end to; abolish or kill. —**liq·ui·da'tion** *n.* —**liq'ui·da'tor** *n.*

liq·uor (lĭk'ər) *n.* 1. An alcoholic beverage made by distillation rather than by fermentation. 2. A liquid substance or solution. [Lat., a liquid.]

li·ra (lîr'ə, lē'rä) *n., pl.* **li·re** (lîr'ā, lē'rä) or -**ras.** See table at **currency.** [Ital.]

li·sen·te (lē-sĕn'tā) *n., pl.* -**te.** See table at **currency.** [Sotho.]

lisle (līl) *n.* A fine, smooth, tightly twisted thread spun from long-stapled cotton. [< *Lisle* (Lille), France.]

lisp (lĭsp) *n.* A speech defect or mannerism, esp. one in which *s* and *z* are pronounced (*th*) and (*th*). [< OE *wlisp.*] —**lisp** *v.* —**lisp'er** *n.*

lis·some (lĭs'əm) *adj.* Limber; nimble; lithe. [< LITHESOME.] —**lis'some·ly** *adv.* —**lis'some·ness** *n.*

list¹ (lĭst) *n.* A printed or written series of the names of persons or things, often arranged in a particular order. —*v.* 1. To make a list of; itemize. 2. To enter in a list. [< OItal. *lista*, of Gmc. orig.]

list² (lĭst) *n.* An inclination to one side, as of a ship; tilt. [Orig. unknown.] —**list** *v.*

lis·ten (lĭs'ən) *v.* 1. To make an effort to hear something. 2. To pay attention. [< OE *hlystan.*] —**lis'ten·er** *n.*

list·ing (lĭs'tĭng) *n.* 1. A list. 2. An entry in a list.

list·less (lĭst'lĭs) *adj.* Lacking energy or enthusiasm; lethargic. [Prob. OE *list*, ability + -LESS.] —**list'less·ly** *adv.* —**list'less·ness** *n.*

list price *n.* A basic published price, often subject to discount.

lit¹ (lĭt) *v.* A *p.t.* & *p.p.* of **light¹.**

lit² (lĭt) *v.* A *p.t.* & *p.p.* of **light².**

lit·a·ny (lĭt'n-ē) *n., pl.* -**nies.** 1. A prayer consisting of phrases recited by a leader alternating with responses by the congregation. 2. A repetitive recital. [< Gk. *litaneia*, entreaty.]

li·tchi (lē'chē) *n.* Also **li·chee.** 1. A Chinese tree that bears edible fruit. 2. Also **litchi nut.** The thin-shelled, fleshy fruit of the litchi. [Chin. *li⁴ zhī¹*]

li·ter (lē'tər) *n.* Also *chiefly Brit.* **li·tre.** A metric unit of volume, approx. 1.056 liquid quarts or 0.908 dry quart. [< Gk. *litra*, a unit of weight.]

lit·er·a·cy (lĭt'ər-ə-sē) *n.* The ability to read and write.

lit·er·al (lĭt'ər-əl) *adj.* 1. Upholding the exact meaning of a word or the words of a text. 2. Word for word; verbatim: *a literal translation.* 3. Concerned chiefly with facts; prosaic. 4. Of or expressed by letters. [< Lat. *littera*, letter.] —**lit'er·al·ly** *adv.* —**lit'er·al·ness** *n.*

lit·er·ar·y (lĭt'ə-rĕr'ē) *adj.* 1. Of or relating to literature. 2. **a.** Found in or appropriate to

literature: *a literary style.* **b.** Employed chiefly in writing rather than speaking: *literary language.* [Lat. *litterarius.*] —**lit'er·ar'i·ness** *n.*

lit·er·ate (lĭt'ər-ĭt) *adj.* 1. Able to read and write. 2. Skillful in the use of words. 3. Knowledgeable; well-read. [< Lat. *litteratus.*] —**lit'er·ate** *n.*

lit·er·a·ti (lĭt'ə-rä'tē) *pl.n.* Distinguished writers and scholars in general. [Ital.]

lit·er·a·ture (lĭt'ər-ə-chŏŏr', -chər) *n.* 1. Imaginative or creative writing. 2. The body of written work produced by scholars or researchers in a given field: *medical literature.* 3. Printed material of any kind, as for a political campaign. [< LLat. *litteratura.*]

lith- *pref.* Var. of **litho-.**

-lith *suff.* Stone or rock: *monolith.* [< Gk. *lithos*, stone.]

lithe (līth, līth) *adj.* **lith·er, lith·est.** 1. Readily bent; supple. 2. Graceful. [< OE *līthe.*] —**lithe'ly** *adv.* —**lithe'ness** *n.*

lithe·some (līth'səm, līth'-) *adj.* Lithe; lissome.

-lithic *suff.* Stone: *Neolithic.* [-LITH + -IC.]

lith·i·um (lĭth'ē-əm) *n.* *Symbol* Li A soft, silvery, highly reactive metallic element, used as a heat transfer medium, in thermonuclear weapons, and in various alloys. Atomic number 3; atomic weight 6.939.

litho- or **lith-** *pref.* Stone: *lithograph.* [< Gk. *lithos*, stone.]

lith·o·graph (lĭth'ə-grăf') *n.* A print produced by lithography. —**lith'o·graph'** *v.* —**li·thog'ra·pher** (lĭ-thŏg'rə-fər) *n.* —**lith'o·graph'ic** or **lith'o·graph'i·cal** *adj.* —**lith'o·graph'i·cal·ly** *adv.*

li·thog·ra·phy (lĭ-thŏg'rə-fē) *n.* A printing process in which the printing surface, often a metal plate, is treated so that ink will stick only to those parts that are to be printed.

Lith·u·a·ni·an (lĭth'ōō-ā'nē-ən) *n.* 1. An inhabitant or native of Lithuania. 2. The Baltic language of the Lithuanians. —**Lith'u·a'ni·an** *adj.*

lit·i·gant (lĭt'ĭ-gənt) *n.* One who is engaged in a lawsuit.

lit·i·gate (lĭt'ĭ-gāt') *v.* -**gat·ed**, -**gat·ing.** To engage in or subject to legal proceedings. [Lat. *litigare.*] —**lit'i·ga'tion** *n.* —**lit'i·ga'tor** *n.*

li·ti·gious (lĭ-tĭj'əs) *adj.* Given to or characterized by lawsuits. —**li·ti'gious·ly** *adv.* —**li·ti'gious·ness** *n.*

lit·mus (lĭt'məs) *n.* A blue powder, derived from certain lichens, that changes from blue to red in an acid solution and from red to blue in an alkaline solution. [Of Scand. orig.]

litmus paper *n.* White paper impregnated with litmus, used to distinguish acid and alkaline solutions.

li·tre (lī'tər) *n.* *Chiefly Brit.* Var. of **liter.**

lit·ter (lĭt'ər) *n.* 1. A couch mounted between shafts, used to carry a person from place to place. 2. A stretcher for the sick or wounded. 3. Straw or other material used as bedding for animals. 4. Young animals produced at one birth by a single mother. 5. Carelessly scattered scraps of waste material. —*v.* 1. To make untidy by discarding rubbish carelessly. 2. To scatter (litter) about. [< Lat. *lectus*, bed.] —**lit'ter·er** *n.*

lit·ter·bug (lĭt'ər-bŭg') n. Slang. One who litters public areas.

lit·tle (lĭt'l) adj. **-tler** or **less** (lĕs), **-tlest** or **least** (lēst). **1.** Small in size, quantity, or degree. **2. a.** Short in extent or duration; brief: little time. **b.** Unimportant; trivial; insignificant. **3.** Without much force; weak. **4.** Narrow; petty. **5.** Without much power or influence. **6. a.** Appealing; endearing: a little rascal. **b.** Contemptible. —adv. **less, least.** Not much: He sleeps little. —n. A small quantity: Give me a little. —idiom. **little by little.** Gradually. [< OE lȳtel.] —**lit'tle·ness** n.

Little Dipper n. Ursa Minor.

lit·to·ral (lĭt'ər-əl) adj. Of or existing on a shore. —n. A shore or coastal region. [< Lat. litus, shore.]

lit·ur·gy (lĭt'ər-jē) n., pl. **-gies.** The prescribed form for a religious service; ritual. [< Gk. leitouria, public service.] —**li·tur'gi·cal** (lĭ-tûr'jĭ-kəl) adj.

liv·a·ble (lĭv'ə-bəl) adj. Also **live·a·ble. 1.** Suitable to live in; habitable. **2.** Endurable.

live¹ (lĭv) v. **lived, liv·ing. 1.** To have life; continue to remain alive. **2.** To reside. **3.** To pass; spend: live a full life. **4.** To pass life in a particular manner. **5.** To remain in human memory, usage, or general acceptance. —phrasal verbs. **live down.** To bear the shame of over a period of time. **live with.** To put up with; resign oneself to. [< OE libban.]

live² (lĭv) adj. **1.** Having life; living. **2.** Broadcast while actually being performed. **3.** Of current interest. **4.** Glowing; burning. **5.** Not yet exploded: live ammunition. **6.** Carrying an electric current. [< ALIVE.]

live·li·hood (lĭv'lē-hŏŏd') n. Means of support; subsistence. [< OE līflād.]

live·long (lĭv'lông', -lŏng') adj. Complete; whole: the livelong day. [ME lefe long, dear long.]

live·ly (lĭv'lē) adj. **-li·er, -li·est. 1.** Full of life, energy, or activity; vigorous. **2.** Full of spirit; animated: a lively tune. **3.** Intense; keen: a lively discussion. **4.** Cheerful. **5.** Bouncing readily upon impact, as a ball. —adv. In a vigorous, energetic, or spirited manner. —**live'li·ness** n.

liv·en (lĭ'vən) v. To make or become lively or livelier.

liv·er (lĭv'ər) n. A large gland in the abdomen of vertebrates that secretes bile and acts in the formation of blood and the metabolism of carbohydrates, fats, proteins, minerals, and vitamins. [< OE lifer.]

liv·er·wort (lĭv'ər-wûrt', -wôrt') n. **1.** Any of various green nonflowering plants related to the mosses. **2.** The hepatica.

liv·er·wurst (lĭv'ər-wûrst', -wŏŏrst') n. A sausage made of or containing ground liver.

liv·er·y (lĭv'ə-rē, lĭv'rē) n., pl. **-ies. 1.** A uniform worn by the male servants of a household. **2. a.** The stabling and care of horses. **b.** The hiring out of horses and carriages. [< OFr. livree, delivery.] —**liv'er·ied** adj. —**liv'ery·man** n.

lives (lĭvz) n. Pl. of **life.**

live·stock (lĭv'stŏk') n. Domestic animals, such as cattle or horses, raised for home use or for profit.

live wire (lĭv) n. **1.** A wire carrying electric current. **2.** Slang. A vivacious, alert, or energetic person.

liv·id (lĭv'ĭd) adj. **1.** Discolored, as from a bruise. **2.** Ashen or pale, as from anger. [< Lat. lividus.] —**li·vid'i·ty** (lĭ-vĭd'ĭ-tē) or **liv'id·ness** n. —**liv'id·ly** adv.

liv·ing (lĭv'ĭng) adj. **1.** Possessing life; alive. **2.** In active function or use: a living language. **3.** True to life; real. —n. **1.** The condition or action of maintaining life. **2.** A manner or style of life. **3.** A livelihood.

  Syns: living, keep, livelihood, maintenance, subsistence, support, sustenance n.

living room n. A room for general use in a private residence.

liz·ard (lĭz'ərd) n. **1.** Any of various reptiles having a long, scaly body, four legs, and a tapering tail. **2.** Leather made from the skin of a lizard. [< Lat. lacerta.]

lla·ma (lä'mə) n. A South American mammal raised for its wool and for carrying loads. [< Quechua.]

llama

lla·no (lä'nō, län'ō) n., pl. **-nos.** A large, grassy plain in Latin America. [< Lat. planus, level.]

lo (lō) interj. Used to attract attention or to show surprise. [< OE lā.]

load (lōd) n. **1. a.** A supported weight or mass. **b.** The overall force to which a structure is subjected. **2.** Material transported by a vehicle, person, or animal. **3.** The share of work allocated to or required of an individual, machine, or group. **4.** A heavy responsibility; burden. **5.** Often **loads.** Informal. A large amount or quantity. —v. **1.** To place (a load) in or on (e.g. a structure or conveyance). **2.** To take on or receive a load. **3.** To weigh down; burden; oppress. **4.** To charge (a firearm) with ammunition. **5.** To insert film, tape, etc. into (a holder or magazine). **6.** To raise the power demand in (a circuit). [< OE lād.] —**load'er** n.

loaf¹ (lōf) n., pl. **loaves** (lōvz). A shaped mass of bread or other food baked in one piece. [< OE hlāf.]

loaf² (lōf) v. To spend (time) lazily or aimlessly. [Orig. unknown.] —**loaf'er** n.

loam (lōm) n. Soil consisting mainly of sand, clay, silt, and organic matter. [< OE lām, clay.] —**loam'y** adj.

loan (lōn) n. **1.** A sum of money lent at interest. **2.** Anything lent for temporary use. —v. To lend. [< ON lān.] —**loan'er** n.

loan-word (lōn'wûrd') n. Also **loan·word.** A word borrowed from another language and at least partially naturalized.

loath (lōth, lŏth) adj. Unwilling; reluctant. [< OE lath, loathsome.]

loathe (lōth) v. **loathed, loath·ing.** To dislike greatly; abhor. [< OE lāthian.] —**loath'er** n.

loath·ing (lō'thǐng) *n.* Extreme dislike; abhorrence.

loath·some (lōth'səm, lōth'-) *adj.* Repulsive; disgusting. —**loath'some·ly** *adv.* —**loathe'some·ness** *n.*

loaves (lōvz) *n.* Pl. of **loaf¹**.

lob (lŏb) *v.* **lobbed, lob·bing.** To hit, throw, or propel (something) in a high arc. [Prob. of LG orig.] —**lob** *n.*

lob·by (lŏb'ē) *n., pl.* **-bies.** **1.** A hall, foyer, or waiting room in a hotel, apartment house, theater, etc. **2.** A group of private persons engaged in influencing legislation. —*v.* **-bied, -by·ing.** To seek to influence (legislators) on behalf of a special interest. [Med. Lat. *lobium,* gallery, of Gmc. orig.] —**lob'by·ist** *n.*

lobe (lōb) *n.* A rounded projection, esp. a projecting anatomical part such as the fleshy lower part of the ear. [< Gk. *lobos.*] —**lo'bar** *adj.* —**lobed** *adj.*

lo·bot·o·my (lō-bŏt'ə-mē, lə-) *n., pl.* **-mies.** A surgical operation that severs one or more frontal lobes of the brain.

lob·ster (lŏb'stər) *n.* **1.** A large, edible marine crustacean with five pairs of legs, of which the first pair is large and clawlike. **2.** Any of several related crustaceans. [< OE *loppestre.*]

lo·cal (lō'kəl) *adj.* **1.** Of a limited area or place: *local governments.* **2.** Making many stops: *a local train.* **3.** Limited to part of the body. —*n.* **1.** A public conveyance that stops at all stations. **2.** A local branch of an organization, esp. of a labor union. [< Lat. *locus,* place.] —**lo'cal·ly** *adv.*

lo·cale (lō-kǎl', -kǎl') *n.* A locality, with reference to some event. [< Lat. *locus,* place.]

lo·cal·i·ty (lō-kǎl'ǐ-tē) *n., pl.* **-ties.** **1.** A certain neighborhood, place, or region. **2.** A site of an event.

lo·cal·ize (lō'kə-līz') *v.* **-ized, -iz·ing.** To restrict or be restricted to a particular area or part. —**lo'cal·i·za'tion** *n.*

lo·cate (lō'kāt', lō-kāt') *v.* **-cat·ed, -cat·ing.** **1.** To determine the position of. **2.** To find by searching: *locate the source of error.* **3.** To situate or place. **4.** To become established; settle. [Lat. *locare,* to place.] —**lo'ca'tor** *n.*

lo·ca·tion (lō-kā'shən) *n.* **1.** The act or process of locating. **2.** A place where something is located. **3.** A site away from a motion-picture studio at which a scene is filmed.

loch (lŏkh, lŏk) *n. Scot.* **1.** A lake. **2.** An arm of the sea similar to a fjord. [< Sc. Gael.]

lo·ci (lō'sī') *n.* Pl. of **locus**.

lock¹ (lŏk) *n.* **1.** A key- or combination-operated mechanism used to secure a door, lid, etc. **2.** A section of a canal closed off with gates for raising or lowering the water level. **3.** A mechanism in a firearm for exploding its charge of ammunition. —*v.* **1.** To fasten or become fastened with a lock. **2. a.** To confine or safeguard by putting behind a lock. **b.** To put in jail: *locked up the suspect.* **3.** To clasp or embrace tightly. **4.** To entangle in struggle or battle. **5.** To become entangled; interlock. **6.** To jam together so as to make unmovable. **7.** To become rigid or unmovable. [< OE *loc,* bolt, and *loca,* enclosure.]

lock² (lŏk) *n.* A strand or curl of hair. [< OE *locc.*]

lock·er (lŏk'ər) *n.* **1.** An enclosure that can be locked, esp. one at a public place for the safekeeping of clothing and valuables. **2.** A flat storage trunk. **3.** A refrigerated cabinet or room for storing frozen foods.

lock·et (lŏk'ĭt) *n.* A small ornamental case for a keepsake, usu. worn on a chain about the neck.

lock·jaw (lŏk'jô') *n.* **1.** Tetanus. **2.** A symptom of tetanus in which the jaw is held tightly closed by a spasm of muscles.

lock·out (lŏk'out') *n.* The closing down of a plant by an employer to force the workers to meet his terms.

lock·smith (lŏk'smĭth') *n.* One who makes or repairs locks.

lock step *n.* A marching technique in which the marchers follow each other closely.

lo·co (lō'kō) *adj. Slang.* Mad; insane. [Sp.]

lo·co·mo·tion (lō'kə-mō'shən) *n.* The act or capability of moving from place to place.

lo·co·mo·tive (lō'kə-mō'tĭv) *n.* A self-propelled engine that moves railroad cars. —*adj.* Also **lo·co·mo·tor** (-mō'tər). Of or involved in locomotion.

lo·co·weed (lō'kō-wēd') *n.* Any of several plants of the western and central United States that are poisonous to livestock.

lo·cus (lō'kəs) *n., pl.* **-ci** (-sī'). **1.** A place. **2.** *Math.* The set or arrangement of all points that satisfy specified conditions. [Lat.]

lo·cust (lō'kəst) *n.* **1.** A grasshopper that travels in destructive swarms. **2.** A cicada. **3.** A tree with featherlike compound leaves, clusters of fragrant white flowers, and hard, durable wood. [< Lat. *locusta.*]

locust

lo·cu·tion (lō-kyōo'shən) *n.* **1.** A particular word, phrase, or expression. **2.** Style of speaking; phraseology. [< Lat. *loqui,* to speak.]

lode (lōd) *n.* A vein of mineral ore deposited between layers of rock. [< OE *lād,* way.]

lode·star (lōd'stär') *n.* A star that is used as a point of reference, esp. the North Star. [ME *lodesterre.*]

lode·stone (lōd'stōn') *n.* A magnetized piece of magnetite. [Obs. *lode,* course + STONE.]

lodge (lŏj) *n.* **1.** A cottage or cabin, often rustic, used as a temporary abode or shelter: *a ski lodge.* **2.** An inn. **3.** A North American Indian living unit such as a wigwam. **4. a.** A local chapter of certain fraternal organizations. **b.** The meeting hall of such a society. —*v.* **lodged, lodg·ing.** **1.** To provide with or rent quarters temporarily, esp. for sleeping. **2.** To live in a rented room or rooms. **3.** To register (a charge): *lodge a complaint.* **4.** To vest (authority or power). **5.** To be or become embedded. [< OFr. *loge*, of Gmc. orig.] —**lodge'a·ble** *adj.*

lodg·er (lŏj'ər) *n.* One who rents and lives in a furnished room or rooms; roomer.

lodg·ing (lŏj'ĭng) *n.* **1.** Sleeping accommodations. **2. lodgings.** Rented rooms.

lo·ess (lō'əs, lĕs, lōōs) *n.* A fine-grained silt or clay, thought to be deposited by the wind. [G. *Löss.*]

loft (lôft, lŏft) *n.* **1.** A large, usu. unpartitioned floor in a commercial building. **2.** An open space under a roof; attic. **3.** A gallery or balcony, as in a church. **4.** A high arc given to a struck or thrown object —*v.* **1.** To put, store, or keep in a loft. **2.** To send in a high arc. [< ON *lopt*, upstairs room.]

loft·y (lôf'tē, lŏf'-) *adj.* **-i·er, -i·est. 1.** Of imposing height; towering. **2.** Exalted; noble. **3.** Arrogant; haughty. —**loft'i·ly** *adv.* —**loft'i·ness** *n.*

log¹ (lôg, lŏg) *n.* **1.** A trunk or section of a trunk of a fallen or felled tree. **2.** A device used to determine the speed of a ship through water. **3.** A record of a ship's or aircraft's speed, progress, etc. **4.** A regularly kept record; journal. —*v.* **logged, log·ging. 1.** To cut (trees) into logs. **2. a.** To enter in a ship's or aircraft's log. **b.** To travel a (specified distance, time, or speed). [ME.] —**log'ger** *n.*

log² (lôg, lŏg) *n.* Logarithm. —**log** *suff.* Var. of **-logue.**

lo·gan·ber·ry (lō'gən-bĕr'ē) *n.* An edible, blackberrylike red fruit. [< James H. *Logan* (1841–1928).]

log·a·rithm (lôg'ə-rĭth'əm, lŏg'ə-) *n.* The exponent that indicates the power to which a fixed number, the base, must be raised to produce a given number. [Gk. *logos,* reason + *arithmos,* number.] —**log'a·rith'mic** (-rĭth'mĭk) or **log'a·rith'mi·cal** *adj.* —**log'a·rith'mi·cal·ly** *adv.*

loge (lōzh) *n.* **1.** A small compartment, esp. a box in a theater. **2.** The front rows of a theater's mezzanine. [< OFr., lodge.]

log·ger·head (lô'gər-hĕd', lŏg'ər-) *n.* A marine turtle with a large, beaked head. —*idiom.* **at loggerheads.** In a head-on dispute. [Prob. dial. *logger,* wooden block + HEAD.]

log·ic (lŏj'ĭk) *n.* **1.** The study of the principles of reasoning. **2.** Valid reasoning, esp. as distinguished from invalid or irrational argumentation. [< Gk. *logos,* reason.] —**lo·gi'cian** (lō-jĭsh'ən) *n.*

log·i·cal (lŏj'ĭ-kəl) *adj.* **1.** Of, using, or agreeing with logic. **2.** Showing consistency of reasoning. **3.** Reasonable. —**log'i·cal·ly** *adv.* —**log'i·cal·ness** *n.*

lo·gis·tics (lō-jĭs'tĭks) *n.* (*used with a sing. verb*). The procurement, distribution, maintenance, and replacement of materiel and personnel. [< Gk. *logistikos,* of calculation.] —**lo·gis'tic** or **lo·gis'ti·cal** *adj.*

log·jam (lôg'jăm', lŏg'-) *n.* **1.** A mass of floating logs crowded immovably together. **2.** A deadlock; impasse.

lo·go·type (lō'gə-tīp', lŏ'-, lŏg'ə-) *n.* Also **lo·go** (lō'gō). A distinctive trademark or symbol of a company, publication, etc. [Gk. *logos,* word + TYPE.]

log·roll·ing or **log-roll·ing** (lôg'rō'lĭng, lŏg'-) *n.* The trading of influence or votes among legislators to achieve passage of projects of interest to one another. —**log'roll'er** *n.*

—**logue** or **-log** *suff.* Speech or discourse: *travelogue.*

lo·gy (lō'gē) *adj.* **-gi·er, -gi·est.** Sluggish; lethargic. [Perh. < Du. *log,* heavy.] —**lo'gi·ness** *n.*

—**logy** *suff.* **1.** Discourse; expression: *phraseology.* **2.** Science; theory; study: *geology.* [< Gk. *logos,* word.]

loin (loin) *n.* **1. a.** *Anat.* The part of the side and back between the ribs and pelvis. **b.** A cut of meat from this part of an animal. **2. loins.** The region of the thighs and groin. [< Lat. *lumbus.*]

loin·cloth (loin'klôth', -klŏth') *n.* A strip of cloth worn around the loins.

loi·ter (loi'tər) *v.* **1.** To stand idly about; linger aimlessly. **2.** To proceed slowly or with many stops. **3.** To dawdle: *loiter over a job.* [ME *loiteren.*] —**loi'ter·er** *n.*

loll (lŏl) *v.* **1.** To recline indolently. **2.** To hang or droop laxly. [< MDu. *lollen,* to doze.] —**loll'ing·ly** *adv.*

lol·li·pop (lŏl'ē-pŏp') *n.* Also **lol·ly·pop.** A piece of hard candy on the end of a stick. [Perh. dial. *lolly,* tongue + POP¹.]

lone (lōn) *adj.* **1.** Solitary: *a lone tree.* **2.** Isolated; unfrequented. [< ALONE.]

lone·ly (lōn'lē) *adj.* **-li·er, -li·est. 1. a.** Sad at being alone. **b.** Producing such sadness. **2.** Without companions; solitary. **3.** Empty of people; unfrequented. —**lone'li·ness** *n.*

lon·er (lō'nər) *n. Informal.* One who avoids other people.

lone·some (lōn'səm) *adj.* **1.** Sad at feeling alone. **2.** Offering solitude; secluded. —**lone'some·ly** *adv.* —**lone'some·ness** *n.*

long¹ (lông, lŏng) *adj.* **-er, -est. 1.** Having great length. **2.** Of relatively great duration: *a long time.* **3.** Of a specified length or duration: *a mile long; an hour long.* **4.** Concerned with distant issues; far-reaching: *a long view.* **5.** Risky; chancy: *long odds.* **6.** Having an abundance or excess: *long on hope.* —*adv.* **1.** For an extended period of time. **2.** For or throughout a specified period: *all night long.* **3.** At a distant point of time: *long before we were born.* —*n.* A long time. —*idioms.* **as (or so) long as.** Inasmuch as; since. **no longer.** Not now as formerly; no more: *He no longer smokes.* [< OE *lang.*]

Syns: long, extended, lengthy *adj.*

long² (lông, lŏng) *v.* To wish earnestly; yearn. [< OE *langian.*]

long·bow (lông'bō', lŏng'-) *n.* A wooden, hand-drawn bow 5 to 6 ft. long.

longbow

long distance *n.* Telephone service between distant points. —**long'-dis'tance** *adj. & adv.*

lon·gev·i·ty (lŏn-jĕv'ĭ-tē) *n.* **1.** Long life. **2.** Long duration. [< Lat. *longaevus,* ancient.]

long·hair (lông'hâr', lŏng'-) *n. Informal.* One

dedicated to the arts and esp. to classical music. —**long'hair'** or **long'haired'** *adj.*

long-hand (lông'hând', lŏng'-) *n.* Handwriting in which the letters are joined together; cursive writing.

long-horn (lông'hôrn', lŏng'-) *n.* One of a breed of long-horned cattle formerly bred in the southwestern United States.

long-ing (lông'ĭng, lŏng'-) *n.* A persistent yearning or desire. —*adj.* Affected by longing. —**long'ing-ly** *adv.*

lon-gi-tude (lŏn'jĭ-tōōd', -tyōōd') *n.* Angular distance east or west, gen. measured with respect to the prime meridian at Greenwich, England. [< Lat. *longitudo.*] —**lon'gi-tu'di-nal** *adj.* —**lon'gi-tu'di-nal-ly** *adv.*

long jump *n.* A jump made for distance.

long-lived (lông'līvd', -lĭvd', lŏng'-) *adj.* Having a long life. —**long'-lived'ness** *n.*

long-play-ing (lông'plā'ĭng, lŏng'-) *adj.* Of or relating to a microgroove phonograph record that turns at 33⅓ revolutions per minute.

long-range (lông'rānj', lŏng'-) *adj.* 1. Involving a long span of time: *long-range planning.* 2. Of or designed for great distances.

long-shore-man (lông'shôr'mən, -shōr'-, lŏng'-) *n.* A dock worker who loads and unloads ships.

long shot *n.* An entry, as in a horse race, with little chance of winning.

long-stand-ing (lông'stăn'dĭng, lŏng'-) *adj.* Of long duration.

long-suf-fer-ing (lông'sŭf'ər-ĭng, lŏng'-) *adj.* Patiently enduring pain or difficulties. —**long'-suf'fer-ing-ly** *adv.*

long-term (lông'tûrm', lŏng'-) *adj.* In effect for or involving a number of years.

long ton *n.* A ton weighing 2,240 pounds, or approx. 1,016 kilograms.

long-wind-ed (lông'wĭn'dĭd, lŏng'-) *adj.* Wearisomely talkative. —**long'-wind'ed-ly** *adv.* —**long'-wind'ed-ness** *n.*

look (lŏŏk) *v.* 1. To use the eyes to see. 2. To focus one's gaze or attention: *looked toward the river.* 3. To search. 4. To seem or appear to be: *These bananas look ripe.* 5. To face in a specified direction. 6. To have an appearance in conformity with: *look one's age.* —*phrasal verbs.* **look after.** To take care of. **look down on** (or **upon**). To regard with contempt or condescension. **look into.** To investigate. **look on.** 1. To be a spectator. 2. To consider; regard. **look out.** To be on guard. **look over.** To inspect, esp. in a casual way. **look up.** 1. To search for and find, as in a reference book. 2. To locate and call upon; visit. 3. *Informal.* To improve. **look up to.** To admire. —*n.* 1. The action of looking; a gaze or glance. 2. Appearance or aspect. 3. **looks.** Physical appearance, esp. when pleasing. [< OE *lōcian.*] —**look'er** *n.*

look-ing glass (lŏŏk'ĭng) *n.* A mirror.

look-out (lŏŏk'out') *n.* 1. The act of observing or keeping watch. 2. A high place that commands a wide view for observation. 3. A person assigned to keep watch.

loom¹ (lōŏm) *v.* 1. To come into view as a massive, distorted, or indistinct image. 2. To appear imminent and usu. threatening. [Orig. unknown.]

loom² (lōŏm) *n.* A machine on which cloth is

produced by interweaving thread or yarn at right angles. [< OE *gelōma,* tool.]

loon¹ (lōōn) *n.* A diving bird with mottled plumage and an eerie, laughlike cry. [Of Scand. orig.]

loon² (lōōn) *n.* A simple-minded or mad person. [ME *louen,* rogue.]

loon-y (lōō'nē) *adj.* **-i-er, -i-est.** *Informal.* Crazy; insane. —**loon'i-ness** *n.* —**loon'y** *n.*

loop (lōōp) *n.* 1. A length of line, thread, etc., that is folded over and joined at the ends. 2. A roughly oval, closed, or nearly closed turn or figure. —*v.* 1. To form or form into a loop or loops. 2. To fasten, join, or encircle with a loop or loops. [ME *loupe.*]

loop-hole (lōōp'hōl') *n.* 1. A small hole or slit in a wall. 2. A means of evasion. [Med. Lat. *loupa,* loophole + HOLE.]

loose (lōōs) *adj.* **loos-er, loos-est.** 1. Not tightly fastened or secured. 2. Free from confinement. 3. Not tightly stretched; slack. 4. Not tight-fitting. 5. Not bound, packaged, or gathered together. 6. Not strict or exact: *a loose translation.* 7. Lacking a sense of restraint or responsibility: *loose talk.* 8. Licentious; immoral. —*adv.* In a loose manner. —*v.* **loosed, loos-ing.** 1. To set free; release. 2. To undo, untie, or unwrap. 3. To make less tight, firm, or compact; loosen. 4. To relax. 5. To let fly (a missile). [< ON *lauss.*] —**loose'ly** *adv.* —**loose'ness** *n.*

Syns: loose, lax, relaxed, slack *adj.*

loos-en (lōō'sən) *v.* 1. To make or become loose or looser. 2. To free from restraint, pressure, or strictness. —**loos'en-er** *n.*

loot (lōōt) *n.* 1. Valuables pillaged in time of war; spoils. 2. Goods stolen or illicitly obtained. —*v.* 1. To plunder; pillage. [< Skt. *lotram,* plunder.] —**loot'er** *n.*

lop (lŏp) *v.* **lopped, lop-ping.** 1. To cut off branches or twigs from; trim. 2. To cut off (a part), esp. with a single swift blow. [Perh. < ME *loppe,* small branches.] —**lop'per** *n.*

lope (lōp) *v.* **loped, lop-ing.** To run or ride with a steady, easy gait. —*n.* A steady, easy gait. [< ON *hlaupa.*] —**lop'er** *n.*

lop-sid-ed (lŏp'sī'dĭd) *adj.* Heavier, larger, or higher on one side than on the other. —**lop'sid'ed-ly** *adv.* —**lop'sid'ed-ness** *n.*

lo-qua-cious (lō-kwā'shəs) *adj.* Very talkative. [< Lat. *loqui,* to speak.] —**lo-qua'cious-ly** *adv.* —**lo-qua'cious-ness** or **lo-quac'i-ty** (-kwăs'ĭ-tē) *n.*

lord (lôrd) *n.* 1. A person having dominion over others; ruler or master. 2. The owner of a feudal estate. 3. **Lord.** *Chiefly Brit.* The general masculine title of nobility and other rank. 4. **Lord.** God. —*v.* To play the lord; domineer: *lording it over the newcomers.* [< OE *hlāford.*]

lord-ly (lôrd'lē) *adj.* **-li-er, -li-est.** 1. Of or suitable for a lord. 2. Dignified; noble. 3. Arrogant; overbearing. —**lord'li-ness** *n.*

lord-ship (lôrd'shĭp') *n.* 1. **Lordship.** A form of address for a British nobleman, judge, or bishop. 2. The rank or domain of a lord.

Lord's Prayer *n.* The prayer taught by Jesus to his disciples.

lore (lôr, lōr) *n.* Accumulated fact, tradition, or belief about a specific subject. [< OE *lār.*]

lor·gnette (lôrn-yĕt′) *n.* Eyeglasses or opera glasses with a short handle. [< OFr. *lorgne*, squinting.]

lorn (lôrn) *adj.* Forsaken; forlorn. [< OE *leosan*, to suffer a loss.]

lor·ry (lôr′ē, lŏr′ē) *n., pl.* **-ries.** Chiefly Brit. A motor truck. [Orig. unknown.]

lose (lōōz) *v.* **lost** (lôst, lŏst), **los·ing.** *v.* 1. To be unable to find; mislay. 2. To be unable to maintain or keep. 3. To be deprived of: *lose a friend.* 4. To fail to win; be defeated. 5. To fail to take advantage of: *lose a chance.* 6. To rid oneself of. 7. To allow (oneself) to become engrossed. 8. To result in the loss of: *Failure to reply lost her a job.* 9. To suffer loss. **—phrasal verb. lose out.** To fail or be defeated. [< OE *lōsian.*] **—los′er** *n.*

loss (lôs, lŏs) *n.* 1. The act or fact of losing or having lost. 2. One that is lost. 3. **losses.** People who are killed, wounded, or captured. **—idiom. at a loss.** Perplexed; puzzled. [< OE *los.*]

loss leader *n.* A commodity offered at cost or less than cost to attract customers.

lost (lôst, lŏst) *v. p.t. & p.p.* of **lose.** **—adj.** 1. Strayed or missing. 2. Not won or likely to be won. 3. Gone or passed away. 4. Uncertain; bewildered: *felt lost in the new school.* 5. Absorbed.

lot (lŏt) *n.* 1. An object used in making a determination by chance. 2. The use of lots for selection. 3. One's fortune in life; fate. 4. A number of people or things. 5. Often **lots.** A large amount or number. 6. A piece of land having fixed boundaries. [< OE *hlot.*]

Lo·thar·i·o (lō-thâr′ē-ō′, -thä′rē-ō′) *n., pl.* **-os.** An amoral seducer of women. [< *Lothario*, a character in *The Fair Penitent* by Nicholas Rowe (1674–1718).]

lo·ti (lō′tē) *n., pl.* **-ti.** See table at **currency.** [Sotho.]

lo·tion (lō′shən) *n.* A liquid medicine or cosmetic applied to the skin. [< Lat. *lotio,* a washing.]

lot·ter·y (lŏt′ə-rē) *n., pl.* **-ies.** A contest in which winners are selected in a drawing of lots. [Prob. < Du. *lot,* lot.]

lo·tus (lō′təs) *n.* **a.** An Oriental water lily with pinkish flowers and large leaves. **b.** Any of several similar or related plants. 2. A fruit said in Greek legend to produce a drugged, indolent state in those who eat it. [< Gk. *lōtos,* name of several plants.]

lotus

loud (loud) *adj.* **-er, -est.** 1. Marked by high volume and intensity of sound. 2. Producing or capable of producing a sound of high volume and intensity. 3. Gaudy; flashy: *a loud necktie.* [< OE *hlūd.*] **—loud** or **loud′ly** *adv.* **—loud′ness** *n.*

loud-mouth (loud′mouth′) *n.* A person whose speech is loud, irritating, and often indiscreet. **—loud′mouthed′** (-mou*th*d′, -moutht′) *adj.*

loud-speak·er or **loud-speak·er** (loud′spē′kər) *n.* A device that converts electric signals to sound and projects the sound.

Lou·i·si·an·a French (lōō-ē′zē-ăn′ə) *n.* French as spoken by descendants of the original French settlers of Louisiana.

lounge (lounj) *v.* **lounged, loung·ing.** To stand, sit, or lie in a lazy, relaxed way. **—n.** 1. A comfortably furnished waiting room, as in a hotel or theater. 2. A long couch. [Orig. unknown.] **—loung′er** *n.*

lour (lou′ər) *v. & n.* Var. of **lower¹.**

louse (lous) *n.* 1. *pl.* **lice** (līs). A small, wingless insect that lives as a parasite on various animals, including man. 2. *pl.* **lous·es.** *Slang.* A mean or despicable person. **—v. loused, lous·ing.** *Slang.* To bungle: *louse up a contract.* [< OE *lūs.*]

lous·y (lou′zē) *adj.* **-i·er, -i·est.** 1. Infested with lice. 2. *Slang.* **a.** Mean; nasty. **b.** Inferior; worthless. **—lous′i·ly** *adv.* **—lous′i·ness** *n.*

lout (lout) *n.* An awkward, stupid person. [Perh. < OE *lūtan,* to bend.] **—lout′ish** *adj.*

lou·ver (lōō′vər) *n.* Also **lou·vre.** 1. An opening fitted with fixed or movable slanted slats. 2. One of the slats of a louver. [Med. Lat. *luvarium,* hole in the roof.] **—lou′vered** *adj.*

love (lŭv) *n.* 1. Intense affection and warm feeling for another. 2. Strong sexual desire for another person. 3. A strong fondness or enthusiasm. 4. A beloved person. 5. A zero score in tennis. **—v. loved, lov·ing.** 1. To feel love for. 2. To like or desire enthusiastically. **—idioms. in love.** Feeling love; enamored. **make love.** 1. To copulate. 2. To embrace and caress. [< OE *lufu.*] **—lov′a·ble** or **love′a·ble** *adj.* **—love′less** *adj.* **—love′less·ly** *adv.* **—love′less·ness** *n.*

love·bird (lŭv′bûrd′) *n.* A small parrot often kept as a cage bird.

love·lorn (lŭv′lôrn′) *adj.* Deprived of love or one's lover. **—love′lorn′ness** *n.*

love·ly (lŭv′lē) *adj.* **-li·er, -li·est.** 1. Having pleasing or attractive qualities; beautiful. 2. Enjoyable; delightful. **—love′li·ness** *n.*

love·mak·ing (lŭv′mā′kĭng) *n.* 1. Courtship. 2. Sexual activity between lovers.

lov·er (lŭv′ər) *n.* 1. One who loves another. 2. One who is fond of or devoted to something: *a nature lover.* 3. **lovers.** A couple in love with each other. 4. **lovers.** A sexual partner.

love·sick (lŭv′sĭk′) *adj.* 1. Pining with love. 2. Expressing a lover's yearning. **—love′sick′ness** *n.*

lov·ing (lŭv′ĭng) *adj.* Feeling or showing love. **—lov′ing·ly** *adv.*

loving cup *n.* A large, ornamental cup, often given as an award in sporting events.

low¹ (lō) *adj.* **-er, -est.** 1. Having little height. 2. Of less than usual height or depth. 3. Below average, as in amount, degree, or intensity. 4. **a.** Having a pitch that corresponds to a relatively small number of cycles per second. **b.** Not loud; hushed. 5. Inferior, as in status. 6. Morally base. 7. Sad; depressed. 8. Of small value or quality. 9. Depreciatory; disparaging. **—adv.** 1. At, in, or to a low position or level. 2. Softly; quietly. 3. With or at a low pitch. **—n.** 1. A low level, position, or degree. 2. A mass of atmospheric air that exerts less pressure than the air around it. 3. The gear configuration that produces the lowest range of output speeds, as in an automotive transmission. [< ON *lágr.*] —**low'ness** *n.*

low² (lō) *v.* To moo. [< OE *hlōwan.*] —**low** *n.*

low-boy (lō'boi') *n.* A low, tablelike chest of drawers.

low-brow (lō'brou') *n.* *Informal.* A person with uncultivated tastes. —**low'brow** *adj.*

low-down (lō'doun') *n.* *Slang.* Full information; all the facts.

low-down (lō'doun') *adj.* Mean; despicable.

low-er¹ (lou'ər) *v.* Also **lour.** 1. To look angry; scowl. 2. To appear dark or threatening, as the sky. [ME *louren.*] —**low'er** *n.*

low-er² (lō'ər). Compar. of **low.** —*adj.* 1. Below someone or something, as in rank, position, etc. 2. **Lower.** *Geol. & Archaeol.* Being an earlier division of the period named. 3. Denoting the larger house of a bicameral legislature. —*v.* 1. To let or move something down to a lower level. 2. To make or become less; reduce or diminish.

Syns: *lower, cheapen, downgrade, mark down, reduce v.*

lower case *n.* Small letters as distinguished from capital letters. —**low'er-case'** *adj.*

lower class *n.* The group in society of low social and economic status, ranking below the middle class. —**low'er-class'** *adj.*

lowest common denominator *n.* The least common multiple of the denominators of a set of fractions.

low frequency *n.* A radio-wave frequency in the range from 30 to 300 kilohertz.

Low German *n.* 1. Any of the German dialects spoken in northern Germany. 2. Any of the Germanic languages of continental Europe except Scandinavian and High German.

low-key (lō'kē') *adj.* Also **low-keyed** (-kēd'). Restrained, as in style or quality.

low-land (lō'lənd) *n.* An area of relatively low land.

low-ly (lō'lē) *adj.* **-li-er, -li-est.** 1. Having a low rank or position. 2. Humble; meek. —**low'li-ness** *n.* —**low'ly** *adv.*

low-mind-ed (lō'mīn'dĭd) *adj.* Exhibiting coarseness and vulgarity of mind. —**low'mind'ed-ly** *adv.* —**low'mind'ed-ness** *n.*

low profile *n.* Unobtrusive, restrained behavior or activity.

low relief *n.* Sculptural relief that projects very little from the background.

low tide *n.* 1. The tide at its lowest ebb. 2. The time of this ebb.

lox¹ (lŏks) *n.* Smoked salmon. [< OHG *lahs, salmon.*]

lox² (lŏks) *n.* Liquid oxygen. [L(IQUID) OX(Y-GEN).]

loy-al (loi'əl) *adj.* 1. Steadfast in allegiance, as to one's homeland. 2. Faithful to a person, ideal, or custom. [< Lat. *legalis,* legal.] —**loy'al-ly** *adv.* —**loy'al-ty** or **loy'al-ness** *n.*

loy-al-ist (loi'ə-lĭst) *n.* A supporter of the lawful government during a revolt.

loz-enge (lŏz'ənj) *n.* 1. A flat, diamond-shaped figure. 2. A small, often lozenge-shaped piece of medicated candy. [< OFr. *losenge.*]

LP (ĕl'pē') *n.* A long-playing record.

LSD (ĕl'ĕs-dē') *n.* A powerful drug, lysergic acid diethylamide, $C_{20}H_{25}N_3O_2$, that induces hallucinations.

Lu The symbol for the element lutetium.

lu-au (lōō-ou') *n.* A Hawaiian feast.

lu-bri-cant (lōō'brĭ-kənt) *n.* Any of various materials, such as grease, machine oil, or graphite, that reduce friction when applied as a coating to moving parts. —**lu'bri-cant** *adj.*

lu-bri-cate (lōō'brĭ-kāt') *v.* **-cat-ed, -cat-ing.** To apply a lubricant to. [Lat. *lubricare.*] —**lu'bri-ca'tion** *n.* —**lu'bri-ca'tor** *n.*

lu-bri-cous (lōō'brĭ-kəs) *adj.* Also **lu-bri-cious** (lōō-brĭsh'əs). 1. Characterized by lewdness. 2. Elusive. 3. Slippery. [Lat. *lubricus,* slippery.] —**lu-bric'i-ty** (-brĭs'ĭ-tē) *n.*

lu-cid (lōō'sĭd) *adj.* 1. Easily understood; clear. 2. Clear-minded; rational. 3. Translucent. [< Lat. *lucidus.*] —**lu-cid'i-ty** or **lu'cid-ness** *n.* —**lu'cid-ly** *adv.*

Lu-ci-fer (lōō'sə-fər) *n.* In Christian tradition, the archangel cast from Heaven for leading a revolt of the angels; Satan.

Lu-cite (lōō'sīt'). A trademark for a transparent, thermoplastic acrylic resin.

luck (lŭk) *n.* 1. The chance happening of good or bad events; fortune. 2. Good fortune. [< MDu. *luc.*] —**luck'less** *adj.*

luck-y (lŭk'ē) *adj.* **-i-er, -i-est.** Having, bringing, or resulting from good luck. —**luck'i-ly** *adv.* —**luck'i-ness** *n.*

lu-cra-tive (lōō'krə-tĭv) *adj.* Producing wealth; profitable. [< Lat. *lucrativus.*] —**lu'cra-tive-ly** *adv.* —**lu'cra-tive-ness** *n.*

lu-cre (lōō'kər) *n.* Money; profits. [< Lat. *lucrum.*]

lu-cu-brate (lōō'kyə-brāt') *v.* **-brat-ed, -brat-ing.** To stay up late to study. [< Lat. *lucubrare,* to work at night by lamplight.] —**lu'cu-bra'tion** *n.*

lu-di-crous (lōō'dĭ-krəs) *adj.* Laughable because of obvious absurdity or incongruity. [Lat. *ludicrus,* sportive.] —**lu'di-crous-ly** *adv.* —**lu'di-crous-ness** *n.*

lug¹ (lŭg) *v.* **lugged, lug-ging.** To drag or haul with great difficulty. [ME *luggen,* of Scand. orig.]

lug² (lŭg) *n.* 1. An earlike handle or projection on a vessel or machine used as a hold or support. 2. A nut, esp. one closed at one end to serve as a cap. 3. *Slang.* A clumsy fool. [ME *lugge,* earflap.]

lug-gage (lŭg'ĭj) *n.* Baggage, esp. suitcases. [Prob. LUG¹ + (BAG)GAGE.]

lu-gu-bri-ous (lōō-gōō'brē-əs, -gyōō'-) *adj.* Mournful or sad, esp. to a ridiculous degree. [Lat. *lugubris.*] —**lu-gu'bri-ous-ly** *adv.* —**lu-gu'bri-ous-ness** *n.*

Luke (lōōk) *n.* See table at **Bible.**

luke-warm (lōōk'wôrm') *adj.* 1. Mildly warm; tepid. 2. Halfhearted: *a lukewarm welcome.* [ME *leukwarm.*] —**luke'warm'ly** *adv.* —**luke'warm'ness** *n.*

lull (lŭl) *v.* 1. To cause to sleep or rest; soothe. 2. To deceive into trustfulness. —*n.* A relatively calm or inactive period. [ME *lullen.*]

lul-la-by (lŭl'ə-bī') *n., pl.* **-bies.** A song with which to lull a child to sleep. [Perh. LULL + (BYE-)BY(E).]

lum-ba-go (lŭm-bā'gō) *n.* A painful form of rheumatism that affects the muscles and tendons of the lower back. [Lat.]

lum-bar (lŭm'bər, -bär') *adj.* Of or located in

the part of the back and sides between the lowest ribs and the hips. [< Lat. *lumbus*, loin.]

lum·ber¹ (lŭm'bər) *n.* **1.** Timber sawed into boards and planks. **2.** Heavy, useless material. —*v.* To cut down (trees) and prepare as marketable timber. [Perh. < LUMBER².] —**lum'ber·er** *n.*

lum·ber² (lŭm'bər) *v.* To walk or move with heavy clumsiness. [ME *lomeren*.]

lum·ber·jack (lŭm'bər-jăk') *n.* One who fells trees and transports the timber to a mill.

lum·ber·yard (lŭm'bər-yärd') *n.* An establishment that sells lumber and other building materials from a yard.

lu·mi·nar·y (lōō'mə-nĕr'ē) *n., pl.* **-ies. 1.** An object, as a celestial body, that gives light. **2.** A notable person in a specific field. [< Lat. *lumen*, light.] —**lu'mi·nar·y** *adj.*

lu·mi·nes·cence (lōō'mə-nĕs'əns) *n.* **1.** The production of light without heat, as in fluorescence. **2.** Light that is produced in this way. [Lat. *lumen*, light + -ESCENCE.] —**lu'mi·nes'cent** *adj.*

lu·mi·nous (lōō'mə-nəs) *adj.* **1.** Emitting light. **2.** Full of light; illuminated. **3.** Intelligible; clear. [< Lat. *lumen*, light.] —**lu'mi·nos'i·ty** (-nŏs'ĭ-tē) *or* **lu'mi·nous·ness** *n.* —**lu'mi·nous·ly** *adv.*

lum·mox (lŭm'əks) *n.* An oaf; lout. [Orig. unknown.]

lump¹ (lŭmp) *n.* **1.** An irregularly shaped mass or piece. **2.** An abnormal swelling or bump in a part of the body. **3.** **lumps.** Punishment that is deserved. —*adj.* **1.** Formed into lumps: *lump sugar.* **2.** Not divided into parts: *a lump sum.* —*v.* To put together in a single group or pile. [ME.] —**lump'i·ness** *n.* —**lump'y** *adj.*

lump² (lŭmp) *v. Informal.* To tolerate: *like it or lump it.* [Orig. unknown.]

lu·na·cy (lōō'nə-sē) *n., pl.* **-cies. 1.** Insanity. **2.** Foolish conduct. [< LUNATIC.]

lu·nar (lōō'nər) *adj.* Of, involving, caused by, or affecting the moon. [< Lat. *luna*, moon.]

lu·na·tic (lōō'nə-tĭk) *adj.* **1.** Insane. **2.** Of or for the insane. **3.** Wildly or giddily foolish. [< Lat. *luna*, moon.] —**lu'na·tic** *n.*

lunch (lŭnch) *n.* A meal eaten at midday. [Perh. < Sp. *lonja*, slice.] —**lunch** *v.* —**lunch'er** *n.*

lunch·eon (lŭn'chən) *n.* A lunch, esp. a party at which lunch is served. [Prob. < LUNCH.]

lunch·eon·ette (lŭn'chə-nĕt') *n.* A small restaurant that serves simple meals.

lung (lŭng) *n.* Either of two spongy, saclike thoracic organs in most vertebrates, functioning to remove carbon dioxide from the blood and provide it with oxygen. [< OE *lungen.*]

lunge (lŭnj) *n.* **1.** A sudden thrust or pass, as with a sword. **2.** A sudden forward movement. —*v.* **lunged, lung·ing.** To move with a lunge. [< Fr. *allonger.*] —**lung'er** *n.*

lung·fish (lŭng'fĭsh') *n.* Any of several tropical freshwater fishes that have lungs as well as gills.

lu·pine (lōō'pĭn) *n.* Also **lu·pin.** A plant with long clusters of variously colored flowers. [< Lat. *lupinus*, wolflike.]

lu·pus (lōō'pəs) *n.* Any of several diseases of the skin and mucous membranes, many causing disfiguring lesions. [< Lat., wolf.]

lurch¹ (lûrch) *v.* **1.** To stagger. **2.** To roll or pitch suddenly, as a ship. [Orig. unknown.] —**lurch** *n.*

lurch² (lûrch) *n.* A difficult position. [< OFr. *lourche*, soundly defeated.]

lure (lōōr) *n.* **1.** Something that attracts with the prospect of pleasure or reward. **2.** An artificial bait used in catching fish. —*v.* **lured, lur·ing.** To attract by temptation; entice. [< OFr., of Gmc. orig.]

lure

lu·rid (lōōr'ĭd) *adj.* **1.** Horrible; gruesome. **2.** Stressing violence or sensational elements. [Lat. *luridus*, pale.] —**lu'rid·ly** *adv.* —**lu'rid·ness** *n.*

lurk (lûrk) *v.* **1.** To lie in wait, as in ambush. **2.** To move furtively. [ME *lurken*, of Scand. orig.]

lus·cious (lŭsh'əs) *adj.* **1.** Pleasant and sweet to taste or smell; delicious. **2.** Sensually appealing. [ME *lucius.*] —**lus'cious·ly** *adv.* —**lus'cious·ness** *n.*

lush¹ (lŭsh) *adj.* **-er, -est. 1.** Characterized by luxuriant growth or vegetation. **2.** Luxurious; opulent. [ME *lusch*, soft.] —**lush'ly** *adv.* —**lush'ness** *n.*

lush² (lŭsh) *n. Slang.* A drunkard. [Orig. unknown.]

lust (lŭst) *n.* **1.** Intense, excessive, or unrestrained sexual desire. **2.** An overwhelming craving. —*v.* To have an inordinate desire, esp. sexual desire. [< OE, desire.] —**lust'ful** *adj.* —**lust'ful·ly** *adv.* —**lust'ful·ness** *n.*

lus·ter (lŭs'tər) *n.* Also *chiefly Brit.* **lus·tre. 1.** Soft reflected light; sheen. **2.** Brilliance or radiance. **3.** Splendor. [< Lat. *lustrare*, to brighten.] —**lus'trous** (-trəs) *adj.* —**lus'trous·ly** *adv.* —**lus'trous·ness** *n.*

lust·y (lŭs'tē) *adj.* **-ier, -iest.** Full of vigor; robust. —**lust'i·ly** *adv.* —**lust'i·ness** *n.*

lute (lōōt) *n.* A stringed instrument that has a fretted fingerboard and a body shaped like half a pear. [< Ar. *al-'ud.*] —**lut'ist** *or* **lu·ta·nist** (lōōt'n-ĭst) *n.*

lu·te·ti·um (lōō-tē'shē-əm, -shəm) *n.* Also **lu·te·ci·um.** *Symbol* **Lu** A silvery-white rare-earth element used in nuclear technology. Atomic number 71; atomic weight 174.97. [Lat. *Lutetia*, ancient name of Paris + -IUM.]

Lu·ther·an (lōō'thər-ən) *adj.* Of or relating to the branch of the Protestant Church adhering to the views of Martin Luther. —**Lu'ther·an** *n.* —**Lu'ther·an·ism** *n.*

lux·u·ri·ant (lŭg-zhŏŏr'ē-ənt, lŭk-shŏŏr'-) *adj.* **1.** Growing abundantly, vigorously, or lushly. **2.** Exuberantly elaborate; ornate; florid. —**lux·u'ri·ance** *n.* —**lux·u'ri·ant·ly** *adv.*

lux·u·ri·ate (lŭg-zhŏŏr'ē-āt', lŭk-shŏŏr'-) *v.* **-at·ed, -at·ing.** To take luxurious pleasure; indulge oneself. —**lux·u'ri·a'tion** *n.*

lux·u·ri·ous (lŭg-zhŏŏr'ē-əs, lŭk-shŏŏr'-) *adj.* **1.** Marked by luxury. **2.** Fond of or accustomed to luxury. —**lux·u'ri·ous·ly** *adv.*

Syns: *luxurious, lavish, lush, luxuriant, opulent, palatial, plush, rich* **adj.**

lux·u·ry (lŭg'zhə-rē, lŭk'shə-) *n., pl.* **-ries.** 1. Something not necessary that provides comfort or enjoyment. 2. The enjoyment of sumptuous living. [< Lat. *luxus*.]

Lw The symbol for the element lawrencium.

lwei (lwā) *n., pl.* **lwei.** See table at **currency**. [Of Bantu orig.]

-ly¹ *suff.* 1. Characteristic of or resembling: *sisterly.* 2. Recurring at a specified interval of time: *monthly.* [< OE *-lic.*]

-ly² *suff.* 1. In a specified manner: *gradually.* 2. At a specified interval of time: *daily.* [< OE *-lice.*]

ly·ce·um (lī-sē'əm) *n.* 1. A hall in which lectures, concerts, etc., are presented. 2. An organization sponsoring such presentations. [< Gk. *Lukeion*, Aristotle's school.]

lye (lī) *n.* 1. The liquid obtained by leaching wood ashes. 2. Potassium hydroxide. 3. Sodium hydroxide. [< OE *lēag.*]

lymph (lĭmf) *n.* A clear, watery, sometimes faintly yellowish liquid that contains white blood cells and some red blood cells and acts to remove bacteria and certain proteins from the tissues, transport fat from the intestines, and supply lymphocytes to the blood. [Lat. *lympha*, water.]

lym·phat·ic (lĭm-făt'ĭk) *adj.* Of or relating to lymph or the lymphatic system. —*n.* A vessel that conveys lymph.

lymphatic system *n.* The interconnected system of spaces and vessels between tissues and organs by which lymph is circulated.

lymph node *n.* Any of numerous oval or round bodies that supply lymphocytes to the circulatory system and remove bacteria and foreign particles from the lymph.

lym·pho·cyte (lĭm'fə-sīt') *n.* A white blood cell formed in lymphoid tissue.

lym·phoid (lĭm'foid') *adj.* Of lymph, lymphatic tissue, or the lymphatic system.

lynch (lĭnch) *v.* To execute, esp. to hang, without due process of law. [Perh. < Charles *Lynch* (1736–96).] —**lynch'er** *n.*

lynx (lĭngks) *n.* A wildcat with thick, soft fur, a short tail, and tufted ears. [< Gk. *lunx.*]

lynx-eyed (lĭngks'īd') *adj.* Keen of vision.

Ly·ra (lī'rə) *n.* A constellation in the Northern Hemisphere.

lyre (līr) *n.* A stringed instrument of the harp family, used esp. in ancient Greece. [< Gk. *lura.*]

lyr·ic (lĭr'ĭk) or **lyr·i·cal** (-ĭ-kəl) *adj.* 1. Of or relating to poetry that is a direct, often songlike expression of the poet's thoughts and feelings. 2. Exuberant; unrestrained. —*n.* 1. A lyric poem. 2. **lyrics.** The words of a song. [< Gk. *lura*, lyre.] —**lyr'i·cal·ly** *adv.* —**lyr'i·cism** (-sĭz'əm) *n.*

lyr·i·cist (lĭr'ĭ-sĭst) *n.* A person who writes lyrics.

ly·ser·gic acid (lī-sûr'jĭk, lĭ-) *n.* A crystalline alkaloid, $C_{16}H_{16}N_2O_2$, derived from ergot and used in medical research. [< Gk. *lusis*, loosening + ERG(OT) + -IC.]

lysergic acid di·eth·yl·am·ide (dī'ĕth-əl-ăm'-ĭd') *n.* LSD.

ly·sin (lī'sĭn) *n.* A specific antibody that acts to destroy blood cells, tissues, or microorganisms. [Gk. *lusis*, a loosening + -IN.]

-lysis *suff.* Decomposition or dissolving: *hydrolysis.* [< Gk. *lusis*, loosening.]

-lyte *suff.* A substance decomposable by a specified process: *electrolyte.* [< Gk. *lutos*, soluble.]

Mm

m or **M** (ĕm) *n., pl.* **m's** or **Ms.** 1. The 13th letter of the English alphabet. 2. The 13th in a series. 3. **M** The Roman numeral for 1,000.

Ma'am (măm). Madam.

ma·ca·bre (mə-kä'brə, -bər) *adj.* Suggesting the horror of death and decay; gruesome; ghastly. [< OFr. *(danse de)* ℵ *ιcabre*, (dance of) Death.]

mac·ad·am (mə-kăd'əm) *n.* A pavement of layers of compacted small stones, usu. bound with tar or asphalt. [< John L. *McAdam* (1756–1836).] —**mac·ad'am·ize'** *v.*

mac·a·ro·ni (măk'ə-rō'nē) *n., pl.* **-ni** or **-nies.** A paste of wheat flour pressed into hollow tubes or other shapes, dried, and prepared for eating by boiling. [< dial. Ital. *maccarone.*]

mac·a·roon (măk'ə-rōōn', măk'ə-rōōn') *n.* A chewy cookie made with sugar, egg whites, and almond paste or coconut. [< dial. Ital. *maccarone*, small cake, macaroni.]

ma·caw (mə-kô') *n.* A large, often brightly colored tropical American parrot. [Port. *macaú.*]

macaw

Mac·ca·bees (măk'ə-bēz') *n.* See table at **Bible.** —**Mac'ca·be'an** *adj.*

mace¹ (mās) *n.* 1. A heavy medieval war club with a spiked metal head. 2. A ceremonial staff used as a symbol of authority. [< OFr.]

mace² (mās) n. An aromatic spice made from the dried seed covering of the nutmeg. [< Gk. makir, a kind of spice.]

mac·er·ate (măs′ə-rāt′) v. **-at·ed, -at·ing.** **1.** To soften or separate by soaking or steeping. **2.** To emaciate usu. by starvation. [Lat. macerare.] **—mac′er·a′tion** n. **—mac′er·a′tor** or **mac′er·at′er** n.

Mach or **mach** (mäk) n. Mach number.

ma·chete (mə-shĕt′ē, -chĕt′ē) n. A large, broad-bladed knife used esp. for cutting vegetation. [Sp.]

Mach·i·a·vel·li·an (măk′ē-ə-vĕl′ē-ən) adj. Suggestive of or characterized by the principles of expediency, deceit, and cunning attributed to Niccolò Machiavelli. **—Mach′i·a·vel′li·an** n. **—Mach′i·a·vel′li·an·ism** n.

mach·i·na·tion (măk′ĭ-nā′shən, măsh′ĭ-) n. Often **machinations.** A crafty, intricate, or secret plot, usu. intended to achieve an evil purpose. **—mach′i·nate′** v. **—mach′i·na′tor** n.

ma·chine (mə-shēn′) n. **1. a.** A system formed and connected to alter, transmit, and direct applied forces to accomplish a specific objective. **b.** A simple device, as a lever, pulley, or inclined plane, that alters an applied force. **2.** A system or device, as an electronic computer, that assists in the performance of a human task. **3.** A person who acts or performs a task mechanically, without thinking or intelligence. **4.** A powerful political group whose members appear to be under the control of one or more leaders. **—v. -chined, -chin·ing.** To cut, shape, or finish by machine. [< Gk. mēkhos, means.]

machine gun n. A gun, often mounted, that fires rapidly and repeatedly. **—ma·chine′·gun′** v. **—machine gunner** n.

ma·chin·er·y (mə-shē′nə-rē, -shēn′rē) n., pl. **-ies.** **1.** Machines or machine parts in general. **2.** The working parts of a particular machine. **3.** A system with related elements that operate together: the machinery of modern society.

ma·chin·ist (mə-shē′nĭst) n. One who makes, operates, or repairs machines.

ma·chis·mo (mä-chēz′mō) n. An exaggerated sense of masculinity. [Sp.]

Mach number or **mach number** n. The ratio of the speed of an object to the speed of sound in the surrounding medium. [< Ernst Mach (1836–1916).]

ma·cho (mä′chō′) adj. Characterized by machismo. **—n.,** pl. **-chos.** **1.** Machismo. **2.** A male characterized by machismo. [Sp.]

mack·er·el (măk′ər-əl, măk′rəl) n., pl. **-el** or **-els.** Any of several widely distributed marine food fishes. [< OFr. maquerel.]

mack·i·naw (măk′ə-nô′) n. A short coat of heavy woolen material, usu. plaid. [< Mackinaw City, Michigan.]

mack·in·tosh (măk′ĭn-tŏsh′) n. Also **mac·in·tosh.** Chiefly Brit. A raincoat. [< Charles Macintosh (1766–1843).]

mac·ra·mé (măk′rə-mā′) n. Coarse lacework made by weaving and knotting cords into a pattern. [< Ar. miqramah, striped cloth.]

macro- pref. **1.** Large: macroscopic. **2.** Long: macrobiotics. **3.** Inclusive: macroeconomics. [< Gk. makros, large.]

mac·ro·bi·ot·ics (măk′rō-bī-ŏt′ĭks) n. (used with a sing. verb). **1.** The theory or practice of promoting longevity. **2.** A method purporting to promote longevity, principally by means of diet. **—mac′ro·bi·ot′ic** adj.

mac·ro·cosm (măk′rō-kŏz′əm) n. **1.** The en-

tire world; universe. **2.** A system regarded as an entity containing subsystems. [< Med. Lat. macrocosmus.] **—mac′ro·cos′mic** adj.

mac·ro·ec·o·nom·ics (măk′rō-ĕk′ə-nŏm′ĭks, -ē′kə-) n. (used with a sing. verb). The study of the overall aspects and workings of a national economy.

ma·cron (mā′krŏn′, -krən) n. A mark (ˉ) placed over a vowel to indicate a long sound, as the (ā) in make. [< Gk. makros, long.]

mac·ro·scop·ic (măk′rə-skŏp′ĭk) or **mac·ro·scop·i·cal** (-ĭ-kəl) adj. Large enough to be observed or examined by the naked eye.

mad (măd) adj. **mad·der, mad·dest.** **1.** Suffering from a disorder of the mind; insane. **2.** Informal. Feeling or showing strong liking or enthusiasm: mad about science-fiction movies. **3.** Feeling anger or resentment. **4.** Lacking restraint, reason, or judgment. **5.** Marked by extreme excitement, confusion, or agitation; frantic: a mad scramble for the bus. **6.** Affected by rabies. [< OE gemād.] **—mad′ly** adv. **—mad′man** n. **—mad′ness** n. **—mad′wom′an** n.

Mad·am (măd′əm) n. **1.** pl. **Mes·dames** (mā-däm′). A title of courtesy used as a form of address to a woman. **2.** madam. A woman who manages a house of prostitution.

Ma·dame (mə-däm′, măd′əm) n., pl. **Mes·dames** (mā-däm′). A married woman in a French-speaking area. [< OFr. ma dame, my lady.]

mad·cap (măd′kăp′) n. A rash or impulsive person. **—mad′cap′** adj.

mad·den (măd′n) v. **1.** To make frantic or insane. **2.** To make or become angry. **—mad′den·ing·ly** adv.

mad·der (măd′ər) n. **1.** An Old World plant with small, yellow flowers and a red, fleshy root. **2.** A red dye obtained from the root of the madder. [< OE mædere.]

made (mād) v. p.t. & p.p. of **make.**

Mad·e·moi·selle (măd′ə-mə-zĕl′) n. A young girl or unmarried woman in a French-speaking area. [< OFr. ma demoiselle, my young lady.]

made-to-or·der (mād′tŏŏ-ôr′dər) adj. **1.** Made in accordance with particular instructions. **2.** Very suitable.

made-up (mād′ŭp′) adj. **1.** Fictitious; fabricated: a made-up story. **2.** Marked by the use of cosmetics or make-up: a made-up actress.

mad·house (măd′hous′) n. **1.** Formerly, an insane asylum. **2.** Informal. A place of great disorder.

mad·ras (măd′rəs, mə-drăs′, -drăs′) n. A fine cotton cloth, usu. with a plaid, striped, or checked pattern. [< Madras, India.]

mad·ri·gal (măd′rĭ-gəl) n. **1.** An unaccompanied vocal composition for two or more voices in simple harmony. **2.** A polyphonic part song, usu. unaccompanied. [Ital. madrigale.]

mael·strom (māl′strəm) n. **1.** A large and violent whirlpool. **2.** A situation that resembles a maelstrom in violence, turbulence, etc. [Du.]

maes·tro (mīs′trō) n., pl. **-tros** or **-tri** (-trē). A master in an art, esp. a composer, conductor, or music teacher. [Ital.]

Ma·fi·a (mä′fē-ə) n. **1.** A secret terrorist organization in Sicily. **2.** A criminal organization believed active since the late 19th cent. [< dial. Ital. mafia, boldness.]

Ma·fi·o·so (mä′fē-ō′sō) n., pl. **-si** (-sē′). A member of the Mafia. [Ital.]

mag·a·zine (măg′ə-zēn′, măg′ə-zēn′) n. **1.** A

place where ammunition is stored. **2.** A periodical containing articles, pictures, etc. **3.** A usu. detachable compartment to hold cartridges for a firearm. **4.** A compartment in a camera for holding film. [< Ar. *makhzan*, storehouse.]

ma·gen·ta (mə-jĕn'tə) *n.* A bright purplish red. [< *Magenta*, Italy.] —**ma·gen'ta** *adj.*

mag·got (măg'ət) *n.* The legless, soft-bodied larva of an insect, as the housefly. [ME *magot.*] —**mag'got·y** *adj.*

Ma·gi (mā'jī') *pl.n.* The three wise men of the East who paid homage to the infant Jesus. [< Pers. *maguš*, sorcerer.]

mag·ic (măj'ĭk) *n.* **1.** The art or alleged art of controlling natural events, effects, or forces by invoking charms, ꞁells, etc. **2.** The use of sleight of hand and other tricks to entertain. **3.** A mysterious quality that seems to enchant. [< Pers. *maguš*, sorcerer.] —**mag'ic** or **mag'i·cal** *adj.* —**mag'i·cal·ly** *adv.* —**ma·gi'cian** *n.* **Syns:** *magic, sorcery, witchcraft, wizardry n.*

ma·gis·te·ri·al (măj'ĭs-tîr'ē-əl) *adj.* **1. a.** Authoritative; commanding. **b.** Dictatorial; dogmatic. **2.** Of a magistrate or his official functions. [< Lat. *magister*, master.] —**mag'is·te'ri·al·ly** *adv.*

mag·is·trate (măj'ĭs-trāt', -trĭt) *n.* A civil officer with power to administer the law. [Lat. *magistratus.*]

mag·ma (măg'mə, măg'-) *n., pl.* **-ma·ta** (-mä'tə) or **-mas.** The molten matter under the earth's crust, from which igneous rock is formed by cooling and hardening. [< Gk., unguent.]

Mag·na Char·ta or **Mag·na Car·ta** (măg'nə kär'tə) *n.* The charter of English political and civil liberties granted in 1215.

mag·nan·i·mous (măg-năn'ə-məs) *adj.* Generous and noble, esp. in forgiving. [Lat. *magnanimus.*] —**mag'na·nim'i·ty** (-nə-nĭm'ĭ-tē) *n.* —**mag·nan'i·mous·ly** *adv.* —**mag·nan'i·mous·ness** *n.*

mag·nate (măg'nāt') *n.* A powerful or influential person. [< Lat. *magnus*, great.]

mag·ne·sia (măg-nē'zhə, -shə) *n.* A white, powdery compound, MgO, used in high-temperature refractories, electric insulation, and as a laxative and antacid. [< Gk. *Magnēs*, of Magnesia, an ancient city in Asia Minor.]

mag·ne·si·um (măg-nē'zē-əm, -shəm) *n. Symbol* **Mg** A light, silvery, moderately hard metallic element that burns with a brilliant white flame, used in lightweight structural alloys. Atomic number 12; atomic weight 24.312. [< MAGNESIA.]

mag·net (măg'nĭt) *n.* **1.** A body, as of metal, ore, etc., that attracts iron and certain other materials. **2.** One that attracts. [< Gk. *Magnēs (lithos)*, (stone) of Magnesia.]

mag·net·ic (măg-nĕt'ĭk) *adj.* **1.** Of or relating to magnetism or magnets. **2.** Having the properties of a magnet; exhibiting magnetism. **3.** Relating to the magnetic poles of the earth. **4.** Capable of being magnetized or of being attracted by a magnet. **5.** Exerting attraction: *a magnetic personality.* —**mag·net'i·cal·ly** *adv.*

magnetic field *n.* A region of space, as that around a magnet or an electric current, in which a detectable force is exerted on a magnetic body at any point.

magnetic needle *n.* A light, needle-shaped magnet, usu. suspended from a pivot, that aligns itself with a magnetic field around it.

magnetic north *n.* The direction to which the north-seeking pole of a magnetic needle points.

magnetic pole *n.* **1.** Either of two points or regions in a magnet at which the magnet's field is strongest. **2.** Either of two points on the earth, close to but not coinciding with the geographic poles, where the earth's magnetic field is most intense.

magnetic recording *n.* The recording of a signal, such as sound or computer instructions, in the form of a magnetic pattern.

magnetic tape *n.* A plastic tape coated with a magnetic material such as iron oxide for use in magnetic recording.

mag·ne·tism (măg'nə-tĭz'əm) *n.* **1.** The properties, ꞁfects, etc., associated with the presence of magnetic ꞁields. **2.** The study of magnets and their effects. **3.** The force exerted by a magnetic field. **4.** Power to attract, fascinate, or influence: *the magnetism of money.*

mag·ne·tite (măg'nə-tīt') *n.* A magnetic black iron oxide, Fe_3O_4, an important ore of iron.

mag·ne·tize (măg'nə-tīz') *v.* **-tized, -tiz·ing.** **1.** To make magnetic. **2.** To attract. —**mag·net·i·za'tion** *n.* —**mag'net·iz'er** *n.*

mag·ne·to (măg-nē'tō) *n., pl.* **-tos.** A small generator of alternating current that works by means of permanent magnets, used in the ignition systems of some internal-combustion engines. [< *magnetoelectric machine.*]

mag·ne·tom·e·ter (măg'nə-tŏm'ə-tər) *n.* An instrument for measuring the intensity of magnetic fields, esp. of the earth's magnetic field.

mag·nif·i·cent (măg-nĭf'ĭ-sənt) *adj.* **1.** Splendid in appearance; grand: *a magnificent cathedral; a magnificent view.* **2.** Grand, imposing, or noble in character; exalted. **3.** Outstanding; superlative; exceptional. [< Lat. *magnificus.*] —**mag·nif'i·cence** *n.* —**mag·nif'i·cent·ly** *adv.*

mag·ni·fy (măg'nĭ-fī') *v.* **-fied, -fy·ing.** **1.** To make greater in size, extent, or effect; enlarge. **2.** To exaggerate. **3.** To increase the apparent size of, esp. by means of a lens. **4.** To glorify. [< Lat. *magnificare.*] —**mag'ni·fi·ca'tion** *n.* —**mag'ni·fi'er** *n.*

magnifying glass *n.* A lens that enlarges the image of an object seen through it.

mag·ni·tude (măg'nĭ-tōōd', -tyōōd') *n.* **1.** Greatness, esp. in size or extent. **2.** Greatness in significance or influence. **3.** The relative brightness of a celestial body designated on a numerical scale. [< Lat. *magnitudo.*]

mag·no·lia (măg-nōl'yə) *n.* A tree or shrub with large, showy white, pink, purple, or yellow flowers. [< Pierre *Magnol* (1638–1715).]

mag·num o·pus (măg'nəm ō'pəs) *n.* A great work, esp. the greatest single work of an artist, writer, or composer. [Lat.]

mag·pie (măg'pī) *n.* **1.** A long-tailed, loud-voiced, chiefly black and white bird related to the crows and jays. **2.** A person who chatters constantly. [*Mag*, a nickname for *Margaret* + *pie*, magpie.]

Mag·yar (măg'yär, mäg'-) *n.* **1.** A member of

the principal ethnic group of Hungary. **2.** The Finno-Ugric language of the Magyars that is the official language of Hungary. —**Mag'yar** *adj.*

ma·ha·ra·jah or **ma·ha·ra·ja** (mä'hə-rä'jə, -zhə) *n.* A king or prince in India. [< Skt. *mahārājā.*]

ma·ha·ra·ni or **ma·ha·ra·nee** (mä'hə-rä'nē) *n.* A queen or princess in India. [< Skt. *mahārājñī.*]

ma·ha·ri·shi (mä'hə-rē'shē, mə-härə-shē) *n.* A Hindu teacher of mysticism and spiritual knowledge. [Skt. *mahārṣi.*]

Ma·hat·ma (mä-hät'mä, mə-hät'mə) *n.* A Hindu title of respect for a man renowned for spirituality. [Skt. *mahātman.*]

Ma·hi·can (mə-hē'kən) *n., pl.* **-can** or **-cans.** Also **Mo·hi·can** (mō-, mə-). **1. a.** A tribe or confederacy of Indians that formerly lived between the upper Hudson River Valley and Lake Champlain. **b.** A member of the Mahican tribe or confederacy. **2.** The Algonquian language of the Mahican.

ma·hog·a·ny (mə-hŏg'ə-nē) *n., pl.* **-nies. 1. a.** A tropical American tree with hard, reddish-brown wood. **b.** The wood of such a tree. **2. a.** Any of several similar trees. **b.** The wood of any of these trees. [Orig. unknown.]

Mah·rat·i or **Mah·rat·ti** (mə-rä'tē, t. Vars. of **Marathi.**

maid (mād) *n.* **1.** A girl or an unmarried woman. **2.** A female servant. [< MAIDEN.]

maid·en (mād'n) *n.* An unmarried girl or woman. —*adj.* **1.** Of, pertaining to, or befitting a maiden. **2.** First or earliest: *a maiden voyage.* [< OE *mægden.*] —**maid'en·hood** *n.*

maid·en·hair (mād'n-hâr') *n.* A fern having feathery fronds with fan-shaped leaflets.

maid of honor *n., pl.* **maids of honor.** The chief unmarried female attendant of a bride.

Mai·du (mī'dōō) *n., pl.* **-du** or **-dus. 1. a.** An Indian tribe formerly living in the Sacramento Valley area of California. **b.** A member of this tribe. **2.** The Penutian language of the Maidu. —**Mai'du** *adj.*

mail[1] (māl) *n.* **1. a.** Materials, as letters and packages, handled in a postal system. **b.** Postal material for a specific person or organization. **2.** A postal system. —*v.* To send by mail. [< OFr. *male,* bag, of Gmc. orig.] —**mail'er** *n.*

mail[2] (māl) *n.* Flexible armor made of small overlapping metal rings, loops of chain, or scales. [< Lat. *macula,* mesh.]

mail·box (māl'bŏks') *n.* **1.** A public box for deposit of mail. **2.** A private box for the delivery of mail.

mail·man (māl'măn', -mən) *n.* One who carries and delivers mail.

mail order *n.* An order for goods or services that is received and filled through the mail.

mail-order house (māl'ôr'dər) *n.* A business establishment that is primarily organized to promote, receive, and fill requests for merchandise or services through the mail.

maim (mām) *v.* **1.** To disable; mutilate; cripple. **2.** To impair. [< OFr. *mahaignier.*]

main (mān) *adj.* **1.** Most important; principal; major. **2.** Exerted to the utmost; sheer: *by main strength.* —*n.* **1.** The principal pipe or conduit in a system for conveying water, gas, oil, etc. **2.** Physical strength: *might and main.* —**idiom. in the main.** On the whole; mostly. [< OE *mægen.*] —**main'ly** *adv.*

main·land (mān'lănd', -lənd) *n.* The principal land mass of a country or continent.

main·line (mān'līn') *v.* **-lined, -lin·ing.** *Slang.* To inject narcotics directly into a vein.

main·mast (mān'məst) *n.* The principal mast of a sailing ship.

main·sail (mān'səl) *n.* The largest sail set on the mainmast of a sailing ship.

main·spring (mān'spring') *n.* **1.** The principal spring mechanism in a device, esp. in a watch or clock. **2.** A motivating force.

main·stay (mān'stā') *n.* **1.** A rope that supports a mainmast. **2.** A principal support.

main·stream (mān'strēm') *n.* The prevailing current or direction of a movement or influence. —**main'stream'** *adj. & v.*

main·tain (mān-tān') *v.* **1.** To continue; carry on. **2.** To preserve or retain. **3.** To keep in good repair. **4.** To provide for; support. **5.** To defend or sustain. **6.** To assert or declare. [< Lat. *manu tenēre,* to hold in the hand.] —**main·tain'a·ble** *adj.* —**main'te·nance** (-tə-nəns) *n.*

maî·tre d'hô·tel (mā'trə dō-tĕl') *n., pl.* **maî·tres d'hô·tel** (mā'trə dō-tĕl'). **1.** A head steward. **2.** A headwaiter. [Fr.]

maize (māz) *n.* Corn. [< Taino *mahiz.*]

ma·jes·ty (măj'ĭs-tē) *n., pl.* **-ties. 1.** The greatness and dignity of a sovereign. **2.** Supreme authority or power. **3. Majesty.** A title used in speaking of or to a sovereign monarch: *Your Majesty.* **4.** Regal dignity, splendor, and grandeur. [< Lat. *majestas.*] —**ma·jes'tic** *adj.* —**ma·jes'ti·cal·ly** *adv.*

ma·jor (mā'jər) *adj.* **1.** Greater in importance, rank, or extent. **2.** Serious or dangerous: *a major illness.* **3.** *Mus.* Of or based on a major scale. —*n.* **1.** A military officer ranking next above a captain. **2. a.** The principal field of specialization of a college student. **b.** A student specializing in such a field. —*v.* To pursue academic studies in a major field. [< Lat. *greater.*]

ma·jor-do·mo (mā'jər-dō'mō) *n., pl.* **-mos.** A head steward or butler. [< Med. Lat. *major domus.*]

major general *n.* A military officer who ranks next above a brigadier general.

ma·jor·i·ty (mə-jôr'ĭ-tē, -jŏr'-) *n., pl.* **-ties. 1.** A number more than half of the total number of a given group. **2.** The number of votes cast in an election above the total number of all other votes cast. **3.** The status of legal age.

major league *n.* A league of principal importance in professional sports, esp. baseball. —**ma'jor-league'** *adj.*

ma·jor-med·i·cal (mā'jər-mĕd'ĭ-kəl) *adj.* Of, relating to, or being a type of insurance plan that covers most of the medical bills of major illnesses.

major scale *n.* A diatonic scale having half steps between the 3rd and 4th and the 7th and 8th tones.

make (māk) *v.* **made** (mād), **mak·ing. 1.** To create; construct; form; shape. **2.** To cause to be, become, or seem. **3.** To compel. **4.** To appoint. **5.** To perform. **6.** To do; execute. **7.** To arrive at. **8.** To acquire. **9.** To achieve; attain. **10.** To prepare. **11.** To provide. **12.** To develop into. **13.** To admit of being transformed into. **14.** To constitute. **15.** To behave or act in a specified manner. **16.** To set out; proceed. —*phrasal verbs.* **make out. 1.** To see with difficulty: *could barely make out the lighthouse through the fog.* **2.** To grasp the meaning of; understand. **3.** To write out or draw up. **4.** *Slang.* To get along well; succeed. **5.** *Slang.* To neck; pet. **make over. 1.** To redo; renovate. **2.** To transfer the ownership of, usu. by legal means. **make up. 1. a.** To produce or create by assembling. **b.** To think up or imagine: *made up an excuse.* **2.** To constitute. **3.** To compensate, as for a mistake or omission. **4.** To decide: *make up one's mind.* **5.** To resolve a personal quarrel. **6.** To apply cosmetics. —*n.* **1.** The style or manner in which a thing is made. **2. A** specific line of manufactured goods. —*idioms.* **make believe.** To pretend. **make do.** To manage or get along with what is available. **make good. 1.** To carry out successfully; achieve. **2.** To pay back. **3.** To succeed: *make good in the big city.* **make way.** To give room for passage. **on the make. 1.** Aggressively seeking social or financial self-improvement. **2.** *Slang.* Eagerly pursuing sexual conquests or encounters. [< OE *macian*.] —**mak'er** *n.*

Syns: *make, construct, fabricate, fashion, manufacture, shape* v.

make-be-lieve (māk'bĭ-lēv') *n.* Playful or fanciful pretense. —**make'-be-lieve'** *adj.*

make-shift (māk'shĭft') *n.* A temporary expedient or substitute. —**make'shift'** *adj.*

make-up (māk'ŭp') *n.* Also **make-up. 1.** The way in which something is arranged or constructed. **2.** The mental, physical, or moral qualities that constitute a personality; disposition. **3.** Cosmetics applied esp. to the face.

ma-ku-ta (mä-kōō'tä) *n.* Pl. of **likuta.**

mal- *pref.* Bad; badly: *maladjustment.* [< Lat.]

Mal-a-chi (măl'ə-kī') *n.* See table at **Bible.**

mal-a-chite (măl'ə-kīt') *n.* A green to nearly black mineral carbonate of copper, $CuCO_3 \cdot Cu(OH)_2$, used for decorative objects. [< Gk. *molokhitis.*]

mal-ad-just-ment (măl'ə-jŭst'mənt) *n.* Faulty or poor adjustment. —**mal'ad-just'ed** *adj.*

mal-a-droit (măl'ə-droit') *adj.* Lacking in dexterity; clumsy. —**mal'a-droit'ly** *adv.* —**mal'a-droit'ness** *n.*

mal-a-dy (măl'ə-dē) *n.,* pl. **-dies.** A disease, disorder, or ailment. [< Lat. *male habitus,* in poor condition.]

Mal-a-gas-y (măl'ə-găs'ē) *n.,* pl. **-gas-y** or **-gas-ies. 1.** A native of Madagascar. **2.** The Austronesian language of the Malagasy. —**Mal'a-gas'y** *adj.*

mal-aise (măl-āz') *n.* A vague feeling of illness or depression. [Fr.]

ma-la-mute (mä'lə-myōōt', măl'ə-) *n.* A dog

developed in Alaska as a sled dog, with a thick coat and a bushy tail. [*Malemute,* an Alaskan Eskimo people.]

mal-a-prop-ism (măl'ə-prŏp-ĭz'əm) *n.* A humorous misuse of a word. [< *Mrs. Malaprop,* a character in *The Rivals,* a play by Richard B. Sheridan.]

mal-a-pro-pos (măl'ăp-rə-pō') *adv.* Inappropriately; inopportunely. [Fr. *mal à propos.*] —**mal'a-pro-pos'** *adj.*

ma-lar-i-a (mə-lâr'ē-ə) *n.* An infectious disease characterized by cycles of chills, fever, and sweating, transmitted by the bite of an infected mosquito. [Ital. *mal'aria,* foul air, malaria.] —**ma-lar'i-al** *adj.*

ma-lar-key (mə-lär'kē) *n.* Also **ma-lar-ky.** *Slang.* Exaggerated or foolish talk; nonsense. [Orig. unknown.]

Mal-a-thi-on (măl'ə-thē'ŏn'). A trademark for the organic compound $C_{10}H_{19}O_6PS_2$, used as an insecticide.

Ma-lay (mā'lā', mə-lā') *n.* **1.** One of a people inhabiting the Malay Peninsula and adjacent areas. **2.** The Indonesian language of the Malays. —*adj.* **1.** Of or pertaining to the Malays or their language. **2.** Of or pertaining to Malaya or Malaysia. —**Ma-lay'an** *adj.* & *n.*

Mal-a-ya-lam (măl'ə-yä'ləm) *n.* A Dravidian language of the Malabar coast in southwestern India.

mal-con-tent (măl'kən-tĕnt') *adj.* Discontented. —*n.* A discontented person.

male (māl) *adj.* **1.** Of, pertaining to, or designating the sex that produces spermatozoa for fertilizing ova. **2.** Characteristic of the male sex; masculine. **3.** Designed for i..sertion into a hollow bore or socket. —*n.* A male animal or plant. [< Lat. *mas.*] —**male'ness** *n.*

Mal-e-cite (măl'ĭ-sīt') *n.,* pl. **-cite** or **-cites. 1. a.** A tribe of Indians formerly inhabiting New Brunswick and northeastern Maine. **b.** A member of this tribe. **2.** The Algonquian language of the Malecites.

mal-e-dic-tion (măl'ĭ-dĭk'shən) *n.* A curse. [< Lat. *maledicere,* to curse.]

mal-e-fac-tor (măl'ə-făk'tər) *n.* **1.** A criminal. **2.** An evildoer. [< Lat.] —**mal'e-fac'tion** (-făk'shən) *n.*

ma-lef-ic (mə-lĕf'ĭk) *adj.* **1.** Baleful. **2.** Malicious. [Lat. *maleficus.*]

ma-lef-i-cence (mə-lĕf'ə-səns) *n.* **1.** An evil or harmful act. **2.** The quality or condition of being harmful or evil. [Lat. *maleficentia.*] —**ma-lef'i-cent** *adj.*

ma-lev-o-lent (mə-lĕv'ə-lənt) *adj.* Having or showing ill will; malicious. [Lat. *malevolens.*] —**ma-lev'o-lence** *n.* —**ma-lev'o-lent-ly** *adv.*

Syns: *malevolent, evil, malicious, malign, malignant, mean, nasty, poisonous, venomous, vicious, wicked* adj.

mal-fea-sance (măl-fē'zəns) *n.* *Law.* Misconduct or wrongdoing, esp. by a public official. [MAL- + OFr. *faisance,* doing.]

mal-for-ma-tion (măl'fôr-mā'shən) *n.* An abnormal or irregular structure or form. —**mal-formed'** *adj.*

mal-func-tion (măl-fŭngk'shən) *v.* To fail to function normally. —**mal-func'tion** *n.*

mal-ice (măl'ĭs) *n.* The desire to harm others or to see others suffer; spite. [< Lat. *malus,*

malamute

bad.] —**ma·li'cious** adj. —**ma·li'cious·ly** adv. —**ma·li'cious·ness** n.

ma·lign (mə-līn') v. To speak evil of; slander; defame. —adj. 1. Malevolent. 2. Harmful in influence or effect; injurious. [< Lat. *malignus,* harmful.] —**ma·lign'er** n.

ma·lig·nant (mə-lĭg'nənt) adj. 1. Showing great malevolence. 2. Highly injurious; pernicious. 3. Designating an abnormal growth that tends to spread. —**ma·lig'nan·cy** n. —**ma·lig'nant·ly** adv.

ma·lig·ni·ty (mə-lĭg'nə-tē) n., pl. **-ties.** 1. a. Intense ill will or hatred; malice. b. An act or feeling of great malice. 2. The condition or quality of being evil or injurious.

ma·lin·ger (mə-lĭng'gər) v. To feign illness or injury to avoid duty or work. [< Fr. *malingre,* sickly.] —**ma·lin'ger·er** n.

mall (môl, măl) n. 1. A shady public walk or promenade. 2. A walk lined with stores and closed to vehicles. 3. A median strip dividing a roadway. [< *The Mall,* London.]

mal·lard (măl'ərd) n. A wild duck of which the male has a green head and neck. [< OFr. *malarde.*]

mal·le·a·ble (măl'ē-ə-bəl) adj. 1. Capable of being shaped or formed, as by hammering or pressure. 2. Tractable; pliable. [< Med. Lat. *malleare,* to hammer.] —**mal'le·a·bil'i·ty** or **mal'le·a·ble·ness** n. —**mal'le·a·bly** adv.

mal·let (măl'ĭt) n. 1. A short-handled hammer, usu. with a cylindrical head of wood. 2. A similar long-handled hammer used to strike a ball, as in croquet and polo. [< Lat. *malleus,* hammer.]

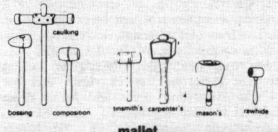

caulking

boxing   composition   tinsmith's carpenter's   mason's   rawhide

mallet

mal·le·us (măl'ē-əs) n., pl. **mal·le·i** (măl'ē-ī', -ē-ē'). The largest of three small bones in the middle ear. [Lat., hammer.]

mal·low (măl'ō) n. Any of various related plants with showy pink or white flowers. [< Lat. *malva.*]

mal·nour·ished (măl-nûr'ĭsht) adj. Inadequately nourished.

mal·nu·tri·tion (măl'nōō-trĭsh'ən, -nyōō-) n. Insufficient and poor nutrition.

mal·oc·clu·sion (măl'ə-klōō'zhən) n. Faulty closure of teeth.

mal·o·dor·ous (măl-ō'dər-əs) adj. Having a bad smell. —**mal·o'dor·ous·ly** adv. —**mal·o'dor·ous·ness** n.

mal·prac·tice (măl-prăk'tĭs) n. Improper or negligent conduct or treatment, esp. by a physician. —**mal'prac·ti'tion·er** n.

malt (môlt) n. 1. Soaked, sprouted, and dried grain, usu. barley, used chiefly in brewing and distilling. 2. An alcoholic beverage brewed from malt. 3. Malted milk (sense 2). [< OE *mealt.*] —**malt'y** adj.

malt·ed milk (môl'tĭd) n. 1. A soluble powder made of dried milk, malted barley, and wheat flour. 2. Also **malt** or **malted.** A beverage made by mixing malted milk with milk and sometimes ice cream and flavoring.

mal·tose (môl'tōs', -tōz') n. A sugar, $C_{12}H_{22}O_{11} \cdot H_2O$.

mal·treat (măl-trēt') v. To treat cruelly or roughly. —**mal·treat'ment** n.

ma·ma (mä'mə, mə-mä') n. Also **mam·ma.** Mother. [Of baby-talk orig.]

mam·ba (mäm'bə) n. A venomous tropical African snake. [Zulu *i-mâmbà.*]

mam·bo (mäm'bō) n., pl. **-bos.** A dance of Latin-American origin similar to the rumba. [Sp. (Cuba).] —**mam'bo** v.

mam·mal (măm'əl) n. Any of a group of warm-blooded vertebrate animals, including man, characterized by the presence of hair and by milk-producing glands in the females. [< Lat. *mamma,* breast.] —**mam·mal'i·an** (mă-mā'lē-ən) adj. & n.

mam·ma·ry (măm'ər-ē) adj. Of or pertaining to a breast or milk-producing organ.

mam·mon (măm'ən) n. Also **Mammon.** Money personified as a false god. [< Aram. *māmônā,* riches.]

mam·moth (măm'əth) n. An extinct elephant once found throughout the Northern Hemisphere. —adj. Huge; gigantic. [Obs. R. *mammot'.*]

man (măn) n., pl. **men** (mĕn). 1. An adult male human being. 2. A human being; person. 3. Mankind. 4. A man having the qualities considered characteristic of manhood. 5. A male employee or worker. 6. A husband, lover, or sweetheart. 7. Any of the pieces used in board games, as chess. —v. **manned, man·ning.** 1. To supply or furnish with men for work, defense, etc. 2. To fortify or strengthen. —*idiom.* **to a man.** Including everyone; without exceptions. [< OE.]

Usage: The use of *man* to mean "a human being, regardless of sex" has a long history, but many feel that the sense of "male" is predominant over that of "person." Therefore many occupational titles in which *man* occurs as an element are being replaced, sometimes officially, by terms that are neutral. For example, *firefighter* is often used instead of *fireman,* or *Member of Congress* instead of *Congressman.*

man about town n., pl. **men about town.** A worldly and socially knowledgeable man who frequents fashionable places.

man·a·cle (măn'ə-kəl) n. Often **manacles.** 1. A device for shackling the hands; handcuff. 2. Something that confines or restrains. —v. **-cled, -cling.** To restrain with or as if with manacles. [< Lat. *manicula,* little hand.]

man·age (măn'ĭj) v. **-aged, -ag·ing.** 1. To direct, control, or handle. 2. To administer or regulate. 3. To make submissive. 4. To contrive or arrange. 5. To get along. [Ital. *maneggiare,* ult. < Lat. *manus,* hand.] —**man'age·a·bil'i·ty** n. —**man'age·a·ble** adj. —**man'age·a·bly** adv.

man·age·ment (măn'ĭj-mənt) n. 1. The act, manner, or practice of managing. 2. The person or persons who manage an organization. 3. Executive ability.

man·ag·er (măn'ĭj-ər) n. 1. One who manages. 2. One in charge of the training and performance of an athlete or team. —**man'a·ge'ri·al** (-ĭ-jîr'ē-əl) adj. —**man'a·ge'ri·al·ly** adv. —**man'ag·er·ship** n.

ma·ña·na (mä-nyä'nä) n. Some indefinite time in the future. [Sp., tomorrow]. —**ma·ña'na** adv.

man·a·tee (măn′ə-tē′) *n.* An aquatic, primarily tropical mammal. [Sp. *manati.*]

Man·chu (măn′chōō, măn-chōō′) *n., pl.* **-chu** or **-chus.** 1. One of a nomadic Mongoloid people, native to Manchuria, who conquered China in 1644 and established a dynasty that was overthrown by revolution in 1911. 2. The Tungusic language of the Manchu. —**Man′chu** *adj.*

man·da·mus (măn-dā′məs) *n. Law.* A writ issued by a superior court ordering a public official or body or a lower court to perform a specified duty. [Lat., we order.]

Man·dan (măn′dăn′) *n., pl.* **-dan** or **-dans.** 1. a. A tribe of Indians that inhabited the Missouri River valley in North Dakota. b. A member of this tribe. 2. The Siouan language of the Mandan.

man·da·rin (măn′də-rĭn) *n.* 1. In imperial China, a high-ranking public official. 2. **Mandarin.** Chinese (sense 2.b.). [< Skt. *mantrī,* counselor.]

man·date (măn′dāt′) *n.* 1. An authoritative command or instruction. 2. a. A commission from the League of Nations authorizing a nation to administer a territory. b. A region under administration. [< Lat. *mandare,* to command.] —**man′date′** *v.* —**man′da·tor** *n.*

man·da·to·ry (măn′də-tôr′ē, -tōr′ē) *adj.* 1. Of, pertaining to, or holding a mandate. 2. Required; obligatory.

man·di·ble (măn′də-bəl) *n.* A jaw or jawlike part, esp. the lower jaw in vertebrates. [< Lat. *mandere,* to chew.] —**man·dib′u·lar** (măn-dĭb′yə-lər) *adj.*

Man·din·go (măn-dĭng′gō) *n., pl.* **-gos** or **-goes.** 1. A member of any of various Negroid peoples inhabiting the region of the upper Niger River valley of western Africa. 2. A language or dialect of the Mandingos.

man·do·lin (măn′də-lĭn′, măn′də-lĭn′) *n.* A stringed musical instrument with a usu. pearshaped body and a fretted neck. [< Gk. *pandoura,* three-string lute.]

man·drake (măn′drāk′) *n.* 1. A Eurasian plant with a branched root thought to resemble the human body, once widely believed to have magical powers. 2. The May apple. [< Gk. *mandragas.*]

man·drel or **man·dril** (măn′drəl) *n.* 1. A spindle or axle used to secure or support material being machined. 2. A metal core around which wood and other materials may be cast or shaped. [Prob. < Fr. *mandrin,* lathe.]

man·drill (măn′drĭl) *n.* A large African monkey, with brilliant facial markings in the adult male. [MAN + *drill,* a kind of monkey.]

mane (mān) *n.* 1. The long hair growing from the neck of a horse, male lion, etc. 2. A long, thick growth of human hair. [< OE *manu.*]

ma·nège (mă-nĕzh′) *n.* Also **ma·nege.** The art of training or riding horses. [< Ital. *maneggiare,* to manage.]

ma·nes or **Ma·nes** (mā′nēz, mā′nās′) *pl.n.* In ancient Rome, the deified spirits of the dead. [Lat.]

ma·neu·ver (mə-nōō′vər, -nyōō′-) *n.* 1. a. A strategic or tactical military movement. b. Often **maneuvers.** A large-scale military training exercise that simulates combat. 2. A physical movement that requires skill. 3. An adroit and clever move; stratagem. —*v.* 1. To perform a military maneuver. 2. To use clever tactics or stratagems. 3. To manipulate or guide adroitly to a desired position or goal. [< Lat. *manu operari,* to work by hand.] —**ma·neu′ver·a·bil′i·ty** *n.* —**ma·neu′ver·a·ble** *adj.*

man·ful (măn′fəl) *adj.* Courageous and resolute. —**man′ful·ly** *adv.* —**man′ful·ness** *n.*

man·ga·nese (măng′gə-nēz′, -nēs′) *n. Symbol* **Mn** A gray-white, brittle metallic element. Atomic number 25; atomic weight 54.9380. [< Ital.]

mange (mānj) *n.* A contagious skin disease esp. of domestic animals, characterized by itching and loss of hair. [< OFr. *mangier,* to eat.] —**mang′y** *adj.*

man·ger (măn′jər) *n.* A trough or open box in which feed for livestock is placed. [< Lat. *mandere,* to chew.]

man·gle¹ (măng′gəl) *v.* **-gled, -gling.** 1. To batter, hack, or cut. 2. To ruin or spoil; botch. [< AN *mangler.*] —**man′gler** *n.*

man·gle² (măng′gəl) *n.* A laundry machine for pressing fabrics. [Du. *mangel.*]

mangle²   mangrove

man·go (măng′gō) *n., pl.* **-goes** or **-gos.** 1. A tropical evergreen tree that bears edible fruit. 2. The fruit of the mango, with sweet, juicy, yellow-orange flesh. [< Tamil *mānkāy.*]

man·grove (măng′grōv′, măng′grōv′) *n.* A tropical evergreen tree or shrub that has stiltlike roots and stems and forms dense thickets in tidal regions. [< Taino *mangle.*]

man·han·dle (măn′hăn′dəl) *v.* To handle roughly.

Man·hat·tan (măn-hăt′n, mən-) *n.* A cocktail made from vermouth and whiskey. [< *Manhattan,* a borough of New York City.]

man·hole (măn′hōl′) *n.* A hole through which an underground structure, such as a sewer, can be entered.

man·hood (măn′hŏŏd) *n.* 1. The condition of being an adult male. 2. The qualities, such as courage and vigor, usu. attributed to a man. 3. Men collectively.

man·hour (măn′our′) *n.* A unit of production equal to the work a person can produce in one hour.

man·hunt (măn′hŭnt′) *n.* An organized search for a person, usu. a fugitive criminal.

ma·ni·a (mā′nē-ə, mān′yə) *n.* 1. An intense enthusiasm; craze. 2. A mental disorder characterized by excessive physical activity and emotional excitement. [< Gk.]

–mania *suff.* An exaggerated or unreasonable desire or enthusiasm for: *balletomania.* [< MANIA.]

In the following list, the English meaning is

indicated for the form with which **-mania** is combined:

acromania (heights)
ailuromania (cats)
cynomania (dogs)
gymnomania (nudity)
hedonomania (pleasure)
heliomania (sunbathing)
hippomania (horses)
hypnomania (sleep)
necromania (death)
noctimania (night)
ochlomania (crowds)
ophidiomania (reptiles)
ornithomania (birds)
pharmacomania (medicines)
sitomania (food)
xenomania (foreigners)
zoomania (animals)

ma·ni·ac (mā′nē-ăk′) n. 1. An insane person; lunatic. 2. One with an excessive enthusiasm for something. [< Gk. *maniakos*, maniacal.] —**ma′ni·ac′** or **ma·ni′a·cal** (mə-nī′ə-kəl) adj.

man·ic (măn′ĭk) adj. Of, relating to, or characterized by mania.

man·ic-de·pres·sive (măn′ĭk-dĭ-prĕs′ĭv) adj. Characterized by alternating periods of manic excitement and severe depression. —n. A manic-depressive person.

man·i·cot·ti (măn′ĭ-kŏt′ē) n. Tubular pasta with a filling, as of ricotta cheese. [Ital.]

man·i·cure (măn′ĭ-kyŏŏr′) n. Treatment of the hands and fingernails. —v. **-cured, -curing.** 1. To give a manicure to. 2. To trim closely. [Fr.] —**man′i·cur′ist** n.

man·i·fest (măn′ə-fĕst′) adj. Clearly apparent to the sight or understanding; obvious. —v. To show plainly. —n. A list of cargo or passengers. [< Lat. *manifestus.*] —**man′i·fest·ly** adv.

man·i·fes·ta·tion (măn′ə-fĕs-tā′shən) n. A demonstration; display.

man·i·fes·to (măn′ə-fĕs′tō) n., pl. **-toes** or **-tos.** A public declaration of principles or intentions. [Ital.]

man·i·fold (măn′ə-fōld) adj. 1. Of many and diverse kinds. 2. Having many features or forms. —n. A pipe with several openings for making multiple connections. —v. 1. To make several copies of. 2. To multiply.

man·i·kin or **man·ni·kin** (măn′ĭ-kĭn) n. 1. A little man; dwarf. 2. Var. of **mannequin.** [< MDu. *mannekijn.*]

Ma·nil·a hemp (mə-nĭl′ə) n. The fiber of the abaca, used for making rope, cordage, and paper. [< *Manila*, Philippines.]

Manila paper n. Strong paper, usu. buff in color.

ma·nip·u·late (mə-nĭp′yə-lāt′) v. **-lat·ed, -lat·ing.** 1. To operate or manage by skilled use esp. of the hands. 2. To influence or manage skillfully. 3. To manage artfully or deceitfully for personal advantage. [< Lat. *manipulus*, handful.] —**ma·nip′u·la′tion** n. —**ma·nip′u·la′tive** or **ma·nip′u·la·to′ry** (-lə-tôr′ē, -tōr′ē) adj. —**ma·nip′u·la′tor** n.

man·kind (măn′kīnd′, -kīnd′) n. 1. The human race. 2. Men as distinguished from women.

man·ly (măn′lē) adj. **-li·er, -li·est.** Having qualities gen. attributed to a man. —**man′li·ness** n.

man-made (măn′mād′) adj. Made by man; synthetic.

man·na (măn′ə) n. 1. In the Old Testament, the food miraculously provided for the Israel-ites in the wilderness during their flight from Egypt. 2. Something badly needed that comes unexpectedly. [< Heb. *mān.*]

man·ne·quin (măn′ĭ-kĭn) n. Also **man·i·kin.** 1. A life-size representation of the human body, used for fitting or displaying clothes. 2. A woman who models clothes. [< MDu. *mannekijn*, manikin.]

man·ner (măn′ər) n. 1. **a.** A way or style of doing something. **b.** The way in which something is done or happens. 2. A person's characteristic bearing or behavior. 3. **manners.** Socially proper behavior. 4. Practice, style, or method in the arts. 5. Kind; sort. —**idiom. in a manner of speaking.** In a way; so to speak. [< Lat. *manus*, hand.]

man·nered (măn′ərd) adj. 1. Having manners of a particular kind: *ill-mannered.* 2. Artificial; affected: *mannered speech.*

man·ner·ism (măn′ər-ĭz′əm) n. 1. A peculiarity of behavior or manner. 2. An exaggerated or affected trait or habit.

man·ner·ly (măn′ər-lē) adj. Displaying good manners; polite. —**man′ner·li·ness** n.

man·nish (măn′ĭsh) adj. Resembling, typical of, or appropriate to a man. —**man′nish·ly** adv. —**man′nish·ness** n.

man-of-war (măn′ə-wôr′) n., pl. **men-of-war.** A warship.

ma·nom·e·ter (mă-nŏm′ĭ-tər) n. An instrument for measuring the pressure of liquids and gases. [Gk. *manos*, sparse + **-METER.**] —**man′o·met′ric** (măn′ə-mĕt′rĭk) or **man′o·met′ri·cal** adj.

man·or (măn′ər) n. 1. The landed estate of a feudal lord. 2. A landed estate. 3. The main house of an estate. [< Lat. *manēre*, to dwell.] —**ma·no′ri·al** (mă-nôr′ē-əl, -nōr′-) adj.

man·pow·er (măn′pou′ər) n. 1. The power of human physical effort. 2. The total number of people available for work or service.

man·qué (män-kā′) adj. Unsuccessful; frustrated: *an artist manqué.* [< Lat. *mancus*, maimed.]

man·sard (măn′särd) n. A roof that has two slopes on all four sides, with the lower slope steeper than the upper. [< François *Mansart* (1598–1666).]

manse (măns) n. The residence of a minister, esp. a Presbyterian minister. [< Lat. *manēre*, to dwell.]

man·sion (măn′shən) n. A large, stately house. [< Lat. *manēre*, to dwell.]

man-sized (măn′sīzd′) adj. Also **man-size** (-sīz′). *Informal.* Very large.

man·slaugh·ter (măn′slô′tər) n. The unlawful killing of another without malice or the intent to do injury.

man·tel (măn′təl) n. Also **man·tle.** 1. A facing around a fireplace. 2. A mantelpiece. [< Lat. *mantellum*, cloak.]

man·tel·piece (măn′təl-pēs′) n. The projecting shelf over a fireplace.

man·til·la (măn-tē′ə, -tĭl′ə) n. A scarf, often of lace, worn over the head and shoulders by Spanish and Latin-American women. [Sp.]

man·tis (măn′tĭs) n., pl. **-es** or **-tes** (-tēz). A predatory grasshopperlike insect with powerful forelimbs that are often folded in a praying position. [< Gk., prophet.]

man·tis·sa (măn-tĭs′ə) n. The decimal part of a logarithm. [Lat., counterweight.]

man·tle (măn′təl) n. 1. A loose, sleeveless outer garment. 2. Something that covers, envelops, or conceals. 3. A sheath of threads that gives off a strong light when heated by a flame. **4.** The layer of the earth between the crust and the core. **5.** Var. of **mantel.** —v. **-tled, -tling.** To cover with or as with a mantle. [< Lat. *mantellum*, cloak.]

man·tra (mŭn'trə) n. *Hinduism.* A sacred formula used as an incantation or prayer. [Skt. *mantraḥ.*]

man·u·al (măn'yōō-əl) adj. **1.** Of, pertaining to, or operated by the hands. **2.** Requiring physical rather than mental effort. —n. **1.** A small book of instructions. **2.** *Mil.* Prescribed movements in the handling of a weapon. [< Lat. *manus,* hand.] —**man·u·al·ly** adv.

manual alphabet n. An alphabet of hand signals used for communication by deaf-mutes.

manual alphabet

man·u·fac·to·ry (măn'yə-făk'tər-ē) n., pl. **-ries.** A factory. [MANUFAC(TURE) + -ORY.]

man·u·fac·ture (măn'yə-făk'chər) v. **-tured, -tur·ing. 1.** To make or process from raw materials, esp. with the use of machinery. **2.** To make up; fabricate. —n. **1.** The act or process of manufacturing. **2.** A manufactured product. [< LLat. *manufactus,* handmade.] —**man·u·fac'tur·er** n.

man·u·mit (măn'yōō-mĭt') v. **-mit·ted, -mit·ting.** To free from slavery. [< Lat. *manumittere.*]

ma·nure (mə-nŏŏr', -nyŏŏr') n. Material used to fertilize soil, esp. animal excrement. —v. **-nured, -nur·ing.** To apply manure to. [< Med. Lat. *manuoperari,* to till.]

man·u·script (măn'yə-skrĭpt') n. **1.** A typewritten or handwritten version of a book or other work. **2.** A book or other composition written by hand. —adj. Handwritten or typewritten as opposed to printed. [< Med. Lat. *manuscriptus,* handwritten.]

man·y (mĕn'ē) adj. **more** (môr, mōr), **most** (mōst). Amounting to or consisting of a large, indefinite number: *many friends.* —n. (used with a pl. verb). A large, indefinite number. —pron. (used with a pl. verb). A large number of persons or things. [< OE *manig.*]

Ma·o·ism (mou'ĭz'əm) n. The Communist political philosophy and practice developed in China chiefly by Mao Zedong. —**Ma·o·ist** n.

Ma·o·ri (mou'rē) n., pl. **-ri** or **-ris. 1.** A member of the aboriginal people of New Zealand. **2.** The Austronesian language of the Maori. —**Ma·o·ri** adj.

map (măp) n. A representation, usu. on a plane surface, of a region. —v. **mapped, mapping. 1.** To make a map of. **2.** To plan in detail: *mapped out an ad campaign.* [< Lat. *mappa,* napkin.] —**map'mak'er** n. —**map'per** n.

ma·ple (mā'pəl) n. **1.** A tree or shrub with lobed leaves and winged seeds borne in pairs.

2. The hard, close-grained wood of a maple. [< OE *mapul.*]

maple syrup n. A sweet syrup made from boiling down the sap of the sugar maple.

mar (mär) v. **marred, mar·ring.** To damage, deface, or spoil. [< OE *mierran.*]

mar·a·bou (măr'ə-bōō') n. **1.** A large Old World stork. **2.** The long, downy feathers of the marabou, used esp. as trimming on women's clothing. [< Ar. *murābit.*]

ma·ra·ca (mə-rä'kə) n. A percussion instrument consisting of a hollow gourd that contains pebbles or dried beans. [Port. *maracá.*]

mar·a·schi·no (măr'ə-skē'nō, -shē'nō) n. A liqueur made from the juice and crushed pits of a bitter cherry. [Ital.]

maraschino cherry n. A preserved cherry flavored with maraschino.

Ma·ra·thi (mə-rä'tē) n. Also **Mah·rat·i** or **Mah·rat·ti.** The major Indic language in the state of Maharashtra, India.

mar·a·thon (măr'ə-thŏn') n. **1.** A long-distance race, esp. one on foot. **2.** A test or contest of endurance. [< *Marathon,* Greece.]

ma·raud (mə-rôd') v. To rove in search of plunder. [Fr. *marauder.*] —**ma·raud'er** n.

mar·ble (mär'bəl) n. **1.** A sometimes streaked metamorphic rock, chiefly calcium carbonate, used esp. in sculpture and architecture. **2. a.** A little ball made of a hard substance such as glass, used in children's games. **b. marbles.** (used with a sing. verb). A game played with marbles. **3. marbles.** *Slang.* Common sense: *Have you lost your marbles?* [< Gk. *marmaros.*] —**mar'ble** v. —**mar'bly** adj.

mar·bling (mär'blĭng) n. A mottling or streaking that resembles marble, esp. in meat.

march¹ (märch) v. **1.** To walk or cause to walk with an even, measured gait, usu. keeping pace with others. **2.** To walk in a purposeful or determined manner. **3.** To advance or proceed with steady movement. **4.** To traverse by marching. —n. **1.** The act of marching. **2.** The distance or period of time covered by marching. **3.** A measured, even step. **4.** Forward movement; progression. **5.** *Mus.* A composition in strongly accented, usu. duple rhythm to accompany marching. —**idiom. on the march.** Moving ahead; advancing. [< OFr. *marchier.*]

march² (märch) n. A border region; frontier. [< OFr. *marche,* of Gmc. orig.]

March (märch) n. The 3rd month of the year, having 31 days. See table at **calendar.** [< Lat. *Martius (mensis),* (month) of Mars.]

mar·chion·ess (mär'shən-ĭs, mär'shə-nĕs') n. **1.** The wife of a marquis. **2.** A woman who holds the rank of marquis in her own right. [Med. Lat. *marchionissa.*]

Mardi gras (mär'dē grä') n. Shrove Tuesday, often celebrated by parades. [Fr.]

mare¹ (mâr) n. A female horse or related animal. [< OE *mere.*]

ma·re² (mä'rā) n., pl. **ma·ri·a** (-rē·ə). *Astron.* Any of the large, dark regions on the moon or Mars. [Lat., sea.]

mar·ga·rine (mär'jə-rĭn) n. A butter substitute made of a blend of hydrogenated vegetable oils mixed with emulsifiers, vitamins, and coloring matter. [Fr.]

mar·ga·ri·ta (mär'gə-rē'tə) n. A cocktail made

with tequila and lemon or lime juice. [Sp.]

mar·gin (mär′jən) *n.* **1.** An edge and the area that adjoins it; border. **2.** The space bordering the written or printed area on a page. **3.** An extra amount allowed beyond what is needed: *a margin of safety.* **4.** A quantity or degree of advantage: *a margin of 500 votes.* [< Lat. *margo*.] **—mar′gin·al** *adj.* **—mar′gin·al·ly** *adv.*

mar·gi·na·li·a (mär′jə-nā′lē-ə) *pl.n.* Notes in a margin.

mar·i·gold (mār′ə-gōld′, mâr′-) *n.* A widely cultivated plant with showy yellow or orange flowers. [ME.]

mar·i·jua·na or **mar·i·hua·na** (mār′ə-wä′nə) *n.* **1.** The hemp plant. **2.** The dried flower clusters and leaves of the hemp plant smoked for an intoxicating effect. [Mex. Sp. *marihuana.*]

ma·rim·ba (mə-rĭm′bə) *n.* A large xylophone with resonators. [Of African orig.]

ma·ri·na (mə-rē′nə) *n.* A boat basin that has docks, supplies, and repair facilities for small boats. [< Lat. *marinus,* marine.]

mar·i·nade (mār′ə-nād′) *n.* A spiced liquid in which food is soaked before cooking. [< Sp. *marinar,* to marinate.]

mar·i·nate (mār′ə-nāt′) *v.* **-nat·ed, -nat·ing.** To soak in a marinade. [< MARINADE.]

ma·rine (mə-rēn′) *adj.* **1.** Of or relating to the sea. **2.** Of or pertaining to shipping or trade by sea. **3.** Of or pertaining to sea navigation. **—n.** **1.** A soldier serving on a ship. **2.** A picture of the sea. [< Lat. *mare,* sea.]

Marine Corps *n.* A branch of the U.S. armed forces composed chiefly of amphibious troops.

mar·i·ner (mār′ə-nər) *n.* A sailor.

mar·i·o·nette (mār′ē-ə-nĕt′) *n.* A jointed puppet manipulated by strings. [Fr.]

mar·i·tal (mār′ə-təl) *adj.* Of or relating to marriage. [< Lat. *maritus,* married.] **—mar′i·tal·ly** *adv.*

mar·i·time (mār′ə-tīm′) *adj.* **1.** Located on or near the sea. **2.** Of commerce or navigation on the sea. [< Lat. *maritimus.*]

mar·jo·ram (mär′jər-əm) *n.* An aromatic plant with leaves used for seasoning. [< Med. Lat. *majorana.*]

mark[1] (märk) *n.* **1.** A visible trace or impression on something, as a spot, dent, or line. **2.** A written or printed symbol: *punctuation mark.* **3.** A grade, as in school. **4.** A name, stamp, etc., placed on an article to signify ownership, quality, etc. **5.** A visible indication of some quality, property, etc. **6.** A standard or criterion of quality. **7.** Quality; note; importance. **8.** A target. **9.** That which one wishes to achieve; goal. **10.** An object or point that serves as a guide. **—v.** **1.** To make a visible impression (on). **2.** To form, distinguish, or separate by making a visible impression on. **3.** To pay attention to. **4.** To characterize; set off. **5.** To grade (school papers). **—phrasal verbs. mark down.** To reduce in price. **mark up.** To increase the selling price. **—idiom. mark time. 1.** To keep time by moving the feet as in marching without moving forward. **2.** To make little or no progress. [< OE *mearc.*] **—mark′er** *n.*

mark[2] (märk) *n.* **1.** See table at currency. **2.** The deutsche mark. [< OE *marc,* unit of weight.]

Mark (märk) *n.* See table at **Bible.**

mark·down (märk′doun′) *n.* **1.** A reduction of

price. **2.** The amount by which a price has been reduced.

marked (märkt) *adj.* **1.** Having an identifying mark. **2.** Noticeable; distinctive. **—mark′ed·ly** (mär′kĭd-lē) *adv.*

mar·ket (mär′kĭt) *n.* **1. a.** A public gathering for buying and selling goods. **b.** The public place in which a market is held. **2.** A retail store that sells a particular type of merchandise: *a meat market.* **3.** Trade or commerce, esp. in a particular commodity: *the international coffee market.* **4. a.** A region or country where goods may be sold. **b.** A particular group of buyers: *the college market.* **5.** The extent or degree of demand. **—v.** **1.** To sell. **2.** To offer for sale. **3.** To purchase provisions. [< Lat. *merx,* merchandise.] **—mar′ket·a·bil′i·ty** *n.* **—mar′ket·a·ble** *adj.*

mar·ket·place (mär′kĭt-plās′) *n.* **1.** A public place in which a market is set up. **2.** Commercial activity or trade.

market price *n.* Also **market value.** The prevailing price of a commodity in the open market.

mark·ka (märk′kä′) *n., pl.* **-kaa** (-kä′). See table at currency. [Finn.]

marks·man (märks′mən) *n.* One skilled at shooting a weapon, esp. a gun. **—marks′man·ship′** *n.*

mark·up (märk′ŭp′) *n.* **1.** A raise in price. **2.** The amount added to the cost of an item to figure the selling price.

marl (märl) *n.* Clay containing calcium carbonate, used as fertilizer. [< Lat. *marga.*]

mar·lin (mär′lən) *n.* A large saltwater game fish resembling the swordfish. [< MARLINESPIKE.]

mar·line·spike (mär′lən-spīk′) *n.* Also **mar·lin·spike.** A pointed metal spike, used to separate strands of rope in splicing.

mar·ma·lade (mär′mə-lād′) *n.* A preserve made with the pulp and rind esp. of citrus fruits. [< Gk. *melimelon,* a kind of apple.]

mar·mo·re·al (mär-môr′ē-əl, -mōr′ē-əl) *adj.* Of or suggestive of marble: *marmoreal rigidity.* [< Lat. *marmoreus.*]

mar·mo·set (mär′mə-sĕt′, -zĕt′) *n.* Any of various small tropical American monkeys with soft fur and a long tail. [< OFr., a kind of monkey.]

marmoset

mar·mot (mär′mət) *n.* Any of various stocky, short-legged burrowing rodents, such as the woodchuck. [Fr. *marmotte.*]

ma·roon[1] (mə-rōōn′) *v.* **1.** To abandon, as on a deserted island. **2.** To leave (a person) helpless. [< Am. Sp. *cimarrón,* fugitive slave.]

ma·roon² (mə-rōōn′) *n.* A dark purplish red. [< Ital. *marrone*.] —**ma·roon′** *adj.*

mar·quee (mär-kē′) *n.* **1.** A large tent, used chiefly for outdoor entertainment. **2.** A rooflike structure that projects over an entrance, as to a theater. [Fr. *marquise*, marquee, marquise.]

mar·que·try (mär′kə-trē) *n., pl.* **-tries.** Decoration made by inlaying pieces of material, such as wood, into a veneer surface. [< OFr. *marqueter*, to checker, of Gmc. orig.]

mar·quis (mär′kwis) *n., pl.* **-es** *or* **-quis.** A nobleman who ranks below a duke. [< OFr. *marche*, boundary, of Gmc. orig.]

mar·quise (mär-kēz′) *n.* A marchioness. [Fr.]

mar·qui·sette (mär′ki-zĕt′, mär′kwĭ-) *n.* A sheer mesh fabric used esp. for curtains. [< Fr. *marquise*, marquee.]

mar·riage (măr′ĭj) *n.* **1.** The condition of being married; wedlock. **2.** A wedding ceremony. **3.** A close or intimate union. —**mar·riage·a·ble** *adj.*

mar·row (măr′ō) *n.* **1.** The soft material that fills the cavities inside bones. **2.** The essential part. [< OE *mearg.*]

mar·ry (măr′ē) *v.* **-ried, -ry·ing. 1.** To take as a husband or wife. **2.** To unite as husband and wife. **3.** To enter into a close relationship. [< Lat. *maritus*, married.] —**mar′ried** *adj.* & *n.*

Mars (märz) *n.* **1.** *Rom. Myth.* The god of war. **2.** The 4th planet of the solar system in order of increasing distance from the sun.

marsh (märsh) *n.* An area of low-lying, wet land. [< OE *mersc.*] —**marsh′y** *adj.*

mar·shal (mär′shəl) *n.* **1.** A Federal or city official who carries out court orders. **2.** The head of a city police or fire department. **3.** A person in charge of a ceremony. **4.** A military officer of the highest rank in some countries. **5.** A high official in a royal household or court. —*v.* **-shaled** *or* **-shalled, -shal·ing** *or* **-shal·ling. 1.** To place in methodical or proper order. **2.** To conduct ceremoniously; usher. [< OFr. *mareschall*, military commander, of Gmc. orig.]

marsh·mal·low (märsh′mĕl′ō, -măl′ō) *n.* A confection made of corn syrup, gelatin, sugar, and starch, and dusted with powdered sugar. [< MARSH MALLOW.]

marsh mallow *n.* A plant with showy pink flowers and a root used in confectionery and medicine.

marsh marigold *n.* A North American swamp plant with bright yellow flowers.

marsh·y (mär′shē) *adj.* **-i·er, -i·est. 1.** Of or like a marsh; swampy. **2.** Growing in or native to a marsh. —**marsh′i·ness** *n.*

mar·su·pi·al (mär-sōō′pē-əl) *n.* Any of a group of mammals, including the kangaroo and opossum, of which the females have an abdominal pouch in which the newly born young are fed and sheltered. [< Gk. *marsupion*, pouch.] —**mar·su′pi·al** *adj.*

mart (märt) *n.* A market. [< MDu.]

mar·ten (mär′tn) *n., pl.* **-ten** *or* **-tens. 1.** A thick-furred, weasellike mammal. **2.** The fur of the marten. [< Med. Lat. *martrina*, of Gmc. orig.]

mar·tial (mär′shəl) *adj.* **1.** Of, pertaining to, or suggesting war or a warrior: *martial music.*

2. Pertaining to or connected with military life. [< Lat. *Mars*, Mars.] —**mar′tial·ly** *adv.*

martial law *n.* Rule by military authorities imposed upon a civilian population during an emergency.

Mar·tian (mär′shən) *adj.* Of or pertaining to the planet Mars. —*n.* A hypothetical inhabitant of the planet Mars.

mar·tin (mär′tn) *n.* Any of several birds resembling and closely related to the swallows. [Prob. < the name *Martin.*]

mar·ti·net (mär′tə-nĕt′) *n.* A rigid disciplinarian. [< Jean *Martinet* (d. 1672).]

mar·tin·gale (mär′tən-gāl′) *n.* A strap of a horse's harness designed to prevent a horse from throwing its head back. [OFr.]

mar·ti·ni (mär-tē′nē) *n., pl.* **-nis.** A cocktail usu. made of gin or vodka and dry vermouth. [Orig. unknown.]

mar·tyr (mär′tər) *n.* **1.** One who chooses to suffer death rather than renounce a religious principle. **2.** One who makes great sacrifices for a cause or principle. **3.** One who endures great suffering. [< Gk. *martus*, witness.] —**mar′tyr** *v.* —**mar′tyr·dom** *n.*

mar·vel (mär′vəl) *n.* A cause of surprise, admiration, or wonder. —*v.* **-veled** *or* **-velled, -vel·ing** *or* **-vel·ling.** To become filled with wonder, surprise, or astonishment. [< Lat. *mirabilis*, wonderful.]

mar·vel·ous (mär′vəl-əs) *adj.* **1.** Causing wonder or astonishment. **2.** Miraculous. **3.** Of the highest kind or quality; splendid. —**mar′vel·ous·ly** *adv.* —**mar′vel·ous·ness** *n.*

Marx·ism (märk′sĭz′əm) *n.* The political, social, and economic doctrines of Karl Marx in which the class struggle is held to be the fundamental force that will lead to the establishment of a classless society. —**Marx′ist** *n.*

marz·i·pan (mär′zə-păn′, märt′sə-păn′) *n.* A confection made of ground almonds, sugar, and egg whites. [< Ital. *marzapane.*]

mas·cara (măs-kăr′ə) *n.* A cosmetic applied to color the eyelashes. [< Ital. *maschera.*]

mas·cot (măs′kŏt, -kət) *n.* A person, animal, or object believed to bring good luck. [< LLat. *masca*, witch.]

mas·cu·line (măs′kyə-lĭn) *adj.* **1.** Of or pertaining to the male sex. **2.** Characteristic of or suitable to a man: *a masculine voice.* **3.** *Gram.* Of, designating, or constituting the gender of words or grammatical forms that usu. denote or refer to males. —*n.* **1.** The masculine gender. **2.** *Gram.* A word or word form of the masculine gender. [< Lat. *masculus.*] —**mas·cu·line·ly** *adv.* —**mas′cu·lin′i·ty** (măs′kyə-lĭn′ĭ-tē) *n.*

ma·ser (mā′zər) *n. Physics.* A device that converts electromagnetic radiation from a wide range of frequencies to one or more discrete frequencies of highly amplified microwave radiation. [M(ICROWAVE) A(MPLIFICATION BY) S(TIMULATED) E(MISSION OF) R(ADIATION).]

mash (măsh) *n.* **1.** A fermentable starchy mixture from which alcohol can be distilled. **2.** A mixture of ground grain and nutrients fed to livestock. **3.** A soft, pulpy mass. —*v.* **1.** To convert (malt or grain) into mash. **2.** To convert into a soft, pulpy mixture. [< OE *max.*] —**mash′er** *n.*

mask (măsk, mäsk) *n.* **1.** A covering worn on

the face to disguise or conceal identity. **2.** A figure of a head worn by actors in Greek and Roman drama. **3.** A protective covering for the face or head. **4.** A sculptured or molded representation of a face or head. **5.** The facial markings of certain animals. **6.** Something that disguises or conceals. —v. **1.** To cover with or as with a mask. **2.** To disguise or conceal. [< Ital. *maschera*.]

mask

mas·o·chism (măs′ə-kĭz′əm) n. **1.** An abnormal condition in which sexual satisfaction is largely derived from abuse or physical pain. **2.** The deriving of pleasure from being mistreated in some way. [< Leopold von Sacher-*Masoch* (1836–95).] —**mas′o·chist** n. —**mas′o·chis′tic** (-kĭs′tĭk) adj. —**mas′o·chis′ti·cal·ly** adv.

ma·son (mā′sən) n. **1.** One who builds or works with stone or brick. **2. Mason.** A Freemason. [< OFr., of Gmc. orig.]

Ma·son·ic (mə-sŏn′ĭk) adj. Of or pertaining to Freemasons or Freemasonry.

Mason jar n. A wide-mouthed glass jar with a screw top, used for home canning and preserving. [< John L. *Mason* (1832–1902).]

ma·son·ry (mā′sən-rē) n., pl. -**ries.** **1.** The trade or work of a mason. **2.** Stonework or brickwork. **3. Masonry.** Freemasonry.

masque (măsk, mäsk) n. **1.** An allegorical dramatic entertainment, popular in the 16th and early 17th cent. **2.** A masquerade. [Fr. < Ital. *maschera*, mask.]

mas·quer·ade (măs′kə-rād′) n. **1.** A costume ball or party at which masks and costumes are worn. **2.** A false outward show or pretense. —v. -**ad·ed, -ad·ing.** **1.** To wear a mask or disguise, as at a masquerade. **2.** To have a deceptive appearance. [< OSp. *mascarada*.] —**mas′quer·ad′er** n.

mass (măs) n. **1.** A unified body of matter with no specific shape. **2.** A large but unspecified amount or number. **3.** The major part of something; majority. **4.** The physical volume or bulk of a solid body. **5.** *Physics.* The amount of matter contained in a physical body that is the measure of a body's resistance to acceleration, different from but proportional to its weight. **6. the masses.** The body of common people. —v. To gather or form into a mass. [< Gk. *maza.*]

Mass or **mass** (măs) n. In Roman Catholic and some Protestant churches, the celebration of the Eucharist. [< Lat. *mittere*, to send.]

Mas·sa·chu·set (măs′ə-chōō′sĭt, -zĭt) n., pl. -**set** or -**sets.** Also **Mas·sa·chu·sett** pl. -**sett** or -**setts.** **1. a.** A large tribe of Indians who lived on or near Massachusetts Bay. **b.** A member

of this tribe. **3.** The Algonquian language of the Massachuset.

mas·sa·cre (măs′ə-kər) n. **1.** A savage and indiscriminate wholesale killing. **2.** *Informal.* A severe defeat, as in sports. [OFr.] —**mas′sa·cre** v.

mas·sage (mə-säzh′) n. The rubbing or kneading of parts of the body to aid circulation or to relax the muscles. [< Ar. *massa*, he touched.] —**mas·sage′** v.

mas·seur (mă-sûr′) n. A man who gives massages professionally. [Fr.]

mas·seuse (mă-sœz′) n. A woman who gives massages professionally. [Fr.]

mas·sive (măs′ĭv) adj. **1.** Consisting of or making up a large mass. **2.** Impressive in quantity, scope, degree, intensity, or scale. —**mas′sive·ly** adv. —**mas′sive·ness** n.

mass medium n., pl. **mass media.** A means of public communication reaching a large audience.

mass number n. The total number of neutrons and protons in an atomic nucleus.

mass-pro·duce (măs′prə-dōōs′, -dyōōs′, -prō-) v. To manufacture goods in large quantities, esp. by using assembly-line techniques. —**mass production** n.

mast (măst, mäst) n. **1.** A tall vertical spar that rises from the keel of a sailing vessel to support the sails and rigging. **2.** A vertical pole. [< OE *mæst.*]

mas·tec·to·my (măs-tĕk′tə-mē) n., pl. -**mies.** Surgical removal of a breast. [Gk. *mastos*, breast + -ECTOMY.]

mas·ter (măs′tər, mäs′-) n. **1.** One having control over others; employer; owner. **2.** The captain of a merchant ship. **3.** A teacher or tutor. **4.** One highly skilled, as in a trade. **5. Master.** A title preceding the name of a boy too young to be addressed as Mister. **6. a.** A college or university degree granted to a person who has completed at least one year of study beyond the bachelor's degree. **b.** One holding such a degree. —v. **1.** To make oneself a master of (an art, craft, or science). **2.** To overcome or subdue. [< Lat. *magister.*]

mas·ter·ful (măs′tər-fəl, mäs′-) adj. **1.** Given to playing the master; imperious. **2.** Expert; skillful. —**mas′ter·ful·ly** adv.

master key n. A key that opens several different locks.

mas·ter·ly (măs′tər-lē, mäs′-) adj. Indicating the knowledge or skill of a master. —adv. With the skill of a master.

mas·ter·mind (măs′tər-mīnd′, mäs′-) n. One who plans and directs an important project. —**mas′ter·mind′** v.

master of ceremonies n. One who acts as host at a formal event or program of varied entertainment.

mas·ter·piece (măs′tər-pēs′, mäs′-) n. **1.** An outstanding work of art or craft. **2.** Something done with skill or brilliance.

master sergeant n. A U.S. noncommissioned officer of the next to highest rating.

mas·ter·stroke (măs′tər-strōk′, mäs′-) n. A masterly achievement or action.

mas·ter·work (măs′tər-wûrk′, mäs′-) n. A masterpiece.

mas·ter·y (măs′tər-ē, mäs′-) n., pl. -**ies.** **1.** The consummate skill or knowledge of a master. **2.** The status of a master. **3.** Full command or control, as of a subject or situation.

mast·head (măst′hĕd′, mäst′-) n. **1.** The top of a ship's mast. **2.** The listing in a newspaper, magazine, etc., of information about its staff and operation.

mas·tic (măs′tĭk) *n.* A pastelike cement, esp. one made with powdered lime or brick and tar. [< Gk. *mastikhē*, a kind of tree.]

mas·ti·cate (măs′tə-kāt′) *v.* **-cat·ed, -cat·ing.** To chew. [< Gk. *mastikhān*, to grind the teeth.] —**mas′ti·ca′tion** *n.* —**mas′ti·ca′tor** *n.* —**mas′ti·ca·to′ry** (-kə-tôr′ē, -tōr′ē) *adj.*

mas·tiff (măs′tĭf) *n.* A large dog with a short brownish coat. [< Lat. *mansuetus*, tamed.]

mastiff

mas·to·don (măs′tə-dŏn′) *n.* An extinct elephantlike mammal. [Gk. *mastos*, nipple + Gk. *odous*, tooth.]

mas·toid (măs′toid′) *n.* The mastoid process. —*adj.* Of or near the mastoid process. [Gk. *mastos*, breast + -OID.]

mastoid process *n.* The rear portion of the temporal bone on each side of the head behind the ear.

mas·tur·ba·tion (măs′tər-bā′shən) *n.* Excitation of the genital organs, usu. to orgasm, by means other than sexual intercourse. [< Lat. *masturbari*, to masturbate.] —**mas′tur·bate′** *v.*

mat¹ (măt) *n.* 1. A flat piece of material used as a protective covering. 2. A floor pad to protect athletes, as in wrestling. 3. A thickly tangled mass. —*v.* **mat·ted, mat·ting.** 1. To cover, protect, or decorate with a mat. 2. To interweave or tangle into a thick mass. [< LLat. *matta.*]

mat² (măt) *n.* 1. A border placed around a picture to serve as a frame or contrast between the picture and a frame. 2. Also **matte.** A dull, often rough finish, as on glass, metal, or paper. —*adj.* Also **matte.** Having a dull finish. [< Fr., dull.] —**mat** *v.*

mat·a·dor (măt′ə-dôr′) *n.* One who kills the bull in a bullfight. [< Lat. *mactare*, to sacrifice.]

match¹ (măch) *n.* 1. One equal or similar to another. 2. Two persons or things that harmonize. 3. A game or contest. 4. A marriage or arrangement of marriage. —*v.* 1. To be or make similar or equal to. 2. To harmonize with. 3. To place in competition with. 4. To join in marriage. [< OE *gemæcca*, mate.] —**match′er** *n.*

match² (măch) *n.* A narrow strip of flammable material coated on one end with a substance that ignites easily. [< Gk. *muxa*, lamp wick.]

match·book (măch′bŏŏk′) *n.* A small folder containing matches.

match·less (măch′lĭs) *adj.* Having no equal. —**match′less·ly** *adv.*

match·mak·er (măch′mā′kər) *n.* 1. One who

arranges marriages. 2. One who arranges athletic competitions, esp. in boxing.

mate¹ (māt) *n.* 1. One of a matched pair: *the mate to this glove.* 2. A spouse. 3. One of a pair of breeding animals. 4. A close associate. 5. A deck officer on a merchant ship ranking below the master. —*v.* **mat·ed, mat·ing.** 1. To join closely; pair. 2. To unite in marriage. 3. To pair for breeding. [< MLG.]

mate² (māt) *Chess.* —*n.* A checkmate. —*v.* **mat·ed, mat·ing.** To checkmate. [< Pers. *māt*, helpless.]

ma·té (mä′tā′) *n.* A mildly stimulant beverage made from the dried leaves of a South American tree. [< Quechua *mate.*]

ma·te·ri·al (mə-tîr′ē-əl) *n.* 1. The substance from which something is or can be made. 2. **materials.** Tools or apparatus for the performance of a given task. —*adj.* 1. Of, composed of, or pertaining to physical substances. 2. Of or affecting physical well-being: *material comforts.* 3. Of or concerned with the physical as distinct from the intellectual or spiritual. 4. Substantial; important; essential: *a material consideration.* [< Lat. *materia*, matter.] —**ma·te′ri·al·ly** *adv.*

ma·te·ri·al·ism (mə-tîr′ē-əl-ĭz′əm) *n.* 1. The philosophical doctrine that physical matter is the only reality in the universe and that everything else, including thought, feeling, mind, and will, can be explained in terms of physical laws. 2. Excessive regard for worldly and material concerns. —**ma·te′ri·al·ist** *n.* —**ma·te′ri·al·is′tic** *adj.* —**ma·te′ri·al·is′ti·cal·ly** *adv.*

ma·te·ri·al·ize (mə-tîr′ē-ə-līz′) *v.* **-ized, -iz·ing.** 1. To become or cause to become real or actual. 2. To take shape or form, esp. bodily form; appear as if from nowhere. —**ma·te′ri·al·i·za′tion** *n.*

ma·te·ri·el or **ma·té·ri·el** (mə-tîr′ē-ĕl′) *n.* The equipment, apparatus, and supplies of an organization, esp. of a military force. [Fr.]

ma·ter·nal (mə-tûr′nəl) *adj.* 1. Relating to or characteristic of a mother or motherhood; motherly. 2. Inherited from or related to through one's mother. [< Lat. *mater*, mother.] —**ma·ter′nal·ly** *adv.*

ma·ter·ni·ty (mə-tûr′nə-tē) *n.* The condition of being a mother; motherhood.

math (măth) *n.* Mathematics.

math·e·mat·ics (măth′ə-măt′ĭks) *n.* (*used with a sing. verb*). The study of numbers, their forms, arrangements, and sets, and their relationships and properties. [< Gk. *mathēma*, science.] —**math′e·mat′i·cal** *adj.* —**math′e·mat′i·cal·ly** *adv.* —**math′e·ma·ti′cian** (-mə-tĭsh′ən) *n.*

mat·i·nee or **mat·i·née** (măt′n-ā′) *n.* A dramatic or musical performance given in the afternoon. [< Lat. *matutinus*, of the morning.]

mat·ins (măt′ĭnz) *n.* (*used with a sing. or pl. verb*). Often **Matins.** In the Anglican Church, the service of morning worship. [< Med. Lat. (*vigiliae*) *matutinae*, morning (vigils).]

matri- *pref.* Mother: *matrilineal.* [< Lat. *mater.*]

ma·tri·arch (mā′trē-ärk′) *n.* A woman who rules a family, clan, or group. —**ma′tri·ar′chal** or **ma′tri·ar′chic** *adj.* —**ma′tri·ar′chy** *n.*

mat·ri·cide (măt′rə-sīd′) *n.* 1. The act of killing one's mother. **2.** One who kills his mother. —**mat'ri·ci'dal** (-sīd'l) *adj.*

ma·tric·u·late (mə-trĭk'yə-lāt') *v.* **-lat·ed, -lat·ing.** To enroll in a group, esp. a college or university. [< Lat. *matrix*, womb.] —**ma·tric'u·la'tion** *n.*

mat·ri·lin·e·al (măt'rə-lĭn'ē-əl) *adj.* Of, relating to, or tracing ancestral descent through the maternal line.

mat·ri·mo·ny (măt'rə-mō'nē) *n., pl.* **-nies.** The act or condition of being married. [< Lat. *matrimonium.*] —**mat'ri·mo'ni·al** *adj.* —**mat'ri·mo'ni·al·ly** *adv.*

ma·trix (mā'trĭks) *n., pl.* **-tri·ces** (-trə-sēz', măt'rĭ-) or **-es. 1.** A situation, substance, object, etc., within which something is contained, originates, or develops. **2.** A mold or die, as for casting or shaping metal. [< Lat. *womb.*]

ma·tron (mā'trən) *n.* **1.** A married woman, esp. a woman in middle age or older. **2.** A woman who supervises a public institution, such as a prison. [< Lat. *matrona.*] —**ma'tron·li·ness** *n.* —**ma'tron·ly** *adj.* & *adv.*

matron of honor *n., pl.* **matrons of honor.** A married woman who serves as chief attendant of the bride at a wedding.

matte (măt) *n.* Var. of **mat**² (sense 2). —*adj.* Var. of **mat**².

mat·ter (măt'ər) *n.* **1. a.** Something that occupies space, has weight, and can be perceived by one or more senses; the substance of which a physical body is constituted. **b.** An entity displaying gravitation and inertia when at rest as well as when in motion. **2.** A specific type of substance: *inorganic matter.* **3.** The substance of thought or expression. **4.** A subject of concern or action. **5.** A difficulty: *What's the matter?* **6.** An indefinite quantity: *a matter of a few cents.* **7.** Something written or printed —*v.* To be of importance. —**idioms. as a matter of fact.** In fact; actually. **no matter.** Regardless of. [< Lat. *materia.*]

mat·ter-of-fact (măt'ər-əv-făkt') *adj.* Adhering strictly to facts; literal. —**mat'ter-of-fact'ly** *adv.* —**mat'ter-of-fact'ness** *n.*

Mat·thew (măth'yōō) *n.* See table at **Bible.**

mat·ting (măt'ĭng) *n.* **1.** A coarse fabric used for covering floors and similar purposes. **2.** Mats in general.

mat·tock (măt'ək) *n.* A digging tool with a blade set at right angles to the handle. [< OE *mattuc.*]

mat·tress (măt'rĭs) *n.* A pad of heavy cloth filled with soft material, used as or on a bed. [< Ar. *maṭraḥ*, place where something is thrown.]

ma·ture (mə-tyŏŏr', -tŏŏr', -chŏŏr') *adj.* **-tur·er, -tur·est. 1.** Having reached full growth or development. **2.** Fully developed; ripe: *a mature wine; a mature cheese.* **3.** Worked out fully by the mind; perfected. **4.** Payable; due: *a mature bond.* —*v.* **-tured, -tur·ing.** To bring or come to full development; ripen. [< Lat. *maturus.*] —**ma·ture'ly** *adv.* —**ma·tur'i·ty** or **mat'u·ra'tion** *n.*

mat·zo (mät'sə) *n., pl.* **-zoth** (-sōth', -sōt', -sōs') or **-zos** (-səz, -səs, -sōz'). A brittle, flat piece of unleavened bread, eaten esp. during Passover. [< Heb. *maṣṣāh.*]

maud·lin (môd'lĭn) *adj.* Excessively sentimental. [< Mary *Magdalen*, who was frequently depicted as a tearful penitent.]

maul (môl) *n.* A heavy, long-handled hammer used to drive stakes, piles, or wedges. —*v.* **1.** To beat, bruise, or tear. **2.** To handle roughly; mishandle. [< Lat. *malleus.*] —**maul'er** *n.*

maun·der (môn'dər, män'-) *v.* **1.** To talk incoherently or aimlessly. **2.** To move or act aimlessly or vaguely. [Prob. imit.]

mau·so·le·um (mô'sə-lē'əm, mô'zə-) *n., pl.* **-ums** or **-le·a** (-lē'ə). A large, stately tomb or a building housing such a tomb or tombs. [< the satrap *Mausolus* (d. 353 B.C.).]

mauve (mōv) *n.* A light reddish or grayish purple. [< Lat. *malva*, mallow.] —**mauve** *adj.*

mav·er·ick (măv'ər-ĭk, măv'rĭk) *n.* **1.** An unbranded range calf or colt. **2.** An independent person, esp. in politics. [< Samuel A. *Maverick* (1803–70).]

maw (mô) *n.* **1.** The stomach, mouth, or gullet of a voracious animal. **2.** An opening that gapes. [< OE *maga.*]

mawk·ish (mô'kĭsh) *adj.* Excessively and obnoxiously sentimental. [< ME *mawke*, maggot.] —**mawk'ish·ly** *adv.* —**mawk'ish·ness** *n.*

max·il·la (măk-sĭl'ə) *n., pl.* **max·il·lae** (-măk-sĭl'ē) or **-las.** One of a pair of bones forming the upper jaw. [< Lat., jawbone.] —**max'il·lar** (măk'sə-lər, măk-sĭl'ər) or **max'il·lar'y** (-sə-lĕr'ē) *adj.*

max·im (măk'sĭm) *n.* A concise formulation of a fundamental principle or rule of conduct. [< Med. Lat. *(propositio) maxima*, greatest (principle).]

max·i·mal (măk'sə-məl) *adj.* Of or being a maximum. —**max'i·mal·ly** *adv.*

max·i·mize (măk'sə-mīz') *v.* **-mized, -miz·ing.** To make as great as possible.

max·i·mum (măk'sə-məm) *n., pl.* **-mums** or **-ma** (-mə). **1.** The greatest possible quantity, degree, or number. **2.** An upper limit allowed by law or other authority. —*adj.* The greatest or highest possible. [< Lat. *maximus*, greatest.]

may (mā) *v.* past tense **might** (mīt). Used as an auxiliary followed by an infinitive without *to*, or in reply to a question or suggestion, with the infinitive understood. Used to indicate: **1.** A requesting or granting of permission: *May I take a swim? You may.* **2.** Possibility: *It may rain this afternoon.* **3.** Ability or capacity: *If I may be of service.* **4.** Desire or fervent wish: *Long may he live.* **5.** Contingency, purpose, or result, used in clauses introduced by *that* or so *that: expressing ideas so that the average man may understand.* [< OE *magan*, to be able.]

May (mā) *n.* The 5th month of the year, having 31 days. See table at **calendar.** [< *Maia*, a Roman goddess.]

Ma·ya (mä'yə) *n., pl.* **-yas** or **-ya. 1.** A member of a race of Indians whose southern Mexico and Central America whose civilization reached its height around A.D. 1000. **2.** The Mayan language of the Mayas.

Ma·yan (mä'yən, mī'ən) *adj.* Of the Mayas, their language, or their culture. —*n.* **1.** A Maya. **2.** A linguistic stock of Central America that includes Maya.

May apple *n.* A North American plant with a single, nodding white flower, oval yellow fruit, and poisonous roots, leaves, and seeds.

may·be (mā'bē) *adv.* Perhaps; possibly.

May Day *n.* **1.** May 1, a traditional holiday in celebration of spring. **2.** May 1, regarded in a number of places as an international holiday to celebrate labor organizations.

may·flow·er (mā'flou'ər) n. Any of various spring-blooming flowers, esp. the arbutus.

may·hem (mā'hěm', mā'əm) n. 1. Law. The crime of willfully maiming or crippling a person. 2. A willful violent destruction. 3. A condition of usu. riotous disorder or confusion; havoc. [< OFr. mahaignier, to maim.]

may·n't (mā'ənt, mānt). May not.

may·on·naise (mā'ə-nāz') n. A creamy dressing of egg yolks, olive oil, lemon juice or vinegar, and seasonings. [Fr.]

may·or (mā'ər, mâr) n. The chief official of a city, town, or borough. [< Lat. major, greater.] —**may'or·al** adj. —**may'or·al·ty** n.

May·pole or **may·pole** (mā'pōl') n. A pole decorated with streamers, flowers, etc., that May Day celebrants hold while dancing.

maze (māz) n. 1. An intricate, usu. confusing network of walled or hedged pathways; labyrinth. 2. A confusing or intricate condition or situation. [< OE āmasian, to bewilder.]

ma·zur·ka (mə-zûr'kə, -zōōr'kə) n. 1. A lively Polish dance. 2. Music for a mazurka.

Md The symbol for the element mendelevium.

me (mē) pron. The objective case of I, used: 1. As the direct object of a verb: They blamed me. 2. As the indirect object of a verb: Give me the letter. 3. As the object of a preposition: She addressed it to me. [< OE mē.]

mead (mēd) n. An alcoholic beverage made from fermented honey and water. [< OE medu.]

mead·ow (měd'ō) n. A tract of grassland used as pasture or for growing hay. [< OE mæd.]

mead·ow·lark (měd'ō-lärk') n. A bird with a cone-shaped bill, noted for its song.

mea·ger (mē'gər) adj. 1. Thin; lean. 2. Deficient in quantity, extent, or quality: a meager allowance. [< Lat. macer.] —**mea'ger·ly** adv. —**mea'ger·ness** n.

meal¹ (mēl) n. 1. Coarsely ground edible grain. 2. Any similar granular substance. [< OE melu.] —**meal'y** adj.

meal² (mēl) n. The food served and eaten in one sitting. [< OE mæl.]

meal·time (mēl'tīm') n. The usual time for eating a meal.

meal·y-mouthed (mē'lē-mouthd', -moutht') adj. Unwilling to speak directly or simply.

mean¹ (mēn) v. **meant** (měnt), **mean·ing.** 1. a. To be defined as; denote. b. To act as a symbol of; represent. 2. To intend to convey or indicate: What do you mean by that look? 3. To have as a purpose or intention. 4. To have as a consequence: Friction means heat. 5. To be of a specified importance; matter: Advice meant little to him. [< OE mænan, to tell of.]

mean² (mēn) adj. **-er, -est.** 1. Low in quality or grade. 2. Low in social status. 3. Ignoble; base; petty. 4. Low in value or amount. 5. Miserly. 6. Lacking elevating human qualities, as kindness and good will. 7. Informal. Ill-tempered. 8. Slang. Hard to cope with. [< OE gemæne, common.] —**mean'ly** adv. —**mean'ness** n.

mean³ (mēn) n. 1. The middle point or state between two extremes. 2. Moderation. 3. Math. a. A number that represents a set of numbers in a way determined by a rule involving all members of the set; average.

b. The arithmetic mean. 4. **means.** A course of action or instrument by which some act can be accomplished or some end achieved. 5. **means.** Money, property, or other wealth. —adj. Occupying a middle or intermediate position between two extremes. —**idioms. by all means.** Without fail; certainly. **by no means.** In no sense; certainly not. [< Lat. medius, middle.]

Usage: In the sense of "financial resources," *means* takes a plural verb: *His means are more than adequate.* In the sense of "a method of achieving an end," it may take a singular or plural verb; the choice of a modifier such as *any* or *all* generally determines the number of the verb: *Every means was tried. There are several means at our disposal.*

me·an·der (mē-ăn'dər) v. 1. To follow a winding or circuitous course. 2. To wander aimlessly and idly. —n. A circuitous turn or winding, as of a stream or path. [< Gk. Maiandros, a river in Asia Minor.]

mean·ing (mē'nĭng) n. 1. Something that is signified; sense. 2. Something that one wishes to convey, esp. by language. 3. Intent; purpose: *couldn't understand the meaning of his action.* —**mean'ing·ful** adj. —**mean'ing·less** adj.

meant (měnt) v. p.t. & p.p. of mean¹.

mean·time (mēn'tīm') n. The time between one occurrence and another. —adv. Meanwhile.

mean·while (mēn'hwīl') n. The intervening time. —adv. In the intervening time.

mea·sles (mē'zəlz) n. (used with a sing. verb). 1. An acute, contagious viral disease, characterized by coughing, fever, and red spots on the skin. 2. Any of several milder diseases similar to measles. [Of MLG orig.]

mea·sly (mēz'lē) adj. **-sli·er, -sli·est.** Slang. Contemptibly small: *a measly tip.*

meas·ure (mězh'ər) n. 1. The dimensions, quantity, or capacity of anything as ascertained by measuring. 2. A reference standard or sample used for the quantitative comparison of properties. 3. A unit specified by a scale, as an inch, or by variable conditions, as a day's march. 4. A device, such as a marked tape, used for measuring. 5. An act of measuring. 6. A criterion. 7. Extent or degree. 8. A limited amount or degree. 9. An action taken as a means to an end. 10. A legislative bill or enactment. 11. Poetic meter. 12. Mus. The metrical unit between two bars on the staff; bar. —v. **-ured, -ur·ing.** 1. To ascertain or mark off the dimensions, quantity, or capacity of. 2. To have a specified measure: *a room measuring 10 by 12 feet.* 3. To bring into opposition: *measured her power with that of her rival.* 4. To choose with care; weigh: *measured his words.* —**phrasal verb. measure up.** 1. To be the equal of. 2. To have the necessary qualifications: *a candidate who didn't measure up.* —**idioms. for good measure.** In addition to the amount required. **in great (or large) measure.** To a great extent. [< Lat. mensura.] —**meas'ur·a·ble** adj. —**meas'ure·ment** n. —**meas'ur·er** n.

measuring worm n. An inchworm.

meat (mēt) n. 1. The edible flesh of an animal, esp. a mammal. 2. The edible, fleshy, inner part of something: *crab meat; walnut meats.* **3.** Solid food: *meat and drink.* **4.** The principal or essential part; gist: *the meat of an argument.* [< OE *mete*, food.] **—meat′i•ness** *n.* **—meat′y** *adj.*

mec•ca (měk′ə) *n.* A place regarded as a desirable goal: *a museum that was a mecca for connoisseurs.* [< *Mecca*, Saudi Arabia.]

me•chan•ic (mĭ-kǎn′ĭk) *n.* A worker skilled in making, using, or repairing machines.

me•chan•i•cal (mĭ-kǎn′ĭ-kəl) *adj.* **1.** Of or pertaining to machines or tools. **2.** Operated or produced by a machine. **3.** Suggestive of or appropriate for performance by a machine: *mechanical tasks.* **4.** Of, pertaining to, or in accordance with the science of mechanics. [< Gk. *mēkhanē*.] **—me•chan′i•cal•ly** *adv.* **—me•chan′i•cal•ness** *n.*

mechanical drawing *n.* A drawing made by the use of instruments such as compasses or triangles.

me•chan•ics (mĭ-kǎn′ĭks) *n.* (*used with a sing. or pl. verb*). **1.** The analysis of the action of forces on matter or material systems. **2.** The development, production, operation, and use of machines and structures. **3.** The functional and technical aspects of an activity: *The mechanics of football are learned with practice.*

mech•a•nism (měk′ə-nĭz′əm) *n.* **1. a.** A machine or mechanical device. **b.** The arrangement of connected parts in a machine. **2.** A system of parts that operate or interact like those of a machine. **3.** A process or means by which something is done or comes into being.

mech•a•nis•tic (měk′ə-nĭs′tĭk) *adj.* Pertaining to mechanics as a branch of physics. **—mech′a•nis′ti•cal•ly** *adv.*

mech•a•nize (měk′ə-nīz′) *v.* **-nized, -niz•ing. 1.** To equip with machinery. **2.** To make automatic or mechanical. **—mech′a•ni•za′tion** *n.*

med•al (měd′l) *n.* **1.** A flat piece of metal, often in the form of a coin, issued to commemorate an event or person or to reward bravery or achievement. **2.** A metal disk that bears a religious figure or symbol. [< Lat. *metallum*, metal.]

med•al•ist (měd′l-ĭst) *n.* **1.** One who designs or makes medals. **2.** A recipient of a medal.

me•dal•lion (mə-dǎl′yən) *n.* **1.** A large medal. **2.** Something resembling a large medal, such as a decorative tablet. [< Ital. *medaglione.*]

med•dle (měd′l) *v.* **-dled, -dling.** To intrude in the affairs of others; interfere. [< Lat. *miscēre*, to mix.] **—med′dler** (měd′lər, měd′l-ər) *n.* **—med′dle•some** *adj.* **—med′dle•some•ness** *n.*

me•di•a (mē′dē-ə) *n.* A pl. of **medium.**

me•di•ae•val (mē′dē-ē′vəl, měd-ē′vəl) *adj.* Var. of **medieval.**

me•di•al (mē′dē-əl) *adj.* Of, pertaining to, or situated in the middle. [< Lat. *medius.*] **—me′di•al•ly** *adv.*

me•di•an (mē′dē-ən) *adj.* **1.** Of, at, or toward the middle; medial. **2.** Of or lying in the plane that divides a symmetrical organism into right and left halves. **—n. 1.** A median point, plane, line, or part. **2.** A line that joins a vertex of a triangle to the midpoint of the opposite side. [< Lat. *medius.*]

median strip *n.* A strip that divides opposing traffic lanes of a highway.

me•di•ate (mē′dē-āt′) *v.* **-at•ed, -at•ing.** To act as an intermediary, esp. to seek to resolve (differences) between two or more conflicting parties. [< LLat. *mediare*, to be in the middle.] **—me′di•a′tion** *n.* **—me′di•a′tor** *n.*

med•ic (měd′ĭk) *n. Informal.* A person, such as a physician or member of the medical corps, trained to provide medical care. [Lat. *medicus*, doctor.]

Med•i•caid (měd′ĭ-kād′) *n.* Also **med•i•caid.** A government program that provides medical care for people whose income is below a certain level. [MEDIC(AL) + AID.]

med•i•cal (měd′ĭ-kəl) *adj.* Of or pertaining to the science or practice of medicine. [< Lat. *medicus*, doctor.] **—med′i•cal•ly** *adv.*

me•dic•a•ment (mĭ-dĭk′ə-mənt, měd′ĭ-kə-) *n.* A medicine. [Lat. *medicamentum.*]

Med•i•care (měd′ĭ-kâr′) *n.* Also **med•i•care.** A government program that provides medical care for the elderly. [MEDI(CAL) + CARE.]

med•i•cate (měd′ĭ-kāt′) *v.* **-cat•ed, -cat•ing. 1.** To treat with medicine. **2.** To add a medicinal substance to.

med•i•ca•tion (měd′ĭ-kā′shən) *n.* **1.** The act or process of medicating. **2.** A medicine.

me•dic•i•nal (mə-dĭs′ə-nəl) *adj.* Of or having the properties of medicine; healing; curative. **—me•dic′i•nal•ly** *adv.*

med•i•cine (měd′ĭ-sən) *n.* **1. a.** The scientific study of diagnosing, treating, or preventing disease. **b.** The branch of this science that deals with treatment by means other than surgery. **2.** A substance used to treat disease. [< Lat. *medicina.*]

medicine man *n.* A person believed by North American Indians to possess the power to cure disease.

med•i•co (měd′ĭ-kō′) *n., pl.* **-cos.** *Informal.* A doctor or medical student. [Ital. and Sp.]

me•di•e•val (mē′dē-ē′vəl, měd′ē′vəl) *adj.* Also **me•di•ae•val.** Of, pertaining to, or typical of the Middle Ages. [< Lat. *medium*, middle + Lat. *aevum*, age.] **—me′di•e′val•ist** *n.* **—me′di•e′val•ly** *adv.*

Medieval Greek *n.* The Greek language from about 800 to 1500.

Medieval Latin *n.* The Latin language from about 700 to 1500.

me•di•o•cre (mē′dē-ō′kər) *adj.* Of moderate to low quality; average. [Lat. *mediocris.*] **—me′di•oc′ri•ty** (-ŏk′rĭ-tē) *n.*

med•i•tate (měd′ĭ-tāt′) *v.* **-tat•ed, -tat•ing. 1.** To reflect upon; contemplate. **2.** To engage in contemplation. [Lat. *meditari.*] **—med′i•ta′tion** *n.* **—med′i•ta′tive** *adj.* **—med′i•ta′tive•ly** *adv.* **—med′i•ta′tive•ness** *n.* **—med′i•ta′tor** *n.*

me•di•um (mē′dē-əm) *n., pl.* **-di•a** (-dē-ə) or **-ums. 1.** A position, choice, or course of action midway between extremes. **2.** An intervening substance through which something is transmitted or carried on. **3.** An agency by means of which something is accomplished, conveyed, or transferred. **4.** *pl.* **media.** A means of mass communication. **5.** *pl.* **mediums.** One thought to have powers of communicating with the spirits of the dead. **6.** An environment in which something functions and thrives. **7.** A means of expression as determined by the materials or creative methods involved. **—adj.** Occurring midway between extremes; intermediate: *low, medium, and high speeds.* [< Lat. *medius*, middle.]

med•ley (měd′lē) *n., pl.* **-leys. 1.** A confused mixture. **2.** A musical arrangement of several songs or melodies. [< OFr. *medlee.*]

me•dul•la (mə-dŭl′ə) *n., pl.* **-las** or **-dul•lae** (-dŭl′ē′). **1.** *Anat.* The inner core of certain

GUIDE TO THE METRIC SYSTEM
MEASUREMENT UNITS
Length

Unit	Number of Meters	Approximate U.S. Equivalent	
myriameter	10,000	6.2	miles
kilometer	1,000	0.62	mile
hectometer	100	109.36	yards
dekameter	10	32.81	feet
meter	1	39.37	inches
decimeter	0.1	3.94	inches
centimeter	0.01	0.39	inch
millimeter	0.001	0.04	inch

Area

Unit	Number of Square Meters	Approximate U.S. Equivalent	
square kilometer	1,000,000	0.3861	square mile
hectare	10,000	2.47	acres
are	100	119.60	square yards
centare	1	10.76	square feet
square centimeter	0.0001	0.115	square inch

Volume

Unit	Number of Cubic Meters	Approximate U.S. Equivalent	
dekastere	10	13.10	cubic yards
stere	1	1.31	cubic yards
decistere	0.10	3.53	cubic feet
cubic centimeter	0.000001	0.061	cubic inch

Mass and Weight

Unit	Number of Grams	Approximate U.S. Equivalent	
metric ton	1,000,000	1.1	tons
quintal	100,000	220.46	pounds
kilogram	1,000	2.2046	pounds
hectogram	100	3.527	ounces
dekagram	10	0.353	ounce
gram	1	0.035	ounce
decigram	0.10	1.543	grains
centigram	0.01	0.154	grain
milligram	0.001	0.015	grain

Capacity

Unit	Number of Liters	Approximate U.S. Equivalent Cubic	
kiloliter	1,000	1.31	cubic yards
hectoliter	100	3.53	cubic feet
dekaliter	10	0.35	cubic foot
liter	1	61.02	cubic inches

MEASUREMENT (continued)

Capacity

Unit	Number of liters	Approximate U.S. Equivalent
deciliter	0.10	6.1 cubic inches
centiliter	0.01	0.6 cubic inch
milliliter	0.001	0.06 cubic inch
		Dry
hectoliter	100	2.84 bushels
decaliter	10	1.14 pecks
liter	1	0.908 quart
deciliter	0.10	0.18 pint
		Liquid
decaliter	10	2.64 gallons
liter	1	1.057 quarts
deciliter	0.10	0.21 pint
centiliter	0.01	0.338 fluid ounce
milliliter	0.001	0.27 fluid dram

METRIC CONVERSION CHART — APPROXIMATIONS

When You Know	Multiply By	To Find
Length		
millimeters	0.04	inches
centimeters	0.4	inches
meters	3.3	feet
meters	1.1	yards
kilometers	0.6	miles
inches	25	millimeters
inches	2.5	centimeters
feet	30	centimeters
yards	0.9	meters
miles	1.6	kilometers
Area		
square centimeters	0.16	square inches
square meters	1.2	square yards
square kilometers	0.4	square miles
hectares (10,000m^2)	2.5	acres
square inches	6.5	square centimeters
square feet	0.09	square meters
square yards	0.8	square meters
square miles	2.6	square kilometers
acres	0.4	hectares
Mass and Weight		
grams	0.035	ounce
kilograms	2.2	pounds
tons (100kg)	1.1	short tons
ounces	28	grams
pounds	0.45	kilograms
short tons (2000 lb)	0.9	tons

MEASUREMENT *(continued)*

Volume

milliliters	0.2	teaspoons
milliliters	0.06	tablespoons
milliliters	0.03	fluid ounces
liters	4.2	cups
liters	2.1	pints
milliliters	0.2	teaspoons
milliliters	0.06	tablespoons
milliliters	0.03	fluid ounces
liters	4.2	cups
liters	2.1	pints
liters	1.06	quarts
liters	0.26	gallons
cubic meters	35	cubic feet
cubic meters	1.3	cubic yards
teaspoons	5	milliliters
tablespoons	15	milliliters
fluid ounces	30	milliliters
cups	0.24	liters
pints	0.47	liters
quarts	0.95	liters
gallons	3.8	liters
cubic feet	0.03	cubic meters
cubic yards	0.76	cubic meters

Speed

miles per hour	1.6	kilometers per hour
kilometers per hour	0.6	miles per hour

Temperature (exact)

Celsius temp.	9/5, +32	Fahrenheit temp.
Fahrenheit temp.	− 32, 5/9 × remainder	Celsius temp.

---

vertebrate body structures, such as the marrow of bone. **2.** The medulla oblongata. [< Lat.] **—me·dul′lar** or **med′ul·lar′y** (mĕd′ə-lĕr′-ē, mə-dŭl′ə-rē) *adj.*

medulla ob·lon·ga·ta (ŏb′lŏng-gä′tə) *n., pl.* **medulla ob·lon·ga·tas** or **medullae ob·lon·ga·tae** (-tē). The nerve tissue at the base of the brain that controls respiration, circulation, and certain other bodily functions. [NLat., oblong medulla.]

meed (mēd) *n. Archaic.* A well-deserved reward. [< OE *mēd.*]

meek (mēk) *adj.* **-er, -est. 1.** Patient and humble. **2.** Submissive. [< ON *mjūkr,* soft.] **—meek′ly** *adv.* **—meek′ness** *n.*

meer·schaum (mîr′shəm, -shôm) *n.* A fine, claylike, heat-resistant mineral used esp. to make tobacco pipes. [G.]

meet¹ (mēt) *v.* **met** (mĕt), **meet·ing. 1.** To come upon; encounter. **2.** To be present at the arrival of: *meet a train.* **3.** To be introduced (to). **4.** To come into conjunction (with). **5.** To come into the company of, as for a conference. **6.** To come to the notice of: *more than meets the eye.* **7.** To cope or contend effectively with. **8.** To satisfy completely; fulfill. **9.** To come together: *Let's meet tonight.* *—n.* A meeting or contest. [< OE *mētan.*]

meet² (mĕt) *adj.* **-er, -est.** *Archaic.* Fitting; proper. [< OE *gemǣte.*] **—meet′ly** *adv.*

meet·ing (mē′tĭng) *n.* **1.** A coming together; assembly. **2.** A place where things join; junction.

mega- *pref.* **1.** One million (10⁶): *megacycle.* **2.** Large: *megalith.* [< Gk. *megas,* great.]

meg·a·cy·cle (mĕg′ə-sī′kəl) *n.* **1.** One million cycles. **2.** Megahertz.

meg·a·hertz (mĕg′ə-hûrtz) *n., pl.* **-hertz.** One million cycles per second.

meg·a·lith (mĕg′ə-lĭth′) *n.* A very large stone used in various prehistoric monuments. **—meg′a·lith′ic** *adj.*

megalo- *pref.* Exaggeratedly large or great: *megalomania.* [< Gk. *megas,* great.]

meg·a·lo·ma·ni·a (mĕg′ə-lō-mā′nē-ə, -mān′yə

---

n. A mental disorder characterized by feelings of great personal power or omnipotence. —**meg'a·lo·ma'ni·ac'** *n.* —**meg'a·lo·ma·ni'a·cal** (-mə-nī'ə-kəl) *adj.*

meg·a·lop·o·lis (měg'ə-lŏp'ə-lĭs) *n.* A large, thickly populated region, esp. one that contains several large cities in close proximity. [MEGALO- + Gk. *polis,* city.] —**meg'a·lo·pol'i·tan** (-lō-pŏl'ĭ-tən) *adj.*

meg·a·phone (měg'ə-fōn') *n.* A funnel-shaped device used to project the voice.

megaphone

meg·a·ton (měg'ə-tŭn') *n.* A unit of explosive force equal to that of one million tons of TNT.

mei·o·sis (mī-ō'sĭs) *n., pl.* **-ses** (-sēz'). The cell division in sexually reproducing organisms that reduces the number of chromosomes in reproductive cells. [< Gk. *meiōsis,* diminution.] —**mei·ot'ic** (mī-ŏt'ĭk) *adj.* —**mei·ot'i·cal·ly** *adv.*

melan- *pref.* Var. of **melano-**.

mel·an·cho·li·a (měl'ən-kō'lē-ə) *n.* A mental condition characterized by feelings of severe depression. [< LLat., melancholy.]

mel·an·chol·ic (měl'ən-kŏl'ĭk) *adj.* 1. Subject to melancholy; depressed. 2. Of or afflicted with melancholia.

mel·an·chol·y (měl'ən-kŏl'ē) *n.* 1. Sadness; depression. 2. Pensive reflection. —*adj.* 1. Sad; gloomy. 2. Pensive; thoughtful. [< Gk. *melankholia.*]

mé·lange (mā-länzh') *n.* Also **me·lange.** A mixture. [Fr.]

mel·a·nin (měl'ə-nĭn) *n.* A dark-brown or black pigment of animals and plants.

melano- or **melan-** *pref.* Black or dark: *melanoma.* [< Gk. *melas.*]

mel·a·no·ma (měl'ə-nō'mə) *n., pl.* **-mas** or **-ma·ta** (-mə-tə). A dark-pigmented malignant tumor.

Mel·ba toast (měl'bə) Very thinly sliced crisp toast. [< Dame Nellie *Melba* (1861–1931).]

meld¹ (měld) *v.* To declare or display (a playing card or combination of cards) for a score in a card game. —*n.* A combination of cards to be declared for a score. [< OHG *meldōn,* to announce.]

meld² (měld) *v.* To be or cause to be blended. [Blend of MELT and WELD.]

me·lee (mā'lā', mā-lā') *n.* Also **mê·lée** (mě-lā'). 1. A confused fight; brawl. 2. A confused mingling of people or things. [< Lat. *miscēre,* to mix.]

mel·io·rate (měl'yə-rāt', mē'lē-ə-) *v.* **-rat·ed, -rat·ing.** To make or become better; improve. [< Lat. *melior,* better.] —**mel'io·ra'tion** *n.* —**mel'io·ra'tive** *adj.* & *n.*

mel·lif·lu·ous (mə-lĭf'lōō-əs) *adj.* Flowing in a smooth or sweet manner. [< Lat. *mellifluus.*] —**mel·lif'lu·ous·ly** *adv.* —**mel·lif'lu·ous·ness** *n.*

mel·low (měl'ō) *adj.* **-er, -est.** 1. Soft, sweet, and full-flavored because of ripeness. 2. Rich and full in flavor as a result of being properly aged: *a mellow wine.* 3. Gently and maturely dignified. 4. Relaxed and at ease. 5. Slightly and pleasantly high or intoxicated. —*v.* To make or become mellow. [ME *melowe.*] —**mel'low·ly** *adv.* —**mel'low·ness** *n.*

me·lo·de·on (mə-lō'dē-ən) *n.* A small reed organ. [G. *Melodion.*]

me·lo·di·ous (mə-lō'dē-əs) *adj.* 1. Tuneful. 2. Agreeable to hear. —**me·lo'di·ous·ly** *adv.* —**me·lo'di·ous·ness** *n.*

mel·o·dra·ma (měl'ə-drä'mə, -drăm'ə) *n.* 1. A work, such as a play or motion picture, that relies heavily upon suspense, sensational events, coincidence, and conventional sentiment instead of characterization. 2. Melodramatic situations, behavior, or events. [Fr. *mélodrame,* musical drama.]

mel·o·dra·mat·ic (měl'ə-drə-măt'ĭk) *adj.* 1. Of, relating to, or typical of melodrama. 2. Exaggerated or distorted to heighten sensation. —**mel'o·dra·mat'i·cal·ly** *adv.*

mel·o·dy (měl'ə-dē) *n., pl.* **-dies.** 1. A pleasing succession or arrangement of sounds. 2. A rhythmic sequence of single tones organized so as to make up a musical phrase. [< Gk. *melōidia.*] —**me·lod'ic** (mə-lŏd'ĭk) *adj.*

mel·on (měl'ən) *n.* Any of several fruits, as a cantaloupe or watermelon, having a hard rind and juicy flesh. [< Gk. *mēlopepōn.*]

melt (mělt) *v.* 1. To change or be changed from a solid to a liquid state usu. as a result of heat or pressure. 2. To dissolve. 3. To disappear or cause to disappear gradually. 4. To pass or cause to pass gradually or imperceptibly; blend. 5. To make or become gentle or mild. [< OE *meltan.*] —**melt'a·ble** *adj.* —**melt'er** *n.*

melting point *n.* The temperature at which a solid becomes a liquid at standard atmospheric pressure.

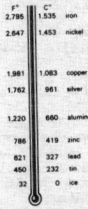

°F	C°	
2,795	1,535	iron
2,647	1,453	nickel
1,981	1,083	copper
1,762	961	silver
1,220	660	aluminum
786	419	zinc
621	327	lead
450	232	tin
32	0	ice

melting point

mem (měm) *n.* The 13th letter of the Hebrew alphabet. See table at **alphabet.** [Heb.]

mem·ber (měm'bər) *n.* 1. An element or part of a whole. 2. A bodily part, organ, or limb, as of a human or animal. 3. One who belongs to a group or organization. 4. One elected to a legislative body. [< Lat. *membrum.*]

mem·ber·ship (měm'bər-shĭp') *n.* 1. The condition of being a member. 2. All the members of a group or association.

mem·brane (měm'brān') *n.* 1. A thin, flexible layer of animal or plant tissue covering or separating structures or organs. 2. A thin sheet of natural or synthetic material through which dissolved substances can pass, as in osmosis. [Lat. *membrana*, skin.] —**mem'bra·nous** (-brə-nəs) *adj.*

me·men·to (mə-měn'tō) *n., pl.* **-tos** or **-toes.** A reminder of the past; souvenir. [< Lat., imper. of *meminisse*, to remember.]

mem·o (měm'ō) *n., pl.* **-os.** A memorandum.

mem·oir (měm'wär', -wôr') *n.* **1. memoirs.** An autobiography or biography. **2.** A written reminder. **3.** The report of the proceedings of a learned society. [< Lat. *memoria*, memory.]

mem·o·ra·bil·i·a (měm'ər-ə-bĭl'ē-ə, -bĭl'yə) *pl.n.* Things worthy of remembrance. [< Lat. *memorabilis*, memorable.]

mem·o·ra·ble (měm'ər-ə-bəl) *adj.* Worth remembering: *a memorable occasion.* —**mem'o·ra·bly** *adv.*

mem·o·ran·dum (měm'ə-răn'dəm) *n., pl.* **-dums** or **-da** (-də). **1.** A short note written as a reminder. **2.** A written record, note, or communication, as in a business office. [Lat., thing to be remembered.]

me·mo·ri·al (mə-môr'ē-əl, mə-mōr'-) *n.* **1.** Something, such as a monument or a holiday, established to preserve the memory of a person or an event. **2.** A written statement of facts or a formal petition. —*adj.* Commemorative. —**me·mo'ri·al·ize'** *v.*

Memorial Day *n.* May 30, a U.S. holiday officially celebrated on the last Monday in May in honor of servicemen killed in war.

mem·o·rize (měm'ə-rīz') *v.* **-rized, -riz·ing.** To commit to memory; learn by heart. —**mem'o·ri·za'tion** *n.* —**mem'o·riz'er** *n.*

mem·o·ry (měm'ə-rē) *n., pl.* **-ries. 1.** The mental capacity to retain and recall past experience. **2.** A remembrance; recollection. **3.** All that a person can remember. **4.** Something remembered of a person, thing, or event. **5.** The period of time covered by remembrance or recollection. **6.** A unit of a computer that stores data for retrieval. [< Lat. *memoria.*]

men (měn) *n.* Pl. of **man.**

men·ace (měn'ĭs) *n.* **1.** A threat. **2.** A troublesome or annoying person. —*v.* **-aced, -ac·ing.** To threaten. [< Lat. *minari*, to threaten.] —**men'ac·ing·ly** *adv.*

mé·nage (mā-näzh') *n.* Also **me·nage.** A household. [Fr.]

me·nag·er·ie (mə-nǎj'ə-rē, mə-nǎzh'-) *n.* A collection of wild animals on exhibition. [Fr. *ménagerie.*]

mend (měnd) *v.* **1.** To make right; restore; repair. **2.** To reform or improve. **3.** To improve in health or heal. —*n.* A mended place. —*idiom.* **on the mend.** Improving in health; recuperating. [< ME *amenden*, to amend.] —**mend'er** *n.*

men·da·cious (měn-dā'shəs) *adj.* **1.** Untruthful. **2.** False; untrue. [< Lat. *mendax.*] —**men·da'cious·ly** *adv.* —**men·dac·i·ty** (-dǎs'ĭ-tē) *n.*

men·de·le·vi·um (měn'də-lē'vē-əm) *n. Symbol* **Md** An artificially produced radioactive element. Atomic number 101; mass numbers 255 and 256. [< Dmitri *Mendeleev* (1834-1907).]

men·di·cant (měn'dĭ-kənt) *adj.* Depending on alms for a living. —*n.* **1.** A beggar. **2.** A mendicant friar. [< Lat. *mendicare*, to beg.]

me·ni·al (mē'nē-əl, měn'yəl) *adj.* **1.** Pertaining to or appropriate for a servant. **2.** Of or pertaining to work regarded as servile: *menial tasks.* —*n.* A domestic servant. [< AN *meine*, household servants.] —**me'ni·al·ly** *adv.*

men·in·gi·tis (měn'ĭn-jī'tĭs) *n.* Inflammation of any or all of the meninges of the brain and spinal cord, usu. caused by a bacterial infection. [MENING(ES) + -ITIS.]

me·ninx (mē'nǐngks) *n., pl.* **me·nin·ges** (mə-nĭn'jēz). Any of the membranes enclosing the brain and spinal cord in vertebrates. [< Gk. *mēninx*, membrane.] —**me·nin'ge·al** *adj.*

me·nis·cus (mə-nǐs'kəs) *n., pl.* **-nis·ci** (-nǐs'ī') or **-es. 1.** A crescent-shaped body. **2.** The curved upper surface of a liquid in a container. [< Gk. *mēniskos*, crescent.]

men·o·pause (měn'ə-pôz') *n.* The cessation of menstruation that occurs usu. between the ages of 45 and 50. [Gk. *meis, měn-*, moon + PAUSE.]

men·ses (měn'sēz') *pl.n.* The material discharged from the uterus in menstruation. [< Lat. *mensis*, month.]

men·stru·al (měn'strōō-əl) *adj.* Relating to menstruation. [< Lat. *menstruus.*]

men·stru·ate (měn'strōō-āt') *v.* **-at·ed, -at·ing.** To undergo menstruation. [Lat. *menstruare.*]

men·stru·a·tion (měn'strōō-ā'shən) *n.* A process occurring at approx. 28-day intervals in women from puberty through middle age, in which blood and cell debris are discharged from the uterus through the reproductive tract if fertilization has not taken place.

men·su·ra·ble (měn'sər-ə-bəl, -shər-) *adj.* Capable of being measured. [< Lat. *mensura*, measure.] —**men'su·ra·bil'i·ty** *n.*

men·su·ra·tion (měn'sə-rā'shən, -shə-) *n.* The process, act, or technique of measuring.

-ment *suff.* Product, means, action, or state: *measurement.* [< Lat. *-mentum*, n. suffix.]

men·tal (měn'tl) *adj.* **1.** Pertaining to the mind. **2.** Done or performed by the mind. [< Lat. *mens*, mind.] —**men'tal·ly** *adv.*

mental age *n.* A measure of mental development, as determined by intelligence tests, gen. restricted to children and expressed as the age at which a given level is average.

mental deficiency *n.* Subnormal mental ability and intelligence, reflected in difficulty with learning, that results from genetic causes or brain damage.

men·tal·i·ty (měn-tǎl'ĭ-tē) *n., pl.* **-ties. 1.** Intellectual capability or endowment; intelligence. **2.** A habitual way of thinking.

men·thol (měn'thôl') *n.* A white, crystalline, organic compound, $CH_3C_6H_9(C_3H_7)OH$, used in perfumes, as a mild anesthetic, and as a flavoring. [Lat. *mentha*, mint + -OL.] —**men'tho·lat'ed** *adj.*

men·tion (měn'shən) *v.* To refer to incidentally or briefly. [< Lat. *mentio*, remark.] —**men'tion** *n.*

men·tor (měn'tôr', -tər) *n.* A wise and trusted counselor or teacher. [< *Mentor*, a tutor in Homer's *Odyssey.*]

men·u (měn'yōō, mān'-) *n.* A list of dishes to be served or available for a meal or a series of meals. [Fr.]

---

me·ow (mē-ou′) n. The cry of a cat. —**me·ow′** v.

me·phi·tis (mə-fī′tĭs) n. **1.** An offensive smell; stench. **2.** A foul-smelling gas emitted from the earth. [Lat.] —**me·phit′ic** (-fĭt′ĭk) adj. —**me·phit′i·cal·ly** adv.

-mer suff. Var. of **-mere**.

mer·can·tile (mûr′kən-tēl′, -tīl′) adj. Of or pertaining to merchants or trade; commercial. [< Ital.]

mer·ce·nar·y (mûr′sə-nĕr′ē) adj. **1.** Motivated only by a desire for money or material gain. **2.** Hired for service in a foreign army. [< Lat. merces, pay.] —**mer′ce·nar′y** n.

mer·cer (mûr′sər) n. Chiefly Brit. A dealer in textiles. [< Lat. merx, merchandise.]

mer·cer·ize (mûr′sə-rīz′) v. **-ized, -iz·ing.** To treat (cotton thread) with sodium hydroxide, so as to shrink the fiber and increase its luster, strength, and ability to hold dyes. [< John Mercer (1791-1866).]

mer·chan·dise (mûr′chən-dīz′, -dīs′) n. Goods that may be bought or sold in commerce; commodities. —v. (-dīz′) **-dised, -dis·ing.** To buy and sell (goods). [< Lat. mercari, to trade.] —**mer′chan·dis′er** n.

mer·chant (mûr′chənt) n. **1.** One whose occupation is buying and selling goods for profit. **2.** A shopkeeper. [< Lat. mercari, to trade.]

mer·chant·man (mûr′chənt-mən) n. A ship used in commerce.

merchant marine n. **1.** A nation's ships engaged in commerce. **2.** The personnel of the merchant marine.

mer·cu·ri·al (mər-kyŏor′ē-əl) adj. **1.** Of, containing, or caused by the action of the element mercury. **2.** Quick and changeable in character. [< Lat. Mercurius, Mercury.] —**mer·cu′ri·al·ly** adv.

mer·cu·ric (mər-kyŏor′ĭk) adj. Pertaining to or containing bivalent mercury.

mer·cu·rous (mər-kyŏor′əs, mûr′kyə-rəs) adj. Pertaining to or containing monovalent mercury.

mer·cu·ry (mûr′kyə-rē) n., pl. **-ries. 1.** Symbol **Hg** A silvery-white poisonous metallic element that is liquid at room temperature, used in thermometers, barometers, vapor lamps, and batteries and in the preparation of chemical pesticides. Atomic number 80; atomic weight 200.59. **2. Mercury.** Rom. Myth. The god of commerce, travel, and thievery, who served as messenger to the other gods. **3. Mercury.** The smallest of the planets and the one nearest the sun, having a sidereal period of revolution about the sun of 88.0 days at a mean distance of 36.2 million miles, a mean radius of approx. 1,500 miles, and a mass approx. 0.05 that of Earth. [< Lat. Mercurius, Mercury.]

mer·cy (mûr′sē) n., pl. **-cies. 1.** Compassionate treatment of an offender, enemy, etc.; clemency. **2.** A disposition to be kind and forgiving. **3.** A fortunate occurrence. [< Lat. merces, reward.] —**mer′ci·ful** adj. —**mer′ci·ful·ly** adv. —**mer′ci·less** adj. —**mer′ci·less·ly** adv.

mere (mîr) adj. superl. **mer·est.** Being nothing more than what is specified: a mere boy; a mere trifle. [< Lat. merus, pure.] —**mere′ly** adv.

-mere or **-mer** suff. Part; segment: isomer. [< Gk. meros, part.]

mer·e·tri·cious (mĕr′ĭ-trĭsh′əs) adj. Attracting attention in a vulgar manner. [< Lat.

meretrix, prostitute.] —**mer′e·tri′cious·ly** adv. —**mer′e·tri′cious·ness** n.

mer·gan·ser (mər-găn′sər) n. A fish-eating duck with a slim, hooked bill. [Lat. mergus, diver + Lat. anser, goose.]

merganser

merge (mûrj) v. **merged, merg·ing.** To blend together or cause to be absorbed so as to lose identity. [Lat. mergere, to plunge.]

merg·er (mûr′jər) n. An act or result of merging, esp. the union of two or more commercial interests or corporations.

me·rid·i·an (mə-rĭd′ē-ən) n. **1. a.** A great circle on the earth's surface that passes through both geographic poles. **b.** Either half of such a circle lying between the poles. **2.** A great circle that passes through the two poles of the celestial sphere and the point directly overhead. **3.** The highest point or stage; zenith. [< Lat. meridies, midday.] —**me·rid′i·an** adj.

me·ringue (mə-răng′) n. A dessert topping or pastry shell made of stiffly beaten and baked egg whites and sugar. [Fr. méringue.]

me·ri·no (mə-rē′nō) n., pl. **-nos. 1.** A sheep of a breed having fine, soft wool. **2.** A soft, lightweight fabric made of merino wool. [Sp.]

mer·it (mĕr′ĭt) n. **1.** Value, excellence, or superior quality. **2.** Often **merits.** An aspect of a person's character deserving approval or disapproval. **3. a.** The intrinsic right or wrong of any matter. **b.** The actual facts of a legal matter. —v. To earn; deserve. [< Lat. meritus, p.p. of merēre, to deserve.]

mer·i·to·ri·ous (mĕr′ĭ-tôr′ē-əs, -tōr′-) adj. Deserving reward or praise; having merit. [Lat. meritorius, earning money.] —**mer′i·to′ri·ous·ly** adv.

mer·maid (mûr′mād′) n. A fabled sea creature with the head and upper body of a woman and the tail of a fish. [ME meremaide.] —**mer′man′** n.

mer·ri·ment (mĕr′ĭ-mənt) n. Amusement; gaiety; fun.

mer·ry (mĕr′ē) adj. **-ri·er, -ri·est. 1.** Full of high-spirited gaiety; jolly. **2.** Characterized by fun and gaiety; festive. **3.** Pleasurable; entertaining. [< OE myrige.] —**mer′ri·ly** adv. —**mer′ri·ness** n.

   Syns: merry, gala, glad, happy, joyful, joyous adj.

mer·ry-go-round (mĕr′ē-gō-round′) n. **1.** A revolving circular platform with seats, usu. in the form of wooden animals, ridden for amusement. **2.** A whirl or swift round of activity.

mer·ry·mak·ing (mĕr′ē-mā′kĭng) n. **1.** Participation in a festive celebration. **2.** Fun and gaiety; festivity. —**mer′ry·mak′er** n.

me·sa (mā′sə) n. A flat-topped hill with cliff-like sides. [< Lat. mensa, table.]

mes·cal (mĕ-skăl′) n. A spineless, globe-shaped cactus with buttonlike tubercles that are the source of the drug mescaline. [< Nahuatl *mexcalli*, liquor made from agave.]

mes·ca·line (mĕs'kə-lēn') *n.* An alkaloid drug that produces hallucinations and abnormal mental states.

Mes·dames (mā-däm') *n.* **1.** Pl. of **Madam** (sense 1). **2.** Pl. of **Madame.**

Mes·de·moi·selles (mā'də-mə-zĕl', mād'mwə-) *n.* Pl. of **Mademoiselle.**

mesh (mĕsh) *n.* **1.** Any of the open spaces in a net, sieve, or wire screen. **2.** A net or network. **3.** The engagement of two sets of gear teeth. —*v.* **1.** To entangle or ensnare. **2.** To engage or become engaged, as gear teeth. [Prob. < MDu. *maesche.*]

mesh·work (mĕsh'wûrk') *n.* Meshes; network.

mes·mer·ize (mĕz'mə-rīz', mĕs'-) *v.* **-ized, -iz·ing.** To hypnotize. [< Franz *Mesmer* (1734-1815).] —**mes'mer·ism** *n.* —**mes'mer·iz'er** *n.*

mes·o- *pref.* Middle: *Mesolithic.* [< Gk. *mesos.*]

Mes·o·lith·ic (mĕz'ə-lĭth'ĭk, mĕs'-) *adj.* Pertaining to the period between the Paleolithic and Neolithic ages, marked by the appearance of the bow and of cutting tools. —*n.* The Mesolithic Age.

mes·o·sphere (mĕz'ə-sfîr', mĕs'-) *n.* The portion of the atmosphere above the stratosphere.

mes·quite (mĕ-skēt', mĕs'-) *n.* A thorny, pod-bearing shrub of North America. [< Nahuatl *mizquitl.*]

mess (mĕs) *n.* **1.** A disorderly mass or accumulation; jumble. **2.** A confusing state of affairs. **3.** An unappetizing amount, usu. of food: *a mess of fish.* **4. a.** A group who regularly eat meals together. **b.** A room or hall where such meals are served. **c.** A meal eaten there. —*v.* **1.** To make disorderly or dirty; clutter. **2.** To bungle, mismanage, or botch. **3.** To interfere; meddle: *Don't mess with my plans.* [< Lat. *missus,* course of a meal.]

mes·sage (mĕs'ĭj) *n.* **1.** A communication transmitted from one person or group to another. **2.** A basic theme or meaning. [< Lat. *missus,* p.p. of *mittere,* to send.]

Mes·sei·gneurs (mā'sān-yœr') *n.* Pl. of **Monseigneur.**

mes·sen·ger (mĕs'ən-jər) *n.* One who transmits messages or performs errands. [< OFr. *messagier.*]

messenger RNA *n.* An RNA that carries genetic information required for protein synthesis.

Mes·si·ah (mə-sī'ə) *n.* **1.** The expected deliverer and king of the Jews. **2.** Jesus Christ. **3.** messiah. An expected deliverer or savior. [Aram. *méshíha* or Heb. *máshíah.*] —**Mes·si·an'ic** *adj.*

Mes·sieurs (mā-syœr') *n.* Pl. of **Monsieur.**

mess·y (mĕs'ē) *adj.* **-i·er, -i·est.** Untidy; dirty; disordered. —**mess'i·ly** *adv.* —**mess'i·ness** *n.*

met (mĕt) *v.* p.t. & p.p. of **meet.**

meta- *pref.* **1.** Changed or transferred: *metastasis.* **2.** Situated behind: *metacarpus.* [< Gk. *meta,* beside, after.]

me·tab·o·lism (mə-tăb'ə-lĭz'əm) *n.* **1.** The physical and chemical processes that living things carry on to maintain life. **2.** The func-

tioning of a specific substance within the living body: *iodine metabolism.* [< Gk. *metabolē,* change.] —**met'a·bol'ic** (mĕt'ə-bŏl'ĭk) *adj.* —**me·tab'o·lize'** *v.*

met·a·car·pus (mĕt'ə-kär'pəs) *n.* The part of the hand between the wrist and fingers or forefoot between the ankle and toes that contains five bones.

met·al (mĕt'l) *n.* **1.** Any of a category of chemical elements, as copper, iron, or gold, with certain characteristic properties such as luster, malleability, ductility, and conductivity of electricity and heat. **2.** An alloy of two or more metals. **3.** Basic character; mettle. [< Gk. *metallon.*] —**me·tal'lic** (mə-tăl'ĭk) *adj.* —**me·tal'li·cal·ly** *adv.*

met·al·lur·gy (mĕt'l-ûr'jē) *n.* The science or technology of extracting metals from ores, purifying them, and making useful objects from them. [< Gk. *metallourgos,* miner.] —**met'al·lur'gic** or **met'al·lur'gi·cal** *adj.* —**met'al·lur'gist** *n.*

met·al·work (mĕt'l-wûrk') *n.* Artistic work done in metal. —**met'al·work'er** *n.* —**met'al·work'ing** *n.*

met·a·mor·phic (mĕt'ə-môr'fĭk) *adj.* **1.** Of or relating to metamorphosis. **2.** Of, pertaining to, involving, or changed by metamorphism.

met·a·mor·phism (mĕt'ə-môr'fĭz'əm) *n.* **1.** A change in composition, texture, or structure of rock masses, caused by great heat, pressure, etc. **2.** Metamorphosis.

met·a·mor·phose (mĕt'ə-môr'fōz', -fōs') *v.* **-phosed, -phos·ing.** To change or be changed by metamorphosis.

met·a·mor·pho·sis (mĕt'ə-môr'fə-sĭs) *n., pl.* **-ses** (-sēz'). **1.** A transformation, as by magic. **2.** A pronounced change in appearance, character, etc. **3.** *Biol.* Marked changes in form and mode of life during development to maturity, as in insects. [Gk. *metamorphósis.*]

met·a·phor (mĕt'ə-fôr', -fər) *n.* A figure of speech in which a term that ordinarily designates an object or idea is used to designate a dissimilar object or idea in order to suggest comparison or analogy, as in the phrase *evening of life.* [< Gk. *metaphora.*] —**met'a·phor'ic** or **met'a·phor'i·cal** *adj.* —**met'a·phor'i·cal·ly** *adv.*

met·a·phys·i·cal (mĕt'ə-fĭz'ĭ-kəl) *adj.* **1.** Of or pertaining to metaphysics. **2.** Based on speculative or abstract reasoning. **3.** Abstruse. —**met'a·phys'i·cal·ly** *adv.*

met·a·phys·ics (mĕt'ə-fĭz'ĭks) *n.* (used with a sing. verb). The branch of philosophy that systematically investigates first causes and the nature of ultimate reality. [Med. Lat. *metaphysica,* the title of Aristotle's treatise on the subject.] —**met'a·phy·si'cian** (-fə-zĭsh'ən) *n.*

me·tas·ta·sis (mə-tăs'tə-sĭs) *n., pl.* **-ses** (-sēz'). The spreading of a disease from its original location to one or more places elsewhere in the body, as in cancer. —**me·tas'ta·size'** *v.* —**met'a·stat'ic** (mĕt'ə-stăt'ĭk) *adj.*

met·a·tar·sus (mĕt'ə-tär'səs) *n., pl.* **-si** (-sī'). The middle part of the foot, composed of the five bones between the toes and tarsus, that forms the instep. —**met'a·tar'sal** *adj.*

mete¹ (mēt) *v.* **met·ed, met·ing.** To deal out; allot. [< OE *metan.*]

mete² (mēt) *n.* A boundary: *metes and bounds.* [< Lat. *meta.*]

me·tem·psy·cho·sis (mə-těm'sĭ-kō'sĭs, mět'-əm-sī-) *n., pl.* **-ses** (-sēz'). The transmigration of souls. [Gk. *metempsukhōsis.*]

me·te·or (mē'tē-ər, -ôr') *n.* 1. The luminous trail or streak that appears in the sky when a fragment of solid material is made incandescent by the earth's atmosphere. 2. A meteoroid. [< Gk. *meteōros,* high in the air.]

me·te·or·ic (mē'tē-ôr'ĭk, -ŏr'-) *adj.* 1. Of, pertaining to, or formed by meteors. 2. Resembling a meteor in speed or brilliance: *a meteoric rise to fame.*

me·te·or·ite (mē'tē-ə-rīt') *n.* The solid material of a meteoroid that survives passage through the atmosphere and reaches the earth's surface.

me·te·or·oid (mē'tē-ə-roid') *n.* Any of numerous celestial bodies, ranging in size from minute specks to huge asteroids, that appear as meteors when entering the earth's atmosphere.

me·te·or·ol·o·gy (mē'tē-ə-rŏl'ə-jē) *n.* The science dealing with the phenomena of the atmosphere, esp. weather conditions. —**me'te·or·o·log'i·cal** (-ər-ə-lŏj'ĭ-kəl) or **me'te·or·o·log'ic** *adj.* —**me'te·or'o·log'i·cal·ly** *adv.* —**me'te·or·ol'o·gist** *n.*

me·ter¹ (mē'tər) *n. Also chiefly Brit.* **me·tre.** 1. A measured rhythmic pattern used in verse. 2. **a.** The division of music into measures or bars. **b.** A specific division of this kind. [ME, ult. < Gk. *metron.*]

me·ter² (mē'tər) *n. Also chiefly Brit.* **me·tre.** The basic unit of length in the metric system, equal to 39.37 inches. [Fr. *mètre* < Gk. *metron,* measure.]

me·ter³ (mē'tər) *n.* Any of various devices designed to measure or indicate and record or regulate. —*v.* 1. To measure or regulate with a meter. 2. To imprint with postage by means of a postage meter or other similar device. [< -METER.]

-meter *suff.* A measuring device: *barometer.* [< Gk. *metron,* measure.]

me·ter-kil·o·gram-sec·ond system (mē'tər-kĭl'ə-grăm-sĕk'ənd) *n.* A system of measurement using the meter, the kilogram, and the second as basic units of length, mass, and time.

meter maid *n.* A policewoman who writes parking tickets.

meth·a·done hydrochloride (měth'ə-dōn'). An organic compound, $C_{21}H_{27}NO \cdot HCL$, used as an analgesic and in treating heroin addiction.

meth·ane (měth'ān') *n.* An odorless, colorless, flammable gas, CH_4, that is the major component of natural gas, used as a fuel and in the production of a wide variety of organic compounds. [METH(YL) + -ANE.]

meth·a·nol (měth'ə-nôl', -nŏl') *n.* A colorless, flammable liquid, CH_3OH, used as an antifreeze, solvent, fuel, and denaturant for ethanol. [METHAN(E) + -OL.]

meth·od (měth'əd) *n.* 1. A systematic means or manner of procedure; regularity. 2. Orderly and systematic arrangement; regularity. [< Gk. *methodos.*] —**meth'od·i·cal** (mə-thŏd'ĭ-kəl) or **me·thod'ic** *adj.*

Meth·od·ist (měth'ə-dĭst) *n.* A member of a Protestant denomination founded in 18th-cent. England on the teachings of John and Charles Wesley and characterized by an emphasis on the doctrines of free grace and individual responsibility. —**Meth'od·ism** *n.* —**Meth'od·ist** *adj.*

meth·od·ol·o·gy (měth'ə-dŏl'ə-jē) *n., pl.* **-gies.** 1. The system of principles and procedures applied to a science or discipline. 2. The branch of logic dealing with the general principles of the formation of knowledge. —**meth'od·o·log'i·cal** (měth'ə-də-lŏj'ĭ-kəl) *adj.*

meth·yl (měth'əl) *n.* The univalent organic radical CH_3. [< Gk. *methu,* wine.]

methyl alcohol *n.* Methanol.

me·tic·u·lous (mə-tĭk'yə-ləs) *adj.* Extremely or excessively careful and precise: *a meticulous worker.* [Lat. *meticulosus,* timid.] —**me·tic'u·lous·ness** *n.*

mé·tier (mā-tyā') *n.* 1. An occupation, trade, or profession. 2. One's specialty. [Fr.]

me·tre¹ (mē'tər) *n. Chiefly Brit.* Var. of **meter¹.**

me·tre² (mē'tər) *n. Chiefly Brit.* Var. of **meter².**

met·ric (mět'rĭk) *adj.* Of, designating, or using the metric system.

met·ri·cal (mět'rĭ-kəl) *adj.* 1. Of, pertaining to, or composed in musical or poetic meter. 2. Of or pertaining to measurement. [< Gk. *metrikos.*] —**met'ri·cal·ly** *adv.*

met·ri·ca·tion (mět'rĭ-kā'shən) *n.* Conversion to the metric system of weights and measures.

metric system *n.* A decimal system of weights and measures based on the meter as a standard of length and the kilogram as a standard of mass or weight, with other units, such as the liter for volume and the are for area, being derived from these.

metric ton *n.* A unit of mass equal to 1,000 kilograms.

met·ro·nome (mět'rə-nōm') *n.* A device that marks time at precise, adjustable intervals. [Gk. *metron,* measure + Gk. *nomos,* rule.] —**met'ro·nom'ic** (mět'rə-nōm'ĭk) *adj.*

me·trop·o·lis (mə-trŏp'ə-lĭs) *n.* 1. A major city, esp. the capital or the largest city of a country, state, or region. 2. A large urban center of culture, trade, etc. [< Gk. *mētropolis,* mother city.] —**met'ro·pol'i·tan** (mět'rə-pŏl'ĭ-tn) *adj.*

-metry *suff.* Science or process of measuring: *photometry.* [< Gk. *metron,* measure.]

met·tle (mět'l) *n.* 1. Courage and fortitude; spirit. 2. Inherent quality of character and temperament. [< METAL.] —**met'tle·some** *adj.*

mew (myōō) *v.* To make the high-pitched, crying sound of a cat; meow. [ME *mewen.*] —**mew** *n.*

mews (myōōz) *pl.n.* (*used with a sing. verb*). A small street with private stables, now mostly converted into small apartments. [< the *Mews* at Charing Cross, London.]

Mex·i·can (měk'sĭ-kən) *n.* A native or inhabitant of Mexico. —*adj.* Of or pertaining to Mexico or to its inhabitants, their language, or their culture.

Mexican Spanish *n.* Spanish as used in Mexico.

mez·za·nine (měz'ə-nēn', měz'ə-nēn') *n.* 1. A partial story between two main stories of a building. 2. The lowest balcony in a theater or the first few rows of the balcony. [< Ital. *mezzano,* middle.]

mez·zo-so·pran·o (mět'sō-sə-prăn'ō, -prä'nō, měd'zō-) *n., pl.* **-os.** Also **mez·zo.** 1. A woman's singing voice with a range between soprano and contralto. **2.** A woman with such a voice. [Ital.]

Mg The symbol for magnesium.

mi (mē) *n.* The 3rd tone of the diatonic scale. [Med. Lat.]

mi·as·ma (mī-ăz′mə, mē-) *n., pl.* **-mas** or **-ma·ta** (-mə-tə). **1.** A poisonous vapor formerly thought to rise from swamps and cause disease. **2.** A noxious atmosphere or influence. [Gk. < *miainein*, to pollute.] **—mi·as′mal** or **mi·as′mic** *adj.*

mi·ca (mī′kə) *n.* Any of a group of chemically and physically related silicate minerals, common in igneous and metamorphic rocks. [< Lat., grain.]

Mi·cah (mī′kə) *n.* Also **Mi·che·as** (mī-kē′əs). See table at **Bible.**

mice (mīs) *n.* Pl. of **mouse.**

Mic·mac (mĭk′măk′) *n., pl.* **-mac** or **-macs.** **1. a.** A tribe of Indians formerly inhabiting eastern Canada. **b.** A member of this tribe. **2.** The Algonquian language of the Micmac.

mi·cra (mī′krə) *n.* A pl. of **micron.**

micro- *pref.* **1.** Small: *microbe.* **2.** Abnormally small: *microcephaly.* **3.** Requiring or involving a microscope: *microsurgery.* **4.** One-millionth (10-6): *microsecond.* [< Gk. *mikros,* small.]

mi·crobe (mī′krōb′) *n.* A minute life form; microorganism. [MICRO- + Gk. *bios,* life.] **—mi·cro′bi·al** (-krō′bē-əl) or **mi·cro′bic** *adj.*

mi·cro·bi·ol·o·gy (mī′krō-bī-ŏl′ə-jē) *n.* The science of microorganisms. **—mi′cro·bi′o·log′i·cal** (-ə-lŏj′ĭ-kəl) or **mi′cro·bi′o·log′ic** *adj.* **—mi′cro·bi′o·log′i·cal·ly** *adv.* **—mi′cro·bi·ol′o·gist** *n.*

mi·cro·bus (mī′krō-bŭs′) *n.* A station wagon in the shape of a small bus.

mi·cro·ceph·a·ly (mī′krō-sĕf′ə-lē) *n.* Abnormal smallness of the head. [MICRO- + Gk. *kephalē,* head.] **—mi′cro·ce·phal′ic** (-sə-făl′ĭk) *n. & adj.* **—mi′cro·ceph′a·lous** *adj.*

mi·cro·cir·cuit (mī′krō-sûr′kĭt) *n.* An electric circuit consisting of miniaturized components. **—mi′cro·cir′cuit·ry** (-kĭ-trē) *n.*

mi·cro·com·put·er (mī′krō-kəm-pyōō′tər) *n.* A very small computer built around a microprocessor.

mi·cro·cosm (mī′krō-kŏz′əm) *n.* A diminutive, representative world; a system analogous to a much larger system in constitution, configuration, or development. [< Gk. *mikros kosmos,* small world.] **—mi′cro·cos′mic** or **mi′cro·cos′mi·cal** *adj.*

mi·cro·ec·o·nom·ics (mī′krō-ĕk′ə-nŏm′ĭks, -ē′kə-) *n. (used with a sing. verb).* The branch of economics that deals with specific areas of activity.

mi·cro·e·lec·tron·ics (mī′krō-ĭ-lĕk-trŏn′ĭks) *n. (used with a sing. verb).* The branch of electronics dealing with miniature components. **—mi′cro·e·lec·tron′ic** *adj.*

mi·cro·fiche (mī′krō-fēsh′) *n.* A sheet of microfilm containing rows of pages in reduced form. [Fr.]

mi·cro·film (mī′krə-fĭlm′) *n.* **1.** A film on which documents are photographed greatly reduced in size. **2.** A reproduction on microfilm. **—mi′cro·film′** *v.*

mi·cro·groove (mī′krō-grōōv′) *n.* A long-playing phonograph record. [Orig. a trademark.]

mi·crom·e·ter (mī-krŏm′ĭ-tər) *n.* A device for measuring minute distances.

mi·cron (mī′krŏn′) *n., pl.* **-crons** or **-cra** (-krə). A unit of length equal to one-millionth (10-6) of a meter. [< Gk. *mikros,* small.]

mi·cro·or·gan·ism (mī′krō-ôr′gə-nĭz′əm) *n.* An animal or plant of microscopic size, esp. a bacterium or a protozoan.

mi·cro·phone (mī′krə-fōn′) *n.* A device that converts sound waves into an electric current, usu. fed into an amplifier, recorder, or broadcast transmitter.

mi·cro·pro·ces·sor (mī′krō-prŏs′ĕs-ər) *n.* A semiconductor central processing unit usu. contained on a single integrated circuit chip.

mi·cro·scope (mī′krə-skōp′) *n.* An instrument that uses a combination of lenses to produce magnified images of small objects, esp. of objects too small to be seen by the naked eye. **—mi′cro·scop′ic** (-skŏp′ĭk) or **mi′cro·scop′i·cal** *adj.* **—mi′cro·scop′i·cal·ly** *adv.*

mi·cros·co·py (mī-krŏs′kə-pē) *n.* **1.** The study or use of microscopes. **2.** Investigation using a microscope. **—mi·cros′co·pist** *n.*

mi·cro·sec·ond (mī′krə-sĕk′ənd) *n.* A unit of time equal to one-millionth (10-6) of a second.

mi·cro·sur·ger·y (mī′krō-sûr′jə-rē) *n.* Minute surgery on living structures, as by use of microscopes and lasers. **—mi′cro·sur′gi·cal** *adj.*

mi·cro·wave (mī′krə-wāv′) *n.* An electromagnetic wave with a wavelength in the range from approx. 1 centimeter to 1 meter.

microwave oven *n.* An oven in which microwaves are used to heat food by acting on water molecules.

mid (mĭd) *adj.* Middle; central. [< OE *midd.*]

mid- *pref.* Middle: *midpoint.* [< MID.]

mid·air (mĭd-âr′) *n.* A point in the middle of the air. **—mid·air′** *adj.*

mid·brain (mĭd′brān′) *n.* The middle region of the vertebrate brain.

mid·day (mĭd′dā′) *n.* Noon. **—mid′day′** *adj.*

mid·dle (mĭd′l) *n.* **1.** An area or point equally distant from extremes or limits. **2.** The waist. *—adj.* **1.** Equally distant from extremes or limits; central. **2.** Intermediate; in-between. **3.** Medium; moderate. [< OE *middel.*]

middle age *n.* The time of human life between 40 and 60. **—mid′dle-aged′** *adj.*

Middle Ages *pl.n.* The period in European history between antiquity and the Renaissance, regarded as dating from A.D. 476 to 1453.

Middle America *n.* **1.** That part of the U.S. middle class thought of as being conservative in values and attitudes. **2.** The American heartland, thought of as being made up of small towns, small cities, and suburbs. **—Middle American** *n. & adj.*

middle class *n.* The members of society that occupy a social and economic position intermediate between the laborers and the wealthy. **—mid′dle-class′** *adj.*

Middle Dutch *n.* Dutch from the middle of the 12th cent. through the 15th cent.

middle ear *n.* The tympanic membrane together with the malleus, incus, and stapes and the structure that encloses them.

Middle English *n.* English from the 12th cent. through the 15th cent.

ă pat ā pay â care ä father ĕ pet ē be ĭ pit ī tie î pier ŏ pot ō toe ô paw, for oi noise ŏŏ took ōō boot ou out th thin th this ŭ cut û urge yōō abuse zh vision ə about, item, edible, gallop, circus

Middle High German *n.* High German from the 11th cent. through the 15th cent.

Middle Low German *n.* Low German from the middle of the 13th cent. through the 15th cent.

mid·dle·man (mĭd'l-măn') *n.* An intermediary or go-between, esp. one who buys from producers and sells to retailers or consumers.

middle management *n.* A group of persons occupying intermediate managerial positions. —**middle manager** *n.*

middle-of-the-road (mĭd'l-əv-thə-rōd') *adj.* Advocating or pursuing a course of action midway between extremes, esp. in politics.

middle school *n.* A school usu. including grades five through eight.

mid·dle·weight (mĭd'l-wāt') *n.* A boxer or wrestler weighing between 147 and 160 pounds.

mid·dling (mĭd'lĭng) *adj.* Of medium size, quality, or condition. —*adv.* Fairly; moderately. [ME *mydlyn.*] —**mid'dling·ly** *adv.*

mid·dy (mĭd'ē) *n., pl.* -**dies.** **1.** *Informal.* A midshipman. **2.** Also **middy blouse.** A woman's or child's loose blouse with a sailor collar.

midge (mĭj) *n.* A small, gnatlike fly. [< OE *mycg.*]

midg·et (mĭj'ĭt) *n.* **1.** An extremely small person. **2.** Something very small of its kind.

mid·land (mĭd'lənd) *n.* The middle or interior part of a specific country or region. —**mid'land** *adj.*

mid·night (mĭd'nīt') *n.* The middle of the night; 12 o'clock at night.

midnight sun *n.* The sun as seen at midnight during the summer within the Arctic or Antarctic Circle.

mid·point (mĭd'point') *n.* The point at or near the middle.

mid·riff (mĭd'rĭf) *n.* **1.** The diaphragm. **2.** The outer part of the human body that extends from the chest to the waist. [< OE *midhrif.*]

mid·ship·man (mĭd'shĭp'mən, mĭd-shĭp'mən) *n.* A student training to be an officer in the U.S. Navy or Coast Guard.

midst (mĭdst) *n.* **1.** The middle position or part; center. **2.** The condition of being surrounded by or enveloped in something. —*prep.* Among. [ME *middest.*]

mid·sum·mer (mĭd'sŭm'ər) *n.* **1.** The middle of the summer. **2.** The summer solstice, about June 21. —**mid'sum'mer** *adj.*

mid·term (mĭd'tûrm') *n.* **1.** The middle of a term, as of a school or a political office. **2.** An examination given at the middle of a school term.

mid·town (mĭd'toun') *n.* The central part of a city. —**mid'town'** *adj.*

mid·way (mĭd'wā') *n.* The area of a fair, carnival, or circus where side shows and other amusements are located. —*adv. & adj.* In the middle; halfway.

mid·week (mĭd'wēk') *n.* The middle of the week. —**mid'week'** *adj.* —**mid'week'ly** *adj. & adv.*

mid·wife (mĭd'wīf') *n.* A woman who assists women during childbirth. [ME *mid,* with + ME *wif,* woman.] —**mid'wife'ry** (-wīf'rē, -wī'fə-rē) *n.*

mid·win·ter (mĭd'wĭn'tər) *n.* **1.** The middle of the winter. **2.** The winter solstice, about Dec. 22. —**mid'win'ter** *adj.*

mid·year (mĭd'yîr') *n.* **1.** The middle of a year.

2. An examination given in the middle of a school year. —**mid'year'** *adj.*

mien (mēn) *n.* Bearing; manner; appearance. [< *demean,* behavior.]

miff (mĭf) *v.* To offend; upset. [Orig. unknown.]

might[1] (mīt) *n.* **1.** Tremendous power. **2.** Great physical strength. [< OE *miht.*]

might[2] (mīt) *v.* Used as an auxiliary to indicate a condition contrary to fact, a weaker or more remote probability than *may,* or to express a higher degree of politeness than *may.* [< OE *magan,* to be able.]

might·y (mī'tē) *adj.* -**i·er,** -**i·est.** **1.** Powerful. **2.** Pre-eminent. —*adv. Informal.* Very. —**might'i·ly** *adv.* —**might'i·ness** *n.*

mi·gnon·ette (mĭn'yə-nĕt') *n.* A plant cultivated for its small, fragrant greenish flowers. [Fr. < *mignon,* small.]

mi·graine (mī'grān') *n.* A severe, recurrent headache, usu. affecting only one side of the head. [< Gk. *hēmikrania,* pain in half of the head.]

mi·grant (mī'grənt) *n.* **1.** One that migrates. **2.** One who travels from place to place in search of work. [< Lat. *migrare,* to migrate.] —**mi'grant** *adj.*

mi·grate (mī'grāt') *v.* -**grat·ed,** -**grat·ing.** **1.** To move from one country or region and settle in another. **2.** To move regularly from one region to another. [< Lat. *migrare,* to migrate.] —**mi·gra'tion** *n.* —**mi'gra·tion·al** *adj.* —**mi'gra·to'ry** (-grə-tôr'ē, -tōr'ē) *adj.*

mi·ka·do (mĭ-kä'dō) *n., pl.* -**dos.** The emperor of Japan. [J.]

mike (mīk) *n. Informal.* A microphone.

mil[1] (mĭl) *n.* A unit of length equal to one-thousandth (10^{-3}) of an inch. [< Lat. *mille,* thousand.]

mil[2] (mĭl) *n.* See table at **currency.** [< Lat. *mille,* thousand.]

mild (mīld) *adj.* -**er,** -**est.** **1.** Gentle or meek in disposition or behavior. **2.** Not extreme; moderate. **3.** Not sharp or strong in taste or odor. [< OE *milde.*] —**mild'ly** *adv.* —**mild'ness** *n.*

mil·dew (mĭl'dōō', -dyōō') *n.* A white or grayish coating formed by fungi on plant leaves, cloth, paper, etc. [< OE *mīdēaw.*] —**mil'dew** *v.* —**mil'dew·y** *adj.*

mile (mīl) *n.* **1.** A unit of length equal to 5,280 feet, 1,760 yards, or 1,609.34 meters. **2.** A nautical mile. **3.** An air mile. [< Lat. *mille,* thousand.]

mile·age (mī'lĭj) *n.* **1.** Distance measured or expressed in miles. **2.** Service or wear estimated by or as by miles used or traveled. **3.** An allowance for travel expenses established at a specified rate per mile.

mile·post (mīl'pōst') *n.* A post set up to indicate distance in miles, as on a highway.

mile·stone (mīl'stōn') *n.* **1.** A stone milepost. **2.** A turning point.

mi·lieu (mēl-yœ') *n.* Environment; surroundings. [< OFr., center.]

mil·i·tant (mĭl'ĭ-tənt) *adj.* **1.** Engaged in combat. **2.** Combative and aggressive. —*n.* A militant person. [< Lat. *militare,* to serve as a soldier.] —**mil'i·tan·cy** *n.* —**mil'i·tant·ly** *adv.*

mil·i·ta·rism (mĭl'ĭ-tə-rĭz'əm) *n.* The glorification of a professional military class or policies arising from its predominance in state affairs. —**mil'i·ta·rist** *n.* —**mil'i·ta·ris'tic** *adj.* —**mil'i·ta·ris'ti·cal·ly** *adv.*

mil·i·ta·rize (mĭl'ĭ-tə-rīz') *v.* -**rized,** -**riz·ing.**

1. To equip or train for war. **2.** To imbue with militarism. —**mil′i·ta·ri·za′tion** n.

mil·i·tar·y (mĭl′ĭ-tĕr′ē) adj. Of, pertaining to, or associated with soldiers, armed forces, or war. —n. Armed forces. [< Lat. miles, soldier.] —**mil′i·tar′i·ly** (-târ′ə-lē) adv.

mil·i·tate (mĭl′ĭ-tāt′) v. -tat·ed, -tat·ing. To have force as evidence. [Lat. militare, to serve as a soldier.]

mi·li·tia (mĭ-lĭsh′ə) n. A military force that is not a part of the regular armed forces but is on call for service in an emergency. [Lat., warfare.] —**mi·li′tia·man** n.

milk (mĭlk) n. **1. a.** A whitish liquid secreted by the mammary glands of female mammals to nourish their young. **b.** Cows' milk used as food by human beings. **2.** A liquid that resembles milk: coconut milk. —v. **1.** To draw milk from (a female mammal). **2.** To draw out or extract from as if by milking. [< OE milc.] —**milk′er** n. —**milk′i·ness** n. —**milk′y** adj.

milk·maid (mĭlk′mād′) n. A girl or woman who milks cows.

milk·man (mĭlk′măn′) n. A man who sells or delivers milk.

milk of magnesia n. A milky white liquid suspension of magnesium hydroxide, Mg(OH)₂, used as an antacid and laxative.

milk shake n. A whipped beverage made of milk, flavoring, and usu. ice cream.

milk·sop (mĭlk′sŏp′) n. A man who lacks manly qualities.

milk tooth n. Any of the temporary first teeth of a young mammal.

milk·weed (mĭlk′wēd′) n. A plant with milky juice and pods that split open to release downy seeds.

Milky Way n. The galaxy in which the solar system is located, visible as a broad, luminous band that stretches across the night sky.

mill¹ (mĭl) n. **1.** A building or establishment equipped with machinery for grinding grain. **2.** A device for grinding or crushing. **3.** A structure equipped with machinery for processing materials; factory. **4.** A place that turns out something routinely and in large quantities: a diploma mill. —v. **1.** To grind or crush in or as if in a mill. **2.** To move around in a confused or disorderly manner. —idiom. **run of the mill.** Ordinary; commonplace. [< Lat. mola, millstone.]

mill¹

mill² (mĭl) n. A monetary unit equal to one-thousandth of a U.S. dollar. [< Lat. mille, thousand.]

mill·dam (mĭl′dăm′) n. **1.** A dam to make a millpond. **2.** A millpond.

mil·len·ni·um (mĭ-lĕn′ē-əm) n., pl. -ums or -ni·a (-ē-ə). **1.** A period of 1,000 years. **2.** In the New Testament, the thousand-year reign of Christ on earth. **3.** A hoped-for period of joy, prosperity, and peace. [< Lat. mille, thousand + Lat. annus, year.] —**mil·len′ni·al** (-lĕn′ē-əl) adj.

mil·le·pede (mĭl′ə-pēd′) n. Var. of **millipede**.

mill·er (mĭl′ər) n. One who operates or owns a mill, esp. a grain mill.

mil·let (mĭl′ət) n. **1.** A grass cultivated for its edible seed and for hay. **2.** The white seeds of this plant. [< Lat. milium.]

milli- pref. One-thousandth (10⁻³): millimeter. [< Lat. mille, thousand.]

mil·liard (mĭl′yərd, -yärd′, mĭl′ē-ärd′) n. Chiefly Brit. A billion. [Fr.]

mil·li·bar (mĭl′ə-bär′) n. A unit of atmospheric pressure equal to 1,000 dynes per square centimeter. [MILLI- + bar, a unit of pressure.]

mil·lieme (mēl-yĕm′, mē-yĕm′) n. See table at currency. [Prob. < Fr. millième, thousandth.]

mil·li·gram (mĭl′ĭ-grăm′) n. A unit of mass or weight equal to one-thousandth (10⁻³) of a gram.

mil·li·li·ter (mĭl′ə-lē′tər) n. A unit of fluid volume or capacity equal to one-thousandth (10⁻³) of a liter.

mil·li·me·ter (mĭl′ə-mē′tər) n. A unit of length equal to one-thousandth (10⁻³) of a meter or 0.0394 inch.

mil·li·ner (mĭl′ə-nər) n. One who makes or sells women's hats. [< obs. Milaner, a native of Milan, Italy.] —**mil′li·ner′y** n.

mil·lion (mĭl′yən) n., pl. -lion or -lions. **1.** The cardinal number equal to 1,000 × 1,000. **2.** Often **millions.** An indefinitely large number. [< Lat. mille, thousand.] —**mil′lion** adj.

mil·lion·aire (mĭl′yə-nâr′) n. One whose wealth amounts to a million or more units of currency. [Fr. millionnaire.]

mil·lionth (mĭl′yənth) n. **1.** The ordinal number one million in a series. **2.** One of a million equal parts. —**mil′lionth** adj.

mil·li·pede or **mil·le·pede** (mĭl′ə-pēd′) n. A crawling, plant-eating arthropod with a long, segmented body and legs attached in double pairs to most of its body segments. [Lat. millepeda, a kind of insect.]

mil·li·sec·ond (mĭl′ĭ-sĕk′ənd) n. A unit of time equal to one-thousandth (10⁻³) of a second.

mill·pond (mĭl′pŏnd′) n. A pond formed by a dam to supply power for operating a mill.

mill·race (mĭl′rās′) n. **1.** The fast-moving stream of water that drives a mill wheel. **2.** A channel for the water driving a mill wheel.

mill·stone (mĭl′stōn′) n. **1.** One of a pair of large, circular stones used to grind grain. **2.** A heavy burden.

mill·stream (mĭl′strēm′) n. **1.** The water in a millrace. **2.** Millrace (sense 1).

milque·toast (mĭlk′tōst′) n. A meek, timid person. [< Caspar Milquetoast, a comic-strip character created by Harold T. Webster (1885-1952).]

milt (mĭlt) n. The sperm of fishes. [Prob. < MDu. milte.]

ă pat ā pay â care ä father ĕ pet ē be ĭ pit ī tie î pier ŏ pot ō toe ô paw, for oi noise ŏŏ took
ōō boot ou out th thin th this ŭ cut û urge yōō abuse zh vision ə about, item, edible, gallop, circus

mime (mīm) *n.* **1.** The art of pantomime. **2.** A performer in pantomime. **3.** A mimic. —*v.* **mimed, mim·ing. 1.** To mimic; ape. **2.** To act or portray in pantomime. [< Gk. *mimos,* imitator.] —**mim′er** *n.*

mim·e·o·graph (mĭm′ē-ə-grăf′) *n.* A duplicator that makes copies of written, drawn, or typed material from a stencil fitted around an inked drum. [Orig. a trademark.] —**mim′e·o·graph′** *v.*

mi·me·sis (mĭ-mē′sĭs, mī-) *n.* The appearance, often due to hysteria, of symptoms of a disease not actually present. [< Gk. *mimeisthai,* to imitate.]

mi·met·ic (mĭ-mĕt′ĭk, mī-) *adj.* Of, pertaining to, or using mimicry. [< Gk. *mimētikos.*] —**mi·met′i·cal·ly** *adv.*

mim·ic (mĭm′ĭk) *v.* **-icked, -ick·ing. 1.** To imitate closely, as in speech, expression, or gesture; ape. **2.** To ridicule by imitating; mock. **3.** To resemble closely; simulate. —*n.* One that mimics. —*adj.* Of or pertaining to mimicry. [< Gk. *mimikos,* imitative.] —**mim′ick·er** *n.*

mim·ic·ry (mĭm′ĭ-krē) *n., pl.* **-ries.** The act or practice of mimicking; imitation.

mi·mo·sa (mĭ-mō′sə, -zə) *n.* Any of various shrubs or trees with compound leaves and ball-like clusters of small flowers. [< Gk. *mimos,* imitator.]

min·a·ret (mĭn′ə-rĕt′) *n.* A tall, slender tower on a mosque. [< Ar. *manārat.*]

min·a·to·ry (mĭn′ə-tôr′ē, -tōr′ē) *adj.* Menacing; threatening. [< Lat. *minari,* to menace.] —**min′a·to′ri·ly** *adv.*

mince (mĭns) *v.* **minced, minc·ing. 1.** To cut into very small pieces. **2.** To pronounce in an affected way. **3.** To refrain from the forthright use of: *Let's not mince words; the man is a liar.* **4.** To walk in a prim or affected way. [< Lat. *minuere,* to lessen.] —**minc′er** *n.* —**minc′ing·ly** *adv.*

mince·meat (mĭns′mēt′) *n.* A mixture of finely chopped apples, spices, and sometimes meat, used esp. as a pie filling. —*idiom.* **make mincemeat of.** *Slang.* To ruin or destroy completely.

mind (mīnd) *n.* **1.** The consciousness that originates in the brain and directs mental and physical behavior. **2.** Memory; recollection. **3.** Conscious thoughts; attention. **4.** Opinion or intentions. **5.** Intellect; intelligence. **6.** One considered with regard to intellectual ability. **7.** Mental or emotional health; sanity. —*v.* **1.** To attend to; heed. **2.** To obey. **3.** To take care of; tend. **4.** To be careful about. **5.** To be concerned or troubled (about); object (to). —*idiom.* **piece of (one's) mind.** *Informal.* A sharply worded rebuke. [< OE *gemynd.*]

mind-blow·ing (mīnd′blō′ĭng) *adj. Slang.* **1.** Producing hallucinations. **2.** Intensely affecting the emotions. —**mind′-blow′er** *n.*

mind-bog·gling (mīnd′bŏg′lĭng) *adj. Informal.* Overwhelming.

mind-ex·pand·ing (mīnd′ĭk-spăn′dĭng) *adj.* Psychedelic.

mind·ful (mīnd′fəl) *adj.* Aware; heedful. —**mind′ful·ly** *adv.* —**mind′ful·ness** *n.*

mind·less (mīnd′lĭs) *adj.* **1.** Lacking intelligence, sense, or purpose. **2.** Careless; heedless. —**mind′less·ly** *adv.* —**mind′less·ness** *n.*

mine¹ (mīn) *n.* **1.** An excavation in the earth to extract minerals, as metals, coal, or salt. **2.** A deposit of ore or minerals. **3.** An abundant source. **4. a.** A tunnel dug under an enemy position. **b.** An explosive device, either buried in the ground or floating in the water, detonated by contact or by a time fuse. —*v.* **mined, min·ing. 1.** To dig from or as from a mine. **2.** To dig a mine (in). **3.** To lay explosive mines in or under. **4.** To undermine; subvert. [< OFr.] —**min′a·ble** or **mine′a·ble** *adj.* —**min′er** *n.*

mine² (mīn) *pron.* Used to indicate the one or ones belonging to me: *If you can't find your hat, take mine. The green boots are mine.* [< OE *mīn.*]

mine·field (mīn′fēld′) *n.* An area in which explosive mines have been placed.

min·er·al (mĭn′ər-əl) *n.* **1.** A natural inorganic substance with a definite chemical composition and characteristic physical structure. **2. a.** An element, such as gold or silver. **b.** A mixture of inorganic compounds, such as granite. **c.** An organic derivative, such as coal or petroleum. **3.** A substance that is neither animal nor vegetable; inorganic matter. **4.** An ore. [< MINE¹.] —**min′er·al** *adj.* —**min′er·al·i·za′tion** *n.* —**min′er·al·ize′** *v.*

min·er·al·o·gy (mĭn′ə-rŏl′ə-jē, -răl′-) *n.* The scientific study of minerals. —**min′er·a·log′i·cal** (-ər-ə-lŏj′ĭ-kəl) *adj.* —**min′er·a·log′i·cal·ly** *adv.* —**min′er·al′o·gist** *n.*

mineral oil *n.* A refined oil distilled from petroleum, used esp. as a laxative.

mineral water *n.* Water containing dissolved minerals or gases.

Mi·ner·va (mĭ-nûr′və) *n. Rom. Myth.* The goddess of wisdom, the arts, and warfare.

min·e·stro·ne (mĭn′ĭ-strō′nē) *n.* A thick soup that contains beans, pasta, and assorted vegetables. [Ital. < *minestrare,* to serve.]

mine sweeper *n.* A ship equipped for detecting, removing, or neutralizing explosive mines.

min·gle (mĭng′gəl) *v.* **-gled, -gling.** To mix together in close association. [< OE *mengan,* to mix.] —**min′gler** *n.*

mini (mĭn′ē) *n.* **1.** Something distinctly smaller than others of its class. **2.** A miniskirt.

mini- *pref.* Miniature: *minicar.* [< MINIATURE.]

min·i·a·ture (mĭn′ē-ə-chŏŏr′, mĭn′ə-, -chər) *n.* **1.** A very small copy or model. **2.** A very small, detailed painting. —*adj.* Very small. [Ital. *miniatura,* illumination of manuscripts.] —**min′i·a·tur·i·za′tion** *n.* —**min′i·a·tur·ize′** *v.*

miniature
From Jeanne d'Evreux's book of hours, illuminated by Jean Pucelle. Actual size 3½ by 2 7/10 inches.

miniature golf *n.* A simplified version of golf played on a miniature course.

min·i·bike (mĭn′ē-bīk′) *n.* A small motorbike.

min·i·bus (mĭn'ē-bŭs') *n.* A small bus.

min·i·car (mĭn'ē-kär') *n.* A subcompact car.

min·i·com·put·er (mĭn'ē-kəm-pyōō'tər) *n.* A small computer with more memory and higher execution speed than a microcomputer.

min·im (mĭn'əm) *n.* 1. A unit of fluid measure equal to one-sixtieth of a fluid dram. 2. A very small amount. [< Lat. *minimus*, least.]

min·i·mal (mĭn'ə-məl) *adj.* Least in amount or degree. —**min'i·mal·ly** *adv.*

minimal art *n.* Nonrepresentational art consisting chiefly of geometric shapes and forms. —**minimal artist** *n.*

min·i·mize (mĭn'ə-mīz') *v.* **-mized, -miz·ing.** To reduce to or represent as having minimum importance or value.

min·i·mum (mĭn'ə-məm) *n., pl.* **-mums** or **-ma** (-mə). 1. The least possible quantity or degree. 2. The lowest quantity, degree, or number reached or permitted. [< Lat. *minimus*, least.] —**min'i·mum** *adj.*

minimum wage *n.* The lowest wage, set by law or contract, that can be paid for a specified job.

min·ion (mĭn'yən) *n.* A usu. servile follower or dependent. [< OFr. *mignot*, darling.]

min·i·se·ries (mĭn'ē-sîr'ēz) *n.* 1. A sequence of episodes making up a televised drama. 2. A short series, as of athletic contests.

min·i·skirt (mĭn'ē-skûrt') *n.* An extremely short skirt.

min·is·ter (mĭn'ī-stər) *n.* 1. A person authorized to perform religious functions in a church. 2. The head of a governmental department. 3. A diplomat ranking below an ambassador. 4. One who serves as an agent for another. —*v.* To attend to the wants and needs of others. [< Lat., servant.] —**min'is·te'ri·al** (-stîr'ē-əl) *adj.* —**min'is·trant** (-strənt) *adj. & n.* —**min'is·tra'tion** *n.* —**min'is·tra'tive** *adj.*

min·is·try (mĭn'ī-strē) *n., pl.* **-tries.** 1. The act of ministering or serving. 2. a. The profession of a minister of religion. b. The clergy. c. The term of service of a minister of religion. 3. a. A governmental department headed by a minister. b. The building in which it is housed. c. The position, duties, or term of a government minister.

mink (mĭngk) *n., pl.* **mink** or **minks.** 1. A semiaquatic weasellike mammal with soft, thick, lustrous, brownish fur. 2. The fur of the mink. [ME *mynk*.]

min·now (mĭn'ō) *n., pl.* **-now** or **-nows.** Any of several small, freshwater fish often used as bait. [ME *meneu*.]

mi·nor (mī'nər) *adj.* 1. Lesser or smaller in amount, size, or importance. 2. Not in seriousness or danger. 3. Not of legal age: *a minor child.* 4. *Mus.* Of or based on a minor scale. —*n.* 1. One who has not yet reached legal age. 2. a. A secondary area of academic study. b. A student studying a minor: *a chemistry minor.* 3. *Mus.* A minor key, scale, or interval. 4. *Sports.* **minors.** The minor leagues. —*v.* To pursue academic studies in a minor field. [< Lat.]

mi·nor·i·ty (mī-nôr'ī-tē, -nŏr'-, mī-) *n., pl.* **-ties.** 1. The smaller in number of two groups forming a whole. 2. A group that differs, as in race, religion, or ethnic background, from the larger group of which it is a part. 3. The condition or period of being under legal age. —**mi·nor'i·ty** *adj.*

minority leader *n.* The leader of the minority party in a legislature.

minor league *n.* A league of professional sports clubs other than the major leagues. —**mi'nor-league'** *adj.*

minor scale *n. Mus.* A diatonic scale having a minor third between the 1st and 3rd notes.

min·ster (mĭn'stər) *n.* 1. A monastery church. 2. A large, important church; cathedral. [< LGk. *monastērion*, monastery.]

min·strel (mĭn'strəl) *n.* 1. A medieval traveling musician. 2. A performer in a minstrel show. [< LLat. *ministerialis*, official in the imperial household.]

minstrel show *n.* A formerly popular variety show in which performers, often in blackface, sing, dance, tell jokes, and perform comic skits.

mint¹ (mĭnt) *n.* 1. A place where money is manufactured by a government. 2. A large amount, esp. of money. —*v.* 1. To produce (money) by stamping metal. 2. To invent; make up: *mint phrases.* —*adj.* In original condition; unused. [< Lat. *moneta*.] —**mint'age** *n.*

mint² (mĭnt) *n.* 1. Any of various related plants, many of which yield an aromatic oil used for flavoring. 2. A candy flavored with mint. [< Gk. *minthē*.] —**mint'y** *adj.*

mint julep *n.* A drink made of bourbon, sugar, crushed mint leaves, and ice.

min·u·end (mĭn'yōō-ĕnd') *n.* A number from which another number is to be subtracted. [< Lat. *minuendum*, thing to be diminished.]

min·u·et (mĭn'yōō-ĕt') *n.* 1. A stately dance that originated in 17th-cent. France. 2. Music for a minuet. [< Lat. *minutus*, small.]

mi·nus (mī'nəs) *prep.* 1. *Math.* Reduced by; less: *Seven minus four equals three.* 2. *Informal.* Lacking; without. —*adj.* 1. *Math.* Negative or on the negative part of a scale: *a minus value.* 2. Slightly lower or less than a specified norm: *a grade of B minus.* —*n.* 1. The minus sign. 2. A negative number or quantity. 3. A loss, deficiency, or disadvantage. [< Lat., less.]

min·us·cule (mĭn'ə-skyōōl', mĭ-nŭs'kyōōl') *adj.* Very small; minute. [< Lat. *minusculus*, very small.] —**mi·nus'cu·lar** (mĭ-nŭs'kyə-lər) *adj.*

minus sign *n.* The symbol (–), as in 4 – 2=2, used to indicate subtraction or a negative quantity.

min·ute¹ (mĭn'ĭt) *n.* 1. a. A unit of time equal to one-sixtieth of an hour or 60 seconds. b. A unit of angular measurement equal to one-sixtieth of a degree or 60 seconds. 2. A short interval of time; moment. 3. A specific point in time. 4. **minutes.** An official record of the proceedings at a meeting of an organization. [< Lat. *minutus*, small.]

mi·nute² (mī-nōōt', -nyōōt', mĭ-) *adj.* 1. Exceptionally small; tiny. 2. Insignificant; trifling. 3. Characterized by close examination. [Lat. *minutus*.] —**min·ute'ly** *adv.* —**min·ute'ness** *n.*

---

min·ute·man or **Min·ute·man** (mĭn′ĭt-măn′) *n.* A Revolutionary War militiaman ready to fight on a minute's notice.

minuteman

Drawing of the minuteman statue in Concord, Massachusetts

mi·nu·ti·a (mĭ-nŏō′shē-ə, -nyŏō′-, -shə) *n., pl.* **-ti·ae** (-shē-ē′). A small or trivial detail. [Lat., smallness.]

minx (mĭngks) *n.* An impudent or flirtatious girl. [Orig. unknown.]

Mi·o·cene (mī′ə-sēn′) *adj.* Of or belonging to the geologic time, rock series, or sedimentary deposits of the 4th epoch of the Tertiary period. —*n.* The Miocene epoch. [Gk. *meiōn*, less + -CENE.]

mir·a·cle (mĭr′ə-kəl) *n.* 1. An extraordinary or unusual event that is considered to be a manifestation of divine or supernatural power. 2. One that excites admiration, awe, or wonder. [< Lat. *miraculum.*] —**mi·rac·u·lous** (mĭ-răk′yə-ləs) *adj.* —**mi·rac·u·lous·ly** *adv.* —**mi·rac·u·lous·ness** *n.*

mi·rage (mĭ-räzh′) *n.* 1. An optical phenomenon that creates the illusion of water often with inverted reflections of distant objects. 2. Something that is illusory or insubstantial. [< Lat. *mirari*, to wonder at.]

mire (mīr) *n.* 1. A bog. 2. Deep, slimy soil or mud. —*v.* **mired, mir·ing.** 1. To sink or cause to sink in mire. 2. To soil with mud. [< ON *mȳrr.*] —**mir′y** *adj.*

mir·ror (mĭr′ər) *n.* 1. A surface capable of reflecting enough undiffused light to form a virtual image of an object placed in front of it. 2. Something that gives a true picture of something else. —*v.* To reflect in or as in a mirror. [< Lat. *mirari*, to wonder at.]

mirth (mûrth) *n.* Gaiety; merriment. [< OE *myrgth.*] —**mirth′ful** *adj.* —**mirth′ful·ly** *adv.* —**mirth′ful·ness** *n.*

mis- *pref.* 1. Bad; badly; wrong; wrongly: *misconduct.* 2. Failure; lack: *misfire.* [< OE, and < Lat. *minus*, less.]

mis·ad·ven·ture (mĭs′əd-vĕn′chər) *n.* A misfortune; mishap.

mis·al·li·ance (mĭs′ə-lī′əns) *n.* An unsuitable marriage.

mis·an·thrope (mĭs′ən-thrōp′, mĭz′-) *n.* One who hates mankind. [< Gk. *misanthropos*, hating mankind.] —**mis·an·throp′ic** (-thrŏp′ĭk) *adj.* —**mis·an·thro·py** (mĭs-ăn′thrə-pē, mĭz′-) *n.*

mis·ap·ply (mĭs′ə-plī′) *v.* To apply wrongly. —**mis·ap·pli·ca′tion** *n.*

mis·ap·pre·hend (mĭs′ăp′rĭ-hĕnd′) *v.* To misunderstand. —**mis·ap′pre·hen′sion** *n.*

mis·ap·pro·pri·ate (mĭs′ə-prō′prē-āt′) *v.* To appropriate dishonestly for one's own use. —**mis′ap·pro′pri·a′tion** *n.*

mis·be·got·ten (mĭs′bĭ-gŏt′n) *adj.* Illegally begotten, esp. illegitimate.

mis·be·have (mĭs′bĭ-hāv′) *v.* To behave badly. —**mis·be·hav′ior** *n.*

mis·cal·cu·late (mĭs-kăl′kyə-lāt′) *v.* To calculate wrongly; misjudge. —**mis·cal′cu·la′tion** *n.*

mis·call (mĭs-kôl′) *v.* To call by a wrong name.

mis·car·riage (mĭs-kăr′ĭj) *n.* 1. Mismanagement. 2. Premature expulsion of a nonviable fetus from the uterus.

mis·car·ry (mĭs-kăr′ē) *v.* 1. To go wrong. 2. To abort.

mis·cast (mĭs-kăst′) *v.* To cast in an unsuitable role.

mis·ce·ge·na·tion (mĭs′ĭ-jə-nā′shən, mĭ-sĕj′ə-) *n.* Marriage, cohabitation, or interbreeding between persons of different races. [< Lat. *miscēre*, to mix + Lat. *genus*, race.]

mis·cel·la·ne·ous (mĭs′ə-lā′nē-əs) *adj.* Made up of many different parts, elements, or characteristics. [Lat. *miscellaneus.*] —**mis·cel·la·ne·ous·ly** *adv.*

mis·cel·la·ny (mĭs′ə-lā′nē) *n., pl.* **-nies.** 1. A collection of various items or ingredients. 2. A collection of diverse literary works.

mis·chance (mĭs-chăns′) *n.* 1. Bad luck. 2. A mishap.

mis·chief (mĭs′chĭf) *n.* 1. A cause of discomfiture or annoyance. 2. An inclination to play pranks. 3. Injury caused by a specified human agency. [< OFr. *meschef*, misfortune.]

mis·chie·vous (mĭs′chə-vəs) *adj.* 1. Playful, teasing, or troublesome. 2. Causing harm or injury. —**mis′chie·vous·ly** *adv.* —**mis′chie·vous·ness** *n.*

mis·ci·ble (mĭs′ə-bəl) *adj. Chem.* Capable of being mixed in all proportions. [< Lat. *miscēre*, to mix.] —**mis′ci·bil′i·ty** *n.*

mis·con·ceive (mĭs′kən-sēv′) *v.* To interpret incorrectly. —**mis′con·ceiv′er** *n.* —**mis′con·cep′tion** (-sĕp′shən) *n.*

mis·con·duct (mĭs-kŏn′dŭkt′) *n.* 1. Improper conduct or behavior. 2. Dishonest or bad management. —*v.* (mĭs′kən-dŭkt′). 1. To behave improperly. 2. To manage poorly or dishonestly.

mis·con·strue (mĭs′kən-strōō′) *v.* To misinterpret. —**mis′con·struc′tion** (-strŭk′shən) *n.*

mis·count (mĭs-kount′) *v.* To count incorrectly. —*n.* (mĭs′kount′). An inaccurate count.

mis·cre·ant (mĭs′krē-ənt) *n.* An evildoer; villain. [< OFr. *mescroire*, to disbelieve.] —**mis′cre·ant** *adj.*

mis·cue (mĭs-kyōō′) *n.* A blunder or mistake. —**mis·cue′** *v.*

mis·deed (mĭs-dēd′) *n.* A wicked act.

mis·de·mean·or (mĭs′dĭ-mē′nər) *n.* 1. A misdeed. 2. *Law.* An offense of less seriousness than a felony.

mis·di·rect (mĭs′dĭ-rĕkt′, -dī-) *v.* To direct incorrectly. —**mis′di·rec′tion** *n.*

mis·do (mĭs-dōō′) *v.* To do wrongly. —**mis·do′er** *n.*

mise en scène (mēz äN sĕn′) *n.* 1. The setting and staging of a play. 2. A setting or environment. [Fr., putting on stage.]

mi·ser (mī′zər) *n.* A grasping, avaricious person, esp. one who hoards money. [< Lat., wretched.] —**mi′ser·li·ness** *n.* —**mi′ser·ly** *adj.*

mis·er·a·ble (mĭz′ər-ə-bəl, mĭz′rə-bəl) *adj.* 1. Very unhappy; wretched. 2. Causing distress or discomfort. **3.** Wretchedly poor; squalid. **4.** Of poor quality; inferior. [< Lat. *miserabilis.*] —**mis'er·a·ble·ness** n. —**mis'er·a·bly** adv.

mis·er·y (mĭz'ə-rē) n., pl. -**ies.** **1.** Prolonged or extreme suffering; wretchedness. **2.** An affliction or deprivation. [< Lat. *miseria.*]

mis·file (mĭs-fīl') v. To file incorrectly.

mis·fire (mĭs-fīr') v. **1.** To fail to fire, explode, or ignite at the proper time. **2.** To fail to achieve an intended result. —**mis'fire'** n.

mis·fit (mĭs'fĭt', mĭs-fĭt') n. **1.** A poor fit. **2.** A maladjusted person.

mis·for·tune (mĭs-fôr'chən) n. **1.** Bad fortune. **2.** A mishap.

mis·giv·ing (mĭs-gĭv'ĭng) n. Often **misgivings.** A feeling of doubt or suspicion.

mis·gov·ern (mĭs-gŭv'ərn) v. To govern badly. —**mis·gov'ern·ment** n.

mis·guide (mĭs-gīd') v. To give misleading direction to; lead astray. —**mis·guid'ance** n. —**mis·guid'ed·ly** adv. —**mis·guid'er** n.

mis·han·dle (mĭs-hăn'dl) v. To deal with clumsily or inefficiently.

mis·hap (mĭs'hăp', mĭs-hăp') n. An unfortunate accident.

mis·hear (mĭs-hîr') v. To hear incorrectly.

mish·mash (mĭsh'măsh') n. A hodgepodge. [< MASH.]

mis·in·form (mĭs'ĭn-fôrm') v. To give false or inaccurate information to. —**mis'in·form'ant** n. —**mis·in'for·ma'tion** n.

mis·in·ter·pret (mĭs'ĭn-tûr'prĭt) v. To explain or understand incorrectly. —**mis'in·ter'pre·ta'tion** n.

mis·judge (mĭs-jŭj') v. To judge incorrectly. —**mis·judg'ment** n.

mis·lay (mĭs-lā') v. To put in a place that is afterward forgotten; lose.

mis·lead (mĭs-lēd') v. **1.** To lead in the wrong direction. **2.** To lead into error. **3.** To deceive.

mis·like (mĭs-līk') v. To dislike. —n. Dislike.

mis·man·age (mĭs-măn'ĭj) v. To manage badly or improperly; botch. —**mis·man'age·ment** n.

mis·match (mĭs-măch') v. To match unsuitably, esp. in marriage. —**mis'match'** n.

mis·name (mĭs-nām') v. To call by a wrong name.

mis·no·mer (mĭs-nō'mər) n. A wrong or inappropriate name. [< OFr. *mesnommer,* to misname.]

mi·sog·a·my (mĭ-sŏg'ə-mē) n. Hatred of marriage. [Gk. *misein,* to hate + -GAMY.] —**mi·sog'a·mist** n.

mi·sog·y·ny (mĭ-sŏj'ə-nē) n. Hatred of women. [Gk. *misogunia.*] —**mi·sog'y·nist** n. —**mi·sog'y·nis'tic** or **mi·sog'y·nous** adj.

mis·place (mĭs-plās') v. **1. a.** To put in a wrong place. **b.** To mislay. **2.** To bestow on a wrong object: *misplaced her trust.* —**mis·place'ment** n.

mis·play (mĭs'plā') n. A wrong or inept play in a game. —**mis·play'** v.

mis·print (mĭs-prĭnt') v. To print incorrectly. —**mis·print'** n.

mis·pro·nounce (mĭs'prə-nouns') v. To pronounce incorrectly. —**mis'pro·nun'ci·a'tion** (-nŭn'sē-ā'shən) n.

mis·quote (mĭs-kwōt') v. To quote incorrectly. —**mis·quo·ta'tion** (-kwō-tā'shən) n.

mis·read (mĭs-rēd') v. **1.** To read incorrectly. **2.** To misinterpret.

mis·rep·re·sent (mĭs-rĕp'rĭ-zĕnt') v. To represent falsely or misleadingly. —**mis·rep're·sen·ta'tion** n.

mis·rule (mĭs-rōōl') v. To misgovern. —**mis·rule'** n.

miss¹ (mĭs) v. **1.** To fail to hit, reach, or otherwise make contact with. **2.** To fail to perceive or understand. **3.** To fail to achieve or obtain. **4.** To fail to attend or perform. **5.** To omit. **6.** To avoid. **7.** To discover or feel the absence of. **8.** To misfire. —n. **1.** A failure to hit or succeed. **2.** A misfire. [< OE *missan.*]

miss² (mĭs) n. **1. a. Miss.** A title of courtesy used before the name of an unmarried woman. **b.** A word used without a name in speaking to an unmarried woman: *I beg your pardon, miss.* **2.** An unmarried woman. [< MISTRESS.]

mis·sal (mĭs'əl) n. A book containing the prayers and responses necessary for celebrating the Roman Catholic Mass. [< Med. Lat. *missalis,* of the Mass.]

mis·shape (mĭs-shāp') v. To shape badly; deform. —**mis·shap'en** adj.

mis·sile (mĭs'əl) n. **1.** An object or weapon that is projected at a target. **2.** A guided missile. **3.** A ballistic missile. [< Lat. *mittere,* to let go.] —**mis'sile·ry** n.

miss·ing (mĭs'ĭng) adj. Absent; lost; lacking.

mis·sion (mĭsh'ən) n. **1.** A body of envoys to a foreign country. **2.** A body of missionaries, their ministry, or the place of its exercise. **3.** A permanent diplomatic office in a foreign country. **4.** A combat assignment. **5.** A function or task. [< Lat. *mittere,* to send.]

mis·sion·ar·y (mĭsh'ə-nĕr'ē) n., pl. -**ies.** **1.** One sent to do religious or charitable work in a territory or foreign country. **2.** A propagandist for a belief or cause. —**mis'sion·ar'y** adj.

mis·sive (mĭs'ĭv) n. A written message. [< Med. Lat. *(littere) missivus,* (letter) sent.]

Mis·sou·ri (mĭ-zŏor'ē) n., pl. -**ri** or -**ris.** **1. a.** A tribe of Indians once inhabiting northern Missouri. **b.** A member of this tribe. **2.** The Siouan language of the Missouri.

mis·spell (mĭs-spĕl') v. To spell incorrectly. —**mis·spell'ing** n.

mis·spend (mĭs-spĕnd') v. To spend improperly; squander.

mis·state (mĭs-stāt') v. To state wrongly or falsely. —**mis·state'ment** n.

mis·step (mĭs-stĕp') n. **1.** A wrong step. **2.** A mistake in conduct or behavior.

mist (mĭst) n. **1.** A mass of tiny droplets of water in the atmosphere. **2.** Water vapor condensed on and clouding a surface. **3.** Fine drops of a liquid, as perfume, sprayed into the air. **4.** Something that dims or obscures; haze. —v. To make or become misty or obscured. [< OE.]

mis·take (mĭ-stāk') n. **1.** An error or blunder. **2.** A misconception or misunderstanding. [< ON *mistaka,* to take in error.] —**mis·tak'a·ble** adj. —**mis·tak'a·bly** adv. —**mis·take'** v.

mis·tak·en (mĭ-stā'kən) adj. **1.** Wrong in

opinion, understanding, or perception. **2.** Misunderstood. —**mis·tak'en·ly** *adv.*

Mis·ter (mĭs'tər) *n.* **1.** A title of courtesy used before the name of a man and usu. abbreviated Mr. **2. mister.** *Informal.* A word used without a name in speaking to a man: *Watch out, mister.* [< MASTER.]

mis·tle·toe (mĭs'əl-tō') *n.* A plant growing as a parasite on trees and having leathery evergreen leaves and waxy white berries. [< OE *mistletān.*]

mis·treat (mĭs-trēt') *v.* To abuse. —**mis·treat'ment** *n.*

mis·tress (mĭs'trĭs) *n.* **1.** A woman in a position of authority, control, or ownership. **2.** A country enjoying hegemony: *mistress of the seas.* **3.** A woman who has a habitual sexual relationship with a man to whom she is not married. **4. Mistress.** *Archaic.* Mrs. [< OFr. *maistresse.*]

mis·tri·al (mĭs-trī'əl, -trīl') *n.* *Law.* **1.** A trial declared invalid because of a procedural error. **2.** An inconclusive trial.

mis·trust (mĭs-trŭst') *n.* Lack of trust; suspicion. —*v.* To regard with suspicion or doubt. —**mis·trust'ful** *adj.* —**mis·trust'ing·ly** *adv.*

mist·y (mĭs'tē) *adj.* **-i·er, -i·est. 1.** Consisting of or resembling mist. **2.** Obscured or clouded by or as if by mist. **3.** Vague. —**mist'i·ly** *adv.* —**mist'i·ness** *n.*

mis·un·der·stand (mĭs'ŭn-dər-stănd') *v.* To understand incorrectly; misinterpret.

mis·un·der·stand·ing (mĭs'ŭn-dər-stăn'dĭng) *n.* **1.** A failure to understand correctly. **2.** A disagreement; quarrel.

mis·use (mĭs-yōōz') *v.* **1.** To use wrongly or incorrectly. **2.** To mistreat; abuse. —*n.* (mĭs-yōōs'). Wrong or improper use; misapplication.

mite¹ (mīt) *n.* Any of various small, spiderlike, often parasitic organisms. [< OE *mīte.*]

mite² (mīt) *n.* **1.** A very small amount of money or contribution. **2.** A tiny thing or amount. [< MDu., a small coin.]

mi·ter (mī'tər) *n.* **1.** A tall, pointed hat with peaks in front and back, worn esp. by bishops. **2.** A miter joint. [< Gk. *mitra,* headband.]

miter

miter joint *n.* A joint made by fitting together two beveled edges to form a 90° corner.

mit·i·gate (mĭt'ĭ-gāt') *v.* **-gat·ed, -gat·ing.** To make or become less severe or intense; moderate. [< Lat. *mitigare.*] —**mit'i·ga·ble** (-gə-bəl) *adj.* —**mit'i·ga'tion** *n.* —**mit'i·ga'tive**

(-gə'tĭv) or **mit'i·ga·to·ry** (-gə-tôr'ē, -tōr'ē) *adj.* —**mit'i·ga'tor** *n.*

mi·to·sis (mī-tō'sĭs) *n.* *Biol.* **1.** The sequential differentiation and segregation of replicated chromosomes in a cell nucleus that precedes complete cell division. **2.** The sequence of processes by which a cell divides to form two daughter cells having the normal number of chromosomes. [Gk. *mitos,* thread + -OSIS.] —**mi·tot'ic** (-tŏt'ĭk) *adj.* —**mi·tot'i·cal·ly** *adv.*

mitt (mĭt) *n.* **1.** A woman's glove that extends over the hand but only partially covers the fingers. **2.** A mitten. **3.** A baseball glove, esp. the one used by a catcher or a first baseman. [< MITTEN.]

mit·ten (mĭt'n) *n.* A covering for the hand that has one section for the thumb and another for all four fingers. [< OFr. *mitaine.*]

mitz·vah (mĭts'və) *n., pl.* **-voth** (-vōt', -vōth', -vōs') or **-vahs.** Also **mits·vah.** *Judaism.* **1.** A command of the Law. **2.** A worthy deed. [Heb. *miṣwāh.*]

mix (mĭks) *v.* **1.** To combine or blend so that the constituent parts are indistinguishable. **2.** To form by blending. **3.** To combine or join: *mix joy with sorrow.* **4.** To crossbreed. **5.** To associate socially. —*phrasal verb.* **mix up. 1.** To confuse. **2.** To throw into disorder; jumble. **3.** To involve: *mixed up in a robbery.* —*n.* A packaged mixture, as of baking ingredients. [< Lat. *miscēre.*] —**mix'a·ble** or **mix'i·ble** *adj.*

mixed bag *n.* A varied assortment.

mixed drink *n.* A cocktail made of one or more kinds of liquor combined with other ingredients, usu. shaken or stirred.

mixed-me·di·a (mĭkst'mē'dē-ə) *adj.* Multimedia.

mixed number *n.* A number, such as 7½, equal to the sum of an integer and a fraction.

mix·er (mĭk'sər) *n.* **1.** One that mixes, esp. a mechanical device that mixes substances or ingredients. **2.** A sociable person. **3.** An informal party arranged to give people an opportunity to get acquainted. **4.** A beverage, as ginger ale, added to an alcoholic drink.

mix·ol·o·gy (mĭk-sŏl'ə-jē) *n.* The study or skill of preparing mixed drinks. —**mix·ol'o·gist** *n.*

mix·ture (mĭks'chər) *n.* **1.** Something produced by mixing. **2.** Something consisting of diverse elements. **3.** The act of mixing or condition of being mixed. **4.** *Chem.* A blend of substances not chemically bound to each other. [< Lat. *miscēre,* to mix.]

mix-up (mĭks'ŭp') *n.* A confused situation; a muddle.

miz·zen (mĭz'ən) *n.* Also **miz·en. 1.** A fore-and-aft sail set on the mizzenmast. **2.** A mizzenmast. [Prob. ult. < Lat. *medianus,* middle.]

miz·zen·mast (mĭz'ən-məst, -măst') *n.* Also **miz·en·mast.** The 3rd mast aft on sailing ships carrying three or more masts.

Mn The symbol for the element manganese.

mne·mon·ic (nĭ-mŏn'ĭk) *adj.* Assisting or designed to assist the memory. —*n.* A device, as a formula or rhyme, used to assist the memory. [< Gk. *mnēmonikos,* of memory.] —**mne·mon'i·cal·ly** *adv.*

Mo The symbol for the element molybdenum.

moan (mōn) *n.* A low, sustained, mournful sound, as of sorrow or pain. [ME *mone,* complaint.] —**moan** *v.*

moat (mōt) *n.* A wide, deep ditch, usu. filled with water, surrounding a medieval town or castle. [< OFr. *mote,* mound.]

mob (mŏb) n. 1. A large, disorderly crowd. 2. The masses; common people. 3. *Informal.* An organized gang of hoodlums. —v. **mobbed, mob·bing.** 1. To crowd around and jostle or attack. 2. To crowd into a (place). [< Lat. *mobile* (*vulgus*), fickle (crowd).]

mo·bile (mō′bəl, -bēl′, -bīl′) adj. 1. Capable of moving or of being moved. 2. Changing quickly from one condition to another. —n. (mō′bēl′). A sculpture consisting of parts that move, esp. in response to air currents. [< Lat. *mobilis*.] —mo·bil′i·ty (mō-bĭl′ĭ-tē) n.

mobile home n. A house trailer used as a permanent home.

mo·bi·lize (mō′bə-līz′) v. **-lized, -liz·ing.** 1. To make mobile or capable of movement. 2. To assemble and prepare for war or a similar emergency. —mo′bi·li·za′tion n.

mob·ster (mŏb′stər) n. A member of a criminal gang.

moc·ca·sin (mŏk′ə-sĭn) n. 1. A soft leather slipper or shoe. 2. A water moccasin. [Natick *mohkussin.*]

mo·cha (mō′kə) n. 1. A rich, pungent, choice Arabian coffee. 2. Coffee flavoring. [< *Mocha*, a port of Yemen.]

mock (mŏk) v. 1. To treat with scorn or contempt; deride. 2. To imitate, as in sport or derision. —adj. Simulated; sham. [< OFr. *mocquer.*] —**mock′er** n. —**mock′er·y** n. —**mock′ing·ly** adv.

mock-he·ro·ic (mŏk′hĭ-rō′ĭk) adj. Satirizing or burlesquing the heroic manner, style, or character: *a mock-heroic poem.* —**mock′-he·ro′i·cal·ly** adv.

mock·ing·bird (mŏk′ĭng-bûrd′) n. A gray and white songbird common in the southern United States.

mock orange n. Any of several deciduous shrubs with white, usu. fragrant flowers.

mock-up or **mock·up** (mŏk′ŭp′) n. A scale model, often full-sized, of a machine, structure, etc., used for demonstration, study, or testing.

mod (mŏd) n. Fashionable style of dress. —adj. Stylishly up-to-date. [< MODERN.]

mode (mōd) n. 1. a. A manner, way, or method of doing or acting. b. A particular form, variety, or manner. c. A given condition of functioning; status: *a spacecraft in the recovery mode.* 2. The current fashion or style. 3. *Mus.* Any of certain arrangements of the diatonic tones of an octave. [< Lat. *modus.*]

mod·el (mŏd′l) n. 1. A miniature representation of an existing object. 2. A preliminary pattern. 3. A tentative description of a theory or system that accounts for all of its known properties. 4. A type or design. 5. An example to be emulated. 6. One who poses for an artist or photographer. 7. A mannequin. —v. **-eled** or **-elled, -el·ing** or **-el·ling.** 1. To plan or construct. 2. To display (clothes) by wearing. 3. To work as a model. [< Lat. *modus,* measure.] —**mod′el·er** n.

mod·er·ate (mŏd′ər-ĭt) adj. 1. Not excessive or extreme. 2. Temperate. 3. Average; mediocre. 4. Opposed to radical views or measures. —n. One who holds moderate views or opinions. —v. (mŏd′ə-rāt′) **-at·ed, -at·ing.** 1. To make or become less violent, severe, or extreme. 2. To preside over as a moderator.

[Lat. *moderatus,* p.p. of *moderare,* to regulate.] —**mod′er·ate·ly** adv. —**mod′er·a′tion** n.

mod·er·a·tor (mŏd′ə-rā′tər) n. 1. One that moderates. 2. A presiding officer.

mod·ern (mŏd′ərn) adj. 1. Of, pertaining to, or characteristic of recent times or the present. 2. Up-to-date. [< Lat. *modernus.*] —**mod′ern** n. —**mod·ern′i·ty** (mō-dûr′nĭ-tē) n. —**mod′ern·i·za′tion** n. —**mod′ern·ize′** v. —**mod′ern·ly** adv.

Modern English n. English since about 1500.

Modern Greek n. Greek since the early 16th cent.

Modern Hebrew n. The Hebrew language used in Israel at the present time.

mod·ern·ism (mŏd′ər-nĭz′əm) n. A theory, practice, or belief that is peculiar to modern times. —**mod′ern·ist** n. —**mod′ern·is′tic** adj.

mod·est (mŏd′ĭst) adj. 1. Having or showing a moderate estimation of oneself. 2. Shy; reserved. 3. Decent. 4. Unpretentious. 5. Moderate; not extreme: *a modest charge.* [< Lat. *modestus.*] —**mod′est·ly** adv. —**mod′es·ty** n.

Syns: *modest, demure, diffident, shy* **adj.**

mod·i·cum (mŏd′ĭ-kəm) n. A small amount. [< Lat. *modicus,* moderate.]

mod·i·fy (mŏd′ə-fī′) v. **-fied, -fy·ing.** 1. To change; alter. 2. To make or become less extreme, severe, or strong. 3. *Gram.* To qualify or limit the meaning of. [< Lat. *modificare.*] —**mod′i·fi′a·ble** adj. —**mod′i·fi·ca′tion** n. —**mod′i·fi′er** n.

mod·ish (mō′dĭsh) adj. Stylish; fashionable. —**mod′ish·ly** adv. —**mod′ish·ness** n.

mo·diste (mō-dēst′) n. One who makes, designs, or deals in ladies' fashions. [Fr.]

mod·u·late (mŏj′ə-lāt′, mŏd′yə-) v. **-lat·ed, -lat·ing.** 1. To regulate; temper. 2. To change or vary the pitch, intensity, or tone of. 3. *Mus.* To pass from one tonality to another by harmonic progression. 4. *Electronics.* To vary the frequency, amplitude, phase, or other characteristic of (a carrier wave). [Lat. *modulari.*] —**mod′u·la′tion** n. —**mod′u·la′tive** or **mod′u·la·to′ry** adj. —**mod′u·la′tor** n.

mod·ule (mŏj′ool, mŏd′yool) n. 1. A standardized unit or component, gen. having a defined function in a system. 2. *Electronics.* A self-contained assembly used as a component of a larger system, as a stage in a computer. 3. A self-contained unit of a spacecraft that performs a specific task. [< Lat. *modus,* measure.] —**mod′u·lar** adj.

mo·dus op·er·an·di (mō′dəs ŏp′ə-răn′dē, -dī′) n. The method by which one operates. [Lat.]

mo·dus vi·ven·di (vĭ-vĕn′dē, -dī′) n. A way of life. [Lat.]

Mo·gul (mō′gəl, mō-gŭl′) n. 1. A follower or a descendant of the Mongols who conquered India in 1526. 2. A Mongol or Mongolian. 3. **mogul.** A very rich or powerful person.

mo·hair (mō′hâr′) n. 1. The soft, silky hair of the Angora goat. 2. A fabric made of Angora hair. [< Ar. *mukhayyar.*]

Mo·ham·med·an (mō-hăm′ĭ-dən) adj. Moslem. —**Mo·ham′med·an** n. —**Mo·ham′med·an·ism** n.

Mo·hawk (mō′hôk′) n., pl. **-hawk** or **-hawks.** 1. a. A tribe of Indians who occupied the territory from the Mohawk River to the St. Lawrence. b. A member of this tribe. 2. The

---

ă pat ā pay â care ä father ĕ pet ē be ĭ pit ī tie î pier ŏ pot ō toe ô paw, for oi noise ōō took ōō boot ou out th thin th this ŭ cut û urge yōō abuse zh vision ə about, item, edible, gallop, circus

Iroquoian language of the Mohawk. —**Mo'-hawk'** *adj.*

Mo·he·gan (mō-hē'gən) *n.*, *pl.* **-gan** or **-gans.**
1. A tribe of Algonquian-speaking Indians, formerly living in eastern Connecticut. 2. A member of the Mohegan. —**Mo·he'gan** *adj.*

Mo·hi·can (mō-hē'kən, mə-) *n.* Var. of **Mahican.**

Mohs scale (mōz) *n.* A scale for determining the hardness of a mineral ranging from 1 for the softest to 10 for the hardest. [< Friedrich *Mohs* (1773–1839).]

moi·e·ty (moi'ĭ-tē) *n.*, *pl.* **-ties.** 1. A half. 2. A part, portion, or share. [< LLat. *medietas.*]

moil (moil) *v.* To toil. [< OFr. *moillier,* to moisten.] —**moil'** *n.*

moi·ré (mwä-rā') *n.* 1. Cloth, esp. silk, with a watered or wavy pattern. 2. A watered pattern pressed on cloth by engraved rollers. [Fr. < *moirer,* to water.] —**moi·ré'** *adj.*

moist (moist) *adj.* **-er, -est.** Slightly wet; damp. [< Lat. *mucidus,* moldy.] —**moist'en** *v.* —**moist'ly** *adv.* —**moist'ness** *n.*

mois·ture (mois'chər) *n.* Diffused or condensed liquid; dampness. —**mois'tur·ize'** *v.* —**mois'tur·iz'er** *n.*

mol (mōl) *n.* Var. of **mole⁴.**

mo·lar (mō'lər) *n.* A tooth with a broad crown for grinding food, located behind the bicuspids. [Lat. *molaris.*] —**mo'lar** *adj.*

mo·las·ses (mə-lăs'ĭz) *n.* A thick, brownish syrup produced as a by-product in refining sugar. [< LLat. *mellaceum,* must.]

mold¹ (mōld) *n.* 1. A hollow form or matrix for shaping a liquid or plastic substance. 2. A frame or model for shaping or forming something. 3. Something made in or shaped on a mold. 4. General shape or form. 5. Distinctive shape, character, or type. —*v.* To shape in or on a mold. [< Lat. *modulus,* a small measure.] —**mold'a·ble** *adj.*

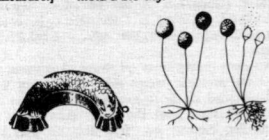

mold¹   mold²

mold² (mōld) *n.* 1. Any of various fungous growths formed on the surface of organic matter. 2. A fungus that causes mold. —*v.* To become moldy. [ME *molde.*]

mold³ (mōld) *n.* Loose soil rich in humus. [< OE *molde.*]

mold·er (mōl'dər) *v.* To decay or crumble into dust. [Prob. of Scand. orig.]

mold·ing (mōl'dĭng) *n.* 1. An object that is molded. 2. The process of shaping in a mold. 3. An ornamental strip used to decorate a surface.

mold·y (mōl'dē) *adj.* **-i·er, -i·est.** 1. Covered with or containing mold. 2. Musty or stale. —**mold'i·ness** *n.*

mole¹ (mōl) *n.* A small congenital growth on the human skin, usu. slightly raised and dark. [< OE *māl.*]

mole² (mōl) *n.* A small, burrowing mammal with minute eyes, a narrow snout, and silky fur. [ME *molle.*]

mole³ (mōl) *n.* A massive jetty or breakwater. [< Lat. *moles.*]

mole⁴ (mōl) *n.* Also **mol** (mōl). *Chem.* The amount of a substance that has a weight in grams numerically equal to the molecular weight of the substance. [G. *Mol.*]

molecular biology *n.* The study of the structure and development of biological systems in terms of the physics and chemistry of their molecular constituents.

molecular weight *n.* *Chem.* The sum of the atomic weights of the atoms in a molecule.

mol·e·cule (mŏl'ĭ-kyōōl') *n.* 1. A stable configuration of atomic nuclei and electrons bound together by electrostatic and electromagnetic forces, the simplest structural unit that displays the characteristic physical and chemical properties of a compound. 2. A small particle; tiny bit. [< Lat. *moles,* mass.] —**mo·lec'u·lar** (mə-lĕk'yə-lər) *adj.*

mole·hill (mōl'hĭl') *n.* A small mound of loose earth thrown up by a burrowing mole.

mole·skin (mōl'skĭn') *n.* 1. The fur of a mole. 2. A sturdy napped cotton fabric.

mo·lest (mə-lĕst') *v.* 1. To interfere with or annoy. 2. To accost or harass sexually. [< Lat. *molestare.*] —**mo'les·ta'tion** (mō'lĕs-tā'shən) *n.* —**mo·lest'er** *n.*

moll (mōl) *n. Slang.* A female companion of a gangster. [< *Moll,* nickname for *Mary.*]

mol·li·fy (mŏl'ə-fī') *v.* **-fied, -fy·ing.** 1. To placate; calm. 2. To soften or ease. [< Lat. *mollificare,* to make soft.] —**mol'li·fi·ca'tion** *n.*

mol·lusk (mŏl'əsk) *n.* Any of a large group of soft-bodied, usu. shell-bearing invertebrates, including the snails, oysters, and clams. [< Lat. *mollis,* soft.]

mol·ly·cod·dle (mŏl'ē-kŏd'l) *n.* A pampered person. —*v.* **-dled, -dling.** To spoil by pampering. [Brit. slang *molly,* milksop + CODDLE.]

Mo·lo·tov cocktail (mŏl'ə-tôf', mō'lə-) *n.* An incendiary bomb made of a bottle filled with flammable liquid and a rag wick. [< Vyacheslav *Molotov* (1890–1981).]

molt (mōlt) *v.* To shed an outer covering, as feathers or skin, for replacement by a new growth. —*n.* The process of molting. [< Lat. *mutare,* to change.]

mol·ten (mōl'tn) *adj.* Made liquid and glowing by heat; melted. [< OE (*ge*)*molten.*]

mo·lyb·de·num (mə-lĭb'də-nəm) *n. Symbol* **Mo** A hard, gray metallic element used to toughen steel alloys. Atomic number 42; atomic weight 95.94. [< Gk. *molubdos,* lead.]

mom (mŏm) *n. Informal.* Mother. [< MAMA.]

mo·ment (mō'mənt) *n.* 1. A brief interval of time. 2. A specific point in time: *He is reading at the moment.* 3. A particular period of importance or excellence. 4. Importance. [< Lat. *momentum.*]

Syns: *moment, flash, instant, jiffy, minute, second, trice* **n.**

mo·men·tar·y (mō'mən-tĕr'ē) *adj.* 1. Lasting only a brief time. 2. Occurring at every moment. —**mo'men·tar'i·ly** *adv.* —**mo'men·tar'i·ness** *n.*

mo·men·tly (mō'mənt-lē) *adv.* From moment to moment.

mo·men·tous (mō-mĕn'təs) *adj.* Of great importance or significance. —**mo·men'tous·ly** *adv.* —**mo·men'tous·ness** *n.*

mo·men·tum (mō-mĕn'təm) *n.*, *pl.* **-ta** (-tə) or **-tums.** 1. The product of a body's mass and linear velocity. 2. Impetus. [Lat., movement.]

mon- *pref.* Var. of **mono-.**

mon·arch (mŏn'ərk, -ärk') *n.* 1. A hereditary

sovereign, as a king or queen. **2.** One that presides over or rules. **3.** A large orange and black butterfly. [< Gk. *monarkhēs.*] —**mo·nar'chal** (mə-när'kəl) *or* **mo·nar'chic** *adj.* —**mo·nar'chal·ly** *or* **mo·nar'chi·cal·ly** *adv.*

mon·ar·chism (mŏn'ər-kĭz'əm) *n.* **1.** The principles of monarchy. **2.** Belief in or advocacy of monarchy. —**mon'ar·chist** (-kĭst) *n.* —**mon'ar·chis'tic** *adj.*

mon·ar·chy (mŏn'ər-kē) *n., pl.* **-chies. 1.** Government by a monarch. **2.** A country ruled by a monarch.

mon·as·ter·y (mŏn'ə-stĕr'ē) *n., pl.* **-ies.** The dwelling place of a community of monks. [< LGk. *monastērion.*] —**mon'as·te'ri·al** (-stĭr'ē-əl, -stĕr'-) *adj.*

mo·nas·tic (mə-nās'tĭk) *or* **mo·nas·ti·cal** (-tĭ-kəl) *adj.* Of, pertaining to, or characteristic of monasteries or monks or their way of life. —**mo·nas'ti·cism** *n.*

mon·au·ral (mŏn-ôr'əl, mŏ-nôr'-) *adj.* **1.** Designating sound reception by one ear. **2.** Using a single channel to record, store, or reproduce sound; monophonic.

Mon·day (mŭn'dē, -dā') *n.* The 2nd day of the week. [< OE *Mōnandæg.*]

Mo·nel (mō-nĕl') *n.* A trademark for an alloy of nickel, copper, iron, and manganese.

mon·e·tar·y (mŏn'ĭ-tĕr'ē, mŭn'-) *adj.* **1.** Of or pertaining to money. **2.** Of or pertaining to a nation's currency or coinage. [Lat. *monetarius.*] —**mon'e·tar'i·ly** (-târ'ə-lē) *adv.*

mon·e·tize (mŏn'ĭ-tīz', mŭn'-) *v.* **-tized, -tiz·ing. 1.** To establish as legal tender. **2.** To coin into money.

mon·ey (mŭn'ē) *n., pl.* **-eys** *or* **-ies. 1.** A commodity that is legally established as an exchangeable equivalent of all other commodities and used as a measure of their comparative market value. **2.** The official currency issued by a government. **3.** Assets and property considered in terms of their monetary value; wealth. **4.** Profit or loss measured in money. [< Lat. *moneta.*]

mon·ey·ed (mŭn'ēd) *adj.* Also **mon·ied. 1.** Wealthy. **2.** Representing or arising from money or wealth.

mon·ey·lend·er (mŭn'ē-lĕn'dər) *n.* One whose business is lending money at interest.

mon·ey·mak·ing (mŭn'ē-mā'kĭng) *n.* Acquisition of money —*adj.* **1.** Engaged in acquiring wealth. **2.** Profitable. —**mon'ey·mak'er** *n.*

money order *n.* An order for the payment of a specified amount of money, usu. issued and payable at a bank or post office.

mon·ger *n.* A dealer. [< Lat. *mango.*]

mon·go (mŏng'gō) *n., pl.* **-go.** See table at **currency.** [Mongolian.]

Mon·gol (mŏng'gəl, -gŏl', mŏn'-) *n.* **1.** A member of one of the nomadic tribes of Mongolia or a native of Mongolia. **2.** Mongolian (sense 3). **3.** A member of the Mongoloid ethnic group.

Mon·go·li·an (mŏng-gō'lē-ən, -gŏl'yən, mŏn'-) *n.* **1.** A native or inhabitant of Mongolia. **2.** A member of the Mongoloid ethnic division. **3.** Any of the Mongolic languages of Mongolia. —**Mon·go'li·an** *adj.*

Mon·gol·ic (mŏng-gŏl'ĭk, mŏn-) *n.* A sub-

family of the Altaic language family that includes Mongolian. —*adj.* **1.** Of or pertaining to the Mongoloid ethnic division. **2.** Of or pertaining to Mongolic.

mon·gol·ism *or* **Mon·gol·ism** (mŏng'gə-lĭz'-əm, mŏn'-) *n.* Down's syndrome.

Mon·gol·oid (mŏng'gə-loid', mŏn'-) *adj.* **1.** Pertaining to a major ethnic division of the human species having yellowish-brown to white skin color. **2.** Characteristic of or like a Mongol. **3.** **mongoloid.** Characterized by, affected with, or relating to Down's syndrome. —**Mon'gol·oid'** *n.*

mon·goose (mŏng'gōōs', mŏn'-) *n., pl.* **-goos·es.** Any of various weasellike, chiefly African or Asian mammals noted for their ability to kill venomous snakes. [Marathi *mangūs.*]

mon·grel (mŭng'grəl, mŏng'-) *n.* A plant or animal, esp. a dog, of mixed breed. [Prob. < ME *mong,* mixture.] —**mon'grel** *adj.*

mon·ied (mŭn'ēd) *adj.* Var. of **moneyed.**

mon·ies (mŭn'ēz) *n.* A pl. of **money.**

mon·i·ker *or* **mon·ick·er** (mŏn'ĭ-kər) *n. Slang.* A personal name. [Orig. unknown.]

mo·nism (mō'nĭz'əm, mŏn'ĭz'-) *n.* A metaphysical theory that all reality is composed of and reducible to one substance. —**mo'nist** *n.* —**mo·nis'tic** (mō-nĭs'tĭk, mŏ-) *adj.*

mo·ni·tion (mō-nĭsh'ən, mə-) *n.* A warning or admonition. [< Lat. *monēre,* to warn.]

mon·i·tor (mŏn'ĭ-tər) *n.* **1.** A student who assists a teacher. **2.** A device used to record or control a process. **3.** A screen used to watch or check the picture being broadcast or picked up by a camera. —*v.* To check, watch, or keep track of, often by means of an electronic device. [Lat., one who warns.] —**mon'i·to'ri·al** (-tôr'ē-əl, -tōr'-) *adj.*

mon·i·to·ry (mŏn'ĭ-tôr'ē, -tōr'ē) *adj.* Giving a warning.

monk (mŭngk) *n.* A member of a religious brotherhood living in a monastery. [< LGk. *monakhos.*] —**monk'ish** *adj.* —**monk'ish·ly** *adv.*

mon·key (mŭng'kē) *n., pl.* **-keys.** Any member of the primates except man, esp. one of the long-tailed small- to medium-sized species as distinguished from the larger apes and the smaller lemurs. —*v. Informal.* To play or tamper with something. [Prob. of LG orig.]

mon·key·shine (mŭng'kē-shīn') *n.* Often **monkeyshines.** *Slang.* A prank.

monkey wrench *n.* A hand tool with adjustable jaws for turning nuts.

monks·hood (mŭngks'hŏŏd') *n.* Any of various often poisonous plants with hooded flowers.

mon·o¹ (mŏn'ō) *n.* Mononucleosis.

mon·o² (mŏn'ō) *adj.* Monaural (sense 2).

mono- *or* **mon-** *pref.* One; single; alone: *monochromatic.* [< Gk. *monos,* single.]

mon·o·chro·mat·ic (mŏn'ə-krō-măt'ĭk) *adj.* Of only one color. —**mon'o·chro·mat'i·cal·ly** *adv.*

mon·o·chrome (mŏn'ə-krōm') *n.* **1.** A painting or drawing done in different shades of one color. **2.** The technique of executing monochromes. [MONO- + Gk. *khrōmē,* color.] —**mon'o·chro'mic** (-krō'mĭk) *adj.*

ă pat ā pay â care ä father ĕ pet ē be ĭ pit ī tie î pier ŏ pot ō toe ô paw, for oi noise ŏŏ took
ŏŏ boot ou out th thin th this ŭ cut û urge yŏŏ abuse zh vision ə about, item, edible, gallop, circus

mon·o·cle (mŏn′ə-kəl) *n.* An eyeglass for one eye. [< Lat. *monoculus*, having one eye.]

monocle

mon·o·cot·y·le·don (mŏn′ə-kŏt′l-ēd′n) *n.* Also **mon·o·cot** (mŏn′ə-kŏt′). A plant, as a grass, with a single embryonic seed leaf that appears at germination. —**mon′o·cot′y·le′don·ous** *adj.*

mo·noc·u·lar (mō-nŏk′yə-lər, mə-) *adj.* 1. Having one eye. 2. Adapted for use by only one eye.

mon·o·dy (mŏn′ə-dē) *n., pl.* **-dies.** An ode or elegy. [< Gk. *monōidia*.] —**mo·nod′ic** (mə-nŏd′ĭk) —**mon′o·dist** (mŏn′ə-dĭst) *n.*

mo·nog·a·my (mə-nŏg′ə-mē) *n.* Marriage to only one person at a time. —**mo·nog′a·mist** *n.* —**mo·nog′a·mous** *adj.* —**mo·nog′a·mous·ly** *adv.*

mon·o·gram (mŏn′ə-grăm) *n.* A design composed of one or more initials of a name. —*v.* **-grammed** or **-gramed, -gram·ming** or **-gram·ing.** To mark with a monogram. —**mon′o·gram·mat′ic** (-grə-măt′ĭk) *adj.*

mon·o·graph (mŏn′ə-grăf) *n.* A scholarly book or article on a specific and usu. limited subject. —**mo·nog′ra·pher** *n.* —**mon′o·graph′ic** *adj.*

mon·o·lin·gual (mŏn′ə-lĭng′gwəl) *adj.* Using or knowing only one language. —**mon′o·lin′gual** *n.*

mon·o·lith (mŏn′ə-lĭth) *n.* 1. A large block of stone used in architecture or sculpture. 2. A large organization that acts as a powerful unit. —**mon′o·lith′ic** *adj.*

mon·o·logue (mŏn′ə-lôg′, -lŏg′) *n.* 1. A long speech. 2. A soliloquy. 3. A series of jokes delivered by a comedian. [Fr.] —**mo·nol′o·gist** (mə-nŏl′ə-jĭst, mŏn′ə-lô′gĭst, -lŏg′ĭst) *n.*

mon·o·ma·ni·a (mŏn′ō-mā′nē-ə, -mān′yə) *n.* 1. Obsession with one idea. 2. An intense preoccupation with one subject. —**mon′o·ma′ni·ac′** *n.* —**mon′o·ma·ni′a·cal** (-mə-nī′ə-kəl) *adj.*

mon·o·mer (mŏn′ə-mər) *n.* Any molecule that can be chemically bound as a unit of a polymer. —**mon′o·mer′ic** (-mĕr′ĭk) *adj.*

mo·no·mi·al (mō-nō′mē-əl, mə-) *n.* 1. A mathematical expression consisting of only one term. 2. *Biol.* A taxonomic name consisting of a single word. [MON(O)- + (BI)N)OMIAL.] —**mo·no′mi·al** *adj.*

mon·o·nu·cle·o·sis (mŏn′ō-nōō′klē-ō′sĭs, -nyōō′-) *n.* An infectious disease characterized by an abnormally large number of leukocytes with single nuclei in the bloodstream. [MONO- + NUCLE(US) + -OSIS.]

mon·o·phon·ic (mŏn′ə-fŏn′ĭk) *adj.* Monaural (sense 2).

mon·o·plane (mŏn′ə-plān′) *n.* An airplane with only one pair of wings.

mo·nop·o·ly (mə-nŏp′ə-lē) *n., pl.* **-lies.** 1. Exclusive ownership or control, as of a given commodity or business activity. 2. **a.** A company or group having such control. **b.** A commodity or service thus controlled. [< Gk. *monopōlion*, sole selling rights.] —**mo·nop′o·list** *n.* —**mo·nop′o·lis′tic** *adj.* —**mo·nop′o·li·za′tion** *n.* —**mo·nop′o·lize′** *v.*

mon·o·rail (mŏn′ə-rāl′) *n.* A single-rail railway system.

mon·o·so·di·um glu·ta·mate (mŏn′ə-sō′dē-əm glōō′tə-māt′) *n.* Sodium glutamate.

mon·o·syl·la·ble (mŏn′ə-sĭl′ə-bəl) *n.* A word of one syllable. —**mon′o·syl·lab′ic** (-sĭ-lăb′ĭk) *adj.* —**mon′o·syl·lab′i·cal·ly** *adv.*

mon·o·the·ism (mŏn′ə-thē-ĭz′əm) *n.* The doctrine or belief that there is only one God. —**mon′o·the′ist** *n.* —**mon′o·the·is′tic** *adj.*

mon·o·tone (mŏn′ə-tōn′) *n.* A succession of sounds or words uttered in a single tone of voice or sung at a single pitch.

mo·not·o·nous (mə-nŏt′n-əs) *adj.* 1. Unvarying in tone or pitch. 2. Repetitiously dull. —**mo·not′o·nous·ly** *adv.* —**mo·not′o·nous·ness** *n.* —**mo·not′o·ny** *n.*

mon·o·type (mŏn′ə-tīp′) *n. Biol.* The sole member of a group, such as a species that also constitutes a genus. —**mon′o·typ′ic** (-tĭp′ĭk) *adj.*

mon·o·va·lent (mŏn′ə-vā′lənt) *adj.* Univalent. —**mon′o·va′lence** or **mon′o·va′len·cy** *n.*

mon·ox·ide (mə-nŏk′sīd′) *n.* An oxide containing one oxygen atom in each molecule.

Mon·sei·gneur (mŏn′sān-ycer′) *n., pl.* **Mes·sei·gneurs** (mā′sān-ycer′). A French title of honor given to princes and prelates.

Mon·sieur (mə-syœ′) *n., pl.* **Mes·sieurs** (mā-syœ′). A French title of courtesy prefixed to the name or title of a man.

Mon·si·gnor (mŏn-sēn′yər) *n., pl.* **-gnors** or **-ri** (-rē). Also **mon·si·gnor.** *Rom. Cath. Ch.* A title given to certain officials or dignitaries. [Ital.]

mon·soon (mŏn-sōōn′) *n.* A wind system that influences large climatic regions and reverses direction seasonally, esp. the Asiatic system that produces dry and wet seasons in India and southern Asia. [< Ar. *mausim*, season.]

mon·ster (mŏn′stər) *n.* 1. An animal or plant that is structurally abnormal or grotesquely deformed. 2. A very large animal, plant, or object. 3. One who inspires horror or disgust. —*adj.* Gigantic; huge. [< Lat. *monstrum*, portent.] —**mon·stros′i·ty** (-strŏs′ĭ-tē) *n.* —**mon′strous** *adj.* —**mon′strous·ly** *adv.* —**mon′strous·ness** *n.*

mon·strance (mŏn′strəns) *n. Rom. Cath. Ch.* A vessel in which the Host is held. [< Lat. *monstrare*, to show.]

mon·tage (mŏn-täzh′, môn-) *n.* 1. A composite photograph or other artistic composition consisting of several superimposed components. 2. A rapid sequence of thematically related scenes or images that exhibits different aspects of the same idea or situation. [Fr.]

Mon·tes·so·ri method (mŏn′tĭ-sôr′ē, -sōr′ē) *n.* A method of instructing children that stresses development of a child's own initiative. [< Maria *Montessori* (1870–1952).]

month (mŭnth) *n.* 1. One of the 12 divisions of a year. 2. A period extending from a date in one calendar month to the corresponding date in the following month. 3. **a.** A period of four weeks. **b.** A period of 30 days. 4. One twelfth of a tropical year. [< OE *mōnath*.]

month·ly (mŭnth′lē) *adj.* 1. Occurring, appearing, or payable every month. 2. Continuing or lasting for a month. —*adv.* Once a month; every month. —*n., pl.* **-lies.** A publication appearing once each month.

mon·u·ment (mŏn′yə-mənt) *n.* 1. A structure erected as a memorial. 2. A tombstone. 3. A structure preserved for its historical or aesthetic significance. 4. An outstanding and enduring achievement. 5. An exceptional example. [< Lat. *monumentum.*]

mon·u·men·tal (mŏn′yə-mĕn′tl) *adj.* 1. Of, resembling, or serving as a monument. 2. Impressively large and sturdy. 3. Of outstanding significance. 4. Enormous and outrageous. —**mon·u·men′tal·ly** *adv.*

moo (mōō) *n.* The deep, throaty sound made by a cow. [Imit.] —**moo** *v.*

mooch (mōōch) *v. Slang.* To obtain free; beg. [< OFr. *muchier.*] —**mooch′er** *n.*

mood¹ (mōōd) *n.* 1. A state of mind or feeling. 2. Inclination or disposition. [< OE *mŏd.*]

mood² (mōōd) *n. Gram.* A set of verb forms used to indicate the factuality or likelihood of the action or condition expressed. [< MODE.]

mood·y (mōō′dē) *adj.* **-i·er, -i·est.** 1. Given to changeable emotional states. 2. Gloomy; uneasy. —**mood′i·ly** *adv.* —**mood′i·ness** *n.*

moon (mōōn) *n.* 1. The natural satellite of the earth, varying in distance from the earth between 221,600 and 252,950 miles and having a mean diameter of 2,160 miles, a mass approx. one-eightieth that of the earth, and an average period of revolution around the earth of 29 days 12 hours 44 minutes. 2. Any natural satellite revolving around a planet. 3. The moon as seen at a particular time in its cycle of phases: *a full moon.* 4. A month. 5. A disk, globe, or crescent resembling the moon. —*v.* To wander about in a dreamy or aimless manner. [< OE *mōna.*]

moon·beam (mōōn′bēm′) *n.* A ray of moonlight.

moon·light (mōōn′līt′) *n.* The light of the moon. —*v. Informal.* To work at a second job, often at night. —**moon′light′er** *n.*

moon·lit (mōōn′līt′) *adj.* Of or under moonlight.

moon·shine (mōōn′shīn′) *n.* 1. Moonlight. 2. *Informal.* Foolish talk. 3. *Slang.* Illegally distilled whiskey. —*v.* **-shined, -shin·ing.** *Slang.* To distill liquor illegally. —**moon′-shine′** *adj.* —**moon′shin′er** *n.*

moon shot *n.* The launching of a spacecraft to the moon.

moon·stone (mōōn′stōn′) *n.* A form of feldspar valued as a gem for its pearly translucent luster.

moon·struck (mōōn′strŭk′) *adj.* 1. Mentally unbalanced. 2. Distracted with romantic sentiment. [< the belief that moonlight causes insanity.]

moor¹ (mōōr) *v.* To secure or make fast, as with cables or anchors. [< MLG *mōren.*] —**moor′age** (-ĭj) *n.*

moor² (mōōr) *n.* A broad tract of open, often boggy land, usu. covered with low shrubs. [< OE *mōr.*]

Moor (mōōr) *n.* 1. One of a Moslem people of mixed Berber and Arab descent, now living chiefly in northern Africa. 2. One of a Moslem people who invaded Spain in the 8th cent. —**Moor′ish** *adj.*

moor·ing (mōōr′ĭng) *n.* 1. A place at which a vessel or aircraft can be moored. 2. Often **moorings.** Elements providing stability or security.

moose (mōōs) *n., pl.* **moose.** A very large deer of northern North America, having broad, flattened antlers. [Natick *moos.*]

moot (mōōt) *adj.* 1. Subject to debate; arguable. 2. *Law.* Without legal significance. [< OE *mōt,* assembly.]

moot court *n.* A mock court where hypothetical cases are tried for the training of law students.

mop (mŏp) *n.* A household implement made of absorbent material attached to a handle and used for cleaning floors. —*v.* **mopped, mop·ping.** To wash or wipe with or as if with a mop. —*phrasal verb.* **mop up.** 1. *Mil.* To clear (an area) of remaining enemy troops after a victory. 2. To complete a task or action. [ME *mappe.*]

mope (mōp) *v.* **moped, mop·ing.** To be gloomy or dejected. [Orig. unknown.] —**mop′er** *n.* —**mop′ing·ly** *adv.*

mo·ped (mō′pĕd′) *n.* A motor-driven vehicle resembling a motorbike that can be pedaled. [MO(TOR) + PED(AL).]

mop·pet (mŏp′ĭt) *n.* A young child. [< ME *mop,* child.]

mop-up (mŏp′ŭp′) *n.* The act of disposing of remaining details after the completion of a task or action.

mo·raine (mə-rān′) *n.* An accumulation of boulders, stones, or other debris carried and deposited by a glacier. [Fr.]

mor·al (môr′əl, mŏr′-) *adj.* 1. Of or concerned with the discernment or instruction of what is good and evil. 2. Being or acting in accordance with established standards of good behavior. 3. Arising from conscience. 4. Having psychological rather than tangible effects. 5. Based on likelihood rather than evidence. —*n.* 1. The principle taught by a story or event. 2. **morals.** Rules or habits of conduct, esp. sexual conduct. [< Lat. *moralis.*] —**mor′al·ly** *adv.*

mo·rale (mə-răl′) *n.* The state of mind of an individual or group in regard to confidence, cheerfulness, and discipline. [Fr.]

mor·al·ist (môr′ə-lĭst, mŏr′-) *n.* 1. A teacher or student of ethics. 2. A person who follows a system of moral principles. —**mor′a·lis′tic** *adj.* —**mor′al·is′ti·cal·ly** *adv.*

mo·ral·i·ty (mə-răl′ĭ-tē, mô-) *n., pl.* **-ties.** 1. The quality of being moral. 2. A system of conduct based on principles of right and wrong. 3. Virtuous conduct.

mor·al·ize (môr′ə-līz′, mŏr′-) *v.* **-ized, -iz·ing.** To think about or discuss moral issues. —**mor′al·i·za′tion** *n.* —**mor′al·iz′er** *n.*

mo·rass (mə-răs′, mô-) *n.* 1. An area of low-lying, soggy ground; a bog or marsh. 2. A difficult or perplexing situation. [< OFr. *maresc.*]

mor·a·to·ri·um (môr′ə-tôr′ē-əm, -tōr′-, mŏr′-) *n., pl.* **-ums** or **-to·ri·a** (-tôr′ē-ə, -tōr′-). 1. *Law.* An authorization to a debtor permitting temporary suspension of payments. 2. A deferment or delay of any action. [< LLat. *moratorius*, delaying.]

mo·ray (môr′ā, mə-rā′) *n.* Any of various often voracious tropical marine eels. [< Gk. *muraina*.]

mor·bid (môr′bĭd) *adj.* **1.** Of, relating to, or caused by disease. **2.** Characterized by preoccupation with unwholesome matters. **3.** Gruesome; grisly. [Lat. *morbidus*, diseased.] —**mor′bid·ly** *adv.* —**mor′bid·ness** *n.*

mor·bid·i·ty (môr-bĭd′ĭ-tē) *n., pl.* **-ties.** **1.** The condition or quality of being morbid. **2.** The rate of occurrence of a disease.

mor·da·cious (môr-dā′shəs) *adj.* **1.** Given to biting. **2.** Caustic; sarcastic. [< Lat. *mordax*.] —**mor·da′cious·ly** *adv.* —**mordac′i·ty** (-dăs′ĭ-tē) *n.*

mor·dant (môr′dnt) *adj.* **1.** Bitingly sarcastic. **2.** Incisive and trenchant. [< Lat. *mordēre*, to bite.] —**mor′dan·cy** *n.* —**mor′dant·ly** *adv.*

more (môr, mōr) *adj. superl.* **most** (mōst). **1. a.** Greater in number. **b.** Greater in size, amount, extent, or degree. **2.** Additional; extra: *We brought more food.* —*n.* A greater or additional quantity, number, degree, or amount. —*adv.* **1.** To or in a greater extent or degree. Used to form the comparative of many adjectives and adverbs: *more difficult; more intelligently.* **2.** In addition; again. —**idiom. more or less. 1.** Approximately; about. **2.** To an undetermined degree. [< OE *māra.*]

mo·rel (mə-rĕl′, mō-) *n.* An edible mushroom with a brownish, spongelike cap. [< OFr. *morille.*]

more·o·ver (môr-ō′vər, mōr-, môr′ō′vər, mōr′-) *adv.* Beyond what has been said; further; besides.

mo·res (môr′āz′, mōr′-, -ēz′) *pl.n.* The customs and rules of a particular social group that are gen. regarded as essential to its survival. [Lat., customs.]

Mor·gan (môr′gən) *n.* Any of a breed of light American saddle and trotting horses. [< Justin *Morgan* (1747–98).]

morgue (môrg) *n.* **1.** A place where the bodies of persons found dead are temporarily kept. **2.** A file in a newspaper or magazine office for storing old issues and reference material. [Fr.]

mor·i·bund (môr′ə-bŭnd′, mōr′-) *adj.* At the point of death. [Lat. *moribundus.*] —**mor′i·bun′di·ty** *n.* —**mor′i·bund′ly** *adv.*

Mor·mon (môr′mən) *n.* A member of the Church of Jesus Christ of Latter-day Saints. —**Mor′mon** *adj.* —**Mor′mon·ism** *n.*

morn (môrn) *n. Poet.* Morning. [< OE *morgen.*]

morn·ing (môr′nĭng) *n.* The first or early part of the day, esp. from sunrise to noon.

morn·ing-glo·ry (môr′nĭng-glôr′ē, -glōr′ē) *n.* Any of various twining vines with funnelshaped flowers that close late in the day.

mo·roc·co (mə-rŏk′ō) *n., pl.* **-cos.** A soft, grainy-textured goatskin leather. [< *Morocco.*]

mo·ron (môr′ŏn′, mōr′-) *n.* A mentally retarded person with a mental age between 7 and 12 years. [< Gk. *mōros*, stupid.] —**moron′ic** (mə-rŏn′ĭk) *adj.*

mo·rose (mə-rōs′, mō-) *adj.* Sullenly melancholy. [Lat. *morosus.*] —**mo·rose′ly** *adv.* —**mo·rose′ness** *n.*

-morph *suff.* **1.** Form; shape; structure: *isomorph.* **2.** Morpheme: *allomorph.* [< Gk. *morphē*, shape.]

mor·pheme (môr′fēm′) *n.* A linguistic unit that has meaning and that cannot be divided into smaller meaningful parts. [Fr. *morphème.*] —**mor·phem′ic** *adj.* —**mor·phem′i·cal·ly** *adv.*

mor·phine (môr′fēn′) *n.* A powerfully addictive narcotic drug extracted from opium, used as an anesthetic and sedative. [< Lat. *Morpheus*, the god of dreams.]

morpho- *pref.* **1.** Shape; form; structure: *morphogenesis.* **2.** Morpheme: *morphology.* [< Gk. *morphē*, shape.]

mor·pho·gen·e·sis (môr′fə-jĕn′ĭ-sĭs) *n.* Evolutionary or embryological development of the structure of an organism or part. —**mor′pho·ge·net′ic** (-jə-nĕt′ĭk) or **mor′pho·gen′ic** (-jĕn′ĭk) *adj.*

mor·phol·o·gy (môr-fŏl′ə-jē) *n.* **1.** The biological study of the form and structure of organisms. **2.** *Ling.* The study of word formation, including the origin and function of inflections and derivations. —**mor′pho·log′i·cal** (môr′fə-lŏj′ĭ-kəl) or **mor′pho·log′ic** *adj.* —**mor′pho·log′i·cal·ly** *adv.*

mor·ris (môr′ĭs, mŏr′-) *n.* An English folk dance in which a story is acted by costumed dancers. [< ME *More*, Moor.]

Morris chair *n.* A large easy chair with an adjustable back and removable cushions. [< William *Morris* (1834–96).]

mor·row (môr′ō, mŏr′ō) *n.* **1.** The following day. **2.** *Archaic.* The morning. [< OE *morgen.*]

Morse code (môrs) *n.* A code, used esp. in telegraphy, in which letters of the alphabet

A	·—	V	···—
B	—···	W	·——
C	—·—·	X	—··—
D	—··	Y	—·——
E	·	Z	——··
F	··—·	Á	·——·—
G	——·	Ä	·—·—
H	····	É	··—··
I	··	Ñ	——·——
J	·———	Ö	———·
K	—·—	Ü	··——
L	·—··	1	·————
M	——	2	··———
N	—·	3	···——
O	———	4	····—
P	·——·	5	·····
Q	——·—	6	—····
R	·—·	7	——···
S	···	8	———··
T	—	9	————·
U	··—	0	—————
. (comma)			——··——
. (period)			·—·—·—
?			··——··
:			———···
;			—·—·—·
/			—··—·
- (hyphen)			—····—
apostrophe			·————·
parenthesis			—·——·—
underline			··——·—

Morse code

and numbers are represented by combinations of short and long sounds, light, or written dots and dashes. [< Samuel F.B. *Morse* (1791–1872).]

mor·sel (môr′səl) *n.* **1.** A small piece of food. **2.** A tasty tidbit. [< Lat. *mordēre*, to bite.]

mor·tal (môr′tl) *adj.* **1.** Liable or subject to death. **2.** Causing death; fatal. **3.** Fought to the death. **4.** Unrelentingly antagonistic; implacable. **5.** Like the fear of death: *mortal terror.* **6.** *Rom. Cath. Ch.* Causing spiritual death and eternal damnation: *a mortal sin.* —*n.* A human being. [< Lat. *mortalis.*] —**mor′tal·ly** *adv.*

mor·tal·i·ty (môr-tăl′ĭ-tē) *n., pl.* **-ties. 1.** The condition of being subject to death. **2.** Frequency of number of deaths in proportion to a population; death rate.

mor·tar (môr′tər) *n.* **1.** A receptacle made of a hard material in which substances are crushed or ground with a pestle. **2.** A muzzleloading cannon used to fire shells in high trajectories. **3.** A mixture of cement or lime with sand and water, used in building. [< Lat. *mortarium.*]

mor·tar·board (môr′tər-bôrd′, -bôrd′) *n.* **1.** A square board used to hold and carry mortar. **2.** An academic cap with a flat square top and a tassel.

mort·gage (môr′gĭj) *n.* **1.** A legal pledge of property to a creditor as security for the payment of a loan or other debt. **2.** A contract or deed specifying the terms of a mortgage. —*v.* **-gaged, -gag·ing.** To pledge (property) as security for the payment of a debt. [< OFr.]

mort·gag·ee (môr′gə-jē′) *n.* The holder of a mortgage.

mort·ga·gor (môr′gə-jôr′, môr′gə-jər) *n.* One who mortgages his or her property.

mor·ti·cian (môr-tĭsh′ən) *n.* An undertaker. [MORT(UARY) + -ICIAN.]

mor·ti·fy (môr′tə-fī′) *v.* **-fied, -fy·ing. 1.** To shame; humiliate. **2.** To discipline (one's body and appetites) by self-denial. **3.** To cause gangrene or become gangrenous. [< LLat. *mortificare*, to cause to die.] —**mor′ti·fi·ca′tion** *n.* —**mor′ti·fy′ing·ly** *adv.*

mor·tise (môr′tĭs) *n.* A cavity, usu. rectangular, in a piece of wood, stone, or other material, prepared to receive a tenon of another piece so as to join the two. [< OFr. *mortoise.*]

mor·tu·ar·y (môr′chōō-ĕr′ē) *n., pl.* **-ies.** A place where corpses are prepared or kept prior to burial or cremation. [< Lat. *mortuarius*, of burial.]

mo·sa·ic (mō-zā′ĭk) *n.* A picture or decorative design made by setting small colored pieces of glass or tile in cement. [< Gk. *mouseios*, of the Muses.] —**mo·sa′ic** *adj.*

mo·sey (mō′zē) *v. Informal.* To amble along slowly. [Orig. unknown.]

Mos·lem (mŏz′ləm, mŏs′-). Also **Mus·lim** (mŭz′ləm, mŏŏz′-, mŏŏs′-). —*adj.* Of Islam. —*n.* A believer in or adherent of Islam.

mosque (mŏsk) *n.* A Moslem house of worship. [< Ar. *masjid.*]

mos·qui·to (mə-skē′tō) *n., pl.* **-toes** or **-tos.** Any of various winged insects of which the females suck blood and in some species transmit diseases. [< Lat. *musca*, fly.]

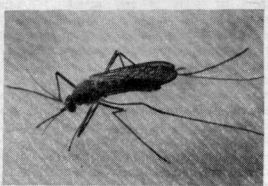

mosquito

Mos·qui·to (mō-skē′tō) *n., pl.* **-to** or **-tos. 1.** A South American Indian people living in Nicaragua and Honduras. **2.** The language of the Mosquito.

mosquito net *n.* A fine net used to keep out mosquitoes.

moss (môs, mŏs) *n.* Any of various small, green, nonflowering plants often forming a dense, matlike growth. [< OE *mos.*] —**moss′i·ness** *n.* —**moss′y** *adj.*

most (mōst) *adj.* **1. a.** Greatest in number. **b.** Largest in amount, size, or degree. **2.** In the greatest number of instances: *Most fish have fins.* —*n.* **1.** The greatest amount, quantity, or degree; the largest part. **2.** The largest number; majority: *Most of these stones are worthless.* —*adv.* **1.** In the highest degree, quantity, or extent. Used to form the superlative of many adjectives and adverbs: *most honest; most impatiently.* **2.** Very: *a most impressive book.* **3.** *Informal.* Almost: *Most everyone agrees.* —**idioms. at (the) most.** At the absolute limit: *four miles at the most.* **for the most part.** Mostly; mainly. **make the most of.** To use as advantageously as possible. [< OE *mæst.*]

-most *suff.* **1.** Most: *innermost.* **2.** Nearest: *aftermost.* [< ME *-mest.*]

most·ly (mōst′lē) *adv.* For the most part; almost entirely.

Usage: In speech and informal writing *mostly* is sometimes used to mean "in the greatest degree," but this usage is best avoided in formal style: *Those most* (not *mostly) affected are farmers.*

mot (mō) *n.* A short, witty saying. [< Lat. *muttum*, grunt.]

mote (mōt) *n.* A speck, esp. of dust. [< OE *mot.*]

mo·tel (mō-tĕl′) *n.* A hotel for motorists, usu. opening directly on a parking area. [Blend of MOTOR and HOTEL.]

mo·tet (mō-tĕt′) *n.* A polyphonic musical composition, often based on a religious text. [< OFr.]

moth (môth, mŏth) *n., pl.* **moths** (môthz, mŏthz, môths, mŏths). Any of various insects related to and resembling the butterflies but gen. night-flying and with featherlike antennae. [< OE *moththe.*]

moth·ball (môth′bôl′, mŏth′-) *n.* **1.** A marble-sized ball of camphor or naphthalene, stored with clothes to repel moths. **2.** Protective storage: *warships put into mothballs.*

moth-eat·en (môth′ĕt′n, mŏth′-) *adj.* **1.** Eaten away by moths. **2.** Old-fashioned or run-down.

moth·er (mŭ*th*′ər) *n.* **1.** A female parent. **2.** A creative source; origin: *Necessity is the mother of invention.* **3.** A woman having some of the responsibilities of a mother: *a class mother.* —*adj.* **1.** Being a mother: *a mother hen.* **2.** Characteristic of a mother: *mother love.* **3.** Native: *one's mother tongue.* —*v.* **1.** To give birth to; be the mother of. **2.** To care for; nourish and protect. [< OE *mōdor.*] —**moth′er·hood′** *n.* —**moth′er·less** *adj.* —**moth′er·li·ness** *n.* —**moth′er·ly** *adj.*

moth·er-in-law (mŭ*th*′ər-ĭn-lô′) *n., pl.* **moth·ers-in-law.** The mother of one's spouse.

moth·er·land (mŭ*th*′ər-lănd′) *n.* One's native land.

moth·er-of-pearl (mŭ*th*′ər-əv-pûrl′) *n.* The pearly internal layer of certain mollusk shells, used to make decorative objects; nacre.

mother superior *n.* The head of a religious community of women.

mother tongue *n.* One's native language.

moth·proof (mŏth′prōōf′, môth′-) *adj.* Resistant to moths. —**moth′proof′** *v.*

mo·tif (mō-tēf′) *n.* A recurrent thematic element used in the development of a musical, artistic, or literary work. [< OFr., motive.]

mo·tile (mōt′l, mō′tĭl′) *adj.* Moving or having the power to move spontaneously. [< MOTION.] —**mo·til′i·ty** (mō-tĭl′ĭ-tē) *n.*

mo·tion (mō′shən) *n.* **1.** The action or process of change of position. **2.** A significant movement of a part of the body; gesture. **3.** A formal proposal put to vote under parliamentary procedures. —*v.* **1.** To signal to or direct by making a gesture. **2.** To make a gesture signifying something, such as agreement. [< Lat. *movēre*, to move.] —**mo′tion·less** *adj.* —**mo′tion·less·ly** *adv.*

motion picture *n.* A series of filmed images projected on a screen in rapid succession to create the illusion of motion and continuity. —**mo′tion-pic′ture** *adj.*

motion sickness *n.* Nausea, vomiting, and often dizziness caused by motion, as from riding in a vehicle.

mo·ti·vate (mō′tə-vāt′) *v.* **-vat·ed, -vat·ing.** To stir to action; provide with a motive. —**mo′ti·va′tion** *n.* —**mo′ti·va′tion·al** *adj.*

mo·tive (mō′tĭv) *n.* **1.** An impulse that causes one to act in a particular manner. **2.** (*also* mō-tēv′). A motif. —*adj.* Causing or able to cause motion. [< LLat. *motivus*, causing to move.]

mot·ley (mŏt′lē) *adj.* **1.** Having components of great variety; heterogeneous; varied. **2.** Having or exhibiting many colors; multicolored. [< OE *mot*, speck.]

mo·tor (mō′tər) *n.* **1.** Something that imparts or produces motion. **2.** A device that converts any form of energy into mechanical energy, esp. a device that converts electric current into mechanical power. —*adj.* **1.** Causing or producing motion. **2.** Driven by or having a motor. **3.** Of or for motor vehicles: *motor oil.* **4.** *Physiol.* Relating to movements of the muscles. —*v.* To travel in a motor vehicle. [Lat.] —**mo′tor·i·za′tion** *n.* —**mo′tor·ize′** *v.*

mo·tor·bike (mō′tər-bīk′) *n.* **1.** A lightweight motorcycle. **2.** A bicycle powered by an attached motor.

mo·tor·boat (mō′tər-bōt′) *n.* A boat propelled by an internal-combustion engine.

mo·tor·cade (mō′tər-kād′) *n.* A procession of automobiles. [MOTOR + (CAVAL)CADE.]

mo·tor·car (mō′tər-kär′) *n.* An automobile.

motor court *n.* A motel.

mo·tor·cy·cle (mō′tər-sī′kəl) *n.* A vehicle with two wheels in tandem, propelled by an internal-combustion engine. —*v.* **-cled, -cling.** To ride on or drive a motorcycle. —**mo′tor·cy′clist** (-sī′klĭst) *n.*

motor inn *n.* An urban motel usu. having several stores and a guest parking lot.

mo·tor·ist (mō′tər-ĭst) *n.* One who drives or rides in an automobile.

motor lodge *n.* A motel.

mo·tor·man (mō′tər-mən) *n.* One who drives a streetcar, locomotive, or subway train.

motor scooter *n.* A small two-wheeled vehicle with a low-powered gasoline engine.

motor vehicle *n.* Any self-propelled motor-powered vehicle that travels on wheels but does not run on rails.

mot·tle (mŏt′l) *v.* **-tled, -tling.** To cover with spots or streaks of different shades or colors. [< MOTLEY.]

mot·to (mŏt′ō) *n., pl.* **-toes** or **-tos.** A brief sentence, phrase, or word used to express a principle, goal, or ideal. [Ital. < Lat. *muttum*, grunt.]

moue (mōō) *n.* A grimace; pout. [< OFr.]

mound (mound) *n.* **1.** A pile or bank of earth, sand, or rocks. **2.** A natural elevation, as a small hill. **3.** *Baseball.* The slightly elevated pitcher's area in the center of the diamond. [Orig. unknown.]

mount¹ (mount) *v.* **1.** To climb or ascend. **2.** To get up on: *mount a horse.* **3.** To increase in amount, degree, extent, intensity, or number. **4.** To place in an appropriate setting, as for display, study, etc. **5. a.** To set (guns) in position. **b.** To launch and carry out: *mount an attack.* —*n.* **1.** A horse or other animal on which to ride. **2.** An object to which another is affixed for accessibility, display, or use. [< Lat. *mons*, mountain.] —**mount′a·ble** *adj.*

mount² (mount) *n.* A mountain or hill. [< Lat. *mons.*]

moun·tain (moun′tən) *n.* A natural elevation of the earth's surface greater in height than a hill. [< Lat. *montanus*, of a mountain.]

mountain ash *n.* Any of various deciduous trees with clusters of small white flowers and bright orange-red berries.

moun·tain·eer (moun′tə-nîr′) *n.* **1.** An inhabitant of a mountainous area. **2.** One who climbs mountains for sport. —*v.* To climb mountains for sport.

mountain goat *n.* A hoofed mammal of northwestern North America, with short, curved black horns and thick yellowish-white hair and beard.

mountain laurel *n.* An evergreen shrub of eastern North America, with leathery, poisonous leaves and pink or white flowers.

mountain lion *n.* A large tawny cat of mountainous regions of the Western Hemisphere.

moun·tain·ous (moun′tə-nəs) *adj.* **1.** Having many mountains. **2.** Giant; massive.

mountain range *n.* A series of mountain ridges.

moun·tain·side (moun′tən-sīd′) *n.* The sloping side of a mountain.

moun·tain·top (moun′tən-tŏp′) *n.* The top of a mountain.

moun·te·bank (moun′tə-băngk′) *n.* **1.** A peddler of quack medicines. **2.** An imposter or swindler. [< Ital. *monta im banco*, he gets up onto the bench.]

mount·ing (moun'tĭng) *n.* A supporting structure or frame: *a mounting for a gem.*

mourn (môrn, mōrn) *v.* To express or feel sorrow (for or over). [< OE *murnan.*] —**mourn'er** *n.*

mourn·ful (môrn'fəl, mōrn'-) *adj.* 1. Feeling or expressing grief. 2. Arousing or suggesting grief. —**mourn'ful·ly** *adv.* —**mourn'ful·ness** *n.*

mourn·ing (môr'nĭng, mōr'-) *n.* 1. Expression of grief. 2. Clothes worn as a sign of grief for the dead. 3. The period during which a death is mourned. —**mourn'ing·ly** *adv.*

mourning dove *n.* A wild dove of North America, noted for its plaintive call.

mouse (mous) *n., pl.* **mice** (mīs). Any of numerous small, usu. long-tailed rodents, some of which live in or near human dwellings. —*v.* (mouz) **moused, mous·ing.** To hunt or catch mice. [< OE *mūs.*] —**mous'er** (mou'zər) *n.*

mouse-trap (mous'trăp') *n.* A trap for catching mice.

mousse (mōōs) *n.* A chilled dessert made with whipped cream, gelatin, and flavoring. [Fr.]

mous·tache (mŭs'tăsh', mə-stăsh') *n.* Var. of **mustache.**

mous·y (mou'sē, -zē) *adj.* **-i·er, -i·est.** 1. Mouselike in color or appearance. 2. Timid and unnoticeable. —**mous'i·ness** *n.*

mouth (mouth) *n., pl.* **mouths** (mouthz). 1. *Anat.* The body opening and related organs with which food is taken in, chewed, and swallowed and sounds and speech are articulated. 2. A natural opening, such as the part of a river that empties into a larger body of water or the entrance to a harbor, canyon, etc. 3. The opening through which a container is filled or emptied. —*v.* (mouth). 1. To utter in a meaninglessly declamatory manner. 2. To put, take, or move around in the mouth. —*phrasal verb.* **mouth off.** *Slang.* To complain, criticize, or brag loudly. [< OE *mūth.*] —**mouth'ful** *n.*

mouth

A. Tongue
B. Palatine tonsil
C. Soft palate
D. Uvula
E. Mandible
F. Hyoid bone
G. Epiglottis

mouth organ *n.* A harmonica.

mouth-piece (mouth'pēs') *n.* 1. A part of an instrument that functions in or near the mouth. 2. A protective device worn over the teeth by athletes. 3. *Informal.* A spokesman.

mouth-to-mouth (mouth'tə-mouth') *adj.* Of, relating to, or being a method of artificial resuscitation in which the rescuer's mouth is placed directly over the victim's and air is thereby forced into the victim's lungs.

mouth-wash (mouth'wŏsh', -wôsh') *n.* An antiseptic, usu. flavored liquid for cleaning the mouth and breath.

move (mōōv) *v.* **moved, mov·ing.** 1. To change in position from one point to another. 2. To transfer (a piece) in a board game. 3. To settle in a new place. 4. To change hands commercially: *Furs move slowly in summer.* 5. To affect deeply. 6. To take action. 7. To make a formal motion in parliamentary procedure. 8. To cause (the bowels) to evacuate. —*phrasal verbs.* **move in.** To occupy as a residence or place of business. **move in on.** To attempt to seize control of. —*n.* 1. The act of moving. 2. A change of residence or place of business. 3. *Board Games.* **a.** The act of moving a piece. **b.** A player's turn to move a piece. 4. A calculated action to achieve an end. —*idioms.* **get a move on.** *Informal.* To get going. **on the move.** Traveling about or making progress. [< Lat. *movēre.*] —**mov'a·bil'i·ty** or **mov'a·ble·ness** *n.* —**mov'a·ble** or **move'a·ble** *adj.* —**mov'a·bly** *adv.*

move·ment (mōōv'mənt) *n.* 1. **a.** An act of moving; a change in position. **b.** A maneuver in which military units are moved toward a tactical or strategic objective. 2. The activities of a group toward the achievement of a specific goal: *the labor movement.* 3. Activity, esp. in business or commerce. 4. An evacuation of the bowels. 5. *Mus.* A primary section of a composition. 6. A mechanism that produces or transmits motion, as the works of a watch.

mov·er (mōō'vər) *n.* 1. One that moves. 2. One whose occupation is transporting furnishings.

mov·ie (mōō'vē) *n. Informal.* 1. A motion picture. 2. **movies. a.** A showing of a motion picture. **b.** The motion-picture industry. [< MOVING PICTURE.]

moving picture *n.* A motion picture.

mow¹ (mō) *v.* **mowed, mowed** or **mown** (mōn), **mow·ing.** 1. To cut down (e.g. grain or grass) with a scythe or machine. 2. To cut (such growth) from. —*phrasal verb.* **mow down.** To destroy in great numbers, as in battle. [< OE *māwan.*] —**mow'er** (mō'ər) *n.*

mow² (mou) *n.* A place for storing hay or grain. [< OE *mūwa.*]

mox·ie (mŏk'sē) *n. Slang.* The ability to face difficulty with spirit; nerve; guts. [< *Moxie,* a trademark for a soft drink.]

moz·za·rel·la (mŏt'sə-rĕl'ə, mōt'-) *n.* A soft, white Italian cheese with a mild flavor. [< Ital. *mozza,* slice.]

Mr. (mĭs'tər) *n., pl.* **Messrs.** The abbreviated form of the title *Mister* when used with names.

Mrs. (mĭs'ĭz) *n. pl.* **Mmes.** A title of courtesy used in speaking of a married woman, preceding the woman's surname.

Ms. or **Ms** (mĭz) *n., pl.* **Mses.** or **Mss.** A title of courtesy used before a woman's surname or before her given name and surname without regard to her marital status. [Blend of Miss and Mrs.]

Usage: As a title of respect for a woman without regard to her marital status, Ms. is the equivalent of *Mr.*, the courtesy title for a man: *Ms. Smith; Ms. Judith Smith. Ms.* should not be used when a woman is addressed by her husband's given name and surname: *Ms. Green,* but not *Ms. Paul Green.* Though controversial when first introduced, *Ms.* has come to be used widely in business, professional, and many social contexts.

mu (myōō, mōō) *n.* The 12th letter in the Greek alphabet. See table at **alphabet.** [Gk.]

much (mŭch) *adj.* **more, most.** Great in quantity, degree, or extent: *much rain.* —*n.* 1. A large quantity or amount. 2. Something remarkable or important: *not much of a leader.* —*adv.* **more, most.** 1. To a great degree or extent: *much easier.* 2. Just about; almost: *much the same.* [< OE *mycel.*]

mu·ci·lage (myōō'sə-lĭj) *n.* A sticky substance used as an adhesive. [< Lat. *mucus, mucus.*] —**mu'ci·lag'i·nous** (-lăj'ə-nəs) *adj.*

muck (mŭk) *n.* 1. A moist, sticky mixture, esp. of mud and filth. 2. Moist animal dung. 3. Dark, fertile soil containing putrid vegetable matter. —*v. Informal.* To soil or make dirty with or as if with muck. —*phrasal verb.* **muck up.** *Informal.* To botch. [< ON *mykr.*] —**muck'y** *adj.*

muck·rake (mŭk'rāk') *v.* **-raked, -rak·ing.** To search for and expose wrongdoing or corruption. —**muck'rak'er** *n.*

mu·cous (myōō'kəs) *adj.* Producing or secreting mucus. [Lat. *mucosus.*]

mucous membrane *n.* The membrane lining all bodily channels that communicate with the air, the glands of which secrete mucus.

mu·cus (myōō'kəs) *n.* The viscous liquid secreted as a protective lubricant coating by glands in the mucous membrane. [Lat.]

mud (mŭd) *n.* 1. Wet, sticky, soft earth. 2. Slanderous or defamatory charges. [ME *mudde.*] —**mud'di·ly** *adv.* —**mud'di·ness** *n.* —**mud'dy** *adj. & v.*

mud·dle (mŭd'l) *v.* **-dled, -dling.** 1. To make turbid; muddy. 2. To mix confusedly; jumble. 3. To mix up (the mind), as with alcohol; confuse. 4. To mismanage or bungle. —*phrasal verb.* **muddle through.** To accomplish in a confused, blundering fashion. —*n.* A jumble; mess. [Poss. < MDu. *moddelen.*] —**mud'dler** *n.*

mud·guard (mŭd'gärd') *n.* A shield over a vehicle's wheel.

mud puppy *n.* Any of various aquatic salamanders with prominent external gills.

mud·sling·er (mŭd'slĭng'ər) *n.* One who makes slanderous charges about an opponent. —**mud'sling'ing** *n.*

mud turtle *n.* A freshwater turtle found throughout the Western Hemisphere.

mu·ez·zin (myōō-ĕz'ĭn, mōō-) *n.* A Moslem crier who calls the faithful to prayer, usu. from a minaret. [Ar. *mu'adhdhin.*]

muff¹ (mŭf) *v.* To perform clumsily; bungle. [Orig. unknown.] —**muff** *n.*

muff² (mŭf) *n.* A cylindrical cover open at both ends, used to keep the hands warm. [< Med. Lat. *muffla.*]

muf·fin (mŭf'ĭn) *n.* A small, cup-shaped bread, usu. served hot. [Prob. < LG *muffen,* cakes.]

muf·fle (mŭf'əl) *v.* **-fled, -fling.** 1. To wrap up snugly for warmth or protection. 2. To wrap or pad in order to deaden a sound. 3. To deaden (a sound). 4. To suppress: *muffle political opposition.* [< Med. Lat. *muffla,* glove.]

muf·fler (mŭf'lər) *n.* 1. A heavy scarf worn around the neck for warmth. 2. A device that absorbs noise, esp. that of an internal-combustion engine.

muf·ti (mŭf'tē) *n.* Civilian dress. [< Ar. *muftī,* judge.]

mug¹ (mŭg) *n.* A cylindrical drinking vessel, often having a handle. [Orig. unknown.]

mug² (mŭg) *Slang.* —*n.* 1. The face of a person. 2. A grimace. 3. A hoodlum. —*v.* **mugged, mug·ging.** To waylay and beat severely, usu. with intent to rob. [Prob. < MUG¹.] —**mug'ger** *n.*

mug·gy (mŭg'ē) *adj.* **-gi·er, -gi·est.** Warm and very humid. [< ME *muggen,* to drizzle.] —**mug'gi·ly** *adv.* —**mug'gi·ness** *n.*

Mu·ham·mad·an (mō-hăm'ĭ-dən) *n.* A Moslem. —**Mu·ham'mad·an** *adj.* —**Mu·ham'mad·an·ism** *n.*

Mu·har·ram (mōō-har'əm) *n.* The 1st month of the Moslem calendar. See table at **calendar.** [Ar. *muḥarram.*]

muk·luk (mŭk'lŭk') *n.* 1. A soft Eskimo boot made of reindeer skin or sealskin. 2. A slipper similar to a mukluk. [Eskimo *muklok,* large seal.]

mu·lat·to (mōō-lăt'ō, -lä'tō, myōō-) *n.,* *pl.* **-tos** or **-toes.** A person having one white and one black parent. [< Lat. *mulus,* mule.]

mul·ber·ry (mŭl'bĕr'ē, -bə-rē) *n.* 1. A tree bearing sweet reddish or purplish berrylike fruit. 2. The fruit of the mulberry tree. [ME *mulberrie.*] —**mul'ber·ry** *adj.*

mulch (mŭlch) *n.* A protective covering, as of leaves or hay, placed around plants to prevent evaporation of moisture and freezing of roots and to control weeds. —*v.* To cover with a mulch. [< ME *melsch,* soft.]

mulct (mŭlkt) *n.* A fine or similar penalty. —*v.* 1. To penalize by fining. 2. To swindle or defraud. [< Lat. *mulcta.*]

mule¹ (myōōl) *n.* 1. The sterile hybrid offspring of a male ass and female horse. 2. *Informal.* A stubborn person. [< Lat. *mulus.*]

mule¹

mule² (myōōl) *n.* An open slipper that leaves the heel bare. [< Lat. *mulleus (calceus),* red (shoe).]

mule deer *n.* A long-eared hoofed mammal of western North America.

mule·skin·ner (myōōl'skĭn'ər) *n. Informal.* A muleteer.

mu·le·teer (myōō′lə-tîr′) n. A driver of mules.

mull¹ (mŭl) v. To heat and spice (a beverage, as wine). [Orig. unknown.]

mull² (mŭl) v. To ponder or ruminate: mull over a plan. [< ME mul, dust.]

mul·lah (mŭl′ə, mōōl′ə) n. A Moslem religious teacher or leader, esp. one trained in law. [< Ar. mawlā, master.]

mul·lein (mŭl′ən) n. Any of various tall plants with closely clustered yellow flowers and downy leaves. [< OFr. moleine.]

mul·let (mŭl′ĭt) n., pl. -let or -lets. Any of various saltwater and freshwater edible fishes. [< Gk. mullos.]

mul·lion (mŭl′yən) n. A vertical strip dividing the panes of a window. [< Lat. medianus, middle.]

multi- pref. 1. Many; much; multiple: multicolored. 2. a. More than one: multiparous. b. More than two: multilateral. [< Lat. multus, much.]

Usage: Many compounds other than those entered here may be formed with multi-. In forming compounds multi- is normally joined to the following word or element without space or hyphen: multiangular. However, if the second element begins with i, it is separated with a hyphen: multi-infection.

mul·ti·cel·lu·lar (mŭl′tĭ-sĕl′yə-lər) adj. Containing many cells. **—mul′ti·cel′lu·lar′i·ty** (-lăr′ĭtē) n.

mul·ti·col·ored (mŭl′tĭ-kŭl′ərd) adj. Having many colors.

mul·ti·cul·tur·al (mŭl′tĭ-kŭl′chər-əl) adj. Of, relating to, or intended for several cultures.

mul·ti·di·men·sion·al (mŭl′tĭ-dĭ-mĕn′shə-nəl) adj. Of, relating to, or having several dimensions. **—mul′ti·di·men′sion·al′i·ty** n.

mul·ti·di·rec·tion·al (mŭl′tĭ-dĭ-rĕk′shə-nəl) adj. Reaching in many directions.

mul·ti·dis·ci·pli·nar·y (mŭl′tĭ-dĭs′ə-plə-nĕr′ē) adj. Involving or utilizing several academic disciplines at once.

mul·ti·eth·nic (mŭl′tē-ĕth′nĭk) adj. Of or including a variety of ethnic groups.

mul·ti·fac·et·ed (mŭl′tə-făs′ĭ-tĭd, -tē-) adj. Having several facets.

mul·ti·fam·i·ly (mŭl′tĭ-făm′ə-lē) adj. Of or intended for use by several families.

mul·ti·far·i·ous (mŭl′tə-fâr′ē-əs) adj. Having great variety; of many parts or kinds. [Lat. multifarius.] **—mul′ti·far′i·ous·ly** adv. **—mul′ti·far′i·ous·ness** n.

mul·ti·form (mŭl′tə-fôrm′) adj. Having many forms, shapes, or appearances.

mul·ti·lane (mŭl′tə-lān′, -tē-) adj. Having several lanes: a multilane highway.

mul·ti·lat·er·al (mŭl′tĭ-lăt′ər-əl) adj. 1. Having many sides. 2. Involving more than two governments or parties. **—mul′ti·lat′er·al·ly** adv.

mul·ti·lay·ered (mŭl′tĭ-lā′ərd) adj. Consisting of several layers or levels.

mul·ti·lev·el (mŭl′tĭ-lĕv′əl) adj. Having several levels: a multilevel garage.

mul·ti·lin·gual (mŭl′tə-lĭng′gwəl) adj. 1. Of, including, or written in several languages. 2. Using or able to use several languages. **—mul′ti·lin′gual·ism** n.

mul·ti·me·di·a (mŭl′tĭ-mē′dē-ə) adj. Including or involving several media: a multimedia advertising campaign. **—mul′ti·me′di·a** n.

mul·ti·mil·lion·aire (mŭl′tĭ-mĭl′yə-nâr′) n. One whose assets equal many millions of dollars.

mul·ti·na·tion·al (mŭl′tĭ-năsh′ən-əl, -năsh′nəl) adj. Of, relating to, or involving more than one country: a multinational corporation.

mul·tip·a·rous (mŭl-tĭp′ər-əs) adj. 1. Having borne more than one child. 2. Giving birth to more than one offspring at one time.

mul·ti·ple (mŭl′tə-pəl) adj. Having, pertaining to, or consisting of more than one individual, element, or part. **—n.** Math. A quantity into which another quantity may be divided with zero remainder. [< Lat. multipulus.]

mul·ti·ple-choice (mŭl′tə-pəl-chois′) adj. Offering a number of answers from which the correct one is to be chosen.

multiple sclerosis n. A degenerative disease of the central nervous system, in which hardening of tissue occurs.

multiple star n. Three or more stars that appear as one to the naked eye.

mul·ti·plex (mŭl′tə-plĕks′) adj. 1. Multiple; manifold. 2. Of or being a communication system that can simultaneously transmit two or more messages on the same circuit or radio channel. [Lat.] **—mul′ti·plex′** v.

mul·ti·pli·cand (mŭl′tə-plĭ-kănd′) n. The number that is or is to be multiplied by another. [Lat. multiplicandum, thing to be multiplied.]

mul·ti·pli·ca·tion (mŭl′tə-plĭ-kā′shən) n. 1. The act or process of multiplying. 2. The reproduction of plants and animals. 3. Math. The operation of adding a number to itself a designated number of times. **—mul′ti·pli·ca′tive** adj.

mul·ti·plic·i·ty (mŭl′tə-plĭs′ə-tē) n., pl. -ties. 1. The condition of being various or multiple. 2. A large number. [< Lat. multiplicitas.]

mul·ti·pli·er (mŭl′tə-plī′ər) n. Math. A number by which another number is multiplied.

mul·ti·ply (mŭl′tə-plī′) v. -plied, -ply·ing. 1. To increase in amount, number, or degree. 2. Math. To perform multiplication (on). 3. To breed; reproduce. [< Lat. multiplicare.]

mul·ti·pur·pose (mŭl′tə-pûr′pəs) adj. Having several purposes.

mul·ti·ra·cial (mŭl′tē-rā′shəl) adj. Of, involving, or acting on behalf of several races: a multiracial coalition.

mul·ti·sense (mŭl′tĭ-sĕns′) adj. Having multiple meanings.

mul·ti·stage (mŭl′tĭ-stāj′) adj. Functioning by stages: a multistage rocket.

mul·ti·sto·ry (mŭl′tĭ-stôr′ē, -stōr′ē) adj. Having several stories: a multistory building.

mul·ti·tude (mŭl′tĭ-tōōd′, -tyōōd′) n. A great, indefinite number. [< Lat. multitudo.] **—mul′ti·tu′di·nous** adj. **—mul′ti·tu′di·nous·ly** adv.

mul·ti·va·lent (mŭl′tĭ-vā′lənt, mŭl-tĭv′ə-lənt) adj. Polyvalent. **—mul′ti·va′lence** n.

mul·ti·vi·ta·min (mŭl′tə-vī′tə-mĭn) adj. Containing many vitamins. **—n.** A multivitamin preparation.

mum¹ (mŭm) adj. Not talking. [ME.]

mum² (mŭm) n. Informal. A chrysanthemum.

mum·ble (mŭm′bəl) v. -bled, -bling. To speak or utter indistinctly by lowering the voice or partially closing the mouth. [ME momelen.] **—mum′ble** n. **—mum′bler** n.

ă pat ā pay â care ä father ĕ pet ē be ĭ pit ī tie î pier ŏ pot ō toe ô paw, for oi noise ōō took ōō boot ou out th thin th this ŭ cut û urge yōō abuse zh vision ə about, item, edible, gallop, circus

mum·bo jum·bo (mŭm′bō jŭm′bō) n. 1. An object or idol believed to have supernatural powers. 2. An obscure ritual or incantation. 3. Confusing or meaningless activity or language. [Prob. of Mandingo orig.]

mum·mer (mŭm′ər) n. One who acts or plays in a mask or costume. [< OFr. momer, to pantomime.] —**mum′mery** n.

mum·my (mŭm′ē) n., pl. -ies. A body embalmed after death, as by the ancient Egyptians. [< Ar. mūmiyā, embalming ointment.] —**mum′mi·fi·ca′tion** n. —**mum′mi·fy′** v.

mumps (mŭmps) pl.n. (used with a sing. or pl. verb). A contagious viral disease, marked by a painful swelling esp. of the salivary glands, and sometimes, of the ovaries or testes. [< dial. mump, grimace.]

munch (mŭnch) v. To chew noisily. [ME monchen.]

mun·dane (mŭn-dān′, mŭn′dān′) adj. 1. Of this world; worldly. 2. Typical of or concerned with the ordinary. [< LLat. mundanus.] —**mun·dane′ly** adv.

mu·nic·i·pal (myōō-nĭs′ə-pəl) adj. 1. Of or pertaining to a municipality. 2. Having local self-government. [Lat. municipalis.] —**mu·nic′i·pal·ly** adv.

mu·nic·i·pal·i·ty (myōō-nĭs′ə-păl′ĭ-tē) n., pl. -ties. A political unit, as a city or town, incorporated for local self-government.

mu·nif·i·cent (myōō-nĭf′ĭ-sənt) adj. Extremely liberal in giving; very generous. [< Lat. munificens.] —**mu·nif′i·cence** n. —**mu·nif′i·cent·ly** adv.

mu·ni·tions (myōō-nĭsh′əns) pl.n. War materiel. [< Lat. munire, to defend.]

mu·ral (myŏŏr′əl) n. A painting applied directly to a wall or ceiling. [< Lat. murus, wall.] —**mu′ral·ist** n.

murder (mûr′dər) n. The unlawful killing of one human being by another, esp. with malice aforethought. —v. 1. To kill (a human being) unlawfully. 2. To mar or spoil by ineptness; mutilate: murder the English language. 3. Slang. To defeat decisively. [< OE morthor.] —**mur′der·er** n.

 Syns: murder, hit, kill, knock off, liquidate, rub out, slay, waste, wipe out, zap v.

mur·der·ous (mûr′dər-əs) adj. 1. Capable of, guilty of, or intending murder. 2. Characteristic of murder; brutal. 3. Informal. Very difficult or dangerous: a murderous exam. —**mur′der·ous·ly** adv. —**mur′der·ous·ness** n.

murk (mûrk) n. Darkness; gloom. [< OE mirce.] —**murk′i·ly** adv. —**murk′i·ness** n. —**murk′y** adj.

mur·mur (mûr′mər) n. 1. A low, indistinct, and continuous sound. 2. A grumbled complaint. 3. Med. An abnormal sound in the heart, lungs, or blood vessels. —v. To make a low, continuous sound. [< Lat.] —**mur′mur·er** n.

mus·cat (mŭs′kăt′, -kət) n. A sweet white grape used for making wine or raisins. [< LLat. muscus, musk.]

mus·ca·tel (mŭs′kə-tĕl′) n. A rich, sweet wine made from muscat grapes. [< OProv. muscat, musky.]

mus·cle (mŭs′əl) n. 1. A tissue composed of fibers capable of contracting and relaxing to effect bodily movement. 2. A contractile organ consisting of muscle tissue. 3. Muscular strength. 4. Power; force. —v. -cled, -cling. To force one's way. [< Lat. mus, mouse.]

mus·cle-bound (mŭs′əl-bound′) adj. Having stiff, overdeveloped muscles, as from excessive exercise.

mus·cu·lar (mŭs′kyə-lər) adj. 1. Of, pertaining to, or consisting of muscles. 2. Having well-developed muscles. [< Lat. musculus, muscle.] —**mus′cu·lar′i·ty** (-lăr′ĭ-tē) n. —**mus′cu·lar·ly** adv.

muscular dystrophy n. A chronic, noncontagious disease of unknown cause in which gradual but irreversible muscular deterioration results in complete incapacitation.

mus·cu·la·ture (mŭs′kyə-lə-chŏŏr′, -chər) n. The system of muscles of an animal or a body part. [Fr.]

muse (myōōz) v. mused, mus·ing. To ponder, consider, or deliberate at length. [< Med. Lat. mus, snout.] —**mus′er** n.

Muse (myōōz) n. 1. Gk. Myth. Any of nine daughters of Zeus, each of whom presided over a different art or science. 2. muse. A source of inspiration, esp. of a poet.

mu·se·um (myōō-zē′əm) n. A place in which works of artistic, historical, and scientific value are exhibited. [< Gk. mouseios, of the Muses.]

mush (mŭsh) n. 1. Boiled cornmeal. 2. Something thick, soft, and pulpy. 3. Informal. Maudlin sentimentality. [Prob. < MASH.] —**mush′i·ness** n. —**mush′y** adj.

mush·room (mŭsh′rŏŏm′, -rŏŏm′) n. Any of various fleshy fungi with a stalk topped by an umbrella-shaped cap. —v. To grow or spread rapidly. [< OFr. musseron.]

mu·sic (myōō′zĭk) n. 1. The art of organizing sound so as to elicit an aesthetic response in a listener. 2. Vocal or instrumental sounds having some degree of rhythm, melody, and harmony. 3. A musical composition or body of such compositions. 4. Aesthetically pleasing or harmonious sound or a combination thereof. [< Gk. mousikē (tekhnē), (art) of the Muses.]

mu·si·cal (myōō′zĭ-kəl) adj. 1. Of, pertaining to, or producing music. 2. Melodious. 3. Set to or accompanied by music. 4. Devoted to or skilled in music. —n. A musical comedy. —**mu′si·cal·ly** adv.

musical comedy n. A play in which dialogue is interspersed with songs and dances.

mu·si·cale (myōō′zĭ-kăl′) n. A program of music performed at a social gathering. [< Fr. (soirée) musicale, musical (evening).]

music box n. A box containing a mechanical device that produces music.

music hall n. A vaudeville theater.

mu·si·cian (myōō-zĭsh′ən) n. One skilled in composing or performing music. —**mu·si′cian·ly** adj. —**mu·si′cian·ship′** n.

mu·si·col·o·gy (myōō′zĭ-kŏl′ə-jē) n. The historical and scientific study of music. —**mu′si·col′o·gist** n.

musk (mŭsk) n. An odorous substance secreted by an Asian deer or produced synthetically, used in perfumery. [< Pers. mushk.] —**musk′i·ness** n. —**musk′y** adj.

mus·ket (mŭs′kĭt) n. A smoothbore, long-barreled shoulder gun. [< Ital. moschetto.] —**mus′ket·eer′** n.

mus·ket·ry (mŭs′kĭ-trē) n. 1. Muskets in general. 2. Musketeers.

Mus·kho·ge·an (mŭs-kō′gē-ən) n. A family of North American Indian languages that includes Chickasaw, Choctaw, Creek, and Seminole.

musk·mel·on (mŭsk′mĕl′ən) n. Any of several

varieties of edible melon, as the cantaloupe, with a rough rind and juicy flesh.

musk ox *n.* A large, shaggy, horned mammal of northern Canada and Greenland.

musk·rat (mŭs′krăt′) *n., pl.* **-rat** or **-rats. 1.** An aquatic North American rodent with dense brown fur. **2.** The fur of the muskrat.

Mus·lim (mŭz′ləm, mŏŏs′-, mŏŏz′-) *n.* Var. of **Moslem.**

mus·lin (mŭz′lĭn) *n.* A sturdy, plain-weave cotton fabric. [< Ital. *mussoline*, of Mosul, a town in Iraq.]

muss (mŭs) *v.* To make messy or untidy; rumple. —*n.* Disorder; mess. [Prob. < MESS.] —**muss′i·ly** *adv.* —**muss′i·ness** *n.* —**muss′y** *adj.*

mus·sel (mŭs′əl) *n.* Any of various narrow-shelled bivalve mollusks, esp. an edible marine species. [< OE *muscelle.*]

Mus·sul·man (mŭs′əl-mən) *n., pl.* **-men** or **-mans.** *Archaic.* A Moslem.

must¹ (mŭst) *v.* Used as an auxiliary to indicate: **1.** Necessity or obligation: *You must register in order to vote.* **2.** Probability: *It must be midnight.* **3.** Certainty or inevitability: *All good things must come to an end.* **4.** Insistence: *I must repeat, you are wrong.* —*n.* An absolute requirement. [< OE *mōtan*, to be allowed.]

must² (mŭst) *n.* Staleness. [< MUSTY.]

must³ (mŭst) *n.* Unfermented or fermenting fruit juice. [< Lat. *mustum.*]

mus·tache (mŭs′tăsh′, mə-stăsh′) *n.* Also **mous·tache.** The hair growing on the upper lip of a human being. [< Gk. *mustax.*]

mus·tang (mŭs′tăng′) *n.* A wild horse of the western North American plains. [Sp. *mesteñ*, stray animal.]

mus·tard (mŭs′tərd) *n.* **1.** Any of various plants with yellow flowers and often pungent seeds. **2.** A condiment made from powdered mustard seeds. **3.** A dark brownish yellow. [< Lat. *mustum*, new wine.]

mustard gas *n.* An oily volatile liquid, $(ClCH_2CH_2)_2S$, used in warfare as a gaseous blistering agent.

mus·ter (mŭs′tər) *v.* **1.** To summon or assemble (troops). **2.** To gather up: *muster up courage.* —*phrasal verbs.* **muster in.** To enlist (someone) in military service. **muster out.** To discharge (someone) from military service. —*n.* A gathering, esp. of troops, as for inspection or roll call. [< Lat. *monstrare*, to show.]

must·n't (mŭs′ənt) Must not.

must·y (mŭs′tē) *adj.* **-i·er, -i·est.** Having a stale or moldy odor. [< MOIST.] —**must′i·ness** *n.*

mu·ta·ble (myōō′tə-bəl) *adj.* **1.** Subject to change. **2.** Prone to change; fickle. —**mu·ta·bil′i·ty** or **mu·ta·ble·ness** *n.* —**mu′ta·bly** *adv.*

mu·tant (myōōt′nt) *n.* An organism differing from the parental strain as a result of mutation. —**mu′tant** *adj.*

mu·tate (myōō′tāt′, myōō-tāt′) *v.* **-tat·ed, -tat·ing.** To undergo or cause to undergo change or alteration by or as if by mutation. [Lat. *mutare.*] —**mu′ta·tive** (-tā′tĭv, -tə-tĭv) *adj.*

mu·ta·tion (myōō-tā′shən) *n.* **1.** An alteration or change, as in nature, form, or quality.

2. *Biol.* Any heritable alteration of an organism.

mute (myōōt) *adj.* **mut·er, mut·est. 1.** Incapable of producing speech or vocal sound. **2.** Not speaking or spoken; silent. —*n.* **1.** A person incapable of speech, esp. one both deaf and mute. **2.** A device used to muffle or soften the tone of a musical instrument. —*v.* **mut·ed, mut·ing.** To soften the sound, color, or shade of. [< Lat. *mutus.*] —**mute′ly** *adv.* —**mute′ness** *n.*

mu·ti·late (myōōt′l-āt′) *v.* **-lat·ed, -lat·ing. 1.** To deprive of a limb or other essential part. **2.** To disfigure by seriously damaging a part. [Lat. *mutilare.*] —**mu′ti·la′tion** *n.* —**mu′ti·la′tive** *adj.* —**mu′ti·la′tor** *n.*

mu·ti·ny (myōōt′n-ē) *n., pl.* **-nies.** Open rebellion against constituted authority, esp. by military personnel against their superior officers. [< Lat. *movēre*, to move.] —**mu′ti·neer′** *n.* —**mu′ti·nous** *adj.* —**mu′ti·nous·ly** *adv.* —**mu′ti·nous·ness** *n.* —**mu′ti·ny** *v.*

mutt (mŭt) *n. Slang.* A mongrel dog. [< *muttonhead*, fool.]

mut·ter (mŭt′ər) *v.* **1.** To speak or utter indistinctly and in low tones. **2.** To complain or grumble. —*n.* A low, indistinct utterance. [ME *muttren.*] —**mut′ter·er** *n.*

mut·ton (mŭt′n) *n.* The flesh of a full-grown sheep. [< OFr. *moton.*]

mutton chops *pl.n.* Side-whiskers narrow at the temples and wide and rounded at the bottom.

mu·tu·al (myōō′chōō-əl) *adj.* **1.** Having the same feelings each for the other: *mutual friends.* **2.** Given and received in equal amounts: *mutual concern.* **3.** Possessed in common: *mutual interests.* [< Lat. *mutuus.*] —**mu′tu·al′i·ty** *n.* —**mu′tu·al·ly** *adv.*

mutual fund *n.* An investment company that by the sale of its shares acquires funds to invest in a variety of securities.

muu·muu (mōō′mōō′) *n.* A loose dress. [Hawaiian *mu′u mu′u.*]

Mu·zak (myōō′zăk′). A trademark for recorded background music transmitted by wire on a subscription basis.

muz·zle (mŭz′əl) *n.* **1.** The usu. projecting jaws and nose of certain animals. **2.** A device fitted over an animal's snout to prevent biting or eating. **3.** The front end of the barrel of a firearm. —*v.* **-zled, -zling. 1.** To put a muzzle on (an animal). **2.** To restrain (someone) from expressing opinions. [< LLat. *musum*, snout.]

muzzle

muz·zle·load·er (mŭz′əl-lō′dər) n. A firearm loaded through the muzzle. **—muz′zle·load·ing** adj.

my (mī) pron. The possessive case of I, used attributively: my work. —interj. Used to express surprise, pleasure, or dismay. [< OE mīn.]

my·as·the·ni·a gra·vis (mī′ăs-thē′nē-ə grăv′ĭs) n. An inherited disease characterized by progressive muscular weakness and fatigue caused by degeneration of muscle fibers. [Gk. mus, muscle + Gk. asthenia, weakness + Lat. gravis, serious.]

my·ce·li·um (mī-sē′lē-əm) n., pl. **-li·a** (-lē-ə). The vegetative part of a fungus, consisting of a mass of branching, threadlike filaments that forms its main growing structure. [MYC(O)- + Gk. hēlos, wart.] **—my·ce′li·al** adj.

-mycete suff. Fungus: actinomycete. [< Gk. mukēs.]

-mycin suff. A substance derived from a fungus: streptomycin. [MYC(O)- + -IN.]

myco- or **myc-** pref. Fungus: mycology. [< Gk. mukēs.]

my·col·o·gy (mī-kŏl′ə-jē) n. The branch of botany that deals with fungi. **—my′co·log′i·cal** (mī′kə-lŏj′ĭ-kəl) or **my′co·log′ic** adj. **—my·col′o·gist** n.

myel- pref. Spinal cord; marrow: myeloma. [< Gk. muelos, marrow.]

my·e·lin (mī′ə-lĭn) n. Also **my·e·line** (mī′ə-lĭn, -lēn′). A white, fatty material that sheathes certain nerve fibers.

my·e·lo·ma (mī′ə-lō′mə) n., pl. **-mas** or **-ma·ta** (-mə-tə). A malignant tumor of the bone marrow.

my·na (mī′nə) n. Any of various Asian birds related to the starlings. [< Skt. madanah, passion.]

my·o·car·di·um (mī′ō-kär′dē-əm) n. The muscle tissue of the heart. [< Gk. mus, muscle + Gk. kardia, heart.] **—my′o·car′di·al** adj.

my·o·pi·a (mī-ō′pē-ə) n. 1. A visual defect in which distant objects appear blurred because their images are focused in front of the retina rather than on it; nearsightedness. 2. Shortsightedness in thinking or planning. [Gk. muōpia.] **—my·op′ic** (mī-ŏp′ĭk, -ō′pĭk) adj. **—my·op′i·cal·ly** adv.

myr·i·ad (mĭr′ē-əd) n. Constituting a very large, indefinite number. **—n.** A vast number. [< Gk. murias, ten thousand.]

myr·i·a·me·ter (mĭr′ē-ə-mē′tər) n. A unit of length equal to 10,000 meters. [Gk. myrias, ten thousand + METER.]

Myr·mi·don (mûr′mĭ-dŏn′, -dən) n. 1. Gk. Myth. One of a legendary people of ancient Thessaly who were followers of Achilles in the Trojan War. 2. **myrmidon**. A follower who carries out orders without question.

myrrh (mûr) n. An aromatic gum resin obtained from several Asian or African trees and shrubs and used in perfume and incense. [< Gk. murrha.]

myr·tle (mûr′tl) n. 1. An Old World shrub with pink or white flowers and blackish berries. 2. A trailing vine with evergreen leaves and usu. blue flowers. [< Gk. murtos.]

my·self (mī-sĕlf′) pron. 1. That one identical with me. Used: **a.** Reflexively: I hurt myself. **b.** For emphasis: I myself was responsible. 2. My normal or proper state: I am just not myself these days. [< OE mē self.]
Usage: In informal speech reflexive pronouns like myself and yourself are often used for emphasis in compound subjects and objects: My husband and myself are undecided. He will assign the territory to John and yourself. According to the Usage Panel such constructions should be avoided in writing.

mys·ter·y (mĭs′tə-rē) n., pl. **-ies.** 1. Something that cannot be explained or understood. 2. The quality associated with the unexplained, secret, or unknown. 3. A piece of fiction dealing with a puzzling crime. 4. A religious truth revealed through Christ to the elect. [< Gk. mustērion, secret rite.] **—mys·te′ri·ous** adj. **—mys·te′ri·ous·ly** adv. **—mys·te′ri·ous·ness** n.

mystery play n. A medieval drama based on episodes in the life of Christ. [< ME mystery, trade.]

mys·tic (mĭs′tĭk) adj. 1. Of or pertaining to sacred mysteries, rites, or practices; occult. 2. Mysterious; enigmatic. 3. Of or pertaining to mystics or mysticism. **—n.** One who believes in or practices mysticism. [< Gk. mustikos.]

mys·ti·cal (mĭs′tĭ-kəl) adj. 1. Of, pertaining to, or characteristic of mystics, mysticism, or sacred mysteries. 2. Spiritually symbolic. **—mys′ti·cal·ly** adv. **—mys′ti·cal·ness** n.

mys·ti·cism (mĭs′tĭ-sĭz′əm) n. A spiritual discipline aiming at union with the divine through deep meditation or contemplation.

mys·ti·fy (mĭs′tə-fī′) v. **-fied, -fy·ing.** 1. To perplex; bewilder. 2. To make obscure or mysterious. [Fr. mystifier.] **—mys′ti·fi·ca′tion** n. **—mys′ti·fi′er** n. **—mys′ti·fy′ing·ly** adv.

mys·tique (mĭ-stēk′) n. A body of mystical attitudes and beliefs associated with a particular person, thing, or idea: the mystique of power. [< Fr., mystical.]

myth (mĭth) n. 1. A traditional story presenting supernatural beings, ancestors, or heroes that serve as primordial types in a primitive view of the world. 2. A fictitious or imaginary story, person, or thing. 3. A false belief. [< Gk. muthos.] **—myth′i·cal** or **myth′ic** adj. **—myth′i·cal·ly** adv.

myth·mak·er (mĭth′mā′kər) n. One who creates myths or mythical situations. **—myth′mak·ing** n.

my·thol·o·gy (mĭ-thŏl′ə-jē) n., pl. **-gies.** 1. A body of myths about the origin and history of a people. 2. The study of myths. **—myth′o·log′i·cal** (mĭth′ə-lŏj′ĭ-kəl) adj. **—myth′o·log′i·cal·ly** adv. **—my·thol′o·gist** n.

Nn

n or **N** (ĕn) *n., pl.* **n's** or **N's.** The 14th letter of the English alphabet.

N The symbol for the element nitrogen.

Na The symbol for the element sodium. [< NLat. *natrium,* ult. < Gk. *nitron,* soda.]

nab (năb) *v.* **nabbed, nab·bing.** *Slang.* **1.** To seize and arrest. **2.** To grab. [Perh. < dial. *nap,* to seize.]

na·bob (nā′bŏb′) *n.* A man of wealth or prominence. [< Ar. *na'ib,* deputy.]

na·celle (nə-sĕl′) *n.* A streamlined enclosure on an aircraft for housing an engine or sheltering the crew. [Fr., ult. < Lat. *navis,* ship.]

na·cre (nā′kər) *n.* Mother-of-pearl. [< Ar. *naqqārah,* drum.] —**na′cre·ous** (-krē-əs) *adj.*

Na-Den·e (nä-dĕn′ē) *n.* Also **Na-Dé·né.** A phylum of North American Indian languages spoken in western North America from Alaska to Mexico.

na·dir (nā′dər, -dîr′) *n.* **1.** A point on the celestial sphere diametrically opposite the zenith. **2.** The lowest point. [< Ar. *naḍīr assamt,* opposite the zenith.]

nae (nā) *adv. Scot.* **1.** No. **2.** Not.

nag¹ (năg) *v.* **nagged, nag·ging. 1.** To annoy by constant scolding, complaining, or urging. **2.** To torment persistently, as by anxiety. **3.** To scold, complain, or find fault constantly: *nagged at the child.* —*n.* One who nags. [Prob. of Scand. orig.] —**nag′ger** *n.* —**nag′ging·ly** *adv.*

nag² (năg) *n.* A horse, esp. an old or worn-out horse. [ME.]

Na·hua·tl (nä′wät′l) *n., pl.* **-tl** or **-tls. 1. a.** A group of Mexican and Central American Indian tribes, including the Aztecs. **b.** A member of any of these tribes. **2.** The Uto-Aztecan language of the Nahuatl.

Na·hum (nā′həm, nā′əm) *n.* See table at Bible.

nai·ad (nā′ăd, -ăd′, nī′-) *n., pl.* **-ads** or **-a·des** (-ə-dēz′). *Gk. Myth.* One of the nymphs living in brooks, springs, and fountains. [Gk. *naias.*]

nail (nāl) *n.* **1.** A slim, pointed piece of metal, often with a head, hammered into wood or other material as a fastener. **2.** A fingernail or toenail. —*v.* **1.** To fasten with or as with nails. **2.** To cover, enclose, or shut by fastening with nails: *nail up a window.* **3.** *Slang.* To

nail

seize; catch: *The police nailed the thief.* **4.** *Informal.* To strike; hit. —*phrasal verb.* **nail down.** To settle clearly and definitely. [< OE *nægl.*] —**nail′er** *n.*

nain·sook (nān′sŏŏk′) *n.* A soft, light cotton material. [< Hindi *nainsukh,* pleasant.]

nai·ra (nī′rə) *n.* See table at **currency.** [< *Nigeria.*]

na·ive or **na·ïve** (nä-ēv′) *adj.* **-iv·er, -iv·est.** Also **na·if** or **na·ïf** (nä-ēf′). Lacking worldliness and sophistication; artless; ingenuous. [< Lat. *nativus,* natural.] —**na·ive′ly** *adv.* —**na·ive′ness** *n.*

na·ive·té or **na·ïve·té** (nä′ēv-tā′) *n.* Also **na·ive·ty** or **na·ïve·ty** (nä-ēv′ĭ-tē) *n.* **-ties. 1.** The quality of being naive. **2.** A naive statement or action. [Fr.]

na·ked (nā′kĭd) *adj.* **1.** Without clothing; nude. **2.** Without covering. **3.** Without addition, disguise, or embellishment: *naked fear.* [< OE *nacod.*] —**na′ked·ly** *adv.* —**na′ked·ness** *n.*

naked eye *n.* The eye unassisted by an optical instrument.

nam·by-pam·by (năm′bē-păm′bē) *adj.* **1.** Insipid and sentimental. **2.** Lacking vigor or decisiveness. [< *Namby-Pamby,* a satire on Ambrose Philips (1675?-1749) by Henry Carey (d. 1743).] —**nam′by-pam′by** *n.*

name (nām) *n.* **1.** A word or words by which an entity is designated. **2.** A disparaging designation: *Names will never hurt me.* **3.** Appearance rather than reality: *a democracy in name only.* **4.** Reputation; renown. **5.** *Informal.* One that is famous. —*v.* **named, nam·ing. 1.** To give a name to. **2.** To mention, specify, or identify by name. **3.** To nominate or appoint. **4.** To specify or fix: *named the time and date.* —**idioms. in the name of. 1.** For the sake of. **2.** By the authority of. **to (one's) name.** Among one's possessions. [< OE *nama.*] —**nam′a·ble** or **name′a·ble** *adj.* —**nam′er** *n.*

Syns: name, appellation, cognomen, denomination, designation *n.*

name·less (nām′lĭs) *adj.* **1.** Having no name. **2.** Not known by name; anonymous. **3.** Inexpressible; indescribable. —**name′less·ly** *adv.* —**name′less·ness** *n.*

name·ly (nām′lē) *adv.* That is to say; specifically.

name·sake (nām′sāk′) *n.* One named after another.

nan·keen (-kēn′) *n.* Also **nan·kin** (năn-kēn′, -kĭn′). A sturdy yellow or buff cotton cloth. [< *Nanjing* (Nanking), China.]

nanny goat *n.* A female goat. [< *Nanny,* nickname for *Ann.*]

nap¹ (năp) *n.* A brief sleep, usu. during the day. —*v.* **napped, nap·ping. 1.** To doze or sleep for a brief period. **2.** To be unprepared. [< OE *hnappian.*]

nap² (năp) *n.* A fuzzy surface on cloth or leather. [< MDu. *noppe*.] —**nap'less** *adj.*

na·palm (nā'päm') *n.* 1. An aluminum soap that is mixed with gasoline to make a jelly. 2. A jelly that consists of gasoline mixed with napalm, used in flame throwers and fire bombs. [*Na(phthenate)* + *palm(itate)*, substances used in its composition.]

nape (nāp) *n.* The back of the neck. [ME.]

na·per·y (nā'pǝ-rē) *n.* Household linen, esp. table linen. [< Lat. *mappa*, napkin.]

naph·tha (năf'thǝ, năp'-) *n.* A colorless flammable liquid, obtained from crude petroleum, used as a solvent and a raw material for gasoline. [Gk.]

naph·tha·lene (năf'thǝ-lēn', năp'-) *n.* A white crystalline compound, $C_{10}H_8$, used to manufacture dyes, moth repellents, explosives, and solvents. [NAPHTH(A) + AL(COHOL) + -ENE.]

nap·kin (năp'kĭn) *n.* 1. A piece of cloth or absorbent paper, used while eating to protect one's clothes or wipe one's lips or fingers. 2. A cloth or towel. [< Lat. *mappa*.]

narc or **nark** (närk) *n.* *Slang.* A narcotics agent.

nar·cis·sism (när'sĭ-sĭz'ǝm) *n.* Excessive admiration of oneself. [< NARCISSUS.] —**nar'cis·sist** *n.* —**nar'cis·sis'tic** *adj.*

nar·cis·sus (när-sĭs'ǝs) *n.*, *pl.* **-es** or **-cis·si** (-sĭs'ī', -sĭs'ē). 1. A widely cultivated plant having grasslike leaves and white or yellow flowers with a cup-shaped or trumpet-shaped central crown. 2. **Narcissus.** *Gk. Myth.* A youth who fell in love with his own image in a pool of water and was transformed into a flower. [Gk. *narkissos*.]

nar·co·sis (när-kō'sĭs) *n.*, *pl.* **-ses** (-sēz'). Deep unconsciousness produced by a drug. [Gk. *narkōsis*, a numbing.]

nar·cot·ic (när-kŏt'ĭk) *n.* A drug that dulls the senses, induces sleep, and becomes addictive with prolonged use. [< Gk. *narkōtikos*, numbing.] —**nar·cot'ic** *adj.* —**nar·cot'i·cal·ly** *adv.*

nar·co·tize (när'kǝ-tīz') *v.* **-tized, -tiz·ing.** 1. To place under the influence of a narcotic. 2. To put to sleep; lull.

nard (närd) *n.* Spikenard. [< Gk. *nardos*.]

nar·is (nâr'ĭs) *n.*, *pl.* **-es** (-ēz). An opening in the nasal cavity of a vertebrate; nostril. [Lat.]

Nar·ra·gan·set (năr'ǝ-găn'sĭt) *n.*, *pl.* **-set** or **-sets.** 1. a. A tribe of Indians that formerly inhabited the area of Rhode Island. b. A member of this tribe. 2. The Algonquian language of the Narraganset. —**Nar'ra·gan'set** *adj.*

nar·rate (när'āt', nă-rāt') *v.* **-rat·ed, -rat·ing.** To give an account or commentary. [Lat. *narrare*.] —**nar·ra'tion** *n.* —**nar·ra'tor** *n.*

nar·ra·tive (năr'ǝ-tĭv) *n.* 1. A story or description of actual or fictional events. 2. The act, technique, or process of narrating. —**nar'ra·tive** *adj.* —**nar'ra·tive·ly** *adv.*

nar·row (năr'ō) *adj.* **-er, -est.** 1. Of small or slender width. 2. Limited in area or scope; cramped. 3. Lacking flexibility; rigid. 4. Barely sufficient: *a narrow margin of victory.* —*v.* To make or become narrow or narrower. —*n.* **narrows.** A narrow body of water connecting two larger ones. [< OE *nearu*.] —**nar'row·ly** *adv.* —**nar'row·ness** *n.*

nar·row-mind·ed (năr'ō-mīn'dĭd) *adj.* Lacking breadth of view or tolerance; bigoted. —**nar'row-mind'ed·ly** *adv.* —**nar'row-mind'ed·ness** *n.*

nar·whal (när'wǝl) *n.* A whalelike mammal of arctic seas, with a long, spirally twisted tusk. [< ON *náhvalr.*]

narwhal
Female (*above*) and male (*below*)

na·sal (nā'zǝl) *adj.* 1. Of or relating to the nose. 2. Uttered so that most of the air is exhaled through the nose: *a nasal twang.* [< Lat. *nasus*, nose.] —**na·sal'i·ty** (-zăl'ĭ-tē) *n.* —**na'sal·ly** *adv.*

nas·cent (năs'ǝnt, nā'sǝnt) *adj.* Coming into existence; in the process of emerging. [< Lat. *nasci*, to be born.] —**nas'cence** *n.*

na·stur·tium (nǝ-stûr'shǝm, nă-) *n.* A plant with showy orange or yellow flowers and pungent leaves and seeds. [Lat., a kind of cress.]

nas·ty (năs'tē) *adj.* **-ti·er, -ti·est.** 1. Disgustingly dirty; filthy; foul. 2. Malicious; spiteful. 3. Unpleasant: *nasty weather.* 4. Painful and dangerous: *a nasty accident.* [ME *nasti*, of Scand. orig.] —**nas'ti·ly** *adv.* —**nas'ti·ness** *n.*

na·tal (nāt'l) *adj.* 1. Of, relating to, or accompanying birth. 2. Of or pertaining to the time or place of one's birth. [< Lat. *natus*, p.p. of *nasci*, to be born.]

na·tal·i·ty (nā-tăl'ĭ-tē, nǝ-) *n.*, *pl.* **-ties.** Birthrate.

na·ta·to·ri·um (nā'tǝ-tôr'ē-ǝm, -tōr', năt'ǝ-) *n.*, *pl.* **-ums** or **-to·ri·a** (-tôr'ē-ǝ, -tōr'-). An indoor swimming pool. [< Lat. *natare*, to swim.]

Natch·ez (năch'ĭz) *n.*, *pl.* **-ez.** 1. a. A tribe of Indians formerly living in the area of Mississippi. b. A member of this tribe. 2. The Muskhogean language of the Natchez. —**Natch'ez** *adj.*

Na·tick (nā'tĭk) *n.* A dialect of Massachuset.

na·tion (nā'shǝn) *n.* 1. An aggregation of people organized under a single government. 2. A federation or tribe, esp. one composed of North American Indians. [< Lat. *natio*.] —**na'tion·hood** *n.*

na·tion·al (năsh'ǝ-nǝl, năsh'nǝl) *adj.* 1. Of, relating to, or belonging to a nation as a whole. 2. Characteristic of or peculiar to the people of a nation. —*n.* A citizen of a particular nation. —**na'tion·al·ly** *adv.*

National Guard *n.* The military reserve unit of each U.S. state, equipped by the federal government and subject to the call of either the federal or state government.

na·tion·al·ism (năsh'ǝ-nǝ-lĭz'ǝm, năsh'nǝ-) *n.* 1. Devotion to the interests or culture of a particular nation. 2. Aspirations for national independence. —**na'tion·al·ist** *n.* —**na'tion·al·is'tic** *adj.* —**na'tion·al·is'ti·cal·ly** *adv.*

na·tion·al·i·ty (năsh'ǝ-năl'ĭ-tē) *n.*, *pl.* **-ties.** 1. The status of belonging to a particular nation by origin, birth, or naturalization. 2. A people having common origins or traditions and often constituting a nation.

na·tion·al·ize (năsh′ə-nə-līz′, năsh′nə-) v. **-ized, -iz·ing. 1.** To convert from private to governmental ownership and control. **2.** To make national. **—na′tion·al·i·za′tion** n.

national monument n. A landmark, structure, or site of historic interest maintained by a national government for enjoyment or study by the public.

national park n. An area of land maintained by a national government for the recreational and cultural use of the public.

na·tion·wide (nā′shən-wīd′) adj. Throughout a whole nation.

na·tive (nā′tĭv) adj. **1.** Inborn; innate. **2.** Being such by birth or origin. **3.** One's own by birth: *one's native language.* **4.** Originating or produced in a certain place; indigenous. *—n.* **1.** One born in or connected with a place by birth. **2. a.** An original inhabitant. **b.** A lifelong resident. **3.** Something, esp. an animal or a plant, that is native to a particular place. [< Lat. *nativus.*] **—na′tive·ly** adv. **—na′tive·ness** n.

Native American n. An American Indian.

Usage: Native American is the term many now prefer to designate the original inhabitants of the Western Hemisphere. Usage, however, varies according to tribe and region; in Canada and Alaska, *American Indian* is still preferred as the term for all indigenous inhabitants other than the Eskimos.

na·tiv·i·ty (nə-tĭv′ĭ-tē, nā-) n., pl. **-ties. 1.** Birth, esp. the conditions or circumstances of being born. **2. Nativity. a.** The birth of Jesus. **b.** Christmas. [< Lat. *nativitas.*]

nat·ty (năt′ē) adj. **-ti·er, -ti·est** *Informal.* Neat, trim, and smart. [Perh. < ME *net,* neat.] **—nat′ti·ly** adv. **—nat′ti·ness** n.

nat·u·ral (năch′ər-əl, năch′rəl) adj. **1.** Present in or produced by nature; not artificial. **2.** Of, relating to, or concerning nature. **3.** Conforming to the usual course of nature: *a natural death.* **4. a.** Inherent; innate. **b.** Distinguished by innate qualities or aptitudes. **5.** Free from affectation. **6.** Consonant with particular circumstances; expected and accepted. **7.** *Mus.* Not sharped or flatted. *—n.* **1.** *Informal.* One obviously suited or qualified: *a natural for the job.* **2.** *Mus.* The sign (♮) placed before a note to cancel a preceding sharp or flat. **—nat′u·ral·ness** n.

natural gas n. A mixture of hydrocarbon gases, principally methane, occurring with petroleum deposits and used as a fuel and in the manufacture of organic compounds.

natural history n. The study of natural objects and organisms and their origins and interrelationships.

nat·u·ral·ism (năch′ər-ə-lĭz′əm, năch′rə-) n. **1.** Factual or realistic representation, esp. in art and literature. **2.** The view that all phenomena can be explained in terms of natural causes and laws. **—nat′u·ral·is′tic** adj.

nat·u·ral·ist (năch′ər-ə-lĭst, năch′rə-) n. **1.** One who specializes in natural history, esp. in the study of plants and animals in their natural environments. **2.** One who believes in and follows the tenets of naturalism.

nat·u·ral·ize (năch′ər-ə-līz′, năch′rə-) v. **-ized, -iz·ing. 1.** To grant full citizenship to. **2.** To adopt into general use. **3.** To adapt or acclimate (a plant or animal) to life in a new environment. **—nat′u·ral·i·za′tion** n.

nat·u·ral·ly (năch′ər-ə-lē, năch′rə-) adv. **1.** In a natural manner. **2.** By nature; inherently. **3.** Without a doubt; of course.

natural resource n. A material source of wealth, such as timber, fresh water, or a mineral deposit, that occurs in a natural state.

natural science n. A science, such as biology, chemistry, or physics, based chiefly on objective quantitative hypotheses.

natural selection n. The principle that individuals possessing characteristics advantageous for survival in a specific environment constitute an increasing proportion of their species in that environment with each succeeding generation.

na·ture (nā′chər) n. **1.** The intrinsic character of a person or thing. **2.** The order, disposition, and essence of all entities composing the physical universe. **3.** The physical world, including living things, natural phenomena, etc. **4.** The primitive state of existence. **5.** Kind; type: *something of that nature.* **6.** Disposition; temperament: *a sweet nature.* [< Lat. *natura.*] **—na′tured** adj.

naught (nôt) n. Also **nought. 1.** Nothing. **2.** A cipher; zero. [< OE *nāwiht.*]

naugh·ty (nô′tē) adj. **-ti·er, -ti·est. 1.** Disobedient; mischievous: *a naughty child.* **2.** Improper. **—naugh′ti·ly** adv. **—naugh′ti·ness** n.

nau·se·a (nô′zē-ə, -zhə, -sē-ə, -shə) n. **1.** A stomach disturbance characterized by a feeling of the need to vomit. **2.** Extreme disgust. [< Gk. *nausia,* seasickness.]

nau·se·ate (nô′zē-āt′, -zhē-, -sē-, -shē-) v. **-at·ed, -at·ing.** To feel or cause to feel nausea or queasiness. **—nau′se·at′ing·ly** adv. **—nau′se·a′tion** n.

nau·seous (nô′shəs, -zē-əs) adj. **1.** Causing nausea; sickening. **2.** Feeling nausea. **—nau′seous·ly** adv.

nau·ti·cal (nô′tĭ-kəl) adj. Of, relating to, or characteristic of ships, shipping, seamen, or navigation. [< Gk. *naus,* ship.] **—nau′ti·cal·ly** adv.

nautical mile n. A unit of length used in sea and air navigation equal to 1,852 meters or about 6,076 feet.

nau·ti·lus (nôt′l-əs) n., pl. **-es** or **-li** (-lī′). A tropical marine mollusk with a partitioned spiral shell. [< Gk. *nautilos,* sailor.]

Nav·a·ho (năv′ə-hō′, näv′ə-) n., pl. **-ho** or **-hos** or **-hoes.** Also **Nav·a·jo** pl. **-jo** or **-jos** or **-joes. 1. a.** A group of Indians occupying an extensive reservation in parts of New Mexico, Arizona, and Utah. **b.** A member of this group. **2.** The Athapascan language of the Navaho. **—Nav′a·ho′** adj.

na·val (nā′vəl) adj. Of, pertaining to, or possessing a navy.

nave (nāv) n. The central part of a church. [< Lat. *navis,* ship.]

na·vel (nā′vəl) n. The mark on the abdomen of mammals where the umbilical cord was attached during gestation. [< OE *nafela.*]

navel orange n. An orange with a navellike formation opposite the stem end.

nav·i·ga·ble (năv′ĭ-gə-bəl) adj. **1.** Deep or wide enough to provide passage for vessels.

2. Capable of being steered. —**nav'i-ga-bil'i-ty** or **nav'i-ga-ble-ness** n. —**nav'i-ga-bly** adv.

nav-i-gate (năv'ĭ-gāt') v. **-gat-ed, -gat-ing.** 1. To control the course of a ship or aircraft. 2. To voyage over water in a boat or ship; sail. 3. *Informal.* To make one's way; walk. [Lat. *navigare.*] —**nav'i-ga'tion** n. —**nav'i-ga'tion-al** adj. —**nav'i-ga'tor** n.

na-vy (nā'vē) n., pl. **-vies.** 1. All of a nation's warships. 2. Often **Navy.** A nation's entire military organization for sea warfare and defense. [< Lat. *navis,* ship.]

navy blue n. A dark blue. [< the color of the British naval uniform.] —**na'vy-blue'** adj.

nay (nā) adv. 1. No. 2. And moreover: *He was ill-favored, nay, hideous.* —n. 1. A denial. 2. A negative vote. [< ON *nei.*]

Na-zi (năt'sē, nät'-) n., pl. **-zis.** A member or supporter of the fascist National Socialist German Workers' Party, brought to power in 1933 under Adolf Hitler. —**Na'zi** adj. —**Na'zism** or **Na'zi-ism** n.

Nb The symbol for the element niobium.

Nd The symbol for the element neodymium.

Ne The symbol for the element neon.

Ne-an-der-thal (nē-ăn'dər-thôl', -tôl', nā-än'dər-täl') adj. 1. Of, pertaining to, or designating an extinct primitive man of the Stone Age. 2. Crude, primitive, or boorish. [< *Neanderthal,* a valley near Düsseldorf, West Germany.]

neap tide (nēp) n. A tide of lowest range. [< OE *nēp(flōd),* neap (tide).]

near (nîr) adv. **-er, -est.** 1. To, at, or within a short distance or interval in space or time. 2. Almost; nearly: *near exhausted by the heat.* 3. With or in a close relationship. —adj. **-er, -est.** 1. Close in time, space, position, or degree: *near equals.* 2. Closely related; intimate. 3. Failing or succeeding by a small margin: *a near miss.* 4. Closer of two or more. —prep. Close to: *an inn near London.* —v. To come closer or closer to; draw near. [< OE *nēah.*] —**near'ness** n.

Syns: *near, close, immediate, nearby, nigh* adj.

near-by (nîr'bī') adj. & adv. Not far away; adjacent.

near-ly (nîr'lē) adv. Almost but not quite.

near-sight-ed (nîr'sī'tĭd) adj. Unable to see distant objects clearly; myopic. —**near'sight'ed-ly** adv. —**near'sight'ed-ness** n.

neat (nēt) adj. **-er, -est.** 1. Orderly and clean; tidy. 2. Skillfully executed; adroit: *a neat turn of phrase.* 3. Not diluted with other substances: *neat whiskey.* 4. *Slang.* Wonderful; terrific: *a neat party.* [< Lat. *nitidus,* elegant.] —**neat'ly** adv. —**neat'ness** n.

Syns: *neat, orderly, shipshape, tidy, trim* adj.

neath or **'neath** (nēth) prep. *Poet.* Beneath.

neat's-foot oil (nēts'foot') n. A light, yellow oil obtained from the feet and shinbones of cattle, used chiefly to process leather. [< *neat,* cow.]

neb (nĕb) n. 1. a. A beak of a bird. b. A nose; snout. 2. A nib. [< OE.]

neb-u-la (nĕb'yə-lə) n., pl. **-lae** (-lē', -lī') or **-las.** *Astron.* A diffuse mass of interstellar gas or dust. [Lat., cloud.] —**neb'u-lar** adj.

neb-u-lize (nĕb'yə-līz') v. **-lized, -liz-ing.** To convert (a liquid) to a fine spray. —**neb'u-li-za'tion** n. —**neb'u-liz'er** n.

neb-u-los-i-ty (nĕb'yə-lŏs'ĭ-tē) n., pl. **-ties.** 1. The condition or quality of being nebulous. 2. A nebula.

neb-u-lous (nĕb'yə-ləs) adj. 1. Lacking definite form or limits; vague. 2. Of or characteristic of a nebula. —**neb'u-lous-ly** adv. —**neb'u-lous-ness** n.

nec-es-sar-i-ly (nĕs'ĭ-sâr'ə-lē) adv. Of necessity; inevitably.

nec-es-sar-y (nĕs'ĭ-sĕr'ē) adj. 1. Absolutely essential; indispensable. 2. a. Inevitably or unavoidably determined. b. Logically inevitable. 3. Required, as by obligation, compulsion, or convention. —n., pl. **-ies.** Something that is indispensable or necessary. [< Lat. *necesse.*]

ne-ces-si-tate (nə-sĕs'ĭ-tāt') v. **-tat-ed, -tat-ing.** To make necessary or unavoidable. —**ne-ces'si-ta'tion** n.

ne-ces-si-tous (nə-sĕs'ĭ-təs) adj. Needy; destitute. —**ne-ces'si-tous-ly** adv.

ne-ces-si-ty (nə-sĕs'ĭ-tē) n., pl. **-ties.** 1. a. The condition or quality of being necessary. b. Something that is necessary. 2. The force exerted by circumstance. 3. Pressing or urgent need. [< Lat. *necessitas.*]

neck (nĕk) n. 1. The part of the body joining the head to the trunk. 2. The part of a garment around or near the neck. 3. A relatively narrow elongation or connecting part: *the neck of a bottle; a neck of land.* 4. a. The length of the head and neck of a horse: *won by a neck.* b. *Slang.* A narrow margin by which a competition is won or lost. —**idiom.** **neck and neck.** Even in a race or contest. —v. *Slang.* To kiss and caress. [< OE *hnecca.*] —**necked** adj.

neck-er-chief (nĕk'ər-chĭf) n. A kerchief worn around the neck.

neck-lace (nĕk'lĭs) n. An ornament worn around the neck.

neck-line (nĕk'līn') n. The line formed by the edge of a garment at the neck.

neck-tie (nĕk'tī') n. A narrow band of fabric worn around the neck and tied in a knot or bow.

necro- or **necr-** pref. Death or the dead: *necrology.* [< Gk. *nekros,* corpse.]

ne-crol-o-gy (nə-krŏl'ə-jē, nĕ-) n., pl. **-gies.** 1. A list of people who have died, esp. in the recent past. 2. An obituary. —**nec'ro-log'ic** (nĕk'rə-lŏj'ĭk) or **nec'ro-log'i-cal** adj. —**ne-crol'o-gist** n.

nec-ro-man-cy (nĕk'rə-măn'sē) n. 1. The art that professes to conjure up and commune with the spirits of the dead in order to predict the future. 2. Black magic; sorcery. [NECRO- + Gk. *manteia,* divination.] —**nec'ro-man'cer** n. —**nec'ro-man'tic** adj.

ne-crop-o-lis (nə-krŏp'ə-lĭs, nĕ-) n., pl. **-es** or **-leis** (-lās'). A large and elaborate cemetery esp. of an ancient city. [NECRO- + Gk. *polis,* city.]

ne-cro-sis (nə-krō'sĭs, nĕ-) n., pl. **-ses** (-sēz'). The pathologic death of living tissue. —**ne-crot'ic** (-krŏt'ĭk) adj.

nec-tar (nĕk'tər) n. 1. *Gk. & Rom. Myth.* The drink of the gods. 2. A delicious drink. 3. A sweet liquid secreted by flowers. [< Gk. *nektar.*] —**nec'tar-ous** adj.

nec-tar-ine (nĕk'tə-rēn') n. A smooth-skinned variety of peach. [< obs. *nectarine,* sweet as nectar.]

née or **nee** (nā) adj. Born: *Mary Smith, née Jones.* [< Fr. *naître,* to be born.]

need (nēd) n. 1. A lack of something required or desirable. 2. Necessity; obligation. 3. Something required or wanted; requisite. 4. Poverty. —v. 1. Used with an infinitive to express necessity or obligation: *He needs to* *study.* **2.** To want urgently; require. **3.** To be in want. **—*idiom.* If need be.** If necessary. [< OE *nēod.*]

Usage: Need, as an auxiliary verb, is not inflected in the 3rd person singular present tense in negative statements and questions: *He need not come. Need it have happened?*

need·ful (nēd'fəl) *adj.* Necessary; required. **—need'ful·ly** *adv.* **—need'ful·ness** *n.*

nee·dle (nēd'l) *n.* **1. a.** A slender sewing implement, made of steel with a point at one end and an eye at the other to hold thread. **b.** Any of various implements similar in shape and use, as a knitting needle. **2.** A stylus used to transmit vibrations from the grooves of a phonograph record. **3.** A slender pointer or indicator, as on a dial. **4.** A hypodermic needle. **5.** A stiff, narrow leaf, as of a pine. **6.** A fine, sharp projection, as a spine of a sea urchin. *—v.* **-dled, -dling.** *Informal.* To goad, provoke, or tease. [< OE *nǣdl.*]

nee·dle·point (nēd'l-point') *n.* **1.** Decorative needlework on canvas. **2.** A type of lace worked on paper patterns with a needle.

needlepoint

need·less (nēd'lĭs) *adj.* Not needed; unnecessary. **—need'less·ly** *adv.* **—need'less·ness** *n.*

nee·dle·work (nēd'l-wûrk') *n.* Work, esp. embroidery, done with a needle. **—nee'dle·work'er** *n.*

need·n't (nēd'nt). Need not.

needs (nēdz) *adv.* Necessarily: *He must needs go.* [< OE *nēde.*]

need·y (nē'dē) *adj.* **-i·er, -i·est.** Being in need; impoverished. **—need'i·ness** *n.*

ne'er (nâr) *adv. Poetic.* Never.

ne'er-do-well (nâr'dōō-wěl') *n.* A worthless, irresponsible person. **—ne'er-do-well'** *adj.*

ne·far·i·ous (nə-fâr'ē-əs) *adj.* Evil; wicked. [< Lat. *nefas,* sin.] **—ne·far'i·ous·ly** *adv.* **—ne·far'i·ous·ness** *n.*

ne·gate (nə-gāt') *v.* **-gat·ed, -gat·ing.** **1.** To make ineffective or invalid. **2.** To deny. [Lat. *negare,* to deny.]

ne·ga·tion (nə-gā'shən) *n.* **1.** The act of negating. **2.** A negative statement.

neg·a·tive (něg'ə-tĭv) *adj.* **1.** Expressing negation, refusal, or denial. **2.** Not positive or constructive: *negative criticism.* **3.** Pertaining to or denoting a quantity less than zero or a quantity, number, angle, velocity, or direction in a sense opposite to another indicated or understood to be positive. **4.** Pertaining to or denoting electric charge of the same sign as that of an electron, designated by the symbol (-). *—n.* **1.** A negative word, statement, or concept. **2.** The side opposing the opinion

upheld by the affirmative side in a debate. **3. a.** An image in which the light areas of the object rendered appear dark and the dark areas appear light. **b.** A film, plate, or other photographic material containing such an image. *—v.* **-tived, -tiv·ing.** **1.** To refuse to approve; veto. **2.** To deny; contradict. **—neg'a·tive·ly** *adv.* **—neg'a·tive·ness** or **neg'a·tiv'i·ty** *n.*

neg·a·tiv·ism (něg'ə-tĭ-vĭz'əm) *n.* A habitual attitude of skepticism or resistance to the beliefs, suggestions, or instructions of others. **—neg'a·tiv·ist** *n.* **—neg'a·tiv·is'tic** *adj.*

ne·glect (nĭ-glĕkt') *v.* **1.** To ignore; disregard. **2.** To fail to care for or give proper attention to. **3.** To fail to do through carelessness or oversight. *—n.* **1.** The act or an example of neglecting. **2.** The condition of being neglected. [Lat. *neglegere.*] **—ne·glect'er** or **ne·glec'tor** *n.*

ne·glect·ful (nĭ-glĕkt'fəl) *adj.* Marked by neglect; heedless. **—ne·glect'ful·ly** *adv.* **—ne·glect'ful·ness** *n.*

neg·li·gee (něg'lǐ-zhā', něg'lĭ-zhā') *n.* A woman's long, loose dressing gown. [Fr.]

neg·li·gence (něg'lǐ-jəns) *n.* **1.** The condition or quality of being negligent. **2.** *Law.* The omission or neglect of any reasonable precaution, care, or action.

neg·li·gent (něg'lǐ-jənt) *adj.* **1.** Habitually guilty of neglect. **2.** Extremely careless or casual. [< Lat. *neglegere,* to neglect.] **—neg'li·gent·ly** *adv.*

neg·li·gi·ble (něg'lǐ-jə-bəl) *adj.* Worthy of neglect; trifling. **—neg'li·gi·bil'i·ty** *n.* **—neg'li·gi·bly** *adv.*

ne·go·ti·a·ble (nĭ-gō'shə-bəl, -shē-ə-) *adj.* **1.** Capable of being negotiated. **2.** Capable of being legally transferred from one person to another. **—ne·go'tia·bil'i·ty** *n.*

ne·go·ti·ate (nĭ-gō'shē-āt') *v.* **-at·ed, -at·ing.** **1.** To confer with another in order to come to terms. **2.** To arrange by conferring: *negotiate a contract.* **3.** To transfer title to or ownership of (e.g. documents) to another party in return for value received. **4.** To succeed in going over, accomplishing, or coping with: *negotiate a sharp curve.* [< Lat. *negotium,* business.] **—ne·go'ti·a'tion** *n.* **—ne·go'ti·a'tor** *n.*

ne·gri·tude (něg'rǐ-tōōd', -tyōōd', něg'rǐ-) *n.* Awareness of and pride in the culture and history of blacks. [< Fr. *négritude.*]

Ne·gro (nē'grō) *n., pl.* **-groes.** **1.** A member of the Negroid ethnic division of the human species. **2.** A person of Negro descent. **—Ne'gro** *adj.*

Ne·groid (nē'groid') *adj.* Of, relating to, or designating a major ethnic division of the human species whose members are characterized by brown to black pigmentation and often by tightly curled hair. **—Ne'groid** *n.*

Ne·he·mi·ah (nē'hə-mī'ə, nē'ə-) *n.* See table at Bible.

neigh (nā) *n.* The long, high-pitched sound made by a horse. [< OE *hnǣgan,* to neigh.] **—neigh** *v.*

neigh·bor (nā'bər) Also *chiefly Brit.* **neigh·bour.** *n.* One who lives or is located near another. *—v.* To lie close to; live or be situated close by. [< OE *nēahgebūr.*]

neigh·bor·hood (nā'bər-hōōd') *n.* **1.** A district

or area with distinctive characteristics. **2.** The people who live in a particular area or district. **—idiom. in the neighborhood of.** Near or approximately: *in the neighborhood of a million dollars.*

neigh·bor·ly (nā′bər-lē) *adj.* Of or showing the feelings of a friendly neighbor. **—neigh′bor·li·ness** *n.*

nei·ther (nē′thər, nī′-) *adj.* Not either; not one nor the other: *Neither shoe fits comfortably.* **—pron.** Not either one; not the one nor the other: *Neither of them fits.* **—conj. 1.** Used with *nor* to mark two negative alternatives; not either: *They had neither seen nor heard of us.* **2.** Nor: *So you don't have a job? Neither do I.* [< OE *nāwther.*]

Usage: According to the traditional rule, the pronoun *neither* is construed as singular: *Neither of the houses is* (not *are*) *finished.* Accordingly, a pronoun that refers to *neither* should also be singular: *Neither of the authors is likely to reveal his* (not *their*) *indentity.*

nel·son (něl′sən) *n.* A wrestling hold in which the user places an arm under the opponent's arm and applies pressure with the palm of the hand against the opponent's back. [Orig. unknown.]

nem·e·sis (něm′ĭ-sĭs) *n., pl.* **-ses** (-sēz′). **1.** *Nemesis. Gk. Myth.* The goddess of retributive justice or vengeance. **2.** One that is the cause of just punishment or retribution; avenger. **3.** Just punishment; retributive justice. **4.** An unbeatable rival.

neo- *pref.* New or recent: *neoplasm.* [< Gk. *neos,* new.]

ne·o·clas·si·cism (nē′ō-klăs′ĭ-sĭz′əm) *n.* A revival of classical aesthetics and forms, esp. in art, music, literature. **—ne′o·clas′sic** or **ne′o·clas′si·cal** *adj.*

ne·o·dym·i·um (nē′ō-dĭm′ē-əm) *n.* **Symbol Nd** A bright, metallic, rare-earth element, used for coloring glass and in some lasers. Atomic number 60; atomic weight 144.24. [NEO- + (*di*)*dymium,* a mixture of rare-earth elements.]

Ne·o·lith·ic (nē′ə-lĭth′ĭk) *adj.* Of or denoting the period of human culture that began around 10,000 B.C. in the Middle East and was characterized by the introduction of farming and the making and use of fairly advanced stone tools and implements. **—n.** The Neolithic Age.

ne·ol·o·gism (nē-ŏl′ə-jĭz′əm) *n.* A newly coined word or expression.

ne·on (nē′ŏn′) *n.* **Symbol Ne** An inert, gaseous element occurring in the atmosphere to the extent of 18 parts per million, and used in display and television tubes. Atomic number 10; atomic weight 20.183. [< Gk. *neos,* new.]

ne·o·phyte (nē′ə-fīt′) *n.* **1.** A recent convert. **2.** A beginner; novice. [< Gk. *neophutos.*]

ne·o·plasm (nē′ə-plăz′əm) *n.* An abnormal new growth of tissue; tumor. **—ne′o·plas′tic** *adj.*

ne·o·prene (nē′ə-prēn′) *n.* A tough synthetic rubber that is resistant to the effects of oils, solvents, heat, and weather. [NEO- + PR(O-PYL) + -ENE.]

Nep·al·ese (nĕp′ə-lēz′, -lēs′) *n., pl.* **-ese. 1.** A native or resident of Nepal. **2.** The Indic language of Nepal. **—Nep′al·ese′** *adj.*

ne·pen·the (nĭ-pĕn′thē) *n.* **1.** A legendary drug of ancient times, used as a remedy for grief. **2.** Something that eases suffering or sorrow. [Gk. *nēpenthes (pharmakon),* grief-banishing (drug).]

neph·ew (něf′yōō) *n.* A son of one's brother, sister, brother-in-law, or sister-in-law. [< Lat. *nepos.*]

neph·rite (něf′rīt′) *n.* A white to dark green variety of jade. [G. *Nephrit.*]

ne·phrit·ic (nə-frĭt′ĭk) *adj.* Of or pertaining to the kidneys.

ne·phri·tis (nə-frī′tĭs) *n.* Inflammation of the kidneys.

nephro- or **nephr-** *pref.* The kidney: *nephritis.* [< Gk. *nephros,* kidney.]

nep·o·tism (nĕp′ə-tĭz′əm) *n.* Preference or patronage given to relatives. [< Lat. *nepos,* nephew.] **—nep′o·tist** *n.*

Nep·tune (nĕp′tōōn′, -tyōōn′) *n.* **1.** *Rom. Myth.* The god of the sea. **2.** The 8th planet from the sun, having a sidereal period of revolution around the sun of 164.8 years at a mean distance of 14,000 miles, and a density 17.2 times that of Earth. **—Nep·tu′ni·an** *adj.*

nep·tu·ni·um (nĕp-tōō′nē-əm, -tyōō′-) *n.* **Symbol Np** A silvery, metallic, naturally radioactive element, found in trace quantities in uranium ores and produced synthetically by nuclear reactions. Atomic number 93; longest-lived isotope Np 237. [< NEPTUNE, the planet.]

nerve (nûrv) *n.* **1.** Any of the bundles of fibers interconnecting the central nervous system and the organs or parts of the body, capable of transmitting both sensory stimuli and motor impulses from one part of the body to another. **2. a.** Patience; endurance. **b.** Forcefulness; stamina. **c.** Courage. **d.** *Informal.* Audacity; effrontery. **3. nerves.** Nervous agitation caused by fear, anxiety, or stress; hysteria. **—v.** nerved, nerv·ing. To give strength or courage to. [Lat. *nervus.*]

nerve center *n.* A source or focus of power or control.

nerve gas *n.* A poisonous gas used in warfare that attacks the respiratory and central nervous systems.

nerve·less (nûrv′lĭs) *adj.* **1.** Lacking strength or energy. **2.** Calm; poised. **—nerve′less·ly** *adv.* **—nerve′less·ness** *n.*

nerve-rack·ing (nûrv′răk′ĭng) *adj.* Also **nerve-wrack·ing.** Intensely distressing.

nerv·ous (nûr′vəs) *adj.* **1.** Of, affecting, or having to do with the nerves or the nervous system. **2.** High-strung; jittery. **3.** Uneasy; anxious. **4.** Spirited: *a nervous, vibrant prose.* **—nerv′ous·ly** *adv.* **—nerv′ous·ness** *n.*

nervous breakdown *n.* A severe mental or emotional disorder.

nervous system *n.* A coordinating mechanism in most multicellular animals that regulates internal functions and responses to stimuli.

nerv·y (nûr′vē) *adj.* **-i·er, -i·est. 1.** Impudently confident; brazen. **2.** Marked by strength, energy, or endurance. **3.** Jumpy; nervous.

-ness *suff.* State, quality, or condition: *brightness.* [< OE.]

nest (nĕst) *n.* **1. a.** A container or shelter made by a bird for holding its eggs and young. **b.** A similar shelter, as for an insect, fish, or animal. **2. a.** A snug, cozy place. **3.** A den; haunt. **4.** A set of objects that can be stacked together. **—v. 1.** To build or occupy a nest. **2.** To fit or place snugly together. [< OE.]

nest egg *n.* A reserve sum of money.

nes·tle (nĕs′əl) *v.* **-tled, -tling. 1. a.** To settle snugly and comfortably. **b.** To lie in a sheltered location. **2.** To snuggle contentedly. [< OE *nestlian,* to make a nest.] **—nes′tler** *n.*

nest·ling (nĕst′lĭng) *n.* A bird too young to leave its nest.

net¹ (nĕt) *n.* **1.** An openwork meshed fabric. **2.** Something made of net, as a device used to capture animals or act as a barrier: *a fishing net; a mosquito net.* **3.** A barrier strung between two posts to divide a tennis, badminton, or volleyball court in half. **4.** Something that entraps. *—v.* **net·ted, net·ting.** To catch or surround in or as if in a net. [< OE *nett.*]

net² (nĕt) *adj.* **1.** Remaining after all deductions or adjustments have been made: *net profit.* **2.** Final; ultimate. *—n.* A net amount. *—v.* **net·ted, net·ting.** To bring in or clear as profit. [ME, neat.]

neth·er (nĕth′ər) *adj.* Lower or under: *the nether regions of the earth.* [< OE *nither,* down.]

net·tle (nĕt′l) *n.* A plant with toothed leaves covered with stinging hairs. *—v.* **-tled, -tling.** To annoy; irritate. [< OE *netele.*]

net·work (nĕt′wûrk′) *n.* **1.** An open fabric or structure in which cords, threads, or wires cross at regular intervals. **2.** A system or pattern made up of interconnecting parts. **3.** A chain of interconnected radio or television broadcasting stations, usu. sharing a large proportion of their programs.

neu·ral (nŏor′əl, nyŏor′-) *adj.* Of or pertaining to the nerves or nervous system.

neu·ral·gia (nŏo-rălʹjə, nyŏo-) *n.* Intense pain that occurs along a nerve. [NEUR(O)- + Gk. *algos,* pain.] **—neu·ralʹgic** *adj.*

neu·ras·the·ni·a (nŏor′əs-thē′nē-ə, nyŏor′-) *n.* A condition marked by fatigue, loss of energy and memory, and feelings of inadequacy. [NEUR(O)- + Gk. *asthenia,* weakness.] **—neu′ras·then′ic** (-thĕn′ĭk) *adj.* **—neu′·ras·then′i·cal·ly** *adv.*

neu·ri·tis (nŏo-rī′tĭs, nyŏo-) *n.* Inflammation of a nerve. **—neu·rit′ic** (-rĭt′ĭk) *adj.*

neuro- or **neur-** *pref.* Nerve or nervous system: *neuritis.* [< Gk. *neuron,* nerve.]

neu·rol·o·gy (nŏo-rŏl′ə-jē, nyŏo-) *n.* The medical science of the nervous system and its diseases and disorders. **—neu′ro·log′i·cal** *adj.* **—neu·rol′o·gist** *n.*

neu·ron (nŏor′ŏn′, nyŏor′-) *n.* Also **neu·rone** (-ōn′). A nerve cell consisting of a nucleated portion and cytoplasmic extensions, the cell body, the dendrites, and axons. [Gk. nerve.] **—neu·ron′ic** (-rŏn′ĭk) *adj.*

neu·ro·sis (nŏo-rō′sĭs, nyŏo-) *n., pl.* **-ses** (-sēz′). A disorder in which the function of the mind or emotions is disturbed with no apparent physical cause. **—neu·rot′ic** *adj. & n.* **—neu·rot′i·cal·ly** *adv.*

neu·ter (nŏo′tər, nyŏo′-) *adj.* **1.** *Gram.* Neither masculine nor feminine in gender. **2.** Lacking sex glands or sex organs. *—n.* **1.** *Gram.* **a.** The neuter gender. **b.** A neuter word. **2. a.** A castrated or spayed animal. **b.** An animal or plant with undeveloped sex glands or organs, as a worker in a colony of ants or bees. [< Lat., neither.] **—neu′ter** *v.*

neu·tral (nŏo′trəl, nyŏo′-) *adj.* **1.** Not allied with, supporting, or favoring any side in a war, dispute, or contest. **2.** Belonging to neither side nor party. **3.** Designating a color

with no hue; achromatic. **4.** *Chem.* Neither acid nor alkaline. **5.** *Physics.* Having a net electric charge of zero. *—n.* **1.** One that is neutral. **2.** A neutral color. **3.** A position in which a set of gears is disengaged. **—neu′tral·ly** *adv.*

neu·tral·ism (nŏo′trə-lĭz′əm, nyŏo′-) *n.* Neutrality. **—neu′tral·ist** *n.*

neu·tral·i·ty (nŏo-trăl′ĭ-tē, nyŏo-) *n.* The quality or condition of being neutral, esp. nonparticipation in war.

neu·tral·ize (nŏo′trə-līz′, nyŏo′-) *v.* **-ized, -iz·ing.** To make neutral or ineffective. **—neu′·tral·i·za′tion** *n.* **—neu′tral·iz′er** *n.*

neu·tri·no (nŏo-trē′nō, nyŏo-) *n., pl.* **-nos.** Either of two electrically neutral subatomic particles that interact weakly with matter. [Ital.]

neu·tron (nŏo′trŏn′, nyŏo′-) *n.* An electrically neutral subatomic particle having a mass 1,839 times that of the electron, stable when bound in an atomic nucleus, and having a mean lifetime of approx. 16.6 minutes as a free particle. [NEUTR(AL) + -ON.]

nev·er (nĕv′ər) *adv.* **1.** At no time; on no occasion; not ever. **2.** Not at all; in no way. [< OE *næfre.*]

nev·er·more (nĕv′ər-môr′, -mōr′) *adv.* Never again.

nev·er·the·less (nĕv′ər-thə-lĕs′) *adv.* None the less; however.

ne·vus (nē′vəs) *n., pl.* **-vi** (-vī′). A congenital growth or mark on the skin, such as a birthmark. [Lat. *naevus.*] **—ne′void′** (nē′void′) *adj.*

new (nŏo, nyŏo) *adj.* **-er, -est. 1. a.** Not old; recent. **b.** Used for the first time. **2.** Recently become known. **3.** Unfamiliar. **4.** Unaccustomed. **5.** Begun afresh. **6.** Refreshed; rejuvenated. **7.** Different and distinct from what was before. **8. a.** Modern; current. **b.** In the most recent form, period, or development of something: *New Latin.* *—adv.* Freshly; recently. [< OE *nīwe.*] **—new′ness** *n.*

new·born (nŏo′bôrn′, nyŏo′-) *adj.* **1.** Recently born. **2.** Reborn.

new·com·er (nŏo′kŭm′ər, nyŏo′-) *n.* One who has only recently arrived.

New Deal *n.* The programs and policies for economic recovery and reform, relief, and social security, introduced during the 1930's by President Franklin D. Roosevelt and his administration. **—New Dealer** *n.*

new·el (nŏo′əl, nyŏo′-) *n.* **1.** The upright support at the center of a circular staircase. **2.** A post at the bottom or landing of a staircase. [< OFr. *novel.*]

new·fan·gled (nŏo′făng′gəld, nyŏo′-) *adj.* New; novel. [< ME *neuefangel,* fond of novelty.]

New Latin *n.* Latin as used from 1500 to the present.

new·ly (nŏo′lē, nyŏo′-) *adv.* **1.** Lately; recently. **2.** Once more; anew. **3.** In a new or different way.

new·ly·wed (nŏo′lē-wĕd′, nyŏo′-) *n.* One recently married.

new math *n.* Also **new mathematics.** Mathematics based on set theory.

new moon *n.* **1.** The phase of the moon that occurs as it passes between the earth and the sun and is invisible or visible only as a thin crescent at sunset. **2.** The crescent moon.

---

news (nōōz, nyōōz) *pl.n. (used with a sing. verb).* **1.** Recent events and happenings. **2.** Written or broadcast information about recent events. **3.** Newsworthy material.

news·boy (nōōz'boi', nyōōz'-) *n.* A boy who sells or delivers newspapers.

news·cast (nōōz'kăst', nyōōz'-) *n.* A broadcast of news events. [NEWS + (BROAD)CAST.] **—news'cast'er** *n.*

news·let·ter (nōōz'lĕt'ər, nyōōz'-) *n.* A report, usu. giving news or information of interest to a special group.

news·man (nōōz'măn', -mən, nyōōz'-) *n.* One who gathers, reports, or edits news.

news·pa·per (nōōz'pā'pər, nyōōz'-) *n.* A publication, usu. issued daily or weekly, that contains current news, editorials, feature articles, and advertisements.

news·pa·per·man (nōōz'pā'pər-măn', nyōōz'-) *n.* One who owns or is employed on a newspaper. **—news'pa·per·wom'an** *n.*

news·print (nōōz'prĭnt', nyōōz'-) *n.* A cheap, thin paper used esp. for newspapers.

news·reel (nōōz'rēl', nyōōz'-) *n.* A short motion picture of recent events.

news·stand (nōōz'stănd', nyōōz'-) *n.* A stand where newspapers and periodicals are sold.

news·wor·thy (nōōz'wûr'thē, nyōōz'-) *adj.* Interesting or significant enough to be included in a news report. **—news'wor'thi·ness** *n.*

news·y (nōō'zē, nyōō'-) *adj.* **-i·er, -i·est.** *Informal.* Full of news; informative.

newt (nōōt, nyōōt) *n.* Any of several small, semiaquatic salamanders. [ME *an eute.*]

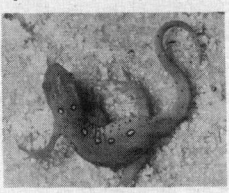

newt

New Testament *n.* The second of the two main divisions of the Christian Bible, recording the life, acts, and teachings of Christ and his followers. See table at **Bible.**

new·ton (nōōt'n, nyōōt'n) *n.* A unit of force equal to the force needed to accelerate a mass of 1 kilogram 1 meter per second per second. [< Sir Isaac *Newton* (1642–1727).]

New World *n.* The Western Hemisphere; North and South America and adjacent islands.

New Year's Day *n.* The first day of the year, Jan. 1.

next (nĕkst) *adj.* **1.** Immediately preceding or following in time, order, or sequence. **2.** Closest in space or position; adjacent. **—***adv.* **1.** In the time, position, or order immediately following. **2.** On the first subsequent occasion. **—***prep.* Close to; nearest. [< OE *nēahst.*]

nex·us (nĕk'səs) *n., pl.* **-us** or **-us·es.** **1.** A means of connection; bond; link. **2.** A connected series or group. [Lat.]

Nez Perce (nĕz' pûrs') *n., pl.* **Nez Perce** or **Nez Perc·es** (pûr'sĭz). **1. a.** A tribe of Indians formerly occupying much of the Pacific Northwest. **b.** A member of this tribe. **2.** The Sahaptin language of the Nez Perce.

ngul·trum (ĕn-gŭl'trəm, ĕng-) *n.* See table at **currency.** [Native word in Bhutan.]

ngwee (ĕn-gwē') *n., pl.* **ngwee.** See table at **currency.** [Of Bantu orig.]

Ni The symbol for the element nickel.

ni·a·cin (nī'ə-sĭn) *n.* Nicotinic acid. [NI(CO-TINIC) AC(ID) + -IN.]

nib (nĭb) *n.* The point of a pen. [Perh. < NEB.]

nib·ble (nĭb'əl) *v.* **-bled, -bling. 1.** To bite (at) gently and repeatedly. **2.** To take small or hesitant bites. [Orig. unknown.] **—nib'bler** *n.*

nice (nīs) *adj.* **nic·er, nic·est. 1.** Pleasing; appealing. **2.** Considerate; well-mannered. **3.** Respectable; virtuous. **4.** Proper; seemly. **5.** Fastidious; exacting. **6. a.** Showing or requiring sensitive discernment. **b.** Done with skill. [< Lat. *nescire,* to be ignorant.] **—nice'ly** *adv.* **—nice'ness** *n.*

ni·ce·ty (nī'sĭ-tē) *n., pl.* **-ties. 1.** Precision or accuracy. **2.** A fine point, small detail, or subtle distinction. **3.** An elegant or refined feature: *the niceties of civilized life.*

niche (nĭch, nēsh) *n.* **1.** A recess in a wall, as for holding a statue. **2.** A situation or activity specially suited to a person's abilities or character. [< Lat. *nidus,* nest.]

nick (nĭk) *n.* A shallow cut, notch, or chip on a surface. **—***v.* To cut a nick or notch in. **—idiom. in the nick of time.** Just at the critical moment. [ME *nik.*]

nick·el (nĭk'əl) *n.* **1.** *Symbol* **Ni** A silvery, hard, ductile, ferromagnetic metallic element used in alloys, in corrosion-resistant surfaces and batteries, and for electroplating. Atomic number 28; atomic weight 58.71. **2.** A U.S. coin worth five cents. [< G. *Kupernickel,* copper demon.]

nick·el·o·de·on (nĭk'ə-lō'dē-ən) *n.* **1.** An early movie house charging an admission price of five cents. **2.** A juke box. [NICKEL + (MEL)O-DEON.]

nickel silver *n.* A silvery alloy of copper, zinc, and nickel.

nick·name (nĭk'nām') *n.* **1.** A descriptive name used instead of or along with the real name of a person, place, or thing. **2.** A familiar or shortened form of a proper name. [< ME *an ekename,* an additional name.] **—nick'name'** *v.*

nic·o·tine (nĭk'ə-tēn') *n.* A poisonous alkaloid, $C_5H_4NC_4H_7NCH_3$, derived from the tobacco plant and used in medicine and as an insecticide. [Fr.]

nic·o·tin·ic acid (nĭk'ə-tĭn'ĭk) *n.* A member of the vitamin B complex, C_5H_4NCOOH, occurring in living cells and synthesized for use in treating pellagra.

niece (nēs) *n.* A daughter of one's brother, sister, brother-in-law, or sister-in-law. [< Lat. *neptis.*]

nif·ty (nĭf'tē) *adj.* **-ti·er, -ti·est.** *Slang.* Very good; first-rate. [Orig. unknown.]

nig·gard (nĭg'ərd) *n.* A stingy person; miser. **—***adj.* Stingy; miserly. [ME *nigard,* of Scand. orig.]

nig·gard·ly (nĭg'ərd-lē) *adj.* **1.** Stingy. **2.** Scanty; meager. **—***adv.* Stingily. **—nig'gard·li·ness** *n.*

nig·gling (nĭg'lĭng) *adj.* **1.** Fussy; fastidious. **2.** Petty. **3.** Requiring close attention to details. [Orig. unknown.] **—nig'gling·ly** *adv.*

nigh (nī) *adv.* **-er, -est.** Near in time, space, or

relationship. —*adj.* Close; near. —*prep.* Near. [< OE *nēah.*]

night (nīt) *n.* **1.** The period between sunset and sunrise, esp. the hours of darkness. **2.** Nightfall. **3.** Darkness. [< OE *niht.*]

night blindness *n.* Subnormal vision in poor light. —**night′blind′** *adj.*

night-cap (nīt′kăp′) *n.* **1.** A cloth cap worn esp. in bed. **2.** A usu. alcoholic drink taken before bedtime. **3.** The last event in a day's competition.

night-clothes (nīt′klōz′, -klōthz′) *pl.n.* Clothes worn in bed.

night-club (nīt′klŭb′) *n.* An establishment that stays open late at night and provides food, drink, and entertainment.

night crawler *n.* An earthworm that crawls out from the ground at night.

night-dress (nīt′drĕs′) *n.* A nightgown.

night-fall (nīt′fôl′) *n.* The coming of darkness.

night-gown (nīt′goun′) *n.* A loose garment worn to bed.

night-hawk (nīt′hôk′) *n.* **1.** A nocturnal bird with buff to black mottled feathers. **2.** *Informal.* A night owl.

night-in-gale (nīt′n-gāl′, nī′tĭng-) *n.* A brownish European songbird noted for its melodious nocturnal song. [< OE *nihtegale.*]

nightingale

night-life (nīt′līf′) *n.* Social activities pursued in the evening.

night-ly (nīt′lē) *adj.* Occurring, done, or used at night or every night. —**night′ly** *adv.*

night-mare (nīt′mâr′) *n.* **1.** An extremely frightening dream. **2.** An event or experience that is intensely distressing. [ME *nihtmare,* female incubus.] —**night′mar′ish** *adj.*

night owl *n.* One who habitually stays up late.

night school *n.* A school that holds classes in the evening.

night-shade (nīt′shăd′) *n.* Any of several related plants, such as the potato, morning glory, and belladonna. [< OE *nihtscada.*]

night-shirt (nīt′shûrt′) *n.* A long shirt worn in bed.

night-stick (nīt′stĭk′) *n.* A club carried by a policeman.

night-time (nīt′tīm′) *n.* The time between sunset and sunrise.

night-y (nī′tē) *n., pl.* **-ies.** *Informal.* A nightgown.

ni-hil-ism (nī′ə-lĭz′əm, nī′hə-, nē′-) *n.* **1.** A doctrine that all values are baseless, that nothing is knowable or can be communicated, and that life itself is meaningless. **2.** The belief that destruction of existing political or social institutions is necessary for future improvement. [< Lat. *nihil,* nothing.] —**ni′hil-ist** *n.* —**ni′hil-is′tic** *adj.*

ni-hil-i-ty (nī-hĭl′ĭ-tē, nē-) *n.* Nonexistence; nothingness. [< Lat. *nihil,* nothing.]

-nik *suff.* One associated with or characterized by: *beatnik.* [Of Slavic orig.]

nil (nĭl) *n.* Nothing; zero. [Lat. *nihil.*]

nim-ble (nĭm′bəl) *adj.* **-bler, -blest. 1.** Quick and light in movement or action; deft. **2.** Quick and clever in understanding or responding. [ME *nemel.*] —**nim′ble-ness** *n.* —**nim′bly** *adv.*

nim-bus (nĭm′bəs) *n., pl.* **-bi** (bī′) or **-es. 1.** A radiant light that appears about the head in the representation of a deity or saint. **2.** A uniformly gray rain cloud. [Lat., cloud.]

nim-rod (nĭm′rŏd′) *n.* A hunter. [< *Nimrod,* a hunter in the Old Testament.]

nin-com-poop (nĭn′kəm-pŏŏp′, nĭng′-) *n.* A foolish person; blockhead. [Orig. unknown.]

nine (nīn) *n.* **1.** The cardinal number equal to the sum of 8 + 1. **2. a.** A set of nine persons or things. **b.** A baseball team. [< OE *nigon.*] —**nine** *adj. & pron.*

nine-teen (nīn′tēn′) *n.* The cardinal number equal to the sum of 18 + 1. —**nine′teen′** *adj. & pron.*

nine-teenth (nīn′tēnth′) *n.* **1.** The ordinal number that matches the number 19 in a series. **2.** One of 19 equal parts. —**nine′teenth′** *adj. & adv.*

nine-ti-eth (nīn′tē-ĭth) *n.* **1.** The ordinal number that matches the number 90 in a series. **2.** One of 90 equal parts. —**nine′ti-eth** *adj. & adv.*

nine-ty (nīn′tē) *n., pl.* **-ties.** The cardinal number equal to 9 × 10. —**nine′ty** *adj. & pron.*

nin-ny (nĭn′ē) *n., pl.* **-nies.** A fool; simpleton. [Perh. < INNOCENT.]

ninth (nīnth) *n.* **1.** The ordinal number that matches the number 9 in a series. **2.** One of nine equal parts. **3.** *Mus.* An interval equal to an octave plus a whole step or a half step. —**ninth** *adj. & adv.*

ni-o-bi-um (nī-ō′bē-əm) *n.* *Symbol* Nb A silvery, soft, ductile, metallic element used in steel alloys, arc welding, and superconductivity research. Atomic number 41; atomic weight 92.906. [< *Niobe,* a character in Greek myth.]

nip¹ (nĭp) *v.* **nipped, nip-ping. 1.** To seize and pinch or bite. **2.** To remove by or as by nipping. **3.** To sting with the cold. **4.** To stop the growth or development of. **5.** *Slang.* **a.** To snatch up hastily. **b.** To steal. —*n.* **1.** A small bite or pinch. **2.** A small amount. **3.** Sharp, stinging cold. [< MDu. *nipen.*]

nip² (nĭp) *n.* A small amount of liquor. —*v.* **nipped, nip-ping.** To drink (liquor) in small amounts. [Prob. < Du. *nippen,* to sip.]

nip-per (nĭp′ər) *n.* **1.** One that nips. **2.** **nippers.** A pincerlike tool. **3.** A pincerlike part, as the claw of a lobster.

nip-ple (nĭp′əl) *n.* **1.** A small projection of a mammary gland containing the outlets of the milk ducts. **2.** Something resembling a nipple, esp. a soft rubber cap used on a baby's bottle. [< obs. *neble,* dim. of NEB.]

nip-py (nĭp′ē) *adj.* **-pi-er, -pi-est. 1.** Sharp or biting. **2.** Bitingly cold.

nir-va-na (nĭr-vä′nə, nûr-) *n.* **1.** Often **Nirvana.** *Buddhism.* The state of absolute blessedness, characterized by release from the cycle of reincarnations and attained through the extinction of the self. **2.** Great harmony, stability, or joy. [Skt. *nirvāṇam.*]

Ni-san (nĭs′ən, nē-sän′) *n.* In the Hebrew calendar, the 7th month of the civil year and the 1st of the religious year. See table at **calendar.** [Heb. *Nīsān.*]

Ni-sei (nē-sā′, nē′sā′) *n., pl.* **-sei** or **-seis.** One born in America of parents who emigrated from Japan. [J.]

nit (nĭt) *n.* The egg or young of a parasitic insect, such as a louse. [< OE *hnitu.*] —**nit′ty** *adj.*

ni-ter (nī′tər) *n.* Also *chiefly Brit.* **ni-tre.** **1.** Potassium nitrate. **2.** Sodium nitrate. [< Gk. *nitron,* soda, of Semitic orig.]

nit-pick (nĭt′pĭk′) *v. Informal.* To be concerned with petty details. —**nit′-pick′er** *n.*

ni-trate (nī′trāt′) *n.* **1.** A salt or ester of nitric acid. **2.** Fertilizer consisting of sodium nitrate or potassium nitrate. —*v.* **-trat-ed, -trat-ing.** To treat with nitric acid or with a nitrate, usu. to change an organic compound into a nitrate. —**ni-tra′tion** *n.*

nitric acid *n.* A transparent, corrosive liquid, HNO_3, used in the production of fertilizers, explosives, and rocket fuels.

ni-tride (nī′trīd′) *n.* A compound containing nitrogen with another, more electropositive element.

ni-tri-fi-ca-tion (nī′trə-fĭ-kā′shən) *n.* A process in which ammonia present in soil is oxidized by bacteria to form nitrites that are oxidized by other bacteria to form nitrates.

ni-tri-fy (nī′trə-fī′) *v.* **-fied, -fy-ing. 1.** To treat or combine with nitrogen or compounds containing nitrogen. **2.** To carry on nitrification.

ni-trite (nī′trīt′) *n.* A salt or ester of nitrous acid.

nitro- or **nitr-** *pref.* **1.** Nitrate: *nitric acid.* **2. a.** Nitrogen: *nitrify.* **b.** Containing the univalent group NO_2: *nitrite.* [< Gk. *nitron,* soda.]

ni-tro-cel-lu-lose (nī′trō-sĕl′yə-lōs′) *n.* A cottonlike substance derived from cellulose treated with sulfuric and nitric acids, used in explosives, plastics, and rocket fuels.

ni-tro-gen (nī′trə-jən) *n. Symbol* **N** A nonmetallic element that constitutes nearly four-fifths of the air by volume, occurring as a colorless, odorless, almost inert gas in various minerals and in all proteins. Atomic number 7; atomic weight 14.0067. —**ni-trog′e-nous** (nī-trŏj′ə-nəs) *adj.* —**ni′trous** *adj.*

ni-tro-glyc-er-in or **ni-tro-glyc-er-ine** (nī′trō-glĭs′ər-ĭn) *n.* A thick, pale-yellow, explosive liquid, $C_3N_3H_5O_9$, used in dynamite and in medicine.

nitrous oxide *n.* A colorless, sweet, inorganic gas, N_2O, used as a mild anesthetic.

nit-ty-grit-ty (nĭt′ē-grĭt′ē, nĭt′ē-grĭt′ē) *n. Slang.* The specific or practical details. [Orig. unknown.]

nit-wit (nĭt′wĭt′) *n. Informal.* A stupid or silly person.

nix (nĭks) *Slang.* —*n.* Nothing. —*adv.* No. —*v.* To forbid; veto. [< G. *nichts,* nothing.]

no¹ (nō) *adv.* **1.** Not so. Used to express refusal, denial, or disagreement. **2.** Not at all. Used with the comparative: *no better; no more.* **3.** Not: *whether or no.* —*n., pl.* **noes.** A negative response. [< OE *nā.*]

no² (nō) *adj.* **1.** Not any; not one. **2.** Not at all. [< OE *nān,* none.]

Usage: When *no* introduces a compound phrase, its elements should be connected with *or* rather than *nor: He has no training or interest in chemistry* (not *nor interest*).

No The symbol for the element nobelium.

no-bel-i-um (nō-bĕl′ē-əm, -bē′lē-) *n. Symbol* **No** A synthetic radioactive element produced in trace amounts. Atomic number 102; longest-lived isotope No 254. [< *Nobel* Institute at Stockholm.]

No-bel Prize (nō-bĕl′) *n.* Any of six international prizes awarded annually by the Nobel Foundation for outstanding achievements in physics, chemistry, physiology or medicine, literature, economics, and the promotion of peace. —**No-bel′ist** *n.*

no-bil-i-ty (nō-bĭl′ĭ-tē) *n., pl.* **-ties. 1.** A class of persons distinguished by high birth or rank. **2.** Noble rank or status. **3.** The quality or condition of being noble. [< Lat. *nobilitas.*]

no-ble (nō′bəl) *adj.* **-bler, -blest. 1.** Of, in, or belonging to the nobility. **2.** Having or showing qualities of high moral character. **3. a.** Exalted: *a noble ideal.* **b.** Majestic; imposing: *noble mountain peaks.* —*n.* A member of the nobility. [< Lat. *nobilis.*] —**no′ble-ness** *n.* —**no′bly** *adv.*

no-ble-man (nō′bəl-mən) *n.* A man of noble rank. —**no′ble-wom′an** *n.*

no-blesse o-blige (nō-blĕs′ ō-blēzh′) *n.* Kind and generous behavior considered to be the responsibility of persons of high birth or rank. [Fr.]

no-bod-y (nō′bŏd′ē, -bə-dē) *pron.* No person; no one. —*n., pl.* **-ies.** A person of no importance.

noc-tur-nal (nŏk-tûr′nəl) *adj.* **1.** Of, relating to, or occurring in the night. **2.** Active at night. [< Lat. *nocturnus < nox,* night.] —**noc-tur′nal-ly** *adv.*

noc-turne (nŏk′tûrn′) *n.* A work of art, esp. a musical composition for the piano, intended to suggest or evoke the feelings associated with night. [Fr.]

nod (nŏd) *v.* **nod-ded, nod-ding. 1.** To lower the head quickly, as in agreement or drowsiness. **2.** To express by bowing the head. **3.** To be momentarily inattentive. **4.** To sway or bend downward. [ME *nodden.*] —**nod** *n.* —**nod′der** *n.*

node (nōd) *n.* **1.** A protuberance or swelling. **2.** An often knoblike marking on a plant stem where a leaf, bud, or stem is attached. **3.** *Physics.* A point or region of minimum or zero amplitude in a periodic system. [Lat. *nodus,* knot.] —**nod′al** *adj.*

nod-ule (nŏj′ŏol) *n.* A small, knoblike lump or protuberance. —**nod′u-lar** (-ə-lər) *adj.*

No-el or **No-el** (nō-ĕl′) *n.* **1.** Christmas. **2.** *noël* or **noel.** A Christmas carol. [< Lat. *natalis (dies),* (day) of birth.]

no-fault (nō′fôlt′) *adj.* **1.** Of or indicating a system of automobile insurance in which accident victims are compensated by their insurance companies without assignment of blame. **2.** Of or indicating a type of divorce in which no blame is assigned.

nog-gin (nŏg′ĭn) *n.* **1.** A small mug or cup. **2.** A small drink of liquor equal to one-quarter of a pint. **3.** The head. [Orig. unknown.]

noise (noiz) *n.* **1.** Sound or a sound that is loud, unpleasant, or unexpected. **2.** Sound of any kind. **3.** A loud outcry or commotion. **4.** *Physics.* Persistent interference in an electronic signal. —*v.* **noised, nois·ing.** To spread the rumor or report of. [< Gk. *nausia,* seasickness.] —**noise'less** *adj.* —**noise'less·ly** *adv.*

noise·mak·er (noiz'mā'kər) *n.* One that makes noise, esp. a device, as a form, used to make noise at a party.

noi·some (noi'səm) *adj.* **1.** Offensive; foul. **2.** Harmful or dangerous. [ME *noisom.*] —**noi'some·ly** *adv.* —**noi'some·ness** *n.*

nois·y (noi'zē) *adj.* **-i·er, -i·est. 1.** Making noise. **2.** Full of noise. —**nois'i·ly** *adv.* —**nois'i·ness** *n.*

no·lo con·ten·de·re (nō'lō kən-tĕn'də-rē) *n. Law.* A plea made by the defendant in a criminal action that is equivalent to an admission of guilt but allows the defendant to deny the charges in other proceedings. [Lat., I do not wish to contend.]

no·mad (nō'măd') *n.* **1.** One of a group of people who have no permanent home and move about from place to place. **2.** A wanderer. [< Gk. *nomas,* wandering around for pasture.] —**no·mad'ic** *adj.*

no man's land *n.* **1.** An unclaimed or unowned piece of land. **2.** The unoccupied area between two opposing entrenched armies. **3.** An area of uncertainty or ambiguity.

nom de guerre (nŏm' də gâr') *n.* A pseudonym. [Fr., war name.]

nom de plume (nŏm' də plōōm') *n.* A pen name. [Fr.]

no·men·cla·ture (nō'mən-klā'chər, nō-mĕn'klə-) *n.* A system of names used in an art or science. [Lat. *nomenclatura.*]

nom·i·nal (nŏm'ə-nəl) *adj.* **1.** Of or like a name or names. **2.** Existing in name only and not in actuality. **3.** Insignificant; trifling. [< Lat. *nomen,* name.] —**nom'i·nal·ly** *adv.*

nom·i·nate (nŏm'ə-nāt') *v.* **-nat·ed, -nat·ing.** To propose as a candidate, as for election or office. —**nom'i·na'tion** *n.* —**nom'i·na'tor** *n.*

nom·i·na·tive (nŏm'ə-nə-tĭv) *adj.* Of, relating to, or belonging to a grammatical case that usu. indicates the subject of a verb. —*n.* The nominative case.

nom·i·nee (nŏm'ə-nē') *n.* One who has been nominated. [NOMIN(ATE) + -EE¹.]

-nomy *suff.* A system of laws governing or a body of knowledge about a specified field: *astronomy.* [< Gk. *nomos,* law.]

non- *pref.* Not: *nonconductor.* [< Lat. *non.*] *Usage:* Many compounds other than those entered here may be formed with *non-.* In forming compounds, *non-* is normally joined with the following element without space or hyphen: *nonnutritive.* However, if the second element begins with a capital letter, it is separated with a hyphen: *non-French.*

non·age (nŏn'ĭj, nō'nĭj) *n.* **1.** Legal minority. **2.** A period of immaturity.

non·a·ge·nar·i·an (nŏn'ə-jə-nâr'ē-ən, nō'nə-) *adj.* Being between 90 and 100 years old. [< Lat. *nonagenarius.*] —**non'a·ge·nar'i·an** *n.*

non·a·ligned (nŏn'ə-līnd') *adj.* Not in alliance with other nations or power blocs. —**non'a·lign'ment** *n.*

nonce (nŏns) *n.* The present or particular occasion: *for the nonce.* [< ME *for then anes,* for the one.]

non·cha·lant (nŏn'shə-länt') *adj.* Cool, carefree, and casually unconcerned. [< OFr. *non-*

non·a·ban'don·ment *n.*
non·ab·di·ca'tion *n.*
non·ab·o·li'tion *n.*
non·a·bra'sive *adj.*
non·a·bridg'ment *n.*
non·ab·so·lute' *adj. & n.*
non·ab·sorb'ent *adj. & n.*
non·ab·sorp'tion *n.*
non·ab·stain'er *n.*
non·ab'stract *adj. & n.*
non·a·bu'sive *adj.*
non·ac·a·dem'ic *adj.*
non·ac·cel'er·a'tion *n.*
non·ac'cent *n.*
non·ac·cept'ance *n.*
non·ac·ces'so·ry *adj. & n.*
non·ac·ci·den'tal *adj. & n.*
non·ac·com'mo·dat'ing *adj.*
non·ac·cord' *n.*
non·ac·cu·mu·la'tion *n.*
non·ac'id *n.*
non·ac·qui·es'cent *adj.*
non·ac·quit'tal *n.*
non·ac'tion *n.*
non·ac'tive *adj.*
non·ac'tu·al *adj.*
non·a·cute' *adj.*
non·a·dapt'a·ble *adj.*
non·ad·dic'tive *adj.*
non·a·dept' *adj.*
non·ad·her'ence *n.*
non·ad·he'sive *adj.*

non·ad·ja'cent *adj.*
non·ad·jec'ti'val *adj.*
non·ad·join'ing *adj.*
non·ad·just'a·ble *adj.*
non·ad·min·is·tra'tive *adj.*
non·ad·mis'sion *n.*
non·a·dult' *adj. & n.*
non·ad·vance'ment *n.*
non·ad·van·ta'geous *adj.*
non·ad·ven'tur·ous *adj.*
non·ad·ver'bi·al *adj.*
non·aes·thet'ic *adj.*
non·af·fec·ta'tion *n.*
non·af·fil'i·a'tion *n.*
non·Af'ri·can *adj. & n.*
non·al'co·hol'ic *adj.*
non·a·pol'o·get'ic *adj.*
non·ap·par'ent *adj.*
non·ap·pear'ance *n.*
non·ap·pre'ci·a'tion *n.*
non·ap·proach'a·ble *adj.*
non·a'que·ous *adj.*
non·ar·bi·trar'y *adj.*
non·ar·o·mat'ic *adj.*
non·Ar'yan *n. & adj.*
non·as·ser'tive *adj.*
non·as·sim·i·la'tion *n.*
non·ath'lete *n.*
non·a·tom'ic *adj.*
non·at·tach'ment *n.*
non·at·tain'a·ble *adj.*

non·at·ten'dance *n.*
non·at·trib'u·tive *adj. & n.*
non·au·to·mat'ic *adj.*
non·bac·te'ri·al *adj.*
non-Bap'tist *n.*
non·ba'si·cal *adj.*
non·beau'ty *n.*
non·be'ing *n.*
non·be·liev'er *n.*
non·be·nev'o·lent *adj.*
non-Bib'li·cal *adj.*
non-Brit'ish *adj.*
non·bus'y *adj.*
non·caf'feine' *n.*
non·cak'ing *adj.*
non·can'cer·ous *adj.*
non·ca·non'i·cal *adj.*
non·cap·i·tal·is'tic *adj.*
non·car·niv'o·rous *adj.*
non·cat·e·gor'i·cal *adj.*
non-Cath'o·lic *adj. & n.*
non'-Cau·ca'sian *adj. & n.*
non·ce·les'tial *adj.*
non·cel'lu·lar *adj.*
non-Celt'ic *adj.*
non·cer·e·mo'ni·al *adj.*
non·cer'ti·fied' *adj.*
non·chem'i·cal *adj.*
non'-Chi·nese' *adj. & n.*
non-Chris'tian *adj. & n.*
non·cit'i·zen *n.*
non·civ'i·lized' *adj.*

chaloir, to be unconcerned.] —**non'cha·lance'**
n. —**non'cha·lant·ly** *adv.*

non·com (nŏn'kŏm') *n. Informal.* A noncommissioned officer.

non·com·bat·ant (nŏn'kəm-băt'nt, nŏn-kŏm'-bə-tənt) *n.* **1.** A member of the armed forces whose duties exclude fighting. **2.** A civilian in wartime.

non·com·mis·sioned officer (nŏn'kə-mĭsh'-ənd) *n.* An enlisted member of the armed forces appointed to a subordinate rank, such as sergeant or corporal.

non·com·mit·tal (nŏn'kə-mĭt'l) *adj.* Not indicating preference or purpose.

non com·pos men·tis (nŏn kŏm'pəs měn'tĭs) *adj. Law.* Not of sound mind; not legally responsible. [Lat., not in control of the mind.]

non·con·duc·tor (nŏn'kən-dŭk'tər) *n.* A substance that conducts little or no electricity or heat. —**non'con·duc'tive** *adj.*

non·con·form·ist (nŏn'kən-fôr'mĭst) *n.* One who does not conform to accepted customs, beliefs, or practices. —**non'con·form'i·ty** *n.*

non·de·script (nŏn'dĭ-skrĭpt') *adj.* Lacking in distinctive qualities. [NON- + Lat. *descriptus*, p.p. of *describere*, to describe.] —**non'de·script'** *n.*

none (nŭn) *pron.* **1.** No one; nobody. **2.** Not any. **3.** No part: *none of his business.* —*adv.* In no way; not at all. [< OE *nān*.]

non·en·ti·ty (nŏn-ĕn'tĭ-tē) *n., pl.* **-ties.** **1.** One of no importance or significance. **2.** Something that does not exist, or that exists only in the imagination.

nones (nōnz) *pl.n.* In the ancient Roman calendar, the 7th day of March, May, July, or

October, and the 5th day of the other months. [< Lat. *nonus*, ninth.]

none·such (nŭn'sŭch') *n.* A person or thing without equal. —**none'such'** *adj.*

none·the·less (nŭn'thə-lĕs') *adv.* Nevertheless; however.

non·e·vent (nŏn'ĭ-vĕnt') *n. Slang.* An anticipated event that does not occur or that proves anticlimactic.

non·ex·ist·ent (nŏn'ĭg-zĭs'tənt) *adj.* Not existing. —**non'ex·ist'ence** *n.*

non·fat (nŏn'făt') *adj.* Lacking fat solids or having the fat content removed.

non·fic·tion (nŏn-fĭk'shən) *n.* Literary works other than fiction. —**non·fic'tion·al** *adj.*

non·he·ro (nŏn-hîr'ō) *n.* An antihero.

no·nil·lion (nō-nĭl'yən) *n.* **1.** The cardinal number equal to 10³⁰. **2.** *Chiefly Brit.* The cardinal number equal to 10⁵⁴. [Fr.] —**no·nil'lion** *adj.*

no·nil·lionth (nō-nĭl'yənth) *n.* The ordinal number that matches nonillion in a series. —**no·nil'lionth** *adj. & adv.*

non·in·ter·ven·tion (nŏn'ĭn-tər-věn'shən) *n.* Failure or refusal to intervene, esp. in the affairs of another nation. —**non'in·ter·ven'·tion·ist** *n.*

non·met·al (nŏn-mět'l) *n.* Any of the elements, such as oxygen or sulfur, that lack the characteristics of a metal. —**non'me·tal'lic** (nŏn'mə-tăl'ĭk) *adj.*

non·pa·reil (nŏn'pə-rěl') *adj.* Having no equal; peerless. —*n.* **1.** One that has no equal; paragon. **2.** A small, flat chocolate drop covered with white pellets of sugar. [< OFr.]

non·par·ti·san (nŏn-pär'tĭ-zən) *adj.* Not parti-

non'clas·si·fi·ca'tion *n.*
non'cler'i·cal *adj.*
non'clin'i·cal *adj.*
non'co·er'cive *adj.*
non'co·he'sive *adj.*
non'col·laps'i·ble *adj.*
non'col·le'giate *adj.*
non'com·bus'ti·ble *adj. & n.*
non'com·mer'cial *adj. & n.*
non'com·mu'ni·ca·ble *adj.*
non'com·mu·nist *n. & adj.*
non'com·pen·sa'tion *n.*
non'com·pe'tent *adj.*
non'com·pe'tent·ly *adv.*
non'com·pet'i·tive *adj.*
non'com·pet'i·tive·ness *n.*
non'com·ple'tion *n.*
non'com·pli'ance *n.*
non'com·pli'ant *adj. & n.*
non'com·pres'sion *n.*
non'com·pul'sion *n.*
non'con·cur'rence *n.*
non'con·cur'rent *adj.*
non'con·den·sa'tion *n.*
non'con·fi·den'tial *adj.*
non'con·fine'ment *n.*
non'con·flic'tive *adj.*
non'con·ges'tion *n.*
non'-Con·gres'sion·al *adj.*
non'con·nec'tive *adj. & n.*
non'con·scious *adj.*
non'con·sec'u·tive *adj.*
non'con·sent' *n.*
non'con·ser'va·tive *adj. & n.*
non'con·sid·er·a'tion *n.*

non'con·spir·a'tor *n.*
non'con·sult·a'tive *adj.*
non'con·ta'gious *adj.*
non'con·tem'po·rar'y *adj. & n.*
non'con·tin'u·ous *adj.*
non'con·tra·band' *n. & adj.*
non'con·tra·dic'tion *n.*
non'con·tri·bu'tion *n.*
non'con·trib'u·tor *n.*
non'con·tro·ver'sial *adj.*
non'con·ver'gence *n.*
non'con·ver'sion *n.*
non'con·vic'tion *n.*
non'co·op·er·a'tion *n.*
non'co·or'di·na'tion *n.*
non'cor'po·rate *adj.*
non'cor·rec'tive *adj. & n.*
non'cor·re·la'tion *n.*
non'cos'mic *adj.*
non'crea'tive *adj.*
non'cred'i·ble *adj.*
non'crim'i·nal *adj. & n.*
non'cul'pa·ble *adj.*
non'cul'ture *n.*
non'cu'mu·la·tive *adj.*
non'cur'rent *adj.*
non'cur·tail'ment *n.*
non'cus'tom·ar'y *adj.*
non'dair'y *adj.*
non'de·cay'ing *adj.*
non'de·cep'tive *adj.*
non'de·liv'er·y *n.*
non'dem·o·crat'ic *adj.*
non'de·nom'i·na'tion·al *adj.*
non'de·part·men'tal *adj.*

non'de·par'ture *n.*
non'de·pen'dence *n.*
non'de·pos'i·tor *n.*
non'de·pre·ca'tion *n.*
non'de·riv'a·tive *adj. & n.*
non'de·rog'a·to'ry *adj.*
non'de·struc'tive *adj.*
non'de·tach'a·ble *adj.*
non'det·ri·men'tal *adj.*
non'de·vel'op·ment *n.*
non'de·vi·a'tion *n.*
non'de·vo'tion·al *adj.*
non'di·a·lec'tal *adj.*
non'di·dac'tic *adj.*
non'dif·fer·en·ti·a'tion *n.*
non'di·gest'i·ble *adj.*
non'di·rec'tion·al *adj.*
non'dis·cern'ment *n.*
non'dis·ci·pli·nar'y *adj.*
non'dis·crim'i·na'tion *n.*
non'dis·pos'al *n.*
non'dis·rup'tive *adj.*
non'dis·si'dence *n.*
non'dis·tinc'tive *adj.*
non'dis·tri·bu'tion *n.*
non'di·ver'gence *n.*
non'di·ver·si·fi·ca'tion *n.*
non'di·vis'i·ble *adj.*
non'doc·tri·nal *adj.*
non'doc·u·men'ta·ry *adj. & n.*
non'dog·mat'ic *adj.*
non'do·mes'tic *adj. & n.*
non'dra·mat'ic *adj.*
non'drink'er *n.*
non'dry'ing *adj.*
non'ec·cle'si·as'ti·cal *adj.*

san, esp. not influenced by one political party.

non·per·son (nŏn-pûr'sən) *n.* A person whose obliteration from the memory of the public is sought, esp. by governmental action.

non·plus (nŏn-plŭs') *v.* **-plussed** or **-plused, -plus·ing** or **-plus·ing.** To bewilder; perplex. [< Lat. *non plus,* no more.]

non·prof·it (nŏn-prŏf'ĭt) *adj.* Not seeking profit.

non·pro·lif·er·a·tion (nŏn'prə-lĭf'ə-rā'shən) *adj.* Of, involving, or calling for cessation of the proliferation of nuclear weapons.

non·rep·re·sen·ta·tion·al (nŏn-rĕp'rĭ-zən-tā'shə-nəl) *adj.* Not objectively representing objects.

non·res·i·dent (nŏn-rĕz'ĭ-dənt) *adj.* Not living in a particular place. **—non·res'i·dent** *n.*

non·re·stric·tive (nŏn'rĭ-strĭk'tĭv) *adj. Gram.* Of or designating a descriptive word, clause, or phrase that is not essential to the meaning of the sentence and that is set off by commas.

non·sched·uled (nŏn-skĕj'ōōld) *adj.* Not having a regular schedule of passenger or cargo flights.

non·sec·tar·i·an (nŏn'sĕk-târ'ē-ən) *adj.* Not limited to or associated with a particular religious denomination.

non·sense (nŏn'sĕns', -səns) *n.* **1.** Behavior or language that is foolish or absurd. **2.** Something of little or no importance or usefulness. **—non·sen'si·cal** (nŏn-sĕn'sĭ-kəl) *adj.* Foolish; silly; absurd. **—non·sen'si·cal·ly** *adv.*

non se·qui·tur (nŏn sĕk'wĭ-tər, -tōōr') *n.* A statement that does not follow logically from what preceded it. [Lat., it does not follow.]

non·skid (nŏn'skĭd') *adj.* Designed to prevent or resist skidding.

non·stan·dard (nŏn-stăn'dərd) *adj.* **1.** Varying from or not adhering to the standard. **2.** Of, relating to, or indicating a level of language usage that is usu. avoided by educated speakers and writers.

non·stop (nŏn'stŏp') *adj.* Performed or accomplished without a stop. **—non'stop'** *adv.*

non·suit (nŏn-sōōt') *n. Law.* A judgment given against a plaintiff for failure to prosecute his case or to introduce sufficient evidence.

non·sup·port (nŏn'sə-pôrt', -pōrt') *n. Law.* Failure to provide financial support to one's dependents.

non trop·po (nŏn trŏ'pō) *adv. & adj. Mus.* Moderately. [Ital.]

non·un·ion (nŏn-yōōn'yən) *adj.* **1.** Not belonging to a labor union. **2.** Not recognizing a labor union or employing union members.

non·vi·o·lence (nŏn-vī'ə-ləns) *n.* The doctrine or practice of rejecting violence in favor of peaceful tactics as a means of gaining esp. political ends. **—non·vi'o·lent** *adj.* **—non·vi'o·lent·ly** *adv.*

noo·dle¹ (nōōd'l) *n. Slang.* The head. [Poss. < *noddle.*]

noo·dle² (nōōd'l) *n.* A narrow, ribbonlike strip of dried dough, usu. made of flour, eggs, and water. [G. *Nudel.*]

nook (nōōk) *n.* **1.** A small corner, esp. in a room. **2.** A hidden or secluded spot. [ME *nok,* prob. of Scand. orig.]

noon (nōōn) *n.* Twelve o'clock in the daytime; midday. [< OE *nōn,* ninth hour after sunrise < Lat. *nonus,* ninth.]

---

non·ec·lec'tic *adj.*
non·ec·o·nom'ic *adj.*
non·ed'i·ble *adj. & n.*
non·ed·i·to'ri·al *adj.*
non·ed·u·ca·ble *adj.*
non·ed·u·ca'tion·al *adj.*
non·ef·fec'tive *adj.*
non·ef·fer·ves'cent *adj.*
non·ef·fi'cien·cy *n.*
non·e·las'tic *adj.*
non·e·lect' *n.*
non·e·lec'tion *n.*
non·e·lec'tive *adj.*
non·e·lec'tric *adj.*
non·el·e·men'ta·ry *adj.*
non·e·lim'i·na'tion *adj.*
non·e·mo'tion·al *adj.*
non·em·pir'i·cal *adj.*
non·en·cy'clo·pe'dic *adj.*
non·en·force'a·ble *adj.*
non-Eng'lish *adj. & n.*
non·en'ter·pris'ing *adj.*
non'-E·pis'co·pa'lian *adj. & n.*
non·e'qual *adj. & n.*
non·e'quiv·a·lent *adj. & n.*
non·e'ra·sure *n.*
non·e·rot'ic *adj.*
non·er·u'dite' *adj.*
non·es·sen'tial *adj. & n.*
non·es·thet'ic *adj.*
non·e·ter'nal *adj.*
non·eth'i·cal *adj.*

non·eth·no·log'i·cal *adj.*
non'-Eu·clid'e·an *adj.*
non'-Eu·ro·pe'an *adj. & n.*
non·e·vac'u·a'tion *n.*
non·e·va'sion *n.*
non·e·va'sive *adj.*
non·e·vic'tion *n.*
non·ev·o·lu'tion·ar'y *adj.*
non·ex·pan'sive *adj.*
non·ex·pend'a·ble *adj.*
non·ex·per'i·men'tal *adj.*
non·ex·plo'sive *adj. & n.*
non·ex'tant *adj.*
non·ex·ter'nal *adj.*
non·ex'tinct' *adj.*
non·ex·tra·di'tion *n.*
non·ex·tra'ne·ous *adj.*
non·fa·ce'tious *adj.*
non·fac'tu·al *adj.*
non·fan'ta·sy *n.*
non·fas'cist *n. & adj.*
non·fas·tid'i·ous *adj.*
non·fa'tal *adj.*
non·fat'ten·ing *adj.*
non·fed'er·al *adj.*
non·fer'rous *adj.*
non·fer'tile *adj.*
non·fes'tive *adj.*
non·feu'dal *adj.*
non·fig'ur·a·tive *adj.*
non·fi·nan'cial *adj.*
non·fi'nite *adj. & n.*

non·fire'proof *adj.*
non·flam'ma·ble *adj.*
non·for'mal *adj.*
non·for'tu·i·tous *adj.*
non·fra·ter'nal *adj.*
non·fraud'u·lent *adj.*
non·free'dom *n.*
non·French' *adj. & n.*
non·fre'quent *adj.*
non·ful·fill'ment *n.*
non·func'tion·al *adj.*
non·fun·da·men'tal *adj. & n.*
non·gas'e·ous *adj.*
non·ge·lat'i·nous *adj.*
non·ge·net'ic *adj.*
non·gov·ern·men'tal *adj.*
non·gre·gar'i·ous *adj.*
non·hab'it·a·ble *adj.*
non·hab'it·u·al *adj.*
non·haz'ard·ous *adj.*
non·hea'then *n. & adj.*
non·he·red'i·tar'y *adj.*
non·he·ret'i·cal *adj.*
non·he·ro'ic *adj.*
non·his·tor'ic *adj.*
non·ho·mo·ge'ne·ous *adj.*
non·hos'tile *adj.*
non·hu'man *adj.*
non·hu'man·ness *n.*
non·hu'mor·ous *adj.*
non·i·den'ti·cal *adj.*
non·i·den'ti·ty *n.*

ă pat ā pay â care ä father ĕ pet ē be ĭ pit ī tie î pier ŏ pot ō toe ô paw, for oi noise ōō took
ōō boot ou out th thin th this ŭ cut û urge yōō abuse zh vision ə about, item, edible, gallop, circus

noon·day (nŏon'dā') n. Noon.

no one pron. No person; nobody.

noon·time (nŏon'tīm') n. Noon.

noose (nŏos) n. A loop formed in a rope by means of a slipknot so that it binds tighter as the rope is pulled. [ME nose.]

Noot·ka (nŏot'kə, nŏot'-) n. **1. a.** A tribe of Indians living in western Canada and northwestern Washington. **b.** A member of this tribe. **2.** The Wakashan language of the Nootka. —**Noot'ka** adj.

no-par (nŏ'pär') adj. Also **no-par-val·ue** (văl'-yŏo). Without face value: a no-par stock certificate.

nope (nŏp) adv. Slang. No. [< NO¹.]

nor (nôr, nər when unstressed) conj. And not; or not; not either: They are neither able nor willing to help. [ME.]

Nor·dic (nôr'dĭk) adj. Of or belonging to the division of the Caucasoid group of the human species that is most predominant in Scandinavia. [< OE north, north.] —**Nor'dic** n.

norm (nôrm) n. A standard, model, or pattern regarded as typical for a specific group. [Lat. norma, carpenter's square.]

nor·mal (nôr'məl) adj. **1.** Conforming to a usual or typical standard: normal room temperature; one's normal weight. **2. a.** Of average intelligence and development. **b.** Free from physical or emotional disorder. —n. **1.** Something normal; standard. **2.** The usual state, amount, or degree. —**nor'mal·cy** n. —**nor·mal'i·ty** n. —**nor'mal·ly** adv.

nor·mal·ize (nôr'mə-līz') v. **-ized, -iz·ing.** To make normal. —**nor'mal·i·za'tion** n. —**nor'mal·iz'er** n.

normal school n. A school that trains teachers, chiefly for the elementary grades.

Nor·man (nôr'mən) n. **1.** A member of a Scandinavian people who conquered Normandy in the 10th cent. **2.** A member of a people of Norman and French blood who conquered England in 1066. **3.** A native of Normandy. —**Nor'man** adj.

Norman French n. The dialect of Old French used in Normandy.

nor·ma·tive (nôr'mə-tĭv) adj. Of, relating to, or prescribing a norm. —**nor'ma·tive·ly** adv. —**nor'ma·tive·ness** n.

Norse (nôrs) adj. **1.** Of or relating to ancient Scandinavia, its people, or its language. **2. a.** Of or relating to western Scandinavia or the languages of its inhabitants. **b.** Norwegian. —**Norse** n.

Norse·man (nôrs'mən) n. A member of any of the ancient Scandinavian peoples.

north (nôrth) n. **1. a.** The direction along a meridian 90° counterclockwise from east. **b.** The cardinal point on the mariner's compass located at 0°. **2.** Often **North.** An area or region lying to the north of a particular point. —adj. To, toward, of, from, facing, or in the north. —adv. In, from, or toward the north. [< OE.]

north·east (nôrth-ēst') n. **1.** The direction that is 45° counterclockwise from east and 45° clockwise from north. **2.** An area or region lying to the northeast of a particular point. —**north·east'** adj. & adv. —**north·east'ern** adj. —**north·east'ward** adv. & n. —**north·east'ward·ly** adj. & adv.

north·east·er (nôrth-ē'stər; nôr-ē'stər) n. A storm or gale from the northeast.

---

north·east·er·ly (nôrth-ē′stər-lē) *adj.*
1. Toward or in the northeast. 2. From the
northeast. —**north·east′er·ly** *adv.*

north·east·ward (nôrth-ēst′wərd) *adv.* Also
north·east·wards (-wərdz). Toward the northeast.

north·er·ly (nôr′thər-lē) *adj.* 1. In or toward
the north. 2. From the north, as a wind.
—**north′er·ly** *adv.*

north·ern (nôr′thərn) *adj.* 1. Of, in, or toward
the north. 2. From the north. 3. Characteristic of or found in northern regions. [< OE
northerne.]

north·ern·er (nôr′thər-nər) *n.* A native or inhabitant of a northern region.

Northern Hemisphere *n.* The half of the
earth north of the equator.

northern lights *pl.n.* The aurora borealis.

North Pole *n.* 1. The northern end of the
earth's axis of rotation. 2. The point, about
one degree from the star Polaris, at which the
earth's axis of rotation intersects the celestial
sphere.

North Star *n.* Polaris.

north·ward (nôrth′wərd) *adv.* Also **north·
wards** (-wərdz). To or toward the north.
—**north′ward** *adj.* —**north′ward·ly** *adj & adv.*

north·west (nôrth-wĕst′) *n.* 1. The direction
that is 45° counterclockwise from north and
45° clockwise from west. 2. An area or region
lying to the northwest of a particular point.
—**north·west** *adj. & adv.* —**north·west′ern** *adj.*

north·west·er·ly (nôrth-wĕs′tər-lē) *adj.*
1. Toward or in the northwest. 2. From the
northwest. —**north·west′er·ly** *adv.*

north·west·ward (nôrth-wĕst′wərd) *adv.* Also
north·west·wards (-wərdz). To or toward the
northwest. —**north·west′ward** *adj. & n.*
—**north·west′ward·ly** *adj & adv.*

Nor·we·gian (nôr-wē′jən) *n.* 1. A native or
inhabitant of Norway. 2. The Germanic language of the Norwegians. —**Nor·we′gian** *adj.*

nose (nōz) *n.* 1. The structure on the face
that contains the nostrils and organs of smell
and forms the beginning of the respiratory
tract. 2. The sense of smell. 3. The ability to
detect things, as if by smell. 4. Something
resembling a nose, as the forward end of an
airplane. —*v.* **nosed, nos·ing.** 1. To find out
by or as if by smell. 2. To touch with the
nose; nuzzle. 3. To move or advance cautiously. 4. To pry curiously. —*Idioms.* **on the
nose.** Exactly; precisely. **under (someone's)
nose.** In plain view of. [< OE *nosu.*]

nose

A. Frontal sinuses
B. Sphenoid sinus
C. Pharyngeal tonsil
D. Eustachian tube

nose·bleed (nōz′blēd′) *n.* Bleeding from the
nostrils.

---

non′par·lia·men′ta·ry *adj.*
non′pa·ro′chi·al *adj.*
non′par′tial *adj.*
non′par·tic′i·pant *n.*
non′par·tic′i·pat′ing *adj.*
non′par·tic′i·pa′tion *n.*
non′pa·ter′nal *adj.*
non′path·o·gen′ic *adj.*
non′pay′ment *n.*
non′per·cep′tu·al *adj.*
non′per·form′ance *n.*
non′pe·ri·od′i·cal *adj. & n.*
non′per·ish·a·ble *adj. & n.*
non′per·ma·nent *adj.*
non′per·me·a·ble *adj.*
non′per·pet′u·ral *adj.*
non′per·sist′ence *n.*
non′per·sist′ent *adj.*
non′phil·an·throp′ic *adj.*
non′phys′i·cal *adj.*
non′phys·i·o·log′i·cal *adj.*
non′plan·e′tar·y *adj.*
non′po·et′ic *adj.*
non′poi′son·ous *adj.*
non′po·lit′i·cal *adj.*
non′po′rous *adj.*
non′pred′a·to′ry *adj.*
non′pre·dict′a·ble *adj.*
non′pref·er·en′tial *adj.*
non′pre·scrip′tion *adj.*

non′pres·i·den′tial *adj.*
non′prev′a·lent *adj.*
non′priest′ly *adj.*
non′pro·duc′er *n.*
non′pro·duc′tive *adj.*
non′pro·fes′sion·al *adj. & n.*
non′pro·fi′cien·cy *n.*
non′pro·gres′sive *adj. & n.*
non′pro·lif′ic *adj.*
non′pro·por′tion·al *adj.*
non′pro·pri′e·ty *n.*
non′pro·tec′tion *n.*
non-Prot′es·tant *n. & adj.*
non′psy·chic *adj. & n.*
non·pub′lic *adj.*
non·ra′cial *adj.*
non·rad′i·cal *adj. & n.*
non·ra′tion·al *adj.*
non′re·ac′tive *adj.*
non′re·ceiv′a·ble *adj. & n.*
non′re·cip′ro·cal *adj. & n.*
non′rec·og·ni′tion *n.*
non′rec·tan′gu·lar *adj.*
non′re·cur′rent *adj.*
non′re·deem′a·ble *adj.*
non′re·gen′er·a′tive *adj.*
non′reg·i·men′tal *adj.*
non′reg·is·tra′tion *n.*
non′re·li′ance *n.*
non′re·lig′ious *adj.*

non′re·mu′ner·a′tive *adj.*
non′re·new′a·ble *adj.*
non′re·pay′a·ble *adj.*
non′re·pen′tant *adj.*
non′re·pet′i·tive *adj.*
non′rep·re·hen′si·bly *adv.*
non′rep·re·sen·ta′tion *n.*
non′rep·re·sen·ta′tive *n. & adj.*
non′re·pro·duc′tive *adj.*
non′re·sem′blance *n.*
non′res·i·den′tial *adj.*
non′re·sid′u·al *adj.*
non′re·sis′tance *n.*
non′re·sis′tant *adj. & n.*
non′re·solv′a·ble *adj.*
non′re·ten′tion *n.*
non′re·ten′tive *adj.*
non′re·tir′ing *adj.*
non′re·turn′a·ble *adj.*
non′re·vers′i·ble *adj.*
non′re·volt′ing *adj.*
non′rhe·tor′i·cal *adj.*
non·rig′id *adj.*
non·ri′val *n.*
non-Ro′man *adj. & n.*
non·ru′ral *adj.*
non′sac·ra·men′tal *adj.*
non·sa′cred *adj.*
non·sal′a·ble *adj.*
non·sal′a·ried *adj.*

---

nose cone *n.* The forward, usu. separable end of a rocket or guided missile.

nose dive *n.* **1.** A very steep dive made by an airplane. **2.** A sudden plunge. —**nose′-dive** *v.*

nose-gay (nōz′gā′) *n.* A small bunch of flowers. [ME.]

nos-tal-gia (nŏ-stăl′jən, nə-) *n.* A bittersweet longing for things, persons, or situations of the past. [Gk. *nostos*, home + Gk. *algos*, pain.] —**nos-tal′gic** *adj.*

nos-tril (nŏs′trəl) *n.* Either of the external openings of the nose. [< OE *nosthyrl*.]

nos-trum (nŏs′trəm) *n.* A quack medicine or remedy. [Lat., our own.]

nos-y (nō′zē) *adj.* **-i-er, -i-est**. Also **nos-ey**. Prying; inquisitive. [< NOSE.] —**nos′i-ness** *n.*

not (nŏt) *adv.* In no way; to no degree. Used to express negation, denial, refusal, or prohibition: *I will not go. You may not have any.* [< OE *nōwiht*.]

no-ta be-ne (nō′tä bĕn′ē). Used to direct attention to something particularly important. [Lat., note well.]

no-ta-ble (nō′tə-bəl) *adj.* Worthy of notice; remarkable; striking. —*n.* A person of distinction or of great reputation. —**no′ta-bil′i-ty** *n.* —**no′ta-bly** *adv.*

no-ta-rize (nō′tə-rīz′) *v.* **-rized, -riz-ing.** To witness and authenticate as a notary public. —**no′ta-ri-za′tion** *n.*

no-ta-ry (nō′tə-rē) *n., pl.* **-ries.** A notary public. [< Lat. *notarius*, stenographer.]

notary public *n., pl.* **notaries public.** A person legally empowered to witness and certify documents, take affidavits and depositions, and administer oaths.

no-ta-tion (nō-tā′shən) *n.* **1. a.** The use of standard symbols or figures to represent quantities, tones, or values. **b.** A system of such symbols or figures. **2.** A brief note or record.

notch (nŏch) *n.* **1.** A V-shaped cut. **2.** A narrow pass between mountains. **3.** A level or degree. —*v.* **1.** To cut a notch in. **2.** To record by or as if by making notches. [< OFr. *ochier*, to notch.]

note (nōt) *n.* **1.** A brief written record or communication. **2.** A formal diplomatic or official communication. **3.** A commentary to a passage in a text. **4. a.** A piece of paper currency. **b.** A promissory note. **5.** *Mus.* **a.** A tone of definite pitch. **b.** The symbol of such a tone in musical notation. **6.** A musical call or cry, as of a bird. **7.** An indication of some quality or aspect: *a note of suspicion.* **8.** Importance; consequence. **9.** Notice; observation —*v.* **noted, noting.** **1.** To observe carefully; notice; perceive. **2.** To write down; make a note of. **3.** To make particular mention of; remark. [Lat. *nota*, mark.]

note-book (nōt′book′) *n.* A book of blank pages for notes.

not-ed (nō′tĭd) *adj.* Well-known; famous.

note-wor-thy (nōt′wûr′thē) *adj.* Deserving notice or attention; remarkable. —**note′wor′thi-ness** *n.*

noth-ing (nŭth′ĭng) *n.* **1.** No thing; not anything. **2.** No part; no portion: *Nothing remains of its former glory.* **3.** One of no interest or importance. **4.** Absence of anything perceptible; nonexistence: *The sound faded into nothing.* **5.** Zero. —*adv.* Not at all: *He looks nothing like me.* [< OE *nāthing*.]

Usage: Nothing takes a singular verb, even when it is followed by a phrase containing a plural noun or pronoun: *Nothing except your fears stands* (not *stand*) *in your path.*

noth-ing-ness (nŭth′ĭng-nĭs) *n.* **1.** The condi-

---

non′scho-las′tic *adj.*
non′sci-en-tif′ic *adj.*
non′scor′ing *adj.*
non′sea′son-al *adj.*
non′sec-re-tar′i-al *adj.*
non′sec′u-lar *adj.*
non′seg-men′tal *adj.*
non′se-lec′tive *adj.*
non-Sem′ite *n.*
non′sen-a-to′ri-al *adj.*
non′sen-si-tive *adj.*
non′sen′su-ral *adj.*
non′ser′vile *adj.*
non′sex′u-al *adj.*
non′sig-nif′i-cant *adj.*
non′slip′per-y *adj.*
non-smok′er *n.*
non-smok′ing *adj.*
non-so′cial *adj.*
non-so′cial-ist *n.*
non′sol′vent *n.*
non′spar′ing *adj.*
non′spar′kling *adj.*
non′spe-cif′ic *adj.*
non′spec-tac′u-lar *adj.*
non′spec′u-la′tive *adj.*
non′spher′i-cal *adj.*
non′spir′i-tu-ral *adj. & n.*
non′spon-ta′ne-ous *adj.*
non′sport′ing *adj.*
non′stand′ard-ized′ *adj.*
non′sta′tion-ar′y *adj.*
non-stat′u-to′ry *adj.*

non′stick′ *adj.*
non′stim-u-la′tion *n.*
non′stra-te′gic *adj.*
non′stretch′a-ble *adj.*
non′stri′at-ed *adj.*
non′strik′er *n.*
non′struc′tur-al *adj.*
non′sub-mis′sive *adj.*
non′sub-scrib′er *n.*
non′suc-cess′ *n.*
non′sup-port′er *n.*
non′sur′gi-cal *adj.*
non′sus-tain′ing *adj.*
non′sym-pa-thet′ic *adj.*
non′sym′pa-thy *n.*
non′sym-phon′ic *adj.*
non′symp-to-mat′ic *adj.*
non′syn′chro-nous *adj.*
non′syn-tac′tic *adj.*
non′sys-tem-at′ic *adj.*
non-talk′a-tive *adj.*
non′tech′ni-cal *adj.*
non′tem′po-ral *adj.*
non′ter-ri-to′ri-al *adj.*
non′tex′tur-al *adj.*
non′the-at′ri-cal *adj.*
non′ther′mal *adj.*
non′think′er *n.*
non′tox′ic *adj.*
non′tra-di′tion-al *adj.*
non′trag′ic *adj.*
non′trans-fer′a-ble *adj.*

non′tran-si′tion-al *adj.*
non′trans-par′ent *adj.*
non-triv′i-al *adj.*
non-truth′ *n.*
non′tur-ber′cu-lar *adj.*
non′typ′i-cal′ *adj.*
non′ty-po-graph′ic *adj.*
non′ty-po-graph′i-cal *adj.*
non′un-der-stand′a-ble *adj.*
non′un-der-stand′ing *adj. & n.*
non-u′ni-form′ *adj.*
non′u-ni-ver′sal *adj. & n.*
non-ur′ban *adj.*
non-us′er *n.*
non′u-til′i-tar′i-an *adj.*
non′va-lid′i-ty *n.*
non-val′ue *n.*
non′vas′cu-lar *adj.*
non′ven-om-ous *adj.*
non′ver′bal *adj.*
non-ver′ti-cal *adj.*
non-vet′er-an *n.*
non′vi-o-la′tion *n.*
non-vis′ur-al *adj.*
non-vi′tal *adj.*
non-vo′cal *adj.*
non′vo-ca′tion-al *adj.*
non′vol′a-tile *adj.*
non-vol′un-tar′y *adj.*
non-vot′er *n.*
non-white′ *n. & adj.*
non-work′er *n.*
non-yield′ing *adj.*

tion or quality of being nothing; nonexistence. **2.** Empty space; void.

no·tice (nō'tĭs) *n.* **1.** Attention; observation. **2.** Respectful attention or consideration. **3.** A usu. formal announcement. **4.** A written or printed announcement. **5.** A critical review, as of a book. —*v.* **-ticed, -tic·ing. 1.** To observe. **2.** To comment on; mention. [< Lat. *notus,* p.p. of *noscere,* to come to know.]

no·tice·a·ble (nō'tĭ-sə-bəl) *adj.* **1.** Readily observed; evident. **2.** Deserving of notice. —**no'tice·a·bly** *adv.*

no·ti·fy (nō'tə-fī') *v.* **-fied, -fy·ing. 1.** To give notice to; inform. **2.** To give notice of; proclaim. [< Lat. *notificare,* to make known.] —**no'ti·fi·ca'tion** *n.* —**no'ti·fi'er** *n.*

no·tion (nō'shən) *n.* **1.** A conception; idea. **2.** A belief; opinion. **3.** A fanciful impulse; whim. **4. notions.** Small useful items, such as needles, buttons, or thread. [Lat. *notio.*] —**no'tion·al** *adj.*

no·to·ri·ous (nō-tôr'ē-əs, -tōr'-) *adj.* Known widely and usu. unfavorably. [< Lat. *notus,* known.] —**no·to'ri·e·ty** (-tə-rī'ĭ-tē) *n.* —**no·to'ri·ous·ly** *adv.*

no-trump (nō'trŭmp') *n.* In bridge and other card games, a declaration to play a hand without a trump suit. —**no'-trump'** *adj.*

not·with·stand·ing (nŏt'wĭth-stăn'dĭng, -wĭth-) *prep.* In spite of. —*adv.* All the same; nevertheless. —*conj.* In spite of the fact that; although.

nou·gat (nōō'gət) *n.* A candy made from nuts and honey or sugar. [< Prov.]

nought (nôt) *n.* Var. of **naught.**

noun (noun) *n.* A word used to name a person, place, thing, quality, or action. [< Lat. *nomen,* name.]

nour·ish (nûr'ĭsh, nŭr'-) *v.* **1.** To provide with substances necessary for life and growth. **2.** To foster the development of; promote. [< Lat. *nutrire.*] —**nour'ish·ing** *adj.* —**nour'ish·ment** *n.*

nou·veau riche (nōō'vō rēsh') *n., pl.* **nou·veaux riches** (nōō'vō rēsh'). One who has recently become rich. [Fr., new rich.]

no·va (nō'və) *n., pl.* **-vae** (-vē) or **-vas.** A star that suddenly increases greatly in brightness and then returns to its original appearance over a period of time. [< Lat. *novus,* new.]

nov·el[1] (nŏv'əl) *n.* A fictional prose narrative of considerable length, typically having a plot that is unfolded by the actions, speech, and thoughts of the characters. [Ital. *(storia) novella,* new (story).] —**nov'el·ist** *n.* —**nov·el·is'tic** *adj.*

nov·el[2] (nŏv'əl) *adj.* Strikingly new or unusual. [< Lat. *novellus,* dim. of *novus,* new.] —**nov'el·ly** *adv.*

nov·el·ette (nŏv'ə-lĕt') *n.* A short novel.

nov·el·ize (nŏv'ə-līz') *v.* **-ized, -iz·ing.** To convert into a novelistic format. —**nov'el·i·za'tion** *n.*

no·vel·la (nō-vĕl'ə) *n., pl.* **-las** or **-vel·le** (-vĕl'ē). A short novel. [Ital.]

nov·el·ty (nŏv'əl-tē) *n., pl.* **-ties. 1.** The quality of being novel. **2.** Something new and unusual; newness. **3. novelties.** Small mass-produced articles, as trinkets.

No·vem·ber (nō-vĕm'bər) *n.* The 11th month

of the year, having 30 days. See table at **calendar.** [< Lat., ninth month.]

no·ve·na (nō-vē'nə) *n., pl.* **-nas** or **-nae** (-nē). *Rom. Cath. Ch.* A nine-days' devotion. [< Lat. *novem,* nine.]

nov·ice (nŏv'ĭs) *n.* **1.** A beginner. **2.** One who has entered a religious order, but has not yet taken the final vows. [< Lat. *novus,* new.]

no·vi·ti·ate (nō-vĭsh'ē-ĭt, -āt') *n.* **1.** The period of being a novice. **2.** A place where novices live. **3.** A novice. [Med. Lat. *noviciatus,* ult. < Lat. *novus,* new.]

now (nou) *adv.* **1.** At the present time. **2.** Very recently. **3.** Very soon. **4.** At this point in the series of events; then. **5.** In these circumstances; as things are. **6.** Used esp. to introduce a command, reproof, or request: *Now pay attention.* —*conj.* Since; seeing that. —*n.* The present time or moment. —*adj. Informal.* Of the present time; current: *the now generation.* [< OE *nū.*]

now·a·days (nou'ə-dāz') *adv.* During the present time. [ME *nou a daies,* on this day.]

no·way (nō'wā') *adv.* Also **no·ways** (-wāz'). Nowise.

no·where (nō'hwâr', -wâr') *adv.* **1.** Not anywhere. **2.** To no place or result. —*n.* A remote, unknown, or nonexistent place.

no·wise (nō'wīz') *adv.* In no way, manner, or degree; not at all.

nox·ious (nŏk'shəs) *adj.* Injurious to health or morals. [< Lat. *noxa,* damage.]

noz·zle (nŏz'əl) *n.* A projecting part with an opening through which something is discharged. [Dim. of NOSE.]

Np The symbol for the element neptunium.

nth (ĕnth) *adj.* **1.** Corresponding in order to an indefinitely large whole number. **2.** Highest; utmost: *to the nth degree.*

nu (nōō, nyōō) *n.* The 13th letter of the Greek alphabet. See table at **alphabet.** [Gk.]

nu·ance (nōō-äns', nyōō-, nōō'äns', nyōō'-) *n.* A subtle or slight degree of difference, as in meaning, color, or tone. [< OFr. *nuer,* to show different shades.]

nub (nŭb) *n.* **1.** A lump or knob. **2.** The essence; core. [< MLG *knubbe,* knot on a tree.] —**nub'by** *adj.*

nub·bin (nŭb'ĭn) *n.* Something, as an ear of corn, stunted or imperfectly developed. [Dim. of NUB.]

nu·bile (nōō'bəl, -bīl', nyōō'-) *adj.* Of a marriageable age. [< Lat. *nubilis.*]

nu·cle·ar (nōō'klē-ər, nyōō'-) *adj.* **1.** *Biol.* Of, relating to, or forming a nucleus. **2.** *Physics.* Of or concerning atomic nuclei. **3.** Of or using nuclear energy or nuclear weapons.

nuclear energy *n.* Energy that is released from an atomic nucleus, esp. by fission, fusion, or radioactive decay.

nuclear fission *n.* Fission.

nuclear fusion *n.* Fusion.

nuclear reaction *n.* A reaction that alters the energy, composition, or structure of an atomic nucleus.

nuclear reactor *n.* A device in which a nuclear chain reaction is started and controlled.

nu·cle·ate (nōō'klē-ĭt, nyōō'-) *adj.* Having a nucleus or nuclei. —*v.* (nōō'klē-āt', nyōō'-) **-at·ed, -at·ing.** —*v.* **1.** To bring together into or form a nucleus. **2.** To act as a nucleus for. [NUCLE(O)- + -ATE[1].] **—nu·cle·a'tion** n.

nu·cle·ic acid (nŏŏ-klē'ĭk, nyŏŏ-). A member of either of two groups of complex chemical compounds found in all living cells.

nucleo— or **nucle—** pref. Nucleus: nucleon. [< NUCLEUS.]

nu·cle·o·lus (nŏŏ-klē'ə-ləs, nyŏŏ-) n., pl. **-li** (-lī'). Also **nu·cle·ole** (nŏŏ'klē-ōl', nyŏŏ'-). Biol. A small body of protein and ribonucleic acid in the nucleus of a cell. [Lat., dim. of nucleus, kernel.] **—nu·cle'o·lar** (-lər) adj.

nu·cle·on (nŏŏ'klē-ŏn', nyŏŏ'-). A proton or a neutron, esp. as part of an atomic nucleus. **—nu·cle·on'ic** adj.

nu·cle·on·ics (nŏŏ-klē-ŏn'ĭks, nyŏŏ'-) n. (used with a sing. verb). The branch of science that deals with the application of nuclear energy.

nu·cle·us (nŏŏ'klē-əs, nyŏŏ'-) n., pl. **-cle·i** (-klē-ī') or **-es.** **1.** A central or essential part around which other parts are grouped or collected; core. **2.** Biol. A structure within a living cell that contains the cell's hereditary material and controls metabolism, growth, and reproduction. **3.** Physics. The central, positively charged core of an atom, composed of protons and neutrons, and containing almost all of the mass of the atom. [Lat., kernel < nux, nut.]

nu·clide (nŏŏ'klīd', nyŏŏ'-) n. Physics. An atomic nucleus specified by its atomic number, atomic mass, and energy state. **—nu·clid'ic** (nŏŏ-klĭd'ĭk, nyŏŏ-) adj.

nude (nŏŏd, nyŏŏd) adj. Without clothing; naked. **—n.** **1.** The unclothed human figure, esp. in artistic representation. **2.** The condition of being unclothed. [Lat. nudus.] **—nu'di·ty** n.

nudge (nuj) v. **nudged, nudg·ing.** To push against gently, esp. in order to gain attention. [Prob. of Scand. orig.] **—nudge** n.

nud·ism (nŏŏ'dĭz'əm, nyŏŏ'-) n. The belief in or practice of going nude. **—nu'dist** n.

nu·ga·to·ry (nŏŏ'gə-tôr'ē, -tōr'ē, nyŏŏ'-) adj. **1.** Of little or no importance; trifling. **2.** Without force; invalid. [< Lat. nugae, jokes.]

nug·get (nŭg'ĭt) n. A small lump, esp. of gold. [< nug, lump.]

nui·sance (nŏŏ'səns, nyŏŏ'-) n. Something that is inconvenient, annoying, or unpleasant. [< OFr., ult. < Lat. nocēre, to harm.]

null (nŭl) adj. **1.** Having no legal force; invalid. **2.** Of no consequence; insignificant. **3.** Amounting to nothing. [< Lat. nullus.] **—null'i·ty** n.

nul·li·fy (nŭl'ə-fī') v. **-fied, -fy·ing. 1.** To make null; invalidate. **2.** To counteract. **—nul'li·fi·ca'tion** n.

numb (nŭm) adj. **-er, -est. 1.** Insensible, as from excessive chill. **2.** Stunned, as from shock. [< OE niman, to seize.] **—numb** v. **—numb'ly** adv. **—numb'ness** n.

num·ber (nŭm'bər) n. **1. a.** A member of the set of positive integers. **b.** A member of any of the further sets of mathematical objects that can be derived from the positive integers. **2. numbers.** Arithmetic. **3.** A numeral or series of numerals designating a specific object. **4.** A specific quantity composed of equal units. **5.** Quantity of units: The crowd was small in number. **6.** A multitude. **7.** One item in a sequence or series. **8. Numbers.** See table at Bible. **—v. 1.** To add up to. **2.** To count or enumerate. **3.** To include in or be one of a

group. **4.** To assign a number to. **5.** To limit in number. [< Lat. numerus.]

Usage: Number may take either a singular or plural verb. It takes a singular verb when preceded by the: The number of skilled workers is small. It takes a plural verb when preceded by a: A number of the workers are unskilled.

num·ber·less (nŭm'bər-lĭs) adj. Innumerable; countless.

nu·mer·a·ble (nŏŏ'mər-ə-bəl, nyŏŏ'-) adj. Capable of being counted; countable. [< Lat. numerus, number.]

nu·mer·al (nŏŏ'mər-əl, nyŏŏ'-) n. A symbol or mark used to represent a number. **—nu'mer·al** adj.

nu·mer·ate (nŏŏ'mə-rāt', nyŏŏ'-) v. **-at·ed, -at·ing.** To count; number. **—nu'mer·a'tion** n.

nu·mer·a·tor (nŏŏ'mə-rā'tər, nyŏŏ'-) n. The number written above the line in a common fraction.

nu·mer·i·cal (nŏŏ-mĕr'ĭ-kəl, nyŏŏ-) adj. Also **nu·mer·ic** (-ĭk). Of, relating to, represented by, or representing a number. **—nu·mer'i·cal·ly** adv.

nu·mer·ol·o·gy (nŏŏ'mə-rŏl'ə-jē, nyŏŏ'-) n. The study of the occult meanings of numbers. **—nu'mer·ol'o·gist** n.

nu·mer·ous (nŏŏ'mər-əs, nyŏŏ'-) adj. Consisting of many persons or items. **—nu'mer·ous·ly** adv.

Usage: Numerous is not used as a pronoun in standard English. Therefore, expressions like numerous of the firemen should be avoided.

nu·mis·mat·ics (nŏŏ'mĭz-măt'ĭks, -mĭs-, nyŏŏ'-) n. (used with a sing. verb). The collection or study of money and medals. [< Gk. numisma, current coin.] **—nu·mis·mat'ic** adj. **—nu·mis'ma·tist** n.

num·skull (nŭm'skŭl') n. A stupid person; blockhead. [NUM(B) + SKULL.]

nun[1] (nŭn) n. A woman who belongs to a religious order. [< LLat. nonna.]

nun[2] (nŏŏn) n. The 14th letter of the Hebrew alphabet. See table at alphabet. [Heb. nûn.]

nun·ci·o (nŭn'sē-ō', nŏŏn'-) n., pl. **-os.** A papal ambassador or representative. [< Lat. nuntius, messenger.]

nun·ner·y (nŭn'ə-rē) n., pl. **-ies.** A convent.

nup·tial (nŭp'shəl, -chəl) adj. Of or relating to marriage or the wedding ceremony. **—n. nuptials.** A wedding ceremony. [< Lat. nuptus, p.p. of nubere, to take a husband.]

nurse (nûrs) n. **1.** One trained to care for the sick. **2.** One employed to take care of a child; nursemaid. **—v. nursed, nurs·ing. 1.** To suckle. **2.** To serve as a nurse (for). **3.** To treat: nurse a cough. **4.** To take special care of; foster. **5.** To bear in the mind: nursing a grudge. **6.** To treat carefully. [< Lat. nutrix.] **—nurs'er** n.

nurse·maid (nûrs'mād') n. Also **nurs·er·y·maid** (nûr'sə-rē-mād', nûrs'rē-). A woman employed to take care of children.

nurs·er·y (nûr'sə-rē, nûrs'rē) n., pl. **-ies. 1.** A room set apart for the children. **2. a.** A nursery school. **b.** A place for the temporary care of children. **3.** A place where plants are grown, esp. for sale.

nurs·er·y·man (nûr'sə-rē-mən, nûrs'rē-) n. One who owns or works in a nursery for plants.

nursery school n. A school for children who are too young for kindergarten.

nurs·ling (nûrs′lĭng) n. 1. A nursing infant or young animal. 2. A carefully nurtured person or thing.

nur·ture (nûr′chər) n. 1. Something that nourishes; sustenance; food. 2. Training; rearing. —v. -tured, -tur·ing. 1. To nourish. 2. To educate; train. 3. To cultivate; foster. [< Lat. *nutrire*, to suckle.] —**nur′tur·er** n.

nut (nŭt) n. 1. a. A fruit or seed with a hard shell and an inner kernel. b. The often edible kernel itself. 2. *Slang.* a. A crazy or eccentric person. b. An enthusiast. 3. A small block of metal or wood that has a threaded hole in its center and is designed to screw onto and hold a matching bolt or screw. 4. *Mus.* A ridge of wood at the top of the fingerboard or neck of stringed instruments, over which the strings pass. [< OE *hnutu.*]

nut·crack·er (nŭt′krăk′ər) n. An implement used to crack nuts.

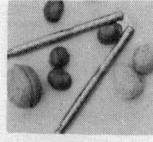

nutcracker   nutmeg

nut·meat (nŭt′mēt′) n. The edible kernel of a nut.

nut·meg (nŭt′mĕg′) n. The hard, aromatic seed of a tropical tree used as a spice when grated or ground. [Prob. < OFr. *nois mugede.*]

nu·tri·a (nōō′trē-ə, nyōō′-) n. The thick, brownish fur of a beaverlike South American rodent. [Sp.]

nu·tri·ent (nōō′trē-ənt, nyōō′-) adj. Providing nourishment. [< Lat. *nutrire*, to feed.] —**nu′tri·ent** n.

nu·tri·ment (nōō′trə-mənt, nyōō′-) n. Something that nourishes.

nu·tri·tion (nōō-trĭsh′ən, nyōō-) n. The process of nourishing or being nourished, esp. the process by which a living organism assimilates and uses food. —**nu·tri′tion·al** adj. —**nu′tri·tive** (-trĭ-tĭv′) adj.

nu·tri·tion·ist (nōō-trĭsh′ə-nĭst, nyōō-) n. One who specializes in the study of nutrition.

nu·tri·tious (nōō-trĭsh′əs, nyōō-) adj. Providing nourishment. [< Lat. *nutrix*, nurse.] —**nu·tri′tious·ly** adv. —**nu·tri′tious·ness** n.

nuts (nŭts) adj. *Slang.* 1. Crazy; insane. 2. Extremely enthusiastic. —interj. *Slang.* A word used to express disappointment, contempt, or refusal. [< NUT.]

nut·shell (nŭt′shĕl′) n. The shell of a nut. —idiom. **in a nutshell.** In a few words.

nut·ty (nŭt′ē) adj. -ti·er, -ti·est. 1. Full of or tasting like nuts. 2. *Slang.* Crazy. —**nut′ti·ly** adv. —**nut′ti·ness** n.

nuz·zle (nŭz′əl) v. -zled, -zling. 1. To rub or push against gently with the nose or snout. 2. To nestle together. [< NOSE.]

ny·lon (nī′lŏn′) n. 1. Any of various very strong, elastic synthetic resins. 2. Cloth or yarn made from nylon. 3. **nylons.** Stockings made of nylon. [Coined by its inventors, E. I. duPont de Nemours & Co., Inc.]

nymph (nĭmf) n. 1. *Gk. & Rom. Myth.* One of the female spirits dwelling in woodlands and waters. 2. A young, incompletely developed form of certain insects that goes through a series of gradual changes before reaching the adult stage. [< Gk. *numphē.*]

Oo

o or **O** (ō) n., pl. **o's** or **O's.** 1. The 15th letter of the English alphabet. 2. A zero. 3. Something shaped like the letter O.

O¹ (ō) interj. 1. Used before the name of a person or thing being formally addressed: *Hear us, O Lord.* 2. Used to express surprise or strong emotion: *O my goodness!*

Usage: *O* is used chiefly in religious or poetic invocations: *O God on High! O mighty ocean!* It is always capitalized and is never followed directly by punctuation. The interjection *oh* can stand alone or as part of a sentence to express strong emotions or merely a reflective pause: *Oh! What a horse! Oh, I see.* It is only capitalized when it is the first word of a sentence and is usually followed by a comma or, when the emphasis is strong, by an exclamation point.

O² The symbol for the element oxygen.

oaf (ōf) n. A stupid or clumsy person. [< ON *alfr*, elf.] —**oaf′ish** adj. —**oaf′ish·ly** adv. —**oaf′ish·ness** n.

oak (ōk) n. 1. Any of various trees bearing acorns as fruit. 2. The hard, durable wood of the oak. [< OE *āc.*] —**oak′en** adj.

oa·kum (ō′kəm) n. Hemp or jute fiber, sometimes treated with tar, used for caulking ships. [< OE *ācumba.*]

oar (ôr, ōr) n. 1. A long pole with a blade at one end, used to row or steer a boat. 2. An oarsman. [< OE *ār.*]

oar·lock (ôr′lŏk′, ōr′-) n. A U-shaped device used to hold an oar in place.

oars·man (ôrz′mən, ōrz′-) n. One who rows a boat, esp. in a racing crew.

o·a·sis (ō-ā′sĭs) n., pl. -ses (-sēz′). A fertile or green spot in a desert. [Gk.]

oat (ōt) n. Often **oats.** 1. A cereal grass widely cultivated for its edible seeds. 2. The seeds of this plant. [< OE *āte.*] —**oat′en** adj.

oath (ōth) *n., pl.* **oaths** (ōthz, ōths). **1.** A formal promise to fulfill a pledge, often calling upon God as witness. **2.** A blasphemous use of a sacred name. [< OE *āth.*]

oat·meal (ōt′mēl′) *n.* **1.** Meal made from oats; ground or rolled oats. **2.** A porridge made from ground or rolled oats.

O·ba·di·ah (ō′bə-dī′ə) *n.* See table at **Bible.**

ob·bli·ga·to (ŏb′lĭ-gä′tō) *n., pl.* **-tos** or **-ti** (-tē). *Mus.* An accompaniment that is an integral, indispensable part of a piece. [Ital.]

ob·du·rate (ŏb′dŏŏ-rĭt, -dyŏŏ-) *adj.* Hardened against influence or feeling; unyielding. [< Lat. *obdurare,* to harden.] **—ob′du·ra·cy** *n.* **—ob′du·rate·ly** *adv.* **—ob′du·rate·ness** *n.*

o·be·di·ent (ō-bē′dē-ənt) *adj.* Obeying or inclined to obey. [< Lat. *oboedire,* to obey.] **—o·be′di·ence** *n.* **—o·be′di·ent·ly** *adv.*

o·bei·sance (ō-bā′səns, ō-bē′-) *n.* **1.** A gesture, as a bow, expressing respect. **2.** Great deference. [< OFr. *obeir,* to obey.] **—obei′sant** *adj.*

ob·e·lisk (ŏb′ə-lĭsk′) *n.* A tall, four-sided shaft of stone, usu. tapering to a pyramidal point. [< Gk. *obeliskos.*]

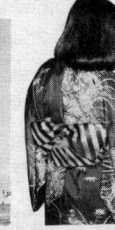

obelisk   **obi**

o·bese (ō-bēs′) *adj.* Fat; corpulent. [Lat. *obesus,* p.p. of *obedere,* to devour.] **—o·be′si·ty** or **o·bese′ness** *n.*

o·bey (ō-bā′) *v.* **1.** To carry out the commands of. **2.** To comply with (a command, order, or request). [< Lat. *oboedire.*] **—o·bey′er** *n.*
Syns: *obey, comply, follow, mind* v.

ob·fus·cate (ŏb′fə-skāt′, ŏb-fŭs′kāt′, əb-) *v.* **-cat·ed, -cat·ing. 1.** To make indistinct or dark. **2.** To confuse or becloud. [LLat. *obfuscare.*] **—ob′fus·ca′tion** *n.* **—ob·fus′ca·to′ry** (ŏb-fŭs′kə-tôr′ē, -tōr′ē, əb-) *adj.*

o·bi (ō′bē) *n.* A wide sash worn with a Japanese kimono. [J., belt.]

o·bit (ō′bĭt, ŏ-bĭt′) *n. Informal.* An obituary.

o·bi·ter dic·tum (ō′bĭ-tər dĭk′təm) *n., pl.* **obiter dic·ta** (-tə). An incidental remark or observation. [Lat., something said in passing.]

o·bit·u·ar·y (ō-bĭch′ōō-ěr′ē) *n., pl.* **-ies.** A death notice, usu. with a brief biography of the deceased. [Med. Lat. *obituarius,* (report) of death.] **—o·bit′u·ar′y** *adj.*

ob·ject¹ (əb-jĕkt′) *v.* **1.** To present a dissenting or opposing argument. **2.** To feel or express disapproval. [< Lat. *obicere.*] **—ob·jec′tion** *n.* **—ob·jec′tor** *n.*

ob·ject² (ŏb′jĭkt, -jĕkt′) *n.* **1.** Something perceptible by the senses; a material thing. **2.** Something intelligible or perceptible by the mind. **3.** Something serving as a focus of attention or action. **4.** The purpose of a specific action. **5.** *Gram.* A noun that receives or is affected by the action of a verb or that follows and is governed by a preposition. [< Lat. *objectus,* p.p. of *obicere,* to oppose.]

ob·jec·tion·a·ble (əb-jĕk′shə-nə-bəl) *adj.* Arousing disapproval; offensive. **—ob·jec′tion·a·bil′i·ty** *n.* **—ob·jec′tion·a·bly** *adv.*

ob·jec·tive (əb-jĕk′tĭv) *adj.* **1.** Of or having to do with a material object as distinguished from a mental concept, idea, or belief. **2.** Having actual existence. **3. a.** Uninfluenced by emotion or personal prejudice. **b.** Based on observable phenomena. **4.** *Gram.* Denoting the case of a noun or pronoun serving as the object of a verb or preposition. **5.** Serving as the goal of a course of action. **—n. 1.** Something worked toward or striven for; goal. **2.** *Gram.* The objective case or a noun or pronoun in the objective case. **3.** The lens in an optical system that is closest to the object. **—ob·jec′tive·ly** *adv.* **—ob·jec′tive·ness** *n.* **—ob′jec·tiv′i·ty** (ŏb′jĕk-tĭv′ĭ-tē) *n.*

object lesson *n.* A lesson taught by concrete examples.

ob·jet d'art (ŏb′zhĕ′ där′) *n., pl.* **ob·jets d'art** (ŏb′zhĕ′ där′). An object of artistic merit. [Fr.]

ob·jur·gate (ŏb′jər-gāt′, ŏb-jûr′gāt′) *v.* **-gat·ed, -gat·ing.** To rebuke harshly. [Lat. *objurgare.*] **—ob′jur·ga′tion** *n.*

ob·late (ŏb′lāt′, ŏb-lāt′) *adj.* Compressed along or flattened at the poles: *oblate spheroid.* [Med. Lat. *oblatus.*] **—ob′late·ly** *adv.* **—ob′late·ness** *n.*

ob·la·tion (ə-blā′shən, ŏ-blā′-) *n.* The ritual of offering something to a deity. [< Lat. *oblatus,* p.p. of *offerre,* to offer.] **—ob·la′tion·al** *adj.*

ob·li·gate (ŏb′lĭ-gāt′) *v.* **-gat·ed, -gat·ing.** To bind, compel, or constrain by a legal or moral tie. [< Lat. *obligare.*] **—ob′li·ga′tor** *n.*

ob·li·ga·tion (ŏb′lĭ-gā′shən) *n.* **1.** The act of binding oneself by a social, legal, or moral tie. **2.** Something, as a contract or promise, that constrains one to a certain course of action. **3.** The constraining power of a law, promise, contract, or sense of duty. **4.** The fact or condition of being indebted to another for a favor received.

o·blig·a·to·ry (ə-blĭg′ə-tôr′ē, -tōr′ē, ŏb′lĭ-gə-) *adj.* **1.** Legally or morally constraining. **2.** Compulsory. **—o·blig′a·to′ri·ly** *adv.*

o·blige (ə-blīj′) *v.* **o·bliged, o·blig·ing. 1.** To constrain. **2.** To make indebted by physical, legal, or moral means. **3.** To do a service or favor for. [< Lat. *obligare.*] **—o·blig′er** *n.* **—o·blig′ing·ly** *adv.* **—o·blig′ing·ness** *n.*

o·blique (ō-blēk′, ə-blēk′) *adj.* **1. a.** Slanting or sloping. **b.** *Geom.* Neither parallel nor perpendicular. **2.** Indirect or evasive; not straightforward. **—n.** Something oblique. [< Lat. *obliquus.*] **—o·blique′ly** *adv.* **—o·blique′ness** *n.* **—o·bliq′ui·ty** *n.*

o·blit·er·ate (ə-blĭt′ə-rāt′) *v.* **-at·ed, -at·ing. 1.** To destroy completely. **2.** To wipe out; erase. [< Lat. *obliterare.*] **—o·blit′er·a′tion** *n.* **—o·blit′er·a′tive** (-ə-rā′tĭv, -ər-ə-tĭv) *adj.* **—o·blit′er·a′tor** *n.*

o·bliv·i·on (ə-blĭv′ē-ən) *n.* **1.** The condition of being completely forgotten. **2.** Forgetfulness. [< Lat. *oblivisci,* to forget.]

o·bliv·i·ous (ə-blĭv′ē-əs) *adj.* **1.** Lacking all memory of something; forgetful. **2.** Unaware or unmindful. **—o·bliv′i·ous·ly** *adv.* **—o·bliv′i·ous·ness** *n.*

ob·long (ŏb′lông′, -lŏng′) *adj.* **1.** Having one of two perpendicular dimensions, as length or width, greater than the other; rectangular.

2. *Bot.* Elongated. [< Lat. *oblongus.*] —**ob′-long** *n.*

ob·lo·quy (ŏb′lə-kwē) *n., pl.* **-quies.** **1.** Abusive or slanderous language. **2.** Ill repute; disgrace. [< Lat. *obloqui,* to speak against.]

ob·nox·ious (ŏb-nŏk′shəs, əb-) *adj.* Highly disagreeable or offensive; odious. [< Lat. *obnoxius,* punishable.] —**ob·nox′ious·ly** *adv.* —**ob·nox′ious·ness** *n.*

o·boe (ō′bō) *n.* A slender woodwind instrument with a conical bore and a double-reed mouthpiece. [< Fr. *hautbois.*] —**o′bo·ist** *n.*

ob·scene (ŏb-sēn′, əb-) *adj.* **1.** Offensive to accepted standards of decency. **2.** Inciting lustful feelings. **3.** Offensive to the senses. [< Lat. *obscenus.*] —**ob·scene′ly** *adv.* —**ob·scen′i·ty** (-sēn′ĭ-tē) *n.*

ob·scur·ant·ism (ŏb-skyŏŏr′ən-tĭz′əm, əb-, ŏb′skyŏŏ-răn′tĭz′əm) *n.* **1.** Deliberate abstruseness. **2.** Opposition to free inquiry or the advancement of knowledge. —**ob·scur′ant·ist** *n.*

ob·scure (ŏb-skyŏŏr′, əb-) *adj.* **-scur·er, -scur·est.** **1.** Dark; gloomy. **2.** Indistinctly heard or perceived. **3.** Out of sight; hidden. **4.** Not famous or well-known. **5.** Difficult to understand. —*v.* **-scured, -scur·ing.** **1.** To make indistinct or unclear. **2.** To conceal from view; hide. [< Lat. *obscurus.*] —**ob·scure′ly** *adv.* —**ob·scure′ness** or **ob·scu′ri·ty** *n.*

ob·se·qui·ous (ŏb-sē′kwē-əs, əb-) *adj.* Servilely compliant; fawning. [< Lat. *obsequiosus.*] —**ob·se′qui·ous·ly** *adv.* —**ob·se′qui·ous·ness** *n.*

ob·se·quy (ŏb′sĭ-kwē) *n., pl.* **-quies.** A funeral rite or ceremony. [< Lat. *obsequium,* compliance.]

ob·serv·ance (əb-zûr′vəns) *n.* **1.** The act of observing or complying with something prescribed, as a law or custom. **2.** The keeping or celebrating of a holiday or other ritual occasion. **3.** Observation.

ob·serv·ant (əb-zûr′vənt) *adj.* **1.** Quick to observe or take notice; alert. **2.** Diligent in observing~a law, custom, duty, or principle. —**ob·serv′ant·ly** *adv.*

ob·ser·va·tion (ŏb′zər-vā′shən) *n.* **1.** The act of observing or the condition of being observed. **2.** Something that has been observed. **3.** A comment; remark. —**ob′ser·va′tion·al** *adj.* —**ob′ser·va′tion·al·ly** *adv.*

ob·ser·va·to·ry (əb-zûr′və-tôr′ē, -tōr′ē) *n., pl.* **-ries.** A building equipped for making observations of astronomical, meteorological, or other natural phenomena.

ob·serve (əb-zûrv′) *v.* **-served, -serv·ing.** **1.** To perceive; notice. **2.** To watch attentively. **3.** To make a systematic or scientific observation of. **4.** To say by way of comment or remark. **5.** To adhere to or abide by. **6.** To keep or celebrate according to custom. [< Lat. *observare.*] —**ob·serv′a·ble** *adj.* —**ob·serv′a·ble·ness** *n.* —**ob·serv′a·bly** *adv.* —**ob·serv′er** *n.*

ob·sess (əb-sĕs′, ŏb-) *v.* To occupy the mind of excessively. [< Lat. *obsidēre,* to possess.]

ob·ses·sion (əb-sĕsh′ən, ŏb-) *n.* **1.** Compulsive preoccupation with a fixed idea or an unwanted feeling. **2.** An idea or emotion causing such preoccupation. —**ob·ses′sion·al** *adj.* —**ob·ses′sive** *adj.* —**ob·ses′sive·ly** *adv.*

ob·sid·i·an (ŏb-sĭd′ē-ən) *n.* An acid-resistant, lustrous volcanic glass, usu. black or banded. [< Lat. *obsidianus.*]

ob·so·les·cent (ŏb′sə-lĕs′ənt) *adj.* Becoming obsolete. [< Lat. *obsolescere,* to grow old.] —**ob′so·les′cence** *n.* —**ob′so·les′cent·ly** *adv.*

ob·so·lete (ŏb′sə-lēt′, ŏb′sə-lēt′) *adj.* **1.** No longer in use or fashion. **2.** No longer useful or functioning. [Lat. *obsoletus,* p.p. of *obsolescere,* to wear out.] —**ob′so·lete′ly** *adv.* —**ob′so·lete′ness** *n.*

ob·sta·cle (ŏb′stə-kəl) *n.* One that stands in the way of or holds up progress toward a goal. [< Lat. *obstaculum.*]

ob·ste·tri·cian (ŏb′stĭ-trĭsh′ən) *n.* A physician specializing in obstetrics.

ob·stet·rics (ŏb-stĕt′rĭks, əb-) *n.* *(used with a sing. verb).* The branch of medicine concerned with childbirth and the care of women during and after pregnancy. [< Lat. *obstetrix,* midwife.] —**ob·stet′ric** or **ob·stet′ri·cal** *adj.* —**ob·stet′ri·cal·ly** *adv.*

ob·sti·nate (ŏb′stə-nĭt) *adj.* **1.** Tenaciously unwilling to yield. **2.** Difficult to manage, control, or subdue. [< Lat. *obstinare,* to persist.] —**ob′sti·na·cy** (-nə-sē) or **ob′sti·nate·ness** *n.* —**ob′sti·nate·ly** *adv.*

Syns: *obstinate, bullheaded, dogged, hardheaded, headstrong, intractable, intransigent, perverse, pigheaded, refractory, stubborn, tough, willful* adj.

ob·strep·er·ous (əb-strĕp′ər-əs, ŏb-) *adj.* Noisily defiant; unruly. [Lat. *obstreperus.*] —**ob·strep′er·ous·ly** *adv.* —**ob·strep′er·ous·ness** *n.*

ob·struct (əb-strŭkt′, ŏb-) *v.* **1.** To block (a passage) with obstacles. **2.** To impede; retard. **3.** To get in the way of; hide, as a view. [< Lat. *obstructus,* p.p. of *obstruere,* to block.] —**ob·struct′er** or **ob·struc′tor** *n.* —**ob·struc′tive** *adj.*

ob·struc·tion (əb-strŭk′shən, ŏb-) *n.* **1.** An obstacle. **2.** An act or an instance of obstructing. **3.** The causing of delay.

ob·struc·tion·ist (əb-strŭk′shə-nĭst, ŏb-) *n.* One who systematically obstructs or interrupts progress. —**ob·struc′tion·ism** or **ob·struc′tion·is′tic** *adj.*

ob·tain (əb-tān′, ŏb-) *v.* **1.** To succeed in gaining; get or acquire. **2.** To be established or accepted. [< Lat. *obtinēre.*] —**ob·tain′a·ble** *adj.* —**ob·tain′er** *n.*

ob·trude (əb-trōŏd′, ŏb-) *v.* **-trud·ed, -trud·ing.** **1.** To force (oneself or one's ideas) upon others. **2.** To thrust out; push forward. [Lat. *obtrudere.*] —**ob·trud′er** *n.* —**ob·tru′sion** (əb-trōŏ′zhən, ŏb-) *n.* —**ob·tru′sive** (-trōŏ′sĭv) *adj.* —**ob·tru′sive·ly** *adv.* —**ob·tru′sive·ness** *n.*

ob·tuse (ŏb-tōŏs′, -tyōŏs′, əb-) *adj.* **1.** Not sharp, pointed, or acute; blunt. **2.** Slow to apprehend or perceive. [< Lat. *obtusus,* p.p. of *obtundere,* to blunt.] —**ob·tuse′ly** *adv.* —**ob·tuse′ness** *n.*

obtuse angle *n.* An angle greater than 90° and less than 180°.

ob·verse (ŏb-vûrs′, əb-, ŏb′vûrs′) *adj.* **1.** Facing the observer. **2.** Serving as a counterpart or complement. —*n.* (ŏb′vûrs′, ŏb-vûrs′, əb-). **1.** The side of a coin or medal that bears the principal stamp or design. **2.** A counterpart or complement. [Lat. *obversus*, p.p. of *obvertere*, to turn toward.] —**ob·verse'ly** *adv.*

ob·vi·ate (ŏb'vē-āt') *v.* **-at·ed, -at·ing.** To prevent by making unnecessary. [LLat. *obviare*.] —**ob'vi·a'tion** *n.* —**ob'vi·a'tor** *n.*

ob·vi·ous (ŏb'vē-əs) *adj.* Easily perceived or understood; apparent. [Lat. *obvius*.] —**ob'vi·ous·ly** *adv.* —**ob'vi·ous·ness** *n.*

oc·a·ri·na (ŏk'ə-rē'nə) *n.* A small bulb-shaped terra-cotta or plastic wind instrument with a mouthpiece and finger holes. [< Ital. *oca*, goose.]

oc·ca·sion (ə-kā'zhən) *n.* **1.** An event or happening, esp. a significant event. **2.** The time of an occurrence. **3.** A favorable time; opportunity. **4.** Something that brings on an action. **5.** Ground; reason. **6.** Need; necessity. —*v.* To provide occasion. —**Idiom. on occasion.** From time to time. [< Lat. *occidere*, to fall down.]

oc·ca·sion·al (ə-kā'zhə-nəl) *adj.* **1.** Occurring from time to time. **2.** Occurring on or created for a special occasion. —**oc·ca'sion·al·ly** *adv.*

Oc·ci·dent (ŏk'sə-dĭnt, -dĕnt') *n.* Europe and the Western Hemisphere. [< Lat. *occidere*, to set.] —**Oc'ci·den'tal** *adj. & n.*

oc·cip·i·tal (ŏk-sĭp'ĭ-tl) *adj.* Of the occiput or the occipital bone. —*n.* The occipital bone.

occipital bone *n.* A curved, trapezoidal, compound bone that forms the lower posterior part of the skull.

oc·ci·put (ŏk'sə-pət) *n., pl.* **-ci·pi·ta** (ŏk-sĭp'-ĭ-tə) or **-puts.** The back of the skull, esp. the occipital area. [Lat.]

oc·clude (ə-klood') *v.* **-clud·ed, -clud·ing. 1.** To close or shut off; obstruct. **2.** *Chem.* To absorb or adsorb in great quantities. **3.** To close so that the opposing tooth surfaces meet. [Lat. *occludere*.] —**oc·clu'sion** *n.*

oc·cult (ə-kŭlt', ŏ-kŭlt', ŏk'ŭlt') *adj.* **1.** Of or relating to supernatural influences, phenomena, or knowledge. **2.** Beyond human understanding. **3.** Available only to the initiate; secret. [< Lat. *occulere*, to conceal.] —**oc·cult'** *n.* —**oc·cult'ly** *adv.* —**oc·cult'ness** *n.*

oc·cult·ism (ə-kŭl'tĭz'əm, ŏ-kŭl'-, ŏk'əl-tĭz'əm) *n.* **1.** The study of the supernatural. **2.** A belief in supernatural powers. —**oc·cult'ist** *n.*

oc·cu·pan·cy (ŏk'yə-pən-sē) *n., pl.* **-cies. 1.** The act of occupying or condition of being occupied. **2.** The period during which something is occupied.

oc·cu·pant (ŏk'yə-pənt) *n.* One who occupies a position or place.

oc·cu·pa·tion (ŏk'yə-pā'shən) *n.* **1.** An activity that serves as one's regular source of livelihood. **2.** The act of occupying or state of being occupied. **3.** The invasion, conquest, and control of a nation or territory by a foreign military force. —**oc'cu·pa'tion·al** *adj.* —**oc'cu·pa'tion·al·ly** *adv.*

occupational therapy *n.* Therapy in which the principal element is some form of productive or creative activity.

oc·cu·py (ŏk'yə-pī') *v.* **-pied, -py·ing. 1.** To seize possession of and maintain control over (a place or region). **2.** To fill or take (time or space). **3.** To dwell or reside in. **4.** To hold or fill (an office). **5.** To engage or busy (oneself). [< Lat. *occupare*.] —**oc'cu·pi'er** *n.*

oc·cur (ə-kûr') *v.* **-curred, -cur·ring. 1.** To take place. **2.** To be found to exist or appear. **3.** To come to mind. [Lat. *occurrere*, to run to meet.] —**oc·cur'rence** *n.*

o·cean (ō'shən) *n.* **1.** The entire body of salt water that covers about 72% of the earth's surface. **2.** Often **Ocean.** Any of the principal divisions of this body of water: *the Atlantic Ocean.* **3.** A great expanse or amount. [< Gk. *okeanos*, a great river encircling the earth.] —**o'ce·an'ic** (ō'shē-ăn'ĭk) *adj.*

o·cean·ar·i·um (ō'shə-nâr'ē-əm) *n., pl.* **-i·ums** or **-i·a** (-ē-ə). A large aquarium for the study or display of marine life.

o·cean·og·ra·phy (ō'shə-nŏg'rə-fē) *n.* The exploration and scientific study of the ocean. —**o'cean·og'ra·pher** *n.* —**o'cean·o·graph'ic** (-nə-grăf'ĭk) or **o'cean·o·graph'i·cal** *adj.*

oc·e·lot (ŏs'ə-lŏt', ō'sə-) *n.* A spotted wild cat of the southwestern United States and Central and South America. [< Nahuatl *ocelotl*.]

ocelot

o·cher (ō'kər) *n.* Also **o·chre. 1.** Any of several earthy mineral oxides of iron mingled with varying amounts of clay and sand, occurring in yellow, brown, or red, and used as pigments. **2.** A yellowish or brownish orange. [< Gk. *ōkhros*, pale yellow.] —**o'cher·ous** (ō'-kər-əs) or **o'chery** (ō'krē) *adj.*

o'clock (ə-klŏk') *adv.* Of or according to the clock: *three o'clock.* [< *of the clock*.]

oct- or **octa-** *pref.* Eight: *octane.* [< Gk. *oktō,* and < Lat. *octo.*]

oc·ta·gon (ŏk'tə-gŏn') *n.* A polygon with eight sides and angles. —**oc·tag'o·nal** *adj.* —**oc·tag'o·nal·ly** *adv.*

oc·ta·he·dron (ŏk'tə-hē'drən) *n., pl.* **-drons** or **-dra** (-drə). A polyhedron with eight surfaces.

oc·tane (ŏk'tān') *n.* **1.** Any of various hydrocarbons with the formula C_8H_{18}. **2.** Octane number.

octane number *n.* A numerical measure of the antiknock properties of motor fuel, based on the percentage by volume of one particular octane in a standard reference fuel.

oc·tant (ŏk'tənt) *n.* One-eighth of a circle or of the arc of a circle. [Lat. *octans.*]

oc·tave (ŏk'tĭv, -tāv') *n.* **1.** *Mus.* The interval of eight diatonic degrees between two musical tones. **2.** Any group or series of eight. [< Lat. *octavus,* eighth.]

oc·ta·vo (ŏk-tā'vō, -tä'-) *n., pl.* **-vos. 1.** The page size (from 5 × 8 inches to 6 × 9½ inches) of a book composed of printer's sheets folded into eight leaves. **2.** A book composed of pages of this size. [< Lat. *octavus,* eighth.]

oc·tet (ŏk-tĕt') *n.* Also **oc·tette. 1.** A musical composition written for eight voices or instruments. **2.** A group of eight. [Ital. *ottetto.*]

Oc·to·ber (ŏk-tō'bər) *n.* The 10th month of the year, having 31 days. See table at **calendar.** [< Lat., 8th month.]

oc·to·ge·nar·i·an (ŏk'tə-jə-nâr'ē-ən) *n.* One

between 80 and 90 years of age. [< Lat. *octogenarius*, containing 80.]

oc·to·pus (ŏk'tə-pəs) *n., pl.* **-es** or **-pi** (-pī'). A marine mollusk with a rounded, saclike body and eight sucker-bearing tentacles. [< Gk. *oktopous*, eight-footed.]

oc·u·lar (ŏk'yə-lər) *adj.* **1.** Pertaining to the eye. **2.** Visual. —*n.* The eyepiece of an optical instrument. [LLat. *ocularis*.]

oc·u·list (ŏk'yə-list) *n.* **1.** An ophthalmologist. **2.** An optometrist. [Fr. *oculiste*.]

OD (ō'dē') *Slang.* —*n.* **1.** An overdose of a narcotic drug. **2.** One who has taken an overdose. —*v.* **OD'd, OD'ing.** To overdose.

odd (ŏd) *adj.* **-er, -est. 1. a.** Strange; unusual. **b.** Eccentric in conduct. **2.** In addition to what is usual, regular, or approximated: *odd jobs; 40-odd persons.* **3.** Being one of an incomplete pair or set; extra. **4.** Not divisible by two. [< ON *oddi*, odd number.] —**odd'ly** *adv.* —**odd'ness** *n.*

Usage: When *odd* is used to indicate a few more than a given number, it is used only with round numbers and should be preceded by a hyphen in order to avoid ambiguity: *thirty-odd guests.*

odd·ball (ŏd'bôl') *n. Informal.* An eccentric person.

odd·i·ty (ŏd'ĭ-tē) *n., pl.* **-ties. 1.** One that is odd. **2.** The condition of being odd.

odd·ment (ŏd'mənt) *n.* Something left over.

odds (ŏdz) *pl.n.* **1.** An advantage given to a weaker side in a contest to equalize the chances of the participants. **2.** A ratio expressing the probability of an event or outcome. **3.** The likelihood that one thing will occur rather than another: *The odds are that the candidate will win on the first ballot.* —*Idiom.* **at odds.** In disagreement.

odds and ends *pl.n.* Miscellaneous items.

ode (ōd) *n.* A lyric poem often addressed to a praised object or person and characterized by exalted style. [< Gk. *aoidē*, song.]

-ode *suff.* Way; path: *electrode.* [< Gk. *hodos.*]

O·din (ō'dĭn) *n. Norse Myth.* The ruler of the gods.

o·di·ous (ō'dē-əs) *adj.* Offensive, hateful, or repugnant; abhorrent. —**o'di·ous·ly** *adv.* —**o'di·ous·ness** *n.*

o·di·um (ō'dē-əm) *n.* **1.** The condition or quality of being odious. **2.** Disgrace resulting from hateful conduct. [Lat., hatred.]

o·dom·e·ter (ō-dŏm'ĭ-tər) *n.* An instrument that indicates distance traveled by a vehicle. [Fr. *odomètre.*]

o·don·tol·o·gy (ō'dŏn-tŏl'ə-jē) *n.* The study of the anatomy, growth, and diseases of the teeth. [Gk. *odous*, tooth + -LOGY.] —**o·don'·to·log'i·cal** (-tə-lŏj'ĭ-kəl) *adj.* —**o·don'to·log'i·cal·ly** *adv.* —**o'don·tol'o·gist** *n.*

o·dor (ō'dər) *n.* Also chiefly Brit. **o·dour. 1.** The property or quality of a thing that is perceived by the sense of smell; scent. **2.** Esteem; repute. [< Lat.] —**o'dor·less** *adj.* —**o'·dor·less·ly** *adv.* —**o'dor·ous** *adj.* —**o'dor·ous·ly** *adv.* —**o'dor·ous·ness** *n.*

o·dor·if·er·ous (ō'də-rĭf'ər-əs) *adj.* Having or giving off an odor. [< Lat. *odorifer.*] —**o'dor·if'er·ous·ly** *adv.* —**o'dor·if'er·ous·ness** *n.*

O·dys·seus (ō-dĭs'yōōs', ō-dĭs'ē-əs) *n. Gk. Myth.* The hero of Homer's *Odyssey.*

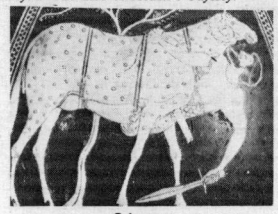

Odysseus
Detail from a 5th-century B.C.
Attic vase painting

od·ys·sey (ŏd'ĭ-sē) *n.* A long, adventurous wandering. [< ODYSSEUS.]

Oed·i·pus complex (ĕd'ə-pəs, ē'də-) *n. Psychoanal.* Libidinal feelings in a child, esp. a male child, for the parent of the opposite sex. [< *Oedipus*, a character in Greek myth who married his mother.] —**oed'i·pal** *adj.*

o'er (ôr, ōr) *prep. & adv. Poet.* Over.

of (ŭv, ŏv; əv *when unstressed*) *prep.* **1.** From. **2.** Owing to: *died of tuberculosis.* **3.** Away from. **4.** So as to be separated or relieved from: *robbed of their dignity.* **5.** From the total or group comprising. **6.** Composed or made from. **7.** Associated with or adhering to. **8.** Belonging or connected to. **9.** Possessing; having: *a person of honor.* **10.** Containing or carrying. **11.** Specified as; named or called: *a depth of ten feet; the Garden of Eden.* **12.** Centering on or directed toward. **13.** Produced by; issuing from. **14.** Characterized or identified by. **15.** With reference to; about. **16.** Set aside for; taken up by: *a day of rest.* **17.** Before; until: *five minutes of two.* **18.** During or on: *of recent years.* [< OE.]

Usage: The "double genitive," as in *a friend of my father's,* is a usage well supported by literary precedent and should be regarded as acceptable at all levels of the spoken or written language.

off (ôf, ŏf) *adv.* **1.** At or to a distance from a nearer place. **2.** Distant in time. **3.** So as to be unattached, disconnected, or removed. **4.** So as to be smaller, fewer, or less. **5.** So as to be away from work or duty. —*adj.* **1.** More distant or removed. **2.** Not on, attached, or connected. **3.** Not continuing, operating, or functioning. **4.** No longer existing or effective; canceled. **5.** Fewer, smaller, or less. **6.** Inferior. **7.** In a specified condition: *well off.* **8.** In error. **9.** Absent or away from work or duty: *I'm off Tuesday.* —*prep.* **1.** So as to be removed or distant from. **2.** Away or relieved from: *off duty.* **3. a.** By consuming: *living off honey.* **b.** With the means provided by: *living off my pension.* **4.** Extending or branching out from. **5.** Below the usual level of: *off your game.* **6.** Abstaining from. **7.** Seaward of: *a mile off Sandy Hook.* —*v. Slang.* To take the life of. —*Idiom.* **off and on.** Intermittently. [< OE *of.*]

Usage: The preposition *off* should not be

followed by *of: He stepped off* (not *off of*) *the platform.*

of·fal (ô'fəl, ŏf'əl) *n.* **1.** Waste parts, esp. of a butchered animal. **2.** Refuse; rubbish. [ME.]

off·beat (ôf'bēt', ŏf'-) *n.* An unaccented beat in a musical measure. —*adj.* (ôf'bēt', ŏf'-). *Slang.* Unconventional.

off-col·or (ôf'kŭl'ər, ŏf'-) *adj.* **1.** Varying from the expected or required color. **2.** In bad taste: *an off-color joke.*

of·fend (ə-fĕnd') *v.* **1.** To create anger, resentment, or annoyance in. **2.** To be displeasing or disagreeable (to). **3.** To sin. [< Lat. *offendere.*] —**of·fend'er** *n.*

of·fense (ə-fĕns') *n.* Also chiefly Brit. **of·fence.** **1.** The act of offending. **2.** Any violation of a moral or social code. **3.** A crime. **4.** (ŏf'ĕns'). The act of attacking or assaulting. **5.** (ŏf'ĕns'). The attacker, as in a game or contest. [< Lat. *offendere,* to offend.] —**of·fen'sive** *adj.* —**of·fen'sive·ly** *adv.* —**of·fen'sive·ness** *n.*

of·fer (ô'fər, ŏf'ər) *v.* **1.** To present for acceptance or rejection. **2.** To present for sale. **3.** To propose as payment; bid. **4.** To present as an act of worship. **5.** To provide; furnish; afford. **6.** To produce or introduce on the stage. [< Lat. *offerre.*] —**of'fer** *n.* —**of'fer·er** or **of'fer·or** *n.*
Syns: *offer, extend, present, proffer, tender, volunteer v.*

of·fer·ing (ô'fər-ĭng, ŏf'ər-) *n.* **1.** The act of making an offer. **2.** Something offered. **3.** A presentation made to a deity as an act of religious worship or sacrifice.

of·fer·to·ry (ô'fər-tôr'ē, -tōr'ē, ŏf'ər-) *n., pl.* **-ries.** **1.** Often **Offertory.** The part of the Eucharist at which bread and wine are offered to God. **2.** A collection of offerings at a religious service. [< Lat. *offerre,* to offer.]

off·hand (ôf'hănd', ŏf'-) *adv. & adj.* Without preparation or forethought; impromptu. —**off'hand'ed·ly** *adv.* —**off'hand'ed·ness** *n.*

of·fice (ô'fĭs, ŏf'ĭs) *n.* **1. a.** A place in which services, clerical work, and professional duties are carried out. **b.** The staff working in such a place. **2.** A duty or function assigned to or assumed by someone. **3.** A position of authority given to a person, as in a government or other organization. **4.** A branch of the U.S. government ranking just below a department. **5.** A public position: *seek office.* **6.** Often **offices.** A favor. **7.** *Eccles.* A ceremony, usu. prescribed by liturgy, esp. a rite for the dead. [< Lat. *officium,* duty.]

of·fice-hold·er (ô'fĭs-hōl'dər, ŏf'ĭs-) *n.* One who holds a public office.

of·fi·cer (ô'fĭ-sər, ŏf'ĭ-) *n.* **1.** One who holds an office of authority or trust. **2.** One holding a commission in the armed forces. **3.** One licensed in the merchant marine as master, mate, chief engineer, or assistant engineer. **4.** A police officer.

of·fi·cial (ə-fĭsh'əl) *adj.* **1.** Of, pertaining to, or authorized by a proper authority; authoritative. **2.** Formal or ceremonious: *an official banquet.* —*n.* **1.** One who holds an office or position. **2.** A referee in a sport. —**of·fi'cial·dom** *n.* —**of·fi'cial·ly** *adv.*

of·fi·cial·ism (ə-fĭsh'ə-lĭz'əm) *n.* Rigid adherence to official regulations, forms, and procedures.

of·fi·ci·ate (ə-fĭsh'ē-āt') *v.* **-at·ed, -at·ing.** **1.** To perform the duties and functions of an office or position of authority, esp. as a priest, minister, or rabbi at a religious service. **2.** To

serve as referee or umpire in a sport. —**of·fi'ci·a'tion** *n.* —**of·fi'ci·a'tor** *n.*

of·fi·cious (ə-fĭsh'əs) *adj.* Excessively forward in offering one's services or advice to others. [Lat. *officiosus.*] —**of·fi'cious·ly** *adv.* —**of·fi'cious·ness** *n.*

off·ing (ô'fĭng, ŏf'ĭng) *n.* The near or immediate future: *in the offing.*

off·ish (ô'fĭsh, ŏf'ĭsh) *adj.* Distant and reserved in manner; aloof. —**off'ish·ly** *adv.* —**off'ish·ness** *n.*

off-lim·its (ôf-lĭm'ĭts, ŏf-) *adj.* Forbidden to a designated group.

off-line (ôf'līn', ŏf'-) *adj. Computer Sci.* Not controlled by a central computer.

off·load (ôf'lōd', ŏf'-) *v.* **1.** To launch (e.g. a rocket) with propellant tanks less than fully loaded so as to alter the vehicle's center of gravity. **2.** To unload.

off·print (ôf'prĭnt', ŏf'-) *n.* A separately printed reproduction or excerpt from a publication. —**off'print'** *v.*

off-sea·son (ôf'-sē'zən, ŏf'-) *n.* A time period of lessened activity.

off·set (ôf'sĕt', ŏf'-) *n.* **1.** Something that balances, counteracts, or compensates. **2.** *Archit.* A ledge or recess in a wall. **3.** A bend, as in a pipe or bar, made so as to reach around an obstruction. **4.** Printing by indirect image transfer. —*v.* (ôf-sĕt', ŏf-) **-set, -set·ting.** **1.** To counterbalance or compensate for. **2.** To print by offset. **3.** To make or form an offset in (a wall, bar, or pipe).

off·shoot (ôf'shōōt', ŏf'-) *n.* Something that branches out or originates from a particular source, as a shoot from a plant stem.

off·shore (ôf'shôr', -shōr', ŏf'-) *adj.* **1.** Away from the shore. **2.** At a distance from the shore. —**off'shore'** *adv.*

off·side (ôf'sīd', ŏf'-) *adj.* Also **off side. 1.** In front of the ball before the play in football has properly begun. **2.** Illegally ahead of the ball or puck in an attacking zone.

off·spring (ôf'sprĭng', ŏf'-) *n., pl.* **-spring** or **-springs. 1.** Progeny; young. **2.** Something that results from something else. [< OE *ofspring.*]

off-stage (ôf'stāj', ŏf'-) *adj. & adv.* Away from the area of a stage visible to the audience.

off-the-rec·ord (ôf'thə-rĕk'ərd, ŏf'-) *adj. & adv.* Not for publication or attribution.

off-the-wall (ôf'thə-wôl', ŏf'-) *adj. Informal.* Very unconventional; bizarre.

off-track betting (ôf'trăk', ŏf'-) *n.* A system of placing bets away from a racetrack.

off-white (ôf'hwīt', -wīt', ŏf'-) *n.* A grayish or yellowish white. —**off'-white'** *adj.*

off year *n.* **1.** A year in which no major political elections are held. **2.** A year of reduced activity or production.

oft (ôft, ŏft) *adv.* Often. [< OE.]

of·ten (ô'fən, ŏf'ən, ôf'tən, ŏf'-) *adv.* Frequently; repeatedly. [< OE *oft.*]

of·ten·times (ô'fən-tīmz', ŏf'ən-, ôf'tən-, ŏf'-) *adv.* Often.

O·gla·la (ō-glä'lə) *n., pl.* **-la** or **-las. 1. a.** A tribe of Indians inhabiting the area west of the Missouri River in South Dakota. **b.** A member of this tribe. **2.** The Siouan language of the Oglala.

o·gle (ō'gəl, ŏ'gəl) *v.* **o·gled, o·gling.** To stare at, esp. impertinently, flirtatiously, or amorously. [Poss. < LG *oegeln.*] —**o'gler** *n.*

o·gre (ō'gər) *n.* **1.** A fabled man-eating giant

or monster. **2.** A cruel or brutish person.
[Fr.] —**o'gre·ish** (ō'gər-ĭsh, ō'grĭsh) *adj.*

oh (ō) *interj.* **1.** Used to express strong emotion, as surprise, fear, anger, or pain. **2.** Used to indicate understanding or acknowledgment: *Oh, I see.*—See Usage note at O¹.

ohm (ōm) *n.* A unit of electrical resistance equal to that of a conductor in which a current of one ampere is produced by a potential of one volt across its terminals. [< Georg S. *Ohm* (1787–1854).]

-oid *suff.* **1.** Resembling: *fibroid.* **2.** One that resembles something specified or has a specified quality: *humanoid.* [< Gk. *eidos*, shape.]

oil (oil) *n.* **1.** Any of numerous mineral, vegetable, and synthetic substances and animal and vegetable fats that are gen. slippery, combustible, viscous, liquid or liquefiable at room temperatures, soluble in various organic solvents such as ether, but not in water, and used in a great variety of products, esp. lubricants and fuels. **2.** Petroleum. **3.** A substance with an oily consistency. **4.** An oil color. **5.** An oil painting. —*v.* To lubricate, supply, or cover with oil. [< Gk. *elaion*, olive oil.]

oil·cloth (oil'klôth', -klŏth') *n.* A fabric treated with clay, oil, and pigments to make it waterproof.

oil color *n.* A pigment for making oil paint.

oil field *n.* An area containing underground petroleum deposits.

oil paint *n.* A paint in which the vehicle is a drying oil.

oil painting *n.* **1.** A painting done in oil colors. **2.** The art or practice of painting with oil colors.

oil shale *n.* A black or dark-brown shale containing hydrocarbons that yield petroleum by distillation.

oil·skin (oil'skĭn') *n.* **1.** Cloth treated with oil so that it is waterproof. **2.** A garment made of oilskin.

oil slick *n.* A thin film of oil on water.

oil well *n.* A well from which petroleum flows or is pumped.

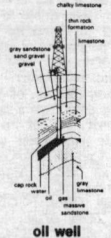

oil well

oil·y (oi'lē) *adj.* **-i·er, -i·est. 1.** Of or like oil. **2.** Impregnated with oil; greasy. **3.** Unctuous. —**oil'i·ly** *adv.* —**oil'i·ness** *n.*

oint·ment (oint'mənt) *n.* A thick, often oily substance made to be rubbed on the skin for cosmetic or medicinal purposes. [< Lat. *unguentum.*]

O·jib·wa (ō-jĭb'wä', -wə) *n., pl.* **-wa** or **-was.** Also **O·jib·way** (ō-jĭb'wä') *pl.* **-way** or **-ways. 1. a.** A tribe of Indians inhabiting regions of the United States and Canada around Lake Superior. **b.** A member of this tribe. **2.** The Algonquian language of the Ojibwa.

O.K. or **OK** or **o·kay** (ō'kā', ō-kā') *Informal.* —*n., pl.* **O.K.'s** or **OK's** or **o·kays.** Approval; agreement. —*v.* **O.K.'d** or **OK'd** or **o·kayed, O.K.'ing** or **OK'ing** or **o·kay·ing.** To approve or endorse. —*interj.* Used to express approval or agreement. —*adj.* Acceptable; fine. —*adv.* Acceptably. [Prob. abbr. of *oll korrect*, slang respelling of *all correct.*]

o·kra (ō'krə) *n.* **1.** A tall plant with edible, mucilaginous green pods. **2.** The pods of this plant, used esp. in soups. [Twi *nkruma.*]

-ol *suff.* An alcohol or phenol: *ethanol.* [< ALCOHOL.]

old (ōld) *adj.* **old·er** or **eld·er** (ĕl'dər), **old·est** or **eld·est** (ĕl'dĭst). **1.** Having lived or existed for a long time; far advanced in years or life. **2.** Made long ago; not new. **3.** Characteristic of an aged person. **4.** Mature; sensible. **5.** Having a specified age. **6.** Belonging to or being of an earlier time: *my old classmates.* **7.** Dear or cherished through long acquaintance: *good old Bob.* —*n.* Former times; yore: *days of old.* [< OE *eald.*] —**old'ness** *n.*

old country *n.* The native country of an immigrant.

old·en (ōl'dən) *adj.* Old. [< OE *eald.*]

Old English *n.* English from the middle of the 5th to the beginning of the 12th cent.

old-fash·ioned (ōld'făsh'ənd) *adj.* Outdated.

Old French *n.* French from the 9th to the early 16th cent.

old guard *n.* The conservative, often reactionary element of a class, society, or political group.

Old High German *n.* High German from the middle of the 9th to the end of the 11th cent.

old·ie (ōl'dē) *n.* Something old, esp. a popular song of the past.

Old Irish *n.* Irish from 725 to about 950.

Old Italian *n.* The Italian language until the middle of the 16th cent.

old-line (ōld'līn') *adj.* **1.** Conservative; reactionary. **2.** Traditional.

old master *n.* **1.** A distinguished European artist from around 1500 to the early 1700's. **2.** A work by an old master.

Old Norse *n.* The Germanic language of the Scandinavian peoples until the middle of the 14th cent.

Old North French *n.* The northern dialects of Old French.

Old Persian *n.* An ancient form of Persian recorded in inscriptions from the 6th to the 5th cent. B.C.

Old Provençal *n.* Provençal until the middle of the 16th cent.

old school *n.* A group committed to traditional ideas or practices. —**old'-school'** *adj.*

Old Spanish *n.* The Spanish language until the middle of the 16th cent.

old·ster (ōld'stər) *n. Informal.* An old or elderly person.

Old Testament *n.* The first of the two main divisions of the Christian Bible, containing the Hebrew Scriptures. See table at **Bible.**

old-tim·er (ōld'tī'mər) *n. Informal.* **1.** One who has served in or belonged to an organization for a long time. **2.** Something very old.

old wives' tale *n.* A bit of superstitious folklore.

old-world (ōld'wûrld') *adj.* **1.** Antique; old-fashioned; quaint. **2. Old-World.** Of or belonging to the Old World.

Old World *n.* The Eastern Hemisphere, esp. Europe.

ole– *pref.* Var. of **oleo-.**

o·le·ag·i·nous (ō'lē-ăj'ə-nəs) *adj.* **1.** Containing or consisting of oil. **2.** Unctuous. [< Lat. *oleginus,* of the olive tree.] —**o'le·ag'i·nous·ly** *adv.* —**o'le·ag'i·nous·ness** *n.*

o·le·an·der (ō'lē-ăn'dər, ō'lē-ăn'-) *n.* A poisonous, chiefly tropical shrub with clusters of white or reddish flowers. [Med. Lat.]

o·le·ic acid (ō-lē'ĭk) *n.* An oily liquid, $CH_3(CH_2)_7CH:CH(CH_2)_7COOH$, occurring in animal and vegetable oils.

o·le·o (ō'lē-ō') *n., pl.* **-os.** Margarine.

oleo– or **ole–** *pref.* Oil: *oleomargarine.* [< Gk. *elaion,* olive oil.]

o·le·o·mar·ga·rine (ō'lē-ō-mär'jər-ĭn, -jə-rēn') *n.* Margarine.

ol·fac·tion (ŏl-făk'shən, ōl-) *n.* **1.** The sense of smell. **2.** The act of smelling. [< Lat. *olfacere,* to smell.]

ol·fac·to·ry (ŏl-făk'tə-rē, -trē, ōl-) *adj.* Of or relating to the sense of smell. [Lat. *olfactorius.*]

ol·i·gar·chy (ŏl'ĭ-gär'kē) *n., pl.* **-chies.** **1. a.** Government by the few. **b.** Those making up such a government. **2.** A state governed by oligarchy. —**ol'i·garch'** *n.* —**ol'i·gar'chic** or **ol'i·gar'chi·cal** or **ol'i·gar'chal** *adj.*

oligo– or **olig–** *pref.* Few: *oligarchy.* [< Gk. *oligos.*]

Ol·i·go·cene (ŏl'ĭ-gō-sēn') *adj.* Of or belonging to the geologic time, rock series, or sedimentary deposits of the 3rd epoch of the Tertiary period. —*n.* The Oligocene epoch.

o·li·o (ō'lē-ō') *n., pl.* **-os.** A mixture; hodgepodge. [< Sp. *olla,* pot.]

ol·ive (ŏl'ĭv) *n.* **1.** A semitropical evergreen tree having an edible fruit, yellow flowers, and leathery leaves. **2.** The small fruit of the olive, important as a food and a source of oil. **3.** A dull yellowish green. [< Gk. *elaia.*] —**ol'ive** *adj.*

O·lym·pic games (ō-lĭm'pĭk) *pl. n.* **1.** An ancient Greek festival of athletic competitions and other contests held every four years in Olympia in honor of Zeus. **2.** A modern international athletic competition held every four years.

O·lym·pics (ō-lĭm'pĭks) *pl.n.* Olympic games (sense 2).

-oma *suff.* Tumor: *myeloma.* [< Gk. *-ōma,* n. suffix.]

O·ma·ha (ō'mə-hô', -hä') *n., pl.* **-ha** or **-has.** **1.** A tribe of Siouan-speaking Indians of northeastern Nebraska. **2.** A member of the Omaha.

om·buds·man (ŏm'bŭdz'mən, -bōōdz'-) *n.* **1.** A government official, esp. in Scandinavian countries, who investigates citizens' complaints against the government or its functionaries. **2.** One that investigates complaints, as from consumers, and assists in achieving fair settlements. [< ON *umbodhsmadhr,* steward.] —**om'buds'man·ship** *n.*

o·me·ga (ō-mĕg'ə, ō-mē'gə, ō-mā'-) *n.* The 24th and final letter of the Greek alphabet. See table at **alphabet.** [Gk. *ō mega,* large o.]

om·e·let (ŏm'ə-lĭt, ŏm'lĭt) *n.* Also **om·e·lette.** A dish of beaten eggs cooked and folded, often around a filling. [< Lat. *lamella,* thin metal plate.]

o·men (ō'mən) *n.* A sign of future good or evil. [Lat.]

om·i·cron (ŏm'ĭ-krŏn', ō'mĭ-) *n.* The 15th letter of the Greek alphabet. See table at **alphabet.** [Gk. *o mikron,* small o.]

om·i·nous (ŏm'ə-nəs) *adj.* **1.** Being or pertaining to an evil omen; foreboding; portentous. **2.** Menacing; threatening. [Lat. *ominosus.*] —**om'i·nous·ly** *adv.* —**om'i·nous·ness** *n.*

o·mit (ō-mĭt') *v.* **o·mit·ted, o·mit·ting. 1.** To leave out; fail to include. **2.** To fail to do; neglect. [< Lat. *omittere.*] —**o·mis'si·ble** *adj.* —**o·mis'sion** (-mĭsh'ən) *n.*

omni– *pref.* All: *omnidirectional.* [< Lat. *omnis.*]

om·ni·bus (ŏm'nĭ-bŭs') *n., pl.* **-bus·es.** A bus. —*adj.* Including or covering many things or classes: *an omnibus law.* [< Lat., for all.]

om·ni·di·rec·tion·al (ŏm'nĭ-dĭ-rĕk'shə-nəl, -dī-) *adj.* Capable of transmitting or receiving signals in all directions.

om·nip·o·tent (ŏm-nĭp'ə-tənt) *adj.* Having unlimited power, authority, or force. —*n.* **Omnipotent.** God. —**om·nip'o·tence** *n.* —**om·nip'o·tent·ly** *adv.*

om·ni·pres·ent (ŏm'nĭ-prĕz'ənt) *adj.* Present everywhere. —**om'ni·pres'ence** *n.*

om·nis·cient (ŏm-nĭsh'ənt) *adj.* Having total knowledge; knowing everything. [Med. Lat. *omnisciens.*] —**om·nis'cience** *n.* —**om·nis'cient·ly** *adv.*

om·ni·um-gath·er·um (ŏm'nē-əm-găth'ər-əm) *n.* A miscellany; hodgepodge. [< Lat. *omnium,* of all + GATHER.]

om·niv·o·rous (ŏm-nĭv'ər-əs) *adj.* **1.** *Zool.* Eating both animal and vegetable substances. **2.** Taking in everything available: *an omnivorous reader.* —**om·niv'o·rous·ly** *adv.* —**om·niv'o·rous·ness** *n.*

on (ŏn, ôn) *prep.* **1.** Used to indicate: **a.** Position upon. **b.** Contact with. **c.** Location at or along. **d.** Proximity. **e.** Attachment to or suspension from. **2.** Used to indicate motion or direction toward. **3.** Used to indicate: **a.** Occurrence during: *on July third.* **b.** The particular occasion or circumstance: *On entering the room, I saw them.* **c.** The exact time: *on the hour.* **4.** Used to indicate: **a.** The object affected by an action: *The spotlight fell on the actress.* **b.** The agent of a specified action: *I cut my foot on the broken glass.* **c.** The agency of a specified action: *talk on the telephone.*

Olympic games

The opening of the 1980 Olympic games in Lake Placid, New York

5. Used to indicate a source or basis: *live on bread and water.* **6.** Used to indicate: **a.** The state, condition, or process of: *on leave; on fire.* **b.** The purpose of: *travel on business.* **c.** A means of conveyance: *ride on a train.* **d.** Availability by means of: *beer on tap.* **e.** Association with: *a doctor on the staff.* **f.** Addition or repetition: *error on error.* **g.** The ground or basis for: *on principle.* **7.** Concerning; about: *a book on astronomy.* **8.** In the possession of; with: *I haven't a cent on me.* **9.** At the expense of: *drinks on the house.* —*adv.* **1.** In or into a position of being attached to or covering something. **2.** In the direction of: *We looked on while the ship docked.* **3.** Forward or ahead in space or time: *The army moved on to the next town.* **4.** In a continuous course. **5.** In or into performance or operation. [< OE.]

Usage: In constructions in which *on* is an adverb attached to a verb, it should not be joined with *to* and written as the single word *onto: moved on to* (not *onto) new topics.*

-on *pref.* **1.** Subatomic unit: *baryon.* **2.** Unit; quantum: *photon.* [< ION.]

once (wŭns) *adv.* **1.** One time only: *once a day.* **2.** At one time in the past; formerly. **3.** At any time; ever. —*n.* A single occurrence; one time: *You can go this once.* —*conj.* As soon as; when. —**idioms. all at once. 1.** All at the same time. **2.** Suddenly. **at once. 1.** All together; simultaneously. **2.** Immediately. **once and for all.** Finally; conclusively. **once in a while.** Now and then. [< OE ān, one.]

once-o·ver (wŭns'ō'vər) *n. Informal.* A quick but thorough look or examination.

on·col·o·gy (ŏn-kŏl'ə-jē) *n.* The scientific study of tumors. [Gk. *onkos,* mass + -LOGY.]

on·com·ing (ŏn'kŭm'ĭng, ôn'-) *adj.* Approaching.

one (wŭn) *adj.* **1.** Being a single entity or being; individual. **2.** Of a single kind or nature; undivided. **3.** Designating an unspecified person or thing. **4.** Single in kind; alike or the same. —*n.* **1.** The cardinal number represented by the symbol 1, designating the first such unit in a series. **2.** A single individual; unit. —*pron.* **1.** A single member of a group or class. **2.** An unspecified person; anyone. [< OE ān.] —**one'ness** *n.*

Usage: The construction *more than one* is always singular, despite the fact that logic would seem to require a plural verb: *More than one of my students is entering the competition.*

-one *suff.* A ketone or an analogous oxygen-containing compound: *acetone.* [< -ENE.]

O·nei·da (ō-nī'də) *n., pl.* **-da** or **-das. 1. a.** An Indian tribe orig. inhabiting New York state. **b.** A member of this tribe. **2.** The Iroquoian language of the Oneida.

on·er·ous (ŏn'ər-əs, ō'nər-) *adj.* Troublesome or oppressive; burdensome. [< Lat. *onerosus.*] —**on'er·ous·ly** *adv.* —**on'er·ous·ness** *n.*

one·self (wŭn-sĕlf') *pron.* **1.** A person's own self. Used: **a.** Reflexively: *forget oneself.* **b.** For emphasis: *One must take the initiative oneself.* **2.** One's normal, healthy condition.

one-shot (wŭn'shŏt') *adj.* **1.** Effective after only one attempt. **2.** Being the only one and unlikely to be repeated.

one-sid·ed (wŭn'sī'dĭd) *adj.* **1.** Biased: *a one-sided view.* **2.** Unequal: *a one-sided contest.* —**one'-sid'ed·ly** *adv.* —**one'-sid'ed·ness** *n.*

one-time (wŭn'tīm') *adj.* Also **one-time.** At or in some past time; former.

one-to-one (wŭn'tə-wŭn') *adj.* **1.** *Math.* Pairing each element of a set uniquely with an element of another set. **2.** Characterized by proportional amounts on both sides.

one-track (wŭn'trăk') *adj.* Obsessed by a single idea or purpose.

one-up (wŭn'ŭp') *v. Informal.* To practice one-upmanship on.

one-up·man·ship (wŭn-ŭp'măn-shĭp') *n. Informal.* The practice of keeping one step ahead of a competitor.

one-way (wŭn'wā') *adj.* Moving or permitting movement or travel in one direction only: *a one-way street; a one-way ticket.*

on·go·ing (ŏn'gō'ĭng, ôn'-) *adj.* Currently going on; progressing.

on·ion (ŭn'yən) *n.* **1.** A plant widely cultivated for its pungent edible bulb. **2.** The bulb of this plant. [< Lat. *unio.*]

on·ion·skin (ŭn'yən-skĭn') *n.* A thin, strong, translucent paper.

on-line (ŏn'līn', ôn'-) *adj.* **1.** *Computer Sci.* Controlled by a central computer. **2.** Ongoing: *on-line projects.*

on·look·er (ŏn'lŏŏk'ər, ôn'-) *n.* A spectator. —**on'look'ing** *adj.*

on·ly (ŏn'lē) *adj.* Alone in its kind or class; sole: *an only child.* —*adv.* **1.** Without anyone or anything else; alone. **2. a.** No more than; at least; just. **b.** Merely. **3.** Exclusively; solely. —*conj.* But; except. [< OE ānlīc.]

Usage: Only is often used as a conjunction equivalent in meaning to *but: They would have called, only the phone was out of order.* This example is considered unacceptable in writing by a large majority of the Usage Panel.

on·o·mat·o·poe·ia (ŏn'ə-măt'ə-pē'ə) *n.* The formation or use of words, as *buzz* or *cuckoo,* that imitate what they denote. [< Gk. *onomatopoiia.*] —**on'o·mat'o·poe'ic** (-pē'ĭk) or **on'o·mat'o·po·et'ic** (-pō-ĕt'ĭk) *adj.* —**on'o·mat'o·po·et'i·cal·ly** *adv.*

On·on·da·ga (ŏn'ən-dô'gə, -dä'gə) *n., pl.* **-ga** or **-gas. 1. a.** A tribe of Indians formerly inhabiting upper New York state and Ontario. **b.** A member of the Onondaga. **2.** The Iroquoian language of the Onondaga. —**On'on·da'gan** *adj.*

on·rush (ŏn'rŭsh', ôn'-) *n.* **1.** A forward rush. **2.** An assault. —**on'rush'ing** *adj.*

on·set (ŏn'sĕt', ôn'-) *n.* **1.** An onslaught. **2.** A beginning.

on·shore (ŏn'shôr', -shōr', ôn'-) *adj.* **1.** Moving or directed toward the shore. **2.** Located or operating on the shore. **3.** Domestic: *onshore oil drilling.* —**on'shore'** *adv.*

on·slaught (ŏn'slôt', ôn'-) *n.* A violent attack. [< MDu. *aenslag.*]

on·to (ŏn'tŏō', ôn'-, ŏn'tə, ôn'-) *prep.* **1.** On top of; upon. **2.** *Informal.* Aware of: *I'm onto your schemes.*

onto- or **ont-** *pref.* **1.** Existence; being: *ontology.* **2.** Organism: *ontogeny.* [< Gk. *ōn,* pr.p. of *einai,* to be.]

on·tog·e·ny (ŏn-tŏj'ə-nē) *n., pl.* **-nies.** The course of development of an individual organism. —**on'to·ge·net'ic** (ŏn'tə-jə-nĕt'ĭk) *adj.*

on·tol·o·gy (ŏn-tŏl'ə-jē) *n.* The systematic study of being. —**on'to·log'i·cal** (ŏn'tə-lŏj'-ĭ-kəl) *adj.*

o·nus (ō'nəs) *n.* **1.** A burden. **2.** Blame. [Lat.]

on·ward (ŏn'wərd, ŏn'-) *adv.* Also **on·wards** (-wərdz). In a direction or toward a position that is ahead; forward. —**on'ward** *adj.*

-onym *suff.* Word; name: *antonym.* [< Gk. *onuma,* name.]

on·yx (ŏn'ĭks) *n.* A chalcedony that occurs in bands of different colors. [< Gk. *onux.*]

oo- *pref.* Egg; ovum: *oogenesis.* [< Gk. *ōion,* egg.]

o·o·cyte (ō'ə-sīt') *n.* **1.** A cell, derived from an oogonium, that undergoes meiosis and produces an ovum. **2.** A female gamete in certain protozoa.

oo·dles (ōōd'lz) *pl.n. Informal.* A great amount. [Orig. unknown.]

o·o·gen·e·sis (ō'ə-jĕn'ĭ-sĭs) *n. Biol.* The enlargement and meiotic division of an oogonium that produces an ovum.

o·o·go·ni·um (ō'ə-gō'nē-əm) *n., pl.* **-ni·a** (-nē-ə) or **-ums.** **1.** *Biol.* One of the cells that form the bulk of ovarian tissue. **2.** *Bot.* A female reproductive structure in certain fungi. [< OE *A.* gk. *gonos,* seed.]

o·o·lite (ō'ə-līt') *n.* **1.** A small, round, calcareous grain found in rock as limestones and dolomites. **2.** Rock, usu. limestone, composed of such grains. —**o'o·lit'ic** (-lĭt'ĭk) *adj.*

o·ol·o·gy (ō-ŏl'ə-jē) *n.* The branch of ornithology that deals with birds' eggs. —**o'o·log'ic** (ō'ə-lŏj'ĭk) or **o'o·log'i·cal** *adj.* —**o'o·log'i·cal·ly** *adv.* —**o·ol'o·gist** *n.*

oomph (ōōmf) *n. Slang.* **1.** Spirit; vigor. **2.** Sex appeal. [Orig. unknown.]

ooze[1] (ōōz) *v.* **oozed, ooz·ing.** **1.** To flow or leak out slowly; exude. **2.** To disappear or ebb slowly. [< OE *wōs,* juice.] —**ooze** *n.* —**ooz'i·ness** *n.* —**ooz'y** *adj.*

ooze[2] (ōōz) *n.* Soft, thin mud or mudlike sediment, as on the floor of oceans and lakes. [< OE *wase.*] —**ooz'i·ness** *n.* —**ooz'y** *adj.*

o·pal (ō'pəl) *n.* A translucent mineral of hydrated silicon dioxide, often used as a gem. [< Skt. *upalaḥ.*] —**o'pal·ine'** (ō'pə-līn', -lēn') *adj.*

o·pal·es·cence (ō'pə-lĕs'əns) *n.* A milky iridescence like that of an opal. —**o'pal·esce'** *v.* —**o'pal·es'cent** *adj.*

o·paque (ō-pāk') *adj.* **1. a.** Impenetrable by light. **b.** Not reflecting light; dull. **2.** Obtuse; dense. [< Lat. *opacus,* dark.] —**o·pac'i·ty** (-păs'ĭ-tē) or **o·paque'ness** *n.* —**o·paque'ly** *adv.*

op art *n.* Optical art.

op-ed page (ŏp'ĕd') *n.* A newspaper section opposite the editorial page that features articles expressing personal viewpoints. [OP(PO-SITE) + ED(ITORIAL).]

o·pen (ō'pən) *adj.* **1.** Allowing unobstructed entrance and exit; not shut or closed; spacious. **2.** Having no cover; exposed. **3.** Not sealed, tied, or folded. **4.** Having gaps, spaces, or intervals. **5.** Accessible to all; unrestricted. **6.** Susceptible; vulnerable. **7.** Available; obtainable. **8.** Ready to transact business. **9.** Unoccupied. **10.** Frank; candid. —*v.* **1.** To become or cause to become open; release from a closed position. **2.** To remove obstructions from; clear. **3.** To spread out or apart. **4.** To remove the cover or wrapping from; expose; undo. **5.** To begin; initiate; commence. **6.** To make available. **7.** To make or become more responsive or understanding. **8.** To reveal the secrets of. **9.** To come into view; become revealed. —*phrasal verb.* **open up.** *Informal.* To speak or act freely and unrestrainedly. —*n.* **1. the open.** The outdoors. **2.** A tournament or contest for both professionals and amateurs. —**o'pen·ly** *adv.* —**o'pen·ness** *n.*

o·pen-air (ō'pən-âr') *adj.* Outdoor: *an open-air concert.*

o·pen-end (ō'pən-ĕnd') *adj.* Also **o·pen-end·ed** (-ĕn'dĭd). Having no limit.

o·pen-eyed (ō'pən-īd') *adj.* **1.** Having the eyes wide open. **2.** Watchful and alert.

o·pen-hand·ed (ō'pən-hăn'dĭd) *adj.* Giving freely; generous. —**o'pen·hand'ed·ly** *adv.*

o·pen-heart (ō'pən-härt') *adj.* Of or involving surgery in which the heart is open while its normal functions are assumed by external apparatus.

o·pen-hearth (ō'pən-härth') *adj.* Of, used in, or designating a process for producing high-quality steel in a furnace with a heat-reflecting roof.

o·pen·ing (ō'pə-nĭng) *n.* **1.** The act of becoming open or making open. **2.** An open space. **3.** A hole. **4.** The first period or stage. **5.** A first performance. **6.** A series of beginning moves, as in chess. **7.** An opportunity; chance. **8.** An unfilled job or position.

o·pen-mind·ed (ō'pən-mīn'dĭd) *adj.* Receptive to new ideas or to reason. —**o'pen·mind'ed·ly** *adv.* —**o'pen·mind'ed·ness** *n.*

open shop *n.* A business establishment employing both union and nonunion workers.

o·pen·work (ō'pən-wûrk') *n.* Ornamental or structural work containing numerous openings, usu. in set patterns.

op·er·a[1] (ŏp'ər-ə, ŏp'rə) *n.* **1.** A theatrical work consisting of a dramatic performance set to music, usu. with orchestral accompaniment. **2.** A theater designed primarily for operas. [< Lat., work.] —**op'er·at'ic** *adj.*

op·er·a[2] (ō'pər-ə, ŏp'ər-ə) *n.* A pl. of **opus.**

op·er·a·ble (ŏp'ər-ə-bəl, ŏp'rə-) *adj.* **1.** Capable of or suitable for use. **2.** Capable of being treated surgically. —**op'er·a·bil'i·ty** *n.*

opera glasses *pl.n.* Small binoculars for use esp. at a theatrical performance.

opera glasses
Detail from "At the Opera" by
Mary Cassatt

op·er·ate (ŏp'ə-rāt') *v.* **-at·ed, -at·ing.** **1.** To function effectively; work. **2.** To have an effect; act. **3.** To perform surgery. **4.** To run or control the functioning of. [Lat. *operari.*]

op·er·a·tion (ŏp′ə-rā′shən) n. 1. A method or way of operating. 2. The condition of being operative. 3. Med. A surgical procedure for remedying an injury or ailment in a living body. 4. Math. A process performed in a specified sequence and in accordance with specific rules of procedure. 5. A military action or project. —**op′er·a′tion·al** adj. —**op′er·a′tion·al·ly** adv.

op·er·a·tive (ŏp′ər-ə-tĭv, ŏp′rə-, -ə-rā′tĭv) adj. 1. Exerting influence or force. 2. Functioning effectively. 3. Being in operation: operative regulations. 4. Of or involving a surgical operation. —n. 1. A skilled worker, esp. in industry. 2. a. A secret agent. b. A detective. —**op′er·a·tive·ly** adv.

op·er·a·tor (ŏp′ə-rā′tər) n. 1. One who operates a mechanical device. 2. One who operates a business. 3. A symbol that denotes a mathematical operation. 4. Informal. A shrewd and sometimes unscrupulous person.

op·er·et·ta (ŏp′ə-rĕt′ə) n. A theatrical production that has elements of opera but is lighter and more popular in subject and style. [Ital.]

oph·thal·mic (ŏf-thăl′mĭk, ŏp-) adj. Of or relating to the eye.

ophthalmo- or **ophthalm-** pref. Eye; eyeball: ophthalmology. [< Gk. ophthalmos, eye.]

oph·thal·mol·o·gy (ŏf′thăl-mŏl′ə-jē, ŏp′-, -thăl-) n. The medical specialty that deals with the anatomy, functions, pathology, and treatment of the eye. —**oph′thal·mol′o·gist** n.

o·pi·ate (ō′pē-ĭt, -āt′) n. 1. A narcotic containing opium or its derivatives. 2. A narcotic. 3. Something that relaxes or that induces sleep. —adj. (ō′pē-ĭt, -āt′). 1. Consisting of or containing opium. 2. Causing or producing sleep or sedation. [< Lat. opium, opium.]

o·pine (ō-pīn′) v. **o·pined, o·pin·ing.** To hold or state as an opinion. [< Lat. opinari, to suppose.]

o·pin·ion (ə-pĭn′yən) n. 1. A belief held often without positive knowledge or proof. 2. An evaluation based on special knowledge. 3. A judgment or estimation. [< Lat. opinio.]

o·pin·ion·at·ed (ə-pĭn′yə-nā′tĭd) adj. Holding stubbornly to one's own opinions.

o·pi·um (ō′pē-əm) n. A bitter, yellowish-brown, narcotic drug prepared from the dried juice of unripe pods of an Old World poppy. [< Gk. opion.]

o·pos·sum (ə-pŏs′əm) n., pl. **-sum** or **-sums.** Any of various nocturnal, arboreal marsupials

opossum

of the Western Hemisphere. [Powhatan aposoum.]

op·po·nent (ə-pō′nənt) n. One that opposes

another or others. [< Lat. opponere, to oppose.]

op·por·tune (ŏp′ər-tōōn′, -tyōōn′) adj. Occurring at a fitting or appropriate time. [< Lat. opportunus.] —**op′por·tune′ly** adv. —**op′por·tune′ness** n.

op·por·tun·ism (ŏp′ər-tōō′nĭz′əm, -tyōō′-) n. The practice of taking advantage of an opportunity to achieve an end, usu. with little regard for consequences or moral principles. —**op′por·tun′ist** n. —**op′por·tun·is′tic** adj.

op·por·tu·ni·ty (ŏp′ər-tōō′nĭ-tē, -tyōō′-) n., pl. **-ties.** A favorable time or occasion for a certain purpose.

Syns: opportunity, break, chance, occasion, opening n.

op·pose (ə-pōz′) v. **-posed, -pos·ing.** 1. To be in contention or conflict with; resist. 2. To be against. 3. To place in opposition; contrast or counterbalance. [< Lat. opponere, to set against.] —**op·pos′a·ble** adj. —**op·po·si′tion** (ŏp′ə-zĭsh′ən) n. —**op′po·si′tion·al** adj.

op·po·site (ŏp′ə-zĭt, -sĭt) adj. 1. Placed or located directly across from. 2. Facing or moving away from each other. 3. Diametrically opposed: opposite views. —n. One that is opposite or contrary to another. —adv. In an opposite position. —prep. Across from or facing. [< Lat. oppositus, p.p. of opponere, to oppose.] —**op′po·site·ly** adv. —**op′po·site·ness** n.

op·press (ə-prĕs′) v. 1. To burden harshly, unjustly, or tyrannically. 2. To weigh heavily upon the mind or spirit. [< Lat. oppressus, p.p. of opprimere, to press against.] —**op·pres′sion** n. —**op·pres′sor** n.

op·pres·sive (ə-prĕs′ĭv) adj. 1. a. Difficult to bear; harsh. b. Tyrannical. 2. Weighing heavily on the senses or spirits. —**op·pres′sive·ly** adv. —**op·pres′sive·ness** n.

op·pro·bri·ous (ə-prō′brē-əs) adj. 1. Expressing contemptuous scorn. 2. Shameful; infamous. —**op·pro′bri·ous·ly** adv.

op·pro·bri·um (ə-prō′brē-əm) n. 1. Disgrace arising from shameful conduct. 2. Scorn; contempt. 3. A cause of shame. [Lat.]

-opsy suff. Examination: biopsy. [< Gk. opsis, sight.]

opt (ŏpt) v. To make a choice. [Lat. optare.]

op·tic (ŏp′tĭk) adj. Of or relating to the eye or to vision. [< Gk. optikos.]

op·ti·cal (ŏp′tĭ-kəl) adj. 1. Of or relating to sight. 2. Of or relating to optics. 3. Designed to assist sight. —**op′ti·cal·ly** adv.

optical art n. Abstract art that features the use of geometric shapes or patterns, esp. to create optical illusions.

op·ti·cian (ŏp-tĭsh′ən) n. One who makes or sells lenses, eyeglasses, and other optical instruments.

op·tics (ŏp′tĭks) n. (used with a sing. verb). The scientific study of light and vision.

op·ti·mal (ŏp′tə-məl) adj. Most desirable or favorable. —**op′ti·mal·ly** adv.

op·ti·mism (ŏp′tə-mĭz′əm) n. 1. A tendency to expect the best possible outcome or to dwell upon the most hopeful aspects of a situation. 2. The doctrine that this world is the best of all possible worlds. [< Lat. optimus, best.] —**op′ti·mist** n. —**op′ti·mis′tic** adj. —**op′ti·mis′ti·cal·ly** adv.

op·ti·mum (ŏp′tə-məm) *n., pl.* **-ma** (-mə) or **-mums.** The best or most favorable condition, degree, or amount for a particular situation. [Lat., best.] **—op′ti·mum** *adj.*

op·tion (ŏp′shən) *n.* **1.** The power or right of choosing. **2.** A right to buy or sell something at a specified price within a specified time. **3.** Something available as a choice. [< Lat. *optio.*] **—op′tion·al** *adj.* **—op′tion·al·ly** *adv.*

op·tom·e·try (ŏp-tŏm′ĭ-trē) *n.* The profession of examining visual defects and treating them by means of corrective lenses. [Gk. *optos*, visible + -METRY.] **—op·to·met′ric** (ŏp′- tə-mĕt′rĭk) *adj.* **—op·tom′e·trist** *n.*

op·u·lent (ŏp′yə-lənt) *adj.* **1.** Having great wealth. **2.** Abundant; lavish. [Lat. *opulentus.*] **—op′u·lence** *n.* **—op′u·lent·ly** *adv.*

o·pus (ō′pəs) *n., pl.* **o·pe·ra** (ō′pər-ə, ŏp′ər-ə) or **o·pus·es.** A creative work, esp. a musical composition. [Lat., work.]

or (ôr; ər *when unstressed*) *conj.* Used to indicate: **1. a.** An alternative. **b.** The second of two alternatives: *either right or wrong.* **2.** A synonymous or equivalent expression: *acrophobia, or fear of great heights.* **3.** Uncertainty or indefiniteness: *two or three.* [< OE *oththe.*]

-or¹ *suff.* The performer of an action: *investor.* [< Lat. *-or*, and < Lat. *-ator.*]

-or² *suff.* State; quality: *behavior.* [< Lat.]

or·a·cle (ôr′ə-kəl, ŏr′-) *n.* **1. a.** A shrine consecrated to a prophetic god. **b.** The priest at such a shrine. **c.** A prophecy made known at such a shrine. **2.** A wise person. [< Lat. *oraculum.*] **—o·rac′u·lar** (ō-răk′yə-lər, ô-) *adj.*

o·ral (ôr′əl, ōr′-) *adj.* **1.** Spoken rather than written. **2.** Of the mouth: *oral hygiene.* **3.** Used in or taken through the mouth. [< Lat. *os*, mouth.] **—o′ral·ly** *adv.*

or·ange (ôr′ĭnj, ŏr′-) *n.* **1. a.** Any of several evergreen trees that bear white flowers and round fruit. **b.** The fruit of the orange tree, with a yellowish-red rind and a sectioned, edible pulp. **2.** A color between red and yellow in hue. [< Skt. *nāraṅgaḥ.*] **—or′ange** *adj.*

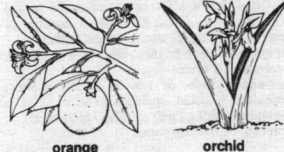

orange   orchid

or·ange·ade (ôr′ĭn-jād′, ŏr′-) *n.* A beverage of orange juice, sugar, and water.

o·rang·u·tan (ō-răng′ə-tăn′, ə-răng′-) *n.* Also **o·rang·ou·tan.** An arboreal anthropoid ape having a shaggy coat and very long arms. [Malay *ōrang hūtan.*]

o·rate (ô-rāt′, ō-rāt′, ôr′āt′, ōr′āt′) *v.* **o·rat·ed, o·rat·ing.** To speak in a dignified and often pompous manner. [< ORATION.]

o·ra·tion (ô-rā′shən, ō-rā′-) *n.* A formal address or speech. [< Lat. *orare*, to speak.]

or·a·tor (ôr′ə-tər, ŏr′-) *n.* **1.** One who delivers an oration. **2.** One skilled in the art of public speaking. **—or′a·tor′i·cal** (-tôr′ĭ-kəl, -tŏr′-) *adj.* **—or′a·tor′i·cal·ly** *adv.*

o·ra·to·ri·o (ôr′ə-tôr′ē-ō′, -tōr′-, ŏr′-) *n., pl.* **-os.** A musical composition for voices and orchestra, usu. with a religious theme, without cos-

tumes, scenery, or dramatic action. [< Ital. *Oratorio*, the Oratory of St. Philip Neri at Rome.]

o·ra·to·ry¹ (ôr′ə-tôr′ē, -tōr′ē, ŏr′-) *n.* **1.** The art of public speaking; rhetoric. **2.** Skill or style in public speaking.

o·ra·to·ry² (ôr′ə-tôr′ē, -tōr′ē, ŏr′-) *n., pl.* **-ries.** A small private chapel. [< Lat. *oratorium (templum)*, (place) of prayer.]

orb (ôrb) *n.* **1.** A sphere. **2.** A celestial body. [< Lat. *orbis.*] **—or·bic′u·lar** (-bĭk′yə-lər) *adj.*

or·bit (ôr′bĭt) *n.* **1.** The path of one celestial body or manmade object as it revolves around another. **2.** The path of a body in a field of force surrounding another body. **3.** A range of activity or influence. *—v.* **1.** To put into or cause to move in an orbit. **2.** To revolve or move in orbit. [< Lat. *orbita.*] **—or′bit·al** *adj.*

or·chard (ôr′chərd) *n.* **1.** An area of land devoted to the cultivation of fruit or nut trees. **2.** The trees cultivated in an orchard. [< OE *ortgeard.*]

or·ches·tra (ôr′kĭ-strə, -kĕs′trə) *n.* **1.** A group of musicians who play together on various musical instruments. **2. a.** The front section of seats on the main floor of a theater. **b.** The entire main floor of a theater. [< Gk. *orkhēstra*, the space in front of a stage.] **—or·ches′tral** (-kĕs′trəl) *adj.* **—or·ches′tral·ly** *adv.*

or·ches·trate (ôr′kĭ-strāt′) *v.* **-trat·ed, -trat·ing.** **1.** To compose or arrange (music) for an orchestra. **2.** To arrange or organize; direct. **—or′ches·tra′tion** *n.* **—or′ches·tra′tor** or **or′ches·trat′er** *n.*

or·chid (ôr′kĭd) *n.* **1. a.** Any of numerous chiefly tropical plants with irregularly shaped flowers. **b.** The flower of one of these plants. **2.** A light reddish purple. [< Gk. *orkhis.*]

or·dain (ôr-dān′) *v.* **1.** To install as a minister, priest, or rabbi. **2.** To order by or as if by decree. **3.** To predestine. [< Lat. *ordinare*, to organize.] **—or·dain′er** *n.* **—or·dain′ment** *n.*

or·deal (ôr-dēl′, ôr′dēl′) *n.* An extremely difficult or painful experience. [< OE *ordāl.*]

or·der (ôr′dər) *n.* **1.** A condition of logical or comprehensible arrangement among the separate elements of a group. **2.** The state, condition, or disposition of a thing. **3. a.** The existing structures of a given society. **b.** The condition in which these structures are maintained and preserved by the rule of law. **4.** A sequence, arrangement, or category of successive things. **5.** The established sequence; customary procedure. **6.** A command or direction. **7.** A commission or instruction to buy, sell, or supply something. **8.** A portion of food requested by a customer at a restaurant. **9. a.** Any of several grades of the Christian ministry. **b. orders.** Ordination. **10.** A monastic institution. **11.** An organization of people bound by some common fraternal bond or social aim. **12.** A group of persons upon whom a government or sovereign has formally conferred honor: *the Order of the Garter.* **13.** Degree of quality; distinction; rank. **14.** Approximate size or magnitude. *—v.* **1.** To issue a command or instruction (to). **2.** To request to be supplied with (something). **3.** To put in a systematic arrangement. **—idioms. in order to.** For the purpose of. **on the order of.** Similar to; like. **to order.** According to the buyer's specifications. [< Lat. *ordo.*]

or·der·ly (ôr′dər-lē) *adj.* **1.** Having a methodi-

cal and systematic arrangement; tidy.
2. Peaceful; well-behaved. —*n., pl.* **-lies.**
1. An attendant in a hospital. **2.** A soldier assigned to attend upon a superior officer. —**or'der·li·ness** *n.*

or·di·nal (ôr'dn-əl) *adj.* Being of a specified position in a numbered series. [< Lat. *ordo,* order.]

ordinal number *n.* A number indicating position in a series or order.

or·di·nance (ôr'dn-əns) *n.* **1.** An authoritative command or order. **2.** A municipal statute or regulation. [< Lat. *ordinare,* to ordain.]

or·di·nar·i·ly (ôr'dn-âr'ə-lē, ôr'dn-ĕr'-) *adv.* As a general rule; usually.

or·di·nar·y (ôr'dn-ĕr'ē) *adj.* **1.** Commonly encountered; usual; normal. **2.** Average in rank, ability, or merit; commonplace. [< Lat. *ordinarius.*] —**or'di·nar'i·ness** *n.*

Syns: *ordinary, average, common, commonplace, plain, unexceptional adj.*

or·di·nate (ôr'dn-ĭt, -āt') *n.* The plane Cartesian coordinate representing the distance from a specified point to the *x*-axis, measured parallel to the *y*-axis. [< Lat. *ordinare,* to order.]

or·di·na·tion (ôr'dn-ā'shən) *n.* The ceremony of ordaining a person to the ministry.

ord·nance (ôrd'nəns) *n.* **1.** Military supplies, esp. weapons and ammunition. **2.** Heavy guns; artillery. [< Lat. *ordinare,* to put in order.]

Or·do·vi·cian (ôr'də-vĭsh'ən) *adj.* Of, pertaining to, or designating the geologic time, system of rocks, and sedimentary deposits of the second period of the Paleozoic era, characterized by the appearance of primitive fishes. —*n.* The Ordovician period. [< the *Ordovices,* an ancient Celtic tribe of northern Wales.]

or·dure (ôr'jər) *n.* Excrement; dung. [< Lat. *horridus,* frightful.]

ore (ôr, ōr) *n.* A mineral or rock from which a valuable constituent, esp. a metal, can be mined or extracted. [< OE *ōra.*]

ö·re (œ'rə) *n., pl.* **ö·re.** See table at **currency.** [Dan. and Norw. *ore* and Swed. *öre.*]

o·re·ad (ôr'ē-ăd', ōr'-) *n.* Gk. Myth. A mountain nymph. [Gk. *Oreias.*]

o·reg·a·no (ə-rĕg'ə-nō', ō-rĕg'-) *n.* An herb seasoning made from the dried leaves of a species of marjoram. [< Gk. *origanon.*]

or·gan (ôr'gən) *n.* **1.** A musical instrument consisting of a number of pipes that sound tones when supplied with air, and a keyboard that operates a mechanism controlling the flow of air to the pipes. **2.** An instrument designed to imitate the organ electronically. **3.** A differentiated part of a living thing, adapted for a specific function. **4.** A body or agency that is part of a larger organization. **5.** A periodical. [< Gk. *organon,* instrument.]

or·gan·dy (ôr'gən-dē) *n., pl.* **-dies.** Also **organ·die.** A fine fabric, as of cotton or silk, usu. with a crisp finish. [Fr. *organdi.*]

or·gan·ic (ôr-găn'ĭk) *adj.* **1.** Of, relating to, or affecting an organ of the body. **2.** Of, relating to, or derived from living organisms. **3.** Using or grown with fertilizers consisting only of natural animal or vegetable matter. **4.** Like an organism in organization or development:

an organic whole. **5.** Of or constituting an integral part of something; fundamental. **6.** *Chem.* Of or relating to carbon compounds. —**or·gan'i·cal·ly** *adv.*

or·gan·ism (ôr'gə-nĭz'əm) *n.* **1.** A living being. **2.** A system similar to a living body: *the social organism.* —**or'gan·is'mal** or **or'gan·is'mic** *adj.*

or·gan·ist (ôr'gə-nĭst) *n.* One who plays the organ.

or·gan·i·za·tion (ôr'gə-nĭ-zā'shən) *n.* **1.** The act of organizing or process of being organized. **2.** The condition or manner of being organized: *a high degree of organization.* **3.** Something that has been organized and functions as a whole. **4.** A group united by a common interest or goal. —**or'gan·i·za'tion·al** *adj.* —**or'gan·i·za'tion·al·ly** *adv.*

or·gan·ize (ôr'gə-nīz') *v.* **-ized, -iz·ing.** **1.** To put together into an orderly, functional, structured whole. **2.** To arrange in a coherent form; systematize. **3.** To arrange by planning and coordinating. **4.** To persuade or form to join a labor union. [< Lat. *organum,* instrument.] —**or'gan·iz'er** *n.*

or·gan·za (ôr-găn'zə) *n.* A sheer, stiff fabric of silk or synthetic material. [Orig. unknown.]

or·gasm (ôr'găz'əm) *n.* The climax of sexual excitement. [< Gk. *orgasmos.*] —**or·gas'mic** or **or·gas'tic** *adj.*

or·gy (ôr'jē) *n., pl.* **-gies.** **1.** A wild revel often marked by unrestrained sexual activity. **2.** Excessive indulgence in something. [< Gk. *orgia.*] —**or'gi·as'tic** (-ăs'tĭk) *adj.*

o·ri·el (ôr'ē-əl, ōr'-) *n.* A projecting bay window supported by brackets. [< Med. Lat. *oriolum,* porch.]

o·ri·ent (ôr'ē-ənt, -ĕnt', ōr'-) *n.* **1.** The east. **2.** Orient. The countries of Asia, esp. of eastern Asia. —*v.* (ôr'ē-ĕnt', ōr'-). **1.** To locate or place in a particular relation to the points of the compass. **2.** To make familiar or acquainted with a situation. [< Lat. *oriri,* to rise.] —**o'ri·en·ta'tion** *n.*

o·ri·en·tal (ôr'ē-ĕn'tl, ōr'-) *adj.* **1.** Eastern. **2.** Often Oriental. Of or characteristic of the Orient. —*n.* Often Oriental. A member of one of the peoples native to the Orient.

o·ri·en·tate (ôr'ē-ĕn-tāt', -ən-, ōr'-) *v.* **-tat·ed, -tat·ing.** To orient.

or·i·fice (ôr'ə-fĭs, ōr'-) *n.* A mouth or vent; opening. [< LLat. *orificium.*]

o·ri·ga·mi (ôr'ĭ-gä'mē) *n.* The Japanese art or process of folding paper.

origami

or·i·gin (ôr'ə-jĭn, ōr'-) *n.* **1.** The primary source or cause of something. **2.** Parentage; ancestry. **3.** A coming into being. **4.** *Math.*

The point of intersection of coordinate axes.
[< Lat. *origo*.]

o·rig·i·nal (ə-rĭj′ə-nəl) *adj.* **1.** Initial; first. **2.** Fresh and unusual; new. **3.** Creative; inventive. —*n.* **1.** The primary form from which varieties arise or copies are made. **2.** An authentic work of art as distinguished from a copy. —**o·rig′i·nal′i·ty** (-năl′ĭ-tē) *n.* —**o·rig′i·nal·ly** *adv.*

o·rig·i·nate (ə-rĭj′ə-nāt′) *v.* **-nat·ed, -nat·ing.** To come or bring into being. —**o·rig′i·na′tion** *n.* —**o·rig′i·na′tor** *n.*

o·ri·ole (ôr′ē-ōl′, ōr′-) *n.* A songbird with bright orange or yellow and black plumage. [< Lat. *aureolus*, golden.]

O·ri·on (ō-rī′ən) *n.* A constellation in the celestial equator near Gemini and Taurus.

ori·son (ôr′ĭ-sən, -zən, ōr′-) *n.* A prayer. [< Lat. *oratio*, speech.]

Orlon (ôr′lŏn′). A trademark for a synthetic acrylic fiber.

or·mo·lu (ôr′mə-lōō′) *n.* An alloy that resembles gold, used esp. to decorate furniture. [Fr. *or moulu*, ground gold.]

or·na·ment (ôr′nə-mənt) *n.* Something that decorates or adorns; embellishment. —*v.* (ôr′nə-měnt′). To decorate; adorn. [< Lat. *ornamentum*.] —**or′na·men′tal** (-měn′təl) *adj.* —**or′na·men·ta′tion** *n.*

or·nate (ôr-nāt′) *adj.* Elaborately ornamented or embellished. [< Lat. *ornare*, to adorn.] —**or·nate′ly** *adv.* —**or·nate′ness** *n.*

or·ner·y (ôr′nə-rē) *adj.* **-i·er, -i·est.** *Informal.* Mean and stubborn. [< ORDINARY.]

or·ni·thol·o·gy (ôr′nə-thŏl′ə-jē) *n.* The scientific study of birds as a branch of zoology. [Gk. *ornis*, bird + -LOGY.] —**or′ni·tho·log′i·cal** (-thə-lŏj′ĭ-kəl) or **or′ni·tho·log′ic** *adj.* —**or′ni·thol′o·gist** *n.*

o·ro·tund (ôr′ə-tŭnd′, ōr′-, ōr′-) *adj.* **1.** Full in sound; sonorous. **2.** Pompous and bombastic. [< Lat. *ore rotundo*, with a round mouth.]

or·phan (ôr′fən) *n.* A child whose parents are dead. [< Gk. *orphanos*, without parents.] —**or′phan** *v.*

or·phan·age (ôr′fə-nĭj) *n.* An institution for the care of orphans.

Or·phe·us (ôr′fē-əs, -fyōōs′) *n. Gk. Myth.* A musician and poet whose music had the power to charm wild beasts.

or·ris·root (ôr′ĭs-rōōt′, -rŏŏt′, ōr′-) *n.* The fragrant root of an Old World iris, used in perfumes and cosmetics. [*orris*, iris + ROOT.]

ortho- *pref.* Correct: *orthodontia.* [< Gk. *orthos.*]

or·tho·don·tia (ôr′thə-dŏn′shə) *n.* The dental specialty and practice of correcting abnormally aligned or positioned teeth. [< ORTHO- + Gk. *odous*, tooth.] —**or′tho·don′tic** *adj.* —**or′tho·don′tist** *n.*

or·tho·don·tics (ôr′thə-dŏn′tĭks) *n.* (used with a sing. verb). Orthodontia.

or·tho·dox (ôr′thə-dŏks′) *adj.* **1.** Adhering to traditional or established beliefs, esp. in religion. **2.** Commonly accepted; customary. **3. Orthodox. a.** Of or relating to Christian churches derived from the church of the Byzantine Empire. **b.** Of or belonging to a branch of Judaism adhering strictly to the ancient Hebrew law. [< Gk. *orthodoxos.*] —**or′tho·dox′y** *n.*

or·thog·ra·phy (ôr-thŏg′rə-fē) *n., pl.* **-phies. 1.** Correct spelling. **2.** The study and formulation of systems of spelling. —**or′tho·graph′ic** (-thə-grăf′ĭk) *adj.* —**or′tho·graph′i·cal·ly** *adv.*

or·tho·pe·dics (ôr′thə-pē′dĭks) *n.* (used with a sing. verb). The branch of medicine that deals with disorders of the bones, joints, and associated muscles. [< ORTHO- + Gk. *pais*, child.] —**or′tho·pe′dic** *adj.* —**or′tho·pe′di·cal·ly** *adv.* —**or′tho·pe′dist** *n.*

-ory *suff.* **1.** Of, pertaining to, or characterized by: *advisory.* **2.** A place or thing used for or connected with: *crematory.* [< Lat. *-orius*, adj. suffix and *-orium*, n. suffix.]

Os The symbol for the element osmium.

O·sage (ō′sāj′, ō-sāj′) *n., pl.* **Osage** or **O·sag·es. 1. a.** A tribe of Indians formerly inhabiting the region between the Missouri and Arkansas rivers. **b.** A member of this tribe. **2.** The Siouan language of the Osage. —**O′sage′** *adj.*

os·cil·late (ŏs′ə-lāt′) *v.* **-lat·ed, -lat·ing. 1.** To swing back and forth steadily. **2.** To waver; vacillate. **3.** *Physics.* To vary between alternate extremes, usu. with a definable period. [< Lat. *oscillare.*] —**os′cil·la′tion** *n.* —**os′cil·la′tor** *n.* —**os′cil·la·to′ry** (-lə-tôr′ē, -tōr′ē) *adj.*

os·cil·lo·scope (ŏ-sĭl′ə-skōp′, ə-sĭl′-) *n.* An electronic instrument that produces an instantaneous visual display or trace of electronic motion on the screen of a cathode-ray tube corresponding to external oscillatory motion. [OSCILL(ATION) + -SCOPE.] —**os·cil′lo·scop′ic** (-skŏp′ĭk) *adj.*

os·cu·late (ŏs′kyə-lāt′) *v.* **-lat·ed, -lat·ing.** To kiss. [Lat. *osculari.*] —**os′cu·la′tion** *n.*

-ose¹ *suff.* Possession of or similarity to: *grandiose.* [< Lat. *-osus.*]

-ose² *suff.* A carbohydrate: *dextrose.* [< GLUCOSE.]

o·sier (ō′zhər) *n.* **1.** A willow with long, rodlike twigs used in basketry. **2.** A twig of such a willow. [< Med. Lat. *osaria*, willow bed.]

-osis *suff.* **1.** A condition or process: *hypnosis.* **2.** A diseased or abnormal condition: *cirrhosis.* [< Gk. *-ōsis*, n. suffix.]

os·mi·um (ŏz′mē-əm) *n. Symbol* **Os** A bluishwhite, hard, metallic element, used as a platinum hardener and as a catalyst in cortisone synthesis. Atomic number 76; atomic weight 190.2. [< Gk. *osmē*, odor.]

os·mo·sis (ŏz-mō′sĭs, ŏs-) *n.* **1.** The diffusion of fluid through a semipermeable membrane until there is an equal concentration of fluid on either side of the membrane. **2.** A gradual process of assimilation or absorption that resembles osmosis. [< Gk. *ōsmos*, thrush.] —**os·mot′ic** (ŏz-mŏt′ĭk, ŏs-) *adj.*

os·prey (ŏs′prē, -prā′) *n., pl.* **-preys.** A large fish-eating hawk with black and white plumage. [< Lat. *avis praedae*, bird of prey.]

os·si·fy (ŏs′ə-fī′) *v.* **-fied, -fy·ing. 1.** To change into bone. **2.** To set into a rigidly conventional pattern. [Lat. *os*, bone + -FY.] —**os′si·fi·ca′tion** *n.*

os·ten·si·ble (ŏ-stěn′sə-bəl, ə-stěn′-) *adj.* Outwardly apparent; seeming; professed. [< Lat. *ostendere*, to show.] —**os·ten′si·bly** *adv.*

os·ten·ta·tion (ŏs′těn-tā′shən, -tən-) *n.* Pretentious or excessive display. [< Lat. *ostentare*, to show.] —**os′ten·ta′tious** *adj.* —**os′ten·ta′tious·ly** *adv.*

os·te·op·a·thy (ŏs′tē-ŏp′ə-thē) *n.* A system that emphasizes manipulation esp. of the bones for treating disease. [Gk. *osteon*, bone + -PATHY.] —**os′te·o·path′** (ŏs′tē-ə-păth′) *n.* —**os′te·o·path′ic** *adj.* —**os′te·o·path′i·cal·ly** *adv.*

os·tler (ŏs′lər) *n.* Var. of **hostler.**

os·tra·cize (ŏs'trə-sīz') v. **-cized, -ciz·ing.** To banish or exclude from a group. [Gk. *ostrakizein*.] **—os'tra·cism** n.

os·trich (ŏs'trĭch, ô'strĭch) n. A large, long-necked flightless African bird with long, bare legs. [< Gk. *strouthiōn*.]

ostrich

oth·er (ŭth'ər) adj. **1. a.** Being the remaining one of two or more. **b.** Being the remaining ones of several. **2.** Different or distinct from what has been mentioned. **3.** Just recent or past: *the other day.* **4.** Additional; extra: *I have no other shoes.* **5.** Alternate; second: *We play tennis every other day.* —n. **1. a.** The remaining one of two or more. **b. others.** The remaining ones of several. **2. a.** A different one: *one hurricane after the other.* **b.** An additional one: *Where is the other?* —pron. Another person or thing. —adv. Otherwise. [< OE *ōther.*]

oth·er·wise (ŭth'ər-wīz') adv. **1.** In another way; differently. **2.** Under other circumstances. **3.** In other respects: *an otherwise logical mind.* —adj. **1.** Other than supposed; different: *The evidence is otherwise.* **2.** Other: *be otherwise than happy.*

oth·er·world·ly (ŭth'ər-wûrld'lē) adj. **1.** Of or characteristic of another world, esp. a mystical world. **2.** Concerned with intellectual or imaginative things. **—oth'er·world'li·ness** n.

-otic suff. **1.** Of, pertaining to, or characterized by a specified process or condition: *narcotic.* **2.** Having a specified disease or abnormal condition: *neurotic.* [< Gk. *-ōtikos,* adj. suffix.]

o·ti·ose (ō'shē-ōs', ō'tē-) adj. **1.** Indolent. **2.** Useless; futile. [Lat. *otiosus.*]

Ot·ta·wa (ŏt'ə-wə, -wä', -wô') n. **1. a.** A group of Indians inhabiting Michigan and southern Ontario. **b.** A member of this group. **2.** The dialect of Ojibwa spoken by the Ottawas.

ot·ter (ŏt'ər) n., pl. **-ter** or **-ters. 1.** An aquatic, carnivorous mammal with webbed feet and dark-brown fur. **2.** The fur of an otter. [< OE *otor.*]

ot·to·man (ŏt'ə-mən) n. **1.** A backless, upholstered sofa or divan. **2.** An upholstered footstool. [< Fr. *ottoman,* Turk.]

ou·bli·ette (ōō'blē-ĕt') n. A dungeon entered through a trap door in the ceiling. [< Fr. *oublier,* to forget.]

ouch (ouch) interj. Used to express sudden pain.

ought (ôt) aux. v. Indicates: **1.** Obligation or duty: *You ought to work harder than that.* **2.** Expediency or prudence: *You ought to wear a raincoat.* **3.** Desirability: *You ought to have*

been there. **4.** Probability or likelihood: *She ought to finish by next week.* [< OE *āhte,* p.t. of *āgan,* to possess.]

Usage: Usages like *he hadn't ought to come* and *she shouldn't ought to say* that are common in many varieties of American English. They should be avoided in written English in favor of the standard equivalent *ought not to.*

ou·gui·ya (ōō-gē'yə) n. See table at **currency.** [Native word in Mauritania.]

ounce (ouns) n. **1. a.** A unit of weight in the U.S. Customary System, an avoirdupois unit equal·to 16 drams or 437.5 grains. **b.** A unit of apothecary weight, equal to 480 grains or 1.097 avoirdupois ounces. **2. a.** A unit of volume or capacity in the U.S. Customary System, used in liquid measure, equal to 8 fluid drams or 1.804 cubic inches. **b.** A unit of volume or capacity in the British Imperial System, used in dry and liquid measure, equal to 1.734 cubic inches. **3.** A tiny bit. [< Lat. *uncia,* a twelfth.]

our (our) pron. The possessive form of **we,** used as a modifier before a noun: *our homework; our greatest setback.* [< OE *ūre.*]

ours (ourz) pron. Used to indicate the one or ones belonging to us: *The house is ours. He is a friend of ours.* [< OE *ūre,* our.]

our·self (our-sĕlf', är-) pron. Myself. Used in royal proclamations or editorial commentaries.

our·selves (our-sĕlvz', är-) pron. **1.** Those identical with us. Used: **a.** Reflexively as the direct object of a verb or the object of a preposition: *We injured ourselves.* **b.** For emphasis: *We ourselves are excluded from the contract.* **2.** Our normal or healthy condition: *We have not been ourselves since he left.* **—idiom. by ourselves. 1.** Alone. **2.** Without help.

-ous suff. **1.** Possessing; full of: *joyous.* **2.** Chem. Occurring with a valence lower than that in a comparable *-ic* system: *ferrous.* [< Lat. *-osus.*]

oust (oust) v. To evict; force out. [< Lat. *obstare,* to hinder.]

oust·er (ou'stər) n. Eviction; expulsion. [< Norman Fr. *ouster,* to oust.]

out (out) adv. **1.** Away or forth from inside. **2.** Away from the center or middle. **3.** Away from a usual place. **4.** Outside: *went out to play.* **5. a.** To exhaustion or depletion: *The supplies have run out.* **b.** To extinction: *The fire has gone out.* **c.** To a finish or conclusion: *Play the game out.* **6.** Into the open: *The moon came out.* **7.** Into circulation: *giving out free passes.* **8.** Into disuse or disfavor. **9.** Baseball. So as to be retired. —adj. **1.** Exterior; external. **2.** Unable to be used; in disrepair: *The power is out.* **3.** Informal. Without an amount possessed previously: *I am out ten dollars.* **4.** Not available for use or consideration: *A taxi is out, because we haven't the money.* —prep. Through; forth from: *He fell out the window.* —n. **1.** One that is out, esp. one who is out of power. **2.** A means of escape. **3.** Baseball. A play in which a batter or base runner is retired. —v. To be revealed; come out: *Truth will out.* **—idioms. on the outs.** Informal. Not on friendly terms;

disagreeing. **out for.** Trying to get or have. [< OE *ūt*.]

out- *pref.* To a surpassing or superior degree: *outdistance.* [< OUT.]
  Usage: Many compounds other than those entered here may be formed with *out-*. In forming compounds, *out-* is joined with the following element without a space or hyphen: *outclass.*

out-and-out (out′n-out′) *adj.* Complete; thoroughging.

out-back (out′băk′) *n.* A wild, remote part esp. of Australia or New Zealand.

out-bid (out-bĭd′) *v.* To bid higher than.

out-board (out′bôrd′, -bōrd′) *adj.* 1. Situated outside the hull of a vessel. 2. Situated toward or nearer the end of an aircraft wing. —**out′board′** *adv.*

out-bound (out′bound′) *adj.* Outward bound.

out-break (out′brāk′) *n.* A sudden eruption.

out-build-ing (out′bĭl′dĭng) *n.* A building separate from but associated with a main building.

out-burst (out′bûrst′) *n.* A sudden, often violent display, as of activity or emotion.

out-cast (out′kăst′) *n.* One who has been excluded from a society. —**out′cast′** *adj.*

out-class (out-klăs′) *v.* To surpass decisively.

out-come (out′kŭm′) *n.* A result; consequence.

out-crop (out′krŏp′) *n. Geol.* A portion of bedrock from a lower stratum that extends up above the soil level. —**out′crop′** *v.*

out-cry (out′krī′) *n.* 1. A loud cry or clamor. 2. A strong protest.

out-dated (out-dā′tĭd) *adj.* Out-of-date; antiquated.

out-dis-tance (out-dĭs′tans) *v.* To go ahead of by a wide margin.

out-do (out-dōō′) *v.* To do better than.

out-door (out′dôr′, -dōr′) *adj.* Also **out-of-door** (out′əv-dôr′, -dōr′). Located in, done in, or suited to the open air.

out-doors (out-dôrz′, -dōrz′). Also **out-of-doors** (out′əv-dôrz′, -dōrz′). —*adv.* In or into the open; outside of a house or shelter. —*n.* The open air; the area outside buildings.

out-doors-man (out-dôrz′mən, -dōrz′-) *n.* One who spends considerable leisure time in outdoor activities.

out-er (ou′tər) *adj.* 1. Located on the outside; external. 2. Farther from the center or middle.

out-er-most (ou′tər-mōst′) *adj.* Farthest out.

outer space *n.* Space beyond the limits of a celestial body or system.

out-face (out-fās′) *v.* **-faced, -fac-ing.** 1. To overcome with a self-assured look. 2. To defy.

out-field (out′fēld′) *n.* The playing area extending outward from a baseball diamond. —**out′field′er** *n.*

out-fit (out′fĭt′) *n.* 1. Clothing or equipment for a special purpose. 2. An association of persons who work together. —*v.* To provide with an outfit. —**out′fit′ter** *n.*

out-flank (out-flăngk′) *v.* 1. To maneuver around the flank of (an opposing force). 2. To gain a tactical advantage over.

out-flow (out′flō′) *n.* 1. The act of flowing out. 2. Something that flows out.

out-fox (out-fŏks′) *v.* To outsmart.

out-go (out′gō′) *n., pl.* **-goes.** Something, esp. money, that goes out.

out-go-ing (out′gō′ĭng) *adj.* 1. Departing; going out. 2. Friendly; sociable.

out-grow (out-grō′) *v.* 1. To grow too large for. 2. To grow too mature for: *outgrew childish games.* 3. To surpass in growth.

out-growth (out′grōth′) *n.* 1. Something that grows out of something else. 2. A result or consequence.

out-guess (out-gĕs′) *v.* To anticipate correctly the plans or actions of.

out-house (out′hous′) *n.* 1. A toilet housed in a small outdoor structure. 2. An outbuilding.

out-ing (ou′tĭng) *n.* 1. An excursion. 2. A walk outdoors.

out-land (out′lănd′, -lənd) *n.* 1. A foreign land. 2. **outlands.** The outlying areas of a country. —**out′land′er** *n.*

out-land-ish (out-lăn′dĭsh) *adj.* 1. Strikingly foreign; unfamiliar. 2. Conspicuously unconventional; bizarre. —**out-land′ish-ly** *adv.* —**out-land′ish-ness** *n.*

out-last (out-lăst′) *v.* To last longer than.

out-law (out′lô′) *n.* 1. A person excluded from normal legal protection and rights. 2. A lawless person. —*v.* 1. To declare illegal. 2. To deprive of the protection of the law. —**out′law-ry** *n.*

out-lay (out′lā′) *n.* 1. The spending or disbursing of money. 2. An amount spent.

out-let (out′lĕt′, -lĭt) *n.* 1. A passage for escape or exit; vent. 2. A means of release or expression, as for energy or talent. 3. A commercial market for goods or services. 4. A receptacle that is connected to a power supply and equipped with a socket for a plug.

out-line (out′līn′) *n.* 1. **a.** A line forming the outer boundary of any object or figure. **b.** Contour; shape. 2. A style of drawing in which objects are represented by their outer edges, without shading. 3. A short summary, description, or account. —*v.* 1. To draw the outline of. 2. To give the main points of; summarize.

out-live (out-lĭv′) *v.* To live longer than; outlast.

out-look (out′lŏŏk′) *n.* 1. **a.** A place where something can be viewed. **b.** The view seen. 2. A point of view or attitude. 3. Prospect; expectation.

out-ly-ing (out′lī′ĭng) *adj.* Distant or remote from a center.

out-ma-neu-ver (out′mə-nōō′vər, -nyōō′-) *v.* 1. To overcome by more artful maneuvering. 2. To excel in maneuverability, as an automobile.

out-mod-ed (out-mō′dĭd) *adj.* 1. Not in fashion. 2. Obsolete.

out-num-ber (out-nŭm′bər) *v.* To be more numerous than.

out *prep.* 1. **a.** From within to the outside of: *ran out of the room.* **b.** From a given condition: *came out of her trance.* **c.** From an origin, source, or cause: *made out of wood.* 2. **a.** In a position or situation beyond the range, boundaries, limits, or sphere of: *She went out of sight.* **b.** In a state or position away from the expected or usual: *out of sorts.* 3. Because of; owing to: *did it out of malice.* 4. With headquarters in: *works out of the main office.* 5. From among: *five out of six votes.*

out-of-bounds (out′əv-boundz′) *adv. & adj.* Beyond the designated boundaries or limits.

out-of-date (out′əv-dāt′) *adj.* Outmoded; old-fashioned.

out-of-door (out'əv-dôr', -dōr') *adj.* Var. of outdoor.

out-of-doors (out'əv-dôrz', -dōrz') *adv. & n.* Var. of outdoors.

out-of-pock·et (out'-əv-pŏk'ĭt) *adj.* Calling for the spending of cash: *out-of-pocket expenses.*

out-of-the-way (out'əv-thə-wā') *adj.* 1. Distant; remote. 2. Unusual.

out-of-town·er (out'əv-tou'nər) *n.* A visitor from another town or city.

out·pa·tient (out'pā'shənt) *n.* A patient who receives treatment at a hospital without being hospitalized.

out·play (out-plā') *v.* To play better than.

out·post (out'pōst') *n.* 1. A detachment of troops stationed at a distance from a main unit of forces. 2. The station occupied by an outpost. 3. An outlying settlement.

out·pour·ing (out'pôr'ĭng, -pōr'-) *n.* Something that pours out or is poured out.

out·put (out'pŏŏt') *n.* 1. Production, esp. the amount of something produced or manufactured during a given time. 2. a. The energy, power, or work produced by a system. b. The information produced by a computer from a specific input. —**out'put'** *v.*

out·rage (out'rāj') *n.* 1. An act of extreme violence or viciousness. 2. An act grossly offensive to decency or morality. 3. Resentful anger. —*v.* **-raged, -rag·ing.** 1. To inflict violence upon. 2. To rape. 3. To produce anger or resentment in. [< Lat. *ultra,* beyond.]

out·ra·geous (out-rā'jəs) *adj.* 1. a. Grossly offensive. b. Disgraceful; shameful. 2. Extravagant; immoderate. —**out·ra'geous·ly** *adv.* —**out·ra'geous·ness** *n.*

Syns: outrageous, atrocious, flagrant, heinous, monstrous, scandalous, shocking adj.

out·rank (out-răngk') *v.* To rank higher than.

ou·tré (ōō-trā') *adj.* Eccentric; bizarre. [< Fr. *outrer,* to go to excess.]

out·reach (out-rēch') *v.* 1. To surpass in reach. 2. To go beyond.

out·rid·er (out'rī'dər) *n.* A mounted attendant.

out·rig·ger (out'rĭg'ər) *n.* 1. A long, thin float attached parallel to a seagoing canoe to prevent it from capsizing. 2. A vessel fitted with an outrigger.

out·right (out'rīt', -rīt') *adv.* 1. Without reservation or qualification. 2. Entirely; wholly. 3. Without delay; straightway. —*adj.* (out'rīt'). 1. Unqualified: *an outright gift.* 2. Thoroughgoing: out-and-out.

out·run (out-rŭn') *v.* 1. To run faster than. 2. To exceed.

out·sell (out-sĕl') *v.* To surpass in sales or selling.

out·set (out'sĕt') *n.* Beginning; start.

out·shine (out-shīn') *v.* 1. To shine brighter than. 2. To exceed.

out·side (out-sīd', out'sīd') *n.* 1. An outer surface or side; exterior. 2. The space beyond a boundary or limit. 3. The utmost limit; maximum: *We'll be leaving in ten days at the outside.* —*adj.* 1. Acting, occurring, originating, or existing at a place beyond certain limits; outer; foreign: *outside assistance.* 2. Of, restricted to, or situated on the outside of an enclosure or boundary; external: *an outside*

door lock. 3. Extreme; uttermost: *The cost exceeded even my outside estimate.* 4. Slight; remote: *an outside chance.* —*adv.* On or into the outside; outdoors: *Let's go outside.* —*prep.* 1. On or to the outer side of: *outside the playing field.* 2. Beyond the limits of: *outside the rules.* 3. With the exception of; except: *no information outside the figures given.*

outside of *prep.* Outside.

out·sid·er (out-sī'dər) *n.* A person who is not part of a certain group or community.

out·size (out'sīz') *n.* An unusual size, esp. a very large size. —**out'size'** or **out'sized'** *adj.*

out·skirts (out'skûrts') *pl.n.* The peripheral parts, as of a city.

out·smart (out-smärt') *v.* To outwit.

out·spend (out-spĕnd') *v.* 1. To spend beyond the limits of. 2. To outdo in spending.

out·spo·ken (out-spō'kən) *adj.* Marked by frankness and lack of reserve. —**out·spo'ken·ly** *adv.* —**out·spo'ken·ness** *n.*

out·spread (out-sprĕd') *v.* To spread out; extend. —**out'spread'** *adj.*

out·stand·ing (out-stăn'dĭng, out'stăn'-) *adj.* 1. Projecting upward or outward. 2. Prominent. 3. Distinguished; excellent. 4. Not paid, settled, or resolved.

out·stretch (out-strĕch') *v.* To extend. —**out'stretched'** *adj.*

out·strip (out-strĭp') *v.* 1. To leave behind; outrun. 2. To exceed; surpass.

out·ward (out'wərd) *adj.* 1. Of or moving toward the outside or exterior. 2. Visible on the surface; superficial. —*adv.* Also **outwards** (-wərdz). Toward the outside. —**out'ward·ly** *adv.*

out·wear (out-wâr') *v.* To wear or last longer than.

out·weigh (out-wā') *v.* 1. To weigh more than. 2. To be more significant than.

out·wit (out-wĭt') *v.* **-wit·ted, -wit·ting.** To gain an advantage over by cleverness or cunning.

out·work¹ (out-wûrk') *v.* To work better or faster than.

out·work² (out'wûrk') *n.* A defensive position that is outside a fortification.

ou·zo (ōō'zō) *n., pl.* **-zos.** An aniseed-flavored Greek liqueur. [Mod. Gk.]

ov- *pref.* Var. of **ovi-.**

o·va (ō'və) *n.* Pl. of **ovum.**

o·val (ō'vəl) *adj.* 1. Egg-shaped. 2. Elliptical. —**o'val** *n.*

o·va·ry (ō'və-rē) *n., pl.* **-ries.** 1. One of a pair of female reproductive glands that produce ova. 2. The part of a pistil containing the ovules. —**o·var'i·an** (ō-vâr'ē-ən) *adj.*

o·vate (ō'vāt') *adj.* Oval; egg-shaped.

o·va·tion (ō-vā'shən) *n.* Enthusiastic and prolonged applause. [< Lat. *ovare,* to rejoice.]

ov·en (ŭv'ən) *n.* A compartment, as in a stove, for baking or heating. [< OE *ofen.*]

ov·en·bird (ŭv'ən-bûrd') *n.* A thrushlike North American warbler that builds a domed nest on the ground.

o·ver (ō'vər) *prep.* 1. Above. 2. On or above and across. 3. On the other side of. 4. Upon. 5. Throughout or during. 6. Along the length of. 7. In excess of; more than. 8. Through the duration of. 9. On account of: *an argument over methods.* —*adv.* 1. Above. 2. a. Across to another or opposite side.

b. Across the edge or brim. **3.** Across an intervening distance. **4.** To a different opinion or allegiance: *win him over.* **5.** To a different person, condition, or title: *sign over land.* **6.** So as to be completely covered: *The river froze over.* **7.** Through; thoroughly: *think it over.* **8. a.** From an upright position. **b.** From an upward to an inverted or reversed position. **9. a.** Again. **b.** In repetition: *ten times over.* **10.** In addition or excess. *—adj.* **1.** Finished: *The war is over.* **2. a.** Upper; higher. **b.** Covering; outer. **3.** In excess: *His estimate was fifty dollars over. —interj.* Used in radio conversations to mark the end of a transmission by one speaker. *—idiom.* **over and above.** In addition to; besides. [< OE *ofer.*]
over- *pref.* Excessive; excessively: *overexpose.* [< OVER.]

Usage: Many compounds other than those entered here may be formed with *over-.* In forming compounds, *over-* is joined with the following element without a space or hyphen: *overrate.*

o·ver·act (ō'vər-ăkt') *v.* To act with unnecessary exaggeration.
o·ver·age¹ (ō'vər-ĭj) *n.* An excess or surplus.
o·ver·age² (ō'vər-āj') *adj.* Older than the proper or required age.
o·ver·all (ō'vər-ôl', ō'vər-ôl') *adj.* **1.** From end to end. **2.** Including everything; comprehensive. *—adv.* (ō'vər-ôl'). Generally.
o·ver·alls (ō'vər-ôlz') *pl.n.* Loose-fitting trousers with a bib front and shoulder straps.
o·ver·arm (ō'vər-ärm') *adj.* Executed with the arm raised above the shoulder.
o·ver·awe (ō'vər-ô') *v.* To subdue or overcome with awe.
o·ver·bal·ance (ō'vər-băl'əns) *v.* **1.** To outweigh. **2.** To throw off balance.

o·ver·bear (ō'vər-bâr') *v.* **1.** To crush or press down upon with physical force. **2.** To prevail over, as if by superior force; dominate.
o·ver·bear·ing (ō'vər-bâr'ĭng) *adj.* Domineering and arrogant. *—o'ver·bear'ing·ly adv.*
o·ver·blown (ō'vər-blōn') *adj.* **1.** Extremely fat. **2.** Inflated; pretentious.
o·ver·board (ō'vər-bôrd', -bōrd') *adv.* Over the side of a boat or ship. *—idiom.* **go overboard.** To show wild or excessive enthusiasm.
o·ver·build (ō'vər-bĭld') *v.* To build beyond the demand or need of.
o·ver·cap·i·tal·ize (ō'vər-kăp'ĭ-tl-īz') *v.* **1.** To provide an excess amount of capital for (a business enterprise). **2.** To estimate the value of (property) too highly. *—o'ver·cap'i·tal·i·za'tion n.*
o·ver·cast (ō'vər-kăst', ō'vər-kăst') *adj.* **1.** Clouded over. **2.** Gloomy; dark.
o·ver·charge (ō'vər-chärj') *v.* **1.** To charge too much. **2.** To fill too full. *—o'ver·charge' n.*
o·ver·cloud (ō'vər-kloud') *v.* To make or become cloudy.
o·ver·coat (ō'vər-kōt') *n.* A heavy coat worn over the ordinary clothing.
o·ver·come (ō'vər-kŭm') *v.* **-came** (-kām'), **-come, -com·ing.** **1.** To defeat; conquer. **2.** To surmount; prevail over. **3.** To overpower, as with emotion. [< OE *ofercuman.*]
o·ver·do (ō'vər-dōō') *v.* **1.** To do too much. **2.** To exaggerate. **3.** To cook too long.
o·ver·dose (ō'vər-dōs') *v.* To give too large a dose to. *—o'ver·dose' n.*
o·ver·draft (ō'vər-drăft') *n.* **1.** The act of overdrawing an account. **2.** The amount overdrawn.
o·ver·draw (ō'vər-drô') *v.* **1.** To withdraw more from (an account) than one has credit for. **2.** To exaggerate or overstate.

o'ver·a·bound' *v.*
o'ver·a·bun'dance *n.*
o'ver·a·bun'dant *adj.*
o'ver·ac'tive *adj.*
o'ver·anx'ious *adj.*
o'ver·at·tached' *adj.*
o'ver·bid' *v.*
o'ver·bur'den *v.*
o'ver·buy *v.*
o'ver·care'ful *adj.*
o'ver·cau'tious *adj.*
o'ver·cau'tious·ly *adv.*
o'ver·cau'tious·ness *n.*
o'ver·chill' *v.*
o'ver·com·pen'sate' *v.*
o'ver·com·pen·sa'tion *n.*
o'ver·con'fi·dence *n.*
o'ver·con'fi·dent *adj.*
o'ver·con'fi·dent·ly *adv.*
o'ver·cool' *v.*
o'ver·cook' *v.*
o'ver·cour'te·ous *adj.*
o'ver·crit'i·cal *adj.*
o'ver·crowd' *v.*
o'ver·dar'ing *adj.*
o'ver·dec'o·rate' *v.*
o'ver·de·mand' *v.*
o'ver·de·vel'op *v.*
o'ver·de·vel'op·ment *n.*
o'ver·de·vot'ed *adj.*
o'ver·de·vo'tion *n.*
o'ver·dil'i·gence *n.*
o'ver·dil'i·gent *adj.*

o'ver·dis'ci·pline *v.*
o'ver·dra·mat'ic *adj.*
o'ver·drink' *v.*
o'ver·ea'ger *adj.*
o'ver·ear'nest *adj.*
o'ver·ear'nest·ly *adv.*
o'ver·eas'y *adj.*
o'ver·eat' *v.*
o'ver·ed'u·cate' *v.*
o'ver·e·lab'o·rate *adj.*
o'ver·el'e·gant *adj.*
o'ver·e·mo'tion·al *adj.*
o'ver·em'pha·sis *n.*
o'ver·em'pha·size' *v.*
o'ver·em·phat'ic *adj.*
o'ver·en·thu'si·as'tic *adj.*
o'ver·es'ti·mate' *v.*
o'ver·ex·cit'a·ble *adj.*
o'ver·ex·cite' *v.*
o'ver·ex·cite'ment *n.*
o'ver·ex·ert' *v.*
o'ver·ex·er'tion *n.*
o'ver·ex·pand' *v.*
o'ver·ex·pan'sion *n.*
o'ver·ex·pect'ant *adj.*
o'ver·ex·tend' *v.*
o'ver·ex·u'ber·ant *adj.*
o'ver·faith'ful *adj.*
o'ver·fa·mil'iar *adj.*
o'ver·fan'ci·ful *adj.*
o'ver·fas·tid'i·ous *adj.*
o'ver·fat'ten *v.*

o'ver·fed' *adj.*
o'ver·feed' *v.*
o'ver·fem'i·nine *adj.*
o'ver·fierce' *adj.*
o'ver·fill' *v.*
o'ver·fond'ness *n.*
o'ver·frank' *adj.*
o'ver·free'ly *adv.*
o'ver·fre'quent *adj.*
o'ver·full' *adj.*
o'ver·full'ness *n.*
o'ver·fur'nish *v.*
o'ver·gen'er·al·ize' *v.*
o'ver·gen'er·ous *adj.*
o'ver·gift'ed *adj.*
o'ver·glad' *adj.*
o'ver·gra'cious *adj.*
o'ver·grate'ful *adj.*
o'ver·greas'y *adj.*
o'ver·hard' *adj.*
o'ver·hard'en *v.*
o'ver·harsh' *adj.*
o'ver·hast'y *adj.*
o'ver·heat' *v.*
o'ver·help'ful *adj.*
o'ver·hon'est *adj.*
o'ver·i·de'al·ism *n.*
o'ver·im·ag'i·na·tive *adj.*
o'ver·im·press' *v.*
o'ver·in·clined' *adj.*
o'ver·in·dulge' *v.*
o'ver·in·dul'gence *n.*
o'ver·in·dul'gent *adj.*

o·ver·dress (ō'vər-drĕs') v. To dress too formally or elaborately for an occasion.

o·ver·drive (ō'vər-drīv') n. A gearing mechanism of an automotive engine that increases the ratio of drive shaft to engine speed in a given speed range.

o·ver·due (ō'vər-dōō', -dyōō') adj. 1. Being unpaid after becoming due. 2. Past due; late.

o·ver·ex·pose (ō'vər-ĭk-spōz') v. To expose too long or too much. —**o'ver·ex·po'sure** n.

o·ver·flow (ō'vər-flō') v. 1. To flow over the top, brim, or bounds (of). 2. To spread or cover over. —n. (ō'vər-flō'). 1. A flood. 2. An excess; surplus. 3. An outlet through which excess liquid may escape.

o·ver·grow (ō'vər-grō') v. 1. To spread over with growth. 2. To grow too large for. 3. To grow beyond normal size. —**o'ver·grown'** adj. —**o'ver·growth'** n.

o·ver·hand (ō'vər-hănd') adj. Also **o·ver·hand·ed** (ō'vər-hăn'dĭd). Executed with the hand above the level of the shoulder. —**o'ver·hand'** adv. & n.

o·ver·hang (ō'vər-hăng') v. 1. To project or extend beyond. 2. To threaten or menace; loom over. —**o'ver·hang'** n.

o·ver·haul (ō'vər-hôl', ō'vər-hôl') v. 1. To examine carefully and make repairs. 2. To overtake. —**o'ver·haul'** n.

o·ver·head (ō'vər-hĕd') adj. 1. Located or functioning above the level of the head. 2. Of or relating to the operating expenses of a business concern. —n. (ō'vər-hĕd'). The operating expenses of a business, such as rent, utilities, and taxes. —**o'ver·head'** adv.

o·ver·hear (ō'vər-hîr') v. To hear without being noticed or addressed by the speaker.

o·ver·joyed (ō'vər-joid') adj. Filled with joy; delighted.

o·ver·kill (ō'vər-kĭl') n. 1. Nuclear destructive capacity exceeding the amount needed to destroy an enemy. 2. An excessive action or response.

o·ver·land (ō'vər-lănd', -lənd) adj. Over or across land. —**o'ver·land'** adv.

o·ver·lap (ō'vər-lăp') v. 1. To extend over and cover part of. 2. To have something in common with. —**o'ver·lap'** n.

o·ver·lay (ō'vər-lā') v. To lay or spread over or upon. —**o'ver·lay'** n.

o·ver·look (ō'vər-lōōk') v. 1. To look over from above. 2. To afford a view over. 3. To fail to notice or consider. 4. To ignore deliberately or indulgently; disregard. 5. To look over; examine. 6. To supervise.

o·ver·lord (ō'vər-lôrd') n. A lord having supremacy over other lords.

o·ver·ly (ō'vər-lē) adv. To an excessive degree.

o·ver·mas·ter (ō'vər-măs'tər) v. To overcome.

o·ver·match (ō'vər-măch') v. 1. To be more than the match of. 2. To match with a superior opponent.

o·ver·much (ō'vər-mŭch') adj. Too much. —adv. In excess.

o·ver·night (ō'vər-nīt') adj. 1. Of, lasting for, or remaining during a night. 2. Sudden: an overnight success. —adv. (ō'vər-nīt'). 1. During or for the length of the night. 2. Suddenly.

o·ver·pass (ō'vər-păs') n. A roadway or bridge that crosses above another.

o·ver·play (ō'vər-plā') v. 1. To overact. 2. To overestimate the strength of (one's position).

---

o'ver·in·flate' v.
o'ver·in·fla'tion n.
o'ver·in'flu·en'tial adj.
o'ver·in·sist'ence n.
o'ver·in·sist'ent adj.
o'ver·in·sure' v.
o'ver·in'tel·lec'tu·al adj.
o'ver·in·tense' adj.
o'ver·in'ter·est n.
o'ver·in·vest' v.
o'ver·jeal'ous adj.
o'ver·keen' adj.
o'ver·kind' adj.
o'ver·large' adj.
o'ver·late' adj.
o'ver·lav'ish adj.
o'ver·lax' adj.
o'ver·lib'er·al adj.
o'ver·live'ly adj.
o'ver·loud' adj.
o'ver·long' adj. & adv.
o'ver·loud' adj.
o'ver·loy'al adj.
o'ver·mag'ni·fy v.
o'ver·man'y adj.
o'ver·ma·ture' adj.
o'ver·meek' adj.
o'ver·mer'ci·ful adj.
o'ver·might'y adj.
o'ver·mix' v.
o'ver·mod'est adj.

o'ver·moist' adj.
o'ver·mois'ten v.
o'ver·mort'gage v.
o'ver·near' adj.
o'ver·neat' adj.
o'ver·neg·lect' v.
o'ver·nerv'ous adj.
o'ver·nour'ish v.
o'ver·o·bese' adj.
o'ver·o·blige' v.
o'ver·ob·se'qui·ous adj.
o'ver·of·fi'cious adj.
o'ver·op'ti·mis'tic adj.
o'ver·or'nate' adj.
o'ver·par·tic'u·lar adj.
o'ver·pas'sion·ate adj.
o'ver·pas'sion·ate·ly adv.
o'ver·pa·tri·ot'ic adj.
o'ver·pay' v.
o'ver·pes'si·mis'tic adj.
o'ver·plain' adj.
o'ver·pol'ish v.
o'ver·pop'u·lar adj.
o'ver·pop'u·la'tion n.
o'ver·pop'u·lous adj.
o'ver·pre·cise' adj.
o'ver·press' v.
o'ver·print'ed adj.
o'ver·pro·cras'ti·na'tion n.
o'ver·pro·duce' v.
o'ver·pro·duc'tive adj.

o'ver·pro·lif'ic adj.
o'ver·prom'i·nent adj.
o'ver·prompt' adj.
o'ver·proud' adj.
o'ver·pro·vide' v.
o'ver·pro·voke' v.
o'ver·pub'lic adj.
o'ver·pun'ish v.
o'ver·pun'ish·ment n.
o'ver·quan'ti·ty n.
o'ver·quick' adj.
o'ver·qui'et adj.
o'ver·ra'tion·al adj.
o'ver·re·act' v.
o'ver·re·ac'tion n.
o'ver·read'y adj.
o'ver·re'al·is'tic adj.
o'ver·re·fined' adj.
o'ver·re·fine'ment n.
o'ver·re·flec'tive adj.
o'ver·re·li'ant adj.
o'ver·re·lig'ious adj.
o'ver·re·served' adj.
o'ver·re·strain' v.
o'ver·rich' adj.
o'ver·rife' adj.
o'ver·right'eous adj.
o'ver·rig'id adj.
o'ver·rig'or·ous adj.
o'ver·ripe' adj.
o'ver·rip'en v.

---

o·ver·pow·er (ō'vər-pou'ər) v. **1.** To overcome by superior force. **2.** To overwhelm.

o·ver·rate (ō'vər-rāt') v. To overestimate the merits of.

o·ver·reach (ō'vər-rēch') v. **1.** To reach or extend over or beyond. **2.** To miss by reaching too far or attempting too much. **3.** To defeat (oneself) by going too far. —**o'ver·reach'er** n.

o·ver·ride (ō'vər-rīd') v. **1.** To ride across. **2.** To trample upon. **3.** To prevail over. **4.** To declare null and void; set aside.

o·ver·rule (ō'vər-rōōl') v. **1.** To rule against. **2.** To invalidate.

o·ver·run (ō'vər-rŭn') v. **1.** To spread or swarm over in great numbers. **2.** To run or extend beyond; exceed. **3.** To defeat and spread out over or through. **4.** To overflow. —n. (ō'vər-rŭn'). **1.** An act of overrunning. **2.** The amount by which something overruns.

o·ver·seas (ō'vər-sēz', ō'vər-sēz') adv. Beyond the sea; abroad. —**o'ver·seas'** adj.

o·ver·see (ō'vər-sē') v. **1.** To supervise. **2.** To examine; inspect.

o·ver·se·er (ō'vər-sē'ər) n. A supervisor; superintendent.

o·ver·sexed (ō'vər-sĕkst') adj. Exhibiting an unusually large sexual appetite.

o·ver·shad·ow (ō'vər-shăd'ō) v. **1.** To cast a shadow over. **2.** To surpass in importance.

o·ver·shoe (ō'vər-shōō') n. An outer shoe worn as protection from water, snow, or cold.

o·ver·shoot (ō'vər-shōōt') v. **1.** To shoot over or beyond. **2.** To miss by or as if by shooting: *overshot his goal.*

o·ver·sight (ō'vər-sīt') n. **1.** An unintentional omission or mistake. **2.** Supervision.

o·ver·size (ō'vər-sīz') adj. Also **o·ver·sized** (ō'-vər-sīzd'). Larger than usual.

o·ver·skirt (ō'vər-skûrt') n. A skirt worn over another.

o·ver·sleep (ō'vər-slēp') v. To sleep beyond the usual or appointed time.

o·ver·state (ō'vər-stāt') v. To exaggerate. —**o'ver·state'ment** n.

o·ver·stay (ō'vər-stā') v. To stay beyond the limits or duration of.

o·ver·step (ō'vər-stĕp') v. To go beyond.

o·ver·stock (ō'vər-stŏk') v. To stock too much of. —**o'ver·stock'** n.

o·ver·stuffed (ō'vər-stŭft') adj. **1.** Stuffed too much. **2.** Thickly upholstered.

o·ver·sub·scribe (ō'vər-səb-skrīb') v. To subscribe for in excess of the available supply. —**o'ver·sub·scrip'tion** (-skrĭp'shən) n.

o·vert (ō-vûrt', ō'vûrt') adj. Open and observable; not concealed. [< OFr., p.p. of *ovrir,* to open.] —**o'vert·ly** adv.

o·ver·take (ō'vər-tāk') v. To catch `up with.

over-the-coun·ter (ō'vər-*thə*-koun'tər) adj. **1.** Not listed or available on an officially recognized stock exchange. **2.** Sold legally without a prescription.

o·ver·throw (ō'vər-thrō') v. **1.** To overturn. **2.** To bring about the downfall of. **3.** To throw over or beyond. —**o'ver·throw'** n.

o·ver·time (ō'vər-tīm') n. **1. a.** Working hours in addition to those of the regular schedule. **b.** The payment for such work. **2.** Playing time beyond the set time limit of an athletic contest. —**o'ver·time'** adv.

o·ver·tone (ō'vər-tōn') n. `1. A harmonic. **2.** A suggestion; hint.

o'ver·rough' adj.
o'ver·rude' adj.
o'ver·sad' adj.
o'ver·sale' n.
o'ver·salt' v.
o'ver·salt'y adj.
o'ver·sat'u·rate' v.
o'ver·sat'u·ra'tion n.
o'ver·scent'ed adj.
o'ver·scru'pu·lous adj.
o'ver·scru'pu·lous·ness n.
o'ver·sea'son v.
o'ver·sea'soned adj.
o'ver·se·cure' adj.
o'ver·sell' v.
o'ver·sen'si·tive adj.
o'ver·sen'ti·men'tal adj.
o'ver·se'ri·ous adj.
o'ver·se·vere' adj.
o'ver·sharp' adj.
o'ver·short' adj.
o'ver·short'en v.
o'ver·shrink' v.
o'ver·si'lent adj.
o'ver·sim'ple adj.
o'ver·sim·plic'i·ty n.
o'ver·sim·pli·fi·ca'tion n.
o'ver·sim·pli'fy v.
o'ver·skep'ti·cal adj.
o'ver·slow' adj.
o'ver·small' adj.
o'ver·smooth' adj.
o'ver·soak' v.
o'ver·soft' adj.
o'ver·sol'emn adj.

o'ver·so·lic'i·tous adj.
o'ver·so·phis'ti·cat'ed adj.
o'ver·so·phis'ti·ca'tion n.
o'ver·spar'ing adj.
o'ver·spar'ing·ly adv.
o'ver·spe'cial·i·za'tion n.
o'ver·spe'cial·ize' v.
o'ver·spec'u·late' v.
o'ver·spec'u·la'tion n.
o'ver·spec'u·la'tive adj.
o'ver·spend' adj.
o'ver·stim'u·late' v.
o'ver·stim'u·la'tion n.
o'ver·strain' v.
o'ver·stress' v.
o'ver·stretch' v.
o'ver·striv'ing adj. & n.
o'ver·sub'tle adj.
o'ver·sub'tle·ty n.
o'ver·suf·fi'cient adj.
o'ver·su'per·sti'tious adj.
o'ver·sure' adj.
o'ver·sus·pi'cious adj.
o'ver·sus·pi'cious·ly adv.
o'ver·sweet' adj.
o'ver·sys'tem·at'ic adj.
o'ver·talk'a·tive adj.
o'ver·talk'a·tive·ness n.
o'ver·tax' v.
o'ver·tax·a'tion n.
o'ver·teach' v.
o'ver·tech'ni·cal adj.
o'ver·te·na'cious adj.
o'ver·ten'der adj.
o'ver·ten'der·ness n.

o'ver·tense' adj.
o'ver·ten'sion n.
o'ver·thick' adj.
o'ver·thin' adj.
o'ver·thought'ful adj.
o'ver·thrift'y adj.
o'ver·tight' adj.
o'ver·tire' v.
o'ver·train' v.
o'ver·truth'ful adj.
o'ver·use' v.
o'ver·val'u·a·ble adj.
o'ver·val'ue v.
o'ver·ri'e·ty n.
o'ver·ve'he·ment adj.
o'ver·ven'ti·late' v.
o'ver·ven'tur·ous adj.
o'ver·vig'or·ous adj.
o'ver·vi'o·lent adj.
o'ver·warm' adj.
o'ver·warmed' adj.
o'ver·weak' adj.
o'ver·wet' adj.
o'ver·will'ing adj.
o'ver·wise' adj.
o'ver·wor'ry v.
o'ver·write' v.
o'ver·writ'ten adj.
o'ver·young' adj.
o'ver·youth'ful adj.
o'ver·zeal' n.
o'ver·zeal'ous adj.
o'ver·zeal'ous·ly adv.
o'ver·zeal'ous·ness n.

o·ver·top (ō′vər-tŏp′) v. 1. To tower above. 2. To surpass in importance.

o·ver·ture (ō′vər-chŏŏr′, -chər) n. 1. a. An instrumental introduction to an extended musical work. b. An independent instrumental composition of similar form. 2. A first offer or proposal. [< Lat. apertura, an opening.]

o·ver·turn (ō′vər-tûrn′) v. 1. To turn over; upset. 2. To overthrow.

o·ver·view (ō′vər-vyōō′) n. A comprehensive view; survey.

o·ver·ween·ing (ō′vər-wē′nĭng) adj. 1. Arrogant; overbearing. 2. Excessive; immoderate.

o·ver·weigh (ō′vər-wā′) v. 1. To outweigh. 2. To overburden.

o·ver·weight (ō′vər-wāt′) adj. Weighing more than is normal or allowed.

o·ver·whelm (ō′vər-hwĕlm′, -wĕlm′) v. 1. To submerge; engulf. 2. To overcome; overpower. 3. To upset; overthrow. —**o′ver·whelm′ing·ly** adv.

o·ver·work (ō′vər-wûrk′) v. 1. To work too hard or too long. 2. To use too often or to excess: overwork a metaphor.

o·ver·wrought (ō′vər-rôt′) adj. 1. Nervous or excited. 2. Extremely elaborate.

ovi- or **ov-** pref. Egg or ovum: oviduct. [< Lat. ovum, egg.]

o·vi·duct (ō′vĭ-dŭkt′) n. A tube through which ova travel from an ovary.

o·vip·a·rous (ō-vĭp′ər-əs) adj. Producing eggs that hatch outside the body.

o·void (ō′void′) adj. Also **o·voi·dal** (ō-void′l). Egg-shaped. —n. Something egg-shaped.

o·vu·late (ō′vyə-lāt′, ŏv′yə-) v. To produce or discharge ova. [< OVULE.] —**o′vu·la′tion** n.

o·vule (ō′vyōōl, ŏv′yōōl) n. A minute structure that after fertilization becomes a plant seed. [< Lat. ovum, egg.] —**o′vu·lar** (ō′-vyə-lər, ŏv′yə-) adj.

o·vum (ō′vəm) n., pl. **o·va** (ō′və). The female reproductive cell of animals. [Lat., egg.]

owe (ō) v. **owed, ow·ing.** 1. To have to pay or repay. 2. To be morally obligated to: I owe him an apology. 3. To be in debt to. 4. To be indebted for. 5. To bear (a certain feeling) toward a person. [< OE āgan, to possess.]

ow·ing to prep. Because of; on account of.

owl (oul) n. A usu. night-flying bird of prey with a large head, a short, hooked bill, and a disklike face. [< OE ūle.] —**owl′ish** adj.

owl·et (ou′lĭt) n. A young owl.

own (ōn) adj. Of or belonging to oneself. —n. Something that belongs to one. —v. 1. To have or possess. 2. To acknowledge or admit. —**idiom. on (one's) own.** Completely independent. [< OE āgen.] —**own′er** n. —**own′er·ship** n.

ox (ŏks) n., pl. **ox·en** (ŏk′sən). 1. An adult castrated bull. 2. A bovine mammal. [< OE oxa.]

ox·al·ic acid (ŏk-săl′ĭk) n. A poisonous, crystalline organic acid, $HOOCCOOH \cdot 2H_2O$,

used as a cleansing agent and bleach. [< Lat. oxalis, a kind of plant.]

ox·blood (ŏks′blŭd′) n. A deep reddish brown.

ox·bow (ŏks′bō′) n. 1. A U-shaped collar for a draft ox. 2. A U-shaped bend in a river.

ox·ford (ŏks′fərd) n. A low shoe that laces over the instep. [< Oxford, England.]

ox·i·dant (ŏk′sĭ-dənt) n. A chemical reagent that oxidizes.

ox·i·da·tion (ŏk′sĭ-dā′shən) n. 1. The combination of a substance with oxygen. 2. A reaction in which the atoms in an element lose electrons and the element's valence is correspondingly increased. —**ox′i·da′tive** adj. —**ox′i·da′tive·ly** adv.

ox·ide (ŏk′sīd′) n. A binary compound of an element or radical with oxygen. —**ox·id′ic** (ŏk-sĭd′ĭk) adj.

ox·i·dize (ŏk′sĭ-dīz′) v. **-dized, -diz·ing.** 1. To combine with oxygen. 2. To increase the positive charge or valence of (an element) by removing electrons. 3. To coat with oxide. —**ox′i·diz′er** n.

oxy- pref. Oxygen, esp. additional oxygen: oxyacetylene. [< OXYGEN.]

ox·y·a·cet·y·lene (ŏk′sē-ə-sĕt′l-ĭn, -ēn′) adj. Containing a mixture of acetylene and oxygen, as commonly used in metal welding and cutting torches.

ox·y·gen (ŏk′sĭ-jən) n. Symbol **O** A colorless, odorless, tasteless gaseous element that constitutes 21 per cent of the atmosphere by volume, is essential for plant and animal respiration, and is required for nearly all combustion and combustive processes. Atomic number 8; atomic weight 15.9994. [Fr. oxygène.] —**ox′y·gen′ic** (ŏk′sĭ-jĕn′ĭk) adj.

ox·y·gen·ate (ŏk′sĭ-jə-nāt′) v. **-at·ed, -at·ing.** To treat, combine, or infuse with oxygen. —**ox′y·gen·a′tion** n.

oxygen tent n. A canopy placed over the head and shoulders of a patient to provide a continuous flow of oxygen.

ox·y·mo·ron (ŏk′sĭ-môr′ŏn′, -mōr′-) n., pl. **-mo·ra** (-môr′ə, -mōr′ə). A figure of speech in which incongruous or contradictory terms are combined, as in "a deafening silence." [< Gk. oxumōros, pointedly foolish.]

oys·ter (oi′stər) n. Any of several often edible bivalve mollusks with an irregularly shaped shell. [< Gk. ostreon.]

o·zone (ō′zōn′) n. 1. A blue, gaseous allotrope of oxygen, O_3, derived or formed naturally from diatomic oxygen by electric discharge or exposure to ultraviolet radiation, used to purify and deodorize air, to sterilize water, and as a bleach. 2. Informal. Fresh, pure air. [< Gk. ozein, to smell.]

o·zo·no·sphere (ō-zō′nə-sfîr′) n. A region of the upper atmosphere, between 10 and 20 miles in altitude, containing a relatively high concentration of ozone that absorbs solar ultraviolet radiation.

Pp

p or **P** (pē) *n., pl.* **p's** or **P's**. The 16th letter of the English alphabet.

P The symbol for the element phosphorus.

Pa The symbol for the element protactinium.

pa·an·ga (päng'gə) *n.* See table at currency. [Tongan.]

pab·u·lum (păb'yə-ləm) *n.* A usu. soft food. [Lat.]

pace (pās) *n.* **1. a.** A step made in walking. **b.** The distance spanned by such a step. **2.** Rate of movement or progress. **3.** A horse's gait in which both feet on one side move together. —*v.* **paced, pac·ing. 1.** To walk or cover at a slow pace. **2.** To measure by counting paces. **3.** To set or regulate the rate of speed for. **4.** To train (a horse) in a particular gait, esp. the pace. [< Lat. *passus.*] —**pac'er** *n.*

pace·mak·er (pās'mā'kər) *n.* **1.** One that sets the pace, as in a race. **2. a.** A mass of specialized muscle fibers of the heart that regulate the heartbeat. **b.** Any of several usu. miniaturized and surgically implanted electronic devices used to regulate or aid in regulation of the heartbeat.

pach·y·derm (păk'ĭ-dûrm') *n.* A large, thick-skinned mammal, as the elephant or rhinoceros. [< Gk. *pakhudermos,* thick-skinned.]

pach·y·san·dra (păk'ĭ-săn'drə) *n.* A low-growing plant with evergreen leaves, cultivated as a ground cover. [< Gk. *pakhus,* thick + Gk. *aner,* man.]

pa·cif·ic (pə-sĭf'ĭk) *adj.* **1.** Tending to diminish conflict. **2.** Peaceful; tranquil.

pac·i·fi·er (păs'ə-fī'ər) *n.* **1.** One that pacifies. **2.** A rubber or plastic nipple for a baby to suck on.

pac·i·fism (păs'ə-fĭz'əm) *n.* Opposition to war or violence as a means of resolving disputes. —**pac'i·fist** *n.* —**pac'i·fis'tic** *adj.*

pac·i·fy (păs'ə-fī') *v.* **-fied, -fy·ing. 1.** To ease the anger or agitation of; calm. **2.** To reduce to peaceful submission; subdue. [< Lat. *pacificare.*] —**pac'i·fi·ca'tion** *n.*

pack (păk) *n.* **1. a.** A collection of items tied up or wrapped; bundle. **b.** A container for carrying a bundle esp. on the back. **2.** A set of related items, as playing cards. **3.** A large number or amount; heap. **4.** A group or gang of people or animals. **5.** An absorbent material, such as gauze, applied to parts of the body. —*v.* **1.** To fold, roll, or combine into a pack. **2. a.** To put into a protective receptacle. **b.** To stow luggage or belongings for transportation or storage. **3.** To crowd together tightly; cram. **4.** To compact firmly. **5.** *Informal.* To carry: *pack a pistol.* **6.** To send or be sent off abruptly or without ceremony. **7.** To rig (a voting panel) to be fraudulently favorable: *pack the jury.* [ME.]

pack·age (păk'ĭj) *n.* **1.** A parcel or bundle. **2.** A proposition or offer made up of several items each of which must be accepted: *a benefits package.* —*v.* **-aged, -ag·ing.** To put or make into a package.

package store *n.* A store that sells sealed bottles of alcoholic beverages for consumption away from its premises.

pack·er (păk'ər) *n.* One who packs goods, esp. food products, for transportation and sale.

pack·et (păk'ĭt) *n.* **1.** A small package or bundle. **2.** A regularly scheduled passenger and cargo boat.

pack·ing (păk'ĭng) *n.* **1.** The processing and packaging of food products. **2.** Material used to prevent breakage or seepage.

pack rat *n.* Any of various small North American rodents that collect and store food and a variety of objects.

pact (păkt) *n.* A formal agreement; treaty. [< Lat. *pactum.*]

pad¹ (păd) *n.* **1.** Something soft that serves as a cushion. **2.** A number of sheets of writing paper glued together at one end; tablet. **3.** The floating leaf of an aquatic plant. **4.** The cushionlike flesh on the underpart of the foot of an animal. **5.** *Slang.* A person's apartment. —*v.* **pad·ded, pad·ding. 1.** To provide with padding or a pad. **2.** To expand unnecessarily or fictitiously. [Orig. unknown.]

pad² (păd) *v.* **pad·ded, pad·ding.** To go about quietly on foot. [Prob. < MDu. *paden,* to walk along a path.]

pad·ding (păd'ĭng) *n.* Material that is used to pad.

pad·dle¹ (păd'l) *n.* **1.** A wooden implement with a flat blade used to propel a small boat such as a canoe. **2.** An implement used for stirring, mixing, or turning. **3.** A board of a paddle wheel. **4.** A light wooden racket used in table tennis. —*v.* **-dled, -dling. 1.** To move or propel through water with or as if with a paddle. **2.** To stir or beat with a paddle. [ME *padell,* implement used for cleaning a plowshare.]

pad·dle² (păd'l) *v.* **-dled, -dling.** To move the hands or feet about in shallow water. [Orig. unknown.]

paddle wheel *n.* A wheel with paddles on its rim, used to propel a ship.

pad·dock (păd'ək) *n.* A usu. fenced area in which horses are kept, as for grazing or for preparation and display before a race. [< OE *pearroc.*]

pad·dy (păd'ē) *n., pl.* **-dies.** An irrigated or flooded field where rice is grown. [Malay *padi.*]

paddy wagon *n.* A police van for taking suspects into custody. [< *Paddy,* offensive term for an Irishman.]

pad·lock (păd'lŏk') *n.* A lock with a U-shaped bar that can be passed through the staple of a hasp and then snapped shut. [ME *padlok.*] —**pad'lock'** *v.*

pa·dre (pä'drā, -drē) *n. Informal.* **1.** A priest. **2.** A military chaplain. [< Lat. *pater,* father.]

pae·an (pē'ən) *n.* A song of joyful praise or exultation. [< Gk. *paiōn,* hymn praising Apollo.]

pa·gan (pā′gən) n. One who is not a Christian, Moslem, or Jew; heathen. [< Lat. *paganus*, country-dweller.] **—pa′gan** adj. **—pa′gan·ism** n.

page¹ (pāj) n. One employed to run errands or carry messages, as in a hotel. —v. **paged, pag·ing.** To summon by calling the name of. [< OItal. *paggio*.]

page² (pāj) n. A leaf or one side of a leaf, as of a book, letter, or manuscript. —v. **paged, pag·ing.** To number the pages of. [< Lat. *pagina*.]

pag·eant (pāj′ənt) n. An elaborate and colorful public spectacle. [< Med. Lat. *pagina*, scene of a play.] **—pag′eant·ry** n.

pag·i·na·tion (pāj′ə-nā′shən) n. 1. The system with which pages are numbered. 2. The arrangement and number of pages, as in a book. **—pag′i·nate′** v.

pa·go·da (pə-gō′də) n. A many-storied Buddhist tower. [Port. *pagode*.]

paid (pād) v. p.t. & p.p. of **pay.**

pail (pāl) n. A cylindrical vessel with a handle; bucket. [< OE *pægel*.]

pain (pān) n. 1. An unpleasant sensation arising from injury, disease, or emotional disorder. 2. Suffering or distress. 3. **pains.** Trouble; effort. 4. *Informal.* A nuisance. 5. Penalty: *under pain of death.* —v. To cause or suffer pain. [< Gk. *poinē*, penalty.] **—pain′ful** adj. **—pain′ful·ly** adv. **—pain′less** adj. **—pain′less·ly** adv.

pain·kil·ler (pān′kil′ər) n. Something, as a drug, that relieves pain. **—pain′kill′ing** adj.

pains·tak·ing (pānz′tā′king) adj. Taking pains; careful. **—pains′tak′ing·ly** adv.

paint (pānt) n. 1. a. A mixture of a pigment in a liquid, spread on a surface as a decorative or protective coating. b. The dry film formed by such a mixture applied to a surface. 2. Make-up. —v. 1. To represent with or as if with paint. 2. To coat or decorate with paint. 3. To use cosmetics or apply cosmetics to. 4. To practice the art of painting. [< Lat. *pingere*, to paint.] **—paint′er** n.

paint·brush (pānt′brŭsh′) n. A brush for applying paint.

paint·ing (pān′ting) n. 1. The process, art, or occupation of working with paints. 2. A picture or design in paint.

pair (pâr) n., pl. **pairs** or **pair.** 1. Two corresponding persons or items similar in form or function. 2. Something composed of two corresponding parts: *a pair of pliers.* 3. Two persons or animals considered together. —v. 1. To arrange in pairs. 2. To form a pair. [< Lat. *paria*.]

pai·sa (pī-sä′) n., pl. **-sa** (-sä′) or **-sas.** See table at **currency.** [Hindi *paisā.*]

pais·ley (pāz′lē) adj. Made of a soft wool fabric with a colorful pattern of abstract, curved shapes. [< *Paisley,* Scotland.]

Pai·ute (pī′yŏōt′) n., pl. **-ute** or **-utes.** 1. a. Either of two distinct Indian peoples, the Northern Paiute and the Southern Paiute, who formerly lived in the southwestern United States. b. A member of either of the Paiute peoples. 2. The Shoshonean language of the Paiute. **—Pai′ute′** adj.

pa·ja·mas (pə-jä′məz, -jăm′əz) pl.n. Also chiefly *Brit.* **py·ja·mas.** A loose-fitting garment consisting of trousers and a jacket, worn for sleeping or lounging. [Hindi *pāejāma,* loose-fitting trousers.]

pal (păl) n. *Informal.* A friend; chum. [< Skt. *bhrātr,* brother.]

pal·ace (păl′ĭs) n. 1. The official residence of a royal person. 2. A large or splendid residence; mansion. [< Lat. *palatium.*] **—pa·la′tial** (pə-lā′shəl) adj.

pal·a·din (păl′ə-dĭn) n. A paragon of chivalry; knightly champion. [< Lat. *palatium,* palace.]

pal·an·quin (păl′ən-kēn′) n. A covered litter for one person carried on poles on the shoulders of two or four men. [< Skt. *palyankaḷ,* bed.]

palanquin

pal·at·a·ble (păl′ə-tə-bəl) adj. 1. Agreeable to the taste. 2. Acceptable to the mind or sensibilities. [< PALATE.]

pal·ate (păl′ĭt) n. 1. The roof of the mouth, consisting of a hard, bony front backed by the fleshy soft palate. 2. The sense of taste. [< Lat. *palatum.*] **—pal′a·tal** (-ə-təl) adj.

pa·lat·i·nate (pə-lăt′n-āt′, -ĭt) n. The territory of a palatine.

pal·a·tine (păl′ə-tīn′) n. 1. A title of various administrative officials of the late Roman and Byzantine empires. 2. A feudal lord delegated with royal powers within his own domain. —adj. 1. Of or pertaining to a palace. 2. Of or pertaining to a palatine or palatinate. 3. Having royal powers or privileges. [< Lat. *palatium,* palace.]

pa·la·ver (pə-lăv′ər, -lä′vər) n. Long and often idle chatter. [< Gk. *parabolē,* comparison.] **—pa·la′ver** v.

pale¹ (pāl) n. 1. A stake or pointed stick; picket. 2. The area enclosed by a fence or boundary. **—idiom. beyond the pale.** Beyond the limits of what is safe, accepted, or protected. [< Lat. *palus.*]

pale² (pāl) adj. **pal·er, pal·est.** 1. Whitish in complexion; pallid. 2. Of a low intensity of color; light: *pale pink.* 3. Of a low intensity of light; dim: *a pale moon.* —v. **paled, pal·ing.** To become or cause to become pale. [< Lat. *pallēre,* to be pale.] **—pale′ness** n.

paleo– pref. Ancient or prehistoric: *paleography.* [< Gk. *palaios,* ancient.]

Pa·le·o·cene (pā′lē-ə-sēn′) adj. Of or belonging to the geologic time, rock series, or sedimentary deposits of the first epoch of the Tertiary period. —n. The Paleocene epoch.

pa·le·og·ra·phy (pā′lē-ŏg′rə-fē) n. The study of ancient written documents. **—pa′le·og′ra-**

pher n. —pa'le·o·graph'ic (-ə-grăf'ĭk) or pa'le·o·graph'i·cal adj.

Pa·le·o·lith·ic (pā'lē-ə-lĭth'ĭk) adj. Of or belonging to the period of human culture beginning with the earliest chipped stone tools, about 750,000 years ago, until the beginning of the Mesolithic, about 15,000 years ago. —n. The Paleolithic Age.

pa·le·on·tol·o·gy (pā'lē-ŏn-tŏl'ə-jē, -ən-) n. The study of fossils and ancient life forms. —pa'le·on'to·log'ic (-ŏn'tə-lŏj'ĭk) or pa'le·on'to·log'i·cal adj. —pa'le·on·tol'o·gist n.

Pa·le·o·zo·ic (pā'lē-ə-zō'ĭk) adj. Of or belonging to the geologic time, rock series, or sedimentary deposits of the era preceding the Mesozoic, divided into seven periods from the Cambrian to the Permian. —n. The Paleozoic era.

pal·ette (păl'ĭt) n. 1. A board, typically with a hole for the thumb, upon which an artist mixes colors. 2. The range of colors on a palette. [< Lat. pala, shovel.]

palette pallet¹

pal·imp·sest (păl'ĭmp-sĕst') n. Vellum or parchment that has been written upon several times, often with remnants of earlier, imperfectly erased writing still visible. [< Gk. palimpsēstos, scraped again.]

pal·in·drome (păl'ĭn-drōm') n. A word, phrase, or sentence that reads the same backward and forward, as A man, a plan, a canal, Panama! [< Gk. palindromos, running back again.]

pal·ing (pā'lĭng) n. 1. A pale; picket. 2. Pointed sticks used in making fences. 3. A fence of pales.

pal·i·sade (păl'ĭ-sād') n. 1. A high fence of stakes forming a defensive barrier. 2. A line of lofty, steep cliffs, usu. along a river. [< Lat. palus, stake.]

pall¹ (pôl) n. 1. A cloth covering for a coffin or bier. 2. A coffin. 3. Something that produces a gloomy effect or atmosphere. [< Lat. pallium, cloak.]

pall² (pôl) v. 1. To become insipid, boring, or wearisome. 2. To cloy; satiate. [ME pallen, to grow faint.]

pal·la·di·um (pə-lā'dē-əm) n. Symbol **Pd** A soft, ductile, steel-white, tarnish-resistant, metallic element alloyed for use in electric contacts, jewelry, nonmagnetic watch parts, and surgical instruments. Atomic number 46; atomic weight 106.4. [< the asteroid Pallas.]

pall·bear·er (pôl'bâr'ər) n. One of the persons carrying or attending the coffin at a funeral.

pal·let¹ (păl'ĭt) n. A portable platform for storing or moving cargo or freight. [< Lat. pala, shovel.]

pal·let² (păl'ĭt) n. A narrow, hard bed or straw-filled mattress. [< Lat. palea, chaff.]

pal·li·ate (păl'ē-āt') v. -at·ed, -at·ing. 1. To make (an offense or crime) seem less serious; excuse. 2. To alleviate without curing. [<

Lat. pallium, cloak.] —pal'li·a'tion n. —pal'li·a'tive adj. & n.

pal·lid (păl'ĭd) adj. 1. Pale in complexion or color; wan. 2. Lacking in vitality; lifeless. [< Lat. pallēre, to be pale.]

pal·lor (păl'ər) n. Paleness, esp. of the face.

palm¹ (päm) n. The inner surface of the hand from the wrist to the fingers. —v. To conceal in the palm of the hand. —phrasal verb. **palm off.** To dispose of fraudulently. [< OFr. paume < Lat. palma, palm of hand, palm tree.]

palm² (päm) n. 1. Any of various chiefly tropical trees usu. having an unbranched trunk with a crown of large featherlike or fanlike leaves. 2. a. A symbol of victory or success. b. Triumph; victory. [< OE < Lat. palma, palm tree, palm of hand.]

pal·mate (păl'māt', păl'-, păl'māt') adj. Also **palm·at·ed** (-mā'tĭd). Resembling a hand with the fingers extended.

pal·met·to (păl-mĕt'ō) n., pl. -tos or -toes. Any of several small palms with fan-shaped leaves. [Sp. palmito.]

palm·is·try (pä'mĭ-strē) n. The practice or art of telling fortunes from the lines, marks, and patterns on the palms of the hands. [< ME pawmestrie.] —palm'ist n.

Palm Sunday n. The Sunday before Easter, commemorating Christ's triumphal entry into Jerusalem.

palm·y (pä'mē) adj. -i·er, -i·est. 1. Of, pertaining to, or covered with palm trees. 2. Prosperous; flourishing.

pal·o·mi·no (păl'ə-mē'nō) n., pl. -nos. A horse with a golden or tan coat and a lighter mane and tail. [Am. Sp. < Sp., dove-colored.]

pal·pa·ble (păl'pə-bəl) adj. 1. Capable of being touched or felt; tangible. 2. Easily perceived; obvious. [< Lat. palpare, to touch.] —pal'pa·bly adv.

pal·pate (păl'pāt') v. -pat·ed, -pat·ing. To examine by touching as a diagnostic aid. [Lat. palpare, to touch.] —pal·pa'tion n.

pal·pi·tate (păl'pĭ-tāt') v. -tat·ed, -tat·ing. To beat rapidly and irregularly; throb. [< Lat. palpare, to touch.] —pal'pi·ta'tion n.

pal·sy (pôl'zē) n., pl. -sies. 1. Paralysis. 2. Loss of power to feel or control movement in a part of the body. [< Gk. paralusis.] —pal'sied adj.

pal·ter (pôl'tər) v. 1. To talk or act insincerely; equivocate. 2. To be capricious; trifle. 3. To quibble. [Orig. unknown.]

pal·try (pôl'trē) adj. -tri·er, -tri·est. 1. Petty; trifling. 2. Worthless; trashy. 3. Contemptible; vile. [< obs. paltry, trash.]

pam·pa (păm'pə) n., pl. -pas (-pəz, -pəs). A nearly treeless grassland area of South America. [Am. Sp. < Quechua, plain.]

pam·per (păm'pər) v. To treat with excessive indulgence; coddle. [ME pamperen.]

pam·phlet (păm'flĭt) n. A usu. short publication with a paper cover and no binding. [< Pamphilus, a short Latin poem of the 12th cent.] —pam'phlet·eer' (-flĭ-tîr') n.

pan (păn) n. 1. A wide, shallow, open container for household purposes. 2. A shallow container similar to a pan. —v. panned, pan·ning. 1. To wash (gravel or earth) in a pan to separate precious metal. 2. Informal. To criticize harshly. —phrasal verb. **pan out.** Informal. To turn out well; be successful. [< OE panne.]

Pan (păn) *n. Gk. Myth.* The god of woods, fields, and flocks.

pan- *pref.* All: *panchromatic.* [Gk. < *pas,* all.]

pan·a·ce·a (păn'ə-sē'ə) *n.* A remedy for all diseases, evils, or difficulties; cure-all. [< Gk. *panakēs,* all-healing.]

pa·nache (pə-năsh', -näsh') *n.* **1.** A bunch of feathers or a plume, esp. on a helmet. **2.** Dash; verve. [< Lat. *pinna,* feather.]

Pan·a·ma (păn'ə-mä') *n.* A hand-plaited hat made from the leaves of a palmlike tropical American plant.

Pan-A·mer·i·can (păn'-əmĕr'ī-kən) *adj.* Of or pertaining to North, South, and Central America collectively.

pan·a·tel·a (păn'ə-tĕl'ə) *n.* A long, slender cigar. [Sp.]

pan-broil (păn'broil') *v.* To cook over direct heat in an uncovered, usu. ungreased skillet.

pan·cake (păn'kāk') *n.* A thin cake made of batter fried on a skillet until brown.

pan·chro·mat·ic (păn'krō-măt'ĭk) *adj.* Sensitive to all colors, as film.

pan·cre·as (păng'krē-əs, păn'-) *n.* A long, soft, irregularly shaped gland that produces insulin and discharges enzymes into the bloodstream. [Gk. *pankreas.*] —**pan'cre·at'ic** (-ăt'ĭk) *adj.*

pan·da (păn'də) *n.* **1.** A bearlike black and white mammal of the mountains of China and Tibet. **2.** A raccoonlike mammal related to the panda. [Fr.]

panda

pan·dem·ic (păn-dĕm'ĭk) *adj.* **1.** Widespread; general. **2.** Prevalent over a wide geographic area, as a disease. [< Gk. *pandēmos,* of all the people.] —**pan·dem'ic** *n.*

pan·de·mo·ni·um (păn'də-mō'nē-əm) *n.* Wild uproar or noise; tumult. [< *Pandæmonium,* capital of Hell in Milton's *Paradise Lost.*]

pan·der (păn'dər) *n.* **1.** A go-between or liaison in sexual intrigues; procurer. **2.** A pimp. **3.** One who caters to the lower tastes and desires of others or exploits their weaknesses. —*v.* To act as a pander. [< *Pandare,* character in Chaucer's *Troilus and Criseyde.*]

Pan·do·ra (păn-dôr'ə, -dōr'ə) *n. Gk. Myth.* The first woman, who opened a box containing all the ills that could plague mankind.

pan·dow·dy (păn-dou'dē) *n., pl.* **-dies.** Sliced apples baked with sugar and spices in a deep dish, with a thick top crust. [Orig. unknown.]

pane (pān) *n.* A sheet of glass, esp. in a window or door. [< Lat. *pannus,* cloth.]

pan·e·gyr·ic (păn'ə-jĭr'ĭk, -jī'rĭk) *n.* Elaborate praise; encomium. [< Gk. *panēgurikos,* of a public assembly.] —**pan'e·gyr'i·cal** *adj.* —**pan'e·gyr'ist** *n.*

pan·el (păn'əl) *n.* **1.** A flat, usu. rectangular raised, recessed, or framed piece, esp. of wood, forming part of a surface into which it is set. **2.** A board with instruments or controls. **3. a.** A list or group of persons chosen for jury duty. **b.** A group of persons participating in a discussion or television game show. —*v.* **-eled** or **-elled, -el·ing** or **-el·ling.** To cover, furnish, or decorate with panels. [< Lat. *pannus,* cloth.]

pan·el·ing (păn'ə-lĭng) *n.* Panels, esp. decorative panels.

pan·el·ist (păn'ə-lĭst) *n.* A member of a panel.

panel truck *n.* A small delivery truck with a fully enclosed body.

pang (păng) *n.* A sudden, sharp sensation, as of pain. [Orig. unknown.]

pan·han·dle¹ (păn'hăn'dl) *v.* **-dled, -dling.** *Informal.* To beg, esp. on the streets. —**pan'han'dler** *n.*

pan·han·dle² (păn'hăn'dl) *n.* A narrow strip of territory projecting from a larger area.

pan·ic (păn'ĭk) *n.* A sudden, overpowering, often contagious terror. —*v.* **-icked, -ick·ing.** To affect or be affected with panic. [< Gk. *panikos,* of Pan, a god who aroused terror among people in lonely places.] —**pan'ick·y** *adj.*

panic button *n.* **1.** A device for setting off an alarm in an emergency. **2.** *Slang.* A hasty, emotional response.

pan·i·cle (păn'ĭ-kəl) *n.* A loosely and irregularly branched flower cluster. [< Lat. *panus,* tuft.] —**pan'i·cled** *adj.*

Pan·ja·bi (pŭn-jä'bē, -jäb'ē) *n.* Var. of Punjabi.

pan·jan·drum (păn-jăn'drəm) *n.* A person of importance. [< the *Grand Panjandrum,* character in a story by Samuel Foote.]

pan·nier (păn'yər, păn'ē-ər) *n.* A large wicker basket, esp. one carried on the back. [< Lat. *panarium,* breadbasket.]

pannier

pan·o·ply (păn'ə-plē) *n., pl.* **-plies.** **1.** The complete arms and armor of a warrior. **2.** Something that covers or protects. **3.** A magnificent array. [Gk. *panoplia.*]

pan·o·ram·a (păn'ə-răm'ə, -rä'mə) *n.* **1.** An unlimited view over a wide area. **2.** A picture unrolled before the spectator's eyes. [PAN- + Gk. *horama,* sight.] —**pan'o·ram'ic** *adj.*

pan·sy (păn'zē) *n., pl.* **-sies.** A garden plant having flowers with rounded, velvety petals of

---

various colors. [< OFr. *pensée,* pansy, thought.]

pant (pănt) *v.* 1. To breathe rapidly in short gasps, as after exertion. 2. To utter hurriedly or breathlessly. 3. To yearn. —*n.* A short, labored breath; gasp. [< Gk. *phantasioun,* to cause to imagine.] —**pant'ing·ly** *adv.*

pan·ta·loons (păn'tl-ōōnz') *pl.n.* Trousers. [< OItal. *Pantalone,* a comic character portrayed as an old man in tight trousers.]

pan·the·ism (păn'thē-ĭz'əm) *n.* The belief that God and nature are one. —**pan'the·ist** *n.* —**pan'the·is'tic** *adj.*

pan·the·on (păn'thē-ŏn', -ən) *n.* 1. A temple dedicated to all gods. 2. All the gods of a people. 3. A public building commemorating and dedicated to the great persons of a nation. [< Gk. *pantheion.*]

pan·ther (păn'thər) *n.* A large wild cat, esp. a leopard or mountain lion. [< Gk. *panthēr.*]

pant·ies (păn'tēz) *pl.n.* Short underpants for women or children. [< PANTS.]

pan·to·mime (păn'tə-mīm') *n.* 1. Expression of something by facial gestures and body movement alone. 2. A play or entertainment presented in pantomime. —*v.* -**mimed,** -**mim·ing.** To represent by or express oneself in pantomime. [< Gk. *pantomimos,* pantomimic actor.] —**pan'to·mim'ic** (-mĭm'ĭk) *adj.* —**pan'to·mim'ist** (-mī'mĭst, -mĭm'ĭst) *n.*

pan·try (păn'trē) *n., pl.* -**tries.** A small room or closet for storing food, dishes, etc. [< AN *pantrie,* bread closet.]

pants (pănts) *pl.n.* 1. A pair of trousers. 2. A pair of underpants. [< PANTALOONS.]

pant·y·hose (păn'tē-hōz') *pl.n.* A woman's undergarment consisting of stockings and underpants in one piece.

pant·y·waist (păn'tē-wāst') *n.* A weak man; sissy. [< *pantywaist,* a child's undergarment.]

pap (păp) *n.* Soft, easily digested food, as for infants. [ME.]

pa·pa (pä'pə, pə-pä') *n.* Father. [Fr.]

pa·pa·cy (pä'pə-sē) *n., pl.* -**cies.** 1. The office and jurisdiction of a pope. 2. The period of time during which a pope is in office. 3. **Papacy.** The system of church government headed by the pope. [< LLat. *papa,* pope.]

pa·pal (pä'pəl) *adj.* Of or pertaining to the pope or his office. [< LLat. *papa,* pope.]

pa·paw (pô'pô') *n.* Also **paw·paw.** 1. A North American tree with fleshy, edible fruit. 2. The fruit of the papaw. [Prob. < Sp. *papaya,* papaya.]

pa·pa·ya (pə-pä'yə) *n.* The large, yellow, edible fruit of a tropical American tree. [Sp., of Cariban orig.]

pa·per (pä'pər) *n.* 1. **a.** A thin material made from cellulose pulp derived mainly from wood and rags, and used for writing, printing, drawing, wrapping, and covering walls. **b.** A single sheet of this material. 2. **a.** An official document. **b. papers.** Documents establishing the identity of the bearer. 3. A newspaper. 4. An essay, report, or scholarly dissertation. —*v.* To cover with wallpaper. [< Gk. *papuros,* papyrus.] —**pa'per·y** *adj.*

pa·per·back (pä'pər-băk') *n.* A book with a flexible paper binding.

pa·per·board (pä'pər-bôrd', -bōrd') *n.* Cardboard.

pa·per·hang·er (pä'pər-hăng'ər) *n.* One who applies wallpaper. —**pa'per·hang'ing** *n.*

pa·per·weight (pä'pər-wāt') *n.* A small heavy object for holding down loose papers.

pa·pier-mâ·ché (pä'pər-mə-shā', păp'yā-) *n.* A material made from waste paper mixed with glue or paste that can be molded when wet. [Fr.]

pa·pil·la (pə-pĭl'ə) *n., pl.* -**pil·lae** (-pĭl'ē). A small, nipplelike projection, as on the tongue. [< Lat., nipple.] —**pap'il·lar'y** (păp'ə-lĕr'ē, pə-pĭl'ə-rē) *adj.*

pa·pist (pä'pĭst) *n. Offensive.* A Roman Catholic. [< LLat. *papa,* pope.]

pa·poose (pă-pōōs', pə-) *n.* A North American Indian infant or young child. [Algonquian *papoos.*]

pa·pri·ka (pă-prē'kə, pə-, păp'rĭ-kə) *n.* A mild powdered seasoning made from sweet red peppers. [Hung., ult. < Gk. *peperi,* pepper.]

Pap test (păp) *n.* A test in which a smear of a bodily secretion, esp. from the cervix, is immediately fixed and examined to detect cancer in an early stage. [< George *Papanicolaou* (1883-1962).]

pa·py·rus (pə-pī'rəs) *n., pl.* -**es** or -**ri** (-rī'). 1. A tall, grasslike water, plant of northern Africa. 2. Paper made from the pith or stems of the papyrus. [< Gk. *papuros.*]

par (pär) *n.* 1. An accepted or normal average. 2. An equal status, level, or footing. 3. The number of golf strokes considered necessary to complete a hole. 4. A face value, as of a stock or bond. [< Lat., equal.]

pa·ra (pä-rä', pä'rä) *n.* See table at currency. [Turk.]

para- or **par-** *pref.* 1. Near or beside: *parathyroid gland.* 2. Outside or beyond: *parapsychology.* 3. Resembling or similar to: *paratyphoid.* 4. Subsidiary; assistant: *paralegal.* [< Gk. *para,* beside.]

par·a·ble (păr'ə-bəl) *n.* A simple story illustrating a moral or religious lesson. [< Gk. *parabolē.*]

pa·rab·o·la (pə-răb'ə-lə) *n.* A plane curve formed by the locus of points equidistant from a fixed line and a fixed point not on the line. [< Gk. *parabolē.*] —**par'a·bol'ic** (păr'ə-bŏl'ĭk) *adj.*

par·a·chute (păr'ə-shōōt') *n.* An umbrella-shaped device used esp. to retard free fall from an aircraft or to slow speeding vehicles. [Fr.] —**par'a·chute'** *v.* —**par'a·chut'ist** *n.*

pa·rade (pə-rād') *n.* 1. A public procession held on a festive or ceremonial occasion. 2. A formal review of troops. 3. A long line or succession. 4. An elaborate or ostentatious display: *a parade of riches.* —*v.* -**rad·ed,** -**rad·ing.** 1. To march in or as if in a parade. 2. To exhibit ostentatiously; flaunt. 3. To promenade, esp. in a public place. [< Lat. *parare,* to prepare.] —**pa·rad'er** *n.*

par·a·digm (păr'ə-dĭm', -dĭm) *n.* 1. An example or model. 2. A list of all the inflectional forms of a word taken as an illustrative example. [< Gk. *paradeigma.*] —**par'a·dig·mat'ic** (-dĭg-măt'ĭk) *adj.*

par·a·dise (păr'ə-dīs', -dīz') *n.* 1. Often **Paradise.** Heaven. 2. A place or condition of perfect happiness or beauty. [< Pers. *pairi-daēza.*] —**par'a·dis'i·ac'** (-dīz'ē-ăk') or **par'a·di·si'a·cal** (-dĭ-sī'ə-kəl, -zī'-) *adj.*

par·a·dox (păr'ə-dŏks') *n.* 1. A statement that appears to contradict itself or be contrary to common sense but that may be true. 2. One with apparently contradictory aspects. [< Gk. *paradoxos,* conflicting with expectation.] —**par'a·dox'i·cal** *adj.* —**par'a·dox'i·cal·ly** *adv.*

par·af·fin (păr'ə-fĭn) *n.* 1. A waxy, white or

colorless solid hydrocarbon mixture used to make candles, wax paper, lubricants, and sealing materials. **2.** *Chiefly Brit.* Kerosene. [Lat. *parum*, too little + Lat. *affinis*, associated with.] —**par'af·fin** v.

par·a·gon (păr'ə-gŏn', -gən) n. A model of excellence or perfection. [< Gk. *parakonan*, to sharpen.]

par·a·graph (păr'ə-grăf') n. **1.** A distinct division of a written work consisting of one or more sentences on a single idea or aspect of a subject. **2.** A mark, (¶), used to indicate a new paragraph. —v. To divide or arrange in paragraphs. [< Gk. *paragraphos*, line in a dialogue showing a change in speakers.]

par·a·keet (păr'ə-kēt') n. A small parrot with a long, tapering tail. [OFr. *paroquet*.]

par·a·le·gal (păr'ə-lē'gəl) adj. Of, pertaining to, or being a person with specialized training who assists a lawyer. —**par'a·le'gal** n.

par·al·lax (păr'ə-lăks') n. An apparent change in the direction of an object, caused by a change in the viewer's position. [< Gk. *parallassein*, to change.]

par·al·lel (păr'ə-lĕl', -ləl) adj. **1.** Moving or lying in the same plane, always separated by the same distance and not intersecting. **2.** Matching feature for feature; corresponding. —n. **1.** Any of a set of parallel curves, lines, or surfaces. **2. a.** Something closely resembling or analogous to something else. **b.** A comparison indicating resemblance or analogy. **3.** Any of the imaginary lines of the earth's surface parallel to the equator, representing a given latitude. —v. **-leled** or **-lelled**, **-lel·ing** or **-lel·ling**. **1.** To be or extend parallel to. **2.** To be similar or analogous to. [< Gk. *parallelos*.] —**par'al·lel·ism** n.

par·al·lel·o·gram (păr'ə-lĕl'ə-grăm') n. A four-sided plane figure with opposite sides parallel.

pa·ral·y·sis (pə-răl'ĭ-sĭs) n., pl. **-ses** (-sēz'). Loss or impairment of the ability to feel sensation in or to move a part of the body. [< Gk. *paralusis*.] —**par'a·lyt'ic** (păr'ə-lĭt'ĭk) adj. & n.

par·a·lyze (păr'ə-līz') v. **-lyzed**, **-lyz·ing**. **1.** To affect with paralysis. **2.** To make inoperative or powerless.

par·a·me·ci·um (păr'ə-mē'shē-əm, -sē-) n., pl. **-ci·a** (-shē-ə, -sē-ə) or **-ums**. A usu. oval aquatic protozoan that moves by means of cilia. [< Gk. *paramēkēs*, oblong.]

par·a·med·ic (păr'ə-mĕd'ĭk) n. One who is trained to supply emergency medical treatment or to assist medical professionals. —**par'a·med'i·cal** adj.

pa·ram·e·ter (pə-răm'ĭ-tər) n. **1.** A variable or arbitrary constant appearing in a mathematical expression each value of which restricts or determines the specific form of the expression. **2.** *Informal.* **a.** A fixed limit or boundary; constant. **b.** A characteristic element. —**par'a·met'ric** (-mĕt'rĭk) adj.

par·a·mil·i·tary (păr'ə-mĭl'ĭ-tĕr-ē) adj. Of, pertaining to, or designating forces organized after a military pattern, esp. as an auxiliary military force.

par·a·mount (păr'ə-mount') adj. **1.** Of greatest concern or importance. **2.** Supreme in rank, power, or authority. [AN *paramont*.]

par·a·mour (păr'ə-mōōr') n. A lover, esp. in an illicit relationship. [< OFr. *par amour*, by way of love.]

par·a·noi·a (păr'ə-noi'ə) n. A serious mental disorder characterized by well-rationalized delusions of persecution or of grandeur. [< Gk., madness.] —**par'a·noi'ac'** (-ăk', -ĭk) adj. & n. —**par'a·noid'** (păr'ə-noid') adj. & n.

par·a·pet (păr'ə-pĭt, -pĕt') n. **1.** A low wall or railing, as along the edge of a roof or balcony. **2.** An embankment protecting soldiers from enemy fire. [< Ital. *parapetto*, chest-high wall.]

parapet

parasol

par·a·pher·na·lia (păr'ə-fər-nāl'yə, -fə-) n. *(used with a sing. or pl. verb)*. **1.** Personal belongings. **2.** The articles used in an activity; equipment. [< Gk. *parapherna*, married woman's property exclusive of her dowry.]

par·a·phrase (păr'ə-frāz') n. A restatement of a text or passage in other words, often to clarify meaning. [< Gk. *paraphrasis*.] —**par'a·phrase'** v.

par·a·ple·gi·a (păr'ə-plē'jē-ə, -jə) n. Complete paralysis of the lower half of the body. [< Gk. *paraplēssein*, to strike on one side.] —**par'a·ple'gic** (-jĭk) adj. & n.

par·a·pro·fes·sion·al (păr'ə-prə-fĕsh'ə-nəl) n. One who is trained to assist a professional.

par·a·psy·chol·o·gy (păr'ə-sī-kŏl'ə-jē) n. The study of phenomena such as telepathy and clairvoyance. —**par'a·psy·chol'o·gist** n.

par·a·site (păr'ə-sīt') n. **1.** An often harmful organism that lives on or in a different organism. **2.** A person who takes advantage of the generosity of others. [< Gk. *parasitos*.] —**par'a·sit'ic** (-sĭt'ĭk) adj. —**par'a·sit·ism** (-sī-tĭz'əm, -sĭ-) n. —**par'a·sit·ize'** (-sī-tīz') v.

par·a·si·tol·o·gy (păr'ə-sī-tŏl'ə-jē, -sĭ-) n. The scientific study of parasites and parasitism. —**par'a·si·tol'o·gist** n.

par·a·sol (păr'ə-sôl', -sŏl') n. A light, usu. small umbrella carried as a protection against the sun. [< Oltal. *parasole*.]

par·a·sym·pa·thet·ic nervous system (păr'ə-sĭm'pə-thĕt'ĭk) n. The part of the autonomic nervous system that inhibits or opposes the physiological effects of the sympathetic nervous system.

par·a·thy·roid gland (păr'ə-thī'roid') n. Any of four small glands that lie in pairs adjacent to the thyroid gland and secrete a hormone that controls the metabolism of calcium and phosphorus.

par·a·troops (păr'ə-trōōps') pl.n. Troops trained and equipped to parachute from an aircraft. [PARA(CHUTE) + TROOPS.] —**par'a·troop'er** n.

par·a·ty·phoid (păr'ə-tī'foid') n. An acute

food poisoning similar to but less severe than typhoid fever.

par·boil (pär'boil') v. To cook partially by boiling briefly. [< LLat. *perbullire,* to boil thoroughly.]

par·cel (pär'səl) n. 1. Something wrapped up or packaged; package. 2. A portion or plot of land, usu. a division of a larger area. 3. A group of people or things; collection. —v. **-celed** or **-celled, -cel·ing** or **-cel·ling.** 1. To divide into portions and distribute. 2. To make into a parcel; package. [< Lat. *particula,* portion.]

parcel post n. The branch of the postal service that handles and delivers parcels.

parch (pärch) v. 1. To make very dry, esp. with intense heat. 2. To make thirsty. [ME *parchen.*]

parch·ment (pärch'mənt) n. 1. The skin of a sheep or goat prepared as a material to write on. 2. Something written on a sheet of parchment. [< OFr. *parchemin.*]

par·don (pär'dn) v. 1. To release from further punishment. 2. To pass over (an offense) without punishment. 3. To forgive; excuse. —n. 1. Exemption from the penalties of an offense or crime. 2. Forgiveness, as for a discourtesy. [< LLat. *perdonare,* to give wholeheartedly.] —**par'don·a·ble** adj.

par·don·er (pär'dn-ər) n. 1. One who pardons. 2. A medieval ecclesiastic authorized to raise money by granting papal indulgences to contributors.

pare (pâr) v. **pared, par·ing.** 1. To remove the outer covering or skin of; peel. 2. To reduce by or as if by paring: *pared the budget.* [< Lat. *parare,* to prepare.]

par·e·gor·ic (pär'ĭ-gôr'ĭk, -gŏr'-) n. Camphorated tincture of opium, taken chiefly for the relief of diarrhea or intestinal pain. [< Gk. *parēgoros,* consoling.]

par·ent (pâr'ənt, păr'-) n. 1. A father or mother. 2. A forefather; ancestor. 3. The source or cause of something; origin. [< Lat. *parere,* to give birth.] —**par'ent·age** (-ən-tĭj) n. —**pa·ren'tal** (pə-rĕn'tl) adj. —**par'ent·hood'** n.

pa·ren·the·sis (pə-rĕn'thĭ-sĭs) n., pl. **-ses** (-sēz'). 1. Either of the upright curved lines, ( ), used to mark off explanatory or qualifying remarks. 2. A qualifying or amplifying phrase, word, or sentence placed within a passage. [< Gk., insertion.] —**par·en·thet'i·cal** (păr'ən-thĕt'ĭ-kəl) or **par·en·thet'ic** (-thĕt'ĭk) adj. —**par·en·thet'i·cal·ly** adv.

pa·re·sis (pə-rē'sĭs, păr'ĭ-) n. Slight or partial paralysis. [< Gk.]

par ex·cel·lence (pär' ĕk-sə-läns') adj. Being of the highest degree; pre-eminent. [Fr., by excellence.]

par·fait (pär-fā') n. 1. A frozen dessert made of cream, eggs, sugar, and flavoring. 2. A dessert of layers of ice cream, fruit, various toppings, and whipped cream. [< Lat. *perfectus,* perfect.]

pa·ri·ah (pə-rī'ə) n. One who has been excluded from society; outcast. [Tamil *paṛaiyan.*]

pa·ri·e·tal (pə-rī'ĭ-təl) adj. 1. Of, pertaining to, or forming the wall of a hollow structure or bodily cavity. 2. Dwelling or having authority within the walls or buildings of a college. [< Lat. *paries,* wall.]

pari-mu·tu·el (pär'ĭ-myōō'chōō-əl) n. A system of betting on races in which the winners

divide the net amount bet, minus management expenses, in proportion to the sums they have wagered. [Fr. *pari mutuel.*]

par·ing (pâr'ĭng) n. Something pared off: *cucumber parings.*

pari pas·su (pär'ē päs'ōō) adv. At the same pace or rate. [Lat.]

par·ish (pär'ĭsh) n. 1. An administrative division of a diocese that has its own church. 2. A civil district in Louisiana corresponding to a county in other states. 3. The members of an ecclesiastical parish. [< LGk. *paroikos,* Christian < Gk., neighbor.]

pa·rish·ion·er (pə-rĭsh'ə-nər) n. A member or resident of a parish.

par·i·ty (pär'ĭ-tē) n., pl. **-ties.** 1. Equality, as in amount or value. 2. A fixed relative value between two different kinds of currency. 3. A level for farm-product prices maintained by governmental support. [< Lat. *par,* equal.]

park (pärk) n. 1. An area of land set aside for public use, as for recreation. 2. A stadium or enclosed playing field: *a baseball park.* 3. A place for storing or leaving vehicles. —v. To put or leave (a vehicle) for a time in a certain location. [< OFr. *parc,* enclosure.]

par·ka (pär'kə) n. A warm fur or cloth jacket with a hood. [R., pelt.]

Par·kin·son's disease (pär'kĭn-sənz) n. A progressive nervous disease of later life, characterized by muscular tremor, slowing of movement, partial facial paralysis, and impaired muscular control. [After James *Parkinson* (1755–1824).]

park·way (pärk'wā') n. A broad landscaped highway.

par·lance (pär'ləns) n. A particular manner of speaking: *legal parlance.* [< Med. Lat. *parabolare,* to talk.]

par·lay (pär'lā') n. A bet on two or more successive events at once, with the winnings of one, plus the original stake, to be risked on the next. [< Ital. *parolo,* a set of dice.] —**par'lay** v.

par·ley (pär'lē) n., pl. **-leys.** A discussion or conference, esp. between opponents. [< LLat. *parabola,* discourse.] —**par'ley** v.

par·lia·ment (pär'lə-mənt) n. 1. A legislative assembly. 2. **Parliament.** The national legislature of various countries, esp. the United Kingdom. [< OFr. *parler,* to talk.] —**par'lia·men'ta·ry** (-mĕn'tə-rē, -mĕn'trē) adj.

par·lia·men·tar·i·an (pär'lə-mĕn-târ'ē-ən) n. An expert in parliamentary procedures, rules, or debate.

par·lor (pär'lər) n. Also chiefly Brit. **par·lour.** 1. A room in a private home set apart for the entertainment of visitors. 2. A business establishment: *beauty parlor.* [< OFr. *parler,* to talk.]

par·lous (pär'ləs) adj. Perilous; dangerous. [ME < *perilous,* perilous.] —**par'lous·ly** adv.

Par·me·san (pär'mĭ-zăn', -zän', -zən) n. A hard, dry Italian cheese usu. served grated as a condiment. [Orig. a trademark.]

par·mi·gia·na (pär'mĭ-jä'nə) adj. Made of or covered with Parmesan: *eggplant parmigiana.* [< Ital., of Parma, Italy.]

pa·ro·chi·al (pə-rō'kē-əl) adj. 1. Of, pertaining to, or supported by a church parish. 2. Narrow in scope; provincial: *parochial attitudes.* [< LLat. *parochia,* parish.] —**pa·ro'chi·al·ism** n. —**pa·ro'chi·al·ly** adv.

parochial school n. A school supported by a church parish.

par·o·dy (păr'ə-dē) *n., pl.* **-dies. 1.** A satirical imitation, as of a literary or musical work. **2.** Travesty: *a parody of justice.* [< Gk. *parōidia.*] **—par'o·dist** *n.* **—par'o·dy** *v.*

pa·role (pə-rōl') *n.* **1.** The release of a prisoner before his term has expired on condition of good behavior. **2.** Word of honor; promise. **—v. -roled, -rol·ing.** To release (a prisoner) on parole. [Fr., promise.] **—pa·rol'ee'** *n.*

pa·rot·id gland (pə-rŏt'ĭd) *n.* Either of the salivary glands located below and ahead of each ear. [< Gk. *parōtis,* tumor near the ear.]

-parous *suff.* Giving birth to or bearing: *multiparous.* [< Lat. *parere,* to give birth to.]

par·ox·ysm (păr'ək-sĭz'əm) *n.* **1.** A sudden outburst, as of emotion. **2.** A spasm or fit; convulsion. [< Gk. *paroxusmos.*] **—par'ox·ys'mal** (-məl) *adj.*

par·quet (pär-kā') *n.* **1. a.** The part of the main floor of a theater in front of the balcony. **b.** The main floor of a theater; orchestra. **2.** A floor made of parquetry. [< OFr. *parc,* enclosure.]

par·quet·ry (pär'kĭ-trē) *n., pl.* **-ries.** Wood, often of contrasting colors, worked into an inlaid pattern.

par·ri·cide (păr'ĭ-sīd') *n.* **1.** One who murders his father, mother, or a near relative. **2.** The act committed by a parricide. [Lat. *parricida.*] **—par'ri·cid'al** (-sīd'l) *adj.*

par·rot (păr'ət) *n.* **1.** Any of various chiefly tropical birds with a short, hooked bill, brightly colored plumage, and sometimes the ability to mimic human speech. **2.** One who mindlessly imitates the words or actions of another. **—v.** To repeat or imitate without meaning or understanding. [Prob. < *Perrot,* dim. of *Pierre,* Peter.]

parrot fever *n.* Psittacosis.

par·ry (păr'ē) *v.* **-ried, -ry·ing. 1.** To deflect or ward off. **2.** To avoid skillfully; evade. [< Ital. *parare,* to defend.] **—par'ry** *n.*

parse (pärs) *v.* **parsed, pars·ing.** To describe a word or group of words by stating its part of speech, form, and function in a sentence. [< Lat. *pars,* part.]

par·si·mo·ny (pär'sə-mō'nē) *n.* Extreme or excessive frugality; stinginess. [< Lat. *parcere,* to spare.] **—par'si·mo'ni·ous** *adj.* **—par'si·mo'ni·ous·ly** *adv.*

pars·ley (pär'slē) *n.* A plant with finely divided curled leaves used as a seasoning and garnish. [< Gk. *petroselinon.*]

pars·nip (pär'snĭp') *n.* **1.** A strong-scented plant cultivated for its long, edible root. **2.** The root of the parsnip. [< Lat. *pastinaca.*]

par·son (pär'sən) *n.* A clergyman in charge of a parish. [< Lat. *persona,* character.]

par·son·age (pär'sə-nĭj) *n.* The official residence provided by a church for its parson.

part (pärt) *n.* **1.** A portion, division, or segment of a whole. **2.** An essential component: *a machine part.* **3.** A role, as in a play. **4.** One's share in a responsibility or obligation; duty. **5. a.** One of the individual melodic lines for a particular musical instrument or voice. **b.** A written representation of such a line. **6.** A side in a dispute or controversy. **7.** Often **parts.** A region, land, or territory. **8.** A dividing line formed by combing the hair in different directions. **—v. 1.** To divide or

break into separate parts. **2.** To separate by or as if by coming between; put or keep apart. **3.** To comb (the hair) into a part. **4.** To go away; separate: *parted as friends.* **5.** To leave; depart. **—phrasal verb. part with.** To give up; relinquish: *hated to part with a penny.* **—adv.** In part; partially: *part yellow, part green.* [< Lat. *pars.*]

par·take (pär-tāk') *v.* **-took** (-tŏŏk'), **-tak·en** (-tā'kən), **-tak·ing. 1.** To take part; participate. **2.** To take a portion. [< *part taker,* partaker.] **—par·tak'er** *n.*

par·terre (pär-târ') *n.* A flower garden whose beds form a pattern. [< OFr. *par terre,* on the ground.]

par·the·no·gen·e·sis (pär'thə-nō-jĕn'ĭ-sĭs) *n.* Reproduction without conjunction of gametes of opposite sexes. [Gk. *parthenos,* virgin + -GENESIS.] **—par'the·no·ge·net'ic** (-jə-nĕt'ĭk) *adj.* **—par'the·no·ge·net'i·cal·ly** *adv.*

par·tial (pär'shəl) *adj.* **1.** Not total; incomplete. **2.** Favoring one person or side over another; biased. **3.** Particularly fond: *partial to Chinese cooking.* **—par'ti·al'i·ty** (-shē-ăl'ĭ-tē, -shăl'ĭ-) *n.* **—par'tial·ly** *adv.*

par·tic·i·pate (pär-tĭs'ə-pāt') *v.* **-pat·ed, -pat·ing.** To take part; join or share with others. [< Lat. *particeps,* partaker.] **—par·tic'i·pant** (-pənt) *n.* **—par·tic'i·pa'tion** *n.* **—par·tic'i·pa'tor** *n.* **—par·tic'i·pa·to'ry** (-pə-tôr'ē, -tōr'ē) *adj.*

par·ti·ci·ple (pär'tĭ-sĭp'əl) *n.* A nominal form of a verb that is used with an auxiliary verb to indicate certain tenses and that can also function independently as an adjective. [< Lat. *participium.*] **—par'ti·cip'i·al** (-ē-əl) *adj.*

par·ti·cle (pär'tĭ-kəl) *n.* **1.** A very small piece or part; speck. **2.** A very small amount. **3.** A subatomic particle. **4.** Any of a class of words, including many prepositions and conjunctions, that have little meaning but help specify, connect, or limit the meanings of other words. [< Lat. *particula.*]

par·ti-col·ored (pär'tē-kŭl'ərd) *adj.* Having different parts or sections colored differently. [Obs. *parti,* parti-colored + COLORED.]

par·tic·u·lar (pər-tĭk'yə-lər) *adj.* **1.** Of, pertaining to, or associated with a single person, group, thing, or category. **2.** Separate and distinct from others; specific. **3.** Exceptional; special: *of particular interest.* **4.** Giving or demanding close attention to details; fussy. **—n.** An individual item, fact, or detail. [< Lat. *particula,* dim. of *pars,* part.] **—par·tic'u·lar'i·ty** (-lăr'ĭ-tē) *n.* **—par·tic'u·lar·ly** *adv.*

par·tic·u·lar·ize (pər-tĭk'yə-lə-rīz') *v.* **-ized, -iz·ing. 1.** To state or enumerate in detail; itemize. **2.** To give particulars.

part·ing (pär'tĭng) *n.* **1.** The act of separating or dividing. **2.** A departure or leave-taking. **—adj.** Done, given, or said on departing: *a parting gift.*

par·ti·san (pär'tĭ-zən) *n.* **1.** A strong supporter of a party, cause, faction, person, or idea. **2.** A guerrilla. [< Lat. *pars,* part.] **—par'ti·san** *adj.* **—par'ti·san·ship'** *n.*

par·tite (pär'tīt') *adj.* Divided into parts. [< Lat. *partire,* to divide.]

par·ti·tion (pär-tĭsh'ən) *n.* **1. a.** The act or process of dividing something into parts. **b.** The condition of being divided into parts.

2. Something that separates or divides, as a wall separating one part of a building from another. —v. 1. To divide into parts, pieces, or sections. 2. To separate or divide by means of a partition.

part·ly (pärt′lē) adv. In part; to some extent.

part·ner (pärt′nər) n. 1. A person associated with another in some common activity, esp.: **a.** One of two or more persons who together own a business. **b.** A spouse or mate. **c.** Either of two persons dancing together. **d.** A person playing on the same team as another. 2. An ally. [< Lat. pars, part.] —**part′ner·ship′** n.

Syns: partner, ally, associate, colleague, confederate n.

part of speech n. Any of the traditional grammatical classes into which words are placed according to their function in a sentence, as a noun, verb, etc.

par·took (pär-tŏŏk′) v. p.t. of partake.

par·tridge (pär′trĭj) n., pl. -tridg·es or -tridge. Any of several plump-bodied game birds. [< Gk. perdix.]

partridge

part-time (pärt′tīm′) adj. For or during less than the customary time: a part-time job. —**part′-time′** adv.

par·tu·ri·tion (pär′chŏŏ-rĭsh′ən, -cho̵-) n. The act of giving birth; childbirth. [< Lat. parturire, to be in labor.]

part·way (pärt′wā′) adv. In part; to a certain degree.

par·ty (pär′tē) n., pl. -ties. 1. A social gathering. 2. A group of persons participating in a specific activity or task. 3. A political group organized to promote and support its principles and candidates. 4. A person or group involved in a legal proceeding. 5. A participant: refused to be a party to the dispute. [< OFr. partir, to divide.]

party line n. 1. A telephone circuit used by two or more subscribers. 2. The official policies of a political party to which loyal members are expected to adhere.

par·ve·nu (pär′və-nŏŏ′, -nyŏŏ′) n. One who has suddenly become powerful or wealthy without the background or culture appropriate to his new status. [Fr. < parvenir, to arrive.]

pas (pä) n., pl. **pas** (pä, päz). A ballet step or series of steps. [Fr.]

pa·sha (pä′shə, păsh′ə) n. A former high-ranking Turkish civil official. [Turk. paşa.]

Pash·to (pŭsh′tō) n. Also **Push·to** (-tō). An Iranian language, one of two official languages of Afghanistan.

pass (păs) v. 1. To move on or ahead; proceed. 2. To run; extend: The river passes through town. 3. To cause to move: passed her hand over the fabric. 4. To move over, past, or beyond. 5. To transfer or be transferred from one to another; circulate. 6. To be communicated, exchanged, transferred, or conveyed. 7. To elapse or allow to elapse. 8. To come to an end; be terminated. 9. To take place; happen. 10. To be allowed to happen without challenge: let a remark pass. 11. To undergo or cause to undergo a test, trial, or course of study with favorable results. 12. To be accepted as something different. 13. To approve or be approved, as by a legislature. 14. To express a legal judgment. 15. Sports. To transfer (the ball or puck) to a teammate. 16. To decline to bid in a card game. 17. To hand over to someone else: pass the bread. 18. To discharge (bodily wastes); excrete. —phrasal verbs. **pass out** To lose consciousness. **pass up** Informal. To turn down; refuse. —n. 1. The act of passing. 2. A narrow passage between mountains. 3. **a.** A permit, ticket, or authorization to come or go at will or without charge. **b.** Written leave of absence from military duty. 4. A sweep or run by a military aircraft over a target area. 5. An attempt; effort. 6. A situation, esp. a difficult or threatening one; predicament. 7. A sexual invitation or overture. [< Lat. passus, p.p. of pandere, to stretch out.]

Usage: The past tense and past participle of pass is passed (several months passed or centuries have passed), and past is the corresponding adjective (in past centuries), adverb (drove past), and preposition (past midnight).

pass·a·ble (păs′ə-bəl) adj. 1. Capable of being passed, traversed, or crossed. 2. Satisfactory but not outstanding. —**pass′a·bly** adv.

pas·sage (păs′ĭj) n. 1. The act or process of passing. 2. A journey, esp. by water. 3. The right to travel, as on a ship. 4. A channel, duct, or path through, over, or along which something may pass. 5. Enactment or approval of a legislative measure. 6. A portion or section, as from a literary work or musical composition.

pas·sage·way (păs′ĭj-wā′) n. A corridor.

Pas·sa·ma·quod·dy (păs′ə-mə-kwŏd′ē) n., pl. -dy or -dies. 1. **a.** A tribe of Indians formerly inhabiting Maine and New Brunswick, Canada. **b.** A member of this tribe. 2. The Algonquian language of the Passamaquoddy.

pass·book (păs′bŏŏk′) n. A bankbook.

pas·sé (pä-sā′) adj. 1. Out-of-date; old-fashioned. 2. Past one's prime. [< Fr. passer, to pass.]

pas·sen·ger (păs′ən-jər) n. A person traveling in a vehicle or conveyance. [< OFr. passager.]

passe partout (păs′ pär-tŏŏ′) n. Something enabling one to pass or go everywhere. [Fr.]

pass·er·by (păs′ər-bī′, păs′ər-bī′) n., pl. **pass·ers·by**. A person who passes by, often by chance.

pas·ser·ine (păs′ə-rīn′) adj. Of or pertaining to the great order of birds consisting chiefly of perching birds and songbirds. [< Lat. passer, sparrow.]

pas·sim (păs′ĭm) adv. Throughout; frequently. [Lat.]

pass·ing (păs′ĭng) adj. 1. Of brief duration; transitory. 2. Superficial; casual. 3. Satisfactory. —n. 1. The act of one that passes. 2. Death.

pas·sion (păsh′ən) n. 1. A powerful emotion

or appetite. **2. a.** Ardent love. **b.** Strong sexual desire; lust. **c.** The object of such love or desire. **3. a.** Boundless enthusiasm. **b.** The object of such enthusiasm. **4. Passion.** The sufferings of Christ following the Last Supper and including the Crucifixion. [< Lat. *passus*, p.p. of *pati*, to suffer.] —**pas'sion·ate** *adj.* —**pas'sion·less** *adj.*

pas·sive (păs'ĭv) *adj.* **1.** Not active but acted upon. **2.** Accepting without resistance; submissive. **3.** *Gram.* Denoting a verb form or voice used to indicate that the grammatical subject is the object of the action. —*n. Gram.* **1.** The passive voice. **2.** A verb or construction in the passive voice. [< Lat. *passivus*, capable of suffering.] —**pas'sive·ly** *adv.* —**pas·siv'i·ty** (pă-sĭv'ĭ-tē) or **pas'sive·ness** *n.*

pass·key (păs'kē') *n.* A master key.

Pass·o·ver (păs'ō'vər) *n.* A Jewish festival celebrated in the spring and commemorating the Exodus from Egypt.

pass·port (păs'pôrt', -pōrt') *n.* An official governmental document that certifies the identity and citizenship of an individual traveling abroad. [Fr. *passeport*.]

pass·word (păs'wûrd') *n.* A secret word or phrase spoken to a guard to gain admission.

past (păst) *adj.* **1.** No longer current; over. **2.** Having existed or occurred in an earlier time; bygone. **3. a.** Earlier than the present time; ago: *forty years past.* **b.** Just gone by: *in the past month.* **4.** *Gram.* Of or denoting a verb tense or form used to express an action or condition prior to the time it is expressed. —*n.* **1.** The time before the present. **2.** A person's history, background, or former activities. **3.** *Gram.* **a.** The past tense. **b.** A verb form in the past tense. —*adv.* So as to pass by or go beyond: *He walked past.* —*prep.* **1.** By and beyond: *walk past the theater.* **2.** Beyond in position, time, extent, or amount. [ME < p.p. of *passen*, to pass.]

pas·ta (pä'stə) *n.* **1.** Paste or dough made of flour and water, as in macaroni and ravioli. **2.** A prepared dish of pasta. [Ital. < LLat.]

paste (päst) *n.* **1.** A smooth, viscous adhesive, as that made of flour and water. **2.** Dough, as that used in making pastry. **3.** A food made by pounding or grinding: *almond paste.* **4.** Moistened clay used in making porcelain or pottery. **5.** A hard, brilliant glass used in making artificial gems. —*v.* **past·ed, past·ing.** **1.** To cause to adhere by applying paste. **2.** *Slang.* To punch; hit. [< LLat. *pasta*.]

paste·board (päst'bôrd', -bōrd') *n.* A thin, firm material made of sheets of paper pasted together.

pas·tel (pă-stĕl') *n.* **1. a.** A dried paste made of ground and mixed pigment. **b.** A crayon of pastel. **2.** A picture or sketch drawn with a pastel crayon. **3.** A light or pale tint. [LLat. *pastellus*, woad < *pasta*, paste.]

pas·tern (păs'tərn) *n.* The part of a horse's foot between the fetlock and hoof. [< OFr. *pasturon* < *pasture*, pasture.]

pas·teur·i·za·tion (păs'chə-rĭ-zā'shən) *n.* The process of destroying most disease-producing microorganisms and limiting fermentation in liquids such as milk and beer by partial or complete sterilization. [< Louis *Pasteur* (1822–95).] —**pas'teur·ize'** (păs'chə-rīz') *v.*

pas·tiche (pă-stēsh', pä-) *n.* A dramatic, literary, or musical piece made up of selections from various works. [< Ital. *pasticcio*.]

pas·tille (pă-stēl') *n.* Also **pas·til** (păs'tĭl). A small medicated or aromatic tablet; lozenge. [< Lat. *pastillus*.]

pas·time (păs'tīm') *n.* An activity that occupies one's time pleasantly.

pas·tor (păs'tər) *n.* A Christian minister who is the leader of a congregation. [< Lat., shepherd.] —**pas'tor·ate** (-tər-ĭt) *n.*

pas·tor·al (păs'tər-əl) *adj.* **1.** Of or pertaining to shepherds, herdsmen, etc. **2.** Of or pertaining to rural life. **3.** Of or pertaining to a pastor or his duties. —*n.* A literary or other artistic work that portrays rural life, usu. in an idealized manner.

pas·to·rale (păs'tə-räl', -răl', päs'-) *n.* A musical composition with a pastoral theme. [Ital.]

past participle *n.* A participle that indicates completed action and that is used as an adjective and to form the passive voice and the perfect tenses.

pas·tra·mi (pə-strä'mē) *n.* A highly seasoned smoked cut of beef, usu. from the breast or shoulder. [Yiddish < Rum. *pastramă.*]

pas·try (pā'strē) *n., pl.* **-tries.** **1.** A baked paste of flour, water, and shortening used for the crusts of such foods as pies and tarts. **2.** Baked foods made with pastry.

pas·tur·age (păs'chər-ĭj) *n.* **1.** Grass or other plants eaten by grazing animals. **2.** Grazing land.

pas·ture (păs'chər) *n.* **1.** Plants such as grass eaten by grazing animals. **2.** A piece of land on which animals graze. —*v.* **-tured, -tur·ing.** **1.** To herd (animals) into a pasture to graze. **2.** To graze. [< Lat. *pastus*, p.p.p. of *pascere*, to feed.]

pas·ty (pā'stē) *adj.* **-i·er, -i·est.** **1.** Resembling paste, as in color. **2.** Pale and unhealthy-looking.

pat (păt) *v.* **pat·ted, pat·ting.** **1. a.** To tap lightly with a flat implement. **b.** To stroke gently, esp. as a gesture of affection. **2.** To mold by tapping lightly with the hands or a flat implement. —*n.* **1.** A light stroke or tap. **2.** The sound made by a pat. **3.** A small mass: *a pat of butter.* —*adj.* **1.** Precisely suited. **2.** Prepared and ready for use: *a pat answer.* **3.** Facile; glib. —*adv.* **1.** Without changing position; steadfastly: *standing pat.* **2.** Perfectly; precisely: *had the instructions down pat.* [< ME *patte*, a light blow.] —**pat'ly** *adv.* —**pat'ness** *n.*

pa·ta·ca (pə-tä'kə) *n.* See table at **currency.** [Port.]

patch (păch) *n.* **1.** A small piece of material affixed to another piece to conceal or reinforce a weakened or worn area. **2.** A cloth badge affixed to a sleeve to indicate the military unit to which one belongs. **3. a.** A dressing or bandage for a wound. **b.** A small shield of cloth worn over an injured eye. **4.** A small piece of land. **5.** A small area that differs from the whole: *a patch of blue sky.* —*v.* **1.** To put a patch on. **2.** To repair or put together, esp. hastily. —*phrasal verb.* **patch up.** To settle: *patched up a quarrel.* [ME *pacche.*]

patch test *n.* A test for allergic sensitivity

made by applying a suspected allergen to the skin with a small surgical pad.

patch·work (păch′wûrk′) n. Material consisting of pieces of various colors, shapes, and sizes.

pate (pāt) n. The head, esp. the top of the head. [ME.]

pâ·té (pä-tā′, pă-) n. A seasoned meat paste. [< OFr. *paste*, paste.]

pa·tel·la (pə-tĕl′ə) n., pl. **-tel·lae** (-tĕl′ē). A flat, triangular bone located at the front of the knee joint; kneecap. [Lat.] **—pa·tel′lar** or **pa·tel′late** (-tĕl′ĭt, -āt′) adj.

pat·en (păt′n) n. 1. A plate, esp. one used to hold the Eucharistic bread. 2. A thin disk of metal. [< Gk. *patanē*, plate.]

pat·ent (păt′nt) n. 1. A grant made by a government to an inventor, assuring him the sole right to make, use, and sell his invention for a certain period of time. 2. Something that is protected by a patent. —adj. 1. Open to general inspection: *letters patent*. 2. (*also* pāt′nt). Obvious; plain: *patent insincerity*. 3. Protected by a patent. —v. 1. To obtain a patent on. 2. To grant a patent to. [< Lat. *patēre*, to be open.] **—pat′ent·ee′** (păt′n-tē′) n.

patent leather n. Leather with a smooth, hard, glossy surface. [< its being made by a once-patented process.]

pa·ter·fa·mil·i·as (pā′tər-fə-mĭl′ē-əs, pä′tər-) n., pl. **pa·tres·fa·mil·i·as** (pä′trēz-). 1. The father of a family. 2. The male head of a household. [Lat.]

pa·ter·nal (pə-tûr′nəl) adj. 1. Of or characteristic of a father; fatherly. 2. Received or inherited from a father. 3. Of the father's side of a family. [< Lat. *pater*, father.] **—pa·ter′nal·ly** adv.

pa·ter·nal·ism (pə-tûr′nə-lĭz′əm) n. A policy or practice of treating or governing people in a fatherly manner, esp. by providing for their needs without giving them responsibility. **—pa·ter·nal·is′tic** adj.

pa·ter·ni·ty (pə-tûr′nĭ-tē) n. 1. The fact or condition of being a father; fatherhood. 2. Descent on a father's side.

path (păth, päth) n., pl. **paths** (păthz, päthz, păths, päths). 1. A trodden track or way. 2. A course; route. [< OE *paeth*.] **—path′less** adj.

pa·thet·ic (pə-thĕt′ĭk) adj. Expressing or arousing pity, sympathy, or tenderness. [< Gk. *pathos*, suffering.] **—pa·thet′i·cal·ly** adv.

path·find·er (păth′fīn′dər, päth′-) n. One who discovers a way through or into unexplored regions.

patho– pref. Disease or suffering: *pathogen*. [< Gk. *pathos*, suffering.]

path·o·gen (păth′ə-jən) n. An agent that causes disease, esp. a microorganism such as a bacterium. **—path′o·gen′ic** (-jĕn′ĭk) adj.

pa·thol·o·gy (pă-thŏl′ə-jē, pä-) n., pl. **-gies**. 1. The scientific study of the nature of disease. 2. The anatomic or functional manifestations of disease. **—path′o·log′i·cal** (păth′ə-lŏj′ĭ-kəl) adj. **—pa·thol′o·gist** n.

pa·thos (pā′thŏs′) n. A quality in something or someone that arouses feelings of pity, sympathy, tenderness, or sorrow in another. [Gk., suffering.]

path·way (păth′wā′, päth′-) n. A path.

-pathy suff. 1. Feeling; perception: *telepathy*. 2. a. Disease; a diseased condition: *psychopathy*. b. A system of treating disease: *homeopathy*. [< Gk. *pathos*, suffering.]

pa·tience (pā′shəns) n. 1. The quality, capacity, or fact of being patient. 2. The game solitaire.

pa·tient (pā′shənt) adj. 1. Enduring affliction with calmness. 2. Tolerant; understanding. 3. Persevering; steadfast. —n. One under medical treatment. [< Lat. *pati*, to endure.] **—pa′tient·ly** adv.

pa·ti·na (păt′n-ə, pə-tē′nə) n. A thin layer of corrosion, usu. brown or green, that appears on copper or copper alloys as a result of oxidation. [Ital.]

pa·ti·o (păt′ē-ō′) n., pl. **-os**. 1. An inner, roofless courtyard. 2. A recreation area, usu. paved, next to a residence. [Sp.]

pat·ois (păt′wä′) n., pl. **-ois** (-wäz′). 1. A regional dialect. 2. Illiterate or substandard speech. 3. Jargon; cant. [< OFr.]

patri– pref.: *patricide*. [Lat. < *pater*.]

pa·tri·arch (pā′trē-ärk′) n. 1. The male leader of a family or tribe. 2. An ecclesiastical dignitary, esp. in Eastern churches. 3. A very old and venerable man; elder. **—pa′tri·ar′chal** or **pa′tri·ar′chic** adj. **—pa′tri·ar′chate** (-kĭt, -kāt′) n. **—pa′tri·ar′chy** n.

pa·tri·cian (pə-trĭsh′ən) n. A person of high rank; aristocrat. **—pa·tri′cian** adj.

pat·ri·cide (păt′rĭ-sīd′) n. 1. The act of murdering one's father. 2. One who murders his father. **—pat′ri·cid′al** (-sīd′l) adj.

pat·ri·mo·ny (păt′rə-mō′nē) n., pl. **-nies**. An inheritance, esp. from one's father. [< Lat. *patrimonium*.] **—pat′ri·mo′ni·al** adj.

pa·tri·ot (pā′trē-ət, -ŏt′) n. One who loves, supports, and defends his country. [< Gk. *patris*, fatherland.] **—pa′tri·ot′ic** (-ŏt′ĭk) adj. **—pa′tri·ot·ism** (-ə-tĭz′əm) n.

pa·tris·tic (pə-trĭs′tĭk) adj. Of or pertaining to the early church fathers or their writings. [PATR(I-) + -IST + -IC.]

pa·trol (pə-trōl′) n. 1. a. The action of moving about an area for observation or security. b. A person or group who performs such an action. 2. A military unit sent out to reconnoiter. —v. **-trolled**, **-trol·ling**. To engage in a patrol (of). [< OFr. *patouiller*, to paddle around in mud.]

pa·trol·man (pə-trōl′mən) n. A policeman who patrols an assigned area.

patrol wagon n. A police truck used to convey prisoners.

pa·tron (pā′trən) n. 1. One who supports, protects, or champions; benefactor: *a patron of the arts*. 2. A regular customer. [< Lat. *patronus*.] **—pa′tron·ess** n.

pa·tron·age (pā′trə-nĭj, păt′rə-) n. 1. Support from a patron. 2. The trade of customers. 3. Customers; clientele. 4. The power of appointing people to governmental positions.

pa·tron·ize (pā′trə-nīz′, păt′rə-) v. **-ized**, **-iz·ing**. 1. To be a patron to; support. 2. To treat in an offensively condescending way. **—pa′tron·iz′ing·ly** adv.

pat·ro·nym·ic (păt′rə-nĭm′ĭk) n. A name received from a paternal ancestor, esp. one formed by an affix. [< Gk. *patrōnumikos*, of a patronymic.] **—pat′ro·nym′ic** adj.

pa·troon (pə-trōōn′) n. A landholder granted certain feudal powers, esp. in New York under Dutch colonial rule. [Du., ult. < Lat. *pater*, father.]

pat·sy (păt′sē) n., pl. **-sies**. Slang. One who is cheated or victimized. [Orig. unknown.]

pat·ter¹ (păt′ər) v. To make a succession of quick light taps. [< PAT.] **—pat′ter** n.

pat·ter² (păt'ər) v. To chatter glibly or mechanically. —n. 1. The jargon of a particular group; cant. 2. Glib, rapid speech, as of an auctioneer. [ME *patren.*]

pat·tern (păt'ərn) n. 1. An artistic or decorative design. 2. A model to be followed in making things. 3. A composite of traits or characteristics. 4. An ideal worthy of imitation. 5. A representative sample; specimen. —v. To make, mold, form, or design by following a pattern. [< Med. Lat. *patronus,* pattern, patron.]

pat·ty (păt'ē) n., pl. -ties. 1. A small flattened cake of chopped food. 2. A small pie. [Fr. *pâté.*]

pau·ci·ty (pô'sĭ-tē) n. Smallness of quantity or number. [< Lat. *paucus,* few.]

paunch (pônch, pänch) n. The belly, esp. a potbelly. [< Lat. *pantex.*] —**paunch'y** adj.

pau·per (pô'pər) n. An extremely poor person, esp. one living on public charity. [Lat., poor.] —**pau'per·ism** n. —**pau'per·ize'** (-pə-rīz') v.

pause (pôz) v. **paused, paus·ing.** To cease or suspend an action for a time; linger or hesitate. —n. 1. A temporary stop in action or speech. 2. A hesitation. 3. Mus. A sign indicating that a note or rest is to be held. 4. A reason for hesitation. [< Gk. *pauein,* to stop.]

pave (pāv) v. **paved, pav·ing.** To cover with a hard, smooth surface for travel. —idiom. **pave the way.** To make progress or development easier. [< Lat. *pavire,* to stamp.]

pave·ment (pāv'mənt) n. 1. A paved surface. 2. The material of which a pavement is made.

pa·vil·ion (pə-vĭl'yən) n. 1. An ornate tent. 2. A temporary, often open structure, as in a park, used for amusement or shelter. 3. An annex of a building. [< Lat. *papilio.*]

pav·ing (pā'vĭng) n. Pavement.

paw (pô) n. 1. The clawed foot of an animal, as a dog. 2. Informal. A human hand. —v. 1. To strike, touch, or scrape with a paw or forefoot. 2. To handle clumsily or rudely. 3. To make clumsy, grasping motions with the hands. [< OFr. *powe,* of Gmc. orig.]

pawl (pôl) n. A hinged or pivoted device adapted to fit into a notch of a ratchet wheel to impart forward or prevent backward motion. [Poss. < Du. *pal.*]

pawl
Left: Ratchet wheel with pawl
Right: Diagram

pawn¹ (pôn) n. 1. Something given as security for a loan; pledge. 2. The condition of being held as a pledge. —v. To give or deposit as security for money borrowed. [< OFr. *pan.*]

pawn² (pôn) n. 1. A chessman of the lowest value. 2. One used to further the purposes of another. [< Med. Lat. *pedo,* foot soldier.]

pawn·bro·ker (pôn'brō'kər) n. One who lends money on personal property left as security. —**pawn'bro'king** n.

Paw·nee (pô-nē') n., pl. **-nee** or **-nees.** 1. a. A confederation of four Plains Indian tribes in the region of Kansas and Nebraska, now living on a reservation in Oklahoma. b. A member of this confederation. 2. The Caddoan language of the Pawnee.

pawn·shop (pôn'shŏp') n. The shop of a pawnbroker.

paw·paw (pô'pô') n. Var. of papaw.

pay (pā) v. **paid** (pād), **pay·ing.** 1. To recompense for goods or services. 2. To discharge (a debt or obligation); settle. 3. To requite. 4. To yield as return. 5. To be profitable or worthwhile (to). 6. To bear the cost of or suffer the consequences of. 7. To give or bestow. 8. To make (a visit or call). —adj. 1. Requiring payment to operate: a pay phone. 2. Yielding something valuable, as gold in mining. —n. 1. The act of paying or fact of being paid. 2. Something paid, as a salary or wages. [Med. Lat. *pacare,* ult. < Lat. *pax,* peace.] —**pay'a·ble** adj. —**pay·ee'** (pā-ē') n. —**pay'er** n.

pay·check (pā'chĕk') n. 1. A check issued to an employee in payment of salary or wages. 2. Salary.

pay·load (pā'lōd') n. The total load, as of cargo and passengers, that a vehicle, as an aircraft or spacecraft, can carry.

pay·mas·ter (pā'măs'tər) n. One in charge of paying wages and salaries.

pay·ment (pā'mənt) n. 1. The act of paying. 2. An amount that is paid.

pay·off (pā'ôf', -ŏf') n. 1. Full payment, as of a salary. 2. Informal. a. Final settlement or reckoning. b. The climax of a narrative or sequence of events. 3. Final retribution or revenge. 4. Informal. A bribe.

pay·roll (pā'rōl') n. 1. A list of employees and the wages due to each. 2. The total sum of money to be paid to employees on a payroll.

Pb The symbol for the element lead. [< Lat. *plumbum,* lead.]

Pd The symbol for the element palladium.

pe (pā) n. The 17th letter of the Hebrew alphabet. See table at **alphabet.** [Heb. *peh.*]

pea (pē) n. 1. A vine cultivated for its round edible seeds enclosed in green pods. 2. A seed of the pea. 3. Any of several plants related to the pea. [< Gk. *pison.*]

peace (pēs) n. 1. a. The absence of war or other hostilities. b. An agreement or treaty to end hostilities. 2. Freedom from quarrels and disagreement; harmony. 3. Public security: disturbing the peace. 4. Calm; serenity: peace of mind. [< Lat. *pax.*] —**peace'a·ble** adj. —**peace'a·bly** adv. —**peace'ful** adj. —**peace'ful·ly** adv. —**peace'ful·ness** n.

peace·keep·ing (pēs'kē'pĭng) n. The preservation of peace, esp. the international supervision of a truce between hostile nations.

peace·mak·er (pēs'mā'kər) n. One who makes peace, esp. by settling disputes.

peace officer n. A law officer, such as a sheriff, responsible for maintaining civil peace.

peace-time (pēs'tīm') *n.* A time of absence of war.

peach (pēch) *n.* **1. a.** A small tree with pink flowers and edible fruit. **b.** The sweet, juicy fruit of the peach, with downy reddish or yellowish skin. **2.** A light yellowish pink. [< Lat. *persicum.*]

pea-cock (pē'kŏk') *n.* The male peafowl, having brilliant blue or green plumage and long tail feathers that can be spread in a fanlike form. [Lat. *pavo,* peacock + COCK[1].]

pea-fowl (pē'foul') *n.* A large Asiatic pheasant. [PEA(COCK) + FOWL.]

pea-hen (pē'hĕn') *n.* The female peafowl.

peak (pēk) *n.* **1.** A tapering point that projects upward. **2. a.** The top of a mountain. **b.** A mountain. **3.** The visor of a cap. **4.** The point of greatest development, value, height, or intensity. —*v.* To bring to or form a peak. [Prob. < *pike,* a hill with a pointed summit.]

peak-ed (pē'kĭd) *adj.* Pale and sickly in appearance. [< *peak,* to become sickly.]

peal (pēl) *n.* **1.** A ringing of bells. **2.** A set of tuned bells; carillon. **3.** A loud noise or series of noises: *peals of laughter.* —*v.* To sound or cause to sound in a peal; ring. [< ME *apel,* appeal.]

pea-nut (pē'nŭt', -nət) *n.* **1.** A pealike vine bearing brittle-shelled pods that ripen underground. **2.** The edible, nutlike, oily seed of the peanut vine.

pear (pâr) *n.* **1.** A widely cultivated tree with glossy leaves, white flowers, and edible fruit. **2.** The fruit of the pear, spherical at the base and tapering toward the stem end. [< Lat. *pirum.*]

pearl (pûrl) *n.* **1.** A smooth, often rounded lustrous deposit formed in the shells of certain oysters and other mollusks and valued as a gem. **2.** Mother-of-pearl; nacre. **3.** One likened to a pearl in beauty or value. **4.** A yellowish white. [< Lat. *perna,* sea mussel.] —**pearl'y** *adj.*

peas-ant (pĕz'ənt) *n.* **1.** A member of the sup. European class of agricultural workers. **2.** A countryman; rustic. **3.** An uncouth, crude, or ill-bred person; boor. [< LLat. *pagensis,* inhabitant of a district.] —**peas'ant-ry** *n.*

peat (pēt) *n.* Partially carbonized vegetable matter, as moss, found in bogs and used esp. as fuel. [< Med. Lat. *peta.*] —**peat'y** *adj.*

peb-ble (pĕb'əl) *n.* **1.** A small stone worn smooth and usu. round by erosion. **2.** A crinkled surface, as on leather. —*v.* **-bled, -bling.** To impart a rough, grainy surface to (leather or paper). [< OE *papolstān.*] —**peb'bly** *adj.*

pe-can (pĭ-kän', -kăn') *n.* **1.** A tree of the southern United States with deeply furrowed bark and edible nuts. **2.** The nut of the pecan. [Algonquian *paccan.*]

pec-ca-dil-lo (pĕk'ə-dĭl'ō) *n., pl.* **-loes** or **-los.** A minor offense. [Sp.]

pec-ca-ry (pĕk'ə-rē) *n., pl.* **-ries.** A piglike tropical American mammal with long, dark bristles. [< Cariban *pakira.*]

peck¹ (pĕk) *v.* **1.** To strike, form, or make strokes with or as with the beak. **2.** To pick up with the beak. **3.** To kiss briefly and casually. —*n.* **1.** A stroke or mark made with the beak. **2.** A light, quick kiss. [ME *pecken.*]

peck² (pĕk) *n.* **1.** A unit of volume or capacity in the U.S. system, used in dry measure, equal to 8 quarts or 537.605 cubic inches. **2.** A unit of volume or capacity in the British

Imperial System, used in dry and liquid measure, equal to 554.84 cubic inches. [< OFr. *pek.*]

pecking order *n.* **1.** A hierarchy within flocks of poultry in which each member submits to pecking by the stronger or more aggressive members and has the privilege of pecking the weaker members. **2.** A hierarchy in a human group.

pec-tin (pĕk'tĭn) *n.* Any of a group of colloidal substances found in ripe fruits and used to jell various foods, drugs, and cosmetics. [< Gk. *pēktikos,* coagulating.] —**pec'tic** *adj.*

pec-to-ral (pĕk'tər-əl) *adj.* Of or pertaining to the breast or chest. [< Lat. *pectus,* breast.]

pec-u-late (pĕk'yə-lāt') *v.* **-lated, -lating.** To embezzle. [< Lat. *peculari.*] —**pec'u-la'tion** *n.*

pe-cu-liar (pĭ-kyōōl'yər) *adj.* **1.** Unusual or eccentric; odd. **2.** Distinct and particular. **3.** Belonging exclusively to one group or person. [< Lat. *peculiaris,* of private property.] —**pe-cu'li-ar'i-ty** (-kyōō'lē-ăr'ĭ-tē, -kyōōl-yăr'-) *n.* —**pe-cu'liar-ly** *adv.*

pe-cu-ni-ar-y (pĭ-kyōō'nē-ĕr'ē) *adj.* Of or pertaining to money. [< Lat. *pecunia,* wealth.]

ped- *pref.* Var. of **pedo-.**

-ped or **-pede** *suff.* Foot or feet: *biped.* [< Lat. *pes,* foot.]

ped-a-gogue (pĕd'ə-gŏg') *n.* A schoolteacher. [< Gk. *paidagōgos.*]

ped-a-go-gy (pĕd'ə-gō'jē, -gŏj'ē) *n.* The art, profession, or study of teaching. —**ped'a-gog'ic** (-gŏj'ĭk, -gō'jĭk) or **ped'a-gog'i-cal** *adj.* —**ped'a-gog'i-cal-ly** *adv.*

ped-al (pĕd'l) *n.* A lever operated by the foot, as on a musical instrument or a machine. —*adj.* Of or pertaining to a foot or footlike part. —*v.* **-aled** or **-alled, -aling** or **-alling.** **1.** To use or operate a pedal. **2.** To ride a bicycle. [< Lat. *pedalis,* of the foot.]

ped-ant (pĕd'nt) *n.* **1.** One who stresses trivial details of learning. **2.** One who parades his learning. [< OItal. *pedante.*] —**pe-dan'tic** (pĭ-dăn'tĭk) *adj.* —**pe-dan'ti-cal-ly** *adv.* —**ped'ant-ry** (pĕd'n-trē) *n.*

ped-dle (pĕd'l) *v.* **-dled, -dling.** To travel about selling (goods). [< ME *pedlere,* peddler.] —**ped'dler** *n.*

-pede *suff.* Var. of **-ped.**

ped-er-as-ty (pĕd'ə-răs'tē) *n.* Sexual relations between a man and a boy. [Gk. *paiderastēs,* lover of boys.] —**ped'er-ast** *n.*

ped-es-tal (pĕd'ĭ-stəl) *n.* A support or base, as for a column or statue. [< OItal. *pie di stallo,* foot of a stall.]

pe-des-tri-an (pĭ-dĕs'trē-ən) *n.* One traveling on foot. —*adj.* **1.** Going or performed on foot. **2.** Commonplace; ordinary. [< Lat. *pedester,* going on foot.]

pe-di-at-rics (pē'dē-ăt'rĭks) *n. (used with a sing. verb).* The branch of medicine that deals with the care of infants and children and the treatment of their diseases. —**pe'di-at'ric** *adj.* —**pe'di-a-tri'cian** (-ə-trĭsh'ən) *n.*

ped-i-cure (pĕd'ĭ-kyŏŏr') *n.* **1.** Cosmetic care of the feet and toenails. **2.** A single cosmetic treatment of the feet and toenails. [Fr. *pédicure.*] —**ped'i-cur'ist** *n.*

ped-i-gree (pĕd'ĭ-grē') *n.* **1.** A line of ancestors; ancestry; lineage. **2.** A list or record of ancestors, as of a purebred animal. [< OFr. *pie de grue,* crane's foot < the claw-shaped lines used in family trees.] —**ped'i-greed'** *adj.*

ped-i-ment (pĕd'ə-mənt) *n.* A wide, low triangular decorative element, as over the door of a building. [Prob. < PYRAMID.]

pedo- or **ped-** *pref.* Child: *pediatrics.* [< Gk. *pais.*]

pe·dom·e·ter (pǐ-dǒm′ǐ-tər) *n.* An instrument that measures the approximate distance traveled on foot by registering the number of steps taken.

peek (pēk) *v.* 1. To glance quickly. 2. To look or peer furtively, as from a place of concealment. [ME *piken.*] —**peek** *n.*

peel (pēl) *n.* The skin or rind, esp. of a fruit. —*v.* 1. To strip the skin, rind, or bark from; pare. 2. To remove by or as if by peeling; pull off. 3. To lose or shed skin, rind, or bark. 4. To come off in thin strips or pieces. [< Lat. *pilare,* to deprive of hair.] —**peel′er** *n.*

peen (pēn) *n.* The often wedge-shaped or ball-shaped end of a hammerhead opposite the flat striking surface. [Prob. of Scand. orig.]

peep¹ (pēp) *v.* To utter a short, soft, high-pitched sound, as of a baby bird. —*n.* A weak sound or utterance. [ME *pepen.*] —**peep′er** *n.*

peep² (pēp) *v.* 1. To peek furtively, as through a small aperture. 2. To become visible gradually. —*n.* 1. A quick or furtive look. 2. A first glimpse or appearance. [ME *pepen.*] —**peep′er** *n.*

peep·hole (pēp′hōl′) *n.* A small hole through which one may peep.

peer¹ (pîr) *v.* 1. To look intently, searchingly, or with difficulty. 2. To be partially visible. [Perh. < APPEAR.]

peer² (pîr) *n.* 1. One who has equal standing with another. 2. A nobleman. [< Lat. *par,* equal.] —**peer′age** *n.* —**peer′ess** *n.*

peer·less (pîr′lĭs) *adj.* Without peer; unmatched. —**peer′less·ly** *adv.*

peeve (pēv) *v.* **peeved, peev·ing.** To annoy or vex. —*n.* 1. A vexation; grievance. 2. A resentful mood. [< PEEVISH.]

pee·vish (pē′vĭsh) *adj.* Irritable; querulous. [ME *pevish,* spiteful.] —**pee′vish·ly** *adv.* —**pee′vish·ness** *n.*

pee·wee (pē′wē) *n.* One that is noticeably or unusually small. [Prob. var. of WEE.]

peg (pĕg) *n.* 1. A small cylindrical pin, as of wood, used to fasten things or to fit a hole. 2. A projection used as a support or as a boundary marker. 3. A degree or notch. 4. A throw, as of a baseball. 5. A pretext or occasion. —*v.* **pegged, peg·ging.** 1. To put or insert a peg into. 2. To mark with pegs. 3. To fix (a price) at a certain level. 4. *Informal.* To classify; categorize. 5. To throw. 6. To work steadily; persist: *pegging away at the job.* [ME *pegge.*]

peg·ma·tite (pĕg′mə-tīt′) *n.* A coarse-grained igneous rock, largely granite. [< Gk. *pēgma,* framework.] —**peg·ma·tit′ic** (-tĭt′ĭk) *adj.*

peig·noir (pān-wär′, pĕn-) *n.* A woman's loose-fitting dressing gown. [Fr.]

pe·jo·ra·tive (pǐ-jôr′ə-tǐv, -jŏr′-, pĕj′ə-rā′tĭv) *adj.* Tending to make or become worse; disparaging or downgrading. [< Lat. *pejor,* worse.]

Pe·king·ese (pē′kǐ-nēz′, -nēs′) *n.* Also **Pe·kin·ese.** A small, short-legged, long-haired dog with a flat nose. [< *Peking* (Beijing), China.]

pe·koe (pē′kō) *n.* Black tea made from relatively small leaves. [Dial. Chin. *peh ho.*]

pe·lag·ic (pə-lăj′ĭk) *adj.* Of or pertaining to open oceans or seas. [< Gk. *pelagos,* sea.]

pelf (pĕlf) *n.* Wealth or riches. [< OFr. *pelfre,* booty.]

pel·i·can (pĕl′ĭ-kən) *n.* A large, web-footed bird with a large pouch under the lower bill used for catching and holding fish. [< Gk. *pelekan.*]

pel·la·gra (pə-lăg′rə, -lā′grə) *n.* A chronic niacin-deficiency disease marked by skin eruptions and digestive and nervous disturbances. [Ital.] —**pel·lag′rous** *adj.*

pel·let (pĕl′ĭt) *n.* 1. A small, solid or densely packed ball or mass, as of medicine. 2. A bullet or piece of small shot. [< Lat. *pila,* ball.]

pell-mell (pĕl′mĕl′) *adv.* Also **pell-mell.** 1. In a jumbled, confused manner. 2. In disorderly haste; headlong. [Fr. *pêle-mêle.*]

pel·lu·cid (pə-lōō′sĭd) *adj.* 1. Transparent. 2. Very clear, as in meaning. [< Lat. *pellucēre,* to shine through.] —**pel·lu′cid·ly** *adv.* —**pel·lu′cid·ness** *n.*

pelt¹ (pĕlt) *n.* An animal skin, esp. with the fur or hair still on it. [ME.]

pelt² (pĕlt) *v.* To strike repeatedly with or as with blows or missiles. [ME *pelten.*]

pel·vis (pĕl′vĭs) *n., pl.* **-vis·es** or **-ves** (-vēz′). A basin-shaped skeletal structure that rests on the lower limbs and supports the spinal column. [< Lat., basin.] —**pel′vic** *adj.*

pem·mi·can (pĕm′ĭ-kən) *n.* Also **pem·i·can.** A food prepared from dried meat pounded into paste and mixed with fat. [Cree *pimikân.*]

pen¹ (pĕn) *n.* An instrument for writing or drawing with ink. —*v.* **penned, pen·ning.** To write, esp. with a pen. [< Lat. *penna,* feather.]

pen² (pĕn) *n.* A small, fenced enclosure, esp. for animals. —*v.* **penned** or **pent** (pĕnt), **pen·ning.** To confine in or as if in a pen. [< OE *penn.*]

pen³ (pĕn) *n. Slang.* A penitentiary.

pe·nal (pē′nəl) *adj.* Of or pertaining to punishment, esp. for breaking the law. [< Lat. *poena,* penalty.] —**pe′nal·ly** *adv.*

pe·nal·ize (pē′nə-līz′, pĕn′ə-) *v.* **-ized, -iz·ing.** To subject to a penalty.

pen·al·ty (pĕn′əl-tē) *n., pl.* **-ties.** 1. A punishment for a crime or offense. 2. Something required as a forfeit when the terms of an agreement are not met. 3. A punishment, handicap, or disadvantage resulting from an action or condition.

pen·ance (pĕn′əns) *n.* 1. An act performed to show repentance or sorrow for a sin. 2. *Eccles.* A sacrament that includes contrition, confession to a priest, acceptance of punishment, and absolution. [< Lat. *paenitens,* penitent.]

Pe·na·tes (pĭ-nā′tēz′, -nä′-) *pl.n.* The Roman gods of the household.

pence (pĕns) *n. Chiefly Brit.* A pl. of **penny.**

pen·chant (pĕn′chənt) *n.* A strong inclination; liking. [Fr. < *pencher,* to incline.]

pen·cil (pĕn′səl) *n.* 1. A writing implement consisting of a thin stick of graphite, often encased in wood. 2. Something shaped or used like a pencil: *an eyebrow pencil.* —*v.* **-ciled** or **-cilled, -cil·ing** or **-cil·ling.** To write, draw, or mark with a pencil. [< Lat. *penicillus,* brush.]

pen·dant (pĕn'dənt) *n.* Also **pen·dent.** Something suspended from something else, esp. an ornament. —*adj.* Var. of **pendent.** [< Lat. *pendēre,* to hang.]

pen·dent (pĕn'dənt) *adj.* Also **pen·dant.** Hanging down; suspended. —*n.* Var. of **pendant.** [< Lat. *pendēre,* to hang.] —**pen'dent·ly** *adv.*

pend·ing (pĕn'dĭng) *adj.* **1.** Not yet decided or settled. **2.** Impending. —*prep.* **1.** While in process of; during. **2.** While awaiting; until. [< Fr. *pendant,* during.]

pen·du·lar (pĕn'jə-lər, pĕnd'yə-) *adj.* Swinging back and forth like a pendulum.

pen·du·lous (pĕn'jə-ləs, pĕnd'yə-) *adj.* Hanging loosely; sagging. [< Lat. *pendēre,* to hang.]

pen·du·lum (pĕn'jə-ləm, pĕnd'yə-) *n.* A body suspended from a fixed support so that it swings freely back and forth under the influence of gravity. [< Lat. *pendēre,* to hang.]

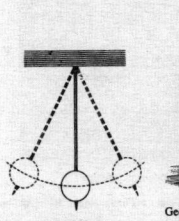

pendulum

George Miksch Sutton
penguin

pe·ne·plain (pē'nə-plān') *n.* Also **pe·ne·plane.** A large, nearly flat eroded land surface. [Lat. *pene,* almost + PLAIN.]

pe·nes (pē'nēz') *n.* A pl. of **penis.**

pen·e·trate (pĕn'ĭ-trāt') *v.* **-trat·ed, -trat·ing. 1.** To enter into; pierce. **2.** To enter into and permeate. **3.** To grasp the inner significance of; understand. **4.** To see through. **5.** To affect deeply. [Lat. *penetrāre.*] —**pen'e·tra·ble** *adj.* —**pen'e·tra'tion** *n.*

pen·e·trat·ing (pĕn'ĭ-trā'tĭng) *adj.* **1.** Piercing; sharp: *a penetrating chill.* **2.** Keenly perceptive; discerning: *a penetrating mind.* —**pen'e·trat'ing·ly** *adv.*

pen·guin (pĕn'gwĭn) *n.* A flightless saltwater bird of cool regions of the Southern Hemisphere, with flipperlike wings and webbed feet. [Poss. < Welsh *pen gwyn,* white head.]

pen·i·cil·lin (pĕn'ĭ-sĭl'ĭn) *n.* Any of several antibiotic compounds obtained from certain molds or produced synthetically and used to prevent or treat a variety of diseases and infections. [< Lat. *penicillus,* brush.]

pen·in·su·la (pə-nĭn'sə-lə, -nĭns'yə-) *n.* A long projection of land into water. [Lat.] —**pen·in'su·lar** *adj.*

pe·nis (pē'nĭs) *n., pl.* **-nis·es** or **-nes** (-nēz'). The male organ of copulation and urination. [Lat.]

pen·i·tent (pĕn'ĭ-tənt) *adj.* Feeling or expressing sorrow for misdeeds or sins; repentant. —*n.* One who is penitent. [< Lat. *paenitēre,* to repent.] —**pen'i·tence** *n.* —**pen'i·ten'tial** (-tĕn'shəl) *adj.* —**pen'i·tent·ly** *adv.*

pen·i·ten·tia·ry (pĕn'ĭ-tĕn'shə-rē) *n., pl.* **-ries.** A prison for those convicted of major crimes. —*adj.* Of, pertaining to, or incurring imprisonment in a penitentiary. [< Lat. *paenitens,* penitent.]

pen·knife (pĕn'nīf') *n.* A small pocketknife.

pen·man (pĕn'mən) *n.* **1.** A copyist; scribe. **2.** An expert in penmanship. **3.** An author; writer.

pen·man·ship (pĕn'mən-shĭp') *n.* The art, skill, or style of handwriting. [Finn.]

pen name *n.* Also **pen-name** (pĕn'nām'). A literary pseudonym.

pen·nant (pĕn'ənt) *n.* **1.** A long, tapering flag used on ships for signaling or for identification. **2.** A flag similar to a pennon. **3.** A flag that serves as the emblem of a championship. [Blend of PENDANT and PENNON.]

pen·ni (pĕn'ē) *n., pl.* **-nis** or **pen·ni·a** (pĕn'ē-ə). See table at **currency.** [Finn.]

pen·ni·less (pĕn'ĭ-lĭs) *adj.* Entirely without money.

pen·non (pĕn'ən) *n.* A long, narrow banner borne on a lance. [< Lat. *penna,* wing.]

Penn·syl·va·nia Dutch (pĕn'səl-vān'yə, -vā'nē-ə) *n.* **1.** The descendants of German and Swiss immigrants who settled in Pennsylvania in the 17th and 18th cent. **2.** The dialect of High German spoken by the Pennsylvania Dutch.

Penn·syl·va·nian (pĕn'səl-vān'yən, -vā'nē-ən) *adj.* Of or belonging to the geologic time, system of rocks, or sedimentary deposits of the 6th period of the Paleozoic era. —*n.* The Pennsylvanian period.

pen·ny (pĕn'ē) *n., pl.* **-nies** or *chiefly Brit.* **pence** (pĕns). **1.** See table at **currency. 2.** Any of various coins of small denomination. **3.** A sum of money. [< OE *penig,* an English coin.]

penny pincher *n. Informal.* One who is very stingy with money; miser. —**pen'ny-pinch'ing** *adj. & n.*

pen·ny·roy·al (pĕn'ē-roi'əl) *n.* An aromatic plant of the mint family with hairy leaves and small bluish flowers.

pen·ny·weight (pĕn'ē-wāt') *n.* A unit of troy weight equal to 24 grains, 1/20 of a troy ounce, or approx. 1.555 grams.

pen·ny·wise (pĕn'ē-wīz') *adj.* Careful or wise in dealing only with small sums of money or small matters.

Pe·nob·scot (pə-nŏb'skət, -skŏt') *n., pl.* **-scot** or **-scots. 1. a.** A tribe of Indians formerly inhabiting central Maine. **b.** A member of this tribe. **2.** The Algonquian language of the Penobscot. —**Pe·nob'scot** *adj.*

pe·nol·o·gy (pē-nŏl'ə-jē) *n.* The theory and practice of prison management and criminal rehabilitation. [Lat. *poinē,* penalty + -LOGY.] —**pe'no·log'i·cal** (-lŏj'ĭ-kəl) *adj.* —**pe·nol'o·gist** *n.*

pen·sion (pĕn'shən) *n.* A sum of money paid regularly, esp. as a retirement benefit. —*v.* To grant a pension to. [< Lat. *pensio,* payment.]

pen·sion·er (pĕn'shə-nər) *n.* One who receives a pension.

pen·sive (pĕn'sĭv) *adj.* Wistfully or sadly thoughtful; reflective. [< Lat. *pensare,* freq. of *pendere,* to weigh.] —**pen'sive·ly** *adv.* —**pen'sive·ness** *n.*

pent (pĕnt) *v.* A *p.t.* & *p.p.* of **pen².** —*adj.* Penned or shut up; closely confined.

penta– or **pent–** *pref.* Five: *pentameter.* [Gk. < *pente,* five.]

pen·ta·gon (pĕn′tə-gŏn′) *n.* A polygon with five sides and five interior angles. **—pen·tag′o·nal** (-tăg′ə-nəl) *adj.*

pen·tam·e·ter (pĕn-tăm′ĭ-tər) *n.* A line of verse composed of five metrical feet.

Pen·te·cost (pĕn′tĭ-kôst′, -kŏst′) *n.* A Christian festival commemorating the descent of the Holy Ghost upon the disciples; Whitsunday. [< Gk. *pentēkostē (hēmera),* 50th (day).] **—Pen′te·cos′tal** *adj.*

pent·house (pĕnt′hous′) *n.* **1.** An apartment or dwelling on the roof of a building. **2.** A shed or sloping roof attached to the side of a building or wall. [< Med. Lat. *appendicum,* appendage.]

pe·nul·ti·mate (pĭ-nŭl′tə-mĭt) *adj.* Next to last. [< Lat. *penultimus.*] **—pe·nul′ti·mate** *n.*

pe·nu·ri·ous (pĭ-nŏŏr′ē-əs, -nyŏŏr′-) *adj.* **1.** Miserly; stingy. **2.** Extremely poor; needy.

pen·u·ry (pĕn′yə-rē) *n.* Extreme poverty; destitution. [< Lat. *penuria.*]

Pe·nu·ti·an (pə-nŏŏ′tē-ən, -shən) *n.* A stock of Indian languages spoken in Pacific coastal areas from California to British Columbia.

pe·on (pē′ŏn′) *n.* **1.** An unskilled laborer or farm worker in Latin America. **2.** One bound in servitude to a creditor. [< Med. Lat. *pedo,* foot soldier.] **—pe′on·age** (-ə-nĭj) *n.*

pe·o·ny (pē′ə-nē) *n., pl.* **-nies.** A garden plant with large pink, red, or white flowers. [< Gk. *paiōnia.*]

peo·ple (pē′pəl) *n., pl.* **-ple. 1.** Human beings. **2.** A body of persons living in the same country under one national government: *the American people.* **3.** *pl.* **-ples.** A group sharing a common religion, culture, language, or inherited condition of life. **4. the people. a.** The mass of ordinary persons; populace. **b.** Citizens, as of a nation; electorate. **5.** Persons subordinate or loyal to a superior. **—v. -pled, -pling.** To furnish with a population; populate. [< Lat. *populus.*]

Usage: The possessive form of *people* is *people's (the people's rights)* except when *people* is used in the plural to denote two or more groups considered to be political or cultural entities: *the Slavic peoples' history.*

pep (pĕp) *Informal.* **—n.** Energy; vim. **—v. pepped, pep·ping.** To impart pep to; invigorate. [< PEPPER.] **—pep′py** *adj.*

pep·per (pĕp′ər) *n.* **1. a.** The small, pungent berry of a tropical Asian vine, used as a condiment. **b.** The vine itself. **2. a.** The podlike or bell-shaped fruit of several bushy plants related to the pepper, used as a vegetable or condiment. **b.** A plant bearing such fruit. **—v. 1.** To season or sprinkle with or as if with pepper. **2.** To sprinkle or shower with missiles. [< Skt. *pippali,* berry.]

pep·per·corn (pĕp′ər-kôrn′) *n.* A dried berry of the pepper vine.

pep·per·mint (pĕp′ər-mĭnt′) *n.* **1.** An aromatic plant with downy leaves that yield a pungent oil. **2.** A candy flavored with the oil of the peppermint plant.

pep·per·y (pĕp′ə-rē) *adj.* **1.** Of, like, or containing pepper; pungent. **2.** Hot-tempered; feisty. **3.** Vivid and fiery: *a peppery speech.*

pep·sin (pĕp′sĭn) *n.* **1.** A digestive enzyme in gastric juice that catalyzes the breakdown of protein to peptides. **2.** A substance containing pepsin and used as a digestive aid. [< Gk. *pepsis,* digestion.]

pep·tic (pĕp′tĭk) *adj.* **1.** Of, relating to, or assisting digestion. **2.** Induced by or associated with the action of digestive secretions: *a peptic ulcer.* [< Gk. *peptein,* to digest.]

Pe·quot (pē′kwŏt′) *n., pl.* **-quot** or **-quots. 1. a.** A tribe of Indians formerly living in southern New England. **b.** A member of this tribe. **2.** The Algonquian language of the Pequot. **—pe′quot** *adj.*

per (pûr) *prep.* **1.** By means of. **2.** To, for, or by each. **3.** According to. [Lat.]

per– *pref.* Containing a large or the largest possible proportion of an element: *peroxide.* [< Lat. *per,* through.]

per·am·bu·late (pə-răm′byə-lāt′) *v.* **-lat·ed, -lat·ing.** To walk about; stroll. [Lat. *perambulari.*] **—per·am′bu·la′tion** *n.*

per·am·bu·la·tor (pə-răm′byə-lā′tər) *n. Chiefly Brit.* A baby carriage.

perambulator

per an·num (pər ăn′əm) *adv.* By the year; annually. [Lat.]

per·cale (pər-kāl′) *n.* A close-woven cotton cloth used esp. to make sheets. [< Pers. *pargālah.*]

per cap·i·ta (pər kăp′ĭ-tə) *adv. & adj.* Per person. [Med. Lat., by heads.]

per·ceive (pər-sēv′) *v.* **-ceived, -ceiv·ing. 1.** To become aware of through the senses. **2.** To observe; detect. **3.** To achieve understanding of. [< Lat. *percipere.*] **—per·ceiv′a·ble** *adj.* **—per·ceiv′a·bly** *adv.*

per cent. Also **per·cent** (pər-sĕnt′). **—adv.** For or out of each hundred. **—n., pl. per cent** or **percent. 1.** One part in a hundred. **2.** A percentage. [Lat. *per centum,* by the hundred.]

Usage: *Per cent* is generally used with a specific figure. The number of its verb is governed by the number of the following noun, whether expressed or understood.

per·cent·age (pər-sĕn′tĭj) *n.* **1.** A fraction or ratio with 100 fixed and understood as the denominator. **2.** A proportion or share in relation to a whole. **3.** Odds; probability. **4.** *Informal.* Advantage; gain.

per·cen·tile (pər-sĕn′tīl′) *n.* A number that divides the range of a set of data so that a given percentage lies below this number.

per·cep·ti·ble (pər-sĕp′tə-bəl) *adj.* Capable of being perceived. **—per·cep′ti·bil′i·ty** *n.* **—per·cep′ti·bly** *adv.*

per·cep·tion (pər-sĕp′shən) *n.* **1.** The process, act, or result of perceiving. **2.** The ability to

perceive; insight or understanding. [< Lat. *perceptus,* p.p. of *percipere,* to perceive.]

per·cep·tive (pər-sĕp′tĭv) *adj.* **1.** Of or pertaining to perception. **2. a.** Having the ability to perceive. **b.** Marked by discernment. **—per·cep′tive·ly** *adv.*

per·cep·tu·al (pər-sĕp′chōō-əl) *adj.* Of, based on, or involving perception. **—per·cep′tu·al·ly** *adv.*

perch[1] (pûrch) *n.* **1.** A rod or branch serving as a roost for a bird. **2.** A place for resting or sitting. *—v.* To alight or rest on a perch; roost. [< Lat. *pertica.*]

perch[2] (pûrch) *n., pl.* **perch** or **-es. 1.** A freshwater food fish. **2.** Any of various fishes related or similar to the perch. [< Gk. *perkē.*]

per·chance (pər-chăns′) *adv.* Perhaps.

per·cip·i·ent (pər-sĭp′ē-ənt) *adj.* Marked by or capable of perception. [< Lat. *percipere,* to perceive.] **—per·cip′i·ence** *n.*

per·co·late (pûr′kə-lāt′) *v.* **-lat·ed, -lat·ing. 1.** To pass or cause to pass through a porous substance. **2.** To make (coffee) in a percolator. [Lat. *percolare.*] **—per′co·la′tion** *n.*

per·co·la·tor (pûr′kə-lā′tər) *n.* A coffeepot in which boiling water is forced repeatedly up through a center tube to filter through ground coffee.

per·cus·sion (pər-kŭsh′ən) *n.* **1. a.** The striking together of two bodies, esp. when noise is produced. **b.** The sound, vibration, or shock caused by percussion. **2.** The act of detonating a cap in a firearm. **3. a.** A musical instrument in which sound is produced by striking, as a drum. **b.** Percussion instruments collectively. [< Lat. *percussus,* p.p. of *percutere,* to strike hard.]

per di·em (pər dē′əm) *adv.* Per day. *—n.* An allowance for daily expenses. [Lat.]

per·di·tion (pər-dĭsh′ən) *n.* **1.** Eternal damnation. **2.** Hell. [< Lat. *perdere,* to lose.]

per·e·gri·nate (pĕr′ə-grə-nāt′) *v.* **-nat·ed, -nat·ing.** To travel from place to place. [Lat. *peregrinari.*] **—per′e·gri·na′tion** *n.* **—per′e·gri·na′tor** *n.*

per·emp·to·ry (pə-rĕmp′tə-rē) *adj.* **1.** *Law.* Precluding further debate or action. **2.** Not admitting contradiction or refusal; imperative. **3.** Expressing a command; urgent. **4.** Dictatorial; imperious. [LLat. *peremptorius.*] **—per·emp′to·ri·ly** *adv.* **—per·emp′to·ri·ness** *n.*

per·en·ni·al (pə-rĕn′ē-əl) *adj.* **1.** Lasting for a year or many years. **2. a.** Lasting indefinitely; perpetual. **b.** Continually recurring. *—n.* A plant that continues to live for several or many years. [< Lat. *perennis.*] **—per·en′ni·al·ly** *adv.*

per·fect (pûr′fĭkt) *adj.* **1.** Lacking nothing essential. **2.** Being without defect; flawless. **3.** Accurate; exact. **4.** Complete; utter: *a perfect fool.* **5.** *Gram.* Of or being a verb form expressing action completed prior to a fixed point of reference in time. *—n. Gram.* **1.** The perfect tense. **2.** A verb or verb form in this tense. *—v.* (pər-fĕkt′). To make perfect. [< Lat. *perficere,* to finish.] **—per′fect·ly** *adv.* **—per′fect·ness** *n.*

Usage: Perfect traditionally has been considered an absolute term and therefore not subject to comparison with *more, less,* and other modifiers of degree. The comparative form nonetheless must be regarded as entirely correct, especially when *perfect* is used to mean "ideal for the purpose," as in *A more perfect solution could not be found.*

per·fect·i·ble (pər-fĕk′tə-bəl) *adj.* Capable of becoming or being made perfect. **—per·fect′i·bil′i·ty** *n.*

per·fec·tion (pər-fĕk′shən) *n.* **1.** The quality or condition of being perfect. **2.** The process or act of perfecting. **3.** One that is considered perfect.

per·fec·tion·ism (pər-fĕk′shə-nĭz′əm) *n.* A tendency to set extremely high standards and to be dissatisfied with anything less. **—per·fec′tion·ist** *n.*

per·fi·dy (pûr′fĭ-dē) *n., pl.* **-dies.** Deliberate breach of faith; treachery. [< Lat. *perfidus,* treacherous.] **—per·fid′i·ous** (pər-fĭd′ē-əs) *adj.* **—per·fid′i·ous·ly** *adv.*

per·fo·rate (pûr′fə-rāt′) *v.* **-rat·ed, -rat·ing. 1.** To pierce, punch, or bore a hole or holes in. **2.** To pierce or stamp with rows of holes to allow easy separation. [Lat. *perforare.*] **—per′fo·ra′tion** *n.*

per·force (pər-fôrs′, -fōrs′) *adv.* By necessity; necessarily.

per·form (pər-fôrm′) *v.* **1.** To carry through to completion; accomplish. **2.** To carry out; fulfill. **3.** To give a public presentation, as of a dramatic or musical work. [< OFr. *parfornir.*] **—per·form′er** *n.*

per·form·ance (pər-fôr′məns) *n.* **1.** The act or manner of performing. **2.** A presentation before an audience. **3.** Something performed; accomplishment or deed.

per·fume (pûr′fyōōm′, pər-fyōōm′) *n.* **1.** A fragrant liquid, as one distilled from flowers or prepared by synthetic means. **2.** A pleasing scent or odor. *—v.* (pər-fyōōm′) **-fumed, -fum·ing.** To fill with fragrance. [< OItal. *parfumare,* to fill with smoke.]

per·fum·er·y (pər-fyōō′mə-rē) *n., pl.* **-ies. 1.** Perfumes in general. **2.** An establishment that makes or sells perfumes.

per·func·to·ry (pər-fŭngk′tə-rē) *adj.* Done or acting routinely and with little interest or care. [< Lat. *perfungi,* to get through with.] **—per·func′to·ri·ly** *adv.* **—per·func′to·ri·ness** *n.*

per·go·la (pûr′gə-lə) *n.* An arbor or passageway with a roof of trelliswork. [< Lat. *pergula.*]

per·haps (pər-hăps′) *adv.* Maybe; possibly.

peri- *pref.* **1.** About, around, encircling, or enclosing: *periscope.* **2.** Near: *perihelion.* [< Gk. *peri,* near, around.]

per·i·gee (pĕr′ə-jē) *n.* The point nearest the earth in the orbit of the moon or a satellite. [< Gk. *perigeios,* near the earth.]

per·i·he·lion (pĕr′ə-hēl′yən) *n., pl.* **-lia** (-yə). The point nearest the sun in the orbit of a celestial body such as a planet. [PERI- + *hēlios,* sun.]

per·il (pĕr′əl) *n.* **1.** Danger. **2.** Something that endangers. [< Lat. *periculum.*] **—per′il·ous** *adj.* **—per′il·ous·ly** *adv.*

pe·rim·e·ter (pə-rĭm′ĭ-tər) *n.* **1.** A closed curve bounding a plane area. **2.** The outer boundary of an area.

pe·ri·od (pîr′ē-əd) *n.* **1.** An interval of time characterized by the occurrence of certain conditions or events. **2.** A unit of geologic time longer than an epoch and shorter than an era. **3.** An interval regarded as a developmental phase; stage. **4.** Any of various arbitrary temporal units, as of an academic day. **5.** An instance of menstruation. **6.** A point at which something is ended; completion. **7. a.** The full pause at the end of a spoken sentence. **b.** A punctuation mark (.) indicating a full stop, placed esp. at the end of declarative sentences. —*adj.* Of, belonging to, or representing a certain historical age or time: *a period piece.* [< Gk. *periodos,* circuit.]

pe·ri·od·ic (pîr'ē-ŏd'ĭk) *adj.* 1. Having periods or repeated cycles. 2. Happening or appearing at regular intervals. 3. Taking place now and then; intermittent. —**pe'ri·od'i·cal·ly** *adv.*

pe·ri·od·i·cal (pîr'ē-ŏd'ĭ-kəl) *adj.* 1. Periodic. 2. a. Published at regular intervals of more than one day. b. Of or relating to a publication issued at such intervals. —*n.* A periodical publication.

periodic table *n. Chem.* A tabular arrangement of the elements according to their atomic numbers.

per·i·o·don·tal (pĕr'ē-ō-dŏn'tl) *adj.* Of or designating tissue and structures surrounding and supporting the teeth. [< PERI- + Gk. *odous,* tooth.] —**per'i·o·don'tal·ly** *adv.* —**per'i·o·don'tist** *n.*

per·i·pa·tet·ic (pĕr'ə-pə-tĕt'ĭk) *adj.* 1. Walking about from place to place. 2. Carried on while walking from place to place. [< Gk. *peripatein,* to walk about.]

pe·riph·er·al (pə-rĭf'ər-əl) *adj.* 1. Of or on the periphery. 2. Relatively unimportant. —**pe·riph'er·al·ly** *adv.*

pe·riph·er·y (pə-rĭf'ə-rē) *n., pl.* **-ies.** 1. The outermost region within a precise boundary. 2. The region immediately beyond a precise boundary. 3. A zone constituting an imprecise boundary. 4. A perimeter (sense 1). [< Gk. *peripherēs,* carrying around.]

pe·riph·ra·sis (pə-rĭf'rə-sĭs) *n., pl.* **-ses** (-sēz'). Circumlocution. [< Gk.]

per·i·scope (pĕr'ĭ-skōp') *n.* An optical instrument in which mirrors or prisms allow observation of objects not in a direct line of sight. —**per'i·scop'ic** (-skŏp'ĭk) or **per'i·scop'i·cal** *adj.*

per·ish (pĕr'ĭsh) *v.* 1. To die, esp. in a violent or untimely manner. 2. To disappear gradually. [< Lat. *perire.*]

per·ish·a·ble (pĕr'ĭ-shə-bəl) *adj.* Liable to decay or spoil easily. —*n.* Often **perishables.** Things, such as foods, that spoil or decay easily. —**per'ish·a·bil'i·ty** or **per'ish·a·ble·ness** *n.* —**per'ish·a·bly** *adv.*

per·i·stal·sis (pĕr'ĭ-stôl'sĭs, -stăl'-) *n., pl.* **-ses** (-sēz'). Wavelike muscular contractions that propel contained matter along tubular organs, as in the alimentary canal. [< Gk. *peristellein,* to wrap around.] —**per'i·stal'tic** (-stôl'tĭk, -stăl'-) *adj.* —**per'i·stal'ti·cal·ly** *adv.*

per·i·style (pĕr'ĭ-stīl') *n.* A series of columns surrounding a building or enclosing a court. [< Gk. *peristulon.*]

per·i·to·ne·um (pĕr'ĭ-tə-nē'əm) *n., pl.* **-ne·a** (-nē'ə). Also **per·i·to·nae·um.** The membrane lining the walls of the abdominal cavity. [< Gk. *peritonaios,* stretched across.] —**per'i·to·ne'al** *adj.*

per·i·to·ni·tis (pĕr'ĭ-tə-nī'tĭs) *n.* Inflammation of the peritoneum.

per·i·wig (pĕr'ĭ-wĭg') *n.* A wig. [< OFr. *perruque.*]

per·i·win·kle¹ (pĕr'ĭ-wĭng'kəl) *n.* A small edible marine snail with a cone-shaped shell. [Prob. < OE *pinewincle.*]

per·i·win·kle² (pĕr'ĭ-wĭng'kəl) *n.* A trailing blue-flowered myrtle. [< Lat. *pervinca.*]

per·jure (pûr'jər) *v.* **-jured, -juring.** To testify falsely under oath. [< Lat. *perjurare.*] —**per'jur·er** *n.* —**per'ju·ry** *n.*

perk¹ (pûrk) *v.* To raise, as the head, smartly and quickly. —*phrasal verb.* **perk up.** 1. To regain or cause to regain one's good spirits or liveliness. 2. To add to the appearance of; spruce up. [< ONFr. *perquer,* to perch.] —**perk'i·ness** *n.* —**perk'y** *adj.*

perk² (pûrk) *n. Informal.* Often **perks.** A perquisite.

perm (pûrm) *n. Informal.* A permanent.

per·ma·frost (pûr'mə-frôst', -frŏst') *n.* Permanently frozen subsoil in frigid regions. [PERMA(NENT) + FROST.]

per·ma·nent (pûr'mə-nənt) *adj.* Fixed and lasting. —*n.* A long-lasting hair setting. [< Lat. *permanēre,* to endure.] —**per'ma·nence** or **per'ma·nen·cy** *n.* —**per'ma·nent·ly** *adv.*

permanent press *adj.* Of, pertaining to, or made from a fabric that is chemically treated so it will dry without wrinkles.

per·me·a·ble (pûr'mē-ə-bəl) *adj.* Capable of being permeated. —**per'me·a·bil'i·ty** *n.* —**per'me·a·bly** *adv.*

per·me·ate (pûr'mē-āt') *v.* **-at·ed, -at·ing.** 1. To spread or flow throughout; pervade. 2. To pass through openings or small gaps of. [Lat. *permeare.*] —**per'me·a'tion** *n.* —**per'me·a'tive** *adj.*

Per·mi·an (pûr'mē-ən) *adj.* Of or belonging to the geologic time, system of rocks, or sedimentary deposits of the 7th and last period of the Paleozoic era. —*n.* The Permian period. [< *Perm,* a region in the USSR.]

per·mis·si·ble (pər-mĭs'ə-bəl) *adj.* Allowable. —**per·mis'si·bil'i·ty** or **per·mis'si·ble·ness** *n.* —**per·mis'si·bly** *adv.*

per·mis·sion (pər-mĭsh'ən) *n.* Consent, esp. formal consent. [< Lat. *permittere,* to permit.]

per·mis·sive (pər-mĭs'ĭv) *adj.* 1. Granting permission. 2. Lenient; tolerant. —**per·mis'sive·ly** *adv.* —**per·mis'sive·ness** *n.*

per·mit (pər-mĭt') *v.* **-mit·ted, -mit·ting.** 1. To allow; consent to. 2. To afford opportunity to. —*n.* (pûr'mĭt, pər-mĭt'). A document granting permission. [Lat. *permittere.*] —**per·mit'ter** *n.*

per·mu·ta·tion (pûr'myōō-tā'shən) *n.* 1. A transformation. 2. The act of altering a given set of objects in a group. 3. *Math.* An ordered arrangement of all or some of the elements of a set. [< Lat. *permutare,* to thoroughly change.] —**per'mu·ta'tion·al** *adj.*

per·ni·cious (pər-nĭsh'əs) *adj.* Destructive; deadly. [< Lat. *pernicies,* destruction.] —**per·ni'cious·ly** *adv.* —**per·ni'cious·ness** *n.*

pernicious anemia *n.* A severe anemia associated with failure to absorb vitamin B_{12} and characterized by the presence of abnormally large red blood cells, gastrointestinal disturbances, and lesions of the spinal cord.

per·o·rate (pĕr'ə-rāt') *v.* **-rat·ed, -rat·ing.** 1. To conclude a speech, esp. with a formal summing up. 2. To speak at great length; declaim. [Lat. *perorare,* to harangue at length.] —**per'o·ra'tion** (pĕr'ə-rā'shən) *n.*

per·ox·ide (pə-rŏk'sīd') *n. Chem.* 1. Hydrogen peroxide. 2. A compound containing oxygen that yields hydrogen peroxide with an acid, such as sodium peroxide. —v. -id-ed, -id-ing. To treat or bleach with peroxide.

per·pen·dic·u·lar (pûr′pən-dĭk′yə-lər) *adj.* 1. Intersecting at or forming right angles. 2. At right angles to the horizontal; vertical. [< Lat. *perpendiculum*, plumb line.] —per·pen·dic′u·lar *n.* —per·pen·dic′u·lar′i·ty (-lăr′ĭ-tē) *n.* —per′pen·dic′u·lar·ly *adv.*

per·pe·trate (pûr′pĭ-trāt′) *v.* -trat-ed, -trat-ing. 1. To be guilty of; commit. 2. To carry out; perform. [Lat. *perpetrare*, to accomplish.] —per′pe·tra′tion *n.* —per′pe·tra′tor *n.*

per·pet·u·al (pər-pĕch′ōō-əl) *adj.* 1. Lasting forever. 2. Lasting for an indefinitely long time. 3. Ceaselessly repeated. [< Lat. *perpetuus*, continuous.] —per·pet′u·al·ly *adv.* —per·pet′u·al·ness *n.*

per·pet·u·ate (pər-pĕch′ōō-āt′) *v.* -at-ed, -at-ing. 1. To make perpetual. 2. To prolong the existence of. —per·pet′u·a′tion *n.* —per·pet′u·a′tor *n.*

per·pe·tu·i·ty (pûr′pĭ-tōō′ĭ-tē, -tyōō′-) *n.,* pl. -ties. The quality or condition of being perpetual.

per·plex (pər-plĕks′) *v.* To confuse or puzzle; bewilder. [< Lat. *perplexus*, perplexed.] —per·plex′i·ty *n.*

per·qui·site (pûr′kwĭ-zĭt) *n.* 1. A payment or profit received in addition to a regular wage or salary. 2. A tip; gratuity. 3. Something claimed as an exclusive right. [< Lat. *perquisitus*, p.p. of *perquirere*, to search for.]

per se (pər sā′, sē′) *adv.* In or by itself; as such. [Lat.]

per·se·cute (pûr′sĭ-kyōōt′) *v.* -cut-ed, -cut-ing. 1. To oppress or harass with ill-treatment. 2. To annoy persistently. [< Lat. *persecutus*, p.p. of *persequi*, to pursue.] —per′se·cu′tion *n.* —per′se·cu′tor *n.*

Per·seph·o·ne (pər-sĕf′ə-nē) *n. Gk. Myth.* The queen of the underworld.

Persephone

per·se·vere (pûr′sə-vîr′) *v.* -vered, -ver-ing. To persist in or remain constant to a purpose, idea, or task in spite of obstacles. [< Lat. *perseverare*.] —per′se·ver′ance *n.* —per′se·ver′ing·ly *adv.*

Per·sian (pûr′zhən) *n.* 1. A native or inhabitant of ancient Persia or modern Iran. 2. a. Any of the Iranian languages of the Persians in use during various historical periods. b. The modern Iranian language of Iran and western Afghanistan. —Per′sian *adj.*

Persian cat *n.* A domestic cat with long silky fur.

Persian lamb *n.* The glossy, tightly curled fur obtained from a young lamb of the karakul sheep.

per·si·flage (pûr′sə-fläzh′) *n.* Light, jesting or teasing talk. [Fr. *persifler*, to banter.]

per·sim·mon (pər-sĭm′ən) *n.* 1. A tree with hard wood and orange-red, edible fruit.

2. The fruit of a persimmon tree. [Of Algonquian orig.]

per·sist (pər-sĭst′) *v.* 1. To hold firmly and steadfastly to a purpose or undertaking despite obstacles. 2. To continue in existence. [Lat. *persistere*.] —per·sist′ence *n.* —per·sist′ent *adj.* —per·sist′ent·ly *adv.*

per·snick·e·ty (pər-snĭk′ĭ-tē) *adj.* Fastidious. [Orig. unknown.]

per·son (pûr′sən) *n.* 1. A human being. 2. The living body of a human being. 3. The personality of a human being; self. 4. *Gram.* Any of three groups of pronouns with corresponding verb inflections that distinguish between the speaker (first person), the individual addressed (second person), and the individual or thing spoken of (third person). [< Lat. *persona*.]

per·son·a·ble (pûr′sə-nə-bəl) *adj.* Pleasing in appearance or personality. —per′son·a·ble·ness *n.*

per·son·age (pûr′sə-nĭj) *n.* A person of distinction.

per·son·al (pûr′sə-nəl) *adj.* 1. Of a particular person; private. 2. Done in person: *a personal appearance.* 3. Pertaining to the body of a human being. 4. Pertaining to an individual, esp. in an offensive way: *a highly personal remark.* 5. *Law.* Pertaining to a person's movable property. 6. Indicating grammatical person. —n. A personal item or notice in a newspaper. —per′son·al·ly *adv.*

personal effects *pl.n.* Privately owned items, as keys, a wallet, or a watch, regularly worn or carried on the person.

per·son·al·i·ty (pûr′sə-năl′ĭ-tē) *n.,* pl. -ties. 1. The quality or condition of being a person. 2. The totality of distinctive traits of an individual. 3. The personal traits that make one socially appealing. 4. *Informal.* A celebrity. 5. Often **personalities.** An offensive personal remark: *Let's not engage in personalities.*
Usage: Personality, meaning "celebrity," occurs often in speech and journalistic writing. In more formal writing, however, it is considered unacceptable by a majority of the Usage Panel.

per·son·al·ize (pûr′sə-nə-līz′) *v.* -ized, -iz-ing. 1. To personify. 2. To have printed, engraved, or monogrammed with one's name or initials. —per′son·al·i·za′tion *n.*

personal property *n. Law.* Temporary or movable property.

per·so·na non gra·ta (pər-sō′nə nŏn grä′tə, grăt′ə) *adj.* Unacceptable or unwelcome, esp. to a foreign government. [Lat., an unacceptable person.]

per·son·i·fy (pər-sŏn′ə-fī′) *v.* -fied, -fy-ing. 1. To think of or represent (e.g. an inanimate object) as a person. 2. To be the embodiment or perfect example of. —per·son′i·fi·ca′tion (-fī-kā′shən) *n.* —per·son′i·fi′er *n.*

per·son·nel (pûr′sə-nĕl′) *n.* 1. The body of persons employed by or active in an organization. 2. An administrative division of an organization concerned with this body of persons. [Fr.]
Usage: Personnel is a collective noun and never refers to an individual; therefore it is unacceptable when used with a numeral. It is acceptable, however, to use another qualifying word: *A number of armed forces personnel* (not *six armed forces personnel*) *testified.*

per·spec·tive (pər-spĕk′tĭv) *n.* 1. Any of various techniques for representing three-dimensional objects and depth relationships on a two-dimensional surface. **2.** The relationship of aspects of a subject to each other and to a whole: *a perspective of history.* **3.** Point of view. [< Lat. *perspicere,* to inspect.] —**per·spec'tive·ly** *adv.*

per·spi·cac·i·ty (pûr'spĭ-kăs'ĭ-tē) *n.* Acuteness of perception or understanding. [< Lat. *perspicere,* to see through.] —**per·spi·ca'cious** (-kā'shəs) *adj.* —**per·spi·ca'cious·ly** *adv.* —**per·spi·ca'cious·ness** *n.*

per·spic·u·ous (pər-spĭk'yōō-əs) *adj.* Clearly expressed or presented; easy to understand; lucid. [< Lat. *perspicere,* to see through.] —**per·spi·cu'i·ty** (-kyōō'ĭ-tē) *n.* —**per·spic'u·ous·ly** *adv.* —**per·spic'u·ous·ness** *n.*

per·spi·ra·tion (pûr'spə-rā'shən) *n.* **1.** The saline moisture excreted through the pores of the skin by the sweat glands; sweat. **2.** The act or process of perspiring.

per·spire (pər-spīr') *v.* **-spired, -spir·ing.** To excrete perspiration through the pores of the skin. [< Lat. *perspirare,* to breathe through.]

per·suade (pər-swād') *v.* **-suad·ed, -suad·ing.** **1.** To cause (someone) to do something by means of argument, reasoning, or entreaty. **2.** To make (someone) believe something. [Lat. *persuadēre.*] —**per·suad'a·ble** *adj.* —**per·suad'er** *n.* —**per·sua'sive** *adj.* —**per·sua'sive·ly** *adv.* —**per·sua'sive·ness** *n.*

per·sua·sion (pər-swā'zhən) *n.* **1.** The act of persuading or condition of being persuaded. **2.** The ability to persuade. **3.** A body of religious beliefs: *worshipers of various persuasions.*

pert (pûrt) *adj.* **-er, -est.** **1.** Impudently bold. **2.** High-spirited. **3.** Trim and stylish; jaunty. [< Lat. *apertus,* p.p. of *aperire,* to open.] —**pert'ly** *adv.* —**pert'ness** *n.*

per·tain (pər-tān') *v.* **1.** To have reference; relate. **2.** To belong as an adjunct or accessory. **3.** To be suitable. [< Lat. *pertinēre.*]

per·ti·na·cious (pûr'tn-ā'shəs) *adj.* **1.** Holding firmly to a purpose, belief, or opinion. **2.** Stubbornly persistent. [< Lat. *pertinax.*] —**per·ti·na'cious·ly** *adv.* —**per·ti·na'cious·ness** *n.* —**per·ti·nac'i·ty** (-ăs'ĭ-tē) *n.*

per·ti·nent (pûr'tn-ənt) *adj.* Relating to a specific matter; relevant. [< Lat. *pertinēre,* to pertain.] —**per'ti·nence** or **per'ti·nen·cy** *n.* —**per'ti·nent·ly** *adv.*

per·turb (pər-tûrb') *v.* To disturb greatly; make uneasy or anxious. [< Lat. *perturbare.*] —**per·tur·ba'tion** (pûr'tər-bā'shən) *n.*

per·tus·sis (pər-tŭs'ĭs) *n.* Whooping cough. [Lat. *per-* (intensive) + Lat. *tussis,* cough.] —**per·tus'sal** *adj.*

pe·ruse (pə-rōōz') *v.* **-rused, -rus·ing.** To read or examine, esp. with great care. [ME *perusen,* to use up.] —**pe·rus'al** *n.* —**pe·rus'er** *n.*

per·vade (pər-vād') *v.* **-vad·ed, -vad·ing.** To spread throughout; permeate. [Lat. *pervadere.*] —**per·va'sion** (-vā'zhən) *n.* —**per·va'sive** (-vā'sĭv, -zĭv) *adj.* —**per·va'sive·ly** *adv.* —**per·va'sive·ness** *n.*

per·verse (pər-vûrs') *adj.* **1.** Directed away from what is right or good; perverted. **2.** Obstinately persisting in an error or fault. **3.** Cranky; peevish. [< Lat. *perversus,* p.p. of *pervertere,* to pervert.] —**per·verse'ly** *adv.* —**per·verse'ness** or **per·ver'si·ty** *n.*

per·ver·sion (pər-vûr'zhən) *n.* **1.** The act of perverting or condition of being perverted. **2.** A deviant sexual practice.

per·vert (pər-vûrt') *v.* **1.** To corrupt or debase. **2.** To misuse. **3.** To interpret incorrectly. —*n.* (pûr'vûrt'). One who practices sexual perversion. [< Lat. *pervertere.*] —**per·vert'ed** *adj.* —**per·vert'er** *n.*

per·vi·ous (pûr'vē-əs) *adj.* **1.** Open to passage; permeable. **2.** Open to arguments, ideas, or change. [Lat. *pervius.*] —**per·vi·ous·ly** *adv.* —**per·vi·ous·ness** *n.*

pe·se·ta (pə-sā'tə) *n.* See table at **currency.** [Sp., dim. of *peso,* peso.]

pe·se·wa (pā-sā'wä) *n., pl.* **-wa** or **-was.** See table at **currency.** [Native word in Ghana.]

pes·ky (pĕs'kē) *adj.* **-ki·er, -ki·est.** Annoying; troublesome. [Prob. < PEST.] —**pes'ki·ly** *adv.* —**pes'ki·ness** *n.*

pe·so (pā'sō, pĕs'ō) *n., pl.* **-sos.** See table at **currency.** [Sp.]

pes·si·mism (pĕs'ə-mĭz'əm) *n.* **1.** A tendency to take the gloomiest possible view of a situation. **2.** The belief that the evil in the world outweighs the good. [< Lat. *pessimus,* worst.] —**pes'si·mist** *n.* —**pes'si·mis'tic** *adj.* —**pes'si·mis'ti·cal·ly** *adv.*

pest (pĕst) *n.* **1.** An annoying person or thing; nuisance. **2.** An injurious plant or animal. [< Lat. *pestis,* plague.]

pes·ter (pĕs'tər) *v.* To harass with petty annoyances; bother. [Prob. < OFr. *empestrer,* to hobble.] —**pes'ter·er** *n.*

pes·ti·cide (pĕs'tĭ-sīd') *n.* A chemical used to kill pests, esp. insects and rodents. —**pes'ti·cid'al** *adj.*

pes·tif·er·ous (pĕ-stĭf'ər-əs) *adj.* **1.** Producing, causing, or contaminated with an infectious disease. **2.** *Informal.* Bothersome; annoying. —**pes·tif'er·ous·ly** *adv.*

pes·ti·lence (pĕs'tə-ləns) *n.* A fatal epidemic disease, esp. bubonic plague.

pes·ti·lent (pĕs'tə-lənt) *adj.* Also **pes·ti·len·tial** (pĕs'tə-lĕn'shəl). **1.** Tending to cause death. **2.** Likely to cause an epidemic disease. [< Lat. *pestis,* plague.]

pes·tle (pĕs'əl, pĕs'təl) *n.* A club-shaped hand tool for grinding or mashing substances in a mortar. [< Lat. *pistillum.*]

pet[1] (pĕt) *n.* **1.** An animal kept for amusement or companionship. **2.** An object of the affections. **3.** A favorite: *teacher's pet.* —*adj.* **1.** Kept as a pet. **2.** Especially cherished or indulged. —*v.* **pet·ted, pet·ting.** **1.** To stroke or caress gently. **2.** To engage in amorous fondling and caressing. [Orig. unknown.] —**pet'ter** *n.*

pet[2] (pĕt) *n.* A fit of bad temper or pique. [Orig. unknown.]

pet·al (pĕt'l) *n.* A separate segment of a flower corolla. [< Gk. *petalon,* leaf.] —**pet'aled** or **pet'alled** *adj.*

pe·tard (pə-tärd') *n.* A small bell-shaped bomb formerly used to blow apart a gate or wall. —*idiom.* **hoist with (or by) (one's) own petard.** Harmed by one's own cleverness. [< Lat. *pedere,* to break wind.]

pet·cock (pĕt'kŏk') *n.* A small valve used to drain pipes. [Perh. PET(TY) + COCK[1].]

pe·ter (pē'tər) *v.* **1.** To come to an end slowly;

diminish. **2.** To become exhausted. [Orig. unknown.]

Pe·ter (pē′tər) n. See table at **Bible**.

Peter Principle n. The notion that a corporate employee will advance to his or her highest level of incompetence and will remain there.

pet·i·ole (pĕt′ē-ōl′) n. *Bot.* The stalk by which a leaf is attached to a stem. [< LLat. *petiolus,* fruit stalk.]

pet·it (pĕt′ē) adj. Also **pet·ty.** *Law.* Lesser; minor: *petit larceny.* [< OFr., small.]

pe·tite (pə-tēt′) adj. Small, slender, and trim. [Fr.]

pet·it four (pĕt′ē fôr′, fōr′, fŏŏr′, pə-tē′) n., pl. **pet·its fours** or **pet·it fours** (pĕt′ē fôrz′, fōrz′, fŏŏrz′, pə-tē′) n. A small, rich, frosted tea cake. [Fr.]

pe·ti·tion (pə-tĭsh′ən) n. **1.** A solemn request; an entreaty. **2.** A formal document containing such a request. —v. **1.** To address a petition to. **2.** To request formally. **3.** To make an entreaty: *petition for retrial.* [< Lat. *petere,* to request.] —**pe·ti′tion·ar′y** (pə-tĭsh′ə-nĕr′ē) adj. —**pe·ti′tion·er** n.

pet·it jury (pĕt′ē) n. Also **pet·ty jury.** A jury of 12 persons that sits at civil and criminal trials.

pet·it mal (pĕt′ē mäl′, măl′) n. A mild form of epilepsy characterized by frequent but transient lapses of consciousness and only rare spasms or falling. [Fr.]

pet·it point (pĕt′ē point′) n. Needlepoint done with a small stitch. [Fr.]

pet·rel (pĕt′rəl) n. Any of various small, blackish sea birds. [Orig. unknown.]

pet·ri·fy (pĕt′rə-fī′) v. **-fied, -fy·ing. 1.** To convert (wood or other organic matter) into a stony replica by structural impregnation with dissolved minerals. **2.** To cause to become stonelike; deaden. **3.** To stun or paralyze with terror. [OFr. *petrifier.*] —**pet′ri·fac′tion** (pĕt′rə-făk′shən) or **pet·ri·fi·ca·tion** (-fĭ-kā′shən) n.

petro- or **petri-** or **petr-** pref. **1.** Rock; stone: *petrology.* **2.** Petroleum: *petrochemical.* [< Gk. *petra,* rock, and *petros,* stone.]

pet·ro·chem·i·cal (pĕt′rō-kĕm′ĭ-kəl) n. A chemical derived from petroleum or natural gas. —**pet′ro·chem′i·cal** adj.

pet·ro·dol·lar (pĕt′rō-dŏl′ər) n. A unit of hard currency, as a dollar, held by oil-exporting countries.

pe·trog·ra·phy (pə-trŏg′rə-fē) n. The description and classification of rocks. —**pe·trog′ra·pher** n. —**pet′ro·graph′ic** (pĕt′rə-grăf′ĭk) or **pet′ro·graph′i·cal** —**pet′ro·graph′i·cal·ly** adv.

pet·rol (pĕt′rəl) n. *Chiefly Brit.* Gasoline. [Fr. *(essence de) pétrole,* (essence of) petroleum.]

pet·ro·la·tum (pĕt′rə-lā′təm) n. A colorless-to-amber gelatinous semisolid, obtained from petroleum and used in lubricants and medicinal ointments. [< Med. Lat. *petroleum,* petroleum.]

pe·tro·le·um (pə-trō′lē-əm) n. A natural, yellow-low-to-black, thick, flammable liquid hydrocarbon mixture found principally beneath the earth's surface and processed for fractions including natural gas, gasoline, naphtha, kerosene, fuel and lubricating oils, paraffin wax, and asphalt. [Med. Lat.]

petroleum jelly n. Petrolatum.

pe·trol·o·gy (pə-trŏl′ə-jē) n. The study of the origin, composition, structure, and alteration of rocks. —**pet′ro·log′ic** (pĕt′rə-lŏj′ĭk) or **pet′-**

ro·log′i·cal adj. —**pet′ro·log′i·cal·ly** adv. —**pe·trol′o·gist** n.

pet·ro·pol·i·tics (pĕt′rō-pŏl′ĭ-tĭks) n. *(used with a sing. or pl. verb).* The control of petroleum sales to achieve geopolitical and economic objectives.

pet·ti·coat (pĕt′ē-kōt′) n. A skirt, esp. a woman's slip or underskirt. [ME *petycote.*]

pet·ti·fog·ger (pĕt′ē-fŏg′gər, -fôg′gər) n. A petty, quibbling, unscrupulous lawyer. [Orig. unknown.]

pet·tish (pĕt′ĭsh) adj. Ill-tempered; petulant. [Prob. < PET[2].] —**pet′tish·ly** adv.

pet·ty (pĕt′ē) adj. **-ti·er, -ti·est. 1.** Small, trivial, or insignificant in quantity or quality. **2.** Of contemptibly narrow mind or views. **3.** Spiteful; mean. **4.** *Law.* Var. of **petit.** [< OFr. *petit,* small.] —**pet′ti·ly** adv. —**pet′ti·ness** n.

petty cash n. A small fund of money for incidental expenses, as in an office.

petty jury n. Var. of **petit jury.**

petty officer n. A noncommissioned naval officer.

pet·u·lant (pĕch′ŏŏ-lənt) adj. Unreasonably irritable or ill-tempered; peevish. [< Lat. *petulans.*] —**pet′u·lance** or **pet′u·lan·cy** n. —**pet′u·lant·ly** adv.

pe·tu·nia (pə-tōōn′yə, -tyōōn′-) n. A cultivated plant with funnel-shaped variously colored flowers. [< Tupi *petyn.*]

pew (pyōō) n. A bench for the congregation in a church. [< Lat. *podium,* balcony.]

pe·wee (pē′wē) n. A small, brownish North American bird. [Imit. of its song.]

pew·ter (pyōō′tər) n. An alloy of tin with various amounts of antimony, copper, and lead, used for kitchen utensils and tableware. [< OFr. *peutre.*] —**pew′ter** adj.

pe·yo·te (pā-ō′tē) n. **1.** Mescal. **2.** A hallucinatory drug derived from mescal. [< Nahuatl *peyotl.*]

pfen·nig (fĕn′ĭg) n., pl. **-nigs** or **pfen·ni·ge** (fĕn′ĭ-gə). See table at **currency.** [G.]

PG (pē′jē′) adj. Indicating a motion-picture rating allowing admission of persons of all ages but suggesting parental guidance in the case of children. [P(ARENTAL) G(UIDANCE).]

pH n. *Chem.* A measure of the acidity or alkalinity of a solution, numerically equal to 7 for neutral solutions, increasing with increasing alkalinity and decreasing with increasing acidity. [P(OTENTIAL) OF) H(YDROGEN).]

pha·e·ton (fā′ĭ-tn) n. A light, open, four-wheeled carriage, usu. drawn by a pair of horses. [Fr. *phaéton.*]

phaeton

-phage *suff.* One that eats: *bacteriophage.* [< Gk. *phagein,* to eat.]

pha·lanx (fā'lăngks') *n., pl.* **-lanx·es** or **pha·lan·ges** (fə-lăn'jēz, fā-). **1.** A formation of infantry carrying overlapping shields and long spears, developed by Philip II of Macedonia in the 4th cent. B.C. **2.** A close-knit or compact group. **3.** *pl.* **phalanges.** A bone of a finger or toe. [< Gk.]

phal·a·rope (făl'ə-rōp') *n.* Any of several small wading shore birds. [< Gk. *phalaros,* having a white spot + Gk. *pous,* foot.]

phal·lus (făl'əs) *n., pl.* **-li** (-ī') or **-es.** **1.** The penis. **2.** A representation or symbol of the penis. [< Gk. *phallos.*] —**phal'lic** *adj.*

phan·tasm (făn'tăz'əm) *n.* A phantom. [< Gk. *phantasma.*] —**phan·tas'mal** (făn-tăz'məl) or **phan·tas'mic** (-mĭk) *adj.*

phan·tas·ma·go·ri·a (făn-tăz'mə-gôr'ē-ə, -gōr'-) *n.* A fantastic sequence of haphazardly associative imagery, as in dreams. [Poss. < Gk. *phantasma,* phantasm + Gk. *agora,* assembly.] —**phan·tas'ma·go'ric** or **phan·tas'ma·go'ri·cal** *adj.*

phan·ta·sy (făn'tə-sē) *n.* Var. of **fantasy.**

phan·tom (făn'təm) *n.* **1.** Something apparently seen, heard, or sensed, but having no physical reality; ghost; specter. **2.** An illusory mental image. [< Gk. *phantasma.*] —**phan'tom** *adj.*

Phar·aoh (fâr'ō, fā'rō) *n.* Also **phar·aoh.** A king of ancient Egypt. —**Phar'a·on'ic** (fâr'ā-ŏn'ĭk) *adj.*

phar·i·see (făr'ĭ-sē) *n.* **1. Pharisee.** A member of an ancient Jewish sect that emphasized strict interpretation and observance of the Mosaic law. **2.** A hypocritically self-righteous person. [< Aram. *perīshayyā.*] —**phar'i·sa'ic** (-sā'ĭk) *adj.* —**phar'i·sa'i·cal·ly** *adv.* —**Phar'i·sa'i·cal·ness** *n.*

phar·ma·ceu·ti·cal (făr'mə-sōō'tĭ-kəl) or **phar·ma·ceu·tic** (-tĭk) *adj.* Of pharmacy or pharmacists. —*n.* A pharmaceutical product or preparation. [< Gk. *pharmakeutikos.*] —**phar'ma·ceu'ti·cal·ly** *adv.*

phar·ma·cist (făr'mə-sĭst) *n.* A person trained in pharmacy; druggist.

pharmaco- *pref.* Drug: *pharmacology.* [< Gk. *pharmakon,* drug.]

phar·ma·col·o·gy (făr'mə-kŏl'ə-jē) *n.* The science of drugs, including their composition, uses, and effects. —**phar'ma·co·log'ic** (-kə-lŏj'ĭk) or **phar'ma·co·log'i·cal** *adj.* —**phar'ma·co·log'i·cal·ly** *adv.* —**phar'ma·col'o·gist** *n.*

phar·ma·co·poe·ia (făr'mə-kə-pē'ə) *n., pl.* **-ias.** **1.** A book that contains an official list of medicinal drugs together with information on their preparation and use. **2.** A collection or stock of drugs. [PHARMACO- + Gk. *poiein,* to make.] —**phar'ma·co·poe'ial** (-pē'əl) *adj.*

phar·ma·cy (făr'mə-sē) *n., pl.* **-cies.** **1.** The art of preparing and dispensing drugs. **2.** A drugstore. [< Gk. *pharmakeia.*]

pharyngo- or **pharyng-** *pref.* Pharynx: *pharyngoscope.* [< Gk. *pharunx,* throat.]

phar·yn·gol·o·gy (făr'ĭn-gŏl'ə-jē) *n.* The medical study of the pharynx and its diseases.

pha·ryn·go·scope (fə-rĭng'gə-skōp') *n.* An instrument used to examine the pharynx. —**phar'yn·gos'co·py** (făr'ĭn-gŏs'kə-pē) *n.*

phar·ynx (făr'ĭngks) *n., pl.* **pha·ryn·ges** (fə-rĭn'jēz) or **-ynx·es.** The section of the digestive tract that extends from the nasal cavities to the larynx, there becoming continuous with the esophagus. [Gk. *pharunx,* throat.] —**pha·ryn'ge·al** (fə-rĭn'jē-əl, fâr'ĭn-jē'əl) *adj.*

phase (fāz) *n.* **1.** One of a sequence of apparent forms. **2.** A distinct stage of development. **3.** A temporary pattern of behavior: *a passing phase.* **4.** One of the cyclically recurring apparent forms of the moon or a planet. —*v.* **phased, phas·ing.** To plan or carry out systematically in phases. —**phrasal verbs. phase in.** To introduce in stages. **phase out.** To eliminate in stages. [< Gk. *phasis,* phase of the moon.]

pheas·ant (fĕz'ənt) *n.* Any of various longtailed, often brightly colored chickenlike birds. [< Gk. *phasianos,* of the Phasis River in the Caucasus.]

phe·nix (fē'nĭks) *n.* Var. of **phoenix.**

pheno- or **phen-** *pref.* **1.** Showing; displaying: *phenotype.* **2.** Related to or derived from benzene: *phenol.* [< Gk. *phainein,* to show.]

phe·no·bar·bi·tal (fē'nō-bär'bĭ-tôl') *n.* A white, shiny, crystalline compound, $C_{12}H_{12}N_2O_3$, used in medicine as a sedative and hypnotic.

phe·nol (fē'nôl', -nōl') *n.* A caustic, poisonous, white, crystalline compound, C_6H_5OH, derived from benzene and used in various resins, plastics, disinfectants, and pharmaceuticals.

phe·nom·e·non (fĭ-nŏm'ə-nŏn') *n., pl.* **-na** (-nə) or **-nons.** **1.** An occurrence or fact that can be perceived by the senses. **2. a.** An unusual fact or occurrence. **b.** A person outstanding for an extreme quality or achievement. [< Gk. *phainesthai.*] —**phe·nom'e·nal** *adj.* —**phe·nom'e·nal·ly** *adv.*

phe·no·type (fē'nə-tīp') *n.* **1.** The environmentally and genetically determined observable appearance of an organism. **2.** An individual or group of organisms exhibiting a particular phenotype. —**phe'no·typ'ic** (-tĭp'ĭk) or **phe'no·typ'i·cal** *adj.* —**phe'no·typ'i·cal·ly** *adv.*

pher·o·mone (fĕr'ə-mōn') *n.* A chemical secreted by an animal that serves to communicate to another of the same species and elicit a specific behavioral response. [Gk. *pherein,* to carry + (HOR)MONE.]

phi (fī) *n.* The 21st letter of the Greek alphabet. See table at **alphabet.** [< Gk. *phei.*]

phi·al (fī'əl) *n.* A vial. [< Gk. *phialē,* shallow vessel.]

Phi Be·ta Kap·pa (fī' bā'tə kăp'ə) *n.* An honorary fraternity whose members are chosen on the basis of high academic standing. [< the initials of the Greek motto *philosophia biou kubernētēs,* philosophy the guide of life.]

phi·lan·der (fĭ-lăn'dər) *v.* To engage in love affairs frivolously or casually. [< Gk. *philandros,* loving men.] —**phi·lan'der·er** *n.*

phi·lan·thro·py (fĭ-lăn'thrə-pē) *n., pl.* **-pies.** **1.** The effort to increase the well-being of mankind, as by charitable donations. **2.** Love of mankind in general. **3.** A charitable action or institution. [< Gk. *philanthrōpos,* loving mankind.] —**phil'an·throp'ic** (fĭl'ən-thrŏp'ĭk) or **phil'an·throp'i·cal** (-ĭ-kəl) *adj.* —**phi·lan'thro·pist** *n.*

---

phi·lat·e·ly (fĭ-lăt'l-ē) n. The collection and study of postage stamps and related materials. [Fr. *philatélie*.] —**phil'a·tel'ic** (fĭl'ə-tĕl'ĭk) adj. —**phil·at'e·list** n.

-phile or **-phil** suff. One that loves or has a strong affinity or preference for: *audiophile*. [< Gk. *philos*, loving.]

Phi·le·mon (fĭ-lē'mən, fī-) n. See table at **Bible**.

phil·har·mon·ic (fĭl'här-mŏn'ĭk, fĭl'ər-) adj. Of or relating to a symphony orchestra. —n. Also **Philharmonic**. A symphony orchestra or the group that supports it. [< Ital. *filarmonico*.]

-philia suff. Tendency towards: *hemophilia*. [< Gk. *philia*, friendship.]

Phi·lip·pi·ans (fĭ-lĭp'ē-ənz) pl.n. (used with a sing. verb). See table at **Bible**.

phi·lip·pic (fĭ-lĭp'ĭk) n. A passionate speech intended to arouse opposition; tirade. [< *Philip* of Macedonia (359–336 B.C.).]

Phil·is·tine (fĭl'ĭ-stēn', fĭ-lĭs'tĭn, -tēn') n. 1. A member of an ancient people in Palestine. 2. Also **philistine**. One who is annoyingly indifferent to artistic and cultural values. —adj. 1. Of the ancient Philistines. 2. Also **philistine**. Boorish; uncultured.

phil·o·den·dron (fĭl'ə-dĕn'drən) n., pl. -drons or -dra (-drə). Any of various climbing tropical American plants often cultivated as house plants. [< Gk. *philodendros*, loving trees.]

phi·lol·o·gy (fĭ-lŏl'ə-jē) n. 1. Historical linguistics. 2. Literary study or classical scholarship. [< Gk. *philologos*, loving learning.] —**phil'o·log'ic** (fĭl'ə-lŏj'ĭk) or **phil'o·log'i·cal** adj. —**phil'o·log'i·cal·ly** adv. —**phil·lol'o·gist** or **phi·lol'o·ger** n.

phi·los·o·pher (fĭ-lŏs'ə-fər) n. 1. A specialist in philosophy. 2. One who lives by a particular philosophy. 3. One who is calm and rational under any circumstances. [< Gk. *philosophos*, loving wisdom.]

phi·los·o·phize (fĭ-lŏs'ə-fīz') v. -phized, -phizing. To speculate in a philosophical manner. —**phi·los'o·phiz'er** n.

phi·los·o·phy (fĭ-lŏs'ə-fē) n., pl. -phies. 1. a. Speculative inquiry concerning the source and nature of human knowledge. b. A system of ideas based on such thinking. 2. *Archaic*. The investigation of natural phenomena: *natural philosophy*. 3. The sciences and liberal arts, excluding medicine, law, and theology: *Doctor of Philosophy*. 4. A basic theory concerning a particular subject: *philosophy of education*. 5. The set of values of an individual, culture, etc. —**phil'o·soph'i·cal** (fĭl'ə-sŏf'ĭ-kəl) or **phil·o·soph'ic** (-ĭk) adj. —**phil'o·soph'i·cal·ly** adv.

phil·ter (fĭl'tər) n. Also **phil·tre**. 1. A love potion. 2. Any magic potion or charm. [< Gk. *philtron*.]

phle·bi·tis (flĭ-bī'tĭs) n. Inflammation of a vein. —**phle·bit'ic** (-bĭt'ĭk) adj.

phleb·o- or **phleb-** pref. Vein: *phlebitis*. [< Gk. *phleps*.]

phle·bot·o·my (flĭ-bŏt'ə-mē) n., pl. -mies. The therapeutic practice of opening a vein to draw blood.

phlegm (flĕm) n. Stringy, thick mucus produced in the respiratory tract. [< Gk. *phlegma*, clammy humor of the body.] —**phlegm'y** (flĕm'ē) adj.

phleg·mat·ic (flĕg-măt'ĭk) or **phleg·mat·i·cal** (-ĭ-kəl) adj. Having or suggesting a calm,

stolid temperament; unemotional. [< Gk. *phlegma*, clammy humor of the body.]

phlo·em (flō'ĕm') n. *Bot.* The food-conducting tissue of vascular plants. [< Gk. *phloios*, bark.]

phlox (flŏks) n., pl. phlox or phlox·es. A plant with clusters of white, red, or purple flowers. [< Gk., a kind of flower.]

-phobe suff. One who fears or is averse to something: *xenophobe*.

pho·bi·a (fō'bē-ə) n. A persistent, abnormal, or illogical fear of something. [< -PHOBIA.] —**pho'bic** (-bĭk) adj.

-phobia suff. An intense, abnormal, or illogical fear: *acrophobia*. [< Gk. *phobos*, fear.]

In the following list, the English meaning is indicated for the form which **-phobia** is combined:

acrophobia	(heights)
aerophobia	(drafts)
agoraphobia	(open spaces)
ailurophobia	(cats)
algophobia	(pain)
androphobia	(men)
anthropophobia	(society)
claustrophobia	(enclosed spaces)
cynophobia	(dogs)
erotophobia	(love)
gymnophobia	(nudity)
gynephobia	(women)
haphephobia	(touching)
hedenophobia	(pleasure)
hemophobia	(blood)
hydrophobia	(water)
icthyophobia	(fish)
mysophobia	(infection)
necrophobia	(death)
nyctophobia	(night)
ochlophobia	(crowds)
ophidiophobia	(snakes)
phonophobia	(noise)
pyrophobia	(fire)
sitophobia	(food)
xenophobia	(foreigners)
zoophobia	(animals)

phoe·be (fē'bē) n. A small, grayish North American bird. [Imit. of its song.]

Phoe·ni·cian (fə-nĭsh'ən, -nē'shən) n. 1. A native, inhabitant, or subject of ancient Phoenicia. 2. The Semitic language of ancient Phoenicia. —**Phoe·ni'cian** adj.

phoe·nix (fē'nĭks) n. Also **phe·nix**. *Myth.* A bird that consumed itself by fire after 500 years and rose renewed from its ashes. [< Gk. *phoinix*.]

phon- pref. Var. of phono-.

phone (fōn) *Informal.* —n. A telephone. —v. phoned, phon·ing. To telephone. [< TELEPHONE.]

-phone suff. 1. Sound: *allophone*. 2. Device that receives or emits sound: *radiophone*. [< Gk. *phōnē*.]

pho·neme (fō'nēm') n. *Ling.* One of the smallest units of speech that distinguish one utterance or word from another. [< Gk. *phōnēma*, utterance.] —**pho·ne'mic** (fə-nē'mĭk, fō-) adj. —**pho·ne'mi·cal·ly** adv.

pho·net·ic (fə-nĕt'ĭk) adj. 1. Pertaining to phonetics. 2. Representing the sounds of speech with a set of distinct symbols, each denoting a single sound. [< Gk. *phōein*, to speak.] —**pho·net'i·cal·ly** adv.

pho·net·ics (fə-nĕt'ĭks) n. (used with a sing. verb). The branch of linguistics dealing with the study of the sounds of speech.

phon·ics (fŏn'ĭks) n. (used with a sing. verb).
1. The study of sound; acoustics. 2. The use of elementary phonetics in the teaching of reading.

phono- or **phon-** pref. Sound; voice; speech: phonology. [< Gk. phōnē.]

pho·no·graph (fō'nə-grăf') n. A machine that reproduces sound recorded on a grooved disc. —pho'no·graph'ic adj.

pho·nol·o·gy (fə-nŏl'ə-jē, fō-) n. The study of sound changes in a language. —pho'no·log'ic (fō'nə-lŏj'ĭk) or pho'no·log'i·cal adj. —pho'no·log'i·cal·ly adv. —pho·nol'o·gist n.

pho·ny (fō'nē) adj. -ni·er, -ni·est. Also pho·ney. Informal. Not genuine or real; fake. [Orig. unknown.] —pho'ny n.

-phony suff. Sound: telephony. [< Gk. phōnē.]

-phore suff. Bearer; carrier: chromatophore. [< Gk. pherein, to bear.]

-phoresis suff. Transmission: electrophoresis. [< Gk. phorein, to carry.]

phos- pref. Light: phosgene. [< Gk. phōs, light.]

phos·gene (fŏs'jēn', fŏz'-) n. A colorless volatile liquid or gas, COCl₂, used as a poison gas and in making glass, dyes, resins, and plastics.

phos·phate (fŏs'fāt') n. 1. Chem. A salt or ester of phosphoric acid. 2. A fertilizer containing phosphorus compounds. [PHOSPH(O-RUS) + -ATE².] —phos·phat'ic (fŏs-făt'ĭk) adj.

phos·phor (fŏs'fər, -fôr') n. 1. A substance that can be stimulated to emit light by incident radiation. 2. Something exhibiting phosphorescence. [< PHOSPHORUS.]

phos·pho·res·cence (fŏs'fə-rĕs'əns) n. 1. Persistent emission of light following exposure to and removal of incident radiation. 2. Organically generated light emission. —phos'pho·resce' v. —phos'pho·res'cent adj. —phos'pho·res'cent·ly adv.

phos·phor·ic acid (fŏs-fôr'ĭk, -fŏr'-) n. A clear colorless liquid, H₃PO₄, used in fertilizers, soaps, and detergents.

phos·pho·rus (fŏs'fər-əs) n. 1. Symbol P A highly reactive, poisonous, nonmetallic element used in safety matches, pyrotechnics, incendiary shells, fertilizers, glass, and steel. Atomic number 15; atomic weight 30.9738. 2. A phosphorescent substance. [< Gk. phōs-phoros, bringing light.] —phos·phor'ic (fŏs-fôr'ĭk, -fŏr'-) adj. —phos'pho·rous (fŏs'-fər-əs, fŏs-fôr'əs, -fôr'-). adj.

pho·to (fō'tō) n., pl. -tos. Informal. A photograph. —pho'to v.

photo- or **phot-** pref. 1. Light: photosynthesis. 2. Photographic: photomontage. 3. Photoelectric: photoemission. [< Gk. phōs, light.]

pho·to·chem·is·try (fō'tō-kĕm'ĭ-strē) n. The chemistry of the interactions of radiant energy and chemical systems. —pho'to·chem'i·cal adj.

pho·to·com·po·si·tion (fō'tō-kŏm'pə-zĭsh'ən) n. The preparation of manuscript for printing by the projection of images of type characters on photographic film. —pho'to·com·pose' v. —pho'to·com·pos'er n.

pho·to·cop·y (fō'tō-kŏp'ē) v. To make a photographic reproduction of (printed or pictorial material). —n. A photographic reproduction. —pho'to·cop'i·er n.

pho·to·du·pli·cate (fō'tō-dōō'plĭ-kāt', -dyōō'-) v. To photocopy. —pho'to·du·pli·cate (-kĭt) n. —pho'to·du'pli·ca'tion n.

pho·to·e·lec·tric (fō'tō-ĭ-lĕk'trĭk) or pho·to·e·lec·tri·cal (-trĭ-kəl) adj. Pertaining to electrical effects, esp. increased electrical conduction, caused by illumination.

photoelectric cell n. An electronic device with an electrical output that varies in response to the intensity of incident radiation.

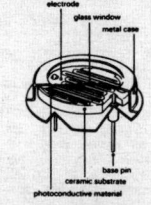

photoelectric cell

pho·to·e·lec·tron (fō'tō-ĭ-lĕk'trŏn') n. An electron that is released in photoemission.

pho·to·e·mis·sion (fō'tə-ĭ-mĭsh'ən) n. The emission of photoelectrons, esp. from metallic surfaces.

pho·to·en·grav·ing (fō'tō-ĕn-grā'vĭng) n. 1. The process of reproducing graphic material by photographing it on a metal plate and then etching the plate for printing. 2. A reproduction made by this method. —pho'to·en·grave' v. —pho'to·en·grav'er n.

pho·to·es·say (fō'tō-ĕs'ā) n. A photographic commentary on a particular subject. —pho'to·es'say·ist n.

photo finish n. A race so closely contested that the winner must be determined by a photograph taken of the finish.

pho·to·flash (fō'tō-flăsh) n. A flash bulb.

pho·to·gen·ic (fō'tə-jĕn'ĭk) adj. Attractive as a subject for photography. —pho'to·gen'i·cal·ly adv.

pho·to·graph (fō'tə-grăf') n. An image formed on a light-sensitive surface by a camera and developed chemically to produce a positive print. —v. 1. To take a photograph of. 2. To be the subject for photographs.

pho·to·graph·ic (fō'tə-grăf'ĭk) or pho·to·graph·i·cal (-ĭ-kəl) adj. 1. Pertaining to photography or a photograph. 2. Used in photography. 3. Like a photograph, as in accuracy or detail. —pho'to·graph'i·cal·ly adv.

pho·tog·ra·phy (fə-tŏg'rə-fē) n. 1. The process or technique of creating images on light-sensitive surfaces. 2. The art, practice, or profession of taking and printing photographs. —pho·tog'ra·pher n.

pho·to·gra·vure (fō'tə-grə-vyŏŏr') n. The process of printing from an intaglio plate, etched according to a photographic image.

pho·to·jour·nal·ism (fō'tō-jûr'nə-lĭz'əm) n. Journalism employing photographs primarily.

—pho·to·jour'nal·ist *n.* —pho·to·jour'nal·is'tic *adj.*

pho·tom·e·try (fō-tŏm'ĭ-trē) *n.* The measurement of the intensity, brightness, or other properties of light. —pho'to·met'ric (fō'tə-mĕt'rĭk) or pho'to·met'ri·cal *adj.*

pho·to·mi·cro·graph (fō'tō-mī'krə-grăf') *n.* A photograph made through a microscope. —pho'to·mi'cro·graph' *v.* —pho'to·mi'cro·graph'ic *adj.* —pho'to·mi·crog'ra·phy (-krŏg'rə-fē) *n.*

pho·to·mon·tage (fō'tō-mŏn-täzh', -mŏn-) *n.* 1. The technique of making a picture by assembling pieces of photographs, often with other graphic material. 2. A composite picture produced by this technique.

pho·ton (fō'tŏn') *n.* The quantum of electromagnetic energy, gen. regarded as a discrete particle with zero mass, no electric charge, and an indefinitely long lifetime. —pho'ton'ic *adj.*

pho·to·play (fō'tō-plā) *n.* A play filmed or arranged for filming as a motion picture.

pho·to·sen·si·tive (fō'tō-sĕn'sĭ-tĭv) *adj.* Sensitive to light. —pho'to·sen·si·tiv'i·ty *n.*

pho·to·sphere (fō'tə-sfîr') *n.* The surface of a star, esp. of the sun. —pho'to·spher'ic (-sfîr'ĭk, -sfĕr'-) *adj.*

Pho·to·stat (fō'tə-stăt'). A trademark for a device used to make quick, direct-reading negative or positive copies.

pho·to·syn·the·sis (fō'tō-sĭn'thĭ-sĭs) *n.* The process by which chlorophyll-containing cells in green plants use the energy of light to synthesize carbohydrates from carbon dioxide and water. —pho'to·syn'the·size' (-sĭn'thə-sīz) *v.* —pho'to·syn·thet'ic (-sĭn-thĕt'ĭk) *adj.* —pho'to·syn·thet'i·cal·ly *adv.*

pho·to·tro·pism (fō-tŏt'rə-pĭz'əm) *n. Biol.* Growth or movement in response to light. —pho'to·trop'ic (fō'tə-trŏp'ĭk) *adj.* —pho'to·trop'i·cal·ly *adv.*

phrase (frāz) *n.* 1. A sequence of words intended to have meaning. 2. A brief, cogent expression. 3. Two or more words in sequence that form a syntactic unit or group of syntactic units, less completely predicated than a sentence. 4. *Mus.* A segment of a composition, usu. consisting of several measures. —*v.* phrased, phras·ing. 1. To express orally or in writing. 2. *Mus.* To render in phrases. [< Gk. *phrasis,* style of speech.] —phras'al *adj.* —phras'al·ly *adv.*

phra·se·ol·o·gy (frā'zē-ŏl'ə-jē) *n., pl.* -gies. The way in which words and phrases are used. —phra'se·o·log'i·cal (-ə-lŏj'ĭ-kəl) *adj.*

phre·net·ic (frə-nĕt'ĭk) *adj.* Var. of frenetic. —phrenia *suff.* Mental disorder: *schizophrenia.* [< Gk. *phrēn,* mind.]

phre·nol·o·gy (frĭ-nŏl'ə-jē) *n.* The practice of studying character and mental capacity from the shape and irregularities of the human skull. [Gk. *phrēn,* mind + -LOGY.] —phren'o·log'ic (frĕn'ə-lŏj'ĭk, frē'nə-) or phren'o·log'i·cal *adj.* —phre·nol'o·gist *n.*

phy·la (fī'lə) *n.* Pl. of phylum.

phy·lac·ter·y (fĭ-lăk'tə-rē) *n., pl.* -ies. *Judaism.* Either of two small leather boxes that contain strips of parchment inscribed with quotations from the Hebrew Scriptures, with one strapped to the forehead and the other to the left arm by Jewish men during morning worship. [< Gk. *phulaktērion,* safeguard.]

phylactery

—phyll *suff.* Leaf: *chlorophyll.* [< Gk. *phullon.*]

phyl·lo·tax·y (fĭl'ə-tăk'sē) *n.* Also phyl·lo·tax·is (fĭl'ə-tăk'sĭs). *Bot.* The arrangement of leaves on a stem. [Gk. *phullon,* leaf + Gk. *taxis,* arrangement.]

phy·log·e·ny (fī-lŏj'ə-nē) *n., pl.* -nies. The evolutionary development of an animal or plant species. [Gk. *phulon,* race + -GENY.] —phy'lo·ge·net'ic (fī'lō-jə-nĕt'ĭk) or phy'lo·gen'ic (-jĕn'ĭk) *adj.* —phy'lo·ge·net'i·cal·ly *adv.*

phy·lum (fī'ləm) *n., pl.* -la (-lə). 1. One of the broad categories, esp. of the animal kingdom, used in the classification of organisms. 2. A large division of genetically related families of languages or linguistic stocks. [< Gk. *phulon,* class.]

physi– *pref.* Var. of physio–.

phys·ic (fĭz'ĭk) *n.* 1. A medicine or drug. 2. A cathartic. —*v.* -icked, -ick·ing. To act upon as a cathartic. [< Lat. *physica,* natural medicine.]

phys·i·cal (fĭz'ĭ-kəl) *adj.* 1. Of or pertaining to the body. 2. Of material things. 3. Of or pertaining to matter and energy or the sciences dealing with them, esp. physics. —*n.* A physical examination. —phys'i·cal·ly *adv.*

physical education *n.* Instruction in the care and development of the human body, stressing athletics and hygiene.

physical geography *n.* The study of the structure and phenomena of the earth's surface.

physical science *n.* Any of the sciences, such as physics, chemistry, and geology, that analyzes the nature and properties of energy and nonliving matter.

physical therapy *n.* The treatment of disease and injury by mechanical means such as exercise, heat, light, and massage. —physical therapist *n.*

phy·si·cian (fĭ-zĭsh'ən) *n.* A medical doctor.

phys·i·cist (fĭz'ĭ-sĭst) *n.* A scientist who specializes in physics.

phys·ics (fĭz'ĭks) *n. (used with a sing. verb).* The science of matter and energy and of the interactions between the two.

physio– or physi– *pref.* 1. Nature; natural: *physiography.* 2. Physical: *physiotherapy.* [< Gk. *phusis,* nature.]

phys·i·og·no·my (fĭz'ē-ŏg'nə-mē, -ŏn'ə-mē) *n., pl.* -mies. Facial features, esp. when regarded as revealing character. [< Gk. *phusiognomonia.*] —phys'i·og·nom'ic (fĭz'ē-ŏg-nŏm'ĭk, fĭz'ē-ə-nŏm'ĭk) or phys'i·og·nom'i·cal *adj.* —phys'i·og·nom'i·cal·ly *adv.*

phys·i·og·ra·phy (fĭz'ē-ŏg'rə-fē) *n.* Physical geography. —phys'i·og'ra·pher *n.* —phys'i·o·

graph·ic (-ə-grăf'ĭk) or **phys'i·o·graph'i·cal** *adj.* —**phys'i·o·graph'i·cal·ly** *adv.*

phys·i·ol·o·gy (fĭz'ē-ŏl'ə-jē) *n.* 1. The biological science of life processes, activities, and functions. 2. The vital processes of an organism. —**phys'i·o·log'i·cal** (-ə-lŏj'ĭ-kəl) *adj.* —**phys'i·o·log'i·cal·ly** *adv.* —**phys'i·ol'o·gist** *n.*

phys·i·o·ther·a·py (fĭz'ē-ō-thĕr'ə-pē) *n.* Physical therapy. —**phys'i·o·ther'a·peu'tic** (-thĕr'-ə-pyōō'tĭk) *adj.*

phy·sique (fĭ-zēk') *n.* The body, considered as to its proportions, muscular development, and appearance. [Fr.]

–phyte *suff.* A plant with a specified character or habitat: *saprophyte*. [< Gk. *phuton*, plant.]

pi¹ (pī) *n., pl.* **pis.** 1. The 16th letter of the Greek alphabet. See table at **alphabet.** 2. *Math.* A transcendental number, approx. 3.14159, representing the ratio of the circumference to the diameter of a circle. [Gk. *pei*.]

pi² (pī) *n., pl.* **pies.** *Printing.* Jumbled type. [Orig. unknown.]

pi·a·nis·si·mo (pē'ə-nĭs'ə-mō') *adv. Mus.* Very softly or quietly. [Ital.] —**pi'a·nis'si·mo'** *adj.*

pi·an·ist (pē-ăn'ĭst, pē'ə-nĭst) *n.* One who plays the piano.

pi·an·o¹ (pē-ăn'ō, -ä'nō) *n., pl.* **-os.** A musical keyboard instrument with hammers that strike wire strings. [Ital. < *pianoforte*, pianoforte.]

pi·an·o² (pē-ä'nō) *adv. Mus.* Softly; quietly. [Ital.] —**pi·a'no** *adj. & n.*

pi·an·o·for·te (pē-ăn'ō-fôr'tā, -tē, -fôrt', -ä'nō-) *n.* A piano. [Ital.< *piano e forte*, soft and loud.]

pi·as·ter (pē-ăs'tər, -ä'stər) *n.* Also **pi·as·tre.** See table at **currency.** [Fr. *piastre*.]

pi·az·za (pē-ăz'ə, -ä'zə) *n.* A verandah; porch. [Ital.]

pi·ca (pī'kə) *n.* 1. A printer's unit of type size, equal to 12 points or about ⅙ inch. 2. A type size for typewriters, providing 10 characters to the inch. [Prob. < Med. Lat., list of church services.]

pic·a·dor (pĭk'ə-dôr') *n., pl.* **-dors** or **-do·res** (-dôr'ēz). A horseman in a bullfight who lances the bull's neck muscles. [Sp. < *picar*, to prick.]

pic·a·resque (pĭk'ə-rĕsk', pē'kə-) *adj.* Of or involving clever rogues or adventurers. [< Sp. *picaro*, rogue.]

pic·a·yune (pĭk'ē-yōōn') *adj.* 1. Of little value or importance; paltry. 2. Petty; mean. [< Prov. *picaioun*, small coin.]

pic·co·lo (pĭk'ə-lō') *n., pl.* **-los.** A small flute pitched an octave above a regular flute. [Ital.]

pick¹ (pĭk) *v.* 1. To select from a group. 2. To gather in; harvest. 3. a. To remove the outer covering of; pluck. b. To tear off bit by bit. 4. To poke at with the fingers. 5. To break up or detach with a pointed instrument. 6. To pierce with a sharp instrument. 7. To steal the contents of. 8. To open (a lock) without the use of the key. 9. To make (one's way) carefully. 10. To provoke: *pick a fight.* —**phrasal verbs. pick off.** To shoot after singling out. **pick on.** To tease or bully. **pick out.** 1. To choose or select. 2. To discern from the surroundings; distinguish. **pick up.** 1. To take on (e.g. passengers or freight). 2. To change for the better; improve. 3. To take into custody; arrest. 4. To receive or intercept: *pick up radio signals.* 5. To learn without great effort; choice. 2. The best or choicest part. —**idiom. pick and choose.** To decide with great care. [Prob. < Lat. *picus*, woodpecker.] —**pick'er** *n.*

pick² (pĭk) *n.* 1. A tool for breaking hard surfaces, consisting of a curved bar sharpened at both ends and fitted to a long handle. 2. A plectrum. [ME *pik*.]

pick·ax or **pick·axe** (pĭk'ăks') *n.* A pick in which one end of the head is pointed and the other has a chisellike edge. [< OFr. *picois*.]

pick·er·el (pĭk'ər-əl, pĭk'rəl) *n., pl.* **-el** or **-els.** A North American freshwater fish related to the pike. [ME *pikerel*, dim. of *pik*, pike.]

pick·et (pĭk'ĭt) *n.* 1. A pointed stake driven into the ground to support a fence, secure a tent, tether an animal, etc. 2. *Mil.* A detachment of one or more soldiers on guard against enemy approach. 3. A person or persons stationed outside a building, as during a strike or boycott, to express grievance or protest. —*v.* 1. To enclose, secure, or tether with pickets. 2. *Mil.* To guard with pickets. 3. To post a picket or pickets at a strike or demonstration. 4. To function as a picket. [< OFr. *piquet*.] —**pick'et·er** *n.*

picket fence *n.* A fence of pointed, upright pickets.

picket line *n.* A line or procession of people picketing a place of business or otherwise staging a public protest.

pick·ings (pĭk'ĭngz) *pl.n.* 1. Something that is or may be picked. 2. Leftovers. 3. A share of spoils.

pick·le (pĭk'əl) *n.* 1. A food, as a cucumber, preserved and flavored in a solution of brine or vinegar. 2. A solution of brine or vinegar, often spiced, for preserving and flavoring food. 3. *Informal.* A troublesome or difficult situation. —*v.* **-led, -ling.** To preserve or flavor in a solution of brine or vinegar. [ME *pekille.*]

pick-me-up (pĭk'mē-ŭp') *n. Informal.* A drink taken as a stimulant.

pick·pock·et (pĭk'pŏk'ĭt) *n.* One who steals from pockets or purses.

pick·proof (pĭk'prōōf') *adj.* Impervious to picking: *a pickproof lock.*

pick·up (pĭk'ŭp') *n.* 1. The action or process of picking up. 2. One that is picked up. 3. Ability to accelerate rapidly. 4. *Electronics.* a. The part of a phonograph that changes the variations of the record groove into an electrical signal to be amplified as it is fed to a loudspeaker. b. The tone arm of a record player. 5. *Radio & TV.* a. The reception of light or sound waves for conversion to electrical impulses. b. The apparatus used for such reception. c. A telecast originating outside of a studio. d. The apparatus for transmitting a broadcast from an outside place to the broadcasting station. 6. A pickup truck.

pickup truck *n.* A light truck with an open body and low sides.

pick·y (pĭk'ē) *adj.* **-i·er, -i·est.** *Informal.* Fussy; meticulous.

pic·nic (pĭk'nĭk) *n.* 1. A meal eaten outdoors

on an excursion. **2.** *Slang.* An easy task. —*v.* **-nicked, -nick·ing.** To go on a picnic. [Fr. *piquenique.*] —**pic'nick·er** *n.*

pi·cot (pē'kō, pē-kō') *n.* A small loop forming an ornamental edging, as on ribbon. [< OFr.]

pic·to·ri·al (pĭk-tôr'ē-əl, -tōr'-) *adj.* **1.** Characterized by or composed of pictures. **2.** Illustrated by pictures. —*n.* An illustrated periodical. [< Lat. *pictor,* painter.] —**pic·to'ri·al·ly** *adv.*

pic·ture (pĭk'chər) *n.* **1.** A visual representation or image painted, drawn, photographed, or otherwise rendered on a flat surface. **2.** A vivid verbal description. **3.** One that bears a striking resemblance to another. **4.** One that typifies or embodies an emotion, state of mind, or mood. **5.** The chief circumstances; situation. **6.** A motion picture. **7.** An image or series of images on a television or movie screen. —*v.* **-tured, -tur·ing.** **1.** To make a visible representation or picture of. **2.** To visualize. **3.** To describe vividly in words. [< Lat. *pictura.*]

pic·tur·esque (pĭk'chə-rĕsk') *adj.* **1.** Of or suggesting a picture. **2.** Unusually or quaintly attractive. **3.** Strikingly expressive or vivid: *picturesque language.* —**pic'tur·esque'ly** *adv.* —**pic'tur·esque'ness** *n.*

picture window *n.* A large, usu. single-paned window.

pid·dling (pĭd'lĭng) *adj.* Trifling; trivial. [Orig. unknown.]

pidg·in (pĭj'ĭn) *n.* A simplified mixture of two or more languages, used for communication between groups speaking different languages. [< PIDGIN ENGLISH.] —**pidg'in** *adj.*

Pidgin English *n.* Also **pidgin English.** A pidgin based on English that is used as a trade language in parts of Eastern Asia and Melanesia. [< *business English.*]

pie¹ (pī) *n.* A baked pastry shell filled with fruit, meat, etc., and often covered with a crust. [ME.]

pie² (pī) *n.* Var. of PI².

pie·bald (pī'bôld') *adj.* Spotted or patched: *a piebald horse.* [*pie,* magpie + BALD.]

piece (pēs) *n.* **1.** A unit or element of a larger quantity or class; portion. **2.** An artistic, musical, or literary work. **3.** An instance; specimen. **4.** One's mind: *speak one's piece.* **5.** A coin or counter. **6.** A figure used in a game. **7.** A firearm, esp. a rifle. **8.** A given distance: *down the road a piece.* —*v.* **pieced, piec·ing.** **1.** To mend by adding a piece to. **2.** To join the pieces of. —*idioms.* **go to pieces.** To lose one's self-control; break down. —**of a piece.** Of the same kind, type, or group. [< Med. Lat. *pecia.*]

pièce de ré·sis·tance (pē-ĕs' də rā'zē-stäns') *n.* **1.** The principal dish of a meal. **2.** An outstanding accomplishment. [Fr.]

piece·meal (pēs'mēl') *adv.* Piece by piece. —*adj.* Made piece by piece. [ME *pecemele.*]

piece of eight *n.* An obsolete Spanish silver coin.

piece·work (pēs'wûrk') *n.* Work paid for by the piece. —**piece'work'er** *n.*

pied (pīd) *adj.* Piebald. [< ME *pie,* magpie.]

pied-à-terre (pyā-dä-târ') *n., pl.* **pieds-à-terre** (pyä-dä-târ'.) A second or temporary lodging. [Fr.]

pie-plant (pī'plănt') *n.* Rhubarb.

pier (pîr) *n.* **1.** A platform extending from a shore over water, used to secure, protect, and provide access to ships or boats. **2.** A support

for the spans of a bridge. **3.** *Archit.* Any of various vertical supporting structures. [< Med. Lat. *pera.*]

pierce (pîrs) *v.* **pierced, pierc·ing.** **1.** To cut or pass through with or as if with a sharp instrument. **2.** To perforate. **3.** To penetrate through. [< Lat. *pertundere,* to bore through.] —**pierc'er** *n.* —**pierc'ing·ly** *adv.*

pi·e·ty (pī'ĭ-tē) *n., pl.* **-ties.** **1.** Devotion and reverence, esp. to God and family. **2.** A pious act or thought. [< Lat. *pietas,* dutiful conduct.]

pi·e·zo·e·lec·tric·i·ty (pē-ā'zō-ĭ-lĕk-trĭs'ĭ-tē, pē-ăt'sō-) *n.* The generation of electricity or of electric polarity in dielectric crystals subjected to mechanical stress and, conversely, the generation of stress in such crystals subjected to an applied voltage. [Gk. *piezein,* to squeeze + ELECTRICITY.] —**pi·e'zo·e·lec'tric** or **pi·e'zo·e·lec'tri·cal** *adj.*

pif·fle (pĭf'əl) *v.* **-fled, -fling.** To talk or act in a foolish or futile way. —*n.* Nonsense. [Orig. unknown.]

pig (pĭg) *n.* **1.** A hoofed mammal with short legs, bristly hair, and a blunt snout used for digging, esp. one of a kind raised for meat. **2.** A person regarded as being piglike, greedy, or gross. **3.** An oblong block of metal, chiefly iron or lead, poured from a smelting furnace. **4.** *Offensive Slang.* A police officer. [ME *pigge.*]

pi·geon (pĭj'ən) *n.* **1.** Any of various related birds with a deep-chested body, a small head, and short legs, esp. a common, often domesticated species. **2.** *Slang.* One easily swindled. [< Lat. *pipio,* young chirping bird.]

pi·geon·hole (pĭj'ən-hōl') *n.* A small compartment, as in a desk. —*v.* **-holed, -hol·ing.** **1.** To place or file in a pigeonhole. **2.** To categorize. **3.** To put aside and ignore.

pi·geon-toed (pĭj'ən-tōd') *adj.* Having the toes turned inward.

pig·gish (pĭg'ĭsh) *adj.* **1.** Like a pig; dirty. **2.** Greedy. **3.** Pigheaded. —**pig'gish·ly** *adv.* —**pig'gish·ness** *n.*

pig·gy·back (pĭg'ē-băk') *adv.* **1.** On the shoulders or back. **2.** By a method of transportation in which truck trailers are carried on trains. [Orig. unknown.] —**pig'gy·back'** *adj.*

pig·head·ed (pĭg'hĕd'ĭd) *adj.* Stubborn. —**pig'head'ed·ly** *adv.* —**pig'head'ed·ness** *n.*

pig iron *n.* Crude iron cast in blocks or pigs.

pig Latin *n.* A jargon formed by the transposition of the initial consonant to the end of a word and the suffixation of an additional syllable, as *igpay atinlay* for *pig Latin.*

pig·let (pĭg'lĭt) *n.* A young pig.

pig·ment (pĭg'mənt) *n.* **1.** A coloring substance or matter. **2.** *Biol.* A substance, as chlorophyll or hemoglobin, that produces a characteristic color in plant or animal tissue. [Lat. *pigmentum.*] —**pig'men·tar·y** (-mən-tĕr'ē) *adj.*

pig·men·ta·tion (pĭg'mən-tā'shən) *n.* Coloration of animal or plant tissues by pigment.

pig·my (pĭg'mē) *n. & adj.* Var. of pygmy.

pig·pen (pĭg'pĕn') *n.* **1.** A pen for pigs. **2.** A dirty place.

pig·skin (pĭg'skĭn') *n.* **1.** The skin of a pig or leather made from it. **2.** *Informal.* A football.

pig·sty (pĭg'stī') *n.* A pigpen.

pig·tail (pĭg'tāl') *n.* A braid of hair. —**pig'-tailed'** *adj.*

pike¹ (pīk) *n.* A long spear formerly used by infantry. [< Lat. *picus,* woodpecker.]

pike² (pīk) *n., pl.* **pike** or **pikes.** A narrow-bodied freshwater game and food fish with a long snout. [ME.]

pike³ (pīk) *n.* A turnpike. [< TURNPIKE.]

pike⁴ (pīk) *n.* A spike or sharp point. [< OE *pīc.*]

pi·ker (pī′kər) *n. Slang.* A stingy, petty person. [Orig. unknown.]

pi·laf or **pi·laff** (pī-läf′, pē-) *n.* A steamed rice dish cooked with bits of meat, shellfish, or vegetables. [Turk. *pilāw.*]

pi·las·ter (pĭ-lăs′tər, pī-lăs′-) *n.* A rectangular column, usu. ornamental, that is set into a wall. [< Med. Lat. *pilastrum.*]

pile¹ (pīl) *n.* **1.** A quantity of objects in a heap. **2.** A large accumulation or quantity. **3.** A funeral pyre. **4.** A nuclear reactor. —*v.* **piled, pil·ing. 1.** To stack in or form a pile. **2.** To load with a pile. **3.** To move in a disorderly mass or group: *pile out of a car.* [< Lat. *pila, pillar.*]

pile² (pīl) *n.* A heavy beam driven into the earth as a support for a structure. [< Lat. *pilum, spear.*]

pile³ (pīl) *n.* Cut or uncut loops of yarn forming the surface of certain fabrics, as carpeting. [< Lat. *pilus, hair.*] —**piled** *adj.*

pile·at·ed woodpecker (pī′lē-ā′tĭd) *n.* A large North American woodpecker with black and white plumage and a red crest. [< Lat. *pileus, felt cap.*]

pile driver *n.* A machine that drives piles into the ground.

piles (pīlz) *pl.n.* Hemorrhoids. [< Lat. *pila, ball.*]

pile-up (pīl′ŭp′) *n.* A serious collision of several motor vehicles.

pil·fer (pĭl′fər) *v.* To steal; filch. [< OFr. *pelfre, boot.*] —**pil′fer·age** *n.* —**pil′fer·er** *n.*

pil·grim (pĭl′grĭm, -grəm) *n.* **1.** One who goes on a pilgrimage. **2.** A traveler. **3.** **Pilgrim.** One of the English Puritans who migrated to New England in 1620. [< Lat. *peregrinus,* foreigner.]

pilgrim
"Pilgrims Going to Church" by
George Henry Boughton

pil·grim·age (pĭl′grə-mĭj) *n.* **1.** A journey to a sacred place or shrine. **2.** A long journey or search.

pill (pĭl) *n.* **1.** A small pellet or tablet of medicine. **2. the pill.** *Informal.* An oral contraceptive. **3.** Something distasteful or unpleasant but necessary. **4.** *Slang.* An ill-natured person. [< Lat. *pila, ball.*]

pil·lage (pĭl′ĭj) *v.* **-laged, -lag·ing. 1.** To plunder. **2.** To take as spoils. —*n.* **1.** The act of

pillaging. **2.** Spoils. [< OFr. *piller,* to plunder.] —**pil′lag·er** *n.*

pil·lar (pĭl′ər) *n.* **1.** A slender, freestanding, vertical support; column. **2.** One occupying a central or responsible position. [< Lat. *pilla.*]

pill-box (pĭl′bŏks′) *n.* **1.** A small box for pills. **2.** A roofed concrete emplacement esp. for a machine gun.

pil·lion (pĭl′yən) *n.* A seat for an extra rider behind the saddle on a horse or motorcycle. [< Lat. *pellis, skin.*]

pil·lo·ry (pĭl′ə-rē) *n., pl.* **-ries.** A wooden framework with holes for the head and hands, in which offenders were formerly locked to be exposed to public scorn as punishment. —*v.* **-ried, -ry·ing. 1.** To put in a pillory as punishment. **2.** To expose to ridicule and abuse. [< OFr. *pilori.*]

pil·low (pĭl′ō) *n.* **1.** A cloth case stuffed with something soft and used to cushion the head during sleep. **2.** A decorative cushion. —*v.* **1.** To rest (one's head) on or as if on a pillow. **2.** To serve as a pillow for. [< Lat. *pulvinus.*] —**pil′low·y** *adj.*

pil·low·case (pĭl′ō-kās′) *n.* A removable pillow covering.

pi·lot (pī′lət) *n.* **1.** One who flies or is licensed to fly an aircraft. **2.** A licensed specialist who steers ships in and out of port or through dangerous waters. **3.** A ship's helmsman. **4.** A guide or leader. **5.** A television program produced as a prototype of a prospective series. **6.** A small-scale experimental model. —*v.* **1.** To serve as the pilot of. **2.** To steer or control the course of. [< OItal. *pilota.*]

pi·lot·age (pī′lə-tĭj) *n.* The act or business of piloting.

pi·lot·house (pī′lət-hous′) *n.* An enclosed area on the deck or bridge of a vessel from which the vessel is controlled.

pilot light *n.* A small jet of gas that is kept burning in order to ignite a gas burner, as in a stove.

Pilt·down man (pĭlt′doun′) *n.* A supposed early genus and species of man postulated from bones allegedly found in an early Pleistocene gravel bed between 1909 and 1915 and proved in 1953 to have been a forgery. [< *Piltdown* Common, East Sussex, England.]

Pi·ma (pē′mə) *n., pl.* **-ma** or **-mas. 1. a.** A tribe of Indians living in southern Arizona and northern Mexico. **b.** A member of the Pima. **2.** The Uto-Aztecan language of the Pima. —**Pi′man** *adj.*

pi·men·to (pĭ-mĕn′tō) *n., pl.* **-tos.** Also **pi·mien·to** (pĭ-mĕn′tō, -myĕn′-). A mild-flavored red pepper. [< LLat. *pigmentum, pigment.*]

pimp (pĭmp) *n.* One who procures customers for a prostitute. —*v.* To serve as a pimp. [Orig. unknown.]

pim·per·nel (pĭm′pər-nĕl′, -nəl) *n.* A plant with red, purple, or white flowers that close in bad weather. [< Lat. *piper, pepper.*]

pim·ple (pĭm′pəl) *n.* A small swelling of the skin, sometimes containing pus. [ME *pinple.*] —**pim′pled** or **pim′ply** *adj.*

pin (pĭn) *n.* **1.** A short, straight, stiff piece of wire with a blunt head and a sharp point, used esp. for fastening. **2.** Something resembling a pin in shape or use, as a hairpin. **3.** An ornament fastened to the clothing by a clasp. **4.** A slender, cylindrical piece of wood or metal for holding, fastening, or supporting. **5.** One of the wooden clubs at which the ball is aimed in bowling. **6.** *Golf.* The pole bearing a pennant to mark a hole. **7. pins.** The legs. —*v.* **pinned, pin·ning. 1.** To fasten or secure with or as if with a pin. **2.** To make completely dependent: *pinned all our hopes on winning.* **3.** To hold fast; immobilize. **4.** To oblige (someone) to make a definite response. —*phrasal verb.* **pin on.** To attribute (a wrongdoing or crime). —*idiom.* **on pins and needles.** In a state of suspense or anxiety. [< OE *pinn.*]

pin·a·fore (pĭn′ə-fôr′, -fōr′) *n.* A sleeveless, apronlike garment. [PIN + *afore*, before.]

pince-nez (păns-nā′, păns-) *n.*, *pl.* **pince-nez** (-nāz′, -nā′). Eyeglasses clipped to the bridge of the nose. [Fr.]

pin·cers (pĭn′sərz) *pl.n.* Also **pin·chers** (pĭn′-chərz). **1.** A grasping tool with a pair of jaws and handles that are pivoted together to work in opposition. **2.** The jointed, prehensile claws of certain arthropods, as the lobster. [< OFr. *pincier*, to pinch.]

pinch (pĭnch) *v.* **1.** To squeeze between the thumb and a finger, the jaws of a tool, etc. **2.** To squeeze or bind (a part of the body) painfully. **3.** To wither or shrivel. **4.** To be miserly. **5.** *Slang.* To steal. **6.** *Slang.* To arrest. —*n.* **1.** The act of pinching. **2.** An amount that can be held between thumb and forefinger. **3.** A difficult or straitened circumstance. **4.** An emergency. [< OFr. *pincier.*] —**pinch′er** *n.*

pinch-hit (pĭnch′hĭt′) *v.* **1.** *Baseball.* To bat in place of a scheduled player. **2.** *Informal.* To substitute for another. —**pinch hitter** *n.*

pin·cush·ion (pĭn′koosh′ən) *n.* A cushion in which pins are stuck when not in use.

pine¹ (pīn) *n.* **1.** Any of various cone-bearing evergreen trees with needle-shaped leaves in clusters. **2.** The wood of such a tree. [< Lat. *pinus.*]

pine² (pīn) *v.* **pined, pin·ing. 1.** To suffer longing; yearn. **2.** To wither away from longing or grief. [< Gk. *poinē*, punishment.]

pin·e·al body (pĭn′ē-əl, pī′nē-) *n.* A small glandlike body of uncertain function found in the brain.

pine·ap·ple (pīn′ăp′əl) *n.* **1.** A tropical American plant with swordlike leaves and a large, fleshy, edible fruit. **2.** The fruit of the pineapple. [ME, pine cone.]

pine needle *n.* The needle-shaped leaf of a pine tree.

pin·ey (pī′nē) *adj.* Var. of **piny**.

ping (pĭng) *n.* A brief, high-pitched sound, as that made by a bullet striking metal. [Imit.] —**ping** *v.*

Ping-Pong (pĭng′pŏng′, -pông′) A trademark for table tennis.

pin·head (pĭn′hĕd′) *n.* **1.** The head of a pin. **2.** Something small or insignificant. **3.** *Slang.* A stupid person. —**pin′head′ed** *adj.*

pin·hole (pĭn′hōl′) *n.* A tiny puncture made by or as if by a pin.

pin·ion¹ (pĭn′yən) *n.* A bird's wing. —*v.* **1.** To restrain or immobilize by binding the wings or arms. **2.** To fix in one place. [< Lat. *pinna.*]

pin·ion² (pĭn′yən) *n.* A small cogwheel that engages or is engaged by a larger cogwheel or a rack. [< Lat. *pecten*, comb.]

pink¹ (pĭngk) *n.* **1.** Any of various plants re-

lated to the carnation, often cultivated for their fragrant flowers. **2.** A light red. **3.** The highest degree of excellence: *in the pink of health.* [Orig. unknown.] —**pink** *adj.* —**pink′ish** *adj.* —**pink′ness** *n.*

pink² (pĭngk) *v.* **1.** To stab lightly. **2.** To decorate with a pattern of small holes. **3.** To cut with pinking shears. [ME *pinken.*]

pink-eye (pĭngk′ī′) *n.* Also **pink eye.** Acute contagious conjunctivitis.

pink·ie (pĭng′kē) *n.* Also **pinky** *pl.* **-ies.** The little finger. [Prob.< Du. *pink.*]

pinking shears *pl.n.* Sewing scissors with notched blades, used to finish edges of cloth with a scalloped or zigzag pattern for decoration or to prevent raveling.

pink·o (pĭng′kō) *n.*, *pl.* **-os.** *Slang.* One in sympathy with Communist doctrine.

pin money *n.* Money for incidental expenses.

pin·nace (pĭn′əs) *n.* **1.** A small sailing boat. **2.** A ship's boat. [OFr. *pinace.*]

pin·na·cle (pĭn′ə-kəl) *n.* **1.** A small turret or spire on a roof or buttress. **2.** A tall, pointed formation. **3.** The highest point; acme. [LLat. *pinnaculum*, dim. of Lat. *pinna*, wing.]

pin·nate (pĭn′āt′) *adj.* Featherlike, as compound leaves with leaflets along each side of a stalk. [< Lat. *pinna*, feather.]

pi·noch·le (pē′nŭk′əl, -nŏk′-) *n.* Also **pi·noc·le.** A card game for two to four persons, played with a deck of 48 cards. [Orig. unknown.]

pi·ñon (pĭn′yən, -yōn′) *n.* Also **pin·yon.** A pine tree bearing edible, nutlike seeds. [Sp., pine cone.]

pin·point (pĭn′point′) *n.* An extremely small thing or spot; particle. —*v.* **1.** To pierce. **2.** To locate and identify precisely.

pin·prick (pĭn′prĭk′) *n.* **1.** A slight puncture made by or as if by a pin. **2.** A minor annoyance.

pins and needles *pl.n.* Tingling felt in a part of the body that has been numbed from lack of circulation.

pin·stripe (pĭn′strīp′) *n.* **1.** A thin stripe on a fabric. **2.** A fabric with thin stripes.

pint (pīnt) *n.* **1.** A U.S. Customary System unit of volume or capacity, equal to 16 fluid ounces or 28.875 cubic inches. **2.** A U.S. Customary System unit of volume or capacity, used in dry measure, equal to ½ quart or 33.6 cubic inches. **3.** A British Imperial System unit of volume or capacity, used in dry and liquid measure, equal to 34.678 cubic inches. **4. a.** A container with a pint capacity. **b.** The amount it will hold. [< OFr. *pinte*, a unit of volume.]

pin·tail (pĭn′tāl′) *n.*, *pl.* **-tails** or **-tail.** A duck with gray, brown, and white plumage and a sharply pointed tail.

pin·to (pĭn′tō) *n.*, *pl.* **-tos** or **-toes.** A horse with irregular spots or markings. [Am. Sp.]

pin·up (pĭn′ŭp′) *n.* A picture to be pinned up on a wall, esp. a photograph of an attractive girl. —**pin′up′** *adj.*

pin·wheel (pĭn′hwēl′, -wēl′) *n.* **1.** A toy consisting of colored vanes pinned to the end of a stick so as to revolve like a wind. **2.** A firework that forms a rotating wheel of colored flames.

pin·y (pī′nē) *adj.* **-i·er, -i·est.** Also **pine·y. 1.** Consisting of or covered with pines. **2.** Of or like pines, esp. in odor.

Pin·yin or **pin·yin** (pĭn′yĭn′, -yĭn′) *n.* A system for translating Chinese ideograms into the

English alphabet. [Chin. *pin¹ yin¹*, spelling of the sound.]

pin·yon (pĭn'yən, -yōn') *n.* Var. of **piñon**.

pi·o·neer (pī'ə-nîr') *n.* **1.** One who ventures into unknown or unclaimed territory to settle. **2.** An innovator. [OFr. *pionier*, foot soldier.] **—pi·o·neer'** *v.*

pi·ous (pī'əs) *adj.* **1.** Reverently observant of religion; devout. **2.** Solemnly hypocritical. **3.** Devotional. **4.** High-minded. **5.** Commendable; worthy. [Lat. *pius*, dutiful.] **—pi'ous·ly** *adv.* **—pi'ous·ness** *n.*

pip¹ (pĭp) *n.* A small fruit seed, as of an orange. [< PIPPIN.]

pip² (pĭp) *n.* A dot on dice or dominoes. [Orig. unknown.]

pip³ (pĭp) *n.* A short, high-pitched radio signal. [Orig. unknown.]

pip⁴ (pĭp) *n.* **1.** A disease of birds. **2.** A minor or imaginary human ailment. [< Lat. *pituita*.]

pipe (pīp) *n.* **1.** A hollow cylinder or tubular conveyance for a fluid or gas. **2.** A tube of wood or clay with a mouthpiece at one end and a small bowl at the other, used for smoking. **3. a.** A tubular part or organ. **b. pipes.** *Informal.* The human respiratory system. **4. a.** A tubular wind instrument, such as a flute. **b.** Any of the tubes in an organ. **5. pipes. a.** A small wind instrument, consisting of tubes of different lengths bound together: *pipes of Pan.* **b.** A bagpipe. *—v.* **piped, pip·ing.** **1.** To convey (liquid or gas) by means of pipes. **2.** To play (a tune) on pipes. **3.** To make a shrill sound. **—phrasal verbs. pipe down.** *Slang.* To be quiet. **pipe up.** To speak up. [< Lat. *pipare*, to chirp.]

pipe dream *n.* A wishful, fantastic hope. [< the fantasies induced by smoking opium.]

pipe·line (pīp'līn') *n.* **1.** A conduit of pipe for the conveyance of water or petroleum products. **2.** A channel by which secret information is transmitted. **3.** A line of supply. **—pipe'line'** *v.*

pipe organ *n.* An organ (sense 1).

pip·er (pī'pər) *n.* A person who plays on a pipe. **—idiom. pay the piper.** To bear the consequences of one's actions.

pi·pette (pī-pĕt') *n.* Also **pi·pet.** A tube, open at both ends and often graduated, used for transferring liquids.

pip·ing (pī'pĭng) *n.* **1.** A system of pipes. **2.** A narrow band of material, used as a trimming on fabric.

pip·pin (pĭp'ĭn) *n.* Any of several varieties of apple. [< OFr. *pepin*.]

pip·squeak (pĭp'skwēk') *n.* A small and insignificant person.

pi·quant (pē'kənt, -känt', pē-känt') *adj.* **1.** Pleasantly pungent. **2.** Appealingly provocative. [< OFr. *piquer*, to pierce.] **—pi'quan·cy** or **pi'quant·ness** *n.* **—pi'quant·ly** *adv.*

pique (pēk) *n.* Resentment or vexation arising from wounded pride or vanity. *—v.* **piqued, piqu·ing.** **1.** To cause to feel resentment. **2.** To provoke; arouse. [< OFr. *piquer*, to pierce.]

pi·qué (pī-kā', pē'kā') *n.* A fabric with various patterns of wales. [< OFr. *piquer*, to pierce.]

pi·ra·nha (pī-rän'yə, -rän'-) *n.* Also **pi·ra·ña.** A sharp-toothed tropical American freshwater fish that often attacks and destroys living animals. [< Tupi.]

piranha

pi·rate (pī'rĭt) *n.* **1.** One who robs at sea or plunders the land from the sea. **2.** One who makes use of or reproduces the patented or copyrighted work of another illicitly or without permission. [< Gk. *peiratēs*.] **—pi'ra·cy** *n.* **—pi'rate** *v.* **—pi·rat'ic** (pī-răt'ĭk) or **pi·rat'i·cal** *adj.* **—pi·rat'i·cal·ly** *adv.*

pir·ou·ette (pĭr'ōō-ĕt') *n.* A full turn of the body on the tip of the toe or on the ball of the foot. [< OFr. *pirouet*, spinning top.] **—pir'ou·ette'** *v.*

pis·ca·to·ri·al (pĭs'kə-tôr'ē-əl, -tōr'-) *adj.* Of or relating to fishing. [< Lat. *piscis*, fish.] **—pis'ca·to'ri·al·ly** *adv.*

Pi·sces (pī'sēz) *n.* **1.** A constellation in the equatorial region of the Northern Hemisphere. **2.** The 12th sign of the zodiac.

pis·mire (pĭs'mīr', pĭz'-) *n.* An ant. [ME *pissemyre*.]

pis·ta·chi·o (pĭ-stăsh'ē-ō', -stä'shē-ō') *n., pl.* **-os.** **1.** A tree bearing hard-shelled, edible nuts with a green kernel. **2.** Also **pistachio nut.** The nut of this tree. [< Pers. *pistah*.]

pis·til (pĭs'təl) *n.* The seed-bearing reproductive organ of a flower. [< Lat. *pistillum*, pestle.]

pis·tol (pĭs'təl) *n.* A firearm designed to be held and fired with one hand. [< Czech *pišťala*, pipe.]

pis·tol-whip (pĭs'təl-hwĭp', -wĭp') *v.* **1.** To beat with a pistol barrel. **2.** To attack violently.

pis·ton (pĭs'tən) *n.* A solid cylinder or disk that fits snugly into a cylinder and moves back and forth under fluid pressure. [< Ital. *pistone*, large pestle.]

pit¹ (pĭt) *n.* **1.** A relatively deep hole in the ground. **2.** A trap; pitfall. **3.** Hell. **4.** An enclosed space in which animals are placed for fighting. **5. a.** A natural depression in the surface of the body. **b.** A small indentation in the skin left by disease or injury; pockmark. **6.** The musicians' section directly in front of the stage of a theater. **7.** The section of an exchange where trading in a specific commodity is carried on. **8.** A refueling area at an auto racecourse. **9. the pits.** *Slang.* The worst imaginable. *—v.* **pit·ted, pit·ting.** **1.** To make cavities, depressions, or scars in. **2.** To place in contest against another. [< OE *pytt.*]

pit² (pĭt) *n.* The single, hard-shelled seed of certain fruits, as a peach or cherry; stone. *—v.* **pit·ted, pit·ting.** To extract pits from (fruit). [< MDu.]

pit·a·pat (pĭt'ə-păt') *v.* **-pat·ted, -pat·ting.** To

make a repeated tapping sound. —n. A series of quick steps, taps, or beats. [Imit.]

pitch¹ (pĭch) n. Any of various thick, dark, sticky substances obtained from the distillation residue of coal tar, wood tar, or petroleum, used for waterproofing, roofing, caulking, and paving. [< Lat. *pix*.]

pitch² (pĭch) v. 1. To throw in a specific, intended direction; hurl. 2. To throw (a baseball) from the mound to the batter. 3. To put up or in position; establish. 4. To fix firmly; implant. 5. To fix the level of. 6. To plunge; fall forward. 7. To set at a specified pitch or level. 8. To dip bow and stern alternately, as a ship in rough seas. —*phrasal verb.* **pitch in.** To set to work vigorously, esp. in cooperation with others. —n. 1. An act of pitching. 2. a. A downward slant. b. The degree of such a slant. 3. A point or stage of development. 4. Lowness or highness of a complex sound, such as a musical tone, that is dependent mostly on frequency. 5. a. The distance traveled by a screw in a single revolution. b. The distance between two corresponding points on adjacent screw threads or gear teeth. 6. *Slang.* A set talk designed to persuade. [ME *pichen*.]

pitch-black (pĭch′blăk′) adj. Extremely black.

pitch-blende (pĭch′blĕnd′) n. A brownish-black mineral, the principal ore of uranium. [G. *Pechblende*.]

pitch-dark (pĭch′därk′) adj. Extremely dark.

pitch·er¹ (pĭch′ər) n. *Baseball.* One who pitches.

pitch·er² (pĭch′ər) n. A vessel for liquids, with a handle and a lip or spout for pouring. [< Med. Lat. *bicarius*, goblet.]

pitcher plant n. Any of various insectivorous plants with leaves modified to form pitcherlike organs that attract and trap insects.

pitch·fork (pĭch′fôrk′) n. A large fork with widely spaced prongs for pitching hay and breaking ground.

pitch pipe n. A small pipe sounded to give the pitch for a piece of music or for tuning an instrument.

pit·e·ous (pĭt′ē-əs) adj. Arousing pity; pathetic. —**pit′e·ous·ly** adv. —**pit′e·ous·ness** n.

pit·fall (pĭt′fôl′) n. 1. A trap made by digging a hole in the ground and concealing its opening. 2. Any danger or difficulty not anticipated.

pith (pĭth) n. 1. *Bot.* The soft, spongelike substance in the center of stems and branches of many plants. 2. The essential or central part. 3. Force; strength. [< OE *pitha*.]

pith·y (pĭth′ē) adj. **-i·er, -i·est.** 1. Of or resembling pith. 2. Precise and meaningful. —**pith′i·ly** adv. —**pith′i·ness** n.

pit·i·a·ble (pĭt′ē-ə-bəl) adj. Arousing pity. —**pit′i·a·ble·ness** n. —**pit′i·a·bly** adv.

pit·i·ful (pĭt′i-fəl) adj. 1. Arousing pity; pathetic. 2. So inferior or insignificant as to be contemptible. —**pit′i·ful·ly** adv. —**pit′i·ful·ness** n.

pit·i·less (pĭt′i-lĭs) adj. Having no pity; without mercy. —**pit′i·less·ly** adv. —**pit′i·less·ness** n.

pi·ton (pē′tŏn′) n. A metal spike with an eye or ring through which to pass a rope, used in mountain climbing as a hold. [< OFr., nail.]

pit stop n. 1. A stop at a pit during an auto race, usu. for fuel or for a tire change. 2. *Informal.* A rest stop during a trip.

pit·tance (pĭt′ns) n. A small amount or portion, esp. of money. [< Med. Lat. *pietantia*, donation to a monastery.]

pit·ter-pat·ter (pĭt′ər-păt′ər) n. A rapid series of light, tapping sounds. [Imit.] —**pit′ter-pat′ter** v.

pi·tu·i·tary (pĭ-tōō′ĭ-tĕr′ē, -tyōō′-) n., pl. **-ies.** *Anat.* The pituitary gland. [< Lat. *pituitarius*, of phlegm.] —**pi·tu′i·tar′y** adj.

pituitary gland n. A small, oval endocrine gland attached to the base of the vertebrate brain, the secretions of which control the other endocrine glands and influence growth, metabolism, and maturation.

pit·y (pĭt′ē) n., pl. **-ies.** 1. a. Sorrow aroused by the misfortune of another. b. Condescending sympathy. 2. A regrettable or disagreeable fact or necessity. —v. **-ied, -y·ing.** To feel pity (for). [< Lat. *pius*, dutiful.]

piv·ot (pĭv′ət) n. 1. A short rod or shaft about which a related part rotates or swings. 2. One that determines the direction or effect of something. 3. A wheeling movement made as if on a pivot. —v. To turn or cause to turn on or as if on a pivot. [< OFr.] —**piv′ot·al** adj. —**piv′ot·al·ly** adv.

pix (pĭks) n. Var. of pyx.

pix·y (pĭk′sē) n., pl. **-ies.** Also **pix·ie.** A fairylike or elfin creature. [Orig. unknown.]

piz·za (pēt′sə) n. An Italian baked dish consisting of a pielike crust covered usu. with a spiced mixture of tomatoes and cheese. [Ital.]

piz·ze·ri·a (pēt′sə-rē′ə) n. A place where pizzas are made and sold.

piz·zi·ca·to (pĭt′sĭ-kä′tō) adj. *Mus.* Played by plucking the strings of an instrument. [Ital.] —**piz′zi·ca′to** adv. & n.

plac·ard (plăk′ärd′, -ərd) n. 1. A poster for public display. 2. A nameplate, as on the door of a house. —v. 1. To announce on a placard. 2. To post placards on or in. [< OFr. *plaquart*, official document.]

pla·cate (plā′kāt′, plăk′āt′) v. **-cat·ed, -cat·ing.** To allay the anger of; appease. [Lat. *placare*.] —**plac′a·bil′i·ty** (plăk′ə-bĭl′ĭ-tē, plā′kə-) n. —**plac′a·ble** adj. —**plac′a·bly** adv. —**pla·cat′er** n. —**pla·ca′tion** (plă-kā′shən, plā-) n. —**pla·ca·to·ry** (-kə-tôr′ē, -tōr′ē) or **pla·ca′tive** adj.

place (plās) n. 1. A portion of space; an area with or without definite boundaries. 2. An area occupied by or set aside for someone or something. 3. A definite location. 4. Often **Place.** A public square or a short street in a town. 5. A table setting. 6. A position regarded as possessed by someone or something else; stead: *I was chosen in his place.* 7. A relative position in a series; standing: *fourth place.* —v. **placed, plac·ing.** 1. To put in some particular position; set. 2. To appoint to a post. 3. To rank (someone or something) in an order or sequence. 4. To make: *place a telephone call.* 5. To request formally: *place an order.* 6. To finish in second place or among the first three finishers in a race. —*idiom.* **go places.** *Informal.* To be successful. [< Gk. *plateia* (*hodos*), broad (street).]

pla·ce·bo (plə-sē′bō) n., pl. **-bos** or **-boes.** 1. A substance containing no medication, given merely to humor a patient. 2. An inactive substance used as a control in an experiment. [Lat., I shall please.]

place kick n. *Football.* A kick, as for a field goal, for which the ball is held or propped up in a fixed position. —**place′-kick′** v.

place mat n. A decorative and protective mat

for a single setting of dishes and silver at mealtime.

place·ment (plās'mənt) n. 1. a. The act of placing or arranging. b. The condition of being placed or arranged. 2. The act or business of finding jobs, lodgings, or other positions for applicants.

pla·cen·ta (plə-sĕn'tə) n., pl. -tas or -tae (-tē). A vascular, membranous organ that develops in female mammals during pregnancy, lining the uterine wall and partially enveloping the fetus, to which it is attached by the umbilical cord. [< Lat., flat cake.] —**pla·cen'tal** adj.

plac·er (plăs'ər) n. A deposit of sand or gravel left by a river or glacier, containing particles of valuable minerals. [Sp. < plaza, place.]

plac·id (plăs'ĭd) adj. Outwardly calm or composed. [< Lat. placēre, to please.] —**pla·cid'i·ty** (plə-sĭd'ĭ-tē) or **plac'id·ness** n. —**plac'id·ly** adv.

plack·et (plăk'ĭt) n. A slit in a garment. [Orig. unknown.]

pla·gia·rize (plā'jə-rīz') v. -rized, -riz·ing. To steal and use (the ideas or writings of another) as one's own. [< Lat. plagiarius, plunderer.] —**pla'gia·rism** n. —**pla'gia·rist** or **pla'gia·riz'er** n.

plague (plāg) n. 1. A pestilence, affliction, or calamity. 2. A cause for annoyance; nuisance. 3. A highly infectious, usu. fatal epidemic disease, esp. bubonic plague. —v. **plagued, plagu·ing.** To harass, pester, or annoy. [< Gk. plēgē, wound.] —**plagu'er** n.

plaid (plăd) n. 1. A rectangular woolen scarf of a checked or tartan pattern worn over one shoulder by Scottish Highlanders. 2. A tartan or checked pattern, esp. in cloth. [Sc. Gael. plaide.] —**plaid'ed** adj.

plain (plān) adj. -er, -est. 1. Free from obstructions; open to view; clear. 2. Easily understood; clearly evident. 3. Uncomplicated; simple. 4. Straightforward. 5. Not mixed with other substances; pure. 6. Common in rank or station; ordinary. 7. Not pretentious; unsophisticated. 8. Having little ornamentation or decoration. 9. Unattractive. —n. An extensive, level, treeless area of land. —adv. In a clear or intelligible manner. [< Lat. planus, flat.] —**plain'ly** adv. —**plain'ness** n.

plain-clothes man (plān'klōz') n. Also **plain-clothes·man** (plān'klōz'mən). A member of a police force who wears civilian clothes on duty.

Plains Indian n. A member of any of the tribes of North American Indians that once inhabited the plains of the central United States and Canada.

plain-spo·ken (plān'spō'kən) adj. Frank; straightforward. —**plain'spo'ken·ness** n.

plaint (plānt) n. 1. A complaint. 2. A lamentation. [< Lat. plangere, to lament.]

plain·tiff (plān'tĭf) n. The party that institutes a suit in a court. [< OFr. plaintif, plaintive.]

plain·tive (plān'tĭv) adj. Expressing sorrow; mournful. —**plain'tive·ly** adv. —**plain'tive·ness** n.

plait (plāt, plăt) n. A braid, esp. of hair. —v. To braid. [< Lat. plicare, to fold.]

plan (plăn) n. 1. A detailed scheme or method for the accomplishment of an object. 2. A proposed or tentative project or goal. 3. An outline or sketch, esp. a drawing or diagram made to scale. —v. **planned, plan·ning.** 1. To formulate, draw up, or make a plan or plans. 2. To intend. [< Lat. plantare, to plant.] —**plan'ner** n.

pla·nar (plā'nər) adj. 1. Of or in a plane. 2. Flat. —**pla·nar'i·ty** (plə-năr'ĭ-tē) n.

plane¹ (plān) n. 1. A surface containing all the straight lines connecting any two points on it. 2. A flat or level surface. 3. A level of development. 4. An airplane. 5. A supporting surface of an airplane. [Lat. planum.]

plane² (plān) n. A carpenter's tool for smoothing and leveling wood. —v. **planed, plan·ing.** To smooth or finish with or as if with a plane. [Lat. planus, flat.] —**plan'er** n.

plane³ (plān) n. A sycamore or related tree, with ball-shaped seed clusters and leaves resembling those of the maple. [< Gk. platus, broad.]

plan·et (plăn'ĭt) n. A nonluminous celestial body illuminated by light from a star around which it revolves. [< Gk. planēs, wanderer.]

plan·e·tar·i·um (plăn'ĭ-târ'ē-əm) n., pl. -ums or -i·a (-ē-ə). 1. An apparatus or model representing the solar system. 2. A device for projecting images of celestial bodies on the inner surface of a dome. 3. A building or room containing such a device.

plan·e·tar·y (plăn'ĭ-tĕr'ē) adj. 1. Of or resembling a planet. 2. Worldwide; global.

plan·gent (plăn'jənt) adj. 1. Having a deep, reverberating sound. 2. Plaintive. [< Lat. plangere, to strike.] —**plan'gen·cy** n. —**plan'gent·ly** adv.

plank (plăngk) n. 1. A thick piece of lumber. 2. One of the articles of a political platform. —v. 1. To cover with planks. 2. To bake or broil and serve (fish or meat) on a board. 3. To put or set down with force. [< Lat. planca.]

plank·ton (plăngk'tən) n. Plant and animal organisms, gen. microscopic, that float in bodies of water. [< Gk. planktos, wandering.] —**plank·ton'ic** (-tŏn'ĭk) adj.

Planned Parenthood (plănd). A service mark for an organization that provides family planning services.

plant (plănt) n. 1. An organism characteristically having cellulose cell walls, growing by synthesis of inorganic substances, and lacking the power of locomotion. 2. A plant without a permanent woody stem, as distinguished from a tree or shrub. 3. A factory. 4. The buildings, equipment, and fixtures of an institution. —v. 1. To place in the ground to grow. 2. To sow or supply with or as if with seeds or plants. 3. To fix or set firmly in position. 4. To establish. 5. To implant in the mind. 6. To place for the purpose of spying or deception. [< Lat. planta.] —**plant'a·ble** adj.

plan·tain¹ (plăn'tən) n. A weedy plant with a dense spike of small, greenish or whitish flowers. [< Lat. plantago.]

plan·tain² (plăn'tən) n. A bananalike tropical plant or its fruit. [Sp. plantano, plane tree.]

plan·ta·tion (plăn-tā'shən) n. 1. A group of cultivated trees or plants. 2. A large estate or

---

ă pat ā pay â care ä father ĕ pet ē be ĭ pit ī tie î pier ŏ pot ō toe ô paw, for oi noise ōō took ōō boot ou out th thin th this ŭ cut û urge yōō abuse zh vision ə about, item, edible, gallop, circus

farm on which crops are grown and harvested, usu. by resident workers.

plant·er (plăn'tər) *n.* **1.** One that plants. **2.** The owner or manager of a plantation. **3.** A decorative container for plants.

plaque (plăk) *n.* **1.** An ornamented or engraved plate, slab, or disk used for decoration or on a monument for information. **2.** A small ornament or a badge of membership. **3.** A deposit that builds up on a tooth or on the inner wall of a blood vessel. [< MDu. *placken,* to patch.]

plash (plăsh) *n.* A light splash. [Prob. imit.] **—plash** *v.*

-plasm *suff.* Material forming cells or tissue: *cytoplasm.* [< PLASMA.]

plas·ma (plăz'mə) *n.* **1.** The clear, yellowish fluid portion of blood, lymph, or intramuscular fluid, in which cells are suspended. **2.** The fluid portion of milk from which the curd has been separated; whey. **3.** *Physics.* An electrically neutral, highly ionized gas composed of ions, electrons, and neutral particles. **4.** Protoplasm or cytoplasm. [< Gk., image.] **—plas·mat·ic** (plăz-măt'ĭk) or **plas·mic** *adj.*

plas·min (plăz'mĭn) *n.* An enzyme in plasma that dissolves fibrin and other blood-clotting factors.

plasmo- or **plasm-** *pref.* Plasma: *plasmin.* [< PLASMA.]

plas·mol·y·sis (plăz-mŏl'ĭ-sĭs) *n.* Shrinkage or contraction of the protoplasm in a cell, esp. a plant cell, caused by loss of water through osmosis. **—plas·mo·lyt·ic** (plăz'mə-lĭt'ĭk) *adj.* **—plas·mo·lyt'i·cal·ly** *adv.*

plas·ter (plăs'tər) *n.* **1.** A paste that hardens to a smooth solid and is used for coating walls and ceilings. **2.** Plaster of Paris. **3.** A pastelike mixture applied to a part of the body for healing or cosmetic purposes. **—v. 1.** To cover with or as if with plaster. **2.** To cover conspicuously or to excess. [< Gk. *emplastron,* medical dressing.] **—plas'ter·er** *n.*

plas·ter·board (plăs'tər-bôrd', -bŏrd') *n.* A thin, rigid board composed of layers of fiberboard or paper, bonded to a plaster core and used to cover walls and ceilings.

plaster of Paris *n.* Any of a group of gypsum cements, essentially hemihydrated calcium sulfate, $CaSO_4 \cdot 1/2H_2O$, a white powder that forms a paste when mixed with water and hardens into a solid.

plas·tic (plăs'tĭk) *adj.* **1.** Capable of being shaped or formed; pliable. **2.** Relating to or dealing with shaping or modeling. **3.** Made of plastic. **—n.** Any of various complex organic compounds produced by polymerization, capable of being molded, extruded, or cast into various shapes and films or drawn into filaments used as textile fibers. [< Gk. *plassein,* to mold.] **—plas'ti·cal·ly** *adv.* **—plas·tic'i·ty** *n.*

plastic surgery *n.* Surgery to remodel, repair, or restore injured or defective tissue or body parts. **—plastic surgeon** *n.*

plate (plāt) *n.* **1.** A smooth, flat, relatively thin, rigid body of uniform thickness. **2. a.** A sheet of hammered, rolled, or cast metal. **b.** A flat piece of metal on which something is engraved. **3.** *Printing.* **a.** A sheet of material converted into a printing surface, such as an electrotype. **b.** An impression taken from such a surface. **c.** A full-page book illustration, often in color. **4.** A sheet of glass or metal on which a photographic image can be recorded. **5.** A thin metallic or plastic support fitted to the gums to anchor artificial teeth. **6.** *Baseball.* Home base or plate, usu. a flat piece of heavy rubber. **7.** A shallow dish from which food is served or eaten. **8.** Food and service for one person at a meal. **9.** Household utensils made of or covered with a precious metal. **—v. plat·ed, plat·ing 1.** To cover with a thin layer of metal. **2.** To armor. [< Gk. *platus,* flat.]

pla·teau (plă-tō') *n., pl.* **-teaus** or **-teaux** (-tōz'). **1.** An elevated, level expanse of land. **2.** A stable period or condition. [< OFr., *plate.]

plate glass *n.* A strong rolled and polished sheet glass.

plate·let (plāt'lĭt) *n.* A protoplasmic disk, smaller than a red blood cell, found in the blood of vertebrates and important in promoting coagulation.

plat·en (plăt'n) *n.* **1.** A flat metal plate that positions the paper and holds it against the inked type in a printing press. **2.** The roller on a typewriter. [< OFr. *platine,* metal plate.]

plat·form (plăt'fôrm') *n.* **1.** A horizontal surface higher than an adjoining area. **2.** A formal declaration of the policy of a group, as a political party. [OFr. *plate-forme,* diagram.]

plat·ing (plā'tĭng) *n.* **1.** A thin layer or coating of metal, as gold or silver. **2.** A covering or layer of metal plates.

plat·i·num (plăt'n-əm) *n. Symbol* **Pt** A silverwhite, corrosive-resistant, metallic element used in electrical components, jewelry, dentistry, electroplating, and as a catalyst. Atomic number 78; atomic weight 195.09. [< Sp. *plata,* silver.]

plat·i·tude (plăt'ĭ-tōōd', -tyōōd') *n.* A trite remark, statement, or idea. [Fr. < *plat,* flat.] **—plat·i·tu'di·nous** *adj.* **—plat·i·tu'di·nous·ly** *adv.*

Pla·ton·ic (plə-tŏn'ĭk, plā-) *adj.* **1.** Of or characteristic of Plato or his philosophy. **2.** Often **platonic.** Transcending physical desire; spiritual. **—Pla·ton'i·cal·ly** *adv.*

pla·toon (plə-tōōn') *n.* **1.** A subdivision of a military company usu. consisting of two or more squads. **2.** A body of persons working together. [Fr. *peloton.]

plat·ter (plăt'ər) *n.* **1.** A large, shallow dish or plate. **2.** *Slang.* A phonograph record. [< OFr. *plate,* plate.]

plat·y·pus (plăt'ĭ-pəs) *n., pl.* **-es.** A semiaquatic, egg-laying Australian mammal with webbed feet and a snout resembling a duck's bill. [< Gk. *platupous,* flat-footed.]

platypus

plau·dit (plô'dĭt) *n.* An expression of praise. [< Lat. *plaudere,* to applaud.]

plau·si·ble (plô′zə-bəl) adj. Apparently valid or likely. [< Lat. plausus, p.p. of plaudere, to applaud.] —**plau′si·bil′i·ty** or **plau′si·ble·ness** n. —**plau′si·bly** adv.

play (plā) v. 1. To occupy oneself in amusement, sport, or other recreation. 2. To take part in (a game or sport). 3. To act or perform in jest. 4. To toy; trifle. 5. To act in a specified way: play fair. 6. To act or perform (a role). 7. To perform (on a musical instrument). 8. To be performed: Othello is playing next week. 9. To move lightly or irregularly: The breeze played on the water. 10. To pretend to be. 11. To compete against in a game. 12. a. To occupy (a position) in a game: playing first base. b. To employ (a player) in a game or position. c. To use (e.g. a card) in a game. 13. To manipulate: played the two opponents against each other. 14. To bet or wager. 15. To cause (e.g. a record) to emit sounds. —**phrasal verbs. play back.** To replay (a record or tape). **play down.** To minimize the importance of. **play on** (or **upon**). To take advantage of (another's feelings). **play up.** Informal. To emphasize or publicize. **play up to.** To curry favor with. —n. 1. a. A literary work written for the stage. b. The performance of such a work. 2. Activity engaged in for enjoyment or recreation. 3. Fun. 4. The act or manner of playing a game or sport. 5. A method of dealing with people: fair play. 6. A move in a game: It's your play. 7. Sports. Legitimate use: The ball was in play. 8. Action or use: the play of the imagination. 9. Free movement, as of mechanical parts. —**idioms. play ball.** Informal. To cooperate. **play both ends against the middle.** To maneuver between two antagonists to get what one wants. **play hardball.** To use rough or unscrupulous tactics to gain an end. [< OE plegan.] —**play′a·ble** adj.

pla·ya (plī′ə) n. A flat area at the bottom of a desert basin, sometimes temporarily covered with water. [Sp. < Med. Lat. plagia, shore.]

play-act (plā′ăkt′) v. 1. To play a role in a dramatic performance. 2. To make believe. 3. To behave affectedly or artificially.

play·back (plā′băk′) n. The act or process of replaying a record or tape.

play·bill (plā′bĭl′) n. A poster announcing a theatrical performance.

Play·bill (plā′bĭl′). A trademark for a program of a theatrical performance.

play·boy (plā′boi′) n. A wealthy man devoted to the pleasures of nightclubs, sports, and women.

play-by-play (plā′bī-plā′) adj. Being a detailed running commentary, as of the action of a sports event.

play·er (plā′ər) n. 1. One who participates in a game or sport. 2. An actor. 3. A musician.

player piano n. A mechanically operated piano using a perforated roll to control the keys.

play·ful (plā′fəl) adj. 1. Full of fun; frolicsome. 2. Humorous; jesting. —**play′ful·ly** adv. —**play′ful·ness** n.

play·go·er (plā′gō′ər) n. One who attends the theater.

play·ground (plā′ground′) n. An outdoor area for recreation and play.

playing card n. A card marked with its rank and suit belonging to any of several decks used in playing various games.

play·mate (plā′māt′) n. A companion in play.

play-off (plā′ôf′, -ŏf′) n. Sports. A final game or series of games played to determine a championship.

play·pen (plā′pĕn′) n. A portable enclosure in which a baby can be left to play.

play·room (plā′rōōm′, -rŏŏm′) n. A room designed for recreation or play.

play·thing (plā′thĭng′) n. A toy.

play·wright (plā′rīt′) n. One who writes plays.

pla·za (plä′zə, plăz′ə) n. A public square or similar open area in a town or city. [Sp., ult. < Gk. platus, broad.]

plea (plē) n. 1. An appeal or entreaty. 2. An excuse; pretext. 3. Law. The answer of the accused to a charge or indictment. [< OFr. plaid, lawsuit.]

plea-bar·gain (plē′bär′gən) v. To make an agreement to plead guilty to a lesser charge so as to avoid being tried for a more serious one. —**plea′-bar′gain·ing** n.

plead (plēd) v. **plead·ed** or **pled** (plĕd), **pleading.** 1. To appeal earnestly; implore. 2. To argue for or against something. 3. To submit as an excuse or defense. 4. To put forward a plea in a court of law. 5. To argue or present (a case) in a court. [< OFr. plaidier.] —**plead′a·ble** adj. —**plead′er** n. —**plead′ing·ly** adv.

pleas·ant (plĕz′ənt) adj. -er, -est. 1. Pleasing; agreeable; delightful. 2. Pleasing or favorable in manner; amiable: a pleasant disposition. —**pleas′ant·ly** adv. —**pleas′ant·ness** n.

Syns: pleasant, enjoyable, pleasing, pleasurable adj.

pleas·ant·ry (plĕz′ən-trē) n., pl. -ries. A pleasant, entertaining, or humorous remark.

please (plēz) v. **pleased, pleas·ing.** 1. To make glad; give enjoyment or satisfaction to. 2. To be the will or desire of: may it please the court. 3. To be willing to. 4. To like; wish: Do whatever you please. [< Lat. placēre.] —**pleas′er** n. —**pleas′ing** adj.

·pleas·ur·a·ble (plĕzh′ər-ə-bəl) adj. Agreeable; gratifying. —**pleas′ur·a·ble·ness** n. —**pleas′ur·a·bly** adv.

pleas·ure (plĕzh′ər) n. 1. Enjoyment; satisfaction. 2. A source of enjoyment. 3. One's preference, wish, or choice: What is your pleasure?

pleat (plēt) n. A fold in cloth made by doubling the material upon itself. [< PLAIT.] —**pleat** v.

plebe (plēb) n. A freshman at a military academy. [< Lat. plebs, common people.]

ple·be·ian (plǐ-bē′ən) adj. Common; vulgar. —n. One who is common or crude. [< Lat. plebs, common people.] —**ple·be′ian·ism** n.

pleb·i·scite (plĕb′ĭ-sīt′) n. A direct vote by an entire people on an important issue. [< Lat. plebiscitum.]

plebs (plĕbz) n., pl. **ple·bes** (plē′bēz′). 1. The common people of ancient Rome. 2. The populace. [Lat.]

plec·trum (plĕk′trəm) n., pl. -**trums** or -**tra** (-trə). Also **plec·tron** (plĕk′trŏn′). A small, thin piece of metal, plastic, bone, or other material, used to play a stringed instrument. [< Gk. plēktron.]

pled (plĕd) v. A *p.t.* & *p.p.* of **plead**.

pledge (plĕj) n. 1. A formal promise. 2. Something considered as security to guarantee payment of a debt or an obligation. 3. One who has been accepted for membership in a fraternity. —v. **pledged, pledg·ing.** 1. To promise solemnly. 2. To bind by or as if by a pledge. 3. To deposit as security. 4. To promise to join (e.g. a club). [< LLat. *plevium,* of Gmc. orig.] —**pledg′er** n.

Plei·a·des (plē′ə-dēz′) *pl.n. Astron.* An open star cluster in the constellation Taurus, consisting of several hundred stars, of which six are visible to the naked eye.

Pleis·to·cene (plī′stə-sēn′) adj. Of or belonging to the geologic time, rock series, or sedimentary deposits of the earlier of the two epochs of the Quaternary period. —n. The Pleistocene epoch. [Gk. *pleistos,* most + -CENE.]

ple·na·ry (plē′nə-rē, plĕn′ə-) adj. 1. Full; absolute: *a diplomat with plenary powers.* 2. Attended by all qualified members. [< Lat. *plenus.*] —**ple′na·ri·ly** adv.

plen·i·po·ten·ti·ary (plĕn′ə-pə-tĕn′shē-ĕr′ē, -sha-rē) adj. Invested with full powers. —n., pl. -ies. A diplomatic agent, as an ambassador, fully authorized to represent a government. [< LLat. *plenipotens.*]

plen·i·tude (plĕn′ĭ-tōōd′, -tyōōd′) n. Abundance; fullness. [< Lat. *plenus,* full.]

plen·te·ous (plĕn′tē-əs) adj. 1. Abundant; plentiful. 2. Producing or yielding in abundance. —**plen′te·ous·ly** adv. —**plen′te·ous·ness** n.

plen·ti·ful (plĕn′tĭ-fəl) adj. 1. Existing in great quantity; abundant. 2. Providing or producing an abundance. —**plen′ti·ful·ly** adv. —**plen′ti·ful·ness** n.

plen·ty (plĕn′tē) n. 1. A large quantity or amount; abundance: *goods in plenty.* 2. A condition of general abundance or prosperity. [< Lat. *plenus,* full.]

pleth·o·ra (plĕth′ər-ə) n. Superabundance; excess. [< Gk. *plēthōra.*] —**ple·thor′ic** (plə-thôr′ĭk, -thŏr′-) adj. —**ple·thor′i·cal·ly** adv.

pleu·ri·sy (plŏŏr′ĭ-sē) n. Inflammation of the membranous sacs that enclose the lungs. [< Gk. *pleura,* rib, side.] —**pleu·rit′ic** (-rĭt′ĭk) adj.

Plex·i·glas (plĕk′sĭ-glăs′, -gläs′). A trademark for a light, permanently transparent, weather-resistant thermoplastic.

plex·us (plĕk′səs) n., pl. -us or -us·es. *Anat.* A structure in the form of a network, esp. of nerves, blood vessels, or lymphatics: *the solar plexus.* [< Lat., p.p. of *plectere,* to plait.]

pli·a·ble (plī′ə-bəl) adj. 1. Easily bent or shaped; flexible. 2. Easily influenced, persuaded, or swayed. [< Lat. *plicare,* to fold.] —**pli′a·bil′i·ty** or **pli′a·ble·ness** n. —**pli′a·bly** adv.

pli·ant (plī′ənt) adj. 1. Easily bent or flexed; supple. 2. Receptive to change; adaptable. [< Lat. *plicare,* to fold.] —**pli′an·cy** (-ən-sē) n. —**pli′ant·ly** adv.

pli·ers (plī′ərz) *pl.n.* (*used with a sing. or pl. verb*). A tool with a pair of pivoted jaws, used for gripping, bending, and cutting.

plight¹ (plīt) n. A condition of difficulty or adversity. [< Lat. *plicare,* to fold.]

plight² (plīt) v. To promise or bind by a solemn pledge, esp. to betroth. [< OE *pliht.*] —**plight′er** n.

plinth (plĭnth) n. A block or slab upon which a pedestal, column, or statue is placed. [< Gk. *plinthos,* tile.]

Pli·o·cene (plī′ə-sēn′) adj. Of or belonging to the geologic time, rock series, or sedimentary deposits of the last of the five epochs of the Tertiary period. —n. The Pliocene epoch. [Gk. *pleiōn,* more + -CENE.]

plod (plŏd) v. **plod·ded, plod·ding.** 1. To walk heavily or laboriously; trudge. 2. To work perseveringly or monotonously. [Imit.] —**plod′der** n. —**plod′ding·ly** adv.

plop (plŏp) v. **plopped, plop·ping.** 1. To fall with a sound like that of an object falling into water. 2. To drop or sink heavily. [Imit.]

plot (plŏt) n. 1. A small piece of ground. 2. The series of events that constitute the action of a narrative or drama. 3. A secret plan; scheme. —v. **plot·ted, plot·ting.** 1. To represent graphically, as on a chart. 2. To devise secretly; conspire. [< OE.] —**plot′less** adj. —**plot′less·ness** n. —**plot′ter** n.

Syns: plot, collusion, conspiracy, intrigue, scheme n.

plov·er (plŭv′ər, plō′vər) n., pl. -ers or -er. Any of various relatively small, short-billed wading birds. [< Lat. *pluvia,* rain.]

plow (plou). Also *chiefly Brit.* **plough.** —n. 1. A farm implement used for breaking up soil and cutting furrows. 2. An implement of similar function, as a snowplow. —v. 1. To break and turn up (earth) with a plow. 2. To move or proceed forcefully: *plowed through the crowd.* —*phrasal verbs.* **plow back.** To reinvest (e.g. profits) in one's business. **plow into.** *Informal.* To strike forcefully. **plow under.** To overwhelm. [< OE *plōh,* a unit of land area.] —**plow′er** n.

plow·boy (plou′boi′) n. 1. A boy who guides a team of animals in plowing. 2. A country boy.

plow·share (plou′shâr′) n. The cutting blade of a plow.

ploy (ploi) n. A stratagem to obtain an advantage over an opponent. [Orig. unknown.]

pluck (plŭk) v. 1. To pull off or out; pick. 2. To pull the hair or feathers from. 3. To sound (the strings of an instrument) by pulling and releasing them. —n. 1. The act of plucking. 2. Resourceful courage; spirit. [< OE *pluccian.*] —**pluck′er** n.

pluck·y (plŭk′ē) adj. -i·er, -i·est. Courageous; brave. —**pluck′i·ly** adv. —**pluck′i·ness** n.

plug (plŭg) n. 1. An object used to stop a hole. 2. a. A fitting, commonly with metal prongs for insertion in a fixed socket, used to make electric connections. b. A spark plug. 3. A fireplug. 4. A portion of chewing tobacco. 5. *Informal.* A favorable public mention, as of a product or person. —v. **plugged, plug·ging.** 1. To fill (a hole) tightly with or as with a plug. 2. To connect to a socket by means of a plug. 3. *Slang.* To hit with a bullet. 4. *Informal.* To make favorable public mention of (e.g. a product). 5. *Informal.* To work doggedly at some activity. [< MDu. *plugge.*] —**plug′ger** n.

plum (plŭm) n. 1. A smooth-skinned, fleshy fruit with a hard-shelled pit. 2. A tree bearing such fruit. 3. Something esp. desirable, as a good position. [< Gk. *proumnon.*]

plum·age (plōō′mĭj) n. The feathers of a bird.

plumb (plŭm) n. 1. A weight suspended from the end of a line, used to determine water depth. 2. Such a device used to establish a true vertical. —adj. 1. Exactly vertical. 2. *In-*

formal. Utter; sheer: *a plumb fool.* —*v.* **1.** To test the alignment or angle of with a plumb. **2.** To determine the depth of; sound. [< Lat. *plumbum,* lead.] —**plumb'a·ble** *adj.*

plumb·er (plŭm'ər) *n.* One who installs and repairs pipes and plumbing.

plumb·ing (plŭm'ĭng) *n.* **1.** The pipes, fixtures, and other apparatus of a water or sewage system. **2.** The work or trade of a plumber.

plumb line *n.* A line from which a weight is suspended to determine depth or verticality.

plume (plōōm) *n.* **1.** A feather, esp. a large and showy one. **2.** Something resembling a feather: *a plume of smoke.* —*v.* **plumed, plum·ing. 1.** To decorate with or as if with plumes. **2.** To pride or congratulate (oneself). [< Lat. *pluma.*] —**plum'y** *adj.*

plum·met (plŭm'ĭt) *v.* To drop straight down; plunge. [< Lat. *plumbum,* lead.]

plump¹ (plŭmp) *adj.* **-er, -est.** Well-rounded and full in form; chubby. —*v.* To make or become plump. [Prob. < MLG *plomp,* dull.] —**plump'ly** *adv.* —**plump'ness** *n.*

plump² (plŭmp) *v.* **1.** To drop abruptly or heavily. **2.** To give full support or praise. —*n.* **1.** A heavy or abrupt fall. **2.** The sound of such a fall. —*adv.* **1.** With a heavy impact. **2.** Straight down or ahead. [MLG *plumpen.*]

plun·der (plŭn'dər) *v.* To rob of goods by force, esp. in time of war; pillage. —*n.* Property stolen by fraud or force; booty. [< MHG, household goods.] —**plun'der·er** *n.*

plunge (plŭnj) *v.* **plunged, plung·ing. 1.** To thrust or throw oneself forcefully into a substance or place. **2.** To enter or cast suddenly into a given condition, situation, or activity. **3.** To descend steeply or suddenly. **4.** *Informal.* To speculate or gamble extravagantly. [< OFr. *plonger,* ult. < Lat. *plumbum,* lead.] —**plunge** *n.*

plung·er (plŭn'jər) *n.* **1.** A machine part that operates with a repeated thrusting or plunging movement. **2.** A device consisting of a rubber suction cup at the end of a stick, used to unclog drains and pipes.

plunk (plŭngk) *Informal.* —*v.* **1.** To pluck (the strings of a musical instrument). **2.** To throw, place, or drop heavily or abruptly. **3.** To emit a hollow, twanging sound. —*n.* **1.** A short, hollow, twanging sound. **2.** A heavy blow or stroke. [Imit.] —**plunk'er** *n.*

plu·per·fect (plōō-pûr'fĭkt) *Gram.* —*adj.* Of or designating a verb tense used to express action completed prior to a specified or implied past time. —*n.* **1.** The pluperfect tense. **2.** A verb or form in this tense. [< LLat. *plus quam perfectum,* more than perfect.]

plu·ral (plŏŏr'əl) *Gram.* —*adj.* Of or relating to a form that designates more than one of the things specified. —*n.* **1.** The plural number or form. **2.** A word or term in this form. [< Lat. *plus,* more.] —**plu'ral·ly** *adv.*

plu·ral·i·ty (plŏŏ-răl'ĭ-tē) *n., pl.* **-ties. 1.** In a contest of more than two candidates, the number of votes cast for the winner if this number is less than half the total votes cast. **2.** The number by which the vote of a winning candidate is more than that of the closest opponent.

plus (plŭs) *prep.* **1.** Added to. **2.** Increased by; along with: *wages plus bonuses.* —*adj.* **1.** Positive, as on a scale or in polarity. **2.** Being in addition to what is expected or specified. —*n.* **1.** A symbol (+) used to indicate addition or a positive quantity. **2.** A favorable factor. [Lat., more.]

Usage: **Plus** as a preposition does not have the conjunctive force of *and.* Therefore when *plus* is used after a singular subject, the verb remains singular: *2 plus 2 equals 4.*

plush (plŭsh) *n.* A fabric with a thick, deep pile. —*adj.* Luxurious. [< Lat. *pilus,* hair.] —**plush'ly** *adv.* —**plush'i·ness** *n.* —**plush'y** *adv.* —**plush'y** *adj.*

Plu·to (plōō'tō) *n.* **1.** *Rom. Myth.* The god of the dead. **2.** The 9th and farthest planet from the sun, with a sidereal period of revolution about the sun of 248.4 years, 2.8 billion miles distance at perihelion and 4.6 billion miles at aphelion, and a diameter approx. half that of the earth.

plu·toc·ra·cy (plōō-tŏk'rə-sē) *n., pl.* **-cies. 1.** Government by the wealthy. **2.** A wealthy class that controls a government. [Gk. *ploutos,* wealth + **-CRACY.**] —**plu'to·crat'** (-tə-krăt') *n.* —**plu'to·crat'ic** or **plu'to·crat'i·cal** *adj.* —**plu'to·crat'i·cal·ly** *adv.*

plu·ton·ic (plōō-tŏn'ĭk) *adj. Geol.* Of deep igneous or magmatic origin: *plutonic water.* [< PLUTO.]

plu·to·ni·um (plōō-tō'nē-əm) *n. Symbol* **Pu** A naturally radioactive, silvery metallic element, used as a reactor fuel and in nuclear weapons. Atomic number 94; longest-lived isotope Pu 244. [< PLUTO.]

plu·vi·al (plōō'vē-əl) *adj.* **1.** Of or relating to rain. **2.** Marked by abundant rain. [< Lat. *pluvia,* rain.]

ply¹ (plī) *v.* **plied, ply·ing. 1.** To join together, as by molding or twisting. **2.** To double over (e.g. cloth). —*n., pl.* **plies. 1.** A layer, as of cloth, paperboard, or wood. **2.** One of the strands twisted together to make yarn, rope, or thread. [< Lat. *plicare,* to fold.]

ply² (plī) *v.* **plied, ply·ing. 1.** To use diligently, as a tool or weapon. **2.** To engage in, as a trade. **3.** To traverse or sail over regularly. **4.** To continue supplying: *plying guests with food.* [< APPLY.]

Plym·outh Rock (plĭm'əth) *n.* An American breed of fowl raised for both meat and eggs.

ply·wood (plī'wŏŏd') *n.* A building material made of layers of wood glued tightly together. [PLY¹ + WOOD.]

Pm The symbol for the element promethium.

pneu·mat·ic (nōō-măt'ĭk, nyōō'-) or **pneu·mat·i·cal** (-ĭ-kəl) *adj.* Of, operated by, or filled with air or another gas. [< Gk. *pneuma,* wind.] —**pneu·mat'i·cal·ly** *adv.*

pneu·mo·coc·cus (nōō'mə-kŏk'əs, nyōō'-) *n., pl.* **-coc·ci** (-kŏk'sī', -kŏk'ī'). A bacterium that causes pneumonia. [Gk. *pneuma,* breath + **-COCCUS.**] —**pneu'mo·coc'cal** (-kŏk'əl) *adj.*

pneu·mo·nia (nōō-mōn'yə, nyōō-) *n.* An acute or chronic disease marked by inflammation of the lungs and caused by viruses, bacteria, and physical and chemical agents. [< Gk. *pleumōn,* lung.] —**pneu·mon'ic** *adj.*

Po The symbol for the element polonium.

poach¹ (pōch) *v.* To cook in simmering liquid. [< OFr. *pochier (des oeufs)*, to put (egg yolks) in pockets.] —**poach'er** *n*.

poach² (pōch) *v*. **1.** To trespass on another's property in order to take fish or game. **2.** To take (fish or game) illegally. [OFr. *pocher*, to trample, of Gmc. orig.] —**poach'er** *n*.

pock (pŏk) *n*. **1.** A pustule caused by smallpox or a similar eruptive disease. **2.** A mark or scar left in the skin by such a pustule; pockmark. [< OE *pocc*.]

pock·et (pŏk'ĭt) *n*. **1.** A pouch with an open edge sewed into or onto a garment. **2.** A receptacle or cavity. **3.** Financial means. **4.** A small isolated or protected area or group. —*adj*. **1.** Suitable for carrying in a pocket. **2.** Tiny; miniature. —*v*. **1.** To place in or as if in a pocket. **2.** To take possession of for oneself, esp. dishonestly. [< ONFr. *poke*, bag, of Gmc. orig.] —**pock'et·ful** *n*.

pock·et·book (pŏk'ĭt-bŏŏk') *n*. **1.** A wallet; billfold. **2.** A handbag. **3.** Financial resources.

pock·et·knife (pŏk'ĭt-nīf') *n*. A small knife with a blade or blades and sometimes other implements folding into the handle.

pocket veto *n*. The indirect veto of a bill by an executive through retention of the unsigned bill until legislative adjournment.

pock·mark (pŏk'märk') *n*. A pitlike scar left on the skin by smallpox or another eruptive disease. —**pock'marked'** *adj*.

po·co (pō'kō) *adv*. *Mus*. Somewhat: *poco allegro*. [Ital.]

pod (pŏd) *n*. **1.** *Bot*. A seed vessel, as of a pea or bean, that splits open. **2.** A housing that encloses an externally mounted part of an aircraft. [Prob. < obs. *cod*, bag.]

-pod or **-pode** *suff*. Foot: *gastropod*. [< Gk. *pous*, foot.]

po·di·a·try (pə-dī'ə-trē) *n*. The study and treatment of foot ailments. [Gk. *pous*, foot + -IATRY.] —**po·di'a·trist** *n*.

po·di·um (pō'dē-əm) *n*., *pl*. **-di·a** (-dē-ə) or **-ums**. An elevated platform for an orchestra conductor, lecturer, etc. [< Gk. *podion*, base.]

po·em (pō'əm) *n*. A verbal composition having the suggestive power to engage the feelings and imagination, typically through the highly structured patterning and movement of sound, rhythm, and meaning characteristic of verse. [< Gk. *poiēma*.]

po·e·sy (pō'ĭ-zē, -sē) *n*. *Archaic*. Poetry. [< Gk. *poiēsis*.]

po·et (pō'ĭt) *n*. A writer of poems. [< Gk. *poiētēs*.] —**po'et·ess** (-ĭ-tĭs) *n*.

po·et·as·ter (pō'ĭ-tăs'tər) *n*. An inferior poet. [POET + -aster, partially resembling.]

po·et·ic (pō-ĕt'ĭk) or **po·et·i·cal** (-ĭ-kəl) *adj*. Of, relating to, or characteristic of poetry. —**po·et'i·cal·ly** *adv*.

poetic justice *n*. The rewarding of virtue and the punishing of vice in a manner that is particularly and often ironically fitting.

poetic license *n*. The liberty taken, esp. by an artist or writer, in deviating from conventional form or fact to achieve a desired effect.

poet laureate *n*., *pl*. **poets laureate** or **poet laureates**. **1.** A poet appointed by the British sovereign to a lifetime position as chief poet of the kingdom. **2.** A poet held to be the most excellent in a nation or region.

po·et·ry (pō'ĭ-trē) *n*. **1.** The art or work of a poet. **2.** Verse as distinguished from prose. **3.** The quality characteristic of the poetic experience.

po·grom (pə-grŭm', -grŏm', pō'grəm) *n*. An organized massacre of a minority group, esp. Jews. [R.]

poi (poi, pō'ē) *n*. A Hawaiian food made from cooked taro root pounded to a paste and often fermented. [Hawaiian.]

poign·ant (poin'yənt) *adj*. **1.** Keenly distressing to the mind or feelings: *poignant anxiety*. **2.** Affecting; touching: *poignant memories*. [< Lat. *pungere*, to prick.] —**poign'ance** or **poign'an·cy** *n*. —**poign'ant·ly** *adv*.

poin·ci·an·a (poin'sē-ăn'ə, -ä'nə) *n*. Any of various tropical trees with large orange or red flowers. [< M. de *Poinci*, 17th-cent. governor of the French Antilles.]

poin·set·ti·a (poin-sĕt'ē-ə, -sĕt'ə) *n*. A tropical American shrub with showy, usu. scarlet bracts beneath the small yellow flowers. [< Joe Roberts *Poinsett* (1799–1851).]

point (point) *n*. **1.** The sharp or tapered end of something. **2.** A tapering extension of land projecting into water. **3.** A dimensionless geometric object having no property but location. **4.** A position or place. **5.** A specified degree, condition, or limit. **6.** A specific moment in time. **7.** An important, essential, or primary factor or idea. **8.** A purpose; reason. **9.** An individual item or element. **10.** A distinctive characteristic or quality. **11.** A single unit, as in counting, rating, or measuring. **12.** An electrical contact, esp. one in the distributor of an automobile engine. **13.** A unit equal to one dollar, used to quote or state the current prices esp. of stocks or commodities. —*v*. **1.** To direct or aim. **2.** To bring to notice: *pointed out the landmarks*. **3.** To indicate the position or direction of with or as with the finger. **4.** To give emphasis to; stress: *pointed up the difference*. —**idioms**. **beside the point**. Irrelevant. **in point of**. With reference to. **stretch a point**. **1.** To make an exception. **2.** To exaggerate. **to the point**. Precisely relevant. [< Lat. *punctus*, p.p. of *pungere*, to pierce.]

point·blank (point'blăngk') *adj*. **1. a.** So close to a target that a weapon can be aimed directly at it: *pointblank range*. **b.** Close enough so that missing the target is unlikely. **2.** Straightforward; blunt. —*adv*. **1.** With a straight aim: *fired pointblank*. **2.** Without hesitation or equivocation: *answer pointblank*. [Orig. unknown.]

point·ed (poin'tĭd) *adj*. **1.** Having a point. **2.** Pertinent; incisive. **3.** Obviously directed at or referring to a particular object: *a pointed comment*. **4.** Clearly evident or conspicuous; marked: *a pointed lack of interest*. —**point'ed·ly** *adv*. —**point'ed·ness** *n*.

point·er (poin'tər) *n*. **1.** An indicator, as on a watch or balance. **2.** A long stick for indicating objects esp. on a chart or blackboard. **3.** A hunting dog with a short, smooth coat. **4.** A suggestion; piece of advice.

poin·til·lism (point'tl-ĭz'əm, pwăn'-) *n*. A painting technique characterized by the application of paint in small dots that blend together when seen from a distance. [Fr. < *pointille*, small dot.] —**poin'til·list** *n*. & *adj*. —**poin'til·lis'tic** *adj*.

point·less (point'lĭs) *adj*. Meaningless; irrelevant. —**point'less·ly** *adv*. —**point'less·ness** *n*.

point of no return *n*. **1.** The point in flight beyond which an aircraft must proceed, there being insufficient fuel to return to the takeoff point. 2. The point in a course of action beyond which reversal is impossible.

point-of-sale (point′əv-sāl′) *adj.* Of or being the physical place where an item is purchased: *point-of-sale displays.*

point of view *n.* 1. The position from which something is observed or considered. 2. One's manner of viewing things; attitude.

poise (poiz) *v.* **poised, pois·ing.** To balance or be balanced. —*n.* 1. Balance; stability. 2. a. Composure. b. Dignity of manner. [< OFr. *poiser,* to weigh.]

poi·son (poi′zən) *n.* A substance that causes injury, illness, or death, esp. by chemical means. —*v.* 1. To give poison to; kill or harm with poison. 2. To make poisonous. 3. To have a harmful influence on; corrupt or ruin. [< Lat. *potio,* drink.] —**poi′son·er** *n.* —**poi′son·ous** *adj.* —**poi′son·ous·ly** *adv.*

poison ivy *n.* A North American plant having leaflets in groups of three and causing a rash on contact.

poison oak *n.* A North American shrub that is related to poison ivy and causes a rash on contact.

poison sumac *n.* A swamp shrub of the southeastern United States, with compound leaves that cause a rash on contact.

poke (pōk) *v.* **poked, pok·ing.** 1. To push or jab, as with a finger or stick. 2. To make (a hole or pathway) by or as if by prodding or thrusting. 3. To thrust forward; appear. 4. To pry or meddle. 5. To search curiously; rummage. —*n.* A push, thrust, or jab. —*idiom.* **poke fun at.** To make fun of. [ME *poken.*]

pok·er¹ (pō′kər) *n.* A metal rod used to stir a fire.

pok·er² (pō′kər) *n.* Any of various card games played by two or more players who bet on the value of their hands. [Orig. unknown.]

poke·weed (pōk′wēd′) *n.* A tall North American plant with small white flowers, blackish-red berries, and a poisonous root, the young shoots of which are sometimes eaten as greens. [Algonquian (Virginia) *pakon,* any plant used for dyeing + WEED.]

po·key (pō′kē) *n., pl.* **-keys.** *Slang.* Jail. [Orig. unknown.]

pok·y (pō′kē) *adj.* **-i·er, -i·est.** Also **poke·y, pok·i·er, pok·i·est.** *Informal.* Dawdling; slow. [< POKE.]

po·lar (pō′lər) *adj.* 1. Of, measured from, or referred to a pole or poles. 2. Of or near the North or South Pole. 3. Occupying or characterized by opposite extremes.

polar bear *n.* A large, white bear of Arctic regions.

polar bear

Po·lar·is (pō-lâr′ĭs, -lăr′-) *n.* A star at the end of the handle of the Little Dipper and almost at the north celestial pole.

po·lar·i·ty (pō-lâr′ĭ-tē, -lär′-) *n., pl.* **-ties.** 1. Intrinsic polar separation, alignment, or orientation, esp. of a physical property. 2. The manifestation of two opposing tendencies. 3. An indicated polar extreme.

po·lar·ize (pō′lə-rīz′) *v.* **-ized, -iz·ing.** 1. To impart polarity to. 2. To cause to concentrate about two opposing positions. 3. To acquire polarity. —**po′lar·iz′a·ble** *adj.* —**po′lar·i·za′tion** *n.* —**po′lar·iz′er** *n.*

Po·lar·oid (pō′lə-roid′). A trademark for a specially treated, transparent plastic capable of polarizing light passing through it and used in glare-reducing optical devices.

pole¹ (pōl) *n.* 1. Either axial extremity of any axis through a sphere. 2. The North Pole or the South Pole. 3. A magnetic pole. 4. Either of two oppositely charged terminals, as in an electric cell or battery. 5. Either of two opposing forces. [< Gk. *polos.*]

pole² (pōl) *n.* A long, slender piece of wood or other material. —*v.* **poled, pol·ing.** 1. To propel with a pole, as a boat. 2. To use ski poles to maintain or gain speed. [< Gk. *palus,* stake.]

pole-ax or **pole-axe** (pōl′ăks′) *n.* A long-handled battle-ax. [ME *pollax.*]

pole·cat (pōl′kăt′) *n.* 1. A weasellike Old World mammal. 2. A skunk. [ME *polcat.*]

po·lem·ic (pə-lěm′ĭk) *n.* 1. A controversy, argument, or refutation. 2. **polemics.** *(used with a sing. or pl. verb).* The art or practice of argumentation or controversy. [< Gk. *polemos.*] —**po·lem′ic** or **po·lem′i·cal** *adj.* —**po·lem′i·cal·ly** *adv.* —**po·lem′i·cist** *n.*

pole-star (pōl′stär′) *n.* Polaris.

pole vault *n.* An athletic field event in which the contestant jumps or vaults over a high crossbar with the aid of a long pole. —**pole′vault′** *v.* —**pole′-vault′er** *n.*

po·lice (pə-lēs′) *n., pl.* **-lice.** 1. a. A government department established to maintain order, enforce the law, and prevent and detect crime. b. *(used with a pl. verb).* The members of such a department. 2. A group of persons resembling the police force of a community in function: *campus police.* 3. Soldiers assigned to a specified maintenance duty: *kitchen police.* —*v.* **-liced, -lic·ing.** 1. To control or keep in order with or as with police. 2. To make (e.g. a military area) neat and orderly. [< Gk. *polis,* city.]

police dog *n.* A guard dog.

police force *n.* Police (sense 1.a.).

po·lice·man (pə-lēs′mən) *n.* A man who is a member of a police force.

police state *n.* A political unit in which the government exercises rigid control over the social, economic, and political life, esp. by means of a secret police force.

police station *n.* The headquarters of a police force.

po·lice·wom·an (pə-lēs′wŏŏm′ən) *n.* A woman who is a member of a police force.

pol·i·cy¹ (pŏl′ĭ-sē) *n., pl.* **-cies.** 1. A general principle or plan that guides the actions taken by a person or group. 2. Care and skill in managing one's affairs or advancing one's interests; prudence; shrewdness. [< Gk. *politeia,* government.]

pol·i·cy² (pŏl'ĭ-sē) *n., pl.* **-cies. 1.** A written contract or certificate of insurance. **2.** A form of gambling; numbers. [< Gk. *apodeixis,* proof.]

pol·i·cy·hold·er (pŏl'ĭ-sē-hōl'dər) *n.* One who holds an insurance contract or policy.

pol·i·cy·mak·ing or **pol·i·cy·mak·ing** (pŏl'ĭ-sē-mā'kĭng) *n.* The top-level development of policy esp. of a government. **—pol'i·cy·mak'er** *n.*

po·li·o (pō'lē-ō') *n.* Poliomyelitis.

po·li·o·my·e·li·tis (pō'lē-ō-mī'ə-lī'tĭs) *n.* An infectious viral disease that occurs mainly in children and in its acute forms attacks the central nervous system and produces paralysis, muscular atrophy, and often death. [Gk. *polios,* gray + MYELITIS.]

pol·ish (pŏl'ĭsh) *v.* **1.** To make smooth or shiny, as by abrasion or rubbing. **2.** To remove flaws from; perfect; refine. **—*phrasal verb.* polish off.** *Informal.* To finish or dispose of quickly. **—*n.* 1.** Smoothness or shininess of surface. **2.** A substance used to shine a surface. **3.** Elegance of style or manners. [< Lat. *polire.*] **—pol'ish·er** *n.*

Po·lish (pō'lĭsh) *adj.* Of Poland, its inhabitants, or their language or culture. **—*n.*** The Slavic language of the Poles.

pol·it·bu·ro (pŏl'ĭt-byŏŏr'ō, pə-lĭt'-) *n.* The chief political and executive committee of a Communist party. [R.]

po·lite (pə-līt') *adj.* **-lit·er, -lit·est. 1.** Marked by consideration and courteous manners. **2.** Refined; cultivated. [< Lat. *polire,* to polish.] **—po·lite'ly** *adv.* **—po·lite'ness** *n.*

Syns: *polite, civil, courteous, genteel, mannerly adj.*

po·li·tesse (pŏl'ĭ-tĕs', pō'lĭ-) *n.* Courteous formality. [Fr.]

pol·i·tic (pŏl'ĭ-tĭk) *adj.* **1.** Shrewd and tactful. **2.** Prudent; judicious. [< Gk. *polis,* city.] **—pol'i·tic·ly** *adv.*

po·lit·i·cal (pə-lĭt'ĭ-kəl) *adj.* **1.** Of or pertaining to government or politics. **2.** Characteristic of political parties or politicians. **—po·lit'i·cal·ly** *adv.* **—po·lit'i·cize'** (pə-lĭt'ĭ-sīz') *v.*

political science *n.* The study of the processes and principles of government and political institutions.

pol·i·ti·cian (pŏl'ĭ-tĭsh'ən) *n.* **1.** One actively involved in politics, esp. party politics. **2.** One who holds or seeks a political office.

pol·i·tick (pŏl'ĭ-tĭk') *v.* To engage in or talk politics.

po·lit·i·co (pə-lĭt'ĭ-kō') *n., pl.* **-cos.** A politician. [< Ital., political.]

pol·i·tics (pŏl'ĭ-tĭks') *n.* **1.** *(used with a sing. verb).* The art or science of political government. **2.** *(used with a sing. verb).* The policies or affairs of a government. **3.** *(used with a pl. verb).* Intrigue or maneuvering within a group: *office politics.* **4.** *(used with a pl. verb).* One's general position or attitude on political subjects.

pol·i·ty (pŏl'ĭ-tē) *n., pl.* **-ties.** An organized society, as a nation, having one specific form of government. [< Gk. *politēs,* citizen.]

pol·ka (pōl'kə, pō'kə) *n.* **1.** A lively round dance performed by couples. **2.** Music for this dance. [Pol.]

pol·ka dot (pō'kə) *n.* One of a number of dots forming a regular pattern on cloth.

poll (pōl) *n.* **1. a.** The casting and registering of votes in an election. **b.** The number of votes cast or recorded. **c.** Often **polls.** The place where votes are cast and registered. **2.** A canvassing of persons to analyze public opinion on a particular question. **—*v.* 1. a.** To receive (a given number of votes). **b.** To receive or record the votes of. **2.** To canvass (persons) to survey public opinion. **3.** To cut off; trim; clip. [< MLG *polle,* head.] **—poll'er** *n.*

pol·len (pŏl'ən) *n.* The powderlike material produced by the anthers of flowering plants, and functioning as the male element in fertilization. [Lat., dust.]

pollen count *n.* The average number of pollen grains, usu. of ragweed, in a cubic yard or other standard volume of air over a 24-hour period at a specified time and place, used to estimate the possible severity of hay-fever attacks.

pol·li·nate (pŏl'ə-nāt') *v.* **-nat·ed, -nat·ing.** To fertilize by transferring pollen from an anther to a stigma of (a plant or flower). **—pol'li·na'tion** *n.* **—pol'li·na'tor** *n.*

pol·li·wog (pŏl'ē-wŏg', -wŏg') *n.* Also **pol·ly·wog.** A tadpole. [ME *polwygle.*]

poll·ster (pōl'stər) *n.* One who takes public-opinion surveys.

poll tax *n.* A tax on persons rather than on property, often imposed as a requirement for voting.

pol·lute (pə-lōōt') *v.* **-lut·ed, -lut·ing.** To make impure or unclean; contaminate. [< Lat. *polluere.*] **—pol·lut'ant** or **pol·lut'er** *n.* **—pol·lu'tion** (-lōō'shən) *n.*

Pol·lux (pŏl'əks) *n.* A bright star in the constellation Gemini.

po·lo (pō'lō) *n.* A game played by two teams on horseback, equipped with long-handled mallets for driving a wooden ball. [Of Tibeto-Burman orig.] **—po'lo·ist** *n.*

po·lo·naise (pŏl'ə-nāz', pō'lə-) *n.* **1.** A stately, marchlike Polish dance in triple time. **2.** Music for or in the style of this dance. [< Med. Lat. *Polonia,* Poland.]

po·lo·ni·um (pə-lō'nē-əm) *n.* Symbol **Po** A naturally radioactive metallic element that occurs in minute quantities as a product of radium disintegration and is produced by bombarding bismuth or lead with neutrons. Atomic number 84; longest-lived isotope Po 210. [< Med. Lat. *Polonia,* Poland.]

polo shirt *n.* A knitted pullover sport shirt.

pol·ter·geist (pōl'tər-gīst') *n.* A noisy, usu. mischievous ghost. [G.]

pol·troon (pŏl-trōōn') *n. Archaic.* A coward. [< OItal. *poltrone.*] **—pol·troon'er·y** *n.*

poly- *pref.* **1.** More than one; many; much: *polychrome.* **2.** More than usual; excessive; abnormal: *polydipsia.* **3.** Polymer; polymeric: *polyethylene.* [< Gk. *polus,* many.]

pol·y·chrome (pŏl'ĭ-krōm') *adj.* Having or decorated in many colors. [POLY- + Gk. *khrōma,* color.] **—pol'y·chro·mat'ic** (pŏl'ĭ-krō-măt'ĭk) or **pol'y·chro'mic** (-krō'mĭk) *adj.* **—pol'y·chrome** *n.*

pol·y·clin·ic (pŏl'ĭ-klĭn'ĭk) *n.* A clinic that treats all types of diseases and injuries.

pol·y·dip·si·a (pŏl'ē-dĭp'sē-ə) *n.* Excessive or abnormal thirst. [POLY- + Gk. *dipsa,* thirst.] **—pol'y·dip'sic** *adj.*

pol·y·es·ter (pŏl'ē-ĕs'tər) *n.* Any of numerous synthetic resins.

pol·y·eth·yl·ene (pŏl'ē-ĕth'ə-lēn') *n.* A synthetic resin, used esp. in the form of films and sheets.

po·lyg·a·my (pə-lĭg′ə-mē) n. The condition or practice of having more than one spouse at a time. —**po·lyg′a·mist** (-mĭst) n. —**po·lyg′a·mous** (-məs) adj. —**po·lyg′a·mous·ly** adv.

pol·y·glot (pŏl′ĭ-glŏt′) n. One with a reading, writing, or speaking knowledge of several languages. [POLY- + Gk. glōtta, tongue.]

pol·y·gon (pŏl′ĭ-gŏn′) n. A closed plane figure bounded by three or more line segments. —**po·lyg′o·nal** (pə-lĭg′ə-nəl) adj. —**po·lyg′o·nal·ly** adv.

pol·y·graph (pŏl′ĭ-grăf′) n. An instrument that records changes in such physiological processes as heartbeat, blood pressure, and respiration, often used in lie detection. —**pol′y·graph′ic** adj.

po·lyg·y·ny (pə-lĭj′ə-nē) n. The condition or practice of having more than one wife at a time. [POLY- + Gk. gunē, woman.] —**po·lyg′y·nous** adj.

pol·y·he·dron (pŏl′ĭ-hē′drən) n., pl. -**drons** or -**dra** (-drə). A solid bounded by polygons. —**pol′y·he′dral** adj.

pol·y·math (pŏl′ĭ-măth′) n. A person of great and varied learning. [< Gk. polumathēs, knowing much.] —**pol′y·math′ic** or **pol′y·math′ic** adj.

pol·y·mer (pŏl′ə-mər) n. Any of numerous natural and synthetic compounds of usu. high molecular weight consisting of repeated linked units, each a relatively light and simple molecule. —**pol′y·mer′ic** (pŏl′ə-mĕr′ĭk) adj.

po·lym·er·ize (pə-lĭm′ə-rīz′, pŏl′ə-mə-) v. -**ized**, -**iz·ing**. To unite two or more monomers to form a polymer. —**po·lym′er·i·za′tion** (-ər-ĭ-zā′shən) n.

pol·y·no·mi·al (pŏl′ĭ-nō′mē-əl) adj. Of or consisting of more than two names or terms. —n. An algebraic function of two or more summed terms, each term consisting of a constant multiplier and one or more variables raised, in general, to integral powers. [POLY- + (BI)NOMIAL.]

pol·yp (pŏl′ĭp) n. 1. Zool. An organism, such as a hydra or coral, having a cylindrical body and an oral opening usu. surrounded by tentacles. 2. Pathol. A growth protruding from the mucous lining of an organ. [< Gk. polupous, octopus.] —**pol′yp·oid** adj.

po·lyph·o·ny (pə-lĭf′ə-nē) n., pl. -**nies**. The simultaneous combination of two or more independent melodic parts. —**pol′y·phon′ic** (pŏl′ē-fŏn′ĭk) adj. —**pol′y·phon′i·cal·ly** adv.

pol·y·sac·cha·ride (pŏl′ĭ-săk′ə-rīd′) n. A group of nine or more monosaccharides joined by bonds such as starch or cellulose.

pol·y·sty·rene (pŏl′ĭ-stī′rēn′) n. A hard, rigid, dimensionally stable, clear thermoplastic polymer.

pol·y·syl·la·ble (pŏl′ĭ-sĭl′ə-bəl) n. A word of more than three syllables. —**pol′y·syl·lab′ic** (-sĭ-lăb′ĭk) adj. —**pol′y·syl·lab′i·cal·ly** adv.

pol·y·tech·nic (pŏl′ĭ-tĕk′nĭk) adj. Of or dealing with many arts or sciences. —n. A school specializing in industrial arts and applied sciences.

pol·y·the·ism (pŏl′ĭ-thē-ĭz′əm) n. The worship of or belief in more than one god. —**pol′y·the′ist** n. —**pol′y·the·is′tic** adj.

pol·y·un·sat·u·rat·ed (pŏl′ē-ŭn-săch′ə-rā′tĭd) adj. Pertaining to long-chain carbon compounds, esp. fats, with many unsaturated bonds.

pol·y·u·re·thane (pŏl′ē-yŏŏr′ə-thān′) n. Any of various thermoplastic or thermosetting resins used in coatings and in adhesives, foams, and electrical insulation.

pol·y·va·lent (pŏl′ĭ-vā′lənt) adj. 1. Containing, sensitive to, or interacting with more than one kind of antigen, antibody, toxin, or microorganism. 2. Chem. a. Having more than one valence. b. Having a valence of 3 or higher. —**pol′y·va′lence** or **pol′y·va′len·cy** n.

pol·y·vi·nyl chloride (pŏl′ē-vī′nəl) n. A common thermoplastic resin, used in a wide variety of manufactured products.

po·made (pə-mād′, -mäd′, pō-) n. A perfumed hair ointment. —v. -**mad·ed**, -**mad·ing**. To apply pomade to. [Ital. pomata.]

pome·gran·ate (pŏm′grăn′ĭt, pŭm′-) n. 1. A fruit with a tough reddish rind and many seeds enclosed in juicy, red pulp. 2. A tree bearing such fruit. [< OFr. pome grenate.]

pom·mel (pŭm′əl, pŏm′-) n. 1. A knob on the hilt of a sword. 2. The upper front part of a saddle. —v. -**meled** or -**melled**, -**mel·ing** or -**mel·ling**. To beat; pummel. [< Lat. pomum, fruit.]

pomp (pŏmp) n. 1. Magnificent display; splendor. 2. Ostentatious display. [< Gk. pompē, procession.]

pom·pa·dour (pŏm′pə-dôr′, -dōr′) n. A hair style formed by sweeping the hair straight up from the forehead. [< the Marquise de Pompadour (1721–64).]

pom·pa·no (pŏm′pə-nō′, pŭm′-) n., pl. -**no** or -**nos**. A food fish of tropical and temperate Atlantic waters. [Sp. pámpano salpa, a kind of fish.]

pom·pom (pŏm′pŏm′) n. Also **pom·pon** (-pŏn′). 1. A tuft of material, as wool or feathers, worn as a decoration. 2. A buttonlike flower of some chrysanthemums and dahlias. [Fr. pompon.]

pom-pom (pŏm′pŏm′) n. An automatic, rapid-fire antiaircraft gun usu. mounted on ships. [Imit.]

pom·pous (pŏm′pəs) adj. 1. Self-important; pretentious. 2. Characterized by pomp or stately display. —**pom·pos′i·ty** (-pŏs′ĭ-tē) n. —**pom′pous·ly** adv. —**pom′pous·ness** n.

pon·cho (pŏn′chō) n., pl. -**chos**. 1. A blanketlike cloak with a hole in the center for the head. 2. A similar garment used as a raincoat. [Am. Sp.]

pond (pŏnd) n. A still body of water, smaller than a lake. [< OE pund-, enclosure.]

pon·der (pŏn′dər) v. 1. To consider carefully. 2. To meditate; reflect. [< Lat. ponderare.] —**pon′der·a·bil′i·ty** n. —**pon′der·a·ble** adj. —**pon′der·er** n.

pon·der·o·sa pine (pŏn′də-rō′sə) n. A tall timber tree of western North America, with long, dark-green needles. [Lat. ponderosus, ponderous + PINE.]

pon·der·ous (pŏn′dər-əs) adj. 1. Extremely heavy; massive; huge. 2. Lacking fluency; dull. [< Lat. pondus, weight.] —**pon′der·os′i·ty** (-də-rŏs′ĭ-tē) or **pon′der·ous·ness** n. —**pon′der·ous·ly** adv.

---

pon·gee (pŏn-jē′, pŏn′jē′) n. A soft, thin silk cloth. [Chin. *ben³zhi¹*.]

pon·iard (pŏn′yərd) n. A dagger. [< Lat. *pugnus*, fist.]

pons (pŏnz) n., pl. **pon·tes** (pŏn′tēz). Anat. Any slender tissue joining two parts of an organ. [Lat., bridge.]

pon·tiff (pŏn′tĭf) n. 1. The pope. 2. A bishop. [< Lat. *pontifex*, high priest.]

pon·tif·i·cal (pŏn-tĭf′ĭ-kəl) adj. Of or pertaining to a pope or bishop. —n. **pontificals.** The vestments and insignia of a pontiff. —**pon·tif′i·cal·ly** adv.

pon·tif·i·cate (pŏn-tĭf′ĭ-kĭt, -kāt′) n. The office or term of office of a pontiff. —v. (pŏn-tĭf′ĭ-kāt′) -cat·ed, -cat·ing. 1. To administer the office of a pontiff. 2. To speak or behave pompously. —**pon·tif′i·ca′tion** n. —**pon·tif′i·ca′tor** n.

pon·toon (pŏn-tōōn′) n. 1. A flat-bottomed boat or other structure used to support a floating bridge. 2. A float on a seaplane. [< Lat. *ponto*, boat bridge.]

po·ny (pō′nē) n., pl. **-nies.** A small horse. [Prob. < Lat. *pullus*, foal.]

po·ny·tail (pō′nē-tāl′) n. A hair style in which the hair is drawn back and fastened so that it hangs like a horse's tail.

pooch (pōōch) n. Slang. A dog. [Orig. unknown.]

poo·dle (pōōd′l) n. A dog with thick, curly hair. [G. *Pudel*.]

pooh (pōō) interj. Used to express disdain.

Pooh-Bah (pōō′bä′) n. 1. A pompous, ostentatious, ineffective official. 2. One holding high office. [< the character in Gilbert and Sullivan's *The Mikado*.]

pooh-pooh (pōō′pōō, pōō-pōō′) v. Informal. To express contempt or disdain for.

pool¹ (pōōl) n. 1. A small pond. 2. A puddle of any liquid. 3. A deep place in a river or stream. 4. A swimming pool. [< OE *pōl*.]

pool² (pōōl) n. 1. In certain gambling games, the total amount staked by all players. 2. A grouping of resources for the common advantage of the participants. 3. An agreement between competing business concerns to establish certain controls for common profit. 4. Any of several games played on a six-pocket billiard table. —v. 1. To combine (money, funds, or interests) for mutual benefit. 2. To join or form a pool. [Fr. *poule*, stakes.]

pool·room (pōōl′rōōm′, -rōōm′) n. A place for the playing of pool or billiards.

pool table n. A six-pocket billiard table on which pool is played.

poop¹ (pōōp) n. Naut. 1. The stern superstructure of a ship. 2. A poop deck. [< Lat. *puppis*.]

poop² (pōōp) v. Slang. To become or cause to become exhausted. [Orig. unknown.]

poop deck n. The aftermost deck of a ship.

poor (pōōr) adj. **-er, -est. 1. a.** Having little or no money. **b.** Destitute. **2.** Inferior; inadequate; inefficient. **3. a.** Lacking desirable elements or constituents. **b.** Undernourished; lean. **4.** Lacking in value. **5.** Humble. **b.** Pitiable. [< Lat. *pauper*.] —**poor′ly** adv. —**poor′ness** n.

Syns: poor, broke, destitute, indigent, needy, penniless, penurious, strapped adj.

Usage: Poor is an adjective, not an adverb. In formal usage it should not be used to qualify a verb as in *did poor* or *never played*

poorer. In such examples *poorly* and *more poorly* are required.

poor box n. A box, esp. in a church, for collecting alms.

poor·house (pōōr′hous′) n. A publicly supported establishment for paupers.

poor-mouth (pōōr′mouth′, -mou*th*′) v. To claim poverty as an excuse for one's behavior or position.

pop¹ (pŏp) v. **popped, pop·ping. 1.** To make or cause to make a short, sharp, explosive sound. **2.** To burst open with such a sound. **3.** To appear abruptly. **4.** To open the eyes wide suddenly. **5.** To put or thrust suddenly: *popped the candy into my mouth.* **6.** To shoot with a pistol or other firearm. —n. **1.** A sudden sharp, explosive sound. **2.** A shot with a firearm. **3.** A nonalcoholic carbonated beverage. [ME *poppen*.]

pop² (pŏp) n. Informal. Father. [< PAPA.]

pop³ (pŏp) adj. Informal. 1. Relating to or specializing in popular music: *a pop singer.* 2. Suggestive of pop art. [< POPULAR.]

pop art n. A form of art that depicts objects of everyday life and adapts techniques of commercial art.

pop·corn (pŏp′kôrn′) n. A variety of corn with hard kernels that burst to form white, irregularly shaped puffs when heated.

pope (pŏp) n. Often Pope. The bishop of Rome and head of the Roman Catholic Church. [< LGk. *pappas*, father.]

pop-eyed (pŏp′īd′) adj. Having bulging eyes.

pop fly n. Baseball. A short high fly ball.

pop·gun (pŏp′gŭn′) n. A toy gun operating by compressed air to fire corks or pellets.

pop·in·jay (pŏp′ĭn-jā′) n. A vain, supercilious person. [< Ar. *babaghā*, parrot.]

pop·lar (pŏp′lər) n. Any of several trees with triangular leaves and soft wood. [< Lat. *populus*.]

pop·lin (pŏp′lĭn) n. A ribbed fabric used in making clothing and upholstery. [Ital. *papalino*, papal.]

pop·o·ver (pŏp′ō′vər) n. A light, puffy, hollow muffin made with eggs, milk, and flour.

pop·py (pŏp′ē) n., pl. **-pies.** Any of various plants with showy red, orange, or white flowers, and a milky white juice. [< Lat. *papaver*.]

pop·py·cock (pŏp′ē-kŏk′) n. Senseless talk. [Dial. Du. *pappekak*.]

Pop·sl·cle (pŏp′sĭ-kəl, -sĭk′əl). A trademark for colored, flavored ice molded into a rectangle with two flat sticks for handles.

pop-top (pŏp′tŏp′) adj. Designating or made with a tab that can be pulled up or off to make an opening. —**pop-top′** n.

pop·u·lace (pŏp′yə-ləs) n. 1. The common people; masses. 2. A population. [Lat. *populus*, the people.]

pop·u·lar (pŏp′yə-lər) adj. 1. Widely liked or appreciated. 2. Of, representing, or carried on by the people at large. 3. Accepted by or suited to the people in general. [Lat. *popularis*, of the people.] —**pop′u·lar′i·ty** (-lăr′ĭ-tē) n. —**pop′u·lar·ly** adv.

popular front n. A political coalition of democratic and revolutionary parties opposing reaction and fascism.

pop·u·lar·ize (pŏp′yə-lə-rīz′) v. **-ized, -iz·ing.** To make or become popular. —**pop′u·lar·i·za′tion** n. —**pop′u·lar·iz′er** n.

pop·u·late (pŏp′yə-lāt′) v. **-lat·ed, -lat·ing.** 1. To supply with inhabitants. 2. To inhabit. [< Lat. *populus*, people.]

pop·u·la·tion (pŏp'yə-lā'shən) n. 1. The total number of the people inhabiting a specified area. 2. The set of individuals, items, or data from which a statistical sample is taken. 3. All the plants or animals of the same kind living in a particular region.

population explosion n. Great expansion of a biological population, esp. the unchecked growth in human population due to decreased infant mortality and increased adult longevity.

pop·u·lism (pŏp'yə-lĭz'əm) n. A philosophy opposing the concentration of power in the hands of corporations, government bureaucracies, and the rich. —**pop'u·list** n.

pop·u·lous (pŏp'yə-ləs) adj. Thickly settled or populated. —**pop'u·lous·ly** adv. —**pop'u·lous·ness** n.

por·ce·lain (pôr'sə-lĭn, pôr'-, pôrs'lĭn, pôrs'-) n. 1. A hard, white, translucent ceramic. 2. An object made of porcelain. [< Oltal. porcellana.]

porch (pôrch, pōrch) n. 1. A platform, usu. with a separate roof, at an entrance to a house. 2. A gallery or room attached to the outside of a building; verandah. [< Lat. porticus, portico.]

por·cine (pôr'sīn') adj. Of or resembling swine or a pig. [Lat. porcinus.]

por·cu·pine (pôr'kyə-pīn') n. Any of various rodents characteristically covered with long, sharp quills. [< OFr. porc espin, spiny pig.]

porcupine

pore¹ (pôr, pōr) v. pored, por·ing. 1. To gaze steadily or earnestly. 2. To read or study carefully and attentively. 3. To meditate deeply; ponder. [ME pouren.]

pore² (pôr, pōr) n. A minute opening, as in an animal's skin or a plant leaf, esp. for the passage of fluid. [< Gk. poros.]

pork (pôrk, pōrk) n. The flesh of a pig or hog used as food. [< Lat. porcus, pig.]

pork barrel n. Slang. A government project or appropriation benefiting a specific locale and a legislator's constituents.

pork·er (pôr'kər, pōr'-) n. A fattened young pig.

por·no (pôr'nō) n. Also **porn** (pôrn). Slang. Pornography.

por·nog·ra·phy (pôr-nŏg'rə-fē) n. Written or pictorial matter intended to arouse sexual feelings. [< Gk. pornographos, writing about prostitutes.] —**por·nog'ra·pher** n. —**por'no·graph'ic** (pôr'nə-grăf'ĭk) adj.

po·rous (pôr'əs, pōr'-) adj. 1. Having or full of pores. 2. Admitting the passage of gas or liquid through pores or interstices. —**po·ros'i·ty** (pə-rŏs'ĭ-tē) n. —**po'rous·ly** adv.

por·phy·ry (pôr'fə-rē) n., pl. -ries. A fine-grained igneous rock containing relatively large crystals, esp. of feldspar or quartz. [< Gk. porphurītēs.]

por·poise (pôr'pəs) n. A marine mammal related to the whales but smaller, usu. having a blunt snout and a triangular dorsal fin. [< Med. Lat. porcopiscis.]

por·ridge (pôr'ĭj, pŏr'-) n. Boiled cereal, esp. oatmeal, usu. eaten with milk. [< POTTAGE.]

por·rin·ger (pôr'ĭn-jər, pŏr'-) n. A shallow cup or bowl with a handle. [< OFr. potager.]

port¹ (pôrt, pōrt) n. 1. A town with a harbor. 2. A harbor. [< Lat. portus.]

port² (pôrt, pōrt) n. The left-hand side of a ship or aircraft facing forward. —adj. Of, pertaining to, or on the port. —v. To turn or shift (the helm of a vessel) to the left. [Orig. unknown.]

port³ (pôrt, pōrt) n. 1. A porthole. 2. An opening, as in a cylinder, for the passage of steam or fluid. [< Lat. porta, gate.]

port⁴ (pôrt, pōrt) n. A rich sweet fortified wine. [< Oporto, Portugal.]

port·a·ble (pôr'tə-bəl, pōr'-) adj. 1. Capable of being carried. 2. Easily moved. [< LLat. portabilis.] —**port'a·bil'i·ty** n. —**port'a·ble** n.

port·age (pôr'tĭj, pōr'-, pôr-täzh') n. 1. The carrying of boats and supplies overland between two waterways. 2. A track or route used for portage. —v. -aged, -ag·ing. To transport by portage. [< Lat. portare, to carry.]

por·tal (pôr'tl, pōr'-) n. A doorway or entrance. [< Lat. porta, gate.]

port·cul·lis (pôrt-kŭl'ĭs, pōrt-) n. A grating in the gateway of a fortified place that can be lowered in case of attack. [< OFr. porte coleïce, sliding door.]

porte-co·chère or **porte-co·chere** (pôrt'kō-shâr', pōrt'-) n. A porch roof projecting over a driveway at the entrance to a building and providing shelter for those getting in and out of vehicles. [Fr. porte cochère, coach door.]

por·tend (pôr-tĕnd', pōr-) v. 1. To serve as an omen or warning of; presage. 2. To indicate or suggest. [< Lat. portendere.]

por·tent (pôr'tĕnt', pōr'-) n. 1. An indication of something about to occur; omen. 2. Something amazing or marvelous; prodigy. [Lat. portentum.]

por·ten·tous (pôr-tĕn'təs, pōr-) adj. 1. Of, pertaining to, or constituting a portent. 2. Exciting wonder and awe; prodigious. 3. Pretentiously weighty; pompous. —**por·ten'tous·ly** adv. —**por·ten'tous·ness** n.

por·ter¹ (pôr'tər, pōr'-) n. 1. One employed to carry travelers' luggage. 2. A railroad employee who waits on passengers. [< LLat. portator.]

por·ter² (pôr'tər, pōr'-) n. Chiefly Brit. A gatekeeper; doorman. [< Lat. portarius.]

por·ter³ (pôr'tər, pōr'-) n. A dark beer made from browned or charred malt. [< porter's beer.]

por·ter·house (pôr'tər-hous', pōr'-) n. A cut of beef with a T-bone and a sizable piece of tenderloin.

port·fo·li·o (pôrt-fō′lē-ō′, pōrt-) *n.*, *pl.* **-os.**
1. A portable case for holding loose drawings or papers. 2. The office or post of a cabinet member or minister of state. 3. An itemized list of the investments and securities owned by an investor. [Ital. *portafoglio.*]

port·hole (pôrt′hōl′, pōrt′-) *n.* A small, usu. circular window in the side of a ship.

por·ti·co (pôr′tĭ-kō′, pōr′-) *n.*, *pl.* **-coes** or **-cos.** A porch or walkway with a roof supported by columns, often leading to the entrance of a building. [< Lat. *porticus.*]

por·tière or **por·tiere** (pôr-tyâr′, pōrt-) *n.* A heavy curtain hung across a doorway. [Fr.]

por·tion (pôr′shən, pōr′-) *n.* 1. A part of a whole. 2. A part allotted to a person or group. 3. A woman's dowry. 4. A person's lot or fate. —*v.* 1. To distribute in portions. 2. To provide with a portion. [< Lat. *portio.*]

Port·land cement (pôrt′lənd, pōrt′-) *n.* A cement made by heating and pulverizing a mixture of limestone and clay. [< *Portland*, England.]

port·ly (pôrt′lē, pōrt′-) *adj.* **-li·er, -li·est.** Comfortably stout; corpulent. [< *port*, mien.]
—**port′li·ness** *n.*

port·man·teau (pôrt-măn′tō, pôrt-, pōrt′-mǎn-tō′, pōrt′-) *n.*, *pl.* **-teaus** or **-teaux** (-tōz). A large leather suitcase with two hinged compartments. [< OFr. *portemanteau.*]

port of call *n.* A port where ships dock in the course of voyages to load or unload cargo, obtain supplies, or undergo repairs.

port of entry *n.* A place where travelers or goods may enter or leave a country under official supervision.

por·trait (pôr′trĭt, -trāt′, pōr′-) *n.* A likeness of a person, as a painting or photograph, esp. one showing the face. [< OFr. *portraire*, to portray.]

por·trait·ist (pôr′trə-tĭst, pōr′-) *n.* One who makes portraits.

por·trai·ture (pôr′trĭ-chŏŏr′, -chər, pōr′-) *n.* The practice or art of making portraits.

por·tray (pôr-trā′, pōr-) *v.* 1. To depict pictorially. 2. To describe in words. 3. To represent dramatically, as on stage. [< Lat. *protrahere*, to reveal.] —**por·tray′al** *n.*

Por·tu·guese (pôr′chə-gēz′, -gēs′, pōr′-chə-gēz′, -gēs′, pōr′-) *n.*, *pl.* **-guese.** 1. A native or inhabitant of Portugal. 2. The Romance language of Portugal and Brazil. —**Por′tu·guese′** *adj.*

Portuguese man-of-war *n.* A chiefly tropical marine organism with a bluish, bladderlike float and numerous long stinging tentacles.

por·tu·lac·a (pôr′chə-lǎk′ə, pōr′-) *n.* A tropical plant with fleshy stems and leaves cultivated for its showy flowers. [< Lat., *purslane.*]

pose (pōz) *v.* **posed, pos·ing.** 1. To assume or cause to assume a particular position or posture, as in sitting for a portrait. 2. To place in a specific position; set. 3. To affect a particular attitude. 4. To present or put forward: *pose a threat; pose a question.* —*n.* 1. A bodily attitude or position, esp. one assumed in modeling. 2. A false appearance or attitude; pretense. [< Gk. *pausis*, pause.]

Po·sei·don (pō-sīd′n) *n.* Gk. Myth. The god of the sea.

pos·er¹ (pō′zər) *n.* One who poses.

pos·er² (pō′zər) *n.* A baffling question. [< *pose*, to puzzle.]

po·seur (pō-zûr′) *n.* One who affects an attitude, esp. to impress others. [< OFr. *poser*, to pose.]

posh (pŏsh) *adj. Informal.* Fashionable. [Orig. unknown.]

pos·it (pŏz′ĭt) *v.* To put forward as a fact or assumption; postulate. [< Lat. *positus*, p.p. of *ponere*, to place.]

po·si·tion (pə-zĭsh′ən) *n.* 1. A place or location. 2. The appropriate place. 3. a. The way in which something or someone is placed. b. The arrangement of bodily parts; posture. 4. A situation relative to circumstances: *in an awkward position.* 5. A point of view. 6. A post of employment; job. 7. Status; rank. —*v.* To place in position. [< Lat. *ponere*, to place.] —**po·si′tion·al** *adj.* —**po·si′tion·er** *n.*

pos·i·tive (pŏz′ĭ-tĭv) *adj.* 1. Characterized by or displaying affirmation: *a positive answer.* 2. Explicitly expressed: *a positive demand.* 3. Admitting of no doubt; irrefutable. 4. Certain; confident. 5. Real and not fictitious. 6. Pertaining to or designating: a. A quantity greater than zero. b. A quantity, number, angle, or direction opposite to another designated as negative. 7. Pertaining to or designating electric charge of a sign opposite to that of an electron. 8. Having the areas of light and dark in their original and normal relationship, as in a photographic print made from a negative. 9. *Gram.* Of or denoting the simple uncompared degree of an adjective or adverb. —*n.* 1. A photographic image in which the lights and darks appear as they do in nature. 2. *Gram.* The positive degree of an adjective or adverb. [< Lat. *positivus*, formally laid down.] —**pos′i·tive·ly** *adv.* —**pos′i·tive·ness** *n.*

pos·i·tron (pŏz′ĭ-trŏn′) *n.* The antiparticle of the electron. [POSI(TIVE) + (ELEC)TRON.]

pos·se (pŏs′ē) *n.* A group of people summoned by a sheriff to aid in law enforcement. [< Med. Lat. *posse comitatus*, force of the county.]

pos·sess (pə-zĕs′) *v.* 1. To have as property; own. 2. To have as an attribute. 3. To exert influence or control over; dominate. [< Lat. *possidere.*] —**pos·ses′sor** *n.*

pos·ses·sion (pə-zĕsh′ən) *n.* 1. The act or fact of possessing. 2. The state of being possessed. 3. One that is owned or possessed. 4. Self-control. 5. The state of being dominated, as by evil spirits.

pos·ses·sive (pə-zĕs′ĭv) *adj.* 1. Having or showing a desire to control or dominate: *a possessive mother.* 2. *Gram.* Of or designating a noun or pronoun case that indicates possession. —*n.* 1. The possessive case. 2. A possessive word or form. —**pos·ses′sive·ness** *n.*

pos·si·ble (pŏs′ə-bəl) *adj.* 1. Capable of happening, existing, or being done. 2. Capable of occurring or being true. 3. Potential. [< Lat. *possibilis.*] —**pos′si·bil′i·ty** *n.* —**pos′si·bly** *adv.*

pos·sum (pŏs′əm) *n.* An opossum.

post¹ (pōst) *n.* 1. A stake set upright in the ground to serve as a marker or support. 2. Something resembling a post. —*v.* 1. To put up for public view. 2. To announce by or as if by posters. 3. To put up signs on (property) warning against trespassing. 4. To publish (a name) on a list. [< Lat. *postis.*]

post² (pōst) *n.* 1. A military base where troops are stationed. 2. An assigned position or station, as of a sentry. 3. A position of employment. 4. A trading post. —*v.* 1. To assign to a specific position or station. 2. To put forward; present: *post bail.* [< Lat. *positum* < *ponere*, to place.]

post³ (pōst) *n.* **1.** A rider on a mail route; courier. **2.** *Chiefly Brit.* **a.** A governmental system for transporting and delivering mail. **b.** A post office. —*v.* **1.** To travel quickly; hasten. **2.** To mail (a letter). **3.** To inform of the latest news. **4.** *Accounting.* To make entries in (a ledger). [< OItal. *posta*, relay station, ult. < Lat. *ponere*, to place.]

post– *pref.* **1.** Later; subsequent to: *postgraduate.* **2.** Behind; posterior to: *postnasal.* [< Lat. *post*, after.]

post·age (pō'stĭj) *n.* The charge for mailing an item.

post·al (pō'stəl) *adj.* Of or pertaining to the post office or mail service.

postal card *n.* A postcard.

post·card or **post card** (pōst'kärd') *n.* A card used for sending messages through the mail without an envelope.

post chaise *n.* A closed, four-wheeled, horse-drawn carriage.

post·date (pōst-dāt') *v.* **-dat·ed, -dat·ing.** **1.** To put a date on (a check, letter, or document) that is later than the actual date. **2.** To occur later than; follow in time.

post·doc·tor·al (pōst-dŏk'tər-əl) *adj.* Of, pertaining to, or engaged in academic study beyond the level of a doctor's degree.

post·er (pō'stər) *n.* A placard, bill, or announcement posted to advertise or publicize something.

pos·te·ri·or (pŏ-stîr'ē-ər, pō-) *adj.* **1.** Located behind a part or toward the rear of a structure. **2.** Following in time; later. —*n.* The buttocks. [< Lat. *posterus*, next.]

pos·ter·i·ty (pŏ-stĕr'ĭ-tē) *n.* **1.** Future generations. **2.** All of a person's descendants. [< Lat. *posteritas.*]

pos·tern (pō'stərn, pŏs'tərn) *n.* A rear gate, esp. in a fort or castle. [< LLat. *posterula.*]

Post Exchange A trademark for a store on a military base that sells to military personnel and their families.

post·grad·u·ate (pōst-grăj'ōō-ĭt, -āt') *adj.* Of, pertaining to, or pursuing studies beyond the bachelor's degree. —*n.* A person engaged in postgraduate studies.

post·haste (pōst'hāst') *adv.* With great speed; rapidly. [< *post, haste,* a direction on letters.]

post·hu·mous (pŏs'chə-məs) *adj.* **1.** Occurring or continuing after one's death. **2.** Published after the author's death. **3.** Born after the death of the father. [< Lat. *postumus.*] —**post'hu·mous·ly** *adv.*

post·hyp·not·ic suggestion (pōst'hĭp-nŏt'ĭk) *n.* A suggestion made to a hypnotized person specifying an action to be performed in a subsequent waking state.

pos·til·ion (pō-stĭl'yən, pə-) *n.* Also **pos·til·lion.** One who rides the left-hand lead horse to guide the team drawing a coach. [< Ital. *postiglione.*]

post·lude (pōst'lōōd') *n.* An organ voluntary played at the end of a church service. [POST- + (PRE)LUDE.]

post·man (pōst'mən) *n.* A mailman.

post·mark (pōst'märk') *n.* An official mark stamped on mail that cancels the stamp and records the date and place of mailing. —**post'mark'** *v.*

post·mas·ter (pōst'mǎs'tər) *n.* A government official in charge of a post office.

postmaster general *n., pl.* **postmasters general.** The executive head of a national postal service.

post me·rid·i·em (pōst' mə-rĭd'ē-əm) *adj.* After noon. [Lat.]

post·mor·tem (pōst-môr'təm) *adj.* **1.** Occurring or done after death. **2.** Of a postmortem examination. —*n.* **1.** A postmortem examination. **2.** *Informal.* An analysis or review of a completed event. [< Lat. *post mortem,* after death.]

postmortem examination *n.* An autopsy.

post·na·sal (pōst-nā'zəl) *adj.* Of, in, or from the area in back of the nose.

post·na·tal (pōst-nāt'l) *adj.* Occurring after birth.

post office *n.* **1.** The public department responsible for the transportation and delivery of the mails. **2.** A local office where mail is processed and stamps are sold.

post·op·er·a·tive (pōst-ŏp'ər-ə-tĭv, -ŏp'rə-, -ŏp'ə-rā'-) *adj.* Happening or done after surgery.

post·paid (pōst'pād') *adj.* With the postage paid in advance.

post·par·tum (pōst-pär'təm) *adj.* Following childbirth. [< Lat. *post partum,* after birth.]

post·pone (pōst-pōn', pōs-pōn') *v.* **-poned, -pon·ing.** To delay until a future time; put off. [< Lat. *postponere.*] —**post·pone'ment** *n.*

post·script (pōst'skrĭpt', pōs'skrĭpt') *n.* A message added at the end of a letter after the writer's signature. [Lat. *postscriptum.*]

pos·tu·lant (pŏs'chə-lənt) *n.* A candidate for admission into a religious order. [< Lat. *postulare,* to demand.]

pos·tu·late (pŏs'chə-lāt') *v.* **-lat·ed, -lat·ing.** To assume or claim as true, esp. as a basis of an argument. —*n.* (-lĭt, -lāt'). Something assumed without proof as being self-evident or gen. accepted. [Lat. *postulare.*] —**pos'tu·la'tion** *n.*

pos·ture (pŏs'chər) *n.* **1.** A position or attitude of the body or bodily parts. **2.** A condition; state: *the nation's military posture.* **3.** A frame of mind; attitude. —*v.* **-tured, -tur·ing.** To assume an exaggerated or unnatural pose or mental attitude. [< Lat. *positura,* position.] —**pos'tur·er** *n.*

post·war (pōst'wôr') *adj.* Occurring after a war.

po·sy (pō'zē) *n., pl.* **-sies.** **1.** A flower or bunch of flowers. **2.** *Archaic.* A brief verse or sentimental phrase. [< POESY.]

pot (pŏt) *n.* **1.** A round vessel esp. for cooking. **2.** Something resembling a pot in appearance or function. **3.** The total amount staked by all the players in one hand of a card game. **4.** *Informal.* A common fund to which the members of a group contribute. **5.** *Slang.* Marijuana. —*v.* **pot·ted, pot·ting.** **1.** To place or plant in a pot. **2.** To cook or preserve in a pot. —*idiom.* **go to pot.** *Informal.* To deteriorate. [< OE *pott.*]

po·ta·ble (pō'tə-bəl) *adj.* Fit to drink. [< LLat. *potabilis.*]

pot·ash (pŏt'ăsh') *n.* **1.** Potassium carbonate.

2. Potassium hydroxide. **3.** Any of several compounds containing potassium, esp. soluble compounds, used chiefly in fertilizers. [< obs. *pot ashes*.]

po·tas·si·um (pə-tăs′ē-əm) *n.* **Symbol K** A soft, silver-white, light, highly or explosively reactive metallic element found in or converted to a wide variety of salts used esp. in fertilizers and soaps. Atomic number 19; atomic weight 39.102. [< POTASH.]

potassium bromide *n.* A white crystalline solid or powder, KBr, used as a sedative and in photographic emulsion.

potassium carbonate *n.* A transparent, white, granular powder, K_2CO_3, used in making glass, pigments, ceramics, and soaps.

potassium hydroxide *n.* A caustic solid, KOH, used as a bleach and in the manufacture of liquid detergents and soaps.

potassium nitrate *n.* A transparent white crystalline compound, KNO_3, used to pickle meat and in the manufacture of explosives, matches, and fertilizers.

po·ta·tion (pō-tā′shən) *n.* **1.** The act of drinking. **2.** A drink, esp. an alcoholic beverage. [< Lat. *potare*, to drink.]

po·ta·to (pə-tā′tō) *n., pl.* **-toes.** **1.** The starchy, edible tuber of a widely cultivated plant. **2.** The plant itself. [< Taino *batata*.]

potato chip *n.* A thin slice of potato fried in deep fat until crisp and then salted.

Pot·a·wat·o·mi (pŏt′ə-wŏt′ə-mē) *n., pl.* **-mi** or **-mis.** **1. a.** A tribe of Indians inhabiting Michigan. **b.** A member of this tribe. **2.** The Algonquian language of the Potawatomi.

pot·bel·ly (pŏt′bĕl′ē) *n.* A protruding belly. **—pot′bel′lied** *adj.*

pot·boil·er (pŏt′boi′lər) *n.* A sensational literary or artistic work of poor quality produced only for profit.

pot cheese *n.* Cottage cheese.

po·tent (pōt′nt) *adj.* **1.** Possessing strength; powerful. **2.** Having a strong effect or influence; cogent. **3.** Capable of producing strong physiological or chemical effects. **4.** Able to perform sexually. Used of a male. [< Lat. *potens*.] **—po′ten·cy** *n.* **—po′tent·ly** *adv.*

po·ten·tate (pōt′n-tāt′) *n.* One who has the power and position to rule over others; monarch. [< Lat. *potentatus*, power.]

po·ten·tial (pə-tĕn′shəl) *adj.* Capable of being but not yet realized; latent. **—n.** **1.** Capacity for growth, development, or progress. **2.** The potential energy of a unit charge by virtue of its location in an electric field; voltage. **—po·ten′ti·al′i·ty** (-shē-ăl′ī-tē) *n.* **—po·ten′tial·ly** *adv.*

pot·head (pŏt′hĕd′) *n. Slang.* One who habitually smokes marijuana.

poth·er (pŏth′ər) *n.* **1.** A commotion; disturbance. **2.** A fuss. [Orig. unknown.]

pot·hole (pŏt′hōl′) *n.* A large hole, esp. in a road surface.

pot·hook (pŏt′hŏŏk′) *n.* A hooked piece of iron for hanging a pot or kettle over a fire.

po·tion (pō′shən) *n.* A liquid dose, esp. of medicinal, magic, or poisonous content. [< Lat. *potare*, to drink.]

pot·luck (pŏt′lŭk′) *n.* Whatever food happens to be available for a meal, esp. when offered to a guest.

pot·pie (pŏt′pī′) *n.* A meat or poultry stew with a crust or dumplings.

pot·pour·ri (pō′pŏŏ-rē′) *n.* **1.** A combination of diverse elements. **2.** A fragrant mixture of dried flower petals and spices. [Fr. *pot pourri.*]

pot roast *n.* Beef that is browned and then cooked until tender in a covered pot.

pot·sherd (pŏt′shûrd′) *n.* A fragment of broken pottery. [ME *potschoord*.]

pot shot *n.* **1.** A shot fired without taking careful aim or fired at a target within easy range. **2.** A criticism made without careful thought and aimed at a handy target.

pot·tage (pŏt′ĭj) *n.* A thick soup or stew of vegetables and often meat. [< OFr. *potage*.]

pot·ter¹ (pŏt′ər) *n.* One who makes pottery.

potter¹

pot·ter² (pŏt′ər) *v. Chiefly Brit.* To putter. [< dial. *potler*.]

pot·tery (pŏt′ə-rē) *n., pl.* **-ies.** **1.** Objects, such as vases, pots, bowls, or plates, shaped from moist clay and hardened by heat. **2.** The craft or occupation of a potter. **3.** The place where pottery is made.

pouch (pouch) *n.* **1.** A small bag used esp. for carrying loose pipe tobacco. **2.** A mailbag, esp. one for diplomatic dispatches. **3.** A saclike structure, as the external abdominal pocket in which marsupials carry their young. **—v.** To assume or cause to assume the form of a pouch or pouchlike cavity. [< OFr. *pouche*, of Gmc. orig.]

poul·ter·er (pōl′tər-ər) *n.* A poultry dealer.

poul·tice (pōl′tĭs) *n.* A moist, soft, usu. heated mass spread on cloth and applied to an aching or inflamed part of the body. [< Gk. *poltos*, porridge.] **—poul′tice** *v.*

poul·try (pōl′trē) *n.* Domestic fowls, such as chickens, turkeys, or ducks, raised for meat or eggs. [< OFr. *pouleterie*.]

pounce (pouns) *v.* **pounced, pounc·ing.** To spring or swoop suddenly so as to seize something. [< ME, predatory bird's talon.] **—pounce** *n.*

pound¹ (pound) *n., pl.* **pounds** or **pound.** **1. a.** A unit of avoirdupois weight equal to 16 ounces, 7,000 grains, or 453.592 grams. **b.** A unit of apothecary weight equal to 5,760 grains or 373.242 grams. **2.** A unit of weight differing in various countries and times. **3.** A British unit of force equal to the weight of a standard one-pound mass where the local acceleration of gravity is 32.174 feet per second per second. **4.** See table at **currency.** [< Lat. *pondo*, a unit of weight.]

pound² (pound) *v.* **1.** To strike heavily with repeated blows. **2.** To beat to a powder or pulp; pulverize or crush. **3.** To instill by persistent and emphatic repetition; drill. **4.** To move along heavily and noisily. **5.** To pulsate rapidly and heavily. [< OE *pūnian*.]

pound³ (pound) *n.* A public enclosure for the confinement of stray animals. [ME.]

pound·age (poun'dĭj) n. Weight measured in pounds.

pound cake n. A rich cake containing eggs and orig. made with a pound each of flour, butter, and sugar.

pound-fool·ish (pound'fŏŏl'ĭsh) adj. Unwise in dealing with large sums of money or large matters.

pour (pôr, pōr) v. 1. To flow or cause to flow in a flood or steady stream. 2. To supply abundantly, as if in a stream or flood. 3. To rain heavily. [ME pouren.] —pour'er n.

pour·boire (pŏŏr-bwär') n. Money given as a gratuity; tip. [< Fr. pour boire, for drinking.]

pout (pout) v. 1. To protrude the lips in an expression of displeasure. 2. To show displeasure or disappointment; sulk. [ME pouten.] —pout n. —pout'er n.

pov·er·ty (pŏv'ər-tē) n. 1. Lack of money or material comforts; want. 2. Deficiency in amount; scantiness. 3. Unproductiveness; infertility. [< Lat. paupertas.]

pov·er·ty-strick·en (pŏv'ər-tē-strĭk'ən) adj. Destitute; poor.

pow·der (pou'dər) n. 1. A substance consisting of ground, pulverized, or otherwise finely dispersed solid particles. 2. Any of various cosmetic or medicinal preparations in the form of powder. 3. An explosive mixture such as gunpowder. —v. 1. To reduce to powder; pulverize. 2. To dust or cover with or as if with powder. [< Lat. pulvis.] —pow'der·i·ness n. —pow'der·y adj.

powder puff n. A soft pad for applying powder to the skin.

powder room n. A lavatory for women.

pow·er (pou'ər) n. 1. The ability or capacity to act or perform effectively. 2. A specific capacity, faculty, or aptitude: had the power of concentration. 3. Strength or force capable of being exerted; might. 4. The ability or capacity to exercise control; authority. 5. A nation having influence or control over others. 6. Physical strength. 7. The rate at which work is done, commonly measured in units such as the watt and horsepower. 8. Electricity. 9. Math. An exponent. 10. A measure of the magnification of an optical instrument. —v. To supply with power, esp. mechanical power. [< OFr. poeir, to be able.] —pow'er·ful adj. —pow'er·ful·ly adv. —pow'er·less adj. —pow'er·less·ly adv.

pow·er·boat (pou'ər-bōt') n. A motorboat.

pow·er·house (pou'ər-hous') n. 1. A station for the generating of electricity. 2. One possessing great force or energy.

power of attorney n. A legal authorization to act as another's attorney or agent.

power plant n. 1. All the equipment that constitutes a unit power source. 2. A complex of structures and machinery for generating power, esp. electric power.

Pow·ha·tan (pou'ə-tăn') n., pl. -tan or -tans. 1. a. One of various tribes of Indians formerly inhabiting eastern Virginia. b. A member of one of these tribes. 2. The Algonquian language of the Powhatan.

pow·wow (pou'wou') n. 1. A North American Indian ceremony in which divine help is invoked. 2. Informal. A gathering, meeting, or conference. [Of Algonquian orig.]

pox (pŏks) n. A disease, as smallpox, characterized by purulent skin eruptions. [< POCK.]

Pr The symbol for the element praseodymium.

prac·ti·ca·ble (prăk'tĭ-kə-bəl) adj. Capable of being effected, done, or executed; feasible. —prac'ti·ca·bil'i·ty n. —prac'ti·ca·bly adv.

prac·ti·cal (prăk'tĭ-kəl) adj. 1. Serving or capable of serving a purpose; useful. 2. Acquired through or qualified by practice or action rather than theory or speculation: practical knowledge. 3. Level-headed, efficient, and unspeculative; sensible. 4. Being actually so; virtual. [< Gk. praktikos.] —prac'ti·cal'i·ty (-kăl'ĭ-tē) n. —prac'ti·cal·ly adv.

Syns: practical, functional, handy, serviceable, useful, utilitarian adj.

practical joke n. A prank played on a person to make him seem or feel foolish.

practical nurse n. A nurse who has completed a practical nursing program and who is licensed by a state to provide routine patient care under the direction of a registered nurse or a physician.

prac·tice (prăk'tĭs) n. 1. A habitual or customary action or way of doing something. 2. a. Repeated performance of an activity in order to acquire or perfect a skill. b. Proficiency resulting from repeated exercise. 3. The act or process of doing something; performance. 4. The exercise of an occupation or profession. 5. The business of a professional person. 6. A habitual action. —v. -ticed, -tic·ing. Also chiefly Brit. prac·tise, -tised, -tis·ing. 1. To do or perform habitually or customarily; make a habit of: practice restraint. 2. To exercise or perform repeatedly in order to acquire or perfect a skill. 3. To work at, esp. as a profession: practice law. 4. To carry out; apply. [< Gk. praktikos, practical.]

prac·ti·tio·ner (prăk-tĭsh'ə-nər) n. One who practices an occupation, profession, or technique. [OFr. practicien.]

prae·tor (prē'tər) n. An ancient Roman magistrate ranking below a consul. [Lat.] —prae·to'ri·an (-tôr'ē-ən, -tōr'-) adj.

prag·mat·ic (prăg-măt'ĭk) or **prag·mat·i·cal** (-ĭ-kəl) adj. 1. Concerned with facts or actual occurrences; practical. 2. Of or pertaining to pragmatism. [< Gk. pragma, deed.] —prag·mat'i·cal·ly adv.

prag·ma·tism (prăg'mə-tĭz'əm) n. A method of solving problems and affairs by practical means. —prag'ma·tist n.

prai·rie (prâr'ē) n. An extensive area of flat or rolling grassland, as in central North America. [< Lat. pratum, meadow.]

prairie dog n. A burrowing rodent of west-central North America with yellowish fur and a barklike call.

prairie schooner n. A canvas-covered wagon used by pioneers crossing the North American prairies.

praise (prāz) n. 1. An expression of warm approval, admiration, or commendation. 2. The extolling of a deity, ruler, or hero. —v. praised, prais·ing. 1. To commend. 2. To extol. [< Lat. pretium, price.]

Syns: praise, acclaim, applaud, commend, laud v.

praise·wor·thy (prāz'wûr'thē) adj. Meriting praise; commendable.

pra·line (prā'lēn', prä'-) n. A crisp confection made of nut kernels stirred in boiling sugar syrup. [< Count du Plessis-*Praslin* (1598–1675).]

pram (prăm) n. Chiefly Brit. A perambulator.

prance (prăns) v. pranced, pranc·ing. 1. To spring forward on the hind legs, as a spirited horse does. 2. a. To move about in a lively manner; caper. b. To strut. [ME *prauncer*.] —pranc'er n. —pranc'ing·ly adv.

prank (prăngk) n. A mischievous trick. [Orig. unknown.] —prank'ster n.

pra·se·o·dym·i·um (prā'zē-ō-dĭm'ē-əm, -sē-) n. Symbol **Pr** A soft, silvery, malleable, ductile rare-earth element used to color glass yellow and in metallic alloys. Atomic number 59; atomic weight 140.907. [Gk. *prasios*, leek-green + E. *didymium*, a metal mixture.]

prate (prāt) v. prat·ed, prat·ing. To talk idly and at length; chatter. [ME *praten*.]

prat·fall (prăt'fôl') n. A fall on the buttocks. [*prat*, buttocks + FALL.]

prat·tle (prăt'l) v. -tled, -tling. To talk idly or meaninglessly; babble. —n. Childish or meaningless sounds; babble. [< PRATE.]

prawn (prôn) n. An edible crustacean related to and resembling the shrimps. [ME *prayne*.]

pray (prā) v. 1. To utter or address a prayer to a deity. 2. To make a fervent request for something. 3. To beseech; implore. [< Lat. *precari*, to entreat.]

prayer (prâr) n. 1. An expression of thoughts, hopes, or needs directed to a deity. 2. A special formula of words used in praying. 3. The act of praying. 4. Often **prayers.** A religious service in which praying predominates. 5. An earnest appeal, request, or plea. 6. The slightest chance or hope, as for survival. [< Med. Lat. *precaria*.]

prayer·ful (prâr'fəl) adj. 1. Inclined to pray frequently; devout. 2. Solemnly sincere; earnest. —prayer'ful·ly adv.

praying mantis n. A green or brownish insect that while at rest folds its front legs as if in prayer.

pre- pref. 1. a. Earlier; prior to: *prehistoric.* b. Preparatory; preliminary: *premedical.* c. In advance: *prepay.* 2. Anterior; in front of: *premolar.* [< Lat. *prae*, before.]

preach (prēch) v. 1. To urge acceptance of or compliance with. 2. To deliver a sermon. 3. To give moral advice, esp. in a tiresome manner. [< Lat. *praedicare*, to proclaim.] —preach'er n.

pre·am·ble (prē'ăm'bəl) n. A preliminary part, esp. the introduction to a formal document that explains its purpose. [< LLat. *praeambulus*, walking in front.]

pre·am·pli·fi·er (prē-ăm'plə-fī'ər) n. An electronic circuit or device that detects and amplifies weak signals, esp. from a radio receiver, for subsequent amplification stages.

pre·ar·range (prē'ə-rānj') v. To arrange in advance. —pre'ar·range'ment n.

preb·end (prĕb'ənd) n. 1. A clergyman's stipend drawn from a special endowment belonging to his cathedral or church. 2. The endowment providing a prebend. [< Lat. *praebēre*, to grant.]

preb·en·dar·y (prĕb'ən-dĕr'ē) n., pl. -ies. A clergyman who receives a prebend.

Pre·cam·bri·an (prē-kăm'brē-ən) adj. Of or belonging to the oldest and largest division of

geologic time, preceding the Cambrian and characterized by the appearance of primitive forms of life. —n. The Precambrian era.

pre·can·cer·ous (prē-kăn'sər-əs) adj. Exhibiting a likelihood of becoming cancerous.

pre·car·i·ous (prĭ-kâr'ē-əs) adj. 1. Dangerously lacking in stability. 2. Subject to chance or uncertain conditions. [< Lat. *precarius*, obtained by entreaty.] —pre·car'i·ous·ly adv. —pre·car'i·ous·ness n.

pre·cau·tion (prĭ-kô'shən) n. An action taken in advance to protect against possible failure or danger. [< Lat. *praecavēre*, to beware.] —pre·cau'tion·ar'y (-shə-nĕr'ē) adj.

pre·cede (prĭ-sēd') v. -ced·ed, -ced·ing. To come or be before in time, place, or rank. [< Lat. *praecedere*.]

prec·e·dence (prĕs'ĭ-dəns, prĭ-sēd'ns) n. The act, state, or right of preceding; priority.

prec·e·dent (prĕs'ĭ-dnt) n. 1. Something that may be used as an example in dealing with subsequent similar cases. 2. Convention or custom. —adj. pre·ce·dent (prĭ-sēd'nt, prĕs'ĭ-dnt). Preceding; prior.

pre·ced·ing (prĭ-sē'dĭng) adj. Existing or coming before; previous.

pre·cen·tor (prĭ-sĕn'tər) n. One who directs the singing of a church choir or congregation. [< Lat. *praecinere*, to sing before.]

pre·cept (prē'sĕpt') n. A rule or principle imposing a standard of action or conduct. [< Lat. *praeceptum*.]

pre·cep·tor (prĭ-sĕp'tər, prē'sĕp'-) n. A teacher; instructor.

pre·cinct (prē'sĭngkt') n. 1. a. A district of a city patrolled by a unit of the police force. b. An election district of a city or town. 2. Often **precincts.** A place or enclosure marked off by definite limits. 3. **precincts.** Neighborhood; environs. [< Lat. *praecingere*, to encircle.]

pre·ci·os·i·ty (prĕsh'ē-ŏs'ĭ-tē) n., pl. -ties. Extreme meticulousness or overrefinement.

pre·cious (prĕsh'əs) adj. 1. Of high cost or worth; valuable. 2. Dear; beloved. 3. Affectedly dainty or overrefined. [< Lat. *pretiosus*.] —pre'cious·ly adv.

prec·i·pice (prĕs'ə-pĭs) n. An extremely steep or overhanging cliff. [< Lat. *praeceps*, headlong.]

pre·cip·i·tant (prĭ-sĭp'ĭ-tnt) adj. 1. Rushing or falling headlong. 2. Impulsive in thought or action; rash. 3. Abrupt or unexpected; sudden. —pre·cip'i·tance or pre·cip'i·tan·cy n.

pre·cip·i·tate (prĭ-sĭp'ĭ-tāt') v. -tat·ed, -tat·ing. 1. To hurl downward. 2. To cause to happen before anticipated or required: *precipitate a crisis.* 3. To condense and fall as rain or snow. 4. Chem. To cause (a solid substance) to be separated from a solution. —adj. (-tĭt, -tāt'). 1. Speeding headlong; moving rapidly and heedlessly. 2. Acting with excessive haste or impulse. 3. Occurring suddenly or unexpectedly. —n. (-tāt', -tĭt). Chem. A solid or solid phase chemically separated from a solution. [< Lat. *praecipitare*.] —pre·cip'i·tate·ly adv. —pre·cip'i·tate·ness n.

Usage: Precipitate applies primarily to rash, overhasty human actions. *Precipitous* is used primarily of physical steepness, as in a *precipitous slope,* or in the figurative extension of such literal use, as in a *precipitous drop in interest rates.*

pre·cip·i·ta·tion (prĭ-sĭp'ĭ-tā'shən) n. 1. A headlong fall or rush. 2. Abrupt or impulsive haste. **3. a.** Water that falls as rain or snow. **b.** The amount of this in a specific area within a specific period. **4.** *Chem.* The production of a precipitate.

pre·cip·i·tous (prĭ-sĭp′ĭ-təs) *adj.* **1. a.** Like a precipice; extremely steep. **b.** Having precipices: *a precipitous bluff.* **2.** Precipitate. —**pre·cip′i·tous·ly** *adv.*

pré·cis (prā-sē′) *n., pl.* **pré·cis** (-sēz′). A concise summary of essential facts; abstract. [< OFr. *precis,* precise.] —**pré·cis′** *v.*

pre·cise (prĭ-sīs′) *adj.* **1.** Clearly expressed or delineated; definite. **2.** Exactly corresponding to what is indicated; correct. **3.** Strictly distinguished from others; very: *at that precise moment.* **4.** Conforming strictly to rule or proper form. [< Lat. *praecisus,* p.p. of *praecidere,* to shorten.] —**pre·cise′ly** *adv.* —**pre·cise′ness** *n.*

pre·ci·sion (prĭ-sĭzh′ən) *n.* The state or quality of being precise.

pre·clude (prĭ-klōōd′) *v.* **-clud·ed, -clud·ing.** **1.** To make impossible; prevent. **2.** To exclude; debar. [Lat. *praecludere.*]

pre·co·cious (prĭ-kō′shəs) *adj.* Characterized by unusually early development or maturity, esp. in mental aptitude. [< Lat. *praecox,* premature.] —**pre·co′cious·ly** *adv.* —**pre·coc′i·ty** (-kŏs′ĭ-tē) *n.*

pre·con·ceive (prē′kən-sēv′) *v.* To form an opinion or conception of beforehand. —**pre′con·cep′tion** (-sĕp′shən) *n.*

pre·con·di·tion (prē′kən-dĭsh′ən) *n.* A prerequisite. —*v.* To condition, train, or accustom in advance.

pre·cook (prē-kōōk′) *v.* To cook in advance or cook partially before final cooking.

pre·cur·sor (prĭ-kûr′sər, prē′kûr′-) *n.* **1.** One that precedes and indicates or announces another; forerunner. **2.** An ancestor; predecessor. [Lat. *praecursor.*]

pre·da·cious or **pre·da·ceous** (prĭ-dā′shəs) *adj.* Living by seizing prey; predatory. [< Lat. *praedari,* to plunder.]

pre·date (prē-dāt′) *v.* To antedate.

pred·a·tor (prĕd′ə-tər, -tôr′) *n.* **1.** An animal that preys upon others. **2.** One who plunders or abuses others for his own profit. [Lat.]

pred·a·to·ry (prĕd′ə-tôr′ē, -tōr′ē) *adj.* **1.** Of, pertaining to, or characterized by plunder: *a predatory war.* **2.** Preying on other animals; predacious. —**pred′a·to′ri·ness** *n.*

pre·de·cease (prē′dĭ-sēs′) *v.* To die before (another person).

pred·e·ces·sor (prĕd′ĭ-sĕs′ər, prē′dĭ-) *n.* One that precedes another in time, esp. in an office or position. [< LLat. *praedecessor.*]

pre·des·ti·na·tion (prē-dĕs′tə-nā′shən) *n.* **1.** The act whereby God is believed to have foreordained all things. **2.** The doctrine that God has foreordained all things, esp. the salvation of individual souls.

pre·des·tine (prē-dĕs′tĭn) *v.* To decide or decree in advance; foreordain.

pre·de·ter·mine (prē′dĭ-tûr′mĭn) *v.* To determine or decide in advance. —**pre′de·ter′mi·na′tion** *n.*

pred·i·ca·ble (prĕd′ĭ-kə-bəl) *adj.* Capable of being stated or predicated.

pre·dic·a·ment (prĭ-dĭk′ə-mənt) *n.* A trouble-

some or embarrassing situation. [< LLat. *praedicamentum.*]

pred·i·cate (prĕd′ĭ-kāt′) *v.* **-cat·ed, -cat·ing.** **1.** To base or establish: *predicate an argument on the facts.* **2.** To affirm as an attribute or quality: *predicate the perfectibility of mankind.* —*n.* (-kĭt). The part of a sentence or clause that expresses what is stated about the subject. [Lat. *praedicare,* to proclaim.] —**pred′i·ca′tion** *n.* —**pred′i·ca′tive** *adj.*

pre·dict (prĭ-dĭkt′) *v.* To state, tell about, or make known in advance; foretell. [< Lat. *praedicere.*] —**pre·dict′a·ble** *adj.* —**pre·dict′a·bly** *adv.* —**pre·dic′tion** *n.*

pre·di·gest (prē′dī-jĕst′, -dī-) *v.* To subject to partial digestion.

pre·di·lec·tion (prĕd′l-ĕk′shən, prēd′l-) *n.* A disposition in favor of something; preference. [< Med. Lat. *praediligere,* to prefer.]

pre·dis·pose (prē′dĭ-spōz′) *v.* **1.** To make (someone) inclined to something in advance. **2.** To make susceptible or liable. —**pre·dis′po·si′tion** *n.*

pre·dom·i·nant (prĭ-dŏm′ə-nənt) *adj.* **1.** Having superior authority or importance. **2.** Most common, numerous, or noticeable; prevalent. —**pre·dom′i·nance** *n.* —**pre·dom′i·nant·ly** *adv.*

pre·dom·i·nate (prĭ-dŏm′ə-nāt′) *v.* **-nat·ed, -nat·ing.** **1.** To be of greater power, importance, or quantity. **2.** To have authority, power, or controlling influence; prevail. [< Lat. *praedominari,* to subdue beforehand.] —**pre·dom′i·nate·ly** (-nĭt-lē) *adv.* —**pre·dom′i·na′tion** *n.*

pree·mie (prē′mē) *n. Informal.* An infant born prematurely. [< PREMATURE.]

pre·em·i·nent or **pre·em·i·nent** (prē-ĕm′ə-nənt) *adj.* Superior to all others; outstanding. [< Lat. *praeeminēre,* to excel.] —**pre·em′i·nence** *n.* —**pre·em′i·nent·ly** *adv.*

pre·empt or **pre·empt** (prē-ĕmpt′) *v.* **1.** To settle on (public land) so as to obtain the right to buy before others. **2.** To appropriate or seize for oneself before others. **3.** To be presented in place of. [< Lat. *praeemere,* to buy beforehand.] —**pre·emp′tion** *n.* —**pre·emp′tive** *adj.* —**pre·emp′tive·ly** *adv.*

preen (prēn) *v.* **1.** To smooth or clean (feathers) with the beak. **2.** To dress or groom (oneself) with care; primp. **3.** To take pride or satisfaction in (oneself). [ME *preinen.*]

pre·ex·ist or **pre·ex·ist** (prē′ĭg-zĭst′) *v.* To exist before. —**pre′-ex·ist′ence** *n.* —**pre′-ex·ist′ent** *adj.*

pre·fab (prē′făb′) *n.* A prefabricated part or structure.

pre·fab·ri·cate (prē-făb′rĭ-kāt′) *v.* To construct in standard sections that can be easily shipped and assembled. —**pre·fab′ri·ca′tion** *n.*

pref·ace (prĕf′ĭs) *n.* An introductory statement, as to a book; foreword. —*v.* **-aced, -ac·ing.** To introduce by, serve as, or provide with a preface. [< Lat. *praefatio.*] —**pref·a·to′ry** (-ə-tôr′ē, -tōr′ē) *adj.*

pre·fect (prē′fĕkt′) *n.* **1.** A high administrative official. **2.** A student officer, esp. in a private school. [< Lat. *praefectus.*] —**pre·fec′ture** (-fĕk′chər) *n.*

pre·fer (prĭ-fûr′) *v.* **-ferred, -fer·ring.** **1.** To choose as more desirable; like better. **2.** To file before a legal authority: *prefer charges.* [< Lat. *praeferre.*]

pref·er·a·ble (prĕf′ər-ə-bəl) *adj.* More desirable; preferred. —**pref′er·a·bly** *adv.*

pref·er·ence (prĕf′ər-əns) *n.* **1.** The exercise of choice. **2.** A liking for something over another. **3.** One that is preferred. —**pref′er·en′tial** (-ə-rĕn′shəl) *adj.*

pre·fer·ment (prĭ-fûr′mənt) *n.* The condition of being singled out for promotion or favored treatment.

pre·fig·ure (prē-fĭg′yər) *v.* **1.** To presage; foreshadow. **2.** To imagine in advance. —**pre·fig′ure·ment** *n.*

pre·fix (prē′fĭks′, prē-fĭks′) *v.* To put or fix before: *prefixed the title "Dr." to his name.* —*n.* (prē′fĭks′). An affix put before a word, changing or modifying its meaning. [OFr. *prefixer.*]

pre·flight (prē′flīt′) *adj.* Preparing for or occurring prior to flight.

preg·na·ble (prĕg′nə-bəl) *adj.* Vulnerable to seizure or capture: *a pregnable fort.* [< Lat. *prehendere,* to take.] —**preg′na·bil′i·ty** *n.*

preg·nant (prĕg′nənt) *adj.* **1.** Carrying a developing fetus within the uterus. **2.** Fraught with significance or implication; meaningful. [< Lat. *praegnans.*] —**preg′nan·cy** *n.*

pre·heat (prē-hēt′) *v.* To heat beforehand.

pre·hen·sile (prĭ-hĕn′sĭl, -sīl′) *adj.* Adapted for seizing or holding, esp. by wrapping around: *a prehensile tail.* [< Lat. *prehendere,* to seize.]

pre·his·tor·ic (prē′hĭ-stôr′ĭk, -stŏr′-) *adj.* Also **pre·his·tor·i·cal** (-ĭ-kəl). Of, pertaining to, or belonging to the era before recorded history. —**pre·his·tor′i·cal·ly** *adv.*

pre·judge (prē-jŭj′) *v.* To judge beforehand without having adequate evidence. —**pre·judg′er** *n.* —**pre·judg′ment** or **pre·judge′ment** *n.*

prej·u·dice (prĕj′ə-dĭs) *n.* **1.** A strong feeling for or against something formed before one knows the facts; bias. **2.** Irrational hostility toward members of a particular race, religion, or group. **3.** Harm or injury. —*v.* **-diced, -dic·ing. 1.** To cause (someone) to have a prejudice. **2.** To do harm to; injure: *prejudiced his own cause.* [< Lat. *praejudicium.*] —**prej′u·di′cial** (-dĭsh′əl) *adj.*

prel·ate (prĕl′ĭt) *n.* A high-ranking clergyman, as a bishop. [< Lat. *praelatus,* p.p. of *praeferre,* to carry before.] —**prel′a·cy** (-ə-sē) *n.*

pre·lim·i·nar·y (prĭ-lĭm′ə-nĕr′ē) *adj.* Prior to the main matter, action, or business; introductory. —*n., pl.* **-ies.** Something that leads to or serves as preparation for a main event, action, or business. [< Med. Lat. *praeliminaris.*] —**pre·lim′i·nar′i·ly** (-nâr′ə-lē) *adv.*

prel·ude (prĕl′yōōd, prā′lōōd′) *n.* **1.** An introductory performance, event, or action. **2.** *Mus.* A piece or movement that acts as an introduction to the main theme or a larger work. [< Lat. *praeludere,* to play beforehand.]

pre·mar·i·tal (prē-mâr′ĭ-tl) *adj.* Taking place or existing prior to marriage.

pre·ma·ture (prē′mə-tōōr′, -tyōōr′, -chōōr′) *adj.* Occurring, born, done, or existing prior to the customary, correct, or assigned time; early. —**pre′ma·ture′ly** *adv.*

pre·med (prē′mĕd′) *adj. Informal.* Premedical. —**pre′med′** *n.*

pre·med·i·cal (prē-mĕd′ĭ-kəl) *adj.* Preparing for or leading to the study of medicine.

pre·med·i·tate (prē-mĕd′ĭ-tāt′) *v.* To plan, arrange, or plot in advance. —**pre·med′i·ta′tion** *n.*

pre·men·stru·al (prē-mĕn′strōō-əl) *adj.* Of, pertaining to, or occurring in the period just prior to menstruation.

pre·mier (prĭ-mîr′, prĭ-mîr′) *n.* **1.** First in status or importance; chief. **2.** First to occur or exist; earliest. —*n.* (prĭ-mîr′). A prime minister. [< Lat. *primus,* first.]

pre·mière (prĭ-mîr′, prĭm-yâr′) *n.* A first public presentation, as of a play. —*v.* **-mièred, -mièr·ing.** To present or receive a first public presentation. [Fr., first.]

prem·ise (prĕm′ĭs) *n.* **1.** A proposition upon which an argument is based or from which a conclusion is drawn. **2. premises.** Land and the buildings on it. [< Lat. *praemittere,* to set in front.]

pre·mi·um (prē′mē-əm) *n.* **1.** A prize; reward. **2.** A sum of money paid in addition to a regular amount. **3.** An amount charged in addition to the standard or usual price. **4.** An unusually high value: *put a premium on hard work.* **5.** An amount paid, often in installments, for an insurance policy. [Lat. *praemium,* profit.]

pre·mo·lar (prē-mō′lər) *n.* One of eight bicuspid teeth located in pairs between the canines and molars.

pre·mo·ni·tion (prē′mə-nĭsh′ən, prĕm′ə-) *n.* **1.** An advance warning; forewarning. **2.** A presentiment; foreboding. [< Lat. *praemonēre,* to forewarn.] —**pre·mon′i·to′ry** (-mŏn′ĭ-tôr′ē, -tōr′ē) *adj.*

pre·na·tal (prē-nāt′l) *adj.* Existing or occurring prior to birth. —**pre·na′tal·ly** *adv.*

pre·oc·cu·py (prē-ŏk′yə-pī′) *v.* **1.** To occupy completely the mind or attention of; engross. **2.** To occupy or take possession of in advance or before another. —**pre·oc′cu·pa′tion** (-pā′shən) *n.*

pre·or·dain (prē′ôr-dān′) *v.* To decree or ordain in advance; foreordain.

pre·pack·age (prē-păk′ĭj) *v.* To wrap or package (products) before marketing.

prep·a·ra·tion (prĕp′ə-rā′shən) *n.* **1.** The act or process of preparing. **2.** Readiness. **3.** Often **preparations.** Preliminary measures. **4.** A substance, as a medicine, prepared for a particular purpose.

pre·par·a·to·ry (prĭ-pâr′ə-tôr′ē, -tōr′ē, -pâr′-) *adj.* Serving to prepare.

preparatory school *n.* A secondary school, usu. private, preparing students for college.

pre·pare (prĭ-pâr′) *v.* **-pared, -par·ing. 1.** To make ready. **2.** To put together from various elements or ingredients. **3.** To fit out; equip. [< Lat. *praeparare.*]

pre·par·ed·ness (prĭ-pâr′ĭd-nĭs) *n.* The condition of being prepared, esp. for war.

pre·pay (prē-pā′) *v.* To pay or pay for beforehand. —**pre·pay′ment** *n.*

pre·pon·der·ate (prĭ-pŏn′də-rāt′) *v.* **-at·ed, -at·ing.** To be greater in power, weight, or importance. [< Lat. *praeponderare.*] —**pre·pon′der·ance** *n.* —**pre·pon′der·ant** *adj.*

prep·o·si·tion (prĕp′ə-zĭsh′ən) *n.* In some languages, a word that indicates the relation of a substantive to a verb, an adjective, or another substantive, as English *at, by, in, to, from,* and *with.* [< Lat. *praeponere,* to place in front.] —**prep′o·si′tion·al** *adj.*

Usage: There is nothing inherently wrong

about ending a sentence with a preposition, although such placement may be awkward or may provide a weak ending: *It was a place he planned to spend a lot of time in.* Often the final position is the only natural one for the preposition, as in *We have much to be thankful for*, and rephrasing the sentence would only result in an awkward or stilted effect.

pre·pos·sess (prē'pə-zĕs') v. **1.** To influence beforehand; prejudice; bias. **2.** To impress favorably in advance.

pre·pos·sess·ing (prē'pə-zĕs'ĭng) adj. Impressing favorably; pleasing: *a prepossessing manner.*

pre·pos·ter·ous (prĭ-pŏs'tər-əs) adj. Contrary to nature, reason, or common sense; absurd. [Lat. *praeposterus*.] —**pre·pos'ter·ous·ly** adv. —**pre·pos'ter·ous·ness** n.

prep·pie or **prep·py** (prĕp'ē) n., pl. **-pies.** *Informal.* **1.** A student in a preparatory school. **2.** A student or young adult whose manner and dress are traditional and conservative.

prep school n. *Informal.* A preparatory school.

pre·puce (prē'pyōōs) n. The foreskin. [< Lat. *praeputium.*]

pre·re·cord (prē'rĭ-kôrd') v. To record (a radio or television program) at an earlier time for later use.

pre·req·ui·site (prē-rĕk'wĭ-zĭt) adj. Required as a prior condition. —**pre·req'ui·site** n.

pre·rog·a·tive (prĭ-rŏg'ə-tĭv) n. An exclusive right or privilege. [< Lat. *praerogativus*, asked first.]

pres·age (prĕs'ĭj) n. **1.** An indication or warning of a future occurrence; omen. **2.** A presentiment; foreboding. —v. **pre·sage** (prĭ-sāj', prĕs'ĭj), **-saged, -sag·ing.** **1.** To indicate or warn of in advance; portend. **2.** To foretell or predict. [< Lat. *praesagium.*]

pres·by·ter (prĕz'bĭ-tər, prĕs'-) n. **1.** An elder in the Presbyterian Church. **2.** A priest or minister in various other churches. [< Gk. *presbuteros*, elder.]

pres·by·te·ri·an (prĕz'bĭ-tîr'ē-ən, prĕs'-) **1.** Of or pertaining to ecclesiastical government by presbyters. **2. Presbyterian.** Of or pertaining to a Protestant church governed by presbyters and traditionally Calvinistic in doctrine. —n. A member or adherent of a Presbyterian Church. —**pres'by·te'ri·an·ism** n.

pres·by·ter·y (prĕz'bĭ-tĕr'ē, prĕs'-) n., pl. **-ies.** **1.** A court in Presbyterian churches composed of the ministers and representative elders of a particular locality. **2.** The section of a church reserved for the clergy.

pre·school (prē'skōōl') adj. Of, pertaining to, or designed for a child of nursery-school age. —**pre'school'er** n.

pre·science (prē'shəns, prē'shē-əns, prĕsh'əns, prĕsh'ē-əns) n. Knowledge of actions or events before they occur. [< Lat. *praescire*, to know beforehand.] —**pre'scient** adj.

pre·scribe (prĭ-skrīb') v. **-scribed, -scrib·ing. 1.** To set down as a rule or guide. **2.** To order or recommend the use of a remedy or treatment. [< Lat. *praescribere*, to appoint.] —**pre·scrip'tive** (-skrĭp'tĭv) adj.

pre·scrip·tion (prĭ-skrĭp'shən) n. **1.** The act of prescribing. **2. a.** A written instruction for the preparation and administration of a medicine. **b.** A prescribed medicine.

pres·ence (prĕz'əns) n. **1.** The condition or fact of being present. **2.** The area immediately surrounding someone. **3.** One that is present. **4. a.** A manner of carrying oneself; bearing. **b.** The quality of self-assurance and confidence.

pres·ent¹ (prĕz'ənt) n. **1.** A moment or period in time intermediate between past and future; now. **2.** *Gram.* **a.** The verb tense expressing action in the present. **b.** A verb form in this tense. **3. presents.** *Law.* The document or instrument in question. —adj. **1.** Being or occurring at the present: *his present difficulties.* **2.** Being at hand. **3.** *Gram.* Of, pertaining to, or denoting a verb tense or form that expresses present time. [< Lat. *praesens*, pr.p. of *praeesse*, to be present.]

pre·sent² (prĭ-zĕnt') v. **1.** To introduce, esp. formally. **2.** To bring before the public: *present a play.* **3. a.** To make a gift or award of. **b.** To make a gift to; bestow. **4.** To offer for inspection or consideration. **5.** To aim or direct (a weapon) in a particular direction. **6.** *Law.* To bring (a charge or indictment) against someone. —n. **pres·ent** (prĕz'ənt). Something presented; gift. [Lat. *praesentare.*] —**pre·sent'a·ble** adj. —**pre·sent'a·bly** adv. —**pres'en·ta'tion** n.

pres·ent-day (prĕz'ənt-dā') adj. Current.

pre·sen·ti·ment (prĭ-zĕn'tə-mənt) n. A sense of something about to occur; premonition. [< Lat. *praesentire*, to feel beforehand.]

pres·ent·ly (prĕz'ənt-lē) adv. **1.** In a short time; soon. **2.** At this time or period; now. *Usage:* Presently may be used to mean "soon" and, confusingly, may also be used to mean "at the present time." Care should be taken to see that its meaning is clear from the context.

present participle n. A participle that expresses present action or condition and is sometimes used as an adjective formed in English by adding *-ing* to the infinitive.

pre·serv·a·tive (prĭ-zûr'və-tĭv) n. Something used to preserve, esp. a chemical used in foods to inhibit spoilage. —**pre·serv'a·tive** adj.

pre·serve (prĭ-zûrv') v. **-served, -serv·ing. 1.** To protect from injury or peril. **2.** To keep or maintain intact. **3.** To treat or prepare so as to prevent decay. —n. **1.** Often **preserves.** Fruit cooked with sugar to protect against decay or fermentation. **2.** An area maintained for the protection of wildlife or natural resources. [< LLat. *praeservare*.] —**pres'er·va'tion** (prĕz'ər-vā'shən) n. —**pre·serv'er** n.

pre·set (prē'sĕt') v. To set beforehand.

pre·shrunk (prē'shrŭngk') adj. Also **pre·shrunk.** Shrunk during manufacture to minimize subsequent shrinkage.

pre·side (prĭ-zīd') v. **-sid·ed, -sid·ing. 1.** To hold the position of authority, esp. to act as chairperson. **2.** To possess or exercise authority or control. [< Lat. *praesidēre*, to hold authority.]

pres·i·dent (prĕz'ĭ-dənt, -dĕnt') n. **1.** One appointed or elected to preside: *president of the assembly.* **2.** Often **President.** The chief executive of a republic, esp. of the United States.

3. The chief officer of an organization, as a corporation. —**pres'i·den·cy** n. —**pres'i·den'tial** (-dĕn'shəl) adj.

pre·soak (prē-sōk') v. To soak before washing. —n. (prē'sōk'). A cycle on an automatic washing machine for presoaking clothes.

pre·sort (prē-sôrt') v. To sort (mail) according to Zip Codes before delivering to a post office.

press (prĕs) v. **1.** To exert steady weight or force (against); bear down (on). **2.** To squeeze the juice or other contents from. **3. a.** To smooth or reshape by applying steady force. **b.** To iron: *press a suit.* **4.** To try hard to persuade. **5.** To place in trying circumstances; harass: *pressed for time.* **6.** To carry on vigorously; prosecute. **7.** To advance eagerly; push forward. **8.** To assemble in large numbers; crowd. —n. **1.** Any of various machines or devices that apply pressure. **2.** A printing press. **3.** A place or establishment where matter is printed. **4.** The method, art, or business of printing. **5. a.** Printed matter, esp. newspapers and magazines. **b.** The people involved with the collection, editing, and presentation of news. **c.** The matter dealt with by the news media, esp. comment and criticism. **6.** A large gathering; throng. **7.** The act of applying pressure. **8.** The pressure or urgency of business or affairs. **9.** The set of proper creases in a garment or fabric, formed by ironing. **10.** A storage closet; cupboard. [< Lat. *premere.*] —**press'er** n.

press agent n. A person employed to arrange advertising and publicity, as for an actor or business.

press conference n. An interview held for newsmen by a political figure or celebrity.

press·ing (prĕs'ĭng) adj. Demanding immediate attention; urgent.

press·man (prĕs'mən, -măn') n. A printing press operator.

press·room (prĕs'rōōm', -rŏŏm') n. **1.** The room in a printing establishment that contains the presses. **2.** A room that reporters can use.

pres·sure (prĕsh'ər) n. **1.** The act of pressing or the condition of being pressed. **2.** The application of continuous force by one body upon another that it is touching. **3.** Force applied over a surface measured as force per unit of area. **4.** A constraining influence: *under pressure to resign.* **5.** Urgent claim or demand: *under the pressure of business.* —v. -**sured,** -**sur·ing.** To exert pressure on. [< Lat. *premere,* to press.]

pressure group n. A group that exerts pressure, esp. on legislators, to advance or protect its interests.

pressure suit n. A garment worn in high-altitude aircraft or in spacecraft to compensate for low-pressure conditions.

pres·sur·ize (prĕsh'ə-rīz') v. -**ized,** -**iz·ing.** To maintain normal air pressure in (an enclosure, as an aircraft or submarine). —**pres'sur·i·za'tion** n.

pres·ti·dig·i·ta·tion (prĕs'tĭ-dĭj'ĭ-tā'shən) n. Sleight of hand. [< Fr. *prestidigateur,* juggler.] —**pres'ti·dig'i·ta'tor** n.

pres·tige (prĕ-stēzh', -stēj') n. Status or esteem in the eyes of others; repute. [< Lat. *prestigiae,* tricks.] —**pres·tig'ious** (prĕ-stĭj'əs, -stē'jəs) adj. —**pres·tig'ious·ly** adv.

pres·to (prĕs'tō) adv. **1.** *Mus.* In rapid tempo. **2.** Suddenly; at once. [Ital.] —**pres'to** adj.

pre·sume (prĭ-zōōm') v. -**sumed,** -**sum·ing.** **1.** To take for granted; assume. **2.** To take on oneself without authority or permission; dare. **3.** To take unwarranted advantage of something. [< Lat. *praesumere.*] —**pre·sum'a·ble** adj. —**pre·sum'a·bly** adv.

pre·sump·tion (prĭ-zŭmp'shən) n. **1.** Boldly arrogant or offensive behavior or language; effrontery. **2. a.** A belief based on reasonable evidence; assumption or supposition. **b.** A condition or basis for accepting or presuming. —**pre·sump'tive** adj.

pre·sump·tu·ous (prĭ-zŭmp'chŏŏ-əs) adj. Impertinently forward or confident; arrogant. —**pre·sump'tu·ous·ly** adv. —**pre·sump'tu·ous·ness** n.

pre·sup·pose (prē'sə-pōz') v. **1.** To suppose in advance. **2.** To require or involve necessarily as an antecedent condition. —**pre'sup·po·si'tion** (-sŭp'ə-zĭsh'ən) n.

pre·teen (prē'tēn') adj. Of, pertaining to, or being a preadolescent child. —**pre'teen'** n.

pre·tend (prĭ-tĕnd') v. **1.** To put on a false show (of); feign. **2.** To claim or allege insincerely or falsely; profess. **3.** To put forward a claim: *pretends to the throne.* [< Lat. *praetendere,* to assert.] —**pre·tend'er** n.

pre·tense (prē'tĕns', prĭ-tĕns') n. Also *chiefly Brit.* **pre·tence.** **1.** A false appearance or action intended to deceive. **2.** A false reason or excuse; pretext. **3.** An outward appearance: *not even a pretense of a fair trial.* **4.** A claim, esp. without foundation. **5.** Ostentation; pretentiousness. [< Lat. *praetendere,* to assert.]

pre·ten·sion (prĭ-tĕn'shən) n. **1.** A claim, esp. when unrealistic or immodest. **2.** Outward show; ostentation.

pre·ten·tious (prĭ-tĕn'shəs) adj. **1.** Claiming or demanding distinction or merit. **2.** Making an extravagant outward show; ostentatious. —**pre·ten'tious·ly** adv. —**pre·ten'tious·ness** n.

pret·er·it or **pret·er·ite** (prĕt'ər-ĭt) adj. Denoting the verb tense that expresses a past or completed action. [< Lat. *praeteritus,* p.p. of *praeterire,* to pass.] —**pret'er·it** n.

pre·ter·nat·u·ral (prē'tər-năch'ər-əl) adj. **1.** Transcending the normal course of nature. **2.** Supernatural. [< Lat. *praeter naturam,* beyond nature.] —**pre'ter·nat'u·ral·ly** adv. —**pre'ter·nat'u·ral·ness** n.

pre·text (prē'tĕkst') n. A purpose or excuse given to hide the real reason for something. [< Lat. *praetextum* < *praetexere,* to disguise.]

pret·ti·fy (prĭt'ĭ-fī') v. -**fied,** -**fy·ing.** To make pretty. —**pret'ti·fi·ca'tion** n.

pret·ty (prĭt'ē) adj. -**ti·er,** -**ti·est.** **1.** Pleasing or attractive in a graceful or delicate way. **2.** Excellent; fine. Often used ironically: *a pretty mess you've made of everything.* **3.** *Informal.* Considerable in size or extent: *a pretty fortune.* —adv. To a fair degree; moderately: *a pretty good student.* —v. -**tied,** -**ty·ing.** *Informal.* To make pretty. [< OE *prættig,* cunning.] —**pret'ti·ly** adv. —**pret'ti·ness** n.

pret·zel (prĕt'səl) n. A glazed biscuit, salted on the outside, usu. baked in the form of a loose knot or stick. [G.]

pre·vail (prĭ-vāl') v. **1.** To be victorious; triumph. **2.** To win out; succeed. **3.** To be common or frequent. **4.** To predominate. [< Lat. *praevalēre,* to be stronger.] —**pre·vail'er** n. —**pre·vail'ing·ly** adv.

prev·a·lent (prĕv'ə-lənt) adj. Commonly occurring or existing; widespread. [< Lat. *prae-*

valere, to be stronger.] —**prev'a·lence** *n.*
—**prev'a·lent·ly** *adv.*

pre·var·i·cate (prĭ-văr'ĭ-kāt') *v.* **-cat·ed, -cat·ing.** To stray from or evade the truth; equivocate. [Lat. *praevaricari.*] —**pre·var'i·ca'tion** *n.* —**pre·var'i·ca'tor** *n.*

pre·vent (prĭ-vĕnt') *v.* **1.** To keep from happening; avert: *prevent spoilage.* **2.** To keep from doing something; hinder: *prevent him from making a mistake.* [< Lat. *praevenire.*] —**pre·vent'a·ble** or **pre·vent'i·ble** *adj.* —**pre·ven'tion** *n.*

pre·ven·tive (prĭ-vĕn'tĭv) *adj.* Also **pre·ven·ta·tive** (-tə-tĭv). **1.** Designed or used to prevent or ward off; precautionary. **2.** Thwarting or warding off illness or disease; prophylactic. —**pre·ven'tive** *n.*

pre·view (prē'vyōō) *n.* Also **pre·vue.** **1.** An advance showing, as of a motion picture, prior to public presentation. **2.** The presentation of several scenes advertising a forthcoming motion picture. **3.** An advance experience; foretaste. —*v.* To view or exhibit in advance.

pre·vi·ous (prē'vē-əs) *adj.* Existing or occurring prior to something else; earlier. [Lat. *praevius,* going before.] —**pre'vi·ous·ly** *adv.*

pre·vi·sion (prĭ-vĭzh'ən) *n.* **1.** Foreknowledge; prescience. **2.** A prediction.

pre·war (prē'wôr') *adj.* Existing or occurring before a war.

prey (prā) *n.* **1.** An animal hunted or caught for food; quarry. **2.** A victim. **3.** The act of seizing animals for food. —*v.* **1.** To hunt, catch, or eat as prey. **2.** To victimize. **3.** To have a harmful effect. [< Lat. *praeda.*]

price (prīs) *n.* **1.** The amount of money asked or given for something. **2.** The cost at which something is obtained. **3.** Value or worth. —*v.* **priced, pric·ing.** **1.** To fix or establish a price for. **2.** To find out the price of. [< Lat. *pretium.*]

price·less (prīs'lĭs) *adj.* **1.** Of inestimable worth; invaluable. **2.** Highly amusing.

price war *n.* A period of intense competition in which each competitor tries to cut retail prices below those of the others.

prick (prĭk) *n.* **1. a.** The act of pricking. **b.** The sensation of being pricked. **2.** A small mark or puncture made by a pointed object. **3.** A sharp or pointed object, as a thorn. —*v.* **1.** To stab or puncture lightly. **2.** To affect sharply with a mental or emotional pang. **3.** To mark or delineate by means of small punctures. —*idiom.* **prick up (one's) ears.** **1.** To raise one's ears erect, as certain animals do. **2.** To listen with attentive interest. [< OE *prica,* puncture.]

prick·er (prĭk'ər) *n.* A thorn; brier.

prick·le (prĭk'əl) *n.* **1.** A small, sharp spine or thorn. **2.** A slight stinging sensation. —*v.* **-led, -ling.** **1.** To prick, as with a thorn. **2.** To tingle. [< OE *pricel.*] —**prick'ly** *adj.*

prickly heat *n.* A noncontagious skin disease caused by inflammation of the sweat glands.

prickly pear *n.* **1.** A cactus with bristly flattened or cylindrical joints and showy, usu. yellow flowers. **2.** The edible fruit of a prickly pear.

prickly pear

pride (prīd) *n.* **1.** Proper and justified self-respect. **2.** Pleasure or satisfaction taken in work, achievements, or possessions. **3.** A cause or source of pride. **4.** Conceit; arrogance. **5.** A group of lions. —*v.* **prid·ed, prid·ing.** To indulge in self-esteem; glory. [< OFr. *prud,* brave.] —**pride'ful** *adj.* —**pride'ful·ly** *adv.*

prie-dieu (prē-dyœ') *n., pl.* **-dieus** or **-dieux** (-dyœz'). A low desk with space for a book above and with a foot piece below for kneeling in prayer. [< Fr. *prie Dieu,* pray God.]

priest (prēst) *n.* In the Roman Catholic, Eastern Orthodox, Anglican, and certain other Christian churches, a member of the second grade of clergy ranking below a bishop but above a deacon and having authority to pronounce absolution and administer all sacraments save that of ordination. [< Gk. *presbuteros,* elder.] —**priest'ess** *n.* —**priest'hood** *n.* —**priest'ly** *adj.*

prig (prĭg) *n.* An overprecise, smug, or narrow-minded person. [Orig. unknown.] —**prig'gish** *adj.* —**prig'gish·ly** *adv.*

prim (prĭm) *adj.* **prim·mer, prim·mest.** Precise or proper to the point of affectation. [Orig. unknown.] —**prim'ly** *adv.* —**prim'ness** *n.*

pri·ma·cy (prī'mə-sē) *n., pl.* **-cies.** **1.** The state of being first or foremost. **2.** The office or rank of an ecclesiastical primate. [< Lat. *primas,* leader.]

pri·ma don·na (prē'mə dŏn'ə, prĭm'ə) *n., pl.* **prima donnas.** **1.** The leading female soloist in an opera company. **2.** A temperamental or conceited person. [Ital.]

pri·ma fa·cie (prī'mə fā'shē, fā'shə) *adv.* At first sight; before closer inspection. [Lat.] —**pri'ma-fa'cie** *adj.*

pri·mal (prī'məl) *adj.* **1.** Being first in time; original. **2.** Of first importance; primary.

pri·mar·i·ly (prī-mĕr'ə-lē, -mâr'-) *adv.* **1.** At first; originally. **2.** Chiefly; principally.

pri·ma·ry (prī'mĕr'ē, -mə-rē) *adj.* **1. a.** Occurring first in time or sequence; original. **b.** Preparatory. **2.** Of first rank, quality, or importance. **3.** Not derived from something else: *primary sources of information.* **4.** Immediate; direct. **5.** Fundamental; basic. —*n., pl.* **-ries.** **1.** One that is first in time, order, or importance. **2.** A preliminary election in which voters nominate party candidates for office.

Syns: *primary, capital, cardinal, chief, dominant, first, foremost, main, paramount, pre-eminent, premier, prime, principal, top* **adj.**

primary school *n.* A school including the first three or four grades and sometimes kindergarten.

pri·mate (prī′māt′) *n.* 1. (*also* -mĭt) A bishop of highest rank in a province or country. 2. One of the group of mammals that includes the monkeys, apes, and man. [< Lat. *primatus,* leader.]

prime (prīm) *adj.* 1. Being first, as in quality, importance, rank, or time: *her prime concern.* 2. Of, pertaining to, or being a prime number. —*n.* 1. The earliest or beginning stage of something. 2. Springtime. 3. The period or phase of ideal or peak condition. 4. The best or most choice part of something. 5. A prime number. —*v.* **primed, prim·ing.** 1. To load (a gun or mine) for firing. 2. To prepare for operation, as by pouring water into a pump. 3. To prepare for painting by covering with an undercoat. 4. To prepare with information; coach. [< Lat. *primus.*]

prime meridian *n.* The zero meridian from which longitude east and west is measured.

prime minister *n.* 1. A chief minister appointed by a ruler. 2. The chief executive of a parliamentary democracy. —**prime minister·ship** *or* **prime ministry** *n.*

prime number *n.* A number that has itself and unity as its only factors.

prim·er¹ (prĭm′ər) *n.* 1. An elementary textbook. 2. A book that covers the basics of a subject. [< Lat. *primarius,* first.]

prim·er² (prī′mər) *n.* 1. One that primes. 2. A coat of paint or size used to prime a surface. 3. A device for detonating an explosive charge.

pri·me·val (prī-mē′vəl) *adj.* Of or pertaining to the first or earliest ages; primitive. [< Lat. *primaevus,* young.]

prim·i·tive (prĭm′ĭ-tĭv) *adj.* 1. Of or pertaining to an early or original stage or state of development. 2. Characterized by simplicity or crudity; unsophisticated. 3. Of or pertaining to early stages in the evolution of human culture. 4. Self-taught. —*n.* 1. A member of a primitive society. 2. **a.** A self-taught artist. **b.** An artist that has or affects a primitive style. [< Lat. *primitivus.*] —**prim′i·tive·ly** *adv.* —**prim′i·tive·ness** *n.*

prim·i·tiv·ism (prĭm′ĭ-tĭ-vĭz′əm) *n.* The style of primitive artists, esp. painters.

pri·mo·gen·i·tor (prī′mō-jĕn′ĭ-tər) *n.* The earliest ancestor; forefather. [Med. Lat.]

pri·mo·gen·i·ture (prī′mō-jĕn′ĭ-chŏŏr′, -chər) *n.* 1. The state of being the first-born child of the same parents. 2. The right of the eldest son to inherit his parents' entire estate. [Med. Lat. *primogenitura.*]

pri·mor·di·al (prī-môr′dē-əl) *adj.* Being, happening, developing, or existing first; primeval. [< Lat. *primordius.*]

primp (prĭmp) *v.* To dress or groom oneself with considerable attention to detail. [Orig. unknown.]

prim·rose (prĭm′rōz′) *n.* Any of several plants that have tubular flowers with five lobes. [< Med. Lat. *prima rosa,* first rose.]

prince (prĭns) *n.* 1. A hereditary ruler; king. 2. A male member of a royal family. 3. An outstanding man in a group or class: *a merchant prince.* [< Lat. *princeps.*] —**prince′dom** *n.* —**prince′ly** *adj.*

prin·cess (prĭn′sĭs, -sĕs′, prĭn-sĕs′) *n.* 1. A female member of a royal family. 2. The consort of a prince.

prin·ci·pal (prĭn′sə-pəl) *adj.* First or foremost in importance; chief. —*n.* 1. The head of an elementary or high school. 2. A main participant. 3. A person having a leading or starring role, as in a play. 4. **a.** Capital, as distinguished from revenue. **b.** A sum of money owed as a debt, upon which interest is calculated. 5. *Law.* **a.** A person who empowers another to act as his representative. **b.** The person having prime responsibility for an obligation. [< Lat. *principalis.*] —**prin′ci·pal·ly** *adv.* —**prin′ci·pal·ship′** *n.*

prin·ci·pal·i·ty (prĭn′sə-păl′ĭ-tē) *n., pl.* **-ties.** The territory, position, or jurisdiction of a prince; sovereignty.

principal parts *pl.n.* The main forms of the verb from which all other forms are derived.

prin·ci·ple (prĭn′sə-pəl) *n.* 1. A basic truth, law, or assumption. 2. **a.** A rule or standard of personal conduct. **b.** Moral or ethical standards or judgments. 3. A fixed or predetermined rule; policy. 4. A rule or law concerning the functioning of natural phenomena or mechanical processes. 5. A basic source. [< Lat. *principium.*]

prin·ci·pled (prĭn′sə-pəld) *adj.* Motivated by or based on moral or ethical principles.

prink (prĭngk) *v.* To primp. [Prob. < *prank,* to adorn.]

print (prĭnt) *n.* 1. A mark or impression made by pressure. 2. Something marked with an impression. 3. **a.** Lettering or other impressions produced in ink. **b.** Printed matter, such as newsprint. **c.** The condition or form of matter so produced. 4. A design or picture reproduced by printing. 5. A photographic image transferred to a surface, as paper, usu. from a negative. 6. A fabric with a stamped dyed pattern. —*v.* 1. To press (e.g., a mark or design) onto a surface. 2. To make an impression on or in (a surface), as with a stamp. 3. To produce by means of pressed type on a paper surface. 4. To publish: *print books.* 5. To write in characters similar to those commonly used in print. 6. To produce (a positive photograph) by passing light through a negative onto sensitized paper. —*phrasal verb.* **print out.** To print as a computer function; produce printout. [< Lat. *premere,* to press.] —**print′er** *n.*

print·a·ble (prĭn′tə-bəl) *adj.* 1. Capable of being printed or of producing a print. 2. Fit for publication.

printed circuit *n.* An electric circuit formed by depositing a conducting metal on an insulating surface.

print·ing (prĭn′tĭng) *n.* 1. The process, art, or business of producing printed material. 2. Matter that is printed. 3. All the copies of a book or other publication that are printed at one time.

printing press *n.* A machine that transfers images onto paper or similar medium by contact with an inked surface.

print·out (prĭnt′out′) *n.* The printed output of a computer.

pri·or¹ (prī′ər) *adj.* 1. Earlier in time or order. 2. Taking precedence in importance or value. [Lat.] —**pri·or′i·ty** (-ôr′ĭ-tē, -ŏr′-) *n.*

pri·or² (prī′ər) *n.* A monastic officer in charge of a priory. [< Lat., superior.] —**pri′or·ess** *n.*

pri·or·i·tize (prī-ôr′ĭ-tīz′, -ŏr′-) *v.* **-tized, -tiz·ing.** To arrange or deal with in order of importance. [PRIORIT(Y)+ -IZE.]

Usage: In spite of the fact that many consider *prioritize* to be bureaucratic jargon and so avoid its use, in recent times it has become firmly established in the language.

prior to *prep.* Before.

pri·o·ry (prī'ə-rē) *n., pl.* **-ies.** A monastery or convent governed by a prior or prioress.

prism (prĭz'əm) *n.* 1. A polyhedron with parallel, congruent polygons as bases and parallelograms as sides. 2. A homogeneous transparent solid, usu. with triangular bases and rectangular sides, used to produce or analyze a continuous spectrum. 3. A cut-glass object, as a pendant of a chandelier. [< Gk. *prisma.*] —**pris·mat·ic** (-măt'ĭk) *adj.*

pris·on (prĭz'ən) *n.* A place of confinement for persons convicted or accused of crimes. [< Lat. *prehensio,* capture.]

pris·on·er (prĭz'ə-nər, prĭz'nər) *n.* 1. A person held in custody or captivity, esp. in a prison. 2. A person deprived of freedom of action or expression.

pris·sy (prĭs'ē) *adj.* **-si·er, -si·est.** Finicky, fussy, and prudish. [Blend of PRIM and SISSY.] —**pris'si·ness** *n.*

pris·tine (prĭs'tēn', prĭ-stēn') *adj.* 1. Of the earliest time or condition; primitive or original. 2. Remaining in a pure state; uncorrupted. [Lat. *pristinus.*]

prith·ee (prĭth'ē, prĭth'ē) *interj.* Archaic. Please. [< *I pray thee.*]

pri·va·cy (prī'və-sē) *n., pl.* **-cies.** 1. The condition of being secluded or isolated from others. 2. Secrecy.

pri·vate (prī'vĭt) *adj.* 1. Secluded from the sight, presence, or intrusion of others. 2. Of or confined to one person; personal. 3. Not available for public use, control, or participation. 4. Belonging to a particular person or group. 5. Not holding an official or public position. 6. Intimate; secret. —*n.* An enlisted person ranking below private first class in the Army or Marine Corps. [Lat. *privatus,* not in public life.] —**pri'vate·ly** *adv.*

pri·va·teer (prī'və-tîr') *n.* A ship privately owned and manned but authorized to attack and capture enemy vessels. 2. The commander or one of the crew of a privateer.

private first class *n.* An enlisted person ranking below corporal and above private in the Army or Marine Corps.

pri·va·tion (prī-vā'shən) *n.* 1. Lack of the basic necessities or comforts of life. 2. The state of being deprived; deprivation. [< Lat. *privare,* to deprive.]

priv·et (prĭv'ĭt) *n.* A shrub with small, dark-green leaves, widely used for hedges. [Orig. unknown.]

priv·i·lege (prĭv'ə-lĭj) *n.* A special right, immunity, or benefit granted to or enjoyed by an individual or group. —*v.* **-leged, -leg·ing.** To grant a privilege to. [< Lat. *privilegium,* law affecting one person.]

priv·i·leged (prĭv'ə-lĭjd) *adj.* 1. Enjoying or having a privilege. 2. Legally exempt from disclosure; confidential.

priv·y (prĭv'ē) *adj.* 1. Made a participant in a secret. 2. Belonging to a person, as a sovereign, in his private rather than his official capacity. —*n., pl.* **-ies.** 1. A latrine. 2. An outhouse. [< OFr. *prive,* secret.]

prize¹ (prīz) *n.* 1. Something offered or won

as an award in a competition or a game of chance. 2. Something worth striving for or aspiring to. —*adj.* 1. Offered or given as a prize. 2. Worthy of a prize. 3. Outstanding. —*v.* **prized, priz·ing.** To value highly; esteem. [< Lat. *pretium.*]

prize² (prīz) *n.* Something, esp. an enemy ship, captured during wartime. [< OFr. *prise.*]

prize³ (prīz) *v.* **prized, priz·ing.** To pry². [< OFr. *prise,* grasp.]

prize·fight (prīz'fīt') *n.* A professional boxing match. —**prize'fight'er** *n.* —**prize'fight'ing** *n.*

prize·win·ner (prīz'wĭn'ər) *n.* One that wins a prize. —**prize'win'ning** *n.*

pro¹ (prō) *n., pl.* **pros.** 1. An argument in favor of something. 2. One who takes an affirmative position. —*adv.* In favor; affirmatively. [< Lat., *for.*]

pro² (prō) *Informal.* —*n., pl.* **pros.** 1. A professional. 2. An expert. —*adj.* Professional. [< Lat. *pro,* for.]

pro–¹ *pref.* Acting in the place of: *procaine hydrochloride.* [< Lat. *pro,* for.]

pro–² *pref.* In front of: *prognathous.* [< Gk. *pro.*]

prob·a·bil·i·ty (prŏb'ə-bĭl'ĭ-tē) *n., pl.* **-ties.** 1. The quality or condition of being probable; likelihood. 2. A probable situation, condition, or event. 3. *Math.* A number expressing the likelihood of occurrence of a specific event.

prob·a·ble (prŏb'ə-bəl) *adj.* 1. Likely to happen or to be true. 2. Relatively likely but not certain; plausible. [< Lat. *probabilis,* provable.] —**prob'a·bly** *adv.*

pro·bate (prō'bāt') *n.* Legal establishment of the validity of a will. —*v.* **-bat·ed, -bat·ing.** To establish the validity of (a will). [< Lat. *probare,* to prove.]

pro·ba·tion (prō-bā'shən) *n.* 1. A trial period in which a person's fitness, as for membership in a group, is tested. 2. The release of a convicted offender on condition of good behavior. [< Lat. *probare,* to test.] —**pro·ba'tion·al** or **pro·ba'tion·ar'y** (-shə-nĕr'ē) *adj.*

pro·ba·tion·er (prō-bā'shə-nər) *n.* A person on probation.

pro·ba·tive (prō'bə-tĭv) *adj.* 1. Serving to test or try. 2. Furnishing evidence or proof.

probe (prōb) *n.* 1. An object or device used to investigate an unknown configuration, condition, or region: *a space probe.* 2. A slender instrument used to examine a cavity, esp. a wound or bodily cavity. 3. A thorough examination or investigation. —*v.* **probed, prob·ing.** 1. To explore or examine with a probe. 2. To examine or investigate thoroughly. [< Lat. *probare,* to test.]

pro·bi·ty (prō'bĭ-tē) *n.* Integrity; honesty. [< Lat. *probitas.*]

prob·lem (prŏb'ləm) *n.* 1. A question or situation that presents uncertainty, perplexity, or difficulty. 2. A source of trouble or annoyance. 3. A question put forward for consideration or solution. [< Gk. *problēma.*]

prob·lem·at·ic (prŏb'lə-măt'ĭk) or **prob·lem·at·i·cal** (-ĭ-kəl) *adj.* Having the puzzling, uncertain, or debatable character of a problem. —**prob'lem·at'i·cal·ly** *adv.*

pro·bos·cis (prō-bŏs'ĭs) *n., pl.* **-cis·es** or **-bos·ci·des** (-bŏs'ĭ-dēz'). A long, flexible snout, as the trunk of an elephant. [< Gk. *proboskis.*]

pro·caine hydrochloride (prō'kān') *n.* A

white crystalline powder, $C_{13}H_{20}O_2N_2$·HCl, used as a local anesthetic. [PRO-1 + (CO)-CAINE.]

pro·ce·dure (prə-sē'jər) n. 1. A way of performing or effecting something. 2. A series of steps; course of action. 3. A set of established forms for conducting business or public affairs. [< Lat. *procedere*, to proceed.] —**pro·ce'du·ral** (-jər-əl) adj. —**pro·ce'du·ral·ly** adv.

pro·ceed (prō-sēd', prə-) v. 1. To continue, esp. after an interruption. 2. To undertake and carry on an action or process. 3. To progress in an orderly manner; advance. 4. To issue forth; originate. 5. To institute and conduct legal action. [< Lat. *procedere*.]

pro·ceed·ing (prō-sē'dĭng, prə-) n. 1. A course of action; procedure. 2. A transaction. 3. **proceedings. a.** Events; doings. **b.** A record of business carried on by an organization. **c.** Legal action.

pro·ceeds (prō'sēdz') pl.n. The amount of money derived from a commercial or fundraising venture.

proc·ess¹ (prŏs'ĕs', prō'sĕs') n. 1. A series of steps, actions, or operations used to bring about a desired result. 2. A series of natural changes by which something passes from one condition to another. 3. *Law.* **a.** A summons or writ to appear in court. **b.** The entire course of a legal action. 4. A part that extends or projects from an organ or organism; appendage. —v. 1. To put through the steps of a process. 2. To prepare, treat, or convert by subjecting to a special process. [< Lat. *processus*, advance.] —**proc'es·sor** n.

proc·ess² (prə-sĕs') v. To move along in or as if in a procession. [< PROCESSION.]

pro·ces·sion (prə-sĕsh'ən) n. A group of persons, vehicles, or objects moving along in an orderly and usu. formal manner.

pro·ces·sion·al (prə-sĕsh'ə-nəl) n. Music intended to be played or sung during a procession, esp. a religious procession.

pro·claim (prō-klām', prə-) v. To announce officially and publicly. [< Lat. *proclamare*.] —**proc'la·ma'tion** (prŏk'lə-mā'shən) n.

pro·cliv·i·ty (prō-klĭv'ĭ-tē) n., pl. -**ties.** A natural inclination; propensity. [Lat. *proclivitas*.]

pro·con·sul (prō-kŏn'səl) n. 1. An ancient Roman provincial governor of consular rank. 2. A high administrator in one of the European colonial empires. [< Lat. *pro consule*, for the consul.] —**pro·con'su·lar** (-sə-lər) adj. —**pro·con'su·late** (-sə-lĭt) n.

pro·cras·ti·nate (prə-krăs'tə-nāt', prō-) v. -**nat·ed, -nat·ing.** To put off, esp. habitually, doing something until a future time. [< Lat. *procrastinare*.] —**pro·cras'ti·na'tion** n. —**pro·cras'ti·na'tor** n.

pro·cre·ate (prō'krē-āt') v. -**at·ed, -at·ing.** To beget offspring; reproduce. [Lat. *procreare*.] —**pro'cre·a'tion** n. —**pro'cre·a'tive** adj. —**pro'cre·a'tor** n.

pro·crus·te·an (prō-krŭs'tē-ən) adj. 1. Forcing conformity by ruthless or arbitrary means. 2. Marked by merciless disregard for individual differences or special circumstances. [< *Procrustes*, a giant in Greek myth who stretched or shortened captives to make them fit his iron beds.]

proc·tor (prŏk'tər) n. One appointed to supervise students, as during examinations. [< Lat. *procurator*, procurator.] —**proctor** v. —**proc·to'ri·al** (-tôr'ē-əl, -tōr'-) adj.

proc·u·ra·tor (prŏk'yə-rā'tər) n. An adminis-

trator, esp. of a minor province of ancient Rome. [< Lat.]

pro·cure (prō-kyōōr', prə-) v. -**cured, -cur·ing.** 1. To obtain; acquire. 2. To bring about; effect. 3. To obtain (a woman) to serve as a prostitute. [< Lat. *procurare*, to manage.] —**pro·cur'er** n.

Pro·cy·on (prō'sē-ŏn', prŏs'ē-) n. A double star in the constellation Canis Minor.

prod (prŏd) v. **prod·ded, prod·ding.** 1. To jab or poke with a pointed instrument. 2. To rouse to action; stir. [Orig. unknown.] —**prod** n.

prod·i·gal (prŏd'ĭ-gəl) adj. 1. Recklessly wasteful; extravagant. 2. Profuse; lavish. [< Lat. *prodigus*.] —**prod'i·gal** n. —**prod'i·gal'i·ty** (-găl'ĭ-tē) n. —**prod'i·gal·ly** adv.

pro·di·gious (prə-dĭj'əs) adj. 1. Impressively great in size, force, or extent; enormous. 2. Extraordinary; marvelous. [Lat. *prodigiosus*.] —**pro·di'gious·ly** adv.

prod·i·gy (prŏd'ĭ-jē) n., pl. -**gies.** 1. A person, esp. a child, with exceptional talent. 2. Something extraordinary or rare; marvel. [Lat. *prodigium*, omen.]

pro·duce (prə-dōōs', -dyōōs', prō-) v. -**duced, -duc·ing.** 1. To bring forth; yield. 2. To create by mental or physical effort. 3. To manufacture. 4. To give rise to; bring about. 5. To bring forward; exhibit. 6. *Geom.* To extend (an area or volume) or lengthen (a line). —n. (prŏd'ōōs, -yōōs, prō'dōōs, -dyōōs). Something produced, esp. farm products collectively. [Lat. *producere*.] —**pro·duc'er** n.

prod·uct (prŏd'əkt) n. 1. Something produced naturally or by labor. 2. The result obtained by performing multiplication. [< Lat. *producere*, to produce.]

pro·duc·tion (prə-dŭk'shən, prō-) n. 1. The act or process of producing. 2. Something produced; product. 3. The total number of products; output. —**pro·duc'tive** adj. —**pro·duc'tive·ly** adv. —**pro·duc·tiv'i·ty** (prō'dŭk-tĭv'ĭ-tē, prŏd'-ək-) or **pro·duc'tive·ness** n.

pro·em (prō'ĕm') n. A short introduction; preface. [< Gk. *prooimion*, prelude.]

prof (prŏf) n. *Informal.* A professor.

pro·fane (prō-fān', prə-) adj. 1. Showing contempt or irreverence for what is sacred; blasphemous. 2. Nonreligious; secular. 3. Vulgar; coarse. —v. -**faned, -fan·ing.** 1. To treat with irreverence; blaspheme. 2. To put to an improper, unworthy, or degrading use; abuse. [< Lat. *profanus*.] —**prof·a·na'tion** (prŏf'ə-nā'shən) n. —**pro·fan'a·to·ry** (-făn'ə-tôr'ē, -tōr'ē) adj. —**pro·fane'ly** adv. —**pro·fane'ness** n.

pro·fan·i·ty (prō-făn'ĭ-tē, prə-) n., pl. -**ties.** 1. The condition or quality of being profane. 2. Profane language or its use.

pro·fess (prə-fĕs', prō-) v. 1. To affirm. 2. To make a pretense of. 3. To have or claim skill in or knowledge of. 4. To affirm belief in. [Lat. *profiteri*.] —**pro·fess'ed·ly** (-fĕs'ĭd-lē) adv.

pro·fes·sion (prə-fĕsh'ən) n. 1. An occupation, esp. one requiring training and specialized study. 2. The body of qualified persons engaged in an occupation or field. 3. The act or an instance of professing; declaration. 4. An avowal of faith in a religion.

pro·fes·sion·al (prə-fĕsh'ə-nəl) adj. 1. Of, pertaining to, characteristic of, or engaged in a profession. 2. Engaged in a specific activity as a source of livelihood. —n. A person following a profession. —**pro·fes'sion·al·ly** adv.

pro·fes·sion·al·ism (prə-fĕsh'ə-nə-lĭz'əm) *n.* Professional status, methods, character, or standards.

pro·fes·sion·al·ize (prə-fĕsh'ə-nə-līz') *v.* **-ized, -iz·ing.** To make professional. **—pro·fes'sion·al·i·za'tion** *n.*

pro·fes·sor (prə-fĕs'ər) *n.* **1.** A teacher of the highest rank in an institution of higher learning. **2.** A teacher or instructor. **—pro·fes'sor·ate** *n.* **—pro·fes·so·ri·al** (prō'fĭ-sôr'ē-əl, -sôr'-, prŏf'ĭ-) *adj.* **—pro·fes'sor·ship'** *n.*

prof·fer (prŏf'ər) *v.* To present for acceptance; offer; tender. [< OFr. *proffrir.*] **—prof'fer** *n.*

pro·fi·cient (prə-fĭsh'ənt) *adj.* Expert in an art, skill, or branch of learning; adept. [< Lat. *proficere,* to make progress.] **—pro·fi'cien·cy** *n.* **—pro·fi'cient·ly** *adv.*

pro·file (prō'fīl') *n.* **1.** A side view of an object or structure, esp. of a human head. **2.** A brief biographical essay. **—v. -filed, -fil·ing.** To draw or write a profile of. [< Ital. *profilare,* to draw in outline.]

prof·it (prŏf'ĭt) *n.* **1.** A gain or return; benefit. **2.** The money made in a business venture, sale, or investment after all expenses have been met. **—v. 1.** To make a gain or profit. **2.** To be advantageous; benefit. [< Lat. *profectus.*] **—prof'it·a·ble** *adj.* **—prof'it·a·bly** *adv.*

prof·i·teer (prŏf'ĭ-tîr') *n.* One who makes excessive profits, esp. on commodities in short supply. **—prof'i·teer** *v.*

prof·li·gate (prŏf'lĭ-gĭt, -gāt') *adj.* **1.** Recklessly wasteful or extravagant. **2.** Completely given over to self-indulgence and vice; dissolute. [< Lat. *profligare,* to ruin.] **—prof'li·ga·cy** (-gə-sē) *n.* **—prof'li·gate** *n.*

pro for·ma (prō fôr'mə) *adj.* Done as a matter of or according to form. [< Lat.]

pro·found (prə-found', prō-) *adj.* **-er, -est. 1.** Extending to or coming from a great depth; deep. **2.** Coming as if from the depths of one's being: *profound contempt.* **3.** Thoroughgoing; far-reaching. **4.** Penetrating beyond what is superficial or obvious. **5.** Absolute; complete: *a profound silence.* [< Lat. *profundus.*] **—pro·found'ly** *adv.* **—pro·fun'di·ty** (-fŭn'dĭ-tē) *n.*

pro·fuse (prə-fyoōs', prō-) *adj.* Given or coming forth abundantly; extravagant. [< Lat. *profusus,* p.p. of *profundere,* to pour forth.] **—pro·fuse'ly** *adv.* **—pro·fu'sion** (-fyoō'zhən) or **pro·fuse'ness** *n.*

pro·gen·i·tor (prō-jĕn'ĭ-tər) *n.* **1.** A direct ancestor. **2.** An originator of a line of descent. [< Lat.]

prog·e·ny (prŏj'ə-nē) *n.* Children or descendants; offspring. [< Lat. *progenies.*]

pro·ges·ter·one (prō-jĕs'tə-rōn') *n.* A female hormone, $C_{21}H_{30}O_2$, produced by the ovary prior to implantation of the fertilized ovum. [PRO-1 + GE(STATION) + STER(OL) + -ONE.]

prog·na·thous (prŏg'nə-thəs) *adj.* Having jaws that project beyond the upper part of the face. [< PRO-2 + Gk. *gnathos,* jaw.]

prog·no·sis (prŏg-nō'sĭs) *n., pl.* **-ses** (-sēz'). A prediction, esp. of the probable course of a disease. [< Gk. *prognōsis.*]

prog·nos·tic (prŏg-nŏs'tĭk) *n.* **1.** An omen; portent. **2.** A prediction; prophecy. [< Gk. *prognōstikos,* predicting.] **—prog·nos'tic** *adj.*

prog·nos·ti·cate (prŏg-nŏs'tĭ-kāt') *v.* **-cat·ed, -cat·ing.** To predict on the basis of present indications. **—prog·nos'ti·ca'tion** *n.* **—prog·nos'ti·ca'tor** *n.*

pro·gram (prō'grăm', -grəm) *n.* Also *chiefly Brit.* **pro·gramme. 1.** A listing of the order of events and other information, as for a public presentation. **2.** A public presentation; performance. **3.** A list of procedures; schedule. **4. a.** A procedure for solving a problem, including collection of data, processing, and presentation of results. **b.** Such a procedure coded for a computer. **—v. -grammed** or **-gramed, -gram·ming** or **-gram·ing. 1.** To include in a program. **2.** To provide (a computer) with a set of instructions. [< Gk. *programma,* public notice.] **—pro'gram·mat'ic** (prō'grə-măt'ĭk) *adj.* **—pro'gram'mer** or **pro'gram·er** *n.*

prog·ress (prŏg'rĕs', -rĭs) *n.* **1.** Movement toward a goal. **2.** Steady improvement, as of a civilization. **—v. pro·gress** (prə-grĕs'). **1.** To advance; proceed. **2.** To move toward a more advanced stage. [< Lat. *progressus.*]

pro·gres·sion (prə-grĕsh'ən) *n.* **1.** Progress. **2.** Advance. **3.** A series (an image) of events; sequence.

pro·gres·sive (prə-grĕs'ĭv) *adj.* **1.** Moving forward; advancing. **2.** Proceeding in steps or by stages. **3.** Promoting or favoring political reform; liberal. **4.** *Pathol.* Continuously spreading or increasing in severity. **5.** Designating a verb tense or form that expresses an action or condition in progress. **—n.** A partisan of reform in fields such as politics and education. **—pro·gres'sive·ly** *adv.* **—pro·gres'sive·ness** *n.*

pro·hib·it (prō-hĭb'ĭt, prə-) *v.* **1.** To forbid by authority. **2.** To prevent or debar. [< Lat. *prohibēre.*] **—pro·hib'i·to·ry** *adj.*

pro·hi·bi·tion (prō'ə-bĭsh'ən) *n.* **1.** The act of prohibiting. **2.** The forbidding by law of the manufacture, transportation, and sale of alcoholic beverages. **—pro'hi·bi'tion·ist** *n.*

pro·hib·i·tive (prō-hĭb'ĭ-tĭv, prə-) *adj.* **1.** Prohibiting; forbidding. **2.** Preventing or discouraging purchase or use. **—pro·hib'i·tive·ly** *adv.*

proj·ect (prŏj'ĕkt', -ĭkt) *n.* **1.** A plan or proposal; scheme. **2.** An undertaking requiring concerted effort. **—v. pro·ject** (prə-jĕkt'). **1.** To thrust outward or forward; protrude or cause to protrude. **2.** To throw forward; hurl. **3.** To direct (one's voice) so as to be heard clearly at a distance. **4.** To form a plan or intention for. **5.** To cause (an image) to appear upon a surface. [< Lat. *projectus,* p.p. of *proicere,* to throw out.] **—pro·jec'tion** *n.*

pro·jec·tile (prə-jĕk'təl, -tīl') *n.* **1.** A fired, thrown, or otherwise projected object, as a bullet. **2.** A self-propelling missile, as a rocket.

pro·jec·tion·ist (prə-jĕk'shə-nĭst) *n.* **1.** One who operates a motion-picture projector. **2.** A mapmaker.

pro·jec·tor (prə-jĕk'tər) *n.* A device for projecting an image onto a screen.

pro·le·gom·e·non (prō'lĭ-gŏm'ə-nŏn', -nən) *n., pl.* **-na** (-nə). An introductory remark. [Gk.]

pro·le·tar·i·an (prō'lĭ-târ'ē-ən) *n.* A member of the proletariat. [< Lat. *proletarius,* Roman citizen of the lowest class.] —**pro'le·tar'i·an** *adj.* —**pro'le·tar'i·an·ism** *n.*

pro·le·tar·i·at (prō'lĭ-târ'ē-ət) *n.* The class of industrial wage earners who must earn their living by selling their labor. [Fr. *prolétariat.*]

pro·lif·er·ate (prə-lĭf'ə-rāt') *v.* **-at·ed, -at·ing.** To reproduce, increase, or produce new growth or parts rapidly and repeatedly, as cells. [< Lat. *prolifer,* producing offspring.] —**pro·lif'er·a'tion** *n.*

pro·lif·ic (prə-lĭf'ĭk) *adj.* **1.** Producing offspring or fruit in abundance. **2.** Producing abundant works or results. [< Lat. *proles,* offspring.] —**pro·lif'i·cal·ly** *adv.*

pro·lix (prō-lĭks', prō'lĭks') *adj.* Wordy and tedious; verbose. [< Lat. *prolixus,* abundant.] —**pro·lix'i·ty** (-lĭk'sĭ-tē) *n.* —**pro·lix'ly** *adv.*

pro·logue (prō'lôg', -lŏg') *n.* An introduction, as to a play. [< Lat. *prologus.*]

pro·long (prə-lông', -lŏng') *v.* **1.** To lengthen in duration; protract. **2.** To lengthen in extent. [< LLat. *prolongare.*] —**pro'lon·ga'tion** (prō'lông-gā'shən) *n.*

prom (prŏm) *n.* A formal dance held for a high-school or college class. [< PROMENADE.]

prom·e·nade (prŏm'ə-nād', -näd') *n.* **1.** A leisurely walk; stroll. **2.** A place for a promenade. **3.** A formal march by the guests at the opening of a ball. —*v.* **-nad·ed, -nad·ing.** To go on a leisurely walk. [< LLat. *prominare,* to drive forward.]

Pro·me·the·us (prə-mē'thē-əs, -thyōōs) *n. Gk. Myth.* A Titan who stole fire from Olympus and gave it to man.

Prometheus
17th-century German sculpture

pro·me·thi·um (prə-mē'thē-əm) *n. Symbol* **Pm** A radioactive rare-earth element. Atomic number 61; longest-lived isotope Pm 145. [< PROMETHEUS.]

prom·i·nence (prŏm'ə-nəns) *n.* **1.** The condition or quality of being prominent. **2.** Something prominent; projection.

prom·i·nent (prŏm'ə-nənt) *adj.* **1.** Projecting outward; protuberant. **2.** Readily evident; conspicuous. **3.** Well-known; eminent. [< Lat. *prominēre,* to project.] —**prom'i·nent·ly** *adv.*

pro·mis·cu·ous (prə-mĭs'kyōō-əs) *adj.* **1.** Consisting of diverse and unrelated parts or individuals. **2.** Lacking standards of selection, esp. engaging in sexual intercourse indiscriminately with more than one partner. [Lat. *miscuus.*] —**prom'is·cu'i·ty** (prŏm'ĭ-skyōō'ĭ-tē, prō'mĭ-) or **pro·mis'cu·ous·ness** *n.* —**pro·mis'cu·ous·ly** *adv.*

prom·ise (prŏm'ĭs) *n.* **1.** A declaration assuring that one will or will not do something. **2.** Something promised. **3.** Indication of something forthcoming, esp. future excellence or success. —*v.* **-ised, -is·ing. 1.** To make a

promise (of). **2.** To afford a basis for expecting. **3.** To give indication of in advance: *clouds that promise rain.* [< Lat. *promittere,* to promise.] —**prom'is·er** *n.*

prom·is·ing (prŏm'ĭ-sĭng) *adj.* Likely to excel, succeed, or develop in a desirable manner. —**prom'is·ing·ly** *adv.*

prom·is·so·ry (prŏm'ĭ-sôr'ē, -sōr'ē) *adj.* Containing or involving a promise.

promissory note *n.* A written promise to pay or repay a specified sum of money at a stated time or on demand.

prom·on·to·ry (prŏm'ən-tôr'ē, -tōr'ē) *n., pl.* **-ries.** A high ridge of land or rock jutting out into a body of water. [< Lat. *promuntorium.*]

pro·mote (prə-mōt') *v.* **-mot·ed, -mot·ing. 1.** To raise in position or rank. **2.** To contribute to the progress or growth of; further. **3.** To urge the adoption of; advocate. **4.** To attempt to sell or popularize. [< Lat. *promovēre,* to advance.] —**pro·mo'tion** *n.* —**pro·mo'tion·al** *adj.*

pro·mot·er (prə-mō'tər) *n.* **1.** An active supporter; advocate. **2.** A finance and publicity organizer, as of a boxing match.

prompt (prŏmpt) *adj.* **-er, -est. 1.** On time; punctual. **2.** Done without delay. —*v.* **1.** To urge to action; incite. **2.** To give rise to; inspire. **3.** To give a cue to, as in a theater. [< Lat. *promptus,* ready.] —**prompt'er** *n.* —**prompt'i·tude'** (prŏmp'tĭ-tōōd', -tyōōd') or **prompt'ness** *n.* —**prompt'ly** *adv.*

prompt·book (prŏmpt'bŏŏk') *n.* An annotated script used by a theater prompter.

prom·ul·gate (prŏm'əl-gāt', prō-mŭl'-) *v.* **-gat·ed, -gat·ing.** To make known or put into effect by public declaration, as a decree or law. [Lat. *promulgare.*] —**prom'ul·ga'tion** *n.* —**prom'ul·ga'tor** *n.*

prone (prōn) *adj.* **1.** Lying with the front or face downward. **2.** Having a tendency; inclined. [< Lat. *pronus.*] —**prone'ness** *n.*

prong (prông, prŏng) *n.* **1.** A sharply pointed part, as a tine of a fork. **2.** A sharply pointed projection. [ME *pronge,* forked instrument.]

prong·horn (prông'hôrn', prŏng'-) *n.* A small deer that resembles an antelope and is found on western North American plains.

pro·noun (prō'noun') *n.* One of a class of words that function as substitutes for nouns.

pro·nounce (prə-nouns') *v.* **-nounced, -nounc·ing. 1.** To produce (a word or speech sound); articulate. **2.** To state officially or formally; declare. [< Lat. *pronuntiare,* to declare.] —**pro·nounce'a·ble** *adj.* —**pro·nun'ci·a'tion** (-nŭn'sē-ā'shən) *n.*

pro·nounced (prə-nounst') *adj.* Strongly marked; distinct.

pro·nounce·ment (prə-nouns'mənt) *n.* A formal declaration or statement.

pron·to (prŏn'tō) *adv. Informal.* Without delay; quickly. [Sp.]

pro·nun·ci·a·men·to (prə-nŭn'sē-ə-měn'tō) *n., pl.* **-tos.** An authoritative declaration; proclamation. [Sp. *pronunciamiento.*]

proof (prōōf) *n.* **1.** The evidence establishing the truth or validity of something. **2.** Conclusive demonstration of something. **3.** The act of proving the truth or validity of something; test. **4.** A trial impression, as of an engraved plate. **5.** A trial print of a photograph. **6.** The alcoholic content of a liquor, expressed as a given number of parts of alcohol per 200 parts of liquor. —*adj.* **1.** Fully resistant; impervious: *proof against fire.* **2.** Of standard alcoholic strength. [< LLat. *proba.*]

-proof *suff.* Impervious to or able to withstand: *waterproof.* [< PROOF.]

proof·read (prōōf'rēd') *v.* **-read** (-rēd'), **-reading.** To mark corrections in a printer's proof while reading against an original manuscript. **—proof'read'er** *n.*

prop¹ (prŏp) *n.* A support used to keep something from falling. [ME *proppe.*] **—prop** *v.*

prop² (prŏp) *n.* A stage property.

prop³ (prŏp) *n. Informal.* A propeller.

prop·a·gan·da (prŏp'ə-găn'də) *n.* **1.** The systematic propagation of a given doctrine. **2.** Ideas, information, or other material disseminated to win people over to a given doctrine. [< Lat. *propagare,* to propagate.] **—prop'a·gan'dist** *n.* **—prop'a·gan·dis'tic** *adj.* **—prop'a·gan·dize'** *v.*

prop·a·gate (prŏp'ə-gāt') *v.* **-gat·ed, -gat·ing.** **1.** To reproduce or cause to reproduce; breed. **2.** To make known; publicize. **3.** *Physics.* To move or cause to move through a medium. [Lat. *propagare.*] **—prop'a·ga'tion** *n.*

pro·pane (prō'pān') *n.* A gas, C₃H₈, found in natural gas and petroleum and widely used as a fuel. [PROP(IONIC ACID) + -ANE.]

pro·pel (prə-pĕl') *v.* **-pelled, -pel·ling.** **1.** To cause to move or continue in motion. **2.** To urge ahead; impel. [< Lat. *propellere.*]

pro·pel·lant (prə-pĕl'ənt) *n.* Also **pro·pel·lent.** Something that propels, as an explosive charge or a rocket fuel. **—pro·pel'lant** *adj.*

pro·pel·ler (prə-pĕl'ər) *n.* Also **pro·pel·lor.** A device for propelling aircraft or boats, esp. one with radiating blades mounted on a revolving power-driven shaft.

pro·pen·si·ty (prə-pĕn'sĭ-tē) *n., pl.* **-ties.** An innate inclination; bent. [< Lat. *propendere,* to be inclined.]

prop·er (prŏp'ər) *adj.* **1.** Suitable; appropriate. **.2.** Characteristically belonging to a person or thing: *regained his proper frame of mind.* **3.** Called for by rules or conventions; correct. **4.** Decorous; seemly. **5.** In the strict sense of the term: *the city proper.* [< Lat. *proprius,* one's own.] **—prop'er·ly** *adv.*

proper noun *n.* A noun that is the name of a particular person, place, or thing.

prop·er·tied (prŏp'ər-tēd) *adj.* Owning land or securities, esp. as a principal source of income.

prop·er·ty (prŏp'ər-tē) *n., pl.* **-ties.** **1.** Something, esp. land, owned by someone. **2.** A characteristic trait, quality, or attribute. **3.** Ownership. **4.** A movable object, other than costumes and scenery, that is used in a play. [< Lat. *proprietas,* ownership.]

proph·e·cy (prŏf'ĭ-sē) *n., pl.* **-cies.** **1.** A prediction. **2.** The inspired utterance of a prophet. [< Gk. *prophēteia.*]

proph·e·sy (prŏf'ĭ-sī') *v.* **-sied, -sy·ing.** **1.** To reveal by divine inspiration. **2.** To predict. [< Gk. *prophēteia,* prophecy.] **—proph'e·si'er** *n.*

proph·et (prŏf'ĭt) *n.* **1.** One who speaks by divine inspiration. **2.** A predictor or soothsayer. **3.** The chief spokesman of a movement or cause. [< Gk. *prophētēs.*] **—proph'et·ess** *n.*

pro·phet·ic (prə-fĕt'ĭk) or **pro·phet·i·cal** (-ĭ-kəl) *adj.* Of, pertaining to, or of the nature

of a prophet or prophecy. **—pro·phet'i·cal·ly** *adv.*

pro·phy·lac·tic (prō'fə-lăk'tĭk, prŏf'ə-) *adj.* Acting against or preventing something, esp. disease. **—n.** A prophylactic medicine, device, or measure, esp. a condom. [Gk. *prophulaktikos.*]

pro·phy·lax·is (prō'fə-lăk'sĭs, prŏf'ə-) *n., pl.* **-lax·es** (-lăk'sēz'). Steps taken to maintain health and prevent disease. [< Gk. *prophulaktikos,* prophylactic.]

pro·pin·qui·ty (prə-pĭng'kwĭ-tē) *n.* **1.** Nearness; proximity. **2.** Kinship. [< Lat. *propinquitas.*]

pro·pi·ti·ate (prō-pĭsh'ē-āt') *v.* **-at·ed, -at·ing.** To conciliate; appease. [Lat. *propitiare.*] **—pro·pi'ti·a'tion** *n.* **—pro·pi'ti·a'tor** *n.* **—pro·pi'ti·a·to'ry** (-ə-tôr'ē, -tōr'ē) *adj.*

pro·pi·tious (prə-pĭsh'əs) *adj.* Favorable; auspicious. [< Lat. *propitius,* favorable.] **—pro·pi'tious·ly** *adv.*

pro·po·nent (prə-pō'nənt) *n.* One who argues in support of something; advocate. [< Lat. *proponere,* to propose.]

pro·por·tion (prə-pôr'shən, -pōr'-) *n.* **1.** A part considered in relation to another part or to the whole. **2.** A relationship between things or parts of things with respect to comparative magnitude, quantity, or degree. **3.** A relationship between quantities, such that if one varies, another varies as a multiple of the first; ratio. **4.** Harmonious relation; balance. **5.** Often **proportions.** Dimensions; size. **—v.** **1.** To adjust so that proper relations between parts are attained. **2.** To form with symmetry. [< Lat. *pro portione,* for its share.] **—pro·por'tion·al** *adj.* **—pro·por'tion·al·ly** *adv.* **—pro·por'tion·ate** *adj.* **—pro·por'tion·ate·ly** *adv.*

pro·pose (prə-pōz') *v.* **-posed, -pos·ing.** **1.** To put forward for consideration; suggest. **2.** To present or nominate (a person) for a position, office, or membership. **3.** To intend; plan. **4.** To make an offer, esp. of marriage. [< Lat. *proponere.*] **—pro·pos'er** *n.* **—pro·pos'er** *n.*

prop·o·si·tion (prŏp'ə-zĭsh'ən) *n.* **1. a.** Something offered for consideration; proposal. **b.** A sexual proposal. **2.** A subject for discussion or analysis. **3.** A matter to be dealt with; undertaking. **—v.** *Informal.* To make a proposal to, esp. a sexual proposal. **—prop'o·si'tion·al** *adj.*

pro·pound (prə-pound') *v.* To put forward for consideration; set forth. [< Lat. *proponere,* to propose.]

pro·pri·e·tar·y (prə-prī'ĭ-tĕr'ē) *adj.* **1.** Of, pertaining to, or characteristic of a proprietor. **2.** Exclusively owned, made, and sold by one holding a trademark or patent. [LLat. *proprietarius.*]

pro·pri·e·tor (prə-prī'ĭ-tər) *n.* An owner. **—pro·pri'e·tor·ship'** *n.* **—pro·pri'e·tress** *n.*

pro·pri·e·ty (prə-prī'ĭ-tē) *n., pl.* **-ties.** **1.** The quality or condition of being proper. **2.** Conformity to prevailing rules and conventions. **3. proprieties.** The rules and conventions of polite society. [< Lat. *proprietas,* ownership.]

pro·pul·sion (prə-pŭl'shən) *n.* **1.** The process of propelling. **2.** A driving force. [< Lat. *propellere,* to drive forward.] **—pro·pul'sive** *adj.*

pro ra·ta (prō rä'tə, răt'ə, rā'tə) *adv.* In pro-

PROOFREADERS' MARKS

Instruction	Mark in Margin	Mark in Type	Corrected Type
Delete	ℓ	the good word	the word
Insert indicated material	good	the word	the good word
Let it stand	stet	the good word	the good word
Make capital	cap	the word	the Word
Make lower case	lc	The Word	the Word
Set in small capitals	sc	See word.	See WORD.
Set in italic type	ital	The word is word.	The word is *word*.
Set in roman type	rom	the *word*	the word
Set in boldface type	bf	the entry word	the entry **word**
Set in lightface type	lf	the entry **word**	the entry word
Transpose	tr	the word good	the good word
Close up space	⌒	the wo rd	the word
Delete and close up space	⌀	the wØord	the word
Spell out	sp	2 words	two words
Insert: space	#	theword	the word
period	⊙	This is the word	This is the word.
comma	ˆ	words words, words	words, words, words
hyphen	=	word for word test	word-for-word test
colon	⊙	The following words	The following words:
semicolon	;	Scan the words skim the words.	Scan the words; skim the words.
apostrophe	⌄	Johns words	John's words
quotation marks	⌄/⌄/	the word word	the word "word"
parentheses	(/)/	The word word is in parentheses.	The word (word) is in parentheses.
brackets	[/]/	He read from the Word the Bible.	He read from the Word [the Bible].
en dash	N	1964 1972	1964-1972
em dash	M/M/	The dictionary how often it is needed belongs in every home.	The dictionary—how often it is needed—belongs in every home.
superior type	⌄	$2 = 4$	$2^2 = 4$
inferior type	⌃	HO	H_2O
asterisk	⌄	word	word*

PROOFREADERS' MARKS

Instruction	Mark in Margin	Mark in Type	Corrected Type
dagger	†	a word$_\wedge$	a word†
double dagger	‡	words and words$_\wedge$	words and words‡
section symbol	§	$_\wedge$Book Reviews	§Book Reviews
virgule	/	either$_\wedge$or	either/or
Start paragraph	¶	"Where is it?" $_\wedge$"It's on the shelf."	"Where is it?" "It's on the shelf."
Run in	*run in*	The entry word is printed in boldface. The pronunciation follows.	The entry word is printed in boldface. The pronunciation follows.
Turn right side up	ꝺ	th♭word	the word
Move left	⊏	⊏ the word	the word
Move right	⊐	the word	the word
Move up	⌐	th⌷word	the word
Move down	⌣	th⌷word	the word
Align	‖	the word the word the word	the word the word the word
Straighten line	⸗	the word	the word
Wrong font	*wf*	th♭word	the word
Broken type	✕	th♭word	the word

portion. [< Lat. *pro rata (parte)*, according to the calculated (share).]

pro·rate (prō-rāt′, prō′rāt′) *v.* **-rat·ed, -rat·ing.** To divide, distribute, or assess proportionately. [< PRO RATA.] **—pro·ra′tion** *n.*

pro·rogue (prō-rōg′) *v.* **-rogued, -rogu·ing.** To discontinue a session of (a legislative body). [< Lat. *prorogare*, to prolong.] **—pro′ro·ga′tion** *n.*

pro·sa·ic (prō-zā′ĭk) *adj.* **1.** Matter-of-fact. **2.** Lacking in imagination or interest; dull. [LLat. *prosaicus*] **—pro·sa′i·cal·ly** *adv.*

pro·sce·ni·um (prō-sē′nē-əm) *n., pl.* **-ni·a** (-nē-ə). The area of a theater located between the curtain and the orchestra. [Lat. < Gk. *proskēnion.*]

pro·scribe (prō-skrīb′) *v.* **-scribed, -scrib·ing.** **1.** To prohibit; forbid. **2.** To outlaw. [Lat. *proscribere.*] **—pro·scrip′tion** (-skrĭp′shən) *n.* **—pro·scrip′tive** *adj.*

prose (prōz) *n.* Ordinary speech or writing as distinguished from verse. [< Lat. *prosa (oratio)*, straightforward (discourse).]

pros·e·cute (prŏs′ĭ-kyōot′) *v.* **-cut·ed, -cut·ing.** **1.** To initiate and conduct a legal action

against. **2.** To press to completion; pursue determinedly: *prosecuting a war.* [< Lat. *prosecutus*, p.p. of *prosequi*, to follow up.] **—pros′e·cu′tion** *n.* **—pros′e·cu′tor** *n.*

pros·e·lyte (prŏs′ə-līt′) *n.* A new convert to a religion or doctrine. **—***v.* **-lyt·ed, -lyt·ing.** To proselytize. [< Gk. *prosēlutos.*]

pros·e·ly·tize (prŏs′ə-lə-tīz′) *v.* **-tized, -tiz·ing.** To convert from one belief or faith to another. **—pros′e·ly·tiz′er** *n.*

pros·o·dy (prŏs′ə-dē) *n.* The study of the metrical structures of verse. [< Gk. *prosōidia*, singing in accord.] **—pro·sod′ic** (prə-sŏd′ĭk) *adj.* **—pro·sod′i·cal·ly** *adv.*

pros·pect (prŏs′pĕkt′) *n.* **1.** Something expected or foreseen; possibility. **2.** prospects. Chances for success. **3. a.** A potential customer or purchaser. **b.** A potential candidate. **4.** The direction in which something faces; outlook. **5.** A scene; view. **—***v.* To explore or search about, esp. for mineral deposits. [< Lat. *prospectus*, view.] **—pros′pec·tor** *n.*

pro·spec·tive (prə-spĕk′tĭv) *adj.* Likely to occur; expected. **—pro·spec′tive·ly** *adv.*

pro·spec·tus (prə-spĕk′təs) *n., pl.* **-es.** A formal summary of a proposed business or other venture, sent out to prospective participants or buyers. [Lat., view.]

pros·per (prŏs'pər) v. To be successful; thrive. [< Lat. *prosperare*.]
   Syns: prosper, boom, flourish, thrive *v.*

pro·sper·i·ty (prŏ-spĕr'ĭ-tē) n., pl. **-ties.** The condition of being prosperous; success, esp. financial success.

pros·per·ous (prŏs'pər-əs) adj. 1. Having success; flourishing. 2. Propitious; favorable. —**pros'per·ous·ly** adv.

pros·tate (prŏs'tāt') n. A gland in male mammals composed of muscular and glandular tissue that surrounds the urethra at the bladder. [< Gk. *prostatēs*.]

pros·the·sis (prŏs-thē'sĭs) n., pl. **-ses** (-sēz'). An artificial device used to replace a part of the body, such as a tooth or limb. [< Gk., addition.] —**pros·thet'ic** (-thĕt'ĭk) adj.

pros·ti·tute (prŏs'tĭ-tōōt', -tyōōt') n. One who performs sexual acts with others for pay. —v. **-tut·ed, -tut·ing.** 1. To offer (oneself or another) for sexual acts in return for pay. 2. To devote (oneself or one's talents) to an unworthy cause. [Lat. *prostituta*.] —**pros'ti·tu'tion** n.

pros·trate (prŏs'trāt') v. **-trat·ed, -trat·ing.** 1. To put or throw down in a posture of humility or adoration. 2. To lay low; overcome. —adj. 1. Lying face down, as in humility or adoration. 2. Lying down full-length. 3. Physically or emotionally incapacitated; helpless. [< Lat. *prostratus*, p.p. of *prosternere*, to prostrate.] —**pros·tra'tion** n. —**pros'tra'tor** n.

prot- pref. Var. of proto-.

pro·tac·tin·i·um (prō'tăk-tĭn'ē-əm) n. Symbol **Pa** A rare radioactive element chemically similar to uranium. Atomic number 91; longest-lived isotope Pa 231.

pro·tag·o·nist (prō-tăg'ə-nĭst) n. 1. The leading character in a story or drama. 2. A leading figure, esp. of a cause; champion. [Gk. *prōtagōnistēs*.]

pro·te·an (prō'tē-ən, prō-tē'-) adj. Readily taking on different shapes or forms. [< *Proteus*, a Greek sea god who could change his shape at will.]

pro·tect (prə-tĕkt') v. To keep from harm, attack, or injury; guard. [< Lat. *protegere*.] —**pro·tec'tive** adj. —**pro·tec'tive·ly** adv.

pro·tec·tion (prə-tĕk'shən) n. 1. The act of protecting or condition of being protected. 2. One that protects. 3. A tariff system protecting domestic industries from foreign competition. —**pro·tec'tion·ism** n.

pro·tec·tor (prə-tĕk'tər) n. 1. One who protects. 2. One ruling a kingdom during the absence, minority, or illness of a monarch. —**pro·tec'tor·ship'** n.

pro·tec·tor·ate (prə-tĕk'tər-ĭt) n. 1. a. A relationship of partial control by a superior power over a dependent country or region. b. A dependent country or region in such a relationship. 2. The rule, office, or period of rule of a protector.

pro·té·gé (prō'tə-zhā') n. One whose welfare or career is promoted by an influential person. [Fr. < p.p. of *protéger*, to protect.]

pro·tein (prō'tēn', -tē-ĭn) n. Any of a group of complex organic compounds that contain amino acids as their basic structural units, occur in all living matter, and are essential for the growth and repair of animal tissue. [< LGk. *proteios*, primary.]

pro tem (prō těm') adv. Pro tempore.

pro tem·po·re (prō těm'pə-rē) adv. For the time being; temporarily. [Lat.]

pro·test (prə-tĕst', prō-) v. 1. To express strong objection (to), esp. formally or publicly. 2. To promise or affirm solemnly. —n. (prō'tĕst'). 1. The act of protesting, esp. formal expression of disapproval or objection. 2. An individual or collective gesture or display of disapproval. [< Lat. *protestari*.] —**prot'es·ta'tion** (prŏt'ĭ-stā'shən) n. —**pro·test'er** n. —**pro·test'ing·ly** adv.

Prot·es·tant (prŏt'ĭ-stənt) n. 1. A Christian belonging to a sect descending from those that broke away from the Roman Catholic Church in the 16th cent. 2. **prot·es·tant** (also prə-tĕs'tənt). One who protests. —**Prot'es·tant·ism** n.

proto- or **prot-** pref. Earliest: prototype. [< Gk. *prōtos*, first.]

pro·to·col (prō'tə-kôl', -kōl', -kŏl') n. 1. The forms of ceremony and etiquette observed by diplomats and heads of state. 2. The first copy of a treaty or other document prior to its ratification. 3. A preliminary draft or record of a transaction. [< LGk. *prōtokollon*, table of contents.]

Pro·to-In·do-Eu·ro·pe·an (prō'tō-ĭn'dō-yŏŏr'-ə-pē'ən) n. The earliest reconstructed stage of Indo-European.

pro·ton (prō'tŏn') n. A stable, positively charged subatomic particle with a mass 1,836 times that of the electron. [Gk. *prōton*, first.]

pro·to·plasm (prō'tə-plăz'əm) n. A complex, jellylike colloidal substance constituting the living matter of plant and animal cells. —**pro'to·plas'mic** (-plăz'mĭk) or **pro'to·plas'mal** (-məl) adj.

pro·to·type (prō'tə-tīp') n. An original form or model on which later examples are based. —**pro'to·typ'al** (-tī'pəl) or **pro'to·typ'ic** (-tĭp'ĭk) or **pro'to·typ'i·cal** adj.

pro·to·zo·an (prō'tə-zō'ən) n., pl. **-ans** or **-zo·a** (-zō'ə). Any of the single-celled, usu. microscopic organisms belonging to a group that includes the most primitive forms of animal life. —**pro'to·zo'an** or **pro'to·zo'ic** (-zō'ĭk) adj.

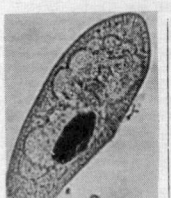
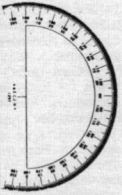

protozoan   protractor

pro·tract (prō-trăkt', prə-) v. To draw out; prolong. [< Lat. *protractus*, p.p. of *protrahere*, to lengthen.] —**pro·trac'tion** n.

pro·trac·tor (prō-trăk'tər) n. A semicircular instrument for measuring and constructing angles.

pro·trude (prō-trōōd') v. **-trud·ed, -trud·ing.** To push or jut outward; project. [Lat. *protrudere*.] —**pro·tru'sion** n. —**pro·tru'sive** adj.

pro·tu·ber·ance (prō-tōō'bər-əns, -tyōō'-) n. Something that protrudes; bulge or knob. [<

Lat. *protuberare*, to swell out.] —**pro·tu'ber·ant** *adj.* —**pro·tu'ber·ant·ly** *adv.*

proud (proud) *adj.* -**er**, -**est**. 1. Feeling pleasurable satisfaction. 2. Occasioning pride; gratifying: *a proud moment.* 3. Full of self-respect and independence of spirit: *too proud to ask for help.* 4. Highly respected; honored: *a proud name.* 5. Stately; majestic. 6. Haughty; arrogant. [< LLat. *prode*, advantageous.] —**proud'ly** *adv.* —**proud'ness** *n.*

prove (proov) *v.* **proved**, **proved** or **proven** (proo'vən), **prov·ing.** 1. To establish the truth or validity of by evidence or argument. 2. To determine the quality of by testing; try out. 3. To be shown to be; turn out. [< Lat. *probare.*] —**prov'a·ble** *adj.*

Syns: *prove, authenticate, confirm, demonstrate, show, substantiate, validate, verify* v.

Usage: The form *proved* is the preferred form of the past participle: *He has proved his point. Proven* is more widely employed as an adjective used immediately before the noun it modifies: *a proven talent.*

prov·e·nance (prŏv'ə-nəns) *n.* Place of origin; source. [< Lat. *provenire*, to originate.]

Pro·ven·çal (prō'vən-säl', prŏv'ən-) *n.* 1. A native or inhabitant of Provence, France. 2. The Romance language of Provence. —**Pro·ven'çal'** *adj.*

prov·en·der (prŏv'ən-dər) *n.* 1. Dry food for livestock. 2. Food; provisions. [< Lat. *praebenda*, support.]

pro·ve·nience (prə-vēn'yəns, -vē'nē-əns) *n.* A source or origin. [< Lat. *provenire*, to originate.]

prov·erb (prŏv'ûrb') *n.* 1. A short, popular saying expressing a well-known truth or fact. 2. **Proverbs.** (*used with a sing. verb*). See table at **Bible.** [< Lat. *proverbium.*] —**pro·ver'bi·al** (prə-vûr'bē-əl) *adj.*

pro·vide (prə-vīd') *v.* -**vid·ed**, -**vid·ing.** 1. To furnish; supply. 2. To make available; afford. 3. To set down as or make a stipulation. 4. To take measures in preparation: *provide against emergencies.* 5. To supply means of subsistence: *provide for one's family.* [< Lat. *providere*, to prepare for.] —**pro·vid'er** *n.*

pro·vid·ed (prə-vī'dĭd) *conj.* On the condition that; if.

prov·i·dence (prŏv'ĭ-dəns, -dĕns') *n.* 1. Foresight. 2. Economy. 3. a. Divine care and guardianship. b. **Providence.** God.

prov·i·dent (prŏv'ĭ-dənt, -dĕnt') *adj.* 1. Providing for future needs or events. 2. Frugal; economical. —**prov'i·dent·ly** *adv.*

prov·i·den·tial (prŏv'ĭ-dĕn'shəl) *adj.* 1. Of, pertaining to, or resulting from divine providence. 2. Fortunate; opportune. —**prov'i·den'tial·ly** *adv.*

prov·ince (prŏv'ĭns) *n.* 1. A territory governed as an administrative or political unit of a country or empire. 2. **provinces.** Areas of a country situated away from the capital or population center. 3. A comprehensive area of knowledge, activity, etc.; sphere. [< Lat. *provincia.*]

pro·vin·cial (prə-vĭn'shəl) *adj.* 1. Of or pertaining to a province. 2. Limited in perspective; narrow and self-centered: *provincial attitudes.* —**pro·vin'cial·ism** *n.*

proving ground *n.* A place for testing new devices or theories.

pro·vi·sion (prə-vĭzh'ən) *n.* 1. The act of providing. 2. Something that is provided. 3. Often **provisions.** A stock of food and other necessary supplies. 4. A preparatory measure. 5. A stipulation, as in a will. —*v.* To supply with provisions. [< Lat. *providere*, to prepare for.] —**pro·vi'sion·er** *n.*

pro·vi·sion·al (prə-vĭzh'ə-nəl) *adj.* Provided for the time being pending permanent arrangements. —**pro·vi'sion·al·ly** *adv.*

pro·vi·so (prə-vī'zō) *n., pl.* -**sos** or -**soes.** A clause in a document making a qualification or condition. [< Med. Lat. *proviso quod*, provided that.]

prov·o·ca·tion (prŏv'ə-kā'shən) *n.* 1. The act of provoking. 2. An action that provokes.

pro·voc·a·tive (prə-vŏk'ə-tĭv) *adj.* 1. Tending to arouse curiosity or interest. 2. Tending to irritate or arouse resentment. —**pro·voc'a·tive·ly** *adv.* —**pro·voc'a·tive·ness** *n.*

pro·voke (prə-vōk') *v.* -**voked**, -**vok·ing.** 1. To incite to anger or resentment. 2. To stir to action. 3. To bring on by inciting: *provoke a fight.* [< Lat. *provocare*, to challenge.]

Syns: *provoke, arouse, excite, galvanize, goad, impel, incite, inflame, inspire, instigate, kindle, motivate, move, rouse, spur, stimulate* v.

pro·vost (prō'vōst', prŏv'əst) *n.* A chief administrative officer, as in some colleges. [< Lat. *praepositus*, superintendent.]

provost marshal (prō'vō) *n.* The head of military police in a U.S. Army command.

prow (prou) *n.* The forward part of a ship's hull; bow. [< Gk. *prōira.*]

prow·ess (prou'ĭs) *n.* 1. Bravery and resourcefulness, esp. in battle. 2. Exceptional skill; excellence. [< OFr. *prou*, brave.]

prowl (proul) *v.* To roam about stealthily, as in search of prey. [ME *prollen.*] —**prowl** *n.* —**prowl'er** *n.*

prowl car *n.* A police squad car.

prox·i·mate (prŏk'sə-mĭt) *adj.* 1. Nearest; next. 2. Approximate. [< Lat. *proximare*, to come near.]

prox·im·i·ty (prŏk-sĭm'ĭ-tē) *n.* Nearness; closeness. [< Lat. *proximitas.*]

prox·i·mo (prŏk'sə-mō') *adv.* Of or in the following month. [< Lat. *proximo mense*, in the next month.]

prox·y (prŏk'sē) *n., pl.* -**ies.** 1. A person authorized to act for another. 2. a. The authority to act for another. b. The written authorization for such action. [< Lat. *procurare*, to take care of.]

prude (prood) *n.* One who is too concerned with being or seeming to be proper and virtuous. [< OFr. *preudefemme*, virtuous woman.] —**prud'er·y** *n.* —**prud'ish** *adj.* —**prud'ish·ly** *adv.* —**prud'ish·ness** *n.*

pru·dent (prood'nt) *adj.* 1. Wise in handling practical matters. 2. Careful in regard to one's own interests; provident. 3. Careful about one's conduct; circumspect. [< Lat. *prudens.*] —**pru'dence** *n.* —**pru·den'tial** (proo-dĕn'shəl) *adj.* —**pru'dent·ly** *adv.*

prune¹ (proon) *n.* A partially dried plum. [< Lat. *prunum*, plum.]

prune² (proon) *v.* **pruned**, **prun·ing.** 1. To cut off parts or branches of (e.g. a shrub) to

---

ă pat ā pay â care ä father ĕ pet ē be ĭ pit ī tie î pier ŏ pot ō toe ô paw, for oi noise ŏŏ took ŏŏ boot ou out th thin th this ŭ cut û urge yŏŏ abuse zh vision ə about, item, edible, gallop, circus improve shape or growth. **2.** To remove or cut out as superfluous. [< OFr. *proignier.*]

pru·ri·ent (prŏŏr'ē-ənt) *adj.* Characterized by or arousing an interest in sexual matters. [< Lat. *prurire,* to itch.] —**pru'ri·ence** *n.*

pry¹ (prī) *v.* **pried, pry·ing.** To look or inquire closely or curiously; snoop. [ME *prien.*]

pry² (prī) *v.* **pried, pry·ing. 1.** To raise, move, or force open with a lever. **2.** To obtain with difficulty. —*n., pl.* **pries.** Something, as a crowbar, used to apply leverage. [< PRIZE³.]

psalm (säm) *n.* **1.** A sacred song; hymn. **2. Psalms.** *(used with a sing. verb).* See table at **Bible.** [< Gk. *psalmos.*] —**psalm'ist** *n.*

Psal·ter (sôl'tər) *n.* Also **psal·ter.** A book containing the Book of Psalms or a particular version of, musical setting for, or selection from it. [< Gk. *psaltērion,* harp.]

pseu·do (sŏŏ'dō) *adj.* False; fake. [< PSEUDO-.]

pseudo– *pref.* False; deceptive: *pseudonym.* [< Gk. *pseudos,* falseness.]

pseu·do·nym (sŏŏd'n-ĭm') *n.* A fictitious name, esp. a pen name. —**pseu·don'y·mous** (sŏŏ-dŏn'ə-məs) *adj.*

psi (sī, psī) *n.* The 23rd letter of the Greek alphabet. See table at **alphabet.** [< Gk. *psei.*]

psit·ta·co·sis (sĭt'ə-kō'sĭs) *n.* A virus disease of parrots and related birds that is communicable to human beings. [Gk. *psittakos,* parrot + -OSIS.]

pso·ri·a·sis (sə-rī'ə-sĭs) *n.* A chronic skin disease characterized by inflammation and white scaly patches. [< Gk. *psōriasis.*]

psych (sīk) *Informal. —n.* Psychology. *—v.* **1.** To put into the right psychological frame of mind. **2.** To undermine the confidence of by psychological means.

psych– *pref.* Var. of **psycho–.**

psy·che (sī'kē) *n.* **1.** The soul or spirit as distinguished from the body. **2.** The mind functioning as the center of thought, feeling, and behavior. [< Gk. *psukhē.*]

psy·che·del·ic (sī'kĭ-dĕl'ĭk) *adj.* Of, inducing, or marked by hallucinations and distortions of perception. [< PSYCHE + Gk. *dēlos,* clear.] —**psy'che·del'ic** *n.*

psy·chi·a·try (sī-kī'ə-trē, sĭ-) *n.* The medical study, diagnosis, and treatment of mental illness. —**psy·chi·at'ric** (sī'kē-ăt'rĭk) *adj.* —**psy·chi'a·trist** *n.*

psy·chic (sī'kĭk) or **psy·chi·cal** (-kĭ-kəl) *adj.* **1.** Of or pertaining to the psyche. **2.** Of or caused by phenomena, such as extrasensory perception and mental telepathy, that are not explainable by known natural laws. *—n.* **1.** A person apparently responsive to psychic forces. **2.** A medium. —**psy'chi·cal·ly** *adv.*

psycho– or **psych–** *pref.* The mind: *psychology.* [< Gk. *psukhē,* soul.]

psy·cho·ac·tive (sī'kō-ăk'tĭv) *adj.* Affecting the mind or mental processes, as a drug.

psy·cho·a·nal·y·sis (sī'kō-ə-năl'ĭ-sĭs) *n.* **1.** An analytic technique that uses free association, dream interpretation, and analysis of feelings and behavior to investigate mental disorders. **2.** A psychiatric therapy incorporating the techniques of psychoanalysis. —**psy'cho·an'a·lyst** (-ăn'ə-lĭst) *n.* —**psy'cho·an'a·lyt'ic** (-ăn'-ə-lĭt'ĭk) or **psy'cho·an'a·lyt'i·cal** *adj.* —**psy'cho·an'a·lyze'** (-līz') *v.*

psy·cho·dra·ma (sī'kō-drä'mə, -drăm'ə) *n.* A psychotherapeutic and analytic technique in which individuals are assigned roles to be spontaneously enacted.

psy·cho·gen·ic (sī'kō-jĕn'ĭk) *adj.* Originating in the mind or in mental activities or conditions. —**psy'cho·gen'i·cal·ly** *adv.*

psy·chol·o·gy (sī-kŏl'ə-jē) *n., pl.* **-gies. 1.** The science of mental processes and behavior. **2.** The emotional and behavioral characteristics, as of an individual or group. —**psy'cho·log'i·cal** (-kə-lŏj'ĭ-kəl) *adj.* —**psy'cho·log'i·cal·ly** *adv.* —**psy·chol'o·gist** *n.*

psy·cho·path (sī'kə-păth') *n.* A person with a severe personality disorder, esp. one manifested in aggressively antisocial behavior. —**psy'cho·path'ic** *adj.* —**psy'chop'a·thy** *n.*

psy·cho·sis (sī-kō'sĭs) *n., pl.* **-ses** (-sēz'). Any of a class of serious mental disorders in which the mind cannot function normally and the ability to deal with reality is impaired or lost. —**psy·chot'ic** (-kŏt'ĭk) *adj. & n.*

psy·cho·so·mat·ic (sī'kō-sə-măt'ĭk) *adj.* **1.** Of or pertaining to phenomena that are both physiological and psychological. **2.** Of or pertaining to a partially or wholly psychogenic disease or physiological disorder.

psy·cho·ther·a·py (sī'kō-thĕr'ə-pē) *n.* The psychological treatment of mental, emotional, and nervous disorders. —**psy'cho·ther'a·peu'tic** (-pyŏŏ'tĭk) *adj.* —**psy'cho·ther'a·pist** *n.*

Pt The symbol for the element platinum.

ptar·mi·gan (tär'mĭ-gən) *n., pl.* **-gan** or **-gans.** A grouselike bird of northern regions, with feathered feet. [< Sc. Gael. *tarmachan.*]

PT boat (pē-tē') *n.* A fast, lightly armed vessel used to torpedo enemy shipping. [P(ATROL) T(ORPEDO) BOAT.]

pter·o·dac·tyl (tĕr'ə-dăk'təl) *n.* An extinct flying reptile. [Gk. *pteron,* wing + Gk. *daktulos,* finger.]

pto·maine (tō'mān', tō-mān') *n.* Also **ptomain.** Any of various basic nitrogenous materials, some poisonous, produced by the putrefaction and decomposition of protein. [< Gk. *ptōma,* corpse.]

ptomaine poisoning *n.* Food poisoning caused by bacteria or bacterial toxins.

Pu The symbol for the element plutonium.

pub (pŭb) *n.* A tavern; bar. [< PUBLIC HOUSE.]

pu·ber·ty (pyŏŏ'bər-tē) *n.* The stage of maturation in which an individual becomes physiologically capable of sexual reproduction. [< Lat. *pubertas.*] —**pu'ber·tal** *adj.*

pu·bes·cent (pyŏŏ-bĕs'ənt) *adj.* **1.** Covered with short hairs or soft down. **2.** Reaching or having reached puberty. [< Lat. *pubescere,* to reach puberty.] —**pu·bes'cence** *n.*

pu·bic (pyŏŏ'bĭk) *adj.* Of, pertaining to, or in the region of the pubis or pubes.

pu·bis (pyŏŏ'bĭs) *n., pl.* **-bes** (-bēz'). The forward portion of either of the hipbones, at the juncture forming the front arch of the pelvis. [< Lat., groin.]

pub·lic (pŭb'lĭk) *adj.* **1.** Of, concerning, or affecting the community or the people. **2.** Maintained for or used by the people or community: *a public park.* **3.** Participated in or attended by the people or community: *public worship.* **4.** Connected with or acting on behalf of the people or community: *public office.* **5.** Generally or widely known. *—n.* **1.** The community or the people as a whole. **2.** A group of people sharing a common interest: *the reading public.* [< Lat. *publicus.*] —**pub'lic·ly** *adv.*

pub·lic-ad·dress system (pŭb'lĭk-ə-drĕs') *n.*

An electronic amplification apparatus used for broadcasting in public areas.

pub·li·can (pŭb'lĭ-kən) n. 1. *Chiefly Brit.* The keeper of a public house. 2. A tax collector in the ancient Roman Empire. [< Lat. *publicanus*, tax collector.]

pub·li·ca·tion (pŭb'lĭ-kā'shən) n. 1. The act or process of publishing. 2. An issue of printed material.

public domain n. 1. Land owned and controlled by a government. 2. The status of publications, products, and processes that are not protected under patent or copyright.

public house n. *Chiefly Brit.* A licensed tavern or bar.

pub·li·cist (pŭb'lĭ-sĭst) n. One who publicizes, esp. a press or publicity agent.

pub·lic·i·ty (pŭ-blĭs'ĭ-tē) n. 1. Information disseminated to attract public notice. 2. Public interest, notice, or notoriety.

pub·li·cize (pŭb'lĭ-sīz') v. **-cized, -ciz·ing.** To give publicity to.

public relations pl.n. 1. Methods and activities employed to promote a favorable relationship with the public. 2. The degree of success obtained in achieving a favorable relationship with the public.

public school n. 1. In the United States, a tax-supported school providing free education for children of a community or district. 2. In Great Britain, a private boarding school for pupils between the ages of 13 and 18.

pub·lic-spir·it·ed (pŭb'lĭk-spĭr'ĭ-tĭd) adj. Motivated by or showing devotion to the good of the general public.

public television n. Noncommercial television that provides programs, esp. of an educational nature, for the public.

pub·lish (pŭb'lĭsh) v. 1. To prepare and issue (printed material) for public distribution or sale. 2. To bring to the attention of the public; announce. [< Lat. *publicare*, to make public.] —**pub'lish·a·ble** adj. —**pub'lish·er** n.

puck (pŭk) n. A hard rubber disk used in ice hockey. [Prob. < dial. *puck*, to strike.]

Puck (pŭk) n. A mischievous sprite in English folklore.

puck·er (pŭk'ər) v. To gather into wrinkles or folds. —n. A wrinkle or fold. [Perh. < POCKET.]

puck·ish (pŭk'ĭsh) adj. Mischievous; impish.

pud·ding (pŏŏd'ĭng) n. A sweet dessert, usu. boiled, steamed, or baked, with a soft, smooth consistency. [< Lat. *botulus*, sausage.]

pud·dle (pŭd'l) n. A small pool of liquid, as of water. [< OE *pudd*, ditch.]

pud·dling (pŭd'lĭng) n. The purification of impure metal, esp. pig iron, by agitation of a molten bath of the metal in an oxidizing atmosphere.

pu·den·dum (pyŏŏ-dĕn'dəm) n., pl. **-da** (-də). The external genital organs, esp. of a woman. [Lat., thing to be ashamed of.]

pudg·y (pŭj'ē) adj. **-i·er, -i·est.** Short and fat; chubby. [Orig. unknown.]

pueb·lo (pwĕb'lō) n., pl. **-los.** 1. A flat-roofed community dwelling built of stone or adobe by Indian tribes of the southwestern United States. 2. **Pueblo.** A member of a tribe, such as the Hopi or Zuñi, inhabiting pueblos. [Sp., people, pueblo.]

pu·er·ile (pyŏŏ'ər-əl, pyŏŏr'əl) adj. Immature; childish. [< Lat. *puer*, boy.] —**pu·er·il'i·ty** (pyŏŏ'ə-rĭl'ĭ-tē) n.

pu·er·per·al (pyŏŏ-ûr'pər-əl) adj. Of or pertaining to childbirth. [Lat. *puerperus*, bearing young.]

puff (pŭf) n. 1. a. A short, forceful discharge, as of air or smoke. b. A short, explosive sound produced by a puff. 2. A swelling or rounded protuberance. 3. A soft pad for applying cosmetic powder. 4. A light, flaky pastry, often filled with custard or cream. 5. An expression of exaggerated or deliberately flattering praise. —v. 1. To blow in puffs. 2. To breathe forcefully and rapidly; pant. 3. To emit puffs, as of smoke or vapor. 4. To swell or seem to swell. 5. To fill with pride or conceit. 6. To praise or publicize exaggeratedly. [< OE *pyff.*] —**puff'i·ly** adv. —**puff'i·ness** n. —**puff'y** adj.

puff·ball (pŭf'bôl') n. A ball-shaped fungus that releases dustlike spores when broken open.

puf·fin (pŭf'ĭn) n. A black and white northern sea bird with a flattened, brightly colored bill. [ME *poffoun*.]

pug¹ (pŭg) n. 1. A small, short-haired dog with a square, flat muzzle. 2. A short, turned-up nose. [Orig. unknown.]

pug¹

pug² (pŭg) n. *Slang.* A boxer. [< PUGILIST.]

pu·gi·lism (pyŏŏ'jə-lĭz'əm) n. Boxing. [< Lat. *pugil*, boxer.] —**pu'gi·list** n. —**pu'gi·lis'tic** (-lĭs'tĭk) adj.

pug·na·cious (pŭg-nā'shəs) adj. Having a quarrelsome disposition; combative. [< Lat. *pugnax.*] —**pug·nac'i·ty** (-năs'ĭ-tē) n.

pu·is·sance (pwĭs'əns, pyŏŏ'ĭ-səns) n. Power; might. [< OFr.] —**puis'sant** adj.

puke (pyŏŏk) v. **puked, puk·ing.** To vomit. [Prob. imit.]

pul (pŏŏl) n., pl. **puls** or **pu·li** (pŏŏ'lē). See table at **currency.** [Pers. *pūl.*]

pul·chri·tude (pŭl'krĭ-tŏŏd', -tyŏŏd') n. Physical beauty. [< Lat. *pulchritudo.*] —**pul'chri·tu'di·nous** (-tŏŏd'n-əs, -tyŏŏd'-) adj.

pule (pyŏŏl) v. **puled, pul·ing.** To whine; whimper. [Perh. < Fr. *piauler.*]

pull (pŏŏl) v. 1. To apply force to so as to draw (something) toward the source of the force. 2. To remove from a fixed position; extract. 3. To tug; jerk. 4. To rip or tear; rend. 5. To stretch. 6. To strain, esp. injuriously. 7. To move: *pulled over to the side of* *the road.* **8.** *Informal.* To perform, esp. with skill: *pull a stunt.* **9.** To draw out (a knife or gun). **10.** To produce (a print or impression) from type. —*phrasal verbs.* **pull off.** To do or accomplish in spite of difficulties. **pull through.** To come or bring successfully through difficulty. **pull up.** To come or bring to a stop. —*n.* **1.** The action or process of pulling. **2.** Force exerted in pulling. **3.** A force that attracts or draws; attraction. **4.** Something used for pulling. **5.** *Slang.* A means of gaining special advantage; influence. **6.** *Informal.* Ability to draw or attract; appeal. [< OE *pullian.*] —**pull′er** *n.*

pull·back (pŏŏl′băk′) *n.* An orderly troop withdrawal.

pul·let (pŏŏl′ĭt) *n.* A young hen. [< Lat. *pullus.*]

pul·ley (pŏŏl′ē) *n., pl.* **-leys. 1.** A simple machine used to change the direction and point of application of a pulling force, esp. for lifting weight, consisting essentially of a wheel with a grooved rim in which a pulled rope or chain is run. **2.** A wheel turned by or driving a belt. [< OFr. *polie.*]

Pull·man (pŏŏl′mən) *n.* A railroad parlor car or sleeping car. [< George M. *Pullman* (1831-97).]

pull·out (pŏŏl′out′) *n.* A pullback.

pull·o·ver (pŏŏl′ō′vər) *n.* A garment, esp. a sweater, put on by being drawn over the head.

pul·mo·nary (pŏŏl′mə-nĕr′ē, pŭl′-) *adj.* Of or involving the lungs. [< Lat. *pulmo,* lung.]

pulp (pŭlp) *n.* **1.** A soft, moist mass of matter. **2.** The soft, moist part of a vegetable or fruit. **3.** A mixture of cellulose material, such as wood, paper, and rags, ground up and moistened to make paper. **4.** The soft inner structure of a tooth, containing nerve tissue and blood vessels. **5.** A magazine containing sensational subject matter and usu. printed on rough, coarse paper. [Lat. *pulpa.*] —**pulp′i·ness** *n.* —**pulp′y** *adj.*

pul·pit (pŏŏl′pĭt, pŭl′-) *n.* An elevated platform, lectern, or stand used in preaching or conducting a religious service. [< Lat. *pulpitum,* platform.]

pulp·wood (pŭlp′wŏŏd′) *n.* Soft wood used in making paper pulp.

pul·sar (pŭl′sär′) *n. Astron.* Any of several very short-period variable galactic radio sources. [PULSE + (QUAS)AR.]

pul·sate (pŭl′sāt′) *v.* **-sat·ed, -sat·ing.** To expand and contract rhythmically; throb. [Lat. *pulsare.*] —**pul·sa′tion** *n.*

pulse (pŭls) *n.* **1.** The rhythmical throbbing of the arteries produced by the regular contractions of the heart. **2.** A short and temporary change in electrical energy or wave energy. —*v.* **pulsed, puls·ing.** To pulsate. [< Lat. *pulsus < pellere,* to beat.]

pul·ver·ize (pŭl′və-rīz′) *v.* **-ized, -iz·ing. 1.** To reduce or be reduced to a powder or dust. **2.** To demolish. [< LLat. *pulverizare.*]

pu·ma (pyŏŏ′mə) *n.* The mountain lion. [< Quechua *poma.*]

pum·ice (pŭm′ĭs) *n.* A porous, lightweight volcanic rock used as an abrasive and polish. [< Lat. *pumex.*]

pum·mel (pŭm′əl) *v.* **-meled** or **-melled, -mel·ing** or **-mel·ling.** To strike repeatedly; pound. [< POMMEL.]

pump¹ (pŭmp) *n.* A device for transferring a liquid or gas from a source or container

through tubes or pipes to another container or receiver. —*v.* **1.** To raise or cause to flow with a pump. **2.** To inflate with gas by means of a pump. **3.** To remove the water or air from. **4.** To move up and down in the manner of a pump handle. **5.** To propel, eject, or insert with or as if with a pump. **6.** To question closely or persistently. [ME *pumpe.*] —**pump′er** *n.*

pump² (pŭmp) *n.* A low-cut shoe without fastenings. [Orig. unknown.]

pum·per·nick·el (pŭm′pər-nĭk′əl) *n.* A dark, coarse rye bread. [G.]

pump·kin (pŭmp′kĭn, pŭm′-, pŭng′-) *n.* **1.** A large, round fruit with a thick, orange-yellow rind and numerous seeds. **2.** A vine bearing pumpkins. [< Gk. *pepōn,* ripe.]

pun (pŭn) *n.* A humorous use of a word involving two interpretations of the meaning. —*v.* **punned, pun·ning.** To make a pun. [Orig. unknown.]

punch¹ (pŭnch) *n.* **1.** A tool for piercing or stamping. **2.** A tool for forcing a pin, bolt, or rivet in or out of a hole. —*v.* To perforate or make with a punch. [< PUNCHEON¹.]

punch² (pŭnch) *v.* **1.** To hit with a sharp blow of the fist. **2.** To herd (cattle). —*n.* **1.** A blow with the fist. **2.** Vigor or drive. [ME *punchen.*] —**punch′er** *n.*

punch³ (pŭnch) *n.* A sweetened beverage of fruit juices, often spiced, usu. with wine or liquor. [Perh. < Skt. *pañca,* five.]

punch card *n.* A card punched with a pattern of holes or notches to represent data for use in a computer.

pun·cheon¹ (pŭn′chən) *n.* **1.** A short, wooden upright used in structural framing. **2.** A piece of broad, roughly dressed timber. [< Lat. *pungere,* to prick.]

pun·cheon² (pŭn′chən) *n.* A cask with a capacity of 84 U.S. gallons or approx. 318 liters. [OFr. *poinçon.*]

punch line *n.* The climax of a joke or humorous story.

punc·til·i·o (pŭngk-tĭl′ē-ō′) *n., pl.* **-os. 1.** A fine point of etiquette. **2.** Precise observance of formalities. [Ital. *punctiglio.*]

punc·til·i·ous (pŭngk-tĭl′ē-əs) *adj.* Marked by precise observance of the finer points of etiquette and formal conduct. —**punc·til′i·ous·ly** *adv.*

punc·tu·al (pŭngk′chŏŏ-əl) *adj.* Acting or arriving at an appointed time; prompt. [< Lat. *punctum,* point.] —**punc′tu·al′i·ty** (-ăl′ĭ-tē) *n.* —**punc′tu·al·ly** *adv.*

punc·tu·ate (pŭngk′chŏŏ-āt′) *v.* **-at·ed, -at·ing. 1.** To provide (a text) with punctuation. **2.** To interrupt periodically. **3.** To stress; emphasize. [< Lat. *punctum,* point.]

punc·tu·a·tion (pŭngk′chŏŏ-ā′shən) *n.* **1.** The use of standard marks and signs in writing and printing to separate words into sentences, clauses, and phrases in order to clarify meaning. **2.** The marks used in punctuating.

punc·ture (pŭngk′chər) *v.* **-tured, -tur·ing. 1.** To pierce with or as if with a sharp or pointed object. **2.** To deflate by or as if by piercing. —*n.* **1.** An act of puncturing. **2.** A hole made by puncturing. [< Lat. *punctura,* a pricking.]

pun·dit (pŭn′dĭt) *n.* A learned or authoritative person. [< Skt. *panditaḥ,* learned man.]

pun·gent (pŭn′jənt) *adj.* **1.** Affecting the organs of taste or smell with a sharp, acrid sensation. **2.** Biting; caustic: *pungent satire.*

[< Lat. *pungere*, to prick.] —**pun'gen·cy** (-jən-sē) *n.* —**pun'gent·ly** *adv.*

Pu·nic (pyōō'nĭk) *adj.* Of or pertaining to ancient Carthage.

pun·ish (pŭn'ĭsh) *v.* **1.** To subject to penalty for a crime or fault. **2.** To inflict a penalty for (an offense). **3.** To injure; hurt. [< Lat. *punire.*] —**pun'ish·a·ble** *adj.*

pun·ish·ment (pŭn'ĭsh-mənt) *n.* **1. a.** An act of punishing. **b.** The condition of being punished. **2.** A penalty imposed for wrongdoing. **3.** Rough handling.

pu·ni·tive (pyōō'nĭ-tĭv) *adj.* Inflicting or designed to inflict punishment. [< Lat. *punire*, to punish.]

Pun·ja·bi (pŭn-jä'bē, -jäb'ē) *n.* Also **Pan·ja·bi.** **1.** A native of the Punjab. **2.** An Indic language spoken in the Punjab.

punk¹ (pŭngk) *n.* Dry, decayed wood used as tinder. [Orig. unknown.]

punk² (pŭngk) *Slang.* —*n.* **1.** An inexperienced youth. **2.** A young tough; hoodlum. **3.** Punk rock. —*adj.* Of poor quality; inferior. [Orig. unknown.]

punk rock *n.* A form of hard-driving rock music characterized by an extremely bitter treatment of alienation and social unrest. —**punk rocker** *n.*

pun·ster (pŭn'stər) *n.* A person given to making puns.

punt¹ (pŭnt) *n.* An open, flat-bottomed boat with squared ends, propelled by a long pole. —*v.* To propel (a boat) with a pole. [< Lat. *ponto*, pontoon.]

punt² (pŭnt) *n.* A kick in which a football is dropped and kicked before touching the ground. —*v.* To kick by means of a punt. [Orig. unknown.]

pu·ny (pyōō'nē) *adj.* **-ni·er, -ni·est.** Of inferior size, strength, or importance; weak. [< OFr. *puisne*, lower in rank.]

pup (pŭp) *n.* **1.** A young dog; puppy. **2.** The young of certain other animals, as the seal. [< PUPPY.]

pu·pa (pyōō'pə) *n.,* *pl.* **-pae** (-pē') or **-pas.** The inactive stage in the metamorphosis of an insect, between the larval and adult forms. [< Lat., girl.] —**pu'pal** *adj.*

pu·pil¹ (pyōō'pəl) *n.* A student supervised by a teacher. [< Lat. *pupus*, boy.]

pu·pil² (pyōō'pəl) *n.* The dark circular aperture in the center of the iris of the eye. [< Lat. *pupilla.*]

pup·pet (pŭp'ĭt) *n.* **1.** A small figure of a person or animal moved by strings or wires; marionette. **2.** A doll. **3.** One whose behavior is determined by the will of others. [< Lat. *pupa*, doll.]

pup·pet·eer (pŭp'ĭ-tîr') *n.* One who operates and entertains with puppets.

pup·py (pŭp'ē) *n.,* *pl.* **-pies.** A young dog; pup. [< Lat. *pupa*, doll.]

pur·blind (pûr'blīnd') *adj.* **1.** Nearly or partly blind. **2.** Slow in understanding or discernment; dull. [ME *pur blind*, totally blind.] —**pur'blind'ness** *n.*

pur·chase (pûr'chĭs) *v.* **-chased, -chas·ing.** To obtain in exchange for money or its equivalent; buy. —*n.* **1.** Something that is purchased. **2.** The act or an instance of purchasing. **3.** A secure grasp or hold. [<

OFr. *pourchacier*, to pursue.] —**pur'chas·a·ble** *adj.* —**pur'chas·er** *n.*

pur·dah (pûr'də) *n.* The practice observed by Hindus and some Moslems of secluding women. [< Pers. *pardah*, veil.]

pure (pyōōr) *adj.* **pur·er, pur·est.** **1.** Having a uniform composition; not mixed: *pure oxygen.* **2.** Free from adulterants or impurities; not tainted. **3.** Free from contaminants; clean. **4.** Complete; utter: *pure folly.* **5.** Without faults; perfect. **6.** Chaste; virgin. **7.** Theoretical rather than applied: *pure science.* [< Lat. *-purus*, clean.] —**pure'ly** *adv.* —**pur'i·ty** *n.*

pure-bred (pyōōr'brĕd') *adj.* Of a strain established through breeding many generations of unmixed stock. —**pure'bred'** *n.*

pu·rée (pyōō-rā', pyōōr'ā) *v.* **-reed, -ree·ing.** To rub (food) through a strainer so that it becomes a fine pulp or thick liquid. —*n.* Food prepared by puréeing. [< OFr. *purer*, to purify.]

pur·ga·tion (pûr-gā'shən) *n.* The act of purging or state of being purged.

pur·ga·tive (pûr'gə-tĭv) *adj.* Tending to purge, esp. tending to cause evacuation of the bowels. —*n.* A purgative agent or medicine.

pur·ga·to·ry (pûr'gə-tôr'ē, -tōr'ē) *n.,* *pl.* **-ries.** **1.** *Rom. Cath. Ch.* A state of temporary punishment in which the souls of those who have died in grace must expiate their sins. **2.** A place or condition of expiation, suffering, or remorse. —**pur'ga·to'ri·al** (-tôr'ē-əl, -tōr'-) *adj.*

purge (pûrj) *v.* **purged, purg·ing.** **1.** To purify, esp. of sin, guilt, or defilement. **2.** To rid of persons considered undesirable, esp. by harsh methods: *purge a political party.* **3.** To undergo or cause evacuation of the bowels. —*n.* **1.** The act, process, or result of purging. **2.** Something that purges, esp. a purgative. [< Lat. *purgare*, to cleanse.]

pu·ri·fy (pyōōr'ə-fī') *v.* **-fied, -fy·ing.** To make or become pure. [< Lat. *purificare.*] —**pu'ri·fi·ca'tion** *n.* —**pu'ri·fi'er** *n.*

pu·rine (pyōōr'ēn') *n.* **1.** A colorless crystalline compound, $C_5H_4N_4$, used in organic synthesis and metabolism studies. **2.** Any of a group of naturally occurring organic compounds derived from or having molecular structures related to purine, including uric acid, adenine, and guanine. [G. *Purin.*]

pur·ism (pyōōr'ĭz'əm) *n.* Strict observance of or insistence upon traditional correctness, esp. of language. —**pur'ist** *n.* —**pu·ris'tic** *adj.*

pu·ri·tan (pyōōr'ĭ-tn) *n.* **1.** **Puritan.** A member of a 16th- and 17th-cent. English Protestant group advocating simplification of the ceremonies of the Church of England. **2.** One who advocates or practices a strict moral code and regards luxury or pleasure as sinful. [< LLat. *puritas*, purity.] —**pu'ri·tan'i·cal** (-tăn'ĭ-kəl) *adj.*

purl¹ (pûrl) *v.* To flow or ripple with a murmuring sound. —*n.* The sound made by or as if by water purling. [Prob. of Scand. orig.]

purl² (pûrl) *v.* To knit with an inverted stitch. —*n.* An inverted knitting stitch. [Orig. unknown.]

pur·lieu (pûr'lyōō, pûr'lōō) *n.* **1.** An outlying area. **2. purlieus.** Outskirts; environs. [< OFr. *poraler*, to traverse.]

ă pat ā pay â care ä father ĕ pet ē be ĭ pit ī tie î pier ŏ pot ō toe ô paw, for oi noise ōō took ōō boot ou out th thin th this ŭ cut û urge yōō abuse zh vision ə about, item, edible, gallop, circus

pur·loin (pər-loin', pûr'loin') v. To steal; filch. [< Norman Fr. *purloigner*, to remove.]

pur·ple (pûr'pəl) n. 1. Any of a group of colors produced by mixing red and blue pigments or dyes. 2. Purple cloth worn as a symbol of royalty or high office. —*adj.* 1. Of the color purple. 2. Elaborate and ornate: *purple prose.* —v. **-pled, -pling.** To make or become purple. [< Gk. *porphura*, a shellfish yielding purple dye.] —**pur'plish** *adj.*

pur·port (pər-pôrt', -pōrt') v. To have or present the appearance, often false, of being or intending; profess. —n. (pûr'pôrt', -pōrt'). An apparent meaning or purpose. [< Med. Lat. *purportare*, to extend.] —**pur·port'ed·ly** (-pôr'tĭd-lē, -pōr'-) *adv.*

pur·pose (pûr'pəs) n. 1. A result or effect that is intended or desired; intention. 2. Determination; resolution. —v. **-posed, -posing.** To resolve on; intend to do. [< Lat. *proponere*, to propose.] —**pur'pose·ful** *adj.* —**pur'pose·ful·ly** *adv.* —**pur'pose·less** *adj.* —**pur'pose·less·ly** *adv.* —**pur'pose·ly** *adv.*

purr (pûr) n. The softly vibrant sound made by a contented cat. [Imit.] —**purr** *v.*

purse (pûrs) n. 1. A bag or pouch for carrying money and often other small articles. 2. Wealth or resources; money. 3. A sum of money offered as a present or prize. —v. **pursed, pursing.** To pucker. [< Gk. *bursa*, leather.]

purs·er (pûr'sər) n. The officer in charge of money matters on board a ship.

purs·lane (pûr'slĭn, -slān') n. A trailing weed with small yellow flowers and fleshy leaves that are sometimes used in salads. [Prob. < Lat. *portulaca*.]

pur·su·ance (pər-sōō'əns) n. A carrying out or putting into effect.

pur·su·ant to (pər-sōō'ənt) prep. In accordance with.

pur·sue (pər-sōō') v. **-sued, -suing.** 1. To follow in an effort to overtake or capture; chase. 2. To strive to gain or accomplish. 3. To proceed along; follow: *pursue a winding course.* 4. To be engaged in: *pursue a hobby.* [< Lat. *prosequi.*] —**pur·su'er** n.

pur·suit (pər-sōōt') n. 1. The act or an instance of pursuing. 2. A vocation, hobby, or other activity regularly engaged in. [< OFr. *poursuivre*, to pursue.]

pu·ru·lent (pyōōr'ə-lənt, pyōōr'yə-) *adj.* Containing or secreting pus. [Lat. *purulentus.*] —**pu'ru·lence** n.

pur·vey (pər-vā') v. To supply (e.g. food or information); furnish: *purvey provisions for an army.* [< Lat. *providēre*, to provide.] —**pur·vey'ance** n. —**pur·vey'or** n.

pur·view (pûr'vyōō) n. 1. The extent or range of function, power, or competence; scope. 2. Range of vision, comprehension, or experience; outlook. [< OFr. *porveeir*, to provide.]

pus (pŭs) n. A viscous, yellowish-white fluid formed in infected tissue, consisting chiefly of leukocytes, cellular debris, and liquefied tissue elements. [Lat.]

push (pŏŏsh) v. 1. To exert force against (an object) to move it. 2. To move (an object) by pushing; thrust. 3. To urge forward; promote: *push a cause.* 4. To urge insistently; pressure. 5. *Slang.* a. To promote or sell (a product). b. To sell (a narcotic) illegally. —n. 1. The act of pushing; thrust. 2. A vigorous or insistent effort; drive. 3. A provocation to

action; stimulus. 4. *Informal.* Persevering energy; enterprise. [< Lat. *pulsare*, to beat.]

push button n. A small button that activates an electric circuit.

push-but·ton (pŏŏsh'bŭt'n) *adj.* Operated by or as if by push buttons; automatic: *push-button warfare.*

push·cart (pŏŏsh'kärt') n. A light cart pushed by hand.

push·er (pŏŏsh'ər) n. One that pushes, esp. one who sells drugs illegally.

push·o·ver (pŏŏsh'ō'vər) n. 1. Something easily accomplished. 2. One that is easily defeated or taken advantage of.

Push·tu (pŭsh'tōō) n. Var. of **Pashto.**

push-up (pŏŏsh'ŭp') n. A strengthening exercise performed by lying with the face and palms to the floor and pushing the body up and down with the arms.

push·y (pŏŏsh'ē) *adj.* **-i·er, -i·est.** *Informal.* Offensively forward or aggressive. —**push'i·ly** *adv.* —**push'i·ness** n.

pu·sil·lan·i·mous (pyōō'sə-lăn'ə-məs) *adj.* Lacking courage; cowardly. [LLat. *pusillanimis.*] —**pu·sil·la·nim'i·ty** (-lə-nĭm'ĭ-tē) n. —**pu·sil·lan'i·mous·ly** *adv.*

puss[1] (pŏŏs) n. *Informal.* A cat. [Orig. unknown.]

puss[2] (pŏŏs) n. *Slang.* The face. [< OIr. *bus*, lip.]

puss·y[1] (pŏŏs'ē) n., pl. **-ies.** *Informal.* A cat.

pus·sy[2] (pŭs'ē) *adj.* **-si·er, -si·est.** Resembling or containing pus.

pus·sy·cat (pŏŏs'ē-kăt') n. A cat.

pus·sy·foot (pŏŏs'ē-fŏŏt') v. 1. To move stealthily or cautiously. 2. *Slang.* To avoid committing oneself.

pussy willow n. A North American shrub with silky catkins.

pus·tule (pŭs'chōōl', -tyōōl') n. A slight, inflamed elevation of the skin filled with pus. [< Lat. *pustula*, blister.] —**pus'tu·lar** *adj.*

put (pŏŏt) v. **put, put·ting.** 1. To place in a specified position; set. 2. To cause to be in a specified condition. 3. To subject: *put him to a lot of trouble.* 4. To attribute: *put a false interpretation on events.* 5. To estimate: *put the time at five o'clock.* 6. To impose or levy: *put a tax on cigarettes.* 7. To hurl with an overhand pushing motion: *put the shot.* 8. To bring up for consideration or judgment: *put a question.* 9. To express; state. 10. To render in a specified language; translate. 11. To adapt. 12. To apply: *put our minds to it.* 13. To proceed: *The ship put into the harbor.* —**phrasal verbs. put across.** To state so as to be understood or accepted. **put down.** 1. To suppress: *put down an uprising.* 2. *Slang.* To criticize or reject. **put in.** 1. To interpose: *putting in a good word for me.* 2. To spend (time) at a location or job: *put in six years of work.* **put out.** 1. To annoy or anger. 2. To put to trouble or inconvenience. [ME *putten.*]

pu·ta·tive (pyōō'tə-tĭv) *adj.* Generally regarded as such; supposed. [LLat. *putativus.*]

put-down (pŏŏt'doun') n. *Slang.* A critical or slighting remark.

put-on (pŏŏt'ŏn', -ŏn') *adj.* Pretended; feigned. —n. *Slang.* 1. The act of misleading someone, esp. for amusement. 2. Something intended as a hoax or joke; spoof.

put·out (pŏŏt'out') n. *Baseball.* A play that causes a batter or base runner to be out.

pu·tre·fy (pyōō'trə-fī') v. **-fied, -fy·ing.** 1. To decompose or cause to decompose; rot. 2. To make or become gangrenous. [< Lat. *putre-facere*, to make rotten.] **—pu'tre·fac'tion** (-făk'shən) *n.* **—pu'tre·fac'tive** (-făk'tĭv) *adj.*

pu·tres·cent (pyōō-trĕs'ənt) *adj.* Becoming putrid; putrefying. [< Lat. *putrescere*, to grow rotten.] **—pu·tres'cence** *n.*

pu·trid (pyōō'trĭd) *adj.* **1.** Decayed; rotten. **2.** Corrupt; vile. [Lat. *putridus.*] **—pu·trid'i·ty** (-trĭd'ĭ-tē) *n.*

putsch (pŏŏch) *n.* A sudden and secret attempt by a group to overthrow a government. [G.]

putt (pŭt) *n.* A golf stroke made in an effort to place the ball into the hole. [< PUT.] **—putt** *v.*

put·tee (pŭ-tē', pŭt'ē) *n.* **1.** A strip of cloth wound spirally around the lower leg. **2.** A leather garter for the lower leg. [< Skt. *paṭṭikā.*]

putt·er¹ (pŭt'ər) *n.* **1.** A short, stiff-shafted golf club used for putting. **2.** A golfer who is putting.

putt·er² (pŭt'ər) *v.* To move or act aimlessly or ineffectually. [< POTTER.] **—putt'er·er** *n.*

put·ty (pŭt'ē) *n., pl.* **-ties.** A doughlike cement made by mixing whiting and linseed oil, used esp. to fill holes in woodwork and to secure panes of glass. **—v. -tied, -ty·ing.** To fill, cover, or secure with putty. [< OFr. *potee,* a potful.]

puz·zle (pŭz'əl) *v.* **-zled, -zling. 1.** To cause uncertainty and indecision in; perplex. **2.** To be perplexed. **3.** To ponder over a problem in an effort to solve or understand it. **4.** To clarify or solve by reasoning or study. **—n. 1.** Something that puzzles. **2.** A toy, game, or device that tests ingenuity. [Orig. unknown.] **—puz'zle·ment** *n.* **—puz'zler** *n.*

py·a (pĕ-ä') *n.* See table at currency. [Burmese.]

pyg·my (pĭg'mē) *n., pl.* **-mies.** Also **pig·my. 1.** One of unusually small size; dwarf. **2.** **Pygmy.** A member of any of several African and Asian peoples with a hereditary stature of from four to five feet. [< Gk. *pugmē,* the length from the elbow to the knuckles.] **—pyg'my** *adj.*

py·ja·mas (pə-jä'məz, -jăm'əz) *pl.n. Chiefly Brit.* Var. of **pajamas.**

py·lon (pī'lŏn') *n.* **1.** A monumental gateway, esp. one in the form of a pair of flat-topped pyramids that serves as the entrance to an Egyptian temple. **2.** A tower that marks a turning point in an air race. **3.** A steel tower that supports high-tension wires. [Gk. *pulōn,* gateway.]

py·or·rhe·a or **py·or·rhoe·a** (pī'ə-rē'ə) *n.* Inflammation of the gum and tooth sockets leading to loosening of the teeth. [Gk. *puon,* pus + -RRHEA.] **—py'or·rhe'al** *adj.*

pyr·a·mid (pĭr'ə-mĭd) *n.* **1.** A polyhedron with a polygonal base and triangular faces that meet in a common vertex. **2.** A massive structure with a rectangular base and four triangular faces that culminate in a single apex. **—v.**

1. To place or build in or as if in the shape of a pyramid. **2.** To increase rapidly and on a widening base. [< Gk. *puramis.*] **—py·ram'i·dal** (pĭ-răm'ĭ-dl) *adj.*

pyramid

pyre (pīr) *n.* A combustible pile for burning a corpse as a funeral rite. [< Gk. *pura.*]

py·re·thrum (pī-rē'thrəm) *n.* **1.** Any of several Old World plants cultivated for its showy flowers. **2.** The dried flowers of a pyrethrum used as an insecticide. [Gk. *purethron,* a kind of plant.]

Py·rex (pī'rĕks'). A trademark for any of various types of heat-resistant and chemical-resistant glass.

py·rim·i·dine (pī-rĭm'ĭ-dēn', pĭ-) *n.* **1.** A liquid and crystalline organic base, $C_4H_4N_2$. **2.** Any of several basic compounds, such as uracil, that has a molecular structure similar to pyrimidine and is found in living matter as a nucleotide component.

py·rite (pī'rīt') *n.* A yellow to brown mineral sulfide, FeS_2, used as a source of iron and sulfur. [< PYRITES.] **—py·rit'ic** (pī-rĭt'ĭk) *adj.*

py·ri·tes (pī-rī'tēz, pĭ-) *n., pl.* **-tes.** Any of various natural metallic sulfides, esp. of iron. [< Gk. *puritēs (lithos),* fire (stone).]

pyro- *pref.* Fire or heat: *pyrotechnics.* [< Gk. *pur,* fire.]

py·rol·y·sis (pī-rŏl'ĭ-sĭs) *n.* Chemical change caused by heat. **—py·ro·lyt·ic** (pī'rə-lĭt'ĭk) *adj.*

py·ro·ma·ni·a (pī'rō-mā'nē-ə, -mān'yə) *n.* The uncontrollable impulse to start fires. **—py·ro·ma'ni·ac'** (-mā'nē-ăk') *n.*

py·rom·e·ter (pī-rŏm'ĭ-tər) *n.* A thermometer for measuring high temperatures.

py·ro·tech·nics (pī'rə-tĕk'nĭks) *pl.n.* **1.** A fireworks display. **2.** A brilliant display, as of eloquence. **—py·ro·tech'nic** or **py·ro·tech'ni·cal** *adj.*

Pyr·rhic victory (pĭr'ĭk) A victory won with staggering losses. [< the victory of *Pyrrhus* (319-272 B.C.), King of Epirus, over the Romans in 279 B.C.]

py·thon (pī'thŏn', -thən) *n.* A large, nonvenomous Old World snake that coils around and suffocates its prey. [< Gk. *Puthōn,* mythological Greek serpent.]

pyx (pĭks) *n.* Also **pix. 1.** A container in which supplies of wafers for the Eucharist are kept. **2.** A container in which the Eucharist is carried to the sick. [< Gk. *puxis,* box.]

Qq

q or **Q** (kyōō) *n.*, *pl.* **q's** or **Q's.** The 17th letter of the English alphabet.

qin·tar (kĭn-tär') *n.* Var. of **quintar.**

qoph (kōf) *n.* The 19th letter of the Hebrew alphabet. See table at **alphabet.** [Heb. *qōph*.]

quack¹ (kwăk) *n.* The characteristic sound of a duck. [Imit.] —**quack** *v.*

quack² (kwăk) *n.* **1.** One who pretends to have medical knowledge. **2.** A charlatan. [< obs. Du. *quacksalver*.] —**quack'er·y** *n.*

quad¹ (kwŏd) *n. Informal.* A quadrangle (sense 2).

quad² (kwŏd) *n.* A quadruplet.

quadr– *pref.* Var. of **quadri–.**

quad·ran·gle (kwŏd'răng'gəl) *n.* **1.** A plane figure consisting of four points, no three of which are collinear, connected by straight lines. **2.** A rectangular area surrounded by buildings. [< LLat. *quadrangulum*.]

quad·rant (kwŏd'rənt) *n.* **1.** *Geom.* **a.** A quarter of a circle; an arc of 90°. **b.** The area bounded by a quarter circle and two perpendicular radii. **2.** A navigational and astronomical instrument, used to measure altitude and the angular distance between an object and the horizon. [< Lat. *quadrans*, quarter.]

quad·ra·phon·ic (kwŏd'rə-fŏn'ĭk) *adj.* Of or used in a sound-reproduction system with four transmission channels. [QUADR(I)– + PHONIC.]

quad·rat·ic (kwŏ-drăt'ĭk) *adj.* Of or containing mathematical quantities of the second degree and no higher. [< Lat. *quadratus*, p.p.s of *quadrare*, to make square.] —**quad·rat'ic** *n.*

quad·ren·ni·al (kwŏ-drĕn'ē-əl) *adj.* **1.** Happening once in four years. **2.** Lasting for four years. [< Lat. *quadrennium*, period of four years.] —**quad·ren'ni·al·ly** *adv.*

quadri– or **quadru–** or **quadr–** *pref.* Four: *quadrilateral.* [Lat.]

quad·ri·lat·er·al (kwŏd'rə-lăt'ər-əl) *n.* A four-sided polygon. —*adj.* Having four sides.

qua·drille (kwŏ-drĭl', kwə-, kə-) *n.* **1.** A square dance composed by four couples. **2.** Music for a quadrille. [< Fr., one of four divisions of an army.]

quad·ri·par·tite (kwŏd'rə-pär'tīt') *adj.* **1.** Consisting of or divided into four parts. **2.** Involving four participants.

quad·ru·ped (kwŏd'rə-pĕd') *n.* A four-footed animal.

quad·ru·ple (kwŏ-drōō'pəl, -drŭp'əl, kwŏd'rə-pəl) *adj.* **1.** Having four parts. **2.** Multiplied by four; fourfold. —*n.* A number or amount four times as many or as much as another. —*v.* **-pled, -pling.** To multiply or increase by four. [< Lat. *quadruplus*.]

quad·ru·plet (kwŏ-drŭp'lĭt, -drōō'plĭt, kwŏd'rə-plĭt) *n.* **1.** A group of four. **2.** One of four offspring born in a single birth.

quad·ru·pli·cate (kwŏ-drōō'plĭ-kĭt) *adj.* Multiplied by four; quadruple. —*n.* One of a set or group of four. —*v.* (-kāt') **-cat·ed, -cat·ing.** To quadruple. [< Lat. *quadruplicare*, to multiply by four.] —**quad·ru'pli·ca'tion** *n.*

quaff (kwŏf, kwăf, kwôf) *v.* To drink heartily. [Orig. unknown.] —**quaff** *n.* —**quaff'er** *n.*

quag·mire (kwăg'mīr', kwŏg'-) *n.* **1.** Land with a soft, muddy surface that yields when stepped on. **2.** A difficult or precarious situation. [*quag*, marsh + MIRE.]

qua·hog (kwŏ'hŏg', -hŏg', kwô'-, kō'-) *n.* An edible, hard-shelled clam of the North American Atlantic coast. [Narraganset *poquaûhock*.]

quail¹ (kwāl) *n.*, *pl.* **quail** or **quails.** Any of various small, short-tailed chickenlike game birds. [< Med. Lat. *quaccula*.]

quail¹

George Miksch Sutton

quail² (kwāl) *v.* To shrink back in fear; cower. [ME *quailen*, to give way.]

quaint (kwānt) *adj.* **-er, -est. 1.** Charmingly old-fashioned. **2.** Unfamiliar or unusual; strange. [< Lat. *cognitus*, p.p.s of *cognoscere*, to learn.] —**quaint'ly** *adv.* —**quaint'ness** *n.*

quake (kwāk) *v.* **quaked, quak·ing. 1.** To shake or tremble. **2.** To shiver or tremble, as from cold or fear. —*n.* **1.** An instance of quaking. **2.** An earthquake. [< OE *cwacian*.] —**quak'y** *adj.*

Quak·er (kwā'kər) *n.* A member of the Society of Friends. —**Quak'er·ism** *n.*

qual·i·fi·ca·tion (kwŏl'ə-fĭ-kā'shən) *n.* **1.** The act of qualifying or condition of being qualified. **2.** A quality or ability that suits a person for a particular position or task. **3.** A restriction or limitation.

qual·i·fy (kwŏl'ə-fī') *v.* **-fied, -fy·ing. 1.** To describe; characterize. **2.** To make competent or eligible for an office, position, etc. **3.** To declare competent or capable; certify. **4.** To limit or restrict. **5.** To make less harsh. **6.** To modify the meaning of (a word or phrase). [< Med. Lat. *qualificare*, to attribute a quality to.] —**qual'i·fi'er** *n.*

qual·i·ta·tive (kwŏl'ĭ-tā'tĭv) *adj.* Of, pertaining to, or concerning quality: *qualitative analysis.* —**qual'i·ta'tive·ly** *adv.*

qual·i·ty (kwŏl'ĭ-tē) *n.*, *pl.* **-ties. 1.** The essential character of something; nature. **2.** A characteristic or attribute; property. **3.** Degree of excellence. **4.** High social position. [< Lat. *qualitas*.]

qualm (kwŏm, kwôm) *n.* **1.** A sudden feeling of sickness, faintness, etc. **2.** Doubt or mis-

giving; uneasiness. **3.** A pang of conscience. [Orig. unknown.]
Syns: *qualm, compunction, misgiving, reservation, scruple* n.

quan·da·ry (kwŏn'də-rē, -drē) n., pl. **-ries.** A condition of uncertainty or doubt; dilemma. [Orig. unknown.]

quan·ti·ta·tive (kwŏn'tĭ-tā'tĭv) adj. Of, pertaining to, or expressed as the measurement of quantity. **—quan'ti·ta'tive·ly** adv.

quan·ti·ty (kwŏn'tĭ-tē) n., pl. **-ties. 1.** A specified or indefinite number or amount. **2.** A large amount or number: *produce oil in quantity.* [< Lat. *quantitas.*]

quan·tum (kwŏn'təm) n., pl. **-ta** (-tə). **1.** A quantity or amount. **2.** A small, indivisible unit of energy. [< Lat. *quantus,* how great.]

quantum theory n. Physics. A theory of atomic and subatomic interaction based on the behavior of the photon as both a wave and a particle.

quar·an·tine (kwôr'ən-tēn', kwŏr'-) n. **1. a.** A period of time during which one suspected of carrying a contagious disease is detained. **b.** A place for such detention. **2.** A condition of enforced isolation. —v. **-tined, -tin·ing.** To isolate in or as if in quarantine. [< Lat. *quadraginta,* 40.]

quark (kwôrk) n. One of a group of hypothetical subatomic particles with fractional electric charges, proposed as the fundamental units of matter. [Coined by Murray Gell-Mann (b. 1929).]

quar·rel (kwôr'əl, kwŏr'-) n. **1.** An angry dispute; argument. **2.** A cause for a dispute. —v. **-reled** or **-relled, -rel·ing** or **-rel·ling. 1.** To engage in a quarrel. **2.** To find fault. [< Lat. *querela,* complaint.] **—quar'rel·some** adj. **—quar'rel·some·ness** n.

quar·ry¹ (kwôr'ē, kwŏr'ē) n., pl. **-ries. 1.** A hunted animal. **2.** The object of a hunt or pursuit. [< OFr. *cuiree,* entrails of a beast given to the hounds.]

quar·ry² (kwôr'ē, kwŏr'ē) n., pl. **-ries.** An open excavation from which stone is obtained. [< Lat. *quadrus,* square.] **—quar'ri·er** n. **—quar'ry** v.

quart (kwôrt) n. **1. a.** A unit of volume or capacity in the U.S. Customary System, used in liquid measure, equal to 2 pints or .946 liter. **b.** A unit of volume or capacity in the U.S. Customary System, used in dry measure, equal to 2 pints or 1.101 liters. **c.** A unit of volume or capacity in the British Imperial System, used in liquid and dry measure, equal to 1.201 U.S. liquid quarts, 1.032 U.S. dry quarts, or 69.354 cubic inches. **2.** A container having a capacity of one quart. [< Lat. *quartus,* fourth.]

quar·ter (kwôr'tər) n. **1.** One of four equal parts of something. **2.** A U.S. or Canadian coin equal to one-fourth of the dollar. **3.** One-fourth of an hour; 15 minutes. **4.** quarters. A place of residence. **5.** A district of a city. **6.** An unspecified direction, person, or group of persons: *information from the highest quarters.* **7.** Mercy; clemency. —v. **1.** To divide into four equal or equivalent parts. **2.** To dismember. **3.** To furnish with or occupy lodgings. —adj. Equal to or being a quarter. **—idiom. at close quarters.** At close range. [< Lat. *quartarius.*]
Usage: With reference to the time of day, *a* in the following phrases is optional: *(a) quarter of* (or *to* or *before*) *ten; (a) quarter past* (or *after*) *five.*

quar·ter·back (kwôr'tər-băk') n. Football. An offensive backfield player who usu. calls the play signals. **—quar'ter·back'** v.

quar·ter·deck (kwôr'tər-dĕk') n. The rear area of a ship's upper deck.

quarter horse n. A strong, muscular saddle horse able to run short distances at high speed. [< its being trained for quarter-mile races.]

quarter horse

quar·ter·ly (kwôr'tər-lē) adj. Occurring at regular three-month intervals. —adv. At three-month intervals. —n., pl. **-lies.** A quarterly publication.

quar·ter·mas·ter (kwôr'tər-măs'tər) n. **1.** A military officer responsible for the food, clothing, and equipment of troops. **2.** A petty officer responsible for the navigation of a ship.

quar·tet (kwôr-tĕt') n. Also **quar·tette. 1.** A group of four. **2.** A musical composition for four voices or instruments. [< Lat. *quartus,* fourth.]

quar·to (kwôr'tō) n., pl. **-tos. 1.** The page size obtained by folding a whole sheet into four leaves. **2.** A book composed of quarto pages. [< Lat. *quartus,* fourth.]

quartz (kwôrts) n. A hard, crystalline, vitreous mineral silicon dioxide, SiO_2, found worldwide as a component of sandstone and granite or as pure crystals. [G. *Quarz.*]

quartz·ite (kwôrt'sīt') n. A metamorphic rock that results from the compression of quartz sandstone.

qua·sar (kwā'zär', -sär') n. Any of several classes of starlike objects that emit radio waves and visible radiation. [QUAS(I) + (STELL)AR.]

quash (kwŏsh, kwôsh) v. **1.** Law. To set aside or annul: *quash an indictment.* **2.** To put down or suppress forcibly and completely. [< LLat. *cassare.*]

qua·si (kwā'zī', -sī', kwä'zē, -sē) adj. Having a resemblance or likeness to something. [Lat., as if.]

quasi– pref. Almost or somewhat: *quasi-stellar object.* [< Lat. *quasi,* as if.]

qua·si-stel·lar object (kwā'zī-stěl'ər, -sī-, kwä'zē-, -sě-). A quasar.

Qua·ter·nary (kwŏt'ər-něr'ē, kwə-tûr'nə-rē) *adj.* Of or belonging to the geologic time, system of rocks, or sedimentary deposits of the second period of the Cenozoic era. —*n.* The Quaternary period.

quat·rain (kwŏt'rān', kwŏ-trān') *n.* A poem or stanza of four lines. [< Lat. *quattuor*, four.]

quat·re·foil (kăt'ər-foil', kăt'rə-) *n.* A representation of a flower with four petals or a leaf with four leaflets. [ME *quaterfoile*.]

qua·ver (kwā'vər) *v.* 1. To shake or tremble. 2. To speak tremulously or shakily. [ME *quaveren*.] —**qua'ver** *n.* —**qua'ver·y** *adj.*

quay (kē) *n.* A wharf. [< OFr. *quai*.]

quea·sy (kwē'zē) *adj.* -**si·er**, -**si·est.** 1. Nauseated. 2. Uneasy; troubled. 3. Squeamish or fastidious. [ME *coisy*.] —**quea'si·ly** *adv.* —**quea'si·ness** *n.*

Quech·ua (kěch'wə) *n., pl.* -**ua** or -**uas.** 1. A member of a tribe of Indians of central Peru. 2. The language of the Quechua and other Indian peoples of South America. —**Quech'uan** *adj.*

queen (kwēn) *n.* 1. The wife or widow of a king. 2. A female ruler. 3. A woman who is eminent or supreme in a given domain. 4. The most powerful chess piece. 5. A playing card bearing the figure of a queen. 6. The fertile, fully developed female in a colony of bees, ants, etc. [< OE *cwēn*.] —**queen'li·ness** *n.* —**queen'ly** *adj.*

queen mother *n.* A dowager queen who is the mother of the reigning monarch.

queer (kwîr) *adj.* 1. Deviating from the expected or normal; strange. 2. Eccentric. —*v. Slang.* To ruin or thwart. [Orig. unknown.] —**queer'ly** *adv.* —**queer'ness** *n.*

quell (kwěl) *v.* 1. To put down forcibly; suppress. 2. To pacify. [< OE *cwellan*, to kill.]

quench (kwěnch) *v.* 1. To put out; extinguish. 2. To suppress; squelch. 3. To slake; satisfy. 4. To cool (hot metal) by thrusting in liquid. [< OE *ācwencan*.] —**quench'a·ble** *adj.*

quer·u·lous (kwěr'ə-ləs, kwěr'yə-) *adj.* 1. Given to complaining; peevish. 2. Expressing a complaint. [Lat. *querulus*.] —**quer'u·lous·ly** *adv.* —**quer'u·lous·ness** *n.*

que·ry (kwîr'ē) *n., pl.* -**ries.** 1. A question; inquiry. 2. A doubt in the mind; reservation. 3. A question mark. —*v.* -**ried,** -**ry·ing.** To question. [< Lat. *quaerere*, to ask.]

quest (kwěst) *n.* 1. A search; pursuit. 2. A chivalrous expedition undertaken by a medieval knight. [< Lat. *quaerere*, to seek.]

ques·tion (kwěs'chən) *n.* 1. An expression of inquiry made to elicit information. 2. A subject open to doubt or controversy. 3. A difficult matter; issue. 4. A subject or proposal under consideration. 5. Uncertainty; doubt. —*v.* 1. To put a question to; ask questions. 2. To interrogate, as a witness. 3. To express doubt about. —*Idiom.* **out of the question.** Not to be considered; unthinkable. [< Lat. *quaerere*, to ask.] —**ques'tion·er** *n.* —**ques'tion·ing·ly** *adv.*

ques·tion·a·ble (kwěs'chə-nə-bəl) *adj.* 1. Open to doubt; uncertain. 2. Of dubious morality or respectability. —**ques'tion·a·bil'i·ty** *n.* —**ques'tion·a·bly** *adv.*

question mark *n.* A punctuation symbol (?) written at the end of a sentence or phrase to indicate a direct question.

ques·tion·naire (kwěs'chə-nâr') *n.* A set of questions asked of a number of people in order to gather statistical information. [Fr.]

quet·zal (kět-säl') *n., pl.* -**zals** or -**za·les** (-sä'lās). 1. A Central American bird with brilliant bronze-green and red plumage. 2. See table at **currency.** [< Nahuatl *quetzalli*, large, brilliant tail feather.]

queue (kyōō) *n.* 1. A line of people or vehicles. 2. A long braid of hair worn hanging down the back of the neck. —*v.* **queued, queu·ing.** To form or wait in a line: *We queued up for tickets.* [< Lat. *cauda*, tail.]

quib·ble (kwĭb'əl) *v.* -**bled,** -**bling.** To make trivial distinctions or objections, esp. in order to evade an issue. [Perh. < obs. *quib*, equivocation.] —**quib'bler** *n.* —**quib'bler** *n.*

quick (kwĭk) *adj.* -**er,** -**est.** 1. Moving or acting rapidly; speedy. 2. Occurring or achieved in a brief space of time. 3. Understanding, thinking, or learning with speed; bright. 4. Hasty or sharp in reacting. —*n.* 1. Sensitive flesh, as under the fingernails. 2. The most sensitive aspect of the emotions: *an insult that cut to the quick.* 3. The living: *the quick and the dead.* [< OE *cwicu*, alive.] —**quick'ly** *adv.* —**quick'ness** *n.*

Usage: Both *quick* and *quickly* can be used as adverbs: *Come quick! When he heard the news, he returned quickly.* In writing *quickly* is preferred.

quick·en (kwĭk'ən) *v.* 1. To make or become more rapid; accelerate. 2. To revive; come to life. 3. To excite and stimulate.

quick-freeze (kwĭk'frēz') *v.* To freeze (food) so rapidly that natural flavor and nutritional value are preserved.

quick·ie (kwĭk'ē) *n. Informal.* Something made or done rapidly.

quick·sand (kwĭk'sănd') *n.* A soft, shifting mass of loose sand mixed with water that yields easily to pressure and in which a heavy object tends to sink.

quick·sil·ver (kwĭk'sĭl'vər) *n.* The element mercury. [< OE *cwicseolfor*.]

quick·step (kwĭk'stěp') *n.* A march to accompanying military quick time.

quick-tem·pered (kwĭk'těm'pərd) *adj.* Easily angered.

quick time *n.* A military marching pace of 120 steps per minute.

quick-wit·ted (kwĭk'wĭt'ĭd) *adj.* Mentally alert and sharp. —**quick'-wit'ted·ly** *adv.*

quid[1] (kwĭd) *n.* A piece of something chewable, as tobacco. [< OE *cwidu*, cud.]

quid[2] (kwĭd) *n., pl.* **quid** or **quids.** *Brit. Slang.* A pound sterling. [Orig. unknown.]

quid pro quo (kwĭd' prō kwō') *n.* Something given in exchange for something else. [Lat., something for something.]

qui·es·cent (kwī-ĕs'ənt, kwē-) *adj.* Inactive or still; dormant. [< Lat. *quiescere*, to be quiet.] —**qui·es'cence** *n.* —**qui·es'cent·ly** *adv.*

qui·et (kwī'ĭt) *adj.* -**er,** -**est.** 1. Silent; hushed. 2. Unmoving; still. 3. Untroubled; peaceful. 4. Not showy; unobtrusive. —*n.* The quality or condition of being quiet. —*v.* To become or cause to become quiet. [< Lat. *quietus*.] —**qui'et·ly** *adv.* —**qui'et·ness** *n.*

qui·e·tude (kwī'ĭ-tōōd', -tyōōd') *n.* Tranquillity or repose.

qui·e·tus (kwī-ē'təs) *n.* 1. Death. 2. A final discharge, as of a debt. [< Med. Lat. *quietus est,* he is discharged.]

quill (kwĭl) *n.* **1.** The hollow main shaft of a feather. **2.** A large, stiff feather. **3.** A writing pen made from a quill. **4.** A sharp hollow spine, as of a porcupine. [ME *quille.*]

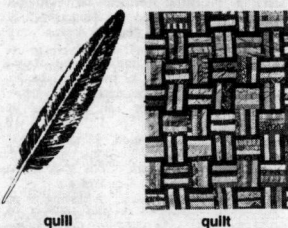

quill   quilt

quilt (kwĭlt) *n.* A padded coverlet for a bed. [< Lat. *culcita,* mattress.] **—quilt** *v.* **—quilt'ed** *adj.* **—quilt'ing** *n.*

quince (kwĭns) *n.* A tree with white flowers and aromatic, applelike fruit that is edible only when cooked. [< Lat. *cotoneum.*]

qui·nine (kwī'nīn') *n.* A bitter, colorless, crystalline powder, $C_{20}H_{24}N_2O_2 \cdot 3H_2O$, derived from certain cinchona barks and used to treat malaria. [< Sp. *quina,* cinchona bark.]

quin·quen·ni·al (kwĭn-kwĕn'ē-əl, kwĭng-) *adj.* **1.** Happening once every five years. **2.** Lasting for five years. [< Lat. *quinquennium,* period of five years.]

quin·sy (kwĭn'zē) *n.* An acute inflammation of the tonsils and the surrounding tissue, often leading to the formation of an abscess. [< Gk. *kunankhē.*]

quint (kwĭnt) *n.* A quintuplet.

quin·tal (kwĭn'tl) *n.* A metric unit of mass equal to 100 kilograms. [< Ar. *quinṭār,* a unit of weight, ult. < Lat. *centum,* hundred.]

quin·tar (kĕn-tär') *n.* Also **qin·tar** (kĭn-). See table at **currency.** [Albanian *qintar.*]

quin·tes·sence (kwĭn-tĕs'əns) *n.* **1.** The purest, most essential element of something. **2.** The most perfect or typical instance. [< Med. Lat. *quinta essentia,* fifth essence.] **—quin'tes·sen'tial** (kwĭn'tĭ-sĕn'shəl) *adj.*

quin·tet (kwĭn-tĕt') *n.* Also **quin·tette.** **1.** A group of five. **2.** A musical composition for five voices or instruments. [< Lat. *quintus,* fifth.]

quin·til·lion (kwĭn-tĭl'yən) *n.* **1.** The cardinal number equal to 10^{18}. **2.** *Chiefly Brit.* The cardinal number equal to 10^{30}. [Lat. *quintus,* fifth + (M)ILLION.] **—quin·til'lion** *adj.* **—quin·til'lionth** *n. & adj.*

quin·tu·ple (kwĭn-tōō'pəl, -tyōō'-, -tŭp'əl, kwĭn'tə-pəl) *adj.* **1.** Having five parts. **2.** Multiplied by five; fivefold. **—n.** A number or amount five times as many or as much as another. **—v. -pled, -pling.** To multiply or increase by five. [< Lat. *quīntus,* five.]

quin·tu·plet (kwĭn-tŭp'lĭt, -tōō'plĭt, -tyōō'plĭt, kwĭn'tə-plĭt) *n.* **1.** A group of five. **2.** One of five offspring born in a single birth.

quin·tu·pli·cate (kwĭn-tōō'plĭ-kĭt, -tyōō'-) *adj.* Multiplied by five; quintuple. **—n.** One of a set or group of five. **—v.** (-kāt') **-cat·ed, -cat·ing.** To quintuple. [Prob. < QUINTUPLE.]

quip (kwĭp) *n.* A brief, witty, or sarcastic remark. **—v. quipped, quip·ping.** To make quips. [< obs. *quippy.*]

quire (kwīr) *n.* A set of 24 or sometimes 25 sheets of paper of the same size and stock. [< Lat. *quaterni,* set of four.]

quirk (kwûrk) *n.* **1.** A sudden sharp turn or twist. **2.** A peculiarity of behavior or action; idiosyncrasy. [Orig. unknown.] **—quirk'i·ness** *n.* **—quirk'y** *adj.*

quirt (kwûrt) *n.* A short-handled riding whip with a lash of braided rawhide. [Perh. < Sp. *cuerda,* whip.]

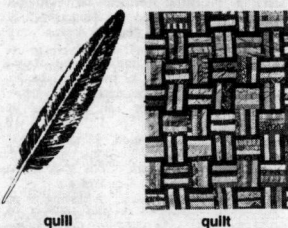

quirt   quiver²

quis·ling (kwĭz'lĭng) *n.* A traitor who collaborates with an invading enemy, esp. as a member of a puppet government. [< Vidkun Quisling (1887–1945).]

quit (kwĭt) *v.* **quit** or **quit·ted, quit·ting. 1.** To depart from; leave. **2.** To give up; relinquish. **3.** To stop. [< Lat. *quietus,* at rest.]

quite (kwīt) *adv.* **1.** Completely; altogether. **2.** Actually; really. **3.** Somewhat; rather: *quite angry.* [< Lat. *quietus,* freed of.]

quits (kwĭts) *adj.* Even with, as by payment or revenge. [Prob. < Lat. *quietus,* freed of.]

quit·tance (kwĭt'ns) *n.* **1.** Release from a debt. **2.** Something given as recompense. [< OFr. *quiter,* to free.]

quit·ter (kwĭt'ər) *n.* One who gives up easily.

quiv·er¹ (kwĭv'ər) *v.* To shake or cause to shake with a trembling motion. [ME *quiveren.*] **—quiv'er** *n.*

quiv·er² (kwĭv'ər) *n.* A case for holding arrows. [< OFr. *cuivre,* of Gmc. orig.]

qui vive (kē vēv') *n.* A sentinel's challenge. **—idiom. on the qui vive.** On the alert; vigilant; watchful. [Fr., (long) live who?]

quix·ot·ic (kwĭk-sŏt'ĭk) *adj.* Impractically romantic or idealistic. [< Don Quixote, hero of a romance by Miguel de Cervantes.] **—quix·ot'i·cal·ly** *adv.*

quiz (kwĭz) *n., pl.* **quiz·zes.** A short oral or written examination. **—v. quizzed, quiz·zing.** To question closely; interrogate. [Orig. unknown.] **—quiz'zer** *n.*

quiz·zi·cal (kwĭz'ĭ-kəl) *adj.* **1.** Suggesting puzzlement. **2.** Teasing; mocking. **—quiz·zi·cal'i·ty** (-kăl'ĭ-tē) *n.* **—quiz'zi·cal·ly** *adv.*

quoin (koin, kwoin) *n.* **1.** An exterior angle of a wall or building. **2.** A block forming a quoin. [< *coin,* corner.]

quoit (kwoit, koit) *n.* **1.** **quoits** (*used with a sing. verb*). A game in which flat rings of iron or rope are pitched at a peg. **2.** One of the rings used in quoits. [ME *coite.*]

quon·dam (kwŏn′dəm, -dăm′) *adj.* That once was; former. [< Lat., formerly.]

quo·rum (kwôr′əm, kwōr′-) *n.* The minimum number of members of a committee or organization who must be present for the valid transaction of business. [< Lat., of whom.]

quo·ta (kwō′tə) *n.* **1. a.** An allotment. **b.** A production assignment. **2.** The maximum number or proportion, esp. of persons, that may be admitted, as to a nation, group, or institution. [< Lat. *quotus,* of what number.]

quot·a·ble (kwō′tə-bəl) *adj.* Worth quoting.

quo·ta·tion (kwō-tā′shən) *n.* **1.** The act of quoting. **2.** A passage that is quoted. **3.** The quoting of current prices and bids for securities and goods.

quotation mark *n.* Either of a pair of punctuation marks (" " or ' ') used to mark the beginning and end of a passage attributed to another and repeated word for word.

quote (kwōt) *v.* **quot·ed, quot·ing. 1.** To repeat or copy the words of (another), with acknowledgment of the source. **2.** To cite as illustration or proof. **3.** To state (a price) for securities, goods, or services. —*n.* **1.** A quotation. **2.** A quotation mark. [< Lat. *quotus,* of what number.] —**quot′er** *n.*

Usage: Quote is the appropriate verb to use to refer to the act of repeating the exact words of a speech or text. If the repetition is less than exact, *cite* is preferable.

quoth (kwōth) *v. Archaic.* Uttered; said. [< OE *cwæth.*]

quo·tid·i·an (kwō-tĭd′ē-ən) *adj.* **1.** Occurring or recurring daily. **2.** Commonplace. [< Lat. *quotidianus.*]

quo·tient (kwō′shənt) *n.* The number that results from the division of one number by another. [< Lat. *quotiens,* how many times.]

qu·rush (kŏŏ′rəsh) *n., pl.* **-rush** or **-es.** See table at **currency.** [Ar. *qurūš.*]

Rr

r or **R** (är) *n., pl.* **r's** or **R's.** The 18th letter of the English alphabet.

Ra The symbol for the element radium.

rab·bet (răb′ĭt) *n.* A cut or groove along or near the edge of a piece of wood that allows another piece to fit into it to form a joint. —*v.* **1.** To cut a rabbet in. **2.** To join by a rabbet. [< OFr. *rabattre,* to beat down.]

rab·bi (răb′ī′) *n., pl.* **-bis. 1.** The ordained spiritual leader of a Jewish congregation. **2.** Formerly, a person authorized to interpret Jewish law. [Heb.] —**rab·bin′i·cal** (rə-bĭn′ĭ-kəl) or **rab·bin′ic** *adj.*

rab·bin·ate (răb′ĭn-ət′) *n.* The office or function of a rabbi.

rab·bit (răb′ĭt) *n., pl.* **-bits** or **-bit. 1.** A long-eared, short-tailed burrowing mammal with soft fur. **2.** The fur of a rabbit. [ME *rabet.*]

rab·ble (răb′əl) *n.* **1.** A mob. **2.** A group regarded contemptuously. [ME, pack of animals.]

rab·ble-rous·er (răb′əl-rou′zər) *n.* A demagogue.

Rab·bi (rŭ′bē) *n.* Also **Ra·bi·a** (rə-bē′ə). Either the 3rd or the 4th month of the Moslem calendar. See table at **calendar.** [Ar. *rabī*′, spring.]

rab·id (răb′ĭd) *adj.* **1.** Of or afflicted with rabies. **2.** Overzealous; fanatical. **3.** Raging; furious. [Lat. *rabidus.*] —**rab′id·ly** *adv.* —**rab′id·ness** *n.*

ra·bies (rā′bēz) *n.* An infectious, often fatal viral disease of most mammals that attacks the central nervous system and is transmitted by the bite of an infected animal. [< Lat., rage.]

rac·coon (ră-kōōn′) *n., pl.* **-coons** or **-coon. 1.** A North American mammal with a bushy, black-ringed tail. **2.** The fur of the raccoon. [Algonquian *arathkone.*]

raccoon

race[1] (rās) *n.* **1.** A group of people distinguished by genetically transmitted physical characteristics. **2.** A group of people united by a common history, nationality, or tradition. **3.** A subspecies, breed, or strain of plants or animals. [Fr., generation.]

race[2] (rās) *n.* **1.** A contest of speed. **2.** A contest for supremacy: *the Presidential race.* **3.** Steady or rapid onward movement. **4. a.** A strong or swift current of water. **b.** The channel of such a current. —*v.* **raced, rac·ing. 1.** To compete in a race (with). **2.** To rush. **3.** To operate too rapidly. [< ON *rās.*] —**rac′er** *n.*

race·course (rās′kôrs′) *n.* A racetrack.

race·horse (rās′hôrs′) *n.* A horse bred and trained to race.

ra·ceme (rā-sēm′, rə-) *n.* A flower cluster with flowers arranged singly along a common main stem. [Lat. *racemus,* bunch of grapes.]

race·track (rās′trăk′) *n.* A course laid out for racing.

ra·cial (rā′shəl) *adj.* **1.** Of, pertaining to, or based on race: *racial characteristics.* **2.** Arising from or occurring between races. —**ra′cial·ly** *adv.*

rac·ism (rā′sĭz′əm) *n.* **1.** The belief that some races are inherently better than others. **2.** Racial prejudice or discrimination. —**rac'ist** n.

rack (răk) n. **1.** A framework, stand, or bar on which to hold, display, or hang something. **2.** A metal bar with teeth that mesh with those of a pinion or gearwheel. **3.** An instrument of torture on which the victim's body was stretched. —v. **1.** To torture by means of the rack. **2.** To torment. **3.** To strain with great effort: *rack one's brain.* —*phrasal verb.* **rack up.** *Slang.* To score. [Prob. < MDu. *rakke,* framework.]

rack•et¹ (răk'ĭt) n. Also **rac•quet.** A light bat that consists of an oval frame with a tight interlaced network of strings and a handle, used to strike a ball in certain games. [< Ar. *râhet,* palm of the hand.]

rack•et² (răk'ĭt) n. **1.** A loud noise; clamor. **2.** A dishonest or fraudulent business. [Orig. unknown.]

rack•et•eer (răk-ĕt-tîr') n. One who extorts money esp. from a business by threatening harm or violence.

rac•on•teur (răk'ŏn-tûr', -ən-) n. One who tells stories and anecdotes with skill and wit. [< OFr.]

rac•quet•ball (răk'ĭt-bôl') n. A court game identical to handball but utilizes a short strung racket and a larger, softer ball.

rac•y (rā'sē) adj. **-i•er, -i•est. 1.** Pungent; piquant. **2.** Vigorous; lively. **3.** Slightly improper; risqué. [< RACE¹.]

ra•dar (rā'där') n. A device for detecting distant objects and determining such features as position, velocity, or size by analysis of radio waves reflected from their surfaces. [RA(DIO) D(ETECTING) A(ND) R(ANGING).]

ra•dar•scope (rā'där-skōp') n. The viewing screen of a radar receiver. [RADAR + (OSCILLO)SCOPE.]

ra•di•al (rā'dē-əl) adj. **1.** Of, pertaining to, or arranged like rays or radii. **2.** Having or characterized by parts radiating from a common center. **3.** Moving or directed along a radius. [< Lat. *radius,* ray.] —**ra'di•al•ly** adv.

radial engine n. An internal-combustion engine with radially arrayed cylinders.

ra•di•ant (rā'dē-ənt) adj. **1.** Sending forth light or heat. **2.** Consisting of or transmitted as radiation. **3.** Filled with happiness or joy. **4.** Glowing; bright. [< Lat. *radiare,* to radiate.] —**ra'di•ance** or **ra'di•an•cy** n. —**ra'di•ant•ly** adv.

radiant energy n. Energy transferred by radiation, esp. by an electromagnetic wave.

ra•di•ate (rā'dē-āt') v. **-at•ed, -at•ing. 1.** To send forth rays. **2.** To issue in rays. **3.** To spread out from or as if from a center. [Lat. *radiare.*]

ra•di•a•tion (rā'dē-ā'shən) n. **1.** The act or process of radiating. **2.** *Physics.* **a.** The emission and movement of waves, atomic particles, etc., through space or other media. **b.** The waves or particles that are emitted.

radiation sickness n. An often fatal illness caused by overexposure to radiation, characterized by nausea, diarrhea, and changes in blood chemistry.

ra•di•a•tor (rā'dē-ā'tər) n. **1.** A heating device for the circulation of steam or hot water. **2.** A cooling device, as in an automotive engine.

rad•i•cal (răd'ĭ-kəl) adj. **1.** Fundamental; basic. **2.** Carried to the farthest limit; extreme. **3.** Advocating extreme or revolutionary changes, esp. in politics or government. —n. **1.** One who advocates political and social revolution. **2.** *Math.* **a.** The root of a quantity as indicated by the radical sign. **b.** The sign √ placed before a quantity to indicate that its root is to be extracted. **3.** *Chem.* A group of atoms that behaves as a unit in chemical reactions and is only stable as a part of a compound. [< LLat. *radicalis,* having roots.] —**rad'i•cal•ly** adv. —**rad'i•cal•ness** n.

rad•i•cal•ism (răd'ĭ-kə-lĭz'əm) n. The doctrines or practices of political radicals.

rad•i•cal•ize (răd'ĭ-kə-līz') v. **-ized, -iz•ing.** To make radical or more radical. —**rad'i•cal•i•za'tion** n.

ra•di•i (rā'dē-ī') n. A pl. of **radius.**

ra•di•o (rā'dē-ō') n., pl. **-os. 1.** The use of electromagnetic waves lying between about 10 kilocycles/second and 300,000 megacycles/second to carry messages or information between points without the use of wires. **2.** The equipment used for transmitting or receiving radio signals. **3.** Transmission of radio broadcasts, esp. as an industry. —v. To transmit a message to or communicate with by radio. [< RADIOTELEGRAPHY.]

radio- pref. **1.** Radiant energy; radiation: *radiometer.* **2.** Radioactive: *radiocarbon.* **3.** Radio: *radiotelephone.* [< RADIATION.]

ra•di•o•ac•tiv•i•ty (rā'dē-ō-ăk-tĭv'ĭ-tē) n. The spontaneous emission of radiation, either directly from unstable atomic nuclei or as a consequence of a nuclear reaction. —**ra'di•o•ac'tive** adj. —**ra'di•o•ac'tive•ly** adv.

radio astronomy n. The study of celestial objects and phenomena by observation and analysis of emitted or reflected radio frequency waves.

ra•di•o•car•bon (rā'dē-ō-kär'bən) n. A radioactive isotope of carbon, esp. carbon 14.

radio frequency n. A frequency in the range within which radio waves may be transmitted, from about 10 kilocycles/second to about 300,000 megacycles/second.

ra•di•o•gram (rā'dē-ō-grăm') n. A message transmitted by radiotelegraphy.

ra•di•o•graph (rā'dē-ō-grăf') n. An image produced by radiation other than visible light, esp. by x-rays. —v. To make a radiograph of. —**ra'di•o•graph'ic** adj. —**ra'di•o•graph'i•cal•ly** adv. —**ra'di•og'ra•phy** (-ŏg'rə-fē) n.

ra•di•o•i•so•tope (rā'dē-ō-ī'sə-tōp') n. A radioactive isotope.

ra•di•ol•o•gy (rā'dē-ŏl'ə-jē) n. The use of ionizing radiation, esp. of x-rays, in medical diagnosis and treatment. —**ra'di•o•log'i•cal** (-ə-lŏj'ĭ-kəl) adj. —**ra'di•ol'o•gist** n.

ra•di•o•man (rā'dē-ō-măn') n. A radio technician or operator.

ra•di•om•e•ter (rā'dē-ŏm'ĭ-tər) n. A device used to detect and measure radiation. —**ra'di•o•met'ric** (-ō-mĕt'rĭk) adj. —**ra'di•om'e•try** n.

ra•di•o•phone (rā'dē-ō-fōn') n. A radiotelephone.

ra•di•o•sonde (rā'dē-ō-sŏnd') n. An instrument carried aloft, chiefly by balloon, to gather and transmit meteorological data. [RADIO- + Fr. *sonde,* sounding line.]

ă pat ā pay â care ä father ĕ pet ē be ĭ pit ī tie î pier ŏ pot ō toe ô paw, for oi noise ŏŏ took ōō boot ou out th thin th this ŭ cut û urge yōō abuse zh vision ə about, item, edible, gallop, circus

ra·di·o·te·leg·ra·phy (rā′dē-ō-tə-lĕg′rə-fē) *n.* Wireless telegraphy in which messages are sent by radio. **—ra′di·o·tel′e·graph′** (-tĕl′ĭ-grăf′) *n.*

ra·di·o·tel·e·phone (rā′dē-ō-tĕl′ə-fōn′) *n.* A telephone system in which messages are sent by radio waves instead of wires. **—ra′di·o·te·leph′o·ny** (-tə-lĕf′ə-nē) *n.*

radio telescope *n.* A very sensitive radio receiver used to detect and analyze radio waves that reach the earth from space.

ra·di·o·ther·a·py (rā′dē-ō-thĕr′ə-pē) *n.* The treatment of disease with radiation.

radio wave *n.* A radio-frequency electromagnetic wave.

rad·ish (răd′ĭsh) *n.* **1.** A plant with a thickened, edible root. **2.** The pungent root of the radish plant. [< Lat. *radix*, root.]

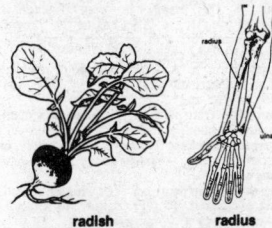

radish   radius

ra·di·um (rā′dē-əm) *n. Symbol* **Ra** A rare, white, highly radioactive metallic element, used in radiotherapy, as a neutron source, and as a constituent of luminescent paints. Atomic number 88; longest-lived isotope Ra 226. [< RADIUM.]

ra·di·us (rā′dē-əs) *n., pl.* **-di·i** (-dē-ī′) *or* **-es.** **1. a.** A line segment that joins the center of a circle with any point on its circumference. **b.** A line segment that joins the center of a sphere with any point on its surface. **2. a.** A radius used as a measure of circular area. **3.** The shorter and thicker of the two bones that make up the forearm. [Lat., ray.]

ra·don (rā′dŏn′) *n. Symbol* **Rn** A colorless, radioactive, inert gaseous element formed by disintegration of radium and used in radiotherapy. Atomic number 86; atomic weight 222. [< RADIUM.]

raf·fi·a (răf′ē-ə) *n.* A fiber from the leaves of an African palm, used esp. for mats or baskets. [Malagasy *rafia.*]

raff·ish (răf′ĭsh) *adj.* **1.** Vulgar; showy. **2.** Rakish; jaunty. [Prob. < ME *raf*, rubbish.] **—raff′ish·ly** *adv.* **—raff′ish·ness** *n.*

raf·fle (răf′əl) *n.* A lottery in which a number of persons buy chances on a prize. **—v. -fled, -fling.** To dispose of in a raffle. [< OFr. *raffle*, act of seizing.]

raft¹ (răft) *n.* A floating platform usu. made of logs or planks fastened together and used for transport or travel over water. [< ON *raptr*, beam.] **—raft** *v.*

raft² (răft) *n. Informal.* A great number or amount. [< *raff*, trash.]

raf·ter (răf′tər) *n.* One of the sloping beams that support a roof. [< OE *ræfter.*]

rag¹ (răg) *n.* A scrap of cloth. [< ON *rögg.*]

rag² (răg) *v.* **ragged, rag·ging.** *Slang.* **1.** To tease; taunt. **2.** To scold. [Orig. unknown.]

rag³ (răg) *n.* A ragtime composition.

rag·a·muf·fin (răg′ə-mŭf′ĭn) *n.* A dirty or unkempt child. [< *Ragamoffyn*, demon in *Piers Plowman*, a 14th-cent. poem.]

rage (rāj) *n.* **1.** Violent anger. **2.** A fad; craze. **—v. raged, rag·ing. 1.** To be intensely or violently angry. **2.** To move or act with great violence. **3.** To spread or prevail uncontrolled. [< Lat. *rabies.*]

rag·ged (răg′ĭd) *adj.* **1.** Tattered. **2.** Dressed in tattered clothes. **3.** Having a rough surface or edges. **4.** Imperfect: *a ragged performance.* **—rag′ged·ly** *adv.* **—rag′ged·ness** *n.*

rag·lan (răg′lən) *n.* A garment with slanted shoulder seams and sleeves extending in one piece to the neckline. [< 1st Baron *Raglan* (1788–1855).]

ra·gout (ră-gōō′) *n.* A meat and vegetable stew. [< Fr. *ragoûter*, to renew the appetite.]

rag·time (răg′tīm′) *n.* A style of jazz in which a syncopated melody is played against a steadily accented accompaniment. [Perh. < *ragged time.*]

rag·weed (răg′wēd′) *n.* Any of several weeds whose profuse pollen is one of the chief causes of hay fever.

raid (rād) *n.* A surprise attack, invasion, or forcible entry. **—v.** To make a raid on. [< OE *rād*, ride.] **—raid′er** *n.*

rail¹ (rāl) *n.* **1.** A horizontal bar or timber supported by vertical posts, as in a fence. **2.** A bar used as a track for a vehicle, such as a railroad car. **3.** A railroad: *transported goods by rail.* **—v.** To enclose or supply with a rail. [< Lat. *regula*, rod.]

rail² (rāl) *v.* To complain bitterly or abusively. [< LLat. *ragere*, to bray.] **—rail′er** *n.*

rail³ (rāl) *n.* A brownish, short-winged marsh bird. [< OFr. *raale.*]

rail·ing (rā′lĭng) *n.* A structure, as a fence, made of rails.

rail·ler·y (rā′lə-rē) *n., pl.* **-ies.** Good-natured teasing or ridicule. [< OFr. *railler*, to rail.]

rail·road (rāl′rōd′) *n.* **1.** A road composed of parallel steel rails supported by ties and providing a track for trains. **2.** The entire system of a railroad together with its assets, such as the land, stations, and rolling stock. **—v. 1.** To transport by railroad. **2.** *Informal.* **a.** To rush or push through quickly in order to prevent careful consideration. **b.** To convict without a fair trial or on false charges. **—rail′road′er** *n.* **—rail′road′ing** *n.*

rail·way (rāl′wā′) *n.* **1.** A railroad. **2.** A track providing a pathway for wheeled vehicles.

rai·ment (rā′mənt) *n.* Clothing; garments. [< OFr. *araiement*, array.]

rain (rān) *n.* **1.** Water that condenses from atmospheric vapor and falls to the earth as drops. **2.** A rapid or heavy fall of objects. **—v.** To fall or release as or like rain. **—phrasal verb. rain out.** To postpone or interrupt because of rain. [< OE *rēn.*] **—rain′i·ness** *n.* **—rain′y** *adj.*

rain·bow (rān′bō′) *n.* An arc of color seen opposite the sun, as after rain, caused by sunlight refracted by rain or mist.

rain check *n.* **1.** A ticket stub entitling the holder to admission to a performance that has been rescheduled because of rain. **2.** An authorization entitling a customer to purchase an item at a later date for the sale price. **rain·coat** (rān′kōt′) *n.* A waterproof or water-resistant coat.

rain·drop (rān′drŏp′) *n.* A drop of rain.

rain·fall (rān'fôl') n. 1. A fall of rain; a shower. 2. *Meteorol.* The amount of water, usu. measured in inches, that falls over a given area during a given time.

rain forest n. A dense evergreen forest in a tropical region with an annual rainfall of at least 100 inches.

rain·mak·ing (rān'mā'kĭng) n. The technique or action of producing or trying to produce rain by artificial methods. —**rain'mak'er** n.

rain·storm (rān'stôrm') n. A storm accompanied by rain.

rain·wa·ter (rān'wô'tər, -wŏt'ər) n. Water that falls as rain.

raise (rāz) v. **raised, rais·ing.** 1. To elevate; lift. 2. To erect; build. 3. To cause to arise or appear. 4. To increase, as in size or worth. 5. To improve in rank or status. 6. To breed. 7. To bring up; rear. 8. To bring forward for consideration. 9. To arouse or stir up. 10. To collect: *raise money.* 11. To make puffy and light. 12. To end (a siege). —n. 1. An increase in amount. 2. An increase in salary. [< ON *reisa.*]
  Syns: *raise, boost, elevate, hoist, lift, uplift* v.
  Usage: *Raise* is properly used as a transitive verb: *He raised the window.* For intransitive uses *rise* is standard: *The sun will rise at 6:37 tomorrow morning.*

rai·sin (rā'zĭn) n. A sweet dried grape. [< Lat. *racemus,* bunch of grapes.]

rai·son d'ê·tre (rā'zŏN dĕt'rə) n. Reason for being. [Fr.]

Ra·jab (rŭj'əb) n. The 7th month of the Moslem year. See table at **calendar.** [Ar.]

ra·jah or **ra·ja** (rä'jə) n. An Indian prince. [< Skt. *rājan,* king.]

rake¹ (rāk) n. A long-handled garden tool with a row of projecting teeth at its head. —v. **raked, rak·ing.** 1. To gather, smooth, loosen, or scrape with or as if with a rake. 2. To gain rapidly and in abundance: *rake in profits.* 3. To revive or bring to light: *rake up old gossip.* 4. To search or examine thoroughly: *rake through a drawer.* 5. To shoot heavy gunfire along the length of. [< OE *raca.*] —**rak'er** n.

rake² (rāk) n. A dissolute man; roué. [< *rakehell,* scoundrel.] —**rak'ish** adj.

rake³ (rāk) n. A slant or inclination from the horizontal or perpendicular. [Orig. unknown.]

rake-off (rāk'ôf', -ŏf') n. *Slang.* A percentage or share of the profits of an enterprise, esp. one accepted as a bribe.

rak·ish¹ (rā'kĭsh) adj. Morally loose; corrupt. —**rak'ish·ly** adv. —**rak'ish·ness** n.

rak·ish² (rā'kĭsh) adj. 1. Having a trim, streamlined appearance. 2. Gay and showy; jaunty. [Prob. < RAKE³.] —**rak'ish·ly** adv. —**rak'ish·ness** n.

ral·ly (răl'ē) v. **-lied, -ly·ing.** 1. To call together for a common purpose; assemble. 2. To restore to order. 3. To rouse from inactivity or decline. —n., pl. **-lies.** 1. The act of rallying. 2. A mass meeting or assembly to generate enthusiasm. 3. A notable rise in stock-market prices and active trading after a decline. [< OFr. *rallier.*]

ram (răm) n. 1. A male sheep. 2. A bar used to drive, batter, or crush by forceful impact. —v. **rammed, ram·ming.** 1. To strike or force

against with a heavy impact. 2. To force into place. 3. To cram; stuff. [< OE *ramm.*]

Ram·a·dan (răm'ə-dän') n. 1. The 9th month of the Moslem year, spent in fasting from sunrise to sunset. See table at **calendar.** 2. The fast engaged in during Ramadan. [Ar. *Ramaḍān.*]

ram·ble (răm'bəl) v. **-bled, -bling.** To wander aimlessly; roam. —n. A leisurely stroll. [Prob. < ME *romen,* to roam.]

ram·bler (răm'blər) n. 1. One that rambles. 2. A climbing rose with many small flowers.

ram·bunc·tious (răm-bŭngk'shəs) adj. Boisterous; unruly. [Prob. < Lat. *robustus,* strong.]

ram·ie (răm'ē) n. A textile fiber obtained from the stems of an Asian plant. [Malay *rami.*]

ram·i·fy (răm'ə-fī') v. **-fied, -fy·ing.** To branch out. [< OFr. *ramifier.*] —**ram'i·fi·ca'tion** n.

ram·jet (răm'jĕt') n. A jet engine that propels by igniting fuel with air taken in and compressed by the engine.

ramp (rămp) n. A sloping passage or roadway that connects different levels. [< OFr. *ramper,* to rear up.]

ram·page (răm'pāj') n. A course of violent, frenzied action or behavior. —v. (răm-pāj') **-paged, -pag·ing.** To move about wildly or violently. [Sc.] —**ram·pa'geous** adj. —**ram·pag'er** n.

ram·pant (răm'pənt) adj. Growing or spreading unchecked. [< OFr. *ramper,* to rear up.] —**ram'pan·cy** n. —**ram'pant·ly** adv.

ram·part (răm'pärt', -pərt) n. A wall or embankment raised as protection against attack. [< OFr. *ramparer,* to fortify.]

ram·rod (răm'rŏd') n. 1. A metal rod used to force the charge into a muzzleloading firearm. 2. A rod used to clean the barrel of a firearm.

ram·shack·le (răm'shăk'əl) adj. Shoddily constructed; rickety. [< ME *ransaken,* to ransack.]

ran (răn) v. p.t. of **run.**

ranch (rănch) n. 1. A large farm, esp. one on which cattle, sheep, or horses are raised. 2. A large farm on which a particular crop or kind of animal is raised. —v. To work on or manage a ranch. [< OFr. *ranger,* to put in place.] —**ranch'er** n.

ranch house n. A rectangular, one-story house with a low-pitched roof.

ran·cid (răn'sĭd) adj. Having the unpleasant odor or taste of decomposed oils or fats; rank. [Lat. *rancidus.*] —**ran·cid'i·ty** or **ran'cid·ness** n.

ran·cor (răng'kər) n. Deep-seated ill will. [< Lat., rancid smell.] —**ran'cor·ous** adj. —**ran'cor·ous·ly** adv.

rand (rănd) n. See table at **currency.** [Afr.]

ran·dom (răn'dəm) adj. Having no particular pattern or purpose; haphazard. [< OFr. *randon.*] —**ran'dom·ly** adv. —**ran'dom·ness** n.

rang (răng) v. p.t. of **ring².**

range (rānj) n. 1. **a.** The extent of perception, knowledge, experience, or ability. **b.** The area, sphere, or scope of activity or occurrence. 2. The extent of variation: *price range.* 3. The maximum distance that a missile can travel. 4. A place for shooting at targets. 5. Open land on which livestock wander and

---

graze. **6.** The act of roaming. **7.** An extended series forming a row or line. **8.** A cooking stove. —*v.* **ranged, rang·ing. 1.** To arrange in order, esp. in rows or lines. **2.** To classify. **3.** To explore. **4.** To roam freely. **5.** To extend in a particular direction. **6.** To vary within limits. [< OFr. *renge*, series.]
   Syns: *range, extent, orbit, reach, realm, scope, sphere, sweep* n.

rang·er (rān'jər) *n.* **1.** One that ranges. **2. Ranger.** A member of a group of soldiers trained to make raids. **3.** A person who patrols and guards forest land.

rang·y (rān'jē) *adj.* **-i·er, -i·est.** Long-legged and slender.

ra·ni (rä'nē) *n., pl.* **-nis.** Also **ra·nee.** The wife of a rajah. [< Skt. *rājñī.*]

rank¹ (răngk) *n.* **1.** Relative position or status in a group. **2.** Official position. **3.** Eminent position. **4.** A row, line, or series. **5.** A line esp. of soldiers standing side by side in close order. **6. ranks.** Enlisted men. —*v.* **1.** To place in rows or ordered formation. **2.** To classify. **3.** To hold a particular rank. **4.** To take precedence over. [< OFr. *renc.*]

rank² (răngk) *adj.* **-er, -est. 1.** Growing profusely and with excessive vigor. **2.** Strong and unpleasant in odor. [< OE *ranc*, strong.] —**rank'ly** *adv.* —**rank'ness** *n.*

rank and file *n.* **1.** The common soldiers of an army. **2.** The ordinary members of a group or organization, as distinguished from the leaders and officers.

rank·ing (răng'kĭng) *adj.* Having a high or the highest rank.

ran·kle (răng'kəl) *v.* **-kled, -kling. 1.** To cause irritation or resentment. **2.** To become sore or inflamed. [< OFr. *rancler.*]

ran·sack (răn'săk') *v.* **1.** To search thoroughly. **2.** To pillage. [< ON *rannsaka.*] —**ran'sack·er** *n.*

ran·som (răn'səm) *n.* **1.** The release of a person held captive in return for payment. **2.** The price demanded or paid for the release of a captive. [< Lat. *redemptio*, a buying back.] —**ran'som** *v.* —**ran'som·er** *n.*

rant (rănt) *v.* To speak violently, loudly, and at length. [Prob. < Du. *ranten*.] —**rant'er** *n.*

rap¹ (răp) *v.* **rapped, rap·ping. 1.** To hit sharply. **2.** To utter sharply. **3.** *Slang.* To find fault with; criticize. —*n.* **1.** A sudden, sharp blow. **2.** A reprimand. **3.** *Slang.* Blame or responsibility. [ME *rappen.*]

rap² (răp) *v.* **rapped, rap·ping.** To talk freely and openly. [Poss. < RAPPORT.]

ra·pa·cious (ra·pā'shas) *adj.* **1.** Greedy; avaricious. **2.** Existing by feeding on live prey. **3.** Voracious; ravenous. [< Lat. *rapax.*] —**ra·pa'cious·ly** *adv.* —**ra·pa'cious·ness** or **ra·pac'i·ty** (ra·păs'ĭ-tē) *n.*

rape¹ (rāp) *n.* **1.** The crime of forcing a person to submit to sexual intercourse. **2.** The act of seizing and carrying off by force; abduction. **3.** Profanation. [< Lat. *rapere*, to seize.] —**rape** *v.* —**rap'ist** *n.*

rape² (rāp) *n.* A plant with oil-rich seeds used as fodder. [< Lat. *rapa*, turnip.]

rap·id (răp'ĭd) *adj.* **-er, -est.** Very fast; swift. —*n.* Often **rapids.** An extremely fast-moving part of a river. [Lat. *rapidus.*] —**ra·pid'i·ty** (ra·pĭd'ĭ-tē) or **rap'id·ness** *n.* —**rap'id·ly** *adv.*

rapid eye movement *n.* The rapid, periodic, jerky movement of the eyes during the stages of the sleep cycle when dreaming takes place.

ra·pi·er (rā'pē-ər, răp'yər) *n.* A sword with a double-edged blade. [< OFr. (*espee*) *rapiere*, rapier (sword).]

rap·ine (răp'ĭn) *n.* The seizure of property by force; plunder. [< Lat. *rapina.*]

rap·port (ră-pôr', -pôr', rə-) *n.* A relationship, esp. one of mutual trust and harmony. [< OFr. *raporter*, to bring back.]

rap·proche·ment (ră'prôsh-mäN') *n.* **1.** The establishment of cordial relations. **2.** Cordial relations. [< Fr. *rapprocher*, to bring together.]

rap·scal·lion (răp-skăl'yən) *n.* A rascal; scamp. [< RASCAL.]

rapt (răpt) *adj.* **1.** Enthralled; enraptured. **2.** Deeply absorbed; engrossed. [< Lat. *raptus*, p.p. of *rapere*, to seize.]

rap·ture (răp'chər) *n.* A state of ecstasy. [< Lat. *rapere*, to seize.] —**rap'tur·ous** *adj.* —**rap'tur·ous·ly** *adv.*

ra·ra a·vis (râr'ə ā'vĭs) *n., pl.* **ra·ra a·vis·es** or **ra·rae a·ves** (râr'ē ā'vēz). A rare person or thing. [Lat., rare bird.]

rare¹ (râr) *adj.* **rar·er, rar·est. 1.** Infrequently occurring; uncommon. **2.** Extraordinary; special. **3.** Thin in density; rarefied: *the rare air of high altitudes.* [< Lat. *rarus.*] —**rare'ly** *adv.* —**rare'ness** *n.* —**rar'i·ty** *n.*

rare² (râr) *adj.* **rar·er, rar·est.** Not cooked through. [< OE *hrēr.*] —**rare'ness** *n.*

rare-earth element (râr'ûrth') *n.* Any of the metallic elements with atomic numbers ranging from 57 through 71.

rar·e·fy (râr'ə-fī', răr'-) *v.* **-fied, -fy·ing. 1.** To make or become thin, less compact, or less dense. **2.** To purify or refine. [< Lat. *rarefacere.*] —**rar'e·fac'tion** *n.*

ras·cal (răs'kəl) *n.* **1.** A dishonest or unscrupulous person. **2.** A mischievous person. [< OFr. *rascaille*, person of low station.] —**ras·cal'i·ty** *n.* —**ras'cal·ly** *adv.*

rash¹ (răsh) *adj.* **-er, -est.** Acting without forethought or due caution; too hasty. [ME *rasche*, active.] —**rash'ly** *adv.* —**rash'ness** *n.*

rash² (răsh) *n.* **1.** An eruption of the skin. **2.** An outbreak of many occurrences within a brief period: *a rash of burglaries.* [Poss. < Lat. *radere*, to scratch.]

rash·er (răsh'ər) *n.* **1.** A thin slice of bacon fried or broiled. **2.** A serving of thin slices of bacon. [Orig. unknown.]

rasp (răsp) *n.* A coarse file with raised, pointed projections. —*v.* **1.** To file or scrape with or as if with a rasp. **2.** To speak in a grating voice. **3.** To grate upon (e.g. nerves). [< OFr. *rasper*, to scrape.] —**rasp'er** *n.*

rasp·ber·ry (răz'bĕr'ē) *n.* **1. a.** The sweet, usu. red berry of certain prickly, shrubby plants. **b.** A plant bearing such berries. **2.** *Slang.* A jeering or contemptuous sound made by protruding and vibrating the tongue between the lips. [Obs. *raspis*, raspberry + BERRY.]

raspberry   **ratchet**
            Wheel and pawl

rat (răt) *n.* **1.** Any of various long-tailed, often destructive rodents similar to but larger than the mouse. **2.** *Slang.* A despicable person, esp. one who betrays or informs on his associates. —*v.* **rat·ted, rat·ting. 1.** To hunt for or catch rats. **2.** *Slang.* To betray one's associates. [< OE *ræt.*]

ratch·et (răch'ĭt) *n.* A mechanism consisting of a pawl, or hinged catch, that engages the sloping teeth of a wheel or bar and permits motion in one direction only. [< OFr. *rocquet,* head of a lance.]

rate¹ (răt) *n.* **1.** A quantity measured with respect to a standard or norm. A quantitative measure of a part to a whole; proportion: *the birth rate.* **3.** A charge or payment calculated with respect to another sum or standard. **4.** A level of quality; rank. —*v.* **rat·ed, rat·ing. 1.** To estimate the value of; appraise. **2.** To classify or be classified. **3.** To regard; consider. **4.** *Informal.* To merit; deserve. **5.** *Informal.* To have status or importance. —*idiom.* **at any rate.** Whatever happens; in any case. **2.** At least. [< Med. Lat. *pro rata parte,* according to an estimated part.]

rate² (răt) *v.* **rat·ed, rat·ing.** To berate; scold. [ME *raten.*]

rate of exchange *n.* The ratio at which the unit of currency of one country may be exchanged for the unit of currency of another country.

rath·er (răth'ər, rä'thər) *adv.* **1.** Preferably. **2.** More accurately or correctly. **3.** On the contrary. **4.** With more reason. **5.** Somewhat. [< OE *hrathor.*]

raths·kel·ler (rät'skĕl·ər, răth'-) *n.* A restaurant that is in the style of the cellar of a German city hall and serves beer. [Obs. G., restaurant in a city hall basement.]

rat·i·fy (răt'ə-fī') *v.* **-fied, -fy·ing.** To give formal approval and acceptance to. [< Med. Lat. *ratificare.*] —**rat'i·fi·ca'tion** *n.*

rat·ing (rä'tĭng) *n.* **1.** A classification assigned according to standing or rank. **2.** An estimate of financial status and ability to pay back debts: *a good credit rating.*

ra·tio (rä'shō, -shē-ō') *n., pl.* **-tios. 1.** *Math.* The relative size of two quantities expressed as the quotient of one divided by the other. **2.** Relation in degree or number between two things. [Lat., calculation.]

ra·ti·oc·i·nate (răsh'ē-ŏs'ə-nāt') *v.* **-nat·ed, -nat·ing.** To reason methodically and logically. [Lat. *ratiocinare.*] —**ra'ti·oc'i·na'tion** *n.* —**ra'ti·oc'i·na'tive** *adj.* —**ra'ti·oc'i·na'tor** *n.*

ra·tion (răsh'ən, rä'shən) *n.* **1. a.** A fixed share. **b.** An allotment of food for one day. **2. rations.** Food. —*v.* **1.** To supply with rations. **2.** To restrict to limited allotments. [< Lat. *ratio,* calculation.]

ra·tio·nal (răsh'ə-nəl) *adj.* **1.** Having or using the ability to reason. **2.** Of or pertaining to reason. **3.** Of sound mind; sane. **4.** *Math.* Of, relating to, or being a rational number. —*n.* A rational number. [Lat. *rationalis.*] —**ra'tio·nal·ly** *adv.*

ra·tio·nale (răsh'ə-năl') *n.* **1.** The fundamental reason for something. **2.** An exposition of underlying principles or beliefs.

ra·tio·nal·ism (răsh'ə-nə-lĭz'əm) *n.* The theory that the exercise of reason provides the only valid basis for action or belief. —**ra'tio·nal·ist** *n.* —**ra'tio·nal·is'tic** *adj.* —**ra'tio·nal·is'ti·cal·ly** *adv.*

ra·tio·nal·i·ty (răsh'ə-năl'ĭ-tē) *n., pl.* **-ties.** The quality or condition of being rational.

ra·tio·nal·ize (răsh'ə-nə-līz') *v.* **-ized, -iz·ing. 1.** To interpret or explain from a rational standpoint. **2.** To cause to appear reasonable or rational. **3.** To devise reasonable but untrue explanations for (e.g. one's behavior). —**ra'tio·nal·i·za'tion** *n.*

rational number *n.* A number that is an integer or a quotient of two integers.

rat·line (răt'lĭn) *n.* Also **rat·lin.** Any of the small ropes fastened horizontally to the shrouds of a ship and forming a ladder for going aloft. [Orig. unknown.]

rat·tan (ră-tăn', rə-) *n.* Any of various climbing palms of tropical Asia, with long, tough, slender stems that are used to make wickerwork. [Malay *rotan.*]

rat·tle (răt'l) *v.* **-tled, -tling. 1.** To make or cause to make a succession of short, sharp sounds. **2.** To chatter rapidly and in an animated way. **3.** *Informal.* To fluster; unnerve. —*n.* **1.** Short, sharp sounds produced in rapid succession. **2.** A device, as a baby's toy, that rattles when shaken. **3.** One of the dry, horny rings at the end of a rattlesnake's tail. [< MLG *rattelen.*]

rat·tler (răt'lər) *n.* A rattlesnake.

rat·tle·snake (răt'l-snāk') *n.* A poisonous New World snake with a series of dry, horny rings at the end of the tail.

rat·tling (răt'lĭng) *Informal.* —*adj.* **1.** Animated; brisk. **2.** Very good. —*adv.* Especially: *a rattling good time.*

rat·ty (răt'ē) *adj.* **-ti·er, -ti·est. 1.** Characteristic of or infested by rats. **2.** *Slang.* Disreputable; shabby.

rau·cous (rô'kəs) *adj.* **1.** Rough-sounding; harsh. **2.** Boisterous; disorderly. [Lat. *raucus.*] —**rau'cous·ly** *adv.* —**rau'cous·ness** *n.*

rav·age (răv'ĭj) *v.* **-aged, -ag·ing.** To destroy, devastate, or despoil. —*n.* The act of ravaging. **2.** Severe damage. [< OFr. *ravir,* to ravish.] —**rav'ag·er** *n.*

rave (rāv) *v.* **raved, rav·ing. 1.** To speak wildly or irrationally. **2.** To roar; rage. **3.** To speak with wild enthusiasm. —*n.* **1.** The act or an example of raving. **2.** *Informal.* An extravagantly enthusiastic opinion or review. [< ONFr. *raver.*]

rav·el (răv'əl) *v.* **-eled** or **-elled, -el·ing** or **-el·ling. 1.** To separate the fibers or threads of (e.g. cloth); unravel; fray. **2.** To tangle or complicate. —*n.* **1.** A raveling. **2.** A loose thread. **3.** A tangle. [< Du. *rafel,* loose thread.] —**rav'el·er** *n.*

rav·el·ing (răv'ə-lĭng) *n.* Also **rav·el·ling.** A thread or fiber that has become separated from a woven material.

ra·ven (rā'vən) *n.* A large crowlike bird with a croaking cry. —*adj.* Black and shiny. [< OE *hræfn.*]

rav·en·ous (răv'ə-nəs) *adj.* **1.** Extremely hungry. **2.** Predatory. **3.** Greedy for gratification. —**rav'en·ous·ly** *adv.* —**rav'en·ous·ness** *n.*

ra·vine (rə-vēn') *n.* A deep, narrow cut in the earth's surface, esp. one worn by water. [< Lat. *rapina,* rapine.]

rav·i·o·li (răv'ē-ō'lē, rä'vē-) *pl.n.* Small casings of pasta with various fillings, as of chopped meat or cheese. [< Ital. *rava*, turnip.]

rav·ish (răv'ĭsh) *v.* 1. To seize and take by force. 2. To rape. 3. To enrapture. [< Lat. *rapere*, to seize.] —**rav'ish·er** *n.* —**rav'ish·ment** *n.*

rav·ish·ing (răv'ĭ-shĭng) *adj.* Entrancing.

raw (rô) *adj.* **-er, -est.** 1. In a natural condition; not processed or refined: *raw wool.* 2. Uncooked. 3. Inexperienced; unskilled. 4. Having tissue below the skin exposed: *a raw wound.* 5. Unpleasantly damp and chilly: *raw weather.* 6. Cruel and unfair: *a raw deal.* 7. Outspoken; crude. —**Idiom. in the raw.** 1. In a crude or unrefined state: *nature in the raw.* 2. *Informal.* Nude; naked. [< OE *hrēaw.*] —**raw'ly** *adv.* —**raw'ness** *n.*

raw·boned (rô'bōnd') *adj.* Having a lean, gaunt frame with prominent bones.

raw·hide (rô'hīd') *n.* 1. The untanned hide of cattle. 2. A whip or rope made of rawhide.

ray¹ (rā) *n.* 1. a. A thin line or narrow beam of light or other radiation. 2. A small amount; trace. 3. a. A straight line extending from a point. b. A part or structure having this form. [< Lat. *radius.*]

ray² (rā) *n.* Any of various marine fishes with horizontally flattened bodies and narrow tails. [< Lat. *raia.*]

ray²

ray·on (rā'ŏn') *n.* 1. A synthetic fiber produced by forcing a cellulose solution through fine holes and solidifying the resulting filaments. 2. Fabric woven or knit from rayon. [< RAY¹.]

raze (rāz) *v.* **razed, raz·ing.** To tear down or demolish. [< Lat. *radere*, to scrape.]

ra·zor (rā'zər) *n.* A sharp-edged cutting instrument used esp. for shaving. [< Lat. *radere*, to scrape.]

razz (răz) *v. Slang.* To ridicule; heckle. [< RASPBERRY.]

Rb The symbol for the element rubidium.

re¹ (rā) *n. Mus.* A syllable representing the second tone of the diatonic scale. [< Med. Lat.]

re² (rē, rā) *prep.* Concerning; in reference to; in the case of. [Lat., ablative of *res*, thing.]

Re The symbol for the element rhenium.

re– *pref.* 1. Back: *replace.* 2. Again: *reactivate.* 3. Used as an intensive: *refine.* [< Lat. *re–*.]
Usage: In forming compounds *re–* is normally joined with the following element without space or hyphen: *reopen.* If the second element begins with an *e*, *re–* may be separated from it by a hyphen (*re-entry*) although such compounds may also have acceptable variants that are written solid. The hyphen is also used as a means of differentiation if the formation of a compound with *re–* would result in a term that resembles another, more common term: *re-creation*, meaning "creation anew."

reach (rēch) *v.* 1. To stretch out or extend (a bodily part). 2. To touch, take hold of, or try to grasp (something) by extending a bodily part, esp. the hand. 3. To get to or arrive at. 4. To succeed in communicating with. 5. To extend or carry as far as. 6. To aggregate or amount to. —*n.* 1. The act or power of stretching or thrusting out. 2. The extent or distance something can reach. 3. An unbroken expanse. [< OE *rǣcan.*] —**reach'er** *n.*

re·act (rē-ăkt') *v.* 1. To act in response to a stimulus or prompting. 2. To act in opposition to some former condition or act. 3. To take part in or undergo chemical change.

re·ac·tance (rē-ăk'təns) *n.* Opposition to the flow of alternating electric current caused by the inductance and capacitance in a circuit.

re·ac·tant (rē-ăk'tənt) *n.* A substance that participates in a chemical reaction.

re·ac·tion (rē-ăk'shən) *n.* 1. A response to a stimulus or the state resulting from such a response. 2. A reverse or opposing action.

re·a·ban'don *v.*
re'ab·sorb' *v.*
re'ab·sorp'tion *n.*
re'ac·cept' *v.*
re'ac·com'mo·date' *v.*
re'ac·com'pa·ny *v.*
re'ac·cuse' *v.*
re'ac·quire' *v.*
re·ac'ti·vate' *v.*
re·ac'ti·va'tion *n.*
re'a·dapt' *v.*
re'ad·dress' *v.*
re'ad·journ' *v.*
re'ad·journ'ment *n.*
re'ad·just' *v.*
re'ad·just'ment *n.*
re'ad·mis'sion *n.*
re'ad·mit' *v.*
re'ad·mit'tance *n.*
re'a·dopt' *v.*
re'a·dorn' *v.*
re'ad·vance' *v.*

re'af·firm' *v.*
re'a·lign' *v.*
re'a·lign'ment *n.*
re·an'i·mate' *v.*
re·an'i·ma'tion *n.*
re'an·nex' *v.*
re'a·noint' *v.*
re'ap·pear' *v.*
re'ap·pear'ance *n.*
re'ap·ply' *v.*
re'ap·point' *v.*
re'ap·point'ment *n.*
re'ap·por'tion *v.*
re'ap·por'tion·ment *n.*
re·ar'gue *v.*
re·ar'gu·ment *n.*
re·arm' *v.*
re·ar'ma·ment *n.*
re'ar·range' *v.*
re'ar·range'ment *n.*
re'as·cend' *v.*
re'as·cent' *n.*

re'as·sem'ble *v.*
re'as·sem'bly *n.*
re'as·sert' *v.*
re'as·ser'tion *n.*
re'as·sign' *v.*
re'as·sim'i·late' *v.*
re'as·sim'i·la'tion *n.*
re'as·so'ci·ate' *v.*
re'as·sume' *v.*
re'as·sump'tion *n.*
re'at·tach' *v.*
re'at·tack' *v.*
re'at·tain' *v.*
re'at·tempt' *v.*
re'a·vow' *v.*
re'a·wake' *v.*
re'a·wak'en *v.*
re·bill' *v.*
re·bind' *v.*
re·bloom' *v.*
re·blos'som *v.*
re·boil' *v.*

3. Opposition to progress or liberalism. 4. A chemical change or transformation. 5. A nuclear reaction.

re·ac·tion·ar·y (rē-ăk'shə-nĕr'ē) adj. Opposing progress, reform, or change. —n., pl. **-ies.** An opponent of progress or liberalism.

re·ac·tive (rē-ăk'tĭv) adj. 1. Tending to be responsive or to react to a stimulus. 2. Of or marked by reaction.

re·ac·tor (rē-ăk'tər) n. 1. One that reacts. 2. A nuclear reactor.

read (rēd) v. **read** (rĕd), **read·ing.** 1. To comprehend the meaning of (written or printed words or symbols). 2. To speak aloud the words of (something written or printed). 3. To determine the intent or mood of: *read my mind.* 4. To derive a special meaning from or give a special significance to: *read hostility into her silence.* 5. To foretell or predict. 6. To perceive, receive, or comprehend (e.g. a signal or message). 7. To study: *read law.* 8. To learn by reading. 9. To indicate or register: *The dial reads 0°.* 10. To have a particular wording. 11. To contain a specific meaning. —*Idiom.* **read between the lines.** To find an implicit or hidden meaning that is not actually expressed. [< OE *rǣdan.*] —**read·a·bil'i·ty** or **read'a·ble·ness** n. —**read'a·ble** adj. —**read'er** n.

read·i·ly (rĕd'l-ē) adv. 1. Promptly. 2. Willingly. 3. Easily.

read·ing (rē'dĭng) n. 1. The act or practice of a reader. 2. Written or printed material. 3. A public recitation of literary or other written material. 4. A personal interpretation or appraisal. 5. The specific form of a particular

passage in a text. 6. Information indicated, as by a gauge.

read-out (rēd'out') n. Presentation of computer data from calculations or storage.

read·y (rĕd'ē) adj. **-i·er, -i·est.** 1. Prepared or available for action or use. 2. Inclined; willing. 3. Quick in understanding or responding. —v. **-ied, -y·ing.** To make ready; prepare. [< OE *rǣde.*] —**read'i·ness** n.

read·y-made (rĕd'ē-mād') adj. Already made, prepared, or available: *ready-made clothes.*

re·a·gent (rē-ā'jənt) n. A substance used in a chemical reaction to detect, measure, examine, or produce other substances.

re·al (rē'əl, rēl) adj. 1. Not imaginary, fictional, or pretended; actual. 2. Authentic or genuine. 3. Essential; basic: *The real subject is people.* 4. Serious: *in real trouble.* 5. *Law.* Of or pertaining to stationary or fixed property, as buildings or land. [< LLat. *realis.*]

real estate n. Land, including all the natural resources and permanent buildings on it.

re·al·ism (rē'ə-lĭz'əm) n. 1. Concern with facts and things as they actually are. 2. The depiction of reality, as in painting, sculpture, or literature. —**re'al·ist** n. —**re'al·is'tic** adj. —**re'al·is'ti·cal·ly** adv.

re·al·i·ty (rē-ăl'ĭ-tē) n., pl. **-ties.** 1. The condition or quality of being real or true. 2. Something that is real.

re·al·ize (rē'ə-līz') v. **-ized, -iz·ing.** 1. To comprehend completely or correctly. 2. To make real or actual. 3. To obtain or bring in as profit. —**re'al·iz'a·ble** adj. —**re'al·i·za'tion** n. —**re'al·iz'er** n.

---

re·broad'cast' v. & n.	re·con'quer v.	re'de·vel'op·ment n.
re·build' v.	re·con'quest n.	re'di·gest' v.
re·bur'y v.	re'con·se'crate' v.	re'dis'count' v.
re·car'ry v.	re'con·sol'i·date' v.	re'dis·cov'er v.
re·cast' v. & n.	re'con·sti·tute' v.	re'dis·cov'er·y n.
re·cel'e·brate' v.	re'con·sti·tu'tion n.	re'dis·solve' v.
re·chal'lenge v.	re'con·vene' v.	re'dis·till' v.
re·charge' v.	re'con·vert' v.	re'dis·trib'ute v.
re·char'ter v.	re'con·vey' v.	re'dis·tri·bu'tion n.
re·check' v.	re·cop'y v.	re'di·vide' v.
re·choose' v.	re'cor·o·na'tion n.	re'di·vi'sion n.
re·chris'ten v.	re·cross' v.	re·do' v.
re·cir'cle v.	re·crown' v.	re·dou'ble v.
re·cir'cu·late' v.	re·crys'tal·li·za'tion n.	re'draft' n.
re·clasp' v.	re·crys'tal·lize' v.	re·draw' v.
re·clean' v.	re·cul'ti·vate' v.	re·drive' v.
re·clothe' v.	re'cy·cle v.	re·dry' v.
re·coin' v.	re·dec'o·rate' v.	re·dye' v.
re·coin'age n.	re·dec'o·ra'tion n.	re·ech'o n. & v.
re'col·lect' v.	re·ded'i·ca'tion n.	re·ed'it v.
re·col'o·nize' v.	re'de·feat' v. & n.	re·ed'u·cate' v.
re·col'or v.	re·de·fine' v.	re·ed'u·ca'tion n.
re'com·bine' v.	re'de·liv'er v.	re'e·lect' v.
re'com·mence' v.	re'de·mand' v.	re'e·lec'tion n.
re'com·mis'sion v.	re'dem·on·strate' v.	re·el'e·vate' v.
re·com·mit' v.	re·de·ny' v.	re'em·bark' v.
re·com·mit'ment n.	re'de·pos'it v. & n.	re'em·bod'y v.
re'com·pose' v.	re'de·scend' v.	re'em·brace' v.
re'con·dense' v.	re'de·scent' n.	re'e·merge' v.
re'con·di'tion v.	re'de·scribe' v.	re'e·mer'gence n.
re'con·duct' v.	re'de·ter'mine v.	re'em'i·grate' v.
re'con·firm' v.	re'de·vel'op v.	re'en·act' v.

ă pat ā pay â care ä father ĕ pet ē be ĭ pit ī tie î pier ŏ pot ō toe ô paw, for oi noise ōō took
ōō boot ou out th thin th this ŭ cut û urge yōō abuse zh vision ə about, item, edible, gallop, circus

re·al·ty (rē′əl-tē, rē′lē) *adv.* 1. In reality. 2. Truly.

realm (rĕlm) *n.* 1. A kingdom. 2. A field, sphere, or province: *the realm of science.* [< Lat. *regimen*, government.]

real number *n.* A member of the set of rational or irrational numbers.

real time *n.* 1. The actual time in which a physical process under computer study or control occurs. 2. *Computer Sci.* The time required for a computer to solve a problem, measured from the time data are fed in to the time a solution is received.

Re·al·tor (rē′əl-tər, -tôr′). A collective mark for a real-estate agent affiliated with the National Association of Realtors.

re·al·ty (rē′əl-tē) *n.*, *pl.* **-ties.** Real estate.

ream¹ (rēm) *n.* 1. A quantity of paper, now 500 or 516 sheets. 2. **reams.** A large amount. [< Ar. *rizmah*, bundle.]

ream² (rēm) *v.* 1. To shape, enlarge, or clean out (e.g. a hole) with or as if with a reamer. 2. To remove (material) by reaming. [Orig. unknown.]

ream·er (rē′mər) *n.* A tool used to shape, enlarge, or clean out holes.

reap (rēp) *v.* 1. To cut and gather (grain or a similar crop). 2. To gather a crop from; harvest. 3. To gain as a reward, esp. as a result of effort. [< OE *rīpan.*]

reap·er (rē′pər) *n.* 1. One who reaps. 2. A machine for harvesting.

rear¹ (rîr) *n.* 1. The back or hind part. 2. The part of a military deployment farthest from the fighting front. *—adj.* Of, at, or located in the rear. [Poss. < REARWARD.]

rear² (rîr) *v.* 1. To care for during the early years of life. 2. To lift upright. 3. To build; erect. 4. To raise; breed: *reared sheep.* 5. To rise on the hind legs, as a horse. [< OE *rǣran*, to lift up.]

rear admiral *n.* A naval officer ranking above a captain.

rear·most (rîr′mōst′) *adj.* Farthest in the rear; in the last position.

rear·ward (rîr′wərd) *adv.* Also **rear·wards** (-wərdz). Toward, to, or at the rear. *—rear·ward adj.*

rea·son (rē′zən) *n.* 1. The basis or motive for an action, decision, feeling, or belief. 2. An underlying fact or cause that provides logical sense for a premise or occurrence. 3. The capacity for rational thought, inference, or discrimination. 4. A normal mental state; sanity: *lost his reason.* *—v.* 1. To use the faculty of reason; think logically. 2. To talk or argue logically and persuasively. 3. To determine or conclude by logical thinking. *—idioms.* **by reason of.** Because of. **within reason.** Within the bounds of good sense or practicality. [< Lat. *ratio*, calculation.] *—rea′son·er n.* *—rea′son·ing n.*

rea·son·a·ble (rē′zə-nə-bəl) *adj.* 1. Capable of reasoning; rational. 2. In accordance with reason; logical. 3. Moderate: *reasonable prices.* *—rea′son·a·ble·ness n.* *—rea′son·a·bly adv.*

re·as·sure (rē′ə-shŏŏr′) *v.* 1. To restore confidence to. 2. To assure again. *—re·as·sur′ance n.* *—re·as·sur′ing·ly adv.*

re·bate (rē′bāt′) *n.* A deduction from an amount to be paid or a return of part of an

---

re′·en·act′ment *n.*
re′·en·cour′age *v.*
re′·en·cour′age·ment *n.*
re′·en·dow′ *v.*
re′·en·gage′ *v.*
re′·en·gage′ment *n.*
re′·en·grave′ *v.*
re′·en·list′ *v.*
re′·en·list′ment *n.*
re′·en·slave′ *v.*
re·en′ter *v.*
re′·e·rect′ *v.*
re′·es·tab′lish *v.*
re′·es·tab′lish·ment *n.*
re′·e·val′u·ate′ *v.*
re′·e·val·u·a′tion *n.*
re′·ex·am′i·na′tion *n.*
re′·ex·am′ine *v.*
re′·ex·change′ *v.*
re′·ex·hib′it *v.*
re′·ex·pel′ *v.*
re′·ex·pe′ri·ence *v.*
re′·ex·port′ *v.*
re·face′ *v.*
re·fash′ion *v.*
re·fas′ten *v.*
re·fer′ti·lize′ *v.*
re·fin′ish *v.*
re·fire′ *v.*
re·flow′ *v.*
re·flow′er *v.*
re·fold′ *v.*
re·forge′ *v.*
re·for′mu·late′ *v.*
re·for′ti·fi·ca′tion *n.*
re·for′ti·fy *v.*

re·frame′ *v.*
re·freeze′ *v.*
re·fu′el *v.*
re·fur′nish *v.*
re·gath′er *v.*
re·gear′ *v.*
re·ger′mi·nate′ *v.*
re·ger′mi·na′tion *n.*
re·gild′ *v.*
re·glaze′ *v.*
re·glue′ *v.*
re·grade′ *v.*
re·graft′ *v.*
re·grant′ *v.*
re·group′ *v.*
re·han′dle *v.*
re·hear′ing *n.*
re·heat′ *v.*
re·heel′ *v.*
re·hire′ *v.*
re·ig′nite′ *v.*
re′·im·plant′ *v.*
re′·im·port′ *v.*
re′·im·pose′ *v.*
re′·im·po·si′tion *n.*
re′·im·preg′nate *v.*
re′·im·press′ *v.*
re′·im·print′ *v.*
re′·im·pris′on *v.*
re′·im·pris′on·ment *n.*
re′·in·cite′ *v.*
re′·in·au′gu·rate′ *v.*
re′·in·cor′po·rate′ *v.*
re′·in·cur′ *v.*
re′·in·duce′ *v.*
re′·in·fect′ *v.*

re′·in·fec′tion *n.*
re′·in·flame′ *v.*
re′·in·form′ *v.*
re′·in·fuse′ *v.*
re′·in·hab′it *v.*
re′·in·oc′u·late′ *v.*
re′·in·oc·u·la′tion *n.*
re′·in·scribe′ *v.*
re′·in·sert′ *v.*
re′·in·ser′tion *n.*
re′·in·spect′ *v.*
re′·in·spec′tion *n.*
re′·in·spire′ *v.*
re′·in·stall′ *v.*
re′·in·stal·la′tion *n.*
re′·in·struct′ *v.*
re′·in·sure′ *v.*
re′·in·te·grate′ *v.*
re′·in·te·gra′tion *n.*
re′·in·ter′ *v.*
re′·in·ter′ro·gate′ *v.*
re′·in·tro·duce′ *v.*
re′·in·tro·duc′tion *n.*
re′·in·vent′ *v.*
re′·in·vest′ *v.*
re′·in·ves′ti·gate′ *v.*
re′·in·ves·ti·ga′tion *n.*
re′·in·vest′ment *n.*
re′·in·vig′or·ate′ *v.*
re′·in·vig·or·a′tion *n.*
re′·in·vite′ *v.*
re′·in·volve′ *v.*
re·is′sue *n.* & *v.*
re·judge′ *v.*
re·kin′dle *v.*
re·la′bel *v.*

amount paid. —v. (rĕ'băt', rĭ-bāt') **-bat-ed,
-bat-ing.** To deduct or return (an amount) from a payment or bill. [< OFr. *rebattre*, to reduce.]

re-bel (rĭ-bĕl') v. **-belled, -bel-ling. 1.** To refuse loyalty to or oppose by force an established government or ruling authority. **2.** To resist or oppose an authority or established convention. **3.** To feel or express strong unwillingness or repugnance. —n. **reb-el** (rĕb'əl). One who rebels or is in rebellion. [< Lat. *rebellare.*]

re-bel-lion (rĭ-bĕl'yən) n. **1.** An uprising intended to change or overthrow an existing government or ruling authority. **2.** An act or show of defiance toward an authority or established convention.
Syns: rebellion, insurgence, insurrection, mutiny, revolt, uprising **n.**

re-bel-lious (rĭ-bĕl'yəs) adj. **1.** Participating in or inclined toward a rebellion. **2.** Resisting control; unruly. **—re-bel'lious-ly** adv. **—re-bel'lious-ness** n.

re-birth (rē-bûrth', rē'bûrth') n. **1.** A second or new birth. **2.** A renaissance; revival.

re-born (rē-bôrn') adj. Born again.

re-bound (rē'bound', rĭ-) v. **1.** To spring or bounce back after hitting or colliding with something. **2.** To recover, as from disappointment. —n. (rē'bound', rĭ-bound'). **1.** A springing or bounding back. **2.** *Sports.* A rebounding hockey puck or basketball.

re-buff (rĭ-bŭf') n. A blunt or abrupt repulse or refusal. —v. To refuse bluntly or abruptly; snub. [< Oltal. *ribuffo*, reprimand.]

re-buke (rĭ-byōōk') v. **-buked, -buk-ing.** To criticize sharply; reprimand. [< ONFr. *rebuker.*] **—re-buke'** n.

re-bus (rē'bəs) n. A puzzle composed of words or syllables that appear in the form of pictures. [Lat., by things.]

re-but (rĭ-bŭt') v. **-but-ted, -but-ting.** To refute, esp. by offering opposing evidence or arguments, as in a legal case. [< OFr. *reboter.*] **—re-but'tal** n. **—re-but'ter** n.

re-cal-ci-trant (rĭ-kăl'sĭ-trənt) adj. Stubbornly resistant to authority or guidance. [< Lat. *recalcitrare*, to kick back.] **—re-cal'ci-trance** or **re-cal'ci-tran-cy** n.

re-call (rĭ-kôl') v. **1.** To call back; ask or order to return. **2.** To remember or recollect. **3.** To cancel, take back, or revoke. **4.** To bring back; restore. —n. (rĭ-kôl', rē'kôl'). **1.** The act of recalling. **2.** The ability to remember; recollection. **3.** The act of revoking. **4.** The act of removing a public official from office by popular vote. **—re-call'a-ble** adj.

re-cant (rĭ-kănt') v. To make a formal denial or disavowal of (e.g. a previously held belief.) [Lat. *recantare.*] **—re'can-ta'tion** n. **—re-cant'er** n.

re-cap¹ (rē-kăp') v. To restore (a used automobile tire) by vulcanizing and cementing new rubber onto the worn tread. —n. (rē'-kăp'). A recapped tire.

re-cap² (rē'kăp', rĭ-kăp') v. **-capped, -cap-ping.** To summarize. —n. A summary. [< RECAPITULATE.]

re-ca-pit-u-late (rē'kə-pĭch'ə-lāt') v. **-lat-ed, -lat-ing.** To repeat in concise form; summarize. [< LLat. *recapitulare.*] **—re'ca-pit'u-la'tion** n. **—re'ca-pit'u-la'tive** adj.

re-cap-ture (rē-kăp'chər) v. **1.** To capture again; retake or recover. **2.** To recall: *an attempt to recapture the past.*

re-cede (rĭ-sēd') v. **-ced-ed, -ced-ing. 1.** To move back or away; retreat. **2.** To slope backward. **3.** To become or seem to become more distant. [Lat. *recedere.*]

re-ceipt (rĭ-sēt') n. **1.** The act or fact of receiving something. **2.** receipts. The quantity or amount of something received. **3.** A written acknowledgment that specifies something has been received. **4.** *Regional.* A recipe. —v. **1.** To mark (a bill) as paid. **2.** To give a receipt for. [< Lat. *recipere*, to receive.]

re-ceiv-a-ble (rĭ-sē'və-bəl) adj. **1.** Capable of being received. **2.** Awaiting or requiring payment; due.

re-ceive (rĭ-sēv') v. **-ceived, -ceiv-ing. 1.** To take or acquire (something given, offered, or transmitted); get. **2.** To meet with; experi-

---

ă pat ā pay â care ä father ĕ pet ē be ĭ pit ī tie î pier ŏ pot ō toe ô paw, for oi noise ŏŏ took ōō boot ou out th thin th this ŭ cut û urge yōō abuse zh vision ə about, item, edible, gallop, circus

ence. **3.** To take in, hold, or contain. **4.** To greet or welcome: *receive guests.* **5.** To convert incoming electromagnetic waves into pictures or sounds. [< Lat. *recipere.*]

re·ceiv·er (rĭ-sē'vər) *n.* **1.** One that receives. **2.** A person appointed by a court to hold and administer the property of others pending litigation. **3.** A device, as part of a radio, television set, or telephone, that receives incoming electromagnetic signals and converts them into perceptible forms.

re·ceiv·er·ship (rĭ-sē'vər-shĭp') *n. Law.* **1.** The office or functions of a receiver. **2.** The condition of being held by a receiver.

re·cent (rē'sənt) *adj.* **1.** Of, belonging to, or occurring at a time immediately prior to the present. **2.** Modern; new. [Lat. *recens,* fresh.] —**re'cent·ly** *adv.* —**re'cent·ness** *n.*

re·cep·ta·cle (rĭ-sĕp'tə-kəl) *n.* **1.** A container. **2.** *Elect.* A fitting connected to a power supply and equipped to receive a plug. [< Lat. *receptare,* to receive again.]

re·cep·tion (rĭ-sĕp'shən) *n.* **1.** The act or process of receiving or being received. **2.** A welcome, greeting, or acceptance: *a favorable reception.* **3.** A social function: *a wedding reception.* **4. a.** The receiving of electromagnetic signals. **b.** The quality of the signals received. [Lat. *receptio.*]

re·cep·tion·ist (rĭ-sĕp'shə-nĭst) *n.* One employed chiefly to receive callers and answer the telephone.

re·cep·tive (rĭ-sĕp'tĭv) *adj.* **1.** Capable of receiving. **2.** Ready or willing to receive favorably. —**re·cep'tive·ly** *adv.* —**re·cep'tiv'i·ty** or **re·cep'tive·ness** *n.*

re·cep·tor (rĭ-sĕp'tər) *n.* A nerve ending specialized to sense or receive stimuli.

re·cess (rē'sĕs', rĭ-sĕs') *n.* **1. a.** A cessation of customary activities. **b.** The period of such cessation. **2.** A remote, secret, or hidden place. **3.** An indentation or small hollow. —*v.* **1.** To place in a recess. **2.** To make a recess in. **3.** To suspend for a recess. [Lat. *recessus.*]

re·ces·sion (rĭ-sĕsh'ən) *n.* **1.** The act of withdrawing. **2.** The filing out of clergy and choir members after a church service. **3.** A moderate, temporary decline in economic activity.

re·ces·sion·al (rĭ-sĕsh'ə-nəl) *n.* A hymn that accompanies the exit of the clergy and choir after a service.

re·ces·sive (rĭ-sĕs'ĭv) *adj.* **1.** Tending to go backward or recede. **2.** *Genetics.* Incapable of being manifested when occurring with a dominant form of a gene. —**re·ces'sive·ly** *adv.*

re·cid·i·vism (rĭ-sĭd'ə-vĭz'əm) *n.* A tendency to relapse into a former pattern of behavior, esp. a tendency to return to criminal habits. [< Lat. *recidere,* to fall back.] —**re·cid'i·vist** *n.* —**re·cid'i·vis'tic** *adj.*

rec·i·pe (rĕs'ə-pē) *n.* A formula for preparing something, esp. food or a medical prescription. [< Lat., imper. of *recipere,* to receive.]

re·cip·i·ent (rĭ-sĭp'ē-ənt) *n.* One that receives. [< Lat. *recipere,* to receive.]

re·cip·ro·cal (rĭ-sĭp'rə-kəl) *adj.* **1.** Given or shown in return: *reciprocal trade concessions.* **2.** Experienced, felt, or done by both sides; mutual. —*n.* **1.** Something reciprocal to something else. **2.** *Math.* Either of a pair of numbers whose product is 1. [Lat. *reciprocus,* alternating.] —**re·cip'ro·cal·ly** *adv.* —**re·cip'ro·cal·ness** *n.*

re·cip·ro·cate (rĭ-sĭp'rə-kāt') *v.* **-cat·ed, -cat·ing.** **1.** To give or take mutually; interchange. **2.** To show or feel in return. **3.** To make a return for something given or done. —**re·cip'ro·ca'tion** *n.* —**re·cip'ro·ca'tive** *adj.* —**re·cip'ro·ca'tor** *n.*

rec·i·proc·i·ty (rĕs'ə-prŏs'ĭ-tē) *n.* **1.** A reciprocal condition or relationship. **2.** A mutual exchange or interchange of favors, esp. the exchange of rights or privileges of trade between nations.

re·cit·al (rĭ-sīt'l) *n.* **1.** The act of reciting publicly. **2.** A narration. **3.** A performance of music or dance, esp. by a solo performer.

rec·i·ta·tion (rĕs'ĭ-tā'shən) *n.* **1.** The act of reciting. **2.** The oral delivery of prepared lessons by a pupil during a class period.

---

re·ra'di·ate' *v.*	re·sift' *v.*	re·tie' *v.*
re·read' *v.*	re·sol'der *v.*	re'trans·late' *v.*
re're·cord' *v.*	re·sole' *v.*	re·trav'erse *v.*
re·rise' *v.*	re·so·lid'i·fy' *v.*	re·type' *v.*
re·roll' *v.*	re·sow' *v.*	re'u·ni·fi·ca'tion *n.*
re·route' *v.*	re·spell' *v.*	re·u'ni·fy' *v.*
re·sad'dle *v.*	re·spread' *v.*	re·use' *v.*
re·sail' *v.*	re·stack' *v.*	re·u'til·ize' *v.*
re·sale *n.*	re·state' *v.*	re·ut'ter *v.*
re·sa·lute' *v.*	re·state'ment *n.*	re·val'u·ate' *v.*
re·seal' *v.*	re·stip'u·late' *v.*	re·val'u·a'tion *n.*
re·seat' *v.*	re'stip·u·la'tion *n.*	re·val'ue *v.*
re·seed' *v.*	re·stock' *v.*	re·var'nish *v.*
re·seek' *v.*	re·strength'en *v.*	re'ver·i·fi·ca'tion *n.*
re·seg're·gate' *v.*	re·string' *v.*	re·ver'i·fy' *v.*
re·seize' *v.*	re·strive' *v.*	re'vin·di·cate' *v.*
re·sei'zure *n.*	re·stud'y *n. & v.*	re·vin'di·ca'tion *n.*
re·self' *v.*	re'sub·ject' *v.*	re·vis'it *v.*
re·set' *v. & n.*	re'sub·jec'tion *n.*	re·voice' *v.*
re·set'tle *v.*	re·sum'mon *v.*	re·warm' *v.*
re·set'tle·ment *n.*	re·sum'mons *n.*	re·wash' *v.*
re·shape' *v.*	re·sup'ply' *v.*	re·weigh' *v.*
re·sharp'en *v.*	re'sur·vey' *v. & n.*	re·wind' *v.*
re·ship' *v.*	re·teach' *v.*	re·wire' *v.*
re·ship'ment *n.*	re·tell' *v.*	re·work' *v.*
re·shuf'fle *v.*	re·test' *v.*	re·zone' *v.*

rec·i·ta·tive (rĕs'ĭ-tə-tēv') *n.* 1. A musical style, used in opera and oratorio, in which the text is declaimed in the rhythm of natural speech. 2. A passage in the style of recitative. [< Lat. *recitare*, to recite.]

re·cite (rĭ-sīt') *v.* -cit·ed, -cit·ing. 1. To repeat (something rehearsed or memorized), esp. before an audience. 2. To tell in detail. [< Lat. *recitare*.] **—re·cit'er** *n.*

reck·less (rĕk'lĭs) *adj.* 1. Careless. 2. Headstrong; rash. [< OE *rēcelēas.*] **—reck'less·ly** *adv.* **—reck'less·ness** *n.*

reck·on (rĕk'ən) *v.* 1. To count or calculate. 2. To regard as. 3. *Informal.* To think or assume. [< OE *gerecenian*, to explain.]

reck·on·ing (rĕk'ə-nĭng) *n.* 1. The act of counting. 2. A statement of an amount due. 3. The calculation of the position of a ship, aircraft, etc.

re·claim (rĭ-klām') *v.* 1. To make (e.g. land) usable for growing crops or living on. 2. To extract (useful substances) from waste products. 3. To reform. [< Lat. *reclamare*, to entreat.] **—re·claim'a·ble** *adj.* **—re·claim'er** *n.* **—rec'la·ma'tion** (rĕk'lə-mā'shən) *n.*

re·cline (rĭ-klīn') *v.* -clined, -clin·ing. To assume or cause to assume a leaning or prone position. [< Lat. *reclinare*.]

rec·luse (rĕk'lōōs, rĭ-klōōs') *n.* One who lives in solitude and seclusion. [< Lat. *reclusus*, p.p. of *recludere*, to close off.] **—re·clu'sive** (-sĭv, -zĭv) *adj.*

rec·og·ni·tion (rĕk'əg-nĭsh'ən) *n.* 1. The act of recognizing or the condition of being recognized. 2. An acknowledgment, as of a claim. 3. Attention or favorable notice.

re·cog·ni·zance (rĭ-kŏg'nĭ-zəns, -kŏn'ĭ-) *n.* An obligation of record committing a person to perform a particular act, as to appear in court. **—re·cog'ni·zant** *adj.*

rec·og·nize (rĕk'əg-nīz') *v.* -nized, -niz·ing. 1. To know or identify from past experience or knowledge. 2. To acknowledge or accept. 3. To approve of or appreciate: *recognize services rendered.* [< Lat. *recognoscere.*] **—rec'og·niz'a·ble** *adj.* **—rec'og·niz'a·bly** *adv.*

re·coil (rĭ-koil') *v.* 1. To move or jerk back, as a gun upon firing. 2. To shrink back in fear or dislike. [< OFr. *reculer.*] **—re·coil'** (rē'koil', rĭ-koil') *n.* **—re·coil'er** *n.*

rec·ol·lect (rĕk'ə-lĕkt') *v.* To recall to mind; remember. [< Lat. *recolligere*, to gather up.] **—rec'ol·lec'tion** *n.*

re·com·bi·nant DNA (rē-kŏm'bĭ-nənt) *n.* DNA that has been artificially prepared by combining DNA fragments from different species.

re·com·bi·na·tion (rē-kŏm'bĭ-nā'shən) *n.* The formation in offspring of genetic combinations not present in parents.

rec·om·mend (rĕk'ə-mĕnd') *v.* 1. To commend to another as worthy or desirable; endorse. 2. To advise or counsel. 3. To make attractive or acceptable. [< Med. Lat. *recommendare.*] **—rec'om·mend'a·ble** *adj.* **—rec'om·men·da'tion** *n.*

rec·om·pense (rĕk'əm-pĕns') *v.* -pensed, -pens·ing. To give as compensation to or for. **—n.** 1. Amends made for damage, loss, etc. 2. Payment in return for services. [< LLat. *recompensare.*]

rec·on·cile (rĕk'ən-sīl') *v.* -ciled, -cil·ing. 1. To restore friendship between. 2. To settle, as a dispute. 3. To bring (oneself) to accept. 4. To make compatible or consistent: *reconcile different points of view.* [< Lat. *reconciliare.*] **—rec'on·cil'a·bil'i·ty** *n.* **—rec'on·cil'a·ble** *adj.* **—rec'on·cile'ment** or **rec'on·cil'i·a'tion** (-sĭl'ē-ā'shən) *n.* **—rec'on·cil'er** *n.* **—rec'on·cil'i·a·to'ry** (-sĭl'ē-ə-tôr'ē, -tōr'ē) *adj.*

rec·on·dite (rĕk'ən-dīt', rĭ-kŏn'dīt') *adj.* 1. Abstruse. 2. Concealed; hidden. [Lat. *reconditus*, p.p. of *recondere*, to put away.] **—rec'on·dite'ly** *adv.* **—rec'on·dite'ness** *n.*

re·con·nais·sance (rĭ-kŏn'ə-səns, -zəns) *n.* An inspection or exploration of an area, esp. one made to gather military information. [< OFr.]

re·con·noi·ter (rē'kə-noi'tər, rĕk'ə-) *v.* To make a preliminary survey or inspection (of). [< OFr. *reconnoistre*, to recognize.] **—re'con·noi'ter·er** *n.*

re·con·sid·er (rē'kən-sĭd'ər) *v.* To consider again, esp. with intent to modify a previous decision. **—re'con·sid·er·a'tion** *n.*

re·con·struct (rē'kən-strŭkt') *v.* To construct again; restore.

re·con·struc·tion (rē'kən-strŭk'shən) *n.* 1. The act or result of reconstructing. 2. **Reconstruction.** The period (1865–77) during which the Confederate states were controlled by the federal government before being readmitted to the Union.

rec·ord (rĕk'ərd) *n.* 1. A written account of events or facts. 2. Something on which such an account is made. 3. Information on a particular subject collected and preserved: *the coldest day on record.* 4. The known history of performance. 5. The best performance known, as in a sport. 6. A disk structurally coded to reproduce sound; phonograph record. **—v.** *re·cord* (rĭ-kôrd'). 1. To set down for preservation in a record. 2. To register or indicate. 3. To register (sound) in permanent form on a record or a tape. **—idioms. off the record.** Not for publication. **on record.** Known to have taken or stated a certain position. [< Lat. *recordari*, to remember.]

re·cord·er (rĭ-kôr'dər) *n.* 1. One that records: *a tape recorder.* 2. A flute with eight finger holes and a whistlelike mouthpiece.

re·cord·ing (rĭ-kôr'dĭng) *n.* Something on which sound is recorded, as a magnetic tape or phonograph record.

re·count (rĭ-kount') *v.* To narrate the facts or particulars of; tell in detail. [< OFr. *reconter.*]

re·count (rē-kount') *v.* To count again. **—n.** (rē'kount', rē-kount'). A second count, as of votes.

re·coup (rĭ-kōōp') *v.* 1. To receive an equivalent for. 2. To reimburse. 3. To regain. [< OFr. *recouper*, to cut back.]

re·course (rē'kôrs', -kōrs', rĭ-kôrs', -kōrs') *n.* 1. A turning or applying to a person or thing for aid or protection. 2. One that is turned to for help or support. [< Lat. *recursus*, a running back.]

re·cov·er (rĭ-kŭv'ər) *v.* 1. To get back; regain. 2. To regain a normal or usual condition, as of health. 3. To receive a favorable judgment in a lawsuit. [< Lat. *recuperare.*] **—re·cov'er·a·ble** *adj.* **—re·cov'er·y** *n.*

Syns: recover, mend, rally, recuperate v.

rec·re·ant (rĕk'rē-ənt) *adj.* **1.** Unfaithful. **2.** Craven or cowardly. —*n.* **1.** A disloyal person. **2.** A coward. [< OFr. *recroire*, to remember.]

rec·re·ate (rĕk'rē-āt') *v.* **-at·ed, -at·ing.** To refresh mentally or physically. [< Lat. *recreare.*]

re·cre·ate (rē'krē-āt') *v.* To create again or anew. —**re'·cre·a'tion** *n.*

rec·re·a·tion (rĕk'rē-ā'shən) *n.* Refreshment of one's mind or body through some activity that amuses or stimulates; play. —**rec're·a'tion·al** *adj.*

re·crim·i·nate (rĭ-krĭm'ə-nāt') *v.* **-nat·ed, -nat·ing.** To counter one accusation with another. [Med. Lat. *recriminare.*] —**re·crim'i·na'tion** *n.*

re·cru·desce (rē'krōō-dĕs') *v.* **-desced, -desc·ing.** To break out anew after a dormant or inactive period, as a disease. [Lat. *recrudescere.*] —**re'cru·des'cence** *n.* —**re'cru·des'cent** *adj.*

re·cruit (rĭ-krōōt') *v.* **1.** To seek out and engage (persons) for work or service. **2.** To strengthen or raise (an armed force). **3.** To renew or restore (health or vitality). —*n.* A newly engaged member of a military force or organization. [< OFr. *recroistre,* to grow again.] —**re·cruit'er** *n.* —**re·cruit'ment** *n.*

rec·tan·gle (rĕk'tăng'gəl) *n.* A parallelogram with an angle of 90°. [Med. Lat. *rectangulum.*] —**rec·tan'gu·lar** *adj.* —**rec·tan'gu·lar·i·ty** (-lăr'ĭ-tē) *n.* —**rec·tan'gu·lar·ly** *adv.*

rec·ti·fy (rĕk'tə-fī') *v.* **-fied, -fy·ing.** To set right; correct. [< Med. Lat. *rectificare.*] —**rec'ti·fi·ca'tion** *n.* —**rec'ti·fi'er** *n.*

rec·ti·lin·e·ar (rĕk'tə-lĭn'ē-ər) *adj.* Moving in, bounded by, or characterized by a straight line or lines. [< LLat. *rectilineus.*]

rec·ti·tude (rĕk'tĭ-tōōd', -tyōōd') *n.* Moral uprightness. [< LLat. *rectitudo.*]

rec·to (rĕk'tō) *n., pl.* **-tos.** A right-hand page. [Lat. *recto (folio),* (the page) being right.]

rec·tor (rĕk'tər) *n.* **1.** A clergyman in charge of a parish. **2.** *Rom. Cath. Ch.* A priest serving as head of a seminary or university. **3.** The principal of certain schools, colleges, or universities. [Lat., director.]

rec·to·ry (rĕk'tə-rē) *n., pl.* **-ries.** A rector's dwelling.

rec·tum (rĕk'təm) *n., pl.* **-tums** or **-ta** (-tə). The lower end of the alimentary canal, extending from the colon to the anus. [NLat. *rectum (intestinum),* straight (intestine).] —**rec'tal** *adj.*

re·cum·bent (rĭ-kŭm'bənt) *adj.* Lying down; reclining. [< Lat. *recumbere,* to lie down.]

re·cu·per·ate (rĭ-kōō'pə-rāt', -kyōō'-) *v.* **-at·ed, -at·ing.** To return to health or strength; recover. **2.** To recover from a loss. [Lat. *recuperare.*] —**re·cu'per·a'tion** *n.* —**re·cu'per·a·tive** (-pə-rā'tĭv, -pər-ə-tĭv) *adj.*

re·cur (rĭ-kûr') *v.* **-curred, -cur·ring.** To happen, come up, or show up again or repeatedly. [Lat. *recurrere.*] —**re·cur'rence** *n.* —**re·cur'rent** *adj.* —**re·cur'rent·ly** *adv.*

red (rĕd) *n.* **1.** Any of a group of colors whose hue resembles that of blood. **2.** A red pigment or dye. **3.** Often **Red.** A revolutionary, esp. a Communist. —*adj.* **red·der, red·dest. 1.** Of the color red. **2.** Being or having distinctive parts that are reddish in color: *a red fox.* **3.** Ruddy or flushed in complexion. **4.** Often **Red.** **a.** Revolutionary. **b.** Of, directed by, or favoring Communists. —*idiom.*

in the red. Operating at a loss; in debt. [< OE *rēad.*] —**red'ness** *n.*

red blood cell *n.* Any of the cells in the blood, disk-shaped and lacking nuclei, that contain hemoglobin and give the blood its red color.

red-blood·ed (rĕd'blŭd'ĭd) *adj.* Strong or virile. —**red'-blood'ed·ness** *n.*

red·breast (rĕd'brĕst') *n.* A bird with a red breast, esp. the robin.

red·coat (rĕd'kōt') *n.* A British soldier during the American Revolution and the War of 1812.

red·den (rĕd'n) *v.* To make or become red.

red·dish (rĕd'ĭsh) *adj.* Mixed or tinged with red; somewhat red. —**red'dish·ness** *n.*

re·deem (rĭ-dēm') *v.* **1.** To recover ownership of by paying a specified sum. **2.** To pay off, as a promissory note. **3.** To turn in (e.g. coupons or trading stamps) and receive something in exchange. **4.** To set free; rescue. **5.** To save from sin. **6.** To make up for: *redeemed his earlier mistake.* [< Lat. *redimere.*] —**re·deem'a·ble** *adj.* —**re·deem'er** *n.*

re·demp·tion (rĭ-dĕmp'shən) *n.* The act of redeeming or the condition of being redeemed. [< Lat. *redimere,* to redeem.] —**re·demp'tion·al** or **re·demp'tive** *adj.*

red-hand·ed (rĕd'hăn'dĭd) *adv. & adj.* In the act of doing or having just done something wrong: *caught red-handed.*

red·head (rĕd'hĕd') *n.* A person with red hair.

red herring *n.* Something that draws attention away from the subject under notice or discussion. [< the use of red herring to distract hunting dogs from the scent.]

red-hot (rĕd'hŏt') *adj.* **1.** Glowing hot; very hot. **2.** New; recent: *red-hot information.*

re·dis·trict (rē-dĭs'trĭkt) *v.* To divide again, as into administrative or election districts.

red-let·ter (rĕd'lĕt'ər) *adj.* Memorably happy: *a red-letter day.* [< the use of red letters to mark feast days in church calendars.]

red·o·lent (rĕd'l-ənt) *adj.* **1.** Having or emitting a pleasant odor; scented. **2.** Suggestive; reminiscent: *an administration redolent of machine politics.* [< Lat. *redolēre,* to smell.] —**red'o·lence** *n.*

re·doubt (rĭ-dout') *n.* A defensive fortification. [< Med. Lat. *reductus,* concealed place.]

re·doubt·a·ble (rĭ-dou'tə-bəl) *adj.* **1.** Awesome; formidable. **2.** Worthy of respect or honor. [< OFr. *redouter,* to dread.] —**re·doubt'a·bly** *adv.*

re·dound (rĭ-dound') *v.* **1.** To have an effect or consequence. **2.** To contribute; accrue. [< Lat. *redundare,* to overflow.]

re·dress (rĭ-drĕs') *v.* **1.** To set right; remedy or rectify. **2.** To make amends for. —*n.* (rē'drĕs', rĭ-drĕs') **1.** Satisfaction for wrong done; reparation. **2.** Correction. [< OFr. *redresser.*]

red snapper *n.* Any of several marine food fishes with red or reddish bodies.

red tape *n.* Official forms and procedures, esp. when needlessly complex and time-consuming. [< its former use in tying British official documents.]

red tide *n.* Ocean waters colored by the proliferation of red, one-celled, plantlike animals in sufficient numbers to kill fish.

re·duce (rĭ-dōōs', -dyōōs') v. **-duced, -duc·ing.** **1.** To lessen in extent, amount, number, degree, or price; diminish. **2.** To gain control of; conquer. **3.** To put in order systematically. **4.** To separate into orderly components by analysis. **5.** To bring to a certain condition: *reduce marble to dust.* **6.** *Chem.* **a.** To decrease the valence of (an atom) by adding electrons. **b.** To deoxidize. **c.** To add hydrogen to. **d.** To change to a metallic state; smelt. **7.** To lose weight, as by dieting. [< Lat. *reducere,* to bring back.] **—re·duc'er** n. **—re·duc'i·bil'i·ty** n. **—re·duc'i·ble** adj. **—re·duc'i·bly** adv. **—re·duc'tion** (-dŭk'shən) n. **—re·duc'tive** adj.

re·dun·dant (rĭ-dŭn'dənt) adj. **1.** Exceeding what is necessary or natural; superfluous. **2.** Needlessly repetitive; verbose. [< Lat. *redundare,* to overflow.] **—re·dun'dan·cy** n. **—re·dun'dant·ly** adv.

re·du·pli·cate (rĭ-dōō'plĭ-kāt', -dyōō'-) v. **-cat·ed, -cat·ing.** *Ling.* To double (the initial syllable or all of a root word) to form a new word. [LLat. *reduplicare.*] **—re·du'pli·ca'tion** n. **—re·du'pli·ca'tive** adj.

red·wood (rĕd'wōōd') n. **1.** A very tall evergreen tree of coastal California. **2.** The soft, reddish wood of this tree.

reed (rēd) n. **1.** Any of several tall, hollow-stemmed swamp or marsh grasses. **2.** a. A strip of cane or metal, used in the mouthpiece of certain instruments, that produces tone by vibration. **b.** A woodwind instrument played with a reed. [< OE *hrēod.*] adj. **—reed'i·ness** n. **—reed'y** adj.

reef¹ (rēf) n. A strip or ridge of rocks, sand, or coral at or near the surface of water. [MDu. *rif,* poss. < ON, ridge.]

reef² (rēf) n. A portion of a sail rolled and tied down to lessen the area exposed to the wind. **—v.** To reduce the size of (a sail) by tucking in a part. [< ON *rif,* ridge.]

reef·er (rē'fər) n. *Slang.* A marijuana cigarette. [Prob. < REEF².]

reek (rēk) v. **1.** To smoke, steam, or fume. **2.** To be pervaded by something unpleasant. **3.** To give off a strong and unpleasant odor. **—n.** **1.** A stench. **2.** Vapor; steam. [< OE *rēocan.*]

reel¹ (rēl) n. **1.** A cylinder, spool, or frame that turns on an axis and is used for winding rope, tape, etc. **2.** The quantity of material wound on one reel. **3.** a. A fast dance of Scottish origin. **b.** The music for this dance. **—v.** **1.** To wind upon a reel. **2.** To recover by

reel¹

winding on a reel: *reel in a marlin.* [< OE *hrēol.*]

reel² (rēl) v. **1.** To be thrown off balance or fall back. **2.** To stagger or lurch, as from drunkenness. **3.** To be in a confused condition. [ME *relen.*]

re·en·try or **re·en·try** (rē-ĕn'trē) n., pl. **-tries.** **1.** The act of re-entering. **2.** The return of a missile or spacecraft into the earth's atmosphere.

re·fec·to·ry (rĭ-fĕk'tə-rē) n., pl. **-ries.** A room where meals are served. [LLat. *refectorium.*]

re·fer (rĭ-fûr') v. **-ferred, -fer·ring.** **1.** To direct to a source for help or information. **2.** To assign or attribute. **3.** To direct the attention of. **4.** To pertain; apply. **5.** To allude or make reference. [< Lat. *referre.*] **—ref·er·a·ble** (rĕf'ər-ə-bəl, rĭ-fûr'-) adj. **—re·fer'ral** n.

ref·er·ee (rĕf'ə-rē') n. **1.** One to whom something is referred for settlement; arbitrator. **2.** *Sports.* An official who supervises play and enforces the rules. **—v.** **-reed, -ree·ing.** To act as referee.

ref·er·ence (rĕf'ər-əns, rĕf'rəns) n. **1.** An act of referring. **2.** Relation; regard; respect. **3.** An allusion or mention. **4.** A note in a publication directing the reader to another source of information. **5.** a. One who is in a position to recommend another, as for a job. **b.** A statement about a person's character or qualifications.

ref·er·en·dum (rĕf'ə-rĕn'dəm) n., pl. **-dums** or **-da** (-də). **1.** The submission of a proposed public measure or actual statute to a direct popular vote. **2.** Such a vote. [Lat., thing to be referred.]

re·fill (rē-fĭl') v. To fill again. **—n.** (rē'fĭl'). **1.** A replacement for the used contents of a container. **2.** A second or subsequent filling. **—re·fill'a·ble** adj.

re·fine (rĭ-fīn') v. **-fined, -fin·ing.** **1.** To reduce to a pure state; purify. **2.** To free from coarse characteristics. **3.** To improve. [RE- + *fine,* to make pure.] **—re·fin'er** n.

re·fined (rĭ-fīnd') adj. **1.** Free from coarseness or vulgarity. **2.** Free of impurities. **3.** Precise to a fine degree; exact.

Syns: *refined, cultivated, cultured, urbane, well-bred* adj.

re·fine·ment (rĭ-fīn'mənt) n. **1.** a. An act of refining. **b.** The condition of being refined. **2.** An improvement. **3.** Fineness of thought or expression. **4.** A subtle distinction.

re·fin·er·y (rĭ-fī'nə-rē) n., pl. **-ies.** An industrial plant for purifying a crude substance, such as petroleum.

re·flect (rĭ-flĕkt') v. **1.** To throw or bend back (e.g. light) from a surface. **2.** To mirror or be mirrored. **3.** To reveal as through a mirror; manifest. **4.** To think or consider seriously. **5.** To bring blame or discredit. [< Lat. *reflectere,* to bend back.] **—re·flec'tion** n. **—re·flec'tive** adj. **—re·flec'tive·ly** adv.

re·flec·tor (rĭ-flĕk'tər) n. One that reflects, esp. a surface that reflects radiation.

re·flex (rē'flĕks') adj. **1.** Turned, thrown, or bent backward. **2.** Involuntary: *a reflex neural response.* **—n.** **1.** Reflection or an image produced by reflection. **2.** An involuntary, unlearned, or instinctive response to a stimulus. [Lat. *reflexus,* p.p. of *reflectere,* to reflect.]

re·flex·ive (rǐ-flěk'sǐv) *adj. Gram.* **1.** Designating a verb having an identical subject and direct object, as *dressed* in the sentence *She dressed herself.* **2.** Designating the pronoun used as the direct object. **—re·flex'ive** *n.* **—re·flex'ive·ly** *adv.* **—re·flex'ive·ness** *or* **re·flex·iv'i·ty** *n.*

re·for·est (rē-fôr'ĭst, -fŏr'-) *v.* To replant with trees. **—re·for'es·ta'tion** *n.*

re·form (rǐ-fôrm') *v.* **1.** To improve by correction of error or removal of defects. **2.** To abolish abuse or malpractice in. **3.** To give up irresponsible or immoral practices. *—n.* **1.** An act, process, or example of reforming; improvement. **2.** A movement that attempts to institute reform without revolutionary change. **3.** Moral improvement. [< Lat. *reformare.*] **—re·form'a·ble** *adj.* **—re·for'ma·tive** *adj.* **—re·formed'** *adj.* **—re·form'er** *n.*

ref·or·ma·tion (rěf'ər-mā'shən) *n.* **1.** The act of reforming or condition of being reformed. **2. Reformation.** The political and religious rebellion in 16th-cent. Europe that resulted in the separation of the Protestant churches from the Roman Catholic Church. **—ref'or·ma'tion·al** *adj.*

re·for·ma·to·ry (rǐ-fôr'mə-tôr'ē, -tōr'ē) *n., pl.* **-ries.** A penal institution for young offenders.

re·fract (rǐ-frăkt') *v.* To deflect by refraction. [< Lat. *refractus,* p.p. of *refringere,* to break off.]

re·frac·tion (rǐ-frăk'shən) *n.* The bending or deflection of the path of a wave, as of light or sound, as it passes between mediums with different characteristics. **—re·frac'tive** *adj.* **—re·frac'tive·ly** *adv.* **—re·frac'tive·ness** *or* **re·frac·tiv'i·ty** (rē'frăk-tǐv'ĭ-tē) *n.*

re·frac·to·ry (rǐ-frăk'tə-rē) *adj.* **1.** Obstinate; unmanageable. **2.** Difficult to melt, refine, shape, or work. *—n., pl.* **-ries.** Any of various heat-resistant materials, such as alumina, silica, or magnesite. **—re·frac'to·ri·ly** *adv.* **—re·frac'to·ri·ness** *n.*

re·frain¹ (rǐ-frān') *v.* To hold oneself back; forbear: *refrain from singing.* [< Lat. *refrenare,* to restrain.]

re·frain² (rǐ-frān') *n.* A phrase or verse repeated at intervals throughout a song or poem. [< OFr. *refraindre,* to resound.]

re·fresh (rǐ-frěsh') *v.* **1.** To revive or become revived with or as if with rest, food, or drink. **2.** To make cool, clean, or damp; freshen. **3.** To rouse; stimulate: *refresh one's memory.* **—re·fresh'er** *n.* **—re·fresh'ing** *adj.* **—re·fresh'ing·ly** *adv.*

re·fresh·ment (rǐ-frěsh'mənt) *n.* **1.** The act of refreshing or condition of being refreshed. **2.** Something that refreshes. **3. refreshments.** A light meal or snack.

re·frig·er·ant (rǐ-frǐj'ər-ənt) *n.* A substance, such as air, ammonia, water, or carbon dioxide, used to produce refrigeration.

re·frig·er·ate (rǐ-frǐj'ə-rāt') *v.* **-at·ed, -at·ing.** **1.** To cool or chill (a substance). **2.** To preserve (food) by chilling. [Lat. *refrigerare.*] **—re·frig'er·a'tion** *n.*

re·frig·er·a·tor (rǐ-frǐj'ə-rā'tər) *n.* A cabinet used for refrigerating and freezing food.

ref·uge (rěf'yōōj) *n.* **1.** Protection or shelter, as from danger or hardship. **2.** A haven or sanctuary. [< Lat. *refugium.*]

ref·u·gee (rěf'yōō-jē') *n.* One who flees to find refuge from oppression or persecution.

re·ful·gent (rǐ-fŏŏl'jənt, -fŭl'-) *adj.* Shining radiantly; brilliant. [< Lat. *refulgēre,* to shine.] **—re·ful'gence** *n.*

re·fund (rǐ-fŭnd', rē'fŭnd') *v.* To return or repay; give back. *—n.* (rē'fŭnd'). **1.** A repayment of funds. **2.** The amount repaid. [< Lat. *refundere,* to pour back.] **—re·fund'a·ble** *adj.*

re·fur·bish (rē-fûr'bǐsh) *v.* To make clean, bright, or fresh again. **—re·fur'bish·ment** *n.*

re·fuse¹ (rǐ-fyōōz') *v.* **-fused, -fus·ing.** To decline to do, accept, allow, or give. [< Lat. *refusus,* p.p. of *refundere,* to pour back.] **—re·fus'al** *n.*

ref·use² (rěf'yōōs) *n.* Anything discarded or rejected as useless or worthless; trash; rubbish. [< OFr. *refus,* rejection.]

re·fute (rǐ-fyōōt') *v.* **-fut·ed, -fut·ing.** To prove to be false or erroneous; disprove. [Lat. *refutare.*] **—re·fut'a·ble** *adj.* **—re·fut'a·bly** *adv.* **—re·fut'er** *n.*

re·gain (rē-gān') *v.* **1.** To get back again. **2.** To reach again.

re·gal (rē'gəl) *adj.* Of or befitting a king; royal. [< Lat. *regalis.*] **—re'gal·ly** *adv.*

re·gale (rǐ-gāl') *v.* **-galed, -gal·ing.** **1.** To delight or entertain. **2.** To entertain sumptuously. [< OFr. *regaler.*]

re·ga·lia (rǐ-gāl'yə) *n.* (*used with a sing. or pl. verb).* **1.** The emblems and symbols of royalty. **2.** The distinguishing symbols of a rank, office, etc. **3.** Magnificent or fancy attire; finery. [< Lat. *regalis,* of a king.]

re·gard (rǐ-gärd') *v.* **1.** To look at attentively; watch. **2.** To look upon or consider: *I regard him as a fool.* **3.** To have great affection or admiration for. **4.** To have reference to; concern. *—n.* **1.** A look or gaze. **2.** Careful thought or attention; concern; heed. **3.** Respect, favor, or esteem. **4. regards.** Good wishes: *send one's regards.* **5.** Reference or relation: *in regard to this case.* **6.** A particular point: *I agree in this regard.* [< OFr. *regarder.*] **—re·gard'ful** *adj.* **—re·gard'ful·ly** *adv.*

Usage: *Regard* is traditionally used as a singular in the phrase *in* (or *with) regard* (not *regards) to.*

re·gard·ing (rǐ-gär'dǐng) *prep.* In reference to; concerning.

re·gard·less (rǐ-gärd'lǐs) *adj.* Heedless; unmindful: *regardless of the consequences.* *—adv.* In spite of everything; anyway: *She loved him regardless.* **—re·gard'less·ly** *adv.*

re·gat·ta (rǐ-gä'tə, -gä'tə) *n.* A boat race or an organized series of boat races. [Ital.]

re·gen·cy (rē'jən-sē) *n., pl.* **-cies.** **1.** The office, area of jurisdiction, or government of a regent or regents. **2.** The period during which a regent governs.

re·gen·er·ate (rǐ-jěn'ə-rāt') *v.* **-at·ed, -at·ing.** **1.** To reform spiritually or morally. **2.** To form, construct, or create anew. *—adj.* (-ər-ĭt). **1.** Spiritually or morally revitalized. **2.** Restored; refreshed. **—re·gen'er·a'tion** *n.* **—re·gen'er·a'tive** **—re·gen'er·a'tor** *n.*

re·gent (rē'jənt) *n.* **1.** One who rules during the minority, absence, or disability of a sovereign. **2.** One serving on a governing board, as of a state university. [< Lat. *regere,* to rule.] **—re'gent** *adj.*

reg·i·cide (rěj'ĭ-sīd') *n.* **1.** The killing of a king. **2.** One who kills a king. [Lat. *rex,* king + -CIDE.] **—reg'i·cid'al** (-sīd'l) *adj.*

re·gime (rā-zhēm', rǐ-) *n.* **1.** A government in power; administration. **2.** A regimen. [< Lat. *regimen,* government.]

reg·i·men (rĕj′ə-mən, -mĕn′) n. 1. Governmental rule or control. 2. A system of therapy or course of treatment. [< Lat.]

reg·i·ment (rĕj′ə-mənt) n. A military unit of ground troops consisting of at least two battalions. —v. (-mĕnt′). 1. To put into order; systematize. 2. To force uniformity and discipline upon. [< LLat. regimentum, rule.] —reg′i·men′tal (-mĕn′tl) adj. —reg′i·men′tal·ly adv. —reg′i·men·ta′tion n.

regiment
Soldiers storming Fort Wagner on
July 18, 1863

re·gion (rē′jən) n. 1. A large, usu. continuous segment of a surface or space; area. 2. A section or area of the body: the abdominal region. [< Lat. regere, to direct.]

re·gion·al (rē′jə-nəl) adj. 1. Of, relating to, or characteristic of a large geographic area. 2. Of, relating to, or characteristic of a particular region. —re′gion·al·ly adv.

reg·is·ter (rĕj′ĭ-stər) n. 1. a. A formal or official recording of items, names, or actions. b. A book for such entries. 2. A device that automatically records or displays a quantity or number: a cash register. 3. A grill-like device through which heated or cooled air is released into a room. 4. The range or part of a range of an instrument or voice. —v. 1. To record officially. 2. To indicate, as on a scale. 3. To show; reveal: a face that registers no emotion. 4. To cause (mail) to be officially recorded by payment of a fee. 5. To have one's name officially placed on a list of eligible voters. [< LLat. regesta.] —reg′is·tra·ble (-strə-bəl) adj.

registered nurse n. A graduate trained nurse who has passed a state registration exam.

reg·is·trar (rĕj′ĭ-strär′, rĕj′ĭ-strär′) n. An official of a college or corporation who keeps records.

reg·is·tra·tion (rĕj′ĭ-strā′shən) n. 1. The act or process of registering. 2. The number of persons or things registered; enrollment. 3. A document certifying registration.

reg·is·try (rĕj′ĭ-strē) n., pl. -tries. 1. Registration. 2. A place where registers are kept.

re·gress (rĭ-grĕs′) v. To go back; return, esp. to a previous condition. —n. (rē′grĕs′). Return or withdrawal. [< Lat. regressus, p.p. of regredi, to go back.] —re·gres′sive adj.

re·gres·sion (rĭ-grĕsh′ən) n. 1. Backward movement. 2. Relapse to a less perfect or developed state.

re·gret (rĭ-grĕt′) v. -gret·ted, -gret·ting. 1. To feel sorry, disappointed, or distressed about.

2. To mourn. —n. 1. Distress over a desire unfulfilled or an action performed or not performed. 2. An expression of grief or disappointment. 3. regrets. A polite refusal of an invitation. [< OFr. regretter, to lament.] —re·gret′ful adj. —re·gret′ful·ly adv. —re·gret′ful·ness n. —re·gret′ta·ble adj. —re·gret′ta·bly adv.

reg·u·lar (rĕg′yə-lər) adj. 1. Customary, usual, or normal. 2. Orderly or symmetrical. 3. Conforming to set procedure, principle, or discipline. 4. Methodical; well-ordered. 5. Evenly spaced; periodic. 6. Constant; not varying. 7. Formally correct; proper. 8. Complete; thorough: a regular villain. 9. Informal. Good; nice: a regular guy. 10. Gram. Belonging to a standard mode of inflection or conjugation. 11. Geom. a. Having equal sides and angles. b. Having faces that are congruent regular polygons and congruent polyhedral angles. 12. Belonging to or constituting the permanent army of a nation. —n. A soldier belonging to a regular army. [< Lat. regularis, according to rule.] —reg′u·lar′i·ty (rĕg′yə-lăr′ĭ-tē) n. —reg′u·lar·ly adv.

reg·u·late (rĕg′yə-lāt′) v. -lat·ed, -lat·ing. 1. To control or direct according to a rule. 2. To adjust or control (e.g. a flow) so as to remain within certain limits: regulate traffic. 3. To adjust for accurate and proper functioning. [LLat. regulare.] —reg′u·la′tive adj. —reg′u·la′tor n. —reg′u·la·to′ry (-lə-tôr′ē, -tōr′ē) adj.

reg·u·la·tion (rĕg′yə-lā′shən) n. 1. The act of regulating. 2. A principle, rule, or law designed to govern behavior. 3. A governmental order having the force of law.

re·gur·gi·tate (rē-gûr′jĭ-tāt′) v. -tat·ed, -tat·ing. To surge back, esp. to cast up (partially digested food); vomit. [Med. Lat. regurgitare.] —re·gur′gi·ta′tion n.

re·ha·bil·i·tate (rē′hĭ-bĭl′ĭ-tāt′) v. -tat·ed, -tat·ing. 1. To restore to useful life through education and therapy. 2. To reinstate the good name or former rank of. [Med. Lat. rehabilitare.] —re′ha·bil′i·ta′tion n. —re′ha·bil′i·ta′tive adj.

re·hash (rē-hăsh′) v. To repeat, rework, or rewrite: rehashed their old disagreement. —re′hash′ n.

re·hears·al (rĭ-hûr′səl) n. 1. The act or process of rehearsing, esp. in preparation for a public performance. 2. A session devoted to rehearsing.

re·hearse (rĭ-hûrs′) v. -hearsed, -hears·ing. 1. To practice in preparation for a public performance. 2. To train and prepare by means of rehearsals. 3. To retell or recite. [< OFr. rehercer, to repeat.]

reign (rān) n. 1. a. The exercise of sovereign power. b. The term during which sovereignty is held. 2. Dominance or prevalence: the reign of reason. —v. 1. To exercise sovereignty. 2. To be prevalent. [< Lat. regnum.]

re·im·burse (rē′ĭm-bûrs′) v. -bursed, -burs·ing. To pay back. [RE- + obs. imburse, to pay.] —re′im·burse′ment n.

rein (rān) n. 1. Often reins. A long, narrow leather strap attached to the bit of a bridle and used by a rider or driver to control a horse or other animal. 2. Means of guidance, restraint, or control. —v. 1. To check or hold back. **2.** To guide or control. —*Idiom.* **give (tree) rein to.** To release from restraints. [< Lat. *retinēre*, to retain.]

re·in·car·nate (rē'ĭn-kär'nāt') *v.* **-nat·ed, -nat·ing.** To be reborn in another body. —**re·in'-car·na'tion** *n.*

rein·deer (rān'dîr') *n.* A large deer of arctic regions, with branched antlers. [< ON *hreindȳri.*]

re·in·force (rē'ĭn-fôrs', -fōrs') *v.* **-forced, -forc·ing. 1.** To strengthen; support. **2.** To strengthen with additional troops or equipment. [RE- + *inforce,* var. of ENFORCE.] —**re'in·force'ment** *n.*

re·in·state (rē'ĭn-stāt') *v.* **-stat·ed, -stat·ing.** To restore to a previous condition or position. —**re'in·state'ment** *n.*

re·it·er·ate (rē-ĭt'ə-rāt') *v.* To say over again; repeat. —**re·it'er·a'tion** *n.* —**re·it'er·a'tive** *adj.*

re·ject (rĭ-jĕkt') *v.* **1.** To be unwilling to accept, recognize, or make use of; repudiate. **2.** To refuse to grant; deny. **3.** To throw out; discard. —*n.* (rē'jĕkt'). One that has been rejected. [< Lat. *rejectus,* p.p. of *reicere,* to throw back.] —**re·jec'tion** *n.*

Syns: reject, decline, dismiss, refuse, spurn *v.*

re·joice (rĭ-jois') *v.* **-joiced, -joic·ing.** To feel or be joyful. [< OFr. *rejoir.*] —**re·joic'er** *n.*

re·join (rĭ-join') *v.* To respond; answer. [< OFr. *rejoindre.*]

re·join (rĭ-join') *v.* To come or join together again.

re·join·der (rĭ-join'dər) *n.* An answer, esp. in response to a reply. [< OFr. *rejoindre,* to answer.]

re·ju·ve·nate (rĭ-jŏŏ'və-nāt') *v.* **-nat·ed, -nat·ing.** To restore the youthful vigor or appearance of. [RE- + Lat. *juvenis,* a youth.] —**re·ju've·na'tion** *n.*

re·lapse (rĭ-lăps') *v.* **-lapsed, -laps·ing.** To fall back or revert to a former state, esp. to regress after partial recovery from an illness. —*n.* (rē'lăps', rĭ-lăps'). The act or result of relapsing. [< Lat. *relapsus,* p.p. of *relabi,* to slide back.]

re·late (rĭ-lāt') *v.* **-lat·ed, -lat·ing. 1.** To narrate or tell. **2.** To bring into logical or natural association. **3.** To have connection, relation, or reference. **4.** *Informal.* To interact with others in a meaningful way. [< Lat. *relatus,* p.p. of *referre,* to refer.]

re·lat·ed (rĭ-lā'tĭd) *adj.* **1.** Connected; associated. **2.** Connected by kinship, marriage, or common origin.

re·la·tion (rĭ-lā'shən) *n.* **1.** A logical or natural association between two or more things. **2.** The connection of people by blood or marriage; kinship. **3.** A relative. **4. relations.** Dealings or associations with others: *social relations; diplomatic relations.* **5.** Reference; regard. **6.** The act of telling or narrating. —**re·la'tion·ship'** *n.*

rel·a·tive (rĕl'ə-tĭv) *adj.* **1.** Relevant; connected; related. **2.** Considered in comparison to or dependent on something else. **3.** *Gram.* Referring to or qualifying an antecedent. —*n.* **1. a.** A person related by kinship. **b.** A thing related to or connected with another. **2.** *Gram.* A relative term. —**rel'a·tive·ly** *adv.* —**rel'a·tive·ness** *n.*

relative clause *n.* A dependent clause introduced by a relative pronoun.

relative humidity *n.* The ratio of the amount of water vapor in the air at a specific temper-

ature to the maximum capacity of the air at that temperature.

rel·a·tiv·i·ty (rĕl'ə-tĭv'ĭ-tē) *n.* **1.** The condition or quality of being relative. **2.** *Physics.* **a.** Special relativity. **b.** General relativity.

re·lax (rĭ-lăks') *v.* **1.** To make or become less tight. **2.** To make or become less severe or strict. **3.** To relieve from effort or strain. **4.** To take one's ease; rest. **5.** To become less formal, aloof, or tense. [< Lat. *relaxare.*] —**re'lax·a'tion** *n.* —**re·lax'er** *n.*

re·lay (rē'lā', rĭ-lā') *n.* **1.** A fresh team or crew to relieve others in work, a journey, etc. **2.** The act of relaying. **3.** A relay race. **4.** A device that responds to a small current or voltage change by activating switches or other devices in an electric circuit. —*v.* **1.** To pass or send along from one group or station to another: *relay a message.* **2.** To supply with fresh relays. [< OFr. *relaier,* to leave behind.]

relay race *n.* A race between two or more teams in which each team member runs only part of the race and then is relieved by another teammate.

re·lease (rĭ-lēs') *v.* **-leased, -leas·ing. 1.** To set free from confinement, restraint, or bondage; liberate. **2.** To free; unfasten. **3.** To allow performance, sale, publication, or circulation of. **4.** To relinquish (e.g. a claim). —*n.* **1.** The act of releasing; liberation. **2.** A device or catch for locking or releasing a mechanism. [< Lat. *relaxare,* to relax.] —**re·leas'a·ble** *adj.* —**re·leas'er** *n.*

rel·e·gate (rĕl'ĭ-gāt') *v.* **-gat·ed, -gat·ing. 1.** To send or consign, esp. to a less important place, position, or condition. **2.** To assign to a particular category. **3.** To refer for decision or performance. **4.** To banish; exile. [Lat. *relegare,* to send away.] —**rel'e·ga'tion** *n.*

re·lent (rĭ-lĕnt') *v.* To become softened or gentler in attitude, temper, or determination. [ME *relenten.*]

re·lent·less (rĭ-lĕnt'lĭs) *adj.* **1.** Unyielding; pitiless. **2.** Steady and persistent. —**re·lent'-less·ly** *adv.* —**re·lent'less·ness** *n.*

rel·e·vant (rĕl'ə-vənt) *adj.* Having to do with the matter at hand; to the point. [< Lat. *relevare,* to lift up.] —**rel'e·vance** or **rel'e·van·cy** *n.* —**rel'e·vant·ly** *adv.*

Syns: relevant, applicable, germane, material, pertinent *adj.*

re·li·a·ble (rĭ-lī'ə-bəl) *adj.* Able to be relied upon; dependable. —**re·li'a·bil'i·ty** or **re·li'a·ble·ness** *n.* —**re·li'a·bly** *adv.*

re·li·ance (rĭ-lī'əns) *n.* **1.** The act of relying; dependence. **2.** Confidence; trust. **3.** One depended on. —**re·li'ant** *adj.* —**re·li'ant·ly** *adv.*

rel·ic (rĕl'ĭk) *n.* **1.** An object or custom surviving from a culture or period that has disappeared. **2.** A keepsake. **3.** An object of religious veneration. **4. relics.** A corpse; remains. [< Lat. *reliquiae,* remains.]

re·lief (rĭ-lēf') *n.* **1.** Ease from or lessening of pain or discomfort. **2.** Something that lessens pain, anxiety, etc. **3.** Assistance given to the needy, the aged, or disaster victims. **4.** The projection of figures or forms from a flat background, as in sculpture. **5.** The variations in elevation of an area of the earth's surface. [< Lat. *relever,* to relieve.]

relief map *n.* A map that shows the physical features of land, as with contour lines.

relief pitcher *n.* *Baseball.* A pitcher who regularly stands ready to replace another pitcher during a game.

re·lieve (rĭ-lēv′) v. **-lieved, -liev·ing. 1.** To lessen or alleviate; ease. **2.** To free from pain, anxiety, fear, etc. **3.** To aid. **4.** To take something from the possession of. **5.** To free from a specified duty by providing a replacement. **6.** To make less unpleasant or monotonous. **7.** To make distinct through contrast. [< Lat. *relevare.*] **—re·liev′er** n.

re·li·gion (rĭ-lĭj′ən) n. **1. a.** An organized system of beliefs and rituals centering on a supernatural being or beings. **b.** Adherence to such a system. **2.** A belief upheld or pursued with zeal and devotion. [< Lat. *religio.*]

re·li·gious (rĭ-lĭj′əs) adj. **1.** Of or relating to religion. **2.** Adhering to or manifesting religion; pious; godly. **3.** Scrupulous; conscientious. **4.** Of or belonging to a monastic order. **—**n., pl. **-ious.** A person belonging to a monastic order, as a monk or nun. **—re·lig′ious·ly** adv. **—re·lig′ious·ness** n.

re·lin·quish (rĭ-lĭng′kwĭsh) v. **1.** To retire from; leave; abandon. **2.** To put aside or desist from. **3.** To surrender; renounce. **4.** To release. [< Lat. *relinquere,* to leave behind.] **—re·lin′quish·er** n. **—re·lin′quish·ment** n.

rel·i·quar·y (rĕl′ĭ-kwĕr′ē) n., pl. **-ies.** A receptacle for keeping or displaying sacred relics. [< Lat. *reliquiae,* remains.]

reliquary
12th-century Spanish

rel·ish (rĕl′ĭsh) n. **1.** An appetite for something; appreciation. **2.** Pleasure; zest. **3.** A spicy or savory condiment served with other food. **4.** The flavor of a food, esp. when appetizing. **—**v. **1.** To take pleasure in; enjoy. **2.** To like the flavor of. [< Lat. *relaxare,* to relax.] **—rel′ish·a·ble** adj.

re·live (rē-lĭv′) v. To undergo again, esp. by means of the imagination.

re·luc·tant (rĭ-lŭk′tənt) adj. **1.** Unwilling; averse: *reluctant to help.* **2.** Marked by unwillingness: *a reluctant admission.* [< Lat. *reluctari,* to struggle against.] **—re·luc′tance** or **re·luc′tan·cy** n. **—re·luc′tant·ly** adv.

re·ly (rĭ-lī′) v. **-lied, -ly·ing. 1.** To depend: *relied on the rope to hold him.* **2.** To trust confidently: *rely on the children to behave.* [< Lat. *religare,* to bind fast.]

REM (rĕm) n. Rapid eye movement.

re·main (rĭ-mān′) v. **1.** To continue without change of condition, quality, or place. **2.** To stay or be left over after the removal, departure, or destruction of others. **3.** To be left as still to be dealt with: *A cure remains to be found.* **4.** To endure or persist. [< Lat. *remanēre,* to stay behind.]

re·main·der (rĭ-mān′dər) n. **1.** The remaining part; the rest. **2. a.** In division, the dividend minus the product of the divisor and quotient. **b.** In subtraction, the difference. **3.** The copies of a book remaining with a publisher after sales have fallen off. **—**v. To sell (books) as remainders, usu. at a reduced price. [< OFr. *remaindre,* to remain.]

re·mains (rĭ-mānz′) pl.n. **1.** All that is left after other parts have been taken away. **2.** A corpse.

re·mand (rĭ-mănd′) v. To send back (a person in custody) to prison, to another court, or to another agency for further proceedings. [< LLat. *remandare,* to send back word.] **—re·mand′ment** n.

re·mark (rĭ-märk′) n. **1.** A casual statement; comment. **2.** The act of noticing or observing. **—**v. **1.** To make a remark; comment. **2.** To take notice of; observe. [< OFr. *remarquer,* to notice.]

re·mark·a·ble (rĭ-mär′kə-bəl) adj. **1.** Worthy of notice. **2.** Extraordinary; uncommon. **—re·mark′a·ble·ness** n. **—re·mark′a·bly** adv.

re·me·di·al (rĭ-mē′dē-əl) adj. Intended to correct something, esp. a deficiency. **—re·me′di·al·ly** adv.

rem·e·dy (rĕm′ĭ-dē) n., pl. **-dies. 1.** A medicine or therapy that relieves pain, cures disease, or corrects a disorder. **2.** Something that corrects an evil, fault, or error. **—**v. **-died, -dy·ing. 1.** To relieve or cure. **2.** To counteract or rectify. [< Lat. *remedium.*]

re·mem·ber (rĭ-mĕm′bər) v. **1.** To recall to the mind; think of again. **2.** To retain in the mind. **3.** To keep (someone) in mind. **4.** To mention (someone) to another as sending greetings. [< LLat. *rememorari.*]

re·mem·brance (rĭ-mĕm′brəns) n. **1.** The act of remembering or state of being remembered. **2.** A memorial. **3.** The length of time over which one's memory extends. **4.** Something remembered; reminiscence. **5.** A memento or souvenir.

re·mind (rĭ-mīnd′) v. To cause (someone) to remember. **—re·mind′er** n.

rem·i·nisce (rĕm′ə-nĭs′) v. **-nisced, -nisc·ing.** To recollect and tell of past experiences or events. [< REMINISCENT.]

rem·i·nis·cence (rĕm′ə-nĭs′əns) n. **1.** The act or process of recalling the past. **2.** A memory. **3.** Often **reminiscences.** A narration of past experiences.

rem·i·nis·cent (rĕm′ə-nĭs′ənt) adj. **1.** Of or containing reminiscence. **2.** Recalling to the mind; suggestive. [< Lat. *reminisci,* to recollect.] **—rem′i·nis′cent·ly** adv.

re·miss (rĭ-mĭs′) adj. Lax in attending to duty; negligent. [< Lat. *remissus,* slack.] **—re·miss′ly** adv. **—re·miss′ness** n.

re·mis·si·ble (rĭ-mĭs′ə-bəl) adj. Capable of being remitted or forgiven. **—re·mis′si·bil′i·ty** n. **—re·mis′si·bly** adv.

re·mis·sion (rĭ-mĭsh′ən) n. **1.** The act of remitting or condition of being remitted. **2.** A lessening of intensity or seriousness, as of a disease.

re·mit (rĭ-mĭt′) v. **-mit·ted, -mit·ting. 1.** To send

583 · remittance | rental

(money). **2. a.** To cancel (a penalty or punishment). **b.** To pardon; forgive. **3.** To relax; slacken. **4.** To diminish; abate. [< Lat. *remittere*.] —**re·mit'ta·ble** *adj.* —**re·mit'tal** *n.* —**re·mit'ter** *n.*

re·mit·tance (rĭ-mĭt'ns) *n.* Money or credit sent to someone.

re·mit·tent (rĭ-mĭt'nt) *adj.* Characterized by temporary abatements in severity.

rem·nant (rĕm'nǝnt) *n.* **1.** Something left over; remainder. **2.** A surviving trace or vestige. [< OFr. *remaindre*, to remain.]

re·mod·el (rē-mŏd'l) *v.* To rebuild in order to improve; renovate. —**re·mod'el·er** *n.*

re·mon·strance (rĭ-mŏn'strǝns) *n.* The act or an instance of remonstrating.

re·mon·strate (rĭ-mŏn'strāt', rĕm'ǝn-) *v.* **-strated, -strating.** To say or plead in protest, objection, or reproof. [Med. Lat. *remonstrare*, to demonstrate.] —**re·mon'stra·tion** (rĭ-mŏn'strā'shǝn, rĕm'ǝn-) *n.* —**re·mon'stra·tive** (-strǝ-tĭv) *adj.*

rem·o·ra (rĕm'ǝr-ǝ) *n.* Any of several saltwater fishes that have a sucking disk on the head with which they attach themselves to sharks, whales, or the hulls of ships. [Lat., delay.]

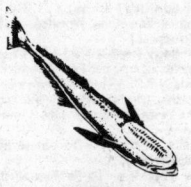

remora

re·morse (rĭ-môrs') *n.* Bitter regret or guilt for past misdeeds. [< Lat. *remordēre*, to bite again.] —**re·morse'ful** *adj.* —**re·morse'ful·ly** *adv.* —**re·morse'ful·ness** *n.*

re·morse·less (rĭ-môrs'lĭs) *adj.* Having no pity or compassion; merciless. —**re·morse'less·ly** *adv.* —**re·morse'less·ness** *n.*

re·mote (rĭ-mōt') *adj.* **-moter, -motest. 1.** Located far away. **2.** Distant in time. **3.** Barely discernible; slight. **4.** Being distantly related: *a remote cousin.* **5.** Distant in manner; aloof. [Lat. *remotus*, p.p. of *removēre*, to move away.] —**re·mote'ly** *adv.* —**re·mote'ness** *n.*

remote control *n.* The control of an activity, process, or machine from a distance, esp. by radio or electricity.

re·move (rĭ-mōōv') *v.* **-moved, -moving. 1.** To move from a position occupied; convey from one place to another. **2.** To take away; extract; do away with. **3.** To dismiss from office. **4.** To change one's residence; move. —*n.* **1.** The act of removing. **2.** Distance or degree away or apart. [< Lat. *removēre*, to move back.] —**re·mov'a·ble** *adj.* —**re·mov'a·bly** *adv.* —**re·mov'al** *n.* —**re·mov'er** *n.*

re·mu·ner·ate (rĭ-myōō'nǝ-rāt') *v.* **-ated, -ating.** To pay for goods provided, services rendered, or losses incurred. [Lat. *remunerare*.] —**re·mu'ner·a'tion** *n.* —**re·mu'ner·a'tive** *adj.* —**re·mu'ner·a'tor** *n.*

ren·ais·sance (rĕn'ĭ-säns', -zäns', rĭ-nā'sǝns) *n.* **1.** A rebirth or revival. **2. Renaissance.**

a. The humanistic revival of classical art, literature, and learning in Europe. **b.** The period of this revival, roughly from the 14th through the 16th cent. **3.** Often **Renaissance.** A period of revived intellectual or artistic achievement. [< OFr.]

re·nal (rē'nǝl) *adj.* Of or near the kidneys. [< Lat. *renes*, kidneys.]

re·nas·cent (rĭ-nás'ǝnt, -nā'sǝnt) *adj.* Showing renewed growth or vigor. [< Lat. *renasci*, to be born again.] —**re·nas'cence** *n.*

rend (rĕnd) *v.* **rent** (rĕnt) **or rended, rending. 1.** To tear apart or into pieces violently; split. **2.** To remove forcibly. **3.** To penetrate and disturb as if by tearing. **4.** To distress painfully. [< OE *rendan.*] —**rend'er** *n.*

ren·der (rĕn'dǝr) *v.* **1.** To submit: *render a bill.* **2.** To give or make available: *render assistance.* **3.** To give what is due. **4.** To represent in a verbal or artistic form. **5.** To translate. **6.** To cause to become; make: *renders me helpless.* **7.** To liquefy (fat) by heating. [< OFr. *rendre.*] —**ren'der·er** *n.*

ren·dez·vous (rän'dā-vōō', -dǝ-) *n., pl.* **-vous** (-vōōz'). **1.** A prearranged meeting place. **2.** A prearranged meeting. **3.** A popular gathering place. —*v.* To meet together at a specified time and place. [< OFr. *rendez vous*, present yourselves.]

ren·di·tion (rĕn-dĭsh'ǝn) *n.* **1.** The act of rendering. **2.** An interpretation or performance of a musical or dramatic work. **3.** A translation. [< OFr. *rendre*, to give back.]

ren·e·gade (rĕn'ĭ-gād') *n.* **1.** One who rejects a religion, cause, allegiance, or group for another; traitor. **2.** An outlaw. [< Med. Lat. *renegare*, to deny.] —**ren'e·gade'** *adj.*

re·nege (rĭ-nĭg', -nĕg') *v.* **-neged, -neging. 1.** To fail to carry out a promise or commitment. **2.** *Card Games.* To fail to follow suit when able and required by the rules to do so. [Med. Lat. *renegare*, to deny.] —**re·neg'er** *n.*

re·new (rĭ-nōō', -nyōō') *v.* **1.** To make new or as if new again; restore. **2.** To take up again; resume. **3.** To grant or obtain for the extension of: *renew a contract.* —**re·new'a·ble** *adj.* —**re·new'al** *n.*

ren·min·bi (rĕn'mĭn-bē') *n.* See table at currency. [Chin. *ren² min² bi⁴*.]

ren·net (rĕn'ĭt) *n.* An extract from the lining of a calf's stomach, used to curdle milk in making cheese or junket. [ME.]

ren·nin (rĕn'ĭn) *n.* A milk-coagulating enzyme produced from rennet. [RENN(ET) + -IN.]

re·nounce (rĭ-nouns') *v.* **-nounced, -nouncing. 1.** To give up, esp. by formal announcement. **2.** To reject; disown. [< Lat. *renuntiare.*] —**re·nounce'ment** *n.*

ren·o·vate (rĕn'ǝ-vāt') *v.* **-vated, -vating.** To restore to an earlier condition. [< Lat. *renovare.*] —**ren'o·va'tion** *n.* —**ren'o·va'tor** *n.*

re·nown (rĭ-noun') *n.* Widespread honor and fame; celebrity. [< OFr. *renomer*, to make famous.] —**re·nowned'** *adj.*

rent¹ (rĕnt) *n.* Periodic payment made by one in return for the right to use the property of another. —*v.* **1.** To pay for and obtain use of (another's property). **2.** To be for rent. [< OFr. *rente.*] —**rent'a·ble** *adj.* —**rent'er** *n.*

rent² (rĕnt) *v.* A *p.t.* & *p.p.* of **rend.** —*n.* An opening made by rending; rip.

rent·al (rĕn'tl) *n.* **1.** An amount paid out or taken in as rent. **2.** Property available for renting. **3.** The act of renting.

re·nun·ci·a·tion (rĭ-nŭn'sē-ā'shən) n. The act or practice of renouncing. [< Lat. *renuntiare*, to renounce.] —**re·nun'ci·a'tive** or **re·nun'ci·a·to'ry** (-ə-tôr'ē, -tōr'ē) adj.

re·or·der (rē-ôr'dər) v. 1. To rearrange. 2. To order (the same goods) again. —**re·or'der** n.

re·or·gan·ize (rē-ôr'gə-nīz') v. To organize again or anew, as a business after a bankruptcy. —**re·or'gan·i·za'tion** n. —**re·or'gan·iz'er** n.

rep¹ (rĕp) n. A ribbed or corded fabric. [Fr. *reps.*]

rep² (rĕp) n. *Informal.* A representative.

re·pair¹ (rĭ-pâr') v. 1. To restore to sound condition after damage or injury. 2. To set right; remedy. 3. To renew or refresh. —n. 1. The work or act of repairing. 2. General condition after use or repairing: *in good repair.* 3. Often **repairs.** An instance of repairing. [< Lat. *reparare.*] —**re·pair'a·ble** adj. —**re·pair'er** n.

re·pair² (rĭ-pâr') v. To betake oneself; go. [< LLat. *repatriare*, to return to one's country.]

re·pair·man (rĭ-pâr'măn', -mən) n. One whose occupation is making repairs.

rep·a·ra·ble (rĕp'ər-ə-bəl) adj. Capable of being repaired.

rep·a·ra·tion (rĕp'ə-rā'shən) n. 1. The act or process of making amends. 2. Something done or paid to make amends. 3. **reparations.** Compensation, esp. that required from a nation for damage inflicted during a war. [< Lat. *reparare*, to repair.] —**re·par'a·tive** (rĭ-pâr'ə-tĭv) or **re·par'a·to'ry** (-tôr'ē, -tōr'ē) adj.

rep·ar·tee (rĕp'ər-tē', -tā', -är-) n. 1. A swift, witty reply. 2. Conversation characterized by repartee. [< OFr. *repartir*, to retort.]

re·past (rĭ-păst') n. 1. A meal. 2. The food eaten or provided at a meal. [< OFr. *repaistre*, to feed.]

re·pa·tri·ate (rē-pā'trē-āt') v. **-at·ed, -at·ing.** To return to the country of birth or citizenship: *repatriate war refugees.* [Lat. *repatriare*, to return to one's country.] —**re·pa'tri·ate** (-trē-ət, -āt') n. —**re·pa'tri·a'tion** n.

re·pay (rĭ-pā') v. 1. To pay back (money). 2. To return; requite: *repaid anger with indignation.* —**re·pay'a·ble** adj. —**re·pay'ment** n.

re·peal (rĭ-pēl') v. To withdraw or annul officially or formally. [< OFr. *rapeler.*] —**re·peal'** n. —**re·peal'er** n.

re·peat (rĭ-pēt') v. 1. To say or do (something) again. 2. To manifest or express in the same way or words: *History repeats itself.* —n. 1. The act of repeating. 2. Something repeated. [< Lat. *repetere*, to return.] —**re·peat'a·ble** adj. —**re·peat'er** n.

re·peat·ed (rĭ-pē'tĭd) adj. Said, done, or occurring again and again. —**re·peat'ed·ly** adv.

re·pel (rĭ-pĕl') v. **-pelled, -pel·ling.** 1. To drive back; ward off or keep away. 2. To cause aversion or distaste in. 3. To be incapable of absorbing or mixing with. 4. To present an opposing force to: *Electric charges of the same sign repel one another.* [< Lat. *repellere.*]

Syns: repel, disgust, nauseate, revolt, sicken v.
Usage: Both repel and repulse mean "to drive back or off." Only repel, however, is used to mean "to cause distaste or aversion in": *We were repelled by the noise and filth.*

re·pel·lent (rĭ-pĕl'ənt) adj. 1. Serving or tending to repel. 2. Repulsive. 3. Resistant to some substance. —n. 1. A substance used to repel insects. 2. A substance for making a surface resistant to something. —**re·pel'lence** or **re·pel'len·cy** n.

re·pent (rĭ-pĕnt') v. 1. To feel regret for (what one has done or failed to do). 2. To feel contrition for one's sins and to abjure sinful ways. [< OFr. *repentir.*] —**re·pen'tance** n. —**re·pen'tant** adj. —**re·pen'tant·ly** adv. —**re·pent'er** n.

re·per·cus·sion (rē'pər-kŭsh'ən, rĕp'ər-) n. 1. An indirect effect produced by an event or action. 2. A reciprocal action. 3. A reflection, esp. of sound. [< Lat. *repercutere*, to cause to rebound.] —**re'per·cus'sive** adj.

rep·er·toire (rĕp'ər-twär') n. 1. The stock of songs, plays, etc., that a person or company is prepared to perform. 2. The skills, aptitudes, or special accomplishments of a person or group. [Fr. *répertoire.*]

rep·er·to·ry (rĕp'ər-tôr'ē, -tōr'ē) n., pl. **-ries.** 1. A repertoire. 2. A theater in which a resident company presents plays from a specified repertoire, usu. in alternation. 3. A place, as a storehouse, where a stock of things is kept; repository. [LLat. *repertorium.*] —**rep'er·to'ri·al** adj.

rep·e·ti·tion (rĕp'ĭ-tĭsh'ən) n. 1. The act of repeating. 2. Something repeated. [< Lat. *repetere*, to repeat.]

rep·e·ti·tious (rĕp'ĭ-tĭsh'əs) adj. Characterized by repetition, esp. needless repetition. —**rep'e·ti'tious·ly** adv. —**rep'e·ti'tious·ness** n.

re·pet·i·tive (rĭ-pĕt'ĭ-tĭv) adj. Marked by repetition. —**re·pet'i·tive·ly** adv. —**re·pet'i·tive·ness** n.

re·phrase (rē-frāz') v. To phrase again, esp. in a clearer way.

re·pine (rĭ-pīn') v. To be discontented; complain; fret.

re·place (rĭ-plās') v. 1. To put back in place. 2. To take or fill the place of. —**re·place'a·ble** adj. —**re·place'ment** n. —**re·plac'er** n.

re·play (rē-plā') v. To play (a record, video tape, etc.) again. —**re'play'** n.

re·plen·ish (rĭ-plĕn'ĭsh) v. To fill or make complete again. [< OFr. *replenir.*] —**re·plen'ish·er** n. —**re·plen'ish·ment** n.

re·plete (rĭ-plēt') adj. 1. Plentifully supplied; abounding. 2. Filled to satiation; gorged. [< Lat. *repletus*, p.p. of *replēre*, to refill.] —**re·ple'tion** or **re·plete'ness** n.

rep·li·ca (rĕp'lĭ-kə) n. A copy or close reproduction. [< Lat. *replicare*, to repeat.]

rep·li·cate (rĕp'lĭ-kāt') v. **-cat·ed, -cat·ing.** 1. To make a replica of; duplicate. 2. To fold over or bend back upon itself. [Lat. *replicare.*] —**rep'li·ca'tion** n.

re·ply (rĭ-plī') v. **-plied, -ply·ing.** To say or give as an answer. —n., pl. **-plies.** An answer; response. [< Lat. *replicare*, to repeat.] —**re·pli'er** n.

re·port (rĭ-pôrt', -pōrt') n. 1. An account that is prepared or presented, usu. in formal or organized form. 2. Rumor. 3. Reputation. 4. An explosive noise. —v. 1. To make or present an account of (something). 2. To relate or tell about; present. 3. To complain about or make known to the proper authorities. **4.** To serve as a reporter. **5.** To present oneself: *report for duty.* [< Lat. *reportare,* to carry back.]

report card *n.* A report of a student's progress presented periodically to a parent or guardian.

re·port·ed·ly (rĭ-pôr'tĭd-lē, -pôr'-) *adv.* By report; supposedly.

re·port·er (rĭ-pôr'tər, -pôr'-) *n.* One who reports, esp. a writer of news stories. **—rep'or·to'ri·al** (rĕp'ər-tôr'ē-əl, -tôr'-, rē'pər-) *adj.*

re·pose¹ (rĭ-pōz') *n.* **1. a.** The act of resting; a rest. **b.** The condition of being at rest; relaxation. **2.** Calmness; tranquillity. **—v. -posed, -pos·ing. 1.** To lie at rest; relax. **2.** To be supported by something. [< Lat. *repausare,* to relax.] **—re·pose'ful** *adj.* **—re·pose'ful·ly** *adv.*

re·pose² (rĭ-pōz') *v.* **-posed, -pos·ing.** To place (faith, trust, etc.): *They repose their hopes in him.* [< Lat. *reponere.*]

re·pos·i·to·ry (rĭ-pŏz'ĭ-tôr'ē, -tōr'ē) *n., pl. -ries.* A place where things may be put for safekeeping.

re·pos·sess (rē'pə-zĕs') *v.* To regain possession of (property). **—re'pos·ses'sion** *n.*

rep·re·hend (rĕp'rĭ-hĕnd') *v.* To reprove; blame; censure. [< Lat. *reprehendere.*] **—rep're·hen'sion** *n.*

rep·re·hen·si·ble (rĕp'rĭ-hĕn'sə-bəl) *adj.* Deserving of rebuke or censure; blameworthy. **—rep're·hen'si·bil'i·ty** *n.* **—rep're·hen'si·bly** *adv.*

rep·re·sent (rĕp'rĭ-zĕnt') *v.* **1.** To stand for; symbolize. **2.** To depict; portray. **3.** To serve as an example of. **4.** To describe as having a certain identity. **5.** To serve as the authorized delegate or agent for. [< Lat. *repraesentare,* to show.] **—rep're·sent'a·bil'i·ty** *n.* **—rep're·sent'a·ble** *adj.*

Syns: *represent, embody, epitomize, exemplify, personify, symbolize, typify* v.

rep·re·sen·ta·tion (rĕp'rĭ-zĕn-tā'shən, -zən-) *n.* **1.** The act of representing or the condition of being represented, esp. in a legislative body. **2.** Something that represents. **3.** A statement, as of facts or arguments. **—rep're·sen·ta'tion·al** *adj.*

rep·re·sen·ta·tive (rĕp'rĭ-zĕn'tə-tĭv) *n.* **1.** A typical example, esp. of a class. **2.** A delegate or agent acting on behalf of another. **3. Representative.** A member of the U.S. House of Representatives or of a state legislature. **—adj. 1.** Of, relating to, or based on political representation. **2.** Serving as a typical example. **—rep're·sen'ta·tive·ly** *adv.* **—rep're·sen'ta·tive·ness** *n.*

re·press (rĭ-prĕs') *v.* **1.** To hold back; restrain: *repress a laugh.* **2.** To suppress; quell: *repress a rebellion.* **3.** To keep out of the conscious mind. [< Lat. *repressus,* p.p. of *reprimere,* to repress.] **—re·pres'i·ble** *adj.* **—re·pres'sion** *n.* **—re·pres'sive** *adj.* **—re·pres'sive·ly** *adv.* **—re·pres'sor** *n.*

re·prieve (rĭ-prēv') *n.* **1.** The postponement of a punishment. **2.** Temporary relief, as from pain. **—v. -prieved, -priev·ing.** To postpone the punishment of. [< Lat. *reprehendere,* to hold back.]

rep·ri·mand (rĕp'rĭ-mănd') *n.* A severe or formal rebuke. **—v.** To rebuke or censure severely; criticize. [< Lat. *reprimere,* to repress.]

re·print (rē'prĭnt') *n.* **1.** A new or additional printing of a book. **2.** A separately printed excerpt. **—re·print'** *v.* **—re·print'er** *n.*

re·pris·al (rĭ-prī'zəl) *n.* Retaliation for an injury with the intent of inflicting at least as much injury in return. [< Lat. *reprehendere,* to reprehend.]

re·prise (rĭ-prēz') *n. Mus.* A repetition of an original theme. [< OFr. *reprendre,* to take back.]

re·proach (rĭ-prōch') *v.* To rebuke severely or sternly; blame. **—n. 1.** Rebuke; blame. **2.** Disgrace; shame. [< OFr. *reprochier.*] **—re·proach'a·ble** *adj.* **—re·proach'ful** *adj.* **—re·proach'ful·ly** *adv.*

rep·ro·bate (rĕp'rə-bāt') *n.* A morally unprincipled person. [< Lat. *reprobare,* to reprove.] **—rep'ro·ba'tion** *n.*

re·pro·duce (rē'prə-dōōs', -dyōōs') *v.* **-duced, -duc·ing. 1.** To produce a counterpart, image, or copy of. **2.** To produce offspring. **3.** To produce again or anew; re-create. **4.** To undergo copying. **—re'pro·duc'er** *n.* **—re'pro·duc'i·ble** *adj.* **—re'pro·duc'tion** (-dŭk'shən) *n.* **—re'pro·duc'tive** (-dŭk'tĭv) *adj.* **—re'pro·duc'tive·ly** *adv.*

re·proof (rĭ-prōōf') *n.* Blame for a fault.

re·prove (rĭ-prōōv') *v.* **-proved, -prov·ing. 1.** To rebuke; scold. **2.** To find fault with. [< LLat. *reprobare,* to disapprove.] **—re·prov'ing·ly** *adv.*

rep·tile (rĕp'tĭl, -tīl') *n.* Any of various coldblooded vertebrates, as a snake or crocodile, that are covered with scales or horny plates. [< Lat. *reptus,* p.p. of *repere,* to creep.] **—rep·til'i·an** (-tĭl'ē-ən, -tĭl'yən) *adj. & n.*

reptile
A rattlesnake

re·pub·lic (rĭ-pŭb'lĭk) *n.* **1.** A government in which the head of state is usu. a president. **2.** A country governed by the elected representatives of its people. [< Lat. *respublica.*]

re·pub·li·can (rĭ-pŭb'lĭ-kən) *adj.* **1.** Of, relating to, or advocating a republic. **2. Republican.** Of or belonging to the Republican Party. **—n. 1.** An advocate of a republican form of government. **2. Republican.** A member or a supporter of the Republican Party. **—re·pub'li·can·ism** *n.*

Republican Party *n.* One of the two major U.S. political parties.

re·pu·di·ate (rĭ-pyōō'dē-āt') *v.* **-at·ed, -at·ing. 1.** To reject the validity of. **2.** To refuse to recognize, acknowledge, or pay. [Lat. *repudiare.*] **—re·pu'di·a'tion** *n.* **—re·pu'di·a'tor** *n.*

re·pug·nant (rĭ-pŭg'nənt) *adj.* **1.** Offensive; distasteful. **2.** Contrary; antagonistic. [< Lat. *repugnare,* to oppose.] **—re·pug'nance** *n.* **—re·pug'nant·ly** *adv.*

re·pulse (rĭ-pŭls') *v.* **-pulsed, -puls·ing. 1.** To drive back; repel. **2.** To repel with rudeness, coldness, or denial. **—n. 1.** The act of repulsing or condition of being repulsed. **2.** A rejection. [< Lat. *repulsus,* p.p. of *repellere,* to repel.] **—re·pul'sion** *n.*

re·pul·sive (rĭ-pŭl'sĭv) *adj.* **1.** Causing repugnance or disgust. **2.** Tending to repel or drive off. **—re·pul'sive·ly** *adv.* **—re·pul'sive·ness** *n.*

rep·u·ta·ble (rĕp'yə-tə-bəl) *adj.* Having a good reputation. **—rep'u·ta·bly** *adv.*

rep·u·ta·tion (rĕp'yə-tā'shən) *n.* **1.** The general opinion of a person or thing held by others or the public. **2.** The condition of being held in high esteem.

re·pute (rĭ-pyōōt') *n.* Reputation or esteem. —*v.* **-put·ed, -put·ing.** To believe; regard. [< Lat. *reputare,* to think over.]

re·put·ed (rĭ-pyōō'tĭd) *adj.* Generally supposed. **—re·put'ed·ly** *adv.*

re·quest (rĭ-kwĕst') *v.* **1.** To ask for. **2.** To ask of: *requested him to leave.* —*n.* **1.** An act or example of asking. **2.** Something requested. **3.** The condition of being sought after: *information available on request.* [< Lat. *requirere.*]

req·ui·em (rĕk'wē-əm, rē'kwē-) *n.* **1. Requiem. a.** A mass sung for the dead. **b.** A musical composition for such a mass. **2.** A hymn, composition, or service for the dead. [< Lat. *requies,* rest.]

re·quire (rĭ-kwīr') *v.* **-quired, -quir·ing.** **1.** To need. **2.** To demand; insist upon. [< Lat. *requirere.*] **—re·quire'ment** *n.*

req·ui·site (rĕk'wĭ-zĭt) *adj.* Required; necessary. —*n.* A necessity. [< Lat. *requisitus,* p.p. of *requirere,* to require.]

req·ui·si·tion (rĕk'wĭ-zĭsh'ən) *n.* **1.** A formal request for something that is needed. **2.** The condition of being needed or in use. **—req'ui·si'tion** *v.*

re·quite (rĭ-kwīt') *v.* **-quit·ed, -quit·ing.** **1.** To make repayment or return for. **2.** To avenge. [RE- + obs. *quite,* to pay.] **—re·quit'al** *n.* **—re·quit'er** *n.*

re·run (rē'rŭn') *n.* A repetition, esp. of a recorded performance. **—re·run'** *v.*

re·scind (rĭ-sĭnd') *v.* To void; repeal. [Lat. *rescindere.*] **—re·scind'a·ble** *adj.* **—re·scind'er** *n.* **—re·scis'sion** (-sĭzh'ən) *n.*

res·cue (rĕs'kyōō) *v.* **-cued, -cu·ing.** To save, as from danger. [< OFr. *rescourre.*] **—res'cue** *n.* **—res'cu·er** *n.*

re·search (rĭ-sûrch', rē'sûrch') *n.* Careful study of a subject, esp. scholarly or scientific study of a given field or problem. [< OFr. *recercher,* to seek out.] **—re·search'** *v.* **—re·search'er** *n.*

re·sec·tion (rĭ-sĕk'shən) *n.* The surgical removal of part of an organ or structure.

re·sem·blance (rĭ-zĕm'bləns) *n.* A similarity, esp. in appearance.

re·sem·ble (rĭ-zĕm'bəl) *v.* **-bled, -bling.** To have a similarity to. [< OFr. *resembler.*]

re·sent (rĭ-zĕnt') *v.* To feel angry or bitter about. [Obs. Fr. *resentir,* to feel strongly.] **—re·sent'ful** *adj.* **—re·sent'ful·ly** *adv.* **—re·sent'ment** *n.*

res·er·va·tion (rĕz'ər-vā'shən) *n.* **1.** The act of reserving. **2.** A limiting qualification or condition. **3.** A tract of public land set apart for a special purpose. **4.** An arrangement by which accommodations are held for one.

re·serve (rĭ-zûrv') *v.* **-served, -serv·ing.** **1.** To set aside for future use. **2.** To set apart for a

particular person or use. **3.** To retain; defer: *reserve judgment.* —*n.* **1.** Something saved for future use. **2.** The condition of being reserved: *funds held in reserve.* **3.** Self-restraint; reticence. **4.** A reservation of public land. **5.** Often **reserves.** The part of a country's armed forces that is not part of the regular military force. [< Lat. *reservare,* to keep back.]

re·served (rĭ-zûrvd') *adj.* **1.** Held for a particular person or persons. **2.** Quiet and restrained in manner. **—re·serv'ed·ly** (rĭ-zûr'vĭd-lē) *adv.* **—re·serv'ed·ness** *n.*

res·er·voir (rĕz'ər-vwär', -vwôr', -vôr') *n.* **1.** A body of water stored for public use. **2.** A reserve supply. [Fr. *réservoir.*]

resh (rĕsh) *n.* The 20th letter of the Hebrew alphabet. See table at **alphabet.** [Heb. *rēsh.*]

re·side (rĭ-zīd') *v.* **-sid·ed, -sid·ing.** **1.** To live in a place; dwell. **2.** To be inherently present: *the power that resides in the electorate.* [< Lat. *residēre,* to sit back.] **—re·sid'er** *n.*

res·i·dence (rĕz'ĭ-dəns) *n.* **1.** The place in which one lives. **2.** The act or a period of residing somewhere.

res·i·den·cy (rĕz'ĭ-dən-sē, -dĕn'-) *n., pl.* **-cies.** A period of specialized clinical training for a physician.

res·i·dent (rĕz'ĭ-dənt, -dĕnt') *n.* **1.** One who makes his home in a particular place. **2.** A physician serving a residency. **—res'i·dent** *adj.*

res·i·den·tial (rĕz'ĭ-dĕn'shəl) *adj.* **1.** Relating to or having residence. **2.** Containing or suitable for homes.

re·sid·u·al (rĭ-zĭj'ōō-əl) *adj.* Of, characteristic of, or remaining as a residue. —*n.* **1.** A residue; remainder. **2.** Payment made to a performer for each rerun of a television show.

res·i·due (rĕz'ĭ-dōō', -dyōō') *n.* The part left after something is removed; remainder. [< Lat. *residuus,* remaining.]

re·sign (rĭ-zīn') *v.* **1.** To give over or submit (oneself). **2.** To give up (a position); quit. **3.** To relinquish (a privilege, right, or claim) formally. [< Lat. *resignare,* to unseal.]

res·ig·na·tion (rĕz'ĭg-nā'shən) *n.* **1.** The act of resigning. **2.** A formal statement that one is resigning. **3.** Acceptance; submission.

re·signed (rĭ-zīnd') *adj.* Acquiescent. **—re·sign'ed·ly** (rĭ-zī'nĭd-lē) *adv.*

re·sil·ient (rĭ-zĭl'yənt) *adj.* **1.** Capable of returning to an original shape after being bent, stretched, or compressed; elastic. **2.** Recovering quickly, as from misfortune or illness. [< Lat. *resilire,* to leap back.] **—re·sil'ience** or **re·sil'ien·cy** *n.*

res·in (rĕz'ĭn) *n.* **1.** A viscous substance of plant origin, as rosin or amber, used principally in varnishes, adhesives, synthetic plastics, and pharmaceuticals. **2.** Any of various artificial substances similar to natural resins. [< Lat. *resina.*] **—res'in·ous** (rĕz'ə-nəs) *adj.*

re·sist (rĭ-zĭst') *v.* **1.** To strive or work against; oppose. **2.** To withstand. [< Lat. *resistere.*] **—re·sist'er** *n.* **—re·sist'i·ble** *adj.*

re·sis·tance (rĭ-zĭs'təns) *n.* **1.** The act or capacity of resisting. **2.** A force that opposes or retards. **3.** *Elect.* The opposition that a material body offers to the passage of an electric current. **4.** Often **Resistance.** An underground organization engaged in the struggle for national liberation in a country under military occupation or totalitarian domination. —re·sis'tant *adj.*

re·sis·tor (rĭ-zĭs'tər) *n.* An electric circuit element used to provide resistance.

res·o·lute (rĕz'ə-lōōt') *adj.* Characterized by firmness, determination, and often loyalty. [Lat. *resolutus,* p.p. of *resolvere,* to resolve.] —res'o·lute'ly *adv.* —res'o·lute'ness *n.*

res·o·lu·tion (rĕz'ə-lōō'shən) *n.* **1.** The quality of being resolute. **2.** Something that has been resolved. **b.** A formal statement of a decision voted, as by a legislature. **3.** A solving, as of a problem or puzzle.

re·solve (rĭ-zŏlv') *v.* -solved, -solv·ing. **1.** To make a firm decision about. **2.** To decide or express by formal vote. **3.** To separate (something) into constituent parts. **4.** To find a solution to. **5.** To dispel: *resolve a conflict.* —*n.* **1.** Firmness of purpose; resolution. **2.** A determination or decision. [< Lat. *resolvere,* to untie.] —re·solv'a·ble *adj.*

re·solved (rĭ-zŏlvd') *adj.* Fixed in purpose; determined.

res·o·nance (rĕz'ə-nəns) *n.* **1.** The quality or condition of being resonant. **2.** *Physics.* The increased response of an electric or mechanical system to a periodic driving force oscillating at the frequency at which the system tends to oscillate naturally. **3.** The intensification of sound, esp. of musical tones, by sympathetic vibrations.

res·o·nant (rĕz'ə-nənt) *adj.* **1.** Continuing to sound; echoing. **2.** Of or exhibiting resonance. **3.** Having a full, pleasing sound. —res'o·nant·ly *adv.*

res·o·nate (rĕz'ə-nāt') *v.* -nat·ed, -nat·ing. **1.** To exhibit resonance. **2.** To resound. [< Lat. *resonare,* to resound.]

res·o·na·tor (rĕz'ə-nā'tər) *n.* A hollow chamber that permits internal resonant oscillation of electromagnetic or acoustical waves of specific frequencies.

re·sort (rĭ-zôrt') *v.* **1.** To have recourse: *resorted to force.* **2.** To go customarily or frequently. —*n.* **1.** A place where people go for relaxation or recreation. **2.** Recourse. **3.** One turned to for aid or relief. [< OFr. *resortir,* to go out again.]

re·sound (rĭ-zound') *v.* **1.** To be filled with sound; reverberate. **2.** To sound loudly. [< Lat. *resonare.*] —re·sound'ing·ly *adv.*

re·source (rē'sôrs', -sōrs', -zôrs', -zōrs', rĭ-) *n.* **1.** A source of support or help. **2.** The ability to deal with a situation effectively. **3.** re·sources. Means; assets. **4.** A natural resource. [< Lat. *resurgere,* to rise again.]

re·source·ful (rĭ-sôrs'fəl, -sōrs'-, -zôrs'-, -zōrs'-) *adj.* Clever and imaginative, esp. in dealing with a difficult situation. —re·source'ful·ly *adv.* —re·source'ful·ness *n.*

re·spect (rĭ-spĕkt') *n.* **1.** Deferential or high regard; esteem. **2.** re·spects. Expressions of consideration or deference: *pay one's respects.* **3.** A particular aspect; detail. **4.** Relation; reference: *with respect to his request.* —*v.* **1.** To have esteem for. **2.** To avoid violation of. **3.** To concern. [< Lat. *respectus,* p.p.s of *respicere,* to look back.] —re·spect'er *n.* —re·spect'ful *adj.* —re·spect'ful·ly *adv.* —re·spect'ful·ness *n.*

re·spect·a·ble (rĭ-spĕk'tə-bəl) *adj.* **1.** Worthy of respect or esteem. **2.** Correct or proper in conduct. **3.** Moderately good. **4.** Consider-

able in amount, number, or size: *a respectable sum of money.* **5.** Acceptable in appearance; presentable. —re·spect'a·bil'i·ty *n.* —re·spect'a·bly *adv.*

re·spect·ing (rĭ-spĕk'tĭng) *prep.* In relation to.

re·spec·tive (rĭ-spĕk'tĭv) *adj.* Individual; particular: *They took their respective seats.*

re·spec·tive·ly (rĭ-spĕk'tĭv-lē) *adv.* Each in the order named.

res·pi·ra·tion (rĕs'pə-rā'shən) *n.* **1.** The act or process of inhaling and exhaling. **2.** The metabolic process by which an organism takes in oxygen and releases carbon dioxide and other products of oxidation. —res'pi·ra·to·ry (-pər-ə-tôr'ē, -tōr'ē) *adj.*

res·pi·ra·tor (rĕs'pə-rā'tər) *n.* **1.** An apparatus for artificial respiration. **2.** A device worn over the mouth or nose to protect the respiratory tract.

re·spire (rĭ-spīr') *v.* -spired, -spir·ing. **1.** To engage in respiration. **2.** To breathe. [< Lat. *respirare,* to breathe again.]

res·pite (rĕs'pĭt) *n.* **1.** A short interval of rest or relief. **2.** A postponement. [< Lat. *respectus,* refuge.]

re·splen·dent (rĭ-splĕn'dənt) *adj.* Shining with splendor. [< Lat. *resplendēre,* to shine brightly.] —re·splen'dence *n.* —re·splen'dent·ly *adv.*

re·spond (rĭ-spŏnd') *v.* **1.** To reply; answer. **2.** To act in return. **3.** To react positively. [Lat. *respondēre.*]

re·spon·dent (rĭ-spŏn'dənt) *n.* One who responds, esp. a defendant in divorce or equity cases. —re·spon'dent *adj.*

re·sponse (rĭ-spŏns') *n.* **1.** The act of responding; answer. **2.** A reaction to a specific stimulus. [< Lat. *responsum.*]

re·spon·si·bil·i·ty (rĭ-spŏn'sə-bĭl'ĭ-tē) *n., pl.* -ties. **1.** The condition or fact of being responsible. **2.** A thing or person that one is responsible for.

re·spon·si·ble (rĭ-spŏn'sə-bəl) *adj.* **1.** Liable to be called to account for something. **2.** Being the cause or source of something. **3.** Dependable; reliable; trustworthy. **4.** Involving important duties or obligations. —re·spon'si·ble·ness *n.* —re·spon'si·bly *adv.*

Syns: responsible, accountable, amenable, answerable, liable *adj.*

re·spon·sive (rĭ-spŏn'sĭv) *adj.* Readily reacting. —re·spon'sive·ly *adv.* —re·spon'sive·ness *n.*

rest[1] (rĕst) *n.* **1.** A period of inactivity, relaxation, or sleep. **2.** Absence of activity or motion. **3.** *Mus.* **a.** An interval of silence equal to a note of the same time value. **b.** The symbol indicating a rest. **4.** Something serving as a support. —*v.* **1.** To refresh (oneself). **2.** To sleep. **3.** To be, become, or remain temporarily quiet or inactive. **4. a.** To be supported: *a clock resting on the shelf.* **b.** To place or lay: *rest it against the wall.* **5.** To be imposed as a responsibility. **6.** To depend or rely. [< OE.] —rest'er *n.*

rest[2] (rĕst) *n.* **1.** Something left over; remainder. **2.** (*used with a pl. verb*). The others remaining: *The rest are coming later.* [< Lat. *restare,* to stay behind.]

res·tau·rant (rĕs'tər-ənt, -tə-ränt') *n.* A place where meals are served to the public. [< OFr. *restorer,* to restore.]

res·tau·ra·teur (rĕs'tər-ə-tûr') *n.* The owner or manager of a restaurant. [Fr.]

rest·ful (rĕst´fəl) *adj.* **1.** Offering rest. **2.** Pleasant and soothing: *restful colors.* —**rest´ful·ly** *adv.* —**rest´ful·ness** *n.*

rest home *n.* An establishment where elderly or sick people reside and are cared for.

res·ti·tu·tion (rĕs´tĭ-tōō´shən, -tyōō´-) *n.* **1.** The act of restoring something to the rightful owner. **2.** The act of making good for loss, damage, or injury. [< Lat. *restituere,* to restore.]

res·tive (rĕs´tĭv) *adj.* **1.** Impatiently restless; uneasy. **2.** Difficult to control; unruly. [< Lat. *restare,* to keep back.] —**res´tive·ly** *adv.* —**res´tive·ness** *n.*

rest·less (rĕst´lĭs) *adj.* **1.** Without rest or sleep: *a restless night.* **2. a.** Unable or reluctant to rest or be still. **b.** Feeling nervous tension. **3.** Never still: *the restless sea.* —**rest´less·ly** *adv.* —**rest´less·ness** *n.*

res·to·ra·tion (rĕs´tə-rā´shən) *n.* **1.** The act of restoring or condition of being restored. **2.** Something that has been restored, as a renovated building.

re·stor·a·tive (rĭ-stôr´ə-tĭv, -stōr´-) *adj.* Tending to renew or restore something. —*n.* Something that restores health or strength.

re·store (rĭ-stôr´, -stōr´) *v.* **-stored, -storing. 1.** To bring back into existence or use. **2.** To bring back to a previous or original condition. **3.** To give back; make restitution of. [< Lat. *restaurare.*] —**re·stor´er** *n.*

re·strain (rĭ-strān´) *v.* **1.** To check; hold back. **2.** To deprive of freedom. **3.** To limit or restrict. [< Lat. *restringere,* to bind back.] —**re·strain´a·ble** *adj.* —**re·strain´er** *n.*

re·straint (rĭ-strānt´) *n.* **1.** The act of restraining. **2.** The condition of being restrained. **3.** Something that holds back or restrains. **4.** Moderation in action or expression.

re·strict (rĭ-strĭkt´) *v.* To keep within limits; confine. [< Lat. *restrictus,* p.p. of *restringere,* to bind back.] —**re·stric´tive** *adj.* —**re·stric´tive·ly** *adv.*

re·stric·tion (rĭ-strĭk´shən) *n.* **1.** The act of restricting or the condition of being restricted. **2.** Something that restricts.

rest room *n.* A public lavatory.

re·sult (rĭ-zŭlt´) *v.* **1.** To come about as a consequence. **2.** To have a particular outcome. —*n.* A consequence; outcome. [< Lat. *resultare,* to leap back.] —**re·sult´ant** *adj.* & *n.*

re·sume (rĭ-zōōm´) *v.* **-sumed, -suming. 1.** To begin again or continue after interruption. **2.** To occupy or take again. [< Lat. *resumere.*] —**re·sump´tion** (-zŭmp´shən) *n.*

ré·su·mé (rĕz´ŏŏ-mā´, rĕz´ŏŏ-mā´) *n.* A summary, esp. of work experience, submitted when applying for a job. [Fr.]

re·sur·gent (rĭ-sûr´jənt) *adj.* Rising or tending to rise again. [< Lat. *resurgere,* to rise again.] —**re·sur´gence** *n.*

res·ur·rect (rĕz´ə-rĕkt´) *v.* **1.** To raise from the dead. **2.** To bring back into notice or use.

res·ur·rec·tion (rĕz´ə-rĕk´shən) *n.* **1. a.** Revival; rebirth. **2. Resurrection. a.** The rising again of Christ on the 3rd day after the Crucifixion. **b.** The rising again of the dead at the Last Judgment. [< Lat. *resurrectus,* p.p. of *resurgere,* to rise again.]

re·sus·ci·tate (rĭ-sŭs´ĭ-tāt´) *v.* **-tat·ed, -tat·ing.** To return to life or consciousness; revive.

[Lat. *resuscitare.*] —**re·sus´ci·ta´tion** *n.* —**re·sus´ci·ta´tor** *n.*

re·tail (rē´tāl´) *n.* The sale of commodities to the general public. —*v.* To sell at retail. [< OFr. *retaillier,* to cut up.] —**re´tail´** *adj.* & *adv.* —**re´tail´er** *n.*

re·tain (rĭ-tān´) *v.* **1.** To keep or hold in one's possession. **2.** To keep or hold in a particular place, condition, or position. **3.** To keep in mind; remember. **4.** To hire (e.g. a lawyer) by the payment of a fee. **5.** To keep in one's service or pay. [< Lat. *retinēre.*] —**re·tain´a·ble** *adj.* —**re·tain´ment** *n.*

re·tain·er (rĭ-tā´nər) *n.* **1.** One that retains. **2. a.** An attendant in a feudal household. **b.** A servant. **3.** A fee paid to engage the services of a professional.

re·take (rē-tāk´) *v.* **1.** To take again. **2.** To photograph again. —*n.* (rē´tāk´.) A rephotographed scene.

re·tal·i·ate (rĭ-tāl´ē-āt´) *v.* **-at·ed, -at·ing.** To return like for like, esp. to take revenge. [Lat. *retaliare.*] —**re·tal´i·a´tion** *n.* —**re·tal´i·a·to´ry** (-ə-tôr´ē, -tōr´ē) *adj.*

re·tard (rĭ-tärd´) *v.* To slow the progress of; impede or delay. [< Lat. *retardare.*]

re·tar·da·tion (rē´tär-dā´shən) *n.* **1.** The act or the condition of being retarded. **2.** The amount or time of delay or hindrance. **3.** Mental deficiency.

re·tard·ed (rĭ-tär´dĭd) *adj.* Slow or backward in mental or emotional development.

retch (rĕch) *v.* To try to vomit. [Ult. < OE *hrǣcan.*]

re·ten·tion (rĭ-tĕn´shən) *n.* **1.** The act of retaining or condition of being retained. **2.** The capacity to retain. [< Lat. *retentus,* p.p. of *retinēre,* to retain.] —**re·ten´tive** *adj.* —**re·ten´tive·ness** *n.*

ret·i·cent (rĕt´ĭ-sənt) *adj.* **1.** Disinclined to speak out; quiet. **2.** Reserved in style. [< Lat. *reticēre,* to keep silent.] —**ret´i·cence** *n.* —**ret´i·cent·ly** *adv.*

ret·i·na (rĕt´n-ə) *n., pl.* **-nas** *or* **-nae** (-n-ē´.) A delicate multilayer light-sensitive membrane that lines the inside of the eyeball and is connected to the brain by the optic nerve. [< Med. Lat. *retina.*] —**ret´i·nal** *adj.*

ret·i·nue (rĕt´n-ōō´, -yōō´) *n.* A group of attendants that accompany a person of rank. [< OFr. *retenir,* to retain.]

re·tire (rĭ-tīr´) *v.* **-tired, -tiring. 1.** To go away; depart, as for rest or seclusion. **2.** To go to bed. **3.** To withdraw from business or public life. **4.** To remove from active service: *retire an old career officer.* **5.** To withdraw troops. **6.** To take out of circulation: *retire bonds.* **7.** *Baseball.* To put out (a batter). [OFr. *retirer.*] —**re·tire´ment** *n.*

re·tired (rĭ-tīrd´) *adj.* **1.** Secluded. **2.** Withdrawn from business or public life.

re·tir·ing (rĭ-tīr´ĭng) *adj.* Reserved; shy. —**re·tir´ing·ly** *adv.* —**re·tir´ing·ness** *n.*

re·tool (rē-tōōl´) *v.* To provide with new tools, machinery, or equipment.

re·tort¹ (rĭ-tôrt´) *v.* **1.** To reply to, esp. in a quick, direct manner. **2.** To retaliate; pay back. —*n.* A quick, clever reply. [< Lat. *retortus,* p.p. of *retorquēre,* to bend back.]

re·tort² (rĭ-tôrt´, rē´tôrt´) *n.* A laboratory vessel used for distilling or decomposing sub

---

ă pat ā pay â care ä father ĕ pet ē be ĭ pit ī tie î pier ŏ pot ō toe ô paw, for oi noise ŏŏ took
ŏŏ boot ou out th thin th this ŭ cut û urge yŏŏ abuse zh vision ə about, item, edible, gallop, circus

stances by heat. [OFr. *retorte*, ult. < Lat. *retorquēre*, to bend back.]

re·touch (rē-tŭch′) v. **1.** To touch up. **2.** *Photog.* To change, esp. by removing flaws.

re·trace (rē-trās′) v. To trace again.

re·tract (rī-trăkt′) v. **1.** To take back; recant: *retract an accusation.* **2.** To draw back or in. [< Lat. *retractare*, to handle again.] —**re·tract′a·ble** or **re·tract′i·ble** adj. —**re·trac′tion** (rē-trăk′shən) n.

re·trac·tile (rī-trăk′tĭl, -tīl′) adj. Capable of being drawn back or in.

re·tread (rē-trĕd′) v. **-tread·ed, -tread·ing.** To fit a new tread on. —n. (rē′trĕd′) A retreaded tire.

re·treat (rī-trēt′) n. **1.** The act of withdrawing, esp. from danger or difficulty. **2.** A safe, secluded place; refuge. **3.** A period of retirement, esp. for religious meditation. **4. a.** The withdrawal of a military force from an enemy attack. **b.** The signal for such a withdrawal. **5.** *Mil.* A trumpet call that signals the lowering of the flag. —v. To make a retreat; withdraw. [< Lat. *retrahere*, to draw back.]

re·trench (rī-trĕnch′) v. **1.** To cut down; reduce. **2.** To reduce expenses; economize. [< OFr. *retrenchier.*] —**re·trench′ment** n.

ret·ri·bu·tion (rĕt′rə-byōō′shən) n. Something given or demanded in response, esp. punishment. [< Lat. *retribuere*, to pay back.] —**re·trib′u·tive** (rī-trĭb′yə-tĭv) or **re·trib′u·to·ry** (-tôr′ē, -tōr′ē) adj.

re·trieve (rī-trēv′) v. **-trieved, -triev·ing.** **1.** To get or bring back; regain. **2.** To find and carry back (game that has been shot). [< OFr. *retrover.*] —**re·triev′a·ble** adj. —**re·triev′a·bly** adv. —**re·triev′al** n.

re·triev·er (rī-trē′vər) n. **1.** One that retrieves. **2.** Any of several breeds of dog developed and trained to retrieve game.

retriever

retro- pref. Backward or back: *retrorocket.* [< Lat. *retro.*]

ret·ro·ac·tive (rĕt′rō-ăk′tĭv) adj. Effective on or applying to an earlier date. —**ret′ro·ac′tive·ly** adv.

ret·ro·fire (rĕt′rō-fīr′) v. To fire a retrorocket.

ret·ro·grade (rĕt′rə-grād′) adj. **1.** Moving or tending backward. **2.** Reverting to an inferior condition. —v. **-grad·ed, -grad·ing.** **1.** To move backward. **2.** To decline; deteriorate. [< Lat. *retrogradus.*]

ret·ro·gress (rĕt′rə-grĕs′, rĕt′rə-grĕs′) v. To move backward, esp. to an earlier, inferior, or less complex condition. [< Lat. *retrogressus*, p.p. of *retrogradi*, to go backward.] —**ret′ro·gres′sion** n. —**ret′ro·gres′sive** adj. —**ret′ro·gres′sive·ly** adv.

ret·ro·rock·et (rĕt′rō-rŏk′ĭt) n. A rocket engine used to slow, stop, or reverse the motion of an aircraft, missile, or spacecraft.

ret·ro·spect (rĕt′rə-spĕkt′) n. A contemplation

of things in the past. [< Lat. *retrospectus*, p.p. of *retrospicere*, to look back at.] —**ret′ro·spec′tion** n. —**ret′ro·spec′tive** adj. —**ret′ro·spec′tive·ly** adv.

re·turn (rī-tûrn′) v. **1.** To go or come back. **2.** To answer; respond. **3.** To send, put, or carry back. **4.** To give in reciprocation. **5.** To bring in (profit); yield. **6.** To deliver (a verdict). **7.** To re-elect to an office or position. —n. **1.** The act of returning. **2.** Something that is returned. **3.** A periodic recurrence. **4.** A reply; response; answer. **5.** A profit or yield. **6.** An official report: *a tax return.* —adj. **1.** Of, relating to, or involving a return. **2.** Given, sent, or done in return: *a return visit.* [< OFr. *retourner.*] —**re·turn′a·ble** adj. —**re·turn′er** n.

re·turn·ee (rī-tûr′nē′) n. One who has returned, as from military service.

re·un·ion (rē-yōōn′yən) n. **1.** The act or an example of reuniting. **2.** A reuniting of the members of a group.

re·u·nite (rē′yōō-nīt′) v. To bring or come together again.

rev (rĕv) *Informal.* —n. A revolution, as of a motor. —v. **revved, rev·ving.** To increase the speed of.

re·vamp (rē-vămp′) v. To make over; revise.

re·veal (rī-vēl′) v. **1.** To make known. **2.** To display or show clearly. [< Lat. *revelare.*]

rev·eil·le (rĕv′ə-lē) n. A signal, as on a drum or bugle, given in the morning to awaken soldiers. [< OFr. *reveiller*, to wake.]

rev·el (rĕv′əl) v. **-eled** or **-elled, -el·ing** or **-el·ling.** **1.** To take part in unrestrained festivities. **2.** To take great pleasure. —n. An unrestrained party or celebration. [< Lat. *rebellare*, to rebel.] —**rev′el·er** or **rev′el·ler** n. —**rev′el·ry** n.

rev·e·la·tion (rĕv′ə-lā′shən) n. **1.** Something that is revealed, esp. something surprising. **2.** An act of revealing. **3. Revelation.** See table at **Bible.** [< Lat. *revelare*, to reveal.] —**rev′e·la·to′ry** (-lə-tôr′ē, -tōr′-) adj.

re·venge (rī-vĕnj′) v. **-venged, -veng·ing.** To inflict punishment in return for (injury or insult); avenge. —n. **1.** The act of revenging. **2.** A desire for revenge. **3.** An opportunity to get even. [< LLat. *revindicare.*] —**re·venge′ful** adj. —**re·veng′er** n.

rev·e·nue (rĕv′ə-nōō′, -nyōō′) n. **1.** The income of a government. **2.** Income from investments. [< Lat. *revenire*, to return.]

re·ver·ber·ate (rī-vûr′bə-rāt′) v. **-at·ed, -at·ing.** To echo; resound. [Lat. *reverberare*, to cause to rebound.] —**re·ver·ber·a′tion** n.

re·vere (rī-vîr′) v. **-vered, -ver·ing.** To regard with great respect or devotion. [Lat. *reverērī.*] —**re·ver′er** n.

rev·er·ence (rĕv′ər-əns) n. **1.** Profound honor and respect. **2.** An act of respect, such as a bow or curtsy. **3. Reverence.** A title of respect for a clergyman. —v. **-enced, -enc·ing.** To feel reverence for.

rev·er·end (rĕv′ər-ənd) adj. **1.** Worthy of reverence. **2.** Often **Reverend.** Designating a member of the clergy. —n. *Informal.* A cleric or minister. [< Lat. *reverērī*, to revere.]

rev·er·ent (rĕv′ər-ənt) adj. Feeling or showing reverence. —**rev′er·ent·ly** adv.

rev·er·en·tial (rĕv′ə-rĕn′shəl) adj. Reverent. —**rev′er·en′tial·ly** adv.

rev·er·ie (rĕv′ə-rē) n. **1.** Abstracted thought. **2.** A daydream. [< OFr. *rêver*, to dream.]

re·ver·sal (rī-vûr′səl) n. An act or instance

of reversing. **2.** A change from better to worse.

re·verse (rĭ-vûrs′) *adj.* **1.** Turned backward in position, direction, or order. **2.** Causing backward movement: *a reverse gear.* —*n.* **1.** The opposite or contrary of something. **2.** The back or rear of something. **3.** A change to an opposite position, condition, or direction, esp. a change for the worse. **4.** A mechanism for reversing movement, as a gear in an automobile. —*v.* **-versed, -vers·ing. 1.** To turn to the opposite direction or position. **2.** To exchange the positions of; transpose. **3.** *Law.* To revoke or annul. **4.** To turn or move in the opposite direction. **5.** To reverse the action of an engine. [< Lat. *revertere,* to revert.] —**re·vers′er** *n.* —**re·vers′i·ble** *adj. & n.*

  Syns: reverse, invert, transpose *v.*

re·vert (rĭ-vûrt′) *v.* **1.** To return to a former condition, practice, or belief. **2.** *Law.* To go back to the possession of a former owner or his heirs. [< Lat. *revertere.*] —**re·ver′sion** *n.* —**re·ver′sion·ar·y** (-vûr′zhə-nĕr′-ē) *adj.*

re·view (rĭ-vyōō′) *v.* **1.** To look over or study (material) again. **2.** To look back on. **3.** To give a critical report on. **4.** *Law.* To examine again, esp. in a higher court. **5.** To conduct a formal inspection of: *reviewed the squadron.* —*n.* **1.** A re-examination or reconsideration. **2.** A summary or survey. **3.** The act of re-studying. **4.** An inspection or examination for the purpose of evaluation. **5. a.** A critical estimate of a work or performance. **b.** A periodical devoted primarily to critical reviews. **6.** A formal military inspection. **7.** *Law.* A re-examination of an action or determination. [OFr. *revoir.*]

re·view·er (rĭ-vyōō′ər) *n.* One who reviews, esp. a newspaper or magazine critic.

re·vile (rĭ-vīl′) *v.* **-viled, -vil·ing.** To subject to abusive language. [< OFr. *reviler.*] —**re·vile′-ment** *n.* —**re·vil′er** *n.*

re·vise (rĭ-vīz′) *v.* **-vised, -vis·ing. 1.** To review (a text) in order to improve or correct. **2.** To change or modify. [Lat. *revisere,* to visit again.] —**re·vis′er** or **re·vi′sor** *n.* —**re·vi′sion** (-vĭzh′ən) *n.*

re·vi·sion·ism (rĭ-vĭzh′ə-nĭz′əm) *n.* Advocacy of the revision of an accepted, usu. long-standing view, theory, or doctrine, esp. a revision of historical events and movements. —**re·vi′sion·ist** *n.*

re·vi·tal·ize (rē-vīt′l-īz′) *v.* To give new life or vigor to. —**re·vi′tal·i·za′tion** *n.*

re·viv·al (rĭ-vī′vəl) *n.* **1.** The act of reviving or condition of being revived. **2.** A new presentation, as of a play. **3.** A meeting or series of meetings for the purpose of reawakening religious faith.

re·vive (rĭ-vīv′) *v.* **-vived, -viv·ing. 1.** To bring or come back to life or consciousness. **2.** To impart or regain health or vigor. **3.** To restore to use or notice. [< Lat. *revivere,* to live again.] —**re·viv′er** *n.*

re·viv·i·fy (rē-vĭv′ə-fī′) *v.* **-fied, -fy·ing.** To give new life to. —**re·viv′i·fi·ca′tion** *n.*

rev·o·ca·ble (rĕv′ə-kə-bəl) *adj.* Capable of being revoked.

re·voke (rĭ-vōk′) *v.* **-voked, -vok·ing.** To make void by withdrawing or canceling; annul. [<

Lat. *revocare,* to call back.] —**rev′o·ca′tion** *n.* —**re·vok′er** *n.*

re·volt (rĭ-vōlt′) *v.* **1.** To attempt to overthrow the authority of the state; rebel. **2.** To oppose or refuse to accept something. **3.** To fill with disgust; repel. —*n.* An uprising; rebellion. [< Lat. *revolvere,* to turn over.]

re·volt·ing (rĭ-vōl′tĭng) *adj.* Repulsive; abhorrent. —**re·volt′ing·ly** *adv.*

rev·o·lu·tion (rĕv′ə-lōō′shən) *n.* **1. a.** Movement in an orbit around a point, esp. as distinguished from rotation on an axis. **b.** A spinning or rotation about an axis. **c.** A single complete cycle of motion about a point in a closed path. **2.** A momentous change in a situation: *the revolution in physics.* **3.** A sudden political overthrow brought about from within a given system. [< Lat. *revolutus,* p.p. of *revolvere,* to turn over.]

rev·o·lu·tion·ar·y (rĕv′ə-lōō′shə-nĕr′ē) *adj.* **1.** Pertaining to revolution. **2.** Promoting revolution; radical. —*n., pl.* **-ies.** One who is engaged in or promotes revolution.

rev·o·lu·tion·ist (rĕv′ə-lōō′shə-nĭst) *n.* A revolutionary.

rev·o·lu·tion·ize (rĕv′ə-lōō′shə-nīz′) *v.* **-ized, -iz·ing.** To change radically or drastically.

re·volve (rĭ-vŏlv′) *v.* **-volved, -volv·ing. 1.** To orbit a central point. **2.** To turn on an axis; rotate. **3.** To recur periodically. [< Lat. *revolvere,* to roll back.] —**re·volv′a·ble** *adj.*

re·volv·er (rĭ-vŏl′vər) *n.* A pistol with a revolving cylinder that places the cartridges one at a time in a position to be fired.

re·vue (rĭ-vyōō′) *n.* A show consisting of usu. satirical skits, songs, and dances. [< OFr. *revoir,* to review.]

re·vul·sion (rĭ-vŭl′shən) *n.* **1.** A sudden, strong feeling of disgust or loathing. **2.** A withdrawing or turning away from something. [< Lat. *revulsus,* p.p. of *revellere,* to tear back.]

re·ward (rĭ-wôrd′) *n.* Something, such as money, that is given or offered for some special service, such as the return of a lost article or the capture of a criminal. —*v.* **1.** To give a reward to. **2.** To give a reward in return for. [< ONFr. *rewarder.*]

re·word (rē-wûrd′) *v.* To state or express again in different words.

re·write (rē-rīt′) *v.* To write again, esp. in a different or improved form.

Rh The symbol for the element rhodium.

Rhae·to-Ro·man·ic (rē′tō-rō-măn′ĭk) *n.* Also **Rhae·to-Ro·mance** (-rō-măns′). A Romance language of southern Switzerland, northern Italy, and the Tyrol. —**Rhae·to-Ro·man′ic** or **Rhae·to-Ro·mance′** *adj.*

rhap·so·dize (răp′sə-dīz′) *v.* **-dized, -diz·ing.** To express oneself rhapsodically.

rhap·so·dy (răp′sə-dē) *n., pl.* **-dies. 1.** Excessively enthusiastic expression of feeling in speech or writing. **2.** *Mus.* A composition of irregular form. [< Gk. *rhapsōidos,* singer of epic poems.] —**rhap·sod′ic** (-sŏd′ĭk) *adj.* —**rhap·sod′i·cal·ly** *adv.*

rhe·a (rē′ə) *n.* A flightless, three-toed South American bird resembling the ostrich. [< *Rhea,* a character in Roman myth.]

rhe·ni·um (rē′nē-əm) *n. Symbol* **Re** A rare dense, silvery-white metallic element used for electrical contacts and with tungsten for high-

---

temperature thermocouples. Atomic number 75; atomic weight 186.2. [< Lat. *Rhenus,* Rhine.]

rhe·o·stat (rē′ə-stăt′) *n.* A variable resistor used to control the flow of current in an electric current. [Gk. *rheos,* current + -STAT.] —**rhe′o·stat′ic** *adj.*

rhe·sus monkey (rē′səs) *n.* A brownish monkey of India, often used in biological research. [< Lat. *Rhesus,* mythological king of Thrace.]

rhet·o·ric (rĕt′ər-ĭk) *n.* 1. The art of effective expression and the persuasive use of language. 2. Affected or pretentious language. [< Gk. *rhētōr,* public speaker.] —**rhe·tor′i·cal** (rĭ-tôr′ĭ-kəl, -tŏr-) *adj.* —**rhet′o·ri′cian** (rĕt′ə-rĭsh′ən) *n.*

rhetorical question *n.* A question to which no answer is expected.

rheum (rōōm) *n.* A watery mucous discharge esp. from the eyes or nose. [< Gk. *rheuma.*] —**rheum′y** *adj.*

rheu·mat·ic (rōō-măt′ĭk) *adj.* Of, pertaining to, or afflicted with rheumatism. —*n.* One afflicted with rheumatism.

rheumatic fever *n.* A severe infectious disease occurring chiefly in children, characterized by fever and painful inflammation of the joints, and frequently resulting in permanent damage to the heart.

rheu·ma·tism (rōō′mə-tĭz′əm) *n.* Any of several diseased conditions of the muscles, tendons, joints, bones, or nerves, that cause pain and disability. [< Gk. *rheuma,* rheum.]

rheu·ma·toid arthritis (rōō′mə-toid′) *n.* A chronic disease marked by stiffness and inflammation of the joints.

Rh factor *n.* Any of several substances in red blood cells capable of causing a severe antigenic reaction. [< RH(ESUS MONKEY).]

rhine·stone (rīn′stōn′) *n.* An imitation diamond made of paste or glass. [< the *Rhine* River.]

rhi·no (rī′nō) *n., pl.* **-nos.** A rhinoceros.

rhi·noc·er·os (rī-nŏs′ər-əs) *n.* A large, thick-skinned, herbivorous mammal of Africa and Asia, with one or two upright horns on the snout. [< Gk. *rhinokerōs.*]

rhinoceros

rhi·zome (rī′zōm′) *n.* A rootlike plant stem that sends out roots below and leaves or shoots above. [< Gk. *rhiza,* root.]

Rh negative *adj.* Lacking an Rh factor.

rho (rō) *n.* The 17th letter of the Greek alphabet. See table at **alphabet.** [Gk. *rhō.*]

rho·di·um (rō′dē-əm) *n. Symbol* **Rh** A hard, durable, silvery-white metallic element used to form high-temperature alloys with plati-

num. Atomic number 45; atomic weight 102.905. [Gk. *rhodon,* rose + -IUM.]

rho·do·den·dron (rō′də-dĕn′drən) *n.* An evergreen shrub with clusters of pink, white, or purplish flowers. [< Gk. *oleander.*]

rhom·boid (rŏm′boid′) *n.* A parallelogram with oblique angles and unequal adjacent sides.

rhom·bus (rŏm′bəs) *n., pl.* **-es** or **-bi** (-bī′). A parallelogram with usu. oblique angles and four equal sides. [< Gk. *rhombos.*] —**rhom′bic** *adj.*

Rh positive *adj.* Containing an Rh factor.

rhu·barb (rōō′bärb′) *n.* 1. A plant with long, fleshy, edible leafstalks. 2. *Slang.* A noisy argument. [Prob. < LLat. *rha barbarum,* barbarian rhubarb.]

rhyme (rīm). Also **rime.** —*n.* 1. Correspondence of terminal sounds of words or lines of verse. 2. Poetry or verse in rhyme. 3. A word that corresponds with another in terminal sound. —*v.* **rhymed, rhym·ing.** 1. To form a rhyme. 2. To compose rhymes or verse. 3. To use as a rhyme. [< Gk. *rhuthmos,* rhythm.] —**rhym′er** *n.*

rhythm (rĭth′əm) *n.* 1. A movement or action characterized by a regularly recurring element. 2. *Mus.* A pattern formed by a series of notes or beats of different lengths and stresses. 3. Metrical movement as regulated by the alternation of long and short or accented and unaccented syllables. [< Gk. *rhuthmos.*] —**rhyth′mi·cal** (-mĭ-kəl) or **rhyth′mic** *adj.* —**rhyth′mi·cal·ly** *adv.*

rhythm and blues *n.* A kind of music developed by black Americans that combines blues and jazz, characterized by a strong simple rhythm.

rhythm method *n.* A birth-control method dependent on continence during the period of female ovulation.

ri·al (rē-ôl′, -äl′) *n.* See table at **currency.** [Pers.]

rib (rĭb) *n.* 1. One of the paired, curved bones extending from the spine to or toward the breastbone in most vertebrates. 2. Something similar to a rib that shapes or supports. 3. A raised ridge in fabric. —*v.* **ribbed, rib·bing.** 1. To shape, support, or provide with a rib or ribs. 2. To make with ridges. 3. To tease. [< OE.] —**ribbed** *adj.*

rib·ald (rĭb′əld) *adj.* Vulgar and indecent. [< OFr. *riber,* to be wanton, of Gmc. orig.] —**rib′ald·ry** *n.*

rib·bon (rĭb′ən) *n.* 1. A narrow strip of fabric, finished at the edges and used for trimming or tying. 2. **ribbons.** Tatters; rags. 3. An inked strip of cloth, polyethylene, etc., in a typewriter. [< OFr. *riban,* of Gmc. orig.]

ri·bo·fla·vin (rī′bō-flā′vĭn) *n.* A crystalline orange-yellow pigment, $C_{17}H_{20}O_6N_4$, the principal growth-promoting factor in the vitamin B complex, found in milk, leafy vegetables, meat, and egg yolks and produced synthetically. [RIBO(SE) + Lat. *flavus,* yellow.]

ri·bo·nu·cle·ic acid (rī′bō-nōō-klē′ĭk, -nyōō-) *n.* RNA. [RIBO(SE) + NUCLEIC ACID.]

ri·bose (rī′bōs′) *n.* A crystalline sugar, $C_5H_{10}O_5$, occurring as a component of nucleic acids. [< G. *Ribonsäure,* acid from which ribose is obtained.]

ri·bo·some (rī′bə-sōm′) *n.* A spherical cytoplasmic RNA-containing particle active in the synthesis of protein. [RIBO(SE) + -SOME[3].] —**ri′bo·so′mal** *adj.*

rice (rīs) *n.* **1.** A cereal grass cultivated extensively in warm climates. **2.** The starchy seed of the rice plant, used as a food. [< Gk. *oruza.*]

rich (rĭch) *adj.* **-er, -est. 1.** Possessing great material wealth. **2.** Having great worth or value: *a rich harvest.* **3.** Magnificent; sumptuous. **4. a.** Abundant: *rich in tradition.* **b.** Abounding, esp. in natural resources: *a rich land.* **5.** Extremely productive. **6.** Containing a large amount of choice ingredients, as butter, sugar, or eggs. **7. a.** Pleasantly full and mellow: *a rich tenor voice.* **b.** Warm and strong in color. **8.** Containing a large proportion of fuel to air: *a rich mixture.* [< OE *rīce.*] —**rich′ly** *adv.* —**rich′ness** *n.*

rich·es (rĭch′ĭz) *pl.n.* Valuable or precious possessions. [< OFr. *richesse.*]

Rich·ter scale (rĭk′tər) *n.* A logarithmic scale used to express the magnitude of an earthquake. [< Charles F. *Richter* (b. 1900).]

rick (rĭk) *n.* A stack, as of hay or straw. [< OE *hrēac.*]

rick·ets (rĭk′ĭts) *n. (used with a sing. verb).* A disease of the young that results from a lack of vitamin D in the diet and is characterized by defective bone growth. [Orig. unknown.]

rick·et·y (rĭk′ĭ-tē) *adj.* **-i·er, -i·est. 1.** Likely to break or fall apart; shaky. **2.** Of or having rickets. [< RICKETS.]

rick·ey (rĭk′ē) *n., pl.* **-eys.** A drink of soda water, lime juice, sugar, and usu. gin. [Prob. < the name *Rickey.*]

rick·shaw or **rick·sha** (rĭk′shô′) *n.* A jinriksha.

ric·o·chet (rĭk′ə-shā′) *v.* **-cheted** (-shād′) or **-chet·ted** (-shĕt′ĭd), **-chet·ing** (-shā′ĭng) or **-chet·ting** (-shĕt′ĭng). To rebound from a surface. [Fr.] —**ric′o·chet′** *n.*

ri·cot·ta (rĭ-kŏt′ə) *n.* An Italian soft cheese that resembles cottage cheese. [Ital.]

rid (rĭd) *v.* **rid** or **rid·ded, rid·ding.** To make free: *rid the streets of litter.* [< ON *rythja.*] —**rid′dance** *n.*

rid·dle¹ (rĭd′l) *v.* **-dled, -dling. 1.** To pierce with numerous holes; perforate. **2.** To spread throughout: *a theory riddled with flaws.* [< OE *hriddel,* sieve.]

rid·dle² (rĭd′l) *n.* **1.** A puzzling question or statement requiring thought to answer or understand. **2.** Something perplexing. [< OE *rædelse.*]

ride (rīd) *v.* **rode** (rōd), **rid·den** (rĭd′n), **rid·ing. 1.** To sit on and be conveyed by an animal. **2.** To be conveyed in a vehicle. **3.** To travel over a surface: *This car rides well.* **4.** To float or move on or as on water. **5.** To sit on and drive. **6.** To be supported or carried upon. **7.** To take part in or do by riding: *rode his last race.* **8.** To cause to be carried: *rode him out of town.* **9.** *Informal.* To tease or ridicule. —**phrasal verb. ride out.** To survive: *ride out a storm.* —*n.* **1.** An act of riding, as on an animal or in a vehicle. **2.** A path or way made for riding. **3.** Something, as at an amusement park, that one rides for pleasure or excitement. [< OE *rīdan.*]

rid·er (rī′dər) *n.* **1.** One who rides. **2.** A clause added to a legislative bill. **3.** An amendment or addition to a document or record.

ridge (rĭj) *n.* **1.** The line formed by the junction of two sloping surfaces: *the ridge of a roof.* **2.** A long, narrow land elevation. **3.** A long, narrow, or crested part, esp. of the body: *the ridge of the nose.* **4.** A raised strip of plowed ground. —*v.* **ridged, ridg·ing.** To mark with, form into, or provide with ridges. [< OE *hrycg.*] —**ridg′y** *adj.*

ridge·pole (rĭj′pōl′) *n.* A horizontal beam at the ridge of a roof, to which the upper ends of the rafters are attached.

ridgepole

rid·i·cule (rĭd′ĭ-kyōōl′) *n.* Words or actions intended to evoke contemptuous laughter at a person or thing. —*v.* **-culed, -cul·ing.** To make fun of. [< Lat. *ridiculus,* laughable.]
Syns: *ridicule, deride, gibe, mock, taunt v.*

ri·dic·u·lous (rĭ-dĭk′yə-ləs) *adj.* Deserving or inspiring ridicule; absurd or preposterous. —**ri·dic′u·lous·ly** *adv.* —**ri·dic′u·lous·ness** *n.*

ri·el (rē-ĕl′) *n.* See table at **currency.** [Orig. unknown.]

rife (rīf) *adj.* **rif·er, rif·est. 1.** Widespread; prevalent. **2.** Abounding; full: *rife with corruption.* [< OE *rȳfe.*]

riff (rĭf) *n.* A constantly repeated rhythmic phrase esp. in jazz. [Orig. unknown.]

riff·raff (rĭf′răf′) *n.* **1.** Worthless or disreputable persons. **2.** Rubbish; trash. [< OFr. *rif et raf,* one and all.]

ri·fle¹ (rī′fəl) *n.* A firearm with a long barrel containing spiral grooves. —*v.* **-fled, -fling.** To cut spiral grooves within. [< OFr. *rifler,* to scratch.]

ri·fle² (rī′fəl) *v.* **-fled, -fling. 1.** To search with intent to steal. **2.** To rob. [< OFr. *rifler,* to plunder.] —**ri′fler** *n.*

rift (rĭft) *n.* **1. a.** A fault, as in a system of rock. **b.** A narrow break or crack in a rock. **2.** A break in friendly relations. —*v.* To split or cause to split open. [ME, of Scand. orig.]

rig (rĭg) *v.* **rigged, rig·ging. 1.** To fit out; equip. **2.** To equip (a ship) with rigging. **3.** *Informal.* To dress, clothe, or adorn. **4.** To make or equip in a makeshift manner. **5.** To manipulate dishonestly: *rig a prizefight.* —*n.* **1.** The arrangement of masts, spars, and sails on a sailing vessel. **2.** Equipment or gear for a particular purpose. **3.** A vehicle with its horses. **4.** *Informal.* An outfit. [ME *riggen.*]

rig·a·ma·role (rĭg′ə-mə-rōl′) *n.* Var. of **rigmarole.**

rig·ging (rĭg′ĭng) *n.* **1.** The system of ropes, chains, and tackle used to support and control the masts, sails, and yards of a sailing vessel. **2.** The supporting material for construction work.

right (rīt) *n.* **1. a.** The side opposite the left. **b.** The direction of this side. **2.** Often **Right.** The persons who adhere to traditional attitudes and beliefs and hold conservative political views. **3.** Something that is morally and ethically proper, just, or good. **4.** A just or legal claim or title: *the right to vote.* —*adj.*

---

1. a. Of or located on the side opposite the left. **b.** Toward this side: *a right turn*. **2.** Often **Right**. Of or relating to the political right. **3.** Intended to be worn facing outward: *the right side of the dress*. **4.** In accordance with fact, reason, or truth; correct: *the right answer*. **5.** Morally correct or justifiable: *the right thing to do*. **6.** Advantageous, desirable, or suitable: *in the right place at the right time*. **7.** Fitting; proper: *just right for the part*. —*adv.* **1.** To or on the right. **2.** In a straight line; directly. **3.** In a correct manner; properly. **4.** Exactly; just: *right where he was standing*. **5.** Immediately: *right after breakfast*. **6.** Very: *the Right Reverend Mr. Smith*. **7.** Used as an intensive: *kept right on going.* —*v.* **1.** To restore to or regain an upright position. **2.** To put in or restore to a proper state. **3.** To redress: *right a wrong.* —*idioms.* **by right (or rights).** Justly; properly. **to rights.** In a satisfactory condition. [< OE *riht*.] —**right'ness** *n.*

right angle *n.* An angle of 90° formed by two lines perpendicular to each other. —**right'-an'gled** *adj.*

right·eous (rī'chəs) *adj.* Morally right; just. [< OE *rihtwīs*.] —**right'eous·ly** *adv.* —**right'eous·ness** *n.*

right field *n. Baseball.* The part of the outfield that is to the right as viewed from home plate. —**right fielder** *n.*

right·ful (rīt'fəl) *adj.* **1.** Right or proper; just. **2.** Having or held by a just or proper claim. —**right'ful·ly** *adv.* —**right'ful·ness** *n.*

right-hand (rīt'hănd') *adj.* **1.** Located on or directed toward the right side. **2.** Of or done by the right hand. **3.** Indispensable; reliable.

right-hand·ed (rīt'hăn'dĭd) *adj.* **1.** Using the right hand more skillfully than the left. **2.** Done with or made for the right hand. **3.** Clockwise. —**right'-hand'ed** *or* **right'-hand'ed·ly** *adv.* —**right'-hand'ed·ness** *n.*

right·ist (rī'tĭst) *n.* A political conservative or reactionary.

right·ly (rīt'lē) *adv.* **1.** In a correct manner; properly. **2.** With honesty; justly.

right of way *n.* Also **right-of-way** (rīt'əv-wā') *pl.* **rights-of-way** *or* **right-of-ways.** **1.** *Law.* **a.** The right to pass over property owned by another. **b.** The path or thoroughfare on which such passage is made. **2.** The strip of land over which facilities such as highways, railroads, or power lines are built. **3.** The customary or legal right of a person, vessel, or vehicle to pass before another.

right-on (rīt'ŏn', -ôn') *adj. Slang.* Up-to-date and sophisticated; trendy.

right wing *n.* A division holding conservative views within a larger political group. —**right winger** *n.*

rig·id (rĭj'ĭd) *adj.* **1.** Not bending; stiff; inflexible. **2.** Not moving; fixed. **3.** Harsh; severe. [< Lat. *rigēre*, to be stiff.] —**ri·gid'i·ty** *or* **rig'id·ness** *n.* —**rig'id·ly** *adv.*

Syns: *rigid, inflexible, stiff, unbending, unyielding adj.*

rig·ma·role (rĭg'mə-rōl') *n.* Also **rig·a·ma·role** (-ə-mə-rōl'). **1.** Meaningless speech; nonsense. **2.** A complicated procedure. [< ME *rageman rolle*, scroll used in a game of chance.]

rig·or (rĭg'ər) *n.* **1.** Strictness; severity. **2.** A trying condition; hardship. **3.** A shivering or trembling, as from a chill. [< Lat.] —**rig'or·ous** *adj.* —**rig'or·ous·ly** *adv.*

rig·or mor·tis (rĭg'ər môr'tĭs) *n.* Muscular stiffening after death. [Lat., stiffness of death.]

rile (rīl) *v.* **riled, ril·ing.** To anger or irritate. [< ROIL.]

rill (rĭl) *n.* A small brook. [LG *rille*.]

rim (rĭm) *n.* **1.** The border or edge of something. **2.** The outer part of a wheel around which the tire is rolled. —*v.* **rimmed, rim·ming.** To furnish with a rim. [< OE *rima*.]

rime¹ (rīm) *n.* A frost or granular ice coating; hoarfrost. [< OE *hrīm*.] —**rim'y** *adj.*

rime² (rīm) *n. & v.* Var. of **rhyme.**

rind (rīnd) *n.* A tough outer covering, as the bark of a tree or the skin of a fruit. [< OE.]

ring¹ (rĭng) *n.* **1.** A circular object, form, or arrangement with a vacant circular center. **2.** A small circular band, often of precious metal, worn on a finger. **3.** An enclosed area in which exhibitions, sports, or contests take place. **4.** Boxing. **5.** A group of persons acting for their own gain. —*v.* **1.** To surround with or as if with a ring; encircle. **2.** To form a ring. **3.** *Games.* To toss a ring over (a peg). [< OE *hring*.]

ring² (rĭng) *v.* **rang** (răng), **rung** (rŭng), **ring·ing.** **1.** To give forth a clear, resonant sound when caused to vibrate. **2.** To cause (e.g. a bell) to sound. **3.** To sound a bell in order to summon someone. **4.** To have a character suggestive of a particular quality: *a perception that rings true.* **5.** To resound. **6.** To hear a persistent humming or buzzing: *ears ringing from the blast.* **7.** To call (someone) on the telephone. —*phrasal verb.* **ring up.** To record: *ring up a sale.* —*n.* **1.** The sound created by or as if by a bell. **2.** A loud sound that is continued or repeated. **3.** A telephone call. **4.** A particular quality: *His offer has a suspicious ring.* [< OE *hringan*.]

ring·er (rĭng'ər) *n.* **1.** One that sounds a bell or chime. **2.** *Slang.* A contestant entered dishonestly into a competition. **3.** *Slang.* One who bears a striking resemblance to another.

ring·lead·er (rĭng'lē'dər) *n.* A leader, esp. of a group involved in unlawful activities.

ring·let (rĭng'lĭt) *n.* A lock of hair. **2.** A small circle or ring.

ring·mas·ter (rĭng'măs'tər) *n.* A person in charge of the performances in a circus ring.

ring·side (rĭng'sīd') *n.* A place providing a close view, esp. at a prizefight.

ring·worm (rĭng'wûrm') *n.* A contagious skin disease caused by a fungus and resulting in ring-shaped itching patches.

rink (rĭngk) *n.* **1.** An area surfaced with smooth ice for skating. **2.** A smooth floor suited for roller-skating. [< OFr. *renc*, line, of Gmc. orig.]

rinse (rĭns) *v.* **rinsed, rins·ing.** **1.** To wash lightly. **2.** To remove with water. —*n.* **1.** The act of rinsing. **2.** The liquid used in rinsing. **3.** A solution used in coloring the hair. [< Lat. *recens*, fresh.] —**rins'er** *n.*

ri·ot (rī'ət) *n.* **1.** Public uproar or disturbance. **2.** A disturbance of the peace. **3.** A profuse display. **4.** Unrestrained merrymaking; revelry. **5.** *Slang.* An extremely funny person or thing. —*v.* **1.** To take part in a riot. **2.** To engage in uncontrolled revelry. [< OFr. *rioter*, to quarrel.] —**ri'ot·ous** *adj.* —**ri'ot·ous·ly** *adv.* —**ri'ot·ous·ness** *n.*

rip (rĭp) *v.* **ripped, rip·ping.** **1.** To tear or become torn apart. **2.** To split or saw (wood) along the grain. **3.** To remove by pulling or tearing roughly. **4.** To move quickly or violently. **5.** To attack or censure. —*phrasal verb.* **rip off.** *Slang.* **1.** To steal. **2.** To exploit. —*n.* A torn or split place; tear. [ME *rippen*.] —**rip′per** *n.*

rip·cord (rĭp′kôrd′) *n.* A cord pulled to release a parachute from its pack.

ripe (rīp) *adj.* **rip·er, rip·est. 1.** Fully grown and developed; mature: *a ripe melon.* **2.** Fully prepared; ready. **3.** Suitable; opportune: *The time is ripe.* [< OE *rīpe.*] —**ripe′ness** *n.*

rip·en (rī′pən) *v.* To make or become ripe.

rip-off (rĭp′ôf′, -ŏf′) *n. Slang.* **1.** A theft. **2.** An act of exploitation.

ri·poste (rĭ-pōst′) *n.* **1.** *Fencing.* A quick thrust given after parrying an opponent's lunge. **2. a.** A retaliatory maneuver. **b.** A retort. [< Ital. *riposta,* answer.] —**ri·poste′** *v.*

rip·ple (rĭp′əl) *v.* **1.** A small wave or undulation. **2.** A sound like rippling water: *a ripple of laughter.* —*v.* **-pled, -pling. 1.** To form small waves on the surface. **2.** To rise and fall gently in tone or volume. [Orig. unknown.]

rip·saw (rĭp′sô′) *n.* A coarse-toothed saw used for cutting wood along the grain.

rise (rīz) *v.* **rose** (rōz), **ris·en** (rĭz′ən), **ris·ing. 1.** To move from a lower to a higher position. **2.** To get up from a sitting or lying position. **3.** To get out of bed. **4.** To increase in size, volume, or level. **5.** To increase in number, amount, or value. **6.** To increase in intensity, force, or speed. **7.** To advance in status, rank, or condition. **8.** To slope or extend upward. **9.** To become visible above the horizon. **10.** To come back to life. **11.** To come into existence; spring up. **12.** To rebel. —*n.* **1.** An act of rising; ascent. **2.** An upward slope. **3.** The appearance of the sun or other heavenly body above the horizon. **4.** An increase in volume, size, or height. **5.** An increase, as in amount, value, or intensity. **6.** An improvement in status, rank, or condition. **7.** An origin; beginning. **8.** An angry reaction. [< OE *rīsan.*]

Syns: rise, ascend, climb, mount, soar *v.*

Usage: Either *rise* or *arise* may be used in the sense "to get out of bed."

ris·er (rī′zər) *n.* **1.** One who rises, esp. from sleep. **2.** The vertical part of a stair step.

ris·i·bil·i·ty (rĭz′ə-bĭl′ĭ-tē) *n., pl.* **-ties. 1.** Often **risibilities.** The ability or tendency to laugh. **2.** Laughter; hilarity.

ris·i·ble (rĭz′ə-bəl) *adj.* **1.** Capable of laughing or inclined to laugh. **2.** Causing laughter; funny. [< Lat. *risus,* p.p. of *rīdēre,* to laugh.] —**ris′i·bly** *adv.*

risk (rĭsk) *n.* The possibility of harm or loss; danger. —*v.* **1.** To expose to a chance of loss or damage: *risked her life.* **2.** To incur the risk of: *risk an accident.* [< Ital. *risco.*] —**risk′y** *adj.*

ris·qué (rĭ-skā′) *adj.* Suggestive of or bordering on indelicacy or impropriety. [Fr. < *risquer,* to risk.]

rite (rīt) *n.* **1.** The prescribed form for conducting a religious or other solemn ceremony. **2.** A ceremonial act. [< Lat. *rītus.*]

rit·u·al (rĭch′ōō-əl) *n.* **1.** The form for a ceremony. **2.** A system of ceremonies. **3.** Often **rituals.** A ceremonial act or a series of such acts. **4.** A customary procedure. [< Lat. *ri-*

tuālis, of rites.] —**rit′u·al** *adj.* —**rit′u·al·ism** *n.* —**rit′u·al·is′tic** *adj.* —**rit′u·al·is′ti·cal·ly** *adv.* —**rit′u·al·ly** *adv.*

ritz·y (rĭt′sē) *adj.* **-i·er, -i·est.** *Slang.* Elegant; fashionable. [< the *Ritz* hotels.]

ri·val (rī′vəl) *n.* **1.** One who competes with or attempts to outdo another. **2.** One that equals another. —*v.* **-valed** or **-valled, -val·ing** or **val·ling. 1.** To attempt to equal or surpass. **2.** To be a match for. [< Lat. *rivalis,* one sharing a stream.] —**ri′val** *adj.* —**ri′val·ry** *n.*

rive (rīv) *v.* **rived, rived** or **riv·en** (rĭv′ən), **riv·ing. 1.** To tear apart; rend. **2.** To split; cleave. [< ON *rīfa.*]

riv·er (rĭv′ər) *n.* A relatively large natural stream of water. [< Lat. *ripa,* bank.]

riv·er·side (rĭv′ər-sīd′) *n.* The bank or side of a river.

riv·et (rĭv′ĭt) *n.* A metal bolt or pin, with a head on one end, that is used to join two or more objects by passing through a hole in each piece and whose headless end is then hammered to form another head. —*v.* **1.** To fasten with or as if with a rivet. **2.** To engross or hold (e.g. the attention). [< OFr. *river,* to attach.] —**riv′et·er** *n.*

riv·u·let (rĭv′yə-lĭt) *n.* A small brook or stream. [< Lat. *rivus,* stream.]

ri·yal (rē-ôl′, -äl′) *n.* See table at **currency.** [Ar. *riyāl.*]

ri·yal-o·ma·ni (rē-ôl′ō-mä′nē, rē-äl′-) *n.* See table at **currency.** [Ar. *riyāl 'umānīy,* riyal of Oman.]

Rn The symbol for the element radon.

RNA (är′ĕn-ā′) *n.* Ribonucleic acid, a universal polymeric constituent of all living cells, consisting of a single-stranded chain of alternating phosphate and ribose units with the bases adenine, guanine, cytosine, and uracil bonded to the ribose, the structure and base sequence of which are determinants of protein synthesis. [R(IBO)N(UCLEIC) A(CID).]

roach¹ (rōch) *n.* A European freshwater fish. [< OFr. *roche.*]

roach² (rōch) *n.* A cockroach.

road (rōd) *n.* **1.** An open way for the passage of vehicles, persons, and animals. **2.** A path; course. —*idiom.* **on the road.** Traveling. [< OE *rād,* the act of riding.]

road·bed (rōd′bĕd′) *n.* **1.** The foundation upon which railroad tracks are laid. **2.** The foundation and surface of a road.

road·block (rōd′blŏk′) *n.* **1.** A blockade set up on a road. **2.** An obstacle or hindrance.

road·house (rōd′hous′) *n.* An inn, restaurant, or nightclub located on a road outside a city.

road·run·ner (rōd′rŭn′ər) *n.* A swift-running, long-tailed, crested bird of southwestern North America.

road·side (rōd′sīd′) *n.* The area bordering a road. —**road′side′** *adj.*

road·ster (rōd′stər) *n.* An open automobile for two people.

road·way (rōd′wā′) *n.* A road, esp. the part over which vehicles travel.

road·work (rōd′wûrk′) *n.* Outdoor long-distance running as a form of exercise or conditioning.

roam (rōm) *v.* To move or travel (through) purposelessly. [ME *romen.*] —**roam′er** *n.*

roan (rōn) *adj.* Having a chestnut, bay, or

sorrel coat thickly sprinkled with white or gray: *a roan horse.* —*n.* A roan animal. [< OSp. *roano.*]

roar (rôr) *v.* **1.** To utter a loud, deep, prolonged sound, esp. in distress, rage, or excitement. **2.** To utter or express with a loud, deep, prolonged sound. **3.** To laugh loudly or excitedly. —*n.* A roaring sound or cry. [< OE *rārian.*] —**roar'er** *n.*

roast (rōst) *v.* **1.** To cook with dry heat. **2.** To expose to great or excessive heat. **3.** To heat (ore) in a furnace in order to dehydrate, purify, or oxidize. **4.** *Informal.* To criticize or ridicule harshly. —*n.* **1.** A cut of meat roasted or suitable for roasting. **2.** An outing at which food is cooked by roasting. [< OFr. *rostir,* of Gmc. orig.]

rob (rŏb) *v.* **robbed, rob·bing. 1.** To steal (from). **2.** To deprive of something. [< OFr. *rober.*] —**rob'ber** *n.* —**rob'ber·y** *n.*

robe (rōb) *n.* **1.** A long, loose, flowing garment, esp. one worn to show office or rank. **2.** A bathrobe or dressing gown. **3.** A blanket or covering for the lap and legs. —*v.* **robed, rob·ing.** To dress in a robe. [< OFr., of Gmc. orig.]

rob·in (rŏb'ĭn) *n.* **1.** A North American songbird with a rust-red breast and gray and black upper plumage. **2.** A small Old World bird with an orange breast and a brown back. [< the name *Robin.*]

robin

ro·bot (rō'bŏt, -bŏt) *n.* **1.** A machine that resembles a human being and is capable of performing human tasks. **2.** A person who works or follows orders mechanically. **3.** A machine or device that works automatically. [Czech < *robota,* work.]

ro·bust (rō-bŭst', rō'bŭst) *adj.* **1.** Full of health and vigor. **2.** Marked by richness and fullness. [< Lat. *robur,* strength, oak.] —**ro·bust'ly** *adv.* —**ro·bust'ness** *n.*

rock¹ (rŏk) *n.* **1. a.** A relatively hard, naturally occurring material of mineral origin. **b.** A fragment of such material; stone. **2.** *Geol.* A naturally formed mineral mass forming part of the earth's crust. **3.** One that is firm, stable, or dependable. **4.** *Slang.* A large gem, esp. a diamond. —*idiom.* **on the rocks. 1.** In or into ruin. **2.** Served over ice cubes. [< ONFr. *roque.*]

rock² (rŏk) *v.* **1.** To move back and forth or from side to side in a rhythmic motion. **2.** To shake violently, as from a shock. —*n.* **1.** A rhythmic, swaying motion. **2.** Rock 'n' roll. [< OE *roccian.*]

rock-and-roll (rŏk'ən-rōl') *n.* Var. of **rock 'n' roll.**

rock-bound (rŏk'bound') *adj.* Hemmed in by or bordered with rocks.

rock·er (rŏk'ər) *n.* **1.** A rocking chair. **2.** A curved piece upon which something, as a cradle, rocks. **3.** A machine part that has a rocking motion.

rock·et (rŏk'ĭt) *n.* **1. a.** A device propelled by ejection of matter, esp. by the high-velocity ejection of gaseous combustion products. **b.** An engine that propels in this manner; rocket engine. **2.** A rocket-propelled explosive weapon. —*v.* To move swiftly, as a rocket. [Ital. *rocchetta,* dim. of *rocca,* distaff.]

rock·et·ry (rŏk'ĭ-trē) *n.* The science and technology of rocket design, construction, and flight.

rock·ing chair (rŏk'ĭng) *n.* A chair mounted on rockers or springs.

rocking horse *n.* A toy horse mounted upon rockers.

rock 'n' roll (rŏk'ən-rōl') *n.* Also **rock-and-roll.** A form of popular music having a strongly accented beat and combining elements of blues, country, and folk music.

rock-ribbed (rŏk'rĭbd') *adj.* **1.** Rocky. **2.** Stern and unyielding.

rock salt *n.* Common salt in large masses.

rock wool *n.* Fireproof fibers made by shooting steam through molten rock, used as insulation.

rock·y¹ (rŏk'ē) *adj.* **-i·er, -i·est. 1.** Consisting of or full of rocks. **2.** Resembling or suggesting rock; unyielding. —**rock'i·ness** *n.*

rock·y² (rŏk'ē) *adj.* **-i·er, -i·est. 1.** Inclined to sway or totter; shaky. **2.** Weak, dizzy, or nauseated. —**rock'i·ness** *n.*

ro·co·co (rə-kō'kō, rō'kə-kō') *adj.* **1.** Of an artistic style characterized by fanciful, asymmetric ornamentation. **2.** Overly elaborate; ornate. [Fr.] —**ro·co'co** *n.*

rod (rŏd) *n.* **1.** A straight, thin stick or bar. **2. a.** A stick used to punish by whipping. **b.** Punishment. **3.** A fishing rod. **4.** A measuring stick. **5.** A linear measure equal to 5.5 yards, 16.5 feet, or 5.03 meters. **6.** *Slang.* A handgun. [< OE *rodd.*]

rode (rōd) *v.* *p.t.* of **ride.**

ro·dent (rōd'nt) *n.* Any of various related mammals, as a mouse, rat, or beaver, that have large incisors adapted for gnawing or nibbling. [< Lat. *rodere,* to gnaw.]

ro·de·o (rō'dē-ō', rō-dā'ō) *n.,* *pl.* **-os. 1.** A cattle roundup. **2.** A competition featuring cowboy skills. [Sp. < *rodear,* to surround.]

roe¹ (rō) *n.* The eggs of a fish, often with the membranes in which they are held. [ME *row.*]

roe² (rō) *n.* Also **roe deer.** A small, delicately formed Eurasian deer. [< OE *rā.*]

roent·gen (rĕnt'gən, rŭnt'-) *n.* A unit used to measure the intensity of exposure to x-rays, gamma rays, and similar ionizing radiation. [< Wilhelm K. *Roentgen* (1845–1923).]

rog·er (rŏj'ər) *interj.* Used in radio communications to indicate a message has been received. [< the name *Roger,* code word for letter *r.*]

rogue (rōg) *n.* **1.** An unprincipled person; scoundrel. **2.** A mischievous person; scamp. [Orig. unknown.] —**rog'uer·y** *n.* —**rog'uish** *adj.* —**rog'uish·ly** *adv.* —**rog'uish·ness** *n.*

roil (roil) *v.* **1.** To make muddy or cloudy by stirring up sediment. **2.** To irritate; vex. [Orig. unknown.]

role *or* **rôle** (rōl) *n.* **1.** A character played esp. by an actor. **2.** A function. [< OFr. *rolle,* roll of parchment.]

roll (rōl) *v.* **1.** To move by turning over and

over. **2.** To move on wheels. **3.** To gain momentum. **4.** To go by; elapse. **5.** To turn over and over: *roll in the mud.* **6.** To advance with a rising and falling motion, as waves. **7.** To move or rock from side to side, as a ship. **8.** To make a deep, prolonged, surging sound, as thunder. **9.** To rotate: *roll one's eyes.* **10.** To pronounce or utter with a trill: *roll one's r's.* **11.** To wrap (something) round and round upon itself or around something else. **12.** To envelop or enfold in a covering. **13.** To spread, compress, or flatten by applying pressure with a roller. **14.** To throw (dice) in craps or other games. —*phrasal verb.* **roll back.** To reduce (prices or wages) to a previous lower level. —*n.* **1.** An instance of rolling. **2.** A quantity of something rolled up in the form of a cylinder. **3.** A piece of parchment or paper that can be or is rolled up; scroll. **4.** A list of names of persons belonging to a given group. **5. a.** A small rounded portion of bread. **b.** A food that is prepared by rolling up: *an egg roll.* **6.** A rolling, swaying, or rocking motion. **7.** A deep reverberation or rumble. **8.** A rapid succession of short sounds: *a drum roll.* [< Lat. *rota*, wheel.]
roll·back (rōl′băk′) *n.* A reduction of prices or wages to a previous lower level.
roll call *n.* The reading aloud of a list of names to determine who is present.
roll·er (rō′lər) *n.* **1.** A small wheel, as on a caster. **2.** A cylinder around which something is wound. **3.** A heavy cylinder used to level or crush. **4.** A cylinder for applying paint, ink, etc., onto a surface. **5.** A heavy wave that breaks on the coast.
roller coaster *n.* A sharply banked railway in an amusement park with small open cars.
roller skate *n.* A skate having four small wheels instead of a runner or runners. —**roll′-er-skate′** *v.*
rol·lick (rōl′ĭk) *v.* To romp; frolic. [Orig. unknown.] —**rol′lick·ing** *adj.*
rolling pin *n.* A smooth cylinder for rolling out dough.
ro·ly-po·ly (rō′lē-pō′lē) *adj.* Short and plump. [< ROLL.]
ro·maine (rō-mān′) *n.* A variety of lettuce with long leaves that form a head. [Fr., Roman.]
Ro·man (rō′mən) *n.* **1.** A native or inhabitant of Rome, esp. ancient Rome. **2.** The Latin language. **3. roman.** *Printing.* The most common style of type, characterized by upright letters. **4. Romans.** (*used with a sing. verb*). See table at Bible. —*adj.* **1.** Of or pertaining to Rome and its people, esp. ancient Rome. **2.** Latin. **3.** Of or pertaining to the Roman Catholic Church. **4. roman.** Of, set, or printed in roman.
Roman candle *n.* A firework consisting of a tube from which balls of fire are ejected.
Roman Catholic *adj.* Of or pertaining to the Roman Catholic Church. —*n.* A member of the Roman Catholic Church.
Roman Catholic Church *n.* The Christian church that is organized in a hierarchical structure of bishops and priests with the pope in Rome at its head.
ro·mance (rō-măns′, rō′măns′) *n.* **1. a.** A medieval narrative telling of the adventures of

chivalric heroes. **b.** A long, fictitious tale of heroes and extraordinary or mysterious events. **c.** A quality suggestive of the adventure and idealized exploits found in such tales. **2.** A story or film dealing with a love affair. **3. a.** A love affair. **b.** Romantic involvement; love. **4.** Inclination toward the romantic or adventurous; romantic spirit. **5. Romance.** The Romance languages. —*adj.* **Romance.** Of or relating to the Romance languages. —*v.* (rō-măns′) **-manced, -manc·ing.** To carry on a love affair with; woo. [< OFr. *romans*, ult. < Lat. *Roma*, Rome.]
Romance languages *pl.n.* A group of languages that developed from Latin, including French, Italian, Portuguese, Rumanian, and Spanish.
Ro·man·esque (rō′mə-nĕsk′) *adj.* Of or designating a style of European architecture prevalent from the 9th to the 12th cent. —**Ro′man·esque′** *n.*
Ro·ma·ni·an (rō-mā′nē-ən, -mān′yən) *n.* Var. of Rumanian.
Roman numeral *n.* Any of the numerals formed with the characters I, V, X, L, C, D, and M in the ancient Roman system of numeration.
Ro·mansch (rō-mänsh′, -mänsh′) *n.* Also **Ro·mansh.** The Rhaeto-Romanic dialects of eastern Switzerland and neighboring parts of Italy.
ro·man·tic (rō-măn′tĭk) *adj.* **1.** Of or characteristic of romance. **2.** Inclined to dream of adventure, heroism, or love. **3.** Imaginative but impractical. **4.** Of love or a love affair. **5.** Of romanticism in the arts. —*n.* **1.** A romantic person. **2.** A romanticist. —**ro·man′ti·cal·ly** *adv.*
ro·man·ti·cism (rō-măn′tĭ-sĭz′əm) *n.* An artistic and intellectual movement that originated in the late 18th cent. and stressed strong emotion, imagination, freedom from classical correctness in art forms, and rebellion against social conventions. —**ro·man′ti·cist** *n.*
ro·man·ti·cize (rō-măn′tĭ-sīz′) *v.* **-cized, -ciz·ing.** **1.** To interpret romantically. **2.** To think in a romantic way. —**ro·man′ti·ci·za′tion** *n.*
Rom·a·ny (rŏm′ə-nē, rō′mə-) *n.,* *pl.* **-ny** or **-nies.** **1.** A Gypsy. **2.** The Indic language of the Gypsies. —**Rom′a·ny** *adj.*
romp (rŏmp) *v.* **1.** To play in a boisterous manner. **2.** *Slang.* To win a race easily. [< OFr. *ramper*, to rear up.] —**romp** *n.*
romp·er (rŏm′pər) *n.* **1.** One that romps. **2. rompers.** A loose-fitting one-piece playsuit, worn esp. by small children.
rood (rōōd) *n.* **1.** A cross or crucifix. **2.** A measure of land equal to ¼ acre or 40 square rods. [< OE *rōd.*]
roof (rōōf, rŏŏf) *n.* **1.** The exterior covering on the top of a building. **2.** The top covering of anything. **3.** The upper part of the mouth. —*v.* To cover with a roof. [< OE *hrōf.*] —**roof′er** *n.* —**roof′less** *adj.*
roof·ing (rōō′fĭng, rŏŏf′ĭng) *n.* Materials used in constructing a roof.
rook¹ (rŏŏk) *n.* An Old World bird related to the crow. —*v. Slang.* To cheat; swindle. [< OE *hrōc.*]
rook² (rŏŏk) *n.* A chess piece that may move

I	1
II	2
III	3
IV	4
V	5
VI	6
VII	7
VIII	8
IX	9
X	10
XI	11
XII	12
XIII	13
XIV	14
XV	15
XVI	16
XVII	17
XVIII	18
XIX	19
XX	20
XXI	21
XXIX	29
XXX	30
XL	40
XLVIII	48
IL	49
L	50
LX	60
XC	90
XCVIII	98
IC	99
C	100
CI	101
CC	200
D	500
DC	600
CM	900
M	1,000
MDCLXVI	1666
MCMLXX	1970

Roman numeral

horizontally or vertically across any number of unoccupied squares. [< Pers. *rukh.*]
rook·er·y (rŏŏk′ə-rē) *n., pl.* **-ies**. The breeding ground of rooks and various animals, as seals.
rook·ie (rŏŏk′ē) *n. Slang.* **1.** An untrained recruit. **2.** A beginner; novice. [< RECRUIT.]
room (rŏŏm, rŏŏm) *n.* **1.** Open space. **2. a.** An area of a building set off by walls or partitions. **b.** The people present in such an area: *The whole room laughed.* **3. rooms.** Living quarters. **4.** Suitable opportunity: *no room for error.* —*v.* To occupy a room; lodge. [< OE *rūm.*] —**room′ful′** *adj.* —**room′i·ness** *n.* —**room′y** *adj.*
room·er (rŏŏ′mər, rŏŏm′ər) *n.* A lodger.
room·ette (rŏŏ-mĕt′, rŏŏm-ĕt′) *n.* A small compartment in a railroad sleeping car.
room·ing house (rŏŏ′mĭng, rŏŏm′ĭng) *n.* A house where lodgers can rent rooms.
room·mate (rŏŏm′māt′, rŏŏm′-) *n.* A person with whom one shares a room or apartment.
roost (rŏŏst) *n.* **1.** A perch on which birds rest. **2.** A place where birds perch. —*v.* To perch for the night. [< OE *hrōst.*]

roost·er (rŏŏ′stər) *n.* The adult male of the common domestic fowl.
root¹ (rŏŏt, rŏŏt) *n.* **1. a.** The usu. underground portion of a plant that serves as support and draws and stores food. **b.** A similar underground plant part, such as a tuber. **2.** The part of an organ or body structure, as a hair, that is embedded in other tissue. **3.** A base or support. **4.** A source; origin. **5.** The essential part; core. **6.** *Ling.* **a.** In etymology, a word or word element from which other words are formed. **b.** In morphology, a base to which prefixes and suffixes may be added. **7.** *Math.* A number that when used as a factor in multiplication a given number of times produces a specified product. —*v.* **1.** To send forth a root or roots. **2.** To implant or become firmly established by or as if by roots. **3.** To pull up by or as if by the roots. [< ON *rōt.*] —**root′less** *adj.* —**root′less·ness** *n.*
root² (rŏŏt, rŏŏt) *v.* **1.** To dig with or as with the snout or nose. **2.** To rummage for something. [< OE *wrōtan.*]
root³ (rŏŏt, rŏŏt) *v.* **1.** To give encouragement to; cheer. **2.** To lend support to. [Poss. < *rout,* to make a loud noise.] —**root′er** *n.*
root beer *n.* A carbonated soft drink made from extracts of certain plant roots.
rope (rōp) *n.* **1.** A heavy, strong cord made of twisted strands of fiber, wire, or other material. **2.** A string of items attached by or as by twisting or braiding: *a rope of onions.* **3. ropes.** *Informal.* Specialized techniques or procedures: *learning the ropes.* —*v.* **roped, rop·ing. 1.** To tie or fasten with or as if with a rope. **2.** To enclose with a rope. **3.** To lasso. —*idiom.* **on the ropes.** Nearing total collapse or ruin. [< OE *rāp.*]
Roque·fort (rōk′fərt). A trademark for a cheese made from ewes' milk and ripened in caves.
Ror·schach test (rôr′shäk′, -shäKH) *n.* A psychological personality test in which a subject's interpretations of ten standard abstract designs are used to measure emotional health and intellectual functioning. [< Hermann Rorschach (1884–1922).]
ro·sa·ry (rō′zə-rē) *n., pl.* **-ries**. *Rom. Cath. Ch.* **1.** A series of prayers. **2.** A string of beads on which these prayers are counted. [Med. Lat. *rosarium.*]
rose¹ (rōz) *n.* **1. a.** Any of numerous shrubs or vines with prickly stems and variously colored, often fragrant flowers. **b.** The flower of any of these plants. **2.** A deep pink. [< Lat. *rosa.*] —**rose** *adj.*
rose² (rōz) *v. p.t.* of **rise.**
ro·sé (rō-zā′) *n.* A pink, light table wine. [Fr., pink.]
ro·se·ate (rō′zē-ĭt, -āt′) *adj.* **1.** Rose-colored. **2.** Cheerful; optimistic; rosy.
rose·bud (rōz′bŭd′) *n.* The bud of a rose.
rose·bush (rōz′bŏŏsh′) *n.* A shrub that bears roses.
rose-col·ored (rōz′kŭl′ərd) *adj.* **1.** Having a rose color. **2.** Optimistic or overoptimistic.
rose·mary (rōz′mâr′ē) *n., pl.* **-ies**. An aromatic evergreen shrub with grayish-green leaves used as a seasoning and in manufacturing perfume. [< Lat. *ros marinus,* sea dew.]
ro·sette (rō-zĕt′) *n.* An ornament, as of ribbon or silk, that resembles a rose.
rose water *n.* A fragrant preparation made by steeping rose petals in water, used in cosmetics and cooking.

rose·wood (rōz′wŏŏd′) n. The hard reddish or dark wood of a tropical tree, used in cabinetwork.

Rosh Ha·sha·nah (rōsh′ hə-shä′nə, rōsh′) n. The Jewish New Year, celebrated in late September or early October.

Ro·si·cru·cian (rō′zĭ-krōō′shən, rōz′ĭ-) n. A member of an international fraternity of religious mysticism devoted to the application of esoteric religious doctrine to modern life. —**Ro′si·cru′cian·ism** n.

ros·in (rŏz′ĭn) n. A translucent resin derived from the sap of various pine trees, used on the bows of certain stringed instruments to prevent slipping and in a wide variety of manufactured products. [< RESIN.]

ros·ter (rŏs′tər, rô′stər) n. 1. A list of names. 2. A list of the members of a group, esp. of military officers and enlisted personnel enrolled for active duty. [Du. rooster.]

ros·trum (rŏs′trəm, rô′strəm) n., pl. -trums or -tra (-trə). A raised platform for public speaking. [Lat., beak.]

ros·y (rō′zē) adj. -i·er, -i·est. 1. Having a rose color. 2. Bright; promising. —**ros′i·ly** adv. —**ros′i·ness** n.

rot (rŏt) v. **rot·ted, rot·ting.** To decompose; decay. —n. 1. a. The process of rotting. b. Something rotting or rotted. 2. A plant or animal disease characterized by the breakdown of tissue. 3. Something foolish, meaningless, or worthless. [< OE rotian.]

ro·ta·ry (rō′tə-rē) adj. 1. Of or involving rotation, esp. axial rotation. 2. Having a part that rotates. —n., pl. -ries. 1. A rotary machine. 2. A traffic circle. [< Lat. rota, wheel.]

ro·tate (rō′tāt′) v. -tat·ed, -tat·ing. 1. To turn or spin on an axis. 2. To alternate in sequence. [Lat. rotare.] —**ro·tat′a·ble** adj. —**ro·ta′tor** n. —**ro·ta′to·ry** (-tə-tôr′ē, -tōr′ē) adj.

ro·ta·tion (rō-tā′shən) n. 1. Motion in which the path of every point in the moving object is a circle or circular arc centered on a specified axis, esp. on an internal axis. 2. A single complete cycle on such a motion; revolution. 3. Uniform sequential variation; alternation. —**ro·ta′tion·al** adj.

rote (rōt) n. 1. Memorization usu. achieved by repetition without understanding. 2. Mechanical routine or repetition. [ME.]

ro·tis·ser·ie (rō-tĭs′ə-rē) n. An appliance with a rotating spit for cooking food. [< OFr. rostir, to roast.]

ro·to·gra·vure (rō′tə-grə-vyŏŏr′) n. 1. A printing process in which an image or impression is produced on a surface from an etched copper cylinder in a rotary press. 2. Material produced by rotogravure. [Lat. rota, wheel + GRAVURE.]

ro·tor (rō′tər) n. 1. A rotating part of a machine or device. 2. An assembly of airfoils that rotates, as in a helicopter. [< ROTATOR.]

rot·ten (rŏt′n) adj. -er, -est. 1. Marked by rot or decay; putrid. 2. Morally corrupt; despicable. 3. Very bad; wretched. [< ON rotinn.] —**rot′ten·ly** adv. —**rot′ten·ness** n.

ro·tund (rō-tŭnd′) adj. Rounded in shape; plump. [Lat. rotundus.] —**ro·tun′di·ty** n.

ro·tun·da (rō-tŭn′də) n. 1. A round building or hall, esp. one with a dome. 2. A large room with a high ceiling. [< Lat. rotundus, round.]

rou·ble or **ru·ble** (rōō′bəl) n. See table at currency. [R. rubl'.]

rou·é (rōō-ā′) n. A lecherous, dissipated man; rake. [Fr. < rouer, to break on the wheel.]

rouge (rōōzh) n. 1. A red or pink cosmetic used to color the cheeks or lips. 2. A fine reddish powder used to polish gems or metal. [< Lat. rubeus, red.] —**rouge** v.

rough (rŭf) adj. -er, -est. 1. a. Having a bumpy, irregular surface; not smooth or even. b. Coarse or shaggy to the touch. 2. Stormy; turbulent. 3. Marked by violence or force; harsh: rough handling. 4. Difficult; taxing. 5. Harsh to the ear. 6. Crude and unmannerly; uncouth. 7. Not polished or refined; crude. 8. Not complete or exact: a rough drawing. —n. 1. Rugged, overgrown ground, esp. the uncleared part of a golf course along the fairways. 2. A crude, unmannerly person; rowdy. —v. 1. To make rough; roughen. 2. To treat roughly or with physical violence. 3. To make or do in a rough or incomplete form: rough out a house plan. —idiom. rough it. To live without comforts or conveniences. [< OE rūh.] —**rough′ly** adv. —**rough′ness** n.

rough·age (rŭf′ĭj) n. Coarse, indigestible food that stimulates intestinal peristalsis.

rough·en (rŭf′ən) v. To make or become rough.

rough-hew (rŭf′hyōō′) v. 1. To hew or shape roughly, without finishing. 2. To make in rough form.

rough·house (rŭf′hous′) n. Rowdy, rough play or behavior. —**rough′house′** v.

rough·neck (rŭf′nĕk′) n. A rough, unruly person; rowdy.

rou·lade (rōō-läd′) n. A slice of meat rolled around a filling and cooked. [Fr. < rouler, to roll.]

rou·lette (rōō-lĕt′) n. 1. A gambling game played on a rotating wheel with numbered slots in which a ball will come to rest. 2. A tool with a rotating toothed disk for making rows of dots or rows of perforations. [< OFr., ult. < Lat. rota, wheel.]

Rou·ma·ni·an (rōō-mā′nē-ən, -mān′yən) n. Var. of Rumanian.

round (round) adj. -er, -est. 1. Spherical; globular; ball-shaped. 2. Circular. 3. Curved. 4. Complete; full: a round dozen. 5. Expressed or designated as a whole number or integer; not fractional. 6. Approximate; not exact: a round estimate. —n. 1. Something round, as a circle, disk, globe, or ring. 2. A cut of beef between the rump and shank. 3. A complete course, succession, or series: a round of parties. 4. Often rounds. A course of customary or prescribed actions, duties, or places. 5. A single distribution, as of drinks. 6. A single outburst of applause. 7. a. A single shot or volley. b. Ammunition for a single shot; a cartridge. 8. A period of play or action in various sports. 9. Mus. A musical form in which the same melody is repeated by successive overlapping voices. —v. 1. To make or become round. 2. To make or become plump. 3. To bring to completion or perfection. 4. To go or pass around. 5. To make a turn around or to the other side of. 6. To encompass;

surround. —*phrasal verb.* **round up. 1.** To collect together in a roundup. **2.** To gather or bring together. —*adv.* Around. —*prep.* **1.** Around. **2.** Throughout: *a plant that grows round the year.* —*idiom.* **in the round. 1.** With the stage in the center of the audience. **2.** Fully shaped so as to stand free of a background. [< Lat. *rotundus.*] —**round′ish** *adj.* —**round′ness** *n.*

round·a·bout (round′ə-bout′) *adj.* Not direct; circuitous.

roun·de·lay (roun′də-lā′) *n.* A poem or song with a recurring refrain. [OFr. *rondelet.*]

round·house (round′hous′) *n.* **1.** A circular building for housing and switching locomotives. **2.** A punch or swing delivered with a sweeping movement.

round·ly (round′lē) *adv.* **1.** In the form of a circle or sphere. **2.** Fully or thoroughly. **3.** Bluntly; frankly.

round robin *n.* A tournament in which each contestant is matched in turn against every other contestant.

round-shoul·dered (round′shōl′dərd) *adj.* Having the shoulders and upper back rounded.

round table *n.* A conference at which a number of people discuss a given topic.

round-the-clock (round′thə-klŏk′) *adj.* Throughout the entire day; continuous.

round trip *n.* A trip to a place and back.

round·up (round′ŭp′) *n.* **1.** The gathering together of cattle on the range. **2.** A gathering together of persons or things. **3.** A summary.

round·worm (round′wûrm′) *n.* A nematode.

rouse (rouz) *v.* **roused, rous·ing. 1.** To arouse from sleep, unconsciousness, or inactivity. **2.** To stir up, as to anger or action; excite. [ME *rowsen,* to shake feathers.]

roust·a·bout (rou′stə-bout′) *n.* An unskilled laborer, esp. on a dock or in an oil field. [< ROUSE + ABOUT.]

rout¹ (rout) *n.* **1.** A disorderly retreat or flight. **2.** An overwhelming defeat. —*v.* **1.** To put to disorderly flight or retreat. **2.** To defeat overwhelmingly. [< Lat. *ruptus,* p.p. of *rumpere,* to break.]

rout² (rout) *v.* **1.** To search; rummage. **2.** To gouge out. **3.** To drive or force out; eject. [< ROOT².] —**rout′er** *n.*

route (rōōt, rout) *n.* **1. a.** A road or course for traveling. **b.** A means of reaching a goal. **2.** A customary or fixed course of travel. —*v.* **rout·ed, rout·ing. 1.** To send by a particular route. **2.** To schedule the order of (a sequence of procedures). [< OFr.]

rou·tine (rōō-tēn′) *n.* **1.** A prescribed and detailed course of action. **2.** A set of customary and often mechanically performed procedures or activities. —*adj.* **1.** In accordance with established procedure. **2.** Not special; ordinary. [< ROUTE.] —**rou·tine′ly** *adv.*

rove¹ (rōv) *v.* **roved, rov·ing.** To wander about at random; roam. [ME *roven,* to shoot at a random mark.] —**rov′er** *n.*

rove² (rōv) *v.* A *p.t.* & *p.p.* of **reeve.**

row¹ (rō) *n.* **1.** A series of persons or things placed next to each other, usu. in a straight line. **2.** A continuous line of buildings along a street. [< OE *rāw.*]

row² (rō) *v.* **1.** To propel (a boat) with or as if with oars. **2.** To travel or carry in a rowboat. —*n.* A trip or excursion in a rowboat. [< OE *rōwan.*] —**row′er** *n.*

row³ (rou) *n.* A noisy quarrel or fight. —*v.* To take part in a row. [Orig. unknown.]

row·an (rou′ən) *n.* A small, deciduous tree with white flowers and orange-red berries. [Of Scand. orig.]

row·boat (rō′bōt′) *n.* A small boat propelled by oars.

row·dy (rou′dē) *n., pl.* **-dies.** A rough, disorderly person. —*adj.* **-di·er, -di·est.** Noisy and disorderly; rough. [Prob. < ROW³.] —**row′di·ness** or **row′dy·ism** *n.* —**row′dy·ish** *adj.*

row·el (rou′əl) *n.* A sharp-toothed wheel inserted into the end of the shank of a spur. [< Lat. *rota,* wheel.] —**row′el** *v.*

roy·al (roi′əl) *adj.* **1.** Of or pertaining to a sovereign. **2.** Befitting a king; stately. [< Lat. *regalis* < *rex,* king.] —**roy′al·ly** *adv.*

royal blue *n.* A deep to vivid blue.

roy·al·ist (roi′ə-list) *n.* A supporter of monarchical government.

roy·al·ty (roi′əl-tē) *n., pl.* **-ties. 1.** Monarchs and their families collectively. **2.** The status or authority of monarchs. **3.** Royal quality or bearing; kingliness. **4. a.** A share paid to an author or composer out of the profits from the sale or performance of his work. **b.** A share paid to an inventor or proprietor for the right to use his invention or services.

-rrhea or **-rrhoea** *suff.* Abnormal or excessive flow or discharge: *pyorrhea.* [< Gk. *rhoia,* a flowing.]

Ru The symbol for the element ruthenium.

rub (rŭb) *v.* **rubbed, rub·bing. 1.** To apply pressure and friction to (a surface). **2.** To apply friction and with friction upon a surface. **3.** To contact or cause to contact repeatedly and with friction; scrape. **4.** To become or cause to become chafed or irritated. —*phrasal verbs.* **rub down.** To massage. **rub off.** To be transferred by contact or proximity. **rub out.** *Slang.* To murder. —*n.* **1.** An act of rubbing. **2.** An obstacle or difficulty; catch. [ME *rubben.*]

rub·ber¹ (rŭb′ər) *n.* **1.** An amorphous, elastic, solid substance, made from the milky sap of various tropical plants. **2.** Any of numerous synthetic elastic materials similar to natural rubber. **3.** Often **rubbers.** A low overshoe made of rubber. **4.** *Slang.* A condom. —**rub′bery** *adj.*

rub·ber² (rŭb′ər) *n.* **1.** In various games and sports, a series of games of which a majority must be won to terminate the play. **2.** Also **rubber game.** A game that breaks a tie in a series. [Orig. unknown.]

rub·ber·ize (rŭb′ə-rīz′) *v.* **-ized, -iz·ing.** To coat, treat, or impregnate with rubber.

rub·ber·neck (rŭb′ər-nĕk′) *v.* To gawk or stare. —**rub′ber·neck′** *n.*

rubber stamp *n.* **1.** A piece of rubber with raised characters, used to make ink impressions. **2.** One that gives quick endorsement of a policy without assessing its merit.

rub·ber-stamp (rŭb′ər-stămp′) *v.* To endorse or approve without question or deliberation.

rub·bing (rŭb′ing) *n.* An image of a raised or indented surface made by placing paper over the surface and rubbing a marking agent.

rub·bish (rŭb′ish) *n.* **1.** Something discarded as refuse; trash. **2.** Foolish talk; nonsense. [< AN *robbous.*]

rub·ble (rŭb′əl) *n.* **1.** Fragments of rock or masonry. **2.** Irregular fragments or pieces of rock used in masonry. [ME *rubel.*]

rub·down (rŭb'doun') n. A massage.

rube (rōōb) n. Slang. An unsophisticated rustic. [Prob. < Rube, nickname for Reuben.]

ru·bel·la (rōō-bĕl'ə) n. German measles. [< Lat. rubellus, reddish.]

ru·bi·cund (rōō'bĭ-kănd) adj. Reddish in complexion; ruddy. [Lat. rubicundus.] —ru'bi·cun'di·ty (-kŭn'dĭ-tē) n.

ru·bid·i·um (rōō-bĭd'ē-əm) n. Symbol Rb A soft silvery-white alkali element used in photocells and in the manufacture of vacuum tubes. Atomic number 37; atomic weight 85.47. [< Lat. rubidus, red < the red lines in its spectrum.]

ru·ble (rōō'bəl) n. Var. of rouble.

ru·bric (rōō'brĭk) n. 1. A title, heading, or initial letter, usu. printed in red lettering. 2. A title or heading of a statute or chapter in a code of law. 3. A class or category. 4. A direction in a missal, hymnal, or other liturgical book. [< Lat. ruber, red.]

ru·by (rōō'bē) n., pl. -bies. 1. A deep-red, translucent corundum, highly valued as a precious stone. 2. A deep red. [< Lat. rubeus, red.] —ru'by adj.

ruck·sack (rŭk'săk', rōōk'-) n. A knapsack. [G.]

ruck·us (rŭk'əs) n. Informal. A noisy disturbance; commotion. [Blend of ruction, a riotous disturbance + RUMPUS.]

rud·der (rŭd'ər) n. A vertically hinged plate mounted at the rear of a vessel or aircraft for steering. [< OE rōther.]

rud·dy (rŭd'ē) adj. -di·er, -di·est. 1. Having a healthy, reddish color. 2. Reddish; rosy. [< OE rudig.] —rud'di·ness n.

rude (rōōd) adj. rud·er, rud·est. 1. Primitive; not civilized. 2. Ill-mannered; discourteous. 3. Makeshift; crude. 4. Sudden and jarring: a rude shock. [< Lat. rudis, unformed.] —rude'ly adv. —rude'ness n.

Syns: *rude, discourteous, ill-mannered, impolite, unmannerly adj.*

ru·di·ment (rōō'də-mənt) n. 1. A fundamental element, principle, or skill. 2. Often rudiments. Something in an incipient or undeveloped form: *the rudiments of social behavior in children.* [< Lat. rudis, unformed.] —ru'di·men'ta·ry (-mĕn'tə-rē) adj.

rue[1] (rōō) v. rued, ru·ing. To feel remorse or sorrow for. [< OE hrēowan.] —rue'ful adj. —rue'ful·ly adv. —rue'ful·ness n.

rue[2] (rōō) n. An aromatic Eurasian plant yielding an oil formerly used in medicine. [< Gk. rhutē.]

ruff (rŭf) n. 1. A stiffly starched circular collar worn in the 16th and 17th cent. 2. A collarlike projection around the neck, as of feathers on a bird. [Perh. < RUFFLE.]

ruf·fi·an (rŭf'ē-ən, rŭf'yən) n. A tough or rowdy fellow. [OFr.]

ruf·fle (rŭf'əl) n. 1. A strip of frilled or closely pleated fabric used for trimming or decoration. 2. A ruff. 3. A slight discomposure. 4. A ripple. —v. -fled, -fling. 1. a. To disturb the smoothness or regularity of. b. To annoy. 2. To pleat or gather (fabric) into a ruffle. 3. To erect (the feathers). 4. To discompose; fluster. [< ME ruffelen, to roughen.]

rug (rŭg) n. A piece of heavy fabric used to cover a floor. [Of Scand. orig.]

rug
Oriental rug

rug·by (rŭg'bē) n. Also Rugby football. A form of football in which forward passing, substitution of players, and time-outs are not permitted. [< Rugby School, England.]

rug·ged (rŭg'ĭd) adj. 1. Having a rough, irregular surface. 2. Tempestuous; stormy. 3. Demanding great effort or ability. 4. Vigorously healthy; hardy. [ME, shaggy, of Scand. orig.] —rug'ged·ly adv. —rug'ged·ness n.

ru·in (rōō'ĭn) n. 1. a. Severe destruction or disintegration. b. The cause of such destruction. 2. Often ruins. The remains of something destroyed, disintegrated, or decayed. —v. 1. To reduce to ruin. 2. To harm irreparably. 3. To reduce to poverty or bankruptcy. [< Lat. ruina, ruin.] —ru'in·a'tion n. —ru'in·ous adj. —ru'in·ous·ly adv.

rule (rōōl) n. 1. Governing power. 2. An authoritative direction for conduct or procedure; regulation. 3. A usual or customary course of action or behavior. 4. A statement that describes what is true in most or all cases. 5. A standard method or procedure. 6. A straightedge; ruler. —v. ruled, rul·ing. 1. To exercise control (over); govern. 2. To dominate; hold sway over. 3. To decide judicially; decree. 4. To mark with straight parallel lines. —phrasal verb. rule out. To exclude. [< Lat. regula.]

rul·er (rōō'lər) n. 1. One that rules or governs. 2. A straight-edged strip, as of wood or metal, for drawing straight lines and measuring lengths.

rul·ing (rōō'lĭng) adj. Exercising control; governing. —n. An official decision, esp. a judicial one.

rum (rŭm) n. An alcoholic liquor distilled from fermented molasses or sugar cane. [Perh. < obs. rumbullion.]

Ru·ma·ni·an (rōō-mā'nē-ən, -mān'yən) n. Also Ro·ma·ni·an (rō-) or Rou·ma·ni·an (rōō-). 1. An inhabitant or native of Rumania. 2. The Romance language of the Rumanian people. —Ru·ma'ni·an adj.

rum·ba (rŭm'bə, rōōm'-) n. A rhythmical dance that originated in Cuba or an adaptation of it. [Am. Sp.] —rum'ba v.

rum·ble (rŭm'bəl) v. -bled, -bling. 1. To make a deep, long, rolling sound. 2. To move or proceed with a rumbling sound. 3. Slang. To participate in a gang fight. —n. 1. A deep, long, rolling sound. 2. A widespread murmur of discontent. **3.** *Slang.* A gang fight. [ME *romblen*.]

ru·mi·nant (rōō'mə-nənt) *n.* Any of various hoofed, cud-chewing mammals, including cattle, sheep, goats, and deer. —*adj.* **1.** Chewing cud. **2.** Meditative; contemplative.

ru·mi·nate (rōō'mə-nāt') *v.* **-nat·ed, -nat·ing. 1.** To chew cud. **2.** To meditate at length; muse. [Lat. *ruminare < rumen,* throat.] —**ru'mi·na'tion** *n.* —**ru'mi·na'tive** *adj.*

rum·mage (rŭm'ĭj) *v.* **-maged, -mag·ing. 1.** To discover by searching thoroughly. **2.** To make an energetic, usu. hasty search. [< OFr. *arumer,* to stow.] —**rum'mage** *n.*

rummage sale *n.* A sale of assorted second-hand objects.

rum·my (rŭm'ē) *n.* A card game in which the object is to obtain sets of three or more cards of the same rank or suit. [Orig. unknown.]

ru·mor (rōō'mər) *n.* Also *chiefly Brit.* **ru·mour. 1.** A report of uncertain origin and truthfulness. **2.** Hearsay. [< Lat.] —**ru'mor'** *v.*

rump (rŭmp) *n.* **1. a.** The fleshy hindquarters of an animal. **b.** A cut of meat from this part. **2.** The human buttocks. **3.** The last or inferior part. [ME *rumpe,* of Scand. orig.]

rum·ple (rŭm'pəl) *v.* **-pled, -pling.** To wrinkle or form into folds or creases. [< MDu. *rompelen.*] —**rum'ple** *n.* —**rum'ply** *adj.*

rum·pus (rŭm'pəs) *n.* A noisy disturbance. [Orig. unknown.]

rumpus room *n.* A family room.

run (rŭn) *v.* **ran** (răn), **run, run·ning. 1.** To move on foot at a pace faster than the walk. **2.** To retreat rapidly; flee. **3.** To move without hindrance or restraint. **4.** To make a short, quick trip. **5.** To swim in large numbers, as in migrating. **6. a.** To hurry; hasten. **b.** To have frequent recourse to someone or something. **7.** To take part in a race. **8.** To compete for elected office. **9.** To finish a race in a specified position. **10.** To move freely, as by rolling or sliding. **11.** To be in operation. **12.** To go regularly. **13.** To sail or steer before the wind or on an indicated course. **14.** To flow in a steady stream. **15.** To melt and flow. **16.** To flow and spread. **17.** To be wet with: *streets running with blood.* **18.** To overflow. **19.** To discharge; drain. **20.** To surge, as waves. **21.** To extend, stretch, or reach. **22.** To spread or climb, as vines. **23.** To spread rapidly. **24.** To be valid in a given area: *The ordinance runs only to the county line.* **25.** To unravel along a line. **26.** To continue. **27.** To pass. **28.** To persist or recur. **29.** *Law.* **a.** To be effective. **b.** To be concurrent with: *Fishing tickets run with the ownership of land.* **30. a.** To accumulate or accrue. **b.** To become payable. **31.** To be expressed in a given way. **32.** To tend or incline. **33.** To be channeled. **34.** To vary or range in quality, price, size, proportion, etc. **35.** To come into or out of a specified condition. —*phrasal verbs.* **run along.** To go away; leave. **run away with. 1.** To win by a large margin. **run down. 1.** To stop because of lack of force or power. **2.** To become tired. **3.** To collide with and knock down. **4.** To chase and capture. **5.** To disparage. **6.** To trace to a source. **run in.** To take into legal custody. **run off. 1.** To print or duplicate. **run out.** To become used up. **run out of.** To exhaust the supply. **run through. 1.** To pierce. **2.** To use up. **3.** To examine or rehearse quickly. —*n.* **1. a.** A pace faster than the

walk. **b.** A gait faster than the canter. **2.** An act of running. **3. a.** A distance covered by or as if by running. **b.** The time taken to cover it. **4.** A quick trip or visit. **5.** *Baseball.* **a.** The process of scoring a point by running from home plate around the bases and back to home plate. **b.** The point so scored. **6.** A shoaling or migrating of fish prior to spawning. **7.** Unrestricted freedom or use of: *the run of the library.* **8. a.** A journey between points on a scheduled route. **b.** The time taken to cover this distance. **9.** A continuous period of operation by a machine, factory, etc. **10.** A movement or flow, as of fluid or sand. **11.** A pipe or channel through which something flows: *a mill run.* **12.** A continuous length or extent of something. **13.** The direction, configuration, or lie of something: *the run of the grain in leather.* **14.** An outdoor enclosure for domestic animals or poultry. **15.** A length of torn or unraveled stitches in a knitted fabric. **16.** An unbroken series or sequence. **17.** An unbroken sequence of theatrical performances. **18.** A series of unexpected and urgent demands by customers: *a run on a bank.* **19. a.** In certain games, a continuous set or sequence, as of playing cards in one suit. **b.** A successful sequence of shots or points. **20.** A sustained state or condition: *a run of good luck.* **21.** A trend or tendency. **22.** An average type, group, or category; majority: *the broad run of votes.* —*idioms.* **in the long run.** In the final analysis or outcome. **on the run. 1.** In hiding. **2.** Hurrying busily from place to place. [< OE *rinnan.*]

run·a·bout (rŭn'ə-bout') *n.* A small, usu. open automobile, carriage, or motorboat.

runabout

run·a·round (rŭn'ə-round') *n.* Deception, usu. in the form of evasive excuses.

run·a·way (rŭn'ə-wā') *n.* **1.** One who has run away. **2.** *Informal.* An easy victory. —*adj.* **1.** Escaping or having escaped from captivity. **2.** Out of control or proper confinement. **3.** Easily won.

run·down (rŭn'doun') *n.* A summary or résumé. —*adj.* **1.** Old and decayed. **2.** Tired or listless. **3.** Unwound and not running.

rune (rōōn) *n.* **1.** One of the letters of an alphabet used by ancient Germanic peoples. **2.** A magic charm. [< OE *rūn.*] —**ru'nic** *adj.*

rung¹ (rŭng) *n.* **1.** A bar forming a step of a ladder. **2.** A crosspiece supporting the legs or back of a chair. **3.** The spoke in a wheel. [< OE *hrung.*]

rung² (rŭng) *v. p.p.* of **ring².**

run-in (rŭn'ĭn') *n.* A quarrel; argument; fight.

run·let (rŭn'lĭt) *n.* A rivulet.

run·nel (rŭn'əl) *n.* **1.** A rivulet; brook. **2.** A narrow channel, as for water. [< OE *rynel.*]

run·ner (rŭn'ər) *n.* **1.** One who runs. **2. a.** One who competes in a race. **b.** A jogger. **c.** *Baseball.* One who runs the bases.

d. *Football.* One who carries the ball. **3.** A messenger. **4. a.** A smuggler. **b.** A vessel engaged in smuggling. **5.** A device in or on which a mechanism slides or moves, as the blade of a skate. **6.** A long narrow carpet. **7.** *Bot.* **a.** A creeping stem that roots at intervals along its length. **b.** A plant having such a stem.

run·ner-up (rŭn′ər-ŭp′, rŭn′ər-ŭp′) *n.* One that takes second place.

run·ning (rŭn′ĭng) *n.* **1.** The act or action of one that runs. **2.** The sport or exercise of someone who runs. —*adj.* Continuous. —*adv.* Consecutively.

running light *n.* One of several lights on a ship or aircraft to indicate position and size.

run·ny (rŭn′ē) *adj.* **-ni·er, -ni·est.** Inclined to run or flow.

run-off (rŭn′ôf′, -ŏf′) *n.* An extra competition held to break a tie.

run-of-the-mill (rŭn′əv-thə-mĭl′) *adj.* Not special; average.

runt (rŭnt) *n.* **1.** An undersized animal, esp. the smallest animal of a litter. **2.** An unusually small person. [Orig. unknown.] —**runt′i·ness** *n.* —**runt′y** *adj.*

run-through (rŭn′thrōō′) *n.* A complete but rapid review or rehearsal.

run·way (rŭn′wā′) *n.* **1.** A path, channel, or track over which something runs. **2.** A narrow walkway extending from a stage into an auditorium. **3.** A strip on which aircraft take off and land.

ru·pee (rōō-pē′, rōō′pē) *n.* See table at **currency.** [Hindi *rupaīyā*.]

ru·pi·ah (rōō-pē′ə) *n., pl.* **-ah** or **-ahs.** See table at **currency.** [Hindi *rupaīya.*]

rup·ture (rŭp′chər) *n.* **1.** The act or process of breaking open or bursting. **2.** A hernia. [< Lat. *ruptus*, p.p. of *rumpere*, to break.] —**rup′ture** *v.*

ru·ral (rōōr′əl) *adj.* Of or pertaining to the country as opposed to the city. [< Lat. *rus*, country.] —**ru′ral·ly** *adv.*

ruse (rōōs, rōōz) *n.* An action or device meant to confuse or mislead; deception. [< OFr. *ruser*, to drive back.]

rush¹ (rŭsh) *v.* **1.** To move or act swiftly; hurry. **2.** To attack; charge. **3.** To perform with great haste. —*n.* **1.** A swift forward movement. **2.** A great flurry of activity or press of business. **3.** A sudden attack; onslaught. **4.** A rapid, often noisy flow or passage. —*adj.* Requiring or marked by haste or urgency: *a rush job.* [< Lat. *recusare*, to object to.] —**rush′er** *n.*

Syns: *rush, dart, dash, hasten, hurry, hustle, race, run, scoot, scurry, speed, tear, whiz, zip, zoom* v.

rush² (rŭsh) *n.* A grasslike marsh plant with hollow or pithy stems. [< OE *rysc.*]

rusk (rŭsk) *n.* Sweet raised bread dried and browned in an oven. [Sp. *rosca*, coil.]

rus·set (rŭs′ĭt) *n.* **1.** A reddish brown. **2.** A coarse reddish-brown to brown homespun cloth. **3.** A winter apple with a rough reddish-brown skin. [< Lat. *russus*, red.] —**rus′set** *adj.*

Rus·sian (rŭsh′ən) *n.* **1.** A native or inhabitant of Russia. **2.** The Slavic language of the Russian people. —**Rus′sian** *adj.*

rust (rŭst) *n.* **1.** Any of various reddish-brown oxides formed on iron and iron-containing materials by low-temperature oxidation in the presence of water. **2.** Any of various metallic coatings formed by corrosion. **3.** A plant disease caused by various parasitic fungi and characterized by reddish or brownish spots on leaves and stems. **4.** A reddish brown. —*v.* **1.** To corrode. **2.** To deteriorate through inactivity or neglect. [< OE *rūst.*] —**rust′y** *adj.*

rus·tic (rŭs′tĭk) *adj.* **1.** Typical of country life. **2.** Unsophisticated; simple. **3.** Made of rough tree branches: *rustic furniture.* —*n.* **1.** A rural person. **2.** A crude, coarse, or simple person. [< Lat. *rus*, country.] —**rus′ti·cal·ly** *adv.* —**rus·tic′i·ty** (-tĭs′ĭ-tē) *n.*

rus·ti·cate (rŭs′tĭ-kāt′) *v.* **-cat·ed, -cat·ing.** To go to or live in the country. —**rus′ti·ca′tion** *n.* —**rus′ti·ca′tor** *n.*

rus·tle (rŭs′əl) *v.* **-tled, -tling.** **1.** To move with soft fluttering or crackling sounds. **2.** To cause to make such sounds. **3.** *Informal.* To make or get quickly: *rustle up a dinner.* **4.** To steal (cattle). [ME *rustlen.*] —**rus′tle** *n.* —**rus′tler** *n.* —**rus′tling·ly** *adv.*

rut¹ (rŭt) *n.* **1.** A sunken track or groove made by the passage of vehicles. **2.** A habitual, unvaried way of living or acting. [Poss. < OFr. *route*, way.] —**rut** *v.* —**rut′ty** *adj.*

rut² (rŭt) *n.* A recurring sexually active condition of certain male animals, such as deer. [< Lat. *rugire*, to roar.]

ru·ta·ba·ga (rōō′tə-bā′gə) *n.* A turniplike plant with a thick, bulbous, edible root. [Dial. Swed. *rotabagge.*]

Ruth (rōōth) *n.* See table at **Bible.**

ru·the·ni·um (rōō-thē′nē-əm) *n.* *Symbol* **Ru** A hard white acid-resistant metallic element used to harden platinum and palladium for jewelry and in alloys for electrical contacts. Atomic number 44; atomic weight 101.07. [< Med. Lat. *Ruthenia*, Russia.]

ruth·less (rōōth′lĭs) *adj.* Having no compassion or pity; merciless. [ME *ruthe*, compassion + **-LESS.**] —**ruth′less·ly** *adv.* —**ruth′less·ness** *n.*

-ry *suff.* Var. of **-ery.**

rye (rī) *n.* **1.** A widely cultivated cereal grass. **2.** The grain of this plant, used in making flour and whiskey and for livestock feed. **3.** Whiskey made from rye. [< OE *ryge.*]

ă pat   ā pay   â care   ä father   ĕ pet   ē be   ĭ pit   ī tie   î pier   ŏ pot   ō toe   ô paw, for   oi noise   ŏŏ took   ōō boot   ou out   th thin   th this   ŭ cut   û urge   yōō abuse   zh vision   ə about, item, edible, gallop, circus

Ss

s or **S** (ĕs) *n., pl.* **s's** or **S's.** 1. The 19th letter of the English alphabet. 2. Something shaped like the letter S.

S The symbol for the element sulfur.

–s¹ *suff.* Used to form plural nouns: *letters.* [< OE *-as.*]

–s² *suff.* Used to form the 3rd person sing. present tense of all regular and most irregular verbs: *looks, holds.* [< OE *-es, -as.*]

–s³ *suff.* Used to form adverbs: *caught unawares.* [< OE *-es,* genitive suffix.]

–'s *suff.* Used to indicate the possessive case: *nation's.* [< OE *-es,* genitive suffix.]

Sab·bath (săb'əth) *n.* 1. The 7th day of the week, Saturday, observed as a day of rest and worship by the Jews and some Christian sects. 2. The 1st day of the week, Sunday, observed as a day of rest and worship by most Christians. [< Heb. *shabbāth.*]

sab·bat·i·cal year (sə-băt'ĭ-kəl) *n.* Also **sabbatical.** A leave of absence, often paid and usu. granted, as to a professor, every 7th year for research, travel, or rest. [< Gk. *sabbatikos,* of the Sabbath.]

sa·ber (sā'bər) *n.* Also *chiefly Brit.* **sa·bre.** 1. A heavy cavalry sword with a one-edged, slightly curved blade. 2. A two-edged fencing sword. [< obs. G. *sabel.*]

Sa·bin vaccine (sā'bĭn) *n.* An oral vaccine taken as immunization against poliomyelitis. [< Albert B. *Sabin* (b. 1906).]

sa·ble (sā'bəl) *n.* 1. A weasellike mammal of northern Eurasia, having soft, dark fur. 2. The valuable fur of this animal. 3. a. The color black. b. **sables.** Black garments worn in mourning. [< OFr.] —**sa'ble** *adj.*

sab·o·tage (săb'ə-täzh') *n.* 1. The damaging of property or the hindering of production so as to obstruct productivity or normal functioning. 2. An underhand effort to defeat or harm an endeavor; deliberate subversion. [< OFr. *saboter,* to sabotage.] —**sab'o·tage'** *v.*

sab·o·teur (săb'ə-tûr') *n.* One who commits sabotage. [Fr.]

sa·bra (sä'brə) *n.* A native-born Israeli. [Heb. *ṣabēr.*]

sa·bre (sā'bər) *n. Chiefly Brit.* Var. of **saber.**

sac (săk) *n.* A pouchlike plant or animal structure. [< Lat. *saccus,* bag.]

Sac (săk) *n.* Var. of **Sauk.**

sacchar– *pref.* Sugar: *saccharin.* [< Skt. *śarkarā.*]

sac·cha·rin (săk'ər-ĭn) *n.* A very sweet, white crystalline powder, $C_7H_5NO_3S$, used as a calorie-free sweetener.

sac·cha·rine (săk'ər-ĭn, -ə-rēn', -ə-rīn') *adj.* 1. Of, relating to, or of the nature of sugar or saccharin. 2. Cloyingly sweet.

sac·er·do·tal (săs'ər-dōt'l, săk'-) *adj.* Of or pertaining to priests or the priesthood.

sa·chem (sā'chəm) *n.* The chief of a tribe or confederation of some North American Indians. [Narraganset *sâchim,* chief.]

sa·chet (să-shā') *n.* A small packet of perfumed powder used to scent clothes or linens. [< Lat. *saccus,* bag.]

sack¹ (săk) *n.* 1. a. A large bag of strong, coarse material. b. A similar container of paper or plastic. 2. A short, loose-fitting coat or dress. 3. *Slang.* Dismissal from employment. 4. *Slang.* A bed. —*v.* 1. To place in a sack. 2. *Slang.* To discharge from employment. [< Gk. *sakkos.*]

sack² (săk) *v.* To loot or pillage. [< OFr. (mettre a) *sac,* (to put in) a sack.] —**sack** *n.*
Syns: *sack, loot, pillage, plunder, ravage v.*

sack·cloth (săk'klôth', -klŏth') *n.* 1. A rough, coarse cloth. 2. A garment of sackcloth, worn as a symbol of mourning or penitence.

sac·ra·ment (săk'rə-mənt) *n.* 1. Any of the rites of the Christian church considered to have been instituted by Christ, such as the Eucharist or baptism. 2. **Sacrament.** The consecrated elements of the Eucharist. [< Lat. *sacramentum,* oath.] —**sac'ra·men'tal** (-měn'tal) *adj.* —**sac'ra·men'tal·ly** *adv.*

sa·cred (sā'krĭd) *adj.* 1. Dedicated to or set apart for worship. 2. Made or declared holy. 3. Worthy of religious veneration. 4. Dedicated or devoted exclusively to a single use or person. 5. Worthy of reverence or respect. 6. Of or pertaining to religious as opposed to secular things. [< Lat. *sacer.*] —**sa'cred·ly** *adv.* —**sa'cred·ness** *n.*

sacred cow *n.* One that is immune to criticism.

sac·ri·fice (săk'rə-fīs') *n.* 1. The offering of something to a deity. 2. a. The forfeiture of something highly valued for the sake of someone or something considered to have a greater value or claim. b. Something so forfeited. 3. a. A relinquishing of something at less than its presumed value. b. A loss so sustained. —*v.* **-ficed, -fic·ing.** 1. To offer as a sacrifice. 2. To forfeit something for something else considered of greater value. To sell or give away at a loss. [< Lat. *sacrificium.*] —**sac'ri·fic'er** *n.* —**sac'ri·fi'cial** (-fĭsh'əl) *adj.* —**sac'ri·fi'cial·ly** *adv.*

sac·ri·lege (săk'rə-lĭj) *n.* The misuse, theft, desecration, or profanation of something sacred. [< Lat. *sacrilegium.*] —**sac'ri·le'gious** (-lĭj'əs, -lē'jəs) *adj.* —**sac'ri·le'gious·ly** *adv.* —**sac'ri·le'gious·ness** *n.*

sac·ris·tan (săk'rĭ-stən) *n.* 1. One in charge of a sacristy. 2. A sexton. [< Med. Lat. *sacristanus.*]

sac·ris·ty (săk'rĭ-stē) *n., pl.* **-ties.** A room in a church for sacred vessels and vestments. [< Med. Lat. *sacristia.*]

sac·ro·il·i·ac (săk'rō-ĭl'ē-ăk', săk'rō-) *n.* The region of the lower back in which the sacrum and the ilium join. [< SACRUM + ILIUM.] —**sac'ro·il'i·ac** *adj.*

sac·ro·sanct (săk'rō-săngkt') *adj.* Inviolably sacred. [Lat. *sacrosanctus,* consecrated with religious ceremonies.] —**sac'ro·sanc'ti·ty** *n.*

sa·crum (sā'krəm) *n., pl.* **-cra** (-krə). A triangular bone that forms the posterior section of the pelvis.

sad (săd) *adj.* **sad·der, sad·dest.** 1. Sorrowful;

unhappy. **2.** Deplorable; sorry. [< OE *sæd, sated.*] **—sad'ly** *adv.* **—sad'ness** *n.*

sad·den (săd'n) *v.* To make or become sad.

sad·dle (săd'l) *n.* **1.** A leather seat for a rider, fastened to the back of an animal. **2.** A padded seat, as on a bicycle. **3.** A cut of meat, consisting of part of the backbone and both loins. *—v.* **-died, -dling. 1.** To put a saddle on. **2.** To load or burden; encumber. **—idiom. in the saddle.** In control. [< OE *sadol.*]

sad·dle·bag (săd'l-băg') *n.* A pouch that hangs from the saddle of a motorcycle or bicycle.

Sad·du·cee (săj'ə-sē, săd'yə-) *n.* An ancient Jewish priestly sect that opposed the Pharisees. **—Sad'du·ce'an** (-sē'ən) *adj.* **—Sad'du·cee'ism** *n.*

sa·de or **sa·dhe** (sä'də, -dē, tsä'-) *n.* The 18th letter of the Hebrew alphabet. See table at **alphabet.** [Heb. *ṣadhe.*]

sa·dism (să'dĭz'əm, săd'ĭz'-) *n. Psychol.* The association of sexual satisfaction with the infliction of pain on others. **2.** Delight in cruelty. [< Comte Donatien de *Sade* (1740–1814).] **—sa'dist** *n.* **—sa·dis'tic** (sə-dĭs'tĭk) *adj.* **—sa·dis'ti·cal·ly** *adv.*

Sa·far (sə-fär') *n.* Also **Sa·phar.** The 2nd month of the Moslem calendar. See table at **calendar.** [Ar.]

sa·fa·ri (sə-fä'rē) *n., pl.* **-ris.** An overland expedition, esp. in Africa. [Ar. *safarīy,* journey.]

safe (sāf) *adj.* **safer, safest. 1.** Not apt to cause or incur danger or harm. **2.** Unhurt: *safe and sound.* **3.** Free from risk: *a safe bet.* **4.** Affording protection: *a safe place.* **5.** *Baseball.* Reaching a base without being put out. *—n.* A container for storing valuables. [< Lat. *salvus,* healthy.] **—safe'ly** *adv.* **—safe'ness** *n.*

safe·con·duct (sāf'kŏn'dŭkt) *n.* A document assuring unmolested passage, as through enemy territory.

safe·crack·er (sāf'krăk'ər) *n.* One who forces open safes to steal the contents.

safe·de·pos·it box (sāf'dĭ-pŏz'ĭt) *n.* A box, usu. in a bank vault, for the safe storage of valuables.

safe·guard (sāf'gärd') *n.* A precautionary measure or device. *—v.* To ensure the safety of; protect.

safe·keep·ing (sāf'kē'pĭng) *n.* Protection; care.

safe·ty (sāf'tē) *n., pl.* **-ties. 1.** Freedom from danger, risk, or injury. **2.** A protective device, as the lock on a firearm. **3.** A football play in which the offensive team downs the ball behind its own goal line, resulting in two points for the defensive team.

safety glass *n.* A shatterproof composite of two sheets of glass with an intermediate layer of plastic.

safety match *n.* A match that can be lighted only by being struck against a chemically prepared friction surface.

safety pin *n.* A pin in the form of a clasp, with a sheath to cover and hold the point.

safety razor *n.* A razor in which the blade is fitted into a holder with guards to prevent cutting of the skin.

safety valve *n.* A valve, as in a steam boiler,

that automatically opens when pressure reaches a dangerous level.

saf·flow·er (săf'lou'ər) *n.* A plant with flowers yielding a dyestuff and seeds used in a cooking oil. [< Ar. *asfar,* a yellow plant.]

saf·fron (săf'rən) *n.* **1.** The dried orange-yellow stigmas of a kind of crocus, used to color and flavor food and as a dye. **2.** An orange-yellow. [< Ar. *za'farān.*] **—saf'fron** *adj.*

sag (săg) *v.* **sagged, sag·ging. 1.** To droop, hang downward, or settle from weight or slackness. **2.** To diminish in strength. **3.** To decline, as in value or price. [ME *saggen.*] **—sag** *n.*

sa·ga (sä'gə) *n.* **1.** An Icelandic prose narrative of the 12th and 13th cent. **2.** A long heroic narrative. [ON.]

sa·ga·cious (sə-gā'shəs) *adj.* Shrewd and wise. [< Lat. *sagax.*] **—sa·ga'cious·ly** *adv.* **—sa·gac'i·ty** (-găs'ĭ-tē) *n.*

sage¹ (sāj) *n.* A venerable, wise person. *—adj.* **sag·er, sag·est.** Judicious; wise. [< Lat. *sapere,* to be wise.] **—sage'ly** *adv.* **—sage'ness** *n.*

sage² (sāj) *n.* **1.** An aromatic plant with grayish-green leaves used as seasoning. **2.** Sagebrush. [< Lat. *salvia.*]

sage·brush (sāj'brŭsh') *n.* An aromatic shrub of arid regions of western North America.

Sag·it·tar·i·us (săj'ĭ-târ'ē-əs) *n.* **1.** A constellation in the Southern Hemisphere. **2.** The 9th sign of the zodiac.

sa·go (sā'gō) *n., pl.* **-gos.** A powdery starch obtained from the trunks of an Asian palm. [Malay *sagu.*]

sa·gua·ro (sə-gwä'rō, sə-wä'rō) *n., pl.* **-ros.** Also **sa·hua·ro** (sə-wä'rō). A large branching cactus of southwestern North America. [Mex. Sp.]

Sa·hap·tin (sä-hăp'tĭn) *n., pl.* **-tin** or **-tins. 1.** A member of an Indian people of Idaho, Washington, and Oregon. **2.** The language of the Sahaptin.

sa·hib (sä'ĭb, sä'hĭb) *n.* Master; sir. Used as a title of respect for Europeans in colonial India. [Hindi *ṣāhib,* master.]

said (sĕd) *v. p.t. & p.p.* of **say.** *—adj.* Aforementioned.

Usage: The adjective *said* is seldom appropriate to any but legal or business contexts, in which it is equivalent to *aforesaid:* *the said property* (as previously named in a lease or contract). Otherwise the use of *said* as an adjective is usually unnecessary.

sail (sāl) *n.* **1.** A length of shaped fabric that catches the wind and propels or aids in maneuvering a vessel. **2.** A sailing ship. **3.** A trip in a sailing craft. **4.** Something resembling a sail. *—v.* **1.** To move across the surface of water by means of a sail. **2.** To travel by water in a vessel. **3.** To start out on a voyage. **4.** To operate a sailing craft; navigate or manage (a vessel). **5.** To glide through the air; soar. [< OE *segl.*]

sail·board (sāl'bôrd', -bōrd') *n.* A small, light sailboat with a flat hull that carries one or more people.

sail·boat (sāl'bōt') *n.* A small boat propelled by a sail or sails.

sail·fish (sāl'fĭsh') *n.* A large marine fish with

---

a large dorsal fin and a spearlike projection from the upper jaw.

sail·or (sā'lər) *n.* **1.** One who serves in a navy or works on a ship as a crew member. **2.** A straw hat with a flat top and brim.

sail·plane (sāl'plān') *n.* A light glider used esp. for soaring. **—sail'plane'** *v.* **—sail'plan'er** *n.*

saint (sānt) *n.* **1.** A person considered holy and worthy of public veneration, esp. one who has been canonized. **2.** A very virtuous person. **—v.** To canonize. [< Lat. *sanctus*, sacred.] **—saint'dom** *n.* **—saint'ed** *adj.* **—saint'hood'** *n.* **—saint'li·ness** *n.* **—saint'ly** *adj.*

Saint Ber·nard (bər-närd') *n.* A large, strong dog orig. used in the Swiss Alps to rescue lost travelers. [< the hospice of *Saint Bernard.*]

Saint Bernard

saith (sĕth, sā'ŏth) *v. Archaic.* 3rd person sing. present tense of **say.**

sake¹ (sāk) *n.* **1.** Purpose; end: *for the sake of argument.* **2.** Advantage; good: *for your own sake.* [< OE *sacu.*]

sa·ke² (sä'kē) *n.* Also **sa·ki.** A Japanese liquor made from fermented rice. [J.]

sa·laam (sə-läm') *n.* An Oriental obeisance performed by bowing low while placing the right palm on the forehead. [Ar. *salām*, peace.] **—sa·laam'** *v.*

sa·la·cious (sə-lā'shəs) *adj.* Lewd; bawdy. [< Lat. *salax*, lustful.] **—sa·la'cious·ly** *adv.* **—sa·la'cious·ness** *or* **sa·lac'i·ty** (-lăs'ĭ-tē) *n.*

sal·ad (săl'əd) *n.* A dish usu. consisting of raw green vegetables tossed with a dressing. [< Lat. *sal*, salt.]

sal·a·man·der (săl'ə-măn'dər) *n.* **1.** A small, lizardlike amphibian. **2.** A portable stove used to heat or dry buildings under construction. [< Gk. *salamandra.*]

sa·la·mi (sə-lä'mē) *n.* A highly spiced salted sausage. [< Lat. *sal*, salt.]

sal·a·ried (săl'ə-rēd) *adj.* Earning or yielding a salary.

sal·a·ry (săl'ə-rē, săl'rē) *n., pl.* **-ries.** Regular compensation for services or work. [< Lat. *salarium*, money given to Roman soldiers for the purchase of salt.]

sale (sāl) *n.* **1.** The exchange of property or ownership for money. **2.** Demand; ready market. **3.** Availability for purchase. **4.** An auction. **5.** A special disposal of goods at lowered prices. [< ON *sala.*] **—sal'a·bil'i·ty** (sā'lə-bĭl'ĭ-tē) *n.* **—sal'a·ble** *or* **sale'a·ble** *adj.*

sales·clerk (sālz'klûrk') *n.* One employed to sell goods in a store.

sales·man (sālz'mən) *n.* A man employed to sell merchandise in a store or in a designated territory. **—sales'man·ship'** *n.* **—sales'wom·an** *n.*

sales·peo·ple (sālz'pē'pəl) *pl.n.* Persons engaged in selling.

sales·per·son (sālz'pûr'sən) *n.* A salesman or saleswoman.

sales tax *n.* A tax levied on the price of goods and services.

sal·i·cyl·ic acid (săl'ĭ-sĭl'ĭk) *n.* A white crystalline acid, $C_7H_6O_3$, used in making aspirin. [< Fr. *salicyle*, the radical of salicylic acid.]

sa·li·ent (sā'lē-ənt, sāl'yənt) *adj.* **1.** Projecting or jutting beyond a line or surface. **2.** Striking; conspicuous. [< Lat. *salire*, to leap.] **—sa'li·ence** *or* **sa'li·en·cy** *n.* **—sa'li·ent·ly** *adv.* **—sa'li·ent·ness** *n.*

sa·line (sā'lēn', -lĭn') *adj.* Of or containing salt. [Lat. *salinus.*] **—sa·lin'i·ty** (sə-lĭn'ĭ-tē) *n.*

Sa·lish (sā'lĭsh) *n.* Also **Sa·lish·an** (-lĭ-shən). **1.** A family of Indian languages of the northwestern United States and British Columbia. **2.** The Indians speaking languages of this family. **—Sa'lish·an** *adj.*

sa·li·va (sə-lī'və) *n.* The watery, slightly alkaline fluid secreted into the mouth by the salivary glands. [Lat.] **—sal'i·var'y** (săl'ə-vĕr'ē) *adj.*

sal·i·vate (săl'ə-vāt') *v.* **-vat·ed, -vat·ing.** To secrete or produce saliva. **—sal'i·va'tion** *n.*

Salk vaccine (sôlk) *n.* A killed-virus vaccine used to immunize against poliomyelitis. [< Jonas Salk (b. 1914).]

sal·low¹ (săl'ō) *adj.* **-er, -est.** Of a sickly yellow color. [< OE *salo.*] **—sal'low·ness** *n.*

sal·low² (săl'ō) *n.* Any of several European willows. [< OE *sealh.*]

sal·ly (săl'ē) *n., pl.* **-lies. 1.** A sudden assault from a defensive position. **2.** A quick witticism; quip. **3.** A short excursion; jaunt. [< Lat. *salire*, to leap.] **—sal'ly** *v.*

salm·on (săm'ən, să'mən) *n., pl.* **-on** *or* **-ons. 1.** Any of various large food and game fishes of northern waters, usu. with pinkish flesh. **2.** A yellowish pink or pinkish orange. [< Lat. *salmo.*] **—salm'on** *adj.*

sal·mo·nel·la (săl'mə-nĕl'ə) *n., pl.* **-la** *or* **-las** *or* **-lae** (-lē). Any of various bacteria, many of which cause disease in warm-blooded animals. [< Daniel E. *Salmon* (1850–1914).]

sa·lon (sə-lŏn', să-lŏn') *n.* **1.** An elegant drawing room. **2.** An assemblage of persons, usu. of social or intellectual distinction, who frequent the home of a particular person. **3.** A stylish commercial establishment: *a beauty salon.* [< Ital. *sala*, hall.]

sa·loon (sə-lōōn') *n.* **1.** A bar; tavern. **2.** A large lounge or ballroom on a ship. [< Ital. *sala*, hall.]

salt (sôlt) *n.* **1.** A colorless or white crystalline solid, chiefly sodium chloride, used as a food seasoning and preservative. **2.** A chemical compound formed by replacing all or part of the hydrogen ions of an acid with one or more metallic ions. **3. salts.** Any of various mineral salts used as cathartics. **4.** An element that gives flavor or zest. **5.** Sharp, lively wit; pungency. **6.** *Informal.* A veteran sailor. **—adj. 1.** Tasting of salt. **2.** Preserved with salt. **—v. 1.** To add salt to. **2.** To preserve with salt. **—phrasal verb. salt away.** To put aside; save. **—idiom. with a grain of salt.** With skepticism. [< OE *sealt.*] **—salt'i·ly** *adv.* **—salt'i·ness** *n.* **—salt'y** *adj.*

salt·box (sôlt'bŏks') *n.* A house with two stories in front and one in back and a roof with a long rear slope.

salt·cel·lar (sôlt'sĕl'ər) *n.* A small container

for holding and dispensing salt. [< ME *salt saler*.]

sal·tine (sŏl-tēn′) *n.* A thin salted cracker.

salt lick *n.* A block or deposit of exposed salt that animals lick.

salt·pe·ter (sŏlt′pē′tər) *n.* 1. Potassium nitrate. 2. Sodium nitrate. [< Med. Lat. *salpetra*.]

salt·shak·er (sŏlt′shā′kər) *n.* A container for sprinkling table salt.

salt·water (sŏlt′wô′tər, -wŏt′ər) *adj.* Consisting of or inhabiting salt water.

sa·lu·bri·ous (sə-lōō′brē-əs) *adj.* Favorable to health. [< Lat. *salubris*.] **—sa·lu′bri·ous·ly** *adv.* **—sa·lu′bri·ous·ness** or **sa·lu′bri·ty** (-brĭ-tē) *n.*

sal·u·tary (săl′yə-tĕr′ē) *adj.* 1. Beneficial: *salutary advice.* 2. Wholesome. [< Lat. *salutaris*.] **—sal′u·tar′i·ly** *adv.* **—sal′u·tar′i·ness** *n.*

sal·u·ta·tion (săl′yə-tā′shən) *n.* An expression of greeting, good will, or courtesy.

sa·lute (sə-lōōt′) *v.* **-lut·ed, -lut·ing.** 1. To greet. 2. To recognize (a military superior) with a prescribed gesture. 3. To honor formally. **—n.** 1. A greeting. 2. A prescribed military display of honor or greeting. [< Lat. *salutare*.] **—sa·lut′er** *n.*

sal·vage (săl′vĭj) *n.* 1. The rescue of a ship. 2. Money paid to those who aid in a ship's rescue. 3. The act of saving imperiled property. 4. Rescued property. **—v. -vaged, -vag·ing.** To save from loss or destruction. **—sal′vage·a·ble** *adj.* **—sal′vag·er** *n.*

sal·va·tion (săl-vā′shən) *n.* 1. Preservation or deliverance from evil or difficulty. 2. A means or cause of such deliverance. 3. Deliverance from the power or penalty of sin; redemption. [< Lat. *salvare*, to save.] **—sal·va′tion·al** *adj.*

salve (săv, säv) *n.* A soothing or healing ointment. **—v. salved, salv·ing.** To soothe or heal with or as if with salve. [< OE *sealf*.]

sal·ver (săl′vər) *n.* A serving tray. [< LLat. *salvare*, to save.]

sal·vi·a (săl′vē-ə) *n.* Any of various plants with showy scarlet or blue flowers. [< Lat., sage.]

sal·vo (săl′vō) *n., pl.* **-vos** or **-voes.** 1. A simultaneous discharge of firearms. 2. A sudden outburst. [< Ital. *salva*, salute.]

sa·mar·i·um (sə-mâr′ē-əm, -măr′-) *n.* Symbol **Sm** A silvery or pale-gray metallic rare-earth element used in laser materials, in infrared absorbing glass, and as a neutron absorber. Atomic number 62; atomic weight 150.35. [< Colonel von *Samarski*, a 19th-cent. Russian mine official.]

same (sām) *adj.* 1. Being the very one; identical. 2. Similar or corresponding. **—adv.** In like or identical manner. **—pron.** 1. One identical with another. 2. The one previously mentioned. [< ON *samr*.] **—same′ness** *n.*

Syns: *same, identical, selfsame, very* adj.

Usage: Only in legal contexts is *same* or the *same* used as a substitute for *it* or *they*. Therefore, in general, avoid sentences like *The charge is $5; please remit same.*

sa·mekh (sä′mĕk) *n.* The 15th letter of the Hebrew alphabet. See table at **alphabet.** [Heb. *sāmekh*.]

Sa·mo·an (sə-mō′ən) *n.* 1. A native or inhabi-

tant of Samoa. 2. The Polynesian language of the Samoans. **—Sa·mo′an** *adj.*

sam·o·var (săm′ə-vär′) *n.* A metal urn with a spigot, used to boil water for tea. [R.]

Sam·o·yed (săm′ə-yĕd′) *n.* 1. A member of a Ural-Altaic nomadic people of the north-central USSR. 2. A Uralic language spoken by the Samoyed people. 3. A working dog of a breed orig. developed in northern Eurasia. **—Sam′o·yed′ic** *adj.*

sam·pan (săm′păn′) *n.* A flat-bottomed Oriental skiff. [Chin. *san¹ ban³*.]

sampan

sam·ple (săm′pəl) *n.* 1. A portion, piece, or segment representative of a whole. 2. *Statistics.* A set of elements analyzed to estimate the characteristics of a population. **—v. -pled, -pling.** To take a sample of, esp. in order to test or analyze. [< OFr. *essample*, example.]

sam·pler (săm′plər) *n.* 1. One employed to appraise samples. 2. A piece of cloth embroidered with various designs.

sam·pling (săm′plĭng) *n.* A sample (sense 2).

Sam·u·el (săm′yōō-əl) *n.* See table at Bible.

sam·u·rai (săm′ōō-rī′) *n., pl.* **-rai** or **-rais.** The military aristocracy of feudal Japan or one of its members. [J., warrior.]

san·a·to·ri·um (săn′ə-tôr′ē-əm, -tōr′-) *n., pl.* **-ums** or **-to·ri·a** (-tôr′ē-ə, -tōr′-). 1. An institution for the treatment of chronic diseases. 2. A sanitarium. [< LLat. *sanatorius*, curative.]

sanc·ta (săngk′tə) *n.* A pl. of **sanctum.**

sanc·ti·fy (săngk′tə-fī′) *v.* **-fied, -fy·ing.** 1. To reserve for sacred use; consecrate. 2. To make holy; purify. [< LLat. *sanctificare*.] **—sanc′ti·fi·ca′tion** *n.* **—sanc′ti·fi′er** *n.*

sanc·ti·mo·ny (săngk′tə-mō′nē) *n.* Hypocritical piety. [< Lat. *sanctimonia*, sacredness.] **—sanc′ti·mo′ni·ous·ly** *adv.* **—sanc′ti·mo′ni·ous·ness** *n.*

sanc·tion (săngk′shən) *n.* 1. Authoritative permission or approval. 2. A penalty intended to enforce compliance or conformity. 3. A coercive measure adopted usu. by several nations against a nation violating international law. **—v.** To authorize, approve, or encourage. [< Lat. *sanctus*, sacred.]

sanc·ti·ty (săngk′tĭ-tē) *n., pl.* **-ties.** 1. Holiness of life; saintliness. 2. Sacredness or inviolability: *the sanctity of the family.* [< Lat. *sanctitas*.]

sanc·tu·ar·y (săngk′chōō-ĕr′ē) *n., pl.* **-ies.** A consecrated place, as of a house of worship.

2. A place of refuge, asylum, or protection. [< LLat. *sanctuarium.*]

sanc·tum (săngk′təm) *n., pl.* **-tums** or **-ta** (-tə). 1. A sacred or holy place. 2. A private room or study. [< Lat. *sanctus,* sacred.]

sand (sănd) *n.* 1. Loose, granular, gritty particles of disintegrated rock, finer than gravel and coarser than dust. —*v.* 1. To polish or scour with sand or sandpaper. 2. To fill up (a harbor) with sand. [< OE.] —**sand′er** *n.* —**sand′i·ness** *n.* —**sand′y** *adj.*

san·dal (săn′dəl) *n.* 1. A shoe consisting of a sole fastened to the foot by thongs or straps. 2. A low-cut shoe with an ankle strap. [< Gk. *sandalon.*]

san·dal·wood (săn′dəl-wŏŏd′) *n.* 1. An Asian tree with aromatic wood used for carving and in perfumery. 2. The wood of this tree. [< Gk. *santalon,* sandalwood + WOOD.]

sand·bag (sănd′băg′) *n.* A bag filled with sand, used esp. in piles to form protective walls. —*v.* 1. To put sandbags in or around. 2. To coerce.

sand·bar (sănd′bär′) *n.* A ridge of sand in a river or off a shore.

sand·blast (sănd′blăst′) *n.* A blast of air carrying sand at high velocity, as for cleaning stone or glass. —**sand′blast′** *v.* —**sand′blast′er** *n.*

sand·box (sănd′bŏks′) *n.* A box filled with sand for children to play in.

sand dollar *n.* Any of various thin, circular echinoderms of sandy ocean bottoms of the northern Atlantic and Pacific.

sand·hog (sănd′hôg′, -hŏg′) *n.* One who works in a caisson in the construction of underwater tunnels.

sand·lot (sănd′lŏt′) *n.* A vacant lot used by children for sports. —**sand′lot′** *adj.*

sand·man (sănd′măn′) *n.* A character in folklore who puts children to sleep by sprinkling sand in their eyes.

sand·pa·per (sănd′pā′pər) *n.* Heavy paper coated on one side with an abrasive material, used for smoothing. —**sand′pa′per** *v.*

sand·pip·er (sănd′pī′pər) *n.* Any of various small, usu. long-billed shore birds.

sand·stone (sănd′stōn′) *n.* Variously colored sedimentary rock composed chiefly of sandlike quartz.

sand·storm (sănd′stôrm′) *n.* A strong wind carrying clouds of sand.

sand trap *n.* A sand-filled depression serving as a hazard on a golf course.

sand·wich (sănd′wĭch, săn′-) *n.* Two or more slices of bread with a filling placed between them. —*v.* To insert or fit tightly. [< the 4th Earl of *Sandwich* (1718–92).]

sane (sān) *adj.* **san·er, san·est.** 1. Mentally healthy. 2. Rational: *a sane approach.* [Lat. *sanus.*] —**sane′ly** *adv.* —**sane′ness** or **san′i·ty** (săn′ĭ-tē) *n.*

sang (săng) *v.* A *p.t.* of **sing.**

sang-froid (sän-frwä′) *n.* Composure; imperturbability. [Fr.]

san·gri·a (săng-grē′ə, săn-) *n.* A cold drink made of red wine mixed with fruit juice and sugar. [Sp. *sangría* < Lat. *sanguis,* blood.]

san·gui·nary (săng′gwə-nĕr′ē) *adj.* 1. Bloody. 2. Bloodthirsty. —**san′gui·nar′i·ly** *adv.*

san·guine (săng′gwĭn) *adj.* 1. Ruddy, as the complexion. 2. Optimistic; cheerful. [< Lat. *sanguineus,* blood.] —**san′guine·ly** *adv.* —**san′guine·ness** or **san·guin′i·ty** (-gwĭn′ĭ-tē) *n.* —**san·guin′e·ous** (-gwĭn′ē-əs) *adj.*

san·i·tar·i·um (săn′ĭ-târ′ē-əm) *n., pl.* **-ums** or **-i·a** (-ē-ə). 1. A health resort. 2. A sanatorium.

san·i·tary (săn′ĭ-tĕr′ē) *adj.* 1. Of or used to preserve health. 2. Clean; hygienic. [< Lat. *sanitas,* health.]

san·i·ta·tion (săn′ĭ-tā′shən) *n.* 1. The formulation and application of public health measures. 2. The disposal of sewage and garbage.

san·i·tize (săn′ĭ-tīz′) *v.* **-tized, -tiz·ing.** 1. To make sanitary. 2. To make more acceptable by removing unpleasant or offensive elements from: *sanitized the movie script for family viewing.*

sank (săngk) *v.* A *p.t.* of **sink.**

sans (sănz) *prep.* Without. [< OFr.]

San·skrit (săn′skrĭt′) *n.* An ancient Indic language, the classical literary language of India. —**San′skrit·ist** *n.*

San·ta Claus (săn′tə klôz′) *n.* The personification of the spirit of Christmas, usu. represented as a fat old man with a white beard and a red suit. [< dial. Du. *Sinterklaas.*]

sap¹ (săp) *n.* 1. The watery fluid that circulates through a plant, carrying food and other substances to the tissues. 2. Health and energy; vitality. 3. *Slang.* A gullible person; fool. [< OE *sæp.*]

sap² (săp) *v.* **sapped, sap·ping.** 1. To undermine the foundations of. 2. To deplete or weaken gradually. [< OFr. *sappe,* an undermining.]

sa·pi·ent (sā′pē-ənt) *adj.* Wise; discerning. [< Lat. *sapere,* to be wise.] —**sa′pi·ence** *n.* —**sa′pi·ent·ly** *adv.*

sap·ling (săp′lĭng) *n.* A young tree.

sap·per (săp′ər) *n.* A military engineer.

sap·phire (săf′īr′) *n.* 1. Any of several relatively pure forms of corundum, esp. a blue form used as a gemstone. 2. A corundum gem. 3. The blue color of a gem sapphire. [< Gk. *sappheiros.*]

sap·py (săp′ē) *adj.* **-pi·er, -pi·est.** 1. Full of sap; juicy. 2. *Slang.* Silly; foolish.

sap·ro·phyte (săp′rə-fīt′) *n.* A plant that lives on dead or decaying organic matter. [Gk. *sapros,* rotten + -PHYTE.] —**sap′ro·phyt′ic** (-fĭt′ĭk) *adj.*

sap·suck·er (săp′sŭk′ər) *n.* A small North American woodpecker that drills into trees to drink the sap.

Sar·a·cen (săr′ə-sən) *n.* A member of a pre-Islamic nomadic people of the Syrian and northern Arabian deserts.

sa·ran (sə-răn′) *n.* Any of various thermoplastic resins used to make packaging films, corrosion-resistant pipes, and fiber for fabrics. [< *Saran,* a former U.S. trademark.]

sar·casm (sär′kăz′əm) *n.* 1. A mocking or ironic remark. 2. The use of sarcasm. [Gk. *sarkasmos.*] —**sar·cas′tic** (-kăs′tĭk) *adj.* —**sar·cas′ti·cal·ly** *adv.*

sar·co·ma (sär-kō′mə) *n., pl.* **-ma·ta** (-mə-tə) or **-mas.** A malignant tumor arising from nonepithelial connective tissues. [Gk. *sarkōma,* fleshy excrescence.]

sar·coph·a·gus (sär-kŏf′ə-gəs) *n., pl.* **-gi** (-jī′). A stone coffin. [< Gk. *sarkophagos,* flesh-eating.]

sar·dine (sär-dēn′) *n.* A small herring or related fish, often canned in oil. [< Lat. *sardina.*]

sar·don·ic (sär-dŏn′ĭk) *adj.* Scornfully mocking. [< Gk. *sardonios.*] —**sar·don′i·cal·ly** *adv.*

sa·ri (sä'rē) n., pl. **-ris.** A lightweight, wrapped garment worn by women of India and Pakistan. [< Skt. *śāṭī.*]

sa·rong (sə-rông', -rŏng') n. A length of brightly colored cloth worn by both men and women in Malaysia, Indonesia, and the Pacific islands. [Malay.]

sar·sa·pa·ril·la (săs'pə-rĭl'ə, sär'sə-pə-) n. 1. The dried roots of a tropical American plant, used as a flavoring. 2. A soft drink flavored with sarsaparilla. [Sp. *zarzaparrilla.*]

sar·to·ri·al (sär-tôr'ē-əl, -tōr'-) adj. 1. Pertaining to tailors or tailoring. 2. Pertaining to clothing, esp. men's. [< Lat. *sartor,* tailor.]

sash¹ (săsh) n. A band worn about the waist or over the shoulder. [Ar. *shāsh,* muslin.]

sash² (săsh) n. A frame in which the panes of a window or door are set. [< Fr. *châssis,* frame.]

sa·shay (să-shā') v. *Informal.* To strut or flounce. [< Fr. *chassé,* a dance step.]

sass (săs) *Informal.* —n. Impertinence; back talk. —v. To talk back to. [< SASSY.]

sas·sa·fras (săs'ə-frăs') n. 1. A North American tree with irregularly lobed leaves and aromatic bark. 2. The dried root bark of the sassafras tree, used as flavoring. [Sp. *sasafrás.*]

sas·sy (săs'ē) adj. **-si·er, -si·est.** Impudent. [< SAUCY.] —**sas'si·ly** adv. —**sas'si·ness** n.

sat (săt) v. p.t. & p.p. of **sit.**

Sa·tan (sāt'n) n. The Devil. [< Heb. *śāṭan.*]

sa·tang (sə-täng') n., pl. **-tang.** See table at **currency.** [Thai *satān.*]

sa·tan·ic (sə-tăn'ĭk) or **sa·tan·i·cal** (-ĭ-kəl) adj. 1. Pertaining to or suggestive of Satan. 2. Fiendishly cruel or evil.

satch·el (săch'əl) n. A small valise or bag. [< Lat. *saccellus.*]

sate (sāt) v. **sat·ed, sat·ing.** 1. To satisfy completely or fully. 2. To indulge to excess; surfeit. [Prob. < OE *sadian.*]

sa·teen (să-tēn') n. A cotton fabric with a satin finish. [< SATIN.]

sat·el·lite (săt'l-īt') n. 1. *Astron.* A relatively small body orbiting a planet. 2. A manmade object intended to orbit a celestial body. 3. A servile attendant or follower. 4. A nation dominated politically by another. [< Lat. *satelles,* attendant.]

sa·ti·ate (sā'shē-āt') v. **-at·ed, -at·ing.** 1. To satisfy fully. 2. To gratify to excess. [Lat. *satiare.*] —**sa'ti·a'tion** n.

sa·ti·e·ty (sə-tī'ĭ-tē) n. The condition of being sated. [< Lat. *satietas,* sufficiency.]

sat·in (săt'n) n. A smooth, close-woven, glossy fabric. [< OFr.] —**sat'in·y** adj.

sat·in·wood (săt'n-wŏŏd') n. An East Indian tree with yellowish close-grained wood.

sat·ire (săt'īr') n. 1. An artistic work that attacks human vice or foolishness with irony, derision, or wit. 2. Irony or caustic wit used to expose or attack human folly. [< Lat. *satira.*] —**sa·tir'i·cal** (sə-tĭr'ĭ-kəl) or **sa·tir'ic** adj. —**sa·tir'i·cal·ly** adv. —**sat'i·rist** (săt'ə-rĭst) n.

sat·i·rize (săt'ə-rīz') v. **-rized, -riz·ing.** To ridicule by satire.

sat·is·fac·tion (săt'ĭs-făk'shən) n. 1. **a.** Gratification of a desire, need, or appetite. **b.** The pleasure derived from such gratification.

2. Reparation; atonement. 3. Compensation; amends.

sat·is·fac·to·ry (săt'ĭs-făk'tə-rē) adj. Giving satisfaction. —**sat'is·fac'to·ri·ly** adv. —**sat'is·fac'to·ri·ness** n.

sat·is·fy (săt'ĭs-fī') v. **-fied, -fy·ing.** 1. To gratify or fulfill a need or desire. 2. To relieve of doubt or question; assure. 3. To fulfill or discharge an obligation. 4. To conform to the requirements of. 5. To give satisfaction. [< Lat. *satisfacere.*] —**sat'is·fi'er** n. —**sat'is·fy'ing·ly** adv.

sa·trap (sā'trăp', săt'răp') n. A subordinate ruler. [< OPers. *khshathrapāvā,* protector of the people.]

sat·u·rate (săch'ə-rāt') v. **-rat·ed, -rat·ing.** To soak or fill thoroughly. [Lat. *saturare.*] —**sat'u·ra·ble** (-ər-ə-bəl) adj. —**sat'u·ra'tion** n. —**sat'u·ra'tor** n.

Sat·ur·day (săt'ər-dē, -dā') n. The 7th day of the week. [< OE *sæternesdæg.*]

Saturday night special n. *Informal.* A handgun.

Sat·urn (săt'ərn) n. 1. *Rom. Myth.* The god of agriculture. 2. The 6th planet from the sun, having a diameter of 74,000 miles, a mass 95 times that of Earth, and an orbital period of 29.5 years at a mean distance of about 886,000,000 miles.

sat·ur·nine (săt'ər-nīn') adj. Morose and sardonic.

sat·yr (săt'ər, sā'tər) n. 1. *Gk. Myth.* A woodland deity often depicted with the ears, legs, and horns of a goat. 2. A lecher. [< Gk. *saturos.*] —**sa·tyr'ic** (sə-tĭr'ĭk) or **sa·tyr'i·cal** adj.

sauce (sôs) n. 1. A liquid dressing served with food. 2. Cooked fruit. 3. *Informal.* Impudence. 4. *Slang.* Alcoholic liquor. —v. **sauced, sauc·ing.** 1. To flavor with sauce. 2. To add zest to. 3. *Informal.* To be impudent to. [< Lat. *salsa,* salted.]

sauce·pan (sôs'păn') n. A long-handled cooking pan.

sau·cer (sô'sər) n. A small, shallow dish for holding a cup. [< OFr. *sausse,* sauce.]

sau·cy (sô'sē) adj. **-ci·er, -ci·est.** 1. Impudent. 2. Pert. —**sau'ci·ly** adv. —**sau'ci·ness** n.

sau·er·bra·ten (sour'brät'n) n. A pot roast of beef marinated in vinegar before cooking. [G.]

sau·er·kraut (sour'krout') n. Shredded cabbage salted and fermented in its own juice. [G.]

Sauk (sôk) n., pl. **Sauk** or **Sauks.** Also **Sac** (săk, sôk) pl. **Sac** or **Sacs.** 1. **a.** A tribe of Indians living orig. in Michigan, Wisconsin, and Illinois and now settled in Iowa and Oklahoma. **b.** A member of this tribe. 2. The Algonquian language of the Sauk.

sau·na (sou'nə, sô'-) n. A steambath in which steam is often produced by water thrown on heated rocks. [Finn.]

saun·ter (sôn'tər) v. To walk leisurely. —n. A leisurely stroll. [Prob. < ME *santren,* to muse.]

-saur suff. Lizard: brontosaur. [< Gk. *sauras.*]

sau·sage (sô'sĭj) n. Finely chopped and seasoned meat stuffed into a casing. [< LLat. *salsicius,* prepared by salting.]

sau·té (sō-tā′, sô-) v. **-téed, -té·ing.** To fry lightly in fat. [< Fr. *sauter*, to leap.]

sau·terne (sō-tûrn′, sô-) n. A delicate, sweet white wine. [< *Sauternes*, France.]

sav·age (săv′ĭj) adj. **1.** Not domesticated or cultivated; wild. **2.** Not civilized; primitive. **3.** Ferocious; fierce. —n. **1.** A primitive or uncivilized person. **2.** A brutal person. **3.** A rude person. —v. **-aged, -ag·ing.** To attack violently or brutally. [< Lat. *silvaticus*, of the woods.] —**sav′age·ly** adv. —**sav′age·ry** n.

sa·van·na (sə-văn′ə) n. Also **sa·van·nah.** A flat, treeless grassland of tropical or subtropical regions. [< Taino *zabana*.]

sa·vant (sə-vänt′,) n. A learned person. [< Fr. *savoir*, to know.]

save¹ (sāv) v. **saved, sav·ing. 1.** To rescue from danger. **2.** To preserve or safeguard. **3.** To set aside for future use; store. **4.** To prevent waste. **5.** To avoid fatigue, wear, or damage; spare. **6.** To deliver from sin. [< LLat. *salvare*.] —**sav′er** n.

save² (sāv) prep. With the exception of; except. —conj. Except; but. [< Lat. *salvo*.]

sav·ing (sā′vĭng) adj. **1.** Redeeming: *saving graces.* **2.** Economical. —n. **1.** Preservation or rescue. **2.** Economy. **3. savings.** Money saved. —prep. With the exception of. —conj. Except; save.

savings account n. A bank account that draws interest.

savings bank n. A bank that receives, invests, and pays interest on savings accounts.

sav·ior (sāv′yər) n. Also chiefly Brit. **sav·iour.** One who saves or preserves. [< LLat. *salvator.*]

sa·voir-faire (săv′wär-fâr′) n. Social skill or tact. [Fr.]

sa·vor (sā′vər) n. Also chiefly Brit. **sa·vour.** —n. **1.** Taste or aroma. **2.** A specific taste, smell, or quality. —v. **1.** To have a particular savor. **2.** To taste with zest; relish. [< Lat. *sapor.*] —**sa′vor·er** n.

sa·vor·y¹ (sā′və-rē) adj. **1.** Appetizing to the taste or smell. **2.** Piquant, pungent, or salty to the taste. —**sa′vor·i·ness** n.

sa·vor·y² (sā′və-rē) n., pl. **-ies.** An aromatic herb used as a seasoning. [< Lat. *satureia.*]

sav·vy (săv′ē) Slang. —v. **-vied, -vy·ing.** To understand. —n. Practical understanding. [< Sp. *sabe (usted),* (you) know.]

saw¹ (sô) n. A cutting tool having a thin metal blade or disk with a sharp-toothed edge. —v. **sawed, sawed** or **sawn** (sôn), **saw·ing.** To cut with or as if with a saw. [< OE *sagu.*] —**saw′er** n.

saw² (sô) n. A familiar and often trite saying. [< OE *sagu,* speech.]

saw³ (sô) v. p.t. of **see¹.**

saw·buck (sô′bŭk′) n. **1.** A sawhorse, esp. one with X-shaped legs. **2.** Slang. A ten-dollar bill.

saw·dust (sô′dŭst′) n. The small waste particles that result from sawing.

sawed-off (sôd′ôf′, -ŏf′) adj. **1.** Having one end sawed off: *a sawed-off shotgun.* **2.** Slang. Shorter than average height.

saw·horse (sô′hôrs′) n. A rack or trestle used to support wood being sawed.

saw·mill (sô′mĭl′) n. A mill where lumber is cut into boards.

sawn (sôn) v. p.p. of **saw¹.**

saw·yer (sô′yər) n. One employed to saw wood. [ME *sawier.*]

sax (săks) n. Informal. A saxophone.

sax·i·frage (săk′sə-frĭj, -frāj′) n. Any of numerous plants with small flowers and leaves that often form a basal rosette. [< LLat. *saxifragus,* rock-breaking.]

Sax·on (săk′sən) n. **1.** A member of a Germanic tribal group that inhabited northern Germany and invaded England in the 5th cent. with the Angles and Jutes. **2.** The Germanic language of the Saxons. —**Sax′on** adj.

sax·o·phone (săk′sə-fōn′) n. A wind instrument with a single-reed mouthpiece and a usu. curved conical metal tube. [< Adolphe *Sax* (1814-94).] —**sax′o·phon′ist** n.

say (sā) v. **said** (sĕd), **say·ing. 1.** To utter aloud. **2.** To express in words. **3.** To state; declare. **4.** To recite. **5.** To allege. **6.** To indicate; show: *The clock said noon.* **7.** To estimate or suppose. —n. **1.** A turn or chance to express an opinion. **2.** Authority. —adv. **1.** Approximately. **2.** For instance. [< OE *secgan.*] —**say′er** n.

say·ing (sā′ĭng) n. An adage or proverb.

say-so (sā′sō′) n., pl. **-sos.** Informal. **1.** An unsupported statement or assurance. **2.** An authoritative assertion. **3.** The right or authority to decide.

Sb The symbol for the element antimony.

Sc The symbol for the element scandium.

scab (skăb) n. **1.** The crustlike surface that forms on a healing wound. **2.** One who takes the place of a worker who is on strike. —v. **scabbed, scab·bing. 1.** To form or become covered with a scab. **2.** Informal. To work as a scab. [< ON *skabb.*]

scab·bard (skăb′ərd) n. A sheath, as for a dagger or sword. [< AN *escaubers.*]

scab·by (skăb′ē) adj. **-bi·er, -bi·est. 1.** Having or covered with scabs. **2.** Afflicted with scabies. —**scab′bi·ly** adv. —**scab′bi·ness** n.

sca·bies (skā′bēz′) n. (used with a sing. verb). A contagious skin disease caused by a mite and characterized by intense itching. [Lat., itch.] —**sca′bi·et′ic** (-ĕt′ĭk) adj.

scab·rous (skăb′rəs, skā′brəs) adj. Rough or harsh. [Lat. *scabrosus.*]

scads (skădz) pl.n. Informal. A large number. [Orig. unknown.]

scaf·fold (skăf′əld, -ōld′) n. **1.** A platform, esp. a temporary one used by construction workers. **2.** A platform for the execution of condemned prisoners. [< ONFr. *escafaut.*]

scal·a·wag (skăl′ə-wăg′) n. Informal. A scoundrel. [Orig. unknown.]

scald (skôld) v. **1.** To burn with or as with hot liquid or steam. **2.** To subject to or treat with boiling water. **3.** To heat (a liquid) almost to the boiling point. —n. An injury caused by scalding. [< LLat. *excaldare,* to wash in hot water.]

scale¹ (skāl) n. **1. a.** One of the small platelike structures forming the external covering esp. of fishes, reptiles, etc. **b.** A similar structure or part. **2.** A dry, thin flake of epidermis shed from the skin. **3.** A small, thin piece. **4.** Also **scale insect.** A destructive insect that forms and remains under waxy scales on plants. **5.** A flaky oxide film formed on a metal. —v. **scaled, scal·ing. 1.** To clear or strip of scale or scales. **2.** To remove or come off in layers or scales. **3.** To become encrusted. [< OFr. *escale,* shell.] —**scal′i·ness** n. —**scal′y** adj.

scale² (skāl) n. **1.** A system of ordered marks at fixed intervals used in measurement. **2.** A progressive classification, as of size, amount, importance, or rank. **3.** A relative level or degree. **4.** *Mus.* An ascending or descending series of tones proceeding by a specified scheme of intervals. —*v.* **scaled, scal·ing.** **1.** To climb up with or as if with a ladder. **2.** To reproduce in accordance with a scale. **3.** To adjust according to a proportion. [< Lat. *scalae,* stairs.]

scale³ (skāl) *n.* Often **scales.** An instrument or machine for weighing. [< ON *skāl,* bowl.]

sca·lene (skā'lēn', skā-lēn') *adj.* Having three unequal sides. [< Gk. *skalēnos,* uneven.]

scal·lion (skăl'yən) *n.* A young onion with a small bulb. [< Lat. *Ascalonia (caepa),* (onion) of Ascalon, a port in Palestine.]

scal·lop (skŏl'əp, skăl'-) *n.* **1.** A bivalve marine mollusk with a fan-shaped ridged shell. **2.** The edible muscle of a scallop. **3.** One of a series of curved projections forming an ornamental border. **4.** A thin, boneless slice of meat. —*v.* **1.** To border with scallops. **2.** To bake in a casserole with milk or a sauce and often with bread crumbs. [< OFr. *escalope,* shell.] —**scal·lop·er** *n.*

scallop
Shell

scalp (skălp) *n.* The skin covering the top of the human head. —*v.* **1.** To cut or tear the scalp from. **2.** *Informal.* To buy and resell (tickets) at an excessively high price. [ME.] —**scalp·er** *n.*

scal·pel (skăl'pəl, skăl-pĕl') *n.* A small surgical knife with a thin, sharp blade. [Lat. *scalpellum.*]

scamp (skămp) *n.* A rogue; rascal. [< obs. *scamp,* to go about idly.]

scam·per (skăm'pər) *v.* To run nimbly. [Prob. < Flem. *scamperen,* to decamp.] —**scam·per** *n.* —**scam·per·er** *n.*

scan (skăn) *v.* **scanned, scan·ning.** **1.** To examine closely. **2.** To look over quickly. **3.** To analyze (verse) into metrical patterns. **4.** *Electronics.* To move a finely focused beam of light or electrons in a systematic pattern over (a surface) to reproduce, or sense and subsequently transmit, an image. —*n.* An act or an instance of scanning. [< Lat. *scandere,* to climb.] —**scan'ner** *n.*

scan·dal (skăn'dl) *n.* **1.** Public disgrace. **2.** Outrage; shame. **3.** Malicious gossip. [< Gk. *skandalon.*] —**scan'dal·ous** *adj.* —**scan'dal·ous·ly** *adv.*

scan·dal·ize (skăn'dl-īz') *v.* **-ized, -iz·ing.** To offend the moral standards of. —**scan'dal·i·za'tion** *n.*

scandal sheet *n.* A newspaper that habitually prints scandalous stories.

Scan·di·na·vi·an (skăn'də-nā'vē-ən, -nāv'yən) *n.* **1.** A native or inhabitant of Scandinavia. **2.** A branch of Germanic including Norwegian, Swedish, Danish, and Icelandic. —**Scan'di·na'vi·an** *adj.*

scan·di·um (skăn'dē-əm) *n.* Symbol **Sc** A silvery-white, very lightweight metallic element found in various rare minerals. Atomic number 21; atomic weight 44.956. [< Lat. *Scandia,* Scandinavia.]

scan·sion (skăn'shən) *n.* The analysis of verse into metrical patterns. [< Lat. *scandere,* to climb.]

scant (skănt) *adj.* **-er, -est.** **1.** Deficient in quantity or amount; meager. **2.** Being just short of a specific measure. —*v.* **1.** To skimp. **2.** To limit, as in amount; stint. [< ON *skant,* short.] —**scant'ly** *adv.* —**scant'ness** *n.*

scant·ling (skănt'lĭng, -lĭn) *n.* A small piece of timber, esp. one used as an upright in a building frame. [< OFr. *escantillon,* carpenter's gauge.]

scant·y (skăn'tē) *adj.* **-i·er, -i·est.** **1.** Barely sufficient. **2.** Deficient; insufficient. —**scant'i·ly** *adv.* —**scant'i·ness** *n.*

-scape *suff.* Scene; view: *seascape.* [< LANDSCAPE.]

scape·goat (skāp'gōt') *n.* One bearing blame for others. [(E)SCAPE + GOAT.]

scap·u·la (skăp'yə-lə) *n., pl.* **-lae** (-lē') or **-las.** The shoulder blade. [Lat.] —**scap'u·lar** *adj.*

scar (skär) *n.* **1.** A mark left on the skin after an injury or wound has healed. **2.** A lingering sign of damage. —*v.* **scarred, scar·ring.** To mark or become marked with a scar. [< Gk. *eskhara,* hearth.] —**scar'less** *adj.*

scar·ab (skăr'əb) *n.* **1.** A large black beetle, regarded as a symbol of the soul by the ancient Egyptians. **2.** A representation of a scarab beetle. [< Lat. *scarabaeus.*]

scarce (skârs) *adj.* **scarc·er, scarc·est.** **1.** Infrequently seen or found. **2.** Not plentiful or abundant. [< Lat. *excerpere,* to pick out.] —**scarce'ness** or **scar'ci·ty** *n.*

scarce·ly (skârs'lē) *adv.* **1.** By a small margin; just; barely. **2.** Almost not; hardly. **3.** Certainly not.

Usage: Scarcely has the force of a negative; therefore it is not properly used with another negative: *I could* (not *couldn't*) *scarcely believe it.* A clause following *scarcely* may be introduced by *when* or *before* but not by *than: The meeting had scarcely begun when (or before) it was interrupted.*

scare (skâr) *v.* **scared, scar·ing.** To frighten or become frightened. —*n.* **1.** A fright. **2.** Panic. [< ON *skjarr,* timid.] —**scar'er** *n.*

scare·crow (skâr'krō') *n.* A crude figure set up in a cultivated area to scare birds away.

scarf (skärf) *n., pl.* **scarfs** or **scarves** (skärvz). **1.** A piece of cloth, worn about the neck, shoulders, or head. **2.** A runner, as for a bureau or table. [< ONFr. *escarpe,* sash.]

scar·la·ti·na (skär'lə-tē'nə) *n.* A usu. mild form of scarlet fever. [< Med. Lat. *scarlata,* scarlet.]

scar·let (skär'lĭt) *n.* A bright red or red-orange. [< Pers. *sāqalāt,* a kind of rich cloth.] —**scar·let** *adj.*

scarlet fever *n.* An acute contagious disease caused by a streptococcus, occurring predominantly among children and characterized by a scarlet skin eruption and high fever.

scarp (skärp) *n.* A steep slope; cliff. [Ital. *scarpa.*]

scar·y (skâr'ē) *adj.* **-i·er, -i·est** *Informal.* **1.** Frightening. **2.** Easily scared; very timid.

scat (skăt) *v.* **scat·ted, scat·ting.** *Informal.* To go away hastily. [Orig. unknown.]

scath·ing (skā'thǐng) *adj.* Extremely severe or harsh. [< ON *skadha,* to injure.]

sca·tol·o·gy (skə-tŏl'ə-jē, skă-) *n.* An interest in obscenity, esp. in literature. [Gk. *skato-,* excrement + -LOGY.] **—scat·o·log'i·cal** (skăt'-ə-lŏj'ĭ-kəl) *adj.*

scat·ter (skăt'ər) *v.* **1.** To disperse. **2.** To distribute loosely by or as if by sprinkling or strewing. [ME *scatteren.*] **—scat'ter·er** *n.*
    Syns: scatter, dispel, disperse, dissipate *v.*

scat·ter·brain (skăt'ər-brān') *n.* A flighty, disorganized person. **—scat'ter·brained'** *adj.*

scat·ter·ing (skăt'ər-ĭng) *n.* A sparse distribution: *a scattering of applause.*

scatter rug *n.* A small rug.

scat·ter·shot (skăt'ər-shŏt') *adj.* Randomly wide-ranging: *scattershot criticism.*

scav·enge (skăv'ĭnj) *v.* **-enged, -eng·ing. 1.** To act as a scavenger. **2.** To search through for salvageable material. [< SCAVENGER.]

scav·en·ger (skăv'ĭn-jər) *n.* **1.** An animal that feeds on dead or decaying matter. **2.** One who scavenges. [< AN *scawage,* toll levied on foreign merchants.]

sce·nar·i·o (sĭ-nâr'ē-ō', -năr'-) *n., pl.* **-os. 1.** A script or an outline of the plot of a motion picture. **2.** An outline of possible future events. [< Lat. *scaenarius,* of the stage.] **—sce·nar'ist** *n.*

scene (sēn) *n.* **1.** A prospect; view. **2.** The setting of an action. **3.** A subdivision of an act of a play. **4.** A unit of continuous related action in a film. **5.** The scenery for a dramatic presentation. **6.** A display of temper. **7.** *Slang.* A sphere of given activity: *the drug scene.* [< Gk. *skēnē,* stage.]

scen·er·y (sē'nə-rē) *n.* **1.** A landscape. **2.** The painted backdrops on a theatrical stage. **—sce'nic** *adj.* **—sce'ni·cal·ly** *adv.*

scent (sĕnt) *n.* **1.** A distinctive odor. **2.** A perfume. **3.** The trail of a hunted animal or fugitive. **—v. 1.** To smell; hunt by smell. **2.** To detect as if by smelling: *scent danger.* **3.** To fill with a scent. [< Lat. *sentire,* to feel.]

scep·ter (sĕp'tər) *n.* Also *chiefly Brit.* **scep·tre.** A staff carried by a sovereign as an emblem of authority. [< Gk. *skēptron,* staff.]

scep·tic (skĕp'tĭk) *n.* Var. of **skeptic.**

scep·ti·cism (skĕp'tĭ-sĭz'əm) *n.* Var. of **skepticism.**

sched·ule (skĕj'ŏŏl, -ŏŏ-əl, skĕj'əl) *n.* **1.** A list of items. **2.** A program. **3.** A timetable. **4.** A production plan. **—v. -uled, -ul·ing. 1.** To enter on a schedule. **2.** To make up a schedule for. **3.** To plan for a certain time. [< Lat. *scheda,* papyrus leaf.]

sche·mat·ic (skē-măt'ĭk) *adj.* Pertaining to or in the form of a scheme or diagram. **—n.** A structural diagram, esp. of an electrical or mechanical system.

scheme (skēm) *n.* **1.** A systematic plan or design. **2.** An orderly combination of elements: *a color scheme.* **3.** A plot. **—v. schemed, schem·ing. 1.** To contrive a plan or scheme for. **2.** To plot. [< Gk. *skhēma,* form.] **—schem'er** *n.*

scher·zo (skĕr'tsō) *n., pl.* **-zos** or **-zi** (-tsē).

Mus. A lively movement commonly in ¾ time. [Ital.]

Schick test (shĭk) *n.* A skin test of susceptibility to diphtheria. [< Bela *Schick* (1877–1967).]

schil·ling (shĭl'ĭng) *n.* See table at **currency.** [G.]

schism (sĭz'əm, skĭz'-) *n.* A separation or division into factions, esp. within a religious body. [< Gk. *skhisma.*] **—schis·mat'ic** (-măt'-ĭk) *adj.* **—schis·mat'i·cal·ly** *adv.*

schist (shĭst) *n.* A metamorphic rock consisting of laminated, often flaky, parallel layers. [< Gk. *skhistos,* split.] **—schis'tose** (shĭs'tōs') or **schis'tous** (-təs) *adj.*

schizo- or **schiz-** *pref.* **1.** Split: *schizophrenia.* **2.** Schizophrenia: *schizoid.* [< Gk. *skhizein,* to split.]

schiz·oid (skĭt'soid') *adj.* Characteristic of or resembling schizophrenia. **—n.** A schizophrenic.

schiz·o·phre·ni·a (skĭt'sə-frē'nē-ə) *n.* A psychosis characterized by withdrawal from reality and by highly variable behavioral and intellectual disturbances. **—schiz'o·phren'ic** (-frĕn'ĭk) *adj.* & *n.*

schle·miel (shlə-mēl') *n. Slang.* A dolt. [Yiddish *shlumiel.*]

schlep (shlĕp) *v.* **schlepped, schlep·ping.** *Slang.* To carry clumsily or with difficulty; lug. [Yiddish *shleppen,* to drag.]

schmaltz (shmälts) *n.* Also **schmalz.** *Slang.* Sentimental art or music. [Yiddish *shmalts,* melted fat.] **—schmaltz'y** *adj.*

schnapps (shnäps, shnăps) *n.* Any of various strong liquors. [G. *Schnaps.*]

schnau·zer (shnou'zər, shnout'sər) *n.* A dog with a wiry gray coat and a blunt muzzle. [G.]

schol·ar (skŏl'ər) *n.* **1.** A learned person. **2.** A pupil or student. **3.** A student holding a scholarship. [< LLat. *scholaris,* of a school.] **—schol'ar·li·ness** *n.* **—schol'ar·ly** *adv.*

schol·ar·ship (skŏl'ər-shĭp') *n.* **1.** The knowledge or discipline of a scholar. **2.** A grant awarded to a student.

scho·las·tic (skə-lăs'tĭk) *adj.* Of or pertaining to schools or scholarship. [< Gk. *skholastikos.*] **—scho·las'ti·cal·ly** *adv.*

school[1] (skŏŏl) *n.* **1.** An institution for instruction and learning. **2.** The student body of an educational institution. **3.** The process of being educated. **4.** A group of persons under common influence or sharing a unifying belief. **—v. 1.** To instruct. **2.** To train; discipline. [< Gk. *skholē.*]

school[2] (skŏŏl) *n.* A large group of fish or other aquatic animals swimming together. [< MDu. *schole,* troop.]

school·boy (skŏŏl'boi') *n.* A boy attending school.

school·girl (skŏŏl'gûrl') *n.* A girl attending school.

school·marm (skŏŏl'märm') *n. Informal.* A woman who teaches school. [SCHOOL + dial. *marm,* madam.]

school·mas·ter (skŏŏl'măs'tər) *n.* A man who teaches school.

school·mis·tress (skŏŏl'mĭs'trĭs) *n.* A woman who teaches school.

school·room (skŏŏl'rŏŏm', -rŏŏm') *n.* A classroom.

school·teach·er (skŏŏl'tē'chər) *n.* One who teaches in a school below the college level.

schoo·ner (skōō'nər) n. 1. A ship with two or more fore-and-aft-rigged masts, the mainmast being taller than the foremast. 2. A large beer glass, gen. holding a pint or more. [Orig. unknown.]

schooner

schot·tische (shŏt'ĭsh) n. 1. A round dance similar to the polka. 2. Music for a schottische. [G.]

schuss (shŏŏs) v. To ski a fast, straight, downhill course. —n. 1. A straight, steep skiing course. 2. The act of schussing. [G.]

schwa (shwä) n. 1. A vowel sound that in English often occurs in an unstressed syllable, as the sound of *a* in *alone* or *e* in *linen*. 2. The symbol (ə) often used to represent schwa. [< Heb. *shewā'.*]

sci·at·i·ca (sī-ăt'ĭ-kə) n. Chronic neuralgic pain in the area of the hip or thigh. [< LLat., of the hip.]

sci·ence (sī'əns) n. 1. The observation, identification, description, experimental investigation, and theoretical explanation of natural phenomena. 2. A methodological activity, discipline, or study. 3. An activity that appears to require study and method. 4. Knowledge, esp. knowledge gained through experience. [< Lat. *scientia*, knowledge.] —**sci·en·tif·ic** (sī'ən-tĭf'ĭc) adj. —**sci·en·tif·i·cal·ly** adv.

science fiction n. Fiction in which actual or potential scientific developments form part of the plot. —**sci·ence-fic·tion** adj.

sci·en·tist (sī'ən-tĭst) n. One who has expert knowledge of one or more sciences.

sci-fi (sī'fī') n. Informal. Science fiction.

scim·i·tar (sĭm'ĭ-tər, -tär') n. A curved Oriental sword. [Ital. *scimitarra.*]

scin·til·la (sĭn-tĭl'ə) n. A small amount; trace. [Lat., spark.]

scin·til·late (sĭn'tə-lāt') v. -lat·ed, -lat·ing. To give off sparks; sparkle. [Lat. *scintillare.*] —**scin·til·la'tion** n.

sci·on (sī'ən) n. 1. A descendant or heir. 2. A detached plant shoot used in grafting. [< OFr. *cion.*]

scis·sors (sĭz'ərz) n. (used with a sing. or pl. verb). A cutting implement of two blades joined by a swivel pin that allows the cutting edges to be opened and closed. [< LLat. *cisorium*, cutting instrument.]

scissors kick n. A swimming kick used chiefly with the side stroke in which the legs are snapped together like scissors.

scle·ra (sklîr'ə, sklĕr'ə) n. The tough fibrous

tissue covering all of the eyeball except the cornea. [< Gk. *sklēros*, hard.]

scle·ro·sis (sklə-rō'sĭs) n., pl. -ses (-sēz'). A thickening or hardening of a body part, esp. from tissue overgrowth or disease. [< Gk. *sklērōsis.*] —**scle·rot·ic** (-rŏt'ĭk) adj.

scoff (skŏf, skŏf) v. To treat with derision; mock. —n. An expression of derision or scorn; jeer. [ME *scoffen.*] —**scoff'er** n.

scold (skōld) v. To reprimand harshly. —n. One who persistently rails against others. [< ME *scolde*, an abusive person.] —**scold'er** n.
Syns: scold, bawl out, castigate, chew out, rebuke, reprimand, reproach, reprove, upbraid v.

sconce (skŏns) n. A wall bracket for candles or lights. [< OFr. *esconse*, hiding place.]

scone (skōn, skŏn) n. A round, soft, doughy pastry. [Perh. < Du. *schoonbrood*, fine white bread.]

scoop (skōōp) n. 1. A small, shovellike utensil. 2. The bucket or shovel of a steam shovel or dredge. 3. The amount taken with one scoop. 4. Slang. An exclusive news story acquired by luck or initiative. —v. 1. To take up with or as with a scoop. 2. To hollow out. 3. Slang. To outmaneuver in acquiring a news story. [< MDu. *schope.*] —**scoop'er** n.

scoot (skōōt) v. To go speedily. [Prob. of Scand. orig.]

scoot·er (skōō'tər) n. 1. A child's vehicle consisting of a long footboard mounted on two end wheels controlled by an upright steering handle attached to the front wheel. 2. A motor scooter.

scope (skōp) n. 1. The range of one's perceptions, thoughts, or actions. 2. Breadth or opportunity to function. 3. The area covered by a given activity or subject. [< Gk. *skopos*, target.]

-scope suff. An instrument for observing: *microscope.* [< Gk. *skopein*, to see.]

sco·pol·a·mine (skō-pŏl'ə-mēn', -mĭn) n. A thick, syrupy, colorless alkaloid, $C_{17}H_{21}NO_4$, used as a sedative and truth serum. [G. *Scopolamin.*]

scor·bu·tic (skôr-byōō'tĭk) or **scor·bu·ti·cal** (-tĭ-kəl) adj. Related to, resembling, or afflicted with scurvy. [< LLat. *scorbutus*, scurvy.] —**scor·bu'ti·cal·ly** adv.

scorch (skôrch) v. 1. To burn the surface of. 2. To wither or parch. —n. 1. A slight or surface burn. 2. Discoloration caused by heat. [ME *scorchen.*] —**scorch'er** n.

score (skôr, skōr) n. 1. A notch or incision. 2. A record of points made in a competitive event. 3. A result of a test or examination. 4. A debt. 5. A reason; account. 6. A group of 20 items. 7. The written form of a musical composition. 8. The music for a theatrical production or film. 9. Informal. The realities of a situation: *doesn't know the score.* —v. **scored, scor·ing.** 1. To mark with lines or notches. 2. To gain (a point) in a game or contest. 3. To record the score in a contest. 4. To achieve; win. 5. To evaluate and assign a grade to. 6. Mus. a. To orchestrate. b. To arrange for a specific instrument. [< ON *skor.*] —**scor'er** n.

scorn (skôrn) n. 1. Contempt or disdain. 2. Derision. —v. To consider or treat as contemptible; disdain. [< ME *scornen*, to de-

spise.] —**scorn'ful** adj. —**scorn'ful-ly** adv.
—**scorn'ful-ness** n.
Scor-pi-o (skôr'pē-ō') n. **1.** A constellation in
the Southern Hemisphere. **2.** The 8th sign of
the zodiac.
scor-pi-on (skôr'pē-ən) n. An arachnid with
an erectile tail tipped with a venomous sting.
[< Gk. *skorpios*.]

scorpion

Scot (skŏt) n. **1.** A native or inhabitant of
Scotland. **2.** A member of the ancient Gaelic
tribe that migrated to northern Great Britain
from Ireland in about A.D. 500.
scotch (skŏch) v. **1.** To cut or scratch. **2.** To
cripple. **3.** To put an end to; stifle. [< AN
escocher, to notch.]
Scotch (skŏch) n. **1.** The people of Scotland.
2. A smoky-flavored whiskey distilled in Scotland. —**Scotch** adj.
Scotch-I-rish (skŏch-ī'rĭsh) adj. Of or relating
to the people of Northern Ireland who are
descendants of Scottish settlers.
Scotch-man (skŏch'mən) n. A Scot.
scot-free (skŏt'frē') adj. Free from obligation
or penalty. [< ME *scot*, tax.]
Scots (skŏts) adj. Scottish. —n. The English
dialect of Scotland.
Scots-man (skŏts'mən) n. A Scot.
Scot-tish (skŏt'ĭsh) adj. Of or characteristic of
Scotland, its people, or its language. —n.
1. Scots. **2.** The people of Scotland.
Scottish Gaelic n. The Gaelic language of
Scotland.
Scottish terrier n. A terrier with a heavy-set
body, short legs, blunt muzzle, and a dark,
wiry coat.
scoun-drel (skoun'drəl) n. A villain. [Orig.
unknown.]
scour¹ (skour) v. **1.** To clean by scrubbing
vigorously, as with an abrasive. **2.** To scrub
something in order to clean it. [< LLat. *excu-
rare*, to clean out.]
scour² (skour) v. **1.** To search through or over
thoroughly. **2.** To move swiftly; run. [ME
scouren.]
scourge (skûrj) n. **1.** A whip. **2.** Any instrument for inflicting severe punishment. **3.** A
cause of great suffering or harm. —v.
scourged, *scourg-ing*. **1.** To beat or whip severely; flog. **2.** To punish severely; excoriate.
3. To devastate; ravage. [< OFr. *escorgier*, to
whip.] —**scourg'er** n.
scout¹ (skout) n. **1.** One sent out to gather
information. **2.** A sentinel. **3.** One who seeks
out persons with talent, as in sports or entertainment. **4. a.** A Boy Scout. **b.** A Girl Scout.
—v. **1.** To reconnoiter. **2.** To observe and
evaluate. [< Lat. *ascultare*, to listen.]
—**scout'er** n.
scout² (skout) v. To reject with contempt or
derision. [Of Scand. orig.]

scout-mas-ter (skout'măs'tər) n. The adult
leader of a troop of Boy Scouts.
scow (skou) n. A flat-bottomed boat with
square ends. [Du. *schouw*.]
scowl (skoul) v. To wrinkle or contract the
brow, as in anger or disapproval. —n. A
look of anger or strong disapproval. [ME
scoulen.] —**scowl'er** n.
scrab-ble (skrăb'əl) v. **-bled, -bling. 1.** To
grope about frenetically with the hands. **2.** To
scribble. **3.** To struggle. [MDu. *schrabblen*.]
—**scrab'ble** n.
scrag-gly (skrăg'lē) adj. **-gli-er, -gli-est.** Ragged; unkempt. [< *scrag*, a scrawny animal.]
scrag-gy (skrăg'ē) adj. **-gi-er, -gi-est. 1.** Jagged; rough. **2.** Bony and lean. [< *scrag*, a
scrawny animal.] —**scrag'gi-ness** n.
scram (skrăm) v. **scrammed, scram-ming.**
Slang. To leave at once. [< SCRAMBLE.]
scram-ble (skrăm'bəl) v. **-bled, -bling. 1.** To
move or climb hurriedly. **2.** To compete fran-
tically. **3.** To mix haphazardly. **4.** To fry
(eggs) while mixing and stirring together.
5. *Electronics.* To distort (a signal) so as to
render it unintelligible without a special receiver. [Blend of obs. *scamble*, to struggle for,
and *cramble*, to crawl.] —**scram'ble** n.
—**scram'bler** n.
scrap¹ (skrăp) n. **1.** A small bit or fragment.
2. scraps. Leftover food. **3.** Discarded construction material, such as metal. —v.
scrapped, *scrap-ping*. **1.** To break down into
parts for disposal or salvage. **2.** To discard as
useless. [< ON *skrap*, trifles.]
scrap² (skrăp) *Informal.* —v. *scrapped,*
scrap-ping. To fight or quarrel. —n. A
quarrel. [Orig. unknown.] —**scrap'per** n.
—**scrap'pi-ly** adv. —**scrap'pi-ness** n.
—**scrap'py** adj.
scrap-book (skrăp'bŏŏk') n. A book with
blank pages for mounting pictures and other
mementos.
scrape (skrāp) v. **scraped, scrap-ing. 1.** To
rub (a surface) with considerable pressure.
2. To draw (a hard or abrasive object) forcefully over a surface. **3.** To abrade, smooth,
injure, or remove by this procedure. **4.** To
come into abrasive contact. **5.** To rub or
move with a grating noise. **6.** To amass or
produce with difficulty: *scraped together the
money.* —n. **1.** The act or result of scraping.
2. a. A predicament. **b.** A scuffle. [< ON
skrapa.] —**scrap'er** n.
scratch (skrăch) v. **1.** To make a shallow cut
or mark with something sharp. **2.** To use the
nails or claws to dig, scrape, or wound. **3.** To
rub (the skin) to relieve itching. **4.** To strike
out or cancel (a word, name, or passage) by
or as if by drawing lines through. —n. A
mark or wound produced by scratching.
—adj. **1.** Done or made by chance. **2.** Assembled at random; haphazard. —**idioms. from
scratch.** From the beginning. **up to scratch.**
Informal. Up to standard. [ME *scracchen*.]
—**scratch'er** n. —**scratch'i-ly** adv. —**scratch'-
i-ness** n. —**scratch'y** adj.
scrawl (skrôl) v. To write hastily or illegibly.
—n. Irregular, illegible handwriting. [Perh. <
obs. *scrawl*, to gesticulate.] —**scrawl'y** adj.
scraw-ny (skrô'nē) adj. **-ni-er, -ni-est.** Gaunt
and bony; skinny. [Orig. unknown.]
—**scraw'ni-ness** n.
scream (skrēm) v. **1.** To cry out loudly and
shrilly, as from pain or fear. **2.** To have a
blatantly arresting effect. —n. **1.** A long,

loud, piercing cry or sound. **2.** *Slang.* One that is hilariously funny. [ME *scremen.*] **—scream'er** *n.*

screech (skrēch) *n.* **1.** A shriek. **2.** A sound that resembles a screech. [< ON *skraekja,* to screech.] **—screech** *v.* **—screech'y** *adj.*

screech owl *n.* Any of various small North American owls with ear tufts and a quavering, whistlelike call.

screen (skrēn) *n.* **1.** Something that serves to divide, conceal, or protect, as a movable room partition. **2.** A coarse sieve. **3.** A window insertion of framed mesh used to keep out insects. **4. a.** The white or silver surface on which a picture is projected for viewing. **b.** The motion-picture industry. **—v. 1.** To provide with a screen. **2.** To conceal or protect. **3.** To separate with or as if with a sieve. **4.** To show on a screen, as a motion picture. [< MDu. *scherm,* shield.] **—screen'er** *n.*

screen-play (skrēn'plā') *n.* The script for a motion picture.

screen test *n.* A brief motion-picture sequence filmed to test the ability of an aspiring movie actor or actress. **—screen'-test'** *v.*

screen-writ-er (skrēn'rī'tər) *n.* A writer of screenplays.

screw (skrōō) *n.* **1.** A metal pin with incised thread or threads, having a broad slotted head so that it can be driven as a fastener by turning it with a screwdriver. **2.** A propeller. **—v. 1.** To fasten, tighten, adjust, or attach by or as if by means of a screw. **2.** To turn or twist. **3.** To become attached by means of screw threads. **4.** *Slang.* To take advantage of; cheat. **—phrasal verb. screw up.** *Slang.* To make a mess of; bungle. [< Lat. *scrofa,* sow.] **—screw'er** *n.*

screw-ball (skrōō'bôl') *n.* **1.** *Baseball.* A pitched ball curving in the direction opposite to a normal curve ball. **2.** *Slang.* An eccentric or crazy person.

screw-driv-er (skrōō'drī'vər) *n.* A tool used to turn screws. **2.** A cocktail of vodka and orange juice.

screw-y (skrōō'ē) *adj.* **-i-er, -i-est.** *Slang.* **1.** Eccentric; crazy. **2.** Ludicrously odd.

scrib-ble (skrĭb'əl) *v.* **-bled, -bling.** To write hastily or carelessly. [< Lat. *scribere,* to write.] **—scrib'bler** *n.*

scribe (skrīb) *n.* **1.** A public clerk. **2.** A professional copyist of manuscripts. **3.** A writer. [< Lat. *scriba.*]

scrim-mage (skrĭm'ĭj) *n.* **1.** A rough-and-tumble struggle; scuffle. **2.** *Football.* **a.** The action from the time the ball is snapped until it is out of play. **b.** A practice game. [< SKIRMISH.] **—scrim'mage** *v.*

scrimp (skrĭmp) *v.* To economize severely. [Perh. < Scand. orig.] **—scrimp'i-ly** *adv.* **—scrimp'i-ness** *n.* **—scrimp'y** *adj.*

scrim-shaw (skrĭm'shô') *n.* **1.** The art of carving on ivory, bone, or shells. **2.** An article made in this way. [Orig. unknown.]

scrip¹ (skrĭp) *n.* Paper money issued for temporary, emergency use. [< SCRIPT.]

scrip² (skrĭp) *n.* A provisional certificate that entitles the holder to a fractional share of stock or of other property. [< *subscription receipt,* receipt for a portion of a loan.]

script (skrĭpt) *n.* **1.** Handwriting as distin-

guished from print. **2.** Cursive writing. **3.** The text of a play, broadcast, or motion picture. [< Lat. *scriptum.*]

Scrip-ture (skrĭp'chər) *n.* **1.** Often **Scriptures.** **a.** A sacred writing, esp. the Bible. **b.** A passage from such a writing. **2. scripture.** A statement regarded as authoritative. [< Lat. *scriptura,* act of writing.] **—Scrip'tural** or **scrip'tural** *adj.*

script-writ-er (skrĭpt'rī'tər) *n.* One who writes scripts.

scriv-en-er (skrĭv'ə-nər) *n.* A scribe, writer, or author. [< Lat. *scriba.*]

scrod (skrŏd) *n.* A young cod or haddock. [Poss. < obs. Du. *schrood,* shred.]

scroll (skrōl) *n.* **1.** A roll of parchment, papyrus, etc., used esp. for writing a document. **2.** Ornamentation that resembles a scroll. [< OFr. *escroue,* strip of parchment.]

Scrooge (skrōōj) *n.* A mean, miserly person. [< the character Ebenezer *Scrooge* in Dickens' *A Christmas Carol.*]

scro-tum (skrō'təm) *n., pl.* **-ta** (-tə) or **-tums.** The external sac of skin enclosing the testes. [Lat.] **—scro'tal** (skrōt'l) *adj.*

scrounge (skrounj) *v.* **scrounged, scroung-ing.** *Slang.* **1.** To forage about in an effort to acquire (something) free. **2.** To wheedle. [< dial. *scrunge,* to steal.] **—scroung'er** *n.*

scrub¹ (skrŭb) *v.* **scrubbed, scrub-bing. 1.** To rub hard, as with a brush, in order to clean. **2.** To clean by hard rubbing. [< MDu. *schrobben.*] **—scrub** *n.* **—scrub'ber** *n.*

scrub² (skrŭb) *n.* **1.** A growth of stunted vegetation. **2.** An undersized, poorly developed plant or animal. **3.** A player not on the first team. [ME.] **—scrub'by** *adj.*

scruff (skrŭf) *n.* The back of the neck. [Orig. unknown.]

scruf-fy (skrŭf'ē) *adj.* **-fi-er, -fi-est.** Shabby; dirty. [< obs. *scruff,* scurf.] **—scruf'fi-ly** *adv.* **—scruf'fi-ness** *n.*

scrump-tious (skrŭmp'shəs) *adj.* *Slang.* Delicious. [Perh. < SUMPTUOUS.]

scrunch (skrŭnch, skrōōnch) *v.* **1.** To crush or squeeze. **2.** To hunch. **3.** To make a crunching sound. [< CRUNCH.] **—scrunch** *n.*

scru-ple (skrōō'pəl) *n.* **1.** Ethical objection to certain actions; dictate of conscience. **2.** A unit of apothecary weight equal to 20 grains. [< Lat. *scrupus,* rough stone.]

scru-pu-lous (skrōō'pyə-ləs) *adj.* **1.** Having scruples; principled. **2.** Conscientious; careful. **—scru'pu-los'i-ty** (-lŏs'ĭ-tē) or **scru'pu-lous-ness** *n.* **—scru'pu-lous-ly** *adv.*

scru-ti-nize (skrōōt'n-īz') *v.* **-nized, -niz-ing.** To examine with great care. **—scru'ti-niz'er** *n.*

scru-ti-ny (skrōōt'n-ē) *n., pl.* **-nies.** A close, careful examination. [Lat. *scrutinium.*]

scu-ba (skōō'bə) *n.* An apparatus containing compressed air used by divers to breathe underwater. [S(ELF) + C(ONTAINED) + U(NDER-WATER) + B(REATHING) + A(PPARATUS).]

scud (skŭd) *v.* **scud-ded, scud-ding.** To move along swiftly and easily: *clouds scudding across the sky.* **—n.** Wind-driven clouds or mist. [Prob. of Scand. orig.]

scuff (skŭf) *v.* **1.** To scrape with the feet. **2.** To scrape and roughen the surface of. **—n. 1.** The act or result of scuffing. **2.** A flat, backless house slipper. [Prob. of Scand. orig.]

scuf-fle (skŭf′əl) v. **-fled, -fling. 1.** To fight confusedly at close quarters. **2.** To shuffle. —n. A disorderly struggle at close quarters. [Prob. of Scand. orig.] **—scuf′fler** n.

scull (skŭl) n. **1.** An oar used for rowing a boat from the stern. **2.** One of a pair of short-handled oars used by a single rower. **3.** A small, light boat for racing. —v. To propel (a boat) with a scull or sculls. [ME sculle.]

scul-ler-y (skŭl′ə-rē) n., pl. **-ies.** A room adjoining a kitchen for washing dishes or other chores. [< OFr. escuelier, keeper of dishes.]

sculpt (skŭlpt) v. To sculpture. [< Lat. sculpere, to carve.]

sculp-tor (skŭlp′tər) n. One who sculptures.

sculp-tress (skŭlp′trĭs) n. A woman who sculptures.

sculp-ture (skŭlp′chər) n. **1.** The art or practice of shaping three-dimensional figures or designs, as by carving wood, chiseling stone, modeling clay, or casting metal. **2.** A work created in this manner. —v. **-tured, -tur-ing. 1.** To shape (stone, metal, wood, etc.) into sculpture. **2.** To represent in sculpture. **3.** To ornament with sculpture. [Lat. sculptura.] **—sculp′tur-al** adj. **—sculp′tur-al-ly** adv.

scum (skŭm) n. **1.** A filmy layer of impure matter on the surface of a liquid or body of water. **2.** Refuse or worthless matter. **3.** An element of society regarded as being vile or worthless. [< MDu. schūm.]

scup-per (skŭp′ər) n. A deck-level opening in the side of a ship to allow water to run off. [ME skopper.]

scurf (skûrf) n. Flakes of dry skin, as dandruff. [< OE.] **—scurf′i-ness** n. **—scurf′y** adj.

scur-ri-lous (skûr′ə-ləs) adj. Vulgar; abusive. [< Lat. scurrilis, jeering.] **—scur-ril′i-ty** (skə-rĭl′ĭ-tē) or **scur′ri-lous-ness** n. **—scur′ri-lous-ly** adv.

scur-ry (skûr′ē) v. **-ried, -ry-ing. 1.** To scamper. **2.** To rush. [Prob. < hurry-scurry.]

scur-vy (skûr′vē) n. A disease caused by a vitamin C deficiency, characterized by soft, bleeding gums, bleeding under the skin, and extreme weakness. —adj. **-vi-er, -vi-est.** Contemptible. [< SCURF.]

scut-tle¹ (skŭt′l) n. A small hatch in a ship's deck or bulkhead. —v. **-tled, -tling. 1.** To sink (a ship) by boring holes in the bottom. **2.** Informal. To discard; abandon. [< OFr. escoutille.]

scut-tle² (skŭt′l) n. A pail for carrying coal. [< Lat. scutella.]

scut-tle³ (skŭt′l) v. **-tled, -tling.** To run hastily; scurry. [< SCUD.]

scut-tle-butt (skŭt′l-bŭt′) n. Slang. Gossip; rumor. [SCUTTLE¹ + butt, cask.]

scythe (sīth) n. A tool with a long, curved blade and a long, bent handle, used for mowing or reaping. [< OE sīthe.] **—scythe** v.

Se The symbol for the element selenium.

sea (sē) n. **1. a.** The continuous body of salt water that covers most of the surface of the earth. **b.** A region of water within an ocean. **c.** A large body of water completely or partially landlocked. **d.** A body of fresh water. **2.** The condition of the ocean's surface: a high sea; choppy seas. **3.** A vast number, expanse, or extent: a sea of advancing troops. **—idiom. at sea. 1.** On the ocean. **2.** At a loss; perplexed. [< OE sǣ.]

sea anemone n. Any of various marine or-

ganisms with a flexible, cylindrical body and numerous tentacles.

Sea-bee (sē′bē′) n. A member of one of the U.S. Navy's construction battalions. [Pronunciation of cee bee, the initials of construction battalion.]

sea-board (sē′bôrd′, -bōrd′) n. Land that borders or is near the sea; seacoast. [SEA + obs. board, border.]

sea-far-er (sē′fâr′ər) n. A sailor.

sea-food (sē′fŏod′) n. Edible fish or shellfish from the sea.

sea-go-ing (sē′gō′ĭng) adj. Made or used for ocean voyages: a seagoing barge.

sea gull n. A gull, esp. one appearing near coastal areas.

sea horse n. A small marine fish with a horselike head and a body covered with bony plates.

sea horse   sea lion

seal¹ (sēl) n. **1. a.** A die or signet with a raised or engraved design, used to stamp an impression on a substance such as wax or lead. **b.** The impression made. **c.** A small disk or wafer bearing such a mark and used to fasten shut or authenticate a document. **2.** Something that serves to authenticate or confirm. **3.** An adhesive agent used to close or fasten. **4.** An airtight or watertight closure or fitting. **5.** A small decorative paper sticker. —v. **1.** To affix a seal to so as to prove authenticity or attest to accuracy, quality, etc. **2.** To close with or as with a seal; make fast. **3.** To establish or determine irrevocably. [< Lat. sigillum.] **—seal′a-ble** adj. **—seal′er** n.

seal² (sēl) n. **1.** An aquatic mammal with a torpedo-shaped body and limbs in the form of flippers. **2.** Also **seal-skin** (sēl′skĭn′). The pelt or fur of a seal. —v. To hunt seals. [< OE seolh.] **—seal′er** n.

sea-lane (sē′lān′) n. A sea route.

sea level n. The level of the ocean's surface, esp. the mean level halfway between high and low tide.

sea lion n. A brown seal of Pacific waters.

seam (sēm) n. **1. a.** A line formed by sewing together two pieces of material. **b.** A similar line, ridge, or groove. **2.** A line across a surface, as a fissure or wrinkle. **3.** A thin layer or stratum, as of coal. —v. **1.** To join with or as if with a seam. **2.** To mark with a wrinkle or other line: a face seamed with age. [< OE sēam.]

sea-man (sē′mən) n. **1.** A sailor. **2.** An enlisted person ranking below petty officer in the U.S. Navy.

sea-man-ship (sē′mən-shĭp′) n. Skill in handling or navigating a boat or ship.

seam-stress (sēm′strĭs) n. A woman who sews, esp. one who earns a living by sewing.

seam-y (sē′mē) adj. **-i-er, -i-est. 1.** Having or

showing seams. **2.** Rough and raw; sordid. **—seam'i·ness** n.

sé·ance (sā'äns') n. A meeting at which persons attempt to communicate with the dead. [< OFr. *seoir*, to sit.]

sea·plane (sē'plān') n. An aircraft equipped with floats for taking off from or landing on water.

sea·port (sē'pôrt', -pōrt') n. A port with facilities for seagoing ships.

sea power n. **1.** A nation having significant naval strength. **2.** Naval strength.

sear (sîr) v. **1.** To make or become withered. **2.** To scorch or burn the surface of. —*adj.* Var. of **sere.** [< OE *sēarian.*]

search (sûrch) v. **1.** To make a thorough examination of in order to find something; explore. **2.** To make a careful investigation of; probe. **3.** To make a thorough check of; scrutinize. [< Lat. *circare*, to go around.] **—search** n. **—search'er** n.

search·light (sûrch'līt') n. **1.** A powerful light equipped with a reflector to produce a bright beam. **2.** The beam so produced.

search warrant n. A warrant giving legal authorization to search a specified place, as for unlawful property.

sea·scape (sē'skāp') n. A view of the sea.

Sea Scout n. A member of a program designed to train Boy Scouts in seamanship.

sea·shell (sē'shĕl') n. The shell of a saltwater mollusk.

sea·shore (sē'shôr', -shōr') n. Land by the sea.

sea·sick·ness (sē'sĭk'nĭs) n. Nausea and other discomforts resulting from the motion of a vessel at sea. **—sea'sick'** adj.

sea·side (sē'sīd') n. The seashore.

sea snake n. Any of several venomous tropical saltwater snakes.

sea·son (sē'zən) n. **1.** One of the four equal divisions of the year, spring, summer, autumn, and winter. **b.** The two divisions of the year, rainy and dry, in tropical climates. **2.** A period of the year devoted to or marked by certain activities or events: *the hunting season; the hurricane season.* —*v.* **1.** To enhance the flavor of (food) by adding salt, spices, etc. **2.** To add zest or interest to. **3.** To dry (lumber) until usable; cure. **4.** To make fit through experience. [< Lat. *satio*, act of sowing.] **—sea'son·al** adj. **—sea'son·al·ly** adv.

sea·son·a·ble (sē'zə-nə-bəl) adj. **1.** Suitable for the time or the season. **2.** Occurring at the proper time. **—sea'son·a·bly** adv.

sea·son·ing (sē'zə-nĭng) n. An ingredient used to flavor food.

seat (sēt) n. **1.** Something that may be sat on, as a chair. **2.** A place in which one may sit. **3.** A part on which a person rests in sitting: *a bicycle seat.* **4. a.** The buttocks. **b.** That part of a garment covering the buttocks. **5. a.** The place where anything is located or based: *the seat of intelligence.* **b.** A center of authority; capital. **6.** Membership, as in a legislature. —*v.* **1.** To place in or on a seat. **2.** To have or provide seats for. [< ON *sæti.*]

seat belt n. A safety strap that holds a person securely in a seat, as in a car.

sea·train (sē'trān') n. A seagoing vessel capable of carrying a railroad train.

sea urchin n. A marine organism with a spiny globular shell.

sea wall n. An embankment to prevent erosion of a shore.

sea·ward (sē'wərd) adv. Also **sea·wards** (-wərdz). Toward the sea. **—sea'ward** adj.

sea·way (sē'wā') n. **1.** A sea route. **2.** An inland waterway for ocean shipping.

sea·weed (sē'wēd') n. Any of various large or branching marine algae.

sea·wor·thy (sē'wûr'thē) adj. Fit or safe for sailing. **—sea'wor'thi·ness** n.

se·ba·ceous (sĭ-bā'shəs) adj. Of or secreting fat. [< Lat. *sebum*, tallow.]

se·cant (sē'kănt', -kənt) n. *Geom.* A straight line intersecting a curve at two or more points. [< Lat. *secare*, to cut.]

se·cede (sĭ-sēd') v. **-ced·ed, -ced·ing.** To withdraw formally from membership in an organization, association, or union. [Lat. *secēdere*, to separate.]

se·ces·sion (sĭ-sĕsh'ən) n. The act of seceding. [Lat. *secessio.*] **—se·ces'sion·ism** n. **—se·ces'sion·ist** n.

se·clude (sĭ-klōōd') v. **-clud·ed, -clud·ing. 1.** To set apart from others; isolate. **2.** To screen from view. [< Lat. *secludere.*] **—se·clu'sion** (-klōō'zhən) n. **—se·clu'sive** (-sĭv, -zĭv) adj.

sec·ond¹ (sĕk'ənd) n. **1.** A unit of time equal to 1/60 of a minute. **2.** A short period of time. **3.** *Geom.* A unit of angular measure equal to 1/60 of a minute of arc. [< Med. Lat. (*pars minuta*) *secunda*, second (small part).]

sec·ond² (sĕk'ənd) adj. **1.** Next after the first. **2.** Inferior to another; subordinate. —*n.* **1. a.** The ordinal number that matches the number 2 in a series. **b.** One of two equal parts. **2.** One that is next after the first. **3.** The forward gears in an automobile transmission having the 2nd highest ratio. **4.** Often **seconds.** Merchandise of inferior quality. **5.** The official attendant of a contestant in a duel or boxing match. —*v.* **1.** To attend as an aide or assistant. **2.** To promote or encourage. **3.** To endorse (a motion or nomination). [< Lat. *secundus*, following.] **—sec'ond** or **sec'ond·ly** adv.

sec·on·dary (sĕk'ən-dĕr'ē) adj. **1. a.** One step removed from the first; not primary. **b.** Inferior; minor. **2.** Derived from what is original: *a secondary source.* **3.** Of or relating to education between elementary school and college. —*n., pl.* **-ies.** One that acts in an auxiliary or subordinate capacity. **—sec'on·dar'i·ly** (-dâr'ə-lē) adv.

secondary sex characteristic n. Any of the genetically transmitted physical or behavioral characteristics, as growth of facial hair or breast development, that distinguish males and females of the same species and do not have a direct relation to reproduction.

second base n. *Baseball.* **1.** The base across the diamond from home plate, to be touched second by a runner. **2.** The position played by a second baseman.

second baseman n, *Baseball.* The infielder who is positioned near and usu. to the first-base side of second base.

sec·ond-class (sĕk'ənd-klăs') adj. **1.** Of the class below the first or best. **2.** Inferior.

sec·ond-de·gree burn (sĕk′ənd-dĭ-grē′) *n.* A burn that blisters the skin.

second fiddle *n.* A secondary or subordinate role.

sec·ond-guess (sĕk′ənd-gĕs′) *v.* 1. To criticize (a decision) after the outcome is known. 2. To outguess. **—sec′ond-guess′er** *n.*

sec·ond·hand (sĕk′ənd-hănd′) *adj.* 1. Previously used; not new. 2. Dealing in used merchandise. 3. Not original; borrowed.

second lieutenant *n.* An officer in the U.S. Army and Marine Corps of the lowest commissioned grade.

second person *n. Gram.* A set of forms used in referring to the person addressed.

sec·ond-rate (sĕk′ənd-rāt′) *adj.* Inferior.

sec·ond-string (sĕk′ənd-strĭng′) *adj.* Of or being a substitute, as on a ball team.

second wind *n.* Restored energy or strength.

se·cre·cy (sē′krĭ-sē) *n.* 1. The condition or quality of being secret. 2. The ability to keep secrets.

se·cret (sē′krĭt) *adj.* 1. Concealed from general knowledge or view; kept hidden. 2. Operating covertly: *a secret agent.* 3. Beyond ordinary understanding; mysterious. *—n.* 1. Something kept hidden from others. 2. Something beyond understanding; mystery. [< Lat. *secretus.*] **—se′cret·ly** *adv.*
Syns: *secret, clandestine, covert, hush-hush, undercover* **adj.**

sec·re·tar·i·at (sĕk′rĭ-târ′ē-ĭt) *n.* 1. The department administered by a governmental secretary. 2. The position of a governmental secretary.

sec·re·tar·y (sĕk′rĭ-tĕr′ē) *n., pl.* **-ies.** 1. One employed to handle correspondence and do clerical work. 2. An officer of an organization in charge of minutes of meetings, important records, correspondence, etc. 3. An official presiding over an administrative department of government. 4. A writing desk. [< Med. Lat. *secretarius,* confidential officer.] **—sec′re·tar′i·al** (-târ′ē-əl) *adj.*

sec·re·tary-gen·er·al (sĕk′rĭ-tĕr′ē-jĕn′ər-əl) *n., pl.* **sec·re·tar·ies-gen·er·al.** A high-ranking executive officer, as in the United Nations.

se·crete¹ (sĭ-krēt′) *v.* **-cret·ed, -cret·ing.** To generate and separate out (a substance) from cells or bodily fluids. [< Lat. *secernere,* to separate.] **—se·cre′tion** *n.* **—se·cre′tor** *n.* **—se·cre′to·ry** (-krē′tə-rē) *adj.*

se·crete² (sĭ-krēt′) *v.* **-cret·ed, -cret·ing.** To conceal; hide. [< SECRET.]

se·cre·tive (sē′krə-tĭv, sĭ-krē′-) *adj.* Close-mouthed. **—se′cre·tive·ness** *n.*

Secret Service *n.* A branch of the U.S. Treasury Department concerned with the suppression of counterfeiters and the protection of the President.

sect (sĕkt) *n.* 1. A group of people forming a distinct unit within a larger group by virtue of common beliefs or practices. 2. A schismatic religious body. 3. A religious denomination. [< Lat. *secta,* faction.]

-sect *suff.* Cut; divide: *bisect.* [< Lat. *secare,* to cut.]

sec·tar·i·an (sĕk-târ′ē-ən) *adj.* 1. Of a sect or sects. 2. Narrow in outlook. *—n.* 1. A member of a sect. 2. One characterized by narrow-mindedness. **—sec·tar′i·an·ism** *n.*

sec·tion (sĕk′shən) *n.* 1. A component part or subdivision; portion. 2. The representation of a solid object as it would appear if cut by an intersecting plane, so that the internal structure is displayed. *—v.* To separate or divide into parts. [< Lat. *secare,* to cut.]

sec·tion·al (sĕk′shə-nəl) *adj.* 1. Of or pertaining to a particular section or district. 2. Composed of or divided into component sections: *sectional furniture.* **—sec′tion·al·ly** *adv.*

sec·tion·al·ism (sĕk′shə-nə-lĭz′əm) *n.* Excessive devotion to local interests and customs. **—sec′tion·al·ist** *n.*

sec·tor (sĕk′tər, -tôr′) *n.* 1. *Geom.* The part of a circle bound by two radii and one of the arcs that they intercept. 2. A military zone of action. 3. A division of something: *the private business sector.* [< Lat., cutter.]

sec·u·lar (sĕk′yə-lər) *adj.* 1. Worldly rather than spiritual. 2. Not related to religion. 3. Not living in a religious community. [< Lat. *saecularis.*] **—sec′u·lar′i·ty** (-lâr′ĭ-tē) *n.* **—sec′u·lar·ly** *adv.*

sec·u·lar·ize (sĕk′yə-lə-rīz′) *v.* **-ized, -iz·ing.** 1. To convert from religious to civil or lay use, ownership, or control. 2. To make secular. **—sec′u·lar·i·za′tion** *n.*

se·cure (sĭ-kyŏor′) *adj.* **-cur·er, -cur·est.** 1. Free from danger; safe. 2. Free from fear or doubt. 3. Assured; certain. *—v.* **-cured, -cur·ing.** 1. To guard from danger or risk of loss. 2. To make firm. 3. To make certain; guarantee. 4. To acquire. [< Lat. *securus.*] **—se·cure′ly** *adv.* **—se·cure′ment** *n.* **—se·cure′ness** *n.* **—se·cur′er** *n.*

se·cu·ri·ty (sĭ-kyŏor′ĭ-tē) *n., pl.* **-ties.** 1. Safety. 2. Confidence. 3. Anything that gives or assures safety. 4. Something deposited or given to guarantee fulfillment of an obligation; pledge. 5. **securities.** Stocks or bonds. 6. Measures adopted to guard against attack, theft, or disclosure.

security blanket *n.* Something that dispels anxiety.

se·dan (sĭ-dăn′) *n.* 1. A closed car with two or four doors and a front and rear seat. 2. Also **sedan chair.** An enclosed chair carried on poles by two bearers. [Orig. unknown.]

se·date¹ (sĭ-dāt′) *adj.* **-dat·er, -dat·est.** Serenely deliberate in character or manner. [< Lat. *sedare,* to settle.] **—se·date′ly** *adv.* **—se·date′ness** *n.*

se·date² (sĭ-dāt′) *v.* **-dat·ed, -dat·ing.** To administer a sedative to. [< SEDATIVE.] **—se·da′tion** *n.*

sed·a·tive (sĕd′ə-tĭv) *adj.* Having a soothing, calming, or quieting effect. *—n.* A sedative medicine or drug. [< Lat. *sedare,* to settle.]

sed·en·tar·y (sĕd′n-tĕr′ē) *adj.* Characterized by much sitting: *sedentary work.* [Lat. *sedentarius.*] **—sed′en·tar′i·ness** *n.*

Se·der (sā′dər) *n.* The Jewish feast commemorating the exodus of the Israelites from Egypt, usu. celebrated on the 1st evening of Passover. [Heb. *sēdher.*]

sedge (sĕj) *n.* Any of various grasslike plants growing chiefly in wet places. [< OE *secg.*]

sed·i·ment (sĕd′ə-mənt) *n.* Material that settles to the bottom of a liquid. [Lat. *sedimentum,* a settling.] **—sed′i·men·ta′tion** *n.*

sed·i·men·ta·ry (sĕd′ə-mĕn′tə-rē, -mĕn′trē) *adj.* 1. Of or resembling sediment. 2. *Geol.* Of rocks formed from sediment.

se·di·tion (sĭ-dĭsh′ən) *n.* Conduct or language that incites others to rebel against the state.

[< Lat. *seditio*.] **—se·di'tious** *adj.* **—se·di'-tious·ly** *adv.* **—se·di'tious·ness** *n.*

se·duce (sǐ-dōōs', -dyōōs') *v.* **-duced, -duc·ing.**
1. To entice into wrongful conduct; corrupt.
2. To induce to have sexual intercourse. 3. To attract, esp. by enticement. [< Lat. *seducere*, to lead away.] **—se·duc'er** *n.* **—se·duc'tion** (-dǔk'shən) *n.* **—se·duc'tive** *adj.*

sed·u·lous (sĕj'ə-ləs) *adj.* Diligent; industrious. [Lat. *sedulus*.] **—sed·u·lous·ly** *adv.* **—sed·u·lous·ness** *n.*

see¹ (sē) *v.* **saw** (sô), **seen** (sēn), **see·ing.**
1. To perceive with the eye; have the power of sight. 2. To understand; comprehend. 3. To regard; view. 4. To believe possible; imagine.
5. To foresee. 6. To undergo: *I've seen hard times.* 7. To find out; ascertain. 8. To take note of. 9. To meet regularly, as in dating.
10. To visit or consult: *seeing a lawyer.*
11. To escort; attend: *see someone to the door.*
12. To make sure: *Please see that it gets done.* **—phrasal verb. see through.** To understand the true character of. [< OE *sēon.*]

see² (sē) *n.* The position, authority, or jurisdiction of a bishop. [< Lat. *sedes*, residence.]

seed (sēd) *n., pl.* **seeds** or **seed.** 1. A fertilized plant ovule containing an embryo capable of developing a new plant. 2. Seeds collectively. 3. A source or germ. 4. Offspring. 5. Ancestry. **—v.** 1. To plant seeds in. 2. To remove seeds from. **—idiom. go (or run) to seed.** 1. To pass into the seed-bearing stage. 2. To deteriorate. [< OE *sǣd.*]

seed·ling (sēd'lĭng) *n.* A young plant that has sprouted from a seed.

seed·y (sē'dē) *adj.* **-i·er, -i·est.** 1. Having many seeds. 2. Shabby; run-down. **—seed'i·ly** *adv.* **—seed'i·ness** *n.*

see·ing (sē'ĭng) *conj.* Inasmuch as.

Seeing Eye. A trademark for a dog trained to lead a blind person.

seek (sēk) *v.* **sought** (sôt), **seek·ing.**
1. To search for. 2. To endeavor to obtain or reach. 3. To try: *sought to escape.* [< OE *sēcan.*] **—seek'er** *n.*

seem (sēm) *v.* 1. To give the impression of being; appear. 2. To appear to one's own mind. 3. To be evident. 4. To appear to exist. [< ON *sæma*, to conform to.]

seem·ing (sē'mĭng) *adj.* Apparent: *her seeming friendliness.* **—seem'ing·ly** *adv.* **—seem'ing·ness** *n.*

seem·ly (sēm'lē) *adj.* **-li·er, -li·est.** 1. Proper; suitable. 2. Of pleasing appearance. [< ON *sœmiligr.*] **—seem'li·ness** *n.*

seen (sēn) *v. p.p.* of **see¹.**

seep (sēp) *v.* 1. To pass slowly through small openings. 2. To enter, depart, or spread gradually. [< OE *sipian.*] **—seep'age** *n.*

seer (sē'ər) *n.* 1. A prophet. 2. A clairvoyant. [ME.]

seer·suck·er (sîr'sŭk'ər) *n.* A light, thin fabric with a crinkled surface and striped pattern. [< Pers. *shīr-o-shakar.*]

see·saw (sē'sô') *n.* 1. A long plank balanced on a central support so that with a person riding on either end, one end goes up as the other goes down. 2. The game of riding a seesaw. 3. A back-and-forth or up-and-down movement. [< SAW¹.] **—see'saw'** *v.*

seesaw

seethe (sēth) *v.* **seethed, seeth·ing.** 1. To bubble or churn while or as if while boiling. 2. To be violently agitated. [< OE *sēothan.*]

seg·ment (sĕg'mənt) *n.* A part into which something can be divided; subdivision or section. **—v.** (sĕg-mĕnt'). To divide or become divided into segments. [Lat. *segmentum.*] **—seg·men'tal** *adj.* **—seg·men·ta'tion** *n.*

seg·re·gate (sĕg'rĭ-gāt') *v.* **-gat·ed, -gat·ing.** 1. To separate or isolate from others or from a main body or group. 2. To impose the separation of (a race or class) from the rest of society. [< Lat. *segregare.*] **—seg're·ga'tion** *n.* **—seg're·ga'tion·ist** *n.* **—seg're·ga'tor** *n.*

sen·ior (sēn'yər', sēn'yôr') *n.* A feudal lord. [< Lat. *senior*, older.] **—sei·gnio'ri·al** *adj.*

seine (sān) *n.* A large fishing net held in a vertical position in the water by means of weights and floats. **—v. seined, sein·ing.** To fish for or catch with a seine. [< Gk. *sagēnē.*]

seis·mic (sīz'mĭk) *adj.* Of or caused by an earthquake. **—seis'mi·cal·ly** *adv.* **—seis·mic'i·ty** (sīz-mĭs'ĭ-tē) *n.*

seismo- or **seism-** *pref.* Earthquake: *seismograph.* [< Gk. *seismos.*]

seis·mo·graph (sīz'mə-grăf') *n.* An instrument for automatically detecting and measuring earthquakes and other ground vibrations. **—seis·mog'ra·pher** (sīz-mŏg'rə-fər) *n.* **—seis'mo·graph'ic** *adj.* **—seis·mog'ra·phy** *n.*

seis·mol·o·gy (sīz-mŏl'ə-jē) *n.* The geophysical science of earthquakes and of the mechanical properties of the earth. **—seis·mo·log'ic** (-mə-lŏj'ĭk) or **seis'mo·log'i·cal** *adj.* **—seis'mo·log'i·cal·ly** *adv.* **—seis·mol'o·gist** *n.*

seize (sēz) *v.* **seized, seiz·ing.** 1. To grasp suddenly and forcibly. 2. To have a sudden effect upon; overwhelm. 3. *Law.* To take into custody; confiscate. [< OFr. *seisir.*]

sei·zure (sē'zhər) *n.* 1. The act of seizing or being seized. 2. A sudden, often acute paroxysm, as an epileptic convulsion.

sel·dom (sĕl'dəm) *adv.* Not often; rarely. [< OE *seldan.*] **—sel'dom·ness** *n.*

se·lect (sǐ-lĕkt') *v.* To choose from among several; pick out. **—adj.** Also **se·lect·ed** (sǐ-lĕk'tĭd). 1. Singled out; chosen. 2. Of special quality; preferred. [< Lat. *seligere.*] **—se·lec'tive** *adj.* **—se·lec'tiv'i·ty** *n.* **—se·lect'ness** *n.* **—se·lec'tor** *n.*

se·lec·tee (sǐ-lĕk'tē') *n.* One who is selected.

se·lec·tion (sǐ-lĕk'shən) *n.* 1. The act of selecting or the fact of being selected. 2. One that has been selected. 3. A literary or musical text chosen for reading or performance.

4. A process that promotes the continued existence of certain organisms in competition with others.

selective service *n.* A system for calling up individuals for compulsory military service.

se·lect·man (sĭ-lĕkt′mən) *n.* One of a governing board of town officials elected in many New England towns.

se·le·ni·um (sĭ-lē′nē-əm) *n.* *Symbol* **Se** A nonmetallic element resembling sulfur, used as a semiconductor and in xerography. Atomic number 34; atomic weight 78.96. [< Gk. *selēnē*, moon.]

self (sĕlf) *n.*, *pl.* **selves** (sĕlvz). **1.** The total being of one person; the individual. **2.** Individuality. **3.** One's own interests, welfare, or advantage. —*pron.* Myself, yourself, himself, or herself. —*adj.* **1.** Of the same character throughout. **2.** Of the same material as the article with which it is used: *a self belt.* [< OE.]

self- *pref.* **1.** Oneself; itself: *self-control, selfless.* **2.** Automatic; automatically: *self-winding.* [< OE.]

Usage: Many compounds other than those entered here may be formed with *self-*. When *self-* precedes a word that can stand alone, it is joined with a hyphen: *self-deception.* In the rare cases when *self-* is combined with a form that cannot stand alone, it is joined without space or hyphen: *selfhood.*

self-ab·sorbed (sĕlf′əb-sôrbd′, -zôrbd′) *adj.* Absorbed in oneself. —**self′-ab·sorp′tion** *n.*

self-ad·dressed (sĕlf′ə-drĕst′) *adj.* Addressed to oneself.

self-ag·gran·dize·ment (sĕlf′ə-grăn′dĭz-mənt) *n.* The practice of making oneself greater, as in importance.

self-ap·point·ed (sĕlf′ə-poin′tĭd) *adj.* Appointed by oneself.

self-as·ser·tion (sĕlf′ə-sûr′shən) *n.* The act of asserting one's own rights, wishes, or views. —**self′-as·ser′tive** *adj.*

self-as·sured (sĕlf′ə-shŏŏrd′) *adj.* Having or showing confidence in oneself. —**self′-as·sur′ance** *n.*

self-cen·tered (sĕlf′sĕn′tərd) *adj.* Selfish; egocentric. —**self′-cen′tered·ly** *adv.* —**self′-cen′tered·ness** *n.*

self-com·posed (sĕlf′kəm-pōzd′) *adj.* Possessing or displaying control over one's emotions.

self-con·fessed (sĕlf′kən-fĕst′) *adj.* By one's own admission.

self-con·fi·dence (sĕlf′kŏn′fĭ-dəns) *n.* Confidence in oneself or one's abilities. —**self′-con′fi·dent** *adj.* —**self′-con′fi·dent·ly** *adv.*

self-con·scious (sĕlf′kŏn′shəs) *adj.* Uncomfortably conscious of one's appearance or manner; ill at ease. —**self′-con′scious·ly** *adv.* —**self′-con′scious·ness** *n.*

self-con·tained (sĕlf′kən-tānd′) *adj.* **1.** Complete in itself. **2. a.** Possessing or displaying self-control. **b.** Reserved.

self-con·trol (sĕlf′kən-trōl′) *n.* Control of one's emotions, desires, or actions. —**self′-con·trolled′** *adj.*

self-de·cep·tion (sĕlf′dĭ-sĕp′shən) *n.* The act of deceiving oneself or the state of being deceived by oneself.

self-de·feat·ing (sĕlf′dĭ-fē′tĭng) *adj.* Injurious to one's or its own purposes or welfare.

self-de·fense (sĕlf′dĭ-fĕns′) *n.* **1.** Defense against attack on oneself, one's property, or one's reputation. **2.** *Law.* The right to protect oneself against violence or threatened violence with whatever force or means are reasonably necessary.

self-de·ni·al (sĕlf′dĭ-nī′əl) *n.* Sacrifice of one's own comfort or gratification. —**self′-de·ny′ing** *adj.* —**self′-de·ny′ing·ly** *adv.*

self-de·struct (sĕlf′dĭ-strŭkt′) *v.* To destroy oneself or itself. —*n.* A mechanism for causing a device to destroy itself.

self-de·struc·tion (sĕlf′dĭ-strŭk′shən) *n.* The destruction of oneself, esp. suicide. —**self′-de·struc′tive** *adj.* —**self′-de·struc′tive·ness** *n.*

self-de·ter·mi·na·tion (sĕlf′dĭ-tûr′mə-nā′shən) *n.* **1.** Freedom to decide matters for oneself. **2.** The right of a people to determine its own political status.

self-dis·ci·pline (sĕlf′dĭs′ə-plĭn) *n.* Training and control of oneself usu. for personal improvement.

self-doubt (sĕlf′dout′) *n.* Lack of confidence in oneself.

self-ed·u·cat·ed (sĕlf′ĕj′ə-kā′tĭd) *adj.* Educated by oneself, without formal instruction. —**self′-ed′u·ca′tion** *n.*

self-ef·fac·ing (sĕlf′ĭ-fā′sĭng) *adj.* Not drawing attention to oneself; modest. —**self′-ef·face′ment** *n.*

self-em·ployed (sĕlf′ĕm-ploid′) *adj.* Earning an income directly from one's own business or profession rather than as the employee of another. —**self′-em·ploy′ment** *n.*

self-es·teem (sĕlf′ĭ-stēm′) *n.* Satisfaction with oneself.

self-ev·i·dent (sĕlf′ĕv′ĭ-dənt) *adj.* Requiring no proof or explanation. —**self′-ev′i·dence** *n.* —**self′-ev′i·dent·ly** *adv.*

self-ex·plan·a·to·ry (sĕlf′ĭk-splăn′ə-tôr′ē, -tōr′ē) *adj.* Needing no explanation.

self-ex·pres·sion (sĕlf′ĭk-sprĕsh′ən) *n.* Expression of one's own personality, as through speech or art.

self-fer·til·i·za·tion (sĕlf′fûr′tl-ĭ-zā′shən) *n.* Fertilization of a plant or animal by itself.

self-ful·fill·ing (sĕlf′fŏŏl-fĭl′ĭng) *adj.* **1.** Achieving self-fulfillment. **2.** Achieving fulfillment as a result of having been expected or predicted: *a self-fulfilling prophecy.*

self-ful·fill·ment (sĕlf′fŏŏl-fĭl′mənt) *n.* Fulfillment of oneself.

self-gov·ern·ment (sĕlf′gŭv′ərn-mənt) *n.* **1.** Political independence; autonomy. **2.** Democracy. —**self′-gov′erned** *adj.* —**self′-gov′ern·ing** *adj.*

self-hard·en·ing (sĕlf′här′dn-ĭng) *adj.* Of or pertaining to materials that harden without special treatment.

self-heal (sĕlf′hēl′) *n.* Any of several plants believed to have healing powers, esp. a low-growing plant with tightly clustered violet-blue flowers.

self-help (sĕlf′hĕlp′) *n.* The act or an example of providing for oneself rather than relying on help from others.

self-im·age (sĕlf′ĭm′ĭj) *n.* One's conception of oneself.

self-im·por·tance (sĕlf′ĭm-pôr′tns) *n.* An excessively high opinion of one's own importance. —**self′-im·por′tant** *adj.*

self-im·posed (sĕlf′ĭm-pōzd′) *adj.* Imposed by oneself.

self-in·crim·i·na·tion (sĕlf′ĭn-krĭm′ə-nā′shən) *n.* Incrimination of oneself, esp. by furnishing evidence that could make one liable to criminal prosecution. —**self′-in·crim′i·nat′ing** *adj.* —**self′-in·crim′i·na·to·ry** (-nə-tôr′ē, -tōr′ē) *adj.*

self-in·duced (sĕlf'ĭn-dōōst', -dyōōst') adj. 1. Induced by oneself. 2. *Elect.* Produced by self-induction.

self-in·duc·tion (sĕlf'ĭn-dŭk'shən) n. The generation by a changing current of an electromotive force in the same circuit tending to counteract such change.

self-in·dul·gence (sĕlf'ĭn-dŭl'jəns) n. Excessive indulgence of one's own appetites and desires. **—self'-in·dul'gent** adj. **—self'-in·dul'gent·ly** adv.

self-in·flict·ed (sĕlf'ĭn-flĭk'tĭd) adj. Inflicted on oneself. **—self'-in·flic'tion** n.

self-in·struc·tion·al (sĕlf'ĭn-strŭk'shə-nəl) adj. Relating to or designed for independent study.

self-in·ter·est (sĕlf'ĭn'trĭst, -ĭn'tər-ĭst) n. 1. Personal advantage or interest; gain. 2. Selfish regard for one's personal advantage or interest. **—self'-in'ter·est·ed** adj.

self·ish (sĕl'fĭsh) adj. Concerned only with oneself. **—self'ish·ly** adv. **—self'ish·ness** n. **Syns:** *selfish, self-absorbed, self-centered, self-seeking* **adj.**

self-knowl·edge (sĕlf'nŏl'ĭj) n. Knowledge of one's own nature, abilities, and limitations.

self·less (sĕlf'lĭs) adj. Without concern for oneself; unselfish. **—self'less·ly** adv. **—self'less·ness** n.

self-made (sĕlf'mād') adj. 1. Successful as a result of one's own efforts. 2. Made by oneself or itself.

self-mail·er (sĕlf'mā'lər) n. A folder that can be mailed without being enclosed in an envelope. **—self'-mail'ing** adj.

self-pit·y (sĕlf'pĭt'ē) n. Often excessive pity for oneself. **—self'-pit'y·ing** adj. **—self'-pit'y·ing·ly** adv.

self-pol·li·na·tion (sĕlf'pŏl'ə-nā'shən) n. The transfer of pollen from the anther to the stigma of the same flower.

self-por·trait (sĕlf'pôr'trĭt, -trāt, pōr'-) n. A portrait of oneself made by oneself.

self-pos·ses·sion (sĕlf'pə-zĕsh'ən) n. Full command of one's feelings and behavior; presence of mind. **—self'-pos·sessed'** adj.

self-pres·er·va·tion (sĕlf'prĕz'ər-vā'shən) n. The instinct to preserve oneself from harm or destruction.

self-pro·claimed (sĕlf'prō-klāmd', -prə-) adj. Proclaimed by oneself.

self-pro·pelled (sĕlf'prə-pĕld') adj. Containing its own means of propulsion.

self-re·al·i·za·tion (sĕlf'rē'ə-lĭ-zā'shən) n. The fulfillment by oneself of one's potential.

self-reg·u·lat·ing (sĕlf'rĕg'yə-lā'tĭng) adj. Regulating itself or itself without outside control. **—self'-reg·u·la'tion** n.

self-re·li·ance (sĕlf'rĭ-lī'əns) n. Reliance on one's own resources. **—self'-re·li'ant** adj. **—self'-re·li'ant·ly** adv.

self-re·proach (sĕlf'rĭ-prōch') n. The act of blaming oneself for a fault or mistake. **—self'-re·proach'ful** adj.

self-re·spect (sĕlf'rĭ-spĕkt') n. Proper respect for oneself. **—self'-re·spect'ing** adj.

self-re·straint (sĕlf'rĭ-strānt') n. Restraint imposed on one's emotions, desires, or conduct; self-control.

self-right·eous (sĕlf'rī'chəs) adj. Smugly sure of one's righteousness. **—self'-right'eous·ly** adv. **—self'-right'eous·ness** n.

self-ris·ing flour (sĕlf'rī'zĭng) n. A commercially produced mixture made up of flour and leavening.

self-sac·ri·fice (sĕlf'săk'rə-fīs') n. Sacrifice of one's personal interests or well-being for the sake of others. **—self'-sac'ri·fic'ing** adj.

self·same (sĕlf'sām') adj. The very same; identical. **—self'same'ness** n.

self-sat·is·fac·tion (sĕlf'săt'ĭs-făk'shən) n. Smug satisfaction with oneself.

self-sat·is·fied (sĕlf'săt'ĭs-fīd') adj. Feeling or exhibiting self-satisfaction.

self-seal·ing (sĕlf'sē'lĭng) adj. 1. Capable of sealing itself: *a self-sealing tire.* 2. Capable of being sealed without moisture: *a self-sealing envelope.*

self-seek·ing (sĕlf'sē'kĭng) adj. Concerned only for oneself. **—self'-seek'er** n.

self-serv·ice (sĕlf'sûr'vĭs) adj. Requiring patrons or users to help themselves: *a self-service elevator.*

self-serv·ing (sĕlf'sûr'vĭng) adj. Furthering one's own interests: *a self-serving statement.*

self-styled (sĕlf'stīld') adj. As designated by oneself.

self-suf·fi·cient (sĕlf'sə-fĭsh'ənt) adj. Also **self-suf·fic·ing** (-fī'sĭng). Providing for oneself without help. **—self'-suf·fi'cien·cy** n.

self-sup·port (sĕlf'sə-pôrt', -pōrt') n. Support of oneself without the help of others. **—self'-sup·port'ing** adj.

self-will (sĕlf'wĭl') n. Willfulness; obstinacy. **—self'-willed'** adj.

self-wind·ing (sĕlf'wīn'dĭng) adj. Winding automatically.

Sel·juk (sĕl'jōōk, sĕl-jōōk') adj. Also **Sel·ju·ki·an** (-jōō'kē-ən). 1. Of any of several Turkish dynasties of the 11th, 12th, and 13th cent. 2. Of a Turkish people ruled by a Seljuk dynasty. **—Sel'juk'** n.

sell (sĕl) v. **sold** (sōld), **sell·ing.** 1. To exchange for money or its equivalent. 2. To offer for sale: *sells textiles.* 3. To be sold or be on sale. 4. To promote the sale of. 5. To attract prospective buyers: *an item that sells well.* 6. To convince: *sold me on the idea.* **—phrasal verb. sell out.** *Slang.* To betray. [< OE *sellan,* to give.] **—sell'er** n.

Syns: *sell, handle, market, merchandise, retail, vend* **v.**

sell-out (sĕl'out') n. 1. The act of selling out. 2. An event for which all the tickets have been sold. 3. *Slang.* One who betrays.

selt·zer (sĕlt'sər) n. 1. A natural effervescent spring water of high mineral content. 2. Soda water. [G. *Selterser (Wasser),* (water) of Nieder Selters, a district in West Germany.]

sel·vage (sĕl'vĭj) n. Also **sel·vedge.** The edge of a fabric woven to prevent raveling. [ME.]

selves (sĕlvz) n. Pl. of **self.**

se·man·tic (sə-măn'tĭk) adj. Pertaining to meaning, esp. in language. [Gk. *sēmantikos,* significant.]

se·man·tics (sə-măn'tĭks) n. (used with a sing. verb). The study of meaning, esp. in language.

sem·a·phore (sĕm'ə-fôr', -fōr') n. An apparatus or system for making visual signals, as with flags, lights, or movable arms. **—v.**

-phored, -phor·ing. To send (a message) by or as if by semaphore. [Gk. *sēma*, sign + -PHORE.]

semaphore

sem·blance (sĕm′bləns) *n.* 1. An outward or token appearance; show. 2. A likeness; resemblance. 3. The barest trace. [< OFr. *sembler*, to resemble.]

se·men (sē′mən) *n.* A whitish fluid of the male reproductive organs, which carries spermatozoa; sperm. [< Lat., seed.]

se·mes·ter (sə-mĕs′tər) *n.* One of two terms, each from 15 to 18 weeks long, into which an academic year is often divided. [< Lat. *(cursus) semestris*, (period) of six months.]

semi-¹ (sĕm′ē, sĕm′ī) *n.* A semitrailer.

semi- *pref.* 1. Half: *semicircle.* 2. Partial; partially: *semiconscious.* 3. Occurring twice during: *semimonthly.* [Lat., half.]

Usage: Many compounds other than those entered here may be formed with *semi-*. In forming compounds, *semi-* is normally joined with the following element without space or hyphen: *semiannual.* However, if the second element begins with a capital letter or with *i*, it is separated with a hyphen: *semi-American-ized, semi-idle.*

sem·i·an·nu·al (sĕm′ē-ăn′yōō-əl) *adj.* Happening or issued twice a year.

sem·i·au·to·mat·ic (sĕm′ē-ô′tə-măt′ĭk) *adj.* Partially automatic. —*n.* A semiautomatic firearm.

sem·i·cir·cle (sĕm′ē-sûr′kəl) *n.* A half of a circle as divided by a diameter. —**sem′i·cir′cu·lar** (-kyə-lər) *adj.*

semicircular canal *n.* Any of the three tubular and looped structures in the inner ear, functioning together in the maintenance of a sense of balance and orientation.

sem·i·co·lon (sĕm′ē-kō′lən) *n.* A mark of punctuation (;) indicating a degree of separation intermediate in value between the comma and the period.

sem·i·con·duc·tor (sĕm′ē-kən-dŭk′tər) *n.* Any of various solid crystalline substances, such as germanium or silicon, that have electrical conductivity greater than insulators but less than good conductors.

sem·i·fi·nal (sĕm′ē-fī′nəl) *adj.* Immediately preceding the final, as in a series of competitions. —*n.* A semifinal competition. —**sem′i·fi′nal·ist** *n.*

sem·i·month·ly (sĕm′ē-mŭnth′lē) *adj.* Occurring or appearing twice a month.

sem·i·nal (sĕm′ə-nəl) *adj.* 1. Of or relating to semen. 2. Of a creative nature; capable of originating or stimulating growth and development. [< Lat. *seminalis.*]

sem·i·nar (sĕm′ə-när′) *n.* 1. A small group of advanced students engaged in special study or original research. 2. The course of study of a seminar. [< Lat. *seminarium*, seed plot.]

sem·i·nar·y (sĕm′ə-nĕr′ē) *n., pl.* **-ies.** A school for training priests, ministers, or rabbis. —**sem′i·nar′i·an** (sĕm′ə-nâr′ē-ən) *n.*

Sem·i·nole (sĕm′ə-nōl′) *n., pl.* **-nole** or **-noles.** 1. a. A tribe of Indians formerly living in Alabama and Florida. b. A member of this tribe. 2. The Muskhogean language of the Seminole. —**Sem′i·nole′** *adj.*

sem·i·per·me·a·ble (sĕm′ē-pûr′mē-ə-bəl) *adj.* 1. Partially permeable. 2. Permeable to some molecules in a mixture but not to all.

sem·i·pre·cious (sĕm′ē-prĕsh′əs) *adj.* Of somewhat less value than precious: *semiprecious gemstones.*

sem·i·pri·vate (sĕm′ē-prī′vĭt) *adj.* Shared with other occupants.

sem·i·pro (sĕm′ē-prō′) *adj. Informal.* Semiprofessional. —**sem′i·pro′** *n.*

sem·i·pro·fes·sion·al (sĕm′ē-prə-fĕsh′ə-nəl) *adj.* 1. Taking part in a sport for pay but not on a full-time basis. 2. Composed of or engaged in by semiprofessional players. —*n.* A semiprofessional player.

sem·i·skilled (sĕm′ē-skĭld′, sĕm′ī-) *adj.* Possessing minimal skills.

sem·i·sol·id (sĕm′ē-sŏl′ĭd, sĕm′ī-) *adj.* Intermediate in properties, esp. in rigidity, between solids and liquids. —*n.* A semisolid substance.

Sem·ite (sĕm′īt′) *n.* One of a group of Middle Eastern peoples that includes chiefly the Jews and Arabs.

Se·mit·ic (sə-mĭt′ĭk) *adj.* 1. Of or pertaining to the Semites, esp. Jewish or Arabic. 2. Pertaining to a subfamily of the Afro-Asiatic language family that includes Arabic and Hebrew. —*n.* 1. The Semitic subfamily of languages. 2. Any of the Semitic languages.

Sem·i·tism (sĕm′ĭ-tĭz′əm) *n.* 1. Semitic traits, attributes, or customs. 2. A predisposition in favor of the Jews.

sem·i·tone (sĕm′ē-tōn′) *n. Mus.* An interval equal to half a tone in the diatonic scale. —**sem′i·ton′ic** (-tŏn′ĭk) *adj.*

sem·i·trail·er (sĕm′ē-trā′lər) *n.* A trailer with rear wheels only, supported in front by the truck tractor.

sem·i·vow·el (sĕm′ē-vou′əl) *n.* A letter or vocal sound having the sound of a vowel but used as a consonant, as *y* and *w.*

sem·i·week·ly (sĕm′ē-wēk′lē) *adj.* Occurring or appearing twice a week.

sem·i·year·ly (sĕm′ē-yîr′lē) *adj.* Appearing or occurring twice a year.

sen¹ (sĕn) *n., pl.* **sen.** See table at **currency.** [J.]

sen² (sĕn) *n., pl.* **sen.** See table at **currency.** [Indonesian *sén.*]

sen·ate (sĕn′ĭt) *n.* 1. a. The upper house in a bicameral legislature. b. The highest council of state of the ancient Roman republic and empire. 2. The building or hall in which a senate meets. 3. A governing body of some colleges and universities. [< Lat. *senatus.*]

sen·a·tor (sĕn′ə-tər) *n.* A member of a senate. —**sen′a·to′ri·al** (-tôr′ē-əl, -tōr′-) *adj.* —**sen′a·to′ri·al·ly** *adv.*

send (sĕnd) *v.* **sent** (sĕnt), **send·ing.** 1. To cause to be conveyed by an intermediary to a destination. 2. a. To direct to go on a mission. b. To enable to go. 3. To command or request to go. **4.** To cause to depart. **5.** To emit. **6.** To direct or propel with force. **7.** To cause to take place or befall. **8. a.** To put into a given state or condition. **b.** *Slang.* To transport with delight; thrill. [< OE *sendan.*] —**send'er** *n.*

Syns: *send, dispatch, forward, route, ship, transmit* v.

send-off (sĕnd'ôf', -ŏf') *n.* A demonstration of affection and good wishes, as for a person about to begin a journey.

se-ne (sā'nā) *n., pl.* -ne. See table at **currency**. [Samoan.]

Sen-e-ca (sĕn'ĭ-kə) *n., pl.* -ca or -cas. **1. a.** A tribe of Indians formerly inhabiting western New York. **b.** A member of this tribe. **2.** The Iroquoian language of the Seneca.

se-nes-cent (sĭ-nĕs'ənt) *adj.* Aging; elderly. [< Lat. *senescere,* to grow old.] —**se-nes'cence** *n.*

se-nile (sē'nīl', sĕn'īl') *adj.* **1.** Characteristic of or proceeding from old age. **2.** Mentally and physically deteriorating with old age. [< Lat. *senilis.*] —**se-nile'ly** *adv.* —**se-nil'i-ty** (sĭ-nĭl'ĭ-tē) *n.*

sen-ior (sēn'yər) *adj.* **1.** Of or designating the older of two persons of the same name. **2.** Above others in age, rank, or length of service. **3.** Of the 4th and last year of high school or college. —*n.* **1.** A senior person. **2.** A student in the 4th year. [Lat., older.]

senior citizen *n.* A person of or over the age of retirement.

senior high school *n.* A high school usu. comprising grades 10, 11, and 12.

sen-ior-i-ty (sēn-yôr'ĭ-tē, -yŏr'-) *n., pl.* -ties. **1.** The condition of being senior. **2.** Precedence over others because of length of service.

sen-i-ti (sĕn'ĭ-tē) *n., pl.* -ti. See table at **currency**. [Tongan.]

sen-na (sĕn'ə) *n.* **1.** A plant with compound leaves and yellow flowers. **2.** The dried leaves of such a plant, used as a cathartic. [< Ar. *sanā'.*]

se-ñor (sān-yôr', -yōr') *n., pl.* **se-ño-res** (sān-yôr'ās, -yōr'-). The Spanish title of courtesy for a man, equivalent to English *Mr.*

se-ño-ra (sān-yôr'ə, -yōr'-) *n., pl.* **se-ño-ras** (sān-yôr'əs, -yōr'-). The Spanish title of courtesy for a woman, equivalent to English *Mrs.*

se-ño-ri-ta (sān'yə-rē'tə) *n.* The Spanish title of courtesy for an unmarried woman or girl, equivalent to English *Miss.*

sen-sa-tion (sĕn-sā'shən, sən-) *n.* **1.** A perception associated with stimulation of a sense organ. **2.** A vague or indefinite feeling. **3. a.** A condition of intense interest and excitement. **b.** A cause of such excitement. —**sen'sa'tion-al-ly** *adv.*

sen-sa-tion-al-ism (sĕn-sā'shə-nə-lĭz'əm, sən-) *n.* The use of lurid or exaggerated details in writing, art, or politics. —**sen-sa'tion-al-ist** *n.* —**sen-sa'tion-al-is'tic** *adj.*

sense (sĕns) *n.* **1.** Any of the functions of hearing, sight, smell, touch, and taste. **2.** The faculty of external or self-perception exemplified by these functions. **3. senses.** The faculties of sensation as means of providing physical gratification and pleasure. **4.** A feeling or perception either through the senses or the intellect. **5.** Correct judgment. **6. a.** Import; point. **b.** Lexical meaning. —*v.* **sensed, sens-ing. 1.** To become aware of; perceive. **2.** To understand. **3.** To detect something automatically: *sense radioactivity.* [Lat. *sensus.*]

sense-less (sĕns'lĭs) *adj.* **1.** Without sense or meaning; purposeless. **2.** Foolish. **3.** Unconscious. —**sense'less-ly** *adv.* —**sense'less-ness** *n.*

sen-si-bil-i-ty (sĕn'sə-bĭl'ĭ-tē) *n., pl.* -ties. **1.** The ability to feel or perceive. **2.** Keen perception. **3.** Delicate sensitivity to. **4.** The aptness of plant organisms and instruments to be affected by environment.

sen-si-ble (sĕn'sə-bəl) *adj.* **1.** Perceptible by the senses or the mind. **2.** Easily perceived; appreciable. **3.** Able to feel or perceive. **4.** Cognizant; aware. **5.** Acting with or showing good sense. —**sen'si-ble-ness** *n.* —**sen'si-bly** *adv.*

Syns: *sensible, logical, rational, reasonable* adj.

sen-si-tive (sĕn'sĭ-tĭv) *adj.* **1.** Capable of perceiving. **2.** Responsive to external conditions or stimulation. **3.** Aware of and responsive to the feelings of others. **4.** Quick to take offense; touchy. **5.** Easily irritated. **6.** Easily altered. **7.** Registering very slight differences or changes: *a sensitive barometer.* **8.** Concerned with classified government information. [< Lat. *sensus,* sense.] —**sen'si-tive-ly** *adv.* —**sen'si-tiv'i-ty** or **sen'si-tive-ness** *n.*

sen-si-tize (sĕn'sĭ-tīz') *v.* -tized, -tiz-ing. To make or become sensitive or more sensitive. —**sen'si-ti-za'tion** *n.* —**sen'si-tiz'er** *n.*

sen-sor (sĕn'sər, -sôr') *n.* A device, as a photoelectric cell, that detects and responds to a signal or stimulus.

sen-so-ry (sĕn'sə-rē) *adj.* Pertaining to the senses.

sen-su-al (sĕn'shōō-əl) *adj.* **1.** Of or affecting the senses. **2. a.** Pertaining to the gratification of the physical appetites. **b.** Suggesting sexuality. **c.** Carnal rather than intellectual. **3.** Sensory. —**sen'su-al-ist** *n.* —**sen'su-al-is'tic** *adj.* —**sen'su-al'i-ty** or **sen'su-al-ness** *n.* —**sen'su-al-i-za'tion** *n.* —**sen'su-al-ize'** *v.* —**sen'su-al-ly** *adv.*

sen-su-ous (sĕn'shōō-əs) *adj.* **1.** Pertaining to, derived from, or appealing to the senses. **2.** Highly appreciative of the pleasures of sensation. —**sen'su-ous-ly** *adv.* —**sen'su-ous-ness** *n.*

sent (sĕnt) *v. p.t. & p.p.* of **send.**

sen-tence (sĕn'təns) *n.* **1.** A grammatical unit comprising a word or group of words that usu. consists of at least one subject and a finite verb or verb phrase. **2. a.** A judgment, esp. a decision as to the punishment of a convicted person. **b.** The penalty imposed. —*v.* -tenced, -tenc-ing. To pass sentence on. [< Lat. *sententia,* opinion.] —**sen-ten'tial** (sĕn-tĕn'shəl) *adj.* —**sen'ten'tial-ly** *adv.*

sen-ten-tious (sĕn-tĕn'shəs) *adj.* **1.** Terse and forceful in expression. **2.** Given to pompous moralizing. [Lat. *sententiosus,* full of meaning.] —**sen-ten'tious-ly** *adv.* —**sen-ten'tious-ness** *n.*

sen-tient (sĕn'shənt) *adj.* **1.** Having sense perception. **2.** Experiencing sensation. [< Lat. *sentire,* to feel.] —**sen'tient-ly** *adv.*

sen-ti-ment (sĕn'tə-mənt) *n.* **1. a.** A cast of

mind regarding something. **b.** An opinion about a specific matter; view. **2.** A thought or attitude based on emotion rather than reason. **3.** The emotional import of something. [< Lat. *sentire,* to feel.]

sen·ti·men·tal (sĕn′tə-mĕn′tl) *adj.* **1. a.** Characterized or swayed by sentiment. **b.** Affectedly or extravagantly emotional. **2.** Appealing to the sentiments, esp. to romantic feelings. **—sen′ti·men′tal·ism** or **sen′ti·men′tal′i·ty** *n.* **—sen′ti·men′tal·ize** *v.* **—sen′ti·men′tal·ly** *adv.*

sen·ti·nel (sĕn′tə-nəl) *n.* A guard; sentry. [< Ital. *sentinella.*]

sen·try (sĕn′trē) *n., pl.* **-tries. 1.** A guard, esp. a soldier posted to prevent passage of unauthorized persons. **2.** The duty of a sentry. [Perh. < obs. *sentery,* sanctuary.]

se·pal (sē′pəl) *n.* One of the leaflike segments of a flower calyx. [< Gk. *skepē,* covering.] **—se′paled** or **sep′a·lous** (sĕp′ə-ləs) *adj.*

sepal

sep·a·ra·ble (sĕp′ər-ə-bəl, sĕp′rə-) *adj.* Capable of being separated. **—sep′a·ra·bil′i·ty** *n.* **—sep′a·ra·bly** *adv.*

sep·a·rate (sĕp′ə-rāt′) *v.* **-rat·ed, -rat·ing. 1. a.** To set, keep, or come apart; divide or become divided; disunite. **b.** To sort. **2.** To differentiate between; distinguish. **3.** To remove from a mixture or combination; isolate. **4.** To part, as a married couple, by decree. **5.** To part company; disperse. *—adj.* (sĕp′ər-ĭt, sĕp′rĭt). **1.** Set apart; detached. **2.** Existing by itself; independent. **3.** Dissimilar; distinct. **4.** Not shared; individual. *—n.* (sĕp′ər-ĭt, sĕp′rĭt). A garment, such as a skirt or blouse, that is one of a group designed to be worn in various combinations. [< Lat. *separare.*] **—sep′a·rate·ly** *adv.* **—sep′a·rate·ness** *n.*

Syns: *separate, break up, divide, part, partition, section, segment* v.

sep·a·ra·tion (sĕp′ə-rā′shən) *n.* **1. a.** The act or process of separating. **b.** The state of being separated. **2.** The place where a division or parting occurs. **3.** A formal agreement to live separately.

sep·a·ra·tist (sĕp′ər-ə-tĭst, sĕp′rə-, sĕp′ə-rā′tĭst) *n.* One who advocates political or religious separation. **—sep′a·ra·tism** *n.* **—sep′a·ra·tis′tic** *adj.*

sep·a·ra·tor (sĕp′ə-rā′tər) *n.* **1.** One that separates. **2.** A device for separating cream from milk.

se·pi·a (sē′pē-ə) *n.* **1.** A dark-brown pigment. **2.** A dark brown. [< Gk. *sēpia,* cuttlefish.] **—se′pi·a** *adj.*

sep·sis (sĕp′sĭs) *n.* The presence of pathogenic organisms, or their toxins, in the blood or tissues. [Gk. *sēpsis,* putrefaction.]

Sep·tem·ber (sĕp-tĕm′bər) *n.* The 9th month

of the year, having 30 days. See table at **calendar.** [< Lat., the seventh month.]

sep·tic (sĕp′tĭk) *adj.* **1.** Pertaining to sepsis. **2.** Causing sepsis. [< Gk. *sēptikos,* putrefying.]

sep·ti·ce·mi·a (sĕp′tĭ-sē′mē-ə) *n.* A systemic disease caused by pathogenic organisms or their toxins in the bloodstream.

septic tank *n.* A sewage-disposal tank in which waste material is decomposed by anaerobic bacteria.

sep·til·lion (sĕp-tĭl′yən) *n.* **1.** The cardinal number equal to 10^{24}. **2.** *Chiefly Brit.* The cardinal number equal to 10^{42}. [Fr.] **—sep·til′lion** *adj.* **—sep·til′lionth** *adj. & n.*

Sep·tu·a·gint (sĕp′chŏŏ-ə-jĭnt′, sĕp′tōō-) *n.* A pre-Christian Greek translation of the Old Testament. [Lat. *septuaginta,* 70 (from the traditional number of its translators).]

sep·ul·cher (sĕp′əl-kər) *n.* Also *chiefly Brit.* **sep·ul·chre.** **1.** A burial vault; tomb. **2.** A receptacle for sacred relics. *—v.* To place in or as if in a sepulcher. [< Lat. *sepulcrum.*] **—se·pul′chral** (sə-pŭl′krəl) *adj.* **—se·pul′chral·ly** *adv.*

se·quel (sē′kwəl) *n.* **1.** Something that follows; continuation. **2.** A literary work that continues an earlier narrative. **3.** A consequence. [< Lat. *sequela.*]

se·quence (sē′kwəns) *n.* **1.** A following of one thing after another; succession. **2.** An order of succession; arrangement. **3.** A related or continuous series. [< Lat. *sequi,* to follow.] **—se·quen′tial** (sĭ-kwĕn′shəl) *adj.* **—se·quen′ti·al′i·ty** *n.* **—se·quen′tial·ly** *adv.*

se·ques·ter (sĭ-kwĕs′tər) *v.* **1.** To set apart; segregate. **2.** To withdraw into seclusion. [< Lat., *depository.*]

se·quin (sē′kwĭn) *n.* A small shiny ornamental disk used on clothing; spangle. [< Ar. *sikkah,* coin die.]

se·quoi·a (sĭ-kwoi′ə) *n.* A very tall, massive evergreen tree of the mountains of California. [< *Sequoya* (George Guess), d. 1843.]

se·ra (sĭr′ə) *n.* A pl. of **serum.**

se·ra·glio (sĭ-răl′yō, -răl′-) *n., pl.* **-glios. 1.** A harem. **2.** A sultan's palace. [Ital. *serraglio.*]

se·ra·pe (sə-rä′pē) *n.* A woolen poncho worn esp. by Latin-American men. [Mex. Sp.]

ser·aph (sĕr′əf) *n., pl.* **-aphs** or **-a·phim** (-ə-fĭm). An angel. [< Heb. *śārāph.*] **—se·raph′ic** (sə-răf′ĭk) *adj.*

Serb (sûrb) *n.* A Serbian.

Ser·bi·an (sûr′bē-ən) *n.* **1.** A member of a southern Slavic people of Serbia and Yugoslavia. **2.** A Serbo-Croatian. **3.** Serbo-Croatian as spoken in Serbia. **—Ser′bi·an** *adj.*

Ser·bo-Cro·a·tian (sûr′bō-krō-ā′shən) *n.* **1.** The Slavic language of the Serbians and Croatians. **2.** A native speaker of Serbo-Croatian. **—Ser′bo-Cro·a′tian** *adj.*

sere (sĭr) *adj.* Also **sear.** Withered. [< OE *sēar.*]

ser·e·nade (sĕr′ə-nād′, sĕr′ə-nād′) *n.* A musical performance given to honor or express love for someone. *—v.* (sĕr′ə-nād′) **-nad·ed, -nad·ing.** To perform a serenade (for). [< Ital. *serenata.*]

ser·en·dip·i·ty (sĕr′ən-dĭp′ĭ-tē) *n.* The faculty of making valuable discoveries by accident. [< the fairy tale *The Three Princes of Serendip.*] **—ser′en·dip′i·tous** *adj.*

se·rene (sə-rēn′) *adj.* **1.** Unruffled; tranquil; dignified. **2.** Unclouded; bright. [Lat. *sere-*

nus.] **—se·rene'ly** adv. **—se·rene'ness** or **se·ren'i·ty** (sə-rĕn'ĭ-tē) n.

serf (sûrf) n. A slave, esp. a member of the lowest feudal class in medieval Europe, bound to the land. [< Lat. *servus*, slave.] **—serf'dom** n.

serge (sûrj) n. A cloth of worsted or worsted and wool. [< Lat. *serica*, silks.]

ser·geant (sär'jənt) n. **1. a.** Any of several ranks of noncommissioned officers in the U.S. Army, Air Force, or Marine Corps. **b.** A person holding any of these ranks. **2. a.** The rank of police officer next below a captain, lieutenant, or inspector. **b.** A person holding this rank. [< Lat. *servire*, to serve.] **—ser'gean·cy** n.

sergeant at arms n., pl. **sergeants at arms.** An officer appointed to keep order, as at the meetings of a legislature.

sergeant major n., pl. **sergeants major** or **sergeant majors. 1.** A noncommissioned officer serving as chief administrative assistant of a headquarters unit of the U.S. Army, Air Force, or Marine Corps. **2.** *Chiefly Brit.* A noncommissioned officer of the highest rank.

se·ri·al (sîr'ē-əl) adj. **1.** Of, forming, or arranged in a series. **2.** Published or produced in installments. *—n.* A work published or produced in installments. **—se'ri·al·i·za'tion** n. **—se'ri·al·ize'** v. **—se'ri·al·ly** adv.

se·ries (sîr'ēz) n., pl. **series. 1. a.** A group of events related by order of occurrence. **b.** A group of thematically connected works or performances. **2.** A group of related objects. [Lat.]

ser·if (sĕr'ĭf) n. In printing, a fine line finishing off the main strokes of a letter. [Perh. < Du. *schreef*, line.]

serif

serrate
Serrate leaf

se·ri·o·com·ic (sîr'ē-ō-kŏm'ĭk) or **se·ri·o·com·i·cal** (-ĭ-kəl) adj. Both serious and comic.

se·ri·ous (sîr'ē-əs) adj. **1.** Grave in character, quality, or manner; sober. **2.** Sincere; earnest. **3.** Concerned with important rather than trivial matters. **4.** Difficult. **5.** Causing anxiety; critical. [Lat. *seriosus.*] **—se'ri·ous·ly** adv. **—se'ri·ous·ness** n.

ser·mon (sûr'mən) n. **1.** A religious discourse delivered as part of a church service. **2.** A lengthy and tedious reproof or exhortation. [< Lat. *sermo*, discourse.] **—ser'mon·ize'** v. **—ser'mon·iz'er** n.

se·rol·o·gy (sĭ-rŏl'ə-jē) n. The medical study of serum. [SER(UM) + -LOGY.] **—se'ro·log'ic** (sîr'ə-lŏj'ĭk) or **se'ro·log'i·cal** adj. **—se·rol'o·gist** n.

se·rous (sîr'əs) adj. Containing, secreting, or resembling serum. [< SERUM.]

ser·pent (sûr'pənt) n. A snake. [< Lat. *serpens.*]

ser·pen·tine (sûr'pən-tēn', -tīn') adj. Snakelike, as in form, movement, or behavior.

ser·rate (sĕr'āt') adj. Also **ser·rat·ed** (-ā'tĭd). Edged with notched, toothlike projections: *a serrate leaf.* [Lat. *serratus*, saw-shaped.] **—ser·ra'tion** n.

ser·ried (sĕr'ēd) adj. Pressed together in rows; in close order. [< OFr. *serrer*, to crowd.]

se·rum (sîr'əm) n., pl. **-rums** or **se·ra** (sîr'ə). **1.** The clear yellowish fluid obtained upon separating whole blood into its solid and liquid components. **2.** The fluid from the tissues of immunized animals, used esp. as an antitoxin. [Lat.]

ser·vant (sûr'vənt) n. One employed to perform domestic or other services.

serve (sûrv) v. **served, serv·ing. 1.** To work for; be a servant to. **2.** To act in a particular capacity. **3.** To place food before; wait on. **4.** To provide goods and services for. **5.** To be of assistance to. **6.** To spend or complete (time), as in prison or elective office. **7.** To undergo military service for. **8.** To requite. **9.** To meet a need. **10.** To be used by or be of use to. **11.** To give homage to. **12.** To present (a legal writ or summons). **13.** To put (a ball) in play, as in tennis. *—n.* The right, manner, or act of serving, as in a court game. [< Lat. *servire.*] **—serv'er** n.

serv·ice (sûr'vĭs) n. **1.** The occupation or duties of a servant. **2.** The act or means of serving. **3.** A government department and its employees: *civil service.* **4.** The armed forces of a nation, or any branch thereof. **5.** Duties performed as an occupation. **6.** Installation, maintenance, or repairs provided or guaranteed by a dealer or manufacturer. **7.** A set of dishes or utensils. **8.** A serve in a game. *—v.* **-iced, -ic·ing. 1.** To maintain and repair: *service a car.* **2.** To provide services to. [< Lat. *servitium*, servitude.]

serv·ice·a·ble (sûr'vĭs-ə-bəl) adj. **1.** Ready for service; usable. **2.** Wearing well; durable. **—serv'ice·a·bil'i·ty** or **serv'ice·a·ble·ness** n. **—serv'ice·a·bly** adv.

serv·ice·man (sûr'vĭs-măn', -mən) n. **1.** A member of the armed forces. **2.** Also **service man.** One whose work is the maintenance and repair of equipment.

service station n. A gas station.

serv·ile (sûr'vəl, -vīl') adj. Slavish in character; abjectly submissive. [< Lat. *servilis.*] **—serv'ile·ly** adv. **—serv'ile·ness** or **ser·vil'i·ty** (sər-vĭl'ĭ-tē) n.

serv·ing (sûr'vĭng) n. A helping of food or drink.

serv·i·tor (sûr'vĭ-tər, -tôr') n. An attendant. [< Lat.] **—serv'i·tor·ship'** n.

serv·i·tude (sûr'vĭ-tood', -tyood') n. Submission to a master; slavery. [< Lat. *servitudo.*]

ser·vo (sûr'vō) n., pl. **-vos. 1.** A servomechanism. **2.** A servomotor.

ser·vo·mech·a·nism (sûr'vō-mĕk'ə-nĭz'əm) n. A feedback mechanism used in the automatic control of a mechanical device.

ser·vo·mo·tor (sûr'vō-mō'tər) n. A motor or

piston supplying power to a servomechanism. [Lat. *servus,* slave + MOTOR.]

ses·a·me (sĕs'ə-mē) n. 1. An Asian plant bearing small, edible, oil-rich seeds. 2. The seeds of this plant. [< Gk. *sésamē.*]

ses·qui·cen·ten·ni·al (sĕs'kwĭ-sĕn-tĕn'ē-əl) adj. Pertaining to a period of 150 years. —n. A 150th anniversary or its celebration. [Lat. *sesqui-,* one and a half + CENTENNIAL.]

ses·qui·pe·da·li·an (sĕs'kwĭ-pə-dā'lē-ĭn, -dāl'yən) adj. Also **ses·quip·e·dal** (sĕ-skwĭp'ĭ-dəl). 1. Long and ponderous; polysyllabic. 2. Given to using long words. —n. A long word. [< Lat. *sesquipedalis,* of a foot and a half in length.]

ses·sile (sĕs'ĭl', -əl) adj. Bot. Attached directly at the base: *sessile leaves.* [Lat. *sessilis,* of sitting.]

ses·sion (sĕsh'ən) n. 1. a. A meeting of a legislative or judicial body. b. A series of such meetings. c. The duration of such a series of meetings. 2. The part of a year or of a day during which a school holds classes. [< Lat. *sessio.*] —**ses'sion·al** adj.

ses·tet (sĕ-stĕt') n. The last six lines of a sonnet. [Ital. *sestetto.*]

set¹ (sĕt) v. **set, set·ting.** 1. To put into a specified position or state. 2. To put into a stable position; fix. 3. To restore to a proper and normal state. 4. To adjust, as for proper functioning. 5. To arrange tableware on (a table) preparatory to eating. 6. To apply curlers and clips to (one's hair) in order to style. 7. To arrange (type) into words and sentences preparatory to printing; compose. 8. To prescribe, establish, or assign. 9. To put forth as a model to be emulated. 10. To put in a mounting; mount. 11. To cause to sit. 12. To sit on eggs, as a hen. 13. To affix (a price or value). 14. To disappear below the horizon, as the sun. 15. To diminish or decline; wane. 16. To become fixed; harden or congeal. —*phrasal verbs.* **set about.** To begin. **set aside.** 1. To reserve for a special purpose. 2. To annul. **set back.** To slow down the progress of a set. **set down.** To put in writing. **set forth.** To utter or express. **set off.** To embark on a trip. **set off.** 1. To give rise to; cause to occur. 2. To indicate as being different; distinguish. 3. To direct attention to by contrast; accentuate. **set on** (or **upon**). To attack or direct to attact. **set out.** To begin any procedure or progress; start. **set up.** 1. To arrange; assemble. 2. To found; establish. 3. To place in a position of authority. 4. To provide with the necessary means or money. —*adj.* 1. Fixed or established. 2. Stereotyped. 3. Fixed and rigid. 4. Unyielding; firm. 5. Ready. —*n.* 1. The act or process of setting. 2. The condition resulting from setting. [< OE *settan.*]

Usage: Set in most cases is a transitive verb: *He set the plate on the table.* Sit generally is an intransitive verb: *He sits in the last row.*

set² (sĕt) n. 1. A group of persons or things connected by or collected for their similar appearance, interest, importance, etc.: *a chess set.* 2. A group of circumstances, situations, or events treated as a whole: *a set of experiences.* 3. A group of books published as a unit. 4. a. The scenery constructed for a theatrical performance. b. The enclosure in which a motion picture or broadcast is being filmed or videotaped; studio. 5. The receiving apparatus assembled to operate a radio or television. 6. Math. A collection of distinct elements. 7. In tennis and other games, a group of games constituting one division or unit of a match. [< Lat. *secta,* sect.]

set·back (sĕt'băk') n. An unexpected check in progress; reverse.

set·off (sĕt'ôf', -ŏf') n. 1. Anything that sets off something else by contrast. 2. Anything that offsets or compensates.

set piece n. 1. A piece of freestanding stage scenery. 2. A literary or artistic work characterized by a formal pattern. 3. A carefully planned and executed operation, esp. a military one.

set·screw (sĕt'skrōō') n. A screw used to hold two parts in a position relative to each other without motion.

set·tee (sĕ-tē') n. 1. A wooden bench with a high back. 2. A small sofa. [Perh. < settle, bench.]

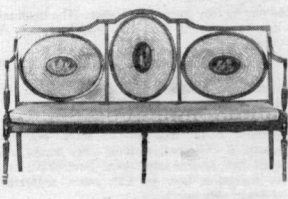

settee
18th-century English

set·ter (sĕt'ər) n. A long-haired dog orig. trained to hunt game.

set theory n. The study of the mathematical properties of sets.

set·ting (sĕt'ĭng) n. 1. The act of one that sets. 2. The context in which a situation is set. 3. A jewelry mounting. 4. The scenery for a theatrical performance. 5. The descent of the sun or other celestial body below the horizon.

set·tle (sĕt'l) v. **-tled, -tling.** 1. To put into order; arrange or fix definitely as desired. 2. To establish residence in. 3. To restore calmness or comfort to. 4. a. To come or cause to come to rest, sink, or become compact. b. To cause (a liquid) to become clear by forming a sediment. 5. To stabilize; assure. 6. a. To make compensation for (a claim). b. To pay (a debt). 7. To decide (e.g. a lawsuit) by mutual agreement. [< OE *setlan.*] —**set'tler** n.

set·tle·ment (sĕt'l-mənt) n. 1. The act or process of settling. 2. a. Establishment, as of a person in a business or of people in a new region. b. A newly colonized region. 3. A small community. 4. An adjustment or other understanding reached. 5. Also **settlement house.** A welfare center providing community services in an underprivileged area.

set-to (sĕt'tōō') n., pl. **-tos.** A brief but usu. heated contest.

set-up (sĕt'ŭp') n. 1. Informal. Arrangement; plan. 2. Often **setups.** Informal. The ingredients for serving mixed drinks. 3. Slang. a. A contest prearranged to result in an easy or faked victory. b. An endeavor that is intentionally made easy.

sev·en (sĕv'ən) n. 1. The cardinal number equal to the sum of 6 + 1. 2. The 7th in a set or sequence. [< OE *seofon.*] —**sev'en** *adj. & pron.*

seven deadly sins *pl.n.* The sins of pride, lust, envy, anger, covetousness, gluttony, and sloth.

sev·en·teen (sĕv'ən-tēn') *n.* **1.** The cardinal number equal to the sum of 16 + 1. **2.** The 17th in a set or sequence. —**sev'en·teen'** *adj. & pron.*

sev·en·teenth (sĕv'ən-tēnth') *n.* **1.** The ordinal number that matches the number 17 in a series. **2.** One of 17 equal parts. —**sev'en·teenth'** *adj. & adv.*

sev·enth (sĕv'ənth) *n.* **1.** The ordinal number that matches the number 7 in a series. **2.** One of 7 equal parts. —**sev'enth** *adj. & adv.*

seventh heaven *n.* A state of great joy.

sev·en·ti·eth (sĕv'ən-tē-ĭth) *n.* **1.** The ordinal number that matches the number 70 in a series. **2.** One of 70 equal parts. —**sev'en·ti·eth** *adj. & adv.*

sev·en·ty (sĕv'ən-tē) *n., pl.* **-ties.** The cardinal number equal to 7 × 10. —**sev'en·ty** *adj. & pron.*

sev·er (sĕv'ər) *v.* **1.** To divide or separate into parts. **2.** To cut or break from a whole. **3.** To break off; dissolve: *sever diplomatic ties.* [< Lat. *separare,* separate.]

sev·er·al (sĕv'ər-əl, sĕv'rəl) *adj.* **1.** Being of a number more than two or three, but not many. **2.** Different; various: *They parted and went their several ways.* —*n.* Several persons or things; a few. [< Lat. *separ,* separate.] —**sev'er·al·ly** *adv.*

sev·er·ance (sĕv'ər-əns) *n.* **1. a.** The act or process of severing. **b.** The condition of being severed. **2.** Extra pay given an employee upon leaving a job.

se·vere (sə-vîr') *adj.* **-ver·er, -ver·est.** **1.** Unsparing and harsh in treating others; stern; strict. **2.** Maintained rigidly: *severe accuracy.* **3.** Austere or dour; forbidding. **4.** Extremely plain; conservatively presented. **5.** Extreme; intense: *a severe storm.* **6.** Trying; rigorous. [< Lat. *severus.*] —**se·vere'ly** *adv.* —**se·vere'ness** *or* **se·ver'i·ty** (-vĕr'ə-tē) *n.*

sew (sō) *v.* **sewed, sewn** (sōn) *or* **sewed, sew·ing.** **1.** To make, repair, or fasten with a needle and thread. **2.** To close, fasten, or attach with stitches. —*phrasal verb.* **sew up.** *Informal.* To complete with success. [< OE *seowian.*]

sew·age (sōō'ĭj) *n.* Waste carried off with ground water in sewers or drains. [SEW(ER) + -AGE.]

sew·er (sōō'ər) *n.* An artificial, usu. underground conduit for carrying off sewage or rainwater. [< OFr. *sewiere.*]

sew·er·age (sōō'ər-ĭj) *n.* **1.** A system of sewers. **2.** The removal of waste materials by sewers. **3.** Sewage.

sew·ing (sō'ĭng) *n.* The article upon which one is working with needle and thread; needlework.

sex (sĕks) *n.* **1. a.** The property or quality by which organisms are classified according to their reproductive function. **b.** Either of two divisions, designated male and female, of this classification. **2.** Males or females collectively. **3.** The sexual urge or instinct as it manifests itself in behavior. **4.** Sexual intercourse. [< Lat. *sexus.*] —**sex'less** *adj.*

sex·a·ge·nar·i·an (sĕk'sə-jə-nâr'ē-ən) *n.* A person between 60 and 70 years old. [< Lat. *sexagenarius.*] —**sex'a·ge·nar'i·an** *adj.*

sex chromosome *n.* Either of a pair of chromosomes, usu. designated X or Y, in the germ cells of human beings, most animals, and some plants, that combine to determine the sex of an individual, XX resulting in a female and XY in a male.

sex hormone *n.* Any of various animal hormones affecting the growth or function of the reproductive organs.

sex·ism (sĕk'sĭz'əm) *n.* Discrimination by members of one sex against the other, esp. by men against women, based on the assumption that one sex is superior. —**sex'ist** *adj. & n.*

sex-linked (sĕks'lĭngkt') *adj.* Carried by a sex chromosome, esp. an X chromosome: *a sex-linked gene.* **2.** Sexually determined: *a sex-linked trait.* —**sex linkage** *n.*

sex·tant (sĕk'stənt) *n.* A navigational instrument used for measuring the altitudes of celestial bodies. [< Lat. *sextans,* sixth part.]

sex·tet (sĕk-stĕt') *n.* **1. a.** A group of six musicians. **b.** A composition written for six musicians. **2.** A group of six persons or things. [< SESTET.]

sex·til·lion (sĕk-stĭl'yən) *n.* **1.** The cardinal number written 10²¹. **2.** *Chiefly Brit.* The cardinal number written 10³⁶. [Fr.] —**sex·til'lion** *adj.* —**sex·til'lionth** *adj. & adv.*

sex·ton (sĕk'stən) *n.* One responsible for the care and upkeep of church property. [< Med. Lat. *sacristanus.*]

sex·tu·ple (sĕk-stōō'pəl, -styōō'-, -stŭp'əl, sĕk'stōō-pəl) *v.* **-pled, -pling.** To multiply or be multiplied by six. —*adj.* **1.** Having six parts. **2.** Multiplied by six. —*n.* A number six times larger than another. [Prob. Lat. *sex,* six + (QUIN)TUPLE.] —**sex'tu·ply** *adv.*

sex·tu·plet (sĕk-stŭp'lĭt, -stōō'plĭt, -styōō'-, sĕk'stōō-plĭt) *n.* One of six offspring delivered at one birth. [SEXTU(PLE) + (TRI)PLET.]

sex·u·al (sĕk'shōō-əl) *adj.* **1.** Of or involving sex, the sexes, or the sex organs and their functions. **2.** Having a sex or sexual organs. **3.** Implying or symbolizing erotic desires or activity. **4.** Pertaining to or designating reproduction involving the union of male and female gametes. [LLat. *sexualis.*] —**sex'u·al·ly** *adv.*

sexual intercourse *n.* Coitus, esp. between human beings.

sex·u·al·i·ty (sĕk'shōō-ăl'ĭ-tē) *n.* **1.** The condition of being characterized and distinguished by sex. **2.** Concern with sex. **3.** The quality of possessing a sexual character or potency.

sex·y (sĕk'sē) *adj.* **-i·er, -i·est.** *Informal.* Arousing or intending to arouse sexual desire or interest. —**sex'i·ness** *n.*

Sha·ban (shə-bän') *n.* Also **Shaa·ban.** The 8th month of the year in the Moslem calendar. See table at calendar. [Ar. *sha'bān.*]

shab·by (shăb'ē) *adj.* **-bi·er, -bi·est.** **1.** Threadbare; worn-out. **2.** Wearing worn garments; seedy. **3.** Dilapidated; deteriorated. **4.** Despicable; mean. [< obs. *shab,* scab.] —**shab'bi·ly** *adv.* —**shab'bi·ness** *n.*

---

shack (shăk) *n.* A small, crudely built cabin. [< Nahuatl *xacalli*, adobe hut.]

shack·le (shăk'əl) *n.* 1. A metal fastening, usu. one of a pair, for encircling and confining the ankle or wrist of a prisoner or captive; fetter; manacle. 2. Often **shackles.** Something that confines or restrains. —*v.* **-led, -ling.** To put shackles on; fetter. [< OE *sceacel.*] —**shack'ler** *n.*

shad (shăd) *n., pl.* **shad** or **shads.** A food fish that swims up streams from marine waters to spawn. [< OE *sceadd.*]

shade (shād) *n.* 1. **a.** Diminished or partial light; comparative darkness or obscurity. **b.** An area or space of such partial darkness or obscurity. 2. Cover or shelter from the sun or its rays. 3. **shades.** *Slang.* Sunglasses. 4. The degree to which a color is mixed with black or otherwise darkened. 5. A slight variation; nuance. 6. A small amount; trace. —*v.* **shad·ed, shad·ing.** 1. To screen from light or heat. 2. To obscure or darken. 3. To represent or produce degrees of darkness in (a picture). 4. To change or vary by slight degrees. [< OE *sceadu.*]

shad·ow (shăd'ō) *n.* 1. A partially or totally unilluminated area, caused by an object blocking rays of light. 2. The outline of an object that casts a shadow. 3. Gloom or an influence that causes gloom. 4. A shaded area in a picture. 5. A phantom; ghost. 6. A faint indication. 7. A remnant. 8. A slight trace. —*v.* 1. To cast a shadow on; shade. 2. To make gloomy or dark. 3. To represent vaguely or mysteriously. 4. To darken in a painting; shade in. 5. To follow after, esp. in secret. [< OE *sceaduwe.*] —**shad'ow·er** *n.* —**shad'ow·i·ness** *n.* —**shad'ow·y** *adj.*

shad·ow·box (shăd'ō-bŏks') *v.* To spar with an imaginary opponent.

shadow cabinet *n.* A group of leaders of a parliamentary opposition expected to hold positions in the official cabinet once their party returns to power.

shad·y (shā'dē) *adj.* **-i·er, -i·est.** 1. Full of shade. 2. Hidden. 3. Of dubious character or honesty; questionable. —**shad'i·ly** *adv.* —**shad'i·ness** *n.*

shaft (shăft) *n.* 1. The long, narrow stem or body of a spear or arrow. 2. A spear or arrow. 3. Something suggestive of a missile in appearance or effect. 4. The handle of any of various tools or implements. 5. A long, cylindrical bar, esp. one that rotates and transmits power: *a drive shaft.* 6. A long, narrow passage, duct, or conduit. [< OE *sceaft.*]

shag (shăg) *n.* 1. A tangle or mass, esp. of matted hair. 2. Cloth with a coarse, long nap. [< OE *sceagga,* matted hair.]

shag·gy (shăg'ē) *adj.* **-gi·er, -gi·est.** 1. Having long, rough hair or wool. 2. Bushy and matted. 3. Poorly groomed.

shah (shä) *n.* The title of the former hereditary monarchs of Iran. [Pers. *shāh.*]

shake (shāk) *v.* **shook** (shŏŏk), **shak·en** (shā'kən), **shak·ing.** 1. To move or cause to move to and fro with short jerky movements. 2. To vibrate or rock; tremble. 3. To cause to stagger or waver; unsettle. 4. To remove or dislodge by or as if by jerky movements. 5. To brandish or wave. 6. To clasp (hands or another's hand) in greeting or leave-taking or as a sign of agreement. —*phrasal verbs.* **shake down.** *Informal.* 1. To extort money from. 2. To make a thorough search of. **shake off.**

To free oneself from. **shake up.** *Informal.* 1. To unnerve; agitate. 2. To rearrange drastically. —*n.* 1. An act of shaking. 2. A beverage in which the ingredients are mixed by shaking: *a milk shake.* —**idioms. no great shakes.** *Slang.* Ordinary; mediocre. **shake a leg.** *Slang.* To hurry. [< OE *sceacan.*] —**shak'a·ble** or **shake'a·ble** *adj.* —**shak'er** *n.* —*Syns:* **shake, quake, quaver, quiver, shiver, shudder, tremble, tremor** *v.*

shake·down (shāk'doun') *n.* 1. *Informal.* An extortion of money, as by blackmail. 2. *Informal.* A thorough search. 3. A period of appraisal followed by adjustments to improve efficiency or functioning. —*adj.* Designed to test the performance of a ship or airplane: *a shakedown cruise.*

Shak·er (shā'kər) *n.* A member of a religious sect practicing communal living and observing celibacy.

Shake·speare·an or **Shake·spear·i·an** (shāk-spîr'ē-ən) *adj.* Of or like Shakespeare, his works, or his style.

shake·up (shāk'ŭp') *n.* *Informal.* A thorough reorganization.

shak·o (shăk'ō, shā'kō, shä'-) *n., pl.* **-os** or **-oes.** A stiff, cylindrical military dress hat with a short visor and a plume. [< Hung. *csákó (süveg),* pointed (cap).]

shak·y (shā'kē) *adj.* **-i·er, -i·est.** 1. Trembling or quivering. 2. Unsteady or weak. —**shak'i·ly** *adv.* —**shak'i·ness** *n.*

shale (shāl) *n.* A rock composed of layers of claylike, fine-grained sediments. [< OE *scealu.*]

shale oil *n.* Crude oil obtained from oil shale by heating and distillation.

shall (shăl) *v. p.t.* **should** (shŏŏd). Used as an auxiliary followed by an infinitive to indicate: 1. Simple futurity: *I shall be 28 tomorrow.* 2. **a.** Determination or promise: *I shall not give in.* **b.** Inevitability: *We shall have to repay those debts.* **c.** Command or compulsion: *You shall not go.* [< OE *sceal.*]

Usage: The traditional rules require that *shall* be used with the first person to indicate simple futurity and that *will* be used for that same purpose with the second and third persons. However, these rules are rarely observed in American English even at the most formal levels, and the widespread practice of using *will* to indicate futurity with all three persons is acceptable to a majority of the Usage Panel.

shal·lot (shə-lŏt', shăl'ət) *n.* 1. An onionlike plant with an edible bulb divided into sections. 2. The bulb of this plant. [< OFr. *eschaloigne.*]

shallot   shamrock

shal·low (shăl'ō) *adj.* **-er, -est.** 1. Measuring little from bottom to top or surface; not deep. 2. Lacking depth, as in intellect or significance. —*n.* A shallow part of a body of

water. [ME *schalowe*.] —**shal'low·ly** *adv.*
—**shal'low·ness** *n.*

sha·lom (shä-lōm', shə-) *interj.* Used as a greeting or farewell. [Heb. *shālōm*, peace.]

shalt (shălt) *v. Archaic.* 2nd person sing. present tense of **shall.**

sham (shăm) *n.* 1. Something false or empty purporting to be genuine. 2. One who assumes a false character. —*adj.* Not genuine; fake. —*v.* **shammed, sham·ming.** To put on a false appearance; feign. [Perh. < SHAME.] —**sham'mer** *n.*

sha·man (shä'mən, shā'-) *n.* 1. A priest of shamanism. 2. A medicine man among certain North American Indian tribes. [< Skt. *śramaṇas.*]

sha·man·ism (shä'mə-nĭz'əm, shā'-) *n.* The religious practices of certain peoples of northern Asia who believe that good and evil spirits pervade the world and can be summoned through inspired priests acting as mediums. —**sha'man·ist** *n.* —**sha'man·is'tic** *adj.*

sham·ble (shăm'bəl) *v.* **-bled, -bling.** To walk in an awkward, lazy, or unsteady manner, shuffling the feet. [< *shamble*, ungainly.] —**sham'ble** *n.*

sham·bles (shăm'bəlz) *pl.n.* (*used with a sing. verb*) A scene or condition of complete disorder or destruction. [< dial. *shamble*, table for display of meat.]

shame (shām) *n.* 1. A painful emotion caused by a strong sense of guilt, embarrassment, unworthiness, or disgrace. 2. Capacity for such a feeling: *Have you no shame?* 3. One that brings dishonor, disgrace, or condemnation. 4. Disgrace; ignominy. 5. A great disappointment. —*v.* **shamed, sham·ing.** 1. To cause to feel shame. 2. To bring dishonor or disgrace upon. 3. To force by making ashamed: *shamed into an apology.* [< OE *sceamu.*] —**shame'ful** *adj.* —**shame'ful·ly** *adv.* —**shame'ful·ness** *n.*

shame·faced (shām'fāst') *adj.* 1. Indicative of shame: *a shamefaced explanation.* 2. Bashful; shy. [< OE *sceamfæst.*] —**shame'fac'ed·ly** (-fā'sĭd-lē) *adv.* —**shame'fac'ed·ness** *n.*

shame·less (shām'lĭs) *adj.* Without shame; brazen. —**shame'less·ly** *adv.* —**shame'less·ness** *n.*

sham·my (shăm'ē) *n.* Var. of **chamois** (sense 2).

sham·poo (shăm-pōō') *n., pl.* **-poos.** 1. A preparation of soap or detergent used to wash the hair and scalp. 2. Any of various cleaning agents for rugs or upholstery. 3. The act or process of washing or cleaning with shampoo. [< Hindi *cāpnā*, to press.] —**sham·poo'** *v.*

sham·rock (shăm'rŏk') *n.* A plant, as a clover, having leaves with three leaflets, considered the national emblem of Ireland. [Ir. Gael. *seamrog.*]

shang·hai (shăng-hī') *v.* 1. To kidnap (a man) for service aboard a ship, esp. after drugging him. 2. To compel (someone) to do something, esp. by fraud or force. [< *Shanghai*, China.]

shank (shăngk) *n.* 1. The part of the human leg between the knee and ankle or the corresponding part in other vertebrates. 2. A cut of meat from the leg of an animal. 3. The section of a tool or instrument connecting the

functioning part and handle. [< OE *sceanca.*]

shan't or **sha'nt** (shănt, shänt). Shall not.

shan·tung (shăn-tŭng') *n.* A heavy silk fabric with a rough, nubby surface. [< *Shantung* (Shandong), China.]

shan·ty (shăn'tē) *n., pl.* **-ties.** A shack. [Prob. < Can. Fr. *chantier.*]

shape (shāp) *n.* 1. The outline or characteristic surface configuration of a thing; contour; form. 2. The contour of a person's body; figure. 3. Developed or definite form. 4. A form or condition in which something may exist or appear. —*v.* **shaped, shap·ing.** 1. To give a particular form to. 2. To take a definite form; develop. —*phrasal verb.* **shape up.** *Informal.* 1. To develop; turn out. 2. To improve. [< OE *gesceap.*] —**shap'er** *n.*

shape·less (shāp'lĭs) *adj.* Having no shape. —**shape'less·ly** *adv.* —**shape'less·ness** *n.*

shape·ly (shāp'lē) *adj.* **-li·er, -li·est.** Having a pleasing shape. —**shape'li·ness** *n.*

shard (shärd) *n.* A fragment of a brittle substance. [< OE *sceard.*]

share¹ (shâr) *n.* 1. A part or portion belonging to a person or group. 2. A fair or full portion. 3. Any of the equal parts into which the capital stock of a corporation or company is divided. —*v.* **shared, shar·ing.** 1. To divide and parcel out in shares; apportion. 2. To participate in, use, or experience in common. [< OE *scearu.*] —**shar'er** *n.*

share² (shâr) *n.* A plowshare. [< OE *scēar.*]

share·crop·per (shâr'krŏp'ər) *n.* A tenant farmer who gives a share of his or her crop to the landlord as rent.

share·hold·er (shâr'hōl'dər) *n.* One that owns or holds a share or shares of stock; stockholder.

shark (shärk) *n.* 1. Any of various often large and voracious marine fishes with tough skin and small, toothlike scales. 2. A ruthless, greedy, or dishonest person. [Orig. unknown.]

shark·skin (shärk'skĭn') *n.* 1. A shark's skin or leather made from it. 2. A fabric with a smooth, shiny surface.

sharp (shärp) *adj.* **-er, -est.** 1. Having a thin edge or a fine, acute point. 2. Not rounded or blunt; pointed: *a sharp nose.* 3. Abrupt; sudden. 4. Clear; distinct. 5. Shrewd; astute. 6. Artful; underhand. 7. Alert. 8. Intense; biting. 9. Sudden and shrill. 10. Intense; severe: *a sharp pain.* 11. Angular; not rounded. 12. *Mus.* a. Raised in pitch by a semitone from the corresponding natural tone or key: *a C sharp.* b. Above the proper pitch: *a sharp note.* 13. *Slang.* Attractive or stylish. —*adv.* 1. In a sharp manner. 2. Punctually; exactly. 3. *Mus.* Above the proper pitch. —*n.* 1. *Mus.* a. A note or tone that is a semitone higher than a corresponding natural note or tone. b. A sign (#) indicating this. 2. *Informal.* A shrewd cheater. [< OE *scearp.*] —**sharp'ly** *adv.* —**sharp'ness** *n.*

sharp·en (shär'pən) *v.* To make or grow sharp or sharper. —**sharp'en·er** *n.*

sharp·shoot·er (shärp'shōō'tər) *n.* An expert marksman.

shat·ter (shăt'ər) *v.* To break or burst suddenly into pieces, as with a violent blow. [< OE *sceaterian.*]

---

shat·ter·proof (shăt′ər-prōōf′) *adj.* Impervious to shattering.

shave (shāv) *v.* **shaved**, **shaved** or **shav·en** (shā′vən), **shav·ing.** 1. To remove (the beard or other body hair) from with a razor. 2. To remove thin slices of or from. 3. To cut or scrape into thin slices. 4. To come close to or graze in passing. —*n.* The act, process, or result of shaving. —*idiom.* **close shave.** *Informal.* A narrow escape. [< OE *sceafan.*]

shav·er (shā′vər) *n.* 1. An electric or mechanical device used to shave. 2. *Informal.* A small child, esp. a boy.

shawl (shôl) *n.* A square or oblong piece of cloth worn as a covering for the head, neck, and shoulders. [< Pers. *shāl.*]

Shaw·nee (shô-nē′) *n., pl.* **-nee** or **-nees.** 1. a. A tribe of Indians formerly living in the central Ohio valley. b. A member of this tribe. 2. The Algonquian language of the Shawnee.

Shaw·wal (shə-wäl′) *n.* The 10th month of the Moslem year. See table at **calendar.** [Ar. *shawwāl.*]

shay (shā) *n. Informal.* A chaise. [< CHAISE.]

she (shē) *pron.* The 3rd person sing. pronoun in the nominative case, feminine gender. 1. Used to represent the female person last mentioned. 2. Used traditionally of certain objects and institutions, such as ships and nations. —*n.* A female animal or person: *Is the cat a she?* [Prob. < OE *sēo,* fem. of *sē,* that one.]

sheaf (shēf) *n., pl.* **sheaves** (shēvz). 1. A bound bundle of cut stalks, esp. of grain. 2. Any collection held or bound together. [< OE *scēaf.*]

shear (shîr) *v.* **sheared**, **sheared** or **shorn** (shôrn, shōrn), **shear·ing.** 1. To remove (fleece, hair, etc.) by cutting or clipping with a sharp instrument. 2. To remove the hair or fleece from. 3. To cut with or as if with shears. 4. To divest or deprive. [< OE *sceran.*] —**shear′er** *n.*

shears (shîrz) *pl.n.* 1. Large-sized scissors. 2. Any of various other implements or machines that cut with scissorslike action. [< OE *scēara,* scissors.]

sheath (shēth) *n., pl.* **sheaths** (shē*th*z, shēths). 1. A case for the blade of a knife, sword, etc. 2. Any of various coverings or structures resembling a sheath. 3. A close-fitting dress. [< OE *scēath.*]

sheathe (shē*th*) *v.* **sheathed**, **sheath·ing.** To insert into or provide with a sheath.

shed¹ (shĕd) *v.* **shed**, **shed·ding.** 1. To pour forth or cause to pour forth: *shed tears.* 2. To give off: *shed light.* 3. To repel without allowing penetration: *A duck's feathers shed water.* 4. To lose by a natural process: *shed leaves; a snake shedding its skin.* —*idiom.* **shed blood.** To take life; kill. [< OE *scēadan,* to divide.] —**shed′der** *n.*

shed² (shĕd) *n.* A small structure for storage or shelter. [< obs. *shadde.*]

she'd (shēd) 1. She had. 2. She would.

sheen (shēn) *n.* Glistening brightness; shininess. [< OE *scīene.*]

sheep (shēp) *n., pl.* **sheep.** 1. A hoofed, thick-fleeced mammal widely domesticated for wool and meat. 2. One who is meek and submissive. [< OE *scēap.*]

sheep·ish (shē′pĭsh) *adj.* Embarrassed and apologetic: *a sheepish grin.* —**sheep′ish·ly** *adv.* —**sheep′ish·ness** *n.*

sheep·skin (shēp′skĭn′) *n.* 1. The skin of a sheep. 2. A diploma.

sheer¹ (shîr) *v.* To swerve from a course. [Perh. < SHEAR.]

sheer² (shîr) *adj.* **-er, -est.** 1. Thin and transparent: *a sheer fabric.* 2. Undiluted; pure: *sheer delight.* 3. Perpendicular or nearly so. [< ME *schir,* free from guilt.] —**sheer′ly** *adv.* —**sheer′ness** *n.*

sheet¹ (shēt) *n.* 1. A rectangular piece of cotton or similar material serving as a basic article of bedding. 2. A broad, thin, usu. rectangular piece of material. [< OE *scēte.*]

sheet² (shēt) *n.* 1. A rope or chain attached to one or both of the lower corners of a sail, serving to move or extend it. 2. **sheets.** The spaces at either end of an open boat, in front of and behind the seats. [< OE *scēata,* corner of a sail.]

Sheet·rock (shēt′rŏk′). A trademark for plasterboard.

sheik (shēk, shāk) *n.* An Arab chief. [Ar. *shaik,* old man.] —**sheik′dom** *n.*

shek·el (shĕk′əl) *n.* 1. Any of several ancient units of weight, esp. a Hebrew unit equal to about half an ounce. 2. The chief silver coin of the Hebrews, weighing one shekel. 3. See table at **currency.** [Heb. *sheqel.*]

shelf (shĕlf) *n., pl.* **shelves** (shĕlvz). 1. A flat, usu. rectangular structure of a rigid material fixed at right angles to a wall or other vertical surface and used to hold or store objects. 2. Something resembling a shelf, such as a balcony or a ledge of rock. [ME.]

shelf life *n.* The length of time that a product may be stored without deterioration.

shell (shĕl) *n.* 1. a. The usu. hard outer covering that encases certain organisms. b. A similar outer covering on an egg, fruit, or nut. 2. Something resembling a shell, esp.: a. A framework or exterior, as of a building. b. A thin layer of pastry. c. A long, narrow racing boat propelled by oarsmen. 3. A projectile or piece of ammunition. —*v.* 1. To remove the shell of; shuck. 2. To fire shells at; bombard. —*phrasal verb.* **shell out.** *Informal.* To pay (money). [< OE *scell.*] —**shell′er** *n.*

she'll (shēl). 1. She will. 2. She shall.

shel·lac (shə-lăk′) *n.* 1. A purified lac formed into flakes and used in varnishes, paints, sealing wax, and phonograph records. 2. A thin varnish made by dissolving flake shellac in denatured alcohol. —*v.* **-lacked, -lack·ing.** 1. To apply shellac (to). 2. *Slang.* To defeat decisively. [SHEL(L) + LAC.]

shell·fire (shĕl′fīr′) *n.* The firing of artillery projectiles.

shell·fish (shĕl′fĭsh′) *n.* An aquatic animal having a shell or shell-like external covering.

shell shock *n.* A nervous disorder resulting from trauma suffered in combat. —**shell′-shocked′** *adj.*

shel·ter (shĕl′tər) *n.* 1. a. Something that provides cover or protection, as from the weather. b. A refuge; haven. 2. The condition of being covered or protected. —*v.* To provide cover or protection for. [Orig. unknown.] —**shel′ter·er** *n.*

shelve (shĕlv) *v.* **shelved, shelv·ing.** 1. To place on a shelf. 2. To put aside; postpone.

shelves (shĕlvz) *n.* Pl. of **shelf.**

she·nan·i·gan (shə-năn′ĭ-gən) *n. Informal.* 1. A crafty trick. 2. Often **shenanigans.** Mischief. [Orig. unknown.]

shep·herd (shĕp′ərd) *n.* One who herds,

guards, and cares for sheep. —*v.* To herd, guard, or care for as or in the manner of a shepherd. [< OE *scēaphirde.*] —**shep'herd·ess** *n.*

shepherd's pie *n.* A casserole of cooked cubes of beef or lamb with gravy, topped by mashed potatoes.

sher·bet (shûr'bĭt) *n.* A sweet, frozen, often fruit-flavored dessert containing fruit, milk, and egg whites or gelatin. [< Ar. *sharbah,* drink.]

sher·iff (shĕr'ĭf) *n.* The chief law-enforcement official of a county. [< OE *scīrgerēfa.*]

Sher·pa (shûr'pə) *n., pl.* **-pa** or **-pas.** A member of a Tibetan people living in northern Nepal.

sher·ry (shĕr'ē) *n., pl.* **-ries.** A fortified, amber-colored wine, ranging from very dry to sweet. [< *Xeres,* Spain.]

Shet·land (shĕt'lənd) *n.* A fine yarn made from the wool of sheep raised in the Shetland Islands and used for knitting and weaving.

Shetland pony *n.* A small, compactly built pony of a breed originating in the Shetland Islands.

She·vat (shə-vät') *n.* Also **She·bat** (-bät', -vät'). The 5th month of the Hebrew calendar. See table at **calendar.** [Heb. *shĕbhāt.*]

shib·bo·leth (shĭb'ə-lĭth, -lĕth') *n.* A slogan or saying, esp. one distinctive of a particular group. [Heb. *shibbōleth.*]

shield (shēld) *n.* 1. An article of protective armor carried on the forearm. 2. A means of defense; protection. 3. Something resembling a shield. —*v.* 1. To protect or defend with or as with a shield. 2. To cover up; conceal. [< OE *scild.*] —**shield'er** *n.*

shield law *n.* A law protecting journalists from being forced to reveal confidential sources of information.

shi·er (shī'ər) *adj.* A compar. of **shy¹.**

shi·est (shī'ĭst) *adj.* A superl. of **shy¹.**

shift (shĭft) *v.* 1. To move or transfer from one place or position to another. 2. To change; switch: *shift tactics.* 3. To change gears in an automobile. 4. To get along; manage: *shift for myself.* —*n.* 1. A change from one place or position to another; transfer. 2. A change of direction or form. 3. a. A group of workers on duty at the same time. b. The working period of such a group: *the night shift.* 4. A mechanism for changing gears, as in an automobile. 5. a. A loosely fitting dress that hangs straight from the shoulders. b. A woman's undergarment; slip; chemise. 6. A stratagem; trick. [< OE *sciftan,* to arrange.] —**shift'er** *n.*

shift·less (shĭft'lĭs) *adj.* Lacking ambition or purpose; lazy. —**shift'less·ly** *adv.* —**shift'less·ness** *n.*

shift·y (shĭf'tē) *adj.* **-i·er, -i·est.** 1. Tricky; crafty. 2. Suggestive of craft or guile. —**shift'i·ly** *adv.* —**shift'i·ness** *n.*

shill (shĭl) *n. Slang.* A secret accomplice to a swindler. [Orig. unknown.]

shil·le·lagh (shə-lā'lē) *n.* A club or cudgel. [< *Shillelagh,* Ireland.]

shil·ling (shĭl'ĭng) *n.* See table at **currency.** [< OE *scilling.*]

shil·ly-shal·ly (shĭl'ē-shăl'ē) *v.* **-lied, -ly·ing.**

To put off acting; hesitate or waver. [< *shall I.*] —**shil'ly-shal'li·er** *n.*

shim (shĭm) *n.* A thin, often tapered piece of material used for leveling or filling space, as between a chair leg and the floor. [Orig. unknown.]

shim·mer (shĭm'ər) *v.* To shine with a flickering light. —*n.* A flickering or tremulous light; glimmer. [< OE *scimerian.*] —**shim'mery** *adj.*

shim·my (shĭm'ē) *n., pl.* **-mies.** 1. Abnormal vibration or wobbling, as in the chassis of an automobile. 2. *Informal.* A chemise. —*v.* **-mied, -my·ing.** To vibrate or wobble. [< CHEMISE.]

shin¹ (shĭn) *n.* The front part of the leg below the knee and above the ankle. —*v.* **shinned, shin·ning.** To climb by gripping and pulling alternately with the hands and legs. [< OE *scinu.*]

shin² (shēn) *n.* The 22nd letter of the Hebrew alphabet. See table at **alphabet.** [Heb. *shîn.*]

shin·dig (shĭn'dĭg') *n. Slang.* A festive party or celebration. [Prob. < *shindy,* uproar.]

shine (shīn) *v.* **shone** (shōn) or **shined, shin·ing.** 1. To emit light; be radiant. 2. To reflect light; glint or glisten. 3. To perform conspicuously well; excel. 4. To direct or cast the light of. 5. To make glossy or bright by polishing. —*n.* 1. Brightness; radiance. 2. A shoeshine. 3. Fair weather: *rain or shine.* —*idiom.* **take a shine to.** To like spontaneously. [< OE *scīnan.*]

shin·er (shī'nər) *n.* 1. *Slang.* A black eye. 2. A small, silvery fish.

shin·gle¹ (shĭng'gəl) *n.* 1. A thin oblong piece of wood or other material laid in overlapping rows to cover the roofs or sides of houses. 2. *Informal.* A small signboard, as one indicating a doctor's office. —*v.* **-gled, -gling.** 1. To cover (a roof or building) with shingles. 2. To cut (hair) short and close to the head. [< Lat. *scandula.*] —**shin'gler** *n.*

shin·gle² (shĭng'gəl) *n.* 1. Beach gravel consisting of large smooth pebbles. 2. A beach covered with such gravel. [Sc. *chyngill.*] —**shin'gly** *adj.*

shin·gles (shĭng'gəlz) *pl.n.* (*used with a sing. or pl. verb*). A painful virus infection marked by skin eruption along a nerve path on one side of the body. [< Lat. *cingulus,* belt.]

shin·ny (shĭn'ē) *v.* **-nied, -ny·ing.** To climb by shinning.

Shin·to (shĭn'tō) *n.* Also **Shin·to·ism** (-ĭz'əm) *n.* The traditional religion of Japan, marked by the worship of nature spirits and ancestors. —**Shin'to·ist** *n.*

shin·y (shī'nē) *adj.* **-i·er, -i·est.** Bright; glistening. —**shin'i·ness** *n.*

ship (shĭp) *n.* 1. A large vessel built for deep-water navigation. 2. A three-masted sailing vessel with square mainsails on all masts. 3. A ship's company. 4. An airplane, airship, or spacecraft. —*v.* **shipped, ship·ping.** 1. To place or take on board a ship. 2. To send or cause to be transported. 3. To take in (water) over the side. [< OE *scip.*] —**ship'per** *n.*

-ship *suff.* 1. Quality or condition: *friendship.* 2. Status, rank, or office: *professorship.* 3. Art or skill: *penmanship.* [< OE *-scipe.*]

ship·board (shĭp'bôrd', -bōrd') *n.* A ship.

ship·build·ing (shĭp′bĭl′dĭng) n. The business of constructing ships. —**ship′build′er** n.

ship·mas·ter (shĭp′măs′tər) n. The commander or captain of a merchant ship.

ship·mate (shĭp′māt′) n. A fellow sailor.

ship·ment (shĭp′mənt) n. 1. The act of transporting goods. 2. The goods or cargo transported.

ship·ping (shĭp′ĭng) n. 1. The act or business of transporting goods. 2. The body of ships belonging to one port, industry, or country.

ship·shape (shĭp′shāp′) adj. Neatly arranged; orderly; tidy. —**ship′shape′** adv.

ship·wreck (shĭp′rĕk′) n. 1. The remains of a wrecked ship. 2. The destruction of a ship, as by storm or collision. —v. To cause to suffer shipwreck. [< OE scipwræc, jetsam.]

ship·yard (shĭp′yärd′) n. A yard where ships are built or repaired.

shire (shīr) n. One of the counties of Great Britain. [< OE scīr.]

shirk (shûrk) v. To evade or avoid (work or duty). [Orig. unknown.] —**shirk′er** n.

shirr (shûr) v. 1. To gather (cloth) into parallel rows. 2. To cook (eggs) by baking until set. —n. A decorative gathering of cloth into parallel rows. [Orig. unknown.]

shirt (shûrt) n. 1. A garment for the upper part of the body, typically having a collar, sleeves, and a front opening. 2. An undershirt. [< OE scyrte.]

shirt·waist (shûrt′wāst′) n. A woman's dress with the bodice styled like a tailored shirt.

shish ke·bab (shĭsh′ kə-bŏb′) n. A dish of pieces of seasoned meat, often with onions, tomatoes, or green peppers, roasted and served on skewers. [Turk. şiş kebabıı.]

Shi·va (shē′və) n. The Hindu god of destruction and reproduction.

Shiva

shiv·er¹ (shĭv′ər) v. To shudder or shake from or as if from cold. [ME chiveren.] —**shiv′er** n.

shiv·er² (shĭv′ər) v. To break or cause to break suddenly into fragments or splinters; shatter. [< ME scivre, fragment.]

shoal¹ (shōl) n. 1. A shallow. 2. A sandbank or sandbar. [< OE sceald, shallow.]

shoal² (shōl) n. 1. A large group. 2. A school of fish. [Prob. < MLG schōle.]

shoat (shōt) n. Also **shote**. A young pig. [ME shote.]

shock¹ (shŏk) n. 1. A violent collision or impact. 2. a. Something that jars the mind or emotions as if with a violent, unexpected blow. b. The disturbance of mental or emotional equilibrium caused by such a blow. 3. A severe offense to a person's sense of propriety or decency; outrage. 4. Pathol. A gen. temporary physiological reaction to bodily trauma, usu. characterized by marked loss of blood pressure and the depression of vital signs. 5. The sensation and muscular spasm caused by an electric current passing through the body or through a bodily part. —v. 1. To strike with great surprise and agitation. 2. To offend; disgust. 3. To induce a state of shock in (a living organism). 4. To subject to an electric shock. [< OFr. choquer, to strike.] —**shock′er** n.

shock² (shŏk) n. 1. A number of sheaves of grain stacked upright in a field for drying. 2. A bushy mass: a shock of fair hair. [ME schocke.] —**shock′er** n.

shock absorber n. Any of various devices to absorb mechanical shocks, esp. one used in automobiles.

shock·ing (shŏk′ĭng) adj. 1. Highly disturbing emotionally. 2. Highly offensive; distasteful. —**shock′ing·ly** adv.

shock therapy n. The inducing of shock by electric current or drugs, sometimes with convulsions, as a therapy for mental illness.

shock troops pl.n. Highly experienced and specially trained military personnel used to lead attacks.

shock wave n. A large-amplitude compression wave, such as that produced by an explosion, caused by supersonic motion of a body in a medium.

shod·dy (shŏd′ē) adj. **-di·er, -di·est.** 1. Made of or containing inferior material. 2. Imitative; ersatz. 3. Dishonest; shabby: a shoddy trick. [Orig. unknown.] —**shod′di·ly** adv. —**shod′di·ness** n.

shoe (shōo) n. 1. A durable covering for the human foot. 2. A horseshoe. 3. The outer covering, casing, or tread of a pneumatic rubber tire. 4. The part of a brake that presses against the wheel or drum to retard its motion. —v. **shod** (shŏd), **shoe·ing.** To furnish or fit with shoes. [< OE schōh.]

shoe·horn (shōo′hôrn′) n. A curved tool used at the heel to help slip on a shoe.

shoe·lace (shōo′lās′) n. A string or cord used for lacing and fastening shoes.

shoe·mak·er (shōo′mā′kər) n. One who makes or repairs shoes as an occupation. —**shoe′mak′ing** n.

shoe·string (shōo′strĭng′) n. A shoelace. —adj. Cut long and slender: shoestring potatoes. —**idiom. on a shoestring.** With very little money.

shoe·tree (shōo′trē′) n. A foot-shaped form inserted into a shoe to preserve its shape.

sho·gun (shō′gən) n. A member of a group of Japanese military leaders who, until 1868, exercised absolute rule. [J. shōgun, general.]

shone (shōn) v. p.t. & p.p. of **shine.**

shoo (shōo) interj. Used to scare away something. —v. To drive or scare away, as by crying "shoo."

shoo-in (shōo′ĭn′) n. Informal. A sure winner.

shook (shŏok) v. p.t. of **shake.**

shook-up (shŏok-ŭp′) adj. Slang. Upset; shaken.

shoot (shōot) v. **shot** (shŏt), **shoot·ing.** 1. To hit, wound, or kill with a missile. 2. To discharge (a missile) from a weapon. 3. To discharge (a weapon); go off. 4. To move or send forth swiftly. 5. To pass over or through swiftly: shoot the rapids. 6. To record on film. 7. To project or cause to project or protrude. 8. To put forth; begin to grow; sprout. 9. To propel (e.g. a ball) toward its objective.

—*phrasal verb.* **shoot up. 1.** *Informal.* To grow or get taller rapidly. **2.** *Slang.* To inject (a narcotic drug) directly into a vein. —*n.* **1.** The young growth arising from a germinating seed; sprout. **2.** A shooting match or tournament. [< OE *scēotan.*] —**shoot'er** *n.*

shooting star *n.* A briefly visible meteor.

shop (shŏp) *n.* **1.** A small retail store. **2.** A place where goods are manufactured; factory. **3.** A commercial or industrial establishment. **4.** A workshop. —*v.* **shopped, shop·ping.** To visit stores to inspect and buy merchandise. [< OE *sceoppa,* stall.] —**shop'per** *n.*

shop·keep·er (shŏp'kē'pər) *n.* An owner or manager of a shop.

shop·lift·er (shŏp'lĭf'tər) *n.* One who steals goods on display in a store. —**shop'lift'** *v.* —**shop'lift'ing** *n.*

shopping center *n.* A group of stores forming a central retail market, as in a suburban area.

shopping mall *n.* **1.** An urban shopping center limited to pedestrians. **2.** A shopping center with stores facing an enclosed walkway for pedestrians.

shop steward *n.* A union member chosen by fellow workers to represent them in dealings with management.

shop·talk (shŏp'tôk') *n.* Talk concerning one's business or occupation.

shop·worn (shŏp'wôrn', -wōrn') *adj.* **1.** Tarnished, frayed, faded, or otherwise defective from being on display in a store. **2.** Trite; hackneyed.

shore[1] (shôr, shōr) *n.* The land along the edge of a body of water, such as an ocean, sea, or lake. [ME *schore.*]

shore[2] (shôr, shōr) *v.* **shored, shor·ing.** To prop up, as with an inclined timber. [ME *schoren.*]

shore·line (shôr'līn', shōr'-) *n.* The line marking the edge of a body of water.

shorn (shôrn, shōrn) *v.* A *p.p.* of **shear.**

short (shôrt) *adj.* **-er, -est. 1.** Having little length. **2.** Having little height. **3.** Having a small extent in time. **4.** Inadequate; insufficient: *water in short supply.* **5.** Lacking in length or amount. **6.** Rudely brief; curt. **7.** Containing shortening; crisp: *short pastry.* **8.** Designating a particular pronunciation of the letters for vowel sounds, as the sound of (ă) in *pan.* —*adv.* **1.** Abruptly; quickly. **2.** Concisely. **3.** Without reaching a goal or target. **4.** Unawares: *caught short.* —*n.* **1.** Anything that is short. **2. shorts. a.** Short trousers extending to the knee or above. **b.** Men's undershorts. **3.** *Elect.* A short circuit. —*v.* To cause a short circuit in. [< OE *scort.*] —**short'ness** *n.*

short·age (shôr'tĭj) *n.* A deficiency in amount.

short·cake (shôrt'kāk') *n.* A cake made with rich biscuit dough, split and filled with fruit.

short·change (shôrt'chānj') *v.* **1.** To give less than the right change to. **2.** To swindle, cheat, or trick. —**short'chang'er** *n.*

short circuit *n.* A low-resistance connection, often unintended, between two points in an electric circuit. —**short'-cir'cuit** *v.*

short·com·ing (shôrt'kŭm'ĭng) *n.* A deficiency or flaw.

short cut *n.* **1.** A more direct route than the customary one. **2.** A means of saving time or effort.

short·en (shôr'tn) *v.* To make or become short or shorter. —**short'en·er** *n.*

short·en·ing (shôr'tn-ĭng, shôrt'nĭng) *n.* A fat, such as butter or lard, used to make cake or pastry rich and flaky.

short·fall (shôrt'fôl') *n.* **1.** A shortage. **2.** The amount by which a supply falls short. **3.** A monetary deficit.

short·hand (shôrt'hănd') *n.* A system of rapid handwriting employing symbols to represent words, phrases, and letters; stenography.

short·lived (shôrt'līvd', -lĭvd') *adj.* Living or lasting only a short time.

short·ly (shôrt'lē) *adv.* **1.** In a short time; soon. **2.** In a few words; concisely.

short order *n.* Food quickly prepared and served, as in a diner.

short-range (shôrt'rānj') *adj.* **1.** Extending only briefly into the future: *short-range goals.* **2.** Capable of reaching only a short distance: *short-range weapons.*

short shrift *n.* **1.** A short respite, as from death. **2.** Unsympathetic treatment.

short·sight·ed (shôrt'sī'tĭd) *adj.* **1.** Nearsighted; myopic. **2.** Lacking foresight. —**short'sight'ed·ness** *n.*

short·stop (shôrt'stŏp') *n. Baseball.* **1.** The field position between second and third bases. **2.** The player who occupies this position.

short story *n.* A relatively brief fictional prose composition that usu. develops a single theme or mood.

short subject *n.* A brief film shown with a featured motion picture.

short-tem·pered (shôrt'tĕm'pərd) *adj.* Easily angered.

short-term (shôrt'tûrm') *adj.* **1.** Involving or occurring over a short time period. **2.** Pertaining to a financial transaction based on a time period usu. of less than one year.

short ton *n.* A ton (sense 1.b.).

short wave *n.* An electromagnetic wave with wavelength of 80 meters or less. —**short'wave'** (shôrt'wāv') *adj.*

Sho·sho·ne (shō-shō'nē) *n., pl.* **-ne** or **-nes.** Also **Sho·sho·ni** *pl.* **-ni** or **-nis. 1. a.** A tribe of Indians, formerly occupying parts of the western United States. **b.** A member of this tribe. **2.** The Uto-Aztecan language of the Shoshone.

Sho·sho·ne·an (shō-shō'nē-ən) *n.* An Indian linguistic group of western North America, comprising most of the Uto-Aztecan languages found in the United States. —**Sho'sho'ne·an** *adj.*

shot[1] (shŏt) *n.* **1.** The firing or discharge of a weapon. **2.** *pl.* **shot.** A bullet or similar missile fired from a weapon. **3.** A throw, hit, or drive in any of several games. **4.** A marksman. **5.** Scope; range. **6.** An attempt, guess, or opportunity. **7.** The heavy metal ball that is put for distance in the shot-put. **8.** A photograph or single cinematic view. **9.** A hypodermic injection. **10.** A drink of liquor, esp. a jigger. [< OE *scot.*]

shot[2] (shŏt) *v., p.t. & p.p.* of **shoot.**

shote (shōt) *n.* Var. of **shoat.**

shot·gun (shŏt'gŭn') *n.* A shoulder-held firearm that fires multiple pellets through a smooth bore.

shot-put (shŏt'pŏŏt') n. 1. An athletic event in which the shot is thrown for distance. 2. The ball used in this event. —**shot'-put'ter** n.

should (shŏŏd) v. p.t. of **shall.** Used to express obligation, necessity, probability, or contingency.

shoul-der (shōl'dər) n. 1. Anat. a. The part of the body between the neck and upper arm or forelimb. b. The joint connecting the arm or forelimb with the trunk. 2. **shoulders.** The two shoulders and the area of the back between them. 3. The edge or ridge running on either side of a roadway. —v. 1. To carry on or as if on the shoulders. 2. To push with or as if with the shoulders. [< OE sculdor.]

shoulder blade n. The scapula.

should-n't (shŏŏd'nt). Should not.

shouldst (shŏŏdst) v. Also **should-est** (shŏŏd'ĭst). Archaic. 2nd person sing. past tense of **shall.**

shout (shout) n. A loud cry, often expressing strong emotion or a command. [ME shoute.] —**shout** v. —**shout'er** n.

shove (shŭv) v. **shoved, shov-ing.** To push forcefully or rudely. —**phrasal verb. shove off.** 1. To set a beached boat afloat. 2. Informal. To leave. —n. The act of shoving, esp. a rude push. [< OE scūfan.] —**shov'er** n.

shov-el (shŭv'əl) n. 1. A tool with a handle and scoop for picking up dirt, snow, etc. 2. A large mechanical device with a jawed scoop for heavy digging or excavation. —v. -**eled** or -**elled, -el-ing** or -**el-ling.** 1. To dig into or move with a shovel. 2. To convey or set down in a hasty or careless way; unload. [< OE scofl.]

show (shō) v. **showed, shown** (shōn) or **showed, show-ing.** 1. To cause or allow to be seen; display. 2. To conduct; guide. 3. To point out; demonstrate. 4. To manifest; reveal. 5. To grant; confer. 6. To instruct. 7. To be visible or evident. 8. To finish third or better for betting purposes. —**phrasal verbs. show off.** To behave in an ostentatious or conspicuous manner. **show up.** 1. To expose or reveal (e.g. faults or defects). 2. To be clearly visible. 3. To put in an appearance; arrive. —n. 1. A display; demonstration. 2. An appearance; semblance. 3. A spectacle. 4. A public exhibition or entertainment. 5. Informal. An affair or undertaking: a poor show. 6. Third place or better for betting purposes. [< OE scēawian, to look at.]

Syns: show, demonstrate, display, evidence, evince, exhibit, manifest v.

show business n. The entertainment industry or arts.

show-case (shō'kās') n. 1. A display case, as in a store or museum. 2. A setting for advantageous display. —v. -**cased, -cas-ing.** To display or feature prominently.

show-down (shō'doun') n. An event or circumstance that forces an issue to a conclusion.

show-er (shou'ər) n. 1. A brief fall of rain, hail, or sleet. 2. An outpouring: a shower of abuse. 3. A party held to honor and present gifts to someone. 4. A bath in which water is sprayed on the bather. —v. 1. To sprinkle; spray. 2. To bestow abundantly. 3. To fall or pour down in a shower. 4. To take a shower. [< OE scūr.]

show-ing (shō'ĭng) n. 1. A presentation or display. 2. Performance: a poor showing.

show-man (shō'mən) n. 1. A theatrical producer. 2. A person with a flair for the dramatic. —**show'man-ship'** n.

shown (shōn) v. A p.p. of **show.**

show-off (shō'ôf', -ŏf') n. 1. Ostentatious display or behavior. 2. An exhibitionist.

show-piece (shō'pēs') n. Something exhibited as an outstanding example of its kind.

show place n. A place viewed for its beauty or historical interest.

show room n. A room in which merchandise is on display.

show-stop-per (shō'stŏp'ər) n. One that evokes so much audience applause that a performance is temporarily halted.

show-y (shō'ē) adj. -**i-er, -i-est.** Making a conspicuous display; ostentatious; flashy. —**show'i-ly** adv. —**show'i-ness** n.

shrank (shrăngk) v. A p.t. of **shrink.**

shrap-nel (shrăp'nəl) n., pl. -**nel.** 1. An artillery shell containing metal balls, fused to explode in the air above enemy troops. 2. Shell fragments from any high-explosive shell. [< General Henry Shrapnel (1761–1842).]

shred (shrĕd) n. 1. A long, irregular strip cut or torn off. 2. A small amount; particle: not a shred of truth in the story. —v. **shred-ded** or **shred, shred-ding.** To cut or tear into shreds. [< OE scrēade.] —**shred'der** n.

shrew (shrōō) n. 1. A very small mouselike mammal with a pointed nose. 2. A scolding, sharp-tempered woman. [< OE scrēawa.] —**shrew'ish** adj.

shrewd (shrōōd) adj. 1. Discerning; astute. 2. Artful; cunning. [< ME shrew, rascal.] —**shrewd'ly** adv. —**shrewd'ness** n.

Syns: shrewd, astute, cagey, slick adj.

shriek (shrēk) n. A shrill outcry; screech. [< ME shriken, to shriek.] —**shriek** v.

shrift (shrĭft) n. Archaic. The act of shriving. [< OE scrift.]

shrike (shrīk) n. A carnivorous bird with a hooked bill, often impaling its prey on thorns. [< OE scrīc, thrush.]

shrill (shrĭl) adj. -**er, -est.** High-pitched and piercing. —v. To produce a shrill sound. [ME shrille.] —**shrill'ness** n. —**shrill'ly** adv.

shrimp (shrĭmp) n., pl. **shrimp** or **shrimps.** 1. A small, often edible marine crustacean. 2. Slang. A small or unimportant person. [ME shrimpe.]

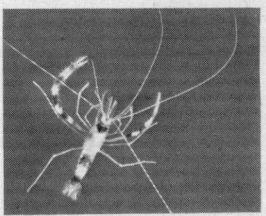

shrimp

shrine (shrīn) n. 1. A container for sacred relics. 2. The tomb of a saint. 3. A site or object revered for its associations. [< Lat. scrinium, case for books and papers.]

shrink (shrĭngk) v. **shrank** (shrăngk) or **shrunk**

(shrŭngk), **shrunk** or **shrunk·en** (shrŭng′kən), **shrink·ing.** 1. To draw together or contract from heat, moisture, or cold. 2. To dwindle. 3. To draw back; recoil. —*n. Slang.* A psychiatrist. [< OE *scrincan.*] —**shrink′a·ble** *adj.* —**shrink′age** *n.*

shrive (shrīv) *v.* **shrove** (shrōv) or **shrived, shriv·en** (shrīv′ən) or **shrived, shriv·ing.** To confess and give absolution to (a penitent). [< Lat. *scribere,* to write.]

shriv·el (shrĭv′əl) *v.* **-eled** or **-elled, -el·ing** or **-el·ling.** 1. To shrink and wrinkle, often in drying. 2. To cause to shrivel. [Orig. unknown.]

shroud (shroud) *n.* 1. A cloth used to wrap a body for burial. 2. Something that conceals, protects, or screens. 3. One of a set of lines stretched from the masthead to a vessel's sides to support the mast. —*v.* To screen; hide. [< OE *scrūd,* garment.]

shrub (shrŭb) *n.* A low, woody plant with several stems. [< OE *scrybb.*] —**shrub′by** *adj.*

shrub·ber·y (shrŭb′ə-rē) *n., pl.* **-ies.** A group or planting of shrubs.

shrug (shrŭg) *v.* **shrugged, shrug·ging.** To raise (the shoulders) as a gesture of doubt, disdain, or indifference. —*phrasal verb.* **shrug off.** 1. To minimize. 2. To get rid of. [ME *shruggen.*] —**shrug** *n.*

shrunk (shrŭngk) *v.* A *p.t.* & *p.p.* of **shrink.**

shrunk·en (shrŭng′kən) *v.* A *p.p.* of **shrink.**

shuck (shŭk) *n.* A husk or shell. —*v.* 1. To remove the husk or shell from. 2. *Informal.* To cast off; shed. —*interj.* **shucks.** Used to express disappointment or annoyance. [Orig. unknown.]

shud·der (shŭd′ər) *v.* 1. To tremble convulsively, as from fear or aversion. 2. To vibrate; quiver. [ME *shoddren.*] —**shud′der** *n.*

shuf·fle (shŭf′əl) *v.* **-fled, -fling.** 1. To move with a shambling, idle gait. 2. To move (something) from one place to another. 3. To mix together in a disordered, haphazard fashion. 4. To mix together (playing cards, tiles, or dominoes) to change their order. [Prob. < LG *schüffeln,* to walk clumsily.] —**shuf′fle** *n.* —**shuf′fler** *n.*

shuf·fle·board (shŭf′əl-bôrd′, -bōrd′) *n.* A game in which disks are pushed along a smooth, level surface toward numbered squares. [< obs. *shove-board.*]

shun (shŭn) *v.* **shunned, shun·ning.** To keep away from deliberately. [< OE *scunian,* to abhor.] —**shun′ner** *n.*

shunt (shŭnt) *n.* 1. The act of turning aside or moving to an alternate course. 2. A railroad switch. 3. A low-resistance alternative path for a portion of an electric current. —*v.* 1. To cause to turn or move aside or onto another course: *shunting traffic around a bottleneck.* 2. To provide or divert (current) by means of a shunt. [ME *shunten,* to flinch.]

shush (shŭsh) *interj.* Used to demand silence. —*v.* To silence by saying "shush."

shut (shŭt) *v.* **shut, shut·ting.** 1. To move (a door, lid, valve, etc.) into closed position. 2. To block passage or access to. 3. To confine. 4. To close (a business establishment). 5. To move or be moved to a closed position; close. —*phrasal verbs.* **shut down.** 1. To halt operation of. 2. To stop operating, esp. auto-

matically. **shut out.** 1. To keep from entering. 2. To prevent (a team) from scoring any runs or points. **shut up.** 1. To cause to be silent. 2. To be or become silent. [< OE *scyttan.*]

shut-down (shŭt′doun′) *n.* 1. A temporary closing of an industrial plant. 2. A cessation of operation.

shut·eye (shŭt′ī′) *n. Slang.* Sleep.

shut-in (shŭt′ĭn′) *n.* One confined indoors by illness or disability. —**shut′-in′** *adj.*

shut·out (shŭt′out′) *n.* A game in which one side does not score.

shut·ter (shŭt′ər) *n.* 1. A hinged cover or screen for a window. 2. A device that opens and shuts the lens aperture of a camera. —*v.* To furnish or close with a shutter.

shut·tle (shŭt′l) *n.* 1. A device used in weaving to carry the thread back and forth. 2. A device for holding the thread esp. in tatting or in a sewing machine. 3. A train, bus, or plane making short, frequent trips between two points. —*v.* **-tled, -tling.** To move back and forth by or as if by a shuttle. [< OE *scytel,* dart.]

shut·tle·cock (shŭt′l-kŏk′) *n.* A rounded cork or similar material with a crown of feathers, used in badminton.

shy¹ (shī) *adj.* **shi·er** or **shy·er, shi·est** or **shy·est.** 1. Easily startled; timid. 2. Bashfully reserved; modest. 3. Distrustful; cautious. 4. *Informal.* Short; lacking. —*v.* **shied, shy·ing.** 1. To move suddenly, as if startled. 2. To draw back, as from fear. [< OE *scēoh.*] —**shy′er** *n.* —**shy′ly** *adv.* —**shy′ness** *n.*

shy² (shī) *v.* **shied, shy·ing.** To throw with a swift sideways motion. [Perh. < *shy¹.*]

shy·ster (shī′stər) *n. Slang.* An unethical or unscrupulous lawyer or politician. [Perh. < *Scheuster,* an unscrupulous 19th-cent. lawyer.]

Si The symbol for the element silicon.

Si·a·mese (sī′ə-mēz′, -mēs′) *n., pl.* **-mese.** Thai. —**Si′a·mese′** *adj.*

Siamese twin *n.* One of a pair of twins born with their bodies joined together.

sib·i·lant (sĭb′ə-lənt) *adj.* Producing or having a hissing sound. —*n.* A sibilant speech sound, such as (s) or (z). [< Lat. *sibilare,* to hiss.]

sib·ling (sĭb′lĭng) *n.* One of two or more persons having the same parents. [< OE.]

sib·yl (sĭb′əl) *n.* A female prophet. [< Gk. *Sibulla,* prophetess.] —**sib′yl·line′** (-ə-līn′, -lēn′) *adj.*

sic¹ (sĭk, sēk) *adv.* Thus; so. Used in written texts to indicate that a surprising word or fact is not a mistake and should be read as it stands. [Lat.]

sic² (sĭk) *v.* **sicced, sic·cing.** To urge to attack or chase. [< SEEK.]

sick (sĭk) *adj.* **-er, -est.** 1. a. Ailing; ill; unwell. b. Nauseated. 2. Of or for sick persons: *sick leave.* 3. a. Mentally ill or disturbed. b. Morbid or unwholesome. 4. a. Deeply distressed; upset. b. Disgusted; revolted. c. Weary; tired: *sick of it all.* d. Pining; longing. [< OE *sēoc.*] —**sick′ness** *n.*

sick·bay (sĭk′bā′) *n.* The hospital and dispensary of a ship.

sick·bed (sĭk′bĕd′) *n.* A sick person's bed.

sick·en (sĭk′ən) *v.* To make or become sick.

ă pat ā pay â care ä father ĕ pet ē be ĭ pit ī tie î pier ŏ pot ō toe ô paw, for oi noise ōō took ōō boot ou out th thin th this ŭ cut û urge yōō abuse zh vision ə about, item, edible, gallop, circus

sick·en·ing (sĭk′ə-nĭng) adj. 1. Causing sickness. 2. Revolting or disgusting. —**sick′en·ing·ly** adv.

sick·le (sĭk′əl) n. A tool with a curved blade attached to a short handle, for cutting grain or tall grass. [< Lat. secula.]

sickle

sidecar

sickle cell anemia n. A hereditary anemia characterized by the presence of oxygen-deficient, abnormally crescent-shaped red blood cells, episodic pain, and leg ulcers.

sick·ly (sĭk′lē) adj. -li·er, -li·est. 1. Prone to sickness; frail. 2. Of or associated with sickness: a sickly pallor. 3. Nauseating; sickening. 4. Feeble; weak.

side (sīd) n. 1. A surface of an object, esp. a surface joining a top and a bottom. 2. Either of the two surfaces of a flat object, such as a piece of paper. 3. The left or right half in reference to a vertical axis, as of the body. 4. The space immediately next to someone or something: stood at her side. 5. An area separated from another by some intervening line, barrier, or other feature: on this side of the Atlantic. 6. One of two or more opposing groups, teams, or sets of opinions. 7. A distinct aspect of something: the cruel side of her nature. 8. Line of descent. —adj. 1. Located on a side: a side door. 2. From or to one side; oblique: a side view. 3. Minor; incidental: a side interest. 4. Supplementary: a side benefit. —v. **sid·ed, sid·ing.** To align oneself with a particular side. —**idioms. on the side.** In addition to the main portion, occupation, or arrangement. **side by side.** Next to each other. **take sides.** To associate oneself with a faction or cause. [< OE sīde.]

side·arm (sīd′ärm′) adj. Thrown with or marked by a sweep of the arm between shoulder and hip height. —**side′arm′** adv.

side arm n. A small weapon carried at the side or waist.

side·board (sīd′bôrd′, -bōrd′) n. A piece of dining-room furniture with drawers for linens and tableware.

side·burns (sīd′bûrnz′) pl.n. Growths of hair down the sides of the face in front of the ears. [< Ambrose E. Burnside (1824–81).]

side·car (sīd′kär′) n. A one-wheeled passenger car attached to the side of a motorcycle.

side effect n. A secondary, usu. undesirable effect, esp. of a drug.

side·kick (sīd′kĭk′) n. Slang. A close companion; pal.

side·light (sīd′līt′) n. Incidental information.

side·line (sīd′līn′) n. 1. A line along either of the two sides of a playing court or field, marking its limits. 2. A secondary job, activity, or line of merchandise. —v. **-lined, -lin·ing.** To remove or keep from active participation.

side·long (sīd′lông′, -lŏng′) adj. Directed to one side; sideways: a sidelong glance. —**side′long′** adv.

side·man (sīd′măn′) n. An instrumentalist in a band.

si·de·re·al (sī-dîr′ē-əl) adj. Of, concerned with, or measured by the stars: sidereal time. [< Lat. siderus.]

side·sad·dle (sīd′săd′l) n. A saddle designed so that a rider may sit with both legs on one side of the horse. —adv. On a sidesaddle.

side show n. 1. A minor show offered in addition to the main attraction. 2. A diverting spectacle.

side·step (sīd′stĕp′) v. 1. To step out of the way of. 2. To evade; skirt.

side stroke n. A swimming stroke in which a person swims on one side and thrusts his arms forward alternately while performing a scissors kick.

side·swipe (sīd′swīp′) v. -swiped, -swip·ing. To strike along the side in passing. —n. A glancing blow.

side·track (sīd′trăk′) v. 1. To switch from a main track to a siding. 2. To divert from a main issue or course. —n. A railroad siding.

side·walk (sīd′wôk′) n. A usu. paved walk along the side of a road.

side wall n. A side surface of an automobile tire.

side·ways (sīd′wāz′) adv. 1. Toward or from one side. 2. With one side forward. —adj. Toward or from one side.

sid·ing (sī′dĭng) n. 1. A short section of railroad track connected by switches with a main track. 2. Material, as shingles, used for surfacing a frame building.

si·dle (sīd′l) v. -dled, -dling. To move sideways or edge along. [< SIDELONG.]

siege (sēj) n. 1. The surrounding and blockading of a town or fortress by an army bent on capturing it. 2. A prolonged attack, as of illness. [< Lat. sedēre, to be seated.]

si·er·ra (sē-ĕr′ə) n. A rugged range of mountains having a jagged outline. [Sp. < Lat. serra, saw.]

si·es·ta (sē-ĕs′tə) n. An afternoon rest or nap. [< Lat. sexta (hora), 6th (hour).]

sieve (sĭv) n. A utensil of wire mesh or closely perforated metal, used for straining, sifting, or draining. [< OE sife.]

sift (sĭft) v. 1. To put through a sieve to separate fine from coarse particles. 2. To pass through or as through a sieve. 3. To examine closely and carefully: sift through the evidence. [< OE siftan.] —**sift′er** n.

sigh (sī) v. 1. To exhale in a long, audible breath, as in sorrow or relief. 2. To feel longing or grief. —n. The act or sound of sighing. [< OE sīcan.]

sight (sīt) n. 1. The ability to see. 2. The act or fact of seeing. 3. The field of a person's vision. 4. A view. 5. Something worth seeing. 6. Informal. Something unsightly. 7. A device used to assist aim by guiding the eye, as on a firearm. —v. 1. To see within one's field of vision: sight land. 2. To take aim with. [< OE sihth.]

sight·ed (sī′tĭd) adj. Having sight.

sight·ly (sīt′lē) adj. -li·er, -li·est. Pleasing to see; handsome. —**sight′li·ness** n.

sight-read (sīt′rēd′) v. To read or perform, as music, without preparation or prior acquaintance. —**sight′-read′er** n.

sight·see·ing (sīt′sē′ĭng) n. The act of touring places of interest. —**sight′se′er** n.

sig·ma (sĭg′mə) n. The 18th letter of the Greek alphabet. See table at **alphabet.** [Gk.]

sign (sīn) n. **1.** Something that suggests the existence of a fact, condition, or quality; indication. **2.** An action or gesture used to convey an idea. **3.** A board, poster, or placard displayed to convey information or a direction. **4.** A conventional figure or device that stands for a word, phrase, or operation. **5.** An omen; presage. **6.** Astrol. One of the 12 divisions of the zodiac. —v. **1.** To affix one's signature to. **2.** To write (one's signature). **3.** To approve or ratify (a document) by affixing a signature, seal, or other mark. **4.** To hire by obtaining a signature on a contract. **5.** To relinquish or transfer title to by signature. **6.** To express or signify with a sign. —phrasal verbs. **sign off.** To stop broadcasting. **sign up.** To volunteer one's services; enlist. [< Lat. signum.] —**sign′er** n.

Syns: sign, evidence, indication, indicator, manifestation, mark, symptom, token n.

sig·nal (sĭg′nəl) n. **1.** A sign, gesture, device, or other indicator serving as a means of communication. **2. a.** An impulse or fluctuating electric quantity, such as voltage or current, the variations of which represent coded information. **b.** Information so represented. —adj. Remarkable; conspicuous. —v. **-naled** or **-nalled, -nal·ing** or **-nal·ling. 1.** To make a signal or signals (to). **2.** To relate or make known by signals. [< Lat. signalis, of a sign.] —**sig′nal·ly** adv.

sig·nal·ize (sĭg′nə-līz′) v. **-ized, -iz·ing. 1.** To make remarkable or noticeable. **2.** To point out particularly.

sig·na·to·ry (sĭg′nə-tôr′ē, -tōr′ē) adj. Bound by a signed agreement. —n., pl. **-ries.** One that signs or has signed a treaty or other agreement.

sig·na·ture (sĭg′nə-chŏŏr′, -chər) n. **1.** The name of a person as written by that person. **2.** A distinctive mark, characteristic, or sound effect. **3.** A symbol on a musical staff used to indicate tempo. [< Lat. signare, to mark with a sign.]

sign·board (sīn′bôrd′, -bōrd′) n. A board bearing a sign.

sig·net (sĭg′nĭt) n. A seal, esp. a seal used to stamp official documents. [< OFr.]

sig·nif·i·cance (sĭg-nĭf′ĭ-kəns) n. **1.** The condition or quality of being significant. **2.** The sense of something; meaning. **3.** Implied meaning; suggestiveness.

sig·nif·i·cant (sĭg-nĭf′ĭ-kənt) adj. **1.** Having or expressing a meaning; meaningful. **2.** Suggestive: a significant glance. **3.** Important; notable. [< Lat. significare.] —**sig·nif′i·cant·ly** adv.

sig·ni·fy (sĭg′nə-fī′) v. **-fied, -fy·ing. 1.** To serve as a sign or symbol of; betoken. **2.** To make known; indicate. [< Lat. significare.] —**sig′ni·fi·ca′tion** n. —**sig′ni·fi′er** n.

sign language n. A system of communication by means of hand gestures.

sign·post (sīn′pōst′) n. **1.** A post supporting a sign. **2.** An indicator; guide.

Sikh (sēk) n. A member of a monotheistic religious sect of India founded in the 16th cent. —**Sikh** adj. —**Sikh′ism** n.

si·lage (sī′lĭj) n. Green fodder that has been stored and fermented in a silo.

si·lence (sī′ləns) n. **1.** The absence of sound; stillness. **2.** The absence or avoidance of speech or noise. **3.** Refusal or failure to speak out. —v. **-lenced, -lenc·ing. 1.** To make silent. **2.** To suppress.

si·lenc·er (sī′lən-sər) n. A device muffling the sound of a firearm.

si·lent (sī′lənt) adj. **1.** Making no sound or noise; quiet. **2.** Not disposed to speak; taciturn. **3.** Unable to speak; mute. **4.** Not voiced or expressed; tacit. **5.** Unpronounced, as the b in subtle. [< Lat. silēre, to be silent.] —**si′lent·ly** adv.

sil·hou·ette (sĭl′ŏŏ-ĕt′) n. **1.** A drawing consisting of the outline of something, usu. filled in with a solid color. **2.** An outline. —v. **-et·ted, -et·ting.** To cause to be seen as a silhouette; outline. [< Étienne de Silhouette (1709–67).]

silhouette

sil·i·ca (sĭl′ĭ-kə) n. A crystalline compound, SiO_2, that occurs abundantly as quartz, sand, and other minerals. [< Lat. silex, flint.]

sil·i·cate (sĭl′ĭ-kāt′, -kĭt) n. A compound that contains silicon, oxygen, and a metallic or organic radical.

si·li·ceous (sĭ-lĭsh′əs) adj. Containing or resembling silica. [Lat. siliceus, of flint.]

sil·i·con (sĭl′ĭ-kən, -kŏn′) n. Symbol **Si** A nonmetallic element that occurs extensively in the earth's crust, has both an amorphous and a crystalline allotrope, and is used in glass, semiconducting devices, concrete, brick, refractories, pottery, and silicones. Atomic number 14; atomic weight 28.086. [< SILICA.]

sil·i·cone (sĭl′ĭ-kōn′) n. Any of a group of semi-inorganic polymers based on the structural unit R_2SiO, where R is an organic group, characterized by wide-range thermal stability and used in adhesives, lubricants, protective coatings, and synthetic rubber.

sil·i·co·sis (sĭl′ĭ-kō′sĭs) n. Fibrosis of the lungs caused by long-term inhalation of silica dust.

silk (sĭlk) n. **1. a.** The fine, glossy fiber produced by a silkworm to form its cocoon. **b.** A similar fine fiber produced by spiders or by certain insect larvae. **2.** Thread or fabric made from the fiber produced by silkworms. [< OE sioloc.] —**silk′en** adj. —**silk′i·ness** n. —**silk′y** adj.

silk screen n. A stencil method in which ink is forced through a design-bearing screen of silk or other fabric onto the printing surface. —**silk′-screen′** v.

sill (sĭl) n. A horizontal support that holds up the upright part of a frame, esp. the base of a window. [< OE *sylle*, threshold.]

sil·ly (sĭl′ē) adj. **-li·er, -li·est.** 1. Showing a lack of good sense; foolish; stupid. 2. Frivolous. [< OE *gesǣlig*, blessed.] —**sil′li·ness** n.

si·lo (sī′lō) n., pl. **-los.** 1. A tall, cylindrical structure in which fodder is stored. 2. An underground shelter for a missile. [< Gk. *siros*, pit for storing grain.]

silt (sĭlt) n. Fine mineral particles found at the bottom of bodies of water. —v. To fill or become filled with silt. [ME *cylte*.]

Si·lu·ri·an (sĭ-lŏŏr′ē-ən, sī-) adj. Of or belonging to the geologic time, system of rocks, or sedimentary deposits of the 3rd period of the Paleozoic era. —n. The Silurian period.

sil·ver (sĭl′vər) n. 1. *Symbol* **Ag** A lustrous, white, ductile, malleable metallic element, highly valued for jewelry, tableware, and other ornamental use and widely used in coinage, photography, dental and soldering alloys, electrical contacts, and printed circuits. Atomic number 47; atomic weight 107.870. 2. Coins made of silver. 3. Tableware and other articles made of or plated with silver. 4. A light, shiny, or metallic gray. —adj. 1. Of the color silver. 2. Eloquent; persuasive: *a silver tongue.* 3. Of or designating a 25th anniversary. —v. To cover, plate, or decorate with silver or a similar lustrous substance. [< OE *siolfor*.]

silver bromide n. A pale-yellow crystalline compound, AgBr, used as the light-sensitive component on photographic films.

sil·ver·fish (sĭl′vər-fĭsh′) n. A silvery, wingless insect that often damages bookbindings and starched clothing.

silver iodide n. A pale-yellow powder, AgI, used in artificial rainmaking, photography, and medicine.

silver nitrate n. A poisonous, colorless crystalline compound, AgNO₃, used in photography, mirror manufacturing, hair dyeing, silver plating, and medicine.

sil·ver·smith (sĭl′vər-smĭth′) n. One who makes, repairs, or replates articles of silver.

sil·ver·ware (sĭl′vər-wâr′) n. Articles made of or plated with silver, esp. tableware.

sil·ver·y (sĭl′vər-ē) adj. 1. Containing or coated with silver. 2. Resembling or suggestive of silver. —**sil′ver·i·ness** n.

sim·i·an (sĭm′ē-ən) adj. Of or like an ape or monkey. —n. An ape or monkey. [< Lat. *simia*, ape.]

sim·i·lar (sĭm′ə-lər) adj. Showing some resemblance; alike though not identical. [< Lat. *similis*, like.] —**sim′i·lar′i·ty** (-lăr′ĭ-tē) n. —**sim′i·lar·ly** adv.

sim·i·le (sĭm′ə-lē) n. A figure of speech in which two essentially unlike things are compared, often in a phrase introduced by *like* or *as*, as in *eyes like stars.* [< Lat., like.]

si·mil·i·tude (sĭ-mĭl′ĭ-tōōd′, -tyōōd′) n. Similarity; resemblance. [< Lat. *similitudo.*]

sim·mer (sĭm′ər) v. 1. To cook gently below or just at the boiling point. 2. To be filled with barely controlled emotion; seethe. —*phrasal verb.* **simmer down.** To become calm after anger or excitement. —n. The condition or process of simmering. [ME *simperen.*]

si·mo·ny (sĭm′ə-nē, sī′mə-) n. The buying or selling of ecclesiastical pardons, offices, or emoluments. [< *Simon* Magus, who tried to buy spiritual powers from the Apostle Peter.]

sim·pa·ti·co (sĭm-pä′tĭ-kō′, -păt′ĭ-) adj. 1. Compatible. 2. Attractive; pleasing. [Ital.]

sim·per (sĭm′pər) v. To smile in a silly or self-conscious manner. [Of Scand. orig.] —**sim′per** n. —**sim′per·er** n.

sim·ple (sĭm′pəl) adj. **-pler, -plest.** 1. Having only a single part or unit. 2. Not involved or complicated; easy. 3. Bare; mere: *a simple "yes" or "no."* 4. Not ornate or adorned: *a simple dress.* 5. Unassuming or unpretentious. 6. Humble or lowly in condition or rank. 7. Not important or significant; trivial. 8. Having or manifesting little sense or intellect. [< Lat. *simplus.*]

sim·ple-mind·ed (sĭm′pəl-mīn′dĭd) adj. 1. Not sophisticated; naive. 2. Stupid or silly. 3. Mentally defective. —**sim′ple-mind′ed·ly** adv. —**sim′ple-mind′ed·ness** n.

sim·ple·ton (sĭm′pəl-tən) n. A silly or stupid person; fool. [< SIMPLE.]

sim·plic·i·ty (sĭm-plĭs′ĭ-tē) n., pl. **-ties.** 1. The property, condition, or quality of being simple. 2. Absence of luxury or showiness; plainness. 3. Absence of affectation or pretense. 4. Foolishness. [< Lat. *simplicitas.*]

sim·pli·fy (sĭm′plə-fī′) v. **-fied, -fy·ing.** To make simple or simpler. —**sim′pli·fi·ca′tion** n. —**sim′pli·fi′er** n.

sim·ply (sĭm′plē) adv. 1. In a simple manner; plainly. 2. Merely; just. 3. Absolutely; altogether: *simply delicious.*

sim·u·late (sĭm′yə-lāt′) v. **-lat·ed, -lat·ing.** 1. To have or take on the appearance of. 2. To pretend; feign. [Lat. *simulare.*] —**sim′u·la′tion** n. —**sim′u·la′tor** n.

si·mul·cast (sī′məl-kăst′, sĭm′əl-) v. To broadcast simultaneously by FM and AM radio or by radio and television. [SIMUL(TANEOUS) + (BROAD)CAST.] —**sī′mul·cast′** n.

si·mul·ta·ne·ous (sī′məl-tā′nē-əs, sĭm′əl-) adj. Happening, existing, or done at the same time. [Lat. *simul*, at the same time + (IN-STAN)TANEOUS.] —**sī′mul·ta′ne·ous·ly** adv. —**sī′mul·ta′ne·ous·ness** or **sī′mul·ta·ne′i·ty** (-tə-nē′ĭ-tē, -nā′-) n.

sin¹ (sĭn) n. 1. A transgression of a religious or moral law. 2. A serious offense or fault. —v. **sinned, sin·ning.** To commit a sin. [< OE *synn.*] —**sin′less** adj. —**sin′ner** n.

sin² (sēn, sĭn) n. The 21st letter of the Hebrew alphabet. See table at **alphabet.** [Heb.]

since (sĭns) adv. 1. From then until now or between then and now: *He left town and hasn't been here since.* 2. Before now; ago: *long since forgotten.* —conj. 1. During the time after which: *He hasn't been home since he graduated.* 2. Continuously from the time when: *He hasn't spoken since he sat down.* 3. As a result of the fact that: *Since you're not interested, I won't tell you.* —prep. From that time in the past: *Since last month's upset, the team has been winning.* [< OE *siththan.*]

sin·cere (sĭn-sîr′) adj. **-cer·er, -cer·est.** Without false appearance or nature; true. [Lat. *sincerus.*] —**sin·cere′ly** adv. —**sin·cer′i·ty** (-sĕr′ĭ-tē) n.

si·ne·cure (sī′nĭ-kyŏŏr′, sĭn′ĭ-) n. A salaried position that requires little or no work. [< Med. Lat. *sine cura*, without care (of souls).]

si·ne di·e (sī′nĭ dī′ē, sĭn′ā dē′ā) adv. Without a future time specified; indefinitely. [Lat., without a day.]

si·ne qua non (sĭn′ĭ kwä nŏn′, nŏn′, sī′nĭ kwä nŏn′) n. An indispensable condition or element. [Lat., without which not.]

sin·ew (sĭn′yōō) n. 1. A tendon. 2. Vigorous strength. [< OE *sinu*.] —**sin′ew·y** adj.

sin·ful (sĭn′fəl) adj. Marked by or full of sin; wicked. —**sin′ful·ly** adv. —**sin′ful·ness** n.

sing (sĭng) v. **sang** (săng) or **sung** (sŭng), **sung, sing·ing.** 1. To utter a series of words or sounds in musical tones. 2. To render in tones with musical inflections of the voice. 3. To proclaim or extol, esp. in verse. 4. To bring to a specified state by singing: *sang him to sleep.* 5. *Slang.* To give information or evidence against someone. —n. A gathering of people for group singing. [< OE *singan.*] —**sing′er** n.

singe (sĭnj) v. **singed, singe·ing.** 1. To burn slightly; scorch. 2. To burn off the feathers or bristles of. [< OE *sengan.*]

Sin·gha·lese (sĭng′gə-lēz′, -lēs′) n., pl. **-lese.** Also **Sin·ha·lese** (sĭn′hə-). 1. A people constituting the major portion of the population of Sri Lanka. 2. The Indic language of the Singhalese. —**Sin′gha·lese′** adj.

sin·gle (sĭng′gəl) adj. 1. One only; lone; solitary. 2. Consisting of one form or part. 3. Separate; individual: *every single one of them.* 4. Designed to accommodate one person: *a single bed.* 5. Unmarried. —n. 1. A separate thing or person; individual. 2. An accommodation for one person. 3. An unmarried person. 4. A one-dollar bill. 5. *Baseball.* A one-base hit. 6. **singles.** A match between two players in tennis and other games. —v. **-gled, -gling.** 1. To choose or distinguish from among others: *singled out for praise.* 2. Baseball. To make a one-base hit. [< Lat. *singulus.*] —**sin′gle·ness** n.

Syns: single, discrete, individual, separate, singular *adj.*

sin·gle-breast·ed (sĭng′gəl-brĕs′tĭd) adj. Closing with a narrow overlap and fastened with a single row of buttons: *a single-breasted jacket.*

sin·gle-hand·ed (sĭng′gəl-hăn′dĭd) adj. 1. Working or done without help; unassisted. 2. Having, using, or requiring only one hand. —**sin′gle-hand′ed·ly** adv.

sin·gle-mind·ed (sĭng′gəl-mīn′dĭd) adj. 1. Having one overriding purpose or opinion. 2. Steadfast. —**sin′gle-mind′ed·ly** adv. —**sin′gle-mind′ed·ness** n.

singles bar n. A bar patronized esp. by unmarried people.

sin·gle·ton (sĭng′gəl-tən) n. A single thing, esp. a playing card that is the only one of its suit in a player's hand. [< SINGLE.]

sin·gly (sĭng′glē) adv. 1. Alone. 2. One by one; individually.

sing·song (sĭng′sŏng′, -sŏng′) n. Monotonous regularity of rhythm or rhyme. —**sing′song′** adj.

sin·gu·lar (sĭng′gyə-lər) adj. 1. Being only one; single. 2. *Gram.* Denoting a single person or thing or a group considered as one. 3. Extraordinary; rare: *singular good fortune.* 4. Very strange; peculiar. —n. *Gram.* The form taken by a word indicating one person or thing or a group considered as one. [<

Lat. *singularis,* single.] —**sin′gu·lar′i·ty** (-lăr′ĭ-tĕ) or **sin′gu·lar·ness** n. —**sin′gu·lar·ly** adv.

Sin·ha·lese (sĭn′hə-lēz′, -lēs′) n. Var. of **Singhalese.**

sin·is·ter (sĭn′ĭ-stər) adj. 1. Suggesting an evil force or motive. 2. Promising trouble; ominous. [< Lat., on the left.] —**sin′is·ter·ly** adv.

sink (sĭngk) v. **sank** (săngk) or **sunk** (sŭngk), **sunk** or **sunk·en** (sŭng′kən), **sink·ing.** 1. To submerge beneath the surface or descend to the bottom of a liquid or soft substance. 2. To descend slowly or in stages. 3. To force into the ground. 4. To dig or drill (a mine or well) in the earth. 5. To pass into a worsened physical condition; approach death. 6. To become weaker, quieter, or less forceful. 7. To diminish or decline. 8. To penetrate the mind; become understood: *The facts sank in finally.* 9. To invest. 10. To get the ball into the hole or basket, as in golf, pool, or basketball. —n. A basin fixed to a wall or floor and having a drainpipe and gen. a piped water supply. [< OE *sincan.*] —**sink′a·ble** adj.

sink·er (sĭng′kər) n. A weight used for sinking fishing lines or nets.

sink·hole (sĭngk′hōl′) n. A natural depression in a land surface communicating with an underground passage, gen. occurring in limestone regions and formed by solution or collapse of a cavern roof.

sinking fund n. A fund accumulated to pay off a public or corporate debt.

Sino- pref. Chinese: Sinology. [< Ar. *Sīn,* China.]

Si·nol·o·gy (sī-nŏl′ə-jē, sĭ-) n. The study of the Chinese language, literature, and people. —**Si·nol′o·gist** n.

Si·no-Ti·bet·an (sī′nō-tĭ-bĕt′n, sĭn′ō-) n. A linguistic group that includes Tibeto-Burman.

sin·u·ous (sĭn′yōō-əs) adj. Having many curves or turns; winding. [Lat. *sinuosus.*] —**sin′u·os′i·ty** (-ŏs′ĭ-tĕ) n. —**sin′u·ous·ly** adv.

si·nus (sī′nəs) n. 1. A depression or cavity formed by a bending or curving. 2. Any of various air-filled cavities in the bones of the skull, esp. one that connects with the nostrils. [Lat., curve.]

si·nus·i·tis (sī′nə-sī′tĭs) n. Inflammation of a sinus membrane, esp. in the nasal region.

Si·on (sī′ən) n. Var. of **Zion.**

Siou·an (sōō′ən) n. A large family of North American Indian languages spoken over an extensive area of the Midwest. —**Siou′an** adj.

Sioux (sōō) n., pl. **Sioux.** 1. a. A group of tribes of Plains Indians formerly living in the Dakotas, Minnesota, and Nebraska. b. A member of any of these tribes. 2. Any of the Siouan languages of these tribes. —**Sioux** adj.

sip (sĭp) v. **sipped, sip·ping.** To drink delicately and in small quantities. —n. 1. The act of sipping. 2. A small quantity of liquid sipped. [ME *sippen.*]

si·phon (sī′fən). Also **sy·phon.** —n. A pipe or tube in the form of an inverted U, filled with liquid and arranged so that the pressure of the atmosphere forces liquid from a container to flow through the tube, over a barrier, and into a lower container. —v. To draw off through or as if through a siphon. [< Gk. *siphōn,* tube.]

ă pat ā pay â care ä father ĕ pet ē be ĭ pit ī tie î pier ŏ pot ō toe ô paw, for oi noise ōō took
ōō boot ou out th thin th this ŭ cut û urge yōō abuse zh vision ə about, item, edible, gallop, circus

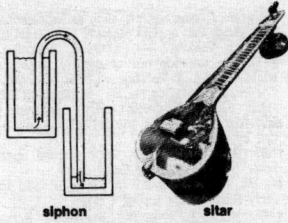

siphon   **sitar**

sir (sûr) *n.* **1.** Often **Sir.** A polite form of address used instead of a man's name. **2. Sir.** A title of honor used before the name of baronets and knights. [< **SIRE.**]

sire (sīr) *n.* **1.** A father or forefather. **2.** The male parent of an animal. **3.** *Archaic.* A title and form of address to a superior. —*v.* **sired, sir-ing.** To beget. [< Lat. *senior,* older.]

si-ren (sī'rən) *n.* **1.** Often **Siren.** *Gk. Myth.* One of a group of sea nymphs whose sweet singing lured sailors to their destruction. **2.** A beautiful or captivating woman. **3.** A device for making a loud whistling or wailing sound as a signal or warning. [< Gk. *Seirēn.*]

Siri-us (sîr'ē-əs) *n.* A star in the constellation Canis Major, the brightest star in the night sky.

sir-loin (sûr'loin') *n.* A cut of meat from the upper part of the loin. [OFr. *surlonge.*]

si-roc-co (sĭ-rŏk'ō) *n., pl.* **-cos. 1.** A hot south or southeast wind of southern Europe that originates in the Sahara. **2.** A warm southerly wind. [< Ar. *sharq,* east.]

sirup (sĭr'əp, sûr'-) *n.* Var. of **syrup.**

sis (sĭs) *n. Informal.* Sister.

si-sal (sī'zəl, -səl) *n.* A cordage fiber obtained from the leaves of a Mexican plant. [< *Sisal,* Mexico.]

sis-sy (sĭs'ē) *n., pl.* **-sies. 1.** An effeminate boy or man. **2.** A timid person. [< **SIS.**]

sis-ter (sĭs'tər) *n.* **1.** A female having the same mother and father as another person. **2.** A female who shares a common ancestry, allegiance, or purpose with another. **3. Sister.** A nun. —*adj.* Of the same kind or design: *sister ships.* [< OE *sweostor.*] —**sis'ter-ly** *adj.*

sis-ter-hood (sĭs'tər-hŏŏd') *n.* **1.** The relationship of being a sister or sisters. **2.** The quality of being sisterly. **3.** A group of women united by a common purpose.

sis-ter-in-law (sĭs'tər-ĭn-lô') *n., pl.* **sis-ters-in-law. 1.** The sister of one's husband or wife. **2.** The wife of one's brother. **3.** The wife of the brother of one's spouse.

sit (sĭt) *v.* **sat** (săt), **sit-ting. 1.** To rest with the body supported on the buttocks or hindquarters. **2.** To perch, as a bird. **3.** To rest on and cover eggs for hatching. **4.** To maintain a seated position on (a horse). **5.** To be situated; lie. **6.** To pose for an artist or photographer. **7.** To be in session. **8.** To remain inactive or unused. **9.** To baby-sit. **10.** To cause to sit; seat. —*phrasal verbs.* **sit in on.** To attend or participate in. **sit on.** *Informal.* To suppress or repress: *sit on the evidence.* **sit up.** To become suddenly alert. —*Idiom.* **sit tight.** *Informal.* To be patient and await the next move. [< OE *sittan.*] —**sit'ter** *n.*

si-tar (sĭ-tär') *n.* A stringed instrument used in Hindu music, with a long, fretted neck and usu. 6 or 7 playing strings. [Hindi *sitār.*] —**si-tar'ist** *n.*

sit-down (sĭt'doun') *n.* **1.** A work stoppage in which the workers refuse to leave their place of employment until they reach an agreement. **2.** An obstruction of normal activity, as of an office, by the act of a large group sitting down to express a grievance or protest.

site (sīt) *n.* The place or plot of land where something was, is, or is to be located. —*v.* **sit-ed, sit-ing.** To situate or locate. [< Lat. *situs,* place.]

sit-in (sĭt'ĭn') *n.* A work stoppage in which the workers refuse to leave their place of employment until their demands are considered or met.

sit-ting (sĭt'ĭng) *n.* **1.** A period during which one is seated and occupied with a single activity. **2.** A term or session, as of a legislature.

sit-u-ate (sĭch'ōō-āt') *v.* **-at-ed, -at-ing.** To place in a certain spot; locate. [Med. Lat. *situare.*]

sit-u-a-tion (sĭch'ōō-ā'shən) *n.* **1.** Location; position. **2.** A state of affairs. **3.** A job. —**sit'u-a'tion-al** *adj.*

situation comedy *n.* A humorous television series with a continuing cast of characters.

sit-up (sĭt'ŭp') *n.* A form of exercise in which a person lying on his back rises to a sitting position without the support of the arms.

Si-van (sĭv'ən) *n.* The 9th month of the Hebrew year. See table at **calendar.** [Heb. *sîwān.*]

six (sĭks) *n.* **1.** The cardinal number equal to the sum of 5 + 1. **2.** The 6th in a set or sequence. **3.** Something having six parts, units, or members, esp. a motor vehicle having six cylinders. —*Idiom.* **at sixes and sevens.** In a state of confusion or disorder. [< OE *siex.*] —**six** *adj. & pron.*

six-pack (sĭks'păk') *n.* Six units of a commodity, esp. six containers of a beverage sold in a pack.

six-shoot-er (sĭks'shōō'tər) *n. Informal.* A revolver that fires six times.

six-teen (sĭk'stēn') *n.* **1.** The cardinal number equal to the sum of 15 + 1. **2.** The 16th in a set or sequence. —**six-teen'** *adj. & pron.*

six-teenth (sĭk'stēnth') *n.* **1.** The ordinal number that matches the number 16 in a series. **2.** One of 16 equal parts. —**six-teenth'** *adj. & adv.*

sixth (sĭksth) *n.* **1.** The ordinal number that matches the number 6 in a series. **2.** One of six equal parts. **3.** *Mus.* **a.** An interval of six degrees in a diatonic scale. **b.** A tone separated by this interval from a given tone. **c.** The harmonic combination of two tones separated by this interval. **d.** The sixth tone of a diatonic scale. —**sixth** *adj. & adv.*

six-ti-eth (sĭks'stē-ĭth) *n.* **1.** The ordinal number that matches the number 60 in a series. **2.** One of 60 equal parts. —**six'ti-eth** *adj. & adv.*

six-ty (sĭk'stē) *n., pl.* **-ties.** The cardinal number equal to 6 × 10. —**six'ty** *adj. & pron.*

siz-a-ble (sī'zə-bəl) *adj.* Also **size-a-ble.** Of considerable size; fairly large. —**siz'a-bly** *adv.*

size¹ (sīz) *n.* **1.** The physical dimensions, magnitude, or extent of something. **2.** Any of a series of graduated dimensions whereby manufactured articles are classified. —*v.* **sized, siz-ing.** To arrange according to size.

—*phrasal verb.* **size up.** To make an estimate or judgment of. [< OFr. *sise.*]

size² (sīz) *n.* A gluey substance used as a glaze or filler for materials such as paper, cloth, or wall surfaces. —*v.* **sized, siz·ing.** To treat or coat with size. [ME *syse.*]

siz·ing (sī'zĭng) *n.* A glaze or filler; size.

siz·zle (sĭz'əl) *v.* **-zled, -zling.** 1. To make the hissing sound of frying fat. 2. To seethe with anger. 3. To be very hot. —*n.* A hissing sound. [Imit.] —**siz'zle** *n.*

skate¹ (skāt) *n.* 1. A shoe or metal frame having a bladelike metal runner fixed to its sole, enabling the wearer to glide over ice. 2. A roller skate. [< ONFr. *escace,* stilt.] —**skate** *v.* —**skat'er** *n.*

skate² (skāt) *n.* A saltwater fish having a flattened body with fins that form winglike lateral extensions. [< ON *skata.*]

skate·board (skāt'bôrd', -bōrd') *n.* A short, narrow board mounted on roller-skate wheels. —**skate'board'** *v.*

skeet (skēt) *n.* A form of trapshooting in which clay targets are used to simulate birds in flight. [< ON *skjōta,* to shoot.]

skein (skān) *n.* A length of thread or yarn wound in a loose, long coil. [< OFr. *escaigne.*]

skel·e·ton (skĕl'ĭ-tn) *n.* 1. **a.** The internal supporting structure of a vertebrate, composed of bone and cartilage. **b.** A hard external supporting and protecting structure, as of a crustacean or turtle. 2. A supporting structure or framework. 3. An outline or sketch. [< Gk. *skeletos,* dried up.] —**skel'e·tal** *adj.*

skeleton key *n.* A key that can open many different locks.

skep·tic (skĕp'tĭk) *n.* Also **scep·tic.** 1. One who habitually doubts, questions, or disagrees. 2. One inclined to skepticism in philosophical or religious matters. [< Gk. *skeptesthai,* to examine.] —**skep'ti·cal** *adj.* —**skep'ti·cal·ly** *adv.*

skep·ti·cism (skĕp'tĭ-sĭz'əm) *n.* Also **scep·ti·cism.** 1. A doubting or questioning attitude or state of mind. 2. The philosophical doctrine that absolute knowledge is impossible. 3. Doubt or disbelief of religious tenets.

sketch (skĕch) *n.* 1. A hasty or undetailed drawing or painting. 2. A brief outline, as of a book to be completed. 3. **a.** A brief essay or literary composition. **b.** A short scene or play, often satirical in tone. —*v.* To make a sketch (of). [< Ital. *schizzo.*] —**sketch'i·ly** *adv.* —**sketch'i·ness** *n.* —**sketch'y** *adj.*

skew (skyōō) *v.* To turn or place at an angle; slant. —*adj.* Turned or placed to one side. —*n.* A slant. [< ONFr. *eskiuer,* to avoid.]

skew·er (skyōō'ər) *n.* A long pin used to secure or suspend food during cooking. [< dial. *skiver.*] —**skew'er** *v.*

ski (skē) *n., pl.* **skis** or **ski.** One of a pair of long, flat runners attached to a boot for gliding over snow. —*v.* **skied, ski·ing.** To travel on skis, esp. as a sport. [< ON *skith.*] —**ski'er** *n.* —**ski'ing** *n.*

skid (skĭd) *n.* 1. The act of slipping or sliding over a surface. 2. **a.** A plank or log used for sliding or rolling heavy objects. **b.** A small platform for stacking merchandise to be moved. 3. A runner forming part of the land-

ing gear of some aircraft, such as helicopters. 4. A wedge that applies pressure to a wheel to brake a vehicle. —*v.* **skidded, skid·ding.** 1. To slip or slide out of control sideways while moving. 2. To slide without revolving: *The wheel skidded on the ice.* —**idiom. on the skids.** *Slang.* In decline. [Orig. unknown.]

skid row *n. Slang.* A squalid district inhabited by derelicts.

skiff (skĭf) *n.* A small, flat-bottomed open boat. [< Ital. *schifo,* of Gmc. orig.]

ski lift *n.* A power-driven conveyor used to carry skiers to the top of a slope.

skill (skĭl) *n.* 1. Proficiency; expertness. 2. An art, trade, or technique, esp. one that requires use of the hands or body. [< ON *skil.*] —**skilled** *adj.*

skil·let (skĭl'ĭt) *n.* A frying pan. [ME *skelet.*]

skill·ful (skĭl'fəl) *adj.* Also *chiefly Brit.* **skil·ful.** 1. Possessing or exercising skill. 2. Characterized by or requiring skill. —**skill'ful·ly** *adv.* —**skill'ful·ness** *n.*

skim (skĭm) *v.* **skimmed, skim·ming.** 1. To remove floating matter from (a liquid). 2. To remove (floating matter) from a liquid. 3. To glide or pass quickly and lightly over. 4. To read or glance through quickly or superficially. [ME *skymmen.*]

skim milk *n.* Milk from which the cream has been removed.

skimp (skĭmp) *v.* 1. To do carelessly or with poor material. 2. To be extremely sparing with; scrimp. [Poss. < SCRIMP.]

skimp·y (skĭm'pē) *adj.* **-i·er, -i·est.** 1. Inadequate in size or amount; scanty. 2. Stingy; niggardly. —**skimp'i·ly** *adv.*

skin (skĭn) *n.* 1. The membranous tissue that forms the outer covering of an animal. 2. An animal hide or pelt. 3. An outer layer or covering, as the rind of fruit. —*v.* **skinned, skin·ning.** 1. To remove skin from. 2. To injure by scraping. 3. *Slang.* To cheat; swindle. —**idiom. by the skin of (one's) teeth.** By the smallest margin. [< ON *skinn.*] —**skin'less** *adj.*

skin diving *n.* Underwater swimming, often with flippers, a face mask, and a snorkel or scuba. —**skin'-dive'** *v.* —**skin diver** *n.*

skin flick *n.* A pornographic film.

skin·flint (skĭn'flĭnt') *n.* A miser.

skin·ny (skĭn'ē) *adj.* **-ni·er, -ni·est.** Very thin. —**skin'ni·ness** *n.*

skin·ny-dip (skĭn'ē-dĭp') *v. Informal.* To swim in the nude. —**skin'ny-dip'ping** *n.*

skip (skĭp) *v.* **skipped, skip·ping.** 1. To leap or spring lightly (over). 2. To ricochet. 3. To pass from point to point omitting what intervenes. 4. To pass over, omit, or disregard. 5. To be promoted beyond (the next grade or level). 6. *Informal.* To leave hastily: *skip town.* —*n.* 1. A gait in which hops and steps alternate. 2. A passing over or omission. [ME *skippen.*] —**skip'ping·ly** *adv.*

skip·per (skĭp'ər) *n.* The master of a ship. [< MDu. *schipper.*]

skir·mish (skûr'mĭsh) *n.* A minor encounter in war. [< OFr. *eskermir,* to fight with a sword.] —**skir'mish** *v.* —**skir'mish·er** *n.*

skirt (skûrt) *n.* 1. The part of a garment, such as a dress, that hangs from the waist down. 2. A separate garment hanging from the waist down. —*v.* **1.** To lie along the edge of; border. **2.** To pass around the edge or border of. **3.** To evade or avoid: *skirt the issue.* [< ON *skyrta,* shirt.]

skit (skĭt) *n.* A short, usu. comic theatrical sketch. [Orig. unknown.]

ski tow *v.* A ski lift.

skit·ter (skĭt′ər) *v.* To skip, glide, or move lightly or rapidly along a surface. [Prob. < dial. *skite,* to run rapidly.]

skit·tish (skĭt′ĭsh) *adj.* **1.** Excitable or nervous. **2.** Capricious; undependable. [ME.] —**skit′tish·ly** *adv.* —**skit′tish·ness** *n.*

skiv·vy (skĭv′ē) *n., pl.* -**vies.** *Slang.* **1.** A man's undershirt. **2. skivvies.** A man's underwear consisting of undershirt and shorts. [Orig. unknown.]

skulk (skŭlk) *v.* **1.** To lurk; lie in hiding. **2.** To move about stealthily. [ME *skulken,* of Scand. orig.] —**skulk′er** *n.*

skull (skŭl) *n.* The bony framework of the head. [ME *skulle.*]

skull·cap (skŭl′kăp′) *n.* A light, close-fitting, brimless cap.

skull·dug·ger·y (skŭl-dŭg′ə-rē) *n.* Also **skul·dug·ger·y.** Crafty deception or trickery. [Orig. unknown.]

skunk (skŭngk) *n.* **1.** A New World mammal having black and white fur and ejecting an ill-smelling secretion if startled. **2.** *Slang.* A despicable person. —*v.* *Slang.* To defeat overwhelmingly. [Massachuset *squnck.*]

skunk cabbage *n.* A North American swamp plant having ill-smelling minute flowers enclosed in a mottled greenish or purplish spathe.

sky (skī) *n., pl.* **skies. 1.** The upper atmosphere, seen as a hemisphere above the earth. **2.** The heavenly regions. [< ON *skȳ,* cloud.]

sky·cap (skī′kăp′) *n.* A porter at an airport.

sky·dive (skī′dīv′) *v.* To jump from an airplane, performing various maneuvers before opening a parachute. —**sky′div′er** *n.* —**sky′div·ing** *n.*

sky-high (skī′hī′) *adv.* **1.** To a very high level: *garbage piled sky-high.* **2.** To pieces; apart: *blew the bridge sky-high.* —*adj.* Extremely high: *sky-high prices.*

sky·jack (skī′jăk′) *v.* To hijack (an airplane in flight). [SKY + (HI)JACK.] —**sky′jack′er** *n.* —**sky′jack′ing** *n.*

sky·lark (skī′lärk′) *n.* An Old World bird noted for its singing while in flight. —*v.* To romp; frolic.

sky·light (skī′līt′) *n.* A window in a roof or ceiling that admits daylight.

sky·line (skī′līn′) *n.* **1.** The horizon. **2.** An outline seen against the horizon.

sky·rock·et (skī′rŏk′ĭt) *n.* A firework that ascends high into the air, where it explodes brilliantly. —*v.* To rise rapidly or suddenly.

sky·scrap·er (skī′skrā′pər) *n.* A very tall building.

sky·ward (skī′wərd) *adv.* Also **sky·wards** (-wərdz). Toward the sky: *turn skyward.* —**sky′ward** *adj.*

sky·writ·ing (skī′rī′tĭng) *n.* Writing formed in the sky by releasing a visible vapor from a flying airplane. —**sky′writ′er** *n.*

slab (slăb) *n.* **1.** A broad, flat, somewhat thick piece or slice. **2.** An outside piece cut from a log when squaring it for lumber. [ME *slabbe.*]

slack (slăk) *adj.* -**er,** -**est. 1.** Not lively; sluggish. **2.** Not busy or active. **3.** Not taut or firm; loose. **4.** Careless; negligent. —*v.* **1.** To make or become slack. **2.** To slake (lime). —*n.* **1.** Something slack or hanging loose. **2.** A period of little activity; lull. **3. slacks.** Trousers for casual wear. [< OE *slæc.*] —**slack′ly** *adv.* —**slack′ness** *n.*

slack·en (slăk′ən) *v.* To make or become slack.

slack·er (slăk′ər) *n.* One who shirks work or duty.

slag (slăg) *n.* The glassy mass left by the smelting of metallic ore. [MLG *slagge.*]

slain (slān) *v.* *p.p.* of **slay.**

slake (slāk) *v.* **slaked, slak·ing. 1.** To cause to lessen or subside; quench. **2.** To combine (lime) chemically with water or moist air. [< OE *slacian.*]

sla·lom (slä′ləm) *n.* A skiing race along a downhill zigzag course. [Norw.]

slam[1] (slăm) *v.* **slammed, slam·ming. 1.** To shut with force and loud noise. **2.** To put, throw, or strike so as to produce a loud noise. —*n.* A loud noise produced by a forceful impact. [Perh. of Scand. orig.]

slam[2] (slăm) *n.* In certain card games, such as bridge, the winning of all the tricks or all but one during the play of one hand. [Orig. unknown.]

slan·der (slăn′dər) *n.* A false and malicious statement or report that damages the reputation or well-being of another. —*v.* To utter slander (about). [< Gk. *skandalon,* trap.] —**slan′der·er** *n.* —**slan′der·ous** *adj.* —**slan′der·ous·ly** *adv.*

slang (slăng) *n.* A nonstandard vocabulary of striking and often short-lived coinages, expressions, and figures of speech. [Orig. unknown.] —**slang′i·ly** *adv.* —**slang′i·ness** *n.* —**slang′y** *adj.*

slant (slănt) *v.* **1.** To incline; slope. **2.** To present in a way that conforms with a particular outlook. —*n.* **1.** A sloping plane, direction, or course. **2.** A particular bias. [ME *slenten.*] —**slant′ing·ly** *adv.* —**slant′wise′** *adv.* & *adj.*

slap (slăp) *n.* A smacking blow made with the open hand. **b.** The sound so made. **2.** An insult. —*v.* **slapped, slap·ping. 1.** To give a slap to. **2.** To criticize or insult sharply. [LG *slapp.*] —**slap′per** *n.*

slap-dash (slăp′dăsh′) *adj.* Hasty; careless. —**slap′dash′** *adv.*

slap-stick (slăp′stĭk′) *n.* Comedy marked by loud and boisterous farce.

slash (slăsh) *v.* **1.** To cut with violent sweeping strokes. **2.** To make a gash or slit in. **3.** To reduce drastically. —*n.* **1. a.** A sweeping stroke made with a sharp instrument. **b.** A cut made by such a stroke. **2.** A virgule. [ME *slashen.*] —**slash′er** *n.*

slat (slăt) *n.* A flat, narrow strip, as of metal or wood. [< OFr. *esclat,* splinter.]

slate (slāt) *n.* **1. a.** A fine-grained rock that splits into thin, smooth-surfaced layers. **b.** A piece of slate cut for use as a roofing tile or writing surface. **2.** A list of the candidates of a particular political party running for various offices. —*v.* **slat·ed, slat·ing. 1.** To cover with slate. **2.** To schedule. [< OFr. *esclate,* splinter.]

slath·er (slăth′ər) *v. Informal.* To spread thickly or lavishly. [Orig. unknown.]

slat·tern (slăt′ərn) *n.* A slovenly woman. [Perh. < dial. *slatter,* to slop.] —**slat′tern·li·ness** *n.* —**slat′tern·ly** *adj.*

slaugh·ter (slô′tər) *n.* **1.** The killing of animals for food. **2.** The killing of a large number of people; massacre. —*v.* **1.** To butcher (animals) for food. **2.** To kill brutally or in large numbers. [ME, of Scand. orig.] —**slaugh′ter·er** *n.*

slaugh·ter·house (slô′tər-hous′) *n.* A place where animals are butchered.

Slav (släv) *n.* A member of one of the Slavic-speaking peoples of eastern Europe.

slave (släv) *n.* **1.** A person who is owned by and forced to work for someone else. **2.** A person completely controlled by a specified influence, emotion, etc. —*v.* **slaved, slav·ing.** To work like a slave. [< Med. Lat. *Sclavus,* Slav.]

slav·er (slăv′ər, slä′vər) *v.* To drool; slobber. [Prob. < ON *slafra.*] —**slav′er** *n.*

slav·er·y (slā′və-rē, slāv′rē) *n.* **1.** The condition of being a slave; bondage. **2.** The practice of owning slaves. **3.** A condition of hard work and subjection.

Slav·ic (slä′vĭk, slāv′ĭk) *adj.* Of or pertaining to the Slavs or their languages. —*n.* A branch of the Indo-European language family that includes Bulgarian, Czech, Polish, Russian, Serbo-Croatian, and Slovak.

slav·ish (slā′vĭsh) *adj.* **1.** Like or befitting a slave; servile: *slavish devotion.* **2.** Showing no originality: *a slavish copy.* —**slav′ish·ly** *adv.* —**slav′ish·ness** *n.*

slaw (slô) *n.* Coleslaw.

slay (slā) *v.* **slew** (slōō), **slain** (slān), **slay·ing.** To kill by violent means. [< OE *slēan.*] —**slay′er** *n.*

slea·zy (slē′zē) *adj.* **-zi·er, -zi·est. 1.** Thin; flimsy. **2.** Cheap; shoddy. [Orig. unknown.] —**slea′zi·ly** *adv.* —**slea′zi·ness** *n.*

sled (slĕd) *n.* **1.** A vehicle mounted on runners, used for moving over ice and snow. **2.** A light wooden frame mounted on runners, used by children for coasting over snow or ice. —*v.* **sled·ded, sled·ding.** To ride or convey by a sled. [< MLG *sledde.*]

sledge¹ (slĕj) *n.* A vehicle on low runners used for transporting loads across snow and ice. [MDu. *sleedse.*]

sledge² (slĕj) *n.* A sledgehammer. [OE *slecg.*]

sledge·ham·mer (slĕj′hăm′ər) *n.* A long, heavy hammer, usu. wielded with both hands.

sleek (slēk) *adj.* **-er, -est. 1.** Smooth and lustrous as if polished; glossy. **2.** Neat, trim, and graceful. **3.** Healthy or well-fed; thriving. **4.** Polished or smooth in behavior. —*v.* To make glossy or smooth. [< SLICK.] —**sleek′ly** *adv.* —**sleek′ness** *n.*

sleep (slēp) *n.* **1.** A natural, periodic condition of rest characterized by unconsciousness and lessened responsiveness to external stimuli. **2.** A condition, as of inactivity or unconsciousness, similar to sleep. —*v.* **slept** (slĕpt), **sleep·ing. 1.** To be in or as if in a state of sleep. **2.** To be in a condition resembling sleep. **3.** To pass by sleeping. [< OE *slæp.*]

sleep·er (slē′pər) *n.* **1.** One that sleeps. **2.** A sleeping car. **3.** *Informal.* Something that becomes unexpectedly popular or successful.

sleeping bag *n.* A warmly lined zippered bag in which one may sleep outdoors.

sleeping car *n.* A railroad car with accommodations for sleeping.

sleeping pill *n.* A sedative in the form of a pill or capsule.

sleeping sickness *n.* An infectious disease of tropical Africa transmitted by the tsetse fly and characterized by fever and lethargy.

sleep·less (slēp′lĭs) *adj.* **1.** Unable to sleep. **2.** Without sleep: *a sleepless night.* **3.** Always alert or in motion. —**sleep′less·ly** *adv.* —**sleep′less·ness** *n.*

sleep·walk·ing (slēp′wô′kĭng) *n.* The act of walking in one's sleep. —**sleep′walk′er** *n.*

sleep·y (slē′pē) *adj.* **-i·er, -i·est. 1.** Ready for sleep; drowsy. **2.** Quiet; inactive. —**sleep′i·ly** *adv.* —**sleep′i·ness** *n.*

sleet (slēt) *n.* **1.** Frozen or partially frozen rain. **2.** An icy glaze. —*v.* To shower sleet. [ME *slete.*] —**sleet′y** *adj.*

sleeve (slēv) *n.* **1.** The part of a garment that covers the arm. **2.** A tubular part into which a piece of equipment fits. —*idiom.* **up (one's) sleeve.** Hidden but ready to be used. [< OE *slēf.*] —**sleeve′less** *adj.*

sleigh (slā) *n.* A light vehicle mounted on runners for use on snow or ice, usu. drawn by a horse. —*v.* To ride in or drive a sleigh. [< MDu. *slēde.*]

sleigh

sleight (slīt) *n.* **1.** Dexterity; skill. **2.** A trick; stratagem. [< ON *slœgdh.*]

sleight of hand *n.* A trick performed so quickly that the manner of execution cannot be observed.

slen·der (slĕn′dər) *adj.* **-er, -est. 1.** Having little width in proportion to the height or length. **2.** Meager; inadequate: *slender wages.* [ME *sclendre.*] —**slen′der·ly** *adv.* —**slen′der·ness** *n.*

slen·der·ize (slĕn′də-rīz′) *v.* **-ized, -iz·ing.** To make or become slender.

slept (slĕpt) *v. p.t. & p.p.* of **sleep.**

sleuth (slōōth) *n. Informal.* A detective. [< SLEUTHHOUND.] —**sleuth** *v.*

sleuth·hound (slōōth′hound′) *n.* **1.** A bloodhound. **2.** A detective. [ME.]

slew¹ (slōō) *n.* Also **slue.** *Informal.* A large amount or number. [Ir. Gael. *sluag.*]

slew² (slōō) *v. p.t.* of **slay.**

slew³ (slōō) *v. & n.* Var. of **slue¹.**

slice (slīs) *n.* **1.** A thin, broad piece cut from a larger object. **2.** A portion or share. **3.** A knife with a broad, thin, flexible blade. **4.** *Sports.* **a.** A stroke that causes a ball to curve off course to the right or, if the player is left-handed, to the left. **b.** The course followed by such a ball. —*v.* **sliced, slic·ing.** **1.** To cut or divide with or as if with a knife. **2.** To cut or remove from a larger piece. **3.** To hit (a ball) with a slice. [< OFr. *eslicer,* to splinter.] —**slice′a·ble** *adj.* —**slic′er** *n.*

slick (slĭk) *adj.* **-er, -est. 1.** Smooth and glossy. **2.** Deftly executed; adroit. **3.** Shrewd; crafty. **4.** Superficially attractive but without depth. —*n.* **1.** A smooth or slippery surface or area: *an oil slick.* **2.** *Informal.* A magazine printed on glossy paper. —*v.* To make smooth or glossy. [ME *slike.*]

slick·er (slĭk′ər) *n.* **1.** A loose, glossy raincoat. **2.** *Informal.* A person with stylish clothing and manners.

slide (slīd) *v.* **slid** (slīd), **slid·ing. 1.** To move or cause to move over a surface while maintaining continuous contact. **2.** To glide. **3.** To slip or skid. **4.** To go back to a less favorable or less worthy condition. **5.** *Baseball.* To drop down and skid into a base. —*n.* **1.** A sliding movement or action. **2.** A smooth surface or track for sliding. **3.** A part that operates by sliding, as the bolt in certain locks. **4.** An image, usu. photographic, formed on a transparent piece of material for projection on a screen. **5.** A small glass plate for mounting microscope specimens. **6.** The fall of a mass of ice, snow, or rocks down a slope. [< OE *slīdan.*]

Syns: slide, coast, drift, glide, slip v.

slid·er (slīd′ər) *n.* **1.** One that slides. **2.** *Baseball.* A pitch that moves like a fast ball but breaks slightly downward at the last moment.

slide rule *n.* A device that consists of two rules marked with logarithmic scales and arranged to slide along each other, used in performing mathematical operations.

sliding scale *n.* A scale in which indicated prices, taxes, or wages vary in accordance with some other factor, as wages with the cost-of-living index.

sli·er (slī′ər) *adj.* A compar. of *sly.*

sli·est (slī′ĭst) *adj.* A superl. of *sly.*

slight (slīt) *adj.* **-er, -est. 1.** Small in size, degree, or amount. **2.** Of small importance; trifling. **3.** Frail; delicate. —*v.* **1.** To treat as if of slight importance. **2.** To snub or insult. **3.** To neglect. —*n.* An act of pointed disrespect or discourtesy. [ME, slender, of Scand. orig.] —**slight′ly** *adv.* —**slight′ness** *n.*

slim (slĭm) *adj.* **slim·mer, slim·mest. 1.** Small in girth or thickness; slender. **2.** Scanty; meager. —*v.* **slimmed, slim·ming.** To make or become slim. [MDu. *slimp,* bad.] —**slim′ly** *adv.* —**slim′ness** *n.*

slime (slīm) *n.* A moist, sticky substance or coating. [< OE *slīm.*] —**slim′y** *adj.*

sling (slĭng) *n.* **1.** A belt, rope, or chain in which loads are placed to be hoisted, secured, or carried. **2.** A band of cloth looped around the neck to support an injured arm or hand. **3.** A weapon made from a looped strap in which a stone is hurled. —*v.* **slung** (slŭng), **sling·ing. 1.** To hurl with a swinging motion; fling. **2.** To place, carry, or move in a sling. [ME.] —**sling′er** *n.*

sling·shot (slĭng′shŏt′) *n.* A Y-shaped stick with an elastic strap attached to the prongs, used for flinging stones.

slink (slĭngk) *v.* **slunk** (slŭngk), **slink·ing.** To move in a furtive manner. [< OE *slincan.*]

slink·y (slĭng′kē) *adj.* **-i·er, -i·est. 1.** Stealthy; furtive. **2.** *Informal.* Sinuous and sleek.

slip¹ (slĭp) *v.* **slipped, slip·ping. 1.** To move quietly and stealthily. **2.** To slide accidentally; lose one's balance. **3.** To slide out of place or from one's grasp. **4.** To get away (from); escape unnoticed. **5.** *Informal.* To decline in ability, strength, or keenness. **6.** *Informal.* To decline; fall off. **7.** To place or insert smoothly and quietly. **8.** To put on or remove (clothing) easily or quickly. —*phrasal verb.* **slip up.** *Informal.* To make a mistake; err. —*n.* **1.** The act of slipping. **2.** A slight error or oversight. **3.** A docking place for a ship between two piers. **4.** A woman's undergarment of various lengths. **5.** A pillowcase. —*idioms.* **give (someone) the slip.** *Slang.* To escape the company of. **let slip.** To say unintentionally or thoughtlessly. **slip one over on.** *Informal.* To hoodwink; dupe. [ME *slippen.*]

slip² (slĭp) *n.* **1.** A part of a plant cut or broken off for grafting or planting. **2.** A youthful, slender person. **3.** A small piece of paper. [ME *slippe,* strip.]

slip·case (slĭp′kās′) *n.* A protective box for a book.

slip·cover (slĭp′kŭv′ər) *n.* A fitted, removable, usu. cloth cover for a piece of upholstered furniture.

slip·knot (slĭp′nŏt′) *n.* A knot made with a loop so that it slips easily along the rope or cord around which it is tied.

slip-on (slĭp′ŏn′, -ôn′) *n.* A piece of clothing easily slipped on and off.

slip·page (slĭp′ĭj) *n.* **1.** A slipping. **2.** Loss of motion or power due to slipping.

slipped disk *n.* An injury that results from the shifting out of position of one of the cushioning disks between the spinal vertebrae.

slip·per (slĭp′ər) *n.* A light, low shoe that may be slipped on and off easily.

slip·per·y (slĭp′ə-rē) *adj.* **-i·er, -i·est. 1.** Causing or tending to cause sliding or slipping. **2.** Hard to capture or pin down; elusive. [< OE *slipor.*] —**slip′per·i·ness** *n.*

slip·shod (slĭp′shŏd′) *adj.* **1.** Poorly made or done; careless. **2.** Shabby; seedy.

slip-up (slĭp′ŭp′) *n.* *Informal.* An error; mistake.

slit (slĭt) *n.* A long, narrow cut, tear, or opening. [ME *slitte.*] —**slit** *v.*

slith·er (slĭth′ər) *v.* **1.** To slip and slide. **2.** To move along by gliding, as a snake does. [< OE *slidrian.*] —**slith′er·y** *adj.*

sliv·er (slĭv′ər) *n.* A sharp-ended, thin piece; splinter. [< ME *slyven,* to split.] —**sliv′er** *v.*

slob (slŏb) *n.* *Informal.* A crude or slovenly person. [Ir. Gael. *slab,* mud.]

slob·ber (slŏb′ər) *v.* **1.** To let saliva or food dribble from the mouth. **2.** To express emotion in an exaggerated way. [ME *sloberen.*] —**slob′ber** *n.* —**slob′ber·er** *n.*

sloe (slō) *n.* The tart, blue-black, plumlike fruit of the blackthorn. [< OE *slā.*]

slog (slŏg) *v.* **slogged, slog·ging. 1.** To walk with a slow, plodding gait. **2.** To work or toil for long hours. [Orig. unknown.]

slo·gan (slō′gən) *n.* **1.** A phrase expressing the aims or nature of an enterprise, team, or other group; motto. **2.** A battle cry of the Scottish clans. **3.** A catch phrase used in advertising or promotion. [< Gael. *sluaghghairm,* battle cry.]

sloop (slōōp) *n.* A single-masted, fore-and-aft-rigged sailing boat with a mainsail and a jib. [Du. *sloep.*]

sloop

slop (slŏp) *n.* **1.** Liquid spilled or splashed. **2.** Soft mud or slush. **3.** Unappetizing, watery food or soup. **4.** Often **slops.** Waste food used to feed pigs or other animals; swill. —*v.* **slopped, slop·ping.** To spill or splash messily. [ME *sloppe,* a kind of garment.]

slope (slŏp) *v.* **sloped, slop·ing.** To incline upward or downward. —*n.* **1.** An inclined line, surface, plane, or stretch of ground. **2.** A deviation from the horizontal or the amount of such deviation. [< ME, *sloping.*]

slop·py (slŏp′ē) *adj.* **-pi·er, -pi·est. 1.** Muddy; slushy. **2.** Untidy; messy. **3.** Carelessly done.

slosh (slŏsh) *v.* To splash or flounder, as in water or another liquid. —*n.* Slush. [< SLUSH.] —**slosh′y** *adj.*

slot (slŏt) *n.* **1.** A long, narrow groove or opening. **2.** *Informal.* A suitable position or niche. [< OFr. *esclot,* hollow between the breasts.]

sloth (slôth, slōth, slŏth) *n.* **1.** Laziness; indolence. **2.** A slow-moving, arboreal mammal of tropical America. [< OE *slāw,* slow.] —**sloth′ful** *adj.*

slot machine *n.* A coin-operated vending or gambling machine.

slouch (slouch) *n.* **1.** An awkward, drooping posture or gait. **2.** A lazy or incompetent person. [Orig. unknown.] —**slouch** *v.* —**slouch′er** *n.*

slouch hat *n.* A soft hat with a broad, flexible brim.

slough¹ (slōō, slou) *n.* **1.** A hollow, usu. filled with mud. **2.** A state of deep despair. [< OE *slōh.*]

slough² (slŭf) *n.* **1.** Dead tissue separated from a living structure. **2.** An outer layer or covering that is shed. —*v.* To shed or cast off; discard. [ME *slughe.*]

Slo·vak (slō′väk′, -văk′) *n.* **1.** A member of a Slavic people living in Slovakia. **2.** The Slavic language of the Slovaks. —**Slo′vak′** or **Slo·vak′i·an** *adj.*

slov·en (slŭv′ən) *n.* A habitually untidy or careless person. [ME *sloveyn.*]

slov·en·ly (slŭv′ən-lē) *adj.* **-li·er, -li·est. 1.** Untidy; messy. **2.** Careless; slipshod: *slovenly work.* —**slov′en·li·ness** *n.* —**slov′en·ly** *adv.*

slow (slō) *adj.* **-er, -est. 1. a.** Not moving or able to move quickly. **b.** Marked by a low speed or tempo: *a slow waltz.* **2.** Taking or

requiring a long time. **3. a.** Registering a time or rate behind or below the correct one. **b.** Tardy. **4.** Sluggish; inactive. **5.** Dull; boring. **6.** Not quick to understand: *a slow student.* —*adv.* Slowly. —*v.* **1.** To make or become slow or slower. **2.** To delay; retard. [< OE *slāw.*] —**slow′ly** *adv.* —**slow′ness** *n.*
Syns: *slow, dilatory, laggard, poky, tardy* **adj.**
Usage: Slow sometimes occurs as an adverb in speech and informal writing: *Drive slow! Slow* is also the idiomatic form in certain set expressions, as in *My watch runs slow.* Otherwise, in formal writing *slowly* is preferable.

slow·down (slō′doun′) *n.* A slackening of pace, esp. an intentional slowing down of production.

slow motion *n.* A motion-picture technique in which action is projected at a slower-than-normal pace.

sludge (slŭj) *n.* **1.** Mud, mire, or ooze. **2.** Slushy matter or sediment precipitated by the treatment of sewage. [Perh. < dial. *slutch,* mire.] —**sludg′y** *adj.*

slue¹ (slōō). Also **slew.** —*v.* **slued, slu·ing.** To turn or twist to the side. —*n.* The act of sluing. [Orig. unknown.]

slue² (slōō) *n.* Var. of **slew¹.**

slug¹ (slŭg) *n.* **1. a.** A lump of metal. **b.** A round bullet. **2.** *Informal.* A shot of liquor. **3.** A small metal disk used in place of a coin. [Prob. < SLUG².]

slug² (slŭg) *n.* A terrestrial gastropod mollusk having an elongated body with no shell. [ME *slugge,* sluggard.]

slug³ (slŭg) *v.* **slugged, slug·ging.** To strike heavily, esp. with the fist. —*n.* A hard, heavy blow. [Perh. < SLUG¹.] —**slug′ger** *n.*

slug·gard (slŭg′ərd) *n.* A lazy person. [ME *sluggart.*] —**slug′gard·ly** *adj.*

slug·gish (slŭg′ĭsh) *adj.* **1.** Slow; inactive. **2.** Dull; lazy. **3.** Slow to perform or respond. [Prob. < ME *sluggen,* to be lazy.] —**slug′gish·ly** *adv.* —**slug′gish·ness** *n.*

sluice (slōōs) *n.* **1. a.** A manmade channel for water with a gate to regulate the flow. **b.** The gate itself. **2.** A sluiceway. **3.** A long inclined trough, as for floating logs. —*v.* **sluiced, sluic·ing. 1.** To wash with a sudden flow of water; flush. **2.** To draw off by a sluice. **3.** To send down a sluice. [< Lat. *excludere,* to shut out.]

sluice
Hells Canyon Dam in Idaho

sluice·way (slōōs′wā′) *n.* An artificial channel for carrying off excess water.

slum (slŭm) *n.* A heavily populated urban

area characterized by poverty, poor housing, and squalor. —*v.* **slummed, slum·ming. 1.** To visit a slum, esp. from curiosity. **2.** *Slang.* To live in or as if in rough or squalid conditions. [Orig. unknown.]

slum·ber (slŭm′bər) *v.* **1.** To sleep or doze. **2.** To be dormant or quiescent. —*n.* **1.** Sleep. **2.** A state of inactivity or dormancy. [Prob. < OE *slūma*, sleep.] —**slum′ber·er** *n.*

slum·ber·ous (slŭm′bər-əs) *adj.* Also **slum·brous** (-brəs). **1.** Sleepy; drowsy. **2.** Quiet; tranquil. **3.** Inducing sleep.

slum·lord (slŭm′lôrd′) *n. Informal.* A landlord of slum property, esp. one who allows the property to deteriorate.

slump (slŭmp) *v.* **1.** To decline or sink suddenly. **2.** To droop; slouch. [Prob. of Scand. orig.] —**slump** *n.*

slung (slŭng) *v. p.t. & p.p.* of **sling.**

slunk (slŭngk) *v. p.t. & p.p.* of **slink.**

slur (slûr) *v.* **slurred, slur·ring. 1.** To pass over lightly or carelessly. **2.** To pronounce indistinctly. **3.** To disparage. **4.** *Mus.* To glide over (a series of notes) smoothly without a break. —*n.* **1.** A disparaging remark; aspersion. **2.** *Mus.* A curved line connecting notes to indicate that they are to be played or sung legato. [< ME *sloor*, mud.]

slurp (slûrp) *v.* To eat or drink noisily. [Du. *slurpen.*] —**slurp** *n.*

slush (slŭsh) *n.* **1.** Partially melted snow or ice. **2.** Soft mud; slop. **3.** Sentimental drivel. [Perh. of Scand. orig.] —**slush′i·ness** *n.* —**slush′y** *adj.*

slush fund *n.* A fund used to finance corrupt practices, such as bribery or graft. [< *slush*, discarded material sold for the benefit of a ship's crew.]

slut (slŭt) *n.* **1.** A slovenly woman. **2.** A prostitute. [ME *slutte.*] —**slut′tish** *adj.*

sly (slī) *adj.* **sli·er** or **sly·er, sli·est** or **sly·est. 1.** Stealthily clever; cunning. **2.** Secretive. **3.** Underhand; deceitful. **4.** Mischievous; arch. —**idiom. on the sly.** Secretly. [< ON *slœgr.*] —**sly′ly** *adv.* —**sly′ness** *n.*

Sm The symbol for the element samarium.

smack¹ (smăk) *v.* **1.** To make a sound by pressing together the lips and pulling them apart quickly. **2.** To kiss or slap noisily. —*n.* **1.** The loud, sharp sound of smacking the lips. **2.** A noisy kiss. **3.** A sharp blow or loud slap. —*adv.* Directly; straight: *hit him smack in the face.* [Prob. of MLG orig.]

smack² (smăk) *n.* **1.** A distinctive flavor. **2.** A suggestion or trace. —*v.* **1.** To have the flavor of. **2.** To suggest: *This smacks of foul play.* [< OE *smæc.*]

smack³ (smăk) *n.* A sloop-rigged fishing boat. [Du. *smak.*]

small (smôl) *adj.* **-er, -est. 1.** Little in size, quantity, or extent. **2.** Insignificant; trivial. **3.** Operating on a limited scale: *a small farmer.* **4.** Soft; low: *a small voice.* **5.** Not fully grown; very young. **6.** Petty: *a small mind.* **7.** Belittled; humiliated. —*adv.* **1.** In small pieces: *Cut it up small.* **2.** Softly. **3.** In a small manner. —*n.* Something smaller than the rest, esp. the narrowest part of the back. [< OE *smæl.*] —**small′ness** *n.*

small arms *pl.n.* Firearms that can be carried in the hand.

small intestine *n.* The part of the alimentary canal between the outlet of the stomach and the large intestine.

small·pox (smôl′pŏks′) *n.* An acute, highly

infectious viral disease characterized by high fever and pustules that form pockmarks.

small talk *n.* Casual or light conversation.

small-time (smôl′tīm′) *adj. Informal.* Insignificant; minor. —**small′tim′er** *n.*

smarm·y (smär′mē) *adj.* **-mi·er, -mi·est.** Marked by an exaggerated or insincere earnestness. [< dial. *smarm,* to gush.]

smart (smärt) *adj.* **-er, -est. 1. a.** Intelligent; bright. **b.** Amusingly clever; witty. **c.** Impertinent: *a smart answer.* **2.** Quick and energetic: *a smart pace.* **3.** Marked by sharpness in dealings; shrewd. **4.** Fashionable; elegant: *a smart restaurant.* —*v.* **1.** To cause or feel a sharp, stinging pain. **2.** To be the source of such a pain: *The first-aid spray smarts.* **3.** To feel mental distress. [< OE *smeart,* stinging.] —**smart′ly** *adv.* —**smart′ness** *n.*

smart al·eck (ăl′ĭk) *n. Informal.* An offensively arrogant person. [SMART + *Aleck,* nickname for *Alexander.*] —**smart′-al′eck·y** *adj.*

smart·en (smär′tn) *v.* **1.** To make or become smart or smarter. **2.** To make or become more brisk or lively.

smash (smăsh) *v.* **1.** To break or be broken into pieces. **2.** To throw or dash violently so as to shatter or crush. **3.** To strike with a heavy blow; hit. —*n.* **1.** The act or sound of smashing or the condition of having been smashed. **2.** Total destruction; ruin. **3.** A collision or crash. **4.** *Sports.* A powerful, usu. overhand stroke. **5.** A resounding success. —*adj. Informal.* Very successful. [Perh. blend of SMACK and CRASH.] —**smash′er** *n.*

smash-up (smăsh′ŭp′) *n.* **1.** A total collapse or defeat; failure. **2.** A serious collision between vehicles.

smat·ter·ing (smăt′ər-ĭng) *n.* **1.** Superficial or piecemeal knowledge. **2.** A small, scattered amount. [< *smatter,* to dabble in.]

smear (smîr) *v.* **1.** To spread, cover, or stain with a sticky or dirty substance. **2.** To smudge or soil. **3.** To slander; vilify. —*n.* **1.** A smudge or blot. **2.** Vilification; slander. [< OE *smerian,* to anoint.] —**smear′y** *adj.*

smell (smĕl) *v.* **smelled** or **smelt** (smĕlt), **smell·ing. 1.** To notice the odor of by the sense organs of the nose. **2.** To have or emit an odor. **3.** To suggest evil or corruption. —*n.* **1.** The olfactory sense. **2.** The odor of something; scent. **3.** The act or an example of smelling. **4.** A distinctive quality; an aura: *the smell of success.* [ME *smellen.*]

smelling salts *pl.n.* A preparation based on spirits of ammonia, sniffed to relieve faintness.

smell·y (smĕl′ē) *adj.* **-i·er, -i·est.** Having an unpleasant odor.

smelt¹ (smĕlt) *v.* To melt or fuse (ores), separating the metallic constituents. [MLG *smelten.*]

smelt² (smĕlt) *n., pl.* **smelts** or **smelt.** A small silvery food fish. [< OE.]

smelt³ (smĕlt) *v.* A *p.t. & p.p.* of **smell.**

smelt·er (smĕl′tər) *n.* Also **smelt·ery** (-tə-rē). **1.** An establishment for smelting. **2.** A worker who smelts ore.

smidg·en (smĭj′ən) *n.* Also **smidg·in.** *Informal.* A very small quantity or portion; bit. [< dial. *smitch,* particle.]

smi·lax (smī′lăks′) *n.* A climbing vine that has glossy foliage and is used as a floral decoration. [< Gk., bindweed.]

smile (smīl) *n.* **1.** A facial expression formed by

an upward curving of the corners of the mouth and indicating pleasure, affection, or amusement. —*v.* **smiled, smil·ing. 1.** To have or form a smile. **2.** To express approval. **3.** To express with a smile. [< ME *smilen*, to smile.] —**smil'ing·ly** *adv.*

Syns: *smile, beam, grin* v.

smirch (smûrch) *v.* **1.** To soil or stain. **2.** To dishonor or defame. [ME *smorchen.*] —**smirch** *n.*

smirk (smûrk) *v.* To smile in an obnoxious, superior, or simpering manner. [< OE *smearcian*, to smile.] —**smirk** *n.* —**smirk'er** *n.*

smite (smīt) *v.* **smote** (smōt), **smit·ten** (smit'n) or **smote**, **smit·ing. 1.** To inflict a heavy blow on. **2.** To kill by or as if by blows. **3.** To afflict. [< OE *smītan.*] —**smit'er** *n.*

smith (smith) *n.* A metalworker, esp. a blacksmith. [< OE.]

smith·er·eens (smĭth'ə-rēnz') *pl.n. Informal.* Pieces; bits. [Ir. Gael. *smidirīn.*]

smith·y (smĭth'ē, smĭth'ē) *n., pl.* **-ies.** A blacksmith's shop. [< ON *smidhja.*]

smock (smŏk) *n.* A loose outer garment worn over other clothes to protect them. —*v.* To decorate (fabric) with stitched gathers in a honeycomb pattern. [< OE *smoc.*]

smog (smŏg) *n.* Fog mixed and polluted with smoke. [Blend of SMOKE and FOG.] —**smog'gy** *adj.*

smoke (smōk) *n.* **1.** The vapor made up of small particles of matter from incomplete burning of materials such as wood or coal. **2.** A cloud of fine particles. **3.** The act of smoking a form of tobacco or other plant material. **4.** Tobacco in any form that can be smoked. —*v.* **smoked, smok·ing. 1.** To emit smoke. **2.** To emit smoke excessively. **3.** To draw in and exhale smoke from a cigarette, cigar, pipe, etc. **4.** To preserve (meat or fish) by exposure to smoke. **5.** To fumigate. **6.** *Slang.* To perform at the utmost capacity. —*phrasal verb.* **smoke out.** To force out of hiding by or as if by the use of smoke. [< OE *smoca.*] —**smoke'less** *adj.* —**smok'er** *n.* —**smok'i·ness** *n.* —**smok'y** *adj.*

smoke screen *n.* **1.** A mass of dense smoke used to conceal military operations. **2.** Something used to conceal plans or intentions.

smoke·stack (smōk'stăk') *n.* A large vertical pipe through which combustion gases and smoke are discharged.

smol·der (smōl'dər). Also **smoul·der.** —*v.* **1.** To burn with little smoke and no flame. **2.** To exist in a suppressed state. —*n.* Thick smoke resulting from a slow fire. [ME *smolderen.*]

smooch (smōoch) *Slang.* —*n.* A kiss. —*v.* To kiss. [Perh. imit.]

smooth (smōoth) *adj.* **-er, -est. 1.** Free from irregularities, roughness, or projections. **2.** Having a fine texture or consistency. **3.** Having an even or gentle motion. **4.** Having no obstructions or difficulties. **5.** Ingratiating: *smooth talk.* —*v.* **1.** To make or become smooth. **2.** To rid of hindrances, difficulties, etc. **3.** To soothe; make calm. [< OE *smōth.*] —**smooth'er** *n.* —**smooth'ly** *adv.* —**smooth'ness** *n.*

smor·gas·bord (smôr'gəs-bôrd', -bōrd') *n.* A

buffet meal featuring a varied number of dishes. [Swed. *smörgåsbord.*]

smote (smōt) *v. p.t. & a p.p.* of **smite.**

smoth·er (smŭth'ər) *v.* **1.** To kill by depriving of oxygen. **2.** To conceal or suppress: *smothered a sob.* **3.** To cover thickly. [< ME *smorther*, dense smoke.]

smoul·der (smōl'dər) *v. & n.* Var. of **smolder.**

smudge (smŭj) *v.* **smudged, smudg·ing.** To smear or blur. —*n.* **1.** A blotch or smear. **2.** A smoky fire used as a protection against insects or frost. [ME *smogen.*] —**smudg'i·ly** *adv.* —**smudg'i·ness** *n.* —**smudg'y** *adj.*

smug (smŭg) *adj.* **smug·ger, smug·gest.** Self-satisfied or complacent. [< MLG *smuck*, neat.] —**smug'ly** *adv.* —**smug'ness** *n.*

smug·gle (smŭg'əl) *v.* **-gled, -gling. 1.** To convey illicitly or by stealth. **2.** To import or export without paying lawful customs charges or duties. [LG *smuggeln.*] —**smug'gler** *n.*

smut (smŭt) *n.* **1. a.** A particle of dirt. **b.** A smudge. **2.** Obscene speech or writing. **3.** Any of various plant diseases caused by fungi that form black, powdery masses. [< ME *smotten*, to besmirch.] —**smut'ti·ness** *n.* —**smut'ty** *adj.*

Sn The symbol for the element tin. [< Lat. *stannum*, tin.]

snack (snăk) *n.* A light meal. [< ME *snaken*, to bite.] —**snack** *v.*

snaf·fle (snăf'əl) *n.* A jointed bit for a horse. [Orig. unknown.]

sna·fu (snă-fōo') *n., pl.* **-fus.** *Slang.* A chaotic or confused situation. [S(ITUATION) N(ORMAL) A(LL) F(OULED) U(P)]

snag (snăg) *n.* **1.** A sharp or jagged protuberance. **2.** A tree or a part of a tree that sticks out above a water surface. **3.** An unforeseen or hidden obstacle. —*v.* **snagged, snag·ging. 1.** To get caught by or as if by a snag. **2.** *Informal.* To catch or get quickly or unexpectedly. **3.** To hinder; impede. [Prob. of Scand. orig.]

snail (snăl) *n.* An aquatic or terrestrial mollusk with a spirally coiled shell and a distinct head. [< OE *snægel.*]

snake (snāk) *n.* **1.** Any of various scaly, legless, sometimes poisonous reptiles with a long, tapering body. **2.** A sneaky, untrustworthy person. **3.** A long, flexible wire used for clearing drains and sewers. —*v.* **snaked, snak·ing.** To move, drag, or pull in a snakelike manner. [< OE *snaca.*] —**snak'i·ly** *adv.* —**snak'y** *adj.*

snake oil *n.* A worthless preparation fraudulently peddled as a cure for many ills.

snap (snăp) *v.* **snapped, snap·ping. 1.** To make or cause to make a sharp cracking sound. **2.** To break suddenly with a sharp sound. **3.** To give way abruptly. **4.** To bite or seize with a snatching motion. **5.** To speak abruptly or sharply. **6.** To move smartly. **7.** To flash or sparkle. **8.** *Football.* To pass the ball so as to initiate a play. **9.** To open or close with a click. —*n.* **1.** A sharp cracking sound. **2.** A sudden breaking or release of something under pressure. **3.** A clasp, catch, or other fastening device. **4.** A thin, crisp cooky. **5.** Briskness; energy. **6.** A spell of cold weather. **7.** *Football.* The passing of the ball that initiates each play. [MLG *snappen*, to seize.] —**snap′pi·ly** adv. —**snap′pi·ness** n. —**snap′pish** adj. —**snap′py** adj.

snap bean n. A bean, such as the string bean, cultivated for its crisp, edible pods.

snap·drag·on (snăp′drăg′ən) n. A cultivated plant with showy clusters of two-lipped, variously colored flowers.

snap·per (snăp′ər) n. 1. One that snaps. 2. pl. **-per** or **-pers.** Any of numerous marine fishes prized as food and game fishes.

snapping turtle n. Any of several freshwater turtles with a rough shell and powerful hooked jaws.

snap·shot (snăp′shŏt′) n. An informal photograph taken with a small camera.

snare[1] (snâr) n. 1. A trap, often consisting of a noose, used for capturing birds and small animals. 2. Something that entangles the unwary. [< ON snara.] —**snare** v.

snare[2] (snâr) n. Any of the wires or cords stretched across the lower head of a drum to increase reverberation. [Prob. < Du. snaar, string.]

snarl[1] (snärl) v. 1. To growl while baring the teeth. 2. To speak angrily or threateningly. [< obs. snar, to growl.] —**snarl** n. —**snarl′er** n. —**snarl′ing·ly** adv.

snarl[2] (snärl) n. A tangle. —v. 1. To tangle or knot. 2. To confuse. [Prob. < SNARE[1].]

snatch (snăch) v. 1. To try to grasp or seize. 2. To seize or grab. —n. 1. The act of snatching. 2. A brief period. 3. A bit or fragment: a snatch of a song. [ME snacchen, to snap at.] —**snatch′er** n.

snaz·zy (snăz′ē) adj. **-zi·er, -zi·est.** Fashionable and flashy or showy. [Perh. a blend of SNAPPY and JAZZY.]

sneak (snēk) v. To move, give, or take in a quiet, stealthy way. —n. 1. A stealthy or underhanded person. 2. An instance of sneaking. [Orig. unknown.] —**sneak′i·ly** adv. —**sneak′i·ness** n. —**sneak′y** adj.

Syns: sneak, creep, glide, lurk, prowl, skulk, slide, slink, slip, steal v.

sneak·er (snē′kər) n. A usu. canvas sports shoe with rubber soles.

sneer (snîr) n. A slight raising of one corner of the upper lip, expressive of contempt. [Perh. of LG orig.] —**sneer** v. —**sneer′er** n. —**sneer′ful** adj.

sneeze (snēz) v. **sneezed, sneez·ing.** To expel air forcibly from the mouth and nose in an explosive, involuntary spasm. [< OE fnēosan.] —**sneeze** n.

snick·er (snĭk′ər) n. Also **snig·ger** (snĭg′ər). A nasty, slightly stifled laugh. [Imit.] —**snick·er** v. —**snick′er·ing·ly** adv.

snide (snīd) adj. **snid·er, snid·est.** Slyly disparaging. [Orig. unknown.]

sniff (snĭf) v. 1. To inhale a short, audible breath through the nose. 2. To indicate ridicule, contempt, or doubt. 3. To detect by or as if by sniffing. [ME sniffen.] —**sniff** n. —**sniff′er** n. —**sniff′ing·ly** adv.

snif·fle (snĭf′əl) v. **-fled, -fling.** 1. To breathe audibly through a congested nose. 2. To whimper. —n. 1. An act or sound of sniffling. 2. **the sniffles.** Informal. A condition, such as a cold, that makes one sniffle. [< SNIFF.] —**snif′fler** n.

snif·ter (snĭf′tər) n. A goblet that narrows at the top, used esp. in serving brandy. [< ME snifteren, to sniff.]

snig·ger (snĭg′ər) n. Var. of **snicker.**

snip (snĭp) v. **snipped, snip·ping.** To cut or

clip with short, quick strokes. —n. 1. A small cut made with scissors or shears. 2. A small piece clipped off. [LG snippen, to snap.]

snipe (snīp) n., pl. **snipe** or **snipes.** 1. Any of various long-billed, brownish wading birds. 2. A shot, esp. a gunshot, from a concealed place. —v. **sniped, snip·ing.** 1. To shoot at persons from a concealed place. 2. To make nasty attacks. [ME.] —**snip′er** n.

George Miksch Sutton
snipe

snip·pet (snĭp′ĭt) n. A tidbit or morsel.

snip·py (snĭp′ē) adj. **-pi·er, -pi·est.** Impertinent; fresh; impudent.

snit (snĭt) n. Slang. A state of agitation. [Orig. unknown.]

snitch (snĭch) v. Slang. 1. To steal. 2. To turn informer. [Orig. unknown.] —**snitch′er** n.

sniv·el (snĭv′əl) v. **-eled** or **-elled, -el·ing** or **-el·ling.** 1. To complain or whine tearfully. 2. To run at the nose, esp. while crying. [ME snyvelen, to run at the nose.] —**sniv′el** n.

snob (snŏb) n. One who is convinced of and flaunts his social superiority. [Obs. snob, a lower-class person.] —**snob′ber·y** n. —**snob′bish** adj. —**snob′bish·ly** adv. —**snob′bish·ness** n.

snook·er (snook′ər) n. A pocket billiards game in which 15 red and 6 nonred balls are used. [Orig. unknown.]

snoop (snoop) Informal. —v. To pry furtively. —n. One who snoops. [Du. snoepen, to eat on the sly.] —**snoop′er** n. —**snoop′i·ness** n. —**snoop′y** adj.

snoot (snoot) n. Slang. A snout or nose.

snoot·y (snoo′tē) adj. **-i·er, -i·est.** Informal. Snobbish; haughty.

snooze (snooz) v. **snoozed, snooz·ing.** Informal. To take a nap. [Orig. unknown.] —**snooze** n.

snore (snôr, snōr) v. **snored, snor·ing.** To breathe with a rough grating noise while sleeping. [ME snoren, to snort.] —**snore** n. —**snor′er** n.

snor·kel (snôr′kəl) n. 1. A J-shaped tube used by skin divers for breathing with the face underwater. 2. A retractable tube that can be extended from a submarine, used to draw in air and expel waste gases while submerged. [G. Schnorchel.] —**snor′kel** v.

snort (snôrt) n. 1. To exhale or inhale forcibly and noisily through the nostrils. 2. To make an abrupt noise expressive of scorn or anger. —n. 1. An act or sound of snorting. 2. A small amount or dose, esp. a small drink. [ME snorten.] —**snort′er** n.

snot (snŏt) n. Slang. 1. Nasal mucus; phlegm. 2. An untrustworthy, devious, or malicious person. [< OE gesnot.]

snout (snout) n. 1. The projecting nose or facial part of an animal's muzzle. 2. Slang. The human nose. [ME snute.]

snow (snō) n. 1. Translucent crystals of ice

that form from water vapor in the atmosphere. —v. A falling of snow; snowstorm. —v. **1.** To fall to the earth as snow. **2.** To cover or close off with snow. **3.** *Slang.* To overwhelm or deceive with talk or information, esp. with flattery. [< OE *snāw.*] —**snow'y** *adj.*

snow•ball (snō'bôl') *n.* A mass of soft, wet snow packed into a ball. —v. **1.** To throw snowballs. **2.** To grow rapidly in significance, importance, or size.

snow•bank (snō'băngk') *n.* A large mass of snow.

snow•bound (snō'bound') *adj.* Confined, blocked, or isolated by heavy snow.

snow•drift (snō'drĭft') *n.* A large mass of snow banked up by the wind.

snow•drop (snō'drŏp') *n.* A bulbous plant with nodding white flowers.

snow•fall (snō'fôl') *n.* **1.** A fall of snow. **2.** The amount of snow that falls in a given area over a given time.

snow•flake (snō'flāk') *n.* A single flake or crystal of snow.

snow•mo•bile (snō'mō-bēl') *n.* A small vehicle with skilike runners in front and tanklike treads, used for traveling on snow.

snow•plow (snō'plou') *n.* A plowlike device used to remove snow.

snow•shoe (snō'shōō') *n.* A racket-shaped frame with interlaced strips, attached to the shoe to prevent sinking into deep snow. —**snow'shoe'** *v.*

snow•storm (snō'stôrm') *n.* A storm marked by heavy snowfall.

snow tire *n.* A tire with a deeply grooved tread to provide traction on snow.

snub (snŭb) *v.* **snubbed, snub•bing.** **1.** To slight by ignoring or behaving coldly. **2.** To dismiss or turn down in a decisive way. **3.** To check suddenly the movement of (a rope or cable running out). —*n.* A deliberate slight. [< ON *snubba,* to rebuke.]

snub-nosed (snŭb'nōzd') *adj.* Having a short, turned-up nose.

snuff¹ (snŭf) *v.* **1.** To inhale through the nose. **2.** To sniff. —*n.* Finely pulverized tobacco for snorting up the nostrils. —**Idiom. up to snuff.** *Informal.* Up to standard. [Prob. < MDu. *snuffen,* to snuffle.]

snuff² (snŭf) *v.* **1.** To cut off the charred portion of (a candlewick). **2.** To extinguish; put out. [ME *snoffe.*]

snuf•fle (snŭf'əl) *v.* **-fled, -fling. 1.** To breathe or sniff noisily, as through a blocked nose. **2.** To sniffle. [Prob. < LG *snuffelen.*] —**snuf'fle** *n.*

snug (snŭg) *adj.* **snug•ger, snug•gest. 1.** Comfortably sheltered; cozy. **2.** Small but well-arranged: *a snug apartment.* **3.** Close-fitting; tight. [Perh. < Scand. orig.] —**snug** or **snug'ly** *adv.* —**snug'ness** *n.*

snug•gle (snŭg'əl) *v.* **-gled, -gling.** To nestle or cuddle. [< SNUG.]

so (sō) *adv.* **1.** In the manner expressed or indicated; thus: *got stuck and remained so.* **2.** To such an extent: *I'm so happy that I could cry.* **3.** To a great extent: *It's so cold.* **4.** Consequently; as a result. **5.** Thereabouts: *The student fare is only $10 or so.* **6.** Too; also; likewise: *She likes the book and so do I.* **7.** Then; apparently. **8.** In truth; indeed.

—*adj.* True; factual. —*conj.* With the result or consequence that: *He failed to show up, so we went without him.* —*interj.* Used to express surprise or comprehension. —**Idioms. so as to.** In order to: *Mail your packages early so as to be sure they arrive in time.* **so that.** In order that. [< OE *swā.*]

Usage: In formal writing the conjunction *so* is preferably followed by *that* when it introduces a clause stating the purpose of or reason for an action: *He stayed a day longer so that he could avoid the holiday traffic.* However, when used to introduce a clause stating a result or consequence, *so* generally stands alone: *The holiday traffic was unusually heavy, so he stayed a day longer.*

soak (sōk) *v.* **1.** To make thoroughly wet by or as if by being immersed; steep. **2.** To absorb. **3.** To be immersed. **4.** To penetrate or permeate; seep. —*n.* **1.** The act or process of soaking. **2.** *Slang.* A drunkard. [< OE *socian.*] —**soak'er** *n.*

soap (sōp) *n.* **1.** A cleansing agent made from an alkali acting on natural oils and fats. **2.** *Slang.* A soap opera. —*v.* To treat or cover with soap. [< OE *sāpe.*] —**soap'i•ly** *adv.* —**soap'i•ness** *n.* —**soap'y** *adj.*

soap opera *n.* A usu. daytime radio or television serial drama. So called because of orig. sponsorship by soap companies.]

soap•stone (sōp'stōn') *n.* Steatite.

soar (sôr, sōr) *v.* **1.** To rise, fly, or glide high in the air. **2.** To climb swiftly or powerfully. [< OFr. *esorer.*]

sob (sŏb) *v.* **sobbed, sob•bing.** To weep aloud with convulsive gasping. [ME *sobben.*] —**sob** *n.* —**sob'bing•ly** *adv.*

so•ber (sō'bər) *adj.* **-er, -est. 1.** Abstemious or temperate. **2.** Not intoxicated. **3.** Serious or grave: *a sober expression.* **4.** Without frivolity, excess, or exaggeration. **5.** Marked by self-control or sanity; reasonable. —*v.* To make or become sober. [< Lat. *sobrius.*] —**so'ber•ly** *adv.* —**so'ber•ness** *n.*

so•bri•e•ty (sō-brī'ĭ-tē) *n.* **1.** Seriousness or gravity; solemnity. **2.** Absence of alcoholic intoxication.

so•bri•quet (sō'brĭ-kā', -kĕt') *n.* **1.** A nickname. **2.** An assumed name. [Fr.]

so-called (sō'kôld') *adj.* So named or designated, often incorrectly.

soc•cer (sŏk'ər) *n.* A game in which two 11-member teams seek to propel the ball into the opposing team's goal by kicking it or by

soccer

using any part of the body except the arms and hands. [< *association football.*]

so·cia·ble (sō'shə-bəl) *adj.* **1.** Liking the company of others; friendly. **2.** Providing occasion for friendly social relations. —*n.* A social. [< Lat. *sociabilis.*] —**so·cia·bil'i·ty** *or* **so'cia·ble·ness** *n.* —**so'cia·bly** *adv.*

so·cial (sō'shəl) *adj.* **1.** Living together in communities or groups: *social insects.* **b.** Of or typical of such a way of life: *social activities.* **2.** Of or in society. **3.** Sociable or companionable. **4.** Marked by or promoting friendly social relations: *a social gathering.* **5.** Of or occupied with welfare work. —*n.* An informal social gathering. [Lat. *socialis*, of companionship.] —**so'cial·ly** *adv.*

social disease *n.* Venereal disease.

so·cial·ism (sō'shə-lĭz'əm) *n.* A system or theory of social organization in which the producers possess both political power and production and distribution means. —**so'cial·ist** *n.* —**so'cial·is'tic** *adj.*

so·cial·ite (sō'shə-līt') *n.* One prominent in fashionable society.

so·cial·ize (sō'shə-līz') *v.* **-ized, -iz·ing. 1.** To place under public ownership or control. **2.** To convert or adapt to social needs. **3.** To take part in social activities. —**so'cial·i·za'tion** *n.* —**so'cial·iz'er** *n.*

socialized medicine *n.* The provision of medical and hospital care for the people at nominal cost through government regulation of health services and tax subsidies.

social science *n.* Any of the sciences, such as sociology, psychology, or anthropology, that study society or the relationships between the individual and society.

social security *n.* A government program that provides monthly payments to the elderly and others, financed by payments made both by employers and employees.

social work *n.* Organized public efforts to aid the poor and counsel those with special problems. —**social worker** *n.*

so·ci·e·ty (sə-sī'ĭ-tē) *n., pl.* **-ties. 1.** Human beings in general. **2.** A group of people with a common culture or way of life. **3.** A group of people who unite to share a common interest. **4.** The rich and fashionable social class. **5.** Companionship; company. **6.** *Biol.* A community of organisms. [< Lat. *societas.*] —**so·ci'e·tal** (-təl) *adj.*

Society of Friends *n.* A Christian sect founded in about 1650 in England that rejects ritual, formal sacraments, a priesthood, and violence.

socio- *pref.* **1.** Society: *sociology.* **2.** Social: *socioeconomic.* [< Lat. *socius*, fellow.]

so·ci·o·ec·o·nom·ic (sō'sē-ō'-ĕk'ə-nŏm'ĭk, -ē'kə-, -shē-) *adj.* Both social and economic.

so·ci·ol·o·gy (sō'sē-ŏl'ə-jē, -shē-) *n.* The study of the origins, organization, institutions, and development of human society. —**so'ci·o·log'ic** (-ə-lŏj'ĭk) *or* **so'ci·o·log'i·cal** *adj.* —**so'ci·ol'o·gist** *n.*

sock¹ (sŏk) *n., pl.* **socks** *or* **sox** (sŏks). A short stocking. [< Lat. *soccus*, a kind of shoe.]

sock² (sŏk) *v. Slang.* To strike forcefully; punch. [Orig. unknown.] —**sock** *n.*

sock·et (sŏk'ĭt) *n.* An opening or cavity into which something fits. [< OFr. *soc*, plowshare.]

So·crat·ic (sə-krăt'ĭk, sō-) *adj.* Of or pertaining to Socrates, his followers, or his method of trying to arrive at the truth by asking questions. —**So·crat'i·cal·ly** *adv.*

sod (sŏd) *n.* Grass-covered surface soil held together by matted roots. —*v.* **sod·ded, sod·ding.** To cover with sod. [< MLG *sode.*]

so·da (sō'də) *n.* **1. a.** Any of various forms of sodium carbonate. **b.** Chemically combined sodium. **2. a.** Carbonated water. **b.** A flavored, carbonated soft drink. **c.** A drink made from carbonated water, ice cream, and usu. flavoring. [Med. Lat.]

soda pop *n.* Soda (sense 2.b.).

soda water *n.* Water charged with carbon dioxide under pressure.

sod·den (sŏd'n) *adj.* **1.** Thoroughly soaked; saturated. **2.** Soggy and heavy. **3.** Bloated and dull, esp. from drink. [ME *soden*, p.p. of *sethen*, to seethe.] —**sod'den·ly** *adv.* —**sod'den·ness** *n.*

so·di·um (sō'dē-əm) *n. Symbol* **Na** A soft, light, extremely malleable silver-white metallic element, used esp. in the production of a wide variety of industrially important compounds. Atomic number 11; atomic weight 22.99. [SOD(A) + -IUM.]

sodium bicarbonate *n.* A white crystalline compound, $NaHCO_3$, used esp. in making beverages and baking soda.

sodium borate *n.* A crystalline compound, $Na_2B_4O_7 \cdot 10H_2O$, used in the manufacture of glass, detergents, and pharmaceuticals.

sodium carbonate *n.* **1.** A white powdery compound, Na_2CO_3, used in the manufacture of sodium compounds, ceramics, detergents, and soap. **2.** Any of various hydrated carbonates of sodium.

sodium chloride *n.* A colorless crystalline compound, NaCl, used in the manufacture of chemicals and as a food preservative and seasoning; salt.

sodium glu·ta·mate (glōō'tə-māt') *n.* A white crystalline compound used for seasoning food. [SODIUM + GLUT(EN) + *am*(ide) + -ATE².]

sodium hydroxide *n.* An alkaline compound, NaOH, used in chemicals and soaps and in petroleum refining.

sodium nitrate *n.* A white crystalline compound, $NaNO_3$, used in explosives and tobacco.

sod·om·y (sŏd'ə-mē) *n.* **1.** Anal copulation of one male with another. **2.** Anal or oral copulation with a member of the opposite sex. **3.** Copulation with an animal. [< *Sodom*, a city in ancient Palestine.]

so·fa (sō'fə) *n.* A long upholstered seat with a back and arms. [Ar. *sufah*, dais.]

sofa

soft (sôft, sŏft) *adj.* **-er, -est. 1.** Not hard or firm; offering little resistance. **2.** Out of condition; flabby. **3.** Smooth or fine to the touch. **4.** Not loud, harsh, or irritating. **5.** Not brilliant or glaring; subdued. **6.** Mild; balmy: *a soft breeze.* **7. a.** Of a gentle disposition; yielding. **b.** Affectionate. **c.** Not stern; lenient. **8.** *Informal.* Simple; feeble: *soft in the head.* **9.** *Informal.* Easy: *a soft job.* **10.** Apt to change, fluctuate, or devaluate. **11.** Having low dissolved mineral content: *soft water.* —*adv.* Gently; softly. [< OE *sōfte*, pleasant.] —**soft′ly** *adv.* —**soft′ness** *n.*

soft-ball (sôft′bôl′, sŏft′-) *n.* **1.** A variation of baseball played with a larger, softer ball. **2.** The ball used in this game.

soft drink *n.* A nonalcoholic beverage.

soft-en (sô′fən, sŏf′ən) *v.* To make or become soft or softer. —**soft′en-er** *n.*

soft-heart-ed (sôft′här′tĭd, sŏft′-) *adj.* Easily moved; tender; merciful. —**soft′heart′ed-ly** *adv.* —**soft′heart′ed-ness** *n.*

soft landing *n.* The landing of a space vehicle at a velocity low enough to prevent damage.

soft palate *n.* The movable fold that hangs from the back of the hard palate and closes off the nasal cavity from the mouth cavity during swallowing or sucking.

soft-ped-al (sôft′pĕd′l, sŏft′-) *v.* **-aled** or **-alled,** **-al-ing** or **-al-ling.** *Informal.* To make less emphatic or obvious.

soft sell *n.* A subtly persuasive method of selling or advertising.

soft-shell clam (sôft′shĕl′, sŏft′-) *n.* An edible clam with a thin, elongated shell.

soft soap *n.* *Informal.* Cajolery; flattery. —**soft′-soap′** *v.*

soft-ware (sôft′wâr′, sŏft′-) *n.* *Computer Sci.* Written or printed data, as programs, routines, and symbolic languages, essential to the operation and maintenance of computers.

soft-wood (sôft′wŏŏd′, sŏft′-) *n.* **1.** The wood of a coniferous tree. **2.** A coniferous tree.

soft-y (sôf′tē, sŏf′-) *n., pl.* **-ies.** *Informal.* One who is overly sentimental, trusting, or lenient.

sog-gy (sŏg′ē, sô′gē) *adj.* **-gi-er, -gi-est.** Saturated with moisture; soaked. [< dial. *sog,* to soak.] —**sog′gi-ly** *adv.* —**sog′gi-ness** *n.*

soil¹ (soil) *n.* **1.** The top layer of the earth's surface, suitable for the growth of plant life. **2.** Earth or ground. **3.** Country; region: *native soil.* [< Lat. *solium,* seat.]

soil² (soil) *v.* **1.** To make or become dirty. **2.** To disgrace; tarnish. **3.** To corrupt; defile. —*n.* **1. a.** The condition of being soiled. **b.** A stain. **2.** Manure, esp. human excrement, used as fertilizer. [< OFr. *souiller.*]

soi-ree or **soi-rée** (swä-rā′) *n.* An evening party or reception. [< Fr. *soir,* evening.]

so-journ (sō′jûrn′, sō-jûrn′) *v.* To stay for a time. —*n.* A temporary stay. [< OFr. *sojorner.*] —**so′journ′er** *n.*

sol¹ (sōl) *n.* *Mus.* The 5th tone of a diatonic scale. [Med. Lat.]

sol² (sōl, sŏl) *n., pl.* **so-les** (sō′lās). See table at **currency.** [Sp.]

sol-ace (sŏl′əs) *n.* **1.** Comfort in sorrow or distress; consolation. **2.** Something that furnishes comfort or consolation. [< Lat. *solari,* to comfort.] —**sol′ace** *v.*

so-lar (sō′lər) *adj.* **1.** Of or proceeding from the sun: *solar rays.* **2.** Using or operating by energy derived from the sun. **3.** Measured with respect to the sun: *the solar year.* [< Lat. *sol,* sun.]

solar battery *n.* An electric battery that consists of solar cells connected together.

solar cell *n.* A semiconductor device that converts solar radiation into electrical energy, often used in space vehicles.

solar flare *n.* A temporary outburst of gases from a small area of the sun's surface.

so-lar-i-um (sō-lâr′ē-əm, -lär′-) *n., pl.* **-i-a** (-ē-ə) or **-i-ums.** A room, gallery, or glassed-in porch exposed to the sun. [Lat., terrace.]

solar plexus *n.* **1.** The large network of nerves located behind the stomach. **2.** *Informal.* The pit of the stomach.

solar system *n.* The sun together with the nine planets and all other celestial bodies that orbit the sun.

solar wind *n.* The flow of charged atomic particles that radiates from the sun.

sold (sōld) *v.* *p.t. & p.p.* of **sell.**

sol-der (sŏd′ər, sō′dər) *n.* **1.** Any of various alloys, mainly of tin and lead, applied in the molten state to join metallic parts. **2.** Something that joins or cements. —*v.* To join or repair with or as if with solder. [< Lat. *solidare,* to make solid.] —**sol′der-er** *n.*

sol-dier (sōl′jər) *n.* **1.** One who serves in an army. **2.** An enlisted person as distinguished from an officer. **3.** An active follower. —*v.* To be or serve as a soldier. [< OFr. *soulde,* pay.] —**sol′dier-ly** *adj.*

soldier of fortune *n.* One who serves in an army for monetary gain or love of adventure.

sol-diery (sōl′jə-rē) *n., pl.* **-ies.** **1.** A body of soldiers. **2.** The military profession.

sole¹ (sōl) *n.* **1.** The undersurface of the foot. **2.** The undersurface of a shoe or boot. —*v.* **soled, sol-ing.** To furnish (a shoe or boot) with a sole. [< Lat. *solea,* sandal.]

sole² (sōl) *adj.* Single; only. [< Lat. *solus.*] —**sole′ly** *adv.*

sole³ (sōl) *n., pl.* **sole** or **soles.** Any of various chiefly marine flatfishes valued as food. [< Lat. *solea,* sandal, flatfish.]

sol-e-cism (sōl′ĭ-sĭz′əm, sŏl′ĭ-) *n.* **1.** A nonstandard usage or grammatical construction. **2.** A violation of etiquette. [< Gk. *soloikos,* speaking incorrectly.]

sol-emn (sŏl′əm) *adj.* **1.** Deeply earnest; grave. **2.** Performed with full ceremony. **3.** Gloomy; somber. [< Lat. *sollemnis,* customary.] —**so-lem′ni-ty** (sə-lĕm′nĭ-tē) or **sol′emn-ness** *n.* —**sol′emn-ly** *adv.*

sol-em-nize (sŏl′əm-nīz′) *v.* **-nized, -niz-ing.** **1.** To celebrate or observe with solemnity. **2.** To perform with formal ceremony. —**sol′em-ni-za′tion** *n.*

so-le-noid (sō′lə-noid′) *n.* A coil of insulated wire in which a magnetic field is established when an electric current is passed through it. [< Gk. *sōlēnoeidēs,* pipe-shaped.]

so-lic-it (sə-lĭs′ĭt) *v.* **1.** To seek to obtain: *solicit votes.* **2.** To entreat; importune. **3.** To entice; tempt. [< Lat. *sollicitare.*] —**so-lic′i-ta′tion** *n.*

so-lic-i-tor (sə-lĭs′ĭ-tər) *n.* **1.** One who solicits. **2.** The chief law officer of a city, town, or government department. **3.** *Chiefly Brit.* A lawyer who is not a member of the bar and who may be heard only in the lower courts.

so-lic-i-tous (sə-lĭs′ĭ-təs) *adj.* **1.** Concerned; attentive. **2.** Eager. [Lat. *sollicitus,* troubled.] —**so-lic′i-tous-ly** *adv.* —**so-lic′i-tous-ness** *n.*

---

so·lic·i·tude (sə-lĭs′ĭ-tōōd′, -tyōōd′) *n.* Care; concern.

sol·id (sŏl′ĭd) *adj.* **-er, -est. 1.** Having a definite shape and volume; not liquid or gaseous. **2.** Not hollowed out. **3.** Being the same substance or color throughout. **4.** Having or dealing with three dimensions: *solid figures.* **5.** Of good quality and substance. **6.** Financially sound. **7.** Upstanding and dependable. **8.** Sound; reliable. **9.** Acting together; unanimous. —*n.* **1.** A solid substance. **2.** A geometric figure that has three dimensions. [< Lat. *solidus,* not hollow.] —**so·lid′i·ty** (sə-lĭd′-ĭ-tē) *or* **sol′id·ness** *n.* —**sol′id·ly** *adv.*

sol·i·dar·i·ty (sŏl′ĭ-dăr′ĭ-tē) *n., pl.* **-ties.** A unity of interests, purposes, or sympathies among a group.

so·lid·i·fy (sə-lĭd′ə-fī′) *v.* **-fied, -fy·ing.** To make or become solid or united. —**so·lid′i·fi·ca′tion** *n.*

sol·id-state (sŏl′ĭd-stāt′) *adj.* **1.** Of or concerned with the physical properties of crystalline solids. **2.** Based on or using transistors or related semiconductor devices.

so·lil·o·quize (sə-lĭl′ə-kwīz′) *v.* **-quized, -quiz·ing.** To deliver a soliloquy.

so·lil·o·quy (sə-lĭl′ə-kwē) *n., pl.* **-quies. 1.** A dramatic discourse in which a character reveals his thoughts in the form of a monologue. **2.** The act of speaking to oneself. [LLat. *soliloquium.*]

sol·ip·sism (sŏl′ĭp-sĭz′əm, sō′lĭp-) *n.* The philosophical theory that the self is the only reality. [Lat. *solus,* alone + Lat. *ipse,* self + -ISM.] —**sol′ip·sist** *n.* —**sol′ip·sis′tic** *adj.*

sol·i·taire (sŏl′ĭ-târ′) *n.* **1.** A gemstone set alone, as in a ring. **2.** A card game played by one person. [< Lat. *solitarius,* solitary.]

sol·i·tar·y (sŏl′ĭ-tĕr′ē) *adj.* **1.** Existing or living alone. **2.** Happening or done alone. **3.** Remote; secluded. **4.** Single; sole. [< Lat. *solus,* alone.] —**sol′i·tar′i·ly** *adv.* —**sol′i·tar′i·ness** *n.*

sol·i·tude (sŏl′ĭ-tōōd′, -tyōōd′) *n.* **1.** The condition of being alone; isolation. **2.** A lonely or secluded place. [< Lat. *solus,* alone.]

so·lo (sō′lō) *n., pl.* **-los. 1.** A musical composition for an individual voice or instrument, with or without accompaniment. **2.** A performance or accomplishment by a single individual. —*v.* To perform a solo. [Ital.] —**so′lo** *adj. & adv.* —**so′lo·ist** *n.*

so·lon (sō′lən) *n.* A wise lawgiver. [< *Solon,* Athenian statesman (c. 600 B.C.).]

so long *interj. Informal.* Used to express farewell.

sol·stice (sŏl′stĭs, sōl′-) *n.* Either of the two times of year when the sun reaches an extreme of its northward or southward motion. [< Lat. *solstitum.*] —**sol·sti′tial** (-stĭsh′əl) *adj.*

sol·u·ble (sŏl′yə-bəl) *adj.* **1.** Capable of being dissolved. **2.** Capable of being solved or explained. [< Lat. *solvere,* to loosen.] —**sol′u·bil′i·ty** *n.* —**sol′u·bly** *adv.*

sol·ute (sŏl′yōōt′, sō′lōōt′) *n.* A substance dissolved in another substance. —*adj.* In solution; dissolved. [< Lat. *solutus,* p.p. of *solvere,* to loosen.]

so·lu·tion (sə-lōō′shən) *n.* **1. a.** A mixture of two or more substances that appears to be uniform throughout except at the molecular level and is capable of forming by itself when the substances are in contact. **b.** The act or process of forming a solution. **2.** The method or process of solving a problem. **3.** The answer to or disposition of a problem.

solve (sŏlv) *v.* **solved, solv·ing.** To find a solution to. [< Lat. *solvere,* to loosen.] —**solv′a·ble** *adj.* —**solv′er** *n.*

sol·vent (sŏl′vənt) *adj.* **1.** Able to meet financial obligations. **2.** Capable of dissolving another substance. —*n.* A liquid capable of dissolving another substance. [< Lat. *solvere,* to loosen.] —**sol′ven·cy** *n.*

so·mat·ic (sō-măt′ĭk, sə-) *adj.* Of the body, esp. as distinguished from a bodily part, the mind, or the environment; physical. [< Gk. *soma,* body.]

som·ber (sŏm′bər) *adj.* Also **som·bre. 1.** Dark; gloomy. **2.** Melancholy; dismal. [Fr. *sombre.*]

som·bre·ro (sŏm-brâr′ō) *n., pl.* **-ros.** A large, broad-brimmed straw or felt hat worn esp. in Mexico and the American Southwest. [Sp.]

some (sŭm) *adj.* **1.** Being an unspecified number or quantity: *some people; some sugar.* **2.** Unknown or unspecified by name: *Some student left you this note.* **3.** *Informal.* Considerable; remarkable: *He is some cook.* —*pron.* An indefinite or unspecified number or quantity. —*adv.* **1.** Approximately; about. **2.** *Informal.* Somewhat. [< OE *sum,* a certain one.]

-some¹ *suff.* Characterized by a specified state, quality, or action: *quarrelsome.* [< OE *-sum.*]

-some² *suff.* Body: *chromosome.* [< Gk. *soma.*]

-some³ *suff.* A group of a specified number: *threesome.* [< ME *sum,* some.]

some·bod·y (sŭm′bŏd′ē, -bŭd′ē, -bə-dē) *pron.* An unspecified person; someone. —*n. Informal.* A person of importance.

some·day (sŭm′dā′) *adv.* At some time in the future.

some·how (sŭm′hou′) *adv.* **1.** In some way or other. **2.** For some reason.

some·one (sŭm′wŭn′, -wən) *pron.* Some person; somebody. —*n. Informal.* A somebody.

som·er·sault (sŭm′ər-sôlt′) *n.* An acrobatic stunt in which the body rolls in a complete circle, heels over head. [OFr. *sombresault.*] —**som′er·sault** *v.*

some·thing (sŭm′thĭng) *pron.* An unspecified or not definitely known thing. —*n. Informal.* A remarkable or important thing or person. —*adv.* Somewhat. —**idioms. something else.** *Informal.* One that is special or remarkable. **something of.** To some extent.

some·time (sŭm′tīm′) *adv.* **1.** At an indefinite or unstated time. **2.** At an indefinite time in the future. —*adj.* Former.

some·times (sŭm′tīmz′) *adv.* Now and then.

some·way (sŭm′wā′) *adv.* Also **some·ways** (-wāz′). *Informal.* **1.** Somehow. **2.** For some reason or other.

some·what (sŭm′hwŏt′, -wŏt′, -hwət, -wət′) *adv.* To some extent or degree; rather.

some·where (sŭm′hwĕr′, -wĕr′) *adv.* **1.** At, in, or to a place not specified or known. **2.** To a place or state of further development or progress. —*n.* An unspecified place.

som·me·lier (sŭm′əl-yā′) *n.* A wine steward in a restaurant. [Fr.]

som·nam·bu·lism (sŏm-năm′byə-lĭz′əm) *n.* The act of walking while asleep. [Lat. *somnus,* sleep + AMBUL(ANT) + -ISM.] —**som·nam′bu·late′** (-lāt′) *v.* —**som·nam′bu·list** *n.*

som·no·lent (sŏm′nə-lənt) *adj.* Drowsy; sleepy. [< Lat. *somnus,* sleep.] —**som′no·lence** *n.* —**som′no·lent·ly** *adv.*

son (sŭn) *n.* **1.** A male offspring. **2.** A male

descendant. **3.** A male associated with a place or cause. **4. the Son.** Christ. [< OE *sunu.*]

so·nar (sō'när') *n.* A system or apparatus that uses reflected sound waves to detect and locate underwater objects. [SO(UND) NA(VIGATION) R(ANGING).]

so·na·ta (sə-nä'tä) *n.* An instrumental musical composition written in three or four movements. [Ital.]

song (sông, sŏng) *n.* **1.** A brief musical composition written for singing. **2.** The act or art of singing. **3.** A melodious utterance. **4. a.** Poetry. **b.** A lyric poem. —**idiom. for a song.** At a low price. [< OE *sang.*]

song·bird (sông'bûrd', sŏng'-) *n.* A bird with a melodious song or call.

Song of Sol·o·mon (sŏl'ə-mən) *n.* See table at **Bible.**

Song of Songs *n.* See table at **Bible.**

song·ster (sông'stər, sŏng'-) *n.* A singer or songwriter.

song·writ·er (sông'rī'tər, sŏng'-) *n.* One who writes lyrics or melodies for songs.

son·ic (sŏn'ĭk) *adj.* Of or relating to sound or its speed of propagation. [< Lat. *sonus,* sound.]

sonic boom *n.* A loud, transient explosive sound caused by the shock wave preceding an aircraft traveling at a supersonic speed.

son-in-law (sŭn'ən-lô') *n., pl.* **sons-in-law.** The husband of one's daughter.

son·net (sŏn'ĭt) *n.* A 14-line poetic form, usu. in iambic pentameter, with a fixed rhyme pattern. [< OProv. *sonet.*]

so·no·rous (sə-nôr'əs, -nōr'-, sŏn'ər-) *adj.* **1.** Having or producing sound, esp. full, deep, or rich sound. **2.** Impressive; grandiloquent: *sonorous prose.* [< Lat. *sonor,* sound.] —**so·nor'i·ty** *n.* —**so·no'rous·ly** *adv.*

soon (sōōn) *adv.* -**er,** -**est. 1. a.** In the near future. **b.** Within a short time; quickly. **2.** Early. **3.** Quickly; fast. **4.** Gladly; willingly: *I'd just as soon leave right now.* [< OE *sōna.*]

Usage: *No sooner* as a comparative adverb should be followed by *than,* not *when,* as in *No sooner had he left than she called.*

soot (sŏōt, sŏōt, sŭt) *n.* A black powdery substance, chiefly carbon, produced by the incomplete combustion of fuel. [< OE *sōt.*] —**soot'i·ness** *n.* —**soot'y** *adj.*

sooth (sōōth) *n. Archaic.* Truth; reality. [< OE *sōth.*]

soothe (sōōth) *v.* **soothed, sooth·ing. 1.** To calm or quiet. **2.** To ease or relieve the pain of. [< OE *sōthian,* to verify.] —**sooth'er** *n.* —**sooth'ing·ly** *adv.*

sooth·say·er (sōōth'sā'ər) *n.* One who foretells events.

sop (sŏp) *v.* **sopped, sop·ping. 1.** To dip, soak, or drench in a liquid. **2.** To take up by absorption. —*n.* Something yielded to placate or soothe; bribe. [< OE *sopp,* dipped bread.]

soph·ism (sŏf'ĭz'əm) *n.* **1.** A seemingly reasonable argument that is actually invalid. **2.** Deceptive or fallacious argumentation. [< Gk. *sophos,* clever.] —**soph'ist** *n.* —**so·phis'tic** or **so·phis'ti·cal** *adj.* —**so·phis'ti·cal·ly** *adv.*

so·phis·ti·cate (sə-fĭs'tĭ-kāt') *v.* -**cat·ed,** -**cat·ing. 1.** To cause to become less naive. **2.** To make more complex or advanced. —*n.* (-kĭt). A sophisticated person. —**so·phis'ti·ca'tion** *n.*

so·phis·ti·cat·ed (sə-fĭs'tĭ-kā'tĭd) *adj.* **1.** Having acquired worldly knowledge or refinement. **2.** Elaborate, complex, or complicated: *a sophisticated machine.* **3.** Appealing to the tastes of sophisticates: *a sophisticated play.*

soph·ist·ry (sŏf'ĭ-strē) *n., pl.* -**tries.** Plausible but faulty or misleading argumentation.

soph·o·more (sŏf'ə-môr', -mōr') *n.* A second-year student in an American college or high school. [Gk. *sophos,* wise + *mōros,* foolish.]

soph·o·mor·ic (sŏf'ə-môr'ĭk, -mōr'-, -mŏr'-) *adj.* **1.** Of or characteristic of a sophomore. **2.** Immature and overconfident.

sop·o·rif·ic (sŏp'ə-rĭf'ĭk) *adj.* **1.** Causing sleep. **2.** Drowsy. —*n.* A sleep-inducing drug. [< Lat. *sopor,* sleep.]

so·pran·o (sə-prăn'ō, -prä'nō) *n., pl.* -**os. 1.** The highest singing voice of a woman or young boy. **2.** A singer having a soprano voice. **3.** A part written for a soprano voice. [Ital.]

sor·cer·y (sôr'sə-rē) *n., pl.* -**ies.** The use of supernatural power; witchcraft. [< Lat. *sors,* lot.] —**sor'cer·er** *n.* —**sor'cer·ess** *n.*

sor·did (sôr'dĭd) *adj.* **1.** Filthy; foul. **2.** Depressingly squalid; wretched. **3.** Morally degraded; vile; base. [< Lat. *sordēre,* to be dirty.] —**sor'did·ly** *adv.* —**sor'did·ness** *n.*

sore (sôr, sōr) *adj.* **sor·er, sor·est. 1.** Painful or tender. **2.** Feeling pain; hurting. **3.** Causing sorrow or distress; grievous. **4.** Angry; offended. —*n.* An open injury, wound, ulcer, etc. **2.** A source of pain or distress. [< OE *sār.*] —**sore'ly** *adv.* —**sore'ness** *n.*

sor·ghum (sôr'gəm) *n.* An Old World grass cultivated as grain and forage or as a source of syrup. [< Ital. *sorgo.*]

so·ror·i·ty (sə-rôr'ĭ-tē, -rōr'-) *n., pl.* -**ties.** A club for women, esp. one at a college. [< Lat. *soror,* sister.]

sor·rel[1] (sôr'əl, sŏr'-) *n.* Any of several plants with acid-tasting leaves. [< OFr. *sur,* sour.]

sor·rel[2] (sôr'əl, sŏr'-) *n.* **1.** A yellowish or reddish brown. **2.** A horse of this color. [< OFr. *sor,* reddish-brown.] —**sor'rel** *adj.*

sor·row (sôr'ō, sŏr'ō) *n.* **1.** Mental suffering because of loss or injury. **2.** Something that causes sadness or grief. —*v.* To grieve. [< OE *sorg.*] —**sor'row·ful** *adj.* —**sor'row·ful·ly** *adv.* —**sor'row·ful·ness** *n.*

sor·ry (sôr'ē, sŏr'ē) *adj.* -**ri·er,** -**ri·est. 1.** Feeling or expressing sympathy or regret. **2.** Poor; wretched: *a sorry excuse.* **3.** Grievous; sad. [< OE *sār,* sore.] —**sor'ri·ness** *n.*

sort (sôrt) *n.* **1.** A group or collection of similar persons or things; kind. **2.** Type; quality. **3.** Manner; style. —*v.* To arrange according to class, kind, or size. —**idioms. of sorts.** Of an inferior kind. **out of sorts.** *Informal.* **1.** Somewhat ill. **2.** In a bad mood. **sort of.** *Informal.* Somewhat; rather. [Prob. < Lat. *sors,* lot.]

sor·tie (sôr'tē, sôr-tē') *n.* **1.** An armed attack made from a place surrounded by enemy forces. **2.** A flight of a combat warplane. [< OFr. *sortir,* to go out.] —**sor'tie** *v.*

S O S (ĕs'ō-ĕs') *n.* A call for help or rescue. [< the letters represented by a radio distress signal.]

so-so (sō′sō′) *adj.* Mediocre. **—so′-so′** *adv.*

sot (sŏt) *n.* A drunkard. [< OE *sott*, fool.] **—sot′tish** *adj.*

So-tho (sō′tō) *n.* **1.** A group of Bantu languages spoken in southern Africa. **2.** Any of the Sotho languages.

sou-brette (sōō-brĕt′) *n.* A saucy, coquettish lady's maid in comedies or comic opera. [< Prov. *soubret*, conceited.]

souf-flé (sōō-flā′) *n.* A light, fluffy baked dish made with egg yolks and beaten egg whites. [< Lat. *sufflare*, to puff up.]

sough (sŭf, sou) *v.* To make a soft murmuring sound. [< OE *swōgan.*] **—sough** *n.*

sought (sŏt) *v. p.t. & p.p.* of **seek**.

soul (sōl) *n.* **1.** The animating and vital principle in a person often conceived as an immaterial entity that survives death. **2.** A spirit; ghost. **3.** A human being. **4.** The central or vital part of something. **5.** A person considered as the embodiment of an intangible quality: *the soul of discretion.* **6.** A person's emotional or moral nature. **7.** Emotional or expressive intensity, esp. in music. *—adj. Slang.* Of or derived from blacks and their culture. [< OE *sāwol.*]

soul-ful (sōl′fəl) *adj.* Full of or expressing a deep feeling. **—soul′ful-ly** *adv.* **—soul′ful-ness** *n.*

sound¹ (sound) *n.* **1. a.** A vibratory disturbance, with frequency in the approximate range between 20 and 20,000 cycles per second, capable of being heard. **b.** The sensation stimulated in the organs of hearing by such a disturbance. **c.** Such sensations collectively. **2.** A distinctive noise. **3.** An articulation made by the vocal apparatus. **4.** Recorded material, as for a motion picture. **5.** A conveyed impression; implication. *—v.* **1.** To make or cause to make a sound. **2.** To seem to be: *sounds reasonable.* **3.** To summon or signal by a sound. **4.** To examine (a bodily organ or part) by causing to emit sound. [< Lat. *sonus.*]

sound² (sound) *adj.* **-er, -est. 1.** Free from defect or damage. **2.** Solid. **3.** Secure or safe. **4.** Based on valid reasoning. **5.** Thorough; complete: *a sound thrashing.* **6.** Deep and undisturbed: *a sound sleep.* **7.** *Law.* Valid; legal: *sound title.* [< OE *gesund.*] **—sound′ly** *adv.* **—sound′ness** *n.*

sound³ (sound) *n.* A long body of water, wider than a strait or a channel, that usu. connects larger bodies of water. [< OE *sund*, sea, and < ON *sund*, strait.]

sound⁴ (sound) *v.* **1.** To measure the depth of (water). **2.** To try to learn the attitudes or opinions of. **3.** To dive swiftly downward, as a whale. [< OFr. *sonde*, a line for measuring water depth.] **—sound′er** *n.* **—sound′ing** *n.*

sounding board *n.* **1.** A thin board forming the upper portion of the resonant chamber in a musical instrument. **2.** A suspended structure designed to reflect a speaker's voice to the audience. **3.** A device or means serving to spread or popularize opinions.

sound-less (sound′lĭs) *adj.* Having or making no sound; quiet; silent. **—sound′less-ly** *adv.*

sound-proof (sound′prōōf′) *adj.* Allowing little or no audible sound to penetrate. *—v.* To make soundproof.

sound-track (sound′trăk′) *n.* **1.** The narrow strip at one side of a motion-picture film that carries the sound recording. **2.** A recording of the music from a motion picture.

soup (sōōp) *n.* A liquid food prepared from meat, fish, or vegetable stock with various other ingredients added. *—phrasal verb.* **soup up.** *Slang.* To add greater speed potential to. [< OFr. *soupe*, broth, of Gmc. orig.]

soup-çon (sōōp-sŏn′) *n.* A very small amount. [Fr.]

soup-y (sōō′pē) *adj.* **-i-er, -i-est. 1.** Having the consistency or appearance of soup. **2.** Foggy.

sour (sour) *adj.* **-er, -est. 1.** Having a sharp or acid taste. **2.** Spoiled; rancid. **3.** Bad-tempered. **4.** Unpleasant; disagreeable. *—v.* To make or become sour. [< OE *sūr.*] **—sour′ly** *adv.* **—sour′ness** *n.*

sour-ball (sour′bôl′) *n.* A round piece of hard, tart candy.

source (sôrs, sōrs) *n.* **1.** A point of origin. **2.** The beginning of a stream of water. **3.** One that supplies information. [< Lat. *surgere*, to rise.]

sour-dough (sour′dō′) *n.* Sour fermented dough used as leaven for bread.

souse (sous) *v.* **soused, sous-ing. 1.** To plunge in a liquid. **2.** To drench. **3.** To steep. **4.** *Slang.* To make intoxicated. *—n.* **1.** The act or process of sousing. **2. a.** Food steeped in pickle, esp. pork trimmings. **b.** Brine. **3.** *Slang.* A drunkard. [< OFr. *sous*, pickled meat, of Gmc. orig.]

south (south) *n.* **1. a.** The direction along a meridian 90° clockwise from the east. **b.** The cardinal point on the mariner's compass 180° clockwise from north. **2.** Often **South.** An area or region lying to the south of a particular point. **3. the South.** The southern part of the United States, esp. the states that fought for the Confederacy during the Civil War. *—adj.* To, toward, of, from, facing, or in the south. *—adv.* In, from, or toward the south. [< OE *sūth.*]

south-east (south-ēst′, sou-ēst′) *n.* **1.** The direction that is 45° clockwise from east and 45° clockwise from south. **2.** An area or region lying to the southeast of a particular point. **—south-east′** *adj. & adv.* **—south-east′ern** *adj.*

south-east-er (south-ē′stər, sou-ē′-) *n.* A storm or gale from the southeast.

south-east-er-ly (south-ē′stər-lē, sou-ē′-) *adj.* **1.** To or in the southeast. **2.** From the southeast. **—south-east′er-ly** *adv.*

south-east-ward (south-ēst′wərd, sou-ēst′-) *adv.* Also **south-east-wards** (-wərdz). Toward the southeast. **—south-east′ward** *adj. & n.* **—south-east′ward-ly** *adj. & adv.*

south-er-ly (sŭth′ər-lē) *adj.* **1.** In or toward the south. **2.** From the south. **—south′er-ly** *adv.*

south-ern (sŭth′ərn) *adj.* **1.** Of, in, or toward the south. **2.** From the south. **3.** Characteristic of or found in southern regions. [< OE *sūtherne.*]

south-ern-er (sŭth′ər-nər) *n.* A native or inhabitant of a southern region.

south-paw (south′pô′) *n.* A left-handed person, esp. a baseball pitcher. *—adj.* Left-handed.

South Pole *n.* **1.** The southern end of the earth's axis of rotation. **2.** The celestial zenith of the heavens as viewed from the south terrestrial pole.

south-ward (south′wərd, sŭth′ərd) *adv.* Also **south-wards** (south′wərdz, sŭth′ərdz). To or toward the south. **—south′ward** *adj.* **—south′ward-ly** *adj. & adv.*

south·west (south-wĕst′, sou-wĕst′) *n.* **1.** The direction that is 45° clockwise from south and 45° clockwise from west. **2.** An area or region lying to the southwest of a particular point. —**south·west′** *adj. & adv.* —**south′·west′ern** *adj.*

south·west·er (south-wĕs′tər, sou-wĕs′tər) *n.* Also **sou′west·er** (sou-wĕs′tər). **1.** A storm or gale from the southwest. **2.** A waterproof hat with a broad brim in back.

south·west·er·ly (south-wĕs′tər-lē, sou-wĕs′-) *adj.* **1.** To or in the southwest. **2.** From the southwest. —**south·west′er·ly** *adv.*

south·west·ward (south-wĕst′wərd, sou-wĕst′-) *adv.* Also **south·west·wards** (-wərdz). To or toward the southwest. —**south·west′ward** *adj.* —**south·west′ward·ly** *adj. & adv.*

sou·ve·nir (sōō′və-nîr′) *n.* Something serving as a token of remembrance; memento. [< Fr., to recall.]

sov·er·eign (sŏv′ər-ən, sŏv′rən) *n.* **1.** The chief of state in a monarchy. **2.** A former British gold coin worth one pound. —*adj.* **1.** Paramount; supreme. **2.** Having supreme rank or power. **3.** Independent: *a sovereign state.* **4.** Excellent. [< Lat. *super,* above.]

sov·er·eign·ty (sŏv′ər-ən-tē, sŏv′rən-) *n., pl.* **-ties.** **1.** Supremacy of authority or rule. **2.** Royal rank, authority, or power. **3.** Complete independence and self-government.

so·vi·et (sō′vē-ĕt′, -ĭt, sŏv′ē-) *n.* **1.** A popular elected legislative assembly in the Soviet Union. **2.** **Soviets.** The people and government of the Soviet Union. [R. *sovet.*]

sow[1] (sō) *v.* **sowed, sown** (sōn) or **sowed, sow·ing.** **1.** To plant (seeds) to produce a crop. **2.** To scatter with or as if with seed. **3.** To spread; propagate. [< OE *sāwan.*] —**sow′er** *n.*

sow[2] (sou) *n.* An adult female pig. [< OE *sugu.*]

sox (sŏks) *n.* A pl. of **sock**[1].

soy (soi) *n.* **1.** The soybean. **2.** Also **soy sauce.** A brown, salty liquid condiment made from soybeans. [Jap. *jiang*[4] *you*[2].]

soy·bean (soi′bēn′) *n.* An Asiatic bean cultivated for forage and for its nutritious, edible seeds.

spa (spä) *n.* **1.** A mineral spring. **2.** A resort area having mineral springs. [< *Spa,* Belgium.]

space (spās) *n.* **1. a.** A set of points or elements satisfying specified geometric conditions. **b.** The three-dimensional field of everyday experience or its infinite extension. **2. a.** The expanse in which the solar system, stars, and galaxies exist; universe. **b.** The distance between two points or the area or volume between specified boundaries. **3.** A blank or empty area. **4.** A particular area, as an accommodation on a train. **5. a.** A period or interval of time. **b.** A little while. —*v.* **spaced, spac·ing.** To arrange or organize with spaces between. [< Lat. *spatium,* distance.] —**spac′er** *n.*

space·craft (spās′krăft′) *n., pl.* **-craft.** A vehicle designed to be launched into space.

space flight *n.* Flight beyond the atmosphere of earth.

space heater *n.* A small, usu. portable device used to heat an enclosed area.

space·man (spās′măn′) *n.* One who travels in outer space; astronaut.

space·ship (spās′shĭp′) *n.* A spacecraft.

space shuttle *n.* A space vehicle designed to transport astronauts between the earth and an orbiting space station.

space shuttle
The space shuttle Orbiter 101
"Enterprise" separates from its 747
carrier aircraft

space station *n.* A large manned satellite placed in permanent orbit around the earth.

space suit *n.* A protective pressurized suit designed to allow the wearer to move about freely in space.

space walk *n.* An excursion by an astronaut outside a spacecraft in space; extravehicular activity. —**space walk** *v.* —**space walker** *n.*

spa·cious (spā′shəs) *adj.* Large in range, extent, or scope. —**spa′cious·ly** *adv.* —**spa′cious·ness** *n.*

spade[1] (spād) *n.* A digging tool with a long handle and a flat blade. —*v.* **spad·ed, spad·ing.** To dig with a spade. [< OE *spadu.*]

spade[2] (spād) *n.* Any of a suit of playing cards marked with a black figure shaped like an inverted heart with a short stalk at the bottom. [< Gk. *spathē,* broad blade.]

spade·work (spād′wûrk′) *n.* Preparatory work necessary to a project or activity.

spa·dix (spā′dĭks) *n., pl.* **-di·ces** (-dĭ-sēz′). A clublike stalk bearing tiny flowers, often surrounded by a sheathlike spathe. [< Gk., broken-off palm branch.]

spa·ghet·ti (spə-gĕt′ē) *n.* Pasta consisting of long, solid strings. [Ital., pl. dim. of *spago,* string.]

spake (spāk) *v.* Archaic. *p.t.* of **speak**.

span[1] (spăn) *n.* **1.** The distance between two points or extremities. **2. a.** The distance between vertical supports of a horizontal structural part. **b.** A section of a bridge extending from one vertical support to another. **3.** A unit of measure equal to about 9 inches. **4.** A period of time: *a span of four hours.* —*v.* **spanned, span·ning.** **1.** To measure by or as if by the extended hand. **2.** To extend across. [< OE *spann,* a unit of measurement.]

span[2] (spăn) *n.* A pair of harnessed or matched animals, such as oxen. [< MDu. *spannen,* to fetter.]

span·gle (spăng′gəl) *n.* A small, often circular piece of shiny metal or plastic used esp. on garments for decoration. —*v.* **-gled, -gling.** To decorate with or as with spangles. [ME *spangele.*]

Span·iard (spăn′yərd) *n.* A native or inhabitant of Spain.

---

span·iel (spăn'yəl) *n.* A dog with drooping ears, short legs, and silky, wavy hair. [< OFr. *espaignol*, Spanish dog.]

Span·ish (spăn'ĭsh) *n.* **1. the Spanish.** The people of Spain. **2.** The Romance language of Spain and most of Central and South America. —*adj.* Of Spain, the Spanish, or their language.

Span·ish-A·mer·i·can (spăn'ĭsh-ə-mĕr'ĭ-kən) *n.* **1.** A native or inhabitant of a country of Spanish America. **2.** A U.S. resident whose native language is Spanish. —**Span·ish-A·mer·i·can** *adj.*

Spanish fly *n.* **1.** A European blister beetle. **2.** A preparation produced from the Spanish fly and formerly used as a medicine and an aphrodisiac.

Spanish moss *n.* A plant of the southeastern United States and tropical America that grows on trees in long, threadlike tangled masses.

spank (spăngk) *v.* To slap on the buttocks with the open hand. [Perh. imit.] —**spank** or **spank'ing** *n.*

spank·ing (spăng'kĭng) *adj.* **1.** *Informal.* Exceptional of its kind; remarkable. **2.** Brisk and fresh: *a spanking breeze.* [Orig. unknown.]

spar¹ (spär) *n.* A wooden or metal pole used to support sail rigging. [< ON *sperra*, beam.]

spar² (spär) *v.* **sparred, spar·ring. 1.** To box, esp. for practice. **2.** To bandy words about; wrangle. [ME *sparren*, to strike rapidly.]

spare (spâr) *v.* **spared, spar·ing. 1. a.** To treat mercifully; deal with leniently. **b.** To refrain from harming or destroying. **2.** To save from experiencing or doing something; exempt. **3.** To use with restraint or frugality. **4.** To do without. —*adj.* **spar·er, spar·est. 1. a.** Kept in reserve: *a spare tire.* **b.** Extra: *spare cash.* **c.** Free for other use; unoccupied: *spare time.* **2. a.** Without excess; meager. **b.** Thin or lean. —*n.* **1.** A replacement, such as a tire, reserved for future need. **2.** The knocking down of all ten bowling pins with two successive rolls of the ball. [< OE *sparian*, to leave unharmed.] —**spare'ness** *n.*

spare·ribs (spâr'rĭbz') *pl.n.* A cut of pork consisting of the lower ribs with most of the meat trimmed off. [< MLG *ribbespēr.*]

spar·ing (spâr'ĭng) *adj.* Thrifty; frugal. —**spar'ing·ly** *adv.*

spark¹ (spärk) *n.* **1.** A glowing particle, as one thrown off from a burning substance. **2. a.** A brief flash of light, esp. one produced by electric discharge. **b.** A short pulse or flow of electric current. **3.** A quality or factor with latent potential; seed: *the spark of genius.* —*v.* **1.** To produce or give off sparks. **2.** To rouse to action: *sparked a desire for freedom.* [< OE *spærca.*]

spark² (spärk) *n.* **1.** A young dandy. **2.** A suitor. —*v.* To court or woo. [Perh. of Scand. orig.]

spar·kle (spär'kəl) *v.* **-kled, -kling. 1.** To give off or reflect flashes of light; glitter. **2.** To be brilliant or witty. **3.** To release gas bubbles; effervesce. —*n.* **1.** A small spark or glowing particle. **2.** Effervescence. **3.** Animation; vivacity. [ME *sparklen.*] —**spar'kler** *n.*

spark plug *n.* A device in an internal-combustion-engine cylinder that ignites the fuel mixture by means of an electric spark.

spark plug

spat³

spar·row (spăr'ō) *n.* Any of various small birds with grayish or brownish plumage. [< OE *spearwa.*]

sparrow hawk *n.* A small falcon or hawk that preys on small birds and animals.

sparse (spärs) *adj.* **spars·er, spars·est.** Occurring, growing, or settled at widely spaced intervals. [Lat. *sparsus,* p.p. of *spargere,* to scatter.] —**sparse'ly** *adv.* —**sparse'ness** or **spar'si·ty** (spär'sĭ-tē) *n.*

spasm (spăz'əm) *n.* **1.** A sudden, involuntary muscular contraction. **2.** A sudden burst of energy, activity, or emotion. [< Gk. *spasmos.*] —**spas·mod·ic** (spăz-mŏd'ĭk) *adj.* —**spas·mod'i·cal·ly** *adv.*

spas·tic (spăs'tĭk) *adj.* Of, pertaining to, or affected by muscular spasms. —*n.* A person suffering from chronic muscular spasms. [< Gk. *spastikos.*] —**spas'ti·cal·ly** *adv.*

spat¹ (spăt) *v.* A *p.t.* & *p.p.* of **spit¹.**

spat² (spăt) *n., pl.* **spat** or **spats.** The larval stage of a bivalve mollusk, as an oyster. [Orig. unknown.]

spat³ (spăt) *n.* A gaiter covering the upper shoe and the ankle. [< *spatterdash.*]

spat⁴ (spăt) *n.* A brief, petty quarrel. —*v.* **spat·ted, spat·ting.** To engage in a spat. [Orig. unknown.]

spate (spāt) *n.* A sudden flood, rush, or outpouring. [ME.]

spathe (spāth) *n.* A leaflike organ that encloses or spreads from the base of the spadix of certain plants, such as the calla. [< Gk. *spathē,* broad blade.]

spa·tial (spā'shəl) *adj.* Of or relating to space. [< Lat. *spatium,* space.] —**spa'tial·ly** *adv.*

spat·ter (spăt'ər) *v.* **1.** To scatter in drops or small splashes. **2.** To spit off small splashes; splatter. —*n.* **1.** The act or sound of spattering. **2.** A drop or splash of something spattered. [Perh. of LG orig.]

spat·u·la (spăch'ə-lə) *n.* An implement with a flexible blade used esp. to spread, mix, or lift soft material. [< Gk. *spathē,* broad blade.]

spav·in (spăv'ĭn) *n.* A disease affecting the hock joint of horses. [< OFr. *espavin.*] —**spav'ined** *adj.*

spawn (spôn) *n.* **1.** The eggs of aquatic animals such as fishes, oysters, or frogs. **2.** Offspring, esp. when produced in large numbers. —*v.* **1.** To produce offspring. **2.** To produce offspring in large numbers. **3.** To give rise to; engender. [< AN *espaundre.*]

spay (spā) *v.* To remove the ovaries of (a female animal). [< OFr. *espeer,* to cut with a sword.]

speak (spēk) *v.* **spoke** (spōk), **spo·ken** (spō'kən), **speak·ing. 1.** To utter words; talk. **2.** To converse. **3.** To deliver an address or lecture; make a speech. **4.** To converse in or be able to converse in (a language). [< OE *sprecan.*]

speak·eas·y (spēk'ē'zē) *n., pl.* **-ies.** A place for the illegal sale of alcoholic drinks.

speak·er (spē'kər) *n.* **1.** One who speaks. **2.** One who delivers a public speech. **3.** The presiding officer of a legislative assembly.

spear (spîr) *n.* **1.** A weapon consisting of a long shaft with a sharply pointed head. **2.** A sharp, barbed shaft used esp. for spearing fish. **3.** A slender stalk, as of asparagus. —*v.* To pierce or stab with or as with a spear. [< OE *spere.*]

spear·head (spîr'hĕd') *n.* **1.** The sharpened head of a spear. **2.** The leading forces in a military attack. **3.** The driving force in an action or endeavor. —**spear'head'** *v.*

spear·mint (spîr'mĭnt') *n.* A common mint widely used as a flavoring.

spe·cial (spĕsh'əl) *adj.* **1.** Surpassing what is common or usual; exceptional. **2.** Distinct among others of a kind; singular. **3.** Peculiar to a specific person or thing; particular. **4.** Having a limited or specific function, application, or scope. **5.** Additional; extra. —*n.* **1.** One that is special. **2.** Something designed for a particular occasion: *a television special.* **3.** A featured attraction, as a reduced price: *a special on lamb chops.* [< Lat. *species,* appearance.] —**spe'cial·ly** *adv.*

spe·cial·ist (spĕsh'ə-lĭst) *n.* One who devotes himself to a particular branch of study or research.

spe·cial·ize (spĕsh'ə-līz') *v.* **-ized, -iz·ing.** **1.** To concentrate on a particular study, activity, or product: *specialized in pediatrics.* **2.** *Biol.* To adapt to a specific environment or function. —**spe'cial·i·za'tion** *n.*

special relativity The physical theory of time and space developed by Albert Einstein.

spe·cial·ty (spĕsh'əl-tē) *n., pl.* **-ties.** **1.** A pursuit, occupation, service, or product in which one specializes. **2.** An aspect of medicine to which physicians confine their practice. **3.** A special feature or characteristic; peculiarity.

spe·cie (spē'shē, -sē) *n.* Coined money; coin. [< Lat. *(in) specie,* (in) kind.]

spe·cies (spē'shēz, -sēz) *n., pl.* **-cies.** **1. a.** A fundamental category of taxonomic classification consisting of organisms capable of interbreeding. **b.** An organism belonging to such a category. **2.** A kind, variety, or type. [Lat., a kind.]

spe·cif·ic (spĭ-sĭf'ĭk) *adj.* **1.** Explicitly set forth; definite. **2.** Of, pertaining to, characterizing, or distinguishing a species. **3.** Intended for, applying to, or acting upon a particular thing, esp. effective in the treatment of a particular disease. —*n.* A specific remedy. [Med. Lat. *specificus.*] —**spe·cif'i·cal·ly** *adv.* —**spec'i·fic'i·ty** (spĕs'ə-fĭs'ĭ-tē) *n.*

spec·i·fi·ca·tion (spĕs'ə-fĭ-kā'shən) *n.* **1.** Something that is specified. **2.** Often **specifications.** A detailed and exact statement of particulars, esp. a statement prescribing materials, dimensions, and workmanship for something to be built, installed, or manufactured.

specific gravity *n.* The ratio of the mass of a solid or liquid material to the mass of an equal volume of distilled water at 4°C or of a gas to an equal volume of air or hydrogen under prescribed conditions of temperature and pressure.

spec·i·fy (spĕs'ə-fī') *v.* **-fied, -fy·ing.** To state explicitly and unambiguously. [< Med. Lat. *specificare.*]

spec·i·men (spĕs'ə-mən) *n.* An element or a part taken as representative of an entire set or whole; sample. [Lat., example.]

spe·cious (spē'shəs) *adj.* Seemingly attractive, true, plausible, or correct but actually not so; deceptive. [< Lat. *speciosus,* attractive.] —**spe'cious·ly** *adv.* —**spe'cious·ness** *n.*

speck (spĕk) *n.* **1.** A small spot or mark. **2.** A particle. —*v.* To mark with specks. [< OE *specca.*]

speck·le (spĕk'əl) *n.* A small spot; speck. —*v.* **-led, -ling.** To mark or cover with or as if with speckles. [ME *spakle.*]

spec·ta·cle (spĕk'tə-kəl) *n.* **1.** A public performance or display. **2. spectacles.** A pair of eyeglasses. [Lat. *spectaculum < spectare,* to watch.] —**spec'ta·cled** *adj.*

spec·tac·u·lar (spĕk-tăk'yə-lər) *adj.* Of the nature of a spectacle; sensational. —*n.* A lavish spectacle.

spec·ta·tor (spĕk'tā'tər) *n.* One who attends and views an event; observer. [Lat.]

spec·ter (spĕk'tər) *n.* Also *chiefly Brit.* **spec·tre.** **1.** A ghost; phantom; apparition. **2.** A threatening or haunting possibility: *the specter of nuclear war.* [< Lat. *spectrum,* appearance.]

spec·tra (spĕk'trə) *n.* A pl. of **spectrum.**

spec·tral (spĕk'trəl) *adj.* **1.** Of or resembling a specter; ghostly. **2.** Of, pertaining to, or produced by a spectrum.

spectro– *pref.* Spectrum: *spectrograph.* [< SPECTRUM.]

spec·tro·gram (spĕk'trə-grăm') *n.* A graph or photograph of a spectrum.

spec·tro·graph (spĕk'trə-grăf') *n.* **1.** A spectroscope equipped to photograph spectra. **2.** A spectrogram. —**spec'tro·graph'ic** *adj.* —**spec'tro·graph'i·cal·ly** *adv.* —**spec·trog'ra·phy** (-trŏg'rə-fē) *n.*

spec·trom·e·ter (spĕk-trŏm'ĭ-tər) *n.* **1.** A spectroscope equipped to measure the wavelengths of radiation observed by it. **2.** An instrument used to measure the index of refraction. —**spec'tro·met'ric** (-trə-mĕt'rĭk) *adj.*

spec·tro·scope (spĕk'trə-skōp') *n.* Any of various instruments for resolving and observing or recording spectra. —**spec'tro·scop'ic** (-skŏp'ĭk) or **spec'tro·scop'i·cal** *adj.* —**spec'tro·scop'i·cal·ly** *adv.* —**spec·tros'co·pist** (spĕk-trŏs'kə-pĭst) *n.* —**spec·tros'co·py** *n.*

spec·trum (spĕk'trəm) *n., pl.* **-tra** (-trə) or **-trums.** **1.** The distribution of a characteristic of a physical system or phenomenon, esp. the distribution of energy emitted by a radiant source, as an incandescent body, arranged in order of wavelengths. **2.** A broad sequence or range: *the whole spectrum of contemporary thought.* [Lat., appearance.]

spec·u·late (spĕk'yə-lāt') *v.* **-lat·ed, -lat·ing.** **1.** To meditate on a given subject; reflect. **2.** To engage in risky business ventures that offer the chance of large profits. [Lat. *speculari,* to observe.] —**spec'u·la'tion** *n.* —**spec'u·la·tive** *adj.* —**spec'u·la·tor** *n.*

speech (spēch) *n.* **1.** The act of speaking.

---

2. The capacity to speak. 3. Vocal communication; conversation. 4. The manner in which one speaks. 5. A talk or address, esp. one delivered to an audience. 6. The language or dialect of a nation or region. [< OE *spæc*.] —**speech'less** *adj.*

speed (spēd) *n.* 1. The rate or a measure of the rate of motion. 2. A rate of action, activity, or performance. 3. Rapidity; swiftness. 4. A transmission gear in a motor vehicle. 5. *Slang.* An amphetamine drug. 6. *Archaic.* Prosperity or success. —*v.* **sped** (spēd) or **speed·ed, speed·ing.** 1. To move rapidly. 2. To increase the speed or rate of; accelerate. 3. To drive at a high or illegal rate of speed. [< OE *spēd*, success.] —**speed'er** *n.* —**speed'i·ly** *adv.* —**speed'y** *adj.*

speed·boat (spēd'bōt') *n.* A fast motorboat.

speed·om·e·ter (spē-dŏm'ĭ-tər, spĭ-) *n.* 1. An instrument for indicating speed, as of an automobile. 2. An odometer.

speed-up (spēd'ŭp') *n.* Acceleration of production without increase in pay.

speed·way (spēd'wā') *n.* 1. A course for automobile racing. 2. A road designed for fast-moving traffic.

speed·well (spēd'wĕl') *n.* A low-growing plant with clusters of small, usu. blue flowers.

spell¹ (spĕl) *v.* **spelled** or **spelt** (spĕlt), **spell·ing.** 1. To name or write in order the letters of (a word or part of a word). 2. To mean; signify. —*phrasal verb.* **spell out.** To make explicit; specify. [< OFr. *espeller*, to read letter by letter, of Gmc. orig.]

spell² (spĕl) *n.* 1. An incantational word or formula. 2. A bewitched state. 3. A state of compelling attraction. [< OE, story.]

spell³ (spĕl) *n.* 1. A short, indefinite period of time. 2. *Informal.* A period of weather of a particular kind. 3. One's turn at work; shift. 4. *Informal.* A period of illness or indisposition. —*v.* To relieve (someone) from work temporarily. [< OE *spelian*, to represent.]

spell·bind (spĕl'bīnd') *v.* To hold under or as if under a spell; enchant.

spell·bind·er (spĕl'bīn'dər) *n.* An eloquent orator.

spell·er (spĕl'ər) *n.* 1. One who spells. 2. A textbook to teach spelling.

spelt (spĕlt) *v.* A *p.t.* & *p.p.* of **spell¹.**

spe·lun·ker (spĭ-lŭng'kər, spē'lŭng'kər) *n.* One who explores and studies caves. [< Lat. *spēlunx*, cave.] —**spe·lun'king** *n.*

spend (spĕnd) *v.* **spent, spend·ing.** 1. To use up; expend. 2. To pay out (money); disburse. 3. To wear out; exhaust. 4. To pass (time). 5. To waste; squander. [< Lat. *expendēre*, to expend, and < Lat. *dispendere*, to weigh out.] —**spend'er** *n.*

spend·thrift (spĕnd'thrĭft') *n.* One who spends money wastefully. [SPEND + THRIFT, accumulated wealth (obs.)]

spent (spĕnt) *adj.* Depleted of energy, force, or strength; exhausted.

sperm (spûrm) *n.* 1. A spermatozoon. 2. Semen. [< Gk. *sperma*, sperm.] —**sper·mat'ic** (spər-măt'ĭk) *adj.*

sper·mat·o·zo·on (spər-măt'ə-zō'ŏn', spûr'-mə-tə-, -ən) *n.*, *pl.* **-zo·a** (-zō'ə). The fertilizing gamete of a male animal. [*spermato-*, sperm + -ZOON.]

sperm whale *n.* A whale that has a large head and a long, narrow lower jaw. [< *spermaceti*, a waxy substance obtained from a sperm whale.]

spew (spyōō) *v.* 1. To vomit. 2. To force out in a stream; eject. [< OE *spiwan*.]

sphag·num (sfăg'nəm) *n.* Any of various pale or ashy mosses whose decomposed remains form peat. [< Gk. *sphagnos*, a kind of moss.]

sphe·noid (sfē'noid') *n.* A compound bone with winglike processes, situated at the base of the skull. —*adj.* Wedge-shaped. [< Gk. *sphēnoeidēs*, wedge-shaped.]

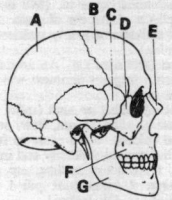

sphenoid

A. Parietal
B. Frontal
C. Sphenoid
D. Zygomatic
E. Nasal
F. Maxilla
G. Mandible

sphere (sfîr) *n.* 1. A three-dimensional surface all points of which are equidistant from a fixed point. 2. Something shaped like a sphere; ball. 3. A planet, star, or other heavenly body. 4. An area of power, control, or influence; domain. [< Gk. *sphaira*, ball.] —**spher'i·cal** (sfîr'ĭ-kəl, sfĕr'-) *adj.* —**spher'i·cal·ly** *adv.*

sphe·roid (sfîr'oid', sfĕr'-) *n.* A three-dimensional geometric surface generated by rotating an ellipse on or about one of its axes. —**sphe·roid'al** (-oid'l) *adj.*

sphinc·ter (sfĭngk'tər) *n.* A ringlike muscle that maintains constriction of a bodily passage or orifice. [< Gk. *sphingein*, to bind tight.]

sphinx (sfĭnks) *n.*, *pl.* **-es** or **sphin·ges** (sfĭn'jēz'). 1. *Egypt. Myth.* A figure having the body of a lion and the head of a man, ram, or hawk. 2. *Gk. Myth.* A winged monster with the head of a woman and the body of a lion that destroyed all who could not answer its riddle. 3. A mysterious or enigmatic person. [Gk.]

spice (spīs) *n.* 1. An aromatic or pungent plant substance, as cinnamon or peppers, used as flavoring. 2. Something that adds zest or interest. [< LLat. *species*, spices < Lat., appearance.] —**spice** *v.* —**spic'y** *adj.*

spick-and-span (spĭk'ən-spăn') *adj.* Also **spic-and-span.** 1. Neat and clean; spotless. 2. Brand-new. [*spick*, spike + *spannew*, entirely new.]

spic·ule (spĭk'yōōl) *n.* A small needlelike structure or part. [Lat. *spiculum*, dim. of *spica*, spike.]

spi·der (spī'dər) *n.* 1. Any of various eight-legged arachnids that have a body divided into two parts and that spin webs to trap insects. 2. A cast-iron frying pan with a long handle. [< OE *spīthra*.] —**spi'dery** *adj.*

spiel (spēl) *n. Slang.* A lengthy, usu. extravagant speech or argument intended to be persuasive. [G., play.] —**spiel** *v.*

spig·ot (spĭg′ət) *n.* A faucet. [ME.]

spike¹ (spīk) *n.* 1. A large, heavy nail. 2. A sharp-pointed projection, as one in the sole of a shoe for traction. —*v.* **spiked**, **spik·ing.** 1. To secure or provide with a spike. 2. To impale, pierce, or injure with a spike. 3. To put an end to; quash: *spike a plot.* 4. *Slang.* To add alcoholic liquor to. [ME *spyk.*]

spike² (spīk) *n.* 1. An ear of grain. 2. A long cluster of stalkless or nearly stalkless flowers. [< Lat. *spica.*]

spike·nard (spīk′närd′) *n.* An aromatic plant from which a fragrant ointment was obtained in ancient times.

spill (spĭl) *v.* **spilled** or **spilt** (spĭlt), **spill·ing.** 1. To cause or allow to run, flow, or fall out. 2. To shed (blood). 3. To cause to fall. 4. To come to the ground suddenly and involuntarily. —*n.* 1. An act of spilling, esp. a fall, as from a horse. 2. An amount spilled. 3. Something spilled. [< OE *spillan.*]

spill·way (spĭl′wā′) *n.* A channel for reservoir overflow.

spin (spĭn) *v.* **spun** (spŭn), **spin·ning.** 1. a. To draw out and twist (fibers) into thread. b. To form (thread or yarn) by spinning. 2. To form thread from a fluid emitted from the body. 3. To relate, esp. imaginatively: *spin a story.* 4. To rotate or cause to rotate swiftly; twirl. 5. To reel; whirl. 6. To ride or drive rapidly. —*n.* 1. A swift whirling motion. 2. *Informal.* A short drive in a vehicle. [< OE *spinnan.*] —**spin′ner** *n.*

spin·ach (spĭn′ĭch) *n.* A plant cultivated for its dark-green edible leaves. [< Ar. *isfānākh.*]

spi·nal (spī′nəl) *adj.* Of, pertaining to, or near the spine or spinal cord; vertebral. —**spi′nal·ly** *adv.*

spinal canal *n.* The passage formed by the successive openings in the vertebrae through which the spinal cord and its membranes pass.

spinal column *n.* In vertebrate animals, the series of vertebrae enclosing the spinal cord and forming the main support of the body; backbone.

spinal cord *n.* The part of the central nervous system that extends from the brain through the spinal canal.

spin·dle (spĭn′dl) *n.* 1. A slender, rounded rod or stick on which fibers are twisted into thread and on which the spun thread is wound. 2. Any of various slender revolving mechanical parts. [< OE *spinel.*]

spin·dly (spĭn′dlē) *adj.* **-dli·er**, **-dli·est.** Long, thin, and often weak.

spin·drift (spĭn′drĭft′) *n.* Wind-blown sea spray. [Obs. *spoon*, to drive back and forth + DRIFT.]

spine (spīn) *n.* 1. The spinal column of a vertebrate. 2. A sharp-pointed, projecting plant or animal part, as a thorn or quill. [< Lat. *spina.*] —**spine′less** *adj.* —**spin′y** *adj.*

spi·nel (spĭ-nĕl′) *n.* Any of several hard minerals valued as a gem. [< Lat. *spina*, thorn.]

spin·et (spĭn′ĭt) *n.* 1. A small upright piano. 2. A small harpsichord with a single keyboard. [< Ital. *spinetta.*]

spin·na·ker (spĭn′ə-kər) *n.* A large triangular sail set on a spar that swings out opposite the mainsail. [Orig. unknown.]

spinning jenny *n.* An early machine with several spindles used to spin fibers into thread or yarn.

spinning wheel *n.* A device for making yarn or thread, consisting of a foot- or hand-driven wheel and a single spindle.

spin-off (spĭn′ôf′, -ŏf′) *n.* Also **spin-off.** A product or enterprise derived from a larger or more complex one.

spin·ster (spĭn′stər) *n.* A woman who has remained single beyond the conventional age of marrying. [ME *spinnester.*] —**spin′ster·hood′** *n.*

spi·ral (spī′rəl) *n.* 1. The two-dimensional path formed by a point moving around a fixed center at an increasing or decreasing distance. 2. a. A three-dimensional curve moving about a central axis; helix. b. Something having the form of such a curve. 3. A continuously accelerating increase or decrease. —*adj.* 1. Of or resembling a spiral. 2. Coiling in a constantly changing plane; helical. —*v.* **-raled** or **-ralled**, **-ral·ing** or **-ral·ling.** 1. To take a spiral form or course. 2. To rise or fall with steady acceleration. [< Gk. *speira*, coil.] —**spi′ral·ly** *adv.*

spi·rant (spī′rənt) *n.* A fricative. [< Lat. *spirare*, to breathe.] —**spi′rant** *adj.*

spire (spīr) *n.* 1. The top part or point of something that tapers upward. 2. A formation or structure that tapers to a point at the top, as a steeple. [< OE *spīr.*] —**spir′y** *adj.*

spir·it (spĭr′ĭt) *n.* 1. The animating or life-giving principle within a living being; soul. 2. The part of a human being associated with the mind and feelings as distinguished from the physical body. 3. The real sense or significance of something. 4. A person. 5. A prevailing mood or attitude: *a spirit of rebellion.* 6. **Spirit.** The Holy Ghost. 7. A supernatural being; ghost. 8. Mood or emotional state. 9. Vivacity and courage. 10. Strong loyalty or dedication. 11. Often **spirits.** An alcohol solution of an essential or volatile substance. 12. **spirits.** An alcoholic beverage. —*v.* To carry off mysteriously or secretly. [< Lat. *spiritus*, breath.] —**spir′it·less** *adj.*

Syns: *spirit, brio, dash, élan, esprit, liveliness, pep* n.

spir·it·ed (spĭr′ĭ-tĭd) *adj.* Characterized by vigor or courage.

spir·i·tu·al (spĭr′ĭ-chōō-əl) *adj.* 1. Of, pertaining to, or consisting of spirit. 2. Ecclesiastical; sacred. —*n.* A religious folk song of black American origin. —**spir′i·tu·al′i·ty** (-ăl′ĭ-tē) *n.* —**spir′i·tu·al·ize′** (-ə-līz′) *v.* —**spir′i·tu·al·ly** *adv.*

spir·i·tu·al·ism (spĭr′ĭ-chōō-ə-lĭz′əm) *n.* The belief that the dead communicate with the living, usu. through a medium. —**spir′i·tu·al·ist** *n.* —**spir′i·tu·al·is′tic** *adj.*

spir·i·tu·ous (spĭr′ĭ-chōō-əs) *adj.* Of or containing alcohol.

spi·ro·chete (spī′rə-kēt′) *n.* Also **spi·ro·chaete.** Any of various slender, twisted microorganisms, including those causing syphilis. [Gk. *speira*, coil + Gk. *khaitē*, long hair.]

spirt (spûrt) *n. & v. Chiefly Brit.* Var. of **spurt.**

spit¹ (spĭt) *v.* **spat** (spăt) or **spit, spit·ting.**
1. To eject (saliva) from the mouth; expectorate. **2.** To eject as if by spitting. —*n.* **1.** Saliva, esp. when expectorated; spittle. **2.** The act of spitting. [< OE *spittan.*]

spit² (spĭt) *n.* **1.** A slender, pointed rod on which meat is impaled for broiling. **2.** A narrow point of land extending into a body of water. —*v.* **spit·ted, spit·ting.** To impale on or as if on a spit. [< OE *spitu.*]

spit·ball (spĭt′bôl′) *n.* **1.** A piece of paper chewed and shaped into a lump for use as a projectile. **2.** An illegal baseball pitch in which the ball is moistened on one side.

spite (spīt) *n.* Malice or ill will prompting an urge to hurt or thwart. —*v.* **spit·ed, spit·ing.** To treat with malice. —*idiom.* **in spite of.** Regardless of; despite. [ME.] —**spite′ful** *adj.* —**spite′ful·ly** *adv.* —**spite′ful·ness** *n.*

spit·tle (spĭt′l) *n.* Spit; saliva. [< OE *spǣtl.*]

spit·tle·bug (spĭt′l-bŭg′) *n.* Any of various insects whose nymphs form frothy masses of liquid on plant stems.

spit·toon (spĭ-tōōn′) *n.* A vessel for spitting into. [< SPIT¹.]

splash (splăsh) *v.* **1.** To dash or scatter (a liquid) about in masses. **2.** To dash liquid upon. **3.** To fall into or move through liquid with the sound of splashing. —*n.* **1.** The act or sound of splashing. **2.** A flying mass of liquid. **3.** A marking produced by or as if by scattered liquid. [< PLASH.] —**splash′er** *n.* —**splash′i·ness** *n.* —**splash′y** *adj.*

splash·down (splăsh′doun′) *n.* The landing of a missile or spacecraft in the ocean.

splat¹ (splăt) *n.* A slat of wood, as one in the middle of a chair back. [Orig. unknown.]

splat² (splăt) *n.* A slapping noise. [Imit.]

splat·ter (splăt′ər) *v.* To spatter. [Blend of SPLASH and SPATTER.] —**splat′ter** *n.*

splay (splā) *adj.* **1.** Spread or turned out. **2.** Clumsy; awkward. —*v.* **1.** To spread out or apart, esp. clumsily. **2.** To slant or slope. [< ME *displayen,* to display.] —**splay** *n.*

splay·foot (splā′fŏŏt′) *n.* A deformity characterized by abnormally flat and turned-out feet. —**splay′foot·ed** *adj.*

spleen (splēn) *n.* **1.** One of the largest lymphoid structures, an organ on the left side below the diaphragm, functioning as a blood filter and to store blood. **2.** Ill temper. [< Gk. *splēn.*]

splen·did (splĕn′dĭd) *adj.* **1.** Brilliant with light or color; radiant. **2.** Grand; magnificent. **3.** Glorious; illustrious. **4.** Excellent. [< Lat. *splendēre,* to shine.] —**splen′did·ly** *adv.*

splen·dif·er·ous (splĕn-dĭf′ər-əs) *adj.* Splendid. [< Med. Lat. *splendiferus.*]

splen·dor (splĕn′dər) *n.* Also *chiefly Brit.* **splen·dour. 1.** Great light or luster; brilliance. **2.** Magnificence; grandeur. [Lat. < *splendēre,* to shine.]

sple·net·ic (splĭ-nĕt′ĭk) *adj.* **1.** Of or pertaining to the spleen. **2.** Ill-humored; irritable. [< Gk. *splēn,* spleen.]

splen·ic (splĕn′ĭk) *adj.* Of or near the spleen. [< Gk. *slēn,* spleen.]

splice (splīs) *v.* **spliced, splic·ing. 1. a.** To join (e.g. lengths of wire or film) at the ends. **b.** To join (ropes) by interweaving strands. **2.** To join (pieces of wood) by overlapping and binding. [MDu. *splissen.*] —**splice** *n.*

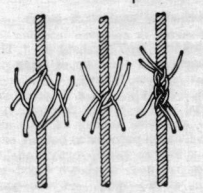

splice
Left to right: Three steps in
making a splice

splint (splĭnt) *n.* **1.** A rigid device used to prevent motion of a joint or the ends of a fractured bone. **2.** A thin, flexible wooden strip, as one used in making baskets. [< MLG *splinte,* splinter.]

splin·ter (splĭn′tər) *n.* A sharp, slender piece, as of wood, bone, or glass, split or broken off from a main body. —*v.* To form or cause to form splinters. [< MDu.]

split (splĭt) *v.* **split, split·ting. 1.** To divide, esp. into lengthwise sections. **2.** To break, burst, or rip apart with force; rend. **3.** To part company; disunite. **4.** To divide and share: *split a meal.* **5.** To separate into layers or sections. **6.** *Slang.* To leave, esp. abruptly. —*n.* **1.** The act or result of splitting. **2.** A breach or rupture in a group. [< MDu. *splitten.*]

split-lev·el (splĭt′lĕv′əl) *adj.* Having the floor levels of adjoining rooms separated by about a half story: *a split-level ranch house.*

split personality *n.* A form of hysteria in which an individual manifests two or more relatively distinct identities.

split·ting (splĭt′ĭng) *adj.* Very severe: *a splitting headache.*

splotch (splŏch) *n.* An irregularly shaped stain, spot, or blotch. [Perh. blend of SPOT and BLOTCH.] —**splotch** *v.* —**splotch′y** *adj.*

splurge (splûrj) *n.* An extravagant expense or luxury. [Orig. unknown.] —**splurge** *v.*

splut·ter (splŭt′ər) *v.* **1.** To make a spitting sound. **2.** To speak hastily and unclearly, as when angry. [Perh. < SPUTTER.] —**splut′ter** *n.*

spoil (spoil) *v.* **spoiled** or **spoilt** (spoilt), **spoil·ing. 1.** To impair the value or quality of; damage. **2.** To impair the completeness, perfection, or unity of. **3.** To disrupt; disturb. **4.** To overindulge so as to harm the character. **5.** *Archaic.* To plunder; despoil. **6.** To become tainted or rotten; decay. **7.** To have a craving: *spoiling for a fight.* —*n.* **spoils. 1.** Goods or property seized by force; plunder. **2.** Political patronage enjoyed by a successful candidate or party. [< Lat. *spolium,* booty.] —**spoil′age** *n.*

spoil·er (spoi′lər) *n.* **1.** One that spoils. **2.** A long, narrow hinged plate on the upper surface of an airplane wing whose position affects the lift.

spoil·sport (spoil′spôrt′) *n.* One who spoils the pleasure of others.

spoke¹ (spōk) *n.* **1.** One of the rods connecting the hub and rim of a wheel. **2.** A rung of a ladder. [< OE *spāca.*]

spoke² (spōk) *v.* *p.t. & archaic p.p.* of **speak.**

spo·ken (spō′kən) *v.* *p.p.* of **speak.**

spokes·man (spōks′mən) *n.* One who speaks

on behalf of another or others. **—spokes'-wom'an** n.

spo·li·a·tion (spō'lē-ā'shən) n. **1.** The act of plundering. **2.** The state of being plundered. [< Lat. *spolium*, booty.]

sponge (spŭnj) n. **1. a.** A primitive marine animal with a porous skeleton. **b.** The porous, absorbent skeleton of such an animal, used for such purposes as bathing or cleaning. **c.** A substance with spongelike qualities. **2.** A gauze pad used to absorb blood and other fluids, as in surgery. —v. **sponged, sponging. 1.** To moisten, wipe, or clean with a sponge. **2.** To fish for sponges. **3.** *Slang.* To live by relying on another's generosity. [< Gk. *sphongos.*] **—spong'y** adj.

sponge cake n. A light cake containing no shortening.

sponge rubber n. A soft, porous rubber used in toys, cushions, gaskets, etc.

spon·sor (spŏn'sər) n. **1.** One who assumes responsibility for a person or thing. **2.** A godparent. **3.** A business enterprise that pays for a radio or television program, usu. in return for advertising time. [Lat. < *spondēre*, to pledge.] **—spon'sor** v. **—spon'sor·ship** n.

spon·ta·ne·ous (spŏn-tā'nē-əs) adj. **1.** Happening or arising without apparent external cause. **2.** Voluntary; unpremeditated: *spontaneous applause.* [< Lat. *sponte*, voluntarily.] **—spon'ta·ne'i·ty** (-tə-nē'ĭ-tē, -nā'-) n. **—spon·ta'ne·ous·ly** adv.

spontaneous combustion n. The breaking into flame of combustible material, such as oily rags, as a result of heat generated within the material by slow oxidation.

spoof (spōōf) n. **1.** A hoax. **2.** A gentle satirical imitation; light parody. [< *Spoof*, a trademark for a card game characterized by nonsense and hoaxing.] **—spoof** v.

spook (spōōk) *Informal.* n. **1.** A ghost. **2.** A secret agent; spy. —v. **1.** To haunt. **2.** To frighten. [Du.] **—spook'i·ly** adv. **—spook'i·ness** n. **—spook'y** adj.

spool (spōōl) n. A cylinder on which thread, yarn, wire, tape, ribbon, or film is wound. [< MDu. *spoele.*]

spoon (spōōn) n. **1.** A utensil consisting of a small, shallow bowl on a handle, used in preparing, serving, or eating food. **2.** A shiny, curved metallic fishing lure. —v. **1.** To lift, scoop up, or carry with or as if with a spoon. **2.** *Informal.* To make love by kissing or caressing. [< OE *spōn*, chip of wood.] **—spoon'ful** (-fōōl) n.

spoon·bill (spōōn'bĭl') n. Any of several long-legged wading birds having a long, flat bill with a broad tip.

spoon·er·ism (spōō'nə-rĭz'əm) n. An unintentional transposition of sounds in language, as *Let me sew you to your sheet* for *Let me show you to your seat.* [< William A. Spooner (1844–1930).]

spoon-fed (spōōn'fĕd') adj. **1.** Fed with a spoon. **2.** Given no chance to think or act independently.

spoor (spōōr) n. The track or trail of an animal. [< MDu.]

spo·rad·ic (spə-răd'ĭk) adj. Occurring at irregular intervals. [< Gk. *sporas*, scattered.] **—spo·rad'i·cal·ly** adv.

spore (spôr, spōr) n. A usu. single-celled reproductive structure or resting stage, as of a fern, fungus, or bacterium. [< Gk. *spora*, seed.]

spor·ran (spôr'ən, spŏr'-) n. A pouch worn at the front of the kilt by Scottish Highlanders. [< Gk. *bursa*, leather.]

sport (spôrt, spōrt) n. **1.** An active pastime; diversion. **2.** A specific diversion, usu. involving physical exercise and having a set form and body of rules; game. **3.** Light mockery. **4.** One known for the manner of his acceptance of defeat or criticism: *a good sport.* **5.** *Informal.* One who lives a gay, extravagant life. **6.** *Genetics.* A mutation. —v. **1.** To play; frolic. **2.** To joke or trifle. **3.** To display or show off. —adj. Of, pertaining to, or appropriate for sport: *a sport shirt.* [< ME *sporten*, to amuse.] **—sport'y** adj.

sport·ing (spôr'tĭng, spōr'-) adj. **1.** Used in or appropriate for sports. **2.** Characterized by sportsmanship. **3.** Of or associated with gambling. **4.** Offering a fair hope of success: *a sporting chance.* **—sport'ing·ly** adv.

sport·ive (spôr'tĭv, spōr'-) adj. Playful; frolicsome. **—sport'ive·ly** adv. **—sport'ive·ness** n.

sports·cast (spôrts'kăst', spōrts'-) n. A broadcast of a sports event or of sports news. **—sports'cast·er** n.

sports·man (spôrts'mən, spōrts'-) n. **1.** One who participates in sports. **2.** One who abides by the rules and accepts victory or defeat graciously. **—sports'wom'an** n.

sports·man·ship (spôrts'mən-shĭp', spōrts'-) n. The qualities and conduct befitting a sportsman.

sports·writ·er (spôrts'rī'tər) n. One who writes about sports, esp. for a newspaper or magazine.

sport·y (spôr'tē, spōr'-) adj. **-i·er, -i·est.** *Informal.* **1.** Appropriate to sport. **2.** Casual; carefree.

spot (spŏt) n. **1.** A mark on a surface, as a stain, differing sharply in color from the surroundings. **2.** A position; location. **3.** *Informal.* A situation, esp. a troublesome one. —v. **spot·ted, spot·ting. 1.** To mark or become marked with spots. **2.** To locate precisely. **3.** To discern; detect. —adj. Made, paid, or delivered immediately: *spot cash.* [ME.] **—spot'less** adj. **—spot'less·ly** adv. **—spot'less·ness** n. **—spot'ta·ble** adj.

spot-check (spŏt'chĕk') v. To subject to a check conducted at random or limited to a few instances. **—spot check** n.

spot·light (spŏt'līt') n. **1. a.** A strong beam of light that illuminates only a small area, as on a stage. **b.** A lamp that produces this light. **2.** Public attention or prominence. **—spot'light'** v.

spot·ter (spŏt'ər) n. One, as a military lookout, that looks for and reports something.

spot·ty (spŏt'ē) adj. **-ti·er, -ti·est.** Lacking consistency; uneven, as in quality.

spou·sal (spou'zəl, -səl) n. Often **spousals.** Marriage; nuptials.

spouse (spous, spouz) n. One's husband or wife. [< Lat. *sponsus*, p.p. of *spondēre*, to betroth.]

spout (spout) v. **1.** To gush forth or discharge

---

rapidly or continuously. **2.** To speak or utter volubly and pompously. —*n.* **1.** A tube or pipe through which liquid is discharged. **2.** A continuous stream of liquid. [ME *spouten.*]

sprain (sprān) *n.* A painful injury caused by a wrenching or laceration of the ligaments of a joint. —*v.* To cause a sprain in (a muscle or joint). [Orig. unknown.]

sprang (sprăng) *v.* A *p.t.* of **spring.**

sprat (sprăt) *n.* **1.** A small saltwater food fish of northeastern Atlantic waters. **2.** A young herring. [< OE *sprott.*]

sprawl (sprôl) *v.* **1.** To sit or lie with the limbs spread out awkwardly. **2.** To spread out haphazardly. [< OE *sprēawlian.*] —**sprawl** *n.*

spray¹ (sprā) *n.* **1.** Liquid moving in a mass of dispersed droplets or mist. **2.** A fine jet of liquid discharged from a pressurized container. **b.** A pressurized container, as an atomizer. —*v.* **1.** To disperse (a liquid) in a spray. **2.** To apply a spray to (a surface). [< MDu. *sprayen,* to sprinkle.] —**spray'er** *n.*

spray² (sprā) *n.* A branch bearing buds, flowers, or berries. [ME.]

spray gun *n.* A device used to apply a liquid as a spray.

spread (sprĕd) *v.* **spread, spread·ing.** **1.** To open or be extended more fully; stretch. **2.** To separate or become separated more widely; open out. **3.** To distribute over a surface in a layer; apply. **4.** To extend or cause to extend over a considerable area; distribute widely. **5.** To become or cause to become widely known. **6.** To prepare (a table) for eating. —*n.* **1.** The act or process of spreading. **2.** An open area of land; expanse. **3.** The extent or limit to which something is or can be spread; range. **4.** A cloth covering for a bed or table. **5.** *Informal.* An abundant meal laid out on a table. **6.** A food to be spread on bread or crackers. **7.** Printed material that extends across facing pages or adjacent columns. **8.** A difference, as between two figures or totals. [< OE *sprǣden.*] —**spread'er** *n.*

Syns: *spread, diffuse, disperse, distribute, radiate, scatter, strew* v.

spree (sprē) *n.* An overindulgence in an activity, esp. a bout of drinking. [Perh. < Sc. *spreath,* cattle raid.]

spri·er (sprī'ər) *adj.* A compar. of **spry.**

spri·est (sprī'ĭst) *adj.* A superl. of **spry.**

sprig (sprĭg) *n.* A small twig or shoot of a plant. [ME *sprigge.*]

spright·ly (sprīt'lē) *adj.* **-li·er, -li·est.** Lively and brisk; animated. [< SPRITE.]

spring (sprĭng) *v.* **sprang** (sprăng) or **sprung** (sprŭng), **sprung, spring·ing.** **1.** To move upward or forward suddenly; leap. **2.** To emerge suddenly. **3.** To shift position suddenly. **4.** To arise from a source; develop. **5.** To be or become warped or bent, as wood. **6.** To release from a checked or held position; actuate: *spring a trap.* **7.** To present unexpectedly: *spring a surprise.* —*n.* **1.** An elastic device, esp. a coil of wire, that regains its original shape after being compressed or extended. **2.** Elasticity; resilience. **3.** The act of springing. **4.** A natural fountain or flow of water. **5.** A source or origin. **6.** The season of the year between winter and summer. [< OE *springan.*] —**spring'i·ly** *adv.* —**spring'i·ness** *n.* —**spring'y** *adj.*

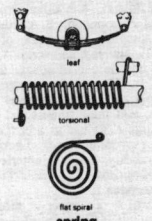

leaf

torsional

flat spiral

spring

spring·board (sprĭng'bôrd', -bōrd') *n.* A flexible board used by gymnasts or divers.

spring fever *n.* A feeling of laziness, rejuvenation, or yearning that may affect people at the advent of spring.

spring tide *n.* The tide gen. having the greatest rise and fall, occurring at the new moon and the full moon.

spring·time (sprĭng'tīm') *n.* The season of spring.

sprin·kle (sprĭng'kəl) *v.* **-kled, -kling.** To scatter in drops or small particles. —*n.* **1.** A light, sparse rainfall. **2.** A small amount. [ME *sprenklen.*] —**sprin'kler** *n.*

sprin·kling (sprĭng'klĭng) *n.* A small amount.

sprint (sprĭnt) *n.* A short race run at top speed. —*v.* To run at top speed. [Of Scand. orig.] —**sprint'er** *n.*

sprite (sprīt) *n.* **1.** An elf or pixie. **2.** A specter or ghost. [< Lat. *spiritus,* spirit.]

sprock·et (sprŏk'ĭt) *n.* **1.** Any of various toothlike projections arranged on a wheel rim to engage the links of a chain. **2.** A wheel with sprockets. [Orig. unknown.]

sprout (sprout) *v.* **1.** To begin to grow; give off shoots or buds. **2.** To grow or develop quickly. —*n.* A young plant growth, as a bud or shoot. [< OE *sprūten.*]

spruce¹ (sprōōs) *n.* **1.** A cone-bearing evergreen tree with short pointed needles and soft wood. **2.** The wood of a spruce. [< obs. *Spruce fir,* Prussian fir.]

spruce² (sprōōs) *adj.* **spruc·er, spruc·est.** Neat, trim, or dapper in appearance. —*v.* **spruced, spruc·ing.** To make or become spruce. [Perh. < obs. *Spruce leather,* Prussian leather.]

sprung (sprŭng) *v.* A *p.t.* and the *p.p.* of **spring.**

spry (sprī) *adj.* **spri·er** or **spry·er, spri·est** or **spry·est.** Active; nimble. [Perh. of Scand. orig.]

spud (spŭd) *n.* **1.** A sharp tool resembling a spade. **2.** *Informal.* A potato. [ME *spudde,* short knife.]

spume (spyōōm) *n.* Froth on a liquid; foam. [< Lat. *spuma.*] —**spum'y** *adj.*

spu·mo·ne (spōō-mō'nē) *n.* Also **spu·mo·ni.** Ice cream of different flavors in layers, often with nuts and candied fruits. [Ital.]

spun (spŭn) *v. p.t. & p.p.* of **spin.**

spun glass *n.* Fiber glass.

spunk (spŭngk) *n. Informal.* Spirit; pluck. [Sc. Gael. *spong,* tinder.] —**spunk'y** *adj.*

spur (spûr) *n.* **1.** One of a pair of spiked devices attached to a rider's heels and used to urge the horse forward. **2.** An incentive; stimulus. **3.** A narrow, pointed attachment or projection, as on the back of a bird's leg or on certain flowers. **4.** A ridge projecting from the side of a mountain. **5.** A side track that connects with the main track of a railroad system. —v. **spurred, spurring. 1.** To urge (a horse) by the use of spurs. **2.** To incite; stimulate. [< OE *spura.*] —**spurred** *adj.*

spurge (spûrj) *n.* Any of various plants with milky juice and small flowers. [< OFr. *espurgier,* to purge < its use as a purgative.]

spu·ri·ous (spyŏŏr'ē-əs) *adj.* Lacking authenticity or validity; false; counterfeit. [< Lat. *spurius,* illegitimate.] —**spu'ri·ous·ly** *adv.* —**spu'ri·ous·ness** *n.*

spurn (spûrn) *v.* To reject or refuse disdainfully; scorn. [< OE *spurnan.*] —**spurn'er** *n.*

spurt (spûrt). Also *chiefly Brit.* **spirt.** —n. **1.** A sudden and forcible gush, as of water. **2.** A sudden short burst of energy or activity. —v. **1.** To burst forth. **2.** To force out in a burst; squirt. [< OE *spryttan,* to sprout.]

sput·nik (sప్ŏŏt'nĭk, spŏŏt'-) *n.* An artificial earth satellite launched by the USSR. [R. *sputnik (zemlyi),* fellow traveler (of Earth).]

sput·ter (spŭt'ər) *v.* **1.** To spit out small particles in short bursts. **2.** To make a sporadic coughing noise. **3.** To utter words in a hasty or confused fashion. [Prob. of LG orig.] —**sput'ter** *n.* —**sput'ter·er** *n.*

spu·tum (spyŏŏ'təm) *n., pl.* **-ta** (-tə). Expectorated matter including saliva and substances from the respiratory tract. [Lat. < *spuere,* to spit.]

spy (spī) *n., pl.* **spies. 1.** A secret agent employed by a state to obtain intelligence relating to enemies at home or abroad. **2.** One who secretly watches others. —v. **spied, spying. 1.** To observe secretly and closely with hostile intent. **2.** To catch sight of; see. **3.** To investigate; pry. [< OFr. *espier,* to watch, of Gmc. orig.]

spy·glass (spī'glăs') *n.* A small telescope.

squab (skwŏb) *n.* A young pigeon. [Prob. of Scand. orig.]

squab·ble (skwŏb'əl) *n.* A trivial quarrel. [Prob. of Scand. orig.] —**squab'ble** *v.*

squad (skwŏd) *n.* **1.** A small group of persons organized for a specific purpose. **2.** The smallest unit of military personnel, usu. about ten persons. [< OSp. *escuadra,* or < OItal. *squadra.*]

squad car *n.* A police patrol car connected by radiotelephone with headquarters.

squad·ron (skwŏd'rən) *n.* **1.** A group of naval vessels constituting two or more divisions of a fleet. **2.** The basic air force tactical unit. [Ital. *squadrone.*]

squal·id (skwŏl'ĭd) *adj.* **1.** Having a dirty or wretched appearance. **2.** Morally repulsive; sordid. [< Lat. *squalidus.*] —**squal'id·ly** *adv.* —**squal'id·ness** *n.*

squall¹ (skwôl) *n.* A loud, harsh outcry. [Prob. of Scand. orig.] —**squall** *v.*

squall² (skwôl) *n.* A brief, sudden, and violent windstorm, often with rain or snow. [Prob. of Scand. orig.] —**squall'y** *adj.*

squal·or (skwŏl'ər) *n.* The state or quality of being squalid. [Lat. < *squalus,* filthy.]

squan·der (skwŏn'dər) *v.* To use or spend wastefully or extravagantly. [Orig. unknown.]

square (skwâr) *n.* **1.** A rectangle with four equal sides. **2.** Something shaped like a

square. **3.** An instrument for drawing or testing right angles. **4.** The product of a number or quantity multiplied by itself. **5. a.** An open area at the intersection of two or more streets. **b.** A rectangular space enclosed by streets; block. **6.** *Slang.* One characterized by rigid conventionality. —*adj.* **squar·er, squar·est. 1.** Having four equal sides and four right angles. **2.** Forming a right angle. **3. a.** Expressed in units measuring area: *square feet.* **b.** Having a specified length in each of two equal dimensions. **4.** Like a square in form: *a square jaw.* **5.** Honest; direct: *a square answer.* **6.** Just; equitable: *a square deal.* **7.** Paid-up; settled. **8.** Even; tied. **9.** *Slang.* Rigidly conventional. —v. **squared, squaring. 1.** To cut to a square or rectangular shape. **2.** To bring into balance; settle: *square a debt.* **3.** To multiply (a number, quantity, or expression) by itself. **4.** To agree or conform; balance. [Ult. < Lat. *quadrus.*] —**square'ly** *adv.* —**square'ness** *n.*

square dance *n.* A dance in which sets of four couples form squares. —v. **square'-dance'** *v.* —**square'-danc'er** *n.*

square rig *n.* A sailing-ship rig with rectangular sails set approx. at right angles to the keel line from horizontal yards. —**square'-rigged'** *adj.*

square-rig·ger (skwâr'rĭg'ər) *n.* A square-rigged vessel.

square root *n.* A divisor of a quantity that when squared gives the quantity.

squash¹ (skwŏsh, skwôsh) *n.* **1.** A fleshy fruit related to the pumpkins and the gourds, eaten as a vegetable. **2.** A plant that bears squash. [< Massachuset *askŏŏtasquash.*]

squash² (skwŏsh, skwôsh) *v.* **1.** To press, squeeze, or flatten to a pulp; crush. **2.** To suppress; quash. —*n.* **1.** The impact or sound of a soft body dropping against a surface. **2.** A crush or press, esp. of people. **3.** A game played in a walled court with a racket and a hard rubber ball. [OFr. *esquasser.*] —**squash'i·ness** *n.* —**squash'y** *adj.*

squat (skwŏt) *v.* **squat·ted** or **squat, squatting. 1.** To sit on one's heels. **2. a.** To settle on unoccupied land without legal claim. **b.** To settle on public land in order to acquire title to it. —*adj.* **squat·ter, squat·test. 1.** Seated in a squatting position. **2.** Short and thick. —*n.* The act or posture of squatting. [< OFr. *esquatir,* to crush.] —**squat'ter** *n.*

squaw (skwô) *n.* A North American Indian woman. [Massachuset *squa.*]

squawk (skwôk) *v.* **1.** To utter a loud screech. **2.** *Slang.* To make a loud or insistent protest. [Perh. blend of *squall,* a loud cry and SQUEAK.] —**squawk** *n.*

squeak (skwēk) *v.* To utter, speak in, or make a thin, high-pitched cry or sound. [ME *squeken.*] —**squeak** *n.* —**squeak'i·ly** *adv.* —**squeak'i·ness** *n.* —**squeak'y** *adj.*

squeal (skwēl) *v.* **1.** To utter with or produce a loud, shrill cry or sound. **2.** *Slang.* To turn informer. —*n.* A loud, shrill cry or sound. [ME *squelen.*] —**squeal'er** *n.*

squea·mish (skwē'mĭsh) *adj.* **1. a.** Easily nauseated. **b.** Nauseated. **2.** Easily offended or disgusted. [< AN *escoymous.*] —**squea'mish·ness** *n.*

squee-gee (skwē′jē′) n. A T-shaped implement with a rubber blade set across a handle, used esp. to remove excess water from a surface, as a window. [Perh. < SQUEEZE.] —squee′gee′ v.

squeeze (skwēz) v. **squeezed, squeez-ing.** 1. To press together; compress. 2. To exert pressure. 3. To extract by applying pressure: *squeeze juice from a lemon.* 4. To force by pressure; cram. —n. 1. An act of squeezing. 2. An amount squeezed. [< OE cwȳsan.] —squeez′er n.

squelch (skwĕlch) v. 1. To crush completely; suppress. 2. To silence, as with a crushing remark. 3. To make or move with a splashing, squashing, or sucking sound. [Imit.] —squelch n.

squib (skwĭb) n. 1. A firecracker, esp. one that burns but does not explode. 2. A brief, sometimes witty literary effort. [Prob. imit.]

squid (skwĭd) n., pl. **squids** or **squid.** A marine mollusk with a long body and ten arms surrounding the mouth. [Orig. unknown.]

squid   squirrel

squig-gle (skwĭg′əl) n. A small wiggly mark or scrawl. —v. **-gled, -gling.** To squirm and wriggle. [Blend of SQUIRM and WRIGGLE.] —squig′gly adj.

squint (skwĭnt) v. 1. **a.** To look with the eyes partly open. **b.** To close (the eyes) partly. 2. To be cross-eyed. [ME asquint, with a sidelong glance.] —squint n.

squire (skwīr) n. 1. A young nobleman attendant upon and ranked next below a knight. 2. An English country gentleman. 3. A judge or other local dignitary. 4. A man who escorts a woman; gallant. —v. **squired, squiring.** To attend as an escort or squire. [< OFr. esquier.]

squirm (skwûrm) v. 1. To twist about in a wriggling motion; writhe. 2. To feel or exhibit signs of humiliation or embarrassment. [Perh. imit.] —squirm n. —squirm′er n. —squirm′y adj.

squir-rel (skwûr′əl, skwŭr′-) n. 1. Any of various tree-climbing rodents with gray or reddish-brown fur and a long, bushy tail. 2. The fur of a squirrel. [< Gk. skiouros.]

squirt (skwûrt) v. To eject liquid in a thin swift stream. —n. 1. **a.** A device used to squirt. **b.** The liquid squirted. 2. *Informal.* An insignificant but impudent and esp. young person. [ME squirten.]

Sr The symbol for the element strontium.

-st suff. Var. of **-est²**.

stab (stăb) v. **stabbed, stab-bing.** 1. To pierce or wound with or as if with a pointed weapon. 2. To lunge with or as if with a pointed weapon; thrust. —n. 1. A thrust made with a pointed weapon. 2. A wound

inflicted by stabbing. 3. An attempt; effort. [< ME stabbe, a stab wound.]

sta-bi-lize (stā′bə-līz′) v. **-lized, -liz-ing.** 1. To make or become more stable. 2. To maintain the stability of. —sta′bi-li-za′tion n.

sta-ble¹ (stā′bəl) adj. **-bler, -blest.** 1. Resistant to sudden change, as of position or condition. 2. Maintaining equilibrium. 3. Long-lasting; enduring. 4. **a.** Consistently dependable. **b.** Emotionally well-balanced and sound. [< Lat. stabilis.] —sta-bil′i-ty (stə-bĭl′ĭ-tē) n. —sta′bly adv.

sta-ble² (stā′bəl) n. 1. A building for the shelter and feeding of domestic animals, esp. horses. 2. All the racehorses of a single owner. —v. **-bled, -bling.** To put or keep (an animal) in a stable. [< Lat. stabulum.]

stac-ca-to (stə-kä′tō) adj. Composed of abrupt, distinct parts or sounds: *staccato applause.* [Ital., p.p. of staccare, to detach.] —stac-ca′to n. & adv.

stack (stăk) n. 1. A large, usu. conical pile, as of straw. 2. An orderly pile, esp. one arranged in layers. 3. **a.** A chimney or flue. **b.** A vertical exhaust pipe. 4. **stacks.** The area of a library in which most of the books are shelved. 5. *Informal.* A large quantity. —v. 1. To arrange in a stack; pile. 2. To prearrange the order of (playing cards) so as to cheat. —phrasal verb. **stack up.** To measure up; compare. [< ON stakkr.]

sta-di-um (stā′dē-əm) n., pl. **-di-a** (-dē-ə) or **-ums.** A large, often unroofed structure in which athletic events are held. [< Gk. stadion, racetrack.]

staff (stăf) n. 1. pl. **staffs** or **staves** (stāvz). A pole, rod, or stick used as an aid in walking, as a weapon, or as a symbol of authority. 2. pl. **staffs. a.** A group of assistants to an executive or military commander. **b.** The personnel of an enterprise. 3. pl. **staffs** or **staves.** The set of horizontal lines on which musical notes are written. —v. To provide with a staff of employees. [< OE stæf.]

staff-er (stăf′ər) n. *Informal.* A member of a staff.

stag (stăg) n. An adult male deer. —adj. For or attended by men only: *a stag party.* —adv. Not in the company of a female date: *go stag.* [< OE stagga.]

stage (stāj) n. 1. A raised platform, as a workmen's scaffold. 2. **a.** The raised platform on which theatrical performances are presented. **b.** The acting profession. 3. The scene or setting of an event of note. 4. A resting place on a journey. 5. A stagecoach. 6. A level, degree, or period of time in the course of a process; step. 7. One of the successive propulsion units of a rocket. —v. **staged, stag-ing.** 1. To exhibit, present, or perform on or as if on a stage. 2. To arrange and carry out: *stage an invasion.* [Ult. < Lat. stare, to stand.]

stage-coach (stāj′kōch′) n. A horse-drawn vehicle formerly used to transport mail and passengers.

stag-ger (stăg′ər) v. 1. To move or cause to move unsteadily; totter. 2. To begin to lose confidence; waver. 3. To overwhelm with emotion or surprise. 4. To arrange in alternating or overlapping time periods or positions. —n. 1. A tottering or reeling motion. 2. **staggers** (used with a sing. verb). A disease of animals, esp. horses, characterized by stag-

gering and falling. [< ON *staka,* to push.]
—**stag'ger·er** *n.* —**stag'ger·ing·ly** *adv.*

stag·ing (stā'jǐng) *n.* **1.** A temporary platform; scaffold. **2.** The process of producing and directing a stage play.

stag·nant (stāg'nənt) *adj.* **1.** Not moving or flowing; motionless. **2.** Lacking liveliness or briskness; sluggish. [< Lat. *stagnum,* swamp.] —**stag'nan·cy** *n.* —**stag'nant·ly** *adv.*

stag·nate (stāg'nāt') *v.* **-nat·ed, -nat·ing.** **1.** To be or become stagnant. **2.** To fail to change or develop. —**stag·na'tion** *n.*

stag·y (stā'jē) *adj.* **-i·er, -i·est.** Having a theatrical quality. —**stag'i·ly** *adv.* —**stag'i·ness** *n.*

staid (stād) *adj.* **-er, -est.** Restrained and sober; sedate. [< obs. p.p. of STAY.]

stain (stān) *v.* **1.** To discolor, soil, or spot. **2.** To corrupt; taint. **3.** To color with a penetrating liquid dye or tint. —*n.* **1.** A spot or smudge of foreign matter. **2.** A blemish on one's name; stigma. **3.** A liquid substance, as a dye, used to stain. [< OFr. *desteindre,* to deprive of color, and < ON *steina,* to paint.] —**stain'less** *adj.*

stainless steel *n.* Any of various steels alloyed with sufficient chromium to be resistant to rusting and corrosion.

stair (stâr) *n.* **1. stairs.** A series or flight of steps; staircase. **2.** One of a flight of steps. [< OE *stæger.*]

stair·case (stâr'kās) *n.* A flight of steps and its supporting structure.

stair·way (stâr'wā) *n.* A flight of stairs.

stair·well (stâr'wěl) *n.* A vertical shaft around which a staircase has been built.

stake (stāk) *n.* **1.** A pointed piece, as of wood, driven into the ground and used as a marker, barrier, or support. **2. a.** A post to which a condemned person is bound for execution by burning. **b.** Execution by burning. **3.** Often **stakes.** **a.** Money or property risked in a wager or gambling game. **b.** The award or prize in a contest or race. **4.** A share or interest in an enterprise. —*v.* **staked, stak·ing.** **1.** To mark the location or boundaries of with or as if with stakes. **2.** To fasten to a stake. **3.** To gamble; risk. **4.** To provide with needed capital; finance. [< OE *staca.*]

stake·out (stāk'out') *n.* Police surveillance of an area, building, or person.

sta·lac·tite (stə-lǎk'tīt') *n.* A deposit, usu. of calcite or aragonite, that projects downward from the roof of a cavern. [< Gk. *stalaktos,* dripping.]

sta·lag·mite (stə-lǎg'mīt') *n.* A deposit, usu. of calcite or aragonite, that projects upward from the floor of a cavern. [< Gk. *stalagmos,* dripping.]

stale (stāl) *adj.* **stal·er, stal·est.** **1.** Having lost freshness or flavor: *stale beer.* **2.** Lacking in originality or spontaneity; trite. —*v.* **staled, stal·ing.** To make or become stale. [ME, well-aged (as beer).]

stale·mate (stāl'māt') *n.* A situation in which further progress is impossible; deadlock. [Obs. *stale,* stalemate + MATE².] —**stale'mate'** *v.*

stalk¹ (stôk) *n.* **1.** A stem that supports a plant or plant part. **2.** A slender or elongated support or structure. [ME.]

stalk² (stôk) *v.* **1.** To walk with a stiff or

haughty gait. **2.** To move menacingly. **3.** To track (game). [< OE *(be)stealcian,* to walk softly.] —**stalk'er** *n.*

stall (stôl) *n.* **1.** A compartment for one animal in a barn or stable. **2.** A small compartment or booth for selling wares. **3.** A pew in a church. —*v.* **1.** To bring or come to a standstill accidentally: *stall an engine.* **2.** To employ delaying tactics (against). [< OE *steall,* cattle stall.]

stal·lion (stăl'yən) *n.* An uncastrated adult male horse. [< OFr. *estalon,* of Gmc. orig.]

stal·wart (stôl'wərt) *adj.* **1.** Physically strong; sturdy. **2.** Resolute; uncompromising. [< OE *stælwierthe,* serviceable.]

sta·men (stā'mən) *n.* The pollen-producing reproductive organ of a flower. [Lat., thread.]

stam·i·na (stăm'ə-nə) *n.* Physical or moral power of endurance. [Lat., pl. of *stamen,* thread.]

stam·i·nate (stăm'ə-nət, -nāt') *adj.* **1.** Having a stamen or stamens. **2.** Bearing stamens but lacking pistils.

stam·mer (stăm'ər) *v.* To speak with involuntary pauses and repetitions of sounds. [< OE *stamerian.*] —**stam'mer** *n.* —**stam'mer·er** *n.*

stamp (stămp) *v.* **1.** To bring (the foot) down forcibly. **2.** To thrust the foot forcibly downward. **3.** To imprint or impress with a mark, design, or seal. **4.** To affix an adhesive stamp to. **5.** To form or cut out with a mold, form, or die. **6.** To identify, characterize, or reveal. —*n.* **1.** The act of stamping. **2. a.** An implement or device used to stamp. **b.** The impression or shape stamped. **3.** A mark, design, or seal indicating ownership, approval, or completion. **4.** A postage stamp. **5.** An identifying or characterizing mark. [ME *stampen.*]

stam·pede (stăm-pēd') *n.* A sudden headlong rush, as of startled animals or a crowd of people. —*v.* **-ped·ed, -ped·ing.** To participate in or cause a stampede. [Sp. *estampida,* uproar.] —**stam·ped'er** *n.*

stance (stăns) *n.* The posture of a standing person. [< Lat. *stare,* to stand.]

stanch¹ (stônch, stănch) *v.* Also **staunch.** To stop or check the flow of a (bodily fluid, esp. blood). [< Lat. *stare,* to stand.]

stanch² (stônch, stănch) *adj.* Var. of **staunch¹.**

stan·chion (stăn'chən) *n.* An upright pole or post. [< Lat. *stare,* to stand.]

stand (stănd) *v.* **stood** (stood), **stand·ing.** **1.** To take, cause to take, or maintain an upright position on the feet. **2.** To assume a particular position: *stand straight.* **3.** To remain stable, valid, or intact. **4.** To be situated, placed, or ranked. **5.** To remain unchanged or stationary. **6.** To tolerate; endure. **7.** To be subjected to; undergo: *stand trial.* —*phrasal verbs.* **stand in.** To substitute. **stand out.** To be prominent or outstanding. **stand up.** *Informal.* To fail to keep an appointment with. —*n.* **1.** The act of standing. **2.** A ceasing of work or activity; standstill. **3.** A stop on a performance tour. **4.** A witness stand. **5.** A booth, stall, or counter for the display of goods for sale. **6.** A parking space reserved for taxis. **7.** A position or opinion one is prepared to defend: *take a stand.* **8. stands.** The bleachers at a playing field or stadium. **9.** A rack or prop for holding things upright. **10.** A group or growth of tall plants or trees. [< OE *standan.*]

stan·dard (stăn'dərd) *n.* **1.** A flag, banner, or ensign. **2.** An acknowledged basis for comparing or measuring; criterion. **3.** A degree or level of requirement, excellence, or attainment. **4.** A pedestal, stand, or base. [< OFr. *estandard*, of Gmc. orig.] —**stan'dard** *adj.*

stan·dard-bear·er (stăn'dərd-bâr'ər) *n.* One who is in the vanguard of a political or religious movement.

stan·dard·ize (stăn'dər-dīz') *v.* **-ized, -iz·ing.** To make, adjust, or adapt to fit a standard. —**stan'dard·i·za'tion** *n.*

standard of living *n.* A measure of the goods and services affordable by and available to a person or country.

standard time *n.* The time in any of 24 time zones, usu. the mean solar time at the central meridian of each zone.

stand·by (stănd'bī') *n., pl.* **-bys.** **1.** One that is ready and available for service or substitution. **2.** One that can always be depended on.

stand-in (stănd'ĭn') *n.* **1.** One who takes the place of an actor while lights and camera are adjusted. **2.** A substitute.

stand·ing (stăn'dĭng) *adj.* **1.** Standing upright. **2.** Performed from an upright position: *a standing jump.* **3.** Remaining in effect or existence; permanent: *a standing army.* —*n.* **1.** A relative position in a group; rank. **2.** Status; reputation. **3.** Persistence in time; duration.

stand-off (stănd'ôf', -ŏf') *n.* A tie, as in a contest; draw.

stand·off·ish (stănd-ô'fĭsh, -ŏf'ĭsh) *adj.* Unfriendly; aloof.

stand·out (stănd'out') *n.* One that is outstanding or excellent.

stand·pipe (stănd'pīp') *n.* A large vertical pipe into which water is pumped in order to produce a desired pressure.

stand·point (stănd'point') *n.* A position from which things are considered; point of view.

stand-still (stănd'stĭl') *n.* A halt.

stank (stăngk) *v.* A *p.t.* of **stink.**

stan·za (stăn'zə) *n.* One of the divisions of a poem composed of two or more lines. [Ital.]

sta·pes (stā'pēz') *n., pl.* **-pes** or **sta·pe·des** (stə-pē'dēz'). A small bone of the inner ear, shaped somewhat like a stirrup. [< Med. Lat., stirrup.]

staph·y·lo·coc·cus (stăf'ə-lō-kŏk'əs) *n., pl.* **-coc·ci** (-kŏk'sī', -kŏk'ī'). Any of various spherical parasitic bacteria occurring in grapelike clusters causing infections such as septicemia. [Gk. *staphulē*, bunch of grapes + -COCCUS.] —**staph'y·lo·coc'cal** (-kŏk'əl) or **staph'y·lo·coc'cic** (-kŏk'sĭk, -kŏk'ĭk) *adj.*

sta·ple¹ (stā'pəl) *n.* **1.** A major product or commodity. **2.** A major part, element, or feature. **3.** Raw material. **4.** The fiber of cotton, wool, or flax, graded as to length and fineness. —*adj.* **1.** Regularly grown or produced in large quantities. **2.** Principal; leading. [< MDu. *stapel*, emporium.]

sta·ple² (stā'pəl) *n.* **1.** A U-shaped metal loop with pointed ends, driven into a surface to hold something, as a bolt or wire. **2.** A thin piece of wire having the shape of a square bracket, used to fasten thin material, as paper. [< OE *stapol*, post.] —**sta'ple** *v.* —**sta'pler** *n.*

star (stär) *n.* **1. a.** A celestial object that consists of extremely hot gases and emits radi-

ation and light. **b.** A luminous, relatively stationary celestial body visible from the earth, esp. at night. **2. stars. a.** The celestial bodies regarded as determining and influencing human events. **b.** Fate; fortune. **3.** A graphic design representing a star. **4.** An asterisk. **5. a.** An actor who plays a leading role. **b.** An outstanding and widely admired performer. —*v.* **starred, star·ring.** **1.** To ornament with stars. **-2.** To mark with an asterisk. **3.** To play the leading role in a theatrical production. [< OE *steorra.*] —**star'dom** *n.* —**star'less** *adj.* —**star'ry** *adj.*

star·board (stär'bərd) *n.* The right-hand side of a ship or aircraft as one faces forward. [< OE *stēorbord.*] —**star'board** *adj. & adv.*

starch (stärch) *n.* **1.** A carbohydrate, $(C_6H_{10}O_5)_n$, found notably in corn, potatoes, wheat, and rice and commonly prepared as a white, tasteless powder. **2.** Any of various substances, including natural starch, used to stiffen fabrics. **3.** A food with a high starch content. —*v.* To stiffen with starch. [< ME *sterchen*, to stiffen.] —**starch'i·ness** *n.* —**starch'y** *adj.*

stare (stâr) *v.* **stared, star·ing.** To look with a steady, often wide-eyed gaze. [< OE *starian.*] —**stare** *n.* —**star'er** *n.*

star·fish (stär'fĭsh) *n.* A marine animal having a star-shaped form with five radiating arms.

starfish

star·gaze (stär'gāz') *v.* **-gazed, -gaz·ing.** **1.** To gaze at the stars. **2.** To daydream. —**star'gaz·er** *n.*

stark (stärk) *adj.* **-er, -est.** **1.** Bare; blunt: *stark truth.* **2.** Complete or utter; extreme: *stark poverty.* **3.** Harsh in appearance; grim: *stark cliffs.* —*adv.* Utterly. [< OE *stearc*, severe.] —**stark'ly** *adv.* —**stark'ness** *n.*

star·let (stär'lĭt) *n.* A young actress publicized as a future star.

star·light (stär'līt') *n.* The light given by the stars.

star·ling (stär'lĭng) *n.* An Old World bird with dark, often iridescent plumage, widely naturalized in North America. [< OE *stærline.*]

star·lit (stär'lĭt') *adj.* Illuminated by starlight.

Stars and Stripes *n.* (*used with a sing. or pl. verb*). The flag of the United States.

start (stärt) *v.* **1.** To commence; begin. **2.** To move suddenly and involuntarily: *started at the noise.* **3.** To set into motion, operation, or activity. **4.** To enter in a race. **5.** To found; establish. —*n.* **1. a.** A beginning; commencement. **b.** A place or time of beginning. **2.** A sudden, involuntary movement. **3.** A quick, brief spurt of effort or activity. [< OE *styrtan*, to leap up.] —**start'er** *n.*

star·tle (stär'tl) *v.* **-tled, -tling.** **1.** To cause to make a sudden, involuntary movement, as in fright. **2.** To become startled. [< OE *steartlian,* to kick.] **—star′tling·ly** *adv.*

starve (stärv) *v.* **starved, starv·ing. 1.** To die or cause to die from prolonged lack of food. **2.** To suffer or cause to suffer from deprivation: *starving for affection.* **3.** *Informal.* To be hungry. [< OE *steorfan,* to die.] **—star·va′-tion** *n.*

starve·ling (stärv′lĭng) *n.* One that is starving or being starved.

stash (stăsh) *v.* To hide or store away in a secret place. [Orig. unknown.] **—stash** *n.*

—stasis *suff.* A stable state or a balance: *homeostasis.* [< Gk. *stasis,* standstill.]

—stat *suff.* Stationary: *thermostat.* [< Gk. *-statēs,* one that causes to stand.]

state (stāt) *n.* **1.** A condition of being. **2.** A mental or emotional condition. **3. a.** A body of people living under a single independent government; nation. **b.** The territory of such a government. **4.** One of the political and geographic subdivisions of a federated country, as the United States. **5.** A social position; rank. **—v. stat·ed, stat·ing.** To set forth in words; declare. [< Lat. *status,* condition.] **—state′hood** *n.*

state house *n.* The building in which a state legislature holds sessions.

state·ly (stāt′lē) *adj.* **-li·er, -li·est. 1.** Dignified; formal. **2.** Majestic; lofty. **—state′li·ness** *n.*

state·ment (stāt′mənt) *n.* **1.** The act of stating. **2.** Something stated. **3.** A written summary of a financial account.

state·room (stāt′rōōm′, -rŏŏm′) *n.* A private compartment on a ship or train.

state·side (stāt′sīd′) *adj.* Of, pertaining to, or in the continental United States. **—state′side′** *adv.*

states·man (stāts′mən) *n.* **1.** A leader in national or international affairs. **2.** A political leader regarded as a disinterested promoter of the public good. **—states′man·like′** *adj.* **—states′man·ship** *n.* **—states′wom·an** *n.*

stat·ic (stăt′ĭk) *adj.* **1.** Not moving, active, or in motion; at rest. **2.** Of, pertaining to, or producing stationary charges; electrostatic. **3.** Of, pertaining to, or produced by random radio noise. **—n. 1.** Random noise, as crackling in a radio receiver or specks on a television screen, produced by atmospheric disturbances. **2.** *Slang.* **a.** Interference. **b.** Angry criticism. [< Gk. *statikos,* causing to stand.] **—stat′i·cal·ly** *adv.*

sta·tion (stā′shən) *n.* **1.** The place where a person or thing stands or is assigned to stand. **2.** The place from which a service is provided or operations are directed. **3.** A stopping place along a transportation route, esp. a depot. **4.** Social position; status. **5.** An establishment equipped for radio or television transmission. **—v.** To assign to a station; post. [< Lat. *stare,* to stand.]

sta·tion·ar·y (stā′shə-nĕr′ē) *adj.* **1.** Not moving; fixed. **2.** Unchanging.

station break *n.* An intermission in a radio or television program for identification of the network or station.

sta·tion·er (stā′shə-nər) *n.* One who sells stationery. [Med. Lat. *statio,* shop.]

sta·tion·er·y (stā′shə-nĕr′ē) *n.* Writing materials, as pens, paper, and envelopes.

station wagon *n.* An automobile that has an extended interior with a third seat or luggage platform and a tailgate.

sta·tis·tic (stə-tĭs′tĭk) *n.* A numerical datum. **—sta·tis′ti·cal** (-tĭ-kəl) *adj.* **—sta·tis′ti·cal·ly** *adv.*

sta·tis·tics (stə-tĭs′tĭks) *n.* **1.** *(used with a sing. verb).* The mathematics of the collection, organization, and interpretation of numerical data. **2.** *(used with a pl. verb).* A collection of numerical data. [G. *Statistik,* political science, ult. < Lat. *status,* state.] **—stat′is·ti′cian** (stăt′ĭ-stĭsh′ən) *n.*

stat·u·ar·y (stăch′ōō-ĕr′ē) *n., pl.* **-ies.** Statues collectively.

stat·ue (stăch′ōō) *n.* A likeness of a person or thing sculpted in a solid substance. [< Lat. *statuere,* to erect.]

stat·u·esque (stăch′ōō-ĕsk′) *adj.* Suggestive of a statue, as in proportion or dignity; stately.

stat·u·ette (stăch′ōō-ĕt′) *n.* A small statue.

stat·ure (stăch′ər) *n.* **1.** Natural height, as of a person, in an upright position. **2.** A level reached, as by achievement; status. [< Lat. *statura.*]

sta·tus (stā′təs, stăt′əs) *n.* **1.** The legal character or condition of a person or thing. **2.** A stage in progress or development. **3.** A relative position, esp. a high relative position, as in a social system. [Lat., condition.]

sta·tus quo (stā′təs kwō′, stăt′əs) *n.* The existing condition or state of affairs. [Lat., state in which.]

stat·ute (stăch′ōōt) *n.* A law enacted by a legislature. [< Lat. *statuere,* to decree.]

statute mile *n.* The standard mile, 5,280 feet.

stat·u·to·ry (stăch′ə-tôr′ē, -tōr′ē) *adj.* Enacted, regulated, or authorized by statute.

staunch¹ (stônch, stänch) *adj.* **-er, -est.** Also **stanch. 1.** Firm and steadfast; true. **2.** Well-built; strong. [< OFr. *estanchier,* to stanch.] **—staunch′ly** *adv.* **—staunch′ness** *n.*

Usage: Staunch is more common than *stanch* as the spelling of the adjective, but *stanch* is more common than *staunch* as the spelling of the verb.

staunch² (stônch, stänch) *v.* Var. of **stanch¹.**

stave (stāv) *n.* **1.** A narrow strip of wood forming part of the sides of a structure such as a barrel or tub. **2.** A staff or cudgel. **3.** A stanza. **—v. staved** or **stove** (stōv), **stav·ing. 1.** To break in or puncture the staves of. **2.** To break or smash a hole in. **3.** To keep or hold off; repel: *stave off hunger.* [< STAVES.]

staves (stāvz) *n.* A pl. of **staff.**

stay¹ (stā) *v.* **1.** To remain or cause to remain in a given place or condition. **2.** To stop; halt. **3.** To wait; pause. **4.** To hold on; endure. **5.** To postpone; delay. **6.** To satisfy or appease temporarily: *stay his hunger.* **—n. 1.** A stop or pause. **2.** A brief period of residence or visiting. [< Lat. *stare,* to stand.]

stay² (stā) *v.* To brace, support, or prop up. **—n. 1.** A support or brace. **2.** A strip of bone, plastic, or metal used to stiffen a garment or part. **3.** stays. A corset. [< OFr. *estaie,* support, of Gmc. orig.]

stay³ (stā) *n.* A heavy rope or cable used as a

support, as for a ship's mast. —v. To brace or support with stays. [< OE *stæg*.]

staying power n. The ability to endure or last.

stead (stĕd) n. 1. The place, position, or function of another person. 2. Advantage: *stood her in good stead.* [< OE *stede*.]

stead·fast (stĕd′făst′) adj. 1. Fixed or unchanging; steady. 2. Firmly loyal or constant. —**stead′fast′ly** adv. —**stead′fast′ness** n.

stead·y (stĕd′ē) adj. **-i·er, -i·est.** 1. Firm in position or place; stable. 2. Direct and unfaltering; sure. 3. Having a continuous movement, quality, or pace: *a steady wind.* 4. Calm and controlled: *steady nerves.* 5. Reliable. —v. **-ied, -y·ing.** To make or become steady. —**stead′i·ly** adv. —**stead′i·ness** n. —**stead′y** adv.

steak (stāk) n. A slice of meat, esp. beef, typically cut thick and across the muscle grain. [< ON *steik*.]

steal (stēl) v. **stole** (stōl), **sto·len** (stō′lən), **steal·ing.** 1. To take away without right or permission. 2. To get or effect secretly or artfully. 3. To move, happen, or elapse stealthily or unobtrusively. 4. *Baseball.* To advance (a base) by running during the delivery of a pitch. —n. 1. The act of stealing. 2. *Slang.* A bargain. [< OE *stelan*.] —**steal′er** n.

stealth (stĕlth) n. 1. The act of moving, proceeding, or acting in a covert way. 2. Furtiveness; covertness. [ME *stelth.*]

stealth·y (stĕl′thē) adj. **-i·er, -i·est.** Marked by or done with stealth; furtive. —**stealth′i·ly** adv. —**stealth′i·ness** n.

steam (stēm) n. 1. a. The vapor phase of water. b. The mist of cooling water vapor. 2. Power; energy. —v. 1. To produce or emit steam. 2. To become or rise up as steam. 3. To move or be powered by steam. 4. To expose to steam, as in cooking. [< OE *stēam*, vapor.] —**steam′i·ness** n. —**steam′y** adj.

steam·boat (stēm′bōt′) n. A steamship.

steam engine n. An engine that converts the heat energy of pressurized steam into mechanical energy, esp. one in which steam expands in a closed cylinder to drive a piston.

steam·er (stē′mər) n. 1. A steamship. 2. A container in which something is steamed. 3. A soft-shell clam.

steam·fit·ter (stēm′fĭt′ər) n. One whose occupation is the installation and repair of heating, ventilating, or refrigerating systems.

steam·roll·er (stēm′rō′lər) n. A machine with a heavy roller used esp. for smoothing road surfaces. —v. 1. To smooth with a steamroller. 2. To defeat or silence ruthlessly; crush.

steam·ship (stēm′shĭp′) n. A large vessel propelled by steam-driven screws or propellers.

steam shovel n. A steam-driven machine for digging.

ste·a·tite (stē′ə-tīt′) n. A massive, white-to-green talc used in paints, ceramics, and insulation. [< Gk. *steatitis*, a precious stone.]

steed (stēd) n. A horse, esp. a spirited mount. [< OE *stēda*, stallion.]

steel (stēl) n. 1. Any of various hard, strong, durable, malleable alloys of iron and carbon. 2. A quality suggestive of steel: *nerves of steel.* 3. Something made of steel, as a sword. —v. 1. To cover, edge, or point with steel. 2. To make hard or strong; brace. [< OE *stȳle*.] —**steel′y** adj.

steel wool n. Fine fibers of woven or matted steel used esp. for scouring.

steep¹ (stēp) adj. **-er, -est.** 1. Sharply sloped; precipitous. 2. Excessive; exorbitant: *a steep price.* [< OE *stēap*, lofty.] —**steep′ly** adv. —**steep′ness** n.

steep² (stēp) v. 1. To soak or be soaked in liquid, esp. in order to extract a given property. 2. To saturate: *steeped in knowledge.* [ME *stepen.*]

steep·en (stē′pən) v. To make or become steeper.

stee·ple (stē′pəl) n. 1. A tall tapering tower rising from the roof of a building, as a church. 2. A spire. [< OE *stēpel*, tall tower.]

stee·ple·chase (stē′pəl-chās′) n. A horse race across open country or over an obstacle course. —**stee′ple·chas′er** n.

steeplechase

stee·ple·jack (stē′pəl-jăk′) n. A worker on steeples or very high structures.

steer¹ (stîr) v. 1. To guide by means of a device such as a rudder. 2. To direct the course of. 3. To follow a course of action. 4. To be capable of being steered. [< OE *stīeran*.] —**steers′man** n.

steer² (stîr) n. A young ox, esp. one castrated before sexual maturity and raised for beef. [< OE *stēor*.]

steer·age (stîr′ĭj) n. 1. The action or practice of steering. 2. The section of a passenger ship providing the cheapest accommodations.

stein (stīn) n. An earthenware mug. [G.]

stel·lar (stĕl′ər) adj. 1. Of, relating to, or consisting of stars. 2. a. Of or relating to a star performer. b. Outstanding. [< Lat. *stella*, star.]

stem¹ (stĕm) n. 1. a. The main supporting part of a plant; stalk. b. A stalk supporting another plant part, as a leaf or flower. 2. Something that resembles a stem, as the slender upright support of a wineglass. 3. A main line of descent; stock. 4. The part of a word to which affixes are added. 5. The prow of a vessel. —v. **stemmed, stem·ming.** 1. To extend like a stem; branch out. 2. To derive or originate; spring. 3. To make headway against (a force such as a tide). [< OE *stefn*, prow.]

stem² (stĕm) v. **stemmed, stem·ming.** To hold back or stop by or as if by damming. [< ON *stemma.*]

stem·ware (stĕm′wâr′) n. Glassware mounted on a stem.

stench (stĕnch) n. A strong and foul odor; stink. [< OE *stenc*, odor.]

sten·cil (stĕn′səl) n. A sheet of material in which lettering or a design has been cut so that ink or paint applied to the sheet will reproduce the pattern on the surface beneath. —v. **-ciled** or **-cilled, -cil·ing** or **-cil·ling.** To mark or produce with a stencil. [< OFr. *estenceler*, to adorn with bright colors.]

ste·nog·ra·phy (stə-nŏg′rə-fē) *n.* The art or process of writing in shorthand. [Gk. *stenos*, narrow + -GRAPHY.] —**ste·nog′ra·pher** *n.* —**sten′o·graph′ic** (stĕn′ə-grăf′ĭk) *adj.* —**sten′o·graph′i·cal·ly** *adv.*

sten·to·ri·an (stĕn-tôr′ē-ən, -tōr′-) *adj.* Extremely loud. [< *Stentor*, a loud-voiced herald in Homer's *Iliad*.]

step (stĕp) *n.* **1. a.** The single complete movement of raising and putting down one foot in the act of walking. **b.** A manner of walking. **2.** A short distance. **3. a.** A fixed rhythm or pace, as in marching. **b.** Conformity with the rhythm, pace, views, or attitudes of others: *out of step with the times.* **4. a.** A rest for the foot in climbing up or down. **b. steps.** Stairs. **5. a.** One of a series of actions or measures taken to achieve a goal. **b.** One of the stages of a process. **6.** A degree of progress or a grade or rank in a scale, as of value. —*v.* **stepped, step·ping. 1.** To put or press the foot down. **2.** To shift or move by or as if by taking steps. **3.** To walk, esp. a short distance. **4.** To measure by pacing. —*phrasal verbs.* **step down.** To reduce, esp. in stages: *stepping down the electric power.* **step up.** To increase, esp. in stages: *step up production.* [< OE *stæpe.*]

step- *pref.* Related through remarriage rather than by blood: *stepbrother.* [< OE *stēop-.*]

step·broth·er (stĕp′brŭth′ər) *n.* The son of one's stepparent by a previous marriage.

step·child (stĕp′chīld′) *n.* The child of one's spouse by a former marriage.

step·daugh·ter (stĕp′dô′tər) *n.* The daughter of one's spouse by a former marriage.

step·fa·ther (stĕp′fä′thər) *n.* The husband of one's mother by a later marriage.

step·lad·der (stĕp′lăd′ər) *n.* A portable ladder with a hinged supporting frame.

step·moth·er (stĕp′mŭth′ər) *n.* The wife of one's father by a later marriage.

step·par·ent (stĕp′pâr′ənt, -pâr′-) *n.* A stepfather or stepmother.

steppe (stĕp) *n.* A vast semiarid grass-covered plain, as in southeastern Europe and Siberia. [R. *step′.*]

step·ping-stone (stĕp′ĭng-stōn′) *n.* An advantageous position for advancement toward a goal.

step·sis·ter (stĕp′sĭs′tər) *n.* The daughter of one's stepparent by a previous marriage.

step·son (stĕp′sŭn′) *n.* The son of one's spouse by a former marriage.

step-up (stĕp′ŭp′) *n.* An increase, as in size or amount.

-ster *suff.* **1.** One that is associated with, participates in, makes, or does: *songster.* **2.** One that is: *youngster.* [< OE *-estre.*]

stere (stîr) *n.* A unit of volume equal to one cubic meter. [< Gk. *stereos*, solid.]

ste·re·o (stĕr′ē-ō′, stîr′-) *n., pl.* **-os. 1.** A stereophonic sound-reproduction system. **2.** Stereophonic sound. —**ste′re·o′** *adj.*

stereo- *pref.* **1.** Solid; solid body: *stereotype.* **2.** Three-dimensional: *stereoscope.* [< Gk. *stereos*, solid.]

ster·e·o·phon·ic (stĕr′ē-ə-fŏn′ĭk, stîr′-) *adj.* Of or used in a sound-reproduction system that

uses two or more separate channels to give a more natural distribution of sound. —**ster′e·o·phon′i·cal·ly** *adv.*

ster·e·o·scope (stĕr′ē-ə-skōp′, stîr′-) *n.* An optical instrument used to impart a three-dimensional effect to two photographs of the same scene taken at slightly different angles and viewed through two eyepieces. —**ster′e·o·scop′ic** *adj.* —**ster′e·o·scop′i·cal·ly** *adv.*

ster·e·os·co·py (stĕr′ē-ŏs′kə-pē, stîr′-) *n.* The viewing of objects as three-dimensional.

ster·e·o·type (stĕr′ē-ə-tīp′, stîr′-) *n.* **1.** A metal printing plate cast from a matrix that is molded from a raised printing surface, such as type. **2.** A conventional and usu. oversimplified conception or belief. **3.** One considered typical of a kind and without individuality. —*v.* **1.** To make a stereotype from. **2.** To form a fixed, unvarying idea about. —**ster′e·o·typ′ic** (-tĭp′ĭk) or **ster′e·o·typ′i·cal** *adj.*

ster·ile (stĕr′əl, -īl′) *adj.* **1.** Incapable of reproducing sexually. **2.** Producing little or no vegetation. **3.** Free from microorganisms. **4.** Not productive or effective. [< Lat. *sterilis*, unfruitful.] —**ste·ril′i·ty** (stə-rĭl′ĭ-tē) *n.*

ster·il·ize (stĕr′ə-līz′) *v.* **-ized, -iz·ing.** To make sterile. —**ster′il·i·za′tion** *n.* —**ster′il·iz′er** *n.*

ster·ling (stûr′lĭng) *n.* **1.** British money. **2.** Sterling silver. —*adj.* **1.** Consisting of or relating to British money. **2.** Made of sterling silver. **3.** Of the highest quality. [ME, silver penny.]

sterling silver *n.* An alloy of 92.5% silver with copper or another metal.

stern¹ (stûrn) *adj.* **-er, -est. 1.** Firm or unyielding; inflexible. **2.** Grave or severe in manner or appearance; austere. **3.** Inexorable; relentless. [< OE *styrne.*] —**stern′ly** *adv.* —**stern′ness** *n.*

stern² (stûrn) *n.* The rear part of a ship or boat. [ME *sterne.*]

ster·num (stûr′nəm) *n., pl.* **-na** (-nə) or **-nums.** A long, flat bone located in the center of the chest and serving as a support for the ribs; breastbone. [< Gk. *sternon.*]

ster·oid (stîr′oid′, stĕr′-) *n.* Any of a large class of naturally occurring, fat-soluble organic compounds based on a structure having 17 carbon atoms bound in a ring, including many hormones and sterols. [STER(OL) + -OID.]

ster·ol (stîr′ôl′, stĕr′-) *n.* Any of a group of predominantly unsaturated solid alcohols of the steroid group, as cholesterol, occurring in the fatty tissues of plants and animals. [< CHOLESTEROL.]

stet (stĕt) *n.* A printer's term directing that matter marked for omission or correction is to be retained. —*v.* **stet·ted, stet·ting.** To nullify a correction or omission previously made in (printed matter) by marking with the word *stet* and underlining with dots. [Lat., let it stand.]

steth·o·scope (stĕth′ə-skōp′) *n.* An instrument used to listen to sounds produced within the body. [Gk. *stēthos*, chest + -SCOPE.]

ste·ve·dore (stē′və-dôr′, -dōr′) *n.* One employed in loading and unloading ships. [< Sp. *estivar*, to pack.]

stew (stōō, styōō) v. 1. To cook (food) by simmering or boiling slowly. 2. *Informal.* To worry; fret. —n. 1. A dish cooked by stewing, esp. a mixture of meat or fish and vegetables with stock. 2. *Informal.* Mental agitation. [< OFr. *estuver,* to bathe in hot water.]

stew·ard (stōō′ərd, styōō′-) n. 1. One who manages another's property, finances, or other affairs. 2. One in charge of the household affairs of a large estate, hotel, club, or resort. 3. An officer on a ship in charge of provisions and dining arrangements. 4. An attendant, esp. a male, on a ship or airplane. [< OE *stigweard.*] —**stew′ard·ess** n. —**stew′ard·ship′** n.

stick (stĭk) n. 1. A long, slender piece of wood, esp. a branch cut or fallen from a tree. 2. A sticklike implement, as a cane or baton, used for a particular purpose. 3. Something having the shape of a stick. 4. **sticks.** *Informal.* Rural, remote country. 5. A stiff, listless, or boring person. —v. **stuck** (stŭk), **stick·ing.** 1. To pierce, puncture, or penetrate with a pointed instrument. 2. To fix on a pointed object; impale. 3. To fasten or hold fast with or as with an adhesive material; adhere (to). 4. To put, thrust, or poke into a specified place or position. 5. To be or become fixed or embedded in place. 6. To be at or come to a standstill. 7. To persist, endure, or persevere. 8. *Informal.* To remain; linger: *Stick around until I get back.* 9. To be blocked, checked, or obstructed. 10. To project or protrude. —*phrasal verb.* **stick up.** To rob, esp. at gunpoint. [< OE *sticca.*]

stick·er (stĭk′ər) n. 1. One that sticks, esp. a gummed or adhesive label.

stick·ler (stĭk′lər) n. One who insists on meticulous observance of detail.

stick shift n. An automobile gearshift operated by hand.

stick-to-it·ive·ness (stĭk-tōō′ĭ-tĭv-nĭs) n. *Informal.* Unwavering tenacity; perseverance.

stick·up (stĭk′ŭp′) n. *Slang.* A robbery, esp. at gunpoint.

stick·y (stĭk′ē) adj. **-i·er, -i·est.** 1. Sticking or tending to stick; adhesive. 2. Warm and humid. 3. *Informal.* Painful or difficult: *a sticky situation.* —**stick′i·ly** adv. —**stick′i·ness** n.

stiff (stĭf) adj. **-er, -est.** 1. Difficult to bend or stretch; rigid. 2. Not moving or operating easily; not limber: *a stiff joint.* 3. Taut; tense. 4. Rigidly or excessively formal, awkward, or constrained. 5. Not liquid, loose, or fluid: *a stiff dough.* 6. Strong, swift, and steady in force or movement: *a stiff drink.* 7. Potent: *a stiff drink.* 8. Difficult; arduous. 9. Harsh; severe. —n. *Slang.* A corpse. [< OE *stīf.*] —**stiff′ly** adv. —**stiff′ness** n.

stiff·en (stĭf′ən) v. To make or become stiff or stiffer. —**stiff′en·er** n.

stiff-necked (stĭf′nĕkt′) adj. Stubborn; unyielding.

sti·fle (stī′fəl) v. **-fled, -fling.** 1. To kill by preventing respiration; smother. 2. To keep or hold back; suppress. 3. To die of suffocation. [ME *stuflen.*]

stig·ma (stĭg′mə) n. 1. *pl.* **-mas** or **stig·ma·ta** (stĭg-mä′tə, stĭg′mə-tə). A mark or token of shame or disgrace. 2. *pl.* **-mas.** The sticky tip of a flower pistil on which pollen is deposited. 3. **stigmata.** Marks or sores resembling the Crucifixion wounds of Christ. [< Gk., tattoo mark.] —**stig·mat′ic** (stĭg-mǎt′ĭk) adj.

stig·ma·tize (stĭg′mə-tīz′) v. **-tized, -tiz·ing.**
1. To characterize or brand as disgraceful or ignominious. 2. To mark with a stigma.

stile (stīl) n. A set or series of steps for crossing a fence or wall. [< OE *stigel.*]

sti·let·to (stĭ-lĕt′ō) n., *pl.* **-tos** or **-toes.** A small dagger with a slender, tapering blade. [Ital., dim. of *stilo,* dagger.]

still¹ (stĭl) adj. **-er, -est.** 1. Free from sound; silent. 2. Motionless. 3. Free from disturbance; tranquil. —n. 1. Silence; calm. 2. A static photograph, esp. one from a scene of a motion picture. —adv. 1. Without movement; motionlessly: *stand still.* 2. Now as before; yet: *still awake.* 3. In increasing amount or degree: *still further complaints.* 4. All the same; nevertheless. —conj. But yet; nevertheless. —v. 1. To make or become still. 2. To allay; calm. [< OE.] —**still′ness** n.

still² (stĭl) n. 1. An apparatus for distilling liquids, esp. alcohols. 2. A distillery. [< ME *distillen,* to distill.]

still·birth (stĭl′bûrth′) n. The birth of a dead fetus.

still·born (stĭl′bôrn′) adj. Born dead.

still life n., *pl.* **still lifes.** A painting or picture of inanimate objects.

stilt (stĭlt) n. 1. Either of a pair of long, slender poles, each equipped with a raised footrest to permit walking elevated above the ground. 2. Any of various tall posts or pillars used as support, as for a dock. [ME *stilte.*]

stilt·ed (stĭl′tĭd) adj. Stiffly or artificially formal; pompous. —**stilt′ed·ly** adv.

stim·u·lant (stĭm′yə-lənt) n. 1. An agent, such as a drug, that temporarily excites or accelerates the function of the body or one of its systems or parts. 2. A stimulus or incentive. 3. An alcoholic beverage. —**stim′u·lant** adj.

stim·u·late (stĭm′yə-lāt′) v. **-lat·ed, -lat·ing.** To rouse to activity or to increased action or interest; stir. [Lat. *stimulare,* to goad.] —**stim′u·la′tion** n. —**stim′u·la′tive** adj.

stim·u·lus (stĭm′yə-ləs) n., *pl.* **-li** (-lī′). Something that stimulates; incentive or spur. [Lat., goad.]

Syns: *stimulus, catalyst, impetus, impulse, incentive, motivation, spur, stimulant* n.

sting (stĭng) v. **stung** (stŭng), **sting·ing.** 1. To pierce or wound painfully with or as if with a sharp-pointed structure or organ. 2. To feel or cause to feel a sharp, smarting pain. 3. To cause to suffer keenly. —n. 1. The act of stinging. 2. The wound or pain caused by or as if by stinging. 3. A sharp piercing organ or part, as of certain insects. [< OE *stingan.*] —**sting′er** n.

stin·gy (stĭn′jē) adj. **-gi·er, -gi·est.** 1. Giving or spending reluctantly. 2. Scanty or meager. [Obs. *stingy,* stinging < STING.] —**stin′gi·ly** adv. —**stin′gi·ness** n.

Syns: *stingy, cheap, close, mean, miserly, niggardly, parsimonious, penurious, tight, tight-fisted* adj.

stink (stĭngk) v. **stank** (stăngk) or **stunk** (stŭngk), **stunk, stink·ing.** 1. To emit or cause to emit a strong, offensive odor. 2. To be highly offensive or abhorrent. —n. A strong, offensive odor; stench. [< OE *stincan.*] —**stink′er** n.

stink·bug (stĭngk′bŭg′) n. Any of numerous insects that emit a foul odor.

stint (stĭnt) v. 1. To be sparing with; limit or restrict, as in amount or number. 2. To be frugal or sparing. —n. 1. An amount of work to be performed within a given period of time. **2.** A limitation or restriction. [< OE *styntan*, to blunt.] **—stint'er** n.

sti·pend (stī'pĕnd', -pənd) n. A fixed or regular payment or allowance. [< Lat. *stipendium*, tax.]

stip·ple (stĭp'əl) v. **-pled, -pling. 1.** To draw or engrave in dots or short touches rather than lines. **2.** To apply (paints, for example) in dots or short touches. [< Du. *stip*, dot.] **—stip'ple** n.

stip·u·late (stĭp'yə-lāt') v. **-lat·ed, -lat·ing. 1.** To specify or demand as a condition of an agreement. **2.** To guarantee in an agreement. [Lat. *stipulari*, to bargain.] **—stip'u·la'tion** n. **—stip'u·la'tor** n.

stir¹ (stûr) v. **stirred, stir·ring. 1.** To pass an implement through in circular motions so as to mix or cool. **2.** To change or cause to change position slightly. **3.** To rouse, as from sleep or indifference. **4.** To provoke or instigate: *stir up trouble.* **5.** To move or affect strongly. **—n. 1.** An act of stirring. **2.** A disturbance or commotion: *cause a stir.* [< OE *styrian*, to excite.] **—stir'rer** n.

stir² (stûr) n. *Slang.* Prison. [Orig. unknown.]

stir-fry (stûr'frī') v. To fry quickly in a small amount of oil while stirring continuously.

stir·ring (stûr'ĭng) adj. **1.** Rousing; exciting. **2.** Active; lively. **—stir'ring·ly** adv.

stir·rup (stûr'əp, stĭr'-) n. A loop or ring hung from a horse's saddle to support the rider's foot. [< OE *stigrāp.*]

stitch (stĭch) n. **1. a.** A link, loop, or knot formed by a threaded needle in sewing or surgical suturing. **b.** A single loop of yarn around an implement such as a knitting needle. **2.** A method of sewing, knitting, or crocheting: *a purl stitch.* **3.** A sudden sharp pain. **—v. 1.** To fasten, join, or ornament with stitches. **2.** To sew. [< OE *stice*, sting.] **—stitch'er** n.

stoat (stōt) n. The ermine, esp. in its brown color phase. [ME *stote.*]

stock (stŏk) n. **1.** A supply accumulated for future use. **2.** The total merchandise kept on hand by a commercial establishment. **3.** Domestic animals; livestock. **4. a.** The capital that a corporation raises through the sale of shares. **b.** A certificate showing ownership of a stated number of shares. **5. a.** The original progenitor of a family line or group of descendants. **b.** Ancestry or lineage. **c.** A group, as of organisms or languages, descended from a common ancestor. **6.** The raw material out of which something is made. **7.** The broth from boiled meat or fish, used in preparing soup, gravy, or sauces. **8.** A supporting structure, block, handle, or frame. **9. stocks.** A pillory. **10.** A company of actors and technicians attached to a single theater and performing in repertory. **—v. 1.** To provide with stock. **2.** To keep and store a supply: *stocked up on sugar.* **—adj. 1.** Kept regularly available for sale or use. **2.** Commonplace; ordinary: *a stock answer.* [< OE *stocc*, tree trunk.]

stock·ade (stŏ-kād') n. A barrier or enclosure made of strong posts or timbers driven upright in the ground, used for protection or imprisonment. [< Sp. *estaca*, stake, of Gmc. orig.]

stock·bro·ker (stŏk'brō'kər) n. One who acts as an agent in buying and selling securities. **—stock'bro'ker·age** n.

stock car n. An automobile of a standard make modified for racing.

stock exchange n. **1.** A place where stocks, bonds, or other securities are bought and sold. **2.** An association of stockbrokers.

stock·hold·er (stŏk'hōl'dər) n. One who owns stock in a company.

stock·i·net (stŏk'ə-nĕt') n. Also **stock·i·nette.** An elastic knitted fabric used esp. in making undergarments and bandages. [< *stocking net.*]

stock·ing (stŏk'ĭng) n. A close-fitting, usu. knitted covering for the foot and leg. [< obs. *stock.*]

stock market n. **1.** A stock exchange. **2.** The business transacted at a stock exchange.

stock·pile (stŏk'pīl') n. A supply of material stored for future use. **—stock'pile'** v.

stock·y (stŏk'ē) adj. **-i·er, -i·est.** Compact and solidly built; thickset. **—stock'i·ness** n.

stock·yard (stŏk'yärd') n. A large yard in which livestock are kept until being shipped or slaughtered.

stodg·y (stŏj'ē) adj. **-i·er, -i·est. 1.** Lacking excitement or interest; dull. **2.** Prim or pompous; stuffy. **3.** Heavy; indigestible. [< *stodge*, to cram.] **—stodg'i·ly** adv. **—stodg'i·ness** n.

sto·ic (stō'ĭk) n. A person seemingly indifferent to or unaffected by pleasure or pain. **—adj.** Also **sto·i·cal** (-ĭ-kəl). Indifferent to or unaffected by pleasure or pain. [< Gk. *stōikos*, a person whose philosophy held that all occurrences were the unavoidable result of divine will.] **—sto'i·cal·ly** adv. **—sto'i·cism** n.

stoke (stōk) v. **stoked, stok·ing. 1.** To stir up and feed (a fire, furnace, etc.). **2.** To tend a fire, furnace, etc. [< Du. *stoken*, to poke.] **—stok'er** n.

stole¹ (stōl) n. **1.** A long scarf worn by some clergymen while officiating. **2.** A long scarf of cloth or fur worn about the shoulders by women. [< Gk. *stolē*, garment.]

stole² (stōl) v. p.t. of **steal.**

sto·len (stō'lən) v. p.p. of **steal.**

stol·id (stŏl'ĭd) adj. Having or showing little emotion; impassive. [Lat. *stolidus*, stupid.] **—sto·lid'i·ty** (stə-lĭd'ĭ-tē) n. **—stol'id·ly** adv.

stom·ach (stŭm'ək) n. **1.** A large saclike digestive organ of the alimentary canal, located in vertebrates between the esophagus and the small intestine. **2.** *Informal.* The abdomen or belly. **3.** An appetite for food. **4.** A desire or inclination. **—v.** To bear; tolerate. [< Gk. *stomakhos.*]

stom·ach·ache (stŭm'ə-kāk') n. Pain in the abdomen.

stom·ach·er (stŭm'ə-kər) n. A decorative garment formerly worn over the chest and stomach, esp. by women.

sto·mach·ic (stə-māk'ĭk) adj. Beneficial to or stimulating digestion in the stomach. **—sto·mach'ic** n.

stomp (stŏmp, stômp) v. To tread heavily (on). [< STAMP.]

stone (stōn) n. **1.** A naturally hardened mass

of earthy or mineral matter; rock. **2.** A small piece of rock. **3.** A precious stone; gem. **4.** The hard covering enclosing the kernel in certain fruits, such as the cherry. **5.** A mineral concretion in a hollow organ, as in the kidney. **6.** *pl.* **stone.** A British unit of weight equivalent to 14 pounds avoirdupois. —*v.* **stoned, ston·ing. 1.** To pelt or kill with stones. **2.** To remove the stones or pits from. [< OE *stān.*] —**ston'i·ly** *adv.* —**ston'i·ness** *n.* —**ston'y** *adj.*

Stone Age *n.* The earliest known period of human culture, characterized by the use of stone tools.

stoned (stōnd) *adj. Slang.* **1.** Intoxicated; drunk. **2.** Under the influence of a mind-altering drug.

stone·wall (stōn'wôl') *v. Informal.* To refuse to answer or cooperate (with); resist.

stone·ware (stōn'wâr') *n.* A heavy, nonporous pottery.

stood (stŏŏd) *v. p.t. & p.p.* of **stand.**

stooge (stōōj) *n.* **1.** The straight man to a comedian. **2.** One who allows himself to be used by another. **3.** A stool pigeon. [Orig. unknown.]

stool (stōōl) *n.* **1.** A usu. backless and armless seat. **2.** A low bench or support for the feet. **3.** Waste matter expelled in a bowel movement. [< OE *stōl.*]

stool pigeon *n.* **1.** A pigeon used as a decoy. **2.** *Slang.* An informer or decoy, esp. a spy for the police.

stoop¹ (stōōp) *v.* **1.** To bend forward and down. **2.** To lower or debase oneself; condescend. —*n.* The act or habit of stooping. [< OE *stūpian.*]

stoop² (stōōp) *n.* A small porch, platform, or staircase at the entrance of a house. [Du. *stoep,* front verandah.]

stop (stŏp) *v.* **stopped, stop·ping. 1.** To close (an opening) by covering, filling in, or plugging. **2.** To bring or come to an end or a halt. **3.** To obstruct or prevent the flow or passage of. **4.** To restrain; prevent. **5.** To desist from; cease. **6.** To adjust a vibrating medium to produce a desired pitch. **7.** To remain temporarily in a place; stay. —*n.* **1.** The act of stopping or the condition of being stopped. **2.** A finish; end. **3.** A stay or visit. **4.** A place stopped at. **5.** Something that obstructs, blocks, or plugs up. **6.** A mark of punctuation, esp. a period. **7.** A tuned set of pipes, as in an organ. [< LLat. *stuppare,* to stop with a tow, ult. < Gk. *stuppē,* tow.] —**stop'·page** *n.*

Syns: *stop, arrest, cease, check, discontinue, halt, stay* v.

stop·gap (stŏp'găp') *n.* A temporary expedient.

stop·light (stŏp'līt') *n.* A traffic signal.

stop·o·ver (stŏp'ō'vər) *n.* A stop or stopping place in the course of a journey.

stop·per (stŏp'ər) *n.* A device, as a plug, inserted to close an opening.

stop·watch (stŏp'wŏch') *n.* A timepiece with a hand that can be started and stopped by pushing a button to measure duration of time.

stor·age (stôr'ĭj, stōr'-) *n.* **1.** The act of storing or the condition of being stored. **2.** A space for storing. **3.** The price charged for keeping goods stored.

storage battery *n.* A group of reversible or rechargeable electric cells acting as a unit.

store (stôr, stōr) *n.* **1.** A place where merchandise is offered for sale; shop. **2.** A stock or supply reserved for future use. **3.** A warehouse or storehouse. —*v.* **stored, stor·ing. 1.** To reserve or put away for future use. **2.** To fill, supply, or stock. **3.** To deposit or receive in a storehouse or warehouse for safekeeping. [< Lat. *instaurare,* to restore.]

store·front (stôr'frŭnt', stōr'-) *n.* **1.** The side of a store facing a street. **2.** A street-level front room in a store building.

store·house (stôr'hous', stōr'-) *n.* **1.** A building in which goods are stored; warehouse. **2.** An abundant supply.

store·keep·er (stôr'kē'pər, stōr'-) *n.* One who keeps a retail store or shop; shopkeeper.

store·room (stôr'rōōm', -rŏŏm', stōr'-) *n.* A room in which things are stored.

sto·rey (stôr'ē, stōr'ē) *n. Chiefly Brit.* Var. of **story².**

sto·ried (stôr'ēd, stōr'-) *adj.* Celebrated or famous in history or story.

stork (stôrk) *n.* A large wading bird with long legs and a long straight bill. [< OE *storc.*]

storm (stôrm) *n.* **1.** An atmospheric disturbance with strong winds and heavy rain, snow, or hail. **2.** A strong or violent outburst or disturbance. **3.** A violent, sudden attack on a fortified place. —*v.* **1. a.** To blow with great force. **b.** To rain, snow, or hail violently. **2.** To be extremely angry. **3.** To rush or move violently or angrily. **4.** To try to capture by a violent, sudden attack. [< OE.] —**storm'y** *adj.*

sto·ry¹ (stôr'ē, stōr'ē) *n., pl.* **-ries. 1.** An account of an event or series of events; narrative. **2.** A tale. **3.** A short fictional literary composition. **4.** A statement of facts; report. **5.** An anecdote. **6.** A lie. [< Gk. *historia.*]

sto·ry² (stôr'ē, stōr'ē) *n., pl.* **-ries.** Also *chiefly Brit.* **sto·rey** *pl.* **-reys. 1.** A horizontal division of a building. **2.** The set of rooms on the same level of a building. [< Med. Lat. *historia,* a row of windows with pictures on them < STORY¹.]

sto·ry·tell·er (stôr'ē-těl'ər, stōr'-) *n.* A person who tells stories. —**sto'ry·tell'ing** *n.*

sto·tin·ki (stō-tĭng'kē) *n., pl.* **-ki.** See table at currency. [Bulgarian.]

stoup (stōōp) *n.* A basin for holy water in a church. [< ON *staup,* bucket.]

stout (stout) *adj.* **-er, -est. 1.** Resolute or bold in character; valiant. **2.** Physically strong and vigorous; robust. **3.** Substantial; solid. **4.** Thickset; fat. —*n.* A strong, very dark beer or ale. [< OFr. *estout,* of Gmc. orig.] —**stout'ly** *adv.* —**stout'ness** *n.*

stout·heart·ed (stout'här'tĭd) *adj.* Bold and courageous; dauntless. —**stout'heart'ed·ly** *adv.* —**stout'heart'ed·ness** *n.*

stove¹ (stōv) *n.* An apparatus that uses electricity or burns fuel to furnish heat, as for cooking. [< MLG, heated room.]

stove² (stōv) *v.* A *p.t. & p.p.* of **stave.**

stove·pipe (stōv'pīp') *n.* **1.** A pipe used to conduct smoke from a stove into a chimney flue. **2.** A tall silk hat.

stow (stō) *v.* **1.** To put or store away compactly. **2.** To fill by packing tightly. —*phrasal verb.* **stow away.** To be a stowaway. [< OE *stōw,* place.]

stow·a·way (stō'ə-wā') *n.* One who hides on a vehicle to obtain free passage.

stra·bis·mus (strə-bĭz'məs) *n.* A visual defect in which both eyes cannot be simultaneously focused on an objective because of imbalance of the eye muscles. [< Gk. *strabizein*, to squint.] —**stra·bis'mal** or **stra·bis'mic** *adj.*

strad·dle (străd'l) *v.* **-dled, -dling.** 1. To sit, stand, or move astride (of). 2. To appear to favor both sides of (an issue). [< STRIDE.] —**strad'dle** *n.* —**strad'dler** *n.*

strafe (străf, străf) *v.* **strafed, straf·ing.** To attack with machine-gun fire from low-flying aircraft. [G. *strafen*, to punish.]

strag·gle (străg'əl) *v.* **-gled, -gling.** 1. To stray or fall behind. 2. To spread out in a scattered group. [ME *straglen*.] —**strag'gler** *n.* —**strag'gly** *adj.*

straight (străt) *adj.* **-er, -est.** 1. Extending continuously in the same direction without curving. 2. Having no waves or bends. 3. Erect; upright. 4. Direct and candid. 5. Uninterrupted. 6. Correct or accurate. 7. Honest; fair. 8. Neatly arranged; orderly. 9. Undiluted or unmixed: *straight whiskey.* 10. *Slang.* a. Conventional or conservative. b. Heterosexual. —*adv.* In a straight course or manner. —*n.* 1. Something that is straight. 2. A straightaway. 3. A numerical sequence of five cards in a poker hand. 4. *Slang.* a. A heterosexual person. b. A conventional person. —*Idioms.* **go straight.** To reform after having been a criminal. **straight away** (or **off**). Immediately. [ME < *streechen*, to stretch.] —**straight'ly** *adv.* —**straight'ness** *n.*

straight angle *n.* An angle of 180°.

straight-a·way (străt'ə-wā') *n.* A straight course or stretch of road or track, esp. the stretch of a race course between the last turn and the finish. —*adv.* At once; immediately.

straight·edge (străt'ěj') *n.* A rigid object with a straight edge for testing or drawing straight lines.

straight·en (străt'n) *v.* To make or become straight. —*phrasal verb.* **straighten out.** To reform or correct. —**straight'en·er** *n.*

straight·for·ward (străt-fôr'wərd) *adj.* 1. Direct. 2. Honest; frank. —*adv.* Also **straightforwards** (-wərdz). In a straightforward course or manner. —**straight'for'ward·ness** *n.*

straight jacket *n.* Var. of **straitjacket.**

straight man *n.* An actor who serves as a foil for a comedian.

straight·way (străt'wā', -wā') *adv.* At once.

strain¹ (strān) *v.* 1. To pull, draw, or stretch tight. 2. To exert, tax, or be taxed to the utmost. 3. To injure or become injured by overexertion. 4. To stretch or force beyond the proper or legitimate limit. 5. To strive hard. 6. To pass through a strainer or other filtering agent. —*n.* 1. The act of straining or the condition of being strained. 2. A great effort, force, or tension. 3. A deformation produced by stress. [< Lat. *stringere*, to bind tightly.]

strain² (strān) *n.* 1. The collective descendants of a common ancestor. 2. Ancestry; lineage. 3. *Biol.* A group of organisms of the same species, having distinctive characteristics but not usu. considered a separate variety. 4. A characteristic tendency. 5. Often **strains.** A musical passage or tune. 6. A trace; suggestion. [< OE *stréon.*]

strain·er (strā'nər) *n.* 1. A filter, sieve, or

similar device used to separate liquids from solids. 2. One that strains.

strait (strāt) *n.* 1. A narrow passage of water joining two larger bodies of water. 2. Often **straits.** A difficult or perplexing position. —*adj.* **-er, -est.** *Archaic.* 1. Narrow. 2. Strict, rigid, or righteous. [< Lat. *strictus*, p.p. of *stringere*, to bind tightly.]

strait·en (strāt'n) *v.* 1. To make narrow or restricted. 2. To put into difficulties or distress.

strait·jack·et (strāt'jăk'ĭt) *n.* Also **straight jacket.** A jacketlike garment used to bind the arms tightly as a means of restraining a violent patient or prisoner.

strait-laced (strāt-lāst') *adj.* Excessively strict in behavior or morality; prudish.

stra·mo·ni·um (strə-mō'nē-əm) *n.* The dried leaves of the jimsonweed, used in treating asthma. [NLat.]

strand¹ (strănd) *n.* A shore, esp. on an ocean. —*v.* 1. To drive or be driven aground. 2. To bring into or be left in a difficult or helpless position. [< OE.]

strand² (strănd) *n.* 1. Each of the fibers or filaments that are twisted together to form a rope, cable, etc. 2. A ropelike string, as of beads or pearls. [ME *strond.*]

strange (strānj) *adj.* **strang·er, strang·est.** 1. Not previously known; unfamiliar. 2. Differing from the usual; striking or odd. 3. Uncomfortable or peculiar. 4. Not of one's own or a particular locality or kind; alien. 5. Lacking experience. [< Lat. *extraneus.*] —**strange'ly** *adv.* —**strange'ness** *n.*

Syns: strange, different, new, unaccustomed, unfamiliar *adj.*

strang·er (strān'jər) *n.* 1. One with whom one is not acquainted. 2. A foreigner, newcomer, or outsider.

stran·gle (străng'gəl) *v.* **-gled, -gling.** 1. a. To kill by choking or suffocating. b. To smother. 2. To suppress; stifle. [< Lat. *strangulare.*] —**stran'gler** *n.*

stran·gu·late (străng'gyə-lāt') *v.* **-lat·ed, -lat·ing.** 1. To strangle. 2. *Pathol.* To constrict so as to cut off the flow of blood or other fluid. [Lat. *strangulare* < Gk. *strangalan.*] —**stran'gu·la'tion** *n.*

strap (străp) *n.* A long, narrow strip of leather or other material, often with a fastener for binding, fastening, or clamping. —*v.* **strapped, strap·ping.** 1. To fasten or secure with a strap. 2. To beat with a strap. 3. To strop. [< STROP.]

strap·less (străp'lĭs) *adj.* Without a strap or straps. —*n.* A strapless garment.

strapped (străpt) *adj.* *Informal.* Lacking money.

strap·ping (străp'ĭng) *adj.* Tall and sturdy.

stra·ta (strā'tə, străt'ə) *n.* A pl. of **stratum.**

strat·a·gem (străt'ə-jəm) *n.* 1. A maneuver designed to deceive or surprise an enemy. 2. A scheme designed to obtain a goal. [< Gk. *stratēgēma.*]

strat·e·gy (străt'ə-jē) *n., pl.* **-gies.** 1. The overall planning and conduct of large-scale military operations. 2. The art or skill of using stratagems as in politics or business. 3. A plan of action. —**stra·te'gic** (strə-tē'jĭk) *adj.* —**stra·te'gi·cal·ly** *adv.* —**strat'e·gist** *n.*

ă pat ā pay â care ä father ĕ pet ē be ĭ pit ī tie î pier ŏ pot ō toe ô paw, for oi noise ŏŏ took
ōō boot ou out th thin th this ŭ cut û urge yŏŏ abuse zh vision ə about, item, edible, gallop, circus

stra·ti (strā'tī, străt'ī) *n.* Pl. of **stratus.**

strat·i·fy (străt'ə-fī') *v.* -**fied,** -**fy·ing.** To form, arrange, or deposit in layers or strata. —**strat'i·fi·ca'tion** *n.*

strat·o·sphere (străt'ə-sfîr') *n.* The part of the atmosphere above the troposphere. [STRA-T(UM) + SPHERE.] —**strat·o·spher'ic** (-sfîr'ĭk, -sfĕr'-) *adj.*

stra·tum (strā'təm, străt'əm) *n., pl.* -**ta** (-tə) or -**tums.** **1.** A horizontal layer of any material, esp. a formation containing a number of layers of rock of the same kind of material. **2.** A level of society composed of people with similar social, cultural, or economic status. [Lat. *stratum,* a covering.]

stra·tus (strā'təs, străt'əs) *n., pl.* -**ti** (strā'tī, străt'ī). A low-altitude cloud resembling a horizontal layer of fog. [< Lat., p.part. of *sternere,* to spread.]

straw (strô) *n.* **1. a.** Stalks of grain after threshing. **b.** A single stalk of such grain. **2.** A narrow paper or plastic tube used to drink or suck up liquids. **3.** Something of little value or substance. —*adj.* Yellowish in color. [< OE *strēaw.*]

straw·ber·ry (strô'bĕr'ē) *n.* **1.** A low-growing plant with white flowers and red, fleshy, edible fruit. **2.** The fruit of the strawberry.

straw boss *n.* A temporary boss or foreman.

straw vote *n.* An unofficial vote or poll.

stray (strā) *v.* **1. a.** To wander beyond established limits; roam. **b.** To become lost. **2.** To wander about or meander. **3.** To go astray; err. **4.** To digress. —*n.* One that has strayed, esp. a lost domestic animal. —*adj.* **1. a.** Straying or having strayed; out of place. **b.** Lost. **2.** Scattered or separate. [< OFr. *es-traier.*] —**stray'er** *n.*

streak (strēk) *n.* **1.** A line, mark, or band differentiated by color or texture from its surroundings. **2.** A trace or tendency. **3.** An unbroken stretch; run. —*v.* **1.** To mark with or form a streak. **2.** To move at high speed; rush. [< OE *strica.*] —**streak'i·ly** *adv.* —**streak'i·ness** *n.* —**streak'y** *adj.*

stream (strēm) *n.* **1.** A small body of running water flowing over the earth's surface. **2.** A steady current of a fluid. **3.** A steady flow or succession. —*v.* **1.** To flow in or as if in a stream. **2.** To pour forth or give off a stream. **3.** To move in large numbers. **4.** To extend, wave, or float outward. **5.** To leave a continuous trail of light. [< OE *strēam.*]

stream·er (strē'mər) *n.* **1.** A long, narrow flag or banner. **2.** A long, narrow strip of material. **3.** A newspaper headline that runs across a full page.

stream·line (strēm'līn') *v.* -**lined,** -**lin·ing.** **1.** To construct so as to offer the least resistance to the flow of a fluid. **2.** To improve the efficiency of. —**stream'lined'** *adj.*

street (strēt) *n.* **1.** A public thoroughfare in a city or town. **2.** The people who live or work along a street. [LLat. *strata* < Lat. *sternere,* to extend.]

street·car (strēt'kär') *n.* A public passenger car operated on rails along the streets of a city.

street·walk·er (strēt'wô'kər) *n.* A prostitute.

strength (strĕngkth, strĕngth) *n.* **1.** The quality of being strong. **2.** The power to resist force, strain, or stress; toughness; solidity. **3.** The power to sustain or resist an attack. **4.** Power or capability. **5.** Moral courage or power. **6.** Effective or binding force: the *strength of an argument.* **7.** Degree of concentration, distillation, or saturation; potency. **8.** Intensity. **9.** Military or organizational force in terms of numbers: *at half strength.* [< OE *strengthu.*]

strength·en (strĕngk'thən, strĕng'-) *v.* To make or become strong or stronger. —**strength'en·er** *n.*

stren·u·ous (strĕn'yōō-əs) *adj.* **1.** Requiring great effort, energy, or exertion. **2.** Vigorously active. [Lat. *strenuus.*] —**stren'u·ous·ly** *adv.* —**stren'u·ous·ness** *n.*

strep throat (strĕp) *n.* A throat infection caused by streptococci, characterized by fever and inflamed tonsils. [*Strep* < STREPTOCOC-CAL.]

strep·to·coc·cus (strĕp'tə-kŏk'əs) *n., pl.* -**coc·ci** (-kŏk'sī', -kŏk'ī'). Any of various rounded bacteria that occur in pairs or chains and are often a cause of disease. [Gk. *streptos,* twisted + -COCCUS.] —**strep'to·coc'cal** or **strep'to·coc'cic** *adj.*

strep·to·my·cin (strĕp'tə-mī'sĭn) *n.* An antibiotic, $C_{21}H_{39}N_7O_{12}$, produced from mold cultures and used esp. to combat tuberculosis. [Gk. *streptos,* twisted + Gk. *mukes,* fungus + -IN.]

stress (strĕs) *n.* **1.** Importance, significance, or emphasis placed upon something. **2.** *Physics.* An applied force or system of forces that tends to strain or deform a body. **3.** Mental or emotional pressure. **4.** The relative force with which a sound is spoken. **5.** The relative emphasis given a syllable or word in a metrical pattern. **6.** *Mus.* An accent. —*v.* **1.** To place emphasis on. **2.** To subject to mechanical stress. **3.** To subject to pressure or strain. **4.** To pronounce with a stress. [< Lat. *strictus,* p.p. of *stringere,* to bind tightly.]

stretch (strĕch) *v.* **1. a.** To lengthen, widen, or distend by pulling. **b.** To become lengthened, widened, or distended. **2.** To cause to extend across a given space. **3.** To make taut; tighten. **4.** To reach or put forth; extend: *He stretched out his hand.* **5.** To extend (oneself) at full length in a prone position. **6.** To flex one's muscles. **7.** To strain. **8.** To cause to suffice; make do with. **9.** To extend the limits of credulity, conscience, etc. **10.** To prolong. —*n.* **1.** The act of stretching or the condition of being stretched. **2.** The extent to which something can be stretched. **3.** A continuous length, area, or expanse. **4.** A straight section of a racecourse or track, esp. that leading to the finish line. **5. a.** A continuous period of time. **b.** *Informal.* A final stage. **6.** *Slang.* A term of imprisonment. —*adj.* Elastic: *a stretch sock.* [< OE *streccan.*] —**stretch'a·ble** *adj.* —**stretch'y** *adj.*

stretch·er (strĕch'ər) *n.* **1.** One that stretches. **2.** A litter, usu. of canvas, used to transport the disabled.

strew (strōō) *v.* **strewed, strewed** or **strewn** (strōōn), **strew·ing. 1.** To spread here and there; scatter. **2.** To cover (a surface) with things scattered or sprinkled. **3.** To be dispersed over. [< OE *strewian.*]

stri·a (strī'ə) *n., pl.* **stri·ae** (strī'ē). **1.** A thin, narrow groove or channel. **2.** A thin line or band. [Lat.] —**stri'at·ed** (-ā'tĭd) *adj.* —**stri·a'tion** *n.*

strick·en (strĭk'ən) *v.* A p.p. of **strike.** —*adj.* **1.** Struck or wounded, as by a projectile. **2.** Afflicted, as with emotion or disease.

strict (strĭkt) *adj.* -**er,** -**est. 1.** Precise; exact.

2. Complete; absolute: *strict loyalty.* **3.** Kept within narrow limits: *a strict application of a law.* **4.** Imposing an exacting discipline. **5.** Rigorous; stringent. [Lat. *strictus,* p.p. of *stringere,* to bind tightly.] —**strict′ly** *adv.* —**strict′ness** *n.*

stric·ture (strĭk′chər) *n.* **1.** Something that restrains or restricts. **2.** An adverse criticism. **3.** *Pathol.* An abnormal narrowing of a duct or passage.

stride (strīd) *v.* **strode** (strōd), **strid·den** (strĭd′n), **strid·ing.** To walk with long steps. —*n.* **1.** The act or manner of striding. **2.** A single long step. **3.** Often **strides.** An advance. [< OE *strīdan.*] —**strid′er** *n.*

stri·dent (strīd′nt) *adj.* Having a shrill, harsh, and grating sound or effect. [< Lat. *strīdēre,* to make a harsh sound.] —**stri′dence** or **stri′den·cy** *n.* —**strid′ent·ly** *adv.*

strife (strīf) *n.* **1.** Bitter, often violent dissension or conflict. **2.** A contention or struggle between rivals. [< OFr. *estriver,* to fight, of Gmc. orig.]

strike (strīk) *v.* **struck** (strŭk), **struck** or **strick·en** (strĭk′ən), **strik·ing. 1. a.** To hit sharply, as with the hand, fist, or a weapon. **b.** To inflict (a blow). **2.** To collide (with) or crash into. **3.** To attack or begin an attack. **4.** To afflict suddenly with a disease. **5.** To impress by stamping or printing. **6.** To produce by hitting some agent, as a key on a musical instrument. **7.** To indicate by a percussive sound: *The clock struck nine.* **8.** To produce (a flame or spark) by friction. **9.** To eliminate: *struck out the error.* **10.** To come upon; discover. **11.** To reach; fall upon. **12.** To impress abruptly or freshly: *strikes me as a good idea.* **13.** To cause (an emotion) to penetrate deeply. **14. a.** To make or conclude (a bargain). **b.** To achieve (a balance). **15.** To fall into or assume (a pose). **16.** To proceed, esp. in a new direction; set out; head. **17.** To engage in a strike against an employer. —*phrasal verbs.* **strike out.** *Baseball.* **1.** To pitch three strikes to (a batter), putting him out. **2.** To be put out in such a way. **strike up. 1.** To start to play vigorously. **2.** To initiate or begin. —*n.* **1.** An act of striking. **2.** An attack. **3.** A work stoppage by employees in support of demands upon their employer. **4.** A sudden achievement or discovery. **5.** *Baseball.* A pitched ball counted against the batter, typically one swung at and missed or one judged to have passed through the strike zone. **6.** *Bowling.* The knocking down of all the pins with the first ball in a frame. [< OE *strīcan,* to stroke.] —**strik′er** *n.*

strike-break·er (strīk′brā′kər) *n.* One hired to help break a strike.

strike·out (strīk′out′) *n. Baseball.* An act of striking out.

strike zone *n. Baseball.* The area over home plate through which a pitch must pass to be called a strike.

strik·ing (strī′kĭng) *adj.* Immediately or vividly impressive. —**strik′ing·ly** *adv.*

string (strĭng) *n.* **1.** A cord usu. made of fiber, thicker than thread. **2.** Something shaped into a long, thin line. **3.** A set of objects threaded together: *a string of beads.* **4.** A series; sequence. **5.** *Mus.* **a.** A stretched cord that is struck, plucked, or bowed to produce tones. **b. strings.** Instruments having such strings. **6.** Often **strings.** A limiting or hidden condition. —*v.* **strung** (strŭng), **string·ing. 1.** To fit or furnish with a string or strings: *string a guitar.* **2.** To thread on a string. **3.** To arrange in a series. **4.** To fasten, tie, or hang with a string or strings. **5.** To extend; stretch out. [< OE *streng.*] —**string′i·ness** *n.* —**string′y** *adj.*

string bean *n.* **1.** A narrow, green, edible bean pod. **2.** A plant bearing such pods.

strin·gent (strĭn′jənt) *adj.* **1.** Imposing rigorous standards; severe. **2.** Constricted; tight. **3.** Characterized by scarcity of money or credit. [< Lat. *stringere,* to bind tightly.] —**strin′gen·cy** *n.* —**strin′gent·ly** *adv.*

string·er (strĭng′ər) *n.* **1.** One that strings. **2.** A heavy horizontal timber used for any of several connective or supportive purposes. **3.** A part-time correspondent for a news publication.

strip¹ (strĭp) *v.* **stripped, strip·ping. 1. a.** To remove the covering from. **b.** To undress. **2.** To deprive, as of honors or rank; divest. **3.** To remove all excess details from. **4.** To dismantle piece by piece. **5.** To damage or break the threads or teeth of (a nut, gear, etc.). **6.** To rob or plunder. [< OE *strīpan.*]

strip² (strĭp) *n.* **1.** A long, narrow piece. **2.** A comic strip. **3.** An airstrip. [Perh. < STRIPE.]

stripe (strīp) *n.* **1.** A long, narrow band that is different, as in color or texture, from the surrounding material or surface. **2.** A strip of cloth or braid worn on a uniform to indicate rank, awards, etc. **3.** Sort; kind. —*v.* **striped, strip·ing.** To mark with a stripe. [Poss. < MDu. *stripe.*]

strip·ling (strĭp′lĭng) *n.* An adolescent youth. [ME.]

strive (strīv) *v.* **strove** (strōv) or **strived, striv·en** (strĭv′ən) or **strived, striv·ing. 1.** To exert much effort or energy. **2.** To struggle; contend. [< OFr. *estriver,* of Gmc. orig.]

strobe light (strōb) *n.* A flash lamp that produces very short, intense flashes of light. [< STROBOSCOPE.]

stro·bo·scope (strō′bə-skōp′) *n.* Any of various instruments used to make moving objects appear stationary by intermittent illumination or observation. [Gk. *strobos,* a whirling round + -SCOPE.] —**stro′bo·scop′ic** (-skŏp′ĭk) *adj.*

strode (strōd) *v. p.t.* of **stride.**

stroke (strōk) *n.* **1.** An impact; blow. **2.** A single complete movement, as in swimming. **3.** A single movement or mark made by a pen, brush, etc. **4.** A movement of a piston or similar machine part from one end of its travel to the other. **5.** An effective or inspired idea or act. **6. a.** A sudden, severe onset of a disease or disorder. **b.** Apoplexy. —*v.* **stroked, strok·ing.** To rub lightly. [ME.]

stroll (strōl) *v.* To walk at a leisurely pace: *strolling in the park.* [Prob. dial. G. *strollen.*] —**stroll** *n.* —**stroll′er** *n.*

strong (strông) *adj.* **-er, -est. 1.** Physically powerful; muscular. **2.** In good or sound health; robust. **3.** Capable of enduring stress or strain. **4.** Intense in degree or quality. **5.** Forceful or persuasive. **6.** Extreme; drastic.

7. Having a specified number of units or members. [< OE *strang*.] —**strong'ly** *adv.*

strong-arm (strŏng'ärm') *adj. Informal.* Coercive: *strong-arm tactics.*

strong-box (strŏng'bŏks') *n.* A stoutly made safe.

strong-hold (strŏng'hōld') *n.* A fortress.

stron·ti·um (strŏn'chē-əm, -tē-əm) *n. Symbol* **Sr** A soft, silvery, easily oxidized metallic element used in fireworks and various alloys. Atomic number 38; atomic weight 87.62. [< *Strontian*, Scotland.]

strontium 90 *n.* A radioactive isotope of strontium with a half-life of 28 years, found in nuclear fallout.

strop (strŏp) *n.* A flexible strip of leather or canvas used to sharpen a razor. —*v.* **stropped, strop·ping.** To sharpen (a razor) on a strop. [< Gk. *strophion*, band of leather.]

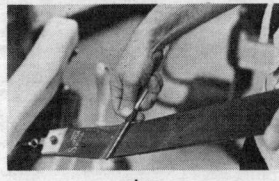

strop

stro·phe (strō'fē) *n.* A stanza of a poem. [Gk. *strophē*, movement of the chorus.] —**stro'phic** (strō'fĭk, strŏf'ĭk) *adj.*

strove (strōv) *v.* A *p.t.* of **strive.**

struck (strŭk) *v. p.t. & p.p.* of **strike.** —*adj.* Shut down by a labor strike.

struc·ture (strŭk'chər) *n.* **1.** Something made up of parts that are put together in a particular way. **2.** The way in which parts are arranged or put together to form a whole. **3.** Something constructed, as a building or bridge. —*v.* **-tured, -tur·ing.** To give form or arrangement to. [< Lat. *structus*, p.p. of *struere*, to construct.] —**struc'tur·al** *adj.* —**struc'tur·al·ly** *adv.*

stru·del (strōōd'l) *n.* A pastry made with a filling rolled up in a thin sheet of dough and baked. [G.]

strug·gle (strŭg'əl) *v.* **-gled, -gling. 1.** To make a strenuous effort; strive. **2.** To compete or contend against. **3.** To progress with great difficulty. —*n.* **1.** Strenuous effort or striving. **2.** A contest; battle. [ME *struglen*.] —**strug'gler** *n.*

strum (strŭm) *v.* **strummed, strum·ming.** To play idly on (a stringed musical instrument) by plucking the strings with the fingers. [Perh. blend of STRING and THRUM.]

strum·pet (strŭm'pĭt) *n.* A whore. [ME.]

strung (strŭng) *v. p.t. & p.p.* of **string.**

strut (strŭt) *v.* **strut·ted, strut·ting.** To walk in a stiff, pompous manner. —*n.* **1.** A stiff, self-important gait. **2.** A bar or rod used to brace a structure against forces applied from the side. [< OE *strūtian*, to stand out stiffly.] —**strut'ter** *n.* —**strut'ting·ly** *adv.*

strych·nine (strĭk'nĭn', -nĭn, -nēn') *n.* A poisonous white crystalline substance, $C_{21}H_{22}N_2O_2$, derived from some plants and used as a poison and medicinally as a stimulant. [< Gk. *strukhnos*, a kind of nightshade.]

stub (stŭb) *n.* **1.** A short blunt remaining end.

2. a. The part of a check or receipt retained as a record. **b.** The part of a ticket returned as a voucher of payment. —*v.* **stubbed, stub·bing.** To strike (one's toe or foot) against something. [< OE *stybb*.]

stub·ble (stŭb'əl) *n.* **1.** The short, stiff stalks, as of grain, that remain on a field after harvesting. **2.** Something resembling stubble. [< Lat. *stipula*, straw.] —**stub'bly** *adj.*

stub·born (stŭb'ərn) *adj.* **1.** Unreasonably determined to exert one's will; obstinate. **2.** Persistent. **3.** Difficult to handle or work with. [ME *stuborn*.] —**stub'born·ly** *adv.* —**stub'born·ness** *n.*

stub·by (stŭb'ē) *adj.* **-bi·er, -bi·est.** Short and stocky.

stuc·co (stŭk'ō) *n., pl.* **-coes** or **-cos.** A durable plaster or cement finish for exterior walls. —*v.* To finish or decorate with stucco. [Ital., of Gmc. orig.]

stuck (stŭk) *v. p.t. & p.p.* of **stick.**

stuck-up (stŭk'ŭp') *adj. Informal.* Snobbish; conceited.

stud¹ (stŭd) *n.* **1.** An upright post in the framework of a wall for supporting sheets of lath, wallboard, etc. **2.** A small knob, nail head, etc. fixed in and slightly projecting from a surface. **3.** A small ornamental button, as on a dress shirt. —*v.* **stud·ded, stud·ding. 1.** To construct or set with a stud or studs. **2.** To strew. [< OE *studu*.]

stud² (stŭd) *n.* **1.** A male animal, esp. a stallion, kept for breeding. **2.** *Slang.* A virile man. [< OE *stōd*, stable for breeding.]

stud·book (stŭd'bŏŏk') *n.* A book registering the pedigrees of thoroughbred animals.

stud·ding (stŭd'ĭng) *n.* **1.** Studs, esp. for walls. **2.** Lumber cut for studs.

stu·dent (stōōd'nt, styōōd'-) *n.* **1.** One who attends a school, college, or university. **2.** One who makes a study of something. [< Lat. *studēre*, to study.]

stud·ied (stŭd'ēd) *adj.* Carefully contrived; calculated.

stu·di·o (stōō'dē-ō', styōō'-) *n., pl.* **-os. 1.** An artist's workroom. **2.** A place where an art is taught or studied: *a dance studio.* **3.** A room or building for motion-picture, television, or radio productions. [< Lat. *studium*, study.]

studio apartment *n.* A small apartment consisting of one main living space, a kitchen, and a bathroom.

studio couch *n.* A couch that can serve as a bed.

stu·di·ous (stōō'dē-əs, styōō'-) *adj.* **1.** Devoted to study. **2.** Earnest; purposeful. —**stu'di·ous·ly** *adv.* —**stu'di·ous·ness** *n.*

stud·y (stŭd'ē) *n., pl.* **-ies. 1.** The act or process of studying. **2.** A detailed examination. **3.** A branch of knowledge. **4.** A room intended or equipped for studying. —*v.* **-ied, -y·ing. 1.** To apply one's mind purposefully in order to gain knowledge or understanding of (a subject). **2.** To take (a course) at a school. **3.** To inquire into; investigate. **4.** To examine closely; scrutinize. [< Lat. *studium* < *studēre*, to study.] —**stud'i·er** *n.*

stuff (stŭf) *n.* **1.** The material out of which something is made or formed; substance. **2.** Unspecified material: *Put that stuff over there.* **3.** Worthless objects. **4.** Foolish or empty words or ideas. **5.** *Chiefly Brit.* Cloth, esp. woolens, of which clothing may be made. —*v.* **1. a.** To pack tightly. **b.** To block or stop up; plug. **2.** To fill with an appropriate stuffing. **3.** To eat to excess. [< OFr. *estoffer*, to equip.]

stuffed shirt *n. Informal.* A stiff, pompous person.

stuff·ing (stŭf′ĭng) *n.* Something used to stuff or fill, esp. padding put in cushions or food put inside meat or vegetables.

stuff·y (stŭf′ē) *adj.* **-i·er, -i·est. 1.** Lacking sufficient ventilation. **2.** Blocked: *a stuffy nose.* **3.** Strait-laced; stodgy. —**stuff′i·ness** *n.*

stul·ti·fy (stŭl′tə-fī′) *v.* **-fied, -fy·ing. 1.** To stifle: *stultify free thought.* **2.** To cause to appear stupid or inconsistent. [Lat. *stultus*, foolish + -FY.] —**stul′ti·fi·ca′tion** *n.*

stum·ble (stŭm′bəl) *v.* **-bled, -bling. 1. a.** To trip and almost fall. **b.** To move unsteadily. **c.** To act or speak falteringly or clumsily. **2.** To make a mistake; blunder. **3.** To come upon accidentally. [ME *stumblen.*] —**stum′ble** *n.* —**stum′bler** *n.*

stumbling block *n.* An obstacle or impediment.

stump (stŭmp) *n.* **1.** The part of a tree trunk left in the ground after the tree has fallen or been cut down. **2.** A part that remains after the main part has been cut off or worn away. **3.** A platform or other place used for political speeches. —*v.* **1.** To clear stumps from (land). **2.** To travel about (an area) making political speeches. **3.** To walk in a stiff, heavy manner. **4.** To puzzle; baffle. [< MLG.] —**stump′er** *n.* —**stump′y** *adj.*

stun (stŭn) *v.* **stunned, stun·ning. 1.** To daze or render senseless, as by a blow. **2.** To stupefy; shock. [< OFr. *estoner.*]

stung (stŭng) *v. p.t. & p.p.* of **sting.**

stunk (stŭngk) *v.* A *p.t. & p.p.* of **stink.**

stun·ning (stŭn′ĭng) *adj.* **1.** Surprising or astonishing. **2.** Strikingly attractive. —**stun′ning·ly** *adv.*

stunt¹ (stŭnt) *v.* To check the growth or development of. [Perh. of Scand. orig.] —**stunt′ed·ness** *n.*

stunt² (stŭnt) *n.* **1.** A feat displaying unusual skill or daring. **2.** Something unusual done for publicity. [Orig. unknown.]

stu·pe·fy (stōō′pə-fī′, styōō′-) *v.* **-fied, -fy·ing. 1.** To dull the senses of. **2.** To amaze; astonish. [Lat. *stupēre*, to be stunned + -FY.] —**stu′pe·fac′tion** (-făk′shən) *n.*

stu·pen·dous (stōō-pĕn′dəs, styōō-) *adj.* **1.** Of astounding force, volume, degree, etc.: *stupendous risks.* **2.** Of tremendous size. [< Lat. *stupēre*, to be stunned.] —**stu·pen′dous·ly** *adv.*

stu·pid (stōō′pĭd, styōō′-) *adj.* **-er, -est. 1.** Slow to apprehend. **2.** Showing a lack of intelligence. **3.** Uninteresting; dull. [< Lat. *stupēre*, to be stunned.] —**stu·pid′i·ty** *n.* —**stu′pid·ly** *adv.*

Syns: **stupid**, *dense, dumb, obtuse, thick adj.*

stu·por (stōō′pər, styōō′-) *n.* **1.** A condition of reduced sensibility; daze. **2.** A condition of mental or moral apathy. [Lat. < *stupēre*, to be stunned.] —**stu′por·ous** *adj.*

stur·dy (stûr′dē) *adj.* **-di·er, -di·est. 1.** Substantially built; strong. **2.** Healthy and vigorous. [< OFr. *estourir*, to stun.] —**stur′di·ly** *adv.* —**stur′di·ness** *n.*

stur·geon (stûr′jən) *n.* A large food fish with roe that is a source of caviar. [< OFr. *estourgeon*, of Gmc. orig.]

stut·ter (stŭt′ər) *v.* To speak with involuntary hesitations and repetitions of sounds. —*n.* The act or habit of stuttering. [< ME *stutten.*] —**stut′ter·er** *n.* —**stut′ter·ing·ly** *adv.*

sty¹ (stī) *n., pl.* **sties. 1.** An enclosure for pigs. **2.** A very dirty or untidy place. [< OE *stig.*]

sty² (stī) *n., pl.* **sties.** Inflammation of an oil-producing gland of an eyelid. [< OE *stīgan*, to rise.]

style (stīl) *n.* **1.** The way or manner in which something is said or done. **2.** Sort; kind; type. **3.** Individuality expressed in one's actions and tastes. **4.** Elegance. **5. a.** The current fashion. **b.** A particular fashion. **6.** A customary manner of presenting printed material, including usage, punctuation, spelling, typography, and arrangement. **7.** A slender, pointed writing instrument; stylus. —*v.* **styled, styl·ing. 1.** To call or name; designate. **2.** To make consistent with rules of style. **3.** To arrange or design. [< Lat. *stilus.*] —**sty·lis′tic** (stī-lĭs′tĭk) *adj.* —**sty·lis′ti·cal·ly** *adv.*

styl·ish (stī′lĭsh) *adj.* Conforming to the current style; fashionable. —**styl′ish·ly** *adv.* —**styl′ish·ness** *n.*

styl·ist (stī′lĭst) *n.* **1.** A writer or speaker who cultivates an artful literary style. **2.** A designer of or expert on styles.

styl·ize (stī′līz′) *v.* **-ized, -iz·ing.** To conform or restrict to a particular style.

sty·lus (stī′ləs) *n., pl.* **-lus·es** or **-li** (-lī′). **1.** A sharp, pointed instrument used for writing, marking, or engraving. **2.** A phonograph needle. [Lat. *stilus.*]

sty·mie (stī′mē) *v.* **-mied, -mie·ing** or **-my·ing.** To block; thwart. [Orig. unknown.]

styp·tic (stĭp′tĭk) *adj.* Contracting the blood vessels so as to check bleeding; astringent. [< Gk. *stuphein*, to contract.] —**styp′tic** *n.*

Sty·ro·foam (stī′rə-fōm′). A trademark for a light, resilient polystyrene plastic.

suave (swäv) *adj.* **suav·er, suav·est.** Smoothly gracious in social manner. [< Lat. *suavis*, agreeable.] —**suave′ly** *adv.* —**suave′ness** or **suav′i·ty** *n.*

sub¹ (sŭb) *n. Informal.* A submarine.

sub² (sŭb) *Informal.* A substitute. —*v.* **subbed, sub·bing.** To act as a substitute.

sub- *pref.* **1.** Under or beneath: *submarine.* **2.** Subordinate; secondary: *subplot.* **3.** Short of or less than: *subtropical.* **4.** Subordinate part: *subset.* [< Lat. *sub*, under.]

Usage: Many compounds other than those entered here may be formed with *sub-.* In forming compounds, *sub-* is normally joined with the following element without space or hyphen: *subbasement.*

sub·al·tern (sŭb-ôl′tərn) *n.* A subordinate. [LLat. *subalternus.*]

sub·a·tom·ic (sŭb′ə-tŏm′ĭk) *adj.* **1.** Pertaining to the constituents of the atom. **2.** Participating in reactions characteristic of these constituents.

sub·com·mit·tee (sŭb′kə-mĭt′ē) *n.* A subordinate committee made up of members from the main committee.

sub·com·pact (sŭb-kŏm′păkt′) *n.* An automobile smaller than a compact.

sub·con·scious (sŭb-kŏn′shəs) *adj.* Beneath

ā pat   ā pay   â care   ä father   ĕ pet   ē be   ĭ pit   ī tie   î pier   ŏ pot   ō toe   ô paw, for   oi noise   ŏŏ took
ōō boot   ou out   th thin   th this   ŭ cut   û urge   yōō abuse   zh vision   ə about, item, edible, gallop, circus

the threshold of consciousness. —**sub·con'·scious** n. —**sub·con'·scious·ly** adv. —**sub·con'·scious·ness** n.

sub·con·ti·nent (sŭb'kŏn'tə-nənt) n. A large land mass, such as India, that is separate to some degree but is still part of a continent.

sub·con·tract (sŭb'kŏn'trăkt') n. A contract that assigns some of the obligations of an original contract to another party. —**sub'·con'tract'** v.

sub·cul·ture (sŭb'kŭl'chər) n. A cultural subgroup within a larger cultural group.

sub·cu·ta·ne·ous (sŭb'kyōō-tā'nē-əs) adj. Just beneath the skin. —**sub'cu·ta'ne·ous·ly** adv.

sub·dea·con (sŭb'dē'kən) n. A clergyman with rank just below that of deacon.

sub·di·vide (sŭb'dĭ-vīd') v. 1. To divide into smaller parts. 2. To divide into many parts, esp. to divide (land) into lots. —**sub'di·vid'er** n. —**sub'di·vi'sion** (-vĭzh'ən) n.

sub·due (səb-dōō', -dyōō') v. -**dued**, -**du·ing**. 1. To conquer and subjugate; vanquish. 2. To quiet or bring under control. 3. To make less intense. [< Lat. *subducere*, to withdraw.] —**sub·du'er** n.

sub·fam·i·ly (sŭb'făm'ə-lē) n. A subdivision of a family, as in taxonomy.

sub·group (sŭb'grōōp') n. A group within a group.

sub·head (sŭb'hĕd') n. 1. Also **sub·head·ing** (-hĕd'ĭng). The title of a subdivision of a printed work. 2. A subordinate heading or title.

sub·hu·man (sŭb'hyōō'mən) adj. 1. Below the human race in evolutionary development. 2. Not fully human.

sub·ject (sŭb'jĭkt) adj. 1. Under the power or authority of another. 2. Prone; disposed: *subject to colds*. 3. Liable to incur or receive: *subject to misinterpretation*. 4. Contingent or dependent: *subject to approval*. —n. 1. One under the rule of another. 2. **a.** A person or thing about which something is said or done; topic. **b.** The main theme of a work of art. 3. A course or area of study. 4. An individual that experiences or is subjected to something. 5. *Gram.* A word, phrase, or clause in a sentence that denotes the doer of the action, the receiver of the action in passive constructions, or that which is described or identified. —v. (səb-jĕkt'). 1. To subdue; subjugate. 2. To render liable; expose: *subjected to infection*. 3. To cause to experience or undergo. [< Lat. *subjectus*, p.p. of *subicere*, to subject.] —**sub·jec'tion** (-jĕk'shən) n.

sub·jec·tive (səb-jĕk'tĭv) adj. 1. **a.** Proceeding from or taking place within an individual's mind and unaffected by the outside world. **b.** Particular to a given individual; personal: *subjective experience*. 2. *Gram.* Of or designating the subject of a verb. —**sub·jec'tive·ly** adv. —**sub'jec·tiv'i·ty** (sŭb'jĕk-tĭv'ĭ-tē) n.

subject matter n. Matter under consideration in a written work or speech.

sub·join (sŭb-join') v. To add at the end; append. [< Lat. *subjungere*.]

sub·ju·gate (sŭb'jə-gāt') v. -**gat·ed**, -**gat·ing**. 1. To bring under dominion; conquer. 2. To make subservient. [< Lat. *subjugare*.] —**sub'·ju·ga'tion** n. —**sub'ju·ga'tor** n.

sub·junc·tive (səb-jŭngk'tĭv) adj. Of a grammatical mood used to express an uncertainty, a wish, or an unlikely condition. [< Lat. *subjunctus*, p.p. of *subjungere*, to subjoin.] —**sub·junc'tive** n.

sub·let (sŭb'lĕt') v. 1. To rent (property one holds by lease) to another. 2. To subcontract (work).

sub·li·mate (sŭb'lə-māt') v. -**mat·ed**, -**mat·ing**. 1. *Chem.* To change from a solid to a gas or from a gas to a solid without becoming a liquid. 2. To express potentially violent or socially unacceptable impulses in a modified, socially acceptable manner. [Lat. *sublimare*, to raise.] —**sub'li·ma'tion** n.

sub·lime (sə-blīm') adj. 1. Exalted; lofty: *sublime poetry*. 2. Of high spiritual, moral, or intellectual worth. 3. Inspiring awe; moving. —v. -**limed**, -**lim·ing**. To sublimate. [Lat. *sublimis*.] —**sub·lime'ly** adv. —**su·blim'i·ty** (sə-blĭm'ĭ-tē) n.

sub·lim·i·nal (sŭb-lĭm'ə-nəl) adj. Below the threshold of conscious perception or awareness. [SUB- + Lat. *limen*, threshold.] —**sub·lim'i·nal·ly** adv.

sub·lu·na·ry (sŭb'lōō'nə-rē) adj. 1. Situated beneath the moon. 2. Of this world; earthly. [LLat. *sublunaris*.]

sub·ma·chine gun (sŭb'mə-shēn') n. A lightweight automatic or semiautomatic gun fired from the shoulder or hip.

sub·ma·rine (sŭb'mə-rēn', sŭb'mə-rēn') adj. Beneath the surface of the water; undersea. —n. 1. A ship that can operate underwater. 2. A hero (sense 4).

submarine

sub·merge (səb-mûrj') v. -**merged**, -**merg·ing**. 1. To place or go under or as if under water or other liquid. 2. To cover with water. [Lat. *submergere*.] —**sub·mer'gence** n. —**sub·mer'gi·ble** adj.

sub·merse (səb-mûrs') v. -**mersed**, -**mers·ing**. To submerge. [< Lat. *submersus*, p.p. of *submergere*, to submerge.] —**sub·mers'i·ble** adj. —**sub·mer'sion** n.

sub·mi·cro·scop·ic (sŭb'mī-krə-skŏp'ĭk) adj. Too small to be resolved by an optical microscope.

sub·mit (səb-mĭt') v. -**mit·ted**, -**mit·ting**. 1. To yield (oneself) to the will or authority of another. 2. To commit (something) to the consideration of another. 3. To offer as a proposition or contention. 4. To allow oneself to be subjected; acquiesce. [< Lat. *submittere*, to set under.] —**sub·mis'sion** n. —**sub·mis'sive** adj. —**sub·mit'tal** n.

sub·nor·mal (sŭb-nôr'məl) adj. Less than normal; below the average. —**sub'nor·mal'i·ty** (-măl'ĭ-tē) n.

sub·or·bit·al (sŭb-ôr'bĭ-tl) adj. Of or involving less than one orbit of the earth.

sub·or·di·nate (sə-bôr'dn-ĭt) adj. 1. Of a lower or inferior class or rank. 2. Subject to the authority or control of another. 3. *Gram.* Dependent on another clause. —n. One that is subordinate. —v. (-nāt') -**nat·ed**, -**nat·ing**.

1. To put in a lower or inferior rank or class. 2. To make subservient. [< Med. Lat. *subordinare*.] **—sub·or′di·nate·ly** *adv.* **—sub·or′di·na′·tion** *n.* **—sub·or′di·na′tive** *adj.*

Syns: *subordinate, inferior, junior, subaltern, underling* n.

sub·orn (sə-bôrn′) *v.* To induce to commit an unlawful act, esp. perjury. [Lat. *subornare*.] **—sub′or·na′tion** *n.*

sub·plot (sŭb′plŏt′) *n.* A subordinate literary plot.

sub·poe·na (sə-pē′nə) *n.* A legal writ requiring appearance in court to give testimony. **—v.** To serve or summon with such a writ. [< Lat. *sub poena*, under penalty.]

sub ro·sa (sŭb rō′zə) *adv.* In secret; privately. [< Lat., under the rose.] **—sub·ro′sa** *adj.*

sub·scribe (səb-skrīb′) *v.* **-scribed, -scrib·ing.** 1. To sign (one's name). 2. To sign one's name to in testimony or consent: *subscribe a will.* 3. To pledge or contribute (a sum of money). 4. To express agreement or approval: *subscribe to a belief.* 5. To contract to receive and pay for a periodical. [< Lat. *subscribere*.] **—sub·scrib′er** *n.*

sub·script (sŭb′skrĭpt′) *n.* A character or symbol written next to and slightly below a letter or number. [< Lat. *subscriptus*, p.p. of *subscribere*, to subscribe.]

sub·scrip·tion (səb-skrĭp′shən) *n.* 1. The signing of one's name, as to a document. 2. A purc se made by signed order, as for issues of a eriodical or a series of performances.

sub·se·quent (sŭb′sĭ-kwənt) *adj.* Following in time or order; succeeding. [< Lat. *subsequi*, to follow close after.] **—sub′se·quent·ly** *adv.*

sub·ser·vi·ent (səb-sûr′vē-ənt) *adj.* 1. Subordinate. 2. Obsequious; servile. [< Lat. *subservire*, to promote.] **—sub·ser′vi·ence** *n.* **—sub·ser′vi·ent·ly** *adv.*

sub·set (sŭb′sĕt′) *n.* A mathematical set contained within another set.

sub·side (səb-sīd′) *v.* **-sid·ed, -sid·ing.** 1. To sink to a lower level. 2. To sink to the bottom; settle. 3. To become less; abate. [Lat. *subsidere*.] **—sub·si′dence** *n.*

sub·sid·i·ary (səb-sĭd′ē-ĕr′ē) *adj.* 1. Serving to assist or supplement. 2. Subordinate. 3. Of or like a subsidy. **—n.,** *pl.* **-ies.** One that is subsidiary, esp. a company owned by another company. **—sub·sid′i·ar′i·ly** (-âr′ə-lē) *adv.*

sub·si·dize (sŭb′sĭ-dīz′) *v.* **-dized, -diz·ing.** To aid or supply with a subsidy.

sub·si·dy (sŭb′sĭ-dē) *n., pl.* **-dies.** Financial assistance, as that granted by a government to a private enterprise. [< Lat. *subsidium*, support.]

sub·sist (səb-sĭst′) *v.* 1. To exist or continue to exist. 2. To maintain life: *subsist on one meal a day.* [Lat. *subsistere*, to stand up.]

sub·sis·tence (səb-sĭs′təns) *n.* 1. The act or means of subsisting. 2. Existence. **—sub·sis′tent** *adj.*

sub·soil (sŭb′soil′) *n.* The layer of earth beneath the surface soil.

sub·son·ic (sŭb′sŏn′ĭk) *adj.* 1. Of less than audible frequency. 2. Of a speed less than that of sound.

sub·stance (sŭb′stəns) *n.* 1. a. Something that has mass and occupies space; matter. b. A material of a particular kind or constitution.

2. The essence; gist. 3. Reality; actuality: *a dream without substance.* 4. Density; body. 5. Material possessions; wealth. [< Lat. *substare*, to be present.]

sub·stan·dard (sŭb′stăn′dərd) *adj.* Failing to meet a standard; below standard.

sub·stan·tial (səb-stăn′shəl) *adj.* 1. Of or having substance; material. 2. Not imaginary; real. 3. Solidly built; strong. 4. Ample; sustaining. 5. Considerable; large: *won by a substantial margin.* 6. Possessing wealth; well-to-do. [< Lat. *substantia*, substance.] **—sub·stan′tial·ly** *adv.*

sub·stan·ti·ate (səb-stăn′shē-āt′) *v.* **-at·ed, -at·ing.** To support with proof or evidence. **—sub·stan′ti·a′tion** *n.*

sub·stan·tive (sŭb′stən-tĭv) *adj.* 1. Substantial; considerable. 2. Of the essence of something; essential. **—n.** A word or group of words functioning as a noun. **—sub′stan·tive·ly** *adv.*

sub·sta·tion (sŭb′stā′shən) *n.* A branch station, as of a post office.

sub·sti·tute (sŭb′stĭ-tōōt′, -tyōōt′) *n.* One that takes the place of another **—v.** **-tut·ed, -tut·ing.** 1. To put or use in place of another. 2. To take the place of another. [< Lat. *substituere*, to substitute.] **—sub′sti·tu′tion** *n.*

sub·stra·tum (sŭb′strā′təm, -străt′əm) *n., pl.* **-ta** or **-tums.** 1. An underlying layer or foundation. 2. Subsoil.

sub·struc·ture (sŭb′strŭk′chər) *n.* The supporting part of a structure; foundation.

sub·sume (səb-sōōm′, -syōōm′) *v.* **-sumed, -sum·ing.** To place in a more comprehensive category. [SUB- + Lat. *sumere*, to take up.] **—sub·sum′a·ble** *adj.*

sub·ter·fuge (sŭb′tər-fyōōj′) *n.* An evasive plan or tactic used to avoid capture or confrontation. [< Lat. *subterfugere*, to flee secretly.]

sub·ter·ra·ne·an (sŭb′tə-rā′nē-ən) *adj.* 1. Situated or operating beneath the earth's surface; underground. 2. Hidden; secret. [< Lat. *subterraneus*.]

sub·ti·tle (sŭb′tīt′l) *n.* 1. A secondary and usu. explanatory title, as of a literary work. 2. A printed translation of the dialogue of a foreign-language film, shown at the bottom of the screen.

sub·tle (sŭt′l) *adj.* **-tler, -tlest.** 1. a. So slight as to be difficult to detect. b. Not obvious; abstruse. 2. Able to make fine distinctions; keen: *a subtle mind.* 3. a. Skillful; clever. b. Sly; devious. [< Lat. *subtilis*.] **—sub′tle·ty** or **sub′tle·ness** *n.* **—sub′tly** *adv.*

sub·to·tal (sŭb′tōt′l) *n.* The total of part of a series of numbers being added. **—sub′to′tal** *v.*

sub·tract (səb-trăkt′) *v.* To take away or deduct, as one number from another. [< Lat. *subtractus*, p.p. of *subtrahere*, to subtract.] **—sub·trac′tion** *n.*

sub·tra·hend (sŭb′trə-hĕnd′) *n.* A quantity to be subtracted from another. [Lat. *subtrahendum*, thing to be subtracted.]

sub·trop·i·cal (sŭb-trŏp′ĭ-kəl) *adj.* Of or being the regions that border the tropics.

sub·trop·ics (sŭb-trŏp′ĭks) *pl.n.* Subtropical regions.

sub·urb (sŭb′ûrb′) *n.* 1. A usu. residential area near a city. 2. **suburbs.** The usu. residential region surrounding a major city. [< Lat. *suburbium*.] —**sub·ur·ban** *adj.*

sub·ur·ban·ite (sə-bûr′bə-nīt′) *n.* One who lives in a suburb.

sub·ur·bi·a (sə-bûr′bē-ə) *n.* **1.** The suburbs. **2.** Suburbanites.

sub·ven·tion (səb-věn′shən) *n.* A subsidy. [< Lat. *subvenire*, to come to help.] —**sub·ven′·tion·ar′y** (-shə-něr′ē) *adj.*

sub·ver·sive (səb-vûr′sĭv, -zĭv) *adj.* Acting to subvert, esp. an established government. —*n.* One who advocates subversive means or policies. —**sub·ver′sive·ly** *adv.* —**sub·ver′sive·ness** *n.*

sub·vert (səb-vûrt′) *v.* **1.** To destroy or overthrow completely; ruin. **2.** To corrupt the morals or character of. [< Lat. *subvertere*.] —**sub·ver′sion** (-vûr′zhən, -shən) *n.* —**sub·vert′er** *n.*

sub·way (sŭb′wā′) *n.* An underground railroad, usu. operated by electricity.

suc·ceed (sək-sēd′) *v.* **1.** To` come next in time or order, esp. to replace another in a position. **2.** To accomplish something attempted. [< Lat. *succedere*.] —**suc·ceed′er** *n.*

suc·cess (sək-sĕs′) *n.* **1.** The achievement of something attempted. **2.** The gaining of fame or prosperity. **3.** One that succeeds. [Lat. *successus* < p.p. of *succedere*, to succeed.] —**suc·cess′ful** *adj.* —**suc·cess′ful·ly** *adv.*

suc·ces·sion (sək-sĕsh′ən) *n.* **1.** The act or process of following in order. **2.** A group of persons or things following in order; sequence. **3.** The sequence, right, or act of succeeding to a title, throne, or estate. —**suc·ces′sion·al** *adj.*

suc·ces·sive (sək-sĕs′ĭv) *adj.* Following in uninterrupted order. —**suc·ces′sive·ly** *adv.*

suc·ces·sor (sək-sĕs′ər) *n.* One that succeeds another.

suc·cinct (sək-sĭngkt′) *adj.* Marked by briefness and clarity of expression; concise. [Lat. *succinctus*, p.p. of *succingere*, to gird from below.] —**suc·cinct′ly** *adv.* —**suc·cinct′ness** *n.*

suc·cor (sŭk′ər) *n.* Assistance or help in time of distress; relief. [< Lat. *succurrere*, to be useful for.] —**suc′cor** *v.*

suc·co·tash (sŭk′ə-tăsh′) *n.* Kernels of corn and lima beans cooked together. [Narraganset *msickquatash*.]

Suc·coth (sŏŏk′əs, -ōt′, -ōs′) *n.* Also **Suk·koth**. A Jewish harvest festival. [< Heb. *sukkāh*, tabernacle.]

suc·cu·lent (sŭk′yə-lənt) *adj.* **1.** Full of juice; juicy. **2.** Having thick, fleshy leaves or stems. —*n.* A succulent plant, as a cactus. [< Lat. *succus*, juice.] —**suc′cu·lence** *n.* —**suc′cu·lent·ly** *adv.*

suc·cumb (sə-kŭm′) *v.* **1.** To yield to something overpowering. **2.** To die. [< Lat. *succumbere*.]

such (sŭch) *adj.* **1.** Of this or that kind or extent. **2.** Similar. —*adv.* **1.** To such a degree: *such a good job.* **2.** Very; especially. —*pron.* **1.** Such a person or persons or thing or things. **2.** Someone or something implied or indicated: *Such are the fortunes of war.* **3.** The like: *pins, needles, and such.* —**idioms. as such. 1.** For example. **2.** Of the stated or implied kind or degree. [< OE *swylc*.]

such·like (sŭch′līk′) *adj.* Of a similar kind; like. —*pron.* Persons or things of such a kind.

suck (sŭk) *v.* **1. a.** To draw (liquid) into the

mouth by inhaling. **b.** To draw from in this manner: *suck a lemon.* **2.** To draw in by or as if by suction. **3.** To suckle. —*n.* The act of sucking. [< OE *sūcan*.]

suck·er (sŭk′ər) *n.* **1.** One that sucks. **2.** *Slang.* A person who is easily deceived. **3.** A lollipop. **4.** A freshwater fish with a thick-lipped mouth adapted for feeding by suction. **5.** An organ or part adapted for clinging by suction. **6.** *Bot.* A secondary shoot arising from the base of a plant. —*v. Slang.* To trick; dupe.

suck·le (sŭk′əl) *v.* **-led, -ling. 1.** To give milk at the breast or udder. **2.** To rear; nourish. [Prob. < SUCKLING.]

suck·ling (sŭk′lĭng) *n.* A young unweaned mammal. [ME *suklinge*.]

su·cre (sōō′krā) *n.* See table at **currency**. [Sp.]

su·crose (sōō′krōs′) *n.* A sugar, $C_{12}H_{22}O_{11}$, found in many plants, mainly sugar cane and sugar beet. [Fr. *sucre*, sugar + -OSE[2].]

suc·tion (sŭk′shən) *n.* **1.** The act or process of sucking. **2.** A force that causes something to be drawn into a space because of the difference between the external and internal pressures. [< Lat. *suctus*, p.p. of *sugere*, to suck.]

sud·den (sŭd′n) *adj.* **1.** Happening quickly and without warning. **2.** Abrupt; hasty. **3.** Rapid; swift. [< Lat. *subitus*.] —**sud′den·ly** *adv.* —**sud′den·ness** *n.*

sudden death *n. Sports.* Extra minutes of play added to a tied game, the winner being the first team to score.

suds (sŭdz) *pl.n.* **1.** Soapy water. **2.** Foam. [Poss. MDu. *sudse*, marsh.] —**suds′y** *adj.*

sue (sōō) *v.* **sued, su·ing. 1.** To institute legal proceedings; bring suit against (a person) for redress of grievances. **2.** To make an appeal or entreaty. [< AN *suer*.]

suede (swād) *n.* Also **suède. 1.** Leather with a soft napped surface. **2.** Fabric made to resemble suede. [< Fr. *Suède*, Sweden.]

su·et (sōō′ĭt) *n.* The hard fat around the kidneys of cattle and sheep, used in cooking and making tallow. [< Lat. *sebum*.]

suf·fer (sŭf′ər) *v.* **1.** To feel pain or distress. **2.** To tolerate or undergo damage or loss. **3.** To appear at a disadvantage: *suffers by comparison.* **4.** To endure or bear. **5.** To permit; allow. [< Lat. *sufferre*.] —**suf′fer·a·ble** *adj.* —**suf′fer·a·bly** *adv.* —**suf′fer·er** *n.*

suf·fer·ance (sŭf′ər-əns, sŭf′rəns) *n.* **1.** Tolerance; endurance. **2.** Sanction or permission implied by failure to prohibit.

suf·fer·ing (sŭf′ər-ĭng, sŭf′rĭng) *n.* Physical or mental pain or distress.

suf·fice (sə-fīs′) *v.* **-ficed, -fic·ing. 1.** To be sufficient (for). **2.** To be capable or competent. [< Lat. *sufficere*.]

suf·fi·cient (sə-fĭsh′ənt) *adj.* As much as is needed; enough. [< Lat. *sufficere*, to suffice.] —**suf·fi′cien·cy** *n.* —**suf·fi′cient·ly** *adv.*

suf·fix (sŭf′ĭks′) *n.* An affix added to the end of a word or stem, serving to form a new word or an inflectional ending. [< Lat. *suffixus*, p.p. of *suffigere*, to affix.]

suf·fo·cate (sŭf′ə-kāt′) *v.* **-cat·ed, -cat·ing. 1.** To kill or destroy by preventing access to oxygen. **2.** To suppress; stifle. [Lat. *suffocare*.] —**suf′fo·ca′tion** *n.*

suf·frage (sŭf′rĭj) *n.* **1.** A vote. **2.** The right or privilege of voting; franchise. [< Lat. *suffragium*.]

suf·fra·gette (sŭf'rə-jĕt') *n.* A woman who advocates suffrage for women.

suffragette
Suffragette pickets in front of the
White House in 1917

suf·fra·gist (sŭf'rə-jĭst) *n.* An advocate of the extension of political voting rights, esp. to women.

suf·fuse (sə-fyōōz') *v.* **-fused, -fus·ing.** To spread through or over: *a room suffused with candlelight.* [< Lat. *suffusus,* p.p. of *suffundere.*] **—suf·fu'sion** *n.* **—suf·fu'sive** *adj.*

Su·fi (sōō'fē) *n.* A member of a Moslem mystic sect. **—Su'fism** (-fĭz'əm) *n.*

sug·ar (shŏŏg'ər) *n.* Any of a class of water-soluble crystalline carbohydrates with a characteristically sweet taste. **—**v.* **1.** To coat, cover, or sweeten with sugar. **2.** To make less distasteful. [< Skt. *śarkarā.*]

sugar beet *n.* A beet with white roots from which sugar is obtained.

sugar cane *n.* A tall grass native to the East Indies, with thick stems that yield sugar.

sug·ar-coat (shŏŏg'ər-kōt') *v.* To cause to seem more appealing or palatable.

sugar maple *n.* A maple tree of eastern North America, with sap that is the source of maple syrup.

sug·ar·plum (shŏŏg'ər-plŭm') *n.* A small ball of candy.

sug·ar·y (shŏŏg'ə-rē) *adj.* **-i·er, -i·est. 1.** Tasting of or resembling sugar. **2.** Deceitfully or cloyingly sweet.

sug·gest (səg-jĕst', sə-jĕst') *v.* **1.** To offer for consideration or action; propose. **2.** To bring or call to mind by association. **3.** To imply. [< Lat. *suggestus,* p.p. of *suggerere.*]
Syns: *suggest, imply, insinuate, intimate* v.

sug·gest·i·ble (səg-jĕs'tə-bəl, sə-jĕs'-) *adj.* Easily influenced by suggestion.

sug·ges·tion (səg-jĕs'chən, sə-jĕs'-) *n.* **1.** The act of suggesting. **2.** Something suggested. **3.** A hint or trace.

sug·ges·tive (səg-jĕs'tĭv, sə-jĕs'-) *adj.* **1.** Tending to suggest thoughts or ideas; provocative. **2.** Tending to suggest something improper or indecent. **—sug·ges'tive·ly** *adv.* **—sug·ges'tive·ness** *n.*

su·i·cide (sōō'ĭ-sīd') *n.* **1.** The act or an instance of intentionally killing oneself. **2.** One who commits suicide. [Lat. *sui,* of oneself + -CIDE.] **—su'i·cid'al** *adj.*

su·i gen·e·ris (sōō'ī jĕn'ər-ĭs, sōō'ē) *adj.* Unique; individual. [< Lat., of its own kind.]

suit (sōōt) *n.* **1.** A set of clothes consisting of a coat and matching trousers or skirt. **2.** A group of related things. **3.** Any of the four sets of playing cards that constitute a deck.

4. *Law.* A proceeding in court to recover a right or claim. **5.** The act or an instance of courtship. **—**v.* **1.** To meet the requirements of. **2.** To make appropriate; adapt. **3.** To be proper for or becoming to. **4.** To please; satisfy. **—idiom. follow suit.** To follow an example. [< OFr. *sieute,* suit, suite.]

suit·a·ble (sōō'tə-bəl) *adj.* Appropriate to a given purpose or occasion. **—suit'a·bil'i·ty** or **suit'a·ble·ness** *n.* **—suit'a·bly** *adv.*
Syns: *suitable, due, just, right* **adj.**

suit·case (sōōt'kās') *n.* A usu. rectangular and flat piece of luggage.

suite (swēt) *n.* **1.** A group of attendants; retinue. **2.** A series of connected rooms used as a unit. **3.** A set of matching furniture. **4.** *Mus.* An instrumental composition consisting of a succession of short pieces or material drawn from a longer work. [< OFr. *sieute,* ult. < Lat. *sequi,* to follow.]

suit·or (sōō'tər) *n.* **1.** One who makes a petition or request. **2.** A man who is courting a woman.

su·ki·ya·ki (sōō'kē-yä'kē, skē-) *n.* A Japanese dish of sliced meat and vegetables fried together. [J.]

Suk·koth (sŏŏk'əs, -ōt', -ōs') *n.* Var. of **Succoth.**

sul·fa drug (sŭl'fə) *n.* Any of a group of synthetic organic compounds used to inhibit bacterial growth and activity. [SULFA(NILAMIDE) + DRUG.]

sul·fa·nil·a·mide (sŭl'fə-nĭl'ə-mīd') *n.* A white, odorless compound, $C_6H_8N_2SO_2$, used to treat various bacterial infections. [SULF(UR) + ANIL(INE) + *amide.*]

sul·fate (sŭl'fāt') *n.* A chemical compound containing the bivalent group SO_4. [SULF(UR) + -ATE².]

sul·fide (sŭl'fīd') *n.* A compound of sulfur with an electropositive element or group. [SULF(UR) + -IDE.]

sul·fur (sŭl'fər) *n.* Also **sul·phur.** *Symbol* **S** A pale-yellow nonmetallic element occurring widely in nature both free and in combined forms, used esp. in rubber vulcanization and in the manufacture of chemicals. Atomic number 16; atomic weight 32.064. [< Lat.]

sulfur dioxide *n.* A colorless, extremely irritating gas or liquid, SO_2, used esp. in the manufacture of sulfuric acid.

sul·fu·ric (sŭl-fyŏŏr'ĭk) *adj.* Of or containing sulfur.

sulfuric acid *n.* A highly corrosive, dense oily liquid, H_2SO_4, used to manufacture a wide variety of chemicals and materials.

sul·fur·ous (sŭl'fər-əs, sŭl-fyŏŏr'əs) *adj.* **1.** Of, relating to, or containing sulfur. **2.** Characteristic of burning sulfur, as in odor.

sulk (sŭlk) *v.* To be sullenly aloof or withdrawn. **—**n.* A mood or display of sulking. [< SULKY¹.]

sulk·y¹ (sŭl'kē) *adj.* **-i·er, -i·est.** Sullenly aloof or withdrawn. [Orig. unknown.] **—sulk'i·ly** *adv.* **—sulk'i·ness** *n.*

sulk·y² (sŭl'kē) *n., pl.* **-ies.** A light two-wheeled vehicle accommodating one person and drawn by one horse. [< SULKY¹ < its having a single seat.]

sul·len (sŭl'ən) *adj.* **-er, -est. 1.** Showing a brooding ill humor; morose. **2.** Gloomy or somber. [< Lat. *solus*, alone.] —**sul'len·ly** *adv.* —**sul'len·ness** *n.*

sul·ly (sŭl'ē) *v.* -**lied**, -**ly·ing.** 1. To soil the cleanness or luster of. 2. To defile; taint. [Prob. < OFr. *souiller*, to soil.]

sul·phur (sŭl'fər) *n.* Var. of **sulfur.**

sul·tan (sŭl'tən) *n.* A ruler esp. of a Moslem country. [< Ar. *-sultãn.*] —**sul'tan·ate'** (-tə-nāt') *n.*

sul·tan·a (sŭl-tăn'ə, -tä'nə) *n.* 1. The wife, mother, sister, or daughter of a sultan. 2. A seedless, pale yellow grape.

sul·try (sŭl'trē) *adj.* -**tri·er**, -**tri·est.** 1. Very hot and humid. 2. Hot; torrid. 3. Sensual; voluptuous. [< SWELTER.] —**sul'tri·ness** *n.*

sum (sŭm) *n.* 1. The result obtained by addition. 2. The whole quantity; aggregate. 3. An amount of money. 4. An arithmetic problem. 5. A summary. —*v.* **summed**, **sum·ming.** To add. —*phrasal verb.* **sum up.** To summarize. [< Lat. *summa.*]

su·mac (sōō'măk', shōō'-) *n.* Also **su·mach.** Any of various shrubs or small trees with compound leaves and greenish flowers followed by usu. red fruits. [< Ar. *summãq.*]

sum·ma·rize (sŭm'ə-rīz') *v.* -**rized**, -**riz·ing.** To make a summary. —**sum'ma·ri·za'tion** *n.*

sum·ma·ry (sŭm'ə-rē) *n.*, *pl.* -**ries.** A condensed statement of the substance or principal points of a larger work. —*adj.* 1. Presented in condensed form; concise. 2. Performed speedily and without ceremony: *summary justice.* [< Lat. *summa*, sum.] —**sum·mar'i·ly** (sə-mâr'ə-lē) *adv.*

sum·ma·tion (sə-mā'shən) *n.* A concluding statement containing a summary of principal points, esp. of a case before a court of law. **sum·mer** (sŭm'ər) *n.* The usu. warmest season of the year, occurring between spring and autumn. —*v.* To pass the summer. [< OE *mor.*] —**sum'mer·y** *adj.*

sum·mer·house (sŭm'ər-hous') *n.* A small, roofed structure in a park or garden.

sum·mit (sŭm'ĭt) *n.* 1. The highest point. 2. The highest degree of achievement or status. [< Lat. *summus*, highest.]

sum·mon (sŭm'ən) *v.* 1. To call together; convene. 2. To send for; request to appear. 3. To order to appear in court. 4. To call forth; rouse: *summoned up a smile.* [< Lat. *sommonēre*, to remind privately.]

sum·mons (sŭm'ənz) *n.*, *pl.* -**mons·es.** 1. A call to appear or do something. 2. *Law.* A notice summoning a person to report to a court.

sump·tu·ous (sŭmp'chōō-əs) *adj.* Of a size suggesting great expense; lavish. [< Lat. *sumptus*, expense.] —**sump'tu·ous·ly** *adv.* —**sump'tu·ous·ness** *n.*

sun (sŭn) *n.* 1. A star that is the center of the solar system, sustains life on Earth with its heat and light, and has a mean distance from Earth of about 93 million miles and a diameter of approx. 864,000 miles. 2. A star that is the center of a planetary system. 3. The radiant energy, esp. heat and visible light, emitted by the sun; sunshine. —*v.* **sunned**, **sun·ning.** To expose to or bask in the sun's rays. [< OE *sunne.*] —**sun'less** *adj.*

sun·bathe (sŭn'bāth') *v.* To expose the body to the direct rays of the sun. —**sun'bath'er** *n.*

sun·beam (sŭn'bēm') *n.* A ray of sunlight.

sun·bon·net (sŭn'bŏn'ĭt) *n.* A woman's wide-brimmed bonnet for shading the face and neck from the sun.

sun·burn (sŭn'bûrn') *n.* An inflammation or blistering of the skin caused by overexposure to direct sunlight. —*v.* To afflict with or be afflicted with sunburn.

sun·burst (sŭn'bûrst') *n.* A design consisting of a central sunlike disk with radiating spires.

sun·dae (sŭn'dē, -dā') *n.* A dish of ice cream with toppings such as syrup, fruits, nuts, and whipped cream. [Orig. unknown.]

Sun·day (sŭn'dē, -dā') *n.* The first day of the week and the Christian Sabbath. [< OE *sunnandæg.*]

sun·der (sŭn'dər) *v.* To break apart; divide. [< OE *sundrian.*]

sun·di·al (sŭn'dī'əl) *n.* An instrument that indicates the time of day by measuring the angle of the sun with a pointer that casts a shadow on a calibrated dial.

sundial

sun·down (sŭn'doun') *n.* Sunset.

sun·dries (sŭn'drēz) *pl.n.* Small miscellaneous items or articles. [< SUNDRY.]

sun·dry (sŭn'drē) *adj.* Various; miscellaneous. [< OE *syndrig*, separate.]

sun·fish (sŭn'fĭsh') *n.* 1. Any of various flat-bodied North American freshwater fishes. 2. Any of several large, round-bodied saltwater fishes.

sun·flow·er (sŭn'flou'ər) *n.* A plant with large yellow-rayed flowers that produce edible seeds rich in oil.

sung (sŭng) *v.* A *p.t.* & the *p.p.* of **sing.**

sun·glass·es (sŭn'glăs'ĭz) *pl.n.* Eyeglasses with tinted lenses to protect the eyes from the sun's glare.

sunk (sŭngk) *v.* A *p.t.* & the *p.p.* of **sink.**

sunk·en (sŭng'kən) *v.* A *p.p.* of **sink.** —*adj.* 1. Depressed, fallen in, or hollowed: *sunken cheeks.* 2. Submerged: *sunken treasure.* 3. Below the surrounding level.

sun lamp *n.* A lamp that emits a wide range of radiation, used in therapeutic and cosmetic treatments.

sun·light (sŭn'līt') *n.* The light of the sun.

sun·lit (sŭn'lĭt') *adj.* Illuminated by the sun.

sun·ny (sŭn'ē) *adj.* -**ni·er**, -**ni·est.** 1. Exposed to or abounding in sunshine. 2. Cheerful; genial. —**sun'ni·ly** *adv.* —**sun'ni·ness** *n.*

sun·rise (sŭn'rīz') *n.* The first appearance of the sun above the horizon.

sun·set (sŭn'sĕt') *n.* The disappearance of the sun below the horizon.

sun·shade (sŭn'shād') *n.* Something, as a parasol, used as a protection from the sun.

sun·shine (sŭn'shīn') *n.* 1. The direct rays from the sun. 2. Happiness or cheerfulness. —**sun'shin'y** *adj.*

sun·spot (sŭn'spŏt') *n.* Any of the relatively dark spots that appear in groups on the surface of the sun.

sun·stroke (sŭn'strōk') *n.* Heat stroke caused by exposure to the sun.

sun·tan (sŭn′tăn′) *n.* A tan color on the skin from exposure to the sun. —**sun′tanned′** *adj.*

sun-up (sŭn′ŭp′) *n.* Sunrise.

sup (sŭp) *v.* **supped, sup·ping.** To have supper; dine. [< OFr. *soup,* soup.]

su·per¹ (sōō′pər) *n. Informal.* A superintendent in an apartment or office building.

su·per² (sōō′pər) *adj. Slang.* Excellent. [SUPER(FINE).]

super- *pref.* 1. Placement above, over, or outside: *superimpose.* 2. Superiority in size, quality, number, or degree: *superfine.* 3. A degree exceeding a norm: *supersonic.* 4. Extra; additional: *superphosphate.* [< Lat. *super,* over, above.]

Usage: Many compounds other than those entered here may be formed with *super-.* In forming compounds *super-* is normally joined with the following element without space or hyphen: *superrefined.* However, if the second element begins with a capital letter, it is separated with a hyphen: *super-American.*

su·per·a·ble (sōō′pər-ə-bəl) *adj.* Capable of being overcome. [< Lat. *superare,* to overcome.] —**su′per·a·bly** *adv.*

su·per·a·bun·dant (sōō′pər-ə-bŭn′dənt) *adj.* More than ample. —**su′per·a·bun′dance** *n.*

su·per·an·nu·at·ed (sōō′pər-ăn′yōō-ā′tĭd) *adj.* 1. Retired or discharged because of age or infirmity. 2. Antiquated; obsolete. [< Med. Lat *superannuari,* to be too old.]

su·perb (sōō-pûrb′, sə-) *adj.* 1. Of unusually high quality; first-rate. 2. Majestic; imposing. [Lat. *superbus,* proud.] —**su·perb′ly** *adv.*

su·per·car·go (sōō′pər-kär′gō) *n., pl.* **-goes** or **-gos.** An officer on a merchant ship who has charge of the cargo. [Sp. *sobrecargo.*]

su·per·charge (sōō′pər-chärj′) *v.* To increase the power (e.g. an engine).

su·per·charg·er (sōō′pər-chär′jər) *n.* A blower or compressor for supplying air under high pressure to the cylinders of an internal-combustion engine.

su·per·cil·i·ous (sōō′pər-sĭl′ē-əs) *adj.* Characterized by haughty scorn; disdainful. [< Lat. *supercilium,* pride.] —**su′per·cil′i·ous·ly** *adv.* —**su′per·cil′i·ous·ness** *n.*

su·per·con·duc·tiv·i·ty (sōō′pər-kŏn′dŭk′tĭv′ĭ-tē) *n.* The complete loss of electrical resistance in certain metals and alloys at temperatures near absolute zero. —**su′per·con·duc′tive** *adj.* —**su′per·con·duc′tor** *n.*

su·per·e·go (sōō′pər-ē′gō, -ĕg′ō) *n.* The consciencelike part of the psyche that develops by the incorporation of the moral standards of the community.

su·per·e·rog·a·to·ry (sōō′pər-ə-rŏg′ə-tôr′ē, -tōr′ē) *adj.* Superfluous; unnecessary.

su·per·fi·cial (sōō′pər-fĭsh′əl) *adj.* 1. Of, affecting, or located on the surface. 2. Concerned with or comprehending only what is apparent or obvious; shallow. 3. **a.** Apparent rather than actual or substantial. **b.** Trivial. [< Lat. *superficies,* surface.] —**su′per·fi′ci·al′i·ty** (-fĭsh′ē-ăl′ĭ-tē) *n.* —**su′per·fi′cial·ly** *adv.*

su·per·fine (sōō′pər-fīn′) *adj.* 1. Of exceptional quality. 2. Overdelicate or refined. 3. Of extra fine texture.

su·per·flu·i·ty (sōō′pər-flōō′ĭ-tē) *n., pl.* **-ties.** 1. The quality or condition of being superflu-

ous. 2. Something that is superfluous. 3. Overabundance.

su·per·flu·ous (sōō-pûr′flōō-əs) *adj.* Beyond what is required or sufficient; extra. [< Lat. *superfluere,* to overflow.] —**su·per′flu·ous·ly** *adv.* —**su·per′flu·ous·ness** *n.*

su·per·high·way (sōō′pər-hī′wā′) *n.* A broad highway for high-speed traffic.

su·per·hu·man (sōō′pər-hyōō′mən) *adj.* 1. Divine; supernatural. 2. Beyond ordinary or normal human ability, power, or experience. —**su′per·hu′man·ly** *adv.*

su·per·im·pose (sōō′pər-ĭm-pōz′) *v.* To lay or place on or over something else. —**su′per·im′po·si′tion** *n.*

su·per·in·tend (sōō′pər-ĭn-tĕnd′) *v.* To have charge of; exercise supervision over; manage. [LLat. *superintendere.*] —**su′per·in·ten′dence** *n.* —**su′per·in·ten′dent** *n.*

su·pe·ri·or (sōō-pîr′ē-ər, sə-) *adj.* 1. Higher in rank, station, or authority. 2. Of a higher nature or kind. 3. Of great value or excellence; extraordinary. 4. Greater in number or amount. 5. Arrogant; haughty. 6. Indifferent or immune. 7. Located higher, as an organ or part. —*n.* 1. One who surpasses another in rank or quality. 2. The head of a religious order or house. [< Lat. *superus,* upper.] —**su·pe′ri·or′i·ty** (-pîr′ē-ôr′ĭ-tē, -ŏr′-) *n.* —**su·pe′ri·or·ly** *adv.*

su·per·la·tive (sōō-pûr′lə-tĭv) *adj.* 1. Of the highest order, quality, or degree. 2. Excessive or exaggerated. 3. *Gram.* Expressing or involving the extreme degree of comparison of an adjective or adverb. —*n.* 1. Something superlative. 2. *Gram.* **a.** The superlative degree. **b.** An adjective or adverb expressing the superlative degree. [< Lat. *superlatus,* excessive.] —**su·per′la·tive·ly** *adv.*

su·per·man (sōō′pər-măn′) *n.* One with more than human powers.

su·per·mar·ket (sōō′pər-mär′kĭt) *n.* A large self-service retail store selling food and household goods.

su·per·nal (sōō-pûr′nəl) *adj.* 1. Celestial; heavenly. 2. Of, coming from, or in the sky. [< Lat. *supernus.*]

su·per·nat·u·ral (sōō′pər-năch′ər-əl) *adj.* 1. Of an order of existence outside the natural world. 2. Attributed to divine power. —**su′per·nat′u·ral·ly** *adv.* —**su′per·nat′u·ral·ness** *n.*

su·per·no·va (sōō′pər-nō′və) *n., pl.* **-vae** (-vē′). A rare celestial phenomenon in which a star explodes, resulting in an extremely bright, short-lived object.

su·per·nu·mer·ar·y (sōō′pər-nōō′mə-rĕr′ē, -nyōō′-) *adj.* Exceeding a fixed or prescribed number; extra. —*n., pl.* **-ies.** 1. One that is in excess of the regular, necessary, or usual number. 2. A theatrical or cinematic performer without a speaking part. [LLat. *supernumerarius.*]

su·per·phos·phate (sōō′pər-fŏs′fāt′) *n.* A fertilizer made by the action of sulfuric acid on phosphate rock.

su·per·pow·er (sōō′pər-pou′ər) *n.* A powerful and influential nation.

su·per·sat·u·rate (sōō′pər-săch′ə-rāt′) *v.* To cause (a chemical solution) to be more highly concentrated than is normally possible under given conditions of temperature and pressure. —su′per·sat′u·ra′tion n.

su·per·scribe (sōō′pər-skrīb′) v. **-scribed, -scrib·ing.** To write (something) on the outside or upper part of. [Lat. *superscribere,* to write over.] —su′per·scrip′tion n.

su·per·script (sōō′pər-skrĭpt′) n. A character placed above and immediately to one side of another. [< Lat. *superscriptus,* p.p. of *superscribere,* to write over.]

su·per·sede (sōō′pər-sēd′) v. **-sed·ed, -sed·ing. 1.** To replace or succeed. **2.** To displace; supplant. [< Lat. *supersedēre,* to desist from.] —su′per·sed′ure n.

su·per·son·ic (sōō′pər-sŏn′ĭk) adj. Of, caused by, or moving at a speed greater than the speed of sound.

su·per·star (sōō′pər-stär′) n. A widely acclaimed star, as in motion pictures or sports, who has great popular appeal.

su·per·sti·tion (sōō′pər-stĭsh′ən) n. **1.** A belief that some action not logically related to a course of events influences its outcome. **2.** A belief, practice, or rite unreasoningly upheld by faith in magic, chance, or dogma. [< Lat. *superstitio.*] —su′per·sti′tious adj. —su′per·sti′tious·ly adv. —su′per·sti′tious·ness n.

su·per·struc·ture (sōō′pər-strŭk′chər) n. A structure literally or figuratively built on top of something else, esp. a part of a ship's structure above the main deck.

su·per·vene (sōō′pər-vēn′) v. **-vened, -ven·ing.** To come or occur as something extraneous, additional, or unexpected. [Lat. *supervenire.*]

su·per·vise (sōō′pər-vīz′) v. **-vised, -vis·ing.** To direct and inspect the work or performance of. [< Med. Lat. *supervisus,* p.p. of *supervidēre,* to look over.] —su′per·vi′sion (-vĭzh′ən) n. —su′per·vi′sor n. —su′per·vi′so·ry (-vī′zə-rē) adj.

su·pine (sōō-pīn′, sōō′pīn′) adj. **1.** Lying on the back or having the face upward. **2.** Lethargic; passive. [Lat. *supinus.*] —su·pine′ly adv. —su·pine′ness n.

sup·per (sŭp′ər) n. An evening meal, esp. a light meal when dinner is taken at midday. [< OFr. *soupe,* soup.]

sup·plant (sə-plănt′) v. To take the place of; supersede. [< Lat. *supplantare,* to trip up.]

sup·ple (sŭp′əl) adj. **-pler, -plest. 1.** Easily bent; pliant. **2.** Agile; limber. **3.** Compliant; submissive. [< Lat. *supplex,* humble.] —sup′ple·ness n. —sup′ply or sup′ple·ly adv.

sup·ple·ment (sŭp′lə-mənt) n. Something added to complete a thing or to make up for a deficiency. —v. (sŭp′lə-mĕnt′). To provide or form a supplement to. [< Lat. *supplēre,* to complete.] —sup′ple·men′ta·ry (-mĕn′tə-rē, -mĕn′trē) or sup′ple·men′tal adj. —sup′ple·men·ta′tion (-mĕn-tā′shən) n.

sup·pli·ant (sŭp′lē-ənt) adj. Asking humbly and earnestly; beseeching. —n. One who supplicates. [< Lat. *supplicare,* to supplicate.]

sup·pli·cant (sŭp′lĭ-kənt) n. One who entreats or supplicates. —adj. Supplicating.

sup·pli·cate (sŭp′lĭ-kāt′) v. **-cat·ed, -cat·ing. 1.** To ask for humbly or earnestly, as by praying. **2.** To beseech; beg. [< Lat. *supplicare.*] —sup′pli·ca′tion n.

sup·ply (sə-plī′) v. **-plied, -ply·ing. 1.** To make available for use; provide. **2.** To furnish or equip with what is needed or lacking. **3.** To fill sufficiently; satisfy: *supply a need.* —n., pl. **-plies. 1.** The act of supplying. **2.** An amount available; stock. **3.** Often **supplies.** Materials or provisions stored and dispensed when needed. **4.** *Econ.* The amount of a commodity available for meeting a demand or for purchase at a given price. [< Lat. *supplēre,* to complete.] —sup·pli′er n.

sup·port (sə-pôrt′, -pōrt′) v. **1.** To hold up or maintain in position. **2.** To be capable of bearing; withstand. **3.** To keep from failing during stress. **4.** To provide for or maintain by supplying with money or other necessities. **5.** To furnish evidence for; substantiate. **6.** To aid or promote the cause of. —n. **1.** The act of supporting or the condition of being supported. **2.** One that supports. **3.** Maintenance or subsistence. [< Lat. *supportare,* to carry.] —sup·port′a·ble adj. —sup·port′er n. —sup·por′tive adj. —sup·por′tive·ly adv.

sup·pose (sə-pōz′) v. **-posed, -pos·ing. 1.** To assume to be true for the sake of argument. **2.** To be inclined to think. **3.** To imply as a necessary condition; presuppose. [< Lat. *suppositus,* p.p. of *supponere,* to substitute.]

sup·posed (sə-pōzd′, -pō′zĭd) adj. Considered to be so, often mistakenly. —sup·pos′ed·ly (-pō′zĭd-lē) adv.

sup·po·si·tion (sŭp′ə-zĭsh′ən) n. **1.** The act of supposing. **2.** An assumption.

sup·pos·i·to·ry (sə-pŏz′ĭ-tôr′ē, -tōr′ē) n., pl. **-ries.** A solid medication designed to melt within a body cavity other than the mouth. [< LLat. *suppositorius,* place under.]

sup·press (sə-prĕs′) v. **1.** To put an end to forcibly; subdue. **2.** To keep from being revealed, published, or circulated. **3.** To hold back; restrain: *suppress a smile.* [< Lat. *suppressus,* p.p. of *supprimere,* to suppress.] —sup·pres′sion n. —sup·pres′sive adj.

sup·pu·rate (sŭp′yə-rāt′) v. **-rat·ed, -rat·ing.** To form or discharge pus. [Lat. *suppurare.*] —sup′pu·ra′tion n.

su·pra·na·tion·al (sōō′prə-năsh′ə-nəl) adj. Of or extending beyond the boundaries or authority of a nation. [Lat. *supra,* beyond + NATIONAL.]

su·prem·a·cist (sōō-prĕm′ə-sĭst) n. One who believes that a certain group is or should be supreme.

su·prem·a·cy (sōō-prĕm′ə-sē) n., pl. **-cies. 1.** The condition or quality of being supreme. **2.** Supreme power.

su·preme (sə-prēm′) adj. **1.** Greatest in power, authority, or rank. **2.** Greatest in importance or quality. **3.** Ultimate; final: *the supreme sacrifice.* [Lat. *supremus,* superl. of *superus,* situated above.] —su·preme′ly adv.

Supreme Court n. **1.** The highest Federal court in the United States. **2.** The highest court in most U.S. states.

Su·qua·mish (sə-kwä′mĭsh, skwä′-) n., pl. **-mish** or **-es. 1. a.** A tribe of Indians of the northwestern Pacific coast, west of Puget Sound. **b.** A member of this tribe. **2.** The Salish language of the Suquamish.

sur- pref. **1.** Over, beyond, or above: *surpass.* **2.** Additional: *surtax.* [< Lat. *super,* over.]

sur·cease (sûr′sēs′, sər-sēs′) n. *Archaic.* Cessation; end.

sur·charge (sûr′chärj′) n. **1.** An additional sum added to the usual amount or cost. **2.** A new value or denomination overprinted on a stamp. —v. **1.** To charge an additional amount. **2.** To overcharge. **3.** To print a surcharge on.

sur·cin·gle (sûr′sĭng′gəl) n. A girth that binds a saddle, pack, or blanket to the body of a horse. [< OFr. *surcengle.*]

sure (shŏŏr) *adj.* **sur·er, sur·est.** **1.** Incapable of being doubted; certain. **2.** Steady; firm: *a sure grip.* **3.** Confident: *sure of victory.* **4. a.** Bound to happen; inevitable. **b.** Destined; bound. **5.** Reliable: *a sure friend.* **—idioms. for sure.** Certainly; without a doubt. **to be sure.** Certainly; indeed. [< Lat. *securus,* safe.] **—sure′ness** *n.*

sure-fire (shŏŏr′fīr′) *adj. Informal.* Bound to be successful.

sure-footed (shŏŏr′fŏŏt′ĭd) *adj.* Not liable to stumble.

sure·ly (shŏŏr′lē) *adv.* **1.** Certainly; without doubt. **2.** With confidence or assurance.

sure·ty (shŏŏr′ĭ-tē) *n., pl.* **-ties.** **1.** The condition of being sure. **2.** Something beyond doubt; certainty. **3.** A guarantee or security. **4.** One who has contracted to be responsible for another.

surf (sûrf) *n.* The offshore waters or waves between the shoreline and the outermost boundaries of the breakers. *—v.* To engage in surfing. [Orig. unknown.] **—surf′er** *n.*

sur·face (sûr′fĭs) *n.* **1.** The outer or topmost boundary of an object. **2.** A superficial or outward appearance. *—adj.* **1.** Of or on a surface. **2.** Superficial. *—v.* **-faced, -fac·ing.** **1.** To form the surface of. **2.** To rise or come to the surface. [Fr.]

surf·board (sûrf′bôrd′, -bōrd′) *n.* A narrow, somewhat rounded board used for surfing.

sur·feit (sûr′fĭt) *v.* To feed or supply to excess; satiate. *—n.* **1.** Overindulgence in food or drink. **2.** The disgust caused by such overindulgence. **3.** An excessive amount. [< OFr. *surfaire,* to overdo.]

surf·ing (sûr′fĭng) *n.* The sport of riding the crests of waves into shore, esp. on a surfboard.

surge (sûrj) *v.* **surged, surg·ing.** **1.** To move in a billowing or swelling manner. **2.** To increase suddenly. *—n.* **1.** A billowing or swelling motion like that of great waves. **2.** A sudden onrush: *a surge of joy.* [< Lat. *surgere,* to rise.]

sur·geon (sûr′jən) *n.* A physician specializing in surgery.

sur·gery (sûr′jə-rē) *n., pl.* **-ies.** **1.** The medical diagnosis and treatment of injury, deformity, and disease by the cutting and removal or repair of bodily parts. **2.** A surgical operating room or laboratory. **3.** The skill or work of a surgeon. [< Gk. *kheirurgos,* working by hand.] **—sur′gi·cal** *adj.* **—sur′gi·cal·ly** *adv.*

sur·ly (sûr′lē) *adj.* **-li·er, -li·est.** Sullenly rude and bad-tempered; gruff. [Obs. *sirly,* masterful < SIR.] **—sur′li·ness** *n.*

sur·mise (sər-mīz′) *v.* **-mised, -mis·ing.** To infer with little evidence; guess. *—n.* An idea or opinion based upon little evidence; conjecture. [< Lat. *supermittere,* to throw on.]

sur·mount (sər-mount′) *v.* **1.** To overcome; conquer. **2.** To ascend and cross to the other side of. **3.** To be above or on top of. **—sur·mount′a·ble** *adj.*

sur·name (sûr′nām′) *n.* One's last or family name as distinguished from a given name.

sur·pass (sər-păs′) *v.* **1.** To go beyond the limit of; transcend. **2.** To be or go beyond; exceed.

Syns: *surpass, exceed, excel, outdo, outshine, outstrip, pass, top, transcend v.*

sur·pass·ing (sər-păs′ĭng) *adj.* Exceptional; superlative. **—sur·pass′ing·ly** *adv.*

sur·plice (sûr′plĭs) *n.* A loose-fitting white gown worn over a cassock by some clergymen. [< Med. Lat. *superpellicium.*]

sur·plus (sûr′pləs) *n.* An amount or quantity in excess of what is needed. *—adj.* Being a surplus. [< Med. Lat. *superplus.*]

sur·prise (sər-prīz′) *v.* **-prised, -pris·ing.** **1.** To encounter suddenly or unexpectedly. **2.** To attack or capture suddenly and without warning. **3.** To astonish by the unexpected. *—n.* **1.** The act of surprising. **2.** A feeling of amazement or wonder. **3.** Something that surprises. [< OFr. *surprendre,* to overcome.] **—sur·pris′er** *n.* **—sur·pris′ing** *adj.* **—sur·pris′ing·ly** *adv.*

sur·re·al·ism (sə-rē′ə-lĭz′əm) *n.* A 20th-cent. literary and artistic movement that attempts to express the workings of the subconscious by fantastic imagery and incongruous juxtaposition of subject matter. **—sur·re′al** or **sur·re′al·is′tic** *adj.* **—sur·re′al·ist** *n.* **—sur·re′al·is′ti·cal·ly** *adv.*

sur·ren·der (sə-rĕn′dər) *v.* **1.** To relinquish possession or control of to another because of demand or force. **2.** To give (oneself) up, as to an emotion: *surrendered himself to grief.* **3.** To give oneself up to another. *—n.* The act of surrendering. [< OFr. *surrendre.*]

sur·rep·ti·tious (sûr′əp-tĭsh′əs) *adj.* Secret and stealthy. [< Lat. *surripere,* to take away secretly.] **—sur·rep·ti′tious·ly** *adv.* **—sur·rep·ti′tious·ness** *n.*

sur·rey (sûr′ē, sŭr′ē) *n., pl.* **-reys.** A horse-drawn four-wheeled vehicle having two seats. [< *Surrey,* England.]

sur·ro·gate (sûr′ə-gĭt, -gāt′, sûr′-) *n.* **1.** A substitute. **2.** A judge in some U.S. states having jurisdiction over the settlement of estates. [< Lat. *surrogare,* to substitute.]

sur·round (sə-round′) *v.* **1.** To extend on all sides of simultaneously; encircle. **2.** To enclose or confine on all sides. [< LLat. *superundare,* to inundate.]

Syns: *surround, circle, compass, encircle, enclose, gird, ring v.*

sur·round·ings (sə-roun′dĭngz) *pl.n.* The external circumstances of something.

sur·tax (sûr′tăks′) *n.* **1.** An additional tax. **2.** A graduated income tax added to the normal income tax.

sur·veil·lance (sər-vā′ləns) *n.* Close observation of a person or group, esp. of one under suspicion. [< Fr. *surveiller,* to watch over.]

sur·vey (sər-vā′, sûr′vā′) *v.* **1.** To examine or look over comprehensively. **2.** To determine the boundaries, area, or elevations of part of the earth's surface by means of measuring angles and distances. *—n.* (sûr′vā′). **1.** A detailed inspection or investigation. **2.** A comprehensive view. **3. a.** The process of surveying land. **b.** A plan or map of surveyed land. [< Med. Lat. *supervidēre,* to look over.] **—sur·vey′or** *n.*

sur·vey·ing (sər-vā′ĭng) *n.* The measurement of dimensional relationships, as of horizontal distances, elevations, directions, and angles, on the earth's surface.

---

sur·vive (sər-vīv′) v. **-vived, -viv·ing.** 1. To remain alive or in existence; endure. 2. To live longer than; outlive. [< LLat. *supervivere*.] **—sur·viv′al** n. **—sur·vi′vor** n.

sus·cep·ti·ble (sə-sĕp′tə-bəl) adj. 1. Easily influenced or affected. 2. Liable; subject: *susceptible to colds.* 3. Capable of accepting or permitting: *susceptible of proof.* [< Lat. *susceptus*, p.p. of *suscipere*, to receive.] **—sus·cep′ti·bil′i·ty** n. **—sus·cep′ti·bly** adv.

sus·pect (sə-spĕkt′) v. 1. To regard as probable; surmise. 2. To distrust or doubt: *suspected their motives.* 3. To think guilty without proof. —n. (sŭs′pĕkt′). One who is suspected, esp. of having committed a crime. —adj. (sŭs′pĕkt′). Open to or viewed with suspicion. [< Lat. *suscipere*, to watch.]

sus·pend (sə-spĕnd′) v. 1. To bar for a period from a privilege, office, or position. 2. To cause to stop for a period; interrupt. 3. a. To hold in abeyance; defer: *suspend judgment.* b. To render ineffective temporarily: *suspend parking regulations.* 4. To hang so as to allow free movement. 5. To support or keep from falling without apparent attachment. [< Lat. *suspendere*, to hang up.]

sus·pend·ers (sə-spĕn′dərz) pl.n. A pair of straps worn over the shoulders to support trousers or a skirt.

sus·pense (sə-spĕns′) n. 1. The condition or quality of being undecided. 2. Anxiety or apprehension resulting from uncertainty. [< Lat. *suspensus*, p.p. of *suspendere*, to hang up.] **—sus·pense′ful** adj.

sus·pen·sion (sə-spĕn′shən) n. 1. The act of suspending or condition of being suspended, esp.: a. A temporary deferment. b. A postponement of judgment or decision. 2. A device from which a mechanical part is suspended. 3. The system of springs and other devices that insulates the chassis of a vehicle from shocks. 4. *Chem.* A relatively coarse, noncolloidal dispersion of solid particles in a liquid.

suspension bridge n. A bridge having the roadway suspended from cables that are usu. supported by towers.

suspension bridge
The Golden Gate Bridge

sus·pi·cion (sə-spĭsh′ən) n. 1. The act of suspecting the existence of something, esp. of something wrong, with little evidence or proof. 2. A faint trace; hint. [< Lat. *suspicere*, to watch.]

sus·pi·cious (sə-spĭsh′əs) adj. 1. Arousing or apt to arouse suspicion. 2. Tending to suspect; distrustful. 3. Expressing suspicion. **—sus·pi′cious·ly** adv.

sus·tain (sə-stān′) v. 1. To keep in existence or effect; maintain. 2. To supply with neces-

sities or nourishment. 3. To keep from falling or sinking. 4. To support the spirits or resolution. 5. To endure or withstand: *sustain hardships.* 6. To experience or suffer (loss or injury). 7. To affirm the validity or justice of: *sustain an objection.* 8. To prove or corroborate; confirm. [< Lat. *sustinēre*, to hold up.] **—sus·tain′a·ble** adj.

sus·te·nance (sŭs′tə-nəns) n. 1. The act of sustaining or condition of being sustained. 2. Something that sustains life or health, esp. food. 3. Means of livelihood. [< OFr. *sustenir*, to sustain.]

su·ture (sōō′chər) n. 1. a. The act of joining together by or as if by sewing. b. The material used in this procedure. 2. A seamless joint or line of junction, as between two bones of the skull. —v. **-tured, -tur·ing.** To join by means of sutures. [< Lat. *sutura*.]

su·ze·rain (sōō′zər-ən, -zə-rān′) n. 1. A feudal lord. 2. A nation that controls another nation in international affairs but allows it domestic sovereignty. [Fr.] **—su′ze·rain·ty** n.

svelte (sfĕlt) adj. **svelt·er, svelt·est.** Slender; lithe; willowy. [< Ital. *svelto*.]

swab (swŏb) n. 1. Absorbent material attached to the end of a stick or wire and used for cleansing or applying medicine. 2. A mop for cleaning decks. 3. *Slang.* A sailor. —v. **swabbed, swab·bing.** To clean or treat with a swab. [Prob. < MDu. *swabbe*, mop.]

swad·dle (swŏd′l) v. **-dled, -dling.** 1. To wrap or bind closely; swathe. 2. To wrap (a baby) in strips of linen or other cloth. [< OE *swæthel*, clothes for swaddling an infant.]

swag (swăg) n. *Slang.* Stolen property; loot. [Prob. < Scand. orig.]

swage (swāj) n. A tool used in bending or shaping cold metal. [< OFr. *souage*, ornamental border.] **—swage** v.

swag·ger (swăg′ər) v. 1. To walk or behave with an insolent air; strut. 2. To brag; bluster. [Prob. < Scand. orig.] **—swag′ger** n. **—swag′ger·er** n.

swagger stick n. A short cane carried esp. by military officers.

Swa·hi·li (swä-hē′lē) n., pl. **-li** or **-lis.** 1. A Bantu language of eastern and central Africa, widely used as a lingua franca. 2. A member of a Bantu people of Zanzibar and the neighboring coastal mainland.

swain (swān) n. 1. A country youth, esp. a young shepherd. 2. A lover. [< ON *sveinn*, boy.]

swal·low¹ (swŏl′ō) v. 1. To cause to pass through the mouth and throat into the stomach. 2. To consume or devour. 3. To bear humbly; tolerate: *swallow an insult.* 4. *Slang.* To believe without question. 5. To take back; retract: *swallow one's words.* —n. 1. The act of swallowing. 2. The amount swallowed at one time. [< OE *swelgan.*] **—swal′low·er** n.

swal·low² (swŏl′ō) n. Any of various birds with long, pointed wings and a usu. notched or forked tail. [< OE *swealewe.*]

swal·low·tail (swŏl′ō-tāl′) n. 1. A deeply forked tail, as of a swallow. 2. Any of various butterflies with a taillike extension at the end of each hind wing.

swam (swăm) v. *p.t.* of **swim.**

swa·mi (swä′mē) n., pl. **-mis.** A Hindu mystic or religious teacher; yogi. [< Skt. *svāmin*, master.]

swamp (swŏmp, swômp) n. A lowland region saturated with water; marsh. —v. 1. To drench in or cover with liquid. **2.** To overwhelm. **3.** To fill or sink (a ship) with water. [Perh. of LG orig.] —**swamp'i·ness** n. —**swamp'y** adj.

swan (swŏn) n. A large aquatic bird with webbed feet, a long slender neck, and usu. white plumage. [< OE.]

swank (swăngk) adj. **-er, -est.** Also **swank·y** (swăng'kē), **-i·er, -i·est. 1.** Imposingly fashionable or elegant. **2.** Ostentatious. [Perh. < MHG swanken, to swing.] —**swank'i·ly** adv. —**swank'i·ness** n.

swan's-down (swŏnz'doun') n. Also **swans·down. 1.** The soft down of a swan. **2.** A soft woolen or cotton fabric.

swan song n. A farewell appearance, declaration, or action.

swap (swŏp) Informal. —v. **swapped, swap·ping.** To exchange one thing for another. —n. An exchange; trade. [ME swappen, to hit < the practice of striking hands in closing a bargain.] —**swap'per** n.

sward (swôrd) n. Land covered with grassy turf. [< OE sweard, skin.]

swarm (swôrm) n. **1.** A large number of insects or other small organisms, esp. when in motion. **2.** A large group of persons or animals. —v. **1. a.** To move in a swarm. **b.** To leave a beehive to form a new colony. **2.** To move in a mass; throng. **3.** To be overrun; teem: a river bank swarming with insects. [< OE swearm.]

swar·thy (swôr'thē) adj. **-thi·er, -thi·est.** Having a dark or sunburned complexion. [< OE sweart.] —**swar'thi·ness** n.

swash (swŏsh, swôsh) v. To move or wash with a splashing sound. [Prob. imit.] —**swash** n.

swash·buck·ler (swŏsh'bŭk'lər, swôsh'-) n. A flamboyant or boastful soldier or adventurer. —**swash'buck'ling** adj. & n.

swas·ti·ka (swŏs'ti·kə) n. **1.** An ancient cosmic or religious symbol, formed by a Greek cross with the ends of the arms bent at right angles. **2.** The emblem of Nazi Germany. [Skt. svastikah, a sign of good luck.]

swat (swŏt) v. **swat·ted, swat·ting.** To deal a sharp blow to. [< SQUAT, to squash (obs.).] —**swat** n. —**swat'ter** n.

swatch (swŏch) n. A sample strip cut from a piece of material. [Orig. unknown.]

swath (swŏth, swôth) n. **1.** The width of a scythe stroke or a mowing-machine blade. **2.** A path made in mowing. **3.** A long strip or width. [< OE swæth, track.]

swathe (swŏth, swôth) v. **swathed, swath·ing.** To wrap or bind with or as with bandages. [< OE swathian.]

sway (swā) v. **1.** To move or cause to move back and forth with a swinging motion. **2.** To lean or bend to one side. **3.** To vacillate. **4.** To exert influence on or control over. —n. **1.** The act of swaying. **2.** Power; dominion. **3.** Influence. [< ME sweyen.]

sway·back (swā'băk') n. An excessive inward or downward curvature of the spine. —**sway'backed'** adj.

swear (swâr) v. **swore** (swôr, swōr), **sworn** (swôrn, swōrn), **swear·ing. 1.** To make a solemn declaration. **2.** To promise; vow. **3.** To use profane language; curse. **4.** To assert un-

der oath. **5.** To administer a legal oath to. **6.** To affirm with great conviction. —**phrasal verbs. swear in.** To administer an oath of office to. **swear off.** To renounce; give up. [< OE swerian.]

sweat (swĕt) v. **sweat·ed** or **sweat, sweat·ing. 1.** To excrete perspiration through the pores in the skin; perspire. **2.** To exude in or become moist with surface droplets. **3.** To collect moisture from the air. **4.** Informal. To work or cause to work long and hard. **5.** Informal. To fret or worry. —**phrasal verb. sweat out.** Slang. To await or endure anxiously. —n. **1.** The product of the sweat glands of the skin. **2.** Any condensation of moisture in the form of droplets on a surface. **3.** The process of sweating or the condition of being sweated. **4.** Informal. An anxious, fretful condition. [< OE swĕtan.] —**sweat'i·ly** adv. —**sweat'i·ness** n. —**sweat'y** adj.

sweat·er (swĕt'ər) n. A knitted or crocheted garment worn on the upper body.

sweat gland n. Any of the numerous small, tubular glands in the skin that excrete perspiration externally through pores.

sweat shirt n. A usu. long-sleeved heavy cotton-jersey pullover.

sweat·shop (swĕt'shŏp') n. A shop or factory where employees work long hours under poor conditions for low wages.

Swede (swēd) n. A native or inhabitant of Sweden. **2.** A person of Swedish descent.

Swed·ish (swē'dish) adj. Of or pertaining to Sweden or to the Swedes or their culture or language. —n. The Germanic language of Sweden.

sweep (swēp) v. **swept** (swĕpt), **sweep·ing. 1.** To clean or clear with or as with a broom. **2.** To touch or brush lightly. **3.** To move, remove, or clear, as by wind or rain. **4.** To traverse with speed or intensity; range throughout: Plague swept Europe. **5. a.** To win all the stages of (a game or contest). **b.** To win overwhelmingly. **6.** To extend gracefully or majestically. —n. **1.** The act or motion of sweeping. **2.** The range or scope encompassed by sweeping. **3.** A reach or extent. **4.** A surging or flowing movement or force. **5.** A curve or contour. **6.** A chimney sweep. **7. a.** The winning of all stages of a game or contest. **b.** A total victory or success. [ME swepen.] —**sweep'er** n.

sweep·ing (swē'pĭng) adj. **1.** Extending over a great area; wide-ranging. **2.** Curving. —n. Often **sweepings.** That which is swept up; debris; litter. —**sweep'ing·ly** adv.

sweep·stakes (swēp'stāks') n., pl. **-stakes.** Also **sweep·stake** (-stāk'). **1.** A lottery in which the participants' contributions form a fund to be awarded as a prize to the winner or winners. **2.** An event or contest, esp. a horse race, whose result determines the winner of such a lottery.

sweet (swēt) adj. **-er, -est. 1.** Having a sugary or pleasing taste. **2.** Pleasing to the senses, feelings, or mind. **3.** Having an agreeable disposition. **4.** Not salty or salted: sweet butter. **5.** Not spoiled, sour, or decaying. —n. **1.** Something that is sweet or contains sugar. **2.** Often **sweets.** Candy. **3.** A dear or beloved

person. [< OE *swēte*.] —**sweet'ly** *adv.*
—**sweet'ness** *n.*

sweet-bread (swēt'brĕd') *n.* The thymus or
pancreas of an animal, used for food.

sweet-bri-er (swēt'brī'ər) *n.* Also **sweet-bri-ar.**
A rose with prickly stems, fragrant leaves,
and pink flowers.

sweet corn *n.* The common edible variety of
corn, with kernels that are sweet when young.

sweet-en (swēt'n) *v.* 1. To make sweet or
sweeter. 2. To make more valuable or attractive. —**sweet'en-er** *n.*

sweet-en-ing (swēt'n-ing) *n.* 1. The act or
process of making sweet. 2. Something used
to sweeten.

sweet-heart (swēt'härt') *n.* 1. One who is
loved by another. 2. A lovable person.

sweet-meat (swēt'mēt') *n.* 1. Candy. 2. Crys-
tallized fruit.

sweet pea *n.* A climbing plant cultivated for
its variously colored, fragrant flowers.

sweet pea   **sweet William**

sweet potato *n.* 1. A tropical American vine
cultivated for its thick, orange-colored, edible
root. 2. The root of this plant, eaten cooked
as a vegetable.

sweet-talk (swēt'tôk') *v.* To coax or cajole
with flattery. —**sweet talk** *n.*

sweet tooth *n. Informal.* A fondness or craving for sweets.

sweet Wil-liam (wĭl'yəm) *n.* A widely cultivated plant with flat, dense clusters of varicolored flowers.

swell (swĕl) *v.* **swelled, swelled** or **swol-len**
(swō'lən), **swell-ing.** 1. To increase in size or
volume. 2. To increase in number, or
intensity. 3. To bulge out; protrude. 4. To fill
or become filled with an emotion: *swelled
with pride.* —*n.* 1. A swollen part. 2. A long
wave that moves continuously without breaking. 3. *Informal.* **a.** A fashionably dressed
person. **b.** A person prominent in fashionable
society. —*adj.* **-er, -est.** 1. *Informal.* Fashionably elegant; smart; stylish. 2. *Slang.* Fine;
excellent. [< OE *swellan.*]

swell-ing (swĕl'ĭng) *n.* 1. The act of expanding. 2. Something that is swollen.

swel-ter (swĕl'tər) *v.* To suffer oppressively
from heat. [< OE *sweltan,* to die.]

swept (swĕpt) *v. p.t. & p.p.* of **sweep.**

swerve (swûrv) *v.* **swerved, swerv-ing.** To
turn aside from a straight course; veer. [<
OE *sweorfan,* to rub.] —**swerve** *n.*

swift (swĭft) *adj.* **-er, -est.** 1. Moving or able
to move with great speed. 2. Occurring or
accomplished quickly. —*n.* Any of various
dark-colored birds with long, narrow wings
and a relatively short tail. [< OE.] —**swift'ly**
adv. —**swift'ness** *n.*

swig (swĭg) *Informal.* —*n.* A large swallow or
draft, as of a liquid; a gulp. —*v.* **swigged,
swig-ging.** To drink with great gulps. [Orig.
unknown.] —**swig'ger** *n.*

swill (swĭl) *v.* 1. To drink greedily or to ex-

cess. 2. To feed (animals) with slop. —*n.*
1. A mixture of liquid and solid food fed to
animals. 2. Garbage; refuse. [< OE *swilian,*
to wash out.]

swim (swĭm) *v.* **swam** (swăm), **swum** (swŭm),
swim-ming. 1. To propel oneself through water by bodily movements. 2. To move as
though gliding through water. 3. To be immersed in or as if in liquid. 4. To have a
dizzy feeling; reel. 5. To cross by swimming.
—*n.* The act or a period of swimming.
—*idiom.* **in the swim.** *Informal.* Participating
in what is current or fashionable. [< OE
swimman.] —**swim'mer** *n.*

swim-ming-ly (swĭm'ĭng-lē) *adv.* Splendidly.

swin-dle (swĭn'dl) *v.* **-dled, -dling.** To cheat or
defraud of money or property. —*n.* The act
or an instance of swindling; fraud. [< G.
schwindeln, to be dizzy.] —**swin'dler** *n.*

swine (swīn) *n., pl.* **swine.** 1. Any of the
hoofed mammals of the family that includes
pigs, hogs, and boars. 2. A contemptible, vicious, or greedy person. [< OE *swīn.*]

swing (swĭng) *v.* **swung** (swŭng), **swing-ing.**
1. To move or cause to move backward and
forward. 2. To walk or move with a swaying
motion. 3. To move in a broad area. 4. To
turn in place, as on a pivot. 5. To hang
freely. 6. To be executed by hanging. 7. To
manage successfully. 8. To have a compelling
or infectious rhythm. 9. To be lively, active,
and up-to-date. —*n.* 1. The act of swinging.
2. The distance traveled while swinging. 3. A
seat suspended from above, on which one
may swing back and forth for amusement.
4. Music based on jazz but usu. employing a
larger band and simpler harmonic and rhythmic patterns. [< OE *swingan,* to flog.]

swipe (swīp) *n.* A heavy, sweeping blow. —*v.*
swiped, swip-ing. 1. To hit with or make a
sweeping blow. 2. *Slang.* To steal; filch.
[Perh. < SWEEP.]

swirl (swûrl) *v.* To rotate or spin in or as if in
a whirlpool or eddy. [ME *swyrl,* eddy.]
—**swirl** *n.* —**swirl'y** *adj.*

swish (swĭsh) *v.* 1. To move with a hissing
sound. 2. To rustle. [Imit.] —**swish** *n.*

Swiss (swĭs) *n., pl.* **Swiss.** A native or inhabitant of Switzerland. —**Swiss** *adj.*

Swiss chard *n.* Chard.

Swiss cheese *n.* A firm white or pale-yellow
cheese with many large holes.

switch (swĭch) *n.* 1. A slender flexible rod,
stick, or twig. 2. A blow given with a switch.
3. A device used to break or open an electrical circuit. 4. A device used to transfer rolling stock from one track to another. 5. A
change or shift from one thing to another.
—*v.* 1. To whip or lash with or as if with a
switch. 2. To transfer, turn, or divert. 3. To
exchange; change. 4. To connect or disconnect by operating a switch. [Perh. < MDu.
swijch, twig.] —**switch'er** *n.*

switch-blade knife (swĭch'blăd') *n.* A pocket
knife with a spring-operated blade.

switch-board (swĭch'bôrd', -bôrd') *n.* A panel
with apparatus for operating electric circuits.

switch hitter *n. Baseball.* A batter who can
hit both right-handed and left-handed.

switch-man (swĭch'mən) *n.* One who operates
a railroad switch.

swiv-el (swĭv'əl) *n.* A link, pivot, or other
fastening that permits free turning of attached
parts. —*v.* **-eled** or **-elled, -el-ing** or **-el-ling.**

To turn or rotate on or as on a swivel. [ME *swyvel*.]

swiz·zle stick (swĭz′əl) *n.* A stick for stirring drinks. [Orig. unknown.]

swol·len (swō′lən) *v.* A *p.p.* of **swell.** —*adj.* Distended; bulging.

swoon (swōōn) *v.* To faint. [Prob. < OE *swōgan,* to suffocate.] —**swoon** *n.*

swoop (swōōp) *v.* To make a sudden sweeping movement, as a bird descending upon its prey. [< OE *swapan,* to sweep.] —**swoop** *n.*

sword (sôrd) *n.* 1. A weapon having a long blade for cutting or thrusting. 2. A symbol of power or authority. 3. The use of force, as in war. [< OE *sweord.*]

sword·fish (sôrd′fĭsh′) *n.* A large marine game and food fish with a long, swordlike extension of the upper jaw.

sword·play (sôrd′plā′) *n.* The action or art of using a sword.

swords·man (sôrdz′mən) *n.* One armed with or skilled in the use of the sword. —**swords′-man·ship′** *n.*

swore (swôr, swōr) *v. p.t.* of **swear.**

sworn (swôrn, swōrn) *v. p.t.* of **swear.**

swum (swŭm) *v. p.p.* of **swim.**

swung (swŭng) *v. p.t. & p.p.* of **swing.**

syb·a·rite (sĭb′ər-īt′) *n.* A person totally devoted to pleasure and luxury. [< *Sybaris,* an ancient Greek city in Italy.] —**syb′a·rit′ic** (-ə-rĭt′ĭk) *adj.*

syc·a·more (sĭk′ə-môr′, -mōr′) *n.* 1. A North American deciduous tree with lobed leaves and ball-like seed clusters. 2. An Old World tree related to the maples. [< Gk. *sukamoros,* a kind of fig tree.]

syc·o·phant (sĭk′ə-fənt, -fănt′) *n.* A servile flatterer of important persons. [< Gk. *sukophantēs,* informer.] —**syc′o·phan·cy** *n.* —**syc′o·phan′tic** (-făn′tĭk) *adj.*

sy·li (sĭl′ē) *n.* See **table** at **currency.** [Native word in Guinea.]

syl·lab·i·cate (sĭ-lăb′ĭ-kāt′) *v.* -**cat·ed,** -**cat·ing.** To form or divide into syllables. —**syl·lab′i·ca′tion** *n.*

syl·lab·i·fy (sĭ-lăb′ə-fī′) *v.* -**fied,** -**fy·ing.** To syllabicate. —**syl·lab′i·fi·ca′tion** *n.*

syl·la·ble (sĭl′ə-bəl) *n.* 1. A unit of spoken language consisting of a single uninterrupted sound forming a whole word, such as *now,* or part of a word, such as *per-* in *person.* 2. One or more letters or phonetic symbols representing a spoken syllable. [< Gk. *sullabē.*] —**syl·lab′ic** *adj.*

syl·la·bus (sĭl′ə-bəs) *n., pl.* -**es** or -**bi** (-bī′). An outline or brief statement of the main points of a text, lecture, or course of study. [Prob. alt. < Gk. *sittuba,* title slip.]

syl·lo·gism (sĭl′ə-jĭz′əm) *n.* A formal argument consisting of a major premise and a minor premise leading to a conclusion. [< Gk. *sullogismos.*] —**syl′lo·gis′tic** *adj.* —**syl′lo·gis′ti·cal·ly** *adv.*

sylph (sĭlf) *n.* 1. An imaginary being believed to inhabit the air. 2. A slim, graceful woman. [NLat. *sylphus.*]

syl·van (sĭl′vən) *adj.* 1. Of, relating to, or characteristic of woods or forest regions. 2. Abounding in trees; wooded. [< Lat. *silva,* forest.]

sym·bi·o·sis (sĭm′bē-ō′sĭs, -bĭ-) *n. Biol.* The relationship or living together of two or more different organisms in a close association, esp. when mutually beneficial. [Gk. *sumbiōsis,* companionship.] —**sym′bi·ot′ic** (-ŏt′ĭk) *adj.* —**sym′bi·ot′i·cal·ly** *adv.*

sym·bol (sĭm′bəl) *n.* 1. Something that represents something else by association, resemblance, or convention. 2. A printed or written sign used to represent an operation, element, quantity, quality, or relation, as in mathematics or music. [< Gk. *sumbolon,* token for identification.] —**sym·bol′ic** (-bŏl′ĭk) *adj.* —**sym·bol′i·cal·ly** *adv.*

sym·bol·ism (sĭm′bə-lĭz′əm) *n.* The representation of things by means of symbols.

sym·bol·ize (sĭm′bə-līz′) *v.* -**ized,** -**iz·ing.** 1. To be or serve as a symbol of. 2. To represent by a symbol. —**sym′bol·i·za′tion** *n.*

sym·me·try (sĭm′ĭ-trē) *n., pl.* -**tries.** 1. Correspondence of form and arrangement of parts on opposite sides of a boundary, such as a plane or line, or around a point or axis. 2. An arrangement with balanced or harmonious proportions. [< Gk. *summetros,* of like measure.] —**sym·met′ric** (sĭ-mĕt′rĭk) or **sym·met′ri·cal** *adj.*

sym·pa·thet·ic (sĭm′pə-thĕt′ĭk) *adj.* 1. Of, expressing, feeling, or resulting from sympathy. 2. In agreement; favorable. —**sym′pa·thet′i·cal·ly** *adv.*

sympathetic nervous system *n.* The part of the autonomic nervous system whose stimulation increases the blood pressure, heart rate, and respiration rate, and, in general, prepares an organism for vigorous activity, as in response to danger.

sym·pa·thize (sĭm′pə-thīz′) *v.* -**thized,** -**thiz·ing.** 1. To feel or express compassion; commiserate. 2. To share or understand another's feelings. —**sym′pa·thiz′er** *n.*

sym·pa·thy (sĭm′pə-thē) *n., pl.* -**thies.** 1. a. A relationship between persons or things in which whatever affects one correspondingly affects the other. b. Mutual understanding or affection. 2. A feeling or expression of pity or sorrow for the distress of another; compassion. 3. Favor; agreement; approval. [< Gk. *sumpatheia.*]

sym·phon·ic (sĭm-fŏn′ĭk) *adj.* 1. Of or having the character or form of a symphony. 2. Harmonious in sound.

sym·pho·ny (sĭm′fə-nē) *n., pl.* -**nies.** 1. A usu. long orchestral composition. 2. A symphony orchestra. 3. Harmony, esp. of sound. [< Gk. *sumphōnia,* harmony.]

symphony orchestra *n.* A large orchestra of string, wind, and percussion sections.

sym·po·si·um (sĭm-pō′zē-əm) *n., pl.* -**ums** or -**si·a** (-zē-ə). 1. A conference for discussion of a particular topic. 2. A collection of writings on a particular topic. [< Gk. *sumposion,* drinking party.]

symp·tom (sĭmp′təm) *n.* 1. A change in normal bodily function, sensation, or appearance, indicating disorder or disease. 2. An indication; sign. [< Gk. *sumptōma.*] —**symp′to·mat′ic** *adj.* —**symp′to·mat′i·cal·ly** *adv.*

syn·a·gogue (sĭn′ə-gŏg′) *n.* 1. A building or place of meeting for Jewish worship and religious instruction. 2. A congregation of Jews. [< Gk. *sunagōgē,* assembly.]

ă pat ā pay â care ä father ĕ pet ē be ĭ pit ī tie î pier ŏ pot ō toe ô paw, for oi noise ōō took ōō boot ou out th thin th this ŭ cut û urge yōō abuse zh vision ə about, item, edible, gallop, circus

SYMBOLS AND SIGNS

+	plus	$\llcorner$	right angle
−	minus	$\triangle$	triangle
±	plus or minus	$\square$	square
∓	minus or plus	$\sqsubset$	rectangle
×	multiplied by	$\square$	parallelogram
÷	divided by	O	circle
=	equal to	$\frown$	arc of circle
≠ or ≢	not equal to	$\perp$	equilateral
≈ or ≑	nearly equal to	$\triangleq$	equiangular
≡	identical with	√	radical; root; square root
≢	not identical with	$\sqrt[3]{}$	cube root
⇔	equivalent	$\sqrt[4]{}$	fourth root
∼	difference	Σ	sum
≅	congruent to	! or ∟	factorial product
>	greater than	∞	infinity
≯	not greater than	∫	integral
<	less than	ƒ	function
≮	not less than	∂ or δ	differential; variation
≧ or ≥	greater than or equal to	π	pi
≦ or ≤	less than or equal to	∴	therefore
		∵	because
| |	absolute value	‾	vinculum (above letter)
∪	logical sum or union	( )	parentheses
∩	logical product or intersection	[ ]	brackets
⊂	is contained in	{}	braces
ε	is a member of; permittivity; mean error	°	degree
:	is to; ratio	′	minute
::	as; proportion	″	second
≐	approaches	$\triangle$	increment
→	approaches limit of	ω	angular frequency; solid angle
∝	varies as	Ω	ohm
||	parallel	μΩ	microhm
⊥	perpendicular	MΩ	megohm
∠	angle	Φ	magnetic flux

SYMBOLS AND SIGNS

Ψ dielectric flux; electrostatic flux

ρ resistivity

Λ equivalent conductivity

ℛ reluctance

→ direction of flow

⇌ electric current

◯ benzene ring

→ yields

⇌ reversible reaction

↓ precipitate

↑ gas

‰ salinity

☉ or ⛢ sun

● or ● new moon

☽ first quarter

○ or ⊗ full moon

☾ last quarter

☿ Mercury

♀ Venus

⊖ or ⊕ Earth

♂ Mars

♃ Jupiter

♄ Saturn

♅ Uranus

♆ Neptune

♇ Pluto

♈ Aries

♉ Taurus

♊ Gemini

♋ Cancer

♌ Leo

♍ Virgo

♎ Libra

♏ Scorpius

♐ Sagittarius

♑ Capricornus

♒ Aquarius

♓ Pisces

☌ conjunction

☍ opposition

△ trine

□ quadrature

∗ sextile

☊ dragon's head, ascending node

☋ dragon's tail, descending node

● rain

∗ snow

⊠ snow on ground

← floating ice crystals

▲ hail

△ sleet

∨ frostwork

⊔ hoarfrost

≡ fog

∞ haze; dust haze

⊤ thunder

< sheet lightning

① solar corona

⊕ solar halo

⌐< thunderstorm

\ direction

O or ⊙ or ① annual

OO or ② biennial

♃ perennial

♂ or ♂ male

♀ female

□ male (in charts)

O female (in charts)

℞ take (from Latin *Recipe*)

ĀĀ or Ā or āā of each (doctor's prescription)

℔ pound

ă pat ā pay â care ä father ĕ pet ē be ĭ pit ī tie î pier ŏ pot ō toe ô paw, for oi noise ŏŏ took ŏŏ boot ou out th thin *th* this ŭ cut û urge yŏŏ abuse zh vision ə about, item, edible, gallop, circus

℥	ounce	@	at
ℨ	dram	*	asterisk
℈	scruple	†	dagger
f℥	fluid ounce	‡	double dagger
fℨ	fluid dram	§	section
♏	minim	☞	index
& or &	and; ampersand	´	acute
℔	per	`	grave
#	number	~	tilde
/	virgule; slash; solidus; shilling	^	circumflex
©	copyright	¯	macron
%	per cent	˘	breve
℅	care of	¨	dieresis
℀	account of	¸	cedilla
		∧	caret

---

syn·apse (sĭn'ăps') *n.* The point at which a nerve impulse passes between neurons. [Gk. *sunapsis*, point of contact.]

sync (sĭngk). Also **synch.** *Informal.* —*n.* Synchronization. —*v.* To synchronize.

syn·chro·mesh (sĭn'krō-mĕsh', sĭn'-) *n.* 1. An automotive gear-shifting system in which the gears are synchronized at the same speeds before engaging to effect a smooth change. 2. A gear in such a system. [SYNCHRO(NIZE) + MESH.] —**syn'chro·mesh'** *adj.*

syn·chro·nize (sĭng'krə-nīz', sĭn'-) *v.* **-nized, -niz·ing.** 1. To occur at or cause to occur at the same time. 2. To operate in unison. 3. To cause to agree exactly in time or rate. 4. To arrange or represent so as to indicate parallel existence or occurrence. [< SYNCHRONOUS.] —**syn'chro·ni·za'tion** *n.* —**syn'chro·niz'er** *n.*

syn·chro·nous (sĭng'krə-nəs, sĭn'-) *adj.* 1. Occurring at the same time. 2. Moving or operating at the same rate. [< Gk. *sunkhronos*.] —**syn'chro·nous·ly** *adv.*

syn·co·pate (sĭng'kə-pāt', sĭn'-) *v.* **-pat·ed, -pat·ing.** To modify (rhythm) by syncopation.

syn·co·pa·tion (sĭng'kə-pā'shən, sĭn'-) *n. Mus.* A shift of accent when a normally weak beat is stressed. [< Gk. *sunkoptein*, to cut short.]

syn·di·cate (sĭn'dĭ-kĭt) *n.* 1. An association of people formed to undertake some duty or transact some business. 2. An agency that sells articles for publication in a number of newspapers or periodicals simultaneously. —*v.* (-kāt') **-cat·ed, -cat·ing.** 1. To organize into a syndicate. 2. To publish through a syndicate. [< Gk. *sundikos*, public advocate.]

syn·drome (sĭn'drōm') *n.* A group of symptoms that collectively characterize a disease or disorder. [Gk. *sundromē*, concurrence of symptoms.]

syn·er·gism (sĭn'ər-jĭz'əm) *n.* Also **syn·er·gy** (-ər-jē). The action of two or more substances, organs, or organisms to achieve an effect of which each is individually incapable. [< Gk. *sunergos*, working together.] —**syn'er·gis'tic** *adj.* —**syn'er·gis'ti·cal·ly** *adv.*

syn·od (sĭn'əd) *n.* 1. A council of churches or church officials. 2. A council; assembly. [< Gk. *sunodos*, meeting.] —**syn'od·al** or **sy·nod'i·cal** *adj.*

syn·o·nym (sĭn'ə-nĭm') *n.* A word that has a meaning identical or very similar to that of another word in the same language. [< Gk. *sunōnumon.*] —**syn·on'y·mi·ty** *n.* —**syn·on'y·mous** (sĭ-nŏn'ə-məs) *adj.* —**syn·on'y·mous·ly** *adv.* —**syn·on'y·my** *n.*

syn·op·sis (sĭ-nŏp'sĭs) *n., pl.* **-ses** (-sēz'). A brief statement or outline of a subject; abstract. [< Gk. *sunopsis*, general view.]

syn·tax (sĭn'tăks') *n.* The way in which words are put together to form constructions, such as phrases and sentences. [< Gk. *suntassein*, to combine.] —**syn·tac'tic** (-tăk'tĭk) or **syn·tac'ti·cal** *adj.*

syn·the·sis (sĭn'thĭ-sĭs) *n., pl.* **-ses** (-sēz'). 1. The combining of separate elements or substances to form a coherent whole. 2. The whole so formed. [< Gk. *suntithenai*, to put together.] —**syn'the·size'** *v.*

syn·thet·ic (sĭn-thĕt'ĭk) *adj.* 1. Of, relating to, involving, or produced by synthesis. 2. Not genuine; artificial. [Gk. *sunthetikos*, component.] —**syn·thet'ic** *n.* —**syn·thet'i·cal·ly** *adv.*

syph·i·lis (sĭf'ə-lĭs) *n.* A chronic infectious venereal disease caused by a spirochete, transmitted usu. in sexual intercourse, and progressing through three stages of increasing severity. [< *Syphilis*, protagonist of a 16th-cent. poem.] —**syph'i·lit'ic** *adj.* & *n.*

sy·phon (sī'fən) *n. & v.* Var. of **siphon.**

sy·ringe (sə-rĭnj', sĭr'ĭnj) *n.* 1. A medical instrument used to inject fluids into the body or draw them from it. 2. A hypodermic syringe. [< Gk. *surinx*, shepherd's pipe.]

syr·up (sĭr'əp, sûr'-) *n.* Also **sir·up.** 1. A thick, sweet, sticky liquid consisting of sugar and water. **2.** The concentrated sap of a plant. [< Ar. *sharāb*.] **—syr'up·y** *adj.*

sys·tem (sĭs'təm) *n.* **1.** A group of interacting elements functioning as a complex whole. **2.** The human body as a functional unit. **3.** A network, as for communications. **4.** A method; procedure. **5.** Regular method; orderliness. [< Gk. *sustēma*.] **—sys'tem·at'ic** *adj.* **—sys'tem·at'i·cal·ly** *adv.*

sys·tem·a·tize (sĭs'tə-mə-tīz') *v.* **-tized, -tiz·ing.** To formulate into or reduce to a system. **—sys'tem·a·ti·za'tion** *n.*

sys·tem·ic (sĭ-stĕm'ĭk) *adj.* **1.** Pertaining to a system or systems. **2.** Of, relating to, or affecting the entire body. **—sys·tem'i·cal·ly** *adv.*

sys·tem·ize (sĭs'tə-mīz') *v.* **-ized, -iz·ing.** To systematize.

systems analysis *n.* The study of an activity by mathematical means to determine its desired end and the most efficient means of obtaining this. **—systems analyst** *n.*

sys·to·le (sĭs'tə-lē) *n.* The rhythmic contraction of the heart, esp. of the ventricles. [Gk. *sustolē*, contraction.] **—sys·tol'ic** (sĭ-stŏl'ĭk) *adj.*

Tt

t or **T** (tē) *n., pl.* **t's** or **T's.** **1.** The 20th letter of the English alphabet. **2.** Something shaped like the letter T. **—idiom. to a T.** Perfectly; precisely.

Ta The symbol for the element tantalum.

tab (tăb) *n.* **1.** A projection attached to an object to aid in opening, handling, or identifying it. **2.** *Informal.* A bill or a check. [Orig. unknown.]

tab·by (tăb'ē) *n., pl.* **-bies.** **1.** A black and grayish striped or mottled domestic cat. **2.** A female domestic cat. [< Ar. *'attābī*, watered silk.]

tab·er·na·cle (tăb'ər-năk'əl) *n.* **1.** Often **Tabernacle.** The portable sanctuary in which the Jews carried the ark of the covenant through the desert. **2.** A receptacle on a church altar containing the consecrated elements of the Eucharist. **3.** A large temple. [< Lat. *taberna*, hut.]

ta·ble (tā'bəl) *n.* **1.** An article of furniture having a flat horizontal surface supported by legs. **2.** An orderly display of data, usu. arranged in rows and columns. **3.** An abbreviated list, as of contents; synopsis. **4.** A slab or tablet, as of stone, bearing an inscription or device. **—v. -bled, -bling.** **1.** To put or place on a table. **2.** To postpone consideration of; shelve. [< Lat. *tabula*, board.]

tab·leau (tă'blō', tă-blō') *n., pl.* **-leaux** (-lōz', -blōz') or **-leaus.** **1.** A vivid or graphic description. **2.** A scene presented on stage by costumed actors who remain silent and motionless as if in a picture. [Fr.]

ta·ble·cloth (tā'bəl-klôth', -klŏth') *n.* A cloth to cover a table, esp. during a meal.

ta·ble d'hôte (tä'bəl dōt') *n., pl.* **ta·bles d'hôte** (tä'bəl dōt'). A full-course meal served at a fixed price in a restaurant. [Fr., table of the host.]

ta·ble·land (tā'bəl-lănd') *n.* A plateau.

ta·ble·spoon (tā'bəl-spōōn') *n.* **1.** A large spoon used for serving food. **2.** A household cooking measure equal to three teaspoons or ½ fluid ounce. **—ta·ble·spoon'ful** *n.*

tab·let (tăb'lĭt) *n.* **1.** A slab or plaque, as of stone or ivory, bearing an inscription. **2.** A

pad of writing paper glued together along one edge. **3.** A small flat pellet of oral medication. [< OFr. *table*, table.]

table tennis *n.* A game similar to tennis but played on a table with wooden paddles and a small celluloid ball.

ta·ble·ware (tā'bəl-wâr') *n.* Dishes, glassware, etc., used in setting a table for a meal.

tab·loid (tăb'loid') *n.* A newspaper of small format presenting the news in condensed form, often with sensational material. [TABL(ET) + -OID.]

ta·boo (tə-bōō', tă-). Also **ta·bu.** **—n., pl.** **-boos.** **1.** A prohibition excluding something from use, approach, or mention because of its sacred and inviolable nature. **2.** A ban attached to something by social custom. **—adj.** Excluded or forbidden from use, approach, or mention. **—v.** To place under taboo. [Tongan *tabu*.]

ta·bor (tā'bər) *n.* A small drum used to accompany a fife. [< OFr. *tabur*.]

tab·u·lar (tăb'yə-lər) *adj.* Organized as a table or list. [< Lat. *tabula*, table.] **—tab'u·lar·ly** *adv.*

tab·u·late (tăb'yə-lāt') *v.* **-lat·ed, -lat·ing.** To arrange in a listed and condensed form, as in a table. [< Lat. *tabula*, table.] **—tab'u·la'tion** *n.* **—tab'u·la'tor** *n.*

ta·chom·e·ter (tə-kŏm'ĭ-tər) *n.* An instrument used to measure speed, esp. rotational speed. [Gk. *takhos*, speed + -METER.] **—tach'o·met'ric** (tăk'ə-mĕt'rĭk) *adj.* **—ta·chom'e·try** *n.*

tac·it (tăs'ĭt) *adj.* **1.** Not spoken: *tacit consent.* **2.** Implied by or inferred from actions or statements. [Lat. *tacitus*, p.p. of *tacēre*, to be silent.] **—tac'it·ly** *adv.* **—tac'it·ness** *n.*

tac·i·turn (tăs'ĭ-tûrn') *adj.* Habitually silent or uncommunicative. [< Lat. *taciturnus*.] **—tac'i·tur·ni·ty** (-tûr'nĭ-tē) *n.* **—tac'i·turn'ly** *adv.*

tack (tăk) *n.* **1.** A short, light nail with a sharp point and a flat head. **2.** The position of a vessel relative to the trim of its sails. **3.** A course of action. **4.** A zigzag course. **5.** A loose, temporary stitch. **—v.** **1.** To fasten or attach with a tack. **2.** To append; add:

3. To change the course of a vessel. [< OFr. *tache*, something that attaches.]

tack·le (tăk′əl) *n.* 1. The equipment used in a sport or occupation, esp. in fishing; gear. 2. (*also* tā′kəl). A system of ropes and blocks for raising and lowering weights. 3. *Football.* a. A lineman stationed between the guard and the end. b. The seizing and throwing to the ground of an opposing player. —*v.* **-led, -ling.** 1. To take on; come to grips with: *tackle a problem.* 2. *Football.* To seize and throw (an opposing player) to the ground. [ME *takel.*] —**tack′ler** *n.*

tack·y¹ (tăk′ē) *adj.* **-i·er, -i·est.** Sticky; gummy. [< TACK.] —**tack′i·ness** *n.*

tack·y² (tăk′ē) *adj.* **-i·er, -i·est.** *Informal.* 1. Rundown; shabby. 2. a. Lacking style; dowdy. b. Vulgar; tawdry: *tacky clothes; a tacky remark.* [< *tacky,* an inferior horse.] —**tack′i·ness** *n.*

ta·co (tä′kō) *n., pl.* **-cos.** A tortilla folded around a filling, as of ground meat or cheese. [Mex. Sp. < Sp., roll.]

tac·o·nite (tăk′ə-nīt′) *n.* A fine-grained sedimentary rock mined as a low-grade iron ore. [< *Taconic* Mountains, New York.]

tact (tăkt) *n.* The ability to appreciate a delicate situation and to do or say the most fitting thing; diplomacy. [< Lat. *tactus,* sense of touch.] —**tact′ful** *adj.* —**tact′less** *adj.*

tac·tic (tăk′tĭk) *n.* 1. A device or expedient for achieving a goal. 2. **tactics** (*used with a sing. verb*). The technique or science of gaining objectives. [< Gk. *taktika,* ult. < *tassein,* to arrange.] —**tac′ti·cal** *adj.* —**tac′ti′cian** *n.*

tac·tile (tăk′təl, -tīl′) *adj.* Of, perceptible to, or proceeding from the sense of touch. [< Lat. *tactus,* sense of touch.] —**tac·til′i·ty** (-tĭl′-ĭ-tē) *n.*

tad·pole (tăd′pōl′) *n.* The aquatic larval stage of a frog or toad, with a tail and external gills. [ME *taddepol.*]

tadpole
Three stages of growth

taf·fe·ta (tăf′ĭ-tə) *n.* A glossy, plain-woven fabric of silk, rayon, or nylon. [< Pers. *tāftah,* woven.]

taf·fy (tăf′ē) *n., pl.* **-fies.** A sweet, chewy candy made of molasses or brown sugar. [Orig. unknown.]

tag¹ (tăg) *n.* 1. A strip of paper, metal, etc., attached to something for purposes of identification, classification, or labeling. 2. A plastic or metal tip on shoelaces. 3. A designation or epithet. —*v.* **tagged, tag·ging.** 1. To label or identify with a tag. 2. To follow closely. [ME *tagge,* a dangling piece of cloth on a garment.] —**tag′ger** *n.*

tag² (tăg) *n.* 1. A children's game in which one player pursues the others until he touches one of them, who in turn becomes the pursuer. 2. *Baseball.* The act of putting another player out by touching him. —*v.* **tagged, tag·ging.** 1. To touch (another player) as in a game of tag. 2. *Baseball.* To touch (a runner) with the ball in order to put him out. [Orig. unknown.] —**tag′ger** *n.*

Ta·ga·log (tə-gä′lŏg, -lôg′) *n., pl.* **-log** or **-logs.**

1. A member of a people native to the Philippines. 2. The Indonesian language of the Tagalog. —**Ta·ga′log** *adj.*

Ta·hi·tian (tə-hē′shən, -hē′tē-ən) *n.* 1. A native or inhabitant of Tahiti. 2. The Polynesian language of Tahiti. —**Ta·hi′tian** *adj.*

tai·ga (tī′gə) *n.* The evergreen forest of Siberia and similar regions in Eurasia and' North America. [R. *taiga.*]

tail (tāl) *n.* 1. The hind part of an animal, esp. when elongated and extending beyond the main part of the body. 2. Something resembling an animal's tail. 3. The bottom, rear, or hindmost part of something. 4. a. The rear of an aircraft. b. An assembly of stabilizing planes and control surfaces in this region. 5. **tails.** The reverse of a coin: *heads or tails.* 6. **tails.** A formal evening costume worn by men. —*v. Informal.* To follow and keep under surveillance. —*adj.* 1. Posterior; hindmost. 2. Coming from behind: *a tail wind.* [< OE *tægel.*]

tail·gate (tāl′gāt′) *n.* A hinged board closing the rear of a truck, wagon, etc. —*v.* **-gat·ed, -gat·ing.** To drive too closely behind (another vehicle).

tail·light (tāl′līt′) *n.* A light mounted on the rear of a vehicle.

tai·lor (tā′lər) *n.* One who makes, repairs, and alters garments. —*v.* 1. To make (a garment). 2. To make, alter, or adapt for a particular purpose. [< Lat. *talea,* a cutting.]

tai·lor-made (tā′lər-mād′) *adj.* Made or as if made to order.

tail·spin (tāl′spĭn′) *n.* 1. The descent of an aircraft in a nose-down spiraling motion. 2. A sudden, steep decline or slump.

Tai·no (tī′nō) *n., pl.* **-no** or **-nos.** 1. An extinct aboriginal Arawakan Indian people of the West Indies. 2. The language of the Taino.

taint (tānt) *v.* 1. To affect slightly with something undesirable. 2. To make poisonous or rotten; infect or spoil. —*n.* 1. A moral defect considered as a stain or spot. 2. An infecting touch, influence, or tinge. [< Lat. *tingere,* to dye.]

ta·ka (tä′kə) *n.* See table at **currency.** [Bengali *ṭākā.*]

take (tāk) *v.* **took** (tŏŏk), **tak·en** (tā′kən), **tak·ing.** 1. To get possession of; capture; seize. 2. To grasp with the hands. 3. To carry with one to another place. 4. To lead or convey to another place. 5. To remove from a place. 6. To charm; captivate. 7. To eat, drink, consume, or inhale. 8. To assume upon oneself; commit oneself to. 9. *Gram.* To govern: *Intransitive verbs take no direct object.* 10. To select; pick out; choose. 11. To use as a means of conveyance or transportation. 12. To occupy: *take a seat.* 13. To require: *It takes money to do that.* 14. To determine through measurement or observation. 15. To write down: *take notes.* 16. To make by photography: *take a picture.* 17. To accept (something owed, offered, or given). 18. To endure: *take criticism.* 19. To follow (e.g. a suggestion). 20. To indulge in; do; perform: *take a step.* 21. To allow to come in; admit. 22. To interpret or react to in a certain manner: *take literally.* 23. To subtract. 24. To commit oneself to the study of: *take a course.* 25. To have the intended effect; work. 26. To become: *take sick.* 27. To make one's way; go. —*phrasal verbs.* **take after.** To resemble. **take**

back. To retract (something stated or written). **take in. 1.** To view: *His eyes took in the whole scene.* **2.** To include or comprise. **3.** To understand. **take off. 1.** To remove, as clothing. **2.** To rise up in flight, as an airplane. **3.** *Informal.* To depart. **take out. 1.** To remove; extract. **2.** *Informal.* To escort, as on a date. **take over.** To assume the control or management of. **take to. 1.** To become fond of. **2.** To begin to do habitually; resort to. **take up. 1.** To begin again. **2.** To develop an interest in. **take up with.** *Informal.* To develop a friendship with. —*n.* **1. a.** The act or process of taking. **b.** The amount taken, esp. at one time. **2.** The money collected as admission to an event. **3.** The uninterrupted running of a camera or other equipment, as in filming a movie. [< ON *taka.*] —**tak'er** *n.*

take-off (tāk'ôf', -ôf') *n.* **1.** The act of leaving the ground. **2.** *Informal.* An imitative caricature or burlesque.

take-o-ver (tāk'ō'vər) *n.* Also **take-o-ver.** The act of seizing control or management.

tak-ing (tā'kǐng) *n.* **1.** The act or process of gaining possession. **2. takings.** Receipts, esp. of money. —*adj.* Attractive.

ta-la (tä'lə) *n.* See table at **currency.** [Samoan.]

talc (tălk) *n.* A fine-grained mineral used in making talcum powder. [< Pers. *talk.*]

tal-cum powder (tăl'kəm) *n.* A fine powder made from purified talc, for use on the skin. [< Med. Lat. *talcum,* talc.]

tale (tāl) *n.* **1.** A report of events or happenings. **2.** A narrative of imaginary events; story. **3.** A piece of gossip, usu. malicious or untrue. [< OE *talu.*]

tale-bear-er (tāl'bâr'ər) *n.* One who spreads malicious gossip. —**tale'bear'ing** *n.*

tal-ent (tăl'ənt) *n.* **1.** A natural or acquired ability; aptitude. **2.** Natural endowment or ability of a superior quality. **3.** A person with such an endowment. **4.** Any of various ancient units of weight and money. [< Gk. *talanton,* unit of money.] —**tal'ent-ed** *adj.*

tal-is-man (tăl'ĭs-mən, -ĭz-) *n.* An object believed to give supernatural powers or protection to its bearer. [< Gk. *telesma,* consecration.] —**tal'is-man'ic** (-măn'ĭk) *adj.*

talk (tôk) *v.* **1.** To articulate words. **2. a.** To converse by means of spoken language. **b.** To converse about. **3.** To speak: *talk French.* **4.** To gossip. **5.** To parley or negotiate. **6.** To consult or confer. **7.** To induce by argument; persuade: *talked her into joining him.* —*phrasal verbs.* **talk back.** To reply rudely. **talk down.** To speak with insulting condescension. **talk over.** To discuss. —*n.* **1.** The act of talking; conversation. **2.** An informal speech. **3.** Hearsay, rumor, or speculation. **4.** A subject of conversation. **5.** A conference. [ME *talken.*]

talk-a-tive (tô'kə-tĭv) *adj.* Inclined to talk a great deal. —**talk'a-tive-ly** *adv.* —**talk'a-tive-ness** *n.*

talk-ing-to (tô'kĭng-tōō') *n., pl.* **-tos.** *Informal.* A scolding.

tall (tôl) *adj.* **-er, -est. 1.** Having greater than ordinary height. **2.** Having a stated height: *a plant three feet tall.* **3.** Fanciful or boastful. **4.** Unusual in length, size, or difficulty: *a tall order to fill.* —*adv.* Straight; proudly: *stand tall.* [< OE *getæl,* swift.] —**tall'ness** *n.*

Syns: *tall, high, lofty, towering adj.*

tal-low (tăl'ō) *n.* A mixture of fats obtained from animals, as cattle or sheep, and used to make candles, soaps, and lubricants. [ME *talow.*] —**tal'low-y** *adj.*

tal-ly (tăl'ē) *n., pl.* **-lies. 1.** A stick on which notches are made to keep a count. **2.** A reckoning or score. —*v.* **-lied, -ly-ing. 1.** To reckon or count. **2.** To correspond; agree. [< Lat. *talea,* stick.]

tal-ly-ho (tăl'ē-hō') *interj.* Used to urge on hounds in fox hunting. [Prob. < OFr. *thialau.*]

Tal-mud (täl'mŏŏd, tăl'məd) *n.* A collection of ancient Rabbinical writings that constitute the basis of religious authority for orthodox Judaism. —**Tal-mu'dic** (tăl-mŏŏ'dĭk, -myŏŏ'-, täl-) or **Tal-mu'di-cal** *adj.* —**Tal'mud-ist** (täl'mŏŏd-ĭst, tăl'məd-) *n.*

tal-on (tăl'ən) *n.* The claw of a bird of prey or other predatory animal. [< Lat. *talus,* ankle.]

ta-ma-le (tə-mä'lē) *n.* An often highly seasoned Mexican dish of fried chopped meat and crushed peppers, wrapped in cornhusks and steamed. [< Nahuatl *tamalli.*]

tam-a-rack (tăm'ə-răk') *n.* An American larch tree. [Of Algonquian orig.]

tam-a-rind (tăm'ə-rĭnd') *n.* **1.** A tropical tree with pulpy, acid-flavored pods. **2.** The fruit of this tree. [< Ar. *tamar hindi.*]

tam-a-risk (tăm'ə-rĭsk') *n.* A shrub or small tree with small, scalelike leaves and clusters of pink flowers. [< Lat. *tamarix.*]

tam-ba-la (täm-bä'lə) *n.* See table at **currency.** [Native word in Malawi.]

tam-bou-rine (tăm'bə-rēn') *n.* A musical instrument consisting of a small drumhead with jingling disks fitted into the rim. [< OFr. *tambour,* drum.]

tame (tām) *adj.* **tam-er, tam-est. 1.** Changed from natural wildness to a manageable state; domesticated. **2.** Gentle; docile. **3.** Insipid; flat. —*v.* **tamed, tam-ing. 1.** To train to live with or be useful to human beings. **2.** To subdue. [< OE *tam.*] —**tame'ly** *adv.* —**tame'ness** *n.* —**tam'er** *n.*

Tam-il (tăm'əl) *n.* **1.** A member of a Dravidian people of southern India and Sri Lanka. **2.** The Dravidian language of the Tamils. —**Tam'il** *adj.*

Tam-muz (tä'mŏŏz') *n.* The 10th month in the Hebrew calendar. See table at **calendar.** [Heb. *Tammūz.*]

tam-o'-shan-ter (tăm'ə-shăn'tər) *n.* A flat-

tam-o'-shanter

topped, tight-fitting Scottish cap. [< the hero of Burns's poem *Tam o'Shanter*.]

tamp (tămp) *v.* To pack down tightly by a succession of blows or taps. [Prob. < *tampion*, a cover for a gun muzzle.]

tam·per (tăm′pər) *v.* **1.** To interfere harmfully; meddle. **2.** To make secret or underhand arrangements: *tamper with a jury.* [< TEMPER.] **—tam′per·er** *n.*

tam·pon (tăm′pŏn′) *n.* A plug of absorbent material inserted into a bodily cavity or wound. [< OFr., of Gmc. orig.]

tan (tăn) *v.* **tanned, tan·ning. 1.** To convert (hide) into leather, esp. by treating with tannin. **2.** To make or become brown by exposure to the sun. **3.** *Informal.* To thrash or beat. **—n. 1.** A light brown. **2.** The brownish color that sun rays impart to the skin. **—adj. tan·ner, tan·nest. 1.** Of the color tan. **2.** Having a suntan. [< Med. Lat. *tannum,* tanbark.]

tan·a·ger (tăn′ə-jər) *n.* Any of various New World birds often having brightly colored plumage. [< Tupi *tangará.*]

tan·bark (tăn′bärk′) *n.* **1.** Tree bark used as a source of tannin. **2.** Shredded bark used to cover a surface such as a circus arena.

tan·dem (tăn′dəm) *n.* **1.** A bicycle built for two. **2.** Two or more persons or objects placed one behind the other and working or acting in conjunction. **3.** A two-wheeled carriage drawn by horses harnessed one behind the other. **—adv.** One behind the other. [< Lat., at last.]

tang (tăng) *n.* **1.** A sharp, distinctive flavor, taste, or odor. **2.** A projection by which a tool is attached to its handle. [ME *tonge,* of Scand. orig.] **—tang′y** *adj.*

tan·ge·lo (tăn′jə-lō′) *n., pl.* **-los.** A citrus fruit that is a cross between a grapefruit and a tangerine. [Blend of TANGERINE and *pomelo,* grapefruit.]

tan·gent (tăn′jənt) *adj.* Making contact at a single point or along a line but not intersecting; touching. **—n. 1.** A line, curve, or surface touching but not intersecting another line, curve, or surface. **2.** A sudden digression or change of course. [< Lat. *tangere,* to touch.] **—tan′gen·cy** *n.* **—tan·gen′tial** (-jěn′shəl) *adj.* **—tan·gen′tial·ly** *adv.*

tan·ge·rine (tăn′jə-rēn′) *n.* A citrus fruit with an easily peeled deep-orange skin. [< *Tangier,* Morocco.]

tan·gi·ble (tăn′jə-bəl) *adj.* **1.** Capable of being touched; material. **2.** Real; concrete. **—n. 1.** Something palpable or concrete. **2. tangibles.** Material assets. [< Lat. *tangere,* to touch.] **—tan′gi·bil′i·ty** or **tan′gi·ble·ness** *n.* **—tan′gi·bly** *adv.*

tan·gle (tăng′gəl) *v.* **-gled, -gling. 1.** To intertwine in a confused mass; snarl. **2.** To be or become entangled. **3.** *Informal.* To contend; wrestle. **—n. 1.** A confused, intertwined mass. **2.** A jumbled or confused condition. [ME *tangilen,* to involve in embarrassment.] **—tan′gler** *n.*

tan·go (tăng′gō) *n., pl.* **-gos.** A Latin-American ballroom dance. [Am. Sp.] **—tan′go** *v.*

tank (tăngk) *n.* **1.** A large container for fluids. **2.** An enclosed, heavily armored combat vehicle mounted with cannon and guns and moving on caterpillar treads. [< Lat. *stagnum,* pond.]

tan·kard (tăng′kərd) *n.* A large drinking cup, usu. with a handle and a hinged cover. [ME.]

tank·er (tăng′kər) *n.* A ship, truck, or plane equipped to transport oil or other liquids in bulk.

tank top *n.* A sleeveless shirt with wide shoulder straps.

tan·ner (tăn′ər) *n.* One who tans hides.

tan·ner·y (tăn′ə-rē) *n., pl.* **-ies.** A place where hides are tanned.

tan·nic acid (tăn′ĭk) *n.* A yellowish to light-brown substance obtained from the fruit and bark of certain plants and used in tanning hides and as a medicine.

tan·nin (tăn′ĭn) *n.* Tannic acid or another substance having similar uses. [< Lat. *tannum,* tanbark.]

Ta·no·an (tä′nō-ən) *n.* An American Indian language family of New Mexico and northeastern Arizona.

tan·ta·lize (tăn′tl-īz′) *v.* **-lized, -liz·ing.** To tease or torment by exposing to view but keeping out of reach something much desired. [< *Tantalus,* mythological Greek king who was punished thus.] **—tan′ta·li·za′tion** *n.* **—tan′ta·liz′er** *n.* **—tan′ta·liz′ing·ly** *adv.*

tan·ta·lum (tăn′tl-əm) *n. Symbol* **Ta** A very hard, heavy, gray metallic element used to make electric-light-bulb filaments, lightning arresters, nuclear reactor parts, and some surgical instruments. Atomic number 73; atomic weight 180.948. [< *Tantalus.*]

tan·ta·mount (tăn′tə-mount′) *adj.* Equivalent in effect or value. [< AN *tant amunter,* to amount to as much.]

tan·trum (tăn′trəm) *n.* A fit of bad temper. [Orig. unknown.]

Tao·ism (tou′ĭz′əm, dou′-) *n.* A Chinese philosophy and religion emphasizing freedom from desire, effortless action, and simplicity. [< Chin. *dao*⁴, way.] **—Tao′ist** *n.* **—Tao·is′tic** *adj.*

tap¹ (tăp) *v.* **tapped, tap·ping. 1.** To strike gently; rap. **2.** To repair (shoe heels or toes) by applying a tap. **—n. 1.** A gentle but audible blow. **2.** A metal plate attached to the toe or heel of a shoe. [ME *tappen.*]

tap² (tăp) *n.* **1.** A faucet; spigot. **2.** Liquor drawn from a tap. **3.** A tool for cutting an internal screw thread. **4.** A makeshift terminal in an electric circuit. **—v. tapped, tap·ping. 1.** To furnish with a spigot or tap. **2.** To pierce in order to draw off liquid. **3.** To draw (liquid) from a vessel or container. **4.** To open outlets from: *tap a water main.* **5. a.** To wiretap. **b.** To establish an electric connection in (a power line). **6.** To cut screw threads in. [< OE *tæppa.*]

tap dance *n.* A dance in which the rhythm is sounded out by the clicking heels and toes of the dancer's shoes. **—tap′-dance′** *v.* **—tap dancer** *n.*

tape (tāp) *n.* **1.** A narrow strip of strong, woven fabric. **2.** A long, narrow, flexible strip of material, such as adhesive tape. **3.** A tape recording. **4.** A string stretched across a finish line. **—v. taped, tap·ing. 1.** To fasten, wrap, or bind with tape. **2.** To measure with a tape measure. **3.** To tape-record. [< OE *tæppe.*]

tape measure *n.* A tape marked off in a scale, used for taking measurements.

ta·per (tā′pər) *n.* **1.** A slender candle or waxed wick. **2.** A gradual decrease in thickness or width of an elongated object. **—v. 1.** To make or become gradually narrower toward one end. **2.** To become gradually smaller; slacken off. [< OE *tapor.*] —**ta′per·ing·ly** *adv.*

tape recorder *n.* A device for recording and playing back sound on magnetic tape.

tape recording *n.* **1.** The act or process of recording on magnetic tape. **2. a.** Magnetized recording tape. **b.** The sound recorded on a magnetic tape. —**tape′-re·cord′** *v.*

tap·es·try (tăp′ĭ-strē) *n., pl.* **-tries.** A heavy textile with a varicolored design woven across the warp, used esp. for a wall hanging. [< Gk. *tapēs,* carpet.] —**tap′es·tried** *adj.*

tape·worm (tāp′wûrm′) *n.* A long, ribbonlike worm that lives as a parasite in the intestines of vertebrates.

tap·i·o·ca (tăp′ē-ō′kə) *n.* A beady starch obtained from cassava root and used for puddings. [< Guarani *tipiog.*]

ta·pir (tā′pər, tə-pîr′) *n.* A tropical American or Asian mammal with a heavy body, short legs, and a fleshy proboscis. [Tupi *tapira.*]

tap·room (tăp′rōōm′, -rŏōm′) *n.* A barroom.

tap·root (tăp′rōōt′, -rŏōt′) *n.* The main root of a plant, growing straight downward from the stem.

taps (tăps) *pl.n. (used with a sing. verb).* A military bugle call blown as an order to put out lights and at funerals and memorial services. [Perh. < obs. *taptoo,* tattoo.]

tar¹ (tär) *n.* A dark, oily, viscid mixture, consisting mainly of hydrocarbons, produced by the destructive distillation of organic substances such as wood, coal, or peat. —*v.* **tarred, tar·ring.** To coat with tar. [< OE *teoru.*]

tar² (tär) *n. Informal.* A sailor. [< TARPAULIN.]

ta·ran·tel·la (tăr′ən-tĕl′ə) *n.* **1.** A lively, whirling dance of southern Italy. **2.** The music for this dance. [Ital. < *Taranto,* Italy.]

ta·ran·tu·la (tə-răn′chə-lə) *n., pl.* **-las** or **-lae** (-lē′). Any of various large, hairy, chiefly tropical spiders capable of inflicting a painful bite. [< OItal. *tarantola* < *Taranto,* Italy.]

tar·dy (tär′dē) *adj.* **-di·er, -di·est. 1.** a. Late. **b.** Dilatory. **2.** Slow; sluggish. [< Lat. *tardus,* slow.] —**tar′di·ly** *adv.* —**tar′di·ness** *n.*

tare¹ (târ) *n.* Any of several weeds that grow in grain fields. [ME.]

tare² (târ) *n.* A deduction from gross weight made to allow for the weight of a container or wrapper. [< Ar. *ṭaraḥa,* the rejected.]

tar·get (tär′gĭt) *n.* **1.** An object with a marked surface that is shot at to test accuracy. **2.** Something aimed or fired at. **3.** An object of criticism, ridicule, or attack. —*v.* To make a target of. [< OFr. *targe,* light shield.]

tar·iff (tär′ĭf) *n.* **1. a.** A list or system of duties imposed on imported or exported goods. **b.** A duty of this kind. **2.** A schedule of rates or fees. [< Ar. *ta′rīf,* notification.]

tarn (tärn) *n.* A small mountain lake. [ME *tarne,* of Scand. orig.]

tar·nish (tär′nĭsh) *v.* **1.** To make or become dull or discolored. **2.** To sully or taint. [OFr. *ternir.*] —**tar′nish** *n.* —**tar′nish·a·ble** *adj.*

ta·ro (tär′ō, tăr′ō) *n., pl.* **-ros.** A tropical plant with broad leaves and a large, starchy, edible root. [Of Polynesian orig.]

tar·ot (tăr′ō) *n.* Any of a set of playing cards used in fortunetelling. [< OItal. *tarocco.*]

tar·pau·lin (tär-pô′lĭn, tär′pə-) *n.* Waterproof canvas used to cover and protect things. [Obs. *tarpawling.*]

tar·pon (tär′pən) *n., pl.* **-pon** or **-pons.** A large, silvery game fish of Atlantic coastal waters. [Orig. unknown.]

tar·ra·gon (tär′ə-gŏn′, -gən) *n.* An aromatic herb with leaves used as seasoning. [Prob. < Ar. *ṭarkhūn.*]

tar·ry (tär′ē) *v.* **-ried, -ry·ing. 1.** To delay or be late; linger. **2.** To stay temporarily; sojourn. [ME *tarien.*] —**tar′ri·er** *n.*

tar·sus (tär′səs) *n., pl.* **-si** (-sī′). The section of the vertebrate foot between the leg and the metatarsus. [< Gk. *tarsos,* ankle.] —**tar′sal** *adj.*

tart¹ (tärt) *adj.* **-er, -est. 1.** Having a sharp, pungent taste; sour. **2.** Caustic; cutting. [< OE *teart,* severe.] —**tart′ly** *adv.* —**tart′ness** *n.*

tart² (tärt) *n.* **1.** A small open pie with a sweet filling. **2.** A prostitute. [< OFr. *tarte.*]

tar·tan (tär′tn) *n.* Any of numerous textile patterns of Scottish origin consisting of stripes of varying widths and colors crossed at right angles against a solid background. [Poss. < OFr. *tertaine,* a kind of fabric.] —**tar′tan** *adj.*

tar·tar (tär′tər) *n.* **1.** A reddish acid material found in the juice of grapes and deposited on the sides of casks during wine-making. **2.** A hard, yellowish deposit on the teeth. [< Med. Lat. *tartaron.*] —**tar·tar′ic** (-tăr′ĭc) *adj.*

Tar·tar (tär′tər) *n.* Also **Ta·tar** (tär′-). **1.** A member of any of the Mongolian peoples who invaded western Asia and eastern Europe in the 13th cent. **2.** A ferocious or violent-tempered person. —**Tar′tar** *adj.*

tartar sauce (tär′tər) *n.* Also **tartare sauce.** Mayonnaise mixed with chopped onion, pickles, etc., and served as a sauce with fish.

task (tăsk) *n.* **1.** A piece of assigned work. **2.** A difficult or tedious undertaking. —*idiom.* **take to task.** To reprimand or censure. [< Med. Lat. *taxare,* to tax.]

task force *n.* A temporary grouping of forces and resources for achieving a specific goal.

task·mas·ter (tăsk′măs′tər) *n.* One who imposes heavy work.

tas·sel (tăs′əl) *n.* **1.** A bunch of loose threads or cords bound at one end and hanging free at the other, used as an ornament on curtains, clothing, etc. **2.** Something resembling this, such as the pollen-bearing flower cluster of a corn plant. —*v.* **-seled, -sel·ing** or **-selled, -sel·ling. 1.** To fringe or decorate with tassels. **2.** To put forth a tassellike blossom. [< OFr.]

tassel

taste (tāst) v. **tast·ed, tast·ing. 1.** To distinguish the flavor of by taking into the mouth. **2.** To eat or drink a small quantity (of). **3.** To experience, esp. for the first time. **4.** To have a distinct flavor: *The milk tastes sour.* —n. **1.** The sense that distinguishes between the sweet, sour, salty, and bitter qualities of something placed in the mouth. **2.** The sensation produced by or as if by something placed in the mouth; flavor. **3.** A small quantity eaten or tasted. **4.** A limited or first experience. **5.** A personal preference or liking. **6.** The ability to perceive what is aesthetically appropriate: *a room furnished with great taste.* [< Lat. *taxare*, to touch.] —**tast·a·ble** adj. —**tast·er** n.

taste bud n. Any of numerous nests of cells on the tongue that are primarily responsible for the sense of taste.

taste·ful (tāst′fəl) adj. Having, showing, or in keeping with good taste. —**taste′ful·ly** adv. —**taste′ful·ness** n.

taste·less (tāst′lĭs) adj. **1.** Lacking flavor; insipid. **2.** Showing or having poor taste. —**taste′less·ly** adv. —**taste′less·ness** n.

tast·y (tā′stē) adj. **-i·er, -i·est.** Having a pleasing flavor. —**tast′i·ly** adv. —**tast′i·ness** n.

tat (tăt) v. **tat·ted, tat·ting.** To make tatting or produce by tatting. [Prob. < TATTING.] —**tat′ter** n.

Ta·tar (tä′tər) n. Var. of **Tartar.**

tat·ter (tăt′ər) n. **1.** A torn and hanging piece, as of cloth; shred. **2. tatters.** Torn and ragged clothing; rags. —v. To make or become ragged. [< ME *tater*, of Scand. orig.]

tat·ter·de·mal·ion (tăt′ər-də-māl′yən, -măl′-) n. A ragamuffin. [Orig. unknown.]

tat·ting (tăt′ĭng) n. **1.** Handmade lace produced by looping and knotting a single strand of heavy thread on a small hand shuttle. **2.** The art of making such lace. [Orig. unknown.]

tat·tle (tăt′l) v. **-tled, -tling. 1.** To reveal the secrets of another. **2.** To chatter idly; prate. [ME *tattlen*, to stammer.] —**tat′tler** n.

tat·tle·tale (tăt′l-tāl′) n. One who tattles on others.

tat·too¹ (tă-tōō′) n. **1.** A call sounded to summon soldiers or sailors to quarters at night. **2.** A rhythmic tapping. [< Du. *taptoe.*]

tat·too² (tă-tōō′) n. A permanent mark or design made on the skin, esp. by a process of pricking and staining with an indelible pigment. —v. To mark (the skin) with a tattoo. [Of Polynesian orig.] —**tat·too′er** n.

tau (tou, tô) n. The 19th letter of the Greek alphabet. See table at **alphabet.** [Gk.]

taught (tôt) v. p.t. & p.p. of **teach.**

taunt (tônt) v. To challenge or deride jeeringly. —n. A scornful or jeering remark. [Prob. < OFr. *tant pour tant*, so much for so much.] —**taunt′er** n. —**taunt′ing·ly** adv.

taupe (tōp) n. A brownish gray. [< Lat. *talpa.*] —**taupe** adj.

Tau·rus (tôr′əs) n. **1.** A constellation in the Northern Hemisphere. **2.** The 2nd sign of the zodiac.

taut (tôt) adj. **-er, -est. 1.** Tight; not slack. **2.** Strained; tense. **3.** Trim; tidy. [ME *toght.*] —**taut′ly** adv. —**taut′ness** n.

tau·tol·o·gy (tô-tŏl′ə-jē) n., pl. **-gies. 1. a.** Needless repetition of the same sense in different words; redundancy. **b.** An instance of such repetition. **2.** A statement that includes all logical possibilities and is therefore always true. [< Gk. *tautologos*, redundant.] —**tau·to·log′i·cal** (tô′tə-lŏj′ĭ-kəl) adj. —**tau·to·log′i·cal·ly** adv.

tav·ern (tăv′ərn) n. **1.** A saloon; bar. **2.** An inn for travelers. [< Lat. *taberna.*]

taw·dry (tô′drē) adj. **-dri·er, -dri·est.** Cheap and gaudy in nature or appearance. —**taw′dri·ly** adv. —**taw′dri·ness** n.

taw·ny (tô′nē) n. A light golden brown. [< Med. Lat. *tannum*, tanbark.] —**taw′ny** adj.

tax (tăks) n. **1.** A charge or contribution required of persons or groups within the domain of a government for its support. **2.** An excessive demand; strain. —v. **1.** To place a tax on (e.g. property). **2.** To exact a tax from. **3.** To make heavy demands upon. **4.** To charge; accuse. [< Med. Lat. *taxare*, to tax < Lat. *tangere*, to touch.] —**tax′a·ble** adj. —**tax·a′tion** n. —**tax′er** n.

tax·i (tăk′sē) n., pl. **-is** or **-ies.** A taxicab. —v. **-ied, -i·ing. 1.** To transport or be transported by taxi. **2.** To move slowly on the ground or water before takeoff or after landing.

tax·i·cab (tăk′sē-kăb′) n. An automobile that carries passengers for a fare. [Fr. *taxe*, charge + CAB.]

tax·i·der·my (tăk′sĭ-dûr′mē) n. The art or process of stuffing and mounting animal skins in lifelike form. [< TAXI- + Gk. *derma*, skin.] —**tax′i·derm′ist** n.

tax·ing (tăk′sĭng) adj. Burdensome.

taxo– or **taxi–** pref. Arrangement or order: *taxonomy.* [< Gk. *taxis.*]

tax·on·o·my (tăk-sŏn′ə-mē) n. The science, laws, or principles of classification, esp. of organisms in categories based on common characteristics. —**tax′o·nom′ic** (-sə-nŏm′ĭk) or **tax′o·nom′i·cal** adj. —**tax′o·nom′i·cal·ly** adv. —**tax·on′o·mist** n.

tax·pay·er (tăks′pā′ər) n. One who pays taxes.

tax shelter n. A financial operation, such as the acquisition of expenses, that reduces taxes on current earnings.

Tb The symbol for the element terbium.

T-bone (tē′bōn′) n. A thick steak taken from the small end of the loin and containing a T-shaped bone.

Tc The symbol for the element technetium.

Te The symbol for the element tellurium.

tea (tē) n. **1. a.** An Asian shrub with evergreen leaves. **b.** The dried, processed leaves of this shrub, steeped in boiling water to make a beverage. **c.** The beverage thus prepared. **2.** A beverage similar to tea. **3.** An afternoon refreshment or social gathering at which tea is taken. [< dial. Chin. *te.*]

tea bag n. A small porous sac holding tea leaves to make an individual serving of tea.

teach (tēch) v. **taught** (tôt), **teach·ing. 1.** To impart knowledge or skill (to). **2.** To instruct in. **3.** To cause to learn by example or experience. [< OE *tǣcan.*] —**teach′a·bil′i·ty** or **teach′a·ble·ness** n. —**teach′a·ble** adj. —**teach′a·bly** adv.

Syns: teach, instruct, train, tutor v.

Usage: Some grammarians have objected to the use of *teach* as a transitive verb with an object denoting an institution of learning, as in *He teaches grade school.* This usage has wide currency, however, and should be regarded as correct.

teach·er (tē′chər) n. One that teaches, esp. a person hired by a school to teach.

teach·ing (tē′chĭng) n. **1.** The work of teachers. **2.** A precept or doctrine.

teak (tēk) *n.* **1.** An Asian tree with hard, durable, yellowish-brown wood. **2.** The wood of the teak tree. [< Malayalam *tēkka.*] —**teak** *adj.*

tea-ket-tle (tē'kĕt'l) *n.* A covered kettle with a handle and a spout for pouring, used to boil water, as for tea.

teal (tēl) *n.* Any of several small wild ducks. [ME *tele.*]

team (tēm) *n.* **1.** Two or more harnessed draft animals. **2.** A group of players in a game. **3.** A group organized to work together. —*v.* **1.** To harness together to form a team. **2.** To form a team. [< OE *tēam.*]

team-mate (tēm'māt') *n.* A fellow member of a team.

team-ster (tēm'star) *n.* **1.** One who drives a team. **2.** A truck driver.

team-work (tēm'wûrk') *n.* Cooperative effort.

tea-pot (tē'pŏt') *n.* A covered pot with a handle and a spout, for making and serving tea.

tear¹ (târ) *v.* **tore** (tôr, tōr), **torn** (tôrn, tōrn), **tear-ing.** **1.** To pull apart or into pieces; rend. **2.** To make (an opening) by ripping. **3.** To lacerate. **4.** To extract or separate forcefully; wrench. **5.** To divide; disunite. **6.** To rush headlong. —*phrasal verb.* **tear down.** To demolish. —*n.* A rip or rent. —*idiom.* **wear and tear.** The damage sustained by an object from continual use. [< OE *teran.*]

tear² (tîr) *n.* **1.** A drop of the clear salty liquid that lubricates the surface between the eyeball and the eyelid. **2.** A drop of liquid or hardened fluid. **3. tears.** The act of weeping. —*v.* To fill with tears. [< OE *tēar.*] —**tear'ful** *adj.* —**tear'ful-ly** *adv.* —**tear'i-ness** *n.* —**tear'y** *adj.*

tear-drop (tîr'drŏp') *n.* A single tear.

tear gas (tîr) *n.* Any of various chemicals that when dispersed irritate the eyes and breathing passages severely.

tear-jerk-er (tîr'jûr'kər) *n. Slang.* A tearfully pathetic story, drama, or performance.

tea-room (tē'rōōm', -rŏŏm') *n.* A restaurant serving tea and other refreshments.

tease (tēz) *v.* **teased, teas-ing.** **1.** To annoy; vex. **2.** To make fun of. **3.** To coax. **4.** To disentangle and dress the fibers of (wool). **5.** To raise the nap of (cloth). **6.** To brush or comb (the hair) toward the scalp for a bouffant effect. [< OE *tǣsan,* to comb apart.] —**teas'er** *n.* —**teas'ing-ly** *adv.*

tea-sel (tē'zəl) *n.* Also **tea-zel** or **tea-zle.** **1.** A plant with thistlelike flowers surrounded by stiff bristles. **2.** The flower head of such a plant, used to raise a nap on fabrics. [< OE *tǣsel.*]

tea-spoon (tē'spōōn') *n.* **1.** A small spoon used esp. with tea, coffee, and desserts. **2.** A household cooking measure equal to ⅓ tablespoon. —**tea'spoon'ful** *n.*

teat (tēt, tīt) *n.* A nipple. [< OFr. *tete,* of Gmc. orig.]

tech-ne-ti-um (tĕk-nē'shē-əm) *n. Symbol* **Tc** A silvery-gray, radioactive metallic element, used as a tracer and to eliminate corrosion in steel. Atomic number 43; specific gravity 11.50. [< Gk. *tekhnētos,* artificial.]

tech-ni-cal (tĕk'nĭ-kəl) *adj.* **1.** Of or derived from technique. **2.** Specialized. **3. a.** Abstract or theoretical. **b.** Scientific. **4.** Formal rather than practical. **5.** Technological. [< Gk. *tekhnikos,* of art.] —**tech'ni-cal-ly** *adv.* —**tech'ni-cal-ness** *n.*

tech-ni-cal-i-ty (tĕk'nĭ-kăl'ĭ-tē) *n., pl.* **-ties.** **1.** The condition or quality of being technical. **2.** Something meaningful or relevant only to a specialist.

tech-ni-cian (tĕk-nĭsh'ən) *n.* An expert in a technical field or process.

Tech-ni-col-or (tĕk'nĭ-kŭl'ər) A trademark for a process used to make pictures in color.

tech-nique (tĕk-nēk') *n.* **1.** The systematic procedure by which a task is accomplished. **2.** Also **tech-nic** (tĕk'nĭk). The degree of skill shown in any performance. [Fr., ult. < Gk. *tekhnē,* skill.]

tech-noc-ra-cy (tĕk-nŏk'rə-sē) *n., pl.* **-cies.** Government by technical scientists and engineers. [Gk. *tekhnē,* skill + -CRACY.] —**tech'-no-crat'** (-nə-krăt') *n.* —**tech'no-crat'ic** *adj.*

tech-nol-o-gy (tĕk-nŏl'ə-jē) *n., pl.* **-gies.** **1.** The application of science, esp. in industry or commerce. **2.** The methods and materials thus used. [Gk. *tekhnē,* skill + -LOGY.] —**tech'no-log'i-cal** (-nə-lŏj'ĭ-kəl) *adj.* —**tech'-no-log'i-cal-ly** *adv.* —**tech-nol'o-gist** *n.*

tec-ton-ics (tĕk-tŏn'ĭks) *n. (used with a sing. verb).* **1.** Construction. **2.** The geology of the earth's structural deformation. [< Gk. *tektōn,* builder.] —**tec-ton'ic** *adj.*

ted-dy bear (tĕd'ē) *n.* A child's toy bear. [< *Teddy,* nickname of *Theodore* Roosevelt (1858–1919).]

te-di-ous (tē'dē-əs) *adj.* Tiresomely long or dull; boring. [< Lat. *taedium,* tedium.] —**te'di-ous-ly** *adv.* —**te'di-ous-ness** *n.*

te-di-um (tē'dē-əm) *n.* Boredom; tediousness. [Lat. *taedium* < *taedēre,* to weary.]

tee (tē) *n.* **1.** A small peg with a concave top for holding a golf ball for an initial drive. **2.** The place from which a player makes his first stroke in golf. —*v.* **teed, tee-ing.** To place (a golf ball) on a tee. —*phrasal verb.* **tee off. 1.** To drive a golf ball from the tee. **2.** *Slang.* To start. **3.** *Slang.* To make or become angry. [Orig. unknown.]

teem (tēm) *v.* To abound or swarm. [< OE *tīeman,* to give birth to.]

teen (tēn) *adj.* Teen-age.

-teen *suff.* Used to form the cardinal numbers 13 through 19. [< OE *-tēne.*]

teen-age (tēn'āj') *adj.* Also **teen-aged** (-ājd'). Of, for, or involving a person or persons aged 13 through 19. —**teen'-ag'er** *n.*

teens (tēnz) *pl.n.* **1.** The numbers that end in *-teen.* **2.** The years of one's life between ages 13 and 19.

tee-ny (tē'nē) *adj.* **-ni-er, -ni-est.** *Informal.* Tiny. [< TINY.]

tee shirt (tē'shûrt') *n.* Var. of **T-shirt.**

tee-ter (tē'tər) *v.* **1.** To move unsteadily; totter. **2.** To seesaw; vacillate. [ME *titeren.*] —**tee'ter** *n.*

tee-ter-tot-ter (tē'tər-tŏt'ər) *n.* A seesaw.

teeth (tēth) *n.* Pl. of **tooth.**

teethe (tēth) *v.* **teethed, teeth-ing.** To grow or cut one's teeth. [< ME *tethe,* teeth.]

tee-to-tal-er (tē-tōt'l-ər) *n.* One who does not drink alcoholic beverages. [*Tee,* pronunciation of first letter in *total* + *total* (abstinence) + -ER¹.] —**tee-to'tal-ism** *n.*

Tef·lon (tĕf′lŏn′). A trademark for a durable plastic used to coat cooking utensils.

tek·tite (tĕk′tīt′) *n.* A dark glassy rock of possibly meteoric origin. [< Gk. *tēktos*, molten.]

tele- *pref.* 1. Distance: *telecommunication.* 2. **a.** Television: *telecast.* **b.** Telegraph: *telegram.* [< Gk. *tēle*, at a distance.]

tel·e·cast (tĕl′ĭ-kăst′) *v.* **-cast** or **-cast·ed, -cast·ing.** To broadcast by television. —*n.* A television broadcast.

tel·e·com·mu·ni·ca·tion (tĕl′ĭ-kə-myōō′nĭ-kā′-shən) *n.* Often **telecommunications** (*used with a sing. verb*). The science and technology of sending messages by electrical or electronic means.

tel·e·gen·ic (tĕl′ə-jĕn′ĭk, -jē′nĭk) *adj.* Presenting an attractive appearance on television. [TELE- + (PHOTO)GENIC.]

tel·e·gram (tĕl′ĭ-grăm′) *n.* A communication sent by telegraph.

tel·e·graph (tĕl′ĭ-grăf′) *n.* 1. A communications system that transmits and receives unmodulated electric impulses, esp. one in which the transmission and reception stations are connected by wires. 2. A telegram. —*v.* To transmit (a message) by telegraph. —**te·leg′ra·pher** (tə-lĕg′rə-fər) or **te·leg′ra·phist** *n.* —**tel′e·graph′ic** *adj.* —**tel′e·graph′i·cal·ly** *adv.* —**te·leg′ra·phy** *n.*

Tel·e·gu (tĕl′ə-gōō′) *n.* A Dravidian language spoken in southeastern India. —**Tel′e·gu** *adj.*

te·lem·e·try (tə-lĕm′ĭ-trē) *n.* The automatic measurement and transmission of data from a distant source to a receiving station. —**tel′e·me′ter** (tĕl′ə-mē′tər) *n.* —**tel′e·met′ric** (tĕl′-ə-mĕt′rĭk) or **tel′e·met′ri·cal** *adj.* —**tel′e·met′ri·cal·ly** *adv.*

tel·e·pa·thy (tə-lĕp′ə-thē) *n.* Communication through means other than the senses. —**tel′e·path′ic** (tĕl′ə-păth′ĭk) *adj.* —**tel′e·path′i·cal·ly** *adv.* —**te·lep′a·thist** *n.*

tel·e·phone (tĕl′ə-fōn′) *n.* An electronic device or system that transmits voice or other acoustic signals to remote locations. —*v.* **-phoned, -phon·ing.** To communicate (with) by telephone. —**tel′e·phon′er** *n.*

te·leph·o·ny (tə-lĕf′ə-nē) *n.* The transmission of sound between distant points, esp. by electronic or electrical means. —**tel′e·phon′ic** (-fŏn′ĭk) *adj.*

tel·e·pho·to (tĕl′ə-fō′tō) *adj.* Of a photographic lens or lens system used to produce a large image of a distant object.

tel·e·play (tĕl′ə-plā′) *n.* A play written for television.

tel·e·scope (tĕl′ĭ-skōp′) *n.* 1. An arrangement of lenses or mirrors or both that gathers light, permitting direct observation or photographic recording of distant objects. 2. Any of various devices used to detect and observe distant objects by their emission or reflection of radiant energy. —*v.* **-scoped, -scop·ing.** 1. To slide inward or outward in overlapping sections, as the cylindrical sections of a small hand telescope. 2. To crush or compress inward. 3. To condense. [< Gk. *teleskopos*, far-seeing.] —**tel′e·scop′ic** (-skŏp′ĭk) *adj.*

tel·e·thon (tĕl′ə-thŏn′) *n.* A long television program, usu. to raise funds for charity. [TELE- + (MARA)THON.]

tel·e·type·writ·er (tĕl′ĭ-tīp′rī′tər) *n.* An electromechanical typewriter that either transmits or receives messages coded in electrical signals.

tel·e·vise (tĕl′ə-vīz′) *v.* **-vised, -vis·ing.** To broadcast (a program) by television. [< TELEVISION.]

tel·e·vi·sion (tĕl′ə-vĭzh′ən) *n.* 1. The transmission and reception of images of moving or stationary objects, usu. with accompanying sound, by electronic means. 2. The receiving apparatus used in this process. 3. The industry of broadcasting programs in this medium.

tell (tĕl) *v.* **told** (tōld), **tell·ing.** 1. To narrate; recount. 2. To express with words. 3. To notify; inform. 4. To command; order. 5. To discern; identify. 6. To have an effect or impact: *In this game every move tells.* —*phrasal verb.* **tell off.** *Informal.* To scold sharply. [< OE *tellan.*] —**tell′a·ble** *adj.*

tell·er (tĕl′ər) *n.* A bank employee who receives and pays out money.

tell·ing (tĕl′ĭng) *adj.* Having force or effect; striking. —**tell′ing·ly** *adv.*

tell·tale (tĕl′tāl′) *n.* One that reveals secrets or hidden information. —**tell′tale′** *adj.*

tel·lu·ri·um (tĕ-lŏŏr′ē-əm, tə-) *n. Symbol* **Te** A brittle, silvery-white metallic element used to alloy stainless steel and lead, in ceramics, and in thermoelectric devices. Atomic number 52; atomic weight 127.60. [< Lat. *tellus*, earth.]

te·mer·i·ty (tə-mĕr′ĭ-tē) *n.* Foolish boldness; rashness. [< Lat. *temere*, rashly.]

tem·per (tĕm′pər) *v.* 1. To soften or moderate. 2. To harden or toughen (a metal), as by alternate heating and cooling. 3. To tune or adjust. —*n.* 1. A habitual condition of the mind or emotions; mood. 2. Calmness; composure. 3. **a.** Irascibility. **b.** An outburst of rage. 4. The degree of hardness. [< Lat. *temperare.*] —**tem′per·a·ble** *adj.* —**tem′per·er** *n.*

tem·per·a (tĕm′pər-ə) *n.* 1. A painting medium in which pigment is mixed with water-soluble glutinous materials such as size or egg yolk. 2. Painting done with this medium. [Ital. < *temperare*, to mingle.]

tem·per·a·ment (tĕm′pər-ə-mənt, -prə-mənt) *n.* 1. The manner of thinking, behaving, and reacting characteristic of a specific individual; disposition. 2. Excessive irritability or sensitiveness. [< Lat. *temperare*, to temper.] —**tem′per·a·men′tal** *adj.* —**tem′per·a·men′tal·ly** *adv.*

tem·per·ance (tĕm′pər-əns, -prəns) *n.* 1. Moderation or self-restraint. 2. Total abstinence from alcoholic beverages.

tem·per·ate (tĕm′pər-ĭt, -prĭt) *adj.* 1. Exercising moderation and self-restraint. 2. Not extreme; moderate. 3. Not subject to extreme hot or cold weather. —**tem′per·ate·ly** *adv.*

tem·per·a·ture (tĕm′pər-ə-chŏŏr′, -chər, tĕm′-prə-) *n.* 1. The degree of hotness or coldness of a body or environment. 2. A body temperature above normal as a result of illness; fever. [< Lat. *temperare*, to temper.]

tem·pered (tĕm′pərd) *adj.* Having a specified temper or disposition.

tem·pest (tĕm′pĭst) *n.* A violent storm. [< Lat. *tempestas.*]

tem·pes·tu·ous (tĕm-pĕs′chōō-əs) *adj.* Tumultuous; stormy. —**tem·pes′tu·ous·ly** *adv.* —**tem·pes′tu·ous·ness** *n.*

tem·plate (tĕm′plĭt) *n.* A pattern or gauge, such as a thin plate, used in making or duplicating something. [< OFr. *temple*, a device in a loom.]

tem·ple¹ (tĕm′pəl) *n.* A building or place dedicated to the worship or the presence of a deity. [< Lat. *templum.*]

tem·ple² (tĕm′pəl) *n.* The flat region on either side of the forehead. [< Lat. *tempus.*]

tem·po (tĕm′pō) *n., pl.* **-pos** or **-pi** (-pē). 1. The relative speed at which music is to be played. 2. Pace. [Ital. < Lat. *tempus,* time.]

tem·po·ral¹ (tĕm′pər-əl, -prəl) *adj.* 1. Of or limited by time. 2. Worldly; secular. [< Lat. *tempus,* time.] —**tem′po·ral·ly** *adv.*

tem·po·ral² (tĕm′pər-əl, -prəl) *adj.* Of or near the temples of the skull. [< Lat. *tempus,* temple of the head.]

tem·po·rar·y (tĕm′pə-rĕr′ē) *adj.* Lasting or used for a limited time only; not permanent. —*n., pl.* **-ies.** A temporary worker. —**tem′po·rar′i·ly** (-rĕr′ə-lē) *adv.*

tem·po·rize (tĕm′pə-rīz′) *v.* **-rized, -riz·ing.** 1. To gain time, as by postponing an action or decision. 2. To yield to current conditions or attitudes; compromise. —**tem′po·ri·za′tion** *n.*

tempt (tĕmpt) *v.* 1. To entice (someone) to commit an unwise or immoral act. 2. To be attractive to. 3. To risk provoking. 4. To incline or dispose. [< Lat. *temptare,* to try.] —**temp·ta′tion** *n.* —**tempt′er** *n.* —**tempt′ress** (tĕmp′trĭs) *n.*

tem·pu·ra (tĕm′pŏŏ-rə, tĕm-pŏŏr′ə) *n.* A Japanese dish of deep-fried vegetables and shrimp or other seafood. [J.]

ten (tĕn) *n.* 1. The cardinal number equal to the sum of 9 + 1. 2. Something having ten parts, units, or members. 3. A playing card marked with ten spots. 4. A ten-dollar bill. [< OE *tīen.*] —**ten** *adj. & pron.*

ten·a·ble (tĕn′ə-bəl) *adj.* Defensible: *a tenable theory.* [< Lat. *tenēre,* to hold.] —**ten′a·bil′i·ty** or **ten′a·ble·ness** *n.* —**ten′a·bly** *adv.*

te·na·cious (tə-nā′shəs) *adj.* 1. Holding firmly; stubborn. 2. Clinging; adhesive. 3. Tending to retain; retentive. [< Lat. *tenax.*] —**te·na′cious·ly** *adv.* —**te·nac′i·ty** (-năs′ə-tē) or **te·na′cious·ness** *n.*

ten·an·cy (tĕn′ən-sē) *n., pl.* **-cies.** 1. The possession or occupancy of lands or buildings by lease or rent. 2. The period of a tenant's occupancy or possession.

ten·ant (tĕn′ənt) *n.* 1. One who temporarily holds or occupies property owned by another. 2. An inhabitant. [< Lat. *tenēre,* to hold.]

Ten Commandments *pl.n.* The ten laws given by God to Moses on Mount Sinai.

tend¹ (tĕnd) *v.* 1. To move or extend in a certain direction. 2. To be likely. 3. To be disposed or inclined. [< Lat. *tendere.*]

tend² (tĕnd) *v.* 1. To look after. 2. To serve at: *tend bar.* 3. To apply one's attention; attend. [< ME *attenden,* to attend.]

ten·den·cy (tĕn′dən-sē) *n., pl.* **-cies.** 1. An inclination to think, act, or behave in a certain way. 2. A drift or trend.

ten·den·tious (tĕn-dĕn′shəs) *adj.* Promoting or implying a particular point of view; biased. [< TENDENCY.]

ten·der¹ (tĕn′dər) *adj.* **-er, -est.** 1. Delicate; fragile. 2. Young and vulnerable. 3. Sensitive or sore. 4. Gentle and loving. 5. Easily moved; sympathetic. [< Lat. *tener.*] —**ten′der·ly** *adv.* —**ten′der·ness** *n.*

ten·der² (tĕn′dər) *n.* 1. A formal offer. 2. Money. —*v.* To offer formally. [< Lat. *tendere,* to hold forth.] —**ten′der·er** *n.*

tend·er³ (tĕn′dər) *n.* 1. One that tends. 2. *Naut.* A ship that services one or more larger ships. 3. A railroad car attached to the locomotive, carrying fuel and water.

ten·der·foot (tĕn′dər-fŏŏt′) *n., pl.* **-foots** or **-feet.** An inexperienced person; novice.

ten·der·heart·ed (tĕn′dər-här′tĭd) *adj.* Compassionate. —**ten′der·heart′ed·ly** *adv.* —**ten′der·heart′ed·ness** *n.*

ten·der·ize (tĕn′də-rīz′) *v.* **-ized, -iz·ing.** To make (meat) tender. —**ten′der·i·za′tion** *n.* —**ten′der·iz′er** *n.*

ten·der·loin (tĕn′dər-loin′) *n.* The tenderest part of a loin of beef or pork.

ten·don (tĕn′dən) *n.* A band of tough, fibrous tissue that connects a muscle with its bony attachment. [< Lat. *tendere,* to stretch.]

ten·dril (tĕn′drəl) *n.* 1. A slender, coiling extension by which a climbing plant clings to a support. 2. Something resembling this. [< OFr. *tendron,* young shoot.]

ten·e·ment (tĕn′ə-mənt) *n.* 1. A building to live in, esp. one intended for rent. 2. A run-down low-rental apartment building whose facilities and maintenance barely meet minimum standards. [< Med. Lat. *tenementum.*]

ten·et (tĕn′ĭt) *n.* A fundamental principle or dogma. [< Lat. *tenēre,* to hold.]

ten-gal·lon hat (tĕn′găl′ən) *n.* A felt hat with an exceptionally tall crown and a wide brim.

ten·nis (tĕn′ĭs) *n.* A game played with rackets and a light ball by two players or two pairs of players on a court divided by a net. [ME *tenetz.*]

ten·on (tĕn′ən) *n.* A projection on a piece of wood shaped for insertion into a mortise to join two pieces together. [< Lat. *tenēre,* to hold.]

ten·or (tĕn′ər) *n.* 1. General sense; drift; purport. 2. **a.** The highest natural voice of an adult male singer. **b.** A singer having such a voice. 3. A part written in the range of a tenor voice. 4. An instrument that sounds within the range of a tenor. [< Lat., uninterrupted course.]

ten·pin (tĕn′pĭn′) *n.* 1. A bowling pin used in playing tenpins. 2. **tenpins** (*used with a sing. verb*). The game of bowling.

tense¹ (tĕns) *adj.* **tens·er, tens·est.** 1. Tightly stretched; taut. 2. Feeling nervous tension. 3. Nerve-racking; suspenseful. —*v.* **tensed, tens·ing.** To make or become tense. [Lat. *tensus,* p.p. of *tendere,* to stretch out.] —**tense′ly** *adv.* —**tense′ness** *n.*

tense² (tĕns) *n.* Any of the inflected forms of a verb that indicate the time and duration or completion of the action or state. [< Lat. *tempus,* time.]

ten·sile (tĕn′səl, -sīl′) *adj.* Of or involving a force that produces stretching. [< Lat. *tensus,* stretched.] —**ten·sil′i·ty** (-sĭl′ĭ-tē) *n.*

ten·sion (tĕn′shən) *n.* 1. The act of stretching or the condition of being stretched. 2. A force tending to produce elongation or extension. 3. **a.** Mental strain. **b.** A strained relation between persons or groups. **c.** Uneasy suspense. 4. Voltage. [< Lat. *tendere,* to stretch.]

ten·sor (tĕn′sər, -sôr′) *n.* A muscle that tenses a part.

tent (tĕnt) *n.* A portable shelter, as of canvas

ă pat ā pay â care ä father ĕ pet ē be ĭ pit ī tie î pier ŏ pot ō toe ô paw, for oi noise ŏŏ took ŏŏ boot ou out th thin *th* this û cut û urge yŏŏ abuse zh vision ə about, item, edible, gallop, circus

stretched over a supporting framework of poles, ropes, and pegs. [< Lat. *tendere*, to stretch.]

ten·ta·cle (tĕn'tə-kəl) *n.* A flexible, unjointed, projecting appendage, as of an octopus or sea anemone. [< Lat. *tentare*, to touch.] —**ten·tac'u·lar** (-tăk'yə-lər) *adj.*

tentacle
Of an octopus

ten·ta·tive (tĕn'tə-tĭv) *adj.* 1. Not final or definite; provisional. 2. Hesitant; uncertain. [< Lat. *tentare*, to try.] —**ten'ta·tive·ly** *adv.* —**ten'ta·tive·ness** *n.*

ten·ter·hook (tĕn'tər-hook') *n.* A hooked nail for securing cloth on a drying framework. —*idiom.* **on tenterhooks.** In a state of suspense or anxiety. [*tenter*, drying framework + HOOK.]

tenth (tĕnth) *n.* 1. The ordinal number that matches the number 10 in a series. 2. One of 10 equal parts. —**tenth** *adj. & adv.*

ten·u·ous (tĕn'yōō-əs) *adj.* 1. Thin; slender. 2. Not dense; rarefied. 3. Unsubstantial; flimsy. [Lat. *tenuis*.] —**ten'u·ous·ly** *adv.* —**ten'u·ous·ness** or **te·nu'i·ty** (tə-nōō'ĭ-tē, -nyōō'-) *n.*

ten·ure (tĕn'yər, -yŏŏr') *n.* 1. The holding of something, as an office; occupation. 2. The terms under which something is held. 3. a. The period of holding. b. Permanence of position. [< Lat. *tenēre*, to hold.]

te·pee (tē'pē) *n.* A cone-shaped tent of skins or bark used by North American Indians. [Dakota *tipi*.]

tep·id (tĕp'ĭd) *adj.* Moderately warm; lukewarm. [< Lat. *tepēre*, to be lukewarm.] —**te·pid'i·ty** (tĕ-pĭd'ĭ-tē) or **tep'id·ness** *n.* —**tep'id·ly** *adv.*

te·qui·la (tə-kē'lə) *n.* An alcoholic liquor distilled from a fleshy-leaved Central American plant. [< *Tequila*, Mexico.]

ter·bi·um (tûr'bē-əm) *n. Symbol* **Tb** A soft, silvery-gray metallic rare-earth element, used in electronics and as a laser material. Atomic number 65; atomic weight 158.924. [< *Ytterby*, Sweden.]

ter·cen·ten·a·ry (tûr'sĕn-tĕn'ə-rē, tər-sĕn'-tə-nĕr'ē) *n., pl.* **-ries.** Also **ter·cen·ten·ni·al** (tûr'sĕn-tĕn'ē-əl). A 300th anniversary. [Lat. *ter*, thrice + CENTENARY.] —**ter'cen·ten'a·ry** *adj.*

term (tûrm) *n.* **1. a.** A limited period of time. **b.** An assigned period for a person to serve. **2. a.** A point of time beginning or ending a period. **b.** A deadline, as for making a payment. **c.** The end of a normal gestation period. **3. a.** A word or phrase having a particular meaning. **b. terms.** Language or manner of expression employed: *no uncertain terms.* **4. terms. a.** Conditions or stipulations:

peace terms. **b.** The relation between two persons or groups: *on speaking terms.* **5.** *Math.* Each of the quantities connected by addition or subtraction signs in an equation or series. —*v.* To designate; call. [< Lat. *terminus*, boundary.]

ter·ma·gant (tûr'mə-gənt) *n.* A scolding woman; shrew. [ME *Termagaunt*, a character in medieval mystery plays.]

ter·mi·nal (tûr'mə-nəl) *adj.* 1. Of or forming the end or boundary. 2. Concluding; final. 3. Of or occurring in a term or each term. 4. Ending in death; fatal. —*n.* 1. A terminating point, limit, or part. 2. A point at which a connection to an electrical component is normally made. 3. A railroad or bus station, esp. a terminus. [< Lat. *terminus*, boundary.] —**ter'mi·nal·ly** *adv.*

ter·mi·nate (tûr'mə-nāt') *v.* **-nat·ed, -nat·ing.** To bring or come to an end; conclude. —**ter'mi·na·ble** (-nə-bəl) *adj.* —**ter'mi·na'tion** *n.* —**ter'mi·na'tive** *adj.* —**ter'mi·na'tor** *n.*

ter·mi·nol·o·gy (tûr'mə-nŏl'ə-jē) *n., pl.* **-gies.** 1. The technical terms of a particular trade, science, or art; nomenclature. 2. The study of nomenclature. [Med. Lat. *terminus*, expression + -LOGY.] —**ter'mi·no·log'i·cal** (-nə-lŏj'-ĭ-kəl) *adj.* —**ter'mi·no·log'i·cal·ly** *adv.*

ter·mi·nus (tûr'mə-nəs) *n., pl.* **-es** or **-ni** (-nī'). 1. The end of something. 2. The final stop at either end of a transportation line. [Lat.]

ter·mite (tûr'mīt') *n.* Any of numerous superficially antlike social insects that feed on wood. [Lat. *termes*, a wood-eating worm.]

tern (tûrn) *n.* Any of various sea birds resembling gulls but usu. smaller and with a forked tail. [Of Scand. orig.]

ter·na·ry (tûr'nə-rē) *adj.* 1. Composed of three or arranged in threes. 2. *Math.* a. Having the base three. b. Involving three variables. [< Lat. *terni*, three each.]

terp·si·cho·re·an (tûrp'sĭ-kə-rē'ən, -kôr'ē-ən, -kōr'-) *adj.* Of dancing. —*n.* A dancer. [< *Terpsichore*, Greek muse of dancing.]

ter·race (tĕr'əs) *n.* 1. A porch or balcony. 2. An open area adjacent to a house, used as an outdoor living area; patio. 3. A raised bank of earth with vertical or sloping sides and a flat top. 4. A row of buildings erected on raised ground or on a sloping site. —*v.* **-raced, -rac·ing.** To form into a terrace. [< Lat. *terra*, earth.]

ter·ra cot·ta (tĕr'ə kŏt'ə) *n.* 1. A hard ceramic clay used in pottery and construction. 2. A brownish orange color. [Ital.] —**ter'ra-cot'ta** *adj.*

ter·ra fir·ma (tĕr'ə fûr'mə) *n.* Dry land. [Lat., solid land.]

ter·rain (tə-rān', tĕ-) *n.* A tract of land; ground. [< Lat. *terra*, earth.]

ter·ra·pin (tĕr'ə-pĭn) *n.* Any of various aquatic North American turtles. [Of Algonquian orig.]

ter·rar·i·um (tə-râr'ē-əm, -rär'-) *n., pl.* **-ums** or **-i·a** (-ē-ə). A closed container in which small plants are grown or small animals, such as turtles or lizards, are kept. [Lat. *terra*, earth + -ARIUM.]

ter·res·tri·al (tə-rĕs'trē-əl) *adj.* 1. Of, relating to, or on the earth. 2. Of or consisting of land as distinguished from water or air. 3. Living or growing on land. —*n.* An inhabitant of the earth. [< Lat. *terra*, earth.] —**ter·res'tri·al·ly** *adv.*

ter·ri·ble (tĕr'ə-bəl) *adj.* 1. Causing terror or

fear; dreadful. **2.** Severe; intense. **3.** Very bad. **2.** Severe; to frighten.] —**ter'ri·ble·ness** n. —**ter'ri·bly** adv.

ter·ri·er (tĕr'ē-ər) n. Any of various usu. small, active dogs orig. bred to hunt burrowing animals. [< Fr. *terrier*, burrow.]

ter·rif·ic (tə-rĭf'ĭk) adj. **1.** Terrifying or frightful. **2.** Very good: *a terrific party.* **3.** Awesome; astounding. **4.** Very great; intense. [Lat. *terrificus.*] —**ter·rif'i·cal·ly** adv.

ter·ri·fy (tĕr'ə-fī') v. **-fied, -fy·ing.** To fill with terror. [Lat. *terrificare.*]

ter·ri·to·ri·al (tĕr'ĭ-tôr'ē-əl, -tōr-) adj. **1.** Of or pertaining to a territory or to its powers of jurisdiction. **2.** Regional; local. —**ter'ri·to'ri·al·ly** adv.

ter·ri·to·ry (tĕr'ĭ-tôr'ē, -tōr'ē) n., pl. **-ries.** **1.** An area of land; region. **2.** The land and waters under the jurisdiction of a government. **3.** Territory. A part of a nation not accorded statehood or provincial status. **4.** The area for which a person is responsible. **5.** A sphere of action or interest; domain. [< Lat. *terra*, land.]

ter·ror (tĕr'ər) n. **1.** Intense, overpowering fear. **2.** A terrifying object or occurrence. **3.** Violence committed by a group to attain a usu. political goal. [Lat. < *terrēre*, to frighten.]

ter·ror·ism (tĕr'ə-rĭz'əm) n. The political use of terror and intimidation. —**ter'ror·ist** n. —**ter'ror·is'tic** adj.

ter·ror·ize (tĕr'ə-rīz') v. **-ized, -iz·ing.** **1.** To fill with terror; terrify. **2.** To coerce by intimidation. —**ter'ror·i·za'tion** n. —**ter'ror·iz'er** n.

ter·ry cloth (tĕr'ē) n. An absorbent cotton fabric with uncut loops forming a pile. [Orig. unknown.]

terse (tûrs) adj. **ters·er, ters·est.** Brief and to the point; concise. [Lat. *tersus*, p.p. of *tergēre*, to wipe off.] —**terse'ly** adv. —**terse'ness** n.

ter·ti·ar·y (tûr'shē-ĕr'ē, -shə-rē) adj. **1.** Third in place, order, degree, or rank. **2.** Tertiary. Of or belonging to the geologic time, system of rocks, and sedimentary deposits of the first period of the Cenozoic era. —n. Tertiary. The Tertiary period. [< Lat. *tertius*, third.]

tes·sel·late (tĕs'ə-lāt') v. **-lat·ed, -lat·ing.** To form into a mosaic pattern. [< Lat. *tessella*, a small cube.] —**tes'sel·la'tion** n.

test (tĕst) n. **1.** A way of examining something to determine its characteristics or effectiveness. **2.** A series of questions or problems designed to measure knowledge or intelligence. **3.** A standard; criterion. [< Lat. *testum*, pot.] —**test** v. —**test'er** n.

tes·ta·ment (tĕs'tə-mənt) n. **1.** A legal document providing for the disposition of personal property after death; will. **2.** Testament. Either of the two main divisions of the Bible, the Old Testament and the New Testament. **3.** A statement of belief. **4.** Convincing evidence. [< Lat. *testis*, witness.]

tes·tate (tĕs'tāt') adj. Having made a legally valid will. [< Lat. *testari*, to make a will.]

tes·ta·tor (tĕs'tā'tər, tĕ-stā'tər) n. One who has made a will. —**tes·ta'trix** n.

tes·ti·cle (tĕs'tĭ-kəl) n. A testis. [< Lat. *testis*.]

tes·ti·fy (tĕs'tə-fī') v. **-fied, -fy·ing.** To make a declaration under oath; give sworn testi-

mony. **2.** To serve as evidence. **3.** To declare publicly. [< Lat. *testificari*.] —**tes'ti·fi'er** n.

tes·ti·mo·ni·al (tĕs'tə-mō'nē-əl, -mōn'yəl) n. **1.** A formal statement testifying to a particular fact. **2.** A written affirmation of another's character or worth. **3.** A tribute. —**tes'ti·mo'ni·al** adj.

tes·ti·mo·ny (tĕs'tə-mō'nē) n., pl. **-nies.** **1. a.** A declaration or affirmation made under oath, esp. in a court of law. **b.** All such declarations in a given legal case. **2.** Evidence in support of a fact or assertion; proof. **3.** A public declaration. [< Lat. *testimonium*.]

tes·tis (tĕs'tĭs) n., pl. **-tes** (-tēz'). The male reproductive gland. [< Lat. *testis*.]

test tube n. A cylindrical clear glass container used in laboratory experiments.

tes·ty (tĕs'tē) adj. **-ti·er, -ti·est.** Irritable; touchy. [< OFr. *teste*, head.] —**tes'ti·ly** adv. —**tes'ti·ness** n.

tet·a·nus (tĕt'n-əs) n. An acute, often fatal infectious disease caused by a bacillus and characterized by rigidity and spasmodic contraction of the voluntary muscles. [< Gk. *tetanos*, stretched.]

tête-à-tête (tāt'ə-tāt') adv. Together without a third person. —n. A private conversation between two people. [Fr.] —**tête-à-tête** adj.

teth (tĕt, tĕs) n. The 9th letter of the Hebrew alphabet. See table at **alphabet.** [Heb. *tēth.*]

teth·er (tĕth'ər) n. **1.** A rope or chain for an animal, allowing it a short radius to move about. **2.** The limit of one's capacity or endurance. [< ON *tjothr*.]

tetra- pref. Four: *tetrahedron*. [Gk.]

tet·ra·cy·cline (tĕt'rə-sī'klēn') n. A yellow crystalline compound, $C_{22}H_{24}N_2O_8$, used as an antibiotic. [TETRA- + CYCL(IC) + -INE[2].]

tet·ra·he·dron (tĕt'rə-hē'drən) n., pl. **-drons** or **-dra** (-drə). A polyhedron with four faces. —**tet'ra·he'dral** adj.

te·tram·e·ter (tĕ-trăm'ĭ-tər) n. A verse line with four metrical feet.

Teu·ton (tōōt'n, tyōōt'n) n. **1.** A member of an ancient people, prob. of Germanic or Celtic origin, who lived in northern Europe until about 100 B.C. **2.** A German.

Teu·ton·ic (tōō-tŏn'ĭk, tyōō-) adj. **1.** Of or relating to the Teutons. **2.** Of or relating to the Germanic languages. —n. Germanic.

Te·vet (tā'vəs, tā-vēt') n. The 4th month of the Hebrew year. See table at **calendar.** [Heb. *tēbhēth.*]

Te·wa (tā'wə, tĕ'wə) n., pl. **-wa** or **-was.** **1. a.** A Tanoan-speaking Indian tribe of New Mexico and northeastern Arizona. **b.** A member of this tribe. **2.** The Tanoan language of the Tewa.

text (tĕkst) n. **1.** The wording or words of something written or printed. **2.** The body of a printed work as distinct from a preface, footnote, or appendix. **3.** A Scriptural passage to be read and expounded upon in a sermon. **4.** The subject matter of a discourse. **5.** A textbook. [< Lat. *textus*.] —**tex'tu·al** (tĕks'chōō-əl) adj.

text·book (tĕkst'bŏŏk') n. A book used for the study of a particular subject.

tex·tile (tĕks'tīl', -stəl) n. **1.** Cloth or fabric, esp. when woven or knitted. **2.** Fiber or yarn

---

ă pat ā pay â care ä father ĕ pet ē be ĭ pit ī tie î pier ŏ pot ō toe ô paw, for oi noise ōō took
ōō boot ou out th thin th this ŭ cut û urge yōō abuse zh vision ə about, item, edible, gallop, circus

for weaving cloth. —*adj.* Of or for textiles. [< Lat. *textus,* p.p. of *texere,* to weave.]

tex·ture (tĕks'chər) *n.* **1.** The appearance of a fabric resulting from the woven arrangement of its yarns or fibers. **2.** The composition or structure of a substance; grain. [Lat. *textura*.] —**tex'tur·al** *adj.* —**tex'tur·al·ly** *adv.*

-th¹ *suff.* Var. of **-eth¹**.

-th² *suff.* Used to form ordinal numbers: *thousandth.* [< OE *-tha.*]

Th The symbol for the element thorium.

thal·a·mus (thăl'ə-məs) *n., pl.* **-mi** (-mī'). A large mass of gray matter that relays sensory stimuli to the cerebral cortex. [< Gk. *thalamos,* inner chamber.] —**tha·lam'ic** (thə-lăm'-ĭk) *adj.*

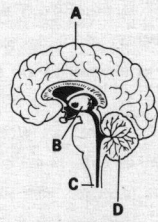

thalamus

A. Cerebrum
B. Thalamus
C. Spinal cord
D. Cerebellum

thal·li·um (thăl'ē-əm) *n. Symbol* **Tl** A soft, malleable, highly toxic metallic element, used in rodent and ant poisons, photoelectric cells, and low-melting glass. Atomic number 81; atomic weight 204.37. [Lat. *thallus,* green shoot (< its green spectral line) + -IUM.]

than (thăn; *thən when unstressed*) *conj.* **1.** Used to introduce the second element or clause of a comparison of inequality: *Pound cake is richer than angel food cake.* **2.** Used to introduce the rejected alternative in statements of preference: *I'd much rather play than work.* [< OE *thanne.*]

thane (thān) *n.* A feudal lord in Scotland. [< OE *thegn.*]

thank (thăngk) *v.* **1.** To express gratitude to. **2.** To credit. [< OE *thancian.*]

thank·ful (thăngk'fəl) *adj.* Grateful. —**thank'ful·ly** *adv.* —**thank'ful·ness** *n.*

thank·less (thăngk'lĭs) *adj.* **1.** Ungrateful. **2.** Not apt to be appreciated: *a thankless task.* —**thank'less·ly** *adv.* —**thank'less·ness** *n.*

thanks (thăngks) *pl.n.* An acknowledgment of a favor, gift, etc. —*interj.* Used to express gratitude. —**idiom. thanks to.** On account of; because of.

thanks·giv·ing (thăngks-gĭv'ĭng) *n.* An act of giving thanks, esp. to God.

Thanksgiving Day *n.* A U.S. national holiday set apart for giving thanks to God, celebrated on the 4th Thursday of Nov.

that (thăt; *thət when unstressed*) *adj., pl.* **those** (thōz). **1.** Being the one indicated or implied. **2.** Being the one farther away or more remote: *This room is warm and that one's cold.* —*pron., pl.* **those. 1.** The one indicated or

implied: *That is my desk.* **2.** Who, whom, or which: *people that I have known; things that have to be done.* **3.** In, on, by, or with which: *She called the day that she arrived.* —*adv.* To such an extent: *Is it that difficult?* —*conj.* **1.** Used to introduce a subordinate clause: *I think that he is coming tonight.* **2.** Used to introduce an exclamatory clause expressing a wish: *Oh, that I might live forever!* [< OE *thæt.*]

thatch (thăch) *n.* Plant stalks or foliage used for roofing. —*v.* To cover with or as if with thatch. [< OE *theccan,* to cover.] —**thatch'er** *n.* —**thatch'y** *adj.*

thaw (thô) *v.* **1.** To change from a frozen solid to a liquid by gradual warming. **2.** To become warm enough for snow and ice to melt. **3.** To become less reserved. —*n.* **1.** The process of thawing. **2.** A period during which ice and snow melt. **3.** A lessening of restraint or tension. [< OE *thawian.*]

the (thē *before a vowel; thə before a consonant*) *def. art.* Used as an adjective before singular or plural nouns and noun phrases that denote particular or usu. previously specified persons or things or before certain nouns and adjectives with generic force. —*adv.* To that extent; by that much: *the sooner the better.* —*prep.* Per; each: *cost a dollar the box.* [< OE *thē.*]

the·a·ter or **the·a·tre** (thē'ə-tər) *n.* **1.** A building for the presentation of motion pictures and dramatic performances. **2.** A similar place with tiers of seats. **3.** Dramatic literature or performance. **4.** A setting for dramatic events. [< Gk. *theatron.*]

the·at·ri·cal (thē-ăt'rĭ-kəl) *adj.* **1.** Of or suitable for the theater. **2.** Affectedly dramatic. —*n.* **theatricals.** Stage performances, esp. by amateurs. —**the·at'ri·cal'i·ty** (-kăl'ĭ-tē) or **the·at'ri·cal·ness** *n.* —**the·at'ri·cal·ly** *adv.*

the·at·rics (thē-ăt'rĭks) *pl.n.* **1.** (*used with a sing. verb*) The art of the theater. **2.** Theatrical effects or mannerisms.

thee (thē) *pron. Archaic.* The objective case of **thou.**

theft (thĕft) *n.* The act of stealing; larceny. [< OE *thiefth.*]

their (thâr; *thər when unstressed*) *pron.* The possessive case of **they.** Used as a modifier before a noun: *their house.* [< ON *theira.*]

theirs (thârz) *pron.* The one or ones belonging to them: *The large packages are theirs.*

the·ism (thē'ĭz'əm) *n.* Belief in the existence of a god or gods. —**the'ist** *n.* —**the·is'tic** or **the·is'ti·cal** *adj.* —**the·is'ti·cal·ly** *adv.*

them (thĕm; *thəm when unstressed*) *pron.* The objective case of **they.** Used as the direct or indirect object of a verb or as the object of a preposition. [< ON *theim* and < OE *them.*]

the·mat·ic (thĭ-măt'ĭk) *adj.* Of, relating to, or being a theme. [Gk. *thematikos.*] —**the·mat'i·cal·ly** *adv.*

theme (thēm) *n.* **1.** A topic of discourse or discussion. **2.** The subject of an artistic work. **3.** A short written composition. **4.** A melody forming the basis of variations or other development in a musical composition. [< Gk. *thema,* proposition.]

theme song *n.* A recurring or distinctive song that is associated with a particular production, character, or performer.

them·selves (thĕm-sĕlvz', thəm-) *pron.* The ones identical to them. Used: **1.** Reflexively as the direct or indirect object of a verb or as the object of a preposition. **2.** For emphasis: *They themselves were unaware of his presence.* —*idiom.* **by themselves.** Alone or without help.

then (thĕn) *adv.* **1.** At that time in the past. **2.** Next in time, space, or order. **3.** At another time in the future. **4.** In that case; accordingly. **5.** In addition; besides. **6.** Yet; on the other hand. —*n.* A particular time or moment. —*adj.* Being so at that time. [< OE *thenne.*]

thence (thĕns, thĕns) *adv.* **1.** From there. **2.** From that circumstance or source. **3.** From that time; thenceforth. [< OE *thanon.*]

thence·forth (thĕns-fôrth′, thĕns-) *adv.* From then on.

thence·for·ward (thĕns-fôr′wərd, thĕns-) *adv.* Also **thence·for·wards** (-wərdz). From that time on; thenceforth.

theo– or **the–** *pref.* A god or gods: *theocracy.* [< Gk. *theos,* god.]

the·oc·ra·cy (thē-ŏk′rə-sē) *n., pl.* **-cies.** **1.** Government by a god regarded as the ruling power or by officials claiming divine sanction. **2.** A state so governed. —**the′o·crat′** *n.* —**the′o·crat′ic** *adj.* —**the′o·crat′i·cal·ly** *adv.*

the·ol·o·gy (thē-ŏl′ə-jē) *n., pl.* **-gies.** **1.** The study of the nature of God and religious truth. **2.** An organized body of opinions concerning God and man's relationship to God. —**the·o′lo·gi·an** (thē′ə-lō′jən) *n.* —**the·o·log′i·cal** (-lŏj′ĭ-kəl) *adj.* —**the·o·log′i·cal·ly** *adv.*

the·o·rem (thē′ər-əm) *n.* **1.** An idea or proposition that is demonstrably true or is assumed to be so. **2.** *Math.* A proposition that is proven or to be proved. [< Gk. *theōrein,* to look at.]

the·o·ret·i·cian (thē′ər-ĭ-tĭsh′ən) *n.* One who formulates, studies, or is expert in the theory of a science or art.

the·o·rize (thē′ə-rīz′) *v.* **-rized, -riz·ing.** To formulate or analyze theories. —**the′o·ri·za′tion** *n.* —**the′o·riz′er** or **the′o·rist** *n.*

the·o·ry (thē′ə-rē) *n., pl.* **-ries.** **1.** A statement or set of statements designed to explain a phenomenon or class of phenomena. **2.** A set of rules or principles designed for the study or practice of an art or discipline. **3.** Abstract thought untested in practice. **4.** An assumption or guess. [< Gk. *theōria.*] —**the′o·ret′i·cal** (-rĕt′ĭ-kəl) *adj.* —**the′o·ret′i·cal·ly** *adv.*

the·os·o·phy (thē-ŏs′ə-fē) *n., pl.* **-phies.** Religious speculation dealing with the mystical apprehension of God. [THEO– + Gk. *sophia,* wisdom.] —**the′o·soph′ic** (-ə-sŏf′ĭk) or **the′o·soph′i·cal** *adj.* —**the′o·soph′i·cal·ly** *adv.* —**the·os′o·phist** *n.*

ther·a·peu·tic (thĕr′ə-pyōō′tĭk) *adj.* Having healing or curative powers. [< Gk. *thera·peuein,* to treat medically.] —**ther′a·peu′ti·cal·ly** *adv.*

ther·a·peu·tics (thĕr′ə-pyōō′tĭks) *n.* (*used with a sing. verb*). The medical treatment of disease. —**ther′a·peu′tist** *n.*

ther·a·py (thĕr′ə-pē) *n., pl.* **-pies.** The treatment of illness or disability. [< Gk. *theraps,* attendant.] —**ther′a·pist** *n.*

there (thâr) *adv.* **1.** At or in that place. **2.** To, into, or toward that place; thither. **3.** At a point of action or time. —*n.* That place. [< OE *thēr.*]

Usage: **There** as an adverb meaning "in that place" comes after the noun in constructions introduced by *that: That boy there is to blame.* While some dialects allow *there* before the noun, as in *that there boy,* this use is inappropriate in formal English.

there·a·bout (thâr′ə-bout′) *adv.* Also **there·a·bouts** (-bouts′). Approximately.

there·af·ter (thâr-ăf′tər) *adv.* After that; from then on.

there·at (thâr-ăt′) *adv.* **1.** At a specified place. **2.** At such time. **3.** By reason of that.

there·by (thâr-bī′) *adv.* By that means.

there·fore (thâr′fôr′, -fōr′) *adv.* For that reason; consequently.

there·from (thâr-frŭm′, -frŏm′) *adv.* From that, this, or it.

there·in (thâr-ĭn′) *adv.* In that place or respect.

there·in·af·ter (thâr′ĭn-ăf′tər) *adv.* In a later or subsequent portion.

there·of (thâr-ŭv′, -ŏv′) *adv.* **1.** Of that or it. **2.** From that cause or origin.

there·on (thâr-ŏn′, -ŏn′) *adv.* **1.** On or upon that or it. **2.** Following that immediately.

there·to (thâr-tōō′) *adv.* To that or it; thereunto.

there·to·fore (thâr′tə-fôr′, -fōr′) *adv.* Up to that time.

there·un·to (thâr′ŭn-tōō′) *adv.* To that or it; thereto.

there·up·on (thâr′ə-pŏn′, -pôn′) *adv.* **1.** Upon that or it. **2.** Immediately following that. **3.** In consequence of that; therefore.

there·with (thâr-wĭth′, -wĭth′) *adv.* **1.** With that. **2.** Immediately thereafter.

there·with·al (thâr-wĭth-ôl′) *adv.* **1.** In addition to that; besides. **2.** *Obs.* Therewith.

ther·mal (thûr′məl) *adj.* Of, using, producing, or caused by heat. —**ther′mal·ly** *adv.*

thermo– *pref.* Heat: *thermodynamics.* [< Gk. *thermos.*]

ther·mo·cou·ple (thûr′mə-kŭp′əl) *n.* A device consisting of two dissimilar metals joined at two points, the potential difference between the two junctions being a measure of their difference in temperature.

ther·mo·dy·nam·ics (thûr′mō-dī-năm′ĭks) *n.* (*used with a sing. verb*). The physics of the relationships between heat and other forms of energy. —**ther′mo·dy·nam′ic** *adj.* —**ther′mo·dy·nam′i·cal·ly** *adv.*

ther·mom·e·ter (thər-mŏm′ĭ-tər) *n.* An instrument for measuring temperature. —**ther′mo·met′ric** or **ther′mo·met′ri·cal** *adj.* —**ther·mom′e·try** *n.*

ther·mo·nu·cle·ar (thûr′mō-nōō′klē-ər) *adj.* **1.** Of or derived from the fusion of atomic nuclei at high temperatures. **2.** Of atomic weapons based on nuclear fusion.

ther·mo·plas·tic (thûr′mə-plăs′tĭk) *adj.* Soft when heated but hard when cooled. —*n.* A thermoplastic material.

Thermos bottle (thûr′məs). A trademark for a vacuum flask.

ther·mo·set·ting (thûr′mō-sĕt′ĭng) *adj.* Becoming permanently hardened or rigid when heated.

ther·mo·stat (thûr′mə-stăt′) *n.* A device that

automatically regulates temperature-controlling equipment, such as furnaces, refrigerators, and air conditioners. —**ther'mo·stat'ic** adj. —**ther'mo·stat'i·cal·ly** adv.

the·sau·rus (thĭ-sôr'əs) n., pl. **-es** or **-sau·ri** (-sôr'ī'). A book of selected words, esp. a dictionary of synonyms. [< Gk. *thēsauros*, treasure.]

these (thēz) pron. Pl. of **this.**

the·sis (thē'sĭs) n., pl. **-ses** (-sēz'). 1. A proposition advanced and maintained by argument. 2. A lengthy essay or treatise resulting from original academic research. [< Gk.]

thes·pi·an (thĕs'pē-ən). Also **Thes·pi·an.** —adj. Of or pertaining to drama; dramatic. —n. An actor or actress. [< *Thespis*, Greek poet of the 6th cent. B.C.]

Thes·sa·lo·ni·ans (thĕs'ə-lō'nē-ənz) pl.n. (used with a sing. verb). See table at **Bible.**

the·ta (thā'tə, thē'-) n. The 8th letter of the Greek alphabet. See table at **alphabet.** [Gk. *thēta*.]

thews (thōōz, thyōōz) pl.n. Sinews or muscles. [< OE *thēaw*, a characteristic.]

they (thā) pron. Those ones. Used as the plural of *he, she,* and *it.* [< ON *their.*]

they'd (thād). 1. They had. 2. They would.

they'll (thāl). They will.

they're (thâr). They are.

they've (thāv). They have.

thi·a·mine (thī'ə-mĭn, -mēn') n. Also **thi·a·min** (-mĭn). A B-complex vitamin, necessary for carbohydrate metabolism, occurring naturally in grains, yeast, and meat. [Gk. *theion,* sulfur + (VIT)AMIN.]

thick (thĭk) adj. **-er, -est.** 1. a. Relatively great in depth or in extent from one surface to the opposite; not thin. b. Measuring in this dimension: *two inches thick.* 2. Thickset. 3. Dense; concentrated. 4. Having a viscous consistency; not transparent or fluid. 5. Having a great number; abounding. 6. Indistinctly articulated. 7. Pronounced; heavy. 8. Lacking mental agility; stupid. 9. *Informal.* Very friendly; intimate. 10. *Informal.* Excessive. —n. 1. The thickest part. 2. The most active or intense part. [< OE *thicce.*] —**thick'ly** adv. —**thick'ness** n.

thick·en (thĭk'ən) v. To make or become thick or thicker. —**thick'en·er** n. —**thick'en·ing** n.

thick·et (thĭk'ĭt) n. A dense growth of shrubs or underbrush. [< OE *thiccet.*]

thick·set (thĭk'sĕt') adj. 1. Having a short, wide body; stocky. 2. Placed closely together.

thick-skinned (thĭk'skĭnd') adj. 1. Having a thick skin. 2. Not easily offended or hurt.

thief (thēf) n., pl. **thieves** (thēvz). One who steals. [< OE *thēof.*]

thieve (thēv) v. **thieved, thiev·ing.** To steal. [< THIEF.] —**thiev'er·y** n.

thigh (thī) n. The portion of the leg between the hip and the knee. [< OE *thēoh.*]

thigh·bone (thī'bōn') n. The femur.

thim·ble (thĭm'bəl) n. A small metal or plastic cup worn to protect the finger in sewing. [< OE *thūma,* thumb.] —**thim'ble·ful** n.

thin (thĭn) adj. **thin·ner, thin·nest.** 1. Having a relatively small distance between opposite sides or surfaces. 2. Not great in diameter or cross section; fine. 3. Lean or slender. 4. Not dense or concentrated; sparse. 5. Not rich or heavy in consistency. 6. Lacking force or substance; flimsy. —v. **thinned, thin·ning.** To become or make thin or thinner. [< OE *thynne.*] —**thin'ly** adv. —**thin'ness** n.

Syns: thin, bony, lanky, lean, scrawny, skinny, slender, spare adj.

thine (thīn) pron. Archaic & Poetic. 1. A possessive form of thou. 2. Used instead of *thy* before an initial vowel or *h: thine enemy.* [< OE *thin.*]

thing (thĭng) n. 1. Something that exists; entity. 2. A tangible object. 3. An inanimate object. 4. A creature. 5. **things.** a. Possessions; belongings. b. The general state of affairs; conditions. 6. An article of clothing. 7. An act, deed, or work. 8. A thought or notion. 9. A piece of information. 10. A matter to be dealt with. 11. A turn of events. 12. *Slang.* A uniquely suitable or satisfying activity: *doing his own thing.* [< OE.]

think (thĭngk) v. **thought** (thôt), **think·ing.** 1. To have as a thought; formulate in the mind. 2. To ponder. 3. To reason. 4. To believe; suppose. 5. To remember; call to mind. 6. To visualize; imagine. 7. To devise or invent. 8. To consider. —*phrasal verb.* **think up.** To devise; invent. [< OE *thencan.*] —**think'a·ble** adj. —**think'a·bly** adv. —**think'er** n.

thin·ner (thĭn'ər) n. A liquid, such as turpentine, mixed with paint to reduce viscosity.

thin-skinned (thĭn'skĭnd') adj. 1. Having a thin rind or skin. 2. Oversensitive.

third (thûrd) n. 1. The ordinal number that matches the number 3 in a series. 2. One of three equal parts. 3. The musical interval formed by two tones of a diatonic scale that are separated by a tone. 4. The next higher gear after second in an automotive transmission. [< OE *thridda.*] —**third** adj. & adv. —**third'ly** adv.

third base n. *Baseball.* 1. The third base to be reached by a runner. 2. The area around the third base that must be defended by a player at that position. —**third baseman** n.

third-degree burn (thûrd'dĭ-grē') n. A severe burn in which the outer layer of skin is destroyed and sensitive nerve endings are exposed.

third person n. A set of grammatical forms used in referring to a person or thing other than the speaker or writer or the one addressed.

Third World n. Also **third world.** Those countries not allied with the Communist or non-Communist blocs.

thirst (thûrst) n. 1. a. A sensation of dryness in the mouth related to a desire to drink. b. The desire to drink. 2. An insistent desire or craving. —v. 1. To be thirsty. 2. To crave; yearn. [< OE *thurst.*] —**thirst'i·ly** adv. —**thirst'i·ness** n. —**thirst'y** adj.

thir·teen (thûr'tēn') n. 1. The cardinal number equal to the sum of 12 + 1. 2. The 13th in a set or sequence. 3. Something having 13 parts, units, or members. [< OE *thrēotīne.*] —**thirteen'** adj. & pron.

thir·teenth (thûr'tēnth') n. 1. The ordinal number that matches the number 13 in a series. 2. One of 13 equal parts. —**thir'teenth'** adj. & adv.

thir·ti·eth (thûr'tē-ĭth) n. 1. The ordinal number that matches the number 30 in a series. 2. One of 30 equal parts. —**thir'ti·eth** adj. & adv.

thir·ty (thûr'tē) n., pl. **-ties.** The cardinal number equal to 3 × 10. [< OE *thrītig.*] —**thir'ty** adj. & pron.

this (*this*) *pron., pl.* **these** (*thēz*). **1.** The person or thing present, nearby, or just mentioned. **2.** What is about to be said. **3.** The one that is nearer than another or the one compared with the other. **4.** The present occasion or time. —*adj., pl.* **these. 1.** Being just mentioned or present. **2.** Being nearer than another or compared with another. **3.** Being about to be stated or described. —*adv.* To this extent. [< OE *thes.*]

Usage: *This* often occurs in speech as an emphatic variant of the definite article *a: I have this terrible headache.* This usage should be avoided in writing.

this·tle (*this'əl*) *n.* Any of various prickly plants with usu. purplish flowers. [< OE *thistel.*]

this·tle·down (*this'əl-doun'*) *n.* The silky down attached to the seeds of a thistle.

thith·er (*thith'ər, thĭth'-*) *adv.* To or toward that place; there. —*adj.* Being on the more distant side; farther. [< OE *thider.*]

thole pin (*thōl*) *n.* A peg set in pairs in the gunwale of a boat to serve as an oarlock. [< OE *tholl.*]

thong (*thông, thŏng*) *n.* A strip of leather used for binding or lashing. [< OE *thwong.*]

tho·rax (*thôr'ăks, thōr'-*) *n., pl.* **-es** or **tho·ra·ces** (*thôr'ə-sēz', thōr'-*). The part of the body between the neck and the diaphragm, partially encased by the ribs; chest. [< Gk. *thōrax.*] —**tho·rac'ic** (*thə-răs'ĭk*) *adj.*

tho·ri·um (*thôr'ē-əm, thōr'-*) *n.* Symbol **Th** A silvery-white metallic element used in magnesium alloys. Atomic number 90; atomic weight 232.038. [< *Thor,* Norse god of thunder.]

thorn (*thôrn*) *n.* **1. a.** A sharp, woody spine protruding from a plant stem. **b.** Any of various shrubs, trees, or plants bearing such spines. **2.** One that causes pain or discomfort. [< OE.] —**thorn'i·ness** *n.* —**thorn'y** *adj.*

thor·ough (*thûr'ō*) *adj.* **1.** Complete in all respects. **2.** Painstakingly careful. [< OE *thuruh,* through.] —**thor'ough·ly** *adv.* —**thor'ough·ness** *n.*

thor·ough·bred (*thûr'ō-brĕd', thûr'ə-, thûr'-*) *adj.* Bred of pure or pedigreed stock. —*n.* **1.** A purebred or pedigreed animal. **2.** Thoroughbred. Any of a breed of horse originating from a cross of Arabian stallions with English mares.

thor·ough·fare (*thûr'ō-fâr', thûr'ə-, thûr'-*) *n.* A main road or public highway.

thor·ough·go·ing (*thûr'ō-gō'ĭng, thûr'ə-, thûr'-*) *adj.* **1.** Complete in all respects. **2.** Absolute; unqualified.

those (*thōz*) *adj.* & *pron.* Pl. of **that.**

thou (*thou*) *pron.* Archaic. The 2nd person sing. in the nominative case, equivalent to **you.** [< OE *thū.*]

though (*thō*) *adv.* However; nevertheless. —*conj.* **1.** Although; while. **2.** Even if. [ME, of Scand. orig.]

thought (*thôt*) *v. p.t.* & *p.p.* of **think.** —*n.* **1.** The process or power of thinking. **2.** An idea. **3.** A body of ideas. **4.** Consideration; attention. **5.** Intention; expectation. **6.** A small amount; bit.

thought·ful (*thôt'fəl*) *adj.* **1.** Contemplative; meditative. **2.** Well thought-out. **3.** Showing regard for others; considerate. —**thought'ful·ly** *adv.* —**thought'ful·ness** *n.*

thought·less (*thôt'lĭs*) *adj.* **1.** Careless; unthinking. **2.** Reckless. **3.** Inconsiderate. —**thought'less·ly** *adv.* —**thought'less·ness** *n.*

thou·sand (*thou'zənd*) *n.* The cardinal number equal to 10 × 100 or 10³. [< OE *thūsend.*] —**thou'sand** *adj.* & *pron.*

thou·sandth (*thou'zəndth, -zənth*) *n.* **1.** The ordinal number that matches the number 1,000 in a series. **2.** One of 1,000 equal parts. —**thou'sandth** *adj.* & *adv.*

thrall (*thrôl*) *n.* **1.** One in bondage, as a slave or serf. **2.** Servitude. [< ON *thrǽll.*] —**thrall'dom** (*-dəm*) or **thral'dom** *n.*

thrash (*thrăsh*) *v.* **1.** To beat or flog with or as with a whip. **2.** To move wildly or violently. **3.** To defeat utterly. [< THRESH.] —**thrash'er** *n.*

thrash·er (*thrăsh'ər*) *n.* A long-tailed New World songbird often having a spotted breast. [Perh. < THRUSH.]

thread (*thrĕd*) *n.* **1.** A fine cord of a fibrous material made of filaments twisted together. **2.** Something like a thread, as in fineness or length. **3.** A helical or spiral ridge on a screw, nut, or bolt. —*v.* **1.** To pass one end of a thread through (e.g. a needle). **2.** To pass cautiously through. **3.** To machine a thread on (a screw, nut, or bolt). [< OE *thrǽd.*] —**thread'er** *n.* —**thread'y** *adj.*

thread·bare (*thrĕd'bâr'*) *adj.* **1.** Having the nap so worn that the threads show through. **2.** Wearing old, shabby clothing. **3.** Hackneyed.

threat (*thrĕt*) *n.* **1.** An expression of an intention to inflict pain, injury, or evil. **2.** One regarded as a possible danger. [< OE *thrēat.*]

threat·en (*thrĕt'n*) *v.* **1.** To utter a threat (against). **2.** To serve as a threat to; endanger. **3.** To portend. **4.** To indicate danger or other harm. —**threat'en·er** *n.* —**threat'en·ing·ly** *adv.*

three (*thrē*) *n.* **1.** The cardinal number equal to the sum of 2 + 1. **2.** The 3rd in a set or sequence. **3.** Something having three parts, units, or members. [< OE *thrī.*] —**three** *adj.* & *pron.*

three-di·men·sion·al (*thrē'dĭ-mĕn'shən-əl*) *adj.* **1.** Of, having, or existing in three dimensions. **2.** Having or appearing to have extension in depth.

three·score (*thrē'skôr', -skōr'*) *adj.* Sixty. —**three'score** *n.*

three·some (*thrē'səm*) *n.* A group of three.

thren·o·dy (*thrĕn'ə-dē*) *n., pl.* **-dies.** A song of lamentation. [Gk. *thrēnos,* lament + Gk. *ōidē,* song.] —**thren'o·dist** *n.*

thresh (*thrĕsh*) *v.* **1.** To beat (cereal plants), as with a flail, to remove the grain or seeds. **2.** To thrash. [< OE *threscan.*] —**thresh'er** *n.*

thresh·old (*thrĕsh'ōld', -hōld'*) *n.* **1.** The piece of wood or stone placed beneath a door. **2.** An entrance. **3.** The beginning; outset. **4.** The lowest level or intensity at which a stimulus can be perceived or can produce a given effect. [< OE *therscold.*]

threw (*thrōō*) *v. p.t.* of **throw.**

thrice (*thrīs*) *adv.* Three times. [< OE *thriga.*]

thrift (*thrĭft*) *n.* Wise economy in the management of money and other resources; frugality.

[< ON, prosperity.] —thrift'i·ly adv. —thrift'i·ness n. —thrift'y adj.

thrill (thrĭl) v. 1. To feel or cause to feel a sudden intense sensation. 2. To quiver or cause to quiver; vibrate. —n. 1. A quivering or trembling. 2. Something that produces great excitement. [< OE thyrlian, to pierce.] —thrill'er n. —thrill'ing·ly adv.

thrive (thrīv) v. throve (thrōv) or thrived, thrived or thriv·en (thrĭv'ən), thriv·ing. 1. To grow or do well; flourish. 2. To prosper. [< ON thrīfa, to seize.] —thriv'er n.

throat (thrōt) n. 1. The portion of the digestive tract lying between the rear of the mouth and the esophagus. 2. The anterior part of the neck. [< OE throte.] —throat'ed adj.

throat·y (thrō'tē) adj. -i·er, -i·est. Sounded or seemingly sounded deep in the throat. —throat'i·ly adv. —throat'i·ness n.

throb (thrŏb) v. throbbed, throb·bing. 1. To beat rapidly or violently; pound. 2. To vibrate rhythmically. [ME throbben.] —throb n. —throb'bing·ly adv.

throe (thrō) n. 1. Often throes. A severe pang or spasm of pain. 2. throes. Agonizing struggle or effort. [< OE thrawe.]

throm·bo·sis (thrŏm-bō'sĭs) n., pl. -ses (-sēz'). The formation or presence of a thrombus.

throm·bus (thrŏm'bəs) n., pl. -bi (-bī'). A blood clot that obstructs a blood vessel or is formed in a chamber of the heart. [< Gk. thrombos, clot.]

throne (thrōn) n. 1. The chair occupied by a sovereign, bishop, etc., on ceremonial occasions. 2. Sovereign power or rank. [< Gk. thronos.]

throng (thrông) n. A large group of people or things crowded together; multitude. —v. 1. To crowd into or around. 2. To move in a throng. [< OE thrang.]

throt·tle (thrŏt'l) n. 1. a. A valve in an internal-combustion engine that regulates the amount of vaporized fuel entering the cylinders. b. A similar valve in a steam engine regulating the amount of steam. 2. A lever or pedal controlling this valve. —v. -tled, -tling. 1. To regulate the speed of (an engine) with a throttle. 2. To strangle; choke. 3. To suppress: tried to throttle the press. [< ME throte, throat.] —throt'tler n.

through (thrōō) prep. 1. In one side and out another side of. 2. In the midst of. 3. By way of. 4. By the means or agency of. 5. Here and there in; around. 6. From the beginning to the end of. 7. Done or finished with. —adv. 1. From one end or side to another end or side. 2. From beginning to end. 3. To a conclusion. 4. Out into the open. —adj. 1. Passing or extending from one end, side, or surface to another. 2. Allowing continuous passage; unobstructed. 3. Finished; done. [< OE thuruh.]

through·out (thrōō-out') prep. In, to, through, or during every part of: throughout the night. —adv. 1. Everywhere. 2. During the entire duration.

through·way (thrōō'wā') n. Var. of thruway.

throve (thrōv) v. A p.t. of thrive.

throw (thrō) v. threw (thrōō), thrown (thrōn), throw·ing. 1. To propel through the air with a swift motion of the arm; fling. 2. To put with or as if with force; hurl. 3. To cast: throw a shadow. 4. To put on or off casually. 5. Informal. To arrange or give: throw a party. 6. Informal. To lose (a contest) purposely.

7. To actuate (a switch or control lever). —phrasal verbs. throw away or out. To discard. throw back. To revert to an earlier stage. throw over. To desert; forsake. throw up. To vomit. —n. 1. The act of throwing. 2. The distance, height, or direction of something thrown. 3. A light coverlet. [< OE thrāwan, to twist.] —throw'er n.

throw·back (thrō'băk') n. A reversion to an earlier type or stage.

thru (thrōō) prep., adv., & adj. Informal. Through.

thrum (thrŭm) v. thrummed, thrum·ming. To play (a stringed instrument) idly or monotonously; strum. [Imit.] —thrum n.

thrush (thrŭsh) n. Any of various songbirds usu. having brownish upper plumage and a spotted breast. [< OE thrÿsce.]

thrust (thrŭst) v. thrust, thrust·ing. 1. To push or drive forcibly. 2. To stab; pierce. 3. To force into a specified condition or situation. 4. To interject. —n. 1. A forceful shove or push. 2. a. A driving force or pressure. b. The forward-directed force developed in a jet or rocket engine as a reaction to the rearward ejection of hot gases. 3. A stab. 4. Outward or lateral stress in a structure. 5. The general tendency; point. [< ON thrÿsta.]

thru·way (thrōō'wā') n. Also through·way. An expressway.

thud (thŭd) n. 1. A dull sound. 2. A blow or fall causing such a sound. [Perh. < OE thyddan, to strike with a weapon.] —thud v.

thug (thŭg) n. A brutal ruffian or hoodlum. [< Skt. sthagah, a cheat.] —thug'ger·y n. —thug'gish adj.

thu·li·um (thōō'lē-əm) n. Symbol Tm A bright silvery rare-earth element, one isotope of which is used in small portable medical x-ray units. Atomic number 69; atomic weight 168.934. [< Thule, the northernmost part of the ancient world.]

thumb (thŭm) n. 1. The short first digit of the hand, opposable to the other four fingers. 2. The part of a glove or mitten that covers the thumb. —v. 1. To soil or wear by handling. 2. Informal. To hitchhike. —idiom. all thumbs. Clumsy. [< OE thūma.]

thumb·nail (thŭm'nāl') n. The nail of the thumb. —adj. Brief: a thumbnail sketch.

thumb·screw (thŭm'skrōō') n. A screw made so it can be turned with the thumb and fingers.

thumb·tack (thŭm'tăk') n. A smooth-headed tack that can be pressed into place with the thumb.

thump (thŭmp) n. 1. A blow with a blunt or heavy instrument. 2. The muffled sound produced by such a blow. —v. 1. To strike with a blunt or dull instrument so as to produce a muffled sound. 2. To pound. [Imit.] —thump'er n.

thun·der (thŭn'dər) n. 1. The explosive sound emitted as a result of the electrical discharge of lightning. 2. A rumbling sound similar to thunder. —v. 1. To produce thunder or similar sounds. 2. To utter loudly. [< OE thunor.] —thun'der·er n. —thun'der·ous adj.

thun·der·bolt (thŭn'dər-bōlt') n. A flash of lightning accompanied by thunder.

thun·der·clap (thŭn'dər-klăp') n. A single sharp crash of thunder.

thun·der·cloud (thŭn'dər-kloud') n. A large, dark cloud that produces thunder and lightning.

thun·der·head (thŭn′dər-hĕd′) *n.* The rounded upper portion of a thundercloud.

thun·der·show·er (thŭn′dər-shou′ər) *n.* A brief rainstorm accompanied by thunder and lightning.

thun·der·storm (thŭn′dər-stôrm′) *n.* An electrical storm accompanied by heavy rain.

thun·der·struck (thŭn′dər-strŭk′) *adj.* Also **thun·der·strick·en** (-strĭk′ən). Astonished; stunned.

Thurs·day (thûrz′dē, -dā′) *n.* The 5th day of the week. [< OE *thunresdæg*.]

thus (thŭs) *adv.* **1.** In this manner. **2.** To a stated degree or extent; so. **3.** Consequently; hence. [< OE.]

thwack (thwăk) *v.* To strike or hit with something flat. [Imit.] —**thwack** *n.*

thwart (thwôrt) *v.* To prevent from taking place; frustrate. —*n.* A seat across a boat, on which the oarsman sits. —*adj.* Transverse. —*adv. & prep. Archaic.* Athwart. [< ON *thverr*, transverse.] —**thwart′er** *n.*

thy (thī) *pron. Archaic & Poetic.* The possessive form of **thou.**

thyme (tīm) *n.* An aromatic plant with leaves used as seasoning. [< Gk. *thumon.*]

thy·mus (thī′məs) *n.* A ductless glandlike structure, situated near the throat, that plays some part in building resistance to disease but is usu. vestigial in adults. [< Gk. *thumos.*] —**thy′mic** *adj.*

thy·roid (thī′roid′) *adj.* Of or relating to the thyroid gland. —*n.* **1.** The thyroid gland. **2.** A dried and powdered preparation of the thyroid gland of certain domestic animals, used in medicine. [Gk. *thureoeidēs.*]

thyroid gland *n.* A two-lobed endocrine gland located in front of and on either side of the trachea in humans and producing a hormone that regulates metabolism.

thy·self (thī-sĕlf′) *pron. Archaic & Poetic.* Yourself.

ti (tē) *n. Mus.* A syllable representing the 7th tone of a diatonic major scale. [< Ital. *si.*]

Ti The symbol for the element titanium.

ti·a·ra (tē-âr′ə, -ăr′ə, -är′ə) *n.* **1.** A bejeweled crownlike ornament, worn on the head by women. **2.** The three-tiered crown worn by the pope. [< Gk., turban.]

Ti·bet·an (tĭ-bĕt′n) *n.* **1.** One of the Mongoloid people of Tibet. **2.** The Tibeto-Burman language of Tibet. —**Ti·bet′an** *adj.*

Ti·bet·o-Bur·man (tĭ-bĕt′ō-bûr′mən) *n.* A branch of the Sino-Tibetan language family that includes Tibetan and Burmese. —**Ti·bet′o-Bur′man** *adj.*

tib·i·a (tĭb′ē-ə) *n., pl.* **-i·ae** (-ē-ē′) or **-as.** The inner and larger of the two bones of the lower leg from the knee to the ankle. [Lat.] —**tib′i·al** *adj.*

tic (tĭk) *n.* A spasmodic ¹muscular contraction, usu. in the face or extremities. [Fr.]

tick¹ (tĭk) *n.* **1.** The recurring clicking sound made by a machine, esp. by a clock. **2.** A light mark used to check off or call attention to an item. [ME *tek.*] —**tick** *v.*

tick² (tĭk) *n.* Any of numerous bloodsucking parasitic arachnids or louselike insects, many of which transmit diseases. [< OE *ticia.*]

tick³ (tĭk) *n.* **1.** The cloth case of a mattress or pillow. **2.** Ticking. [Prob. ult. < Gk. *thēkē,* case.]

tick·er (tĭk′ər) *n.* **1.** A telegraphic printing or display device that receives and records stock-market quotations. **2.** *Slang.* The heart.

ticker tape *n.* The paper strip on which a ticker prints.

tick·et (tĭk′ĭt) *n.* **1.** A paper slip or card indicating that its holder has paid for admission or a service. **2.** A certificate or license. **3.** An identifying tag; label. **4.** A list of candidates endorsed by a political party. **5.** A summons, esp. for a traffic violation. —*v.* **1.** To provide with a ticket. **2.** To attach a tag to; label. [OFr. *estiquet,* short document.]

tick·ing (tĭk′ĭng) *n.* A strong, tightly woven fabric used to make pillow and mattress coverings.

tick·le (tĭk′əl) *v.* **-led, -ling. 1.** To touch (the body) lightly, causing laughter or twitching movements. **2.** To tease or excite pleasurably. **3.** To feel a tingling sensation on the skin. —*n.* The act or sensation of tickling. [ME *tikelen.*] —**tick′ler** *n.*

tick·lish (tĭk′lĭsh) *adj.* **1.** Sensitive to tickling. **2.** Easily offended or upset. **3.** Requiring tactful handling; delicate. —**tick′lish·ly** *adv.* —**tick′lish·ness** *n.*

tick-tack-toe (tĭk′tăk-tō′) *n.* Also **tic-tac-toe.** A game for two, each trying to make a line of three X's or three O's in a boxlike figure with nine spaces.

tid·al (tīd′l) *adj.* Of, having, or affected by tides.

tidal wave *n.* **1.** An unusual rise or incursion of water along the seashore. **2.** An overwhelming manifestation, as of sentiment or opinion.

tid·bit (tĭd′bĭt′) *n.* A choice morsel. [Perh. dial. *tid,* tender + BIT.]

tid·dly·winks (tĭd′lē-wĭngks′) *n. (used with a sing. verb).* A game in which players try to pop small disks into a cup by pressing them on the edge with a larger disk. [Perh. dial. *tiddly,* little + WINK.]

tide (tīd) *n.* **1. a.** The periodic variation in the surface level of the oceans, seas, and other open waters of the earth, caused by the gravitational attraction of the moon and sun. **b.** A specific occurrence of such a variation. **c.** The water that moves in such a variation. **2.** A powerful, periodic movement or trend. **3.** *Archaic.* A time or season. —*v.* **tid·ed, tid·ing. 1.** To rise and fall like the tide. **2.** To drift with the tide. —*phrasal verb.* **tide over.** To

tide
Left: Low tide
Right: High tide

---

support through a difficult period. [< OE *tíd*, season.]

tide·land (tīd'lǎnd') n. Coastal land submerged during high tide.

tide·wa·ter (tīd'wô'tər, -wŏt'ər) n. **1.** Water that flows onto the land at flood tide. **2.** Water affected by tides, esp. in rivers. **3.** Low coastal land drained by tidal streams.

tid·ings (tī'dĭngz) pl.n. Information; news. [Perh. < ON *tidhendi*, events.]

ti·dy (tī'dē) adj. **-di·er, -di·est. 1.** Orderly and neat. **2.** Informal. Substantial; considerable. —v. **-died, -dy·ing.** To put (things) in order. [< TIDE.] —**ti'di·ly** adv. —**ti'di·ness** n.

tie (tī) v. **tied, ty·ing. 1.** To fasten or secure with a cord, rope, or line. **2.** To draw together and knot with strings or laces. **3.** To make (a knot or bow). **4.** To bring together; unite. **5.** To equal (an opponent or his score) in a contest. —phrasal verbs. **tie down.** To restrict. **tie in.** To coordinate. **tie up. 1.** To obstruct. **2.** To be already in use. **3.** To moor. [< OE *tígan*.] —**ti'er** n.
  Syns: **tie, bind, knot, secure** v.

tie-in (tī'ĭn') n. A connection; link.

tier (tîr) n. One of a series of rows placed one above another. [OFr. *tire*, rank.] —**tiered** adj.

tie-up (tī'ŭp') n. A temporary stoppage or delay.

tiff (tĭf) n. **1.** A fit of irritation. **2.** A petty quarrel. [Orig. unknown.] —**tiff** v.

ti·ger (tī'gər) n. A large carnivorous Asian cat having a tawny coat with black stripes. [< Gk. *tigris*.] —**ti'ger·ish** adj. —**ti'gress** n.

tiger lily n. An Asian plant with large, black-spotted reddish-orange flowers.

tight (tīt) adj. **-er, -est. 1.** Of such a close construction, texture, or organization as to be impermeable, esp. by water or air. **2.** Fastened, held, or closed securely. **3.** Compact. **4.** Drawn out; taut. **5.** Snug, often uncomfortably so. **6.** Constricted. **7.** Stingy. **8.** Difficult to deal with or get out of: *a tight spot.* **9.** Closely contested. **10.** Slang. Drunk. —adv. **1.** Firmly; securely. **2.** Soundly: *sleep tight.* [ME, of Scand. orig.] —**tight'ly** adv. —**tight'ness** n.

tight·en (tīt'n) v. To make or become tight or tighter. —**tight'en·er** n.

tight-fist·ed (tīt'fĭs'tĭd) adj. Stingy.

tight-lipped (tīt'lĭpt') adj. **1.** Having the lips pressed together. **2.** Not talkative; close-mouthed.

tight·rope (tīt'rōp') n. A tightly stretched rope on which acrobats perform.

tights (tīts) pl.n. A snug stretchable garment covering the body from the waist or neck down.

tight·wad (tīt'wŏd') n. Slang. A stingy person.

til·de (tĭl'də) n. The diacritical mark (˜) used in Spanish and Portuguese to indicate certain nasal sounds, as in *cañon.* [Sp. < Lat. *titulus*, superscription.]

tile (tīl) n. **1.** A slab, as of baked clay, laid in rows to cover walls, floors, or roofs. **2.** A short length of clay or concrete pipe, used in sewers, drains, etc. **3.** A marked playing piece, as in mahjong. —v. **tiled, til·ing.** To cover or provide with tiles. [< Lat. *tegere*, to cover.] —**til'er** n.

till¹ (tĭl) v. To prepare (land) for the raising of crops by plowing, harrowing, and fertilizing. [< OE *tilian*, to labor.] —**till'a·ble** adj.

till² (tĭl) prep. Until. —conj. Until. [< OE *til.*]

till³ (tĭl) n. A drawer or compartment for money, esp. in a store. [ME *tylle.*]

till·age (tĭl'ĭj) n. **1.** The cultivation of land. **2.** Tilled land.

till·er¹ (tĭl'ər) n. One that tills land.

till·er² (tĭl'ər) n. A lever used to turn a boat's rudder. [< Lat. *tela*, weaver's beam.]

tilt (tĭlt) v. **1.** To slope or cause to slope, as by raising one end; incline; tip. **2.** To thrust (a lance) in a joust. —n. **1.** A slant; slope. **2.** A joust. **3.** A verbal duel. —idiom. **at full tilt.** At full speed. [ME *tylten*, to cause to fall.]

tim·ber (tĭm'bər) n. **1.** Trees or wooded land considered as a source of wood. **2. a.** Wood as a building material. **b.** A dressed piece of wood, esp. a beam in a structure. **c.** A rib in a ship's frame. —interj. Used to warn of a falling tree. [< OE.]

tim·bered (tĭm'bərd) adj. **1. a.** Constructed of or covered with timber. **b.** Built with exposed timbers. **2.** Covered with trees; wooded.

tim·ber·line (tĭm'bər-lĭn') n. Also **timber line.** The altitude beyond which trees do not grow in a mountainous region.

tim·bre (tĭm'bər, tăm'-) n. The quality of a sound that distinguishes it from others of the same pitch and volume. [Ult. < Gk. *tumpanum*, drum.]

time (tīm) n. **1. a.** A nonspatial continuum in which events occur in apparently irreversible succession. **b.** An interval separating two points on this continuum; duration. **c.** A number, as of years, days, or minutes, representing such an interval. **d.** A similar number representing a specific point, as the present, as reckoned from an arbitrary past point. **e.** A system by which such intervals are measured or such numbers reckoned. **2.** Often **times.** A span of years; era. **3.** A suitable or opportune moment. **4.** A designated moment or period: *harvest time.* **5.** One of several instances. **6.** An occasion. **7.** Informal. A prison sentence. **8.** The rate of speed of a measured activity. **9.** The characteristic beat of musical rhythm. —adj. **1.** Of or relating to time. **2.** Constructed to operate at a particular moment: *time bomb.* **3.** Of or relating to installment buying. —v. **timed, tim·ing. 1.** To set the time for (an event or occasion). **2.** To adjust to keep accurate time. **3.** To regulate for orderly sequence of movements or events. **4.** To record, set, or maintain the speed, duration, or tempo of. —idioms. **for the time being.** Temporarily. **from time to time.** Once in a while. **in time. 1.** Before it is too late. **2.** Eventually. **on time. 1.** According to schedule. **2.** By paying in installments. [< OE *tíma*, interval between events.] —**tim'er** n.

time clock n. A device that records the arrival and departure times of employees.

time deposit n. A bank deposit that cannot be withdrawn before a specified date.

time-hon·ored (tīm'ŏn'ərd) adj. Honored because of age or age-old observance.

time·keep·er (tīm'kē'pər) n. One who keeps track of time, as in a sports event.

time·less (tīm'lĭs) adj. **1.** Endless. **2.** Unaffected by time. —**time'less·ly** adv. —**time'less·ness** n.

time·ly (tīm'lē) adj. **-li·er, -li·est.** Occurring at a suitable or opportune moment; well-timed. —**time'li·ness** n.

time-out (tīm'out') n. Also **time out.** A period of suspended play during a game.

time·piece (tīm'pēs') n. An instrument that measures, registers, or records time.

times (tīmz) prep. Multiplied by: *Two times four equals eight.*

time·serv·er (tīm'sûr'vər) n. One who for personal advantage conforms to prevailing opinions. —**time'serv'ing** adj. & n.

time sharing n. 1. A system whereby many users at different locations share a single computer. 2. Joint ownership of vacation property whereby the principals occupy the property individually for set periods of time.

time·worn (tīm'wôrn', -wōrn') adj. 1. Showing the effects of long use or wear. 2. Used too often; trite.

tim·id (tīm'īd) adj. **-er, -est. 1.** Hesitant or fearful. 2. Shy. [< Lat. *timēre*, to fear.] —**ti·mid'i·ty** or **tim'id·ness** n. —**tim'id·ly** adv.

tim·ing (tī'mĭng) n. The regulation of occurrence, pace, or coordination to achieve the most desirable effects.

tim·or·ous (tīm'ər-əs) adj. Fearful; timid. [< Lat. *timēre*, to fear.] —**tim'or·ous·ly** adv. —**tim'or·ous·ness** n.

tim·o·thy (tīm'ə-thē) n. A grass with narrow, cylindrical flower spikes, widely cultivated for hay. [Prob. < *Timothy* Hanson, 18th-cent. American farmer.]

Tim·o·thy (tīm'ə-thē) n. See table at **Bible.**

tim·pa·ni (tīm'pə-nē) pl.n. Also **tym·pa·ni.** A set of kettledrums. [Ital., ult. < Gk. *tumpanum*, drum.] —**tim'pa·nist** n.

tin (tīn) n. 1. *Symbol* **Sn** A malleable, silvery metallic element used to coat other metals to prevent corrosion and in numerous alloys, such as soft solder, pewter, type metal, and bronze. Atomic number 50; atomic weight 118.69. 2. A tin container or box. 3. *Chiefly Brit.* A can for preserved food. —v. **tinned, tin·ning. 1.** To plate or coat with tin. 2. *Chiefly Brit.* To preserve or pack in tins; can. [< OE.]

tinc·ture (tīngk'chər) n. 1. A dyeing substance; pigment. 2. An imparted color; tint. 3. A trace; vestige. 4. An alcohol solution of a nonvolatile medicine: *tincture of iodine.* —v. **-tured, -tur·ing.** To stain or tint with a color. [< Lat. *tinctus*, p.p. of *tingere*, to tinge.]

tin·der (tīn'dər) n. Material that catches fire easily, used for kindling. [< OE *tynder.*]

tin·der·box (tīn'dər-bŏks') n. A metal box for holding tinder.

tine (tīn) n. A pointed part or prong, as of a fork. [< OE *tind.*]

tin·foil (tīn'foil') n. Also **tin foil.** A thin, pliable sheet of tin or a tin alloy.

tinge (tīnj) v. **tinged** (tīnjd), **tinge·ing** or **ting·ing. 1.** To color slightly; tint. 2. To affect slightly. —n. A faint trace, as of color or flavor. [< Lat. *tingere.*]

tin·gle (tīng'gəl) v. **-gled, -gling.** To have or cause a prickling, stinging sensation as from cold or excitement. [ME *tinglen.*] —**tin'gle** n. —**tin'gler** n. —**tin'gly** adj.

tink·er (tīng'kər) n. 1. A traveling mender of metal household utensils. 2. A clumsy worker; bungler. —v. 1. To work as a tinker. 2. To busy oneself aimlessly or meddlesomely, esp. with machine parts. [ME *tinkere.*]

tin·kle (tīng'kəl) v. **-kled, -kling.** To make or cause to make light metallic sounds, as of a

small bell. [ME *tynclen.*] —**tin'kle** n. —**tin'kly** adj.

tin·ny (tīn'ē) adj. **-ni·er, -ni·est. 1.** Of, containing, or suggesting tin. 2. Having a thin metallic sound.

tin·sel (tīn'səl) n. 1. Very thin sheets, strips, or threads of a glittering material used as a decoration. 2. Something showy but basically valueless. [< OFr. *estencele*, spark.] —**tin'sel** adj.

tin·smith (tīn'smĭth') n. One who works with light metal, as tin.

tint (tīnt) n. 1. A shade of a color, esp. a pale or delicate variation. 2. A slight coloration. 3. A trace. 4. A hair dye. —v. To give a tint to. [< Lat. *tinctus*, a dyeing.]

tin·tin·nab·u·la·tion (tīn'tĭ-năb'yə-lā'shən) n. The ringing or sounding of bells. [< Lat. *tintinnabulum*, bell.]

tin·type (tīn'tīp') n. A positive photograph made directly on an iron plate varnished with a thin sensitized film.

ti·ny (tī'nē) adj. **-ni·er, -ni·est.** Extremely small. [ME *tine.*]

-tion suff. Action or process: *adsorption.* [< Lat. *-tio.*]

tip¹ (tĭp) n. 1. An end or extremity. 2. A piece meant to be fitted to the end of something. —v. **tipped, tip·ping. 1.** To furnish with a tip. 2. To cover, decorate, or remove the tip of. [ME.]

tip² (tĭp) v. **tipped, tip·ping. 1.** To knock over or upset; topple. 2. To tilt. 3. To touch or raise (one's hat) in greeting. —n. A tilt or slant. [ME *tipen.*]

tip³ (tĭp) v. **tipped, tip·ping.** To strike gently; tap. [ME *tippen.*] —**tip** n.

tip⁴ (tĭp) n. 1. An extra sum of money given for services rendered; gratuity. 2. A piece of useful advice or information; helpful hint. —v. **tipped, tip·ping.** To give a tip (to). [< slang *tip*, to give.] —**tip'per** n.

tip-off (tĭp'ôf', -ŏf') n. *Informal.* A hint or warning.

tip·pet (tĭp'ĭt) n. A covering for the shoulders, as a cape or scarf. [ME *tipet.*]

tippet

George Miksch Sutton
tit¹

tip·ple (tĭp'əl) v. **-pled, -pling.** To drink alcoholic liquor, esp. habitually. [< ME *tipler*, bartender.] —**tip'pler** n.

tip·ster (tĭp'stər) n. *Informal.* One who sells tips to bettors or speculators.

tip·sy (tĭp'sē) adj. **-si·er, -si·est.** Slightly drunk. —**tip'si·ly** adv. —**tip'si·ness** n.

tip·toe (tĭp'tō') v. To walk or move on or as if on the tips of one's toes. —n. The tip of a toe. —adv. On tiptoe.

tip·top (tip′tŏp′) *n*. The highest point; summit. —*adj*. Excellent; first-rate.

ti·rade (tī′rād′, tī-rād′) *n*. A long, angry, and often abusive speech; diatribe. [Fr.]

tire[1] (tīr) *v*. tired, tir·ing. 1. To make or become weary or fatigued. 2. To make or become bored; lose interest. [< OE *tyrian*.]

tire[2] (tīr) *n*. Also *chiefly Brit*. tyre. 1. A covering for a wheel's rim, usu. rubber and filled with compressed air. 2. A hoop of metal or rubber fitted around a wheel. [ME *tyre*.]

tired (tīrd) *adj*. 1. a. Fatigued. b. Impatient; bored. 2. Hackneyed.

tire·less (tīr′lĭs) *adj*. Untiring. —**tire′less·ly** *adv*. —**tire′less·ness** *n*.

tire·some (tīr′səm) *adj*. Causing fatigue or boredom; tedious. —**tire′some·ly** *adv*. —**tire′some·ness** *n*.

'tis (tĭz) *Archaic & Poetic*. It is.

Tish·ri (tĭsh′rē) *n*. The 1st month of the civil year in the Hebrew calendar. See table at **calendar**. [Heb. *Tishrī*.]

tis·sue (tĭsh′ōō) *n*. 1. *Biol*. a. A group of cells that are similar in form or function. b. Cellular matter in general. 2. A soft, absorbent piece of paper used as a handkerchief. 3. A thin, translucent paper used esp. for packing or wrapping. 4. A fine sheer cloth, such as gauze. 5. A web; network. [< Lat. *texere*, to weave.]

tit[1] (tĭt) *n*. Any of various small Old World birds related to and resembling the New World chickadees. [< TITMOUSE.]

tit[2] (tĭt) *n*. A teat. [< OE.]

ti·tan (tīt′n) *n*. A person of colossal size, strength, or achievement. [< *Titan*, one of a family of giants in Greek myth.]

ti·tan·ic (tī-tăn′ĭk) *adj*. Of enormous size, strength, influence, etc. —**ti·tan′i·cal·ly** *adv*.

ti·ta·ni·um (tī-tā′nē-əm, tĭ-) *n*. *Symbol* **Ti** A strong, low-density, highly corrosion-resistant, lustrous white metallic element used in alloys requiring low weight, strength, and high-temperature stability. Atomic number 22; atomic weight 47.90.

tithe (tīth) *n*. 1. A 10th part of one's income, paid for the support of a church. 2. A 10th part. —*v*. tithed, tith·ing. To pay a tithe of (one's income). [< OE *tēotha*.] —**tith′er** *n*.

tit·il·late (tĭt′ə-lāt′) *v*. -lat·ed, -lat·ing. 1. To tickle. 2. To excite agreeably. [< Lat. *titillare*.] —**tit′il·lat′ing·ly** *adv*. —**tit′il·la′tion** *n*.

ti·tle (tīt′l) *n*. 1. An identifying name given to a book, painting, etc. 2. A claim or right, esp. a legal right to ownership. 3. a. A formal appellation, as of rank or office. b. Such an appellation used to indicate nobility. 4. *Law*. a. Just cause of possession or control. b. The evidence of such means. c. The instrument constituting this evidence, such as a deed. 5. *Sports*. A championship. —*v*. -tled, -tling. To give a title to. [< Lat. *titulus*.]

ti·tled (tīt′əld) *adj*. Having a title, esp. of nobility.

tit·mouse (tĭt′mous′) *n*. A small grayish, crested North American bird. [ME *titmose*.]

tit·ter (tĭt′ər) *v*. To utter a restrained, nervous giggle. [Imit.] —**tit′ter** *n*.

tit·tle (tĭt′l) *n*. The tiniest bit; iota. [< Lat. *titulus*, title.]

tit·u·lar (tĭch′ŏŏ-lər) *adj*. 1. Of, relating to, or constituting a title. 2. In name only; nominal. [< Lat. *titulus*, title.] —**tit′u·lar·ly** *adv*.

Ti·tus (tī′təs) *n*. See table at **Bible**.

tiz·zy (tĭz′ē) *n*., *pl*. -zies. *Slang*. A state of nervous confusion; dither. [Orig. unknown.]

Tl The symbol for the element thallium.

Tlin·git (tlĭng′gĭt, tlĭng′ĭt) *n*., *pl*. -git or -gits. 1. a. A group of Indian seafaring tribes inhabiting the coastal areas of southern Alaska and northern British Columbia. b. A member of any of the Tlingit tribes. 2. A language family of the Na-dene phylum consisting only of the language of the Tlingit.

Tm The symbol for the element thulium.

TNT (tē′ĕn-tē′) *n*. A yellow crystalline compound, $C_7H_5N_3O_6$, used mainly as a high explosive. [*t(ri)n(itro)t(oluene)*.]

to (tōō; *unstressed* tə) *prep*. 1. In a direction toward. 2. In the direction of. 3. Reaching as far as. 4. Toward or reaching the state of. 5. In contact with: *cheek to cheek*. 6. In front of: *face to face*. 7. Through and including; until: *from three to five*. 8. For the attention, benefit, or possession of: *to that end*. 9. For the purpose of: *the belt to this dress*. 10. For or of: *the belt to this dress*. 11. Concerning or regarding: *deaf to her pleas*. 12. In relation with: *parallel to the road*. 13. As an accompaniment to. 14. Composing or constituting: in: *two pints to the quart*. 15. In accord with: *not to my liking*. 16. As compared with: *a score of four to three*. 17. Before: *ten to five*. 18. Used before a verb to indicate the infinitive: *I'd like to go*. —*adv*. 1. Into a shut or closed position: *slammed the door to*. 2. Into consciousness: *He came to*. 3. Into work or application: *Everyone fell to*. 4. *Naut*. Turned into the wind. [< OE *tō*.]

toad (tōd) *n*. A froglike, mostly land-dwelling amphibian with rough, warty skin. [< OE *tādige*.]

toad·stool (tōd′stōōl′) *n*. An inedible or poisonous mushroom.

toad·y (tō′dē) *n*., *pl*. -ies. A servile flatterer; sycophant. —*v*. -led, -y·ing. To be a toady (to).

toast[1] (tōst) *v*. 1. To heat and brown (bread, rolls, etc.). 2. To warm thoroughly. —*n*. Sliced bread heated and browned. [< Lat. *tostus*, p.p. of *torrēre*, to dry.]

toast[2] (tōst) *n*. 1. The act of drinking in honor of a person or thing. 2. The person or thing honored in this way. —*v*. To drink to or propose a toast. [< TOAST[1].]

toast·er (tō′stər) *n*. An electrical appliance used to toast bread.

to·bac·co (tə-băk′ō) *n*., *pl*. -cos or -coes. 1. A plant native to tropical America, having broad leaves used chiefly for smoking. 2. The leaves of this plant processed for use in cigarettes, cigars, pipes, etc. 3. Such products collectively. [Sp. *tabaco*.]

to·bac·co·nist (tə-băk′ə-nĭst) *n*. One who sells cigarettes, cigars, pipe tobacco, etc.

To·bit (tō′bĭt) *n*. See table at **Bible**.

to·bog·gan (tə-bŏg′ən) *n*. A long, narrow, runnerless sled constructed of thin boards curved upward at the front. —*v*. 1. To ride on a toboggan. 2. To decline or fall rapidly. [< Micmac *tobākan*.] —**to·bog′gan·er** or **to·bog′gan·ist** *n*.

toc·sin (tŏk′sĭn) *n*. A warning bell. [< OProv. *tocasenh*.]

to·day (tə-dā′). Also **to·day**. —*adv*. 1. During or on the present day. 2. During or at the present time. —*n*. The present day, time, or age. [< OE *tō dæg*.]

tod·dle (tŏd′l) *v*. -dled, -dling. To walk with

short, unsteady steps, as a small child does. [Orig. unknown.] —**tod′dle** n. —**tod′dler** n.

tod·dy (tŏd′ē) n., pl. **-dies.** A drink consisting of liquor with hot water, sugar, and spices. [Hindi tāṛī, sap of palm.]

to-do (tə-dōō′) n., pl. **-dos** (-dōōz′). Informal. Commotion; stir.

toe (tō) n. **1.** One of the digits of the foot. **2.** The forward part of something worn on the foot. **3.** Anything suggestive of a toe in form, function, or location. —v. **toed, toe·ing.** To touch or kick with the toe. [< OE tā.]

toe·a (toi′ə) n., pl. **toe·a.** See table at **currency.** [Prob. < DOLLAR.]

toe-hold (tō′hōld′) n. A space to support the toe in climbing.

toe-nail (tō′nāl′) n. The nail on a toe.

tof·fee (tôf′ē, tŏf′ē) n. Also **tof·fy** pl. **-fies.** A candy of brown sugar and butter. [< TAFFY.]

to-fu (tō′fōō) n. Bean curd. [J. tōfu.]

to-ga (tō′gə) n. A loose one-piece outer garment worn in public by citizens of ancient Rome. [Lat.] —**to′gaed** (tō′gəd) adj.

to-geth·er (tə-gĕth′ər) adv. **1.** In or into a single group or place. **2.** In relationship to one another. **3.** Regarded collectively. **4.** Simultaneously. **5.** In agreement or cooperation. [< OE tōgedere.] —**to-geth′er·ness** n.

Usage: When together with follows a singular subject to introduce an additional or accompanying element, the verb remains in agreement with the singular subject: The Prime Minister (singular subject), together with his aides, is (singular verb) expected to arrive shortly.

tog·gle switch (tŏg′əl) n. A switch in which a projecting lever with a spring is used to open or close an electric circuit.

togs (tŏgz) pl.n. Clothes: gardening togs. [< Lat. toga, toga.]

toil¹ (toil) v. **1.** To work strenuously. **2.** To proceed with difficulty. —n. Exhausting labor or effort. [< Lat. tudiclare, to stir about.] —**toil′er** n.

toil² (toil) n. Often **toils.** Anything that entangles: in the toils of despair. [< Lat. tela, web.]

toi·let (toi′lĭt) n. **1.** A disposal apparatus used for urination and defecation. **2.** A room or booth containing such an apparatus. **3.** The process of grooming and dressing oneself. [< OFr. toilette, cloth cover for a dressing table.]

toilet paper n. Soft paper for cleansing oneself after defecation or urination.

toi·let·ry (toi′lĭ-trē) n., pl. **-ries.** An article or cosmetic used in dressing or grooming.

toi·lette (twä-lĕt′) n. **1.** The process of dressing or grooming oneself. **2.** A person's dress or style of dress. [Fr.]

to-ken (tō′kən) n. **1.** Something that serves as an indication or representation; sign; symbol. **2.** Something that tangibly signifies authority, validity, etc. **3.** A keepsake. **4.** A piece of stamped metal used as a substitute for currency. —adj. Done as an indication or pledge: a token payment. [< OE tācen.]

to-ken·ism (tō′kə-nĭz′əm) n. Symbolic gestures rather than effective action toward a goal.

told (tōld) v. p.t. & p.p. of **tell.**

tol·er·a·ble (tŏl′ər-ə-bəl) adj. **1.** Endurable.

2. Adequate; passable. —**tol′er·a·bil′i·ty** or **tol′er·a·ble·ness** n. —**tol′er·a·bly** adv.

tol·er·ance (tŏl′ər-əns) n. **1.** The capacity for or practice of recognizing and respecting the opinions, practices, or behavior of others. **2.** The capacity to endure hardship, pain, etc. **3.** Leeway for variation, as from a standard. —**tol′er·ant** adj. —**tol′er·ant·ly** adv.

tol·er·ate (tŏl′ə-rāt′) v. **-at·ed, -at·ing. 1.** To allow without prohibiting or opposing; permit. **2.** To recognize and respect, as contrary opinions or practices. **3.** To put up with; endure. [< Lat. tolerare.] —**tol′er·a′tion** n. —**tol′er·a′tor** n.

toll¹ (tōl) n. **1.** A fixed tax for a privilege, as for passage across a bridge. **2.** A charge for a service, such as a long-distance telephone call. **3.** The amount or extent of loss or destruction, as in a disaster. [< Gk. telōnēs, tax collector.]

toll² (tōl) v. **1.** To sound (a bell) slowly at regular intervals. **2.** To announce or summon by tolling. —n. The sound of a tolling bell. [ME tollen.]

toll-gate (tōl′gāt′) n. A gate barring passage until a toll is collected.

tom (tŏm) n. **1.** A male cat. **2.** A male turkey. [< Tom, nickname for Thomas.]

tom·a·hawk (tŏm′ə-hôk′) n. A light ax formerly used as a tool or weapon by North American Indians. —v. To strike with a tomahawk. [Algonquian tamahaac.]

tomahawk   tom-tom

to·ma·to (tə-mā′tō, -mä′-) n., pl. **-toes. 1.** A fleshy, smooth-skinned reddish fruit eaten in salads or as a vegetable. **2.** A plant bearing such fruit. [< Nahuatl tomatl.]

tomb (tōōm) n. **1.** A vault or chamber for the dead. **2.** A place of burial. [< Gk. tumbos.]

tom·boy (tŏm′boi′) n. A young girl who behaves like an adventurous boy. [Tom, nickname for Thomas + BOY.] —**tom′boy′ish** adj.

tomb·stone (tōōm′stōn′) n. A gravestone.

tom·cat (tŏm′kăt′) n. A male cat.

tome (tōm) n. A book, esp. a large or scholarly one. [< Gk. tomos, roll of papyrus.]

tom·fool·er·y (tŏm′fōō′lə-rē) n. **1.** Foolish behavior. **2.** Nonsense.

to·mor·row (tə-môr′ō, -mŏr′ō) n. **1.** The day following today. **2.** The near future. —adv. On or for the day following today. [< OE tō morgenne, in the morning.]

tom·tit (tŏm′tĭt′) n. A small bird.

tom-tom (tŏm′tŏm′) n. Any of various small-headed drums that are beaten with the hands. [Hindi ṭamṭam.]

–tomy *suff.* A cutting of: *lobotomy.* [< Gk. *temnein,* to cut.]

ton (tŭn) *n.* **1. a.** A U.S. Customary System unit of weight equal to 2,240 pounds; long ton. **b.** A U.S. Customary System unit of weight equal to 2,000 pounds; short ton. **2.** *Informal.* A very large quantity. [< OE *tunne,* large cask.]

to·nal·i·ty (tō-năl′ə-tē) *n., pl.* **-ties.** *Mus.* The arrangement of the tones of a composition in relation to a tonic.

tone (tōn) *n.* **1. a.** A sound of distinct pitch, quality, and duration. **b.** Quality of sound. **2.** *Mus.* The largest interval between adjacent notes of a diatonic scale. **3.** The pitch of a word or phrase. **4.** Manner of expression: *an angry tone of voice.* **5.** A general quality or atmosphere: *the tone of the debate.* **6. a.** A color or shade of color. **b.** Quality of color. **7. a.** The tension in resting muscles. **b.** Normal tissue firmness. —*v.* **toned, ton·ing.** To give a particular tone or inflection to. —*phrasal verbs.* **tone down.** To make less vivid, harsh, etc.; moderate. **tone up.** To make or become brighter, more vigorous, etc. [< Gk. *tonos.*] —**to′nal** *adj.* —**to′nal·ly** *adv.*

Ton·gan (tŏng′gən) *n.* A Polynesian language spoken in Tonga.

tongs (tôngz, tŏngz) *n. (used with a pl. verb).* A grasping device consisting of two arms joined at one end by a pivot or hinge. [< OE *tong.*]

tongue (tŭng) *n.* **1.** The fleshy, movable, muscular organ in the mouth that functions in tasting, speech, and as an aid in chewing and swallowing. **2.** The tongue of an animal, as a cow, used as food. **3.** Anything resembling a tongue in form or function. **4.** A spoken language. **5.** Quality of utterance: *her sharp tongue.* [< OE *tunge.*]

tongue-in-cheek (tŭng′ən-chēk′) *adj.* Meant ironically or facetiously.

tongue-tied (tŭng′tīd′) *adj.* Speechless or confused in expression, as from shyness, embarrassment, or surprise.

ton·ic (tŏn′ĭk) *n.* **1.** Anything that invigorates, refreshes, or restores. **2.** *Mus.* The primary tone of a diatonic scale. —*adj.* **1.** Producing or stimulating physical or mental vigor. **2.** *Mus.* Pertaining to or based on the tonic. [< Gk. *tonos,* tone.]

to·night (tə-nīt′). Also **to-night.** —*adv.* On or during the present or coming night. —*n.* This night or the night of this day. [< OE *tō niht,* at night.]

ton·nage (tŭn′ĭj) *n.* **1.** The number of tons of water a ship displaces afloat. **2.** The capacity of a merchant ship in units of 100 cubic feet. **3.** A charge per ton on cargo. **4.** The total shipping of a country or port, figured in tons. **5.** Weight as measured in tons.

ton·sil (tŏn′səl) *n.* A mass of lymphoid tissue, esp. either of two such masses embedded at the back of the mouth. [Lat. *tonsillae,* tonsils.] —**ton′sil·lar** *adj.*

ton·sil·lec·to·my (tŏn′sə-lĕk′tə-mē) *n., pl.* **-mies.** The surgical removal of one or both tonsils.

ton·sil·li·tis (tŏn′sə-lī′tĭs) *n.* Inflammation of the tonsils.

ton·so·ri·al (tŏn-sôr′ē-əl, -sōr′-) *adj.* Of or relating to a barber or to barbering. [< Lat. *tonsor,* barber.]

ton·sure (tŏn′shər) *n.* **1.** The act of shaving the head, esp. as a preliminary to becoming a monk or priest. **2.** The part of the head so shaven. —*v.* **-sured, -sur·ing.** To shave the head of. [< Lat. *tondēre,* to shear.]

too (tōō) *adv.* **1.** Also; as well. **2.** More than enough; excessively: *study too hard.* **3.** Very; extremely. **4.** *Informal.* Indeed; so. [< OE *tō.*]

took (tōōk) *v. p.t.* of **take.**

tool (tōōl) *n.* **1.** A hand-held implement, as a hammer, saw, or drill. **2.** A machine, such as a lathe, used to cut and shape machinery parts. **3.** A means or instrument. **4.** A dupe. —*v.* **1.** To form, work, or decorate with a tool or tools. **2.** To furnish tools or machinery for (a factory, industry, or shop). **3.** *Informal.* To drive (a vehicle). [< OE *tōl.*]

toot (tōōt) *v.* **1.** To sound (a horn or whistle) in short blasts. **2.** To sound (a blast or series of blasts) on a horn or whistle. —*n.* The act or sound of tooting. [Prob. imit.] —**toot′er** *n.*

tooth (tōōth) *n., pl.* **teeth** (tēth). **1.** One of a set of hard, bonelike structures rooted in sockets in the jaws, used to bite and chew. **2.** A structure or projection resembling a tooth in shape or function, as on a comb, gear, or saw. —*idiom.* **in the teeth of.** Directly against; despite. [< OE *tōth.*] —**toothed** *adj.* —**tooth′less** *adj.*

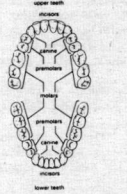

tooth

Left: The upper and lower teeth of
an adult human
Right: Cross section of a human
incisor

tooth·brush (tōōth′brŭsh′) *n.* A brush for cleaning teeth.

tooth·paste (tōōth′pāst′) *n.* A paste for cleaning teeth.

tooth·pick (tōōth′pĭk′) *n.* A small stick for picking food particles from between the teeth.

tooth·some (tōōth′səm) *adj.* Delicious; luscious. —**tooth′some·ly** *adv.* —**tooth′some·ness** *n.*

top¹ (tŏp) *n.* **1.** The uppermost part, point, surface, or end of something. **2.** A lid or cap. **3. a.** The highest rank or position. **b.** The highest degree or pitch; acme; zenith. —*adj.* Of, pertaining to, at, or forming the top. —*v.* **topped, top·ping. 1.** To remove the top from. **2.** To furnish with, form, or serve as a top. **3.** To reach or go over the top of. **4.** To exceed or surpass. —*idioms.* **blow one's top.** *Slang.* To lose one's temper. **on top of. 1.** *Informal.* **a.** In control of. **b.** Fully informed about. **2.** In addition to. **3.** Following closely upon. [< OE *topp.*] —**top′per** *n.*

top² (tŏp) *n.* A child's toy, usu. cone-shaped, made to spin on the pointed end. [< OE.]

to·paz (tō′păz′) *n.* **1.** A hard mineral consisting largely of aluminum silicate and valued as a gem. **2.** Any of various yellow gemstones, esp. a yellow variety of sapphire. [< Gk. *to-pazos.*]

top-coat (tŏp′kōt′) *n.* A lightweight overcoat.

top-er (tō′pər) *n.* A drunkard.

top-flight (tŏp′flīt′) *adj.* First-rate; superior.

top hat *n.* A man's formal hat with a narrow brim and a tall cylindrical crown.

top-heavy (tŏp′hĕv′ē) *adj.* Likely to topple because overloaded at the top. —**top′heav′i-ness** *n.*

top-ic (tŏp′ĭk) *n.* A subject treated in a speech, essay, thesis, conversation, etc. [< Gk. *topos,* place.]

top-i-cal (tŏp′ĭ-kəl) *adj.* 1. Of or relating to current or local events; currently of interest. 2. Local. —**top′i-cal′i-ty** (-kăl′ə-tē) *n.* —**top′i-cal-ly** *adv.*

top-knot (tŏp′nŏt′) *n.* 1. A crest or tuft, as of hair, on the top of the head. 2. A decorative ribbon, bow, etc., worn as a headdress.

top-less (tŏp′lĭs) *adj.* 1. Having no top. 2. Wearing a topless garment.

top-most (tŏp′mōst′) *adj.* Highest; uppermost.

top-notch (tŏp′nŏch′) *adj. Informal.* First-rate; excellent.

topo– *pref.* Place or region. [< Gk. *topos.*]

to-pog-ra-phy (tə-pŏg′rə-fē) *n., pl.* **-phies.** 1. Detailed description or representation of the physical features of a region. 2. The physical features of a region. —**to-pog′ra-pher** *n.* —**top′o-graph′ic** (tŏp′ə-grăf′ĭk) *or* **top′o-graph′i-cal** *adj.* —**top′o-graph′i-cal-ly** *adv.*

top-ping (tŏp′ĭng) *n.* A sauce, frosting, or garnish for food.

top-ple (tŏp′əl) *v.* **-pled, -pling.** 1. To push over; overturn. 2. To totter and fall. [< TOP[1].]

tops (tŏps) *adj. Slang.* First-rate; excellent.

top-sail (tŏp′səl, -sāl′) *n.* A square sail set above the lowest sail on the mast of a square-rigged ship.

top-se-cret (tŏp′sē′krĭt) *adj.* Of the highest level of security classification.

top-side (tŏp′sīd′) *adv.* On or to the upper parts of a ship; on deck.

top-soil (tŏp′soil′) *n.* The surface layer of soil.

top-sy-tur-vy (tŏp′sē-tûr′vē) *adv.* 1. Upside-down. 2. In utter disorder or confusion. —*adj.* In a disordered condition. [Prob. < TOP[1] + obs. *tervy,* to turn.] —**top′sy-tur′vi-ly** *adv.* —**top′sy-tur′vi-ness** *n.*

toque (tōk) *n.* A small, brimless, close-fitting woman's hat. [Fr.]

To-rah (tôr′ə, tōr′ə) *n.* 1. Also **torah.** The body of Jewish literature and oral tradition as a whole. 2. **a.** The Pentateuch. **b.** A scroll on which the Pentateuch is written, used in a synagogue during services.

torch (tôrch) *n.* 1. A portable light produced by the flame of a burning material wound about the end of a stick. 2. A portable apparatus that produces a very hot flame by the combustion of gases, as used in welding. 3. Anything that serves to illuminate or guide. 4. *Chiefly Brit.* A flashlight. 5. *Slang.* An arsonist. [< OFr. *torche.*]

tore (tôr, tōr) *v. p.t.* of **tear**[1].

tor-e-a-dor (tôr′ē-ə-dôr′) *n.* A bullfighter. [Sp.]

tor-ment (tôr′mĕnt′) *n.* 1. Great pain or anguish; agony. 2. A source of harassment or

pain. —*v.* (tôr-mĕnt′, tôr′mĕnt′). 1. To cause to undergo torment. 2. To annoy or harass. [< Lat. *tormentum.*] —**tor-ment′ing-ly** *adv.* —**tor-men′tor** *n.*

torn (tôrn, tōrn) *v. p.p.* of **tear**[1].

Usage: Torn, never *tore,* is the standard past participle of the verb *tear.*

tor-na-do (tôr-nā′dō) *n., pl.* **-does** *or* **-dos.** A violently whirling column of air, usu. accompanied by a funnel-shaped downward extension of a thundercloud and moving destructively over a narrow path. [< Sp. *tronada,* thunderstorm.]

tor-pe-do (tôr-pē′dō) *n., pl.* **-does.** 1. A cigar-shaped, self-propelled underwater projectile, designed to detonate on contact with or in the vicinity of a target. 2. Any of various other explosive devices. —*v.* To attack or destroy with or as with a torpedo. [< Lat., electric ray.]

tor-pid (tôr′pĭd) *adj.* 1. Not active; sluggish; slow. 2. Lethargic; apathetic. [Lat. *torpidus.*] —**tor-pid′i-ty** *n.* —**tor′pid-ly** *adv.*

tor-por (tôr′pər) *n.* 1. A condition of inactivity or insensibility. 2. Lethargy; apathy. [Lat.]

torque (tôrk) *n.* The tendency of a force to produce rotation about an axis. [< Lat. *torquēre,* to twist.]

tor-rent (tôr′ənt, tŏr′-) *n.* 1. A turbulent, swift-flowing stream. 2. A deluge. 3. Any turbulent or overwhelming flow. [< Lat. *torrēre,* to burn.] —**tor-ren′tial** (tô-rĕn′shəl, tə-) *adj.*

tor-rid (tôr′ĭd, tŏr′-) *adj.* 1. Very dry and hot. 2. Passionate. [Lat. *torridus.*] —**tor-rid′i-ty** *or* **tor′rid-ness** *n.* —**tor′rid-ly** *adv.*

tor-sion (tôr′shən) *n.* 1. A twisting or turning. 2. The stress caused when one end of an object is twisted in one direction and the other end is held motionless. [LLat. *torsio.*] —**tor′sion-al** *adj.* —**tor′sion-al-ly** *adv.*

tor-so (tôr′sō) *n., pl.* **-sos.** The trunk of the human body. [Ital.]

tort (tôrt) *n. Law.* Any wrongful act that does not involve a breach of contract and for which a civil suit can be brought. [< Lat. *torquēre,* to twist.]

tor-til-la (tôr-tē′yə) *n.* A thin, round, unleavened Mexican pancake. [< LLat. *torta,* a kind of bread.]

tor-toise (tôr′təs) *n.* A turtle, esp. a land turtle. [< OFr. *tortue.*]

tor-toise-shell (tôr′təs-shĕl′) *n.* The translucent brownish outer covering of certain sea turtles, used to make combs, jewelry, etc.

tor-tu-ous (tôr′chōō-əs) *adj.* 1. Winding; twisting. 2. Devious; deceitful. 3. Complex. [< Lat. *tortuosus.*] —**tor′tu-ous-ly** *adv.* —**tor′tu-ous-ness** *n.*

tor-ture (tôr′chər) *n.* 1. The infliction of severe pain as a means of punishment or coercion. 2. Pain or mental anguish. —*v.* **-tured, -turing.** 1. To subject to torture. 2. To afflict with great pain or anguish. [< Lat. *tortura.*] —**tor′tur-er** *n.* —**tor′tur-ous** *adj.* —**tor′tur-ous-ly** *adv.*

To-ry (tôr′ē, tōr′ē) *n., pl.* **-ries.** 1. A member of the Conservative Party in Great Britain. 2. An American who favored the British side during the American Revolution. [< Ir. Gael. *tōraidhe,* robber.] —**To′ry** *adj.* —**To′ry-ism** *n.*

ă pat ā pay â care ä father ĕ pet ē be ĭ pit ī tie î pier ŏ pot ō toe ô paw, for oi noise ŏŏ took
ōō boot ou out th thin *th* this ŭ cut û urge yōō abuse zh vision ə about, item, edible, gallop, circus

toss (tôs, tŏs) v. **1.** To throw or be thrown to and fro. **2.** To throw lightly. **3.** To move or lift (the head) with rapidity. **4.** To flip a coin to decide something. **5.** To move oneself about vigorously. —n. **1.** An act of tossing. **2.** A rapid lift, as of the head. [Poss. of Scand. orig.] —**toss′er** n.

toss·up (tôs′ŭp′, tŏs′-) n. Informal. An even chance or choice.

tot (tŏt) n. **1.** A small child. **2.** A small amount. [Orig. unknown.]

to·tal (tōt′l) n. **1.** A number or quantity obtained by addition; sum. **2.** A whole quantity; entirety. —adj. **1.** Constituting the whole; entire. **2.** Complete; utter. —v. **-taled** or **-talled, -tal·ing** or **-tal·ling. 1.** To determine the sum of. **2.** To amount to. **3.** To destroy: totaled the car. [< Lat. tōtus, whole.] —**to′tal·ly** adv.

to·tal·i·tar·i·an (tō-tăl′ə-târ′ē-ən) adj. Designating a form of government in which one party exercises absolute control over all spheres of human life and opposition is outlawed. —n. One who supports or favors such a form of government. [TOTAL + (AUTHOR)I·TARIAN.] —**to·tal′i·tar′i·an·ism** n.

to·tal·i·ty (tō-tăl′ə-tē) n., pl. **-ties. 1.** The condition or property of being total. **2.** The aggregate amount.

tote (tōt) v. **tot·ed, tot·ing.** Informal. To haul; carry. [Orig. unknown.] —**tot′er** n.

to·tem (tō′təm) n. **1.** An animal, plant, or natural object that serves as a symbol of a clan or family among certain peoples. **2.** A representation of this. [Ojibwa nintōtēm.] —**to·tem′ic** (tō-tĕm′ĭk) adj.

totem pole n. A post carved and painted with a series of totemic symbols, as among certain North American peoples.

tot·ter (tŏt′ər) v. **1.** To sway as if about to fall. **2.** To walk unsteadily. [< MDu. touteren, to swing.] —**tot′ter** n. —**tot′ter·er** n. —**tot′ter·ing·ly** adv. —**tot′ter·y** adj.

tou·can (tōō′kăn′, -kän′) n. A tropical American bird with brightly colored plumage and a very large bill. [< Tupi tucana.]

touch (tŭch) v. **1.** To cause or permit a part of the body to come in contact with so as to feel. **2.** To be or come into contact. **3.** To tap or nudge lightly. **4.** To partake of: didn't touch her food. **5.** To move by handling. **6.** To adjoin; border. **7.** To come up to; equal. **8.** To treat of a subject, as in a lecture. **9.** To be pertinent to. **10.** To have an effect upon; change. **11.** To move emotionally. —phrasal verbs. **touch down.** To land. **touch off. 1.** To cause to explode. **2.** To incite. **touch up.** To improve by making minor changes. —n. **1.** The act or an instance of touching. **2.** The physiological sense by which bodily contact is registered. **3.** The sensation from a specific contact. **4.** A mark or effect left by a specific contact. **5.** A small amount; trace. **6.** A mild tap or stroke. **7.** A facility; knack. **8.** A characteristic manner of doing something. **9.** Contact or communication: getting in touch. [< OFr. tochier.] —**touch′a·ble** adj. —**touch′a·ble·ness** n. —**touch′er** n. **touch and go** n. A precarious state of affairs. —**touch′-and-go′** adj.

touch·down (tŭch′doun′) n. **1.** Football. A score of six points, made by moving the ball across the opposing team's goal line. **2.** The contact of an aircraft or spacecraft with a landing surface.

tou·ché (tōō-shā′) interj. Used to concede a hit in fencing or a point well made by an opponent in an argument. [Fr., p.p. of toucher, to touch.]

touch·ing (tŭch′ĭng) adj. Eliciting a tender reaction. —**touch′ing·ly** adv.

touch·stone (tŭch′stōn′) n. **1.** A stone used to test the purity of gold or silver. **2.** A test of authenticity or value; criterion.

touch·y (tŭch′ē) adj. **-i·er, -i·est. 1.** Easily offended or annoyed; irritable. **2.** Delicate; precarious. —**touch′i·ly** adv. —**touch′i·ness** n.

tough (tŭf) adj. **-er, -est. 1.** Strong and resilient. **2.** Hard to cut or chew. **3.** Physically rugged. **4.** Severe; harsh. **5.** Aggressive; pugnacious. **6.** Difficult; demanding. **7.** Having a determined will. **8.** Informal. Unfortunate: too bad. —n. A hoodlum. [< OE tōh.] —**tough′ly** adv. —**tough′ness** n.

tough·en (tŭf′ən) v. To make or become tough. —**tough′en·er** n.

tou·pee (tōō-pā′) n. A hair piece worn to cover a bald spot. [< OFr. toup, top.]

tour (tōōr) n. **1.** A comprehensive trip with visits to places of established interest. **2.** A brief trip to or through a place to see or inspect it. **3.** A journey to fulfill a round of engagements in several places: a concert tour. **4.** A period of duty at a single place or job. —v. To make a tour (of). [< Lat. tornus, lathe.]

tour de force (tōōr′ də fôrs′) n. A feat of exceptional strength, virtuosity, or ingenuity. [Fr.]

tour·ism (tōōr′ĭz′əm) n. Tourist travel and accommodation.

tour·ist (tōōr′ĭst) n. One who is traveling for pleasure.

tour·ma·line (tōōr′mə-lĭn, -lēn′) n. A mineral valued, esp. in its green, clear, and blue varieties, as a gemstone. [Singhalese toramalli, carnelian.]

tour·na·ment (tōōr′nə-mənt, tûr′-) n. **1.** A contest composed of a series of elimination games or trials. **2.** A medieval jousting match. [< OFr. torneier, to turn around.]

tour·ney (tōōr′nē, tûr′-) n., pl. **-neys.** A tournament. [< OFr. torneier, to turn around.]

tour·ni·quet (tōōr′nĭ-kĭt, -kā′, tûr′-) n. A device, such as a tight encircling band, used to stop bleeding in an injured limb. [Fr.]

tou·sle (tou′zəl) v. **-sled, -sling.** To disarrange or rumple; dishevel. [ME touselen.]

tout (tout) v. **1.** To obtain and deal in information regarding horse races. **2.** To publicize as being of great worth. —n. One who touts. [ME tuten, to watch.] —**tout′er** n.

tow¹ (tō) v. To draw or pull along behind by a chain or line. —n. **1.** An act of towing or condition of being towed. **2.** Something being towed, as a barge. [< OE togian.] —**tow′age** (tō′ĭj) n. —**tow′er** n.

tow² (tō) n. Short, coarse flax or hemp fibers ready for spinning. [ME.]

to·ward (tôrd, tŏrd, tə-wôrd′) prep. Also **to·wards** (tôrdz, tŏrdz, tə-wôrdz′). **1.** In the direction of. **2.** In a position facing. **3.** Somewhat before in time. **4.** With relation to; regarding. **5.** In furtherance of: a payment toward the house. [< OE tōweard.]

tow·el (tou′əl) n. An absorbent cloth or paper used for wiping or drying. —v. **-eled** or **-elled, -el·ing** or **-el·ling.** To wipe or dry with a towel. [< OFr. toaille.]

tow·el·ing (tou'əl-ĭng) *n.* Any of various fabrics used for making towels.

tow·er (tou'ər) *n.* **1.** A tall building or part of a building. **2.** A tall framework or structure used for observation, signaling, etc. —*v.* To rise to a conspicuous height. [< Gk. *tursis.*]

tow·er·ing (tou'ər-ĭng) *adj.* **1.** Of imposing height. **2.** Outstanding. **3.** Awesomely intense.

tow·head (tō'hĕd') *n.* A person with white-blond hair. —**tow'head'ed** *adj.*

tow·hee (tō'hē, tō·hē') *n.* A North American bird with black, white, and rust-colored plumage. [Imit. of its cry.]

town (toun) *n.* **1.** A population center larger than a village and smaller than a city. **2.** *Informal.* A city. **3.** The commercial district or center of an area. [< OE *tūn,* hamlet.]

town·ship (toun'shĭp') *n.* **1.** A subdivision of a county in most northeastern and Midwestern states. **2.** A public land-surveying unit of 36 square miles.

towns·man (tounz'mən) *n.* **1.** An inhabitant of a town. **2.** A fellow inhabitant of one's town.

towns·peo·ple (tounz'pē'pəl) *pl.n.* The inhabitants or citizens of a town or city.

tow·path (tō'păth', -päth') *n.* A path along a canal or river used by animals towing boats.

tox– *pref.* Poison: *toxemia.* [< Lat. *toxicum.*]

tox·e·mi·a (tŏk-sē'mē-ə) *n.* A condition in which toxins produced by body cells at a local source of infection are contained in the blood. —**tox·e'mic** *adj.*

tox·ic (tŏk'sĭk) *adj.* **1.** Poisonous. **2.** Of or caused by a poison or toxin. —**tox'i·cal·ly** *adv.* —**tox·ic'i·ty** (-sĭs'ə-tē) *n.*

tox·i·col·o·gy (tŏk'sĭ-kŏl'ə-jē) *n.* The study of poisons and the treatment of poisoning. —**tox'i·co·log'i·cal** (-kə-lŏj'ĭ-kəl) *adj.* —**tox'i·co·log'i·cal·ly** *adv.* —**tox'i·col'o·gist** *n.*

tox·in (tŏk'sĭn) *n.* A substance, produced by a plant, animal, or microorganism, that has a protein structure and is capable of causing poisoning when introduced into the body but is also capable of stimulating production of an antitoxin.

toy (toi) *n.* **1.** An object for children to play with. **2.** Something of little importance; trifle. **3.** A very small breed or variety of dog. —*v.* To amuse oneself idly; trifle: *toyed with plans for a world cruise.* —*adj.* **1.** Designed as a toy. **2.** Miniature.

trace¹ (trās) *n.* **1.** A visible mark or sign of the former presence or passage of some person, thing, or event. **2.** A barely perceivable indication of something; touch. **3.** A minute quantity. —*v.* **traced, trac·ing.** **1.** To follow the trail of. **2.** To ascertain the successive stages in the development of. **3.** To locate or discover through inquiry. **4.** To delineate or sketch (a figure). **5.** To form (letters) with special care. **6.** To copy by following lines seen through transparent paper. [ME. track, ult. < Lat. *trahere,* to drag.] —**trace'a·bil'i·ty** or **trace'a·ble·ness** *n.* —**trace'a·ble** *adj.* —**trace'a·bly** *adv.* —**trac'er** *n.*

trace² (trās) *n.* One of two side straps or chains connecting a harnessed draft animal to a vehicle. [< OFr. *trait* < Lat. *trahere,* to haul.]

trac·er·y (trā'sə-rē) *n., pl.* **-ies.** Ornamental work of interlaced and branching lines.

tra·che·a (trā'kē-ə) *n., pl.* **-che·ae** (-kē-ē') or **-as.** A thin-walled tube of cartilaginous and membranous tissue descending from the larynx to the bronchi and carrying air to the lungs. [< Gk. *(artēria) trakheia,* rough (artery).] —**tra'che·al** *adj.*

tra·che·ot·o·my (trā'kē-ŏt'ə-mē) *n., pl.* **-mies.** The surgical procedure of cutting into the trachea through the neck.

track (trăk) *n.* **1.** A mark, as a footprint, left by the passage of something; trace. **2.** A path, route, or course; trail. **3. a.** A road or course, as of cinder, laid out for racing. **b.** Athletic competition on such a course. **4.** A set of parallel rails upon which a train or trolley runs. —*v.* **1.** To follow the footprints or traces of; trail. **2.** To carry on the shoes and deposit as tracks. **3.** To observe or monitor, as by radar. —*phrasal verb.* **track down.** To locate by trailing or searching diligently. —*idioms.* **keep track of.** To remain informed about. **lose track of.** To fail to keep informed about. [< OFr. *trac.*] —**track'a·ble** *adj.* —**track'er** *n.* —**track'less** *adj.*

track and field *n.* Athletic events performed on a running track and the adjacent field.

track and field
Left: Athlete jumping hurdles
Right: Athlete sprinting

track record *n.* A record of performance or accomplishment.

tract¹ (trăkt) *n.* **1.** An expanse of land. **2.** A system of organs and tissues that together perform one specialized function. [Lat. *tractus.*]

tract² (trăkt) *n.* A propaganda pamphlet, esp. one put out by a religious or political group. [< Lat. *tractare,* to discuss.]

trac·ta·ble (trăk'tə-bəl) *adj.* **1.** Easily controlled; governable. **2.** Easily worked; malleable: *tractable metals.* [< Lat. *tractare,* to manage.] —**trac'ta·bil'i·ty** or **trac'ta·ble·ness** *n.* —**trac'ta·bly** *adv.*

trac·tion (trăk'shən) *n.* **1.** The act of drawing or pulling or condition of being drawn or pulled. **2.** Adhesive friction, as of a wheel on a road. **3.** The pulling power of a railroad engine. [< Lat. *trahere,* to pull.]

trac·tor (trăk'tər) *n.* **1.** An automotive vehicle designed for pulling machinery. **2.** A truck having a cab and no body, used for pulling large vehicles.

trade (trād) *n.* **1.** The business of buying and selling goods; commerce. **2.** An exchange of one thing for another. **3.** An occupation, esp. one requiring special skill; craft. **4.** Customers or patrons. —*v.* **trad·ed, trad·ing. 1.** To engage in buying and selling. **2.** To exchange (one thing) for another; barter. **3.** To shop regularly at a given store. [< MLG. *track.*] —**trad'er** *n.*

trade-in (trād'ĭn') *n.* Something accepted as partial payment for a new purchase.

trade·mark (trād'märk') *n.* A name, symbol, or other device identifying a product, legally restricted to the use of the owner or manufacturer. —*v.* **1.** To label (a product) with a trademark. **2.** To register as a trademark.

trade name *n.* **1.** The name by which a commodity, service, process, etc., is known to the trade. **2.** The name under which a business firm operates.

trade-off (trād'ôf', -ŏf') *n.* Also **trade-off.** An exchange in which something desirable, as a benefit or advantage, is given up for another regarded as more desirable.

trades·man (trādz'mən) *n.* **1.** A shopkeeper. **2.** A skilled worker.

trade union *n.* A labor union. —**trade unionism** *n.* —**trade unionist** *n.*

trade winds *pl.n.* A system of winds occupying most of the tropics, blowing northeasterly in the Northern Hemisphere and southeasterly in the Southern Hemisphere.

trading post *n.* A store in a sparsely settled area offering supplies in exchange for local products.

tra·di·tion (trə-dĭsh'ən) *n.* **1.** The passing down of a culture from generation to generation, esp. orally. **2.** A custom handed down. **3.** Any time-honored set of practices, beliefs, etc. [< Lat. *tradere,* to hand over.] —**tra·di'tion·al** *adj.* —**tra·di'tion·al·ism** *n.* —**tra·di'tion·al·ly** *adv.*

tra·duce (trə-dōōs', -dyōōs') *v.* **-duced, -ducing.** To slander; defame. [Lat. *traducere.*] —**tra·duce'ment** *n.* —**tra·duc'er** *n.*

traf·fic (trăf'ĭk) *n.* **1. a.** The commercial exchange of goods; trade. **b.** The quantity of goods traded. **2. a.** The passage of persons, vehicles, or messages through routes of transportation or communication. **b.** The amount, as of vehicles, in transit. **3.** Connections; dealings. —*v.* **-ficked, -ficking.** To carry on trade; have dealings. [< OItal. *trafficare,* to trade.] —**traf'fick·er** *n.*

traffic light *n.* A device that beams lights to control the flow of traffic along a street, highway, etc.

tra·ge·di·an (trə-jē'dē-ən) *n.* An actor of tragic roles. [< OFr. *tragedie,* tragedy.] —**tra·ge'di·enne'** (-ĕn') *n.*

trag·e·dy (trăj'ə-dē) *n., pl.* **-dies. 1.** A dramatic or literary work depicting a protagonist engaged in a morally significant struggle ending in ruin or profound unhappiness. **2.** A dramatic, disastrous event. [< Gk. *tragōidia.*]

trag·ic (trăj'ĭk) or **trag·i·cal** (-ĭ-kəl) *adj.* **1.** Of or having the character of tragedy. **2.** Calamitous; disastrous. **3.** Very sad. [< Gk. *tragikos.*] —**trag'i·cal·ly** *adv.*

trag·i·com·e·dy (trăj'ĭ-kŏm'ə-dē) *n., pl.* **-dies.** A drama that combines elements of both tragedy and comedy. —**trag'i·com'ic** or **trag'i·com'i·cal** *adj.* —**trag'i·com'i·cal·ly** *adv.*

trail (trāl) *v.* **1.** To drag or allow to drag or stream behind, as along the ground. **2.** To follow the traces or scent of; track. **3.** To lag behind (an opponent). **4.** To extend or grow

along the ground or over a surface. **5.** To drift in a tenuous stream, as smoke. **6.** To become gradually fainter: *Her voice trailed off.* —*n.* **1.** Something that trails, esp. something that hangs loose and long. **2. a.** A mark, trace, or path left by a moving body. **b.** The scent of a person or animal. **c.** A path or beaten track. [< Lat. *trahere,* to draw.]

trail·blaz·er (trāl'blā'zər) *n.* **1.** One who blazes a trail. **2.** A leader in a field; pioneer. —**trail'blaz'ing** *adj.*

trail·er (trā'lər) *n.* **1.** One that trails. **2.** A large transport vehicle hauled by a truck or tractor. **3.** A van drawn by a truck or automobile and used as a home.

train (trān) *n.* **1.** Something that follows or is drawn along behind, as the part of a gown that trails. **2.** A staff of followers; retinue. **3.** A long line of moving persons, animals, or vehicles. **4.** A string of connected railroad cars. **5.** An orderly succession of related events or thoughts. —*v.* **1.** To coach in or accustom to some mode of behavior or performance. **2.** To make or become proficient with specialized instruction and practice. **3.** To prepare physically, as with a regimen. **4.** To cause (a plant or one's hair) to take a desired course or shape. [< OFr. *trainer,* to drag.] —**train'a·ble** *adj.* —**train·ee'** *n.* —**train'er** *n.* —**train'ing** *n.*

traipse (trāps) *v.* **traipsed, traips·ing.** *Informal.* To walk about idly. [Orig. unknown.]

trait (trāt) *n.* A distinctive feature, as of character. [< Lat. *trahere,* to drag.]

trai·tor (trā'tər) *n.* One who betrays his country, a cause, or a trust, esp. one who has committed treason. [< Lat. *traditor.*] —**trai'tor·ous** *adj.*

tra·jec·to·ry (trə-jĕk'tə-rē) *n., pl.* **-ries.** The path of a moving particle or body, esp. the flight path of a missile or other projectile. [< Lat. *trajicere,* to throw across.]

tram (trăm) *n.* **1.** *Chiefly Brit.* A streetcar. **2.** An open wagon or car run on tracks in a coal mine. [Perh. < dial. *tram,* shaft of a barrow.]

tram·mel (trăm'əl) *n.* Often **trammels.** Something that restricts activity or free movement; a hindrance. —*v.* **-meled** or **-melled, -mel·ing** or **-mel·ling. 1.** To confine or hinder. **2.** To entrap. [< LLat. *tremaculum,* a kind of net.] —**tram'mel·er** *n.*

tramp (trămp) *v.* **1.** To walk with a firm, heavy step. **2.** To traverse on foot. **3.** To tread down; trample. —*n.* **1.** The sound of heavy walking or marching. **2.** A walking trip. **3.** One who travels aimlessly about as a vagrant. **4.** An immoral woman. **5.** A cargo vessel that has no regular schedule but takes on freight wherever it can be found. [ME *trampen.*] —**tramp'er** *n.*

tram·ple (trăm'pəl) *v.* **-pled, -pling. 1.** To beat down with the feet so as to injure or destroy. **2.** To treat harshly or ruthlessly. —*n.* The act or sound of trampling. [ME *tramplen.*] —**tram'pler** *n.*

tram·po·line (trăm'pə-lēn') *n.* A sheet of strong canvas attached with springs to a metal frame and used for acrobatic tumbling. [< Ital. *trampolino.*] —**tram'po·lin'ist** *n.*

trance (trăns) *n.* **1.** A hypnotic, cataleptic, or ecstatic state. **2.** A state of detachment from one's physical surroundings, as in contemplation. **3.** A dazed state. [< Lat. *transire,* to go across.]

tran·quil (trăn′kwəl) *adj.* **-quil·er** or **-quil·ler**, **-quil·est** or **-quil·lest.** Free from agitation; calm. [Lat. *tranquillus.*] —**tran·quil′li·ty** or **tran·quil′i·ty** *n.* —**tran′quil·ly** *adv.*

tran·quil·ize (trăn′kwə-līz′) *v.* **-ized**, **-iz·ing.** Also **tran·quil·lize**, **-lized**, **-liz·ing.** To make or become tranquil. —**tran′quil·i·za′tion** *n.*

tran·quil·iz·er (trăn′kwə-līz′ər) *n.* A tranquilizing drug.

trans- *pref.* **1.** Across; crossing: *transatlantic.* **2.** Change; transfer: *transliterate.* [Lat. *trans,* across.]

trans·act (trăn-săkt′, -zăkt′) *v.* To carry out or conduct (business or affairs). [< Lat. *transactus,* p.p. of *transigere,* to complete.] —**trans·ac′tor** (trăn-săk′tər, -zăk′tər) *n.*

trans·ac·tion (trăn-săk′shən, -zăk′shən) *n.* **1.** The act or process of transacting. **2.** Something transacted. —**trans·ac′tion·al** *adj.*

trans·at·lan·tic (trăns′ət-lăn′tĭk, trănz′ət-) *adj.* **1.** On the other side of the Atlantic. **2.** Spanning or crossing the Atlantic.

tran·scend (trăn-sĕnd′) *v.* **1.** To exist above and independent of. **2.** To rise above; surpass; exceed. [< Lat. *transcendere.*] —**tran·scen′dence** *n.* —**tran·scen′dent** *adj.*

tran·scen·den·tal (trăn′sĕn-dĕn′tl) *adj.* **1.** Rising above common thought or ideas; exalted; mystical. **2.** Of transcendentalism. —**tran′scen·den′tal·ly** *adv.*

tran·scen·den·tal·ism (trăn′sən-dĕnt′l-ĭz′əm) *n.* The belief or doctrine that knowledge of reality is derived from intuitive sources rather than objective experience. —**tran′scen·den′tal·ist** *n.*

trans·con·ti·nen·tal (trăns′kŏn′tə-nĕn′təl, trănz′-) *adj.* Spanning or crossing a continent.

tran·scribe (trăn-skrīb′) *v.* **-scribed**, **-scrib·ing.** **1. a.** To write or type a copy of. **b.** To write out fully, as from shorthand notes. **2.** To adapt or arrange (a musical composition). **3.** To record for broadcasting at a later date. [Lat. *transcribere,* to copy.] —**tran·scrib′a·ble** *adj.* —**tran·scrib′er** *n.*

tran·script (trăn′skrĭpt′) *n.* Something transcribed; a written or printed copy. [< Lat. *transcriptum.*]

tran·scrip·tion (trăn-skrĭp′shən) *n.* **1.** The act or process of transcribing. **2.** Something transcribed, esp.: **a.** An adaption of a musical composition. **b.** A recorded radio or television program.

tran·sept (trăn′sĕpt′) *n.* Either of the two lateral arms of a cruciform church. [TRANS- + Lat. *saeptum,* partition.]

trans·fer (trăns-fûr′, trăns′fər) *v.* **-ferred**, **-fer·ring.** **1.** To convey, shift, or change from one person or place to another. **2.** To make over the possession or title of to another. **3.** To convey (a drawing or design) from one surface to another. **4.** To change from one train, airplane, or bus to another. —*n.* (trăns′fər). **1.** Also **trans·fer·al** (trăns-fûr′əl). The conveyance of something from one person or place to another. **2.** Also **transferal.** A person or thing that has or has been transferred. **3.** A ticket entitling a passenger to change from one carrier to another. **4.** The conveyance of title or property from one person to another. [< Lat. *transferre.*] —**trans·fer′a·bil′i·ty** *n.*

—**trans·fer′a·ble** *adj.* —**trans·fer′ence** *n.* —**trans·fer′er** *n.*

trans·fig·ure (trăns-fĭg′yər) *v.* **-ured, -ur·ing. 1.** To change radically the appearance or shape of. **2.** To glorify; exalt. [< Lat. *transfigurare.*] —**trans·fig′u·ra′tion** *n.*

trans·fix (trăns-fĭks′) *v.* **1.** To pierce through with or as with a pointed weapon; impale. **2.** To render motionless, as with terror. [< Lat. *transfixus,* p.p. of *transfigere,* to transfix.] —**trans·fix′ion** (-fĭk′shən) *n.*

trans·form (trăns-fôrm′) *v.* **1.** To change markedly in form or appearance. **2.** To change in nature or condition; convert. —**trans·form′a·ble** *adj.* —**trans′for·ma′tion** *n.*

trans·form·er (trăns-fôr′mər) *n.* **1.** One that transforms. **2.** A device used to transfer electric energy from one circuit to another.

trans·fuse (trăns-fyŏŏz′) *v.* **-fused, -fus·ing. 1.** To transfer (liquid) from one vessel into another. **2.** To permeate; instill. **3.** To administer a transfusion of or to. [< Lat. *transfusus,* p.p. of *transfundere,* to pour out.] —**trans·fus′er** *n.*

trans·fu·sion (trăns-fyŏŏ′zhən) *n.* **1.** The act or process of transfusing. **2.** The direct injection of whole blood, plasma, saline solution, etc., into the bloodstream.

trans·gress (trăns-grĕs′, trănz′-) *v.* **1.** To go beyond or over (a limit or boundary). **2.** To act in violation of (a law, commandment, etc.). [< Lat. *transgressus,* p.p. of *transgredi,* to transgress.] —**trans·gres′sion** *n.* —**trans·gres′sive** *adj.* —**trans·gres′sor** *n.*

tran·ship (trăn-shĭp′) *v.* Var. of **transship.**

tran·sient (trăn′shənt, -zhənt, -zē-ənt) *adj.* **1.** Passing away with time; transitory. **2.** Passing through from one place to another; stopping only briefly: *transient workers.* —*n.* One that is transient, esp. a person staying a single night at a hotel or motel. [< Lat. *transire,* to go over.] —**tran′sience** or **tran′sien·cy** *n.* —**tran′sient·ly** *adv.*

tran·sis·tor (trăn-zĭs′tər, trăn-sĭs′-) *n.* **1.** A three-terminal semiconductor device used for amplification, switching, etc. **2.** A radio equipped with transistors. [TRANS(FER) + (RE)SISTOR.] —**tran·sis′tor·ize′** *v.*

tran·sit (trăn′sĭt, -zĭt) *n.* **1. a.** The act of passing over, across, or through. **b.** The conveyance of persons or goods from one place to another, esp. on a local public transportation system. **2.** A surveying instrument that measures angles. [Lat. *transitus.*]

tran·si·tion (trăn-zĭsh′ən, -sĭsh′ən) *n.* An instance or process of changing from one form, state, subject, or place to another. —**tran·si′tion·al** *adj.* —**tran·si′tion·al·ly** *adv.*

tran·si·tive (trăn′sə-tĭv, trăn′zə-) *adj.* Being or using a verb that requires a direct object to complete its meaning. —**tran′si·tive·ly** *adv.* —**tran′si·tive·ness** or **tran·si·tiv′i·ty** *n.*

tran·si·to·ry (trăn′sə-tôr′ē, -tōr′ē, trăn′zə-) *adj.* Existing only briefly. —**tran′si·to′ri·ly** *adv.* —**tran′si·to′ri·ness** *n.*

Syns: *transitory, momentary, passing, short-lived, temporary, transient* **adj.**

trans·late (trăns-lāt′, trănz-, trăns′lāt′, trănz′-) *v.* **-lat·ed, -lat·ing. 1.** To express or admit of being expressed in another language. **2.** To put in simpler terms; explain. **3.** To convey from one form or style to another. **4.** *Phys.* To move from one place to another without rotation. [< Lat. *translatus,* p.p. of *transferre,* to transfer.] **—trans·lat·a·bil′i·ty** or **trans·lat′a·ble·ness** *n.* **—trans·lat′a·ble** *adj.* **—trans·la′tion** *n.* **—trans·la′tor** *n.*

trans·lit·er·ate (trăns-lĭt′ə-rāt′, trănz-) *v.* **-at·ed, -at·ing.** To represent (letters or words) in the characters of another alphabet. [TRANS- + Lat. *littera,* letter + -ATE¹.] **—trans·lit′er·a′tion** *n.*

trans·lu·cent (trăns-lōō′sənt, trănz-) *adj.* Transmitting light but diffusing it sufficiently to cause images to become blurred. [< Lat. *translucēre,* to shine through.] **—trans·lu′cence** or **trans·lu′cen·cy** *n.* **—trans·lu′cent·ly** *adv.*

trans·mi·grate (trăns-mī′grāt′, trănz-) *v.* **-grat·ed, -grat·ing.** To pass into another body after death, as the soul. **—trans·mi·gra′tion** *n.* **—trans·mi′gra·tor** *n.* **—trans·mi′gra·to·ry** (-grə-tôr′ē, -tōr′ē) *adj.*

trans·mis·sion (trăns-mĭsh′ən, trănz-) *n.* **1.** The act or process of transmitting. **2.** Something transmitted. **3. a.** An assembly of gears that links an engine to a driving axle. **b.** A system of gears. **4.** The sending of a signal, as by radio. [< Lat. *transmittere,* to send across.] **—trans·mis′sive** (-mĭs′ĭv) *adj.*

trans·mit (trăns-mĭt′, trănz-) *v.* **-mit·ted, -mit·ting.** **1.** To send from one person, thing, or place to another. **2.** To cause to spread, as an infection. **3.** To impart by heredity. **4.** To send (a signal), as by radio. **5.** To convey (force or energy) from one part of a mechanism to another. [< Lat. *transmittere.*] **—trans·mis′si·ble** or **trans·mit′ta·ble** *adj.* **—trans·mit′tal** *n.*

trans·mit·ter (trăns-mĭt′ər, trănz-) *n.* One that transmits. **2.** Any of various electrical or electronic devices used to originate signals, as in radio or telegraphy.

trans·mute (trăns-myōōt′, trănz-) *v.* **-mut·ed, -mut·ing.** **1.** To change from one form, nature, condition, etc., into another; transform. **2.** To transform (an element) into another by nuclear reactions. [< Lat. *transmutare.*] **—trans·mut·a·bil′i·ty** *n.* **—trans·mut′a·ble** *adj.* **—trans·mut′a·bly** *adv.* **—trans·mu·ta′tion** *n.*

trans·o·ce·an·ic (trăns′ō-shē-ăn′ĭk, trănz′-) *adj.* **1.** Situated beyond the ocean. **2.** Spanning or crossing the ocean.

tran·som (trăn′səm) *n.* **1.** A small hinged window above a door or another window. **2.** A horizontal dividing piece in a window. [ME *traunson,* crossbeam.] **—tran′somed** *adj.*

trans·pa·cif·ic (trăns′pə-sĭf′ĭk) *adj.* **1.** Crossing the Pacific Ocean. **2.** Situated beyond the Pacific Ocean.

trans·par·ent (trăns-pâr′ənt, -păr′ənt) *adj.* **1.** Capable of transmitting light so that objects on the other side can be seen clearly. **2.** Of such texture that objects can be seen on the other side; sheer. **3.** Easily detected; flimsy: *transparent lies.* **4.** Guileless; candid; open. [< Med. Lat. *transparēre,* to appear through.] **—trans·par′en·cy** *n.* **—trans·par′ent·ly** *adv.*

tran·spire (trăn-spīr′) *v.* **-spired, -spir·ing.** **1.** To give off (vapor containing waste products) through pores or stomata. **2.** To become known; come to light. **3.** To happen; occur. [< OFr. *transpirer.*] **—tran′spi·ra′tion** (trăn′-spə-rā′shən) *n.*

Usage: Although *transpire* in the sense of "to happen" is in widespread use, this recent extension of its meaning is unacceptable to a majority of the Usage Panel.

trans·plant (trăns-plănt′, -plänt′) *v.* **1.** To uproot and replant (a growing plant). **2.** To transfer from one place or residence to another. **3.** To transfer (tissue or an organ) from one body, or bodily part, to another. **—trans′plant′** *n.* **—trans′plan·ta′tion** *n.* **—trans·plant′er** *n.*

trans·port (trăns-pôrt′, -pōrt′) *v.* **1.** To carry from one place to another. **2.** To move to strong emotion; enrapture. **3.** To send abroad to a penal colony. *—n.* (trăns′pôrt′, -pōrt′). **1.** The act of transporting; conveyance. **2.** Rapture. **3.** A ship used to transport troops or military equipment. **4.** A vehicle, as an aircraft, used to transport passengers or freight. [< Lat. *transportare.*] **—trans·port′a·bil′i·ty** *n.* **—trans·port′a·ble** *adj.* **—trans′por·ta′tion** *n.* **—trans·port′er** *n.*

trans·pose (trăns-pōz′) *v.* **-posed, -pos·ing.** **1.** To reverse or change the order or place of. **2.** *Mus.* To write or perform (a composition) in a key other than the original. [< Lat. *transponere.*] **—trans·pos′a·ble** *adj.* **—trans·pos′er** *n.* **—trans′po·si′tion** *n.*

trans·sex·u·al (trăns-sĕk′shōō-əl) *n.* A person with a strong desire to become a member of the other sex, sometimes to the point of undergoing a sex-change operation. **—trans·sex′u·al** *adj.* **—trans·sex′u·al′i·ty** *n.*

trans·ship (trăns-shĭp′) *v.* **-shipped, -ship·ping.** Also **tran·ship.** To transfer (cargo) from one vessel or conveyance to another. **—trans·ship′ment** *n.*

tran·sub·stan·ti·ate (trăn′səb-stăn′shē-āt′) *v.* **-at·ed, -at·ing.** **1.** To change (one substance) into another; transmute. **2.** *Theol.* To change the substance of (the Eucharistic bread and wine) into the true presence of Jesus Christ. [Med. Lat. *transubstantiare.*] **—tran′sub·stan′ti·a′tion** *n.*

trans·ver·sal (trăns-vûr′səl, trănz-) *adj.* Transverse. *—n. Geom.* A line that intersects a system of lines. **—trans·ver′sal·ly** *adv.*

trans·verse (trăns-vûrs′, trănz-, trăns′vûrs′, trănz′-) *adj.* Situated or lying across; crosswise. [< Lat. *transvertere,* to direct across.] **—trans·verse′** *n.* **—trans·verse′ly** *adv.*

trap (trăp) *n.* **1.** A device for catching and holding animals. **2.** Any stratagem for betraying, tricking, or exposing an unsuspecting person or group. **3. a.** A device for separating solids or other materials from flowing liquid. **b.** A device for keeping a drain sealed against a backward flow of foul gases. **4.** *Golf.* A land hazard or bunker. **5.** Often **traps.** Musical percussion instruments. **6.** *Slang.* The mouth. *—v.* **trapped, trap·ping.** **1.** To catch in or as if in a trap. **2.** To trap fur-bearing animals, esp. as a business. [< OE *træppe.*] **—trap′per** *n.*

trap door *n.* A hinged or sliding door in a floor or ceiling.

tra·peze (tră-pēz′) *n.* A short horizontal bar hung at the ends of two parallel ropes, used for acrobatic stunts. [< Gk. *trapeza,* table.]

trap·e·zoid (trăp′ə-zoid′) *n.* A quadrilateral with two parallel sides. [Gk. *trapeza,* table + -OID.] **—trap′e·zoi′dal** *adj.*

trap·pings (trăp′ĭngz) *pl.n.* **1.** An ornamental covering for a horse. **2.** Articles of dress or ornamentation. **3.** Outward signs; marks.

trap·shoot·ing (trăp'shōō'tĭng) n. The sport of shooting at clay targets hurled into the air.

trash (trăsh) n. 1. Worthless or discarded material or objects; refuse. 2. Cheap or worthless expressions, ideas, etc. 3. An ignorant or contemptible person. [Orig. unknown.] —**trash'y** adj.

trau·ma (trou'mə, trô'-) n. 1. A bodily wound or injury, esp. one caused by sudden external violence. 2. An emotional shock that causes lasting psychological damage. [Gk.] —**trau·mat'ic** (-măt'ĭk) adj. —**trau·mat'i·cal·ly** adv. —**trau'ma·tize'** v.

tra·vail (trə-vāl', trăv'āl') n. 1. Strenuous exertion; toil. 2. Tribulation or agony; anguish. 3. The labor of childbirth. —v. 1. To toil. 2. To be in the labor of childbirth. [< LLat. tripalium, instrument of torture.]

trav·el (trăv'əl) v. -eled or -elled, -el·ing or -el·ling. 1. To go from one place to another; journey (through). 2. To be transmitted; move, as light. 3. To associate. 4. To move swiftly. —n. 1. The act or process of traveling. 2. travels. A series of journeys. [< OFr. travailler, to toil.] —**trav'el·er** or **trav'el·ler** n.

trav·e·logue (trăv'ə-lôg', -lŏg') n. Also **trav·e·log**. A film or illustrated lecture on travel.

tra·verse (trə-vûrs', trăv'ərs) v. -ersed, -ers·ing. 1. To travel across, over, or through. 2. To move forward and backward over. 3. To move (a gun, telescope, etc.) laterally; swivel. 4. To extend across; cross. —n. (trăv'ərs, trə-vûrs') 1. The act of traversing. 2. Something lying across something else, as a beam or crosspiece. —adj. (trăv'ərs, trə-vûrs') Lying or extending across. [< Lat. transvertere, to direct across.] —**trav'ers·a·ble** —**tra·vers'al** (trə-vûr'səl) n. —**tra·vers'er** n.

trav·er·tine (trăv'ər-tēn', -tĭn) n. A light-colored, porous calcium carbonate deposited from solution in ground or-surface waters. [< Lat. (lapis) Tiburtinus, (stone) of Tibur, town in ancient Italy.]

trav·es·ty (trăv'ĭ-stē) n., pl. -ties. A grotesque imitation; mockery. —v. -tied, -ty·ing. To make a travesty on or of. [< OItal. travestire, to disguise.]

trawl (trôl) n. A large, tapered fishing net, towed along the sea bottom. —v. To fish or catch (fish) with a trawl. [ME trawelle.]

trawl·er (trô'lər) n. A boat used for trawling.

tray (trā) n. A flat, shallow receptacle with a raised edge or rim, used for carrying, holding, or displaying articles. [< OE trēg.]

treach·er·ous (trĕch'ər-əs) adj. 1. Betraying a trust; disloyal; traitorous. 2. Not dependable: a treacherous memory. 3. Not to be trusted; dangerous. —**treach'er·ous·ly** adv. —**treach'er·ous·ness** n.

treach·er·y (trĕch'ə-rē) n., pl. -ies. Willful betrayal of trust; perfidy. [< OFr. trichier, to trick.]

trea·cle (trē'kəl) n. 1. Chiefly Brit. Molasses. 2. Cloying speech or sentiment. [< Gk. thēriakē, antidote for poison.] —**trea'cly** (-klē) adj.

tread (trĕd) v. trod (trŏd), trod·den (trŏd'n) or trod, tread·ing. 1. To walk on, over, or along. 2. To press beneath the foot; trample. 3. To walk; dance. —n. 1. The act, manner, or

sound of treading. 2. The horizontal part of a step in a staircase. 3. The grooved face of an automobile tire. 4. The part of the sole of a shoe that touches the ground. [< OE tredan.] —**tread'er** n.

tread·le (trĕd'l) n. A pedal operated to drive a wheel, as in a sewing machine. [< OE tredel, step of a stair.]

tread·mill (trĕd'mĭl') n. 1. A device operated by walking on an endless belt or on a set of moving steps attached to a wheel. 2. A monotonous routine.

treadmill

trea·son (trē'zən) n. The betrayal of one's country, esp. by giving aid to an enemy. [< Lat. traditio, a giving up.] —**trea'son·ous** adj.

trea·son·a·ble (trē'zən-ə-bəl) adj. Of or involving treason. —**trea'son·a·ble·ness** n. —**trea'son·a·bly** adv.

treas·ure (trĕzh'ər) n. 1. Accumulated or stored wealth in the form of valuables, such as money or jewels. 2. One considered esp. precious or valuable. —v. -ured, -ur·ing. 1. To store up; hoard. 2. To value highly. [< Gk. thēsauros.] —**treas'ur·a·ble** adj.

treas·ur·er (trĕzh'ər-ər) n. One in charge of the funds or revenues of a government, corporation, club, etc. —**treas'ur·er·ship'** n.

treas·ure-trove (trĕzh'ər-trōv') n. 1. Treasure found hidden and not claimed by its owner. 2. A discovery of great value. [AN tresor trove, discovered treasure.]

treas·ur·y (trĕzh'ə-rē) n., pl. -ies. 1. A place where treasure is kept or stored. 2. A place where private or public funds are received, kept, managed, and disbursed. 3. Such funds or revenues. 4. **Treasury.** A governmental department in charge of the public revenue.

treat (trēt) v. 1. To act or behave toward: treated her fairly. 2. To deal with, handle, or cover. 3. To regard or consider in a certain way. 4. To try to cure by administering some remedy or form of therapy. 5. To subject to a process. 6. To entertain at one's own expense. —n. 1. a. Something paid for or provided by someone else. b. An act of treating or turn to treat. 2. A special delight or pleasure. [< Lat. tractare.] —**treat'a·ble** adj. —**treat'er** n.

trea·tise (trē'tĭs) n. A formal, systematic account in writing of some subject. [< OFr. traitier, to treat.]

treat·ment (trēt'mənt) n. 1. The act or manner of treating something. 2. The application of remedies to relieve or cure a disease or disorder.

trea·ty (trē′tē) *n., pl.* **-ties.** A formal agreement between two or more nations. [< Lat. *tractare,* to treat.]

tre·ble (trĕb′əl) *adj.* **1.** Triple. **2.** *Mus.* Of, having, or performing the highest part, voice, or range. **3.** High-pitched; shrill. —*n.* **1.** *Mus.* The highest part, voice, instrument, or range; soprano. **2.** A high, shrill sound or voice. —*v.* **-led, -ling.** To triple. [< Lat. *triplus,* triple.] —**tre′ble·ness** *n.* —**treb′ly** (trĕb′lē) *adv.*

treble clef *n.* A symbol centered on the second line of a musical staff to indicate the position of G above middle C.

tree (trē) *n.* **1.** A usu. tall woody plant with a single main stem or trunk. **2.** Something that resembles a tree: *a clothes tree.* **3.** A diagram showing family relationships. —*v.* **treed, tree·ing.** To chase and force to climb a tree. [< OE *treow.*]

tree of heaven *n.* A tree, the ailanthus.

tre·foil (trē′foil′, trĕf′oil′) *n.* **1.** A plant, as a clover, having compound leaves with three leaflets. **2.** An ornament resembling the leaves of such a plant. [< Lat. *trifolium.*]

trek (trĕk) *v.* **trekked, trek·king.** To make a long, difficult journey. —*n.* A long, difficult journey. [Afr., to travel by ox wagon.] —**trek′ker** *n.*

trel·lis (trĕl′ĭs) *n.* An open latticework used for training climbing plants. [< Lat. *trilix,* woven with three threads.]

trem·ble (trĕm′bəl) *v.* **-bled, -bling.** **1.** To shake involuntarily, as from fear, cold, etc.; shiver. **2.** To feel or express fear or anxiety. —*n.* An act of trembling. [< Lat. *tremulus.*] —**trem′bler** *n.* —**trem′bling·ly** *adv.*

tre·men·dous (trĭ-mĕn′dəs) *adj.* **1.** Capable of making one tremble; terrible. **2. a.** Extremely large; enormous. **b.** *Informal.* Marvelous; wonderful. [Lat. *tremendus.*] —**tre·men′dous·ly** *adv.* —**tre·men′dous·ness** *n.*

trem·o·lo (trĕm′ə-lō′) *n., pl.* **-los.** *Mus.* A vibrating effect produced either by the rapid repetition of a single tone or by the rapid alternation of two tones. [Ital.]

trem·or (trĕm′ər) *n.* **1.** A quick shaking or vibrating movement. **2.** An involuntary trembling motion of the body: *a nervous tremor.* [< Lat.]

trem·u·lous (trĕm′yə-ləs) *adj.* **1.** Vibrating or quivering; trembling. **2.** Timid; fearful. [Lat. *tremulus.*] —**trem′u·lous·ly** *adv.* —**trem′u·lous·ness** *n.*

trench (trĕnch) *n.* **1.** A deep furrow. **2.** A ditch, esp. one embanked with its own soil and used for concealment and protection in warfare. —*v.* **1.** To cut trenches in. **2.** To fortify with trenches. **3.** To verge or encroach. [< OFr. *trenchier,* to dig.]

trench·ant (trĕn′chənt) *adj.* **1.** Keen; incisive. **2.** Forceful; effective. [< OFr. *trenchier,* to cut.] —**trench′an·cy** *n.* —**trench′ant·ly** *adv.*

trench coat *n.* A loose-fitting, belted raincoat with many pockets and flaps.

trench·er (trĕn′chər) *n.* A wooden serving board. [< OFr. *trenchier,* to cut.]

trench fever *n.* An acute infectious fever caused by a microorganism and transmitted by a louse.

trench foot *n.* A foot disorder that resembles frostbite and often afflicts soldiers who must stand in flooded trenches.

trench mouth *n.* A painful form of gingivitis.

trend (trĕnd) *n.* **1.** A general tendency or course; drift. **2.** A direction or movement; flow. —*v.* To have a certain direction or tendency. [< OE *trendan,* to roll.]

trend·y (trĕn′dē) *adj.* **-i·er, -i·est.** *Informal.* Momentarily fashionable; modish. —**trend′i·ly** *adv.* —**trend′i·ness** *n.*

tre·pan (trĭ-păn′) *n.* A trephine. —*v.* **-panned, -pan·ning.** To trephine. [< Gk. *trupanon,* borer.] —**trep′a·na′tion** (trĕp′ə-nā′shən, trĭ-păn′ə′shən) *n.* —**tre·pan′ner** *n.*

tre·phine (trĭ-fīn′) *n.* A surgical saw for cutting out disks of bone, esp. from the skull. —*v.* **-phined, -phin·ing.** To operate on or extract with a trephine. [< Lat. *tres fines,* three ends.] —**treph′i·na′tion** (trĕf′ə-nā′shən) *n.*

trep·i·da·tion (trĕp′ə-dā′shən) *n.* Dread; apprehension. [< Lat. *trepidus,* anxious.]

tres·pass (trĕs′pəs, -păs′) *v.* **1.** To commit an offense or sin; err; transgress. **2.** To infringe upon the privacy or attention of another. **3.** To invade the property or rights of another without consent. —*n.* **1.** A transgression. **2.** The act of trespassing. [< Med. Lat. *transpassare.*] —**tres′pass·er** *n.*

tress (trĕs) *n.* A lock of hair. [< OFr. *tresse.*]

tres·tle (trĕs′əl) *n.* **1.** A horizontal bar held up by two pairs of divergent legs and used as a support. **2.** A framework of vertical, slanted supports and horizontal crosspieces supporting a bridge. [< Lat. *transstrum,* beam.]

trey (trā) *n.* A card or die with three pips. [< Lat. *tres,* three.]

tri– *pref.* **1.** Three: *triangle.* **2. a.** Occurring at intervals of three: *trimonthly.* **b.** Occurring three times during: *triweekly.* [< Lat. *tres* and Gk. *treis.*]

tri·ad (trī′ăd′, -əd) *n.* A group of three persons or things. [< Gk. *trias.*] —**tri·ad′ic** *adj.*

tri·al (trī′əl, trīl) *n.* **1.** The examination of evidence and applicable law to determine the issue of specified charges or claims. **2.** The act or process of testing and trying by use and experience. **3.** An effort or attempt. **4.** A test of patience or endurance. —*adj.* **1.** Of a trial. **2.** Made, done, or used during a test or tests. [< OFr. *trier,* to try.]

tri·an·gle (trī′ăng′gəl) *n.* **1.** The plane figure formed by connecting three points not in a straight line by straight line segments. **2.** Something having the shape of a triangle. **3.** A musical percussion instrument formed of a metal bar bent into a triangle. —**tri·an′gu·lar** *adj.*

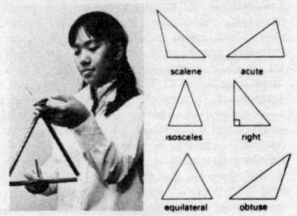

triangle
Left: Percussion instrument
Right: Geometric figures

scalene   acute
isosceles   right
equilateral   obtuse

tri·an·gu·late (trī-ăng′gyə-lāt′) *v.* **-lat·ed, -lat·ing.** To measure by using trigonometry. —**tri·an′gu·la′tion** *n.*

Tri·as·sic (trī-ăs′ĭk) *adj.* Of or belonging to the geologic time, rock systems, and sedimentary deposits of the first period of the Mesozoic era. —*n.* The Triassic period.

tribe (trīb) *n.* 1. A social organization or division comprising several local villages, bands, lineages, or other groups and sharing a common ancestry, language, culture, and name. 2. A group having a common distinguishing characteristic. [< Lat. *tribus*, a division of the Roman people.] —**trib′al** *adj.* —**trib′al·ly** *adv.*

tribes·man (trībz′mən) *n.* A member of a tribe.

trib·u·la·tion (trĭb′yə-lā′shən) *n.* 1. Great affliction or distress. 2. Something that causes such distress. [< Lat. *tribulare*, to oppress.]

tri·bu·nal (trī-byōō′nəl, trĭ-) *n.* 1. A seat or court of justice. 2. A group having the power of determining or judging. [< Lat. *tribunus*, tribune.]

trib·une (trĭb′yōōn′, trī-byōōn′) *n.* 1. An official of ancient Rome chosen by the common people to protect their rights. 2. A protector or champion of the people. [< Lat. *tribunus*.] —**trib′u·nar·y** (trĭb′yə-nĕr′ē) *adj.*

trib·u·tar·y (trĭb′yə-tĕr′ē) *n., pl.* **-ies.** 1. A river or stream that flows into a larger one. 2. One that pays tribute. —*adj.* 1. Flowing into another. 2. Paying tribute. 3. Contributory.

trib·ute (trĭb′yōōt) *n.* 1. A gift or other acknowledgment of gratitude, respect, or admiration. 2. a. A sum of money paid by one ruler or nation to another as acknowledgment of submission or for protection. b. A forced payment. [< Lat. *tributum*.]

trice (trīs) *n.* A very short period of time; instant. [< MDu. *trisen*, to hoist.]

tri·ceps (trī′sĕps′) *n.* A large muscle that runs along the back of the upper arm and serves to extend the forearm. [Lat., three-headed.]

tri·cer·a·tops (trī-sĕr′ə-tŏps′) *n.* A horned plant-eating dinosaur with a bony plate covering the neck. [TRI- + Gk. *keras*, horn + Gk. *ōps*, face.]

trich·i·no·sis (trĭk′ə-nō′sĭs) *n.* A disease caused by eating inadequately cooked pork infested with parasitic worms, characterized by intestinal disorders, fever, muscular swelling, pain, and insomnia. [*trichina*, a parasitic worm + -OSIS.]

trick (trĭk) *n.* 1. A device or action designed to achieve an end by deceptive or fraudulent means; stratagem. 2. A practical joke; prank. 3. A childish act or performance. 4. A peculiar trait; mannerism. 5. The quality necessary to accomplish something easily. 6. A feat requiring special skill or talent. 7. A clever act. 8. *Card Games.* All the cards played in a single round. —*v.* 1. To swindle or cheat; deceive. 2. To ornament or adorn. —*adj.* 1. Involving tricks; tricky. 2. Weak and liable to give way: *a trick knee.* [< ONFr. *trikier*, to deceive.] —**trick′er** *n.*

trick·er·y (trĭk′ə-rē) *n., pl.* **-ies.** The practice or use of tricks; deception.

trick·le (trĭk′əl) *v.* **-led, -ling.** 1. To fall in drops or in a thin, intermittent stream. 2. To proceed slowly or bit by bit. —*n.* 1. The act or condition of trickling. 2. Any slow, small, or irregular quantity. [ME *triklen.*]

trick·ster (trĭk′stər) *n.* One who tricks; deceiver; cheater.

trick·y (trĭk′ē) *adj.* **-i·er, -i·est.** 1. Crafty; sly. 2. Requiring caution or skill. —**trick′i·ly** *adv.* —**trick′i·ness** *n.*

tri·col·or (trī′kŭl′ər) *adj.* *Also* **tri·col·ored** (-ərd). Having three different colors. —*n.* A tricolor flag.

tri·cy·cle (trī′sĭk′əl, -sĭ-kəl) *n.* A three-wheeled vehicle usu. propelled by pedals.

tri·dent (trīd′ənt) *n.* A long, three-pronged spear. [Lat. *tridens.*]

tried (trīd) *v.* *p.t. & p.p.* of **try.** —*adj.* Tested and proved to be trustworthy.

tri·en·ni·al (trī-ĕn′ē-əl) *adj.* 1. Lasting three years. 2. Happening every 3rd year. —*n.* A 3rd anniversary. [< Lat. *triennium*, three years.] —**tri·en′ni·al·ly** *adv.*

tri·fle (trī′fəl) *n.* 1. Something of slight importance or very little value. 2. A small amount. —*v.* **-fled, -fling.** 1. To deal with something as if it were insignificant or valueless. 2. To play or toy with something. 3. To waste (e.g. time or money). [< OFr. *trufle*, trickery.] —**tri′fler** (trī′flər) *n.*

tri·fling (trī′flĭng) *adj.* 1. Of slight importance; insignificant. 2. Frivolous.

tri·fo·cal (trī-fō′kəl) *adj.* Having three focal lengths. —*pl.n.* **trifocals.** Eyeglasses having trifocal lenses.

trig¹ (trĭg) *adj.* 1. Trim; neat; tidy. 2. In good condition. [< ON *tryggr.*]

trig² (trĭg) *n.* Trigonometry.

trig·ger (trĭg′ər) *n.* 1. A lever pressed by the finger to discharge a firearm. 2. A device used to release or activate a mechanism. 3. A stimulus. —*v.* To initiate; activate; set off. [< MDu. *trecker.*]

trig·o·nom·e·try (trĭg′ə-nŏm′ə-trē) *n.* The study of the relations between the sides and angles of triangles. [Gk. *trigōnon*, triangle + -METRY.] —**trig′o·no·met′ric** (-nə-mĕt′rĭk) *adj.* —**trig′o·no·met′ri·cal·ly** *adv.*

trill (trĭl) *n.* 1. A fluttering or tremulous sound; warble. 2. *Mus.* The rapid alternation of two tones either a whole or a half tone apart. 3. *Phon.* a. A rapid vibration of one speech organ against another. b. A speech sound pronounced with such a vibration. —*v.* 1. To sound, sing, or play with a trill. 2. *Phon.* To articulate with a trill. [Ital. *trillo.*]

tril·lion (trĭl′yən) *n.* 1. The cardinal number equal to 10¹². 2. *Chiefly Brit.* The cardinal number equal to 10¹⁸. [TRI- + (M)ILLION.] —**tril′lion** *adj.*

tril·lionth (trĭl′yənth) *n.* 1. The ordinal number that matches the number one trillion in a series. 2. One of a trillion equal parts. —**tril′lionth** *adj. & adv.*

tri·lo·bite (trī′lə-bīt′) *n.* A three-lobed, saltwater arthropod of the Paleozoic era. [< Gk. *trilobos*, three-lobed.]

tril·o·gy (trĭl′ə-jē) *n., pl.* **-gies.** A group of three related artistic works. [Gk. *trilogia.*]

trim (trĭm) *v.* **trimmed, trim·ming.** 1. To make neat or tidy by clipping, smoothing, or pruning. 2. To rid of excess or remove by cutting. 3. To ornament; decorate. 4. a. To adjust (the sails and yards) so that they receive the wind properly. **b.** To balance (a ship) by shifting its cargo or contents. **5.** To balance (an airplane) in flight. —*n.* **1.** State of order or appearance; condition. **2.** Ornamentation. **3.** Excised or rejected material. **4. a.** The readiness of a vessel for sailing. **b.** The balance of a ship. —*adj.* **trim·mer, trim·mest. 1.** In good or neat order. **2.** Having lines of neat and pleasing simplicity. [< OE *trymman,* to arrange.] —**trim′ly** *adv.* —**trim′mer** *n.* —**trim′ness** *n.*

tri·mes·ter (trī-měs′tər) *n.* **1.** A period of three months. **2.** One of three academic terms into which the academic year is sometimes divided. [< Lat. *trimestris,* of three months.]

trim·ming (trĭm′ĭng) *n.* **1.** Something added as decoration. **2.** Something trimmed. **3.** **trimmings.** Accessories; extras.

trine (trīn) *adj.* Threefold; triple. —*n.* A group of three. [< Lat. *trinus.*]

trin·i·ty (trĭn′ə-tē) *n., pl.* **-ties. 1.** A group of three closely related members; triad. **2.** **Trinity.** The Godhead of orthodox Christian belief, constituted by the persons of the Father, Son, and Holy Ghost. [< Lat. *trinitas.*]

trin·ket (trĭng′kĭt) *n.* **1.** A small ornament or piece of jewelry. **2.** A trifle. [Orig. unknown.]

tri·o (trē′ō) *n., pl.* **-os. 1.** A group of three. **2.** *Mus.* **a.** A composition for three performers. **b.** The musicians who perform such a composition. [Ital.]

trip (trĭp) *n.* **1.** A going from one place to another; journey. **2.** *Slang.* An exciting or hallucinatory experience. **3.** A stumble or fall caused by an obstacle or loss of balance. **4. a.** A device for tripping a mechanism. **b.** The action of such a device. —*v.* **tripped, trip·ping. 1.** To stumble or cause to stumble. **2.** To move quickly or nimbly; skip. **3.** To make a mistake; err. **4.** To release or be released, as a catch or trigger. [< MDu. *trippen,* to hop.] —**trip′per** *n.*

tri·par·tite (trī-pär′tīt′) *adj.* **1.** Composed of or divided into three parts. **2.** Involving or done by three parties.

tripe (trīp) *n.* **1.** The stomach lining of cattle or other ruminants, used as food. **2.** *Informal.* Something with no value; rubbish. [< OFr.]

tri·ple (trĭp′əl) *adj.* **1.** Having three parts. **2.** Three times as many or as much. —*n.* **1.** A number or amount three times as great as another. **2.** A group or set of three. **3.** *Baseball.* A hit that enables the batter to reach third base safely. —*v.* **-pled, -pling. 1.** To become or make three times as great in number or amount. **2.** *Baseball.* To hit a triple. [< Lat. *triplus.*] —**tri′ply** *adv.*

trip·let (trĭp′lĭt) *n.* **1.** A group or set of three. **2.** One of three children born at one birth. [**TRIPLE**(E) + (**DOUBL**)**ET.**]

tri·plex (trĭp′lĕks′, trī′plĕks′) *adj.* Triple. [Lat.]

trip·li·cate (trĭp′lĭ-kĭt) *adj.* Made with three identical copies. —*n.* One of a set of three identical objects or copies. —*v.* (trĭp′lĭ-kāt′) **-cat·ed, -cat·ing.** To make three identical copies of. [< Lat. *triplicare,* to triple.] —**trip′li·cate·ly** *adv.* —**trip′li·ca′tion** *n.*

tri·pod (trī′pŏd′) *n.* A three-legged utensil, stool, or stand used for support. [< Lat. *tripous,* three-footed.] —**trip′o·dal** (trĭp′ə-dəl, trī′pŏd′l) *adj.*

trip·tych (trĭp′tĭk) *n.* A three-paneled picture. [< Gk. *triptukhos,* threefold.]

triptych
16th-century Rhenish

tri·sect (trī′sĕkt′, trī-sĕkt′) *v.* To divide into three equal parts. —**tri′sec′tion** (-sĕk′shən) *n.*

trite (trīt) *adj.* **trit·er, trit·est.** Overused and commonplace; lacking interest or originality. [Lat. *tritus,* p.p. of *terere,* to rub out.] —**trite′ly** *adv.* —**trite′ness** *n.*

Syns: *trite, banal, bromidic, commonplace, corny, hackneyed, stereotyped* **adj.**

trit·i·um (trĭt′ē-əm, trĭsh′ē-) *n.* A rare radioactive hydrogen isotope with atomic mass 3. [< Gk. *tritos,* third.]

tri·umph (trī′əmf) *v.* **1.** To be victorious; win; prevail. **2.** To rejoice; exult. —*n.* **1.** The fact or an instance of being victorious; victory. **2.** Exultation. [< Lat. *triumphare.*] —**tri·um′phal** *adj.* —**tri·um′phant** *adj.* —**tri·um′phant·ly** *adv.* —**tri′umph·er** *n.*

tri·um·vir (trī-ŭm′vər) *n., pl.* **-virs** or **-vi·ri** (-və-rī′). One of three men sharing civil authority, as in ancient Rome. [Lat.] —**tri·um′vi·ral** *adj.* —**tri·um′vi·rate** (-vər-ĭt) *n.*

triv·et (trĭv′ĭt) *n.* **1.** A three-legged stand. **2.** A stand or thick plate placed under a hot dish or platter on a table. [< Lat. *tripes,* three-footed.]

triv·i·a (trĭv′ē-ə) *pl.n.* (*used with a sing. or pl. verb*). Insignificant or inessential matters; trivialities; trifles. [< Lat. *trivialis,* trivial.]

triv·i·al (trĭv′ē-əl) *adj.* **1.** Of little importance; trifling. **2.** Ordinary; commonplace. [Lat. *trivialis.*] —**triv′i·al′i·ty** *n.* —**triv′i·al·ly** *adv.*

-trix *suff.* A female connected with a specified thing: *aviatrix.* [Lat.]

tro·che (trō′kē) *n.* A small circular medicinal lozenge. [< Gk. *trokhos,* wheel.]

tro·chee (trō′kē) *n.* A metrical foot of one long or stressed syllable followed by one short or unstressed syllable. [< Gk. *trokhaios.*] —**tro·cha′ic** (-kā′ĭk) *adj.*

trod (trŏd) *v. p.t. & p.p.* of **tread.**

trod·den (trŏd′n) *v.* A *p.p.* of **tread.**

troi·ka (troi′kə) *n.* A small Russian carriage drawn by three horses abreast. [R. *troyka.*]

Tro·jan (trō′jən) *n.* **1.** A native or inhabitant of ancient Troy. **2.** A courageous or hardworking person. —**Tro′jan** *adj.*

troll¹ (trōl) *v.* **1.** To fish by trailing a baited line from behind a slowly moving boat. **2.** To sing in succession the parts of (a round). **3.** To sing heartily. —*n.* **1.** The act of trolling for fish. **2.** A lure used for trolling. **3.** A musical round. [ME *trollen,* to ramble.] —**troll′er** *n.*

troll² (trōl) *n.* A supernatural creature of Scandinavian folklore, often described as living in caves or under bridges. [< ON.]

trol·ley (trŏl′ē) *n., pl.* **-leys.** Also **trol·ly** *pl.*

-lies. 1. An electric car; streetcar. **2.** A wheeled carriage or basket suspended from an overhead track. **3.** A device that collects electric current and transmits it to the motor of an electric vehicle. [Prob. < TROLL¹.]

trolley bus n. An electric bus that receives current from an overhead wire.

trolley car n. A streetcar.

trol·lop (trŏl′əp) n. **1.** A slovenly, untidy woman. **2.** A loose woman; strumpet. [Perh. < TROLL¹.]

trom·bone (trŏm-bōn′, trăm-, trŏm′bōn′) n. A low-pitched brass musical instrument related to the trumpet. [< Ital. *tromba,* trumpet.] **—trom·bon′ist** n.

-tron suff. A device for manipulating subatomic particles: *cyclotron.* [Gk., in suffix.]

troop (trōōp) n. **1.** A group or company of people, animals, or things. **2.** A group of soldiers. **3. troops.** Military units; soldiers. —v. To move or go as a throng. [OFr. *trope.*]

troop·er (trōō′pər) n. **1. a.** A cavalryman. **b.** A cavalry horse. **2.** A mounted policeman. **3.** A state policeman.

troop·ship (trōōp′shĭp′) n. A ship for carrying troops.

trope (trōp) n. A figure of speech. [< Gk. *tropos,* manner.]

tro·phy (trō′fē) n., pl. **-phies.** A prize or memento received as a symbol of victory. [< Gk. *tropaion.*]

-trophy suff. Nutrition; growth: *dystrophy.* [< Gk. *trophē,* food.]

trop·ic (trŏp′ĭk) n. **1.** Either of two parallels of latitude, the *tropic of Cancer* at 23°27′north or the *tropic of Capricorn* at 23°27′south. **2. tropics.** The region of the earth's surface bounded by these latitudes. —adj. Of or concerning the tropics; tropical. [< Gk. *tropikos,* solstice.]

-tropic suff. Turning in response to a specified stimulus: *isotropic.* [< Gk. *tropos,* turn.]

trop·i·cal (trŏp′ĭ-kəl) adj. **1.** Of or characteristic of the tropics. **2.** Hot and humid; torrid. **—trop′i·cal·ly** adv.

tropical year n. The time interval between two successive passages of the sun through the vernal equinox; calendar year.

tro·pism (trō′pĭz′əm) n. The responsive growth or movement of an organism toward or away from an external stimulus. [< Gk. *tropos,* turn.]

tro·po·sphere (trō′pə-sfîr′, trŏp′ə-) n. The lowest region of the earth's atmosphere, characterized by temperatures that decrease with increasing altitude. [Gk. *tropos,* turn + SPHERE.]

-tropy suff. The condition of turning: *allotropy.* [< Gk. *tropos,* turn.]

trot (trŏt) n. **1.** A gait of a four-footed animal in which diagonal pairs of legs move forward together. **2.** A jogging run or quick walk. —v. **trot·ted, trot·ting. 1.** To go or move at a trot. **2.** To proceed rapidly; hurry. [< OFr. *troter,* to trot.] **—trot′ter** n.

troth (trŏth, trōth, trôth) n. **1.** Good faith; fidelity. **2.** One's pledged fidelity; betrothal. [< OE *trēowth.*]

trou·ba·dour (trōō′bə-dôr′, -dōr′, -dōōr′) n. **1.** One of a class of lyric poet-musicians of the 12th and 13th cent. in Provence and northern Italy. **2.** A strolling minstrel. [< OProv. *trobador.*]

trou·ble (trŭb′əl) n. **1.** Difficulty. **2.** Danger or distress. **3.** A source of difficulty, annoyance, or distress. **4.** Inconvenience. **5.** Conflict, disturbance, or unrest. **6.** Failure to perform properly; malfunction or illness. —v. **-led, -ling. 1.** To agitate; stir up. **2.** To afflict with pain or discomfort. **3.** To perturb. **4.** To inconvenience; bother. **5.** To take pains. [< Lat. *turbidus,* confused.] **—trou′bler** n. **—trou′ble·some** adj. **—trou′bling·ly** adv.

trou·ble·mak·er (trŭb′əl-mā′kər) n. One who habitually stirs up trouble.

trou·ble·shoot·er (trŭb′əl-shōō′tər) n. One who locates and eliminates sources of trouble.

trough (trŏf, trôf) n. **1.** A long, narrow, gen. shallow receptacle, esp. one for holding water or feed for animals. **2.** A gutter under the eaves of a roof. **3.** A long, narrow depression, as between waves or ridges. **4.** A low point in a cycle or on a graph. [< OE *trog.*]

trounce (trouns) v. **trounced, trounc·ing. 1.** To thrash; beat. **2.** To defeat decisively. [Orig. unknown.]

troupe (trōōp) n. A company or group, esp. of touring performers. —v. **trouped, troup·ing.** To tour with a theatrical company. [Fr., troop.] **—troup′er** n.

trou·sers (trou′zərz) pl.n. A garment covering the body from the waist to the ankles, divided into sections to fit each leg separately. [< Sc. Gael. *triubhas.*]

trous·seau (trōō′sō, trōō-sō′) n., pl. **-seaux** (-sōz, -sōz′) or **-seaus.** The special wardrobe a bride assembles for her marriage. [< OFr.]

trout (trout) n., pl. **trout** or **trouts.** Any of various chiefly freshwater food and game fishes related to the salmon. [< Gk. *trōktēs,* a kind of seafish.]

trow (trō) v. *Archaic.* To think; suppose. [< OE *trēowian.*]

trow·el (trou′əl) n. **1.** A flat-bladed hand tool used for shaping substances such as cement or mortar. **2.** A small gardening implement with a scoop-shaped blade. [< Lat. *trua,* ladle.]

trowel

Left: Stonemason using a trowel
Right: Different types of trowels

troy (troi) adj. Of or expressed in troy weight. [< *Troyes,* France.]

troy weight n. A system of units of weight in which the grain is the same as in the avoirdupois system and the pound contains 12 ounces, 240 pennyweights, or 5,760 grains.

tru·ant (trōō′ənt) n. **1.** One who is absent without permission, esp. from school. **2.** One who shirks his work or duty. —adj. **1.** Absent without permission. **2.** Idle, lazy, or neglectful. [< OFr., beggar.] **—tru'an·cy** n.

truce (trōōs) n. A temporary cessation of hostilities by agreement; armistice. [< OE *trēow*, pledge.]

truck¹ (trŭk) n. **1.** Any of various heavy automotive vehicles for carrying loads. **2.** A swiveling frame of wheels under each end of a railroad car, streetcar, etc. **3.** A two-wheeled barrow for moving heavy objects by hand. —v. **1.** To drive a truck. **2.** To transport by truck. [Prob. < TRUCKLE.] **—truck'er** n.

truck² (trŭk) v. **1.** To exchange; barter. **2.** To have dealings; traffic. —n. **1.** Garden produce raised for the market. **2.** *Informal.* Worthless articles; rubbish. **3.** *Informal.* Dealings; business. **4.** Barter; exchange. [< OFr. *troquer.*]

truck·age (trŭk'ĭj) n. **1.** Transportation of goods by truck. **2.** A charge for this.

truck·le (trŭk'əl) n. **1.** A small wheel or roller; caster. **2.** A trundle bed. —v. **-led, -ling.** To be submissive; yield weakly. [< Lat. *trochlea,* system of pulleys.] **—truck'ler** n.

truc·u·lent (trŭk'yə-lənt) adj. **1.** Savage and cruel; fierce. **2.** Disposed to fight; pugnacious. [Lat. *truculentus.*] **—truc'u·lence** n. **—truc'u·lent·ly** adv.

trudge (trŭj) v. **trudged, trudg·ing.** To walk in a laborious, heavy-footed way; plod. —n. A long, tedious walk. [Orig. unknown.] **—trudg'er** n.

true (trōō) adj. **tru·er, tru·est. 1.** Consistent with fact or reality; accurate. **2.** Not counterfeit; genuine. **3.** Faithful; loyal. **4.** Rightful; legitimate. **5.** Sincerely felt or expressed. **6.** Exactly conforming to an original or standard. **7.** Determined with reference to the earth's axis, not the magnetic poles: *true north.* —adv. **1.** Rightly; truthfully. **2.** Unswervingly; exactly. **3.** So as to conform to an ancestral type or stock: *breed true.* —v. **trued, tru·ing** or **true·ing.** To adjust so as to conform with a standard. —n. **1. the true.** Truth. **2.** Proper alignment or adjustment: *in or out of true.* [< OE *trēowe*, loyal.] **—true'ness** n.
Syns: true, genuine, real, sincere *adj.*

true-blue (trōō'blōō') adj. Of or marked by unswerving loyalty.

true-love (trōō'lŭv') n. One's beloved; a sweetheart.

truf·fle (trŭf'əl) n. An underground fungus esteemed as a food delicacy. [< Lat. *tuber.*]

tru·ism (trōō'ĭz'əm) n. An obvious truth. **—tru·is'tic** (-ĭs'tĭk) adj.

tru·ly (trōō'lē) adv. **1.** Sincerely; genuinely. **2.** Truthfully; accurately. **3.** Indeed.

trump (trŭmp) n. **1.** A suit the cards of which are declared as outranking all other cards for the duration of a hand. **2.** A card of such a suit. —v. To play a trump card. **—phrasal verb. trump up.** To devise fraudulently. [< TRIUMPH.]

trump·er·y (trŭm'pə-rē) n., pl. **-ies. 1.** Showy but worthless finery. **2.** Nonsense. [< OFr. *tromper,* to deceive.]

trum·pet (trŭm'pĭt) n. **1.** A soprano brass wind instrument that consists of a long metal tube ending in a flared bell. **2.** Something shaped or sounding like a trumpet. **3.** A resounding call. —v. **1.** To play on a trumpet. **2.** To call or proclaim loudly. [< OFr. *tromp,* trumpet.] **—trum'pet·er** n.

trun·cate (trŭng'kāt') v. **-cat·ed, -cat·ing.** To

shorten by or as if by cutting off the end or top. [< Lat. *truncare.*] **—trun·ca'tion** n.

trun·cheon (trŭn'chən) n. A short stick carried by policemen. [< OFr. *truncus,* trunk.]

trun·dle (trŭn'dl) v. **-dled, -dling.** To push on wheels or rollers. [< OE *trendel,* circle.] **—trun'dler** n.

trundle bed n. A low bed on casters that can be rolled under another bed when not in use.

trunk (trŭngk) n. **1.** The main woody stem of a tree. **2.** The human body excluding the head and limbs; torso. **3.** A main body, apart from tributaries or appendages. **4.** A large packing case or box that clasps shut, used as luggage or for storage. **5.** A covered compartment of an automobile, used for luggage and storage. **6.** A proboscis, esp. the long, prehensile proboscis of an elephant. **7. trunks.** Men's shorts worn for swimming or athletics. —adj. Of or designating the main body or line of a system. [< Lat. *truncus.*]

trunk line n. A direct line between two telephone switchboards.

truss (trŭs) n. **1.** A supportive device worn to prevent enlargement of a hernia or the return of a reduced hernia. **2.** A wooden or metal framework used to support a roof, bridge, or similar structure. —v. **1.** To tie up or bind. **2.** To bind or skewer the wings or legs of (a fowl) before cooking. **3.** To support or brace with a truss. [< OFr. *trousser,* to tie.] **—truss'er** n.

trust (trŭst) n. **1.** Firm reliance; confident belief; faith. **2.** One in which confidence is placed. **3.** Custody; care. **4.** One committed into the care of another; charge. **5.** The condition and resulting obligation of having confidence placed in one. **6.** Reliance on something in the future; hope. **7.** A legal arrangement in which property is held by one party for the benefit of another. **8.** A combination of firms for the purpose of reducing competition. —v. **1.** To rely or depend (on); have confidence (in). **2.** To be confident; hope. **3.** To expect with assurance; assume. **4.** To believe. **5.** To entrust. **6.** To grant discretion to confidently. **7.** To extend credit to. —adj. Maintained in trust. [ME *truste.*] **—trust'er** n.

trus·tee (trŭs'tē') n. **1.** A person or agent holding legal title to and administering property for a beneficiary. **2.** A member of a board that directs the funds and policy of an institution. **—trus·tee'ship** n.

trust·ful (trŭst'fəl) adj. Full of trust. **—trust'ful·ly** adv. **—trust'ful·ness** n.

trust·wor·thy (trŭst'wûr'thē) adj. Deserving trust; dependable. **—trust'wor'thi·ly** adv. **—trust'wor'thi·ness** n.

trust·y (trŭs'tē) adj. **-i·er, -i·est.** Dependable; reliable. —n., pl. **-ies.** A trusted person, esp. a convict granted special privileges. **—trust'i·ly** adv. **—trust'i·ness** n.

truth (trōōth) n., pl. **truths** (trōōthz, trōōths). **1.** Conformity to knowledge, fact, or actuality; veracity. **2.** Something that is the case; the real state of affairs. **3.** Reality; actuality. **4.** A statement proven to be or accepted as true. **5.** Sincerity; honesty. [< OE *trēowth.*]

truth·ful (trōōth'fəl) adj. **1.** Consistently telling the truth; honest. **2.** Corresponding to reality. **—truth'ful·ly** adv. **—truth'ful·ness** n.

try (trī) v. **tried, try·ing. 1.** To test in order to determine strength, effect, etc. **2. a.** To examine or hear (evidence or a case) by judicial process. **b.** To put (an accused person) on trial. **3.** To subject to great strain or hardship; tax. **4.** To melt (fat) to separate out impurities; render. **5.** To make an effort (to do something); attempt. **6.** To smooth, fit, or align accurately. —*n., pl.* **tries.** An attempt; effort. [< OFr. *trier*, to pick out.] —**tri'er** *n.*

Usage: Try and is common in speech for *try to,* especially in such expressions as *try and stop me.* This idiom is usually not interchangeable with *try to,* except in informal contexts.

try·ing (trī'ĭng) *adj.* Causing severe strain or distress. —**try'ing·ly** *adv.*

try·out (trī'out') *n.* A competitive test to ascertain the qualifications of applicants, as for a theatrical role.

tryst (trĭst) *n.* **1.** An agreement between lovers to meet. **2.** The meeting or meeting place so arranged. [< OFr. *triste,* an appointed station in hunting.]

tsar (zär) *n.* Var. of **czar.**

tset·se fly (tsĕt'sē, tsĕt'sē) *n.* A bloodsucking African fly that transmits microorganisms causing diseases such as sleeping sickness. [< Tswana *tsetse.*]

Tshi (chwē, chē) *n.* Var. of **Twi.**

T-shirt (tē'shûrt') *n.* Also **tee shirt.** A close-fitting, short-sleeved, collarless shirt.

T-square (tē'skwâr') *n.* A T-shaped ruler used for drawing parallel lines.

tsu·na·mi (tsōō-nä'mē) *n.* A very large ocean wave caused by an underwater earthquake or volcanic eruption. [J.]

Tswa·na (tswä'nə, sä'-) *n., pl.* **-na** or **-nas.** **1.** A Bantu people of southern Africa, living mainly in Botswana. **2.** The Sotho language of the Tswana.

tub (tŭb) *n.* **1.** A round, open, flat-bottomed vessel used for packing, storing, or washing. **2.** A bathtub. [< MLG *tubbe.*]

tu·ba (tōō'bə, tyōō'-) *n.* A large brass wind instrument with a bass pitch and several valves. [< Lat., trumpet.]

tub·by (tŭb'ē) *adj.* **-bi·er, -bi·est.** Short and fat.

tube (tōōb, tyōōb) *n.* **1.** A hollow cylinder that conveys a fluid or functions as a passage. **2.** A flexible cylindrical container sealed at one end and having a screw cap at the other, for pigments, toothpaste, etc. **3.** An electron tube or vacuum tube. **4.** *Chiefly Brit.* A subway. **5.** Often **the tube.** *Informal.* Television. [< Lat. *tubus.*] —**tube'less** *adj.*

tu·ber (tōō'bər, tyōō'-) *n.* **1.** A swollen, usu. underground stem, such as the potato, bearing buds from which new plants sprout. **2.** A swelling; tubercle. [Lat., lump.]

tu·ber·cle (tōō'bər-kəl, tyōō'-) *n.* **1.** A small, knobby prominence or excrescence on the roots of some plants or in the skin or on a bone. **2.** The characteristic lesion of tuberculosis. [Lat. *tuberculum,* little lump.]

tubercle bacillus *n.* A rod-shaped bacterium that causes tuberculosis.

tu·ber·cu·lar (tōō-bûr'kyə-lər, tyōō-) *adj.* **1.** Of or covered with tubercles. **2.** Of or afflicted with tuberculosis.

tu·ber·cu·lin (tōō-bûr'kyə-lĭn, tyōō-) *n.* A substance derived from tubercle bacilli, used

in the diagnosis and treatment of tuberculosis. [Lat. *tuberculum,* tubercle + -IN.]

tu·ber·cu·lo·sis (tōō-bûr'kyə-lō'sĭs, tyōō-) *n.* A communicable disease of man and animals, caused by the tubercle bacillus and manifesting itself in lesions, esp. of the lung. [Lat. *tuberculum,* tubercle + -OSIS.] —**tu·ber·cu·lous** *adj.*

tube·rose (tōōb'rōz', tyōōb'-, tōō'bə-rōz', tyōō'-, -rōs') *n.* A tuber-bearing plant native to Mexico, cultivated for its fragrant white flowers.

tu·bu·lar (tōō'byə-lər, tyōō'-) *adj.* Of or having the form of a tube. —**tu'bu·lar·ly** *adv.*

tuck (tŭk) *v.* **1.** To make one or more folds in. **2.** To thrust or turn in the end or edge of (e.g. a shirt or blanket) in order to secure. **3.** To put in an out-of-the-way and snug place. **4.** To draw in; contract. —*n.* A flattened pleat or fold. [< OE *tūcian,* to torment.]

tuck·er (tŭk'ər) *v. Informal.* To weary; exhaust. [< TUCK.]

-tude *suff.* Condition or quality: *exactitude.* [< Lat. *-tudo.*]

Tues·day (tōōz'dē, tyōōz'-, -dā') *n.* The 3rd day of the week. [< OE *Tīwesdæg,* day of Tiu, a Germanic god.]

tu·fa (tōō'fə, tyōō'-) *n.* The calcareous and siliceous rock deposits of springs, lakes, or ground water. [< Lat. *tofus.*] —**tu·fa'ceous** (-fā'shəs) *adj.*

tuft (tŭft) *n.* A short cluster of hair, feathers, grass, etc., held or growing close together. [ME.] —**tuft'y** *adj.*

tug (tŭg) *v.* **tugged, tug·ging.** **1.** To pull vigorously (at). **2.** To move by pulling with great effort or exertion. **3.** To tow with a tugboat. —*n.* **1.** A strong pull or pulling force. **2.** A tugboat. [ME *tuggen.*] —**tug'ger** *n.*

tug·boat (tŭg'bōt') *n.* A powerful small boat designed for towing larger vessels.

tug of war *n.* **1.** A contest of strength in which two teams tug on opposite ends of a rope, each trying to pull the other across a dividing line. **2.** A struggle for supremacy.

tu·grik (tōō'grĭk) *n.* See table at **currency.** [Mongolian *dughurik.*]

tu·i·tion (tōō-ĭsh'ən, tyōō-) *n.* **1.** A fee for instruction, esp. at a college or private school. **2.** Instruction; teaching. [< Lat. *tueri,* to protect.] —**tu·i'tion·al** *adj.*

tu·la·re·mi·a (tōō'lə-rē'mē-ə, tyōō'-) *n.* An infectious disease transmitted from infected rodents to man and characterized by fever and swelling of the lymph nodes. [< *Tulare* County, California.]

tu·lip (tōō'lĭp, tyōō'-) *n.* A bulb-bearing plant widely cultivated for its showy, variously colored flowers. [< Turk. *tülibend,* turban.]

tulip tree *n.* A tall tree with tuliplike green and orange flowers and soft yellowish, easily worked wood.

tulle (tōōl) *n.* A fine starched net of silk, rayon, or nylon, used for veils, gowns, etc. [< *Tulle,* France.]

tum·ble (tŭm'bəl) *v.* **-bled, -bling.** **1.** To perform acrobatic feats, such as somersaults. **2.** To fall or roll end over end. **3.** To spill or roll out in disorder. **4.** To pitch headlong; fall. **5.** To decline or collapse suddenly. **6.** To cause to fall; bring down. —*n.* **1.** An act of tumbling; a fall. **2.** A condition of confusion or disorder. [< OE *tumbian,* to dance.]

tum·ble-down (tŭm'bəl-doun') *adj.* Dilapidated; rickety.

tum·bler (tŭm'blər) *n.* **1.** An acrobat or gymnast. **2.** A drinking glass without a handle or stem. **3.** The part in a lock that releases the bolt when moved by a key.

tum·ble·weed (tŭm'bəl-wēd') *n.* A densely branched plant that when withered breaks off and is rolled about by the wind.

tum·brel or **tum·bril** (tŭm'brəl) *n.* A two-wheeled cart, esp. one that can be tilted to dump a load. [< OFr. *tomberel.*]

tu·mes·cence (tōō-mĕs'əns) *n.* A swelling or enlarging. [< Lat. *tumescere,* to begin to swell.] —**tu·mes'cent** *adj.*

tu·mid (tōō'mĭd, tyōō'-) *adj.* **1.** Swollen; distended. **2.** Overblown; bombastic. [Lat. *tumidus.*] —**tu·mid'i·ty** *n.* —**tu'mid·ly** *adv.*

tum·my (tŭm'ē) *n., pl.* **-mies.** *Informal.* The stomach. [< STOMACH.]

tu·mor (tōō'mər, tyōō'-) *n.* **1.** A confined mass of tissue that develops without inflammation from normal tissue, but has an abnormal structure and rate of growth and serves no function. **2.** An abnormal swelling within the body. [Lat.] —**tu'mor·ous** *adj.*

tu·mult (tōō'mŭlt, tyōō'-) *n.* **1.** The din and commotion of a great crowd. **2.** Agitation of the mind or emotions. [< Lat. *tumultus.*] —**tu·mul'tu·ous** (tə-mŭl'chōō-əs) *adj.* —**tu·mul'tu·ous·ly** *adv.* —**tu·mul'tu·ous·ness** *n.*

tun (tŭn) *n.* A large cask. [< OE *tunne.*]

tu·na (tōō'nə, tyōō'-) *n., pl.* **-na** or **-nas.** **1.** Any of various often large marine food fishes. **2.** Also **tuna fish.** The canned or commercially processed flesh of such a fish. [< Gk. *thunnos.*]

tun·dra (tŭn'drə) *n.* A treeless area of arctic regions with a permanently frozen subsoil and low-growing vegetation. [R.]

tune (tōōn, tyōōn) *n.* **1.** A melody, esp. a simple one. **2.** Correct musical pitch. **3.** Agreement in musical pitch or key. **4.** Agreement or harmony: *ideas in tune with the times.* **5.** *Electronics.* Adjustment of a receiver or circuit for maximum response to a given signal or frequency. —*v.* **tuned, tun·ing.** **1.** To put into tune. **2.** To adjust for maximum performance. **3.** To adjust a radio or television receiver to receive (a broadcast). [< TONE.] —**tun'a·ble** *adj.* —**tune'less** *adj.* —**tune'less·ly** *adv.* —**tune'less·ness** *n.*

tune·ful (tōōn'fəl, tyōōn'-) *adj.* Full of melody; melodious. —**tune'ful·ly** *adv.* —**tune'ful·ness** *n.*

tun·er (tōō'nər, tyōō'-) *n.* **1.** One that tunes. **2. a.** The part of a radio or television receiver that selects the signal that is to be amplified and demodulated. **b.** A device for use with high-fidelity sound systems, consisting of a radio receiver that lacks only loudspeakers and the amplifiers that drive them.

tune-up (tōōn'ŭp', tyōōn'-) *n.* An adjustment of a motor or engine to put it in efficient working order.

tung·sten (tŭng'stən) *n. Symbol* **W** A hard, brittle, corrosion-resistant gray to white metallic element used in high-temperature structural materials and electrical elements. Atomic number 74; atomic weight 183.85. [Swed.]

Tun·gus (tōōng-gōōz') *n., pl.* **-gus** or **-es.** **1.** A Mongoloid people inhabiting eastern Siberia.

2. The Tungusic language of the Tungus.

Tun·gus·ic (tōōng-gōō'zĭk, tŭn-) *n.* A subfamily of the Altaic language family that includes Tungus and Manchu. —*adj.* Of or pertaining to the Tungus or their language.

tu·nic (tōō'nĭk, tyōō'-) *n.* **1.** A loose-fitting, knee-length garment worn esp. in ancient Greece and Rome. **2.** A fitted outer garment usu. hip-length and often part of a uniform. **3.** A woman's hip-length blouse worn over a skirt or slacks. [Lat. *tunica.*]

tuning fork *n.* A small two-pronged instrument that when struck produces a sound of fixed pitch, used for tuning musical instruments.

tun·nel (tŭn'əl) *n.* An underground or underwater passage. —*v.* **-neled** or **-nelled, -nel·ing** or **-nel·ling.** **1.** To make a tunnel (under or through). **2.** To dig in the form of a tunnel. [< OFr. *tonel,* tubular net.] —**tun'nel·er** or **tun'nel·ler** *n.*

tun·ny (tŭn'ē) *n., pl.* **-ny** or **-nies.** The tuna. [< Gk. *thunnos.*]

Tu·pi (tōō'pē, tōō-pē') *n., pl.* **-pi** or **-pis.** **1.** A member of any of a group of peoples living along the coast of Brazil, in the Amazon River valley, and in Paraguay. **2.** The language of the Tupi. —**Tu'pi·an** *adj.*

tur·ban (tûr'bən) *n.* An eastern headdress consisting of a long scarf wound around the head. [< Pers. *dulband.*]

tur·bid (tûr'bĭd) *adj.* **1.** Having sediment or foreign particles stirred up or suspended: *turbid water.* **2.** Heavy, dark, or dense, as smoke. **3.** In turmoil; muddled: *turbid feelings.* [Lat. *turbidus.*] —**tur'bid·ly** *adv.* —**tur'bid·ness** or **tur'bid'i·ty** *n.*

tur·bine (tûr'bĭn, -bīn') *n.* Any of various machines in which the kinetic energy of a moving fluid is converted to rotational power as the fluid reacts with a series of vanes, paddles, etc., arranged about the circumference of a wheel or cylinder. [< Lat. *turbo,* spinning top.]

tur·bo·jet (tûr'bō-jĕt') *n.* A jet engine with a turbine-driven compressor.

tur·bo·prop (tûr'bō-prŏp') *n.* A turbojet engine used to drive an external propeller. [< *turbopropeller.*]

tur·bot (tûr'bət) *n., pl.* **-bot** or **-bots.** A European flatfish esteemed as food. [< OFr.]

tur·bu·lent (tûr'byə-lənt) *adj.* **1.** Violently agitated or disturbed. **2.** Marked by or causing unrest or disturbance; unruly. [Lat. *turbulentus.*] —**tur'bu·lence** *n.* —**tur'bu·lent·ly** *adv.*

tu·reen (tōō-rēn', tyōō-) *n.* A broad, deep dish with a cover, used esp. for serving soups or stews. [< OFr. *terrine.*]

turf (tûrf) *n.* **1. a.** Surface earth containing a dense growth of grass and its matted roots. **b.** A piece cut from this. **2.** A piece of peat that is burned as fuel. **3. the turf. a.** A racetrack. **b.** The sport or business of racing horses. [< OE.] —**turf'y** *adj.*

tur·gid (tûr'jĭd) *adj.* **1.** Swollen or distended. **2.** Excessively grand in style or language; bombastic. [Lat. *turgidus.*] —**tur·gid'i·ty** or **tur'gid·ness** *n.* —**tur'gid·ly** *adv.*

Turk (tûrk) *n.* **1.** A native or inhabitant of Turkey. **2.** A Moslem.

tur·key (tûr'kē) *n., pl.* **-keys.** **1.** A large, widely domesticated North American bird with a bare wattled head and neck. **2.** The edible flesh of such a bird. [< *Turkey.*]

Turk·ic (tûr'kĭk) *n.* A subfamily of the Altaic

language family that includes Turkish. —*adj.*
1. Of or pertaining to the Turks. **2.** Of or pertaining to Turkic.

Turk·ish (tûr′kĭsh) *adj.* Of or relating to Turkey, the Turks, or their language. —*n.* The Turkic language of Turkey.

Turkish bath *n.* **1.** A steam bath followed by a massage and a cold shower. **2.** An establishment offering such bathing facilities.

tur·mer·ic (tûr′mər-ĭk) *n.* An Indian plant having a rootstock that when powdered is used as a condiment and as a yellow dye. [< Med. Lat. *terra merita.*]

tur·moil (tûr′moil) *n.* Great confusion; extreme agitation. [Orig. unknown.]

turn (tûrn) *v.* **1.** To move around an axis or center; rotate; revolve. **2.** To shape (something) on a lathe. **3.** To give distinctive form to: *turn a phrase.* **4.** To change the position of so as to show another side. **5.** To injure by twisting: *turn an ankle.* **6.** To nauseate or become nauseated; upset. **7. a.** To change the direction or course of: *turn the car left.* **b.** To direct or change one's way or course. **8.** To make a course around or about: *turn the corner.* **9.** To set in a specified way or direction. **10.** To direct (e.g. the attention or interest) toward or away from something: *turn to music.* **11.** To antagonize or become antagonistic. **12.** To send, drive, or let: *turn the dog loose.* **13.** To transform or become transformed; change. **14.** To become: *She turns twelve today.* **15.** To have recourse; resort. **16.** To depend for success or failure; hinge. **17.** To change color. **18.** To make or become sour; ferment. —*phrasal verbs.* **turn down. 1.** To diminish, as the volume of. **2.** To reject or refuse. **turn in. 1.** To hand in; give over. **2.** *Informal.* To go to bed. **turn off. 1.** To stop the operation of. **2.** *Slang.* To affect with dislike or displeasure. **turn on. 1.** To start the operation of: *turn on the light.* **2.** *Slang.* To affect with great pleasure. **b.** To ingest a drug. **turn out. 1.** To shut off, as a light. **2.** To arrive or assemble. **3.** To produce; make. **4.** To result; end up. **turn over. 1.** To think about; consider. **2.** To transfer to another. **turn up. 1.** To increase, as the volume of. **2.** To find or be found. **3.** To arrive; appear. —*n.* **1.** The act of turning or condition of being turned; rotation; revolution. **2.** A change of direction: *a right turn.* **3.** A departure or deviation, as in a trend. **4.** A chance or opportunity to do something. **5.** Natural inclination: *a speculative turn of mind.* **6.** A deed or action: *a good turn.* **7.** A short excursion. **8.** A single wind or convolution, as of wire upon a spool. **9.** A rendering or fashioning: *a turn of phrase.* **10.** A momentary shock or scare. —*idioms.* **by turns.** Alternately. **in turn.** In the proper order. **to a turn.** Perfectly. [< Gk. *tornos,* lathe.] —**turn′er** *n.*

turn·a·bout (tûrn′ə-bout′) *n.* A shift or change in fortune, direction, etc.

turn·coat (tûrn′kōt′) *n.* One who traitorously switches allegiance.

turning point *n.* A decisive moment.

tur·nip (tûr′nĭp) *n.* **1.** A cultivated plant with a large, edible yellow or white root. **2.** The root of this plant. [Perh. TURN + dial. *nepe,* turnip.]

turnip

turtle¹

turn·key (tûrn′kē′) *n.* A jailer.

turn·off (tûrn′ôf′, -ŏf′) *n.* A place for turning off, esp. an exit on a highway.

turn·on (tûrn′ŏn′, -ôn′) *n. Slang.* Something that brings great pleasure or excitement.

turn·out (tûrn′out′) *n.* **1.** The number of people at a gathering; attendance. **2.** An outfit. **3.** A widened section in a road.

turn·o·ver (tûrn′ō′vər) *n.* **1.** The act of turning over; an upset. **2.** An abrupt change; reversal. **3.** A small filled pastry with half- the crust turned back over the other half. **4.** The number of times a particular stock of goods is sold and restocked during a given period. **5.** The amount of business transacted during a given period. **6.** The rate of replacement of workers or personnel. —*adj.* Capable of being turned over.

turn·pike (tûrn′pīk′) *n.* A road, esp. a wide highway with tollgates. [ME *turnepike,* spiked barrier.]

turn·stile (tûrn′stīl′) *n.* A device for controlling passage from one area to another, typically consisting of revolving horizontal arms projecting from a central post.

turn·ta·ble (tûrn′tā′bəl) *n.* **1.** A circular rotating platform used for turning locomotives. **2.** The rotating circular platform of a phonograph.

tur·pen·tine (tûr′pən-tīn′) *n.* A thin, volatile oil, $C_{10}H_{16}$, obtained from the wood or exudate of certain pine trees and used as a paint thinner, solvent, and medicinally as a liniment. [< Gk. *terebinthos,* a kind of tree.]

tur·pi·tude (tûr′pə-tōōd′, -tyōōd′) *n.* Baseness; depravity. [Lat. *turpitudo.*]

tur·quoise (tûr′kwoiz′, -koiz′) *n.* **1.** A blue to blue-green mineral of aluminum and copper, valued as a gemstone. **2.** A light bluish green. [< OFr. *turqueise,* Turkish.] —**tur′quoise′** *adj.*

tur·ret (tûr′ĭt) *n.* **1.** A small tower-shaped projection on a building. **2.** A projecting armored structure, usu. rotating horizontally, containing mounted guns and their gunners, as on a warship or tank. **3.** An attachment for a lathe, consisting of a rotating cylindrical block holding various cutting tools. [< OFr. *tour,* tower.] —**tur′ret·ed** *adj.*

tur·tle¹ (tûrt′l) *n.* Any of various reptiles having beaklike jaws and the body enclosed in a bony or leathery shell. [Perh. < Fr. *tortue.*]

tur·tle² (tûrt′l) *n. Archaic.* A turtledove. [< Lat. *turtur.*]

tur·tle·dove (tûrt′l-dŭv′) *n.* An Old World dove with a soft, purring voice.

tur·tle·neck (tûrt′l-nĕk′) *n.* **1.** A high, close-fitting, turned-down collar. **2.** A garment with such a collar.

Tus·ca·ro·ra (tŭs′kə-rôr′ə, -rōr′ə) *n., pl.* **-ra** or **-ras. 1. a.** A tribe of Indians formerly inhabiting North Carolina and now living in New York and Ontario. **b.** A member of this tribe. **2.** The Iroquoian language of the Tuscarora.

tusk (tŭsk) *n.* A long pointed tooth, as of an elephant or walrus, extending outside of the mouth. [< OE *tūsc.*]

tus·sle (tŭs'əl) *v.* **-sled, -sling.** To fight roughly; scuffle. [< ME *tousen,* to pull roughly.] **—tus'sle** *n.*

tus·sock (tŭs'ək) *n.* A clump or tuft, as of grass. [Orig. unknown.]

tu·te·lage (tōō'tə-lĭj, tyōō'-) *n.* **1.** The function or capacity of a guardian; guardianship. **2.** The function or capacity of a tutor; instruction. **3.** The state of being under a guardian or tutor. [< Lat. *tutela.*] **—tu'te·lar'y** (-lĕr'ē) *adj.*

tu·tor (tōō'tər, tyōō'-) *n.* A private instructor, esp. one who gives additional or remedial instruction. **—v.** To act as a tutor (to). [< Lat.] **—tu·to'ri·al** (tōō-tôr'ē-əl, -tôr'ē-əl, tyōō-) *adj.* **—tu'tor·ship'** *n.*

tut·ti-frut·ti (tōō'tĭ-frōō'tē) *n.* A confection or flavoring that contains a variety of chopped candied fruits. [Ital., all fruits.]

tu·tu (tōō'tōō) *n.* A very short ballet skirt. [Fr.]

tux·e·do (tŭk-sē'dō) *n., pl.* **-dos.** A man's formal or semiformal suit, usu. black with a tailless jacket and a black bow tie. [< *Tuxedo* Park, New York.]

TV (tē'vē') *n.* Television.

TV Dinner. A trademark for a packaged frozen meal that only needs to be heated before serving.

twad·dle (twŏd'l) *n.* Foolish, trivial, or idle talk. [Prob. < dial. *twattle.*] **—twad'dle** *v.* **—twad'dler** *n.*

twain (twān) *n. Poetic.* Two. [< OE *twēgen.*]

twang (twăng) *v.* **1.** To emit or cause to emit a sharp, vibrating sound, as the string of a musical instrument when plucked. **2.** To speak in a sharply nasal tone. **—n.** **1.** A sharp, vibrating sound. **2.** An excessively nasal tone of voice. [Imit.] **—twang'y** *adj.*

tweak (twēk) *v.* To pinch or twist sharply. [< OE *twiccian.*] **—tweak** *n.* **—tweak'y** *adj.*

tweed (twēd) *n.* **1.** A coarse woolen fabric usu. woven of several colors. **2. tweeds.** Clothes made of tweed. [< Sc. *tweel,* twill.] **—tweed'i·ness** *n.* **—tweed'y** *adj.*

tweet (twēt) *n.* A high, chirping sound, as of a small bird. [Imit.] **—tweet** *v.*

tweet·er (twē'tər) *n.* A loudspeaker designed to reproduce high-pitched sounds in a high-fidelity audio system.

tweez·ers (twē'zərz) *pl.n.* A small, usu. metal, pincerlike tool used for plucking or handling small objects. [Obs. *tweezes,* a set of small instruments.]

twelfth (twĕlfth) *n.* **1.** The ordinal number that matches the number 12 in a series. **2.** One of 12 equal parts. **—twelfth** *adj. & adv.*

twelve (twĕlv) *n.* **1.** The cardinal number that is next after the number 11 and equal to the sum of 11 + 1. **2.** The 12th in a series. [< OE *twelf.*] **—twelve** *adj. & pron.*

twelve·month (twĕlv'mŭnth') *n.* A year.

twen·ti·eth (twĕn'tē-ĭth) *n.* **1.** The ordinal number that matches the number 20 in a series. **2.** One of 20 equal parts. **—twen'ti·eth** *adj. & adv.*

twen·ty (twĕn'tē) *n.* The cardinal number equal to 2 x 10. [< OE *twēntig.*] **—twen'ty** *adj. & pron.*

Twi (chwē, chē) *n.* Also **Tshi.** A language of western Africa.

twice (twīs) *adv.* **1.** In two cases or on two occasions; two times. **2.** In doubled degree or amount. [< OE *twiga.*]

twid·dle (twĭd'l) *v.* **-dled, -dling.** **1.** To turn over or around lightly. **2.** To play (with); trifle. **—idiom. twiddle (one's) thumbs.** To do little or nothing; be idle. [Prob. a blend of TWIRL and FIDDLE.] **—twid'dler** *n.*

twig (twĭg) *n.* A small slender branch. [< OE *twigge.*] **—twig'gy** *adj.*

twi·light (twī'līt') *n.* **1.** The time during which the sun is below the horizon but is casting a diffuse light. **2.** The soft, indistinct light of this time, esp. after a sunset. **3.** A period or condition of decline. [ME.]

twill (twĭl) *n.* A fabric with parallel diagonal ribs. [< OE *twilic.*] **—twilled** *adj.*

'twill (twĭl) *Poetic.* It will.

twin (twĭn) *n.* **1.** One of two offspring born at the same birth. **2.** One of two identical or similar things. **3. Twins.** Gemini. **—adj.** **1.** Born at the same birth. **2.** Being one of two identical or similar things: *twin beds.* **3.** Consisting of two identical or similar parts. [< OE *twinn.*]

twin bill *n.* A combination of two similar events, esp. sporting events, presented at one time.

twine (twīn) *n.* A strong string or cord formed of two or more threads twisted together. **—v. twined, twin·ing.** **1.** To twist together; intertwine. **2.** To form by twisting. **3.** To wrap or coil about. **4.** To go in a winding course. [< OE *twīn.*] **—twin'er** *n.*

twinge (twĭnj) *n.* A sharp, sudden physical or emotional pain. **—v. twinged, twing·ing.** To feel or cause to feel a sharp pain. [< OE *twengan,* to pinch.]

twin·kle (twĭng'kəl) *v.* **-kled, -kling.** **1.** To shine with slight, intermittent gleams. **2.** To be bright or sparkling: *Her eyes twinkled.* **—n.** **1.** An intermittent gleam of light. **2.** A sparkle of merriment in the eye. **3.** A brief interval. [< OE *twinclian.*] **—twin'kler** *n.*

twin·kling (twĭng'klĭng) *n.* A brief interval; instant.

twirl (twûrl) *v.* To rotate or revolve briskly; spin. **2.** To twist or wind (around). [Orig. unknown.] **—twirl** *n.*

twist (twĭst) *v.* **1.** To entwine (two or more threads) so as to produce a single strand. **2.** To coil (e.g. vines or rope) about something. **3. a.** To impart a coiling or spiral shape to. **b.** To assume a spiral shape. **4. a.** To turn or open by turning. **b.** To break by turning: *twist off a dead branch.* **5.** To wrench or sprain. **6.** To distort the intended meaning of. **7.** To move in a winding course. **8.** To rotate or revolve. **—n.** **1.** Something twisted or formed by winding. **2.** The act of twisting or condition of being twisted; a spin or twirl. **3.** A spiral curve or turn. **4.** A sprain or wrench, as of a muscle. **5.** An unexpected turn of events. [ME *twisten.*] **—twist'er** *n.*

twit (twĭt) *v.* **twit·ted, twit·ting.** To taunt or tease. [< OE *ætwitan.*]

twitch (twĭch) *v.* To move or cause to move jerkily or spasmodically. **—n.** **1.** A sudden involuntary muscular movement. **2.** A sudden jerk or tug. [ME *twicchen.*]

twit·ter (twĭt'ər) *v.* To make tremulous chirping sounds. —*n.* A tremulous chirping sound. [ME *twiteren.*] —**twit'ter·y** *adj.*

twixt (twĭkst) *prep. & adv. Archaic & Poet.* Betwixt.

two (tōō) *n.* **1.** The cardinal number equal to the sum of 1 + 1. **2.** The 2nd in a set or sequence. **3.** Something having two parts, units, or members. [< OE *twā.*] —**two** *adj. & pron.*

two-base hit (tōō'bās') *n. Baseball.* A hit enabling the batter to reach second base; double.

two-bit (tōō'bĭt') *adj. Slang.* Worth very little; cheap; insignificant. [< TWO BITS.]

two bits *pl.n. Informal.* **1.** Twenty-five cents. **2.** A petty sum.

two-by-four (tōō'bī-fôr', -fōr', tōō'bə-) *n.* A length of lumber measuring 1⅝ inches in thickness and 3⅜ inches in width.

two-faced (tōō'fāst') *adj.* **1.** Having two faces. **2.** Hypocritical or double-dealing; deceitful. —**two'-fac'ed·ly** (tōō'fā'sĭd-lē, -fāst'lē) *adv.* —**two'-fac'ed·ness** *n.*

two-fold (tōō'fōld', -fōld') *adj.* **1.** Having two parts. **2.** Having twice as much or as many; double. —*adv.* Doubly.

two-ply (tōō'plī') *adj.* Made of two layers, thicknesses, or strands.

two-some (tōō'səm) *n.* Two people together; couple.

two-time (tōō'tīm') *v. Slang.* To be unfaithful to. —**two'-tim'er** *n.*

two-way (tōō'wā') *adj.* Affording passage or communication in two directions.

-ty¹ *suff.* A condition or quality: *novelty.* [< Lat. *-tas.*]

-ty² *suff.* A multiple of ten: *eighty.* [< OE *-tig.*]

ty·coon (tī-kōōn') *n. Informal.* A wealthy and powerful businessman; magnate. [J. *taikun,* title of a shogun.]

tyke (tīk) *n.* **1.** A small child, esp. a mischievous one. **2.** A mongrel or cur. [< ON *tīk,* bitch.]

tym·pa·ni (tĭm'pə-nē) *n.* Var. of **timpani.** —**tym'pa·nist** *n.*

tym·pan·ic membrane (tĭm-păn'ĭk) *n.* The eardrum.

tym·pa·num (tĭm'pə-nəm) *n., pl.* **-na** (-nə) or **-nums.** **1.** The middle ear. **2.** The eardrum. [< Gk. *tumpanon,* drum.]

type (tīp) *n.* **1.** A group of persons or things sharing common traits or characteristics; class; category. **2.** One having the characteristics of a group or class: *a type of cactus.* **3.** An example or model; embodiment. **4. a.** A small block of metal bearing a raised character that when inked and pressed upon paper leaves a printed impression. **b.** Such pieces collectively. **5.** Printed or typewritten characters; print. —*v.* **typed, typ·ing. 1.** To classify according to a particular type or class. **2.** To typewrite. **3.** To represent or typify. [< Gk. *tupos,* impression.]

type-cast (tīp'kăst', -käst') *v.* **-cast, -cast·ing.** To cast (an actor) repeatedly in the same kind of part.

type-face (tīp'fās') *n.* A style or design of printing type.

type-script (tīp'skrĭpt') *n.* A typewritten copy, as of a book.

type-set·ter (tīp'sĕt'ər) *n.* **1.** One who sets type; compositor. **2.** A machine used for setting type. —**type'set'ting** *n.*

type-write (tīp'rīt') *v.* To write (something) with a typewriter; type.

type-writ·er (tīp'rī'tər) *n.* A machine that prints characters by means of keys that, when pressed by hand, strike the paper through an inked ribbon.

ty·phoid (tī'foid') *n.* An acute, highly infectious disease caused by a bacillus transmitted by contaminated food or water and characterized by red rashes, high fever, bronchitis, and intestinal hemorrhaging. [TYPH(US) + -OID.] —**ty'phoid'** *adj.*

ty·phoon (tī-fōōn') *n.* A severe tropical hurricane of the western Pacific. [Cant. *tai fung.*]

ty·phus (tī'fəs) *n.* Any of several forms of an infectious disease caused by microorganisms and characterized by severe headache, sustained high fever, depression, delirium, and red rashes. [< Gk. *tuphos,* stupor.] —**ty'phous** (-fəs) *adj.*

typ·i·cal (tĭp'ĭ-kəl) *adj.* **1.** Exhibiting the traits or characteristics peculiar to a kind, group, or category; representative. **2.** Characteristic: *responded with his typical bluntness.* **3.** Conforming to or constituting a type. [< Gk. *tupikos,* impressionable.] —**typ'i·cal·ly** *adv.* —**typ'i·cal·ness** or **typ'i·cal'i·ty** *n.*

typ·i·fy (tĭp'ə-fī') *v.* **-fied, -fy·ing. 1.** To serve as a typical example of. **2.** To represent by an image, form, or model; symbolize. —**typ'i·fi·ca'tion** *n.* —**typ'i·fi'er** *n.*

typ·ist (tī'pĭst) *n.* One who operates a typewriter.

ty·po (tī'pō) *n., pl.* **-os.** *Informal.* A typographical error.

typographical error *n.* A mistake in printed or typewritten copy.

ty·pog·ra·phy (tī-pŏg'rə-fē) *n., pl.* **-phies. 1.** The composition of printed material from movable type. **2.** The arrangement and appearance of printed matter. —**ty·pog'ra·pher** *n.* —**ty'po·graph'i·cal** (tī'pə-grăf'ĭ-kəl) or **ty'po·graph'ic** *adj.*

ty·ran·ni·cal (tĭ-răn'ĭ-kəl, tī-) or **ty·ran·nic** (-răn'ĭk) *adj.* Of or characteristic of a tyrant; despotic. —**ty·ran'ni·cal·ly** *adv.*

tyr·an·nize (tĭr'ə-nīz') *v.* **-nized, -niz·ing. 1.** To rule as a tyrant. **2.** To treat tyrannically. —**tyr'an·niz'er** *n.*

ty·ran·no·saur (tĭ-răn'ə-sôr', tī-) *n.* Also **ty·ran·**

tyrannosaur

no·saur·us (tī-răn′ə-sôr′əs, tī-). A large carnivorous dinosaur with small forelimbs and a large head. [Gk. *turanos,* tyrant + -SAUR.]
tyr·an·nous (tĭr′ə-nəs) *adj.* Despotic; tyrannical. —**tyr·an·nous·ly** *adv.*
tyr·an·ny (tĭr′ə-nē) *n., pl.* -**nies. 1.** A government in which a single ruler is vested with absolute power. **2.** Absolute power, esp. when exercised unjustly or cruelly. **3.** A tyrannical

act. **4.** Extreme harshness or severity; rigor. [< Gk. *turannos,* tyrant.]
ty·rant (tī′rənt) *n.* **1.** An absolute ruler, esp. an oppressive or cruel one. **2.** A tyrannical or despotic person. [< Gk. *turannos.*]
tyre (tīr) *n. Chiefly Brit.* Var. of tire².
ty·ro (tī′rō) *n., pl.* -**ros.** An inexperienced person; beginner. [< Lat. *tiro,* recruit.]
tzar (zär) *n.* Var. of czar.

Uu

u or **U** (yōō) *n., pl.* **u's** or **U's. 1.** The 21st letter of the English alphabet. **2.** Something shaped like the letter U.
U The symbol for the element uranium.
u·biq·ui·tous (yōō-bĭk′wĭ-təs) *adj.* Being or seeming to be everywhere at the same time; omnipresent. [< Lat. *ubique,* everywhere.] —**u·biq′ui·tous·ly** *adv.* —**u·biq′ui·ty** *n.*
U-boat (yōō′bōt′) *n.* A German submarine. [< G. *Unterseeboot.*]
U-bolt (yōō′bōlt′) *n.* A bolt shaped like the letter U, fitted with threads and a nut at each end.

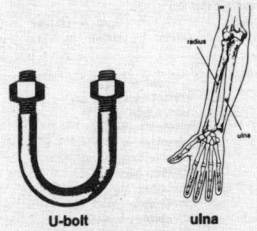

U-bolt   **ulna**

ud·der (ŭd′ər) *n.* The baglike mammary organ of a cow, ewe, or goat, from which milk is taken in suckling or milking. [< OE *ūder.*]
UFO (yōō′ĕf-ō′) *n., pl.* **UFOs** or **UFO's.** An unidentified flying object.
ug·ly (ŭg′lē) *adj.* -**li·er,** -**li·est. 1.** Not pleasing to the eye; unsightly. **2.** Repulsive or offensive in any way; objectionable; unpleasant. **3.** Morally reprehensible; bad. **4.** Threatening; ominous: *ugly weather.* **5.** Cross; disagreeable: *an ugly temper.* [< ON *uggligr,* frightful.] —**ug′li·ness** *n.*
    Syns: ugly, hideous, unsightly *adj.*
u·kase (yōō-kās′, -kāz′, yōō′kās′, -kāz′) *n.* An authoritative order or decree; edict. [< R. *ukaz.*]
U·krain·i·an (yōō-krā′nē-ən) *n.* **1.** An inhabitant or native of the Ukraine. **2.** The Slavic language of the Ukranians. —**U·krain′i·an** *adj.*
u·ku·le·le (yōō′kə-lā′lē, ōō′kə-) *n.* A small four-stringed guitar popularized in Hawaii. [Hawaiian *'ukulele.*]
ul·cer (ŭl′sər) *n.* **1.** An inflamed, often pus-filled lesion resulting in necrosis of the tissue.

2. A corrupting condition or influence. [< Lat. *ulcus.*] —**ul′cer·ous** *adj.*
ul·cer·ate (ŭl′sə-rāt′) *v.* -**at·ed,** -**at·ing.** To affect or become affected with an ulcer. —**ul′-cer·a′tion** *n.* —**ul′cer·a′tive** (-sə-rā′tĭv, -sər-ə-tĭv) *adj.*
-ule *suff.* Small: *nodule.* [< Lat. *-ulus,* dim. suffix.]
ul·na (ŭl′nə) *n., pl.* -**nae** (-nē) or -**nas.** The bone extending from the elbow to the wrist on the side opposite the thumb. [Lat., elbow.] —**ul′nar** *adj.*
ul·ster (ŭl′stər) *n.* A loose, long overcoat. [< *Ulster,* Ireland.]
ul·te·ri·or (ŭl-tîr′ē-ər) *adj.* **1.** Beyond or outside what is evident or admitted: *an ulterior motive.* **2.** Beyond or outside a certain area or region; remoter. [Lat., farther.]
ul·ti·mate (ŭl′tə-mĭt) *adj.* **1.** Completing a series or process; final; conclusive. **2.** Highest possible; greatest; extreme. **3.** Representing the farthest possible extent of analysis or division into parts: *ultimate particle.* **4.** Fundamental; basic; elemental. **5.** Farthest; remotest. —*n.* **1.** The basic or fundamental fact. **2.** The final point; conclusive result. **3.** The maximum; greatest extreme. [< Lat. *ultimus,* last.] —**ul′ti·mate·ly** *adv.* —**ul′ti·mate·ness** *n.*
ul·ti·ma·tum (ŭl′tə-mā′təm, -mä′-) *n., pl.* -**tums** or -**ta** (-tə). A statement of terms that expresses or implies the threat of serious penalties if the terms are not accepted. [< Med. Lat. *ultimatus,* last.]
ul·ti·mo (ŭl′tə-mō′) *adv.* In or of the month before the present one. [Lat. *ultimo (mense),* in the last (month).]
ul·tra (ŭl′trə) *adj.* Going beyond the normal limit; extreme. —*n.* An extremist. [< UL-TRA-.]
ultra- *pref.* **1.** Surpassing a specified limit, range, or scope; beyond: *ultrasonic.* **2.** Exceeding what is common, moderate, or proper; extreme: *ultraconservative.* [< Lat. *ultra,* beyond.]
ul·tra·con·ser·va·tive (ŭl′trə-kən-sûr′və-tĭv) *adj.* Extremely conservative; reactionary. —**ul′tra·con·ser′va·tive** *n.*
ul·tra·high frequency (ŭl′trə-hī′) *n.* A band of radio frequencies from 300 to 3,000 megahertz.
ul·tra·ma·rine (ŭl′trə-mə-rēn′) *n.* **1.** A blue pigment. **2.** A bright deep blue. —*adj.* **1.** Bright deep blue. **2.** Of or from some place

beyond the sea. [< Med. Lat. *ultramarinus,* from the body of the sea.]

ul·tra·mi·cro·scope (ŭl′trə-mī′krə-skōp′) *n.* A microscope with high-intensity illumination used to study very minute objects, such as colloidal particles.

ul·tra·mi·cro·scop·ic (ŭl′trə-mī′krə-skōp′ĭk) *adj.* **1.** Too small to be seen with an ordinary microscope. **2.** Of or relating to an ultramicroscope.

ul·tra·mon·tane (ŭl′trə-mŏn′tān′, -mŏn-tān′) *adj.* **1.** Of or pertaining to peoples or regions lying beyond the mountains. **2.** Supporting the supreme authority of the pope in ecclesiastical and political matters. [Med. Lat. *ultramontanus.*] **—ul′tra·mon′tane′** *n.*

ul·tra·son·ic (ŭl′trə-sŏn′ĭk) *adj.* Pertaining to acoustic frequencies above the range the human ear can hear or above approx. 20,000 cycles per second.

ul·tra·son·ics (ŭl′trə-sŏn′ĭks) *n.* (*used with a sing. verb.*) The scientific study of ultrasonic sound.

ul·tra·vi·o·let (ŭl′trə-vī′ə-lĭt) *adj.* Of electromagnetic radiation with wavelengths between 4,000 angstroms, just shorter than those of visible light, and 40 angstroms, just longer than those of x-rays. **—ul′tra·vi′o·let** *n.*

ul·u·late (ŭl′yə-lāt′) *v.* **-lat·ed, -lat·ing.** To howl, hoot, wail, or lament loudly. [< Lat. *ululare,* to howl.] **—ul′u·la′tion** *n.*

U·lys·ses (yōō-lĭs′ēz) *n.* The Latin name for Odysseus.

um·bel (ŭm′bəl) *n. Bot.* A flat-topped or rounded flower cluster in which the individual flower stalks arise from about the same point on the stem. [< Lat. *umbella,* parasol.]

um·ber (ŭm′bər) *n.* **1.** A natural brown earth composed of oxides of iron, silicon, aluminum, calcium, and manganese, used as pigment. **2.** Any of the shades of brown produced by umber in its various states. **—adj.** Having a brownish hue. [< Lat. *umbra,* shadow.]

um·bil·i·cal (ŭm-bĭl′ĭ-kəl) *adj.* Of, pertaining to, or located near the umbilical cord or navel. **—n.** An umbilical cord.

umbilical cord *n.* The flexible cordlike structure that extends from the navel of a fetus to the placenta, containing blood vessels that supply nourishment to the fetus and remove its wastes.

um·bil·i·cus (ŭm-bĭl′ĭ-kəs, ŭm′bə-lī′kəs) *n., pl.* **-ci** (-sī′). The navel. [< Lat.]

um·bra (ŭm′brə) *n., pl.* **-brae** (-brē). **1.** A dark area, esp. the darkest part of a shadow from which all light is cut off. **2.** The shadow of the moon that falls on a part of the earth where a solar eclipse is total. [Lat., shadow.]

um·brage (ŭm′brĭj) *n.* **1.** Offense; resentment: *took umbrage at their rudeness.* **2.** *Archaic.* Shadow or shade. [< Lat. *umbra,* shadow.]

um·brel·la (ŭm-brĕl′ə) *n.* **1.** A device for protection from the rain or sun, consisting of a usu. cloth cover on a collapsible frame mounted on a handle. **2.** *Zool.* The jellylike rounded mass constituting the major part of the body of most jellyfishes. [< Lat. *umbra,* shade.]

u·mi·ak (ōō′mē-āk′) *n.* A large open Eskimo boat made of skins stretched on a wooden frame. [Eskimo.]

um·laut (ōōm′lout′) *n.* **1. a.** A change in a vowel sound caused by partial assimilation to

un′a·bashed′ *adj.*
un′a·bat′ed *adj.*
un′ab·bre′vi·at′ed *adj.*
un′a·bridged′ *adj.*
un·ac′cent·ed *adj.*
un′ac·cept′a·ble *adj.*
un′ac·cred′it·ed *adj.*
un′ac·knowl′edged *adj.*
un′ac·quaint′ed *adj.*
un′a·dorned′ *adj.*
un′ad·ver′tised′ *adj.*
un′af·fil′i·at′ed *adj.*
un′a·fraid′ *adj.*
un′aid′ed *adj.*
un′a·larmed′ *adj.*
un′a·like′ *adj.*
un′al·lied′ *adj.*
un·al′ter·a·ble *adj.*
un·al′ter·a·bly *adv.*
un·am·big′u·ous *adj.*
un′an·nounced′ *adj.*
un′an·swer·a·ble *adj.*
un·an′tic′i·pat′ed *adj.*
un·ap′par·ent *adj.*
un′ap·peal′ing *adj.*
un′ap·peased′ *adj.*
un·ap′pe·tiz′ing *adj.*
un′ap·pre′ci·at′ed *adj.*
un′ap·pre′cia·tive *adj.*
un·ar′tis′tic *adj.*
un′a·shamed′ *adj.*

un′asked′ *adj.*
un′as·ser′tive *adj.*
un′as·signed′ *adj.*
un′as·sim′i·lat′ed *adj.*
un′as·so′ci·at′ed *adj.*
un′at·tain′a·ble *adj.*
un′at·tempt′ed *adj.*
un′at·tend′ed *adj.*
un′at·test′ed *adj.*
un′at·trac′tive *adj.*
un′at·trib′ut·ed *adj.*
un·au′thor·ized′ *adj.*
un′a·vail′a·ble *adj.*
un′a·venged′ *adj.*
un′a·vowed′ *adj.*
un′a·ward′ed *adj.*
un·bap′tized′ *adj.*
un·bi′ased *adj.*
un·bleached′ *adj.*
un·blem′ished *adj.*
un·block′ *v.*
un·bound′ *adj.*
un·brand′ed *adj.*
un·break′a·ble *adj.*
un·bridge′a·ble *adj.*
un·buck′le *v.*
un·burned′ *adj.*
un·cap′ *v.*
un·cap′i·tal·ized′ *adj.*
un·car′bo·nat′ed *adj.*
un·cared′-for *adj.*
un·car′pet·ed *adj.*

un·cashed′ *adj.*
un·cat′a·logued′ *adj.*
un·caught′ *adj.*
un·cen′sored *adj.*
un·chain′ *v.*
un·chal′lenged *adj.*
un·changed′ *adj.*
un·chang′ing *adj.*
un·chap′er·oned′ *adj.*
un′char·ac·ter·is′tic *adj.*
un′char·ac·ter·is′tic·al·ly *adv.*
un·charged′ *adj.*
un·chas′tened *adj.*
un·checked′ *adj.*
un·cho′sen *adj.*
un·chris′tened *adj.*
un·claimed′ *adj.*
un·clas′si·fied′ *adj.*
un·cleaned′ *adj.*
un·clear′ *adj.*
un·cleared′ *adj.*
un·clench′ *v.*
un·clog′ *v.*
un·clogged′ *adj.*
un·cloud′ed *adj.*
un·clut′tered *adj.*
un·col′lect·ed *adj.*
un·col′ored *adj.*
un·combed′ *adj.*
un′com·bined′ *adj.*
un·com′fort·ed *adj.*
un′com·mer′cial *adj.*

ă pat   ā pay   â care   ä father   ĕ pet   ē be   ĭ pit   ī tie   î pier   ŏ pot   ō toe   ô paw, for   oi noise   ōō took
ōō boot   ou out   th thin   th this   ŭ cut   û urge   yōō abuse   zh vision   ə about, item, edible, gallop, circus

a sound that has been lost in the following syllable. **b.** A vowel sound changed in this manner. **2.** The diacritical mark (¨) placed over a vowel to indicate an umlaut, esp. in German. [G.]

um·pire (ŭm'pīr') *n.* **1.** One appointed to rule on plays in various sports. **2.** One selected to settle a dispute between other persons or groups. [< OFr. *nomper, mediator.*] **—um'pire'** *v.*

ump·teen (ŭmp-tēn', ŭm-) *adj. Informal.* Large but indefinite in number. [Slang *umpty,* dash in Morse code + -TEEN.] **—ump'teenth'** *adj.*

un-[1] *pref.* Not: *unhappy.* [< OE.]

un-[2] *pref.* **1.** Reversal of an action: *unlock.* **2.** Deprivation: *unfrock.* **3.** Release or removal from: *unyoke.* **4.** Used as an intensive: *unloose.* [< OE *on-.*]

Usage: Many compounds are formed with *un-.* Normally *un-* combines with a second element without an intervening hyphen. However, if the second element begins with a capital letter, it is separated with a hyphen: *un-American.*

un·a·ble (ŭn-ā'bəl) *adj.* **1.** Lacking the necessary power, authority, or means. **2.** Incompetent.

un·ac·com·pa·nied (ŭn'ə-kŭm'pə-nēd) *adj.* **1.** Going or acting without a companion. **2.** *Mus.* Performed or scored without accompaniment.

un·ac·count·a·ble (ŭn'ə-koun'tə-bəl) *adj.* **1.** Not able to be explained; inexplicable. **2.** Not responsible. **—un'ac·count'a·bly** *adv.*

un·ac·count·ed (ŭn'ə-koun'tĭd) *adj.* **1.** Not

explained or understood. **2.** Absent with whereabouts unknown.

un·ac·cus·tomed (ŭn'ə-kŭs'təmd) *adj.* **1.** Not customary; unusual. **2.** Unfamiliar.

un·a·dul·ter·at·ed (ŭn'ə-dŭl'tə-rā'tĭd) *adj.* Not mingled or diluted; pure.

un·ad·vised (ŭn'əd-vīzd') *adj.* **1.** Not informed. **2.** Rash; imprudent. **—un'ad·vis'ed·ly** (-vī'zĭd-lē) *adv.*

un·af·fect·ed (ŭn'ə-fĕk'tĭd) *adj.* **1.** Not changed or affected. **2.** Natural or sincere. **—un'af·fect'ed·ly** *adv.* **—un'af·fect'ed·ness** *n.*

un·al·loyed (ŭn'ə-loid') *adj.* **1.** Not in mixture with other metals; pure. **2.** Complete; unqualified.

u·nan·i·mous (yōō-năn'ə-məs) *adj.* **1.** Sharing the same opinions or views. **2.** Based on complete assent or agreement. [Lat. *unanimus.*] **—u'na·nim'i·ty** (-nə-nĭm'ĭ-tē) *n.* **—u·nan'i·mous·ly** *adv.*

un·ap·proach·a·ble (ŭn'ə-prō'chə-bəl) *adj.* **1.** Not friendly; aloof. **2.** Not accessible. **3.** Unequaled.

un·armed (ŭn-ärmd') *adj.* Lacking weapons; defenseless.

un·as·sail·a·ble (ŭn'ə-sā'lə-bəl) *adj.* **1.** Not capable of being disputed or disproven; undeniable. **2.** Impregnable. **—un'as·sail'a·bil'i·ty** *n.* **—un'as·sail'a·bly** *adv.*

un·as·sist·ed (ŭn'ə-sĭs'tĭd) *adj.* **1.** Not assisted; unaided. **2.** *Baseball.* Designating a play handled by only one fielder.

un·as·sum·ing (ŭn'ə-sōō'mĭng) *adj.* Not pretentious; modest. **—un'as·sum'ing·ly** *adv.*

un·at·tached (ŭn'ə-tăcht') *adj.* **1.** Not attached or joined. **2.** Not engaged or married.

---

un·com·pen·sat·ed *adj.*	un·cul·tured *adj.*	un·di·vid·ed *adj.*
un·com·plain·ing *adj.*	un·curbed *adj.*	un·dra·mat·ic *adj.*
un·com·plet·ed *adj.*	un·cured *adj.*	un·dressed *adj.*
un·com·pli·cat·ed *adj.*	un·dam·aged *adj.*	un·drink·a·ble *adj.*
un·com·pli·men·ta·ry *adj.*	un·damped *adj.*	un·du·ti·ful *adj.*
un·com·pre·hend·ing *adj.*	un·dat·ed *adj.*	un·eat·a·ble *adj.*
un·con·cealed *adj.*	un·de·ci·pher·a·ble *adj.*	un·eat·en *adj.*
un·con·fined *adj.*	un·de·clared *adj.*	un·e·co·nom·i·cal *adj.*
un·con·firmed *adj.*	un·de·feat·ed *adj.*	un·ed·i·ble *adj.*
un·con·nect·ed *adj.*	un·de·fend·ed *adj.*	un·ed·i·fy·ing *adj.*
un·con·quered *adj.*	un·de·fined *adj.*	un·ed·u·cat·ed *adj.*
un·con·se·crat·ed *adj.*	un·de·mand·ing *adj.*	un·e·mo·tion·al *adj.*
un·con·sid·ered *adj.*	un·dem·o·crat·ic *adj.*	un·en·closed *adj.*
un·con·sol·i·dat·ed *adj.*	un·de·pend·a·ble *adj.*	un·en·cum·bered *adj.*
un·con·sumed *adj.*	un·de·served *adj.*	un·end·ing *adj.*
un·con·tam·i·nat·ed *adj.*	un·de·serv·ing *adj.*	un·en·dur·a·ble *adj.*
un·con·tend·ed *adj.*	un·de·tect·ed *adj.*	un·en·force·a·ble *adj.*
un·con·test·ed *adj.*	un·de·ter·mined *adj.*	un·en·forced *adj.*
un·con·trolled *adj.*	un·de·terred *adj.*	un·en·gaged *adj.*
un·con·vinced *adj.*	un·de·vel·oped *adj.*	un·en·joy·a·ble *adj.*
un·con·vinc·ing *adj.*	un·dif·fer·en·ti·at·ed *adj.*	un·en·light·ened *adj.*
un·cooked *adj.*	un·dig·ni·fied *adj.*	un·en·light·en·ing *adj.*
un·co·op·er·a·tive *adj.*	un·di·lut·ed *adj.*	un·en·thu·si·as·tic *adj.*
un·co·or·di·nat·ed *adj.*	un·di·min·ished *adj.*	un·en·ti·tled *adj.*
un·cor·rect·ed *adj.*	un·dip·lo·mat·ic *adj.*	un·en·vi·a·ble *adj.*
un·cor·re·lat·ed *adj.*	un·di·rect·ed *adj.*	un·e·quipped *adj.*
un·cor·rob·o·rat·ed *adj.*	un·dis·cern·ing *adj.*	un·eth·i·cal *adj.*
un·cor·rupt·ed *adj.*	un·dis·ci·plined *adj.*	un·ex·ag·ger·at·ed *adj.*
un·count·a·ble *adj.*	un·dis·closed *adj.*	un·ex·celled *adj.*
un·count·ed *adj.*	un·dis·cov·ered *adj.*	un·ex·cep·tion·al *adj.*
un·cov·ered *adj.*	un·dis·guised *adj.*	un·ex·chang·a·ble *adj.*
un·cred·it·ed *adj.*	un·dis·mayed *adj.*	un·ex·cit·ed *adj.*
un·crit·i·cal *adj.*	un·dis·put·ed *adj.*	un·ex·cit·ing *adj.*
un·crowd·ed *adj.*	un·dis·solved *adj.*	un·ex·pired *adj.*
un·crowned *adj.*	un·dis·tin·guished *adj.*	un·ex·plained *adj.*
un·cul·ti·vat·ed *adj.*	un·dis·turbed *adj.*	un·ex·plored *adj.*

un·a·vail·ing (ŭn'ə-vā'lĭng) adj. Useless; unsuccessful.

un·a·void·a·ble (ŭn'ə-voi'də-bəl) adj. Not capable of being avoided; inevitable. —un'a·void'a·bly adv.

un·a·ware (ŭn'ə-wâr') adj. Not aware or cognizant. —adv. Unawares.

un·a·wares (ŭn'ə-wârz') adv. 1. By surprise; unexpectedly. 2. Without intention or forethought.

un·bal·anced (ŭn-băl'ənst) adj. 1. Not in balance or in proper balance. 2. Not mentally sound. 3. Bookkeeping. Not adjusted so that debits and credits correspond.

un·bar (ŭn-bär') v. To open.

un·bear·a·ble (ŭn-bâr'ə-bəl) adj. Unendurable; intolerable. —un·bear'a·bly adv.

un·beat·a·ble (ŭn-bē'tə-bəl) adj. Impossible to surpass or defeat. —un·beat'a·bly adv.

un·beat·en (ŭn-bēt'n) adj. 1. Never defeated. 2. Untrod. 3. Not beaten or pounded.

un·be·com·ing (ŭn-bĭ-kŭm'ĭng) adj. 1. Not appropriate, attractive, or flattering. 2. Indecorous; improper. —un·be·com'ing·ly adv.

un·be·known (ŭn'bĭ-nōn') or un·be·knownst (-nōnst') adj. Occurring or existing without one's knowledge. [UN-¹ + obs. beknown, known.]

un·be·lief (ŭn'bĭ-lēf') n. Lack of belief or faith, esp. in religious matters. —un'be·liev'er n. —un'be·liev'ing adj.

un·be·liev·a·ble (ŭn'bĭ-lē'və-bəl) adj. Not to be believed. —un'be·liev'a·bly adv.

un·bend (ŭn-bĕnd') v. 1. To straighten. 2. To make or become less tense; relax.

un·bend·ing (ŭn-bĕn'dĭng) adj. Not flexible; uncompromising.

un·bid·den (ŭn-bĭd'n) adj. Also un·bid (-bĭd'). Not invited.

un·bind (ŭn-bīnd') v. 1. To untie or unfasten. 2. To release; set free.

un·blink·ing (ŭn-blĭng'kĭng) adj. 1. Without blinking. 2. Without visible emotion. 3. Fearless in facing reality.

un·blush·ing (ŭn-blŭsh'ĭng) adj. 1. Without shame or remorse. 2. Not blushing. —un·blush'ing·ly adv.

un·bolt (ŭn-bōlt') v. To release the bolts of (a door or gate); unlock.

un·born (ŭn-bôrn') adj. Not yet in existence; not born.

un·bos·om (ŭn-bŏŏz'əm, -bōō'zəm) v. 1. To confide; reveal. 2. To relieve (oneself) of troublesome thoughts or feelings.

un·bound·ed (ŭn-boun'dĭd) adj. Having no bounds or limits.

un·bowed (ŭn-boud') adj. 1. Not bowed; unbent. 2. Not subdued.

un·bri·dled (ŭn-brīd'ld) adj. 1. Not fitted with a bridle. 2. Unrestrained.

un·bro·ken (ŭn-brō'kən) adj. 1. Not broken; intact. 2. Uninterrupted; continuous. 3. Not tamed or broken.

un·bur·den (ŭn-bûr'dn) v. To relieve from a burden or trouble.

un·but·ton (ŭn-bŭt'n) v. 1. To unfasten the button or buttons (of). 2. To open or expose as if by unbuttoning.

un·called-for (ŭn-kôld'fôr') adj. 1. Not required or requested. 2. Out of place; impertinent.

un·can·ny (ŭn-kăn'ē) adj. -ni·er, -ni·est. 1. Inexplicable; strange. 2. So keen and perceptive

---

un'ex·posed' adj.
un'ex·pressed' adj.
un'ex·pur·gat·ed adj.
un·fad'ing adj.
un·fal'ter·ing adj.
un·fash'ion·a·ble adj.
un·fas'ten v.
un·fath'om·a·ble adj.
un·fath'omed adj.
un·fea'si·ble adj.
un·fed' adj.
un·fem'i·nine adj.
un·fenced' adj.
un·fer'til·ized' adj.
un·fet'tered adj.
un·fil'led' adj.
un·fil'tered adj.
un·fit'ted adj.
un·flag'ging adj.
un·flat'ter·ing adj.
un·fla'vored adj.
un·fold'ed adj.
un·forced' adj.
un'fore·see'a·ble adj.
un'fore·seen' adj.
un'for·giv'a·ble adj.
un'for·giv'ing adj.
un·for'mu·lat'ed adj.
un·framed' adj.
un·fruit'ful adj.

un'ful·filled' adj.
un·fund'ed adj.
un·fur'nished adj.
un·gen'tle·man·ly adj.
un·gird' v.
un·gov'erned adj.
un·grace'ful adj.
un·grad'ed adj.
un'gram·mat'i·cal adj.
un·guld'ed adj.
un·ham'pered adj.
un·hand'y adj.
un·harmed' adj.
un·har'ness v.
un·heat'ed adj.
un·heed'ed adj.
un·her'ald·ed adj.
un·he·ro'ic adj.
un·hes'i·tat'ing adj.
un·hin'dered adj.
un·hitch' v.
un·hur'ried adj.
un·hurt' adj.
un·hy'gi·en'ic adj.
un·i·den'ti·fied' adj.
un'id·i·o·mat'ic adj.
un'i·mag'i·na·ble adj.
un'i·mag'i·na·tive adj.
un'im·paired' adj.
un'im·por'tant adj.
un'im·pres'sive adj.
un'in·formed' adj.

un'in·hab'i·ta·ble adj.
un'in·hab'it·ed adj.
un'in·spired' adj.
un'in·sured' adj.
un'in·tend'ed adj.
un'in·vit'ed adj.
un'in·vit'ing adj.
un·know'a·ble adj.
un·knowl'edge·a·ble adj.
un·la'beled adj.
un·la'bored adj.
un·lace' v.
un·latch' v.
un·leav'ened adj.
un·li'censed adj.
un·lik'a·ble adj.
un·lim'it·ed adj.
un·lined' adj.
un·list'ed adj.
un·lit'. adj.
un·liv'a·ble adj.
un·lov'a·ble adj.
un·loved' adj.
un·made' adj.
un·man'age·a·ble adj.
un·man'ly adj.
un·manned' adj.
un·marked' adj.
un·mar'ried adj. & n.
un·mas'cu·line adj.
un·matched' adj.

---

as to seem supernatural. —un·can'ni·ly *adv.* —un·can'ni·ness *n.*

un·ceas·ing (ŭn-sē'sĭng) *adj.* Continuous; incessant. —un·ceas'ing·ly *adv.*

un·cer·e·mo·ni·ous (ŭn-sĕr'ə-mō'nē-əs) *adj.* Without the due formalities; abrupt. —un·cer'e·mo'ni·ous·ly *adv.*

un·cer·tain (ŭn-sûr'tn) *adj.* 1. Not having sure knowledge; doubtful. 2. Not capable of being predicted; questionable. 3. Not determined; vague; undecided. 4. Subject to change. —un·cer'tain·ly *adv.*

un·cer·tain·ty (ŭn-sûr'tn-tē) *n.*, *pl.* **-ties.** 1. Lack of certainty. 2. Something that is uncertain.

un·change·a·ble (ŭn-chān'jə-bəl) *adj.* Not capable of being altered.

un·char·i·ta·ble (ŭn-chăr'ĭ-tə-bəl) *adj.* Harsh and unforgiving with regard to others. —un·char'i·ta·ble·ness *n.* —un·char'i·ta·bly *adv.*

un·chart·ed (ŭn-chär'tĭd) *adj.* Not recorded on a map or plan; unexplored; unknown.

un·chaste (ŭn-chāst') *adj.* Not chaste or modest. —un·chaste'ly *adv.*

un·chris·tian (ŭn-krĭs'chən) *adj.* 1. Not Christian. 2. Not in accordance with the Christian spirit.

un·cial (ŭn'shəl, -shē-əl) *adj.* Of or pertaining to a style of writing characterized by somewhat rounded capital letters and found esp. in Greek and Latin manuscripts of the 4th to the 8th cent. [LLat. *uncialis*, inch-high.] —un'cial *n.*

un·cir·cum·cised (ŭn-sûr'kəm-sīzd') *adj.* Not circumcised.

un·civ·il (ŭn-sĭv'əl) *adj.* Impolite; discourteous; rude.

un·civ·i·lized (ŭn-sĭv'ə-līzd') *adj.* Not civilized; barbarous; savage.

un·clad (ŭn-klăd') *adj.* Naked.

un·clasp (ŭn-klăsp') *v.* 1. To release or loosen the clasp of. 2. To release from a grip or embrace.

un·cle (ŭng'kəl) *n.* 1. The brother of one's mother or father. 2. The husband of one's aunt. —*interj. Slang.* Used to express surrender. [< Lat. *avunculus*, maternal uncle.]

un·clean (ŭn-klēn') *adj.* 1. Foul or dirty. 2. Morally impure; sinful. 3. Ceremonially impure. —un·clean'ness *n.*

un·clean·ly (ŭn-klĕn'lē) *adj.* **-li·er, -li·est.** Habitually unclean. —un·clean'ness *n.*

Uncle Sam (săm) *n.* A personification of the United States or the U.S. government, represented as a tall, thin man with a white beard. [< *U.S.*, abbr. of *United States.*]

Uncle Tom (tŏm) *n.* A black held to be too deferential to whites. [< *Uncle Tom*, a slave in Harriet Beecher Stowe's *Uncle Tom's Cabin.*]

un·cloak (ŭn-klōk') *v.* 1. To remove a cloak or cover from. 2. To expose; reveal.

un·close (ŭn-klōz') *v.* To open.

un·clothe (ŭn-klōth') *v.* To remove the clothing or cover from.

un·coil (ŭn-koil') *v.* To unwind or become unwound.

un·com·fort·a·ble (ŭn-kŭm'fər-tə-bəl, -kŭmf'tə-bəl) *adj.* 1. Experiencing discomfort; uneasy. 2. Causing discomfort; disquieting. —un·com'fort·a·bly *adv.*

un·com·mit·ted (ŭn'kə-mĭt'ĭd) *adj.* Not pledged to a specific cause or particular course of action.

---

un·meas'ured *adj.*
un·melt'ed *adj.*
un·men'tioned *adj.*
un·mer'it·ed *adj.*
un·mixed' *adj.*
un·mo·lest'ed *adj.*
un·mov'a·ble *adj.*
un·moved' *adj.*
un·mu'si·cal *adj.*
un·name'a·ble *adj.*
un·named' *adj.*
un·nav'i·ga·ble *adj.*
un·no'tice·a·ble *adj.*
un·no'ticed *adj.*
un'ob·jec'tion·a·ble *adj.*
un'ob·served' *adj.*
un'ob·struct'ed *adj.*
un'ob·tain'a·ble *adj.*
un'of·fi'cial *adj.*
un'of·fi'cial·ly *adv.*
un·o'pened *adj.*
un'op·posed' *adj.*
un·or'ig·i·nal *adj.*
un·or'tho·dox' *adj.*
un·owned' *adj.*
un·paid' *adj.*
un·pal'at·a·ble *adj.*
un·par'don·a·ble *adj.*
un·pas'teur·ized' *adj.*
un·pa'tri·ot'ic *adj.*
un·paved' *adj.*
un'per·turbed' *adj.*
un·pile' *v.*
un·pin' *v.*
un·planned' *adj.*
un·plant'ed *adj.*

un·plowed' *adj.*
un·po·et'ic *adj.*
un·pol'ished *adj.*
un·polled' *adj.*
un·pol·lut'ed *adj.*
un·posed' *adj.*
un·prac'ticed *adj.*
un·prej'u·diced *adj.*
un'pre·med'i·tat'ed *adj.*
un'pre·pos·sess'ing *adj.*
un'pre·sent'a·ble *adj.*
un·pressed' *adj.*
un'pre·vent'a·ble *adj.*
un·proc'essed *adj.*
un'pro·duc'tive *adj.*
un·prom'is·ing *adj.*
un·prompt'ed *adj.*
un'pro·nounce'a·ble *adj.*
un'pro·nounced' *adj.*
un'pro·pi'tious *adj.*
un'pro·tect'ed *adj.*
un·prov'en *adj.*
un'pro·voked' *adj.*
un·pub'lished *adj.*
un·pun'ished *adj.*
un·quench'a·ble *adj.*
un·ques'tion·ing *adj.*
un·read'y *adj.*
un're·al·is'tic *adj.*
un're·al·is'ti·cal·ly *adv.*
un're·al·ized' *adj.*
un·rea'son·ing *adj.*
un're·cord'ed *adj.*
un're·deem'a·ble *adj.*
un·reel' *v.*
un're·fined' *adj.*

un're·gard'ed *adj.*
un·reg'is·tered *adj.*
un·reg'u·lat'ed *adj.*
un're·lat'ed *adj.*
un're·pen'tant *adj.*
un're·port'ed *adj.*
un'rep·re·sen'ta·tive *adj.*
un·re·quit'ed *adj.*
un're·sist'ing *adj.*
un're·solved' *adj.*
un're·spon'sive *adj.*
un're·strict'ed *adj.*
un're·ward'ing *adj.*
un·rhymed' *adj.*
un'ro·man'tic *adj.*
un·safe' *adj.*
un·san'i·tar·y *adj.*
un·sat'is·fac'to·ry *adj.*
un·sat'is·fied' *adj.*
un·sat'u·rat'ed *adj.*
un·scent'ed *adj.*
un·sched'uled *adj.*
un·schol'ar·ly *adj.*
un·sealed' *adj.*
un·sea'soned *adj.*
un·see'ing *adj.*
un·seen' *adj.*
un·sen'ti·men'tal *adj.*
un·serv'ice·a·ble *adj.*
un·shack'le *v.*
un·shad'ed *adj.*
un·shaved' *adj.*
un·shod' *adj.*
un·shorn' *adj.*
un·signed' *adj.*
un·sink'a·ble *adj.*

un·com·mon (ŭn-kŏm'ən) *adj.* **1.** Not common; rare. **2.** Wonderful; remarkable. **—un·com'mon·ly** *adv.*

Syns: uncommon, exceptional, extraordinary, rare, remarkable, singular, unusual *adj.*

un·com·mu·ni·ca·tive (ŭn'kə-myōō'nĭ-kā'tĭv, -kə-tĭv) *adj.* Not tending or willing to talk or to give out information; reserved.

un·com·pro·mis·ing (ŭn-kŏm'prə-mī'zĭng) *adj.* Not making concessions; inflexible.

un·con·cern (ŭn'kən-sûrn') *n.* **1.** Lack of interest; indifference; apathy. **2.** Lack of worry or apprehensiveness.

un·con·cerned (ŭn'kən-sûrnd') *adj.* **1.** Not interested; indifferent. **2.** Not anxious or apprehensive. **—un'con·cern'ed·ly** (-sûr'nĭd-lē) *adv.*

un·con·di·tion·al (ŭn'kən-dĭsh'ə-nəl) *adj.* Without conditions or reservations. **—un'con·di'tion·al·ly** *adv.*

un·con·di·tioned (ŭn'kən-dĭsh'ənd) *adj.* **1.** Unconditional; unrestricted. **2.** *Psychol.* Not the result of learning or conditioning: *an unconditioned reaction.*

un·con·quer·a·ble (ŭn-kŏng'kər-ə-bəl) *adj.* Incapable of being overcome or defeated.

un·con·scion·a·ble (ŭn-kŏn'shə-nə-bəl) *adj.* **1.** Not controlled or guided by conscience. **2.** Beyond what is reasonable; excessive. **—un·con'scion·a·bly** *adv.*

un·con·scious (ŭn-kŏn'shəs) *adj.* **1.** Not accessible to the conscious part of the mind. **2. a.** Temporarily lacking awareness. **b.** Not informed. **3.** Without conscious control; involuntary. **—n.** The part of the mind that operates without conscious awareness and that cannot be directly observed. **—un·con'scious·ly** *adv.* **—un·con'scious·ness** *n.*

un·con·sti·tu·tion·al (ŭn'kŏn-stĭ-tōō'shə-nəl, -tyōō'-) *adj.* Not in accord with the constitution of a country or organization. **—un'con·sti·tu'tion·al'i·ty** *n.* **—un'con·sti·tu'tion·al·ly** *adv.*

un·con·trol·la·ble (ŭn'kən-trō'lə-bəl) *adj.* Not able to be controlled or governed. **—un'con·trol'la·bly** *adv.*

un·con·ven·tion·al (ŭn'kən-vĕn'shə-nəl) *adj.* Not adhering to convention; out of the ordinary. **—un'con·ven'tion·al'i·ty** (-năl'ĭ-tē) *n.* **—un'con·ven'tion·al·ly** *adv.*

un·cork (ŭn-kôrk') *v.* **1.** To draw the cork from. **2.** To free from a constrained state.

un·cou·ple (ŭn-kŭp'əl) *v.* To disconnect.

un·couth (ŭn-kōōth') *adj.* **1.** Crude; unrefined. **2.** Awkward or clumsy; ungraceful. [< OE *uncūth,* strange.]

un·cov·er (ŭn-kŭv'ər) *v.* **1.** To remove the cover from. **2.** To disclose; reveal. **3.** To remove the hat from (one's head) in respect.

un·cross (ŭn-krôs', -krŏs') *v.* To move (one's limbs) from a crossed position.

unc·tion (ŭngk'shən) *n.* **1.** The act of anointing as part of a ceremonial or healing ritual. **2.** An ointment, salve, or oil. **3.** Something that serves to soothe or restore; balm. **4.** Affected or exaggerated earnestness. [< Lat. *unguere,* to anoint.]

unc·tu·ous (ŭngk'chōō-əs) *adj.* **1.** Greasy; oily. **2.** Marked by affected, exaggerated, or insincere earnestness or courtesy. [< Lat. *unctum,* ointment.] **—unc'tu·ous·ly** *adv.* **—unc'tu·ous·ness** *n.*

un·cut (ŭn-kŭt') *adj.* **1.** Not cut. **2.** Not abridged or shortened. **3.** Not ground or polished: *an uncut gem.* **4.** Having the page edge not slit or trimmed: *uncut pages.*

un·daunt·ed (ŭn-dôn'tĭd, -dän'-) *adj.* Not discouraged or disheartened; fearless. **—un·daunt'ed·ly** *adv.*

un·de·ceive (ŭn'dĭ-sēv') *v.* To free from illusion, error, or deception.

un·de·cid·ed (ŭn'dĭ-sī'dĭd) *adj.* **1.** Not yet determined or settled. **2.** Not having reached a decision; uncommitted.

un·de·mon·stra·tive (ŭn'dĭ-mŏn'strə-tĭv) *adj.*

---

un·snap' *v.*
un·snarl' *v.*
un·soiled' *adj.*
un·sold' *adj.*
un·sol'dier·ly *adj.*
un·so·lic'it·ed *adj.*
un·solv'a·ble *adj.*
un·solved' *adj.*
un·sort'ed *adj.*
un·spec'i·fied' *adj.*
un·spoiled' *adj.*
un·sports'man·like' *adj.*
un·stained' *adj.*
un·stat'ed *adj.*
un·stint'ing *adj.*
un·stop'pa·ble *adj.*
un·strap' *v.*
un'sub·stan'ti·at·ed *adj.*
un'suc·cess'ful *adj.*
un'suc·cess'ful·ly *adv.*
un·suit'ed *adj.*
un·sul'lied *adj.*
un'su·per·vised' *adj.*
un'sup·port'ed *adj.*
un'sup·pressed' *adj.*
un·sure' *adj.*
un'sur·passed' *adj.*

un'sus·pect'ed *adj.*
un'sus·pect'ing *adj.*
un'sus·pi'cious *adj.*
un·sweet'ened *adj.*
un·swerv'ing *adj.*
un'sym·met'ri·cal *adj.*
un'sym·pa·thet'ic *adj.*
un'sys·te·mat'ic *adj.*
un'sys·te·mat'i·cal·ly *adv.*
un·taint'ed *adj.*
un·tal'ent·ed *adj.*
un·tamed' *adj.*
un·tapped' *adj.*
un·tar'nished *adj.*
un·taxed' *adj.*
un·teach'a·ble *adj.*
un·ten'a·ble *adj.*
un·test'ed *adj.*
un·thought'ful *adj.*
un·tir'ing *adj.*
un·ti'tled *adj.*
un·touched' *adj.*
un·trace'a·ble *adj.*
un·trained' *adj.*
un·tram'meled *adj.*
un·trav'eled *adj.*
un·tried' *adj.*

un·trimmed' *adj.*
un·trod' *adj.*
un·trou'bled *adj.*
un·trust'wor'thy *adj.*
un·us'a·ble *adj.*
un·var'ied *adj.*
un·var'y·ing *adj.*
un·ver'i·fi'a·ble *adj.*
un·ver'i·fied' *adj.*
un·versed' *adj.*
un·vis'it·ed *adj.*
un·want'ed *adj.*
un·washed' *adj.*
un·watched' *adj.*
un·wa'ver·ing *adj.*
un·weaned' *adj.*
un·wear'a·ble *adj.*
un·wed' *adj.*
un·wel'come *adj.*
un·wom'an·ly *adj.*
un·work'a·ble *adj.*
un·worn' *adj.*
un·wor'ried *adj.*
un·wound'ed *adj.*
un·wrap' *v.*
un·wrin'kled *adj.*
un·yield'ing *adj.*

ă pat ā pay â care ä father ĕ pet ē be ĭ pit ī tie î pier ŏ pot ō toe ô paw, for oi noise ŏŏ took ōō boot ou out th thin th this ŭ cut û urge yōō abuse zh vision ə about, item, edible, gallop, circus

Not given to expressions of feeling; reserved. —**un'de·mon'stra·tive·ness** n.

un·de·ni·a·ble (ŭn'dĭ-nī'ə-bəl) adj. 1. Obviously true; irrefutable. 2. Unquestionably good; outstanding. —**un·de'ni·a·bly** adv.

un·der (ŭn'dər) prep. 1. In a lower position or place than. 2. Beneath the surface of. 3. Beneath the guise of: under a false name. 4. Less than; smaller than: under 20 years of age. 5. Less than the required amount or degree of: under voting age. 6. Inferior to, as in status. 7. Subject to the authority of: living under a dictatorship. 8. Undergoing or receiving the effects of: under intensive care. 9. Subject to the obligation of: under contract. 10. Within the group or classification of: listed under biology. 11. In the process of: under discussion. 12. Because of: under these conditions. —adv. 1. In or into a place below or beneath. 2. From motion or defeat: forced under by bombings. 3. So as to be covered, enveloped, or immersed. 4. Below a quantity, amount, or age. —adj. 1. Lower. 2. Subordinate; inferior. 3. Lower in amount or degree. [< OE.]

under- pref. 1. Below or under: underground. 2. Inferior in rank or importance: undersecretary. 3. Less in degree or quantity than normal: underestimate. [< OE under.]

Usage: Many compounds other than those entered here may be formed with under-. In forming compounds, under- is joined with the following element without space or a hyphen: underrate; undergrow. Note, however, that the adjective under may combine with other words as a unit modifier. In such cases the words are joined by hyphens: an under-the-table deal.

un·der·a·chieve (ŭn'dər-ə-chēv') v. To perform below an expected level of ability or capacity. —**un'der·a·chiev'er** n.

un·der·age (ŭn'dər-āj') adj. Below the customary or required age.

un·der·arm (ŭn'dər-ärm') adj. 1. Located, placed, or used under the arm. 2. Sports. Executed with the hand kept below the level of the shoulder. —adv. With an underarm motion or delivery. —n. The armpit.

un·der·bel·ly (ŭn'dər-bĕl'ē) n. 1. The lowest part of an animal's body. 2. The vulnerable part of something.

un·der·bid (ŭn'dər-bĭd') v. 1. To bid lower than. 2. To bid too low. —**un'der·bid'** n.

un·der·brush (ŭn'dər-brŭsh') n. Small trees, shrubs, etc., that grow beneath the taller trees in a forest.

un·der·car·riage (ŭn'dər-kăr'ĭj) n. 1. A supporting framework, as of an automobile. 2. The landing gear of an aircraft.

un·der·charge (ŭn'dər-chärj') v. To charge (someone) less than is customary or required. —**un'der·charge'** n.

un·der·class·man (ŭn'dər-klăs'mən) n. A student in the freshman or sophomore class at a secondary school or college.

un·der·clothes (ŭn'dər-klōz', -klōŧħz') pl.n. Also **un·der·cloth·ing** (-klō'ŧħĭng). Underwear.

un·der·coat (ŭn'dər-kōt') n. 1. A coat worn beneath another coat. 2. Short hairs or fur concealed by the longer outer hairs of an animal's coat. 3. a. Also **un·der·coat·ing** (-kō'tĭng). A coat of sealing material applied before a final coat. b. A tarlike substance sprayed on the underside of an automobile to prevent rusting. —v. To apply an undercoat.

un·der·cover (ŭn'dər-kŭv'ər) adj. Performed or carried on in secret.

un·der·cur·rent (ŭn'dər-kûr'ənt, -kŭr'-) n. 1. A current below another current or surface. 2. A partly hidden tendency or force often contrary to what is on the surface.

un·der·cut (ŭn'dər-kŭt') v. 1. To make a cut under or below. 2. To sell at a lower price or work for lower wages than (a competitor). 3. To ruin the effectiveness of; undermine. 4. Sports. a. To give backspin to (a ball) by striking downward as well as forward. b. To cut or slice (a ball) with an underarm stroke. —**un'der·cut'** n.

un·der·de·vel·oped (ŭn'dər-dĭ-vĕl'əpt) adj. 1. Not adequately or normally developed. 2. Industrially or economically backward.

un·der·dog (ŭn'dər-dôg', -dŏg') n. 1. One who is expected to lose a contest or struggle. 2. One who is at a disadvantage.

un·der·done (ŭn'dər-dŭn') adj. Not sufficiently cooked or prepared.

un·der·dressed (ŭn'dər-drĕst') adj. 1. Too informally dressed. 2. Wearing insufficient clothing.

un·der·es·ti·mate (ŭn'dər-ĕs'tə-māt') v. To make too low an estimate of the value, amount, or quality of. —**un'der·es'ti·ma'tion** n.

un·der·ex·pose (ŭn'dər-ĭk-spōz') v. To expose (film) to light for too short a time. —**un'der·ex·po'sure** n.

un·der·foot (ŭn'dər-fŏŏt') adv. 1. Below or under the feet. 2. In the way.

un·der·gar·ment (ŭn'dər-gär'mənt) n. A garment that is worn under outer garments.

un·der·go (ŭn'dər-gō') v. 1. To experience; be subjected to. 2. To endure; suffer. [ME undergon, to submit to.]

un·der·grad·u·ate (ŭn'dər-grăj'ŏŏ-ĭt) n. A college or university student who has not yet received a degree.

un·der·ground (ŭn'dər-ground') adj. 1. Below the surface of the earth. 2. Acting or done in secret. 3. Of or describing avant-garde or nonestablishment films, publications, and art. —n. 1. A secret, often nationalist, organization working against a government in power. 2. Chiefly Brit. A subway system. 3. An avant-garde movement or group. —adv. (ŭn'dər-ground'). 1. Below the surface of the earth. 2. In secret; stealthily.

un·der·growth (ŭn'dər-grōth') n. Low-growing plants, saplings, shrubs, etc., beneath trees in a forest.

un·der·hand (ŭn'dər-hănd') adj. 1. Done slyly and secretly; sneaky. 2. Sports. Performed with the hand kept below the level of the shoulder. —adv. 1. With an underhand movement. 2. Slyly and secretly.

un·der·hand·ed (ŭn'dər-hăn'dĭd) adj. Underhand. —**un'der·hand'ed·ly** adv. —**un'der·hand'ed·ness** n.

un·der·lie (ŭn'dər-lī') v. 1. To be located under or below. 2. To be the support or basis for; account for.

un·der·line (ŭn'dər-līn', ŭn'dər-līn') v. 1. To draw a line under; underscore. 2. To emphasize. —**un'der·line'** n.

un·der·ling (ŭn'dər-lĭng) n. A subordinate; inferior.

un·der·ly·ing (ŭn'dər-lī'ĭng) adj. 1. Lying under or beneath. 2. Basic; fundamental. 3. Hidden but implied.

un·der·mine (ŭn'dər-mīn') v. 1. To dig a mine

or tunnel beneath. **2.** To weaken by wearing away gradually or imperceptibly.

un·der·most (ŭn'dər-mōst') *adj.* Lowest in position, rank, or place. *—adv.* Lowest.

un·der·neath (ŭn'dər-nēth') *adv.* **1.** In a place beneath; below. **2.** On the lower face or underside. *—prep.* **1.** Under; below; beneath. **2.** Under the power or control of. *—adj.* Lower; under. *—n.* The part or side below or under. [< OE *underneothan.*]

un·der·nour·ish (ŭn'dər-nûr'ĭsh, -nŭr'-) *v.* To provide with insufficient nourishment. **—un'der·nour'ish·ment** *n.*

un·der·pants (ŭn'dər-pănts') *pl.n.* Pants, shorts, or drawers worn as underwear.

un·der·pass (ŭn'dər-păs') *n.* A passage underneath something, esp. a road under another road or railroad.

underpass

un·der·pay (ŭn'dər-pā') *v.* To pay insufficiently.

un·der·pin·ning (ŭn'dər-pĭn'ĭng) *n.* **1.** A supporting part or structure. **2.** Often **underpinnings.** *Informal.* The legs.

un·der·play (ŭn'dər-plā', ŭn'dər-plāo') *v.* **1.** To minimize the importance of. **2.** To act (a role) subtly or with restraint.

un·der·priv·i·leged (ŭn'dər-prĭv'ə-lĭjd) *adj.* Socially or economically deprived.

un·der·pro·duc·tion (ŭn'dər-prə-dŭk'shən) *n.* Production below full capacity or demand.

un·der·rate (ŭn'dər-rāt') *v.* To judge or rate too low.

un·der·score (ŭn'dər-skôr', -skōr') *v.* **1.** To underline. **2.** To emphasize or stress. **—un'der·score'** *n.*

un·der·sea (ŭn'dər-sē') *adj. & adv.* Beneath the surface of the sea. **—un'der·seas'** *adv.*

un·der·sec·re·tar·y (ŭn'dər-sĕk'rĭ-tĕr'ē) *n.* An official directly subordinate to a cabinet member.

un·der·sell (ŭn'dər-sĕl') *v.* **1.** To sell for a lower price than. **2.** To present in a way that minimizes the value.

un·der·shirt (ŭn'dər-shûrt') *n.* An undergarment worn under a shirt, blouse, etc.

un·der·shoot (ŭn'dər-shōot') *v.* **1.** To shoot a missile short of (a target). **2.** To land an aircraft short of (a landing area).

un·der·shorts (ŭn'dər-shôrts') *pl.n.* Underpants.

un·der·shot (ŭn'dər-shŏt') *adj.* **1.** Driven by water passing from below: *an undershot water wheel.* **2.** Projecting from below.

un·der·side (ŭn'dər-sīd') *n.* The side or surface that is underneath.

un·der·signed (ŭn'dər-sīnd') *n.* The person or persons who have signed at the bottom of a document.

un·der·sized (ŭn'dər-sīzd') *adj.* Also **undersize** (-sīz'). Smaller than the usual, normal, or required size.

un·der·skirt (ŭn'dər-skûrt') *n.* A skirt worn under another.

un·der·slung (ŭn'dər-slŭng') *adj.* Having springs attached to the axles from below, as an auto chassis.

un·der·stand (ŭn'dər-stănd') *v.* **-stood** (-stŏŏd'), **-stand·ing. 1.** To comprehend the meaning and significance of; know. **2.** To know thoroughly through long acquaintance with. **3.** To comprehend the language, sounds, form, or symbols of (a kind of expression). **4.** To know and be tolerant or sympathetic toward. **5.** To learn indirectly, as by hearsay. **6.** To conclude; infer. **7.** To accept as an agreed fact: *It is understood that the fee will be five dollars.* [< OE *understandan.*] **—un'der·stand'a·ble** *adj.* **—un'der·stand'a·bly** *adv.*

Syns: *understand, apprehend, comprehend, fathom, follow, grasp, take in* **v.**

un·der·stand·ing (ŭn'dər-stăn'dĭng) *n.* **1.** The quality of comprehension; discernment. **2.** The faculty by which one understands; intelligence. **3.** Individual or specified judgment or opinion; interpretation. **4.** A reconciliation of differences. **5.** An agreement reached between two or more persons or groups. *—adj.* Tolerant or sympathetic.

un·der·state (ŭn'dər-stāt') *v.* **1.** To state with less completeness or truth than seems warranted by the facts. **2.** To express with restraint or lack of emphasis, esp. for dramatic impact. **—un'der·state'ment** *n.*

un·der·stood (ŭn'dər-stŏŏd') *adj.* **1.** Agreed upon; assumed. **2.** Implicit or implied.

un·der·stud·y (ŭn'dər-stŭd'ē) *v.* **1.** To study or know (a role) so as to be able to replace the regular performer. **2.** To act as an understudy to. *—n.* An actor or actress who understudies.

un·der·take (ŭn'dər-tāk') *v.* **1.** To take upon oneself, as a task. **2.** To pledge or commit oneself to.

un·der·tak·er (ŭn'dər-tā'kər) *n.* One whose business it is to prepare the dead for burial or cremation and to make funeral arrangements.

un·der·tak·ing (ŭn'dər-tā'kĭng) *n.* **1.** Something undertaken; enterprise or venture. **2.** A guarantee or promise. **3.** The occupation of an undertaker.

un·der-the-coun·ter (ŭn'dər-*th*ə-koun'tər) *adj.* Transacted or sold illicitly.

un·der·tone (ŭn'dər-tōn') *n.* **1.** A tone of low pitch or volume. **2.** A pale or subdued color. **3.** A subdued or partly concealed emotional quality.

un·der·tow (ŭn'dər-tō') *n.* A current beneath the surface of a body of water running in a direction opposite to that of the current at the surface.

un·der·val·ue (ŭn'dər-văl'yōō) *v.* **1.** To assign too low a value to. **2.** To have too little regard or esteem for.

un·der·wa·ter (ŭn'dər-wô'tər, -wŏt'ər) *adj.* Used, done, or existing under the surface of water. **—un'der·wa'ter** *adv.*

un·der·wear (ŭn'dər-wâr') *n.* Clothing worn under the outer clothes and next to the skin.

un·der·weight (ŭn'dər-wāt') *adj.* Weighing less than is normal, healthy, or required. —**un'der·weight'** *n.*

un·der·world (ŭn'dər-wûrld') *n.* 1. *Gk. & Rom. Myth.* The world of the dead; Hades. 2. The part of society that is engaged in organized crime.

un·der·write (ŭn'dər-rīt') *v.* 1. To write under, esp. to endorse (a document). 2. To assume financial responsibility for. 3. To sign an insurance policy, thus guaranteeing payment. 4. *Finance.* To agree to buy (stock not yet sold publicly) at a fixed time and price. —**un'der·writ'er** *n.*

un·de·sir·a·ble (ŭn'dĭ-zīr'ə-bəl) *adj.* Not desirable; objectionable. —*n.* One who is considered objectionable. —**un'de·sir'a·bly** *adv.*

un·dies (ŭn'dēz) *pl.n. Informal.* Underwear.

un·dis·crim·i·nat·ing (ŭn'dĭ-skrĭm'ə-nā'tĭng) *adj.* 1. Indiscriminate. 2. Lacking taste or judgment.

un·dis·posed (ŭn'dĭ-spōzd') *adj.* 1. Not removed or resolved. 2. Disinclined; unwilling.

un·do (ŭn-dōō') *v.* 1. To reverse or erase; cancel. 2. To untie, disassemble, or loosen. 3. To open; unwrap. 4. **a.** To cause the ruin of; destroy. **b.** To throw into confusion; unsettle.

un·do·ing (ŭn-dōō'ĭng) *n.* 1. The act of reversing or annulling something. 2. The act of unfastening or loosening. 3. **a.** The act of bringing to ruin. **b.** The cause of ruin.

un·doubt·ed (ŭn-dou'tĭd) *adj.* Accepted as beyond question; undisputed. —**un·doubt'ed·ly** *adv.*

un·dress (ŭn-drĕs') *v.* To remove the clothing of; disrobe; strip. —*n.* 1. Informal attire. 2. Nakedness.

Syns: **undress, disrobe, strip, unclothe** *v.*

un·due (ŭn-dōō', -dyōō') *adj.* 1. Exceeding what is normal or appropriate; excessive. 2. Not proper or legal. 3. Not yet payable or due.

un·du·lant (ŭn'jə-lənt, ŭn'dyə-, ŭn'də-) *adj.* Undulating.

un·du·late (ŭn'jə-lāt', ŭn'dyə-, ŭn'də-) *v.* 1. To move or cause to move in a wavelike motion. 2. To have a wavelike appearance or form. [< LLat. *undulare.*]

un·du·la·tion (ŭn'jə-lā'shən, ŭn'dyə-, ŭn'də-) *n.* 1. A wavelike movement. 2. A wavelike form, outline, or appearance. 3. One of a series of waves or wavelike segments; pulsation.

un·du·ly (ŭn-dōō'lē, -dyōō'-) *adv.* Excessively; immoderately: *unduly fearful.*

un·dy·ing (ŭn-dī'ĭng) *adj.* Endless; everlasting.

un·earned (ŭn-ûrnd') *adj.* 1. Not deserved. 2. Not gained by work or service.

un·earth (ŭn-ûrth') *v.* 1. To dig up; uproot. 2. To bring to public notice; uncover.

un·earth·ly (ŭn-ûrth'lē) *adj.* -**li·er,** -**li·est** 1. Not of the earth; supernatural. 2. Frighteningly unaccountable; unnatural.

un·eas·y (ŭn-ē'zē) *adj.* 1. Lacking ease, comfort, or a sense of security. 2. Affording no ease; difficult. 3. Awkward or unsure in manner: *uneasy with strangers.* —**un·eas'i·ly** *adv.* —**un·eas'i·ness** *n.*

un·em·ployed (ŭn'ĕm-ploid') *adj.* 1. Out of work; jobless. 2. Not being used; idle. —**un'em·ploy'ment** *n.*

un·e·qual (ŭn-ē'kwəl) *adj.* 1. Not the same in any measurable aspect. 2. Asymmetric. 3. Variable; irregular. 4. Not having the required abilities; inadequate. 5. Not fair. —**un·e'qual·ly** *adv.*

un·e·qualed (ŭn-ē'kwəld) *adj.* Not equaled; unrivaled.

un·e·quiv·o·cal (ŭn'ĭ-kwĭv'ə-kəl) *adj.* Not open to doubt or misunderstanding; clear. —**un'e·quiv'o·cal·ly** *adv.*

un·err·ing (ŭn-ûr'ĭng, -ĕr'-) *adj.* Committing no mistakes; consistently accurate. —**un·err'ing·ly** *adv.*

un·es·sen·tial (ŭn'ĭ-sĕn'shəl) *adj.* Not necessary; not of importance; dispensable. —*n.* A nonessential.

un·e·ven (ŭn-ē'vən) *adj.* 1. Not level or smooth. 2. Not straight or parallel. 3. Not uniform or consistent. 4. Not balanced; not fair. —**un·e'ven·ly** *adv.* —**un·e'ven·ness** *n.*

un·e·vent·ful (ŭn'ĭ-vĕnt'fəl) *adj.* Lacking in significant events; without incident. —**un'e·vent'ful·ly** *adv.*

un·ex·am·pled (ŭn'ĭg-zăm'pəld) *adj.* Without precedent; unparalleled.

un·ex·cep·tion·a·ble (ŭn'ĭk-sĕp'shə-nə-bəl) *adj.* Beyond the least reasonable objection.

un·ex·pect·ed (ŭn'ĭk-spĕk'tĭd) *adj.* Coming without warning; unforeseen. —**un'ex·pect'ed·ly** *adv.* —**un'ex·pect'ed·ness** *n.*

un·fail·ing (ŭn-fā'lĭng) *adj.* 1. Not failing or running out; inexhaustible. 2. Constant; reliable. 3. Infallible. —**un·fail'ing·ly** *adv.*

un·fair (ŭn-fâr') *adj.* 1. Not just or evenhanded; biased. 2. Contrary to laws or conventions, esp. in commerce; unethical. —**un·fair'ly** *adv.* —**un·fair'ness** *n.*

Syns: **unfair, inequitable, unequal, unjust** *adj.*

un·faith·ful (ŭn-fāth'fəl) *adj.* 1. Not faithful; disloyal. 2. Adulterous. 3. Not justly representing or reflecting the original; inaccurate. —**un·faith'ful·ly** *adv.* —**un·faith'ful·ness** *n.*

un·fa·mil·iar (ŭn'fə-mĭl'yər) *adj.* 1. Not within one's knowledge; strange. 2. Not acquainted; not conversant. —**un'fa·mil·iar'i·ty** (-mĭl-yăr'ĭ-tē, -mĭl'ē-ăr'-) *n.*

un·fa·vor·a·ble (ŭn-fā'vər-ə-bəl, -fā'vrə-) *adj.* 1. Not favorable or helpful. 2. Negative; adverse. —**un·fa'vor·a·bly** *adv.*

un·feel·ing (ŭn-fē'lĭng) *adj.* 1. Not sympathetic; callous. 2. Having no sensation; insentient. —**un·feel'ing·ly** *adv.*

un·feigned (ŭn-fānd') *adj.* Not pretended; genuine.

un·fet·ter (ŭn-fĕt'ər) *v.* To free from bonds or restraints.

un·fit (ŭn-fĭt') *adj.* 1. Inappropriate. 2. Unqualified. 3. Not in good physical or mental health. —*v.* To make unfit; disqualify. —**un·fit'ly** *adv.* —**un·fit'ness** *n.*

un·flap·pa·ble (ŭn-flăp'ə-bəl) *adj. Slang.* Not easily upset or excited —**un·flap'pa·bil'i·ty** *n.*

un·fledged (ŭn-flĕjd') *adj.* 1. Having incompletely developed feathers and still unable to fly. 2. Inexperienced or immature.

un·flinch·ing (ŭn-flĭn'chĭng) *adj.* Steadfast; resolute. —**un·flinch'ing·ly** *adv.*

un·fold (ŭn-fōld') *v.* 1. To open and spread out. 2. To remove the coverings from. 3. To reveal or be revealed gradually.

un·for·get·ta·ble (ŭn'fər-gĕt'ə-bəl) *adj.* Permanently impressed on one's memory; memorable. —**un'for·get'ta·bly** *adv.*

un·formed (ŭn-fôrmd') *adj.* 1. Having no definite shape or structure. 2. Immature; undeveloped.

un·for·tu·nate (ŭn-fôr'chə-nĭt) *adj.* 1. Unlucky. 2. Causing misfortune; disastrous.

3. Regrettable; inappropriate. —*n.* A victim of bad luck, disaster, poverty, etc. —**un·for′tu·nate·ly** *adv.* —**un·for′tu·nate·ness** *n.*

Syns: *unfortunate, awkward, inappropriate, unhappy adj.*

un·found·ed (ŭn-foun′dĭd) *adj.* Not based on fact or sound observation; groundless.

un·fre·quent·ed (ŭn′frĭ-kwĕn′tĭd, ŭn-frē′kwən-) *adj.* Receiving few or no visitors.

un·friend·ly (ŭn-frĕnd′lē) *adj.* 1. Not disposed to friendship. 2. Unfavorable. —**un·friend′li·ness** *n.*

un·frock (ŭn-frŏk′) *v.* To strip of priestly privileges and functions; defrock.

un·furl (ŭn-fûrl′) *v.* To spread or open out; unroll.

un·gain·ly (ŭn-gān′lē) *adj.* -**li·er**, -**li·est**. Awkward; clumsy. [UN⁻¹ + obs. *gain*, handy + -LY.] —**un·gain′li·ness** *n.*

un·god·ly (ŭn-gŏd′lē) *adj.* 1. Not revering God. 2. Sinful; wicked. 3. *Informal.* Outrageous. —**un·god′li·ness** *n.*

un·gov·ern·a·ble (ŭn-gŭv′ər-nə-bəl) *adj.* Not capable of being governed or controlled.

un·gra·cious (ŭn-grā′shəs) *adj.* 1. Lacking courtesy; rude. 2. Unpleasant; disagreeable. —**un·gra′cious·ly** *adv.* —**un·gra′cious·ness** *n.*

un·grate·ful (ŭn-grāt′fəl) *adj.* 1. Without a feeling of gratitude or appreciation. 2. Disagreeable; repellent. —**un·grate′ful·ly** *adv.* —**un·grate′ful·ness** *n.*

un·guard·ed (ŭn-gär′dĭd) *adj.* 1. Unprotected. 2. Without discretion; imprudent.

un·guent (ŭng′gwənt) *n.* A salve; ointment. [< Lat. *unguentum.*]

un·gu·late (ŭng′gyə-lĭt, -lāt′) *adj.* Having hoofs. [< Lat. *unguis,* claw.]

un·hal·lowed (ŭn-hăl′ōd) *adj.* 1. Not consecrated. 2. Impious; profane.

un·hand (ŭn-hănd′) *v.* To remove one's hand or hands from; let go.

un·hap·py (ŭn-hăp′ē) *adj.* 1. Not happy; sad. 2. Unlucky. 3. Not suitable or tactful. 4. Dissatisfied; disturbed. —**un·hap′pi·ly** *adv.* —**un·hap′pi·ness** *n.*

un·health·y (ŭn-hĕl′thē) *adj.* 1. In ill health; sick. 2. Symptomatic of poor health. 3. Tending to cause poor health. 4. Harmful to character; corruptive. —**un·health′i·ness** *n.*

un·heard (ŭn-hûrd′) *adj.* 1. Not heard. 2. Not given a hearing.

un·heard-of (ŭn-hûrd′ŭv′, -ŏv′) *adj.* 1. Not previously known. 2. Unprecedented.

un·hinge (ŭn-hĭnj′) *v.* 1. To remove from hinges. 2. To unbalance (the mind).

un·ho·ly (ŭn-hō′lē) *adj.* 1. Wicked; immoral. 2. *Informal.* Outrageous; dreadful. —**un·ho′li·ness** *n.*

un·hook (ŭn-hŏok′) *v.* 1. To remove from a hook. 2. To unfasten the hooks of.

un·horse (ŭn-hôrs′) *v.* 1. To cause to fall from a horse. 2. To overthrow or dislodge.

uni- *pref.* One. [< Lat. *unus,* one.]

u·ni·cam·er·al (yŏō′nĭ-kăm′ər-əl) *adj.* Consisting of a single legislative chamber.

u·ni·cel·lu·lar (yŏō′nĭ-sĕl′yə-lər) *adj.* Consisting of one cell: *unicellular microorganisms.*

u·ni·corn (yŏō′nĭ-kôrn′) *n.* A fabled creature usu. represented as a horse with a single spiral horn projecting from its forehead. [< Lat. *unicornis.*]

unicorn   **unicycle**

u·ni·cy·cle (yŏō′nĭ-sī′kəl) *n.* A single-wheeled vehicle usu. propelled by pedals.

un·i·den·ti·fied flying object (ŭn′ī-dĕn′tə-fīd′) *n.* A flying or apparently flying object that cannot be identified as a known aircraft or object or explained as a natural phenomenon.

u·ni·form (yŏō′nə-fôrm′) *adj.* 1. Always the same; unchanging; unvarying. 2. Being the same as another or others; identical. —*n.* A distinctive outfit intended to identify those who wear it as members of a specific group. [< Lat. *uniformis,* of one form.] —**u′ni·for′mi·ty** or **u′ni·form′ness** *n.* —**u′ni·form′ly** *adv.*

u·ni·fy (yŏō′nə-fī′) *v.* -**fied**, -**fy·ing**. To make several into one; consolidate. [< LLat. *unificare.*] —**u′ni·fi·ca′tion** *n.* —**u′ni·fi′er** *n.*

u·ni·lat·er·al (yŏō′nĭ-lăt′ər-əl) *adj.* Of, on, pertaining to, involving, or affecting only one side. —**u′ni·lat′er·al·ly** *adv.*

un·im·peach·a·ble (ŭn′ĭm-pē′chə-bəl) *adj.* Beyond doubt or question. —**un′im·peach′a·bly** *adv.*

un·in·hib·it·ed (ŭn′ĭn-hĭb′ĭ-tĭd) *adj.* Free from inhibition. —**un′in·hib′it·ed·ly** *adv.*

un·in·tel·li·gent (ŭn′ĭn-tĕl′ə-jənt) *adj.* Lacking in intelligence. —**un′in·tel′li·gent·ly** *adv.*

un·in·tel·li·gi·ble (ŭn′ĭn-tĕl′ə-jə-bəl) *adj.* Not capable of being comprehended. —**un′in·tel′li·gi·bly** *adv.*

un·in·ter·est·ed (ŭn-ĭn′trĭs-tĭd, -ĭn′tə-rĕs′tĭd) *adj.* 1. Without an interest, esp. not having a financial interest. 2. Not paying attention; unconcerned.

Syns: *uninterested, incurious, indifferent, unconcerned adj.*

un·ion (yŏōn′yən) *n.* 1. a. The act of uniting. b. A combination thus formed, esp. a confederation of persons, parties, or political entities for mutual interest. c. The condition of being united. 2. a. A partnership in marriage. b. Sexual intercourse. 3. An organization of wage earners formed for the purpose of serving their collective interest with respect to wages and working conditions; labor union. 4. A coupling device for connecting pipes, rods, etc. 5. A design on a flag that symbolizes the union of two or more independent states, regions, etc. 6. **Union.** The United States of America, esp. during the Civil War. [< Lat. *unus,* one.]

un·ion·ism (yŏōn′yə-nĭz′əm) *n.* 1. The principle or theory of forming a union. 2. The principles, theory, or system of a union, esp. a trade union. 3. **Unionism.** Loyalty to the federal government during the Civil War. **—un′-ion•ist** n.

un•ion•ize (yōō′nyə-nīz′) v. **-ized, -iz•ing.** To organize into or cause to join a labor union. **—un′ion•i•za′tion** n.

union jack n. **1.** A flag consisting entirely of a union. **2. Union Jack.** The flag of the United Kingdom.

union shop n. A business or industrial establishment whose employees are required to be union members or to join the union.

u•nique (yōō-nēk′) adj. **1.** Being the only one of its kind. **2.** Being without an equal or equivalent. [< Lat. unicus.] **—u•nique′ly** adv. **—u•nique′ness** n.

Syns: unique, incomparable, matchless, peerless, unequaled, unparalleled, unrivaled adj.

u•ni•sex (yōō′nĭ-sĕks′) adj. Suitable for or common to both males and females.

u•ni•sex•u•al (yōō′nĭ-sĕk′shōō-əl) adj. Of or for only one sex.

u•ni•son (yōō′nĭ-sən, -zən) n. **1. a.** Identity of musical pitch. **b.** The combination of musical parts at the same pitch or in octaves. **2. a.** Speaking of the same words simultaneously by two or more speakers. **b.** Agreement; concord. [< Med. Lat. unisonus, of the same sound.]

u•nit (yōō′nĭt) n. **1.** One regarded as a constituent part of a whole. **2.** A precisely defined quantity in terms of which measurement of quantities of the same kind can be expressed. **3.** A part, device, or module that performs a particular function. [< UNITY.]

U•ni•tar•i•an (yōō′nĭ-târ′ē-ən) n. A member of a Christian denomination that rejects the doctrine of the Trinity and emphasizes freedom and tolerance in religious belief and the autonomy of each congregation. **—U′ni•tar′i•an•ism** n.

u•ni•tar•y (yōō′nĭ-tĕr′ē) adj. **1.** Of or pertaining to a unit. **2.** Whole.

u•nite (yōō-nīt′) v. **u•nit•ed, u•nit•ing. 1.** To bring together so as to form a whole. **2.** To combine (people) in interest, attitude, or action. **3.** To become joined, formed, or combined into a unit. [< LLat. unire.]

unit pricing n. The pricing of goods on the basis of cost per unit of measure.

u•ni•ty (yōō′nĭ-tē) n., pl. **-ties. 1.** The condition of being united into a single whole. **2.** Accord or agreement; concord. **3.** The combination or arrangement of parts into a whole; unification. **4.** An ordering of all elements in a work of art or literature so that each contributes to a unified aesthetic effect. **5.** Singleness of purpose or action; continuity. **6.** Math. The number 1. [< Lat. unitas.]

u•ni•va•lent (yōō′nĭ-vā′lənt) adj. **1.** Having valence 1. **2.** Having only one valence.

u•ni•valve (yōō′nĭ-vălv′) n. A mollusk, esp. a gastropod, that has a single shell. **—u′ni•valve′** adj.

u•ni•ver•sal (yōō′nə-vûr′səl) adj. **1.** Extending to or affecting the entire world; worldwide. **2.** Including, pertaining to, or affecting all members of a class or group. **3.** Applicable or common to all purposes, conditions, or situations. **4.** Of or pertaining to the universe or cosmos; cosmic. **5.** Comprising all or many subjects: a universal genius. **6.** Mechanics. Adapted or adjustable to many sizes or uses. **—u′ni•ver•sal′i•ty** n. **—u′ni•ver′sal•ly** adv.

U•ni•ver•sal•ism (yōō′nə-vûr′sə-lĭz′əm) n.

Theol. The doctrine that all people will ultimately be saved. **—U′ni•ver′sal•ist** n.

universal joint n. A joint that couples a pair of shafts not in the same line so that a rotating motion can be transferred from one to the other.

universal joint

u•ni•verse (yōō′nə-vûrs′) n. **1.** All existing things regarded as a collective entity. **2. a.** The earth. **b.** All human beings. [< Lat. universus, whole.]

u•ni•ver•si•ty (yōō′nə-vûr′sĭ-tē) n., pl. **-ties.** An institution for higher learning with teaching and research facilities comprising a graduate school, professional schools, and an undergraduate division. [< LLat. universitas, guild.]

un•just (ŭn-jŭst′) adj. Violating principles of justice. **—un•just′ly** adv.

un•kempt (ŭn-kĕmpt′) adj. **1.** Not combed. **2.** Not neat or tidy; messy. [UN-1 + kempt, p.p. of dial. kemb, to comb.]

un•kind (ŭn-kīnd′) adj. Not kind; unsympathetic. **—un•kind′li•ness** n. **—un•kind′ly** adv. & adj. **—un•kind′ness** n.

un•know•ing (ŭn-nō′ĭng) adj. Not knowing; uninformed. **—un•know′ing•ly** adv.

un•known (ŭn-nōn′) adj. **1.** Not known; unfamiliar; strange. **2.** Not identified or ascertained. **—un•known′** n.

un•law•ful (ŭn-lô′fəl) adj. Not lawful; illegal. **—un•law′ful•ly** adv. **—un•law′ful•ness** n.

un•lead•ed (ŭn-lĕd′ĭd) adj. Not containing lead: unleaded gasoline.

un•learn (ŭn-lûrn′) v. To put (something learned) out of the mind.

un•learn•ed (ŭn-lûr′nĭd) adj. **1.** Not educated; ignorant or illiterate. **2.** (ŭn-lûrnd′). Not acquired by training or studying.

un•leash (ŭn-lēsh′) v. To release from or as if from a leash.

un•less (ŭn-lĕs′) conj. Except on the condition that. [ME unlesse.]

un•let•tered (ŭn-lĕt′ərd) adj. Not educated; illiterate.

un•like (ŭn-līk′) adj. **1.** Not alike; different; dissimilar. **2.** Not equal. **—prep. 1.** Different from; not like: a sound unlike any other. **2.** Not typical of: It's unlike him not to call. **—un•like′ness** n.

un•like•ly (ŭn-līk′lē) adj. **1.** Not likely; improbable. **2.** Likely to fail. **—un•like′li•hood** or **un•like′li•ness** n.

Syns: unlikely, doubtful, improbable adj.

un•lim•ber (ŭn′lĭm′bər) v. To make ready for action.

un•load (ŭn-lōd′) v. **1. a.** To remove the load or cargo from. **b.** To remove (cargo). **2. a.** To relieve (oneself) of something oppressive; unburden. **b.** To pour forth (one's troubles). **3. a.** To remove the charge from (a firearm).

b. To discharge (a firearm); fire. **4.** To dispose of, esp. by selling in great quantity.

un·lock (ŭn-lŏk′) v. **1. a.** To undo (a lock). **b.** To undo the lock of. **2.** To permit access to: *unlocked her heart.* **3.** To open to solution: *unlock a mystery.*

un·looked-for (ŭn-lŏokt′fôr′) adj. Not looked for or expected; unforeseen.

un·loose (ŭn-lōos′) v. Also **un·loos·en** (-lōo′-sən). **1.** To let loose or unfasten; release. **2.** To relax or ease.

un·luck·y (ŭn-lŭk′ē) adj. **1.** Subjected to or marked by misfortune. **2.** Inauspicious. **3.** Disappointing: *an unlucky choice.* —**un·luck′i·ly** adv.

un·make (ŭn-māk′) v. **1.** To undo the making of. **2.** To deprive of position, rank, or authority. **3.** To ruin; destroy.

un·man·nered (ŭn-măn′ərd) adj. **1.** Without manners; rude. **2.** Without affectations.

un·man·ner·ly (ŭn-măn′ər-lē) adj. Rude; impolite. —**un·man′ner·li·ness** n.

un·mask (ŭn-măsk′) v. **1.** To remove a mask from. **2.** To disclose the true character of; expose.

un·mean·ing (ŭn-mē′nĭng) adj. Meaningless; senseless.

un·men·tion·a·ble (ŭn-měn′shə-nə-bəl) adj. Not fit to be mentioned.

un·mer·ci·ful (ŭn-mûr′sĭ-fəl) adj. **1.** Having no mercy; merciless. **2.** Excessive; extreme: *unmerciful heat.* —**un·mer′ci·ful·ly** adv. —**un·mer′ci·ful·ness** n.

un·mind·ful (ŭn-mīnd′fəl) adj. Careless; forgetful.

un·mis·tak·a·ble (ŭn′mĭ-stā′kə-bəl) adj. Obvious; evident. —**un′mis·tak′a·bly** adv.

un·mit·i·gat·ed (ŭn-mĭt′ĭ-gā′tĭd) adj. **1.** Not diminished or moderated. **2.** Absolute; unqualified.

un·mor·al (ŭn-môr′əl, -mŏr′-) adj. Amoral.

un·nat·u·ral (ŭn-năch′ər-əl, -năch′rəl) adj. **1.** Not in accordance with what usu. occurs in nature. **2.** Strained or affected; artificial. **3.** Against natural feelings or normal or accepted standards. —**un·nat′u·ral·ly** adv. —**un·nat′u·ral·ness** n.

un·nec·es·sar·y (ŭn-něs′ĭ-sěr′ē) adj. Not necessary; needless. —**un·nec′es·sar′i·ly** (-sâr′-ə-lē) adv.

un·nerve (ŭn-nûrv′) v. To cause to lose courage or composure.

un·num·bered (ŭn-nŭm′bərd) adj. **1.** Not numbered; countless. **2.** Not marked with an identifying number.

un·ob·tru·sive (ŭn′əb-trōo′sĭv, -zĭv) adj. Not readily noticed; inconspicuous. —**un·ob·tru′sive·ly** adv. —**un·ob·tru′sive·ness** n.

un·oc·cu·pied (ŭn-ŏk′yə-pīd′) adj. **1.** Not occupied; vacant. **2.** Not busy; idle.

un·or·gan·ized (ŭn-ôr′gə-nīzd′) adj. **1.** Lacking order, system, or unity. **2.** Not unionized.

un·pack (ŭn-păk′) v. **1.** To remove the contents of. **2.** To remove from a container or from packaging.

un·par·al·leled (ŭn-păr′ə-lěld′) adj. Without parallel; unequaled.

un·par·lia·men·ta·ry (ŭn′pär-lə-měn′tə-rē, -měn′trē) adj. Not in accordance with parliamentary procedures.

un·peo·ple (ŭn-pē′pəl) v. To depopulate (an area).

un·per·son (ŭn′pûr′sən) n. A person whose obliteration from the memory of the public is sought, esp. by governmental action.

un·pleas·ant (ŭn-plěz′ənt) adj. **-er, -est.** Not pleasing. —**un·pleas′ant·ly** adv. —**un·pleas′ant·ness** n.

Syns: *unpleasant, disagreeable, offensive* adj.

un·plug (ŭn-plŭg′) v. **1.** To remove a plug, stopper, etc. from. **2.** To disconnect (an electric appliance) by removing its plug from an outlet.

un·plumbed (ŭn-plŭmd′) adj. **1.** Not measured for depth with a plumb line. **2.** Not fully explored or understood.

un·pop·u·lar (ŭn-pŏp′yə-lər) adj. Not popular; not liked or approved of. —**un·pop′u·lar′i·ty** (-lăr′ĭ-tē) n.

un·prec·e·dent·ed (ŭn-prĕs′ĭ-dĕn′tĭd) adj. Without precedent; novel.

un·pre·dict·a·ble (ŭn′prĭ-dĭk′tə-bəl) adj. Not predictable; not capable of being known in advance. —**un′pre·dict′a·bil′i·ty** n. —**un′pre·dict′a·bly** adv.

un·pre·pared (ŭn′prĭ-pârd′) adj. **1.** Not prepared or ready. **2.** Done without preparation; impromptu. —**un′pre·par′ed·ness** n.

un·pre·ten·tious (ŭn′prĭ-tĕn′shəs) adj. Lacking pretention; modest.

un·prin·ci·pled (ŭn-prĭn′sə-pəld) adj. Lacking principles or moral scruples; unscrupulous.

un·print·a·ble (ŭn-prĭn′tə-bəl) adj. Not proper for publication.

un·pro·fes·sion·al (ŭn′prə-fĕsh′ə-nəl) adj. **1.** Not conforming to the standards of a profession. **2.** Without professional skill; amateurish. —**un′pro·fes′sion·al·ly** adv.

un·prof·it·a·ble (ŭn-prŏf′ĭ-tə-bəl) adj. **1.** Not producing a profit. **2.** Serving no purpose; useless.

un·qual·i·fied (ŭn-kwŏl′ə-fīd′) adj. **1.** Lacking the proper or necessary qualifications. **2.** Without reservations.

un·ques·tion·a·ble (ŭn-kwĕs′chə-nə-bəl) adj. Beyond question or doubt; indisputable. —**un·ques′tion·a·bly** adv.

un·qui·et (ŭn-kwī′ĭt) adj. **1.** Uneasy; distraught. **2.** Agitated; turbulent.

un·quote (ŭn′kwōt′) n. A word used to indicate the end of a quotation.

un·rav·el (ŭn-răv′əl) v. **1.** To separate (entangled threads). **2.** To clear up the elements of (something mysterious or baffling); solve.

un·read (ŭn-rĕd′) adj. **1.** Not read, studied, or perused. **2.** Having read little; ignorant.

un·read·a·ble (ŭn-rē′də-bəl) adj. **1.** Illegible. **2. a.** Dull. **b.** Incomprehensible.

un·re·al (ŭn-rē′əl, -rēl′) adj. **1.** Not real or substantial. **2.** Slang. Too good to be true; fantastic. —**un′re·al′i·ty** n.

un·rea·son·a·ble (ŭn-rē′zə-nə-bəl) adj. **1.** Not governed by reason. **2.** Exceeding reasonable limits; exorbitant. —**un·rea′son·a·ble·ness** n. —**un·rea′son·a·bly** adv.

un·re·gen·er·ate (ŭn′rĭ-jĕn′ər-ĭt) adj. **1.** Not spiritually or morally regenerated. **2.** Stubborn.

un·re·lent·ing (ŭn′rĭ-lĕn′tĭng) adj. **1.** Relentless; inexorable. **2.** Not diminishing in intensity, speed, or effort.

ă pat ā pay â care ä father ĕ pet ē be ĭ pit ī tie î pier ŏ pot ō toe ô paw, for oi noise ŏŏ took ōŏ boot ou out th thin th this ŭ cut û urge yŏŏ abuse zh vision ə about, item, edible, gallop, circus

un·re·li·a·ble (ŭn'rĭ-lī'ə-bəl) *adj.* Not reliable or trustworthy. —**un're·li'a·bil'i·ty** *n.* —**un're·li'a·bly** *adv.*

   Syns: *unreliable, undependable, untrustworthy* **adj.**

un·re·mit·ting (ŭn'rĭ-mĭt'ĭng) *adj.* Never slackening; incessant; persistent. —**un're·mit'ting·ly** *adv.*

un·re·served (ŭn'rĭ-zûrvd') *adj.* 1. Not reserved for a particular person. 2. Given without reservation; unqualified: *unreserved praise.* 3. Frank; candid. —**un're·serv'ed·ly** (-zûr'vĭd-lē) *adv.*

un·rest (ŭn-rĕst') *n.* Uneasiness; disquiet: *social unrest.*

un·re·strained (ŭn'rĭ-strānd') *adj.* 1. Not controlled; unchecked. 2. Not constrained; natural.

un·ripe (ŭn-rīp') *adj.* Not fully ripened or formed; immature.

un·ri·valed (ŭn-rī'vəld) *adj.* Unequaled; supreme: *unrivaled skill.*

un·roll (ŭn-rōl') *v.* 1. To unwind and open out (something rolled up). 2. To unfold; reveal.

un·ruf·fled (ŭn-rŭf'əld) *adj.* Not agitated; calm.

un·ru·ly (ŭn-rōō'lē) *adj.* **-li·er, -li·est.** Difficult or impossible to discipline or control; disorderly. [ME *unruly.*]

un·sad·dle (ŭn-săd'l) *v.* 1. To remove the saddle from. 2. To unhorse.

un·said (ŭn-sĕd') *adj.* Not expressed in words; implicit.

un·sa·vory (ŭn-sā'və-rē) *adj.* 1. Having a bad or dull taste; insipid. 2. Distasteful or disagreeable. 3. Morally offensive.

un·scathed (ŭn-skāᵗʰd') *adj.* Unharmed; uninjured.

un·schooled (ŭn-skōōld') *adj.* Not schooled; uninstructed.

un·sci·en·tif·ic (ŭn-sī'ən-tĭf'ĭk) *adj.* Not according to or following the principles of science. —**un'sci'en·tif'i·cal·ly** *adv.*

un·scram·ble (ŭn-skrăm'bəl) *v.* 1. To disentangle; resolve. 2. To restore to a form that can be understood.

un·screw (ŭn-skrōō') *v.* 1. To loosen, adjust, or remove by or as if by turning. 2. To remove the screws from.

un·scru·pu·lous (ŭn-skrōō'pyə-ləs) *adj.* Without scruples or principles; not honorable. —**un·scru'pu·lous·ly** *adv.* —**un·scru'pu·lous·ness** *n.*

un·seal (ŭn-sēl') *v.* To break or remove the seal of; open.

un·sea·son·a·ble (ŭn-sē'zə-nə-bəl) *adj.* 1. Not characteristic of the time of year. 2. Poorly timed; inopportune. —**un·sea'son·a·bly** *adv.*

un·seat (ŭn-sēt') *v.* 1. To remove from a seat, esp. from a saddle. 2. To force out of a position or office.

un·seem·ly (ŭn-sēm'lē) *adj.* Not in good taste; improper; unbecoming.

un·self·ish (ŭn-sĕl'fĭsh) *adj.* Not selfish; generous: *an unselfish nature.* —**un·self'ish·ly** *adv.* —**un·self'ish·ness** *n.*

un·set·tle (ŭn-sĕt'l) *v.* To make unstable; disturb.

un·set·tled (ŭn-sĕt'əld) *adj.* 1. Disordered; disturbed. 2. Not determined or resolved. 3. Not paid or adjusted. 4. Not populated; uninhabited. 5. Not fixed or established, as in a residence or routine.

un·shak·a·ble (ŭn-shā'kə-bəl) *adj.* Not capable of being shaken; firm.

un·shak·en (ŭn-shā'kən) *adj.* Not shaken; firm.

un·sheathe (ŭn-shēᵗʰ') *v.* To draw from or as if from a sheath.

un·sight·ly (ŭn-sīt'lē) *adj.* Unpleasant or offensive to look at; unattractive. —**un·sight'li·ness** *n.*

un·skilled (ŭn-skĭld') *adj.* 1. Lacking skill or technical training. 2. Requiring no training or skill. 3. Crude.

un·skill·ful (ŭn-skĭl'fəl) *adj.* Without skill or proficiency. —**un·skill'ful·ly** *adv.* —**un·skill'·ful·ness** *n.*

un·so·cia·ble (ŭn-sō'shə-bəl) *adj.* Not inclined to seek the company of others. —**un·so'cia·bil'i·ty** *n.*

un·so·phis·ti·cat·ed (ŭn'sə-fĭs'tĭ-kā'tĭd) *adj.* 1. Not sophisticated; naive. 2. Uncomplicated; simple.

un·sound (ŭn-sound') *adj.* 1. Not dependably strong or solid. 2. Not physically healthy; diseased. 3. Not logically founded; fallacious. —**un·sound'ly** *adv.*

un·spar·ing (ŭn-spâr'ĭng) *adj.* 1. Not frugal or thrifty. 2. Unmerciful; severe. —**un·spar'ing·ly** *adv.* —**un·spar'ing·ness** *n.*

un·speak·a·ble (ŭn-spē'kə-bəl) *adj.* 1. Beyond description; inexpressible. 2. Inexpressibly bad or objectionable. —**un·speak'a·bly** *adv.*

   Syns: *unspeakable, abominable, frightful, revolting, shocking, sickening* **adj.**

un·spo·ken (ŭn-spō'kən) *adj.* Not expressed; unsaid: *an unspoken wish.*

un·spot·ted (ŭn-spŏt'ĭd) *adj.* 1. Not marked with spots. 2. Morally unblemished.

un·sta·ble (ŭn-stā'bəl) *adj.* 1. Not steady or firm. 2. a. Of fickle temperament; flighty. b. Mentally unbalanced. 3. Tending to decompose easily, as a chemical compound. 4. a. Decaying after a relatively short time, as an atomic particle. b. Radioactive. —**un·sta'ble·ness** *n.* —**un·sta'bly** *adv.*

un·stead·y (ŭn-stĕd'ē) *adj.* 1. Not securely in place; unstable. 2. Fluctuating; inconstant. 3. Uneven; erratic. —**un·stead'i·ly** *adv.* —**un·stead'i·ness** *n.*

un·stick (ŭn-stĭk') *v.* To free from being stuck.

un·stop (ŭn-stŏp') *v.* 1. To remove a stopper from. 2. To remove an obstruction from.

un·stressed (ŭn-strĕst') *adj.* 1. Not accented or stressed: *an unstressed syllable.* 2. Not emphasized.

un·struc·tured (ŭn-strŭk'chərd) *adj.* 1. Lacking structure. 2. Not regulated or regimented.

un·strung (ŭn'strŭng') *adj.* 1. Having the strings loosened or removed. 2. Emotionally upset; unnerved.

un·stud·ied (ŭn-stŭd'ēd) *adj.* 1. Not contrived; natural. 2. Not having been instructed.

un·sub·stan·tial (ŭn'səb-stăn'shəl) *adj.* 1. Lacking material substance; not real. 2. Flimsy. 3. Insubstantial. —**un'sub·stan'tial·ly** *adv.*

un·suit·a·ble (ŭn-sōō'tə-bəl) *adj.* Not suitable or proper; not appropriate. —**un·suit'a·bly** *adv.*

   Syns: *unsuitable, improper, inappropriate, inapt, malapropos, unbecoming, unfit, unseemly* **adj.**

un·sung (ŭn-sŭng') *adj.* 1. Not sung. 2. Not honored or praised; uncelebrated.

un·tan·gle (ŭn-tăng'gəl) *v.* 1. To disentangle. 2. To clarify; resolve.

un·taught (ŭn-tôt') *adj.* **1.** Not instructed. **2.** Not acquired by instruction.

un·thank·ful (ŭn-thăngk'fəl) *adj.* **1.** Ungrateful. **2.** Unwelcome; thankless.

un·think·a·ble (ŭn-thĭng'kə-bəl) *adj.* Impossible to imagine or consider; inconceivable.

un·think·ing (ŭn-thĭng'kĭng) *adj.* **1.** Inconsiderate or thoughtless. **2.** Not deliberate; inadvertent. **—un·think'ing·ly** *adv.*

un·ti·dy (ŭn-tī'dē) *adj.* Not neat and tidy; sloppy. **—un·ti'di·ly** *adv.* **—un·ti'di·ness** *n.*

un·tie (ŭn-tī') *v.* **1.** To undo or loosen (a knot). **2.** To free from something that binds or restrains.

un·til (ŭn-tĭl') *prep.* **1.** Up to the time of: *danced until dawn.* **2.** Before a specified time: *You can't have the car until tomorrow.* *—conj.* **1.** Up to the time that: *We played until it was dark.* **2.** Before: *You can't leave until your work is finished.* **3.** To the point or extent that: *He talked until he was hoarse.* [ME.]

un·time·ly (ŭn-tīm'lē) *adj.* **1.** Occurring or done at an inappropriate time; inopportune. **2.** Occurring too soon; premature. **—un·time'li·ness** *n.* **—un·time'ly** *adv.*

un·to (ŭn'tōō) *prep.* Archaic. To. [ME.]

un·told (ŭn-tōld') *adj.* **1.** Not told or revealed. **2.** Without limit: *untold suffering.*

un·touch·a·ble (ŭn-tŭch'ə-bəl) *adj.* **1.** Not to be touched. **2.** Out of reach; unobtainable. *—n.* Often **Untouchable.** A member of the lowest Hindu caste, with whom physical contact was considered defiling by Hindus of higher castes.

un·to·ward (ŭn-tôrd', -tōrd', ŭn'tə-wôrd') *adj.* **1.** Unfavorable; unpropitious. **2.** Hard to control; refractory.

un·true (ŭn-trōō') *adj.* **1.** Not true; false. **2.** Deviating from a standard. **3.** Disloyal; unfaithful.

un·truth (ŭn-trōōth') *n.* **1.** A lie. **2.** Lack of truth. **—un·truth'ful** *adj.* **—un·truth'ful·ly** *adv.* **—un·truth'ful·ness** *n.*

un·tu·tored (ŭn-tōō'tərd, -tyōō'-) *adj.* **1.** Having had no formal education. **2.** Unsophisticated; unrefined.

un·twist (ŭn-twĭst') *v.* To loosen or separate (something twisted together) by turning in the opposite direction.

un·used (ŭn-yōōzd', -yōōst') *adj.* **1.** Not in use. **2.** Never having been used. **3.** Not accustomed: *unused to city traffic.*

un·u·su·al (ŭn-yōō'zhōō-əl) *adj.* Not usual, common, or ordinary. **—un·u'su·al·ly** *adv.*

un·ut·ter·a·ble (ŭn-ŭt'ər-ə-bəl) *adj.* **1.** Not capable of being expressed; too profound for expression. **2.** Not capable of being pronounced. **—un·ut'ter·a·ble·ness** *n.* **—un·ut'ter·a·bly** *adv.*

un·var·nished (ŭn-vär'nĭsht) *adj.* **1.** Not varnished. **2.** Presented without any effort to soften or disguise.

un·veil (ŭn-vāl') *v.* **1.** To remove a veil from. **2.** To disclose; reveal.

un·voiced (ŭn-voist') *adj.* **1.** Not expressed or uttered. **2.** *Phonet.* Voiceless.

un·war·rant·ed (ŭn-wôr'ən-tĭd, -wŏr'-) *adj.* Having no justification; groundless.

un·war·y (ŭn-wâr'ē) *adj.* Not alert to danger or deception. **—un·war'i·ly** *adv.* **—un·war'i·ness** *n.*

un·well (ŭn-wĕl') *adj.* Not well; ill.

un·whole·some (ŭn-hōl'səm) *adj.* **1.** Not healthful or healthy. **2.** Morally corrupt. **—un·whole'some·ly** *adv.* **—un·whole'some·ness** *n.*

un·wield·y (ŭn-wēl'dē) *adj.* Difficult to carry or handle because of shape or size.

un·will·ing (ŭn-wĭl'ĭng) *adj.* **1.** Hesitant; reluctant. **2.** Done, given, or said reluctantly. **—un·will'ing·ly** *adv.* **—un·will'ing·ness** *n.*

un·wind (ŭn-wīnd') *v.* **1.** To unroll; uncoil: *unwind a cable.* **2.** To become unrolled or uncoiled. **3.** To relax.

un·wise (ŭn-wīz') *adj.* Lacking wisdom; foolish or imprudent. **—un·wise'ly** *adv.*

un·wit·ting (ŭn-wĭt'ĭng) *adj.* **1.** Not intended; unintentional. **2.** Not knowing; unaware. [ME. unknowing.] **—un·wit'ting·ly** *adv.*

un·wont·ed (ŭn-wŏn'tĭd, -wōn'-, -wŭn'-) *adj.* Not habitual or customary; unusual.

un·world·ly (ŭn-wûrld'lē) *adj.* **1.** Not of this world; spiritual. **2.** Concerned with matters of the spirit or soul. **3.** Not worldly-wise; naive. **—un·world'li·ness** *n.*

un·wor·thy (ŭn-wûr'thē) *adj.* **1.** Insufficient in worth; undeserving. **2.** Not suiting or befitting. **3.** Vile; despicable. **—un·wor'thi·ly** *adv.* **—un·wor'thi·ness** *n.*

un·writ·ten (ŭn-rĭt'n) *adj.* **1.** Not written or recorded. **2.** Forceful or effective through custom; traditional.

un·yoke (ŭn-yōk') *v.* **1.** To release from a yoke. **2.** To separate or disjoin.

up (ŭp) *adv.* **1.** From a lower to a higher position: *moving up.* **2.** In or toward a higher position: *looking up.* **3.** From a reclining to an upright position: *He helped me up.* **4. a.** Above a surface: *come up for air.* **b.** Above the horizon: *The sun came up.* **5.** Into view or consideration: *You never brought this up before.* **6.** In or toward a position conventionally regarded as higher, as on a map: *going up to Canada.* **7.** To or at a higher price. **8.** So as to advance, increase, or improve: *His hopes keep going up.* **9.** With or to a greater pitch or volume. **10.** Into a state of excitement or turbulence: *A great wind came up.* **11.** So as to detach or unearth: *pulling up weeds.* **12.** Apart; into pieces: *tore up the paper.* **13.** Used as an intensive with certain verbs: *cleaning up.* *—adj.* **1.** Moving or directed upward: *an up elevator.* **2.** Being out of bed: *Are you up yet?* **3.** Actively functioning: *He's been up and around for a week.* **4.** *Informal.* Going on; happening: *What's up?* **5.** Being considered: *a contract up for renewal.* **6.** Finished; over: *Time's up!* **7.** *Informal.* Informed, esp. well-informed: *I'm not up on fashions.* **8.** Being ahead of an opponent: *up two games.* **9.** *Baseball.* At bat: *You're up!* *—prep.* **1.** From a lower to or toward a higher point on: *going up a mountain.* **2.** Toward or at a point farther along: *up the road.* **3.** In a direction toward the source of: *up the Hudson.* *—n.* **1.** A rise or ascent. **2.** An upward movement or trend. **3.** *Slang.* A feeling of excitement or euphoria. **—upped, up·ping. 1.** To increase or improve: *he upped his chances for admission with a good interview.* **2.** To raise or lift. **3.** *Informal.* To act suddenly or unexpectedly: *She just upped* *and left.* —**idioms. on the up and up.** Open and honest. **up against.** Confronted with; facing. **up to. 1.** Occupied esp. with scheming or devising. **2.** *Informal.* Primed or prepared for: *Are you up to a game of tennis?* **3.** Dependent upon: *It's up to us.* [< OE *up,* upward and *uppe,* on high.]

up— *pref.* **1.** Up: *uplift.* **2.** Upper: *upmost.* [< OE.]

up-and-com·ing (ŭp'ən-kŭm'ĭng) *adj.* Marked for future success; promising.

U·pan·i·shad (ōō-pän'ĭ-shäd') *n.* Any of a group of philosophical treatises contributing to the theology of ancient Hinduism, elaborating upon the earlier Vedas.

up·beat (ŭp'bēt') *n. Mus.* An unaccented beat, esp. the last beat of a measure. —*adj. Informal.* Optimistic; happy; cheerful.

up·braid (ŭp-brād') *v.* To reprove sharply; scold. [< OE *ūpbrēdan.*] —**up·braid'er** *n.*

up·bring·ing (ŭp'brĭng'ĭng) *n.* The rearing and training received during childhood.

up·com·ing (ŭp'kŭm'ĭng) *adj.* Anticipated; forthcoming.

up·coun·try (ŭp'kŭn'trē) *n.* The interior region of a country. —*adj.* (ŭp'kŭn'trē). Of, located, or coming from the upcountry. —*up'coun'try adv.*

up·date (ŭp-dāt') *v.* To bring up to date. —*up'date' n.*

up·draft (ŭp'drăft') *n.* An upward current of air.

up·end (ŭp-ĕnd') *v.* **1.** To stand, set, or turn on one end. **2.** To overturn or overthrow.

up·grade (ŭp'grād', ŭp-grād') *v.* To raise to a higher rank, grade, or standard. —*n.* (ŭp'grād'). An upward incline.

up·heav·al (ŭp-hē'vəl) *n.* **1.** The process or an example of being heaved upward. **2.** A sudden and violent disturbance or change. **3.** *Geol.* A lifting up of the earth's crust.

up·hill (ŭp'hĭl') *adj.* **1.** Going up a hill or slope. **2.** Long, tedious, or difficult. —*n.* (ŭp'hĭl'). An upward incline. —*adv.* (ŭp'hĭl'). **1.** To or toward higher ground; upward. **2.** Against adversity; with difficulty.

up·hold (ŭp-hōld') *v.* **1.** To hold aloft. **2.** To prevent from falling; support. **3.** To maintain in the face of a challenge. —**up·hold'er** *n.*

up·hol·ster (ŭp-hōl'stər) *v.* To supply (furniture) with stuffing, springs, cushions, and a fabric covering. [< ME *upholden,* to repair.] —**up·hol'ster·er** *n.*

up·hol·ster·y (ŭp-hōl'stər-ē, -hōl'strē) *n., pl.* **-ies. 1.** The materials used in upholstering. **2.** The business of upholstering.

up·keep (ŭp'kēp') *n.* The act or cost of maintenance in proper operation and repair.

up·land (ŭp'lənd, -lănd') *n.* The higher parts of a region or tract of land. —*up'land adj.*

up·lift (ŭp-lĭft') *v.* **1.** To raise up or aloft; elevate. **2.** To raise to a higher social, moral, or intellectual level. —*n.* (ŭp'lĭft'). **1.** The act, process, or result of lifting up. **2.** A movement to improve social, moral, or intellectual standards.

up·most (ŭp'mōst') *adj.* Uppermost.

up·on (ə-pŏn', ə-pôn') *prep.* On.

up·per (ŭp'ər) *adj.* **1.** Higher in place, position, or rank. **2.** Upper. *Geol. & Archaeol.* Being a later division of the period named. —*n.* **1.** The part of a shoe or boot above the sole. **2.** *Slang.* A drug, esp. amphetamine, used as a stimulant.

upper case *n.* Capital letters. —**up'per-case'** *adj.*

up·per-class (ŭp'ər-klăs') *adj.* Of or belonging to an upper social class.

up·per·class·man (ŭp'ər-klăs'mən) *n.* A student in the junior or senior class of a secondary school or college.

upper crust *n.* The highest social class or group.

up·per·cut (ŭp'ər-kŭt') *n. Boxing.* A short swinging punch directed upward, as to an opponent's chin.

upper hand *n.* A position of control or advantage.

up·per·most (ŭp'ər-mōst') *adj.* Highest in position, place, rank, or influence; foremost. —*up'per·most' adv.*

up·pi·ty (ŭp'ĭ-tē) *adj. Informal.* Arrogant.

up·raise (ŭp-rāz') *v.* To raise or lift up; elevate.

up·right (ŭp'rīt') *adj.* **1.** In a vertical position, direction, or stance. **2.** Moral; honorable. —*n.* Something, such as a beam, standing upright. —*up'right' adv.* —*up'right'ly adv.* —*up'right'ness n.*

upright piano *n.* A piano having the strings mounted vertically.

up·ris·ing (ŭp'rī'zĭng) *n.* A revolt; insurrection.

up·roar (ŭp'rôr', -rōr') *n.* A condition of noisy excitement and confusion; tumult. [< MDu. *oproer.*]

up·roar·i·ous (ŭp-rôr'ē-əs, -rōr'-) *adj.* **1.** Causing or accompanied by an uproar. **2.** Causing hearty laughter; hilarious. —*up·roar'i·ous·ly adv.* —*up·roar'i·ous·ness n.*

up·root (ŭp-rōōt', -rŏŏt') *v.* To remove completely by or as if by pulling up the roots. —*up·root'er n.*

uproot

up·set (ŭp-sĕt') *v.* **-set, -set·ting. 1.** To overturn or cause to overturn. **2.** To disturb the usual or normal functioning, order, or course of. **3. a.** To distress or perturb mentally or emotionally. **b.** To distress physically. **4.** To defeat unexpectedly. —*n.* (ŭp'sĕt'). **1. a.** An act of upsetting. **b.** The condition of being upset. **2.** A disturbance of normal order. **3.** A game or competition in which the favorite is defeated. —*adj.* (ŭp-sĕt'). **1.** Overturned; capsized. **2.** Disordered; disturbed. **3.** Distressed; agitated. [ME *upsetter,* to set up.] —*up·set'ter n.*

up·shot (ŭp'shŏt') *n.* The final result; outcome.

up·side-down (ŭp'sīd-doun') *adv.* Also **upside down. 1.** With the upper and lower parts reversed in position. **2.** In or into great disorder. [< ME *up so down,* up as if down.] —*up'side-down' adj.*

up·si·lon (ŭp'sə-lŏn', yōōp'sə-) *n.* The 20th

letter of the Greek alphabet. See table at **alphabet**. [Med. Gk. *u psilon*, simple u.]

up-stage (ŭp'stāj') *adj.* 1. Of the rear of a stage. 2. *Informal.* Haughty; aloof. —*adv.* Toward, to, on, or at the back part of the stage. —*v.* (ŭp-stāj') 1. To make (another actor) face away from the audience by assuming a position upstage. 2. *Informal.* To treat haughtily.

up-stairs (ŭp'stârz') *adv.* 1. Up the stairs. 2. To or on an upper floor. —*adj.* (ŭp'stârz'). Of, relating to, or located on the upper floors. —*n.* (ŭp'stârz'). *(used with a sing. verb).* The upper part of a building.

up-stand-ing (ŭp-stăn'dĭng, ŭp'stăn'-) *adj.* 1. Standing erect. 2. Morally upright; honest.

up-start (ŭp'stärt') *n.* A person who has suddenly risen to wealth or high position, esp. one who is arrogant or self-important.

up-state (ŭp'stāt') *adv.* At, toward, or to that part of a state lying at a distance from and esp. farther north of a large city. —**up'state'** *adj.* & *n.* —**up'stat'er** *n.*

up-stream (ŭp'strēm') *adv.* In, at, or toward the source of a stream or current. —**up'stream'** *adj.*

up-stroke (ŭp'strōk') *n.* An upward stroke.

up-surge (ŭp'sûrj') *n.* A rapid upward swell or rise.

up-swept (ŭp'swĕpt') *adj.* Sweeping upward.

up-swing (ŭp'swĭng') *n.* An upward swing or trend; increase.

up-take (ŭp'tāk') *n.* 1. A passage for drawing up smoke or air. 2. *Informal.* Understanding; comprehension.

up-tight (ŭp'tīt') *adj.* Also **up tight.** *Slang.* 1. Very tense or nervous: *an uptight person.* 2. Conforming rigidly to convention.

up-to-date (ŭp'tə-dāt') *adj.* Reflecting or informed of the latest improvements, facts, or style.

up-town (ŭp'toun') *adv.* In or toward the upper part of a town or city. —*n.* The upper part of a town or city. —**up'town'** *adj.*

up-turn (ŭp'tûrn') *n.* An upward movement, curve, or trend: *an upturn in business.* —*v.* (also ŭp-tûrn'). 1. To turn up or over, as soil. 2. To direct upward.

up-ward (ŭp'wərd) *adv.* Also **up-wards** (-wərdz). In, to, or toward a higher place, level, or position. —**idiom. upward (or upwards) of.** More than; in excess of. [< OE *ūpweard.*] —**up'ward·ly** *adv.*

up-wind (ŭp'wĭnd') *adv.* In or toward the direction from which the wind blows. —**up'wind'** *adj.*

ur- *pref.* Var. of **uro-**.

u-ra-cil (yŏŏr'ə-sĭl) *n.* A nitrogenous pyrimidine base that is one of four bases constituting ribonucleic acids. [UR(O)- + AC(ETIC) + -IL(E).]

U-ral-Al-taic (yŏŏr'əl-ăl-tā'ĭk) *n.* A hypothetical language group including Uralic and Altaic. —**U'ral-Al-ta'ic** *adj.*

U-ra-lic (yŏŏ-răl'ĭk) *n.* Also **U-ra-li-an** (-rā'lē-ən, -răl'ē-ən). A family of languages including the Finno-Ugric and Samoyed languages. —*adj.* Of or designating this language family.

u-ra-ni-um (yŏŏ-rā'nē-əm) *n. Symbol* **U** A heavy silvery-white radioactive metallic ele-

ment, used in research, nuclear fuels, and nuclear weapons. Atomic number 92; atomic weight 238.03. [< URANUS.]

U-ra-nus (yŏŏr'ə-nəs, yŏŏ-rā'nəs) -n. 1. *Gk. Myth.* The earliest supreme god, a personification of the sky. 2. The 7th planet of the solar system in order of distance from the sun, with a diameter of about 29,000 miles, an average distance from the sun of about 1,790 million miles, and a mass 14.6 times that of Earth.

ur-ban (ûr'bən) *adj.* Of, relating to, typical of, or constituting a city. [Lat. *urbanus.*]

ur-bane (ûr'bān') *adj.* Having or showing the refined manners of polite society. [< Lat. *urbanus,* urban.] —**ur'bane'ly** *adv.* —**ur-ban'i-ty** (-băn'ĭ-tē) *n.*

ur-ban-ite (ûr'bə-nīt') *n.* A city dweller.

ur-ban-ize (ûr'bə-nīz') *v.* **-ized, -iz-ing.** To make urban in nature or character. —**ur'ban-i-za'tion** *n.*

ur-chin (ûr'chĭn) *n.* A small, mischievous child. [< Lat. *ericius,* hedgehog.]

Ur-du (ŏŏr'dŏŏ, ûr'-) *n.* An Indic language that is an official language of Pakistan and is widely used in India.

-ure *suff.* 1. An act or process: *erasure.* 2. A function or a body performing a function: *legislature.* [< Lat. *-ura.*]

u-re-a (yŏŏ-rē'ə) *n.* A white crystalline or powdery compound, $CO(NH_2)_2$, found in mammalian urine and other body fluids. [< Lat. *urina,* urine.]

u-re-mi-a (yŏŏ-rē'mē-ə) *n.* An excess of urea in the blood, characterized by headache, nausea, vomiting, and coma.

u-re-ter (yŏŏ-rē'tər, yŏŏr'ĭ-tər) *n.* Either of the long, narrow ducts that carry urine from the kidneys to the urinary bladder. [Gk. *ourētēr.*]

u-re-thra (yŏŏ-rē'thrə) *n., pl.* **-thras** or **-thrae** (-thrē). The duct through which urine is discharged and that serves as the male genital duct. [< Gk. *ourēthra.*] —**u-re'thral** *adj.*

urge (ûrj) *v.* **urged, urg-ing.** 1. To push or drive forward forcefully. 2. To entreat earnestly and repeatedly; exhort. 3. To advocate strongly and persistently. —*n.* An irresistible or impelling force, influence, or desire. [Lat. *urgēre.*]

Syns: *urge, exhort, press, prod, prompt* **v.**

ur-gent (ûr'jənt) *adj.* 1. Requiring immediate action; pressing. 2. Entreating or advocating persistently. —**ur'gen-cy** *n.* —**ur'gent-ly** *adv.*

-urgy *suff.* A technology: *metallurgy.* [< Gk. *ergon,* work.]

u-ric (yŏŏr'ĭk) *adj.* Pertaining to, contained in, or obtained from urine: *uric acid.*

u-ri-nal (yŏŏr'ə-nəl) *n.* 1. A place for urinating. 2. A receptacle for urine. [< LLat.]

u-ri-nal-y-sis (yŏŏr'ə-năl'ĭ-sĭs) *n.* The chemical analysis of urine. [URIN(O)- + (AN)ALYSIS.]

u-ri-nar-y (yŏŏr'ə-nĕr'ē) *adj.* Of or relating to urine or its production, function, or excretion. **urinary bladder** *n.* A muscular membrane-lined sac situated in the anterior part of the pelvic cavity in which urine is stored until excreted.

u-ri-nate (yŏŏr'ə-nāt') *v.* **-nat-ed, -nat-ing.** To discharge urine.

u-rine (yŏŏr'ĭn) *n.* A solution containing body wastes extracted from the blood by the kidneys, stored in the urinary bladder, and discharged from the body through the urethra. [< Lat. *urina*.]

urino- or **urin-** *pref.* Urine: *urinalysis.* [< Lat. *urina.*]

urn (ûrn) *n.* **1.** A vase or pedestal, used esp. to hold the ashes of a cremated body. **2.** A closed metal container with a spigot, used for making and serving tea or coffee. [< Lat. *urna.*]

uro- or **ur-** *pref.* Urine or the urinary tract: *urogenital.* [< Gk. *ouron.*]

u·ro·gen·i·tal (yŏŏr'ō-jĕn'ĭ-tl) *adj.* Of or involving both the urinary and genital functions and organs.

u·rol·o·gy (yŏŏ-rŏl'ə-jē) *n.* The medical study of the physiology and pathology of the urogenital tract. —**u·rol'o·gist** *n.*

Ur·sa Major (ûr'sə) *n.* A constellation that contains the seven stars that form the Big Dipper.

Ursa Minor *n.* A constellation that has the shape of a ladle with the star Polaris at the tip of its handle.

ur·sine (ûr'sīn') *adj.* Of or characteristic of a bear. [< Lat. *ursus*, bear.]

us (ŭs) *pron.* The objective case of **we.** Used: **1.** As the direct object of a verb: *The movie impressed us greatly.* **2.** As the indirect object of a verb: *His father gave us money.* **3.** As the object of a preposition: *Tom sent his regards to us.* [< OE *ūs.*]

us·a·ble (yŏŏ'zə-bəl) *adj.* Also **use·a·ble.** **1.** Capable of being used: *usable waste.* **2.** In a fit condition for use; intact or operative. —**us'a·bil'i·ty** *n.* —**us'a·bly** *adv.*

us·age (yŏŏ'sĭj, -zĭj) *n.* **1.** The act or manner of using. **2.** A customary or habitual practice. **3.** The actual way in which language or its elements, such as words and phrases, are used. [< OFr. *user*, to use.]

Usage. Usage has a more specialized sense than *use*, usually denoting a customary practice, especially with respect to language. Thus, we might say *The term "settee" no longer has wide usage*, but we refer to *the use of synthetic materials in modern dress*, where only the sense of "employment" is intended.

use (yŏŏz) *v.* **used, us·ing.** **1.** To put into service; employ. **2.** To make a habit of employing. **3.** To conduct oneself toward; treat. **4.** *Informal.* To exploit. **5.** To take habitually, as tobacco or alcohol. **6.** Used in the past tense with *to* to express former practice, fact, or condition: *He used to be very fat.* —**phrasal verb. use up.** To consume completely. —*n.* (yŏŏs). **1.** The act of using; employment. **2.** The condition or fact of being used. **3.** The manner of using. **4. a.** The privilege of using something. **b.** The power or ability of using something: *lose the use of one arm.* **5.** The need or occasion to employ. **6.** The quality of being suitable to an end; usefulness. **7.** The goal, object, or purpose for which something is used. **8.** Accustomed or habitual practice; custom. **9.** *Law.* **a.** The enjoyment of property, as by occupying or exercising it. **b.** The benefit or profit of lands and tenements held in trust by another. —**Idiom. used to.** Accustomed to: *We are not used to the cold.* [< Lat. *uti.*]

used (yŏŏzd) *adj.* Not new; secondhand: *a used car.*

use·ful (yŏŏs'fəl) *adj.* Capable of being used

for some beneficial purpose. —**use'ful·ly** *adv.* —**use'ful·ness** *n.*

use·less (yŏŏs'lĭs) *adj.* **1.** Of little or no worth. **2.** Producing no result or effect; vain. —**use'less·ly** *adv.* —**use'less·ness** *n.*

us·er (yŏŏ'zər) *n.* **1.** One that uses. **2.** *Slang.* A drug addict.

ush·er (ŭsh'ər) *n.* **1.** A person who escorts people to their seats, as in a theater. **2.** An official doorkeeper, as in a courtroom or legislative chamber. **3.** An official who precedes persons of rank in a procession, parade, etc. —*v.* **1.** To lead or conduct; escort. **2.** To precede and introduce; serve as the forerunner of. [< Lat. *ostiarius*, doorkeeper.]

u·su·al (yŏŏ'zhŏŏ-əl) *adj.* **1.** Common; ordinary; normal. **2.** Habitual or customary. [< LLat. *usualis.*] —**u'su·al·ly** *adv.* **u'su·al·ness** *n.*

u·su·fruct (yŏŏ'zə-frŭkt', -sə-) *n.* *Law.* The right to utilize and enjoy the profits and advantages of something belonging to another so long as the property is not damaged or altered in any way. [< Lat. *ususfructus.*]

u·su·rer (yŏŏ'zhər-ər) *n.* One who lends money at an exorbitant or unlawful rate of interest. [< Lat. *usura*, interest.]

u·su·ri·ous (yŏŏ-zhŏŏr'ē-əs) *adj.* Practicing, pertaining to, or constituting usury. —**u·su'ri·ous·ly** *adv.* —**u·su'ri·ous·ness** *n.*

u·surp (yŏŏ-sûrp', -zûrp') *v.* To seize and hold by force and without legal right or authority. [< Lat. *usurpare*, to make use of.] —**u'sur·pa'tion** *n.* —**u·surp'er** *n.*

u·su·ry (yŏŏ'zhə-rē) *n., pl.* **-ries.** **1.** The act or practice of lending money at an exorbitant or illegal rate of interest. **2.** An excessive rate of interest, esp. above the legal rate. [< Lat. *usura.*]

Ute (yŏŏt) *n., pl.* **Ute** or **Utes.** **1. a.** A tribe of Indians formerly inhabiting Utah, Colorado, and New Mexico. **b.** A member of this tribe. **2.** The Uto-Aztecan language of the Ute.

u·ten·sil (yŏŏ-tĕn'səl) *n.* **1.** An instrument or container, esp. one used in a household. **2.** A useful instrument or tool. [< Lat. *utensilis*, fit for use.]

utensil
Cooking utensils

u·ter·us (yŏŏ'tər-əs) *n.* A hollow, muscular organ of female mammals, in which a fertilized egg develops and from which the fully formed young emerges during the process of birth. [Lat.] —**u'ter·ine** (-ĭn, -tə-rīn') *adj.*

u·tile (yŏŏ'tĭl, yŏŏ'tīl') *adj.* Useful. [< Lat. *utilis.*]

u·til·i·tar·i·an (yŏŏ-tĭl'ĭ-târ'ē-ən) *adj.* **1.** Of or associated with utility. **2.** Stressing utility rather than beauty. **3.** Believing in or advocating utilitarianism. —*n.* A person who advocates utilitarianism.

u·til·i·tar·i·an·ism (yōō-tĭl′ĭ-târ′ē-ə-nĭz′əm) *n.* The philosophical doctrine that considers utility as the criterion of action and the useful as good or worthwhile, esp. the doctrine that all moral, social, or political action should be directed toward achieving the greatest good for the greatest number of people.

u·til·i·ty (yōō-tĭl′ĭ-tē) *n., pl.* **-ties. 1.** The condition or quality of being useful; usefulness. **2.** A useful article or device. **3.** An organization, such as a telephone company, that provides a public service under governmental regulation. [< Lat. *utilitas.*]

u·til·ize (yōōt′l-īz′) *v.* **-ized, -iz·ing.** To put to use. [< Lat. *utilis,* useful.] —**u′til·iz·a·ble** *adj.* —**u′til·i·za′tion** *n.* —**u′til·iz′er** *n.*

ut·most (ŭt′mōst′) *adj.* **1.** Being or situated at the farthest limit or point; most extreme. **2.** Of the highest or greatest degree, amount, or intensity. [< OE *ūtmest.*] —**ut′most** *n.*

U·to-Az·tec·an (yōō′tō-ăz′tĕk′ən) *n.* **1.** A large language family of North and Central America that includes Ute, Shoshone, Nahuatl, and other languages. **2. a.** A tribe speaking a Uto-Aztecan language. **b.** A member of such a tribe. —**U′to-Az′tec′an** *adj.*

u·to·pi·a (yōō-tō′pē-ə) *n.* **1.** Often **Utopia.** A condition, place, or situation of social or political perfection. **2.** An impractically idealis-

tic goal or scheme. [< Gk. *ou,* no + Gk. *topos,* place.] —**u·to′pi·an** *adj.* & *n.*

ut·ter¹ (ŭt′ər) *v.* **1.** To pronounce; speak. **2.** To give forth as sound: *utter a sigh.* **3.** To put (counterfeit money or a forgery) into circulation. [< MDu. *ūteren.*] —**ut′ter·a·ble** *adj.* —**ut′ter·er** *n.*

ut·ter² (ŭt′ər) *adj.* Complete; absolute: *utter nonsense.* [< OE *ūtera,* outer.] —**ut′ter·ly** *adv.*
   Syns: *utter, all-out, arrant, complete, consummate, flat, out-and-out, outright, positive, pure, sheer, thorough, total, unmitigated, unqualified adj.*

ut·ter·ance (ŭt′ər-əns) *n.* **1. a.** The act of uttering or expressing vocally. **b.** The power of speaking. **2.** Something that is uttered.

ut·ter·ly (ŭt′ər-lē) *adv.* Completely; absolutely; entirely.

ut·ter·most (ŭt′ər-mōst′) *adj.* **1.** Utmost. **2.** Outermost. —**ut′ter·most** *n.*

U-turn (yōō′tûrn′) *n.* A turn, as by a vehicle, reversing the direction of travel.

u·vu·la (yōō′vyə-lə) *n.* The small, conical, fleshy mass of tissue suspended from the center of the soft palate above the back of the tongue. [< LLat., small grape.] —**u′vu·lar** *adj.*

ux·o·ri·ous (ŭk-sôr′ē-əs, -sōr′-, ŭg-zôr′-, -zōr′-) *adj.* Excessively submissive or devoted to one's wife. [< Lat. *uxor,* wife.] —**ux·o′ri·ous·ly** *adv.* —**ux·o′ri·ous·ness** *n.*

Vv

v or **V** (vē) *n., pl.* **v's** or **V's. 1.** The 22nd letter of the English alphabet. **2.** Something shaped like the letter V. **3. V** The Roman numeral for 5.

va·can·cy (vā′kən-sē) *n., pl.* **-cies. 1.** The state of being vacant; emptiness. **2.** An empty space; void. **3.** A position, office, or living space that is unfilled or unoccupied.

va·cant (vā′kənt) *adj.* **1.** Containing nothing; unoccupied; empty. **2. a.** Lacking intelligence; stupid. **b.** Lacking expression; expressionless. **3.** Free from activity; idle. [< Lat. *vacare,* to be empty.] —**va′cant·ly** *adv.*

va·cate (vā′kāt′) *v.* **-cat·ed, -cat·ing. 1.** To make vacant. **2.** *Law.* To make void; annul. [Lat. *vacare,* to be empty.]

va·ca·tion (vā-kā′shən) *n.* A period of time devoted to rest or relaxation, as from work or study. —*v.* To take or spend a vacation. —**va·ca′tion·er** *n.*

vac·ci·nate (văk′sə-nāt′) *v.* **-nat·ed, -nat·ing.** To inoculate with a vaccine in order to give immunity against an infectious disease.

vac·ci·na·tion (văk′sə-nā′shən) *n.* **1.** The act of vaccinating. **2.** A scar left on the skin by vaccinating.

vac·cine (văk-sēn′) *n.* A suspension of weakened or killed microorganisms, as of viruses

or bacteria, used to vaccinate. [Fr. *(virus) vaccine,* (virus) of cowpox.]

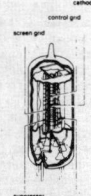

vaccination   vacuum tube

vac·il·late (văs′ə-lāt′) *v.* **-lat·ed, -lat·ing. 1.** To sway to and fro; oscillate. **2.** To waver indecisively between one course of action or opinion and another; waver. [Lat. *vacillare.*] —**vac′il·la′tion** *n.*

va·cu·i·ty (vă-kyōō′ĭ-tē) *n., pl.* **-ties. 1.** The state of being vacuous. **2.** An empty space; vacuum. **3.** Emptiness of mind. **4.** Something, as a remark, that is vacuous.

vac·u·ole (văk′yōō-ōl′) *n.* A small, usu. fluid-filled cavity in the protoplasm of a cell. [Fr.]

vac·u·ous (văk′yŏŏ-əs) *adj.* **1.** Devoid of matter; empty. **2.** Showing a lack of intelligence; stupid. [Lat. *vacuus.*] —**vac′u·ous·ly** *adv.* —**vac′u·ous·ness** *n.*

vac·u·um (văk′yŏŏ-əm, -yŏŏm) *n., pl.* -**ums** or -**u·a** (-yŏŏ-ə). **1.** A space relatively empty of matter. **2.** A state or feeling of emptiness; void. —*v.* To clean with a vacuum cleaner. [< Lat. *vacuus,* empty.]

vacuum cleaner *n.* An electrical appliance that cleans surfaces by means of suction.

vac·u·um-packed (văk′yŏŏ-əm-păkt′, -yŏŏm-, -yəm-) *adj.* Packed in a container with little or no air.

vacuum tube *n.* An electron tube that has an internal vacuum sufficiently high to permit electrons to move with little likelihood of striking any remaining gas molecules.

va·de me·cum (vā′dē mē′kəm) *n., pl.* **va·de me·cums.** Something useful, as a manual, carried about by a person. [Lat., go with me.]

vag·a·bond (văg′ə-bŏnd′) *n.* **1.** One without a permanent home who moves from place to place; wanderer. **2.** A tramp. [< Lat. *vagabundus,* wandering.] —**vag′a·bond** *adj.* —**vag′a·bond·age** *n.*

va·gar·y (və′gə-rē, və-gâr′ē) *n., pl.* -**ies.** A capricious or erratic notion or action; whim. [< Lat. *vagari,* to wander.] —**va·gar′i·ous** *adj.*

va·gi·na (və-jī′nə) *n., pl.* -**nas** or -**nae** (-nē). The passage leading from the external genital orifice to the uterus in female mammals. [Lat., sheath.] —**vag′i·nal** (văj′ə-nəl) *adj.*

va·grant (vā′grənt) *n.* **1.** One who wanders from place to place without a permanent home or livelihood. **2.** *Law.* A person, such as a drunkard, who constitutes a public nuisance. —*adj.* **1.** Wandering from place to place; roving. **2.** Not following a systematic course; random: *vagrant thoughts.* [Prob. < OFr. *wacrer,* to wander, of Gmc. orig.] —**va′gran·cy** *n.*

vague (vāg) *adj.* **vagu·er, vagu·est. 1.** Not clearly expressed or outlined. **2.** Lacking definite shape, form, or character; indistinct. **3.** Indistinctly perceived, understood, or recalled. [< Lat. *vagus.*] —**vague′ly** *adv.* —**vague′ness** *n.*

Syns: *vague, cloudy, foggy, fuzzy, hazy, indefinite, indistinct, misty, unclear* **adj.**

vain (vān) *adj.* -**er,** -**est. 1.** Not successful; futile. **2.** Lacking substance or worth; hollow. **3.** Showing undue preoccupation with one's appearance or accomplishments; conceited. —*idiom.* **in vain. 1.** To no avail; unsuccessfully. **2.** Irreverently or disrespectfully. [< Lat. *vanus.*] —**vain′ly** *adv.*

vain·glo·ry (vān′glôr′ē, -glōr′ē) *n., pl.* -**ries. 1.** Excessive pride and vanity. **2.** Vain and ostentatious display. —**vain·glo′ri·ous** *adj.*

val·ance (văl′əns) *n.* **1.** A short ornamental drapery hung along the top edge, as of a window or canopy. **2.** A decorative frame mounted esp. across the top of a window. [ME *valaunce.*]

vale (vāl) *n.* A valley; dale. [< Lat. *valles.*]

val·e·dic·tion (văl′ĭ-dĭk′shən) *n.* An act or expression of leave-taking. [< Lat. *valedicere,* to say farewell.]

val·e·dic·to·ri·an (văl′ĭ-dĭk-tôr′ē-ən, -tōr′-) *n.* The student, usu. ranking highest in the graduating class, who delivers the farewell address at commencement.

val·e·dic·to·ry (văl′ĭ-dĭk′tə-rē) *n., pl.* -**ries.** A farewell address, esp. at a commencement exercise. —**val′e·dic′to·ry** *adj.*

va·lence (vā′ləns) *n.* **1.** *Chem.* The capacity of an atom or group of atoms to combine in specific proportions with other atoms or groups of atoms. **2.** An integer used to represent this combinatorial capacity. [< Lat. *valēre,* to be strong.]

-valent *suff.* Having a specified valence or valences: *polyvalent.* [< VALENCE.]

val·en·tine (văl′ən-tīn′) *n.* **1.** A usu. sentimental card sent to a lover or friend on Saint Valentine's Day. **2.** A person singled out as one's sweetheart on Saint Valentine's Day.

val·et (văl′ĭt, vă-lā′) *n.* **1.** A male attendant who takes care of a man's clothing and performs personal services. **2.** A hotel employee who performs personal services for patrons. [< OFr. *vaslet,* servant.]

val·e·tu·di·nar·i·an (văl′ĭ-tōŏd′n-âr′ē-ən, -tyōŏd′-) *n.* A person who is constantly concerned with his health. [Lat. *valetudinarius.*] —**val′e·tu′di·nar′i·an·ism** *n.*

Val·hal·la (văl-hăl′ə) *n.* Norse Myth. The great hall of immortality in which the souls of warriors slain heroically were received by the god Odin and enshrined.

val·iant (văl′yənt) *adj.* Possessing, showing, or acting with valor; courageous. [< Lat. *valēre,* to be strong.] —**val′iance** *n.* —**val′iant·ly** *adv.*

val·id (văl′ĭd) *adj.* **1.** Founded on evidence or fact; sound: *a valid objection.* **2.** Legally sound and effective: *a valid passport.* [< Lat. *validus,* strong.] —**va·lid′i·ty** (və-lĭd′ĭ-tē) or **val′id·ness** *n.* —**val′id·ly** *adv.*

Syns: *valid, cogent, solid, sound* **adj.**

val·i·date (văl′ĭ-dāt′) *v.* -**dat·ed,** -**dat·ing. 1.** To make legally valid. **2.** To substantiate; verify. —**val′i·da′tion** *n.*

va·lise (və-lēs′) *n.* A small piece of hand luggage. [Fr. < Ital. *valigia.*]

Val·i·um (văl′ē-əm). A trademark for the tranquilizing drug diazepam.

Val·kyr·ie (văl-kîr′ē, -kī′rē) *n.* Norse Myth. Any of the god Odin's handmaids who hover over battlefields, choosing the heroes to be slain and then conducting their souls to Valhalla.

val·ley (văl′ē) *n., pl.* -**leys. 1.** A long, narrow lowland between ranges of mountains or hills. **2.** A place where two slopes of a roof meet and form a drainage channel. [< Lat. *valles.*]

val·or (văl′ər) *n.* Also *chiefly Brit.* **val·our.** Courage and boldness, as in battle; bravery. [< Lat. *valēre,* to be strong.] —**val′or·ous** *adj.*

val·u·a·ble (văl′yŏŏ-ə-bəl, văl′yə-) *adj.* **1.** Having high monetary or material value. **2.** Of great importance, use, or service. —*n.* Often **valuables.** A valuable personal possession, such as a piece of jewelry.

Syns: *valuable, invaluable, precious, priceless* **adj.**

val·u·ate (văl′yŏŏ-āt′) *v.* -**at·ed,** -**at·ing.** To put a value on; appraise. —**val′u·a′tor** *n.*

val·u·a·tion (văl′yŏŏ-ā′shən) *n.* **1.** The act or process of assessing the value or price of something; appraisal. **2.** The assessed or estimated value of something.

val·ue (văl′yŏŏ) *n.* **1.** A fair equivalent or return for something, as goods or services. **2.** Monetary or material worth. **3.** Worth as measured in usefulness or importance; merit. **4.** A principle, standard, or quality considered inherently worthwhile or desirable. **5.** Precise meaning, as of a word. **6.** An assigned or calculated numerical quantity. **7.** *Mus.* The relative duration of a tone or rest. **8.** The relative darkness or lightness of a color. **9.** The distinctive quality of a speech sound. —*v.* **-ued, -u·ing. 1.** To determine or estimate the value of; appraise. **2.** To regard highly; esteem. **3.** To rate according to relative worth or desirability; evaluate. [< OFr. *valoir*, to be worth.] —**val'ue·less** *adj.*

valve (vălv) *n.* **1.** A membranous bodily structure, as in a vein, that retards or prevents the return flow of a fluid. **2. a.** A mechanical device that regulates gas or liquid flow by blocking and uncovering openings. **b.** The movable control element of such a device. **c.** A device in a brass wind instrument that permits change in pitch through rapid variation of the air column in a tube. **3.** A paired or separable structure or part, as of a mollusk shell or seed pod. [< Lat. *valva*, leaf of a door.] —**valved** *adj.* —**val'vu·lar** (văl'vyə-lər) *adj.*

va·moose (vă-mōōs', vă-) *v.* **-moosed, -moos·ing.** *Slang.* To go away or leave hastily. [< Sp. *vamos*, let's go.]

vamp[1] (vămp) *n.* **1.** The part of a boot or shoe covering the instep and often the toes. **2.** An improvised musical accompaniment. —*v.* **1.** To provide with a new vamp. **2.** To patch up. **3.** To improvise. [< OFr. *avantpie*, sock.]

vamp[2] (vămp) *Informal.* —*n.* An unscrupulous woman who seduces or exploits men with her charms. —*v.* To seduce or exploit in the manner of a vamp. [< VAMPIRE.]

vam·pire (văm'pīr') *n.* **1.** A reanimated corpse that is believed to rise from the grave at night to suck the blood of sleeping persons. **2.** One who preys on others. **3.** Any of various tropical bats thought to feed on the blood of living mammals. [< G. *Vampir*, of Slav. orig.] —**vam'pir·ism** *n.*

van[1] (văn) *n.* **1.** An enclosed truck or wagon for transporting goods or livestock. **2.** *Chiefly Brit.* A closed railroad car for carrying baggage or freight. [< CARAVAN.]

van[2] (văn) *n.* The vanguard.

va·na·di·um (vă-nā'dē-əm) *n. Symbol* **V** A ductile metallic element used as a carbon stabilizer in some steels, as a titanium-steel bonding agent, and as a catalyst. Atomic number 23; atomic weight 50.942. [< ON *Vanadís*, Norse goddess of love and beauty.]

Van Al·len belt (văn ăl'ən) *n.* Either of two zones of high-intensity particulate radiation trapped in the earth's magnetic field and surrounding the planet at various high altitudes. [< James A. *Van Allen* (b. 1914).]

van·dal (văn'dl) *n.* **1.** One who willfully or maliciously defaces or destroys public or private property. **2. Vandal.** A member of a Germanic people who overran Gaul, Spain, northern Africa, and Rome in the 4th and 5th cent. A.D. [< Lat. *Vandalus*, Vandal, of Gmc. orig.]

van·dal·ism (văn'dl-ĭz'əm) *n.* The willful or malicious defacement or destruction of public or private property.

van·dal·ize (văn'dl-īz') *v.* **-ized, -iz·ing.** To de-

stroy or deface (public or private property) willfully or maliciously.

Van·dyke (văn-dīk') *n.* A short, pointed beard. [< Sir Anthony *Vandyke* (1599-1641).]

vane (vān) *n.* **1.** A device that pivots on a vertical spindle to indicate the direction of the wind. **2.** A thin, rigid surface radially mounted along an axis that is turned by or used to turn a fluid. **3.** A metal guidance or stabilizing fin attached to a missile, as the tail of a bomb. [< OE *fana*, flag.]

van·guard (văn'gärd') *n.* **1.** The foremost position in an army. **2.** The foremost or leading position in a trend or movement. [< OFr. *avant-garde.*]

va·nil·la (vă-nĭl'ə) *n.* **1.** Any of various tropical American orchids cultivated for its long, narrow seed pods. **2.** The seed pod of the vanilla. **3.** A flavoring extract obtained from the seed pod of the vanilla. [Sp. *vainilla*, dim. of *vaina*, sheath.]

van·ish (văn'ĭsh) *v.* **-ished, -ish·ing. 1.** To disappear or become invisible, esp. quickly. **2.** To pass out of existence. [< Lat. *evanescere.*] —**van'ish·er** *n.*

van·i·ty (văn'ĭ-tē) *n., pl.* **-ties. 1.** Excessive pride in one's appearance or accomplishments. **2.** The fact or quality of being useless or ineffective; futility. **3.** Something that is vain, futile, or worthless. **4.** A vanity case (sense 2). **5.** A dressing table. [< Lat. *vanus*, vain.]

vanity case *n.* A woman's compact. **2.** A small handbag or case used by women for carrying cosmetics or toiletries.

vanity plate *n.* An automobile license plate bearing a combination of letters or numbers selected by the purchaser.

vanity press *n.* A publisher that publishes a book at the expense of the author.

van·quish (văng'kwĭsh, văn'-) *v.* **1.** To defeat, as in a battle or contest. **2.** To overcome; subdue. [< Lat. *vincere.*] —**van'quish·er** *n.*

van·tage (văn'tĭj) *n.* **1.** An advantage in a competition or conflict; superiority. **2.** Something, as a strategic position, that provides superiority or an advantage. [< OFr. *avantage*, advantage.]

vap·id (văp'ĭd) *adj.* Lacking liveliness, zest, or interest; flat. [Lat. *vapidus*.] —**vap'id·i·ty** (vă-pĭd'ĭ-tē, və-) or **vap'id·ness** *n.* —**vap'id·ly** *adv.*

va·por (vā'pər) *n.* Also *chiefly Brit.* **va·pour. 1.** Fine particles of matter, as fog, suspended in the air. **2.** The gaseous state of a substance that is solid or liquid at normal temperatures. **3.** Something that is unsubstantial, worthless, or fleeting. **4. vapors.** *Archaic.* Depression or hysteria. —*v.* **1.** To give off vapor. **2.** To evaporate. [< Lat.] —**va'por·ish** *adj.*

va·por·ize (vā'pə-rīz') *v.* **-ized, -iz·ing.** To convert or be converted into vapor, esp. by heating. —**va'por·i·za'tion** *n.* —**va'por·iz'er** *n.*

vapor lock *n.* A pocket of vaporized gasoline in the fuel line of an internal-combustion engine that blocks normal flow of fuel.

va·por·ous (vā'pər-əs) *adj.* **1.** Pertaining to or resembling vapor. **2.** Producing vapors; volatile. **3.** Giving off or obscured by vapors; misty. **4.** Insubstantial, vague, or ethereal. —**va'por·ous·ly** *adv.* —**va'por·ous·ness** *n.*

var·i·a·ble (vâr′ē-ə-bəl) *adj.* **1. a.** Liable or likely to vary; changeable. **b.** Inconstant; fickle. **2.** *Biol.* Tending to deviate from an established type; aberrant. —*n.* **1.** Something that is variable. **2.** *Math.* **a.** A quantity capable of assuming any of a set of values. **b.** A symbol representing such a quantity. —**var′·a·bil′i·ty** or **var′i·a·ble·ness** *n.* —**var′i·a·bly** *adv.*

var·i·ance (vâr′ē-əns) *n.* **1. a.** Variation; difference. **b.** The degree of such variation. **2.** A difference of opinion; dispute. **3.** A license to engage in an act contrary to a usual rule.

var·i·ant (vâr′ē-ənt) *adj.* **1.** Exhibiting variation; differing. **2.** Liable to vary; variable. —*n.* Something exhibiting variation in form from another, as a different spelling of the same word.

var·i·a·tion (vâr′ē-ā′shən) *n.* **1.** The act, process, or result of varying. **2.** The extent or degree to which something varies. **3.** Something that is different from another of the same type. **4.** A repetition of a musical theme with changes in harmony, rhythm, or key and often melodic ornamentation.

var·i·col·ored (vâr′ĭ-kŭl′ərd) *adj.* Having a variety of colors.

var·i·cose (vâr′ĭ-kōs′) *adj.* Abnormally dilated and knotted. [< Lat. *varix,* swollen vein.]

var·i·cos·i·ty (vâr′ĭ-kŏs′ĭ-tē) *n., pl.* **-ties.** **1.** A part, as of a vein, that is varicose. **2.** The condition of being varicose.

var·ied (vâr′ēd) *adj.* **1.** Marked by variety; diverse. **2.** Modified; altered. **3.** Varicolored.

var·i·e·gate (vâr′ē-ĭ-gāt′) *v.* **-gat·ed, -gat·ing.** **1.** To change the appearance of, esp. by marking with different colors. **2.** To give variety to. [Lat. *variegare.*] —**var′i·e·ga′tion** *n.*

va·ri·e·ty (və-rī′ĭ-tē) *n., pl.* **-ties.** **1.** The condition or quality of being various or varied; diversity. **2.** A number or collection of different things; assortment. **3.** Something that is distinguished from other things by a specific characteristic or set of characteristics. **4.** An organism, esp. a plant, belonging to a naturally occurring or selectively bred subdivision of a species. [< Lat. *varius,* various.]

var·i·o·rum (vâr′ē-ôr′əm, -ōr′-) *n.* An edition or text, esp. of a classical author, with notes by various scholars or editors and often various versions of the text. [< Lat. *(editio cum notis) variorum,* (edition with the notes) of various persons.]

var·i·ous (vâr′ē-əs) *adj.* **1. a.** Of diverse kinds. **b.** Unlike; different. **2.** More than one; several. **3.** Individual and separate. **4.** Many-sided; versatile. [Lat. *varius.*] —**var′i·ous·ly** *adv.* —**var′i·ous·ness** *n.*

Usage: Various sometimes occurs as a collective noun followed by *of: He spoke to various of the members.* This usage is unacceptable to a great majority of the Usage Panel.

var·let (vär′lĭt) *n.* *Archaic.* **1.** An attendant. **2.** A rascal; knave. [< OFr.]

var·mint (vär′mĭnt) *n.* *Informal.* A person or animal considered undesirable, obnoxious, or troublesome. [< VERMIN.]

var·nish (vär′nĭsh) *n.* **1. a.** An oil-based liquid used to coat a surface with a thin, hard, glossy film. **b.** The smooth coating or finish that results from the application of varnish. **2.** Something that resembles varnish; gloss. **3.** A deceptively attractive external appearance: outward show. —*v.* **1.** To cover with varnish. **2.** To give a deceptively attractive appearance to; gloss. [< OFr. *vernis.*]

var·si·ty (vär′sĭ-tē) *n., pl.* **-ties.** **1.** The principal team representing a university, college, or school, as in sports. **2.** *Chiefly Brit. Slang.* A university. [< UNIVERSITY.]

var·y (vâr′ē) *v.* **-ied, -y·ing.** **1.** To cause or undergo change; modify or alter. **2.** To give variety to; diversify. **3.** To be different; deviate or depart. [< Lat. *variare.*]

vas·cu·lar (văs′kyə-lər) *adj.* Of, characterized by, or containing vessels for the circulation of fluids such as blood, lymph, or sap. [< Lat. *vasculum,* little vessel.]

vas def·er·ens (văs′ dĕf′ər-ənz, -ə-rĕnz′) *n.* The duct in male vertebrate animals that carries sperm from a testis to the ejaculatory duct. [NLat., vessel that carries off.]

vase (vās, vāz, väz) *n.* An open container, as of glass or porcelain, used for holding flowers or for ornamentation. [< Lat. *vas,* vessel.]

va·sec·to·my (vă-sĕk′tə-mē) *n., pl.* **-mies.** Surgical removal of a part of the vas deferens, used as a means of sterilization.

vaso– or **vas–** *pref.* **1.** Blood vessel: *vasoconstriction.* **2.** Vas deferens: *vasectomy.* [< Lat. *vas,* vessel.]

vas·o·con·stric·tion (văs′ō-kən-strĭk′shən) *n.* Constriction of a blood vessel. —**vas′o·con·stric′tor** *n.*

vas·o·dil·a·ta·tion (văs′ō-dĭl′ə-tā′shən, -dĭl′ə-) *n.* Dilatation of a blood vessel. —**vas′o·dil·a′tor** (-dĭl-lā′tər, -dī′-) *n.*

vas·o·mo·tor (văs′ō-mō′tər, vă′sō-) *adj.* Causing or regulating constriction or dilation of blood vessels.

vas·sal (văs′əl) *n.* **1.** One who holds land from a feudal lord and receives protection in return for homage and allegiance. **2.** A subordinate or dependent. [< Med. Lat. *vassus,* of Celt. orig.]

vas·sal·age (văs′ə-lĭj) *n.* **1.** The condition of being a vassal. **2.** The service, homage, and fealty required of a vassal. **3.** Subordination or subjection; servitude.

vast (văst) *adj.* **-er, -est.** Very great in size, amount, intensity, degree, or extent. [Lat. *vastus.*] —**vast′ly** *adv.* —**vast′ness** *n.*

vat (văt) *n.* A large vessel, as a tub or barrel, used to store or hold liquids. [< OE *fæt.*]

vat·ic (văt′ĭk) *adj.* Of or characteristic of a prophet; oracular. [< Lat. *vates,* prophet.]

Vat·i·can (văt′ĭ-kən) *n.* **1.** The official residence of the pope in Vatican City. **2.** The papal government; papacy.

vaude·ville (vôd′vĭl, vôd′-, vô′də-vĭl′) *n.* Stage entertainment consisting of a variety of short acts, as comedy and song-and-dance routines. [< OFr. *vaudevire.*] —**vaude·vil′lian** *n.*

vault¹ (vôlt) *n.* **1.** An arched structure, usu. of masonry, forming a ceiling or roof. **2.** Something resembling a vault. **3.** A room with arched walls and ceiling, esp. when underground, such as a storeroom. **4.** A room or compartment for the safekeeping of valuables.

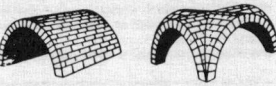

barrel vault   intersecting vault

vault¹

5. A burial chamber. —*v.* To construct, supply, or cover with a vault. [< OFr. *vaute*, ult. < Lat. *volvere*, to turn.]

vault² (vôlt) *v.* To jump or leap (over), esp. with the aid of a support, as the hands or a pole. —*n.* The act of vaulting; leap. [< OItal. *voltare*, ult. < Lat. *volvere*, to turn.] —**vault'er** *n.*

vaunt (vônt, vänt) *v.* To boast; brag. [< Lat. *vanus*, vain.] —**vaunt** *n.* —**vaunt'ing·ly** *adv.*

veal (vēl) *n.* The meat of a calf. [< Lat. *vitulus*, calf.]

vec·tor (vĕk'tər) *n.* **1.** *Math.* A quantity completely specified by a magnitude and a direction. **2.** An organism that carries pathogens from one host to another. [< Lat. *vectus*, p.p. of *vehere*, to carry.] —**vec·to'ri·al** (vĕk-tôr'ē-əl, -tōr'-) *adj.*

Ve·da (vā'də, vē'-) *n.* Any of the oldest sacred writings of Hinduism. [Skt. *vedaḥ.*] —**Ve'dic** *adj.*

Ve·dan·ta (vĭ-dän'tə, -dăn'-) *n.* The system of Hindu philosophy that further develops the implications in the Upanishads that all reality is a single principle. [Skt. *vedantaḥ,* essence of the Veda.]

veep (vēp) *n.* *Slang.* A vice president. [Pronunciation of *V.P.,* abbr. of *vice president.*]

veer (vĭr) *v.* To turn aside from a course, direction, or purpose; swerve. [OFr. *virer.*] —**veer** *n.*

veg·e·ta·ble (vĕj'tə-bəl, vĕj'ĭ-tə-) *n.* **1. a.** A usu. herbaceous plant cultivated for an edible part, as roots, stems, leaves, or flowers. **b.** The edible part of such a plant. **2.** An organism classified as a plant. **3.** A person who leads a monotonous, passive, or merely physical existence. [< LLat. *vegetabilis,* enlivening.] —**veg'e·ta·ble** *adj.*

veg·e·tar·i·an (vĕj'ĭ-târ'ē-ən) *n.* One whose diet consists of grains, plants, and plant products and who eats no meat. —*adj.* **1.** Eating only plants and plant products. **2.** Consisting only of plants and plant products: *a vegetarian diet.* [VEGET(ABLE) + -ARIAN.] —**veg'e·tar'i·an·ism** *n.*

veg·e·tate (vĕj'ĭ-tāt') *v.* **-tat·ed, -tat·ing. 1.** To grow, sprout, or exist as a plant does. **2.** To lead a monotonous, passive, or merely physical existence. [Lat. *vegetare,* to enliven.]

veg·e·ta·tion (vĕj'ĭ-tā'shən) *n.* **1.** The act or process of vegetating. **2.** Plant life collectively, esp. the plants of an area or region.

veg·e·ta·tive (vĕj'ĭ-tā'tĭv) *adj.* **1.** Of, pertaining to, or characteristic of plants or plant growth. **2.** *Biol.* **a.** Of, pertaining to, or capable of growth. **b.** Of, pertaining to, or functioning in processes such as growth or nutrition rather than sexual reproduction. **c.** Of or pertaining to asexual reproduction.

ve·he·ment (vē'ə-mənt) *adj.* **1.** Characterized by forcefulness of expression or intensity of emotion; ardent. **2.** Marked by vigor or energy; violent. [< Lat. *vehemens.*] —**ve'he·mence** *n.* —**ve'he·ment·ly** *adv.*

ve·hi·cle (vē'ĭ-kəl) *n.* **1.** A device for carrying passengers, goods, or equipment. **2.** A medium through which something is conveyed, transmitted, expressed, or achieved. **3.** A substance, such as oil, used as the medium in which active ingredients are applied or administered. [< Lat. *vehere,* to carry.] —**ve·hic'u·lar** (vē-hĭk'yə-lər) *adj.*

veil (vāl) *n.* **1.** A piece of often sheer cloth worn by women over the head, shoulders, and often part of the face. **2.** The vows or life of a nun: *take the veil.* **3.** Something that conceals or obscures: *a veil of secrecy.* —*v.* To cover, conceal, or disguise with or as if with a veil. [< Lat. *velum.*]

veil·ing (vā'lĭng) *n.* **1.** A veil. **2.** Gauzy material used for veils.

vein (vān) *n.* **1.** A vessel through which blood returns to the heart. **2.** One of the branching structures forming the framework of a leaf or an insect's wing. **3.** *Geol.* A long, regularly shaped deposit of an ore; lode. **4.** A long, wavy strip of color, as in marble. **5.** Inherent character or quality; strain. **6.** Style or mode of expression: *talk in a serious vein.* —*v.* To mark, form, or decorate with or as if with veins. [< Lat. *vena.*] —**veined** *adj.*

ve·lar (vē'lər) *adj.* Of or pertaining to a velum, esp. the soft palate.

Vel·cro (vĕl'krō) A trademark for a fastening tape used esp. for cloth products.

veldt (fĕlt, vĕlt) *n.* Also **veld.** Any of the open grasslands of southern Africa. [Afr. *veld.*]

vel·lum (vĕl'əm) *n.* **1.** A fine parchment made from the skins of calf, lamb, or kid and used for the pages and binding of fine books. **2.** A paper resembling vellum. [< OFr. *veel,* calf.]

ve·loc·i·ty (və-lŏs'ĭ-tē) *n., pl.* **-ties. 1.** Rapidity of motion; speed. **2.** *Physics.* The rate per unit of time at which an object moves in a specified direction. [< Lat. *velox,* swift.]

ve·lours or **ve·lour** (və-lōōr') *n., pl.* **-lours** (-lōōr'). A closely napped, velvetlike fabric. [< Lat. *villus,* shaggy hair.]

ve·lum (vē'ləm) *n., pl.* **-la** (-lə). A covering or partition of thin membranous tissue. [< Lat. *veil.*]

vel·vet (vĕl'vĭt) *n.* **1.** A fabric that has a smooth, dense pile and a plain back. **2.** Something resembling velvet, as in smoothness or softness. **3.** The soft covering on the newly developing antlers of deer. [< Lat. *villus,* shaggy hair.] —**vel'vet·y** *adj.*

vel·vet·een (vĕl'vĭ-tēn') *n.* A velvetlike fabric made of cotton. [< VELVET.]

ve·nal (vē'nəl) *adj.* Open to, marked by, or susceptible to bribery; corrupt or corruptible. [< Lat. *venum,* sale.] —**ve·nal'i·ty** (vē-năl'ĭ-tē) *n.* —**ve'nal·ly** *adv.*

ve·na·tion (vē-nā'shən, vĕ-) *n.* The distribution, arrangement, or system of veins. [< Lat. *vena,* vein.]

vend (vĕnd) *v.* To sell, esp. by peddling. [< Lat. *vendere.*]

vend·er (vĕn'dər) *n.* Also **ven·dor. 1.** One who vends; peddler. **2.** A vending machine.

ven·det·ta (vĕn-dĕt'ə) *n.* A bitter feud, esp. between two families. [Ital., revenge.]

vending machine *n.* A coin-operated machine that dispenses small articles.

ve·neer (və-nîr') *n.* **1.** A thin layer of material bonded to and used esp. to cover an inferior material underneath. **2.** Surface show; gloss. —*v.* To overlay with a veneer. [< OFr. *fournir,* to furnish.]

ven·er·a·ble (vĕn'ər-ə-bəl) *adj.* **1.** Worthy of reverence or respect by virtue of dignity, posi-

---

tion, or age. **2.** Commanding respect or reverence by association. [< Lat. *venerari*, to venerate.] —**ven′er·a·bil′i·ty** *n.*

ven·er·ate (vĕn′ə-rāt′) *v.* **-at·ed, -at·ing.** To regard with respect or reverence. [Lat. *venerari.*] —**ven′er·a′tion** *n.*

ve·ne·re·al (və-nîr′ē-əl) *adj.* Of, pertaining to, or transmitted by sexual intercourse. [< Lat. *Venus*, Venus.]

venereal disease *n.* A contagious disease, as syphilis or gonorrhea, transmitted by sexual intercourse.

Ve·ne·tian blind (və-nē′shən) *n.* A window blind consisting of thin horizontal slats that may be raised and lowered and set at a desired angle to regulate the amount of light admitted. [< *Venetian*, of Venice.]

venge·ance (vĕn′jəns) *n.* Retaliation for a wrong or injury; retribution. [< Lat. *vindicare*, to avenge.]

venge·ful (vĕnj′fəl) *adj.* Desiring vengeance; vindictive. —**venge′ful·ly** *adv.* —**venge′ful·ness** *n.*

ve·ni·al (vē′nē-əl, vēn′yəl) *adj.* Capable of being excused or forgiven; pardonable. [< Lat. *venia*, forgiveness.]

ve·ni·re (və-nī′rē) *n.* **1.** A writ summoning prospective jurors. **2.** A panel from which a jury is selected. [< Lat., to come.]

ve·ni·re·man (və-nī′rē-mən) *n.* A person summoned by a venire.

ven·i·son (vĕn′ĭ-sən, -zən) *n.* The flesh of a deer used for food. [< Lat. *venatio*, hunting.]

ven·om (vĕn′əm) *n.* **1.** A poisonous secretion of some animals, as certain snakes or spiders, usu. transmitted by a bite or sting. **2.** Deep hatred; spite. [< Lat. *venenum*, poison.]

ven·om·ous (vĕn′ə-məs) *adj.* **1.** Secreting venom: *a venomous snake.* **2.** Full of venom. **3.** Malicious; spiteful. —**ven′om·ous·ly** *adv.*

ve·nous (vē′nəs) *adj.* **1.** Of or pertaining to veins. **2.** Returning to the heart through the great veins. [< Lat. *vena*, vein.]

vent¹ (vĕnt) *n.* **1.** A means of passage or escape; outlet. **2.** An opening permitting passage or escape, as of a liquid or gas. —*v.* **1.** To discharge through a vent. **2.** To provide with a vent. **3.** To give expression to. [< OFr. *esventer*, to let out air.]

vent² (vĕnt) *n.* A slit at the bottom of a seam, as in a skirt. [< Lat. *findere*, to split.]

ven·ti·late (vĕn′tl-āt′) *v.* **-lat·ed, -lat·ing.** **1.** To admit fresh air into in order to replace stale air. **2.** To circulate (air) through in order to freshen. **3.** To provide with a vent or a similar means of airing. **4.** To expose to public discussion or examination. **5.** To vent: *ventilated her grievances.* [< Lat. *ventilare*, to fan.] —**ven′ti·la′tion** *n.* —**ven′ti·la′tor** *n.*

ven·tral (vĕn′trəl) *adj.* **1.** Of or pertaining to the belly; abdominal. **2.** Of, pertaining to, or situated on or near the anterior part of the human body or the lower surface of the body of an animal. [< Lat. *venter*, belly.] —**ven′tral·ly** *adv.*

ven·tri·cle (vĕn′trĭ-kəl) *n.* A cavity or chamber in an organ, esp. either of the chambers of the heart that contract to pump blood into arteries. [< Lat. *venter*, belly.] —**ven·tric′u·lar** (vĕn-trĭk′yə-lər) *adj.*

ven·tril·o·quism (vĕn-trĭl′ə-kwĭz′əm) *n.* The art or practice of producing vocal sounds so that they seem to come from a source other than the speaker. [< LLat. *ventriloquus*, speaking from the belly.] —**ven·tril′o·quist** *n.*

ven·tril·o·quy (vĕn-trĭl′ə-kwē) *n.* Ventriloquism.

ven·ture (vĕn′chər) *n.* **1.** An undertaking or course of action that involves risk or uncertainty. **2.** Something at risk in a venture; stake. —*v.* **-tured, -tur·ing.** **1.** To expose to danger; risk. **2.** To brave the dangers of. **3.** To express at the risk of denial, criticism, or censure. **4.** To take a risk; dare. [< ME *aventure*, adventure.] —**ven′tur·er** *n.*

ven·ture·some (vĕn′chər-səm) *adj.* **1.** Inclined to take risks; daring. **2.** Involving risk or danger; hazardous. —**ven′ture·some·ly** *adv.* —**ven′ture·some·ness** *n.*

ven·tur·ous (vĕn′chər-əs) *adj.* Venturesome. —**ven′tur·ous·ly** *adv.* —**ven′tur·ous·ness** *n.*

ven·ue (vĕn′yōō) *n.* **1.** The locality where a crime is committed or a cause of legal action occurs. **2.** The locality from which a jury must be called and in which a trial must be held. [< OFr. *venir*, to come.]

Ve·nus (vē′nəs) *n.* **1.** *Rom. Myth.* The goddess of love and beauty. **2.** The second planet from the sun, having an average radius of 3,800 miles, a mass 0.816 times that of Earth, and a sidereal period of revolution about the sun of 224.7 days at a mean distance of approx. 67.2 million miles. —**Ve·nu′sian** (vĭ-nōō′zhən, -nyōō′-) *adj.*

Venus
Detail of "Venus and Adonis" by Veronese

Ve·nus's-fly·trap (vē′nə-sĭz-flī′trăp′) *n.* A plant of boggy areas of the southeastern United States that has hinged leaf blades edged with needlelike bristles that close and entrap insects.

ve·ra·cious (və-rā′shəs) *adj.* **1.** Honest; truthful. **2.** Accurate; precise. [< Lat. *verax.*] —**ve·ra′cious·ly** *adv.* —**ve·ra′cious·ness** *n.*

ve·rac·i·ty (və-răs′ĭ-tē) *n.*, *pl.* **-ties.** **1.** Adherence to the truth; truthfulness. **2.** Conformity to truth or fact; accuracy. **3.** Something that is true. [< Lat. *verax*, true.]

ve·ran·dah or **ve·ran·da** (və-răn′də) *n.* An open porch, usu. roofed, extending along the outside of a building. [Hindi.]

verb (vûrb) *n.* Any of a class of words that express existence, action, or occurrence. [< Lat. *verbum*, word.]

ver·bal (vûr′bəl) *adj.* **1.** Of, pertaining to, or associated with words. **2.** Concerned with words rather than with the facts or ideas they represent. **3.** Expressed in speech; unwritten. **4.** Literal; word for word. **5.** Of, pertaining to, or derived from a verb. —*n.* A noun or adjective derived from a verb and preserving some of the verb's characteristics. [< Lat. *verbum*, word.] —**ver′bal·ly** *adv.*

ver·bal·ize (vûr′bə-līz′) v. **-ized, -iz·ing. 1.** To express in words. **2.** To convert (e.g. a noun) to verbal use. **3.** To be verbose. **—ver′bal·i·za′tion** n.

ver·ba·tim (vər-bā′tĭm) adv. & adj. Word for word; in the same words. [< Med. Lat.]

ver·be·na (vər-bē′nə) n. Any of various plants cultivated for their showy clusters of variously colored, often fragrant flowers. [< Lat., sacred bough.]

ver·bi·age (vûr′bē-ĭj) n. **1.** Excess words; wordiness. **2.** Wording; diction. [< Lat. verbum, word.]

ver·bose (vər-bōs′) adj. Using words in excess of those needed for clarity or precision; wordy. [Lat. verbosus.] **—ver·bos′i·ty** (-bŏs′-ĭ-tē) n.

ver·bo·ten (fər-bōt′n) adj. Strictly forbidden. [G.]

ver·dant (vûr′dənt) adj. **1.** Green with vegetation. **2.** Inexperienced or unsophisticated; green. [< OFr. verd, green.] **—ver′dan·cy** n. **—ver′dant·ly** adv.

ver·dict (vûr′dĭkt) n. **1.** The decision reached by a jury at the conclusion of a trial. **2.** A judgment; conclusion. [< OFr. veirdit.]

ver·di·gris (vûr′dĭ-grēs′, -grĭs) n. A green patina or crust of copper sulfate or copper chloride formed on copper, brass, and bronze exposed to air or sea water for long periods of time. [< OFr. vert-de-Grice, green of Greece.]

ver·dure (vûr′jər) n. **1.** The fresh, vibrant greenness of flourishing vegetation. **2.** Green vegetation. [< OFr. verd, green.]

verge¹ (vûrj) n. **1.** An edge, rim, or margin. **2.** The point beyond which an action or condition is likely to begin or occur; brink. **3.** A rod or staff carried as an emblem of authority or office. **—v.** verged, verg·ing. To border on; approach. [< Lat. virga, rod.]

verge² (vûrj) v. verged, verg·ing. **1.** To slope or incline. **2.** To be in the process of becoming something else. [Lat. vergere.]

verg·er (vûr′jər) n. **1.** One who carries a verge, as before a religious dignitary in a procession. **2.** Chiefly Brit. One in charge of the interior of a church.

ver·i·fy (vĕr′ə-fī′) v. **-fied, -fy·ing. 1.** To prove the truth of; substantiate. **2.** To determine or test the truth or accuracy of. [< Med. Lat. verificare.] **—ver′i·fi′a·ble** adj. **—ver′i·fi·ca′tion** n. **—ver′i·fi′er** n.

ver·i·ly (vĕr′ə-lē) adv. **1.** In truth; in fact. **2.** With confidence; assuredly. [< ME verray, true.]

ver·i·si·mil·i·tude (vĕr′ĭ-sə-mĭl′ĭ-tōōd′, -tyōōd′) n. **1.** The quality of appearing to be true or real; likelihood. **2.** Something that has the appearance of being true or real. [Lat. verisimilitudo.]

ver·i·ta·ble (vĕr′ĭ-tə-bəl) adj. Unquestionable; true or genuine. [< Lat. verus, true.] **—ver′i·ta·bly** adv.

ver·i·ty (vĕr′ĭ-tē) n., pl. **-ties. 1.** The condition or quality of being real, accurate, or correct. **2.** A true statement, principle, or belief. [< Lat. veritas.]

ver·mell n. **1.** (vûr′mĭl). Vermilion. **2.** (vĕr-mā′). Gilded metal, such as silver, bronze, or copper. [< LLat. vermiculus.]

ver·mi·cel·li (vûr′mə-chĕl′ē, -sĕl′ē) n. Pasta made into long threads thinner than spaghetti. [Ital.]

ver·mic·u·lite (vər-mĭk′yə-līt′) n. Any of a group of minerals of varying composition related to the chlorites and used esp. as heat insulation. [Lat. vermiculus, small worm + -ITE.]

ver·mi·form (vûr′mə-fôrm′) adj. Resembling or having the shape of a worm. [Lat. vermis, worm + -FORM.]

vermiform appendix n. The appendix.

ver·mi·fuge (vûr′mə-fyōōj′) n. An agent that expels or destroys intestinal worms. [Lat. vermis, worm + Lat. fuga, flight.]

ver·mil·ion (vər-mĭl′yən) n. Also **ver·mil·lion.** A vivid red to reddish orange color. [< LLat. vermiculus, a kind of red worm.]

ver·min (vûr′mĭn) n., pl. **vermin.** Any of various small animals or insects, such as cockroaches or rats, that are destructive, annoying, or injurious to health. [< Lat. vermis, worm.] **—ver′min·ous** adj.

ver·mouth (vər-mōōth′) n. A white wine flavored with aromatic herbs. [< G. Wermut.]

ver·nac·u·lar (vər-năk′yə-lər) n. **1.** The native language of a country or region, esp. as distinct from literary language. **2.** The idiom of a particular trade or profession: the legal vernacular. [< Lat. vernaculus, native.] **—ver·nac′u·lar** adj.

ver·nal (vûr′nəl) adj. Of, pertaining to, or occurring in the spring. [< Lat. ver, spring.] **—ver′nal·ly** adv.

ver·ni·er (vûr′nē-ər) n. A small scale attached to a main scale to indicate fractional parts of the subdivisions of the main scale. [< Pierre Vernier (1580–1637).]

ve·ron·i·ca (və-rŏn′ĭ-kə) n. The speedwell. [Perh. < the name Veronica.]

ver·sa·tile (vûr′sə-təl, -tĭl′) adj. **1.** Capable of doing many things competently. **2.** Having varied uses or functions. [< Lat. vertere, to turn.] **—ver′sa·til′i·ty** n.

verse (vûrs) n. **1.** Writing arranged according to a metrical pattern; poetry. **2. a.** One line of poetry. **b.** A stanza. **3.** A specific type of metrical composition, as blank verse. **4.** One of the numbered subdivisions of a chapter in the Bible. [< Lat. versus, a line of poetry.]

versed (vûrst) adj. Practiced or skilled; knowledgeable. [< Lat. versari, to occupy oneself.]

ver·si·cle (vûr′sĭ-kəl) n. A verse or sentence spoken or chanted by a priest and followed by a response from the congregation. [< Lat. versiculus.]

ver·si·fy (vûr′sə-fī′) v. **-fied, -fy·ing. 1.** To change from prose into metrical form. **2.** To write verses. [< Lat. versificare.] **—ver′si·fi·ca′tion** n. **—ver′si·fi′er** n.

ver·sion (vûr′zhən, -shən) n. **1.** A description, narration, or account related from a specific point of view. **2.** A translation, esp. of the Bible or of a part of it. **3.** A form or variation of an earlier or original model. **4.** An adaptation of a work of art or literature into another medium or style. [< Lat. vertere, to turn.]

vers li·bre (vĕr lē′brə) n. Free verse. [Fr.]

ver·so (vûr′sō) n., pl. **-sos.** A left-hand page,

as of a book. [Lat. *verso (folio)*, (with the page) turned.]

ver·sus (vûr′səs) *prep.* 1. Against: *the plaintiff versus the defendant.* 2. In contrast with: *death versus dishonor.* [< Lat. *versus,* toward.]

ver·te·bra (vûr′tə-brə) *n., pl.* **-brae** (-brē) or **-bras.** Any of the bones or cartilaginous segments forming the spinal column. [Lat.] **—ver′te·bral** *adj.*

ver·te·brate (vûr′tə-brāt′, -brĭt) *adj.* 1. Having a backbone or spinal column. 2. Of or characteristic of the vertebrates. —*n.* Any of a group of animals, including the fishes, amphibians, reptiles, birds, and mammals, having a segmented bony or cartilaginous spinal column.

ver·tex (vûr′tĕks′) *n., pl.* **-es** or **-ti·ces** (-tĭ-sēz′). 1. The highest point of something; summit. 2. **a.** The point at which the sides of an angle intersect. **b.** The point on a triangle opposite to and farthest away from its base. **c.** A point on a polyhedron common to three or more sides. [Lat. < *vertere,* to turn.]

ver·ti·cal (vûr′tĭ-kəl) *adj.* 1. Perpendicular to the plane of the horizon; directly upright. 2. Of, pertaining to, or situated at the vertex; directly overhead. —*n.* 1. Something, as a line, that is vertical. 2. A vertical position. [< Lat. *vertex,* vertex.] **—ver′ti·cal′i·ty** (-kăl′ĭ-tē) or **ver′ti·cal·ness** *n.* **—ver′ti·cal·ly** *adv.*

ver·tig·i·nous (vər-tĭj′ə-nəs) *adj.* 1. Turning about an axis; revolving. 2. Affected by or tending to produce vertigo; dizzy. [< Lat. *vertigo,* vertigo.] **—ver·tig′i·nous·ly** *adv.*

ver·ti·go (vûr′tĭ-gō′) *n., pl.* **-goes** or **ver·tig·i·nes** (vər-tĭj′ə-nēz′). The sensation of dizziness; giddiness. [Lat. < *vertere,* to turn.]

ver·vain (vûr′vān′) *n.* Any of several plants with slender spikes of small blue, purplish, or white flowers. [< Lat. *verbena,* sacred bough.]

verve (vûrv) *n.* 1. Energy and enthusiasm, as in artistic performance or composition. 2. Liveliness or vivacity; animation. [< OFr., fanciful expression.]

ver·y (vĕr′ē) *adv.* 1. In a high degree; extremely: *very happy.* 2. Truly; absolutely: *the very best way to proceed.* 3. Precisely: *the very same one.* —*adj.* **-i·er, -i·est.** 1. Absolute; utter: *the very end.* 2. Identical; selfsame: *the very questions he asked.* 3. Used as an intensive to emphasize identity: *The very mountains shook.* 4. Precise; exact: *the very center of town.* 5. Mere: *The very mention of the name was frightening.* 6. Actual: *caught in the very act.* [< Lat. *verus,* true.]

very high frequency *n.* A band of radio frequencies between 30 and 300 megahertz.

very low frequency *n.* A band of radio frequencies between 3 and 30 kilohertz.

ves·i·cant (vĕs′ĭ-kənt) *n.* An agent, as mustard gas, that causes blistering. [< Lat. *vesica,* blister.] **—ves′i·cant** *adj.*

ves·i·cle (vĕs′ĭ-kəl) *n.* 1. A small bladderlike cell or cavity. 2. A blister. [< Lat. *vesica,* bladder.] **—ve·sic′u·lar** (və-sĭk′yə-lər) *adj.*

ves·per (vĕs′pər) *n.* 1. **vespers.** A worship service held in the late afternoon or evening. 2. A bell used to summon persons to vespers. 3. *Poet. & Archaic.* Evening. [Lat., evening.]

ves·per·tine (vĕs′pər-tīn′) *adj.* 1. Of, pertaining to, or appearing in the evening. 2. Blooming or becoming active in the evening. [< Lat. *vesper,* evening.]

ves·sel (vĕs′əl) *n.* 1. A ship, large boat, or similar craft. 2. A hollow container, as a

bowl, pitcher, jar, or tank; receptacle. 3. A person considered as a receptacle or agent of a particular quality. 4. *Anat.* A duct or other narrow tube for containing or circulating a bodily fluid. [< Lat. *vas,* container.]

vest (vĕst) *n.* 1. A sleeveless garment, usu. fastening in front, often worn under a suit coat or jacket. 2. *Chiefly Brit.* An undershirt. —*v.* 1. To clothe or dress, esp. with ecclesiastical robes or vestments. 2. To place in the possession of: *vested his estate in his daughter.* 3. To invest with authority or power: *vesting the President with executive powers.* [< Lat. *vestis,* garment.] **—vest′ed** *adj.*

Ves·ta (vĕs′tə) *n. Rom. Myth.* The goddess of the hearth.

ves·tal (vĕs′təl) *adj.* Chaste; pure. —*n.* A woman who is chaste. [< VESTA.]

vested interest *n.* 1. A strong concern for something, such as an institution, from which one expects private benefit. 2. A group that has a vested interest.

ves·ti·bule (vĕs′tə-byōōl′) *n.* 1. A small entrance hall or lobby. 2. An enclosed area at the end of a railroad passenger car. 3. A chamber, opening, or bodily channel that serves as an entrance to another chamber or cavity. [< Lat. *vestibulum.*] **—ves·tib′u·lar** (vĕ-stĭb′yə-lər) *adj.*

ves·tige (vĕs′tĭj) *n.* A visible trace, evidence, or sign of something that no longer exists or appears. [< Lat. *vestigium,* footprint.]

ves·tig·i·al (vĕ-stĭj′ē-əl, -stĭj′əl) *adj.* 1. Of, relating to, or constituting a vestige. 2. Occurring or persisting as a rudimentary or degenerate bodily structure. **—ves·tig′i·al·ly** *adv.*

vest·ment (vĕst′mənt) *n.* 1. A garment, esp. a robe or gown worn as an indication of office. 2. Any of the ritual robes worn by clergymen or assistants at ecclesiastical ceremonies. [< Lat. *vestis,* garment.]

vest-pock·et (vĕst′pŏk′ĭt) *adj.* Small.

ves·try (vĕs′trē) *n., pl.* **-tries.** 1. A room in a church where vestments and sacred objects are stored; sacristy. 2. A meeting room in a church. 3. A committee that administers the temporal affairs of an Episcopal parish. [< Lat. *vestis,* garment.]

ves·try·man (vĕs′trē-mən) *n.* A member of a vestry.

ves·ture (vĕs′chər) *n.* 1. Clothing; apparel. 2. Something that covers or cloaks. [< Lat. *vestis,* garment.]

vet (vĕt) *n. Informal.* 1. A veterinarian. 2. A veteran.

vetch (vĕch) *n.* A climbing or twining plant with featherlike leaves and usu. purple flowers. [< Lat. *vicia.*]

vet·er·an (vĕt′ər-ən, vĕt′rən) *n.* 1. One of long experience in a given activity or capacity. 2. A former member of the armed forces. [< Lat. *vetus,* old.]

Veterans Day *n.* Nov. 11, a holiday celebrated in memory of the armistice ending World War I in 1918 and in honor of veterans of the armed services.

vet·er·i·nar·i·an (vĕt′ər-ə-nâr′ē-ən, vĕt′rə-) *n.* One trained and authorized to treat animals medically.

vet·er·i·nar·y (vĕt′ər-ə-nĕr′ē, vĕt′rə-) *adj.* Of or relating to the diagnosis and treatment of animals. —*n., pl.* **-ies.** A veterinarian. [< Lat. *veterinae,* beasts of burden.]

ve·to (vē′tō) *n., pl.* **-toes.** 1. **a.** The vested

power or constitutional right of a branch of government, esp. of a chief executive, to reject a bill passed by a legislative body and thus prevent or delay its enactment into law. **b.** The exercise of this right. **2.** An authoritative prohibition or rejection of a proposed or intended act. —*v.* **-toed, -to·ing. 1.** To prevent (a legislative bill) from becoming law by exercising the power of veto. **2.** To refuse to consent to; prohibit. [< Lat., I forbid.]

vex (věks) *v.* **1.** To irritate or annoy; bother. **2.** To baffle; puzzle. **3.** To debate at length. [< Lat. *vexare.*]

vex·a·tion (věk-sā′shən) *n.* **1.** The condition of being vexed; annoyance. **2.** One that vexes. —**vex·a′tious** *adj.* —**vex·a′tious·ly** *adv.*

vi·a (vī′ə, vē′ə) *prep.* By way of. [< Lat., road.]

vi·a·ble (vī′ə-bəl) *adj.* **1.** Capable of living or developing under normal or favorable conditions. **2.** Capable of success or continuing effectiveness; practicable. [< Lat. *vita,* life.] —**vi′a·bil′i·ty** *n.* —**vi′a·bly** *adv.*

vi·a·duct (vī′ə-dŭkt′) *n.* A series of spans or arches used to carry a road or railroad over something, as a valley or road. [Lat. *via,* road + (AQUA)DUCT.]

vi·al (vī′əl) *n.* A small container for liquids. [< Gk. *phialē,* shallow vessel.]

vi·and (vī′ənd) *n.* **1.** An article of food. **2.** **-ands.** Provisions; victuals. [< Lat. *vivere,* to live.]

vi·at·i·cum (vī-ăt′ĭ-kəm) *n., pl.* **-ca** (-kə) or **-cums.** The Eucharist given to a dying person or one in danger of death. [Lat., traveling provisions.]

vibes (vībz) *pl.n.* **1.** *Informal.* A vibraphone. **2.** *Slang.* Vibrations (sense 4).

vi·brant (vī′brənt) *adj.* **1.** Showing, marked by, or resulting from vibration; vibrating. **2.** Full of vigor or energy. —**vi′bran·cy** *n.* —**vi′brant·ly** *adv.*

vi·bra·phone (vī′brə-fōn′) *n.* A musical instrument similar to a marimba but with metal bars and rotating disks in the resonators to produce a vibrato. [VIBRA(TE) + -PHONE.] —**vi′bra·phon′ist** *n.*

vibraphone

viburnum

vi·brate (vī′brāt′) *v.* **-brat·ed, -brat·ing. 1.** To move or cause to move back and forth rapidly. **2.** To produce a sound; resonate. **3.** To be moved emotionally; thrill. **4.** To fluctuate; waver. [Lat. *vibrare.*] —**vi′bra′tor** *n.* —**vi′bra·to′ry** (-brə-tôr′ē, -tōr′ē) *adj.*

vi·bra·tion (vī-brā′shən) *n.* **1. a.** The act of vibrating. **b.** The condition of being vibrated. **2.** A rapid linear motion of a particle or of an elastic solid about an equilibrium position. **3.** A single complete vibrating motion. **4. vi·brations.** *Slang.* A distinctive emotional aura or atmosphere capable of being instinctively sensed or experienced. —**vi·bra′tion·al** *adj.*

vi·bra·to (vĭ-brä′tō, vē-) *n., pl.* **-tos.** *Mus.* A small, moderately rapid back-and-forth variation in the pitch of a musical tone that produces a tremulous or pulsating effect. [Ital.]

vi·bur·num (vī-bûr′nəm) *n.* Any of various shrubs or trees having clusters of small white flowers and berrylike red or black fruit. [Lat. *viburnum.*]

vic·ar (vĭk′ər) *n.* **1.** An Anglican clergyman in charge of a parish. **2.** One who represents another; deputy. [< Lat. *vicarius,* a substitute.] —**vi·car′i·al** (vī-kâr′ē-əl) *adj.*

vic·ar·age (vĭk′ər-ĭj) *n.* The residence or benefice of a vicar.

vicar general *n., pl.* **vicars general.** An administrative deputy to a Roman Catholic bishop.

vi·car·i·ous (vī-kâr′ē-əs, vĭ-) *adj.* **1.** Experienced or undergone through sympathetic participation in the experience or feelings of another. **2.** Endured or done by one person substituting for another. **3.** Acting for another. [Lat. *vicarius,* substituting.] —**vi·car′i·ous·ly** *adv.* —**vi·car′i·ous·ness** *n.*

vice[1] (vīs) *n.* **1.** Evil, wickedness, or great immorality. **2.** An evil or immoral practice or habit. **3.** A personal failing; shortcoming. **4.** A flaw or imperfection; defect. [< Lat. *vitium.*]

vice[2] (vīs) *adj.* Acting or having the authority to act as a deputy or substitute for another: *a vice chairman.* —*prep.* **vi·ce** (vī′sē). In place of; replacing. [< Lat. *vicis,* change.]

vice[3] (vīs) *n.* Var. of **vise.**

vice admiral *n.* A naval officer ranking next below an admiral.

vi·cen·ni·al (vī-sěn′ē-əl) *adj.* Happening once every 20 years. [< LLat. *vicennium,* period of 20 years.]

vice president *n.* **1.** An officer ranking next below a president, usu. empowered to assume the president's duties under such conditions as absence, illness, or death. **2.** A deputy of a president, esp. in a corporation, who is in charge of a separate department or location. —**vice-pres′i·den·cy** *n.*

vice·re·gal (vīs-rē′gəl) *adj.* Of or relating to a viceroy.

vice·roy (vīs′roi′) *n.* The governor of a country, province, or colony who rules as the representative of a sovereign or king. [Fr. *viceroi.*] —**vice′roy′al·ty** *n.*

vi·ce ver·sa (vī′sə vûr′sə, vīs vûr′-) *adv.* With the reverse being so; conversely. [Lat., the position being reversed.]

vi·chys·soise (vĭsh′ē-swäz′, vē′shē-) *n.* A thick, creamy potato soup flavored with leeks or onions and usu. served cold. [Fr. < *Vichy,* a town in France.]

vic·i·nage (vĭs′ə-nĭj) *n.* A neighborhood or vicinity. [< Lat. *vicinus,* neighboring.]

vi·cin·i·ty (vĭ-sĭn′ĭ-tē) *n., pl.* **-ties. 1.** The condition of being near; proximity. **2.** A nearby or surrounding area; neighborhood. [< Lat. *vicinus,* neighboring.]

vi·cious (vĭsh′əs) *adj.* **1.** Cruel; malicious.

ă pat ā pay â care ä father ĕ pet ē be ĭ pit ī tie î pier ŏ pot ō toe ô paw, for oi noise ŏŏ took ōō boot ou out th thin *th* this ŭ cut û urge yŏŏ abuse zh vision ə about, item, edible, gallop, circus

2. Evil; wicked. **3.** Savage and dangerous. **4.** Violent; intense. **5.** Characterized by a tendency to worsen. [< Lat. *vitium*, evil.] —**vi′cious·ly** *adv.* —**vi′cious·ness** *n.*

vi·cis·si·tude (vĭ-sĭs′ĭ-tōōd′, -tyōōd′) *n.* **1.** The quality of being changeable; mutability. **2.** Often **vicissitudes.** A sudden or unexpected change or shift. [< Lat. *vicis*, change.]

vic·tim (vĭk′tĭm) *n.* **1.** One who is harmed or killed, as by accident or disease. **2.** One who is tricked, swindled, or injured. **3.** A living being offered as a sacrifice to a deity. [Lat. *victima.*]

vic·tim·ize (vĭk′tə-mīz′) *v.* **-ized, -iz·ing.** To make a victim of. —**vic′tim·i·za′tion** *n.* —**vic′tim·iz′er** *n.*

vic·tim·less (vĭk′tĭm-lĭs) *adj.* Of or pertaining to a crime having no victim.

vic·tor (vĭk′tər) *n.* The winner in a fight, battle, contest, or struggle. [< Lat.]

vic·to·ri·a (vĭk-tôr′ē-ə, -tōr′-) *n.* A low four-wheeled carriage for two with a folding top and an elevated driver's seat in front. [< Queen *Victoria* of England (1819–1901).]

Vic·to·ri·an (vĭk-tôr′ē-ən, -tōr′-) *adj.* **1.** Pertaining or belonging to the period of the reign of Queen Victoria of Great Britain. **2.** Exhibiting qualities usu. associated with the time of Queen Victoria, as prudishness or pompous conservatism. **3.** Being in the highly ornamented, massive style of architecture, decor, and furnishings popular in the 19th-cent. England. —*n.* A person of the Victorian period.

vic·to·ri·ous (vĭk-tôr′ē-əs, -tōr′-) *adj.* **1.** Being the winner in a contest or struggle. **2.** Of, characteristic of, or expressing victory. —**vic′to·ri·ous·ly** *adv.* —**vic′to·ri·ous·ness** *n.*

vic·to·ry (vĭk′tə-rē) *n., pl.* **-ries. 1.** A successful struggle against an opponent or obstacle; triumph. **2.** Final and complete defeat of an enemy in a military engagement.

Syns: *victory, conquest, triumph, win n.*

vict·ual (vĭt′l) *n.* **1.** Food for human consumption. **2. victuals.** Food supplies; provisions. —*v.* **-ualed** or **-ualled, -ual·ing** or **-ual·ling. 1.** To provide with food. **2.** To lay in food supplies. [< Lat. *victus*, nourishment.]

vi·cu·ña or **vi·cu·na** (vĭ-kōōn′yə, -kōōn′ə, -kyōō′nə, və-) *n.* **1.** A South American mammal related to the llama and having fine, silky fleece. **2.** The fleece of the vicuña. **3.** Fabric made from the fleece of the vicuña. [< Quechua *wikuña.*]

vi·de (vī′dē, vē′dā). See. Used to direct a reader's attention: *vide page 64.* [< Lat. *vidēre*, to see.]

vi·de·li·cet (vĭ-dĕl′ĭ-sĭt′, vī-). That is; namely. Used to introduce examples, lists, or items. [Lat., clearly.]

vid·e·o (vĭd′ē-ō′) *adj.* Of or pertaining to television, esp. to televised images. —*n.* **1.** The visual portion of a televised broadcast. **2.** Television. [< Lat. *vidēre*, to see.]

vid·e·o·cas·sette (vĭd′ē-ō-kə-sĕt′, -kă-) *n.* A recording on videotape contained in a cassette that can be played back on a television set.

videocassette recorder *n.* A cassette machine that attaches to and can play back on or record programming from a television set.

vid·e·o·disc (vĭd′ē-ō-dĭsk′) *n.* Also **vid·e·o·disk.** A disc-recording of sounds and images, as of a motion-picture production, that may be played back on a television set. [Orig. a G. trademark.]

videodisc player *n.* A machine that attaches

to and plays back videodiscs on a television set.

video game *n.* An electronic or computerized game played by manipulating images on a television or other display screen.

vid·e·o·tape (vĭd′ē-ō-tāp′) *n.* A magnetic tape used to record television images, usu. together with the associated sound, for subsequent playback and broadcasting. —**vid′e·o·tape′** *v.*

vie (vī) *v.* **vied, vy·ing.** To strive for superiority; contend. [< OFr. *envier*, to challenge.] —**vi′er** *n.*

Vi·et·nam·ese (vē-ĕt′nə-mēz′, -mēs′, vyĕt′-) *n.* **1.** A native or inhabitant of Vietnam. **2.** The language of Vietnam. —**Vi·et′nam·ese′** *adj.*

view (vyōō) *n.* **1.** The act of seeing; sight. **2.** Examination; inspection. **3.** A scene; vista. **4.** A picture of a landscape. **5.** Range or field of sight: *disappeared from view.* **6.** A way of showing or seeing something, as from a particular position or angle: *a side view of the house.* **7.** An opinion; judgment: *her views on education.* **8.** An aim; intention: *laws enacted with the view of providing equal rights.* —*v.* **1.** To look at; see. **2.** To examine; inspect. **3.** To regard; consider. [< Lat. *vidēre*, to see.] —**view′er** *n.*

view·point (vyōō′point′) *n.* A point of view.

vi·ges·i·mal (vī-jĕs′ə-məl) *adj.* Based on or pertaining to 20. [< Lat. *vicesimus*, twentieth.]

vig·il (vĭj′əl) *n.* **1.** A period of alert watchfulness during normal sleeping hours. **2. a.** The eve of a religious festival as observed by devotional watching. **b.** Ritual devotions observed on the eve of a holy day. [< Lat., awake.]

vig·i·lance (vĭj′ə-ləns) *n.* Alert watchfulness.

vig·i·lant (vĭj′ə-lənt) *adj.* On the alert; watchful. —**vig′i·lant·ly** *adv.*

vig·i·lan·te (vĭj′ə-lăn′tē) *n.* A member of an unauthorized group that takes on itself such powers as pursuing and punishing those suspected of being criminals or offenders. [Sp.]

vi·gnette (vĭn-yĕt′, vēn-) *n.* **1.** A decorative design placed at the beginning or end of a book or a chapter of a book or along the border of a page. **2.** A picture that shades off into the surrounding color at the edges. **3.** A brief literary sketch. [< OFr., young wine.]

vig·or (vĭg′ər) *n.* Also *chiefly Brit.* **vig·our. 1.** Physical or mental energy or strength. **2.** Strong feeling; enthusiasm or intensity. **3.** Effectiveness; force. [< Lat.]

vig·or·ous (vĭg′ər-əs) *adj.* **1.** Robust; hardy. **2.** Energetic; lively. —**vig′or·ous·ly** *adv.* —**vig′or·ous·ness** *n.*

Syns: *vigorous, active, brisk, dynamic, energetic, lively, sprightly, spry adj.*

Vi·king or **vi·king** (vī′kĭng) *n.* One of a seafaring Scandinavian people who plundered the coasts of Europe from the 9th to the 11th cent. —**Vi′king** or **vi′king** *adj.*

vile (vīl) *adj.* **vil·er, vil·est. 1.** Hateful; disgusting. **2.** Miserably poor; wretched. **3.** Very unpleasant; objectionable. **4.** Morally low; base. [< Lat. *vilis.*] —**vile′ly** *adv.* —**vile′ness** *n.*

vil·i·fy (vĭl′ə-fī′) *v.* **-fied, -fy·ing.** To speak evil of; defame. [< LLat. *vilificare.*] —**vil′i·fi·ca′tion** *n.* —**vil′i·fi′er** *n.*

vil·la (vĭl′ə) *n.* **1.** A sometimes large and luxurious country estate. **2.** *Chiefly Brit.* A middle-class suburban house. [< Lat.]

vil·lage (vĭl′ĭj) *n.* **1.** A usu. rural settlement smaller than a town. **2.** An incorporated municipality smaller than a town. **3.** The inhabitants of a village. [< Lat. *villa,* country estate.]

vil·lain (vĭl′ən) *n.* **1.** A wicked or evil person; scoundrel. **2.** Var. of **villein.** [< OFr. *vilain,* serf.]

vil·lain·ous (vĭl′ə-nəs) *adj.* **1.** Befitting a villain; wicked or evil. **2.** Very displeasing. —**vil′lain·ous·ly** *adv.* —**vil′lain·ous·ness** *n.*

vil·lain·y (vĭl′ə-nē) *n., pl.* **-ies. 1.** Viciousness of conduct or action. **2.** Baseness of mind or character. **3.** A treacherous or vicious act.

vil·lein (vĭl′ən) *n.* Also **vil·lain.** One of a class of feudal serfs who held the legal status of freemen in their dealings with all persons except their lord. [< VILLAIN.] —**vil′lein·age** *n.*

vim (vĭm) *n.* Liveliness and energy. [< Lat. *vis,* power.]

vin·ai·grette (vĭn′ə-grĕt′) *n.* **1.** A small bottle or container used for holding an aromatic restorative, as smelling salts. **2.** A dressing made of vinegar and oil. [< OFr. *vinaigre,* vinegar.]

vin·ci·ble (vĭn′sə-bəl) *adj.* Capable of being defeated. [< Lat. *vincere,* to conquer.]

vin·di·cate (vĭn′dĭ-kāt′) *v.* **-cat·ed, -cat·ing. 1.** To clear of accusation, blame, suspicion, or doubt with supporting proof. **2.** To substantiate: *vindicated his claim.* **3.** To justify or prove the worth of, esp. in light of later developments. [< Lat. *vindex,* avenger.] —**vin′di·ca′tion** *n.* —**vin′di·ca′tor** *n.*

Syns: *vindicate, absolve, acquit, clear, exonerate v.*

vin·dic·tive (vĭn-dĭk′tĭv) *adj.* **1.** Disposed to seek revenge; vengeful: *a vindictive person.* **2.** Intended to cause pain or harm; spiteful. [< Lat. *vindicta,* vengeance.] —**vin·dic′tive·ly** *adv.* —**vin·dic′tive·ness** *n.*

vine (vīn) *n.* **1. a.** A plant with a flexible stem that climbs, twines around, clings to, or creeps along a surface for support. **b.** The stem of such a plant. **2.** A grapevine. [< Lat. *vinum,* wine.]

vin·e·gar (vĭn′ĭ-gər) *n.* An acid liquid that is basically a dilute solution of acetic acid, obtained by fermentation and used as a condiment and preservative. [< OFr. *vinaigre.*]

vin·e·gar·y (vĭn′ĭ-gə-rē) *adj.* **1.** Of the nature of vinegar; sour. **2.** Unpleasant and irascible in disposition or speech.

vine·yard (vĭn′yərd) *n.* Ground on which grapevines are grown and tended.

vin·i·cul·ture (vĭn′ĭ-kŭl′chər, vī′nĭ-) *n.* The cultivation of grapes; viticulture. [Lat. *vinum,* wine + CULTURE.]

vin·tage (vĭn′tĭj) *n.* **1.** The yield of wine or grapes from a particular vineyard or district in a single season. **2.** Wine, usu. of high quality, identified as to year and vineyard or district of origin. **3.** The harvesting of a grape crop or the initial stages of winemaking. **4.** A year or period of origin: *a vintage car of 1924.* —*adj.* **1.** Of or pertaining to a vintage. **2.** Of very high quality. **3.** Of the best or most distinctive. [< Lat. *vindemia.*]

vint·ner (vĭnt′nər) *n.* A wine merchant. [< Lat. *vinetum,* vineyard.]

vi·nyl (vī′nəl) *n.* Any of various plastics, typically tough, flexible, and shiny, often used for coverings and clothing. [Lat. *vinum,* wine + -YL.]

vi·ol (vī′əl) *n.* A stringed instrument, chiefly of the 16th and 17th cent., with a fretted fingerboard and usu. six strings and played with a bow. [< OProv. *viola.*]

vi·o·la (vē-ō′lə) *n.* A stringed instrument of the violin family, slightly larger than a violin, tuned a fifth lower, and having a deeper, more sonorous tone. [< OProv., viol.] —**vi·o′list** *n.*

vi·o·la·ble (vī′ə-lə-bəl) *adj.* Capable of being violated.

vi·o·late (vī′ə-lāt′) *v.* **-lat·ed, -lat·ing. 1.** To break (e.g. a law); disregard. **2.** To desecrate; profane. **3.** To disturb rudely or improperly; interrupt. **4.** To rape. [< Lat. *violare < vis,* force.] —**vi′o·la′tive** *adj.* —**vi′o·la′tor** *n.*

vi·o·la·tion (vī′ə-lā′shən) *n.* **1.** The act of violating or the condition of being violated. **2.** An instance of violating.

vi·o·lence (vī′ə-ləns) *n.* **1.** Physical force exerted so as to cause damage, abuse, or injury. **2.** An act or instance of violent action or behavior. **3.** Great force or intensity: *the violence of a hurricane.* **4.** Damage; injury, as to meaning or feeling. **5.** Vehemence of feeling or expression; fervor.

vi·o·lent (vī′ə-lənt) *adj.* **1.** Marked by or resulting from great physical force or rough action. **2.** Showing or having great emotional force. **3.** Severe; harsh. **4.** Caused by unexpected force or injury rather than by natural causes: *a violent death.* [< Lat. *violentus < vis,* force.] —**vi′o·lent·ly** *adv.*

vi·o·let (vī′ə-lĭt) *n.* **1.** Any of various low-growing plants with spurred, irregular flowers that are characteristically purplish-blue but sometimes yellow or white. **2.** Any of several plants similar to the violet. **3.** A bluish purple. —*adj.* Bluish purple. [< Lat. *viola.*]

violet

vireo

vi·o·lin (vī′ə-lĭn′) *n.* A stringed instrument that is played with a bow and has four strings tuned at intervals of a fifth, an unfretted fingerboard, and a shallower body than the viol. [< VIOLA.] —**vi′o·lin′ist** *n.*

vi·o·lon·cel·lo (vē′ə-lən-chĕl′ō) *n., pl.* **-los.** A cello. [Ital.] —**vi′o·lon·cel′list** *n.*

VIP (vē′ī-pē′) *n., pl.* **VIPs.** *Informal.* A very important person.

vi·per (vī′pər) *n.* **1.** Any of various venomous Old World snakes. **2.** A poisonous or supposedly poisonous snake. **3.** A treacherous or malicious person. [< Lat. *vipera,* snake.] —**vi′per·ous** *adj.*

vi·ra·go (vĭ-rä′gō) *n., pl.* **-goes** or **-gos.** A noisy, domineering woman. [Lat. < *vir,* man.]

vi·ral (vī′rəl) *adj.* Of, relating to, or caused by a virus.

vir·e·o (vĭr′ē-ō′) *n., pl.* **-os.** Any of several

small grayish or greenish New World birds. [< Lat., a kind of bird.]

vir·gin (vûr′jĭn) n. **1.** A person who has not experienced sexual intercourse. **2.** An unmarried woman who has taken religious vows of chastity. **3. Virgin.** The mother of Jesus. —*adj.* **1.** Of, characteristic of, or suitable to a virgin; modest. **2.** In a pure or natural state: *virgin snow; virgin forests.* [< Lat. *virgo.*] —**vir·gin′i·ty** (vər-jĭn′ĭ-tē) n.

vir·gin·al¹ (vûr′jə-nəl) adj. **1.** Of, relating to, or appropriate to a virgin. **2.** Untouched or unsullied; fresh.

vir·gin·al² (vûr′jə-nəl) n. A small, legless rectangular harpsichord popular in the 16th and 17th cent. [< VIRGIN < its being played by young girls.]

Vir·gin·ia creeper (vər-jĭn′yə) n. A North American climbing vine that has compound leaves with five leaflets and bluish-black, berrylike fruit.

Virginia reel n. A country dance in which couples perform various figures to the instructions called out by a leader.

Vir·go (vûr′gō, vîr′-) n. **1.** A constellation in the region of the celestial equator near Leo and Libra. **2.** The 6th sign of the zodiac.

vir·gule (vûr′gyōōl) n. A diagonal mark (/) used esp. to separate alternatives, as in *and/or,* and to represent the word *per,* as in *miles/hour.* [< Lat. *virgula,* small rod.]

vir·i·des·cent (vĭr′ĭ-dĕs′ənt) adj. Green or slightly green. [Lat. *viridis,* green + -ESCENT.] —**vir′i·des′cence** n.

vir·ile (vĭr′əl) adj. **1.** Of, characteristic of, or befitting a man. **2.** Having or showing traditionally masculine qualities such as strength and vigor. **3.** Capable of performing sexually as a male; potent. [< Lat. *virilis.*] —**vi·ril′i·ty** (vĭ-rĭl′ĭ-tē) n.

vi·rol·o·gy (vī-rŏl′ə-jē) n. The study of viruses and viral diseases. —**vi·rol′o·gist** n.

vir·tu (vər-tōō′, vîr-) n. **1.** A knowledge of or taste for the fine arts. **2.** Objects of art, esp. antique objets d'art. [< Lat. *virtus,* excellence.]

vir·tu·al (vûr′chōō-əl) adj. Existing in effect or essence though not in actual fact or form. [< Lat. *virtus,* capacity.] —**vir′tu·al′i·ty** (-ăl′ĭ-tē) n. —**vir′tu·al·ly** adv.

vir·tue (vûr′chōō) n. **1. a.** Moral excellence and righteousness; goodness. **b.** Conformity to standard morality or mores; rectitude. **2.** Chastity, esp. of a woman. **3.** A particular efficacious or beneficial quality; advantage. **4.** Effective force or power to produce a definite result. —*idiom.* **by virtue of.** On the basis of. [< Lat. *virtus* < *vir,* man.]

vir·tu·os·i·ty (vûr′chōō-ŏs′ĭ-tē) n., pl. **-ties.** The technical skill, fluency, or style of a virtuoso.

vir·tu·o·so (vûr′chōō-ō′sō) n., pl. **-sos** or **-si** (-sē). **1.** A musician with exceptional ability, technique, or style. **2.** A person with exceptional skill or technique in any field, esp. in the performing arts. [Ital.] —**vir′tu·os′ic** (-ŏs′ĭk) adj.

vir·tu·ous (vûr′chōō-əs) adj. **1.** Having or showing virtue; morally good. **2.** Chaste. —**vir′tu·ous·ly** adv.

vir·u·lent (vĭr′yə-lənt, vĭr′ə-) adj. **1.** Extremely poisonous or harmful, as a disease or microorganism. **2.** Bitterly hostile or antagonistic. [< Lat. *virus,* poison.] —**vir′u·lence** n. —**vir′u·lent·ly** adv.

vi·rus (vī′rəs) n. Any of various submicro-

scopic pathogens that consist essentially of a core of a nucleic acid surrounded by a protein coat and are capable of invading and destroying living cells and causing the release of a large number of new particles identical to the original one, thus producing a disease. **2.** A specific pathogen. [Lat., poison.]

vi·sa (vē′zə) n. An official authorization stamped on a passport that permits entry into and travel within a particular country or region. [< Lat. *visus,* p.p. of *vidēre,* to see.]

vis·age (vĭz′ĭj) n. **1.** The face or facial expression of a person. **2.** Appearance; aspect. [< OFr. *vis,* face.]

vis-à-vis (vē′zə-vē′) n., pl. **vis-à-vis.** One opposite or corresponding to another; counterpart. —*adv.* Face to face. —*prep.* Compared with; in relation to. [Fr., face to face.] —**vis′-à-vis′ly** adv.

vis·cer·a (vĭs′ər-ə) pl.n. The internal organs of the body, esp. those contained within the abdomen and thorax. [Lat., pl. of *viscus,* flesh.]

vis·cer·al (vĭs′ər-əl) adj. **1.** Of, situated in, or affecting the viscera. **2.** Intensely emotional.

vis·cid (vĭs′ĭd) adj. Thick and adhesive, as a liquid. [< Lat. *viscum,* birdlime.] —**vis·cid′i·ty** (vĭ-sĭd′ĭ-tē) n. —**vis′cid·ly** adv.

vis·cose (vĭs′kōs′) n. A thick, golden-brown viscous solution derived from cellulose and used in the manufacture of rayon and cellophane. [< Lat. *viscum,* birdlime.]

vis·cos·i·ty (vĭ-skŏs′ĭ-tē) n., pl. **-ties.** The condition, property, or degree of being viscous.

vis·count (vī′kount′) n. A member of the British peerage ranking below an earl and above a baron. [< Med. Lat. *vicecomes.*]

vis·cous (vĭs′kəs) adj. **1.** Tending to resist flow when pressure is applied, as a fluid. **2.** Viscid. [< Lat. *viscum,* birdlime.] —**vis′cous·ly** adv. —**vis′cous·ness** n.

vise (vīs) n. Also **vice.** A clamping device usu. consisting of two jaws closed or opened by a screw or lever, used in carpentry or metalworking to hold a piece in position. [< Lat. *vitis,* vine.]

Vish·nu (vĭsh′nōō) n. *Hinduism.* The second member of the trinity, which includes also Brahma and Shiva.

vis·i·bil·i·ty (vĭz′ĭ-bĭl′ĭ-tē) n., pl. **-ties.** **1.** The fact, condition, or degree of being visible. **2.** The greatest distance to which it is possible to see without aid from instruments under given weather conditions.

vis·i·ble (vĭz′ə-bəl) adj. **1.** Capable of being seen. **2.** Manifest; apparent. [< Lat. *visus,* p.p. of *vidēre,* to see.] —**vis′i·bly** adv.

vi·sion (vĭzh′ən) n. **1.** The faculty of sight. **2.** Unusual foresight. **3.** A mental image produced by the imagination. **4.** Something, as a supernatural sight, perceived through unusual means. **5.** One of extraordinary beauty. —*v.* To see in or as if in a vision. [< Lat. *vidēre,* to see.]

vi·sion·ar·y (vĭzh′ə-nĕr′ē) adj. **1.** Of the nature of a fantasy or dream. **2.** Given to impractical or fanciful ideas. **3.** Not practicable; utopian. —*n., pl.* **-ies.** **1.** One who has visions. **2.** One given to impractical or speculative ideas.

vis·it (vĭz′ĭt) v. **1.** To go or come to see for reasons of business, duty, or pleasure. **2.** To stay with as a guest. **3.** To afflict; assail. **4.** To inflict punishment; avenge. **5.** *Informal.* To converse; chat. —*n.* **1.** An act or instance of visiting. **2.** A stay or sojourn as a guest.

3. An act of visiting in an official capacity. [< Lat. *visitare.*]

vis·i·tant (vĭz'ĭ-tənt) *n.* A visitor; guest.

vis·i·ta·tion (vĭz'ĭ-tā'shən) *n.* 1. A visit, esp. an official inspection or examination. 2. A visit of affliction or blessing regarded as being ordained by God. —**vis'i·ta'tion·al** *adj.*

vis·i·tor (vĭz'ĭ-tər) *n.* One who pays a visit.

vi·sor (vī'zər) *n.* Also **vi·zor.** 1. A projecting part, as on a cap or the windshield of a car, that protects the eyes from sun, wind, or rain. 2. The movable front piece of a helmet. [< OFr. *vis,* face.]

vis·ta (vĭs'tə) *n.* 1. A distant view, esp. one seen through a passage or opening. 2. A mental view of a series of events. [Ital. < *vedere,* to see.]

vi·su·al (vĭzh'ōō-əl) *adj.* 1. Of, serving, or pertaining to the sense of sight. 2. Capable of being seen by the eye; visible. 3. Done or performed by means of the unaided vision. 4. Of or pertaining to instruction by means of vision. [< Lat. *visus,* vision.] —**vi'su·al·ly** *adv.*

vi·su·al·ize (vĭzh'ōō-ə-līz') *v.* **-ized, -iz·ing.** To form a mental image or vision of. —**vi'su·al·i·za'tion** *n.* —**vi'su·al·iz'er** *n.*

vi·ta (vī'tə, vē'-) *n.* An outline of one's personal history and experience, as one submitted when applying for a job. [Lat., life.]

vi·tal (vīt'l) *adj.* 1. Of or characteristic of life. 2. Essential for the continuation of life. 3. Full of life; energetic. 4. Of great importance; essential. —*n.* **vitals.** 1. Essential organs or parts of the body. 2. Essential elements. [< Lat. *vita,* life.] —**vi'tal·ly** *adv.*

vi·tal·i·ty (vī-tăl'ĭ-tē) *n., pl.* **-ties.** 1. An energy, force, or principle that distinguishes the living from the nonliving. 2. The capacity to live, grow, or develop. 3. Vigor; energy.

vi·tal·ize (vīt'l-īz') *v.* **-ized, -iz·ing.** To endow with life, vigor, or energy. —**vi'tal·i·za'tion** *n.* —**vi'tal·iz'er** *n.*

vi·ta·min (vī'tə-mĭn) *n.* Any of various relatively complex organic substances that occur naturally in plant and animal tissue and are essential in small amounts for the control of metabolic processes. [G. *Vitamine.*]

vitamin A *n.* A vitamin or mixture of vitamins occurring principally in fish-liver oils and some yellow and dark-green vegetables, functioning in normal cell growth and development, and responsible in deficiency for hardening and roughening of the skin, night blindness, and degeneration of mucous membranes.

vitamin B *n.* 1. Vitamin B complex. 2. A member of the vitamin B complex.

vitamin B₁₂ *n.* A complex cobalt-containing compound found in liver and widely used to treat pernicious anemia.

vitamin B complex *n.* A group of vitamins important for growth and occurring chiefly in yeast, liver, eggs, and some vegetables.

vitamin C *n.* Ascorbic acid.

vitamin D *n.* Any of several chemically similar compounds obtained from milk, fish, and eggs, required for normal bone growth and used to treat rickets in children.

vitamin E *n.* Any of several chemically related viscous oils found in grains and vegetable oils and used to treat sterility and various

abnormalities of the muscles, red blood cells, liver, and brain.

vitamin K *n.* Any of several natural and synthetic substances essential for the promotion of blood clotting and prevention of hemorrhage.

vi·ti·ate (vĭsh'ē-āt') *v.* **-at·ed, -at·ing.** 1. To make ineffective or worthless. 2. To corrupt morally; debase. 3. To make legally ineffective; invalidate. [Lat. *vitiare.*] —**vi'ti·a'tion** *n.* —**vi'ti·a'tor** *n.*

vit·i·cul·ture (vĭt'ĭ-kŭl'chər) *n.* The cultivation of grapes. [Lat. *vitis,* vine + CULTURE.] —**vit'i·cul'tur·al** *adj.* —**vit'i·cul'tur·ist** *n.*

vit·re·ous (vĭt'rē-əs) *adj.* 1. Of, pertaining to, or resembling glass; glassy. 2. Of or pertaining to the vitreous humor. [Lat. *vitreus.*]

vitreous humor *n.* Clear gelatinous matter that fills the part of the eyeball between the lens and the retina.

vit·ri·fy (vĭt'rə-fī') *v.* **-fied, -fy·ing.** To change into glass or a similar substance, esp. through heat fusion. [< Lat. *vitrum,* glass.] —**vit'ri·fi·ca'tion** *n.*

vit·ri·ol (vĭt'rē-ōl') *n.* 1. a. Sulfuric acid. b. Any of various sulfates of metals. 2. Vituperative feeling or expression. [< LLat. *vitreolus,* of glass.]

vit·ri·ol·ic (vĭt'rē-ōl'ĭk) *adj.* 1. Of, like, or derived from vitriol. 2. Bitterly scathing; caustic.

vit·tles (vĭt'lz) *pl.n. Slang.* Victuals.

vi·tu·per·ate (vī-tōō'pə-rāt', -tyōō'-, vī-) *v.* **-at·ed, -at·ing.** To rail against abusively; berate. [Lat. *vituperare.*] —**vi·tu'per·a'tion** *n.* —**vi·tu'per·a·tive** *adj.*

vi·va (vē'və) *interj.* Used to express acclamation, salute, or applause. [Ital., long live.]

vi·va·ce (vē-vä'chā) *adv. & adj. Mus.* Lively; briskly. Used as a direction. [Ital.]

vi·va·cious (vĭ-vā'shəs, vī-) *adj.* Full of animation and spirit; lively. [< Lat. *vivax.*] —**vi·va'cious·ly** *adv.* —**vi·va'cious·ness** or **vi·vac'i·ty** (vĭ-văs'ĭ-tē, vī-) *n.*

viv·id (vĭv'ĭd) *adj.* 1. Perceived as bright and distinct; brilliant 2. Having intensely bright colors. 3. Full of the freshness of immediate experience. 4. Evoking lifelike mental images. 5. Active in forming lifelike images: *a vivid imagination.* [< Lat. *vivere,* to live.] —**viv'id·ly** *adv.* —**viv'id·ness** *n.*

viv·i·fy (vĭv'ə-fī') *v.* **-fied, -fy·ing.** 1. To impart life to; animate. 2. To make more lively, intense, or striking; enliven. [< LLat. *vivificare.*] —**viv'i·fi·ca'tion** *n.* —**viv'i·fi'er** *n.*

vi·vip·a·rous (vī-vĭp'ər-əs, vī-) *adj.* Giving birth to living young that develop within the mother's body rather than hatching from eggs. [Lat. *viviparus.*] —**vi·vip'a·ri·ty** (vĭv'ə-pǎr'ĭ-tē, vīv'ə-) *n.* —**vi·vip'a·rous·ly** *adv.*

viv·i·sec·tion (vĭv'ĭ-sĕk'shən) *n.* The act of cutting into or dissecting a living animal, esp. for scientific research. [Lat. *vivus,* alive + SECTION.] —**viv'i·sect'** *v.*

vix·en (vĭk'sən) *n.* 1. A female fox. 2. A quarrelsome, sharp-tempered, or malicious woman. [ME *fixen.*] —**vix'en·ish** *adj.*

viz·ard (vĭz'ərd) *n.* A mask. [< VISOR.]

vi·zier (vĭ-zîr') *n.* A high officer in a Moslem government, esp. in the old Turkish Empire. [< Ar. *wazīr.*]

vi·zor (vī′zər) *n.* Var. of **visor**.

vo·ca·ble (vō′kə-bəl) *n.* A word considered as a sequence of sounds or letters rather than as a unit of meaning. [< Lat. *vocare*, to call.]

vo·cab·u·lar·y (vō-kăb′yə-lĕr′ē) *n., pl.* **-ies.** 1. All the words of a language. 2. The sum of words used by a particular person or group. 3. A list of words and phrases, usu. arranged alphabetically and defined or translated; lexicon. [< Lat. *vocabulum*, name.]

vo·cal (vō′kəl) *adj.* 1. Of, for, or pertaining to the voice. 2. Uttered or produced by the voice. 3. Capable of emitting sound or speech. 4. Full of voices; resounding with speech. 5. Quick to speak or criticize; outspoken. —*n.* 1. A vocal sound. 2. A popular piece of music for a singer. [< Lat. *vox*, voice.] —**vo′cal·ly** *adv.*

vocal cords *pl.n.* A pair of muscular bands or folds in the larynx that vibrate when pulled together and when air from the lungs is forced between them, thereby producing vocal sounds.

vo·cal·ic (vō-kăl′ĭk) *adj.* Pertaining to or having the nature of a vowel.

vo·cal·ist (vō′kə-lĭst) *n.* A singer.

vo·cal·ize (vō′kə-līz′) *v.* **-ized, -iz·ing.** 1. To give voice to; articulate. 2. To change (a consonant) into a vowel. 3. To use the voice, esp. to sing. —**vo′cal·i·za′tion** *n.* —**vo′cal·iz′er** *n.*

vo·ca·tion (vō-kā′shən) *n.* 1. A profession, esp. one for which one is specially suited or trained. 2. A strong desire to do a particular type of work, esp. religious work. [< Lat. *vocare*, to call.] —**vo·ca′tion·al** *adj.*

voc·a·tive (vŏk′ə-tĭv) *adj.* Of, pertaining to, or designating a grammatical case indicating the one being addressed. [< Lat. *vocare*, to call.] —**voc′a·tive** *n.*

vo·cif·er·ate (vō-sĭf′ə-rāt′) *v.* **-at·ed, -at·ing.** To cry out vehemently; clamor. [Lat. *vociferari*.] —**vo·cif′er·a′tion** *n.*

vo·cif·er·ous (vō-sĭf′ər-əs) *adj.* Making an outcry; clamorous. —**vo·cif′er·ous·ly** *adv.* —**vo·cif′er·ous·ness** *n.*

vod·ka (vŏd′kə) *n.* A colorless alcoholic liquor distilled from fermented wheat or rye mash, corn, or potatoes. [R., dim. of *voda*, water.]

vogue (vōg) *n.* 1. The current fashion, practice, or style. 2. Popular acceptance or favor; popularity. [Fr.] —**vogu′ish** *adj.*

voice (vois) *n.* 1. **a.** Sound produced by specialized organs in the respiratory tract of a vertebrate, esp. a human being. **b.** Musical sound produced by vibration of the vocal cords. **c.** The ability to produce such sound: *lost his voice.* 2. The organs that produce the voice. 3. A condition, timbre, or quality of vocal sound. 4. A singer: *a chorus of 200 voices.* 5. Any of the melodic parts in a musical composition. 6. **a.** A medium or agency of expression. **b.** The right or opportunity to express a choice or opinion. **c.** A will, desire, or opinion expressed. 7. Something resembling human sound or speech: *the voice of the wind.* 8. *Gram.* A verb form indicating the relation between the subject and the action expressed by the verb. 9. The expiration of air through vibrating vocal cords, used in the production of the vowels and voiced consonants. —*v.* **voiced, voic·ing.** 1. To express or utter; give voice to. 2. To produce (a speech sound) with vibration of the vocal cords. 3. *Mus.* To regulate the tone of: *voice the strings of the piano.* [< Lat. *vox.*]

voice box *n.* The larynx.

voiced (voist) *adj.* 1. Having a voice or a specified kind of voice: *a soft-voiced person.* 2. Expressed by means of the voice. 3. Uttered with vibration of the vocal cords, as the consonant *g.*

voice·less (vois′lĭs) *adj.* 1. Having no voice. 2. Uttered without vibration of the vocal cords, as the consonant *t.* —**voice′less·ly** *adv.* —**voice′less·ness** *n.*

voice-o·ver (vois′ō′vər) *n.* In motion pictures and television, the voice of a narrator who does not appear on camera.

void (void) *adj.* 1. Without legal force or validity; null. 2. Devoid; lacking. 3. Containing no matter; empty. 4. Unoccupied; vacant. 5. Ineffective; useless. —*n.* 1. An empty space; vacuum. 2. A feeling of emptiness, loneliness, or loss. —*v.* 1. To make void; invalidate. 2. **a.** To empty. **b.** To evacuate (body wastes). 3. To leave; vacate. [< Lat. *vacuus*, empty.] —**void′a·ble** *adj.* —**void′er** *n.*

voile (voil) *n.* A sheer fabric of cotton, rayon, wool, or silk, used in making lightweight curtains and clothing. [< Lat. *velum*, covering.]

vol·a·tile (vŏl′ə-tl, -tīl′) *adj.* 1. Changing to vapor readily at normal temperatures and pressures. 2. Changeable, esp.: **a.** Inconstant; fickle. **b.** Tending to erupt into violent action; explosive. **c.** Fleeting; ephemeral. [< Lat. *volare*, to fly.] —**vol′a·til′i·ty** (-tĭl′ĭ-tē) *n.*

vol·a·til·ize (vŏl′ə-tl-īz′) *v.* **-ized, -iz·ing.** 1. To make or become volatile. 2. To evaporate or cause to evaporate.

vol·can·ic (vŏl-kăn′ĭk) *adj.* 1. Of, pertaining to, or resembling a volcano. 2. Powerfully explosive: *a volcanic temper.*

vol·can·ism (vŏl′kə-nĭz′əm) *n.* Volcanic force or activity.

vol·ca·no (vŏl-kā′nō) *n., pl.* **-noes** or **-nos.** 1. An opening in the crust of the earth through which molten rock, dust, ash, and hot gases are ejected. 2. A mountain or other elevation formed by the materials ejected from a volcano. [< Lat. *Vulcanus*, Vulcan.]

volcano

Mount St. Helens in the Cascade Range of Washington erupting in May 1980

vole (vōl) *n.* Any of various rodents resembling rats or mice but with a shorter tail. [Obs. *volemouse.*]

vo·li·tion (və-lĭsh′ən) *n.* 1. An act of willing, choosing, or deciding. 2. The power or capability of choosing; will. 3. A conscious choice; decision. [< Lat. *velle*, to wish.] —**vo·li′tion·al** *adj.* —**vo·li′tion·al·ly** *adv.*

vol·ley (vŏl′ē) *n., pl.* **-leys.** 1. **a.** The simultaneous discharge of a number of missiles. **b.** The missiles discharged. 2. A burst or outburst of many things at once: *a volley of* *questions.* **3. a.** A shot, esp. in tennis, made by striking the ball before it touches the ground. **b.** A continuous series of such shots between opponents. —*v.* **1.** To discharge or be discharged in or as if in a volley. **2.** To strike (a ball) before it touches the ground. [< Lat. *volare*, to fly.] —**vol′ley·er** *n.*

vol·ley·ball (vŏl′ē-bôl′) *n.* **1.** A game played between two teams who hit a ball back and forth over a net with the hands while attempting to score by grounding a ball on the opposing team's court. **2.** The large inflated ball used in this game.

volt (vōlt) *n.* The unit of electric potential and electromotive force equal to the difference of electric potential between two points on a conducting wire carrying a constant current of one ampere when the power dissipated between the points is one watt. [< Count Alessandro *Volta* (1745–1827).]

volt·age (vōl′tĭj) *n.* Electromotive force or potential difference, esp. expressed in volts.

vol·ta·ic (vŏl-tā′ĭk, vōl-, vôl-) *adj.* Of, pertaining to, or producing electricity by chemical action; galvanic.

volt·me·ter (vōlt′mē′tər) *n.* An instrument that measures differences of electric potential in volts.

vol·u·ble (vŏl′yə-bəl) *adj.* Talking readily and fluently; glib. [< Lat. *volubilis*.] —**vol′u·bil′i·ty** *n.* —**vol′u·bly** *adv.*

vol·ume (vŏl′yŏŏm, -yəm) *n.* **1.** A collection of written or printed sheets bound together; book. **2.** One book of a set. **3. a.** The size or extent of a three-dimensional object or region of space. **b.** The capacity of such a region or of a specified container. **4.** An amount: *a decrease in the volume of trade.* **5. a.** The force or intensity of a sound; loudness. **b.** A control for adjusting loudness. [< Lat. *volumen*, a roll of writing.]

vol·u·met·ric (vŏl′yə-mĕt′rĭk) *adj.* Of or pertaining to measurement of volume. [VOLU(ME) + METRIC.] —**vol′u·met′ri·cal·ly** *adv.*

vo·lu·mi·nous (və-lŏŏ′mə-nəs) *adj.* **1.** Having great volume, fullness, size, or number. **2.** Filling or capable of filling many volumes. **3.** Having many coils; winding. [LLat. *voluminosus*, having many folds.] —**vo·lu′mi·nous·ly** *adv.* —**vo·lu′mi·nous·ness** *n.*

vol·un·tar·y (vŏl′ən-tĕr′ē) *adj.* **1.** Arising from one's own free will. **2.** Acting by choice and without constraint or guarantee of reward. **3.** Not accidental; intentional. **4.** Normally controlled by or subject to individual volition. —*n., pl.* **-ies.** A solo organ piece played before and sometimes during or after a church service. [< Lat. *voluntas*, choice.] —**vol′un·tar′i·ly** (-târ′ə-lē) *adv.*
Syns: *voluntary, deliberate, intentional, willful adj.*

vol·un·teer (vŏl′ən-tîr′) *n.* One who performs or gives services of his own free will. —*v.* **1.** To give or offer of one's own accord. **2.** To enter into or offer to enter into an undertaking of one's own free will.

vo·lup·tu·ar·y (və-lŭp′chŏŏ-ĕr′ē) *n., pl.* **-ies.** One whose life is given over to luxury and sensual pleasures. [< Lat. *voluptas*, pleasure.] —**vo·lup′tu·ar·y** *adj.*

vo·lup·tu·ous (və-lŭp′chŏŏ-əs) *adj.* **1.** Of,

marked by, or giving sensual pleasure. **2.** Devoted to or frequently indulging in sensual gratification. **3.** Full and appealing in form. —**vo·lup′tu·ous·ly** *adv.* —**vo·lup′tu·ous·ness** *n.*

vo·lute (və-lŏŏt′) *n.* A spiral, scroll-like formation or decoration. [< Lat. *voluta*, scroll.]

vom·it (vŏm′ĭt) *v.* **1.** To eject or discharge part or all of the contents of the stomach through the mouth. **2.** To eject or discharge in a gush; spew out. —*n.* Matter discharged from the stomach by vomiting. [< Lat. *vomere*.]

voo·doo (vŏŏ′dŏŏ) *n.* **1.** A religious cult of African origin characterized by a belief in sorcery, fetishes, and primitive deities. **2.** A charm, fetish, spell, or curse believed by followers of voodoo to hold magic power. **3.** A person who performs rites at a meeting of followers of voodoo. [< Ewe *vôdú*.] —**voo′-doo·ism** *n.* —**voo′doo·is′tic** *adj.*

vo·ra·cious (vô-rā′shəs, və-) *adj.* **1.** Consuming or greedy for great amounts of food; ravenous. **2.** Exceedingly eager; insatiable. [< Lat. *vorax.*] —**vo·ra′cious·ly** *adv.* —**vo·rac′i·ty** (-răs′ĭ-tē) or **vo·ra′cious·ness** *n.*

-vorous *suff.* Eating or feeding on: *herbivorous.* [< Lat. *vorare*, to devour.]

vor·tex (vôr′tĕks′) *n., pl.* **-es** or **-ti·ces** (-tĭ-sēz′). **1.** Fluid flow, as of water or air, involving rotation about an axis; whirlwind or whirlpool. **2.** Something regarded as drawing into its center all that surrounds it. [Lat. < *vertere*, to turn.] —**vor′ti·cal** (-tĭ-kəl) *adj.*

vo·ta·rist (vō′tər-ĭst) *n.* A votary.

vo·ta·ry (vō′tə-rē) *n., pl.* **-ries. 1. a.** One bound by religious vows. **b.** A devout worshiper. **2.** One fervently devoted to an activity, leader, or ideal. [< Lat. *votus*, p.p. of *vovēre*, to vow.]

vote (vōt) *n.* **1. a.** A formal expression of preference or choice made in or as if in an election. **b.** The means by which such choice is made known, as a raised hand or a ballot. **2.** The number of votes cast in an election or to resolve an issue. **3.** A group of voters: *the labor vote.* **4.** The result of an election. **5.** Suffrage. —*v.* **vot·ed, vot·ing. 1.** To cast a vote. **2.** To endorse, bring into existence, or make available by a vote. **3.** To declare by general consent: *voted the play a success.* [Lat. *votum*, vow.] —**vot′er** *n.*

vo·tive (vō′tĭv) *adj.* Given or dedicated in fulfillment of a vow or pledge. [< Lat. *votum*, vow.]

vouch (vouch) *v.* **1.** To substantiate by supplying evidence; verify. **2.** To furnish a personal guarantee or assurance. **3.** To function or serve as a guarantee; furnish supporting evidence. [< Lat. *vocare*, to call.]

vouch·er (vou′chər) *n.* **1.** One who vouches for another. **2.** A record, as a receipt, of a business transaction.

vouch·safe (vouch-sāf′, vouch′sāf′) *v.* **-safed, -saf·ing.** To grant or give, often as if doing a favor. [ME *vouchen sauf*, to warrant as safe.]

vow (vou) *n.* **1.** An earnest promise or pledge that binds one to a specified act or mode of behavior. **2.** A formal declaration or assertion. —*v.* **1.** To promise or pledge solemnly. **2.** To declare or assert formally. **3.** To make a vow. —**idiom. take vows.** To enter a religious order. [< Lat. *votum* < *vovēre*, to vow.] —**vow′er** *n.*

vow·el (vou'əl) n. 1. A voiced speech sound produced by relatively free passage of the breath through the larynx and mouth. 2. A letter that represents a vowel. [< Lat. (*littera*) *vocalis*, sounding (letter).]

vox pop·u·li (vŏks pŏp'yə-lī') n. Popular opinion. [Lat., voice of the people.]

voy·age (voi'ĭj) n. A long journey, usu. to a foreign or distant land, esp. on a ship but sometimes on an aircraft or spacecraft. —v. **-aged, -ag·ing.** 1. To make a voyage. 2. To sail across; traverse. [< Lat. *via*, road.] **—voy'ag·er** n.

vo·ya·geur (vwä'yä-zhœr', voi'-) n. A woodsman, boatman, or guide, esp. one employed by a fur company. [Fr., traveler.]

Vul·can (vŭl'kən) n. *Rom. Myth.* The god of fire and craftsmanship.

vul·can·ism (vŭl'kə-nĭz'əm) n. Volcanism.

vul·can·ize (vŭl'kə-nīz') v. **-ized, -iz·ing.** To give (rubber or similar materials) greater strength, resistance, or elasticity by combining with sulfur or other additives in the presence of heat and pressure. [< VULCAN.] **—vul'can·i·za'tion** n. **—vul'can·iz'er** n.

vul·gar (vŭl'gər) adj. 1. Lacking good taste, refinement, or cultivation; coarse. 2. Of or associated with the common people. 3. Of, pertaining to, or expressed in language spoken by the common people; vernacular. [< Lat. *vulgus*, common people.] **—vul'gar·ly** adv.

vul·gar·i·an (vŭl-gâr'ē-ən) n. A vulgar person.

vul·gar·ism (vŭl'gə-rĭz'əm) n. 1. a. A vulgar word or phrase; obscenity. b. A word, phrase, or manner of expression used mainly by illiterate persons. 2. Vulgarity.

vul·gar·i·ty (vŭl-găr'ĭ-tē) n., pl. **-ties.** 1. The condition or quality of being vulgar. 2. Something, as an act or expression, that offends good taste or propriety.

vul·gar·ize (vŭl'gə-rīz') v. **-ized, -iz·ing.** 1. To make vulgar; cheapen. 2. To popularize. **—vul'gar·i·za'tion** n. **—vul'gar·iz'er** n.

Vulgar Latin n. The common speech of the ancient Romans, which is distinguished from standard literary Latin and is the ancestor of the Romance languages.

vul·ner·a·ble (vŭl'nər-ə-bəl) adj. 1. Capable of being harmed or injured. 2. Susceptible to danger or attack. 3. Easily affected or hurt, as by criticism or sarcasm. 4. *Bridge.* In a position to receive greater penalties or bonuses after winning one game of a rubber. [< Lat. *vulnerare*, to wound.] **—vul'ner·a·bil'i·ty** n. **—vul'ner·a·bly** adv.

vul·pine (vŭl'pīn') adj. 1. Of, resembling, or characteristic of a fox. 2. Clever; cunning. [< Lat. *vulpes*, fox.]

vul·ture (vŭl'chər) n. 1. Any of various large birds that characteristically have dark plumage and a naked head and neck and that feed on carrion. 2. A greedy, grasping, ruthless person. [< Lat. *vultur.*]

vulture

vul·va (vŭl'və) n., pl. **-vae** (-vē). The external parts of the female genital organs. [Lat., covering.] **—vul'val** or **vul'var** adj.

Ww

w or **W** (dŭb'əl-yōō) n., pl. **w's** or **W's.** 1. The 23rd letter of the English alphabet. 2. Something shaped like the letter W.

W The symbol for the element tungsten. [G. *Wolfram.*]

Wac (wăk) n. A member of the Women's Army Corps of the U.S. Army. [W(OMEN'S) A(RMY) C(ORPS).]

wack·y (wăk'ē) adj. **-i·er, -i·est.** *Slang.* Crazy or silly; nutty. [Orig. unknown.]

wad (wŏd) n. 1. A soft mass of material. 2. A compressed ball, roll, or lump, as of tobacco. 3. A plug, as of cloth, used to hold a powder charge in place, as in a shotgun cartridge. 4. *Informal.* a. A sizable roll of paper money. b. A considerable amount. —v. **wad·ded, wad·ding.** 1. To compress into a wad. 2. To pad, pack, line, or plug with wadding. 3. To hold (shot or powder) in place with a wad. [Orig. unknown.]

wad·ding (wŏd'ĭng) n. 1. Wads collectively. 2. A soft layer of fibrous cotton or wool used for padding or stuffing. 3. Material for wads.

wad·dle (wŏd'l) v. **-dled, -dling.** To walk with short steps that sway the body from side to side, as a duck does. [Prob. < WADE.] **—wad'dle** n.

wade (wād) v. **wad·ed, wad·ing.** 1. To walk in or through a substance, as water, that impedes movement. 2. To make one's way with difficulty and often energetic resolution: *waded through stacks of files.* [< OE *wadan.*]

wad·er (wā'dər) n. 1. One that wades. 2. A

wader

long-legged bird that frequents shallow water. **3. waders.** Waterproof hip boots or trousers.
wa·di (wä′dē) n. In northern Africa and southwestern Asia, a valley, gully, or riverbed that remains dry except during the rainy season. [Ar. *wādī.*]
wa·fer (wä′fər) n. **1.** A thin, crisp cookie, cracker, or candy. **2.** A small, thin disk of unleavened bread used in Communion. **3.** Something resembling a wafer, as a small adhesive seal for papers. [< ONFr. *waufre,* of Gmc. orig.]
waf·fle¹ (wŏf′əl) n. A light, crisp batter cake baked in a waffle iron. [Du. *wafel.*]
waf·fle² (wŏf′əl) v. **-fled, -fling.** *Informal.* To speak or write evasively. [Prob. < obs. *waff,* to yelp.]
waffle iron n. An appliance with hinged, indented metal plates that impress a grid pattern into waffle batter.
waft (wăft, wäft) v. To carry or cause to drift gently and smoothly through the air or over water. —n. **1.** Something, as a scent, carried through the air. **2.** A light breeze. [< MLG *wachten,* to guard.]
wag¹ (wăg) v. **wagged, wag·ging.** To move or cause to move briskly and repeatedly from side to side, and to and fro, or up and down. [ME *waggen.*] —**wag** n.
wag² (wăg) n. A playful or mischievous person; joker. [Orig. unknown.]
wage (wāj) n. **1.** Payment for work done or services rendered. **2. wages** (*used with a sing. or pl. verb*). A suitable return or reward. —v. **waged, wag·ing.** To engage in or carry on (a war or campaign.) [< ONFr., of Gmc. orig.]
wa·ger (wä′jər) n. A bet. —v. To bet. [< ONFr. *wagier,* to pledge.] —**wa′ger·er** n.
wag·ger·y (wăg′ə-rē) n., pl. **-ies. 1.** Waggish behavior or spirit; playfulness. **2.** A playful remark or act.
wag·gish (wăg′ĭsh) adj. Characteristic of a wag; playfully humorous. —**wag′gish·ly** adv.
wag·gle (wăg′əl) v. **-gled, -gling.** To move with short, quick motions; wag. [< WAG¹.] —**wag′gle** n. —**wag′gly** adj.
wag·on (wăg′ən) n. **1.** A four-wheeled usu. horse-drawn vehicle used esp. for transporting loads. **2.** A station wagon. **b.** A police patrol wagon. **3.** A child's low four-wheeled cart. [< MDu. *wagen.*]
wa·gon-lit (vä′gôn-lē′) n., pl. **wa·gons-lits** or **wa·gon-lits** (vä′gôn-lē′). A railroad sleeping car. [Fr.]
wagon train n. A line or group of wagons traveling cross-country.
wag·tail (wăg′tāl′) n. Any of various birds with a long, constantly wagging tail.
wa·hoo (wä′hŏŏ) n., pl. **-hoos.** A shrub or small tree of eastern North America. [Dakota *wáhu.*]
waif (wāf) n. **1. a.** A homeless or forsaken child. **b.** A stray young animal. **2.** Something found and unclaimed. [< ONFr. *waife,* ownerless property.]
wail (wāl) v. **1.** To cry loudly and mournfully, as in grief. **2.** To make a prolonged, high-pitched sound suggestive of a cry. —n. **1.** A long, high-pitched, mournful cry, as of grief. **2.** A sound similar to a wail: *the wail of the wind.* [ME *wailen,* of Scand. orig.]

wail·ful (wāl′fəl) adj. Mournful.
wain (wān) n. A large open farm wagon. [< OE *wægn.*]
wain·scot (wān′skət, -skŏt′, -skōt′) n. **1.** A facing or paneling, usu. of wood, on the walls of a room. **2.** The lower part of an interior wall when finished in a material different from the upper part. [< MDu. *wagenschot.*] —**wain′scot** v.
wain·scot·ing (wān′skə-tĭng, -skŏt′ĭng, -skō′tĭng) n. Also **wain·scot·ting. 1.** A wainscot. **2.** Material for a wainscot.
wain·wright (wān′rīt′) n. A builder and repairer of wagons.
waist (wāst) n. **1.** The part of the human trunk between the bottom of the rib cage and the pelvis. **2. a.** The part of a garment that encircles the waist. **b.** A garment that extends from the shoulders to the waistline, as a blouse. **c.** A child's undershirt. **3.** The middle section or part of something. [ME *wast.*]
waist·band (wāst′bănd′) n. A band encircling the waist, as on trousers.
waist·coat (wĕs′kĭt, wāst′kōt′) n. *Chiefly Brit.* A vest.
waist·line (wāst′līn′) n. **1. a.** The place at which the circumference of the waist is smallest. **b.** The measurement of this circumference. **2.** The point or line at which the skirt and bodice of a dress join.
wait (wāt) v. **1.** To remain inactive in anticipation. **2.** To delay; postpone. **3.** To serve as a waiter or waitress. **4.** To be prepared or ready. —n. A period of time spent in waiting. [< ONFr. *waitier,* to watch.]
Usage: Although *wait on* occurs in some dialects as the equivalent of *wait for,* this expression has not yet become established: *They will wait for* (not *on*) *you if you hurry.*
wait·er (wā′tər) n. **1.** A man who waits on table, as in a restaurant. **2.** A tray.
waiting game n. The stratagem of deferring action in the hope that the passage of time will work in one's favor.
waiting room n. A room, as in a railroad station or doctor's office, for the use of persons waiting.
wait·ress (wā′trĭs) n. A woman who waits on table.
waive (wāv) v. **waived, waiv·ing. 1.** To give up (a claim or right) voluntarily. **2.** To set aside or postpone. [< ONFr. *weyver,* to abandon.]
waiv·er (wā′vər) n. **1.** The intentional relinquishment of a right, claim, or privilege. **2.** A written agreement to waive a right or claim.
Wa·kash·an (wŏ′kə-shăn′, wä-kăsh′ən) n. A family of North American Indian languages spoken by the Nootka and other tribes of Washington and British Columbia.
wake¹ (wāk) v. **woke** (wōk), **waked** (wākt) or *chiefly Brit. & regional* **woke** or **wo·ken** (wō′kən), **waking. 1.** To awaken: *He woke up with a start.* **2.** To keep watch or guard, esp. over a corpse. **3.** To remain awake. **4.** To make aware of; alert. —n. A watch, esp. over the body of a deceased person before burial. [< OE *wacian.*]
wake² (wāk) n. **1.** The visible track left by something, as a ship, moving through water. **2.** The track or course left behind something that has passed. [Of Scand. orig.]

---

wake·ful (wāk'fəl) *adj.* **1. a.** Not sleeping. **b.** Without sleep; sleepless. **2.** Watchful; alert. —**wake'ful·ness** *n.*

wak·en (wā'kən) *v.* **1.** To rouse from sleep; awake. **2.** To rouse from an inactive state. [< OE *wæcnian*.] —**wak'en·er** *n.*

wale (wāl) *n.* **1. a.** A raised ridge in the surface of some fabrics, as corduroy. **b.** The texture of such a ridge. **2.** A ridge raised on the skin by a lash or blow; welt. **3.** *Naut.* One of the heavy planks extending along the sides of a wooden ship. —*v.* **waled, wal·ing.** To mark with wales. [< OE *walu.*]

walk (wôk) *v.* **1.** To move or cause to move on foot at a pace slower than a run. **2.** To pass over, on, or through on foot. **3.** To conduct oneself in a particular manner. **4.** *Baseball.* To go or cause to go to first base after the pitcher has thrown four balls. —*n.* **1.** The act or an instance of walking. **2.** A distance to be covered in walking: *a five-minute walk to town.* **3.** A pathway or sidewalk on which to walk. **4.** A manner of walking; gait, esp. a slow gait of a horse in which the feet touch the ground one after another. **5.** *Baseball.* The automatic advance of a batter to first base after four balls have been pitched. [< OE *wealcan,* to roll.] —**walk'er** *n.*

walk·a·way (wôk'ə-wā') *n.* A contest or victory easily won.

walk·ie-talk·ie (wô'kē-tô'kē) *n.* A portable sending and receiving radio set.

walk-in (wôk'ĭn') *adj.* Large enough to admit entrance, as a closet. —**walk'-in'** *n.*

walking papers *pl.n. Informal.* Notice of discharge or dismissal.

walking stick *n.* **1.** A stick used as an aid in walking. **2.** Any of various insects that have the appearance of twigs or sticks.

walk-on (wôk'ŏn', -ôn') *n.* A minor role in a theatrical production, usu. without speaking lines.

walk-out (wôk'out') *n.* **1.** A strike of workers. **2.** The act of leaving or quitting a meeting, company, or organization as a sign of protest.

walk-o·ver (wôk'ō'vər) *n.* **1.** A horse race with only one horse entered, won by the mere formality of walking the length of the track. **2.** A walkaway.

walk-up (wôk'ŭp') *n.* Also **walk-up.** **1.** An apartment house or office building with no elevator. **2.** An apartment or office in a walkup.

walk·way (wôk'wā') *n.* A passage for walking.

wall (wôl) *n.* **1.** A vertical structure or partition that encloses an area or separates two areas. **2.** A continuous structure forming a rampart and built for defensive purposes. **3.** Something resembling a wall in appearance, function, or construction. —*v.* To enclose, surround, protect, or separate with or as if with a wall. [< Lat. *vallum.*]

wal·la·by (wŏl'ə-bē) *n., pl.* **-bies.** Any of various Australian marsupials related to and resembling the kangaroos but gen. smaller. [Native word in Australia.]

wall·board (wôl'bôrd', -bōrd') *n.* A structural material, as gypsum plaster encased in paper, used to cover interior walls and ceilings.

wal·let (wŏl'ĭt) *n.* A flat pocket-sized folding case for holding paper money, cards, and photographs; billfold. [ME *walet,* knapsack.]

wall·eye (wôl'ī') *n.* **1. a.** An eye abnormally turned away from the center of the face. **b.** An eye in which the cornea is white or opaque. **2.** A North American freshwater food and game fish with large, conspicuous eyes. —**wall'eyed'** *adj.*

wall·flow·er (wôl'flou'ər) *n.* **1. a.** A cultivated plant with fragrant yellow, orange, or brownish flowers. **2.** *Informal.* A person who does not participate in social activity because of shyness or unpopularity.

wal·lop (wŏl'əp) *v.* **1.** To beat soundly; thrash. **2.** To strike with a hard blow; hit. —*n.* **1.** A hard or severe blow. **2. a.** The ability to strike a wallop. **b.** The capacity to create a forceful effect; impact. [< ONFr. *waloper,* to gallop.] —**wal'lop·er** *n.*

wal·lop·ing (wŏl'ə-pĭng) *adj. Informal.* Very large; huge.

wal·low (wŏl'ō) *v.* **1.** To roll around in or as if in mud. **2.** To luxuriate; revel. **3.** To be or become abundantly supplied with something: *wallowing in money.* —*n.* A place, as a mud hole, where animals go to wallow. [< OE *wealwian.*]

wall·pa·per (wôl'pā'pər) *n.* Heavy paper with designs or colors for use as a wall covering. —**wall'pa'per** *v.*

wal·nut (wôl'nŭt', -nət) *n.* **1.** Any of several trees with round, sticky fruit that encloses an edible nut. **2.** The nut of a walnut. **3.** The hard, dark-brown wood of a walnut. [< OE *wealhhnutu.*]

wal·rus (wôl'rəs, wŏl'-) *n., pl.* **-es** or **-rus.** A large Arctic marine mammal with tough, wrinkled skin and large tusks. [Du.]

waltz (wôlts) *n.* **1.** A dance in triple time with a strong accent on the first beat. **2.** Music for the waltz. —*v.* **1.** To dance the waltz (with). **2.** To move lightly and easily: *waltzed out of the room.* **3.** To accomplish a task, chore, or assignment with little effort. [< OHG *walzan,* to roll.] —**waltz'er** *n.*

Wam·pa·no·ag (wăm'pə-nō'ăg') *n., pl.* **-ag** or **-ags. 1. a.** A tribe of Indians, formerly inhabiting eastern Rhode Island and adjacent parts of Massachusetts. **b.** A member of this tribe. **2.** The Algonquian language of the Wampanoag. —**Wam'pa·no'ag** *adj.*

wam·pum (wŏm'pəm, wôm'-) *n.* **1.** Beads made of polished shells strung together into strands or belts formerly used by North American Indians as money or jewelry. **2.** *Informal.* Money. [< Algonquian *wampumpeage,* white strings.]

wan (wŏn) *adj.* **wan·ner, wan·nest. 1.** Unnaturally pale; pallid. **2.** Weak or faint. **3.** Melancholy: *a wan smile.* [< OE *wann,* dark.] —**wan'ly** *adv.* —**wan'ness** *n.*

wand (wŏnd) *n.* **1.** A slender rod carried in a procession as a symbol of office. **2.** A rod used by a magician, diviner, or conjurer. [< ON *vöndr.*]

wan·der (wŏn'dər) *v.* **1.** To move about aimlessly or with no destination or purpose; roam. **2.** To go by an indirect route or at no

wallaby

walnut

set pace. **3.** To stray from a given place, path, group, or subject. **4.** To think or express oneself unclearly or incoherently. [< OE *wandrian.*] **—wan′der·er** *n.* **—wan′der·ing·ly** *adv.*

wandering jew *n.* A trailing plant with usu. variegated foliage that is popular as a house plant.

wan·der·lust (wŏn′dər-lŭst′) *n.* A strong or irresistible impulse to travel. [G.]

wane (wān) *v.* **waned, wan·ing.** **1.** To show a progressively smaller lighted surface, as the moon does when passing from full to new. **2.** To decrease, as in size, strength, or importance. **3.** To draw to a close: *The old year was waning.* —*n.* **1.** The time, phase, or stage during which the moon wanes. **2.** A gradual decrease or decline. [< OE *wanian,* to lessen.]

wan·gle (wăng′gəl) *v.* **-gled, -gling.** **1.** To make, achieve, or get by connivance. **2.** To manipulate or juggle, esp. fraudulently. [Orig. unknown.] **—wan′gler** *n.*

Wan·kel engine (văng′kəl, wăng′-) *n.* A rotary internal-combustion engine in which a triangular rotor performs the functions of the pistons of a conventional engine. [< Felix *Wankel* (b. 1902).]

want (wŏnt, wônt) *v.* **1.** To wish for; desire. **2.** To fail to have; lack. **3.** To have need of; require. **4.** To have need. —*n.* **1.** The condition or quality of lacking a usual or necessary amount. **2.** Pressing need; destitution. **3.** Something needed or wanted; desire. **4.** A defect; fault. [< ON *vanta,* to be lacking.]

want·ing (wŏn′tĭng, wôn′-) *adj.* **1.** Absent; lacking. **2.** Not up to standards or expectations. —*prep.* **1.** Without. **2.** Minus; less.

wan·ton (wŏn′tən) *adj.* **1.** Immoral or unchaste; lewd. **2.** Maliciously cruel; merciless: *wanton killing.* **3.** Sensual. **4.** Extravagant; excessive: *wanton spending.* **5.** Unrestrained; frolicsome. —*n.* A wanton person, esp. an immoral woman. [ME *wantowen.*] **—wan′ton·ly** *adv.* **—wan′ton·ness** *n.*

wap·i·ti (wŏp′ĭ-tē) *n., pl.* **-tis** or **-ti.** A large North American deer with many-branched antlers; elk. [Shawnee.]

war (wôr) *n.* **1.** A state or period of armed conflict between nations or states. **2.** A determined struggle or attack. **3.** A condition of antagonism or conflict. **4.** The techniques or procedures of war; military science. —*v.* **warred, war·ring.** **1.** To wage war. **2.** To struggle, contend, or fight. [< ONFr. *werre,* of Gmc. orig.]

war·ble (wôr′bəl) *v.* **-bled, -bling.** To sing with trills, runs, or other melodic embellishments. —*n.* The act or sound of warbling. [< ONFr. *werble,* a warbling, of Gmc. orig.]

war·bler (wôr′blər) *n.* **1.** Any of various small, often yellowish New World birds. **2.** Any of various small brownish or grayish Old World birds.

war bonnet *n.* A ceremonial headdress used by some North American Plains Indians that consists of a band and a trailing extension decorated with feathers.

war crime *n.* Often **war crimes.** A crime, as genocide, committed during a war. **—war criminal** *n.*

war cry *n.* **1.** A cry uttered by combatants as they attack; battle cry. **2.** A slogan used to rally people to a cause.

ward (wôrd) *n.* **1. a.** A division in a hospital. **b.** A division in a prison. **2.** An administrative division of a city or town, esp. an election district. **3.** A child or incompetent person placed under the care or protection of a guardian or a court. **4. a.** The condition of being under guard; custody. **b.** The act of guarding; guardianship. **5.** A means of protection. —*v.* To turn aside; avert: *warding off colds.* [< OE *weard,* a guarding.]

-ward or **-wards** *suff.* Direction toward: *skyward, westwards.* [< OE *-weard.*]

Usage: Since the suffixes *-ward* or *-wards* both indicate direction, there is no need to use the preposition *to* with either: *The ship is sailing westward* (not *to the westward*).

war dance *n.* A tribal dance performed by certain primitive peoples before a battle or as a celebration after a victory.

war·den (wôr′dn) *n.* **1.** The chief administrative official of a prison. **2.** An official charged with the enforcement of certain laws and regulations: *a game warden.* **3.** A churchwarden. [< ONFr. *warder,* to guard, of Gmc. orig.]

ward·er (wôr′dər) *n.* A guard or watchman. [< ONFr., to guard, of Gmc. orig.]

ward heel·er (hē′lər) *n.* *Slang.* A worker for the local organization of a political machine.

ward·robe (wôr′drōb′) *n.* **1.** A cabinet, closet, or room designed to hold clothes. **2.** Garments collectively, esp. all the clothing belonging to one person. [< ONFr. *warderobe.*]

ward·room (wôrd′rōōm′, -rŏŏm′) *n.* The common recreation area and dining room for the commissioned officers on a warship.

-wards *suff.* Var. of **-ward.**

ward·ship (wôrd′shĭp′) *n.* **1.** The condition of being a ward. **2.** Guardianship; custody.

ware (wâr) *n.* **1.** Articles of the same general kind: *glassware; silverware.* **2.** Pottery or ceramics: *earthenware.* **3. wares.** Articles of commerce; goods. [< OE *waru.*]

ware·house (wâr′hous′) *n.* A place in which goods or merchandise are stored. **—ware′-house′** *v.*

war·fare (wôr′fâr′) *n.* **1.** The act of waging war. **2.** Conflict; struggle. [ME.]

war·fa·rin (wôr′fər-ĭn) *n.* A crystalline compound, $C_{19}H_{16}O_4$, used to kill rodents and medicinally as an anticoagulant. [W(ISCONSIN) A(LUMNI) R(ESEARCH) F(OUNDATION) + *(coum)arin.*]

war·head (wôr′hĕd′) *n.* A section in the forward part of a projectile, as a guided missile, that contains the explosive charge.

war-horse (wôr′hôrs′) *n.* **1.** A horse used in combat; charger. **2.** *Informal.* One who has been through many struggles.

war·like (wôr′līk′) *adj.* **1.** Belligerent; hostile. **2.** Of or pertaining to war. **3.** Threatening or indicating war: *a warlike speech.*

war·lock (wôr′lŏk′) *n.* A male witch, sorcerer, or wizard. [< OE *wǣrloga,* oath-breaker.]

war·lord (wôr′lôrd′) *n.* **1.** A military leader, esp. of a warlike nation. **2.** A military commander exercising civil power in a given region, usu. by force of arms.

warm (wôrm) *adj.* **-er, -est.** **1.** Moderately hot.

2. Giving off or retaining a moderate amount of heat: *the warm sun; a warm sweater.* **3.** Having a sensation of unusually high bodily heat, as from exercise. **4.** Marked by enthusiasm; ardent: *warm support.* **5.** Excited, animated, or emotional: *a warm debate.* **6.** Recently made; fresh: *a warm trail.* **7.** Close to discovering, guessing, or finding something. **8.** *Informal.* Uncomfortable because of danger or annoyance: *Made things warm for the bookies.* —v. **1.** To make or become warm. **2.** To inspire with vitality, enthusiasm, or ardor. **3.** To fill with pleasant emotions: *Her smile warmed me.* **4.** To become ardent, enthusiastic, or animated: *warming to his subject.* —*phrasal verb.* **warm up.** To make or become ready for action, as by exercising or practicing beforehand. [< OE *wearm.*] —**warm′er** n. —**warm′ish** adj. —**warm′ly** adv. —**warm′ness** n.

warm-blood·ed (wôrm′blŭd′ĭd) adj. Maintaining a relatively constant warm body temperature independent of environmental temperature, as a mammal. —**warm′-blood′ed·ness** n.

warm-heart·ed (wôrm′här′tĭd) adj. Kind; friendly. —**warm′-heart′ed·ness** n.

war·mon·ger (wôr′mŭng′gər, -mŏng′-) n. One who advocates or attempts to stir up war. —**war′mon·ger·ing** n.

warmth (wôrmth) n. **1.** The quality or condition of being warm. **2.** Excitement or intensity. [ME.]

warm-up (wôrm′ŭp′) n. An act, procedure, or period of warming up.

warn (wôrn) v. **1.** To make aware of present or potential danger; caution. **2.** To admonish as to action or manners. **3.** To notify to go or stay away. **4.** To notify or inform in advance. [< OE *warnian.*]

warn·ing (wôr′nĭng) n. **1.** Advance notice, as of coming danger. **2. a.** A sign or notice of coming danger. **b.** The act of giving such a sign or notice. —adj. Acting or serving as a warning. —**warn′ing·ly** adv.

warp (wôrp) v. **1.** To twist or become twisted out of shape. **2.** To turn aside or cause to turn aside from a correct, healthy, or true course; pervert or corrupt. **3.** *Naut.* To move (a ship) by hauling on a line that is fastened to or around a piling, anchor, or pier. —n. **1.** The condition of being twisted or bent out of shape. **2.** A distortion or twist. **3.** The threads that run lengthwise in a fabric, crossed at right angles by the woof. [< OE *weorpan,* to throw.]

war paint n. **1.** Colored paints applied to the face or body by certain tribes before going to war. **2.** *Informal.* Cosmetics.

war·path (wôr′păth′, -päth′) n. **1.** The route taken by a party of North American Indians on the attack. **2.** A hostile or belligerent course or mood.

war·plane (wôr′plān′) n. A combat aircraft.

war·rant (wôr′ənt, wŏr′-) n. **1.** Authorization, sanction, or justification. **2.** Something that assures, attests to, or guarantees; proof. **3.** A writ or other order that serves as authorization for something, esp. a judicial writ authorizing a search, seizure, or arrest. **4.** A certificate of appointment given to warrant officers. —v. **1.** To attest to the quality, accuracy, or condition of. **2.** To vouch for. **3. a.** To guarantee (a product). **b.** To guarantee (a purchaser) indemnification against

damage or loss. **4.** To call for; justify. **5.** To authorize or empower. [< ONFr. *warant,* of Gmc. orig.] —**war′rant·a·ble** adj. —**war′rant·a·bly** adv. —**war′ran·tee′** n. —**war′ran·tor** n.

warrant officer n. An officer intermediate in rank between a noncommissioned officer and a commissioned officer, having authority to issue a warrant.

war·ran·ty (wôr′ən-tē, wŏr′-) n., pl. -ties. **1.** Official authorization or sanction. **2.** Justification or valid grounds for an act or course of action. **3.** A legally binding guarantee.

war·ren (wôr′ən, wŏr′-) n. **1.** An area where small game animals, esp. rabbits, live and breed. **2.** An overcrowded place where people live. [< ONFr. *warenne.*]

war·ri·or (wôr′ē-ər, wŏr′-) n. One engaged or experienced in battle. [< ONFr. *werreieur.*]

war·ship (wôr′shĭp′) n. A ship equipped for use in battle.

wart (wôrt) n. **1.** A small, usu. hard growth on the outer skin, esp. one caused by a virus. **2.** A protuberance resembling a wart, as on a plant. [< OE *wearte.*] —**wart′y** adj.

wart hog n. A wild African hog with two pairs of tusks and wartlike protuberances on the face.

war·time (wôr′tīm′) n. A time of war.

war·y (wâr′ē) adj. -i·er, -i·est. **1.** On one's guard; watchful. **2.** Characterized by caution; cautious. [< OE *wær.*] —**war′i·ly** adv. —**war′i·ness** n.

was (wŏz, wŭz; wəz when unstressed) v. 1st and 3rd person sing. past tense of **be**.

wash (wŏsh, wôsh) v. **1.** To cleanse, using water or other liquid, usu. with soap, detergent, etc., by immersing, dipping, rubbing, or scrubbing. **2.** To cleanse oneself. **3.** To rid of corruption; purify. **4.** To make moist or wet. **5.** To flow over, against, or past: *shores washed by ocean tides.* **6.** To sweep or carry away: *The rain had washed them away.* **7.** To erode or destroy by moving water: *The roads were washed out.* **8.** To coat with a watery layer of paint or other coloring substance. **9.** To remove particulate constituents from (as ore) by immersion or agitation with water. **10.** *Informal.* To withstand examination: *Your excuse won't wash.* —n. **1.** An act, process, or period of washing. **2.** A quantity of articles that are to be or have just been washed. **3.** A liquid used in washing or coating. **4. a.** A turbulent flow of water or waves. **b.** The sound of this. **5.** Waste liquid; swill. **6.** The removal or erosion of soil or subsoil by the action of moving water. **7.** *Western U.S.* The dry bed of a stream. [< OE *wacsan.*]

wash·a·ble (wŏsh′ə-bəl, wô′shə-bəl) adj. Capable of being washed without damage.

wash-and-wear (wŏsh′ən-wâr′, wôsh′-) adj. Treated so as to require little or no ironing after being washed.

wash·ba·sin (wŏsh′bā′sĭn) n. A washbowl.

wash·board (wŏsh′bôrd′, -bōrd′, wôsh′-) n. A board with a corrugated surface on which clothes can be rubbed during laundering.

wash·bowl (wŏsh′bōl′, wôsh′-) n. A basin that can be filled with water for use in washing oneself.

wash·cloth (wŏsh′klôth′, -klŏth′, wôsh′-) n. A cloth used for washing the face or body.

washed-out (wŏsht′out′, wôsht′-) adj. **1.** Lacking color; pale. **2.** *Informal.* Exhausted.

wash·er (wŏsh′ər, wô′shər) n. **1.** One that

washes, esp. a machine for washing. **2.** A small disk, as of metal, placed under a nut or at an axle bearing to relieve friction, prevent leakage, or distribute pressure.

wash·er·wom·an (wŏsh′ər-wŏŏm′ən, wô′shər-) *n.* A laundress.

wash·ing (wŏsh′ĭng, wô′shĭng) *n.* **1.** A quantity of articles washed at one time. **2.** The residue after an ore has been washed.

washing soda *n.* A hydrated sodium carbonate, used as a general cleanser.

wash·out (wŏsh′out′, wôsh′-) *n.* **1.** The erosion or carrying away of something, such as a roadbed, by the action of water. **2.** A total failure or disappointment.

wash·room (wŏsh′rŏŏm′, -rŏŏm′, wôsh′-) *n.* A bathroom or lavatory, esp. one in a public place.

wash·stand (wŏsh′stănd′, wôsh′-) *n.* **1.** A stand holding a basin and a pitcher of water for washing. **2.** A stationary bathroom sink.

wash·tub (wŏsh′tŭb′, wôsh′-) *n.* A tub used for soaking or washing clothes.

wash·wom·an (wŏsh′wŏŏm′ən, wôsh′-) *n.* A washerwoman.

wash·y (wŏsh′ē, wô′shē) *adj.* **-i·er, -i·est.** **1.** Watery; diluted. **2.** Lacking intensity or strength.

was·n't (wŏz′ənt, wŭz′-). Was not.

wasp (wŏsp, wôsp) *n.* Any of various insects that have a slender body with a narrow midsection and often inflict a painful sting. [< OE *wæsp.*]

Wasp or **WASP** (wŏsp, wôsp) *n.* A white American Protestant of Anglo-Saxon ancestry. [W(HITE) + A(NGLO)-S(AXON) + P(ROTESTANT).]

wasp·ish (wŏs′pĭsh, wô′spĭsh) *adj.* **1.** Of or suggestive of a wasp. **2.** Easily irritated or annoyed; snappish. **—wasp′ish·ly** *adv.* **—wasp′ish·ness** *n.*

wasp waist *n.* A very slender or tightly corseted waist. **—wasp′-waist′ed** (wŏsp′wās′-tĭd, wôsp′-) *adj.*

was·sail (wŏs′əl, wô-sāl′) *n.* **1. a.** A toast formerly given in drinking someone's health. **b.** The drink used in such toasting. **2.** A festive party or celebration with much drinking. **—v.** To drink to the health of; toast. [< ON *ves heill,* be healthy.] **—was′sail·er** *n.*

Was·ser·mann test (wä′sər-mən) *n.* A diagnostic test for syphilis. [< August Von *Wassermann* (1866–1925).]

wast (wŏst, wŭst) *v. Archaic.* 2nd person sing. past tense of **be.**

wast·age (wā′stĭj) *n.* Loss by deterioration, wear, destruction, use, or wastefulness.

waste (wāst) *v.* **wast·ed, wast·ing.** **1.** To use, consume, or expend thoughtlessly, carelessly, or needlessly; squander. **2.** To lose or cause to lose energy, strength, or vigor: *Disease wasted his body.* **3.** To allow to pass without being used; lose: *waste an opportunity.* **4.** To destroy completely. **—n.** **1. a.** The act or an instance of wasting. **b.** The state of being wasted. **2.** Gradual loss through careless or needless use, action, or practice; wastefulness. **3.** A worthless or useless by-product; refuse. **4.** The undigested residue of food eliminated from the body. **5.** A barren or wild area,

region, or expanse. [< Lat. *vastare,* to make empty.] **—wast′er** *n.*

Syns: *waste, consume, devour, expend, squander v.*

waste·bas·ket (wāst′băs′kĭt) *n.* A container for refuse.

waste·ful (wāst′fəl) *adj.* Characterized by or given to waste; extravagant. **—waste′ful·ly** *adv.* **—waste′ful·ness** *n.*

waste·land (wāst′lănd′) *n.* Uncultivated or desolate land.

waste·pa·per (wāst′pā′pər) *n.* Paper that is discarded after use.

was·trel (wā′strəl) *n.* **1.** One who wastes. **2.** An idler or loafer. [< WASTE.]

watch (wŏch) *v.* **1.** To observe carefully or continuously. **2.** To look and wait expectantly or in anticipation: *watch for an opportunity.* **3.** To be on the lookout or alert; guard. **4.** To stay awake deliberately; keep vigil. **5.** To keep up on or informed about: *watched her progress in college.* **6.** To keep a watchful eye on; tend: *a shepherd watching his sheep.* **—n.** **1.** The act of watching. **2.** A period of close observation. **3.** A person or group of persons serving, esp. at night, to guard or protect. **4.** The post or period of duty of a guard, sentinel, or watchman: *a two-hour watch.* **5.** A small, portable timepiece, esp. one worn on the wrist or carried in the pocket. **6.** *Naut.* **a.** Any of the periods of time during which a part of the crew is assigned to duty. **b.** The members of a ship's crew on duty during a specific watch. [< OE *wæccan.*] **—watch′er** *n.*

Syns: *watch, eye, observe, scrutinize v.*

watch·dog (wŏch′dôg′, -dŏg′) *n.* **1.** A dog trained to guard property. **2.** One who serves as a guardian or protector.

watch·ful (wŏch′fəl) *adj.* Closely observant and alert; vigilant. **—watch′ful·ly** *adv.* **—watch′ful·ness** *n.*

watch·mak·er (wŏch′mā′kər) *n.* One who makes or repairs watches. **—watch′mak′ing** *n.*

watch·man (wŏch′mən) *n.* A man employed to stand guard or keep watch.

watch·tow·er (wŏch′tou′ər) *n.* An observation tower for a guard or lookout.

watch·word (wŏch′wûrd′) *n.* **1.** A prearranged reply to a challenge, as from a guard; password. **2.** A rallying cry; slogan.

wa·ter (wô′tər, wŏt′ər) *n.* **1.** A clear, colorless, odorless, and tasteless liquid, H₂O, that is essential for most plant and animal life and is the most widely used of all solvents. **2.** Any of various forms of water, as rain. **3.** A body of water, as an ocean, lake, river, or stream. **4.** A bodily fluid, as urine, perspiration, or tears. **5.** Any of various liquids that contain and somewhat resemble water. **6.** A wavy finish or sheen, as of a fabric. **7. a.** Clarity and luster of a gem. **b.** Degree; quality: *of the first water.* **—v.** **1.** To sprinkle, moisten, or supply with water. **2.** To supply with drinking water. **3.** To dilute or weaken by or as if by adding water to. **4.** To treat so as to produce a wavy surface effect, as on silk. **5.** To produce or discharge water, as from the eyes: *His mouth watered.* [< OE *wæter.*]

water bed *n.* A bed whose mattress is a large water-filled plastic bag.

ă pat ā pay â care ä father ĕ pet ē be ĭ pit ī tie î pier ŏ pot ō toe ô paw, for oi noise ŏŏ took
ŏŏ boot ou out th thin th this ŭ cut û urge yŏŏ abuse zh vision ə about, item, edible, gallop, circus

wa·ter·borne (wô′tər-bôrn′, -bōrn′, wŏt′ər-) *adj.* Supported or transported by water.

water buffalo *n.* An Asian or African buffalo that has large, spreading horns and is often domesticated.

water buffalo
Water buffalo and calf

water chestnut *n.* 1. A Chinese sedge with an edible corm. 2. The succulent corm of the water chestnut.

water closet *n.* A room or booth containing a toilet and often a sink.

water color *n.* Also **wa·ter·col·or** (wô′tər-kŭl′ər, wŏt′ər-). 1. A paint in which water is mixed with the pigment before use. 2. A painting done in water colors. 3. The art or process of painting with water colors. —**wa·ter colorist** *n.*

wa·ter·course (wô′tər-kôrs′, -kōrs′, wŏt′ər-) *n.* 1. A waterway. 2. The bed or channel of a waterway.

wa·ter·cress (wô′tər-krĕs′, wŏt′ər-) *n.* A plant growing in freshwater ponds and streams and having pungent edible leaves.

wa·ter·fall (wô′tər-fôl′, wŏt′ər-) *n.* A steep descent of water from a height.

wa·ter·fowl (wô′tər-foul′, wŏt′ər-) *n., pl.* **-fowl** or **-fowls.** 1. A swimming bird, as a duck or goose, usu. frequenting freshwater areas. 2. Swimming birds collectively.

wa·ter·front (wô′tər-frŭnt′, wŏt′ər-) *n.* 1. Land that borders a body of water. 2. The district of a town or city that borders the water.

water gap *n.* A cleft in a mountain ridge through which a stream flows.

Wa·ter·gate (wô′tər-gāt′, wŏt′ər-) *n. Informal.* A scandal that involves officials violating public or corporate trust through acts of abuse of power. [< *Watergate,* a building complex in Washington, D.C.]

watering place *n.* A health resort featuring water activities or mineral springs.

wa·ter·ish (wô′tər-ĭsh, wŏt′ər-) *adj.* Watery.

water lily *n.* Any of various aquatic plants with broad floating leaves and showy, variously colored flowers.

water line *n.* Any of several parallel lines on the hull of a ship that indicate the depth to which the ship sinks under various loads.

wa·ter·logged (wô′tər-lôgd′, -lŏgd′, wŏt′ər-) *adj.* So soaked or saturated with water as to be heavy, sluggish, or unwieldy.

wa·ter·loo (wô′tər-lōō′, wŏt′ər-) *n., pl.* **-loos.** A disastrous or crushing defeat. [< *Waterloo,* Belgium.]

wa·ter·mark (wô′tər-märk′, wŏt′ər-) *n.* 1. A mark showing the height to which water has risen. 2. A translucent design impressed on paper during manufacture and visible when the paper is held to the light. —*v.* To mark (paper) with a watermark.

wa·ter·mel·on (wô′tər-mĕl′ən, wŏt′ər-) *n.* 1. An African vine cultivated for its large, edible fruit. 2. The fruit of the watermelon, having a hard green rind and sweet, watery reddish flesh.

water moccasin *n.* A venomous snake of swampy regions of the southern United States.

water ouzel *n.* Any of several small birds that dive into swift-moving streams and feed along the bottom.

water polo *n.* A water sport with two teams that try to pass a ball into the other's goal.

wa·ter·pow·er (wô′tər-pou′ər, wŏt′ər-) *n.* The energy of falling or running water as used for driving machinery, esp. for generating electricity.

wa·ter·proof (wô′tər-prōōf′, wŏt′ər-) *adj.* Impenetrable to or unaffected by water. —*n.* 1. A waterproof material or fabric. 2. *Chiefly Brit.* A raincoat. —*v.* To make waterproof.

wa·ter·re·pel·lent (wô′tər-rĭ-pĕl′ənt, wŏt′ər-) *adj.* Resistant to water but not entirely waterproof.

wa·ter·re·sis·tant (wô′tər-rĭ-zĭs′tənt, wŏt′ər-) *adj.* Water-repellent.

wa·ter·shed (wô′tər-shĕd′, wŏt′ər-) *n.* 1. A ridge of high land dividing two areas drained by different river systems. 2. The region or area that drains into a body of water.

wa·ter·side (wô′tər-sīd′, wŏt′ər-) *n.* Land bordering a body of water.

wa·ter·ski (wô′tər-skē′, wŏt′ər-) *n.* Also **water ski.** A ski used for gliding over water while being towed by a motorboat. —**wa·ter·ski′** *v.* —**wa·ter·ski′er** *n.*

wa·ter·spout (wô′tər-spout′, wŏt′ər-) *n.* 1. A pipe from which water, esp. rainwater, is discharged. 2. A tornado or whirlwind occurring over water and resulting in a whirling column of spray and mist.

water table *n.* The depth or level below which the ground is saturated with water.

wa·ter·tight (wô′tər-tīt′, wŏt′ər-) *adj.* 1. Permitting neither entry nor escape of water. 2. Having no flaws or loopholes: *a watertight alibi.*

wa·ter·way (wô′tər-wā′, wŏt′ər-) *n.* A navigable body of water, as a river, used for travel or transport.

water wheel *n.* A wheel driven by falling or running water, used esp. as a source of power.

water wings *pl.n.* An inflatable device used to support the body of a person learning to swim or swimming.

wa·ter·works (wô′tər-wûrks′, wŏt′ər-) *pl.n.* The water system, including reservoirs, tanks, buildings, pumps, and pipes, of a city or town.

wa·ter·y (wô′tə-rē, wŏt′ər-) *adj.* **-i·er, -i·est.** 1. Filled with, consisting of, or containing water. 2. Resembling or suggestive of water. 3. Diluted: *watery soup.* 4. Without force; insipid: *watery prose.* —**wa′ter·i·ness** *n.*

watt (wŏt) *n.* A unit of power equal to one joule per second, or about ¹/₇₄₆ horsepower. [< James *Watt* (1736–1819).]

watt·age (wŏt′ĭj) *n.* An amount of power, esp. electric power, expressed in watts.

wat·tle (wŏt′l) *n.* 1. **a.** Poles intertwined with twigs, branches, reeds, or similar materials for use in construction, as of walls or fences. **b.** Materials used for such a framework. 2. A fleshy, often brightly colored fold of skin hanging from the neck or throat of certain birds. [< OE *watel*.]

wave (wāv) v. **waved, wav·ing. 1.** To move or cause to move back and forth or up and down in the air. **2.** To signal or make a signal by waving. **3.** To curve or curl: *Her hair waves.* —n. **1.** A ridge or swell moving along the surface of a body of water. **2.** A curve or succession of curves in or on a surface; undulation: *waves of wheat.* **3.** A curve or curl, as in the hair. **4.** A movement up and down or back and forth: *a wave of the hand.* **5.** A surge: *a wave of indignation.* **6.** A persistent meteorological condition: *a heat wave.* **7.** *Physics.* A disturbance or oscillation propagated from point to point in a medium or in space. [< OE *wafian.*]

wave-band (wāv'bănd') n. A range of frequencies, esp. of radio frequencies.

wave-form (wāv'fôrm') n. The mathematical representation of a wave, esp. a graph of deviation at a fixed point versus time.

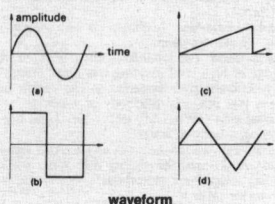

waveform
Single period of common electrical
waveforms: (a) sine wave; (b)
square wave; (c) saw-tooth wave;
(d) triangular wave

wave-length (wāv'lĕngth') n. The distance between two points of identical phase in successive cycles of a periodic wave.

wave-let (wāv'lĭt) n. A small wave; ripple.

wa-ver (wā'vər) v. **1.** To move or swing back and forth; sway. **2.** To show or experience irresolution or indecision; vacillate. **3.** To falter or yield: *His resolve began to waver.* **4.** To tremble or quaver, as a voice. **5.** To flicker or flash, as light. [ME *waveren,* to wander.] —wav'er n. —wa'ver·ing·ly adv.

wav-y (wā'vē) adj. **-i-er, -i-est. 1.** Having or rising in waves: *a wavy sea.* **2.** Marked by wavelike curves; sinuous: *a wavy line.* **3.** Having curls, curves, or undulations: *wavy hair.* —wav'i-ly adv. —wav'i-ness n.

waw (väv, vôv) n. Var. of **vav.**

wax¹ (wăks) n. **1.** Any of various natural unctuous, viscous, or solid heat-sensitive substances, as beeswax, consisting essentially of heavy hydrocarbons or fats. **2.** A waxlike substance found in the ears. **3.** A preparation containing wax and used esp. for polishing. —v. To cover, coat, treat, or polish with wax. [< OE *weax.*]

wax² (wăks) v. **1.** To show a progressively larger light surface, as the moon does in passing from new to full. **2.** To increase gradually in quantity, extent, strength, or intensity.

3. To grow or become: *a speaker waxing eloquent.* [< OE *weaxan.*]

wax bean n. A variety of string bean with yellow pods.

wax-en (wăk'sən) adj. **1.** Made of or covered with wax. **2.** Resembling wax, as in paleness or smoothness: *waxen skin.*

wax myrtle n. A shrub of the southeastern United States that has aromatic evergreen leaves and berrylike fruit with a waxy coating.

wax-wing (wăks'wĭng') n. A crested bird with predominantly brown plumage and waxy red tips on the wing feathers.

wax-work (wăks'wûrk') n. **1.** A figure made of wax, esp. a life-size wax representation of a person. **2. waxworks.** An exhibition of waxwork in a museum.

wax-y (wăk'sē) adj. **-i-er, -i-est. 1.** Resembling wax, as in texture or consistency: *waxy petals.* **2.** Consisting of, full of, or covered with wax. —wax'i-ness n.

way (wā) n. **1.** A manner of doing something. **2.** A method or technique: *a better way of sewing slipcovers.* **3.** A respect, particular, or feature: *improving in many ways.* **4.** A habit, characteristic, or tendency: *Things have a way of happening.* **5.** A usual or customary course of action or state of affairs. **6.** A road, route, path, or passage that leads from one place to another. **7.** Progress or advancement in accomplishing a goal: *worked her way up.* **8.** Room enough to pass or proceed. **9.** Distance: *a short way off the ground.* **10.** A specific direction: *Which way did he go?* **11.** Skill; facility: *has a way with words.* **12.** Wish or will: *if I had my way.* **13.** A course of action: *the easy way out.* **14.** *Informal.* A condition: *in a bad way financially.* **15.** *Informal.* A neighborhood or district: *out your way.* —idioms. by the way. Incidentally. by way of. **1.** Through; via. **2.** As a means of: *by way of celebration.* out of the way. **1.** In a remote location. **2.** Improper. under way. In progress. [< OE *weg,* road.]

way-bill (wā'bĭl') n. A document that contains a list of goods and shipping instructions relative to a shipment.

way-far-er (wā'fâr'ər) n. A person who travels, esp. one who travels on foot. [ME *weyfarere.*] —way'far·ing adj. & n.

way-lay (wā'lā') v. **1.** To lie in wait for and attack from ambush. **2.** To accost or intercept. —way'lay·er n.

way-out (wā'out') adj. *Slang.* Far-out.

-ways suff. Manner, direction, or position: *sideways.* [ME < *weyes,* in such a way.]

ways and means pl.n. Means or methods for increasing the financial resources available to a person or group in order to accomplish a specific end.

way-side (wā'sīd') n. The side or edge of a road.

way station n. A station between major stops on a travel route.

way-ward (wā'wərd) adj. **1.** Stubborn or disobedient; willful: *a wayward boy.* **2.** Irregular; unpredictable. [ME *awayward,* turned away.] —way'ward·ly adv. —way'ward·ness n.

we (wē) pron. **1.** Used to refer to the speaker and another or others. **2.** Used instead of *I* by a sovereign or by a writer. [< OE *wē.*]

weak (wēk) *adj.* **-er, -est.** **1.** Lacking physical strength, force, or energy; feeble. **2.** Likely to fail or break under pressure, stress, weight, or strain. **3.** Lacking strength of character, will, or purpose. **4.** Lacking the usual, proper, or full strength of a component or ingredient: *weak coffee.* **5.** Unable to function well or normally; unsound. **6.** Lacking capacity or capability. **7.** Not persuasive or convincing; inadequate: *a weak defense.* **8.** Lacking power or intensity; faint: *a weak voice; weak light.* **9.** *Ling.* Of, pertaining to, or being a verb that forms the past tense and past participle by means of *-ed, -d,* or *-t.* **10.** Unstressed or unaccented, as a syllable. [< ON *veikr.*] —**weak'ly** *adv.*

weak·en (wē'kən) *v.* To make or become weak or weaker.

weak·fish (wēk'fĭsh') *n.* A marine food and game fish of North Atlantic waters. [Obs. Du. *weekvis.*]

weak-kneed (wēk'nēd') *adj.* Irresolute; timid.

weak·ling (wēk'lĭng) *n.* One who is weak in body, character, or mind.

weak·ly (wēk'lē) *adj.* **-li·er, -li·est.** Feeble; weak.

weak·ness (wēk'nĭs) *n.* **1.** The condition or feeling of being weak. **2.** A defect, fault, or failing. **3.** A special fondness or liking: *a weakness for chocolate.*

weal¹ (wēl) *n.* Prosperity; well-being. [< OE *wela.*]

weal² (wēl) *n.* A welt. [< WALE.]

weald (wēld) *n.* Chiefly *Brit.* **1.** A woodland. **2.** An area of open rolling upland. [< OE.]

wealth (wĕlth) *n.* **1.** A great quantity of money or valuable possessions; riches. **2.** The condition of being rich; affluence. **3.** A profusion or abundance. **4.** All goods and resources having economic value. [< OE *wela.*]

wealth·y (wĕl'thē) *adj.* **-i·er, -i·est.** Having wealth; rich, prosperous, or affluent.

wean (wēn) *v.* **1.** To cause (a young mammal) to give up suckling and accept other food. **2.** To rid of a habit or interest: *wean him from cigarettes.* [< OE *wĕpen.*]

weap·on (wĕp'ən) *n.* **1.** An instrument or device used to attack another or to defend oneself from attack. **2.** A means employed to overcome, persuade, or get the better of another. [< OE *wĕpen.*]

weap·on·ry (wĕp'ən-rē) *n.* Weapons collectively.

wear (wâr) *v.* **wore** (wôr, wōr), **worn** (wôrn, wōrn), **wear·ing.** **1.** To have or put on: *wear a dress; wear a wristwatch.* **2.** To have or carry habitually on one's person: *wear a beard; wear a gun.* **3.** To affect or exhibit: *wear a smile.* **4.** To bear or maintain in a particular manner: *wears her hair long.* **5.** To impair or consume by or as if by long or hard use, friction, or exposure to the elements: *wore the elbows of his jacket.* **6.** To produce by constant use or exposure: *wore hollows in the steps.* **7.** To fatigue, weary, or exhaust: *criticism that wore her patience.* **8.** To endure continual or hard use; last: *That fabric wears well.* **9.** To become by use or attrition: *The gold band wore thin.* **10.** To pass tediously or gradually: *The hours wore on endlessly.* —*phrasal verbs.* **wear down.** To break down the resistance of by relentless pressure: *wear down the opposition.* **wear off.** To diminish gradually and cease having an effect: *The headache wore off.* **wear out. 1.** To make or become unusable through heavy use. **2.** To exhaust: *wore out her welcome.* —*n.* **1.** The act of wearing or state of being worn; use. **2.** Clothing, esp. of a particular kind or for a particular use: *men's wear; evening wear.* **3.** Gradual impairment or diminution resulting from use or attrition: *The rug is beginning to show wear.* **4.** The capacity to withstand use; durability. [< OE *werian.*] —**wear'a·ble** *adj.* —**wear'er** *n.*

wea·ri·some (wîr'ē-səm) *adj.* Causing mental or physical fatigue; tedious. —**wea'ri·some·ly** *adv.* —**wea'ri·some·ness** *n.*

wea·ry (wîr'ē) *adj.* **-ri·er, -ri·est.** **1.** Tired; fatigued. **2.** Expressive of fatigue: *a weary sigh.* **3.** Exhausted of tolerance; impatient: *weary of constant complaints.* —*v.* **-ried, -ry·ing.** To make or become weary; fatigue. [< OE *wērig.*] —**wea'ri·ly** *adv.* —**wea'ri·ness** *n.*

wea·sel (wē'zəl) *n.* **1.** Any of various carnivorous mammals with a long, slender body, short legs, and a long tail. **2.** A sneaky, deceitful person. —*v.* To be evasive; equivocate. [< OE *wesle.*]

weasel   weather vane

weath·er (wĕth'ər) *n.* **1.** The condition of the atmosphere at a given time and place with respect to temperature, humidity, wind velocity, and barometric pressure. **2.** Bad, rough, or stormy atmospheric conditions. —*v.* **1.** To expose to or withstand the action of the weather. **2.** To show the effects of exposure to the weather. **3.** To pass through safely; survive. [< OE *weder.*] —**weath'ered** *adj.*

weath·er-beat·en (wĕth'ər-bēt'n) *adj.* **1.** Worn by exposure to the weather. **2.** Tanned and toughened from exposure to the weather: *weather-beaten hands.*

weath·er·board (wĕth'ər-bôrd', -bōrd') *n.* Clapboard.

weath·er-bound (wĕth'ər-bound') *adj.* Delayed, halted, or kept indoors by bad weather.

weath·er·cock (wĕth'ər-kŏk') *n.* **1.** A weather vane, esp. in the form of a rooster. **2.** One that is fickle.

weath·er·ing (wĕth'ər-ĭng) *n.* Chemical or mechanical processes by which rocks exposed to the weather are broken up.

weath·er·man (wĕth'ər-măn') *n.* One who forecasts or reports weather conditions.

weath·er·proof (wĕth'ər-prōōf') *adj.* Able to withstand exposure to weather without damage. —*v.* To make weatherproof.

weath·er-strip (wĕth'ər-strĭp') *v.* To fit or equip with weather stripping.

weather stripping *n.* A narrow piece of material installed around doors and windows to protect an interior from external temperature extremes.

weather vane *n.* A vane that indicates wind direction.

weave (wēv) *v.* **wove** (wōv) or **weaved, wo·ven** (wō'vən), **weav·ing.** **1. a.** To make (cloth) on a loom by interlacing woof and warp threads: *weave brocade.* **b.** To interlace (strands) into cloth. **2.** To construct by interlacing or interweaving the materials or components of: *weave a basket.* **3.** To combine (elements) into a whole. **4.** To thread in and out through a material or composition: *wove a love theme through the final act.* **5.** To spin (a web) as a spider does. **6.** To move or progress by going from side to side or in and out; wind: *weaving her way through traffic.* **—n.** A pattern or method of weaving: *a twill weave.* [< OE *wefan.*] **—weav'er** *n.*

web (wĕb) *n.* **1.** A fabric being woven on or being removed from a loom. **2.** A latticed or woven structure. **3.** A structure of threadlike filaments spun by a spider. **4.** Something intricately constructed, esp. something that ensnares or entangles: *a web of lies.* **5.** A complex network: *a web of telephone wires.* **6.** A fold of skin or membranous tissue, as that connecting the toes of certain water birds. **7.** The vane of a feather. **8.** A metal sheet or plate, as one connecting the sections of a structural element. **—v. webbed, webbing.** **1.** To provide or cover with a web. **2.** To catch or ensnare in or as if in a web. [< OE.] **—webbed** *adj.*

web·bing (wĕb'ĭng) *n.* Sturdy woven strips of fabric used where strength is required, as for seat belts, brake linings, or upholstery.

web-foot·ed (wĕb'fŏŏt'ĭd) *adj.* Having feet with webbed toes.

wed (wĕd) *v.* **wed·ded, wed** or **wed·ded, wed·ding.** **1.** To take as husband or wife; marry. **2.** To perform the marriage ceremony for. **3.** To bind or join; unite. [< OE *weddian.*]

wed·ding (wĕd'ĭng) *n.* **1.** The ceremony or celebration of a marriage. **2.** The anniversary of a marriage. **3.** A close association or union: *a wedding of ideas.*

wedge (wĕj) *n.* **1.** A triangular metal or wood piece tapered for insertion in a narrow crevice and used for splitting, tightening, securing, or levering. **2.** Something shaped like a wedge: *a wedge of pie.* **3.** Something, as a policy or action, that causes divisiveness or a breach among people. **—v. wedged, wedg·ing.** **1.** To split or force apart with or as if with a wedge. **2.** To fix in place with a wedge. **3.** To crowd or force into a limited space. [< OE *wecg.*]

wed·lock (wĕd'lŏk') *n.* The state of being married; matrimony. [< OE *wedlāc.*]

Wednes·day (wĕnz'dē, -dā') *n.* The 4th day of the week. [< OE *Wōdnesdæg.*]

wee (wē) *adj.* **we·er, we·est.** **1.** Very small; tiny. **2.** Very early: *the wee hours.* [< OE *wǣge,* a weight.]

weed¹ (wēd) *n.* A plant considered troublesome, useless, or unattractive, esp. one growing abundantly in cultivated ground. **—v.** **1.** To remove weeds from. **2.** To remove or get rid of as unsuitable or unwanted: *weed out unqualified applicants.* [< OE *wēod.*] **—weed'er** *n.* **—weed'i·ness** *n.* **—weed'y** *adj.*

weed² (wēd) *n.* **1.** A token of mourning. **2. weeds.** A widow's mourning clothes. [< OE *wǣd,* a garment.]

week (wēk) *n.* **1.** A period of seven days, esp. a period that begins on a Sunday and continues through the next Saturday. **2.** The part of

a calendar week devoted to work, school, or business. [< OE *wicu.*]

week·day (wēk'dā') *n.* **1.** A day of the week except Sunday. **2.** A day that is not part of the weekend.

week·end (wēk'ĕnd') *n.* The end of the week, esp. the period from Friday evening through Sunday evening. **—v.** To spend the weekend.

week·ly (wēk'lē) *adv.* **1.** Once a week. **2.** Every week. **3.** By the week. **—adj.** **1.** Done, happening, coming, or issued once a week or every week. **2.** Computed by the week. **—n.,** *pl.* **-lies.** A publication issued weekly.

ween (wēn) *v.* **weened, ween·ing.** *Archaic.* To think; suppose. [< OE *wenan.*]

weep (wēp) *v.* **wept** (wĕpt), **weep·ing.** **1.** To shed (tears) as an expression of emotion, esp. grief; cry. **2.** To ooze or exude (moisture). [< OE *wēpan.*] **—weep'er** *n.*

weep·ing (wē'pĭng) *adj.* **1.** Tearful. **2.** Having slender, drooping branches.

weep·y (wē'pē) *adj.* **-i·er, -i·est.** Tending to weep; tearful.

wee·vil (wē'vəl) *n.* Any of numerous beetles that characteristically have a downward-curving snout and are destructive to plants and stored plant products. [< OE *wifel.*] **—wee'vil·y** or **wee'vil·ly** *adj.*

weft (wĕft) *n.* **1.** The woof in weaving. **2.** Woven fabric. [< OE *wefta.*]

weigh (wā) *v.* **1.** To determine the weight of by or as if by using a scale or balance. **2.** To consider or balance in the mind; ponder. **3.** *Naut.* To raise (an anchor). **4.** To have or be of a specific weight. **5.** To be considered important; count: *a factor that weighed heavily against her.* **6.** To burden or be a burden on; oppress. **—phrasal verb. weigh in.** To be weighed before participating in a contest or sports event, as a fight. [< OE *wegan.*]

weight (wāt) *n.* **1.** A measure of the heaviness or mass of an object. **2. a.** The gravitational force exerted on an object, equal to the product of the object's mass and the local value of gravitational acceleration. **b.** A unit measure of this force. **c.** A system of such measures. **3.** An object used principally to exert a force by virtue of its gravitational attraction to the earth, esp.: **a.** A solid used as a standard in weighing. **b.** An object used to hold something down. **c.** A heavy object used in weightlifting. **4.** Burden: *the weight of responsibilities.* **5.** The greatest part; preponderance. **6.** Influence; importance. **—v.** **1.** To add heaviness or weight to. **2.** To load down; burden. [< OE *wiht.*]

weight·less (wāt'lĭs) *adj.* **1.** Having little or no weight. **2.** Experiencing little or no gravitational force. **—weight'less·ly** *adv.* **—weight'less·ness** *n.*

weight·lift·ing (wāt'lĭf'tĭng) *n.* The lifting of heavy weights as an exercise or in athletic competition.

weight·y (wā'tē) *adj.* **-i·er, -i·est.** **1.** Heavy. **2.** Of great consequence; important: *a weighty matter.* **3.** Burdensome: *weighty responsibilities.* **4.** Carrying weight; authoritative or influential: *a weighty argument.* **—weight'i·ly** *adv.* **—weight'i·ness** *n.*

weir (wîr) *n.* **1.** A dam across a river or canal to raise, divert, or regulate the flow of the

---

water. 2. A fence, as of branches, placed in a stream to catch fish. [< OE *wer.*]

weird (wîrd) *adj.* **-er, -est. 1.** Suggestive of or concerned with the supernatural; unearthly. **2.** Of an odd, peculiar, or inexplicable character; unusual. [< OE *wyrd,* fate.] —**weird′ly** *adv.* —**weird′ness** *n.*

wel·come (wĕl′kəm) *v.* **-comed, -com·ing. 1.** To greet or entertain cordially or hospitably. **2.** To receive or accept gladly. —*n.* A cordial greeting or hospitable reception. —*adj.* **1.** Greeted, received, or accepted with pleasure. **2.** Freely permitted or invited: *welcome to stay for dinner.* **3.** Used to acknowledge an expression of gratitude: *"Thank you." "You're welcome."* —*interj.* Used to greet a visitor or recent arrival cordially. [< OE *wilcuma,* welcome guest.]

weld (wĕld) *v.* **1.** To join (metal parts) by subjecting to heat and sometimes pressure. **2.** To bring into close association; unite. —*n.* A union or joint produced by welding. [< WELL[1], to weld (obs.).] —**weld′er** *n.*

wel·fare (wĕl′fâr′) *n.* **1.** Health, happiness, or prosperity; well-being. **2.** Organized efforts by a community or an organization for the betterment of the poor. **3.** Public relief. [< ME *wel faren,* to fare well.]

welfare state *n.* A state that assumes responsibility for the welfare of its citizens.

wel·kin (wĕl′kĭn) *n.* The vault of heaven; sky. [< OE *woicen.*]

well[1] (wĕl) *n.* **1.** A deep hole or shaft dug or drilled into the earth to obtain a natural deposit, as water or oil. **2.** A spring; fountain. **3.** A source to be drawn upon. **4.** A container or reservoir, as an inkwell, used to hold a liquid. **5.** A vertical opening that passes through the floors of a building, as for a staircase or an elevator. **6.** An enclosure in a ship's hold for the pumps. —*v.* To rise up and pour forth. [< OE *wælla.*]

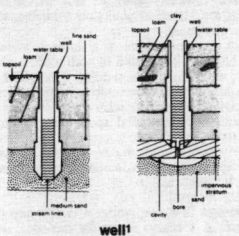

well[1]
Left: Shallow well
Right: Deep well

well[2] (wĕl) *adv.* **bet·ter** (bĕt′ər), **best** (bĕst). **1.** In a good or proper manner; correctly. **2.** Skillfully or proficiently: *plays the piano well.* **3.** Satisfactorily or sufficiently: *slept well.* **4.** Successfully or effectively: *got along well with people.* **5.** In a comfortable or affluent manner: *lived well.* **6.** Favorably: *spoke well of her.* **7.** Thoroughly: *well cooked.* **8.** Perfectly; clearly: *well understood his meaning.* **9.** Considerably: *well after sunset.* **10.** With reason or propriety; properly: *can't very well say no.* **11.** In all likelihood: *His alibi may well be true.* **12.** Prudently: *You would do well to say nothing.* —*adj.* **1. a.** In

good health; not sick. **b.** Cured or healed. **2.** In a satisfactory state; all right: *All is well.* **3. a.** Advisable; prudent: *It would be well not to ask.* **b.** Good; fortunate: *It is well that you stayed.* [< OE *wel.*]

Usage: **As well as,** in the sense of "in addition to," does not have the conjunctive force of *and.* Consequently, a singular subject remains singular and governs a singular verb: *The parent company, as well as its affiliate, was named in the indictment.*

we'll (wĕl). **1.** We will. **2.** We shall.

well-bal·anced (wĕl′băl′ənst) *adj.* **1.** Evenly proportioned or regulated. **2.** Mentally stable; sensible.

well-be·ing (wĕl′bē′ĭng) *n.* The state of being healthy, happy, or prosperous; welfare.

well-born (wĕl′bôrn′) *adj.* Of good lineage or stock.

well-bred (wĕl′brĕd′) *adj.* Having or indicating good upbringing; well-mannered.

well-de·fined (wĕl′dĭ-fīnd′) *adj.* Having definite and distinct lines or features.

well-dis·posed (wĕl′dĭ-spōzd′) *adj.* Disposed to be kindly, friendly, or sympathetic.

well-done (wĕl′dŭn′) *adj.* **1.** Satisfactorily or properly accomplished. **2.** Cooked all the way through.

well-fixed (wĕl′fĭkst′) *adj. Informal.* Financially secure; well-to-do.

well-found·ed (wĕl′foun′dĭd) *adj.* Based on sound judgment, reasoning, or evidence.

well-groomed (wĕl′grōōmd′) *adj.* **1.** Neat and clean in dress and personal appearance. **2.** Carefully cared for.

well-ground·ed (wĕl′groun′dĭd) *adj.* **1.** Adequately versed in a subject. **2.** Having a sound basis; well-founded.

well-heeled (wĕl′hēld′) *adj. Slang.* Well-fixed.

well-man·nered (wĕl′măn′ərd) *adj.* Polite; courteous.

well-mean·ing (wĕl′mē′nĭng) *adj.* Having or prompted by good intentions.

well-nigh (wĕl′nī′) *adv.* Nearly; almost.

well-off (wĕl′ôf′, -ŏf′) *adj.* **1.** In fortunate circumstances. **2.** Well-to-do.

well-read (wĕl′rĕd′) *adj.* Knowledgeable through having read extensively.

well-spo·ken (wĕl′spō′kən) *adj.* **1.** Chosen or expressed with aptness or propriety. **2.** Courteous in speech.

well·spring (wĕl′sprĭng′) *n.* **1.** The source of a stream or spring; fountainhead. **2.** A source of supply.

well-timed (wĕl′tīmd′) *adj.* Occurring or done at an opportune moment.

well-to-do (wĕl′tə-dōō′) *adj.* Prosperous; affluent; well-off.

well-turned (wĕl′tûrnd′) *adj.* **1.** Gracefully formed; shapely: *a well-turned ankle.* **2.** Aptly expressed: *a well-turned phrase.*

well-wish·er (wĕl′wĭsh′ər) *n.* One who wishes another well.

well-worn (wĕl′wôrn′, -wōrn′) *adj.* **1.** Showing signs of much wear or use. **2.** Trite; hackneyed.

welsh (wĕlsh, wĕlch) *v. Slang.* **1.** To swindle a person by not paying a debt or wager. **2.** To fail to fulfill an obligation. [Orig. unknown.] —**welsh′er** *n.*

Welsh (wĕlsh) *n. (used with a pl. verb).* The people of Wales. **2.** The Celtic language of Wales. —**Welsh** *adj.* —**Welsh′man** *n.*

Welsh cor·gi (kôr′gē) *n.* A dog of a breed originating in Wales, with a long body, short legs, and a foxlike head. [< Welsh *corgi*, dwarf dog.]

Welsh rabbit *n.* Also **Welsh rarebit.** A dish made of melted cheese served hot over toast or crackers.

welt (wĕlt) *n.* **1.** A strip of leather stitched between the sole and the upper of a shoe. **2.** A tape or covered cord sewn into a seam as reinforcement or trimming. **3.** A ridge or bump raised on the skin by a blow or an allergic reaction. —*v.* **1.** To reinforce or trim with a welt. **2.** To beat severely. [ME *welte.*]

wel·ter (wĕl′tər) *v.* **1.** To wallow, roll, or writhe. **2.** To lie soaked in a liquid: *welter in blood.* **3.** To roll and surge, as the sea. —*n.* **1.** Turbulence. **2. a.** Confusion; turmoil. **b.** A confused mass; jumble. [ME *welteren.*]

wel·ter·weight (wĕl′tər-wāt′) *n.* A boxer or wrestler who weighs between 136 and 147 pounds, or approx. 62 and 67 kilograms. [Perh. < WELT.]

wen (wĕn) *n.* A cyst containing sebaceous matter. [< OE.]

wench (wĕnch) *n.* **1.** A young woman or girl. **2.** *Archaic.* A female servant. [< OE *wencel*, child.]

wend (wĕnd) *v.* To proceed on or along (one's way). [< OE *wendan*, to turn.]

went (wĕnt) *v. p.t.* of **go.**

wept (wĕpt) *v. p.t. & p.p.* of **weep.**

were (wûr) *v.* **1.** 2nd person sing. past tense of **be. 2.** 1st, 2nd, and 3rd person pl. past tense of **be. 3.** Past subjunctive of **be.**

we're (wîr). We are.

were·n't (wûrnt, wûr′ənt). Were not.

were·wolf (wîr′wŏŏlf′, wûr′-, wâr′-) *n.* A person believed capable of assuming the form of a wolf. [< OE *werewulf.*]

wert (wûrt) *v. Archaic.* 2nd person sing. past tense of **be.**

wes·kit (wĕs′kĭt) *n.* A vest. [< WAISTCOAT.]

west (wĕst) *n.* **1. a.** The direction opposite to the direction in which the earth rotates on its axis. **b.** The point on the mariner's compass 270° clockwise from north. **2.** Often **West.** An area or region lying to the west of a particular point. **3. West.** The part of the earth to the west of Asia and Asia Minor, esp. Europe and the Western Hemisphere; Occident. —*adj.* To, toward, of, from, facing, or in the west. —*adv.* In, from, or toward the west. [< OE.]

west·er·ly (wĕs′tər-lē) *adj.* **1.** In or toward the west. **2.** From the west. —**west′er·ly** *adv.*

west·ern (wĕs′tərn) *adj.* **1.** Of, in, or toward the west. **2.** From the west. **3.** Often **Western. a.** Characteristic of or found in western regions. **b.** Of Europe and the Western Hemisphere: *Western civilization.* —*n.* Often **Western.** A book, motion picture, or television or radio program about cowboys or frontier life. [< OE *westerne.*]

west·ern·er (wĕs′tər-nər) *n.* A native or inhabitant of a western region.

west·ern·ize (wĕs′tər-nīz′) *v.* **-ized, -iz·ing.** To convert to the ways of Western civilization. —**west′ern·i·za′tion** *n.*

west·ward (wĕst′wərd) *adv.* Also **west·wards** (-wərdz). To or toward the west. —**west′ward** *adj.* —**west′ward·ly** *adj. & adv.*

wet (wĕt) *adj.* **wet·ter, wet·test. 1.** Covered,

moistened, soaked, or saturated with a liquid, esp. water. **2.** Rainy. **3.** Not yet dry or firm: *wet paint; wet plaster.* **4.** Allowing or advocating the sale of alcoholic beverages: *a wet county.* —*n.* **1.** Liquid, esp. water. **2.** Moisture. **3.** Rainy weather. **4.** One who advocates the sale of alcoholic beverages. —*v.* **wet** or **wet·ted, wet·ting.** To make or become wet. [< OE *wǣt.*]

wet·back (wĕt′bǎk′) *n.* A Mexican, esp. a laborer, who crosses the U.S. border illegally.

wet blanket *n. Informal.* One that discourages enjoyment or enthusiasm.

weth·er (wĕth′ər) *n.* A castrated male sheep. [< OE.]

wet·land (wĕt′lǎnd′) *n.* A lowland area, as a marsh, that is saturated with moisture.

wet nurse *n.* A woman who suckles another woman's child.

wet suit *n.* A close-fitting permeable suit worn by skin divers to retain body heat.

we've (wēv). We have.

whack (hwǎk, wǎk) *v.* To strike, hit, or slap with a sharp, resounding blow. —*n.* **1.** A sharp, hard blow. **2.** The sound made by a whack. [Imit.]

whale¹ (hwāl, wāl) *n.* **1.** Any of various often very large marine mammals having a gen. fishlike form. **2.** *Informal.* One that is unusually fine, big, or impressive: *a whale of a game.* —*v.* **whaled, whal·ing.** To engage in the hunting of whales. [< OE *hwel.*]

whale² (hwāl, wāl) *v.* **whaled, whal·ing.** To strike repeatedly; thrash. [Orig. unknown.]

whale·boat (hwāl′bōt′, wāl′-) *n.* A long rowboat, pointed at both ends and formerly used in the pursuit and harpooning of whales.

whale·bone (hwāl′bōn′, wāl′-) *n.* **1.** The elastic, hornlike material that forms the plates or strips in the upper jaw of certain whales. **2.** A strip of whalebone, esp. one used to stiffen a corset.

whal·er (hwā′lər, wā′-) *n.* **1.** A person who hunts for whales or works on a whaling ship. **2.** A whaleboat.

wham (hwǎm, wǎm) *n.* **1.** A forceful, resounding blow. **2.** The sound of such a blow; thud. —*v.* **whammed, wham·ming.** To strike or smash into with resounding impact. [Imit.]

wham·my (hwǎm′ē, wǎm′ē) *n., pl.* **-mies.** *Slang.* A supernatural spell; hex. [Perh. < WHAM.]

wharf (hwôrf, wôrf) *n., pl.* **wharves** (hwôrvz, wôrvz) or **wharfs.** A landing place or pier at which vessels may tie up and load or unload. [< OE *hwearf.*]

wharf·age (hwôr′fĭj, wôr′-) *n.* **1.** The use of a wharf. **2.** A charge or fee for this use.

what (hwŏt, hwŭt, wŏt, wŭt; hwət, wət *when unstressed*) *pron.* **1.** Which thing or which particular one of many: *What are we having for supper?* **2.** Which kind, character, or designation: *What are these things?* **3.** One of how much value or significance: *What are possessions to a dying man?* **4. a.** That which or the thing that: *Listen to what I have to say.* **b.** Whatever thing that: *Come what may, I'm staying.* **5.** *Informal.* Something: *I'll tell you what.* —*adj.* **1.** Which one or ones of several or many: *What train do I take?* **2.** Whatever: *We repaired what damage had been done.*

3. How great: *What fools we have been!* —*adv.* How: *What does it matter, after all?* [< OE *hwaet.*]

what-ev-er (hwŏt-ĕv′ər, hwŭt-, wŏt-, wŭt-) *pron.* **1.** Everything or anything that: *Please do whatever you can to help.* **2.** No matter what: *Whatever happens, we'll meet here tonight.* **3.** *Informal.* What: *Whatever does he mean?* —*adj.* Of any number or kind; any: *Whatever needs you have, call on us.*

what-not (hwŏt′nŏt′, hwŭt′-, wŏt′-, wŭt′-) *n.* A set of open shelves to hold small ornaments.

what-so-ev-er (hwŏt′sō-ĕv′ər, hwŭt′-, wŏt′-, wŭt′-) *adj.* Whatever.

wheat (hwēt, wēt) *n.* **1.** A cereal grass widely cultivated for its commercially important grain. **2.** The grain of this plant, ground to produce flour. [< OE *hwǣte.*] —**wheat′en** *adj.*

wheat germ *n.* The vitamin-rich embryo of the wheat kernel, separated before milling for use as a cereal or food supplement.

whee-dle (hwēd′l, wēd′l) *v.* **-dled, -dling.** To persuade, attempt to persuade, or obtain by flattery or cajolery. [Orig. unknown.] —**whee′dler** *n.*

wheel (hwēl, wēl) *n.* **1. a.** A solid disk or rigid circular ring connected to a hub by spokes and designed to turn around an axle or shaft that passes through its center. **b.** Something resembling a wheel in form, appearance, function, or movement. **c.** Something having a wheel as its principal part: *a steering wheel.* **d.** *Informal.* A bicycle. **2. wheels.** Forces that provide energy, movement, or direction: *the wheels of commerce.* **3.** A turn, revolution, or rotation around an axis. **4. wheels.** *Slang.* An automobile. **5.** *Slang.* A very powerful or influential person: *a big wheel at the bank.* —*v.* **1.** To roll, move, or transport on or as if on wheels. **2.** To turn or cause to turn around or as if around a central axis; revolve or rotate. **3.** To turn or whirl around, changing direction; pivot. [< OE *hwēol.*]

wheel-bar-row (hwēl′băr′ō, wēl′-) *n.* A vehicle with handles and usu. one wheel, used to carry small loads.

wheel-base (hwēl′bās′, wēl′-) *n.* The distance from front to rear axle in a motor vehicle.

wheel-chair (hwēl′châr′, wēl′-) *n.* A chair mounted on large wheels for the use of sick or disabled persons.

wheel-er (hwē′lər, wē′-) *n.* **1.** One that wheels. **2.** Something equipped with wheels: *a three-wheeler.*

wheel-er-deal-er (hwē′lər-dē′lər, wē′-) *n.* *Informal.* A sharp operator, esp. in politics or business.

wheel house *n.* A pilothouse.

wheel-wright (hwēl′rīt′, wēl′-) *n.* One whose trade is the building and repairing of wheels.

wheeze (hwēz, wēz) *v.* **wheezed, wheez-ing.** To breathe with difficulty, producing a hoarse whistling sound. —*n.* **1.** A wheezing sound. **2.** An old joke. [Prob. < ON *hvæsa*, to hiss.] —**wheez′er** *n.*

wheez-y (hwē′zē, wē′-) *adj.* **-i-er, -i-est.** **1.** Given to wheezing. **2.** Having or producing a wheezing sound. —**wheez′i-ness** *n.*

whelk (hwĕlk, wĕlk) *n.* Any of various large, sometimes edible marine snails. [< OE *weoloc.*]

whelm (hwĕlm, wĕlm) *v.* To overwhelm. [ME *whelmen*, to turn over.]

whelp (hwĕlp, wĕlp) *n.* **1.** A young offspring

of an animal such as a dog or wolf. **2.** An impudent young fellow. —*v.* To give birth to whelps. [< OE *hwelp.*]

when (hwĕn, wĕn) *adv.* **1.** At what time: *When did you leave?* **2.** At which time: *I know when to leave.* —*conj.* **1.** At the time that: *in April, when the snow melts.* **2.** As soon as: *I'll call you when I get there.* **3.** Whenever: *He's always late when he goes to the barber.* **4.** Whereas; although: *reading comic books when he should be studying.* **5.** Considering that; since: *How are you going to jog when you won't stop smoking?* —*pron.* What or which time: *Since when have you been giving the orders?* —*n.* The time or date: *knew the when but not the where of it.* [< OE *hwenne.*]

Usage: In informal style *when* is often used to mean "a situation in which," as in *A dilemma is when you don't know which way to turn.* This usage is best avoided in formal writing.

whence (hwĕns, wĕns) *adv.* **1.** From what place: *Whence came this man?* **2.** From what origin or source: *Whence comes this splendid feast?* —*conj.* By reason of which; from which. [< OE *hwanon.*]

Usage: Historically, *whence* contained the sense of *from.* Therefore the construction *from whence,* although it occurs in the works of good writers, is often held to be redundant. Examples such as *Tell us the place from whence he came* are unacceptable to a large majority of the Usage Panel.

when-ev-er (hwĕn-ĕv′ər, wĕn-) *adv.* **1.** At whatever time. **2.** When. —*conj.* **1.** At whatever time that. **2.** Every time that.

when-so-ev-er (hwĕn′sō-ĕv′ər, wĕn′-) *adv. & conj.* Whenever.

where (hwâr, wâr) *adv.* **1.** At or in what place, point, or position: *Where is the telephone?* **2.** To what place or end: *Where does this road lead?* **3.** From what place or source: *Where did you get that crazy idea?* —*conj.* **1.** At or in what or which place: *I am going to my room, where I can study.* **2.** In or to a place in which or to which: *She lives where the climate is mild. I will go where you go.* **3.** Wherever: *Where there's smoke, there's fire.* **4.** Whereas: *Mars has two satellites, where Earth has only one.* —*pron.* **1.** What or which place: *Where did they come from?* **2.** The place in, at, or to which: *This is where I found the puppy.* —*n.* The place or occasion. [< OE *hwǣr.*]

where-a-bouts (hwâr′ə-bouts′, wâr′-) *adv.* Where or about where; in, at, or near what location: *Whereabouts do you live?* —*n.* (used with a sing. or pl. verb) The location of someone or something: *I don't know his whereabouts now.*

where-as (hwâr-ăz′, wâr-) *conj.* **1.** It being the fact that; inasmuch as. **2.** While at the same time. **3.** While on the contrary.

where-at (hwâr-ăt′, wâr-) *adv.* **1.** At which place. **2.** Whereupon.

where-by (hwâr-bī′, wâr-) *adv.* By which or by means of which.

where-fore (hwâr′fôr′, -fōr′, wâr′-) *conj.* For which reason or purpose; why. —*adv.* Why. —*n.* A purpose, cause, or reason.

where-in (hwâr-in′, wâr-) *adv.* **1.** In what; how. **2.** In which thing, place, or situation.

where-of (hwâr-ŏv′, -ŭv′, wâr-) *conj.* **1.** Of what: *I know whereof I speak.* **2.** Of which or whom: *a speech whereof I understood nothing.*

where·on (hwâr-ŏn', -ŏn', wâr'-) *conj.* On which.

where·so·ev·er (hwâr'sō-ĕv'ər, wâr'-) *conj.* Archaic. Wherever.

where·to (hwâr-tōō', wâr'-) *conj.* **1.** To which. **2.** To what place or toward what end.

where·up·on (hwâr'ə-pŏn', -pŏn', wâr'-) *conj.* **1.** Upon which. **2.** Following which.

wher·ev·er (hwâr-ĕv'ər, wâr-) *adv.* **1.** In or to whatever place or situation. **2.** Where: *Wherever have you been?* —*conj.* In or to whatever place or situation.

where·with (hwâr'wĭth', -wĭth', wâr'-) *conj.* With which.

where·with·al (hwâr'wĭth-ôl', -wĭth-, wâr'-) *n.* The necessary means, esp. financial means.

wher·ry (hwĕr'ē, wĕr'ē) *n., pl.* **-ries.** A light, swift rowboat built for one person and often used in racing. [ME *whery.*]

wherry   whetstone

whet (hwĕt, wĕt) *v.* **whet·ted, whet·ting. 1.** To sharpen (a knife or other tool); hone. **2.** To stimulate; heighten. [< OE *hwettan.*]

wheth·er (hwĕth'ər, wĕth'-) *conj.* **1.** If it is so that: *Do you know whether the museum is open?* **2.** Whatever the case: *They are wrong whether they realize it or not.* **3.** Either: *He won the fight, whether by skill or luck.* [< OE *hwether.*]

whet·stone (hwĕt'stōn', wĕt'-) *n.* A stone used for whetting cutting tools.

whey (hwā, wā) *n.* The watery part of milk that separates from the curds, as in the process of making cheese. [< OE *hwæg.*] —**whey'ey** *adj.*

which (hwĭch, wĭch) *pron.* **1.** What particular one or ones: *Which is your house?* **2.** The particular one or ones: *Take those which are yours.* **3.** The thing, animal, group of people, or event previously named or implied: *the movie, which was shown later.* **4.** Whichever: *Choose which you like best.* **5.** A thing or circumstance that: *She ignored us, which was a shame.* —*adj.* **1.** What particular one or ones of. **2.** Any one of; whichever. **3.** Being the one or ones previously designated. [< OE *hwilc.*]

which·ev·er (hwĭch-ĕv'ər, wĭch-) *pron.* Whatever one or ones. —*adj.* No matter what or which.

which·so·ev·er (hwĭch'sō-ĕv'ər, wĭch'-) *pron. & adj.* Whichever.

whiff (hwĭf, wĭf) *n.* **1.** A breath or puff, as of air or smoke. **2.** A brief, passing odor carried in the air: *a whiff of buttered popcorn.* **3.** An inhalation, as of perfume. —*v.* **1.** To carry or be carried in whiffs; waft. **2.** To inhale (an odor); smell. [ME *weffe,* offensive smell.]

whif·fle·tree (hwĭf'əl-trē, wĭf'-) *n.* The pivoted horizontal crossbar to which the harness traces of a draft animal are hitched. [< *whippletree,* prob. < WHIP.]

Whig (hwĭg, wĭg) *n.* **1.** A member of a British political party of the 18th and 19th cent. opposed to the Tories. **2.** A supporter of the war against England during the American Revolution. **3.** A member of an American political party formed (1834–55) to oppose the Democratic Party. [Prob. < *Whiggamore,* one of a body of 17th-cent. Scottish insurgents.]

while (hwīl, wīl) *n.* **1.** A period of time: *waited for a while.* **2.** The time, effort, or trouble taken in doing something: *It's not worth my while.* —*conj.* **1.** As long as: *great while it lasted.* **2.** Although: *While he's happy, he's not ecstatic.* **3.** Whereas: *The soles are leather, while the uppers are canvas.* —*v.* **whiled, whil·ing.** To pass (time) idly or pleasantly. [< OE *hwīl.*]

whi·lom (hwī'ləm, wī'-) *adj.* Former: *the whilom Miss Smith.* —*adv.* Archaic. Formerly. [< OE *hwīlum.*]

whilst (hwīlst, wīlst) *conj.* Chiefly Brit. While. [ME *whylst.*]

whim (hwĭm, wĭm) *n.* **1.** A sudden or capricious idea; passing fancy. **2.** Arbitrary thought or impulse: *governed by whim.* [< obs. *whim-wham.*]

whim·per (hwĭm'pər, wĭm'-) *v.* To make soft whining sounds. [Imit.] —**whim'per** *n.* —**whim'per·er** *n.* —**whim'per·ing·ly** *adv.*

whim·si·cal (hwĭm'zĭ-kəl, wĭm'-) *adj.* **1.** Playful, fanciful, or capricious. **2.** Characterized by erratic behavior or unpredictability. [< WHIMSY.] —**whim'si·cal'i·ty** (-kăl'ĭ-tē) *n.* —**whim'si·cal·ly** *adv.*

whim·sy (hwĭm'zē, wĭm'-) *n., pl.* **-sies.** Also **whim·sey** *pl.* **-seys. 1.** An odd or capricious idea; idle fancy. **2.** Something quaint, fanciful, or odd. [< WHIM.]

whine (hwīn, wīn) *v.* **whined, whin·ing. 1.** To utter a plaintive, high-pitched sound, as in pain, fear, complaint, or protest. **2.** To complain in an annoying way. **3.** To produce a sustained noise of relatively high pitch, as a machine does. [< OE *hwīnan,* to make a whizzing sound.] —**whine** *n.* —**whin'er** *n.* —**whin'ing·ly** *adv.*

whin·ny (hwĭn'ē, wĭn'ē) *v.* **-nied, -ny·ing.** To utter the gentle sound characteristic of a horse; neigh. [Prob. imit.] —**whin'ny** *n.*

whip (hwĭp, wĭp) *v.* **whipped** or **whipt, whip·ping. 1.** To strike with repeated strokes, as of a strap; beat. **2.** To punish by or as if by whipping. **3.** To drive, force, or compel by or as if by whipping. **4.** To beat (e.g. eggs) into a froth or foam. **5.** To snatch, pull, or remove suddenly and quickly: *whipped his hat off.* **6.** To wrap or bind (e.g. a rope or rod) with twine or cord to strengthen and protect. **7.** To defeat thoroughly; outdo. **8.** To move briskly or spryly. **9.** To move like a lash; thrash about: *Branches whipped against the windows.* **10.** *Informal.* To prepare quickly: *whipped up a light lunch.* —**phrasal verb. whip up.** To arouse; excite: *whip up enthusiasm.* —*n.* **1.** A flexible instrument, as a thong, used in whipping. **2.** A whipping or lashing blow, motion, or stroke. **3.** A member of a legislature selected by his political party to enforce party discipline and ensure attendance. **4.** A dessert made of sugar, whipped cream or stiffly beaten egg whites, and often fruit. [ME *wippen*.] —**whip'per** *n.*

whip·cord (hwĭp'kôrd', wĭp'-) *n.* **1.** A worsted fabric with a distinct diagonal rib. **2.** A strong twisted or braided cord sometimes used in making whiplashes. **3.** Catgut.

whip·lash (hwĭp'lăsh', wĭp'-) *n.* **1.** The lash of a whip. **2.** An injury to the neck or spine caused by a sudden forward or backward jerk of the head.

whip·per·snap·per (hwĭp'ər-snăp'ər, wĭp'-) *n.* An insignificant and pretentious person, esp. an impudent youth.

whip·pet (hwĭp'ĭt, wĭp'-) *n.* A short-haired, swift-running dog that resembles the greyhound but is smaller. [Prob. < WHIP.]

whipping boy *n.* A scapegoat.

whip·poor·will (hwĭp'ər-wĭl', wĭp'-) *n.* A brownish nocturnal North American bird with a distinctive call. [Imit. of its call.]

whip·saw (hwĭp'sô', wĭp'-) *n.* A narrow two-man crosscut saw. —*v.* **1.** To cut with a whipsaw. **2.** To defeat in two ways at once.

whip·stitch (hwĭp'stĭch', wĭp'-) *v.* To sew with overcast stitches, as in finishing a fabric edge or binding two pieces of fabric together. —*n.* An overcast stitch or stitches.

whipt (hwĭpt, wĭpt) *v.* A *p.t.* & *p.p.* of **whip.**

whir (hwûr, wûr) *v.* **whirred, whir·ring.** To move so as to produce a buzzing or humming sound. —*n.* **1.** A buzzing or vibrating sound. **2.** A bustle; hurry. [ME *whirren.*]

whirl (hwûrl, wûrl) *v.* **1.** To spin, revolve, or rotate rapidly; twirl. **2.** To turn rapidly, changing direction; wheel. **3.** To have the sensation of spinning; reel. **4.** To move or drive rapidly. **5.** To move or drive in a circular or curving course, esp. at high speed. —*n.* **1.** A whirling or spinning motion. **2.** One that whirls or is whirled. **3.** A rapid, dizzying round of events; bustle or rush. **4.** A state of confusion; tumult. **5.** *Informal.* A try: *Let's give it a whirl.* [< ON *hvirfla.*] —**whirl'er** *n.*

whirl·i·gig (hwûr'lĭ-gĭg', wûr'-) *n.* **1.** A toy that whirls, as a pinwheel. **2.** A merry-go-round. **3.** Something that continuously whirls. [ME *whirlegigge.*]

whirl·pool (hwûrl'pōōl', wûrl'-) *n.* Water that is rapidly rotating, as from the convergence of two tides; vortex.

whirl·wind (hwûrl'wĭnd', wûrl'-) *n.* **1.** A column of air that rotates, often violently, about a region of low atmospheric pressure, as a tornado. **2.** A tumultuous, confused rush.

whirl·y·bird (hwûr'lē-bûrd', wûr'-) *n. Slang.* A helicopter.

whisk (hwĭsk, wĭsk) *v.* **1.** To move or cause to move with quick light sweeping motions. **2.** To whip (eggs or cream) lightly. **3.** To move lightly, nimbly, and rapidly. —*n.* **1.** A quick light sweeping motion. **2.** A whisk-broom. **3.** A kitchen utensil used to whip foods by hand. [ME *quhisken.*]

whisk·broom (hwĭsk'brōōm', -brŏōm', wĭsk'-) *n.* A small short-handled broom used esp. to brush clothes.

whisk·er (hwĭs'kər, wĭs'-) *n.* **1. a. whiskers.** The unshaven hair on a man's face that forms the beard and mustache. **b.** A single hair of the beard or mustache. **2.** One of the long bristles or hairs that grow near the mouth of certain animals, such as cats. **3.** *Informal.* A narrow margin: *lost by a whisker.* [< WHISK.] —**whisk'ered** *adj.*

whis·key (hwĭs'kē, wĭs'-) *n., pl.* **-keys.** Also *Scot.* **whis·ky** *pl.* **-kies.** An alcoholic beverage distilled from fermented grain, such as corn, rye, or barley. [< Sc. Gael. *uisge beatha,* water of life.]

whis·per (hwĭs'pər, wĭs'-) *v.* **1.** To speak or utter softly, without full voice. **2.** To tell secretly or privately. **3.** To make a soft rustling sound, as leaves. —*n.* **1.** An act of whispering. **2.** Speech produced by whispering. **3.** Something whispered. **4.** A hint or rumor, as of scandal. [< OE *hwisprian.*]

whist (hwĭst, wĭst) *n.* A game played with 52 cards by two teams of two players each. [Orig. unknown.]

whis·tle (hwĭs'əl, wĭs'-) *v.* **-tled, -tling. 1.** To produce a clear shrill sound by forcing air through the teeth or through an aperture formed by pursing the lips. **2.** To produce a clear shrill sound by blowing on or through a device. **3.** To make a high-pitched sound, esp. when moving swiftly through the air. **4.** To produce by whistling: *whistle a tune.* **5.** To summon, signal, or direct by whistling. —*n.* **1.** A device or instrument for making whistling sounds by means of the breath, air, or steam. **2.** A sound produced by a whistle or by whistling. **3.** A whistling sound, as of an animal or projectile. [< OE *hwistlian.*] —**whis'tler** *n.*

whistle stop *n.* **1.** A town at which a train stops only if signaled. **2.** An appearance of a political candidate in a small town, traditionally on the observation platform of a train.

whit (hwĭt, wĭt) *n.* The least or smallest bit. [< OE *wiht,* thing.]

white (hwīt, wīt) *n.* **1.** An achromatic color of maximum lightness; the opposite of black. **2.** The white or nearly white part of something, as an egg. **3. whites.** White clothes or a white outfit. **4.** A member of a Caucasoid people; Caucasian. —*adj.* **whit·er, whit·est. 1.** Being of nearly of the color white. **2.** Light-colored; pale. **3.** Of, pertaining to, or belonging to an ethnic group having a comparatively pale skin, esp. Caucasoid. **4.** Pale gray or silvery, as from age: *white hair.* **5.** Snowy: *a white Christmas.* **6.** Incandescent: *white heat.* **7.** Pure; innocent. [< OE *hwīt.*]

white ant *n.* A termite.

white·bait (hwīt'bāt', wīt'-) *n.* The young of various fishes, such as the herring, considered a delicacy.

white blood cell *n.* A leukocyte.

white·cap (hwīt'kăp', wīt'-) *n.* A wave with a crest of foam.

white·col·lar (hwīt'kŏl'ər, wīt'-) *adj.* Of or pertaining to workers whose work does not involve manual labor.

white elephant *n.* **1.** A rare whitish or light-gray form of the Asian elephant, often regarded with special veneration in regions of southeastern Asia. **2.** A rare and expensive possession that is of limited usefulness and is financially a burden to maintain. **3.** An article, ornament, or household utensil no longer wanted by its owner.

white·faced (hwīt'fāst', wīt'-) *adj.* **1.** Having a pale face; pallid. **2.** Having a white patch extending from the muzzle to the forehead, as certain animals.

white feather *n.* A sign or symbol of cowardice.

white·fish (hwīt'fĭsh', wīt'-) *n.* Any of various silvery freshwater food fishes.

white flag *n.* A white cloth or flag signaling surrender or truce.

white gold *n.* An alloy of gold and nickel, and sometimes palladium or zinc, that has a platinumlike color.

White House *n.* **1.** The executive mansion of the President of the United States. **2.** The executive branch of the U.S. government.

white lead *n.* A heavy white poisonous compound of lead used in paint pigments.

whit•en (hwīt′n, wīt′n) *v.* To make or become white. **—whit′en•er** *n.*

white•ness (hwīt′nĭs, wīt′-) *n.* The state or quality of being white.

white pine *n.* **1.** A timber tree of eastern North America that has needles in clusters of five and durable, easily worked wood. **2.** The wood of the white pine.

white slave *n.* A woman held unwillingly for purposes of prostitution. **—white slavery** *n.*

white•wall (hwīt′wôl′, wīt′-) *n.* A vehicular tire with a white band on the outer side.

white•wash (hwīt′wŏsh′, -wôsh′, wīt′-) *n.* **1.** A mixture of lime and water, often with whiting, size, or glue added, that is used to whiten structural surfaces. **2.** A concealing or glossing over of flaws or failures. **—v. 1.** To paint or coat with or as with whitewash. **2.** To gloss over (a flaw). **—white′wash′er** *n.*

whith•er (hwĭth′ər, wĭth′-) *adv.* **1.** To what place, result, or condition. **2.** To which specified place or position. **3.** Wherever. [< OE *hwider.*]

whit•ing[1] (hwī′tĭng, wī′-) *n.* A pure white ground chalk used in paints, ink, and putty. [< ME *whit*, white.]

whit•ing[2] (hwī′tĭng, wī′-) *n.* Any of several marine food fishes. [< MDu. *witjing.*]

whit•ish (hwī′tĭsh, wī′-) *adj.* Somewhat white.

whit•low (hwĭt′lō, wĭt′-) *n.* An inflammation of the area around the nail of a finger or toe. [ME *whitflawe.*]

Whit•sun•day (hwĭt′sŭn′dē, -sən-dā′, wĭt′-) *n.* Pentecost. [< OE *hwīta sunnandæg*, white Sunday.]

whit•tle (hwĭt′l, wĭt′l) *v.* **-tled, -tling. 1. a.** To cut small bits or pare shavings from (a piece of wood). **b.** To fashion or shape by whittling. **2.** To reduce or eliminate gradually as if by whittling; pare: *whittled down his expenditures.* [< OE *thwītan.*] **—whit′tler** *n.*

whiz (hwĭz, wĭz). Also **whizz.** *—v.* **whizzed, whiz•zing. 1.** To make a whirring, buzzing, or hissing sound, as of something rushing through air. **2.** To rush past. *—n., pl.* **whiz•zes. 1.** A whizzing sound. **2.** *Slang.* One with remarkable skill: *a whiz at math.* [Imit.]

who (hōō) *pron.* **1.** What or which person or persons: *Who was that on the telephone? I know who called.* **2.** The person or persons that: *The boy who came yesterday is now gone.* [< OE *hwa.*]

Usage: The traditional rules that determine the choice of *who* and *whom* are relatively simple: *who* is used for a grammatical subject and *whom* is used elsewhere. Thus, we write *The actor who played Hamlet was there,* since *who* is the subject of *played.* But we write *To whom did you give the letter?* since *whom* is the object of the preposition *to.* In a complicated sentence, such as *I met the man whom the*

government had tried to get France to extradite, it requires considerable effort and attention to apply the rules correctly. Consequently, few writers or speakers succeed in getting *who* and *whom* right all the time. Furthermore, grammarians since Noah Webster have with great common sense argued that it is excessively pedantic and formal to require a slavish adherence to the traditional rules and so substitute *whom* for *who* in a sentence like *I know who the letter was written to.*

who'd (hōōd). **1.** Who would. **2.** Who had.

who•dun•it (hōō-dŭn′ĭt) *n. Informal.* A detective story. [WHO + DONE + IT.]

who•ev•er (hōō-ĕv′ər) *pron.* Anyone that; no matter who.

whole (hōl) *adj.* **1.** Containing all elements or component parts; complete: *whole milk.* **2.** Not divided or disjoined: *a whole acre of land.* **3.** Sound; healthy. **4.** Constituting the full amount, extent, or duration: *cried the whole trip home.* **5.** *Math.* Not fractional; integral. *—n.* **1.** All of the component parts or elements of a thing. **2.** A complete entity or system. **—idiom. on the whole.** In general. [< OE *hāl.*] **—whole′ness** *n.*

whole•heart•ed (hōl′här′tĭd) *adj.* Without reservation: *wholehearted cooperation.* **—whole′-heart′ed•ly** *adv.* **—whole′heart′ed•ness** *n.*

whole number *n.* An integer.

whole•sale (hōl′sāl′) *n.* The sale of goods in large quantities, as for resale by a retailer. *—adj.* **1.** Of, pertaining to, or engaged in the sale of goods at wholesale. **2.** Sold in large bulk or quantity, usu. at a lower cost. **3.** Performed extensively and indiscriminately: *wholesale destruction.* *—v.* **-saled, -sal•ing.** To sell at wholesale. **—whole′sale′** *adv.* **—whole′sal′er** *n.*

whole•some (hōl′səm) *adj.* **1.** Conducive to mental or physical well-being; salutary: *a wholesome diet.* **2.** Having or indicating a healthy physical or mental condition. **—whole′some•ly** *adv.* **—whole′some•ness** *n.*

whole-wheat (hōl′hwēt′, -wēt′) *adj.* Made from the entire grain of wheat.

who'll (hōl). **1.** Who will. **2.** Who shall.

whol•ly (hō′lē, hōl′lē) *adv.* **1.** Entirely; completely. **2.** Exclusively.

whom (hōōm) *pron.* The objective case of **who.**

whom•ev•er (hōōm-ĕv′ər) *pron.* The objective case of **whoever.**

whom•so•ev•er (hōōm′sō-ĕv′ər) *n.* The objective case of **whosoever.**

whoop (hwōōp, hōōp, wōōp) *n.* **1.** A loud or hooting cry, as of exultation or excitement. **2.** The paroxysmal gasp characteristic of whooping cough. *—v.* **1.** To utter or utter with a whoop. **2.** To gasp, as in whooping cough. **3.** To chase, call, urge on, or drive with a whoop. [ME *whope.*] **—whoop′er** *n.*

whooping cough *n.* A bacterial infection of the lungs and respiratory passages that causes spasms of coughing alternating with paroxysmal gasps.

whooping crane *n.* A large, long-legged nearly extinct North American bird with black and white plumage and a whooping cry.

whoosh (hwōōsh, wōōsh, hwŏŏsh, wŏŏsh) *v.*

To make a gushing or rushing sound. [Imit.] **—whoosh** n.

whop (hwŏp, wŏp) v. **whopped, whop·ping.** To thrash; defeat. —n. A heavy thud or blow. [ME *whappen*.]

whop·per (hwŏp'ər, wŏp'-) n. 1. Something exceptionally big or remarkable. 2. An outrageous lie.

whop·ping (hwŏp'ĭng, wŏp'-) adj. Remarkably big.

whore (hôr, hōr) n. A prostitute. [< OE *hōre.*]

whorl (hwôrl, wôrl, hwûrl, wûrl) n. 1. A coiled, curved, or rounded form, as one of the turns of a spiral shell. 2. An arrangement of three or more parts, as of leaves or petals, radiating from a single point or part. [ME *whorle.*]

who's (hōōz). 1. Who is. 2. Who has.

whose (hōōz) pron. 1. The possessive form of **who.** 2. The possessive form of **which.** [< OE *hwæs.*]

Usage: *Whose* is acceptable on all levels as a possessive form for both persons and things: *The cabinet, whose decoration was typical of the Regency period, was filled with porcelain.*

who·so (hōō'sō) pron. Whoever.

who·so·ev·er (hōō'sō-ĕv'ər) pron. Whoever.

why (hwī, wī) adv. For what purpose, reason, or cause: *Why did you have to leave?* —conj. 1. The reason, cause, or purpose for which: *I know why you left.* 2. On account of which; for which. —n., pl. **whys.** The cause; reason. —interj. Used to express mild indignation, pleasure, surprise, or impatience. [< OE *hwī.*]

Wich·i·ta (wĭch'ə-tô') n., pl. **-ta** or **-tas.** 1. a. A confederacy of Indians, formerly living between the Arkansas River and central Texas. b. A member of the Wichita. 2. The Caddoan language of the Wichita.

wick (wĭk) n. A cord or strand of loosely woven fibers, as in a candle, that draws fuel up to the flame by capillary action. [< OE *wēoce.*]

wick·ed (wĭk'ĭd) adj. **-er, -est.** 1. Morally bad; depraved. 2. Playfully mischievous: *a wicked joke.* 3. Harmful; pernicious: *a wicked cough.* [< ME *wicke.*] **—wick'ed·ly** adv. **—wick'ed·ness** n.

wick·er (wĭk'ər) n. 1. A flexible shoot, as of a willow, used in weaving baskets, articles of furniture, etc. 2. Wickerwork. [ME *wiker.*]

wick·er·work (wĭk'ər-wûrk') n. Woven wicker.

wick·et (wĭk'ĭt) n. 1. *Cricket.* Either of the two sets of three upright sticks that forms the target of the bowler. 2. *Croquet.* An arch through which a player tries to hit the ball. 3. A small door or gate, esp. one built into or near a larger one. 4. A small window or opening, usu. fitted with a grating, as at a ticket window. [< ONFr. *wiket.*]

wick·i·up (wĭk'ē-ŭp') n. A frame hut covered with matting, bark, or brushwood and used by nomadic Indians of North America. [Fox *wikiyapi,* dwelling.]

wide (wīd) adj. **wid·er, wid·est.** 1. Extending over a large area from side to side; broad. 2. Measured from side to side: *a ribbon two inches wide.* 3. Great in range or scope: *a wide selection.* 4. Fully open or extended: *look with wide eyes.* 5. Far, apart, or away from a desired goal, point, or issue. —adv. 1. Over a large area; extensively: *traveling far and wide.* 2. To the full extent; completely: *The door was wide open.* 3. So as to miss the target; astray: *shoot wide.* [< OE *wīd.*] **—wide'ly** adv. **—wide'ness** n.

wide-a·wake (wīd'ə-wāk') adj. 1. Completely awake. 2. Alert; watchful.

wide-eyed (wīd'īd') adj. 1. With the eyes completely open. 2. Ingenuous; naive.

wid·en (wīd'n) v. To make or become wide or wider. **—wid'en·er** n.

wide·spread (wīd'sprĕd') adj. 1. Spread out wide; fully opened. 2. Occurring widely.

wid·geon (wĭj'ən) n., pl. **-geon** or **-geons.** Also *chiefly Brit.* **wi·geon.** A wild duck with brownish plumage and a light head patch. [Orig. unknown.]

wid·ow (wĭd'ō) n. A woman whose husband has died and who has not remarried. —v. To make a widow of. [< OE *widuwe.*] **—wid'ow·hood'** n.

wid·ow·er (wĭd'ō-ər) n. A man whose wife has died and who has not remarried. [ME *widewer.*]

width (wĭdth, wĭtth) n. 1. The condition, quality, or fact of being wide. 2. The measurement of the extent of something from side to side. 3. Something that has a specified width, esp. a piece of fabric measured from selvage to selvage.

wield (wēld) v. 1. To handle or use, esp. capably: *wielding an ax.* 2. To exercise or exert (power or influence). [< OE *wieldan.*]

wie·ner (wē'nər) n. A frankfurter.

wife (wīf) n., pl. **wives** (wīvz). A woman to whom a man is married. [< OE *wīf,* woman.] **—wife'hood'** n. **—wife'ly** adj.

wig (wĭg) n. A covering of artificial or human hair worn on the head for adornment, to conceal baldness, or as a part of a costume. [< PERIWIG.]

wi·geon (wĭj'ən) n. *Chiefly Brit.* Var. of **widgeon.**

wig·gle (wĭg'əl) v. **-gled, -gling.** To move or cause to move with short irregular motions from side to side. [ME *wiglen.*] **—wig'gle** n. **—wig'gler** n. **—wig'gly** adj.

wig·wam (wĭg'wŏm') n. A North American Indian dwelling commonly having an arched or conical framework covered with bark or hides. [Abnaki *wikwam.*]

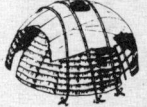

wigwam
Left: Drawing showing structural details
Right: Birch-bark wigwam in Micmac, Nova Scotia

wild (wīld) adj. **-er, -est.** 1. Occurring, growing, or living in a natural state; not cultivated, domesticated, or tamed: *wild plants; a wild pony.* 2. Lacking discipline, restraint, or control; unruly: *wild and delinquent boys.* 3. Full or suggestive of strong, uncontrolled feeling: *wild laughter.* 4. Stormy; turbulent: *wild seas.* 5. Savage; uncivilized. 6. Very extravagant or unlikely; outlandish: *a wild idea.* 7. Deviating from the intended mark or target: *a wild pitch.* 8. Having a value determined by the holder's needs: *playing poker* with *deuces* wild. —*adv.* In a wild manner; out of control: *children running wild.* —*n.* Often **wilds.** An uninhabited or uncultivated region. [< OE *wilde.*] —**wild′ly** *adv.* —**wild′-ness** *n.*

wild-cat (wĭld′kăt′) *n.* **1.** Any of various wild felines of small to medium size, esp. a lynx or bobcat. **2.** A quick-tempered or fierce person. **3.** An oil well drilled in an area not known to yield oil. —*adj.* **1.** Risky or unsound, esp. financially. **2.** Accomplished or operating without official sanction or authority: *a wildcat strike.* —*v.* **-cat-ted, -cat-ting.** To prospect for (oil or minerals) in an area not known to be productive.

wil-de-beest (wĭl′də-bēst′, vĭl′-) *n.* The gnu. [Obs. Afr.]

wil-der-ness (wĭl′dər-nĭs) *n.* An unsettled and uncultivated region left in its natural condition. [< ME *wildēor,* wild beast.]

wild-eyed (wĭld′īd′) *adj.* Glaring in or as if in anger, terror, or madness.

wild-fire (wĭld′fīr′) *n.* A raging fire that travels and spreads rapidly.

wild-fowl (wĭld′foul′) *n.* A bird, as a duck or goose, hunted as game.

wild-goose chase (wĭld′gōōs′) *n.* The hopeless pursuit of something unattainable or imaginary.

wild-life (wĭld′līf′) *n.* Wild animals and vegetation, esp. animals living in a natural undomesticated state.

wild rice *n.* **1.** A tall water grass of northern North America that bears edible brownish seeds. **2.** The seeds of this plant.

wile (wīl) *n.* **1.** A deceitful stratagem or trick. **2.** A disarming or seductive manner, device, or procedure. —*v.* **wiled, wil-ing.** To entice; lure. [ME *wil.*]

will¹ (wĭl) *n.* **1.** The mental faculty by which one deliberately chooses or decides upon a course of action; volition. **2.** An instance of the exercising of the will; choice. **3.** Self-control; self-discipline. **4.** Something desired or decided upon, esp. by a person of authority. **5.** Deliberate intention or wish: *against my will.* **6.** Strong purpose; determination: *the will to win.* **7.** Bearing or attitude toward others; disposition: *a man of good will.* **8.** A legal declaration of how a person wishes his possessions to be disposed of after his death. —*v.* **1.** To bring about, attempt to effect, or decide upon by an act of the will; determine. **2.** To decree; ordain. **3.** To grant in a legal will; bequeath. —*idiom.* **at will.** At one's discretion or pleasure; freely: *wandered about at will.* [< OE *willa.*]

will² (wĭl) *v.* past tense **would** (wōōd). **1.** Used as an auxiliary followed by a simple infinitive to indicate: **a.** Futurity: *They will come later.* **b.** Likelihood or certainty: *You will live to regret it.* **c.** Willingness: *Will you help me?* **d.** Intention: *I will too if I feel like it.* **e.** Requirement or command: *You will report to the supervisor's office.* **f.** Customary or habitual action: *She would spend hours in the kitchen.* **g.** *Informal.* Probability or expectation: *That will be John at the door.* **2.** To wish; desire: *Do what you will with it.* [< OE *wyllan.*]

will-ful (wĭl′fəl) *adj.* Also **wil-ful. 1.** Being in accordance with one's will; deliberate: *willful*

disobedience. **2.** Inclined to impose one's will; obstinate: *a willful child.* —**will′ful-ly** *adv.* —**will′ful-ness** *n.*

wil-lies (wĭl′ēz) *pl.n. Slang.* Feelings of uneasiness. [Orig. unknown.]

will-ing (wĭl′ĭng) *adj.* **1.** Done, accepted, or given readily and without hesitation; voluntary. **2.** Disposed to accept or tolerate; ready. **3.** Acting or ready to act promptly and gladly: *a willing worker.* —**will′ing-ly** *adv.* —**will′ing-ness** *n.*

wil-li-waw (wĭl′ē-wô′) *n.* A violent gust of cold wind blowing seaward from a mountainous coast. [Orig. unknown.]

will-o'-the-wisp (wĭl′ə-thə-wĭsp′) *n.* **1.** A phosphorescent light that hovers over swampy ground at night. **2.** A delusive or misleading goal. [< *Will,* nickname for *William.*]

wil-low (wĭl′ō) *n.* **1.** Any of various trees or shrubs usu. having narrow leaves and slender, flexible twigs. **2.** The wood of a willow tree. [< OE *welig.*]

wil-low-y (wĭl′ō-ē) *adj.* **-i-er, -i-est.** Resembling or suggestive of the slender, flexible branches of a willow: *a tall, willowy girl.*

will power *n.* The ability to carry out one's decisions, wishes, or plans; strength of mind.

wil-ly-nil-ly (wĭl′ē-nĭl′ē) *adv. & adj.* Whether desired or not. [< *will ye, nill ye,* be you willing, be you unwilling.]

wilt¹ (wĭlt) *v.* **1.** To lose or cause to lose freshness and wither; droop. **2.** To lose vigor or force; weaken. **3.** To deprive of energy or courage; enervate. —*n.* Any of various plant diseases characterized by slow or rapid collapse of terminal shoots, branches, or entire plants. [Poss. < ME *welken.*]

wilt² (wĭlt) *v. Archaic.* 2nd person sing. present tense of **will².**

wil-y (wī′lē) *adj.* **-i-er, -i-est.** Full of wile; sly. —**wil′i-ness** *n.*

wim-ble (wĭm′bəl) *n.* Any of numerous hand tools for boring holes. [< AN.]

wim-ple (wĭm′pəl) *n.* A cloth framing the face and drawn into folds beneath the chin, worn by women in medieval times and as part of certain nuns' habits. [< OE *wimpel.*]

win (wĭn) *v.* **won** (wŭn), **win-ning. 1.** To achieve victory over others in or as if in a competition. **2.** To achieve by effort; earn. **3.** To receive as a prize or reward for performance. **4. a.** To succeed in gaining the favor or support of. **b.** To persuade (someone) to marry one. —*n.* A victory, esp. in sports. [< OE *winnan,* to strive.] —**win′ner** *n.*

wince (wĭns) *v.* **winced, winc-ing.** To shrink or start involuntarily, as in pain or distress; flinch. [ME *wincen,* to kick.] —**wince** *n.*

winch (wĭnch) *n.* **1.** A stationary hoisting machine consisting of a drum around which a rope or cable winds as the load is lifted. **2.** The crank used to give motion to a device such as a grindstone. [< OE *wince,* pulley.]

wind¹ (wĭnd) *n.* **1.** A current or stream of air, esp. a natural one that moves along or parallel to the ground. **2.** A strong or prevailing influence or trend; tendency. **3.** A current of air carrying a scent, as of game. **4. winds.** **a.** The wind instruments of an orchestra or band. **b.** Players of wind instruments. **5.** Gas produced in the body during digestion; flatu-

---

ă pat ā pay â care ä father ĕ pet ē be ĭ pit ī tie î pier ŏ pot ō toe ô paw, for oi noise ōō took ōō boot ou out th thin th this ŭ cut û urge yōō abuse zh vision ə about, item, edible, gallop, circus

lence. **6. a.** Respiration. **b.** Breath: *The fall knocked the wind out of him.* **7.** Meaningless or boastful talk. —*v.* **1.** To cause to be out of breath: *The long race winded the runners.* **2.** To catch a scent of: *The dogs winded a rabbit.* **3.** To allow to rest in order to recover breath: *stopped to wind the horses.* —**idiom. get wind of.** To receive hints or intimations of. [< OE.]

wind² (wīnd) *v.* **wound** (wound), **wind·ing. 1.** To coil or be coiled around an object or center once or repeatedly. **2.** To lie or move so as to encircle. **3.** To move or cause to move in a spiral or circular course. **4.** To introduce in a devious or indirect manner; insinuate. **5.** To tighten the spring of (a clock or other mechanism). **6.** To lift or haul, as by means of a windlass. —**phrasal verb. wind up.** *Informal.* **1.** To come or bring to an end; finish. **2.** To arrive in a place or situation as a result of a course of action: *wound up in jail.* **3.** To put -in order; settle. **4.** To swing back the arm in preparation for pitching a baseball. —*n.* A single turn, twist, or curve. [< OE *windan.*] —**wind'er** *n.*

Syns: *wind, coil, curl, entwine, snake, spiral, twine, twist, weave* v.

wind³ (wīnd, wĭnd) *v.* **wind·ed** (wĭn'dĭd, wīn'-) or **wound** (wound), **wind·ing.** To sound (a wind instrument) by blowing. [< WIND¹.]
wind·age (wĭn'dĭj) *n.* The effect of the wind on the course of a projectile.
wind·bag (wĭnd'băg') *n. Slang.* A talkative person who says nothing of importance or interest.
wind-blown (wĭnd'blōn') *adj.* **1.** Blown by the wind. **2.** Having the appearance of having been blown by the wind.
wind·break (wĭnd'brāk') *n.* A hedge, row of trees, or fence serving to lessen or break the force of the wind.
wind·burn (wĭnd'bûrn') *n.* Skin irritation caused by exposure to the wind.
wind-chill factor (wĭnd'chĭl') *n.* The temperature of still air that would have the same effect on the exposed human skin as a given combination of wind speed and air temperature.
wind·fall (wĭnd'fôl') *n.* **1.** Something, as a ripened fruit, that has been blown down by the wind. **2.** A sudden and unexpected piece of good fortune or personal gain.
wind-flow·er (wĭnd'flou'ər) *n.* An anemone.
wind·ing (wīn'dĭng) *adj.* **1.** Turning or twisting; sinuous. **2.** Spiral. —*n.* Material, as wire, wound into a coil or around an object.
wind instrument (wĭnd) *n.* A musical instrument, as a clarinet, trumpet, or flute, sounded by wind, esp. the breath.
wind·jam·mer (wĭnd'jăm'ər) *n.* **1. a.** A sailing ship. **2.** A crew member of a windjammer.
wind·lass (wĭnd'ləs) *n.* Any of various hauling or lifting machines consisting essentially of a drum or cylinder wound with rope and turned by a crank. [< ON *vindáss.*]
wind·mill (wĭnd'mĭl') *n.* A mill or machine powered by a wheel of adjustable blades or vanes that are rotated by the wind.
win·dow (wĭn'dō) *n.* **1.** An opening constructed in a wall in order to admit light or air. **2.** A framework enclosing a window. **3.** A windowpane. **4.** An opening that resembles a window. [< ON *vindauga.*]
win·dow-dress·ing (wĭn'dō-drĕs'ĭng) *n.* Also **window dressing. 1.** The display of merchan-

dise in store windows. **2.** Something used to improve appearances or create a false favorable impression. —**win'dow-dress'er** *n.*
win·dow·pane (wĭn'dō-pān') *n.* A pane of glass in a window.
win·dow-shop (wĭn'dō-shŏp') *v.* To look at merchandise in store windows or showcases without making purchases. —**win'dow-shop'-per** *n.* —**win'dow-shop'ping** *n.*
win·dow-sill (wĭn'dō-sĭl') *n.* The horizontal ledge at the base of a window opening.
wind·pipe (wĭnd'pĭp') *n.* The trachea.
wind·shield (wĭnd'shēld') *n.* A framed pane of transparent material located in front of the occupants of an automobile to protect them from the wind.
wind·sock (wĭnd'sŏk') *n.* A large, tapered, open-ended sleeve pivotally attached to a standard so that it indicates the direction of the wind blowing through it.
wind·storm (wĭnd'stôrm') *n.* A storm with high winds but little or no rain.
wind·swept (wĭnd'swĕpt') *adj.* Exposed to or moved by the force of wind.
wind tunnel (wĭnd) *n.* A chamber through which air is forced at controlled speeds to study its effect on an object.
wind-up (wĭnd'ŭp') *n.* **1. a.** The act of bringing something to a conclusion. **b.** A concluding part; finish. **2.** The movements of a pitcher preparatory to pitching the ball.
wind·ward (wĭnd'wərd) *adj.* Of, situated in, or moving toward the quarter from which the wind blows. —*n.* The direction or quarter from which the wind blows. —**wind'ward** *adv.*
wind·y (wĭn'dē) *adj.* **-i·er, -i·est. 1.** Characterized by or abounding in wind. **2.** Exposed to the wind. **3. a.** Given to prolonged or empty talk. **b.** Wordy, boastful, or bombastic. —**wind'i·ly** *adv.* —**wind'i·ness** *n.*
wine (wīn) *n.* **1. a.** The fermented juice of grapes. **b.** The fermented juice of various other fruits or plants: *dandelion wine.* **2.** A dark purplish red. —*adj.* Dark purplish red. —*v.* **wined, win·ing.** To provide with drink or wine. [< Lat. *vinum.*]
wine·glass (wīn'glăs') *n.* A glass, usu. with a stem, from which wine is drunk.
wine·grow·er (wīn'grō'ər) *n.* One who owns a vineyard and produces wine. —**wine'grow'ing** *adj. & n.*
wine·press (wīn'prĕs') *n.* A vat in which the juice is pressed from grapes.
win·er·y (wī'nə-rē) *n., pl.* **-ies.** An establishment where wine is made.
wing (wĭng) *n.* **1.** One of a pair of specialized organs of flight, as of a bird, bat, or insect. **2.** A structure resembling a wing, as the pectoral fin of a flying fish or a thin or membranous projection on certain seeds. **3.** *Informal.* An arm of a human being. **4.** An airfoil whose principal function is to provide lift, esp. one of a pair of airfoils positioned on each side of the fuselage. **5.** Something that resembles a wing in appearance, function, or position. **6.** A part of a building extending from or attached to the main structure. **7.** One of two sections, as of a political party, holding distinct views; faction. **8.** Often **wings.** The unseen backstage area on either side of a stage. **9.** A unit of military aircraft or aviators. **10.** The left or right flank of an army or navy unit. **11.** Either of the forward positions played near the sideline, esp. in hockey. —*v.* **1.** To fly or soar with or as if

with wings. **2.** To furnish with wings. **3.** To perform or accomplish by flying. **4.** To wound superficially, as in the wing or arm. —**idioms. on the wing.** In the act of flying; in flight. **under (one's) wing.** In one's care or charge. **wing it.** *Informal.* To improvise or ad-lib. [ME *wenge.*] —**wing'less** *adj.*

wing·ding (wĭng'dĭng') *n. Slang.* A lavish or lively party or celebration. [Orig. unknown.]

winged *adj.* **1.** (wĭngd). Having wings or winglike parts: *winged insects.* **2.** (wĭng'ĭd). Seeming to move on or as if on wings: *the winged words of the poet.*

wing·span (wĭng'spăn') *n.* Wingspread.

wing·spread (wĭng'sprĕd') *n.* The distance between the tips of the extended wings, as of a bird, insect, or airplane.

wink (wĭngk) *v.* **1.** To close and open one eye as a signal or suggestion. **2.** To shine fitfully; twinkle. **3.** To close and open the eyes rapidly; blink. —*n.* **1. a.** The act of winking. **b.** The time required for a wink; a very short time. **2.** A brief moment of sleep. —*phrasal verb.* **wink at.** To pretend not to see; ignore intentionally: *winked at corruption.* [< OE *wincian,* to close one's eyes.] —**wink'er** *n.*

Win·ne·ba·go (wĭn'ə-bā'gō) *n., pl.* **-go** or **-gos** or **-goes.** **1. a.** A tribe of Indians inhabiting eastern Wisconsin. **b.** A member of the Winnebago. **2.** The Siouan language of the Winnebago.

win·ning (wĭn'ĭng) *adj.* **1.** Successful; victorious. **2.** Charming: *a winning personality.* —*n.* **1.** Victory. **2.** Often **winnings.** Something that has been won, esp. money won at gambling.

win·now (wĭn'ō) *v.* **1.** To separate the chaff from (grain) by means of a current of air. **2.** To examine closely in order to sort; sift. **3.** To separate (a desirable or undesirable part); eliminate. [< OE *windwian.*] —**win'now·er** *n.*

win·o (wī'nō) *n., pl.* **-os.** *Slang.* One who is habitually drunk on wine.

win·some (wĭn'səm) *adj.* Winning; charming. [< OE *wynsum.*] —**win'some·ly** *adv.* —**win'some·ness** *n.*

win·ter (wĭn'tər) *n.* The usu. coldest season of the year, occurring between autumn and spring. —*adj.* **1.** Of, pertaining to, characteristic of, or occurring in the winter. **2.** Planted in the autumn and harvested in the spring or summer: *winter wheat.* —*v.* **1.** To pass or spend the winter. **2.** To keep, feed, or care for during the winter: *wintered the cattle on the south range.* [< OE.]

win·ter·green (wĭn'tər-grēn') *n.* **1.** A low-growing plant with aromatic evergreen leaves and spicy, edible red berries. **2.** An oil or flavoring obtained from the wintergreen.

win·ter·ize (wĭn'tə-rīz') *v.* **-ized, -iz·ing.** To prepare or equip for winter weather.

win·ter·kill (wĭn'tər-kĭl') *v.* To kill by or die from exposure to cold winter weather.

win·ter·time (wĭn'tər-tīm') *n.* The winter season.

win·try (wĭn'trē) *adj.* **-tri·er, -tri·est.** Also **win·ter·y** (-tə-rē) **-i·er, -i·est.** **1.** Of or like winter; cold: *wintry weather.* **2.** Suggestive of winter; cheerless: *a wintry smile.*

wipe (wīp) *v.* **wiped, wip·ing.** **1.** To rub, as with a cloth or paper, in order to clean or

dry. **2.** To remove by or as if by rubbing; brush: *wiped away the grease.* **3.** To rub, move, or pass over a surface. —*phrasal verb.* **wipe out. 1.** To destroy completely; annihilate. **2.** *Informal.* To murder. **3.** To lose balance and fall or jump off a surfboard. [< OE *wīpian.*] —**wipe** *n.* —**wip'er** *n.*

wire (wīr) *n.* **1.** A usu. flexible metallic strand or rod, often electrically insulated, used chiefly for structural support or to conduct electricity. **2.** A group of wires bundled or twisted together; cable. **3. a.** A telegraph service. **b.** A telegram. **4.** An open telephone connection. **5.** The finish line of a racetrack. **6.** Often **wires.** Hidden influences that affect or control a person or group: *pulled wires to get nominated.* —*v.* **wired, wir·ing.** **1.** To connect or attach with wire. **2.** To equip or provide with electrical wires. **3. a.** To send by telegraph: *wire congratulations.* **b.** To send a telegram to. [< OE *wīr.*]

wire-draw (wīr'drô') *v.* **1.** To draw (metal) into wire. **2.** To treat at great length or with excessive detail.

wire-haired (wīr'hârd') *adj.* Having a coat of stiff, wiry hair.

wire·less (wīr'lĭs) *n.* **1.** A radio telegraph or telephone system. **2.** *Chiefly Brit.* Radio. —*adj.* Having no wire or wires.

wire-pull·er (wīr'pōōl'ər) *n.* One who uses private influence to reach a goal.

wire·tap (wīr'tăp') *n.* A concealed listening or recording device connected to a communications circuit. —*v.* To monitor (a telephone line) by means of a wiretap.

wir·ing (wīr'ĭng) *n.* A system of electric wires.

wir·y (wīr'ē) *adj.* **-i·er, -i·est.** **1.** Wirelike; kinky: *wiry hair.* **2.** Slender but strong: *a wiry physique.* —**wir'i·ness** *n.*

wis·dom (wĭz'dəm) *n.* **1.** Understanding of what is true, right, or lasting. **2.** Common sense; good judgment. **3.** Scholarly learning; knowledge. [< OE *wīsdōm.*]

wisdom tooth *n.* One of four molars, the last on each side of both jaws in human beings.

wise[1] (wīz) *adj.* **wis·er, wis·est.** **1.** Having wisdom; judicious. **2.** Having or showing common sense; prudent. **3.** Having knowledge or awareness; knowing. **4.** Offensively self-assured; fresh: *a wise kid.* **5.** Shrewd; cunning. [< OE *wīs.*] —**wise'ly** *adv.*

Syns: wise, discerning, knowing, sagacious, sage, sapient *adj.*

wise[2] (wīz) *n.* Method or manner of doing; way: *in no wise.* [< OE *wīse.*]

-wise *suff.* **1.** Manner, direction, or position: *clockwise.* **2.** *Informal.* With reference to: *tax-wise.* [< OE *wīse,* manner.]

Usage: The suffix *-wise* has a long history of use in the sense "in the manner or direction of": *slantwise; otherwise.* In recent times *-wise* has been in vogue as a noun suffix meaning "with reference to": *inflationwise.* But the indiscriminate coinage of terms with this suffix can lead to confusion since the exact nature of the intended meaning is not always clear from the context.

wise·a·cre (wīz'ā'kər) *n. Informal.* An offensively self-assured person. [MDu. *wijsseggher,* soothsayer.]

wise·crack (wīz'krăk') *n. Slang.* A clever,

flippant, or witty remark. —**wise′crack′** v.

wish (wĭsh) n. **1.** A desire for something; want. **2.** An expression of a wish. **3.** Something desired or longed for: *got his wish.* —v. **1.** To have or feel a wish; want: *I wish to know; I wish you were here.* **2.** To entertain or express a wish for; bid: *wished her good night.* **3.** To invoke upon: *I wish him luck.* **4.** To request or command by expressing a wish: *The President wishes your presence.* **5.** To impose; foist: *wished a hard job on him.* [< OE *wȳscan,* to wish.] —**wish′er** n.

wish·bone (wĭsh′bōn′) n. The forked bone in front of the breastbone of most birds.

wish·ful (wĭsh′fəl) adj. **1.** Expressing a wish or longing. **2.** Reflecting wishes rather than reality: *wishful thinking.* —**wish′ful·ly** adv. —**wish′ful·ness** n.

wish·y-wash·y (wĭsh′ē-wŏsh′ē, -wô′shē) adj. **-i·er, -i·est.** *Informal.* Lacking in strength or purpose; indecisive. [< WASH.]

wisp (wĭsp) n. **1.** A small bunch or bundle, as of hair. **2.** One that is thin, frail, or slight: *a wisp of a child.* **3.** A faint streak, as of smoke. [ME.] —**wisp′y** adj.

wis·te·ri·a (wĭ-stîr′ē-ə) n. Also **wis·tar·i·a** (-stâr′-). A climbing woody vine with drooping clusters of showy purplish or white flowers. [< Caspar *Wistar* (1761-1818).]

wist·ful (wĭst′fəl) adj. Full of a melancholy yearning; longing: *wistful eyes.* [< obs. *wistly,* intently.] —**wist′ful·ly** adv. —**wist′ful·ness** n.

wit (wĭt) n. **1. a.** The ability to perceive and express humorously the relationship or similarity between seemingly incongruous or disparate things. **b.** A person having this ability. **2.** Often **wits. a.** Understanding; intelligence. **b.** Sound mental faculties; sanity. —**idiom. at (one's wits′ end.** At the limit of one's mental resources; utterly at a loss. [< OE.]

witch (wĭch) n. **1.** A woman who practices sorcery; sorceress. **2.** An ugly, vicious old woman; hag. **3.** *Informal.* A bewitching young woman or girl. [< OE *wicce,* witch, and < OE *wicca,* wizard.]

witch
17th-century witchcraft trial in
Salem, Massachusetts

witch·craft (wĭch′krăft′) n. Black magic; sorcery.

witch doctor n. A medicine man or shaman among primitive peoples or tribes.

witch·er·y (wĭch′ə-rē) n., pl. **-ies. 1.** Sorcery; witchcraft. **2.** Power to charm or fascinate.

witch hazel n. **1.** A North American shrub with yellow flowers that bloom in late autumn or winter. **2.** An alcoholic solution containing an extract of the bark of the witch

hazel that is used as a mild astringent. [ME *wyche,* elm + HAZEL.]

witch-hunt (wĭch′hŭnt′) n. An intensive campaign to search out and harry those whose beliefs and point of view, esp. in politics, are unpopular. —**witch′-hunt′ing** n.

witch·ing (wĭch′ĭng) adj. **1.** Relating to or appropriate for witchcraft: *the witching hour.* **2.** Having power to charm or enchant; bewitching.

with (wĭth, wĭth) prep. **1.** As a companion of; accompanying: *Come with me.* **2.** Next to: *Walk with him and follow me.* **3.** Having: *a man with a beard.* **4.** In a manner characterized by: *done with skill.* **5.** In the opinion of: *if it's all right with you.* **6.** In support of; on the side of: *I'm with you all the way.* **7.** Containing: *coffee with cream.* **8.** By the means or agency of: *eat with a fork.* **9.** In spite of: *With all that talent he's getting nowhere.* **10.** At the same time as: *rising with the sun.* **11.** In regard to: *pleased with her.* **12.** In comparison or contrast to: *a dress identical with the one I saw you wearing.* **13.** Having received: *With your permission, I'll leave.* **14.** In opposition to; against: *wrestling with an opponent.* **15.** As a result or consequence of: *trembling with fear.* **16.** To; onto: *coupled the first car with the second.* **17.** So as to be free of or separated from: *parting with a friend.* **18.** In the course of: *With each moment he got angrier.* **19.** In proportion to: *improving with age.* **20.** As well as: *can sing with the best of them.* [< OE.]

with·al (wĭth-ôl′, wĭth-) adv. **1.** In addition; besides. **2.** Despite that; nevertheless. **3.** *Archaic.* Therewith. [ME.]

with·draw (wĭth-drô′, wĭth-) v. **-drew** (-drōō′), **-drawn** (-drôn′), **-draw·ing. 1.** To take back or away; remove. **2.** To recall; retract: *withdrew his objections.* **3.** To move or draw back; retreat. **4.** To remove oneself from activity, participation, or involvement. [ME *withdrawen.*]

with·draw·al (wĭth-drô′əl, wĭth-) n. **1.** The act or process of withdrawing. **2.** A detachment, as from emotional involvement. **3. a.** Termination of the administration of a habit-forming substance. **b.** The physiological and psychological reactions that take place upon such discontinuation.

with·drawn (wĭth-drôn′, wĭth-) adj. **1.** Socially retiring; shy **2.** Emotionally unresponsive.

withe (wĭth, wĭth, wīth) n. A tough, supple twig, as of willow, used for binding things together. [< OE *withthe.*]

with·er (wĭth′ər) v. **1.** To dry up or shrivel from or as if from lack of moisture. **2.** To lose or cause to lose freshness, strength, or vitality; fade. **3.** To render speechless or incapable of action; stun: *withered her with a glance.* [ME *widderen.*]

with·ers (wĭth′ərz) pl.n. The high point of the back of a horse between the shoulder blades. [Prob. < OE *wither-,* against.]

with·hold (wĭth-hōld′, wĭth-) v. **-held** (-hĕld′), **-hold·ing. 1.** To keep in check; restrain. **2.** To refrain from giving, granting, or permitting: *withhold authorization.* [ME *withholden.*] —**with·hold′er** n.

withholding tax n. A portion of an employee's income withheld by the employer as partial payment of the employee's income tax.

with·in (wĭth-ĭn′, wĭth-) adv. **1.** Inside. **2.** Indoors. **3.** Inside the body or mind; inwardly. —prep. **1.** Inside. **2.** Inside the limits or extent of. **3.** Inside the fixed limits of: *within one's rights.* **4.** In the scope or sphere of. —*n.* An inner position, place, or area: *growing from within.*

with-it (wĭth'ĭt) *adj. Slang.* Up-to-date; hip.

with-out (wĭth-out', wĭth-) *adv.* **1.** In or on the outside. **2.** Outdoors. —*prep.* **1.** Not having; lacking. **2. a.** With no or none of. **b.** Not accompanied by. **3.** Free from. **4.** At, on, to, or toward the outside or exterior of. **5.** With neglect or avoidance of. [< OE *withūtan.*]

with-stand (wĭth-stănd', wĭth-) *v.* **-stood** (-stŏŏd') **-stand-ing.** To oppose successfully; resist or endure. [< OE *withstandan.*]

wit-less (wĭt'lĭs) *adj.* Lacking intelligence or wit; stupid or foolish. —**wit'less-ly** *adv.* —**wit'less-ness** *n.*

wit-ness (wĭt'nĭs) *n.* **1.** One who has seen or heard something. **2.** Something that serves as evidence; sign. **3. a.** One who is called to testify before a court of law. **b.** One who is called upon to be present at a transaction in order to attest to what took place. **4.** An attestation; testimony: *bore witness to the facts.* —*v.* **1.** To be present at or have personal knowledge of. **2.** To serve as or furnish evidence of. **3.** To be the setting or site of. **4.** To attest to the legality or authenticity of by signing one's name. [< OE *witnes.*] —**wit'ness-er** *n.*

wit-ti-cism (wĭt'ĭ-sĭz'əm) *n.* A witty remark or saying. [WITT(Y) + (CRIT)ICISM.]

wit-ty (wĭt'ē) *adj.* **-ti-er, -ti-est.** Having or showing wit; cleverly humorous. —**wit'ti-ly** *adv.* —**wit'ti-ness** *n.*

wives (wīvz) *n.* Pl. of **wife.**

wiz-ard (wĭz'ərd) *n.* **1.** A sorcerer or magician. **2.** *Informal.* A skillful or clever person: *a wizard at mathematics.* [ME *wysard.*]

wiz-ard-ry (wĭz'ər-drē) *n.* **1.** Sorcery. **2.** Skill or cleverness in an endeavor or activity.

wiz-ened (wĭz'ənd) *adj.* Shriveled; withered.

woad (wōd) *n.* **1.** An Old World plant with leaves that yield a blue dye. **2.** The dye obtained from the woad. [< OE *wād.*]

wob-ble (wŏb'əl) *v.* **-bled, -bling.** **1.** To move or cause to move erratically from side to side. **2.** To tremble or quaver, as a sound; shake. **3.** To waver or vacillate, as in one's opinions. [Prob. < LG *wabbeln.*] —**wob'bie** *n.* —**wob'bli-ness** *n.* —**wob'bly** *adj.*

woe (wō) *n.* **1.** Deep sorrow; grief. **2.** Misfortune; calamity: *financial woes.* [< OE *wā,* an interjection expressing dismay.]

woe-be-gone (wō'bĭ-gôn', -gŏn') *adj.* Mournful or sorrowful, esp. in appearance; wretched.

woe-ful (wō'fəl) *adj.* **1.** Afflicted with woe; mournful. **2.** Pitiful or deplorable. —**woe'ful-ly** *adv.*

wok (wŏk) *n.* A metal pan with a convex bottom used esp. in Oriental cooking for frying and steaming. [Cant.]

woke (wōk) *v.* A *p.t.* of **wake[1].**

wo-ken (wō'kən) *v.* A *p.p.* of **wake[1].**

wold (wōld) *n.* An unforested rolling plain. [< OE *weald.*]

wolf (wŏŏlf) *n., pl.* **wolves** (wŏŏlvz). **1.** A carnivorous mammal, chiefly of northern regions, related to and resembling the dogs.

2. A fierce, cruel, predatory person. **3.** *Slang.* A man given to avid amatory pursuit of women. —*v.* To eat voraciously: *wolfed down the hamburger.* [< OE *wulf.*] —**wolf'ish** *adj.* —**wolf'ish-ly** *adv.* —**wolf'ish-ness** *n.*

wolf

wolf-hound (wŏŏlf'hound') *n.* Any of various large dogs orig. trained to hunt wolves.

wol-ver-ine (wŏŏl'və-rēn') *n.* A carnivorous mammal of northern regions with dark fur and a bushy tail. [< WOLF.]

wom-an (wŏŏm'ən) *n., pl.* **wom-en** (wĭm'ĭn). **1.** An adult female human being. **2.** Women collectively; womankind. **3.** Feminine quality or aspect; womanliness. **4.** A female servant. **5.** A mistress; paramour. [< OE *wifmann.*]

wom-an-hood (wŏŏm'ən-hŏŏd') *n.* **1.** The state of being a woman. **2.** Woman's nature. **3.** Womankind.

wom-an-ish (wŏŏm'ə-nĭsh) *adj.* **1.** Characteristic of a woman; womanlike. **2.** Considered appropriate in women but undesirable in men; effeminate.

wom-an-kind (wŏŏm'ən-kīnd') *n.* Female human beings collectively; women.

wom-an-ly (wŏŏm'ən-lē) *adj.* **-li-er, -li-est.** Having or showing qualities or characteristics considered typical of, suitable for, or admirable in women. —**wom'an-li-ness** *n.*

womb (wŏŏm) *n.* **1.** The uterus. **2.** A place where something has its earliest stages of development. [< OE *wamb.*]

wom-bat (wŏm'băt') *n.* An Australian marsupial that somewhat resembles a small bear. [Native word in Australia.]

wom-en (wĭm'ĭn) *n.* Pl. of **woman.**

wom-en-folk (wĭm'ĭn-fōk') *pl.n.* Women.

won[1] (wŭn) *v. p.t. & p.p.* of **win.**

won[2] (wŏn) *n., pl.* **won.** See table at **currency.** [Korean.]

won-der (wŭn'dər) *n.* **1. a.** One that arouses awe, surprise, or admiration; marvel. **b.** The feeling thus aroused. **2.** A feeling of confusion or doubt. —*v.* **1.** To have a feeling of awe or admiration; marvel. **2.** To be filled with curiosity or doubt. **3.** To have doubts or curiosity about. [< OE *wundor.*]

won-der-ful (wŭn'dər-fəl) *adj.* **1.** Capable of exciting wonder; astonishing or marvelous. **2.** Admirable; excellent. —**won'der-ful-ly** *adv.*

won-der-land (wŭn'dər-lănd') *n.* **1.** A marvelous imaginary realm. **2.** A real place or scene that arouses wonder.

won-der-ment (wŭn'dər-mənt) *n.* **1.** Astonishment, awe, or surprise. **2.** A marvel. **3.** Puzzlement or curiosity.

won·drous (wŭn′drəs) *adj.* Wonderful.
—**won′drous·ly** *adv.*

wont (wŏnt, wŏnt) *adj.* Accustomed, apt, or used: *was wont to lend money.* —*n.* Habit; custom: *He joked as was his wont.* [< ME *wonen,* to be accustomed.]

won't (wŏnt). Will not.

wont·ed (wŏn′tĭd, wŏn′-) *adj.* Accustomed; usual.

woo (wōō) *v.* **1.** To seek the affection of, esp. with the hope of marrying. **2.** To seek to gain or achieve. **3.** To entreat; importune. [< OE *wōgian.*] —**woo′er** *n.*

wood (wŏŏd) *n.* **1. a.** The tough, fibrous supporting and water-conducting substance beneath the bark of trees and shrubs. **b.** This substance, often cut and dried, used for various purposes, as building material and fuel. **2.** Often **woods.** A dense growth of trees; forest. **3.** Something made of wood. —*adj.* **1.** Associated with, used on, or containing wood. **2.** Growing or living in woods. —*v.* **1.** To cover with trees. **2.** To supply with wood, esp. for fuel. [< OE *wudu.*]

wood alcohol *n.* Methyl alcohol.

wood·bine (wŏŏd′bīn′) *n.* Any of various climbing vines, as an Old World honeysuckle or the Virginia creeper. [< OE *wudubinde.*]

wood·block (wŏŏd′blŏk′) *n.* A woodcut.

wood·chuck (wŏŏd′chŭk′) *n.* A common North American rodent with a short-legged, heavy-set body and grizzled fur. [< Creek *oček.*]

wood·cock (wŏŏd′kŏk′) *n.* A short-legged, long-billed game bird.

wood·craft (wŏŏd′krăft′) *n.* **1.** The art or skill of working with wood. **2.** Skill and experience in matters pertaining to the woods, as hunting, fishing, or camping.

wood·cut (wŏŏd′kŭt′) *n.* **1.** A piece of wood with an engraved design for printing. **2.** A print made from a woodcut.

wood·cut·ter (wŏŏd′kŭt′ər) *n.* One who cuts wood or trees.

wood·ed (wŏŏd′ĭd) *adj.* Having trees or woods.

wood·en (wŏŏd′n) *adj.* **1.** Made of wood. **2.** Stiff and unnatural; lifeless. **3.** Clumsy and awkward; ungainly. —**wood′en·ly** *adv.* —**wood′en·ness** *n.*

wood·land (wŏŏd′lənd, -lănd′) *n.* Land covered with trees.

wood·peck·er (wŏŏd′pĕk′ər) *n.* Any of various birds that cling to and climb trees and have a chisellike bill for drilling through bark and wood.

wood·pile (wŏŏd′pīl′) *n.* A pile of wood, esp. firewood.

wood·ruff (wŏŏd′rəf, -rŭf′) *n.* A plant with small white flowers and fragrant leaves used as flavoring and in sachets. [< OE *wuderofe.*]

wood·shed (wŏŏd′shĕd′) *n.* A shed in which firewood is stored.

woods·man (wŏŏdz′mən) *n.* One who works or lives in the woods or is skilled in woodcraft; forester.

woods·y (wŏŏd′zē) *adj.* **-i·er, -i·est.** Characteristic or suggestive of the woods.

wood·wind (wŏŏd′wĭnd′) *n.* Any of a group of wind instruments that includes the clarinet, oboe, flute, bassoon, and sometimes the saxophone.

wood·work (wŏŏd′wûrk′) *n.* Something made of wood, esp. wooden interior fittings, as moldings or doors.

wood·y (wŏŏd′ē) *adj.* **-i·er, -i·est. 1.** Consisting of or containing wood. **2.** Of or suggestive of wood. **3.** Covered with trees; wooded.

woof (wŏŏf, wŏŏf) *n.* **1.** The threads in a woven fabric at right angles to the warp threads. **2.** The texture of a fabric. [< OE *ōwef.*]

woof·er (wŏŏf′ər) *n.* A loudspeaker designed to reproduce sounds of low frequency. [< *woof,* bark of a dog.]

wool (wŏŏl) *n.* **1.** The dense, soft, often curly hair of some animals, esp. sheep, used to make yarn, cloth, and clothing. **2.** Yarn, cloth, or clothing made of wool. **3.** Something having the look or feel of wool, as a mass of fine, curled metal strands. [< OE *wull.*]

wool·en (wŏŏl′ən). Also **wool·len.** —*adj.* Of, pertaining to, or consisting of wool. —*n.* Often **woolens.** Wool fabric or clothing.

wool·gath·er·ing (wŏŏl′găth′ər-ĭng) *n.* Absent-minded indulgence in fanciful daydreams. —**wool′gath′er·er** *n.*

wool·ly (wŏŏl′ē) *adj.* **-li·er, -li·est.** Also **wool·y.** **-i·er, -i·est. 1. a.** Pertaining to, consisting of, or covered with wool. **b.** Resembling wool. **2.** Lacking sharp detail; fuzzy: *woolly thinking.* **3.** Characterized by lawlessness and disorder: *a wild and woolly frontier.* —*n., pl.* **-lies.** Also **-ies.** A garment, esp. an undergarment, made of wool.

woo·zy (wŏŏ′zē, wŏŏz′ē) *adj.* **-zi·er, -zi·est. 1.** Confused; muddled. **2.** Dizzy or queasy. [Poss. < *oozy.*] —**woo′zi·ness** *n.*

Worces·ter·shire (wŏŏs′tər-shîr′, -shər). A trademark for a piquant sauce of soy, vinegar, and spices.

word (wûrd) *n.* **1. a.** A spoken sound or group of sounds that communicates a meaning and can be represented graphically. **b.** A graphic representation of a word. **2.** An utterance, remark, or comment. **3. words.** An argument or dispute. **4.** A promise; assurance. **5.** A direction to do something; order. **6.** News; information. **7.** A verbal signal; password. **8. words.** Lyrics; text. **9. Word.** The Scriptures or Gospel. —*v.* To express in words. [< OE.] —**word′less** *adj.* —**word′less·ly** *adv.*

word·age (wûr′dĭj) *n.* **1.** Words. **2.** The number of words used. **3.** Wording.

word·book (wûrd′bŏŏk′) *n.* A lexicon, vocabulary, or dictionary.

word·ing (wûr′dĭng) *n.* The way in which something is expressed; phraseology.

word play *n.* A witty or clever use of words.

word·y (wûr′dē) *adj.* **-i·er, -i·est.** Expressed in or using too many words; verbose. —**word′i·ness** *n.*

wore (wôr, wōr) *v. p.t.* of **wear.**

work (wûrk) *n.* **1.** Physical or mental effort; labor. **2.** Employment: *looking for work.* **3.** The activity by which one makes a living; occupation. **4.** A task or duty. **5.** Workmanship: *slipshod work.* **6. a.** Something that has been produced as a result of effort. **b.** An act; deed: *charitable works.* **c. works.** The output of a creative artist: *the works of Bach.* **d. works.** Engineering structures. **7.** Something being made, studied, or processed. **8. works** (*used with a sing. verb*). A factory, plant, or similar site where industry is carried on: *a steel works.* **9. works.** The essential or operating parts of a mechanism. **10. the works.** *Slang.* The whole lot; everything: *ordered the works, from soup to nuts.* **11.** The transfer of energy to a body by the application of force. —v. 1. To labor; toil. 2. To be employed; have a job. 3. To operate or cause to operate, esp. effectively. 4. To have an influence or effect, as on the feelings. 5. To be changed into a specified state, esp. through gradual or repeated stress, pressure, or movement: *The stitches worked loose.* 6. To force a passage or way. 7. To move or contort, as from emotion or pain. 8. To be formed, shaped, or manipulated: *Copper works easily.* 9. To bring about; accomplish: *work wonders.* 10. To make or force to work: *works his laborers hard.* 11. To form or shape; mold. 12. To solve (a problem) by calculation and reasoning. 13. To achieve (a specified condition) by gradual or repeated effort: *worked herself into a top position with the company.* 14. To arrange; contrive. 15. To excite, rouse, or provoke: *worked the crowd into a frenzy.* 16. To influence or use to advantage; exploit: *worked his contacts.* —phrasal verbs. work on (or upon). 1. To persuade, influence, or affect. 2. To attempt to persuade or influence. work out. 1. To find a solution for; resolve: *worked out his problems.* 2. To prove successful or suitable. 3. To perform athletic exercises. [< OE *weorc.*]

work·a·ble (wûr'kə-bəl) *adj.* 1. Capable of being put into effect; practicable. 2. Capable of being worked. —**work'a·ble·ness** *n.*

work·a·day (wûr'kə-dā') *adj.* 1. Of, pertaining to, or appropriate to working days; everyday. 2. Commonplace; mundane. [< ME *werkeday,* workday.]

work·bench (wûrk'bĕnch') *n.* A sturdy table or bench on which manual work is done, as by a machinist or carpenter.

work·book (wûrk'bŏŏk') *n.* 1. A booklet of problems and exercises to be worked by students directly on its pages. 2. A manual of operating instructions, as for an appliance. 3. A book in which a record of work is kept.

work·day (wûrk'dā') *n.* 1. A day on which work is done. 2. The part of the day during which one works.

work·er (wûr'kər) *n.* 1. One that works. 2. One who works for wages. 3. A sterile female of certain social insects, as the ant or bee, that performs specialized work.

work force *n.* 1. Those workers employed in a specific project; staff. 2. All workers potentially available, as to a nation, project, or industry.

work·horse (wûrk'hôrs') *n.* 1. A horse used for labor rather than for racing or riding. 2. One who works tirelessly.

work·ing (wûr'kĭng) *adj.* 1. Of, used for, or spent in work. 2. Sufficient or adequate for using: *a working knowledge of German.* 3. Capable of being used as the basis of further work.

work·load (wûrk'lōd') *n.* The amount of work assigned or done in a given time period.

work·man (wûrk'mən) *n.* One who performs labor, esp. skilled manual labor, for wages.

work·man·like (wûrk'mən-līk') *adj.* Of or befitting a skilled worker or craftsman.

work·man·ship (wûrk'mən-shĭp') *n.* 1. The art, skill, or technique of a workman. 2. The quality of such art, skill, or technique.

work·out (wûrk'out') *n.* 1. A period of exer-

cise or practice, esp. in athletics. 2. An exhausting task.

work·room (wûrk'rŏŏm', -rŏŏm') *n.* A room where work, esp. manual work, is done.

work·shop (wûrk'shŏp') *n.* 1. An area, room, or establishment in which manual work is done. 2. A regularly scheduled seminar in a specialized field.

work·ta·ble (wûrk'tā'bəl) *n.* A table designed for a specific task or activity, as needlework.

work·week (wûrk'wĕk') *n.* The number of hours worked or required to be worked in one week.

world (wûrld) *n.* 1. The earth. 2. The universe. 3. The earth and its inhabitants. 4. The human race; mankind. 5. The public. 6. A particular part of the earth. 7. A sphere, realm, or domain. 8. A field or sphere of human endeavor: *the world of the arts.* 9. An individual way of life or state of being. 10. Secular life and its concerns: *a man of the world.* 11. A large amount: *did him a world of good.* 12. A planet or other celestial body. [< OE *weorold.*]

world·ly (wûrld'lē) *adj.* **-li·er, -li·est.** 1. Of or devoted to the concerns of this world rather than to spiritual or religious matters. 2. Sophisticated or cosmopolitan; worldly-wise. —**world'li·ness** *n.*

world·ly-wise (wûrld'lē-wīz') *adj.* Experienced in the ways of the world; sophisticated.

world·wide (wûrld'wīd') *adj.* Reaching or extending throughout the world; universal. —**world'wide'** *adv.*

worm (wûrm) *n.* 1. Any of various invertebrates, as an earthworm or tapeworm, that have a long, flexible rounded or flattened body. 2. Any of various insect larvae that have a soft, elongated body. 3. An object or device, as a screw thread, that resembles a worm. 4. An insidiously tormenting or devouring force. 5. A scorned, despised, or weak-willed person. 6. **worms.** Intestinal infestation with worms or wormlike parasites. —v. 1. To move or cause to move with or as with the sinuous crawling motion of a worm. 2. To elicit by devious or artful means: *wormed the truth out of her.* 3. To cure of intestinal worms. [< OE *wyrm.*]

worm-eat·en (wûrm'ĕt'n) *adj.* 1. Bored through or gnawed by worms. 2. Decayed; rotten. 3. Antiquated; decrepit.

worm gear *n.* 1. A gear that consists of a threaded shaft and a wheel with teeth that mesh into it. 2. A worm wheel.

worm wheel *n.* The toothed wheel of a worm gear.

worm·wood (wûrm'wŏŏd') *n.* An aromatic plant that yields a bitter extract used in making absinthe. [< OE *wermōd.*]

worn (wôrn, wōrn) *v.* *p.p.* of **wear.** —*adj.* 1. Affected or impaired by wear or use. 2. Exhausted; spent. 3. Trite; hackneyed.

worn-out (wôrn'out', wōrn'-) *adj.* 1. Used or worn until no longer usable. 2. Thoroughly exhausted; spent.

wor·ri·some (wûr'ē-səm, wŭr'-) *adj.* 1. Causing worry or anxiety. 2. Tending to worry.

wor·ry (wûr'ē, wŭr'ē) *v.* **-ried, -ry·ing.** 1. To feel or cause to feel uneasy or troubled. 2. a. To pull, bite, or tear at repeatedly. b. To touch, press, or handle idly. **3.** To bother; annoy. —*n., pl.* **-ries. 1.** Mental uneasiness or anxiety. **2.** A source of worry. [< OE *wyrgan*, to strangle.] —**wor'ri·er** *n.*

wor·ry·wart (wûr'ē-wôrt', wûr'-) *n. Informal.* One who tends to worry excessively and needlessly.

worse (wûrs). **1.** Compar. of **bad. 2.** Compar. of **ill.** —*adj.* **1.** More inferior, as in quality, condition, or effect. **2.** More severe or unfavorable. —*adv.* In a worse way. —*n.* Something that is worse. [< OE *wyrsa.*]

wors·en (wûr'sən) *v.* To make or become worse.

wor·ship (wûr'shĭp) *n.* **1. a.** Reverent love and respect for a deity or sacred object. **b.** A set of ceremonies or prayers by which this devotion is expressed. **2.** Love of or devotion to a person or thing: *her worship of money.* **3.** Often **Worship.** *Chiefly Brit.* A title of honor used in addressing officials, as magistrates or mayors. —*v.* **-shiped** or **-shipped, -ship·ing** or **-ship·ping. 1.** To honor and love as a deity; venerate. **2.** To love devotedly. **3.** To participate in religious worship. [< OE *weorthscipe*, honor.] —**wor'ship·er** *n.*

wor·ship·ful (wûr'shĭp-fəl) *adj.* **1.** Showing or given to worship. **2.** *Chiefly Brit.* Worthy of honor and respect by virtue of position or rank. Used in titles of respect.

worst (wûrst). **1.** Superl. of **bad. 2.** Superl. of **ill.** —*adj.* **1.** Most inferior, as in quality, condition, or effect. **2.** Most severe or unfavorable. —*n.* Something that is worst. —*adv.* In the worst manner or degree. —*v.* To gain the advantage over; defeat. [< OE *wyrsta.*]

wor·sted (wōōs'tĭd, wûr'stĭd) *n.* **1.** Firmtextured, compactly twisted woolen yarn made from long-staple fibers. **2.** Fabric made from worsted. [ME *worthstede.*]

wort (wûrt, wôrt) *n.* A plant: *liverwort.* [< OE *wyrt.*]

worth (wûrth) *n.* **1.** The quality of something that makes it desirable, useful, or valuable; merit. **2.** The material value of something. **3.** The quantity of something that can be purchased for a specific sum. **4.** Wealth; riches. —*prep.* **1.** Equal in value to something specified. **2.** Having wealth amounting to. **3.** Deserving of; meriting: *a proposal worth considering.* [< OE *weorth.*]

worth·less (wûrth'lĭs) *adj.* **1.** Without worth, use, or value. **2.** Low and despicable. —**worth'less·ness** *n.*

worth·while (wûrth'hwīl', -wīl') *adj.* Sufficiently valuable or important to justify the expenditure of time or effort.

wor·thy (wûr'thē) *adj.* **-thi·er, -thi·est. 1.** Having worth, merit, or value. **2.** Honorable; admirable. **3.** Deserving: *worthy of acclaim.* —*n., pl.* **-thies.** A worthy person. —**wor'thi·ly** *adv.* —**wor'thi·ness** *n.*

would (wŏŏd) *v. p.t.* of **will²**.

would-be (wŏŏd'bē') *adj.* Desiring or pretending to be: *a would-be actor.*

would·n't (wŏŏd'nt). Would not.

wouldst (wŏŏdst) or **would·est** (wŏŏd'ĭst) *v. Archaic.* 2nd person sing. past tense of **will².**

wound¹ (wōōnd) *n.* **1.** An injury, esp. one in which the skin is torn, cut, broken, or pierced. **2.** An injury to the feelings. —*v.* To inflict a wound on. [< OE *wund.*]

wound² (wound) *v. p.t. & p.p.* of **wind².**

wound³ (wound) *v.* A *p.t. & p.p.* of **wind³.**

wove (wōv) *v. p.t.* of **weave.**

wo·ven (wō'vən) *v. p.p.* of **weave.**

wow (wou) *interj.* Used to express wonder, amazement, enthusiasm, etc. —*n. Informal.* An outstanding success. —*v.* To have a strong and usu. pleasurable impact on.

wrack (răk) *n.* **1.** Complete destruction. **2.** Wreckage or a remnant of something destroyed. —*v.* **1.** To cause the ruin of; wreck. **2.** To have a violent or shattering effect on: *Sobs wracked her body.* [< MDu. *wrak.*]

wraith (rāth) *n.* **1.** An apparition of a living person. **2.** The ghost of a dead person. [Orig. unknown.]

wran·gle (răng'gəl) *v.* **-gled, -gling. 1.** To dispute noisily or angrily; bicker. **2.** To win or obtain by argument. **3.** To herd (horses or other livestock). —*n.* A noisy or angry dispute. [ME *wranglen.*] —**wran'gler** *n.*

wrap (răp) *v.* **wrapped** or **wrapt, wrap·ping. 1.** To draw, fold, or wind about in order to cover. **2.** To enclose within a covering; enfold. **3.** To encase and secure (an object), esp. with paper; package. **4.** To clasp, fold, or wind about something. **5.** To envelop or surround, esp. so as to obscure. **6.** To be or cause to be totally absorbed; engross: *wrapped in his studies.* —*phrasal verb.* **wrap up. 1.** To finish; conclude. **2.** To give a brief, comprehensive statement of; summarize. —*n.* **1.** An outer garment worn for warmth. **2.** A wrapping or wrapper. —*idiom.* **under wraps.** Secret or concealed. [ME *wrappen.*]

wrap·a·round (răp'ə-round') *n.* A garment, as a skirt, that is open to the hem and wrapped around the body before being fastened.

wrap·per (răp'ər) *n.* **1.** One that wraps. **2. a.** A cover, as of paper, in which something is wrapped. **b.** The tobacco leaf covering a cigar. **3.** A loose robe or negligee.

wrap·ping (răp'ĭng) *n.* The material in which something is wrapped.

wrap-up (răp'ŭp') *n.* A brief summary, as of the news.

wrasse (răs) *n.* Any of numerous chiefly tropical, often brightly colored marine fishes. [Cornish *wrach.*]

wrath (răth, räth) *n.* **1.** Violent, resentful anger; rage. **2. a.** An action motivated by anger. **b.** Divine retribution. [< OE *wrǣththu.*]

wrath·ful (răth'fəl, räth'-) *adj.* **1.** Filled with wrath; enraged. **2.** Motivated by wrath. —**wrath'ful·ly** *adv.* —**wrath'ful·ness** *n.*

wreak (rēk) *v.* **1.** To inflict (vengeance or punishment). **2.** To express or gratify; vent. [< OE *wrecan.*]

wreath (rēth) *n., pl.* **wreaths** (rēthz, rēths). **1.** A ring or circular band, as of flowers or leaves. **2.** Something resembling a wreath: *a wreath of smoke.* [< OE *writha.*]

wreathe (rēth) *v.* **wreathed, wreath·ing. 1.** To twist or entwine into a wreath or wreathlike shape. **2.** To coil or spiral. **3.** To assume or cause to assume the form of a wreath. [< WREATH.]

wreck (rĕk) *v.* **1.** To destroy accidentally, as by collision. **2.** To tear down or dismantle. **3.** To bring to a state of ruin. —*n.* **1.** The action of wrecking or the condition of being wrecked. **2. a.** The remains of something, as a ship, that has been wrecked. **b.** A shipwreck. **c.** Something, as goods, cast ashore by the sea after a shipwreck. **3.** One that is in a shattered, broken-down, or worn-out state. [< AN *wrec*, of Scand. orig.]

wreck·age (rĕk'ĭj) *n.* **1.** The act of wrecking

or the condition of being wrecked. **2.** The debris of something wrecked.

wreck·er (rĕk'ər) *n.* **1. a.** One that wrecks. **b.** A member of a wrecking or demolition crew. **2. a.** A vehicle or ship employed in recovering or removing a wreck. **b.** Someone who salvages wrecked cargo.

wren (rĕn) *n.* A small, brownish bird that usu. holds the tail upright. [< OE *wrenna.*]

wrench (rĕnch) *n.* **1.** A sudden, forcible twist or turn. **2.** An injury, as to a muscle, produced by twisting or straining. **3.** Any of various tools with fixed or adjustable jaws for gripping, turning, or twisting an object such as a nut. —*v.* **1. a.** To twist or turn suddenly and forcibly. **b.** To twist and sprain (a part of the body). **2.** To force free by pulling; wrest. **3.** To pull at the feelings or emotions of; give pain to. **4.** To distort the original character or import of. [< OE *wrencan,* to twist.]

wrest (rĕst) *v.* **1.** To obtain by or as if by pulling with violent twisting movements. **2.** To gain or take by force. —*n.* A twist or wrench. [< OE *wrǣstan.*] —**wrest'er** *n.*

wres·tle (rĕs'əl) *v.* **-tled, -tling.** **1.** To fight by grappling and attempting to throw one's opponent to the ground. **2.** To struggle to solve or master: *wrestle with a problem.* **3.** To contend against in the sport of wrestling. —*n.* An act of wrestling, esp. a wrestling match. [< OE *wrǣstlian.*] —**wres'tler** *n.*

wres·tling (rĕs'lĭng) *n.* A gymnastic exercise or contest between two competitors who attempt to throw each other by grappling.

wrestling

wretch (rĕch) *n.* **1.** A miserable, unfortunate, or unhappy person. **2.** A base or despicable person. [< OE *wrecca.*]

wretch·ed (rĕch'ĭd) *adj.* **-er, -est.** **1.** Full of or attended by misery or woe. **2.** Of a poor or mean character; dismal. **3.** Hateful or contemptible. **4.** Inferior in performance or quality. [< ME *wrecche,* wretch.] —**wretch'ed·ly** *adv.* —**wretch'ed·ness** *n.*

wri·er (rī'ər) *adj.* A compar. of wry.

wri·est (rī'ĭst) *adj.* A superl. of wry.

wrig·gle (rĭg'əl) *v.* **-gled, -gling.** **1.** To turn or twist with sinuous motions; squirm. **2.** To advance or proceed with sinuous motions. **3.** To insinuate or extricate oneself by sly or subtle means. [< MLG *wriggeln.*] —**wrig'gle** *n.* —**wrig'gly** *adj.*

wrig·gler (rĭg'lər) *n.* **1.** One that wriggles. **2.** The larva of a mosquito.

wring (rĭng) *v.* **wrung** (rŭng), **wring·ing.** **1.** To twist and squeeze, esp. to extract liquid. **2.** To extract by or as if by twisting or compressing; extort: *wring the truth out of a witness.* **3.** To wrench or twist forcibly or painfully: *I'd like to wring his neck.* **4.** To twist or squeeze in distress: *wringing her hands.* **5.** To cause distress or pain to; torment. [< OE *wringan.*]

wring·er (rĭng'ər) *n.* One that wrings, esp. a device in which laundry is squeezed or spun to extract water.

wrin·kle (rĭng'kəl) *n.* **1.** A small furrow, ridge, or crease on a normally smooth surface, as cloth or the skin. **2.** *Informal.* An ingenious new trick or method; innovation. —*v.* **-kled, -kling.** **1.** To make wrinkles in. **2.** To form wrinkles. [< OE *gewrinclian,* to wind.] —**wrin'kly** *adj.*

wrist (rĭst) *n.* **1.** The joint between the hand and forearm. **2.** The system of bones forming the wrist; carpus. [< OE.]

wrist·band (rĭst'bănd') *n.* A band, esp. on a long-sleeved shirt or a wrist watch, that encircles the wrist.

wrist watch *n.* A small watch worn on a band that fastens about the wrist.

writ (rĭt) *n.* **1.** A written order issued by a court directing the person to whom it is addressed to perform or refrain from a specified act. **2.** Something written. [< OE.]

write (rīt) *v.* **wrote** (rōt), **writ·ten** (rĭt'n), **writ·ing.** **1.** To form (letters, symbols, or characters) on a surface with an implement such as a pen or pencil. **2.** To form by inscribing the correct letters, symbols, or words of: *wrote his answers on a sheet of paper.* **3.** To compose and set down, esp. in musical or literary form. **4.** To relate or communicate by writing. **5.** To send a letter or note to. **6.** To communicate by letter; correspond. —*phrasal verbs.* **write in.** To cast a vote for (a candidate not listed on a ballot) by inserting his name. **write off.** **1.** To cancel from accounts as a loss. **2.** To reduce the book value of; depreciate. [< OE *wrītan.*]

write-in (rīt'ĭn') *n.* A vote cast by writing in the name of a candidate not on the ballot.

writ·er (rī'tər) *n.* One that writes, esp. as an occupation.

writer's cramp *n.* A cramp chiefly affecting the muscles of the thumb and two adjacent fingers after prolonged writing.

write-up (rīt'ŭp') *n.* A published account, review, or notice.

writhe (rīth) *v.* **writhed, writh·ing.** To twist or squirm, as in pain. [< OE *wrīthan.*]

writ·ing (rī'tĭng) *n.* **1.** Written form: *Make your request in writing.* **2.** Handwriting. **3.** Something that is written, esp. a literary composition. **4.** The activity, art, or occupation of a writer.

wrong (rông, rŏng) *adj.* **1.** Not correct; erroneous. **2. a.** Contrary to conscience, morality, law, or custom. **b.** Unfair or unjust. **3.** Not required, intended, or wanted. **4.** Not fitting or suitable; inappropriate. **5.** Not in accordance with an established usage, method, or procedure. **6.** Being the side or surface that is less finished or is opposite to the right, principal, or more prominent side. —*adv.* **1.** In a wrong manner; erroneously. **2.** Immorally or unjustly. —*n.* **1.** Something that is wrong.

2. The condition of being mistaken or to blame: *in the wrong.* —*v.* **1.** To treat unjustly, injuriously, or dishonorably. **2.** To discredit unjustly; malign. [ME, of Scand. orig.] —**wrong'ly** *adv.* —**wrong'ness** *n.*

wrong·do·er (rông'dōō'ər, rŏng'-) *n.* One who does wrong. —**wrong'do'ing** *n.*

wrong·ful (rông'fəl, rŏng'-) *adj.* **1.** Wrong; unjust. **2.** Contrary to law; unlawful. —**wrong'ful·ly** *adv.* —**wrong'ful·ness** *n.*

wrong·head·ed (rông'hĕd'ĭd, rŏng'-) *adj.* Persistently and stubbornly wrong. —**wrong'head'ed·ly** *adv.* —**wrong'head'ed·ness** *n.*

wrote (rōt) *v. p.t.* of **write.**

wroth (rôth, rŏth) *adj.* Wrathful; angry. [< OE *wrāth.*]

wrought (rôt) *adj.* **1.** Made, formed, or fashioned. **2.** Shaped by hammering with tools: *wrought silver.*

wrought iron *n.* A highly purified form of iron that is easily shaped, forged, or welded.

wrung (rŭng) *v. p.t. & p.p.* of **wring.**

wry (rī) *adj.* **wri·er** or **wry·er, wri·est** or **wry·est. 1. a.** Twisted or bent to one side; crooked. **b.** Temporarily twisted in an expression of distaste or displeasure: *a wry face.* **2.** Dryly humorous, often with a touch of irony. [< OE *wrigian,* to move.] —**wry'ly** *adv.* —**wry'ness** *n.*

wurst (wûrst, wŏŏrst) *n.* Sausage. [G.]

Wy·an·dot (wī'ən-dŏt') *n., pl.* -**dot** or -**dots.** Also **Wy·an·dotte** *pl.* -**dotte** or -**dottes. 1.** An Indian of a tribe in the Huron confederacy. **2.** The Iroquoian language of the Wyandot.

Xx

x or **X** (ĕks) *n., pl.* **x's** or **X's. 1.** The 24th letter of the English alphabet. **2.** Something shaped like the letter X. **3.** The mark X inscribed to represent the signature of an illiterate person. **4.** The Roman numeral for 10. **5.** An unknown or unnamed quantity, factor, thing, or person. —*v.* **x'd, x'ing.** To delete or cancel with a series of x's: *x'd out the error.*

x-ax·is (ĕks'ăk'sĭs) *n., pl.* **x-ax·es** (-sēz). The horizontal axis of a plane Cartesian coordinate system.

X-chro·mo·some (ĕks'krō'mə-sōm') *n.* The sex chromosome associated with female characteristics, occurring paired in the female and single in the male sex-chromosome pair.

Xe The symbol for the element xenon.

xe·bec (zē'bĕk') *n.* A small three-masted Mediterranean vessel with both square and triangular sails. [< Ar. *shabbāk.*]

xebec

xe·non (zē'nŏn') *n.* Symbol **Xe** A colorless, odorless, highly unreactive gaseous element found in minute quantities in the atmosphere. Atomic number 54; atomic weight 131.30. [< Gk. *xenos,* stranger.]

xen·o·phobe (zĕn'ə-fōb', zē'nə-) *n.* One unduly fearful or contemptuous of strangers or foreigners. [Gk. *xenos,* stranger + -PHOBE.] —**xen'o·pho'bi·a** *n.* —**xen'o·pho'bic** *adj.*

xe·rog·ra·phy (zĭ-rŏg'rə-fē) *n.* A dry photographic or photocopying process in which a negative image formed by a resinous powder on an electrically charged plate is transferred to a sheet of paper and fixed to the paper by heat. [Gk. *xēros,* dry + -GRAPHY.] —**xe'ro·graph'ic** (zîr'ə-grăf'ĭk) *adj.*

xe·ro·phyte (zîr'ə-fīt') *n.* A plant that grows in and is adapted to an environment deficient in moisture. [Gk. *xēros,* dry + -PHYTE.] —**xe'ro·phyt'ic** (-fĭt'ĭk) *adj.*

Xe·rox (zîr'ŏks'). A trademark for a machine or process that produces photocopies by xerography. —*v.* To copy or print with a Xerox machine.

xi (zī, sī) *n.* The 14th letter of the Greek alphabet. See table at **alphabet.** [Gk. *xei.*]

X·mas (krĭs'məs, ĕks'məs) *n. Informal.* Christmas. [< *X,* Greek letter chi, abbr. of *Khristos,* Christ.]

x-ra·di·a·tion (ĕks'rā'dē-ā'shən) *n.* **1.** Treatment with or exposure to x-rays. **2.** Radiation composed of x-rays.

x-ray (ĕks'rā') *n.* Also **X-ray. 1. a.** A relatively high-energy photon with a very short wavelength. **b.** Often **x-rays.** A stream of such photons, used in radiography, radiology, radiotherapy, and research. **2.** A photograph taken with x-rays. —*v.* **1.** To treat with or subject to x-rays. **2.** To photograph with x-rays.

xy·lem (zī'ləm) *n.* The supporting and water-conducting tissue of vascular plants, consisting primarily of woody tissue. [< Gk. *xulon,* wood.]

xy·lo·phone (zī'lə-fōn') *n.* A musical percussion instrument consisting of a mounted row of wooden bars graduated in length to sound a chromatic scale, played with two small mallets. [Gk. *xulon,* wood + -PHONE.] —**xy'lo·phon'ist** *n.*

Yy

y or **Y** (wī) *n.*, *pl.* **y's** or **Y's.** 1. The 25th letter of the English alphabet. 2. Something shaped like the letter Y.

Y The symbol for the element yttrium.

-y¹ *suff.* 1. Characterized by: *rainy.* 2. Like: *summery.* 3. Inclined toward: *sleepy.* [< OE -ig.]

-y² *suff.* 1. Condition; quality: *jealousy.* 2. **a.** Activity: *cookery.* **b.** Instance of a specified action: *entreaty.* 3. **a.** Place for an activity: *cannery.* **b.** Product of an activity: *laundry.* 4. Group: *soldiery.* [< Lat. -ia, and < Gk. -ia.]

-y³ *suff.* 1. Small one: *doggy.* 2. Dear one: *daddy.* [ME.]

yacht (yät) *n.* A relatively small sailing or motor-driven vessel, usu. with smart, graceful lines, used for pleasure cruises or racing. —*v.* To race, sail, or cruise in a yacht. [< obs. Du. *jaghtschip.*]

yacht·ing (yä′tĭng) *n.* The sport of sailing in yachts.

yachts·man (yäts′mən) *n.* One who owns or sails a yacht. —**yachts′man·ship′** *n.*

ya·hoo (yä′hōō, yä′-) *n.* A crude or brutish person. [< the *Yahoos,* a savage race in *Gulliver's Travels* by Jonathan Swift.]

Yah·weh (yä′wā′) *n.* Also **Yah·veh** (-vā′.) A name for God used by the ancient Hebrews.

yak¹ (yäk) *n.* A long-haired bovine mammal of the mountains of central Asia. [Tibetan *gyag.*]

yak² (yäk) *v.* **yakked, yak·king.** *Slang.* To talk or chatter persistently. [Imit.] —**yak** *n.* —**yak′ker** *n.*

yam (yăm) *n.* 1. The starchy edible root of a tropical vine. 2. A sweet potato with reddish flesh. [Port. *inhame.*]

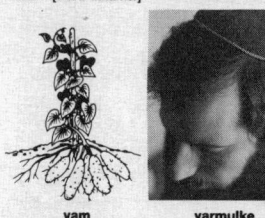

yam   **yarmulke**

yang (yäng) *n.* The active, masculine cosmic principle in Chinese dualistic philosophy. [Chin. *yang²*, sun.]

yank (yăngk) *v.* To pull or extract with or as if with a sudden, forceful movement. —*n.* A sudden vigorous pull; jerk. [Orig. unknown.]

Yank (yăngk) *n. Informal.* A Yankee.

Yan·kee (yăng′kē) *n.* 1. **a.** A native or inhabitant of New England. **b.** A native or inhabi-

tant of a Northern state. 2. A native or inhabitant of the United States. [Orig. unknown.] —**Yan′kee** *adj.*

yap (yăp) *v.* **yapped, yap·ping.** 1. To bark sharply or shrilly; yelp. 2. *Slang.* To talk noisily or stupidly; jabber. —*n.* 1. A sharp, shrill bark; yelp. 2. *Slang.* Noisy, stupid talk; jabbering. 3. *Slang.* The mouth. [Imit.] —**yap′per** *n.*

yard¹ (yärd) *n.* 1. A measure of length equal to 3 feet or 0.9144 meter. 2. A long, tapering pole attached crosswise to a mast to support a sail. [< OE *gerd,* stick.]

yard² (yärd) *n.* 1. A tract of ground adjacent to a building. 2. A tract of ground, often enclosed, set aside for a specific activity. 3. An area where railroad trains are made up and cars are switched, stored, or serviced. 4. An enclosed area for livestock. [< OE *geard,* enclosed area.]

yard·age (yär′dĭj) *n.* The amount or length of something measured in yards.

yard·arm (yärd′ärm′) *n.* Either end of a yard of a square sail.

yard·stick (yärd′stĭk′) *n.* 1. A graduated measuring stick one yard in length. 2. A standard used in making a comparison or judgment.

yar·mul·ke (yär′məl-kə, yä′məl-) *n.* A skullcap worn by male Jews. [Yiddish.]

yarn (yärn) *n.* 1. A continuous strand of twisted fibers, as of wool or cotton, used in weaving or knitting. 2. *Informal.* A long, usu. complicated story. [< OE *gearn.*]

yar·row (yăr′ō) *n.* Any of several plants with finely dissected foliage and flat clusters of usu. white flowers. [< OE *gearwe.*]

yaw (yô) *v.* To turn abruptly or erratically from an intended course; veer: *The ship yawed as the great wave struck it.* [Orig. unknown.] —**yaw** *n.*

yawl (yôl) *n.* 1. A two-masted fore-and-aft-rigged sailing vessel with the shorter mast far to the stern aft of the tiller. 2. A ship's small boat. [MLG *jolle.*]

yawn (yôn) *v.* 1. To open the mouth wide with a deep inward breath, as when sleepy or bored. 2. To open wide; gape. —*n.* An act of yawning. [< OE *geonian.*] —**yawn′er** *n.*

yaws (yôz) *pl.n.* An infectious tropical skin disease characterized by multiple red pimples. [Carib.]

y-ax·is (wī′ăk′sĭs) *n., pl.* **y-ax·es** (-sēz). The vertical axis of a two-dimensional Cartesian coordinate system.

Yb The symbol for the element ytterbium.

Y-chro·mo·some (wī′krō′mə-sōm′) *n.* The sex chromosome associated with male characteristics, occurring with one X-chromosome in the male sex-chromosome pair.

ye¹ (thē) *adj. Archaic.* The. [< the use of *y* for *þ* (th), by early printers.]

ă pat ā pay â care ä father ĕ pet ē be ĭ pit ī tie î pier ŏ pot ō toe ô paw, for oi noise ōō took
ōō boot ou out th thin th this ŭ cut û urge yōō abuse zh vision ə about, item, edible, gallop, circus

ye² (yē) *pron. Archaic.* You (plural). [< OE *gē.*]

yea (yā) *adv.* **1.** Yes; aye. **2.** Indeed; truly. —*n.* **1.** An affirmative statement or vote. **2.** One who votes affirmatively. [< OE *gea.*]

yeah (yĕ′ə, yă′ə, yā′ə) *adv. Informal.* Yes. [< YEA.]

year (yîr) *n.* **1.** The period of time as measured by the Gregorian calendar in which the earth completes a single revolution around the sun, consisting of 365 days, 5 hours, 49 minutes, and 12 seconds of mean solar time divided into 12 months, 52 weeks, and 365 or 366 days. **2.** A period of time, usu. shorter than 12 months, devoted to a special activity: *the academic year.* **3. years.** Age, esp. old age. **4. years.** A long time. [< OE *gēar.*]

year·book (yîr′bŏŏk′) *n.* **1.** A book published every year, containing information about the previous year. **2.** A yearly book published by the graduating class of a school.

year·ling (yîr′lĭng) *n.* An animal that is one year old or has not completed its second year.

year·long (yîr′lông′, -lŏng′) *adj.* Lasting one year.

year·ly (yîr′lē) *adv.* Once a year; annually. —*adj.* Happening once a year; annual.

yearn (yûrn) *v.* **1.** To have a strong or deep desire; long. **2.** To feel deep pity, sympathy, or tenderness. [< OE *gyrnan.*]

yearn·ing (yûr′nĭng) *n.* A deep longing.

year-round (yîr′round′) *adj.* Existing, active, or continuous throughout the year.

yeast (yēst) *n.* **1.** Any of various unicellular fungi capable of fermenting carbohydrates. **2.** Froth produced by and containing yeast cells that is present in or added to fruit juices and other substances in the production of alcoholic beverages. **3.** A commercial preparation containing yeast cells and used esp. as a leavening agent or dietary supplement. **4.** An agent of ferment or activity. [< OE *gist.*] —**yeast′y** *adj.*

yell (yĕl) *v.* To cry out or utter loudly, as in pain, fright, surprise, or enthusiasm; shout. —*n.* **1.** A loud cry; shout. **2.** A rhythmic cheer uttered or chanted in unison by a group. [< OE *giellan.*] —**yell′er** *n.*

yel·low (yĕl′ō) *n.* **1.** The color of ripe lemons or of dandelions. **2.** Something, as the yolk of an egg, of the color yellow. **3. yellows.** Any of various virus plant diseases characterized by yellow or somewhat yellow discoloration. —*adj.* **-er, -est. 1.** Of the color yellow. **2.** Having somewhat yellow skin. **3.** *Slang.* Cowardly. **4.** Exploiting, distorting, or exaggerating news to attract readers; sensational: *yellow journalism.* —*v.* To make or become yellow. [< OE *geolu.*] —**yel′low·ish** *adj.*

yellow fever *n.* An acute infectious disease of subtropical and tropical New World areas, transmitted by a mosquito and characterized by jaundice and dark-colored vomit resulting from hemorrhages.

yellow jack *n.* **1.** Yellow fever. **2.** A yellow flag hoisted by a ship to warn of disease on board.

yellow jacket *n.* A small wasp with yellow and black markings.

yelp (yĕlp) *v.* To utter a sharp, short bark or cry. [< OE *gielpan,* to boast.] —**yelp** *n.*

yen¹ (yĕn) *v. Informal.* A yearning; longing. [Cant. *yan.*] —**yen** *v.*

yen² (yĕn) *n., pl.* **yen.** See table at **currency.** [J. *en.*]

yen·ta (yĕn′tə) *n. Slang.* A gossipy woman, esp. one who pries into the affairs of others. [Yiddish *yente.*]

yeo·man (yō′mən) *n.* **1.** A small independent farmer, esp. a member of a former class of lesser freeholding farmers, below the gentry, in England. **2.** An attendant, servant, or lesser official in a royal or noble household. **3.** A petty officer performing chiefly clerical duties in the U.S. Navy. [ME *yoman.*]

yeo·man·ry (yō′mən-rē) *n.* The class of yeomen; small farmers.

yep (yĕp) *adv. Slang.* Yes.

yes (yĕs) *adv.* It is so; as you say or ask. Used to express affirmation, agreement, positive confirmation, or consent. —*n.* An affirmative reply or vote. [< OE *gese.*]

ye·shi·va or **ye·shi·vah** (yə-shē′və) *n.* **1.** A school where students study the Talmud. **2.** A day school with a curriculum that includes Jewish religion and culture. [Heb. *yĕshībhāh.*]

yes·ter·day (yĕs′tər-dā′, -dē) *n.* **1.** The day before the present day. **2.** Time in the immediate past. —*adv.* **1.** On the day before the present day. **2.** A short while ago. [< OE *giestran dæg.*]

yes·ter·year (yĕs′tər-yîr′) *n.* **1.** The year before this one. **2.** Time past. [YESTER(DAY) + YEAR.]

yet (yĕt) *adv.* **1.** At this time; now. **2.** Up to a specified time; thus far. **3.** In the time remaining; still. **4.** In addition; besides. **5.** Still more; even: *a yet sadder tale.* **6.** Nevertheless: *young yet wise.* **7.** At some future time; eventually. —*conj.* And despite this; nevertheless. [< OE *giĕt.*]

ye·ti (yĕt′ē) *n.* The abominable snowman. [< Tibetan *miti.*]

yew (yōō) *n.* **1.** An evergreen tree or shrub with poisonous flat, dark-green needles and scarlet berries. **2.** The durable fine-grained wood of a yew. [< OE *īw.*]

Yid·dish (yĭd′ĭsh) *n.* A language derived from High German dialects and Hebrew, spoken by Jews, esp. in eastern Europe. —**Yid′dish** *adj.*

yield (yēld) *v.* **1.** To give forth by a natural process; produce. **2.** To furnish or give in return: *an investment that yields 6%.* **3.** To give up possession of; relinquish. **4.** To grant or concede: *yield right of way.* **5.** To give way to pressure, force, or persuasion. **6.** To give way to what is stronger or better; be overcome. —*n.* **1.** An amount yielded, as of a crop. **2.** The profit obtained from investment; return. [< OE *gieldan,* to pay.]

Syns: *yield, bow, capitulate, fold, submit, succumb, surrender* v.

yield·ing (yēl′dĭng) *adj.* **1.** Giving way readily to pressure; not rigid. **2.** Giving in readily; submissive.

yin (yĭn) *n.* The passive, female cosmic element, force, or principle in Chinese dualistic philosophy. [Chin. *yin¹,* moon.]

yip (yĭp) *n.* A sharp, high-pitched bark; yelp. [Imit.] —**yip** *v.*

yip·pee (yĭp′ē) *interj.* A word used to express joy.

-yl *suff.* A chemical radical: *propyl.* [< Gk. *hulē,* matter.]

yod (yŏd, yōōd) *n.* Also **yodh.** The 10th letter of the Hebrew alphabet. See table at **alphabet.** [Heb. *yōdh.*]

yo·del (yōd′l) v. **-deled** or **-delled, -del·ing** or **-del·ling. 1.** To sing so that the voice fluctuates between the normal chest voice and a falsetto. **2.** To sing (a song) by yodeling. [G. *jodeln.*] **—yo′del** n. **—yo′del·er** n.

yo·ga (yō′gə) n. **1.** Often **Yoga.** A Hindu discipline aimed at training the consciousness for a condition of perfect spiritual insight and tranquillity. **2.** A system of exercises practiced as part of yoga to promote control of the body and mind. [Skt. *yogaḥ*, union.]

yo·gi (yō′gē) n., pl. **-gis.** One who practices yoga. [< Skt. *yogī.*]

yo·gurt (yō′gərt) n. Also **yo·ghurt.** A custardlike food made from milk curdled by bacteria. [Turk. *yoğurt.*]

yoke (yōk) n. **1.** A crossbar with two U-shaped pieces that encircle the necks of a pair of draft animals. **2.** pl. **yoke.** A pair of draft animals joined by a yoke. **3.** A frame carried across a person's shoulders with equal loads suspended from each end. **4.** A clamp or vise that holds two parts together. **5.** A fitted part of a garment, such as at the shoulders, to which another part is attached. **6.** Something that connects or joins; bond: *the yoke of matrimony.* **7.** Subjugation; bondage. —v. **yoked, yok·ing. 1.** To fit or join with or as if with a yoke. **2.** To harness a draft animal to. **3.** To connect, join, or bind together. [< OE *geoc.*]

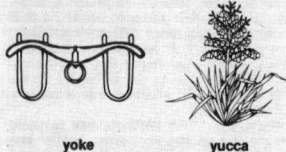

yoke   yucca

yo·kel (yō′kəl) n. A simple country person; bumpkin. [Orig. unknown.]

yolk (yōk) n. **1.** The yellow inner mass of nutritive material in the egg of a bird or reptile. **2.** A greasy substance found in unprocessed sheep's wool. [< OE *geolu*, yellow.]

Yom Kip·pur (yŏm kĭp′ər, yŏm′ kĭ-pŏŏr′) n. The holiest Jewish holiday, celebrated in Sept. or Oct. and observed by fasting, prayer, and atonement.

yon (yŏn) adj. & adv. Archaic. Yonder. [< OE *geon.*]

yon·der (yŏn′dər) adj. Being at an indicated distance, usu. within sight. —adv. In, to, or at that place; over there. [< OE *geond.*]

yore (yôr, yōr) n. Time long past: *days of yore.* [< OE *geāra*, long ago.]

Yo·ru·ba (yō′rŏŏ-bä) n., pl. **-ba** or **-bas. 1.** A member of a West African Negro people living chiefly in southwestern Nigeria. **2.** The language of the Yoruba. **—Yo′ru·ban** adj.

you (yōō) pron. **1.** The person or persons addressed by the speaker: *When can I see you?* **2.** One; anyone: *You can't win them all.* [< OE *ēow.*]

you'd (yōōd). **1.** You had. **2.** You would.

you'll (yōōl). **1.** You will. **2.** You shall.

young (yŭng) adj. **-er, -est. 1.** Being in the early period of life or development; not old. **2.** Having the qualities associated with youth or early life. **3.** Vigorous or fresh; youthful. **4.** Lacking experience; green. —n. **1.** Young persons collectively; youth. **2.** Offspring; brood. [< OE *geong.*]

young·ish (yŭng′ĭsh) adj. Somewhat young.

young·ling (yŭng′lĭng) n. A young person, animal, or plant. **—young′ling** adj.

young·ster (yŭng′stər) n. A young person.

your (yŏŏr, yôr, yōr; yər when unstressed) adj. Of or pertaining to you or yourself: *your wallet; your first rebuff.* [< OE *ēower.*]

you're (yŏŏr; yər when unstressed). You are.

yours (yŏŏrz, yôrz, yōrz) pron. The one or ones belonging to you: *If I can't find my hat, I'll take yours.*

your·self (yŏŏr-sĕlf′, yôr-, yōr-, yər-) pron., pl. **-selves** (-sĕlvz′). That one or ones identical to you. Used: **a.** Reflexively: *hurt yourself; give yourself time; talk to yourself.* **b.** For emphasis: *Do it yourself.*

youth (yōōth) n., pl. **youths** (yōōthz, yōōthz). **1.** The condition or quality of being young. **2.** An early period of development or existence, esp. the time of life before adulthood. **3. a.** A young person, esp. a young man. **b.** Young people collectively. [< OE *geoguth.*]

youth·ful (yōōth′fəl) adj. **1.** Possessing youth; still young. **2.** Characteristic of youth; fresh. **3.** In an early stage of development; new. **—youth′ful·ly** adv. **—youth′ful·ness** n.

you've (yōōv). You have.

yowl (youl) v. To utter a loud, long, mournful cry; howl. [ME *yowlen.*] **—yowl** n.

yo-yo (yō′yō) n., pl. **-yos.** A toy consisting of a flattened spool wound with string that is spun down from and reeled up to the hand by winding and unwinding the string. [Orig. a trademark.]

yt·ter·bi·um (ĭ-tûr′bē-əm) n. Symbol **Yb** A soft bright silvery rare-earth element used as an x-ray source for portable irradiation devices, in some laser materials, and in some special alloys. Atomic number 70; atomic weight 173.04. [< *Ytterby*, Sweden.]

yt·tri·um (ĭt′rē-əm) n. Symbol **Y** A silvery metallic element used to increase the strength of magnesium and aluminum alloys. Atomic number 39; atomic weight 88.905. [< *Ytterby*, Sweden.]

yu·an (yōō′än′) n., pl. **-an** or **-ans.** See table at currency. [Chin. *yuan²*, dollar.]

yuc·ca (yŭk′ə) n. Any of various tall New World plants with a large cluster of white flowers. [Sp. *yuca.*]

Yule or **yule** (yōōl) n. Christmas. [< OE *gēol.*]

Yule log n. A large log traditionally burned in the fireplace at Christmas.

Yule·tide or **yule·tide** (yōōl′tīd′) n. The Christmas season.

yum·my (yŭm′ē) adj. **-mi·er, -mi·est.** Slang. Delicious; delightful.

yurt (yŭrt) n. A circular, domed portable tent used by the nomadic Mongols of Siberia. [R. *yurta.*]

Zz

z or **Z** (zē) *n., pl.* **z's** or **Z's.** The 26th letter of the English alphabet.

Zach·a·ri·as (zăk'ə-rī'əs) *n.* See table at **Bible.**

zaire (zīr, zä-ir') *n.* See table at **currency.** [Port.]

za·ny (zā'nē) *n., pl.* **-nies.** 1. A clown; buffoon. 2. A person given to extravagant, silly, or outlandish behavior. —*adj.* **-ni·er, -ni·est.** 1. Ludicrously comical; clownish. 2. Outlandishly or extravagantly comical; absurd. [Ital. *zani.*] —**za'ni·ly** *adv.* —**za'ni·ness** *n.*

zap (zăp) *v.* **zapped, zap·ping.** *Slang.* To destroy or kill with or as if with a burst of gunfire, flame, or electric current. [Imit.]

zay·in (zā'yĭn, zī'-) *n.* The 7th letter of the Hebrew alphabet. See table at **alphabet.** [Heb.]

zeal (zēl) *n.* Enthusiastic and diligent devotion, as to a cause, ideal, or goal; ardor. [< Gk. *zēlos.*]

zeal·ot (zĕl'ət) *n.* A zealous person, esp. one who is fanatically devoted to a cause. [< Gk. *zēlōtēs.*]

zeal·ous (zĕl'əs) *adj.* Filled with or motivated by zeal; ardent. —**zeal'ous·ly** *adv.* —**zeal'ous·ness** *n.*

ze·bra (zē'brə) *n.* A horselike African mammal with characteristic overall markings of conspicuous dark and whitish stripes. [< OSp. *cebro,* wild ass.]

zebra

ze·bu (zē'byōō, -bōō) *n.* A domesticated Asian or African bovine mammal with a prominent hump and a large dewlap. [Fr. *zébu.*]

Zech·a·ri·ah (zĕk'ə-rī'ə) *n.* See table at **Bible.**

zed (zĕd) *n. Chiefly Brit.* The letter *z.* [< Gk. *zēta.*]

Zeit·geist (tsīt'gīst') *n.* The taste and outlook characteristic of a period or generation.

Zen (zĕn) *n.* A school of Buddhism that asserts that enlightenment can be attained through meditation, self-contemplation, and intuition rather than through the scriptures.

Zend-A·ves·ta (zĕn'də-vĕs'tə) *n.* The sacred writings of Zoroastrianism.

ze·nith (zē'nĭth) *n.* 1. The point on the celestial sphere that is directly above the observer. 2. The part of the sky that is directly overhead. 3. The highest point; acme. [Ar. *samt (arra's),* path (over the head).]

Zeph·a·ni·ah (zĕf'ə-nī'ə) *n.* See table at **Bible.**

zeph·yr (zĕf'ər) *n.* 1. a. The west wind. b. A gentle breeze. 2. Any of various light, soft fabrics, yarns, or garments. [< Gk. *zephuros.*]

zep·pe·lin (zĕp'ə-lĭn) *n.* Also **Zep·pe·lin.** A rigid airship with a long, cylindrical body supported by internal gas cells. [< Count Ferdinand von Zeppelin (1838–1917).]

ze·ro (zîr'ō, zē'rō) *n., pl.* **-ros** or **-roes.** 1. The numerical symbol "0"; cipher. 2. *Math.* a. An element of a set that when added to any other element in the set produces a sum identical with the element to which it is added. b. A cardinal number indicating the absence of any or all units under consideration. c. An ordinal number indicating an initial point or origin. 3. The temperature indicated by the numeral 0 on a thermometer. 4. A nonentity; nobody. 5. The lowest point. —*adj.* 1. Of or being zero. 2. a. Having no measurable or otherwise determinable value. b. Absent, inoperative, or irrelevant. —*v.* **-roed, -ro·ing.** To adjust (an instrument or device) to zero value. —*phrasal verb.* **zero in.** 1. To aim or concentrate firepower on an exact target location. 2. To converge intently; close in: *zero in on the cause of a problem.* [< Ar. *ṣifr.*]

zero hour *n.* The scheduled time for the start of an operation or action, esp. a concerted military attack.

zest (zĕst) *n.* 1. Flavor or interest; piquancy. 2. Spirited enjoyment; gusto. 3. The outermost part of the rind of an orange or lemon, used as flavoring. [Obs. Fr., orange or lemon peel.] —**zest'ful** *adj.* —**zest'ful·ly** *adv.*

ze·ta (zā'tə, zē'-) *n.* The 6th letter of the Greek alphabet. See table at **alphabet.** [< Gk. *zēta.*]

Zeus (zōōs) *n. Gk. Myth.* The principal god of the Greek pantheon, ruler of the heavens and father of the other gods.

zig·zag (zĭg'zăg') *n.* 1. a. A line or course with sharp turns in alternating directions. b. One of a series of such sharp turns. 2. Something, as a design, marked by zigzags. —*adj.* Having a zigzag. —*adv.* In a zigzag manner or pattern. —*v.* **-zagged, -zag·ging.** To move in or form into a zigzag. [Prob. < G. *Zickzack.*]

zilch (zĭlch) *n. Slang.* Zero; nothing. [Orig. unknown.]

zil·lion (zĭl'yən) *n. Informal.* An extremely large indefinite number. [< MILLION.]

zinc (zĭngk) *n. Symbol* **Zn** A bluish-white, lustrous metallic element used to form a wide variety of alloys, including brass, bronze, and various solders, and in galvanizing iron and other metals. Atomic number 30; atomic weight 65.37. —*v.* **zinced** or **zincked, zinc·ing** or **zinck·ing.** To coat or treat with zinc; galvanize. [G. *Zink.*]

zinc ointment *n.* A salve consisting of about 20% zinc oxide with beeswax or paraffin and petrolatum.

zinc oxide *n.* An amorphous white or yellowish powder, ZnO, used as a pigment and in pharmaceuticals and cosmetics.

zing (zĭng) *n.* **1.** A brief high-pitched humming or buzzing sound. **2.** Liveliness; vivacity. —**zing** *v.*

zin·ni·a (zĭn'ē-ə) *n.* A widely cultivated plant with showy, variously colored flowers. [< Johann Gottfried *Zinn* (1727–59).]

Zi·on (zī'ən) *n.* **1. a.** The Jewish people; Israel. **b.** The Jewish homeland as a symbol of Judaism. **2.** A place or religious community regarded as a city of God. **3.** Heaven. **4.** A utopia.

Zi·on·ism (zī'ə-nĭz'əm) *n.* A movement orig. aimed at the re-establishment of a Jewish national homeland and state in Palestine and now concerned with the development of Israel. — **Zi'on·ist** *n.* — **Zi'on·is'tic** *adj.*

zip (zĭp) *n.* **1.** A brief sharp, hissing sound. **2.** *Informal.* Energy; vim. —*v.* **zipped, zip·ping. 1.** To move or act with speed or energy. **2.** To fasten or unfasten with a zipper. [Imit.]

Zip Code. Also **zip code.** A trademark for a system designed to expedite the sorting and delivery of mail by assigning a series of numbers to each delivery area in the United States.

zip·per (zĭp'ər) *n.* A fastening device consisting of parallel rows of metal or nylon teeth on adjacent edges of an opening that are interlocked by a sliding tab. [< ZIP.]

zip·py (zĭp'ē) *adj.* **-pi·er, -pi·est.** Brisk; lively.

zir·con (zûr'kŏn') *n.* A brown to colorless mineral, essentially ZrSiO₄, that is heated, cut, and polished to form a brilliant blue-white gem. [< Ital. *giargone.*]

zir·co·ni·um (zər-kō'nē-əm) *n. Symbol* **Zr** A lustrous, grayish-white, strong, ductile metallic element used chiefly in ceramic and refractory compounds, as an alloying agent, and in nuclear reactors. Atomic number 40; atomic weight 91.22.

zith·er (zĭth'ər, zĭth'-) *n.* A musical instrument with 30 to 40 strings that is played with the fingertips or a plectrum. [< Gk. *kithara,* an ancient musical instrument.] —**zith'er·ist** *n.*

zither

zlo·ty (zlô'tē) *n., pl.* **-ty** or **-tys.** See table at **currency.** [Pol. *złoty.*]

Zn The symbol for the element zinc.

-zoan *suff.* Individual within a taxonomic group: *protozoan.* [< Gk. *zōion,* animal.]

zo·di·ac (zō'dē-ăk') *n.* **1. a.** A band of the celestial sphere, extending about eight degrees to either side of the ecliptic, that represents the path of the principal planets, the moon, and the sun. **b.** In astrology, this band divided into 12 equal parts called signs, each 30° wide, bearing the name of a constellation for which it was orig. named. **2.** A diagram or figure representing the zodiac. [< Gk. *zōidion,* small represented figure.] —**zo·di'a·cal** (zō-dī'ə-kəl) *adj.*

-zoic *suff.* **1.** Relating to a specific kind of animal existence: *protozoic.* **2.** Relating to a specific geologic division: *Paleozoic.* [< Gk. *zōion,* animal.]

zom·bie (zŏm'bē) *n.* Also **zom·bi** *pl.* **-bis. 1. a.** A voodoo snake god. **b.** A supernatural power or spell that according to voodoo belief can enter into and reanimate a corpse. **2.** One who looks or behaves like a reanimated corpse. [< a native African word.]

zon·al (zō'nəl) *adj.* **1.** Of or associated with a zone. **2.** Divided into zones. —**zon'al·ly** *adv.*

zone (zōn) *n.* **1.** An area, region, or division distinguished from adjacent parts by a distinctive feature or character. **2.** Any of the five regions of the surface of the earth that are loosely divided according to prevailing climate and latitude, including the Torrid Zone, the North and South Temperate Zones, and the North and South Frigid Zones. **3.** A section or division of an area or territory: *a residential zone.* **4.** *Archaic.* A belt or girdle. —*v.* **zoned, zon·ing. 1.** To divide into zones. **2.** To designate or mark off into zones. [< Gk. *zōnē,* girdle.] —**zo·na'tion** *n.*

zonked (zŏngkt) *adj. Slang.* Intoxicated by alcohol or a narcotic; high. [Orig. unknown.]

zoo (zōō) *n., pl.* **zoos.** A park or institution in which living animals are kept and exhibited to the public. [< ZOOLOGICAL GARDEN.]

zoo- *pref.* Animal: *zoology.* [< Gk. *zōion.*]

zo·o·ge·og·ra·phy (zō'ō-jē-ŏg'rə-fē) *n.* The biological study of the geographic distribution of animals. —**zo'o·ge·og'ra·pher** *n.* —**zo'o·ge'o·graph'ic** or **zo'o·ge'o·graph'i·cal** (-ĭ-kəl) *adj.*

zo·o·logical garden *n.* A zoo.

zo·ol·o·gy (zō-ŏl'ə-jē) *n., pl.* **-gies. 1.** The biological science of animals. **2.** The animal life of a particular area. **3.** The characteristics of an animal group or category. —**zo'o·log'i·cal** (-ə-lŏj'ĭ-kəl) or **zo'o·log'ic** (-lŏj'ĭk) *adj.* —**zo·ol'o·gist** *n.*

zoom (zōōm) *v.* **1.** To move with a continuous low-pitched buzzing sound. **2.** To climb suddenly and sharply, as in an airplane. **3. a.** To move very quickly. **b.** To move rapidly up or down. **4.** To move rapidly toward or away from a photographic subject: *The camera zoomed in for a close-up.* [Imit.] —**zoom** *n.*

zoom lens *n.* A camera lens whose focal length can be rapidly changed, allowing continuous change in the size of an image.

-zoon *suff.* An individual animal or independently moving organic unit: *spermatozoon.* [< Gk. *zōion.*]

zo·o·spore (zō'ə-spôr', -spōr') *n.* A motile, flagellated asexual spore.

Zo·ro·as·tri·an·ism (zôr'ō-ăs'trē-ə-nĭz'əm) *n.* The ancient Persian religion, founded by the prophet Zoroaster, teaching the worship of the deity Ormazd in the context of a universal struggle between the forces of light and of darkness. —**Zo'ro·as'tri·an** *n. & adj.*

zounds (zoundz) *interj.* Used to express anger, surprise, or indignation.

zoy·si·a (zoi'sē-ə, -zē-ə) *n.* Any of several creeping grasses widely cultivated as a lawn grass. [< Karl von *Zois* (1756–1800).]

Zr The symbol for the element zirconium.

zuc·chet·to (zōō-kĕt'ō, tsōō-) *n., pl.* **-tos.** A small skullcap worn by Roman Catholic clergymen. [Ital.]

zuc·chi·ni (zōō-kē'nē) *n., pl.* **-ni.** A variety of squash with a long, narrow shape and a dark-green rind. [Ital. < *zucca*, gourd.]

Zu·lu (zōō'lōō) *n., pl.* **-lu** or **-lus. 1.** A member of a large Bantu nation of southeastern Africa. **2.** The Bantu language of the Zulus. —**Zu'lu** *adj.*

Zu·ñi (zōōn'yē, zōō'nē) *n., pl.* **-ñi** or **-ñis. 1.** A member of a pueblo-dwelling tribe of Indians of western New Mexico. **2.** The language of the Zuñi.

zwie·back (scē'băk', swī'-, zwĕ'-, zwī'-) *n.* A usu. slightly sweetened bread that is first baked as a loaf and later sliced and oven-toasted [G.]

zy·go·mat·ic bone (zī'gə-măt'ĭk) *n.* A bone in the upper cheek; cheekbone. [< Gk. *zugōma*, bolt.]

zy·gote (zī'gōt') *n.* **1.** The cell formed by the union of two gametes. **2.** The organism that develops from a zygote. [< Gk. *zugoun*, to join.] —**zy·got·ic** (zī-gŏt'ĭk) *adj.*

zy·mur·gy (zī'mûr-jē) *n.* The manufacturing chemistry of fermentation processes in brewing. [Gk. *zumē*, leaven + -URGY.]

Biographical Entries

Biographical entries are listed in alphabetical order. Persons having the same surname are combined in one entry and listed chronologically by date of birth.

A

Aar·on (âr′ən, ăr′-). Hebrew high priest. **—Aar·on′ic** (ă-rŏn′ĭk, âr-ŏn′-) or **Aaron′i·cal** *adj.*

Ab·bott (ăb′ət), Sir **John Joseph Caldwell**. 1821-93. Canadian prime minister (1891-92).

A·bel (ā′bəl). Son of Adam and Eve, killed by his brother, Cain.

Ab·e·lard (ăb′ə-lärd′), **Peter**. 1079-1142. French theologian and philosopher.

A·bra·ham (ā′brə-hăm′). Hebrew patriarch.

Ad·am (ăd′əm). In the Bible, the 1st man.

Ad·ams (ăd′əmz). 1. **Samuel**. 1722-1803. Amer. Revolutionary leader. 2. **John**. 1735-1826. 2nd U.S. President (1797-1801). 3. **John Quincy**. 1767-1848. 6th U.S. President (1825-29). **—Ad′am·so′ni·an** (-sŏ′nē-ən) *adj.*

John Adams

Ad·dams (ăd′əmz), **Jane**. 1860-1935. Amer. social reformer.

Ad·di·son (ăd′ĭ-sən), **Joseph**. 1672-1719. English essayist.

A·den·au·er (ăd′n-ou′ər, äd′-), **Konrad**. 1876-1967. West German statesman.

Ad·ler (ăd′lər, äd′-), **Alfred**. 1870-1937. Austrian psychiatrist.

Aes·chy·lus (ĕs′kə-ləs, ēs′-). 525-456 B.C. Greek dramatist. **—Aes·chy·le′an** *adj.*

Ae·sop (ē′səp′, ē′sŏp′). 6th cent. Greek fabulist. **—Ae·so′pi·an** (ē-sō′pē-ən) or **Ae·sop′ic** (ē-sŏp′ĭk) *adj.*

Ag·as·siz (ăg′ə-sē), **(Jean) Louis (Rodolphe)**. 1807-73. Swiss-born American naturalist.

A·gee (ā′jē), **James**. 1910-55. Amer. author.

Ag·new (ăg′nōō), **Spiro Theodore**. b. 1918. U.S. Vice President (1969-73); resigned.

A·gric·o·la (ə-grĭk′ə-lə), **Gnaeus Julius**. A.D. 37-93. Roman general and politician.

A·grip·pa (ə-grĭp′ə), **Marcus Vipsanius**. 63-12 B.C. Roman general and statesman.

Ag·rip·pi·na (ăg′rə-pī′nə, -pē′-). 13 B.C.?-A.D. 33. Mother of Caligula.

A·gui·nal·do (ä′gē-näl′dō), **Emilio**. 1869-1964. Philippine revolutionary leader.

Ai·ken (ā′kĭn), **Conrad (Potter)**. 1889-1973. Amer. poet.

Ak·bar (ăk′bär, äk′-). "the Great." 1542-1605. Mogul emperor.

A·khe·na·ton or **A·khe·na·ten** (ä′kə-nä′tn, äk′nä′-). Egyptian pharaoh (1375-58 B.C.) and religious reformer.

Al·a·ric (ăl′ə-rĭk). 370?-410. Visigoth king and conqueror of Rome (410).

Al·bee (ôl′bē, ôl′-, ăl′-), **Edward**. Amer. playwright.

Al·bert (ăl′bərt). 1819-61. Prince consort of Queen Victoria of England.

Al·ber·tus Mag·nus (ăl-bûr′təs măg′nəs), Saint. 1206?-80. German theologian.

Al·ci·bi·a·des (ăl′sĭ-bī′ə-dēz′). 450?-404 B.C. Athenian general.

Al·cott (ôl′kət, -kŏt′, ôl′-), **Louisa May**. 1832-88. Amer. author.

Louisa May Alcott

Al·den (ôl′dən), **John**. 1599?-1687. Amer. Pilgrim colonist.

A·lem·bert (ăl′əm-bâr′, ä-län-bēr′), **Jean Le Rond d′**. 1717-83. French Encyclopedist.

Al·ex·an·der I (ăl′ĭg-zăn′dər, -zăn′-). 1777-1825. Czar of Russia (1801-25).

Alexander II. 1818-81. Czar of Russia (1855-81); emancipated serfs (1861).

Alexander III. "the Great." 356-323 B.C. King of Macedonia (336-323). **—Al′ex·an′dri·an** *adj.*

Alexander III. 1845-94. Czar of Russia (1881-94).

Al·fon·so XIII (ăl-fŏn′sō, -zō). 1886-1941. King of Spain (1886-1931, ruled 1902-31); abdicated.

Al·fred (ăl′frĭd). "the Great." 849-99. West Saxon king (871-99) and lawmaker.

A·li (ä-lē′), **Muhammad**. b. 1942. Amer. prizefighter.

Al·len (ăl′ən), **Ethan**. 1738-89. Amer. Revolutionary soldier.

Al·len·de Gos·sens (ä-yĕn′dĕ gŏ′sĕns), **Salvador**. 1908-73. Chilean president (1970-73); died in coup.

Al·va (äl′və), **Duke of**. Also **Al·ba** (-bə). 1508-82. Spanish general and colonial administrator.

A·ma·ti (ä-mä′tē), **Nicolò**. 1596-1684. Italian violin maker.

A·men·ho·tep III (ă'mĕn-hō'tĕp). Egyptian pharaoh (1411?–1375? B.C.).

A·min Da·da (ä-mēn' dä-dä'), **Idi.** b. 1925? Ugandan dictator (1971–79); deposed.

A·mos (ā'məs). 8th cent. B.C. Hebrew prophet.

Am·père (äm'pîr), **Andrè Marie.** 1775–1836. French physicist.

A·mund·sen (ä'mənd-sən), **Roald.** 1872–1928. Norwegian polar explorer.

A·nac·re·on (ə-năk'rē-ən). 572?–488? B.C. Greek poet.

An·ax·ag·o·ras (ăn'ăk-săg'ər-əs). 500?–428 B.C. Greek philosopher.

An·der·sen (ăn'dər-sən), **Hans Christian.** 1805–75. Danish author.

An·der·son (ăn'dər-sən). 1. **Sherwood.** 1876–1941. Amer. author. 2. **Maxwell.** 1888–1959. Amer. playwright. 3. **Marian.** b. 1902. Amer. contralto.

An·dré (ăn'drā), **John.** 1751–80. English soldier; hanged as Revolutionary spy.

An·dre·a del Sar·to (ăn-drā'ä dĕl sär'tō). 1486–1531. Italian painter.

An·drew (ăn'drōō), **Saint.** One of the 12 Apostles.

An·gel·i·co (ăn-jĕl'ĭ-kō), **Fra.** 1387–1455. Italian painter.

Anne (ăn). 1665–1714. Queen of Great Britain (1702–14).

A·nou·ilh (ä-nōō-ē'), **Jean.** b. 1910. French dramatist.

An·tho·ny (ăn'thə-nē), **Saint.** 250?–350? Egyptian ascetic monk.

Anthony, Susan Brownell. 1820–1906. Amer. reformer.

Susan B. Anthony

An·to·ni·nus Pi·us (ăn'tə-nī'nəs pī'əs). A.D. 86–161. Roman emperor (138–61).

An·to·ni·us (ăn-tō'nē-əs), **Marcus.** Mark Antony.

Ap·u·lei·us (ăp'yə-lē'əs), **Lucius.** 2nd cent. Roman satirist.

A·qui·nas (ə-kwī'nəs), **Saint Thomas.** 1225?–74. Italian theologian and philosopher.

Ar·a·fat (är-ä-fät'), **Yasir.** b. 1929. Palestinian leader.

Ar·chi·me·des (är'kə-mē'dēz). 287?–212 B.C. Greek mathematician and physicist. —**Ar'chi·me'de·an** adj.

Ar·is·ti·des (ăr'ĭs-tī'dēz). "the Just." 5th cent. B.C. Athenian general and statesman.

Ar·is·toph·a·nes (ăr'ĭ-stŏf'ə-nēz'). 448?–380? B.C. Athenian dramatist.

Ar·is·tot·le (ăr'ĭ-stŏt'l). 384–322 B.C. Greek philosopher. —**Ar'is·to·te'li·an** (ăr'ĭs-tə-tē'lē-ən, tĕl'yən) adj. & n.

A·ri·us (ə-rī'əs, âr'ē-əs). 256?–336. Greek theologian. —**Ar'i·an** (ăr'ē-ən, âr'-) adj. & n.

Ark·wright (ärk'rīt'), **Sir Richard.** 1732–92. English inventor.

Ar·min·i·us (är-mĭn'ē-əs), **Jacobus.** 1560–1609. Dutch theologian.

Arm·strong (ärm'strông'). 1. (**Daniel) Louis** ("Satchmo"). 1900–71. Amer. jazz musician. 2. **Neil.** b. 1930. Amer. astronaut; 1st to walk on the moon.

Ar·nold (är'nəld). 1. **Benedict.** 1741–1801. Amer. Revolutionary general and traitor. 2. **Matthew.** 1822–88. English poet and critic.

Ar·thur (är'thər), **Chester Alan.** 1830–86. 21st U.S. President (1881–85).

As·quith (ăs'kwĭth), **Herbert Henry.** 1852–1928. British prime minister (1908–16).

As·tor (ăs'tər), **John Jacob.** 1763–1848. German-born Amer. fur trader and capitalist.

At·ti·la (ăt'ə-lə, ə-tĭl'ə). 406?–53. King of the Huns (433?–53).

Att·lee (ăt'lē), **Clement Richard.** 1883–1967. British prime minister (1945–51).

At·tucks (ăt'əks), **Crispus.** 1723?–70. Victim of the Boston Massacre.

Au·den (ôd'n), **Wystan Hugh.** 1907–73. English-born Amer. author.

Au·du·bon (ô'də-bŏn', -bən), **John James.** 1785–1851. Haitian-born Amer. ornithologist and painter.

Au·gus·tine (ô'gə-stēn', ô-gŭs'tĭn), **Saint.** 354–430. Church father and philosopher. —**Au'gus·tin'i·an** (ô'gə-stĭn'ē-ən) adj. & n.

Au·gus·tus (ô-gŭs'təs). "Octavian." 63 B.C.–A.D. 14. 1st Roman emperor. —**Au·gus'tan** adj.

Au·re·li·an (ô-rē'lē-ən, ô-rēl'yən). 212?–75. Roman emperor (270–75).

Aus·ten (ôs'tən), **Jane.** 1775–1817. English novelist.

Aus·tin (ô'stən), **Stephen Fuller.** 1793–1836. Amer. colonizer and Tex. political leader.

B

Bach (bäкн), **Johann Sebastian.** 1685–1750. German composer.

Johann Sebastian Bach

Ba·con (bā'kən). 1. **Roger.** 1214?–94. English scientist and philosopher. 2. **Francis.** 1561–1626. English philosopher, statesman, and essayist. —**Ba·co'ni·an** adj. & n.

Ba·den-Pow·ell (bād'n-pō'əl), **Sir Robert Stephenson Smyth.** 1857–1941. English founder of the Boy Scouts.

Bae·de·ker (bā'dĭ-kər), **Karl.** 1801–59. German guidebook publisher.

Baf·fin (băf'ĭn), **William.** 1584–1622. English explorer.

Ba·ku·nin (bä-kōō'nĭn), **Mikhall.** 1814–76. Russian anarchist.

Bal·an·chine (băl'ən-chēn'), **George.** b. 1904. Russian-born Amer. choreographer.

Bal·bo·a (băl-bō'ə), **Vasco Núñez de.** 1475–1517. Spanish explorer; discovered the Pacific (1513).

Bald·win (bôld'wĭn), **Stanley.** 1867–1947. British prime minister (1923–24, 1924–29, 1935–37).

Bal·four (băl'fŏŏr), **Arthur James.** 1848–1930. British prime minister (1902–5).

Bal·ti·more (bôl'tə-môr, -mŏr), **1st Baron. George Calvert.**

Bal·zac (bôl'zăk', băl'-), **Honoré de.** 1799–1850. French author.

Ban·nis·ter (băn'ĭ-stər), **Roger.** b. 1929. English physician and runner (1st 4-minute mile).

Ba·rab·bas (bə-răb'əs). In the New Testament, prisoner released instead of Jesus at the insistence of the multitude.

?ark·ley (bär'klē), **Alben William.** 1877–1956. U.S. Vice President (1949–53).

3ar·nard (bär'nərd), **Christiaan Neethling.** b. 1923. South African surgeon (1st successful human heart transplant).

3ar·num (bär'nəm), **Phineas Taylor.** 1810–91. Amer. showman.

3ar·ry·more (băr'ĭ-môr', -mŏr'). Family of Amer. actors, including **Lionel Blythe** (1878–1954), **Ethel** (1879–1959), and **John Blythe** (1882–1942).

3ar·thol·di (bär-thôl'dē), **Frédéric Auguste.** 1834–1904. French sculptor.

3ar·thol·o·mew (bär-thŏl'ə-myŏŏ), **Saint.** One of the 12 Apostles.

3art·lett (bärt'lĭt), **John.** 1820–1905. Amer. compiler of *Familiar Quotations.*

Bar·tók (bär'tŏk), **Béla.** 1881–1945. Hungarian composer.

Bar·ton (bärt'n), **Clara.** 1821–1912. Founder of the Amer. Red Cross.

Clara Barton

Ba·ruch (bə-rŏŏk'), **Bernard Mannes.** 1870–1965. Amer. stockbroker and economic and political adviser.

Bath·she·ba (băth-shē'bə, băth'shə-). In the Old Testament, 2nd wife of David and mother of Solomon.

Bau·de·laire (bōd-lâr'), **Charles.** 1821–67. French poet.

Bau·douin I (bō-dwăn'). b. 1930. King of Belgium (since 1951).

Be·a·trix (bē'ə-trĭks). b. 1938. Queen of the Netherlands (since 1980).

Beau·mar·chais (bō-mär-shā'), **Pierre Augustin Caron de.** 1732–99. French author and dramatist.

Beau·mont (bō'mŏnt', -mənt), **Francis.** 1584–1616. English poet and dramatist.

Beau·voir (bō-vwär'), **Simone de.** b. 1908. French writer.

Beck·et (bĕk'ĭt), **Saint Thomas à.** 1118?–70. English Roman Catholic martyr.

Beck·ett (bĕk'ĭt), **Samuel.** b. 1906. Irish author.

Bede (bēd), **Saint.** 673–735. English theologian and historian.

Bee·cher (bē'chər), **Henry Ward.** 1813–87. Amer. clergyman and abolitionist.

Bee·tho·ven (bā'tō-vən), **Ludwig van.** 1770–1827. German composer.

Be·gin (bā'gĭn), **Menachem.** b. 1913. Russian-born Israeli statesman.

Bell (bĕl), **Alexander Graham.** 1847–1922. Scottish-born Amer. inventor.

Bel·li·ni (bə-lē'nē). **1. Giovanni.** 1430?–1516. Italian painter. **2. Vincenzo.** 1801–35. Italian composer.

Bel·low (bĕl'ō), **Saul.** b. 1915. Canadian-born Amer. novelist.

Bel·shaz·zar (bĕl-shăz'ər). In the Old Testament, the last king of Babylon.

Ben·e·dict XIV (bĕn'ə-dĭkt'). 1675–1758. Pope (1740–58).

Benedict XV. 1854–1922. Pope (1914–22).

Benedict of Nur·si·a (nûr'shē-ə, -shə), **Saint.** 480?–543? Italian founder of the Benedictine order.

Be·nét (bĭ-nā'), **Stephen Vincent.** 1898–1943. Amer. poet.

Ben-Gur·i·on (bĕn-gŏŏr'ē-ən), **David.** 1886–1973. Polish-born Israeli statesman.

Ben·ja·min (bĕn'jə-mən). In the Old Testament, ancestor of one of the 12 tribes of Israel.

Ben·nett (bĕn'ĭt), **Richard Bedford.** 1870–1947. Prime minister of Canada (1930–35).

Ben·tham (bĕn'thəm), **Jeremy.** 1748–1832. English philosopher. **—Ben'tham·ite'** *n.*

Ben·ton (bĕnt'n), **Thomas Hart.** 1889–1975. Amer. painter.

Berg·son (bûrg'sən, bĕrg'-), **Henri Louis.** 1859–1941. French philosopher.

Be·ring (bîr'ĭng, bĕr'-), **Vitus.** 1680–1741. Danish navigator and explorer.

Ber·lin (bər-lĭn'), **Irving.** b. 1888. Russian-born Amer. composer.

Ber·li·oz (bĕr'lē-ōz'), **(Louis) Hector.** 1803–69. French composer.

Bern·hardt (bûrn'härt', bĕrn'-), **Sarah.** 1844–1923. French actress.

Ber·ni·ni (bĕr-nē'nē), **Giovanni Lorenzo.** 1598–1680. Italian sculptor, architect, and painter.

Be·thune (bĭ-thŏŏn'), **Mary McLeod.** 1875–1955. Amer. educator.

Mary McLeod Bethune

Bierce (bîrs), **Ambrose (Gwinett).** 1842–1914? Amer. writer.

Bing·ham (bĭng'əm), **George Caleb.** 1811–79. Amer. painter.

Bis·marck (bĭz'märk), **Prince Otto Eduard Leopold von.** 1815–98. 1st chancellor of the German Empire (1871–90).

Bi·zet (bē-zā'), **Georges.** 1838–75. French composer.

Black Hawk (blăk' hôk'). 1767–1838. Amer. Indian leader.

Black Hawk

Black·stone (blăk'stən, -stōn'), Sir **William.** 1723–80. English jurist.

Black·well (blăk'wěl, -wəl), **Elizabeth.** 1821–19lu. English-born Amer. physician.

Blaine (blān), **James Gillespie.** 1830–93. Amer. politician.

Blake (blāk), **William.** 1757–1827. English poet and engraver.

Bligh (blī), **William.** 1754–1817. English naval officer.

Bloom·er (bloō'mər), **Amelia Jenks.** 1818–94. Amer. social reformer.

Boc·cac·cio (bō-kä'chē-ō'), **Giovanni.** 1313–75. Italian author.

Bohr (bōr), **Niels Henrik David.** 1885–1962. Danish physicist.

Bol·eyn (bool'ĭn, bŏ-lĭn'), **Anne.** 1507–36. 2nd wife of Henry VIII; beheaded.

Bo·lí·var (bō'lē'vär'), **Simón.** 1783–1830. South American independence leader.

Bo·na·parte (bō'nə-pärt'). Corsican family, including: **1.** **Joseph.** 1768–1844. King of Naples (1806–8) and Spain (1808–13). **2.** **Napoleon I.** **3.** **Lucien.** 1775–1840. Prince of Canino. **4.** **Louis.** 1778–1846. King of Holland (1806–10). **5.** **Jérôme.** 1784–1860. King of Westphalia (1807).

Boone (boōn), **Daniel.** 1734–1820. Amer. frontiersman.

Booth (boōth). **1.** **William.** 1829–1912. English founder of Salvation Army. **2.** **Edwin Thomas.** 1833–93. Amer. actor. **3.** **John Wilkes.** 1838–65. Amer. actor; assassin of Abraham Lincoln.

John Wilkes Booth

Bor·don (bôrd'n), Sir **Robert Laird.** 1854–1937. Prime minister of Canada (1911–20).

Bor·gia (bôr'jä, -jə). **1.** **Cesare.** 1475?–1507. Italian cardinal and political and military leader. **2.** **Lucrezia.** 1480–1519. Italian noblewoman; patron of the arts.

Bo·ro·din (bôr'ə-dēn'), **Aleksandr Porfirievich.** 1834–87. Russian composer.

Bosch (bŏs, bôs), **Hieronymus.** 1450?–1516. Dutch painter.

Bos·well (bŏz'wěl', -wəl), **James.** 1740–95. Scottish lawyer and writer.

Bot·ti·cel·li (bŏt'ĭ-chěl'ē), **Sandro.** 1444?–1510. Italian painter.

Bour·bon (boōr'bən). French royal family ruling in France, Spain, and Naples.

Bourke-White (bûrk'hwīt', -wīt'), **Margaret.** 1906–71. Amer. photographer.

Bow·ell (bou'l), Sir **Mackenzie.** 1823–1917. Prime minister of Canada (1894–96).

Boyle (boil), **Robert.** 1627–91. English chemist and physicist.

Brad·bur·y (brăd'běr'ē), **Ray Douglas.** b. 1920. Amer. author.

Brad·dock (brăd'ək), **Edward.** 1695–1755. English general in America.

Brad·ford (brăd'fərd), **William.** 1590–1657. English Puritan colonist in America.

Brad·ley (brăd'lē), **Omar Nelson.** 1893–1981. Amer. military leader.

Brad·street (brăd'strēt'), **Anne Dudley.** 1612–72. Amer. colonial poet.

Bra·dy (brā'dē), **Mathew B.** 1823–96. Amer. pioneer photographer.

Bra·he (brä'hē), **Tycho.** 1546–1601. Danish astronomer.

Brahms (brämz), **Johannes.** 1833–97. German composer. **—Brahms'i·an** adj.

Bran·deis (brăn'dīs), **Louis Dembitz.** 1856–1941. Amer. jurist.

Brandt (bränt), **Willy.** b. 1913. West German political leader.

Braque (bräk), **Georges.** 1882–1963. French cubist painter.

Braun (broun, brôn), **Wernher Magnus Maximilian von.** 1912–77. German-born Amer. rocket engineer.

Brecht (brěkt, brěкнт), **Bertolt.** 1898–1956. German playwright.

Breck·in·ridge (brěk'ĭn-rĭj), **John Cabell.** 1821–75. U.S. Vice President (1857–61).

Breu·ghel (broi'gəl). Var. of Brueghel.

Brezh·nev (brězh'něf), **Leonid Ilyich.** 1906–82. Soviet statesman.

Bri·an Bo·ru (brī'ən bô-roō'). 941–1014. King of Ireland (1002–14).

Brit·ten (brĭt'n), **(Edward) Benjamin.** 1913–76. English composer.

Bron·të (brŏn'tē). English family of novelists, including **Charlotte** (1816–55), **Emily Jane** (1818–48), and **Anne** (1820–49).

Brook (broōk), **Rupert.** 1887–1915. English poet.

Brown (broun), **John.** 1800–59. Amer. abolitionist.

Browne (broun), Sir **Thomas.** 1605–82. English physician and author.

Brown·ing (brou'nĭng), **Elizabeth Barrett** (1806–61) and **Robert** (1812–89). English poets.

Bruck·ner (broōk'nər), **Anton.** 1824–96. Austrian composer.

Brue·ghel (broi'gəl), **Pieter.** Also **Brue·gel, Breu·ghel.** 1520?–69. Flemish painter.

Bru·nel·le·schi (broō'nə-lěs'kē), **Filippo.** 1377?–1446. Florentine architect.

Bru·tus (broō'tas), **Marcus Junius.** 85?–42 B.C. Roman political and military leader.

Bry·an (brī'ən), **William Jennings.** 1860–1925. Amer. statesman and lawyer.

Bry·ant (brī'ənt), **William Cullen.** 1794–1878. Amer. poet.

Bu·ber (boō'bər), **Martin.** 1878–1965. Austrian philosopher and Judaic scholar.

Bu·chan·an (byōō-kăn'ən, bə-), James. 1791-1868. 15th U.S. President (1857-61).

James Buchanan

Buck (bŭk), Pearl Sydenstricker. 1892-1973. Amer. author.

Bud·dha (bōō'də, bŏŏd'ə). 563?-483? B.C. Indian philosopher; founder of Buddhism. —Bud'dhist n. & adj.

Buf·fa·lo Bill (bŭf'ə-lō' bĭl'). William Frederick Cody.

Buf·fon (bü-fôn'), Comte Georges Louis Leclerc de. 1707-88. French naturalist.

Bu·kha·rin (bōō-KHä'rĭn), Nikolai Ivanovich. 1888-1938. Russian revolutionary.

Bul·finch (bŏŏl'fĭnch'). 1. Charles. 1763-1844. Amer. architect. 2. Thomas. 1796-1867. Amer. mythologist.

Bul·ga·nin (bōōl-gä'nĭn, -gän'ĭn), Nikolai Aleksandrovich. 1895-1975. Soviet statesman.

Bunche (bŭnch), Ralph Johnson. 1904-71. Amer. diplomat.

Bun·yan (bŭn'yən), John. 1628-88. English preacher and author.

Bur·bank (bûr'băngk'), Luther. 1849-1926. Amer. horticulturist.

Bur·goyne (bər-goin'), John. 1722-92. English general and playwright.

Burke (bûrk), Edmund. 1729-97. British statesman, orator, and philosopher.

Burns (bûrnz), Robert. 1759-96. Scottish poet.

Burn·side (bûrn'sīd'), Ambrose Everett. 1824-81. Amer. general and politician.

Burr (bûr), Aaron. 1756-1836. U.S. Vice President (1801-5).

Aaron Burr

Bur·ton (bûrt'n). 1. Robert. 1577-1640. English clergyman and author. 2. Sir Richard Francis. 1821-90. English Orientalist and adventurer.

Bush (bŏŏsh), George Herbert Walker. b. 1924. U.S. Vice President (since 1981).

But·ler (bŭt'lər), Samuel. 1835-1902. English novelist.

Byrd (bûrd), Richard Evelyn. 1888-1957. Amer. polar explorer.

By·ron (bī'rən), George Gordon. 1788-1824. English poet. —By·ron'ic (bī-rŏn'ĭk) adj. & n.

C

Cab·ot (kăb'ət). 1. John. 1450-98. Italian explorer in English service. 2. Sebastian. 1476?-1557. Italian-born English explorer and cartographer.

Ca·bri·ni (kə-brē'nē), Saint Frances Xavier. 1850-1917. Italian-born Amer. religious leader.

Cad·il·lac (kăd'l-ăk'), Antoine de la Mothe. 1656?-1730. French explorer and colonial administrator.

Caed·mon (kăd'mən). 7th cent. English poet.

Cae·sar (sē'zər), Gaius Julius. 100-44 B.C. Roman statesman, general, and historian. —Cae·sar'e·an or Cae·sar'i·an (sĭ-zâr'ē-ən) adj.

Cain (kān). Son of Adam and Eve; murderer of Abel.

Cal·der (kôl'dər, kŏl'-), Alexander. 1898-1976. Amer. sculptor.

Cal·houn (kăl-hōōn'), John Caldwell. 1782-1850. U.S. Vice President (1825-32) and political philosopher.

Ca·lig·u·la (kə-lĭg'yə-lə). A.D. 12-41. Emperor of Rome (37-41).

Cal·vert (kăl'vərt). Family of English colonists and administrators, including George, 1st Baron Baltimore (1580?-1632); Cecilius, 2nd Baron Baltimore (1605-75); Leonard (1606-47); and Charles, 3rd Baron Baltimore (1637-1715).

Cal·vin (kăl'vĭn), John. 1509-64. French religious reformer.

Cam·o·ëns (kăm'ō-ənz, kə-mŏ'-), Luiz Vaz de. 1524-80. Portuguese poet.

Camp·i·on (kăm'pē-ən), Thomas. 1567-1620. English poet.

Ca·mus (kə-myōō'), Albert. 1913-60. French novelist.

Can·ning (kăn'ĭng), George. 1770-1827. British prime minister (1827).

Ca·nute (kə-nōōt', -nyōōt'). 994?-1035. King of England (1016?-35), Denmark (1018-35), and Norway (1028-35).

Ca·pet (kă'pĭt, kăp'ĭt), Hugh. 940?-96. King of France (987-96). —Ca·pe'tian (kə-pē'shən) adj. & n.

Car·a·cal·la (kăr'ə-kăl'ə). 188-217. Emperor of Rome (211-17).

Ca·ra·vag·gio (kăr'ə-vä'jō), Michelangelo da. 1565?-1609? Italian painter.

Carl XVI Gustav (kärl' gŭs'täv, -täf). b. 1946. King of Sweden (since 1973).

Car·lyle (kär-līl'), Thomas. 1795-1881. Scottish-born historian.

Car·ne·gie (kär'nə-gē, kär-nā'-, -nĕg'ē), Andrew. 1835-1919. Scottish-born Amer. industrialist.

Car·roll (kăr'əl), Lewis. Charles Lutwidge Dodgson.

Car·son (kär'sən), Christopher ("Kit"). 1809-68. Amer. frontiersman.

Car·ter (kär'tər), James Earl (Jimmy), Jr. b. 1924. 39th U.S. President (1977-81).

Car·tier (kär-tyā'), Jacques. 1491-1557. French explorer.

Jimmy Carter

Cart·wright (kärt'rīt'), **Edmund.** 1743–1823. English inventor of the power loom.

Ca·ru·so (kə-rōō'sō), **Enrico.** 1873–1921. Italian-born operatic tenor.

Car·ver (kär'vər), **George Washington.** 1864–1943. Amer. botanist and educator.

Ca·sals (kə-sälz'), **Pablo.** 1876–1973. Spanish-born cellist.

Ca·sa·no·va (kăz'ə-nō'və, kăs'-), **Giovanni Jacopo.** 1725–98. Italian adventurer and author.

Cas·satt (kə-săt'), **Mary.** 1845–1926. Amer. painter.

Cas·tle·reagh (kăs'əl-rā', kă'səl-), Viscount. Robert Stewart. 1769–1822. English statesman.

Cas·tro (kăs'trō), **Fidel.** b. 1927. Cuban revolutionary statesman.

Fidel Castro

Cath·er (kăth'ər), **Willa Sibert.** 1873–1947. Amer. author.

Cath·e·rine I (kăth'rĭn, -ər-ĭn). 1684?–1727. Empress of Russia (1725–27).

Catherine II. "the Great." 1729–96. Empress of Russia (1762–96).

Catherine de Mé·di·cis (də mĕd'ə-chē, mā'də-sēs'). 1519–89. Queen of France (1547–59).

Catherine of Ar·a·gon (ăr'ə-gŏn'). 1485–1536. 1st wife of Henry VIII.

Cat·i·line (kăt'l-īn'). 108?–62 B.C. Roman politician and conspirator.

Ca·to (kā'tō). **1. Marcus Porcius.** "the Elder." 234–149 B.C. Roman consul and censor. **2. Marcus Porcius.** "the Younger." 95–46 B.C. Roman statesman.

Catt (kăt), **Carrie Chapman Lane.** 1859–1947. Amer. suffragist.

Ca·tul·lus (kə-tŭl'əs), **Gaius Valerius.** 1st cent. B.C. Roman poet.

Ca·vour (kə-vōōr', kä-vōōr'), **Conte Camillo Benso di.** 1810–61. Italian political leader.

Cax·ton (kăk'stən), **William.** 1422?–91. 1st English printer.

Cec·il (sĕs'əl). **1. William.** 1st Baron Burghley or Burleigh. 1520–98. English statesman. **2. Robert.** 1st Earl of Salisbury. 1st Viscount Cranborne. 1563?–1612. English statesman.

3. Robert Arthur Talbot Gascoyne. 3rd Marquis of Salisbury. 1830–1903. British prime minister (1885–92, 1895–1902).

Ce·cil·ia (sĭ-sēl'yə), Saint. 3rd cent. Roman martyr.

Cel·li·ni (chə-lē'nē), **Benvenuto.** 1500–71. Italian sculptor.

Cer·van·tes Saa·ve·dra (sər-văn'tĕz sə-vä'drə), **Miguel de.** 1547–1616. Spanish author.

Cé·zanne (sā-zăn'), **Paul.** 1839–1906. French painter.

Cha·gall (shə-gäl'), **Marc.** b. 1887. Russian-born painter.

Cham·ber·lain (chām'bər-lĭn), **(Arthur) Neville.** 1869–1940. British prime minister (1937–40).

Cham·plain (shăm-plān'), **Samuel de.** 1567?–1635. French explorer.

Chap·lin (chăp'lĭn), Sir **Charles Spencer** ("Charlie"). 1889–1977. British-born actor, producer, and director.

Chap·man (chăp'mən), **Frank Michler.** 1864–1945. Amer. ornithologist.

Char·le·magne (shär'lə-mān'). "Charles the Great," "Charles I." 742–814. King of the Franks (768–814); emperor of the West (800–14).

Charles (chärlz). b. 1948. Prince of Wales.

Charles I. 1600–49. King of England (1625–49); beheaded.

Charles II. "the Bald." 823–77. Holy Roman Emperor (875–77); king of France as Charles I (840–77).

Charles II. 1630–85. King of England following the Restoration (1660–85).

Charles V. 1500–58. Holy Roman Emperor (1519–56); king of Spain as Charles I (1516–56).

Charles VII. 1403–61. King of France (1422–61).

Charles IX. 1550–74. King of France (1560–74).

Charles X. 1757–1836. King of France (1824–30); abdicated.

Charles Martel (mär-tĕl'). 689–741. Frankish ruler (715–41).

Châ·teau·bri·and (shä-tō-brē-äɴ'), Vicomte **François René de.** 1768–1848. French author and diplomat.

Chat·ter·ton (chăt'ər-tən), **Thomas.** 1752–70. English poet.

Chau·cer (chô'sər), **Geoffrey.** 1340?–1400. English poet. —**Chau·ce·ri·an** (-shr'ē-ən) adj. & n.

Chee·ver (chē'vər), **John.** 1912–82. Amer. author.

Che·khov (chĕk'ôf', -ôf'), **Anton Pavlovich.** 1860–1904. Russian author.

Che·ops (kē'ŏps). King of Egypt (2900?–2877 B.C.).

Ches·ter·field (chĕs'tər-fēld'), 4th Earl of. Philip Dormer Stanhope. 1694–1773. English statesman and author.

Ches·ter·ton (chĕs'tər-tən), **Gilbert Keith.** 1874–1936. English author.

Chiang Kai-shek (chăng' kī'shĕk', chyăng', jē-äng', jyäng). 1887–1975. Chinese military and political leader.

Cho·pin (shō'păn'), **Frédéric François.** 1810–49. Polish-born composer.

Chou En-lai (jō' ĕn'lī'). Zhou Enlai.

Chris·tie (krĭs'tē), Dame **Agatha.** 1891–1976. English author.

Chris·ti·na (krĭs-tē'nə). 1626–89. Queen of Sweden (1632–54); abdicated.

Chris·to·pher (krĭs'tə-fər), Saint. Legendary 3rd cent. Christian martyr.

Church·ill (chûr′chĭl), **Sir Winston Leonard Spencer.** 1874–1965. British prime minister (1940–45 and 1951–55).

Winston Churchill

Cic·e·ro (sĭs′ə-rō′), **Marcus Tullius.** 106–43 B.C. Roman statesman and orator.

Cid (sĭd), **the.** Rodrigo Díaz de Bivar. 1040?–99. Spanish soldier and epic hero.

Cin·ci·na·tus (sĭn′sə-nă′təs, -năt′əs), **Lucius Quinctius.** 519?–439 B.C. Roman general.

Clark (klärk). **1. George Rogers.** 1752–1818. Amer. frontiersman and military leader. **2. William.** 1770–1838. Amer. military officer and explorer. **3. Charles Joseph ("Joe").** b. 1939. Prime minister of Canada (1979–80).

Clau·di·us I (klô′dē-əs). 10 B.C.–A.D. 54. Roman emperor (41–54).

Clay (klā), **Henry.** 1777–1852. Amer. statesman.

Cle·men·ceau (klĕm′ən-sō′), **Georges.** 1841–1929. French statesman.

Clem·ens (klĕm′ənz), **Samuel Langhorne.** "Mark Twain." 1835–1910. Amer. author and humorist.

Cle·o·pat·ra (klē′ə-păt′rə, -pä′trə, -pă′-). 69–30 B.C. Queen of Egypt (51–49 and 48–30).

Cleve·land (klēv′lənd), **(Stephen) Grover.** 1837–1908. 22nd and 24th U.S. President (1885–89 and 1893–97).

Clin·ton (klĭn′tən). **1. George.** 1739–1812. U.S. Vice President (1805–12). **2. De Witt.** 1769–1828. Amer. political leader.

Clive (klīv), **Robert.** 1725–74. English colonial administrator in India.

Clo·vis I (klō′vĭs). 466?–511. King of the Franks (481–511).

Co·chise (kō′chēs′, -chēz′). 1812?–74. Apache Indian leader.

Co·dy (kō′dē), **William Frederick.** "Buffalo Bill." 1846–1917. Amer. frontier scout and showman.

Co·han (kō′hăn′), **George Michael.** 1878–1942. Amer. singer, playwright, and songwriter.

Coke (kōk), **Sir Edward.** 1552–1634. English jurist.

Col·bert (kôl-bĕr′), **Jean Baptiste.** 1619–83. French statesman.

Cole·ridge (kōl′rĭj), **Samuel Taylor.** 1772–1834. English poet and critic.

Co·lette (kō-lĕt′). Sidonie Gabrielle Claudine Colette. 1873–1954. French novelist.

Col·fax (kōl′făks′), **Schuyler.** 1823–85. U.S. Vice President (1869–73).

Co·lum·bus (kə-lŭm′bəs), **Christopher.** 1451?–1506. Italian navigator in service of Spain; opened New World to exploration.

Com·mo·dus (kŏm′ə-dəs), **Lucius Aelius Aurelius.** 161–92. Roman emperor (180–92).

Con·dor·cet (kôn-dôr-sĕ′), **Marquis de.** Marie Jean Antoine Nicolas Caritat. 1743–94. French mathematician, philosopher, and revolutionary.

Con·fu·cius (kən-fyōō′shəs). 551–479 B.C. Chinese philosopher and teacher. **—Con·fu′cian** *adj.* & *n.*

Con·greve (kŏn′grēv′, kŏng′-), **William.** 1670–1729. English playwright.

Con·rad (kŏn′răd), **Joseph.** 1857–1924. Polish-born English author.

Con·sta·ble (kŭn′stə-bəl, kŏn′-), **John.** 1776–1837. English landscape painter.

Con·stan·tine I (kŏn′stən-tēn). "the Great." 280?–337. Roman emperor (306–37).

Cook (kōōk), **James.** 1728–79. English explorer of the Pacific.

Coo·lidge (kōō′lĭj), **(John) Calvin.** 1872–1933. 30th U.S. President (1923–29).

Calvin Coolidge

Coop·er (kōō′pər), **James Fenimore.** 1789–1851. Amer. novelist.

Co·per·ni·cus (kō-pûr′nə-kəs), **Nicolaus.** 1473–1543. Polish astronomer. **—Co·per′ni·can** *adj.*

Cop·land (kōp′lənd), **Aaron.** b. 1900. Amer. composer.

Cop·ley (kŏp′lē), **John Singleton.** 1738–1815. Amer. painter.

Cor·neille (kôr-nā′), **Pierre.** 1606–84. French dramatist.

Corn·wal·lis (kôrn-wŏl′ĭs), **Charles.** 1st Marquis and 2nd Earl Cornwallis. 1738–1805. English military and political leader.

Co·ro·na·do (kôr′ā-nä′dō, kōr′-), **Francisco Vásquez de.** 1510–54. Spanish explorer.

Co·rot (kô-rō′), **Jean Baptiste Camille.** 1796–1875. French painter.

Cor·reg·gio (kə-rĕj′ō, -ĕ-ō′), **Antonio Allegri da.** 1494–1534. Italian painter.

Cortés (kôr-tĕz′), **Hernando.** Also **Cor·tez.** 1485–1547. Spanish explorer; conquered the Aztecs.

Cou·pe·rin (kōō-prăn′), **François.** 1668–1733. French composer.

Cour·bet (kōōr-bĕ′), **Gustave.** 1819–77. French painter.

Cow·ard (kou′ərd), **Sir Noel Pierce.** 1899–1973. English author and composer.

Cow·ley (kou′lē), **Abraham.** 1618–67. English poet.

Cow·per (kōō′pər, kou′-), **William.** 1731–1800. English poet.

Crabbe (krăb), **George.** 1754–1832. English poet.

Crane (krān). **1. Stephen.** 1871–1900. Amer. writer. **2. (Harold) Hart.** 1899–1932. Amer. poet.

Cran·mer (krăn′mər), **Thomas.** 1489–1556. English religious reformer.

ă pat ā pay â care ä father ĕ pet ē be ĭ pit ī tie î pier ŏ pot ō toe ô paw, for oi noise ōō took
ōō boot ou out th thin th this ŭ cut û urge yōō abuse zh vision ə about, item, edible, gallop, circus

Cra·zy Horse (krä′zē hôrs, hōrs). 1849?-77. Sioux Indian leader.

Cro·ce (krō′chä), **Benedetto.** 1866-1952. Italian philosopher and historian.

Crock·ett (krŏk′ĭt), **David ("Davy").** 1786-1836. American frontiersman; died at the Alamo.

Croe·sus (krē′səs). d. 546 B.C. King of Lydia (560-546).

Crom·well (krŏm′wĕl′, -wəl, krŭm′-), **Oliver.** 1599-1658. English military and religious leader.

Cruik·shank (krŏŏk′shăngk′), **George.** 1792-1878. English illustrator.

Cul·len (kŭl′ən), **Countée.** 1903-46. Amer. poet.

Cum·mings (kŭm′ĭngz), **Edward Estlin.** 1894-1962. Amer. poet.

Cu·rie (kyŏŏr′ē, kyŏō-rē′), **Pierre** (1859-1906) and **Marie** (1867-1934). French chemists.

Cur·tis (kûr′tĭs), **Charles.** 1860-1936. U.S. Vice President (1929-33).

Cus·ter (kŭs′tər), **George Armstrong.** 1839-76. Amer. army officer.

Cu·vi·er (kŏō′vē-ā, kyŏō′-), **Baron Georges Léo·pold.** 1769-1832. French naturalist.

Cyra·no de Ber·ge·rac (sĭr′ə-nō də bûr′jə-răk), **Savinien de.** 1619?-55. French author and duelist.

Cyril (sĭr′əl), **Saint.** 827-69. Greek Christian theologian.

Cy·rus (sĭr′əs). 600?-529 B.C. King of Persia (550-529); founder of the Persian Empire.

D

Da·li (dä′lē), **Salvador.** b. 1904. Spanish artist.

Dal·las (dăl′əs), **George Mifflin.** 1792-1864. U.S. Vice President (1845-49).

Da·na (dä′nə), **Richard Henry.** 1815-82. Amer. author and sailor.

Dan·iel (dăn′yəl). Hebrew prophet.

Dan·te A·li·ghi·eri (dän′tē ä′lē-gyä′rē, -rä). 1265-1321. Italian poet.

Dan·ton (dän-tôn′), **Georges Jacques.** 1759-94. French revolutionary leader.

Dare (dâr), **Virginia.** 1587-? 1st child born in America of English parents.

Da·ri·us I (də-rī′əs). "the Great." 558?-486 B.C. King of Persia (521-486).

Dar·row (dăr′ō), **Clarence Seward.** 1857-1938. Amer. lawyer.

Dar·win (där′wĭn), **Charles Robert.** 1809-82. English evolutionist. —**Dar·win′i·an** adj. & n.

Dau·mier (dō-myā′), **Honoré.** 1808-79. French painter and cartoonist.

Da·vid (dä′vĭd). 2nd king of Judah and Israel (1010?-970? B.C.).

Da·vid (dä-vēd′), **Jacques Louis.** 1748-1825. French painter.

Da·vis (dä′vĭs), **Jefferson.** 1808-89. President of the Confederate States of America (1861-65).

Da·vy (dä′vē), **Sir Humphry.** 1778-1829. English chemist.

Dawes (dôz), **Charles Gates.** 1865-1951. U.S. Vice President (1925-29).

Da·yan (dī-än′, dä-yän′), **Moshe.** 1915-81. Israeli military and political leader.

Debs (dĕbz), **Eugene Victor.** 1855-1926. Amer. labor leader.

De·bus·sy (dĕb′yŏō-sē′, də-byōō′sē), **Claude Achille.** 1862-1918. French composer.

De·ca·tur (dĭ-kā′tər), **Stephen.** 1779-1820. Amer. naval officer.

De·foe (dĭ-fō′), **Daniel.** 1660?-1731. English novelist.

De·gas (də-gä′), **(Hilaire Germain) Edgar.** 1834-1917. French artist.

De Gaulle (də gōl′, gôl′), **Charles.** 1890-1970. French general and statesman.

De·la·croix (də-lä-krwä′), **(Ferdinand Victor) Eu·gène.** 1799-1863. French painter.

de la Mare (də lə mâr′, dĕl′ə mâr′), **Walter John.** 1873-1956. English poet and novelist.

De La Warr (dĕl′ə wâr′), **Baron.** "Lord Delaware." Thomas West. 1577-1618. 1st governor of Virginia (1610-11).

De·li·us (dē′lē-əs), **Frederick.** 1862-1934. English composer.

De Mille (də mĭl′). 1. **Cecil Blount.** 1881-1959. Amer. filmmaker. 2. **Agnes.** b. 1909. Amer. choreographer.

De·moc·ri·tus (dĭ-mŏk′rə-təs). 5th cent. B.C. Greek philosopher.

De·mos·the·nes (dĭ-mŏs′thə-nēz′). 385?-322 B.C. Greek orator.

Deng Xi·ao·ping (dŭng′ ksē-ou-pĭng′). b. 1904. Chinese Communist leader.

De Quin·cey (dĭ kwĭn′sē), **Thomas.** 1785-1859. English essayist.

Des·cartes (dā-kärt′), **René.** 1596-1650. French philosopher and mathematician.

de So·to (dĕ sō′tō), **Hernando.** 1496-1542. Spanish explorer.

de Va·le·ra (dĕv′ə-lĕr′ə, -lîr′ə), **Eamon.** 1882-1975. Amer.-born Irish statesman.

De Vries (də vrēs′), **Hugo.** 1848-1935. Dutch botanist.

Dew·ey (dōō′ē, dyōō′ē). 1. **George.** 1837-1917. Amer. naval officer. 2. **John.** 1859-1952. Amer. philosopher and educator.

Di·as (dē′əs), **Bartholomeu.** Also **Di·az.** 1450?-1500. Portuguese navigator.

Dick·ens (dĭk′ənz), **Charles John Huffam.** 1812-70. English novelist. —**Dick·en′si·an** (dĭ-kĕn′zē-ən) adj.

Dick·in·son (dĭk′ən-sən), **Emily Elizabeth.** 1830-86. Amer. poet.

Di·de·rot (dē′də-rō′), **Denis.** 1713-84. French philosopher and author.

Die·fen·bak·er (dēf′ən-bā′kər), **John George.** 1895-1979. Prime minister of Canada (1957-63).

Di·o·cle·tian (dī′ə-klē′shən). 245-313. Roman emperor (284-305).

Di·og·e·nes (dī-ŏj′ə-nēz′). 412?-323 B.C. Greek philosopher.

Dis·ney (dĭz′nē), **Walter Elias ("Walt").** 1901-66. Amer. cartoonist and motion picture producer.

Dis·rae·li (dĭz-rā′lē), **Benjamin.** 1st Earl of Beaconsfield. 1804-81. British prime minister (1868 and 1874-80).

Dodg·son (dŏj′sən), **Charles Lutwidge.** "Lewis Carroll." 1832-98. English mathematician and author.

Dom·i·nic (dŏm′ə-nĭk), **Saint.** 1170-1221. Spanish-born founder of Dominican order.

Do·mi·tian (də-mĭsh′ən). A.D. 51-96. Roman emperor (81-96).

Don·a·tel·lo (dŏn′ə-tĕl′ō). 1386?-1466. Italian sculptor.

Don·i·zet·ti (dŏn′ĭ-zĕt′ē), **Gaetano.** 1797-1848. Italian composer.

Donne (dŭn), **John.** 1572?-1631. English poet and theologian.

Do·ré (dô-rā′), **(Paul) Gustave.** 1833-83. French artist.

Dos Pas·sos (dŏs păs′ōs), **John Roderigo.** 1896-1970. Amer. novelist.

Dos·to·ev·ski or **Dos·to·yev·sky** (dŏs′tə-yĕf′skē), **Feodor Mikhailovich.** 1821-81. Russian novelist.

Doug·las (dŭg'ləs), **Stephen Arnold.** 1813–61. Amer. political leader.

Doug·lass (dŭg'ləs), **Frederick.** 1817?–95. Amer. abolitionist.

Doyle (doil), **Sir Arthur Conan.** 1859–1930. English physician and novelist.

Dra·co (drā'kō). 7th cent. B.C. Athenian law-giver. —**Dra·co'ni·an** *adj*.

Drake (drāk), **Sir Francis.** 1540?–96. English navigator.

Drei·ser (drī'sər), **Theodore Herman Albert.** 1871–1945. Amer. novelist.

Drey·fus (drā'fəs, drī'-), **Alfred.** 1859–1935. French army officer.

Dry·den (drīd'n), **John.** 1631–1700. English poet, dramatist, and critic.

Du Bar·ry (dōō bär'ē, dyōō), **Comtesse.** Marie-Jeanne Bécu. 1746?–93. French courtesan.

Du Bois (dōō bois'), **William Edward Burghardt.** 1868–1963. Amer. sociologist, author, and educator.

Dud·ley (dŭd'lē), **Robert.** 1st Earl of Leicester. 1532–88. English courtier.

Du·mas (dōō'mä, dū–mä'). **1.** Alexandre. "Dumas père." 1802–70. French playwright and novelist. **2.** Alexandre. "Dumas fils." 1824–95. French author.

Dun·bar (dŭn'bär), **Paul.** 1872–1906. Amer. poet.

Dun·can (dŭng'kən), **Isadora.** 1878–1927. Amer. dancer.

Dü·rer (dōōr'ər), **Albrecht.** 1471–1528. German painter and engraver.

Du·se (dōō'zā), **Eleonora.** 1859–1924. Italian actress.

Dvoř·ák (dvôr'zhäk), **Anton.** 1841–1904. Czech composer.

E

Ea·kins (ā'kĭnz), **Thomas.** 1844–1916. Amer. painter.

Ear·hart (âr'härt'), **Amelia.** 1898–1937? Amer. aviator.

Amelia Earhart

East·man (ēst'mən), **George.** 1854–1932. Amer. inventor.

E·ban (ē'bən), **Abba.** b. 1915. Israeli political leader.

Ed·dy (ĕd'ē), **Mary Baker.** 1821–1910. Amer. founder of the Church of Christ, Scientist.

E·den (ēd'n), **Sir (Robert) Anthony.** Earl of Avon. 1897–1977. British prime minister (1955–57).

Ed·i·son (ĕd'ə-sən), **Thomas Alva.** 1847–1931. Amer. inventor.

Ed·ward (ĕd'wərd). **1.** "the Confessor." 1002?–66. West Saxon king (1043–66). **2.** "the Black Prince." 1330–76. Prince of Wales.

Edward I. 1239–1307. King of England (1272–1307).

Edward II. 1284–1327. King of England (1307–27); murdered.

Edward III. 1312–1377. King of England (1327–77).

Edward IV. 1442–83. King of England (1461–83).

Edward V. 1470–83. King of England (1483); murdered.

Edward VI. 1537–53. King of England (1547–53).

Edward VII. 1841–1910. King of England and emperor of India (1901–10).

Edward VIII. 1894–1972. King of England (1936); abdicated and was created Duke of Windsor.

Ed·wards (ĕd'wərdz), **Jonathan.** 1703–58. Amer. Puritan theologian.

Ein·stein (īn'stīn'), **Albert.** 1879–1955. German-born Amer. physicist.

Ei·sen·how·er (ī'zən-hou'ər), **Dwight David.** 1890–1969. 34th U.S. President (1953–61).

Dwight D. Eisenhower

El·ea·nor of Aq·ui·taine (ĕl'ə-nər, -nôr'; ăk'wĭ-tān'). 1122?–1204. Queen of France; later wife of Henry II of England.

El·gar (ĕl'gär), **Sir Edward William.** 1857–1934. English composer.

E·li·jah (ĭ-lī'jə). Also **E·li·as** (ĭ-lī'əs). 9th cent. B.C. Hebrew prophet.

El·i·ot (ĕl'ē-ət). **1.** **George.** Mary Ann Evans. 1819–80. English novelist. **2.** **T(homas) S(tearns).** 1888–1965. Amer.-born English poet and playwright.

E·li·sha (ĭ-lī'shə). 9th cent. B.C. Hebrew prophet.

E·liz·a·beth (ĭ-lĭz'ə-bəth), **Saint.** In the New Testament, the mother of John the Baptist.

Elizabeth I. 1533–1603. Queen of England and Ireland (1558–1603).

Elizabeth II. b. 1926. Queen of Great Britain and Northern Ireland (since 1952).

El·ling·ton (ĕl'ĭng-tən), **Edward Kennedy** ("Duke"). 1899–1974. Amer. jazz musician.

El·lis (ĕl'ĭs), **(Henry) Havelock.** 1859–1939. English psychologist.

Em·er·son (ĕm'ər-sən), **Ralph Waldo.** 1803–82. Amer. essayist and poet. —**Em'er·so'ni·an** (-sō'nē-ən) *adj*.

En·de·cott (ĕn'dĭ-kət, -kŏt'), **John.** Also **En·di·cott.** 1589–1665. English-born Amer. colonial governor.

Eng·els (ĕng'əls), **Friedrich**. 1820–95. German socialist leader and writer.

Ep·ic·te·tus (ĕp'ĭk-tē'təs). Greek philosopher of the 1st–2nd cent. A.D.

Ep·i·cu·rus (ĕp'ĭ-kyŏŏr'əs). 342?–270 B.C. Greek philosopher. —**Ep'i·cu·re·an** adj. & n.

E·ras·mus (ĭ-răz'məs), **Desiderius**. 1466?–1536. Dutch theologian and scholar.

Eric·son (ĕr'ĭk-sən), **Leif**. Norwegian navigator; discovered Vinland (c. A.D. 1000).

Eric the Red (ĕr'ĭk). 10th cent. Norwegian navigator.

Ernst (ĕrnst), **Max**. 1891–1976. German-born Amer. painter.

Es·sex (ĕs'ĭks), 2nd Earl of. Robert Devereux. 1566–1601. English courtier.

Eth·el·bert (ĕth'əl-bûrt'). 552?–616. Anglo-Saxon king and lawgiver.

Eth·el·red (ĕth'əl-rĕd'). "the Unready." 968?–1016. English king (978–1016).

Eu·clid (yŏŏ'klĭd). 3rd cent. B.C. Greek mathematician. —**Eu·clid'e·an** or **Eu·clid'i·an** adj.

Eu·gé·nie (œ-zhā-nē'). 1826–1920. Empress of France (1853–71) as wife of Napoleon III.

Eu·rip·i·des (yŏŏ-rĭp'ə-dēz'). 480?–406 B.C. Greek dramatist.

Eve (ēv). In the Old Testament, the wife of Adam.

E·ze·ki·el (ĭ-zē'kē-əl). 6th cent. B.C. Hebrew prophet.

Ez·ra (ĕz'rə). 5th cent. B.C. Hebrew high priest.

F

Fahd (fäd), **Fahd ibn Abdel Aziz al- Saud al-**. b. 1922. King of Saudi Arabia (since 1982).

Fair·banks (fâr'băngks), **Charles Warren**. 1852–1918. U.S. Vice President (1905–9).

Fai·sal (fī'səl). 1906?–75. Saudi Arabian king (1964–75); assassinated.

Faisal I. 1885–1933. Iraqi king (1921–33).

Fa·rouk I (fə-rŏŏk'). 1920–65. Egyptian king (1936–52); abdicated.

Far·ra·gut (făr'ə-gət), **David Glasgow**. 1801–70. Amer. naval commander.

Far·rell (făr'əl), **James Thomas**. 1904–79. Amer. novelist.

Faulk·ner (fôk'nər), **William**. Also **Falk·ner**. 1897–1962. Amer. author.

Fawkes (fôks), **Guy**. 1570–1606. English Gunpowder Plot conspirator.

Fer·ber (fûr'bər), **Edna**. 1885–1968. Amer. author.

Ferdi·nand I (fûrd'n-ănd'). 1503–64. King of Bohemia and Hungary (1526–64); Holy Roman Emperor (1556–64).

Ferdinand V. 1452–1516. Spanish king of Aragon, Castile, Sicily, and Naples.

Fer·mi (fâr'mē), **Enrico**. 1901–54. Italian-born Amer. physicist.

Fich·te (fĭкн'tə, fĭкн'-), **Johann Gottlieb**. 1762–1814. German philosopher.

Field·ing (fēl'dĭng), **Henry**. 1707–54. English novelist.

Fill·more (fĭl'môr', -mŏr'), **Millard**. 1800–74. 13th U.S. President (1850–53).

Fitz·ger·ald (fĭts-jĕr'əld), **F(rancis) Scott (Key)**. 1896–1940. Amer. author.

Fitz·Ger·ald (fĭts-jĕr'əld), **Edward**. 1809–83. English poet and translator.

Flau·bert (flō-bâr'), **Gustave**. 1821–80. French novelist. —**Flau·bert'i·an** adj.

Flem·ing (flĕm'ĭng), **Sir Alexander**. 1881–1955. English bacteriologist.

Millard Fillmore

Fletch·er (flĕch'ər), **John**. 1579–1625. English dramatist.

Foch (fôsh, fŏsh), **Ferdinand**. 1851–1929. French army commander.

Fon·teyn (fŏn-tān'), **Dame Margot**. b. 1919. English ballerina.

Ford (fôrd, fōrd). **1. Henry**. 1863–1947. Amer. automobile manufacturer. **2. Gerald Rudolph**. b. 1913. 38th U.S. President (1974–77).

Gerald R. Ford

For·ster (fôr'stər), **E(dward) M(organ)**. 1879–1970. English novelist.

Fos·ter (fôs'tər, fŏs'-), **Stephen Collins**. 1826–64. Amer. composer.

Fou·cault (fŏŏ-kō'), **Jean Bernard Léon**. 1819–68. French physicist.

Fou·rier (fŏŏ-ryā'). **1. Baron Jean Baptiste Joseph**. 1768–1830. French physicist and mathematician. **2. François Marie Charles**. 1772–1837. French utopian socialist.

Fox (fŏks). **1. George**. 1624–91. English founder of the Society of Friends. **2. Charles James**. 1749–1806. English political leader.

Fra·go·nard (frăg'ə-när'), **Jean Honoré**. 1732–1806. French painter.

France (frăns, fräns), **Anatole**. 1844–1924. French author.

Fran·cis I (frăn'sĭs, frän'-). 1494–1547. King of France (1515–47).

Francis II. 1768–1835. Holy Roman Emperor (1792–1806); abdicated; emperor of Austria (1804–35) as Francis I.

Francis Ferdi·nand (fûr'dn-ănd'). 1863–1914. Archduke of Austria.

Francis of As·si·si (ə-sē'zē), **Saint**. 1182?–1226. Italian monk; founder of the Franciscan order.

Franck (frängk), **César Auguste**. 1822–90. Belgian-born French composer.

Fran·co (frăng'kō, fräng'-), **Francisco**. 1892–1975. Spanish general and dictator (1939–75).

Frank·furt·er (frăngk'fər-tər), **Felix**. 1882–1965. Austrian-born Amer. jurist.

Frank·lin (frăngk'lĭn). **1. Benjamin**. 1706–90. Amer. statesman, author, and scientist. **2. Sir John**. 1786–1847. English Arctic explorer.

Franz Jo·sef (fränts′ jō′səf, yō′zĕf). 1830–1916. Emperor of Austria (1848–1916).

Fra·ser (frā′zər), **(John) Malcolm.** b. 1930. Australian statesman.

Fred·er·ick I (frĕd′rĭk). "Barbarossa." 1123?–90. Holy Roman Emperor (1152–90); king of Germany (1152–90); king of Italy (1155–90).

Frederick II. 1194–1250. Holy Roman Emperor (1215–50).

Frederick II. "the Great." 1712–86. King of Prussia (1740–86).

Frederick IX. 1899–1972. King of Denmark (1947–72).

Fré·mont (frē′mŏnt), **John Charles.** 1813–90. Amer. military leader and explorer.

Freud (froid), **Sigmund.** 1856–1939. Austrian neurologist and pioneer psychoanalyst. **—Freud′i·an** adj. & n.

Friml (frĭm′əl), **Rudolf.** 1879–1972. Austrian composer.

Fro·bish·er (frō′bĭ-shər), **Sir Martin.** 1535?–94. English navigator.

Frois·sart (froi′särt), **Jean.** 1333?–1400? French historian.

Fron·te·nac (frŏn′tə-năk′), **Comte Louis de Buade de.** 1620–98. French colonial governor of Canada.

Frost (frôst, frŏst), **Robert Lee.** 1874–1963. Amer. poet.

Ful·ler (fŏŏl′ər), **(Sarah) Margaret.** 1810–50. Amer. editor and reformer.

Ful·ton (fŏŏl′tən), **Robert.** 1765–1815. Amer. inventor.

G

Gad·da·fi (gə-dä′fē). Var. of **Qaddafi.**

Ga·ga·rin (gä-gä′rĭn), **Yuri Alekseyevich.** 1934–68. Soviet cosmonaut; 1st man in space (1961).

Gage (gāj), **Thomas.** 1721–87. British general.

Gains·bor·ough (gānz′bûr′ō, -bər-ə), **Thomas.** 1727–88. English painter.

Gal·ba (găl′bə, gôl′-), **Servius Sulpicius.** 5 B.C.?–A.D. 69. Roman emperor (68–69).

Ga·len (gā′lən). 130?–201? Greek anatomist and physician.

Gal·i·le·o (găl′ə-lē′ō, -lā′ō). 1564–1642. Italian astronomer and philosopher.

Gals·worthy (gôlz′wûr′thē), **John.** 1867–1933. English novelist.

Gal·va·ni (gäl-vä′nē), **Luigi.** 1737–98. Italian physiologist.

Ga·ma (găm′ə), **Vasco da.** 1469?–1524. Portuguese explorer.

Gan·dhi (găn′dē, gän′-). **1. Mohandas Karamchand.** "Mahatma." 1869–1948. Hindu nationalist and spiritual leader; assassinated. **2. Indira Nehru.** b. 1917. Indian political leader.

Gar·field (gär′fēld′), **James Abram.** 1831–81. 20th U.S. President (1881); assassinated.

Gar·i·bal·di (găr′ə-bôl′dē), **Giuseppe.** 1807–82. Italian general and patriot.

Gar·ner (gär′nər), **John Nance.** 1868–1967. U.S. Vice President (1933–41).

Gar·rick (găr′ĭk), **David.** 1717–79. English actor and theater manager.

Gar·ri·son (găr′ĭ-sən), **William Lloyd.** 1805–79. Amer. abolitionist editor.

Gates (gāts), **Horatio.** 1728?–1806. Amer. Revolutionary general.

Gau·guin (gō-găn′), **(Eugène Henri) Paul.** 1848–1903. French painter.

Gau·tier (gō-tyā′), **Théophile.** 1811–72. French poet.

Gay (gā), **John.** 1685–1732. English poet and playwright.

Gen·ghis Khan (jĕng′gĭs kän′, gĕng′-). 1162?–1227. Mongol conqueror.

Geof·frey of Mon·mouth (jĕf′rē; mŏn′məth). 1100?–54. Welsh bishop and historian.

George I (jôrj). 1660–1727. King of Great Britain (1714–27).

George II. 1683–1760. King of Great Britain (1727–60).

George III. 1738–1820. King of Great Britain (1760–1820).

George IV. 1762–1830. King of Great Britain (1820–30).

George V. 1865–1936. King of Great Britain (1910–36).

George VI. 1895–1952. King of Great Britain (1936–52).

Ge·ron·i·mo (jə-rŏn′ə-mō′). 1829–1909. Apache Indian leader.

Ger·ry (gĕr′ē), **Elbridge.** 1744–1814. U.S. Vice President (1813–14).

Gersh·win (gûrsh′wĭn), **George.** 1898–1937. Amer. composer.

Gia·co·met·ti (jä′kə-mĕt′ē), **Alberto.** 1901–66. Swiss sculptor and painter.

Gib·bon (gĭb′ən), **Edward.** 1737–94. English historian.

Gide (zhēd), **André.** 1869–1951. French novelist.

Gid·e·on (gĭd′ē-ən). Hebrew hero in the Old Testament.

Gil·bert (gĭl′bərt), **Sir William S(chwenck).** 1836–1911. English playwright.

Glor·gio·ne (jôr-jō′nā). 1478?–1511. Venetian painter.

Glot·to (jôt′ō). 1266?–1337. Florentine painter and sculptor.

Gi·rau·doux (zhē-rō-dōō′), **Jean.** 1882–1944. French author.

Gis·card d'Es·taing (zhē-skär′ dĕs-tăN′), **Valéry.** b. 1926. French political leader.

Glad·stone (glăd′stŏn′, -stən), **William Ewart.** 1809–98. British prime minister (4 times between 1868 and 1894).

Glenn (glĕn), **John Herschel, Jr.** b. 1921. Amer. astronaut and legislator.

God·dard (gŏd′ərd), **Robert Hutchings.** 1882–1945. Amer. rocket pioneer.

Go·du·nov (gŏd′n-ôf′, gŏŏd′-), **Boris Fedorovich.** 1552–1605. Russian czar (1598–1605).

Goe·thals (gō′thəlz), **George Washington.** 1858–1928. Amer. army engineer.

Goe·the (gœ′tə), **Johann Wolfgang von.** 1749–1832. German author.

Go·gol (gō′gəl), **Nikolai Vasilievich.** 1809–1852. Russian novelist.

Gold·man (gōld′mən), **Emma.** 1869–1940. Russian-born Amer. anarchist.

Gold·smith (gōld′smĭth′), **Oliver.** 1728–74. Irish author.

Go·li·ath (gə-lī′əth). In the Old Testament, Philistine giant killed by David.

Gom·pers (gŏm′pərz), **Samuel.** 1850–1924. English-born Amer. labor leader.

Gor·gas (gôr′gəs), **William Crawford.** 1854–1920. Amer. army surgeon.

ă pat ā pay â care ä father ĕ pet ē be ĭ pit ī tie î pier ŏ pot ō toe ô paw, for oi noise ŏŏ took ōŏ boot ou out th thin th this ŭ cut û urge yŏŏ abuse zh vision ə about, item, edible, gallop, circus

Gor·ki (gôr′kē), **Maksim.** 1868–1936. Russian author.

Gou·nod (goo-nō′), **Charles François.** 1818–93. French composer.

Go·ya (gō′yä), **Francisco José de.** 1746–1828. Spanish artist.

Grac·chus (grăk′əs), **Tiberius Sempronius** (163–133 B.C.) and **Galus Sempronius** (153–121 B.C.). Roman statesmen.

Grace (grās), **Princess. Grace Patricia Kelly.** 1929–82. Amer. actress and princess of Monaco (1956–82).

Gra·ham (grā′əm), **Martha.** b. 1894? Amer. choreographer.

Grandma Mo·ses (mō′zĭz, -zĭs). **Anna Mary Robertson Moses.** 1860–1961. Amer. painter.

Grant (grănt), **Ulysses Simpson.** 1822–85. 18th U.S. President (1869–77).

Ulysses S. Grant

Gra·tian (grā′shən). 359–83. Roman emperor (367–83).

Graves (grāvz), **Robert Ranke.** b. 1895. English author.

Gray (grā), **Thomas.** 1716–71. English poet.

Gre·co (grĕk′ō), **El.** 1541?–1614? Greek-born Spanish artist.

Gree·ley (grē′lē), **Horace.** 1811–72. Amer. journalist and politician.

Greene (grēn). **1. Nathanael.** 1742–86. Amer. Revolutionary general. **2. Graham.** b. 1904. English author.

Greg·o·ry I (grĕg′ə-rē), **Saint. "the Great."** 540?–604. Pope (590–604).

Gregory VII, Saint. 1020?–85. Pope (1073–85).

Gregory XIII. 1502–85. Pope (1572–85).

Grey (grā). **1. Lady Jane.** 1537–54. Queen of England (July 9–19, 1553); executed. **2. Charles.** 1764–1845. British prime minister (1830–34). **3. Sir Edward.** 1862–1933. English statesman. **4. Zane.** 1875–1939. Amer. author.

Grieg (grēg), **Edvard Hagerup.** 1843–1907. Norwegian composer.

Grif·fith (grĭf′ĭth), **D(avid Lewelyn) W(ark).** 1875–1948. Amer. filmmaker.

Grimm (grĭm), **Jakob.** (1785–1863) and **Wilhelm** (1786–1859). German philologists and folklorists.

Gris (grēs), **Juan.** 1887–1927. Spanish painter.

Gro·my·ko (grō-mē′kō), **Andrei Andreevich.** b. 1909. Soviet diplomat.

Gro·pi·us (grō′pē-əs), **Walter Adolph.** 1883–1969. German-born Amer. architect.

Grosz (grōs), **George.** 1893–1959. German-born Amer. artist.

Gro·ti·us (grō′shē-əs), **Hugo.** 1583–1645. Dutch jurist and statesman.

Guar·nie·ri (gwär-nyĕ′rē). Family of Italian violin makers, including **Andrea** (1626–98), **Giuseppe** (1666–1739), and **Pietro** (1655–1728).

Gue·va·ra (gĕ-vä′rä), **Ernesto ("Che").** 1928–67. Argentine-born revolutionary.

Gui·do d'A·rez·zo (gwē′dō dä-rät′tsō). 995?–1050? Italian musical theorist.

Gui·zot (gē-zō′), **François.** 1787–1874. French statesman.

Gus·ta·vus I (gŭ-stā′vəs). 1496–1560. King of Sweden (1523–60).

Gustavus II. "Gustavus Adolphus." 1594–1632. King of Sweden (1611–32).

Gustavus IV. 1778–1837. King of Sweden (1792–1809).

Gustavus V. 1858–1950. King of Sweden (1907–50).

Gustavus VI. 1882–1973. King of Sweden (1950–73).

Gu·ten·berg (goot′n-bûrg′), **Johann.** 1400?–68? German inventor of movable type.

H

Ha·bak·kuk (hə-băk′ək, hăb′ə-kŭk′). Late 7th cent. B.C. Hebrew prophet.

Ha·dri·an (hā′drē-ən). A.D. 76–138. Roman emperor (117–138).

Hag·ga·i (hăg′ē-ī′, hăg′ī′). 6th cent. B.C. Hebrew prophet.

Hai·le Se·las·sie (hī′lē sə-lăs′ē, -lā′sē). 1892–1975. Emperor of Ethiopia (1930–36, 1941–74); deposed.

Hak·luyt (hăk′loot′), **Richard.** 1552?–1616. English geographer.

Hale (hāl). **1. Nathan.** 1755–76. Amer. army officer; hanged by the British for spying. **2. Edward Everett.** 1822–1909. Amer. minister and author.

Hal·ley (hăl′ē), **Edmund.** 1656–1742. English astronomer.

Hals (häls), **Frans.** 1580?–1666. Dutch painter.

Hal·sey (hôl′zē), **William Frederick.** 1882–1959. Amer. naval officer.

Ham (hăm). In the Old Testament, son of Noah.

Ha·mil·car Bar·ca (hə-mĭl′kär bär′kə). 270?–228 B.C. Carthaginian general.

Ham·il·ton (hăm′əl-tən). **1. Alexander.** 1755–1804. Amer. Revolutionary statesman. **2. Edith.** 1867–1963. Amer. scholar and author.

Alexander Hamilton

Ham·lin (hăm′lən), **Hannibal.** 1809–91. U.S. Vice President (1861–65).

Ham·mar·skjöld (hä′mər-shöld′), **Dag Hjalmar Agné Carl.** 1905–61. Swedish diplomat and UN official.

Ham·mu·ra·bi (hä′moo-rä′bē, hăm′ə-). 18th cent. B.C. Babylonian king and lawgiver.

Han·cock (hăn′kŏk′), **John.** 1737–93. Amer. merchant and statesman.

Han·del (hănd′l), **George Frederick.** 1685–1759. German-born English composer.

Han·dy (hăn′dē), **W(illiam) C(hristopher).** 1873–1958. Amer. musician.

Han·na (hăn'ə), Marcus Alonzo ("Mark"). 1837–1904. Amer. politician.

Han·ni·bal (hăn'ə-bəl). 247?–183 B.C. Carthaginian general.

Har·ding (här'dĭng), Warren Gamaliel. 1865–1923. 29th U.S. President (1921–23); died in office.

Warren G. Harding

Har·dy (här'dē), Thomas. 1840–1928. English novelist.

Har·greaves (här'grēvz'), James. d. 1778. English inventor.

Har·old I (här'əld). d. 1040. King of England (1035–40).

Harold II. 1022?–66. King of England (1066).

Har·ris (hăr'ĭs, hâr'-), Joel Chandler. 1848–1908. Amer. author.

Har·ri·son (hăr'ĭ-sən). Amer. political family, including: 1. Benjamin 1726?–91. Revolutionary leader. 2. William Henry. 1773–1841. 9th U.S. President (1841); died in office. 3. Benjamin. 1833–1901. 23rd U.S. President (1889–93).

Harte (härt), (Francis) Bret(t). 1836–1902. Amer. author.

Har·vey (här'vē), William. 1578–1657. English physician and anatomist.

Has·tings (hā'stĭngz), Warren. 1732–1818. English colonial administrator.

Haupt·mann (houpt'män'), Gerhart. 1862–1946. German author.

Haw·thorne (hô'thôrn'), Nathaniel. 1804–64. Amer. author.

Hay·dn (hīd'n), (Franz) Joseph ("Papa"). 1732–1809. Austrian composer.

Hayes (hāz), Rutherford Birchard. 1822–93. 19th U.S. President (1877–81).

Haz·litt (hăz'lĭt), William. 1778–1830. English essayist.

Hearst (hûrst), William Randolph. 1863–1951. Amer. newspaper publisher.

Heath (hēth), Edward Richard George. b. 1916. British prime minister (1970–74).

He·gel (hā'gəl), Georg Wilhelm Friedrich. 1770–1831. German philosopher. —He·ge'li·an (hā-gā'lē-ən) adj. & n.

Hei·deg·ger (hī-dĭg'ər), Martin. 1889–1976. German philosopher.

Hei·fetz (hī'fĭts), Jascha. b. 1901. Russian-born Amer. violinist.

Hei·ne (hī'nə), Heinrich. 1797–1856. German poet and critic.

Hell·man (hĕl'mən), Lillian. b. 1905. Amer. playwright.

Hé·lo·ise (ĕl'ō-ēz', ā-lō-ēz'). 1101?–64? The beloved of Abelard.

Hel·vé·tius (hĕl-vē'shəs), Claude Adrian. 1715–71. French philosopher.

Hem·ing·way (hĕm'ĭng-wā'), Ernest Miller. 1899–1961. Amer. novelist.

Hen·dricks (hĕn'drĭks), Thomas Andrews. 1819–85. U.S. Vice President (1885); died in office.

Hen·ley (hĕn'lē), William Ernest. 1849–1903. English author.

Hen·ry I (hĕn'rē). 1068–1135. King of England (1100–35).

Henry II. 1133–89. King of England (1154–89).

Henry III. 1207–72. King of England (1216–72).

Henry III. 1551–89. King of France (1574–89).

Henry IV. 1050–1106. Holy Roman Emperor and king of Germany (1056–1106).

Henry IV. 1367–1413. King of England (1399–1413).

Henry IV. 1553–1610. King of France (1589–1610).

Henry V. 1387–1422. King of England (1413–22).

Henry VI. 1421–71. King of England (1422–61 and 1470–71).

Henry VII. "Henry Tudor". 1457–1509. King of England (1485–1509).

Henry VIII. 1491–1547. King of England (1509–47).

Henry VIII

Henry, Patrick. 1736–99. Amer. Revolutionary leader.

Her·a·cli·tus (hĕr'ə-klī'təs). 6th cent. B.C. Greek philosopher.

Her·bert (hûr'bərt). 1. George. 1593–1633. English poet. 2. Victor. 1859–1924. Irish-born Amer. composer.

Her·der (hûr'dər), Johann Gottfried von. 1744–1803. German philosopher.

Her·od (hĕr'əd). "the Great". 73?–4 B.C. King of Judea (37–4).

Herod An·ti·pas (ăn'tĭ-păs'). Roman tetrarch of Galilee (4 B.C.–A.D. 40).

He·rod·o·tus (hĭ-rŏd'ə-təs). 5th cent. B.C. Greek historian.

Her·rick (hĕr'ĭk), Robert. 1591–1674. English poet.

Her·schel (hûr'shəl). Family of English astronomers, including Sir William (1738–1822), Caroline Lucretia (1750–1848), and Sir John Frederick William (1792–1871).

Herzl (hĕr'tsəl), Theodor. 1860–1904. Hungarian-born Austrian founder of Zionism.

He·si·od (hē'sē-əd, hĕs'ē-). 8th cent. Greek poet.

Hes·se (hĕs'ə), Hermann. 1877–1962. German author.

Hey·er·dahl (hī'ər-däl'), **Thor.** b. 1914. Norwegian explorer.

Heywood (hā'wŏŏd'), **Thomas.** 1574–1641. English playwright.

Hez·e·ki·ah (hĕz'ĭ-kī'ə). 740?–692? B.C. King of Judah (720?–692?).

Hick·ok (hĭk'ŏk'), **James Butler ("Wild Bill").** 1837–76. Amer. frontier lawman.

Hil·lary (hĭl'ə-rē), **Sir Edmund Percival.** b. 1919. New Zealand-born English mountaineer and explorer.

Hil·ton (hĭl'tn), **James.** 1900–54. English novelist.

Hin·de·mith (hĭn'də-mĭth), **Paul.** 1895–1963. German composer.

Hin·den·burg (hĭn'dən-bûrg'), **Paul von.** 1847–1934. German general and statesman.

Hip·poc·ra·tes (hĭ-pŏk'rə-tēz'). 460?–377? B.C. Greek physician. —**Hip'po·crat'ic** (hĭp'ə-krăt'ĭk) *adj.*

Hi·ro·hi·to (hĭr'ō-hē'tō). b. 1901. Emperor of Japan (since 1926).

Hit·ler (hĭt'lər), **Adolf.** 1889–1945. Austrian-born Nazi dictator.

Ho·bart (hō'bərt, -bärt), **Garret Augustus.** 1844–99. U.S. Vice President (1897–99); died in office.

Hobbes (hŏbz), **Thomas.** 1588–1679. English philosopher.

Ho Chi Minh (hō' chē' mĭn'). 1890–1969. Vietnamese Communist leader.

Hoff·mann (hŏf'mən, hŏf'män'), **Ernst Theodor Amadeus (Wilhelm).** 1776–1822. German author, critic, and composer.

Ho·garth (hō'gärth'), **William.** 1697–1764. English painter and engraver.

Hol·bein (hōl'bīn'). **1. Hans.** 1465?–1524. German painter. **2. Hans. "the Younger".** 1497?–1543. German painter.

Holmes (hōmz, hōlmz). **1. Oliver Wendell.** 1809–94. Amer. physician and author. **2. Oliver Wendell.** 1841–1935. Amer. jurist.

Ho·mer (hō'mər). fl. 850? B.C. Greek epic poet. —**Ho·mer'ic** (hō-mĕr'ĭk) *adj.*

Homer, Winslow. 1836–1910. Amer. painter.

Hook·er (hŏŏk'ər), **Thomas.** 1586?–1647. English Puritan clergyman and Amer. colonizer.

Hoo·ver (hŏŏ'vər). **1. Herbert Clark.** 1874–1964. 31st U.S. President (1929–33). **2. J(ohn) Edgar.** 1895–1972. Amer. FBI director (1924–72).

Herbert Hoover

Hop·kins (hŏp'kĭnz). **1. Mark.** 1813–78. Amer. educator. **2. Gerard Manley.** 1844–89. English poet.

Hor·ace (hôr'ĭs, hŏr'-). 65–8 B.C. Roman poet.

Ho·ro·witz (hôr'ə-wĭts, hŏr'-), **Vladimir.** b. 1904. Russian-born Amer. pianist.

Ho·se·a (hō-zā'ə, -zē'ə). 8th cent. B.C. Hebrew prophet.

Houd·i·ni (hŏŏ-dē'nē), **Harry.** 1874–1926. Amer. magician.

Hou·don (ŏŏ-dôN'), **Jean Antoine.** 1741–1828. French sculptor.

Hous·man (hous'mən), **A(lfred) E(dward).** 1859–1936. English poet.

Hous·ton (hyŏŏ'stən), **Sam(uel).** 1793–1863. Amer. general and politician.

Ho·ward (hou'ərd), **Catherine.** 1520?–42. 5th wife of Henry VIII; executed.

Howe (hou). **1. Elias.** 1819–67. Amer. inventor. **2. Julia Ward.** 1819–1910. Amer. feminist and author.

How·ells (hou'əlz), **William Dean.** 1837–1920. Amer. author and editor.

Hua Guo-feng (hwä' gwŏ'fŭng'). b. 1920. Chinese Communist leader.

Hud·son (hŭd'sən). **1. Henry.** d. 1611. English navigator and Arctic explorer. **2. William Henry.** 1841–1922. English naturalist.

Hughes (hyŏŏz). **1. Charles Evans.** 1862–1948. Amer. jurist. **2. (James) Langston.** 1902–67. Amer. author.

Hu·go (hyŏŏ'gō), **Victor Marie.** 1802–85. French author.

Hull (hŭl), **Cordell.** 1871–1955. Amer. statesman.

Hum·boldt (hŭm'bōlt), **Baron Alexander von.** 1769–1859. German naturalist and explorer.

Hume (hyŏŏm), **David.** 1711–76. Scottish philosopher and historian.

Hum·phrey (hŭm'frē), **Hubert Horatio.** 1911–79. U.S. Vice President (1965–69).

Huss (hŭs), **John.** Also **Jan Hus** (yän' hŏŏs'). 1369?–1415. Bohemian religious reformer.

Hus·sein I (hŏŏ-sān'). b. 1935. King of Jordan (since 1953).

Hutch·in·son (hŭch'ĭn-sən), **Anne.** 1591–1643. English-born Amer. colonist and religious leader.

Hux·ley (hŭk'slē). English family, including: **1. Thomas Henry.** 1825–95. Biologist. **2. Sir Julian Sorell.** 1887–1975. Biologist and author. **3. Aldous Leonard.** 1894–1963. Novelist and critic.

I

Ib·sen (ĭb'sən), **Henrik.** 1828–1906. Norwegian dramatist.

Ig·na·tius Loy·o·la (ĭg-nā'shəs loi-ō'lə), **Saint.** 1491–1556. Spanish soldier and founder of the Society of Jesus.

Inge (ĭnj), **William.** 1913–73. Amer. playwright.

In·gres (ăN'gr'), **Jean Auguste Dominique.** 1780–1867. French painter.

In·no·cent III (ĭn'ə-sənt). 1161–1216. Pope (1198–1216).

Ir·ving (ûr'vĭng), **Washington.** 1783–1859. Amer. author.

Isaac (ī'zək). Hebrew patriarch.

Is·a·bel·la I (ĭz'ə-bĕl'ə). 1451–1501. Queen of Castile and Aragon.

I·sa·iah (ī-zā'ə). 8th cent. B.C. Hebrew prophet.

Ish·er·wood (ĭsh'ər-wŏŏd'), **Christopher.** b. 1904. English-born Amer. author.

I·van III Va·sil·ie·vich (ī'vən və-sĭl'yə-vich'). "the Great." 1440–1505. Grand Duke of Muscovy (1462–1505).

Ivan IV Vasilievich. "the Terrible." 1530–84. Grand Duke of Muscovy (1533–84) and czar of Russia (1547–84).

Ives (īvz), **Charles Edward.** 1874–1954. Amer. composer.

J

Jack·son (jăk′sən). **1. Andrew.** "Old Hickory."
1767–1845. 7th U.S. President (1829–37).
2. Thomas Jonathan ("Stonewall"). 1824–63.
Amer. military leader.

Andrew Jackson

Ja·cob (jā′kəb). Hebrew patriarch.
James (jāmz). **1. William.** 1842–1910. Amer.
philosopher and psychologist. **2. Henry.** 1843–
1916. Amer. novelist and critic.
James, Saint. **1.** "the Less." Traditionally regarded as the brother of Jesus. **2.** "the
Greater." One of the 12 Apostles; martyred.
3. One of the 12 Apostles.
James I. 1566–1625. King of England (1603–
25); as James VI, king of Scotland (1567–1625).
James II. 1633–1701. King of England, Scotland, and Ireland (1685–88).
Jay (jā), **John.** 1745–1829. Amer. statesman
and jurist.
Jef·fer·son (jĕf′ər-sən), **Thomas.** 1743–1826.
3rd U.S. President (1801–9). —**Jef′fer·so′ni·an**
(-sō′nē-ən) *adj. & n.*

Thomas Jefferson

Je·hosh·a·phat (jə-hŏsh′ə-făt′). 9th cent. B.C.
king of Judah.
Jer·e·mi·ah (jĕr′ə-mī′ə). 7th and 6th cent. B.C.
Hebrew prophet.
Jes·se (jĕs′ē). In the Old Testament, father of
King David.
Je·sus (jē′zəs) 4? B.C.–A.D. 29? Founder of
Christianity.
Jez·e·bel (jĕz′ə-bĕl′, -bəl). 9th cent. B.C. queen
of Israel.
Joan of Arc (jōn′; ärk′), Saint. 1412–31.
French heroine and military leader.
Job (jōb). Hebrew patriarch.
Jo·el (jō′əl). 9th cent. B.C. Hebrew prophet.

John (jŏn). 1167?–1216. King of England
(1199–1216).
John, Saint. One of the 12 Apostles.
John XXIII. 1881–1963. Pope (1958–63).
John of Gaunt (gônt, gänt). 1340–99. Duke of
Lancaster.
John Paul I (pôl). 1912–78. Pope (1978).
John Paul II. b. 1920. Pope (since 1978).
John·son (jŏn′sən). **1. Samuel.** 1709–84. Eng-
lish lexicographer and author. **2. Richard Men-
tor.** 1780–1850. U.S. Vice President (1837–41).
3. Andrew. 1808–75. 17th U.S. President
(1865–69). **4. Lyndon Baines.** 1908–73. 36th
U.S. President (1963–69). —**John·so′ni·an**
(- sō′nē-ən) *adj.*

Lyndon B. Johnson

John the Baptist, Saint. 5 B.C. -A.D. 30. Bap-
tizer of Jesus.
Jo·li·et (jō′lē-ĕt′), **Louis.** 1645–1700. French-
Canadian explorer.
Jo·nah (jō′nə). Hebrew prophet.
Jones (jōnz), **John Paul.** 1747–92. Scottish-
born Amer. naval officer.
Jon·son (jŏn′sən), **Ben(jamin).** 1573–1637. Eng-
lish poet and dramatist.
Jo·seph (jō′zəf, -səf). Husband of Mary, the
mother of Jesus.
Jo·sé·phine de Beau·har·nais (zhō-zā-fēn′ də
bō-är-nĕ′). 1763–1814. Empress of the French
as wife of Napoléon I (1804–9).
Joseph of Ar·i·ma·the·a (ăr′ə-mə-thē′ə, ăr′-).
Israelite who buried Jesus.
Jo·se·phus (jō-sē′fəs), **Flavius.** A.D. 37–100?
Jewish historian.
Josh·ua (jŏsh′ōō-ə). Old Testament Hebrew
leader.
Joyce (jois), **James.** 1882–1941. Irish novelist.
Juan Carlos (wän kär′lōs, hwän). b. 1938.
King of Spain (since 1975).
Juá·rez (hwä′rās), **Benito Pablo.** 1806–72.
Mexican revolutionary statesman.
Ju·dah (jōō′də). Hebrew patriarch.
Ju·das (jōō′dəs). "Judas Iscariot." One of the
12 Apostles; betrayer of Jesus.
Jude (jōōd), Saint. One of the 12 Apostles.
Ju·dith (jōō′dĭth). Jewish biblical heroine.
Jul·ian (jōōl′yən). 331–63. Roman emperor
(361–63).
Ju·li·an·a (jōō′lē-ăn′ə). b. 1909. Queen of the
Netherlands (1948–80); abdicated.
Jung (yōōng), **Carl Gustav.** 1875–1961. Swiss
psychologist.
Jus·tin·i·an (jŭ-stĭn′ē-ən). 483–565. Roman
emperor of the East (527–65).
Ju·ve·nal (jōō′və-nəl). A.D. 60?–140? Roman
satirist.

K

Ka·dar (kä′där), **János.** b. 1912. Hungarian statesman.

Kaf·ka (käf′kä), **Franz.** 1883–1924. Austrian novelist. —**Kaf′ka·esque′** (-ĕsk′) *adj.*

Kan·din·sky (kän-dĭn′skē), **Vasili.** 1866–1944. Russian painter.

Kant (känt, känt), **Immanuel.** 1724–1804. German philosopher. —**Kant′i·an** *adj.*

Keats (kēts), **John.** 1795–1821. English poet. —**Keats′i·an** *adj.*

Kel·ler (kĕl′ər), **Helen Adams.** 1880–1968. Amer. author and lecturer.

Kel·logg (kĕl′ŏg, -əg), **Frank Billings.** 1856–1937. Amer. statesman.

Kel·vin (kĕl′vĭn), **1st Baron. William Thomson.** 1824–1907. British physicist and mathematician.

Ke·mal At·a·turk (kĕ-mäl′ ăt′ə-tûrk′). 1881–1938. Turkish soldier and statesman.

Ken·ne·dy (kĕn′ə-dē). **1. John Fitzgerald.** 1917–63. 35th U.S. President (1961–63); assassinated. **2. Robert Francis.** 1925–68. Amer. lawyer and politician; assassinated.

John F. Kennedy

Ken·yat·ta (kĕn-yä′tə), **Jomo.** 1893?–1978. President of Kenya (1963–78).

Kep·ler (kĕp′lər), **Johannes.** 1571–1630. German astronomer.

Ke·ren·sky (kə-rĕn′skē), **Aleksandr Feodorovich.** 1881–1970. Russian revolutionary leader.

Key (kē), **Francis Scott.** 1779–1843. Amer. lawyer and poet; author of "The Star-Spangled Banner."

Keynes (kānz), **John Maynard.** 1883–1946. English economist. —**Keynes′i·an** *adj. & n.*

Kha·lid (KHä-lēd′), **Khalid Abdul Aziz al-Saud al-.** 1913–82. King of Saudi Arabia (1975–82).

Kho·mei·ni (kō-mā′nē, KHō-), **Ayatollah Ruholla.** b. 1900. Iranian leader.

Khru·shchev (krōōsh-chĕf′, -chôf′), **Nikita Sergeyevich.** 1894–1971. Soviet statesman.

Kidd (kĭd), **William.** "Captain Kidd." 1645?–1701. Scottish pirate.

Kier·ke·gaard (kîr′kĭ-gärd′), **Sören Aabye.** 1813–55. Danish philosopher and theologian.

King (kĭng). **1. William Rufus DeVane.** 1786–1853. U.S. Vice President (1853). **2. William Lyon Mackenzie.** 1874–1950. Prime minister of Canada (1921–26, 1926–30, and 1935–48). **3. Martin Luther, Jr.** 1929–68. Amer. civil-rights leader; assassinated.

Kip·ling (kĭp′lĭng), **Rudyard.** 1865–1936. English author.

Kis·sin·ger (kĭs′ĭn-jər), **Henry Alfred.** b. 1923. German-born Amer. statesman.

Klee (klā), **Paul.** 1879–1940. Swiss painter.

Martin Luther King, Jr.

Knel·ler (nĕl′ər), **Sir Godfrey.** 1646–1723. German-born English painter.

Knox (nŏks). **1. John.** 1505–72. Scottish Protestant religious reformer. **2. Henry.** 1750–1806. Amer. Revolutionary soldier and public official.

Koest·ler (kĕst′lər, kœst′-), **Arthur.** 1905–83. Hungarian-born author.

Kos·ci·us·ko (kŏs′ē-ŭs′kō), **Thaddeus.** 1746–1817. Polish general and patriot.

Kos·suth (kŏs′ōōth), **Lajos.** 1802–94. Hungarian statesman.

Ko·sy·gin (kə-sē′gĭn), **Aleksei Nikolaevich.** 1904–80. Soviet statesman.

Ku·blai Khan (kōō′blī kän′). Also **Ku·bla Khan** (-blə). 1216–94. Founder of the Mongol dynasty.

L

La·fay·ette (lä′fē-ĕt′, läf′ē-), **Marquis de.** 1757–1834. French military and political leader.

La Fon·taine (lä fôn-tān′, fôn-tĕn′), **Jean de.** 1621–95. French poet and fabulist.

La·marck (lə-märk′), **Chevalier Jean de.** 1744–1829. French naturalist.

Lamb (lăm), **Charles.** "Elia." 1775–1834. English essayist.

Lang·ley (lăng′lē), **Samuel Pierpont.** 1834–1906. Amer. astronomer and aeronautical pioneer.

Lao·tse (lou′dzŭ′). Also **Lao·tze, Lao·tsu.** 604?–531? B.C. Chinese philosopher.

La·place (lə-pläs′), **Marquis Pierre Simon de.** 1749–1827. French mathematician and astronomer.

La Roche·fou·cauld (lä rôsh-fōō-kō′), **Duc François de.** 1613–80. French author.

La Salle (lə säl′), **Sieur de. Robert Cavelier.** 1643–87. French explorer.

La Tour (lä tōōr′, tōōr′), **Georges de.** 1593–1652. French painter.

Laud (lôd), **William.** 1573–1645. English prelate executed for treason.

La·voi·sier (lä-vwä-zyā′), **Antoine Laurent.** 1743–94. French chemist.

Law·rence (lôr′əns, lŏr′-). **1. Sir Thomas.** 1769–1830. English portraitist. **2. D(avid) H(erbert).** 1885–1930. English author. **3. T(homas) E(dward).** "Lawrence of Arabia." 1888–1935. British soldier and writer.

Laz·a·rus (lăz′ər-əs). In the New Testament, brother of Mary and Martha, believed to have been raised from the dead.

Laz·a·rus (lăz′ər-əs), **Emma.** 1849–87. Amer. poet and philanthropist.

Lear (lîr), **Edward.** 1812–88. English artist and poet.

Lee (lē). **1. Ann.** 1736–84. English religious leader; founded 1st Shaker colony in America (1776). **2. Henry ("Lighthorse Harry").** 1756–

1818. Amer. Revolutionary statesman and commander **3. Robert Edward.** 1807–70. Amer. Confederate commander.

Leib·nitz or **Leib·niz** (līb′nĭts′), **Baron Gottfried Wilhelm von.** 1646–1716. German philosopher and mathematician.

L'En·fant (län-fän′), **Pierre Charles.** 1754–1825. French-born engineer and city planner.

Le·nin (lĕn′ĭn, -ēn′), **V(ladimir) I(lyich).** 1870–1924. Russian revolutionary leader and statesman.

Le·o I (lē′ō), **Saint.** "the Great." 390?–461. Pope (440–61).

Leo III. **Saint.** A.D. 750?–816. Pope (795–816).

Leo X. 1475–1521. Pope (1513–21).

Leo XIII. 1810–1903. Pope (1878–1903).

Le·o·nar·do da Vin·ci (lē′ə-när′dō də vĭn′chē). 1452–1519. Florentine artist and engineer.

Le·o·pold III (lē′ə-pōld′). b. 1901. King of Belgium (1934–51); abdicated.

Les·seps (lĕs′əps), **Vicomte Ferdinand Marie de.** 1805–94. French diplomat; promoted Suez Canal.

Le·vi (lē′vī′). In the Old Testament, son of Jacob.

Lew·is (lōō′ĭs). **1. Meriwether.** 1774–1809. Amer. explorer. **2. John Llewellyn.** 1880–1969. Amer. labor leader. **3. (Harry) Sinclair.** 1885–1951. Amer. novelist. **4. C(live) S(taples).** 1898–1963. English novelist.

Lie (lē), **Trygve Halvdan.** 1896–1968. Norwegian statesman and UN official.

Lin·coln (lĭng′kən), **Abraham.** 1809–65. 16th U.S. President (1861–65); assassinated.

Abraham Lincoln

Lind·bergh (lĭnd′bûrg′, lĭn′-), **Charles Augustus.** 1902–74. Amer. pioneer aviator.

Lind·say (lĭn′zē, lĭnd′-), **(Nicholas) Vachel.** 1879–1931. Amer. poet.

Lin·nae·us (lĭ-nē′əs), **Carolus.** 1707–78. Swedish botanist. —**Lin·nae′an** adj.

Lip·pi (lĭp′ē), **Fra Filippo** or **Lippo** (1406?–69) and **Filippino** (1457?–1504). Florentine painters.

Lis·ter (lĭs′tər), **Joseph.** 1st Baron Lister. 1827–1912. English pioneer surgeon.

Liszt (lĭst), **Franz.** 1811–86. Hungarian composer and pianist.

Liv·ing·stone (lĭv′ĭng-stən), **David.** 1813–73. Scottish medical missionary and African explorer.

Liv·y (lĭv′ē). 59 B.C.–A.D. 17. Roman historian.

Lloyd George (loid′ jôrj′), **David.** 1863–1945. British prime minister (1916–22).

Locke (lŏk), **John.** 1632–1704. English philosopher.

Lon·don (lŭn′dən), **John Griffith ("Jack").** 1876–1916. Amer. author and adventurer.

Long·fel·low (lông′fĕl′ō, lŏng′-), **Henry Wadsworth.** 1807–82. Amer. poet.

Lou·is IX (lōō′ē). "Saint Louis." 1214–70. King of France (1226–70).

Louis XI. 1423–83. King of France (1461–83).

Louis XIII. 1601–43. King of France (1610–43).

Louis XIV. "the Sun King." 1638–1715. King of France (1643–1715).

Louis XV. 1710–74. King of France (1715–74).

Louis XVI. 1754–93. King of France (1774–92); deposed and executed.

Louis XVIII. 1755–1824. King of France (1814–24).

Louis Phi·lippe (fĭ-lĕp′). "the Citizen King." 1773–1850. King of France (1830–48).

Love·lace (lŭv′lās′), **Richard.** 1618–58. English poet.

Low·ell (lō′əl). **1. James Russell.** 1819–91. Amer. poet, essayist, and diplomat. **2. Amy.** 1874–1925. Amer. poet.

Lu·cre·tius (lōō-krē′shəs). 96?–55 B.C. Roman poet and philosopher.

Luke (lōōk), **Saint.** Companion of St. Paul.

Lu·ther (lōō′thər), **Martin.** 1483–1546. German monk; a founder of Protestantism. —**Lu′ther·an** adj. & n.

Lyl·y (lĭl′ē), **John.** 1554?–1606. English novelist and dramatist.

Ly·on (lī′ən), **Mary.** 1797–1849. Amer. educator.

M

Mac·Ar·thur (mək-är′thər), **Douglas.** 1880–1964. Amer. general.

Douglas MacArthur

Ma·cau·lay (mə-kô′lē), **Thomas Babington.** 1800–59. English historian and statesman.

Mac·ca·be·us (măk′ə-bē′əs), **Judas.** d. 160 B.C. Jewish patriot.

Mac·don·ald (mək-dŏn′əld), **Sir John Alexander.** 1815–91. Prime minister of Canada (1867–73 and 1878–91).

Mac·Don·ald (mək-dŏn′əld), **(James) Ramsay.** 1866–1937. British prime minister (1924 and 1929–35).

Mach (mäкн), **Ernst.** 1836–1916. Austrian physicist.

Mach·i·a·vel·li (măk′ē-ə-vĕl′ē), **Niccolò.** 1469–1527. Italian statesman and political theorist. —**Mach′i·a·vel′li·an** adj. & n.

Mac·ken·zie (mə-kĕn′zē). **1. Sir Alexander.** 1764–1820. Scottish explorer. **2. Alexander.** 1822–92. Prime minister of Canada (1873–78).

Mac·Leish (mək-lēsh′), **Archibald.** 1892–1982. Amer. poet and dramatist.

Mac·mil·lan (mək-mĭl′ən), (Maurice) Harold. b. 1894. British prime minister (1957–63).

Mad·i·son (măd′ĭ-sən), James. 1751–1836. 4th U.S. President (1809–17).

James Madison

Mae·ter·linck (mā′tər-lĭngk′), Count Maurice. 1862–1949. Belgian poet and naturalist.

Ma·gel·lan (mə-jĕl′ən), Ferdinand. 1480?–1521. Portuguese navigator.

Mag·say·say (mäg-sī′sī′), Ramón. 1907–57. Philippine statesman.

Mah·ler (mä′lər), Gustav. 1860–1911. Austrian composer.

Mail·er (mā′lər), Norman. b. 1923. Amer. author.

Mail·lol (mä-yôl′), Aristide. 1861–1944. French sculptor.

Mai·mon·i·des (mī-mŏn′ə-dēz′), Moses. 1135–1204. Spanish-born Jewish philosopher.

Ma·kar·i·os III (mä-kä′rē-ôs). 1913–77. Cypriot prelate and statesman.

Mal·a·chi (măl′ə-kī′). 5th cent. B.C. Hebrew prophet.

Mal·a·mud (măl′ə-məd), Bernard. b. 1914. Amer. author.

Mal·lar·mé (mä-lär-mā′), Stéphane. 1842–98. French poet.

Mal·o·ry (măl′ə-rē), Sir Thomas. 15th cent. English author.

Mal·raux (māl-rō′), André. 1901–76. French statesman and author.

Mal·thus (măl′thəs), Thomas Robert. 1766–1834. English economist. —**Mal·thu′sian** (-thōō′zhən) *adj. & n.*

Ma·nas·seh (mə-năs′ə). 7th cent. B.C. king of Judah.

Ma·net (mə-nā′), Edouard. 1832–83. French painter.

Mann (măn). 1. Horace. 1796–1859. Amer. educator. 2. Thomas. 1875–1955. German-born Amer. author.

Man·te·gna (män-tā′nyä), Andrea. 1431–1506. Italian painter.

Mao Ze·dong (mou′ dzŭ′dŏōng′). 1893–1976. Chinese Communist leader.

Ma·rat (mä-rä′), Jean Paul. 1743–93. Swiss-born French revolutionary; assassinated.

Mar·co·ni (mär-kō′nē), Marchese Guglielmo. 1874–1937. Italian engineer and inventor.

Mar·cos (mär′kōs), Ferdinand Edralin. b. 1917. Philippine president (since 1965).

Mar·cus Au·re·li·us An·to·ni·nus (mär′kəs ô-rē′lē-əs ăn′tə-nī′nəs). 121–80. Roman emperor and philosopher.

Mar·ga·ret of An·jou (mär′gə-rət; ăN-zhōō′). 1430–82. Queen of Henry VI of England.

Mar·gre·the II (mär-grā′tə). b. 1940. Queen of Denmark (since 1972).

Ma·ri·a The·re·sa (mə-rē′ə tə-rē′sə, -rā′sə). 1717–80. Queen of Hungary and Bohemia.

Ma·rie An·toi·nette (mə-rē′ ăn′twə-nĕt′). 1755–93. Queen of Louis XVI of France (1774–93); executed.

Mar·in (mär′ĭn), John. 1872–1953. Amer. painter.

Ma·ri·tain (mä-rē-tăN′), Jacques. 1882–1973. French philosopher and critic.

Mar·i·us (mâr′ē-əs), Galus. 155?–86 B.C. Roman general.

Mark (märk), Saint. Author of the 2nd Gospel.

Mark An·to·ny (märk ăn′tə-nē). Also An·tho·ny (-thə-). 83?–30 B.C. Roman general.

Mark·ham (mär′kəm), (Charles) Edwin. 1852–1940. Amer. poet.

Marl·bor·ough (märl′bər-ə, môl′-), 1st Duke of. John Churchill. 1650–1722. English general and statesman.

Mar·lowe (mär′lō), Christopher. 1564–93. English dramatist and poet.

Mar·quand (mär-kwŏnd′), John Phillips. 1893–1960. Amer. author.

Mar·quette (mär-kĕt′), Jacques. 1637–75. French explorer.

Mar·shall (mär′shəl). 1. John. 1755–1835. Amer. statesman and jurist. 2. Thomas Riley. 1854–1925. U.S. Vice President (1913–21). 3. George Catlett. 1880–1959. Amer. soldier, statesman, and diplomat. 4. Thurgood. b. 1908. American jurist.

Mar·tial (mär′shəl). 1st cent. A.D. Roman epigrammatist.

Mar·vell (mär′vəl), Andrew. 1621–78. English poet.

Marx (märks), Karl. 1818–83. German political philosopher and economist. —**Marx′i·an** *adj. & n.* —**Marx′ist** *n.*

Mary (mâr′ē). The mother of Jesus.

Mary I. Mary Tudor. "Bloody Mary." 1516–58. Queen of England and Ireland (1553–58).

Mary II. 1662–94. Queen of England, Scotland, and Ireland (1689–94) with her husband William III.

Mary Mag·da·lene (măg′də-lēn′, -lēn′). A woman cured of evil spirits by Jesus; also identified with the repentant prostitute who anointed Jesus' feet.

Mary Queen of Scots. Mary Stuart. 1542–87. Queen of Scotland; abdicated (1567); beheaded.

Ma·sa·ryk (măs′ə-rĭk), Tomáš Garrigue. 1850–1937. Czech statesman.

Mas·ca·gni (mäs-kä′nyē), Pietro. 1863–1945. Italian composer.

Mase·field (măs′fēld′), John. 1878–1967. English author.

Mas·se·net (măs′ə-nā′), Jules Émile Frédéric. 1842–1912. French composer.

Mas·ters (măs′tərz, mäs′-), Edgar Lee. 1869–1950. Amer. poet.

Math·er (măth′ər, măth′ər), Increase (1639–1723) and Cotton (1663–1728). Amer. clergymen and authors.

Ma·tisse (mä-tēs′), Henri. 1869–1954. French painter.

Mat·thew (măth′yōō), Saint. Apostle and author of the 1st Gospel.

Maugham (môm), W(illiam) Somerset. 1874–1965. English author.

Mau·pas·sant (mō′pə-sänt′, mō-pä-säN′), Guy de. 1850–1893. French author.

Mau·riac (mō-ryäk′), François. 1885–1970. French novelist.

Mau·rois (mô-rwä′), André. 1885–1967. French historian and author.

Max·i·mil·ian (măk′sə-mĭl′yən). 1832–67. Austrian archduke; emperor of Mexico (1864); executed.

Maximilian I. 1459–1519. Holy Roman Emperor (1493–1519).

Max·well (măks′wĕl′, -wəl), **James Clerk.** 1831–79. Scottish physicist.

Maz·a·rin (măz′ə-rĭn), **Jules.** 1602–61. Italian-born French cardinal and statesman.

Maz·zi·ni (mät-tsē′nē), **Giuseppe.** 1805–72. Italian revolutionary patriot.

Mc·Clel·lan (mə-klĕl′ən), **George Brinton.** 1826–85. Amer. general and politician.

Mc·Cor·mick (mə-kôr′mĭk), **Cyrus Hall.** 1809–84. Amer. inventor and manufacturer.

Mc·Kin·ley (mə-kĭn′lē), **William.** 1843–1901. 25th U.S. President (1897–1901); assassinated.

William McKinley

Mead (mēd), **Margaret.** 1901–78. Amer. anthropologist.

Meade (mēd), **George Gordon.** 1815–72. Amer. Union general.

Med·i·ci (mĕd′ĭ-chē′). **1. Cosimo de′.** 1389–1464. Florentine banker, statesman, and art patron. **2. Lorenzo de′.** 1449–92. Florentine statesman, art patron, and author.

Meigh·en (mē′ən), **Arthur.** 1874–1960. Prime minister of Canada (1920–21 and 1926).

Me·ir (mī′ər, mä-ēr′), **Golda.** 1898–1978. Russian-born Amer.-Israeli prime minister (1969–74).

Mel·ville (mĕl′vĭl), **Herman.** 1819–91. Amer. novelist.

Mem·ling (mĕm′lĭng), **Hans.** 1430?–95. Flemish painter.

Me·nan·der (mə-năn′dər). 4th cent. B.C. Greek dramatist.

Men·del (mĕn′dəl), **Gregor Johann.** 1822–84. Austrian botanist.

Men·de·le·ev (mĕn′də-lā′əf), **Dmitri Ivanovich.** 1834–1907. Russian chemist.

Men·dels·sohn (mĕn′dəl-sən), **Felix.** 1809–47. German composer, pianist, and conductor.

Me·not·ti (mə-nôt′ē), **Gian Carlo.** b. 1911. Italian-born Amer. composer.

Mer·ca·tor (mər-kā′tər), **Gerhardus.** 1512–94. Flemish geographer.

Mer·e·dith (mĕr′ə-dĭth), **George.** 1828–1909. English author.

Met·ter·nich (mĕt′ər-nĭkH), **Prince Klemens Wenzel Nepomuk Lothar von.** 1773–1859. Austrian statesman.

Mey·er·beer (mī′ər-bîr′, -bār′), **Giacomo.** 1791–1864. German composer.

Mi·cah (mī′kə). 8th cent. B.C. Hebrew prophet.

Mi·chel·an·ge·lo (mī′kəl-ăn′jə-lō′, mĭk′əl-). 1475–1564. Italian sculptor, painter, architect, and poet.

Mill (mĭl), **John Stuart.** 1806–73. English economist and political theorist.

Mil·lay (mĭ-lā′), **Edna St. Vincent.** 1892–1950. Amer. poet.

Edna St. Vincent Millay

Mil·ler (mĭl′ər), **Arthur.** b. 1915. Amer. playwright.

Mil·let (mĭ-lā′), **Jean François.** 1814–75. French painter.

Milne (mĭln), **A(lan) A(lexander).** 1882–1956. English author.

Mil·ton (mĭl′tən), **John.** 1608–74. English poet.

Min·u·it (mĭn′yōō-wĭt), **Peter.** 1580–1638. Dutch colonial official in America.

Mi·ra·beau (mîr′ə-bō′), **Comte de.** 1749–91. French revolutionary.

Mi·ró (mē-rō′), **Joan.** 1893–1974. Spanish artist.

Mit·ter·and (mē′tə-răN′, -räNd′), **François Maurice.** b. 1916. French statesman.

Mo·di·glia·ni (mō′dē-lyä′nē), **Amedeo.** 1884–1920. Italian painter and sculptor.

Mo·ham·med (mō-hăm′ĭd, -hä′mĭd). Also **Mu·ham·mad** (mōō-). 570?–632. Arab prophet and founder of Islam.

Mo·lière (mōl-yâr′). Jean Baptiste Poquelin. 1622–73. French playwright and actor.

Mol·nár (mōl′när′), **Ferenc.** 1878–1952. Hungarian author.

Mon·dale (mŏn′dāl′), **Walter Frederic.** b. 1928. U.S. Vice President (1977–81).

Mon·dri·an (mŏn′drē-än′), **Piet.** 1872–1944. Dutch painter.

Mo·net (mō-nā′), **Claude.** 1840–1926. French painter.

Mon·mouth (mŏn′məth, mŭn′-), **Duke of.** James Scott. 1649–85. English pretender to the throne.

Mon·roe (mən-rō′), **James.** 1758–1831. 5th U.S. President (1817–25).

James Monroe

Mon·taigne (mŏn-tān′), **Michel Eyquem de.** 1533–92. French essayist.

Mont·calm (mŏnt-käm′), **Marquis Louis Joseph de.** 1712–59. French commander in Canada.

ă pat ā pay â care ä father ĕ pet ē be ĭ pit ī tie ī pier ŏ pot ō toe ô paw, for oi noise ŏŏ took ŏŏ boot ou out th thin th this ŭ cut û urge yŏŏ abuse zh vision ə about, item, edible, gallop, circus

Mon·tes·quieu (mŏn'tə-skyōō'), Baron de la Brède et de. Charles de Secondat. 1689–1755. French political philosopher.

Mon·tes·so·ri (mŏn'tə-sôr'ē, -sōr'ē), Maria. 1870–1952. Italian physician and educator.

Mon·te·zu·ma II (mŏn'tə-zōō'mə). 1480?–1520. Last Aztec emperor of Mexico.

Mont·gom·er·y (mənt-gŭm'rē), Sir Bernard Law. 1887–1976. British army officer.

Moore (mōōr). 1. Marianne Craig. 1887–1972. Amer. poet. 2. Henry. b. 1898. English sculptor.

More (môr, mōr), Saint (Sir) Thomas. 1478–1535. English statesman and author; beheaded.

Mor·gan (môr'gən), J(ohn) P(ierpont). 1837–1913. Amer. financier.

Mor·ris (môr'ĭs, mŏr'-). 1. Robert. 1734–1806. Amer. Revolutionary financier and political leader. 2. Gouverneur. 1752–1816. Amer. diplomat and political leader. 3. William. 1834–96. English poet, artist, and socialist.

Morse (môrs), Samuel Finley Breese. 1791–1872. Amer. artist; promoter of the telegraph.

Mor·ton (môrt'n). Levi Parsons. 1824–1920. U.S. Vice President (1889–93).

Mos·es (mō'zĭz, -zĭs). Hebrew prophet and lawgiver.

Moses, Anna Mary Robertson. "Grandma Moses." 1860–1961. Amer. painter.

Mott (mŏt), Lucretia Coffin. 1793–1880. Amer. social reformer.

Mount·bat·ten (mount-băt'n), Louis. 1st Earl Mountbatten of Burma. 1900–79. British naval officer; assassinated.

Mous·sorg·sky (mə-zôrg'skē), Modest Petrovich. 1835–81. Russian composer.

Mo·zart (mōt'särt), Wolfgang Amadeus. 1756–91. Austrian composer.

Mu·ham·mad (mŏŏ-hăm'ĭd, -hä'mĭd). Var. of Mohammed.

Muir (myŏŏr), John. 1838–1914. Scottish-born Amer. naturalist, explorer, conservationist, and writer.

Mun·ro (mən-rō'), H(ector) H(ugh). "Saki." 1870–1916. English author.

Mu·rat (myŏŏ-rä'), Joachim. 1767?–1815. French marshal; king of Naples (1808–15).

Mu·ril·lo (mŏŏ-rĭl'ō), Bartolomé Esteban. 1617–82. Spanish painter.

Mus·so·li·ni (mōōs'sə-lē'nē), Benito. "Il Duce." 1883–1945. Fascist dictator of Italy (1922–43).

My·ron (mī'rən). 5th cent. B.C. Greek sculptor.

N

Na·bo·kov (nä-bô'kôf), Vladimir Vladimirovich. 1899–1977. Russian-born Amer. novelist and poet.

Na·hum (nā'həm, -əm). 7th cent. B.C. Hebrew prophet.

Nan·sen (năn'sən, nän'-), Fridtjof. 1861–1930. Norwegian Arctic explorer, statesman, and scientist.

Na·pi·er (nā'pē-ər), John. 1550–1617. Scottish mathematician.

Na·po·le·on I (nə-pō'lē-ən, -pōl'yən). Surname, Bonaparte. 1769–1821. Emperor of the French (1804–15). —**Na·po·le·on'ic** adj.

Napoleon III. "Louis Napoleon." 1808–73. Emperor of France (1852–70).

Nash (năsh), Ogden. 1902–71. Amer. poet.

Nas·ser (nä'sər, năs'ər), Gamal Abdel. 1918–70. Egyptian soldier and statesman.

Na·than·ael (nə-thăn'yəl). Bartholomew.

Na·tion (nā'shən), Carry Amelia Moore. 1846–1911. Amer. temperance reformer.

Neb·u·chad·nez·zar II (nĕb'ə-kəd-nĕz'ər, nĕb'-yŏŏ-). King of Babylon (605–562 B.C.).

Nef·er·ti·ti (nĕf'ər-tē'tē). Queen of Egypt in the early 14th cent. B.C.

Ne·he·mi·ah (nē'hə-mī'əh). 5th cent. B.C. Hebrew leader.

Neh·ru (nā'rōō), Jawaharlal. 1889–1964. 1st prime minister of India (1947–64).

Nel·son (nĕl'sən), Viscount Horatio. 1758–1805. English admiral.

Ne·ro (nîr'ō). A.D. 37–68. Roman emperor (54–68).

Nev·el·son (nĕv'əl-sən), Louise. b. 1900. Russian-born Amer. sculptor.

New·man (nōō'mən, nyōō'-), John Henry. 1801–90. English theologian.

New·ton (nōōt'n, nyōōt'n), Sir Isaac. 1642–1727. English mathematician, scientist, and philosopher. —**New·ton'i·an** adj.

Nich·o·las (nĭk'ə-ləs), Saint. Often identified with Santa Claus. 4th-cent. bishop.

Nicholas II. 1868–1918. Czar of Russia (1894–1917); executed.

Nicholas of Cu·sa (kyōō'zə). 1401–64. German cardinal and philosopher.

Nie·buhr (nē'bŏŏr', -bər), Reinhold. 1892–1971. Amer. theologian.

Nie·tzsche (nē'chə, -chē), Friedrich Wilhelm. 1844–1900. German philosopher.

Night·in·gale (nīt'n-gāl', nī'tĭng-), Florence. 1820–1910. English nursing pioneer.

Ni·jin·sky (nə-jĭn'skē, -zhĭn'skē), Vaslav. 1890–1950. Russian-born ballet dancer.

Nils·son (nĭl'sən), Birgit. b. 1918. Swedish operatic soprano.

Nim·itz (nĭm'ĭts), Chester William. 1885–1966. Amer. admiral.

Nix·on (nĭk'sən), Richard Milhous. b. 1913. 37th U.S. President (1969–74); resigned.

Richard M. Nixon

No·ah (nō'əh). Hebrew patriarch.

No·bel (nō-bĕl'), Alfred Bernhard. 1833–96. Swedish chemist, inventor, and philanthropist.

North (nôrth), Frederick. "Lord North." 1732–92. English prime minister (1770–82).

Nos·tra·da·mus (nŏs'trə-dā'məs, -dä'-, nōs'-). 1503–66. French astrologer and physician.

Noyes (noiz), Alfred. 1880–1958. English poet and critic.

O

Oak·ley (ōk'lē), Annie. 1860–1926. Amer. sharpshooter.

O·ba·di·ah (ō'bə-dī'ə). 6th cent. B.C. Hebrew prophet.

O'Ca·sey (ō-kā'sē), Sean. 1880–1964. Irish dramatist.

O·dets (ō-dĕts'), Clifford. 1906–63. Amer. playwright.

Of·fen·bach (ŏ'fən-bäk', ŏf'ən-), Jacques. 1819–80. French composer.

O·gle·thorpe (ō'gəl-thôrp'), James Edward. 1696–1785. English philanthropist and colonizer.

O'Keeffe (ō-kēf'), Georgia. b. 1887. Amer. painter.

O·laf I (ō'ləf). Also O·lav (ō'läv, ō'läf). 969?–1000. King of Norway (995–1000).

Olaf II. "Saint Olaf." 995?–1030. King of Norway (1016–28).

Olaf V. b. 1903. King of Norway (since 1957).

O·mar Khay·yám (ō'mär' kī-yäm', -ăm', ō'mər). 1050?–1123? Persian poet, mathematician, and astronomer.

O'Neill (ō-nēl'), Eugene Gladstone. 1888–1953. Amer. dramatist.

Eugene O'Neill

Op·pen·heim·er (ŏp'ən-hī'mər), J(ulius) Robert. 1904–67. Amer. theoretical physicist.

Or·te·ga y Gas·set (ôr-tě'gä ē gä-sĕt'), José. 1883–1955. Spanish author and philosopher.

Or·well (ôr'wĕl', -wəl), George. Eric Blair. 1903–50. English author.

O·tis (ō'tĭs), James. 1725–83. Amer. Revolutionary leader.

Ot·to I (ŏt'ō). "the Great." 912–73. 1st Holy Roman Emperor (962–73).

Ov·id (ŏv'ĭd). 43 B.C.–A.D. 17? Roman poet.

Ow·en (ō'ĭn), Robert. 1771–1858. Welsh industrialist and reformer.

Ow·ens (ō'ĭnz), Jesse. 1913–80. Amer. Olympic athlete.

P

Pa·de·rew·ski (păd'ə-rĕf'skē, pä'də-), Ignace Jan. 1860–1941. Polish concert pianist and statesman.

Pa·ga·ni·ni (păg'ə-nē'nē, pä'gə-), Nicolò. 1782–1840. Italian violinist and composer.

Pah·la·vi (pä'lä-vē'), Mohammed Riza. Also Pah·le·vi. 1919–79. Shah of Iran (1941–78); deposed.

Paine (pān), Thomas. 1737–1809. English-born Amer. Revolutionary leader.

Pal·la·dio (päl-lä'dyō), Andrea. 1508–80. Italian architect. —Pal·la'di·an (pə-lä'dē-ən) adj.

Palm·er·ston (pä'mər-stən), 3rd Viscount. Henry John Temple. 1784–1865. British prime minister (1855–58 and 1859–65).

Pank·hurst (păngk'hûrst'), Emmeline Goulden. 1858–1928. English suffragist.

Par·a·cel·sus (păr'ə-sĕl'səs), Philippus Aureolus. 1493–1541. Swiss alchemist.

Park (pärk), Mungo. 1771–1806. Scottish explorer in Africa.

Par·ker (pär'kər), Dorothy Rothschild. 1893–1967. Amer. writer.

Park·man (pärk'mən), Francis. 1823–93. Amer. historian.

Par·nell (pär-nĕl', pär'nəl), Charles Stewart. 1846–91. Irish nationalist leader.

Parr (pär), Catherine. 1512–48. Queen of England as 6th wife of Henry VIII.

Pas·cal (păs-kăl'), Blaise. 1623–62. French philosopher and mathematician.

Pas·ter·nak (păs'tər-năk'), Boris Leonidovich. 1890–1960. Russian author.

Pas·teur (pă-stûr'), Louis. 1822–95. French chemist.

Pat·rick (păt'rĭk), Saint. 389?–461? Traditionally, patron saint of Ireland.

Pat·ton (păt'n), George Smith. 1885–1945. Amer. general.

Paul (pôl), ·Saint. A.D. 5?–67? Apostle to the Gentiles. —Paul'ine' (-līn') adj.

Paul III. 1468–1549. Pope (1534–49).

Paul VI. 1897–1978. Pope (1963–78).

Paul·ing (pô'lĭng), Linus Carl. b. 1901. Amer. chemist.

Pav·lov (păv'lŏv, păv'lôf'), Ivan Petrovich. 1849–1936. Russian physiologist.

Pav·lo·va (păv-lō'və, păv-), Anna. 1885–1931. Russian ballerina.

Peale (pēl), Charles Willson. 1741–1827. Amer. painter.

Pear·son (pîr'sən), Lester Bowles. 1897–1972. Prime minister of Canada (1963–68).

Pea·ry (pîr'ē), Robert Edwin. 1856–1920. Amer. naval officer and Arctic explorer.

Peel (pēl), Sir Robert. 1788–1850. British prime minister (1834–35 and 1841–46).

Penn (pĕn), William. 1644–1718. English Quaker leader and colonizer.

Pep·in (pĕp'ĭn). "the Short." 714?–68. King of the Franks (751–68).

Pep·ys (pēps), Samuel. 1633–1703. English diarist.

Per·i·cles (pĕr'ə-klēz'). 495?–429 B.C. Athenian statesman.

Per·kins (pûr'kənz), Frances. 1882–1965. Amer. social reformer and public official.

Pe·rón (pĕ-rōn'). Argentinian popular and political leaders, including Juan Domingo (1895–1974), Maria Eva Duarte de ("Evita"; 1919–52), and Isabel ("Isabelita"; b. 1931).

Per·ry (pĕr'ē), Oliver Hazard (1785–1819) and Matthew Calbraith (1794–1858). Amer. naval officers.

Per·shing (pûr'shĭng), John Joseph ("Black Jack"). 1860–1948. Amer. general.

Pé·tain (pā-tăn'), Henri Philippe. 1856–1951. French soldier and politician.

Pe·ter (pē'tər), Saint. Simon Peter. d. A.D. 67? One of the 12 Apostles.

Peter I. "the Great." 1672–1725. Czar of Russia (1682–1725).

Pe·trarch (pē'trärk'). 1304–74. Italian poet. —Pe·trarch'an (pī-trär'kən) adj.

Phid·i·as (fĭd'ē-əs). 5th cent. B.C. Athenian sculptor.

Phil·ip (fĭl'ĭp). Duke of Edinburgh. b. 1921. Husband of Elizabeth II of Great Britain.

Philip, Saint. One of the 12 Apostles.

Philip II. 382–336 B.C. King of Macedonia (359–336).

Philip II. 1165–1223. King of France (1180–1223).

Philip II. 1527–98. King of Spain (1556–98).

Philip IV. 1268–1314. King of France (1285–1314).

Pi·cas·so (pĭ-kä′sō, pē-), **Pablo.** 1881–1973. Spanish-born painter and sculptor.

Pick·ett (pĭk′ĭt), **George Edward.** 1825–75. Amer. Confederate general.

Pierce (pîrs), **Franklin.** 1804–69. 14th U.S. President (1853–57).

Pi·late (pī′lĭt), **Pontius.** Roman procurator of Judea (A.D. 26?–36?).

Pin·dar (pĭn′dər). 522?–443 B.C. Greek lyric poet. —**Pin·dar′ic** (-dăr′ĭk) adj.

Pi·ran·del·lo (pĭr′ən-dĕl′ō), **Luigi.** 1867–1936. Italian author.

Pi·sis·tra·tus (pĭ-sĭs′trə-təs, pī-). 605?–527 B.C. Ruler of Athens (560–527).

Pis·sar·o (pĭ-sär′ō), **Camille.** 1830–1903. French painter.

Pitt (pĭt). **1. William.** 1st Earl of Chatham. 1708–78. English statesman. **2. William.** 2nd Earl of Chatham. 1759–1806. British prime minister (1783–1801 and 1804–6).

Pi·us V (pī′əs). 1504–72. Pope (1566–72).

Pius IX. 1792–1878. Pope (1846–78).

Pius X. 1835–1914. Pope (1903–14).

Pius XI. 1857–1939. Pope (1922–39).

Pius XII. 1876–1958. Pope (1939–58).

Pi·zar·ro (pĭ-zär′ō), **Francisco.** 1470?–1541. Spanish explorer.

Planck (plängk), **Max Karl Ernst Ludwig.** 1858–1947. German physicist.

Pla·to (plā′tō). 427?–347 B.C. Greek philosopher. —**Pla·ton′ic** (plə-tŏn′ĭk) adj.

Plau·tus (plô′təs), **Titus Maccius.** 254?–184 B.C. Roman playwright.

Plin·y (plĭn′ē). **1.** "the Elder." A.D. 23–79. Roman scholar. **2. Plin·y** "the Younger." A.D. 62–113. Roman consul and orator.

Plu·tarch (plōō′tärk′). A.D. 46?–120? Greek biographer and philosopher.

Po·ca·hon·tas (pō′kə-hŏn′təs). 1595?–1617. Amer. Indian princess.

Poe (pō), **Edgar Allan.** 1809–49. Amer. author.

Polk (pōk), **James Knox.** 1795–1849. 11th U.S. President (1845–49).

Pol·lock (pŏl′ək), **Jackson.** 1912–56. Amer. artist.

Po·lo (pō′lō), **Marco.** 1254?–1324? Venetian traveler to the court of Kublai Khan.

Pom·pa·dour (pŏm′pə-dôr′, -dŏr′), Marquise de. 1721–64. Mistress of Louis XV of France.

Pom·pey (pŏm′pē). 106–48 B.C. Roman statesman and general.

Ponce de Le·ón (pŏns′ də lē′ən), **Juan.** 1460?–1521. Spanish explorer.

Pon·ti·ac (pŏn′tē-ăk′). d. 1769. Ottawa Indian chief.

Pope (pōp), **Alexander.** 1688–1744. English poet and satirist.

Por·ter (pôr′tər, pōr′-). **1. William Sydney.** "O. Henry." 1862–1910. Amer. author. **2. Katherine Anne.** 1890–1980. Amer. author. **3. Cole.** 1893–1964. Amer. composer and lyricist.

Pot·ter (pŏt′ər), **Beatrix.** 1866–1943. English author and illustrator.

Pound (pound), **Ezra Loomis.** 1885–1972. Amer. poet and critic.

Pow·ha·tan (pou′ə-tăn′). 1550?–1618. Amer. Indian chief.

Prax·it·e·les (prăk-sĭt′l-ēz′). 4th cent. B.C. Greek sculptor.

Pres·cott (prĕs′kət), **William Hickling.** 1796–1859. Amer. historian.

Price (prīs), **(Mary) Leontyne.** b. 1927. Amer. operatic soprano.

Priest·ley (prēst′lē), **Joseph.** 1733–1804. English chemist.

Pro·kof·iev (prə-kôf′yəf, -yĕf′), **Sergei Sergeevich.** 1891–1953. Russian composer.

Pro·tag·o·ras (prō-tăg′ər-əs). 481?–411 B.C. Greek philosopher.

Prou·dhon (prōō-dôn′), **Pierre Joseph.** 1809–65. French utopian socialist.

Proust (prōōst), **Marcel.** 1871–1922. French novelist and critic.

Ptol·e·my (tŏl′ə-mē). 2nd cent. Greek astronomer, mathematician, and geographer. —**Ptol′e·ma′ic** (tŏl′ə-mā′ĭk) adj.

Ptolemy I. 367?–283 B.C. King of Egypt (323–285).

Puc·ci·ni (pōō-chē′nē), **Giacomo.** 1858–1924. Italian composer.

Pu·las·ki (pōō-lăs′kē), **Casimir.** 1748?–79. Polish general in the Amer. Revolution.

Pu·lit·zer (pōō′lĭt-sər, pyōō′lĭt-), **Joseph.** 1847–1911. Hungarian-born Amer. newspaper publisher.

Push·kin (pōōsh′kĭn), **Aleksandr Sergeevich.** 1799–1837. Russian poet.

Pym (pĭm), **John.** 1584–1643. English statesman.

Py·thag·o·ras (pĭ-thăg′ər-əs). d. 497 B.C. Greek philosopher. —**Py·thag′o·re′an** (-ə-rē′ən) adj. & n.

Q

Qad·da·fi (kə-dä′fē), **Muammar.** b. 1943. Libyan political leader.

Ques·nay (kĕ-nā′), **François.** 1694–1774. French physician and political economist.

Que·zon (kĕ′sôn′), **Manuel Luis.** 1878–1944. Philippine statesman.

Quin·til·ian (kwĭn-tĭl′yən). 1st cent. A.D. Roman rhetorician.

R

Rab·e·lais (răb′ə-lā), **François.** 1494?–1553. French author. —**Rab′e·lai′se·an** (-zē-ən, zhən) adj.

Rach·ma·ni·noff (răk-mä′nĭ-nôf), **Sergei Vassilievich.** 1873–1943. Russian-born composer and pianist.

Ra·cine (rà-sēn′), **Jean Baptiste.** 1639–99. French playwright.

Rai·nier III (rĕ-nyā′, rā-nîr′). b. 1923. Prince of Monaco (since 1949).

Ra·leigh (rô′lē), **Sir Walter.** 1552?–1618. English navigator, colonizer, and historian.

Ram·e·ses II (răm′ĭ-sēz′). Also **Ram·ses** (răm′sēz). King of Egypt (1292–1225 B.C.).

Ram·say (răm′zē), **Sir William.** 1852–1916. British chemist.

Raph·a·el (răf′ē-əl, rä′fē-). 1483–1520. Italian painter and architect.

Ras·pu·tin (răs-pyōō′tĭn), **Grigori Efimovich.** 1871?–1916. Russian monk; assassinated.

Ra·vel (rə-vĕl′, rä-), **Maurice Joseph.** 1875–1937. French composer.

Ray·burn (rā′bûrn′), **Samuel Taliaferro.** 1882–1961. Amer. legislator.

Rea·gan (rā′gən, rĕ′-), Ronald Wilson. b. 1911. 40th U.S. President (since 1981).

Ronald Reagan

Reed (rēd), Walter. 1851–1902. Amer. army physician.

Re·marque (rə-märk′), Erich Maria. 1898–1970. German-born Amer. novelist.

Rem·brandt (rĕm′brănt). 1606–69. Dutch painter.

Re·noir (rĕn′wär′), Pierre Auguste. 1841–1919. French painter.

Reu·ther (rōō′thər), Walter Philip. 1907–70. Amer. labor leader.

Re·vere (rĭ-vîr′), Paul. 1735–1818. Amer. silversmith, engraver, and Revolutionary patriot.

Reyn·olds (rĕn′əldz), Sir Joshua. 1723–92. English painter.

Rhee (rē), Syngman. 1875–1965. South Korean political leader.

Rhodes (rōdz), Cecil John. 1853–1902. English financier and colonizer.

Ri·car·do (rĭ-kär′dō), David. 1772–1823. English economist.

Rich·ard I (rĭch′ərd). "the Lion-Hearted." 1157–99. King of England (1189–99).

Richard II. 1367–1400. King of England (1377–99).

Richard III. 1452–85. King of England (1483–85).

Rich·ard·son (rĭch′ərd-sən), Samuel. 1689–1761. English author.

Ri·che·lieu (rĭsh′ə-lōō′, rē-shə-lyœ′), Duc de. 1585–1642. French cardinal and statesman.

Rick·o·ver (rĭk′ō-vər), Hyman George. b. 1900. Polish-born Amer. naval officer.

Rim·ski-Kor·sa·kov (rĭm′skē-kôr′sə-kôf), Nikolai Andreevich. 1844–1908. Russian composer.

Ri·ve·ra (rē-vĕ′rä), Diego. 1886–1957. Mexican artist.

Rob·ert I (rŏb′ərt). "the Bruce." 1274–1329. King of Scotland (1306–29).

Robes·pierre (rōbz′pē-âr), Maximilien François Marie Isidore de. 1758–94. French revolutionary leader; guillotined.

Rob·in·son (rŏb′ĭn-sən). 1. Edwin Arlington. 1869–1935. Amer. poet. 2. John Roosevelt ("Jackie"). 1919–72. Amer. baseball player.

Ro·cham·beau (rō-shăm′bō′, rō-shän-bō′), Comte de. 1725–1807. French army officer.

Rock·e·fel·ler (rŏk′ə-fĕl′ər). Family of Amer. businessmen and philanthropists, including: 1. John Davison. 1839–1937. 2. John Davison, Jr. 1874–1960. 3. Nelson Aldrich. 1908–79. U.S. Vice President (1974–77).

Rock·ing·ham (rŏk′ĭng-əm), 2nd Marquis of. 1730–82. English prime minister (1765–66 and 1782).

Ro·din (rō-dăN′), (François) Auguste René. 1840–1917. French sculptor.

Roent·gen (rĕnt′gən, rŭnt′-), Wilhelm Konrad. 1845–1923. German physicist.

Ro·get (rō-zhā′), Peter Mark. 1779–1869. English physician, scholar, and compiler.

Röl·vaag (rōl′väg), Ole Edvart. 1876–1931. Norwegian-born Amer. author.

Rom·berg (rŏm′bərg), Sigmund. 1887–1951. Hungarian-born Amer. composer.

Rom·mel (rŏm′əl), Erwin. 1891–1944. German army officer.

Rom·ney (rŏm′nē, rŭm′-), George. 1734–1802. English painter.

Roo·se·velt (rō′zə-vĕlt, rōz′vĕlt, -vəlt). 1. Theodore. 1858–1919. 26th U.S. President (1901–9). 2. Franklin Delano. 1882–1945. 32nd U.S. President (1933–45). 3. (Anna) Eleanor. 1884–1962. Amer. diplomat, writer, and humanitarian.

Theodore Roosevelt

Franklin D. Roosevelt

Root (rōōt), Elihu. 1845–1937. Amer. statesman.

Rose·crans (rōz′krănz), William Starke. 1819–98. Amer. Union general.

Ross (rôs). 1. Betsy Griscom. 1752–1836. Amer. Revolutionary patriot. 2. Sir James Clark. 1800–62. English polar explorer.

Ros·set·ti (rō-zĕt′ē), Dante Gabriel (1828–82) and Christina Georgina (1830–94). English pre-Raphaelite poets.

Ros·si·ni (rō-sē′nē), Gioacchino Antonio. 1792–1868. Italian composer.

Ros·tand (rō-stäN′), Edmond. 1868–1918. French author.

Roth·schild (rōth′chĭld, rôs-). Family of German bankers, including Meyer Amschel (1743–1812) and Nathan Meyer (1777–1836).

Rou·ault (rōō-ō′), Georges. 1871–1958. French painter.

Rous·seau (rōō-sō′). 1. Jean Jacques. 1712–78.

French author. 2. **Henri ("Le Douanier").** 1844–1910. French painter.

Ru·bens (rōō'bənz), **Peter Paul.** 1577–1640. Flemish painter. —**Ru'ben·esque'** (-ĕsk') *adj.*

Ru·bin·stein (rōō'bən-stīn). 1. **Anton Gregor.** 1829–94. Russian pianist and composer. 2. **Artur.** 1886–1982. Polish-born Amer. pianist.

Ru·dolf I (rōō'dŏlf). 1218–91. Holy Roman Emperor (1273–91).

Ru·pert (rōō'pərt), **Prince.** 1619–82. German-born English military and political leader.

Rus·kin (rŭs'kĭn), **John.** 1819–1900. English author.

Rus·sell (rŭs'əl), **Lord Bertrand Arthur William.** 1872–1970. English philosopher and mathematician.

Ruth (rōōth), **George Herman ("Babe").** 1895–1948. Amer. baseball player.

Ruth·er·ford (rŭth'ər-fərd), **Ernest.** 1871–1937. New Zealand-born English physicist.

S

Sa·bin (sā'bĭn), **Albert Bruce.** b. 1906. Polish-born Amer. physician and microbiologist.

Sac·a·ja·we·a (săk'ə-jə-wē'ə). 1788?–1812. Amer. Indian guide and interpreter for Lewis and Clark.

Sac·co (săk'ō, säk'kō), **Nicola.** 1891–1927. Italian-born Amer. anarchist; executed.

Sa·dat (sə-dăt', -dät'), **Anwar el-.** 1918–81. Egyptian statesman; assassinated.

Sade (säd, säd), **Comte Donatien Alphonse François de. "Marquis de Sade."** 1740–1814. French author and libertine.

Saint-Gau·dens (sānt-gô'dənz), **Augustus.** 1848–1907. Irish-born Amer. sculptor.

Saint Lau·rent (săn lô-răN'), **Louis Stephen.** 1882–1973. Canadian prime minister (1948–57).

Saint-Saëns (săn-säNs'), **(Charles) Camille.** 1835–1921. French composer.

Sa·kha·rov (sä'kə-rôf', -rôv'), **Andrei Dimitrievich.** b. 1921. Russian physicist.

Sal·a·din (săl'ə-dīn). 1138?–93. Sultan of Egypt and Syria.

Sal·in·ger (săl'ən-jər), **J(erome) D(avid).** b. 1919. Amer. author.

Salk (sôlk), **Jonas Edward.** b.1914. Amer. microbiologist.

Sal·lust (săl'əst). 86–34 B.C. Roman historian and politician.

Sam·o·set (săm'ə-sĕt', sə-mōs'ĭt). Early 17th cent. Amer. Indian chief.

Sam·u·el (săm'yōō-əl). 11th cent. B.C. Hebrew prophet.

Sand (sănd), **George.** Amandine Aurore Lucie Dupin. 1804–76. French novelist.

Sand·burg (sănd'bûrg'), **Carl.** 1878–1967. Amer. poet and biographer.

Sang·er (săng'ər), **Margaret Higgins.** 1883–1966. Amer. social reformer.

San·ta An·na or **An·a** (săn'tə än'ə, săn'tä ä'nä), **Antonio López de.** 1795?–1876. Mexican military and political leader.

San·ta·ya·na (săn'tĕ-ăn'ə, -än'ə, săn'tə-yä'nə, sän'-), **George.** 1863–1952. Spanish-born Amer. educator, philosopher, and poet.

Sap·pho (săf'ō). 7th cent. B.C. Greek poet.

Sargent (sär'jənt), **John Singer.** 1856–1925. Amer. painter.

Sargon II (sär'gŏn). d. 705 B.C. King of Assyria (722–705).

Sar·tre (sär'tr'), **Jean Paul.** 1905–80. French philosopher and author.

Saul (sôl). 11th cent. B.C. king of Israel.

Sav·o·na·ro·la (săv'ə-nə-rō'lə), **Girolamo.** 1452–98. Italian religious reformer; burned as a heretic.

Scar·lat·ti (skär-lät'ē), **Alessandro** (1659–1725) and **(Giuseppe) Domenico** (1683–1757). Italian composers.

Schil·ler (shĭl'ər), **Johann Christoph Friedrich von.** 1759–1805. German poet and dramatist.

Schlie·mann (shlē'män'), **Heinrich.** 1822–90. German archaeologist.

Schmidt (shmĭt), **Helmut.** b. 1918. West German statesman.

Schön·berg (shœn'bûrg', -bĕrk'), **Arnold.** 1874–1951. Austrian composer.

Scho·pen·hau·er (shō'pən-hou'ər), **Arthur.** 1788–1860. German philosopher.

Schu·bert (shōō'bərt), **Franz.** 1797–1828. Austrian composer.

Schu·mann (shōō-män'), **Robert.** 1810–56. German composer.

Schwei·tzer (shwīt'sər, shvīt'sər), **Albert.** 1875–1965. French philosopher, missionary physician, and musicologist.

Scip·i·o (skĭp'ē-ō'). 1. **Publius Cornelius. "the Elder."** 237–183 B.C. Roman general. 2. **Publius Cornelius. "the Younger."** 185–129 B.C. Roman consul and general.

Scopes (skōps), **John Thomas.** 1901–70. American teacher; convicted (1925) for teaching evolution.

Scott (skŏt). 1. **Sir Walter.** 1771–1832. Scottish author. 2. **Winfield.** 1786–1866. Amer. military officer. 3. **Dred.** 1795?–1858. Amer. slave; subject of a proslavery decision by Supreme Court (1857). 4. **Robert Falcon.** 1868–1912. English explorer of the Antarctic.

Se·leu·cids (sĭ-lōō'sĭdz). Six dynastic leaders in Asia Minor from 312 B.C. to 64 B.C., esp. **Seleu·cus I** (-kəs), 358?–280 B.C., ruled in Syria (306–280).

Sen·e·ca (sĕn'ə-kə), **Lucius Annaeus.** 4? B.C.–A.D. 65. Roman philosopher and author.

Sen·nach·er·ib (sĕ-năk'ər-ĭb'). King of Assyria (705–681 B.C.).

Se·quoy·a (sĭ-kwoi'ə). 1770?–1843. Cherokee Indian leader.

Se·ton (sē'tən), **Saint Elizabeth Ann Bayley. "Mother Seton."** 1774–1821. Amer. religious leader.

Seu·rat (sœ-rä'), **Georges Pierre.** 1859–91. French painter.

Se·ve·rus (sə-vîr'əs), **Lucius Septimius.** 146–211. Roman emperor (193–211).

Sew·ard (sōō'ərd), **William Henry.** 1801–72. Amer. statesman.

Sey·mour (sē'môr, -mōr), **Jane.** 1509?–37. Queen of England as 3rd wife of Henry VIII.

Shake·speare (shāk'spîr), **William.** 1564–1616. English dramatist and poet. —**Shake·spear'e·an** or **Shake·spear'i·an** *adj. & n.*

Shaw (shô), **George Bernard.** 1856–1950. Irish-born English author. —**Sha'vi·an** (shā'vē-ən) *adj. & n.*

Shel·ley (shĕl'ē). 1. **Percy Bysshe.** 1792–1822. English poet. 2. **Mary Wollstonecraft Godwin.** 1797–1851. English novelist.

Shep·ard (shĕp'ərd), **Alan Bartlett, Jr.** b. 1923. First Amer. astronaut in space (1961).

Sher·i·dan (shĕr'ə-dən). 1. **Richard Brinsley.** 1751–1816. English dramatist. 2. **Philip Henry.** 1831–88. Amer. Union general.

Sher·man (shûr'mən). 1. **Roger.** 1721–93. Amer. statesman and patriot. 2. **William Tecumseh.** 1820–91. Amer. Union commander. 3. **James Schoolcraft.** 1855–1912. U.S. Vice President (1909–12).

Shos·ta·ko·vich (shŏs′tə-kô′vĭch), **Dmitri.** 1906-75. Russian composer.

Si·be·li·us (sĭ-bā′lē-əs, -bāl′yəs), **Jean.** 1865-1957. Finnish composer.

Sid·ney (sĭd′nē), **Sir Philip.** 1554-86. English poet and essayist.

Si·kor·sky (sĭ-kôr′skē), **Igor Ivanovich.** 1889-1972. Russian-born Amer. aviation pioneer.

Si·mon Ze·lo·tes (sī′mən zē-lō′tēz). One of the 12 Apostles.

Sin·clair (sĭn-klâr′), **Upton (Beall).** 1878-1968. Amer. novelist.

Sit·ting Bull (sĭt′ĭng bŏŏl). 1834?-90. Dakota Indian leader.

Smith (smĭth). **1. John.** 1580-1631. English adventurer, colonist in Virginia, and author. **2. Adam.** 1723-90. Scottish political economist. **3. Joseph.** 1805-44. Amer. founder of the Church of Jesus Christ of Latter-day Saints. **4. Alfred Emanuel.** 1873-1944. Amer. political leader. **5. Margaret Chase.** b. 1897. Amer. political leader.

Smith·son (smĭth′sən), **James.** 1765-1829. English chemist and philanthropist.

Smol·lett (smŏl′ĭt), **Tobias George.** 1721-71. English novelist.

Smuts (smŭts), **Jan Christiaan.** 1870-1950. South African military and political leader.

Snow (snō), **C(harles) P(ercy).** 1905-80. English novelist.

Soc·ra·tes (sŏk′rə-tēz′). 470?-399 B.C. Greek philosopher. **—So·crat·ic** (sə-krăt′ĭk) *adj.*

Sol·o·mon (sŏl′ə-mən). 10th cent. B.C. king of Israel.

So·lon (sō′lən), 638?-559 B.C. Athenian statesman and poet.

Sol·zhe·ni·tsyn (sŏl′zhə-nē′tsĭn), **Aleksandr Isaeevich.** b. 1918. Russian author.

Soph·o·cles (sŏf′ə-klēz′). 496?-406 B.C. Greek dramatist.

Sou·sa (sōō′zə, -sə), **John Philip.** 1854-1932. Amer. bandmaster and composer.

South·ey (sŭth′ē), **Robert.** 1774-1843. English poet.

Spar·ta·cus (spär′tə-kəs). d. 71 B.C. Thracian leader of revolt against Rome (73-71).

Spen·cer (spĕn′sər), **Herbert.** 1820-1903. English philosopher.

Spen·ser (spĕn′sər), **Edmund.** 1552?-99. English poet. **—Spen·se′ri·an** (-sîr′ē-ən) *adj.*

Spi·no·za (spĭ-nō′zə), **Baruch.** 1632-77. Dutch philosopher.

Spock (spŏk), **Benjamin McLane.** b. 1903. Amer. pediatrician and educator.

Squan·to (skwän′tō). d. 1622. Indian who befriended Pilgrims at Plymouth Colony.

Staël (stäl), **Madame de. Anne Louise Germaine Neckar.** 1766-1817. French author and literary patron.

Sta·lin (stä′lĭn), **Joseph.** 1879-1953. Soviet Communist revolutionary and political leader.

Stan·dish (stăn′dĭsh), **Myles.** 1584?-1656. English colonial settler in America.

Stan·ley (stăn′lē), **Sir Henry Morton.** 1841-1904. Welsh-born journalist and explorer.

Stan·ton (stăn′tən), **Elizabeth Cady.** 1815-1902. Amer. social reformer.

Steele (stēl), **Sir Richard.** 1672-1729. English essayist.

Stein (stīn), **Gertrude.** 1874-1946. Amer. author.

Stein·beck (stīn′bĕk), **John Ernst.** 1902-68. Amer. novelist.

Sten·dhal (sten-däl′). **Marie Henri Beyle.** 1783-1842. French novelist and biographer.

Ste·phen (stē′vən), **Saint.** 1st cent. Christian martyr.

Stephen of Blois (blwä). 1097?-1154. King of England (1135-54).

Sterne (stûrn), **Laurence.** 1713-68. English novelist.

Steu·ben (stōō′bən, styōō′-), **Baron Friedrich Wilhelm Ludolf Gerhard Augustin von.** 1730-94. Prussian-born Amer. military leader.

Ste·vens (stē′vənz), **Wallace.** 1879-1955. Amer. poet.

Ste·ven·son (stē′vən-sən). **1. Adlai Ewing.** 1835-1914. U.S. Vice President (1893-97). **2. Robert Louis Balfour.** 1850-94. Scottish poet and novelist. **3. Adlai Ewing.** 1900-65. Amer. statesman.

Stone (stōn), **Lucy.** 1818-93. Amer. feminist leader.

Stowe (stō), **Harriet Elizabeth Beecher.** 1811-96. Amer. novelist and reformer.

Strauss (strous, shtrous). Family of Austrian composers, including: **1. Johann.** "the Elder." 1804-49. **2. Johann.** "the Younger," "the Waltz King." 1825-99. **3. Josef.** 1827-70.

Strauss, Richard. 1864-1949. German composer.

Stra·vin·sky (strə-vĭn′skē), **Igor Föodorovich.** 1882-1971. Russian-born Amer. composer.

Strind·berg (strĭnd′bûrg′), **(Johan) August.** 1849-1912. Swedish playwright and novelist.

Stu·art (stōō′ərt, styōō′-). **1. Gilbert Charles.** 1755-1828. Amer. painter. **2. James Ewell Brown ("Jeb").** 1833-64. Amer. Confederate general.

Stuy·ve·sant (stī′və-sənt), **Peter.** 1592-1672. Dutch colonial administrator in America.

Sue·to·ni·us (swĭ-tō′nē-əs). 2nd cent. Roman historian.

Su·kar·no (sōō-kär′nō). 1901-70. Indonesian statesman.

Su·lei·man I (sōō′lā-män). 1490?-1566. Sultan of Turkey (1520-66).

Sul·la (sŭl′ə), **Lucius Cornelius.** 138?-78 B.C. Roman general and dictator.

Sul·li·van (sŭl′ə-vən). **1. Sir Arthur (Seymour).** 1842-1900. English composer of comic operas. **2. Louis Henri or Henry.** 1856-1924. Amer. architect.

Sum·ner (sŭm′nər), **Charles.** 1811-74. Amer. political leader.

Sun Yat-sen (sōōn′ yät′sĕn′). 1866-1925. Chinese revolutionary leader; founder of the Republic of China (1911).

Sur·rey (sûr′ē), **Earl of. Henry Howard.** 1517?-47. English poet.

Suth·er·land (sŭth′ər-lənd), **Joan.** b. 1926. Australian operatic soprano.

Swe·den·borg (swēd′n-bôrg′), **Emanuel.** 1688-1772. Swedish scientist and theologian.

Swift (swĭft), **Jonathan.** "Dean Swift." 1667-1745. English satirist.

Swin·burne (swĭn′bûrn), **Algernon Charles.** 1837-1909. English poet and critic.

Synge (sĭng), **John Millington.** 1871-1909. Irish dramatist.

T

Tac·i·tus (tăs′ə-təs), **Publius Cornelius.** A.D. 55?-118? Roman historian and orator.

Taft (tăft), **William Howard.** 1857–1930. 27th U.S. President (1909–13).

William Howard Taft

Ta·gore (tə-gôr', -gôr'), Sir **Rabindranath.** 1861–1941. Indian poet.

Taine (tān), **Hippolyte Adolphe.** 1828–93. French philosopher and historian.

Tal·ley·rand-Pé·ri·gord (tăl'ē-rănd'pĕr'ə-gôr'), **Charles Maurice de.** 1754–1838. French statesman and diplomat.

Tam·er·lane (tăm'ər-lān'). 1336?–1405. Mongol conqueror.

Tan·cred (tăng'krĕd). 1078?–1112. Norman Crusader.

Ta·ney (tô'nē), **Roger Brooke.** 1774–1864. Amer. jurist.

Tar·king·ton (tär'kĭng-tən), **(Newton) Booth.** 1869–1946. Amer. author.

Tay·lor (tā'lər), **Zachary.** 1784–1850. 12th U.S. President (1849–50).

Tchai·kov·sky (chī-kôf'skē, -kôf'-), **Peter Ilich.** 1840–93. Russian composer.

Te·bal·di (tə-bäl'dē), **Renata.** b. 1922. Italian-born operatic soprano.

Te·cum·seh (tĭ-kŭm'sə, -sē). 1768?–1813. Shawnee Indian leader.

Tel·ler (tĕl'ər), **Edward.** b. 1908. Hungarian-born Amer. physicist.

Ten·ny·son (tĕn'ə-sən), **Alfred.** 1st Baron Tennyson. 1809–92. English poet.

Ter·ence (tĕr'əns). 185–159 B.C. Roman author.

Te·re·sa (tə-rē'sə, -zə, -rā'-), **Mother.** b. 1910. Albanian-born Indian nun.

Te·resh·ko·va (tĕ-rĕsh-kô'və), **Valentina Vladi-mirovna.** b. 1937. Soviet cosmonaut; 1st woman in space.

Tes·la (tĕs'lə), **Nikola.** 1857–1943. Croatian-born Amer. electrical engineer.

Thack·er·ay (thăk'ə-rē, thăk'rē), **William Makepeace.** 1811–63. English novelist.

Tha·les (thā'lēz). 640?–546? B.C. Greek philosopher and geometrician.

Thant (thänt), **U** 1909–74. Burmese diplomat and UN official.

Thatch·er (thăch'ər), **Margaret.** b. 1925. British prime minister (since 1975).

The·oc·ri·tus (thē-ŏk'rə-təs). 3rd cent. B.C. Greek poet.

The·o·do·ra (thē'ə-dôr'ə). 508?–48. Empress of the Eastern Roman Empire.

The·od·o·ric (thē-ŏd'ər-ĭk). 454?–526. Ostrogoth king (474–526).

The·o·do·sius I (thē'ə-dō'shəs). 346?–95. Roman emperor (379–95).

The·re·sa (tə-rē'sə, -rēs'ə), **Saint.** 1515–82. Spanish nun and mystic.

Thes·pis (thĕs'pĭs). 6th cent. B.C. Greek poet.

Thom·as (tŏm'əs), **Saint.** One of the 12 Apostles.

Thomas, Dylan Marlais. 1914–53. Welsh poet.

Thomas à Kem·pis (kĕm'pĭs). 1380–1471. German ecclesiastic and author.

Thomp·son (tŏmp'sən). **1. Benjamin.** 1753–1814. Amer. physicist and philanthropist. **2.** Sir **John Sparrow David.** 1844–94. Canadian prime minister (1892–94).

Tho·reau (thə-rō', thôr'ō), **Henry David.** 1817–62. Amer. essayist.

Thu·cyd·i·des (thōō-sĭd'ə-dēz'). 5th cent. B.C. Greek historian.

Thur·ber (thûr'bər), **James Grover.** 1894–1961. Amer. artist and writer.

Ti·be·ri·us (tī-bîr'ī-əs). 42 B.C.–A.D. 37. Roman emperor (A.D. 14–37).

Tie·po·lo (tē-ĕp'ə-lō'), **Giovanni Battista.** 1696–1770. Italian painter.

Tim·o·thy (tĭm'ə-thē), **Saint.** 1st cent. A.D. Christian leader.

Tin·to·ret·to (tĭn'tə-rĕt'ō), **Il.** 1518–94. Italian painter.

Ti·tian (tĭsh'ən). 1477–1576. Italian painter.

Ti·to (tē'tō). Josip Broz. 1892–1980. Yugoslavian statesman.

Ti·tus (tī'təs). A.D. 40?–81. Emperor of Rome (79–81).

Tocque·ville (tōk'vĭl), **Alexis Charles Henri Maurice Clérel de.** 1805–59. French statesman and historian.

Tol·kien (tōl'kēn'), **J(ohn) R(onald) R(euel).** 1892–1973. English author.

Tol·stoy (tōl'stoi', tôl'-), **Count Leo.** 1828–1910. Russian novelist.

Tomp·kins (tŏm'kənz), **Daniel D.** 1774–1825. U.S. Vice President (1817–25).

Tos·ca·ni·ni (tŏs'kə-nē'nē), **Arturo.** 1867–1957. Italian conductor.

Tou·louse-Lau·trec (tōō-lōōz'lō-trĕk'), **Henri.** 1864–1901. French painter and lithographer.

Tra·jan (trā'jən). A.D. 52–117. Roman emperor (98–117).

Trol·lope (trŏl'əp), **Anthony.** 1815–82. English novelist.

Trots·ky (trŏt'skē), **Leon.** 1879–1940. Russian revolutionary; assassinated in Mexico.

Tru·deau (trōō-dō'), **Pierre Elliott.** b. 1919. Prime Minister of Canada (1968–79 and since 1980).

Tru·man (trōō'mən), **Harry S** 1884–1972. 33rd U.S. President (1945–53).

Harry S Truman

Tub·man (tŭb'mən), **Harriet.** 1820–1913. Amer. abolitionist leader.

Tup·per (tŭp'ər), Sir **Charles.** 1821–1915. Canadian prime minister (1896).

Tur·ge·nev (tōōr-gā'nyəf), **Ivan Sergeevich.** 1818–83. Russian novelist.

Tur·ner (tûr'nər), **Joseph Mallord William.** 1775–1851. English painter.

Tut·ankh·a·men (tōōt'ängk-ä'mən). Late 14 cent. B.C. king of Egypt.

Twain (twān), **Mark.** Samuel Langhorne Clemens.

Harriet Tubman

Ty·ler (tī′lər), **John.** 1790-1862. 10th U.S. President (1841-45).

Tyn·dale (tĭn′dəl), **William.** 1492?-1536. English religious reformer and martyr.

U

Uc·cel·lo (ōō-chĕl′lō), **Paolo.** 1397-1475? Italian painter.

Up·dike (ŭp′dīk), **John (Hoyer).** b. 1932. Amer. author.

Ur·ban II (ûr′bən). 1042?-99. Pope (1088-99).

U·tril·lo (yōō-trĭl′ō), **Maurice.** 1883-1955. French painter.

V

Val·en·tine (văl′ən-tīn′), **Saint.** 3rd cent. Roman Christian martyr.

Va·le·ri·an (və-lîr′ē-ən). Died 269? Emperor of Rome (253-60).

Van Bu·ren (văn byŏŏr′ən), **Martin.** 1782-1862. 8th U.S. President (1837-41).

Martin Van Buren

Van·der·bilt (văn′dər-bĭlt′), **Cornelius.** 1794-1877. Amer. financier.

Van·dyke (văn-dīk′), **Sir Anthony.** Also **Van Dyck.** 1599-1641. Flemish painter.

van Eyck (văn īk′), **Jan.** 1370?-1440? Flemish painter.

van Gogh (văn gō′, gōKH′), **Vincent.** 1853-90. Dutch painter.

Van·zet·ti (văn-zĕt′ē), **Bartolomeo.** 1888-1927. Italian-born Amer. anarchist; executed.

Va·sa·ri (və-zär′ē, -sär′ē), **Giorgio.** 1511-74. Italian artist and architect.

Veb·len (vĕb′lən), **Thorstein Bunde.** 1857-1929. Amer. economist.

Ve·ga (vā′gə), **Lope de.** 1562-1635. Spanish dramatist.

Ve·láz·quez (və-läs′käs, -kəs, -läs′-), **Diego Rodríguez de Silva y.** Also **Ve·lás·quez.** 1599-1660. Spanish painter.

Ver·di (vâr′dē), **Giuseppe.** 1813-1901. Italian composer.

Ver·gil (vûr′jəl). Var. of **Virgil.**

Ver·meer (vər-mâr′, -mîr′), **Jan.** 1632-75. Dutch painter.

Verne (vûrn), **Jules.** 1828-1905. French author.

Ve·ro·ne·se (vā′rō-nā′zā), **Paolo.** 1528-88. Italian painter.

Ver·raz·za·no or **Ver·raz·za·no** (vĕr′ə-zä′nō), **Giovanni da.** 1485?-1528? Italian explorer.

Ves·pa·sian (vĕs-pā′zhən). A.D. 9-79. Emperor of Rome (69-79).

Ves·puc·ci (vĕs-pōō′chē), **Amerigo.** 1451-1512. Italian navigator.

Vic·tor Em·man·u·el I (vĭk′tər ĭ-măn′yōō-əl). 1759-1824. King of Sardinia (1802-21).

Victor Emmanuel II. 1820-78. King of Italy (1861-78).

Vic·to·ri·a (vĭk-tôr′ē-ə, -tōr′ē-ə). 1819-1901. Queen of the United Kingdom of Great Britain and Ireland (1837-1901); empress of India (1876-1901). —**Vic·to′ri·an** adj. & n.

Vil·la (vē′ə, -yä), **Francisco ("Pancho").** 1877?-1923. Mexican revolutionary leader; assassinated.

Vil·lon (vē-yôN′), **François.** 1431-63? French poet.

Vin·cent de Paul (vĭn′sənt də pôl′), **Saint.** 1581?-1660. French priest.

Virgil (vûr′jəl). Also **Ver·gil.** 70-19 B.C. Roman poet. —**Vir·gil′i·an** (-jĭl′ē-ən) adj.

Vi·val·di (vĭ-väl′dē), **Antonio.** 1680?-1743. Italian composer.

Vol·ta (vōl′tä), **Count Alessandro.** 1745-1827. Italian physicist.

Vol·taire (vōl-târ′, vŏl-). **François Marie Arouet.** 1694-1778. French author.

W

Wag·ner (väg′nər), **(Wilhelm) Richard.** 1813-83. German composer. —**Wag·ne′ri·an** adj. & n.

Wald·heim (wôld′hīm), **Kurt.** b. 1918. Austrian diplomat and UN official.

Wa·le·sa (wä-lĕn′sä), **Lech.** b. 1943? Polish labor leader.

Wal·lace (wŏl′ĭs), **Henry Agard.** 1888-1965. U.S. Vice President (1941-45).

Wal·pole (wôl′pōl′, wŏl′-), **Horace.** 4th Earl of Orford. 1717-97. English author.

Wal·ton (wôl′tən), **Izaak.** 1593-1683. English author.

War·ren (wôr′ən, wŏr′-), **Earl.** 1891-1974. Amer. jurist.

Wash·ing·ton (wŏsh′ĭng-tən, wôsh′-). **1. George.** 1732-99. 1st U.S. President (1789-97). **2. Booker Taliaferro.** 1856-1915. Amer. educator. —**Wash′ing·to′ni·an** (-tō′nē-ən) adj.

Watt (wŏt), **James.** 1736-1819. Scottish engineer and inventor.

Wat·teau (wä-tō′, vä-), **Jean Antoine.** 1684-1721. French painter.

Waugh (wô), **Alec** (1898-1981) and **Evelyn** (1903-66). English authors.

Wayne (wān), **Anthony. "Mad Anthony".** 1745-96. Amer. general.

We·ber (vā′bər). **1. Baron Carl Maria Friedrich Ernst von.** 1786-1826. German composer and

---

ă pat ā pay â care ä father ĕ pet ē be ĭ pit ī tie î pier ŏ pot ō toe ô paw, for oi noise ōō took ōō boot ou out th thin th this ŭ cut û urge yōō abuse zh vision ə about, item, edible, gallop, circus

George Washington

conductor. **2. Max.** 1864-1920. German sociologist and economist.

Web·ster (wĕb'stər). **1. John.** 1580?-1625? English dramatist. **2. Noah.** 1758-1843. Amer. lexicographer. · **3. Daniel.** 1782-1852. Amer. statesman.

Wel·ling·ton (wĕl'ĭng-tən), 1st Duke of. Arthur Wellesley. "the Iron Duke." 1769-1852. English soldier and statesman.

Wells (wĕlz), **H(erbert) G(eorge).** 1866-1946. English author.

Wes·ley (wĕs'lē, wĕz'-), **John.** 1703-91. British founder of Methodism.

West (wĕst), **Benjamin.** 1738-1820. Amer. painter.

Wey·den (wīd'n, vīd'n), **Rogier van der.** 1400?-64. Flemish painter.

Whar·ton (hwôrt'n), **Edith Newbold Jones.** 1862-1937. Amer. author.

Wheel·er (hwē'lər), **William Almon.** 1819-87. U.S. Vice President (1877-81).

Whis·tler (hwĭs'lər), **James Abbott McNeill.** 1834-1903. Amer. artist.

White (hwīt, wīt), **Stanford.** 1853-1906. Amer. architect.

White·head (hwĭt'hĕd', wĭt'-), **Alfred North.** 1861-1947. English mathematician and philosopher.

Whit·man (hwĭt'mən), **Walt.** 1819-92. Amer. poet.

Whit·ney (hwĭt'nē), **Eli.** 1765-1825. Amer. inventor and manufacturer.

Whit·ti·er (hwĭt'ē-ər), **John Greenleaf.** 1807-92. Amer. poet.

Wil·ber·force (wĭl'bər-fôrs', -fōrs'), **William.** 1759-1833. English philanthropist and abolitionist.

Wilde (wīld), **Oscar.** 1854-1900. Irish author.

Wil·der (wĭl'dər), **Thornton Niven.** 1897-1975. Amer. author.

Wil·hel·mi·na (wĭl'hĕl-mē'nə). 1880-1962. Queen of the Netherlands (1890-1948); abdicated.

Wil·liam I (wĭl'yəm). "the Conqueror." 1027-87. King of England (1066-87).

William I. "the Silent." 1533-84. Prince of Orange.

William I. 1797-1888. King of Prussia (1861-88) and emperor of Germany (1871-88).

William II. 1056?-1100. King of England (1087-1100).

William II. 1859-1941. Emperor of Germany and king of Prussia (1888-1918); abdicated.

William III. 1650-1702. Stadholder of Holland (1672-1702); king of England (1689-1702).

William IV. 1765-1837. King of Great Britain and Ireland (1830-37).

Wil·liams (wĭl'yəmz). **1. Roger.** 1603?-83. English clergyman in America; founder of Rhode Island. **2. William Carlos.** 1883-1963. Amer. poet and physician. **3. Tennessee.** 1914-83. Amer. dramatist.

Wil·son (wĭl'sən). **1. Henry.** 1812-75. U.S. Vice President (1873-75). **2. (Thomas) Woodrow.** 1856-1924. 28th U.S. President (1913-21). **3. (James) Harold.** b. 1916. British prime minister (1964-70 and 1974-79).

Woodrow Wilson

Win·throp (wĭn'thrəp). Family of English colonial administrators in America, including **John** (1588-1649), **John** (1606-76), and **John** (1638-1707).

Wode·house (wŏŏd'hous'), **P(elham) G(eorge).** 1881-1975. English author.

Wolfe (wŏŏlf). **1. James.** 1727-59. English general. **2. Thomas Clayton.** 1900-38. Amer. novelist.

Wol·sey (wŏŏl'zē), **Thomas.** 1475?-1530. English cardinal and statesman.

Wood (wŏŏd), **Grant.** 1892-1942. Amer. painter.

Woolf (wŏŏlf), **(Adeline) Virginia Stephen.** 1882-1941. English author.

Words·worth (wûrdz'wûrth'), **William.** 1770-1850. English poet.

Wren (rĕn), **Sir Christopher.** 1632-1723. English architect.

Wright (rīt). **1. Wilbur** (1867-1912) and **Orville** (1871-1948). Amer. aviation pioneers. **2. Frank Lloyd.** 1869-1959. Amer. architect.

Wy·att (wī'ət), **Sir Thomas.** 1503-42. English poet.

Wych·er·ley (wĭch'ər-lē), **William.** 1640?-1716. English playwright.

Wyc·liffe (wĭk'lĭf), **John.** 1320?-84. English religious reformer.

Wy·eth (wī'ĭth), **Newell Convers** (1882-1945) and **Andrew Newell** (b. 1917). Amer. painters.

X

Xa·vi·er (zā'vē-ər, zăv'ē-), **Saint Francis.** 1506-52. Spanish Jesuit missionary.

Xen·o·phon (zĕn'ə-fən). 430?-355? B.C. Greek general and historian.

Xerx·es I (zûrk'sēz). 519?-465 B.C. King of Persia (486-465 B.C.).

Y

Yeats (yāts), **William Butler.** 1865-1939. Irish poet and playwright.

Yev·tu·shen·ko (yĕv'tŏŏ-shĕng'kŏ), **Yevgeny Aleksandrovich.** b. 1933. Russian poet.

Young (yŭng), **Brigham.** 1801-77. Amer. Mormon leader.

Z

Zech·a·ri·ah (zĕk'ə-rī'əh). 6th cent. B.C. Hebrew prophet.

Zed·e·ki·ah (zĕd'ə-kī'ə). King of Judah (597-586 B.C.).

Zeng·er (zĕng'ər), **John Peter.** 1697-1746. German-born printer in America.

Ze·no (zē'nō). 342?-270? B.C. Greek Stoic philosopher.

Zeph·a·ni·ah (zĕf'ə-nī'ə). 7th cent. B.C. Hebrew prophet.

Zhou En·lai (jō ĕn-lī'). 1898-1976. Chinese statesman.

Zo·la (zō-lä'), **Émile.** 1840-1902. French novelist.

Zo·ro·as·ter (zôr'ō-ăs'tər, zôr'-). 6th cent. B.C. Persian prophet.

Zwing·li (zwǐng'lē), **Ulrich.** 1484-1531. Swiss religious reformer.

GEOGRAPHICAL ENTRIES

Geographical entries are listed in alphabetical order. Places having the same name are combined in one entry.

A

Aa·chen (ä'kən, ä'ᴋʜən). City of W West Germany. Pop. 242,971.

A·ba·dan (äb'ə-dän', ä'bə-dän'). City of SW Iran. Pop. 296,081.

Ab·er·deen (äb'ər-dēn', ăb'ər-dēn'). Burgh of NE Scotland. Pop. 209,189.

Ab·i·djan (äb'ĭ-jän'). Cap. of Ivory Coast. Pop. 685,800.

A·bruz·zi e Mo·li·se (ä-brōōt'tsē ā mô'lē-zā). Mountainous region of S central Italy.

A·bu Dha·bi (ä'bōō dä'bē). Sheikdom in E Arabia and cap. of United Arab Emirates. Pop. 347,000.

A·ca·pul·co (äk'ə-pōōl'kō). City on the Pacific coast of S Mexico. Pop. 421,100.

Ac·cra (äk'rə, ə-krä'). Cap. of Ghana. Pop. 633,800.

A·con·ca·gua (ä'kōn-kä'gwä). Highest mountain (22,835 ft/6,964.7 m) in the Western Hemisphere, in the Andes of Argentina.

Ac·ti·um (äk'tē-əm, -shē-). Promontory and ancient town of W Greece.

A·da·na (ä'dä-nä'). City of S Turkey. Pop. 568,513.

Ad·dis Ab·a·ba (äd'dĭs ä'bə-bä, äd'ĭs äb'ə-bə). Cap. of Ethiopia. Pop. 1,125,340.

A·de·laide (äd'l-ād'). City of S Australia. Pop. 933,300.

A·den (äd'n, äd'n). Cap. of Southern Yemen, on NW shore of the **Gulf of Aden,** W arm of the Arabian Sea. Pop. 264,326.

Ad·i·ron·dack Mountains (äd'ə-rŏn'däk'). Range of the Appalachian system in NE N.Y., between the St. Lawrence and Mohawk valleys.

Ad·mi·ral·ty (äd'mər-əl-tē). 1. Island in the Alexander Archipelago of SE Alaska. 2. Group of small volcanic islands in the SW Pacific, in the Bismarck Archipelago.

A·dri·at·ic Sea (ä'drē-ăt'ĭk). Arm of the Mediterranean between Italy and the Balkan Peninsula.

Ae·ge·an Sea (ĭ-jē'ən). Arm of the Mediterranean between Greece and Turkey.

Ae·o·lis (ē'ə-lĭs). Ancient region on the W coast of Asia Minor. —**Ae·o'li·an** *adj. & n.*

Af·ghan·i·stan (ăf-găn'ĭ-stän'). Country of S central Asia. Cap. Kabul. Pop. 18,294,000. —**Af'ghan'** *adj. & n.*

Af·ri·ca (ăf'rĭ-kə). 2nd-largest continent, S of Europe between the Atlantic and Indian oceans. —**Af'ri·can** *adj. & n.*

A·ga·na (ä-gä'nyä). Cap. of Guam, on the W coast. Pop. 25,000.

Ag·in·court (ăj'ĭn-kôrt', -kôrt'). Village of N France where Henry V of England defeated the French in 1415.

A·gra (ä'grə). City of N central India; site of the Taj Mahal. Pop. 591,917.

A·gul·has (ə-gŭl'əs), **Cape.** Group of rugged cliffs between the Atlantic and Indian oceans at the S point of Africa.

Ah·mad·a·bad (ä'məd-ə-bäd'). City of NW India. Pop. 1,585,544.

Aisne (ān). River of N France, flowing 165 mi (265.5 km) W to the Oise.

Aix-en-Pro·vence (ăks'än-prō-väns', ĕks'-). City of SE France. Pop. 110,659.

A·jac·cio (ä-yät'chō). Cap. of Corsica, on the W coast. Pop. 50,726.

Ak·kad (äk'äd', ä'kăd'). Region and city of ancient Mesopotamia. —**Ak·kad'i·an** *adj. & n.*

Ak·ron (äk'rən). Industrial city of NE Ohio. Pop. 237,177.

Al·a·bam·a (ăl'ə-băm'ə). 1. State of S U.S. Cap. Montgomery. Pop. 3,890,061. 2. River rising in central Ala. and flowing 315 mi (506.8 km) S to the Gulf of Mexico. —**Al'a·bam'i·an** (-ē-ən) or **Al'a·bam'an** *adj. & n.*

A·lai (ä'lī'). Mountain range of S Central Asian USSR, in the W Tian Shan.

A·la·mein (ăl'ə-mān'), **El.** Village in N Egypt; site of a British victory over the Axis (1942).

Al·a·mo·gor·do (ăl'ə-mə-gôr'dō). City in S central N.Mex.; site of the 1st atomic bomb explosion (1945). Pop. 24,024.

A·las·ka (ə-lăs'kə). 1. State of the U.S., in extreme NW North America. Cap. Juneau. Pop. 400,481. 2. **Gulf of.** N inlet of the Pacific, between the Alaska Peninsula and the Alexander Archipelago. 3. Peninsula of S central Alas., between the Bering Sea and the Pacific. 4. Mountain range of S central Alas., rising to 20,320 ft (6,197.6 m). —**A·las'kan** *adj. & n.*

Al·ba·ni·a (ăl-bā'nē-ə, -bān'yə). Country of SE

Europe, on the Adriatic. Cap. Tirane. Pop. 2,725,000. —**Al·ba'ni·an** *adj. & n.*

Al·ba·ny (ôl'bə-nē). Cap. of N.Y., on the W bank of the Hudson. Pop. 101,727.

Al·be·marle Sound (ăl'bə-märl'). Inland body of generally fresh water in NE N.C.

Al·bert (ăl'bərt), **Lake**. Lake of E central Africa, on the Zaire-Uganda border.

Al·ber·ta (ăl-bûr'tə). Province of W Canada. Cap. Edmonton. Pop. 1,838,037. —**Al·ber'tan** *adj. & n.*

Al·bu·quer·que (ăl'bə-kûr'kē). City of central N.Mex. Pop. 331,767.

Al·ca·traz (ăl'kə-trăz'). Island in San Francisco Bay, W Calif.

Al·dan (ăl-dän'). River of SE Siberian USSR, flowing c. 1,400 mi (2,255 km) to the Lena.

A·lep·po (ə-lĕp'ō). City of NW Syria. Pop. 878,000.

A·leu·tian Islands (ə-lōō'shən). Chain of volcanic islands, extending into the N Pacific in a W arc from the Alaska Peninsula.

Al·ex·an·der Archipelago (ăl'ĭg-zăn'dər). Group of more than 1,000 islands off the SE coast of Alas.

Al·ex·an·dri·a (ăl'ĭg-zăn'drē-ə). **1.** City of Egypt, on the Mediterranean. Pop. 2,409,000. **2.** City of N Va., on the Potomac R. Pop. 103,217. —**Al'ex·an'dri·an** *adj. & n.*

Al·ge·ri·a (ăl-jîr'ē-ə). Country of NW Africa, on the Mediterranean. Cap. Algiers. Pop. 20,050,000. —**Al·ge'ri·an** *adj. & n.*

Al·giers (ăl-jîrz'). Cap. of Algeria, in the N on the Mediterranean. Pop. 1,503,270.

A·li·can·te (ăl'ĭ-kăn'tē). City of SE Spain. Pop. 235,868.

Al·la·ha·bad (ăl'ə-hə-băd'). City of N central India. Pop. 490,622.

Al·le·ghe·ny (ăl'ə-gā'nē). **1. Mountains.** Also **Al·le·ghe·nies** (-nēz). W part of the Appalachian Mts., extending from N Pa. to SW Va. **2.** River rising in N central Pa. and flowing 325 mi (523 km) SW to Pittsburgh, where it joins the Monongahela to form the Ohio.

Al·len·town (ăl'ən-toun'). City of E Pa. Pop. 103,758.

Al·ma-A·ta (ăl'mä-ä'tä). City of SE Central Asian USSR. Pop. 928,000.

Al Ma·nam·ah (ăl mə-năm'ə). Cap. of Bahrain, on the Persian Gulf. Pop. 89,112.

Alps (ălps). Mountain system of S central Europe, rising to 15,771 ft (4,810.2 m).

Al·sace-Lor·raine (ăl'săs-lô-rān', -lŏ-, -săs-). Region of NE France, annexed by Germany (1871) and recovered by France in 1919.

Al·tai Mountains (ăl-tī', ăl'tī). Mountain system of Central Asian USSR, W Mongolia, and N China.

A·ma·ga·sa·ki (ä'mä-gə-sä'kē). Industrial city of S Honshu, Japan. Pop. 523,657.

Am·a·ril·lo (ăm'ə-rĭl'ō). City of N Tex., in the Panhandle. Pop. 149,230.

Am·a·zon (ăm'ə-zŏn', -zən). River of South America, rising in the Peruvian Andes and flowing c. 3,900 mi (6,275 km) N and E through N Brazil to the Atlantic.

A·mer·i·ca (ə-mĕr'ə-kə). **1.** The U.S. **2.** North America, Central America, and South America. —**A·mer'i·can** *adj. & n.*

American Sa·mo·a (sə-mō'ə). U.S. territory in the S Pacific. Cap. Pago Pago. Pop. 32,297.

A·miens (ăm'ē-ənz, ä-myăN'). City of N France. Pop. 131,476.

Am·man (ä'män). Cap. of Jordan, on the N. Pop. 648,587.

A·moy (ä-moi'). City of SE China, on Amoy Is., in Formosa Strait W of Taiwan. Pop. 300,000.

Am·ster·dam (ăm'stər-dăm'). Constitutional cap. of the Netherlands. Pop. 716,919.

A·mu Dar·ya (ä-mōō' där'yə). River of central Asia, rising in the Pamirs and flowing c. 1,600 mi (2,575 km) generally N to the Aral Sea.

A·mund·sen Sea (ä'mŭnd-sən). Part of the S Pacific, off the Antarctic coast.

A·mur (ä-mōōr'). River of NE Asia, flowing c. 1,800 mi (2,895 km) along the USSR-China border.

An·a·heim (ăn'ə-hīm'). City of S Calif. Pop. 221,847.

An·a·to·li·a (ăn'ə-tō'lē-ə, -lyə). Asian Turkey, usu. synonymous with Asia Minor. —**An'a·to'li·an** *adj. & n.*

An·chor·age (ăng'kər-ĭj). City of S Alas. Pop. 173,992.

An·da·lu·sia (ăn'də-lōō'zhə). Region of SW Spain, on the Mediterranean. —**An'da·lu'sian** *adj. & n.*

An·da·man Sea (ăn'də-mən). Arm of the Bay of Bengal, in SE Asia.

Andes (ăn'dēz). Mountain system of W South America, extending from Venezuela to Tierra del Fuego and rising to 22,835 ft (6,964.7 m).

An·dor·ra (ăn-dôr'ə, -dŏr'ə). Country of SW Europe, in the E Pyrenees between France and Spain. Cap. Andorra la Vella. Pop. 32,700. —**An·dor'ran** *adj. & n.*

An·gel Fall (ăn'jəl). Waterfall in SE Venezuela, dropping c. 3,212 ft (980 m).

An·gers (ăn'jərz, äN-zhā'). City of W France. Pop. 137,587.

Ang·kor (ăng'kôr, -kōr). Ruins of Khmer imperial capitals, in NW Cambodia.

An·go·la (ăng-gō'lə). Country of SW Africa. Cap. Luanda. Pop. 7,000,000. —**An·go'lan** *adj. & n.*

An·jou (ăn'jōō', äN-zhōō'). Region and former province of W France.

An·ka·ra (ăng'kər-ə). Cap. of Turkey. Pop. 2,203,729.

Ann (ăn), **Cape**. Peninsula of NE Mass.

An·na·ba (ə-nä'bə). City of NE Algeria. Pop. 313,174.

An·nam (ə-năm', ăn'ăm'). Region and former kingdom of E central Vietnam.

An·nap·o·lis (ə-năp'ə-lĭs). Cap. of Md., on Chesapeake Bay. Pop. 31,740.

An·na·pur·na (ăn'ə-pōōr'nə, -pûr'-). Massif of the Himalayas in N central Nepal; highest elevation, Annapurna I (26,502 ft/8,083.1 m).

Ann Ar·bor (än är'bər). City of SE Mich. Pop. 107,316.

An·shan (än'shän'). City of NE China. Pop. 1,050,000.

Ant·arc·ti·ca (ănt-ärk'tĭ-kə, -är'tĭ-). Continent chiefly within the Antarctic Circle and asymmetrically centered on the South Pole.

Ant·arc·tic Ocean (ănt-ärk'tĭk, -är'tĭk). Waters surrounding Antarctica, the S extensions of the Atlantic, Pacific, and Indian oceans.

An·ti·gua (ăn-tē'gwə, -gə). Island in the West Indies. —**An·ti'guan** *adj. & n.*

An·til·les (ăn-tĭl'ēz). The West Indies except for the Bahamas, separating the Caribbean Sea from the Atlantic.

An·ti·och (ăn'tē-ŏk'). Ancient city of Phrygia, in SW Turkey.

An·ti·sa·na (än'tē-sä'nä). Active volcano, 18,885 ft (5,760 m), in the Andes in N central Ecuador.

Ant·werp (ănt'wərp). Port city of N Belgium. Pop. 194,073.

Ap·en·nines (ăp'ə-nīnz'). Mountain range of Italy, extending along the length of the peninsula.

A·pi·a (ä-pē'ä). Cap. of Western Samoa, on N Upolu Is. Pop. 32, 099.

Ap·pa·la·chi·a (ăp'ə-lā'chē-ə, -chə). Region of E U.S.

Ap·pa·la·chi·an Mountains (ăp'ə-lā'chē-ən, -chən). Mountain system of E North America, extending c. 1,600 mi (2,575 km) from S Que., Canada, to central Ala.

Ap·po·mat·tox (ăp'ə-măt'əks). Town in central Va. where Robert E. Lee surrendered to Ulysses S. Grant on Apr. 9, 1865, bringing the Civil War to a close.

A·qa·ba (ä'kä-bä'). City of SW Jordan at the N end of the **Gulf of Aqaba**, an arm of the Red Sea. Pop. 26,986.

Aq·ui·taine (ăk'wə-tān'). Historical region of SW France.

Aq·ui·ta·ni·a (ăk'wĭ-tā'nē-ə). Roman division of SW Gaul. —**Aq·ui·ta'ni·an** *adj. & n.*

A·ra·bi·a (ə-rā'bē-ə). Peninsula of SW Asia, between the Red Sea and the Persian Gulf.

A·ra·bi·an (ə-rā'bē-ən). **1.** Desert of Egypt between the Nile Valley and the Red Sea. **2. Sea.** NW part of the Indian Ocean bounded by E Africa, Arabia, and W India.

Ar·a·gon (ăr'ə-gŏn'). Region and former kingdom of NE Spain.

Ar·a·guai·a (ä'rə-gwä'yə). River, c. 1,300 mi (2,090 km), of central Brazil.

Ar·al Sea (ăr'əl). Inland sea of Central Asian USSR, E of the Caspian Sea.

Ar·an Islands (ăr'ən). Three islands off the SW coast of Ireland.

Arch·an·gel (ärk'ān'jəl). Arkhangelsk.

Arc·tic (ärk'tĭk, är'tĭk). **1. Archipelago.** Islands in the Arctic Ocean between North America and Greenland. **2. Ocean.** Waters surrounding the North Pole between North America and Eurasia.

Ar·dennes (är-děn'). Forested plateau of N France, SE Belgium, and Luxembourg.

A·re·qui·pa (ä'rĕ-kē'pä). City of S Peru. Metro. pop. 304,653.

Ar·gen·ti·na (är'jən-tē'nə). Country of SE South America. Cap. Buenos Aires. Pop. 27,860,000. —**Ar'gen·tine** *adj.* —**Ar'gen·tin'e·an** (-tĭn'ē-ən) *adj. & n.*

Ar·go·lis (är'gə-lĭs). Region of ancient Greece, in NE Peloponnesus. —**Ar·go'li·an** *adj. & n.*

Ar·gonne (är'gŏn', är-gŏn'). Region of NE France.

Ar·hus (ôr'hōōs'). City of E Jutland, Denmark. Pop. 244,839.

Ar·i·zo·na (ăr'ə-zō'nə). State of SW U.S. Cap. Phoenix. Pop. 2,717,866. —**Ar'i·zo'nan** or **Ar'i·zo'ni·an** *adj. & n.*

Ar·kan·sas (är'kən-sô). **1.** State of S central U.S. Cap. Little Rock. Pop. 2,285,513. **2.** (*also* är-kăn'zəs). River of S central U.S., rising in the Rocky Mts. of central Colo. and flowing c. 1,450 mi (2,335 km) to the Mississippi in SE Ark. —**Ar·kan'san** (-kăn'zən) *adj. & n.*

Ark·han·gelsk (är-KHăn'gĕlsk). City of NW European USSR. Pop. 387,000.

Ar·ling·ton (är'lĭng-tən). County and unincorporated city of N Va., across the Potomac from Washington, D.C. Pop. 152,599.

Ar·me·ni·a (är-mē'nē-ə, -nyə). Ancient country of W Asia, now divided among the USSR, Turkey, and Iran. —**Ar·me'ni·an** *adj. & n.*

Ar·no (är'nō). River of central Italy, flowing c. 150 mi (240 km) to the Ligurian Sea.

A·ru·ba (ə-rōō'bə). Island of the Netherlands Antilles, N of the Venezuelan coast.

A·sa·ma (ä-sä'mä), **Mount.** Active volcano, 8,340 ft (2,543.7 m), of central Honshu, Japan.

A·shan·ti (ə-shän'tē, ə-shăn'-). Region and former kingdom of central Ghana, W Africa.

Ash·kha·bad (ăsh'kə-băd'). City of S Central Asian USSR. Pop. 318,000.

A·sia (ā'zhə, ā'shə). Largest of the earth's continents, occupying the E part of the Eurasian land mass and adjacent islands and separated from Europe by the Ural Mts. —**A'sian** or **A'si·at'ic** *adj. & n.*

Asia Minor. W peninsula of Asia, between the Black Sea and the Mediterranean.

As·syr·i·a (ə-sîr'ē-ə). Ancient empire of W Asia. —**As·syr'i·an** *adj. & n.*

As·tra·khan (ăs'trə-kăn'). City of SE European USSR, on the Volga delta. Pop. 465,000.

A·sun·ción (ä'sōōn-syŏn'). Cap. of Paraguay, in the S. Pop. 462,776.

As·wan (ăs'wän, äs-wän'). City on the E bank of the Nile in S Egypt; site of the **Aswan Dam.** Pop. 144,377.

Ath·a·bas·ca or **Ath·a·bas·ka** (ăth'ə-băs'kə). **1.** Lake of NE Alta. and NW Sask., Canada. **2.** River of Alta., Canada, rising in the Rocky Mts. and flowing 765 mi (1,230.9 km) N into Lake Athabasca.

Ath·ens (ăth'ənz). Cap. of Greece, in the E central part. Pop. 867,023. —**A·the'ni·an** (ə-thē'nē-ən) *adj. & n.*

At·lan·ta (ăt-lăn'tə). Cap. of Ga., in the N part. Pop. 425,022.

At·lan·tic City (ăt-lăn'tĭk). Resort city of SE N.J. Pop. 40,199.

Atlantic Ocean. 2nd largest of the earth's oceans, extending from the Arctic in the N to the Antarctic in the S and from the Americas in the W to Europe and Africa in the E.

At·las Mountains (ăt'ləs). Mountain system of NW Africa, between the Sahara and the Mediterranean.

At·ti·ca (ăt'ĭ-kə). Hinterland of Athens in ancient Greece. —**At'tic** *adj. & n.*

At·tu (ä'tōō). Westernmost of the Aleutian Is. of SW Alas.

Auck·land (ôk'lənd). City of New Zealand, on NW North Is. Metro. pop. 775,000.

Augs·burg (ôgz'bûrg', ouks'bŏŏrk'). City of S West Germany. Pop. 245,940.

Au·gus·ta (ô-gŭs'tə, ə-gŭs'-). Cap. of Me., in the SW. Pop. 21,819.

Aus·ter·litz (ô'stər-lĭts', ous'tər-). Town of S Czechoslovakia.

Aus·tin (ô'stən). Cap. of Tex., in the S central part. Pop. 345,496.

Aus·tral·a·sia (ô'strəl-ā'zhə, -shə). **1.** Islands of Oceania in the S Pacific, together with Australia, New Zealand, New Guinea, and associated islands. **2.** Sometimes, all of Oceania. —**Aus'tral·a'sian** *adj. & n.*

Aus·tra·lia (ô-strāl'yə). **1.** Continent lying SE of Asia between the Pacific and Indian oceans. **2.** Country comprising the continent of Australia, the island of Tasmania, 2 external territories, and a number of dependencies. Cap. Canberra. Pop. 14,423,500. —**Aus·tra'lian** *adj. & n.*

Aus·tra·lian Alps (ô-strāl'yən ălps). Mountain chain in SE Australia.

Aus·tri·a (ô'strē-ə). Country of central Europe.

Cap. Vienna. Pop. 7,456,745. —**Aus'tri·an** adj. & n.

Aus·tri·a-Hun·ga·ry (ô'strē-ə-hŭng'gə-rē). Former dual monarchy (1867–1918) of central Europe, consisting of Austria, Bohemia, and Hungary and parts of Poland, Rumania, Yugoslavia, and Italy. —**Aus'tro-Hun·gar'i·an** (-gär'ē-ən) adj. & n.

Aus·tro·ne·sia (ô'strō-nē'zhə, -shə). Islands in the Pacific, including Indonesia, Melanesia, Micronesia, and Polynesia. —**Aus'tro·ne'sian** adj. & n.

Au·vergne (ō-vêrn', ō-vûrn'). Region of central France.

A·vi·gnon (ä-vē-nyôN'). City on the Rhone in SE France. Pop. 90,786.

A·von (ā'vŏn). River of S central England, flowing past Stratford to the Severn.

A·zer·bai·jan (äz'ər-bī-jän', ä'zər-). Region of SE European USSR.

A·zores (ā'zôrz, ə-zôrz'). Three island groups in the N Atlantic c. 900 mi (1,448 km) W of mainland Portugal.

Az·ov (äz'ôf, -ŏf, ä'zôf), **Sea of.** N arm of the Black Sea.

B

Bab·y·lon (băb'ə-lən, -lŏn'). Cap. of ancient Babylonia, on the Euphrates.

Bab·y·lo·ni·a (băb'ə-lō'nē-ə). Ancient empire in the lower Euphrates valley of SW Asia. —**Bab'y·lo'ni·an** adj. & n.

Bac·tri·a (băk'trē-ə). Ancient country of SW Asia. —**Bac'tri·an** adj. & n.

Ba·den (bäd'n). Region of SW Germany.

Bad·lands (băd'lănz'). Extensive barren region of SW S.Dak. and NW Neb.

Baf·fin Bay (băf'ĭn). Arm of the Atlantic off NE Canada, separating Greenland and **Baffin Is.**

Bagh·dad (băg'dăd'). Also **Bag·dad.** Cap. of Iraq, on the Tigris. Pop. 1,300,000.

Ba·gui·o (bäg'ē-ō'). Summer cap. of the Philippines, on N Luzon Is. Pop. 97,449.

Ba·ha·ma Islands (bə-hä'mə). Also **Ba·ha·mas** (-məz). Island country in the Atlantic SE of Fla. Cap. Nassau. Pop. 168,812. —**Ba·ha'mi·an** (-hä'mē-ən, -hä'-) or **Ba·ha'man** adj. & n.

Bah·rain (bä-rān'). Also **Bah·rein.** Sheikdom and archipelago in the Persian Gulf between Qatar and Saudi Arabia. Cap. Al Manamah. Pop. 350,000. —**Bah·rain'i** adj. & n.

Bai·kal or **Bay·kal** (bī-kôl', -käl'). Lake, 12,160 sq mi (37,494 sq km), of SE Siberian USSR. **Bai·ri·ki** (bī-rē'kē). Cap. of Kiribati, on Tarawa in the W central Pacific. Pop. 17,100.

Ba·ker (bā'kər), **Mount. 1.** Peak, 12,460 ft (3,800.3 m), of N Colo. **2.** Peak, 10,778 ft (3,287.3 m), of the Cascade Range in NW Wash.

Ba·kers·field (bā'kərz-fēld'). City of S central Calif. Pop. 105,611.

Ba·ku (bä-kōō'). City of SW Central Asian USSR, on the Caspian Sea. Pop. 1,030,000.

Bal·e·ar·ic Islands (băl'ē-ăr'ĭk). Island group in the W Mediterranean, E of Spain.

Ba·li (bä'lē). Island of Indonesia, off the E end of Java. —**Ba'li·nese'** (-nēz', -nēs') adj. & n.

Bal·kan (bôl'kən). **1. Mountains.** Also **Bal·kans** (-kənz). Range of mountains extending across N Bulgaria from the Black Sea to the border of Yugoslavia. **2.** Peninsula of SE Europe, bounded by the Mediterranean and Aegean seas to the S, the Adriatic and Ionian seas to the W, and the Black Sea to the E.

Bal·khash (băl-käsh'). Salt lake of SE Central Asian USSR.

Bal·tic Sea (bôl'tĭk). Arm of the Atlantic in N Europe.

Bal·ti·more (bôl'tə-môr', -mōr'). City of Md., on upper Chesapeake Bay. Pop. 786,775. —**Bal'ti·mo're·an** adj. & n.

Ba·ma·ko (băm'ə-kō'). Cap. of Mali, in the SW on the Niger R. Pop. 404,022.

Ban·dar Se·ri Be·ga·wan (bŭn'dər sĕr'ē bə-gä'wən). Cap. of Brunei, in the N. Pop. 37,000.

Ban·dung (băn'dŏong). City of Indonesia, in W Java. Pop. 1,201,730.

Ban·ga·lore (băng'gə-lôr', -lōr'). City of S central India. Pop. 1,540,741.

Bang·kok (băng'kŏk', băng-kŏk'). Cap. of Thailand, in the SW. Pop. 4,178,000.

Ban·gla·desh (băng'glə-dĕsh'). Country of S Asia, between India and Burma. Cap. Dacca. Pop. 88,700,000.

Ban·gor (băng'gôr', -gər). City of S central Me. Pop. 31,643.

Ban·gui (băng-gē'). Cap. of Central African Republic, on the Ubangi R. Pop. 187,000.

Ban·jul (băn-jōōl', băn'jōōl). Cap. of Gambia, on an island at the mouth of the Gambia R. Pop. 45,600.

Bao·tou (bou'tō'). City of N China. Pop. 650,000.

Bar·ba·dos (bär-bā'dōz, -dōs'). Island country of E West Indies. Cap. Bridgetown. Pop. 238,141. —**Bar·ba'di·an** adj. & n.

Bar·ba·ry (bär'bə-rē). Region of N Africa on the Barbary Coast, stretching from Egypt's W border to the Atlantic.

Bar·bu·da (bär-bōō'də). Island of the West Indies, in the Leeward Is. N of Antigua.

Bar·ce·lo·na (bär'sə-lō'nə). City of NE Spain, on the Mediterranean. Pop. 1,902,713.

Ba·rents Sea (bâr'ənts, bä'rənts). Arm of the Arctic Ocean, N of Norway and the USSR.

Ba·ri (bä'rē). City of SE Italy, on the Adriatic. Pop. 387,266.

Bar·na·ul (bär'nä-ōōl'). City of SW Siberian USSR, on the Ob R. Pop. 542,000.

Bar·qui·si·me·to (bär'kē-sē-mē'tō). City of NW Venezuela, W of Caracas. Pop. 430,000.

Bar·ran·quil·la (bär'rän-kē'yä). City of N Colombia, on the Magdalena. Pop. 859,000.

Bar·row (băr'ō), **Point.** Northernmost point of Alas., on the Arctic Ocean.

Ba·sel (bä'zəl). City of NW Switzerland, on the Rhine. Metro. pop. 575,000.

Basque Provinces (băsk). Region of N Spain, on the Bay of Biscay.

Bass Strait (băs). Channel between mainland Australia and Tasmania.

Ba·taan (bə-tăn', -tän'). Peninsula of W Luzon, Philippines.

Bath (băth, bäth). City of SW England. Pop. 83,900.

Bat·on Rouge (băt'n rōōzh'). Cap. of La., on the Mississippi. Pop. 219,486.

Ba·var·i·a (bə-vâr'ē-ə). Region of S West Germany. —**Ba·var'i·an** adj. & n.

Bay·kal (bī-kôl', -käl'). Var. of **Baikal.**

Bay·reuth (bī'roit, bī-roit'). City of S West Germany. Pop. 70,210.

Bear (bâr). River, 350 mi (563.2 km), of N Utah, SW Wyo., and SE Idaho.

Beau·fort Sea (bō'fərt). Part of the Arctic Ocean off NW Canada and NE Alas.

Beau·mont (bō'mŏnt). City of SE Texas. Pop. 118,102.

Bei·jing (bā'jyĭng'). Cap. of China, in the NE. Pop. 5,400,000.

Bei·rut (bā-rōōt'). Cap. of Lebanon, on the E Mediterranean. Pop. 474,870.

Be·lém (bə-lĕm'). City of N Brazil, on the Rio Pará. Pop. 899,400.

Bel·fast (bĕl'făst', bĕl-făst'). Cap. of Northern Ireland, at the head of **Belfast Lough** on the E coast. Pop. 357,600.

Bel·gium (bĕl'jəm). Country of NW Europe. Cap. Brussels. Pop. 9,855,110. —**Bel·gian** (bĕl'jən) *adj. & n.*

Bel·grade (bĕl'grăd', bĕl-grăd'). Cap. of Yugoslavia, in the E on the Danube and Sava rivers. Pop. 770,140.

Be·lize (bə-lēz'). Country of Central America, on the Caribbean. Cap. Belmopan. Pop.127,200.

Bel·mo·pan (bĕl'mə-păn'). Cap. of Belize, in the N central part. Pop. 5,000.

Be·lo Ho·ri·zon·te (bē'lō'rē-zŏn'tĭ). City of E Brazil. Pop. 1,856,800.

Be·lo·rus·sia (bĕl'ō-rŭsh'ə). Region of W central European USSR.

Ben·gal (bĕn-gôl', bĕng-). Region of E India and Bangladesh, on the **Bay of Bengal,** arm of the Indian Ocean between India on the W and Burma on the E. —**Ben·gal'i** *adj. & n.*

Be·ni (bĕ'nē). River, 994 mi (1,599.3 km), of NW and central Bolivia.

Be·nin (bə-nēn'). Country of W Africa, on the **Bight of Benin,** the N section of the Gulf of Guinea. Cap. Porto Novo. Pop. 3,469,000.

Ben Nev·is (bĕn nĕv'ĭs, nĕv'ĭs). Highest elevation, 4,406 ft (1,343.8 m), of Great Britain, in the Grampians of W Scotland.

Ben·xi (bŭn'shē'). City of NE China. Pop. 500,000.

Ber·gen (bûr'gən, bär'-). City of SW Norway, on inlets of the North Sea. Pop. 209,300.

Be·ring Sea (bîr'ĭng, bâr'-). Part of the N Pacific between Siberia and Alas., joined to the Arctic Ocean by the **Bering Strait** (c. 55 mi/90 km wide).

Berke·ley (bûrk'lē). City and educational center of W Calif. Pop. 103,300.

Berk·shire Hills (bûrk'shĭr, -shər). Also **Berkshires** (-shĭrz, -shərz). Range of hills in W Mass.

Ber·lin (bûr-lĭn'). Former cap. of Germany, now a divided city entirely surrounded by East Germany. **East Berlin,** under Soviet control after 1945, became cap. of East Germany in 1949 (pop. 1,128,983). The sectors under American, British, and French control became **West Berlin,** part of West Germany (pop. 1,902,250). —**Ber·lin'er** *n.*

Ber·mu·da (bər-myōō'də). Archipelago and British colony in the Atlantic SE of Cape Hatteras. Cap. Hamilton. Pop. 52,330. —**Bermu'di·an** (-dē·ən) *adj. & n.*

Bern (bûrn, bĕrn). Also **Berne.** Cap. of Switzerland, in the NW. Pop. 141,300.

Ber·nese Alps (bûr-nēz', -nēs'). Range of the Alps in S central Switzerland, rising to 14,032 ft (4,279.8 m).

Bes·kids (bĕs'kĭdz, bĕs-kēdz'). Two mountain ranges in the W Carpathians along the E border of Czechoslovakia.

Bes·sa·ra·bi·a (bĕs'ə-rā'bē·ə). Region of SW European USSR. —**Bes'sa·ra'bi·an** *adj. & n.*

Beth·le·hem (bĕth'lĭ-hĕm, -lē·əm). Town of W Jordan, S of Jerusalem; traditionally, the birthplace of Jesus. Pop. 25,000.

Bhu·tan (bōō-tän', -tăn'). Country of central Asia, in the E Himalayas. Cap. Thimbu. Pop. 1,232,000. —**Bhu'tan·ese'** (-tn-ēz', -ēs') *adj. & n.*

Bi·a·fra (bē-ä'frə, bē-ăf'rə), **Bight of.** Wide inlet of the Gulf of Guinea, off the coasts of Nigeria and Cameroon.

Bia·ly·stok (bē-ä'lĭ-stôk'). City of NE Poland. Pop. 218,700.

Bi·ar·ritz (bē'ə-rĭts'). Resort city of SW France. Pop. 27,595.

Bie·le·feld (bē'lə-fĕlt'). City of N central West Germany. Pop. 312,357.

Big·horn Mountains (bĭg'hôrn'). Range in N central Wyo., part of the Rocky Mts., rising to 13,175 ft (4,018.4 m).

Big Sur (bĭg sûr). Rugged resort region of central Calif. coast.

Bi·ki·ni (bĭ-kē'nē). Atoll in the Marshall Is., in the W central Pacific.

Bil·ba·o (bĭl-bä'ō). City of N Spain. Pop. 452,921.

Bil·lings (bĭl'ĭngz). City of S Mont. Pop. 66,798.

Bim·i·ni (bĭm'ə-nē). Group of small islands in the NW Bahamas.

Bir·ken·head (bûr'kən-hĕd'). Borough of W central England. Pop. 342,300.

Bir·ming·ham (bûr'mĭng-həm', -əm). **1.** City of central England. Pop. 1,033,900. **2.** City of N central Ala. Pop. 284,413.

Bis·cay (bĭs'kā), **Bay of.** Inlet of the Atlantic bordered on the S by Spain and on the E and NE by France.

Bis·cayne Bay (bĭs-kān', bĭs'kān'). Inlet of the Atlantic along the SE coast of Florida.

Bis·marck (bĭz'märk'). **1.** Cap. of N.Dak., in the S central part. Pop. 44,485. **2. Archipelago.** Group of more than 100 islands in the SW Pacific NE of New Guinea.

Bis·sau (bĭ-sou'). Cap. of Guinea-Bissau, on an inlet of the Atlantic. Pop. 71,169.

Black Forest (blăk). Wooded mountain region in SW West Germany.

Black Hills. Mountainous region of SW S.Dak. and NE Wyo.

Black Sea. Large inland sea between Europe and Asia Minor, connected with the Aegean by the Bosporus, the Sea of Marmara, and the Dardanelles.

Blue Nile (blōō nīl). River rising in the highlands of central Ethiopia and flowing c. 1,000 mi (1,610 km) SE and then NW to Khartoum, Sudan, where it joins the White Nile to form the Nile.

Blue Ridge. Range of the Appalachians extending 600 mi (965.4 km) from S Pa. to N Ga.

Bo·chum (bō'KHŏŏm). City of W West Germany, in the Ruhr. Pop. 402,988.

Boe·o·tia (bē-ō'shə). Ancient region of SE Greece, N of Attica and the Gulf of Corinth. —**Boe·o'tian** *adj. & n.*

Bo·go·tá (bō'gə-tä'). Cap. of Colombia, in the central part. Pop. 4,067,000.

Bo Hai (bō' hī'). Inlet of the Yellow Sea in NE China.

Bo·he·mi·a (bō-hē'mē·ə). Region and former kingdom of W Czechoslovakia. —**Bo·he'mi·an** *adj. & n.*

Boi·se (boi'zē, -sē). Cap. of Idaho, in the SW. Pop. 102,145.

ă pat ā pay â care ä father ĕ pet ē be ĭ pit ī tie î pier ŏ pot ō toe ô paw, for oi noise ŏŏ took ōō boot ou out th thin th this ŭ cut û urge yōō abuse zh vision ə about, item, edible, gallop, circus

Bo·liv·i·a (bə-lĭv'ē-ə). Country of W central South America. Caps. La Paz and Sucre. Pop. 4,804,000. —**Bo·liv'i·an** adj. & n.

Bo·lo·gna (bō-lōn'yə, -lō'nyä). City of N Italy. Pop. 471,554.

Bom·bay (bŏm-bā'). Port city of W central India. Pop. 5,970,575.

Bo·nin Islands (bō'nĭn). Archipelago of 15 islands S of Japan.

Bonn (bŏn). Cap. of West Germany, on the Rhine. Pop. 286,184.

Boo·thi·a Peninsula (bōō'thē-ə). Northernmost tip of the North American mainland, in NE Canada W of Baffin Is.

Bor·deaux (bôr-dō'). City of SW France. Pop. 223,131.

Bor·ne·o (bôr'nē-ō'). Island of the Indonesian Archipelago, between the Sulu and Java seas of the W Pacific. —**Bor'ne·an** adj. & n.

Bos·ni·a (bŏz'nē-ə). Region of W central Yugoslavia. —**Bos'ni·an** adj. & n.

Bos·po·rus (bŏs'pər-əs). Narrow strait between European and Asian Turkey, linking the Black Sea with the Sea of Marmara.

Bos·ton (bô'stən, bŏs'tən). Cap. of Mass., in the E. Pop. 562,994. —**Bos·to'ni·an** (bô-stō'nē-ən, bŏs-tō'-) adj. & n.

Both·ni·a (bŏth'nē-ə), **Gulf of.** N arm of the Baltic, between Sweden and Finland.

Bot·swa·na (bŏt-swä'nə). Country of S central Africa. Cap. Gaborone. Pop. 661,000.

Boul·der (bōl'dər). City of N Colo. Pop. 76,685.

Bound·a·ry (boun'drē, -də-rē). Peak, 13,145 ft (4,009.2 m), of SW Nev.

Bourne·mouth (bôrn'məth, bōrn'-, bōōrn'-). Seaside resort of S central England. Pop. 144,200.

Brad·ford (brăd'fərd). Borough of N central England. Pop. 461,600.

Brah·ma·pu·tra (brä'mə-pōō'trə). River of S Asia, rising in SW Tibet and flowing 1,800 mi (2,895 km) to the Bay of Bengal.

Brǎi·la (brə-ē'lä). City of E central Rumania, on the Danube. Pop. 200,435.

Bran·den·burg (brăn'dən-bûrg). Former duchy of N central Germany around which the kingdom of Prussia developed.

Bra·sil·ia (brə-zĭl'yə). Cap. of Brazil, in the central plateau. Pop. 350,000.

Bra·şov (brä-shôv'). City of central Rumania. Pop. 268,256.

Bra·ti·sla·va (brä'tĭ-slä'və, brăt'ĭ-). City of S Czechoslovakia, on the Danube. Pop. 374,860.

Bra·zil (brə-zĭl'). Country of E South America. Cap. Brasília. Pop. 107,145,200. —**Bra·zil'ian** adj. & n.

Braz·os (brăz'əs, brä'zəs). River of E Tex., flowing c. 950 mi (1,528 km) to the Gulf of Mexico.

Braz·za·ville (brăz'ə-vĭl'). Cap. of Congo, on the N bank of the Congo. Pop. 175,000.

Bre·men (brĕm'ən). City of N West Germany, on the Weser R. Pop. 556,128.

Bren·ner Pass (brĕn'ər). Alpine pass between S Austria and NE Italy.

Bre·scia (brĕ'shä). Industrial city of N central Italy. Pop. 212,265.

Brest (brĕst). Also **Brest Li·tovsk** (lə-tôfsk', -tôvsk'). City of W European USSR. Pop. 186,000.

Bridge·port (brĭj'pôrt', -pōrt'). Industrial city of SW Conn. Pop. 142,546.

Bridge·town (brĭj'toun'). Cap. of Barbados, E West Indies. Pop. 8,789.

Brigh·ton (brīt'n). Seaside resort of SE England, on the English Channel. Pop. 152,700.

Bris·bane (brĭz'bən, -bān'). Seaport of SE Australia. Pop. 702,000.

Bris·tol (brĭs'təl). 1. Port city of SW England. Pop. 408,000. 2. **Channel.** Inlet of the Atlantic between Wales and SW England.

Brit·ain (brĭt'n). 1. Great Britain. 2. United Kingdom.

British Co·lum·bi·a (brĭt'ĭsh kə-lŭm'bē-ə). Province of W Canada. Cap. Victoria. Pop. 2,466,608. —**British Co·lum'bi·an** n.

British Isles. Islands off the NW coast of Europe, comprising Great Britain, Ireland, and adjacent smaller islands.

British Vir·gin Islands (vûr'jən). British colony in the West Indies, E of Puerto Rico. Cap. Road Town, on Tortola Is. Pop. 10,484.

Brit·ta·ny (brĭt'n-ē). Region and former province of France on a peninsula between the English Channel and Bay of Biscay. —**Bret'on** (brĕt'n) adj. & n.

Br·no (bûr'nō). City of central Czechoslovakia. Pop. 372,793.

Bronx or **the Bronx** (brŏngks). Borough of New York City, SE N.Y., on the mainland N of Manhattan. Pop. 1,169,115.

Brook·lyn (brŏŏk'lĭn). Borough of New York City, SE N.Y., on W Long Is. Pop. 2,230,936.

Bruges (brōōzh). City of NW Belgium. Pop. 118,243.

Bru·nei (brōō-nī'). Sultanate on the N coast of Borneo. Cap. Bandar Seri Begawan. Pop. 136,256.

Bruns·wick (brŭnz'wĭk). Industrial city E of West Germany. Pop. 261,669.

Brus·sels (brŭs'əlz). Cap. of Belgium, in the N central part. Pop. 143,957.

Bry·ansk (brē-änsk'). City of central European USSR, on the Desna R. Pop. 401,000.

Bu·ca·ra·man·ga (bōō'kä-rä-mäng'gä). City of N central Colombia. Pop. 402,000.

Bu·cha·rest (bōō'kə-rĕst', byōō'-). Cap. of Rumania, in the SE. Pop. 1,858,418.

Bu·da·pest (bōō'də-pĕst'). Cap. of Hungary, in the N central part. Pop. 2,060,000.

Bue·nos Ai·res (bwā'nəs îr'ēz, âr'-, bō'nəs). Cap. of Argentina, in the E on the Río de la Plata. Pop. 2,978,000.

Buf·fa·lo (bŭf'ə-lō'). City of W N.Y., at the NE end of Lake Erie. Pop. 357,870.

Bu·jum·bu·ra (bōō'jam-bōōr'ə, bōō-jōōm'bōōr'-ə). Cap. of Burundi, in the W on Lake Tanganyika. Pop. 157,000.

Bul·gar·i·a (bŭl-gâr'ē-ə, bŏŏl-). Country of SE Europe, on the Black Sea. Cap. Sofia. Pop. 8,846,417. —**Bul·gar'i·an** adj. & n.

Bun·ker Hill (bŭng'kər). Hill in Charlestown, Mass., near site of 1st major Revolutionary War battle (1775).

Bur·gun·dy (bûr'gən-dē). Region and former duchy and province of SE France. —**Bur·gun'di·an** (bər-gŭn'dē-ən) adj. & n.

Bur·ling·ton (bûr'lĭng-tən). City of NW Vt., on Lake Champlain. Pop. 37,712.

Bur·ma (bûr'mə). Country of SE Asia on the E shore of the Bay of Bengal and the Andaman Sea. Cap. Rangoon. Pop. 31,512,000. —**Bur·mese'** (bər-mēz', -mēs') or **Bur'man** adj. & n.

Bur·na·by (bûr'nə-bē). City of SW B.C., Canada, near Vancouver. Pop. 131,599.

Bur·sa (bŏŏr-sä', bŭr'sə). City of NW Turkey, near the Sea of Marmara. Pop. 466,178.

Bu·run·di (bŏŏ-rŏŏn'dē). Country of E central Africa. Cap. Bujumbura. Pop. 3,864,000.

Byd·goszcz (bĭd'gôshch). Industrial city of N Poland. Pop. 343,800.

Byz·an·tine Empire (bĭz'ən-tēn', -tīn'). E part of the later Roman Empire.

By·zan·ti·um (bĭ-zăn'shē-əm, -tē-əm). Ancient Greek city on the site of Istanbul (Constantinople), Turkey.

C

Cá·diz (kā'dĭz, kə-dĭz'). City of SE Spain, on the Gulf of Cádiz, an inlet of the Atlantic. Pop. 156,328.

Caen (kän, käN). City of NW France. Pop. 119,474.

Ca·glia·ri (käl'yə-rē'). Cap. of Sardinia, Italy, on the S coast. Pop. 241,472.

Cai·ro (kī'rō). Cap. of Egypt, on the Nile in the NE. Pop. 5,278,000. —**Cai·rene** (-rēn') adj. & n.

Ca·la·bri·a (kə-lā'brē-ə). Region of S Italy. —**Ca·la'bri·an** adj. & n.

Ca·lais (kă-lā', kăl'ā). Seaport of N France, on the Strait of Dover. Pop. 78,820.

Cal·cut·ta (kăl-kŭt'ə). City of E India, on the Ganges delta. Metro. pop. 9,100,000.

Cal·ga·ry (kăl'gə-rē). City of S Alta., Canada. Pop. 560,618.

Ca·li (kä'lē). City of W Colombia. Pop. 1,293,000.

Cal·i·for·nia (kăl'ə-fôrn'yə, -fôr'nē-ə). **1.** State of SW U.S., on the Pacific. Cap. Sacramento. Pop. 23,668,562. **2.** Gulf of. Inlet of the Pacific, between Lower California and NW Mexico. —**Cal·i·for'nian** adj. & n.

Cal·la·o (kä-yä'ō). Seaport of W Peru, on the Pacific. Pop. 196,919.

Ca·ma·güey (kä'mä-gwā'). City of E central Cuba. Pop. 230,891.

Cam·bo·di·a (kăm-bō'dē-ə). Country of SE Asia, bordering on the Gulf of Siam. Cap. Phnom Penh. Pop. 8,110,000. —**Cam·bo'di·an** adj. & n.

Cam·bridge (kām'brĭj). **1.** City of E central England. Pop. 101,600. **2.** City of E Mass. Pop. 95,322.

Cam·e·roon (kăm'ə-rōōn'). Also **Cam·e·roun** (kăm-rōōn'). Country of W central Africa. Cap. Yaoundé. Pop. 7,663,246.

Cam·pa·gna (käm-pä'nyä). Region of Italy, surrounding Rome.

Cam·pa·nia (kăm-pān'yə, -pā'nē-ə). Region of S Italy, on the Tyrrhenian Sea.

Cam·pi·nas (kăn-pē'nəs). City of SE Brazil, N of São Paulo. Pop. 562,400.

Cam·pos (kăn'pōōs). City of SE Brazil. Pop. 352,500.

Ca·naan (kā'nən). In Biblical times, the part of Palestine between the Jordan R. and the Mediterranean. —**Ca'naan·ite'** adj. & n.

Can·a·da (kăn'ə-də). Country of N North America. Cap. Ottawa. Pop. 22,992,604. —**Ca·na'di·an** (kə-nā'dē-ən) adj. & n.

Ca·na·di·an (kə-nā'dē-ən). River of S central U.S., flowing 906 mi (1,457.8 km) from NE N.Mex. to E Okla.

Ca·nal Zone (kə-năl'). Territory across the Isthmus of Panama, formerly administered by the U.S. for the operation of the Panama Canal.

Ca·nary Islands (kə-nâr'ē). Spanish islands in the Atlantic off the NW coast of Africa.

Ca·nav·er·al (kə-năv'ə-rəl), **Cape.** Sandy promontory of E central Atlantic coast of Fla.

Can·ber·ra (kăn'bər-ə, -bĕr'ə). Cap. of Australia, in the SE part. Pop. 221,000.

Cannes (kăn). Resort city of SE France, on the Mediterranean. Pop. 70,527.

Can·ter·bury (kăn'tər-bĕr'ē). Cathedral city of SE England. Pop. 117,400.

Can·ton (kăn'tŏn', kăn'tŏn'). Guangzhou, China.

Cape Bret·on Island (kăp brĕt'n, brĭt'n). Island of NE N.S., Canada.

Cape Town or **Cape·town** (kāp'toun'). Legislative cap. of South Africa, on the SW tip of Africa. Pop. 697,514.

Cape Verde (vûrd). Island country in the Atlantic W of Senegal. Cap. Praia. Pop. 272,071.

Cap·pa·do·ci·a (kăp'ə-dō'shə, -shē-ə). Ancient region of E Asia Minor, now forming the central part of Turkey. —**Cap'pa·do'cian** adj. & n.

Ca·pri (kä'prē). Mountainous island of Italy, S of the Bay of Naples.

Ca·ra·cas (kə-rä'kəs, -răk'əs). Cap. of Venezuela, in the N near the Caribbean coast. Pop. 1,662,627.

Car·diff (kär'dĭf). City of SE Wales, on Bristol Channel. Pop. 282,000.

Car·ib·be·an Sea (kăr'ə-bē'ən, kə-rĭb'ē-ən). Extension of the Atlantic Ocean, bounded by the coasts of Central and South America and the West Indies.

Car·mel (kär'məl), **Mount.** Ridge extending 13 mi (21 km) across NW Israel to the Mediterranean.

Car·o·line Islands (kăr'ə-lĭn'). Archipelago in the W Pacific E of the Philippines.

Car·pa·thi·an (kär-pā'thē-ən). Mountain system of E Europe, extending in an arc through Czechoslovakia, Hungary, the USSR, and Rumania.

Car·son City (kär'sən). Cap. of Nev., in the SW. Pop. 32,022.

Car·ta·ge·na (kär'tə-gā'nə). **1.** City of NW Colombia, on the Caribbean. Pop. 388,000. **2.** City of SE Spain, on the Mediterranean. Pop. 135,200.

Car·thage (kär'thĭj). Ancient city and state on the N coast of Africa. —**Car'tha·gin'i·an** (-thə-jĭn'ē-ən) adj. & n.

Cas·a·blan·ca (kăs'ə-blăng'kə, kä'sə-bläng'kə). City of NW Morocco, on the Atlantic. Pop. 1,371,300.

Cas·cade Range (kăs-kād'). Also **Cas·cades** (-kādz'). N section of the Sierra Nevada Mts., from NE Calif. to W Ore. and Wash.

Cas·pi·an Sea (kăs'pē-ən). Salt lake, largest inland body of water in the world, between SE Europe and W Asia.

Cas·tile (kăs-tēl'). Region and former kingdom of central and N Spain. —**Cas·til'ian** (kă-stĭl'yən, kə-) adj. & n.

Cat·a·lo·nia (kăt'l-ō'nyə, -nē-ə). Region of NE Spain, bordering on France and the Mediterranean. —**Cat'a·lo'nian** adj. & n.

Ca·ta·nia (kə-tä'nyə, -tä'nē-ə). Port city of E Sicily. Pop. 398,426.

Cats·kill Mountains (kăts'kĭl'). Also **Cats·kills** (-kĭlz). Low mountain range in SE N.Y.

Cau·ca·sus (kô'kə-səs). Region and mountain range of SE European USSR, between the Black and Caspian seas, rising to 18,480 ft (5,636.4 m).

Cay·enne (kī-ĕn', kā-). Cap. of French Guiana, on Cayenne Is., in a river mouth near the Atlantic coast. Pop. 30,461.

ă pat ā pay â care ä father ĕ pet ē be ĭ pit ī tie î pier ŏ pot ō toe ô paw, for oi noise ŏŏ took
ōō boot ou out th thin th this ŭ cut û urge yōō abuse zh vision ə about, item, edible, gallop, circus

Cay·man Islands (kī-mān′, kä-män′, kā′mən).
British-administered group of 3 islands in the
Caribbean NW of Jamaica. Cap. Georgetown.
Pop. 10,652.

Ce·bu (sā-bōō′). **1.** Island in the Visayan Is. of
the Philippines. **2.** City on the E coast of Cebu
Is. Pop. 413,025.

Ce·dar Rap·ids (sē′dər răp′ĭdz). Industrial city
of E central Iowa. Pop. 110,243.

Cen·tral Af·ri·can Republic (sĕn′trəl ăf′rĭ-kən).
Country of central Africa. Cap. Bangui. Pop.
1,637,000.

Central A·mer·i·ca (ə-mĕr′ĭ-kə). Region from
the S boundary of Mexico to the N boundary
of Colombia. **—Central A·mer·i·can** n. & adj.

Cer·ro de Pas·co (sĕr′rō dĕ päs′kō). Mountain,
15,100 ft (4,605.5 m), of central Peru.

Cey·lon (sĭ-lŏn′). Sri Lanka. **—Cey·lo·nese′**
(- nēz′, -nēs′) adj. & n.

Chad (chăd). **1.** Country of N central Africa.
Cap. Ndjamena. Pop. 4,030,000. **2.** Lake in
central Africa, mainly in Chad.

Chal·de·a (kăl-dē′ə). Ancient region of S Babylonia along the Euphrates and the Persian
Gulf. **—Chal·de′an** adj. & n.

Cham·pagne (shăm-pān′). Region and former
province of NE France.

Cham·plain (shăm-plān′), **Lake.** Long, narrow
lake between E N.Y. and W Vt.

Chang·chun (chäng′chŭn′). City of NE China.
Pop. 1,500,000.

Chang·sha (chäng′shä′). City of SE central
China. Pop. 850,000.

Chan·nel Islands (chăn′əl). Group of 9 British
islands in the English Channel off Normandy.

Charles·ton (chärl′stən). Cap. of W.Va., in the
W. Pop. 63,968.

Char·lotte (shär′lət). City of S N.C. Pop.
314,447.

Charlotte A·ma·lie (ə-mäl′yə). Cap. of the U.S.
Virgin Islands, on the S shore of St. Thomas Is.
Pop. 12,220.

Char·lotte·town (shär′lət-toun′). Cap. of P.E.I.,
Canada, on the S coast. Pop. 19,133.

Chartres (shär′trə, shärt). City of N central
France. Pop. 38,928.

Chat·ta·noo·ga (chăt′ə-nōō′gə). City of SE
Tenn., SE of Nashville. Pop. 169,565.

Che·bok·sa·ry (chĭ′bŏk-sä′rĭ). City of E central
European USSR. Pop. 323,000.

Che·lya·binsk (chĭ-lyä′bĭnsk). City of W Siberian USSR. Pop. 1,042,000.

Cheng·chou (jŭng′jō′). Zhengzhou.

Cheng·du (chŭng′dōō′). Also **Cheng·tu.** City of
central China. Pop. 1,800,000.

Ches·a·peake (chĕs′ə-pēk). **1.** City of SE Va.
Pop. 114,226. **2. Bay.** Inlet of the Atlantic in
Va. and Md.

Chey·enne (shī-ăn′, -ĕn′). Cap. of Wyo., in the
SE. Pop. 47,283.

Chi·ba (chē′bä′). City of E Honshu, Japan.
Pop. 712,488.

Chi·ca·go (shə-kä′gō, -kô′gō, -kä′gə). City of
NE Ill., on Lake Michigan. Pop. 3,005,072.
—Chi·ca′go·an n.

Chi·hua·hua (chē-wä′wä). City of N Mexico.
Pop. 369,545.

Chile (chĭl′ē). Country of SW South America,
stretching from Peru to the S tip of the continent. Cap. Santiago. Pop. 10,044,940. **—Chil′e·
an** adj. & n.

Chi·na (chī′nə). **1.** Also **People's Republic of
China.** Country of E central Asia. Cap. Beijing.
Pop. 930,500,000. **2.** Also **Republic of China.**
Taiwan. **3. Sea.** W section of the Pacific, ex-
tending from S Japan to the Malay Peninsula.
—Chi·nese′ adj. & n.

Chit·ta·gong (chĭt′ə-gŏng′). City of SE Bangladesh. Pop. 497,026.

Chong·qing (chŏōng′chyĭng′). Also **Chung·king**
(chōōng′kĭng′, jōōng′gĭng′). City of S central
China, on the Yangtze. Pop. 2,900,000.

Christ·church (krīst′chûrch′). City of E South
Is., New Zealand. Pop. 171,300.

Cin·cin·nat·i (sĭn′sə-năt′ē, -năt′ə). City of SW
Ohio, on the Ohio R. Pop. 385,457.

Cis·al·pine Gaul (sĭs-ăl′pīn′ gôl). Part of ancient Gaul S of the Alps of N Italy.

Ciu·dad Juá·rez (syōō-thäth′ wär′ĕz). City of N
Mexico, on the Rio Grande. Pop. 597,096.

Cleve·land (klēv′lənd). City of NE Ohio, on
Lake Erie. Pop. 573,822.

Clyde (klīd). River rising in S Scotland and
flowing N to the **Firth of Clyde,** an inlet of the
Atlantic.

Coast (kōst). **1. Mountains.** Range in W B.C.,
Canada, and SE Alas. extending c. 1,000 mi
(1,609 km) parallel to the Pacific coast. **2.
Ranges.** Series of ranges of extreme W North
America along the Pacific Coast from Lower
Calif. to SE Alas.

Cod (kŏd), **Cape.** Peninsula in SE Mass.

Coeur d'A·lene (kôr də-lān′). Lake in a resort
area of N Idaho.

Co·logne (kə-lōn′). City of West Germany, on
the Rhine. Pop. 976,136.

Co·lom·bi·a (kə-lŭm′bē-ə). Country of NW
South America. Cap. Bogotá. Pop. 22,551,811.
—Co·lom′bi·an adj. & n.

Co·lom·bo (kə-lŭm′bō). Cap. of Sri Lanka, on
the W coast. Pop. 1,540,000.

Col·o·ra·do (kŏl′ə-rä′dō, -răd′ə). **1.** State of the
W central U.S. Cap. Denver. Pop. 2,888,834.
2. Desert in SE Calif. and NW N.Mex.
3. River rising in N central Colo. and flowing
through Utah and Ariz. to empty into the Gulf
of California. **4.** River rising in NW Tex. and
flowing to the Gulf of Mexico. **—Col′o·ra′dan**
adj. & n.

Colorado Springs. City of central Colo. Pop.
215,150.

Co·lum·bi·a (kə-lŭm′bē-ə). **1.** Cap. of S.C., in the
central part. Pop. 97,100. **2.** River rising in SE
B.C., Canada, and flowing 1,200 mi (1,930.8
km) to the Pacific, forming most of the Wash.-
Ore. border.

Co·lum·bus (kə-lŭm′bəs). **1.** Cap. of Ohio, in
the central part. Pop. 564,871. **2.** City of W
Ga., on the Ala. border. Pop. 169,441.

Com·mon·wealth of Nations (kŏm′ən-wĕlth′).
Association including the United Kingdom, its
dependencies, and many former colonies.

Co·mo (kō′mō). Resort lake in N Italy.

Com·o·ro Islands (kŏm′ə-rō′). Group of islands at the N entrance of Mozambique Channel off E Africa.

Com·mu·nism (kŏm′yə-nĭz′əm), **Mount.** Highest mountain (24,590 ft/7,500 m) in the USSR,
in the Pamirs near the Chinese border.

Con·a·kry (kăn′ə-krē). Cap. of Guinea, on the
Atlantic. Pop. 290,000.

Con·cep·ción (kŏn′sĕp-syōn′). City of W central Chile. Pop. 395,000.

Con·cord (kŏng′kərd). **1.** Town in E Mass; site
of an early battle of the Revolutionary War.
Pop. 16,293. **2.** Cap. of N.H., in the S central
part. Pop. 30,400. **3.** City of W central Calif.
Pop. 103,251.

Con·go (kŏng′gō). **1.** Country of W central Africa. Cap. Brazzaville. Pop. 1,405,000. **2.** 2nd
longest river in Africa (2,900 mi/4,666 km), rising in Zambia and flowing gen. N, W, and
then SW to the Atlantic. **—Con′go·lese′** (-lēz′,
-lēs′) adj. & n.

Con·nect·i·cut (kə-nĕt'ə-kət). **1.** State of the NE U.S. along Long Is. Sound. Cap. Hartford. Pop. 3,105,576. **2.** River of NE U.S., rising in N N.H. and flowing S to Long Is. Sound.

Con·stan·ţa (kŏn-stän'tsä). Seaport of SE Rumania, on the Black Sea. Pop. 267,612.

Con·stan·tine (kŏn'stən-tēn). City of NE Algeria. Pop. 350,183.

Con·stan·ti·no·ple (kŏn'stăn-tə-nō'pəl). Istanbul.

Cook (kŏok). **1. Mount.** Highest mountain (12,349 ft/3,766.5 m) of New Zealand, on South Is. in the Southern Alps. **2. Mount.** One of the St. Elias Mts. of SE Alas. **3.** Inlet of the Pacific in S Alas. **4.** Island group of the S Pacific, NE of New Zealand. **5. Strait.** Channel separating North and South Is. of New Zealand.

Co·pen·ha·gen (kō'pən-hā'gən, -hä'gən). Cap. of Denmark, in the E part. Pop. 1,470,000.

Cor·al (kôr'əl, kŏr'-). Sea of the SW Pacific, NE of Australia and SE of New Guinea.

Cor·dil·le·ras (kôr'dĭl-yâr'əz). **1.** Andes range in W South America. **2.** Complex of ranges in N North America including the Rocky Mts. and the Sierra Nevada and their extension N into Canada and Alas. **3.** Complex of mountain ranges on the W side of the Americas, extending from Alas. to Cape Horn.

Cór·do·ba (kôr'dō-bə, -bä). **1.** City of N central Argentina. Pop. 985,000. **2.** City of S Spain. Pop. 276,255. —**Cor'do·van** adj. & n.

Cor·inth (kôr'ĭnth, kŏr'-). **1.** City of ancient Greece, in the NE Peloponnesus. **2.** Isthmus connecting the Peloponnesus to the rest of Greece.

Cork (kôrk). City of S Ireland. Pop. 138,267.

Corn·wall (kôrn'wôl). Peninsula and region of SW England.

Co·ro·man·del Coast (kôr'ə-măn'dĕl). SE coast of India.

Cor·pus Chris·ti (kôr'pəs krĭs'tē). City of SW Tex. Pop. 231,999.

Cor·reg·i·dor (kə-rĕg'ə-dôr). Island of N Philippines, at the entrance to Manila Bay.

Cor·si·ca (kôr'sĭ-kə). Island of France, in the Mediterranean W of Sardinia. —**Cor'si·can** adj. & n.

Cos·ta Ri·ca (kŏs'tə rē'kə, kô'stə). Country of Central America between Panama and Nicaragua. Cap. San José. Pop. 1,993,800. —**Cos'ta Ri'can** adj. & n.

Côte d'A·zur (dä-zür'). The Mediterranean coast of France.

Co·to·pax·i (kō'tə-pàk'sē). Highest (19,347 ft/5,900.8 m) active volcano in the world, in the Andes of central Ecuador.

Cov·en·try (kŭv'ĭn-trē). City of central England. Pop. 339,300.

Cra·ter (krā'tər). Lake in the crater of an extinct volcano at **Crater Lake National Park** in SW Ore.

Crete (krēt). Greek island in the E Mediterranean. —**Cre'tan** (krēt'ən) adj. & n.

Cri·me·a (krī-mē'ə). Peninsula of extreme S European USSR, extending into the Black Sea. —**Cri·me'an** adj.

Cro·a·tia (krō-ā'shə). Region and former kingdom of SE Europe, along the NE coast of the Adriatic; now part of Yugoslavia. —**Cro·a'tian** adj. & n.

Cu·ba (kyōō'bə). Island country in the Caribbean off the S coast of Fla. Cap. Havana. Pop. 8,553,400. —**Cu'ban** adj. & n.

Cú·cu·ta (kōō'kə-tə, -kōō-tä). City of NE Colombia, near the Venezuelan border. Pop. 355,000.

Cu·lia·cán (kōō'lyä-kän'). City of W Mexico. Pop. 302,200.

Cum·ber·land (kŭm'bər-lənd). **1. Gap.** Pass through the Cumberland Mts. at the junction of the borders of Ky., Va., and Tenn. **2. Plateau** or **Mountains.** W section of the Appalachians, extending along the Va.-Ky. border and into central Tenn.

Cu·ra·çao (kyōō'rə-sō, kōō'rä-sä'ō). Island of the Netherlands Antilles, in the Caribbean off the NW coast of Venezuela.

Cu·ri·ti·ba (kōō'rĭ-tē'bə, kōō'rē-). City of SE Brazil. Pop. 905,800.

Cyc·la·des (sĭk'lə-dēz'). Island group of SE Greece in the S Aegean.

Cy·prus (sī'prəs). Island country in the Mediterranean off S Turkey. Cap. Nicosia. Pop. 639,000. —**Cyp'ri·an** (sĭp'rē-ən) adj. —**Cyp'ri·ot** or **Cyp'ri·ote** (sĭp'rē-ŏt) adj. & n.

Czech·o·slo·va·ki·a (chĕk'ə-slə-vä'kē-ə, -ō-slō-). Country of central Europe. Cap. Prague. Pop. 15,280,148. —**Czech'o·slo'vak** or **Czech·o·slo·va'ki·an** adj. & n.

D

Dac·ca (dăk'ə). Cap. of Bangladesh. Pop. 1,563,517.

Da·ci·a (dā'shē-ə, -shə). Ancient name for the part of Europe corresponding to modern Rumania. —**Da'cian** adj. & n.

Da·ho·mey (də-hō'mē). Benin.

Da·kar (dä-kär'). Cap. of Senegal, on Cape Verde in the W. Pop. 798,792.

Dal·las (dăl'əs). City of NE Tex. Pop. 904,078.

Dal·ma·tia (dăl-mā'shə). Region of Yugoslavia, along the E coast of the Adriatic. —**Dal·ma'tian** adj. & n.

Da·mas·cus (də-măs'kəs). Cap. of Syria, in the SW. Pop. 1,156,000.

Da Nang (dä näng', dä' näng'). City of central Vietnam, on the South China Sea. Pop. 492,194.

Dan·ube (dăn'yōōb). River of SE Europe, rising in the Black Forest of SW West Germany and flowing 1,750 mi (2,815.7 km) E to the Black Sea coast of Rumania. —**Dan·u'bi·an** adj.

Dan·zig (dăn'sĭg, dän'tsĭKH). Gdańsk.

Dar·da·nelles (därd'n-ĕlz'). Strait linking the Sea of Marmara and the Aegean Sea.

Dar es Sa·laam (där' ĕs sə-läm'). Cap. of Tanzania, in the N on the Indian Ocean. Pop. 870,000.

Dar·ling (där'lĭng). River, c. 1,702 mi (2,738.5 km), of SE Australia.

Dav·en·port (dăv'ən-pôrt', -pōrt'). City of E Iowa, on the Mississippi. Pop. 103,264.

Day·ton (dāt'n). City of SW Ohio. Pop. 203,588.

Dead Sea (dĕd). Salt lake between Israel and Jordan; lowest point on earth, 1,302 ft (397.1 m) below sea level.

Death Valley (dĕth). Desert basin in E Calif. and W Nev.; lowest point in the Western Hemisphere, 280 ft (85.4 m) below sea level.

Del-a-ware (dĕl'ə-wâr'). 1. State of the E U. S., on the Atlantic. Cap. Dover. Pop. 595,225. 2. Bay. Inlet of the Atlantic between E Del. and SW N.J. 3. River of NE U.S., rising in SE N.Y. and flowing S to Delaware Bay.

Del-hi (dĕl'ē). City of N central India, on the Jumna R. Pop. 3,706,558.

De-los (dē'lŏs). Island of SE Greece in the central Cyclades.

Del-phi (dĕl'fī'). Ancient town of central Greece, near Mt. Parnassus.

Den-mark (dĕn'märk). Country of N Europe, consisting of a peninsula and an archipelago between the North and Baltic seas. Cap. Copenhagen. Pop. 5,122,065. —**Dan'ish** (dā'nĭsh) *adj. & n.*

Den-ver (dĕn'vər). Cap. of Colo., in the N central part. Pop. 491,396.

Der-by (där'bē). City of S central England. Pop. 215,900.

Des Moines (də moin'). Cap. of Iowa, in the S central part. Pop. 191,003.

De-troit (dĭ-troit'). City of SE Mich., opposite Windsor, Ont. Pop. 1,203,339.

Dev-il's Island (dĕv'əlz). Island in the Caribbean off French Guiana.

Dezh-nev (dĕzh-nyôf'). Cape of extreme NE Far Eastern USSR, on Bering Strait; easternmost point of Asia.

Dhau-la-gi-ri (dou'lə-gĭr'ē). Peak rising to 26,810 ft (8,177 m) in the Himalayas of N central Nepal.

Dia-mond Head (dī'mənd hĕd', dī'-ə-). Promontory, 761 ft (232.1 m) high, on the SE coast of Oahu, Hawaii.

Dien Bien Phu (dyĕn'byĕn'fōō'). Town of NW Vietnam, near the Laos border; site of Vietminh victory over the French (1954).

Di-jon (dē-zhôn'). City of E France, SE of Paris. Pop. 151,705.

Di-na-ric Alps (dĭ-nâr'ĭk ălps). SE range of the Alps, extending along the Adriatic coast of Yugoslavia into N Albania.

District of Co-lum-bi-a (kə-lŭm'bē-ə). Federal district of E U.S., on the Potomac R. between Va. and Md.; coextensive with the city of Washington.

Dja-kar-ta (jə-kär'tə). Cap. of Indonesia, on the NW coast of Java. Pop. 6,400,000.

Dji-bou-ti (jĭ-bōō'tē). 1. Country of E Africa, on the Gulf of Aden. Pop. 150,000. 2. Cap. of Djibouti, in the SE part. Pop. 40,000.

Dne-pro-pe-trovsk (dnyĕ'prə-pə-trôfsk'). City of S European USSR, on the Dnieper. Pop. 1,083,000.

Dnie-per (nē'pər). River of W European USSR, rising near Smolensk and flowing SW to the Black Sea.

Dnies-ter (nē'stər). River of SW European USSR.

Do-dec-a-nese (dō-dĕk'ə-nēs', -nēz'). Islands of SE Greece, in the Aegean between Turkey and Crete.

Do-ha (dō'hə, -hä'). Cap. of Qatar, on the Persian Gulf. Pop. 95,000.

Do-lo-mites (dō'lə-mīts', dŏl'ə-). Range of the E Alps in N Italy.

Dom-i-ni-ca (dŏm'ə-nē'kə, də-mĭn'ī-kə). Island republic in the E Caribbean, between Guadeloupe and Martinique. Cap. Roseau. Pop. 83,100.

Do-min-i-can Republic (də-mĭn'ī-kən). Country occupying the E part of the Caribbean island of Hispaniola. Cap. Santo Domingo. Pop. 5,660,000.

Don (dŏn). River of S European USSR, flowing 1,222 mi (1,966.2 km) into the Sea of Azov.

Do-nets Basin (dō-nĕts'). Industrial region of S European USSR, N of the Sea of Azov.

Dort-mund (dôrt'mənd). City of W West Germany. Pop. 609,954.

Dou-a-la or **Du-a-la** (dōō-ä'lä). City of SW Cameroon, W equatorial Africa, on the Bight of Biafra. Pop. 458,246.

Dou-ro (dō'rōō). River rising in N Spain and flowing W to the Atlantic in N Portugal.

Do-ver (dō'vər). 1. Strait at E end of the English Channel between SE England and N France. 2. Borough of SE England, on the Strait of Dover opposite Calais, France. Pop 34,160. 3. Cap. of Del., in the central part. Pop. 23,512.

Dres-den (drĕz'dən). City of SE East Germany. Pop. 514,508.

Dub-lin (dŭb'lĭn). Cap. of Ireland, on the Irish Sea. Pop. 544,586. —**Dub'lin-er** *n.*

Duis-burg (dūs'bûrk'). City of W West Germany. Pop. 559,066.

Du-luth (də-lōōth'). City of Minn., at the W end of Lake Superior. Pop. 92,811.

Dun-dee (dŭn-dē'). City of E Scotland, on the Firth of Tay. Pop. 190,793.

Du-que de Ca-xi-as (dōō'kə də kə-shē'əsh). City of SE Brazil, on Guanabara Bay NNW of Rio de Janeiro. Pop. 639,100.

Du-ran-go (dōō-räng'gō, dōō-räng'gō). City of N central Mexico, NNW of Guadalajara. Pop. 218,600.

Dur-ban (dûr'bən). City of E South Africa, on the Indian Ocean. Pop. 736,852.

Du-shan-be (dōō-shäm'bə, -shäm'-). City of SW Central Asian USSR, S of Tashkent. Pop. 501,000.

Düs-sel-dorf (dōōs'-əl-dôrf'). City of W West Germany, on the Rhine N of Cologne. Pop. 594,770.

E

East An-gli-a (ēst ăng'glē-ə). Anglo-Saxon kingdom of SE England.

East Berlin (bûr-lĭn'). See **Berlin.**

East-er Island (ē'stər). Island of Chile in the S Pacific; site of a number of ancient massive sculptured heads.

East Ger-ma-ny (jûr'mə-nē). See **Germany.**

East In-dies (ĭn'dēz). 1. The Malay Archipelago. 2. The islands comprising Indonesia.

E-bro (ē'brō). River of NE Spain, flowing c. 575 mi (925 km) to the Mediterranean.

Ec-ua-dor (ĕk'wə-dôr'). Country of NW South America. Cap. Quito. Pop. 7,810,000. —**Ec'ua-dor'e-an** or **Ec'ua-dor'i-an** *adj. & n.*

Ed-in-burgh (ĕd'n-bûr'ə). Cap. of Scotland, in the E on the Firth of Forth. Pop. 455,126.

Ed-mon-ton (ĕd'mən-tən). Cap. of Alta., Canada, in the central part N of Calgary. Pop. 503,773.

E-dom (ē'dəm). Ancient country of SW Asia.

E-gypt (ē'jĭpt). Country of NE Africa and SW Asia. Cap. Cairo. Pop. 40,980,000. —**E-gyp'tian** *adj. & n.*

E-lam (ē'ləm). Ancient kingdom of SW Asia, in present-day SW Iran.

El-ba (ĕl'bə). Italian island off the W coast of Italy.

El-be (ĕl'bə, ĕlb). River of Czechoslovakia, East Germany, and West Germany, flowing to the North Sea.

El-bert (ĕl'bərt), **Mount.** Highest (14,431 ft/ 4,401.5 m) of the U.S. Rocky Mts., in central Colo.

El·brus (ĕl′brŏŏs), **Mount**. Highest mountain of Europe, 18,481 ft (5,636.7 m), in the Caucasus of SE European USSR.

El·burz (ĕl-bŏŏrz′). Mountain range of N Iran, rising to 18,934 ft (5,774.9 m).

E·liz·a·beth (ĭ-lĭz′ə-bəth). City of NE N.J. Pop. 106,201.

El·lis (ĕl′ĭs). Island in Upper New York Bay.

El Pas·o (ĕl păs′ō). City of W Tex., on the Rio Grande. Pop. 425,259.

El Sal·va·dor (ĕl săl′və-dôr′). Country of Central America, on the Pacific. Cap. San Salvador. Pop. 4,360,000. —**El Sal′va·dor′an** *adj. & n.*

Eng·land (ĭng′glənd). Part of the United Kingdom of Great Britain and Northern Ireland, in S Great Britain. Cap. London. Pop. 46,396,100. —**Eng′lish** (glĭsh) *adj. & n.*

Eng·lish Channel (ĭng′glĭsh). Arm of the Atlantic, c. 350 mi (565 km) long, separating England and France.

E·ni·we·tok (ĕn′ĭ-wē′tŏk′, ĕ-nē′wĭ-tŏk′). Atoll in the Marshall Is., in the W central Pacific.

Eph·e·sus (ĕf′ə-səs). Ancient Greek city, in Asia Minor near the Aegean.

E·qua·to·ri·al Guin·ea (ē′kwə-tôr′ē-əl gĭn′ē, ĕk′-wə-). Country of W Africa, including islands in the Gulf of Guinea and mainland Rio Muni. Cap. Malabo. Pop. 320,000.

Er·e·bus (ĕr′ə-bəs), **Mount**. Active volcano on Ross Is., Antarctica.

E·rie (îr′ē). **1.** One of the Great Lakes, between S Ont. and W N.Y., NW Pa., N Ohio, and SE Mich. **2. Canal**. Former artificial waterway extending c. 360 mi (580 km) across central N.Y. from Albany to Buffalo. **3.** City of NW Pa., on Lake Erie SW of Buffalo, N.Y. Pop. 119,123.

Er·i·tre·a (ĕr′ĭ-trē′ə). Region of N Ethiopia, along the Red Sea.

Er Rif or **Er Riff** (ĕr rĭf′). Vars. of Rif.

Erz·ge·bir·ge (ĕrts′gə-bĭr′gə). Mountain range on the border between East Germany and Czechoslovakia.

Es·fa·han (ĕs′fə-hän′) or **Is·fa·han** (ĭs′-). City of central Iran. Pop. 671,825.

Es·sen (ĕs′ən). City of W West Germany, on the Ruhr R. Pop. 652,501.

Es·to·ni·a (ĕ-stō′nē-ə). Region and former country of W European USSR. —**Es·to′ni·an** *adj. & n.*

E·thi·o·pi·a (ē′thē-ō′pē-ə). Country of NE Africa. Cap. Addis Ababa. Pop. 30,400,000. —**E′thi·o′pi·an** *adj. & n.*

Et·na (ĕt′nə), **Mount**. Active volcano in E Sicily.

E·tru·ri·a (ĭ-trŏŏr′ē-ə). Ancient country of W central Italy, now comprising Tuscany and parts of Umbria.

Eu·gene (yŏŏ-jēn′). City of W Ore., S of Salem. Pop. 105,624.

Eu·phra·tes (yŏŏ-frā′tēz). River of SW Asia, flowing c. 1,700 mi (2,735 km) from E central Turkey to the Persian Gulf.

Eur·a·sia (yŏŏ-rā′zhə). Land mass comprising the continents of Europe and Asia. —**Eur·a′sian** *adj. & n.*

Eu·rope (yŏŏr′əp). Continent consisting of the section of the Eurasian land mass that extends W from the Dardanelles, the Black Sea, and the Ural Mts. —**Eu′ro·pe′an** *adj. & n.*

Ev·ans·ville (ĕv′ənz-vĭl, -vəl). City of SW Ind. Pop. 130,496.

Ev·er·est (ĕv′ər-ĭst, ĕv′rĭst), **Mount**. Mountain,

29,028 ft (8,853.5 m), of the central Himalayas on the border of Tibet and Nepal.

Ev·er·glades (ĕv′ər-glādz′). Subtropical swamp on a limestone plateau in S Fla.

F

Faer·oe or **Far·oe** (fâr′ō). Danish islands in the North Atlantic between the Shetlands and Iceland.

Falk·land (fôk′lənd). British islands in the S Atlantic off the SE coast of Argentina.

Far East (fär). SE Asia and the Malay archipelago. —**Far East′ern** *adj. & n.*

Fez (fĕz, fēs). City of N central Morocco. Pop. 744,900.

Fi·ji (fē′jē). Island country of the SW Pacific, comprising c. 320 islands. Cap. Suva. Pop. 618,979. —**Fi′ji·an** *adj. & n.*

Fin·ger Lakes (fĭng′gər). Group of elongated glacial lakes in W central N.Y.

Fin·land (fĭn′lənd). **1.** Country of N Europe. Cap. Helsinki. Pop. 4,758,008. **2. Gulf of.** Arm of the Baltic between Finland and the USSR. —**Finn** (fĭn) *n.* —**Fin′nish** (fĭn′ĭsh) *adj. & n.*

Flan·ders (flăn′dərz). Region of NW Europe, including part of N France and W Belgium, and bordered by the North Sea. —**Flem′ing** (flĕm′ĭng) *n.* —**Flem′ish** (flĕm′ĭsh) *adj. & n.*

Flint (flĭnt). City of SE central Mich. Pop. 159,611.

Flor·ence (flôr′əns, flŏr′-). City on the Arno R. in central Italy. Pop. 462,690. —**Flor′en·tine′** (flôr′ən-tēn′, flŏr′-) *adj. & n.*

Flor·i·da (flôr′ə-də, flŏr′-). **1.** State of the SE U.S. Cap. Tallahassee. Pop. 9,739,992. **2. Straits of.** Sea passage between the Florida Keys, chain of small islands extending SW from Miami to Key West, and Cuba, connecting the Atlantic with the Gulf of Mexico.

Foo·chow (fŏŏ′jō′, -chŏŏ′). Fuzhou.

For·a·ker (fôr′ĭ-kər, fŏr′-), **Mount**. Peak, 17,280 ft (5,270.4 m), of S central Alas.

For·mo·sa (fôr-mō′sə). Taiwan.

For·ta·le·za (fôr′tə-lā′zə). City of NE Brazil, on the Atlantic. Pop. 1,255,600.

Fort-de-France (fôr-də-fräns′). Cap. of Martinique, French West Indies. Pop. 98,807.

Forth (fôrth, fŏrth). River of S central Scotland, flowing c. 60 mi (95 km) to the **Firth of Forth**, inlet of the North Sea extending c. 55 mi (90 km) into SE Scotland.

Fort-La·my (fôr-lä-mē′). Ndjamena.

Fort Lau·der·dale (lô′dər-dāl′). City of SE Fla., N of Miami Beach. Pop. 153,256.

Fort Wayne (wān). City of NE Ind. Pop. 172,196.

Fort Worth (wûrth). City of N Tex. Pop. 385,141.

France (frăns, fräns). Country of W Europe. Cap. Paris. Pop. 53,589,000. —**French** (french) *adj. & n.*

Frank·fort (frăngk′fərt). Cap. of Ky., in the N central part. Pop. 25,973.

Frank·furt (frăngk′fŏŏrt). Also **Frank·furt am Main** (äm mīn′). City of central West Germany. Metro. pop. 1,880,000.

Frank·lin (frăngk′lĭn). Northernmost district of N.W.T., Canada, comprising Baffin Is., other Arctic islands, and Boothia and Melville peninsulas.

Franz Jo·sef Land (fränts′ jō′səf länd, yō′səf länt′). Archipelago in the Arctic Ocean claimed by the USSR.

Fra·ser (frā′zər). River of B.C., Canada, rising in the Rocky Mts. and flowing 850 mi (1,367.6 km) S and then W to the Strait of Georgia at Vancouver.

Fred·er·ic·ton (frĕd′rĭk-tən). Cap. of N.B., Canada, in the SW. Pop. 45,248.

Free·town (frē′toun′). Cap. of Sierra Leone, in the W on the Atlantic. Pop. 274,400.

Fre·mont (frē′mŏnt′). City of W Calif., SE of Oakland. Pop. 131,495.

French Gui·an·a (frĕnch gē-ăn′ə, -ä′nə). French overseas department of NE South America, between Surinam and Brazil. Cap. Cayenne. Pop. 55,125.

French Pol·y·ne·sia (pŏl′ə-nē′zhə, -shə). French overseas territory in the S central Pacific, including the Society, Tubuai, Gambier, Tuamotu, and Marquesas Is. Cap. Papeete, on Tahiti. Pop. 144,000.

Fres·no (frĕz′nō). City of S central Calif. Pop. 218,202.

Fri·sian Islands (frĭzh′ən, frē′zhən). Chain of islands in the North Sea off the coasts of the Netherlands, West Germany, and Denmark.

Fro·ward (frō′wərd, -ərd), **Cape.** Southernmost point of mainland South America, in S Chile on the Strait of Magellan.

Frun·ze (frōōn′zə, -zĕ). City of S Central Asian USSR, WSW of Alma-Ata. Pop. 543,000.

Fu·chou (fōō′jō′, -chou′). Fuzhou.

Fu·ji (fōō′jē). Also **Fu·ji·ya·ma** (fōō′jē-yä′mə). Highest peak (12,389 ft/3,778.6 m) in Japan, in S central Honshu.

Fu·ku·o·ka (fōō′kōō-ō′kä). City of N Kyushu, Japan. Pop. 1,088,617.

Ful·ler·ton (fōōl′ər-tən). City of SW Calif. Pop. 102,034.

Fun·dy (fŭn′dē), **Bay of.** Inlet of the Atlantic between N.B. and SW N.S.

Fu·shun (fōō′shōōn′). City of NE China. Pop. 1,500,000.

Fu·zhou (fōō′jō′). City of SE China, on the Min delta. Pop. 725,000.

G

Ga·bon (gà-bôn′). Country of W central Africa. Cap. Libreville. Pop. 550,000.

Gab·o·ro·ne (gäb′ə-rō′nə). Cap. of Botswana, near the South African border. Pop. 54,000.

Ga·lá·pa·gos (gə-lä′pə-gəs, -läp′ə-). Island group in the Pacific, 650 mi (1,045.8 km) W of Ecuador.

Ga·la·tia (gə-lā′shə, -shē-ə). Ancient country forming part of N central Asia Minor. **—Ga·la′tian** adj. & n.

Ga·li·cia (gə-lĭsh′-ə, -ē-ə). **1.** Historical region of SE Poland and the NW Ukraine. **2.** Region and ancient kingdom of NW Spain. **—Ga·li′cian** adj. & n.

Gal·i·lee (găl′ə-lē′). **1. Sea of.** Freshwater lake, 64 sq mi (165.8 sq km), bordered by Israel, Syria, and Jordan. **2.** Region of N Israel. **—Gal′i·le′an** adj. & n.

Gal·lip·o·li (gə-lĭp′ə-lē). Peninsula of European Turkey.

Gal·ves·ton (găl′və-stən). City of SE Tex., on Galveston Bay, an inlet of the Gulf of Mexico. Pop. 61,902.

Gal·way (gôl′wā′). **1.** Region of W central Ireland. **2.** City of W central Ireland, on Galway Bay, an inlet of the Atlantic. Pop. 36,824.

Gam·bi·a (găm′bē-ə). **1.** Country of W Africa, on the Atlantic. Cap. Banjul. Pop. 610,000. **2.** River of W Africa, flowing 7,700 mi (1,125 km) from N Guinea through SE Senegal and Gambia to the Atlantic. **—Gam′bi·an** adj. & n.

Gan·ges (găn′jēz). River of N India and Bangladesh, flowing 1,560 mi (2,510 km) SE from the Himalayas to the Bay of Bengal.

Garden Grove (gärd′n). City of SW Calif. Pop. 123,351.

Gar·land (gär′lənd). City of NE Tex., near Dallas. Pop. 138,857.

Ga·ronne (gà-rŏn′). River of SW France, rising in the Spanish Pyrenees and flowing 402 mi (646.8 km) NW to the Dordogne.

Gary (gâr′ē). City of NW Ind., on Lake Michigan. Pop. 151,953.

Gas·co·ny (găs′kə-nē). Region and former province of SW France.

Gas·pé (găs-pā′). Peninsula of SE Que., Canada, between Chaleur Bay and the mouth of the St. Lawrence.

Gates·head (gāts′hĕd). Borough of NE England. Pop. 212,200.

Gaul (gôl). Ancient region in Europe S and W of the Rhine, W of the Alps, and N of the Pyrenees, comprising approx. modern France and Belgium.

Ga·za (gä′zə). City of SW Asia, in the **Gaza Strip,** a Mediterranean coastal area (c. 140 sq mi/370 sq km). Pop. 118,272.

Gdańsk (gə-dänsk′, gə-dänsk′). City of N Poland. Pop. 449,200.

Gel·sen·kir·chen (gĕl′zən-kîr′kən, -ᴋᴋən). City of W West Germany, NE of Essen. Pop. 306,323.

Ge·ne·va (jə-nē′və). **1.** City of SW Switzerland, bisected by the Rhone. Metro. pop. 425,000. **2. Lake of.** Lake of SW Switzerland with its S shore in E France.

Gen·o·a (jĕn′ō-ə). Port city of NW Italy. Pop. 782,486.

Georges Bank (jôr′jĭz). Shoal in the Atlantic, E of Cape Cod, Mass.

George·town (jôrj′toun′). **1.** Cap. of Guyana, on the Atlantic. Pop. 72,049. **2.** Cap. of the Caymans, on Grand Cayman Is. Pop. 3,975.

Geor·gia (jôr′jə). **1.** State of the US. Cap. Atlanta. Pop. 5,464,265. **2. Strait of.** Channel between mainland B.C. and Vancouver Is., Canada. **3.** Ancient and medieval kingdom coextensive with present-day Georgian SSR. **4.** Region of SE European USSR. **—Geor′gian** adj. & n.

Ger·ma·ny (jûr′mə-nē). Former state of N central Europe, bordered in the N by the North and Baltic seas and divided in 1949 into the **German Democratic Republic** (East Germany), cap. East Berlin, pop. 16,715,000; and the **German Federal Republic** (West Germany), cap. Bonn, pop. 61,690,000.

Get·tys·burg (gĕt′ĭz-bûrg). Town in S Pa.; site of a Civil War Union victory (1863).

Gha·na (gä′nə). Country of W Africa, on the N shore of the Gulf of Guinea. Cap. Accra. Pop. 11,835,000. **—Gha′na·ian** or **Gha′ni·an** adj. & n.

Ghats (gôts, gäts). Two mountain ranges of S India, the **Eastern Ghats** along the Bay of Bengal coast, and the **Western Ghats** along the Arabian Sea coast.

Ghent (gĕnt). City of NW central Belgium. Pop. 241,695.

Gib·ral·tar (jĭ-brôl′tər). British colony, 2.5 sq mi (6.5 sq km), at the NW end of the **Rock of Gibraltar,** a peninsula on the S central coast of Spain in the **Strait of Gibraltar,** connecting the

Mediterranean and the Atlantic between Spain and N Africa. Pop. 30,000.

Gi·jón (hē-hōn'). City of NW central Spain, on the Bay of Biscay. Pop. 256,904.

Gi·la (hē'lə). River of SW N.Mex. and S Ariz., flowing to the Colorado.

Gil·bert and El·lice Islands (gĭl'bərt; ĕl'ĭs). Former British colony comprised of atolls in the central Pacific; divided into the independent countries of Kiribati and Tuvalu.

Gil·e·ad (gĭl'ē-əd, -ăd'). Mountainous region of Jordan, E of the Jordan R.

Gi·za (gē'zə). City of NE Egypt, on the Nile; site of the Great Pyramids. Pop. 1,246,713.

Gla·cier Bay National Park. Mountain and glacier area, 3,878,269 acres (1,551,307 hectares) of SE Alas., near Juneau.

Glas·gow (glăs'kō, -gō, glăs'-). City of SW Scotland, on the Firth of Clyde. Pop. 794,316.

Glen·dale (glĕn'dāl'). City of SW Calif. Pop. 139,060.

Go·bi (gō'bē). Desert of central Asia, mostly in Mongolia.

Godt·håb (gôt'hôp'). Cap. of Greenland, on the SW coast. Pop. 8,545.

God·win Aus·ten (gŏd'wĭn ôs'tĭn). 2nd highest mountain in the world (28,250 ft/8,616.2 m), in the Karakoram Range of N Pakistan.

Goi·â·ni·a (goi-ä'nē-ə). City of S central Brazil. Pop. 646,000.

Go·lan Heights (gō'lăn'). Hilly area between SW Syria and NE Israel.

Gold Coast (gōld). Coast on the Gulf of Guinea in W Africa along the S shore of Ghana, bordering the Ivory Coast on the W.

Gold·en Gate (gōl'dn). Strait in W central Calif. connecting the Pacific and San Francisco Bay.

Go·mel (gō'mĕl). City of W European USSR. Pop. 393,000.

Go·mor·rah (gə-môr'ə, -môr'ə). Ancient city of Palestine.

Good Hope (gŏŏd hōp'), **Cape of.** Promontory on the SW coast of South Africa.

Gor·ki or **Gor·ky** (gôr'kē). City of E European USSR, on the Volga. Pop. 1,358,000.

Gor·lov·ka (gər-lôf'kə). City of S European USSR, in the Donets Basin Pop. 337,000.

Gö·te·borg (yœ'tə-bôr'ē). Also **Goth·en·burg** (gŏth'ən-bûrg', gŏt'n-). Seaport of SW Sweden. Pop. 434,699.

Got·land (gŏt'lənd). Island of Sweden, in the Baltic Sea off the SE coast.

Gram·pi·ans (grăm'pē-ənz). Mountain range of central Scotland.

Gra·na·da (grə-nä'də). 1. Ancient Moorish kingdom in S Spain. 2. City of S Spain, SE of Córdoba. Pop. 229,108.

Grand Banks (grănd). Also **Grand Bank.** Shoals of the Atlantic off the S and E coasts of Newf., Canada.

Grand Canal. 1. Longest canal in the world, extending c. 1,000 mi (1,610 km) from Tianjin to Hangzhou. 2. Principal waterway of Venice, Italy.

Grand Canyon. Gorge of the Colorado R. in NW Ariz., 217 mi (349.2 km) long; 4-18 mi (6.4-29 km) wide, and c. 1 mi (1.6 km) deep.

Grand Rap·ids (răp'ĭdz). City of SW central Mich. Pop. 181,843.

Graz (gräts). City of SE Austria, SW of Vienna. Pop. 250,900.

Great Bar·ri·er Reef (băr'ē-ər). Largest coral

formation in the world, c. 1,250 mi (2,010 km) long, off the NE coast of Australia.

Great Basin. Desert region of W U.S., comprising most of Nev. and parts of Utah, Calif., Idaho, Wyo., and Ore.

Great Bear Lake. Lake of N central Mackenzie Dist., N.W.T., Canada.

Great Brit·ain (brĭt'n). 1. Island off the W coast of Europe, comprising England, Scotland, and Wales. 2. United Kingdom.

Great·er An·til·les (grā'tər ăn-tĭl'ēz). Island group of the West Indies, including Cuba, Jamaica, Hispaniola, and Puerto Rico.

Great Lakes. Group of 5 freshwater lakes of central North America on either side of the U.S.-Canadian boundary, including Lakes Superior, Huron, Erie, Ontario, and Michigan.

Great Plains. High grassland region of central North America, extending from the Canadian provinces of Alta., Sask., and Man. S into Tex.

Great Rift Valley (rĭft). Geologic depression in SW Asia and E Africa, extending from the valley of the Jordan S to Mozambique.

Great Salt Lake. Saline lake of NW Utah.

Great Slave (slāv). Lake, c. 10,980 sq mi (28,440 sq km), of S N.W.T., Canada; deepest lake (2,015 ft/614.6 m) of North America.

Great Smok·y Mountains (smō'kē). Part of the Appalachians extending along the N.C.-Tenn. boundary.

Greece (grēs). Country of SE Europe, in the S Balkan Peninsula. Cap. Athens. Pop. 8,768,641. —**Gre·cian** (grē'shən) or **Greek** (grēk) *adj. & n.*

Green·land (grēn'lənd, -lănd'). Largest island in the world, c. 840,000 sq mi (2,175,600 sq km), part of Denmark, in the North Atlantic off NE Canada. Cap. Godthåb. Pop. 49,719.

Green Mountains (grēn). Range of the Appalachians, extending from Canada through Vt. to Mass.

Greens·bo·ro (grēnz'bûr'ō). City of N central N.C. Pop. 155,642.

Gre·na·da (grə-nā'də). Southernmost island of the Windward group of the West Indies, part of the country of **Grenada**, including the S Grenadines. Cap. St. George's. Pop. 109,609.

Gren·a·dines (grĕn'ə-dēnz', grĕn'ə-dēnz'). Archipelago in the Windward Is. of the E Caribbean, divided between Grenada and the nation of St. Vincent and the Grenadines.

Gre·no·ble (grə-nō'bəl). City of SE central France. Pop. 166,037.

Groz·ny (grŏz'nē). City of SE European USSR. Pop. 377,000.

Gua·da·la·ja·ra (gwŏd'l-ə-hä'rə). City of SW Mexico, WNW of Mexico City. Pop. 1,813,100.

Gua·dal·ca·nal (gwŏd'l-kə-năl'). Island in the SE Solomon group of the W Pacific.

Gua·de·loupe (gwŏd'l-ōōp'). Overseas department of France, in the Leeward Is. of the West Indies. Cap. Basse-Terre. Pop. 324,530.

Guam (gwŏm). Largest of the Mariana Is., in the W Pacific.

Gua·na·ba·ra Bay (gwä'nə-bä'rə). Inlet of the Atlantic in SE Brazil.

Guang·zhou (gwäng'jō'). City of S China, on a delta near the South China Sea. Pop. 2,300,000.

Guan·tá·na·mo Bay (gwän-tä'nə-mō'). Inlet of the Caribbean in SE Cuba.

Gua·te·ma·la (gwä'tə-mä'lə). 1. Country of N Central America, with coastlines on the Pacific and the Caribbean. Pop. 7,685,000. 2. Also **Guatemala City.** Cap. of Guatemala, in the S central part. Pop. 793,336. —**Gua·te·ma·lan** adj. & n.

Gua·ya·quil (gwī'ə-kēl'). Seaport of W Ecuador, on the **Guayas R.** Pop. 1,022,010.

Guern·sey (gûrn'zē). English island in the SW central English Channel.

Gui·an·a (gē-än'ə, -ä'nə). Region of NE South America, including SE Venezuela, part of N Brazil, and French Guiana, Surinam, and Guyana.

Guin·ea (gĭn'ē). **1.** Country of W central Africa, on the Atlantic. Cap. Conakry. Pop. 5,070,000. **2. Gulf of.** Large inlet of the Atlantic formed by the great bend in the coast of W central Africa. —**Guin·e·an** adj. & n.

Guin·ea-Bis·sau (gĭn'ē-bĭ-sou'). Country of W Africa, on the Atlantic N of Guinea. Cap. Bissau. Pop. 805,000.

Gui·yang (gwā'yäng'). City of SW China, ENE of Kunming. Pop. 800,000.

Gus·ta·vo A. Ma·de·ro (gŏŏs-tä'vō ä'mä-thĕ'rō). City of S central Mexico, N of Mexico City. Pop. 1,182,895.

Guy·a·na (gī-än'ə). Country of NE central South America. Cap. Georgetown. Pop. 921,000.

H

Haar·lem (här'ləm). City of W Netherlands, near the North Sea. Pop. 158,291.

Hague (hāg), **The.** De facto cap. of the Netherlands, in the W near the North Sea. Pop. 456,886.

Hai·fa (hī'fə). City and port of NW Israel. Pop. 229,300.

Hai·phong (hī'fŏng'). City of NE Vietnam, on the Red R. Pop. 400,000.

Hai·ti (hā'tē). Country of the West Indies, on the W part of the island of Hispaniola. Cap. Port-au-Prince. Pop. 5,040,000. —**Hai'tian** adj. & n.

Ha·le·a·ka·la (hä'lä-ä'kä-lä'). Mountain, 10,032 ft (3,059.7 m), in **Haleakala National Park** on E Maui, Hawaii, a dormant volcano containing the largest crater in the world.

Hal·i·fax (hăl'ə-făks'). Cap. of N.S., Canada, on the S coast. Pop. 117,882.

Hal·le (hä'lə). City of S central East Germany. Pop. 232,543.

Ham·burg (hăm'bûrg). City of N West Germany, on the Elbe. Pop. 1,653,043.

Ham·il·ton (hăm'əl-tən). **1.** City of SE Ont., Canada, at the W end of Lake Ontario. Pop. 305,538. **2.** Cap. of Bermuda, on Bermuda Is. Pop. 2,060.

Hamp·ton (hămp'tən). City of SE Va., opposite Norfolk. Pop. 122,617.

Han (hän). River, c. 700 mi (1,126 km), of SE central China.

Hang·zhou (häng'jō'). Also **Hang-chow** (häng'chou', häng'jō'). City of E China, at the head of **Hangzhou Bay,** an inlet of the East China Sea. Pop. 900,000.

Han·no·ver (hä-nō'vər, -fər) or **Han·o·ver** (hăn'ō'vər). City of N West Germany, SE of Bremen. Pop. 535,854.

Ha·noi (hă-noi', hä-). Cap. of Vietnam, in the NE. Pop. 2,000,000.

Har·bin (här'bĭn). City of NE China, in Manchuria. Pop. 2,400,000.

Ha·ri Rud (här'ē rōōd'). River, c. 700 mi (1,125 km) long, of NW Afghanistan, NE Iran, and S Central Asian USSR.

Harpers Ferry (här'pərz). Town of NE W.Va.; site of John Brown's rebellion (1859).

Har·ris·burg (här'ĭs-bûrg', här'-). Cap. of Pa., on the Susquehanna in the SE. Pop. 53,264.

Hart·ford (härt'fərd). Cap. of Conn., in the N central part. Pop. 136,392.

Has·tings (hā'stĭngz). Borough of SE England, on the Strait of Dover, near the site of the Saxon defeat by William the Conqueror (1066). Pop. 74,600.

Hat·ter·as (hăt'ər-əs). Long barrier island off the E coast of N.C., between Pamlico Sound and the Atlantic, with **Cape Hatteras** projecting from the SE part.

Ha·van·a (hə-văn'ə). Cap. of Cuba, in the W. Pop. 1,961,674.

Ha·wai·i (hə-wä'ē, -wä'yə). **1.** Also **Ha·wai·ian Islands** (-wä'yən). State and island group of the U.S., in the central Pacific. Cap. Honolulu. Pop. 965,000. **2.** Largest island of Hawaii, in the SE. —**Ha·wai'ian** (-wä'yən) adj. & n.

Heb·ri·des (hĕb'rə-dēz). Island group in the Atlantic off the W coast of Scotland and divided into the **Inner Hebrides** and the **Outer Hebrides.**

Hei·del·berg (hīd'l-bûrg). City of SW West Germany, on the Neckar R. Pop. 128,773.

Hel·e·na (hĕl'ə-nə). Cap. of Mont., in the W part. Pop. 23,938.

He·li·op·o·lis (hē'lē-ŏp'ə-lĭs). Ancient city of N Egypt, in the Nile Delta.

Hel·les·pont (hĕl'ĭs-pŏnt'). Dardanelles.

Hells Canyon (hĕlz). Gorge of the Snake R., on the Idaho-Ore. border.

Hel·sin·ki (hĕl'sĭng'kē). Cap. of Finland, in the S on the Gulf of Finland. Pop. 484,879.

Her·cu·la·ne·um (hûr'kyə-lā'nē-əm). Ancient city of SW central Italy near Naples.

Her·mo·si·llo (ĕr'mō-sē'yō). City of NW Mexico. Pop. 299,700.

Hi·a·le·ah (hī'ə-lē'ə). City of SE Fla., near Miami. Pop. 145,254.

Hi·ber·ni·a (hī-bûr'nē-ə). Latin. Ireland. —**Hi·ber'ni·an** adj. & n.

Hi·ga·shi-O·sa·ka (hē-gä'shē-ō-sä'kä). City of W central Honshu, Japan, near Osaka. Pop 521,635.

High·lands (hī'ləndz). Mountainous region of N and W Scotland, N of and including the Grampians.

Hi·ma·la·yas (hĭm'ə-lā'əz, hĭ-mäl'yəz). Mountain range of S central Asia, extending c. 1,500 mi (2,415 km) through Kashmir, N India, S Tibet, Nepal, Sikkim, and Bhutan.

Hin·du Kush (hĭn'dōō kōōsh). Mountain range of SW Asia, extending c. 500 mi (805 km) E from NE Afghanistan to N Pakistan.

Hin·du·stan (hĭn'dōō-stän', -stăn'). **1.** N India. **2.** The Indian subcontinent.

Hi·ro·shi·ma (hîr'ə-shē'mə, hĭ-rō'shī-mə). City of SW Honshu, Japan; destroyed by 1st atomic bomb used in warfare (Aug. 6, 1945). Pop. 899,394.

His·pa·nio·la (hĭs'pən-yō'lə). Island of the West Indies E of Cuba, divided between Haiti and the Dominican Republic.

Ho Chi Minh City (hō' chē' mĭn'). City of Vietnam, on the Saigon R. Pop. 3,500,000.

Hok·kai·do (hŏ-kī'dō). 2nd-largest island of Japan, N of Honshu.

Hol·land (hŏl'ənd). The Netherlands.

Hol·ly·wood (hŏl'ē-wŏŏd'). District of Los Angeles, Calif.; center of U.S. motion-picture industry.

Hol·stein (hōl'stīn). Former duchy of Denmark and later Prussia, now part of West Germany.

Ho·ly Ro·man Empire (hō'lē rō'mən). Empire

(962–1806) consisting largely of Germanic states in central and W Europe.

Hon·du·ras (hŏn-dŏŏr'əs, -dyŏŏr'-). Country of NE Central America. Cap. Tegucigalpa. Pop. 3,750,000. —**Hon·dur'an** adj. & n.

Hong Kong (hŏng' kŏng', hŏng' kŏng'). Also **Hong·kong**. British Crown Colony on SE coast of China, including **Hong Kong Is.** and adjacent areas. Cap. Victoria. Pop. 5,265,000.

Ho·ni·a·ra (hō'nē-är'ə). Cap. of the Solomon Is., on NW coast of Guadalcanal. Pop. 14,942.

Hon·o·lu·lu (hŏn'ə-lōō'lōō). Cap. of Hawaii, on the S coast of Oahu. Pop. 365,048.

Hon·shu (hŏn'shōō). Largest island of Japan, located between the Sea of Japan and the Pacific.

Hood (hŏŏd), **Mount**. Volcanic peak, 11,235 ft (3,426.7 m) high, of the Cascade Range in NW Ore.

Hoogh·ly (hōōg'lē). River, c.160 mi (257 km), of E India, the W branch of the Ganges on its delta.

Hor·muz (hôr'mŭz', hôr-mōōz'). Also **Or·muz** (ôr'-, ôr-). **1.** Strait linking the Persian Gulf with the Gulf of Oman. **2.** Island of S Iran, in the Strait of Hormuz.

Horn (hôrn), **Cape**. Headland on an island of Tierra del Fuego, Chile; southernmost point of South America.

Hous·ton (hyōō'stən). Port city of Tex., in the SE. Pop. 1,594,086.

How·rah (hou'rə). City of E India, on the Hooghly R. Pop. 737,877.

Huang (hwäng). Yellow R.

Huas·ca·rán (wäs'kä-rän'). Extinct volcano, 22,205 ft (6,772.5 m), in the Andes of W central Peru.

Hud·son (hŭd'sən). **1.** Bay of the Atlantic in E central Canada. **2.** River, c. 350 mi (505 km), of E N.Y. flowing S to its mouth at New York City.

Hue (hwā, hyōō-ā'). City of central Vietnam, near the South China Sea. Pop. 199,900.

Hum·boldt (hŭm'bōlt). **1.** River, c. 300 mi (485 km), of N Nev. **2.** Ocean current of the S Pacific, flowing N along the coast of Chile and Peru.

Hun·ga·ry (hŭng'gə-rē). Country of central Europe. Cap. Budapest. Pop. 10,945,000. —**Hun·gar'i·an** adj. & n.

Hun·ting·ton Beach (hŭn'tĭng-tən). City of S Calif. Pop. 170,505.

Hunts·ville (hŭnts'vĭl). City of N central Ala. Pop. 142,513.

Hu·ron (hyŏŏr'ən, -ŏn'), **Lake**. 2nd largest of the Great Lakes, between E Mich. and S Ont., Canada.

Hwang (hwäng). Yellow R.

Hyde Park (hīd). Public park in central London, England.

Hy·der·a·bad (hī'dər-ə-bǎd', -bäd'). **1.** City of central India, ESE of Bombay. Pop. 1,607,400. **2.** City of S Pakistan. Pop. 600,796.

I

Ia·şi (yäsh, yä'shē). City of NE Rumania. Pop. 278,545.

I·ba·dan (ē-bä'dän). City of SW Nigeria. Pop. 847,000.

I·be·ri·a (ī-bîr'ē-ə). **1.** The Iberian Peninsula. **2.** Ancient Spain. —**I·be'ri·an** adj. & n.

I·be·ri·an (ī-bîr'ē-ən). Peninsula of SW Europe occupied by Spain and Portugal.

I·bi·za (ē-vē'thä). Spanish island of the Balearics, in the W Mediterranean.

Ice·land (īs'lənd). Island country in the North Atlantic, near the Arctic Circle. Cap. Reykjavik. Pop. 229,000. —**Ice'land·er** n. —**Ice'land'ic** adj.

I·da (ī'də), **Mount**. Highest mountain (8,058 ft/2,457.7 km) of Crete, in the central part.

I·da·ho (ī'də-hō'). State of the NW U.S. Cap. Boise. Pop. 943,935. —**I'da·ho'an** adj. & n.

I·gua·çu (ē'gwə-sōō'). River, c. 380 mi (611 m), of S Brazil, flowing W to the Paraná at the Argentina-Paraguay-Brazil border, just above which it forms **Iguaçu Falls** (2.5 mi/4 km wide).

IJs·sel (ī'səl). Also **IJs·sel**. River of E Netherlands, flowing N from the Rhine to the Ijsselmeer.

IJs·sel·meer (ī'səl-mâr'). Also **IJs·sel·meer**. Lake of NW Netherlands, formed by the diking of the Zuyder Zee.

I·llam·pu (ē-yäm'pōō). Peak, 20,873 ft (6,366.3 m), in the Andes of W Bolivia.

Il·li·nois (ĭl'ə-noi', -noiz'). State of N central U.S. Cap. Springfield. Pop. 11,418,461. —**Il'li·nois'an** adj. & n.

Il·lyr·i·a (ĭ-lîr'ē-ə). Ancient country of S Europe, on the Adriatic. —**Il·lyr'i·an** adj. & n.

In·chon (ĭn'chŏn'). City of NW South Korea, on the Yellow Sea. Pop. 936,497.

In·de·pend·ence (ĭn'dĭ-pĕn'dəns). City of W Mo., E of Kansas City. Pop. 111,806.

In·di·a (ĭn'dē-ə). **1.** Peninsula and subcontinent of S Asia, comprising India, Nepal, Bhutan, Sikkim, Pakistan, and Bangladesh. **2.** Country of S Asia. Cap. New Delhi. Pop. 669,860,000. —**In'di·an** adj. & n.

In·di·an (ĭn'dē-ən). Ocean, c. 28,350,000 sq mi (73,426,500 sq km), extending from S Asia to Antarctica and from E Africa to SE Australia.

In·di·an·a (ĭn'dē-ǎn'ə). State of N central U.S. Cap. Indianapolis. Pop. 5,490,179. —**In'di·an'i·an** n. & adj.

In·di·an·ap·o·lis (ĭn'dē-ə-nǎp'ə-lĭs). Cap. of Ind., in the central part. Pop. 700,807.

In·dies (ĭn'dēz). **1.** East Indies. **2.** West Indies.

In·do·chi·na (ĭn'dō-chī'nə). SE peninsula of Asia, including Vietnam, Laos, Cambodia, Thailand, Burma, and the Malay Peninsula. —**In'do·chi'nese'** adj. & n.

In·do·ne·sia (ĭn'də-nē'zhə, -shə). Country of SE Asia, including Sumatra, Java, Sulawesi, and the Moluccas, parts of Timor, New Guinea, and Borneo, and other islands. Cap. Djakarta. Pop. 153,510,000. —**In'do·ne'sian** adj. & n.

In·dore (ĭn-dôr', -dōr'). City of W central India, NNE of Bombay. Pop. 543,381.

In·dus (ĭn'dəs). River of S central Asia, rising in SW Tibet and flowing 1,900 mi (3,060 km) NW through Tibet, then SW through Pakistan to the Arabian Sea.

In·land (ĭn'lənd). Sea of the Pacific in SE Japan, between Honshu, Shikoku, and Kyushu.

In·ner Mon·go·li·a (ĭn'ər mŏng-gō'lē-ə). Region of NE China.

Inns·bruck (ĭnz'brŏŏk'). City of SW Austria, WSW of Salzburg. Pop. 120,400.

In·side Passage (ĭn'sīd'). Natural waterway

ă pat ā pay â care ä father ĕ pet ē be ĭ pit ī tie î pier ŏ pot ō toe ô paw, for oi noise ŏŏ took
ōō boot ou out th thin th this ŭ cut û urge yŏŏ abuse zh vision ə about, item, edible, gallop, circus

extending c. 950 mi (1,530 km) off the coasts of SE Alas. and W B.C., Canada.

In·tra·coas·tal Waterway (ĭn'trə-kōs'stəl). System of navigation channels and canals along the U.S. Atlantic and Gulf coasts.

I·o·ni·a (ī-ō'nē-ə). Region along the Aegean coast of W Asia Minor. —**I·o'ni·an** adj. & n.

I·o·ni·an (ī-ō'nē-ən). 1. Sea arm of the Mediterranean between W Greece and S Italy and Sicily. 2. Island of W Greece in the Ionian Sea.

I·o·wa (ī'ə-wə). 1. State of N central U.S. Cap. Des Moines. Pop. 2,913,387. 2. River, c. 329 mi (529 km) of N and E Iowa. —**I'o·wan** adj. & n.

I·ran (ĭ-răn', ē-răn'). Country of SW Asia. Cap. Teheran. Pop. 38,940,000. —**I·ra'ni·an** adj. & n.

I·raq (ĭ-răk', ē-räk'). Country of SW Asia. Cap. Baghdad. Pop. 13,230,000. —**I·raq'i** adj. & n.

Ire·land (īr'lənd). 1. Island of the British Isles, in the N Atlantic W of Britain. 2. Country occupying most of Ireland. Cap. Dublin. Pop. 3,455,000. 3. See **Northern Ireland**. —**I'rish** (ī'rĭsh) adj. & n.

I·rish (ī'rĭsh). Sea of the N Atlantic between Britain and Ireland.

Ir·kutsk (ĭr-kōōtsk'). City of SE Siberian USSR. Pop. 561,000.

Ir·ra·wad·dy (ĭr'ə-wä'dē). River of Burma, flowing 1,350 mi (2,172.1 km) S to the Andaman Sea.

Ir·tysh (ĭr'tĭsh). Also **Ir·tish**. River of NW China and W Siberian USSR, flowing c. 2,650 mi (4,265 km) NW to the Ob R.

Ir·ving (ûr'vĭng). Town of NE Tex., near Dallas. Pop. 109,943.

Is·fa·han (ĭs'fə-hän'). Var. of **Esfahan**.

Is·lam·a·bad (ĭs-lä'mə-bäd', ĭz-). Cap. of Pakistan, in the NE. Pop. 77,318.

Is·ra·el (ĭz'rē-əl). Country of SW Asia, on the Mediterranean. Cap. Jerusalem. Pop. 3,920,000. —**Is·rae'li** (ĭz-rā'lē) adj. & n.

Is·tan·bul (ĭs'tän-bōōl', ĭs'tän-). City of Turkey, on the European side of the Bosporus and the Sea of Marmara. Pop. 2,852,539.

It·a·ly (ĭt'ə-lē). Country of S Europe, projecting into the Mediterranean. Cap. Rome. Pop. 57,230,000. —**I·tal'ian** (ĭ-tăl'yən) adj. & n.

Ith·a·ca (ĭth'ə-kə). Island of W Greece, in the Ionian Sea.

I·va·no·vo (ĭ-vä'nô-vô). City of central European USSR, NE of Moscow. Pop. 466,000.

I·vo·ry Coast (ī'və-rē, ī'vrē). Country of W Africa, on the Gulf of Guinea. Cap. Abidjan. Pop. 8,390,000.

I·wo Ji·ma (ē'wō jē'mə). Largest of the Volcano Is. of Japan, in the NW Pacific E of Taiwan.

I·zhevsk (ē'zhĭfsk). City of E central European USSR. Pop. 562,000.

Iz·mir (ĭz-mĭr'). City of W Turkey, on the Aegean. Pop. 753,749.

J

Ja·bal·pur (jŭb'əl-pōōr'). City of central India, SSE of Delhi. Pop. 426,224.

Jack·son (jăk'sən). Cap. of Miss., in the W central part. Pop. 202,895.

Jack·son·ville (jăk'sən-vĭl'). City of NE Fla., near the Atlantic and the Ga. border. Pop. 540,898.

Jaf·fa (jäf'ə, yä'fə). Former city of W central Israel, since 1950 a district of Tel Aviv.

Jai·pur (jī'pōōr'). City of NW India, SW of Delhi. Pop. 615,258.

Ja·kar·ta (jə-kär'tə). Var. of **Djakarta**.

Ja·mai·ca (jə-mā'kə). Island country in the Caribbean, S of Cuba. Cap. Kingston. Pop. 2,137,000. —**Ja·mai'can** n. & adj.

James (jāmz). 1. **Bay**. S arm of Hudson Bay extending between Ont. and Que., Canada. 2. River of Va., flowing 340 mi (547 km) E to Chesapeake Bay.

James·town (jāmz'toun). 1. Cap. of St. Helena in the S Atlantic. Pop. 1,516. 2. Former village of SE Va., 1st permanent English settlement (1607) in the New World.

Ja·pan (jə-păn'). 1. Country of Asia, on an archipelago off the NE coast. Cap. Tokyo. Pop. 117,360,000. 2. **Sea of**. Part of the Pacific between Japan and the Asian mainland. 3. Warm ocean current flowing NE from the Philippine Sea past SE Japan into the N Pacific. —**Jap'a·nese'** (-nĕz', -nēs') adj. & n.

Ja·va (jä'və, jăv'ə). 1. Island of Indonesia SE of Sumatra. 2. Sea of the W Pacific between Java and Borneo. —**Jav'a·nese'** (-nĕz', -nēs') adj. & n.

Jef·fer·son City (jĕf'ər-sən). Cap. of Mo., in the central part on the Missouri R. Pop. 33,619.

Jer·i·cho (jĕr'ĭ-kō'). Ancient city of Palestine, near the N end of the Dead Sea.

Jer·sey (jûr'zē). Largest of the Channel Is. in the English Channel.

Jersey City. City of NE N.J., on the Hudson. Pop. 223,532.

Je·ru·sa·lem (jə-rōō'sə-ləm, -zə-ləm). Cap. of Israel, in the E central part. Pop. 398,200.

Ji·bou·ti (jē-bōō'tē, jĭ-). Var. of **Djibouti**.

Jid·da (jĭd'ə). Also **Jid·dah**. City of W central Saudi Arabia, on the Red Sea. Pop. 561,100.

Ji·lin (jē'lĭn'). City of NE China, E of Changchun. Pop. 775,000.

Ji·nan (jē'nän'). City of E China, on the Yellow R. S of Tianjin. Pop. 1,125,000.

Jodh·pur (jŏd'pōōr'). City of NW India. Pop. 317,612.

Jo·han·nes·burg (jō-hăn'ĭs-bûrg', yō-hä'nĭs-). Largest city of South Africa, in the NE part. Pop. 1,432,643.

Jor·dan (jôrd'n). 1. Country of SW Asia. Cap. Amman. Pop. 2,925,000. 2. River of NE Israel and NW Jordan, flowing c. 200 mi (321.8 km) S through the Sea of Galilee to the Dead Sea. —**Jor·da'ni·an** (jôr-dā'nē-ən) adj. & n.

Juan de Fu·ca Strait (hwän' də fōō'kə). Strait, c. 100 mi (161 km) long, between NW Wash. and Vancouver Is., B.C., Canada.

Ju·dah (jōō'də). Ancient kingdom in S Palestine.

Ju·de·a (jōō-dē'ə). Also **Ju·dae·a**. Ancient region of S Palestine. —**Ju·de'an** also **Ju·dae'an** adj. & n.

Jum·na (jŭm'nə). River of N India, flowing c. 860 mi (1,384 km) SE to the Ganges.

Ju·neau (jōō'nō). Cap. of Alas., in the SE panhandle. Pop. 19,528.

Ju·ra (jōōr'ə, zhū-rä'). Mountain range extending c. 200 mi (322 km) along the French-Swiss border.

Jut·land (jŭt'lənd). Peninsula of N Europe, comprising mainland Denmark and N West Germany.

K

Ka·bul (kä'bōōl). 1. Cap. of Afghanistan, on the Kabul R. (c. 300 mi/483 km) in the E central part. Pop. 318,094.

Ka·go·shi·ma (kä′gō-shē′mä). Port city of S Kyushu, Japan. Pop. 505,077.

Ka·li·nin (kä-lē′nĭn). City of central European USSR, NW of Moscow. Pop. 416,000.

Ka·li·nin·grad (kə-lē′nĭn-grăd). City of extreme W European USSR, on the Baltic. Pop. 361,000.

Kam·chat·ka (kăm-chăt′kə). Peninsula of NE Siberian USSR, between the Sea of Okhotsk and the Bering Sea.

Ka·met (kŭm′ăt′). Mountain, 25,447 ft (7,761.3 m) high, in the Himalayas on the India-Tibet border.

Kam·pa·la (käm-pä′lə). Cap. of Uganda, in the S on Lake Victoria. Pop. 330,700.

Kam·pu·che·a (käm′pə-chē′ə, -pōō-). Cambodia.

Ka·nan·ga (kə-näng′gə). City of S central Zaire. Pop. 601,200.

Kan·chen·jun·ga (kŭn′chən-jŭng′gə). Mountain, 28,146 ft (8,584.5 m), in the Himalayas in Nepal.

Kan·pur (kän′pŏŏr). City of N India, on the Ganges. Pop. 1,154,400.

Kan·sas (kăn′zəs). State of the central U.S. Cap. Topeka. Pop. 2,363,208. —**Kan′san** (kăn′zən) *adj. & n.*

Kansas City. 1. City of NE Kans., on the Missouri R. Pop. 161,087. 2. City of W Mo., WNW of St. Louis. Pop. 448,159.

Kao·hsiung (gou′shyŏŏng′). Port city of SW Taiwan. Pop. 1,172,977.

Ka·ra·chi (kə-rä′chē). City of SE Pakistan, on the Arabian Sea. Pop. 3,498,600.

Ka·ra·gan·da (kär′ə-gən-dä′). City of Central Asian USSR, NNE of Tashkent. Pop. 577,000.

Kar·a·ko·ram (kär′ə-kôr′əm). Mountain range of N Kashmir and SW China.

Karl-Marx-Stadt (kärl-märk′shtät′). City of S East Germany. Pop. 314,951.

Karls·ru·he (kärls′rōō′ə). City of SW West Germany, on the Rhine. Pop. 271,417.

Kar·roo (kə-rōō′, kä-). Semiarid plateau, c. 100,000 sq mi (259,000 sq km), of W South Africa.

Kash·mir (kăsh′mîr, kăsh-mîr′). Former princely state in NW India and NE Pakistan.

Kat·man·du (kät′män-dōō′). Cap. of Nepal, in the central part. Pop. 105,400.

Ka·to·wi·ce (kä′tō-vē′tsě). City of S Poland. Pop. 352,300.

Kat·te·gat (kăt′ĭ-găt′). Strait of the North Sea between E Jutland, Denmark, and SW Sweden.

Kau·ai (kou′ī). Island of Hawaii, NW of Oahu.

Kau·nas (kou′näs′). City of W European USSR, in central Lithuania. Pop. 377,000.

Ka·wa·sa·ki (kä′wə-sä′kē). City of Japan, on the W shore of Tokyo Bay. Pop. 1,040,698.

Ka·zakh (kə-zäk′, kä-). Also **Ka·zakh·stan** (kə-zäk′stän′, -zäk′stän′, kä′-). Region of Central Asian USSR, NE of the Caspian Sea.

Ka·zan (kə-zän′). City of E European USSR, on the Volga E of Moscow. Pop. 1,002,000.

Ken·tuck·y (kən-tŭk′ē). State of E central U.S. Cap. Frankfort. Pop. 3,661,433. —**Ken·tuck′i·an** *adj. & n.*

Ken·ya (kĕn′yə, kēn′-). 1. Country of E central Africa. Cap. Nairobi. Pop. 15,322,000. 2. Extinct volcano, 17,040 ft (5,197.2 m), in central Kenya. —**Ken′yan** *adj. & n.*

Key Largo (lär′gō). Island off S Fla., largest of the Florida Keys.

Key West (wĕst). City of extreme S Fla., on

Key West Is., westernmost of the Florida Keys in the Gulf of Mexico. Pop. 24,292.

Kha·ba·rovsk (kə-bär′əfsk). City of SE Far Eastern USSR, near the Chinese border. Pop. 538,000.

Khar·kov (kär′kôf′, -kôv′). City of S central European USSR, E of Kiev. Pop. 1,464,000.

Khar·toum (kär-tōōm′). Cap. of Sudan, in the E central part. Pop. 333,921.

Kher·son (hĕr-sôn′). City of S European USSR, ENE of Odessa. Pop. 324,000.

Khul·na (kŏŏl′nə). City of SW Bangladesh. Pop. 521,543.

Khy·ber (kī′bər). Pass extending c. 30 mi (48.2 km) through the mountains between Afghanistan and Pakistan.

Kiel (kēl). Seaport of N West Germany, on the Baltic at the head of **Kiel Canal**, artificial waterway connecting the North Sea with the Baltic. Pop. 253,967.

Ki·ev (kē-ěv′, kē′ěf). City of W European USSR, on the Dnieper. Pop. 2,192,000.

Ki·ga·li (kĭ-gä′lē). Cap. of Rwanda, in the central part. Pop. 117,700.

Kil·i·man·ja·ro (kĭl′ə-mən-jär′ō). Highest mountain (19,340 ft/5,898.7 m) in Africa, in NE Tanzania near the border with Kenya.

Kim·ber·ley (kĭm′bər-lē). Diamond-mining center of central South Africa. Pop. 105,258.

Kings·ton (kĭngz′tən). Cap. of Jamaica, on the SE coast. Pop. 665,050.

Kings·town (kĭngz′toun′). Cap. of St. Vincent and the Grenadines, West Indies, on the SW coast of St. Vincent Is. Pop. 17,258.

Kin·sha·sa (kēn-shä′sə). Cap. of Zaire, in the W part on the Congo R. Pop. 2,202,000.

Kirghiz (kĭr-gēz′). Also **Kir·giz** or **Kirghiz·stan** (-gē-stän′). Region of SE Central Asian USSR, bordering on NW China.

Ki·ri·ba·ti (kĭr′ĭ-bäs′, kĭr′ĭ-bäs′). Island country of the W central Pacific, near the equator. Cap. Bairiki. Pop. 56,213.

Ki·rov (kē′rəf). City of E central European USSR, ENE of Moscow. Pop. 392,000.

Ki·san·ga·ni (kē′säng-gä′nē). City of NE Zaire. Pop. 310,705.

Ki·shi·nev (kĭsh′ĭ-nĕf′). City of SW European USSR. Pop. 519,000.

Ki·ta·kyu·shu (kē-tä′kyōō′shōō). City of N Kyushu, Japan. Pop. 1,065,084.

Kitch·e·ner (kĭch′ə-nər). City of S Ont., Canada, WSW of Toronto. Pop. 136,091.

Klon·dike (klŏn′dīk′). Region of E central Y.T., Canada; site of abundant gold deposits.

Knos·sos (nŏs′əs). Ancient city of N Crete.

Knox·ville (nŏks′vĭl′). City of E Tenn., NE of Chattanooga. Pop. 183,139.

Ko·be (kō′bē, -bä′). City of S Japan, on Osaka Bay in S Honshu. Pop. 1,367,392.

Ko·di·ak (kō′dē-ăk). Island in the Gulf of Alaska off the Alaska Peninsula.

Ko·ly·ma (kə-lē′mə, kō-). 1. River of N Far Eastern USSR, flowing c. 1,335 mi (2,148 km) N to the East Siberian Sea. 2. Range of N Far Eastern USSR, extending c. 700 mi (1,126 km) E of the Kolyma R.

Koo·te·nay (kōōt′n-ā′). Also **Koo·te·nai**. River rising in SE B.C., Canada, and flowing 407 mi (654.9 km) S into Mont., through N Idaho, and back into B.C., passing through **Kootenay Lake** before joining the Columbia R.

Ko·re·a (kə-rē′ə, kō-). 1. Former country occupying a peninsula of E central Asia, opposite

Japan, divided since 1948 into: the **People's Democratic Republic of Korea** (unofficially, North Korea), with a pop. of 17,072,000 and its cap. at Pyongyang; and the **Republic of Korea** (unofficially, South Korea), with a pop. of 37,605,000 and its cap. at Seoul. **2. Bay.** Inlet of the Yellow Sea between mainland China and NW North Korea. —**Ko·re'an** *adj. & n.*

Kos·ci·us·ko (kŏs'ē-ŭs'kō), **Mount.** Highest mountain (7,316 ft/2,231.4 m) of Australia, in the SE part of the Australian Alps.

Ko·ši·ce (kô'shĭ-tsĕ). City of E Czechoslovakia, near the Hungarian border. Pop. 200,943.

Kow·loon (kou'lōōn'). City of Hong Kong, on **Kowloon Peninsula** opposite Hong Kong Is. Pop. 749,600.

Kra·ka·to·a (krăk'ə-tō'ə). Volcanic island of Indonesia between Java and Sumatra.

Kra·ków (krä'kou', krăk'ou', krä'kō'). City of S Poland, on the Vistula. Pop. 719,200.

Kras·no·dar (kräs'nə-där). City of SE European USSR, near the Black Sea. Pop. 572,000.

Kras·no·yarsk (kräs'nə-yärsk'). City of S central Siberian USSR, on the Yenisei. Pop. 807,000.

Kre·feld (krā'fĕld', -fĕlt'). City of W West Germany, on the Rhine. Pop. 223,501.

Kri·voy Rog (krĭv'oi rŏg', rôk'). City of SW European USSR, in the Ukraine. Pop. 657,000.

Kru·ger National Park (krōō'gər). Wildlife preserve in NE South Africa.

Kua·la Lum·pur (kwä'lə lōōm'pŏŏr'). Cap. of Malaysia, in the S part of the Malay Peninsula. Pop. 451,728.

Kuang·chow (gwäng'jō'). Guangzhou.

Kui·by·shev (kwē'bə-shĕf'). City of E central European USSR, on the Volga. Pop. 1,226,000.

Ku·ma·mo·to (kōō-mä'mō-tō). Seaport of W central Kyushu, Japan. Pop. 525,613.

Ku·ma·si (kōō-mä'sē). City of S central Ghana, NW of Accra. Pop. 345,117.

Kun·lun (kōōn'lōōn'). Mountain system of W China, on the N edge of the Tibetan plateau.

Kun·ming (kŏŏn'mĭng'). City of S China. Pop. 1,225,000.

Ku·ra (kōō-rä', kōō-). River of NE Turkey and S European USSR, flowing c. 940 mi (1,512 km) NE and SE to the Caspian Sea.

Kurd·i·stan (kûr'dĭ-stăn', kōŏr'dĭ-stän'). Plateau and mountain region of SW Asia.

Ku·rile (kōŏr'ĭl, kōŏ-rēl'). Also **Ku·ril.** Chain of islands of the Soviet Union, between Kamchatka and N Hokkaido, Japan.

Kursk (kōōrsk). City of central European USSR. Pop. 383,000.

Ku·wait (kōō-wāt', -wĭt'). **1.** Country on the Arabian Peninsula at the head of the Persian Gulf. Pop. 1,355,827. **2.** Cap. of Kuwait, in the E central part. Pop. 181,774. —**Ku·wait'i** *adj. & n.*

Kuz·netsk Basin (kōŏz-nĕtsk'). Coal-producing region of W Siberian USSR, E of Novosibirsk.

Kwang·chow (gwäng'jō'). Guangzhou.

Kwang·ju (gwäng'jōō'). City of SW South Korea. Pop. 694,646.

Kwei·yang (gwä'yäng'). Guiyang.

Kyo·to (kē-ō'tō, kyō-). City of S Japan, on S Honshu. Pop. 1,472,993.

Kyu·shu (kē-ōō'shōō, kyōō'shōō'). Southernmost of the 4 main islands of Japan.

L

Lab·ra·dor (lăb'rə-dôr). **1.** Peninsula of NE Canada, between Newf. and Que. **2.** Mainland

territory of Newf., Canada. **3.** Ocean current flowing S from Baffin Bay along the coast of Labrador.

La Co·ru·ña (lä' kô-rōō'nyä). City of NW Spain, on the Atlantic. Pop. 228,637.

La·do·ga (lä'dō-gä', -də-gə). Lake, c. 7,000 sq mi (18,130 sq km), of NW European USSR.

La·gos (lä'gŏs, lā'gŏs). Cap. of Nigeria, in the SW on the Gulf of Guinea. Pop. 1,060,800.

La·hore (lə-hôr', -hōr'). City of NE Pakistan. Pop. 2,022,577.

Lake·wood (lāk'wŏŏd'). City of N central Colo., near Denver. Pop. 112,848.

La·na·i (lä-nä'ē). Island of central Hawaii, W of Maui.

Lan·chou (län'jō'). Lanzhou.

Langue·doc (läNG-dôk'). Former province of S France.

Lan·sing (län'sĭng). Cap. of Mich., in the S central part. Pop. 130,414.

La·nús (lä-nōōs'). City of E Argentina. Pop. 449,824.

Lan·zhou (län'jō'). City of central China, on the Yellow R. Pop. 950,000.

La·os (lä'ōs, lā'ōs, lous). Country of SE Asia. Cap. Vientiane. Pop. 3,760,000. —**La·o'tian** (lā-ō'shən) *n. & adj.*

La Paz (lə päz', päz'). Administrative cap. of Bolivia, in the W part. Pop. 654,713.

Lap·land (lăp'lănd', -lənd). Region of N Scandinavia and NW USSR.

La Pla·ta (lä plä'tä). City of E central Argentina, SE of Buenos Aires. Pop. 435,000.

Las Pal·mas (läs päl'mäs). City of the Canary Is., Spain, on the NE coast of Grand Canary Is. Pop. 357,158.

Las Ve·gas (läs vā'gəs). City of SE Nev. Pop. 164,674.

Lat·in A·mer·i·ca (lăt'ən ə-mĕr'ĭ-kə). Countries of the Western Hemisphere S of the U.S. —**Lat'in-A·mer'i·can** *adj.*

La·ti·um (lā'shē-əm). Ancient country in W central Italy.

Lat·vi·a (lăt'vē-ə). Region and former country of N Europe, on the Baltic. —**Lat'vi·an** *adj. & n.*

Lau·ren·tian Plateau (lə-rĕn'shən). Precambrian plateau extending over E half of Canada.

Lau·sanne (lō-zăn', -zän'). City of W Switzerland, on the N shore of Lake of Geneva. Pop. 128,800.

La·val (lə-văl'). City of S Que., Canada, near Montreal. Pop. 246,243.

Leb·a·non (lĕb'ə-nən). Country of SW Asia, on the E shore of the Mediterranean. Cap. Beirut. Pop. 3,205,000. —**Leb'a·nese'** (-nēz', -nēs') *adj. & n.*

Leeds (lēdz). Borough of N central England. Pop. 724,300.

Lee·ward (lē'wərd). Islands of the West Indies, in the N Lesser Antilles from Virgin Is. SE to Guadeloupe.

Leg·horn (lĕg'hôrn). City of NW Italy, on the Ligurian Sea. Pop. 176,757.

Le Ha·vre (lə hä'vrə). Port city of N France, on the English Channel. Pop. 217,881.

Leices·ter (lĕs'tər). City of central England. Pop. 276,600.

Lei·den (līd'n). Also **Ley·den.** City of SW Netherlands, NE of the Hague. Pop. 103,046.

Leip·zig (līp'sĭg, -sĭk). City of S central East Germany. Pop. 563,980.

Lem·nos (lĕm'nŏs). Island of NE Greece, in the Aegean NW of Lesbos.

Le·na (lē'nə). River of E Siberian USSR, flowing c. 2,670 mi (4,295 km) gen. N to the Laptev Sea.

Len·in·grad (lĕn´ĭn-grăd´). City of NW European USSR. Pop. 4,119,000.

Le·ón (lā-ôn´). 1. Region and former kingdom of NW Spain. 2. City of central Mexico. Pop. 590,000.

Les·bos (lĕz´bŏs, -bōs). Island of E Greece, in the Aegean off the W coast of Turkey.

Le·so·tho (lə-sō´tō). Kingdom of S Africa, enclave within E central South Africa. Cap. Maseru. Pop. 1,360,000.

Les·ser An·til·les (lĕs´ər ăn-tĭl´ēz). Island group in the West Indies extending in an arc from Curaçao to the Virgin Is.

Le·vant (lə-vănt´). Countries bordering on the E Mediterranean.

Lex·ing·ton (lĕk´sĭng-tən). 1. City of N central Ky., ESE of Louisville. Pop. 204,165. 2. Suburb of Boston, Mass., site of 1st Revolutionary War battle (1775).

Ley·den (līd´n). Var. of **Leiden**.

Ley·te (lā´tē, -tā). Island of the E central Philippines, in the Visayan group N of Mindanao.

Lha·sa (lä´sə, läs´ə). City of SW China, traditional cap. of Tibet. Pop. 80,000.

Liao (lyou). River of NE China, flowing c. 900 mi (1,448 km) NE and SW to an arm of the Gulf of Bo Hai.

Li·be·ri·a (lī-bîr´ē-ə). Country of W Africa, on the Gulf of Guinea. Cap. Monrovia. Pop. 1,890,000. —**Li·be´ri·an** adj. & n.

Li·bre·ville (lē´brə-vēl´). Cap. of Gabon, in the NW on the Gulf of Guinea. Pop. 251,000.

Lib·y·a (lĭb´ē-ə). Country of N Africa. Cap. Tripoli. Pop. 13,030,000. —**Lib´y·an** adj. & n.

Liech·ten·stein (lĭk´tən-shtīn´). Principality in central Europe between Austria and Switzerland. Cap. Vaduz. Pop. 26,000.

Li·ège (lē-ĕzh´, -āzh´). City of E Belgium, on the Meuse. Pop. 220,183.

Li·gu·ri·a (lĭ-gyŏŏr´ē-ə). Region of NW Italy, on the Ligurian Sea, an arm of the Mediterranean. —**Li·gu´ri·an** adj. & n.

Li·long·we (lē-lông´wä´). Cap. of Malawi, in the S central part. Pop. 102,924.

Li·ma (lē´mə). Cap. of Peru, in the W central part. Pop. 3,158,417.

Lim·po·po (lĭm-pō´pō). River of SE Africa, rising near Johannesburg in NE South Africa and flowing c. 1,100 m (1,770 km) in NE-SE arc to the Indian Ocean in S Mozambique.

Lin·coln (lĭng´kən). Cap. of Neb., in the SE. Pop. 171,932.

Linz (lĭnts). City of N Austria, on the Danube. Pop. 208,000.

Li·petsk (lē´pĭtsk). City of central European USSR, SSE of Moscow. Pop. 405,000.

Lis·bon (lĭz´bən). Cap. of Portugal, on the Tagus R. Pop. 829,900.

Lith·u·a·ni·a (lĭth´ŏŏ-ā´nē-ə). Region and former country of N Europe, on the Baltic. —**Lith´u·a·ni·an** adj. & n.

Lit·tle Big·horn (lĭt´l bĭg´hôrn´). River, c. 90 mi (145 km), of W Wyo. and S Mont.

Little Rock (rŏk). Cap. of Ark., in the central part. Pop. 153,831.

Liv·er·pool (lĭv´ər-pōōl). Borough NW England, on the Mersey R. Pop. 520,200. —**Liv´er·pud´li·an** (-pŭd´lē-ən) adj. & n.

Łódź (lŏŏj). City of central Poland. Pop. 830,800.

Lo·gan (lō´gən), **Mount**. Peak, 19,850 ft (6,054.3 m), of the St. Elias range in SW Y.T., Canada.

Loire (lwär). Longest river of France, rising in the SE and flowing c. 630 mi (1,014 km) NW to the Bay of Biscay.

Lo·mas de Za·mo·ra (lō´mäs dĕ sä-mō´rä). City of E Argentina, S of Buenos Aires. Pop. 410,806.

Lom·bar·dy (lŏm´bər-dē, lŭm´-). Region of N Italy. —**Lom´bard** adj. & n.

Lo·mé (lō-mā´). Cap. of Togo, in the S on the Gulf of Guinea. Pop. 229,400.

Lo·mond (lō´mənd), **Loch**. Lake in E central Scotland.

Lon·don (lŭn´dən). 1. Cap. of England and of the United Kingdom, on the Thames in SE England. Pop. 6,877,100. 2. City of S Ont., Canada. Pop. 256,789.

Long (lông). Island adjacent to and including sections of New York City.

Long Beach. City of SW Calif., SE of Los Angeles. Pop. 361,334.

Long Island Sound. Arm of the Atlantic between Long Is. and Conn.

Lon·gueil (lông-gāl´, lôn-gē-yē´). City of S Que., Canada, on the St. Lawrence opposite Montreal. Pop. 122,429.

Lor·raine (lô-rān´, lō-). Region and former province of E France.

Los An·ge·les (lôs ăn´jə-ləs, -lēz´, lōs). City of S Calif., on the Pacific. Pop. 2,966,763.

Lou·i·si·an·a (lōō-ē´zē-ăn´ə). 1. State of the S U.S. Cap. Baton Rouge. Pop. 4,203,972. 2. **Purchase**. Territory of the W U.S. extending W from the Mississippi to the Rockies between the Mexican and Canadian borders, purchased from France in 1803.

Lou·is·ville (lōō´ē-vĭl´). City of NW Ky., on the Ohio R. Pop. 298,451.

Lourdes (lōōrd, lōōrdz). Town at the foot of the Pyrenees in SW France; site of a religious shrine. Pop. 17,870.

Low Countries (lō). Belgium, the Netherlands, and Luxembourg.

Lo·yang (lō´yäng´). Luoyang.

Lu·an·da (lōō-än´də). Cap. of Angola, in the W on the Atlantic. Pop. 475,328.

Lub·bock (lŭb´ək). City of NW Tex., S of Amarillo. Pop. 173,979.

Lü·beck (lōō´bĕk). City of NE West Germany. Pop. 222,120.

Lu·bum·ba·shi (lōō´bŏŏm-bä´shē). City of Zaire, in the SE near Zambia. Pop. 404,000.

Lu·cerne (lōō-sûrn´). City of central Switzerland, on NW shore of **Lake of Lucerne**. Pop. 62,400.

Luck·now (lŭk´nou). City of N central India. Pop. 749,239.

Lü·da (lŏŏ´dä). City of NE China, on Korea Bay. Pop. 1,100,000.

Luo·yang (lwō´yäng´). City of E central China, ENE of Xi'an. Pop. 750,000.

Lu·sa·ka (lōō-sä´kə). Cap. of Zambia, in the SE central part. Pop. 641,000.

Lux·em·bourg (lŭk´səm-bûrg´). Also **Lux·em·burg**. 1. Country and grand duchy of W Europe. Pop. 370,000. 2. Also **Luxembourg City**. Cap. of Luxembourg. Pop. 79,300.

Lu·zon (lōō-zŏn´). Largest island of the Philippines, at the N end of the archipelago.

Lvov (lvôf). City of W European USSR. Pop. 676,000.

Lyc·i·a (lĭsh´ē-ə, lĭsh´ə). Ancient country and Roman province on the SW coast of Asia Minor.

Lyd·i·a (lĭd′ē-ə). Ancient country of W central Asia Minor. —**Lyd′i·an** adj. & n.
Ly·on (lē′ŏN′). City of E central France. Pop. 456,716.

M

Maas (mäs). See **Meuse.**
Ma·cao (mə-kou′). Portuguese colony of SE China. Cap. Macao (pop. 241,413). .Pop. 280,000.
Mac·e·do·ni·a (măs′ə-dō′nē-ə). **1.** Also **Mac·e·don** (măs′ə-dŏn′). Ancient kingdom N of Greece. **2.** Balkan region consisting of parts of Greece, Bulgaria, and Yugoslavia. —**Mac′e·do′ni·an** adj. & n.
Ma·chu Pic·chu (mä′chōō pēk′chōō). Ancient fortress city in the Peruvian Andes, NW of Cuzco.
Mac·ken·zie (mə-kĕn′zē). **1.** District of N.W.T., Canada. **2.** River of NW Canada, flowing c. 1,120 mi (1,800 km) into an inlet of the Arctic Ocean.
Mack·i·nac (măk′ĭ-nô′), **Straits of.** Channel between the Upper and Lower peninsulas of Mich., connecting Lakes Huron and Michigan.
Ma·con (mā′kən). City of central Ga., SE of Atlanta. Pop. 116,800.
Mac·quarie (mə-kwôr′ē). River, 590 mi (949.3 km) of New South Wales, Australia.
Mad·a·gas·car (măd′ə-găs′kər). Island country in the Indian Ocean, off the SE coast of Africa. Cap. Antananarivo. Pop. 8,730,000.
Ma·dei·ra (mə-dîr′ə, -dĕr′ə). **1.** Portuguese archipelago in the Atlantic W of Morocco. **2.** River of NW Brazil, flowing c. 900 mi (1,450 km) into the Amazon. —**Ma·dei′ran** adj. & n.
Mad·i·son (măd′ĭ-sən). Cap. of Wis., in the S central part. Pop. 170,616.
Ma·dras (mə-drăs′, -dräs′). City of SE India, on the Bay of Bengal. Pop. 2,469,449.
Ma·dre de Di·os (mä′drĕ dĕ dē-ôs′). River, c. 700 mi (1,125 km), of S Peru and NW Bolivia.
Ma·drid (mə-drĭd′). Cap. of Spain, in the central part. Pop. 3,274,000.
Ma·du·rai (măd′yŏō-rī′). City of S India, SW of Madras. Pop. 548,298.
Mag·da·le·na (măg′də-lā′nə). River rising in SW Colombia, and flowing c. 1,000 mi (1,610 km) gen. N to the Caribbean.
Mag·de·burg (măg′də-bûrg′). City of W East Germany, SW of Berlin. Pop. 276,089.
Ma·gel·lan (mə-jĕl′ən), **Strait of.** Channel between the S tip of South America and Tierra del Fuego.
Mag·ni·to·gorsk (măg-nē′tō-gôrsk′). City of SW Siberian USSR. Pop. 393,000.
Main (mīn, män). River of E West Germany, flowing c. 310 mi (500 km) to the Rhine.
Maine (mān). State of the NE U.S. Cap. Augusta. Pop. 1,124,660.
Mainz (mīnts). City of W central West Germany, SW of Frankfort. Pop. 184,030.
Ma·jor·ca (mə-yôr′kə, -jôr′kə). Largest of the Balearic Is., in the W Mediterranean Sea.
Ma·ka·lu (mŭk′ə-lōō′). Mountain, c. 27,800 ft (8,500 m), in the Himalayas, of NE Nepal.
Ma·ke·yev·ka (mä-kĕ′yəf-kä′). City of S European USSR, NE of Donetsk. Pop. 437,000.
Mal·a·bar Coast (măl′ə-bär′). Region of SW India.
Ma·la·bo (mäl′ə-bō′). Cap. of Equatorial Guinea, on Bioko Is. in the Gulf of Guinea. Pop. 20,000.
Ma·lac·ca (mə-lăk′ə). Strait between Sumatra

and the Malay Peninsula, joining the Andaman and South China seas.
Mál·a·ga (măl′ə-gə). City of S Spain. Pop. 408,458.
Ma·la·wi (mə-lä′wē). Country of SE Africa, bordering on Mozambique and Zambia. Cap. Lilongwe. Pop. 5,975,000. —**Ma·la′wi·an** adj. & n.
Ma·lay (mə-lā′, mā′lā). **1.** Archipelago in the Indian and Pacific oceans, between Australia and SE Asia. **2.** Also **Ma·la·ya** (mə-lā′ə, mā′-). Peninsula of SE Asia, including parts of Malaysia, Thailand, and Burma. —**Ma·lay′an** adj. & n.
Ma·lay·sia (mə-lā′zhə, -shə). Country of SE Asia, consisting of the S Malay Peninsula and N Borneo. Cap. Kuala Lumpur. Pop. 13,650,- 000. —**Ma·lay′sian** adj. & n.
Mal·dives (mäl′dīvz′). Island country in the Indian Ocean SW of Sri Lanka. Cap. Malé. Pop. 136,000. —**Mal·div′i·an** (mäl-dĭv′ē-ən) or **Mal·di′van** (-dī′vən) adj. & n.
Ma·lé (mä′lē). Capital of the Maldives. Pop. 12,000.
Ma·li (mä′lē). Country of W Africa. Cap. Bamako. Pop. 6,660,000.
Mal·lor·ca (mä-yôr′kä). See **Majorca.**
Mal·mö (mäl′mō). City of S Sweden, opposite Copenhagen. Pop. 243,591.
Mal·ta (môl′tə). Island nation in the Mediterranean S of Sicily. Cap. Valletta. Pop. 330,000. —**Mal·tese′** (-tēz′, -tēs′) adj. & n.
Ma·mo·ré (mä′mə-rā′). River, c. 600 mi (965 km), of N Bolivia and Brazil.
Man (măn), **Isle of.** British island in the Irish Sea. —**Manx** (măngks) adj. & n.
Ma·na·gua (mä-nä′gwä). Cap. of Nicaragua, in the W on the shore of **Lake Managua.** Pop. 375,278.
Ma·naus (mə-nous′). City of NW Brazil. Pop. 284,118.
Man·ches·ter (măn′chĕs′tər, -chĭ-stər). **1.** Borough of NW England. Pop. 490,000. **2.** City of SE N.H., S of Concord. Pop. 90,936.
Man·chu·ri·a (măn-chŏŏr′ē-ə). Region of NE China. —**Man·chu′ri·an** adj. & n.
Man·da·lay (măn′də-lā′). City of central Burma, on the Irrawaddy. Pop. 402,000.
Man·hat·tan (măn-hăt′n, mən-). Island and borough of New York City, bounded by the Hudson, Harlem, and East rivers. Pop. 1,427,533.
Ma·ni·la (mə-nĭl′ə). City of SW Luzon, Philippines, on **Manila Bay,** an inlet of the South China Sea. Pop. 1,438,000.
Man·i·to·ba (măn′ĭ-tō′bə). Province of S central Canada. Cap. Winnipeg. Pop. 1,019,000. —**Man′i·to′ban** adj. & n.
Mann·heim (măn′hīm′). City of central West Germany, on the Rhine. Pop. 320,508.
Man·tu·a (măn′tōō-ə, -tyōō-ə). City of N Italy. Pop. 65,574. —**Man′tu·an** adj. & n.
Ma·ra·cai·bo (mär′ə-kī′bō). **1.** Seaport of NW Venezuela. Pop. 651,574. **2.** Largest lake in South America, S of the Gulf of Venezuela.
Ma·ra·ñón (mä′rä-nyōn′). River rising in Peru and flowing c. 1,000 mi (1,610 km) to the Amazon.
Mar del Pla·ta (mär dĕl plä′tə). City of E central Argentina. Pop. 302,282.
Mari·an·a Islands (mär′ē-ăn′ə). Also **Mari·an·as** (-əz). U.S.-administered island group in the W Pacific E of the Philippines.
Mari·time Provinces (măr′ĭ-tīm′). Canadian provinces of N.S., N.B., and P.E.I.
Mar·ma·ra (mär′mə-rə), **Sea of.** Sea between European and Asiatic Turkey.

Marne (märn). River in NE France; scene of battles in World Wars I and II.

Marque·sas Islands (mär-kā′zəz, -səz). Archipelago of volcanic islands of French Polynesia, in the South Pacific.

Mar·ra·kesh or **Mar·ra·kech** (mə-rä′kěsh′, mǎr′ə-kěsh′). City of W central Morocco. Pop. 332,741.

Mar·seilles (mär-sā′). Seaport of SE France. Pop. 908,600.

Mar·shall Islands (mär′shəl). Archipelago of two island chains in the central Pacific N of New Zealand; administered by the U.S.

Mar·tha's Vineyard (mär′thəz). Island off the SE coast of Mass.

Mar·ti·nique (mär′tĭ-nēk′). Island and overseas department of France, in the West Indies. Cap. Fort-de-France. Pop. 333,000. **—Mar′ti·ni′can** n.

Mar·y·land (mâr′ə-lənd). State of the E central U.S. Cap. Annapolis. Pop. 4,216,446. **—Mar′y·land·er** n.

Ma·se·ru (măz′ə-rōō′). Cap. of Lesotho, in the W part. Pop. 14,700.

Mash·had (mäsh-häd′). Meshed.

Mas·sa·chu·setts (măs′ə-chōō′sĭts, -zĭts). 1. State of the NE U.S. Cap. Boston. Pop. 5,737,037. 2. Bay. Inlet of the Atlantic Ocean extending from Cape Ann to Cape Cod.

Mas·sif Cen·tral (mă-sēf′ sĕn-träl′). Plateau region of S central France.

Mas·sive (măs′ĭv), **Mount**. Mountain, 14,418 ft (4,398 m), in W central Colo.

Ma·tsu (mä′tsōō′). Island in Formosa Strait off the SE coast of China.

Mat·ter·horn (mät′ər-hôrn′). Mountain, c. 14,685 ft (4,480 m), on the Italian-Swiss border.

Mau·i (mou′ē). Island of Hawaii, between Hawaii and Molokai.

Mau·na Ke·a (mou′nə kā′ə). Inactive volcano, 13,796 ft (4,208 m), in N central Hawaii Is.

Mau·na Lo·a (lō′ə). Volcanic mountain, 13,680 ft (4,172 m), in S central Hawaii Is.

Mau·re·ta·ni·a (môr′ə-tā′nē·ə). Ancient country of NW Africa including parts of modern Morocco and Algeria. **—Mau′re·ta′ni·an** adj. & n.

Mau·ri·ta·ni·a (môr′ĭ-tā′nē·ə). Country of NW Africa, on the Atlantic. Cap. Nouakchott. Pop. 1,640,000. **—Mau′ri·ta′ni·an** adj. & n.

Mau·ri·tius (mô-rĭsh′əs). Island nation in the SW Indian Ocean. Cap. Port Louis. Pop. 920,000. **—Mau·ri′tian** adj. & n.

May (mā), **Cape**. Peninsula in S N.J., between Delaware Bay and the Atlantic.

Mba·bane (əm-bä-bän′). Cap. of Swaziland, in the NW. Pop. 23,000.

Mc·Kin·ley (mə-kĭn′lē), **Mount**. Highest mountain in North America (20,320 ft/6,197.6 m), in S Alas.

Mead (mēd), **Lake**. Artificial lake on the Nev.-Ariz. border, formed in the Colorado R. by Hoover Dam.

Mec·ca (mĕk′ə). City of W Saudi Arabia; birthplace of Mohammed. Pop. 366,801.

Me·dan (mə-dän′) City of NE Sumatra, Indonesia. Pop. 635,562.

Me·de·llín (mĕd′l-ēn′). City of NW central Colombia. Pop. 1,100,082.

Me·di·a (mē′dē·ə). Ancient country of SW Asia, now the NW region of Iran. **—Me′di·an** adj. & n.

Me·di·na (mə-dē′nə). City of NW Saudi Arabia, N of Mecca. Pop. 198,186.

Med·i·ter·ra·ne·an (mĕd′ə-tə-rā′nē·ən). Inland sea bounded by Africa in the S, Asia in the E, and Europe in the N and W, and connecting with the Atlantic through the Strait of Gibraltar.

Me·kong (mā′kŏng′). River of SE Asia, flowing c. 2,600 mi (4,183 km) through Tibet, Laos, Burma, Thailand, Cambodia, and Vietnam.

Mel·a·ne·sia (mĕl′ə-nē′zhə, -shə). Island group in the SW Pacific NE of Australia. **—Mel′a·ne′sian** adj. & n.

Mel·bourne (mĕl′bərn). Seaport of SE Australia. Metro. pop. 2,603,000.

Mel·ville (mĕl′vĭl). Island of N N.W.T., Canada.

Mem·phis (mĕm′fĭs). 1. Ruined capital of ancient Egypt, on the Nile S of Cairo. 2. City of SW Tenn., on the Mississippi. Pop. 646,356.

Mer·ci·a (mûr′shē·ə, -shə). Anglo-Saxon kingdom extending over most of central England. **—Mer′ci·an** adj. & n.

Mé·ri·da (mĕr′ī-də). City of SE Mexico, in the Yucatán. Pop. 233,900.

Mer·sey (mûr′zē). River rising in NW England and flowing c. 70 mi (113 km) NW to Liverpool.

Me·sa·bi Range (mə-sä′bē). Low hills in NE Minn., noted for vast deposits of ore.

Me·shed (mĕ-shĕd′). City of NE Iran. Pop. 425,000.

Mes·o·po·ta·mi·a (mĕs′ə-pə-tā′mē·ə). Ancient country of SW Asia, between the Tigris and Euphrates rivers. **—Mes′o·po·ta′mi·an** adj. & n.

Mes·si·na (mə-sē′nə). Seaport of NE Sicily, on the Strait of Messina, a narrow channel between Sicily and Italy. Pop. 265,000.

Me·ta (mā′tə). River rising in W central Colombia, flowing c. 650 mi (1,045 km) gen. NE.

Meuse (myōōz, mœz). River rising in E France and flowing c. 560 mi (900 km) through Belgium and the Netherlands to the North Sea.

Mex·i·cal·i (mĕk′sĭ-kăl′ē). City of NW Mexico. Pop. 317,200.

Mex·i·co (mĕk′sĭ-kō′). 1. Country of SW North America. Cap. Mexico City. Pop. 69,381,000. 2. Gulf of. Inlet of the Atlantic S of North America and surrounded by the U.S., Mexico, and Cuba. **—Mex′i·can** (-kən) adj. & n.

Mexico City. Cap. of Mexico, in the central part of the country. Pop. 8,591,750.

Mi·am·i (mī-ăm′ē, -ăm′ə). Resort city of SE Fla. Pop. 346,931.

Miami Beach. Resort city of SE Fla. Pop. 96,298.

Mich·i·gan (mĭsh′ĭ-gən). 1. State of the N U.S. Cap. Lansing. Pop. 9,258,344. 2. Lake. One of the Great Lakes, between Mich. and Wis.

Mi·cro·ne·sia (mī′krō-nē′zhə, -shə). Islands of the W Pacific, E of the Philippines and N of the equator. **—Mi′cro·ne′sian** adj. & n.

Mid·dle East (mĭd′l). Area of SW Asia and NE Africa. **—Mid′dle East′ern** adj. & n.

Middle West. Region of the N central U.S. extending roughly from Ohio W through Iowa, and from the Ohio and Missouri rivers N through the Great Lakes. **—Mid′dle West′ern** adj. **—Mid′dle West′ern·er** n.

Mid·east (mĭd′ēst′). The Middle East. **—Mid′east′ern** n.

Mid·lands (mĭd′ləndz). Region of central England.

Mid·way Islands (mĭd′wā). Coral atoll and

U.S. territory in the central Pacific NW of Hawaii.

Mid·west (mĭd'wĕst'). The Middle West. —**Mid'west'** or **Mid'west'ern** adj. —**Mid'west'ern·er** n.

Mi·lan (mĭ-lăn', -län'). City of N Italy. Pop. 1,724,173. —**Mil'a·nese'** (-nēz', -nēs') adj. & n.

Mi·le·tus (mĭ-lē'tas). Ancient Greek city on the W coast of Asia Minor.

Mil·wau·kee (mĭl-wô'kē). City of SE Wis., on Lake Michigan. Pop. 636,212.

Min·da·na·o (mĭn'də-nä'ō). Island of S Philippines, at the SE extremity of the archipelago.

Min·do·ro (mĭn-dôr'ō, -dōr'ō). Island of W central Philippines.

Mi·nho (mē'nyōō). River rising in NW Spain and flowing c. 210 mi (340 km) SW to the Atlantic.

Min·ne·ap·o·lis (mĭn'ē-ăp'ə-lĭs). City of SE Minn., on the Mississippi. Pop. 370,951.

Min·ne·so·ta (mĭn'ĭ-sō'tə). 1. State of N central U.S. Cap. St. Paul. Pop. 4,077,148. 2. River rising near the Minn.-S.Dak. border and flowing gen. E 332 mi (534 km) to join the Mississippi near St. Paul. —**Min'ne·so'tan** n. & adj.

Mi·nor·ca (mĭ-nôr'kə). Spanish island in the Balearics, NE of Majorca. —**Mi·nor'can** adj. & n.

Minsk (mĭnsk). City of W central European USSR. Pop. 1,215,000.

Mis·sis·sip·pi (mĭs'ĭ-sĭp'ē). 1. State of S U.S. Cap. Jackson. Pop. 2,520,638. 2. River of central U.S., rising in NW Minn. and flowing c. 2,350 mi (3,780 km) SE to the Gulf of Mexico. —**Mis'sis·sip'pi·an** adj. & n.

Mis·sou·ri (mĭ-zŏōr'ē, -zŏōr'ə). 1. State of central U.S. Cap. Jefferson City. Pop. 4,917,444. 2. River of the U.S., rising in the Rockies in W Mont. and flowing c. 2,565 mi (4,127 km) to join the Mississippi N of St. Louis. —**Mis·sou'ri·an** (mĭ-zŏōr'ē-ən) adj. & n.

Mo·ab (mō'ăb'). Ancient kingdom of Jordan. —**Mo'a·bite'** (mō'ə-bīt') adj. & n.

Mo·bile (mō-bēl'). Port city of SW Ala., on **Mobile Bay**, an inlet of the Gulf of Mexico. Pop. 200,452.

Mog·a·dish·o (mŏg'ə-dĭsh'ō). Cap. of Somalia, on the Indian Ocean. Pop. 230,000.

Mo·hen·jo-Da·ro (mō-hĕn'jō-dä'rō). Ruined ancient city on the Indus R. in Pakistan.

Mo·ja·ve (mō-hä'vē). Also **Mo·ha·ve**. Desert region of S California.

Mol·da·vi·a (mŏl-dā'vē-ə). 1. Historical region of E Rumania. 2. Region of SW European USSR.

Mo·lo·kai (mō'lō-kī', mŏl'ə-). Island of Hawaii, between Oahu and Maui.

Mo·luc·ca Islands (mə-lŭk'ə). Island group of E Indonesia between Celebes and New Guinea. —**Mo·luc'can** adj. & n.

Mom·ba·sa (mŏm-bäs'ə, -bä'sä). Seaport of SE Kenya. Pop. 301,000.

Mon·a·co (mŏn'ə-kō', mə-nä'kō). Principality on the Mediterranean coast in the S of France. Cap. Monaco-Ville. Pop. 30,000. —**Mon'a·can** adj. & n.

Mön·chen Glad·bach (mün'kən glăd'bäk). City of W West Germany. Pop. 263,356.

Mon·go·li·a (mŏng-gō'lē-ə, mŏn-). 1. Region of E central Asia, extending from Siberia to N China. 2. Country of N central Asia. Cap. Ulan Bator. Pop. 1,625,000. —**Mon·go'li·an** adj. & n.

Mo·non·ga·he·la (mə-nŏng'gə-hē'lə). River, 128 mi (206 km), of N W.Va. and SW Pa.

Mon·ro·vi·a (mən-rō'vē-ə). Cap. of Liberia, in the NW. Pop. 229,300.

Mon·tan·a (mŏn-tăn'ə). State of the NW U.S. Cap. Helena. Pop. 786,690. —**Mon·tan'an** adj. & n.

Mont Blanc (mônt blängk', môN BLÄN'). Peak, 15,771 ft (4,810 m) high, near the French-Italian border.

Mon·te Car·lo (mŏn'tē kär'lō). Resort town of Monaco. Pop. 9,948.

Mon·te·rey (mŏn'tə-rā'). City of W Calif., on **Monterey Bay**, an inlet of the Pacific. Pop. 27,558.

Mon·ter·rey (mŏn'tə-rā'). City of NE Mexico. Pop. 1,006,200.

Mon·te·vi·de·o (mŏn'tə-vĭ-dā'ō). Cap. of Uruguay, in the S. Pop. 1,229,700.

Mont·gom·er·y (mŏnt-gŭm'ər-ē, -gŭm'rē). Cap. of Ala., in the central part. Pop. 176,860.

Mont·pe·lier (mŏnt-pēl'yər). Cap. of Vt., in the central part. Pop. 8,241.

Mont·pel·lier (môN-pĕ-lyā'). City of S France. Pop. 191,354.

Mon·tre·al (mŏn'trē-ôl'). City of S Que., Canada, on an island in the St. Lawrence R. Pop. 1,080,546.

Mont-Saint-Mi·chel (môN-săN-mē-shĕl'). Small island off the coast of Brittany, NW France.

Mo·ra·vi·a (mə-rä'vē-ə). Region of central Czechoslovakia. —**Mo·ra'vi·an** adj. & n.

Mo·roc·co (mə-rŏk'ō). Kingdom of NW Africa, on the Mediterranean. Cap. Rabat. Pop. 20,050,000. —**Mo·roc'can** adj. & n.

Mor·ris Jes·up (môr'ĭs jĕs'əp, môr'ĭs), **Cape**. World's northernmost point of land, in N Greenland on the Arctic Ocean.

Mos·cow (mŏs'kou', -kō). Cap. of the USSR, in the W central European part. Pop. 8,011,000.

Mo·selle (mō-zĕl'). River rising in NE France and flowing 320 mi (515 km) to join the Rhine.

Mo·sul (mō-sōōl'). City of N Iraq, on the Tigris. Pop. 293,100.

Mo·zam·bique (mō'zăm-bēk'). 1. Country of SE Africa. Cap. Maputo. Pop. 10,460,000. 2. **Channel**. Strait between Mozambique and Madagascar.

Mul·ha·cén (mōō'lä-thĕn'). Mountain, 11,424 ft (3,484 m), of S Spain, in the Sierra Nevada.

Mul·tan (mōōl-tän'). City of E Pakistan. Metro. pop. 542,195.

Mu·nich (myōō'nĭk). City of S West Germany. Pop. 1,293,590.

Mün·ster (mōōn'stər). City of W West Germany. Pop. 262,567.

Mur·chi·son Falls (mûr'chĭ-sən). Series of cascades in the Victoria Nile R., NW Uganda, above Lake Albert.

Mur·cia (môōr'shə). Region and former kingdom of SE Spain.

Mur·mansk (mōōr-mänsk'). City of extreme NW European USSR. Pop. 369,000.

Mur·ray (mûr'ē). River of Australia, rising in the Australian Alps and flowing 1,609 mi (2,589 km) W to the Indian Ocean.

Mur·rum·bidg·ee (mûr'əm-bĭj'ē). River of SE Australia, flowing 1,050 mi (1,689 km) W to the Murray R.

Mus·cat (mŭs'kăt'). Cap. of Oman, on the Gulf of Oman. Pop. 15,000.

Mus·co·vy (mŭs'kə-vē). Principality of Moscow (12th–16th cent.). —**Mus'co·vite'** adj. & n.

Muz·tagh (mōōs-tä'). Mountain, 24,757 ft (7,550 m), in W China near the USSR border.

My·ce·nae (mī-sē'nē). Ancient Greek city, in the NE Peloponnesus. —**My·ce·nae'an** adj. & n.

My·sore (mī-sôr'). City of S India. Pop. 263,131.

N

Nab·a·tae·a (năb'ə-tē'ə). Ancient kingdom of Arabia, in present-day Jordan.

Na·ga·sa·ki (nä'gə-sä'kē). City of W Kyushu, Japan. Pop. 447,091.

Na·go·ya (nä-goi'ä). Seaport of central Honshu, Japan. Pop. 2,087,884.

Nai·ro·bi (nī-rō'bē). Cap. of Kenya, in the S central part. Pop. 835,000.

Na·mi·bia (nə-mĭb'ē-ə). Territory in SW Africa, currently administered by South Africa. **—Na·mĭb'i·an** adj. & n.

Nan·chang (nän'chäng'). City of SE China. Pop. 700,000.

Nan·ga Par·bat (nŭng'gə pûr'bət). Peak, 26,660 ft (8,131.3 m), of NW Kashmir, in the Himalayas.

Nan·jing (nän'jyĭng'). Also **Nan·king** (nän'kĭng'). City of E central China, on the Yangtze. Pop. 1,800,000.

Nantes (nänts). City of W France, on the Loire. Pop. 256,693.

Nan·tuck·et (năn-tŭk'ĭt). Island of Mass., in the Atlantic S of Cape Cod.

Na·ples (nā'pəlz). Seaport of S central Italy. Pop. 1,223,228. **—Na·pol'i·an** adj. & n.

Nar·ra·gan·sett Bay (năr'ə-găn'sĭt). Inlet of the Atlantic extending into S from SE R.I.

Nash·ville (năsh'vĭl'). Cap. of Tenn., in the N central part. Pop. 455,651.

Nas·sau (năs'ô'). Cap. of the Bahamas, on the NE coast of New Providence Is. Pop. 101,503.

Na·tal (nə-tăl', -tôl', -täl'). City of NE Brazil, on the Atlantic N of Recife. Pop. 343,679.

Na·u·ru (nä-ōō'rōō). Atoll and country of the central Pacific, S of the equator and W of Kiribati. Cap. Yaren. Pop. 7,100.

Na·varre (nə-vär'). Former kingdom of SW Europe, extending from N Spain into France.

Naz·a·reth (năz'ə-rĭth). Town of N Israel. Pop. 40,400.

Ndja·me·na (ən-jä'mə-nə). Cap. of Chad, in the SW. Pop. 241,639.

Near East (nîr). Region including the countries of the E Mediterranean, the Arabian Peninsula, and, sometimes, NE Africa. **—Near East'ern** adj. & n.

Ne·bras·ka (nə-brăs'kə). State of the central U.S. Cap. Lincoln. Pop. 1,570,006. **—Ne·bras'kan** adj. & n.

Neg·ev (nĕg'ĕv'). Desert region of S Israel.

Ne·gro (nĕ'grō), **Río** or **Rio**. 1. (also -grōō). River flowing c. 1,400 mi (2,555 km) from E Colombia to the Amazon near Manaus, Brazil. 2. River flowing c. 500 mi (805 km) from S Brazil to the Uruguay R. in central Uruguay.

Ne·me·a (nē'mē-ə). Ancient city of Greece, W of Corinth. **—Ne'me·an** adj. & n.

Ne·pal (nə-pôl', -päl'). Kingdom in the Himalayas between India and Tibet. Cap. Katmandu. Pop. 15,155,000. **—Nep'a·lese'** (-lēz', -lēs') adj. & n.

Ness (nĕs), **Loch**. Lake of N central Scotland.

Neth·er·lands (nĕth'ər-ləndz). Kingdom of NW Europe, on the North Sea. Constitutional cap. Amsterdam; de facto cap. The Hague. Pop. 14,170,000.

Netherlands An·til·les (ăn-tĭl'ēz). Autonomous territory of the Netherlands, in the West Indies. Pop. 246,000. Cap. Willemstad. Pop. 225,000.

Ne·tza·hual·có·yotl (nē-tsä-wäl-kō-yōt'l). City

of S central Mexico, near Mexico City. Pop. 580,438.

Ne·va (nĕ'və). River of NW European USSR, flowing 46 mi (74 km) from Lake Ladoga to the Gulf of Finland.

Ne·vad·a (nə-văd'ə, -vä'də). State of the W U.S. Cap. Carson City. Pop. 799,184. **—Ne·vad'an** adj. & n.

New Am·ster·dam (nōō ăm'stər-dăm', nyōō). Cap. of New Netherland, founded on Manhattan Is. in 1625 and renamed New York after its capture by the English in 1664.

New·ark (nōō'ərk, nyōō'-). City of NE N.J. Pop. 329,248.

New Bruns·wick (brŭnz'wĭk). Province of E Canada. Cap. Fredericton. Pop. 677,250.

New Cal·e·do·ni·a (kăl'ə-dō'nē-ə, -dōn'yə). French overseas territory in the SW Pacific, consisting of **New Caledonia Is.** and several smaller island dependencies. Cap. Nouméa. Pop. 133,233.

New·cas·tle (nōō'kăs'əl, nyōō'-). Also **New·cas·tle-up·on-Tyne** (ə-pŏn'tīn'). Coal-mining center of NE England. Pop. 287,300.

New Del·hi (dĕl'ē). Cap. of India, in the N central part. Pop. 301,801.

New Eng·land (ĭng'glənd). Section of the NE U.S., including Me., N.H., Vt., Mass., Conn., and R.I. **—New Eng'land·er** n.

New·found·land (nōō'fən-lənd, -lănd', nyōō'-). Province of E Canada, including the island of Newfoundland and nearby islands and the mainland area of Labrador with its adjacent islands. Cap. St. John's. Pop. 557,725. **—New'found·land·er** n.

New France (frăns). French colonial territory in North America, including much of SE Canada, the Great Lakes region, and the Mississippi valley.

New Guin·ea (gĭn'ē). Island in the SW Pacific N of Australia; divided politically between Indonesia and Papua New Guinea. **—New Guin·e·an** adj. & n.

New Hamp·shire (hămp'shər, -shĭr', hăm'-). State of the NE U.S. Cap. Concord. Pop. 920,610. **—New Hamp'shir·ite'** n.

New Ha·ven (hā'vən). City of S Conn., on Long Is. Sound. Pop. 126,109.

New Heb·ri·des (hĕb'rə-dēz'). Island group in the S Pacific E of Australia, forming the country of Vanuatu.

New Jer·sey (jûr'zē). State of the E central U.S. Cap. Trenton. Pop. 7,364,158. **—New Jer'sey·ite'** n.

New Mex·i·co (mĕk'sĭ-kō'). State of the SW U.S. Cap. Santa Fe. Pop. 1,299,968. **—New Mex'i·can** n.

New Neth·er·land (nĕth'ər-lənd). Dutch colony (1624–64) along the Hudson and lower Delaware rivers.

New Or·le·ans (ôr'lē-ənz, ôr'lənz, ôr-lēnz'). City of SE La., on the Mississippi. Pop. 557,482.

New·port (nōō'pôrt, -pōrt, nyōō'-). Resort city of SE R.I., on the Atlantic SSE of Providence. Pop. 21,259.

Newport News (nōōz, nyōōz). City of SE Va., opposite Norfolk. Pop. 144,903.

New Prov·i·dence (prŏv'ə-dəns). Island of the Bahamas, in the West Indies.

New Spain (spān). Former Spanish possessions including islands in the West Indies, Central

---

ă pat ā pay â care ä father ĕ pet ē be ĭ pit ī tie î pier ŏ pot ō toe ô paw, for oi noise ōō took
ōō boot ou out th thin th this ŭ cut û urge yōō abuse zh vision ə about, item, edible, gallop, circus

America N of Panama, Mexico, the SW U.S., and the Philippines.

New Swe·den (swē′dn). Swedish colony (1638–55) in North America, extending roughly from the site of present-day Trenton, N.J., S to the mouth of the Delaware R.

New York (yôrk). 1. State of the NE U.S. Cap. Albany. Pop. 17,557,288. 2. City of SE N.Y., at the mouth of the Hudson R. Pop. 7,071,030. —**New York′er** n.

New Zea·land (zē′lənd). Island country in the S Pacific, SE of Australia. Cap. Wellington. Pop. 3,125,000. —**New Zea′land·er** n.

Ni·ag·a·ra (nī-ăg′rə, -ăg′ər-ə). 1. River flowing 34 mi (54.7 km) N from Lake Erie to Lake Ontario. 2. Waterfalls of the Niagara R., consisting of the Canadian or Horseshoe Falls (c. 160 ft/48.8 m high and 2,500 ft/762.5 m wide), and the American Falls (c. 167 ft/50.9 m high and 1,000 ft/305 m wide).

Nia·mey (nyä-mā′). Cap. of Niger, on the Niger R. in the SW. Pop. 225,300.

Ni·cae·a (nī-sē′ə). Ancient city of NW Asia Minor. —**Ni·cae′an** adj.

Nic·a·ra·gua (nĭk′ə-rä′gwə). 1. Country of Central America, S of Honduras. Cap. Managua. Pop. 2,610,000. 2. Largest lake of Central America, in S Nicaragua. —**Nic′a·ra′guan** adj. & n.

Nice (nēs). City of SE France, on the Mediterranean. Pop. 344,481.

Nic·o·bar Islands (nĭk′ə-bär′). Indian island group in the Bay of Bengal.

Nic·o·si·a (nĭk′ə-sē′ə). Cap. of Cyprus, in the N central part. Pop. 121,500.

Ni·ger (nī′jər). 1. Country of W central Africa. Cap. Niamey. Pop. 5,380,000. 2. River of W Africa, flowing c. 2,600 mi (4,185 km) NE and SE to the Gulf of Guinea.

Ni·ge·ri·a (nī-jîr′ē-ə). Country of W Africa, on the Gulf of Guinea. Cap. Lagos. Pop. 78,135,-000. —**Ni·ge′ri·an** adj. & n.

Ni·ko·la·ev (nĭk′ə-lä′yəf). Port of S European USSR, in the Ukraine. Pop. 449,000.

Nile (nīl). Longest river in the world, flowing c. 4,160 mi (6,695 km), through E Africa from its headstream in Burundi to its delta on the Mediterranean in NE Egypt.

Nin·e·veh (nĭn′ə-və). Ancient cap. of Assyria, on the Tigris opposite modern-day Mosul, Iraq.

Ni·te·rói (nē′tĕ-roi′). City of SE Brazil, on Guanabara Bay. Pop. 376,033.

Nizh·ni Ta·gil (nēzh′nī tä-gēl′). City of E European USSR, in the central Urals. Pop. 400,000.

Nome (nōm). Westernmost city of the continental U.S., on Seward Peninsula in W Alas. Pop. 2,301.

Nor·folk (nôr′fək). City of SE Va., SE of Richmond. Pop. 266,979.

Nor·man·dy (nôr′mən-dē). Region and former province of NW France, on the English Channel. —**Nor′man** adj. & n.

North A·mer·i·ca (nôrth ə-mĕr′ə-kə). N continent of the Western Hemisphere, extending from the Colombia-Panama border in the S through Central America, the U.S. (except Hawaii), Canada, and the Arctic Archipelago to the N tip of Greenland. —**North A·mer′i·can** adj. & n.

North Car·o·li·na (kăr′ə-lī′nə). State of the SE U.S. Cap. Raleigh. Pop. 5,874,429. —**North Car′o·lin′i·an** (-lĭn′ē-ən) adj. & n.

North Da·ko·ta (də-kō′tə). State of the N central U.S. Cap. Bismarck. Pop. 652,695. —**North Da·ko′tan** adj. & n.

North·east (nôrth-ēst′). Area of the NE U.S.

including New England, N.Y., and sometimes Pa. and N.J.

North·ern Ire·land (nôr′thərn īr′lənd). Component of the United Kingdom, in the NE part of the island of Ireland. Cap. Belfast. Pop. 1,542,200.

North Sea. Arm of the Atlantic NW of central Europe and E of Great Britain.

North·um·bri·a (nôr-thŭm′brē-ə). Anglo-Saxon kingdom of Britain.

North·west (nôrth-wĕst′). 1. Formerly, area of the U.S. W of the Mississippi and N of the Missouri R. 2. U.S. states of Wash., Ore., and Idaho.

Northwest Passage. Water route from the Atlantic to the Pacific through the Arctic Archipelago of Canada and N of Alas.

Northwest Territories. Region of NW Canada that includes the Arctic Archipelago, the islands in Hudson Bay, and the mainland N of the Canadian provinces and E of Y.T.

Northwest Territory. Historical U.S. region extending from the Ohio and Mississippi rivers to the Great Lakes.

Nor·way (nôr′wā′). Kingdom of N Europe, on the Scandinavian peninsula. Cap. Oslo. Pop. 4,095,000. —**Nor·we′gian** (nôr-wē′jən) adj. & n.

Nor·we·gian Sea (nôr-wē′jən). Part of the Arctic Ocean between Greenland and Norway.

Not·ting·ham (nŏt′ĭng-əm). Borough of central England, N of Leicester. Pop. 278,600.

Nouak·chott (nwäk′shŏt′). Cap. of Mauritania, in the W part. Pop. 134,986.

Nou·mé·a (nōō-mā′ə). Cap. of New Caledonia, on the SW coast of New Caledonia Is. Pop. 56,078.

No·va Sco·tia (nō′və skō′shə). Province and peninsula of SE Canada. Cap. Halifax. Pop. 828,571. —**No′va Sco′tian** adj. & n.

Nov·go·rod (nŏv′gə-rŏd′). City of NW European USSR, SSE of Leningrad. Pop. 192,000.

No·vo·kuz·netsk (nō′və-kōōz-nĕtsk′). City of central Siberian USSR. Pop. 545,000.

No·vo·si·birsk (nō′və-sĭ-bîrsk′). City of S Siberian USSR, on the Ob R. Pop. 1,328,000.

Nu·bi·a (nōō′bē-ə, nyōō′-). Desert region and ancient kingdom in the Nile valley of S Egypt and N Sudan. —**Nu′bi·an** adj. & n.

Nu·bi·an Desert. Desert of NE Sudan, extending E of the Nile to the Red Sea.

Nue·vo La·re·do (nwĕ′vō lä-rē′thō). City of NE Mexico, across the Rio Grande from Laredo, Tex. Pop. 214,200.

Nu·ku·a·lo·fa (nōō′kōō-ə-lō′fə). Cap. of Tonga, in the SW Pacific. Pop. 18,312.

Nu·mid·i·a (nōō-mĭd′ē-ə, nyōō-). Ancient kingdom of N Africa. —**Nu·mid′i·an** adj. & n.

Nu·rem·berg (nōōr′əm-bûrg′, nyōōr′-). City of S West Germany. Pop. 484,184.

Nyas·a (nī-ăs′ə). Lake in SE Africa, between Tanzania, Mozambique, and Malawi.

O

O·a·hu (ō-ä′hōō). Island of Hawaii, between Molokai and Kauai.

Oak·land (ōk′lənd). City of W Calif., opposite San Francisco. Pop. 339,288.

Ob (ōb, ŏb). River, c. 2,300 mi (3,700 km), of W Siberian USSR, flowing N to an inlet of the Arctic Ocean.

O·ber·hau·sen (ō′bər-hou′zən). City of W West Germany, in the Ruhr. Pop. 229,613.

O·ce·an·i·a (ō′shē-ăn′ē-ə, -ä′nē-ə). Islands of the central, W, and S Pacific Ocean, usu. including Australia and New Zealand. —**O'ce·an'i·an** *adj.* & *n.*

O·dense (ō'thən-sə). City of S central Denmark. Pop. 168,528.

O·der (ō'dər). River rising in N central Czechoslovakia and flowing 562 mi (904.3 km) through Poland and East Germany to the Baltic Sea.

O·des·sa (ō-dĕs'ə). City of SW European USSR, on an inlet of the Black Sea. Pop. 1,057,000.

O·hi·o (ō-hī'ō). **1.** State of the N U.S. Cap. Columbus. Pop. 10,797,419. **2.** River formed by the Allegheny and Monongahela rivers at Pittsburgh, Pa., and flowing 981 mi (1,578.4 km) W and SW to the Mississippi in S Ill. —**O·hi'o·an** *adj.* & *n.*

Oise (wäz). River, 186 mi (299.3 km), of S Belgium and N France.

O·ka (ō-kä'). River, c. 925 mi (1,490 km), of central European USSR.

O·ka·van·go (ō'kə-väng'gō). River of W central Africa, flowing c. 1,000 mi (1,610 km) from central Angola to N Botswana.

O·ka·ya·ma (ō'kä-yä'mä). City of SW Honshu, Japan, on the Inland Sea. Pop. 545,737.

O·kee·cho·bee (ō'kē-chō'bē). Lake of SE Fla., with access to the Atlantic via the Okeechobee Waterway.

O·ke·fe·no·kee (ō'kə-fə-nō'kē). Swamp of NE Fla. and SE Ga.

O·khotsk (ō-kŏtsk'), **Sea of.** Arm of the NW Pacific between Kamchatka Peninsula and the Kurile Is.

O·ki·na·wa (ō'kĭ-nou'wə, -nä'wə). Island and island group of the Ryukyu Is., in the W Pacific SW of Japan.

O·kla·ho·ma (ō'klə-hō'mə). State of the SW U.S. Cap. Oklahoma City. Pop. 3,025,266. —**O·kla·ho'man** *adj.* & *n.*

Oklahoma City. Cap. of Okla., in the central part. Pop. 403,213.

Ol·du·vai (ōl'də-vī'). Gorge in N Tanzania; site of fossil remains.

Ol·ives (ŏl'ĭvz), **Mount of.** Also **Ol·i·vet** (ŏl'ə-vĕt'). Ridge of hills E of Jerusalem.

O·lym·pi·a (ō-lĭm'pē-ə). **1.** Plain of NW Peloponnesus, Greece; site of the ancient Olympic games. **2.** Cap. of Wash., at the S end of Puget Sound. Pop. 27,447.

O·lym·pic Peninsula (ō-lĭm'pĭk). Peninsula of NW Wash., between the Pacific Ocean and Puget Sound.

O·lym·pus (ō-lĭm'pəs). Highest mountain in Greece (9,750 ft/2,920 m), mythical home of the Greek gods.

O·ma·ha (ō'mə-hô', -hä'). City of E Neb., on the Missouri R. Pop. 311,681.

O·man (ō-män'). Sultanate at the E tip of the Arabian peninsula, on the **Gulf of Oman,** an arm of the Arabian Sea. Cap. Muscat. Pop. 900,000.

Omsk (ômsk). City of W Siberian USSR. Pop. 1,028,000.

On·tar·i·o (ŏn-târ'ē-ō'). **1.** Province of E central Canada. Cap. Toronto. Pop. 8,264,465. **2.** Easternmost of the Great Lakes, between SE Ont., Canada, and NW N.Y. —**On·tar'i·an** *adj.* & *n.*

O·por·to (ō-pôr'tō, ō-pōr'-). City of NW Portugal. Pop. 335,700.

O·ran (ō-rän', ō-răn'). City of NW Algeria, on the **Gulf of Oran,** an inlet of the Mediterranean. Pop. 485,139.

Or·ange (ôr'ĭnj, ŏr'-). River rising in Lesotho and flowing 1,300 mi (2,090 km) W across South Africa to the Atlantic.

Or·e·gon (ôr'ə-gən, -gŏn', ŏr'-). **1.** State of the NW U.S. Cap. Salem. Pop. 2,632,663. **2.** Territory. Historical region of NW North America. —**Or·e·go'ni·an** (-gō'nē-ən, ōr'-) *adj.* & *n.*

O·rel (ō-rĕl'). City of central European USSR. Pop. 309,000.

O·ri·no·co (ôr'ə-nō'kō, ŏr'-). River rising in SE Venezuela and flowing c. 1,500 mi (2,416 km) W, N, and E to the Atlantic.

Ork·ney Islands (ôrk'nē). Cluster of islands off the NE coast of Scotland.

Or·lan·do (ôr-lăn'dō). Resort city of central Fla. Pop. 128,394.

Or·lé·ans (ôr-lā-äN'). City of N central France. Pop. 106,246.

Or·muz (ôr'mŭz', ôr-mōōz'). Var. of **Hormuz.**

O·sa·ka (ō-sä'kə). City of S Honshu, Japan, on **Osaka Bay,** an inlet of the Pacific. Pop. 2,648,158.

Os·lo (ŏz'lō, ŏs'-). Cap. of Norway, in the SE. Pop. 454,819.

Os·ti·a (ŏs'tē-ə). Ancient city of E central Italy, at the mouth of the Tiber.

O·stra·va (ō'strä-vä). City of N central Czechoslovakia. Pop. 325,473.

Ot·ta·wa (ŏt'ə-wə, -wä', -wô'). Cap. of Canada, on the **Ottawa R.,** c. 700 mi (1,125 km), a major tributary of the St. Lawrence, at the SE tip of Ont. near the U.S. border. Pop. 300,678.

Ot·to·man Empire (ŏt'ə-mən). Turkish empire (1299–1919) in SW Asia, NE Africa, and SE Europe.

Oua·ga·dou·gou (wä'gə-dōō'gōō). Cap. of Upper Volta, in the central part. Pop. 180,000.

Ox·ford (ŏks'fərd). Borough of S central England, on the Thames. Pop. 122,400. —**Ox·o'ni·an** (ŏks-ō'nē-ən) *adj.*

Ox·nard (ŏks'närd). City of S Calif. Pop. 108,195.

O·zark Mountains (ō'zärk). Range of low mountains in SW Mo., NW Ark., and E Okla.

P

Pa·cif·ic (pə-sĭf'ĭk). Earth's largest body of water, extending from the Arctic to the Antarctic and the Americas to Asia and Australia.

Pacific Islands, Trust Territory of the. UN territory in the W Pacific, administered by the U.S. and comprising c. 2,000 islands in the Caroline, Mariana, and Marshall Is.

Pacific North·west (nôrth-wĕst'). Region of the NW U.S., usu. including Wash. and Ore. and sometimes SW B.C., Canada.

Pad·u·a (păj'ōō-ə, păd'yōō-ə). City of NE Italy, W of Venice. Pop. 242,216.

Paes·tum (pĕs'təm). Ancient city of SW Italy.

Pa·go Pa·go (päng'gō päng'gō, päng'ō päng'ō). Cap. of American Samoa, on the S coast of Tutuila Is. Pop. 2,451.

Paint·ed Desert (pān'təd). Plateau area of E central Ariz.

Pak·i·stan (păk'ĭ-stăn', pä'kĭ-stän'). Country of S Asia, on the Arabian Sea. Cap. Islamabad. Pop. 88,610,000. —**Pak'i·stan'i** *adj.* & *n.*

Pa·lem·bang (pä'lĕm-bäng'). City of SE Sumatra, Indonesia. Pop. 582,961.

ă pat ā pay â care ä father ĕ pet ē be ĭ pit ī tie î pier ŏ pot ō toe ô paw, for oi noise ŏŏ took
ōō boot ou out th thin *th* this ŭ cut û urge yōō abuse zh vision ə about, item, edible, gallop, circus

Pa·ler·mo (pä-lĕr′mō). City of NW Sicily. Pop. 693,949.

Pal·es·tine (păl′ĭ-stīn′). Region of SW Asia, on the E shore of the Mediterranean. —**Pal′es·tin′i·an** (-stīn′ē-ən) n.

Pal·i·sades (păl′ə-sādz′). Row of cliffs in NE N.J., along the W bank of the Hudson R.

Pal·ma (päl′mä). City of SW Majorca, in the Balearics. Pop. 287,389.

Pa·mirs (pə-mîrz′). Mountain region of S central Asia, in S Central Asian USSR, bordering on Afghanistan, Kashmir, and China.

Pam·plo·na (păm-plō′nä). City of N Spain. Pop. 175,833.

Pan·a·ma (păn′ə-mä′). 1. A country of SW Central America. Pop. 2,000,000. 2. Also **Panama City.** Cap. of Panama, at the Pacific terminus of the Panama Canal. Pop. 467,000. 3. **Isthmus of.** Isthmus connecting North and South America and separating the Pacific from the Caribbean. 4. **Ship canal,** 51 mi (82 km) long, across the Isthmus of Panama, connecting the Caribbean with the Pacific. —**Pan′a·ma′ni·an** (păn′ə-mä′nē-ən) adj. & n.

Pa·nay (pə-nī′). Island of the Visayan Is., central Philippines.

Pao·tow (bou′tō′). Baotou.

Pa·pal States (pā′pəl). Territories in central Italy ruled by the popes until 1870.

Pap·u·a New Guin·ea (păp′yōō-ə; gĭn′ē). Country occupying the E half of the island of New Guinea. Cap. Port Moresby. Pop. 2,905,000.

Par·a·guay (păr′ə-gwā′, -gwī′). Country of central South America. Cap. Asunción. Pop. 3,100,000. —**Par·a·guay′an** adj. & n.

Pa·ra·í·ba (pä′rə-ē′bə). River, c. 650 mi (1,046 km), of SE Brazil.

Pa·ra·mar·i·bo (păr′ə-măr′ə-bō′). Cap. of Surinam, on the Atlantic. Pop. 102,300.

Pa·ra·ná (păr′ə-nä′). River rising in E central Brazil and flowing c. 2,040 mi (3,282 km) S to the Río de la Plata in E Argentina.

Par·is (păr′ĭs, pä-rē′). Cap. of France, in the NW on the Seine. Pop. 2,050,500. —**Pa·ri′sian** (pə-rē′zhən, -rīzh′ən) adj. & n.

Par·ma (păr′mə). City of N Italy, SE of Milan. Pop. 176,945.

Par·na·í·ba (păr′nə-ē′bə). River, c. 800 mi (1,287 km), of NE Brazil.

Par·nas·sus (păr-năs′əs). Peak, c. 8,060 ft (2,460 m) high, of central Greece N of the Gulf of Corinth.

Par·thi·a (păr′thē-ə). Ancient country of SW Asia, roughly corresponding to NE Iran. —**Par′thi·an** adj. & n.

Pas·a·de·na (păs′ə-dē′nə). 1. City of SW Calif. Pop. 119,374. 2. City of SE Tex. Pop. 112,560.

Pat·er·son (păt′ər-sən). City of NE N.J. Pop. 137,970.

Pat·na (pŭt′nə). City of NE India, on the Ganges. Pop. 473,001.

Peace (pēs). River, c. 945 mi (1,521 km), of N B.C. and N Alta., Canada.

Pearl Harbor (pûrl). Inlet of the Pacific, on the S coast of Oahu, Hawaii.

Pe·cos (pā′kəs). River rising in N central N. Mex. and flowing c. 926 mi (1,490 km) SE to the Rio Grande in W Tex.

Pe·king (pē′kĭng′, bā′jyĭng′). Beijing.

Pe·lée (pə-lā′). Volcano, c. 4,800 ft (1,464 m), on N Martinique, French West Indies.

Pel·o·pon·ne·sus (pĕl′ə-pə-nē′səs). Peninsula S of the Gulf of Corinth and forming the S part of Greece. —**Pel′o·pon·ne′sian** adj. & n.

Pen·ki or **Pen·chi** (bŭn′chē′). Benxi.

Pen·nine Alps (pĕn′īn′). Range of the Alps, in SW Switzerland on the Italian border.

Pennine Chain. Range of hills extending from S Scotland to central England.

Penn·syl·va·nia (pĕn′səl-vān′yə, -vā′nē-ə). State of the E U.S. Cap. Harrisburg. Pop. 11,866,728. —**Penn′syl·va′nian** adj. & n.

Pen·za (pĕn′zə). City of S central European USSR. Pop. 490,000.

Pe·o·ri·a (pē-ô-ôr′ē-ə, -ōr′ē-ə). City of N central Ill. Pop. 124,160.

Per·ga·mum (pûr′gə-məm). Also **Per·ga·mon** (-mŏn′). Ancient Greek city in Asia Minor.

Perm (pĕrm). City of NE European USSR. Pop. 1,008,000.

Per·sep·o·lis (pər-sĕp′ə-lĭs). Ruined city of ancient Persia, in present-day SW Iran.

Per·sia (pûr′zhə). Iran. —**Per′sian** adj. & n.

Persian Gulf (pûr′zhən). Arm of the Arabian Sea between Arabia and SW Iran.

Perth (pûrth). City of SW Australia. Metro. pop. 883,600.

Pe·ru (pə-rōō′). Country of W South America, on the Pacific. Cap. Lima. Pop. 17,995,000. —**Pe·ru′vi·an** adj. & n.

Pe·tra (pē′trə). Ancient city of Edom, in SW Jordan.

Phil·a·del·phi·a (fĭl′ə-dĕl′fē-ə). City of SE Pa., on the Delaware R. Pop. 1,688,210. —**Phil′a·del′phi·an** adj. & n.

Phi·lip·pi (fĭ-lĭp′ī). Ancient town in N central Macedonia, Greece.

Phil·ip·pines (fĭl′ə-pēnz′, fĭl′ə-pēnz′). Country of E Asia, consisting of the **Philippine Is.,** an archipelago in the W Pacific SE of China. Cap. Manila. Pop. 48,200,000. —**Phil′ip·pine** adj.

Philippine Sea (fĭl′ə-pēn′, fĭl′ə-pēn′). Large area of the W Pacific, E of the Philippines and extending NW to Taiwan.

Phnom Penh (pə-nŏm′ pĕn′). Cap. of Cambodia, in the SW part on the Mekong R. Pop. 393,995.

Phoe·ni·cia (fĭ-nĭsh′ə, -nē′shə). Ancient maritime country consisting of city-states along the E coast of the Mediterranean. —**Phoe·ni′cian** adj. & n.

Phoe·nix (fē′nĭks). Cap. of Ariz., in the S central part. Pop. 764,911.

Phryg·i·a (frĭj′ē-ə). Ancient country of W central Asia Minor. —**Phryg′i·an** adj. & n.

Pic·ar·dy (pĭk′ər-dē). Region and former province in N France, extending from the English Channel to the Belgian border.

Pied·mont (pēd′mŏnt′). 1. Region of NW Italy. 2. Low platform in the E U.S. extending E from the Appalachians to the Fall Line and N from Ala. to N.J.

Pierre (pîr). Cap. of S.Dak., in the central part. Pop. 11,973.

Pikes Peak (pīks′). Mountain, 14,110 ft (4,303.6 m), in the Rockies of central Colo.

Pi·rae·us (pī-rē′əs). Chief seaport of Greece, near Athens. Pop. 187,362.

Pi·sa (pē′zə). City of N central Italy, on the Arno R. Pop. 103,772. —**Pi′san** adj. & n.

Pitts·burgh (pĭts′bûrg′). City of SW Pa. Pop. 423,938.

Platte (plăt). River, c. 310 mi (499 km) of S Neb.

Plov·div (plôv′dĭf). City of S Bulgaria. Pop. 342,000.

Plym·outh (plĭm′əth). 1. Borough of SW England, on the English Channel. Pop. 255,500. 2. Town of SE Mass., on **Plymouth Bay,** where the Pilgrims from the *Mayflower* landed (1620). Pop. 35,800.

Po (pō). River of N Italy, flowing c. 405 mi (652 km) E to the Adriatic.

Po Hai (bō′ hī′). Bo Hai.

Po·land (pō′lənd). Country of central Europe, on the Baltic Sea. Cap. Warsaw. Pop. 35,645,-000. —**Po′lish** (-lĭsh) *adj. & n.*

Pol·y·ne·sia (pŏl′ə-nē′zhə, -shə). Group of islands of the central and S Pacific Ocean, extending from New Zealand N to Hawaii and E to Easter Is. —**Pol′y·ne′sian** *adj. & n.*

Pom·er·a·ni·a (pŏm′ə-rā′nē-ə, -rān′yə). Historical region of N central Europe, extending along the S coast of the Baltic.

Pom·pe·ii (pŏm-pā′, -pā′ē). Ancient city of S Italy; destroyed by eruption of Mt. Vesuvius in A.D. 79. —**Pom·pe′ian** *adj. & n.*

Pon·ce (pŏn′sē). City of S Puerto Rico. Pop. 161,260.

Pon·ta Del·ga·da (pōn′tə dĕl-gä′də). Chief city of the Azores, on the SW coast of São Miguel Is. Pop. 21,262.

Pon·tus (pŏn′təs). Ancient region of NE Asia Minor, along the S shore of the Black Sea.

Poo·na (pōō′nə). City of W central India. Pop. 856,105.

Po·po·ca·té·petl (pō′pə-kăt′ə-pĕt′l). Dormant volcano, 17,887 ft (5,455.5 m), of central Mexico.

Port-au-Prince (pôrt′ō-prĭns′, pôrt′-). Cap. of Haiti, in the SW part. Pop. 745,700.

Port Eliz·a·beth (ĭ-lĭz′ə-bəth). City of SE South Africa, on the Indian Ocean. Pop. 392,231.

Port·land (pôrt′lənd, pôrt′-). City of NW Ore., on the Columbia R. Pop. 366,383.

Port Lou·is (lōō′ĭs, lōō′ē, lōō-ē′). Cap. of Mauritius, in the NW part. Pop. 142,853.

Port Mores·by (môrz′bē, môrz′-). Cap. of Papua New Guinea, on SE New Guinea Is. Pop. 106,600.

Pôr·to A·le·gre (pôr′tōō ə-lĕg′rĕ). City of SE Brazil. Pop. 1,183,500.

Port of Spain (spān). Cap. of Trinidad and Tobago, on the NW coast of Trinidad. Pop. 42,950.

Por·to-No·vo (pôr′tō-nō′vō). Cap. of Benin, in the SE part. Pop. 104,000.

Port Sa·id (sä-ēd′). City of NE Egypt, at the Mediterranean end of the Suez Canal. Pop. 271,000.

Ports·mouth (pôrts′məth, pôrts′-). 1. Borough of S England, on the English Channel. Pop. 191,000. 2. City of SE Va., opposite Norfolk. Pop. 104,577.

Por·tu·gal (pôr′chə-gəl, pôr′-). Country of SW Europe, on the Iberian Peninsula. Cap. Lisbon. Pop. 9,980,000. —**Por′tu·guese′** (-gēz′, -gēs′) *adj. & n.*

Po·to·mac (pə-tō′mək). River flowing c. 285 mi (459 km) from NE W.Va. along the Va.-Md. border to Chesapeake Bay.

Pots·dam (pŏts′dăm′). City of central East Germany, near Berlin. Pop. 126,262.

Poz·nań (pōz′nän′yə). City of W central Poland. Pop. 545,600.

Prague (präg). Cap. of Czechoslovakia, in the W part. Pop. 1,193,345.

Pre·to·ri·a (prĭ-tôr′ē-ə, -tōr′-). Administrative cap. of South Africa, in the NE part. Pop. 545,450.

Prince Ed·ward Island (prĭns ĕd′wərd). Island and province of SE Canada, in the S Gulf of

St. Lawrence. Cap. Charlottetown. Pop. 118,229.

Pro·vence (prō-väns′). Region of SE France, on the Mediterranean. —**Pro′ven·çal′** (prō′-vän-säl′) *adj. & n.*

Prov·i·dence (prŏv′ĭ-dəns, -dĕns′). Cap. of R.I., in the NE part. Pop. 156,804.

Prus·sia (prŭsh′ə). Region and former state of N central Europe, including present-day N Germany and N Poland. —**Prus′sian** *adj. & n.*

Pue·bla (pwĕb′lä). City of E central Mexico, ESE of Mexico City. Pop. 678,000.

Pueb·lo (pwĕb′lō). City of S central Colo. Pop. 101,686.

Puer·to Ri·co (pwĕr′tō rē′kō, pôr′-). Island of the West Indies, E of Hispaniola; a self-governing U.S. commonwealth. Cap. San Juan. Pop. 3,187,570. —**Puer′to Ri′can** *adj. & n.*

Pu·get Sound (pyōō′jĭt). Inlet of the Pacific in NW Wash.

Pun·jab (pŭn-jäb′, -jäb′, pŭn′jäb′, -jäb′). Region of NW India and NW Pakistan. —**Pun·ja′bi** *adj. & n.*

Pu·rus (pōō-rōōs′). River of E central Peru and W Brazil, flowing c. 2,100 mi (3,379 km) NE to the Amazon.

Pu·tu·ma·yo (pōō′tōō-mä′yō). River of NW South America, rising in SW Colombia and flowing c. 1,000 mi (1,609 km) along the Colombia-Peru border to the Amazon in NW Brazil.

Pyong·yang (pyŭng′yäng′). Cap. of North Korea, in the SW part. Pop. 840,000.

Pyr·e·nees (pîr′ə-nēz′). Mountain range between France and Spain, extending from the Bay of Biscay to the Mediterranean.

Q

Qa·tar (kä′tär′). Country of E Arabia, on a peninsula in the Persian Gulf. Cap. Doha. Pop. 160,000.

Qing·dao (chyĭng′dou′). City of E China, on the Yellow Sea NNW of Shanghai. Pop. 1,900,000.

Qing·hai (chyĭng′hī′). Salt lake, 1,625 sq mi (4,210 sq km), of N central China.

Qi·qi·har (chē′chē′här′). City of NE China, in Manchuria NW of Harbin. Pop. 1,500,000.

Que·bec (kwĭ-bĕk′). Also **Qué·bec** (kā-). 1. Province of E Canada. Pop. 6,234,445. 2. Cap. of Que., Canada, in the S on the St. Lawrence. Pop. 177,082.

Queens (kwēnz). Borough of New York City, on W Long Is. Pop. 1,891,325.

Que·moy (kē-moi′). Island off SE China; administered by Taiwan.

Que·zon City (kā′zŏn′). City of central Luzon, Philippines, near Manila. Pop. 956,864.

Qui·to (kē′tō). Cap. of Ecuador, on the Andean plateau. Pop. 742,858.

Qum (kōōm). Also **Qom** (kōm). City of W central Iran, SSW of Teheran. Pop. 246,831.

R

Ra·bat (rä-bät′). Cap. of Morocco, on the Atlantic coast. Pop. 367,620.

Rai·nier (rä-nîr′), **Mount**. Volcanic peak, 14,408

ft (4,394.4 m), of the Cascade range in W central Wash.

Ra·leigh (rô′lē, rä′-). Cap. of N.C., in the E central part. Pop. 149,771.

Ran·goon (răng-gōōn′). Cap. of Burma, in the S central part. Pop. 2,276,000.

Re·ci·fe (rə-sē′fə). City of NE Brazil, on the Atlantic. Pop. 1,391,800.

Red (rĕd). 1. River of S central U.S., rising in the Tex. Panhandle and flowing 1,018 mi (1,637.9 km) to the Mississippi. 2. Sea separating the Arabian Peninsula from Africa.

Re·gi·na (ri-jī′nə). Cap. of Sask., Canada, in the S part. Pop. 149,593.

Reims (rēmz). Also **Rheims**. City of NE France. Pop. 178,381.

Re·no (rē′nō). City of W Nev., near the Calif. border. Pop. 100,756.

Ré·un·ion (rē-yōōn′yən). Island of France, in the Indian Ocean SW of Mauritius.

Rey·kja·vík (rā′kyə-vēk′). Cap. of Iceland, in the SW part. Pop. 83,536.

Rhae·ti·a (rē′shē-ə, -shə). Ancient Roman province including present-day E Switzerland and W Austria. —**Rhae′tian** adj. & n.

Rhine (rīn). River of W Europe, rising in E Switzerland and flowing c. 820 mi (1,320 km) N through W West Germany and the Netherlands to the North Sea.

Rhine·land (rīn′lănd′, -lənd). Region along the Rhine in West Germany.

Rhode Island (rōd). State of the NE U.S., on the Atlantic. Cap. Providence. Pop. 947,154. —**Rhode Is′land·er** n.

Rhodes (rōdz). Largest of the Dodecanese Is. of SE Greece, in the Aegean off SW Turkey.

Rho·de·sia (rō-dē′zhə). Zimbabwe. —**Rho·de′sian** adj. & n.

Rhone (rōn). Also **Rhône**. River of SW Switzerland and SE France, flowing c. 505 mi (812 km) to the Mediterranean.

Rich·mond (rĭch′mənd). 1. Cap. of Va., in the E central part. Pop. 219,214. 2. Borough of New York City, coextensive with Staten Is. Pop. 352,121.

Rif (rĭf). Also **Riff, Er Rif** (ĕr rĭf′), or **Er Riff**. Coastal arc of hills in NE Morocco.

Ri·ga (rē′gə). City of W European USSR, on the **Gulf of Riga**, an inlet of the Baltic. Pop. 843,000.

Rio de Ja·nei·ro (rē′ō dā zhə-nâr′ō, jə-, dē). City of SE Brazil on Guanabara Bay. Pop. 5,394,900.

Rio Grande (grănd). River rising in S Colo. and flowing c. 1,885 mi (3,033 km) gen. SE to the Gulf of Mexico, forming much of the U.S.-Mexican border.

Riv·er·side (rĭv′ər-sīd′). City of S Calif., NE of Santa Ana. Pop. 170,876.

Riv·i·er·a (rĭv′ē-âr′ə). Resort area of SE France and NW Italy along the Mediterranean coast.

Ri·yadh (rē-yäd′). Cap. of Saudi Arabia, in the central part. Pop. 666,840.

Ro·a·noke (rō′ə-nōk). 1. City of SW Va., WSW of Richmond. Pop. 100,427. 2. Island off the NE coast of N.C., where Sir Walter Raleigh attempted to found a colony (1585–87).

Roch·es·ter (rŏch′ĕs-tər). City of W N.Y., ENE of Buffalo. Pop. 241,741.

Rock·ford (rŏk′fərd). City of N Ill., WNW of Chicago. Pop. 139,712.

Rocky Mountains (rŏk′ē). Also **Rock·ies** (-ēz). Mountain system of North America, extending c. 3,000 mi (4,800 km) from N Mexico to NW Alas.

Ro·ma·gna (rō-män′yä). Historical region of N central Italy.

Roman Empire (rō′mən). Empire (27 B.C.–A.D. 395) stretching from Britain to North Africa to the Persian Gulf.

Ro·ma·ni·a (rō-mā′nē-ə, -mān′yə). Var. of **Rumania.**

Rome (rōm). Cap. of Italy, on the Tiber in the W central part. Pop. 2,911,671. —**Ro′man** adj. & n.

Ro·sa·rio (rō-zä′rē-ō, -sä′-). City of E central Argentina, on the Paraná. Pop. 810,000.

Ross Sea (rôs). Large inlet of the Pacific, in Antarctica S of New Zealand.

Ros·tock (rŏs′tŏk). City of N East Germany, near the Baltic. Pop. 226,667.

Ros·tov (rə-stôf′, rō-). Also **Ros·tov-on-Don** (-ŏn-dŏn′, -dŏn′). City of E European USSR. Pop. 946,000.

Rot·ter·dam (rŏt′ər-dăm). City of SW Netherlands, SSE of The Hague. Pop. 579,194.

Rou·en (rōō-än′). City of N France, on the Seine NW of Paris. Pop. 114,927.

Ru·bi·con (rōō′bĭ-kŏn). River, 15 mi (24 km), of N central Italy, flowing NE to the Adriatic.

Ru·dolf (rōō′dŏlf′). Lake, c. 2,500 sq mi (6,475 sq km), of NW Kenya.

Ruhr (rōōr). 1. River of NW West Germany, flowing 145 mi (233.3 km) to the Rhine. 2. Industrial region along the Ruhr R.

Ru·ma·ni·a (rōō-mā′nē-ə, -mān′yə). Also **Ro·ma·ni·a** (rō-). Country of SE Europe, N of Bulgaria. Cap. Bucharest. Pop. 22,345,000. —**Ru·ma′ni·an** adj. & n.

Rush·more (rŭsh′môr), **Mount**. Mountain in the Black Hills of W S.Dak.; site of a national memorial with massive carvings.

Rus·sia (rŭsh′ə). 1. Union of Soviet Socialist Republics. 2. Russian Soviet Federated Socialist Republic, extending from the Baltic Sea to the Pacific Ocean. 3. Historically, the Russian Empire under czarist rule until its termination in 1917 by the Russian Revolution. —**Rus′sian** adj. & n.

Ru·the·ni·a (rōō-thē′nē-ə). Historical region of E Europe, in W Ukraine S of the Carpathians.

Rwan·da (rōō-än′də). Country of E central Africa. Cap. Kigali. Pop. 4,780,000. —**Rwan′dan** adj. & n.

Rya·zan (ry-ä-zän′). City of central European USSR, SE of Moscow. Pop. 462,000.

Ry·binsk (rĭ′bĭnsk). City of N central European USSR, on the Volga. Pop. 241,000.

Ryu·kyu (ryōō′kyōō′). Islands of SW Japan, between Kyushu Is. and Taiwan.

S

Saar (sär). River, c. 150 mi (240 km), of NE France and W West Germany.

Saar·land (sär′lănd′). Region of Europe between France and West Germany.

Sac·ra·men·to (săk′rə-mĕn′tō). Cap. of Calif., on the **Sacramento R.** in the N central part. Pop. 275,741.

Sa·ha·ra (sə-hâr′ə, -hä′rə). Vast arid area of N Africa, extending from the Atlantic coast to the Nile valley and from the Atlas Mts. S to the Sudan.

Sai·gon (sī-gŏn′). Ho Chi Minh City.

Saint Bernard (sānt′ bĕr-när′). Two Alpine passes connecting Switzerland and France with Italy: the **Great Saint Bernard** (alt. 8,110 ft/ 2,473.6 m); and the **Little Saint Bernard** (alt. 7,180 ft/2,190 m).

Saint Croix (kroi). One of the U.S. Virgin Is., in the West Indies.

Saint E·li·as (ĭ-lī′əs). Mountains in SW Y.T., Canada, and E Alas.

Saint George's (jôr′jəz). **1. Channel.** Strait between W Wales and SE Ireland. **2.** Also **Saint George** (jôrj). Cap. of Grenada, in the West Indies. Pop. 10,000.

Saint Gott·hard (gŏt′ərd). Mountain group of the Lepontine Alps in central Switzerland.

Saint Hel·ens (hĕl′ənz), **Mount.** Active volcanic peak in SW Wash.

Saint John's (jŏnz′). Cap. of Antigua, on the N coast of the island. Pop. 21,814.

Saint Kitts-Nevis (kĭts-nē′vĭs, -nĕv′ĭs). Island country in the British West Indies. Cap. Basseterre. Pop. 47,457.

Saint Law·rence (lôr′əns, lŏr′-). **1. Gulf of.** Arm of the NW Atlantic off SE Canada, between N.B. and Newf. **2.** River of SE Canada, flowing 744 mi (1,197.1 km) NE from Lake Ontario along the Ont.-N.Y. border and through S Que. to the Gulf of St. Lawrence. **3.** Waterway, 2,342 mi (3,768.3 km) long, consisting of a system of canals, dams, and locks in the St. Lawrence R. and connecting channels between the Great Lakes.

Saint Lou·is (lōō′ĭs, lōō′ē). City of E Mo., on the Mississippi. Pop. 453,085.

Saint Lu·ci·a (lōō′shə, lōō-sē′ə). Island nation of the West Indies, in the E Caribbean. Cap. Castries. Pop. 117,500.

Saint Paul (pôl). Cap. of Minn., in the E adjacent to Minneapolis. Pop. 270,230.

Saint Pe·ters·burg (pē′tərz-bûrg′). **1.** Leningrad. **2.** City of W central Fla., on Tampa Bay. Pop. 236,893.

Saint Thom·as (tŏm′əs). One of the U.S. Virgin Is. in the West Indies.

Saint Vin·cent and the Gren·a·dines (vĭn′sənt; grĕn′ə-dēnz′, grĕn′ə-dēnz′). Island nation of the West Indies, in the E Caribbean. Cap. Kingstown. Pop. 89,129.

Sai·pan (sī-pän′, -păn′, sī′păn). Largest of the Mariana Is. in the W Pacific.

Sa·kai (sä′kī′). City of S Honshu, Japan. Pop. 810,120.

Sa·kha·lin (săk′ə-lēn′). Island of SE Far Eastern USSR, in the Sea of Okhotsk N of Hokkaido, Japan.

Sal·a·man·ca (săl′ə-măng′kə). City of W central Spain. Pop. 144,446.

Sal·a·mis (săl′ə-mĭs). Island of Greece, in an inlet of the Aegean E of Athens.

Sa·lem (sā′ləm). Cap. of Ore., in the NW on the Willamette R. Pop. 89,233.

Sa·ler·no (sä-lâr′nō). City of S Italy. Pop. 161,997.

Salis·bury (sôlz′bĕr′ē, -bə-rē). **1.** Cap. of Zimbabwe, in the NE part. Pop. 118,500. **2. Plain.** Plateau in S central England; site of Stonehenge.

Sa·lon·i·ka (sə-lŏn′ĭ-kə, săl′ə-nē′kə). City of NE Greece, on an arm of the Aegean. Pop. 345,799.

Salt Lake City (sôlt). Cap. of Utah, in the N part. Pop. 163,033.

Sal·va·dor (săl′və-dôr′). City of E Brazil, on the Atlantic. Pop. 1,445,700.

Sal·ween (săl′wēn′). River of SE Asia, rising in E Tibet and flowing c. 1,750 mi (2,816 km) SE to the Gulf of Martaban in Burma.

Salz·burg (sôlz′bûrg′). Resort city of W central Austria. Pop. 139,000.

Sa·mar·i·a (sə-mâr′ē-ə). **1.** Region of ancient Palestine, now in NW Jordan. **2.** Ancient N kingdom of Israel. **3.** Cap. of this kingdom in the 9th cent. B.C. —**Sa·mar′i·tan** (sə-mâr′ĭ-tən) *adj. & n.*

Sam·ar·kand (săm′ər-kănd′). City of S Central Asian USSR, SW of Tashkent. Pop. 481,000.

Sa·mo·a (sə-mō′ə). Island group of the S Pacific, ENE of Fiji; divided between **American Samoa** and **Western Samoa.**

Sa·n'a (sä-nä′). Also **Sa·n'a** or **Sa·naa.** Cap. of Yemen, on the central plateau. Pop. 192,045.

San An·to·ni·o (săn ăn-tō′nē-ō′). City of S central Tex., SSW of Austin. Pop. 785,410.

San Ber·nar·di·no (bûr′nə-dē′nō, -nər-). City of SE Calif. Pop. 116,800.

San Di·e·go (dē-ā′gō). City of S Calif., on the Pacific near the Mexican border. Pop. 875,504.

San Fer·nan·do Valley (fər-năn′dō). Fertile valley in SW Calif.

San Fran·cis·co (frən-sĭs′kō). City of W Calif., on **San Francisco Bay,** an inlet of the Pacific. Pop. 678,974. —**San Fran·cis′can** (-kən *n.*

San Joa·quin (wô-kēn′, wä-kēn′). River f central Calif., rising in the Sierra Nevada and flowing c. 320 mi (515 km) NW through a fertile valley to the Sacramento R.

San Jo·se (hō-zā′). City of W Calif., SE of San Francisco. Pop. 636,550.

San Jo·sé (săn′ hō-zā′). Cap. of Costa Rica, on the central plateau. Pop. 239,800.

San Juan (hwän, wän). Cap. of Puerto Rico, on the NE coast. Pop. 422,701.

San Lu·is Po·to·si (lōō-ēs′ pô′tō-sē′). City of central Mexico. Pop. 315,200.

San Ma·ri·no (mə-rē′nō). **1.** Country within N central Italy, in the Apennines near the Adriatic. Pop. 20,000. **2.** Cap. of this country. Pop. 4,628.

San Sal·va·dor (săl′və-dôr′). Cap. of El Salvador, in the W central part. Pop. 397,100.

San·ta An·a (săn′tə ăn′ə). City of SW Calif., E of Long Beach. Pop. 203,713.

Santa Cruz de Ten·er·ife (krōōz də tĕn′ə-rĭf′). City of the Canary Is., on the NE coast of Tenerife. Pop. 186,949.

Santa Fe (fā′). **1.** Cap. of N.Mex., in the N central part. Pop. 48,899. **2. Trail.** 19th cent. wagon and trade route between Independence, Mo., and Santa Fe, N.Mex.

San·ti·a·go (săn′tē-ä′gō). Cap. of Chile, at the foot of the Andes in the central part. Pop. 3,448,700.

Santiago de Cu·ba (də kyōō′bə). City of SE Cuba, on the Caribbean. Pop. 326,066.

San·to An·dré (săn′tōō än-drĕ′). City of S Brazil, near São Paulo. Pop. 608,800.

San·to Do·min·go (săn′tō də-mĭng′gō). Cap. of the Dominican Republic, in the S part on the Caribbean. Pop. 979,608.

San·tos (săn′təs, săn′tōōsh). City of SE Brazil, on an offshore island in the Atlantic SE of São Paulo. Pop. 440,700.

São Fran·cis·co (soun frən-sĕsh′kōō). River of E Brazil, flowing c. 1,800 mi (2,896 km) NNE and E to the Atlantic.

São Gon·ça·lo (gōōn-sä′lōō). City of SE Brazil, on Guanabara Bay opposite Rio de Janeiro. Pop. 633,200.

São João de Me·ri·tí (zhwoun′ də mə-rē′tĭ, -rē′tē′). City of SE Brazil, near Rio de Janeiro. Pop. 425,800.

São Lu·is (lōō-ēsh′). City of NE Brazil, on an

offshore island in the Atlantic ESE of Belém. Pop. 389,400.

Saône (sōn). River of E central France, flowing c. 268 mi (431 km) SW to the Rhone.

São Pau·lo (pou′lŏō). City of SE Brazil. Pop. 8,407,500.

São To·mé and Prín·ci·pe (tŏō-mě′; prěn′sĕ-pə). Island country in the Gulf of Guinea W of Gabon. Cap. São Tomé (pop. 17,380), on São Tomé Is. Pop. 73,631.

Sap·po·ro (säp-pô′rō). City of SW Hokkaido, Japan. Pop. 1,401,758.

Sar·a·gos·sa (săr′ə-gŏs′ə). City of NE Spain. Pop. 563,375.

Sa·ra·je·vo (sä′rä-yě-vō). City of central Yugoslavia, SW of Belgrade. Pop. 244,045.

Sa·ra·tov (sä-rä′təf). City of S European USSR, on the Volga. Pop. 864,000.

Sar·din·i·a (sär-dǐn′ē-ə). Island of Italy, in the Mediterranean S of Corsica. —**Sar·din′i·an** *adj. & n.*

Sar·dis (sär′dǐs). Ancient city of W Asia Minor, cap. of the Lydian empire.

Sar·gas·so Sea (sär-găs′ō). Section of the North Atlantic between the West Indies and the Azores.

Sar·ma·ti·a (sär-mā′shē-ə, -shə). Ancient region in E Europe between the Vistula and the Volga. —**Sar·ma′tian** *adj. & n.*

Sas·katch·e·wan (săs-kăch′ə-wän′, -wən). Province of S central Canada. Cap. Regina. Pop. 921,323.

Sas·ka·toon (săs′kə-tŏōn′). City of S central Sask., Canada. Pop. 133,750.

Sa·u·di A·ra·bi·a (sä-ōō′dē ə-rā′bē-ə, sou′dē, sô′dē). Kingdom on the Arabian peninsula. Cap. Riyadh. Pop. 7,012,642. —**Sa·u′di or Sa·u′di A·ra′bi·an** *adj. & n.*

Sault Sainte Ma·rie Canals (sōō′ sänt′ mə-rē′). One Canadian and 2 U.S. canals by-passing the rapids of the St. Marys R. between Lakes Huron and Superior.

Sa·van·nah (sə-văn′ə). City of E Ga., at the mouth of the **Savannah R.** (314 mi/505 km). Pop. 141,634.

Sa·voy (sə-voi′). Region and former duchy of SE France, bordering on Switzerland and Italy. —**Sa·voy′ard** (sə-voi′ərd, săv′oi-ärd′) *adj. & n.*

Sax·o·ny (săk′sə-nē). **1.** Former region and duchy of NW Germany. **2.** Former duchy, kingdom, and electorate of central Germany. —**Sax′on** *adj. & n.*

Scan·di·na·vi·a (skăn′də-nā′vē-ə, -nāv′yə). **1.** Peninsula of N Europe occupied by Norway and Sweden. **2.** Norway, Sweden, and Denmark, and sometimes also Iceland, Finland, and the Faeroe Is. —**Scan′di·na′vi·an** *adj. & n.*

Schles·wig (shlěs′wǐg). Region and former duchy of N West Germany and S Denmark.

Scot·land (skŏt′lənd). Constituent country of the United Kingdom of Great Britain and Northern Ireland, in N Great Britain. Cap. Edinburgh. Pop. 5,167,000. —**Scot′tish** *adj. & n.*

Scyth·i·a (sǐth′ē-ə). Ancient region of SW Asia and SE Europe. —**Scyth′i·an** *adj. & n.*

Se·at·tle (sē-ăt′l). City of W central Wash., on Puget Sound. Pop. 493,846.

Seine (sěn). River of N France, flowing c. 480 mi (772 km) gen. NW to its estuary on the English Channel near Le Havre.

Se·leu·ci·a (sǐ-lōō′shē-ə, -shə). Ancient city of Mesopotamia, on the Tigris below modern Baghdad.

Se·ma·rang (sə-mä′räng). City of N Java, Indonesia. Pop. 646,590.

Sen·dai (sěn′dī′). City of NE Honshu, Japan. Pop. 664,799.

Sen·e·gal (sěn′ĭ-gôl′). **1.** River of W Africa, rising in W Mali and flowing c. 1,000 mi (1,609 km) along the Mauritania-Senegal border to the Atlantic. **2.** Country of W Africa, on the Atlantic. Cap. Dakar. Pop. 5,085,388. —**Sen′e·ga·lese′** (-gô′lěz′, -lěs′, -gə-) *adj. & n.*

Seoul (sōl). Cap. of South Korea, in the NW part. Pop. 8,114,000.

Ser·bi·a (sûr′bē-ə). Region and constituent republic of E Yugoslavia. —**Ser′bi·an** *adj. & n.*

Se·vas·to·pol (sə-văs′tə-pōl′). City of SW European USSR, on the Black Sea. Pop. 308,000.

Sev·ern (sěv′ərn). River rising in W Wales and flowing c. 210 mi (338 km) through S England to the Bristol Channel.

Se·ville (sə-vǐl′). City of SW Spain, on the Guadalquivir R. Pop. 630,329.

Sey·chelles (sā-shěl′, -shělz′). Island country in the Indian Ocean E of Tanzania. Cap. Victoria. Pop. 52,437.

Shan·dong (shän′dŏōng′). Also **Shan·tung** (shän′tŭng′, shän′dŏōng′). Peninsula of E China, projecting E between the Gulf of Bo Hai and the Yellow Sea.

Shang·hai (shăng-hī′). City of E China, on the Yangtze estuary. Pop. 8,100,000.

Shan·non (shăn′ən). River, c. 240 mi (386 km), of W Ireland.

Sha·ri (shä′rē). River of N central Africa, rising in the Central African Republic and flowing c. 1,400 mi (2,253 km) NW through S Chad to Lake Chad.

Shas·ta (shăs′tə), **Mount.** Extinct volcano, 14,162 ft (4,319.4 m), in the Cascade Range of N Calif.

Shef·field (shěf′ēld). Borough of N central England, E of Manchester. Pop. 544,200.

Shen·an·do·ah (shěn′ən-dō′ə). River, c. 150 mi (241 km), of N Va. and NE W.Va.

Shen·yang (shŭn′yăng′). City of NE China, ENE of Beijing. Pop. 3,300,000.

Shet·land Islands (shět′lənd). Group of islands in the North Atlantic NE of Scotland.

Shi·jia·zhuang (shœ′jyä′jwäng′). Also **Shih·kia·chwang.** City of NE China, SW of Beijing. Pop. 940,000.

Shi·ko·ku (shē′kô-kŏō′). Island of S Japan, between SW Honshu and E Kyushu.

Shi·raz (shē-räz′). City of SW Iran. Pop. 416,408.

Shreve·port (shrēv′pôrt′, -pōrt′). City of NW La., near the Tex. border. Pop. 205,815.

Si·am (sī-ăm′). **1. Gulf of.** Arm of the South China Sea between the Malay Peninsula and Indochina. **2.** Thailand. —**Si′a·mese′** (sī′ə-mēz′, -mēs′) *adj. & n.*

Si·an (sē′än, shē′-). Xi'an.

Si·ang (shyē-äng′, shyäng). Xiang.

Si·be·ri·a (sī-bîr′ē-ə). Region of N Asian USSR, from the Urals to the Pacific. —**Si·be′ri·an** *adj. & n.*

Sic·i·ly (sǐs′ə-lē). Island of S Italy, in the Mediterranean. —**Si·cil′ian** (sī-sǐl′yən) *adj. & n.*

Si·don (sīd′n). Ancient city of Phoenicia, on the Mediterranean.

Si·en·a (sē-ěn′ə). City of central Italy, S of Florence. Pop. 63,961. —**Si′en·ese′** (sē′ə-nēz′, -nēs′) *adj. & n.*

Si·er·ra Le·one (sē-ěr′ə lē-ōn′). Country of NW Africa, on the Atlantic. Cap. Freetown. Pop. 4,125,000.

Si·er·ra Ma·dre (sē-ěr′ə mä′drā). Mountain system of Mexico, comprising 3 ranges: **1. Sierra Madre del Sur,** in the S along the Pacific. **2. Sierra Madre Oriental,** extending S from the Rio Grande, roughly parallel to the Gulf of Mexico.

3. Sierra Madre Occidental, extending S from the U.S. border, paralleling the Pacific coast.

Sierra Ne·vad·a (sə-nā′də). Mountain range of E Calif., rising to 14,494 ft (4,420.7 m).

Sik·kim (sĭk′ĭm). State of NE India and former kingdom, in the E Himalayas.

Si·le·sia (sī-lē′zhə, -shə, sĭ-). Region of central Europe, chiefly in SW Poland. —**Si·le′sian** adj. & n.

Sim·fe·ro·pol (sĭm′fə-rō′pəl). City of S European USSR, in the Crimea. Pop. 307,000.

Si·nai (sī′nī′). Peninsula between the Gulfs of Suez and Aqaba.

Sin·ga·pore (sĭng′gə-pôr′, sĭng′ə-). 1. Country of SE Asia, comprising **Singapore Is.** and adjacent islands off the S tip of the Malay Peninsula. Pop. 2,465,000. 2. Cap. of this country, on the **Strait of Singapore.**

Sjael·land (shĕl′län). Island of E Denmark, site of Copenhagen.

Skag·er·rak (skăg′ə-răk′). Arm of the North Sea between Norway and Jutland.

Skop·lje (skôp′lĕ′, -lyĕ). City of SE Yugoslavia, in Macedonia. Pop. 312,092.

Sla·vo·ni·a (slə-vō′nē-ə). Region of N Yugoslavia, between the Drava and Sava rivers. —**Sla·vo′ni·an** adj. & n.

Slo·va·ki·a (slō-vä′kē-ə). Region of E Czechoslovakia. —**Slo·vak′i·an** adj. & n.

Smo·lensk (smō-lĕnsk′). City of W central European USSR, on the Dnieper. Pop. 305,000.

Smyr·na (smûr′nə). Izmir.

Snake (snāk). River of the NW U.S., flowing 1,038 mi (1,670 km) W from NW Wyo. to the Columbia in SE Wash.

So·ci·e·ty (sə-sī′ĭ-tē). Islands of French Polynesia, in the S Pacific E of Samoa.

So·co·tra (sə-kō′trə). Island of Southern Yemen, in the Indian Ocean off the Horn of Africa.

Sod·om (sŏd′əm). City of ancient Palestine.

So·fi·a (sō′fē-ə, sō-fē′ə). Cap. of Bulgaria, in the W central part. Pop. 1,047,920.

Sol·o·mon Islands (sŏl′ə-mən). Also **Sol·o·mons** (-mənz). 1. Islands of the W Pacific E of New Guinea, divided between Papua New Guinea and the independent Solomon Is. 2. Nation comprising the Solomons SE of Bougainville. Cap. Honiara. Pop. 225,000.

So·ma·li·a (sō-mä′lē-ə, -mäl′yə). Country of E Africa, on the Indian Ocean. Cap. Mogadishu. Pop. 4,535,000. —**So·ma′li·an** adj. & n.

So·ma·li·land (sō-mä′lē-lănd′). Region of E Africa, including Somalia, Djibouti, and parts of Ethiopia.

Somme (sôm). River, c. 150 mi (241 km), of N France.

Song·hua (sŏong′hwä′). River of Manchuria, NE China, rising near the North Korean border and flowing c. 1,150 mi (1,850 km) NW, E, and NE to the Amur.

Soo Canals (sōō). Sault Ste. Marie Canals.

Soo·chow (sōō′jō′, -chou′). Suzhou.

South Af·ri·ca (south ăf′rĭ-kə). Country of S Africa, on the Atlantic and Indian oceans. Caps. Pretoria, Cape Town. Pop. 29,645,000. —**South Af′ri·can** adj. & n.

South A·mer·i·ca (ə-mĕr′ĭ-kə). S continent of the Western Hemisphere, lying mostly S of the equator. —**South A·mer′i·can** adj. & n.

South·amp·ton (south-hămp′tən, sou-thămp′-). Borough of S central England, on an inlet of the English Channel. Pop. 207,800.

South Bend (bĕnd). City of N Ind. Pop. 109,727.

South Car·o·li·na (kăr′ə-lī′nə). State of the SE U.S., on the Atlantic. Cap. Columbia. Pop. 3,119,208. —**South Car·o·lin′i·an** (-lĭn′ē-ən) adj. & n.

South Chi·na Sea (chī′nə). Section of the W Pacific bordered by SE China, Vietnam, Cambodia, Thailand, Malaysia, Indonesia, and the Philippines.

South Da·ko·ta (də-kō′tə). State of the N central U.S. Cap. Pierre. Pop. 690,178. —**South Da·ko′tan** adj. & n.

South·east A·sia (south-ēst′ ā′zhə, ā′shə). Region gen. considered to include the Philippines, Indochina, Malaysia, Singapore, Indonesia, and Brunei.

South·ern Alps (sŭth′ərn ălps′). Mountain range of W South Is., New Zealand.

South Seas. 1. All seas S of the equator. 2. The S Pacific.

Spain (spān). Country of SW Europe, on the Iberian Peninsula and including the Balearic and Canary Is. Cap. Madrid. Pop. 37,790,000. —**Span′iard** (spăn′yərd) n. —**Span′ish** (spăn′ĭsh) adj. & n.

Spanish Sa·ha·ra (sə-här′ə). Western Sahara.

Spar·ta (spär′tə). Dorian city-state of ancient Greece, in the SE Peloponnesus. —**Spar′tan** adj. & n.

Spo·kane (spō-kăn′). City of NE Wash., near the Idaho border. Pop. 171,300.

Spor·a·des (spôr′ə-dēz′). All the Greek islands in the Aegean, except the Cyclades.

Spring·field (sprĭng′fēld). 1. Cap. of Ill., in the central part. Pop. 99,637. 2. City of SW Mass. Pop. 152,319. 3. City of SW Mo., SE of Kansas City. Pop. 133,116.

Sri Lan·ka (srē läng′kə). Island country in the Indian Ocean SE of India. Cap. Colombo. Pop. 15,470,000. —**Sri Lan′kan** adj. & n.

Stam·ford (stăm′fərd). City of SW Conn., on Long Is. Sound. Pop. 102,453.

Stat·en (stăt′n). Island in New York Bay, coextensive with the New York City Borough of Richmond.

Stock·holm (stŏk′hōlm). Cap. of Sweden, in the E on the Baltic Sea. Pop. 649,384.

Stock·ton (stŏk′tən). City of central Calif., S of Sacramento. Pop. 149,779.

Stoke-on-Trent (stōk′ŏn-trĕnt′). Borough of W central England. Pop. 257,200.

Stras·bourg (străs′bûrg, sträz′-). City of NE France, near the Rhine R. Pop. 253,384.

Strat·ford-on-A·von (străt′fərd-ŏn-ā′vŏn, -ā′vən). Borough of central England; birthplace and burial site of Shakespeare. Pop. 20,080.

Strom·bo·li (strŏm-bō′lē). 1. Island of S Italy, off NE Sicily. 2. Active volcano, 3,038 ft (926.5 m), on Stromboli Is.

Stutt·gart (stŭt′gärt). City of SW West Germany. Pop. 581,989.

Su·chow (shū′jō′). Xuzhou.

Su·cre (sōō′krä). Constitutional cap. of Bolivia, in the S central part. Pop. 62,207.

Su·dan (sōō-dăn′). 1. Region of N Africa, S of the Sahara and N of the equator. 2. Country of NE Africa, S of Egypt. Cap. Khartoum. Pop. 18,630,000. —**Su·da·nese′** (-də-nēz′, -nēs′) adj. & n.

Su·de·ten·land (sōō-dāt′n-lănd′). Region of NW Czechoslovakia along the Polish border.

Su·ez (sōō-ĕz′, sōō′ĕz). 1. **Gulf of.** N arm of the

Red Sea off NE Egypt, W of the Sinai Peninsula. **2.** Isthmus of NE Egypt connecting Africa and Asia and traversed by the **Suez Canal** (107 mi/172 km) from the Mediterranean to the Gulf of Suez. **3.** City of NE Egypt, at the head of the Gulf of Suez. Pop. 204,000.

Su·lu (sŏō'lŏō). **1.** Group of islands in the W Pacific, belonging to the Philippines. **2. Sea.** Section of the W Pacific between the central Philippines and Borneo.

Su·ma·tra (sŏō-mä'trə). Island of Indonesia, in the Indian Ocean W of Malaysia and Borneo. —**Su·ma'tran** adj. & n.

Su·mer (sŏō'mər). Ancient country of Mesopotamia in present-day S Iraq. —**Su·me'ri·an** adj. & n.

Sun·da (sŭn'də, sŏŏn'də). **1. Islands.** W section of the Malay Archipelago, between the South China Sea and the Indian Ocean. **2. Strait.** Channel between Sumatra and Java.

Sun·der·land (sŭn'dər-lənd). Borough of NE England. Pop. 300,800.

Sun·ny·vale (sŭn'ē-vāl'). City of W Calif., near San Jose. Pop. 106,618.

Su·pe·ri·or (sə-pîr'ē-ər). One of the Great Lakes between the U.S. and Canada.

Su·ra·ba·ya (sŏŏr'ə-bī'ə). City of NE Java, Indonesia. Pop. 1,332,249.

Su·ri·nam (sŏŏr'ə-näm). Country of NE South America, on the Atlantic. Cap. Paramaribo. Pop. 425,000.

Su·sa (sŏŏ'sə, -zə). Ruined city of SW Iran; cap. of ancient Elam.

Sus·que·han·na (sŭs'kwə-hăn'ə). River of the NE U.S., rising in central N.Y. and flowing 444 mi (715 km) S to Chesapeake Bay.

Su·va (sŏŏ'vä). Cap. of Fiji, on the SE coast of Viti Levu. Pop. 63,628.

Su·zhou (sŏŏ'jō). City of E China, WNW of Shanghai. Pop. 750,000.

Sverd·lovsk (svĕrd'lôfsk'). City of E European USSR, in the Urals. Pop. 1,225,000.

Swa·bi·a (swä'bē-ə). Historical region of SW Germany. —**Swa'bi·an** adj. & n.

Swan·sea (swän'sē). Borough of S Wales, on an inlet of the Bristol Channel. Pop. 186,900.

Swa·zi·land (swä'zē-lănd'). Country of SE Africa, between South Africa and Mozambique. Cap. Mbabane. Pop. 565,000.

Swe·den (swēd'n). Country on the E part of the Scandinavian Peninsula in N Europe. Cap. Stockholm. Pop. 8,315,010. —**Swede** n. —**Swe'dish** (swē'dĭsh) adj. & n.

Swit·zer·land (swĭt'sər-lənd). Country of central Europe. Cap. Bern. Pop. 6,314,200. —**Swiss** (swĭs) adj. & n.

Syd·ney (sĭd'nē). City of SE Australia, on an inlet of the Tasman Sea. Metro. pop. 3,193,300.

Syr·a·cuse (sĭr'ə-kyŏŏz', -kyŏŏs'). City of central N.Y., ESE of Rochester. Pop. 170,105.

Syr·i·a (sîr'ē-ə). Country of SW Asia, on the E Mediterranean coast. Cap. Damascus. Pop. 8,401,100. —**Syr'i·an** adj. & n.

Szcze·cin (shchě'tsēn). City of NW Poland. Pop. 388,000.

T

Ta·briz (tä-brēz'). City of NW Iran. Pop. 598,576.

Ta·co·ma (tə-kō'mə). City of W central Wash., on an arm of Puget Sound. Pop. 158,501.

Tae·gu (tī-gŏō'). City of SE South Korea. Pop. 1,487,098.

Tae·jon (tī-jŏn'). City of SW South Korea. Pop. 508,574.

Ta·gus (tä'gəs). River rising in E central Spain and flowing c. 585 mi (941 km) NW and SW to the Atlantic at Lisbon, Portugal.

Ta·hi·ti (tə-hē'tē, tä-). One of the Society Is. in French Polynesia. —**Ta·hi'tian** adj. & n.

Ta·hoe (tä'hō). Lake on the Calif.-Nev. border.

Tai·chung (tī'chŏŏng'). City of W central Taiwan. Pop. 585,205.

Tai·nan (tī'nän'). City of SW Taiwan. Pop. 572,590.

Tai·pei (tī'pā'). Cap. of Taiwan, in the N part. Pop. 2,196,237.

Tai·wan (tī'wän'). Island off the SE coast of China, constituting along with the Pescadores and other smaller islands the Republic of China. Cap. Taipei. Pop. 18,055,000. —**Tai'wan·ese'** adj. & n.

Tai·yü·an (tī'yŏō'än'). City of NE China. Pop. 1,350,000.

Tal·la·has·see (tăl'ə-hăs'ē). Cap. of Fla., in the NW part. Pop. 81,548.

Tal·linn (tä'lĭn, tăl'ĭn). City of NW European USSR, in Estonia on the Gulf of Finland. Pop. 436,000.

Tam·pa (tăm'pə). City of W central Fla., on **Tampa Bay,** an inlet of the Gulf of Mexico. Pop. 271,523.

Tam·pi·co (tăm-pē'kō). City of E central Mexico, near the Gulf of Mexico. Pop. 240,600.

Ta·nan·a·rive (tə-năn'ə-rēv'). Antananarivo.

Tan·gan·yi·ka (tăn'gən-yē'kə, tăng'-). **1.** Former country of E central Africa that joined with Zanzibar (1964) to form Tanzania. **2. Lake.** Lake, c. 12,700 sq mi (32,893 km), of E central Africa, between Tanzania and the Congo.

Tan·gier (tăn-jîr'). Also **Tan·giers** (-jîrz'). City of N Morocco. Pop. 187,894.

Tang·shan (täng'shän'). City of NE China. Pop. 650,000.

Tan·za·ni·a (tăn'zə-nē'ə, tăn-zä'nē-ə). Country of E Africa. Cap. Dar es Salaam. Pop. 18,785,000. —**Tan'za·ni'an** adj. & n.

Ta·ran·to (tä'rän-tō). City of SE Italy, on the **Gulf of Taranto,** an arm of the Ionian Sea. Pop. 247,681.

Tar·ta·ry (tär'tə-rē). Region of E Europe and Asia overrun by Tatars in the 13th and 14th cent.

Tash·kent (täsh-kěnt'). City of S Central Asian USSR. Pop. 1,816,000.

Tas·man (tăz'mən). Sea of the S Pacific between Australia and New Zealand.

Tas·ma·ni·a (tăz-mā'nē-ə). Island state off SE Australia. —**Tas·ma'ni·an** adj. & n.

Ta·tra (tä'trä). Range of the Carpathians, along the Czech-Polish border S of Kraków.

Tau·rus (tôr'əs). Range of S Turkey, extending c. 350 mi (565 km) parallel to the Mediterranean coast.

Tbi·li·si (tə-bē-lē'sē). City of S European USSR, on the Kura R. Pop. 1,080,000.

Te·gu·ci·gal·pa (tä-gŏŏ'sē-gäl'pä). Cap. of Honduras, in the S central part. Pop. 316,800.

Te·he·ran (tě'ə-răn', -rän', tā'-). Also **Te·hran** (tě-rän'). Cap. of Iran, in the N central part. Pop. 4,496,159.

Tel A·viv-Jaf·fa (těl'ə-vēv'-jäf'ə, -yä'fə). City of Israel, in the central part on the Mediterranean. Pop. 336,300.

Ten·nes·see (těn'ĭ-sē'). **1.** State of the SE U.S. Cap. Nashville. Pop. 4,590,750. **2.** River of SE U.S., flowing c. 652 mi (1,049 km) from E Tenn. to the Ohio R. —**Ten'nes·se'an** adj. & n.

Te·noch·ti·tlán (tā-nôch'tět-län'). Ancient cap. of the Aztec empire.

Te·ton (tē'tŏn'). Also Te·tons (tē'tŏnz, tĕt'nz). Range of the Rockies in NW Wyo. and SE Idaho, rising to 13,747 ft (4,192.8 m).

Tex·as (tĕk'səs). State of the S central U.S. Cap. Austin. Pop. 14,228,383. —Tex'an adj. & n.

Thai·land (tī'lănd'). Country of SE Asia, on the Gulf of Siam. Cap. Bangkok. Pop. 47,845,000. —Thai adj. & n.

Thames (tĕmz). River of S England, flowing c. 210 mi (337.8 km) E past London to its wide estuary on the North Sea.

Thebes (thēbz). 1. Ancient religious and political cap. of Upper Egypt. 2. Ancient city of E central Greece. —The'ban adj. & n.

Ther·mop·y·lae (thər-mŏp'ə-lē). Pass of E central Greece, SE of Lamia; site of Spartan stand against Persians (480 B.C.).

Thes·sa·ly (thĕs'ə-lē). Ancient region of N central Greece, along the Aegean Sea.

Thim·bu (thĭm'bōō). Also Thim·phu (-pōō'). Cap. of Bhutan. Pop. 8,982.

Tho·hoy·an·dou (tō-hoi'ăn-dōō'). Cap. of Venda, black enclave in NE South Africa.

Thou·sand Islands (thou'zənd). Group of more than 1,500 islands in the St. Lawrence at the outlet of Lake Ontario.

Thrace (thrās). Ancient country in the SE part of the Balkan Peninsula, comprising modern Bulgaria and parts of Greece and Turkey.

Thun·der Bay (thŭn'dər). City of SW Ontario, Can., on Thunder Bay, inlet on the NW shore of Lake Superior. Pop. 112,053.

Tian·jin (tyän'jĭn'). City of NE China, near the Gulf of Bo Hai SE of Beijing. Pop. 4,500,000.

Tian Shan (tyän' shän'). Mountains of central Asia, extending c. 1,500 mi (2,414 km) ENE through S Central Asian USSR and NW China.

Ti·ber (tī'bər). River of central Italy, flowing c. 251 mi (404 km) S and SW through Rome to the Tyrrhenian Sea.

Ti·bes·ti Mas·sif (tĭ-bĕs'tĭ mă-sēf'). Saharan mountain group in N Chad.

Ti·bet (tĭ-bĕt'). Region and former semi-independent theocratic state of SW Asia. —Ti·bet'an adj. & n.

Tier·ra del Fu·e·go (tĭ-ĕr'ə dĕl fōō-ā'gō, fyōō-). 1. Archipelago at the extreme S tip of South America. 2. Main island of this archipelago, divided between Chile and Argentina.

Ti·gris (tī'grĭs). River of SW Asia, rising in E Turkey and flowing c. 1,150 mi (1,850 km) SE to join the Euphrates in S Iraq.

Ti·jua·na (tē-wä'nə). City of NW Mexico. Pop. 535,000.

Tim·buk·tu (tĭm'bŭk-tōō', tĭm-bŭk'tōō). City of central Mali, near the Niger R. Pop. 11,900.

Ti·mor (tē'môr, tē-môr'). Island at the E end of the Indonesian Archipelago.

Ti·ra·ne (tĭ-rä'nə). Also Ti·ra·na (-nä). Cap. of Albania, in the central part. Pop. 192,300.

Ti·ti·ca·ca (tĭt'ĭ-kä'kä). Largest freshwater lake (c. 3,200 sq mi/8,288 sq km) in South America, in the Andes on the Peru-Bolivia border.

To·gli·at·ti (tōl-yä'tē). Also Tol·yat·ti. City of E central European USSR. Pop. 517,000.

To·go (tō'gō). Country of W Africa, on the Gulf of Guinea. Cap. Lomé. Pop. 2,565,000.

To·kyo (tō'kē-ō'). Cap. of Japan, in E central Honshu on Tokyo Bay, a 50 mi (80 km) inlet of the Pacific. Pop. 8,349,209.

To·le·do (tə-lē'dō). 1. City of central Spain, near the Tagus R. Pop. 56,414. 2. City of NW Ohio, on Lake Erie. Pop. 354,635.

Tomsk (tŏmsk, tômsk). City of W central Siberian USSR. Pop. 431,000.

Ton·ga (tŏng'gə). Island nation of the SW Pacific, E of Fiji. Cap. Nukualofa. Pop. 97,000.

Ton·kin (tŏn'kĭn', tŏng'kĭn'). Gulf of. Arm of the South China Sea between Vietnam and S China.

To·pe·ka (tə-pē'kə). Cap. of Kans., in the NE part W of Kansas City. Pop. 115,266.

To·ron·to (tə-rŏn'tō). Cap. of Ont., Canada, on the N shore of Lake Ontario. Pop. 635,685.

Tor·rance (tôr'əns, tŏr'-). City of S Calif., S of Los Angeles. Pop. 131,497.

Tou·louse (tōō-lōōz'). City of SW France. Pop. 373,796.

To·ya·ma (tō-yä'mä). City of W central Honshu, Japan, on Toyama Bay, an inlet of the Sea of Japan. Pop. 305,054.

Tra·fal·gar (trə-făl'gər). Cape on the Atlantic coast of S Spain.

Trans·al·pine Gaul (trăns-ăl'pīn gôl). Section of ancient Gaul NW of the Alps.

Trans·cau·ca·sia (trăns'kô-kā'zhə, trănz'-). Region of the SE USSR between the Caucasus Mts. and the borders of Turkey and Iran.

Trans·kei (trăns-kā', -kī'). Independent black African homeland in SE South Africa, on the Indian Ocean coast. Cap. Umtata. Pop. 2,500,000.

Trans·vaal (trăns-väl', trănz-). Region and province of NE South Africa.

Tran·syl·va·ni·a (trăn'sĭl-vā'nē-ə, -vān'yə). Region of W Rumania. —Tran'syl·va'ni·an adj. & n.

Tran·syl·va·ni·an Alps (trăn'sĭl-vā'nē-ən, -vān'-yən). S section of the Carpathian Mts., extending across central Rumania.

Tren·ton (trĕn'tən). Cap. of N.J., in the W central part on the Delaware R. Pop. 92,124.

Tri·este (trē-ĕst'). Seaport of extreme NE Italy. Pop. 260,291.

Trin·i·dad (trĭn'ə-dăd'). Island off Venezuela. —Trin'i·dad'i·an adj. & n.

Trinidad and To·ba·go (tə-bā'gō). Country of SE West Indies, comprising the islands of Trinidad and Tobago. Cap. Port-of-Spain. Pop. 920,000.

Trip·o·li (trĭp'ə-lē). 1. City of NW Lebanon, on the Mediterranean. Pop. 175,000. 2. Cap. of Libya, in the NW on the Mediterranean. Pop. 551,477.

Troy (troi). Ancient city of NW Asia Minor; site of the Trojan War.

Truk (trŭk, trōōk). Island group in the Caroline Is. in the W Pacific.

Tsi·nan (tsī'nän'). Jinan.

Tsing·tao (chĭng'dou'). Qingdao.

Tsi·tsi·har (chē'chē'här', tsē'tsē'-). Qiqihar.

Tu·a·mo·tu (tōō'ə-mō'tōō). Archipelago of French Polynesia, in the S Pacific E of Tahiti.

Tuc·son (tōō'sŏn'). City of SE Ariz., SSE of Phoenix. Pop. 330,537.

Tu·cu·mán (tōō'kōō-män'). City of NW Argentina. Pop. 375,000.

Tu·la (tōō'lə). City of central European USSR, S of Moscow. Pop. 518,000.

Tul·sa (tŭl'sə). City of NE Okla. Pop. 360,919.

Tu·nis (tōō'nĭs, tyōō'-). Cap. of Tunisia, in the N part on the Mediterranean. Pop. 550,404.

Tu·ni·sia (tōō-nē'zhə, -shə, -nĭzh'ə, -nĭsh'ə, tyōō-). Country of N Africa, on the Mediterranean. Cap. Tunis. Pop. 6,410,000. —**Tu·ni'sian** *adj.* & *n.*

Tu·rin (tōō'rĭn, tyōō'-). City of NW Italy, on the Po R. Pop. 1,160,686.

Tur·key (tûr'kē). Country of SW Asia, between the Mediterranean and Black seas. Cap. Ankara. Pop. 45,955,000. —**Turk'ish** *adj.* & *n.*

Turk·men·i·stan (tûrk'mĕn-ĭ-stăn', -stän'). Region of S Central Asian USSR.

Turks and Cai·cos (tûrks; kī'kŏs). British island groups of the West Indies, SE of the Bahamas.

Tus·ca·ny (tŭs'kə-nē). Rgion of NW Italy. —**Tus'can** *adj.* & *n.*

Tu·va·lu (tōō-väl'ōō, -vär'-). Island country of the W Pacific, N of Fiji. Cap. Funafuti. Pop. 7,500.

Tyre (tīr). Ancient Phoenician city on the E Mediterranean in present-day S Lebanon.

Ty·rol (tĭ-rōl', tī'rōl', tîr'ōl'). Region of the E Alps in W Austria and N Italy. —**Ty'ro·lese'** *adj.* & *n.*

Tyr·rhe·ni·an Sea (tĭ-rē'nē-ən). Section of the Mediterranean between Italy and the islands of Corsica, Sardinia, and Sicily.

U

U·ban·gi (yōō-băng'gē, ōō-bäng'gē). River of central Africa, flowing c. 700 mi (1,125 km) along the NW border of Zaire to the Congo R.

U·fa (ōō-fä'). City of E European USSR, in the Urals. Pop. 986,000.

U·gan·da (yōō-găn'də, ōō-gän'dä). Country of E central Africa. Cap. Kampala. Pop. 12,115,-000. —**U·gan'dan** *adj.* & *n.*

U·kraine (yōō-krān', -krīn', yōō'-krān'). Region of SW European USSR. —**U·krai'ni·an** *adj.* & *n.*

U·lan Ba·tor (ōō'län bä'tôr'). Cap. of Mongolia, in the N central part. Pop. 287,000.

U·lan-U·de (ōō'län-ōō'də). City of S Siberian USSR, E of Lake Baikal. Pop. 305,000.

Ul·ster (ŭl'stər). Region of N Ireland.

Ul·ya·novsk (ōōl-yä'nəfsk). City of E central European USSR, on the Volga. Pop. 473,000.

Um·bri·a (ŭm'brē-ə). Region of central Italy.

Um·ta·ta (ōōm-tä'tə). Cap. of the Transkei, in the W central part. Pop. 25,216.

Un·ga·va (ŭng-gä'və, -gä'və). **1.** Bay. Inlet of Hudson Strait extending into N Que., Canada. **2.** Peninsula of N Que., Canada, between Hudson and Ungava bays.

Un·ion of So·vi·et So·cial·ist Republics (yōōn'yən; sō've-ĕt sō'shə-lĭst). Country of E Europe and N Asia, with coastlines on the Baltic and Black seas and the Arctic and Pacific oceans. Cap. Moscow. Pop. 264,486,000.

U·nit·ed Arab E·mir·ates (yōō-nī'təd är'əb ĕ-mîr'ĭts, -āts'). Country of E Arabia, a federation of 7 sheikdoms on the Persian Gulf and the Gulf of Oman. Cap. Abu Dhabi. Pop. 180,200.

United Kingdom. Also **United Kingdom of Great Brit·ain and Northern Ire·land** (brĭt'n; īr'lənd). Country of W Europe, comprising England, Scotland, Wales, and Northern Ireland. Cap. London. Pop. 55,880,000.

United States. Also **United States of A·mer·i·ca** (ə-mĕr'ĭ-kə). Country of central and NW North America, with coastlines on the Atlantic, Pacific, and Arctic oceans. Cap. Washington, D.C. Pop. 226,504,825.

Up·per Vol·ta (ŭp'ər vōl'tə). Country of W Af-

rica, S of Mali. Cap. Ouagadougou. Pop. 6,390,000.

Ur (ûr, ōōr). Ancient city of Sumer, on a site now in SE Iraq.

U·ral (yōōr'əl). **1.** River of USSR, rising in the S Urals and flowing 1,574 mi (2,533 km) W and S to the Caspian Sea. **2.** Also **U·rals** (yōōr'-əlz). Range of the USSR forming the traditional boundary between Europe and Asia, extending c. 1,500 mi (2,400 km) from the Arctic Ocean S to Kazakhstan.

U·ru·guay (yōōr'ə-gwī', -gwā'). **1.** Country of South America, in the SE on the Atlantic. Cap. Montevideo. **2.** River of SE South America, rising in S Brazil and flowing c. 1,000 mi (1,609 km) to the Río de la Plata. —**U·ru·guay'an** *adj.* & *n.*

U·tah (yōō'tô', -tä'). State of W U.S. Cap. Salt Lake City. Pop. 1,461,037. —**U'tah·an** *adj.* & *n.*

U·trecht (yōō'trĕkt'). City of central Netherlands, SSE of Amsterdam. Pop. 237,037.

Uz·bek·i·stan (ōōz-bĕk'ĭ-stän', -stän', ŭz-). Region of S Central Asian USSR.

V

Va·duz (fä-dōōts'). Cap. of Liechtenstein, on the upper Rhine. Pop. 4,704.

Va·len·ci·a (və-lĕn'shē-ə, -shə). **1.** (və-lĕn'shē-ə, -chə). Region and former kingdom of E Spain, on the Mediterranean S of Catalonia. **2.** City of E Spain, near the Gulf of Valencia, a wide inlet of the Mediterranean. Pop. 750,994. **3.** City of N Venezuela, WSW of Caracas on the W shore of Lake Valencia (125 sq mi/324 sq km). Pop. 455,000.

Va·lla·do·lid (və'lyä-thō-lēth'). City of N central Spain. Pop. 315,486.

Val·let·ta (və-lĕt'ə). Cap. of Malta, on the NE coast. Pop. 14,042.

Val·ley Forge (văl'ē fôrj'). Village of SE Pa.; site of George Washington's winter headquarters (1777–78).

Val·pa·rai·so (văl'pə-rī'zō, -rā'zō). City of W central Chile, on the Pacific. Pop. 248,200.

Van·cou·ver (văn-kōō'vər). **1.** Mount. Mountain, 15,700 ft (4,789 m), in the St. Elias range in SW Y.T., Canada, near the Alas. border. **2.** Island, c. 275 mi (442 km) long, of SW Canada, in the Pacific off SW B.C. mainland. **3.** City of SW B.C., Canada, on the Strait of Georgia opposite Vancouver Is. Pop. 410,188.

Va·nu·a·tu (vä'nōō-ä'tōō). Island country of the S Pacific, E of Australia. Cap. Vila. Pop. 112,596.

Va·ra·na·si (və-rä'nə-sē). City of N central India, on the Ganges. Pop. 583,856.

Var·na (vär'nə). City of E Bulgaria, on the Black Sea. Pop. 286,382.

Vat·i·can City (văt'ĭ-kən). Independent papal state within Rome, Italy. Pop. 723.

Ven·da (vĕn'də). Independent black African homeland in NE South Africa, near the Zimbabwe border. Cap. Thohoyandou. Pop. 525,000.

Ven·e·zue·la (vĕn'ə-zwā'lə, -zwē'lə). Country of N South America, on the Caribbean Sea. Cap. Caracas. Pop. 11,300,000. —**Ven·e·zue'lan** *adj.* & *n.*

Ven·ice (vĕn'ĭs). City of NE Italy, on islets within a lagoon in the Gulf of Venice, a wide inlet of the N Adriatic. Pop. 355,865. —**Ve·ne'tian** (və-nē'shən) *adj.* & *n.*

Ven·tu·ra (vĕn-chûr'ə, -tōōr'ə). City of SW

Calif., on the Pacific W of Los Angeles. Pop. 490,500.

Ve·ra·cruz (vĕr′ə-krōōz′). City of E central Mexico, on the Gulf of Mexico. Pop. 295,300.

Verde (vûrd), **Cape.** Peninsula on the coast of Senegal; westernmost point of the African continent.

Ver·dun (vər-dŭn′). City in NE France; site of prolonged World War I battle (1916). Pop. 23,621.

Vermont (vər-mŏnt′). State of the NE U.S. Cap. Montpelier. Pop. 511,446.

Ve·ro·na (və-rō′nə). City of NE Italy, W of Venice. Pop. 269,763. **—Ver′o·nese′** (vĕr′ə-nēz′, -nēs′) adj. & n.

Ver·sailles (vər-sī′, vĕr-). City of N central France; site of Louis XIV's palace and of the signing of the treaty between the Allies and Germany after World War I (1919). Pop. 94,145.

Ve·su·vi·us (və-sōō′vē-əs). Active volcano, 4,190 ft (1,278 m), in W Italy near Naples.

Vi·chy (vĭsh′ē, vē-shē′). City of central France; seat of the French government during World War II. Pop. 32,117.

Vic·to·ri·a (vĭk-tôr′ē-ə, -tōr′ē-ə). **1.** Lake. Also **Victoria Nyan·za** (nī-ăn′zə, nē-, nyän′zä). Lake, c. 26,830 sq mi (69,490 sq km), of E central Africa, in Uganda, Kenya, and Tanzania. **2.** Falls, c. 420 ft (128 m) high and 1.1 mi (1.7 km) wide, in the Zambesi R. on the Zambia-Zimbabwe border. **3.** Island of N.W.T., Canada, in the Arctic Ocean N of the mainland and S of Parry Channel. **4.** Land. Region of E Antarctica S of New Zealand, bordering the Ross Sea. **5.** Cap. of B.C., Canada, on SE Vancouver Is. and Juan de Fuca Strait. Pop. 62,551. **6.** Cap. of Hong Kong colony, on NW coast of Hong Kong Is. Pop. 1,026,870. **7.** Cap. of the Seychelles, on NE coast of Mahé Is. Pop. 13,622.

Vi·en·na (vē-ĕn′ə). Cap. of Austria, in the NE on the Danube. Pop. 1,572,300. **—Vi′en·nese′** (-nēz′, -nēs′) adj. & n.

Vien·tiane (vyĕn-tyän′). Cap. of Laos, in the N central part on the Mekong R. Pop. 174,229.

Vi·et·nam (vē-ĕt′näm′, -năm′, vyĕt′-). Country of SE Asia, in E Indochina on the South China Sea. Cap. Hanoi. Pop. 53,550,000. **—Vi·et′na·mese′** (-mēz′, -mēs′) adj. & n.

Vi·la (vē′lə). Cap. of Vanuatu, on Efate Is. in the SW Pacific. Pop. 17,400.

Vil·ni·us (vĭl′nē-əs, vēl′-). Also **Vil·na** (vĭl′nə, vēl′-). City of W European USSR, in SE Lithuania. Pop. 492,000.

Vin·son Mas·sif (vĭn′sən mə-sēf′). Peak, 16,860 ft (5,142.3 m), in the Ellsworth Mts. of W Antarctica.

Vir·gin (vûr′jĭn). Islands of the West Indies E of Puerto Rico, divided into the **British Virgin Is.** to the NE and the **Virgin Is. of the United States** to the SW.

Vir·gin·ia (vər-jĭn′yə). State of the E U.S. Cap. Richmond. Pop. 5,346,279. **—Virgin′ian** adj. & n.

Virgin Islands of the United States. SW part of the Virgin Is., 133 sq mi (344 sq km), constituting a U.S. territory. Cap. Charlotte Amalie. Pop. 96,569.

Vi·sa·yan (vē-sä′yən). Also **Vi·sa·yans** (-yənz). Island group of the Philippines, between Luzon and Mindanao.

Vis·tu·la (vĭs′chōō-lə). River of Poland, rising in the Carpathians and flowing 678 mi (1,091 km) NE, NW, and N to the Gulf of Danzig.

Vi·tebsk (vē′tĕpsk, vē-tĕpsk′). City of W European USSR, on the Western Dvina R. NE of Minsk. Pop. 303,000.

Vi·ti Le·vu (vē′tē lā′vōō). Largest of the Fiji Is.

Vlad·i·vos·tok (vlăd′ə-vŏs-tŏk′, -vŏs′tŏk′). City of Far Eastern USSR, on the Sea of Japan. Pop. 558,000.

Vol·ca·no Islands (vŏl-kā′nō). Islands of Japan in the NW Pacific N of the Marianas.

Vol·ga (vŏl′gə). Longest river of Europe, rising NW of Moscow and flowing 2,290 mi (3,684.6 km) E and S to the Caspian Sea.

Vol·go·grad (vŏl′gə-grăd′). City of SE European USSR, on the Volga. Pop. 939,000.

Vol·ta (vŏl′tə). River of W Africa, flowing c. 290 mi (465 km) S through Ghana to the Gulf of Guinea.

Vo·ro·nezh (və-rō′nĭsh). City of central European USSR, on the Don. Pop. 796,000.

Vo·ro·shi·lov·grad (vôr′ə-shē′-ləf-grăd′, vô-rô-shē′ləf-grät′). City of S central European USSR, in the Donets Basin. Pop. 469,000.

Vosges (vōzh). Mountains of NE France, extending c. 120 mi (193 km) along the Rhine.

W

Wa·bash (wô′băsh′). River of E central U.S., rising in W Ohio and flowing c. 475 mi (764 km) W and S across Ind. and on the Ind.-Ill. border to the Ohio R.

Wa·co (wā′kō). City of E central Tex., S of Dallas-Fort Worth. Pop. 101,261.

Wai·ki·ki (wī′kē-kē′, wī′kē-kē′). Resort area of Honolulu, Hawaii.

Wake (wāk). Atoll of the W Pacific, between Hawaii and Guam, belonging to the U.S.

Wales (wālz). Principality of SW Great Britain, W of England; part of the United Kingdom. Pop. 2,774,700. **—Welsh** (wĕlsh) adj. & n.

Wal·lis and Fu·tu·na Islands (wŏl′ĭs; fōō-tōō′nä). Two island groups in the SW Pacific, administered by France. Pop. 12,000.

Warren (wŏr′ən, wôr′-). City of SE Mich. Pop. 161,134.

War·saw (wôr′sô). Cap. of Poland, in the E central part on the Vistula. Pop. 1,576,600.

Wa·satch (wô′săch). Range of the Rockies extending c. 250 mi (402 km) from SE Idaho to S central Utah.

Wash·ing·ton (wŏsh′ĭng-tən, wôsh′-). **1.** State of the NW U.S., on the Pacific. Cap. Olympia. Pop. 4,130,163. **2.** Mount. Highest (6,288 ft/ 1,917.8 m) of the White Mts. in N.H. **—Wash′ing·to′ni·an** (-tō′nē-ən) adj. & n.

Wa·ter·bury (wô′tər-bĕr′ē, -bə-rē, wŏt′ər-). City of W central Conn. Pop. 103,266.

Wa·ter·loo (wô′tər-lōō′). Town of central Belgium, near Brussels; site of Napoleon's final defeat (1815).

Wel·land (wĕl′ənd). Ship canal of SE Ont., Canada, connecting Lakes Ontario and Erie.

Wel·ling·ton (wĕl′ĭng-tən). Cap. of New Zealand, on S North Is. Pop. 137,600.

We·ser (vā′zər). River of West Germany, flowing c. 300 mi (480 km) NW to the North Sea.

Wes·sex (wĕs′ĭks). 5th cent. Anglo-Saxon kingdom of S England.

West·ern Sa·ha·ra (wĕs′tərn sə-hăr′ə). Region

of NW Africa, on the Atlantic coast, partly annexed (1976) and occupied (1979) by Morocco.

West·ern Sa·mo·a (sə-mō′ə). Island nation of the S Pacific, comprising the W half of the Samoa Is. Cap. Apia. Pop. 160,000.

West In·dies (ĭn′dēz). Islands between SE North America and N South America, separating the Caribbean Sea and the Atlantic.

West·pha·lia (wĕst-fāl′yə, -fā′lē-ə). Region of W West Germany E of the Rhine and centered in the Ruhr district. —**West·pha′lian** adj. & n.

West Vir·gin·ia (vûr-jĭn′yə). State of the E central U.S. Cap. Charleston. Pop. 1,949,644. —**West Vir·gin′ian** adj. & n.

Whid·by (hwĭd′bē). Island of NW Wash., in Puget Sound.

White·horse (hwīt′hôrs′). Cap. of the Y.T., Canada, on the Yukon R. Pop. 13,311.

White Mountains (hwīt, wĭt). Range of the Appalachians in N N.H.

White Nile (nīl). Section of the Nile flowing N from Lake No in Sudan.

Whit·ney (hwĭt′nē), **Mount**. 2nd highest elevation (14,495 ft/4,421 m) in the U.S., in the Sierra Nevada of E Calif.

Wich·i·ta (wĭch′ə-tô′). City of S central Kans. Pop. 279,272.

Wies·ba·den (vēs′bäd′n). City of central West Germany, on the Rhine. Pop. 273,267.

Wig·an (wĭg′ən). Borough of NW England, NE of Liverpool. Pop. 311,200.

Wight (wīt), **Isle of**. Island in the English Channel off S central England.

Wil·lem·stad (vĭl′əm-stät). Cap. of the Netherlands Antilles, on the S coast of Curaçao. Pop. 50,000.

Wil·liams·burg (wĭl′yəmz-bûrg). City of SE Va. with restored colonial district, NW of Newport News. Pop. 9,870.

Wind·hoek (vĭnt′hŏŏk). Cap. of Namibia, in the central part. Pop. 61,260.

Wind·sor (wĭn′zər). City of S Ont., Canada, across the Detroit R. from Detroit, Mich. Pop. 197,235.

Wind·ward (wĭnd′wərd). Islands of the SE West Indies, the S group of the Lesser Antilles, from Martinique S to Grenada.

Win·ni·peg (wĭn′ə-pĕg). 1. Cap. of Man., Canada, in the S part. Pop. 610,000. 2. Lake 9,465 sq mi (24,514 sq km) of S central Man., Canada.

Win·ston-Sa·lem (wĭn′stən-sā′ləm). City of N central N.C. Pop. 131,885.

Wis·con·sin (wĭs-kŏn′sən). State of the N central U.S. Cap. Madison. Pop. 4,705,335.

Wit·wa·ters·rand (wĭt-wô′tərz-rănd, wĭt-wŏt′-ərz-). Region of South Africa, in S Transvaal.

Worces·ter (wŏŏs′tər). City of central Mass., W. of Boston. Pop. 161,799.

Wound·ed Knee (wŏŏn′dĭd nē′). Creek of SW S.Dak.; site of last major battle of the Indian Wars (1890).

Wran·gel (răng′gəl). Island of NE Far Eastern USSR, in the Arctic Ocean NW of Bering Strait.

Wran·gell (răng′gəl). 1. Mountains of S Alas., extending c. 100 mi (161 km) from the Copper R. to the Canadian border. 2. **Mount**. Volcano, 14,006 ft (4,272 m), in the Wrangell range of S Alas.

Wro·claw (vrô′tsläf). City of SW Poland, on the Oder R. Pop. 609,100.

Wu·han (wōō′hän′). City of E central China, on the Yangtze. Pop. 3,000,000.

Wup·per·tal (vōōp′ər-täl). City of W West Germany. Pop. 394,605.

Wy·o·ming (wī-ō′mĭng). State of the W U.S. Cap. Cheyenne. Pop. 470,816.

X

Xan·thus (zăn′thəs). Ancient city of Lycia, in present-day SW Turkey.

Xi′an (shyē′än′). City of central China, SW of Beijing. Pop. 1,900,000.

Xi·ang (shyē′äng′). River, c. 715 mi (1,150 km), of SE China.

Xin·gu (shĭng-gōō′). River of central and N Brazil, flowing 1,230 mi (1,979.1 km) to the Amazon.

Xu·zhou (shyōō′jō′). City of E China, NNW of Nanjing. Pop. 800,000.

Y

Yal·ta (yäl′tə, yôl′tə). City of SW European USSR, in S Crimea on the Black Sea. Pop. 81,000.

Ya·lu (yä′lōō). River, c. 500 mi (805 km), forming part of the North Korea-China border.

Yang·tze (yăng′tsē′). Longest river of China and of Asia, flowing c. 3,450 mi (5,550 km) from Tibet to the East China Sea.

Ya·oun·dé (yä-ōōn-dā′). Cap. of Cameroun, in the central part. Pop. 313,706.

Ya·ro·slavl (yə-rō-släv′ly′). City of E European USSR, on the upper Volga. Pop. 603,000.

Yel·low (yĕl′ō). 1. **Sea**. Arm of the Pacific, between the Chinese mainland and Korean Peninsula. 2. River of N China, flowing c. 3,000 mi (4,830 km) to the Gulf of Bo Hai.

Yel·low·knife (yĕl′ō-nīf′). Cap. of N.W.T., Canada, on the N shore of Great Slave Lake. Pop. 9,969.

Yel·low·stone (yĕl′ō-stōn′). 1. River, 671 mi (1,079.6 km) long, of NW Wyo. and Mont. 2. **National Park**. Oldest and largest (2,221,773 acres/899,818 hectares) of U.S. national parks, mostly in NW Wyo.

Yem·en (yĕm′ən, yä′mən). 1. Also **North Yemen**. Country of SW Asia, at the SW tip of the Arabian Peninsula. Cap. Sana. Pop. 5,785,000. 2. Also **Southern Yemen**. Country of SW Asia, at the S edge of the Arabian Peninsula. Cap. Aden. Pop. 1,555,000.

Yen·i·sei (yĕ-nyĭ-syā′). River of central Siberian USSR, flowing c. 2,500 mi (4,025.6 km) to the Kara Sea.

Ye·re·van (yĕ-rĕ-vän′). City of SE European USSR. Pop. 1,036,000.

Yo·ko·ha·ma (yō′kə-hä′mə). City of SE Honshu, Japan, on W shore of Tokyo Bay. Pop. 2,773,322.

Yon·kers (yŏng′kərz). City of SE N.Y., N of New York City. Pop. 195,351.

York (yôrk). 1. **Cape**. Northernmost point of Australia, on Torres Strait at the tip of Cape York Peninsula. 2. Borough of N England, on the Ouse R. ENE of Leeds. Pop. 100,900. 3. W borough of metropolitan Toronto, Ont., Canada, on Lake Ontario. Pop. 134,813.

York·town (yôrk′toun). Village in SE Va.; site of British surrender in the Revolutionary War (1781).

Yo·sem·i·te National Park (yō-sĕm′ə-tē). Area of E central Calif., including **Yosemite Valley** and **Yosemite Falls** (2,425 ft/739.6 m high).

Youngs·town (yŭngz′toun′). City of NE Ohio, near the Pa. border. Pop. 115,436.

Yu·ca·tán (yōō'kə-tăn'). Peninsula, mostly in SE Mexico, separating the Caribbean from the Gulf of Mexico.

Yu·go·sla·vi·a (yōō'gō-slä'vē-ə). Country of SE Europe, on the Adriatic. Cap. Belgrade. Pop. 21,560,000. Cap. Belgrade. —**Yu'go·sla'vi·an** *adj. & n.*

Yu·kon (yōō'kŏn'). 1. River flowing c. 2,000 mi (3,220 km) S Y.T., Canada, through Alas. to the Bering Sea. 2. Territory of NW Canada, E of Alas. Cap. Whitehorse. Pop. 21,836.

Z

Za·greb (zä'grĕb'). City of NW Yugoslavia. Pop. 566,084.

Zaire (zär). Country of W central Africa. Cap. Kinshasa. Pop. 24,222,000.

Zam·be·zi (zăm-bē'zē). River c. 1,700 mi (2,735 km), of central and S Africa.

Zam·bi·a (zăm'bē-ə, zăm'-). Country of S central Africa. Cap. Lusaka. Pop. 5,834,000. —**Zam'bi·an** *adj. & n.*

Zan·zi·bar (zăn'zə-bär'). 1. Region of E Africa, part of Tanzania. 2. Island, 641 sq mi (1,660.2 sq km), off the NE coast of Tanzania.

Za·po·ro·zhe (zə-pə-rô'zhyĕ). City of S European USSR, on the Dnieper. Pop. 799,000.

Zhda·nov (zhdä'nôf'). City of S European USSR. Pop. 507,000.

Zheng·zhou (jŭng'jō'). City of E central China. Pop. 1,100,000.

Zi·bo (dzē'bwŏ'). City of E China, E of Jinan. Metro. pop. 900,000.

Zim·bab·we (zĭm-bä'bwā). Country of S central Africa. Cap. Salisbury. Pop. 7,130,000. —**Zim·bab'we·an** *adj. & n.*

Zu·lu·land (zōō'lōō-lănd'). Historical region and former kingdom of NE South Africa.

Zu·rich (zōōr'ĭk). City of NE Switzerland. Pop. 374,200.

ABBREVIATIONS

A 1. Also **a**. or **A**. acre. 2. ammeter. 3. ampere. 4. area.

a. 1. about. 2. acceleration. 3. adjective. 4. afternoon. 5. *Lat.* anno (in the year). 6. *Lat.* annus (year). 7. anonymous. 8. Also **A**. answer.

A. 1. academician; academy. 2. America; American.

AA 1. Alcoholics Anonymous. 2. antiaircraft.

A.A. Associate in Arts.

AAA American Automobile Association.

A and R artists and repertory.

AAU Amateur Athletic Union.

AB Alberta.

ab. about.

A.B. *Lat.* Artium Baccalaureus (Bachelor of Arts).

ABA also **A.B.A.** American Bar Association.

abb. abbess; abbey; abbot.

abbr. or **abbrev.** abbreviation.

ABC American Broadcasting Company.

ABEND *Computer Sci.* abnormal end of task.

ABM antiballistic missile.

abp. or **Abp.** archbishop.

abr. abridged; abridgment.

abs. 1. absence; absent. 2. absolute; absolutely. 3. abstract.

abt. about.

ac 1. acre. 2. Or **AC** alternating current.

A.C. 1. air corps. 2. *Lat.* ante Christum (before Christ).

a/c account; account current.

acad. academic; academy.

acct. account; accountant.

ack. acknowledge; acknowledgment.

ACLU American Civil Liberties Union.

acpt. acceptance.

actg. acting.

acv actual cash value.

AD active duty.

A.D. *Lat.* anno Domini (in the year of the Lord). Usually small capitals A.D.

ADA Americans for Democratic Action.

ADC also **a.d.c.** aide-de-camp.

add. addendum.

addn. addition; additional.

ad int. *Lat.* ad interim (in the meantime).

adj. 1. adjective. 2. adjunct. 3. adjustment. 4. Also **Adj.** adjutant.

ad loc. *Lat.* ad locum (to, or at, the place).

adm. administrative; administrator.

Adm. admiral; admiralty.

admin. administration; administrator.

ADP automatic data processing.

adv. 1. adverb; adverbial. 2. advertisement. 3. advisory.

advt. advertisement.

AEC Atomic Energy Commission.

AF also **A.F.** 1. air force. 2. audio frequency.

AFB air force base.

Afg. Afghanistan.

AFL 1. Also **A.F. of L.** American Federation of Labor. 2. American Football League.

AFL-CIO also **A.F.L-C.I.O.** American Federation of Labor and Congress of Industrial Organizations.

Afr. Africa; African.

AFT American Federation of Teachers.

aft. afternoon.

AFTRA American Federation of Television and Radio Artists.

A.G. also **AG** 1. adjutant general. 2. attorney general.

agcy. agency.

agr. agricultural; agriculture.

agric. agriculture; agriculturist.

agt. 1. agent. 2. agreement.

A.h or **a-h** ampere-hour.

AHL American Hockey League.

a.i. *Lat.* ad interim (in the meantime).

AK Alaska.
a.k.a. also known as.
AKC American Kennel Club.
AL 1. Alabama. 2. American League. 3. American Legion.
ALA American Library Association.
Ala. Alabama.
Alas. Alaska.
Alb. Albania; Albanian.
alc. alcohol; alcoholic.
Ald. alderman.
alg. algebra.
Alg. Algeria.
alt. 1. alternate. 2. altimeter. 3. altitude.
Alta. Alberta.
am or **AM** amplitude modulation.
Am. America; American.
A.M. 1. airmail. 2. *Lat.* anno mundi (in the year of the world). Usually small capitals A.M. 3. Also **a.m.** *Lat.* ante meridiem (before noon). Usually small capitals A.M. 4. *Lat.* Artium Magister (Master of Arts).
AMA also **A.M.A.** American Medical Association.
Amer. America; American.
Amex American Stock Exchange.
Amn airman.
amp hr. ampere-hour.
amt. amount.
amu *Physics.* atomic mass unit.
an. *Lat.* 1. ante (before). 2. anno (in the year).
anal. 1. analogous; analogy. 2. analysis; analytic.
anat. anatomical; anatomist; anatomy.
And. Andorra.
Ang. Angola.
ann. 1. annals. 2. annual. 3. annuity.
anon. anonymous.
ans. answer.
ant. 1. antenna. 2. antiquarian; antiquity. 3. antonym.
Ant. Antarctica.
anthrop. anthropologic; anthropology.
antiq. 1. antiquarian; antiquary. 2. antiquities. 3. antiquity.
a/o account of.
AP 1. airplane. 2. air police. 3. American plan. 4. antipersonnel. 5. Or **A.P.** Associated Press.
ap. apothecary.
a.p. additional premium.
APB all points bulletin.
APO or **A.P.O.** Army Post Office.
app. 1. apparatus. 2. appendix. 3. applied. 4. apprentice.
appl. applied.
approx. approximate; approximately.
appt appoint; appointment.
apptd. appointed.
Apr. April.
apt. apartment.
AR 1. Also **A/R** account receivable. 2. Arkansas.
ar. arrival; arrive.
Ar. 1. Arabia; Arabian. 2. Arabic.
Arab. 1. Arabia; Arabian. 2. Arabic.
ARC American Red Cross.
arch. 1. archaic; archaism. 2. architect; architectural; architecture.
Archbp. archbishop.
archit. architecture.
archt. architect.
Arg. Argentina; Argentine.
Ariz. Arizona.
Ark. Arkansas.
Arm. Armenia; Armenian.
arr. arrival; arrive.

art. 1. article. 2. artillery.
arty. artillery.
As. Asia; Asian.
a/s airspeed.
ASAP also **asap** as soon as possible.
asb. asbestos.
ASCAP American Society of Composers, Authors, and Publishers.
ASE American Stock Exchange.
asgd. assigned.
asgmt. assignment.
ASL American sign language.
ASPCA American Society for the Prevention of Cruelty to Animals.
assn. association.
assoc. associate; association.
ASSR or **A.S.S.R.** Autonomous Soviet Socialist Republic.
asst. assistant.
asstd. 1. assisted. 2. assorted.
Assyr. Assyrian.
ASTP Army Specialized Training Program.
astrol. astrologer; astrology.
astron. astronomer; astronomy.
AT also **a/t** antitank.
at. atomic.
athl. athlete; athletics.
Atl. Atlantic.
atm *Physics.* atmosphere.
atm. or **atmos.** atmosphere; atmospheric.
at. no. also **at no** atomic number.
ATP *Biochem.* adenosine triphosphate.
att. 1. attached. 2. attention. 3. attorney.
attn. attention.
attrib. attribute; attributive.
atty. attorney.
Atty. Gen. attorney general.
at wt atomic weight.
a.u. or **A.u.** angstrom unit.
aud. audit; auditor.
Aug. August.
Aus. or **Aust.** 1. Australia. 2. Austria.
Austl. Australia; Australian.
auth. 1. authentic. 2. author. 3. authority. 4. authorized.
auto. 1. automatic. 2. automotive.
aux. auxiliary.
AV or **A.V.** audio-visual.
av. 1. Or **Av.** avenue. 2. average. 3. avoirdupois.
a.v. or **a/v** *Lat.* ad valorem (in proportion to the value).
avdp. avoirdupois.
ave. or **Ave.** avenue.
avg. average.
A/W actual weight.
ax. 1. axiom. 2. axis.
AYC American Youth Congress.
AYD American Youth for Democracy.
AYH American Youth Hostels.
AZ Arizona.
az. azure.
Azo. Azores.

b *Physics.* barn.
B baryon number.
b. or **B.** 1. base. 2. book. 3. born.
B. 1. bachelor. 2. bacillus. 3. Baumé scale. 4. Bible. 5. British.
Ba. Bahamas.
B.A. 1. *Lat.* Baccalaureus Artium (Bachelor of Arts). 2. British Academy.
Bab. Babylonia; Babylonian.
bach. bachelor.
bact. bacteria; bacterial.

bacteriol. bacteriologist; bacteriology.
bal. balance.
B and E breaking and entering.
Bap. or **Bapt.** Baptist.
BAR Browning automatic rifle.
bar. barometer; barometric.
Barb. Barbados.
Bart. baronet.
bat. battalion.
Bav. Bavaria; Bavarian.
bb also **b.b.** ball bearing.
BB B'nai B'rith.
BBB Better Business Bureau.
BBC British Broadcasting Corporation.
bbl or **bbl.** barrel.
B.C. 1. before Christ. Usually small capitals
B.C. 2. Or BC British Columbia.
bcd or **BCD** *Computer Sci.* binary coded
decimal.
BCG bacillus Calmette-Guérin (tuberculosis
vaccine).
BD 1. bank draft. 2. Also **b/d** bills
discounted.
bd. 1. board. 2. bound. 3. bundle.
b/d barrels per day.
bd. ft. board foot.
bdl or **bdle.** bundle.
bdrm. bedroom.
BE Board of Education.
B/E bill of exchange.
Bé Baumé scale.
BEC Bureau of Employees' Compensation.
BEF British Expeditionary Force.
bef. before.
Bel or **Belg.** Belgian; Belgium.
bet. between.
BeV *Physics.* billion electron volts.
bf 1. Also **b.f.** or **bf.** boldface. 2. board foot.
b.f. or **B/F** *Accounting.* brought forward.
bg. 1. background. 2. bag.
B.G. Brigadier General.
BH bill of health.
bhd. bulkhead.
BHT butylated hydroxytoluene.
Bhu. Bhutan.
BIA Bureau of Indian Affairs.
Bib. Bible; Biblical.
bibl. or **Bibl.** Biblical.
bibliog. bibliographer; bibliography.
biog. biographer; biographical; biography.
biol. biological; biologist; biology.
bk. 1. bank. 2. book.
bkg. banking.
bkg. background.
bklr. *Printing.* black letter.
bkpg. bookkeeping.
bkpt. bankrupt.
bks. 1. barracks. 2. books.
bl. 1. barrel. 2. black. 3. blue.
B/L bill of lading.
bld. 1. blood. 2. boldface.
bldg. building.
bldr. builder.
B.Lit. or **B.Litt.** *Lat.* Baccalaureus Litterarum
(Bachelor of Literature).
blk. 1. black. 2. block. 3. bulk.
BLS Bureau of Labor Statistics.
blvd. boulevard.
BM basal metabolism.
bm. beam.
b.m. board measure.
BMR basal metabolic rate.
bn. or **Bn.** 1. baron. 2. battalion.
B.N.A. British North America.
Bngl. Bangladesh.
B.O.D. biochemical oxygen demand.
Boh. Bohemia; Bohemian.

Bol. Bolivia.
BOQ Bachelor Officers' Quarters.
bor. borough.
bot. 1. botanical; botanist; botany. 2. bottle.
3. bottom.
Bots. Botswana.
boul. boulevard.
bp boiling point.
BP 1. Or **B/P** bills payable. 2. blood pressure.
bp. bishop.
bpd barrels per day.
bpi bits per inch; bytes per inch.
BPOE also **B.P.O.E.** Benevolent and Protective
Order of Elks.
br. 1. branch. 2. brief. 3. brother. 4. brown.
Br. 1. Breton. 2. Britain; British. 3. Brother
(religious).
B/R bills receivable.
Braz. Brazil; Brazilian.
Br. Gu. British Guiana.
Br. Hond. British Honduras.
Br. I. British India.
brig. brigade; brigadier.
Brig. Gen. brigadier general.
Brit. Britain; British.
bro. brother.
bros. brothers.
Bru. Brunei.
B.S. 1. Bachelor of Science. 2. balance sheet.
3. bill of sale.
BSA Boy Scouts of America.
bsh. bushel.
bsk. basket.
Bt. baronet.
btry. battery.
Btu British thermal unit.
bu. 1. bureau. 2. Or **bu** bushel.
bul. bulletin.
Bul. or **Bulg.** Bulgaria; Bulgarian.
bull. bulletin.
bur. bureau.
Bur. Burma; Burmese.
bus. business.
B.V. Blessed Virgin.
B.V.M. Blessed Virgin Mary.
BW 1. biological warfare. 2. Also **b/w** black
and white.
B.W.I. British West Indies.
bx. box.

c 1. *Physics.* candle. 2. carat. 3. centi-. 4. Or
C *Math.* constant. 5. cubic.
C 1. *Elect.* capacitance. 2. Celsius.
3. centigrade. 4. *Physics.* charge conjugation.
5. coulomb.
c. or **C.** 1. capacity. 2. cape. 3. carton.
4. case. 5. *Baseball.* catcher. 6. cent.
7. centime. 8. century. 9. chapter. 10. church.
11. circa.
C. 1. Catholic. 2. Celtic. 3. chancellor.
4. chief. 5. city. 6. companion. 7. Congress.
8. Conservative. 9. court.
ca 1. centare. 2. circa.
CA 1. California. 2. Also **C.A.** chronological
age.
C.A. Central America.
c/a current account.
CAA or **C.A.A.** Civil Aeronautics Authority.
CAB Civil Aeronautics Board.
C.A.F. cost and freight.
CAI computer-aided instruction.
cal calorie (small).
Cal calorie (large).
cal. 1. calendar. 2. caliber.
Cal. California.

calc. 1. calculation. 2. calculus.
Calif. California.
Cam. Cameroon.
Camb. Cambodia.
can. 1. canceled. 2. canon.
Can. also **Canad.** Canada; Canadian.
canc. canceled; cancellation.
C & W country and western.
Can. Is. Canary Islands.
Cant. Cantonese.
CAP or **C.A.P.** Civil Air Patrol.
cap. 1. capacity. 2. capital (city). 3. capital letter.
caps. 1. capitals (letters). 2. capsule.
Capt. captain.
car. carat.
Card. Cardinal.
CARE Cooperative for American Relief Everywhere.
CAT computerized axial tomography.
cat. catalogue.
cath. 1. cathedral. 2. cathode.
CATV community antenna television.
cav. 1. cavalier. 2. cavalry. 3. cavity.
CB or **C.B.** citizens band.
CBC Canadian Broadcasting Corporation.
C.B.D. cash before delivery.
CBS Columbia Broadcasting System.
CBW chemical and biological warfare.
cc 1. carbon copy. 2. cubic centimeter.
cc. chapters.
C.C.A. Circuit Court of Appeals.
CCC Commodity Credit Corporation.
cckw. counterclockwise.
CCS combined chiefs of staff.
CCTV closed circuit television.
CCU coronary care unit.
ccw. counterclockwise.
CD 1. Also **C/D** certificate of deposit. 2. Also **C.D.** civil defense.
cd. cord.
c.d. cash discount.
CDC Center for Disease Control.
Cdr. commander.
CDT or **C.D.T.** Central Daylight Time.
C.E. 1. chemical engineer. 2. civil engineer. 3. common era.
cen. 1. central. 2. century.
Cen. Afr. Rep. Central African Republic.
cent. 1. centime. 2. central. 3. *Lat.* centum (hundred). 4. century.
CEO also **C.E.O.** chief executive officer.
cert. certificate; certification; certified.
certif. certificate.
CF cystic fibrosis.
cf. 1. calfskin. 2. *Lat.* confer (compare).
c.f. 1. *Baseball.* center field; center fielder. 2. Or **C.F.** cost and freight.
C/F *Accounting.* carried forward.
CFA also **C.F.A.** chartered financial analyst.
c.f.i. or **C.F.i.** cost, freight, and insurance.
cfm or **c.f.m.** cubic feet per minute.
cfs or **c.f.s.** cubic feet per second.
cg centigram.
c.g. 1. center of gravity. 2. Or **C.G.** consul general.
C.G. 1. coast guard. 2. commanding general.
cgs or **CGS** centimeter-gram-second (system of units).
ch chain (measurement).
ch. 1. Or **Ch.** chaplain. 2. chapter. 3. check. 4. Or **Ch.** chief. 5. child; children. 6. Or **Ch.** church.
Ch. China; Chinese.
c.h. or **C.H.** 1. clearing-house. 2. courthouse. 3. customhouse.
chan. channel.

Chanc. 1. chancellor. 2. chancery.
chap. chapter.
char. charter.
Ch.E. chemical engineer.
chem. chemical; chemist; chemistry.
chg. 1. change. 2. charge.
Chin. Chinese.
chl. chloroform.
chm. chairman.
Chr. Christ; Christian.
chron. 1. chronicle. 2. chronological; chronology.
chronol. chronological; chronology.
Ci curie.
CIA Central Intelligence Agency.
CID also **C.I.D.** Criminal Investigation Department (Scotland Yard).
c.i.f. or **C.I.F.** cost, insurance, and freight.
C in C commander in chief.
CIO also **C.I.O.** Congress of Industrial Organizations.
cir or **circ.** circle; circular.
circ. 1. circulation. 2. circumference.
circum. circumference.
cit. 1. citation. 2. cited. 3. citizen.
civ. civil; civilian.
C.J. chief justice.
ck. 1. cask. 2. check. 3. cook.
cl centiliter.
cl. 1. class; classification. 2. clause. 3. clearance.
c.l. 1. Or **C.L.** civil law. 2. common law.
class. 1. classic; classical. 2. classification; classified; classify.
clk. clerk.
clm. column.
clr. clear.
CLU also **C.L.U.** chartered life underwriter.
cm centimeter.
CM center matched.
c.m. 1. circular mil. 2. center of mass. 3. court-martial.
CMA also **C.M.A.** certified medical assistant.
cmd. command.
cmdg. commanding.
Cmdr. commander.
cml. commercial.
cN centinewton.
C/N credit note.
CNS central nervous system.
CO 1. Colorado. 2. Or **c.o.** commanding officer. 3. Or **C.O.** conscientious objector.
co. 1. company. 2. county.
c.o. 1. *Accounting.* carried over. 2. cash order.
c/o also **c.o.** care of.
COD or **C.O.D.** 1. cash on delivery. 2. collect on delivery.
coef. coefficient.
C. of C. chamber of commerce.
C. of E. Church of England.
C. of S. chief of staff.
cog. cognate.
col. 1. collect; collected; collector. 2. college; collegiate. 3. colonial; colony. 4. color. 5. column.
Col. 1. Colombia. 2. colonel. 3. Colorado.
COLA cost-of-living adjustment.
coll. 1. collateral. 2. collect; collection; collector. 3. college; collegiate.
collat. collateral.
Colo. Colorado.
COM computer-output microfilm; computer-output microfilmer.
com. 1. comedy; comic. 2. comma. 3. commentary. 4. commerce; commercial. 5. Or **Com.** commissioner. 6. Or **Com.** committee.

Com. 1. commander. 2. commodore. 3. Communist.
comb. 1. combination. 2. combining. 3. combustion.
comd. command.
comdg. commanding.
Comdr. commander.
Comdt. commandant.
coml. commercial.
comm. 1. commerce. 2. commission; commissioner. 3. Also **Comm.** committee. 4. commonwealth. 5. communication.
Como. commodore.
comp. 1. companion. 2. comparative. 3. compensation. 4. compilation; compiled; compiler. 5. complete. 6. composite; composition; compositor. 7. comprehensive.
compar. comparative.
compd. compound.
Comr. commissioner.
con. 1. concerto. 2. *Law.* conclusion. 3. connection. 4. consolidate; consolidated. 5. Or **Con.** consul. 6. continued.
Con. Congo.
conc. 1. concentrate. 2. concrete.
cond. 1. condition. 2. conductivity. 3. conductor.
conf. 1. conference. 2. confidential.
confed. confederation.
Cong. 1. Congregational. 2. Congress; Congressional.
conj. 1. conjugation. 2. conjunction. 3. conjunctive.
Conn. Connecticut.
cons. 1. consigned; consignment. 2. consonant. 3. Or **Cons.** constable. 4. constitution; constitutional. 5. construction.
Cons. consul.
consol. consolidated.
const. 1. Or **Const.** constable. 2. constant. 3. Or **Const.** constitution. 4. construction.
constr. construction.
cont. 1. containing. 2. contents. 3. continent. 4. continue; continued. 5. contract. 6. contraction. 7. control.
contd. continued.
contemp. contemporary.
contrib. contribution; contributor.
conv. 1. convention. 2. convertible.
coop. cooperative.
cop. copyright.
Cop. Coptic.
cor. 1. correction. 2. correspondence; correspondent; corresponding.
CORE Congress of Racial Equality.
corol. or **coroll.** corollary.
corp. corporation.
corr. 1. correction. 2. correspondence; correspondent.
correl. correlative.
cos cosine.
COS or **C.O.S.** cash on shipment.
cot cotangent.
cp *Physics.* candlepower.
cP centipoise.
CP 1. command post. 2. Communist Party.
cp. compare.
C.P. Cape Province.
CPA also **C.P.A.** certified public accountant.
cpd. compound.
CPI consumer price index.
Cpl. corporal.
cpm cycles per minute.
CPO chief petty officer.
CPR cardiopulmonary resuscitation.
cps 1. characters per second. 2. cycles per second.

Cpt. captain.
CPU central processing unit.
CQ call to quarters.
CR *Psychol.* conditioned reflex; conditioned response.
cr. 1. credit; creditor. 2. crown.
C.R. Costa Rica.
crit. critic; critical; criticism.
CRT cathode-ray tube.
CS 1. capital stock. 2. chief of staff. 3. Christian Science; Christian Scientist. 4. civil service.
cs. case.
C.S.A. Confederate States of America.
CSC civil service commission.
CSF cerebrospinal fluid.
csk. 1. cask. 2. countersink.
CST 1. Or **C.S.T.** Central Standard Time. 2. convulsive shock treatment.
CT 1. Or **C.T.** Central Time. 2. Or **Ct.** Connecticut.
ct. 1. cent. 2. certificate. 3. court.
Ct. count (title).
ctf. certificate.
ctg. or **ctge.** cartage.
ctn cotangent.
ctn. carton.
ctr. 1. center. 2. counter.
cu. or **cu** cubic.
cum. cumulative.
cur. 1. currency. 2. current.
CV cardiovascular.
C.V. Cape Verde.
cvt. convertible.
cw or **CW** continuous wave.
cw. clockwise.
CWO chief warrant officer.
c.w.o. cash with order.
cwt. hundredweight.
CY calendar year.
cyl. cylinder.
CYO Catholic Youth Organization.
Czech. Czechoslovakia; Czechoslovakian.

d 1. day. 2. deci-. 3. *Physics.* deuteron. 4. dextro-.
d. 1. dam. 2. date. 3. daughter. 4. *Lat.* denarius (penny). 5. Or **D.** deputy. 6. died.
D or **D.** democrat; democratic.
D. 1. December. 2. department. 3. *Lat.* Deus (God). 4. Doctor (in academic degrees). 5. *Lat.* Dominus (Lord). 6. duchess. 7. duke. 8. Dutch.
DA 1. delayed action. 2. deposit account.
Da. Danish.
D.A. 1. Also **DA** district attorney. 2. Doctor of Arts.
DAB or **D.A.B.** Dictionary of American Biography.
dag decagram.
DAGC *Electronics.* delayed automatic gain control.
DAH or **D.A.H.** Dictionary of American History.
DAR Daughters of the American Revolution.
DASD direct access storage device.
dat. dative.
DAV Disabled American Veterans.
dB decibel.
DB or **D.B.** daybook.
D.B.E. Dame Commander of the Order of the British Empire.
dbl. double.
dc or **DC** direct current.
DC or **D.C.** District of Columbia.

DCM also **D.C.M.** Distinguished Conduct Medal.
dd. delivered.
D.D. 1. demand draft. 2. dishonorable discharge. 3. *Lat.* Divinitatis Doctor (Doctor of Divinity).
D.D.S. 1. Doctor of Dental Science. 2. Doctor of Dental Surgery.
DE Delaware.
deb. debenture.
dec. 1. deceased. 2. declaration. 3. declension. 4. declination. 5. decrease.
Dec. December.
decd. deceased.
decl. declension.
def. 1. defective. 2. defendant. 3. defense. 4. deferred.
deg or **deg.** degree.
del. 1. delegate; delegation. 2. delete.
Del. Delaware.
dely. delivery.
dem. demurrage.
Dem. Democrat; Democratic.
demon. *Gram.* demonstrative.
Den. Denmark.
denom. denomination.
dent. dental; dentist; dentistry.
dep. 1. depart; departure. 2. department. 3. deponent. 4. deposed. 5. deposit. 6. depot. 7. deputy.
Dep. dependency.
dept. 1. department. 2. deputy.
der. or **deriv.** derivation; derivative.
Des. desert.
det. 1. detach. 2. detachment. 3. detail.
dev. deviation.
DEW distant early warning.
DF direction finder.
DFC also **D.F.C.** Distinguished Flying Cross.
dft. draft.
dg decigram.
DH *Baseball.* designated hitter.
D.H. Doctor of Humanities.
dia. diameter.
diag. 1. diagonal. 2. diagram.
dial. 1. dialect; dialectal. 2. dialectic; dialectical. 3. dialogue.
diam diameter.
dict. 1. dictation. 2. dictionary.
diet. dietetics.
dif. or **diff.** difference; different.
dig. digest.
dil. dilute.
dim. 1. dimension. 2. diminished. 3. diminutive.
dimin. diminutive.
dipl. diplomat; diplomatic.
dir. director.
dis. 1. discount. 2. distance; distant.
disc. discount.
disp. dispensary.
dist. 1. distance; distant. 2. district.
Dist. Atty. district attorney.
distr. distribution; distributor.
div. 1. divergence. 2. diversion. 3. divided; division. 4. dividend.
DJ disc jockey.
D.J. 1. district judge. 2. *Lat.* Doctor Juris (Doctor of Law).
DJIA Dow-Jones Industrial Average.
dkg dekagram.
dkl dekaliter.
dkm dekameter.
dks dekastere.
dl deciliter.
D/L demand loan.

D.Lit. or **D.Litt.** *Lat.* Doctor Litterarum (Doctor of Letters; Doctor of Literature).
DLO dead letter office.
dlr. dealer.
dlvy. delivery.
dm decimeter.
DM 1. *Chem.* adamsite. 2. data management.
D.M.D. *Lat.* Dentariae Medicinae Doctor (Doctor of Dental Medicine).
DMSO dimethylsulfoxide.
DMZ demilitarized zone.
dn. down.
DNC direct numerical control.
do. ditto.
DOA *Med.* dead on arrival.
DOB date of birth.
doc. document.
DOD Department of Defense.
dol. dollar.
dom. 1. domestic. 2. dominant. 3. dominion.
Dom. Dominican.
Dom. Rep. Dominican Republic.
DOS disk-operating system.
doz. dozen.
DP 1. data processing. 2. dew point. 3. Also **D.P.** displaced person. 4. *Baseball.* double play.
DPH Department of Public Health.
D.Ph. or **D.Phil.** Doctor of Philosophy.
dpt. 1. department. 2. deponent.
DPT diphtheria, pertussis, tetanus (vaccine).
DPW Department of Public Works.
dr dram.
DR dead reckoning.
dr. 1. debit. 2. debtor.
Dr. doctor.
dram. dramatic; dramatist.
dr ap apothecaries' dram.
dr avdp avoirdupois dram.
dr t troy dram.
DS data set.
DSC also **D.S.C.** Distinguished Service Cross.
DSM also **D.S.M.** Distinguished Service Medal.
DSO or **D.S.O.** Distinguished Service Order.
d.s.p. *Lat.* decessit sine prole (died without issue).
DST or **D.S.T.** daylight-saving time.
DT or **D.T.** daylight time.
d.t. double time.
D.T.'s delirium tremens.
Du. 1. duke (title). 2. Dutch.
dup. duplicate.
D.V. 1. *Lat.* Deo volente (God willing). 2. *Bible.* Douay Version.
D.V.M. Doctor of Veterinary Medicine.
DW 1. dead weight. 2. distilled water.
DWI driving while intoxicated.
dwt. pennyweight.
dy. 1. delivery. 2. duty.
dyn *Physics.* dyne.
dz. dozen.

e 1. electron. 2. Or **e.** *Baseball.* error.
E 1. Earth. 2. Also **E.** or **e** or **e.** east.
ea. each.
EbN east by north.
EbS east by south.
Ec. Ecuador.
E.C. Established Church.
eccl. or **eccles.** ecclesiastic; ecclesiastical.
Eccles. *Bible.* Ecclesiastes.
ECCS emergency core cooling system.
ECG electrocardiogram.
ECL emitter-coupled logic.
ECM European Common Market.

ecol. ecological; ecology.
econ. economics; economist; economy.
ed. 1. edition; editor. 2. education.
E.D. election district.
edit. edition; editor.
Ed.M. *Lat.* Educationis Magister (Master of Education).
EDP electronic data processing.
EDT or **E.D.T.** Eastern Daylight Time.
educ. education; educational.
e.e. errors excepted.
E.E. electrical engineer; electrical engineering.
EEC European Economic Community.
EEG electroencephalogram; electroencephalograph.
EEO equal employment opportunity.
eff. efficiency.
EFTS electronic funds transfer system.
Eg. Egypt; Egyptian.
e.g. *Lat.* exempli gratia (for example).
EHF extremely high frequency.
EHV extra high voltage.
E.I. East Indian; East Indies.
EKG electrocardiogram; electrocardiograph.
el. elevation.
elec. electric; electrical; electrician; electricity.
elem. elementary.
elev. elevation.
ELF extremely low frequency.
emf or **EMF** electromotive force.
EMT emergency medical technician.
emu electromagnetic unit.
enc. or **encl.** enclosed; enclosure.
ency. or **encyc.** or **encycl.** encyclopedia.
ENE east-northeast.
eng. 1. engine. 2. engineer; engineering.
Eng. England; English.
engin. engineering.
engr. engineer.
Ens. ensign.
e.o. *Lat.* ex officio (by virtue of office).
e.o.m. end of month.
EP 1. extended play. 2. European plan.
Epis. 1. Episcopal; Episcopalian. 2. Epistle.
Episc. Episcopal; Episcopalian.
eq. 1. equal. 2. equation. 3. equivalent.
Equat. Gui. Equatorial Guinea.
equip. equipment.
equiv. equivalency; equivalent.
ER emergency room.
ERA 1. *Baseball.* earned run average. 2. Equal Rights Amendment.
ESE east-southeast.
ESL English as a second language.
ESP extrasensory perception.
esp. especially.
Esq. Esquire (title).
ESR electron spin resonance.
EST or **E.S.T.** Eastern Standard Time.
est. 1. established. 2. *Law.* estate. 3. estimate.
ET 1. Or **E.T.** Eastern Time. 2. elapsed time.
ETA or **e.t.a.** estimated time of arrival.
et al. *Lat.* et alii (and others).
etc. *Lat.* et cetera (and so forth).
ETD or **e.t.d.** estimated time of departure.
Eth. Ethiopia.
etym. or **etymol.** etymological; etymology.
Eur. European; European.
eV electron volt.
EVA extravehicular activity.
evg. evening.
ex. 1. examination. 2. example. 3. except; excepted; exception. 4. exchange. 5. executive. 6. express. 7. extra.
exam. examination.
exc. 1. excellent. 2. except; exception.
Exc. Excellency.

exch. 1. exchange. 2. Or **Exch.** exchequer.
excl. 1. exclamation. 2. exclusive.
exec. 1. executive. 2. executor.
exp *Math.* exponential.
exp. 1. expenses. 2. experiment; experimental. 3. expiration; expired. 4. export; exporter. 5. express.
ext. 1. extension. 2. external; externally. 3. extinct. 4. extra. 5. extract.

f focal length.
F Fahrenheit.
f. 1. or **F** also **f** or **F.** female. 2. Or **F.** *Gram.* feminine.
F. 1. February. 2. French. 3. Friday.
f/ relative aperture of a lens.
FA 1. field artillery. 2. Or **F.A.** fine art.
f.a. fire alarm.
FAA Federal Aviation Administration.
fac. 1. facsimile. 2. faculty.
FAD flavin adenine dinucleotide.
Fahr. Fahrenheit.
Falk. Is. Falkland Islands.
fam. 1. familiar. 2. family.
Far. Faraday.
fath or **fath.** fathom.
fb also **f.b.** fullback.
F.B. 1. foreign body. 2. freight bill.
FBI also **F.B.I.** Federal Bureau of Investigation.
fc foot-candle.
FCA Farm Credit Administration.
FCC Federal Communications Commission.
fcy. fancy.
FD 1. fire department. 2. focal distance.
FDA Food and Drug Administration.
FDIC Federal Deposit Insurance Corporation.
Feb. February.
fec. *Lat.* fecit (he, or she, made or did it).
fed. federal; federated; federation.
fem. female; feminine.
FEP front end processor.
FET field effect transistor.
ff. 1. folios. 2. following.
f.g. *Sports.* field goal; field goals.
FHA Federal Housing Administration.
FHLBB Federal Home Loan Bank Board.
fhp or **f.hp.** friction horsepower.
FICA Federal Insurance Contributions Act.
fict. 1. fiction. 2. fictitious.
fid. fidelity.
FIFO *Accounting.* first in, first out.
fig. 1. figurative; figuratively. 2. figure.
fin. 1. finance; financial. 2. finish.
Fin. Finland; Finnish.
fl fluid.
FL 1. Florida. 2. focal length.
fl. 1. floor. 2. fluid.
Fla. Florida.
fld. field.
fl dr fluid dram.
Flor. Florida.
fl oz fluid ounce.
FM 1. field manual. 2. Or **F.M.** field marshal. 3. or **fm** frequency modulation.
fm. 1. fathom. 2. from.
FMN flavin mononucleotide.
fn. footnote.
FO 1. Or **F.O.** field officer. 2. field order. 3. finance officer. 4. Or **F/O** flight officer. 5. For **F.O.** Foreign Office.
f.o.b. also **F.O.B.** free on board.
FOE Fraternal Order of Eagles.
fol. 1. folio. 2. following.
for. 1. foreign. 2. forest; forestry.

fort. fortification.
fp freezing point.
FPC Federal Power Commission.
fpm or **f.p.m.** feet per minute.
FPO fleet post office.
fps or **f.p.s.** 1. feet per second. 2. frames per second.
fr. from.
Fr. 1. father (clergyman). 2. France; French. 3. friar. 4. Friday.
FRB Federal Reserve Board.
freq. 1. frequency. 2. frequentative.
F.R.G. Federal Republic of Germany.
Fr. Gu. French Guiana.
Fri. Friday.
FRS Federal Reserve System.
frt. freight.
FS 1. Foreign Service. 2. Forest Service.
FSA Federal Security Agency.
FSLIC Federal Savings and Loan Insurance Corporation.
ft foot.
ft. fort; fortification.
FTC Federal Trade Commission.
ft-c foot-candle.
fth. fathom.
ft-lb foot-pound.
fur. furlong.
furn. furnished.
fut. *Gram.* future.
fwd. *Sports.* forward.
FX foreign exchange.
FY fiscal year.
FYI for your information.

g 1. acceleration of gravity. 2. gram.
G *Physics.* gravitation constant.
ga gauge.
GA 1. general agent. 2. Also **G.A.** general assembly. 3. Or **Ga.** Georgia.
G.A. general average.
gal. gallon.
galv. galvanized.
Gam. Gambia.
GAO General Accounting Office.
GAR or **G.A.R.** Grand Army of the Republic.
GAW guaranteed annual wage.
G.B. Great Britain.
GCA ground control approach.
gcd or **g.c.d.** greatest common divisor.
gcf or **g.c.f.** greatest common factor.
GCM Good Conduct Medal.
GCT or **G.c.t.** Greenwich civil time.
gd. good.
G.D.R. German Democratic Republic.
gds. goods.
gen. 1. gender. 2. general; generally. 3. generator. 4. generic. 5. genus.
Gen. general (military rank).
genit. genitive.
genl. general.
geog. geographer; geographic; geography.
geol. geologic; geologist; geology.
geom. geometric; geometry.
ger. gerund.
Ger. German; Germany.
GHQ general headquarters.
gi gill (liquid measure).
GI 1. gastrointestinal. 2. general issue. 3. Also **G.I.** Government Issue.
Gib. Gibraltar.
GIGO *Computer Sci.* garbage in, garbage out.
Gk. Greek.
gl. gloss.
gm gram.

GM or **G.M.** 1. general manager. 2. grand master.
GMT or **G.m.t.** Greenwich mean time.
GMW gram-molecular weight.
GNP gross national product.
GO general order.
GOP or **G.O.P.** Grand Old Party (Republican).
Goth. Gothic.
gov. 1. government. 2. Or **Gov.** governor.
Gov. Gen. governor general.
govt. government.
G.P. or **GP** general practitioner.
GPA grade-point average.
GPO 1. general post office. 2. Government Printing Office.
GPU or **G.P.U.** *Russian.* Gosudarstvennoye Politicheskoye Upravlenie (Government Political Administration).
GQ general quarters.
gr. 1. grade. 2. grain. 3. gross.
Gr. Greece; Greek.
grad. graduate; graduated.
gram. grammar.
Grc. Greece.
Grnld. Greenland.
gro. gross.
gr. wt. gross weight.
GS 1. general staff. 2. ground speed.
GSA General Services Administration.
GSC general staff corps.
GSO general staff officer.
GST or **G.s.t.** Greenwich sidereal time.
Gt. Brit. Great Britain.
gtd. guaranteed.
GU Guam.
Guad. Guadaloupe.
guar. guaranteed.
Guat. Guatemala.
Guin. Guinea.
Guy. Guyana.
gym. gymnasium; gymnastics.
gyn. gynecological; gynecologist; gynecology.

h 1. hour. 2. *Physics.* Planck's constant.
H humidity.
h. 1. Or **H.** hard; hardness. 2. Or **H.** height. 3. Or **H.** high. 4. hundred.
ha hectare.
hab. corp. habeas corpus.
Hai. Haiti.
hb or **hb.** halfback.
Hb hemoglobin.
H.B.M. Her, or His, Britannic Majesty.
H.C. 1. Holy Communion. 2. House of Commons.
hcf or **h.c.f.** highest common factor.
hd. head.
hdbk. handbook.
hdqrs. headquarters.
hdwe. hardware.
HE high explosive.
H.E. 1. His Eminence. 2. Her, or His, Excellency.
Heb. Hebrew.
her. heraldry.
HEW Department of Health, Education, and Welfare.
hex. hexagon; hexagonal.
hf high frequency.
hf. half.
HG also **H.G.** High German.
hgb. hemoglobin.
hgt. height.
hgwy. highway.

H.H. 1. Her, or His, Highness. 2. His Holiness.
HHFA Housing and Home Finance Agency.
HI Hawaii.
H.I. Hawaiian Islands.
hist. historian; historical; history.
H.M. Her, or His, Majesty.
HMS or **H.M.S.** Her, or His, Majesty's Ship.
ho. house.
Hon. 1. Honorable (title). 2. Or **hon.** honorary.
Hond. Honduras.
HOPE Health Opportunity for People Everywhere.
hor. horizontal.
hort. horticultural; horticulture.
hosp. hospital.
hp horsepower.
HPF highest possible frequency.
HQ or **h.q.** headquarters.
hr hour.
h.r. *Baseball.* home run.
H.R. 1. home rule. 2. House of Representatives.
H.R.E. Holy Roman Emperor; Holy Roman Empire.
H.R.H. Her, or His, Royal Highness.
hrs hours.
HS or **H.S.** high school.
H.S.H. Her, or His, Serene Highness.
HST 1. Or **H.S.T.** Hawaiian Standard Time. 2. hypersonic transport.
ht height.
HT 1. Or **H.T.** Hawaiian Time. 2. half time.
Hts. Heights.
HUD or **H.U.D.** Housing and Urban Development.
Hun. or **Hung.** Hungarian; Hungary.
HV 1. high velocity. 2. high-voltage.
hvy. heavy.
HWM high-water mark.
hwy. highway.
hy. henry.
hyp. 1. hypotenuse. 2. hypothesis.
hypoth. hypothesis.
Hz hertz.

I 1. Or **I** *Elect.* current. 2. Or **I.** island; isle.
IA or **Ia.** Iowa.
IAAF International Amateur Athletic Federation.
IAEA International Atomic Energy Agency.
IAS indicated air speed.
ib. or **ibid.** *Lat.* ibidem (in the same place).
ICBM intercontinental ballistic missile.
ICC 1. Indian Claims Commission. 2. Interstate Commerce Commission.
ICE internal-combustion engine.
Ice. or **Icel.** Iceland; Icelandic.
ICU intensive care unit.
ID 1. Or **Id.** Idaho. 2. Also **I.D.** identification.
id. *Lat.* idem (the same).
i.d. inside diameter.
IDP 1. inosine diphosphate. 2. integrated data processing.
IE industrial engineer; industrial engineering.
i.e. *Lat.* id est (that is).
IF or **i.f.** intermediate frequency.
IFF identification, friend or foe.
IFO identified flying object.
Ig immunoglobulin.
IG or **I.G.** inspector general.
ign. ignition.
ihp or **i.hp.** indicated horsepower.
IL Illinois.

ILA International Longshoremen's Association.
ILGWU or **I.L.G.W.U.** International Ladies' Garment Workers' Union.
Ill. illustrated; illustration; illustrator.
Ill. Illinois.
illus. illustrated; illustration; illustrator.
ILO International Labor Organization.
ILS instrument landing system.
IM intramuscular.
IMF International Monetary Fund.
imit. imitate; imitation.
Immun. immunity; immunization.
Immunol. immunology.
imp. 1. imperative. 2. imperfect. 3. imperial. 4. import; imported; importer.
in or **in.** inch.
IN Indiana.
inbd. inboard.
Inc. 1. income. 2. incomplete. 3. Also **Inc.** incorporated. 4. increase.
incl. including; inclusive.
incr. 1. increase; 2. incremental.
ind. 1. independence; independent. 2. index. 3. indigo. 4. industrial; industry.
Ind. 1. India. 2. Indian. 3. Indiana. 4. Indies.
indef. indefinite.
indic. *Gram.* indicative.
Indon. Indonesia; Indonesian.
indus. industrial; industry.
inf. 1. Or **Inf.** infantry. 2. inferior. 3. infinitive.
infin. infinitive.
infl. influence; influenced.
inq. inquiry.
ins. 1. inspector. 2. insulated; insulation. 3. insurance.
insp. inspected; inspector.
inst. 1. instant. 2. Or **Inst.** institute; institution. 3. instrument.
instr. 1. instruction; instructor. 2. instrument.
int. 1. interest. 2. interior. 3. internal.
inter. intermediate.
interj. interjection.
interrog. interrogative.
intl. international.
intr. intransitive.
intro. introduction; introductory.
inv. 1. invented; invention; inventor. 2. invoice.
I/O input/output.
IOOF Independent Order of Odd Fellows.
IPA 1. International Phonetic Alphabet. 2. International Phonetic Association.
ips or **i.p.s.** inches per second.
IQ or **I.Q.** intelligence quotient.
IR 1. information retrieval. 2. infrared.
Ir. Irish.
IRA 1. Individual Retirement Account. 2. Also **I.R.A.** Irish Republican Army.
IRBM Intermediate Range Ballistic Missile.
Ire. Ireland.
irreg. irregular; irregularly.
IRS Internal Revenue Service.
is. or **Is.** island.
ISBN International Standard Book Number.
isl. island.
Isr. Israel; Israeli.
IST insulin shock therapy.
isth. isthmus.
It. Italian; Italy.
ital. italic.
Ital. Italian; Italy.
ITU 1. International Telecommunication Union. 2. International Typographical Union.
IU international unit.
IUD intrauterine device.
IV intravenous; intravenously.
i.w. inside width.

J 1. current density. 2. joule.
J. 1. journal. 2. judge. 3. justice.
JA 1. joint account. 2. Also **J.A.** judge advocate.
JAG also **J.A.G.** Judge Advocate General.
Jam. Jamaica.
Jan. January.
Jap. Japan; Japanese.
Jav. Javanese.
J.C.D. *Lat.* Juris Canonici Doctor (Doctor of Canon Law).
JCL *Computer Sci.* job control language.
JCS or **J.C.S.** Joint Chiefs of Staff.
jct. junction.
JD 1. Justice Department. 2. Also **J.D.** juvenile delinquent.
J.D. *Lat.* Jurum Doctor (Doctor of Laws).
JFK John Fitzgerald Kennedy International Airport.
jg junior grade.
JJ 1. judges. 2. justices.
jnr. junior.
jour. 1. journal; journalist. 2. journeyman.
JP or **J.P.** justice of the peace.
jr. or **Jr.** junior.
J.S.D. *Lat.* Juris Scientiae Doctor (Doctor of Juristic Science).
jt. joint.
jun. or **Jun.** junior.
junc. junction.
JV junior varsity.
jwlr. jeweler.

k 1. karat. 2. kilo-.
K 1. kelvin (temperature unit). 2. Kelvin (temperature scale). 3. kindergarten.
ka cathode.
kc kilocycle.
K.C. 1. King's Counsel. 2. Also **KC** Knights of Columbus.
kcal kilocalorie.
kcs or **kc/s** kilocycles per second.
Ken. Kentucky.
keV kiloelectron volt.
kg kilogram.
kg. keg.
KGB or **K.G.B.** *Russian.* Komitĕt Gosudarstvĕnnoi Bezopasnost'i (Commission of State Security).
KKK or **K.K.K.** Ku Klux Klan.
km kilometer.
kmph kilometers per hour.
kmps kilometers per second.
Knt knight.
K of C Knights of Columbus.
Kor. Korea; Korean.
KP kitchen police.
K.P. Knights of Pythias.
KS Kansas.
kt. karat.
Kuw. Kuwait.
kW kilowatt.
kWh kilowatt-hour.
KY or **Ky.** Kentucky.

l liter.
L also **L.** large.
l. 1. Also **L.** lake. 2. land. 3. late. 4. left. 5. length. 6. line.
L. Latin.
LA or **La.** Louisiana.
L.A. 1. Legislative Assembly. 2. local agent. 3. Also **LA** Los Angeles.

lab. laboratory.
Lab. Labrador.
lang. language.
lat. latitude.
Lat. 1. Latin. 2. Latvia; Latvian.
lav. lavatory.
LB Labrador.
lb. *Lat.* libra (pound).
lc also **l.c.** lower case.
LC 1. landing craft. 2. Or **L.C.** Library of Congress.
L/C letter of credit.
lcd or **l.c.d.** lowest common denominator.
LCL less-than-carload lot.
lcm or **l.c.m.** least common multiple.
LCM landing craft, mechanized.
L.Cpl. lance corporal.
LCS landing craft, support.
LCT landing craft, tank.
ld. load.
Ld. 1. limited. 2. lord (title).
LD learning disability; learning-disabled.
ldg. landing.
lea. 1. league. 2. leather.
Leb. Lebanese; Lebanon.
leg. 1. legal. 2. legislation; legislative; legislature.
legis. legislation; legislative; legislature.
lf 1. Also **l.f.** or **lf.** lightface. 2. low frequency.
LG also **L.G.** Low German.
lg. or **lge.** large.
l.h. also **LH** left hand.
ll link (unit of measurement).
L.I. Long Island.
lib. 1. liberal. 2. librarian; library.
Lib. 1. Liberal. 2. Liberia; Liberian.
Liech. Liechtenstein.
lieut. lieutenant.
LIFO *Accounting.* last in, first out.
lim. limit.
lin. 1. lineal. 2. linear.
ling. linguistics.
liq. 1. liquid. 2. liquor.
lit. 1. liter. 2. literal; literally. 3. literary. 4. literature.
Lit.B. or **Litt.B.** *Lat.* Litterarum Baccalaureus (Bachelor of Letters; Bachelor of Literature).
Lit.D. or **Litt.D.** *Lat.* Litterarum Doctor (Doctor of Letters; Doctor of Literature).
Lith. Lithuania; Lithuanian.
ll or **ll.** lines.
LL.B. *Lat.* Legum Baccalaureus (Bachelor of Laws).
LL.D. *Lat.* Legum Doctor (Doctor of Laws).
LL.M. *Lat.* Legum Magister (Master of Laws).
lm lumen.
LM lunar module.
ln Napierian logarithm.
LNG liquefied natural gas.
loc. cit. *Lat.* loco citato (in the place cited).
long. longitude.
LOOM Loyal Order of Moose.
loq. *Lat.* loquitur (speaks).
LPG liquefied petroleum gas.
LPM or **lpm** lines per minute.
LPN or **L.P.N.** licensed practical nurse.
LSAT Law School Admissions Test.
LSD 1. least significant digit. 2. lysergic acid diethylamide.
lt. light.
Lt. lieutenant.
l.t. or **LT** local time.
Lt. Col. lieutenant colonel.
Lt. Comdr. lieutenant commander.
ltd. or **Ltd.** limited.
Lt. Gen. lieutenant general.
Lt. Gov. lieutenant governor.

Luth. Lutheran.
Lux. Luxembourg.

m 1. Or **M** *Printing.* a. em. b. pica em.
2. *Physics.* mass. 3. meter (measure).
M 1. *Physics.* Mach number. 2. *Chem.* metal.
3. *Physics.* mutual inductance.
m. 1. manual. 2. married. 3. Or **M.** male.
4. Or **M.** masculine. 5. Or **M.** medium. 6. Or
M. meridian. 7. Or **M.** *Lat.* merides (noon).
8. mile. 9. month. 10. morning.
M. 1. majesty. 2. Monday. 3. Monsieur.
mA milliampere.
MA 1. Massachusetts. 2. Also **M.A.** mental age.
M.A. *Lat.* Magister Artium (Master of Arts).
mach. machine; machinery; machinist.
Mad. or **Madag.** Madagascar.
mag. 1. magazine. 2. magnetism. 3. magneto.
4. magnitude.
Maj. major.
Maj. Gen. major general.
Mal. Malay; Malayan.
Mala. Malaysia.
man. manual.
Man. Manitoba.
manuf. or **manufac.** manufacture.
MAP modified American plan.
mar. 1. maritime. 2. married.
Mar. March.
March. marchioness.
marg. margin.
Mart. Martinique.
masc. masculine.
MASH Mobile Army Surgical Hospital.
Mass. Massachusetts.
math. mathematical; mathematician;
mathematics.
max. maximum.
MB Manitoba.
M.B.A. Master of Business Administration.
mc millicurie.
Mc megacycle.
MC 1. Marine Corps. 2. Medical Corps. 3. Or
M.C. Member of Congress.
M.C. or **m.c.** master of ceremonies.
mcf thousand cubic feet.
MD 1. Or **Md.** Maryland. 2. muscular
dystrophy.
M.D. *Lat.* Medicinae Doctor (Doctor of
Medicine).
m/d months after date.
Mdm. Madam.
M.D.S. Master of Dental Surgery.
mdse. merchandise.
ME 1. Or **Me.** Maine. 2. Also **M.E.** Middle
English.
M.E. 1. mechanical engineer; mechanical
engineering. 2. medical examiner.
meas. measurable; measure.
mech. 1. mechanical; mechanics.
2. mechanism.
med. 1. medical; medicine. 2. medieval.
3. medium.
Medit. Mediterranean.
Med. Lat. Medieval Latin.
mem. 1. member. 2. memoir. 3. memorandum.
4. memorial.
mer. meridian.
met. 1. meteorological; meteorology.
2. metropolitan.
metal. or **metall.** metallurgic; metallurgy.
meteor. or **meteorol.** meteorological;
meteorology.
mev or **Mev** million electron volts.
Mex. Mexican; Mexico.

mf medium frequency.
mF millifarad.
M.F.A. Master of Fine Arts.
mfd. manufactured.
mfg. manufacture; manufactured;
manufacturing.
mfr. manufacture; manufacturer.
mg milligram.
M.G. Major General.
Mgr. or **mgr.** manager.
mgt. management.
mH millihenry.
MH Medal of Honor.
MHz megahertz.
MI 1. Michigan. 2. military intelligence.
mi. mile.
MIA missing in action.
Mich. Michigan.
mid. middle.
mil. military; militia.
min. 1. mineralogical; mineralogy.
2. minimum. 3. minor. 4. Or **min** minute.
Minn. Minnesota.
misc. miscellaneous.
Miss. Mississippi.
mks meter-kilogram-second (system of units).
mkt. market.
mktg. marketing.
ml milliliter.
ML also **M.L.** Medieval Latin.
MLA or **M.L.A.** Modern Language
Association.
Mlle. Mademoiselle.
Mlles. Mesdemoiselles.
mm millimeter.
MM. Messieurs.
m.m. *Lat.* mutatis mutandis (with the
necessary changes having been made).
Mme. Madame.
Mmes. Mesdames.
mmf or **m.m.f.** magnetomotive force.
MN 1. magnetic north. 2. Minnesota.
mngr. manager.
MO or **Mo.** Missouri.
mo. month.
m.o. or **M.O.** 1. mail order. 2. medical officer.
3. modus operandi. 4. Also **MO** money order.
mod. 1. moderate. 2. modern.
mol. molecular; molecule.
mol wt molecular weight.
mon. 1. monastery. 2. monetary.
Mon. Monday.
Mong. Mongolia; Mongolian.
Mont. Montana.
Mor. Moroccan; Morocco.
mos. months.
Moz. Mozambique.
mp or **m.p.** melting point.
MP or **M.P.** 1. military police; military
policeman. 2. mounted police.
M.P. Member of Parliament.
mpg or **m.p.g.** miles per gallon.
mph or **m.p.h.** miles per hour.
Mr. Mister.
mRNA messenger RNA.
ms millisecond.
MS 1. Mississippi. 2. multiple sclerosis.
ms. or **MS.** or **ms** manuscript.
M.S. or **M.Sc.** *Lat.* Magister Scientiae (Master
of Science).
msec millisecond.
MSG monosodium glutamate.
msg. message.
Msgr. Monseigneur; Monsignor.
M.Sgt. master sergeant.
MSH melanocyte-stimulating hormone.
mss. or **MSS.** or **mss** manuscripts.

MST or **M.S.T.** Mountain Standard Time.
MT 1. Montana. 2. Or **M.T.** Mountain Time.
mt. or **Mt.** mount; mountain.
m.t. or **M.T.** metric ton.
mtg. 1. meeting. 2. mortgage.
mtge. mortgage.
mtn. mountain.
mts. or **Mts.** mountains.
mun. or **munic.** municipal; municipality.
mus. 1. museum. 2. music; musical; musician.
mV millivolt.
MV 1. mean variation. 2. megavolt. 3. motor vessel.
MVP most valuable player.
mW milliwatt.
MW megawatt.
Mx *Physics.* maxwell.
mxd. mixed.
myth. or **mythol.** mythological; mythology.

n 1. Or **N** *Printing.* en. 2. neutron. 3. Also **N** or **n-** *Chem.* normal.
N 1. Avogadro number. 2. newton. 3. Also **N.** or **n** or **n.** north; northern.
n. 1. *Lat.* natus (born). 2. *Commerce.* net. 3. Or **N.** noon. 4. note. 5. noun. 6. number.
N. 1. Norse. 2. November.
N.A. 1. North America. 2. not applicable. 3. not available.
N.A.A. 1. National Aeronautic Association. 2. National Automobile Association.
NAACP or **N.A.A.C.P.** National Association for the Advancement of Colored People.
NAD nicotinamide-adenine dinucleotide.
NADP nicotinamide-adenine dinucleotide phosphate.
NAM or **N.A.M.** National Association of Manufacturers.
NASA National Aeronautics and Space Administration.
nat. 1. national. 2. native. 3. natural.
natl. national.
NATO North Atlantic Treaty Organization.
NATS Naval Air Transport Service.
naut. nautical.
nav. 1. naval. 2. navigation.
NB or **N.B.** New Brunswick.
n.b. or **N.B.** nota bene.
NBA National Basketball Association.
NBC National Broadcasting Corporation.
NbE north by east.
NBS National Bureau of Standards.
NbW north by west.
NC 1. no charge. 2. Or **N.C.** North Carolina.
NCAA or **N.C.A.A.** National Collegiate Athletic Association.
N.Cal. New Caledonia.
NCC National Council of Churches.
NCO or **N.C.O.** noncommissioned officer.
ND or **N.D.** North Dakota.
n.d. or **N.D.** no date.
N.Dak. North Dakota.
NE 1. Nebraska. 2. Or **N.E.** New England. 3. northeast.
NEA National Education Association.
NEbE northeast by east.
NEbN northeast by north.
Nebr. Nebraska.
neg. negative.
Nep. Nepal.
NET National Educational Television.
Neth. Netherlands.
neur. or **neurol.** neurological; neurology.
neut. 1. neuter. 2. neutral.
Nev. Nevada.

Newf. Newfoundland.
New Hebr. New Hebrides.
New M. New Mexico.
New Test. New Testament.
NF Newfoundland.
n/f no funds.
NFC National Football Conference.
NFL National Football League.
Nfld. Newfoundland.
NG also **N.G.** National Guard.
NGr or **NGr.** New Greek.
NH or **N.H.** New Hampshire.
N.Heb. New Hebrides.
NHI National Health Insurance.
NHL National Hockey League.
Nic. Nicaragua.
Nig. Nigeria.
N.Ire. Northern Ireland.
NIT National Invitational Tournament.
NJ or **N.J.** New Jersey.
NKVD or **N.K.V.D.** *Russian.* Narodny Kommissariat Vnutrennikh Del (People's Commissariat for Internal Affairs).
NL 1. National League. 2. Also **n.l.** new line. 3. Also **N.L.** New Latin.
n.l. *Lat.* non licet (not permitted).
N.L. *Lat.* non liquet (not clear).
NLRB also **N.L.R.B.** National Labor Relations Board.
nm 1. Or **n.m.** nautical mile. 2. nuclear magneton.
NM or **N.M.** New Mexico.
N.Mex. New Mexico.
NNE north-northeast.
NNW north-northwest.
no. or **No.** 1. north; northern. 2. number.
n.o.p. not otherwise provided (for).
Nor. 1. Norman. 2. north. 3. Norway; Norwegian.
norm. normal.
Norw. Norway; Norwegian.
nos. or **Nos.** numbers.
Nov. November.
NOW National Organization for Women.
n.p. no place.
N.P. notary public.
n.p.t. normal pressure and temperature.
NRA also **N.R.A.** National Rifle Association.
NRC Nuclear Regulatory Commission.
ns or **nsec** nanosecond.
NS or **N.S.** Nova Scotia.
n.s. 1. new series. 2. not specified.
n/s not sufficient.
NSC National Security Council.
NSE National Stock Exchange.
n.s.f. or **N.S.F.** not sufficient funds.
N.S.P.C.A. National Society for the Prevention of Cruelty to Animals.
N.S.W. New South Wales.
NT 1. Also **N.T.** New Testament. 2. Northwest Territories.
n.t.p. or **N.T.P.** normal temperature and pressure.
nt. wt. net weight.
num. 1. number. 2. numeral.
numis. or **numism.** numismatic; numismatics.
NV Nevada.
NW northwest.
NWbN northwest by north.
NWbW northwest by west.
n.wt. net weight.
N.W.T. Northwest Territories.
NY or **N.Y.** New York.
NYC or **N.Y.C.** New York City.
NYSE New York Stock Exchange.
N.Z. New Zealand.

O 1. Or **O.** ocean. 2. Or **O.** order.
O. 1. October. 2. Ohio.
o/a on or about.
OAS Organization of American States.
ob. 1. *Lat.* obiit (he, or she, died). 2. *Lat.* obiter (incidentally).
O.B.E. also **OBE** Order of the British Empire.
obj. 1. *Gram.* object; objective. 2. objection.
obl. 1. oblique. 2. oblong.
obs. 1. observation. 2. Or **Obs.** observatory. 3. obsolete. 4. obstetric; obstetrician; obstetrics.
obstet. obstetric; obstetrics.
obv. obverse.
oc. or **Oc.** ocean.
o.c. *Lat.* opere citato (in the work cited).
O.C. Officer Commanding.
o/c overcharge.
OCAS Organization of Central American States.
occ. 1. occident; occidental. 2. occupation.
occas. occasional; occasionally.
OCD Office of Civil Defense.
OCS Officer Candidate School.
Oct. October.
o.d. 1. on demand. 2. outside diameter.
O.D. 1. Doctor of Optometry. 2. officer of the day. 3. Also **o/d** overdraft. 4. overdrawn.
OE also **O.E.** Old English.
OED also **O.E.D.** Oxford English Dictionary.
OEO Office of Economic Opportunity.
off. office; officer; official.
OG or **O.G.** officer of the guard.
OGPU or **O.G.P.U.** *Russian.* Ob'edinyonnoye Gosudarstvennoye Politicheskoye Upravlenie (Unified Government Political Administration).
OH Ohio.
OK Oklahoma.
Okla. Oklahoma.
Om. Oman.
OMB Office of Management and Budget.
ON 1. Also **O.N.** Old Norse. 2. Ontario.
Ont. Ontario.
O.O.D. officer of the deck.
op. 1. Also **Op.** operation. 2. opposite. 3. Also **Op.** opus.
op. cit. *Lat.* opere citato (in the work cited).
OPEC Organization of Petroleum Exporting Countries.
opp. opposite.
opt. 1. optical; optician; optics. 2. optimum. 3. optional.
OR or **Or.** Oregon.
O.R. or **OR** operating room.
orch. orchestra.
ord. 1. order. 2. ordinal. 3. ordinance. 4. ordnance.
ordn. ordnance.
Ore. Oregon.
org. 1. organic. 2. organization; organized.
orig. original; originally.
ornith. ornithologic; ornithology.
orth. orthopedic; orthopedics.
o.s. or **o/s** out of stock.
O.S. ordinary seaman.
OT also **O.T.** Old Testament.
o.t. or **O.T.** 1. occupational therapy. 2. overtime.
OTB off-track betting.
OTC also **O.T.C.** 1. Officer in Tactical Command. 2. Officers' Training Corps.
OTS also **O.T.S.** Officers' Training School.
oz also **oz.** ounce.
oz ap apothecaries' ounce.
oz av or **oz avdp** avoirdupois ounce.
oz t troy ounce.

p momentum.
p. 1. page. 2. part. 3. participle. 4. past. 5. penny. 6. per. 7. pint. 8. Or **P.** president.
PA 1. Or **Pa.** Pennsylvania. 2. public-address system.
p.a. *Lat.* per annum (by the year).
P.A. 1. Or **P/A** power of attorney. 2. press agent. 3. prosecuting attorney.
Pac. or **Pacif.** Pacific.
Pak. Pakistan.
Pal. Palestine.
pam. pamphlet.
Pan. Panama.
P and L profit and loss.
par. 1. paragraph. 2. parallel. 3. parenthesis. 4. parish.
Par. or **Para.** Paraguay.
paren. parenthesis.
parl. parliamentary.
Parl. Parliament.
part. 1. participle. 2. particular.
pass. 1. passage. 2. passive.
pat. patent.
patd. patented.
path. or **pathol.** pathological; pathology.
PAYE or **P.A.Y.E.** 1. pay as you earn. 2. pay as you enter.
payt. payment.
P.B. 1. passbook. 2. prayer book.
PBI protein-bound iodine.
PBS Public Broadcasting System.
PBX also **P.B.X.** private branch (telephone) exchange.
p.c. 1. *Lat.* post cibum (after meals). 2. per cent. 3. Also **p/c** or **P/C** petty cash. 4. post card.
P.C. 1. Past Commander. 2. Police Constable. 3. Post Commander.
p/c or **P/C** prices current.
PCB polychlorinated biphenyl.
PCP phencyclidine.
pct. per cent.
pd. paid.
p.d. or **P.D.** per diem.
P.D. 1. Police Department. 2. postal district.
PDT or **P.D.T.** Pacific Daylight Time.
pe also **p.e.** printer's error.
PE Prince Edward Island.
P.E. 1. physical education. 2. *Statistics.* probable error.
P.E.I. Prince Edward Island.
pen. or **Pen.** peninsula.
P.E.N. International Association of Poets, Playwrights, Editors, Essayists, and Novelists.
Penn. or **Penna.** Pennsylvania.
per. 1. period. 2. person.
perf. 1. perfect. 2. perforated.
perm. permanent.
perp. perpendicular.
pers. 1. person. 2. personal.
Pers. Persia; Persian.
pert. pertaining.
pet. petroleum.
pf. preferred.
Pfc or **Pfc.** private first class.
pfd. preferred.
pg. page.
Pg. Portugal; Portuguese.
P.G. 1. paying guest. 2. postgraduate.
PGA Professional Golfers' Association.
PH also **P.H.** 1. Public Health. 2. Purple Heart.
ph. phase.
PHA Public Housing Administration.
phar. or **Phar.** pharmaceutical; pharmacist; pharmacopoeia; pharmacy.

pharm. or **Pharm.** pharmaceutical; pharmacist; pharmacopoeia; pharmacy.

Ph.D. *Lat.* Philosophiae Doctor (Doctor of Philosophy).

phil. philosopher; philosophical; philosophy.

Phil. Philippines.

Phil. I. or **Phil. Is.** Philippine Islands.

philol. philology.

philos. philosopher; philosophical; philosophy.

phon. 1. phonetic; phonetics. 2. phonology.

photog. photography.

photom. photometry.

phr. phrase.

phren. phrenology.

PHS Public Health Service.

phys. 1. physical. 2. physician. 3. physicist; physics. 4. physiological; physiology.

physiol. physiological; physiology.

P.I. Philippine Islands.

pk. 1. pack. 2. park. 3. peak. 4. Or **pk** peck.

pkg. or **pkge.** package.

pkt. packet.

pl. 1. Or **Pl.** place. 2. plate. 3. plural.

plat. 1. plateau. 2. platform. 3. platoon.

plf. plaintiff.

PLO Palestine Liberation Organization.

plu. plural.

pm also **p-m** phase modulation.

PM or **P.M.** 1. past master. 2. police magistrate. 3. postmaster.

pm. premium.

p.m. also **P.M.** post mortem.

P.M. 1. Also **p.m.** post meridiem. Usually small capitals P.M. 2. Prime Minister.

P.M.G. postmaster general.

pmk. postmark.

pmt. payment.

p.n. or **P/N** promissory note.

pneum. pneumatic; pneumatics.

p.n.g. persona non grata.

po or **p.o.** *Baseball.* putout.

PO or **P.O.** 1. Personnel Officer. 2. Also **p.o.** petty officer. 3. postal order. 4. Also **p.o.** post office.

POE or **P.O.E.** port of entry.

pol. political; politician; politics.

Pol. Poland; Polish.

polit. political; politics.

pop. 1. popular. 2. population.

Port. Portugal; Portuguese.

pos. 1. position. 2. positive.

poss. 1. possession. 2. possessive. 3. possible; possibly.

pot. potential.

POW or **P.O.W.** prisoner of war.

pp. 1. pages. 2. past participle.

p.p. or **P.P.** 1. parcel post. 2. parish priest. 3. past participle. 4. postpaid.

ppd. 1. postpaid. 2. prepaid.

pph. pamphlet.

P.P.S. also **p.p.s.** *Lat.* post postscriptum (additional postscript).

P.Q. or **PQ** Province of Quebec.

PR or **P.R.** 1. public relations. 2. Puerto Rico.

pr. 1. pair. 2. present. 3. price. 4. printing. 5. pronoun.

Pr. 1. priest. 2. prince. 3. Provençal.

prec. preceding.

pred. predicate.

pref. 1. preface; prefatory. 2. preference; preferred. 3. prefix.

prem. premium.

prep. 1. preparation; preparatory; prepare. 2. preposition.

prepd. prepared.

pres. 1. present. 2. president.

Pres. President.

Presb. or **Presby.** Presbyterian.

prf. proof.

prim. 1. primary. 2. primitive.

prin. 1. principal. 2. principle.

print. printing.

priv. 1. private. 2. privative.

PRO also **P.R.O.** public relations officer.

pro. professional.

prob. 1. probable; probably. 2. problem.

proc. 1. proceedings. 2. process.

prod. 1. produce. 2. produced. 3. product; production.

prof. 1. professional. 2. Also **Prof.** professor.

pron. 1. pronominal; pronoun. 2. pronounced; pronunciation.

prop. 1. proper; properly. 2. property. 3. proposition. 4. proprietary; proprietor.

propr. proprietor.

pros. prosody.

Pros. Atty. prosecuting attorney.

Prot. Protestant.

prov. 1. province; provincial. 2. provisional. 3. provost.

P.S. 1. permanent secretary. 2. Police Sergeant. 3. Also **p.s.** postscript. 4. public school.

PSAT Preliminary Scholastic Aptitude Test.

psec picosecond.

pseud. pseudonym.

psf or **p.s.f.** pounds per square foot.

psi or **p.s.i.** pounds per square inch.

PST or **P.S.T.** Pacific Standard Time.

psych. or **psychol.** psychological; psychologist; psychology.

pt. 1. part. 2. payment. 3. pint. 4. point. 5. port.

p.t. *Lat.* pro tempore (temporarily).

P.T. 1. Also **PT** Pacific Time. 2. physical therapy.

PTA or **P.T.A.** Parent-Teacher Association.

ptg. printing.

PTV 1. public television. 2. pay television.

pub. 1. public. 2. publication. 3. published; publisher.

publ. 1. publication. 2. published; publisher.

pvt. or **Pvt.** private.

pyro. pyrotechnics.

q. 1. quart. 2. quarter. 3. quarterly. 4. Also **Q.** quarto. 5. query. 6. question.

qb quarterback.

QC quartermaster corps.

Q.E.D. *Lat.* quod erat demonstrandum (which was to be demonstrated).

Qld. Queensland.

qlty. quality.

QM quartermaster.

QMC quartermaster corps.

QMG Quartermaster General.

qn. question.

qq. questions.

qr. 1. quarter. 2. quarterly. 3. quire.

qt or **qt.** quart.

qt. quantity.

qto. quarto.

qty. quantity.

qu. 1. queen. 2. query. 3. question.

quad. 1. quadrangle. 2. quadrant.

qual. qualitative.

quant. quantitative.

quar. 1. quarter. 2. quarterly.

Que. Quebec.

ques. question.

quot. quotation.

q.v. *Lat.* quod vide (which see).

r 1. Or R radius. 2. Or R *Elect.* resistance.
R 1. *Chem.* gas constant. 2. *Chem.* radical.
3. roentgen (unit of radiation).
r. 1. Or R railroad; railway. 2. range. 3. rare.
4. retired. 5. Or R. right. 6. Or R river. 7. Or
R. road. 8. rod (unit of length).
R. 1. rabbi. 2. rector. 3. regius. 4. Republican.
5. royal.
Ra. Range.
R.A. 1. rear admiral. 2. Or RA Regular Army.
rad. 1. radical. 2. radio. 3. radius.
RAF also R.A.F. Royal Air Force.
R & B rhythm and blues.
R & D research and development.
R and R rest and recreation.
RBC or rbc red blood cell; red blood (cell)
count.
RBE *Physics.* relative biological effectiveness.
rbi also r.b.i. *Baseball.* run batted in.
RC 1. Red Cross. 2. Roman Catholic.
RCAF also R.C.A.F. Royal Canadian Air
Force.
R.C.Ch. Roman Catholic Church.
RCMP also R.C.M.P. Royal Canadian
Mounted Police.
rcpt. receipt.
rct. recruit.
rd rod (unit of length).
RD rural delivery.
rd. 1. Or Rd. road. 2. round.
RDA recommended daily allowance.
RDF radio direction finder.
R.E. or RE real estate.
rec. 1. receipt. 2. record; recording.
3. recreation.
recd. or rec'd. received.
rect. 1. receipt. 2. rectangle; rectangular.
red. reduced; reduction.
ref. 1. referee. 2. reference. 3. referred.
4. reformation; reformed.
refl. 1. reflection; reflective. 2. reflex;
reflexive.
reg. 1. regent. 2. regiment. 3. region.
4. register; registered. 5. registrar. 6. registry.
7. regular; regularly. 8. regulation.
9. regulator.
regd. registered.
regt. regiment.
rel. 1. relating. 2. relative. 3. released.
4. religion; religious.
rem. remittance.
rep. 1. repair. 2. repetition. 3. report.
4. reporter. 5. Or Rep. representative.
6. reprint. 7. Or Rep. republic.
Rep. Republican.
repl. replace; replacement.
repr. representing.
rept. report.
Repub. 1. republic. 2. Republican.
req. 1. require; required. 2. requisition.
reqd. required.
res. 1. research. 2. reserve. 3. residence;
resident; resides. 4. resolution.
Res. 1. Reservation. 2. Reservoir.
ret. 1. retain. 2. retired. 3. return.
rev. 1. revenue. 2. reverse; reversed. 3. review;
reviewed. 4. revise; revision. 5. Or Rev.
revolution.
Rev. reverend (title).
Rev. Ver. *Bible.* Revised Version.
RF radio frequency.
r.f. *Baseball.* right field; right fielder.
RFD also R.F.D. rural free delivery.
r.h. relative humidity.
rhet. rhetoric.
rhp or r.hp. rated horsepower.
RI or R.I. Rhode Island.

R.I.P. *Lat.* requiescat in pace (may he, or she,
rest in peace).
riv. river.
rm. 1. ream. 2. room.
rms root mean square.
RN or R.N. 1. registered nurse. 2. Royal
Navy.
RNA ribonucleic acid.
rnd. round.
ro. rood (measure).
rom also rom. roman (type).
ROM *Computer Sci.* read-only memory.
Rom. 1. Roman. 2. Romance (language).
3. Romania; Romanian.
ROTC Reserve Officers' Training Corps.
rpm or r.p.m. revolutions per minute.
rps or r.p.s. revolutions per second.
rpt. 1. repeat. 2. report.
R.Q. respiratory quotient.
RR also R.R. 1. railroad. 2. rural route.
R.R. Right Reverend.
rRNA ribosomal RNA.
RSV or R.S.V. *Bible.* Revised Standard
Version.
R.S.V.P. or r.s.v.p. *French.* répondez s'il vous
plaît (please reply).
RT radio telephone.
rt. right.
rte. route.
Rt. Hon. Right Honorable.
Rt. Rev. Right Reverend.
Rus. or Russ. Russia; Russian.
RV or R.V. *Bible.* Revised Version.
R.W. 1. Right Worshipful. 2. Right Worthy.
rwy. or ry. railway.

s 1. second (unit of time). 2. second of arc.
3. stere.
S 1. seaman. 2. Also S. or s or s. south;
southern.
s. 1. Or S. school. 2. Or S. sea. 3. see.
4. singular. 5. sister. 6. small. 7. Or S. society.
S. 1. Sabbath. 2. saint. 3. Saturday.
4. Sunday. 5. September.
SA Salvation Army.
s.a. *Lat.* sine anno (without date).
S.A. 1. South Africa. 2. South America.
Sab. Sabbath.
SAC Strategic Air Command.
S.Afr. South Africa.
Sal. El Salvador.
SALT Strategic Arms Limitations Talks.
SAM surface-to-air-missile.
SASE self-addressed stamped envelope.
Sask. Saskatchewan.
SAT Scholastic Aptitude Test.
sat. saturate; saturation.
Sat. Saturday.
Sau. Ar. Saudi Arabia.
S.Austl. South Australia.
Sax. Saxon; Saxony.
S.B. *Lat.* Scientiae Baccalaureus (Bachelor of
Science).
SBA Small Business Administration.
SbE south by east.
SbW south by west.
SC 1. Security Council. 2. Or S.C. South
Carolina.
sc. 1. scale. 2. scene. 3. scruple (weight).
4. science.
Sc. Scotch; Scottish.
s.c. also sc small capitals.
S.C. Supreme Court.
SCC storage connecting circuit.
sch. school.

scl. science; scientific.
SCLC Southern Christian Leadership Conference.
Scot. Scotch; Scotland; Scottish.
scr. scruple (unit of weight).
Script. Scriptural; Scriptures.
sct. scout.
SD 1. sight draft. **2.** Or **S.D.** South Dakota. **3.** special delivery.
sd. sound.
S.Dak. South Dakota.
SDS Students for a Democratic Society.
SE 1. southeast; southeastern. **2.** standard English. **3.** stock exchange.
SEATO Southeast Asia Treaty Organization.
SEbE southeast by east.
SEbS southeast by south.
sec 1. secant. **2.** second. **3.** secondary.
SEC Securities and Exchange Commission.
sec. 1. secretary. **2.** sector.
sect. section.
secy. secretary.
sed. sediment.
sel. select; selected.
SEM scanning electron microscope.
sem. seminary.
Sem. Semitic.
sen. or **Sen. 1.** senate; senator. **2.** senior.
sep. separate; separation.
Sep. September.
Sept. September.
seq. 1. sequel. **2.** *Lat.* sequens (the following).
seqq. *Lat.* sequentia (the following [things]).
ser. 1. serial. **2.** series. **3.** sermon.
Serb. Serbia; Serbian.
serv. 1. servant. **2.** service.
sess. session.
SF science fiction.
Sfc. sergeant first class.
sg specific gravity.
SG surgeon general.
S.G. or **SG** solicitor general.
sgd. signed.
Sgt. sergeant.
Sgt. Maj. sergeant major.
shf or **SHF** superhigh frequency.
shpt. shipment.
shr. share.
SI *French.* Système Internationale d'Unités (International System of Units).
Sib. Siberia; Siberian.
Sic. Sicilian; Sicily.
SIDS sudden infant death syndrome.
slg. 1. signal. **2.** signature.
sing. singular.
S.J. Society of Jesus.
SK Saskatchewan.
SL 1. sea level **2.** south latitude.
S.L. Sierra Leone.
Slav. Slavic.
sld. 1. sailed. **2.** sealed. **3.** sold.
SLIP symmetric list processor.
SLV standard launch vehicle.
SM sergeant major.
sm. small.
S.M.Sgt. Senior Master Sergeant.
s.n. *Lat.* sine nomine (without name).
so. or **So.** south; southern.
s.o. 1. seller's option. **2.** strikeout.
soc. 1. social. **2.** socialist. **3.** society.
sol. 1. solicitor. **2.** soluble. **3.** solution.
Sol. Is. Solomon Islands.
soln. solution.
Som. Somalia.
SOP standard operating procedure.
sop. soprano.
soph. sophomore.

sou. or **Sou.** south; southern.
sov. sovereign (coin).
Sov. Un. Soviet Union.
SP 1. self-propelled. **2.** shore patrol; shore police.
sp. 1. special. **2.** specialist. **3.** species. **4.** specific. **5.** spelling.
Sp. Spain; Spanish.
s.p. *Lat.* sine prole (without issue).
Span. Spanish.
SPCA Society for the Prevention of Cruelty to Animals.
SPCC Society for the Prevention of Cruelty to Children.
spec. 1. special. **2.** specification. **3.** speculation.
specif. specifically.
sp gr specific gravity.
sp ht specific heat.
spp. species (plural).
spr. spring.
s.p.s. *Lat.* sine prole supersite (without surviving issue).
spt. seaport.
sq. 1. squadron. **2.** square.
Sr. 1. Or **sr.** senior. **2.** sister (religious).
SRO standing room only.
SSA Social Security Administration.
SSE south-southeast.
S.Sgt. staff sergeant.
SSR or **S.S.R.** Soviet Socialist Republic.
SSS Selective Service System.
SST supersonic transport.
SSW south-southwest.
ST standard time.
st. 1. stanza. **2.** start. **3.** state. **4.** Or **St** statute. **5.** stet. **6.** stitch. **7.** stone. **8.** Or **St** strait. **9.** Or **St** street.
St. saint.
s.t. short ton.
sta. 1. station. **2.** stationary.
stat. 1. *Lat.* statim (immediately). **2.** stationary. **3.** statistics. **4.** statuary. **5.** statute.
stbd. starboard.
std. standard.
Ste. *French.* sainte (feminine form of saint).
steno or **stenog.** also **sten.** stenographer; stenography.
ster. sterling.
stg. sterling.
stge. storage.
stip. 1. stipend. **2.** stipulation.
stk. stock.
STOL short takeoff and landing.
STP standard temperature and pressure.
STR synchronous transmitter receiver.
str. 1. steamer. **2.** Or **Str.** strait.
stud. student.
sub. 1. subaltern. **2.** substitute. **3.** suburb; suburban.
subj. 1. subject. **2.** subjective. **3.** subjunctive.
subs. subscription.
subst. 1. substantive. **2.** substitute.
Sud. Sudan.
suf. or **suff. 1.** sufficient. **2.** suffix.
Sun. Sunday.
sup. 1. superior. **2.** *Gram.* superlative. **3.** *Gram.* supine.
super. 1. superintendent. **2.** superior.
supp. or **suppl.** supplement; supplementary.
supr. supreme.
supt. or **Supt.** superintendent.
supvr. supervisor.
sur. 1. surface. **2.** surplus.
Sur. Surinam.
surg. surgeon; surgery; surgical.

surr. surrender.
svgs. savings.
sw short wave.
SW southwest.
Sw. Sweden; Swedish.
Swaz. Swaziland.
SWbS southwest by south.
SWbW southwest by west.
Swe. or **Swed.** Sweden; Swedish.
Switz. Switzerland.
sym. 1. symbol. 2. symmetric. 3. symphony.
syn. synonymous; synonym; synonymy.
synd. syndicate.
Syr. 1. Syria; Syrian. 2. Syriac.

t 1. ton. 2. troy (system of weights).
T temperature.
t. 1. teaspoon; teaspoonful. 2. *Gram.* tense.
3. Or **T.** time. 4. *Gram.* transitive.
T. 1. tablespoon; tablespoonful. 2. Tuesday.
tab. table.
TAC Tactical Air Command.
tan tangent.
Tan. Tanzania.
TAS true airspeed.
Tas. or **Tasm.** Tasmania; Tasmanian.
TB also **T.B.** tuberculosis.
t.b. also **T.B.** tubercle bacillus.
tbs. or **tbsp.** tablespoon; tablespoonful.
tchr. teacher.
TD 1. Also **td** touchdown. 2. Also **T.D.**
treasury department.
tech. technical.
technol. technological; technology.
tel. 1. telegram. 2. telegraph; telegraphic.
3. telephone.
teleg. 1. telegram. 2. telegraph; telegraphic;
telegraphy.
temp. 1. temperature. 2. temporary.
Tenn. Tennessee.
ter. territorial; territory.
term. 1. terminal. 2. termination.
terr. territorial; territory.
test. 1. testator. 2. testimony.
Test. Testament.
Teut. Teuton; Teutonic.
Tex. Texas.
tfr. transfer.
t.g. type genus.
TGIF thank God it's Friday.
Th. Thursday.
Thai. Thailand.
theat. theater.
theol. theologian; theological; theology.
therap. therapeutic; therapeutics.
thp or **t.hp.** thrust horsepower.
Thurs. also **Thur.** Thursday.
THz terahertz.
tit. title.
tk. truck.
TKO technical knockout.
tkt. ticket.
t.l. or **t/l** total loss.
TLC tender loving care.
t.l.o. total loss only.
TM trademark.
t.m. true mean.
TN Tennessee.
tn. 1. ton. 2. town. 3. train.
tng. training.
tnpk. turnpike.
TNT trinitrotoluene.
t.o. turnover.
topog. topographic; topography.
tp. township.

t.p. title page.
tpk. turnpike.
TR or **T-R** transmit-receive.
tr. 1. *Gram.* transitive. 2. translated;
translation; translator. 3. transpose;
transposition. 4. treasurer. 5. *Law.* trust;
trustee.
trans. 1. transaction. 2. *Gram.* transitive.
3. translated; translation; translator.
4. transportation. 5. transpose; transposition.
transl. translated; translation.
transp. transportation.
trav. traveler; travels.
treas. treasurer; treasury.
trib. tributary.
trig. also **trigon.** trigonometric; trigonometry.
tripl. triplicate.
tRNA transfer RNA.
trop. tropic; tropical.
trp. troop.
T.Sgt. Technical Sergeant.
TSH thyroid-stimulating hormone.
tsp. teaspoon; teaspoonful.
Tu. Tuesday.
T.U. trade union.
Tues. Tuesday.
Tun. Tunisia; Tunisian.
Tur. or **Turk.** Turkey; Turkish.
TVA Tennessee Valley Authority.
twp. township.
TX Texas.
typ. typographer; typographical; typography.
typo. or **typog.** typographer; typographical;
typography.
typw. typewriter; typewritten.

U *Math.* union.
u. 1. unit. 2. Or **U.** upper.
U. university.
U.A.E. United Arab Emirates.
U.A.R. United Arab Republic.
UAW or **U.A.W.** United Automobile Workers.
u.c. also **UC** upper case.
UCMJ Uniform Code of Military Justice.
Ug. Uganda.
UGT urgent (telegram).
uhf or **UHF** ultrahigh frequency.
U.K. United Kingdom.
ult. 1. ultimate; ultimately. 2. ultimo.
UMW United Mine Workers.
UN or **U.N.** United Nations.
unan. unanimous.
unb. or **unbd.** unbound.
UNESCO United Nations Educational,
Scientific, and Cultural Organization.
UNICEF United Nations International
Children's Emergency Fund.
Unit. Unitarian; Unitarianism.
univ. 1. universal. 2. Or **Univ.** university.
Univ. Universalist.
UPI or **U.P.I.** United Press International.
Ur. Uruguay.
URA Urban Renewal Administration.
US or **U.S.** United States.
USA or **U.S.A.** 1. United States Army.
2. United States of America.
USAF also **U.S.A.F.** United States Air Force.
U.S.C. United States Code.
U.S.C.A. United States Code Annotated.
USCG also **U.S.C.G.** United States Coast
Guard.
USDA United States Department of
Agriculture.
USIA United States Information Agency.
U.S.M. United States Mail.

USMC also **U.S.M.C.** United States Marine Corps.

USN also **U.S.N.** United States Navy.

USNA also **U.S.N.A.** United States Naval Academy.

USO or **U.S.O.** United Service Organizations.

U.S.S. United States Senate.

USSR or **U.S.S.R.** Union of Soviet Socialist Republics.

usu. usually.

UT Utah.

UV ultraviolet.

UW underwriter.

V 1. *Physics.* velocity. 2. victory. 3. *Elect.* volt. 4. volume.

v. 1. verb. 2. verse. 3. version. 4. verso. 5. versus. 6. voice. 7. volume (book). 8. vowel.

V. viscount; viscountess.

VA or **Va.** Virginia.

V.A. 1. Also **VA** Veterans' Administration. 2. vice admiral.

VAB voice answer back.

vac. vacuum.

V.Adm. vice admiral.

val. 1. valley. 2. valuation; value.

VAR visual-aural range.

var. 1. variable. 2. variant. 3. variation. 4. variety. 5. various.

VAT value-added tax.

vb. verb; verbal.

V.C. 1. vice chairman. 2. vice chancellor. 3. vice consul.

vcr. video cassette recorder.

VD also **V.D.** venereal disease.

v.d. vapor density.

VDT visual display terminal.

vel. 1. vellum. 2. velocity.

Ven. venerable.

Venez. Venezuela.

ver. 1. verse. 2. version.

vert. vertical.

vet. 1. veteran. 2. veterinarian; veterinary.

veter. veterinary.

V.F. 1. Also **VF** video frequency. 2. Also **VF** visual field.

VFD volunteer fire department.

VFW also **V.F.W.** Veterans of Foreign Wars.

vhf or **VHF** very high frequency.

VI or **V.I.** Virgin Islands.

V.I. volume indicator.

vic. 1. vicar. 2. vicinity.

Viet. Vietnam; Vietnamese.

vil. village.

Vir. Is. Virgin Islands.

vis. 1. visibility. 2. visual.

Vis. or **Visct.** viscount; viscountess.

VISTA Volunteers in Service to America.

viz. *Lat.* videlicet (namely).

vlf or **VLF** very low frequency.

V.M.D. *Lat.* Veterinariae Medicinae Doctor (Doctor of Veterinary Medicine).

VO verbal order.

vo. verso.

voc. vocative.

vocab. vocabulary.

vol. volume.

vou. voucher.

VP 1. variable pitch. 2. verb phrase. 3. Or **V.P.** vice president.

vs. versus.

V.S. veterinary surgeon.

vss. 1. verses. 2. versions.

V/STOL vertical short takeoff and landing.

VT 1. vacuum tube. 2. variable time. 3. Vermont.

VTOL vertical takeoff and landing.

VTR videotape recorder.

VU volume unit.

Vul. Vulgate.

vulg. vulgar.

Vulg. Vulgate.

vv. verses.

v.v. vice versa.

w or **W** *Physics.* work.

W 1. *Elect.* watt. 2. Also **W.** or **w** or **w.** west; western.

w. 1. week. 2. weight. 3. wide. 4. width. 5. wife. 6. with.

W. 1. Wednesday. 2. Welsh.

WA Washington.

WAAC Women's Army Auxiliary Corps.

WAAF Women's Auxiliary Air Force.

WAC Women's Army Corps.

WAF Women in the Air Force.

war. warrant.

Wash. Washington.

WATS Wide-Area Telephone Service.

W.Aust. Western Australia.

WAVES Women Accepted for Volunteer Emergency Service (U.S. Navy).

w.b. also **W.B.** waybill.

W.B. Weather Bureau.

WBC or **wbc** white blood cell; white blood (cell) count.

WbN west by north.

WbS west by south.

w.c. 1. water closet. 2. without charge.

WCTU or **W.C.T.U.** Women's Christian Temperance Union.

WD or **W.D.** War Department.

wd. 1. wood. 2. word.

Wed. Wednesday.

WH watt-hour.

wh. white.

whf. wharf.

WHO World Health Organization.

W-hr watt-hour.

whsle. wholesale.

WI Wisconsin.

w.i. when issued (financial stock).

W.I. West Indian; West Indies.

WIA wounded in action.

wk. 1. weak. 2. week. 3. work.

wkly. weekly.

WL or **w.l.** wavelength.

WNW west-northwest.

WO or **W.O.** warrant officer.

w/o without.

w.o.c. without compensation.

WP 1. weather permitting. 2. word processing; word processor. 3. Or **w/p** without prejudice.

WPA Work Projects Administration.

wpm or **w.p.m.** words per minute.

wpn. weapon.

WR or **W.r.** Wassermann reaction.

WSW west-southwest.

wt. weight.

WV or **W.Va.** West Virginia.

WW I or **W.W.I** World War I.

WW II or **W.W.II** World War II.

WY or **Wyo.** Wyoming.

x 1. *Math.* abscissa. 2. *Printing.* broken type. 3. by. 4. Or **X** power of magnification. 5. Or

X *Math.* **a.** Unknown number. **b.** algebraic variable.

X **1.** Christ; Christian. **2.** extra. **3.** *Elect.* reactance. **4.** times (multiplied by). **5.** Used to indicate location, as on a map. **6.** Also **x** unknown.

x. ex.

XL **1.** extra large. **2.** extra long.

y *Math.* ordinate.

Y **1.** *Elect.* admittance. **2.** *Physics.* hypercharge. **3. a.** YMCA **b.** YMHA. **c.** YWCA. **d.** YWHA.

y. year.

yd yard (measurement).

yel. yellow.

Yem. Yemen.

yeo. yeoman; yeomanry.

YMCA or **Y.M.C.A.** Young Men's Christian Association.

YMHA or **Y.M.H.A.** Young Men's Hebrew Association.

YOB year of birth.

yr. **1.** year. **2.** younger.

Yug. or **Yugo.** Yugoslavia; Yugoslavian.

YWCA or **Y.W.C.A.** Young Women's Christian Association.

YWHA or **Y.W.H.A.** Young Women's Hebrew Association.

Z **1.** atomic number. **2.** *Elect.* impedance.

z. **1.** zero. **2.** zone.

zool. zoological; zoology.